Current Law

YEAR BOOK
2001

VOLUME TWO

Sweet & Maxwell
A THOMSON COMPANY

AUSTRALIA
LBC Information Services
Sydney

CANADA & USA
Carswell
Toronto

NEW ZEALAND
Brooker's
Auckland

SINGAPORE and MALAYSIA
Sweet & Maxwell Asia
Singapore and Kuala Lumpur

Current Law

YEAR
BOOK 2001

Being a Comprehensive Statement of the Law of 2001

SWEET & MAXWELL EDITORIAL TEAM

James Aidoo-Baidoe	Stephanie Armytage	Shahnaila Aziz
Catherine Berry	Chris Blagg	Sarah Scott
Catherine Collins	Daniel Collins	Robert Crossley
Matthew Davies	James Douse	Lisa Ferguson
Emma Fielden	Heidi Fletcher	Sven Jackson
Jonathan Langtry-Langton		Barbara Loy
Mairead O'Grady	Alix Robinson	Jayne Sykes
Martin Syrett	Nina Taylor	Lynsey Tinch

Carole Webb   Hilary Wyles

SWEET & MAXWELL PRODUCTION TEAM

Joanna Mackinven   Roger Greenwood

Editors

English and Commonwealth Law

MICHAEL BLACK, LL.B., *Solicitor*
PATRICK CLARKE, *Barrister*
CRAIG DUNFORD, *Barrister*
IAN FERRIER, M.A., *Barrister*
SHAUN FERRIS, B.A., *Barrister*
ANN HAND, LL.B. (Hons), *Barrister and Solicitor*
Dr. ALASTAIR HUDSON, LL.B., LL.M., *Barrister*
CHARLES H JOSEPH, B.A., *Barrister, FCI Arb*
EILEEN O'GRADY, LL.B. (Hons), *Barrister*
PETER OSBORNE, PhD, *Solicitor (Ireland and N Ireland)*
JESSICA PENROSE, LL.B., *Solicitor*
WILLIAM VANDYCK, B.A., *Barrister*
GORDON WIGNALL, M.A., *Barrister*

Scotland

MALCOLM THOMSON, Q.C., LL.B.

Damages Awards

DAVID KEMP, Q.C., B.A., *Barrister*
PETER MANTLE, *Barrister*

The Mode of Citation
of the Current Law Year Book is
[2001] C.L.Y. 1282
The 2001 Year Book is published in two volumes.

Published in 2002 by
Sweet & Maxwell Limited of
100 Avenue Road, Swiss Cottage, London NW3 3PF
Typeset by Sweet & Maxwell Limited,
Mytholmroyd, Hebden Bridge
Printed in England by Clays Ltd, St Ives plc.

**A CIP catalogue record for this book is available
from the British Library**

ISBN: 2001 Yearbook: 0-421-79530-1
2001 Yearbook with Case and Legislation Citators: 0-421-79510-7

No forests were destroyed to make this product;
farmed timber was used and then replanted.

ISBN 0-421-79530-1

9 780421 795303 >

PREFACE

The 2001 Current Law Year Book supersedes the issues of *Current Law Monthly Digest* for 2001 and covers the law from January 1 to December 31 of that year.

Jurisdiction

The text of the 2001 Current Law Year Book is divided into three sections respectively: UK, England and Wales and EU, Northern Ireland and Scotland. The European material comprises: cases appearing before the Court of First Instance and European Court of Justice which are published in the reports series and newspapers, and a selection of books.

Cases

The 2001 Current Law Year Book includes digests of 3,447 cases published in over 90 reports series, journals, *The Times* and *Independent* newspapers, transcripts and ex relatione contributions from barristers and solicitors. A number of reports edited by David Kemp Q.C. concerning damages awards in personal injury cases in England and Wales appears under the subject heading DAMAGES and is collated in tabular form together with Scottish personal injuries cases at the beginning of Vol. 1.

The editor thanks those barristers and solicitors who have submitted case reports, many of which demonstrate developments in county court litigation. Whilst all reasonable care is taken in the preparation of the digests it is not possible to guarantee the accuracy of each digest, particularly those cases ex relatione which are not taken from an authorised judgment.

An alphabetical Table of Cases digested in the 2001 Year Book appears at the beginning of Volume 1. The Current Law Case Citator 2001 forms part of the permanent bound volume series for the years 1947-76, 1977-1997, 1998-2001.

Legislation

All public and private Acts of Parliament published in 2001 are abstracted and indexed. All Statutory Instruments, Scottish Statutory Instruments and Statutory Rules of Northern Ireland are abstracted. Cumulative tables of Statutory Instruments, arranged alphabetically, numerically and by subject are published in Vol. 1. Cumulative tables of Statutory Rules of Northern Ireland arranged alphabeticially, numerically and by subject are also published in Vol. 1.

The Current Law Legislation Citators for 2000 and 2001 appear as a separate bound volume and form part of the series of permanent bound volumes for the years 1989-1995, 1996-1999 and 2000-2001.

Books

The full title, reference and author of books of interest to the legal profession published in 2000/2001 are arranged by subject heading. A separate list, arranged by author is included in Volume 2.

Index

The subject-matter index is closely associated with a Legal Taxonomy from Sweet & Maxwell. The 30-year Index from 1947-76 may be found in the 1976 *Current Law Year Book*. The Scottish Index for the years 1972-86 may be found in the Scottish 1986 *Year Book*. Scottish material prior to 1972 can be found in the *Scottish Current Law Year Book Master Volumes*, published in 1956, 1961, 1966 and 1971.

August 2002

CONTENTS

VOLUME 1

THE LAW OF 2001 DIGESTED UNDER TITLES:
Note: Italicised entries refer to Scotland only.

CONTENTS

CURRENT LAW

YEAR BOOK 2001

UK, ENGLAND & WALES & EU

(continued)

HOUSING

3400. Defective premises – closing orders – compensation payable by the local authority following closing order of tenanted property

[Land Compensation Act 1961 s.50(2); Land Compensation Act 1973 s.50(2); Housing Act 1985 s.189(1), s.584A.]

B served a repairs notice under the Housing Act 1985 s.189(1) but the tenant refused to vacate the premises and, after a period during which the works were held in abeyance, a closing order was served in February 1997. A covering letter with the closing order advised the landlord that he was prohibited from reletting the premises after the tenant left until the subject works had been carried out. The tenant was rehoused by the council in June 1997 and the works completed in November 1997 when the property was relet to a different tenant. W, the landlord, then sought compensation for the making of the closing order. It was agreed that the date at which the compensation fell to be assessed was February 1997 but there was a dispute as to the way in which the compensation fell to be assessed under the Housing Act 1985 s.584A. That section provided that the compensation was to be the diminution in the compulsory purchase value of the owner's interest in the premises. The value was further defined as "the compensation which would be payable in respect of the compulsory purchase of that interest if it fell to be assessed in accordance with the Land Compensation Act 1961". The disputes between W and the council were whether (1) the definition provided in the 1985 Act required the amount to be determined by reference only to the Land Compensation Act 1961 or whether the provisions of the Land Compensation Act 1973 could be taken into account; (2) whether account ought to be taken of the prospect of the tenant being rehoused by the council; (3) account ought to be taken of the right to possession that would be obtained by the landlord as a result of the closing order, and (4) the method of calculation of the notional value of the property before and after the closing order. On the basis of W's approach a claim of

£5,413 was made. B argued that no compensation was payable as the notional value after the closing order exceeded the value before the order.

Held, giving judgment for B, that no compensation was payable as there had been no diminution in the compulsory purchase value of the property as a result of the making of the closing order, that (1) the Land Compensation Act 1973 was to be taken into account when assessing compensation as compensation was to be assessed having regard to the whole of the compensation code. The reference in the Housing Act 1985 to the Land Compensation Act 1961 was procedural not substantive in that it indicated that the compensation was to be assessed by the Lands Tribunal; (2) any part of the value attributable to the tenant giving up possession as a result of being re-housed by the council (or to the prospect of that happening) was to be left out of account. The assessment was based on a notional compulsory purchase which would have been made subject to the existing tenancy. Any rehousing would be as a result of the compulsory purchase and would not affect the value at the time of the purchase; (3) however, any value attributable to the landlord obtaining possession as a result of the closing order could be taken into account. It was the landlord's right and obligation to obtain possession after the closing order, and (4) accordingly the value was the difference between the value before the service of the closing order (when the property was tenanted) and the value after the service of the closing order when the freehold interest was still subject to the tenancy but the landlord now had the right to obtain vacant possession and could be expected to do so within six months. On that basis there had been no diminution in the notional value of the property.

WELLS v. BOURNEMOUTH BC [2000] R.V.R. 335, PH Clarke, FRICS, Lands Tr.

3401. Defective premises – local authority housing – failure to disclose defect to subsequent purchaser

[Housing Act 1985 s.562.]

Houses of the Schindler and Hawksley SGS type were designated as defective by the Secretary of State in November 1984, by reason of their construction. NBC published a housing defects notice in January 1985. The cut off date by which those "eligible for assistance" under the Housing Act 1985 was set at April 1985. The house in the instant case was sold by NBC to P in 1972 and P sold it to V in 1982. V would have been a person eligible for assistance under the Act, but she was not aware that the house was affected when she sold it to H in 1987 for £24,000. Its true value because of the defect was £7,075. The truth was discovered following enquiries by a surveyor for H's mortgagee in 1989 and H claimed damages from NBC for breach of statutory duty under s.562. It was held at first instance that NBC had been careless in not discovering the information prior to 1987 and that s.562 created a private law cause of action in certain cases. However, H's claim was refused because H did not fall within the class of persons protected by s.562. H appealed.

Held, dismissing the appeal, that s.562 imposed a duty on housing authorities to give information to enable those eligible for assistance to apply within the cut off period, as set out in the Act. That duty did not extend to future purchasers, as Parliament had intended that knowledge of defective properties would be known to surveyors and mortgagees after that time. As H had acquired an interest in the property after the relevant cut off date they were not eligible for assistance.

HODGE v. NEWPORT BC (2001) 33 H.L.R. 18, Roch, L.J., CA.

3402. Grants – disabled facilities

DISABLED FACILITIES GRANTS AND HOME REPAIR ASSISTANCE (MAXIMUM AMOUNTS) (AMENDMENT) (ENGLAND) ORDER 2001, SI 2001 651; made under the Housing Grants, Construction and Regeneration Act 1996 s.76, s.146. In force: April 2, 2001; £1.50.

This Order amends the Disabled Facilities Grants and Home Repair Assistance (Maximum Amounts) Order 1996 (SI 1996 2888) which prescribes the maximum amount of home repair assistance which a local housing authority may give under the Housing Grants, Construction and Regeneration Act 1996 Part I Ch.III. It increases the maximum amount of home repair assistance for one application from £2,000 to £5,000 and revokes Art.5 of the Order which prescribes the maximum amount of home repair assistance payable in respect of the same dwelling, house-boat or mobile home in any period of three years.

3403. Grants – disabled facilities

DISABLED FACILITIES GRANTS AND HOME REPAIR ASSISTANCE (MAXIMUM AMOUNTS) (AMENDMENT NO.2) (ENGLAND) ORDER 2001, SI 2001 4036; made under the Housing Grants, Construction and Regeneration Act 1996 s.33, s.146. In force: January 21, 2002; £1.50.

This Order amends the Disabled Facilities Grants and Home Repair Assistance (Maximum Amounts) Order 1996 (SI 1996 2888) which prescribes the maximum amount of mandatory disabled facilities grant that a housing authority can be required to pay under the Housing Grants, Construction and Regeneration Act 1996. The Order increases the maximum amount from £20,000 to £25,000 for dwellings or buildings in England.

3404. Grants – disabled facilities – Wales

DISABLED FACILITIES GRANTS AND HOME REPAIR ASSISTANCE (MAXIMUM AMOUNTS) (AMENDMENT) (WALES) ORDER 2001, SI 2001 1275 (W.74); made under the Housing Grants, Construction and Regeneration Act 1996 s.76. In force: April 2, 2001; £1.75.

This Order amends the Disabled Facilities Grants and Home Repair Assistance (Maximum Amounts) Order 1996 (SI 1996 2888), which prescribes the maximum amount of home repair assistance which a local housing authority may give under the Housing Grants, Construction and Regeneration Act 1996 Part I Ch.III, by increasing the maximum amount of home repair assistance for one application from £2,000 to £5,000. In addition, Art.5 of the 1996 Order, which prescribes a maximum amount of home repair assistance payable in respect of the same dwelling, house-boat or mobile home in any period of three years, is revoked.

3405. Grants – housing relocation grants – forms

RELOCATION GRANTS (FORM OF APPLICATION) (AMENDMENT) (ENGLAND) REGULATIONS 2001, SI 2001 780; made under the Housing Grants, Construction and Regeneration Act 1996 s.101, s.132, s.146. In force: April 2, 2001; £1.75.

These Regulations, which amend the Form set out in the Schedule to the Relocation Grants (Form of Application) Regulations 1997 (SI 1997 2847) to be used for an application for relocation grant payable under the Housing Grants, Construction and Regeneration Act 1996 s.131 to s.140, are consequential on those being made by the Housing Renewal Grants (Amendment) Regulations 2001 (SI 2001 739) to the Housing Renewal Grants Regulations 1996 (SI 1996 2890).

3406. Grants – housing relocation grants – forms

RELOCATION GRANTS (FORM OF APPLICATION) (AMENDMENT NO.2) (ENGLAND) REGULATIONS 2001, SI 2001 2385; made under the Housing Grants, Construction and Regeneration Act 1996 s.132, s.146. In force: July 27, 2001; £1.50.

These Regulations amend the Form set out in the Schedule to the Relocation Grants (Form of Application) Regulations 1997 (SI 1997 2847) to be used for an application for a relocation grant under the Housing Grants, Construction and Regeneration Act 1996. The Relocation Grants Regulations 1997 (SI 1997 2764) apply the Housing Renewal Grants Regulations 1996 (SI 1996 2890) as they have effect from time to time. Amendments to the 1996 Regulations by the Housing

Renewal Grants (Amendment No.2) (England) Regulations 2001 (SI 2001 2384) have accordingly necessitated amendments to the Relocation Grants (Form of Application) Regulations 1997 (SI 1997 2847), and these Regulations make the necessary amendments.

3407. **Grants – housing relocation grants – forms – Wales**

RELOCATION GRANTS (FORMS OF APPLICATION) (AMENDMENT) (WALES) REGULATIONS 2001, SI 2001 2072 (W.144); made under the Housing Grants, Construction and Regeneration Act 1996 s.101, s.132, s.146. In force: July 1, 2001; £2.00.

These Regulations amend the Relocation Grants (Form of Application) Regulations 1997 (SI 1997 2847) and the Relocation Grants (Form of Application) (Welsh Form of Application) Regulations 1999 (SI 1999 2315). They amend the bilingual forms to be used for an application for relocation grant payable under the Housing Grants, Construction and Regeneration Act 1996 s.131 to s.140 in Wales.

3408. **Grants – housing relocation grants – forms – Wales**

RELOCATION GRANTS (FORMS OF APPLICATION) (AMENDMENT NO.2) (WALES) REGULATIONS 2001, SI 2001 4008 (W.334); made under the Welsh Language Act 1993, s.26; and the Housing Grants, Construction and Regeneration Act 1996 s.132, s.146. In force: January 11, 2002; £1.75.

These Regulations amend the forms to be used by owner-occupiers and tenants when applying for housing renewal grants under the Housing Grants, Construction and Regeneration Act 1996 and amend the English language form set out in the Schedule to the Relocation Grants (Form of Application) Regulations 1997 (SI 1997 2847).

3409. **Grants – housing renewal grants – forms**

HOUSING RENEWAL GRANTS (PRESCRIBED FORM AND PARTICULARS) (AMENDMENT) (ENGLAND) REGULATIONS 2001, SI 2001 789; made under the Housing Grants, Construction and Regeneration Act 1996 s.2, s.101, s.146. In force: April 2, 2001; £1.75.

These Regulations, which amend the Form set out in the Schedule to the Housing Renewal Grants (Prescribed Form and Particulars) Regulations 1996 (SI 1996 2891) to be used by owner occupiers and tenants when applying for housing renewal grants under the Housing Grants, Construction and Regeneration Act 1996 Part I Ch.1, are consequential on those being made by the Housing Renewal Grants (Amendment) Regulations 2001 (SI 2001 739) and the Housing Renewal Grants Regulations 1996 (SI 1996 2890).

3410. **Grants – housing renewal grants – forms**

HOUSING RENEWAL GRANTS (PRESCRIBED FORM AND PARTICULARS) (AMENDMENT NO.2) (ENGLAND) REGULATIONS 2001, SI 2001 2386; made under the Housing Grants, Construction and Regeneration Act 1996 s.2, s.146. In force: July 27, 2001; £1.50.

These Regulations amend the Form set out in the Schedule to the Housing Renewal Grants (Prescribed Form and Particulars) Regulations 1996 (SI 1996 2891) to be used by owner occupiers and tenants when applying for housing renewal grants under the Housing Grants, Construction and Regeneration Act 1996 Part I Ch.I. The amendments are consequential on those being made by the Housing Renewal Grants (Amendment No.2) (England) Regulations 2001 (SI 2001 2384) to the Housing Renewal Grants Regulations 1996 (SI 1996 2890).

3411. Grants – housing renewal grants – forms – Wales

HOUSING RENEWAL GRANTS (AMENDMENT NO.2) (WALES) REGULATIONS 2001, SI 2001 4007 (W.333); made under the Housing Grants, Construction and Regeneration Act 1996 s.30, s.146. In force: January 11, 2002; £2.00.

These Regulations amend the Housing Renewal Grants Regulations 1996 (SI 1996 2890) which set out the means test for determining the amount of renovation grant and disabled facilities grant which may be paid by local housing authorities to owner-occupier and tenant applicants under the Housing Grants, Construction and Regeneration Act 1996 Ch.I

3412. Grants – housing renewal grants – forms – Wales

HOUSING RENEWAL GRANTS (PRESCRIBED FORMS AND PARTICULARS) (AMENDMENT) (WALES) REGULATIONS 2001, SI 2001 2071 (W.143); made under the Housing Grants, Construction and Regeneration Act 1996 s.2, s.101, s.146. In force: July 1, 2001; £2.00.

These Regulations amend the forms to be used by owner-occupiers and tenants when applying for housing renewal grants under the Housing Grants, Construction and Regeneration Act 1996 Part I Ch.I in Wales contained in the Housing Renewal Grants (Prescribed Form and Particulars) (Welsh Form and Particulars) Regulations 1998 (SI 1998 1113) and the Housing Renewal Grants (Prescribed Form and Particulars) Regulations 1996 (SI 1996 2891).

3413. Grants – housing renewal grants – forms – Wales

HOUSING RENEWAL GRANTS (PRESCRIBED FORMS AND PARTICULARS) (AMENDMENT NO.2) (WALES) REGULATIONS 2001, SI 2001 4006 (W.332); made under the Welsh Language Act 1993 s.26; and the Housing Grants, Construction and Regeneration Act 1996 s.2, s.146. In force: January 11, 2002; £1.75.

These Regulations amend the forms to be used by owner-occupiers and tenants when applying for housing renewal grants under the Housing Grants, Construction and Regeneration Act 1996. In addition, the Regulations amend the English language form set out in the Schedule to the Housing Renewal Grants (Prescribed Form and Particulars) Regulations 1996 (SI 1996 2891).

3414. Grants – housing renewal grants – means test

HOUSING RENEWAL GRANTS (AMENDMENT) (ENGLAND) REGULATIONS 2001, SI 2001 739; made under the Housing Grants, Construction and Regeneration Act 1996 s.30, s.146. In force: April 2, 2001; £2.50.

These Regulations, which amend the Housing Renewal Grants Regulations 1996 (SI 1996 2890), make changes to the means test for determining the amount of renovation grant and disabled facilities grant which may be paid by local housing authorities in respect of applications by owner-occupiers and tenants, under Housing Grants, Construction and Regeneration Act 1996 Part I Ch.1. They remove doubt as to whether persons with whom children or young persons have been placed for fostering may be treated as responsible for them for the purposes of grant applications, increase the "applicable amount" of income that can be received without reduction in grant, provide that working families' tax credit and disabled person's tax credit can be taken into account in calculating the amount of allowable child-care charges for the purposes of the means test and ensure that participants in approved work, such as work trials or work placements, are not treated as being in paid employment for the purposes of the means test. They provide for special rules to be applied to subsistence allowances and discretionary payments made to participants in employment zone programmes established pursuant to the Welfare Reform and Pensions Act 1999 s.60 and increase the threshold at which capital is treated as generating a notional income from £5,000 to £6,000.

3415. Grants – housing renewal grants – means test

HOUSING RENEWAL GRANTS (AMENDMENT NO.2) (FNGLAND) REGULATIONS 2001, SI 2001 2384; made under the Housing Grants, Construction and Regeneration Act 1996 s.30, s.146. In force: July 6, 2001; £1.75.

These Regulations amend the Housing Renewal Grants Regulations 1996 (SI 1996 2890) which set out the means test for determining the amount of renovation grant and disabled facilities grant which may be paid by local housing authorities to owner occupier and tenant applicants under the Housing Grants, Construction and Regeneration Act 1996 Part I Ch.I which are consequential on changes to the Housing Benefit (General) Regulations 1987 (SI 1987 1971) upon which the means test is based.

3416. Grants – housing renewal grants – means test – Wales

HOUSING RENEWAL GRANTS (AMENDMENT) (WALES) REGULATIONS 2001, SI 2001 2073 (W.145); made under the Housing Grants, Construction and Regeneration Act 1996 s.30, s.146. In force: July 1, 2001; £3.00.

These Regulations, which amend the Housing Renewal Grants Regulations 1996 (SI 1996 2890), make changes to the means test for determining the amount of renovation grant and disabled facilities grant which may be paid by local housing authorities in respect of applications by owner-occupiers and tenants, under the Housing Grants, Construction and Regeneration Act 1996 consequential on changes to the Housing Benefit (General) Regulations 1987 (SI 1987 1971) upon which the means test is based.

3417. Grants – housing renovation grants – Wales

HOUSING GRANTS (ADDITIONAL PURPOSES) (WALES) ORDER 2001, SI 2001 2070 (W.142); made under the Housing Grants, Construction and Regeneration Act 1996 s.12, s.17, s.27, s.146. In force: July 1, 2001; £1.75.

This Order provides that the improvement of energy efficiency shall be an additional purpose for which a grant under the Housing Grants, Construction and Regeneration Act 1996 s.12 (renovation grants), s.17 (common parts grants) and s.27 (HMO grants) may be given.

3418. Grants – ownership – equitable interests in land – existence of owner's interest under rental purchase agreement

[Housing Grants, Construction and Regeneration Act 1996 s.101.]

A couple, P, who had applied to their local authority, BMBC, for a disabled facilities grant pursuant to the Housing Grants, Construction and Regeneration Act 1996, sought judicial review of BMBC's decision that they did not have an "owner's interest", as defined in s.101 of the Act, in their home. They argued that they could lay claim to an "owner's interest" if they could establish that they had an equitable interest in their home, and that the rental purchase agreement under which occupied their home gave them such an interest. BMBC argued that rental purchasers could not acquire an "owner's interest" since (1) their possession, whether as licensees or as tenants at will, was precarious; (2) they were not entitled to complete the purchase until the purchase price was paid in full; (3) until completion, their rights were limited to possession of the property, and (4) they were not entitled to apply for specific performance until the rental payments due under the contract had been paid in full.

Held, granting the application for judicial review, that an equitable interest in property was capable of constituting an "owner's interest", *R. v. Tower Hamlets LBC, ex p. Von Goetz* [1999] Q.B. 1019, [1998] C.L.Y. 3050 followed. P had such an interest in their property. The position of a rental purchaser was no less precarious than that of any other kind of purchaser who had not paid the purchase price in full, and in not being entitled to complete until the purchase price was paid in full, the rental purchaser was in no different a position to that of a purchaser under a contract for the sale of land. The terms of the agreement, which included a clause that prohibited P from disposing of or charging the property, showed that in principle the rights of P went beyond mere possession. Furthermore, a party could seek specific performance as soon as contracts had been exchanged, and could do so even though he still had contractual obligations to perform, *Hasham v. Zenab (Executrix of Harji)* [1960] A.C. 316, [1960] C.L.Y. 3282 and *Marks v. Lilley* [1959] 1 W.L.R. 749, [1959] C.L.Y. 3409 applied.

R. v. BRADFORD MBC, *ex p.* PICKERING (2001) 33 H.L.R. 38, Munby, J., QBD.

3419. Homelessness – accommodation – ability of interim accommodation to establish local connection

[Housing Act 1996 s.198, s.199(1)(a).]

HFLBC appealed against a decision ([2001] Q.B. 97, [2000] C.L.Y. 3129) that it was under a duty to provide accommodation for M and his wife. The Court of Appeal had ordered a fresh review of M's application for accommodation consequent to a finding that M and his wife's interim accommodation, allocated pending a decision on their joint application for accommodation, was to be regarded as their normal residence and was sufficient to establish a local connection, notwithstanding M's wife's prior residency in another local authority area. HFLBC contended that the occupation of interim accommodation pending a homelessness application did not qualify as normal residence for the purpose of the Housing Act 1996 s.199(1)(a) and it was entitled under s.198 to refer the application as no local connection had been established.

Held, dismissing the appeal, that the occupation of interim accommodation qualified as M's place of normal residence and was sufficient to establish a local connection. The correct date for determining the existence of a local connection was the date of the decision or review and not the date of the application itself. However in assessing the merits of an application, a reviewing officer could have regard both to material relevant to the period before the initial decision had been made which had come to light only after the initial decision and to matters arising thereafter.

MOHAMED v. HAMMERSMITH AND FULHAM LBC; EALING LBC v. SURDONJA; *sub nom.* MOHAMMED v. HAMMERSMITH AND FULHAM LBC; SURDONJA v. EALING LBC, [2001] UKHL 57, [2001] 3 W.L.R. 1339, Lord Slynn of Hadley, HL.

3420. Homelessness – accommodation – priority need – Wales

HOMELESS PERSONS (PRIORITY NEED) (WALES) ORDER 2001, SI 2001 607 (W.30); made under the Housing Act 1996 s.189. In force: March 1, 2001; £2.00.

Under the Housing Act 1996, local housing authorities have a duty to provide accommodation to those who are homeless, eligible for assistance, and in priority need. The Act sets out descriptions for persons in priority need and also gives the National Assembly for Wales power to specify further descriptions. This Order specifies further descriptions of persons having priority need. These categories are a care leaver or person at particular risk of sexual or financial exploitation, 18 years or over but under the age of 21, a 16 or 17 year old, a person fleeing domestic or threatened domestic violence, a person homeless after leaving the armed forces and a former prisoner homeless after being released from custody.

3421. Homelessness – asylum seekers – temporary admission – eligibility – applicability of international convention

[Immigration and Asylum Act 1971 s.11 (1); Housing Act 1996 Part 7; Immigration and Asylum Act 1999 s.115; Homeless (England) Regulations 2000 (SI 2000 701) Reg.3 Class E; European Convention on Social and Medical Assistance 1953.]

K, a Turkish Kurd, appealed against a decision that she was not entitled to accommodation as a homeless person under the Housing Act 1996 Part 7. K had been granted temporary admission to the United Kingdom pending the outcome of her application for asylum. She claimed that as Turkey was a signatory to the European Convention on Social and Medical Assistance 1953, she came within the provisions of Part 7 of the 1996 Act by virtue of the Homeless (England) Regulations 2000Class E. At first instance it was held that K was excluded from the provisions of the 1996 Act as those to whom the Convention applied were excluded persons by virtue of the Immigration and Asylum Act 1999 s.115. K argued that the Convention had to be given a purposive construction according to international law and as such it should override national provisions.

Held, dismissing the appeal, that K did not qualify under the 1996 Act. In order to come within Reg.3 Class E of the Regulations she had to be "lawfully present" within the UK. Under the Immigration Act 1971 s.11 (1) a person granted temporary admission was treated as though he or she had not entered the UK, and therefore could not be "lawfully present", *Bugdaycay v. Secretary of State for the Home Department* [1987] A.C. 514, [1987] C.L.Y. 1989 applied. The UK courts had to apply and interpret international law, and having done so, the normal rules of precedence applied, *R. (on the application of Bright) v. Central Criminal Court* [2001] 1 W.L.R. 662, [2000] 9 C.L. 138 approved.

KAYA v. HARINGEY LBC, [2001] EWCA Civ 677, [2002] H.L.R. 1, Buxton, L.J., CA.

3422. Homelessness – harassment – lack of priority need – local housing authority required to provide housing to allow for police protection

[Housing Act 1996 s.188(3), s.189(1) (c).]

Following his acquittal on charges of indecent assault, G obtained hostel accommodation in London, but when the local newspaper labelled him a paedophile the hostel terminated his right of occupation. G applied to T on the basis that he was homeless and was told that he did not have a priority need in accordance with the Housing Act 1996 s.189(1) (c). T did however secure hostel accommodation for him in the Midlands but within days of him moving in, the press arrived outside the hostel and the landlord terminated his right of occupation. G returned to London and slept rough. T declined to house G pending the outcome of his statutory review under s.188(3), contending that vulnerability could only arise if the securing of the accommodation could lessen that vulnerability. T's case was that the harassment of G would not be lessened if it housed him and that his circumstances could not therefore give rise to a finding of vulnerability in accordance with s.189(1) (c).

Held, finding in favour of G, that T's argument raised a serious issue that needed to be tried. Having regard to the balance of convenience, T was ordered to house G so that the police could protect him from harassment, which it was difficult for them to do whilst he slept on the streets.

R. v. TOWER HAMLETS LBC, *ex p.* G, August 18, 2000, Judge Newman, QBD. [*Ex rel.* Jon Holbrook, Barrister, 2 Garden court, London].

3423. Homelessness – intentional homelessness – domestic violence – reasonableness of continued occupation

[Housing Act 1996 s.177(1).]

B appealed against the dismissal of her appeal against LCC's decision that she was intentionally homeless. She had left her accommodation after suffering violence and intimidation at the hands of the father of her two young children. LCC maintained that B had deliberately ceased to occupy a property which was available for her occupation and which it was reasonable for her to continue to occupy. In assessing the reasonableness of B's decision to leave the accommodation, the judge had found that LCC was entitled to expect B to secure her own protection through the pursuit of civil or criminal action against her former partner. In response, B maintained that LCC had erred in law as the Housing Act 1996 s.177(1) precluded wider considerations of reasonableness in domestic violence cases.

Held, allowing the appeal, that in situations involving domestic violence, the sole test in determining whether an individual was intentionally homeless was the probability of the occurrence of violence given continued occupation of the property. The issue was one of fact and did not allow for value judgments on an individual's approach to any expected course of action.

BOND v. LEICESTER CITY COUNCIL, [2001] EWCA Civ 1544, [2002] 1 F.C.R. 566, Hale, L.J., CA.

3424. Homelessness – intentional homelessness – local authorities powers and duties – obligation to make proper enquiries

[Housing Act 1996 s.184.]

E appealed against the quashing by the county court of E's finding that K, a Kurdish refugee, had made himself and his family intentionally homeless. E contended that it had not failed in its statutory duty under the Housing Act 1996 s.184 to make proper enquiries by not obtaining more information concerning the claim that K's wife was suffering from depression as a result of being separated from a Turkish community, before concluding that it was not under a duty to provide housing for K, but, that it had, in the circumstances, made all reasonable enquiries and moreover had invited K to make further representations.

Held, allowing the appeal, that EBLC had complied with its statutory duty and that it was reasonable for the local authority to have come to the conclusion that it had.

KACAR v. ENFIELD LBC (2001) 33 H.L.R. 5, Beldam, L.J., CA.

3425. Homelessness – intentional homelessness – settled accommodation – failure of local housing authority to make adequate inquiries

[Housing Act 1996 s.204(3); Human Rights Act 1998 Sch.1 Part I Art.6(1).]

M appealed against a review decision of the local a housing authority. M, and subsequently one of his children, moved in with his parents when his wife excluded him from the matrimonial home. He stayed there for three and a half years until his parents sold their house and emigrated. M applied as homeless under the Housing Act 1996 Part VII. The local housing authority, W, found M's homelessness to have been caused by intentional acts, namely extra marital affairs and criminal behaviour, that resulted in his exclusion from the matrimonial home. On appeal, M argued that his current homelessness was caused by the loss of settled accommodation, being his parents' house, through no fault of his own. In their review decision, W stated that the parents' house had not constituted settled accommodation because it comprised one bedroom and had not been big enough for M and his mother. In a witness statement the reviewing officer said that he had actually considered the parents' house to have been comprised of two bedrooms occupied by five adults and a child.

Held, allowing the appeal and quashing the review decision, that the witness statement should be disregarded because, rather than elucidate the basis for the review decision, it fundamentally altered it, *R. v. Westminster City Council, ex p. Ermakov* [1996] 2 All E.R. 302, [1995] C.L.Y. 2568 applied. W had made inadequate inquiries into the issue of settled accommodation. Further, although W had determined M's civil rights, the court would not rely on the Human Rights Act 1998 Sch.1 Part I Art.6(1) and *Albert v. Belgium* (1983) 5 E.H.R.R. 533 to vary W's decision under s.204(3) of the 1996 Act to the extent of finding M unintentionally homeless. It would be wrong to do this having found that W had not made adequate inquiries into the facts.

MELIM v. CITY OF WESTMINSTER, November 23, 2000, Judge Roger Cooke, CC (Central London). [*Ex rel.* Jon Holbrook, Barrister, 2 Garden Court, Middle Temple, London].

3426. Homelessness – legitimate expectation – assurance of accommodation with security of tenure – requirement for detrimental reliance

NLBC appealed against a ruling that it was obliged to comply with an assurance previously given to B that he and his family would be provided with accommodation possessing security of tenure. NLBC had given the assurance in the erroneous belief that it was obliged to provide security of tenure to refugee applicants who were accepted to be homeless. The court at first instance held that the assurance gave rise to a legitimate expectation with which NLBC were bound to comply. NLBC contended that in such a situation it would only be obliged to comply with such an assurance if the reason for non compliance was improper or, in the alternative, if the recipient had relied upon the assurances given to his detriment.

Held, allowing the appeal in part, that detriment was not a prerequisite to enforcement, *R. v. Secretary of State for Education and Employment, ex p. B (A Minor)* [2000] 1 W.L.R. 1115, [1999] C.L.Y. 1704 applied. In the instant case although there had been no detriment, NLBC had nevertheless been obliged to take B's legitimate expectation into account when exercising its discretion to allocate its housing stock. On the basis that a decision concerning the precise allocation of housing was the preserve of the authority, the declaration previously granted was set aside and replaced with a declaration that NLBC was bound to take the expectation into account when taking a decision upon allocation.

R. (ON THE APPLICATION OF BIBI) v. NEWHAM LBC; R. (ON THE APPLICATION OF AL-NASHED) v. NEWHAM LBC; *sub nom.* R. v. NEWHAM LBC, *ex p.* BIBI; R. v. NEWHAM LBC, *ex p.* AL-NASHED, [2001] EWCA Civ 607, [2002] 1 W.L.R. 237, Schiemann, L.J., CA.

3427. Homelessness – priority needs – spouse as dependant child – right to family life

[Housing Act 1996 s.189; Human Rights Act 1998 Sch.1 Part I Art.8(1).]

The local authority appealed against a decision that E had a priority need for the purposes of the Housing Act 1996 s.189 by reason of his marriage to a 17 year old. E had successfully contended that his wife, who was in full time education, was a dependant child who might reasonably be expected to reside with him within the meaning of s.189(1)(b). The local authority submitted that E's relationship with his wife did not satisfy the requirements of s.189(1)(b) since that subsection applied only to a parent/child relationship.

Held, allowing the appeal, that E's wife was not a dependant child for the purposes of s.189(1)(b) as that subsection concerned a parent/child relationship and did not cover a dependant spouse. E's wife was capable of being a dependant child in respect of her parents but not in respect of E. Further, the determination that E did not have a priority need did not contravene the Human Rights Act 1998 Sch.1 Part I Art.8(1).

EKINCI v. HACKNEY LBC; *sub nom.* HACKNEY LBC v. EKINCI, [2001] EWCA Civ 776, [2002] H.L.R. 2, Pill, L.J., CA.

3428. Homelessness – temporary accommodation – criteria for determining suitability

[Housing Act 1988 s.5; Housing Act 1996 s.188; County Court Rules 1981 (SI 1981 1687) Ord.26 r.17; Civil Procedure Rules 1998 (SI 1998 3132).]

NLBC appealed against a decision ([2000] C.O.D. 133) that its policy on the allocation of temporary accommodation was flawed and that its duty to provide temporary accommodation arose when the order for possession of a property was made. S, a single parent with five children, one of whom had been receiving ongoing treatment at a local hospital, was evicted from her home and, as a homeless person, sought assistance from NLBC. Applying its usual policy on the allocation of temporary accommodation, NLBC concluded that there was no "serious reason" why S could not be accommodated outside its area and allocated her and her children bed and breakfast accommodation in a different county. NLBC defined "serious reasons" as a serious risk to life or health if an applicant and his family were accommodated outside the borough or outside London. S, in applying for judicial review of NLBC's decision, had argued that the accommodation allocated to her was unsuitable.

Held, allowing the appeal in part, that (1) when determining whether temporary accommodation provided to a homeless person under the Housing Act 1996 s.188 was suitable, it was necessary to assess all the characteristics of the accommodation against the background of the needs of the homeless person and his family. It followed that the location of that accommodation would be a relevant factor. In the instant case, NLBC had failed to consider the needs of S and her children, and (2) a person became homeless within the meaning of the 1996 Act only when the warrant for possession of his property was executed, since the County Court Rules 1981 Ord.26 r.17, which had been incorporated into the Civil Procedure Rules 1998, and the Housing Act 1988 s.5 operated so as to prevent a landlord from recovering possession of a property until that had occurred.

R. (ON THE APPLICATION OF SACUPIMA) v. NEWHAM LBC; *sub nom.* R. v. NEWHAM LBC, *ex p.* SACUPIMA [2001] 1 W.L.R. 563, Latham, L.J., CA.

3429. Housing Act 1996 (c.52) – Commencement No.13 Order

HOUSING ACT 1996 (COMMENCEMENT NO.13) ORDER 2001, SI 2001 3164 (C.100); made under the Housing Act 1996 s.232. Commencement details: bringing into force various provisions of the 1996 Act on October 15, 2001; £1.50.

This Order, which brings into operation provisions of the Housing Act 1996 which are not already in force, allows an applicant to apply to the court for a warrant for arrest of a person in breach of an injunction made by virtue of the Housing Act 1996 s.152(6) or s.153 where a power of arrest could have been, but was not attached, and enables a court to remand a person arrested for breach of an injunction.

3430. Housing benefit – rent officers – functions

RENT OFFICERS (HOUSING BENEFIT FUNCTIONS) (AMENDMENT) ORDER 2001, SI 2001 1325; made under the Housing Act 1996 s.122. In force: July 2, 2001; £1.50.

This Order amends the Rent Officers (Housing Benefit Functions) Order 1997 (SI 1997 1984) which confers functions on rent officers, in connection with housing benefit and rent allowance subsidy, and requires them to make determinations and redeterminations in respect of tenancies and licences of dwellings, it extends the relevant criteria that a rent officer must have regard to when determining a single room rent.

3431. Housing benefit – rent officers – functions

RENT OFFICERS (HOUSING BENEFIT FUNCTIONS) (AMENDMENT) ORDER 2001, SI 2001 3561; made under the Housing Act 1996 s.122. In force: November 6, 2001; £1.75.

This Order amends the Rent Officers (Housing Benefit Functions) Order 1997 (SI 1997 1984) and the Rent Officers (Housing Benefit Functions) (Scotland) Order 1997 (SI 1997 1995) which confer functions on rent officers in connection with housing benefit and rent allowance subsidy and require them to make determination in respect of tenancies and licences of dwellings.

3432. Housing benefit – rent officers – functions

RENT OFFICERS (HOUSING BENEFIT FUNCTIONS) (AMENDMENT) (NO.2) ORDER 2001, SI 2001 2317; made under the Housing Act 1996 s.122. In force: July 2, 2001; £1.50.

This Order amends the Rent Officers (Housing Benefit Functions) Order 1997 (SI 1997 1984) which confers functions on rent officers, in connection with housing benefit and rent allowance subsidy, and requires them to make determinations and redeterminations in respect of tenancies and licences of dwellings.

3434. **Local authority housing – children – obligation to provide accommodation suited to needs of disabled child**

[Children Act 1989 s.17.]

A appealed against the refusal of her application for judicial review ([2001] EWHC Admin 376) whereby she sought to compel LBC to provide accommodation suited to the needs of her disabled children. A had three children, two of whom were autistic and had severe learning difficulties. The family resided in a two bedroomed flat with no outside area for the children to play in. An application for a housing transfer resulted in A being awarded "overriding priority" by LBC. Subsequent assessments carried out pursuant to the Children Act 1989 s.17 in relation to A's disabled children identified a need for appropriate accommodation in which they could reside together with A, and their sibling, as a family unit. A contended that s.17(1) imposed a duty on the local authority, enforceable by judicial review, to provide accommodation to meet the assessed needs of her children. The judge had concluded that whilst the local authority possessed the power under s.17(3) and s.17(6) to provide accommodation for the whole family, the duty owed was a general one and not amenable to judicial review.

Held, dismissing the appeal, that in circumstances where a local authority was not obliged to provide residential accommodation to meet the needs of a particular child or children under Part III of the Act or the Housing Acts, it could not be obliged to do so by virtue of s.17 of the Act. Section 17 was not concerned with the provision of accommodation. It could not have been the intention of Parliament to undermine the structure and regime of the Housing legislation by permitting s.17 to override the existing obligation for provision of accommodation in certain specified circumstances.

R. (ON THE APPLICATION OF A) v. LAMBETH LBC; *sub nom.* A v. LAMBETH LBC, [2001] EWCA Civ 1624, [2002] 1 F.L.R. 353, Laws, L.J., CA.

3435. **Local authority housing – introductory tenancies – right to review – compatibility with Convention rights**

[Housing Act 1996 Part V Chapter 1; Human Rights Act 1998 s.4, Sch.1 Part I Art.6, Sch.1 Part I Art.8.]

J, who had been served by the local housing authority, B, with a notice of possession in respect of her introductory tenancy, applied for a declaration pursuant to the Human Rights Act 1998 s.4 that the regime of introductory tenancies provided for by the Housing Act 1996 Part V Chapter 1 was incompatible with certain Convention rights listed under Sch.1 Part I of the 1998 Act. J contended that (1) the regime contravened Art.6 on the basis that the right to review operated by B once a notice of possession had been served did not constitute a hearing by an independent and impartial tribunal and that the power to seek judicial review of any decision reached on review was insufficient protection, and (2) the arrangement fell foul of Art.8 since the right to respect for one's home carried with it protection against eviction other than in accordance with due process of law. The notice of possession having been withdrawn, the court was left to deal with the incompatibility issue.

Held, refusing the declaration, that (1) the review process was not inherently unfair since the reviewing officer was in a position analogous to that of an inspector charged with the determination of planning cases and the scope of the power to judicially review decisions taken by B was adequate, and (2) the extent of the interference with the right to respect for one's home was relevant, sufficient and corresponded to a pressing social need. It was also proportionate and accordingly satisfied all the requirements pursuant to Art.8.

R. (ON THE APPLICATION OF JOHNS) v. BRACKNELL FOREST BC; *sub nom.* R. (ON THE APPLICATION OF JOHNS) v. BRACKNELL FOREST DC (2001) 33 H.L.R. 45, Longmore, J., QBD (Admin Ct).

3436. **Local authority housing – offer and acceptance – suitability of accommodation – discharge of duty – availability of review**

[Housing Act 1996 s.193(3), s.193(5), s.202.]

WCC appealed against the quashing, on the ground of unreasonableness, of its decision that it had discharged its duty to A, who was homeless, under the Housing Act 1996 s.193(3) by offering her temporary accommodation pursuant to s.193(5) and by indicating that it was satisfied that the accommodation was suitable. Her solicitors had written to WCC stating that she had compelling reasons for turning down the accommodation that had been offered. A subsequent review under s.202 had upheld WCC's decision. A relied on *R. v. Kensington and Chelsea RLBC, ex p. Byfield* (1999) 31 H.L.R. 913, [2000] 4 C.L. 344 to contend that had she known she could accept the offer of accommodation and request a review, she would have done so.

Held, allowing the appeal, that since under s.193(5) accommodation could not be offered unless the local authority were satisfied as to its suitability, this should be made clear in the offer. A subsequent refusal by the person to whom the accommodation had been offered discharged the authority's housing duty. For a housing applicant to accept accommodation but then apply for a review on the ground of unsuitability defeated the purpose of s.193(5), which was to enable a local authority to make a single offer of accommodation. Therefore, a review of an offer of accommodation made pursuant to s.193(5) could not be requested once the offer had been accepted, *Byfield* overruled.

ALGHILE v. WESTMINSTER CITY COUNCIL, [2001] EWCA Civ 363, (2001) 33 H.L.R. 57, Tuckey, L.J., CA.

3437. **Multiple occupation – grants – occupation of part of premises by connected person**

[Local Government and Housing Act 1989 s.106(7), s.101(2)(a), s.122(2).]

BLBC appealed against a decision that P, a brother and sister, were not required to repay a housing in multiple occupation grant notwithstanding that a part of the premises forming the subject of the grant had been occupied by the sister within five years of the date of grant. In the grant application P had certified, in accordance with the Local Government and Housing Act 1989 s.106(7), their intention to let part of the house as a residential tenancy to a person who was not a family member. BLBC contended that P had breached a condition of the grant by allowing the sister into occupation of part of the premises within five years of the date of grant in contravention of the s.122(2) of the Act and claimed for the repayment of the grant together with compound interest.

Held, allowing the appeal, that the grant was to be repaid. The grant had been made subject to conditions concerning future occupation of the premises as specified by s.122, which required the premises to be residentially occupied, or available for residential occupation, whether pursuant to a tenancy or a licence, by persons unconnected with P for a period of five years from the initial date of the grant. The occupation by the sister, albeit on a temporary basis and in respect of part of the premises, meant that P had failed to comply with the conditions. It was a requirement of s.122(2) that the whole of the premises must be in or available for residential occupation. The court observed that had P applied for a renovation grant pursuant to s.101(2)(a) of the Act, the grant would have been unaffected by the sister's subsequent occupation of the property.

BRENT LBC v. PATEL [2001] 1 W.L.R. 897, Patten, J., Ch D.

3438. **Possession orders – domestic violence – violence or threat of violence as ground for possession**

[Housing Act 1985 Sch.2 Ground 2A.]

MM continued to occupy a council flat as a secure tenant following the breakdown of his marriage to SM, who had left to live elsewhere. CLBC served a notice seeking possession pursuant to the Housing Act 1985 Sch.2 Ground 2A on the basis that the flat had been occupied by a married couple and one partner had left "because of violence or threats of violence by the other". The case was decided in MM's favour. CLBC appealed, contending that the judge had erred in his interpretation of what was meant by "because of violence or threats of violence". CLBC argued that Ground 2A could be relied on if violence or threats thereof had been only one of a number of causes of the departure of one partner.

Held, dismissing the appeal, that the language of Ground 2A indicated that it was not sufficient for violence to feature as one factor amongst several causes of the departure of one partner, and that the judge had been correct to conclude that violence or threats thereof had to be the real and effective reason for the decision of the partner to leave.

CAMDEN LBC v. MALLETT (2001) 33 H.L.R. 20, Ferris, J., CA.

3439. Possession orders – legal representation – adjournment pending grant of legal aid – right to fair trial

B appealed against an order for possession granted in relation to her council tenancy for alleged noise nuisance. B had submitted an application for legal aid which had not been granted in time for the hearings before the district judge and had accordingly been unrepresented. B contended that the district judge had erred in refusing her request for an adjournment at the preliminary hearing and at the final hearing in view of the fact that her application for legal aid was still being processed and that consequently she had been denied her right to a fair trial.

Held, allowing the appeal and remitting the case for retrial, that given the fact that legal aid was in principle available for housing possession cases, together with the emotional nature of the proceedings and the potential benefits to be gained from legal representation, the judge had been wrong to refuse the request for an adjournment, *Airey v. Ireland (No.1) (A/32)* (1979-80) 2 E.H.R.R. 305 and *Lloyds Bank Plc v. Dix* (Unreported, October 26, 2000) considered.

BATES v. CROYDON LBC, [2001] EWCA Civ 134, [2001] C.P. Rep. 70, Mance, L.J., CA.

3440. Possession orders – suspension – neighbour harassment – availability of injunction

CCC appealed against a ruling granting its application for possession of one of its properties occupied by L, but suspending that order and granting an injunction. The recorder had found that allegations of neighbour harassment had been proven to the requisite standard but had taken the decision to suspend the order on the basis that an injunction order would provide an adequate remedy. CCC submitted that the judge had wrongly balanced the reasonableness of an order for possession against the availability of a potential alternative remedy.

Held, allowing the appeal, that while the recorder had been entitled to take the availability of an injunction into account as one of the relevant factors, her subsequent decision to suspend the possession order was inappropriate and inconsistent with her other findings. In the instant case, it had been found that L and her partner were unlikely to be deterred from committing acts of harassment while on bail and that the effect of the harassment on L's neighbours had been significant.

CANTERBURY CITY COUNCIL v. LOWE (2001) 33 H.L.R. 53, Kay, L.J., CA.

3441. Rehousing – compulsory purchase – extent of compensation payable to protected tenant

A occupied a ground floor flat as a protected tenant for 13 years. The flat had become unfit for human habitation and a closing order was served on the landlord in July 1994. Notices to quit were served by the landlord. In September 1994 WBC, the borough council, offered council rented accommodation of a ground floor flat or a shared ownership scheme. In May 1995 WBC was advised that the landlord had obtained possession orders and offered A a first floor flat, available from June. A viewed the property in July after she had moved into temporary accommodation.

She then moved into the flat in late July. A home loss payment was made to A together with compensation for various agreed items of loss but disputed heads of claim remained. These were (1) kennelling costs for A's dog which was arthritic and which could not move with her into the new first floor flat and so had been housed in with a friend and then in kennels until it died; (2) loss of garden equipment which had been taken and for which A had been paid £50; (3) the costs of temporary accommodation; (4) the loss made by A on the sale of her car which she had to sell in a hurry to raise money to pay for the temporary accommodation; (5) loss of a cooker and refrigerator which had been provided with the old flat but which was not included in the new flat; (6) increased travel costs; (7) loss of a garage so that her car had to be parked on the road where it sustained damage, and (8) disbursements, expenses and interest on loans. WBC offered £400 but A sought about £4,720.

Held, giving judgment for A but awarding WBC's offered amount of £400, that (1) although kennelling costs were not necessarily too remote her claim failed because she had failed to mitigate her losses by accepting the earlier offer from WBC of ground floor accommodation and had left the matter of alternative accommodation until the last minute; (2) A's claim for the loss of garden equipment failed because she had already received money for the garden equipment and could not be paid twice for that; (3) there was no award for temporary accommodation as WBC had acted swiftly when A's need arose and if A had acted promptly there would have been no need for temporary accommodation; (4) A's claim for the loss on the sale of the car failed too. The claims for the cooker and fridge were justified but the amount offered as being too remote and was not a natural consequence of the dispossession; (5) A's claim for the cost of replacing her cooker and fridge was justified but in the absence of any evidence as to cost WBC's offer of £250 was considered reasonable; (6) any extra travel costs were offset by the greater proximity of the new accommodation to the local facilities and A's claim failed; (7) A's claim for damage to her car failed as being unproven and too remote, and (8) A's claim for sundry expenses had been fairly valued by the council at £150. The claim for interest was too remote.

ADAM v. WOKING BC [2000] R.V.R. 329, PR Francis FRICS, Lands Tr.

3442. Right to buy – approved lending institutions

HOUSING (RIGHT TO BUY) (PRIORITY OF CHARGES) (ENGLAND) ORDER 2001, SI 2001 205; made under the Housing Act 1985 s.156. In force: February 19, 2001; £1.50.

This Order specifies two bodies as approved lending institutions for the purposes of the Housing Act 1985 s.156. The bodies thereby also become approved lending institutions for the purposes of s.36 of the 1985 Act and the Housing Act 1996 s.12.

3443. Right to buy – approved lending institutions

HOUSING (RIGHT TO BUY) (PRIORITY OF CHARGES) (ENGLAND) (NO.2) ORDER 2001, SI 2001 3219; made under the Housing Act 1985 s.156. In force: October 15, 2001; £1.50.

This Order specifies six bodies as approved lending institutions for the purposes of the Housing Act 1985 s.156.

3444. Right to buy – approved lending institutions

HOUSING (RIGHT TO BUY) (PRIORITY OF CHARGES) (ENGLAND) (NO.3) ORDER 2001, SI 2001 3874; made under the Housing Act 1985 s.156. In force: December 21, 2001; £1.50.

This Order specifies E-Mex Home Funding Limited as an approved lending institution for the purposes of the Housing Act 1985 s.156 (priority of charges on disposals under the right to buy), in addition to the bodies already specified in that section or in previous Orders. The Company thereby also becomes an approved lending institution for the purposes of s.36 of the 1985 Act (priority of charges on voluntary disposals by local authorities) and the Housing Act 1996 s.12 (priority of charges on voluntary disposals by registered social landlords).

3445. Right to buy – approved lending institutions – Wales

HOUSING (RIGHT TO BUY) (PRIORITY OF CHARGES) (WALES) ORDER 2001, SI 2001 1786 (W.127); made under the Housing Act 1985 s.156. In force: June 1, 2001; £2.00.

This Order specifies two bodies as approved lending institutions for the purposes of the Housing Act 1985 s.156.

3446. Right to buy – electronic communications

HOUSING (RIGHT TO ACQUIRE) (ELECTRONIC COMMUNICATIONS) (ENGLAND) ORDER 2001, SI 2001 3257; made under the Electronic Communications Act 2000 s.8. In force: October 24, 2001; £1.50.

This Order, which amends the Housing Act 1996, provides that the Housing Corporation may use electronic communications to notify a registered social landlord in England that a dwelling is to be regarded as provided by means of a grant.

3447. Right to buy – local authority breach of duty – failure to notify defect – measure of damages

[Housing Act 1985 s.528(1), s.563(1).]

B appealed against an award of damages arising from NBC's sale to her under the right to buy scheme of a defective property. B had purchased the property in 1988 for £10,250, receiving a 59 per cent discount on the market value in line with the scheme. It subsequently came to light that the house was defective because of a design fault, as provided for by the Housing Act 1985 s.528(1). NBC conceded that it had failed in its duty under s.563(1) to inform B of that fact prior to the purchase. B was awarded £6,765 in damages, being the difference between the long term value of the house, assessed at £3,485, and the actual purchase price.

Held, dismissing the appeal, that the judge had taken the right approach to damages. NBC's duty had been to inform B of the defect, and the breach of that duty had not been the cause of the defect. If NBC had not been in breach, B could have decided either not to purchase the house or to have purchased it at a reduced price, an outcome which had been appropriately reflected in the way damages had been calculated at first instance, *Perry v. Sidney Phillips & Son* [1982] 1 W.L.R. 1297, [1982] C.L.Y. 2164 applied.

BERRY v. NEWPORT BC (2001) 33 H.L.R. 19, Roch, L.J., CA.

3448. Right to buy – notices – notice to complete – relevant outstanding matter – change of purchaser

[Housing Act 1985 s.122, s.140, s.140(b), s.141.]

BLBC appealed against a decision that S had complied with a notice served by BLBC under the Housing Act 1985 s.140 in relation to S's application to buy the property of which she was a tenant. In April 1995 S had given notice under s.122 of her wish to buy, and had nominated her daughter A as co-purchaser. BLBC subsequently served a notice to complete under s.140. Within the 56 day time limit S responded to the notice by writing to BLBC informing them that she wished A's name to be removed from the application. BLBC argued that the correspondence did not constitute notice of "relevant outstanding matters" as set out in s.140(1)(b) and that S had therefore failed to respond to the completion notice and had lost her right to buy.

Held, dismissing the appeal, that the written notice given by S had constituted a "relevant outstanding matter" under s.140(b) of the Act and accordingly BLBC's serving of final notice under s.141 was invalid until that outstanding matter had been determined. The fax did not amount to a refusal by S to complete the purchase, but rather a refusal to complete the purchase jointly with her daughter. It followed that since S was entitled, upon receiving the consent of her daughter, to remove her from the right to buy application, such removal should be interpreted as a "relevant outstanding matter". Following acceptance by BLBC of the change of name, the time for S to complete the transaction pursuant to the original s.140 notice would start to run again.

BRENT LBC v. SEBANJOR; *sub nom.* SEBANJOR v. BRENT LBC; SENBANJO v. BRENT [2001] 1 W.L.R. 2374, Pumfrey, J., Ch D.

3449. Right to buy – rate of discount

HOUSING (RIGHT TO ACQUIRE) (DISCOUNT) ORDER 2001, SI 2001 1501; made under the Housing Act 1996 s.17. In force: May 18, 2001; £2.00.

This Order, which revokes the Housing (Right to Acquire) (Discount) Order 2000 (SI 2000 1622), specifies for local authority areas in England the amount of discount for the purposes of the Housing Act 1996 s.16 and s.17 that is available to tenants of registered social landlords who have a right to acquire their homes. The amount of the discount varies according to the area in which the dwelling is situated. In addition, it limits the maximum discount a tenant may receive to 50 per cent of the market value of the dwelling.

3450. Right to buy – rate of discount – Wales

HOUSING (PRESERVATION OF RIGHT TO BUY) (AMENDMENT) (WALES) REGULATIONS 2001, SI 2001 1301 (W.78); made under the Housing Act 1985 s.171C. In force: May 1, 2001; £2.00.

These Regulations amend the Housing (Preservation of Right to Buy) Regulations 1993 (SI 1993 2241) which modify the Housing Act 1985 Part V for cases in Wales where an authority or body disposes of a qualifying dwelling house let to a secure tenant and the tenant's right to buy is preserved by s.171A of that Act. The amendments relate to the calculation of the cost floor which limits the amount of discount a tenant can receive when exercising the right to buy.

HUMAN RIGHTS

3451. Constitutional law – expropriation – discrimination against white farmers – Zimbabwe

[Constitution of Zimbabwe 1979; Land Acquisition Act 1992 (Zimbabwe).]

C sought declarations that M had acted in breach of the Constitution of Zimbabwe 1979 in respect of land acquisition. In 1997, a list of farms was published that M intended to acquire under the Land Acquisition Act 1992 (Zimbabwe), with the purported aim of redressing the balance between white settlers who had laid claim to the land in the nineteenth century, against the interests of local inhabitants. Objections were made to the list under the procedure set out in the Act but that procedure was not followed and in 1998 M made orders under the Act for the acquisition of land included in the list. In 2000 many of the farms were violently taken over by people acting with the apparent encouragement of the government. C argued that its members had been denied the protection of the law in breach of s.18 of the Constitution, had been discriminated against on grounds of colour and political opinion in breach of s.23, that there had been no proper programme of land reform within the meaning of s.16A and that certain farmers had been forced to attend meetings of the ruling party in breach of their right of freedom of association under s.21.

Held, allowing the application, that there had been serious breaches of the farmers' constitutionally protected right and an interdict was granted to prohibit M from taking further steps against farmers, suspended to allow a proper programme of land reform to be put in place. The farmers had been denied proper legal protection. The action encouraged by the government was discriminatory as it targeted white farmers and farm workers of foreign origin, contrary to s.23. The practice of forcing farmers to attend party meetings and the resettlement of that party's supporters on white owned land was discriminatory in terms of political opinion and in breach of the right to freedom of association under s.21. The actions of M did not amount to a proper programme of land reform so that there had been a breach of s.16A.

COMMERCIAL FARMERS UNION v. MINISTER OF LANDS, AGRICULTURE AND RESETTLEMENT 10 B.H.R.C. 1, Gubbay, C.J., Sup Ct (Zim).

3452. **Constitutional law – homelessness – right of access to adequate housing – State's duty to provide – economic constraints – South Africa**

[Constitution of South Africa 1996 s.26.]

SA appealed against an order that it was required to provide G with shelter in accordance with the Constitution of South Africa 1996 s.26. G, along with 389 other adults and 510 children, had moved to privately owned land earmarked for housing development from a shanty town but had been evicted by bailiffs and their possessions had been destroyed. G was then forced to live in temporary shelter on a sports field. G obtained an order that SA should provide housing or shelter and other necessities of life. On appeal, SA argued that it was already complying with its constitutional obligations but was faced with economic difficulties leading to a lack of resources.

Held, allowing the appeal in part, that G had no right to demand immediate housing, but SA had to do more to meet its constitutional obligations. The Constitution had been drafted to make allowances for the economic situation. However, SA was not doing enough to fulfil its duty to work towards providing shelter to all those in extreme need. An order was therefore made requiring SA to develop measures to assist those in desperate need, subject to monitoring by the Human Rights Commission.

SOUTH AFRICA v. GROOTBOOM 10 B.H.R.C. 84, Yacoob, J., Const Ct (SA).

3453. **Detention – disabled persons – degrading treatment – inadequacy of facilities at police station**

[European Convention on Human Rights 1950 Art.3.]

P, a disabled person who was four limb deficient and suffered from kidney problems, brought a complaint claiming that the manner of her detention in police custody had constituted degrading treatment contrary to the European Convention on Human Rights 1950 Art.3. P had been detained following her committal for contempt of court. The cell in which P stayed for her first night of detention contained a wooden bed and mattress which were not adapted to the needs of a disabled person, so that she had to sleep in her wheelchair. The toilet was also inaccessible to her. P had persistently complained of the cold which she felt more acutely as a disabled person. Despite her complaints, P had not been moved to a more suitable cell. For the remainder of her time in detention P was held in a cell where, again, the bed was unsuitable for her special needs, and assistance was required from male officers to lift her onto the toilet. P contended that the detention constituted humiliating and degrading treatment.

Held, granting the application, that P's treatment in custody constituted degrading treatment contrary to Art.3 of the Convention. For a complainant to establish a breach of Art.3, it was necessary to show that the treatment complained of had reached a minimum level of severity which was relative and dependent on all the circumstances of the case. One factor which the court was required to consider was whether the treatment was intended to humiliate the complainant, although the absence of such an intention did not necessarily preclude a complainant from establishing a breach of Art.3. In the instant case the complainant had failed to show an intention to humiliate or debase her, but her detention in circumstances where she was likely to suffer cold, develop sores, and was unable to use the toilet or keep clean, constituted degrading treatment in contravention of Art.3.

PRICE v. UNITED KINGDOM (33394/96) 11 B.H.R.C. 401, J-P Costa (President), ECHR.

3454. Discrimination – disability discrimination – pensions – refusal of disability pension – compatibility with equality rights – Canada

[Canadian Charter of Rights and Freedoms.]

A injured his back at work in 1982 and thereafter was in receipt of a temporary disability allowance. In 1983, he was determined by the Manitoba Workmen's Compensation Board to have a 15 per cent permanent disability and in 1985, was awarded a lump sum payment in full and final settlement. In 1985, it was determined that he was capable of working. Although employed from time to time, he complained that his back condition continued to deteriorate and the disability became permanent in 1993 when, claiming a severe and permanent disability, he applied for a Canada Pension Plan, CPP, disability pension. Because he had failed to make the necessary contributions over a ten-year period A's application was refused by the Minister of Employment and Immigration and again by a review tribunal. A was unsuccessful both before the pension appeals board and the Federal Court of Appeal and appealed to the Supreme Court of Canada on the ground of discrimination.

Held, dismissing the appeal, that CPP retirement benefits were universal but disability benefits were conditional and designed to assist persons with disabilities who were recently in the work force by replacing employment income with a disability pension. A did not have any significant recent attachment to the workforce; thus he did not have recent employment income for which a CPP disability pension could be a substitute. Parliament did not violate Canadian human rights by seeking to benefit individuals with a history of severe and prolonged disability. Furthermore, A was seeking more advantageous treatment than was given to the permanently disabled. A reasonably objective person would not consider the greater allowance made for persons with greater disabilities in terms of CPP contributions marginalised or stigmatised him. Accordingly, CPP did not violate his equality rights.

GRANOVSKY v. MINISTER OF EMPLOYMENT AND IMMIGRATION 10 B.H.R.C. 619, Binnie, J., Sup Ct (Can).

3455. Discrimination – employment – refusal to employ individual diagnosed with HIV – South Africa

H was refused employment as cabin crew by S because he was HIV/AIDS positive. The company acknowledged that its employment policy of refusing such people employment could not be justified on medical grounds and was unfair. The court was asked to decide whether the policy was unconstitutional.

Held, that the practice was unfair discrimination, unconstitutional and could not be justified on commercial or any other grounds.

HOFFMANN v. SOUTH AFRICAN AIRWAYS 10 B.H.R.C. 571, Ngcobo, J., Const Ct (SA).

3456. Discrimination – sexual orientation – Christian university – discriminatory admissions policy – Canada

[Teaching Profession Act RSBC 1996 (Canada) s.4.]

T was a private teacher training college in British Columbia which promoted a Christian world view and required its candidates to sign a community standards document which prohibited homosexuality. British Columbia College of Teachers, B, refused to accredit its teacher education programme pursuant to the Teaching Profession Act RSBC 1996 s.4 on the ground that T discriminated on sexual orientation contrary to British Columbia's human rights legislation. On judicial review the Supreme Court directed B to accredit T and that decision was upheld on appeal. B appealed to the Supreme Court of Canada.

Held, dismissing the appeal, that (1) the suitability for entrance into the profession of teaching had to take into account all features of the education programme at T including human rights and religious freedom and (2) there was nothing in the T's community standards indicating that graduates of T would not treat homosexuals fairly and such students would not be prevented from becoming teachers, and (3) for B to have properly denied accreditation to T, it should have based its concerns on specific rather than speculative evidence involving consideration of the potential future beliefs and conduct of graduates from a teacher education programme taught exclusively at T.

BRITISH COLUMBIA COLLEGE OF TEACHERS v. TRINITY WESTERN UNIVERSITY 10 B.H.R.C 425, McLachlin, C.J., Sup Ct (Can).

3457. **European Court of Human Rights – applications – admissibility in absence of civil right or criminal charge**

[European Convention on Human Rights 1950 Art.6.]

H sought a declaration of admissibility in respect of his application to the Court arising from his appeal to a University academic appeals committee's decision and the rejection, without reasons, of his complaint to the University Visitor.

Held, refusing the application, that the matters complained of did not involve either a civil right or a criminal charge in terms of the European Convention on Human Rights 1950 Art.6.

HANUMAN v. UNITED KINGDOM [2000] E.L.R. 685, AB Baka (President), ECHR.

3458. **Expropriation – compensation – delay in payment – failure to award interest in line with annual inflation**

[European Convention on Human Rights 1950 Protocol 1 Art.1.]

A's land was expropriated as part of a dam building project. She was paid TRL 122,000 in compensation but a study commissioned by the water authority, B, gave a higher value. A successfully applied for an order increasing the compensation by TRL 271,039, with default interest at 30 per cent per annum. B appealed and A cross appealed on the grounds that the basis for calculating the additional loss should have been the rate of inflation, not the rate of statutory interest for delay. Before the appeal court reached its decision, A lodged an application with the European Court of Human Rights, complaining of a breach of the European Convention on Human Rights 1950 Protocol 1 Art.1 due to the delay in paying her compensation. A argued that the payment was made 17 months after the court's final decision and that the rate of interest awarded was inadequate given that the annual rate of inflation was 70 per cent at the time. The appeal court subsequently upheld the first instance judgment.

Held, allowing the application, that A was entitled to be paid as quickly as possible once the initial award had been made. No reason had been given for the 17 months' delay between the final decision and date of payment. The rate of interest awarded meant that the value of the payment decreased when compared with the rate of annual inflation amounting to a breach of Protocol 1 Art.1.

AKKUS v. TURKEY (2000) 30 E.H.R.R. 365, R Bernhardt (President), ECHR.

3459. **Freedom from torture – local authorities powers and duties – social services – child neglect and abuse – failure to protect**

[European Convention on Human Rights 1950 Art.3, Art.6, Art.8, Art.13.]

Z and his three siblings sought relief from the European Court of Human Rights, challenging a decision of the House of Lords that local authorities should not be held liable in respect of the exercise of their statutory duties safeguarding the welfare of children. Z, who had been subjected to severe long term neglect and abuse, argued that the authorities had breached the European Convention on Human Rights 1950 Art.3 which granted freedom from torture or inhuman or degrading treatment. It was not contested that the abuse suffered reached a level of severity prohibited by Art.3 of the Act. The behaviour of the family had been reported to the social services on several occasions, yet they had only acted five years after the first complaint, when the children were placed in emergency care at the insistence of their mother. It was also argued that Z had been denied the right to a fair trial and had not been afforded a remedy in the courts, as guaranteed by Art.13.

Held, granting the application, that the system had failed to protect Z and his siblings, and Art.3 of the Act, which was applicable to situations where ill treatment was administered by private individuals, had been violated, *A v. United Kingdom* [1998] 2 F.L.R. 959, [1998] C.L.Y. 3065 applied. While the role of social services was acknowledged to be a difficult one, the state had clearly failed in its positive obligation to protect the children from ill treatment of which it had, or ought to have had knowledge, *Osman v. United Kingdom* [1999] 1 F.L.R. 193, [1998] C.L.Y. 3102 considered. It was further held that the applicants had been denied an effective remedy following the state's breach of duty, since there had been no procedure in force to enable them to obtain an enforceable award of compensation for the damage suffered, and, therefore, Art.13 of the Act had been breached. The fundamental right enshrined in Art.3 should entitle injured parties to compensation for non-pecuniary damage as part of the range of redress. Damages were awarded accordingly.

Z v. UNITED KINGDOM (29392/95) [2001] 2 F.L.R. 612, L Wildhaber (President), ECHR.

3460. Freedom of association – clubs – selective membership policies – arbitrary exclusion policy

[Human Rights Act 1998 Sch.1 Part I Art.11.]

The RSPCA sought a declaration that its rules permitted it to adopt and administer a selective membership policy whereby it could freely exclude or remove from membership individuals who it suspected would not promote its aims and objectives.

Held, refusing the application, that although a society was justified by virtue of the Human Rights Act 1998 Sch.1 Part I Art.11, which made provision for the right to freedom of association, in excluding from association those whose membership it believed would be damaging to its interests, it was not in the best interests of a large charitable organisation for there to be an arbitrary policy of exclusion which gave the excluded individual no opportunity to make representations in his defence, *Gaiman v. National Association for Mental Health* [1971] Ch. 317, [1970] C.L.Y. 280 considered. If such a membership policy was to be exercised, applicants had to be made aware of it upon receipt of the application form. Furthermore, a rejected applicant had to be invited to make representations as to why his admission to the society was appropriate. A potential member could not, however, maintain an entitlement to join the organisation in reliance upon a right to freedom of expression.

RSPCA v. ATTORNEY GENERAL; *sub nom.* ROYAL SOCIETY FOR THE PREVENTION OF CRUELTY TO ANIMALS v. ATTORNEY GENERAL [2002] 1 W.L.R. 448, Lightman, J., Ch D.

3461. Freedom of association – political parties – dissolution of Turkish political party

[Constitution of Turkey 1982; Law 2820 on the Regulation of Political Parties (Turkey); European Convention on Human Rights 1950 Art.10, Art.11.]

The leaders of OZDEP, a Turkish political party founded in 1992, voted to voluntarily dissolve the party following an application to the Turkish Constitutional Court for its dissolution in 1993 on the ground that OZDEP's aims were contrary to the Constitution and Law 2820 on the regulation of political parties. The court held that OZDEP's aims were capable of undermining the unity and secular nature of the Turkish State. OZDEP challenged this decision, contending that the dissolution and the barring of its leaders from holding office in other political party were contrary to the European Convention on Human Rights 1950 Art.10 and Art.11.

Held, allowing the application, that (1) OZDEP's dissolution, although prescribed by law, interfered with it members' freedom of association in a manner that was not justified in a democratic society; (2) Art.11 had to be considered in the light of Art.10 given the need to express opinions which applied to political parties and their role the proper functioning of democracy, and (3) the incompatibility of OZDEP's aims with current State structures did not mean that it had infringed democratic principles as it was important in a democracy that diverse opinions should be debated, *Socialist Party v. Turkey* (1999) 27 E.H.R.R. 51, [1999] C.L.Y. 3116 applied.

OZDEP v. TURKEY (2001) 31 E.H.R.R. 27, Judge Wildhaber (President), ECHR.

3462. **Freedom of expression – advertisements – Swiss national television – refusal to broadcast advertisement by animal welfare group – Switzerland**

[European Convention on Human Rights 1950 Art.10.]

VT was an association concerned with the protection of animals. It applied to the Swiss national television authority to broadcast an advertisement exhorting reduced meat consumption. The authority was the only medium for national advertising. The authority refused because there was a legal ban on political advertising on TV and radio. There was no such ban on other media. VT complained to the European Court of Human Rights that there was a violation of the European Convention on Human Rights 1950 Art. 10.

Held, allowing the application, that (1) freedom of expression was essential to democratic society and exceptions had to be construed strictly; (2) margins of appreciation were essential in commercial matters but VT's advertisement was outside a regular commercial context; (3) since the ban on political advertising applied only to TV and radio it did not have a pressing social need, and (4) VT had no other means of reaching the entire public on a matter of general interest.

VGT VEREIN GEGEN TIERFABRIKEN v. SWITZERLAND (24699/94) (2002) 34 E.H.R.R. 4, Judge Rozakis (President), ECHR.

3463. **Freedom of expression – Advertising Standards Authority – publication of adjudication**

See MEDIA: R. (on the application of Matthias Rath BV) v. Advertising Standards Authority Ltd. §4409

3464. **Freedom of expression – defamation – comments made in course of public debate**

[European Convention on Human Rights 1950 Art.10.]

N, President of the Norwegian Police Association, complained that his right to freedom of expression under the European Convention on Human Rights 1950 Art.10 had been violated by a finding in the national court that comments he had made to the press were defamatory. Following the publication of a book alleging police brutality in Bergen, a Committee of Inquiry had been set up which had resulted in a report by a criminal law professor, B. B had taken the view that police brutality was potentially even more serious than set out in the book. This had given rise to a heated public debate, in the context of which N's comments had been made, casting doubt on B's motives and claiming that he had fabricated certain allegations. B successfully brought an action for defamation and N had been ordered to pay compensation.

Held, upholding the application, that the freedom of expression was fundamental to a democratic society and included the freedom to express opinions which could offend or disturb. However, the protection of a person's reputation was a strict exception to that right. The national court had been right to find that the comments were potentially damaging to B's reputation, but it was necessary to view them against the background of a public debate involving serious allegations, and of N's role as the representative of the accused officers. N's comments were matters of opinion rather than fact and had been made in response to remarks by B which were themselves capable of being seen as denigrating or offensive. The fact that B had chosen to take part in the debate in such a way had to be put in the balance, with extremes of language having to be tolerated in that context. Further, by the time of the defamation action, some of those who had previously given evidence to the Inquiry had been found to have lied. Taking all those factors into account, N's comments were not out of proportion and should not have been found to be defamatory of B.

NILSEN v. NORWAY (2000) 30 E.H.R.R. 878, L Wildhaber (President), ECHR.

3465. **Freedom of expression – defamation – proportionality of measures applied by domestic court – Slovakia**

[European Convention on Human Rights 1950 Art.10.]

M was allocated a state-owned flat. He was unable to take possession because the husband of the state prosecutor occupied it under separate legal arrangements. M complained by letter to the Prime Minister about the national housing policy and the letter was published in a daily newspaper. The prosecutor and her husband sued for defamation. The court found in their favour because M had not by then acquired the use of the flat and the truthfulness of his allegations was not proven. He was ordered to pay damages and costs of 25 months salary. M complained that his right to freedom of speech under the European Convention on Human Rights 1950 Art. 10 had been breached.

Held, allowing the application, that M's letter raised issues of general interest, namely the housing policy, and taken as a whole his statements were not excessive. Most of the events on which he had relied had already been made public. Furthermore, there was a disparity between the measures complained of and the behaviour they were intended to rectify. Accordingly, the measures applied by the domestic courts in protecting the reputation of others were not proportionate. It followed that there was a violation of Art.10.

MARONEK v. SLOVAKIA (32686/96) 10 B.H.R.C. 558, Judge Rozakis (President), ECHR.

3466. **Freedom of expression – employees – criticism of employer – dismissal disproportionate – Spain**

[European Convention on Human Rights 1950 Art.10.]

B was a Spanish television producer and presenter. He was employed by the Spanish television service, TVE, as a producer. In 1993 several thousand employees of TVE demonstrated against plans to reduce jobs in the public television service. B was dismissed following disciplinary proceedings after he made offensive remarks about the management of TVE during two live radio broadcasts. He complained to the ECHR that his dismissal had violated his right to freedom of expression relying on the European Convention on Human Rights 1950 Art.10.

Held, allowing the application, that (1) Art.10 was not only binding in relations between employer and employee which were governed by public law but might also apply where those relations were governed by private law. Moreover, in certain cases the state was under a positive obligation to protect the right to freedom of expression even against threats from private persons, *Young, James & Webster v. United Kingdom (A/44)* (1982) 4 E.H.R.R. 38 referred to; (2) in the instant case the impugned measure constituted an interference with the exercise of the applicant's right to freedom of expression as protected by Art.10(1). Furthermore, the parties were agreed that the interference was "prescribed by law" and that it pursued a legitimate aim, "the protection of the reputation or rights of others". It therefore satisfied two of the conditions under which an interference might be regarded as justified under Art.10(2). There remained the third condition which required that the interference be "necessary in a democratic society"; (3) the court's task was to determine whether, in all the circumstances, the penalty imposed on the applicant answered a pressing social need and was proportionate to the legitimate aim pursued and whether the reasons adduced by the national authorities in justification of it were relevant and sufficient; (4) in the light of the facts of the case, the court considered that, although the reasons adduced by the state were relevant, they did not show a "pressing social need", and (5) notwithstanding the margin of appreciation enjoyed by the national authorities the dismissal was not proportionate. Consequently there was a violation of Art.10.

BOBO v. SPAIN (39293/98) (2001) 31 E.H.R.R. 50, Judge Pellonpaa (President), ECHR.

3467. **Freedom of expression – harassment – newspapers – duty of state to prevent harassment of newspaper office – Turkey**

[European Convention on Human Rights 1950 Art.10.]

G was a daily newspaper the main office of which was situated in Istanbul. The case concerned the allegations by G that the newspaper was the subject of serious attacks and harassment which forced its eventual closure and for which the Turkish authorities were directly or indirectly responsible. Relying on the European Convention on Human Rights Art.10. G complained to the ECHR that the newspaper had been forced to close because of the attacks and harassment.

Held, allowing the application in part, that (1) freedom of expression was of key importance as a precondition for a functioning democracy. Genuine, effective exercise of this freedom did not depend merely on the State's duty not to interfere, but might require positive measures of protection, even in the sphere of relations between individuals, *X v. Netherlands (A/91)* (1986) 8 E.H.R.R. 235 followed; (2) in determining whether or not a positive obligation existed, regard must be had to the fair balance that had to be struck between the general interests of the Community and the interests of the individual; (3) the fact that the government believed that the newspaper and its staff supported a terrorist organisation and acted as its propaganda tool, did not, even if true, provide a justification for failing to take steps effectively to investigate and, where necessary, provide protection against unlawful acts involving violence; (4) in the instant case the government had failed to comply with its positive obligation to protect the newspaper in the exercise of its freedom of expression; (5) the necessity for any restriction in the exercise of freedom of expression had to be convincingly established. The search operation, as conducted by the authorities in this case, had not been shown to be necessary, in a democratic society, for the implementation of any legitimate aim, *Otto-Preminger Institute v. Austria (A/295-A)* (1995) 19 E.H.R.R. 34, [1995] C.L.Y. 2648 referred to; (6) not only had the press the task of imparting information and ideas on political issues, the public had a right to receive it. Freedom of the press afforded the public one of the best means of discovering and forming an opinion on the ideas and attitudes of public leaders, *Lingens v. Austria (No.2) (A/103)* (1986) 8 E.H.R.R. 407 referred to, and (7) the State had failed to take adequate protective and investigative measures to protect the newspaper's exercise of its freedom of expression and it had imposed measures on the newspaper, through the search and arrest operation and through numerous prosecutions and convictions in respect of issues of the newspaper, which were disproportionate and unjustified in the pursuit of any legitimate aim. As a result of these cumulative factors, the newspaper had ceased publication and there had been a breach of Art.10.

GUNDEM v. TURKEY (23144/93) (2001) 31 E.H.R.R. 49, Judge Pellonpaa, ECHR.

3468. **Freedom of expression – homosexuality – customs seizure of erotic literature – Canada**

[Customs Act 1985 (Canada) s.152(3); Canadian Charter of Rights and Freedoms 1982 s.2(b), s.15(1); Criminal Code (Canada) s.163.]

L appealed against the dismissal of its claim that the Customs Act 1985 violated its right to freedom of expression and equality under the Canadian Charter of Rights and Freedoms 1982 s.2(b) and s.15(1). L, a bookshop catering for the lesbian and gay community, imported erotic literature from the United States. Its shipments were regularly seized or returned by Customs officials on the ground that they contained obscene materials within the meaning of the Criminal Code s.163. L argued that they were being unfairly targeted and that different standards of obscenity were being applied to the materials because they were homosexual rather than heterosexual.

Held, allowing the appeal in part (Iacobucci, J. dissenting in part), that s.152(3) of the 1985 Act was an unlawful limitation of L's right to freedom of expression as far as it put the burden of proving that materials were not obscene on to L. However, the test of "general community tolerance" under the Code was applied equally to heterosexual and homosexual literature. Although the Charter protected freedom of expression, including the freedom to import "expressive material", the state was entitled to limit the influx of obscene material across its borders. L's complaints went to the behaviour of certain Customs officials and to the implementation of the legislation, not to the legislation itself, which was not on its face discriminatory.

LITTLE SISTERS BOOK AND ART EMPORIUM v. MINISTER OF JUSTICE 9 B.H.R.C. 409, Binnie, J., Sup Ct (Can).

3469. **Freedom of expression – injunctions – protection of rights of others – necessity of interference – Austria**

[European Convention on Human Rights 1950 Art.10.]

In June 1988 W, a politician, participated in a protest campaign against the stationing of interceptor fighter planes near Graz airport. Following a subsequent police action, an article was published in a newspaper which the applicant claimed was a political campaign intending to bring him into disrepute. W stated during a press conference: "This is Nazi journalism". That statement was quoted in the Austrian media. The supreme court granted the company which published the newspaper an injunction prohibiting W from repeating that statement. Relying on the European Convention on Human Rights 1950 Art.10, W complained to the ECHR that the injunction amounted to a violation of his right to freedom of expression.

Held, dismissing the application, that it was common ground that the injunction constituted an interference with W's right to freedom of expression as guaranteed by Art.10(1). There was no dispute that the interference was prescribed by law and pursued a legitimate aim, namely the protection of the reputation or rights of others within Art.10(2). The dispute was whether the interference was "necessary in a democratic society"; (2) in reviewing under Art.10 the decisions taken by the national authorities pursuant to their margin of appreciation, the Convention organs had to determine in the light of the case as a whole, whether the interference at issue was proportionate to the legitimate aim pursued and whether the reasons adduced by them to justify the interference were relevant and sufficient *Lingens v. Austria (No.2) (A/103)* (1986) 8 E.H.R.R. 407 referred to; (3) the court had to consider the decision challenged before it, in the light of the case as a whole, including the circumstances in which the applicant made his statement *Oberschlick v. Austria (No.2)* (1998) 25 E.H.R.R. 357, [1998] C.L.Y. 3088 followed; (4) the supreme court duly balanced the interest involved and the detailed reasons given by it were relevant and sufficient for the purposes of Art. 10(2); (5) the injunction was limited to the particular words, and (6) in all the circumstances, the Supreme Court was entitled to consider that the injunction was "necessary in a democratic society" for the protection of the reputation and rights of others.

WABL v. AUSTRIA (24773/94) (2001) 31 E.H.R.R. 51, Judge Costa (President), ECHR.

3470. **Freedom of expression – journalists – justification – publication of derogatory material on former government official – Estonia**

[European Convention on Human Rights 1950 Art.10.]

L, a public official, was the wife of a politician. Both resigned following scandalous conduct. R, a journalist conducted interviews with L for the purpose of publishing her memoirs. Following a dispute between them L obtained an injunction against R preventing publication of his manuscript. R then gave an interview to T, another journalist, who published derogatory material about L. L instituted a private prosecution against T who was convicted and fined ten days' pay. T's appeal was dismissed because the court found his publication to be grossly degrading to L. T complained to the European Court of Human Rights on the ground that his freedom of expression had been violated contrary to the European Convention on Human Rights 1950 Art.10.

Held, dismissing the application, that the measures taken by the domestic court were justified and proportionate to protect the individual rights of L. The impugned remarks related to aspects of L's private life, which she described in her memoirs written in her private capacity. Since L had resigned from her governmental position the use of the impugned terms in relation to her private life was not justified by considerations of public concern nor did they deal with matters of general importance.

TAMMER v. ESTONIA (41205/98) (NO.2) 10 B.H.R.C. 543, Judge Palm (President), ECHR.

3471. **Freedom of expression – media – constitutionality of offence of scandalising court – South Africa**

[Constitution of the Republic of South Africa 1996 s.16, s.35.]

A was an official in the Department of Correctional Services. He was convicted and sentenced in the High Court for scandalising the court, a particular form of contempt of court following comments concerning an order of that court that he had published on behalf of his department. The order in question related to the granting of bail to a prisoner. A obtained permission to appeal to the Constitutional Court to determine (1) whether the law relating to scandalising the court unjustifiably limited the right to freedom of expression enshrined in the Constitution of the Republic of South Africa 1996 s.16 and (2) whether the common law procedure whereby a judge could summon a suspected scandaliser to appear before him to answer to a summary charge of contempt of court fell foul of the fair trial rights guaranteed by the Constitution of the Republic of South Africa 1996 s.35.

Held, that (1) freedom of expression was of the utmost importance in an open and democratic society but was not absolute. The sole aim of the offence of scandalising the court was to preserve the capacity of the judiciary to fulfil its role under the constitution. The test was whether the offending conduct was likely to damage the administration of justice. What was published did not in any way impair the dignity, integrity or standing of the judiciary or of the particular judge. Moreover, as a media spokesman for the department, A was in no position either to execute the order for release on bail, nor to frustrate the order. Thus the statements he made did not seek to challenge the judicial order and did not amount to scandalising the court and (2) the summary procedure, which lacked formal plea procedure, the right to remain silent or the ability to challenge evidence, was manifestly unfair.

SOUTH AFRICA v. MAMABOLO 10 B.H.R.C. 493, Chaskalson (President), Const Ct (SA).

3472. **Freedom of expression – newspapers – damages awarded for libel – substance of article in public interest**

[European Convention on Human Rights 1950 Art.10.]

BT, a newspaper, was ordered to pay damages for libel following the publication of articles revealing complaints by dissatisfied patients following cosmetic surgery conducted by a doctor at his private clinic. BT complained that the judgment was an unjustifiable interference with the right to freedom of expression contrary to the European Convention on Human Rights 1950 Art.10.

Held, allowing the application, that (1) freedom of expression was essential in a democratic society, subject to the restrictions in Art.10(2), which were to be strictly construed, *Sunday Times v. United Kingdom (No.1) (A/30)* (1979-80) 2 E.H.R.R. 245, [1980] C.L.Y. 1385 applied. The freedom applied to both information that was favourably received and to ideas that could offend or disturb; (2) the national authorities had a margin of appreciation when assessing the need for a restriction under Art.10(2), but this was subject to a final ruling by the court on whether the restriction was reconcilable with the freedom in a given context; (3) the press had an essential role in a democratic society, and, although it had to remain within certain bounds regarding the rights and reputation of others and to prevent disclosure of confidential information, it had a duty to impart information that was in the public interest, *Jersild v. Denmark (A/298)*(1995) 19 E.H.R.R. 1, [1995] C.L.Y. 2645 applied; (4) journalistic freedom meant that press coverage could embody elements of exaggeration or provocation, *Prager and Oberschlick v. Austria (A/313)* (1996) 21 E.H.R.R. 1, [1996] C.L.Y. 3144 followed, and (5) in the instant case, the margin of appreciation was restricted in the interests of a democratic society so that BT could impart information of general public concern, *Bladet Tromso v. Norway* (2000) 29 E.H.R.R. 125, [2000] C.L.Y. 3190 followed.

BERGENS TIDENDE v. NORWAY (26132/95) (2001) 31 E.H.R.R. 16, Judge Bratza (President), ECHR.

3473. **Freedom of expression – pornography – possession of child pornography – extent of criminal liability – Canada**

[Criminal Code (Canada) s.163.1 (4); Canadian Charter of Rights and Freedoms 1982 s.2(b), s.7.]

S was charged with possessing child pornography and with possessing such material for distribution, contrary to the Criminal Code s.163.1. S challenged the constitutionality of s.163.1 (4), arguing that the prohibition on simply possessing child pornography violated his right to freedom of expression under the Canadian Charter of Rights and Freedoms 1982 s.2(b). Further, that the risk of imprisonment under such a far reaching legislative provision was contrary to his right to liberty under s.7 of the Charter. Although the Crown accepted that the prohibition on possessing child pornography infringed s.2(b), it argued that it was justifiable under s.1 of the Charter as being necessary to protect children. S's arguments were upheld at first instance and on appeal and the Crown appealed to the Canadian Supreme Court.

Held, allowing the appeal and remitting S for trial, that (1) freedom of expression was a fundamental right and included popular, unpopular and offensive material. The freedom was not absolute, however, and could be subject to legislative restriction in respect of certain forms of expression, as long as such restrictions remained subject to careful scrutiny. While the content of much child pornography reduced its worth in terms of the Charter, it did not wipe it out as free expression included even offensive material. Classification of such material required an objective approach, taking account of the level of explicit activity involving persons under 18 years of age. Section 163.1 (4) was upheld on the ground that the definition of child pornography in s.163.1 excluded material created by an accused acting alone that did not show unlawful sexual acts and was held for purely private purposes.

R. v. SHARPE 10 B.H.R.C. 153, McLachlin, C.J., Sup Ct (Can).

3474. **Freedom of expression – publishers – injunction preventing press reporting of criminal proceedings – validity under ECHR**

[European Convention on Human Rights 1950 Art.6(1), Art.10(2).]

N was a limited company which owned and published a magazine. It complained to the European Court of Human Rights that national court decisions prohibited it from publishing a picture of B who was suspected of involvement in a letter bomb campaign. N argued that the prohibition amounted to a violation of its rights to freedom of expression under the European Convention on Human Rights 1950 Art.10

Held, allowing the application, that (1) it was not for the courts to substitute their own methods of reporting for those of the press. Article 10 protected not only the substance of ideas and information but also the form in which they were conveyed, *Jersild v. Denmark (A/298)* (1995) 19 E.H.R.R. 1, [1995] C.L.Y.

2645 applied; (2) the prohibition on publication of the pictures in the context of reports on criminal proceedings, was an interference with its rights to freedom of expression, which was a breach of Art.10 unless it satisfied the requirements of Art.10(2); (3) the judgments of the domestic courts showed that the injunction against N was intended to protect B against insult and defamation and against violations of the presumption of innocence; thus they had the aim of protecting "the reputation or rights of others" and also the "authority and impartiality of the judiciary" and, therefore, satisfied Art.10(2); (4) although the press must not overstep certain bounds, in particular in respect of the reputation and rights of others or of the proper administration of justice, its duty was nevertheless to impart, in a manner consistent with its obligations and responsibilities, information and ideas on all matters of public interest, *Bladet Tromso v. Norway* (2000) 29 E.H.R.R. 125, [2000] 1 C.L. 241 applied; (5) that duty extended to reporting and commenting on court proceedings and such publicity complied with Art.6(1), which provided that hearings be public; (6) not only did the media have the task of imparting such information and ideas: it had a right to receive them, *Worm v. Austria* (1998) 25 E.H.R.R. 454, [1998] C.L.Y. 3090 applied; (7) the fact that B had a right under Art.6(2) to be presumed innocent until proved guilty was relevant to the balancing of competing interests which the court had to carry out, and (8) the absolute prohibition on publication of B's pictures went further than was needed to protect B. The injunctions granted by the national court were disproportionate to the legitimate aims pursued.

NEWS VERLAGS GmbH & CO KG v. AUSTRIA (31457/97) (2001) 31 E.H.R.R. 8, Palm (President), ECHR.

3475. **Freedom of expression – publishing – conviction for publishing book critical of authorities' actions in south east Turkey**

[European Convention on Human Rights 1950 Art.10 European Convention on Human Rights 1950 Art.14; Prevention of Terrorism Act 1991 (Turkey) s.8.]

A, the author of a book about deaths in south east Turkey attributed to the security forces, was convicted of promoting propaganda against the unity of the State, contrary to the Prevention of Terrorism Act 1991 s.8, for which he was sentenced to 20 months' imprisonment and a fine. He complained that his conviction infringed his right to freedom of expression and was discriminatory on the ground of political opinion, contrary to the European Convention on Human Rights 1950 Art.10 and Art.14.

Held, allowing the application, that (1) having regard to the situation in south east Turkey and the authorities' need to prevent violence, the measures taken against A were in furtherance of the protection of national security and the prevention of crime and disorder; (2) A's book was not neutral in its description of events and it was critical of the authorities' actions. However, Art.10(2) did not allow for the restriction of political speeches or debates on matters of public interest. Furthermore, the limits of permissible criticism were wider where a government was concerned than in relation to private persons or individual politicians; (3) the government's dominant position meant that it had to exercise restraint when resorting to criminal proceedings; (4) A had made his views known via a book, rather than the mass media, which reduced their potential impact on national security and the book itself did not incite violence or armed resistance, and (5) Art.10 had been violated as A's conviction and sentence were disproportionate to the aims being pursued by the government. However, no separate issues arose under Art.10 taken in conjunction with Art.14.

ARSLAN v. TURKEY (23462/94) (2001) 31 E.H.R.R. 9, Judge Wildhaber (President), ECHR.

3476. Freedom of expression – reporting restrictions – law of confidence – existence of exceptional circumstances

[European Convention on Human Rights 1950 Art.10(2).]

V and T, who, at the age of 11, had been convicted of the murder of a child, applied for injunctions protecting them, inter alia, from being identified upon their release from detention. During the period of their detention, injunctions had been made limiting the information that the media could publish. However, those injunctions had expired when V and T reached the age of 18. Both V and T sought injunctions that would run indefinitely.

Held, granting the injunctions, that (1) there was a real possibility that V and T would be in danger of revenge attacks if their identities were disclosed such as to make the instant case an exceptional one. It was apparent from the evidence before the court that a level of hostility and desire for revenge existed amongst certain members of the public; (2) the court was under a positive duty to operate to protect individuals from the criminal acts of others, *Osman v. United Kingdom* [1999] 1 F.L.R. 193, [1998] C.L.Y. 3102 applied; (3) in exceptional cases, the court had jurisdiction to widen the scope of the protection of confidentiality of information, even to the extent of placing restrictions on the press, where if no restrictions were imposed there was a likelihood that the person seeking confidentiality would suffer serious physical injury or even death and no other means of protection was available. Any restriction on the right of the media to publish had to fall within the exceptions established under the European Convention on Human Rights 1950 Art.10(2), and those exceptions were to be given a narrow interpretation, and (4) given that the courts had to act in a way that was compatible with the Convention, the injunctive relief sought would be granted openly against the world.

VENABLES v. NEWS GROUP NEWSPAPERS LTD; THOMPSON v. NEWS GROUP NEWSPAPERS LTD [2001] Fam. 430, Dame Elizabeth Butler-Sloss (President), Fam Div.

3477. Freedom of expression – right to fair trial – published work critical of state policy toward Kurdistan

[European Convention on Human Rights 1950 Art.6(1), Art.7, Art.10; Prevention of Terrorism Act 1991 (Turkey) s.8.]

B and O were convicted of undermining Turkey's territorial integrity under the Prevention of Terrorism Act 1991 s.8 following O's publication of a book written by B that criticised Turkish policy toward Kurdistan. B and O complained to the ECHR that they had not had a fair trial before the Istanbul National Security Court, contrary to the European Convention on Human Rights 1950 Art.6; that their conviction and sentences were contrary to Art.7 and that their right to freedom of expression had been violated, contrary to Art.10.

Held, allowing the reference in part, that (1) Art.7 required that a criminal offence, and the sanctions applicable to it had to be properly defined in law. Although B could have regulated his conduct so as to comply with s.8 of the 1991 Act, in O's case there was no basis for a penalty to be imposed for publishing the book, so that his sentence was contrary to Art.7; (2) as the part of s.8 pertaining to publishers had been repealed by the date of O's conviction, both his conviction and sentence contravened Art.10. In the case of both B and O, the steps taken by the state were disproportionate to the aim pursued and therefore violated Art.10, and (3) the fact that military judges sitting in the security courts remained subject to military discipline and were appointed by the army meant that neither B nor O had not received fair trials before an impartial tribunal, as required by Art.6(1), *Incal v. Turkey* (2000) 29 E.H.R.R. 449, [1998] C.L.Y. 3093 and *Ciraklar v. Turkey* [1998] H.R.C.D. 955 followed.

BASKAYA v. TURKEY (23536/94); OKCUOGLU v. TURKEY (24408/94) (2001) 31 E.H.R.R. 10, Judge Wildhaber (President), ECHR.

3478. Freedom of expression – right to private life – unauthorised publication of photographs – competing considerations

See CIVIL PROCEDURE: Douglas v. Hello Ltd. §567

3479. Freedom of religion – convictions – Muslim leader elected by fellow believers – usurping function of minister

[European Convention on Human Rights 1950 Art.9, Art.10; Criminal Code (Greece).]

S, a Greek citizen and a theology graduate, was elected the Mufti of Rodopi by mosque congregations there in opposition to the Mufti who had been appointed by the government. S was subsequently convicted of usurping the functions of a religious minister and publicly wearing religious robes without the right to do so, contrary to the Criminal Code. He complained that the conviction interfered with his right to exercise his religion together with those who turned to him for spiritual guidance contrary to the European Convention on Human Rights 1950 Art.9 and Art.10.

Held, allowing the application, that (1) S's religious freedom included the right to act in common with others and to teach and worship with those who acknowledged his authority, *Kokkinakis v. Greece (A/260-A)* (1994) 17 E.H.R.R. 397, [1994] C.L.Y. 2419 followed; (2) although freedom of conscience and religion were essential in a democratic society, restriction could be necessary in the interests of other religious groups. However, such restriction had to correspond to a pressing social need and had to be proportionate to a legitimate aim, *Wingrove v. United Kingdom* (1997) 24 E.H.R.R. 1, [1996] C.L.Y. 3143 referred to; (3) punishing S for acting as religious leader of a group that willingly followed him was not compatible with the religious pluralism expected in a democratic society; (4) S's conviction was not justified by reference to a pressing social need so that the interference with his right to practise his religion was contrary to Art.9(2), and (5) there had been no separate breach of Art.10.

SERIF v. GREECE (38178/97) (2001) 31 E.H.R.R. 20, Judge Fischbach (President), ECHR.

3480. Freedom of religion – discrimination – will establishing university bursaries for Roman Catholic students – Canada

[British Columbia Human Rights Code 1996.]

M left by will a sum to fund two university bursaries, subject to the condition that these were to be available to Roman Catholic students. The university sought directions as to the use of the funds that would not discriminate on religious grounds under the British Columbia Human Rights Code 1996

Held, permitting the funds to be used as stipulated by M, that the Code did not apply because M's will established a private relationship between M and the student beneficiaries, not a relationship between the university and its students. Alternatively, even if the Code had applied, the bequest would have been justified given its innocuous nature and the need to uphold testamentary freedom.

McCONNELL (DECEASED), *Re*; *sub nom.* UNIVERSITY OF VICTORIA v. BRITISH COLUMBIA (2000-01) 3 I.T.E.L.R. 24, Maczko, J., Sup Ct (BC).

3481. Freedom of religion – exhumation – right to remove ashes buried in consecrated ground – religious convictions of widow

[Human Rights Act 1998 Sch.1 Part I Art.9.]

S, a widow, sought a faculty for the exhumation of her late husband, J's, ashes which had been buried in consecrated ground at a cemetery in Luton. Neither J nor S had any affinity with the Christian faith. J's funeral had been conducted in the humanist tradition and, thereafter, S had moved to London. S sought the exhumation in order to inter J's ashes at a cemetery closer to her home, contending that her long standing depressive illness and grief had resulted in a decision, which she now regretted, to move away from Luton. S further maintained that had she been aware that the ashes would be interred in ground which had "church associations" she would have regarded that as hypocritical and would not have permitted it to occur.

Held, granting the faculty, that (1) S had, on the basis of her medical condition, failed to discharge the presumption against exhumation on the basis of her medical condition, *Christ Church, Alsager, Re* [1999] Fam. 142, [1998] C.L.Y. 1786 applied, and (2) S had rights under the Human Rights Act 1998 Sch.1 Part I Art.9, which guaranteed a freedom of thought, conscience and religion, and which also encompassed non religious beliefs such as humanism, *Durrington Cemetery, Re* [2001] Fam. 33, [2000] 8 C.L.Y. 216, *Arrowsmith v. United Kingdom* (1981) 3 E.H.R.R. 218 and *Kokkinakis v. Greece (A/260-A)* (1994) 17 E.H.R.R. 397, [1994] C.L.Y. 2419 applied. Accordingly a refusal of the faculty would be incompatible with S's rights under Art.9 to remove J's ashes from a location which was in her view hypocritical and contrary to her humanist beliefs.

CRAWLEY GREEN ROAD CEMETERY, LUTON, *Re* [2001] Fam. 308, Judge Bursell Q.C. (Chancellor), Cons Ct (St Albans).

3482. Freedom of religion – independent schools – constitutionality of ban on corporal punishment – South Africa

[Schools Act 1996 (South Africa) s.10.]

C, an association representing 196 independent Christian schools, appealed against a decision (1999 (4) S.A. 1092) refusing its application for an order declaring the prohibition on corporal punishment in the Schools Act 1996 (South Africa) s.10 to be unconstitutional. C contended that (1) such punishment was biblically ordained; (2) its use had been assented to by the parents of pupils attending the schools it represented, and (3) the ban under s.10 of the Act amounted to an unlawful constraint on the freedom of religion.

Held, dismissing the appeal, that legitimate restrictions on constitutional rights had to be reasonable and capable of justification. Although C's members could expect to have their Christian ethos respected, they in turn were expected to conform to other norms in terms of education and wider society. Whilst it was true that believers should not be forced to choose between the tenets of their faith and obedience to the law, it was reasonable in the instant case for the members' standards of discipline to conform to those chosen by Parliament. The authorities showed that corporal punishment was invasive of a child's rights and dignity, contrary to the paramount principle of child welfare. Further, the state had determined that it was desirable to reduce levels of violence in society in recognition of the excesses of the past.

CHRISTIAN EDUCATION SOUTH AFRICA v. MINISTER OF EDUCATION 9 B.H.R.C. 53, Chaskalson (President), Const Ct (SA).

3483. Freedom of religion – Jewish law – ritual slaughter of animals

[European Convention on Human Rights 1950 Art.9, Art.14.]

JLA, an orthodox Jewish association, complained of a violation of the European Convention on Human Rights 1950 Art.9 in conjunction with Art.14 arising from the refusal to grant its approval to carry out ritual slaughter in a manner acceptable to ultra-orthodox beliefs. The French authorities had refused JLA's application on the basis that A was the organisation authorised for this purpose and exempted from the domestic statutory requirement that animals were to be stunned prior to slaughter.

Held, the majority refusing to uphold the complaint, that by conferring sole authority on A, France had not violated JLA's rights under Art.9 and Art.14. In appointing A as the only permitted ritual slaughterer, France had given practical effect to its undertaking to ensure that there was no violation of the right to manifest religious beliefs through the observance of rites. Further, the method of slaughter was not in dispute and there was no reason why JLA could not reach agreement with A in relation to the inspection and cleaning processes. JLA also imported meat for its members so that it was not necessary for it to carry out its own slaughtering in France.

JEWISH LITURGICAL ASSOCIATION CHA'ARE SHALOM VE TSEDEK v. FRANCE 9 B.H.R.C. 27, L Wildhaber (President), ECHR.

3484. Freedom of religion – racism – teacher publishing anti semitic works in free time – effect on educational system – Canada

[International Covenant on Civil and Political Rights 1966 Art.18, Art.19.]

R was a teacher who published books in his free time containing derogatory views about Judaism. He also took part in media interviews where his views were freely expressed. Although he did not voice his opinions when teaching, a human rights board of inquiry convened as the result of a complaint by a Jewish parent decided that R should be moved to a non teaching role. The transfer was upheld by the Canadian Supreme Court and R complained to the UN Human Rights Committee, contending that his right to express his religious views freely had been violated, contrary to the International Covenant on Civil and Political Rights 1966 Art.18 and Art.19.

Held, dismissing the complaint by a majority, that (1) under Art.19, restrictions on the right to freedom of expression had to be necessary for the protection of others' rights or in the interests of public order or morals; (2) in assessing whether the restrictions placed on R's freedom of expression fulfilled a Covenant purpose the rights of others included both those of individuals as well as society as a whole; (3) statements that raised or reinforced anti semitic feelings could be subject to restriction, *Faurisson v. France* 2 B.H.R.C. 1, [1997] C.L.Y. 2779 applied, and (4) the right to freedom of expression also carried responsibilities which were particularly relevant in an educational setting. The influence of teachers could be restrained to prevent the dissemination of discriminatory views within schools. Therefore, R's removal from a teaching post could be deemed necessary to protect the rights of Jewish children to be educated in a system that was free from prejudice and intolerance.

ROSS v. CANADA 10 B.H.R.C. 219, Judge not applicable, UN Human Rights Committee.

3485. Freedom of religion – religious discrimination – Jehovah's Witness refused admission as accountant – prior conviction by military tribunal

[European Convention on Human Rights 1950 Art.6(1), Art.9, Art.14.]

T, a Greek national and a Jehovah's Witness, was refused admission as an accountant on the basis that he had a military tribunal conviction for refusing to wear military uniform, in respect of which T had served his sentence of four years' imprisonment. T complained to the European Court of Human Rights, contending that there had been a violation of the European Convention on Human Rights 1950 Art.9 and Art.14, in that the refusal to admit him as an accountant because of his conviction failed to take account of his religious beliefs. Further, that the seven year period taken by the domestic courts to determine the matter amounted to a breach of Art.6(1).

Held, allowing the application, that although T had been treated in the same way as another person committing the same offence, the underlying reason for his conviction was his religious beliefs. Therefore, Art.14 and Art.9 had to be considered together. A conviction based on religious belief was not of the same magnitude as one involving dishonesty and therefore the refusal to admit T as an accountant was disproportionate. Art.6(1) had also been breached because of the unreasonable length of time involved, the lack of delay on T's part and the fact that a significant part of the delay was attributable to a backlog of administrative court cases.

THLIMMENOS v. GREECE (34369/97) (2001) 31 E.H.R.R. 15, L Wildhaber (President), ECHR.

3486. **Freedom of religion – religious groups – state interference – compatibility with ECHR – Bulgaria**

[European Convention on Human Rights 1950 Art.6, Art.9, Art.11, Art.13.]

During democratisation in Bulgaria, some of the Muslim community sought to replace their leader G, who had collaborated with the communists, with H. In 1992, the new government declared the election of G as chief mufti void. G unsuccessfully challenged the decision before the Supreme Court. The government subsequently registered H as the new leader. In 1994 supporters of G held another conference at which G was elected leader and in 1995 a new government registered G as leader without any formal notification to H. In March 1995 the government informed H that he had been replaced. He appealed to the Supreme Court but was unsuccessful because the court held that the government had full discretion to register a given religion. H then organised another conference at which he was elected leader and in that capacity requested the government to register his leadership. The government ignored his request. On appeal to the Supreme Court the court held that the government was under a statutory duty to consider the request for registration from H. The government again refused to register H as leader. The Supreme Court held the refusal to be unlawful but the government refused to register H. A new government subsequently registered a new leadership excluding H. H complained that the government was in breach of European Convention on Human Rights 1950 Art.6, Art.9, Art.11 and Art.13.

Held, allowing the application, that (1) H had not established that he did not have adequate remedies before the civil courts and therefore there was no violation of Art.6; (2) Art.9 guaranteed the freedom of expression for religious communities as well as individuals and should be interpreted in the light of Art.11 which operated as a safeguard against freedom from arbitrary state interference; there had been a breach of Art.9; (3) no separate issue arose under Art.11, and (4) there had been no violation of Art.13.

HASAN v. BULGARIA (30985/96) 10 B.H.R.C. 646, Wildhaber (President), ECHR.

3487. **Inhuman treatment – sentencing – death due to criminal negligence – proportionality of mandatory term – Canada**

[Charter of Rights and Freedoms 1982 s.12 (Canada); Criminal Code s.220(a) (Canada).]

M appealed against a Canadian Court of Appeal decision that a four year mandatory sentence imposed on him under the Criminal Code s.220(a) did not constitute cruel and unusual punishment contrary to the Charter of Rights and Freedoms 1982 s.12. M had been convicted of criminal negligence following an incident in which a shotgun that he was holding when intoxicated accidentally discharged, killing his companion.

Held, dismissing the appeal, that the sentence did not violate s.12 of the Charter. To invoke the protection of s.12 it was necessary to examine the subjective effect of the sentence on M as an individual, whilst also taking into account factors such as the aim of the punishment and sentences for comparative criminal acts. M's offence was extremely serious, despite his lack of intention to kill. The deterrent aims of the mandatory sentence were justified in that context and did not constitute cruel and unusual punishment on the facts of the instant case.

MORRISEY v. R. 9 B.H.R.C. 179, Gonthier, J., Sup Ct (Can).

3488. **Parental rights – child protection – provision allowing state to apprehend child where no emergency existed – Canada**

[Canadian Charter of Rights and Fundamental Freedoms 1982 s.7; Child and Family Services Act 1985 (Manitoba) Part III.]

K appealed against the dismissal of her application for a declaration that the Child and Family Services Act 1985 Part III violated her parental rights under the Canadian Charter of Rights and Fundamental Freedoms 1982 s.7. K's first two children had been taken into care by W, and when she gave birth to a third child, J, W applied to apprehend J under s.21 (1) of the 1985 Act by requiring the hospital not to discharge K and J.

Held, dismissing the appeal (Arbour, J. dissenting in part), that apprehension of a child by removing it from its parent was a serious infringement of parental rights, but one that had to be balanced against the state's duty to protect children, particularly in emergency situations. Restricting the state's power to intervene by setting too high a threshold in emergency situations could put children's lives at risk. It was sufficient in such cases that there be a requirement that the matter be brought swiftly before the courts after apprehension. Considered as a whole in the context of child protection the 1985 Act reached that standard and was therefore not unconstitutional.

KLW v. WINNIPEG CHILD AND FAMILY SERVICES 9 B.H.R.C. 370, L'Heureux-Dube, J., Sup Ct (Can).

3489. Property rights – compulsory purchase – expropriation of land by Italian local authority

See REAL PROPERTY: Belvedere Alberghiera Srl v. Italy. §4860

3490. Property rights – taxation – failure to notify tax liability via Official Gazette – accessibility of change imposed by regulations

[European Convention on Human Rights 1950 Protocol 1 Art.1.]

S, a company, complained that its right to peaceful enjoyment of property under the European Convention on Human Rights 1950 Protocol 1 Art.1 had been violated by the imposition of an additional income tax liability by the Czech Republic. The additional liability arose due to S's predecessor changing from single to double entry bookkeeping without increasing the applicable tax base, as required by regulations published in a Finance Ministry Bulletin but not announced in the Official Gazette.

Held, dismissing the application, that although the tax penalty interfered with S's right to property, Protocol 1 Art.1 allowed the Czech Republic to implement laws relating to the payment of taxes. The accounting procedures were contained in regulations made under the relevant national law and were addressed to professional advisers who were used to working in such a way. Although the regulations had not been published in the Official Gazette, they had been set out in the Financial Bulletin, which was a procedure that S's predecessor could be taken to have been familiar with. It was reasonable, therefore, to expect S to take due steps to ensure that it was up to date with current procedures. The regulations were thus sufficiently accessible and there had been no violation of Protocol 1 Art.1.

SPACEK SRO v. CZECH REPUBLIC (2000) 30 E.H.R.R. 1010, Judge Costa (President), ECHR.

3491. Public services – telecommunications services – postal services – technical advisory board

REGULATION OF INVESTIGATORY POWERS (TECHNICAL ADVISORY BOARD) ORDER 2001, SI 2001 3734; made under the Regulation of Investigatory Powers Act 2000 s.13. In force: November 22, 2001; £1.50.

This Order provides for the membership of the Technical Advisory Board established by the Regulation of Investigatory Powers Act 2000 s.13. The Board must be consulted before the Secretary of State makes an order under the 2000 Act, imposing obligations on persons providing public postal services or public telecommunications services, or proposing to do so. The Board also has functions relating to the consideration of notices issued to service providers.

3492. Race discrimination – gypsies – aiding unlawful act

[Race Relations Act 1976 s.20, s.21, s.33(1).]

H, a Romany gypsy, appealed against a decision ([2000] 1 W.L.R. 966, [2000] C.L.Y. 3205) to dismiss her appeal against the dismissal of her claim for damages under the Race Relations Act 1976 s.33(1). H had brought the action against A and L, police officers, who had inaccurately informed the local council from whom she had contracted to hire council owned premises for her wedding reception that there was a risk of disorder owing to the potential large numbers in attendance at the reception. As a result, the council had attempted to unilaterally impose new contract terms whereby H had repudiated the contract and successfully claimed damages against the council under s.20 and s.21 of the Act. H submitted that she was also entitled to claim under s.33(1) of the Act since A and L had knowingly aided the local council to discriminate against them and, for the purposes of the Act, had themselves committed an unlawful act.

Held, dismissing the appeal, that the question whether a person had, within the meaning of s.33(1), aided another to commit an offence was to be determined on the facts of each case but, for a claim to succeed, something more than a general attitude of helpfulness and cooperation was needed. It had not been shown that A and L had knowingly aided the council to unlawfully discriminate against H, given that neither officer had been involved in the council's decision to impose the new contract terms, *Anyanwu v. South Bank Students Union* [2001] UKHL 14, [2001] 1 W.L.R. 638, [2001] 4 C.L. 239 followed.

HALLAM v. AVERY; SMITH v. CHELTENHAM BC; *sub nom.* HALLAM v. CHELTENHAM BC, [2001] UKHL 15, [2001] 1 W.L.R. 655, Lord Bingham of Cornhill, HL.

3493. Race discrimination – statutory duties

RACE RELATIONS ACT 1976 (GENERAL STATUTORY DUTY) ORDER 2001, SI 2001 3457; made under the Race Relations Act 1976 s.71. In force: December 3, 2001; £2.50.

This Order amends the list of bodies and other persons specified in the Race Relations Act 1976 who are subject to the general duty to have due regard, when exercising their functions, to the need to eliminate unlawful racial discrimination and to promote equality of opportunity and good relations between persons of different racial groups. The Order repeals an entry in that list relating to licensing planning committees and updates an entry concerning probation boards. The Order also adds to that list of bodies and other persons specified in the Schedule to the Order, thereby also subjecting those bodies and persons to the general duty.

3494. Race discrimination – statutory duties – Race Equality Scheme

RACE RELATIONS ACT 1976 (STATUTORY DUTIES) ORDER 2001, SI 2001 3458; made under the Race Relations Act 1976 s.71. In force: December 3, 2001; £2.50.

This Order imposes certain bodies and other persons who are subject to the general duty of the Race Relations Act 1976 to have due regard, when exercising their functions, to the need to eliminate unlawful racial discrimination and to promote equality of opportunity and good relations between persons of different racial groups. The duties are imposed for the purpose of ensuring the better performance of the general duty. The Order imposes on a body or other persons specified, a duty to publish, by May 31, 2002, a Race Equality Scheme, that is a Scheme showing how it intends to fulfil the general duty and its duties under this Order. It also imposes on an educational body, duties to prepare, by May 31, 2002, a statement of its race equality policy, to have arrangements in place for fulfilling duties to assess and monitor the impact of its policies on different racial groups, and to fulfil those duties in accordance with such arrangements.

3495. **Race Relations (Amendment) Act 2000 (c.34) – Commencement Order**

RACE RELATIONS (AMENDMENT) ACT 2000 (COMMENCEMENT) ORDER 2001, SI 2001 566 (C.24); made under the Race Relations (Amendment) Act 2000 s.10. Commencement details: bringing into force various provisions of the Act on April 2, 2001; £1.50.

This Order provides for the coming into force of the Race Relations (Amendment) Act 2000 s.2 to s.9 on April 2, 2001. Section 1 of the Act comes into force for the purpose of the imposition of requirements or giving of express authorisations by a Minister of the Crown on March 26, 2001, and for all other purposes on April 2, 2001.

3496. **Regulation of Investigatory Powers Act 2000 (c.23) – Commencement No.2 Order**

REGULATION OF INVESTIGATORY POWERS ACT 2000 (COMMENCEMENT NO.2) ORDER 2001, SI 2001 2727 (C.91); made under the Regulation of Investigatory Powers Act 2000 s.83. Commencement details: bringing into force various provisions of the Act on August 13, 2001; £1.50.

This Order brings into force the Regulation of Investigatory Powers Act 2000 s.71 and s.72, which relate to the issue and effect of codes of practice and the acquisition and disclosure of communications data, for the purposes of Part I Ch.II of that Act.

3497. **Remedies – criminal appeals – prolonged pre trial detention – failure to exhaust domestic remedies for breach of Art.5 – France**

[European Convention on Human Rights 1950 Art.5(3).]

C, a French national, was accused of the rape of his two daughters. C was remanded in custody for two years before he was committed for trial. During this time C made several applications and appeals for his release from detention. C was convicted of rape and sentenced to ten years' imprisonment. C complained to the Commission that his detention prior to trial had been excessively long in violation of the European Convention on Human Rights 1950 Art.5(3). The Commission upheld C's complaint. The French Government maintained that the court should not determine C's complaint since C had not exhausted the domestic remedies available to him.

Held, (by a majority) upholding the French Government's objections, that although the French Court of Cassation could not reassess findings of fact made by the court below it had jurisdiction to review the proceedings as a whole and the reasons given for the court's decision. By failing to appeal to the Court of Cassation regarding his pre-trial detention C had failed to exhaust his domestic remedies. The five dissenting judges took the view that the case law of the Court of Cassation indicated that the question whether a period of detention was excessive was one of fact in respect of which the court lacked jurisdiction. Therefore there was no effective appeal on points of law which C could have made to that court.

CIVET v. FRANCE (29340/95) (2001) 31 E.H.R.R. 38, Judge Wildhaber (President), ECHR.

3498. **Right to fair trial – access to justice – effect of immediate temporary withdrawal of driving licence – Belgium**

[European Convention on Human Rights 1950 Art.6(1).]

E was involved in a road accident, after which his driving licence was temporarily withdrawn on the presumption that he had been driving with a blood-alcohol level above the prescribed limit. Relying on the European Convention on Human Rights 1950 Art.6(1) he complained to the ECHR that the immediate withdrawal of his driving licence without the opportunity to appeal, had deprived him of access to a tribunal.

Held, dismissing the complaint, that (1) Art.6(1) was not applicable unless there was a criminal charge against a particular person; (2) in ascertaining whether there was a "criminal charge", the court had regard to three criteria: the legal classification of the measure in question in national law, the very nature of the measure, and the nature of and degree of severity of the penalty *Pierre-Bloch v. France* (1998) 26 E.H.R.R. 202, [1998] C.L.Y. 3119 applied; (3) the immediate withdrawal of a driving licence was not a measure imposed under the criminal law, since it was a preventive measure designed to take a dangerous driver off the roads for a specific period of time; (4) there was nothing to indicate that its purpose was punitive. Withdrawal of a driving licence could be distinguished from disqualification from driving, a measure ordered by the criminal courts in the context of, and after the outcome of, a criminal prosecution; The impact of withdrawal was not sufficiently substantial to allow it to be classified as a "criminal" penalty; (5) in this case the withdrawal of the applicant's driving licence did not cause him significant prejudice, since he was able to get it back six days after he had handed it over to the police and two days after he had requested its return, and (6) in all the circumstances Art.6 was not applicable under its criminal head. Moreover the applicant had not submitted any evidence in support of his argument that a "civil" right was at issue.

ESCOUBET v. BELGIUM (26780/95) (2001) 31 E.H.R.R. 46, Judge Palm (President), ECHR.

3499. Right to fair trial – access to justice – failure to surrender to custody – right of access to tribunal – France

[European Convention on Human Rights 1950 Art.6(1).]

K, a hospital doctor, was convicted of indecent assault on a patient and sentenced to imprisonment. Following K's unsuccessful appeal against conviction he had lodged an appeal in the Court of Cassation but requested an exemption from the obligation to surrender to custody before the hearing of the appeal on the grounds that he was suffering from tuberculosis. His request was refused and the Court of Cassation ruled that he had forfeited his right to appeal through his failure to surrender to custody. K complained of a breach of his right to a fair trial under the European Convention on Human Rights 1950 Art.6(1).

Held, (by a majority) that the right of access to a court was not an absolute right but could be subject to limitations provided that any such limitation did not affect the essence of the right itself. A limitation had to be in pursuit of a legitimate aim and had to be reasonably proportional in relation to that aim. The French Government's declared aim in imposing the obligation to surrender to custody on prospective appellants to the Court of Cassation was to facilitate the enforcement of the decision under appeal in the event that the appeal was dismissed. However this effectively required the appellant to subject himself in advance to the deprivation of liberty required by the decision under appeal, a decision which could not be considered final until the appeal had been decided, *Omar v. France* (2000) 29 E.H.R.R. 210, [2000] C.L.Y. 3209 applied. Furthermore the appeal procedure itself did not require the attendance of the appellant since the proceedings were mostly conducted on the basis of written pleadings. The forfeiture of the right to appeal was a disproportionately harsh penalty. Accordingly there had been a breach of Art.6(1).

KHALFAOUI v. FRANCE (34791/97) (2001) 31 E.H.R.R. 42, Judge Bratza (President), ECHR.

3500. Right to fair trial – appeals – appellate court's duty to give reasons

[European Convention on Human Rights 1950 Art.6(1).]

R was a lawyer and a member of the Madrid bar, although he worked as a nurse. In 1985 he said that another party had instructed him to carry out non contentious legal work in connection with the purchase of land. He sought payment for his services and when his client failed to pay he brought an action to recover that amount. His claim was dismissed at first instance and appeals to the Audiencia Provincial and the Constitutional Court were dismissed on the ground that there was no evidence that R had carried out the work in the context of judicial proceedings. R complained that the Audiencia Provincial had failed to address his arguments in its judgment so that he had not had a fair hearing in terms of the European Convention on Human Rights 1950 Art.6(1).

Held, refusing the application, that (1) under Art.6(1) judgments were required give the reasons on which they were based, but this duty varied according to the type of decision and the circumstances of the individual case. In dismissing R's appeal, the Audiencia Provincial had merely endorsed the reasons of the first instance court, which was acceptable for the purposes of Art.6(1), and (2) in so far as R's complaint concerned the assessment of the evidence, it was not the court's function to deal with errors of fact or law allegedly committed by a national court, unless Convention rights had been infringed as a result. Furthermore, while Art.6 guaranteed the right to a fair hearing, it did not refer to the admissibility of evidence or the way it should be assessed, which were primarily matters for the national law and the national courts.

GARCIA RUIZ v. SPAIN (30544/96) (2001) 31 E.H.R.R. 22, Judge Wildhaber (President), ECHR.

3501. **Right to fair trial – bias – army law – officers hearing substantive matter also sitting on appeal against committal**

[European Convention on Human Rights 1950 Art.6(1).]

CA, an army officer, was committed for trial for an offence under the Spanish Military Criminal Code. He had unsuccessfully appealed against the order committing him for trial, and was subsequently tried by a tribunal comprising two officers that had refused his appeal against committal. CA then appealed to the Spanish Supreme Court, on the ground that his first appeal had not been conducted in an impartial manner. That appeal was dismissed, and he filed a further appeal with the Spanish Constitutional Court. That appeal was also dismissed and CA complained of a breach of the European Convention on Human Rights 1950 Art.6(1), arguing that he had been denied a hearing before an impartial tribunal. Spain raised a preliminary point that CA had failed to exhaust his domestic remedies by failing to challenge the composition of the tribunal that convicted him.

Held, upholding the complaint, that CA had argued on appeal to the Supreme Court that the tribunal was not impartial because of the presence of the two officers concerned, so the preliminary point could not be upheld. Judicial impartiality was to be assessed on the basis of both subjective and objective tests. Subjectively, judicial impartiality could be presumed in the absence of evidence to the contrary. There was no such evidence in the instant case. However, from an objective standpoint, the appearance of partiality in the eyes of the accused was an important factor to be considered. Decisions taken by the officers concerned at earlier stages in the proceedings could be taken to show that they were of the view that CA had committed the offence, so that CA's fears as to their partiality were objectively justified, *Oberschlick v. Austria (A/204)* (1995) 19 E.H.R.R. 389, [1995] C.L.Y. 2646 applied.

CASTILLO ALGAR v. SPAIN (2000) 30 E.H.R.R. 827, R Bernhardt (President), ECHR.

3502. **Right to fair trial – bias – judicial review – jurisdiction of appellate courts**

See ADMINISTRATIVE LAW: Kingsley v. United Kingdom (35605/97). §96

3503. **Right to fair trial – bias – planning – policy maker acting as adjudicator**

See PLANNING: R. (on the application of Holding & Barnes Plc) v. Secretary of State for the Environment, Transport and the Regions. §4761

3504. Right to fair trial – burden of proof – reversal – defence to supply of drugs charge – retrospective effect of Human Rights Act

[Misuse of Drugs Act 1971 s.5(3), s.28(3)(b)(i); Human Rights Act 1998 s.6(1), Sch.1 Part I Art.6.]

L appealed against a decision of the Court of Appeal ([2001] 2 W.L.R. 211, [2000] 10 C.L. 294) upholding his conviction for possession of cocaine with intent to supply contrary to the Misuse of Drugs Act 1971 s.5(3). At trial, L had maintained that he had been unaware that the bag found in his possession contained cocaine. The judge had directed the jury in accordance with what was accepted to be the law at the time, that in order to establish a defence under s.28(3)(b)(i) of the 1971 Act, L was obliged to establish on the balance of probabilities that he had been unaware that the bag contained a controlled drug. The issue before the House was whether on appeal, in relation to the direction given, L could rely on the retrospective effect of the Human Rights Act 1998 Sch.1 Part I Art.6(2), which conferred on the accused the presumption of innocence.

Held, dismissing the appeal (Lord Steyn dissenting in part), that Parliament had not intended that where a conviction had been secured prior to the implementation of the 1998 Act, a defendant would be entitled to rely upon Convention rights on appeal, *Wilson v. First County Trust Ltd (No.2)* [2001] EWCA Civ 633, [2001] 3 W.L.R. 42, [2001] 6 C.L. 91 considered. If such a situation were permitted, there would be significant potential for confusion and uncertainty. Whilst it was arguable that the legal burden of proof could not be justified under Art.6(2), the s.28(3)(b)(i) test would be compatible with Art.6(2) if interpreted as a reference to the evidential burden alone, *Salabiaku v. France (A/141-A)* (1991) 13 E.H.R.R. 379 considered. Lord Steyn, whilst concurring that the appeal should be dismissed, observed that an appellate court which upheld a conviction that had been obtained in breach of a Convention right would "act" for the purposes of s.6(1) of the 1998 Act in a way that was incompatible with the Convention and therefore unlawfully. Such an interpretation did not involve true retrospectivity.

R. v. LAMBERT (STEVEN); R. v. ALI (MUDASSIR MOHAMMED); R. v. JORDAN (SHIRLEY), [2001] UKHL 37, [2001] 3 W.L.R. 206, Lord Slynn of Hadley, HL.

3505. Right to fair trial – civil servants – unfair dismissal – delay in compensation proceedings

[European Convention on Human Rights 1950 Art.6(1).]

C was unlawfully dismissed from her civil service post, and had applied for compensation from F. The civil proceedings took over eight years to complete. C complained that the delay amounted to a breach of her right to a fair trial within a reasonable time under the European Convention on Human Rights 1950 Art.6(1).

Held, allowing the application and awarding C compensation, that there had been a breach of Art.6. C's claim against F had been in relation to her "economic right" to compensation and not in relation to her employment as a civil servant, and therefore came within Art.6(1). The delay had been the fault of the courts and no adequate explanation for it had been given by F. The delay therefore clearly went beyond what could be described as a "reasonable time".

CAZENAVE DE LA ROCHE v. FRANCE (25549/94) (2001) 33 E.H.R.R. 7, R Bernhardt (President), ECHR.

3506. Right to fair trial – consumer credit agreements – statutory provisions – declaration of incompatibility

See CONSUMER LAW: Wilson v. First County Trust Ltd (No.2). §909

3507. Right to fair trial – criminal appeal – presence of appellant at appeal against detention in mental institution

[European Convention on Human Rights 1950 Art.6.]

After making threats to murder lawyers and judges involved in an earlier criminal prosecution against him, P was ordered to be detained in an institution for the mentally ill. He complained that the Supreme Court had heard his nullity plea and appeal in his absence so that he had been denied a fair trial contrary to the European Convention on Human Rights 1950 Art.6.

Held, dismissing the complaint, that (1) as a general principle, a defendant to a criminal charge should be present at the first instance hearing, but this was not the case on an appeal so that non attendance was not necessarily contrary to Art.6, even if the appellate court had full jurisdiction to review the facts and the law; (2) C's plea of nullity related to procedural and legal matters, such as the dismissal of his requests for further evidence and the state of the legal reasoning. C had been represented by counsel throughout and there were no special circumstances requiring his presence, *Stanford v. UK* Times, March 8, 1994, [1994] C.L.Y. 2398 referred to. Therefore P's absence in respect of the nullity plea did not breach Art.6; (3) the appeal hearing by the Supreme Court was limited to a review of the lower court's findings and an examination, on the court's own motion, of the conditions surrounding P's placement in the institution. Again, P's interests had been represented by counsel and his future condition could be assessed by reference to expert opinion so that P had again failed to show that his absence was contrary to Art.6.

PRINZ v. AUSTRIA (23867/94) (2001) 31 E.H.R.R.12, Judge Costa (President), ECHR.

3508. Right to fair trial – criminal appeal – presence of appellant at appeal hearing

[European Convention on Human Rights 1950 Art.6, Art.25(1).]

C was sentenced to 20 years' imprisonment following his conviction for murder. His plea of nullity and appeal against sentence was heard in his absence and he complained that he had been denied a fair trial under the European Convention on Human Rights 1950 Art.6 and also that his right of individual petition had been hindered, contrary to the former Art.25(1).

Held, allowing the reference in part, that (1) generally the defendant in criminal proceedings was entitled to be present at the hearing, but this did not have the same significance for an appeal. Attendance was not always required therefore to ensure a fair trial in terms of Art.6. In the instant case, however, although C's absence was not an issue in relation to the plea of nullity, the court could not determine the matter properly without assessing C's character and state of mind, so that his presence was required to ensure a fair trial under Art.6(1) and Art.6(3) for sentencing purposes, and (2) on the facts, C had not been hindered in the exercise of his right of petition under the former Art.25(1).

COOKE v. AUSTRIA (25878/94) (2001) 31 E.H.R.R. 11, Judge Costa (President), ECHR.

3509. Right to fair trial – criminal appeals – appellant prevented from attending – public prosecutor present throughout

[European Convention on Human Rights 1950 Art.6.]

B appealed against conviction for theft, for which he had been sentenced to three years' imprisonment. The appeal court decided that it was not necessary for B, who was not represented, to appear in person and his appeal was dismissed. B complained that his right to a fair trial under the European Convention on Human Rights 1950 Art.6(1) and (3)(c) had been violated by denying him the opportunity to defend himself. Further, that the principle of equality of arms had been breached as the public prosecutor had been present throughout.

Held, upholding the complaint unanimously, that generally the presence of the appellant at an appeal hearing was less important than the attendance of the defendant at the initial trial. However, in the instant case, B had intended to give evidence before the appellate court. The prosecutor had attended to ensure that B's appeal was dismissed and not simply to guard the public interest, as contended for by the State.

BELZIUK v. POLAND (2000) 30 E.H.R.R. 614, R Bernhardt (President), ECHR.

3510. **Right to fair trial – criminal charges – conviction for offence different from that originally charged – delay**

[European Convention on Human Rights 1950 Art.6.]

P was convicted by the French courts of aiding and abetting criminal bankruptcy. He had been committed for trial on the charge of criminal bankruptcy and asserted that he was unaware that an alternative verdict was available. Accordingly, P complained that the conviction was contrary to the European Convention on Human Rights 1950 Art.6(3)(a) and Art.6(3)(b). Further, that the duration of the proceedings, which had taken nine years and five months from the date of charge to the judgment date, was unreasonable in terms of Art.6(1).

Held, allowing the complaint, that fairness in criminal proceedings required an assessment of the entire proceedings. An accused was to be given detailed information as to the charges faced and notice of the court proceedings to allow for an adequate defence. French law distinguished the nature of the two offences and it was likely that P would have put forward a different defence had he known that an alternative verdict was possible. As to the length of proceedings, even allowing for the commercial character of the case, it was not unduly complex in nature and P was not responsible for any delay. Furthermore, legislative changes during the proceedings had actually simplified the definition of the offences concerned.

PELISSIER v. FRANCE (2000) 30 E.H.R.R. 715, L Wildhaber (President), ECHR.

3511. **Right to fair trial – criminal evidence – refusal to disclose evidence – public interest immunity**

[European Convention on Human Rights 1950 Art.6(1).]

F appealed against his conviction for conspiracy to rob, possession of a firearm and possession of a prohibited weapon. At the start of the trial, the prosecution had successfully applied ex parte for an order that it would not be required to disclose evidence given by an informant. The trial judge made a second order following an inter partes hearing, relating to the disclosure of statements made by a co-accused, C. F's appeal against the orders was dismissed and he complained to the European Court of Human Rights that non disclosure of the informant's evidence and C's statements rendered his trial unfair under the European Convention on Human Rights 1950 Art.6(1) and (2), as the matters concerned were relevant to his defence. F also argued that he had discovered, after his conviction, that C had previously given false information to obtain reward.

Held, refusing to uphold the complaint, that the right to a fair trial in criminal cases was concerned to ensure equality between prosecution and defence and to maintain the adversarial process. In the instant case, the defence had been informed as to the nature of the prosecution's applications and been allowed to make representations to the judge who had proceeded on the basis that disclosure would be ordered if this would assist the defence. This showed that there had been compliance with Art.6(1) at first instance. Further consideration of the matter on appeal had provided an additional protection for F's rights.

FITT v. UNITED KINGDOM (2000) 30 E.H.R.R. 480, Judge Wlldhaber (President), ECHR.

3512. **Right to fair trial – criminal evidence – refusal to disclose evidence – public interest immunity**

[Interception of Communications Act 1985; European Convention on Human Rights 1950 Art.6(1), Art.6(3).]

J was convicted of importing cannabis resin into the UK concealed in a consignment of meat. J contended that his right to a fair trial under the European Convention on Human Rights 1950 Art.6(1) Art.6(3) had been breached on the basis that the prosecution had made an ex parte application before trial to withhold evidence on public interest immunity grounds. The defence had served a request for information on the prosecution but the trial judge upheld a refusal to disclose information obtained under the Interception of Communications Act 1985. J's appeal on the ground that there had been a failure to disclose all unused evidence was dismissed and he complained to the European Court of Human Rights.

Held, the majority refusing to uphold the complaint, that the right to a fair trial in criminal cases was concerned to ensure equality between prosecution and defence and to maintain the adversarial process. However, there were circumstances where it was appropriate to withhold evidence from the defence in the public interest so as to ensure the secrecy of police investigation methods. It was for the national court to decide on admissibility of evidence and to weigh the public interest favouring non disclosure against the defence's right to disclosure. In the instant case this had been done at both first instance and on appeal, so that J's trial had been fair in terms of Art.6(1) and Art.6(3).

JASPER v. UNITED KINGDOM (2000) 30 E.H.R.R. 441, Judge Wildhaber (President), ECHR.

3513. Right to fair trial – delay – application for pharmacy licence – decision delayed for five years

[European Convention on Human Rights 1950 Art.6(1).]

G applied for a licence to run a pharmacy in September 1988. The proceedings, which became subject to appeal following refusal by the provincial governor, continued for five years and five months until G withdrew his application following an agreement with another pharmacist. He contended that the length of time taken exceeded that which was reasonable in terms of the European Convention on Human Rights 1950 Art.6(1).

Held, allowing the application, that (1) while pharmacists were subject to certain public law requirements, the right to exercise the profession was a civil matter under Art.6(1); (2) reasonableness of the length of proceedings was to be assessed by reference to the circumstances of the case, which included its complexity, conduct of the parties and importance of the right applied for, *Humen v. Poland* (2001) 31 E.H.R.R. 53 referred to, and (3) on the facts, the length of the proceedings as a whole exceeded that which was reasonable in breach of Art.6(1).

GS v. AUSTRIA (26297/95) (2001) 31 E.H.R.R. 21, Judge Kuris (President), ECHR.

3514. Right to fair trial – delay – civil servants – termination of employment – applicability of Art.6(1)

[European Convention on Human Rights 1950 Art.6(1).]

P became a technical adviser to the French Ministry of Cooperation and Development in 1989, in which capacity he was posted to Equatorial Guinea. He was later found to be unfit for service overseas and his name was removed from the Ministry's establishment in March 1990. P challenged this decision in the administrative court by way of an application commenced in May 1990. The application was dismissed in 1995 and P appealed. The appeal was still pending when he complained to the ECHR that his case had not been heard within a reasonable time, contrary to the European Convention on Human Rights 1950 Art.6(1).

Held, refusing the application, that Art.6(1) did not apply, (1) disputes concerning civil service recruitment and termination of service were generally beyond the scope of Art.6(1), *Massa v. Italy (A/265-B)* (1994) 18 E.H.R.R. 266, [1995] C.L.Y. 2629 considered. However, Art.6(1) did apply where remuneration or economic matters were in issue that did not involve public law powers. In determining whether Art.6(1) was applicable it was necessary to consider the type of duties and the extent of the employee's responsibilities. Civil servants whose duties related to specific public service activities involving general interests of the State did not come within Art.6(1) and neither did those who held posts involving the exercise of public law powers. Post retirement pension disputes were covered by Art.6(1), however, as the relationship of trust between former civil servants and the State had ceased and the claimants no longer had the ability to wield sovereign power.

PELLEGRIN v. FRANCE (2001) 31 E.H.R.R. 26, Judge Palm (President), ECHR.

3515. Right to fair trial – delay – compatibility with ECHR

[European Convention on Human Rights 1950 Art.6(1).]

N was severely injured and permanently disabled in a car accident in November 1986. He brought proceedings against three insurance companies on February 26, 1988 which were not concluded for more than 8 years. N complained to the European Court of Human Rights that his right to a fair trial within a reasonable time under the European Convention on Human Rights 1950 Art.6(1) had been violated.

Held, allowing the application and awarding N compensation, that the delay had to be assessed having regard to (1) the complexity of the case, and (2) the conduct of the parties; although some of the delay was attributable to N, over five years of the delay was caused directly by the Danish court. The outcome was important to N because of the seriousness of his injuries and the delay was excessive.

NIELSEN v. DENMARK (33488/96) (2001) 33 E.H.R.R. 9, Judge Rozakis (President), ECHR.

3516. Right to fair trial – delay – compensation for pecuniary and non pecuniary loss – global assessment

[European Convention on Human Rights 1950 Art.6(1).]

C, a Portuguese registered public company, held eight outstanding bills of exchange. It commenced proceedings to recover the sums due in October 1982. However, the proceedings were still pending in April 2000 and C complained that the length of time taken to date breached its right to a fair hearing within a reasonable time under the European Convention on Human Rights 1950 Art.6(1) and sought compensation for pecuniary damage of ESC 20 million and ESC 5 million for non pecuniary damage.

Held, allowing the application in part and ordering global compensation of ESC 1.5 million, that (1) reasonableness in terms of length of proceedings was to be determined by reference to the circumstances of the case, its complexity, along with C's conduct and that of the authorities and the overall values involved, *Silva Pontes v. Portugal (A/286-A)* (1994) 18 E.H.R.R. 156, [1994] C.L.Y. 2392 considered; (2) on the facts taken as a whole, the total period of 17 years and five months that had elapsed so far was not reasonable, *Estima Jorge v. Portugal* [1998] H.R.C.D. 447 considered; (3) contracting states were expected to organise their judicial systems to allow for the determination of civil disputes within a reasonable time; (4) if Art.6(1) was breached in a case where domestic law only allowed for partial reparation, compensation could be awarded under Art.41 at the court's discretion, and (5) a global assessment could be made when compensating for losses actually suffered, pecuniary damage, and assessing the reparation for the loss, non pecuniary damage, where the heads of damage could not be assessed accurately.

COMINGERSOLL SA v. PORTUGAL (2001) 31 E.H.R.R. 31, Judge Wildhaber (President), ECHR.

3517. Right to fair trial – delay – compensation proceedings following miscarriage of justice – Poland

[European Convention on Human Rights 1950 Art.6(1).]

In May 1982, H was arrested by the militia because he had taken part in a street demonstration in Gdansk. He was detained on remand on suspicion of having participated in an illegal assembly and subsequently sentenced to 16 months imprisonment. On appeal in 1993, his conviction was quashed and he was acquitted. In 1996 he was awarded compensation by the Gdansk regional court. Relying on the European Convention on Human Rights 1950 Art.6(1) he complained to the ECHR that the proceedings relating to his claim for compensation for wrongful conviction under martial law and his unjustified detention had been unreasonably long.

Held, dismissing the application, that (1) the reasonableness of the length of proceedings had to be assessed in the light of the particular circumstances of the case having regard to the criteria laid down in the court's case law, in particular the complexity of the case, the conduct of H, the relevant authorities and the importance of what was at stake for the applicant in the litigation, *Styranowski v. Poland* [1998] H.R.C.D. 1001 referred to; (2) certain features of this case were complex. Detailed medical evidence was required. Comprehensive evidence relating to his employment and loss of earnings was required; (3) by the time H initiated the compensation proceedings, his reputation had already been restored because his conviction had been quashed. All that was at stake in those proceedings was a compensation claim; (4) it was true that the regional court took 14 months to prepare the applicant's case for the first hearing and the backlog of similar cases could not be seen as a convincing explanation for the entire length of that period. However, except for that instance of failure to make progress in the proceedings, there was no substantial period of inactivity for which the authorities could be held responsible, and (5) in view of the facts, on the whole, the authorities did not fail to act with all due diligence in the conduct of H's case. The length of the proceedings complained of could not be regarded as unreasonable and there had been no breach of Art.6(1).

HUMEN v. POLAND (26614/95) (2001) 31 E.H.R.R. 53, Judge Rozakis (President), ECHR.

3518.   Right to fair trial – delay – compulsory liquidation – winding up of company – violation of ECHR

[European Convention on Human Rights 1950 Art.6.]

G, a Danish national, owned 90 per cent of the shares in a company registered in Luxembourg which traded in fur and leather products. His wife owned the remaining 10 per cent. In May 1987 the company went into compulsory liquidation. The national court appointed a judge and the official receiver to manage the liquidation and G agreed to assist the receiver. In G's absence the court authorised the receiver to sell the company's assets to satisfy the creditors' claims so far as possible. The liquidation was completed in 1993. G applied to the European Commission of Human Rights 1950 arguing that the delay in completing the liquidation constituted a breach of his human rights under Art.6. The receiver said that the delays had been the result of complex claims by some of the creditors that had to be resolved and proceedings pending in Germany. The Government argued that the liquidation did not involve any civil rights under Art.6; that he was not a victim of any delay; and that only the company itself could make any complaints.

Held, ruling that there had been a breach of Art.6, that (1) the liquidation proceedings involved a determination of a civil right within Art. 6(1); (2) the company was under liquidation and the complaint brought before the court related to the activities of the liquidators, i.e. the official receiver and the Commercial Court. In those circumstances it was not possible for the company, as a legal personality, to bring the case before the Commission; (3) moreover, the applicant held a substantial shareholding of 90 per cent in the company. He was in effect carrying out his business through the company and had, therefore, a direct personal interest in the subject matter of the complaint. Thus the applicant might claim to be a victim of the alleged violation of the ECHR affecting the rights of the limited liability company; (4) the reasonableness of the length of the proceedings had to be assessed in the light of the particular circumstances of the case, having regard to the complexities of the liquidation, G's conduct and the delays caused by the proceedings in Germany, and (5) having regard to the particular circumstances of the case and the overall length of the proceedings lasting six years, the "reasonable time" requirement was not satisfied and there had been a breach of Art.6(1).

GJ v. LUXEMBOURG [2000] B.P.I.R. 1021, AB Baka (President), ECHR.

3519. Right to fair trial – delay – criteria for determining reasonableness

[European Convention on Human Rights 1950 Art.6(1), Art.28(1)(b).]

P, a haemophiliac infected with the HIV virus by blood transfusion, brought proceedings against F in May 1990, seeking compensation for the medical complaints he suffered from because of the HIV infection. The Administrative Court rejected the claim in March 1993 and P's appeal was dismissed in February 1994. P pursued a further appeal before the Conseil d'Etat in April 1994. In December 1994, P lodged an application with the European Court of Human Rights, contending that the delay amounted to a breach of the European Convention on Human Rights 1950 Art 6(1). In June 1995 the Commission noted that P and F had reached a friendly settlement under Art.28(1)(b), resulting from P's acceptance of FF200,000 for non pecuniary damage. P's appeal was subsequently allowed by the Conseil d'Etat in April 1997, which ordered compensation in the sum of £862,250, plus interest.

Held, allowing the application, that in assessing whether the length of proceedings exceeded a reasonable time, consideration had to be given to the state of the proceedings at the start of the period under consideration, to the nature and complexity of the dispute, the conduct of the parties and the seriousness of P's case. On the facts, Art.6 had been breached, notwithstanding the friendly settlement, as the case had been pending before the Conseil d'Etat for more than three years with no explanation for the delay being given.

PAILOT v. FRANCE (2000) 30 E.H.R.R. 328, Thor Vilhjalmsson, ECHR.

3520. Right to fair trial – delay – delay in director disqualification proceedings

[Human Rights Act 1998 Sch.1 Part I Art.6(1).]

E, a former company director, sought a declaration that proceedings issued against him eight and half years previously, were in breach of or incompatible with his Convention right to a fair trial under the Human Rights Act 1998 Sch.1 Part I Art.6(1) and should consequently be struck out. E contended that the proceedings had not been conducted within the reasonable time requirement prescribed by Art.6(1) given that the events giving rise to the proceedings had occurred over ten years previously.

Held, refusing the application, that the proceedings were not incompatible or in breach of the 1998 Act, given that the lapse of time without a hearing was attributable to either the requirements of justice in respect of criminal proceedings or to E's own actions. Even if the proceedings had been found to have breached E's right to a fair trial, the undertaking he had given in accordance with the summary procedure in *Carecraft Construction Co Ltd, Re* [1994] 1 W.L.R. 172, [1993] C.L.Y. 374, to dispose of the proceedings would have been effective as a waiver of his rights under the 1998 Act and had not been induced by misrepresentation, *Carecraft* referred to.

SECRETARY OF STATE FOR TRADE AND INDUSTRY v. EASTAWAY; *sub nom.* BLACKSPUR GROUP PLC, *Re* [2001] 1 B.C.L.C. 653, Sir Robert Andrew Morritt V.C., Ch D (Companies Ct).

3521. Right to fair trial – delay – discrimination in civil service – Cyprus

[European Convention on Human Rights 1950 Art.6(1).]

M applied for a job as Head of Accounts of the Industrial Training Authority (ITA). The only other candidate, who was appointed, was less qualified than M and he sought compensation against the ITA. In the meantime the job in question was abolished. After the decision not to appoint M was declared to be null and void, he brought an action for damages. His action was successful but he appealed on the question of quantum. Final judgement was given on June 20, 1995. M complained to the ECHR about the delay in proceedings and, relying on the European Convention on Human Rights Art.6(1) complained that the time taken to deal with the matter was unreasonable.

Held, allowing the application, that (1) for the purposes of the applicability of Art.6(1) the central issue concerned classification of M's right to compensation following the annulment of the ITA's decision not to hire him; (2) although the court had held that disputes relating to the recruitment of civil servants were as a general rule outside the scope of Art.6(1), in this case the issue of recruitment to a public sector post was not at the heart of the applicant's civil action *Neigel v. France* (2000) 30 E.H.R.R. 310, [2001] 1 C.L. 311 referred to; (3) the applicant brought his civil action against the authorities solely to obtain financial reparation in respect of an administrative Act which he had successfully impugned in his recourse action; (4) the public law features of the civil action did not outweighed the predominantly private law characteristics of the proceedings; (5) when assessing the reasonableness of the length of proceedings in the light of the court's established case law, regard should be had to the fact that the period in respect of which it had jurisdiction began to run from January 1, 1989, when the declaration whereby Cyprus recognised the right of individual petition for the purposes of Art.25 of the Convention took effect. Nevertheless it had to take account of the state of the case on that date in making its determination *Proszak v. Poland* Unreported, December 16, 1997 referred to, and (6) against that background there had been a violation of Art.6(1) in that the applicant's civil rights had not been determined within a reasonable time.

MAVRONICHIS v. CYPRUS (2001) 31 E.H.R.R. 54, R Bernhardt (President), ECHR.

3522. Right to fair trial – delay – dishonest evasion of VAT – delay between end of hearing and decision – legal representation on appeal

[Value Added Tax Act 1983; European Convention on Human Rights 1950 Art.6(1), Protocol 1 Art.1, Protocol 1 Art.13.]

G, a takeaway food shop owner, complained to the European Court of Human Rights following the dismissal of an appeal to the VAT and duties tribunal against a Customs assessment to a penalty for dishonest evasion in respect of underdeclared output tax for the period from November 1, 1986 to October 31, 1989 ([1994] V.A.T.T.R. 125). The decision was affirmed on appeal to the High Court ([1995] S.T.C. 1101, [1995] C.L.Y. 5017) and again by the Court of Appeal ([1996] S.T.C. 463) and G contended that (1) his inability to instruct leading counsel for the Court of Appeal hearing due to lack of legal aid and the nine month delay from the end of the tribunal hearing to the release of its decision breached the European Convention on Human Rights 1950 Art.6(1), and (2) the way the assessment had been reviewed by Customs and the tribunal had violated his rights under Protocol 1 Art.1 and denied him an effective remedy, as required by Art.13.

Held, dismissing the application, that (1) although taken as a whole the penalty was criminal in nature for the purposes of Art.6(1), leading counsel had not been required for the Court of Appeal hearing. The delay on the part of tribunal was justified given the complexities of the case, *Boddaert v. Belgium (A/235D)* (1993) 16 E.H.R.R. 242, [1993] C.L.Y. 2135 and *Katte Klitsche de la Grange v. Italy (A/293-B)* (1995) 19 E.H.R.R. 368, [1995] C.L.Y. 2652 considered, and (2) rights capable of protection under Protocol 1 Art.1 were subject to the proviso that the collection of taxes was not impaired. A wide margin of appreciation was allowed in this respect and the review provided for by the Value Added Tax Act 1983 was more than adequate in Convention terms, *Gasus Dosier und Fordertechnik GmbH v. Netherlands (A/306-B)* (1995) 20 E.H.R.R. 403, [1996] C.L.Y. 3162 applied.

GEORGIOU (T/A MARIOS CHIPPERY) v. UNITED KINGDOM (40042/98) [2001] S.T.C. 80, J-P Costa (President), ECHR.

3523. Right to fair trial – delay – dismissal proceedings lasting nine years – France

[European Convention on Human Rights 1950 Art.6(1).]

F was employed under an individual contract by the Economic Development Department of the Ministry for Economic Affairs. His contract was not renewed owing to his inadequate performance. F challenged his dismissal. The administrative proceedings lasted nine years. Relying on Art.6(1) he complained to the ECHR about the length of the administrative proceedings in respect of that challenge.

Held, allowing the application, that (1) for Art.6(1) in its "civil" limb, to be applicable there must be a dispute over a right that could be said, at least on arguable grounds, to be recognised under domestic law. The dispute must be genuine and serious. It might relate not only to the actual existence of a right but also to its scope and the manner of its exercise. Moreover, the outcome of the proceedings had to be directly decisive for the civil right in question; (2) in the present case the question was whether the right in question was a "civil right" for the purposes of Art.6(1), regard being had to the fact that the proceedings concerned the dismissal of an official working for a public authority, *Pellegrin v. France* [2001] 31 E.H.R.R. 26, [2001] 9 C.L. 343 followed; (3) it was important, with a view to applying Art.6(1), to establish an autonomous interpretation of the term "civil service" which would make it possible to afford equal treatment to public servants in the states party to the Convention, irrespective of the domestic system of employment and, in particular, whatever the nature of the legal relation between the official and the administrative authority; (4) to that end, in order to determine the applicability of Art.6(1) to public servants, whether established or employed under contract, the court should adopt a functional criterion based on the nature of the official's duties and responsibilities; (5) the only disputes excluded from the scope of Art.6(1) were those raised by public servants whose duties were to protect the general interests of the State or other public authorities; (6) in view of the nature of the duties performed in the present case by the applicant and the relatively low level of his responsibilities, he was not carrying out any task which could be said to entail duties designed to safeguard the general interests of the State, and (7) the length of the proceedings complained of was excessive and failed to satisfy the reasonable time requirement and there was a violation of Art.6(1).

FRYDLENDER v. FRANCE (30979/96) (2001) 31 E.H.R.R. 52, Judge Palm (President), ECHR.

3524. Right to fair trial – delay – failure to determine compensation claim within reasonable time

[European Convention on Human Rights 1950 Art.6(1).]

The applicants cultivated land in an area of a land consolidation project. Works were carried out, in close co-operation between the Land Development Commission and water boards, which changed drainage of the applicant's land and caused flooding. The Commission denied liability for the damage to the applicant's land. The applicants brought an action in a regional court in 1993 claiming damages but the case did not come before the court until 1996 and the proceedings were still continuing. A complaint was made to the European Court of Human Rights that there had been a violation of the European Convention on Human Rights 1950 Art.6(1) because the applicants' case was not heard within a reasonable time.

Held, finding a violation of Art.6(1), that (1) the reasonableness of the length of proceedings had to be assessed in the light of the particular circumstances of each case, taking into account the complexity of the case, the parties' conduct and the importance of the outcome to the applicants; (2) even if proceedings were dealt with expeditiously once they started, a reasonable time might still be exceeded if an individual was unable to present his case for a considerable time when there was no good reason for the delay; (3) in the instant case the proceedings had been continuing for nine years and it could not be accepted that the nature of a land consolidation project was such that the applicants' claims could not be examined earlier; (4) although the applicants were responsible for some of the delay, it was not such as to detract from the fact that they had to wait until the end of 1996 before they could put their claims before a court; (5) the situation was hard to reconcile with the need to render justice with the effectiveness and credibility required by the Convention, and (6) the applicants' claim for just satisfaction would be dismissed as out of time, since the details required were not provided in due time.

VAN VLIMMEREN v. NETHERLANDS (25989/94) [2001] R.V.R. 34, L Ferrari Bravo (President), ECHR.

3525. **Right to fair trial – delay – mental patients rights – application for restoration of legal capacity**

[European Convention on Human Rights 1950 Art.6, Art.8.]

M was deprived of his legal capacity in 1983 on the ground that he was suffering from a form of psychosis. It was found that M had been a psychiatric out patient for 20 years at that time and that his condition was exacerbated by dementia. In 1987, M applied for his capacity to be restored and was subsequently subjected to a forcible examination when he refused to be examined voluntarily. M complained about both the length of time taken to determine his application and the forcible examination, contending that these were in breach of the European Convention on Human Rights 1950 Art.6 and Art.8.

Held, allowing the complaint in respect of Art.6, that (1) M was entitled to have his case examined diligently where his capacity was in issue and this included a consideration of the effects of excessive delay. The facts showed that the national courts had not acted with the level of required diligence by Art.6, even allowing the complexity of M's case; (2) the forcible examination interfered with M's rights under Art.8(1) but it served the legitimate aim of protecting his rights in terms of Art8(2) and was not disproportionate given the facts of the case. In determining the necessity of such actions, account had to be taken of the margin of appreciation accorded to the Contracting States and required an objective standard, taking into account all the relevant facts and the necessity of the particular course of action, and (3) the authorities were well placed to determine M's case, as they had direct contact with him and those responsible for his treatment and examination, subject to the court's powers of review under the Convention *Bronda v. Italy* [1998] H.R.C.D. 641 referred to.

MATTER v. SLOVAKIA (2001) 31 E.H.R.R. 32, Judge Rozakis (President), ECHR.

3526. **Right to fair trial – delay – rescission of exclusion order – procedure did not involved right capable of protection**

[European Convention on Human Rights 1950 Art.6(1).]

M, a Tunisian citizen living in France, was made the subject of a deportation order in 1990 on completing a French prison sentence for armed offences against the person. He did not comply with the order and an exclusion order was made against him. In 1994 the deportation order was quashed, but the exclusion order was not rescinded until 1998 and M complained that the length of time taken to rescind the order was unreasonable under the European Convention on Human Rights 1950 Art.6(1).

Held, refusing to uphold the complaint, that Art.6 did not apply. An exclusion order was a legitimate immigration measure that was not related to criminal proceedings. The procedure involved did not constitute a civil right capable of protection under Art.6.

MAAOUIA v. FRANCE (39652/98) (2001) 33 E.H.R.R. 42, Judge Wildhaber (President), ECHR.

3527. **Right to fair trial – delay – solicitors – disciplinary proceedings for professional misconduct lasting seven years – Austria**

[European Convention on Human Rights 1950 Art.6(1).]

WR was an Austrian lawyer. He was convicted in disciplinary proceedings of professional misconduct and unsuccessfully appealed. WR complained to the

Commission that the length of the proceedings, which had lasted seven years, amounted to a violation of his right to a fair trial under the European Convention on Human Rights 1950 Art.6(1).

Held, upholding WR's complaint, that WR's right to practise as a lawyer was a "civil right" within the meaning of Art.6(1). Furthermore Art.6(1) had previously been held to apply to disciplinary proceedings where the right to continue practising a profession was at stake. Even though in the present case WR had only been fined and had not been prevented from continuing to practise as a lawyer, the possible penalties included the suspension of the right to practise. Therefore WR's right to continue practising as a lawyer was at stake in the disciplinary proceedings against him. The overall length of the proceedings was not reasonable and it followed that there had been a breach of Art.6(1).

WR v. AUSTRIA (26602/95) (2001) 31 E.H.R.R. 43, Judge Kuris (President), ECHR.

3528. Right to fair trial – disabled persons – duty of court to take into account particular needs of disabled litigant

[Housing Act 1985 s.376(1); Human Rights Act 1998 Sch.1 Part I Art.6.]

K challenged a decision of the Crown Court to dismiss his appeal against a conviction for wilfully failing to comply with a statutory notice requiring him to execute certain works at his property, contrary to the Housing Act 1985 s.376(1). Having appeared at court without legal representation, K argued that the judge had failed, for the purpose of the appeal hearing, to make allowance for the impact of a stroke, suffered several years previously, on his ability to conduct the hearing and deal with the evidence against him.

Held, granting the application for judicial review and quashing the decision on appeal, that K's right to a fair trial under the Human Rights Act 1998 Sch.1 Part I Art.6 had been breached. It was of vital importance that proceedings were not only fair but also seen to be fair, and in circumstances where a disabled litigant had been kept waiting from 10.00 am until 4.00 pm before the hearing commenced and had not had any opportunity to make closing submissions, the fairness of the proceedings had undoubtedly been compromised.

Observed, that all judges were under a duty to take into account the advice in the Equal Treatment Bench Book concerning persons with disabilities.

R. (ON THE APPLICATION OF KING) v. ISLEWORTH CROWN COURT; *sub nom.* R. v. ISLEWORTH CROWN COURT, *ex p.* KING (MURRAY) [2001] E.H.L.R. 14, Brooke, L.J., QBD.

3529. Right to fair trial – employment – application for reinstatement – claim not involving "civil right" under Art.6

[European Convention on Human Rights 1950 Art.6.]

N was a shorthand typist employed by a local authority, B, who was granted one year's leave of absence for personal reasons in 1983. She was entitled to reinstatement as of right, conditional on a suitable vacancy existing at the time she sought reinstatement. However, no such vacancy existed in 1984 when N applied for reinstatement and she was informed that she had been given unpaid leave of absence pending a suitable vacancy. A subsequent re-application in 1985 was met with the same response and N brought legal proceedings against B in 1986 for reinstatement, but the claim failed and her final appeal was dismissed in 1991. N then complained that she had not had a hearing within a reasonable period of time, contrary to the European Convention on Human Rights 1950 Art. 6.

Held, refusing the application, that reinstatement was a right recognised under domestic law. However, the matter complained of was concerned with N's recruitment and career and did not entail a civil right, as required by Art.6, with the result that it did not apply in the instant case.

NEIGEL v. FRANCE (2000) 30 E.H.R.R. 310, R Ryssdal (President), ECHR.

3530. Right to fair trial – European Space Agency – immunity from prosecution in German Labour Court

[European Convention on Human Rights 1950 Art.6(1); Convention for the Establishment of a European Space Agency 1975.]

B was employed by the European Space Agency, ESA, and commenced proceedings against it in Germany in relation to his employment. The German court claimed that ESA had immunity from prosecution under the Convention for the Establishment of a European Space Agency 1975. B contended that his right to access to a court had been violated by the decision and brought an application claiming that the decision of the German court was in breach of the European Convention on Human Rights 1950 Art.6(1).

Held, dismissing the application, that there had been no breach of Art.6(1). Immunity was necessary to ensure that ESA could operate as an international body and it was therefore a legitimate and proportionate limitation on B's right under Art.6, particularly as B had recourse to ESA's own internal procedures as an effective means of seeking a remedy for his employment complaint. The German court decision was therefore within its margin of appreciation.

BEER v. GERMANY (28934/95) (2001) 33 E.H.R.R. 3, L Wildhaber (President), ECHR.

3531. Right to fair trial – evidence – restitution proceedings – failure to communicate evidence to parties – Czech Republic

[European Convention on Human Rights 1950 Art.6(1).]

K was the successor in title to a Czech company nationalised in 1946. In 1991 the Czech government proposed a privatisation plan and the sale of the company to a foreign company. K brought proceedings claiming restitution alleging flaws in the execution of the nationalisation procedure. The case eventually came before the constitutional court which found against K on the basis of documents which had not been shown to the parties during the hearing. K complained that the proceedings before the constitutional court violated his right to a fair hearing contrary to the European Convention on Human Rights 1950 Art.6(1).

Held, that the gathering of additional evidence by a court was not of itself incompatible with Art.6(1) but the failure to communicate such evidence to the parties was. The concept of a fair hearing implied the right to adversarial proceedings in which the parties should have knowledge of all evidence adduced with a view to influencing the court's decision. In the present case the documentary evidence on which the constitutional court relied was of crucial importance to K's restitution claim. Therefore the failure to allow K the opportunity to comment on the evidence constituted a breach of Art.6(1).

KRCMAR v. CZECH REPUBLIC (35376/97) (2001) 31 E.H.R.R. 41, Judge Bratza (President), ECHR.

3532. Right to fair trial – international law – review of detention – civilians detained during armed conflict

[American Declaration of the Rights and Duties of Man 1948 Art.I, Art.XVII, Art.XXV; Geneva Convention IV 1949.]

C claimed that the US had acted in violation of the American Declaration of the Rights and Duties of Man 1948 in respect of his detention, along with certain others, by US forces during the invasion of Grenada in 1983. C was one of a number of persons detained aboard US warships for between nine to 12 days, prior to being handed over to the Grenadian authorities. C was later convicted of the murder of the former Grenadian Prime Minister and he argued that he had been ill treated during his detention and later denied the right to a fair trial because the US had influenced the Grenadian judiciary so that he had not had a fair trial before an impartial tribunal.

Held, allowing the application, that the Commission had jurisdiction as international laws relating to both human rights and the rights of civilians in time of armed conflict under the Geneva Convention IV 1949 were in issue. The failure of the US to ensure an independent review of C's detention amounted to a violation of Art.I (right to life, liberty and personal security), Art.XVII (right to recognition of juridical personality and civil rights) and Art.XXV (right to protection from arbitrary arrest) of the 1948 Declaration.

COARD v. UNITED STATES 9 B.H.R.C. 150, Bicudo (Vice President), Inter American Commission on Human Rights.

3533. Right to fair trial – just satisfaction – failure to provide report on conviction – reimbursement of costs and expenses – France

[European Convention on Human Rights 1950 Art.6(1).]

S was convicted of criminal offences in connection with his business activities. A report of the conviction were lodged with the civil court which then awarded damages against him. Neither S nor his counsel were provided with copies of the report. Relying on the European Convention on Human Rights Art.6(1). S complained to the ECHR that neither he nor his advisers had been supplied with the reporting judge's report or the Advocate General's submissions prior to the hearing.

Held, allowing the application, that (1) as the report in question had not been supplied to the applicant there had been a violation of Art.6(1), *Reinhardt v. France* (1999) 28 E.H.R.R. 59, [1999] C.L.Y. 3130 followed; (2) it was not for the court to speculate as to what conclusion the criminal division of the Court of Cassation would have reached had not Art.6(1) been breached. Furthermore, no causal link had been established between the violation of that article and the various elements of the alleged pecuniary damage. The claims made in that respect were therefore dismissed; (3) as to non-pecuniary damage, the court considered that its findings of a breach of Art.6(1) provided sufficient just satisfaction, and (4) where the court found that there had been a violation of the convention, it only awarded the applicant the reimbursement of costs and expenses before the domestic courts in so far as such costs and expenses were incurred for the prevention or redress of the violation by those courts *Hertel v. Switzerland* (1999) 28 E.H.R.R. 534, [1999] C.L.Y. 3111 referred to.

SLIMANE-KAID v. FRANCE (29507/95) (2001) 31 E.H.R.R. 48, Judge Bratza, ECHR.

3534. Right to fair trial – legal representation – police stations – inadequate consultation with solicitor in ill equipped cell

[Human Rights Act 1998 Sch.1 Part I Art.6(3)(b).]

M and LR, who had been arrested for separate offences, brought judicial review proceedings against the Commissioner of Police seeking declarations that the Commissioner had breached their right under the Human Rights Act 1998 Sch.1 Part I Art.6(3)(b) to have adequate time and facilities for the preparation of their respective defences. M maintained that he had been forced to consult with his solicitor in an inappropriately equipped and unsanitary cell. He argued that the consultation had lacked privacy owing to a wicket in the cell door, that communication with his solicitor had been difficult and that his solicitor had not found it easy to take notes. LR maintained that he had been compelled to speak with his solicitor using a telephone located on the custody sergeant's desk, which had prevented him from having a full and frank consultation.

Held, refusing the applications, that Convention rights could not be invoked when the deprivation of such rights was merely theoretical and illusory. Instead, the court should have regard to the actual events of a case. In the instant cases, while the conditions for the claimants' consultations had not been ideal, there had been no actual violation of their right to have adequate time and facilities for the preparation of their respective defences. In M's case, there was no evidence that his privacy had been compromised by the wicket in the door. The difficulty that he had experienced in communicating with his solicitor was likely to have resulted from his youth, the fact he was unused to offending and the fact that he had been arrested for serious crimes rather than from the physical conditions in the cell. While ideally every police station should have consultation rooms, thereby avoiding the need for consultations to take place in cells, financial implications prevented this from happening. In LR's case, while the telephone that he had used had not been in the optimum location, it had been LR himself who, anxious to leave the police station quickly, had chosen to have a telephone consultation, and there was no suggestion that anyone had eavesdropped or attempted to eavesdrop on his conversation, *Artico v. Italy (A/37)* (1981) 3 E.H.R.R.1 considered.

R. (ON THE APPLICATION OF M (A CHILD)) v. COMMISSIONER OF POLICE OF THE METROPOLIS; R. (ON THE APPLICATION OF LA ROSE) v. COMMISSIONER OF POLICE OF THE METROPOLIS, [2001] EWHC Admin 553, *The Times*, August 17, 2001, Poole, J., QBD (Admin Ct).

3535. Right to fair trial – legislation – incompatibility – criminal appeals – right of Crown to be joined as party

[Human Rights Act 1998 s.5, Sch.1 Part I Art.6; Youth Justice and Criminal Evidence Act 1999 s.41.]

The Secretary of State for the Home Department petitioned to be joined as a party to the DPP's forthcoming appeal to the House of Lords against a decision of the Court of Appeal (Times, February 13, 2001) in which it had been held that the Youth Justice and Criminal Evidence Act 1999 s.41 did not preclude the cross examination of a rape complainant, or the giving of evidence by a defendant relating to any recent consensual sexual activity between the parties. The point of law that fell to be determined by the House was whether a previous sexual relationship could be relevant to the issue of consent so as to render the restriction on the admission of evidence about a complainant's sexual history under s.41 of the 1999 Act a contravention of a defendant's right to a fair trial under the Human Rights Act 1998 Sch.1 Part I Art.6. The Secretary of State contended that it was appropriate that he should be joined as a party given that the House might make a declaration of incompatibility under s.4 of the 1998 Act.

Held, granting the petition, that it was appropriate for the Crown to be joined as a party in advance of the hearing and before it became entitled to notification under s.5(1) of the 1998 Act. Having regard to the purpose of s.5, where, as in the instant case, the Crown was represented by the DPP, it was necessary to ensure that the appropriate minister should be given an opportunity to participate in the hearing since the role of the prosecutor was different from that of a Government minister carrying out his executive duties. The determination prior to the trial of whether s.41 of the 1999 Act was incompatible with Art.6 was in the best interests of all the parties. The issue was of general public importance. It was therefore clear that argument would be heard concerning compatibility. The Secretary of State had been responsible for the promotion of the 1999 Act and it was accordingly appropriate for him to be joined as a party.

R. v. A (JOINDER OF APPROPRIATE MINISTER) [2001] 1 W.L.R.789, Lord Hope of Craighead, HL.

3536. Right to fair trial – penalties – classification of civil penalties under VAT legislation as "criminal charges"

See VAT: Han (t/a Murdishaw Supper Bar) v. Customs and Excise Commissioners. §5557

3537. Right to fair trial – presumption of innocence – confiscation of property

[Drug Trafficking Act 1994 s.4(3); European Convention on Human Rights 1950 Art.6.]

P complained to the European Court of Human Rights that the statutory assumption under the Drug Trafficking Act 1994 s.4(3) breached his right to the presumption of innocence guaranteed under the European Convention on Human Rights 1950 Art.6. P had been convicted of being involved with the importation of a large amount of cannabis resin following which a confiscation order was made for

£91,400 based on the presumption under s.4(3) of the Act that all property held by a person convicted of a drug trafficking offence within the the preceding six years represented the proceeds of drug trafficking. If P refused to pay he was to serve a further two years' imprisonment consecutive to the nine year term he had received for the offence.

Held, refusing the application, that the statutory presumption did not breach Art.6 since Art.6 did not apply to sentencing and was therefore not applicable to confiscation proceedings. The confiscation procedure was analogous to the determination of the level of fine or the length of a period of imprisonment to impose on a properly convicted offender. Furthermore, the assumption was not applied to facilitate finding the applicant guilty of an offence but was used by the court to assess the amount at which the confiscation order should be fixed. The system also had built in safeguards in that the assessment was carried out by a court with a judicial procedure including a public hearing, advance disclosure of the prosecution case and the opportunity for the applicant to adduce documentary and oral evidence. Most importantly, the assumption could be rebutted if the applicant had shown on the balance of probabilities that the property had not been acquired through the proceeds of drug trafficking.

PHILLIPS v. UNITED KINGDOM (41087/98) 11 B.H.R.C. 280, G Ress (President), ECHR.

3538. Right to fair trial – presumption of innocence – expert evidence based on assumption of guilt

[European Convention on Human Rights 1950 Art.6(1), Art.6(2).]

B was charged with a number of counts of armed robbery. The investigating judge ordered medical, psychiatric and psychological reports, which found that B was both dangerous and unlikely to be successfully rehabilitated. B unsuccessfully applied for a further report. He was subsequently investigated by the same investigating judge for another offence, and the psychiatric expert who had previously reported on him was again commissioned to provide an opinion which came to the same conclusion. B again unsuccessfully sought a second opinion. He was refused leave to appeal against that decision and was committed for trial. At trial, it was formally noted that B had initially admitted his part in an armed robbery and there was positive identification evidence. The experts who prepared the reports gave evidence, after which B requested that a note be entered on the court record to show they had stated his guilt. This was refused and B was convicted. He complained that the proceedings were contrary to the European Convention on Human Rights 1950 Art.6(1) and Art.6(2) and that allowing the experts' evidence without a formal note being entered in the trial record did not accord with the presumption of innocence.

Held, refusing to uphold the complaint, that the experts' opinions were concerned with the question as to whether B was suffering from a disorder in relation to the offences, and this required a consideration of those offences based on an assumption that B had committed them. The opinions did not show that the experts had pre judged the matter and referred to B's denials. B's conviction was based on the totality of the evidence obtained during the investigation, so that the use of the expert's opinions did not breach Art.6(1) or Art.6(2) and the presumption of innocence had been adhered to.

BERNARD v. FRANCE (2000) 30 E.H.R.R. 808, R Bernhardt (President), ECHR.

3539. Right to fair trial – presumption of innocence – refusal to award costs to acquitted defendants – right to judicial review

[Supreme Court Act 1981 s.29(3); Human Rights Act 1998 s.3, Sch.1 Part I Art.6(2).]

R, a company, which had been acquitted of a six count indictment for breach of a fire certificate relating to premises of which it was the freehold owner, sought judicial review of the trial judge's refusal to make a costs award in its favour. R had failed to notify the relevant authorities that it was not the occupier at the time of the charge and had failed to indicate at an early stage that the occupancy point would be relied on in his defence. R submitted that a refusal to pay its costs amounted to a breach of the Human Rights Act 1998 Sch.1 Part I Art.6(2), since such refusal cast doubt on R's innocence. However, owing to a binding House of Lords authority that a refusal to award costs could not be subject to judicial review by virtue of the Supreme Court Act 1981 s.29(3), R was denied a remedy for that breach. R argued that as a consequence of s.3 of the 1998 Act, the court should refuse to follow that decision and s.29 should be construed so as to permit judicial review of any refusal to pay costs.

Held, refusing the application, that (1) the interpretation previously placed upon s.29(3) of the 1981 Act by the House of Lords was not incompatible with any Convention right since there was no Convention right to have all decisions reviewed, notwithstanding that some decisions might breach Convention rights, *Sampson, Re* [1987] 1 W.L.R. 194, [1987] C.L.Y. 2282 followed, and (2) even if the decision was subject to review, in the instant case, the judge's decision was not unreasonable in view of R's failure to indicate the occupation point at an earlier stage causing resources to be wasted in the trial and the judge had therefore been entitled to refuse R its costs from public funds.

R. v. CANTERBURY CROWN COURT, *ex p.* REGENTFORD LTD; *sub nom.* R. (ON THE APPLICATION OF REGENTFORD LTD) v. CANTERBURY CROWN COURT [2001] H.R.L.R. 18, Waller, L.J., QBD (Admin Ct).

3540. **Right to fair trial – presumption of innocence – road traffic offences – specimen tests**

See CRIMINAL LAW: Parker (Lee Christopher) v. DPP. §1067

3541. **Right to fair trial – property rights – expropriation – land taken for road building – delay in settling compensation**

[European Convention on Human Rights 1950 Art.6, Protocol 1 Art.1.]

P complained of violations of his right to peaceful enjoyment of his property under the European Convention on Human Rights 1950 Protocol 1 Art.1 and his right to a fair trial under Art.6. The Greek Government had expropriated land belonging to P and others for the purposes of a major road building programme. The court procedure relating to compensation had taken over five years to complete and P had not been fully compensated for his loss, as a national law provision created a presumption that land owners always benefited from such works.

Held, upholding the application in part, that the length of the court process had not been excessive given the complexity of the case, which had involved the expropriation of a number of plots of land at the same time, and given the fact that the delays in the appeal procedure were not attributable to the Greek Government. The compensation unit price had been fair. However, the presumption under the national law provision created a rigid situation in which a land owner was unable properly to argue his case and was therefore in violation of Protocol 1 Art.1, *Katikaridis v. Greece* (Unreported, November 15, 1996) applied.

PAPACHELAS v. GREECE (2000) 30 E.H.R.R. 923, L Wildhaber (President), ECHR.

3542. **Right to fair trial – remedies – decision to re-license nuclear power plant – access to court**

[European Convention on Human Rights 1950 Art.2, Art.6(1), Art.8, Art.13.]

A, along with others living close to a nuclear power plant, complained in reliance upon the European Convention on Human Rights 1950 Art.6 and Art.13 that they had been denied an effective judicial means of challenging a decision to renew the plant's operating licence. They contended that this meant they had no effective remedy under national law to complain about violations of either their right to life or their right to respect for bodily integrity under Art.2 and Art.8.

Held, dismissing the application, that (1) the connection between the decision to renew the licence and the domestic law rights claimed by A was too tenuous and remote, *Balmer-Schafroth v. Switzerland* (1998) 25 E.H.R.R. 598, [1998] C.L.Y. 3156 applied; (2) A was attempting to derive a means of contesting the use of nuclear energy from Art.6(1), or at the least a means for transferring from the Government to the courts the responsibility for taking the decision on the operation of nuclear power plants, whereas regulation of such plants was a policy matter for each contracting state to be decided according to democratic processes; (3) Art.6(1) required access to a court if there was an arguable claim that a civil right had been unlawfully interfered with. Therefore Art.6(1) did not apply in the instant case as it could not be determined whether the domestic law could protect A from the hypothetical dangers posed by the plant, and (4) Art.13 did not apply either as no arguable grievance had been shown to exist, *Boyle and Rice v. United Kingdom (A/131)* (1988) 10 E.H.R.R. 425, [1989] C.L.Y. 1920 considered.

ATHANASSOGLOU v. SWITZERLAND (27644/95) (2001) 31 E.H.R.R. 13, Judge Palm (President), ECHR.

3543. **Right to fair trial – remedies – excessive detention on remand – inadequate psychiatric treatment – Poland**

[European Convention on Human Rights 1950 Art.3, Art.5(3), Art.6(1), Art.13.]

K, a Polish national suffering from chronic depression and with a diagnosed personality disorder, spent more than two years in detention on remand following his indictment on charges of fraud and forgery. While in detention K twice attempted suicide and underwent numerous psychiatric examinations and made repeated applications and appeals for release. K complained to the Commission alleging that (1) he had not received adequate psychiatric treatment while detained on remand and that this amounted to inhuman and degrading treatment under the European Convention on Human Rights 1950 Art.3; (2) he had been detained for an unreasonably long time contrary to Art.5(3); (3) that his right to a hearing within a reasonable time within the meaning of Art.6(1) had not been respected, and (4) he had no effective domestic remedy under Art.13 to be able to challenge the length of the proceedings against him.

Held, that (1) ill-treatment had to reach a minimum level of severity to constitute a breach of Art.3. Detention on remand was not of itself inhuman or degrading treatment but the state had to ensure that the conditions of detention showed respect for human dignity. In the present case K had regularly sought and obtained medical assistance. There was insufficient evidence to indicate that K's suicide attempts were in any way due to failures on the part of the authorities. On the facts there had been no violation of Art.3; (2) the main reason why K had been detained was the authorities' assessment of the risk that K would abscond together with their reasonable suspicion that he had committed the offences in question. However those reasons became less relevant with the passage of time and there were no other compelling reasons justifying K's pre-trial detention for over two years. Accordingly there had been a violation of Art.5(3); (3) even though the case was a complex one that alone could not justify the length of the proceedings. The fact that K was being held in detention and suffered from serious depression imposed a duty of particular diligence on the courts to administer justice expeditiously. There was insufficient justification for the delays which had occurred and the amount of time taken to conduct the proceedings was not reasonable. Therefore there had been a violation of Art.6(1), and (4) (by a majority) the purpose of Art.13 was to enable individuals to obtain relief through their national courts for human rights violations before invoking the international procedure of the ECHR. Properly construed Art.13 guaranteed an effective remedy before a national authority for an alleged breach of the Art.6(1) requirement that a case should be heard in a reasonable time. In the instant case K had no domestic remedy for enforcing his right to a hearing within a reasonable time and therefore there had been a violation of Art.13.

KUDLA v. POLAND (30210/96) 10 B.H.R.C. 269, Judge Wildhaber (President), ECHR.

3544. Right to fair trial – retrospective legislation – legislation passed during course of proceedings

[European Convention on Human Rights 1950 Art.6.]

During court proceedings concerning the calculation of an additional payment to social security staff, legislation was passed which retrospectively affected the payment's final value. Z argued that the retrospective legislation unfairly affected the court proceedings, contrary to Art.6(1). Further, that the proceedings had not been resolved within a reasonable time.

Held, allowing the application, that (1) although the legislature could adopt retrospective provisions to determine rights established under existing laws, the principle of the rule of law and the right to a fair trial in Art.6 precluded any interference with the administration of justice by the legislature other than in exceptional circumstances, *Stran Greek Refineries v. Greece (A/301-B)* (1995) 19 E.H.R.R. 293, [1995] C.L.Y. 2620 followed; (2) it could not be determined from the facts of the instant case why the conflicting court decisions reached in the course of the proceedings needed legislative intervention. Therefore the legislative intervention was contrary to Art.6(1), and (3) the length of proceedings had to be assessed by reference to the circumstances of the individual case and its complexity, *Vernillo v. France (A/198)* (1991) 13 E.H.R.R. 880 followed. Taking these factors into account, the requirement for the matter to be resolved in a reasonable time under Art.6(1) had been breached by proceedings lasting three years and eight months.

ZIELINSKI v. FRANCE (24846/94, 34165/96 AND 34173/96) (2001) 31 E.H.R.R. 19, Judge Wildhaber (President), ECHR.

3545. Right to fair trial – security for costs – failure to consider applicant's financial means

[European Convention on Human Rights 1950 Art.6.]

A was convicted and imprisoned for offences of armed robbery. A appealed and also lodged civil and criminal actions against two gendarmes who had been part of the investigating team. A alleged perjury, extortion and forgery. A was refused legal aid and an order was made against him requiring him to give security for costs. A complained of a breach of the European Convention on Human Rights 1950 Art.6, on the grounds that he had been refused access to a court. F contended that Art.6 did not apply because there were no civil rights at stake, and that A, who had never sought damages, had pursued the actions merely to bolster his appeals against conviction.

Held, allowing the application, that the proceedings were concerned with a civil right. The amounts of the security for costs orders made against A were manifestly excessive in view of his lack of means and were designed to prevent him from lodging a complaint against the policemen. There had accordingly been a breach of Art.6.

AIT-MOUHOUB v. FRANCE (2000) 30 E.H.R.R. 382, R Bernhardt (President), ECHR.

3546. Right to fair trial – state immunity – alleged assault by foreign soldier – proportionality

[European Convention on Human Rights 1950 Art.6(1).]

M applied to the European Court of Human Rights following a judgment of the Irish Supreme Court that he was not entitled to bring an action for damages against the British Government by reason of state immunity. M claimed that he had been assaulted by a British soldier when re-entering the Irish Republic from Northern Ireland and that he had suffered personal injury as a consequence. M contended that to deny him the right to bring his claim in the Irish courts infringed his right to a fair trial under European Convention on Human Rights 1950 Art.6(1).

Held, refusing the application (Judges Rozakis, Loucaides, Caflisch, Cabral Barreto and Vajic dissenting), that although Art.6(1) was engaged it had not been infringed. The pursuit of harmonious relations between states, which the doctrine of state immunity in civil proceedings was designed to achieve, was a legitimate aim and Convention rights should be interpreted in accordance with rules of international law, including the doctrine of state immunity. Consequently, the application of the doctrine in the instant case could not be regarded as disproportionate. Further, M could have brought the action in Northern Ireland. It was observed that, whilst there was a trend towards limiting state immunity in respect of claims for personal injuries caused by the act or omission of a foreign state, such a trend referred to insurable personal injuries and not to matters reflecting the core activities of the foreign state, such as the acts of its armed forces.

McELHINNEY v. IRELAND (NO.2) (31253/96) (2002) 34 E.H.R.R. 13, L Wildhaber (President), ECHR.

3547. Right to fair trial – suspects – delay in prosecution – violation of ECHR

[European Convention on Human Rights 1950 Art.5(3).]

C had been arrested in Italy and extradited to the Czech Republic in connection with robbery charges. He was held on remand for over three years before conviction. C complained to the European Court of Human Rights that his right to trial within a reasonable time under the European Convention on Human Rights 1950 Art.5(3) had been breached.

Held, allowing the application and awarding C compensation, that there had been a breach of Art.5(3). Although when he was arrested there was a "reasonable suspicion" that C had committed an offence and that he was likely to abscond and therefore needed to be held in custody, this was not sufficient to justify continued detention beyond a certain point. There was no justification for the many delays in prosecuting the case and the Czech Republic had therefore not exercised "special diligence" as required.

CESKY v. CZECH REPUBLIC (33644/96) (2001) 33 E.H.R.R. 8, Judge Costa (President), ECHR.

3548. Right to family life – adoption – child freed for adoption having been placed in care of social services – failure to balance rights of child and parent

[European Convention on Human Rights 1950 Art.6(1), Art.8.]

E's daughter, M, was placed in the temporary care of E's brother soon after E and M arrived in Italy from Greece in October 1988. M was subsequently placed in the care of social services with contact denied to E, who had been diagnosed as psychotic, which manifested itself in hypochondria focused on M. Following appeals by E, a final order was made in October 1995, declaring M free for adoption. E complained that her right to respect for family life had been violated, contrary to the European Convention on Human Rights 1950 Art.8 and that she had been denied a fair trial because of the delay, in breach of Art.6(1).

Held, allowing the application, that (1) the proceedings in the instant case had taken seven years which contravened the requirement for a hearing within a reasonable time under Art.6(1), and (2) taking a child into care was a temporary measure and had the ultimate aim of reuniting parent and child, *Olsson v. Sweden (A/130)* (1989) 11 E.H.R.R. 259, [1988] C.L.Y. 1815 applied. On the facts, however, the authorities had failed to take the necessary steps so that E could re-establish her relationship with M therefore a fair balance had not been struck between M's best interests and E's rights under Art.8.

EP v. ITALY (31127/96) (2001) 31 E.H.R.R. 17, Judge Fischbach (President), ECHR.

3549. Right to family life – care orders – legitimate aim to protect child's welfare

[European Convention on Human Rights 1950 Art.8.]

S had been placed with foster carers as her mother suffered from a serious mental illness, and an order had been made by the youth court of Italy that she was available for adoption. The order was overturned by the Court of Appeal in 1992, but the court stayed its own order to return S to her family as psychiatric evidence showed that immediate return would not be in S's best interests. Following a series of difficult contact visits, the youth court held in 1995 that S should remain with her foster carers and that contact should cease. S's grandfather, B applied to the European Court of Human Rights claiming that his family's right to family life had been violated by the failure of the Italian court to return his granddaughter S to her biological family

Held, dismissing the application, that there had been no breach of the right to family life under the European Convention on Human Rights 1950 Art.8. The interference with family life was in accordance with the law and pursued the legitimate aim of protecting S's welfare, which was the overriding interest. This was "necessary in a democratic society" within the margins of appreciation provided by Art.8. The domestic court was in the best position to judge S's interests and had given due weight to the interests of S's biological family. It had acted within its margin of appreciation.

BRONDA v. ITALY (22430/93) (2001) 33 E.H.R.R. 4, R Bernhardt (President), ECHR.

3550. Right to family life – child abduction – duty of state to assist in return of children to parent with residence

[European Convention on Human Rights 1950 Art.8.]

IZ divorced her husband, D, a Romanian national, in France in 1989 and parental authority was granted to D for their two daughters, with contact to IZ. In 1990 D took the children to live with him in the United States and IZ brought an action in France against D for failing to return the children as arranged without giving prior notice. IZ's application to a French court for the emergency grant of parental authority was refused and parental authority was subsequently granted to both parents on appeal, with the court deciding that the children should reside with IZ with contact to D. D did not comply, but instead obtained a Texan court order cancelling the French decision and granting him residence. IZ succeeded in having this decision overturned, but D then returned to Romania and IZ complained that the Romanian authorities had not taken adequate measures to secure the children's return, contrary to her right to respect for her family life under the European Convention on Human Rights Art.8.

Held, allowing the application, that (1) Art.8 required the national courts to take such steps as were necessary to reunite IZ with her children; (2) the Romanian authorities had an obligation to assist IZ, but this was not absolute, being dependent instead on the facts of the case and the cooperation of the parties. Coercion was to be limited as the interests of all concerned had to be taken into account, with the children's best interests being of prime concern; (3) it was not necessary to decide whether Romanian law gave effective sanctions against D for refusing to comply, as it was for the state to ensure adequate enforcement of Art.8, and (4) in the instant case, the Romanian authorities had failed to make adequate efforts to enforce IZ's right to have the children returned, thereby violating her rights under Art.8.

IGNACCOLO-ZENIDE v. ROMANIA (31679/96) (2001) 31 E.H.R.R. 7, Judge Palm (President), ECHR.

3551. Right to family life – children – care orders – restriction on parental access – failure to attempt family reunion

[European Convention on Human Rights 1950 Art.8, Art.13.]

K suffered from schizophrenia with episodes of psychosis resulting in hospitalisation on several occasions. K cohabited with T and K's son M. At age four M was exhibiting behavioural problems and K agreed that he should enter voluntary care. K later gave birth to another child, J. Immediately after her birth J was placed into emergency care by the authorities on the grounds that K suffered a serious mental illness and T would not be able to safeguard J's development whilst also caring for K. An emergency care order was also made in respect of M. K and T were not told of the proposed action in advance in case K endangered her baby. Supervised access to the children was allowed. The authorities decided to retain M and J in care and they were placed in a children's centre and then with foster parents. For seven years there were a series of reviews of the care arrangements with challenges being made by K and T followed by appeals to the domestic courts when the restrictions on parental access were kept in place. K and T then made an application to the European court of Human Rights contending that their right to a family life under the European Convention on Human Rights 1950 Art.8 had been breached and that there was no effective remedy in the domestic courts contrary to Art.13 of the 1950 Convention.

Held, that there had been a breach of Art.8 in respect of J but not M and that there had been no breach of Art.13. A matter placed on referral before the Grand Chamber would involve the whole case being looked at afresh, the referral would not be limited to specific matters raised as a prerequisite for referral. In deciding whether interference in family life was necessary the court had to consider the varying perceptions in different states but, in every case, the best interests of the child were paramount. The court's task was to review the decision taken. There was a wide margin of appreciation accorded to a state's decision to take a child into care because of the importance of protecting children but a stricter scrutiny was applied to further limitations such as the restriction on parental access. Whilst the making of emergency care orders could be justified in some cases there were no reasons to justify the harsh step of taking J into custody at the moment of birth. That did not apply to M who had already been placed into voluntary care when K and T had realised that they were unable to care for him. A care order was to be regarded as a temporary measure and the ultimate aim ought to be the reuniting of the family. Measures taken under the care order ought to be consistent with that aim. There had been no serious effort towards reuniting the family and that constituted a breach of Art.8. As rights of appeal were available and used by K and T there had been no breach of Art.13.

K v. FINLAND (25702/94) (NO.2); *sub nom.* T v. FINLAND (25702/94) (NO.2) [2001] 2 F.L.R. 707, Wildhaber (President), ECHR.

3552. **Right to family life – deportation – conviction for drug trafficking – links with France outweighed Algerian nationality**

[European Convention on Human Rights 1950 Art.8(2).]

M, an Algerian national, was born in France in 1962 and lived there until his deportation in 1995 following his conviction for drug trafficking. In addition to his parents and siblings, some of whom were French nationals, he also left behind his wife, an Italian national resident in France since 1978, and their three children, who were all French nationals. M complained that his permanent exclusion had interfered with his right to family life, contrary to the European Convention on Human Rights 1950 Art.8(2).

Held, allowing the complaint, that M had shown that his established French private life had been interfered with by the order. The use of deportation in such cases had to strike a balance between crime prevention and the preservation of public order and the individual's rights under Art.8. On the facts, M had no connection with Algeria apart from his nationality, which was outweighed by his French birth, education and upbringing. His links with France were strong in terms of his parents, siblings and his wife and children. Although his conviction weighed against him, his right to family life under Art.8 had been breached by the deportation.

MEHEMI v. FRANCE (2000) 30 E.H.R.R. 739, R Bernhardt (President), ECHR.

3553. Right to family life – deportation – father deported on economic grounds – unable to participate in court ordered access visits

[European Convention on Human Rights 1950 Art.8.]

C had a right of residence in the Netherlands dependent on his marriage and cohabitation with his spouse. The couple had a child, K, but later separated. C was granted an independent residence permit allowing him to work in the Netherlands for one year. C initially did not attempt to see K but later applied to the court for an access arrangement to be established, however the authorities determined that access would be inappropriate. C's next application for a residence permit was refused as he was in receipt of unemployment benefit and also because he was not visiting K. C later began visiting K but the refusal was affirmed on the basis of the need to protect national economic well being. The court ordered trial access visits to take place, but C could not participate because of his detention and later deportation. C applied to the European Court of Human Rights asserting that the authorities had acted in breach of his right to respect for family life under the European Convention on Human Rights 1950 Art.8.

Held, upholding the complaint, that the refusal to extend the residence permit so that trial visits could take place had pre judged the decision on access and C's relationship with K, even if he had separated from the mother, was family life for the purposes of Art.8. Although the interference was in accordance with national law there was no immediate need for C's removal and his deportation prevented his forming a meaningful relationship with K in breach of Art.8.

CILIZ v. NETHERLANDS [2000] 2 F.L.R. 469, E Palm (President), ECHR.

3554. Right to family life – deportation – history of offending – interference justified on public order grounds

[European Convention on Human Rights 1950 Art.8.]

B was born in Morocco and entered France aged five to join his father. He was later convicted of a number of robbery and theft offences. In 1990 he applied to regularise the fact that he did not have a valid residence. B was told that he would be deported on account of his convictions. He sought an order quashing the decision to deport him. The application was dismissed and upheld on appeal. He alleged a violation of the European Convention on Human Rights 1950 Art.8.

Held, refusing the application, that there had been no breach of Art.8. The evidence of B's social and family ties showed that he had a private life in France, with which the deportation order would interfere. However, the offences B had committed were sufficiently serious to warrant the order on public order grounds, and any personal considerations were outweighed as a consequence. Therefore, Art.8 had not been breached.

BOUJLIFA v. FRANCE (2000) 30 E.H.R.R. 419, R Bernhardt (President), ECHR.

3555. Right to family life – illegitimacy – illegitimate child not recognised for purposes of inheriting under father's intestacy

[European Convention on Human Rights 1950 Art.8, Art.14.]

S's father, A, died intestate before he could marry S's mother, C, and prior to S's birth. Two years after his birth, S was granted letters of legitimation but it was held that they were not retrospective in effect, so that S could not inherit from A's estate which passed instead to A's parents and siblings. S and C complained to the European Court of Human Rights, contending that there had been violations of the European Convention of Human Rights 1950 Art.8 and Art 14.

Held, upholding the complaint, that the lack of a legal relationship between S and A did not breach Art.8 on its own. However, the difference in treatment accorded to S, as opposed to a child born to married parents, or recognised by its unmarried father meant that S had been discriminated against. Although the protection of legitimate heirs' rights could justify such a difference in treatment, knowledge of S's existence by A's heirs meant that his exclusion from the inheritance was in breach of Art.8, taken together with Art.14.

CAMP v. NETHERLANDS (28369/95) [2000] 3 F.C.R. 307, E Palm (President), ECHR.

3556. Right to family life – parental contact – refusal of application – dismissal of appeal without hearing

[European Convention on Human Rights 1950 Art.6, Art.8.]

E and M, the parents of C, were not married when they separated. E, the father, paid maintenance for C and there was contact until F complained of inadequate supervision by M when C sustained a broken arm, at which point contact ceased. E's application for a contact order was refused at first instance, and a re-application was also refused at which the court failed to obtain expert psychological evidence, as recommended by the youth officer. E's appeal was dismissed without a hearing and he complained that there had been a breach of his right to family life, contrary to the European Convention on Human Rights 1950 Art.8 and a failure to hold a fair hearing in breach of Art.6.

Held, upholding the complaint, that the denial of contact was an unjust interference with E's right to family life under Art.8. Further, the combined lack of expert evidence and an oral appeal hearing meant that E had been denied a fair hearing in breach of Art.6.

ELSHOLZ v. GERMANY [2000] 2 F.L.R. 486, L Wildhaber (President), ECHR.

3557. Right to family life – parental rights – children placed in residential care for indefinite period

[European Convention on Human Rights 1950 Art.3, Art.6, Art.8.]

M, a Belgian and Italian dual national, had two children, A and B, by her husband, F. They moved to Italy in 1993 but their relationship suffered as a result of F's violence. During 1995 and 1996 a social worker, L, looked after A at weekends voluntarily. In 1997, following a disclosure by A, L was convicted of indecent assault on children. The social service authorities investigated M's family, and M was diagnosed as suffering from personality disorders which allegedly made her care of the children erratic. The children were placed in separate foster care, and then placed together in an agricultural cooperative community, C. M and F's parental rights were suspended and they had no contact with the children for two years. They discovered that some of F's leaders had convictions for sexual and violent offences against community members. M separated from F and was eventually allowed some supervised contact with the children, but following adverse reports from social services this was suspended. M applied to Court, alleging breaches of the European Convention on Human Rights 1950 Art.3, Art.6 and Art.8.

Held, allowing the application in part, that the blocking of contact and delays by social services in allowing contact ordered by the court, constituted a violation of Art.8, as the family situation did not warrant a complete cessation of contact. The indefinite placement at C was also a violation of Art.8 as it drove a wedge between the children and M contrary to their Convention rights. The national court should have taken a more proactive role in ensuring the children's safety and the preservation of their right to family life. There had been no breach of Art.6 of Art.3.

S v. ITALY; G v. ITALY [2000] 2 F.L.R. 771, L Wildhaber (President), ECHR.

3558. Right to liberty – prisoners rights – ill treatment whilst in police custody

[European Convention on Human Rights 1950 Art.3, Art.13.]

T, a Turkish journalist of Kurdish origin was arrested and detained on suspicion of threatening village guards. He was subsequently acquitted of the charges against him. T complained that he was ill-treated while in detention, and that this had not been adequately investigated by the Turkish authorities. He argued that his ill treatment while in police custody violated his rights under the European Convention on Human Rights 1950.

Held, allowing the application in part, that (1) in respect of a person deprived of his liberty, recourse to physical force which had not been made strictly necessary by his own conduct diminished human dignity and was an infringement of Art.3. The conditions in which the applicant was held, and the manner in which he must have been treated in order to leave wounds and bruises on his body, amounted to inhuman and degrading treatment and was a violation of Art.3; (3) where an individual had an arguable claim that he had been tortured or subjected to serious ill-treatment by agents of the State, the notion of an "effective remedy" in Art.13 entailed, in addition to the payment of compensation where appropriate, a thorough and effective investigation capable of leading to the identification and punishment of those responsible and including effective access for the complainant to the investigatory procedure; (4) the investigation in the present case could not properly be described as thorough and effective and there had been a violation of Art.13.

TEKIN v. TURKEY (22496/93) (2001) 31 E.H.R.R. 4, Judge R Bernhardt (President), ECHR.

3559. Right to liberty – right to fair trial – prison disciplinary procedures – extension of sentence

See PENOLOGY: R. (on the application of Greenfield) v. Secretary of State for the Home Department. §4572

3560. Right to liberty and security – arrest – safeguard against arbitrary arrest and detention – reasonable suspicion

[European Convention on Human Rights 1950 Art.5.1 (c), Art.5.3.]

H, an Irish national and member of Sinn Fein, challenged the lawfulness of his arrest on suspicion of committing a terrorist murder. H had been arrested in 1985 and detained by the police for six days and thirteen hours before being released. H contended that (1) the arrest had breached the safeguard against arbitrary arrest and detention as guaranteed by the European Convention on Human Rights 1950 Art.5.1 (c), and (2) his right to be brought promptly before a judge in accordance with Art.5.3 had been breached.

Held, allowing the application in part, that (1) it was an essential component of the safeguard contained in Art.5.1 (c) of the Convention that any suspicion on which an arrest was based should be reasonable and, therefore, based upon objective grounds capable of providing justification to a third party. Terrorist offences were a particular problem since the information used to make the arrest might have been provided by sources which the authorities were anxious to protect. Nevertheless, it was still necessary to provide some information capable of assuring the court that any arrest had been based upon reasonable suspicion. That information did not need to be as compelling as that required to justify a conviction or the bringing of a charge. In the instant case, there had been reasonable suspicion since the arrest had been based upon specific information linking H to the murder, and (2) having regard to the period in which H had been detained without charge, there had been a clear breach of Art.5.3.

O'HARA v. UNITED KINGDOM (37555/97) (2002) 34 E.H.R.R. 32, J-P Costa (President), ECHR.

3561. Right to liberty and security – detention – charge forming basis of detention challenged

[European Convention on Human Rights Art.5(1), Art.5(4).]

D, a Moroccan national living in the Netherlands was arrested there on suspicion of trafficking in persons, an offence carrying a sentence of at least four years' imprisonment. He was correctly informed of the offence when questioned about the matter for which he had been arrested, but he complained that his detention was contrary to the European Convention on Human Rights Art.5(1) as another charge was given for the basis of his detention on the actual detention order. D also sought judicial review of the lawfulness of his detention under Art.5(4).

Held, refusing to uphold the complaint, that the mistake on the detention order was due to a clerical error that D must have been aware of as all other documentation relating to the investigation referred to the offence for which he had been arrested. Further, the investigating judge had considered the legality of his detention for that offence so that Art.5(1) had been complied with. The judge's examination also meant the matter had been determined within a reasonable time period, so that Art.5(4) did not apply.

DOUIYEB v. NETHERLANDS (2000) 30 E.H.R.R. 790, E Palm (President), ECHR.

3562. Right to liberty and security – detention – cult members – false imprisonment – cooperation of police

[European Convention on Human Rights 1950 Art.5(1).]

RB and other members of a religious cult were taken, on the orders of a judge, to a hotel where they were held for 10 days following their arrest. The arrest and detention had been prompted by the actions of the families of the cult members and an anti cult group. While at the hotel, RB and the others were subjected to psychological "deprogramming" and assessment. Upon release the cult members brought actions for false imprisonment. These failed at first instance and on appeal and they complained to the European Court of Human Rights, contending that the detention was contrary to the European Convention on Human Rights 1950 Art.5(1).

Held, upholding the complaint, that Art.5(1) had been violated, as the detention had no basis in law. Although the detention had been carried out at the instigation of the families concerned, it had taken place with the active co-operation of the police so that the state was responsible for the interference with the human rights of the cult members.

BLUME v. SPAIN (2000) 30 E.H.R.R. 632, Judge Pellonpaa (President), ECHR.

3563. Right to liberty and security – detention – detention pending trial – right to fair and independent hearing – Turkey

[European Convention on Human Rights 1950 Art.5(3), Art.5(4), Art.6.]

N, a Bulgarian national worked as a cashier and accountant in a state-owned enterprise. Following an audit N was arrested, detained and charged with misappropriation of funds. She argued, inter alia, that there had been violations of Art.5 in respect of her arrest and detention and that the criminal proceedings against her violated Art.6.

Held, ruling in favour of the claimant, that (1) Art.5(3) provided that everyone arrested or detained should be brought promptly before an independent judge or other authorised officer; (2) the role of the officer was to review the reasons for, and against, detention and to decide, by reference to legal criteria, whether there were reasons to justify detention and to order release if there were not; (3) in the instant case the applicant had been brought before an investigator who did not have power to make a binding decision as to her detention and who was not procedurally independent from the prosecutor. Moreover he was not sufficiently independent and impartial for the purposes of Art.5(3). Accordingly, there had been a violation of Art.5(3); (4) a court examining an appeal against detention had to provide guarantees of a judicial procedure. The proceedings had to be adversarial and always ensure equality of arms between the parties, the prosecutor and the detained person; (5) equality of arms was not ensured if counsel was denied access to those documents in the investigation file which were essential effectively to challenge the lawfulness of his client's detention; (6) while Art.5(4) of the Convention did not impose an obligation on a judge examining an appeal against detention to address every argument in the applicant's submissions, its guarantees would be deprived of their substance if the judge, relying on domestic law and practice, could treat as irrelevant or disregard, facts invoked by the detainee and capable of putting into doubt the existence of the conditions essential for the "lawfulness" of the deprivation of liberty. In the circumstances there had been a violation of Art.5(4); (7) the applicant's claim for loss of earnings suffered during her period of detention was dismissed, and (8) the applicant was entitled to an award of part of her costs incurred as a result of the violations of Art.5(3) and (4) with interest.

NIKOLOVA v. BULGARIA (31195/96) (2001) 31 E.H.R.R. 3, Judge Wildhaber (President), ECHR.

3564. **Right to liberty and security – mental patients – compulsory detention – right to challenge legality under ECHR Art.5(4)**

[European Convention on Human Rights 1950 Art.5(4).]

M was committed to a psychiatric hospital in 1987, as the result of a psychiatric examination that found he was not criminally responsible for the manslaughter of his wife. M's lawyer applied for his release in 1991, but this was refused following a psychiatric examination. Leave to appeal was refused in 1992 and a further request for M's release was lodged in March 1993 and another psychiatric examination was ordered in May 1993. However, this did not take place until February 1994 and the report was not completed until November 1994. This recommended M's continued detention, which was confirmed in two further court decisions of 1996. M contended that the judicial review of his continued detention had taken too long, contrary to the European Convention on Human Rights 1950 Art.5(4).

Held, allowing the application, that (1) the length of time under consideration was one year, eight months and nine days, being the time from Poland's recognition of the right of individual petition on May 1, 1993 until January 9, 1995, when the court dismissed M's release request in reliance upon the November 1994 report; (2) M was entitled to test the legality of his continued detention at regular intervals under Art.5(4), *Luberti v. Italy (A/75)* (1984) 6 E.H.R.R. 440 applied and this also included the right to a timely judicial decision, *Van der Leer v. Netherlands (A/170)* (1990) 12 E.H.R.R. 567, [1990] C.L.Y. 2528 considered, and (4) although the complexity of the issues could be taken into account when determining compliance with Art.5(4), this did not absolve the authorities of their primary obligations under that provision. Further, there had also been a failure to carry out a review of the legality of M's continued detention during the period of the delay.

M v. POLAND (24557/94) (2001) 31 E.H.R.R. 29, Judge Wildhaber (President), ECHR.

3565. **Right to liberty and security – mental patients – detention – delay in hearing discharge application**

See MENTAL HEALTH: R. (on the application of C) v. Mental Health Review Tribunal. §4424

3566. **Right to liberty and security – torture – detention pending deportation – conditions in cell – Greece**

[European Convention on Human Rights 1950 Art.3, Art.5.]

D, a Syrian national, was convicted of drug-related offences in Greece and was ordered to be expelled from Greece. Pending his expulsion he was detained for 17 months, at first in a detention centre and later in a cell at police headquarters in Athens. D complained that during his detention he was confined to an overcrowded cell with inadequate sanitation and insufficient beds and was deprived of fresh air, daylight, hot water and exercise. D claimed that these conditions contravened the European Convention on Human Rights 1950 Art.3 and also invoked Art.5 in relation to the lawfulness and length of his detention.

Held, allowing the application that (1) the Greek government had not denied D's allegations concerning overcrowding and lack of beds. The court relied on a report by the European Committee for the Prevention of Torture and Inhuman or Degrading Treatment or Punishment which corroborated D's allegations. The conditions of D's detention, in particular the serious overcrowding and lack of sleeping facilities together with the amount of time D was detained in those conditions amounted to degrading treatment. Therefore there had been a violation of Art.3, and (2) Art.5 required that a detention should not only have a legal basis in domestic law but also that the quality of the law itself was such that it was sufficiently accessible and precise without risk of arbitrariness. In the present case, the relevant Greek law related to expulsion by administrative order whereas D's expulsion had been ordered by a court. The Greek government had relied on a decision by a public prosecutor that the law applied equally to court orders but that decision did not constitute a law of sufficient "quality" for the purposes of Art.5. Accordingly, D's detention was not lawful and there had been a violation of Art.5.

DOUGOZ v. GREECE (40907/98) 10 B.H.R.C. 306, Judge Costa (President), ECHR.

3567. **Right to life – armed forces – death resulting from disproportionate use of force – Turkey**

[European Convention on Human Rights 1950 Art.2.]

O, a Turkish national, lived in a part of Turkey where a state of emergency had been declared. The Turkish security forces carried out an armed operation in the area during which O's son was killed. The incident was reported to the public prosecutor and an investigation followed but ultimately the supreme administrative court ruled that criminal proceedings would not be brought against any member of the security forces since the identity of the individual responsible for shooting O's son was not known. O complained to the Commission that the security forces' action was a violation of her son's right to life under the European Convention on Human Rights 1950 Art.2.

Held, (by a majority) upholding O's complaint, that (1) contrary to the assertions of the security forces there was insufficient evidence to suggest that they themselves had come under fire or that they had given the necessary verbal warnings before opening fire. The use of force against O's son was disproportionate and unnecessary and amounted to a violation of Art.2, and (2) the investigation into the incident had not been conducted by an independent authority and was deficient in many respects including the omission of a proper post-mortem examination and the failure to make a thorough forensic examination of the scene. Accordingly the investigation was not an effective official investigation capable of leading to the identification and punishment of those responsible for the death of O's son. This also amounted to a violation of Art.2. The Court awarded compensation to O in just satisfaction of her loss.

OGUR v. TURKEY (21594/93) (2001) 31 E.H.R.R. 40, Judge Wildhaber (President), ECHR.

3568. **Right to life – custody – death in custody – Turkish authorities failure to inform father – violation of ECHR**

[European Convention on Human Rights 1950 Art.2, Art.3, Art.5.]

In 1993, T heard that his son, A, had been taken into custody, but T was never able to get satisfactory information from the authorities and no explanation was given as to why A had not been seen since. T brought an action claiming that the disappearance of his son by the Turkish authorities and the anguish that had caused him violated the European Convention on Human Rights 1950 Art.2, Art.3 and Art.5.

Held, allowing the application and awarding T compensation, that given the lapse of time, it had to be presumed that A had died in custody, and the lack of an explanation by the authorities meant that Turkey would be held responsible for his death in violation of Art.2. That Article had also been breached by Turkey's failure to carry out an effective investigation into A's death. The lack of any safeguards and Turkey's failure to acknowledge that A was even being held when there was evidence that he was, amounted to breaches of Art.5. The distress caused to T, given that he had been lied to by Turkey and had no recourse to an effective remedy within the state together with the fact that another of his sons had died in custody, amounted to inhuman and degrading treatment.

TIMURTAS v. TURKEY (23531/94) (2001) 33 E.H.R.R. 6, Judge Palm (President), ECHR.

3569. Right to life – custody – unacknowledged death in custody – breach of fundamental rights – obligation of State to protect right to life – Turkey

[European Convention on Human Rights 1950 Art.2, Art.3.]

C, a Turkish citizen living in South East Turkey, complained that his brother had been detained and tortured by security forces and had since disappeared, presumed dead. C alleged that the events had not been properly investigated by the authorities and claimed justification under the European Convention on Human Rights 1950.

Held, allowing the application, that (1) on the facts, there was sufficient circumstantial evidence to conclude beyond reasonable doubt that the brother had died following his apprehension and unacknowledged detention by security forces, *Kurt v. Turkey* (1999) 27 E.H.R.R. 373, [1999] C.L.Y. 3115 distinguished; (2) Art.2, which safeguarded the right to life, together with Art.3, required, by implication, that there should be some form of effective official investigation when individuals were killed as a result of the use of force, and (3) no explanation had been forthcoming from the authorities as to what had occurred following his apprehension, nor any ground of justification relied on by the government in respect of any use of lethal force by its agents. Liability was therefore attributable to the State. Having regard to the lack of effective procedural safeguards disclosed by the inadequate investigation, the State failed in its obligation to protect his right to life and there had been a violation of Art.2.

CAKICI v. TURKEY (23657/94) (2001) 31 E.H.R.R. 5, Judge Wildhaber (President), ECHR.

3570. Right to life – medical treatment – cessation of invasive treatment – adult of full capacity

See HEALTH: AK (Adult Patient) (Medical Treatment: Consent), *Re*. §2934

3571. Right to life – medical treatment – persistent vegetative state – discontinuance of treatment

[European Convention on Human Rights 1950 Art.2, Art.3.]

A hospital trust sought a declaration that it was entitled to discontinue the administration of artificial hydration and nutrition to M, a patient in a persistent vegetative state. M had been diagnosed as being in a permanent vegetative state in 1997 after having suffered anoxic brain damage and the trust submitted that it would not be in her best interests to continue the treatment.

Held, granting the declaration, that where the continuation of treatment was no longer in the best interests of a patient, action to discontinue that treatment would not constitute an intentional deprivation of life pursuant to the European Convention on Human Rights 1950 Art.2(1). It followed that in the instant case there was no obligation on the state to prolong M's life, *Airedale NHS Trust v. Bland* [1993] A.C. 789, [1993] C.L.Y. 2712 followed. Furthermore, the withdrawal of treatment would not breach the requirement contained in Art.2 to take adequate and appropriate steps to safeguard life as the positive obligation upon a state to protect life was not an absolute obligation to treat a patient if that treatment would be futile, *Osman v. United Kingdom* [1999] 1 F.L.R. 193, [1998] C.L.Y. 3102 applied. Moreover, Art.3, prohibiting torture, was inapplicable as it required the victim to be aware of the inhuman and degrading treatment and, in the instant case, M, as an insensate patient who had been in a persistent vegetative state for in excess of three years, was unaware of the treatment and would also be unaware of its withdrawal.

NHS TRUST A v. M; NHS TRUST B v. H [2001] Fam. 348, Dame Elizabeth Butler-Sloss (President), Fam. Div.

3572. Right to life – prisoners rights – torture – mental health – degrading treatment resulting in death – adequate remedies

[Human Rights Act 1998 Sch 1 Part I Art.2, Art.3, Art.13.]

Following the suicide of her son whilst serving a four month custodial sentence, K applied to the European Court of Human Rights seeking relief. Her son, X, who had been receiving anti-psychotic medication, had been imprisoned after assaulting his girlfriend. During his transfer from the prison health care centre to the main prison, X had badly assaulted two hospital officers and, despite the prison health staff being aware of his problems, he had been further remanded for a period of 28 days, along with a seven day segregation period as punishment. Within 24 hours of that decision, he had hanged himself.

Held, granting the application, that while the prison authorities had made a reasonable response to X's conduct by placing him in hospital care and subject to daily medical supervision, they had shown inadequate concern to maintain records of his progress and had failed to refer him to a psychiatrist for advice regarding his medication and future care. X had been found by the prison doctors to be fit for segregation and there had been no breach of the right to life under the Human Rights Act 1998 Sch 1 Part I Art.2. However, taking into account X's vulnerability and the authorities' obligation to protect his health, the imposition of the further sentence and punishment might have threatened his physical and moral resistance and adversely affected his personality to the extent that it was degrading and inhuman treatment, therefore breaching Art.3. Further, neither X nor his mother had been given the right to an adequate remedy to which they were entitled under Art.13. In particular, the coroner's inquest had been inadequate as it had not provided a remedy for determining the liability of the authorities in respect of the treatment of X nor had it provided a remedy by way of compensation. The Court, therefore, granted the application and awarded compensation of £10,000 in just satisfaction.

KEENAN v. UNITED KINGDOM (27229/95) (2001) 33 E.H.R.R. 38, J-P Costa (President), ECHR.

3573. Right to life – remedies – need for effective investigation

[European Convention on Human Rights 1950 Art.2, Art.13, Art.25(1).]

T brought a complaint alleging that (1) her husband, Z, had been shot by security forces or with their collusion and that the Turkish Government had failed to carry out a proper investigation, in violation of the European Convention on Human Rights 1950 Art.2; (2) there was no effective remedy in Turkish law in violation of Art.13, and (3) her right of individual petition under former Art.25(1) had been interfered with. The Turkish Government contended that T had not exhausted the available domestic remedies.

Held, upholding the application, that the remedies available to T were ineffective. Civil procedure required identification of the perpetrators, which had not been possible in the instant case; administrative remedies, whilst available in theory, had never been pursued by any Turkish citizen and only led to awards of damages. Criminal proceedings would have made little difference to the outcome. In regard to T's complaint: (1) although the Turkish Government had failed to provide all relevant documents to the Commission, which was a serious omission, it was not appropriate to draw from that an inference that Z had been killed by its agents or by others colluding with them. There had been no violation of Art.2 in that respect. However, the obligation under Art.2 to conduct an effective investigation had not been fulfilled. That duty arose regardless of whether the death had been caused by the Government's agents. There had been no full autopsy, no attempt to recover the bullets, no attempt to trace witnesses, nor had any other proper investigative steps been taken, other than the taking of a statement from T a year after the event. There had therefore been a breach of Art.2; (2) despite the lack of conclusive evidence that the Turkish Government's agents were responsible, T had had an arguable case that should have been investigated properly through the criminal procedure. The failure to do so breached Art.13, and (3) the Turkish Government's questioning of T in relation to her application to the Commission, and in particular its inference that she had forged documents, amounted to an unjustified interference with her right of individual petition contrary to the former Art.25(1).

TANRIKULU v. TURKEY (2000) 30 E.H.R.R. 950, L Wildhaber (President), ECHR.

3574. **Right to life – suicide – refusal to give pardon in advance**

See CRIMINAL LAW: R. (on the application of Pretty) v. DPP. §1072

3575. **Right to life – terrorism – investigations into deaths – requirements**

[European Convention on Human Rights 1950 Art.2.]

J and four others petitioned the European Court of Human Rights complaining that the failure of the UK government to carry out proper investigations into the deaths of four individuals who had been killed in the effort to fight terrorism in Northern Ireland constituted a breach of the right to life under the European Convention on Human Rights 1950 Art.2.

Held, allowing the applications, that the obligation to protect life was one of the most fundamental provisions of the Convention which required that there had to be some form of effective investigation when individuals had been killed as a result of the use of force. Any justification for the deprivation of life was to be strictly construed and there were no permitted derogations from the right in peacetime. The investigation did not have to follow a specific form but, whatever form the investigation took, the authorities had to act of their own motion and those involved in the investigation had to be independent from those implicated in the events. The investigation also had to be effective in the sense that it was capable of leading to a determination of whether the force used in such cases was justified in the circumstances and to the identification and punishment of those responsible. To that end, the authorities were required to take reasonable steps available to them to secure relevant evidence, including eye witness testimonials, forensic evidence and conduct an objective analysis of clinical findings to determine the cause of death. In all four cases, the ECHR identified shortcomings in transparency and effectiveness in the investigation which ran counter to the purpose of allaying the suspicion that a "shoot to kill" policy was being operated.

JORDAN v. UNITED KINGDOM (24746/94); KELLY v. UNITED KINGDOM (30054/96); McKERR v. UNITED KINGDOM (28883/95); SHANAGHAN v. UNITED KINGDOM (37715/97) 11 B.H.R.C. 1, J-P Costa (President), ECHR.

3576. **Right to private life – bugging – police surveillance – violation of rights – remedies**

[European Convention on Human Rights 1950 Art.6, Art.8, Art.13.]

G and H made applications in respect of their convictions of conspiracy to commit robbery, following the rejection of their applications for permission to appeal to the Court of Appeal. The police had installed a covert listening device at B's flat after receiving information about an impending armed robbery and, although that robbery was abandoned, G and H were subsequently arrested in a stolen car containing balaclavas and a variety of other suspicious items. Listening devices were also used at the police station to compare G and H's voices with those recorded at the flat. It was submitted that the use of the surveillance devices had infringed the right to respect for private life under the European Convention on Human Rights 1950 Art.8, and the right to an effective remedy under Art.13. Additionally, it was argued that the failure to disclose part of a report, and the use at trial of taped evidence procured by means of covert surveillance, had violated the right to a fair trial under Art.6.

Held, allowing the application in part, that the utilisation by the police of the covert listening devices in the flat and in the police station had breached Art.8(2) of the Convention, *Malone v. United Kingdom (A/82)* [1985] 7 E.H.R.R. 14, *Halford v. United Kingdom* [1997] I.R.L.R. 471, [1997] C.L.Y. 2795, and *Khan v. United Kingdom (35394/97)* [2001] 31 E.H.R.R. 45, [2000] C.L.Y. 3249 considered. Obtaining information regarding the use of a telephone during the investigation of a conspiracy to commit armed robbery was justified under Art.8(2). The domestic courts were not in a position to provide an effective remedy pursuant to Art.13; the complaints investigation procedures did not meet the requisite levels of independence to provide protection against the abuse of authority, and thus the right to an effective remedy had been infringed. Article 6 had not been breached in respect of the non-disclosure as sufficient safeguards had been taken to protect G's and H's interests, and there was no unfairness in leaving the taped evidence to the jury as a thorough summing up had been provided. The method by which the voice samples had been obtained had not infringed G and H's right not to incriminate themselves; voice samples that did not include incriminating evidence were akin to physical samples, such as hair, to which the right did not apply.

PG v. UNITED KINGDOM (44787/98); JH v. UNITED KINGDOM *The Times*, October 19, 2001, J-P Costa (President), ECHR.

3577. **Right to private life – freedom of expression – celebrities – injunction preventing disclosure of address**

[Human Rights Act 1998 Sch.1 Part I Art.8, Art.10.]

M applied inter partes for the continuation of an injunction restraining N from disclosing the address of a property she was buying. M a well known and successful model who had been publicly associated with Sir Paul McCartney argued that in view of a number of disturbing emails she had received, and in the light of the circumstances surrounding the death of John Lennon, and the attack on George Harrison, she was in danger of physical threats or injury. N's editor of "The Sun" had stated that he had no intention of publishing any such item but that he would not give a written assurance as he wished to reserve the right to publish if the story came out through another newspaper first.

Held, discharging the injunction, that the court had a jurisdiction to grant a universal injunction where there was a strong possibility that serious physical harm or death might result otherwise, *Venables v. News Group Newspapers Ltd* [2001] 2 W.L.R. 1038, [2001] 2 C.L. 321 applied. However, it had to weigh N's Convention right to freedom of expression against the potential harm to the applicant and evidence of the latter was insufficient. The availability to the public of the material, the public interest in publication, and any relevant privacy code were other relevant considerations. Furthermore it was unlikely that M's decision to purchase the property had been taken with her personal security as a priority as her location was likely to become available to the public simply as a result of living in a busy and populous town.

MILLS v. NEWS GROUP NEWSPAPERS LTD [2001] E.M.L.R. 41, Lawrence Collins, J., Ch D.

3578. **Right to private life – homosexuality – equalisation of minimum age of consent**

[Human Rights Act 1998 Sch.1 Part I Art.8, Art.14; Sexual Offences (Amendment) Act 2000.]

The parties applied by consent to the European Court of Human Rights to strike out the case of S, a young homosexual male who had brought an action contending that he was the victim of an infringement of the Human Rights Act 1998 Sch.1 Part I Art.8 taken in conjunction with Art.14. The claim had been lodged in regard to the disparity under United Kingdom law between the age of consent for heterosexual and homosexual activities. It was agreed between S and the UK Government that it was appropriate to remove the case from the list following the implementation of the Sexual Offences (Amendment) Act 2000 on January 8, 2001, which equalised the age of consent for homosexual acts between consenting males to the age of 16.

Held, granting the application to strike out, that given that the 2000 Act had removed the risk of prosecution, the application was no longer necessary.

SUTHERLAND v. UNITED KINGDOM (25186/94) *The Times*, April 13, 2001, L Wildhaber (President), ECHR.

3579. Right to private life – homosexuality – investigation and discharge of homosexuals from armed forces – claim for just satisfaction

[European Convention on Human Rights 1950 Art.8, Art.41.]

LP applied to the European Court of Human Rights claiming just satisfaction under the European Convention on Human Rights 1950 Art.41 for violations of Art.8 caused by the nature of investigations into his sexual orientation resulting in his discharge from the Royal Navy, including loss of career prospects, pension rights and legal costs.

Held, allowing the claim in part by awarding LP £19,000 for non pecuniary damage, £94,875 for pecuniary damage, £18,000 for the costs of domestic legal proceedings and £16,000 for the costs of the ECHR proceedings, that (1) certain aspects of the investigation were intrusive and offensive and discharge had fundamentally affected LP's future career prospects; (2) violation of the Convention gave rise to a legal obligation to make reparation that should restore LP, as far as possible, to the situation that pertained prior to the breach. This was not possible in the instant case, however, as precise calculation of the sums involved could not be made because of the uncertain nature of the damage and the significant differences between service and civilian life and qualifications. Discharge had also deprived LP of the armed forces' career resettlement opportunities and he had suffered a major loss in terms of non contributory pension; (3) interest was payable from the point where each element of pecuniary damage occurred, and (4) recovery of legal costs and expenses was limited to those that had been reasonably and necessarily incurred.

LUSTIG-PREAN v. UNITED KINGDOM (NO.2) (2001) 31 E.H.R.R. 23, J-P Costa (President), ECHR.

3580. Right to private life – homosexuality – investigation and discharge of homosexuals from armed forces – claim for just satisfaction

[European Convention on Human Rights 1950 Art.8, Art.13, Art.41.]

Following S's discharge from the UK armed forces as the result of an investigation into her sexual orientation, she claimed just satisfaction for breach of the European Convention on Human Rights 1950 Art.8 and Art.13 under Art.41.

Held, allowing the application in part and awarding £19,000 for non pecuniary loss with £59,000 for pecuniary loss, that (1) certain aspects of the investigation were intrusive and offensive and the discharge had had devastating consequences for S; (2) just satisfaction for past and future loss, including pension rights and lost career prospects was to be determined on an equitable basis; (3) compensation of loss of non contributory pension rights was speculative as the final figure was necessarily dependent on total service and the rank she would have held if she had remained in service, and (4) interest was payable from the point that each element of pecuniary loss accrued.

SMITH v. UNITED KINGDOM (NO.2); GRADY v. UNITED KINGDOM (2001) 31 E.H.R.R. 24, J-P Costa (President), ECHR.

3581. Right to private life – possession orders – harassment of neighbour – proportionality

See LANDLORD AND TENANT: Lambeth LBC v. Howard. §4200

3582. Right to private life – prisoners rights – applicant prisoner held on remand – inhuman and degrading treatment – Greece

[European Convention on Human Rights 1950 Art.3, Art.6(2), Art.8.]

P, a British national who had received treatment for drug addiction, was arrested and detained in Greece for drug-related offences. He was convicted and sentenced to imprisonment and on appeal he was ordered to be expelled from Greece. P complained about the conditions of his detention, the Greek authorities' failure to differentiate between remand and convicted prisoners and the opening of his correspondence from the Commission by the prison authorities.

Held, that (1) the court relied on the findings of the Commission following a visit to the prison where P was detained. P shared a cell with no ventilation which consequently became unbearably hot and in which there was no privacy when using the toilet. Although there was no evidence of a positive intention to humiliate P nevertheless the prison conditions diminished P's human dignity and amounted to degrading treatment within the meaning of the European Convention on Human Rights 1950 Art.3; (2) the failure of the prison authorities to provide a separate regime for remand prisoners did not violate the presumption of innocence and accordingly there had been no violation of Art.6(2), and (3) (by a majority) the opening of the Commission's letters to P had a legal basis in Greek law but could not be justified as being necessary in a democratic society. Accordingly there had been a violation of Art.8.

PEERS v. GREECE (28524/95) (2001) 33 E.H.R.R. 51, Judge Baka (President), ECHR.

3583. Right to private life – prisoners rights – opening of letters by prison social services

[Code of Criminal Procedure (France) Art.D.69.1; European Convention on Human Rights 1950 Art.8.]

D was held on remand and later convicted of murder, for which he was sentenced to 18 years' imprisonment. He complained that during his imprisonment letters from his lawyer, the judicial authorities and prison social services were opened before they reached him and that this was in breach of the European Convention on Human Rights 1950 Art.8.

Held, allowing the application, that the opening of D's correspondence amounted to an interference with his rights under Art.8(1) and did not come within the exception in Art.8(2) as it was not carried out in accordance with the Code of Criminal Procedure Art.D.69.1.

DEMIRTEPE v. FRANCE (2001) 31 E.H.R.R. 28, Judge Bratza (President), ECHR.

3584. Right to private life – sex discrimination – homophobic abuse directed at lesbian teacher

See EMPLOYMENT: Pearce v. Mayfield Secondary School Governing Body. §2315

3585. Right to private life – telephone tapping – details recorded on card index – ineffective remedy

[European Convention on Human Rights 1950 Art.8, Art.13.]

A complained that his right to private life under the European Convention on Human Rights 1950 Art.8 and for an effective remedy under Art.13 had been breached by the tapping of a telephone conversation between himself and a person who had called him from the former Soviet embassy to order an appliance sold by his company. A record of the conversation had been retained on a card index system, noting that A was an embassy contact.

Held, upholding the application, that (1) the surveillance interfered with A's rights under Art.8. The national law relating to such surveillance activities was not sufficiently clear as to allow those who might be affected to be aware of the risk that it could occur. The surveillance did not therefore accord with the law in its fullest sense. The keeping of the card had also interfered with A's right to privacy, and (2) there had been no breach of Art.13 as A had had an effective remedy in the national courts, which had not been invalidated by the fact that his claim in that court had been dismissed.

AMANN v. SWITZERLAND (2000) 30 E.H.R.R. 843, E Palm (President), ECHR.

3586. Right to private life – telephone tapping – third party's telephone line – applicant denied effective remedy

[European Convention on Human Rights 1950 Art.8.]

R had been the subject of an order authorising the tapping of his telephone line. The order was extended by a judge issuing standard form written instructions. As a result of the tapping and interception of R's conversations, L was charged with handling stolen property and was later released subject to judicial supervision. L sought an order that the extensions were invalid, contending that the written instructions had been given without reference to offences capable of justifying the continued tapping. The application was refused and that decision was upheld on appeal, where it was also held that L had no standing to challenge the order allowing the extension. L complained that the decision was in breach of the European Convention on Human Rights 1950 Art.8.

Held, allowing the application, that the tapping of R's line constituted an interference with L's right to a private life and respect for his correspondence. Such interference would contravene Art.8 unless it was in accordance with national law and was in a form that was necessary in a democratic society. The interference in the instant case had a valid legal basis, but exceeded what was necessary as such a requirement presupposed a guarantee against abuse. This was lacking as the finding that L had no standing meant he could not as his own line had not been tapped with the effect that he had been deprived of a remedy.

LAMBERT v. FRANCE (2000) 30 E.H.R.R. 346, R Bernhardt (President), ECHR.

3587. Surveillance – authorisation of surveillance – BBC

REGULATION OF INVESTIGATORY POWERS (BRITISH BROADCASTING CORPORATION) ORDER 2001, SI 2001 1057; made under the Regulation of Investigatory Powers Act 2000 s.47. In force: March 16, 2001; £1.75.

This Order, which applies the Regulation of Investigatory Powers Act 2000 Part II to the carrying out of surveillance to detect whether a television receiver is being used in any residential or other premises, provides for the grant of authorisations for certain forms of surveillance. It provides that certain provisions of the 2000 Act are not to apply to the detection of television receivers, provides for authorisations to be granted by persons holding certain positions within the BBC, if they are satisfied that the authorisation is necessary for preventing or detecting certain offences under the Wireless Telegraphy Act 1949 s.1, or for assessing or collecting sums payable in respect of television licences, modifies the general rules about the grant, renewal and duration of authorisations and provides that authorisations for the detection of television receivers are to last for up to eight weeks and modifies the duty imposed to cancel an authorisation where the requirements that were necessary for its grant or renewal no longer apply.

3588. Surveillance – authorisations – Home Office

REGULATION OF INVESTIGATORY POWERS (DESIGNATION OF PUBLIC AUTHORITIES FOR THE PURPOSES OF INTRUSIVE SURVEILLANCE) ORDER 2001, SI 2001 1126; made under the Regulation of Investigatory Powers Act 2000 s.41. In force: March 22, 2001; £1.50.

This order designates the Home Office as an authority whose activities may require the carrying out of intrusive surveillance and provides that only individuals holding an office, rank or position in Her Majesty's Prison Service may make applications to the Secretary of State for intrusive surveillance authorisations.

3589. Terrorism – derogation – detention of foreign national

HUMAN RIGHTS ACT 1998 (DESIGNATED DEROGATION) ORDER 2001, SI 2001 3644; made under the Human Rights Act 1998 s.14. In force: November 13, 2001; £1.75.

This Order is made in anticipation of the UK making a proposed derogation from the Convention for the Protection of Human Rights and Fundamental Freedoms Art.5 which provides that everyone has the right to liberty and security of person and that no-one shall be deprived of his liberty save in the cases set out in that Article and in accordance with a procedure prescribed by law. The Convention also permits the lawful arrest or detention of a person to prevent his effecting an unauthorised entry into the country or of a person against whom action is being taken with a view to deportation or extradition. The Anti-Terrorism, Crime and Security Bill 2001 contains an extended power to arrest and detain a foreign national where it is intended to remove or deport the person from the UK because the Secretary of State believes that his presence is a risk to national security and suspects him of being an international terrorist, but where such removal or deportation is not for the time being possible. In such cases, detention may be incompatible with the Convention because it is not for the time being possible to take action with a view to deportation. This Order designates the proposed derogation for the purposes of the Human Rights Act 1998.

3590. Terrorism – derogation withdrawal

HUMAN RIGHTS ACT (AMENDMENT) ORDER 2001, SI 2001 1216; made under the Human Rights Act 1998 s.16. In force: April 1, 2001; £1.50.

This Order amends the Human Rights Act 1998 to reflect the withdrawal by the UK Government of the derogation from Art.5(3) of the European Convention on Human Rights 1950 which was originally set out in Sch.3 Part I to that Act. The withdrawal of the derogation was effective from February 26, 2001 and followed the implementation of the Terrorism Act 2000 Sch.8.

3591. Terrorism – right to liberty and security – derogation by the UK

HUMAN RIGHTS ACT 1998 (AMENDMENT NO.2) ORDER 2001, SI 2001 4032; made under the Human Rights Act 1998 s.14. In force: December 20, 2001; £1.75.

This Order is made following the making by the UK of a derogation from the Convention for the Protection of Human Rights and Fundamental Freedoms, agreed by the Council of Europe at Rome on November 4, 1950, which provides that everyone has the right to liberty and security of person and that no-one shall be deprived of his liberty save in the cases specified and in accordance with a procedure prescribed by law. The Anti-Terrorism, Crime and Security Act 2001 contains an extended power to arrest and detain a foreign national where it is intended to remove or deport the person from the UK because the Secretary of State believes that his presence is a risk to national security and suspects him of being an international terrorist, but where such removal or deportation is not for the time being possible. This Order amends the Human Rights Act 1998 to set out the derogation by the UK from the Convention.

3592. Torture – deportation – risk of inhuman treatment if returned – failure to assess risk – right to effective remedy denied

[European Convention on Human Rights 1950 Art.3, Art.13; Convention relating to the Status of Refugees 1951 (United Nations).]

J, an Iranian national, fled to Turkey on a forged passport having been accused of committing adultery in Iran. She was detained in Turkey for the passport offence and recommended for deportation. J lodged an asylum application, which was refused on the basis that she had failed to apply within five days of her arrival. J was subsequently granted refugee status under the Convention relating to the Status of Refugees 1951 and she then lodged an application against her deportation in a Turkish court, which was refused. J applied to the European Court of Human

Rights, contending that there had been violations of the European Convention on Human Rights 1950 Art. 3 and Art.13 since she faced the possibility of death by stoning or flogging if deported to Iran and she had been denied an effective remedy by the Turkish authorities.

Held, allowing the application, that although contracting states had the right to control entry and expel aliens, they were under an obligation not to order an expulsion if there was a real risk of inhuman or degrading treatment in terms of Art.3. On the facts, Turkey had imposed an unreasonable time limit on asylum applications and had not made a proper assessment of the risks J could face if deported. Contracting states had a degree of latitude as to the method of implementation of Art.13, subject to guaranteeing the right to an effective remedy. The failure to assess the risks faced by J upon being returned to Iran meant that Turkey had failed to provide adequate safeguards as required by Art.13.

JABARI v. TURKEY (40035/98) 9 B.H.R.C. 1, Ress (President), ECHR.

3593. Books

Alston, Philip – People's Rights-Reissue. Collected Courses of the Academy of European Law, Vol 9, No 2. Hardback: £40.00. ISBN 0-19-829875-7. Oxford University Press.

Alston, Philip – Peoples' Rights. Collected Courses of the Academy of European Law. Paperback: £16.99. ISBN 0-19-924365-4. Oxford University Press.

Austin, R.C.; Bonner, David; Whitty, Noel – Legal Protection of Civil Liberties. Paperback: £26.95. ISBN 0-406-55511-7. Butterworths Law.

Bailey, S.H.; Harris, D.J.; Jones, B.L. – Civil Liberties-cases and Materials 5th Ed. Paperback: £28.95. ISBN 0-406-90326-3. Butterworths Law.

Bailey, S.H.; Harris, D.J.; Jones, B.L. – Civil Liberties-cases and Materials. 5th Ed. Paperback: £28.95. ISBN 0-406-90326-3. Butterworths Law.

Bouchet-Saulnier, Francois – Practical Guide to Humanitarian Law-1st English Language Ed. Hardback: £65.00. ISBN 0-7425-1062-X. Paperback: £27.00. ISBN 0-7425-1063-8. Rowman & Littlefield Publishers.

Bunker, Matthew D. – Critiquing Free Speech. Hardback: £33.50. ISBN 0-8058-3751-5. Lawrence Erlbaum Associates, Inc.

Chesterman, Simon – Just War or Just Peace? Oxford Monographs in International Law. Hardback: £40.00. ISBN 0-19-924337-9. Oxford University Press.

Clayton, Richard; Tomlinson, Hugh – Fair Trial Rights. Paperback: £27.50. ISBN 0-19-924634-3. Oxford University Press.

Clayton, Richard; Tomlinson, Hugh – Privacy and Freedom of Expression. Paperback: £27.50. ISBN 0-19-924638-6. Oxford University Press.

De Than, Claire; Shorts, Edwin – Human Rights Law in the UK. 2nd Ed. Paperback: £26.95. ISBN 0-421-75460-5. Sweet & Maxwell.

Doolan, Brian – Lawless V Ireland (1957-1961): the First Case Before the European Court of Human Rights. Hardback: £50.00. ISBN 0-7546-2169-3. Dartmouth.

Evans, Carolyn – Freedom of Religion Under the European Convention on Human Rights. Oxford European Human Rights Series. Hardback: £40.00. ISBN 0-19-924364-6. Oxford University Press.

Ewing, Keith David; Gearty, Conor Anthony – Struggle for Civil Liberties. Paperback: £14.99. ISBN 0-19-876251-8. Clarendon Press.

Fenwick, Helen – Civil Liberties and Human Rights. 3rd Ed. Paperback: £24.95. ISBN 1-85941-493-1. Cavendish Publishing Ltd.

Fenwick, Helen – Q&A Civil Liberties and Human Rights. 2nd Ed. Questions and Answers. Paperback: £9.95. ISBN 1-85941-276-9. Cavendish Publishing Ltd.

Fleck, Dieter – Handbook of the Law of Visiting Forces. Hardback: £65.00. ISBN 0-19-826894-7. Oxford University Press.

Fleck, Dieter – Handbook of Humanitarian Law in Armed Conflicts. Paperback: £27.50. ISBN 0-19-829867-6. Oxford University Press.

Fossey, Richard; Jarvis, Robin Garrett; Kemper, Elizabeth A. – Race, the Courts, and Equal Education. Readings on Equal Education, Vol 15. Hardback: £66.95. ISBN 0-404-10115-1. AMS Press.

Franklin, Bob – New Handbook of Children's Rights. 2nd Ed. Hardback: £60.00. ISBN 0-415-25035-8. Paperback: £18.99. ISBN 0-415-25036-6. Routledge, an imprint of Taylor & Francis Books Ltd.

Fredman, Sandra – Discrimination and Human Rights. Collected Courses of the Academy of European Law. Hardback: £40.00. ISBN 0-19-924245-3. Paperback: £16.99. ISBN 0-19-924603-3. Oxford University Press.

Goldrein, Iain; Straker, Tim – Human Rights Torts-judicial Review and Human Rights. Looseleaf/ring bound: £95.00. ISBN 0-406-91721-3. Butterworths Law.

Gordon, Richard; Ward, Tim – Judicial Review and the Human Rights Act. Hardback: £65.00. ISBN 1-85941-430-3. Cavendish Publishing Ltd.

Gordon, Richard; Ward, Tim; Eicke – Strasbourg Case Law: Leading Cases from the European Human Rights Reports. Hardback: £110.00. ISBN 0-421-74240-2. Sweet & Maxwell.

Hayner, Priscilla B. – Unspeakable Truths. Hardback: £16.99. ISBN 0-415-92477-4. Routledge, an imprint of Taylor & Francis Books Ltd.

Hunt, Murray; Singh, Rabinder – Practitioner's Guide to the Impact of the Human Rights Act 1998. Paperback: £22.00. ISBN 1-901362-49-3. Hart Publishing.

Janis, Mark; Kay, Richard; Bradley, Anthony – European Human Rights Law. 2nd Ed. Paperback: £26.99. ISBN 0-19-876569-X. Oxford University Press.

Joseph, Sarah; Schultz, Jenny; Castan, Melissa – International Covenant on Civil and Political Rights: Cases, Materials and Commentary. Hardback: £75.00. ISBN 0-19-826774-6. Oxford University Press.

Kamali – Freedom, Equality and Justice in Islam. Hardback: £35.00. ISBN 1-903682-02-9. The Islamic Texts Society.

Khaled Abou El Fadl – Rebellion and Violence in Islamic Law. Hardback: £47.50. ISBN 0-521-79311-4. Cambridge University Press.

Langlois, Anthony J. – Politics of Justice and Human Rights. Cambridge Asia-Pacific Studies. Hardback: £45.00. ISBN 0-521-80785-9. Paperback: £15.95. ISBN 0-521-00347-4. Cambridge University Press.

Leiser, Burton M.; Campbell, Tom D. – Human Rights in Philosophy and Practice. Applied Legal Philosophy. Hardback: £65.00. ISBN 0-7546-2210-X. Ashgate Publishing Limited.

Lilley, Roy; Newdick, Christopher; Lambden, Paul – Understanding the Human Rights Act. Paperback: £30.00. ISBN 1-85775-494-8. Radcliffe Medical Press.

McGhee, Derek – Homosexuality, Law, and Resistance. Hardback: £55.00. ISBN 0-415-24902-3. Routledge, an imprint of Taylor & Francis Books Ltd.

Mensah, Barbara – European Human Rights Case Summaries 1960-2000. Paperback: £95.00. ISBN 1-85941-649-7. Cavendish Publishing Ltd.

Mulcahy, Leigh-Ann – Human Rights and Civil Practice. Hardback: £150.00. ISBN 0-421-70990-1. Sweet & Maxwell.

Neill, Elizabeth – Rites of Privacy and the Privacy Trade: on the Limits of Protection for the Self. Hardback: £42.50. ISBN 0-7735-2097-X. McGill-Queen's University Press.

Neill, Elizabeth – Rites of Privacy and the Privacy Trade. Paperback: £16.50. ISBN 0-7735-2113-5. McGill-Queen's University Press.

Nousainen, Kevat; Gunnarsson, Asa; Niemi-Kielanen, Johanna; Lundstrom, Karin – Responsible Selves. Hardback: £55.00. ISBN 0-7546-2160-X. Ashgate Publishing Limited.

Peck, Lib; Cooper, Jonathan; Owers, Anne – Developing Key Privacy Rights. Justice-putting Rights Into Practice. Paperback: £15.00. ISBN 1-84113-168-7. Hart Publishing.

Ratner, Steven R.; Abrams, Jason S. – Accountability for Human Rights Atrocities in International Law. Oxford Monographs in International Law. Paperback: £16.99. ISBN 0-19-829871-4. Oxford University Press.

Scott, Craig – Torture As Tort. Hardback: £45.00. ISBN 1-84113-060-5. Hart Publishing.

Simor, Jessica – Human Rights Practice. Hardback: £198.00. ISBN 0-4216-2540-6. Sweet & Maxwell.

Skogly, Sigrun – Human Rights Obligations of theWorld Bank and the International Monetary Fund. Paperback: £65.00. ISBN 1-85941-665-9. Cavendish Publishing Ltd.

Spencer, John; Spencer, Maureen – Human Rights in a Nutshell. Nutshells. Paperback: £5.95. ISBN 0-421-75180-0. Sweet & Maxwell.

Supperstone, Michael; Pitt-Payne,Timothy – Guide to the Freedom of Information Act 2000. Paperback: £35.00. ISBN 0-406-93145-3. Butterworths Law.

Tomlinson, Hugh; Shukla,Vena – Human Rights Cases of the Commonwealth. Hardback: £95.00. ISBN 0-406-91837-6. Butterworths Law.

Tshosa, Onkemetse – National Law and International Human Rights. Law, Social Change and Development Series. Hardback: £50.00. ISBN 0-7546-2175-8. Hardback: £50.00. ISBN 0-7546-2175-8. Ashgate Publishing Limited.

Walker, Campbell – Reading Bills of Rights in Changing Contexts. Hardback: £35.00. ISBN 1-84113-133-4. Hart Publishing.

Wallace, Rebecca M.M. – International Human Rights. 2nd Ed. Paperback: £26.95. ISBN 0-421-71030-6. Sweet & Maxwell.

Ward, Tim; Sedley; Gordon, Richard; Emmerson, Ben – Human Rights Law Reports-UK Cases: Vol 1. 2000. Hardback: £165.00. ISBN 0-421-73910-X. Sweet & Maxwell.

West, Robin – Rights. International Library of Essays in Law and Legal Theory: Second Series-. Hardback:£130.00. ISBN 0-7546-2030-1. Ashgate Publishing Limited.

Whiting, Raymond – Natural Right to die. Contributations in Legal Studies, No101. Hardback: £51.95. ISBN 0-313-31474-8. Greenwood Press.

IMMIGRATION

3594. Appeals – free standing rights – implementation of EC law

IMMIGRATION (EUROPEAN ECONOMIC AREA) (AMENDMENT) REGULATIONS 2001, SI 2001 865; made under the European Communities Act 1972 s.2; and the Immigration and Asylum Act 1999 s.80. In force: April 2, 2001; £1.50.

These Regulations, which amend the Immigration (European Economic Area) Regulations 2000 (SI 2000 2326), correct errors in the definitions of "self-employed person who has ceased activity" by making it clear that the activity referred to is activity in the UK. The Regulations make amendments to take into account the amendments made to the Immigration and Asylum Act 1999 s.65, Sch.4 and the Special Immigration Appeals Commission Act 1997 s.2A by the Race Relations (Amendment) Act 2000. These amendments give a right of appeal to a person who alleges that an authority has, in taking any decision under the Immigration Acts relating to that person's entitlement to enter or remain in the UK, racially discriminated against him and provide that where a person brings an appeal on discrimination grounds, the Secretary of State may certify that appeal was manifestly unfounded.

3595. Asylum – appeals – adjournment – special adjudicator – jurisdiction under Asylum Appeals (Procedure) Rules 1996

[Asylum Appeals (Procedure) Rules1993 (SI19931661) r.10.1; Asylum Appeals (Procedure) Rules1996 (SI1996 2070) r.10.]

B, a citizen of the Ivory Coast, was refused asylum and appeared in person on her appeal to the special adjudicator whereby she sought an adjournment to obtain representation. The special adjudicator decided that there were no real difficulties evident in the case. B had already given her version of events to the immigration officer and could do so again, there were no witnesses for her to cross examine and that he would delay final preparation of his determination to enable B or her advisors to submit documentary evidence as to circumstances in the Ivory Coast. He concluded that he was not satisfied that it was "necessary" to adjourn the hearing within the meaning of Asylum Appeals (Procedure) Rules 1996 r.10, and that therefore he had no jurisdiction to do so. After the IAT refused leave to appeal, B applied for judicial review which was refused on the papers and she re-applied.

Held, dismissing the re-application, that the special adjudicator had correctly analysed and applied r.10 of the 1996 Rules. Tribunal decisions following the case of *Ajeh, Re* (Unreported, August 30, 1996) distinguished, failed to take account of the fact that it was decided on the basis of the Asylum Appeals (Procedure) Rules 1993 r.10.1, which were more permissive of adjournments.

R. v. IMMIGRATION APPEAL TRIBUNAL, *ex p.* BOGOU [2000] Imm. A.R. 494, Kay, J., QBD.

3596. Asylum – appeals – costs – decision of Secretary of State to contest appeal

Following the decision of the Secretary of State to consent to a rehearing subsequent to S being granted permission to appeal against a decision of the Immigration Appeal Tribunal, the court was concerned with the issue of costs.

Held, making no order as to costs, that the Secretary of State should consider as soon as possible whether to contest an appeal against a decision of the IAT so as to minimise costs. It was important that the court did nothing to discourage parties settling judicial review proceedings. Having regard to the conduct of the Secretary of State in the instant case and in particular to the fact that the issue on appeal was one of law in relation to which it might not have been clear until the grounds of appeal had been considered what course to take, it was apparent that he had had regard to the hardship and fairness to S of contesting the appeal. In such circumstances, it was appropriate to make no order as to costs, *R. (on the application of Boxall) v. Waltham Forest LBC* (Unreported, December 21, 2000) applied.

SENGOZ v. SECRETARY OF STATE FOR THE HOME DEPARTMENT, [2001] EWCA Civ 1135, *The Times*, August 13, 2001, Potter, L.J., CA.

3597. Asylum – appeals – criteria for adjournment

[Asylum Appeals (Procedure) Rules 1996 (SI 1996 2070) r.10.]

A, a Sudanese asylum seeker, sought judicial review of a decision by the Immigration Appeal Tribunal to refuse A permission to appeal against the decision of the special adjudicator, S, not to adjourn A's appeal against the dismissal of her asylum application. At the hearing before S, A's counsel had not arrived, but the hearing was allowed to proceed. A claimed that she had been put under unfair pressure by S to proceed.

Held, dismissing the application, that in determining whether or not an adjournment of proceedings was appropriate it was necessary to apply the Asylum Appeals (Procedure) Rules 1996 r.10 and, if required in borderline cases, to apply the guidance found within *R. v. Kingston upon Thames Justices, ex p. Martin (Peter)* [1994] Imm. A.R. 172, [1994] C.L.Y. 3519. Under r.10, the special adjudicator had been obliged to take into account the need for the "just, timely and effective conduct of the proceedings". Applying that principle to the instant case, the special adjudicator had been entirely justified in refusing an adjournment, particularly having regard to the fact that (1) the proceedings had already been adjourned on a previous occasion due to a lack of legal representation; (2) there was no point of law to be argued, and (3) A had been accompanied by her sole witness and had been quite capable of giving evidence and establishing the nature of her case.

R. v. IMMIGRATION APPEAL TRIBUNAL, *ex p.* ALI [2001] Imm. A.R. 67, Jackson, J., QBD.

3598. Asylum – appeals – fear of persecution – criteria governing certification

[Asylum and Immigration Appeals Act 1993 Sch.2 para.5(4)(a); Convention relating to the Status of Refugees 1951.]

G, a Colombian national, applied for judicial review of the decision of a special adjudicator dismissing her appeal against the Secretary of State's refusal of her claim for asylum and upholding the certification of her claim under the Asylum and Immigration Appeals Act 1993 Sch.2 para.5(4)(a). G claimed to be associated with the Hurtado family in Columbia which, due to a longstanding feud, had resulted in her receiving threats upon her life. The special adjudicator disbelieved G's account.

Held, granting the application, that since the aim of certification under Sch.2 para.5(4)(a) of the Act was to exclude asylum seekers from the normal appeal procedure in circumstances where on their own assertions they had no claim to asylum under the Convention relating to the Status of Refugees 1951, it followed that where an asylum seeker claimed a fear of persecution on the basis of facts which, if found to be true, would constitute Convention grounds, he had "show[n] a fear of persecution" and should not be certified. It was apparent that the decision of the special adjudicator, in the instant case, had been made in error due to a misunderstanding of the relevant law, *Secretary of State for the Home Department v. Ziar* [1997] Imm A.R. 456, [1997] C.L.Y. 2834 doubted.

R. (ON THE APPLICATION OF GAVIRA) v. SECRETARY OF STATE FOR THE HOME DEPARTMENT; *sub nom.* GAVIRA v. SECRETARY OF STATE FOR THE HOME DEPARTMENT; R. (ON THE APPLICATION OF GAVIRIA) v. SECRETARY OF STATE FOR THE HOME DEPARTMENT; R. (ON THE APPLICATION OF GAVIRA) v. SPECIAL ADJUDICATOR, [2001] EWHC Admin 250, [2002] 1 W.L.R. 65, Stanley Burnton, J., QBD (Admin Ct).

3599. **Asylum – appeals – human rights – validity of appeal ground – decision appealed against taken prior to coming into force of Human Rights Act 1998**

[Human Rights Act 1998 s.6; Immigration and Asylum Act 1999 s.65(3); Immigration and Asylum Act 1999 (Commencement No.6, Transitional and Consequential Provisions) Order 2000 (SI 2000 2444) Art.3, Sch.2 para.1 (7).]

P, a Sri Lankan Tamil, appealed to the Immigration Appeal Tribunal against the dismissal by a special adjudicator of his appeal against the refusal of his asylum claim. The preliminary point arose as to whether the tribunal had to give consideration to issues under the Human Rights Act 1998 when determining the appeal.

Held, making a starred decision, that although the Immigration and Asylum Act 1999 s.65(3) allowed human rights issues to be raised in current immigration appeals, the Immigration and Asylum Act 1999 (Commencement No.6, Transitional and Consequential Provisions) Order 2000 Art.3 and Sch.2 para.1 (7) prevented the appellate authorities from considering them in decisions taken prior to October 2, 2000. In deciding an appeal, the tribunal could not be said to be doing an act incompatible with the 1998 Act as it was only the Secretary of State's action in removing a failed asylum seeker that actually had direct human rights implications. That having been said, the reality of the situation was that an asylum seeker was potentially under threat of removal throughout the appeal process. If no consideration was given to human rights at any point in that process, both the Secretary of State and the appellate authorities could arguably be acting unlawfully contrary to s.6 of the 1998 Act. However, the tribunal was satisfied by the Secretary of State's assurance that human rights would always be considered at the removal stage, and urged that notices of removal directions should clearly indicate that fact. Adjudicators faced with appeals that included a human rights element where the decision was made prior to October 2, 2000 should hear the appeal, and only dismiss it where human rights was the only issue raised. In the instant case, P had no right to raise human rights issues because the decision to refuse his asylum application was made in 1997.

PARDEEPAN v. SECRETARY OF STATE FOR THE HOME DEPARTMENT [2000] I.N.L.R. 447, Collins, J., IAT.

3600. **Asylum – appeals – Immigration Appeal Tribunal – power to remit "procedurally" – power to delegate appeal to special adjudicator**

[Immigration Act 1971 s.22(2)(a); Asylum and Immigration Appeals Act 1993 s.9(1); Immigration and Asylum Act 1999 Sch.4 para.23; Immigration Appeals

(Procedure) Rules 1984 (SI 1984 2041); Asylum Appeals (Procedure) Rules 1996 (SI 1996 2070) r.17 (2); Immigration and Asylum Appeal (Procedure) Rules 2000 (SI 2000 2333) r.49.]

The Secretary of State applied for judicial review of a decision of the Immigration Appeal Tribunal ([2000] Imm. A.R. 518) that it had jurisdiction to set aside a decision made by another IAT, in the form of a chairman sitting alone, to remit an asylum claim under the Asylum Appeals (Procedure) Rules 1996 r.17 (2) to be heard by a different special adjudicator. The Secretary of State contended that the IAT had erred in finding that in addition to a power of "substantive remittal", it had a power of "procedural remittal" under the Immigration Act 1971 s.22(2) (a) by which it could delegate to a second special adjudicator the hearing of an appeal from another special adjudicator.

Held, granting the application, that there was a single power to remit under s.20 of the Act and s.22(2) (a) merely regulated and reflected that power in s.20 but did not grant a jurisdiction to remit the tribunal's appellate function to a special adjudicator. The decision to remit was a disposal of an appeal and a right to a further appeal from the second SA was preserved. However, that disposal was not a "final determination" for the purposes of the Asylum and Immigration Appeals Act 1993 s.9(1) (now replaced by the Immigration and Asylum Act 1999 Sch.4 para.23) and the outcome of the case was decided by the second SA. Furthermore, there was no power either under the Immigration Appeals (Procedure) Rules 1984 nor under the r.44 of the 1996 Rules (now the Immigration and Asylum Appeal (Procedure) Rules 2000 r.49) to cure an irregularity following a decision, *Akewushola v. Secretary of State for the Home Department* [2000] 1 W.L.R. 2295, [1999] C.L.Y. 3210 applied.

R. (ON THE APPLICATION OF THE SECRETARY OF STATE FOR THE HOME DEPARTMENT) v. IMMIGRATION APPEAL TRIBUNAL, [2001] EWHC Admin 261, [2001] Q.B. 1224, Scott Baker, J., QBD (Admin Ct).

3601. Asylum – appeals – one stop procedure

IMMIGRATION AND ASYLUM APPEALS (ONE-STOP PROCEDURE) (AMENDMENT) REGULATIONS 2001, SI 2001 867; made under the Immigration and Asylum Act 1999 s.74, s.76, s.166. In force: April 2, 2001; £2.00.

These Regulations, which amend the Immigration and Asylum Appeals (One-Stop Procedure) Regulations 2000 (SI 2000 2244) reflect amendments to the Immigration and Asylum Act 1999 by the Race Relations (Amendment) Act 2000. These amendments give a right of appeal to a person who alleges that an authority has, in taking any decision under the Immigration Acts relating to that person's entitlement to enter or remain in the UK, racially discriminated against him. These amendments also provide that a person must include any complaint of racial discrimination in the statement of additional grounds served with the s.74 notice.

3602. Asylum – appeals – procedural impropriety – appearance of unfairness

[Asylum and Immigration Appeals Act 1993 Sch.2 para.5 (5).]

N, a Sri Lankan citizen, appealed against a decision upholding the special adjudicator's refusal of his asylum application. N had described his treatment in Sri Lanka but had been refused asylum, the Secretary of State certifying that he had failed to establish that he had a well founded fear of persecution. At the appeal hearing before the special adjudicator N gave evidence for the first time of having suffered torture in Sri Lanka, which led the special adjudicator to discharge the Secretary of State's certificate under the Asylum and Immigration Appeals Act 1993 Sch.2 para.5 (5), pending his consideration of the substantive case. By the time of his written decision, delivered several months later, he had reached a different conclusion, namely that there was no reasonable likelihood that he had been tortured, or that he would be persecuted, if returned to Sri Lanka. N contended that those two determinations were directly in conflict and could not stand.

Held, allowing the appeal and remitting the case for rehearing before a fresh special adjudicator, that there had been an appearance of unfairness. If the special adjudicator had had any doubt about his final conclusions on the issue of torture, he ought to have refrained from making a decision as to whether to discharge the Secretary of State's certificate until such time as he had reached a final decision on the merits of the case. Para.5(5) had to be applied to all of the material before the special adjudicator, not merely to that relating to the alleged torture and it had been inappropriate to discharge the certificate because that gave the appearance of accepting that the evidence relied upon established a reasonable likelihood of torture.

NANTHAKUMAR v. SECRETARY OF STATE FOR THE HOME DEPARTMENT [2000] I.N.L.R. 480, Lord Woolf, M.R., CA.

3603. Asylum – appeals – procedure

IMMIGRATION AND ASYLUM APPEALS (PROCEDURE) (AMENDMENT) RULES 2001, SI 2001 4014 (L.31); made under the Immigration and Asylum Act 1999 s.58, s.166, Sch.4 para.3, Sch.4 para.4. In force: January 7, 2002; £1.75.

These Rules, which amend the Immigration and Asylum Appeals (Procedure) Rules 2000 (SI 2000 2333), provide that it is the Secretary of State who arranges for documents to be sent to the parties in two circumstances. Firstly, the Secretary of State arranges for the service of the adjudicator's determination where the determination is in relation to a claim for asylum, the claim has been certified by the Secretary of State under the Immigration and Asylum Act 1999 or where the adjudicator has dismissed the appeal. Secondly, the Secretary of State arranges for the service of a decision of the Tribunal to refuse leave to appeal where leave to appeal relates to a claim for asylum, and appellant is not the Secretary of State.

3604. Asylum – appeals – written notice of decision or action

IMMIGRATION AND ASYLUM APPEALS (NOTICES) (AMENDMENT) REGULATIONS 2001, SI 2001 868; made under the Immigration and Asylum Act 1999 s.166, Sch.4 para.1. In force: April 2, 2001; £1.50.

These Regulations, which amend the Immigration and Asylum Appeals (Notices) Regulations 2000 (SI 2000 2246), provide that a notice must be served where a person makes an allegation that an authority racially discriminated against him in taking a decision. These amendments give a right of appeal to a person who alleges that an authority has, in taking any decision under the Immigration Acts relating to that person's entitlement to enter or remain in the UK, racially discriminated against him. In addition, they provide that where a notice is sent outside the UK, it shall be deemed to have been received 28 days after the day it was posted.

3605. Asylum – detainee custody officer certificate – suspension

IMMIGRATION (SUSPENSION OF DETAINEE CUSTODY OFFICER CERTIFICATE) REGULATIONS 2001, SI 2001 241; made under the Immigration and Asylum Act 1999 Sch.11 para.7. In force: April 2, 2001; £1.50.

These Regulations prescribe circumstances in which a detainee custody officer's certificate may be suspended, pending the Secretary of State's decision as to whether to revoke it, under the Immigration and Asylum Act 1999 Sch.11 para.7. The circumstances include where an allegation has been made against the detainee custody officer, where that officer has been charged with a criminal offence or disciplinary action is being taken against him and where it appears that he is by reason or physical or mental illness or for any other reason incapable of satisfactorily carrying out his duties.

3606. **Asylum – educational institutions – health sector bodies – exemptions**

IMMIGRATION AND ASYLUM ACT 1999 (PART V EXEMPTION: EDUCATIONAL INSTITUTIONS AND HEALTH SECTOR BODIES) ORDER 2001, SI 2001 1403; made under the Immigration and Asylum Act 1999 s.84, s.166. In force: April 30, 2001; £2.00.

The Immigration and Asylum Act 1999 s.84 provides for the making of orders specifying categories of person to whom the general prohibition on the provision of immigration advice or services is not to apply. This Order exempts educational institutions and their respective students' unions and also health sector bodies.

3607. **Asylum – government administration – delay in granting refugee status following successful appeal against refusal – illegality**

M, a Turkish citizen, sought a declaration that the delay in granting him refugee status and indefinite leave to remain in the UK following his successful appeal to the special adjudicator had been unlawful.

Held, granting the application for judicial review, that there had been no deliberate delay on the part of the relevant authorities but no procedures had been adopted which enabled priority to be given to asylum applicants who had made successful appeals. The special adjudicator's decision had given M a right to refugee status which the Secretary of State had been under a duty to provide within a reasonable time and the failure to fulfil that duty had been unreasonable in the *Wednesbury* sense, *R. v. Secretary of State for the Home Office, ex p. Phansopkar* [1976] Q.B. 606 applied.

R. v. SECRETARY OF STATE FOR THE HOME DEPARTMENT, *ex p.* MERSIN [2000] I.N.L.R. 511, Elias, J., QBD.

3608. **Asylum – rehearings – jurisdiction – chairman's remittal power – appeals**

[Immigration Act 1971 s.20; Asylum Appeals (Procedure) Rules 1996 (SI 1996 2070) r.17(2).]

Z was refused asylum by the Secretary of State, but his appeal was allowed by a special adjudicator. The Secretary of State was granted leave to appeal, and the matter was listed for a mention before a chairman sitting alone. Z's solicitors indicated that Z was intending to resist the appeal but they did not intend to appear at the mention hearing, although Z in fact attended in person. The chairman took the view that the special adjudicator's decision was flawed and should be remitted to a fresh adjudicator and he accordingly made an order pursuant to the Asylum Appeals (Procedure) Rules 1996 r.17(2). Z's solictors challenged the chairman's decision to remit the appeal.

Held, setting aside the order, that the Immigration Appeal Tribunal could allow an appeal and remit a case for rehearing by an adjudicator under the Immigration Act 1971 s.20, not under the 1996 Rules. Further, if the order was made by a chairman sitting alone who did not hear the appeal, it was interlocutory in nature and could be varied or set aside if it was shown that it should not have been made. However, if the order was made by the IAT determining an appeal it was final in nature and could not be varied or set aside and, in such cases, it could be appealed on to the Court of Appeal.

SECRETARY OF STATE FOR THE HOME DEPARTMENT v. ZENGIN [2000] Imm. A.R. 518, Collins, J. (President), IAT.

3609. **Asylum – voluntary bodies – exemptions**

IMMIGRATION AND ASYLUM ACT 1999 (PART V EXEMPTION: ELIGIBLE VOLUNTARY BODIES AND RELEVANT EMPLOYERS) ORDER 2001, SI 2001 1393; made under the Immigration and Asylum Act 1999 s.84, s.166. In force: April 30, 2001; £1.50.

This Order, which is time limited to January 31, 2002, temporarily exempts two categories of person from the prohibition imposed under the Immigration and Asylum Act 1999 s.84 and the related criminal offence of providing immigration advice or immigration services in breach of this section. These are employees of and volunteers working on behalf of voluntary bodies which have written to the Legal Services Commission before April 30, 2001 to register their firm intention to apply for the Community Legal Service Quality Mark and employers or their staff in cases where the advice or services are provided only to employees or prospective employees who have been granted valid work permits for that employment, and where the advice or services are provided in connection with that employee or their immediate family only.

3610. Asylum seekers – adjudicators – right to fair trial – independence of asylum support adjudicators

[Human Rights Act 1998 Sch.1 Part I Art.6; Immigration and Asylum Act 1999 Part VI, Sch.10; The Asylum Support Regulations 2000 (SI 2000 704) Reg.20.]

H, an Iraqi asylum seeker, challenged the constitutionality of the office of asylum support adjudicators. H contended that (1) asylum support adjudicators determined the civil rights and obligations of asylum seekers within the meaning of the Human Rights Act 1998 Sch.1 Part I Art.6 and as such an asylum support adjudicator appointed by the Home Secretary was not an independent and impartial tribunal, and (2) the chief asylum support adjudicator's refusal of H's appeal against a decision to stop providing him with support under the Immigration and Asylum Act 1999 Part VI should be set aside for an error of law. The Secretary of State maintained that matters determined by asylum support adjudicators were not "civil rights and obligations" within the meaning of Art.6 since the provision of support to asylum seekers under the 1999 Act was discretionary and not mandatory.

Held, granting the application in part, that (1) a destitute asylum seeker receiving support under Part VI of the 1999 Act had a civil right under Art.6 of the Convention to continuation of that support subject to the Asylum Support Regulations 2000 Reg.20 and therefore H had a right to have his appeal against the withdrawal of support heard by an independent and impartial tribunal; (2) asylum support adjudicators were independent for the purposes of Art.6 having regard to the relevant statutory provisions under Sch.10 of the 1999 Act together with a number of non statutory provisions. Furthermore Art.6 did not require the independence of the tribunal to be guaranteed by statute. Although facts establishing the independence of a tribunal had to be made publicly available, none of the information in the instant case could be said to have been unavailable to the public, and (3) the chief asylum support adjudicator's decision should be set aside as an error of law given that the Secretary of State had misconstrued the terms of H's occupancy agreement and therefore had not possessed reasonable grounds for withdrawing H's support.

R. (ON THE APPLICATION OF HUSAIN) v. ASYLUM SUPPORT ADJUDICATOR, [2001] EWHC Admin 852, *The Times*, November 15, 2001, Stanley Burnton, J., QBD (Admin Ct).

3611. Asylum seekers – AIDS – cost of health care – grounds for asylum

[Human Rights Act 1998 Sch.1 Part I Art.3.]

K, a citizen of Uganda who was suffering from AIDS, sought permission to apply for judicial review of the Secretary of State's refusal to grant him asylum. The Secretary of State had refused to grant exceptional permission to remain and had applied the B Division Instructions. K submitted that he should have followed the Asylum Directorate Instructions and, relying on *D v. United Kingdom* (1997) 24 E.H.R.R. 423, [1997] C.L.Y. 2763, he further contended that to be returned to Uganda would be a breach of the Human Rights Act 1998 Sch.1 Part I Art.3.

Held, refusing the application, that the Asylum Directorate Instructions only applied to cases where the appellate system had not been exhausted. On the facts, the Secretary of State had correctly followed the B Division Instructions. In the case of *D* no medical facilities had been available in K's home country; in the instant case it was accepted that treatment was available in Uganda, even if K could not afford such treatment. It was, however, not right to suggest that it would constitute inhuman or degrading treatment to send K back to Uganda on the ground that he might, or might not, be able to afford all the treatment he might require. To accept that submission would be to adopt a rule that any country without a health service which was available free of charge to all people within its boundaries would be a place to which it would be inhuman and degrading to send someone.

K v. SECRETARY OF STATE FOR THE HOME DEPARTMENT [2001] Imm. A.R. 11, Sir Christopher Staughton, CA.

3612. Asylum seekers – conscientious objection – refusal to perform elements of military service – Turkey

[Convention Relating to the Status of Refugees 1951 (United Nations) Art.1A.]

S, a Turkish Kurd who claimed he faced imprisonment if returned to Turkey, as a result of his refusal to complete military service, appealed against a decision ([2000] Imm. A.R. 445, [2000] C.L.Y. 3287) that he was not entitled to asylum. S was not an absolute conscientious objector in that he did not claim that he would refuse to complete military service in all circumstances but objected to the possibility that he might be required to enter into combat against the Kurdish people. S maintained that the tribunal had erred in the manner in which it had approached the issue of partial conscientious objectors, submitting that there existed an internationally recognised fundamental right to refuse to undertake military service on grounds of conscience, applying to both absolute and partial objectors.

Held, dismissing the appeal (Lord Justice Waller dissenting in part), that whilst individual governments were free to treat conscientious objectors as refugees, there was no legal principle establishing a right of conscientious objection to military service, either absolute nor partial, so that a failure to respect such a right might amount to possible grounds for asylum under the Convention Relating to the Status of Refugees 1951 (United Nations). No such right existed no matter how distinct the political basis for objection to partial military service. If objections to military service on political grounds were to bring an objector within Art.1A of the 1951 Convention, there was nothing to prevent those with base political opinion from claiming refugee status. The tribunal, in issuing guidelines for similar cases, had attempted to draw a distinction between "acceptable" and "unacceptable" political opinion which was a difficult and undesirable path for the court to follow and could threaten to undermine the impartiality of the court.

SEPET v. SECRETARY OF STATE FOR THE HOME DEPARTMENT; BULBUL v. SECRETARY OF STATE FOR THE HOME DEPARTMENT; *sub nom.* R. (ON THE APPLICATION OF SEPTET) v. SECRETARY OF STATE FOR THE HOME DEPARTMENT; R. (ON THE APPLICATION OF BULBUL) v. SECRETARY OF STATE FOR THE HOME DEPARTMENT, [2001] EWCA Civ 681, [2001] Imm. A.R. 452, Laws, L.J., CA.

3613. Asylum seekers – criminal conduct – mother convicted of ill treating children – justifiable interference with right to family life

[Human Rights Act 1998 Sch.1 Part I Art.8.]

S, a citizen of the Ivory Coast, sought judicial review of the Secretary of State's refusal to grant her exceptional leave to remain in the United Kingdom. S was a failed asylum seeker and had been convicted of ill-treating her children and sentenced to three years' imprisonment. S's solicitors requested the Secretary of State to grant her exceptional leave to remain in the UK to allow her to have contact with her children. In the light of her history and the fact that she had another daughter in the Ivory Coast, the Secretary of State had refused the application. S submitted that the refusal was unreasonable and breached the Human Rights Act 1998 Sch.1 Part I Art.8.

Held, refusing the application, that taking account of all the matters which had been put to him, the Secretary of State's decision was reasonable. He was entitled to conclude that the disruption to S's family life was justified in the light of the provisions of Art.8(2), and to uphold the Government's immigration policy, which was necessary for the economic well-being of the country and the prevention of crime and disorder.

R. v. SECRETARY OF STATE FOR THE HOME DEPARTMENT, *ex p.* SERI [2001] Imm. A.R. 169, Dyson, J., QBD.

3614. Asylum seekers – dependants – right to education

[Human Rights Act 1998 Sch.1 Part I Art.2.]

H appealed against the dismissal of his application for judicial review of the Secretary of State's decision not to allow him and his family exceptional leave to remain in the UK. H, a Polish national, claimed asylum in the UK in 1994 and his wife and nine year old daughter, L, joined him in 1995. His application was refused and his appeal dismissed, as was his subsequent application for judicial review. H contended that L's right to education under the Human Rights Act 1998 Sch.1 Part I Art.2 would be violated if she were returned to Poland, as she was achieving well in the UK education system and would be prejudiced by returning to a Polish school.

Held, dismissing the appeal, that the right to education while in the UK under Art.2 did not carry with it any right to remain in the UK. It merely encompassed rights to "access such educational establishments as exist" in a state, which was open to L in Poland. She would be faced with no more difficulties than any child who had lived abroad for some time, and given her abilities and her high standard of Polish was unlikely to be disadvantaged. The Secretary of State's decision could thus not be said to be in breach of the limited scope of Art.2 nor to be irrational.

R. (ON THE APPLICATION OF HOLUB) v. SECRETARY OF STATE FOR THE HOME DEPARTMENT; *sub nom.* HOLUB v. SECRETARY OF STATE FOR THE HOME DEPARTMENT; R. v. SECRETARY OF STATE FOR THE HOME DEPARTMENT, *ex p.* HOLUB [2001] 1 W.L.R. 1359, Schiemann, L.J., CA.

3615. Asylum seekers – deportation – discretion to treat as illegal entrant

[Immigration Act 1971 Sch.2 para.8, Sch.2 para.9.]

O, a citizen of Nigeria, sought permission to apply for judicial review of the Secretary of State's decision to remove him from the United Kingdom. O had finally been refused leave to remain on the basis of marriage. He had, at one time, been on temporary admission when the Secretary of State had decided to remove him on the basis that he had no leave to remain. The Secretary of State had elected to treat him, in view of his temporary admission, as a person who had been refused leave to enter under the Immigration Act 1971 Sch.2 para.8. O argued that he should have been treated as an illegal entrant in line with Sch. 2 para.9 as that would have allowed him to benefit from the marriage policy DP/3/96.

Held, refusing the application, that it was for the Secretary of State to decide whether or not he would treat a person in A's position as an illegal entrant. That followed from the settled cases and the different wording of DP/3/96 from that used in earlier policy statements made no difference. Judicial review would serve no purpose.

OLAWALE (TUNJI) v. SECRETARY OF STATE FOR THE HOME DEPARTMENT [2001] Imm. A.R. 20, Kennedy, L.J., CA.

3616. Asylum seekers – deportation – long term overstayer – successful business as basis for leave

[Human Rights Act 1998 Sch.1 Part I Art.8.]

H, a citizen of Cyprus, sought judicial review of the decision by the Secretary of State to deport him. He was a long-term overstayer and after he had gone to ground, he had married and fathered two young children. H had also established a flourishing business. H submitted that, in the circumstances, the decision to deport him was unreasonable and was also a breach of the Human Rights Act 1998 Sch.1 Part I Art.8.

Held, refusing the application, that the business had been set up when H knew he was liable to deportation and he had never had permission to remain as a businessman. The Secretary of State had been fully entitled to carry out the balancing act as he had. Further, the Secretary of State had not breached Art.8, *Abdulaziz v. United Kingdom (A/94)* (1985) 7 E.H.R.R. 471 followed.

R. v. SECRETARY OF STATE FOR THE HOME DEPARTMENT, *ex p.* HAKANSOY (HASAL) [2001] Imm. A.R. 16, Jackson, J., QBD.

3617. Asylum seekers – deportation – quashing of deportation order – impact upon subsisting appeal

[Immigration Act 1971 s.15(1); Asylum and Immigration Appeals Act 1993 s.8(3).]

M, a national of Sierra Leone, who had successfully appealed under the Immigration Act 1971 s.15(1), challenged the Immigration Appeal Tribunal's dismissal of her appeal under the Asylum and Immigration Appeals Act 1993 s.8(3), despite being granted exceptional leave to remain, as she wished to be recognised as a refugee in order to improve her chances of being re-united with her young son who remained in Sierra Leone. M contended that the grant of exceptional leave to remain did not deprive her of the chance to obtain a decision as to whether the prior decision to deport was flawed. The Secretary of State submitted that, for an appeal under s.8(3) of the 1993 Act to be effective, there had to be in existence a decision to make a deportation order.

Held, dismissing the appeal, that, upon a true construction of s.8(3) of the 1993 Act, the decision to make a deportation order was not only a condition precedent to an appeal but was also the subject matter of the appeal. Therefore, the decision of the tribunal could not be impugned and M's success in her first appeal under s.15 of the 1971 Act necessarily resulted in the dismissal of the s.8 appeal, given that it was impossible to quash a deportation order which no longer existed.

MASSAQUOI v. SECRETARY OF STATE FOR THE HOME DEPARTMENT [2001] Imm. A.R. 309, Kennedy, L.J., CA.

3618. Asylum seekers – deportation – risk of torture – compatibility with ECHR

[European Convention on Human Rights 1950 Art.3, Art.13.]

H sought asylum in the United Kingdom having fled from the island of Zanzibar, claiming that he had been detained and tortured because of his connections to the opposition political party in Tanzania. His claim was rejected by the Secretary of State for the Home Department and his appeal dismissed by a special adjudicator on the ground of lack of credibility. Permission to apply for judicial review was refused on the basis that H would be safe in mainland Tanzania. H applied to the European Court of Human Rights claiming that a decision to deport him to Tanzania was in breach of the European Convention on Human Rights 1950 Art.3 and Art.13.

Held, allowing the application and awarding H compensation, that there had been a breach of Art.3 but not of Art.13. Documentary evidence that had been submitted since the special adjudicator's decision largely corroborated H's story, and there was a risk of ill treatment if he were to be deported. Internal flight was not a viable option as the situation in mainland Tanzania was no less dangerous and extradition to Zanzibar was a possibility. Although permission to apply for judicial review had been refused, it was nevertheless an effective remedy and there had therefore been no breach of Art.13.

HILAL v. UNITED KINGDOM (45276/99) (2001) 33 E.H.R.R. 2, Judge Costa (President), ECHR.

3619. Asylum seekers – deportation – without family – right to family life

[European Convention on Human Rights 1950 Art.8.]

R, a Colombian, applied for judicial review of the Secretary of State's decision to confirm his removal from the United Kingdom to Colombia. R had entered the UK with his common law wife with whom he had three children. Both of their asylum applications had been refused and R had also been refused exceptional leave to remain. His wife's application remained outstanding. R had subsequently been convicted of grievous bodily harm, possession of drugs and drink driving. Upon his release from prison, the Secretary of State had confirmed his decision to deport him. R argued that his removal from the UK would breach his right to family life as guaranteed by the European Convention on Human Rights 1950 Art.8.

Held, refusing the application, that to remove R from the UK whilst his wife and children were allowed to remain would pose a serious risk of a breach of his right to family life under Art.8. It would, in addition, be disproportionate to order the removal of R on account of his criminal conviction. R's application, however, would be dismissed in the circumstances and the Secretary of State's undertaking not to deport him until his wife's application for leave to remain had been determined, would be accepted.

R. v. SECRETARY OF STATE FOR THE HOME DEPARTMENT, *ex p.* R *The Times*, November 29, 2000, Gage, J., QBD.

3620. Asylum seekers – detention centres – lawfulness of detention pending determination of application for leave to enter – right to liberty and security

[Immigration Act 1971 Sch.2 Part I para.16; Human Rights Act (1998) Sch.1 Part I Art.5, Art.5(1) (f).]

The Secretary of State appealed against a decision (Daily Telegraph, September 11, 2001) that the detention of S, an asylum seeker, at Oakington Reception Centre contravened his right to liberty and security provided by the Human Rights Act 1998 Sch.1 Part I Art.5. In order to facilitate a speedy and effective process for determining claims, the Secretary of State had introduced a new policy whereby asylum seekers could be detained at Oakington for a period not exceeding ten days whilst their applications were processed. S contended that the fact of his detention was (1) in breach of his Art.5 right, and (2) outside the implicit limitation placed upon the power to detain pending a decision to give or refuse leave to enter conferred by the Immigration Act 1971 Sch.2 Part I para.16.

Held, allowing the appeal, that (1) Art.5(1)(f) of the 1998 Act allowed states to effect lawful arrest or detention in order to prevent the unauthorised entry of aliens but any period of detention should not be unduly prolonged, *Amuur v. France* (1996) 22 E.H.R.R. 533, [1997] C.L.Y. 2766 applied. The test of proportionality required consideration of the length of the period of detention against the background of the conditions of detention and relevant special circumstances. In the instant case, a detention period of about one week was reasonable and proportionate, and (2) the power to detain as provided under Sch.2 Part I para.16 of the 1971 Act persisted only for as long as was reasonably necessary to conduct examinations and hence arrive at a decision on whether to grant leave to enter. A limited detention period was not unreasonable given the need for speedy resolution of asylum claims in the context of a sharp rise in the volume of applications.

R. (ON THE APPLICATION OF SAADI) v. SECRETARY OF STATE FOR THE HOME DEPARTMENT; R. (ON THE APPLICATION OF MAGED) v. SECRETARY OF STATE FOR THE HOME DEPARTMENT; R. (ON THE APPLICATION OF OSMAN (DILSHAD)) v. SECRETARY OF STATE FOR THE HOME DEPARTMENT; R. (ON THE APPLICATION OF MOHAMMED (RIZGAN)) v. SECRETARY OF STATE FOR THE HOME DEPARTMENT, [2001] EWCA Civ 1512, [2002] 1 W.L.R. 356, Lord Phillips of Worth Matravers, M.R., CA.

3621. Asylum seekers – evidence – fresh claims – effect of new representations

The Secretary of State appealed against a decision that the submission of new documentary evidence relating to the likelihood of S, an asylum seeker, facing persecution in the event of his return to Turkey should have been treated as a fresh asylum claim. The judge had found that the new evidence, which dealt with the likelihood of a person returning to Turkey without travel documents or a passport being tortured, was sufficiently different from what had been before the tribunal such that a favourable view might be taken of any new claim. The judge had concluded that the Secretary of State's failure to treat S as making a new asylum application in the light of the new evidence had been *Wednesbury* unreasonable given that such evidence undermined the evidential basis of the tribunal's decision.

Held, dismissing the appeal, that the Secretary of State had been *Wednesbury* unreasonable in not giving consideration to the impact of the new evidence. Whilst the report did not identify S as a person specifically at risk, by implication it included him within that category, *R. v. Secretary of State for the Home Department, ex p. Singh (Manvinder)* [1996] C.O.D. 476 applied and *Ladd v. Marshall* [1954] 1 W.L.R. 1489, [1954] C.L.Y. 2507 considered.

Observed, that two possible "tests" appeared to have emerged in relation to the effect of new evidence on an asylum claim. Such evidence had been found to result in a fresh claim either if any new representations extended beyond the simple provision of additional evidence supporting essentially the same claim, or where the new representations constituted significant, credible and previously unavailable material relevant to a claim, that material being essentially unchallenged. The court considered, however, that it was not appropriate to determine which test was to be preferred.

R. v. SECRETARY OF STATE FOR THE HOME DEPARTMENT, *ex p.* SENKOY; *sub nom.* SECRETARY OF STATE FOR THE HOME DEPARTMENT v. SENKOY, [2001] EWCA Civ 328, [2001] Imm. A.R. 399, Peter Gibson, L.J., CA.

3622.   **Asylum seekers – evidence – nature of evidence required to establish forgery – use of personal knowledge by special adjudicator**

M sought judicial review of the dismissal of his appeal against a refusal to grant him asylum. M contended that the special adjudicator had erred (1) in his conclusion that certain documents relied upon by him in support of his asylum claim had been forged, on the basis of his own experience of working for the UNHCR, rather than on the basis of relevant expert evidence or any other direct evidence, and (2) in using his knowledge of other cases involving Somali nationals to conclude that, in view of his physical appearance, M was not a Somali .

Held, dismissing the appeal, that (1) there was no general requirement that evidence had to be produced by the Home Office before it was possible to conclude that a particular document had been forged. The requirement was only that there should be some evidence in existence, and that test was amply satisfied by M's restricted knowledge of his purported national language and the inconsistencies between the documents produced and M's oral evidence, *Chowdhury v. Entry Clearance Officer (Dhaka)* (Unreported, December 30, 1994) and *Makozo v. Secretary of State for the Home Department* (Unreported, February 12, 1999) considered, and (2) while there were dangers in using personal knowledge in circumstances where it could not easily be objectively verified, the special adjudicator had confirmed that he had dealt with cases involving Somalis regularly over a period of years, and had also taken care to reconcile his conclusion with other evidence in the case.

R. v. IMMIGRATION APPELLATE AUTHORITY, *ex p.* MOHAMMED (MUKHTAR SHALA); *sub nom.* R. v. SPECIAL ADJUDICATOR, *ex p.* MOHAMMED (MUKHTAR SHALA) [2001] Imm. A.R. 162, Newman, J., QBD.

3623.   **Asylum seekers – evidence – recent country report – credibility**

S, a citizen of Sri Lanka, sought judicial review of the Secretary of State's refusal to grant him asylum. S's appeal had been dismissed by a special adjudicator who had not found him a credible witness. The tribunal had refused leave to appeal. S had made representations to the Home Office and the Secretary of State had refused to consider those representations as a fresh claim. S argued that the latest country report, which had not been before the adjudicator, undermined the adverse credibility findings of the special adjudicator.

Held, refusing the application, that it was very unlikely that a country report which contained nothing specifically relating to A could undermine a special adjudicator's credibility findings. The Secretary of State, in applying the acid test laid down by the settled cases, had been entitled to conclude that no fresh claim had been made.

R. v. SECRETARY OF STATE FOR THE HOME DEPARTMENT, *ex p.* SIVARANJAN (SIVAPALAN) [2001] Imm. A.R. 7, Tucker, J., QBD.

3624. Asylum seekers – expert evidence – credibility – reliance on unsourced opinion

E, a citizen of Egypt, sought judicial review of the refusal to grant him permission to appeal from the dismissal by a special adjudicator of his appeal against the refusal by the Secretary of State to grant him asylum. An expert's opinion on conditions in Egypt had been submitted to the adjudicator; however, the opinion was not sourced and, accordingly, it was given little weight. On application for permission to appeal to the Immigration Appeal Tribunal the origin of the opinion was identified, but the tribunal concluded that it should not alter the adjudicator's conclusions, and refused permission. E criticised the approach of the tribunal to the expert's opinion which, inter alia, gave a view on E's credibility.

Held, refusing the application, that the approach by the special adjudicator to the unsourced opinion had been correct. The factual basis on which the report relied was different from that established by the findings of the adjudicator and the tribunal had been entitled to conclude that it would not have affected the adjudicator's conclusions. The opinion included the expert's assessment of E's credibility, but that was inappropriate, being a matter for the special adjudicator.

R. v. IMMIGRATION APPEAL TRIBUNAL, *ex p.* EZ-ELDIN [2001] Imm. A.R. 98, Blofeld, J., QBD.

3625. Asylum seekers – notice – fair hearing – credibility – special adjudicator's function

H, a citizen of Ethiopia who had been refused asylum by the Secretary of State, sought judicial review of the Immigration Appeal Tribunal's refusal to grant him permission to appeal. The Secretary of State had not found H credible although his credibility was not a central issue in the appeal. The special adjudicator had also concluded that he was not credible. H submitted that the adjudicator had been unfair to conclude that his evidence was vague in material respects without putting him on notice and giving him an opportunity to elaborate on it. H relied on para.205 of the UNHCR Handbook and also complained that the adjudicator had not properly assessed the material put before him on the situation in Ethiopia.

Held, refusing the application, that the allegations were ill-founded and represented a serious misunderstanding of the function of the special adjudicator and his duties. He had no obligation, having heard the evidence and found it unsatisfactory, to put H on notice and allow him to start again. None of the material suggested that H would be persecuted because he was Oromo or because of a family connection.

HASSAN (HASSAN NAJEEB) v. IMMIGRATION APPEAL TRIBUNAL [2001] Imm. A.R. 83, Buxton, L.J., CA.

3626. Asylum seekers – passports – certification of claim – validity of passport with missing pages

[Asylum and Immigration Appeals Act 1993 s.5.]

K, a citizen of Kenya, sought permission to apply for judicial review of the Secretary of State's decision to certify his claim for asylum under the Asylum and Immigration Appeals Act 1993 s.5. On his arrival in the United Kingdom, K had produced a passport which had been mutilated by the removal of a number of pages and the Secretary of State had proceeded to certify the case on the basis that K had failed to produce a valid passport and that, following an unsatisfactory interview, A had failed to inform the immigration officer of that fact.

Held, refusing the application, that the passport produced by the applicant was not a valid passport, as required by s.5 para.3. It followed that the Secretary of State had been justified in certifying the applicant's claim for asylum.

R. v. SECRETARY OF STATE FOR THE HOME DEPARTMENT, *ex p.* KARAFU [2001] Imm. A.R. 26, Turner, J., QBD.

3627. Asylum seekers – persecution – attack on pregnant spouse of applicant

F, a Roma citizen of the Czech Republic, appealed against a decision of the Immigration Appeal Tribunal upholding the refusal of his claim for asylum. F alleged that he and his wife had been attacked by skinheads and subjected to racial abuse. The IAT had held that such treatment was not sufficient to warrant a well founded fear of persecution.

Held, allowing the appeal, that the severe ill treatment of the wife or close family of an asylum seeker could amount to the persecution of that asylum seeker. The IAT had not adequately addressed the effect on F of the violent attack on his wife, who had been pregnant at the time, which was capable of constituting grounds for a well founded fear of persecution on his part.

FRANTISEK v. SECRETARY OF STATE FOR THE HOME DEPARTMENT; *sub nom.* KATRINAK v. SECRETARY OF STATE FOR THE HOME DEPARTMENT, [2001] EWCA Civ 832, [2001] 3 F.C.R. 367, Schiemann, L.J., CA.

3628. Asylum seekers – persecution – birth of child in breach of Chinese one child per family policy – Australia

[United Nations Convention relating to the Status of Refugees 1951.]

H, a child aged three, born in Australia of Chinese parents who were unsuccessful in their claim for asylum, appealed against the upholding of M's appeal against a decision remitting H's case back to the Refugee Review Tribunal. H had applied for refugee status in Australia, on the ground that he was a "black child", a child born in breach of China's policy of one child per family, and would be subject to persecution in China, including the denial of access to education and health care. M refused the claim and the tribunal refused H's appeal, on the ground that, although, as a "black child", he was a member of a social group, the potential persecution would not derive from the actions of the authorities towards H himself, but would be directed at his parents for breaching the policy. The Federal Court upheld H's further appeal, directing that the tribunal should reconsider the case on the basis that H came within the definition of a refugee. M appealed to the Full Court which restored the tribunal's decision and also found that "black children" did not constitute a social group.

Held, allowing the appeal, that H was a refugee entitled to protection. China's one child policy had the effect of discriminating against "black children", who were an identifiable group for that reason, and therefore the Full Court had been wrong to find that "black children" were not a social group for the purposes of the United Nations Convention relating to the Status of Refugees 1951. The type of discrimination that H would face would generally be recognised as falling within the definition of persecution, and since he was a member of a social group likely to be subjected to such discrimination, it followed that H came within the scope of the Convention. No adverse intention had to be shown, and the tribunal had erred in holding that it had to be, and in holding that the persecution could be for reasons other than H's status as a "black child".

H (A CHILD) v. MINISTER FOR IMMIGRATION AND MULTICULTURAL AFFAIRS [2000] I.N.L.R. 455, Gleeson, C.J., HC (Aus).

3629. Asylum seekers – persecution – consideration of background evidence of situation in applicant's country of origin – credibility of asylum seeker

S, an Iranian asylum seeker, sought to challenge a refusal of permission to appeal against a decision of a special adjudicator, upholding a refusal of his asylum claim. S contended that the adjudicator's finding as to his lack of credibility was without reason and that in coming to such a conclusion the adjudicator had failed to have regard to relevant material concerning the situation in Iran, particularly in regard to his treatment of evidence concerning an arrest warrant and its lack of relevance or validity.

Held, refusing the application, that while the adjudicator's criticism of S's failure to provide the original arrest warrant had been "naive", his conclusion as to the unreliability of the warrant had been reasonable, he had a full appreciation of the background circumstances within Iran and had been entitled to come to the conclusion he had as to S's credibility, *R. v. Immigration Appeal Tribunal, ex p. Ahmed* [1999] I.N.L.R. 473, [2000] 2 C.L. 321 considered.

R. v. IMMIGRATION APPELLATE AUTHORITY, *ex p.* SHOCKROLLAHY; *sub nom.* R. v. IMMIGRATION APPEAL TRIBUNAL, *ex p.* SHOKROLLAHY [2000] Imm. A.R. 580, Burton, J., QBD.

3630. Asylum seekers – persecution – credibility of evidence

[Asylum and Immigration Appeals Act 1993 Sch.2 para. 5(3)(a).]

S, a Sri Lankan national, sought to challenge a decision of the special adjudicator, upholding the refusal of S's claim for asylum and certifying the claim pursuant to the Asylum and Immigration Appeals Act 1993 Sch.2 para. 5(3)(a). S submitted that the certification had been unlawful and that the adjudicator had erred in her approach to S's credibility and as to the future risk of persecution should S return to Sri Lanka as a failed asylum seeker. Furthermore it was contended that the adjudicator erred in refusing the request for an adjournment of the proceedings for authentication of a letter from the Divisional Secretariat in Sri Lanka which supported some of S's assertions.

Held, refusing the application for judicial review, that the adjudicator had considered all relevant material and had been entitled to reach the conclusions that she had.

R. (ON THE APPLICATION OF SUBATHTHERAN) v. SPECIAL ADJUDICATOR; *sub nom.* R. v. SPECIAL ADJUDICATOR, *ex p.* SUBATHTHERAN, [2001] EWHC Admin 12, [2001] Imm. A.R. 345, Ouseley, J., QBD (Admin Ct).

3631. Asylum seekers – persecution – documentary evidence – forgery – burden of proof

S, a Chinese national, challenged the Immigration Appeal Tribunal's decision not to grant him permission to appeal against the Secretary of State's refusal to grant asylum. The IAT had found that S had no well founded fear of persecution as the authorities had no interest in him. S had evidence, in the form of letters from his family, who advised him not to return home, and from the Chinese police that he was the subject of enquiries by the Chinese authorities concerning his involvement in the democracy demonstrations. S contended that the IAT had erred in finding that the documents were forgeries as the Secretary of State had failed to discharge the burden of proof to disprove the authenticity of documentary evidence. As that was a point with a strong possibility of success, it was submitted that permission should have been granted.

Held, granting the application for judicial review, that the IAT had failed to identify properly the burden of proof point, therefore its decision had been erroneous. The special adjudicator should have examined whether the burden of proof in relation to the authenticity of the documents had been discharged by the Secretary of State, rather than concentrating on S's failure to show that the letters were genuine.

R. v. IMMIGRATION APPEAL TRIBUNAL, *ex p.* SHEN [2000] I.N.L.R. 389, Dyson, J., QBD.

3632. **Asylum seekers – persecution – fear of persecution by non state agents – civil servants – non cooperation with extremist groups**

N, an Algerian, appealed against a decision of the Immigration Appeal Tribunal which had upheld a special adjudicator's decision to refuse her claim for asylum. N, who had been employed as a civil servant in the telegraphic department in Algeria, had been threatened by Islamic insurgents to force her to assist them with their overseas communications. Upon such threats being made, she had fled Algeria. N contended that the law enforcement agencies in Algeria were unable to protect her from persecution from those groups opposed to the government, and that she had a well founded fear of persecution.

Held, allowing the appeal, that (1) a reluctance to cooperate with forces hostile to a government could be construed as a political opinion; (2) authority existed for the granting of asylum to ministers of foreign governments who had fled after the fall of their government to hostile forces. Moreover, asylum could also be granted to ministers who fled before the change of a regime. It followed that it was appropriate that the same protection be afforded to conscientious civil servants, and (3) the tribunal was required to address the question of whether the attacks in Algeria were directed at political opponents of the insurgents and whether it was reasonably likely that a refusal to cooperate with the insurgents might be perceived as an expression of political opinion and lead to persecution. Accordingly, the case would be remitted back for consideration by a differently constituted tribunal.

NOUNE v. SECRETARY OF STATE FOR THE HOME DEPARTMENT [2001] I.N.L.R. 526, Schiemann, L.J., CA.

3633. **Asylum seekers – persecution – homosexuality – violation of right to private life – Pakistan**

[Human Rights Act 1998 Sch.1 Part I.]

T, a Pakistani national, had applied for asylum in the United Kingdom on the grounds that his homosexuality engendered a sufficient fear of persecution if he were to be returned to Pakistan, where homosexuality was a criminal offence and which, under religious law was punishable by death. His application having been refused, he appealed to a special adjudicator, who also dismissed the case. T applied for judicial review of the special adjudicator's decision, arguing (1) that the special adjudicator had failed to consider the case as a whole, placing disproportionate weight on T's non eventful history of homosexuality and not enough on future consequences of his failure to abide by tradition and raise a family, and (2) that the mere existence of the law against homosexuality in Pakistan, given the extreme punishment in the event of breach, amounted to persecution under the European Convention on Human Rights Art.8, whether or not such laws were enforced.

Held, dismissing the application, that (1) it was clear that the special adjudicator had considered all the evidence presented to him. He had been entitled to take account of the fact that T had experienced no persecution in respect of a number of homosexual relationships pursued during a five year period in Pakistan, and that neither his work colleagues, nor his family, were aware of his homosexuality. Thus it was open to the special adjudicator to conclude that T would not behave less discreetly if returned to Pakistan, hence he was unlikely to suffer persecution there, and (2) whilst the criminalisation of homosexuality was contradictory to the principle of Art.8, such that if the law was enforced, an active homosexual living in Pakistan might be described as a refugee, there was no justification for extending that principle to cases where the relevant law was not generally enforced. In the instant case, the special adjudicator had found, as he was entitled to do on the evidence before him, that there was little or no likelihood of T being prosecuted if he returned to Pakistan, thus there was no reason to conclude that he would be persecuted. *Modinos v. Cyprus (A/259)* (1993) 16 E.H.R.R. 485, [1993] C.L.Y. 4360 considered.

R. v. SPECIAL IMMIGRATION ADJUDICATOR, *ex p.* T [2001] Imm. A.R. 187, Goldring, J., QBD.

3634. **Asylum seekers – persecution – insufficient evidence to establish reasonable likelihood of torture**

[Asylum and Immigration Appeals Act 1993 Sch.2, para 5.]

D, an Indian, applied for judicial review of a special adjudicator's decision to uphold the Secretary of State's certificate issued under the Asylum and Immigration Appeals Act 1993 Sch.2 para.5(2) and the Secretary of State's refusal to grant him asylum. D claimed to fear persecution from Khalistan terrorists and the local police on his return to India as a result of beatings he underwent prior to his coming to the UK. D contended that the adjudicator had erred in finding that Sch.2 para.5(5) of the Act did not apply as the adjudicator should have found sufficient evidence of a reasonable likelihood of D having been tortured by the police in India, and also that he had wrongly concluded that there were no Convention grounds to justify allowing the appeal.

Held, refusing the application, that there was insufficient evidence before the adjudicator to enable him to find a reasonable likelihood of torture by the local police and that there was therefore no well founded fear of persecution in the event of a return to India. The adjudicator's decision was a reasonable and lawful one.

R. (ON THE APPLICATION OF DHOTHAR) v. SPECIAL ADJUDICATOR; *sub nom.* R. v. SPECIAL ADJUDICATOR, *ex p.* DHOTHAR [2001] Imm. A.R. 210, Gibbs, J., QBD (Admin Ct).

3635. **Asylum seekers – persecution – interpretation of Convention – differentiated standard of proof under Art.33 – US procedure for determining claims**

[Asylum Act 1996 s.2; Convention Relating to the Status of Refugees 1951 (United Nations) Art.1, Art.33.]

S, who entered the United Kingdom from Ecuador via the USA, was refused asylum by the Secretary of State, who certified his claim under the Asylum Act 1996 s.2, being satisfied that S could safely be returned to the USA. S applied for judicial review of that decision, contending that condition (c) of s.2 of the Act had not been fulfilled, namely that there was no real risk that the US authorities would return him to Ecuador otherwise than in accordance with the Convention Relating to the Status of Refugees 1951 (United Nations). It was contended that US law was not consistent with the true interpretation of the Convention, since an applicant who qualified as a refugee under Art.1 had to establish a clear probability of persecution in order to qualify for mandatory withholding of deportation, which was a higher standard of proof than that required under Art.33. It was submitted that in differentiating between the standard of proof for Art.1 and Art.33, the USA had adopted a position contrary to the Convention's true interpretation. Furthermore, the procedures for determining asylum claims were so unfair that there was a real risk he could be removed in breach of the Convention.

Held, refusing the application, that the correct approach was not to question whether the USA had properly interpreted the Convention as a matter of law, but to consider whether there was a real risk that S would be removed in breach of it. In assessing the risk the Secretary of State had properly considered the administrative practice of the USA, in view of the fact that states were entitled to confer protection against refoulement under Art.33 by legislative or administrative means, *R. v. Secretary of State for the Home Department, ex p. Adan (Lul Omar)* [1999] 3 W.L.R. 1274, [1999] C.L.Y. 3185 distinguished. The exercise of administrative discretion in such cases did not necessarily pose a real risk of return contrary to the Convention. The Secretary of State could not be criticised in his findings regarding the procedural issue, since the holding of a secondary inspection followed by a referral to a credible referral interview in cases where the asylum seeker expressed fears about being returned to their country of origin was a system which complied with the Convention's standards.

R. v. SECRETARY OF STATE FOR THE HOME DEPARTMENT, *ex p.* SALAS [2001] Imm. A.R. 105, Sullivan, J., QBD.

3636. **Asylum seekers – persecution – military service – risks faced by soldiers from terrorism**

[Convention Relating to the Status Refugees 1951 Art.1A(2).]

F, an Algerian national, appealed against the refusal of permission to appeal against the determination of the special adjudicator. The special adjudicator had refused F's application for asylum on the ground that his objection to military service did not amount to a Convention reason. F maintained that should he return to Algeria to complete his military service he would be at risk of attack from the GIA, an Islamic fundamentalist group, and that such risk amounted to persecution from which the state was unable to protect him. It was submitted that the special adjudicator had erred in that he failed to consider whether F was a refugee pursuant to the Convention Relating to the Status of Refugees 1951 Art.1A(2). F contended that (1) upon completion of his military service he would be at risk of harm, and (2) the risks of terrorism faced by serving soldiers and their families amounted to persecution for a Convention reason, notwithstanding that the risks faced by soldiers engaged in a legitimate external conflict would not.

Held, dismissing the appeal, that (1) given that F would not finish his military service for approximately 18 months, too many uncertainties existed as to the future risk of harm for him to be able to claim status as a refugee, and (2) the Convention did not draw a distinction between serving soldiers engaged in a legitimate external conflict and those engaged in internal conflict, such as combatting terrorism. The nature of a soldier's life exposed him to danger. It would not be appropriate to allow an application based on the inadequate protection a state offered to its soldiers from terrorism, given that in so doing a hindrance would be place on that state in offering the same protection to its citizens.

FADLI v. SECRETARY OF STATE FOR THE HOME DEPARTMENT; *sub nom.* R. v. SECRETARY OF STATE FOR THE HOME DEPARTMENT, *ex p.* FADLI; FADLI (APPLICATION FOR JUDICIAL REVIEW), RE; FADIL v. SECRETARY OF STATE FOR THE HOME DEPARTMENT [2001] Imm. A.R. 392, Schiemann, L.J., CA.

3637. **Asylum seekers – persecution – protection of UNMIK and KFOR – state of nationality**

[Convention relating to the Status of Refugees 1951 (United Nations) Art.1A(2), Art.1D.]

D was an ethnic Albanian from Kosovo. The Secretary of State refused his application for asylum on the basis that at the date of the decision, given the presence of the United Nations Interim Administration Mission, UNMIK, and the Kosovo Force, KFOR, he had no well founded fear of persecution in Kosovo. On D's appeal, the special adjudicator concluded that the Convention relating to the Status of Refugees 1951 (United Nations) Art.1D excluded D from protection under the Convention. D appealed, arguing that the protection of KFOR and UNMIK was not for "the protection of his country" within terms of Art.1A(2) of the Convention following *Secretary of State for the Home Department v. Arif* [1999] Imm. A.R. 271, [1999] C.L.Y. 3165 . It followed that the burden shifted to the Secretary of State to show there had been sufficient changes in D's home country in order to remove a well founded fear of persecution.

Held, allowing the appeal and remitting the matter for fresh consideration by way of a starred decision, that D was a Yugoslavian citizen not a citizen of Kosovo for the purposes of the Convention. However, in spite of D's nationality, the protection offered by UNMIK and KFOR in Kosovo was in law capable of being "the protection of his country" under Art.1A(2), so that D's status as a refugee was to be decided under that provision. Further, the reverse burden of proof on the Secretary of State was only relevant where the claimant had been a refugee in the past, *Arif* distinguished. Art.1D did not apply to those in Kosovo who received assistance from UNMIK and KFOR.

DYLI v. SECRETARY OF STATE FOR THE HOME DEPARTMENT [2000] Imm. A.R. 652, CMG Ockelton (Deputy President), IAT.

3638. Asylum seekers – persecution – rape of woman by army officer – discrimination

[Convention relating to the Status of Refugees 1951 (United Nations).]

P, an Angolan citizen, claimed that she had been raped by an Angolan army officer and sought asylum. The Secretary of State refused. Dismissing P's appeal, the special adjudicator concluded that, as there was nothing to suggest that the officer's actions were supported or condoned by the authorities, or that they could not or would not offer P protection, her claim did not bring her within the Convention relating to the Status of Refugees 1951 (United Nations). Following the refusal of her application for permission to apply for judicial review of the Immigration Appeal Tribunal's refusal to grant leave to appeal the special adjudicator's decision, P re-newed her application. She contended that, as a woman, she formed part of a recognisable social group that was liable to be raped and further, that rape was sufficiently serious ill treatment so as to amount to persecution.

Held, refusing the re-application, that it was necessary to show discrimination in order to establish persecution in terms of the Convention and that element was missing in the instant case, *R. v. Immigration Appeal Tribunal, ex p. Shah* [1999] 2 A.C. 629, [1999] C.L.Y. 3172 followed. The facts showed that the P had been raped by the officer acting as an individual who had not been carrying out an official policy that singled out women in that area for discriminatory treatment.

R. v. IMMIGRATION APPEAL TRIBUNAL, *ex p.* PEDRO; *sub nom* PEDRO v. IMMIGRATION APPEAL TRIBUNAL [2000] Imm. A.R. 489, Lord Woolf, M.R., CA.

3639. Asylum seekers – persecution – removal to safe third country – need for autonomous definition of Refugee Convention

[Asylum and Immigration Act 1996 s.2 (2); Convention relating to the Status of Refugees 1951 (United Nations) Art.1 (A) (2).]

A, a Somalian national, sought asylum in the UK after being refused protection in Germany. Although a contracting party to the Convention relating to the Status of Refugees 1951 (United Nations), Germany applied a restrictive interpretation to Art.1A(2) of the Convention so as to deny refugee status to an asylum seeker who feared persecution by non state agents where his home country was unwilling or unable to protect him. The Secretary of State ordered A to return to Germany under the Asylum and Immigration Act 1996 s.2, concluding that it was permissible for Germany to attribute a narrower construction to Art.1A(2) than other contracting states. A's application for judicial review of that decision having been refused, she appealed to the Court of Appeal, which declared ([1999] 3 W.L.R. 1274) the Secretary of State's decision to have been unlawful. The Secretary of State appealed.

Held, dismissing the appeal, that a common autonomous meaning of Art.1 (A) (2) had to be adopted by all contracting states. The concept of persecution was not to be limited to conduct attributable to a state, *Adan (Hassan Hussein) v. Secretary of State for the Home Department* [1999] 1 A.C. 293, [1998] C.L.Y. 3241 followed. There was no material distinction to be made between countries ruled other than by a government and countries where, although a government existed, it was unable to provide the requisite protection to its citizens. In the circumstances, the Secretary of State had been wrong to certify that the conditions of s.2(2) of the Act had been met.

R. (ON THE APPLICATION OF ADAN (LUL OMAR)) v. SECRETARY OF STATE FOR THE HOME DEPARTMENT; R. (ON THE APPLICATION OF AITSEGUER) v. SECRETARY OF STATE FOR THE HOME DEPARTMENT; *sub nom.* R. v. SECRETARY OF STATE FOR THE HOME DEPARTMENT, *ex p.* AITSEGUER; SECRETARY OF STATE FOR THE HOME DEPARTMENT v. ADAN (LUL OMAR); SECRETARY OF STATE FOR THE HOME DEPARTMENT v. AITSEGUER; R. v. SECRETARY OF STATE FOR THE HOME DEPARTMENT, *ex p.* ADAN (LUL OMAR) [2001] 2 A.C. 477, Lord Steyn, HL.

3640. **Asylum seekers – persecution – torture – racist attacks did not constitute persecution**

[Criminal Justice Act 1988 s.134 (1); Asylum and Immigration Appeals Act 1993 Sch.2 para.5; Convention against Torture and other Cruel, Inhuman or Degrading Treatment or Punishment 1984 (United Nations) Art.1 (1).]

R, a Roma gypsy and Polish national, sought judicial review of a decision by a special adjudicator to uphold a certificate granted pursuant to the Asylum and Immigration Appeals Act 1993 Sch.2 para.5. R contended that (1) the special adjudicator had erred in her interpretation of the definition of torture by placing reliance upon definitions found within the Convention against Torture and other Cruel, Inhuman or Degrading Treatment or Punishment 1984 (United Nations) Art.1 (1) and the Criminal Justice Act 1988 s.134 (1), both of which referred to acts by an official or acquiescence by an official. R maintained that those definitions differed from that found within Sch.2 para.5 (5) of the 1993 Act which made no mention of official acts, and (2) under Sch.2 para.5 (5), torture did not have to be linked to the facts of the asylum application but could be "free standing" of the application itself.

Held, refusing the application, that (1) with regard to an asylum seeker's claim to have suffered from "torture" under Sch.2 para.5 (5) of the 1993 Act, such torture had to be either by agents of the state, or where carried out by persons who were not agents of the state, of a kind which that state was not able or disinclined to provide adequate protection against. In the instant case, the issue of action by public officials had played no part in the special adjudicator's determination. The special adjudicator had concluded that, whilst the acts complained of could be categorised as harassment, they could not be defined as acts of torture or persecution. Accordingly, even if the adjudicator had made an error of law, that error would not have vitiated the underlying decision on the merits, *R. v. Secretary of State for the Home Department, ex p. Singh (2000)* (Unreported, March 3, 2000) applied, and (2) it was observed that torture had to be related to the underlying application, *R. v. Immigration Appeal Tribunal, ex p. Brylewicz* (Unreported, March 26, 2000) applied.

R. (ON THE APPLICATION OF ROSZKOWSKI) v. SPECIAL ADJUDICATOR; *sub nom.* R. v. SECRETARY OF STATE FOR THE HOME DEPARTMENT, *ex p.* ROSZKOWSKI; R. v. SPECIAL ADJUDICATOR, *ex p.* ROSZKOWSKI *The Times*, November 29, 2000, Keene, J., QBD (Admin Ct).

3641. **Asylum seekers – persecution – torture by authorities on suspicion of violent terrorist involvement – inference of persecution**

S, a Sri Lankan Tamil, appealed against the refusal of his application for judicial review ([2001] EWHC Admin 109) of a decision to refuse his asylum claim. The special adjudicator had concluded that whilst S's evidence concerning the torture he had been subjected to by the authorities was credible, such torture had not been the result of any political opinion that S might have been believed to have held but had instead resulted from a suspicion that he was involved in violent terrorism. S contended that the special adjudicator had erred and that he should have been found to have a well founded fear of persecution on three Convention grounds, namely imputed political opinion, race and membership of a particular social group. S maintained that imputed political opinion and suspicion of involvement in violent terrorism were not mutually exclusive concepts and that an individual suspected of involvement in violent terrorism could equally have a political opinion imputed to him.

Held, allowing the appeal, that where an individual had been persecuted for his alleged involvement in violent terrorism it did not necessarily follow that he had not been persecuted for his political opinion. Each case had to be assessed on its merits and the particular reason for persecution determined. It was not necessarily the case that excessive and arbitrary punishment for political offences would amount to persecution for Convention purposes but such treatment raised a strong inference that that was in fact the case, *Paramanathan v. Minister for Immigration & Multicultural Affairs* (1998) 160 A.L.R. 24

applied. On the facts of the instant case, there was no evidence that the special adjudicator had addressed the issues on the basis that the torture suffered by S gave rise to an inference of persecution for a Convention reason and it was not clear why he had concluded that S had not been persecuted for reasons of his ethnic origin or imputed political opinion.

R. (ON THE APPLICATION OF SIVAKUMAR) v. IMMIGRATION APPEAL TRIBUNAL; *sub nom.* SIVAKUMAR v. SECRETARY OF STATE FOR THE HOME DEPARTMENT; R. (ON THE APPLICATION OF OF SIVAKUMAR) v. SECRETARY OF STATE FOR THE HOME DEPARTMENT, [2001] EWCA Civ 1196, *The Times*, November 7, 2001, Dyson, L.J., CA.

3642. **Asylum seekers – persecution – women – impact of concession – existence of social group – membership by way of gender and nationality**

[Convention relating to the Status of Refugees 1951 (United Nations) Art.1 (A) (2).]

I, a Lithuanian woman, appealed against the dismissal of her application for judicial review following the refusal of her claim for asylum. I had been habitually abused by her husband and argued that the failure of the authorities to protect her constituted persecution. I contended that although at the hearing before the special adjudicator she had conceded, in the light of the Court of Appeal's decision in *R. v. Immigration Appeal Tribunal, ex p. Shah* [1998] 1 W.L.R. 74, [1997] C.L.Y. 2851, that she was unable to establish membership of a persecuted group under the Convention relating to the Status of Refugees 1951 (United Nations) Art.1A(2), she ought not to be bound by that concession following the reversal of the decision by the House of Lords (*R. v. Immigration Appeal Tribunal, ex p. Shah* [1999] 2 A.C. 629, [1999] C.L.Y. 3172). That judgment had been promulgated two weeks prior to the special adjudicator's determination. I submitted that she should be given a further opportunity to adduce evidence which had only become relevant subsequent to the decision of the House of Lords.

Held, allowing the appeal and remitting the case to a different adjudicator, that I was not bound by her concession at the hearing before the special adjudicator. Although the findings of the House of Lords in *Shah* that Pakistani women could be members of a social group so as to show persecution did not necessarily mean that Lithuanian women were also within the ambit of the Convention, there was a sufficient chance that the special adjudicator would have reached a different conclusion had the decision of the House of Lords been considered, *Horvath v. Secretary of State for the Home Department* [2001] 1 A.C. 489, [2000] C.L.Y. 3319 considered. The special adjudicator's decision was, accordingly, set aside in its entirety, as was the Secretary of State's refusal of exceptional leave to remain, *Shah* considered.

R. (ON THE APPLICATION OF I) v. SPECIAL ADJUDICATOR; *sub nom.* I v. SPECIAL ADJUDICATOR; R. v. SPECIAL ADJUDICATOR, *ex p.* I, [2001] EWCA Civ 1271, *The Times*, September 18, 2001, Schiemann, L.J., CA.

3643. **Asylum seekers – procedural impropriety – failure to provide competent interpreter – entitlement to review**

[Immigration and Asylum Appeals (Procedure) Rules (SI 2000 No 2333) r.16.]

G applied for judicial review of the special adjudicator's dismissal of his asylum appeal. He contended that the special adjudicator should have adjourned the hearing because a competent interpreter had not been provided, and in failing to adjourn he had made a procedural error which the chief adjudicator was obliged to review under the Immigration and Asylum Appeals (Procedure) Rules 2000 r.16. The chief adjudicator had considered the matter to be one of substance, as opposed to procedure, and, on that basis, had declined jurisdiction.

Held, granting the application, that the failure to provide G with a competent interpreter had constituted a procedural error, given that it was related to the means by which evidence might be communicated to the tribunal. Such a failure was of relevance to the special adjudicator's decision and G had been entitled to have the decision reviewed by the chief adjudicator under r.16 of the Rules.

R. (ON THE APPLICATION OF GASHI) v. CHIEF ADJUDICATOR (NEED FOR COMPETENT INTERPRETER), [2001] EWHC Admin 916, *The Times,* November 12, 2001, Judge Wilkie, QBD (Admin Ct).

3644. Asylum seekers – removal – right to family life – power to review Secretary of State's decision

See IMMIGRATION: R. (on the application of Isiko) v. Secretary of State for the Home Department. §3646

3645. Asylum seekers – removal following refusal of application – leave to remain to give evidence in wife's appeal

G, a Colombian national, claimed asylum in the UK and his wife and family applied to remain as his dependants. When G's application was refused, his wife applied for asylum on the ground that there had been a misunderstanding as to the basis for their claim to have a well founded fear of persecution. Her application was refused by the Secretary of State and she appealed. G then sought to resist his own removal, contending that it was necessary for him to remain as he was a witness in his wife's appeal, which had little chance of success if he could not give evidence.

Held, refusing the application, that (1) whether G should be allowed to stay in the UK as a witness was a matter for the Secretary of State which he had not yet had the opportunity to consider; (2) If G was removed he could apply for entry clearance as a visitor so that he could give evidence, *R. v. Secretary of State for the Home Department, ex p. Polat* (Unreported, November 7, 1996) applied, and (3) it was for the adjudicator to decide if G should give written evidence or attend in person. If the latter was decided upon, the adjudicator could also determine whether the appeal should be adjourned to allow G to attend as a witness.

R. v. SECRETARY OF STATE FOR THE HOME DEPARTMENT, *ex p.* GONZALEZ [2001] Imm. A.R. 200, Moses, J., QBD.

3646. Asylum seekers – right to family life – power of court to review decision of Secretary of State

[Human Rights Act 1998 Sch.1 Part I Art.8.]

The Secretary of State appealed against the granting of judicial review of his decision to remove two Ugandan nationals, I and his former wife, S, from the United Kingdom. I had come to the UK in 1990 as a student and in 1992 married S after they had both been declared illegal entrants. They had had a child in 1993. I had also been having a relationship with a British citizen, W, who had had a child in 1995. I had divorced S in 1997 and in 1999 married W whilst he was in prison following his conviction for rape. The Secretary of State had set removal directions for both I and S in 1999. The judge had found that their removal would interfere with their right to family life under the Human Rights Act 1998 Sch.1 Part I Art.8. It was submitted that the judge had been wrong to substitute his own decision for that of the Secretary of State.

Held, allowing the appeal, that the role of the court was to review the decision to ensure that it complied with the Convention Rights, but in doing so it had to bear in mind that there was "an area of discretion permitted to the [decision maker] which need[ed] to be exceeded before an action [could] be categorised as unlawful", *R. (on the application of Mahmood (Amjad)) v. Secretary of State for the Home Department* [2001] 1 W.L.R. 840, [2001] 2 C.L. 342 applied. It was not the function of the court to substitute its own decision. In the instant case, the Secretary of State had taken into account all the circumstances of the case and had been entitled to reach the conclusion that the proper enforcement of immigration control was a sufficient justification for interference in the family lives of the various parties.

R. (ON THE APPLICATION OF ISIKO) v. SECRETARY OF STATE FOR THE HOME DEPARTMENT; *sub nom.* SECRETARY OF STATE FOR THE HOME DEPARTMENT v. ISIKO; R. v. SECRETARY OF STATE FOR THE HOME DEPARTMENT, *ex p.* ISIKO [2001] 1 F.L.R. 930, Schiemann, L.J., CA.

3647. **Asylum seekers – third countries – Germany – alleged persecution by state and non state agents – credibility**

J, a Sri Lankan Tamil, was asked at his immigration interview from whom he feared prosecution. He answered that it was the Sri Lankan army. Later he also alleged that he feared the LTTE who were acting in the form of non state agents. The Secretary of State rejected the latter claim as not being borne out of the evidence, including the fact that fear of the LTTE was not mentioned at interview, and ordered J's return to Germany so that his claim could be considered there. J sought judicial review of that decision, submitting that the finding on credibility was not inappropriate given the questions asked at the interview. J contended that in that regard to the interview, he should have been asked whether he feared the army and then whether he feared the LTTE.

Held, refusing the application, that the Secretary of State had been entitled to make the adverse credibility finding on the facts. The questions asked were perfectly proper and to add to them as suggested would have turned them into leading questions. Further, there would be no difference between the UK and German approach to J's asylum application, *R. v. Secretary of State for the Home Department, ex p. Adan (Lul Omar)* [1999] 3 W.L.R. 1274, [1999] C.L.Y. 3185 considered.

R. v. SECRETARY OF STATE FOR THE HOME DEPARTMENT, *ex p.* JEROMIO [2000] Imm. A.R. 604, Burton, J., QBD.

3648. **Asylum seekers – third countries – Germany – internal flight – compatibility of German approach with Geneva Convention**

[Asylum and Immigration Act 1996 s.2(2)(c); Convention relating to the Status of Refugees 1951 (United Nations).]

Y, a Tamil asylum seeker, appealed against a decision ([2001] EWHC Admin 377) refusing his application challenging the Secretary of State's decision to remove him to Germany, from which country he had entered the United Kingdom. Y contended that the Secretary of State had erred in certifying Germany as a safe country for the purposes of the Asylum and Immigration Act 1996 s.2(2)(c) since (1) Germany's treatment of the question of persecution by non state agents differed from the approach taken by the English authorities and did not accord with the Convention relating to the Status of Refugees 1951 (United Nations); (2) the German authorities might fail to address the issue of persecution by police officers within the context of Art.1A(2) of the Convention, and (3) the German authorities might fail to address the question of internal flight and, to the extent that it was considered, adopted a strict approach which did not accord with the Convention.

Held, dismissing the appeal, that (1) the German approach to the question of persecution by non state agents accorded with the Convention and there was no real risk of the German government refouling Y in breach of the Convention; (2) although the question of police persecution was not considered by the German authorities in the context of the Convention, the requirements of German law were such that adequate consideration was given to the issue, and (3) whilst the German approach to the question of internal flight differed from that adopted by the English authorities, the Convention did not require a unitary approach to be adopted, and the Secretary of State had been entitled to conclude that the German authorities did not return asylum seekers unless the conditions concerning internal flight laid down by the Convention had been met,

R. (on the application of Adan (Lul Omar)) v. Secretary of State for the Home Department [2001] 2 W.L.R. 143, [2001] 1 C.L. 324 considered.

R. (ON THE APPLICATION OF YOGATHAS) v. SECRETARY OF STATE FOR THE HOME DEPARTMENT; R. (ON THE APPLICATION OF THANGARASA) v. SECRETARY OF STATE FOR THE HOME DEPARTMENT, [2001] EWCA Civ 1611, *The Times*, November 15, 2001, Laws, L.J., CA.

3649. Asylum seekers – third countries – Germany – lawfulness of renewing removal certificate previously held unlawful – legitimate expectation

[Asylum and Immigration Act 1996 s.2.]

Z, a Kosovar refugee, appealed against the refusal of his application for judicial review of a decision of the Secretary of State to issue a certificate pursuant to the Asylum and Immigration Act 1996 s.2 requiring his removal to Germany, where he had previously claimed asylum, for the substantive determination of his claim, and a subsequent decision to maintain that certificate. The initial challenge to the Secretary of State's decision had been deferred until the outcome of the Court of Appeal decision in the test case of *R. v. Secretary of State for the Home Department, ex p. Gashi* [1999] Imm. A.R. 415, [1999] C.L.Y. 3187. In that case it had been held that the issue of a certificate, in circumstances similar to those applying to Z, was unlawful. Following that decision a change of circumstances had occurred and the Secretary of State had confirmed his decision to remove Z to Germany. Z contended that as it was accepted that *Gashi* was a test case, the Secretary of State had been bound to apply the same result to his claim. Alternatively, he argued that the decision in *Gashi* had created a legitimate expectation that he would not be removed to Germany.

Held, allowing the appeal, that (1) a change in circumstances following the decision in *Gashi* had meant that the Secretary of State was not precluded from issuing a fresh certificate despite the fact that the original certificate had been rendered invalid, and (2) by deferring Z's application for judicial review until the outcome of the decision in *Gashi* and by then applying for permission to appeal against that decision, the Secretary of State had created a legitimate expectation that Z's substantive claim would be determined in the UK. *Gashi* applied.

R. (ON THE APPLICATION OF ZEQIRI) v. SECRETARY OF STATE FOR THE HOME DEPARTMENT; *sub nom*. R. v. SECRETARY OF STATE FOR THE HOME DEPARTMENT, *ex p.* ZEQIRI, [2001] EWCA Civ 342, [2002] Imm. A.R. 42, Lord Phillips of Worth Matravers, M.R., CA.

3650. Asylum seekers – third countries – Italy – applicant holding Italian residence permit – extended family resident in UK

[European Convention for the Protection of Human Rights and Fundamental Freedoms 1950 Art.8; Convention Determining the State Responsible for Examining Applications for Asylum Lodged in One of the EC Member States 1990.]

G, a Turkish Kurd, arrived in the UK via Italy and applied for asylum on the ground that he faced persecution from the Turkish authorities. The Secretary of State decided to return G and his family to Italy, relying on the terms of the Dublin Convention 1990 and a statement by the Italian authorities that G held an Italian residence permit. G sought judicial review of that decision, arguing that the document he held was not a residence permit under the Dublin Convention. Furthermore, it would be contrary to G's right to family life under the European Convention on Human Rights 1950 Art.8 if he was removed to Italy as members of his extended family were resident here.

Held, refusing the application, that (1) the Secretary of State could rely on the statement by the Italian authorities as to the status of the document; (2) G could not claim a right to come to the UK under Art.8 of the 1950 Convention on the basis that he had extended family members here. The Secretary of State had considered Art.8 when reaching his decision to return G to Italy and there was nothing to show that was a decision he could not properly have reached.

R. v. SECRETARY OF STATE FOR THE HOME DEPARTMENT, *ex p.* GANIDAGLI [2001] Imm. A.R. 202, Owen, J., QBD.

3651. Asylum seekers – third countries – Pakistan – designation as safe country – judicial review of subordinate legislation

[Asylum and Immigration Appeals Act 1993 Sch.2 para.5(2); Asylum (Designated Countries of Destination and Designated Safe Third Countries) Order 1996 (SI 1996 2671).]

The Secretary of State appealed against a decision ([2001] EWHC Admin 7, Times, February 9, 2001) that he had erred in his inclusion and retention of Pakistan on the list of countries designated as appearing to him to be free from a serious risk of persecution and in his decision to accordingly certify J, a Pakistani asylum seeker, as subject to the expedited asylum procedure pursuant to the Asylum and Immigration Appeals Act 1993 Sch.2 para.5(2). The designation of Pakistan had been made via the Asylum (Designated Countries of Destination and Designated Safe Third Countries) Order 1996, which had been debated and approved by both Houses of Parliament. The judge had carried out an evaluation of the evidence that had been available to the Secretary of State and had concluded that the inclusion of Pakistan in the Order had been irrational. The issue arose as to whether, and on what grounds, the court was entitled to review the legality of subordinate legislation.

Held, dismissing the appeal, that (1) subordinate legislation that had been approved by affirmative resolution of both Houses of Parliament could be subject to judicial review on the grounds of illegality, procedural impropriety or *Wednesbury* unreasonableness. The extent of any review on the ground of rationality would be dependent on the nature and purpose of the empowering Act. It was apparent, in the instant case, that the Secretary of State's decision should not be subjected to over zealous scrutiny, and (2) having regard to evidence concerning the treatment of women and of the Ahmadis, a minority religious group, the Secretary of State had been irrational in his conclusion, *R. v. Immigration Appeal Tribunal, ex p. Shah* [1999] 2 A.C. 629, [1999] C.L.Y. 3172 considered.

R. (ON THE APPLICATION OF JAVED) v. SECRETARY OF STATE FOR THE HOME DEPARTMENT; R. (ON THE APPLICATION OF ALI (ZULFIQAR)) v. SECRETARY OF STATE FOR THE HOME DEPARTMENT; R. (ON THE APPLICATION OF ALI (ABID)) v. SECRETARY OF STATE FOR THE HOME DEPARTMENT; *sub nom.* R. v. SECRETARY OF STATE FOR THE HOME DEPARTMENT, *ex p.* ALI; R. v. SECRETARY OF STATE FOR THE HOME DEPARTMENT, *ex p.* JAVED; SECRETARY OF STATE FOR THE HOME DEPARTMENT v. JAVED, [2001] EWCA Civ 789, [2002] Q.B. 129, Lord Phillips of Worth Matravers, M.R., CA.

3652. Asylum seekers – third countries – return to safe third country – legitimate expectations of individuals under Dublin Convention

[Asylum and Immigration Protection Act 1996 s.2; Convention Determining the State Responsible for Examining Applications for Asylum Lodged in One of the EC Member States 1990.]

S, an Afghani national, challenged a decision by the Secretary of State to remove him to Portugal under the Asylum and Immigration Protection Act 1996 s.2. S had been granted a valid Portuguese visa by the Portuguese embassy in Lusaka, endorsed on a false Pakistani passport. S submitted that (1) he had a legitimate expectation that the Dublin Convention 1990 would be applied properly in his case, and that if it was not, he should be able to obtain relief against the Secretary of State's decision, and (2) the Convention had not been applied properly as he did not have a valid visa.

Held, refusing the application for judicial review, that the Dublin Convention was intended to apply between states dealing with asylum applications, rather than to confer rights on an individual, *R. (on the application of Zeqiri) v. Secretary of State for the Home Department* [2001] EWCA Civ 342, Times, March 16, 2001, [2001] 4 C.L. 416 followed. Having refused the application on the first point, the court felt it would be unnecessary to reach a conclusion on the final point, but did state that a visa could be valid even if the document upon which it was stamped was false.

R. (ON THE APPLICATION OF SHAH (AHMED)) v. SECRETARY OF STATE FOR THE HOME DEPARTMENT, [2001] EWHC Admin 197, [2001] Imm. A.R. 419, Collins, J., QBD (Admin Ct).

3653. Channel Tunnel – immigration officers – control zones – entry clearances

CHANNEL TUNNEL (INTERNATIONAL ARRANGEMENTS) (AMENDMENT NO.3) ORDER 2001, SI 2001 1544; made under the Channel Tunnel Act 1987 s.11. In force: in accordance with Art.1 (2); £2.00.

This Order amends the Channel Tunnel (International Arrangements) Order 1993 (SI 1993 1813) to give effect to material provisions of the Additional Protocol which supplement the provisions of the international articles set out in the 1993 Order. A new Art.3A is added which provides that French officers responsible for immigration controls may go about their business in the UK and ensures that they can be provided with the necessary facilities, and a new Art.5A is added to permit UK immigration officers in a supplementary control zone in France to exercise their functions in relation to all persons seeking to board a through train to the UK.

3654. Channel Tunnel – manager of terminal control point – duties

CHANNEL TUNNEL (INTERNATIONAL ARRANGEMENTS) (AMENDMENT NO.4) ORDER 2001, SI 2001 3707; made under the Channel Tunnel Act 1987 s.11. In force: December 10, 2001; £1.75.

This Order amends provisions of the Channel Tunnel (International Arrangements) Order 1993 (SI 1993 1813) which give effect to material provisions of the Additional protocol. The Order clarifies the duty of the occupier or manager of a terminal control point for international services through the Channel Tunnel to provide the necessary facilities for the exercise of functions by French officers in the UK, extends the Race Relations Act 1976 to the exercise of functions by immigration officers in a control zone or supplementary control zone outside the UK and amends the definition of "supplementary control zone" in order to make it clear that the extent of such a zone is determined by mutual agreement between the two Governments. In addition, it extends the power to require a person who has been examined in a supplementary control zone to submit to a further examination, by permitting that further examination to take place before as well as after his arrival in the UK.

3655. Channel Tunnel – prevention of terrorism

CHANNEL TUNNEL (INTERNATIONAL ARRANGEMENTS) (AMENDMENT) ORDER 2001, SI 2001 178; made under the Channel Tunnel Act 1987 s.11. In force: February 19, 2001; £1.75.

This Order amends the Channel Tunnel (International Arrangements) Order 1993 (SI 1993 1813) as a consequence of the repeal of the Prevention of Terrorism (Temporary Provisions) Act 1989 and its replacement by the Terrorism Act 2000, so that the 2000 Act can apply in respect of the Channel Tunnel system.

3656. Channel Tunnel – prevention of terrorism

CHANNEL TUNNEL (INTERNATIONAL ARRANGEMENTS) (AMENDMENT NO.2) ORDER 2001, SI 2001 418; made under the Channel Tunnel Act 1987 s.11. In force: February 19, 2001; £1.75.

This Order which amends the Channel Tunnel (International Arrangements) Order 1993 (SI 1993 1813), amends the codes of practice for examining officers and authorised officers under the Terrorism Act 2000 so that the codes apply to the exercise of their functions in relation to the Channel Tunnel system.

3657. **Citizenship – naturalisation – citizens by descent – application for naturalisation**

[British Nationality Act 1981 s.3(5), s.6.]

The Secretary of State appealed against the decision ([2001] I.N.L.R. 74) that U could apply for naturalisation as a British Citizen under the British Nationality Act 1981 s.6. U was a British citizen by descent under the Act, which meant that any children born to him outside the United Kingdom would not automatically be British citizens. U wished to spend some time in his country of origin, Bangladesh, and sought naturalisation so that he would then be a British citizen otherwise than by descent. The judge had found that U's citizenship was a secondary citizenship with fewer rights as regards children and that nothing in the Act prevented him from applying for naturalisation. The Secretary of State argued that U could not apply for something which he already had, that there were no categories of citizenship, that any perceived disadvantage applied only to U's children, not to U himself, and that any of his children born outside the UK could, in any event, be registered as a British citizen under s.3(5) of the Act.

Held, allowing the appeal, that the judge's decision was flawed. If Parliament had intended for there to be separate categories of citizenship it would have been clearly set out in the Act. Any disadvantage to U's children was dealt with by the provisions of s.3(5). Accordingly, the procedure for naturalisation did not apply to U.

R. (ON THE APPLICATION OF ULLAH (AZAD)) v. SECRETARY OF STATE FOR THE HOME DEPARTMENT; *sub nom.* R. v. SECRETARY OF STATE FOR THE HOME DEPARTMENT, *ex p.* ULLAH (AZAD); SECRETARY OF STATE FOR THE HOME DEPARTMENT v. ULLAH (AZAD), [2001] EWCA Civ 659, [2002] Q.B. 525, Latham, L.J., CA.

3658. **Deportation – bail – detention pending judicial review of deportation order – right to liberty and security**

[Immigration Act 1971 Sch.3, Sch.3 para. 2(3); Bail Act 1976; Supreme Court Act 1981 s.15(3); Human Rights Act 1998 Sch.1 Part I Art.5.]

S, a Turkish national and convicted heroin smuggler, made an application for bail and challenged his detention under the Immigration Act 1971 Sch.3 para.2(3). S was detained in prison pending his appeal to the Court of Appeal against the refusal of his application for judicial review of a deportation order. He contended that (1) by applying analogous provisions contained in the Bail Act 1976, the Court of Appeal had an original jurisdiction to grant him bail, and (2) the power to grant bail should be read into Sch.3 of the 1971 Act to make it compatible with his rights under the Human Rights Act 1998 Sch.1 Part I Art.5.

Held, refusing the application, that (1) the High Court had power in judicial review proceedings to make ancillary orders temporarily releasing an applicant from detention and on an appeal in those proceedings, the Court of Appeal could make a like order by virtue of the Supreme Court Act 1981 s.15(3), *Vilvarajah (Nadarajah) v. Secretary of State for the Home Department* [1990] Imm. A.R. 457, [1991] C.L.Y. 1971 considered. The court was exercising an original jurisdiction and not reviewing the decision of the Secretary of State to direct detention. In the instant case, the Secretary of State had decided on reasonable grounds that there was a serious risk of S absconding and that opinion was entitled to great weight, and (2) it was not necessary to read Sch.3 of the 1971 Act as including a power to grant bail in order for it to be compatible with Art.5 of the Convention. The right to liberty was expressly taken away in the case of a person against whom action was taken with a view to deportation. It could not be said that the exercise by the Secretary of State of his power under para.2(3) to detain S was not in accordance with a procedure prescribed by law and it was always open to the person so detained to seek judicial review of that exercise.

R. (ON THE APPLICATION OF SEZEK) v. SECRETARY OF STATE FOR THE HOME DEPARTMENT (BAIL APPLICATION); *sub nom.* SEZEK v. SECRETARY OF STATE FOR THE HOME DEPARTMENT (BAIL APPLICATION), [2001] EWCA Civ 795, [2002] 1 W.L.R. 348, Peter Gibson, L.J., CA.

3659. **Deportation – mental patients – power of Secretary of State**

[Immigration Act 1971; Mental Health Act 1983 s.48; European Convention on Human Rights 1950 Art.3.]

X, a Maltese national who suffered from paranoid schizophrenia, was detained under the Immigration Act 1971 as an illegal entrant. Whilst his appeal against the refusal of his claim for asylum was pending, the Secretary of State, exercising the powers available to him under the Mental Health Act 1983 s.48, made a transfer direction which resulted in X being detained in hospital for medical treatment. Upon the dismissal of his appeal, the Secretary of State directed that he should be removed from the United Kingdom. His application for judicial review of that decision having been refused (Times, June 14, 2000), X appealed, arguing that his removal would amount to inhuman or degrading treatment in breach of the European Convention on Human Rights 1950 Art.3 since a return to Malta would create an increased risk of suicide or self-harm.

Held, dismissing the appeal, that Parliament had intended that the 1971 Act and the 1983 Act should run in tandem. Accordingly, X's detention in hospital under the provisions of the 1983 Act did not prevent the Secretary of State from directing his removal pursuant to the 1971 Act. The Secretary of State had correctly concluded that his removal would not constitute inhuman of degrading treatment under Art.3.

R. (ON THE APPLICATION OF X) v. SECRETARY OF STATE FOR THE HOME DEPARTMENT; *sub nom.* X v. SECRETARY OF STATE FOR THE HOME DEPARTMENT [2001] 1 W.L.R. 740, Schiemann, L.J., CA.

3660. **Deportation – right to family life – conviction for drug offence – proportionality of interference with Convention right**

[Human Rights Act 1998 Sch.1 Part I Art.8.]

AS, a citizen of Guyana, and MS, a Turkish national, both of whom had been granted indefinite leave to remain in the United Kingdom and both of whom had been convicted of separate offences of being knowingly concerned in the importation of a Class A drug, appealed against the refusal of their applications for judicial review ([2001] Imm. A.R. 324) of the decision of the Secretary of State to make deportation orders against them. In regard to AS, who was married and had a child and step children in the UK, it was submitted that the Secretary of State, having found that "compassionate circumstances" existed, should have asked himself in regard to the interference a deportation order would have on AS's right to family life under the Human Rights Act 1998 Sch.1 Part I Art.8 and in the context of his policy deterring crime and disorder, whether anything other than deportation would have sufficed. In regard to MS, it was argued that he had been in four years of legal employment prior to the making of the deportation order and as a result could rely on the rights established under Decision 1/80 of the Association Council of the European Communities, which related to the rights of Turkish workers in Member States.

Held, dismissing the appeals, that in circumstances where a legitimate aim such as deterring crime and disorder could not be achieved by a method that interfered any less with a Convention right, the decision maker was required, in determining whether to interfere with that right, to strike a fair balance between the legitimate aim and the affected individual's Convention rights and it followed that it was necessary for the court to decide whether a fair balance had been struck, *R. (on the application of Daly) v. Secretary of State for the Home Department* [2001] UKHL 26, [2001] 2 W.L.R. 1622, [2001] 6 C.L. 485 and *R. (on the application of Mahmood (Amjad)) v. Secretary of State for the Home*

Department [2001] 1 W.L.R. 840, [2001] 2 C.L. 342 considered. In regard to AS, the Secretary of State had been entitled to conclude that his involvement in the importation of a Class A drug justified such a serious interference with his right under Art.8. In regard to MS, he did not have any rights under Decision 1/80 since he had not been employed for four years and had ceased to be registered as belonging to the labour force in the UK following his being detained after conviction.

R. (ON THE APPLICATION OF SAMAROO) v. SECRETARY OF STATE FOR THE HOME DEPARTMENT; SEZEK v. SECRETARY OF STATE FOR THE HOME DEPARTMENT; *sub nom.* R. v. SECRETARY OF STATE FOR THE HOME DEPARTMENT, *ex p.* SAMAROO; SAMAROO v. SECRETARY OF STATE FOR THE HOME DEPARTMENT, [2001] EWCA Civ 1139, [2001] U.K.H.R.R. 1150, Dyson, L.J., CA.

3661. Deportation – right to family life – dependant child's continuous seven year residence

[Immigration Act 1971 s.3(5); Human Rights Act 1998 Sch.1 Part I Art.8.]

S, an Indian citizen, sought to quash a decision of the Secretary of State refusing S and his family permission to remain in the UK. S, whose parents had emigrated from India to the UK, had been granted a two year extended leave of stay following the death of his father in 1983. S did not return to India in 1985 but remained in the United Kingdom. His wife and three children joined him in 1992. In the following year S applied for British nationality and indefinite leave to remain in the mistaken belief that the grant of residence would be automatic once he had remained in the country for ten years. His application was refused and he was served with notice of intention to deport in 1996. S contended that the decision to deport his family was contrary to the Secretary of State's discretion pursuant to the Immigration Act 1971 s.3(5) and the published Home Office policy D 5/96 as amended, which provided a concession to deportation for those families whose children had lived in the UK for seven continuous years. S further maintained that in the light of the financial uncertainty of the family in India and the probability that they would no longer reside as a family unit, the Secretary of State's decision infringed the right to a family life under the Human Rights Act 1998 Sch.1 Part I Art.8.

Held, refusing the application, that despite fulfilling the criteria set out in the Home Office policy D 5/96, the Secretary of State had been correct in his conclusion that there had been exceptional circumstances which warranted the deportation of S and his family, namely S's prolonged immigration history, the fact that he had only made himself known to the authorities because of his mistaken belief that after residing in the UK for ten years illegally he would automatically be granted permanent residence, the various devices used by S to prolong his stay and the fact that his son had only resided in the United Kingdom for a continuous period of seven years precisely because of those ploys. Further the Secretary of State had considered all the circumstances which would have affected S's youngest child by his deportation back to India and could not be deemed to have acted irrationally, *R. v. Ministry of Defence, ex p. Smith* [1996] Q.B. 517, [1996] C.L.Y. 383 considered. There had been no breach of the Sch.1 Part I Art.8 as evidence had been presented to indicate that S would be able to support his family once they had been deported to India and there would accordingly be no reason why the family would need to separate..

R. v. IMMIGRATION APPEAL TRIBUNAL, *ex p.* SINGH (TARLOK); *sub nom.* R. v. SECRETARY OF STATE FOR THE HOME DEPARTMENT, *ex p.* SINGH (TARLOK) [2000] Imm. A.R. 508, Jackson, J., QBD.

3662. Deportation – terrorism – threat to national security – standard of proof

R, a Pakistani national with alleged links to an Islamic terrorist group, appealed against the decision of the Court of Appeal ([2000] 3 W.L.R. 1240, [2000] C.L.Y. 3352) allowing the Secretary of State's appeal against the determination of the Special Immigration Appeals Commission ([1999] I.N.L.R. 517). The Commission had allowed R's appeal against the decision of the Secretary of

State to deport him on the basis that he posed a threat to national security. The Court of Appeal had found that in assessing whether an individual posed a risk to national security a global approach should be taken and that on such basis a person was a danger to national security if they engaged in activities of a kind such as to create a risk of adverse repercussions on the security of the United Kingdom.

Held, dismissing the appeal, that a threat to the interests of national security could arise from acts taken against other states and was not limited to activities directly targeted against the UK. It was within the discretion of the Secretary of State to decide whether deportation was "conducive to the public good" and he was entitled to have regard to all the information available to him relating to the actual and potential activities of an individual and in making his decision no particular standard of proof was required. It was necessary that there be material upon which he could reasonably and proportionately determine that it was a real possibility that activities which were harmful to national security might occur but there was no necessity that he be satisfied that such material was proved. It was apparent that the ascertaining of a degree of probability was not relevant when concluding whether deportation should take place for the public good.

SECRETARY OF STATE FOR THE HOME DEPARTMENT v. REHMAN; *sub nom.* REHMAN v. SECRETARY OF STATE FOR THE HOME DEPARTMENT, [2001] UKHL 47, [2001] 3 W.L.R. 877, Lord Slynn of Hadley, HL.

3663. Deportation – time limits – failure to submit grounds of appeal in time – power to review once decision to dismiss leave to appeal taken

[Immigration Act 1971 s.21; Immigration Appeals (Procedure) Rules 1972 (SI 1972 1684) r.44; Immigration Appeals (Procedure) Rules 1984 (SI 1984 2041) r.38.]

N applied for judicial review of a refusal by the Immigration Appeal Tribunal, IAT, to reconsider his application for permission to appeal. A deportation order was made against N after he had overstayed his leave. After his appeal to the adjudicator failed N's solicitors, following the usual practice, submitted an appeal to the IAT on the basis that the grounds for the appeal would follow. The communication from the IAT imposing a time limit for their submission, sent by fax and first class post, did not reach the solicitor in charge of the case. When the time limit passed the IAT dismissed N's application for permission to appeal. N contended that (1) the IAT had a discretion to reconsider his application under the Immigration Appeals (Procedure) Rules 1984 r.38, and (2) that by breaching the requirement contained in the Immigration Appeals (Procedure) Rules 1972 r.44 that all documents should be sent by registered post or recorded delivery, the tribunal had been guilty of procedural unfairness.

Held, refusing the application for judicial review, that (1) it was clear from the wording of r.38 that there was no jurisdiction to re-open the matter after a decision had been taken, *Akewushola v. Secretary of State for the Home Department* [2000] 2 All E.R. 148, [1999] C.L.Y. 3210 applied, and (2) Rule 44 did not require service by registered post or recorded delivery of all documents, but rather, merely authorised it. N's only remedy was to apply to the Secretary of State, who had a residual power under the Immigration Act 1971 s.21 to refer the matter back to the IAT.

R. v. IMMIGRATION APPEAL TRIBUNAL, *ex p.* NELSON [2001] Imm. A.R. 76, Smith, J., QBD.

3664. Detention – detention centres – medical examinations

DETENTION CENTRE (SPECIFIED DISEASES) ORDER 2001, SI 2001 240; made under the Immigration and Asylum Act 1999 Sch.12 para.3. In force: April 2, 2001; £1.75.

This Order specifies certain diseases for the purposes of the Immigration and Asylum Act 1999 Sch.12 para.3, which allows a detainee custody officer at a detention centre to require a detained person to submit to a medical examination at the centre so long as an authorisation is in force and there are reasonable grounds for believing that the individual is suffering from a disease which the Secretary of State considers might endanger the health of others there.

3665. Detention – detention centres – rules

DETENTION CENTRE RULES 2001, SI 2001 238; made under the Immigration and Asylum Act 1999 s.148, s.149, s.152, s.153, s.166, Sch.11 para.2, Sch.12 para.1, Sch.12 para.2, Sch.12 para.3, Sch.13 para.2. In force: April 2, 2001; £3.50.

These Rules, which make provision for the regulation and management of detention centres, provide for matters such as the welfare and privileges of detained person, their religious observance, correspondence, health care and any complaints they wish to make, as well as the use of security measures such as powers of search and removal from association in certain circumstances. They provide for the duties of detainee custody officers, make provision as to the making visits by members of the Visiting Committee and for the making of reports by them to the Secretary of State.

3666. Disclosure – immigration status – information revealed in course of Hague Convention proceedings – court ordering of its own motion

[Hague Convention on the Civil Aspects of International Child Abduction 1980.]
The court of its own motion considered whether immigration information pertaining to the mother, M, that had come to light during an application by the child's father, F, under the Hague Convention 1980 should be disclosed to the Secretary of State for the Home Department. M, on arrival in the UK, had not told the immigration authorities that she had for several years lived in a European country that was not her country of origin before coming to the UK. In the Convention proceedings, the court had held that the child, B, should be returned to that country, being its habitual residence.

Held, directing disclosure of relevant documents, that the due administration of justice required the courts not to tolerate attempts to deceive other bodies operating legal functions, such as the immigration functions performed by the Secretary of State. It was in the public interest to send a clear message that a person appearing before the courts could not expect immunity if a deception by them came to light in the course of unrelated proceedings. The instant case warranted disclosure. As it turned out, M had already disclosed the information to the immigration authorities and all that was therefore required was to direct that the relevant documents in the Convention proceedings be passed to the solicitors acting for M in the immigration appeal.

B (ABDUCTION: FALSE IMMIGRATION INFORMATION), *Re* [2000] 2 F.L.R. 835, Singer, J., Fam Div.

3667. Entry clearances – appeals – family visitor

IMMIGRATION APPEALS (FAMILY VISITOR) (AMENDMENT) REGULATIONS 2001, SI 2001 52; made under the Immigration and Asylum Act 1999 s.60, s.166. In force: January 12, 2001; £1.50.

These Regulations, which amend the Immigration Appeals (Family Visitor) (No.2) Regulations 2000 (SI 2000 2446), reduce the fee that is to be paid by a person who wishes to exercise a right of appeal as a family visitor from £500 to £125 for those who elect an oral hearing, and from £150 to £50 in all other cases.

3668. Entry clearances – convictions – applicant with criminal conviction – residual discretion to permit entry

[Immigration Rules r.320 para.18.]
B sought permission to apply for judicial review of the Secretary of State's decision to allow a boxer, T, to enter the UK for the purpose of a boxing match. B argued that (1) the Secretary of State's instruction to immigration officers to allow T to enter the UK contravened the Immigration Rules r.320 para.18, which provided that permission to enter would not usually be granted to a person who had been

convicted of an offence which was punishable with a term of imprisonment of 12 months or more, and (2) r.320 para.18 reflected an underlying public policy, which dictated that a public statement of disapproval should be made in respect of individuals whose conduct had violated standards of human decency, whether or not evidence existed that the individual concerned showed a continuing propensity to engage in the conduct in question.

Held, refusing permission, that (1) an immigration officer had a residual discretion under r.320 para.18 which permitted him to depart from the usual rule that individuals falling within the ambit of the rule should be refused permission to enter, thus entitling the Secretary of State to give such an instruction, and (2) while the Secretary of State had concentrated in his press statement on the financial consequences of a refusal to allow entry to T to those connected with the fight, he had not ignored the importance of r.320 para.18, and had not been under any obligation to stigmatise T's past behaviour.

R. v. SECRETARY OF STATE FOR THE HOME DEPARTMENT, *ex p.* BINDEL [2001] Imm. A.R. 1, Sullivan, J., QBD.

3669. Entry clearances – dependants – exceptional compassionate circumstances

[Immigration Rules (HC 395) para.317 (i) (f).]

B appealed against the dismissal of her appeal against the refusal of entry clearance following her application to settle in the United Kingdom as a dependent relative. B's parents, together with three of her four siblings, had settled in the United Kingdom and B contended that, as she would be living alone in "the most exceptional compassionate circumstances", she should be granted clearance pursuant to the Immigration Rules (HC 395) para.317 (i) (f).

Held allowing the appeal and remitting the case, that (1) although a family's opportunity to live together in another country might be relevant, it could not be said that the fact that there had been no obstacle to B's family living together in Bangladesh was a crucial determining factor; (2) the fact that B had been voluntarily left behind did not, of itself, mean that she was unable to show that she was alone in exceptional compassionate circumstances; (3) the tribunal had erred by considering whether B's circumstances were exceptional by reference to the category of unmarried Bangladeshi women living alone, and (4) the tribunal had failed properly to consider the evidence of B's relationship with other family members and her marriage prospects.

BEGUM v. ENTRY CLEARANCE OFFICER (DHAKA) [2001] I.N.L.R. 115, Pill, L.J., CA.

3670. Entry clearances – leave to enter – notice of grant or refusal

IMMIGRATION (LEAVE TO ENTER) ORDER 2001, SI 2001 2590; made under the Immigration Act 1971 s.3A. In force: July 18, 2001; £1.75.

This Order permits the Secretary of State to give or refuse leave to enter the UK in specified circumstances and requires notice of any such grant or refusal to be given in writing to the person affected or in such manner as is permitted by the Immigration (Leave to Enter or Remain) Order 2000 (SI 2000 1161). It provides that, in relation to the giving or refusing of leave to enter, the Secretary of State may exercise certain powers exercised by immigration officers under the Immigration Act 1971 Sch.2 and also deals with the situation where an immigration officer has commenced the examination of an arriving passenger but the Secretary of State subsequently gives or refuses leave to enter.

3671. Entry clearances – legitimate expectation – assurance given by High Commission official in Zimbabwe

[Immigration Act 1971 s.4 (1).]

M, a Zimbabwean, sought judicial review of the chief immigration officer's refusal to grant him permission to enter the United Kingdom as a student. M claimed to have secured a place on a computer course at a college in the UK and had tried to obtain entry clearance in Zimbabwe. He maintained that he had been assured by an official at the British High Commission in Harare, whom he believed to have been an entry clearance officer, that, although his application could not be processed in Zimbabwe owing to the commencement date of his course, he would be permitted entry to the UK. M contended that he had had a legitimate expectation that he would be granted leave to enter on the basis of what he had been told in Harare.

Held, dismissing the application, that there was insufficient evidence upon which to base a claim of legitimate expectation. The relevant official may have given M assurance in respect of the fact that his failure to obtain entry clearance in Zimbabwe would not prejudice his application in the UK; such assurance, however, did not fetter the statutory discretion conferred upon the immigration officer by the Immigration Act 1971 s.4(1). Furthermore the official had not been held out as an entry clearance officer by the British High Commission and therefore, M had not been entitled to conclude that she possessed the power to give binding assurances *R. v. Secretary of State for the Home Department, ex p. Oloniluyi* [1989] Imm. A.R. 135, [1991] C.L.Y. 2028 distinguished.

R. v. SECRETARY OF STATE FOR THE HOME DEPARTMENT, *ex p.* MAPERE; *sub nom.* R. v. CHIEF IMMIGRATION OFFICER, *ex p.* MAPERE [2001] Imm. A.R. 89, Sullivan, J., QBD.

3672. **Entry clearances – spouses – foreign spouse seeking indefinite leave to remain – refusal following successful appeal to adjudicator**

[Immigration Act 1971 s.19(3); Immigration Rules (HC 395) para.287.]

B, a Ghanaian citizen, was granted leave to enter the UK on her arrival here in December 1989. She married a British citizen in March 1995 on the strength of which she was granted leave to remain for 12 months as a foreign spouse. Her application for leave to remain for an indefinite period was refused in April 1997 and she successfully appealed against this decision to an adjudicator in December 1998. However, her husband had petitioned for divorce in September 1998 and he obtained a decree absolute on March 14, 2000. The divorce petition was not referred to in the adjudicator's decision of January 25, 1999, which also did not contain any directions, as required by the Immigration Act 1971 s.19(3). The Secretary of State refused to grant B indefinite leave to remain following the adjudicator's decision and B sought judicial review of that decision.

Held, refusing the application, that the grant of indefinite leave to remain to a foreign spouse under the Immigration Rules (HC 395) para.287 required that person to have been admitted to the UK for 12 months, which had to be completed as the spouse of a UK resident. Paragraph 287 was not satisfied at the time of the adjudicator's hearing and it was unclear whether it had been complied with on April 30, 1997, the date B was initially refused indefinite leave to remain. The adjudicator's failure to give directions meant that the Secretary of State did not have to appeal that decision, but could instead consider the facts of the case when the application for leave to remain came before him, *R. v. Secretary of State for the Home Department, ex p. Yousuf (Mohammed)* [1989] Imm. A.R. 554, [1991] C.L.Y. 2041 followed, and on that date the facts showed that B was not entitled to be granted indefinite leave to remain.

R. (ON THE APPLICATION OF BOAFO) v. SECRETARY OF STATE FOR THE HOME DEPARTMENT; *sub nom.* R. v. SECRETARY OF STATE FOR THE HOME DEPARTMENT, *ex p.* BOAFO, [2001] EWHC Admin 782, [2001] Imm. A.R. 361, Stanley Burnton, J., QBD.

3673. **Entry clearances – travel bans – exemptions**

IMMIGRATION (DESIGNATION OF TRAVEL BANS) (AMENDMENT) ORDER 2001, SI 2001 2377; made under the Immigration Act 1971 s.8B. In force: July 4, 2001; £1.75.

This Order amends the Immigration (Designation of Travel Bans) Order 2000 (SI 2000 2724) and revokes the Immigration (Designation of Travel Bans) (Amendment) Order 2000 (SI 2000 3338). It makes amendments by adding to the list of resolutions made by the Security Council of the United Nations

Resolution 1343 (2001) of March 7, 2001, by adding Common Position 2001/155 of February 26, 2001 to the list of instruments made by the Council of the European Union and by removing Common Position 1998/725 from that list.

3674. Freedom of establishment – association agreements – direct effect – right of Member State to restrict entry

[EEC-Poland Association Agreement 1993 Art.44(3).]

Certain questions relating to the interpretation of provisions within the EC-Poland Association Agreement 1993 and other similar agreements in respect of Bulgaria and the Czech republic were referred to the ECJ for a preliminary ruling. The questions had arisen in proceedings before the High Court brought by G, a Polish national, who had applied for judicial review of a decision of the Secretary of State to refuse him leave to remain in the UK on the ground that he did not possess the necessary entry clearance certificate and was thus residing in the UK illegally. G had entered the UK on a six month holiday visa which he had overstayed and had been working in the building industry in contravention of his visa conditions. G sought recognition of the right of establishment in the UK under the Art.44 of the agreement and the question of whether G could rely on Art.44 was referred to the ECJ.

Held, giving the preliminary ruling, that Art.44(3) was sufficiently clear precise and unconditional to have direct effect and conferred rights of entry and residence on Polish nationals who wanted to work in EC countries. However, those rights were not absolute and could be constrained by national rules relating to entry, stay and establishment under Art.58(1). That provision allowed the competent authorities of the host Member State to refuse an application made under Art.44(3) if an applicant had made false claims for the purpose of entering the Member State and was residing illegally. In such a situation the applicant could then be required to submit a new application for establishment.

R. (ON THE APPLICATION OF GLOSZCZUK) v. SECRETARY OF STATE FOR THE HOME DEPARTMENT (C63/99); *sub nom.* R. v. SECRETARY OF STATE FOR THE HOME DEPARTMENT, *ex p.* GLOSZCZUK (C63/99) [2002] All E.R. (EC) 353, GC Rodriguez Iglesias (President), ECJ.

3675. Freedom of movement – visas – Council Regulation

Council Regulation 1091/2001 of 28 May 2001 on freedom of movement with a long-stay visa. [2001] OJ L150/4.

3676. Illegal entrants – carriers liabilities – code of practice for freight shuttle wagons

CARRIERS' LIABILITY (CLANDESTINE ENTRANTS) (CODE OF PRACTICE FOR FREIGHT SHUTTLE WAGONS) ORDER 2001, SI 2001 3233; made under the Immigration and Asylum Act 1999 s.33. In force: October 1, 2001; £1.50.

This Order brings into force a further code of practice issued pursuant to the Immigration and Asylum Act 1999 which is to be followed by any person operating a system for preventing the carriage of clandestine entrants by freight shuttle wagons, and is to be taken into account in determining whether a person who has transported clandestine entrants was operating an effective system for preventing their carriage, and accordingly has a defence to the penalty under the 1999 Act.

3677. Illegal entrants – carriers liabilities – code of practice for rail freight

CARRIERS' LIABILITY (CLANDESTINE ENTRANTS) (CODE OF PRACTICE FOR RAIL FREIGHT) ORDER 2001, SI 2001 312; made under the Immigration and Asylum Act 1999 s.33. In force: March 1, 2001; £1.50.

This Order brings into operation the Code of Practice issued pursuant to the Immigration and Asylum Act 1999 s.33, as applied by the Carriers' Liability (Clandestine Entrants) (Application to Rail Freight) Regulations 2001 (SI 2001

280), on March 1, 2001. This Code of Practice is to be followed by any person operating a system for preventing the carriage of clandestine entrants by rail freight wagons, and is to be taken into account in determining whether a person who has transported clandestine entrants was operating an effective system for preventing their carriage, and accordingly has a defence to the penalty under s.34 of the Act. A Code of Practice in respect of the prevention of the carriage of clandestine entrants by road vehicles was brought into operation by the Carriers' Liability (Clandestine Entrants) (Code of Practice) Order 2000 (SI 2000 684).

3678. Illegal entrants – carriers liabilities – rail freight penalties

CARRIERS' LIABILITY (CLANDESTINE ENTRANTS) (APPLICATION TO RAIL FREIGHT) REGULATIONS 2001, SI 2001 280; made under the Immigration and Asylum Act 1999 s.39, s.43, s.167. In force: in accordance with Reg.1 (1) and (2); £1.75.

These Regulations apply and amend certain provisions of the Immigration and Asylum Act 1999 Part II for the purpose of enabling penalties to be imposed in respect of certain persons who arrive in the UK concealed in a rail freight wagon. They provide the bringing into operation of a code of conduct, and to prescribe such matters as the amount of the penalty, the length of the periods for payment and for serving notice of objection.

3679. Illegal entrants – carriers liabilities – rail freight penalties

CARRIERS' LIABILITY (CLANDESTINE ENTRANTS) (APPLICATION TO RAIL FREIGHT) (AMENDMENT) REGULATIONS 2001, SI 2001 3232; made under the Immigration and Asylum Act 1999 s.39, s.43, s.167. In force: in accordance with Reg.1 (1) and (2); £1.75.

These Regulations, which amend the Carriers' Liability (Clandestine Entrants) (Application to Rail Freight) Regulations 2001 (SI 2001 280), apply certain provisions of the Immigration and Asylum Act 1999 Part II for the purpose of enabling penalties to be imposed in respect of certain persons who arrive in the UK concealed in a rail freight wagon. The Regulations extend the definition of "rail freight wagon" to include certain wagons forming part of the shuttle service operating through the Channel Tunnel.

3680. Illegal entrants – carriers liabilities – rail freight penalties

CARRIERS' LIABILITY (CLANDESTINE ENTRANTS AND SALE OF TRANSPORTERS) (AMENDMENT) REGULATIONS 2001, SI 2001 311; made under the Immigration and Asylum Act 1999 s.32, s.35, s.36, s.166, s.167, Sch.1 para.2, Sch.1 para.5. In force: March 1, 2001; £1.50.

These Regulations amend the Carriers' Liability (Clandestine Entrants and Sale of Transporters) Regulations 2000 (SI 2000 685) concerning the the penalty for carrying clandestine entrants established by, and the sale of transporters under the Immigration and Asylum Act 1999 Part II. The amendments are made in consequence of the extension of that penalty to the carriage of clandestine entrants in rail freight wagons contained in the Carriers' Liability (Clandestine Entrants) (Application to Rail Freight) Regulations 2001 (SI 2001 280). For the purposes of the extension of the penalty to rail freight, these Regulations apply the provisions of SI 2000 685 concerning the amount of penalty, the periods of time within which a penalty must be paid and a notice of objection must be given, the notice of a proposed sale of a transporter, the application of the proceeds of sale and the service of documents.

3681. Illegal entrants – entry via non designated port – notice to illegal entrant – discretion of immigration officer

[Immigration Act 1971 s.3 (1).]

U applied for judicial review of the decision of an immigration officer, IO, to serve him with a Notice to an Illegal Entrant following his arrival in the UK at a non approved port in the rear of a lorry. He contended that (1) his entry had not been unlawful despite being at a non designated port, since he had made it clear at the earliest opportunity that he wished to seek asylum and such entry had been his only means of doing so, therefore the doctrine of necessity or duress applied, and (2) IO had a discretion when deciding whether to serve him with a Notice. IO submitted that a non British citizen entering the country without leave was by virtue of the Immigration Act 1971 s.3(1) an illegal entrant and had to be treated as such.

Held, allowing the application, that (1) U had not been given leave to enter the UK and was therefore by virtue of s.3(1) of the Act an illegal entrant, *R. v. Governor of Ashford Remand Centre, ex p. Bouzagou* [1983] Imm A.R. 69, [1984] C.L.Y. 1765 and *R. v. Secretary of State for the Home Department, ex p. Ali (Ifzal)* [1994] Imm A.R. 69, [1994] C.L.Y. 2494 applied. The doctrines of duress and necessity did not apply in the context of immigration since they were subject to the effect of statute which was clear and unambiguous, and (2) IO did have a discretion not to serve U with a Notice since there was no statutory requirement to do so and by failing to give U the opportunity to explain his presence and state his intentions that discretion had been wrongly exercised.

R. (ON THE APPLICATION OF ULUYOL) v. IMMIGRATION OFFICER [2001] I.N.L.R. 194, Gage, J., QBD (Admin Ct).

3682. Illegal entrants – habeas corpus – abuse of process – finality of litigation

[Immigration Act 1971 s.33(1).]

S, a Pakistani asylum seeker, appealed against the refusal of his application for habeas corpus (Times, December 7, 2000). S had applied for asylum at the end of six months' leave to enter the United Kingdom and was consequently adjudged to be an illegal entrant under the Immigration Act 1971 s.33(1). His asylum application was refused as was his appeal against that refusal and he was refused further leave to appeal. S applied for judicial review of the asylum decisions and, just prior to the hearing, he also applied to review the decision that he was an illegal entrant, some three years and nine months out of time.

Held, dismissing the appeal, that although an application for habeas corpus could be made at any time during detention and the doctrine of res judicata did not apply, it was nevertheless an abuse of process to bring habeas corpus proceedings where matters should have been raised in earlier litigation. It was relevant that S had been released on bail and was thus not being detained, and that he was entitled to a right of appeal from outside the UK.

R. (ON THE APPLICATION OF SHEIKH) v. SECRETARY OF STATE FOR THE HOME DEPARTMENT; *sub nom.* R. v. SECRETARY OF STATE FOR THE HOME DEPARTMENT, *ex p.* SHEIKH; SHEIKH, RE; SHEIK v. SECRETARY OF STATE FOR THE HOME DEPARTMENT; SHEIKH v. SECRETARY OF STATE FOR THE HOME DEPARTMENT [2001] Imm. A.R. 219, Schiemann, L.J., CA.

3683. Illegal entrants – liability – owner of transporter – appropriateness of judicial review proceedings

[Immigration and Asylum Act 1999 s.34, s.35(6), s.37.]

B, the owner of a lorry that had been found to contain 11 illegal immigrants on its arrival into the United Kingdom from France, sought judicial review of a decision by the Secretary of State to uphold a notice of liability to civil penalty issued under the Immigration and Asylum Act 1999 s.35. B had served a notice of objection to the penalty notice pursuant to s.35(6). However, an inspector had responded to that objection indicating that no valid defence under s.34 had been made out. At the judicial review hearing, the Secretary of State raised a preliminary issue in relation to whether a more suitable alternative remedy was available to B under the Act.

Held, refusing the application, that judicial review was not the appropriate remedy. Where a lorry owner considered that he had a valid defence, even if that defence had been rejected by the Secretary of State, he should await the issue of proceedings by the Secretary of State alleging liability and assert his defence in those proceedings. On the same basis, if the Secretary of State applied for the the court's leave to sell a vehicle pursuant to s.37, such leave would not be granted without proof that the penalty was due and the owner was liable to pay but had not done so. In such circumstances, the owner could assert that he had a valid defence under s.34.

R. (ON THE APPLICATION OF BALBO B&C AUTO TRANSPORTI INTERNAZIONALI) v. SECRETARY OF STATE FOR THE HOME DEPARTMENT, [2001] EWHC Admin 195, [2001] 1 W.L.R. 1556, Brooke, L.J., QBD (Admin Ct).

3684. **Illegal entrants – right to family life – retrospective effect of human rights legislation**

[Human Rights Act 1998; European Convention on Human Rights 1950 Art.8(1).]

M appealed against the dismissal of his application for judicial review of a direction that he be removed from the United Kingdom as an illegal entrant. M contended that (1) the court at first instance had erred in its application of the *Wednesbury* criteria and enhanced judicial scrutiny was required where a fundamental freedom such as the right to family life was involved. On the facts, he had complied with the immigration criteria governing applications to enter the UK on grounds of marriage, save for possession of an entry clearance, the purpose of which was to ensure that checks were carried out before the applicant left for the UK. Accordingly, no legitimate purpose would be served by compelling him to return to his native country merely to demonstrate what was already in evidence; (2) the court should address its scrutiny to the Secretary of State's intended act to remove M rather than back to the decision to remove, which had been taken prior to the enactment of the Human Rights Act 1998, and (3) the court had jurisdiction equal to that of the Secretary of State to decide whether M's removal would constitute an infringement of the right to family life under the European Convention on Human Rights 1950 Art.8(1).

Held, dismissing the appeal, that (1) where interference with a fundamental freedom was at issue, the court was required to tailor the level of its scrutiny according to the level of the interference and significant interference with a fundamental freedom would require substantial objective justification, *R. v. Ministry of Defence, ex p. Smith* [1996] Q.B. 517, [1996] C.L.Y. 383, *R. v. Lord Saville of Newdigate, ex p. B (No.2)* [2000] 1 W.L.R. 1855, [1999] C.L.Y. 80 and *R. v. Secretary of State for the Home Department, ex p. Launder (No.2)* [1997] 1 W.L.R. 839, [1997] C.L.Y. 2433 considered; (2) where the court was required to review the legality of an administrative decision already made, it was not part of its duty to go further and review the legality of the decision being made effective in the future, and (3) the 1998 Act did not authorise the court to stand in the shoes of the Secretary of State; there had to be a principled distance between the court's adjudication and the Secretary of State's decision based on his analysis of the case.

R. (ON THE APPLICATION OF MAHMOOD (AMJAD)) v. SECRETARY OF STATE FOR THE HOME DEPARTMENT; *sub nom.* R. v. SECRETARY OF STATE FOR THE HOME DEPARTMENT, *ex p.* MAHMOOD (AMJAD); MAHMOOD (AMJAD) v. SECRETARY OF STATE FOR THE HOME DEPARTMENT [2001] 1 W.L.R. 840, Laws, L.J., CA.

3685. **Immigration and Asylum Act 1999 (c.33) – Commencement No.9 Order**

IMMIGRATION AND ASYLUM ACT 1999 (COMMENCEMENT NO.9) ORDER 2001, SI 2001 239 (C.12); made under the Immigration and Asylum Act 1999 s.170. Commencement details: bringing into force various provisions of the Act on February 19, 2001 and April 2, 2001; £2.50.

This Order brings the Immigration and Asylum Act 1999 s.22 into force on February 19, 2001 for the purposes of laying a draft code before Parliament and of making subordinate legislation. In addition all the provisions of Part VIII, which relates to detention centres and detained persons, Sch.11, which relates to detainee custody officers, Sch.12, which relates to discipline at detention centres and Sch.13, which relates to escort arrangements, are brought into force on April 2, 2001, in so fare as they are not already in force.

3686. Immigration and Asylum Act 1999 (c.33) – Commencement No.10 Order

IMMIGRATION AND ASYLUM ACT 1999 (COMMENCEMENT NO.10) ORDER 2001, SI 2001 1394 (C.49); made under the Immigration and Asylum Act 1999 s.170. Commencement details: bringing into force various provisions of the Act on April 30, 2001 and May 2, 2001; £2.50.

This Order brings the Immigration and Asylum Act 1999 s.22, which inserts a new s.8A into the Immigration and Asylum Act 1996, requiring the Secretary of State to issue a code of practice as to the measures which an employer is to be expected to take or not to take to avoid both unlawful discrimination and the commission of an offence under s.8 of the 1996 Act, on May 2, 2001. The remaining provisions of Part V of the 1999 Act, relating to the creation of a criminal offence of providing immigration advice or services whilst unqualified, laying down the procedure by which the Immigration Services Commissioner may obtain an injunction or interdict where it appears to him that the criminal offence is being committed and is likely to continue otherwise, requiring designated professional bodies to pay fees to the Immigration Services Commissioner for the purpose of financing the regulatory scheme, and providing for disciplinary bodies to make orders suspending or prohibiting persons subject to their jurisdiction from providing immigration advice or services, or restricting such advice or services as appropriate, are brought into force on April 30, 2001.

3687. Immigration Appeal Tribunal – jurisdiction – appeal against abandoned appeal

[Immigration and Asylum Act 1999 s.58; Immigration and Asylum Appeals (Procedure) Rules 2000 (SI 2000 No.2333) r.32, r.33.]

G, a citizen of Lebanon, appealed to a special adjudicator against a refusal to grant him asylum. On September 11, 2000 he and his representative were sent notification of a hearing on October 4, 2000. They were also sent a form requiring details for the hearing which advised them that if the form was returned in time no attendance on October 4 would be required.. The form was returned on time by recorded delivery but was misfiled. As a result, in the absence of the form and with no-one attending the adjudicator treated the appeal as abandoned pursuant to the Immigration and Asylum Appeals (Procedure) Rules 2000 r.32(1). G appealed to the IAT which considered whether there was jurisdiction to hear an appeal against an appeal which had been abandoned.

Held, allowing the appeal and remitting the case for re-hearing, that (1) the tribunal had jurisdiction to hear the appeal. Although the adjudicator's decision was described as a notice it was in reality a determination; (2) if an adjudicator considers that a failure to comply with a direction merits dismissal of an appeal, that should be determined under r.33 as that rule does not require the tribunal to determine whether an appeal should be treated as abandoned.

GREMESTY v. SECRETARY OF STATE FOR THE HOME DEPARTMENT [2001] I.N.L.R. 132, Collins, J., IAT.

3688. Immigration Appeal Tribunal – jurisdiction – witnesses – jurisdiction of tribunal to call witness of its own volition

[Immigration Appeals (Procedure) Rules 1984 (SI 1984/2041) r.27.]

K appealed against a decision of the Immigration Appeal Tribunal upholding an order for his deportation made on the ground that he had obtained leave to remain in the United Kingdom by relying on his marriage to a UK citizen, M, a marriage that he knew to be false. M had made a statutory statement to the effect that she had never married nor met K. The tribunal had summoned M as a witness of its own volition, notwithstanding that both parties were of the opinion that it lacked the jurisdiction to do so. K contended that the tribunal had erred in calling M as it did not have the jurisdiction to summon a witness of its own volition or, alternatively, that the jurisdiction should not have been exercised in this case.

Held, dismissing the appeal, that the IAT had the jurisdiction pursuant to the Immigration Appeals (Procedure) Rules 1984 to summon a witness of its own volition and, more specifically, had the power to call a witness to give evidence. Under r.27 the tribunal could summon a witness if his evidence was relevant to a matter at issue in the appeal. It was implicit in the proviso to that rule that a summons could be issued notwithstanding that it had not been requested by either party. Given the often inadequate representation for litigants before the tribunal, it was appropriate for it to require some evidence to be put before the tribunal prior to it reaching any conclusions. It was, however, desirable that the tribunal use such discretion sparingly, particularly when it had already retired to consider its determination without giving warning that such a course was being considered. In the instant case, the tribunal had been entitled to call M as a witness.

KESSE v. SECRETARY OF STATE FOR THE HOME DEPARTMENT [2001] Imm. A.R. 366, Schiemann, L.J., CA.

3689. Passports – fees

CONSULAR FEES (AMENDMENT) ORDER 2001, SI 2001 3498; made under the Consular Fees Act 1980 s.1. In force: November 30, 2001; £1.75.

This Order amends the Consular Fees (No.2) Order 1999 (SI 1999 3132) so as to prescribe additional fees for the provision of fast-track and premium services for the issuing of passports. In addition, it increases fees for certain specified passports.

3690. Passports – visas – requirements – Council Regulation

Council Regulation 539/2001 of 15 March 2001 listing the third countries whose national must be in possession of visas when crossing the external borders and those whose nationals are exempt from that requirement. [2001] OJ L81/1.

3691. Practice directions – appeals – immigration appeals procedure

[Immigration and Asylum Appeals (Procedure) Rules 2000 (SI 2000 2333).]

The President of the Immigration Appeal Tribunal issued a Practice Direction setting out the procedure for dealing with applications to the tribunal, in particular, applications for permission to appeal, following the Immigration and Asylum Appeals (Procedure) Rules 2000, which came into effect on October 2, 2000 and whichsuperseded all existing Rules. Guidance was given as to how an application for permission to appeal should be made to theTribunal; the time limits involved; applications for review of theTribunal's decision to refuse permission to appeal; variation of grounds of appeal; adjournments; evidence, and citation of authorities.

PRACTICE DIRECTION (IAT: IMMIGRATION AND ASYLUM APPEALS (PROCEDURE) RULES 2000); *sub nom.* PRACTICE DIRECTION (IAT) (2000/4) [2001] Imm. A.R. 172, Collins, J., IAT.

3692. Practice directions – appeals – time limits – proof of delay in service by post

[Interpretation Act 1978 s.7; Asylum Appeals (Procedure) Rules 1996 (SI 1996 2070) r.13(2), r.42(1)(a).]

The President of the Immigration Appeal Tribunal issued a Practice Direction following the decision in *R. v. Secretary of State for the Home Department, ex p. Saleem* [2000] 4 All E.R. 814, [2000] 8 C.L. 406 as to the invalidity of the Asylum Appeals (Procedure) Rules 1996 r.42(1)(a). The effect of the decision in *Asifa Saleem* meant that the Interpretation Act 1978 s.7 now applied so that service was deemed to have occurred at the time a letter including the notice or document would have been delivered in the ordinary course of post, unless the contrary was proved. Applications for leave to appeal would continue to be considered if made in time in accordance with the Asylum Appeals (Procedure) Rules r.13(2) only where they were made no later than seven days after the date of the notice accompanying the determination. After that an application would be assumed to be out of time unless the contrary was proved. As a result, applications made after the time limit has expired must include all material that

could show the determination was not received with two days of its being sent. Applications would not be accepted where an explanation was omitted.
PRACTICE DIRECTION (IAT: SERVICE OF NOTICES); *sub nom.* PRACTICE DIRECTION (IAT) (2000/3) [2000] Imm. A.R. 551, Collins, J., IAT.

3693. Practice directions – Immigration AppealTribunal – appeals and applications – number of required members

The President of the Immigration Appeal Tribunal has issued Practice Direction 2001/1 superseding Practice Direction 2000/1 which sets out the number and type of members that can exercise the tribunal's jurisdiction in certain specified categories of applications and appeals. For appeals in respect of which no specific direction is given, or which is not specified, the tribunal should consist of two or more members, with at least one being legally qualified. However, the President or Deputy President can direct that a particular appeal or category of appeals must be heard by a single legally qualified member or by a tribunal consisting of two or more members none of whom needs to be legally qualified.
PRACTICE DIRECTION (IAT: ALLOCATION OF APPLICATIONS AND APPEALS PURSUANT TO THE IMMIGRATION AND ASYLUM ACT 1999); *sub nom.* PRACTICE DIRECTION (IAT) (2001/1) [2001] Imm. A.R. 359, Collins, J., IAT.

3694. Refugees – fear of persecution by reason of Somali clan membership – Australia

[Convention relating to the Status of Refugees 1951 (United Nations) Art.1A(2).]
I, a Somalian and a member of the Rahanwien clan and the Dabarre subclan, left that country in June 1995 and arrived in Australia in December 1997, where he applied for a protection visa as a refugee in January 1998. The application was refused by a delegate of the Minister, a decision that was affirmed by the Refugee Review Tribunal as it was not satisfied that I had a well founded fear of persecution for the purposes of the Convention relating to the Status of Refugees 1951 (United Nations) Art.1A(2). I's application for a review of that decision was dismissed by the Federal Court, but he succeeded on appeal to the Full Court, which ordered that the case be remitted to the tribunal for a rehearing on the ground that the tribunal had erred by finding a lack of systematic conduct directed against I's clan and subclan. Further, that the tribunal had failed to consider if I's capture and treatment by another clan amounted to persecution in terms of the Convention where it was due to clan affiliations current at that time.The Minister appealed.
Held, allowing the appeal (by majority), that (1) the tribunal had correctly concluded that I did not have a well founded fear of persecution if he was returned to Somalia because of the particular clan or subclan he belonged to. Further, the tribunal could conclude that I's experiences did not form part of the systematic conduct aimed at members of his social groups, and (2) the tribunal had not been misled by use of the terms "civil war" or "civil conflict" in the context of the situation in Somalia. Such terms only served to describe the clan based nature of the conflict and did not mean that its victims were persecuted by reason of their clan membership, *Adan (Hassan Hussein) v. Secretary of State for the Home Department* [1999] 1 A.C. 293, [1998] C.L.Y. 3241 not followed.
MINISTER FOR IMMIGRATION AND MULTICULTURAL AFFAIRS v. IBRAHIM [2001] I.N.L.R. 228, Gleeson, C.J., HC (Aus).

3695. Refugees – temporary protection – burden shared by EU states – draft Council Directive

Proposal for a Council Directive on minimum standards for giving temporary protection in the event of a mass influx of displaced persons and on measures promoting a balance of efforts between Member States in receiving such persons and bearing the consequences thereof. [2000] OJ C311E/251.

3696. **Right of abode – citizenship – effect of parents entering into polygamous marriage**

[Legitimacy Act 1976 s.1 (1); British Nationality Act 1981 s.2(1).]

A appealed against a decision of the Immigration Appeal Tribunal refusing to grant him a right of abode under the British Nationality Act 1981 s.2(1) following his assertion that he had acquired British citizenship as a result of a polygamous marriage in Bangladesh between his mother and his father, a British citizen. A submitted that, when construing the Legitimacy Act 1976 s.1 (1), the tribunal had erred (1) in holding that a belief as to the validity of a marriage was restricted to belief in its validity under English law rather than the law of the country in which the marriage had taken place, and (2) in rejecting his submission that the absence of any reason for his mother to conclude that the marriage was invalid according to English law had been sufficient to discharge the onus upon him to establish her belief as to its validity.

Held, dismissing the appeal, that (1) by reference to the 1976 Act as a whole, it was clear that the validity of the marriage was to be measured by reference to English law alone, and (2) positive evidence as to the belief of the mother in the validity of the marriage was required and accordingly A had failed to discharge that burden.

AZAD v. ENTRY CLEARANCE OFFICER (DHAKA) [2001] Imm. A.R. 318, Jacob, J., CA.

3697. **Books**

Chin, Gabriel J. – Immigration and the Constitution. Hardback: £150.00. ISBN 0-8153-3346-3. Garland Publishing, Inc.

Cohen, Steve – Immigration Controls, the Family and the Welfare State. Paperback: £18.95. ISBN 1-85302-723-5. Jessica Kingsley Publishers.

Dummett, Sir Michael – On Immigration and Refugees. Thinking in Action. Hardback: £30.00. ISBN 0-415-22707-0. Paperback: £7.99. ISBN 0-415-22708-9. Routledge, an imprint of Taylor & Francis Books Ltd.

Gillespie, J. – Immigration Appeals Practice: 2001. Hardback: £100.00. ISBN 0-85308-447-5. Jordans.

Siddique, M.A.B. – International Migration Into the 21st Century. Hardback: £59.95. ISBN 1-84064-531-8. Edward Elgar.

INDUSTRY

3698. **Health and safety at work – equipments – personal protective equipment**

EQUIPMENT AND PROTECTIVE SYSTEMS INTENDED FOR USE IN POTENTIALLY EXPLOSIVE ATMOSPHERES (AMENDMENT) REGULATIONS 2001, SI 2001 3766; made under the European Communities Act 1972 s.2. In force: December 21, 2001; £1.75.

These Regulations amend the Equipment and Protective Systems Intended for Use in Potentially Explosive Atmospheres Regulations 1996 (SI 1996 192) which implemented Directive 94/9 ([1994] OJ L100/1) on the approximation of the laws of the Member States concerning equipment and protective systems intended for use in potentially explosive atmospheres. The Regulations also make amendments to include requirements relating to the activity of "putting into service" in specific situations and make provision that the activity of putting into service shall not be regarded as having taken place in certain circumstances.

3699. **Private Security Industry Act 2001 (c.12)**

This Act makes provision for the regulation of the private security industry. This Act received Royal Assent on May 11, 2001.

3700. Books

Jones, Brian – EMC Management. Paperback: £29.99. ISBN 0-7506-4584-9. Newnes.

Tettenborn, Andrew – Law of Restitution in England and Ireland. 3rd Ed. Paperback: £28.95. ISBN 1-85941-567-9. Cavendish Publishing Ltd.

INFORMATION TECHNOLOGY

3701. Computer contracts – data storage – damage to computerised accounts system – recoverable heads of loss

[Law Reform (Contributory Negligence) Act 1945.]

L, a supplier of computer equipment, attended at E's offices in order to carry out work to a recently installed router for E's email system. L damaged the hard disk of a server on which E's accounts package and data were stored, with the result that E lost "highly valuable accounts data". E had a backup system and had it functioned, then any loss of data could have been corrected within one day. However, the back up system did not function. The system failed because E had purchased and installed the wrong type of tapes, with the result that the relevant data could not be stored.

Held, granting judgment for L, that E was at fault within the meaning of the Law Reform (Contributory negligence) Act 1945 to the extent of 50 per cent, because it had (1) ordered the wrong back-up tapes; (2) failed to check that the back-up tapes were of the correct type; (3) failed to check that the back-up system was working satisfactorily and provided a vital defence against malfunction, and (4) failed to detect or understand the error message which the server produced. On the facts, E had well understood that its business was heavily dependent upon the proper functioning of its computer system and that a back-up system was a vital defence against malfunction. The court determined that it should be common practice in every business which used computers, for the back-up system to be regularly checked for malfunction, and the task of doing so was not to be considered a matter of special expertise or knowledge.

LOGICAL COMPUTER SUPPLIES LTD v. EURO CAR PARKS LTD, June 19, 2001, Richard Fernyhough Q.C., QBD. [*Ex rel.* Nicholas Hill, Barrister, 6 Park Square, Leeds].

3702. Computer records – professional negligence – consultancy services

See NEGLIGENCE: Stephenson Blake (Holdings) Ltd v. Streets Heaver Ltd. §4519

3703. Data protection – health records – access to information – removal of cut off date

DATA PROTECTION (SUBJECT ACCESS) (FEES AND MISCELLANEOUS PROVISIONS) (AMENDMENT) REGULATIONS 2001, SI 2001 3223; made under the Data Protection Act 1998 s.7. In force: October 23, 2001; £1.50.

The Data Protection (Subject Access) (Fees and Miscellaneous Provisions) Regulations 2000 (SI 2000 191) provide the cut off date as October 24, 2001 for the transitional provisions in relation to certain requests relating to accessible records which are health records and which are not exclusively automated or intended for automation. These Regulations make amendments so as to remove October 24, 2001 as the cut off date.

3704. Data protection – Information Commissioner – notification from data controllers

DATA PROTECTION (NOTIFICATION AND NOTIFICATION FEES) (AMENDMENT) REGULATIONS 2001, SI 2001 3214; made under the Data Protection Act 1998 s.19, s.67, Sch.14 para.2. In force: October 23, 2001; £1.50.

These Regulations, which amend the Data Protection (Notification and Notification Fees) Regulations 2000 (SI 2000 188), set out a number of arrangements in respect of the giving of notifications to the Information Commissioner by data controllers under the Data Protection Act 1998 Part III.

3705. Data protection – utilities – use of customer data for marketing purposes – fairness – breach of data protection principles

[Data Protection Act 1984 s.10, Sch.1 Pt 1 Principle 1.]

M supplied mains electricity for domestic and business use. M's customer database incorporated a marking for domestic customers allowing for the automatic insertion of a magazine into their account statement envelopes. The Data Protection Registrar took the view that M was unfairly processing data, contrary to the Data Protection Act 1984 Sch.1 Pt 1 Principle 1, and issued an enforcement notice under s.10. M appealed against the notice, contending that there was no unfairness in using personal data for the purposes of retaining customers and enhancing goodwill. The Registrar maintained that data processing for the promotion of goods and services not connected with M's business was unfair, given the absence of customer consent.

Held, dismissing the appeal, that "fairness" for the purposes of Principle 1 required the interests of customers to be balanced against those of M, a utility similar to a public body supplying an essential service under a statutory framework. In addition, M had a special relationship with many of its customers due to its previous monopoly status. Personal data given for energy supply purposes was being used by M for marketing products unconnected with its business. Although such use would be fair in relation to electrical goods, customers would not have expected their data to be utilised for marketing some items featured in the magazine. However, energy conservation would be a fair use that did not require consent. The enforcement notice would be extended to allow M to obtain customer consent or to modify the magazine.

MIDLANDS ELECTRICITY PLC v. DATA PROTECTION REGISTRAR [1998-99] Info. T.L.R. 217, JAC Spokes Q.C., Data Protection Tribunal.

3706. Books

Brinson, Dianne; Dara-Abrams, Benay; Dara-Abrams, Drew; Masek, Jennifer; McDunn, Ruth; White, Bebo – Exploring E-commerce and Internet Law. Advanced Website Architecture. Paperback: £35.99. ISBN 0-13-085898-6. Prentice Hall PTR.

Ferrera, John; Lichtenstein, Stephen; Reder, Margot – Cyberlaw: Text and Cases. Paperback: £34.99. ISBN 0-324-01297-7. South Western College Publishing.

Frascogna, X.M.; Hetherington, H. Lee; Howell, Shawnasey – Business of Internet Law. Hardback: £15.95. ISBN 0-8230-7735-7. Watson-Guptill Publications.

International IT and Telecoms Law Directory. £60.00. ISBN 1-84311-066-0. LLP Professional Publishing.

Singleton, Susan – Legal Guide to Online Business. Paperback: £9.99. ISBN 1-902646-77-0. Law Pack Publishing.

Taylor, Ian – Procurement of Information Systems. Chandos Business Guides: Purchasing, 1. Paperback: £49.95. ISBN 1-902375-63-7. Paperback: £49.95. ISBN 1-902375-63-7. Chandos Publishing Ltd.

Word XP for Law Firms. Paperback: CD-ROM: £29.99. ISBN 0-7615-3394-X. Prima Tech.

INSOLVENCY

3707. Administration – administration orders – abuse of process – divorce – relevance of underlying motive

[Insolvency Act 1986 s.8(1)(a).]

M, the former wife of I, a director of a company, DJ, applied to set aside an order placing the company in voluntary administration. M and I had previously been involved in a bitterly fought ancillary relief dispute which culminated in an order that I pay to M the sum of £4.875 million. The order further provided that if the specified sum was not paid then I's liability would be satisfied by means of the sale of stock held by DJ, in relation to which the judge was satisfied that I was the beneficial owner and entirely in control. Further findings were made to the effect that I had falsified evidence and sought to mislead the court. M contended that I had systematically set about trying to defeat her legitimate claims and that he had provided false details of his business affairs to the court as part of that strategy. M submitted that DJ was not insolvent and that the petition for an administration order amounted to an abuse of process.

Held, dismissing the application, that (1) on the basis of the available evidence it was clear that as at the date of the making of the administration order, DJ was actually or potentially insolvent so as to fulfil the criteria in the Insolvency Act 1986 s.8(1)(a), and (2) there was no basis for the suggestion that the grant of the petition constituted an abuse of process given that s.8(1)(a) had been satisfied whatever the underlying motives of the various directors. The case of *Nicholas v. Nicholas* [1984] F.L.R. 285, [1984] C.L.Y. 1121 was authority for the proposition that minority interests in a company should be protected before applying the assets of the company in satisfaction of a lump sum owed by a controlling shareholder to his spouse and the situation was analogous to the position of creditors in the instant case, *Nicholas v. Nicholas* followed.

DIANOOR JEWELS LTD (SET ASIDE), Re [2001] 1 B.C.L.C. 450, Blackburne, J., Ch D.

3708. Administration – administration orders – discharge – meaning of "consequential provision"

[Insolvency Act 1986 s.18(3).]

The joint administrators of UCT applied for orders under the Insolvency Act 1986 s.18 for the discharge of an administration order, such discharge to take effect immediately before the passing of a resolution for the winding up of the company. The administrators also sought a direction that they were entitled to retain in a designated trust account those funds necessary to pay any preferential creditor at the date of the administration order since upon entry into voluntary liquidation, the preferential creditors would lose their status as such. The first purpose of the administrative order, namely the advantageous realisation of UCT's assets, had been achieved and no other specified purpose was capable of achievement. The issue arose as to the meaning of the words "consequential provision" for the purposes of s.18(3) of the Act.

Held, granting the application, that a "consequential provision" meant a provision resulting either directly or indirectly from an administrative order being discharged, *Powerstore (Trading) Ltd, Re* [1997] 1 W.L.R. 1280, [1997] C.L.Y. 3051 and *Mark One (Oxford Street) Plc, Re* [1999] 1 W.L.R. 1445, [1999] C.L.Y. 3349 considered. A direction to the administrators could be a "consequential provision" notwithstanding that it would take effect immediately prior to the discharge. In the instant case the direction concerning the trust was a necessary consequence of the application for discharge, given the fact that upon discharge the administrators would cease to act in that capacity. The court did, therefore, have jurisdiction to make such a direction provided that the administrators had power to make the suggested payment to themselves on trust. Since enabling UCT to enter into voluntary liquidation was a position that was most advantageous to its creditors, it followed that the suggested payment was "necessary and incidental" to the performance of the administrators functions pursuant to Sch.1 para.13 of the 1986 Act and was accordingly within their powers.

UCT (UK) LTD (IN ADMINISTRATION), *Re*; *sub nom*. UCT (UK) LTD v. DARGAN [2001] 1 W.L.R. 436, Arden, J., Ch D (Companies Court).

3709. Administration – administrative receivers – motor industry – demand with menaces as reasonable negotiating stance

[Theft Act 1968 s.21.]

T supplied F with an essential manufacturing component on a "just in time" basis. T's administrative receivers exploited the leverage that gave by threatening to halt supply unless F accepted increased prices. F contended that the demand constituted legal and commercial blackmail and sought the appointment of a provisional liquidator, contending that the receivers were placing the existing assets of T's business in jeopardy.

Held, refusing the application, that the action of the receivers was not a demand with menaces according to the legal definition of blackmail under the Theft Act 1968 s.21 because, not only had F failed to establish under s.21 (1) (a) that the receivers had no belief that they had a reasonable ground for the demand, but it was also clear that they, in fact, had a reasonable ground and the position taken was an entirely reasonable negotiating stance to adopt, *Medforth v. Blake* [2000] Ch. 86, [1999] C.L.Y. 3286 followed

FORD AG-WERKE AG v. TRANSTEC AUTOMOTIVE (CAMPSIE) LTD; *sub nom*. TRANSTEC AUTOMOTIVE (CAMPSIE) LTD, *Re* [2001] B.C.C. 403, Jacob, J., Ch D (Companies Ct).

3710. Administration – administrators – refusal to allow company to bring claim – application to Companies Registrar

[Insolvency Act 1986 s.7 (3), s.11 (3) (d).]

C, the administrators of W and the supervisors of a company voluntary arrangement, CVA, entered into by W with its creditors, applied to strike out an application by HS, a wholly owned subsidiary of W, to the Companies Registrar. P, the trustees and beneficiaries of an occupational pension scheme set up by HS, asserted that HS owed a sum in excess of £860,000 to the pension scheme and, further, that W owed approximately £885,000 to HS. HS wished to commence proceedings against W for the recovery of the intercompany debt and sought C's consent to the action. C did not accept that the debts existed at all or in the sums claimed and did not give consent to proceedings against W. HS applied to the Registrar for permission pursuant to the Insolvency Act 1986 s.11 (3) (d) and, further, sought a declaration that the intercompany debt had not been extinguished and a direction that C admit the debt under the CVA. C sought to strike out the application for the declaration and the direction to admit the debt, contending that, since s.11 (3) (d) was the only statutory provision relevant to the application, HS were not entitled to seek declaratory or other relief. HS countered that the application for a declaration and a direction to admit the debt was made under s.7 (3) of the Act against C in their capacity as supervisors of the CVA separately from any application pursuant to s.11 (3) (d).

Held, refusing the application, that C had distinct functions as administrators and as supervisors of the CVA. If these functions were carried out by separate persons, s.7 (3) would give HS the right to complain about acts or admissions of the supervisors and s.11 (3) (d) would entitle them to seek permission to commence proceedings in the absence of the consent of the administrators. Therefore, an application made under s.7 (3) could not be struck out in the instant case merely because an alternative method of achieving a similar end was possible under s.11 (3) (d).

HOLDENHURST SECURITIES PLC v. COHEN [2001] 1 B.C.L.C. 460, Laddie, J., Ch D.

3711. Administration – priorities – classification of rent as administration expense

[Insolvency Act 1986 s.19.]

S owned commercial premises let to a company that had entered into administration. H was appointed administrator and continued trading the business for some months. Thereafter H sold off assets by auction and later petitioned for the winding up of the company which petition was adjourned sine die. S took no action with regard to the property save to demand rent from H. After sums generated during the administration had been used to repay some of the debts, including part of the rent owed to S, and to pay H's agreed remuneration no further funds were available. S argued that it had a priority claim which should have been settled before H withdrew any remuneration. If funds were not available S argued that H should be made personally accountable.

Held, dismissing the claim, that the Insolvency Act 1986 s.19 did not help S because it afforded a priority only to claims arising under new contracts made by the administrator whereas the rent claim arose under a subsisting contract. An administrator was entitled to withdraw agreed remuneration during the currency of the administration and there was nothing in s.19 to preclude this. A court might have required H to pay rent as a precondition of remaining in occupation but S had never made any such application and the court would not make a retrospective order to that effect.

SPRING VALLEY PROPERTIES LTD v. HARRIS; *sub nom.* SALMET INTERNATIONAL LTD (IN ADMINISTRATION), *Re* [2001] B.C.C. 796, Blackburne, J., Ch D.

3712. Agents – liens – entitlement to commission – foreign bankruptcy of principle – Australia

TMA, a Belgian company, was declared bankrupt in Belgium in 1997. R, an Australian shipping agent, had been retained by TMA to recover the proceeds from the sale of two ships, currently held by the Australian court over which TMA had asserted a maritime lien prior to its bankruptcy. R argued that he was entitled to 20 per cent commission from the sale proceeds, under the terms of an oral agreement with TMA. R issued proceedings against TMA, claiming his commission and the Belgian court sought the return of the funds and a stay of R's proceedings.

Held, refusing the request for a stay and return of the sale proceedings, that R had an equitable charge over the funds arising from the commission agreement. The discretion to assist the Belgian court would be refused as R's claim fell to be determined under Australian law and it would be inappropriate to remit the sale proceedings to Belgium without first settling R's claim.

ROLFE v. TRANSWORLD MARINE AGENCY CO NV [2000] B.P.I.R. 822, Tamberlin, J., Fed Ct (Aus) (Sgl judge).

3713. Bankruptcy – administration – assistance from court in external territory – jurisdictional competency – Australia

[Bankruptcy Act 1914 s.122; Bankruptcy Act 1966 (Australia) s.29(4).]

CR, who was declared bankrupt in Australia and owned property in the Cocos Islands, an Australian external territory, appealed against an order obtained by his trustee in bankruptcy, T, at first instance for a letter of assistance pursuant to the Bankruptcy Act 1966 s.29(4) requesting the Islands' Supreme Court to vest CR's property in T, in the exercise of the jurisdiction conferred by the Bankruptcy Act 1914 s.122. CR contended that neither of the courts involved were "British courts" under s.122 of the 1914 Act, so that no valid request for assistance could be made or acceded to.

Held, dismissing the appeal, that it was inappropriate for a court requesting assistance from the court of an external territory to attempt to determine that court's jurisdiction. It was therefore for the Islands' Supreme Court to decide the matter of jurisdiction in response to a request for aid.

CLUNIES-ROSS, *Re* [2000] B.P.I.R. 714, Beaumont, J., Fed Ct (Aus) (Full Ct).

3714. Bankruptcy – administration – assistance to realise assets in foreign jurisdiction – estate comprising revenue debts – Australia

[Bankruptcy Act 1966 (Australia) s.29(2).]

A, who was declared bankrupt in New Zealand, NZ, in 1979 and was the residual beneficiary of his father's estate in Australia, appealed against the successful application by E ((1981) 34 A.L.R. 582), the official assignee in NZ, to realise and collect in assets held by him in Australia. A's interest in the estate, which had not been fully administered on the date of his bankruptcy, was located in New South Wales. A contended that, as half the total debt was due to the NZ revenue authorities, the Australian court should not assist in obtaining payment for another state's revenue debts.

Held, dismissing the appeal, that E was administering A's bankruptcy, not enforcing a foreign revenue claim. The rule against assistance in such cases did not apply in the instant case, as the administration would also benefit A's ordinary creditors. The Bankruptcy Act 1966 s.29(2) permitted assistance to be offered in administering a bankrupt's estate so that the rule A contended for did not apply in any event.

AYRES v. EVANS [2000] B.P.I.R. 697, Fox, J., Fed Ct (Aus) (Full Ct).

3715. Bankruptcy – administration – assistance to vest after acquired property in trustee – Australia

[Bankruptcy Act 1966 (Australia) s.29.]

R moved from New Zealand to Australia in 1988. R was adjudged bankrupt in NZ in 1991 on the basis of a judgment obtained against him by BNZ, which allowed for his discharge in 1994, or earlier on fulfilling certain conditions. BNZ subsequently obtained a bankruptcy order in Australia. R appealed against the second order, contending that it was not necessary, given that it would prevent his early discharge, and that his NZ trustee in bankruptcy could obtain the assistance of the Australian courts to take control of any property R acquired in Australia after the date of the first order. BNZ argued that the second order was necessary to allow such after acquired property to vest in the trustee and to permit examination of R's affairs.

Held, allowing the appeal, that the second bankruptcy order was not required to vest after acquired property in the trustee as the assistance provisions contained in the Bankruptcy Act 1966 s.29 were wide enough to allow the trustee to take possession of such property and to supervise R's affairs, *Hall v. Woolf* (1908) 7 C.L.R. 207 applied restrictively.

RADICH v. BANK OF NEW ZEALAND [2000] B.P.I.R. 783, Einfeld, J., Fed Ct (Aus) (Full Ct).

3716. Bankruptcy – annulment – failure to produce evidence substantiating grounds for annulment

[Insolvency Act 1986 s.282(1)(a).]

W appealed against a decision not to annul a bankruptcy order, following his application under the Insolvency Act 1986 s.282(1)(a), contending that there was additional evidence and that he had failed to appreciate that a bona fide counterclaim exceeding the amount of the debt was a ground to apply for a bankruptcy petition to be dismissed. At the hearing for the annulment, W had not mentioned the possibility of a claim for fraudulent misrepresentation against L.

Held, dismissing the appeal, that (1) W, having failed to produce the appropriate evidence before the Registrar at the time of the annulment application, substantiating the claim that grounds existed for an annulment, would not be permitted to introduce further evidence now, and (2) in any event, the Registrar was entitled to state that he would not have exercised his discretion in W's favour as other evidence had been adduced to show that W was insolvent and had tried to conceal his assets.

SOCIETY OF LLOYD'S v. WATERS [2001] B.P.I.R. 698, Park, J., Ch D.

3717. Bankruptcy – annulment – liability for costs incurred

[Insolvency Act 1986 s.282(1) (a), s.282(1) (b).]

Issues arose in relation to a petition brought by S that B be adjudged bankrupt. There had been some delay between the service of the petition and B's decision to contest it. The parties reached an agreement for the annulment of the bankruptcy. However, this agreement made no provision as to the costs incurred by the trustee in bankruptcy, W.

Held, making an order that S and B should be equally liable for W's costs, that in general if a bankruptcy order was annulled pursuant to the Insolvency Act 1986 s.282(1) (a), the petitioning creditor would be liable for the costs incurred by the trustee in bankruptcy. If such an order was annulled under s.282(1) (b) of the Act, then the bankrupt would be responsible for the trustee's costs in most cases. In the instant case, it was arguable that both S and B were equally responsible for incurring the costs by their respective actions. Further, as S and B were both legally aided, settlement at this stage was preferable on the grounds of public benefit.

BUTTERWORTH v. SOUTTER [2000] B.P.I.R. 582, Neuberger, J., Ch D.

3718. Bankruptcy – appeals – locus standi

H, the trustee in bankruptcy of JP, appealed against a decision that a bankruptcy order against HP, JP's former wife, be quashed and the statutory demand on the basis of which it had been made, set aside. The bankruptcy order had been made as a result of HP's non-payment of taxed costs arising from previous litigation involving herself and H. The quashing order had ultimately been made on the basis that HP had raised new arguments. H contended that HP had had no locus standi to appeal against the judgment on which the order had been made, the right to challenge the judgment vesting in the trustee in bankruptcy.

Held, allowing the appeal and restoring the bankruptcy order, that the judge should not have entertained HP's application to quash the order because a bankrupt possessed no jurisdiction to appeal against the judgment upon which bankruptcy proceedings had been based, *Heath v. Tang* [1993] 1 W.L.R. 1421, [1993] C.L.Y. 222 followed. Even if HP had possessed a right to make the application, any discretion purportedly exercised by the judge in allowing the appeal, had not been exercised judicially.

HUNT v. PEASEGOOD [2001] B.P.I.R. 76, Mummery, L.J., CA.

3719. Bankruptcy – appeals – locus standi of bankrupt – time limits

[Insolvency Act 1986 s.303; Insolvency Rules 1986 (SI 1986 1925) r.6.105.]

S, was declared bankrupt in November 1994. S wished to challenged the order arguing that crucial documentary evidence had not been placed before the court and that the court would not have granted the order if that evidence had been available to it. At first his attempts to appeal were rejected because any rights of action in respect of the judgment now vested in the trustee in bankruptcy and S had no locus standi as a bankrupt. However the court subsequently directed that the trustee should assign the cause of action back to S under Insolvency Act 1986 s.303. By that time the applicant had been discharged from bankruptcy and sought leave to appeal against the 1993 judgment out of time.

Held, dismissing the application, that (1) it was not necessary for the applicant to challenge the 1993 judgment since he had been discharged from bankruptcy and the judgment could not be enforced against him personally; (2) the only steps which the bank could take to enforce the debt were steps in the bankruptcy itself, i.e. by seeking to prove the debt as a creditor in the bankruptcy; (3) the Insolvency Rules 1986 r.6.105 enabled the applicant, a the former bankrupt, to apply to have any decision of the trustees admitting the bank's proof of debt, reversed by the court; (4) r.6.105 allowed the applicant to have the bankruptcy set aside, and (5) if the bank sought to enforce its security against the applicant's dwelling house which was in the joint names of himself and his wife, by proceedings for possession against the wife who had not been party to the bankruptcy proceedings, she could raise the same issues as the applicant without the intervention of the court.

BARCLAYS BANK PLC v. HENSON; BARCLAYS BANK PLC v. STAPLETON [2000] B.P.I.R. 941, Chadwick, L.J., CA.

3720. **Bankruptcy – assignment – assignment of claim against solicitors – trustees in bankruptcy – improper exercise of discretion**

F, a bankrupt, appealed against a decision refusing to set aside the assignment, by S, his trustee in bankruptcy, of a cause of action against PR, F's former solicitors, to PR's own solicitors in consideration of £17,000. The value of the claim against PR was not less than £2,000,000. F contended that S, who had not taken legal advice on the merits of F's claim as there were insufficient assets in F's estate to pay for such advice, had given inadequate consideration to the prospects of success of the claim. S contended that the decision had been a lawful exercise of his discretion with which the court should not interfere.

Held, allowing the appeal, that S had not properly considered the merits of the claim, which was not a hopeless claim, and that the benefit of the assignment to F's creditors was negligible particularly when contrasted with the benefits that could arise from successful prosecution of the claim. The court further held that the judge had erred by holding that he had no jurisdiction to interfere with S's decision. The assignment was set aside and an assignment of the cause of action to F ordered, *Edennote Ltd, Re* [1996] 2 B.C.L.C. 389, [1996] C.L.Y. 3490 considered.

FARYAB (A BANKRUPT) v. SMITH (TRUSTEE IN BANKRUPTCY); FARYAB (A BANKRUPT) v. PHILIP ROSS & CO [2001] B.P.I.R. 246, Robert Walker, L.J., CA.

3721. **Bankruptcy – assignment – causes of action – validity of deed of assignment where events complained of pre dated bankruptcy – Australia**

F was adjudged bankrupt in 1992 and commenced proceedings by way of writ in 1995 against NM to recover sums paid in 1990. F asserted that the cause of action had been assigned under a deed of assignment executed by the Official Trustee. However NM applied for the action to be struck out, contending that the cause of action remained vested in the Official Trustee as it pre dated F's bankruptcy.

Held, allowing the application, that the writ issued in 1995 was a nullity as the cause of action remained with the Official Trustee. The deed did not vest any legal or equitable interest in F as the assignment could not be backdated in respect of a cause of action that accrued prior to F's bankruptcy.

FRANCIS v. MUTUAL LIFE ASSOCIATION OF AUSTRALASIA LTD [2001] B.P.I.R. 480, Ambrose, J., Sup Ct (Qld).

3722. **Bankruptcy – consolidation of estates – trustee in bankruptcy acting as sole administrator – Canada**

[Insolvency Act 1986 s.426.]

It was alleged that W, a Canadian citizen, and a company he controlled, WFSI, had induced fraudulent investments in another of W's companies, U. In 1990, W fled to England where he was later imprisoned for murder. Following W's arrest, the English police seized various moveable assets and foreign bank account details. WFSI was made bankrupt in Canada on the petition of U, with K appointed as trustee. A bankruptcy order was also made against W on the petition of WFSI, with K again appointed trustee. Two classes of creditor were identified, those with claims solely against W, and those with claims against W and WFSI, however WFSI had no assets by the time of the bankruptcy petition. An English county court made an order for assistance in favour of the Canadian court, under the Insolvency Act 1986 s.426 and the English police agreed to deliver up of W's seized assets. K sought orders consolidating W's and WFSI's estates and requests for assistance by foreign courts for the purposes of administration.

Held, allowing the applications, that W's sole creditors would not be unfairly preferred by an order for consolidation, given WFSI's lack of assets. On the facts, requests for assistance were not overly presumptuous. Delivery up and administration should be controlled by K as sole administrator and it was within the accepted boundaries of comity to expect foreign laws to be applied in obtaining the vesting of W's assets in K.

WALKER (ALBERT JOHNSTON), *Re* [2000] B.P.I.R. 930, Browne, J., HC (Ont).

3723. Bankruptcy – coownership – order for sale of property – priority of creditor's interests – existence of exceptional circumstances

[Insolvency Act 1986 s.335A.]

H, the trustee in bankruptcy of KB's estate, sought an order for the sale of a flat owned by KB and her husband, B, as joint tenants. B contended that no sale should be ordered because the equity in the property after discharge of the mortgage would be sufficient only to meet H's expenses. The sale was ordered at first instance and B appealed.

Held, dismissing the appeal, that the judge below had applied the correct principles in dealing with the sale of a jointly owned property, even though the provisions of the Insolvency Act 1986 s.335A had not been mentioned specifically in his judgment. Those principles provided that the creditors' interests had priority where an application for an order for sale was made more than one year after the property had vested in the trustee as was so in the instant case. Such interests could only be displaced in "exceptional circumstances". The fact that the proceeds of sale would be sufficient only to pay the trustee's costs could still result in a benefit to creditors and did not amount to "exceptional circumstances" as it was a common consequence of bankruptcy, *Citro (Domenico) (A Bankrupt), Re* [1991] Ch. 142, [1991] C.L.Y. 261 applied.

HARRINGTON v. BENNETT; *sub nom.* BENNETT, *Re* [2000] B.P.I.R. 630, Lawrence Collins Q.C., Ch D.

3724. Bankruptcy – costs – withdrawal of petition – no prior judgment – costs liability where no application to set aside statutory demand

[Insolvency Rules 1986 (SI 1986 1925) r.6.4.]

BB issued a statutory demand against BJ in respect of debts incurred by BJ in the course of a sole trading business. A bankruptcy petition was presented in January 2001. BJ set out in a detailed statement in April 2001 her grounds for disputing the petition and it was agreed that the petition should be withdrawn. It was subsequently ordered that BB should bear BJ's costs in the bankruptcy proceedings. BB appealed on the grounds that (1) there was provision under the Insolvency Rules 1986 r.6.4 for a debtor to apply for the statutory demand to be set aside and (2) BJ's failure to apply resulted in a perfectly foreseeable and natural increase in costs as a result of the steps taken to issue and deal with the bankruptcy petition. BJ contended that a party issuing proceedings in the insolvency jurisdiction takes the risk that a defence may be available and must bear the costs in those circumstances.

Held, dismissing the appeal, that a party seeking a short cut procedure by issuing in the bankruptcy jurisdiction as opposed to first obtaining judgment, takes the risk that a defence may be available and must bear the debtor's costs in those circumstances. Rule 6.4 of the 1986 Rules provided an opportunity for a debtor to apply to set aside a statutory demand rather than a requirement for such an application to be made.

BORDER BUSINESS SYSTEMS LTD v. JOHN, July 9, 2001, Holland, J., Ch D. [*Ex rel.* Mark Beesley, Barrister, 7 Harrington Street, Liverpool].

3725. Bankruptcy – creditors – reasonable refusal of settlement offer – objective test

[Insolvency Act 1986 s.271 (3).]

D, convicted of fraudulently cheating the Customs and Excise Commissioners of VAT amounting to some £140,000 on services he provided as a barrister, appealed against the making of a bankruptcy order against him on CEC's petition. D contended that the bankruptcy petition should have been dismissed pursuant to the Insolvency Act 1986 s.271(3) as his offer to settle his VAT liability had been unreasonably refused on the grounds that (1) the proposal, comprising the granting of charges over two properties, was the better option for CEC; (2) the offer had been refused because of a rigid institutional policy requiring that CEC concede nothing to a debtor who had defrauded the CEC, and (3) it was not open to CEC to rely on the grounds they had done, as the grounds had not been in their mind at the time of the refusal. CEC asserted that they had given proper consideration to the offer and because of factors such as the existence of a first mortgagee, the failure to produce proper valuations and the length of postponement of payment, they had concluded that it would be more beneficial for a bankruptcy order to be made and for D's assets to be sold for the benefit of creditors generally.

Held, dismissing the appeal, that (1) the test of unreasonableness under s.271 of the Act, was an objective test. Accordingly, a creditor's refusal to accept an offer was unreasonable if it was beyond the range of reasonable responses of a reasonable creditor and a debtor must also be frank and open, providing all the necessary information to enable a creditor to make an informed decision, *Debtor (No.6349 of 1994), Re* [1996] B.P.I.R. 271, *Debtor (No.32 of 1993), Re* [1994] 1 W.L.R. 899, [1994] C.L.Y. 284, applied; (2) it was clear that CEC had viewed D's offer on its merits and had not been constrained by any rigid policy and (3) CEC had been entitled to rely on the grounds that they had, irrespective of whether those factors had been in their mind at the time of the refusal of D's offer, as there were inherent weaknesses in the offer which had to be taken into account by the court in deciding the response of a reasonable hypothetical creditor. In the circumstances, CEC's refusal had been reasonable.

CUSTOMS AND EXCISE COMMISSIONERS v. DOUGALL; *sub nom.* DEBTOR (NO.5795 OF 1998), RE; DOUGALL v. CUSTOMS AND EXCISE COMMISSIONERS [2001] B.P.I.R. 269, Lightman, J., Ch D.

3726. Bankruptcy – debts – loan procured by undue influence – debtor's liability released on discharge from bankruptcy

[Insolvency Act 1986 s.281(3).]

M sought to recover monies loaned to her former solicitor, E, prior to E's bankruptcy. M contended that since she had reposed trust and confidence in E, the loans were deemed by equity to have been made as a result of undue influence. M maintained that the Insolvency Act 1986 s.281(3) could encompass constructive fraud, such as an obligation to repay monies procured by undue influence, and that accordingly E's obligation to repay the monies survived his discharge from bankruptcy.

Held, giving judgment for E, that s.281(3) should be given its natural meaning. Accordingly, the word "fraud" meant actual fraud in the sense of *Derry v. Peek* (1889) L.R. 14 App. Cas. 337. It followed that an obligation to repay monies procured by undue influence was not an obligation "incurred in respect of fraud" for the purposes of s.281(3), and was consequently extinguished upon the debtor's discharge from bankruptcy, *Beaman v. ARTS* [1949] 1 K.B. 550 and *Bartlett v. Barclays Bank Trust Co Ltd (No.2)* [1980] Ch. 515, [1980] C.L.Y. 2403 considered and *Derry* applied..

MANDER v. EVANS [2001] 1 W.L.R. 2378, Ferris, J., Ch D.

3727. Bankruptcy – divorce – right of divorced wife to matrimonial home

[Insolvency Act 1986 s.335A, s.340; Human Rights Act 1988 Sch.1 Part I Art.8.]

B's marriage broke down and a decree nisi was obtained. Whilst negotiations regarding the settlement of the maintenance/property adjustment claim were in progress B's husband was made bankrupt. The trustee claimed a half share of the family home and, after one year, sought and obtained an order for the sale of the home under the Insolvency Act 1986 s.335A. B's request for the postponement of execution pending the outcome of B's claim against her solicitors, was refused by the court at first instance on the basis that any claim was unlikely to raise sufficient money to enable B buy her husband's share of the home. B's appeal was dismissed and she sought permission to appeal.

Held, granting permission to appeal, that there were three serious issues to be considered on appeal namely (1) whether a spouse with a property adjustment order in her favour could be a creditor as defined by the provisions of the 1986 Act thus rendering a transaction in her favour prior to the bankruptcy challengeable under the Act; (2) whether transactions carried out under the terms of an Order of the Family Court could be set aside as transactions at an undervalue and (3) whether the application of 335A might be contrary to the provisions of the Human Rights Act 1988 Sch.1 Part I Art.8.

JACKSON v. BELL, [2001] EWCA Civ 387, [2001] B.P.I.R. 612, Sir Andrew Morritt V.C., CA.

3728. Bankruptcy – garnishee orders – setting aside

[Insolvency Act 1986 s.346; Civil Procedure Rules 1998 (SI 1998 3132) Part 40 r.40.9.]

D underwrote the legal and medical costs of claimants in personal injury actions where the claimants instructed Y to act as their solicitor, resulting in a conditional fee agreement between the claimant client, Y and D being entered into. Following disputes between Y and D. Y was ordered to pay to D £120,000 owed by him to D under the terms of the conditional fee arrangements. There then followed an application against Y for delivery up of litigation files (so that new solicitors could be instructed for the claimant clients) where Y claimed a lien over the papers. The application was compromised on terms including an undertaking by D to pay Y sums representing Y's costs in the actions to date. Payment was to be made if and when the actions were successfully completed. Thereafter the Inland Revenue presented a bankruptcy petition against Y. Knowing of the petition D applied for and were granted four garnishee orders nisi in respect of the contingent debts. The orders were made against the new solicitors instructed by the claimant clients. The orders were subsequently made absolute. A bankruptcy order was made against Y and a trustee appointed. The trustee applied to set aside or vary the garnishee orders and to recover the sums paid to D under the orders before the bankruptcy date.

Held, setting aside the garnishee orders and ordering repayment by D to the trustee, that the court had jurisdiction under the Insolvency Act 1986 s.346 and Civil Procedure Rules 1998 Part 40 r.40.9 to set aside the orders on the application of the trustee. The interests of Y's creditors had been affected by the making of the garnishee orders issued after the presentation of a bankruptcy petition against Y. The trustee accordingly had a right to apply to set aside the orders. The garnishee orders ought not to have been made after the presentation of the bankruptcy petition. Furthermore it was not clear that a contingent debt, before the happening of the contingency was an attachable debt for the purposes of a garnishee order.

INDUSTRIAL DISEASES COMPENSATION LTD v. MARRONS [2001] B.P.I.R. 600, Judge Behrens, Ch D.

3729. Bankruptcy – guarantees – creditor's entitlement to prove in bankruptcy for principal and interest

HL appealed against a decision of the Official Assignee so that proof of debt could be admitted against the bankrupt estate of HK, who had stood as the guarantor for loans made by HL to two companies that had since gone into liquidation. The Official Assignee contended that once receiving and adjudication orders were made against HK, HL became a secured creditor and was therefore obliged to give credit for the value of its security and prove only for the balance of the debt. Further, that HL could not be treated differently from other unsecured creditors who had lodged a proof against HK's estate. Additionally it was contended that HL was not entitled to interest from HK for the period before the demand was made under the guarantee.

Held, allowing the appeal, that (1) HK had agreed to guarantee all amounts outstanding under the loans and HL was entitled to charge contractual interest up to the date that the mortgaged properties were disposed of, notwithstanding the companies' intervening liquidation; (2) the security provided by the companies did not form part of HK's estate; (3) the secured debt carried contractual interest until payment and HL could prove the debt against HK's estate, and (4) following the companies' default, HK became liable for the principal and interest of the debt from the date the loans were disbursed to the date that HL issued the notice of demand.

HO KOK CHEONG, *ex p.* PARIBAS, *Re* [2001] B.P.I.R. 278, Judith Prakash, J., HC (Sing).

3730. **Bankruptcy – individual voluntary arrangements – application by discharged bankrupt**

[Insolvency Act 1986 s.253(3).]

W applied for an Individual Voluntary Arrangement, IVA, in respect of bankruptcy debts from a number of years before from which she had been automatically discharged. She claimed that the payment of the bankruptcy creditors who were to be paid in full could be accomplished more quickly and economically in an IVA rather than by the trustee.

Held, dismissing the application, that the 1986 Act required an individual who sought an IVA to be a person who could petition for his own bankruptcy. Since W had been discharged from the bankruptcy she was no longer a debtor of the bankruptcy creditors and could not petition for her own bankruptcy based on the same debts. She could therefore not apply for an IVA.

WRIGHT v. OFFICIAL RECEIVER [2001] B.P.I.R. 196, District Judge Caddick, CC (Medway).

3731. **Bankruptcy – individual voluntary arrangements – default petition by supervisor**

Four inter linked individual voluntary arrangements were made by E, S, R and A, partners in a family business. The IVAs were to last for four years and provided that the business would continue trading on the basis of an estimated annual profit of £80,000 and further provisions was made for payment by the individuals of an amount representing the monthly equivalent of their share of the annual profit. If, after four years, the contributions did not result in full payment of the debts the IVA provided for the shortfall to be met out of the equities on the properties held by the individuals. At the end of four years it became apparent that the contributions alone were not sufficient to meet the debt and the supervisor pressed for payment out of the equity on the properties. It became apparent that there was insufficient equity in the properties to meet the shortfall, there being negative equity in the properties. A creditors' meeting was called to decide whether bankruptcy petitions ought to be presented. sixty nine per cent of the creditors present voted against bankruptcy but the supervisor presented the petitions in any event.

Held, making the bankruptcy orders sought, that (1) the supervisor was entitled under the terms of the IVA to present the petitions even though the four year period had expired and he was not bound by the outcome of the vote at the creditors' meeting; (2) although the debtors were not in default in making the contributions there had been a serious default in their failure to make available the equity in the properties; (3) it had been implicit within the terms of the IVA that the amounts secured on the properties should not be increased to the detriment of the equity, and (4) in the absence of special circumstances a bankruptcy order would be made.

HARRIS v. GROSS [2001] B.P.I.R. 586, Judge Maddocks, Ch D.

3732. Bankruptcy – insurance policies – vesting of proceeds in trustee

[Insolvency Act 1986.]

R, a bankrupt, appealed against a ruling ([2000] B.P.I.R. 654, [2000] C.L.Y. 3443) that the proceeds of two insurance policies payable upon proof of permanent disablement vested in C, the trustee in bankruptcy. R submitted that entitlement to the policy proceeds was so peculiarly personal to the affected individual that it would inequitable and contrary to the principles underpinning the Insolvency Act 1986 and fell outside the ambit of the bankrupt's estate. Furthermore, that the situation was analogous to the common law exception whereby payments of compensation arising from a tortious claim for pain and suffering or defamation were exempt.

Held, dismissing the appeal, that (1) the proposition advanced was unsupported by authority; (2) the policy itself would have constituted a valuable asset available for distribution to creditors had disablement never occurred and the fact that it had occurred could not logically alter its status, and (3) the payment was dependent upon a contractual right to a sum of money and the policy proceeds did not represent recompense to the bankrupt for personal loss or damage but rather payment on satisfaction of a contractual contingency, *Beckham v. Drake* (1849) 2 H.L. Cas. 579, *Heath v. Tang* [1993] 1 W.L.R. 1421, [1993] C.L.Y. 222 and *Haig v. Aitken* [2001] Ch. 110, [2000] 8 C.L. 422 considered.

CORK v. RAWLINS; *sub nom.* INSOLVENCY ACT 1986, RE; RAWLINS (ALAN JAMES), *Re*, [2001] EWCA Civ 202, [2001] Ch. 792, Peter Gibson, L.J., CA.

3733. Bankruptcy – maintenance orders – costs orders – non provable status of debt

[Magistrates Courts Act 1980 s.65(1)(m); Insolvency Act 1986 s.268, s.270, s.382(1); Insolvency Rules 1986 (SI 1986 1925) r.12.3(2)(a).]

A former wife, W, petitioned for her ex husband's bankruptcy on the basis of maintenance and costs orders made in a German court and registered with the High Court.

Held, dismissing the petition, that the maintenance order came under the definition of family proceedings in the Magistrates Courts Act 1980 s.65(1)(m) and was therefore a non provable debt for the purposes of the Insolvency Rules 1986 r.12.3(2)(a). Similarly, the costs order was an obligation arising out of matrimonial proceedings and was also not provable in bankruptcy under r.13.3(2)(a). Although the Insolvency Act 1986 s.382 did not distinguish between provable and non provable debts, there were no special circumstances under which the petition could proceed as an exercise of the court's discretion. The petition was also irregular as it had been presented at the same time as a statutory demand and s.270 of the 1980 Act only allowed a petition to be presented before the three week period in s.268 had expired if a statutory demand had already been served.

WEHMEYER v. WEHMEYER [2001] 2 F.L.R. 84, Registrar James, Ch D.

3734. Bankruptcy – occupational pensions – council superannuation schemes – time of vesting in trustee

[Insolvency Act 1986 s.436; Local Government Superannuation Regulations 1986 (SI 1986 24).]

P, a former council employee and member of the council's contributory superannuation scheme, appealed against an order ([1999] B.P.I.R. 509) that a lump sum payment and pension, including enhanced benefits, vested in his trustee in bankruptcy. P had been made bankrupt in 1995 and his creditors had received only negligible payments in the bankruptcy. Three years later, and subsequent to the automatic discharge from his bankruptcy, P had been made redundant and had become entitled to an index linked pension and lump sum payment in accordance with the rules of the scheme. The trustee had successfully contended that, apart from the pension attributable to service after the bankruptcy order and an element covering the guaranteed minimum pension payable after pensionable age, the pension benefits vested in him. P submitted that (1) the pension benefits were not "property" within the meaning of the Insolvency Act 1986 s.436, and (2) the pension rights were non assignable under the Local Government Superannuation Regulations 1986.

Held, dismissing the appeal, that (1) the legal right to the basic pension and basic lump sum vested in P prior to the bankruptcy order and was a chose in action within the meaning of the word "property" in s.436 of the Act. The fact that the occasion for the payment of the pension rights did not occur until after the termination of the bankruptcy was irrelevant to the vesting of such rights. Any enhanced discretionary benefits also amounted to property within s.436 as they were "incidental" to the basic pension, and (2) the fact that pension benefits were not assignable under the 1986 Regulations was irrelevant to the question of vesting. P was entitled to the rights which were attributable to his service after bankruptcy since those contributions had been made in the mistaken belief that the pension rights remained vested in him and it would be inequitable for the trustee to take the benefit of such contributions.

PATEL v. JONES; *sub nom.* JONES v. PATEL, [2001] EWCA Civ 779, [2001] B.P.I.R. 919, Mummery, L.J., CA.

3735. **Bankruptcy – pre emption rights – vesting of rights in trustee**

[Insolvency Act 1986 s.436.]

In proceedings commenced by D for a declaration that the right of pre emption granted to R, a bankrupt, over land purchased by D was no longer binding, it fell to the court, upon D's appeal from an interlocutory order, to determine whether the right of pre emption which vested in R at the commencement of the bankruptcy was "property" within the definition in the Insolvency Act 1986 s.436, and if it remained vested in R on his bankruptcy or vested in his trustee.

Held, allowing the appeal, that a right of pre emption was a "thing in action" and was therefore property within the meaning of s.436 of the Act, in spite of the fact that it could be difficult to place a value on it. Such a right was transferable, binding upon the grantor and legally enforceable by the grantee. The right of pre emption vested in R's trustee from the commencement of bankruptcy, *Pritchard v. Briggs* [1980] Ch. 338, [1980] C.L.Y. 1563 distinguished.

DEAR v. REEVES, [2001] EWCA Civ 277, [2002] Ch. 1, Mummery, L.J., CA.

3736. **Bankruptcy – real property – enforcement of sale order abroad – jurisdiction of English court to grant order in personam**

[Brussels Convention on Jurisdiction and the Enforcement of Judgments in Civil and Commercial Matters 1968 Art.16(1).]

P, a bankrupt, appealed against an order ([2000] 2 All E.R. 772, [2000] C.L.Y. 3490) requiring the sale of a property in Portugal, owned jointly by P and his wife, following an application by the trustee in bankruptcy. P submitted that the Brussels Convention 1968 Art.16(1) applied and that as a consequence the proceedings could only be pursued within the Portuguese jurisdiction.

Held, dismissing the appeal, that P could not rely on Art.16(1)(a), which provided that the court of the country where the property was situated would have exclusive jurisdiction "in proceedings which [had] as their object rights in rem in immoveable property", because the trustee's application was a claim "in personam". Furthermore, no factual investigation into the situation in Portugal was required and no issue of Portuguese law or practice arose for determination, *Webb (George Lawrence) v. Webb (Lawrence Desmond) (C294/92)* [1994] Q.B. 696, [1994] C.L.Y. 4798 applied. The court could in appropriate cases exercise its jurisdiction to make orders relating to trust property abroad. There was no justification for arguing that such jurisdiction was to be exercised sparingly, *Hayward (Deceased), Re* [1997] Ch. 45, [1996] C.L.Y. 1111 distinguished.

ASHURST v. POLLARD; *sub nom.* POLLARD v. ASHURST [2001] Ch. 595, Jonathan Parker, L.J., CA.

3737. Bankruptcy – service of process – evidence of delivery – meaning of "returned unsatisfied"

[Insolvency Act 1986 s.268(1) (b).]

S appealed against the refusal of his application for the annulment of his bankruptcy. C had served a writ of fieri facias for costs and recovered various assets from S's business premises. Having received only a nominal sum from the seizure and sale of S's assets, C successfully petitioned for S's bankruptcy. S contended that (1) the sheriff had failed to endorse a proper return on the writ, and (2) he had not been properly served with notice of an adjourned bankruptcy hearing.

Held, allowing the appeal, that (1) "returned unsatisfied" for the purposes of the Insolvency Act 1986 s.268(1) (b) did not have a technical meaning but meant merely proof that the debt had not been satisfied, *Debtor (No.340 of 1992), Re* [1996] 2 All E.R. 211, [1995] C.L.Y. 420 distinguished, and (2) although a copy of the solicitor's letter to S had been exhibited, a failure to aver that it had been sent by first class post to S's address was fatal to the proof of proper service that was a necessary safeguard in bankruptcy cases, *Lex Services v. Johns* (1990) 59 P. & C.R. 427, [1990] C.L.Y. 2782 distinguished.

SKARZYNSKI v. CHALFORD PROPERTY CO LTD [2001] B.P.I.R. 673, Jacob, J., Ch D.

3738. Bankruptcy – trustees in bankruptcy – vesting of negligence claim – requirement for assignment

P appealed against the decision ([2000] B.P.I.R. 506, [2000] C.L.Y. 3738) to refuse its application to strike out a claim brought against it by M, a discharged bankrupt, for damage to her reputation and economic loss allegedly arising from P's negligence. P had acted as the insolvency practitioner for M. P maintained that M had no title to sue them in negligence.

Held, allowing the appeal, that the legal title to a cause of action for personal reputation and status of a bankrupt vested in the trustee in bankruptcy who was accountable to M for damages payable in respect of that part of the claim and accountable to the creditors for damages recovered in respect of economic loss, *Ord v. Upton* [2000] Ch. 352, [2000] C.L.Y. 3440 applied. In order for M to pursue a claim in negligence against P in respect of her personal loss, it was a prerequisite that the trustee assign the right to her since the trustee did not hold the cause of action on a bare trust for M. The judge had erred in treating the trustee as being accountable to M for all the damages recoverable as a result of the action. M was not in a position analogous to an equitable assignee of a chose in action and P was not prevented from asserting the true position that no bare trust existed.

MULKERRINS v. PRICEWATERHOUSECOOPERS; *sub nom.* MULKERRINS v. PRICE WATERHOUSE COOPERS [2001] B.P.I.R. 106, Jonathan Parker, L.J., CA.

3739. Bankruptcy – trustees in bankruptcy – vesting of property in trustee

D, a bank, repossessed properties owned by C which had been provided to D as security. C issued proceedings against D to obtain redelivery of the properties but the proceedings were struck out. C then sought to obtain permission to appeal but, in the meantime, he was adjudged bankrupt. The Official Receiver agreed to the dismissal of the application for leave to appeal. After C's discharge from bankruptcy C sought to commence further actions seeking redelivery of the properties from D.

Held, striking out the claims, that the causes of action had vested in the trustee in bankruptcy. C therefore had no locus standi and could not seek a vesting order in respect of the claims.

KHAN-GHAURI v. DUNBAR BANK PLC [2001] B.P.I.R. 618, Pumfrey, J., Ch D.

3740. Bankruptcy – trustees liability – offshore discretionary trust – transfer of funds by professional trustee – joinder as party in bankruptcy proceedings – Australia

F, the settlor, transferred funds to C, a Jersey resident trust which were subsequently transferred to V trust. The trusts shared the same beneficiaries, none of whom were the settlor, and the same professional trustee was in charge of both trusts. The trustee was accustomed to act on F's wishes, although it was at all material times conceded that it was not obliged to do so. F became bankrupt. His trustee in bankruptcy, W, sought a declaration that the trust funds were held on bare trust for F and applied for the trustee to be joined as a party. F meanwhile applied to be discharged as a party.

Held, dismissing both applications, that (1) the trustee would not be joined as a party in the instant case given the advanced state of the litigation and also because it had earlier been a party and had been discharged with the consent of all parties; (2) F would not be discharged since it was likely that he only sought to be discharged to prevent his evidence in the bankruptcy from being read into the record, and (3) the trustee did not hold the trust funds on a bare trust for F because, even if the transfer of funds to V trust was in breach of trust, the trustee held them on the same terms as for C trust and not for F.

WILY v. FULLER (2000-01) 3 I.T.E.L.R. 321, Hill, J., Fed Ct (Aus) (Sgl judge).

3741. Bankruptcy orders – foreign jurisdictions – recognition of Taiwanese order in Hong Kong

See CONFLICT OF LAWS: Hung v. Miao. §819

3742. Corporate insolvency – fiduciary duty – directors – waiver of entitlement to clawback – company director acting in good faith

Liquidators sought damages for a breach of fiduciary duty arising from the second defendant's agreement, in his capacity as a director of the claimant company, R, to waive that companies entitlement to clawback a sum from the vendors of a company, G. The liquidators contended that by his actions, the second defendant had disposed of the clawback asset for negligible consideration and for an improper purpose. The second defendant submitted that he had agreed to the waiver for a valid commercial reason and had honestly believed that he was acting in the best interest of the company and in accordance with his duties as a director.

Held, giving judgment for the defendant, that the evidence supported the second defendant's submissions.

REGENTCREST PLC (IN LIQUIDATION) v. COHEN [2001] B.C.C. 494, Jonathan Parker, J., Ch D.

3743. Corporate insolvency – liquidation – charges – transactions at an undervalue

[Companies Act 1985 s.395.]

P wanted to purchase a yacht without the acquisition appearing in its balance sheet for a year. M provided finance for yacht purchases. In February 1992 P lent money to M which was used to purchase a yacht. P entered into a rental/operating agreement with M under which P hired the yacht for 12 months from M. The agreement provided that, at the end of 12 months, P would buy the yacht from M at a price equal to the loan, with the loan being repaid by way of set off against the purchase price. Further, that if M became insolvent, P's rights under the agreement would accrue at the date of the insolvency. M's obligations were secured by a mortgage over the yacht, but the charge was not registered under the Companies Act 1985 s.395. M got into financial difficulties. In April 1992 a further agreement was entered into in similar terms, but this time the charge was registered. The purpose of that agreement was to give P the security it should have had under the previous agreement. M went into insolvent liquidation and the liquidator, B, claimed that the second agreement was a transaction at an undervalue, alternatively, a preference, and that the purchase and set off provisions were void as a preference.

Held, finding that P was entitled to the sale proceeds, that, (1) the second agreement did not amount to a transaction at an undervalue because M was not placed in a worse position by reason of it: although its debt to P became secured it remained at the same level, *MC Bacon Ltd (No.1), Re* [1990] B.C.L.C. 324, [1990] C.L.Y. 526 considered, (2) the second agreement was a preference because it put P in a better position than it would have been in but for M's liquidation. However, it would not be set aside because that would merely restart the February agreement and that would not serve any useful purpose, as the purchase and set off provisions were lawful and did not amount to preferences.

MISTRAL FINANCE (IN LIQUIDATION), *Re* [2001] B.C.C. 27, Peter Smith Q.C., Ch D (Companies Court).

3744. **Corporate insolvency – liquidation – contribution – scheme carried out with intent to defraud landlord – liability of directors**

[Insolvency Act 1986 s.213.]

A company had been established in England as part of a road haulage franchise by PM. The managing director, D, assumed onerous leases and was subsequently removed because of the company's poor performance and on suspicion of fraud. PM appointed a new managing director, LB. Together with their solicitors, PM and LB put together a scheme that would allow the company to evade its onerous leasehold obligations. The company's shares were sold at market value to LB's father in law, so that PM and LB ceased to be directors, they then created a new company which acquired the original company's goodwill, thereby allowing them to continue trading under a different name. PM and LB continued to pay trade creditors and informed the landlord, R, that rent would continue to be paid. However, arrears were allowed to build up and the company was later put into liquidation and the liquidator, M, repudiated the lease. R contended that the scheme amounted to knowingly trading with an intent to defraud creditors under the Insolvency Act 1986 s.213 and M sought a declaration as to PM and LB's liability and also contributions from their assets.

Held, allowing the application, that PM and LB had been closely involved in the operation of the business under the scheme and the representation to R as to future payment of rent had been demonstrably false. PM and LB were therefore liable to make a contribution of £17,500 to reflect R's lost rent and a further contribution of £17,500 as a punitive element to reflect their dishonesty. However, their liability was extinguished as their solicitors had previously paid R £75,000 to compromise a claim made against them arising from the same facts.

MORPHITES v. BERNASCONI [2001] 2 B.C.L.C. 1, Anthony Elleray Q.C., Ch D (Companies Court).

3745. **Corporate insolvency – liquidation – director's liability to make restitution**

[Insolvency Act 1986 s.212.]

S, a director of a jewellery company, SB, which had been subject to a creditors' voluntary liquidation following the loss of uninsured jewels, appealed against an order that he should make restitution in the sum of £50,000 pursuant to the Insolvency Act 1986 s.212. S's father, F, who had played an active role in running SB, had purchased the jewellery on credit and had intended to travel to Germany and Italy in order to find a buyer, but the jewels had been lost on a cross-channel ferry. S contended, inter alia, that the trial judge had made a finding of liability against him that was outside the liquidators' pleaded case.

Held, allowing the appeal, that the judge had found S to be negligent and in breach of duty only in that he had abjectly surrendered his director's duties to F, who had effectively acted as the manager of SB. However, the pleaded case against S had, in effect, alleged a breach of duty by S in delegating to his father the power to decide whether the jewellery should be insured and whether it should be taken out of the country without insurance. There had been no evidence adduced to establish that F could not be trusted with such decisions, which related to the day to day management of SB. Accordingly, the pleaded case against S had not been made out and S had been found liable for a breach of duty that had not been alleged against him.

COHEN v. SELBY; *sub nom.* SIMMON BOX (DIAMONDS) LTD, *Re* [2001] 1 B.C.L.C. 176, Chadwick, L.J., CA.

3746. Corporate insolvency – liquidation – loan agreements – dairy farmers – transfer of milk quotas to borrower

D, by its liquidator, appealed against a safe haven order made in respect of the proposed transfers of milk quotas. The milk quotas had been transferred by dairy farmers to F, an associated company of D, as security for monies loaned to those farmers by D. The loan agreements provided that upon discharge of a borrower's indebtedness the quotas would be retransferred. This was to be achieved by the grant of a short term lease over land occupied by F under a tenancy. L, freehold owner of the land leased to F, claimed an entitlement to the milk quotas after the purported forfeiture of F's tenancy by reentry and sought an order for the sale of part of the land. The liquidator contended that the benefit of F's interest in the milk quotas was held on trust for D. The court was asked to determine (1) whether D was entitled to direct F to retransfer a quota to a borrower who had repaid all sums owing under his loan agreement with D; (2) whether D was entitled to direct F to sell a milk quota in the event of the borrower's default; (3) who was entitled to the proceeds of sale from the transfer of a milk quota, and (4) in light of the court's findings in respect of the previous issues, whether the safe haven order was appropriate.

Held, dismissing the appeal, that (1) D was entitled to direct F to retransfer a milk quota to a borrower who had repaid the sums due under the loan agreement whether or not repayment had been effected in accordance with the terms of the agreement; (2) in the absence of an implied term in the agreement between D and the borrower enabling the quota to be sold, a sale of the quota would be inconsistent with the borrower's right to redeem. If a power of sale were to be implied, D would be required to direct a sale of the quota by F subject to the proceeds of sale being applied to the credit of the borrower's account with D; (3) the proceeds of any sale had to be applied to the benefit of the borrower's account with D, and (4) since D had an interest in the land subject to the tenancy by reason of its right to direct the retransfer of the quotas and to require the grant of short term tenancies to the borrowers, the making of the safe haven order had been appropriate, *Bland v. Ingrams Estates Ltd (No.1)* Times, January 18, 2001, [2001] 2 C.L. 423 considered.

SWIFT v. DAIRYWISE FARMS LTD (NO.2), [2001] EWCA Civ 145, [2001] 1 B.C.L.C. 672, Chadwick, L.J., CA.

3747. Corporate insolvency – liquidation – proof of debt – expunging proof after delay when improperly admitted

[Insolvency Rules 1986 r.4.85.]

A was a company used by K as a vehicle for his property investments. It was thought that he was the sole shareholder at the date of his death in 1994. In dealing with his estate the company was wound up. There were seven creditors who submitted proofs of whom (1) M claimed that she had lent money in respect of certain building works; (2) H claimed to be owed money in respect of certain other building works; (3) O claimed to be owed money in respect of services provided for finding suitable properties for K's projects and (4) V claimed to be owed money for the provision of legal services and advice.V was the personal representative of the deceased.The proofs were admitted in 1997. In 1999 K's wife and daughter claimed to own the shares in A.The liquidator then applied to expunge the proofs of M, H, O and V on the basis that the debts were that of the deceased rather than of the company.

Held, expunging three of the proofs, that (1) the burden of proof was on the liquidator who had to show on a balance of probabilities that the proof had been 'improperly' admitted; (2) this did not mean impropriety, but simply that the proof should not, in fact, have been admitted; (3) although there had been delay no estoppel arose and on the facts, it appeared that M, H and V made their agreements with K personally and accordingly their proofs would be expunged. O dealt with A and his proof remained valid and would not be expunged.

ALLARD HOLDINGS LTD, *Re* [2001] 1 B.C.L.C. 404, Hazel Williamson Q.C., Ch D.

3748. **Corporate insolvency – liquidation – schemes of arrangement outside liquidation – division of creditors into classes**

[Companies Act 1985 s.425; Insolvency Rules 1986 (SI 1986 1925) r.4.90.]

L, the liquidators of a company, AA, applied for approval of a scheme of arrangement between AA and its creditors. Although AA was insolvent, L sought to implement the scheme outside of liquidation in order to save costs and maximise returns, allow payment of creditors in their own currencies and improve the range of investment opportunities. The scheme would apply to all unsecured creditors and would bind the Policyholders Protection Board, PPB. It would last for eight years, would survive a winding up order and would include a dispute resolution procedure. The issues before the court were (1) whether the division of creditors into two classes was appropriate; (2) was it appropriate that the scheme be able to survive a winding up order, and (3) the position of PPB.

Held, allowing the application, that the scheme would be approved. (1) Division into classes had to be assessed on the particular circumstances of a case whilst bearing in mind factors of fairness, the influential power of the majority within a class and practical common sense. Applying those tests it was not necessary or helpful in the instant case to divide the classes further, *Sovereign Life Assurance Co (In Liquidation) v. Dodd* [1892] 2 Q.B. 573 applied; (2) the court had power under the Companies Act 1985 s.425 to make a scheme binding after liquidation and therefore it was only common sense that a court should be able to approve such a scheme prior to liquidation, *Bank of Credit and Commerce International SA (In Liquidation) (No.3), Re* [1993] B.C.L.C. 1490, [1994] C.L.Y. 2649 and *Kempe v. Ambassador Insurance Co (In Liquidation)* [1998] 1 W.L.R. 271, [1998] C.L.Y. 3299 applied, and (3) although the scheme in relation to PBB would be in contravention of the provisions of the Insolvency Rules 1986 r.4.90, the court had the power to approve it and it was right in the particular circumstances of this case that that power should be exercised.

ANGLO AMERICAN INSURANCE CO LTD, *Re*; *sub nom.* ANGLO AMERICAN INSURANCE LTD, *Re* [2001] 1 B.C.L.C. 755, Neuberger, J., Ch D (Companies Ct).

3749. **Corporate insolvency – liquidators – assistance – examination of persons named in letters of request issued by Supreme Court of Australia**

[Insolvency Act 1986 s.426.]

The liquidator of DG, a South Australian company, sought orders under the Insolvency Act 1986 s.426 for seven persons to be examined in England by an Australian judge under letters of request issued by the Australian Supreme Court as to matters arising from a 1987 takeover that DG had been involved in. C and three of the others mentioned in the letters objected to the application on the ground that they either worked, or were resident, in Poland and it would be inconvenient for them to travel to England.

Held, allowing the application, that the court had discretion as to whether to accede to the letters of request. Factual errors contained in the letters did not serve to vitiate them, given their intended purpose in determining the truth. Australian law provided the most appropriate forum as all the relevant factors were closely connected with that jurisdiction and the request for assistance was validly made under Australian law, *England v. Smith* [2001] Ch. 419, [2001] C.L.Y. 3463 considered.

DUKE GROUP LTD v. CARVER [2001] B.P.I.R. 459, Jonathan Parker, J., Ch D.

3750. Corporate insolvency – liquidators – consultation – compromise agreement reached between liquidators – duty to consult surety claiming subrogation rights

[Insolvency Act 1986 s.168(5).]

MTL, a company owned and controlled by HA, carried out a substantial part of its business in Nigeria. Following action by the Central Bank of Nigeria, as a result of which payments owed by Nigerians to foreign creditors such as HA were frozen, a number of debts owed to MTL were converted into interest bearing promissory notes. A total of 19 promissory notes were issued and held by BCCI, a bank. A charge was later granted by MTL to BCCI over those promissory notes in relation to which BCCI provided banking services. M, the brothers of HA, held accounts in the joint names of AH with BCCI in Luxembourg. Contractual liens and pledges were entered into through which the sums held in the accounts secured MTL's indebtedness to BCCI. Subsequent to MTL going into liquidation owing BCCI substantial sums, BCCI opted to rely on its own security rather than prove in the liquidation. In exercising its security rights under the liens, BCCI applied the funds held in the accounts of M to discharge part of MTL's indebtedness. Proceedings brought by M for recovery of the moneys were stayed following the appointment of provisional liquidators for BCCI. The liquidator for MTL challenged BCCI's right to all of the promissory notes on the ground that they were not all covered by the charge. After concern had been expressed as to the decline in value of the promissory notes, the liquidators for BCCI sold them with encouragement from M. Protracted negotiations ensued between the liquidators of BCCI and MTL and a compromise agreement was reached, without consultation with M, by which the net sale proceeds were divided. As a result, the moneys taken by BCCI failed to discharge MTL's indebtedness. BCCI, had they taken all the sale proceeds, would have been in a position to repay the moneys taken from M's accounts. M brought proceedings under the Insolvency Act 1986 s.168(5) seeking to set aside the agreement and to gain a declaration that they were entitled to subrogation in respect of BCCI's rights in the promissory notes. The liquidators of BCCI and MTL successfully applied for the proceedings to be struck out, the judge holding that their actions had been reasonable. M appealed, contending that the liquidators had been under a duty to consult them before entering into the compromise agreement.

Held, dismissing the appeal, that (1) as M had been a surety claiming subrogation rights, they were not, for the purpose of s.168(5) of the Act, a "person aggrieved" by the decision of the liquidator, *Edennote Ltd, Re* [1996] 2 B.C.L.C. 389, [1996] C.L.Y. 3490 applied. An outsider to the liquidation who was dissatisfied by the actions of the liquidator could not, except in circumstances where directly affected and without other means of redress, challenge those actions under s.168(5) of the Act, *Hans Place Ltd, Re* [1993] B.C.L.C. 768, [1993] C.L.Y. 2384 considered; (2) the liquidators had been entitled to use their discretion when entering into the compromise agreement and had been under no duty to consult or notify M. The imposition of such an obligation would create a fetter on the freedom of a creditor to exercise the power of sale over a charged property as and in the manner in which he chose, *China and South Seas Bank Ltd v. Tan* [1990] 1 A.C. 536, [1990] C.L.Y. 2440 considered and *Buckingham International Plc (In Liquidation) (No.2), Re* [1998] 2 B.C.L.C. 369, [1999] C.L.Y. 3305 distinguished, and (3) s.168(5) did not enable claims for compensation to be made against a liquidator. Liquidators as agents of a company had no fiduciary duties to the creditors of a company and therefore could not possess any fiduciary obligations in relation to parties who were not creditors notwithstanding that the company for which they were acting might be liable.

MAHOMED v. MORRIS (NO.2) [2000] 2 B.C.L.C. 536, Peter Gibson, L.J., CA.

3751. Corporate insolvency – liquidators – disclosure – refusal by former solicitor to disclose files relating to tax position

The liquidators of a company, L, which was in voluntary liquidation, were replaced by K at the behest of the Inland Revenue, which claimed there was a potential capital gains tax liability of £2.5 million. K sought files held by WM, L's former solicitors that related to its affairs. WM, which was still acting for L's holding company, declined to provide the files unless K gave a personal undertaking not to disclose them to the Revenue. He declined to give such undertaking. WM applied for directions that if the files were passed to K he should not release them without first obtaining a court order.

Held, dismissing the application, that K was entitled to the files by virtue of his position. Although WM had standing as a creditor, it was actually attempting to further the interests of potential debtors, which were inimical to L's creditors. L would not be harmed by the disclosure and a successful claim by the Revenue could lead to a dividend in circumstances where the creditors would otherwise have obtained nothing, *Deloitte & Touche AG v. Johnson* [1999] 1 W.L.R. 1605, [1999] C.L.Y. 3314.

WALKER MORRIS (A FIRM) v. KHALASTCHI [2001] 1 B.C.L.C. 1, Nicholas Strauss Q.C, Ch D (Companies Court).

3752. Corporate insolvency – schemes of arrangement – sanction sought for scheme incorporating provision for adjudicator to resolve all disputes

[Insolvency Act 1986 Sch.4, s.135(4); Human Rights Act 1998 Sch.1 Part I Art.6.]

A company, H, applied for sanction of a scheme of arrangement between H and its creditors. Three questions arose for determination, namely (1) should the court sanction the scheme despite the fact that it contained a clause for the resolution of disputes by a scheme adjudicator and further provided that the adjudicator's decision was final and binding therefore apparently precluding recourse to the courts; (2) did the provision for resolution by the adjudicator infringe the right to fair trial under the Human Rights Act 1998 Sch.1 Part I Art.6, and (3) did the court have power to approve the compromise given that H was only in provisional liquidation.

Held, adjourning the matter pending the hearing of an earlier appeal, that (1) on the face of the scheme there was no limit to the matters that the scheme adjudicator could determine. However, in reality, the adjudicator's powers were limited to issues arising from three clauses and the scheme could easily be modified to make this clear. Despite a clause stating that the adjudicator's decision was final and binding this was only so far as the law permitted. The modifications to the scheme required to make those points clear would not materially affect the scheme as a whole; (2) the scheme would only infringe Art.6 if it was compulsory, but on the facts of the instant case it could not be viewed as genuinely compulsory. Those creditors who had voted at the relevant meeting had voted unanimously in favour of the scheme and therefore it could not be said that the scheme had been imposed upon them. Further, the meeting had been widely publicised and H had taken every step to ensure that the creditors knew of the proposals and had had the opportunity to attend the meeting. In consequence, the risk that creditors would not have been aware of the proposals was minimal, *Bramelid v. Sweden (8588/79, 8589/79)* (1983) 5 E.H.R.R. 249 distinguished, and (3) under the Insolvency Act 1986 Sch.4 the court only had power to sanction compromise if the company was in compulsory liquidation. H was not and did not intend this to happen. However under s.135(4) of the Act the court could confer powers on the provisional liquidator and so grant him power to compromise subject to the sanction of the court.

HAWK INSURANCE CO LTD, *Re* [2001] B.C.C. 57, Arden, J., Ch D (Companies Ct).

3753. **Corporate insolvency – transactions at an undervalue – consideration – commercial reality**

[Insolvency Act 1986 s.238, s.238(4).]

BD appealed against an order, made on an application under the Insolvency Act 1986 s.238, that it should pay £725,000 with interest to P, the liquidator of AJB. It had been found that BD had acquired the business and assets of AJB at an undervalue. The acquisition had been achieved by AJB transferring its business and assets to a subsidiary company, the share capital of which BD had acquired for £1. Both the trial judge ([1998] 1 B.C.L.C. 700, [1998] C.L.Y. 3315) and the Court of Appeal ([1999] 1 W.L.R. 2052, [1999] C.L.Y. 3293) had refused to find that a collateral agreement whereby AJB would be paid four yearly instalments of £312,500 for the rental of computer equipment was consideration for the sale. The covenant for the rental had been sublet to BD by AJB despite an absolute bar in the head lease.

Held, dismissing the appeal, that it was necessary in the instant case to identify for the purposes of s.238(4) the "consideration" rather than the "transaction". Such consideration had included the collateral agreement. However, in valuing that consideration for the purposes of s.238(4), the court should have regard to reality and not speculative suggestion. The collateral agreement was so precarious as to make it worthless, as the headlessors had almost immediately declared the making of it to be a repudiatory breach. It had therefore held no value to BD, and as a result the value of the consideration was restricted to the share sale agreement. It followed accordingly that BD had acquired AJB's business and assets at an undervalue and was liable for the payments due.

PHILLIPS (LIQUIDATOR OF AJ BEKHOR & CO) v. BREWIN DOLPHIN BELL LAWRIE LTD (FORMERLY BREWIN DOLPHIN & CO LTD); *sub nom.* PHILLIPS v. BREWIN DOLPHIN BELL LAWRIE LTD, [2001] UKHL 2, [2001] 1 W.L.R. 143, Lord Scott of Foscote, HL.

3754. **Corporate insolvency – transactions at an undervalue – conspiracy alleged against receivers – world wide Mareva injunction to protect creditor's interests**

[Insolvency Act 1986 s.423.]

D obtained judgment in the estimated sum of £600,000 against PM, a company that was unable to meet its liability and receivers were appointed. All PM's remaining assets were sold for £59,250 to a shell company, A, that assumed its name and to all intents and purposes carried on its business. The former managing director and the chairman of PM became, respectively, managing director and company secretary of A. D sought relief from a transaction at an undervalue under the Insolvency Act 1986 s.423 and alleged conspiracy. D also obtained a world wide ex parte Mareva injunction to protect his rights and S applied to strike out D's statement of claim and for the Mareva injunction to be set aside. The application succeeded in part at first instance ([1999] B.C.C. 836, [1999] C.L.Y. 3292) and the Mareva injunction was discharged. D sought permission to appeal against the discharge of the Mareva injunction.

Held, refusing the application, that the judge at first instance had correctly found that there was no cause of action under s.423 as there was no evidence that the receivers had taken part in the alleged conspiracy. Therefore, the scope of the Mareva injunction was unjustified and D had no prospect of succeeding on appeal against the first instance decision.

DORA v. SIMPER [2000] 2 B.C.L.C. 561, Morritt, L.J., CA.

3755. Corporate insolvency – winding up – compulsory winding up – public interest – companies sub letting properties for housing benefit payments

[Insolvency Act 1986 s.124A.]

The Secretary of State applied for an order to wind up six companies on the ground of public interest under the Insolvency Act 1986 s.124A. The Secretary of State claimed that the companies had operated as a single business, leasing residential properties in order to sublet them to homeless people so as to attract housing benefit payments. It was further submitted that the companies had failed to pay rent due, delayed payments by the use of spurious proceedings and counterclaims, made false statements relating to benefits and the terms and effects of their leases and failed to deliver possession at the end of leases or to keep proper records. Only two companies, E and F, resisted the petition, arguing that they were run independently of the other companies, were solvent and did not deal with the public.

Held, granting the application, that E did have dealings with the public in the form of its tenants and local authorities, and both E's and F's records were inadequate and their businesses were sufficiently intermingled with the other companies so that they could reasonably be regarded as sharing the same defects. It was particularly important that businesses concerned with housing benefits should maintain proper records. Although specific damage to the public interest had not been shown against either E or F, it was in the public interest for all six companies to be wound up, particularly as this would enable them all to be dealt with together so that the liquidator could determine the truth of the situation.

SECRETARY OF STATE FOR TRADE AND INDUSTRY v. LEYTON HOUSING TRUSTEES LTD [2000] 2 B.C.L.C. 808, Carnwath, J., Ch D.

3756. Corporate insolvency – winding up – corporate personality – recovery of costs from company director

[Supreme Court Act 1981 s.51.]

B appealed against an order, made pursuant to the Supreme Court Act 1981 s.51, that he should be personally liable for the Secretary of State's costs in respect of two public interest petitions which sought to wind up two companies effectively owned and controlled by B. The trial judge had found that B, a director of both companies, had acted in his own interests and not those of the company when defending the two petitions, and that the circumstances of the case justified the costs order against B as a non party. B argued that the judge had erred in the exercise of his discretion as there had been no allegations of dishonesty made against him, and he had, he submitted, acted in the best interests of the company as he had been advised that there was a reasonable prospect of defending the petitions. Moreover, the order amounted to lifting the corporate veil and was wrong.

Held, dismissing the appeal, that in the absence of special circumstances, a company director would not be liable for the costs of a winding up petition provided he held a bona fide belief that the company had an arguable defence and that it was in the companies' interest to defend the claim. In the instant case, the judge had been correct to conclude that B had defended the petitions in his own interests and not those of the companies and that he should therefore be liable for the costs of the petitions.

SECRETARY OF STATE FOR TRADE AND INDUSTRY v. BACKHOUSE; *sub nom.* NORTH WEST HOLDINGS PLC (IN LIQUIDATION) (COSTS), *Re*, [2001] EWCA Civ 67, [2001] 1 B.C.L.C. 468, Aldous, L.J., CA.

3757. **Corporate insolvency – winding up – directors – private examination – jurisdiction of Alderney court – examination ordered to aid High Court – Guernsey**

[Insolvency Act 1986 s.426; Insolvency Act 1986 (Guernsey) Order 1989 (SI 1989 2409).]

A winding up order was made against M, a company of which CS and his wife, SS, had formerly been directors. CS and SS were residents of Alderney and the High Court requested the Court of Alderney to aid its examination of M's affairs under the Insolvency Act 1986 s.426 by conducting a private examination of CS and SS and taking control of company papers in their possession. The Court of Alderney obtained the records under an ex parte order. An inter partes hearing was subsequently held, at which SC unsuccessfully requested an adjournment so that they could obtain legal representation. CS unsuccessfully appealed against this refusal to the Royal Court of Guernsey. CS appealed to the Guernsey Court of Appeal.

Held, dismissing the appeal, that the Court of Alderney had authority to carry out a private examination on a request from the High Court, pursuant to s.426(5), under the Insolvency Act 1986 (Guernsey) Order 1989. The court could refuse to act if there were compelling reasons to do so, *Tucker, Re* (Unreported, February 6, 1989) applied, but none were disclosed on the facts of the instant case.

SLINN v. OFFICIAL RECEIVER [2000] B.P.I.R. 847, John Murray Chadwick Q.C., CA (Gue).

3758. **Corporate insolvency – winding up – letter of request to Australian court – transfer of shares held by nominee – Australia**

[Corporations Law (Australia) s.574(3), s.574(5), s.581(3).]

T, a broker on the London Stock Exchange, was the subject of a 1991 English winding up order with S appointed as liquidator. CN, an Australian company, acted on T's behalf and held shares on trust for T and its clients. On CN's dissolution in Australia, such property vested in ASC. S obtained an order from the English court, directing the sale of shares listed as being held by CN and a letter of request from that court to the Australian court sought its assistance in ordering the sale of the shares. S subsequently sought the assistance of the Australian court, including the delivery up of shares not listed in the English court order or the letter of request.

Held, allowing the application with time granted to ASC to consider it position regarding the unlisted shares, that the evidence showed that all the shares now vested in ASC were held on trust for T, and delivery up would have been ordered if this was an Australian liquidation. However, although the Corporations Law s.581(3) allowed orders to be made pursuant to a letter of request, this did not apply to the non listed shares. Therefore an order would be made under s.574(3), reinstating CN, with a direction under s.574(5) for ASC to re transfer the shares it held on the same terms as they had been held by CN as trustee for T and its clients.

SMITH v. AUSTRALIAN SECURITIES COMMISSION [2000] B.P.I.R. 853, Hayne, J., Sup Ct (Vic).

3759. **Corporate insolvency – winding up – undertakings – appointment of provisional liquidators**

FSA applied for a provisional liquidator to be appointed in respect of GM, having presented a petition to wind up GM on the grounds that it had been carrying on an unauthorised investment business, an unauthorised deposit taking business and was insolvent. GM had given undertakings not to deplete the value of its assets, but had breached that undertaking, as well as its duty of disclosure, by making various payments out of bank accounts, including a payment from a previously undisclosed

French bank account. GM submitted that it had received two substantial cheques so that it was no longer insolvent.

Held, granting the application, that no reliance could be placed on the cheques, there being no evidence that the cheques had been presented for payment. GM was still insolvent, and the appointment of the provisional liquidator was ordered to take control of the GM's assets.

GOODWILL MERCHANT FINANCIAL SERVICES LTD, *Re*; *sub nom*. FINANCIAL SERVICES AUTHORITY v. GOODWILL MERCHANT FINANCIAL LTD [2001] 1 B.C.L.C. 259, Sir Andrew Morritt, Ch D (Companies Ct).

3760. **Cross border insolvency – ships – arrest – Belgian trustee seeking release – security for maritime lien – New Zealand**

CV, a ship under arrest in NZ, was owned by A, a Belgian company subject to bankruptcy proceedings in Belgium. Belgian trustees had been appointed to realise A's worldwide assets, including CV. The Belgian court requested recognition of its order in NZ, so that CV could be released and sold outside NZ. However, CV's master and crew claimed security over the ship in the sum of NZD 250,000 for unpaid wages and redundancy payments, which would be lost if CV was released. The trustees agreed that the master and crew should continue to enjoy the same priority they had in NZ if CV was released and for the payment of security to that effect in NZ. In addition, the High Court Registrar sought the reimbursement of expenditure made for the supply of goods and services to CV during the period of its arrest.

Held, that CV was to be released pursuant to the NZ court's duty of assistance, given the compatibility of Belgian and NZ insolvency law. The release was conditional on payment of security in NZ for the claims of the master and crew and reimbursement of the Registrar's expenses. The absolute priority traditionally afforded to maritime liens could be relaxed, given the efficacy of modern communications between ships and their owners and the mutual recognition of jurisdictions in insolvency matters where assets were located at different locations around the world.

TURNERS & GROWERS EXPORTERS LTD v. CORNELIS VEROLME, THE [2000] B.P.I.R. 896, Williams, J., HC (NZ).

3761. **Directors – insolvent companies – application to partnerships**

INSOLVENT PARTNERSHIPS (AMENDMENT) ORDER 2001, SI 2001 767; made under the Insolvency Act 1986 s.411; and the Company Disqualification Act 1986 s.21. In force: April 2, 2001; £2.00.

This Order amends the Insolvent Partnerships Order 1994 (SI 1994 2421) to provide that additional sections of the Company Directors Disqualification Act 1986, are applied to insolvent partnerships where appropriate.

3762. **Directors – insolvent companies – disqualification orders**

INSOLVENT COMPANIES (DISQUALIFICATION OF UNFIT DIRECTORS) PROCEEDINGS (AMENDMENT) RULES 2001, SI 2001 765; made under the Insolvency Act 1986 s.411; and the Company Disqualification Act 1986 s.21. In force: April 2, 2001; £1.50.

These Rules amend the Insolvent Companies (Disqualification of Unfit Directors) Proceedings Rules 1987 (SI 1987 2023) by revoking r.9 which provided for the time when a disqualification order took effect. This is now dealt with in the Company Directors Disqualification Act 1986 s.1 (2), as amended by the Insolvency Act 2000 s.5(2).

3763. **Directors – insolvent companies – reports on directors' conduct**

INSOLVENT COMPANIES (REPORTS ON CONDUCT OF DIRECTORS) (AMENDMENT) RULES 2001, SI 2001 764; made under the Insolvency Act

1986 s.411; and the Company Disqualification Act 1986 s.21. In force: April 2, 2001; £3.00.

These Rules substitute new forms in place of those contained in the Insolvent Companies (Reports on Conduct of Directors) Rules 1996 (SI 1996 1909). The new forms are substantially the same as the previous forms, but contain minor further requirements for information to be provided by office-holders to the Insolvency Practitioners Compliance Unit of the Insolvency Service.

3764. Fees

INSOLVENCY FEES (AMENDMENT) ORDER 2001, SI 2001 761; made under the Insolvency Act 1986 s.415. In force: April 2, 2001; £1.50.

This Order, which amends the Insolvency Fees Order 1986 (SI 1986 2030), prescribes the fee payable in respect of the purchase of Government securities pursuant to a request made by a trustee of a bankrupt's estate under Reg.23A of the Insolvency Regulations 1994 (SI 1994 2507).

3765. Insolvency Act 2000 (c.39) – Commencement No.1 and Transitional Provisions Order

INSOLVENCY ACT 2000 (COMMENCEMENT NO.1 AND TRANSITIONAL PROVISIONS) ORDER 2001, SI 2001 766 (C.27); made under the Insolvency Act 2000 s.16. Commencement details: bringing into force various provisions of the Act on April 2, 2001; £1.75.

This Order provides for the coming into force of the Insolvency Act 2000 s.5 to s.8 and Sch.4, which relate to the disqualification of company directors, s.9, relating to administration orders, s.10, relating to investigation and prosecution of malpractice, s.11, relating to restriction of use of answers obtained under compulsion, s.12, relating to insolvent estates of deceased persons, and s.13, relating to interest on sums held in Insolvency Services Account, together with certain repeals in Sch.5, on April 2, 2001.

3766. Insolvency Act 2000 (c.39) – Commencement No.2 Order

INSOLVENCY ACT 2000 (COMMENCEMENT NO.2) ORDER 2001, SI 2001 1751 (C.59); made under the Insolvency Act 2000 s.16. Commencement details: bringing into force various provisions of the Act on May 11, 2001; £1.50.

This Order provides for the coming into force of the Insolvency Act 2000 s.1 and Sch.1 para.4 insofar as they insert Sch.A1 para.5 and para.45 (1) (2) (3) (5) into the Insolvency Act 1986. The provisions of Sch.A1 introduce the option of a moratorium for a small company whilst directors propose a voluntary arrangement and para.5 of that Schedule allows the Secretary of State to make regulations to modify the qualifications for eligibility of a company for a moratorium.

3767. Insolvency practitioners – removal – move to new firm – notification of creditors

[Insolvency Act 1986; Insolvency Rules 1986 (SI 1986 1925) r.4.102(5), r.4.103(4).]

C, a licensed insolvency practitioner, applied to be removed from 116 of his appointments on the ground that he had moved to a different firm.

Held, granting the application, that C had new commitments and consequently the time he could give to each insolvency was restricted, and in view of the fact that the staff involved with the insolvencies were to remain with his former firm, the refusal of an order would mean more work and expense, *Sankey Furniture Ltd, ex p. Harding, Re* [1995] 2 B.C.L.C. 594, [1996] C.L.Y. 3481 distinguished. It was decided that because of the cost involved in notifying creditors by holding a general meeting or by writing to each creditor individually and the need to keep costs to a minimum, a block advertisement in the London Gazette should be taken, as supported by the Insolvency Rules 1986 r.4.102(5) and r.4.103(4) and the Insolvency Act 1986, *Equity Nominees Ltd, Re* [1999] 2 B.C.L.C.19, [1999] C.L.Y. 3301 not followed.

CORK v. ROLPH *The Times*, December 21, 2000, Neuberger, J., Ch D.

3768. Insolvency proceedings – Insolvency Services Account – balance of accounts

INSOLVENCY (AMENDMENT) REGULATIONS 2001, SI 2001 762; made under the Insolvency Rules 1986 (SI 1986 1925) r.12.1; and the Insolvency Act 1986 s.412, Sch.9 para.30. In force: April 2, 2001; £1.75.

These Regulations amend the Insolvency Regulations 1994 (SI 1994 2507) which make provision for the regulation of administrative matters arising in connection with the winding up of companies and the bankruptcy of individuals in England and Wales. They provide for the investment of funds standing to the credit of bankrupts in the Insolvency Services Account and for the crediting of interest on balances in excess of £2,000 standing to the credit of bankrupts in that Account.

3769. Insolvency proceedings – Insolvency Services Account – trustees powers and duties

INSOLVENCY (AMENDMENT) RULES 2001, SI 2001 763; made under the Insolvency Act 1986 s.412, Sch.9 para.21, Sch.9 para.30. In force: April 2, 2001; £1.50.

These Rules amend the Insolvency Rules 1986 (SI 1986 1925) which set out detailed procedures for the conduct of all company and individual insolvency proceedings in England and Wales under the Insolvency Act 1986. They amend the power to make regulations by ensuring that regulations may be made with respect to the investment of moneys coming into the hands of a trustee of a bankrupt's estate and for the payment of interest on sums which are paid by such a trustee into the Insolvency Services Account.

3770. Insolvency proceedings – winding-up of credit institutions – Council Directive

European Parliament and Council Directive 2001/24 of 4 April 2001 on the reorganisation and winding up of credit institutions. [2001] OJ L125/15.

3771. Insolvency proceedings – winding-up of insurance undertakings – Council Directive

European Parliament and Council Directive 2001/17 of 19 March 2001 on the reorganisation and winding-up of insurance undertakings. [2001] OJ L110/28.

3772. Liquidation – pari passu – hotchpot principle – letter of credit issued prior to liquidation by way of security for court proceedings

T, an insurance company in liquidation, appealed against a ruling that monies paid by its bankers, pursuant to a letter of credit previously issued as security in American court proceedings, to D, an American insurance company, following the entry of judgment in default, were not part of T's assets for the purposes of the liquidation. Proceedings had previously been issued by D against T for alleged breach of a retrocession agreement concluded between the parties. For the purposes of New York insurance law T was considered to be a foreign or alien insurer and had therefore been required to deposit security with the District Court in New York, capable of satisfying any judgment eventually obtained. T contended that D had to bring into account the monies received by way of hotchpot before becoming entitled to receive any dividend in the liquidation, on the basis that a failure to do so would give D an unfair advantage in relation to other creditors and result in an unequal distribution of the available assets.

Held, dismissing the appeal, that the "hotchpot" principle had no application since the monies had been paid pursuant to the letter of credit, security for which had been provided before T went into liquidation. Accordingly the monies received by D had never been monies which would otherwise have been available for distribution in the winding up, *Banco de Portugal v. Waddell* (1879-80) L.R. 5 App. Cas. 161 and *Moor v. Anglo Italian Bank* (1878-79) L.R. 10 Ch. D. 681 applied.

CLEAVER v. DELTA AMERICAN REINSURANCE CO (IN LIQUIDATION), [2001] UKPC 6, [2001] 2 A.C. 328, Lord Scott of Foscote, Privy Council (Cayman Islands).

3773. Liquidators – assignment of contractual obligations

See CONTRACTS: Quadmost Ltd (In Liquidation) v. Reprotech (Pebsham) Ltd. §964

3774. Official Receiver – disclosure to obtain documents for disqualification proceedings

[Insolvency Act 1986 s.235, s.236.]

The Official Receiver appealed against an order ([2001] 1 W.L.R. 730, [2000] C.L.Y. 659) allowing an appeal against an order for the production of documents. The original order had been made under the Insolvency Act 1986 s.236 against former accountants and solicitors of P, a company in liquidation. The Official Receiver had brought disqualification proceedings against a former director of P and the purpose of the application was to obtain evidence for use in the disqualification proceedings. The issue for determination by the court was whether the court had jurisdiction to make an order under s.236 in such circumstances.

Held, dismissing the appeal, that the Official Receiver was not entitled to documents from the former accountants and solicitors of a company in liquidation where the documents were to be used as evidence in disqualification proceedings. In circumstances where a company was not being wound up by the court, the appropriate applicant in any disqualification proceedings was the Secretary of State who was unable to invoke the powers contained in s.235 and s.236 of the Act. The purpose of s.235 and s.236 was to assist the liquidator in the winding up of a company and to assist the Official Receiver in investigating the cause of the company's failure and in preparing his report to the court with the result that the application in the instant case had been brought for an improper purpose.

PANTMAENOG TIMBER CO LTD, *Re*; OFFICIAL RECEIVER v. WADGE RAPPS & HUNT; OFFICIAL RECEIVER v. GRANT THORNTON; OFFICIAL RECEIVER v. MEADE-KING (A FIRM); *sub nom.* OFFICIAL RECEIVER v. HAY; PANTMAENOG TIMBER CO (IN LIQUIDATION), *Re*, [2001] EWCA Civ 1227, [2002] 2 W.L.R. 20, Chadwick, L.J., CA.

3775. Practice directions – appeals – procedure

[Insolvency Rules 1986 (SI 1986 1925) r.7.49; Civil Procedure Rules 1998 (SI 1998 3132) Part 52 r.3.]

A Practice Direction came into force on May 2, 2000, to be read in conjunction with *Practice Direction (Ch D: Insolvency Proceedings) (No.1)* [1999] B.C.C. 727, [1999] C.L.Y. 3318, para.17 of which it revokes. From that date, an appeal from the decision of a district judge or circuit judge of the county court or of a registrar of the High Court lies to a High Court judge. Procedure is governed by the Insolvency Rules 1986 r.7.49, which import the Court of Appeal rules relating to appeals. A further appeal requires the permission of the Court of Appeal. An appeal from the decision of a High Court judge that is not a first appeal requires the permission of either the judge concerned or the Court of

Appeal and is subject to the Civil Procedure Rules 1998 Part 52 r.3. Applications for time extensions in which to appeal must give reasons for the delay. Respondents may seek an order upholding a lower court order on different terms by means of a respondent's notice. An appeal does not constitute a stay against a lower court order unless that court so orders. Appeals are restricted to a review of the lower court decision so that oral evidence will not be heard, or evidence before the lower court examined, unless ordered by the appeal court. Addresses are also given for the lodging of appeal notices at the Royal Courts of Justice and at other appeal venues.

PRACTICE DIRECTION (CH D: INSOLVENCY PROCEEDINGS) (NO.2) [2000] B.C.C. 927, Sir Robert Andrew Morritt V.C., Ch D.

3776. **Sale of assets – receivers – prior court approval – locus standi of disappointed purchaser to appeal – Canada**

The receiver of H applied for and obtained the court's approval for the sale of certain of H's assets to one of the creditors, S. There had been several competing unsuccessful bidders including B. B sought to appeal against the order approving the sale.

Held, refusing permission to appeal, and finding that B had no locus standi to appeal against the order because it was not an interested party, *Crown Trust Co v. Rosenberg* (1986) 60 O.R. (2d) 87 followed. Although B had been heard in the court below it had been in its capacity as a creditor. B had no maintainable interest as an unsuccessful bidder *Royal Bank v. Soundair Corp* (1991) 4 O.R. (3d) 1 (Ont CA) distinguished.

SKYEPHARMA PLC v. HYAL PHARMACEUTICAL CORP [2001] B.P.I.R. 163, O'Connor, J.A., CA (Ont).

3777. **Sale of business – receivers – contractual status on withdrawal of purchaser**

See CONTRACTS: Phoenix International Life Sciences Inc v. Rilett. §962

3778. **Share transfers – creditors – membership of the London Stock Exchange – deprivation of share upon insolvency**

MM, a company in liquidation and a former member of the London Stock Exchange brought an action against LSE, the company of which traders on the exchange were required to be members, seeking reinstatement as a member of the exchange or compensation for the loss of its share in the exchange. Under LSE's articles of association, a member of the exchange was required to acquire a "B" share and to surrender that share upon ceasing to be a member. Article 8 provided that, inter alia, upon a member becoming bankrupt it had to transfer its "B" share back to the exchange. The issue before the court concerned whether such a provision was contrary to the rule as set out in *Harrison, ex p. Jay, Re* (1880) L.R. 14 Ch. D. 19 that a contract, whereby property would remain a person's until their bankruptcy and thereafter transfer to another thus depriving the bankrupt's creditors, was invalid. Shortly after MM had transferred its "B" share back to the exchange, LSE had demutualised. As a result, the "B" share would have had a value of nearly £3 million.

Held, giving judgment for LSE, that having regard to the LSE rules and articles of association, it could not be said that prior to demutualisation the ownership of a "B" share amounted to the ownership of a free standing asset. Under Article 8 it was apparent that a "B" share could only be held by member firms and that pursuant to Article 26, it was for LSE's directors to decide who to elect as member firms. Whilst demutualisation had been under contemplation at the time MM had been required to transfer back to LSE its "B" share, the date at which that decision was formally taken was after the "B" share had been transferred back. It followed that there had been no infringement of the rule, *Bombay Official Assignee v. Shroff* (1932) 48 T.L.R. 443 applied and *Harrison, ex p. Jay, Re, Borland's Trustee v. Steel Bros & Co Ltd* [1901] 1 Ch. 279 and *British*

Eagle International Airlines Ltd v. Compagnie Nationale Air France [1975] 1 W.L.R. 758, [1975] C.L.Y. 320 considered.
MONEY MARKETS INTERNATIONAL STOCKBROKERS LTD (IN LIQUIDATION) v. LONDON STOCK EXCHANGE LTD [2002] 1 W.L.R. 1150, Neuberger, J., Ch D.

3779. Statutory demands – appeals – creditor producing late evidence – failure to attend hearing

C's application to set aside a statutory demand founded on a guarantee was dismissed by the county court. In his initial application to set aside the statutory demand he said he had never signed as a guarantor. In support of that bare assertion nothing was produced by way of forensic examination of the lease and nothing was put forward to suggest who might have forged C's signature. On the day of the hearing, evidence was admitted which sought to suggest who was responsible for the forgery. However the judge was not satisfied that any convincing material had been put forward to the effect that the signature was a forgery. C appealed but the day before the hearing, C wrote to the court saying that he would not be able to attend due to illness and that he had entered into an IVA. A general medical certificate was supplied in support but it did not give any details as to why he was unfit to travel. The creditor, G, sought permission to adduce fresh evidence and an order dismissing the appeal.

Held, granting permission to adduce fresh evidence and dismissing the appeal, that (1) there was no sufficient explanation why C had failed to attend the hearing and the court would accede to G's application to adduce fresh evidence and proceed to hear the matter but leave an ultimate opportunity to C to challenge the decision reached on a prima facie basis. It was all too easy otherwise to obtain a deferment of a decision which in the interests of justice ought to be given as soon as possible; (2) the fact that C had produced evidence before the district judge at such a late stage meant that it was just to permit the creditor to adduce further evidence in answer on appeal, and (3) if C, having consulted his solicitor, considered that there was genuinely a point to be argued on the appeal and had a good credible explanation as to why he was not present at the hearing, either by himself or through a solicitor, then the matter could be considered afresh. On the present material it would be a negation of justice to require the creditor to come back for another hearing.
CEVELLO v. CURRYS GROUP PLC [2000] B.P.I.R. 976, Jacob, J., Ch D.

3780. Statutory demands – setting aside – counterclaims – mutuality

[Insolvency Rules 1986 (SI 1986 1925) r.6.5(4)(a).]
H appealed against the dismissal of his appeal (Times, October 3, 2000, [2000] C.L.Y. 4320) against the refusal of his application to set aside a statutory demand, which had been served on him by B and three other individuals who had formerly been his partners in a firm of solicitors, MJ. The sum claimed in the statutory demand represented H's share of the rent which B and the others were seeking to recover as trustees of MJ. Relying on the Insolvency Rules 1986 r.6.5(4)(a), which enabled the court to set aside a statutory demand if the debtor appeared to have a counterclaim, set off or cross demand equal to, or exceeding the amount of, the debt specified in the statutory demand, H argued that B and his former partners owed him various sums, including his share of a tax repayment and of the proceeds of book debts.

Held, dismissing the appeal (Sir Christopher Staughton concurring as to the outcome but dissenting on the issue of mutuality), that for the purpose of r.6.5(4)(a), a counterclaim or cross demand could not be relied on where the person pursuing it was doing so in a different capacity from that in which the debt referred to in the statutory demand was claimed from him. Whereas the amount claimed in the statutory demand was due to H's former partners personally in their capacity as trustees of MJ, the sums which H was seeking to recover were due from his former partners jointly in their capacity as such. Accordingly, the respective claims of the parties lacked mutuality, *Molesworth, Re* (1907) 51 S.J. 653 applied and *Freeman v. Lomas* (1851) 9 Hare 109, *Debtor (No.87 of 1999), Re* [2000] B.P.I.R. 589, [2000] 3 C.L. 407, *TSB Bank Plc v.*

Platts (No.2) [1998] Lloyd's Rep. Bank. 163, [1998] C.L.Y. 3287 and *Bankruptcy Notice (No.171 of 1934), Re* [1934] Ch. 431 considered.
HURST v. BENNETT (NO.1); *sub nom.* DEBTOR (NO.303 OF 1997), *Re*, [2001] EWCA Civ 182, [2001] 2 B.C.L.C. 290, Arden, L.J., CA.

3781. **Transactions at an undervalue – equitable interests – failure to raise points at previous hearings – abuse of process**

G's wife sought an enquiry into the extent of her beneficial interest in the former matrimonial home and G applied for an earlier order made by the registrar setting aside various transactions on the basis they were at an undervalue, to be set aside. G contended that the property was in negative equity and had not been undervalued.

Held, striking out the applications, that G's wife had failed to raise the issue of a beneficial interest earlier despite relevant applications being before the court, therefore it would be wrong in principle to re-open the enquiry. Further, on the evidence there was no triable issue. G's application was struck out as an abuse of process as G had no interest in any of the transactions covered by the order and therefore no right to be heard. A *Grepe v. Loam* order was made prohibiting G from making any further applications without the permission of the court.

GOPEE v. BEAT [2001] B.P.I.R. 258, Pumfrey, J., Ch D.

3782. **Transactions at an undervalue – gifts – perfection of delivery – intention to defraud creditors**

[Insolvency Act 1986 s.423.]
S applied for summary judgment to strike out LS's claim, brought against her under the Insolvency Act 1986 s.423. S's late husband, AS, a solicitor, had been investigated by LS for serious accounting irregularities and LS sought to recover its costs from AS's estate as a debt. During his lifetime, AS had transferred the matrimonial home, and purportedly its contents, to S. LS contended that (1) the gifts of the house contents to S had not been perfected, and (2) the gifts had been made with the intention of putting the assets outside the reach of creditors and were liable to be set aside.

Held, refusing the application for summary judgment, that (1) LS had no real prospect of showing that the gifts failed for lack of delivery, as the gifts had been transferred to the matrimonial home which, it was accepted, was owned by S, *Cole (A Bankrupt), Re* [1964] Ch. 175, [1963] C.L.Y. 1582 applied, and (2) the manner in which AS had tried to divest himself of his interest in the assets indicated that LS had a real prospect of showing that the gifts had been made with the intention of protecting the assets from the claims of possible creditors.

LAW SOCIETY v. SOUTHALL [2001] B.P.I.R. 303, Hart, J., Ch D.

3783. **Transactions at an undervalue – Inland Revenue – transfer of premises from father to son in consideration of "natural love and affection" – dominant purpose**

[Insolvency Act 1986 s.423.]
The Revenue sought an order setting aside a transfer made by G prior to his death, whereby the beneficial interest in restaurant premises was transferred to his 17 year old son, O, in consideration of "natural love and affection". The Revenue argued that the transaction fulfilled the requirements of the Insolvency Act 1986 s. 423 and should be set aside. O maintained that the purpose of the transaction was that G had wished to secure O's future rather than putting the property beyond the reach of his creditors and because of O's age G had to use the mechanism of a trust.

Held, granting the application, that notwithstanding that G may have intended to secure O's future he had also intended to put assets beyond the reach of his creditors. Where there existed a dual purpose behind the transaction the authorities were undecided on the issue of whether it was necessary to decide which of those two purposes was dominant, *Chohan v. Saggar* [1992] B.C.C. 306, *Lloyds Bank Ltd v. Marcan* [1973] 1 W.L.R. 1387, *Pinewood Joinery v. Starelm Properties Ltd* [1994] B.C.C. 569 and *Arbuthnot Leasing International Ltd v. Havelet Leasing Ltd (No.2)* [1990] B.C.C. 636 considered. However, in the present case, the fact that G chose leave the property in his sole name and no steps were taken until after his death to register O's beneficial interest on the land register were highly significant and did not indicate an overwhelming intention to benefit O at the date of the transaction. Accordingly, the transaction satisfied all the criteria for a transaction at an undervalue pursuant to s.423 and the Revenue was entitled to an order against the insolvent estate.

INLAND REVENUE COMMISSIONERS v. HASHMI [2002] B.P.I.R. 271, Hart, J., Ch D.

3784. Transactions at an undervalue – preferences – limitation period

[Limitation Act 1980 s.8(1), s.9(1); Insolvency Act 1986 s.238, s.239.]

The court was asked to determine as a preliminary issue whether claims brought by A, the liquidator of P Ltd, for orders under the Insolvency Act 1986 s.238 and s.239, had been brought within the relevant limitation period. A had applied to set aside the transfers by P Ltd of the leases of two flats to G, one of its directors. A's application had been issued six years and three months after the order for the winding up of P Ltd had been made.

Held, determining the preliminary issue in favour of A, that (1) an application for an order under s.238 or s.239 was an action on a specialty and was therefore prima facie subject to the limitation period of 12 years set out under the Limitation Act 1980 s.8(1), *Farmizer (Products) Ltd, Re* [1997] 1 B.C.L.C. 589, [1997] C.L.Y. 3056 distinguished; (2) if, however, the application was in substance an application to "recover any sum recoverable" by virtue of those provisions, the six year limitation period prescribed by s.9(1) of the 1980 Act would apply. An application to set aside a payment of money or an application where the only available substantive relief was an order for the payment of money might, for example, be caught by s.9(1); (3) where doubt existed as to whether an application was subject to s.8(1) or s.9(1), the court should look at the reality of the relevant transaction to ascertain the essential nature of the relief being claimed, *West Riding CC v. Huddersfield Corp* [1957] 1 Q.B. 540, [1957] C.L.Y. 2025 applied, and (4) A's application to set aside the transfers of the leases was subject to the limitation period of 12 years under s.8(1). The fact that A might hope to obtain a sum of money at some future date, either by selling the flats once the leases had been revested in P Ltd or by settling the litigation, could not bring the application within s.9(1).

PRIORY GARAGE (WALTHAMSTOW) LTD, *Re* [2001] B.P.I.R. 144, John Randall Q.C., Ch D (Companies Ct).

3785. Transactions at an undervalue – sale of assets – test for determining relevant consideration

[Insolvency Act 1986 s.423.]

J appealed against the granting ([2001] 1 B.C.L.C. 98, [2000] C.L.Y. 3471) of N's application to enforce its security against J. J had granted floating charges over their farm to N, a bank. J got into financial difficulties and set up a company to which they transferred their agricultural assets and granted a tenancy of the farm. The judge had granted N's application on the ground that the transactions had been at undervalue and could therefore be set aside under the Insolvency Act 1986 s.423. J argued that the judge had failed to take into account all the benefits accruing to J, such as the increase in the value of their shares, and, in particular, that he should have adopted the "band of values" approach.

Held, dismissing the appeal, that the judge had taken the right approach. The relevant transactions were the transfer of assets and the granting of the tenancy, which had been entered into in an attempt to avoid liability to N. The only relevant consideration was the money actually paid for those transactions, and not other benefits accruing to J such as the value of shares in the company. The "band of values" test was solely relevant to questions of negligence by valuers and was not appropriate in this context. The judge had been right in ascertaining the actual value of the transaction, and in holding that it had been at an undervalue.

NATIONAL WESTMINSTER BANK PLC v. JONES; *sub nom.* JONES v. NATIONAL WESTMINSTER BANK PLC, [2001] EWCA Civ 1541, [2002] 1 B.C.L.C. 55, Mummery, L.J., CA.

3786. Trustees in bankruptcy – causes of action – abandonment – creditor's loss of set off – New Zealand

[Insolvency Act 1967 (New Zealand) s.86.]

H was adjudged bankrupt with debts of NZD 180,000 for which the Official Assignee could only pay a dividend of NZD 21,000. EJ, a law firm, was owed NZD 13,000 in unpaid fees by H but only received NZD 90 from the Official Assignee. Following H's discharge, his legal adviser informed the Official Assignee that he intended to commence an action against EJ, alleging professional negligence and breach of retainer. The Official Assignee replied to H's adviser on the same day and undertook not to pursue an action against EJ as there were no funds in H's estate. EJ's application to have the Official Assignee's decision quashed under the Insolvency Act 1967 s.86 was refused at first instance and EJ appealed.

Held, allowing the appeal, that the Official Assignee had made a purely administrative decision not to pursue the action and had failed to evaluate the merits of H's proposed action. In doing so, the Official Assignee had not considered whether the action was frivolous or vexatious when he should have been alert to that possibility. Allowing H to commence proceedings against EJ was contrary to the interests of good estate administration and it also prevented EJ from asserting a set off against the balance of H's indebtedness.

JUDD v. OFFICIAL ASSIGNEE [2001] B.P.I.R. 468, Richardson, P., Gault, J., Keith, J., CA (NZ).

3787. Voluntary arrangements – company voluntary arrangements – creditors – enforceability of claim despite existence of CVA

[Insolvency Act 1986 s.7(3).]

AH, a company subject to a company voluntary arrangement, CVA, appealed against a determination that it did not prevent A, a creditor who had agreed to the CVA, from continuing his claim for damages for wrongful dismissal and wrongful detention of chattels. AH submitted that allowing a creditor bound by a CVA to commence proceedings in order to establish his debt would undermine the CVA, and the appropriate remedy was for the creditor to apply to the court under the Insolvency Act 1986 s.7(3). A argued that in the absence of any agreement reached with the supervisor to the CVA, he was entitled to pursue court proceedings.

Held, dismissing the appeal, that as there was no statutory provision which prevented A from continuing with his action, it was necessary to have regard to the terms of the CVA. In the instant case, upon the correct interpretation of its terms, A was not prevented from prosecuting his action against AH, *Sea Voyager Maritime Inc v. Bielecki (t/a Hughes Hooker & Co)* [1999] 1 All E.R. 628, [1998] C.L.Y. 3354 considered.

ALMAN v. APPROACH HOUSING LTD [2001] 1 B.C.L.C. 530, Rimer, J., Ch D.

3788. Voluntary arrangements – company voluntary arrangements – winding up orders – determination by non creditor

[Insolvency Act 1986.]

R, the supervisor of a company voluntary arrangement, CVA, between K and various creditors, applied for a declaration that the funds held by the supervisor were held subject to a trust and were to be applied for the benefit of CVA creditors. L, the liquidator appointed following the winding up of the company, argued that the effect of the winding up order was to terminate the trust in favour of the CVA creditors. L further asserted in the alternative, that the CVA and any trusts had been determined by breaches of the terms of the CVA, and that the money was to be distributed in the company's liquidation.

Held, allowing the application, that examination of the Insolvency Act 1986 did not to lead to the conclusion that a CVA came to an end when a winding up order was made on the petition of a company director or some non CVA creditor, *Excalibur Airways Ltd (In Liquidation), Re* [1998] 1 B.C.L.C. 436, [1998] C.L.Y. 3344 applied. A CVA would determine on a winding up order only if the petitioner was the CVA supervisor or a CVA creditor or where a winding up order had been made in circumstances where the CVA supervisor had failed to bring a petition despite being under an obligation to do so. The money was therefore to be distributed among the CVA creditors.

KUDOS GLASS LTD (IN LIQUIDATION), *Re*; *sub nom*. ROUT v. LEWIS [2001] 1 B.C.L.C. 390, Richard McCombe Q.C., Ch D.

3789. Voluntary arrangements – individual voluntary arrangements – extent of insolvency practitioners duty to scrutinise information provided by debtors

In 1988 P owned numerous nursing homes at the peak of the property market but also had heavy borrowing. When P ran into difficulties and the creditors closed in, P consulted an insolvency practitioner, M. On the basis of a statement of affairs showing a surplus of £900,000 based on property values provided by P, M prepared an IVA which was accepted by the creditors. Following the slump in property values the IVAs were disastrous, leaving P substantially insolvent. P sued M for professional negligence in failing to cater for the possibility that property values might go down, for failing to bind the unsecured element of the debts of secured creditors, for failing to provide for any alternative scheme if the IVA creditors were not paid in full and for failing to provide for the full and final settlement of the creditors' debts.

Held, dismissing the claim, that it was common ground that the standard to be applied was the standards of a competent insolvency practitioner in 1990 when IVAs were rare and untested. M had been entitled to rely on information provided to him by P but he also had a duty to be properly sceptical in respect of any fact which appeared doubtful and required further investigation. Where P had produced independent property valuations M was not to be expected to question them or investigate further. M could not be expected to foresee the forthcoming crash in property values. Even if an alternative dividend payment scheme had been included, on the facts, no dividend would have been paid by P and there would have been no release from the debts.

PITT v. MOND [2001] B.P.I.R. 624, Judge Roger Cooke, Ch D.

3790. Voluntary arrangements – individual voluntary arrangements – nominee's fee – discretionary power of court to refuse – overcharging

O's application for an order permitting an IVA was refused on the ground that the nominee's fee of £2,500 was excessive and that the proposal to make voluntary payments from O's surplus income of £2,500 was not viable. O appealed, contending that there was no power to refuse the application on this basis.

Held, dismissing the appeal, that the court had an unlimited discretion but this should only be exercised in cases of obvious overcharging and after giving the nominee the opportunity to justify that amount. The discretion had been correctly exercised in the instant case, however, given that the judge below had felt that £1,000 was a more appropriate figure.

O'SULLIVAN (JULIE), *Re* [2001] B.P.I.R. 534, Judge Maddocks, Ch D.

3791. Voluntary arrangements – individual voluntary arrangements – secret deal with creditors – entitlement to bankruptcy order

[Insolvency Act 1986 s.262(1), s.276(1)(b).]

S appealed against a finding that CS, a creditor who had voted against his proposal for an individual voluntary arrangement, was entitled to obtain a bankruptcy order against him on the ground that, pursuant to the Insolvency Act

1986 s.276(1)(b), information containing material omissions had been given at a creditors' meeting convened for the purpose of approving the voluntary arrangement. The deputy judge had found that (1) secret payments had been made to two creditors to secure their approval to the voluntary arrangement and that the failure to raise that matter at the creditors' meeting entitled CS to rely on s.276(1)(b), and (2) the secret deal rendered the voluntary arrangement void. S argued that the deputy judge had erred in reaching that conclusion in reliance on principles which applied prior to the implementation of the Act.

Held, dismissing the appeal, that (1) in determining whether a material omission had been made for the purpose of s.276(1)(b), the court had to ask itself whether, had the correct information been supplied, there would have been any material difference to the way in which creditors approached the proposed voluntary arrangement. The deputy judge had been correct to conclude that had the secret deal been disclosed, the creditors' approach to S's voluntary arrangement would have altered. Accordingly, the deputy judge had been right to find that s.276(1)(b) applied. Section 276 enabled creditors to make an informed decision about a proposed voluntary arrangement and mirrored the principles of transparency and good faith that applied to insolvencies under the old law, and (2) the secret deal constituted an irregularity for the purpose of the creditors' meeting. However, the deputy judge had been wrong to rely to such an extent on the older principles at the expense of the statutory regime, and to conclude that the irregularity rendered the voluntary arrangement void. If an individual voluntary arrangement appeared to have been approved at a creditors' meeting, it could only be challenged by the presentation of a bankruptcy petition under s.276(1) or by an application under s.262(1).

CADBURY SCHWEPPES PLC v. SOMJI; *sub nom.* SOMJI v. CADBURY SCHWEPPES PLC [2001] 1 W.L.R. 615, Robert Walker, L.J., CA.

3792. **Voluntary arrangements – individual voluntary arrangements – supervisor for bankruptcy – effect of bankruptcy on distribution of funds**

[Insolvency Act 1986 s.264(1)(c), s.283(3)(a).]

C entered into an individual voluntary arrangement (IVA) with his creditors and J was appointed supervisor. By the terms of the arrangement, the supervisor was to retain any funds held by him on trust for the arrangement creditors with an express provision that such trust was to continue notwithstanding the presentation of a bankruptcy petition. Even though the arrangement would fail if the debtor became bankrupt. After several years the supervisor decided that C was in breach of the terms of the arrangement and petitioned for bankruptcy under the Insolvency Act 1986 s.264(1)(c). R was appointed trustee in bankruptcy. J and R disagreed as to how the funds held by J should be treated. Therefore the court was asked for directions.

Held, declaring that the funds were held on trust for the IVA creditors, that (1) in the absence of clear statutory guidance in respect of distribution of the funds held by the supervisor the terms of the IVA had to be applied. There was express provision about the future of the funds on failure of the IVA. *Halson Packaging Ltd, Re* [1997] B.C.C. 993, [1997] C.L.Y. 3079 followed, and (2) the supervisor held the funds in trust for the creditors and therefore those moneys were excluded pursuant to s.283(3)(a) of the 1986 Act from the bankruptcy. The supervisor had to distribute the funds he held to the creditors of the IVA pursuant to the agreement entered into freely between them and the debtor.

COATH, *Re* [2000] B.P.I.R. 981, District Judge Field, CC (Aylesbury).

3793. **Voluntary arrangements – individual voluntary arrangements – unjust enrichment – novation of previous rights upon implementation of IVA**

P appealed against a finding that he had been unjustly enriched as a result of a payment by a third party in discharge of a debt due from K, who had entered into a voluntary arrangement. K's debts had been assigned to P from the original creditor and represented loans to K and his partner, from the original creditor and secured loans from the bank. As a result of the joint debt arrangement, one half was treated as the several liability of P and his partner and the other half was a secured debt in favour of a bank. The proposals in the individual voluntary arrangement, IVA, did not refer to the debt due to P being secured. P argued that despite voting for the voluntary arrangement, the arrangement had not affected his rights as a secured creditor of K, and that, in any event, the payment could not be recovered by K since it had been made by a third party.

Held, dismissing the appeal, that K's voluntary arrangement had operated to discharge P's debt, and that since both K and the third party had been acting under the mistaken belief that the debt remained due to P, the debt was recoverable by K. The IVA made separate arrangements for the bank in respect of its secured debt and the debt due to P was specifically referred to in the list of unsecured creditors. A necessary implication of the IVA was that if creditors received payment in full, their rights then became novated into the rights conferred upon them by the arrangement. In voting for the IVA, P had agreed to be treated as an unsecured creditor and the effect of the arrangement and its performance by K, was to discharge the original debt and any proprietary rights associated with it. Notwithstanding the fundamental principle that a claimant cannot recover from a defendant, payment which has been made by a third party, subrogation remained an equitable remedy available in cases of unjust enrichment, *Banque Financiere de la Cite SA v. Parc (Battersea) Ltd* [1999] 1 A.C. 221, [1998] C.L.Y. 2521 applied. In the instant case, although the payment to P had been made by a third party, K and his partner were severally liable for the debt which they had mistakenly believed was due to P and to that extent they had agreed to indemnify the third party for the amount for which they were liable.

KHAN v. PERMAYER [2001] B.P.I.R. 95, Morritt, L.J., CA.

3794. Books

Berry, Christopher; Bailey, Edward; Schaw-Miller, Stephen – Personal Insolvency-law and Practice. 3rd Ed. Paperback: £145.00. ISBN 0-406-08153-0. Butterworths Law.

Bridge, Michael; Stevens, Robert – Cross-border Security and Insolvency. Oxford Law Colloquium Series. Hardback: £65.00. ISBN 0-19-829921-4. Oxford University Press.

Davis, Anthony C.R. – Tolley's Taxation on Corporate Insolvency. 4th Ed. Paperback: £46.95. ISBN 1-86012-325-2. Tolley Publishing.

Frieze, Steven – Practice Notes on Insolvency Law. Practice Notes. Paperback: £15.95. ISBN 1-85941-575-X. Cavendish Publishing Ltd.

Lightman, Mr Justice and Moss, Gabr – Law of Receivers and Administrators of Companies. 3rd Ed. Hardback: £135.00. ISBN 0-421-67370-2. Sweet & Maxwell.

INSURANCE

3795. Commercial insurance – burden of proof – policy excluding losses linked with insurrection – looting – Trinidad and Tobago

A retailer, G, sought to recover from its insurers, C, losses sustained during looting and rioting which occurred following an attempted coup against the government of Trinidad and Tobago. C declined to indemnify G on the basis that whilst the policy provided cover in respect of damage resulting from rioting, a special condition in the policy overrode any prima facie liability where losses had occurred as either a direct or indirect consequence of insurrection. Under the terms of the policy, where the insurers maintained that as a result of the special condition the losses sustained were not covered by the terms of the policy, the onus to prove otherwise lay with the insured. G submitted that the fact that an insurrection had occurred did not automatically result in the transfer of the burden of proof and that such transfer would only occur if C could demonstrate that G's losses were sufficiently connected with the insurrection.

Held, giving judgment for C, that the clause in the policy transferring the burden of proof to G was valid and came into operation as soon as an assertion was made by the respondent insurers to the effect that the losses claimed for were not covered by reason of the special condition. Accordingly, G were obliged to establish that there was no sufficient causal connection between the insurrection and the losses incurred, *Levy v. Assicurazione Generali* [1940] A.C. 791 applied and *Spinney's (1948) Ltd v. Royal Insurance Co Ltd* [1980] 1 Lloyd's Rep. 406, [1980] C.L.Y. 1514 considered. The assertion made by CHI was essentially to the effect that the insurrection led to a collapse in public order which allowed looting and damage to occur. Such an assertion was justified on the facts and G had failed to adduce cogent evidence by way of rebuttal, *Spinney's* applied.

GRELL-TAUREL LTD v. CARIBBEAN HOME INSURANCE CO LTD [2000] Lloyd's Rep. I.R. 614, Kangaloo, J., HC (Trin).

3796. Financial services – insurance contracts – EEA passport rights

FINANCIAL SERVICES (EEA PASSPORT RIGHTS) REGULATIONS 2001, SI 2001 1376; made under the European Communities Act 1972 s.2. In force: April 30, 2001; £1.50.

These Regulations, which amend the Financial Services and Markets Act 2000 Sch.3 which makes provision about "passport rights" under the single markets directives relating to financial services, give effect to Council Directive 88/357 [1988] OJ L172/01 and Directive 92/49 [1992] OJ L228/01 relating to the taking up and pursuit of direct insurance other than life assurance and Council Directive 90/619 [1990] OJ L330/50 and Directive 92/96 [1992] OJ L360/01 relating to the taking up and pursuit of the business of direct life assurance relating to the procedure applying to the exercise by UK firms of their passport rights under those directives to provide services in other EEA States.

3797. Fire insurance – fire precautions – applicability of condition – nature of precautions required

L, the owner of premises, sought an indemnity from insurers under a policy of public liability insurance. B had been employed by the manager of the premises, P, to perform a minor roofing repair. P made no enquiries of B as to how the repair was to be effected and no information was volunteered by B. As a result of B's careless use of a blowtorch during the repair, neighbouring premises were badly damaged by fire. The insurers declined to indemnify L on the basis that a condition in the relevant policy prohibiting the use of blowtorches unless stringent safety conditions were complied with, was of application. L contended that the condition was only of application in circumstances where L had actual knowledge that the type of work outlined in the condition was to be undertaken. On the facts, L maintained that P was entirely unaware that a blowtorch was to be used. In the alternative, L argued that it was only bound to comply with the condition in circumstances where it possessed actual or constructive knowledge that work of a type specified by the condition was to be performed.

Held, giving judgment for the insurers, that the policy had to be interpreted on the basis that the condition had been drawn to the attention of relevant staff, namely P as manager of the relevant premises. The condition required that "common care" should be exercised. To exercise "common care" on the facts of the instant case would have involved P either possessing a correct understanding of the work involved, or, in the absence of such understanding, asking B precisely what it was that he proposed to do. Had such an approach been taken and the nature of the work explained, it would have been apparent that "minimum precautions" of the type described in the condition were required before work could commence.

BONNER-WILLIAMS v. PETER LINDSAY LEISURE LTD [2001] 1 All E.R. (Comm) 1140, Judge Richard Seymour Q.C., QBD (T&CC).

3798. Insurance brokers – registration council – dissolution

See FINANCIAL SERVICES. §2752

3799. Insurance claims – consumer hire agreements – entitlement to subrogated claim for hire charges

L sought to recover the cost of hiring a replacement vehicle following a road traffic accident for which F admitted liability. L had a pre-accident contract of insurance with D through K. Under the terms of that insurance, L was entitled to a free hire vehicle in the event of an accident. The replacement vehicle was provided by A, pursuant to an understanding between D and A. L submitted that the vehicle was provided pursuant to the insurance policy and was a subrogated claim. She stated that F had conceded, prior to the issue of proceedings, that D had paid the hire charges, and that her claim was comparable to that where an insurance company paid repair costs on behalf of the insured policy holder. F contended that (1) there was no agreement between L and A and therefore L had no right or remedy against A; (2) since subrogation merely put D "in the shoes of" L, D had no remedy against A as it could not be placed in a better position than L, and (3) repair cases involved direct loss whereas hire charges were a consequential loss.

Held, granting judgment for F, that there was no obligation between L and A. L had suffered no loss and never expected to make payment as she had the benefit of a policy with D. Cases involving subrogated claims for hire charges could be distinguished from cases involving the cost of repairs *Cunningham v. Damon* (Unreported, December 1, 1999), [2000] C.L.Y. 1460 followed.

LATHAM v. FARMER, May 3, 2001, Deputy District Judge Hatch, CC (Canterbury). [*Ex rel.* Azeem Ali, Barrister, Clock Chambers, 78 Darlington Street, Wolverhampton].

3800. Insurance claims – economic loss – liability in negligence and public nuisance – recoverability

J was employed by ABP to carry out dredging works. J insured itself against liabilities to third parties resulting from the dredging works with RB, a Belgian insurance company. Prior to carrying out the works, J conducted a number of tests in relation to the effects of the dredging operations. Upon undertaking the work, however, and contrary to its expectations, considerable siltation occurred, causing interference with use of the river bed. J issued proceedings seeking to recover from RB the sums expended in removing the silt on the ground that having caused the deposits, it had incurred a number of liabilities to third parties falling within the terms of the insurance cover. J conceded that it, as well as ABP, had been negligent toward the third parties and that had it taken proper care, a considerable amount of the siltation would have been avoided. The issue arose as to whether the damage suffered by the third parties constituted a claim for which J or ABP were liable. RB submitted that the majority of the third party claims could not be substantiated, since the claimants lacked proprietary rights in the river bed and the damage claimed was purely economic and therefore irrecoverable.

Held, giving judgment for J, that (1) third party claims in negligence were limited to those claimants who were able to show legal ownership or possessory title to the property damaged by siltation, *Leigh and Sillivan v. Aliakmon Shipping Co Ltd* [1986] A.C. 785, [1986] C.L.Y. 2252 applied; (2) negligence was not an essential element of liability in a nuisance claim. It followed that where a third party had a sufficient interest in the area affected, a claim in nuisance would be made out, *Cambridge Water Co Ltd v. Eastern Counties Leather Plc* [1994] 2 A.C. 264, [1994] C.L.Y. 3410 applied. Given that there was a public right of navigation on the relevant tidal waters in the instant case, any substantial interference with such a right constituted a public nuisance, *Tate & Lyle Industries v. Greater London Council* [1983] 2 A.C. 509, [1983] C.L.Y. 2746 applied. However, it was only open to an individual to undertake an action in public nuisance where he had suffered substantial injury in relation to that suffered by the wider public, *Walsh v. Ervin* [1952] V.L.R. 361 applied; (3) the fact that, with a single exception, the third party claimants had not specified precise losses did not preclude the awarding of general damages. General damages could be awarded in circumstances where the injury suffered had no precise quantification in monetary terms, *Hunter v. Canary Wharf Ltd* [1997] A.C. 655, [1997] C.L.Y. 3865 applied; (4) in respect of third party claims regarding commercial berths, J incurred negligent liability and was entitled to recover all costs in removing silt from the areas, since the berths were not able to operate as a result of the silt deposits. However, J incurred liability in public nuisance only in respect of the claims involving different areas of the river bed. Here the users had suffered purely financial damage, the recovery of which was excluded from cover, and (5) ABP, as conservator of the port, had a duty to maintain rights of navigation and a common law right to recover its costs from J. The majority of the damage was not excluded, as it was negligent damage to property not pure economic loss.

JAN DE NUL (UK) LTD v. ROYALE BELGE NV ; *sub nom* JAN DE NUL (UK) v. AXA ROYALE BELGE (FORMERLY NV ROYALE BELGE) [2000] 2 Lloyd's Rep. 700, Moore-Bick, J., QBD (Comm Ct).

3801. Insurance claims – limit of liability – notification – extent of duty to notify insurer of event likely to lead to claim

C entered into an all risks insurance policy with AI in relation to his business premises, a petrol filling station. The policy incorporated a clause whereby C was required upon the occurrence of any event giving rise or "likely to give rise to a claim" to inform AI of the details within 30 days. Upon receipt of a solicitors letter notifying C of a potential claim, relating to an incident approximately seven months previously in which J had fallen on C's forecourt, he informed AI. J, who had sustained a serious leg injury, subsequently brought an action against C for damages. The action having been compromised, a judge held in Part 20 proceedings that AI could avoid liability on the basis of C's failure to notify them of a likely claim within 30 days. C appealed contending that the mere occurrence of a non trivial injury was not sufficient to establish that an ensuing claim was likely. C argued that at the time of the incident he had not been aware of the extent of J's injuries or that C attributed any fault to him and accordingly had had no reason to suspect a future claim might be made.

Held, allowing the appeal, that the fact that a person fell sustaining an injury did not necessarily mean the incident was likely to give rise to a claim. It followed that the burden resided with an insurer to prove that a claim was likely. It was appropriate to interpret the term "likely to give rise to a claim" under the clause as meaning an event presenting at least a 50 per cent chance that a claim would ensue, *Layher Ltd v. Lowe* 58 Con. L.R. 42, [1997] C.L.Y. 3124 followed. The fact that a later claim did arise was not of itself sufficient to establish that a claim had been likely. In the instant case the judge had erred by inferring the likelihood of a claim by the occurrence of the event itself. C had not been aware of the nature of J's injuries and furthermore had possessed no reason to suspect that he would be held in any way responsible having taken care to inspect the garage forecourt and finding nothing amiss.

JACOBS v. COSTER (T/A NEWINGTON COMMERCIALS SERVICE STATION) [2000] Lloyd's Rep. I.R. 506, Laws, L.J., CA.

3802. Insurance companies – fees

INSURANCE (FEES) REGULATIONS 2001, SI 2001 812; made under the Insurance Companies Act 1982 s.94A, s.96, s.97. In force: April 1, 2001; £2.50.

These Regulations revoke the Insurance (Fees) Regulations 2000 (SI 2000 670) and set out the fees to be paid to the Treasury by insurance companies when they deposit their accounts and other documents as required by the Insurance Companies Act 1982 s.22(1) and by the Council of Lloyd's when the statement in respect of Lloyd's is deposited under s.86(1) of that Act.

3803. Insurance companies – life insurance – reorganisation of business – objections – preemptive costs orders

[Supreme Court Act 1981 s.51; Insurance Companies Act 1982 Sch.2(c) Part 1.]

In proceedings commenced by Axa Sun Life, ASL, seeking sanction for the reorganisation of ASL's and AEL's life insurance business pursuant to the Insurance Companies Act 1982 Sch.2(c) Part 1, M, a policy holder objecting to the proposed scheme, sought a pre-emptive order for costs pursuant to the Supreme Court Act 1981 s.51 in order to pursue his objections through the courts.

Held, granting the application, that a pre-emptive order was appropriate in circumstances where (1) the scheme was a novel one which therefore required the presence of an objector in order that the issue of fairness might be subject to scrutiny by the courts, and (2) the objector represented the interests of a substantial number of pension holders. M represented over 1,400 pension holders who were in an analogous position to minority shareholders as they had given consideration for their interests in the fund, *McDonald v. Horn* [1995] 1 All E.R. 961, [1995] C.L.Y. 3836 and *Wallersteiner v. Moir (No.2)* [1975] Q.B. 373, [1975] C.L.Y. 2602 considered.

AXA EQUITY & LAW LIFE ASSURANCE SOCIETY PLC (NO.1), *Re*; AXA SUN LIFE PLC (NO.1), *Re* [2001] 2 B.C.L.C. 447, Evans-Lombe, J., Ch D.

3804. Insurance companies – reorganisation – valuation of policyholders' expectations – conflict of expert evidence

[Insurance Companies Act 1982 s.49, Sch.2C Part I para.1.]

Pursuant to the Insurance Companies Act 1982 s.49 and Sch.2C Part I para.1, the sanction of the court was sought to a scheme of reorganisation of the life assurance business of two insurance companies. M, a representative policyholder, contended that the scheme was unfair in that the compensation offered for the loss of individual policyholders' potential entitlement to a distribution out of the inherited estate was inadequate. M further submitted that the evidence filed on behalf of the Financial Services Authority, the FSA, and the independent actuary was flawed since the two of them had failed to take into account the reasonable expectations of policyholders and to ensure that the best price possible was obtained, concluding instead that the price offered fell within an unspecified reasonable range.

Held, granting sanction for the scheme, that (1) at the time that they had taken out their individual policies, the policyholders had not had any reasonable expectation that they would receive a distribution out of the inherited estate during the currency of their policy, and (2) in accordance with established authority, where the views of petitioners and objectors were in conflict with those of the FSA and the independent actuary, the court would prefer the evidence of the FSA and the independent actuary. No compelling reason, based on a demonstrable mistake or proven fact, had emerged to militate against such an approach.

AXA EQUITY & LAW LIFE ASSURANCE SOCIETY PLC (NO.2), *Re*; AXA SUN LIFE PLC (NO.2), *Re* [2001] 1 All E.R. (Comm) 1010, Evans-Lombe, J., Ch D.

3805. Insurance contracts – fraud – film finance insurance – exclusion clauses – principal's ability to exclude liability for fraudulent or negligent misstatement

C, a bank, appealed against the determination ([2001] 1 All E.R. (Comm) 719) of certain preliminary issues arising in relation to film finance insurance. C had obtained the benefit of a policy of film finance insurance with HIH, the terms of which were negotiated by brokers, H. C had very little knowledge of the film industry and relied upon H. The policy contained a "truth of statement" clause. HIH refused to accept liability to indemnify under the policy alleging that H had been guilty of non disclosure and fraudulent or negligent misrepresentation. C maintained that (1) the effect of the truth of statement clause was to exclude the duty to "speak" on the part of both C and H since an agent could have no duty to speak in circumstances where such an obligation was not imposed upon the principal, and (2) the effect of the clause was to offer total protection to C against any non disclosure or misrepresentation by H, even if committed fraudulently.

Held, allowing the appeal in part, that (1) if a circumstance was material then there was an obligation of disclosure upon both principal and agent. In circumstances where the duty of disclosure was effectively waived in the case of the principal then the waiver was effective to exclude the obligation to disclose upon the part of the agent also, *SAIL v. Farex* [1995] L.R.L.R. 116 applied, and (2) there was no binding authority providing guidance as to whether a principal could exclude liability for the fraud of his agent. The same public policy considerations did not apply as in the case of a fraud by the principal. Any exclusion would have to be in the clearest possible terms and on the facts of the instant case the clause did not operate to exclude liability for fraud, *S Pearson & Son Ltd v. Dublin Corp* [1907] A.C. 351, *Mair v. Rio Grande Rubber Estates Ltd* [1913] A.C. 853 and *Boyd & Forrest v. Glasgow & South Western Railway Co* 1915 SC 20 considered.

HIH CASUALTY & GENERAL INSURANCE LTD v. CHASE MANHATTAN BANK; CHASE MANHATTAN BANK v. HIH CASUALTY & GENERAL INSURANCE LTD, [2001] EWCA Civ 1250, [2001] 2 Lloyd's Rep. 483, Rix, L.J., CA.

3806. **Insurance contracts – indemnities – costs – scope of boatyard indemnity insurance cover**

[Rules of the Supreme Court 1965 (SI 1965 1776) Ord.14A.]

P sought a determination under the Rules of the Supreme Court 1965 Ord.14A that it was entitled to recover under a boatyard indemnity policy held with E the costs incurred in defending an action brought by a third party. P also sought an interim payment in respect of such costs and/or a proportion of the costs claimed against it by the third party. The action brought against P, which had related to an agreement with the third party to refurbish a yacht, had been settled upon the making of a payment into court by P. Under the policy, P was indemnified against, inter alia, "all costs and expenses of litigation incurred with the written consent of [E] in respect of a claim" brought against it. The issue before the court related to, inter alia, whether certain exclusions applied to such cover.

Held, giving judgment for P, that having regard to the policy wording, P was entitled to an indemnity in relation to the costs and expenses of the litigation brought by the third party. The wording of the policy was clear and detailed three individual indemnities. Such indemnities had to result from those activities or matters set out in various sub clauses. The exclusion clauses were applicable in relation to the entire coverage under the policy. It was, however, apparent that none of the exclusions was relevant to the costs and expenses at issue. Whilst, under the policy, E's consent was required at each major stage of the litigation, it had to be implied that such consent would not be withheld unreasonably, *E Hulton & Co v. Mountain* (1921) 8 Ll. L. Rep. 249 applied. It was apparent that although consent could have been withdrawn, it had not been withdrawn. Given that there was no evidence as to whether the costs incurred by P's solicitors had been reasonable, it was not appropriate to order an interim payment of an amount greater than £30,000.

POOLE HARBOUR YACHT CLUB MARINA LTD v. EXCESS MARINE INSURANCE LTD [2001] Lloyd's Rep. I.R. 580, Thomas, J., QBD (Comm Ct).

3807. **Insurance contracts – indemnities – retrocession pool – liability to indemnify subscriber used as "front"**

LFA sought to set aside the service of a claim form in proceedings commenced by DR seeking reimbursement for payments made by DR under a number of reinsurance contracts. DR and LFA had been involved in an excess of loss reinsurance and retrocession pool managed by Inter Community Reinsurance Agency BV, ICRA. DR maintained that LFA were liable to make payment representing sums paid by DR at a time when it was used to "front" for members of the pool. LFA maintained that since ICRA had not been permitted to use subscribers as fronts for the pool and there had consequently been no obligation to indemnify on the part of those who took advantage of a "front", it was not possible to argue for the existence of an implied retrocession agreement in favour of those pool members used to front risks.

Held, refusing the application, that it was clear that all of the defendants had been aware of the practice of fronting and had never suggested that they were not liable to indemnify the company acting as a front. On the basis of the available evidence it was clearly arguable that the various defendants had ratified the fronting arrangements and an implied obligation to indemnify had accordingly arisen to the extent of their proportionate share of the premium.

DEUTSCHE RUCKVERSICHERUNG AG v. LA FONDARIA ASSICURAZIONI SpA (FORMERLY SOCIETA ITALIA DI ASSICURAZIONI SPA); *sub nom.* DEUTSCHE RUCKVERSICHERUNG AG v. LA FONDIARA ASSICURAZIONI SPA [2001] 2 Lloyd's Rep. 621, David Steel, J., QBD (Comm Ct).

3808. **Insurance policies – cancellation – right to refund – interpretation of policy provisions**

[Road Traffic Act 1988 s.152(1)(c)(iii); Unfair Terms in Consumer Contracts Regulations 1999 (SI 1999 2083) Reg.7 (2).]

After DI, an insurance company, had been placed in provisional liquidation, a group of brokers, the Policyholders' Protection Board and the provisional liquidators negotiated a scheme whereby a majority of the policyholders would receive fresh insurance cover from a new insurer. Before the scheme could be finalised, the court was asked to grant declarations concerning the policyholders' rights under the provisions of their vehicle insurance policies which dealt with cancellation and their right to a refund of premiums paid. Those provisions stipulated as follows: "We ... may cancel this policy if you are given at least [seven] days' notice. You may cancel this policy by writing and telling us ... and at the same time returning the certificate. If you do this, we will return part of your premium for the rest of the period of the insurance, calculated from the date the certificate is received. We will only provide a refund if a claim has not been made under the policy in the current period of insurance". The court was asked to determine whether the policyholder had the right to a refund if it was DI that cancelled the policy and, if the policyholder had such a right, (1) whether it was contractual or restitutionary in nature; (2) whether it arose when the insurance certificate was returned or when DI's notice cancelling the policy expired, and (3) whether it was vitiated if the policyholder had made a claim under the policy.

Held, granting declarations in favour of the policyholders, that (1) the provision entitling DI to cancel the policy was subject to an implied term that, were it to do so, the policyholder would receive a refund. Such a conclusion was supported by the fact that DI did not have to give reasons for cancelling the policy, *Sun Fire Office v. Hart* (1889) L.R. 14 App. Cas. 98 considered; (2) since the policy was a "single risk" policy, the right to a refund was not restitutionary, but contractual. The policyholder's right to a refund in the event of DI cancelling was implied by the express right to a refund enjoyed by the policyholder in the event of his cancelling the policy; (3) the right to a refund arose not on the date when the policyholder returned his certificate but on the expiry of DI's notice cancelling the policy. Such a conclusion was reinforced by comparing the wording and structure of the provisions entitling DI, on the one hand, and the policyholder, on the other, to cancel the policy. While DI remained liable or at least at risk in respect of third party claims pending the return of the certificate, it had the right to avoid such liability by taking proceedings against the policyholder under the Road Traffic Act 1988 s.152(1)(c)(iii), and (4) the right to a refund was not vitiated by the making of a claim under the policy. Such a finding was supported, inter alia, by (a) the layout of the relevant provisions, which indicated that the making of a claim would only affect the policyholder's right to a refund if he cancelled the policy; (b) reasonableness and commercial common sense. It would be unfair if the policyholder were to cancel the policy and claim a refund having already received a benefit under the policy by making a claim. On the other hand, it would not necessarily be fair to disentitle the policyholder who had made a claim from receiving a refund were DI to cancel the policy, especially in cases where it did so without good reason, and (c) the policyholder's ability to rely, given that the relevant provision was unclear, on the contra proferentem rule and/or the Unfair Terms in Consumer Contracts Regulations 1999 Reg.7(2).

DRAKE INSURANCE PLC, *Re* [2001] Lloyd's Rep. I.R. 643, Neuberger, J., Ch D (Companies Ct).

3809. Insurance policies – direct debits – insurer's failure to implement direct debit mandate – negligent liability

See NEGLIGENCE: Weldon v. GRE Linked Life Assurance Ltd. §4490

3810. Insurance policies – exclusion clauses – motor vehicle theft – ordinary meaning to be given to policy wording

NU appealed against a decision (Unreported, October 22, 1999, [2000] C.L.Y. 3810) that pursuant to a policy of motor vehicle insurance it was liable to indemnify H following the theft of his motor vehicle. The vehicle, which had been fitted with an immobiliser, had been driven away from a petrol station whilst H was paying for his petrol. As was his habit, H had left the key in the ignition and the doors unlocked in the belief that the immobiliser provided sufficient protection against theft. H's insurance policy contained a clause excluding liability for loss "arising from theft whilst the ignition keys of your car have been left in or on the car". The deputy judge had found, inter alia, that the words "have been left" were ambiguous and that since the vehicle had been in H's field of vision and he had been in a position to attempt to prevent unauthorised interference with it, the keys had not been left in the car for the purposes of the exclusion clause.

Held, allowing the appeal, that (1) the words "have been left in the car" were to be given their plain and ordinary meaning. The deputy judge had erred in finding them to be ambiguous and in holding that the word "unattended" was to be implied into the exclusion clause, and (2) the fact that the deputy judge had concluded that a robbery had occurred was no justification for arguing that a "theft" had not occurred since theft was an essential ingredient of robbery.

HAYWARD v. NORWICH UNION INSURANCE LTD, [2001] EWCA Civ 243, [2001] 1 All E.R. (Comm) 545, Peter Gibson, L.J., CA.

3811. Insurance policies – financial advice – pensions misselling – interpretation of aggregation clause

B instituted proceedings against G, seeking an indemnity under a policy of professional indemnity insurance following a large number of claims by individual investors who had received negligent pension advice. The relevant policy contained a clause whereby G would only be liable in each individual case for liability exceeding the relevant policy deductible. The clause further provided that a series of third party claims would be aggregated and treated as a single claim for the purposes of the deductible if they had arisen as a result of a "single act or omission (or a related series of acts or omissions)". For the purpose of a preliminary ruling on the interpretation of the clause, B maintained that the misselling of pensions was attributable to a single act or omission, namely the failure to provide proper training to its financial services consultants, and that in those circumstances the claims should be aggregated and treated as one for the purposes of the deductible.

Held, determining the preliminary issue in favour of B, that it was necessary when construing the clause to adopt a common sense approach and to ask whether the dominant cause of the claims was the failure on the part of management to provide the training necessary to enable individual financial services consultants to provide the best advice to investors. On the facts of the instant case it was clear that the claims were an inevitable consequence of the failure to train, and the advice that had to be given by consultants to investors to complete the chain of events was not capable of amounting to a novus actus interveniens. Whether the failure to train was treated as a single act or omission or as a related series of acts or omissions was irrelevant.

LLOYDS TSB GENERAL INSURANCE HOLDINGS LTD v. LLOYDS BANK GROUP INSURANCE CO LTD; ABBEY NATIONAL PLC v. LEE [2001] 1 All E.R. (Comm) 13, Moore-Bick, J., QBD (Comm Ct).

3812. Insurance policies – legal costs insurance – liability of second layer insurer in product liability claim – exhaustion of primary layer by buy out

CI appealed against a decision that it was liable under the second layer insurance policies, when the primary layer insurer exercised a "buy-out" which terminated their liability for the costs of litigation concerning JW, who was the defendant to several product liability claims. CI contended that it was not liable because the "buy-out" did not exhaust the primary layer as no payments had been made in respect of established claims, and that it was entitled to reimbursement of costs paid.

Held, dismissing the appeal, that the "buy-out" had exhausted the primary layer notwithstanding that no payment had been made in respect of established claims, and that CI were liable from the date of the "buy-out" to pay the costs of litigation relating to claims that might fall within the policies, so that there was no requirement for JW to reimburse CI for costs relating to claims outside the policies.

JOHN WYETH & BROS LTD v. CIGNA INSURANCE CO OF EUROPE SA/NV (NO.1), [2001] EWCA Civ 175, [2001] Lloyd s Rep. I.R. 420, Waller, L.J., CA.

3813. Insurance policies – maladministration – basis of liability following prior determination by Ombudsman

RLBC instituted proceedings against its public liability insurers, M, following M's refusal to indemnify RLBC in respect of its liability to former employees as a result of a finding that there had been maladministration of the council pension scheme. M maintained that it was entitled to avoid liability on the basis that the maladministration was equivalent to the crime of misconduct in public office and the relevant policy contained an exclusion for acts of dishonesty on the part of council employees.

Held, determining the preliminary issue in favour of the claimant, that the basis of the liability as between RLBC and its former employees had been determined by the Pensions Ombudsman as maladministration, as this was the only basis upon which he had jurisdiction. Once the extent of liability had been established in a court of competent jurisdiction, it was not open to the parties to challenge in another court the basis upon which that liability had been established. The liability accordingly consisted of negligent acts on the part of council employees, *MDIS Ltd (formerly McDonnell Information Systems Ltd) v. Swinbank* [1999] 2 All E.R. (Comm) 722, [2000] 3 C.L. 414 applied.

REDBRIDGE LBC v. MUNICIPAL MUTUAL INSURANCE LTD [2001] Lloyd's Rep. I.R. 545, Tomlinson, J., QBD (Comm Ct).

3814. Insurance policies – personal injuries – income protection plans – objective test of disability – pain syndrome

H, who suffered from a prolapsed disc and from pain syndrome, appealed against the dismissal of his claim for benefits under two income protection policies issued by AD, which provided for payments in the event of his being wholly unemployable because of disability. The trial judge had concluded that H's disability would not prevent him from working since that disability was partly attributable to H's excessive fears concerning his condition and had resulted in a genuine but mistaken belief that he was unable to return to work. H contended that the judge had been wrong to objectively judge H's disabilities, having already concluded that H had a genuine and subjective belief that his disability was such as to prevent him from working.

Held, dismissing the appeal, that H's belief that he was disabled, however genuine, did not give rise to a valid claim. While it was accepted that functional overlay could aggravate an organic condition, the trial judge, when determining H's capacity to work, had been correct to distinguish between H's condition insofar as it resulted from his pain syndrome and the additional "disability" arising from H's erroneous belief that he was far more disabled than he actually was.

HAGHIRAN v. ALLIED DUNBAR INSURANCE [2001] 1 All E.R. (Comm) 97, Simon Brown, L.J., CA.

3815. Insurance policies – renewal – validity of unilateral amendment by insurance broker to exclusion clause

G, a rail company which had a policy of insurance with A, initially through brokers, F, and latterly through different brokers, J, appealed against a decision that the policy wording originally provided by F remained in force despite a subsequent amendment that G claimed had been effected by J. With the consent of A, F had inserted a clause excluding liability for faulty or defective design, materials or workmanship. The cover was transferred to J, who arranged for the annual renewal and who put forward amended wording to narrow the scope of the exclusion clause to the effect that faulty or defective design, materials or workmanship was covered by the policy if it was caused by persons other than G or any of its employees other than drivers and guards. Following a claim on the policy arising from an incident caused by faulty workmanship unrelated to G or its employees, the judge had accepted A's contention that as the amended wording of the clause had never been agreed, the cover continued on the basis of the original wording of the exclusion clause.

Held, dismissing the appeal, that it would be most unusual for a complex insurance contract to be anything other than a contract in writing signed or initialled by the underwriter. In the instant case, the critical document signed by A and by J confirmed "renewal of the policy". That could only refer to the previous year's terms and not to the wording put forward by J.

GREAT NORTH EASTERN RAILWAY LTD v. AVON INSURANCE PLC; *sub nom.* GNER LTD v. AVON INSURANCE PLC, [2001] EWCA Civ 780, [2001] 2 All E.R. (Comm) 526, Longmore, L.J., CA.

3816. Insurance premium tax – liability – premium for risk of indirect subsidiary – European Community

[Second Council Directive 88/357 on coordination of laws relating to direct insurance other than life insurance Art.2(c), Art.2(d), Art.3.]

The Dutch court referred three questions to the ECJ concerning the interpretation of the Second Council Directive 88/357 Art.2(c), Art.2(d) and Art.3. The questions had arisen in proceedings between K, a company established in the United Kingdom, and the Netherlands State Secretary of Finance relating to a revised assessment to tax in regard to part of the premiums K had paid which covered the business risks of an indirect Dutch subsidiary. The three questions which fell to be determined were: (1) whether Art.2(c) and Art.2(d) permitted a Member State to levy insurance tax on a legal person established in another Member State in relation to premiums paid to an insurer, that insurer also being established in a Member State, for the business insurance of an indirect subsidiary; (2) the consequences to such determination where the policy holder was not the overall parent company, and (3) the effect upon such determination of the insurance premium relating to the risk not being passed on, either entirely or partially, to the indirect subsidiary.

Held, giving a preliminary ruling, that (1) a Member State was permitted under Art.2(c), the final indent of Art.2(d), and Art.3 to levy an insurance tax in relation to premiums which a legal person had paid to an insurer to cover the business risks of an indirect subsidiary; (2) it was of no consequence if the legal person paying the premiums and the legal person whose business risks were covered derived from the same group but were linked by a relationship other than one of parent and subsidiary company, and (3) for the purposes of

Art.2(d), final indent, the method of payment of the premium relating to the risk was immaterial.

KVAERNER PLC v. STAATSSECRETARIS VAN FINANCIEN (C191/99) [2002] Q.B. 385, C Gulmann (President), ECJ.

3817. Legal expenses insurance – indemnities – claim lacking merit – entitlement of insurer to withdraw indemnity

W had an uninsured loss recovery policy with A. Following a road traffic accident in November 1998, in which his car was written off, W relied on his policy to claim the pre-accident value of his car of £523 and his loss of use from the date of the accident until the date he purchased a replacement car for £50 in August 1999. A appointed a solicitor, S, to act for W and to pursue his claim. Liability was eventually settled our of court, W being 20 per cenr to blame. S continued to negotiate a settlement of W's damages claim, however W then wished to include a loss of earnings claim for some £17,000 as he had relied on his car to carry on his trade as a carpenter and he had lost his job in December 1998 as he had no transport. With A's approval, S obtained counsel's opinion on W's prospects which supported the view that there were inherent problems with the merits of W's claim. The third party insurers made a "final offer" of £2,978 in respect of W's total claim in July 1999. S advised both W and A that W's claim for such high loss of earnings flowing from a car of such low value was very dubious and that the offer was a reasonable one which was unlikely to be improved on at trial. A accepted S's advice and stated that, unless W accepted the offer, their indemnity would be withdrawn. S advised W of this fact but W declined to accept the offer. S tried again to improve the offer and as a result the third party increased the offer to £5,200, which W accepted. W then alleged breach of contract against A for withdrawing their indemnity when there was a reasonable prospect of W recovering the full value of his claim at trial.

Held, giving judgment for A, that W was under a duty to mitigate his loss and therefore should have replaced his car much earlier. Accordingly, his claim for loss of use and loss of earnings was unlikely to subsist for more than a few weeks; therefore S's assessment of the dubious merits of W's claim was correct. It was reasonable for A to have relied upon S's advice that the offer of £2,978 should be accepted, thus A had acted properly in withdrawing their indemnity given the term in the contract which stated that both A and W were required to follow the advice of a solicitor appointed in cases of litigation. Moreover, even if the judge had found that £2,978 was too low a settlement and that A was in breach of contract for withdrawing its indemnity at that stage, the final offer of £5,200 accepted by W was almost certainly more than he would have recovered at court and there was effectively no loss suffered by W for which he could sue.

WOODROW v. ALBANY UNINSURED LOSS RECOVERIES LTD, May 3, 2001, Judge Cotram, CC (Shoreditch). [*Ex rel.* Nigel Ffitch, Barrister, Phoenix Chambers, Gray's Inn, London].

3818. Legal expenses insurance – personal injuries – solicitor's duty to investigate insurance position – recoverability of premium

S, who had been injured while travelling as a passenger in a vehicle driven by A and whose claim had been settled for £2,250 together with costs, appealed against the judge's decision to disallow as part of his costs an "after the event", ATE, premium. The judge had found that S should have taken advantage of "before the event", BTE, insurance cover that had been available under A's policy and that it had not been reasonable for him to pay the ATE premium without first checking whether A's policy provided legal expenses insurance cover for his passengers.

Held, allowing the appeal, that (1) if, in a claim not exceeding around £5,000, the claimant had the benefit of BTE cover, he should generally be referred to the relevant BTE insurer; (2) with a view to checking whether BTE cover was available, the claimant's solicitor should ask his client to bring with him to the first interview any relevant motor insurance policy, any household insurance policy and any stand-alone BTE insurance policy of the client and/or any spouse or partner living in the same household. The client should also be asked whether a third party was responsible for paying his costs. The solicitor's enquiries should, however, be proportionate to the value of the claim, and the availability of ATE cover at a modest cost would restrict the extent to which it would be reasonable for his time to be spent in investigating alternative sources of insurance. When acting for a passenger, the solicitor should ask his client to obtain a copy of the driver's insurance policy if that was reasonably practicable. If the driver's policy stated that BTE cover could only be used with his consent, the solicitor should ask his client to obtain such consent; (3) it would not be reasonable to expect a passenger to use BTE cover under the driver's policy where the driver's insurer would have full conduct and control of any claim, thereby denying him the opportunity of instructing a solicitor of his choice, and (4) the court's guidance was not to be treated as an inflexible code. Having regard to the BTE cover that had been available to S under A's policy, it was not reasonable to have expected him to use such cover.

SARWAR v. ALAM; *sub nom.* SAWAR v. ALAM, [2001] EWCA Civ 1401, [2002] 1 W.L.R. 125, Lord Phillips of Worth Matravers, M.R., CA.

3819. **Legal expenses insurance – subrogation – replacement vehicle hire charges – timing of payment of hire charges**

At an assessment of damages hearing, the claimant, LN, sought reimbursement for the cost of hire of a replacement vehicle following a road traffic accident. LN purported to have taken out a legal expenses insurance policy with D, which provided that hire costs would, where there was no fault on the members' part, be borne by D. LN also sought to recover the policy excess of £100. D had an agreement with M whereby M would provide a courtesy car, conduct an enquiry into the accident and commission repairs where necessary. Under that agreement, D was obliged to bear the costs of the hire within six months of receipt of M's invoice. The defendants argued that they were only obliged to discharge L's liabilities and since L had no liability to D or to M in respect of the hire charges, they were not recoverable.

Held, assessing damages, that in essence the claim for hire charges operated by way of subrogation. Subrogation rights existed in circumstances where payment of the hire charges had been made by the insurer prior to the issue of proceedings. Subrogation rights could not be exercised where payment had been made but not until after the issue of proceedings, *Page v. Scottish Insurance Corp Ltd* (1929) 33 Ll. L. Rep. 134 followed and *Yip v. Eckah* (Unreported, November 17, 1999) applied. In the instant case, the payment of the hire charges was made by D to M after proceedings had been issued. In any event, the claimant had not proved at trial that he had paid a premium to D and absent such proof a subrogated claim could not be established and the claim for hire charges failed.

LINTON v. LANCASTER, February 14, 2001, Judge not specified, CC (Doncaster). [*Ex rel.* Morgan Cole, Solicitors, Apex Plaza Commercial Office, Reading].

3820. **Legal expenses insurance – third parties – transference of rights upon insured's bankruptcy**

[Third Parties (Rights against Insurers) Act 1930.]

T, a firm of solicitors who had acted on N's behalf in litigation, sought to recover the balance of its costs from A, an insurer with which T had taken out legal expenses insurance cover. N had been declared bankrupt. The preliminary issue arose as to whether the Third Parties (Rights against Insurers) Act 1930 applied to the right of a litigant, under a legal expenses insurance policy, to payment by an insurer of the costs owed to a solicitor by an insured litigant such that the insured's right would be transferred to the solicitor if they became bankrupt. T submitted that since when entering into the policy of insurance both parties had foreseen that N might become involved in litigation and in so doing be liable to either her legal representatives or those of the opposing party, she had therefore been insured against liabilities to third parties.

Held, determining the preliminary issue in favour of A and dismissing the claim, that the Act, which conferred rights "where a person [was] insured against liabilities to third parties which he [might] incur", was limited to insurance against liabilities that might be incurred by that person due to the operation of the law, whether that be for breach of contract or in tort. It did not extend to liabilities that had been voluntarily undertaken by that person, such as the payment of contractual debts. While such a result was unsatisfactory the solution lay in amendment of the Act. It was observed that it would be expedient if the matter received the attention of the Law Commission.

TARBUCK v. AVON INSURANCE PLC [2001] 3 W.L.R. 1502, Toulson, J., QBD (Comm Ct).

3821. **Lloyd's Names – Chancery Division – practice statement on distribution of estates of deceased Names**

See CIVIL PROCEDURE: Practice Statement (Ch D: Estates of Deceased Lloyd's Names). §625

3822. **Lloyds Names – agreements – participation in syndicate – evidence of written agreement**

P brought an action against W, a Lloyd's Name, for £15,000 representing sums due under two cash calls made in 1996 and 1997. P had been appointed to manage the run off of Lloyd's syndicates, and alleged that W had signed up to the syndicate under which the cash calls had been made. W contended that there was no documentary evidence that her member's agent, KUL, had completed the necessary steps with the managing agency, KSM, to make her a Name on that syndicate.

Held, granting the application, that the proper procedural steps had been taken and W had been a Name on the relevant syndicate. Under the Agency Agreement Byelaw no.8 of 1988 Sched.3, the contractual relationship between a Name and a managing agency did not have to be in writing. Although there were no documents available, the procedural checks made by KUL were normally very thorough and, on a balance of probabilities, it was likely that KUL and KSM had completed the necessary paperwork and that the documents were among those that had gone missing following KSM's liquidation.

P&B (RUN-OFF) LTD v. WOOLLEY [2001] 1 All E.R. (Comm) 1120, Andrew Smith, J., QBD (Comm Ct).

3823. **Lloyds Names – reinsurance contracts – calculation of premium – market regulation – mental harassment**

In proceedings commenced by P, a former Lloyd's name, against L, L sought an order striking out P's claim as disclosing no real prospect of success together with summary judgment on its counterclaim. P sought summary judgment on his claim and dismissal of L's counterclaim. P contended that (1) the Equitas reinsurance premium as calculated by L and payable by P, was manifestly wrong. P maintained that when multiple reserving of the same risk or "double counting" had been identified and accounted for, a substantial reduction in the amount of the premium due was required. Such a reduction had been made in the case of other syndicates operating in a similar market to P's syndicate and in particular those syndicates which were participants in the LMX spiral; (2) L had breached its duty to disclose to P the contents of a report into the management of P's syndicate indicating serious cause for concern or, in the alternative, to close down the managing agents of the syndicate, and (3) the mental health of P's wife had suffered as a result of the action taken by L to recover monies owed to it, such as to constitute the tort of harassment.

Held, striking out P's claim and granting summary judgment to L, that (1) P was required to demonstrate an arguable error in relation to the calculation used by L to formulate the additional premium. P had failed to do so and accordingly clause 5.10 of the reinsurance contract operated to preclude any further challenge to the figures, *Society of Lloyd's v. Fraser* [1998] C.L.C. 1630, [1999] C.L.Y. 3405 applied; (2) L owed no statutory or common law duty to regulate the market and furthermore P had been unable to adduce cogent evidence to establish a prima facie case that L's actions had been motivated by bad faith, *Society of Lloyd's v. Clementson* [1995] 1 C.M.L.R. 693, [1994] C.L.Y. 2684 and *Ashmore v. Corp of Lloyd's (No.2)* [1992] 2 Lloyd's Rep. 620, [1993] C.L.Y. 2407 considered, and (3) whilst conduct designed to result in mental stress culminating in psychiatric harm could amount to the tort of harassment at common law, the conduct complained of had not been calculated to cause such harm but instead constituted a legitimate attempt to recover monies owing, *Khorasandjian v. Bush* [1993] Q.B. 727, [1993] C.L.Y. 3251 considered.

PRICE v. SOCIETY OF LLOYD'S [2000] Lloyd's Rep. I.R. 453, Colman, J., QBD (Comm Ct).

3824. Marine insurance – arson – fraudulent insurance claim – burden of proof

A brought an action for payment under a policy of insurance held with L. A owned a vessel which was insured to the value of £2,100,000. The vessel sank following a fire on board in September 1998. The skipper, D, who had set up the company A and had sole financial interest in the vessel, contended that the fire had started when a loose nut caused diesel fuel to spurt out of the fuel line of an on board generator. L argued that D had started the fire deliberately by spilling diesel fuel into the bilge and then disconnecting the fuel line in order to make it appear to have been an accident.

Held, dismissing the application, that the fire had been started deliberately by D. The burden of proof was on L to show that D's explanation was false, and it had done so, *N Michalos & Sons Maritime SA v. Prudential Assurance Co (The Zinovia)* [1984] 2 Lloyd's Rep. 264, [1984] C.L.Y. 3175 applied. On the evidence, the nut would have been tightened by a spanner and there was therefore no more than a "remote" possibility that it could have loosened by vibration. If it had been loose as described by D it would have caused the generator to stall, which conflicted with D's evidence that the generator continued to run until he switched it off after discovering the fire. D's explanation did not account for how quickly the fire had spread. There was evidence that the vessel was significantly over insured and that D had motives for wishing to scupper the vessel and claim the insurance value.

AQUARIUS FINANCIAL ENTERPRISES INC v. LLOYD'S UNDERWRITERS (THE DELPHINE) [2001] 2 Lloyd's Rep. 542, Toulson, J., QBD (Comm Ct).

3825. Marine insurance – disclosure – pre contract principle of good faith – post contract disclosure

[Marine Insurance Act 1906 s.17, s.39(5).]

U appealed against a decision ([1997] 1 Lloyd's Rep. 361, [1997] C.L.Y. 3152) allowing M's appeal against the rejection ([1995] 1 Lloyd's Rep. 651, [1996] C.L.Y. 3608) of M's claim for constructive total loss after a fire on board its sea vessel. U submitted that (1) its defence under the Marine Insurance Act 1906 s.39(5) should have succeeded given that M had a "blind eye knowledge" of the vessel's unseaworthiness arising from defective engine room dampers and the ship's master's incompetence with the fire extinguishing equipment; (2) the defence under s.17 applied in that reports to which M had access concerning the state of repair of the damper system on the ship should have been disclosed and such non-disclosure was in breach of the principle of utmost good faith. The duty of disclosure continued throughout the contractual relationship, and therefore U had the right to rescind in the contract ab initio, and (3) the principles of good faith and disclosure continued post-contract throughout the litigation, and whilst acknowledging the purpose of litigation was to establish the rights of the parties, M's behaviour during litigation could change its rights and do so retrospectively thereby allowing U to avoid the contract.

Held, dismissing the appeal, that (1) for the s.39(5) defence to succeed, privity in respect of the ship's master's incompetence had to be proved. That was a subjective test and a finding of negligence on the part of the master did not equate to a finding of privity therefore U's defence had to fail; (2) there was a clear distinction between that information which should be disclosed at the pre-contract stage and that disclosed during the performance of the contract. For U's defence under s.17 to succeed, it had to show that M had acted fraudulently in making its claim, and that had not been proved, *Piermay Shipping Co SA and Brandt's Ltd v. Chester (The Michael)* [1979] 2 Lloyd's Rep. 1, [1979] C.L.Y. 2471 applied and *Black King Shipping Corp v. Massie (The Litsion Pride)* [1985] 1 Lloyd's Rep. 437, [1985] C.L.Y. 3208 not followed, and (3) once litigation commenced, the rules of disclosure were governed by the procedural rules, not by s.17, and orders governing the disclosure of documents were at the discretion of the court.

MANIFEST SHIPPING CO LTD v. UNI-POLARIS INSURANCE CO LTD (THE STAR SEA); *sub nom.* MANIFEST SHIPPING & CO LTD v. UNI-POLARIS SHIPPING CO LTD (THE STAR SEA) [2001] UKHL 1, Lord Hobhouse of Woodborough, HL.

3826. Marine insurance – indemnities – alleged failure of assured to disclose material facts

D, the registered owner of a yacht, sought an indemnity from A under a marine insurance policy in respect of the loss of the vessel by fire and consequent sinking at its berth in Spain. A contended that D had failed to disclose factors which were material to the assessment of risk to the yacht, namely that the vessel was beneficially owned by G, a prominent Russian businessman and political activist who was at risk of physical attack and who had engaged security personnel for his protection.

Held, giving judgment for the claimant, that A had failed to discharge the burden of proof upon it. A had failed to establish that, at the time that the policy was taken out, D been aware of, or had been of the opinion that there was a real risk of a physical attack on G or his property. G had been obliged to disclose only facts and circumstances material to the assessment of that risk which would be unknown to the underwriters, *Pan Atlantic Insurance Co Ltd v. Pine Top insurance Co Ltd* [1995] 1 A.C. 501 considered. The evidence demonstrated that there had been no real risk of a physical attack upon G, his family or property. Further, G had engaged security guards to protect his children from abduction rather than for his personal protection or to enhance the security of the yacht.

DECORUM INVESTMENTS LTD v. ATKIN (THE ELENA G) [2001] 2 Lloyd's Rep. 378, David Steel, J., QBD (Comm Ct).

3827. Marine insurance – utmost good faith – fraud – entitlement to avoid policy

[Marine Insurance Act 1906 s.17.]

LU, an insurer, appealed against a decision that a forged letter had not entitled it to avoid the policy for breach of the duty of utmost good faith under the Marine Insurance Act 1906 s.17. LU contended that where the insured had acted dishonestly the insurer was within its rights to avoid the contract and that the full force of s.17 should be invoked.

Held, dismissing the appeal, that only where the dishonesty had been so serious that the insurer would have been entitled to terminate for breach of contract was the remedy of avoidance appropriate, *Manifest Shipping Co Ltd v. Uni-Polaris Insurance Co Ltd (The Star Sea)* [2001] UKHL 1, [2001] 2 W.L.R.

170, [2001] 2 C.L. 373 considered. In the instant case the fraud was irrelevant to the insurer's liability under the policy.

K/S MERC-SCANDIA XXXXII v. LLOYD'S UNDERWRITERS (THE MERCANDIAN CONTINENT); *sub nom.* K/S MERC-SCANDIA XXXXII v. UNDERWRITERS OF LLOYD'S POLICY 25T 105487 (THE MERCANDIAN CONTINENT), [2001] EWCA Civ 1275, [2001] 2 Lloyd's Rep. 563, Longmore, L.J., CA.

3828. **Motor insurance – Motor Insurers Bureau – EC law – uninsured drivers agreement – meaning of "knew or ought to have known"**

[Council Directive 84/5 Art.1 (4) relating to insurance against civil liability in respect of the use of motor vehicles.]

W, who had been injured as a result of the negligent driving of his uninsured brother, appealed against a finding of the Court of Appeal that the phrase "knew or ought to have known" in the MIB agreement implementing Council Directive 84/5 Art.1 (4), which allowed Member States to exclude the right to compensation only where a person "knew" that the vehicle was uninsured, meant that he was excluded from claiming compensation because he had been careless or negligent as to whether his brother was insured.

Held, allowing the appeal (Lord Scott dissenting), that (1) for the purpose of Art.1 (4), "knew" encompassed actual knowledge that the driver was uninsured and the situation where the victim deliberately refrained from finding out whether insurance had been taken out. Since he had merely been careless, W's right to claim compensation was not excluded by Art.1 (4), and (2) the phrase "knew or ought to have known" in the MIB Agreement was intended to mirror the exception permitted by the Directive and therefore had to be interpreted in that context. Accordingly, the exception was to be restrictively construed, as with all exceptions to general principles under EC law, so that carelessness or negligence on the part of the victim did not fall into the permitted exceptions.

WHITE v. WHITE, [2001] UKHL 9, [2001] 1 W.L.R. 481, Lord Nicholls of Birkenhead, HL.

3829. **Motor insurance – policy wordings – validity following disposal of vehicle – replacement vehicle**

D appealed against an order that, upon the true construction of a motor insurance policy issued by ES and despite the sale of D's car during the currency of the policy period, D remained insured to drive any car belonging to third parties with their consent. D brought an action against his insurance brokers, PD, on the basis that they had negligently advised him that his insurance cover remained valid notwithstanding the fact that he had disposed of his vehicle. D contended that his cover under the policy depended upon his retaining either the insured car or a replacement for it. PD contended that (1) no general principle applied and the issue depended on the construction of the particular policy, and (2) "replacement" of the insured car was to be interpreted as meaning the purchase of another car at any time during the policy period, not necessarily immediately after disposal of the old one.

Held, dismissing the appeal, that the central issue was whether cover was conditional upon D's continuing ownership of his own car, the case turning upon the terms of the particular policy. D's submission that the policy had lapsed due to his failure to replace the car was unfounded, as ES had to be taken to have accepted the possibility of a replacement not being obtained at the moment of disposal of the old car and to have agreed nevertheless to provide cover on a continuous basis, given that this was undoubtedly a common situation. The presence of a clause concerning replacement vehicles was highly relevant to the policy in question, *Boss v. Kingston* [1963] 1 W.L.R. 99, [1963] C.L.Y. 3074 distinguished. It was more important to emphasise that insured persons were entitled to clearly worded policies and to the benefit of any ambiguity than to artificially construe the wording of the particular policy.

DODSON v. PETER H DODSON INSURANCE SERVICES [2001] 1 W.L.R. 1012, Mance, L.J., CA.

3830. Motor insurance – subrogation – hire charges – proceedings issued prior to payment

[Civil Procedure Rules 1998 (SI 1998 3132).]

C claimed damages including hire charges from D following a road traffic accident in which liability was not in dispute. Pursuant to her legal expenses insurance with DAS and to an arrangement between DAS and MLG, C was provided with a car by MLG. Proceedings were issued in September 1999. DAS did not pay the hire charges until February 2000. The question of whether DAS could exercise rights of subrogation was dealt with as a preliminary point. D submitted that since DAS had not paid the hire charges before proceedings were issued, DAS was not entitled to exercise subrogated rights, therefore the claim was fatally flawed and was not saved by DAS paying the hire charges at a later date, *Page v. Scottish Insurance Corp Ltd* (1929) 33 Ll.L. Rep. 134 and *Yip v. Eckah* (Unreported, November 17, 1999), [2000] 5 C.L. 385 cited. C submitted that the obligation of DAS under the policy was to provide C with a car, which had been done. Therefore DAS had fulfilled its obligations and it was entitled to exercise subrogation rights. D argued that DAS was obliged not only to provide a car but to pay for it. C submitted that *Page* since it had been decided before the introduction of the Civil Procedure Rules 1998 should be disapplied as it was in the interests of justice and fairness for C to recover a sum for loss of use calculated by reference to the hire charges, *Everson v. Flurry* (Unreported, February 22, 1999), [1999] C.L.Y. 3411 cited. D contended that the introduction of the 1998 Rules did not affect the substantive law of subrogation and the approach of *Everson* on the measure of damages was incompatible with the decision in *Dimond v. Lovell* [2000] 2 W.L.R. 1121, [2000] 6 C.L. 282. *Everson* itself specifically left for future consideration the question of whether DAS could exercise rights of subrogation if it issued proceedings before paying the hire charges.

Held, determining the preliminary issue in favour of D, that DAS was only entitled to subrogated rights in respect of what it had paid. Since DAS had not paid the hire charges before issuing proceedings, it had no subrogated rights, therefore *Page* was still good law, *Yip* followed.

BEALE v. BALAND, July 25, 2000, Deputy District Judge Simpkins, CC (Haywards Heath). [*Ex rel.* Timothy Petts, Barrister, 12 Kings Bench Walk, London].

3831. Motor insurance – third party insurance – standardised system for calculating compensation – European Economic Area

[Act 50 of 1 July 1993 on Tort Damages (Iceland) s.8; Agreement on a European Economic Area 1992; Council Directive 72/166 relating to insurance against civil liability in respect of the use of motor vehicles; Second Council Directive 84/5 relating to insurance against civil liability in respect of the use of motor vehicles.]

HH, then aged 17, sustained head injuries when she was hit by DH's car while riding her bicycle. Under the Tort Damages Act 1993 s.8 compensation paid to accident victims with little or no income was based on an evaluation of medical disability, rather than occupational disability. The national court made a reference to the European Free Trade Association court for a ruling on the compatibility of the compensation system in s.8 with the Agreement on a European Economic Area 1992 and the provisions of Council Directive 72/166, Second Council Directive 84/5 and Third Council Directive 90/232.

Held, finding that s.8 of the 1993 Act was compatible with the Directives, that (1) standardised compensation payable on the basis of medical disability under compulsory third party motor insurance was compatible with EEA law and Directives where victims had little or no earning capacity; (2) the Directives did not provide for a minimum level of compensation in such circumstances, and (3) it was for Member States to determine whether compensation payable under compulsory third party motor insurance should be adjusted to take account of compensation paid to a victim from other sources.

HELGADOTTIR v. HJALTASON (E7/00) [2001] 3 C.M.L.R. 27, Vilhjalmsson (President) f, EFTA.

3832. Motor insurance – unfair contract terms – insurer liable for damage caused by uninsured driver – recovery from insured party

[Road Traffic Act 1988 s.151 (8); Unfair Terms in Consumer Contract regulations 1994 (SI 1994 3159) Reg.6, Sch.2.]

P sought to recover from K a sum in excess of £12,000 pursuant to the Road Traffic Act 1998 s.151 (8). K had left her car in the office car park whilst she went on holiday and left the keys in the office lobby so that the vehicle could be moved by one of her staff if necessary. K also told H that he could drive her car, but only so long as he arranged his own insurance cover. H removed the keys from the lobby and took the car onto a public highway where he was involved in a collision with R's vehicle. At the time of the accident H was uninsured. R issued proceedings against H and judgment was given in R's favour. P, as K's insurers, were obliged to satisfy the judgment. P then issued proceedings against K to recover the sum under s.151 (8) or, in the alternative, to recover under a clause in the insurance contract which provided that "if we are obliged by the laws of any country in which this policy operates to make a payment for which we would not otherwise be liable you must repay the amount to us within 21 days of a formal demand".

Held, giving judgment for the defendant, that (1) K's evidence of the discussion she had had with H was accepted. Therefore, P's claim under s.151 (8) failed becuase permission given subject to a condition which was unfulfilled was no permission at all, *Newbury v. Davis* [1974] R.T.R. 367, [1974] C.L.Y. 3351 followed. Further, by leaving the keys in the lobby, it could not be inferred that any permission to move the vehicle extended to driving it out onto a public highway; (2) it was unclear whether the clause in the contract sought simply to repeat the provisions of s.151 (8) or whether it sought to confer on P a right of recovery regardless of whether or not K had caused or permitted H to use her vehicle. Having regard to the Unfair Terms in Consumer Contract regulations 1994 Reg.6, the meaning of the term was doubtful and accordingly should be given the narrow interpretation which was most favourable to K as a consumer, and (3) in the alternative, if the term was interpreted more widely, it was unfair and P could not rely on it. The term was an indemnity clause and it did not define or circumscribe the insurer's risk or liability, nor did it concern the adequacy of the price. Therefore the court was entitled to assess the fairness of the term under Sch.2 of the Regulations. The term was unfair as it was not individually negotiated, had not been drawn to K's attention and sought to impose an unlimited liability on K, removing her protection under s.151 (8) of the Act, *Director General of Fair Trading v. First National Bank Plc* [2000] Q.B. 672, [2000] C.L.Y. 2595 applied.

PEARL ASSURANCE PLC v. KAVANAGH, June 21, 2001, District Judge Hickman, CC (Milton Keynes). [*Ex rel.* Laurence Jeffrey Deegan, Barrister, Fenners Chambers, 3 Madingley Road, Cambridge].

3833. Motor vehicles – insurance – company cars – records

MOTOR VEHICLES (THIRD PARTY RISKS) (AMENDMENT) REGULATIONS 2001, SI 2001 2266; made under the Road Traffic Act 1988 s.160. In force: July 16, 2001; £1.75.

These Regulations amend the Motor Vehicles (Third Party Risks) Regulations 1972 (SI 1972 1217) by altering the requirements regarding the keeping of records of insurance and securities policies and certificates issued under the Road Traffic Act 1988 and the use of vehicles which is exempt from the normal insurance requirement under s.144 of that Act. The requirements are extended in the case of insurance policies and securities to include particulars of every person whose liability is covered by a policy or security and additional particulars of the vehicles whose use is covered. Records of old insurance policies and securities are required to be kept for a period of seven years after expiry. Copies of any records may be supplied to the Motor Insurers' Bureau or its nominated subsidiary in electronic form and kept by it on a database. In such cases the Bureau or its subsidiary must keep the copy records of expired policies and securities for the same seven-year period and disclose particulars of any record it holds to the Secretary of State or police on request.

3834. **Reinsurance contracts – avoidance – misrepresentation – non disclosure of relevant information concerning fire precautions**

G sought determination of certain preliminary issues as to whether it was entitled to avoid a contract of reinsurance for misrepresentation or non-disclosure. It was alleged that the extent of fire precautions at a building which housed equipment for which the original insurance had been issued had been misrepresented to G, or not fully disclosed.

Held, determining the preliminary issues in favour of T, that it could not be said that false representations had been made in relation to the existence of sophisticated fire fighting systems in the building. It followed that G could not avoid the contract for non disclosure. A reinsurance policy contained an implied term that a reinsurer could not unreasonably withhold its consent to a settlement.

GAN INSURANCE CO LTD v. TAI PING INSURANCE CO LTD (PRELIMINARY ISSUES) [2001] C.L.C. 776, Longmore, J., QBD (Comm Ct).

3835. **Reinsurance contracts – contract terms – clause stipulating all premiums would be held in separate account – resulting trust subsequent to reinsurer's insolvency**

HB, an underwriting syndicate, had entered into a contract of reinsurance with NCR, an Australian reinsurance company, for losses incurred from casualty claims over a twelve month period. The contract incorporated a clause whereby NCR agreed to withhold all premiums owed, after deductions had been made, in a credit fund account administered by BB, a bank. The clause stipulated that the funds held were for use exclusively as collateral for the promulgation of letters of credit. Prior to the issue of a letter of credit NCR appointed an administrator and requested that BB pay out the monies held in the account. HB successfully applied for a freezing order and subsequently issued proceedings claiming entitlement as beneficial owner to the monies held in the account. NCR argued that the letter of credit had been the only security in the agreement, and since it had not been issued at the time of NCR's insolvency, HB was obliged to prove its claim in the Australian liquidation. HB contended that the monies were held either under an express purpose trust, or subsequent to the failure of the purpose of the arrangement, under a resulting trust. An application to strike out elements of NCR's defence having been refused on the ground that it was made too late, HB submitted that the court was not entitled to rely on evidence from the contractual negotiations when construing the agreement.

Held, giving judgment for HB, that (1) evidence deriving from the negotiations prior to the formation of the contract was not admissible in construing the contract. By their nature, negotiations were not illustrative of a consensus between parties and accordingly the court should only have regard to the final document, *Prenn v. Simmonds* [1971] 1 W.L.R. 1381, [1971] C.L.Y. 1711 applied; (2) the contractual clause created an express purpose trust. The monies held in the credit fund account had the single purpose of being "collateral for the issuance of letters of credit". It followed that NCR did not have the freedom to use the monies for its own purposes. The purpose for which the monies were deposited having failed, a resulting trust had arisen, *Barclays Bank Ltd v. Quistclose Investments Ltd* [1970] A.C. 567, [1968] C.L.Y. 459 considered, and (3) the fact that the insolvency regime of another jurisdiction provided a different form of avoidance was not ground for removing the right of a party suing in the English jurisdiction to obtain judgment, *Galbraith v. Grimshaw* [1910] A.C. 508 applied. HB had entered into the contract in good faith and had had no reasonable grounds for believing NCR would become insolvent. It followed that HB was entitled to the monies held in the credit fund account.

HURST-BANNISTER v. NEW CAP REINSURANCE CO LTD [2000] Lloyd's Rep. I.R. 166, John Jarvis Q.C., Ch D.

3836. Reinsurance contracts – contract terms – incorporation of arbitration clause by reference

[Arbitration Act 1996 s.9.]

I applied under the Arbitration Act 1996 s.9 to stay proceedings brought by C, reinsurers, in relation to certain reinsurance contracts. In the proceedings, C sought a declaration that it was off risk at the end of 1997 and rectification of the policy wording. I maintained that C were bound by an arbitration clause in an unexecuted contract document it termed the "Intercaser reinsurance contract". I argued that the signed reinsurance slip had incorporated by reference the terms and conditions of the reinsurance "contract" and that therefore the arbitration clause was binding. C argued that it had not accepted such wording, which was not incorporated into the contract as evidenced by the slip, and that the wording was not incorporated merely by the scratching of the slip.

Held, refusing the application, that general words of incorporation were insufficient to incorporate an arbitration clause as such clauses were regarded as personal to the parties to the agreement and collateral to the main obligations, *Trygg Hansa Insurance Co Ltd v. Equitas Ltd* [1998] 2 Lloyd's Rep. 439, [1998] C.L.Y. 242 applied. In any event, the parties had not properly identified the document whose terms were to be incorporated. The "contract" to which the slip purported to refer did not exist until its terms had been agreed to and the court could not infer that by signing the slip with a reference to the "contract", the parties were thereby intending those terms to be binding without the express approval of the underwriters.

CIGNA LIFE INSURANCE CO OF EUROPE SA NV v. INTERCASER SA DE SEGUROS Y REASEGUROS [2002] 1 All E.R. (Comm) 235, Morison, J., QBD (Comm Ct).

3837. Reinsurance contracts – contract terms – retrocession agreement – meaning of "occurrence"

M, a reinsurer and party to a retrocession agreement with L, appealed against a finding ([2000] 2 All E.R. (Comm) 163, [2000] C.L.Y. 3561) that damage to various shop premises during riots in Indonesia, amounted to a single occurrence for the purposes of the retrocession agreement. A clause in the agreement limited the sum insured to "$5,000,000 per occurrence but in the annual aggregate for flood and earthquake". M contended that (1) despite differences in wording between the policy of reinsurance and the retrocession agreement, clear words would be required to enable a retrocessionaire to aggregate the claims or losses and that such clear wording was only to be found in instances of flood or earthquake, and (2) since the rioting had taken place at disparate times and locations it could not be viewed as a single occurrence even if it had in fact been part of an organised campaign of civil unrest.

Held, allowing the appeal, that (1) the agreement had to be construed in the context of the reinsurance policy. Whilst it was clear that M and L must have reached some agreement upon aggregation, that had only been in relation to flood and earthquake as expressly stated. Under the reinsurance there was reference to "each and every loss, each and every location" and the deductible specified "each loss any one occurrence". The wording of the deductible did not contemplate that an occurrence would encompass more than one location because pursuant to the policy, it could not. Since the deductible clause was exactly the same in the retrocession agreement it could be inferred that "occurrence" had the same meaning, and (2) the fact that riots had been part of an orchestrated campaign but had taken place at differing times and locations militated against a conclusion that they were part of a single occurrence, *Kuwait*

Airways Corp v. Kuwait Insurance Co SAK (No.1) [1996] 1 Lloyd's Rep. 664, [1996] C.L.Y. 3570 considered.

MANN v. LEXINGTON INSURANCE CO [2001] 1 All E.R. (Comm) 28, Waller, L.J., CA.

3838. Reinsurance contracts – jurisdiction – exclusive jurisdiction clauses – incorporation by reference – need for clear language

[Brussels Convention on Jurisdiction and Enforcement of Judgments in Civil and Commercial Matters 1968 Art.17.]

Q applied for a declaration that the English court had no jurisdiction to hear A's claim against it for wrongful termination of a contract of reinsurance. A, a European insurer, was seeking a declaration from the English court that Q had wrongfully purported to cancel the policy before the end of the terms specified in the agreement. Q submitted that the English court had no jurisdiction to grant the declaration because the parties had agreed for the purposes of the Brussels Convention 1968 Art.17 that the French courts would have exclusive jurisdiction. Q claimed that since the underlying insurance contract was governed solely by French law, the reinsurance contract, which provided that "all terms" were to be "as original", was also subject solely to French law.

Held, refusing the application, that an exclusive jurisdiction clause in an insurance contract could be incorporated by reference, so long as the reference was clearly expressed. Jurisdiction clauses were ancillary to the substance of the contract and therefore the form and language of such a reference were of particular importance and the words used had to clearly and precisely demonstrate that the clause was the subject of consensus between the parties, *Colzani v. RUWA Polstereimaschinen GmbH (24/76)* [1976] E.C.R. 1831 [1977] C.L.Y. 1242 applied. Where general words of incorporation by reference were used the court had to look to the commercial background to see which terms were intended to be incorporated. On the facts, the language used was insufficient to satisfy the requirements of Art.17. The reference to "all terms" did not establish that there had been consensus between the parties, as it was clear there were some terms of the original policy which were not intended to apply to the reinsurance, *Benincasa v. Dentalkit Srl (C269/95)* [1998] All E.R. (EC) 135, [1997] C.L.Y. 888 considered.

AIG EUROPE SA v. QBE INTERNATIONAL INSURANCE LTD [2001] 2 All E.R. (Comm) 622, Moore-Bick, J., QBD (Comm Ct).

3839. Reinsurance contracts – liability – non compliance with claims cooperation clause

G appealed and T cross appealed against decisions in a judgment concerning a policy of reinsurance ([2001] C.L.C. 776). The reinsurance was in slip form and included a full reinsurance clause together with a claims cooperation clause which stipulated that it was a precondition to any liability under the policy that "no settlement and/or compromise shall be made and liability admitted without the prior approval" of G, the reinsurer. T had settled the claim with its insured. The judge had found that compliance with the claims cooperation clause was a condition precedent to liability, that a breach could only be substantiated by showing that T had settled or compromised the insured's claim and admitted liability, that if T was in breach of the clause then it could not recover and, since G's approval was a condition precedent to liability, a term would be implied into the contract that approval of a settlement must not be unreasonably withheld. On appeal, the court was asked to determine (1) whether breach of the claims cooperation clause was only established by showing an admission of liability as well as a settlement; (2) whether compliance with the claims cooperation clause was a condition precedent to liability, and (3) whether there was an implied term that G must have reasonable grounds for withholding approval of a settlement.

Held, allowing the appeal in part and dismissing the cross appeal, that (1) there was no requirement for G to establish that there had been both an admission of liability and a settlement since such an interpretation of the claims cooperation clause produced a result which was commercially unrealistic; (2) the wording of the policy clearly showed that compliance with the claims cooperation policy was a condition precedent to liability so that the effect of the breach of the clause was that T could not recover under the reinsurance contract, and (3) the judge had erred in finding that the reinsurance contract contained an implied term that approval of a settlement could not be unreasonably withheld. The right to withhold approval was not unqualified but the only limitations were that it be exercised in good faith, after consideration of the claim as a whole and by reference to the facts giving rise to the particular claim. The court should not substitute itself for the reinsurer. Further, there was no requirement for a reinsurer to be able to establish positively that there were reasonable prospects of defending the claim or procuring a more satisfactory settlement.

GAN INSURANCE CO LTD v. TAI PING INSURANCE CO LTD (NO.2), [2001] EWCA Civ 1047, [2001] 2 All E.R. (Comm) 299, Mance, L.J., CA.

3840. Reinsurance contracts – warranties – use of slip for construction of policy

H, the insurer, appealed and N, the reinsurer, cross appealed against a determination of preliminary issues ([2001] 1 Lloyd's Rep. 378) arising in relation to "pecuniary loss indemnity insurance" provided to indemnify the return on film finance. The preliminary issues had arisen in an action brought by H, which had paid out over $30 million to the investors in a number of films, seeking recovery against the reinsurers. The issues before the court related to, inter alia, whether the wording of the original slip policy had been superseded by that of the policy and whether a term stipulating the number of films to be made constituted a warranty.

Held, dismissing the appeal and cross appeal, that (1) the six film term was a term of the policy wording. There was no rule of law that in circumstances where an earlier contract had been followed by a later contract, or an insurance slip contract had been followed by a policy, it was inadmissible to have regard to the terms of the former, or that the parole evidence rule gave rise to the same effect, *Youell v. Bland Welch & Co Ltd (No.1)* [1992] 2 Lloyd's Rep. 127, [1992] C.L.Y. 2621, *Punjab National Bank v. De Boinville* [1992] 1 W.L.R. 1138, [1992] C.L.Y. 2605, *St Paul Fire & Marine Insurance Co (UK) Ltd v. McConnell Dowell Constructors Ltd* [1993] 2 Lloyd's Rep. 503, [1994] C.L.Y. 2663 and *New Hampshire Insurance Co Ltd v. MGN Ltd (1996)* [1997] L.R.L.R. 24, [1996] C.L.Y. 3572 considered. All the observations in those cases had been obiter dicta. However, it was appropriate to follow a cautious and sceptical approach in seeking assistance from an earlier contract and it was doubtful that the principle that the prior contract was always admissible should be considered a conclusive rule of law. However, in circumstances where it was not common ground that the later contract had been intended to supersede the earlier one, it should always be permissible to have regard to the earlier contract. In regard to the insurance context, it could be said that there was a general presumption that a policy was intended to supersede a slip and that slips tended to set out the contract in shorthand and consequently were neither clear or complete. It followed that there would often be considerable inutility in using a slip as an aid for the construction of the policy. Moreover, given that the status of the slip had been uncertain until recent times, it was not appropriate to seek aid from older case law. It could, however, be said that in the absence of a plea for rectification, a slip could not be used in order to alter or contradict the interpretation of a policy which had superseded a slip. In the instant case, the original slip had not been superseded and accordingly the policy wording had to be read having regard to it, and (2) the six film term was a warranty because it was descriptive of the subject matter and material to the insurance risk. The fact that the word "warranty" or "warranted" was either present or absent in an insurance or reinsurance contract was not conclusive.

HIH CASUALTY & GENERAL INSURANCE LTD v. NEW HAMPSHIRE INSURANCE CO, [2001] EWCA Civ 735, [2001] 2 All E.R. (Comm) 39, Rix, L.J., CA.

3841. Subrogation – fees – engineer's report – absence of proof of payment

C and E were involved in a road traffic accident for which E admitted liability. C claimed, inter alia, the cost of a report from a vehicle engineer which had been necessary to enable C's insurer's to ascertain the extent of the damage to C's vehicle. C contended that the fee could be recovered from E by virtue of the insurer's rights of subrogation.

Held, giving judgment for the defendant, that although the report fee had been reasonably incurred and it could, in principle, be recovered in the manner for which C contended, in the absence of any proof that the fee had been paid, the cost was not recoverable, *Crowe v. Hutt* (Unreported, June 12, 2000), [2000] C.L.Y. 404 and *Coleman v. Stubbs* (Unreported, October 15, 1998), [1998] C.L.Y. 422 distinguished on the ground that those cases concerned reports which had not been prepared for the purposes of litigation.

COLBECK v. ELLIS, February 22, 2001, District Judge Stapeley, CC (Wakefield). [*Ex rel.* Simon Plaut, Barrister, Park Lane Chambers, 19 Westgate, Leeds].

3842. Subrogation – guarantees – exclusion of rights of surety to subrogation

Determination was sought, as a preliminary issue, of whether L's rights of subrogation under a guarantee issued by H to guarantee H's obligations to O had been excluded by the bond's terms. O, which was in the business of providing marine insurance to members, arranged for H to guarantee members' liability to third parties, and in turn provided security to H by way of a bond issued by L. Unknown to L, O later granted H a fixed charge over its book debts, and L continued to issue bonds until liquidators were appointed to O. L submitted that following payment under the bond it was entitled to be subrogated to H's rights to the security from O given under the fixed charge on book debts and to share rateably in the proceeds of such security. H contended that even if such a right to subrogation arose, it was excluded in the instant case by the terms of the bond which stipulated that the indemnity was "separate from any other security or right of indemnity". L submitted that to exclude a right to subrogation required clear words, and that there was no commercial sense in attributing to it a willingness to postpone its rights to subrogation until O's other obligations to H had been discharged in full.

Held, determining the preliminary issue in favour of L, that clear words were needed to exclude or postpone subrogation rights, and that commercial common sense supported L's case. Postponing subrogation until other liabilities had been discharged would have served to extend the liability under the bond, and the practical consequences of this would have enabled both O and H to postpone L's subrogation rights for ever just by creating further liabilities. Accordingly L's rights of subrogation were not excluded by the bond's terms *Butlers Wharf Ltd, Re* [1995] 2 B.C.L.C. 43, [1995] C.L.Y. 2833 applied.

LIBERTY MUTUAL INSURANCE CO (UK) LTD v. HSBC BANK PLC (SUBROGATION) [2001] Lloyd's Rep. Bank. 224, Sir Andrew Morritt V.C., Ch D.

3843. Third party insurance – accidents – deliberate criminal act – public policy

[Road Traffic Act 1988 s.151.]

CI, an insurance company, appealed against a declaration that it was obliged to indemnify F, its insured, in respect of his liability to C. C had sustained injuries following an incident in which F had deliberately reversed his car into a stationary car in a car park. F had subsequently pleaded guilty to criminal damage. CI denied that the incident was an "accident" under the terms of the insurance policy and further that as it had not occurred on the road, it was not covered by the policy, as the policy, whilst meeting the requirements of the law, contained certain common exclusions. In addition, CI argued that there was no statutory obligation to indemnify F. C contended that there was no evidence to suggest that F had sought to deliberately injure her, and that her injuries were discreet from the damage that had been caused to the vehicle. Further, it was argued that on a proper construction of the policy, there was no exclusion of liability arising from incidents that occurred off the road.

Held, allowing the appeal, that as the incident had not happened on the road, C had no rights against CI through the MIB or under the Road Traffic Act 1988 s.151, and CI was not directly liable to her. Any claim therefore only existed as the statutory assignee of F. However, public policy denied F the right to be indemnified against a liability arising from his intentional criminal act, *Gardner v. Moore* [1984] A.C. 548, [1984] C.L.Y. 3050 applied. Further, the word "accident" in the field of compulsory third party insurance was to be narrowly interpreted, and on a true interpretation of the policy, CI was not liable.

CHARLTON v. FISHER; *sub nom.* CHURCHILL INSURANCE v. CHARLTON, [2001] EWCA Civ 112, [2001] 3 W.L.R. 1435, Kennedy, L.J., CA.

3844. Underwriting – risk assessment – negligent misrepresentation – assessment by lead underwriter in accordance with stated criteria

[Misrepresentation Act 1967 s.2(1).]

A, a company of stop loss insurers, made a claim against SF, insurance brokers, pursuant to the Misrepresentation Act 1967 s.2(1). A maintained that material misrepresentations had been made to it in a booklet written by SF, which had induced A to become the stop loss insurer for a large number of Lloyd's Names. A contended that the misrepresentation arose from a statement that SF's lead underwriter, B, would individually assess each of the Names proposing to take out stop loss cover, in accordance with the stated underwriting criteria, when, in fact, he did not do so. A claimed the same measure of damages as that available in fraud, *Royscot Trust Ltd v. Rogerson* [1991] 2 Q.B. 297, [1991] C.L.Y. 1311 cited. SF reserved the right to submit that damages for innocent misrepresentation under s.2(1) of the Act were to be calculated in the same measure as those for negligent misrepresentation.

Held, giving judgment for the defendant, that (1) on the evidence, each risk had been individually assessed and rated. The fact that parts of the process had been delegated to deputies under B's supervision was an inevitable outcome of a process which had been formulated in order to cope with large and increasing numbers of proposals. Overall control of the system had, nevertheless, always remained with B; hence the overall procedure had not been inconsistent with the claims made in the booklet and there was no misrepresentation, and (2) there was little substance to the allegations that the risk had not been assessed in accordance with the stated underwriting criteria. SF's representation was to be construed broadly and, looking at it from that perspective, it had been substantially correct. A representation could be true even if it was not entirely correct, so long as the difference between what was represented and what was correct was not, alone, responsible for inducing the claimant to enter into the contract. A failure in respect of an isolated aspect of the risks assessment was not likely to have influenced A, especially as the ultimate significance of the criteria was to achieve a well spread book of business, and that result had been achieved. The law provided that damages assessed upon the fraud basis were to be awarded where a misrepresentation had induced a contract, *Royscot* applied. It, therefore, followed that the court should take care in finding that a misrepresentation had occurred.

AVON INSURANCE PLC v. SWIRE FRASER LTD [2000] 1 All E.R. (Comm) 573, Rix, J., QBD (Comm Ct).

3845. Books

Bateman, Mike – Tolley's Practical Guide to Risk Assessment. Paperback: £50.00. ISBN 0-7545-0749-1. Tolley Publishing.

Birds, John; Hird, Norma – Birds' Modern Insurance Law. 5th Ed. Paperback: £25.00. ISBN 0-421-71670-3. Sweet & Maxwell.

Hawken, Angela; Carroll, Stephen J.; Abrahamse, Allan F. – Effects of Third-party Bad Faith Doctrine on Automobile Insurance Costs and Compensation. Paperback: £10.95. ISBN 0-8330-3034-5. RAND.

Jess, Digby – Insurance of Commercial Risks: Law and Practice. 3rd Ed. Hardback: £150.00. ISBN 0-421-82440-9. Sweet & Maxwell.

McGee, Andrew – McGee: the Modern Law of Insurance. Hardback: £175.00. ISBN 0-406-90385-9. Butterworths Law.

McGee, Andrew – Modern Law of Insurance. Hardback: £175.00. ISBN 0-406-90385-9. Butterworths Law.

Mildred, Mark – Product Liability: Law and Insurance. Hardback: £190.00. ISBN 1-85978-538-7. LLP Professional Publishing.

Surridge, Robert J.; Scott, Roselyn; Murphy, Brian; James, Natalie; John, Noleen – Houseman and Davies: Law of Life Assurance. 112th Ed. Hardback: £135.00. ISBN 0-406-93589-0. Butterworths Law.

Taylor, Paul; Oliver, Timothy; Pether, Michael – Bingham and Berryman's Motor Claims Cases. 11th Ed. Hardback: £195.00. ISBN 0-406-93230-1. Butterworths Law.

West, Richard – Survival Guide for Claims Handlers. Paperback: £50.00. ISBN 0-406-91342-0. Butterworths Law.

INTELLECTUAL PROPERTY

3846. Copyright – confidential information – Council Directive

European Parliament and Council Directive 2001/29 of 22 May 2001 on the harmonisation of certain aspects of copyright and related rights in the information society. [2001] OJ L167/10.

3847. Copyright – Crown copyright – dominant position – grant of licence – entitlement to charge royalty

[EC Treaty Art.86 (now, after amendment Art.82 EC).]

In proceedings for infringement of copyright commenced by HMSO, AA applied to put in an amended rejoinder and HMSO applied to strike out the existing rejoinder. AA alleged that HMSO were abusing their dominant position concerning information about new roads in breach of the EC Treaty Art.86 (now, after amendment Art.82). AA maintained that (1) the breach arose from the fact that HMSO had requested a royalty fee pursuant to the grant of a licence, and (2) other users of the information such as Ordnance Survey did not pay for the use of the information.

Held, granting the application to strike out the rejoinder and dismissing the application to amend, that (1) no copyright holder was obliged to grant a licence for a nil royalty, *Radio Telefis Eireann v. Commission of the European Communities (C241/91)* [1995] All E.R. (EC) 416, [1995] C.L.Y. 639 considered, and (2) the evidence in relation to other users lacked substance and was misconceived in so far as it related to the Ordnance Survey, which was itself part of the Crown. The fact that one part of the Crown did not charge another part for use of Crown copyright could not amount to discrimination between the Crown itself and third parties.

HM STATIONERY OFFICE v. AUTOMOBILE ASSOCIATION LTD; *sub nom.* HM STATIONERY OFFICE v. AA LTD [2001] E.C.C. 34, Laddie, J., Ch D.

3848. Copyright – database right – bookmakers – websites – derivation – unfair extraction and reutilisation of information – transfer to another medium

[Council Directive 96/9 on the legal protection of databases Art.7(1), Art.7(5).]

B brought an action claiming that W had infringed its database rights under Council Directive 96/9 on the legal protection of databases. B maintained a large and complex computerised database relating to horseracing in the UK, which included genealogical information about horses, and which constantly updated and verified details on racing fixtures. B supplied certain information contained on the database under licence to SIS. W used data and services supplied to it by SIS in order to provide gambling facilities to punters in its betting shops. In February 2000 W launched an internet website allowing punters to access up to date details of races and to place bets. B argued that this information had been derived from its database without its permission and amounted to an extraction and reutilisation of a substantial part of the database contrary to Art.7(1) of the Directive, or, alternatively, that W was making repeated extractions of insubstantial parts of the database contrary to Art.7(5).W contended that derivation had not been proved as the information was available from other sources.

Held, giving judgment for B, that W had infringed B's database right under both Art.7(1) and Art.7(5). As B had made a "substantial investment" in the formation, organisation and upkeep of its database it did come within the protection of the Directive. B was effectively the only body in the country able to supply such detailed up to the minute information on races, and therefore it was nonsensical to suggest that W had obtained the information from other sources. It was not the form alone of the database that was protected under the Directive. The taking of information from a database and ordering it differently was capable of amounting to the use of "parts of the contents" of the database. Given the nature of B's role in UK horseracing the information relating to racing fixtures was highly significant and formed the "core" of the database. It was thus a "substantial" part of the database for the purposes of the Directive. It had been "extracted" as it had been made available to the public by W in another format, namely on the website, and therefore had been "transferred to another medium". It had also been "reutilised". The fact that the information had already been made available to the public was immaterial when considering whether W's use of the data had amounted to "reutilisation" of the data. The regular updating of the database did not have the effect of rendering it into separate databases every time new information was added. It remained one database, and W's use of it on repeated occasions amounted to repeated extractions and reutilisations contrary to Art.7(5).

BRITISH HORSERACING BOARD LTD v. WILLIAM HILL ORGANISATION LTD (NO.2) [2001] 2 C.M.L.R. 12, Laddie, J., Pat Ct.

3849. Copyright – exemptions – entitlement of local authority – nature of activities

[Copyright, Designs and Patents Act 1988 s.67.]

PP, the copyright holder of music played by the local authority in keep fit classes run for the benefit of the public, sought preliminary determination as to whether the local authority was entitled to copyright exemption under the Copyright, Designs and Patents Act 1988 s.67. PP submitted that the local authority was fundamentally wrong in its contention that its function was to promote social welfare on a charitable and non profit making basis.

Held, determining the preliminary issue in favour of PP, that for the purposes of s.67 of the Act, a local authority was not a club, society or other organisation entitled by that section to copyright exemption. Although a local authority could be an "organisation", the nature of its activities placed it outside the scope of s.67, attributing to the words used their everyday meaning. The purpose of a local authority was to discharge administrative and governmental tasks at a local level, and although social and welfare services and fund raising were part of those, it was in a different context to that envisaged by s.67, *Berry v. St Marylebone BC* [1958] Ch. 406, *General Nursing Council for England and Wales v. St Marylebone BC* [1959] A.C. 540, [1959] C.L.Y. 2766 and *National Deposit Friendly Society Trustees v. Skegness Urban DC* [1959] A.C. 293, [1958] C.L.Y. 2844 considered.

PHONOGRAPHIC PERFORMANCE LTD v. SOUTH TYNESIDE MBC [2001] 1 W.L.R. 400, Neuberger, J., Ch D.

3850. Copyright – freedom of expression – conflict between provisions – regard to the facts

[Copyright Designs and Patents Act 1988 s.30, s.171 (3); Human Rights Act 1998 s.3(1), Sch.1 Part I Art.10.]

T, a national newspaper, appealed against a decision ([2001] 2 W.L.R. 967) to grant summary judgment in favour of A, a prominent politician, in a claim for infringement of copyright under the Copyright Designs and Patents Act 1988. A was contemplating publishing his political memoirs and the minute of a meeting with the Prime Minister and other documents were shown in confidence to representatives of newspapers and publishers. T had subsequently published verbatim quotations from the minute. T contended that the court was obliged under the Human Rights Act 1998 s.3(1) to take into consideration the right of freedom of expression under Sch.1 Part I Art.10 in assessing the defences of fair dealing and public interest under s.30 and s.171 (3) of the 1988 Act.

Held, dismissing the appeal, that where in the rare circumstances that the right to freedom of expression came into conflict with the 1988 Act, it was necessary to have close regard to the facts of the individual case. The court was required to apply the 1988 Act in a way that accommodated the right to freedom of expression. However, the freedom of expression did not normally include a right to make free use of another person's work. Where a newspaper felt it necessary to use exact extracts, it was appropriate for it to indemnify the author of such extracts or provide him with any profits that stemmed from the use of them. In the instant case, T's publication of parts of A's minute could not be justified by public interest considerations. It was apparent that T had published for essentially commercial purposes. It was observed that since there was a clear public interest in giving effect to the freedom of expression where such right overrode those rights conferred under the 1988 Act, s.171 (3) did permit the defence of public interest to be raised, *Hyde Park Residence Ltd v. Yelland* [2001] Ch. 143, [2000] C.L.Y. 3573 and *Lion Laboratories Ltd v. Evans* [1985] Q.B. 526 considered.

ASHDOWN v. TELEGRAPH GROUP LTD, [2001] EWCA Civ 1142, [2001] 3 W.L.R. 1368, Lord Phillips of Worth Matravers, M.R., CA.

3851. Copyright – infringement – breach of confidence – husband copying pages of confidential information from wife's diary

[Copyright Designs and Patents Act 1988 s.45.]

A and B had been married to each other. A kept a diary which she said was for her eyes only. She told B she wanted a divorce. At some time thereafter, B read passages from the diary and photocopied two pages of it. B made several further copies, and exhibited one of the copy pages to an affidavit which he swore in the subsequent divorce proceedings. A applied for summary judgment for delivery up of the copy pages, alleging breach of copyright and breach of confidence. B resisted both allegations on the grounds that the copies were made in respect of contemplated and actual court proceedings and did not contain confidential information and that he had a public interest defence.

Held, dismissing the application, that (1) the two pages were a substantial part of the diary; (2) that they were copied for the purpose of judicial proceedings and that B had a realistic prospect of establishing a trial that his use of the copy pages was within the Copyright Designs and Patents Act 1988 s.45, in that the first copying was done after A had said she wanted a divorce, and therefore in contemplation of divorce proceedings, and the second copying (unless done before the divorce petition was issued) had been done in furtherance of actual proceedings *Pro Sieben Media AG v. Carlton UK Television Ltd* [1999] 1 W.L.R. 605, [1999] C.L.Y. 3438 applied, *Auckland Medical Aid Trust v. Commissioner of Police*[1976] 1 N.Z.L.R. 485 considered; (3) the contents of the pages were, on the evidence, confidential. Confidentiality was not, however, a basis for preventing secondary evidence being received of the contents of documents which were not privileged. Confidence was a matter of equity, thereby leaving the court with a discretion as to whether or not to order delivery up; (4) A was however entitled to have the copies safeguarded, and B would be ordered to lodge all copies in his possession with his solicitors, who in turn would undertake to use them only for the purpose of proceedings between the parties, and (5) the diary's content was not such that the court would refuse to enforce copyright or confidence in respect of them on the grounds of immorality, scandal or that they were contrary to family life *Stephens v. Avery* [1988] Ch. 449, [1988] C.L.Y. 3403 applied and *Goddard v. Nationwide Building Society* [1987] Q.B. 670, [1986] C.L.Y. 1516 applied, *Lord Ashburton v. Pape* [1913] 2 Ch. 469, *Webster v. James Chapman & Co* [1989] 3 All E.R. 939, [1990] C.L.Y. 3656 and *Derby & Co Ltd v. Weldon (No.8)* [1991] 1 W.L.R. 73, [1991] C.L.Y. 2861 considered.

A v. B (COPYRIGHT: DIARY PAGES) [2000] E.M.L.R. 1007, Lloyd, J., Ch D.

3852. Copyright – infringement – evidential burden of proof – similarities between designs – inadvertent infringement

S brought an action for alleged infringement of its copyright in a carpet design called "Chamonix" by W through the design of a carpet called "Georgiana". S submitted 21 similarities between the designs as found by its expert witness and argued that, as there was a prima facie case of copying, its action should succeed because W had failed to discharge the evidential burden of giving a detailed account of events leading up to the design for "Georgiana".

Held, giving judgment for W, that a case could not automatically be found against W's designer purely on the basis that he had failed to discharge the burden of proving that his work was independent. The focus had to be on whether the evidence suggested that the design had been copied or not. In the light of the evidence, W had not copied the "Chamonix" design. Furthermore, if a designer received instructions which it was reasonable to expect covered something similar to the copyright work, and then designs were produced without knowledge of the copyright work, one of which was similar to the design, the person selecting the design could not be guilty of a copyright infringement if only a concept was communicated, *Joanna Christina Gleeson and Gleeson Shirt Co v. HR Denne Ltd* [1975] F.S.R. 250, [1975] C.L.Y. 441 followed. The brief to W's designer was incapable of directing him towards the "Chamonix" design and he had demonstrated a sufficient freedom of design.

STODDARD INTERNATIONAL PLC v. WILLIAM LOMAS CARPETS LTD [2001] F.S.R. 44, Pumfrey, J., Ch D.

3853. Copyright – infringement – literary works – animated television films from scripts

[Copyright, Designs and Patents Act 1988 s.16, s.78.]

C worked as a freelance scriptwriter for PFD, a company that made animated films for television. Following a disagreement between C and the director of PFD, C ceased working for the company. C brought an action against PFD alleging that (1) PFD had infringed his copyright in a script he had written based on the story of the Cyclops, which PFD had made into an animated film without his permission; (2) PFD owed him money for work he had done on a script for a film, "The Diploma", and for scripts he had written for an animated series called "Global Bears Rescue", and (3) PFD did not identify C as the author of the Bears scripts. PFD contended that (1) the copyright for the Cyclops story had been purchased, or alternatively the script was not original as it was based on Homer's Odyssey, and furthermore the finished film could not be said to have derived from C's script as it had been reworked by another writer and storyboarded by two different artists consecutively prior to filming; (2) C had been paid the usual amount paid to writers for Bears scripts, and other monies he received from PFD were loans, and (3) C and PFD's secretary, P, had together committed the tort of conversion by removing documents from PFD's possession.

Held, giving judgment for C in part, that (1) there was no evidence that PFD had purchased the copyright of the Cyclops from C. Although based on the ancient work of Homer, C's script was original in the sense that it was different in form and detail and created a new literary work. The process involved in making the film formed a complex but nevertheless unbroken chain from C's script to the finished article and therefore did infringe C's copyright under the Copyright, Designs and Patents Act 1988 s.16, *Harman Pictures, NV v. Osborne* [1967] 1 W.L.R. 723, [1967] C.L.Y. 3169 applied; (2) there was no evidence that monies paid to C were loans. C was however paid the going rate for Bears scripts and was paid for his work on "The Diploma", and was therefore not owed any further sums in respect of those scripts; (3) C had not asserted himself as the author of the relevant Bears scripts under s.78 of the Act and therefore PFD were not at fault for failing to identify him in the credits, and (4) PFD's claim in conversion against C was unfounded, and against P was technically made out, but only nominal damages of £1 would be awarded.

CHRISTOFFER v. POSEIDON FILM DISTRIBUTORS LTD; POSEIDON FILM DISTRIBUTORS LTD v. PAIK; POSEIDON FILM DISTRIBUTORS LTD v. CHRISTOFFER; CHARALAMBOUS v. POSEIDON FILM DISTRIBUTORS LTD [2000] E.C.D.R. 487, Park, J., Ch D.

3854. Copyright – licences of right – factors used to determine royalty – mechanical components with similar competitors

[Copyright, Designs and Patents Act 1988 s.237(2), s.247, Sch.1 para.19(2).]

SE applied for a licence of right under the Copyright, Designs and Patents Act 1988 s.247, pursuant to Sch.1 para.19(2), relating to copyright in design drawings owned by S that pre dated the coming into force date of the Act on August 1, 1989. After protracted correspondence and an interim application by SE following persistent delays by S, S was ordered to produce copies of all its pre 1989 design drawings. In response to this, S produced 17 CAD drawings, but SE did not believe these to be genuine, claiming that S did not have access to CAD equipment before 1989. The royalty rates proposed ranged from three per cent by SE to 12.5 per cent by S.

Held, settling the terms of the licence, that (1) the Comptroller could not settle terms for a licence of right relating to post 1989 drawings and a determination of subsistence of copyright could only be made on an application under s.246. The licence would therefore only relate to the copyright in four pre 1989 design drawings. However, given the doubts as to the possible existence of other pre 1989 drawings, a royalty free licence would be granted in respect of any further drawings that subsequently came to light; (2) there was no requirement under s.237(2) for the parties to have entered into negotiations as to the terms of a licence of right before making an application to the Comptroller to determine such terms, *Roussel-Uclaf's (Clemence & Le Martret) Patent (No.1)* [1987] R.P.C. 109, [1987] C.L.Y. 2800 referred to; (3) terms would be settled on the basis of what would have been agreed between willing parties; (4) as to the royalty rate, those granted in previous cases were not comparable to the facts of the instant case, *Bance Ltd's Licence of Right (Copyright) Application, Re* [1996] R.P.C. 667, [1997] C.L.Y. 1044, *Pioneer Oil Tools Ltd's Licence of Right (Copyright) Application* [1997] R.P.C. 573, [1998] C.L.Y. 3496, *E-UK Controls Ltd's Licence of Right (Copyright) Application* [1998] R.P.C. 833, [1999] C.L.Y. 3448 and *Sterling Fluid System Ltd's Application* [1999] R.P.C. 775, [2000] 2 C.L. 343 considered. S's products were mechanical components competing against similar products and a large proportion of their value consisted of the construction materials used and the manufacturing process, rather than design, which would give a lower royalty than in previous cases; (5) the fact that most of S's sales to date had been in Germany, where its products did not have copyright protection, would also reduce the royalty slightly, and (6) a "norm" for royalty rates should only be adopted as a last resort where all else had failed, as had occurred here. On the basis that the royalty rate should be relatively low, a rate of four per cent was appropriate.

STAFFORD ENGINEERING SERVICES LTD'S LICENCE OF RIGHT (COPYRIGHT) APPLICATION [2000] R.P.C. 797, P Hayward, PO.

3855. Copyright – musical works – failure to obtain licences – breach of agreement – contention assurances gave rise to estoppel

W, a professional musician sought royalties from A arising from the sale of a record created by W using the "sampling" of a well known track recorded by other artists. A counterclaimed for damages contending that W had breached his contract with A by failing to obtain copyright licenses from those artists. W contended that he had acted in reliance on assurances from A that it had been within its rights to issue the track to the public, and therefore the assurances gave rise to a waiver of the strict terms of the agreement. Alternatively, the assurances provided the basis in equity for estopping A from relying on the terms of the agreement.

Held, giving judgment for W, and ordering that A account to W for the royalties to which he was entitled under the contract. The court found that W believed that the licences had already been obtained by A since the assurances given by employees of A were given under the apparent or ostensible authority of A's manager and in house legal adviser. Therefore obtaining the licences was not his responsibility and it would be inequitable to allow A to rely on the agreement, *Brikom Investments Ltd v. Carr* [1979] Q.B. 467, [1979] C.L.Y. 1598 applied.

WALMSLEY v. ACID JAZZ RECORDS LTD [2001] E.C.D.R. 4, Terence Etherton Q.C., Ch D.

3856. Copyright – musical works – joint authorship – extent of contribution – lack of joint intention – Canada

N, a musician, claimed copyright in four songs attributed to a singer, SM, who had had a recording contract with NP at the relevant time. N alleged that he had worked in collaboration with SM in 1988 on four songs, contributing titles and elements of musical composition and arrangement.

Held, dismissing the claim, that N had not shown that he had contributed significant original expression to the songs, either in composition or arrangement, as his input to the creative process had only amounted to proposals that SM had been free to accept or reject. Although joint authorship did not require equality of contribution, on the balance of probabilities there had been no joint intention between N and SM that N's contributions would give rise to joint authorship.

NEUDORF v. NETTWERK PRODUCTIONS LTD [2000] R.P.C. 935, Cohen, J., Sup Ct (BC).

3857. Copyright – newspapers – press cuttings – copying of substantial part – typographical arrangement

[Copyright, Designs and Patents Act 1988 s.16(3)(a).]

NLA appealed against a decision ([2001] Ch. 257, [2000] C.L.Y. 3575) allowing an appeal by MS against a decision that it had been guilty of infringing NLA's copyright. MS subscribed to a press cuttings agency which provided it with relevant items from newspapers. The agency paid a fee to NLA for the right to copy the cuttings. Once received, MS made further copies of the cuttings supplied which were then distributed internally. MS did not possess a licence to make the additional copies. NLA maintained that each copied cutting constituted the copying of a substantial part of the typographical arrangement of the published edition contrary to the Copyright, Designs and Patents Act 1988 s.16(3)(a).

Held, dismissing the appeal, that whilst copying of a literary, dramatic or musical work meant "reproducing the work in any material form", in the case of the typographical arrangement, nothing short of a facsimile copy would suffice. However, the definition of a "published edition" in s.8 of the 1988 Act referring to the "whole or any part of of one or more literary dramatic or musical works" meant that there was no necessary correlation between the concept of a literary, dramatic or musical work and the concept of a published edition, *Nationwide News Pty Ltd v. Copyright Agency Ltd* (1996) 136 A.L.R. 273 applied.

Determination of what constituted a "substantial part" was a qualitative issue dependent not upon the proportion which the copied part bore to the whole but rather whether the copy made had appropriated the presentation and layout of the edition. On the facts of the instant case none of the cuttings made reproduced the layout of any page to such an extent as to constitute a substantial part of the published edition.

NEWSPAPER LICENSING AGENCY LTD v. MARKS & SPENCER PLC, [2001] UKHL 38, [2001] 3 W.L.R. 290, Lord Hoffmann, HL.

3858. Copyright – software – originality of component parts of database system – intended function used to determine protectability – Australia

[Copyright Amendment Act 1984 (Australia) s.10(1).]

DA held the copyright for a database development system, D. PS developed a database development system, PFX, designed to be compatible with D by using the same commands, file structure and function keys. The source code for PFX was written independently of D, and compatibility was achieved by using 225 of the 254 reserved words in D, 192 of which performed the same function. PFX also used the same macros and compression table as D. DA contended that PS's use of these elements had infringed its copyright. DA succeeded at first instance ((1996) 63 F.C.R. 336), but this decision was reversed on appeal ((1997) 75 F.C.R. 108). DA appealed and PS cross appealed against a decision on appeal that PFX's compression table infringed DA's copyright in the corresponding table used in D.

Held, dismissing the appeal and the cross appeal (Gaudron. J dissenting in part), that (1) a computer program consisted of instructions that caused a device to carry out a predetermined function; (2) copyright protection for a computer program under the Copyright Amendment Act 1984 (Australia) s.10(1) required the expression of a language or code that was intended to show either an algorithmic or logical connection between the function to be performed and the physical capabilities of a digital information processing device; (3) programs written in object code enabled functions to be performed directly in terms of the definition in (2), whereas programs written in source code required conversion to another language or code; (4) the reserved words used in D were single instructions that did not constitute a program in their own right as they did not enable a computer to carry out identifiable functions; (5) determining whether reproduction of a large part of a program infringed copyright called for the identification of material features by examining the originality of the part concerned, *Autodesk Inc v. Dyason (No.1)* [1992] R.P.C. 575 and *Autodesk Inc v. Dyason (No.2)* [1993] R.P.C. 259 disapproved. Originality was determined by reference to what was expressed by way of algorithmic or logical connections. In the instant case, the reserved words were neither original nor capable of protection in their compiled form. Similarly, the macros used in D were not capable of protection as computer programs in their own right; (6) the PFX source code was an original expression and did not infringe D's copyright, and (7) D's compression table was a literary work and had been indirectly reproduced in PFX.

DATA ACCESS CORP v. POWERFLEX SERVICES PTY LTD; *sub nom* POWERFLEX SERVICES PTY v. DATA ACCESS CORP [1998-99] Info. T.L.R. 294, Gleeson, C.J., Fed Ct (Aus) (Full Ct).

3859. Design right – infringement – approach to test of substantiality where whole design copied

[Copyright Act 1988 s.16(3).]

DG, who was entitled to copyright in the artwork for a fabric design, appealed against a ruling ([2000] F.S.R. 121, [1999] C.L.Y. 3446) that RW's replication of the design, although very similar to the original, was not an infringing work because those elements which had been copied were not a substantial part of the design within the meaning of the Copyright Act 1988 s.16(3).

Held, allowing the appeal, that (1) in circumstances such as the instant case, where the decision resulted from the application of an ambiguous legal standard to a multitude of factors of varying importance, the appellate court was not permitted to reverses a judge's decision in the absence of an error of principle, *Norowzian v. Arks Ltd (No.2)* [2000] E.C.D.R. 205, [1999] C.L.Y. 3439 applied, and (2) substantiality was a matter of impression principally concerned with a work's derivation. Where it was alleged that an entire design had been copied, a finding that the similarities between the works were of an extent and nature sufficient to support a finding of copying was also likely to be determinative of the issue of substantiality.

DESIGNERS GUILD LTD v. RUSSELL WILLIAMS (TEXTILES) LTD (T/A WASHINGTON DC) [2000] 1 W.L.R. 2416, Lord Bingham of Cornhill, HL.

3860. Design right – infringement – bicycles – stabilisers

[Copyright, Designs and Patents Act 1988 s.51 (3), s.215(2).]

A, a bicycle expert who had been commissioned by W to update and improve its range of bicycle stabilisers, brought claims for damages against W for design right infringement, copyright infringement and misuse of confidential information. A had shown W his design for a universal stabiliser and he claimed that W's new stabiliser kit had been manufactured to his designs which constituted an infringement of his intellectual property rights.

Held, giving judgment for the defendant, that it had been implicit in letters sent by W to A that if A came to the conclusion that a new stabiliser was needed as an addition to or as a substitute for those in the existing range, A would need to indicate the configuration of such a stabiliser. This view was consistent with the commercial reality of the situation. Accordingly, A's design for the universal stabiliser fell squarely within the scope of the work that W had been commissioned to do and he was therefore the first owner of the design rights for the stabiliser in accordance with the Copyright, Designs and Patents Act 1988 s.215(2). A's schematic and engineering drawings were design documents within the meaning of s.51 (3) of the 1988 Act and therefore there had been no infringement of copyright by W. Further, A's claim for misuse of confidential information failed because the right of confidence belonged to W rather than A since W had commissioned the work.

APPS v. WELDTITE PRODUCTS LTD [2001] F.S.R. 39, Ferris, J., Ch D.

3861. Design right – infringement – handle and case of compact folding umbrella

[Copyright, Designs and Patents Act 1988 Part III, s.213(2), s.213(4), s.214(1).]

A, a supplier of umbrellas, claimed entitlement pursuant to the Copyright, Designs and Patents Act 1988 Part III to design rights in the handle and case of a range of compact ladies' folding umbrellas which it marketed. A maintained that its design rights had been infringed by the importation by G of a similar umbrella. G submitted that the handle design was commonplace.

Held, giving judgment for A, that (1) having regard to s.213(2) and s.214(1) of the Act, for a shape or configuration to qualify for a design right it was necessary that it had been consciously designed by an individual. In the instant case both the handle and case had been designed by F, a director of A; (2) the word "commonplace" within s.213(4) of the Act should be given a narrow meaning. Accordingly, the court should be hesitant to exclude statutory protection to a design on the basis that it was commonplace. The exclusion under s.213(4) applied to the shape or configuration of an article rather than the article itself. In the instant case it was apparent that both designs were not commonplace, *Farmers Build Ltd (In Liquidation) v. Carier Bulk Materials Handling Ltd* [2000] E.C.D.R. 42, [1999] C.L.Y. 3463 applied and *Scholes Windows Ltd v. Magnet Ltd (No.1)* [2000] E.C.D.R. 248 considered; (3) there was sufficient similarity between A's umbrellas and the umbrella imported by G to infer that copying had taken place, and (4) G had "reason to believe" that the case was an infringing article at the time it began to import the umbrella. However, in relation to the handle G had "reason to believe" only after A's substituted statement of claim had been served, *LA Gear Inc v. Hi-Tec Sports Plc* [1992] F.S.R. 121, [1992] C.L.Y. 577 considered.

A FULTON CO LTD v. GRANT BARNETT & CO LTD [2001] R.P.C. 16, Park, J., Ch D.

3862. Design right – infringement – originality of garment design

G, a fashion designer, claimed damages against E, her former business partner, contending that E had infringed her copyright and unregistered design right in respect of three garments. Her designs, which commanded a high price in the market, had been described as highly distinctive and possessing a strong signature. E argued that he had created the designs prior to meeting G and had only been influenced by her work.

Held, giving judgment for the claimant in part, that there had been an infringement of G's unregistered design right claim. On the evidence presented, there was a design which G was entitled to protect either by copyright or unregistered design right. For the purpose of both claims, the designs were both "original" and not "commonplace". Given the similarity of the garments in issue, the inevitable inference when the garments were examined was that E had copied the essential elements of the designs from G. However, in relation to the copyright claim, the court found that as the designs were not of "artistic craftmanship", G was not entitled to copyright protection.

GUILD v. ESKANDAR LTD (FORMERLY AMBLEVILLE LTD) [2001] F.S.R. 38, Rimer, J., Ch D.

3863. Design right – infringement – sliding wardrobe doors – type of construction – design and components – applicable exclusions

[Copyright, Designs and Patents Act 1988 s.213, s.246.]

CT designed and manufactured sliding wardrobe door systems comprising mirrored doors with a mirror panel mounted in a frame formed from aluminium extrusions, placed behind wooden mouldings. RW and VC were two of CT's competitors against whom CT commenced actions for design right infringement in respect of his wardrobe door systems. CT referred for determination, under the Copyright, Designs and Patents Act 1988 s.246, whether design right existed.

Held, allowing the reference in part, that design right subsisted in some of the claimed features, as (1) the phrase "any aspect of shape or configuration" in s.213(2) could include materials used in the design, although mere choice of material was excluded by s.213(3); (2) although a given shape or configuration arising from a type of construction could be protected, this would not be the case where a wide range of articles could be produced using the same construction methods, as this was excluded by s.213(3); (3) in the instant case, whilst claims for the overall external appearance of the doors were not based on a type of construction method, claims for the general concept of concealing aluminium extrusions by the use of mouldings were excluded by s.213(3); (4) the "must fit" exclusion under s.213(3)(b)(i) was not restricted to articles designed by the same person; (5) the "must fit" exclusion could also apply to components or features for which there was more than one possible design, *Ocular Sciences Ltd v. Aspect Vision Care Ltd (No.2)* [1997] R.P.C. 289, [1997] C.L.Y. 3894 referred to, and (6) adding mouldings to the aluminium extrusions went beyond mere decorative surface features, so that they were capable of design right protection, *Mark Wilkinson Furniture Ltd v. Woodcraft Designs (Radcliffe) Ltd* [1998] F.S.R. 63, [1997] C.L.Y. 1034 referred to.

CHRISTOPHER TASKER'S DESIGN RIGHT REFERENCES, *Re* [2001] R.P.C. 3, Peter Hayward, PO.

3864. Design right – infringement – window design – commonplace in design field – determination of originality

[Copyright, Designs and Patents Act 1988 s.213(4).]

S, a window design company, appealed against the dismissal of its claim ([2000] E.C.D.R. 248) against M alleging infringement of its unregistered design right in respect of a window which had a decorative horn shaped extension. S contended that the judge had erred in finding that the design had been commonplace in the design field in question at the time of its creation under the Copyright, Designs and Patents Act 1988 s.213(4).

Held, dismissing the appeal, that the judge had correctly concluded that S's design, whilst original in the copyright sense, had lost its originality under s.213(4). For the purpose of determining a design's originality, the relevant design field was not restricted to a consideration of the nature, purpose or material structure of the design nor was a comparison of the design restricted to other designs which were designed at or about the same time. The judge had justifiably considered any similarities and differences between S's window design and other designs from the point of view of a customer rather than a window design expert and had been correct in finding that S's design was commonplace for the purposes of the Act.

SCHOLES WINDOWS LTD v. MAGNET LTD (NO.1), [2001] EWCA Civ 532, [2002] F.S.R. 10, Mummery, L.J., CA.

3865. Designs – convention countries – Bhutan, Nepal and Tonga

DESIGNS (CONVENTION COUNTRIES) (AMENDMENT) ORDER 2001, SI 2001 2125; made under the Registered Designs Act 1949 s.13, s.37. In force: July 11, 2001; £1.50.

This Order, which amends the Designs (Convention Countries) Order 1994 (SI 1994 3219), declares Bhutan, Nepal and Tonga to be convention countries for the purposes of all the provisions of the Registered Designs Act 1949.

3866. Documentary evidence – pharmaceutical industry – disclosure by non party – relevance to issues in dispute

[Civil Procedure Rules 1998 (SI 1998 3132) Part 31 r.31.17.]

N, a pharmaceutical company and the defendant to patent infringement proceedings instituted by the patent holder, AHP, appealed against an order dismissing N's application for F, a non party, to provide disclosure of certain documents pursuant to the Civil Procedure Rules 1998 Part 31 r.31.17. N sought disclosure on the basis that documents retained by F from a previous research project were relevant to the issues of obviousness and novelty of the patent in suit. N submitted that (1) the judge had erred in his conclusion that he had no power to order disclosure because some of the documents held by F would not be relevant. N maintained that in personal injury cases the court was entitled to order disclosure of a class of documents such as medical notes, many of which might be deemed irrelevant to the matters in issue and, by analogy, the court was entitled to disclose the class of documents identified as being held by F; (2) when exercising his discretion, the judge had failed to take into account the attitude of F who had not opposed the application, and (3) there was no substance to the suggestion that the material requested would have no bearing on the issues of novelty and obviousness.

Held, allowing the appeal, that (1) the assertion that certain documents within the class requested were not relevant could not be sustained since their relevance had to be considered in the context of the litigation as a whole; (2) the fact that the costs of compliance were small since the class of documents was small and F had no objection to the order for disclosure, militated in favour of disclosure, and (3) the documents were clearly potentially relevant to the issues of novelty and obviousness.

AMERICAN HOME PRODUCTS CORP v. NOVARTIS PHARMACEUTICALS UK LTD (APPLICATION FOR DISCLOSURE); *sub nom.* AMERICAN HOME

PRODUCTS CORP v. NOVARTIS PHARMACEUTICALS UK LTD (NO. 2), [2001] EWCA Civ 165, [2001] F.S.R. 41, Aldous, L.J., CA.

3867. Internet – domain names – bad faith registration – use of charity's registered trade mark – website critical of charity's activities

LCF, a charity working with disabled people, held the UK registration of a word and device trade mark incorporating the words "Leonard Cheshire". D, a former employee of LCF, registered "www.leonard-cheshire.com" as a domain name and used that website to publish criticisms of LCF's activities. The site carried a notice stating that it was not the site of LCF. D argued that the site was "a work of political interventionist art" and offered it for sale in the sum of £40,000, stating that he intended to use the proceeds to erect a memorial for the disabled. LCF sought the transfer of the website.

Held, allowing the application, that the domain name had been registered and used in bad faith. D had no legitimate right to use the domain name, which was confusingly similar to LCF's trade mark and was likely to attract visitors thinking they were visiting LCF's site, although the true nature of D's site would soon become apparent. While D was entitled to criticise LCF's activities, that was a distinct issue from D's entitlement to use the domain name www.leonard-cheshire.com.

LEONARD CHESHIRE FOUNDATION v. DRAKE [2001] E.T.M.R. 90, Judge not applicable, Arbitration.

3868. Internet – domain names – goodwill – likelihood of confusion – number of "hits" – increased value of site

[Trade Marks Act 1994 s.10(3)(b).]

F registered a domain name for a site which was intended to develop the idea of marketing banners for advertising on the Internet. M, a major international credit card issuer with similar registered domain names for its various businesses, sought an interlocutory injunction restraining F from activating the web site, contending that F had deliberately chosen the acronym in order to take advantage of the goodwill attached to its business and had taken unfair advantage in connection with a dissimilar business contrary to the Trade Marks Act 1994 s.10(3)(b). F contended that his business was entirely different to that of M and there was no likelihood of confusion between the two. M contended that its business customers may well be interested in the idea of using banner advertising and may be misled into believing that F's business had connections with M. Furthermore, by increasing the number of "hits" received by F's site by virtue of its name, the value of the site would increase should he wish to sell it.

Held, granting the application in part, that on the balance of convenience F would not be restrained from using the site, as it was unlikely that visitors to the site would be confused between the two operations. Any individuals interested in using the banner exchange service were likely to be sophisticated Internet users. Furthermore, F had no immediate intention of activating the site, thus the period of restraint involved would be very short and it was open to M to monitor the position. An injunction would not be granted merely on the basis that to do so would cause the defendant no harm. However, F would be restrained from selling or dealing with the domain name, as it would otherwise be open to him to do, at a price possibly enhanced by improper use of M's goodwill, since M had an arguable point on this issue. A sale of the site could lead to an irrecoverable claim for damages or account of profit. An injunction was granted to ensure that F would have to apply to the court if he wished to sell or deal with the domain name prior to trial.

MBNA AMERICA BANK NA v. FREEMAN [2001] E.B.L.R. 13, Nicholas Strauss Q.C., Ch D.

3869. Internet – domain names – registration – bad faith – intended use in connection with legitimate business venture

C claimed ownership of the unregistered marks AVENGERS and THE AVENGERS, having used them commercially since 1960 and since 1966 in the UK and US respectively, during which time it had acquired common law rights in them. In 1995, V registered the internet domain name "avengers.com". Following discussions between C and V, V offered to transfer the domain name to C for $500,000. C considered that V had registered a domain name similar to its marks without legitimate justification, and also alleged that V had been involved in warehousing domain names. C sought the transfer of the domain name under the ICANN rules. V argued that it had set the domain name aside for use in connection with its business, and although the name was not currently in use, over $3 million had been spent on capital equipment. V denied having previously warehoused domain names, and stated that the price have been quoted to deter C, not to realising an unfair profit on the sale of the domain name.

Held, dismissing the claim, that in spite of the similarity between the domain name and C's trade marks, C had not discharged the burden of proving bad faith by V in registering the domain name.

CANAL & IMAGE UK LTD v. VANITYMAIL SERVICES INC [2001] E.T.M.R. 40, Nelson A Diaz, Arbitration.

3870. Internet – domain names – registration – bad faith – motivated by desire for revenge

D owned trade mark registrations for the word GUINNESS in relation to beer. Z had registered a number of domain names incorporating "Guinness" in conjunction with the American slang word "sucks". D sought the transfer of those names, contending that Z had no legitimate interest in their registration, which had been carried out in revenge following earlier proceedings between D and Z. In support of this allegation, D relied on the text of a notice posted by Z on one of his websites signalling his intentions.

Held, allowing the application, that D had shown that Z's registration and use of the domain names was intended to disrupt D's business and draw interest away from D's websites. This, coupled with Z's failure to respond to D's allegations, was evidence of Z's bad faith in registering and using the offending sites.

DIAGEO PLC v. ZUCCARINI (T/A CUPCAKE PATROL) [2001] E.T.M.R. 45, James Bridgeman, Arbitration.

3871. Internet – domain names – registration – bad faith – offer for sale 12 days after registration

C, a Luxembourg company, owned the trade mark RTL in many countries, in respect of television and radio broadcasting services. A merger was announced between C and an English company, P. The announcement, made worldwide via press release and a press conference broadcast live over the internet, referred to the creation of an integrated European broadcasting group, but no name was given. Following German press speculation that the group would be called RTL, T, an American company, registered "rtlgroup.com" as a domain name in New York two days after the press conference. When the newly formed RTL group tried to register "rtlgroup.com" as its domain name, it discovered T's prior registration and T offered to sell the name for $75,000. RTL claimed that T had registered the name in bad faith, and sought arbitration. T asserted that it intended to use the name, which in America meant "right to life", and it could not be expected that RTL's existence and the matters raised in the German press would be known in America.

Held, allowing the application, that T had registered the domain name in bad faith, and it should be transferred to R. The domain name was so close to R's trade mark that confusion was likely. Moreover, the fact of T's name and that the domain had been offered for sale only 12 days after registration were evidence of T's bad faith.

CLT-UFA SA v. THIS DOMAIN IS FOR SALE [2001] E.T.M.R. 43, Jonas Gulliksson, Arbitration.

3872. Internet – domain names – registration – lack of bad faith – protection of registered trade mark by way of infringement proceedings

TH, a UK company, registered the domain name "www.sampdoria.com". UCS, an Italian football club, objected to the registration and requested that TH transfer the name to it. TH refused, stating that it would be against its interests to do so, as the name had been registered for use in connection with an as yet uncompleted website. UCS applied to the WIPO Administrative Panel for the transfer of the domain name, contending that "Sampdoria", which was formed from the contraction of two former football club names, was a registered trade mark and its origins were such that no third party could claim a legitimate use for it. Further, that the terms of TH's refusal implied bad faith on its part.

Held, dismissing the complaint, that UCS had not shown that TH had acted in bad faith by registering a domain name that was identical or likely to be confused with UCS's trade mark, as required by the Uniform Domain Name Dispute Resolution Policy para.4(a). TH had not concealed its identity or sought to profit from the registration. Once the site become operational, it remained open for UCS to protect its registered trade mark by way of an action for infringement on the ground of likelihood of confusion.

UNIONE CALCIO SAMPDORIA SpA v. TITAN HANCOCKS [2000] E.T.M.R. 1017, Judge not applicable, Arbitration.

3873. Internet – domain names – registration in bad faith – celebrity's name constituted unregistered trade mark

H registered the internet domain name writerdomains.com, under which he ran a web page with the stated aim of developing web sites for the world's most famous writers. He listed over 130 such writers, including W. H registered the domain names jeanettewinterson.com, jeanettewinterson.net and jeanettewinterson.org. H was also willing to sell registered domain names to the writers concerned for a fee equivalent to three per cent of their 1999 gross book sales. W filed a complaint with the WIPO Administrative Panel.

Held, allowing the complaint, that the domain names had been registered in bad faith and would be transferred to W. The Uniform Domain Name Dispute Resolution Policy Para.4 required that for W to succeed, H had to have registered a domain name which was identical or confusingly similar to a trade mark or service mark in which she had rights. Such rights were not confined to registered marks and also included unregistered trade marks, such as W's own name.

WINTERSON v. HOGARTH [2000] E.T.M.R. 783, Judge not applicable, Arbitration.

3874. Internet – domain names – registration in bad faith – incorporation of famous trade marks

[Convention for the Protection of Industrial Property Art.6bis; Agreement on Trade-Related Aspects of Intellectual Property Rights including Trade in Counterfeit Goods (TRIPs) Art.16(3).]

C owned a number of well known trade marks, including DIOR, CHRISTIAN DIOR and BABY DIOR. L registered the internet domain names babydior.com and babydior.net, which it offered to sell to C for $150,000. L claimed that "babydior" referred to a purple dinosaur which L had created and intended using for educational purposes. C contended that L had registered the domain names in bad faith, and filed a complaint with the WIPO Administrative Panel.

Held, that the babydior.com and babydior.net domain names had been registered in bad faith and would be transferred to C. Further, C's marks were famous in terms of the Paris Convention Art.6bis and qualified as such for extended protection under the TRIPs Agreement Art.16(3) and L's attempts to sell the domain names to C amounted to a use of those trade marks in bad faith.

CHRISTIAN DIOR COUTURE SA v. LIAGE INTERNATIONAL INC [2000] E.T.M.R. 773, Judge not applicable, Arbitration.

3875. Internet – domain names – registration in bad faith – similarity to well known trade mark – offer to sell for excessive price

L registered the internet domain name scaniabilar.com. S complained, on the basis of its ownership of Swedish and US trade mark registrations for the word mark SCANIA. S contended that its mark was well known in the motor vehicle field and that the addition of the word "bilar", Swedish for car, would lead people to think that L's domain name was actually S's official website. L argued that the word "Scania" was an old word for an area of southern Sweden and that he intended to use the website as a Scandinavian forum for buying and selling of second hand cars. However, L had offered to sell the domain name to Scania for SKR100,000. S considered this to be an excessive sum for a domain name, and submitted a complaint to the WIPO Arbitration and Mediation Center.

Held, that L had registered the domain name scaniabilar.com in bad faith. The SCANIA mark was so well known that L could not reasonably claim to have been unaware of it when he registered his domain name.

SCANIA CV AB v. WESTLYE [2000] E.T.M.R. 767, Judge not applicable, Arbitration.

3876. Internet – domain names – risk of confusion – public likely to be deceived into believing businesses were connected – Ireland

LI had developed online search software to facilitate rapid retrieval of information relating to Ireland. LI devised the names "Localireland" and "Local Ireland", registered a company with the name "Local Ireland" and registered several domain names, including "localireland.com". LI then discovered that LIO had registered a company called "Local Ireland-Online Ltd", and were using the business names "Local Ireland-Online" and "localireland-online", as well as a domain name "localireland-online.com". LI argued that this amounted to passing off and sought interim orders to restrain LIO's conduct. LIO had indicated, following the initiation of proceedings, that its future business would be conducted under the name "Locally Irish" and the domain name "locallyirish.com".

Held, allowing the application, that LI had shown that LIO's use of the names created a high degree of risk that the public would be deceived into believing that LIO's services were connected with LI. The similarity in names and logos would cause confusion so that it was established on the balance of convenience that relief should be granted.

LOCAL IRELAND LTD v. LOCAL IRELAND-ONLINE LTD [2001] E.T.M.R. 42, Herbert, J., HC (Irl).

3877. Passing off – distinctiveness – retail outlet trade names – no evidence of misrepresentation – Singapore

S owned a chain of shops called ONE.99 Shop. The first retail outlet was opened in April 1997, and by the time of the trial S had seven outlets trading in Singapore. All the goods sold in the shops were priced at SD1.99. The logo for the shops showed the words ONE.99 Shop in black on a white background, with the numbers "99" in larger, red type over the word "shop". L was a subsidiary company of a major toy company, R, which was set up in 1992. In September 1997, R began selling goods through joint promotions with retailers for SD1.99, and decided during 1998 to incorporate a retail arm, L, to sell its goods under the fixed SD1.99 concept. L's brand was LIFESTYLE 1.99, shown in a white font against an oval, cyan background. S successfully sued L for passing off at first instance and L appealed.

Held, allowing the appeal, that (1) S had shown that it had acquired goodwill by the date L's first shop opened in September 1998. During the previous 18 months, S had enjoyed a large turnover, with figures showing a total of SD10.4 million over its first 22 months' trading, which was sufficient evidence of goodwill for a retailer selling miscellaneous fixed price goods; (2) the name ONE.99 was clearly descriptive because S sold goods at that price, *McCain International v. Country Fair Foods* [1981] R.P.C. 69, [1981] C.L.Y. 2793 followed; (3) although a descriptive name could become distinctive, a claimant had a heavy burden to discharge when proving that it had acquired a secondary meaning. Furthermore, where a descriptive name was used for the first business of its type, it was difficult to show distinctiveness because the public would inevitably associate the name with that particular business. With descriptive names, a slight difference between the names would be sufficient to distinguish them, *Reddaway v. Banham* [1896] A.C. 199, *Cellular Clothing Co Ltd v. Maxton & Murray* [1899] A.C. 326 and *British Vacuum Cleaner Co Ltd v. New Vacuum Cleaner Co Ltd* [1907] 2 Ch. 312 followed, and (4) the difference in the respective names, in addition to the differences in the appearances of the logos, meant that there was no reasonable probability of deception and there was only minor evidence of confusion in the mind of the public which would pass in time as the businesses continued to trade alongside each other. There was therefore no misrepresentation and so no passing off.

S$1.99 PRIVATE LTD v. LIFESTYLE 1.99 PRIVATE LTD [2001] F.S.R. 10, Yong Pung How, C.J., CA (Sing).

3878. Passing off – exclusive distribution agreements – ownership of goodwill

M, manufacturer of a snoring remedy in the United States, brought a passing off action against P, its exclusive United Kingdom distributor, in a dispute over the trade name, "Snorenz". Each party claimed to own the goodwill in the name. Following the breakdown in relations between the two companies, P approached another manufacturer to produce a snoring remedy and then marketed the product under the name "Snoreeze". M claimed that it owned the goodwill and that misrepresentations by P about the new product connected it with "Snorenz" because of the similar name, packaging and certain statements which were made at the time of its launch.

Held, giving judgment for P, that the goodwill in name and packaging belonged to P because M was not in business in the UK. M were not referred to on the packaging, marketing and sales were carried out by P, and P alone was known and thought of as the source of the product, *Scandecor Development AB v. Scandecor Marketing AB* [1999] F.S.R. 26, [1998] C.L.Y. 3519 applied.

MEDGEN INC v. PASSION FOR LIFE PRODUCTS LTD [2001] F.S.R. 30, Kevin Garnett Q.C., Ch D.

3879. Patents – amendments – disclosure and inspection – level of disclosure required in unopposed application

[Civil Procedure Rules 1998 (SI 1998 3132).]

S, a patentee, applied to amend a patent on the ground that in its existing form the patent was insufficient. The application was unopposed.

Held, allowing the amendment, that having regard to the requirements of the Civil Procedure Rules 1998, particularly the need for active case management and the overriding objective, disclosure of evidence beyond that already disclosed in the statement of reasons was not necessary. As the application was unopposed the level of disclosure required was not as full as for a hearing without notice. The amendment did not extend the protection confirmed by the patent, nor result in additional disclosure, and was formally allowable, *Kimberly Clark Worldwide Inc v. Procter & Gamble Ltd (No.1)* [2000] F.S.R. 235, [2000] 1 C.L. 279 considered.

SWINTEX LTD v. MELBA PRODUCTS LTD [2001] F.S.R. 4, Pumfrey, J., Pat Ct.

3880. Patents – biotechnological inventions

PATENTS (AMENDMENT) RULES 2001, SI 2001 1412; made under the Patents Act 1977 s.123, s.125A. In force: July 6, 2001; £2.50.

These Rules amend the Patents Rules 1995 (SI 1995 2093) to implement European Parliament and Council Directive 98/44 Art.13 and Art.14 on the legal protection of biotechnological inventions. The Articles concern the deposit, access and re-deposit of biological material and amendments are made to the 1995 Rules to more closely align them with the parallel regulations on deposit of biological material under the European Patent Convention.

3881. Patents – convention countries – Bhutan, Nepal and Tonga

PATENTS (CONVENTION COUNTRIES) (AMENDMENT) ORDER 2001, SI 2001 2126; made under the Patents Act 1977 s.90, s.124. In force: July 11, 2001; £1.50.

This Order, which amends the Patents (Convention Countries) Order 1994 (SI 1994 3220), declares Bhutan, Nepal and Tonga to be convention countries for the purposes of the Patents Act 1977 s.5 which affords certain rights of priority to applicants for patents, and this Order extends these rights of priority to applications filed in those countries.

3882. Patents – county court – transfer between courts – relevant considerations

[Civil Procedure Rules 1998 (SI 1998 3132).]

C applied to transfer an action for patent infringement brought by W from the patent county court to the High Court. The action related to two patents, effectively owned by W, concerned with the technology used to manufacture cosmetic contact lenses.

Held, refusing the application, that where the interests of efficiency and expediency so demanded, patent cases should be transferred from the patent county court to the High Court or from the High Court to the patent county court. The Civil Procedure Rules 1998 did not specifically detail how patent business should be distributed and therefore a claimant was free to bring proceedings in the High Court or the county court. Unless a claimant brought proceedings in the county court for inappropriate motives or it was apparent that the county court was not an appropriate forum, the burden of proof was on a defendant to justify a transfer. Where either forum was appropriate, there should be no transfer. The court would have regard to the circumstances of each particular case and to the state of the lists of both courts when considering an application. Account would be taken of, inter alia, the financial position of the parties, the prospective length of the hearing and the degree of complexity and importance of the proceedings, *Mannesmann Kienzle GmbH v. Microsystem Design Ltd* [1992] R.P.C. 569, *Memminger-IRO GmbH v. Trip-Lite Ltd* [1992] R.P.C. 210, [1993] C.L.Y. 3039, *Symbol Technologies Inc v. Opticon Sensors Europe BV (No.2)* [1993] R.P.C. 232 and *Chaplin Patents Holdings Co Inc v. Group Lotus Plc* Times, January 12, 1994, [1994] C.L.Y. 3452 considered.

WESLEY JESSEN CORP v. COOPERVISION LTD *The Times*, July 31, 2001, Neuberger, J., Pat Ct.

3883. Patents – European Patent Court – statement of grounds had to contain specific reasoning

[European Patents Convention 1973 Art.108, Art.123(2).]

A patent application was rejected by the Examining Division on the ground that amended Claim 1 contravened the European Patents Convention 1973 Art.123(2) because a particular feature had been excised. L appealed against that decision on the ground that the decision was said to be contested on the basis that it was clearly wrong, based on the arguments already put forward and the applicants sought to rely on those arguments which they did not repeat. They asserted that this was the exceptional circumstance in which the arguments submitted during the examination were sufficient to demonstrate that the rejection of their patent claim was wrong.

Held, rejecting the application as inadmissible, that (1) the last sentence of the European Patents Convention Art.108 required written statement setting out the grounds of appeal; (2) a written statement of grounds of appeal should state the specific legal and factual reasons why the decision under appeal should be set aside; (3) in the instant case the appeal brief said that the refusal decision was "clearly wrong" without stating specific reasons why this decision was wrong. It only made a general reference to the applicant's arguments submitted before the refusal decision was issued. Thus the applicant had left it entirely to the Board to conjecture why the applicant considered the refusal decision to be defective. It was precisely that situation which the requirement that grounds of appeal should be filed was designed to prevent; and (4) therefore the appeal brief did not comply with Art.108 and would be rejected.

LARSEN/BACKING BOARD (T574/99) [2001] E.P.O.R. 18, Gumbel, European Patent Office (Technical Board of Appeal).

3884. **Patents – European Patent Office – admissibility of amendments – jurisdiction of Technical Board to hear amended applications**

The application related to a polypeptide cartilage inducing factor. By mistake, a certain aminoacid residue in some of the claims had been typed as "Glu" instead of "Gln". A request to correct the mistype was ruled inadmissible following the decision of the Enlarged Board in *CELTRIX/Correction of errors (G11/91)* [1993] E.P.O.R. 245. The applicant appealed and filed a revised main request which excluded the Glu/Gln amendment, but brought in other amendments including amendments unconnected to the Glu/Gln amendment.

Held, allowing the appeal and remitting the application for further consideration by the Examining Division on the basis of the revised main request, that (1) the Examining Board's refusal to admit the amendment was correct, but (2) it was not appropriate at the present stage for the Board to deal with amendments other than minor amendments, and (3) the amended application should be remitted to the Examining Board to be considered on its merits.

CELTRIX/GLU-GLN (T184/91) [2001] E.P.O.R. 28, Lancon, European Patent Office (Technical Board of Appeal).

3885. **Patents – European Patent Office – admissibility of objection based on partiality**

[European Patents Convention 1973 Art.24(1), Art.24(3).]

A patentee D, appealed against a decision of the Opposition Division revoking his patent. K challenged the competence of the chairman of the Board of Appeal arguing that he might not be impartial as he had been a member of the Board of Appeal which had ordered the Examining Division to grant the patent. They also objected to the other members of the Board as being potentially partial in reaching a decision on the competence of the chairman. A newly constituted Board considered the objections.

Held, excluding the original chairman and the legal and technical members of the Board from taking any further part in the appeal (the latter two having recused themselves), that (1) it lay within the competence of the Board in its original composition, i.e. with the participation of the chairman objected to, to consider the admissibility of the objections under the European Patents Convention 1973 Art.24(4) for the purposes of opening the procedure under; (2) Art. 24(3) prescribed only two conditions for admissibility. First, an objection should not be admissible if, while being aware of a reason for objection, the party had taken a procedural step. Secondly, no objection might be based upon the nationality of members. However, even if it was not expressly stated in Art. 24(3) the Convention required as a general rule, that objections be reasoned; (3) under Art.24(1) members of a Board of Appeal were not permitted to take part in a hearing if they had participated in the final decision on the matter in a lower tribunal. In this case that meant that a member would be excluded only if they had participated in the Opposition Division and not in prior proceedings relating to the examination. In those circumstances the objection under Art.24 was not well founded and would be rejected; (4) what was decisive under Art.24(3) was whether there were objective or reasonable reasons to suspect a member of partiality. In this case the issues were identical to those considered by the Board of Appeal in the examination proceedings. The chairman would be compelled to confirm or reject his own previous decision which was the situation which Art.24(3) was enacted to avoid. Therefore the objection under Art.24(3) would be upheld on the particular facts of this case; and (5) finally the other members of the Board should be excluded because an impartial judgment should be seen to be done as well as done. The Board should not include members who had previously been suspected of partiality.

DU PONT/SUSPECTED PARTIALITY (T1028/96); *sub nom.* EI DU PONT DE NEMOURS AND CO'S EUROPEAN PATENT (NO.0203469) [2001] E.P.O.R. 17, F Prols, European Patent Office (Technical Board of Appeal).

3886. Patents – European Patent Office – anti competitive activity – code of practice for professional body – restrictions on comparative advertising

[EC Treaty Art.85(1) (now Art.81 EC); Council Directive 97/55 amending Council Directive 84/450 concerning misleading advertising so as to include comparative advertising. Art.3a; European Patents Convention 1973.]

Under the European Patent Convention 1973 the European Patent Organisation was established to grant patents through the European Patent Office (EPO) and its Administrative Council. Pursuant to the Convention the Administrative Council set up an Institute of Professional Representatives "EPI" over which the Council had disciplinary powers. The EPI is a non-profit-making organisation whose expenditure is derived from members' subscriptions whose objects are to collaborate with the EPO on professional conduct matters and discipline. Everyone on the list of professional representatives is a member of the EPI. The EPI elects a Council which established a Code of Professional Conduct "the Code", which, after various amendments, was submitted to the Commission on October 3, 1997. Council Directive 97/55 Art. 3a restricted anti competitive conduct. The Code (1) permitted comparative advertising provided that it was not misleading; (2) restricted relationships between members. The Commission exempted the Code from the Directive from October 14, 1997 to April 23, 2000. The EPI appealed, contending that either the time limits on the exemption should be removed or the decision annulled.

Held, allowing the appeal in part, and annulling the Commission's decision in so far as it related to relationships between members of the EPI that (1) the EPI had the locus standi to appeal *France v. Commission of the European Communities (C68/94)* [1998] E.C.R. I-1375 followed; (2) that there was a sufficient statement of reasons in the Commission's judgment *Cipeke v. Commission of the European Communities (T84/96)* [1997] E.C.R. II-2081; (3) the Directive could not derogate from EC Treaty Art. 85(1) (now Art.81(1) EC); (4) rules controlling professional bodies did not, as a matter of principle, fall outside the scope of Art. 85(1); (5) the rule against comparative advertising was in breach of Art. 85(1); (6) the restriction on relationships between members was not in breach of Art. 85(1)1; (7) the Commission acted properly in granting the exemption for a limited period until April 23, 2000.

INSTITUTE OF PROFESSIONAL REPRESENTATIVES BEFORE THE EUROPEAN PATENT OFFICE (EPI) v. COMMISSION OF THE EUROPEAN COMMUNITIES (T144/99) [2001] 5 C.M.L.R. 2, Meij (President), CFI.

3887. Patents – European Patent Office – appeals – identification of extent – process claim embodying inventive step

[European Patent Convention 1973 Art.56, Art.104(1).]

T's request in opposition proceedings that product claims relating to a ski boot lining should be maintained on the basis of a set of new process claims was upheld by the Opposition Division. B appealed that decision "in its entirety" and submitted two new documents. B further requested that there should be a referral to the Enlarged Board of Appeal on the point of the legal principle governing the relationship between obviousness and inventive step under the European Patent Convention 1973 Art.56. B also alleged bad faith on T's part during the opposition proceedings so that appeal costs should be apportioned between the parties. T requested the reinstatement of the product claims originally granted. Alternatively, it asked for the acceptance of newly amended sets of process claims.

Held, remitting the case to the first instance, that (1) the extent of an appeal was sufficiently identified if it stated that the first instance decision was appealed in its entirety; (2) T could not reinstate the product claims, but could abandon the request without being taken to have admitted that it could not succeed; (3) one of T's process claims was both novel and involved an inventive step; (4) there should be no referral to the Enlarged Board of Appeal as the legal principle proposed did not conform with Convention requirements, and (5) there was no evidence to substantiate B's allegations of bad faith so that there was no basis to depart from the principle that each party was responsible for its own costs under Art.104(1).

TECNICA/SKI BOOT LINING (T554/98) [2000] E.P.O.R. 475, Hatherly, European Patent Office (Technical Board of Appeal).

3888. Patents – European Patent Office – appeals – refusal of application – acceptance of letter accompanying appeal

The application was refused for lack of an inventive step. AT appealed filing new claims and an accompanying letter stating that the relevant patent claims were to be revised in line with claims proposed by the Examiner, and that the revision would deal with all objections raised.

Held, allowing the appeal that where an applicant, having lodged an appeal, subsequently wrote a letter as described, such letter would suffice as a form of Statement of Grounds of appeal.

AT&T/DIELECTRIC DEPOSITION (T169/98) [2001] E.P.O.R. 29, Shukla, European Patent Office (Technical Board of Appeal).

3889. Patents – European Patent Office – apportionment of costs on withdrawn appeal

A patent was granted in relation to a vehicle testing bench designed to measure the driving torque exerted by the wheels of a vehicle. Opposition had been raised on the grounds of lack of novelty and inventive step. The Opposition Division had rejected the opponent's contentions, and the opponent lodged an appeal. The appeal raised no new grounds of opposition. The holder of the patent, however, lodged a number of new versions of its claims. The opponent notified the Board that it would not be attending the oral hearing of the appeal seven days before the same was due to take place. The holder of the patent sought an apportionment of costs by reason of the opponent's late decision not to attend, and the absence of any fresh contentions on the part of the opponent.

Held, dismissing the appeal but rejecting the application for costs, that the opponent's conduct had not been improper nor an abuse. Hence, there were no special circumstances or culpable behaviour to justify any apportionment of the costs of the appeal.

KABUSHIKI/VEHICLE TESTING BENCH (T06/98) [2001] E.P.O.R. 32, Turrini, European Patent Office (Technical Board of Appeal).

3890. **Patents – European Patent Office – Board of Appeal final decision – alleged procedural violation – lack of remedy under European Patent Convention Art.125**

[European Patent Convention 1973 Art.125; Agreement on Trade-Related Aspects of Intellectual Property Rights 1994.]

Following the revocation on appeal of E's European patent ([1993] E.P.O.R. 253), E made further requests, essentially seeking to review the Board of Appeal's decision. E claimed that its right to a defence and the principle of good faith had been violated since the Board had relied on a document disregarded by the Opposition Division and had introduced fresh grounds for revocation of the patent. E's requests were refused as having no legal basis under the European Patent Convention 1973. Further requests by E resulted in the Legal Board of Appeal referring questions to the Enlarged Board of Appeal concerning the response that could be made to requests founded on alleged procedural violations by a Board of Appeal and whether those could be entered in the Register of European Patents.

Held, that (1) the Convention did not provide an express remedy for challenging Board of Appeal decisions where there was an alleged violation of a fundamental procedural principle; (2) the European Patent Office could take into account the principles of procedural law generally recognised in the Contracting States under Art.125; however, Art.125 could not be construed as providing for the creation of a special means of appeal. Article 125 merely provided a means of supplementing existing procedures where there was a lacuna in the Convention; (3) the Convention was a codified legal system and the legislator was the primary source of law. As a result, the judicial authorities could not substitute their decisions for those of the legislator; (4) the revocation of a European patent, for the first time by a decision of a Board of Appeal, with no means of challenging that decision did not contravene the Agreement on Trade-Related Aspects of Intellectual Property Rights 1994, and (5) accordingly, the response available under the Convention, following requests based on the alleged violation of a fundamental procedural principle and aimed at the revision of a final decision of a Board of Appeal having the force of res judicata, should be refusal on inadmissibility grounds, with no entry relating to such requests being made in the Register of European Patents. Furthermore, the legislator should consider amendment of the Convention to provide for the remedy found to be lacking in the instant case.

ETA/REQUEST WITH A VIEW TO REVISION (G01/97) [2001] E.P.O.R. 1, Messerli, European Patent Office (Enlarged Board of Appeal).

3891. **Patents – European Patent Office – filing date – application filed in Spanish – claim for priority based on Uruguayan application**

[European Patent Convention 1973 Art.14(2), Art.80.]

B, a citizen of Uruguay, filed a European patent application in Spanish at the Spanish patent office claiming the priority of an earlier Uruguayan patent application. The EPO decided that the relevant filing date was the date on which it received the English translation of B's application which was outside the 12-month period for claiming priority. B appealed.

Held, allowing the appeal, that a European patent application filed at the national patent office of any of the Contracting States was treated as having been filed on that date at the EPO. In order to meet the requirements of the European Patent Convention 1973 Art.80 an application had to be made in one of the official languages of the EPO, or in a language authorised by Art.14(2) of the Convention, which included. Spanish. The fact that B did not have her residence or principal place of business in a Contracting State and was not a national of a Contracting State was not relevant for the purposes of Art.80. Accordingly, B's application had been properly filed and she was entitled to claim the priority date of the Uruguayan application.

BENAS DE BRIGANTE/FILING DATE (J15/98) [2001] E.P.O.R. 51, Saisset, European Patent Office (Legal Board of Appeal).

3892. Patents – European Patent Office – opposition – admissibility of additional ground

[European Patent Convention 1973 Art.100.]

BI opposed A's European patent application citing the European Patent Convention 1973 Art.100(a) and (b). During the opposition proceedings, BI sought unsuccessfully to raise an additional ground under Art.100(c). BI appealed.

Held, setting aside the decision of the Opposition Division and remitting the case for further prosecution, that although the Opposition Division had a discretion to admit new grounds, *ROHM & HAAS/Power to examine (G09/91, G10/91)* [1993] E.P.O.R. 485 applied, the Guidelines for Examination in the EPO, Part D, Chapter V, 2.2 stated that the Opposition Division should in general examine any grounds that could prejudice the maintenance of the European patent. It followed that the primary aim of the patent prosecution in first instance proceedings was the avoidance of invalid patents. In the instant case, the Opposition Division should have examined whether the ground raised under Art.100(c) could prejudice the maintenance of the patent and not merely have declared it inadmissible on the grounds that it had been raised too late.

AMGEN/FRESH GROUND OF OPPOSITION (T736/95) [2001] E.P.O.R. 55, Kinkeldey, European Patent Office (Technical Board of Appeal).

3893. Patents – European Patent Office – opposition proceedings – withdrawal of appeal

A patent had been upheld by the Opposition Division. An opponent lodged an appeal. The opponent then withdrew the appeal by fax, received in the EPO at 16.09 hours on the relevant day. At 20.12 hours on the same day, an intervener (the First Intervener) filed notice of intervention by fax. A second intervener (the Second Intervener) served a notice of intervention some weeks later.

Held, deeming the notices of intervention not to have been filed and refunding the interveners' fees, that since withdrawal by a party of his appeal takes immediate effect, then if it is possible to establish the precise time at which the EPO received the requisite notice of withdrawal, then that would constitute the exact moment of withdrawal. It followed that there was no appeal on foot when the First and Second Interveners filed their notices of intervention. Neither notice was, therefore, valid.

UNILEVER/INTERVENTION (T517/97) [2001] E.P.O.R. 30, Burkhart, EPO (Technical Bd App).

3894. Patents – European Patent Office – party filing general authorisation naming professional representative – requirement for appointment

[European Patent Convention 1973 r.85, r.100, r.101, Art.133(2).]

A's European patent application was deemed to be withdrawn following non payment of fees within the time limit specified by the European Patent Convention 1973 r.85(a)(1) and r.85(b). A appealed, contending that the EPO had incorrectly sent notification to its US address and not to that of its European professional representative. The EPO maintained that, at the relevant time, A was not represented by any European professional representative and the issue arose as to whether a general authorisation filed by A and naming several patent agents operated as an appointment of a professional representative, as required by Art.133(2) of the Convention.

Held, dismissing the appeal, that r.100 and r.101 of the Convention distinguished between the appointment of a representative and the mere filing of an authorisation. The latter only established that a representative was able to act on a party's behalf. The EPO could not assume that a representative named in a general authorisation was appointed to act in a specific case. By virtue of Art.133(2) the EPO had to be specifically informed of the person appointed to act as a party's representative in proceedings. As the EPO had not been informed on that basis in the instant case, A was the only person entitled to exercise procedural rights in connection with the proceedings and the notification had been correctly addressed.

ANON/APPOINTMENT OF PROFESSIONAL REPRESENTATIVE (J17/98) [2001] E.P.O.R. 7, Saisset, European Patent Office (Legal Board of Appeal).

3895. **Patents – European Patent Office – party's free choice of evidence – refusal to admit – procedural violation**

[European Patent Convention 1973 Art.117.]

Z opposed a European patent claiming lack of novelty based on public prior use. At the oral proceedings before the Opposition Division, Z sought to call witnesses and requested that an inspection of prior use apparatus be made. The Opposition Division refused to hear the witnesses or conduct an inspection, taking the view that such evidence would add nothing to the documentary evidence and also that it would be unfair to S, the patentee. Z appealed, contending that the Opposition Division's decision amounted to a substantial procedural violation which infringed its right to be heard.

Held, allowing the appeal and remitting the case to the Opposition Division, that (1) under the European Patent Convention 1973 Art.117 parties were free to choose the evidence they wanted to submit. Witness testimony or inspection of a device or process was likely to be of particular assistance in cases where public prior use was at issue; (2) European Patent Office departments of first instance were entitled to exercise a discretion in admitting evidence in certain circumstances and that was only subject to review by a Board of Appeal where the discretion was exercised arbitrarily or without taking account of the right criteria, and (3) in the instant case, the Opposition Division had not found the documentary evidence to be conclusive, the content of the documented prior art was in dispute, and furthermore, it was clear that the Opposition Division had made no attempt to assess the evidence Z wished to admit to determine its relevance to the case. Therefore, the refusal to admit Z's evidence infringed the fundamental right to freely choose evidence under Art.117 and constituted a substantial procedural violation.

STOCKLI/APPARATUS FOR SEPARATING DISC SHAPED OBJECTS (T142/97) [2001] E.P.O.R. 2, Davies, European Patent Office (Technical Board of Appeal).

3896. **Patents – European Patent Office – Patent Cooperation Treaty procedure – examination and protest fees payable to International Preliminary Examining Authority**

[Patent Cooperation Treaty 1970 r.66, r.68.2.]

N appealed against additional examination and protest fees charged by the EPO acting as the International Preliminary Examining Authority, IPEA, under the Patent Cooperation Treaty 1970.

Held, ordering reimbursement of the fees, that the EPO had not followed the correct procedure in its capacity as IPEA. It should first have issued the examiner's opinion under r.66 of the Treaty, giving N an opportunity to respond to the examiner's objections. The next step was to issue an invitation under r.68.2 so that N could either restrict the subject matter of the application or pay additional fees. In the instant case, however, both the opinion and the invitation had been issued simultaneously therefore N had not been able to reply to the IPEA's objections or correct any deficiencies.

NIR RADIATION II (W06/99) [2001] E.P.O.R. 57, Lancon, European Patent Office (Technical Board of Appeal).

3897. **Patents – European Patent Office – procedure – patent owner amending claim – application of reformatio in peius prohibition**

[European Patent Convention 1973 Art.107, Art.123(3).]

3M's European patent application was granted on the basis of an amended claim. NC, the opponent, appealed. In the course of the appeal proceedings, 3M filed an auxiliary request for the deletion of one of the features of the amended claim. The

Board of Appeal considered that 3M's request could be described as appropriate and necessary since it was designed to meet an objection filed by NC on the appeal. However, since the deletion requested by 3M would extend the protection conferred by the patent NC would ultimately be placed in a worse position than if it had not appealed. The Board therefore referred to the Enlarged Board of Appeal the question whether such a request should be rejected and sought clarification of the balance of priorities between the worsening of NC's situation as against the granting of an appropriate and necessary amendment.

Held, that it was a principle of Boards of Appeal case law that no decision should be made which would put an appellant in a worse position than he was in under the decision appealed against, as described in the prohibition reformatio in peius. However, previous cases were in conflict as to whether the application of the prohibition depended on whether the appellant was the opponent or the patent proprietor and in particular where the patent proprietor was a party to the appeal as of right by virtue of the European Patent Convention 1973 Art.107. In principle, a non-appealing party could not file a request going beyond the extent of the appeal as defined in the appellant's request, *BMW/Non appealing party (G09/92)* [1995] E.P.O.R. 169 explained. However a patent proprietor could file a request in appeal proceedings to overcome the deficiency arising where, as in the instant case, the request was filed to meet an objection raised by the appellant that the amendment held allowable by the Opposition Division was in fact inadmissible, with the result that the patent would have to be revoked. In such circumstances, the patent proprietor might be allowed to file a request (1) for an amendment introducing an originally disclosed feature limiting the scope of the patent as maintained; or (2) for an amendment introducing such a feature extending the scope of the patent but within the limits of Art.123(3) of the Convention; or (3) for the deletion of the inadmissible amendment, within the limits of Art.123(3).

3M/REFORMATIO IN PEIUS (G01/99) [2001] E.P.O.R. 50, Messerli, European Patent Office (Enlarged Board of Appeal).

3898. Patents – European Patent Office – reestablishment of rights – missing fee – legitimate expectation

[European Patents Convention 1973 Art.123(2).]

A patent application was refused by the Examining Division on the basis that the amended claims infringed the European Patents Convention 1973 Art.123(2). W appealed and paid the appeal fee. In a letter of July 22, 1999 W admitted late filing of his statement of grounds and requested his appeal be allowed to proceed. The statement of grounds had been meant to be dispatched on July 5 but it had fallen behind a desk until it was discovered on July 22, 1993. Following a call from the European Patent Office, EPO, W believed that its request for restitutio in integrum had been accepted but the EPO decided that the request was inadmissible since the fee was paid outside the time limit. W appealed arguing inter alia that the EPO was under an obligation to warn of impending losses of rights and if necessary to set a new period in which the deficiency could be corrected.

Held, rejecting as inadmissible both the appeal and the request for restitutio in integrum, that (1) the protection of legitimate expectations was a general principle of law and implied that measures taken by the EPO should not violate the reasonable expectations of the parties, *MEDTRONIC/Administrative agreement (G05/88)* [1991] E.P.O.R. 225 applied; (2) however that principle did not impose on a Board an obligation to warn a party of deficiencies within the area of the party's own responsibility. The only reasonable expectation the parties could have was for the Boards to behave with the care and competence normally required by the circumstances; (3) once a case was within the jurisdiction of the Board, the Board had to avoid any action that could undermine the absolute impartiality it had to maintain between applicant, opponent and public in all proceedings. It could not reasonably be expected of the Board to depart, in even the slightest way, from this principle of law, which needed no further substantiation. Each Board was free to decide in any individual case, the level of impartiality it considered appropriate, or even the level of service compatible with its status.

WIGGINS TEAPE/LEGITIMATE EXPECTATION (T690/93) [2001] E.P.O.R. 23, Seidenschwarz, European Patent Office (Technical Board of Appeal).

3899. Patents – European patents – absence of evidence regarding accuracy of publication – apportionment of costs

An application was made for a patent in respect of a method of producing a superconductive film and a device employing that method. An objection to the application for lack of inventive step was upheld in part and both parties appealed. The opponent K, adduced evidence of a relevant disclosure in a document setting out oral presentations made during conference proceedings. Those proceedings had taken place before the priority date but the document had not been published until 10 months after the conference proceedings, one day after the priority date. There was no evidence to confirm how accurately the document reflected what had been said in the oral presentations. K argued for a presumption that the document was accurate and should be accepted at face value. S denied any such presumption and applied for an apportionment of costs as the opponent had not given any reasons for the late filing of evidence on appeal. S also filed a new set of amended claims as its main request.

Held, setting aside the decision and remitting the case to first instance with the order to maintain the patent in amended form, that (1) there was no presumption that conference proceedings published 10 months later were an accurate record; (2) therefore the burden was on the opponent to prove beyond any reasonable doubt that the technical contents of the lecture orally presented on the conference actually corresponded in all details to the respective article published 10 months later on the conference proceedings; (3) unless there was proof to the contrary, a written publication which was supposed to be based on a paper previously read at a public meeting held some time earlier, could not be presumed to be identical to what was orally disclosed but might contain additional information; (4) as K had not produced any evidence appropriate to overcome those doubts, the document did not form state of the art and was therefore disregarded; (5) the problem underlying the opposed patent was providing a method and an apparatus for producing a superconductive thin film exhibiting good crystallisation and adhesion to the substrate. The solution was not suggested by the closest prior art. Thus the solution claimed invoked an inventive step, and (6) as a general rule an apportionment of costs was only ordered where a party had behaved irresponsibly or maliciously. A decision to cite fresh evidence on appeal did not amount to such behaviour and so the application for an apportionment of costs was refused.

SUMITOMO/SUPERCONDUCTIVE FILM (T348/94) [2001] E.P.O.R. 20,Weiss, European Patent Office (Technical Board of Appeal).

3900. Patents – European patents – amendment after grant – reinstatement of items deleted from pre grant application

[European Patent Convention 1973 Art.123(3).]

S, the owner of a European patent, appealed against its revocation for lack of novelty. Amendments submitted on appeal relied on items deleted from the original application documents filed before grant. The opponent, H, claimed that the deletions were of a substantive nature as they reduced the original disclosure to the subject matter retained in the patent specification; the grant of the patent acted in effect as a cut off point after which reinstatement of subject matter deleted before grant would not be possible. It fell to be determined whether the amendments after grant were admissible under the European Patent Convention 1973 Art.123(3).

Held, allowing the appeal and remitting the case for further consideration, that Art.123(3) precluded the amendment of a European patent after grant if it extended the protection conferred by the patent. In general, the grant of a patent had the effect of making pre grant deletions substantive. Where subject matter had either been deleted from the pre grant documents to avoid inconsistencies in the patent specification, or was indicated as no longer relating to the claimed invention, its reinstatement was precluded by Art.123(3). However, S's claim met the requirements of novelty and inventive step stipulated by Art.56.

SOLARTRON/FLUID TRANSDUCER (T1149/97) [2001] E.P.O.R. 3, Steinbrener, European Patent Office (Technical Board of Appeal).

3901. **Patents – European patents – amendments – disclosure – waiver of legal privilege**

[Patents Act 1977 s.75; European Patent Convention 1973 Art.138.]

A appealed against an interlocutory decision in patent proceedings to the effect that while O had waived privilege by disclosing documents to B, A's English lawyers, the court could exercise its discretion under the Patents Act 1977 s.75 to prevent disclosure of the same documents to A's lawyers in the United States. O cross-appealed, contending that its agreement to limited disclosure to B on terms and only for the purposes of its application to amend its patent did not amount to a general waiver of privilege. O also argued that A's opposition to the amendment was an attempt to revoke the patent outside the terms of the European Patent Convention 1973 Art.138.

Held, dismissing the appeal, that (1) practitioners should be made aware that there was no requirement for extensive disclosure on an application to amend and disclosure of only those facts directly relevant to the exercise of the court's discretion was required under the obligation of good faith, and (2) a patentee was not required to waive privilege, *Kimberly Clark Worldwide Inc v. Procter & Gamble Ltd (No.1)* [2000] F.S.R. 235, [2000] 1 C.L. 279 applied. Furthermore, no adverse inference could be drawn against him for not doing so, *WC Wentworth v. JC Lloyd* (Unreported) applied. The disclosure by OGT to B did not amount to the disclosure of any confidential document to an adversary or to a waiver of privilege. The 1973 Convention did not prevent the court from exercising its discretion under s.75 of the 1977 Act to permit an amendment which would validate an otherwise invalid patent.

OXFORD GENE TECHNOLOGY LTD v. AFFYMETRIX INC (NO.2) [2001] R.P.C. 18, Aldous, L.J., CA.

3902. **Patents – European patents – anti-impotence drug – obviousness – anticipation by prior art**

L applied for a declaration of invalidity relating to a European patent registered by P which claimed protection for the medical use of various chemicals, one of which was an active ingredient in the anti-impotence drug Viagra. The patent contained claims that various compounds would result in the "curative or prophylactic treatment of erectile dysfunction". L argued that (1) for the purpose of construing the claims in the patent, it would be sufficient to establish that consumers would use the relevant compound with the intention of treating impotence, and it would not matter if the compound failed to produce the desired effect; (2) in the light of three publications which had appeared in the 18 month period prior to the priority date of the patent, the patent was obvious, and (3) the patent had been anticipated by a publication appearing shortly before the patent's priority date. P argued, inter alia, that Viagra's success was proof of its inventiveness.

Held, giving judgment for L, that (1) the relevant compound had to be effective, at least in some cases, in treating erectile dysfunction, *Bristol Myers Squibb Co v. Baker Norton Pharmaceuticals Inc* (2000) 23(8) I.P.D. 23058, [2000] 7 C.L. 330 applied. If use of the compound was successful in treating the condition, it would not matter whether such success resulted from the use of the compound on its own or from a combination of the compound and another agent; (2) the three publications relied on by L showed that an anti-impotence pill did not represent an unexpected discovery from the standpoint of the notional skilled addressee. The prior art would also have led such a person to use oral administration of the drug. Accordingly, P's patent was invalid for obviousness, *Windsurfing International Inc v. Tabur Marine (Great Britain) Ltd*

[1985] R.P.C. 59 applied, and (3) as regards L's case on anticipation, the scientific study relied on by L failed to show that the chemical referred to therein had achieved a discernible effect on erectile dysfunction. In the circumstances, although the issue was academic, L had failed to establish its case on anticipation.

LILLY ICOS LTD v. PFIZER LTD (NO.1); *sub nom.* PFIZER LTD'S EUROPEAN PATENT (UK) (NO.0702555) [2001] F.S.R. 16, Laddie, J., Pat Ct.

3903. Patents – European patents – appeals – documentary evidence – admissibility

V appealed against a decision of the Opposition Division not to revoke M's patent for a pressure sensor. V contended that the decision should be set aside because new documents had been found which indicated that the claim was invalid for obviousness or lack of novelty.

Held, dismissing the appeal, that an appeal against a refusal to revoke a patent was admissible where the ground for appeal was the citation of new documents, rather than criticism of the decision itself. However, a document would only be admitted where there were sufficient indications showing publication of the document prior to the priority date.

MAGNETTI MARELLI/PRESSURE SENSOR (T708/95) [2001] E.P.O.R. 14, Turrini (Chairman), European Patent Office (Technical Board of Appeal).

3904. Patents – European patents – appeals – reinstatement – time limits – professional adviser suffering serious illness

G's European patent application was rejected on April 4, 1984. Entries in the diary of G's professional representative for filing Grounds of Appeal were inexplicably deleted while he was suffering from medical and mental problems. G applied for re-establishment in 1997.

Held, granting re establishment, that whereas the inexplicable deletion of the diary entries was not in itself a ground for ordering re establishment, there were other exceptional circumstances in the instant case which did justify re establishment of the proceedings.

GEPPERT/ TENSIONING DEVICE (T315/87) [2001] E.P.O.R. 47, Judge not specified, European Patent Office (Technical Board of Appeal).

3905. Patents – European patents – appeals – restricted to defence of patent where no cross appeal

A patent had been maintained by the Opposition Division, allowing the applicant's claims 1 to 3, but disallowing claim 4. An opponent appealed the decision maintaining the patent. The patent holder did not lodge a cross appeal, but did request maintenance of the patent preferably in its original form, but at any rate in the form as amended (i.e. with the disallowed claim 4).

Held, dismissing the appeal but refusing to maintain the patent as granted, that a request by a party which goes beyond the original appeal is not admissible and the patentee in the appeal would be restricted to defending the patent in the amended form in which the Opposition Division had maintained it.

INTERNATIONAL DOME SYSTEMS/BUILDING STRUCTURE (T812/94) [2001] E.P.O.R. 31, Judge not specified, European Patent Office (Technical Board of Appeal).

3906. Patents – European patents – application based on chemical formula – admissibility of re-amended claim

[European Patent Convention 1973 Art.123(2).]

P sought a patent for a group of heteroatom-substituted alkylbenzylaminoquinuclidines, listing numerous possibilities in specific and/or generic form for the substituents around the structural nucleus. The Examining Division rejected the application on the ground that the substantially restricted amended claim contained subject matter not supported by the original claim, contrary to the European Patent Convention 1973 Art.123(2). It held that the lower end of the range of three to six carbon atoms defining the alkyl group of the substituent X in the claim was not supported in the application as filed and that the groups defining the substituent Y in the claim were not supported by the original application. P appealed, submitting a further amendment to claim 1.

Held, allowing the appeal and remitting the case for further prosecution based on the re-amended claim, that (1) the subject matter of the re-amended claim was based on that originally filed. The lower limit of the range specifying the number of carbon atoms had been raised from one to three carbon atoms; (2) the application listed individual alkyl groups, including n-propyl and isopropyl. Since both groups represented the only two possible isomers of an alkyl group with three carbon atoms, their specific disclosure gave a proper basis for claiming three carbon atoms as the lower limit of the range of carbon atoms comprised in the alkyl group; (3) the alternative of substituting that alkyl group by two substituents and the list of those substituents indicated in claim 1 was backed up by claim 2 as filed, and (4) limiting the range of alternative definitions was allowed as the limitation did not single out a particular combination of specific definitions, ie a sub class of compounds not previously mentioned, but maintained the remaining subject matter of the claim as generic lists of alternative definitions that only differing from the original because of their smaller size.

PFIZER/QUINUCLIDINES (T50/97) [2000] E.P.O.R. 533, Nuss, European Patent Office (Technical Board of Appeal).

3907. Patents – European patents – applications – description of subject matter – compliance with EPC requirements

[European Patent Convention 1973 Art.84, Art.123(2).]

The Examining Division refused a European patent application because the word "used" in referring to organic resist in Claim 1 was deleted from that Claim as filed, contrary to the European Patent Convention 1973 Art.123(2). Further, that Claim 1 did not satisfy Art.84 because it did not contain all the essential features of the invention. F appealed.

Held, allowing the appeal, that (1) the original application did not rely on the word "used" in relation to the phrase "for removing a used organic resist on a semiconductor wafer". There was no reason for a skilled person to consider that the invention was limited to "used" resist, and (2) Claim 1 did not lack an essential feature causing it to be unclear in terms of Art.84. It was not the object to be achieved by an invention that defined its essential features, but the measures needed to achieve that object. The features achieving the objects were sufficiently recited in the claims.

FUJITSU/REMOVAL OF ORGANIC RESIST (T311/99) [2000] E.P.O.R. 488, Turrini, European Patent Office (Technical Board of Appeal).

3908. Patents – European patents – applications – third party trade mark used to describe subject matter – sufficient clarity lacking

[European Patent Convention 1973 Art.84, Art.123(2).]

C's European patent application used a third party trade mark as a means of describing material comprised in the claim. The Examining Division refused the claim on the basis that it contravened the European Patent Convention 1973 Art.84 and Art.123(2). C appealed, submitting material that fully explained the subject matter of the trade mark.

Held, dismissing the appeal, that the use of the third party trade mark was insufficiently clear where it covered a number of products which had different compositions and properties at the priority date.

CIUFFO GATTO/TRADE MARK (T480/98) [2000] E.P.O.R. 494, Andries, European Patent Office (Technical Board of Appeal).

3909. Patents – European patents – claims – admissibility – group of chemical compounds

[European Patent Convention 1973 Art.123(2).]

B applied for a patent for a group of benzimidazolone derivatives. The application was rejected on the basis that the substantially restricted amended claim contravened the European Patent Convention 1973 Art.123(2) because the revised group definition was not supported by the application as filed because it relied on an arbitrary selection of subgroups. The Examining Board decided that a skilled reader could not derive from the description of the application whether or not deleted meanings were essential features that had to be maintained in the claim. Further, there had been an impermissible generalisation of the exemplified compounds. B appealed to the Technical Board of Review and submitted an amended Claim 1.

Held, allowing the appeal and remitting the application for further prosecution of the amended Claim 1, that (1) a skilled reader looking for essential features of the disclosed invention would first consider the examples representing the experimental work actually done and the embodiments indicated in the description as the preferred ones; (2) in the instant case he would have come to the conclusion that the subject matter as claimed formed the core of the invention as set out in the application as filed; (3) moreover, the substituents and subgroups defined in the claim did not result from an unallowable generalisation of particular examples. They were actually disclosed in the application as filed, and (4) accordingly the present set of claims complied with the requirements of Art.123(2) because their subject matter was clearly supported by the application as filed.

BOEHRINGER/BENZIMIDAZOLONE (T1052/97) [2000] E.P.O.R. 538, Nuss, European Patent Office (Technical Board of Appeal).

3910. Patents – European patents – disclosure – insufficient to allow skilled person to obtain claimed technical features

E was granted a European patent for antigenic preparations and their isolation. S and L appealed on the grounds of insufficiency of disclosure querying the claimed ratio of proline to glutamic acid determined by amino acid analysis.

Held, setting aside the decision and revoking the patent, that a skilled person would not be able to perform a meaningful measurement of the claimed ratio and would therefore not know whether the relevant protein was present. Since it would not be possible for a skilled person following the instruction of E's patent to obtain without undue difficulty a product having the technical features claimed by E's patent the invention was not sufficiently disclosed by the patent.

EVANS/ANTIGENIC PREPARATIONS (T780/95) [2001] E.P.O.R. 56, Judge not specified, European Patent Office (Technical Board of Appeal).

3911. Patents – European patents – disclosure – late filing of documents admitted to show insufficient disclosure

O was granted a European patent relating to a mouse monoclonal antibody. Notices of Opposition were filed requesting revocation for lack of novelty, lack of inventive step and insufficient disclosure. A month before oral proceedings one of the opponents filed new documents including one published by one of the inventors some years after the filing date. O objected to the late admission of the documents.

Held, allowing the opposition and revoking the patent that (1) although the documents now sought to be relied upon by the opponent had been submitted late, their potential relevance could not be ignored and the material would therefore be admitted and; (2) the Board was satisfied that the recently submitted article showed that the reactivity pattern claimed in the application was erroneous. The patentee must have known of the new data and its likely implications but had failed to disclose them (*ORTHO/Monoclonal antibody*

(T418/89) [1993] E.P.O.R. 338 and *ORTHO/Monoclonal antibody (T495/89)* [1992] E.P.O.R. 48 considered).

ORTHO/ MONOCLONAL ANTIBODY (OKT11) (T498/94) [2001] E.P.O.R. 48, Judge not specified, European Patent Office (Technical Board of Appeal).

3912. Patents – European patents – disclosure – requirements to avoid being burdensome or relying on chance

W held a European patent in respect of a reticulated cellulose product and its production method based on the growth of micro-organisms. A's opposition was rejected and A appealed claiming lack of sufficient disclosure.

Held, allowing the appeal and revoking the patent, that for the purposes of a European patent application an invention had to be disclosed in a sufficiently clear and complete way to enable a person skilled in the art to carry out the patented invention without undue burden and without relying on chance. This applied only in part in this case and there had not been sufficient disclosure in relation to the claim taken as a whole.

WEYERSHAEUSER/CELLULOSE (T727/95) [2001] E.P.O.R. 35, UM Kinkeldy, European Patent Office (Technical Board of Appeal).

3913. Patents – European patents – documentary evidence – novelty of application in comparison with prior art

[European Patent Convention 1973 Art.54(1).]

C's European patent application for a welding device was refused on the grounds of lack of novelty. The Examination Division relied on the abstract of a Japanese document. C appealed.

Held, allowing the appeal, that the reference to the abstract rather than the full document did not constitute a procedural fault. However, an examination of the English translation of the full Japanese document showed that the subject matter of C's application was novel when compared with the prior art, as required by the European Patent Convention 1973 Art.54(1). Accordingly, the decision would be quashed and the case remitted with an order to grant the patent.

COMMISSARIAT A L'ENERGIE ATOMIQUE/WELDING (T243/96) [2001] E.P.O.R. 53, Judge not specified, European Patent Office (Technical Board of Appeal).

3914. Patents – European patents – extension of subject matter – reimbursement of fee – apportionment of costs

The patent in suit related to touch probes. These devices each contained a movable member and a fixed member. Claim 1 in all of the patentee's requests required that a planar spring feature in the devices should operate so as to prevent rotation of the movable member relative to the fixed member. The patent had been granted on a divisional application, and subsequently revoked by the Opposition Division. The patentee sought maintenance of the patent in an amended form, and initiated oral proceedings. Two auxiliary requests were lodged, the second of which was submitted for the first time in the course of the oral proceedings. The purpose of this second request was to meet an objection to the patent lodged by M, the opponent, and the Opposition Division to the effect that Claim 1 lacked features taught as essential in the parent application.

Held, dismissing the patentee's appeal, that (1) the second auxiliary request would be admitted, since its content would not have taken M by surprise; (2) prevention of rotation of the movable member relative to the fixed member was not taught by the parent application, which disclosed only lateral constraint. It was agreed that planar springs could be constructed so as to function in the manner claimed by the patentee, but this function could not be clearly deduced from the schematic drawings and other material forming part of the parent application. The patentee's contention that it had been stated in litigation before a US court that a planar spring did have the rotation preventing property for which the patentee was arguing in the instant proceedings was of no relevance, and (3) since the appeal had been dismissed, the patentee's appeal fee would not be refunded. Further, M's request for an apportionment of costs would be refused, since the Board had found the oral proceedings to be very helpful, and not (as M contended) superfluous.

RENISHAW/TOUCH PROBE (T434/97) [2001] E.P.O.R. 26, Turrini (Chairman), European Patent Office (Technical Board of Appeal).

3915. Patents – European patents – failure to hold oral proceedings

K, the opponent, appealed against a refusal to revoke a patent for lack of inventive step. K filed two new prior art documents. Both parties asked for an oral hearing. The Board held that oral proceedings were inappropriate, and remitted the case to the Opposition Division with a direction for further consideration of admissibility of the prior art, followed (if necessary) by inquiry into inventive step. Following remittal, the Opposition Division rejected the opposition without allowing the parties to make representations on the admissibility of the prior art. K lodged a further appeal.

Held, allowing the appeal and remitting the case to the Opposition Division for a second time, that (1) where the Board had remitted the matter without a substantive hearing, the parties should have been allowed to make submissions on the admissibility of the prior art following remittal, regardless of whether they had made observations thereon during the appeal; (2) the failure by the Opposition Division to invite submissions was a serious procedural violation, and justified an order for the reimbursement to the opponent of the appeal fee, and (3) K had originally requested oral proceedings and, since the remittal proceedings were a continuation of the original proceedings, a decision adverse to K should not have been taken without K having been given an opportunity to be heard.

CESANA/SHOWER CUBICLE (T120/96); *sub nom.* CESANA SPA'S EUROPEAN PATENT (NO.0348653) [2001] E.P.O.R. 13, Judge not specified, European Patent Office (Technical Board of Appeal).

3916. Patents – European patents – failure to pay designation fees by contracting states – withdrawal of designation

[European Patent Convention 1973 Art.67(4), Art.91(4).]

The Enlarged Board of Appeal gave the following opinion (1) without prejudice to the European Patent Convention 1973 Art.67(4) failure to pay the designation fee did not cause a Contracting State to retroactively lose the legal effect of its designation; (2) deemed withdrawal of a designated state under Art.91(4) took effect upon expiry of the time limits laid down. Deemed withdrawal did not occur upon the expiry of the grace period provided for by Rule 85a of the EPC.

DESIGNATION FEES, *Re* (G4/98) [2001] E.P.O.R. 42, Messerli, European Patent Office (Enlarged Board of Appeal).

3917. Patents – European patents – fees – reduction for applicant from state with non EPO language

[European Patent Convention 1973 Art.14, r.6(3).]

A, an Italian company, submitted a written request to the EPO for examination in Italian and requested the 20 per cent reduction in the examination fee in accordance with the European Patent Convention 1973 Art.14(2) and r.6(3). A's request was refused on the ground that the request had not been properly indicated by ticking the pre-printed box on the relevant form. A appealed.

Held, allowing the appeal, that, according to the Guidelines for Examination in the European Patent Office (Part A), as amended following the decision in *ASULAB/Fee reduction (G06/91)* [1993] E.P.O.R. 231, applicants from non-EPO language states wishing to obtain a fee reduction under Art.14 were recommended to file the request for examination in their own language in the request for a grant. However, the Boards of Appeal were bound only by the Convention, not the Guidelines. An examination request was separate from the prior step of filing the patent application and at that time A would not have been in a position to decide whether to prosecute the case and it was entitled to know the outcome of the search report before deciding to request an examination. Article 14 was intended to compensate non EPO language state nationals for having to provide a translation into an official EPO language. A should not therefore be deprived of the right merely because of a failure to tick a pre printed box, *ASULAB/Fee reduction (G06/91)* followed.

AUSIMONT/FEE REDUCTION (J21/98) [2001] E.P.O.R. 8, Saisset, European Patent Office (Legal Board of Appeal).

3918. **Patents – European patents – infringement – lavatory freshener – anticipation by prior art**

[Patents Act 1977 s.75.]

SL was the proprietor of a European patent for a cleansing and freshening unit designed to be suspended from the rim of a toilet bowl, referred to in the art as a rimblock. The essential characteristics of SL's rimblock were that it had a liquid permeable closure in combination with a porous substance. SL alleged that two rimblocks produced by JW infringed its claim in that the devices had liquid permeable closures arranged in the mouth of the reservoir by means of a plastic insert. JW denied infringement and challenged the validity of the patent on the basis of anticipation and obviousness and further contended that the matter disclosed in the patent extended beyond that disclosed in the application as filed rendering the patent void for added matter. SL sought to add additional claims to distinguish the patent more clearly, arguing that they were claims which were dependent on Claim 1. JW countered that the additions were impermissible on the grounds that they did not seek to meet the challenge to invalidity as they did not seek to revise Claim 1.

Held, giving judgment for the defendants, that there had been no infringement of Claim 1 by JW as the plastic insert was not a liquid permeable closure notwithstanding the fact that it was in the mouth of the reservoir. The patent was not invalid on the grounds of anticipation, obviousness or added matter and should not therefore be revoked, *METAL-FREN/Friction pad assembly (T582/91)* [1995] E.P.O.R. 574 applied. The additions proposed by SL had been intended to give them a fall back position should Claim 1 be held to be invalid and to allow such amendment would not be an appropriate exercise of the court's discretion under the Patents Act 1977 s.75, *British Telecommunications, Re (T829/93)* (Unreported) applied.

SARA LEE HOUSEHOLD & BODY CARE UK LTD v. JOHNSON WAX LTD [2001] F.S.R. 17, David Young Q.C., Pat Ct.

3919. **Patents – European patents – inventive step – admissibility of late evidence**

U was granted a patent relating to a process for the preparation of water and oil emulsions, but was subsequently objected to by R on the grounds that its subject matter was not novel and inventive. R requested that the patent be revoked. On appeal to the Board, R cited a fresh document, which was an article in a weekly magazine. U did not object that the magazine was unknown to him and accepted that it represented the nearest prior art.

Held, allowing the appeal and revoking the patent, that (1) there was no negligence on R's part in late filing the article and it could be cited in the proceedings; (2) the decisive step for the assessment of inventive step of the requests was whether a skilled person would have replaced the unmodified egg yolk used in the preparation of the oil in water emulsions with the modified egg yolk as stated in the magazine article, as a means of solving the existing problem, and (3) a skilled person becoming aware of the article would have carried out the recommended step.

UNILEVER/EMULSIONS (T384/94) [2000] E.P.O.R. 469, Judge not specified, European Patent Office (Technical Board of Appeal).

3920. Patents – European patents – inventive step – auxiliary request upheld – problem not capable of solution by nearest prior art

[European Patent Convention 1973 Art.56.]

P obtained a patent for epoxide and rubber based curable compositions that adhered directly to metal. HT opposed the grant on the grounds of lack of novelty and inventive step. The Opposition Division maintained the patent in amended form but HT appealed to the Technical Board of Appeal. In the course of the appeal, P made further amended claims to its main request, including an independent claim not considered by the Opposition Division. P sought the maintenance of the patent as granted by the Opposition Division with minor amendments to the auxiliary request.

Held, allowing the appeal but maintaining the patent in the form of the auxiliary request, that the scope of the new set of claims in the main request was wider than in the original claim and could not be admitted as this would breach the principle of reformatio in peius, *BMW/Non appealing party (G09/92)* [1995] E.P.O.R. 169 applied. However, the auxiliary request was allowable since the amendments it contained did not extend the scope of the claims. The technical problem involved the search for a single composite with a wide latitude for curing temperatures, capable of adhering to a metal substrate and stable when stored. The subject matter involved an inventive step in terms of the European Patent Convention 1973 Art.56 as the nearest prior art did not give a solution to the problem.

PPG/EPOXIDE COMPOSITIONS (T579/94) [2000] E.P.O.R. 584, Judge not specified, European Patent Office (Technical Board of Appeal).

3921. Patents – European patents – inventive step – evidence – time limits – restriction on right to fair hearing – alternative solution to problem

[European Patent Convention 1973 Art.56, Art.114(2).]

K sought revocation of a patent granted in respect of a glide shoe, contending that the problem described by the invention had been solved by the prior art and therefore lacked inventive step. K unsuccessfully attempted to develop a new line of argument in oral proceedings before the Opposition Division, which rejected it on the grounds that it had not been submitted in time, as required by the European Patent Convention 1973 Art.114(2). K appealed to the Technical Board of Appeal.

Held, dismissing the appeal, that (1) although the right to a fair hearing included the right to present facts and evidence to be considered by the decision making body, Art.114(2) limited this right where the evidence was not adduced within the prescribed time limit; (2) Art.114(2) did not, however, refer to "arguments" and the Opposition Division had been wrong to find that the new line of argument had not been submitted in time; (3) Art.56 did not require novelty in respect of the problem to be solved and there was nothing to prevent an alternative solution to a know problem being refused for lack of inventive step, and (4) a consideration of the prior art in the instant case showed that the invention involved an inventive step.

VALMET/GLIDE SHOE (T92/92) [2000] E.P.O.R. 566, Judge not specified, European Patent Office (Technical Board of Appeal).

3922. Patents – European patents – inventive step – examples of use required

An application for a European patent was lodged in respect of non-stick shrink wrapping of packaged items. The initial application related to the wrapping material itself, and was rejected for want of novelty and inventive step. The examples cited of the prior art did not refer to any problem with sticking and the applicant had failed to show that the materials cited in the said examples actually did stick to the items they were to wrap. The applicant appealed, and on appeal changed the basis of the application from one of "product" to one of "use", in which a definition was given of the composition of the inner and outer layers of the wrapping material, the inner layer being non stick.

Held, dismissing the appeal, that although the change in the nature of the application was permissible, and although the revised claim possessed novelty, the non stick nature of the wrapping material was addressing a problem of sticking which did not actually arise. It could not, therefore, be taken into account in assessing the necessary element of inventive step. Since the description in the application did not contain any specific examples, there was no scope for a narrower and more relevant interpretation of the application in relation to the items to be protected by shrink-wrapping.

ROSENLAW/SHRINK WRAPPING (T589/95) [2001] E.P.O.R. 45, Judge not specified, European Patent Office (Technical Board of Appeal).

3923. Patents – European patents – inventive step – genetically modified organisms – state of prior art

[European Patent Convention 1973 Art.56, Art.83, Art.84, Art.123(2), Art.123(3).]

D claimed a patent for a method of preparing Phaffia rhodozyma yeast cells to produce the carotenoid pigment astaxanthin in a specified amount of yeast dry matter by treating a naturally occurring yeast cell with the ethylmethane sulphonate or N-methyl-N'-nitro-N-nitrosoguanide mutagens. B opposed the grant on the ground of lack of inventive step. The Opposition Division gave an interlocutory decision maintaining the patent in amended form on the basis of an auxiliary request. D and B appealed to the Technical Board of Appeal.

Held, setting aside the decision and remitting the case with an order to maintain the patent on the basis of the auxiliary request, limited to specific deposited yeast strains, mutants and derivatives, that (1) in relation to inventive step, it had to be determined what steps the skilled person faced with this problem would have considered, given the state of prior art and general knowledge; (2) in the instant case, the skilled person would have considered mutagenesis techniques to improve astaxanthin yields; (3) such techniques were well known in the art and were chiefly used in strain improvement programmes. The techniques were applied on a trial and error basis so that knowledge of the target organism's genetic structure was not required; (4) mutagenesis was in any case the route of choice as not much was known about Phaffia and both the alternative routes of genetic engineering and protoplast fusions were impractical; (5) in the circumstances, the skilled person faced with this technical problem would have resorted to the method covered by the claim so that there was a lack of inventive step, therefore, the main request was disallowed under the European Patent Convention 1973 Art.56. However, the novelty of the auxiliary request was not contested, limited to the deposited strains, mutants or derivatives and was supported by the application as filed, thus fulfilling Art.123(2) and Art.123(3), and (6) the auxiliary request claims were allowed under Art.56, Art.83 and Art.84 as they embodied a contribution to the art.

DSM/ASTAXANTHIN (T737/96) [2000] E.P.O.R. 557, Kinkeldey, European Patent Office (Technical Board of Appeal).

3924. Patents – European patents – inventive step – knowledge of skilled person – state of prior art

[European Patent Convention 1973 Art.102(3), r.57(a).]

A patent was granted for a flexible composite pipe for transporting high temperature gas and oil. This was opposed on the grounds of lack of novelty and inventive step but it was maintained by the Opposition Division in amended form. The opponent appealed to the Technical Board of Appeal.

Held, allowing the appeal and revoking the patent, that (1) although a patentee could not amend a patent if it was not the appellant, except where the amendment was due to the opponent's appeal, the European Patent Convention 1973 r.57(a) applied to the instant case, so that an amendment could be allowed where it removed deficiencies in a patent to be maintained in amended form under Art.102(3); (2) disclosure of the patent was sufficient where its disclosure and interpretation by the skilled person was decisive; (3) the patent's novelty was due to the fact that the prior art did not disclose the use of a composite pipe, manufactured on conventional equipment, for use in this situation. However, there was no inventive step as the skilled person seeking such a solution would be acquainted with composite pipe manufacture and would also know the range of available materials and their respective properties. Exchanging the lining used in the closest prior art for that claimed in the patent would therefore be an obvious step.

FURUKAWA/FLEXIBLE COMPOSITE PIPE (T1002/95) [2000] E.P.O.R. 544, Judge not specified, European Patent Office (Technical Board of Appeal).

3925. Patents – European patents – inventive step – known ulcer treatment applied to gastritis

Geranylgeranylacetone (GGA) was known as a curative element in the treatment of ulcers. The application related to the use of GGA as an element in an anti gastritis preparation. Gastritis shared the same causative factors as ulcers, on which basis the Examining Division refused the application for lack of inventive step. The applicant appealed.

Held, dismissing the appeal, that even if two diseases share the same cause or origin, that in itself would not preclude an inventive step in respect of a second therapeutic use for a known substance. But if the symptoms of the first disease were the same as, but more serious than, the second disease, then the efficacy of a substance in relation to the more serious disease strongly suggested efficacy in relation to the less serious condition. Given the prior awareness of GGA's effectiveness against ulcers, its use in the anti gastritis preparation the subject of the application lacked an inventive step.

EISAI/ MEDICAMENT FOR GASTRITIS (T913/94) [2001] E.P.O.R. 46, Judge not specified, European Patent Office (Technical Board of Appeal).

3926. Patents – European patents – inventive step – measures to improve yield obvious to person skilled in prior art

R was granted a European patent for a process claiming to improve the yield and selectivity in the manufacture of the chemical 3-(4-methyl-3-cyclohexen-1-yl) butyraldehyde by the hydroformylation of limonene using a rhodium carbonyl complex containing phosphine as a catalyst at an increased temperature and under higher pressure. H sought the revocation of the patent for lack of inventive step. Revocation was refused and H appealed.

Held, allowing the appeal and revoking the patent, that the prior art described the hydroformylation of limonene using a rhodium phosphine catalyst and also the conversion of limonene to butyraldehyde at specified temperatures and pressures. It was therefore obvious to the skilled person understanding the rules governing the rate of reaction that increasing temperature and pressure would improve yield and selectivity.

RUHRCHEMIE/3-(4-METHYL-3-CYCLOHEXEN-1-YL) (T132/86) [2001] E.P.O.R. 5, Judge not specified, European Patent Office (Technical Board of Appeal).

3927. Patents – European patents – inventive step – nail enamel composition – pigment settlement problem known to skilled person

[European Patent Convention 1973 Art.56, Art.100(a).]

R obtained a patent for nail enamel, comprising an inorganic pigment pre coated with a polyorganosiloxane. The examples provided with the application used a commercially available pigment known as "9454" recommended for nail lacquer use. L opposed the patent for lack of inventive step under the European Patent Convention 1973 Art.100(a). However, the Opposition Division held that, in light of the closest prior art, the problem underlying the patent was to prevent pigment settlement and migration and that there was an inventive step, given that the use of pre coated pigments was not obvious in terms of the prior art. L appealed to the Technical Board of Appeal.

Held, allowing the appeal and revoking the patent, that (1) nail enamel compositions were part of the general knowledge of a person skilled in the prior art and were prone to the problem of pigment migration and settling; (2) the problem was to develop an enamel free from such defects. This was solved by a composition using coated inorganic pigment, including commercial available products, and (3) the patent did not comply with Art.56 as the problem was known to the skilled person who would obviously have used a commercial product in solving it and the solution in the instant case did not involve an inventive step.

REVLON/NAIL ENAMEL (T306/93) [2000] E.P.O.R. 575, Judge not specified, European Patent Office (Technical Board of Appeal).

3928. **Patents – European patents – inventive step – novelty – steps required of skilled person to reach subject matter**

The Opposition Division rejected S's opposition to M's European patent application for magnetoresistive materials. S appealed, contending that the invention lacked novelty and inventive step.

Held, setting aside the decision under appeal and remitting the case with an order to maintain the patent in amended form, that (1) the prior art addressed the problem of providing magnetoresistive elements having a large resistance change in a practical low magnetic field and the problem of providing new structures or combinations of materials with unexpected advantages. The composition of the materials as disclosed by M's application were sufficiently different from the specific examples cited in the prior art and were therefore novel. The fact that the prior art mentioned the same alloys as M's patent did not mean that it anticipated the narrower ranges given in M's patent. Since the technical teaching was different, the skilled person would be dissuaded by the prior art from applying it to the range of materials disclosed by M's patent. Furthermore, even assuming that the prior art could include ranges with values outside the specific examples given, the ranges specified by M's patent, taken in combination, could not have been contemplated by the authors of the prior art documents, and (2) in relation to inventive step, although the prior art examples of ferromagnetic layers combined with non magnetic layers fell within the range of M's patent the prior art examples did not disclose the alternately laminated layers described in M's patent. A skilled person would have to carry out a series of steps commencing with the prior art to arrive at the subject matter of M's patent. It was not simply a question of testing other known magnetic alloys. The poor theoretical knowledge available indicated that the discovery of an advantageous combination of materials producing a new effect was not an obvious choice. M's patent therefore involved an inventive step.

MATSUSHITA ELECTRIC INDUSTRIAL/MAGNETORESISTIVE MATERIALS (T610/96) [2001] E.P.O.R. 54, Judge not specified, European Patent Office (Technical Board of Appeal).

3929. **Patents – European patents – inventive step – obviousness**

H was granted a European patent in respect of a manufacturing process for the chemical p-tert.butylbenzaldehyde. The process resulted in substantially increased yields through the substitution of bromine for chlorine as the halogenation agent. B sought the revocation of the patent for lack of inventive step. The novelty of the process was not disputed, but B claimed that it was obvious to the skilled person. B's opposition was rejected on the grounds that the large yield improvement obtained by the process constituted an inventive step. B appealed.

Held, allowing the appeal and revoking the patent, that both stages of the patented process were common knowledge among experts in the field. A skilled person would therefore realise the potential for yield improvement using bromination rather than chlorination. Accordingly, it would be obvious for the skilled person to attempt the process in order to demonstrate such yield improvement. The fact that favourable results were obtained from routine experiments did not constitute an inventive step.

HOECHST/P-TERT.BUTYLBENZALDEHYDE (T199/84) [2001] E.P.O.R. 4, Judge not specified, European Patent Office (Technical Board of Appeal).

3930. **Patents – European patents – inventive step – prior art – new comparative experimental evidence**

E appealed against the failure to grant a patent for a conveyor lubricant. E had filed a document to represent the closest state of the art. The examination division rejected the application for want of inventive step over the document. On appeal E filed new comparative experimental results, demonstrating an improvement on the lubricating performance of the compositions set out in the original document.

Held, allowing the appeal, that the data contained in the original document related only to substances containing 10 or fewer carbon atoms, whereas the substance under application contained between 10 and 18 carbon atoms. The matter would be remitted to the examination division for the inventive step to be considered in the light of all prior art on file.

ECOLAB/CONVEYOR LUBRICANT (T392/96); *sub nom.* ECOLAB INC'S EUROPEAN PATENT APPLICATION (NO.92901186.4) [2001] E.P.O.R. 16, Judge not specified, European Patent Office (Technical Board of Appeal).

3931. **Patents – European patents – inventive step – scope and meaning – obviousness**

The Opposition Division maintained the European patent of A. B appealed on the grounds that the patent lacked novelty and an inventive step.

Held, dismissing the appeal and remitting the case with an order that the patent be maintained that non-obviousness was related to the concept of invention which was technical in character. Arbitrary modifications of no technical relevance might produce a new design, but would not constitute an inventive step and as such would not be patentable.

IBBOTT/ IONIZING FLUIDS (T157/97) [2001] E.P.O.R. 44, Judge not specified, European Patent Office (Technical Board of Appeal).

3932. **Patents – European patents – inventive step – semi conductors – publications intended for qualified professional**

[European Patent Convention 1973 Art.52(1), Art.56.]

T appealed against the refusal of a patent application based on a technical handbook by an author with acknowledged competence in semiconductor devices formed on GaAs substrates, and information in an article with a worldwide reputation, published in a scientific periodical addressed to qualified professionals. The patent was refused on the basis that the subject matter of the claimed patent lacked an inventive step within the meaning of the European Patent Convention 1973 Art.56.

Held, allowing the appeal, that (1) the subject of the application was common general knowledge of the skilled person working in that field; (2) any skilled person attempting to solve a particular problem while designing a device had to bear in mind the elements of the common general knowledge in his field of professional activity; (3) if the design of a device involved any other technical problem which, together with at least one solution, was part of that common general knowledge, skilled persons were supposed to keep themselves aware of the existence of the other technical problem and the available solutions; (4) in the instant case, the technical handbook stated that, contrary to aluminium and titanium, ie the other two metals mentioned in the patent application as envisaged for making gate and extraction electrodes, gold exhibited poor adhesion to gallium arsenide and was highly susceptible to diffusing into that material; (5) only two years could have elapsed between the date of its publication and the priority date claimed in the patent application; (6)

in the circumstances there were strong reasons to believe that, at the priority date, the skilled person involved in the design and production of semiconductor devices formed on GaAs substrates might have been deterred by a technical prejudice from using gold for making the gate and extraction electrodes for a FET, a semi-conductor device with very small dimensions, integrated in such a substrate, and (7) therefore there was an inventive step so that the patent was allowable under Art.52 (1).

TOSHIBA/TRANSISTOR (T378/93) [2000] E.P.O.R. 523, Judge not specified, European Patent Office (Technical Board of Appeal).

3933. Patents – European patents – inventive step – unnecessary amendments

V obtained a European patent relating to vehicle sliding roof. W unsuccessfully sought the revocation of the patent for lack of inventive step and appealed.

Held, allowing the appeal and revoking the patent, that (1) it was permissible in considering the state of the art to refer to documents illustrating both sliding roofs and windows since the two were closely related and both would be understood by a skilled person; (2) V's patent specification claimed to reduce manufacturing costs by using flexible plastic tubing in place of the usual rigid tubing and made allowances for the increased need for support of the flexible tubing; (3) it could be seen from an examination of the state of the art that the use of flexible plastic tubing and the corresponding need for increased support in the roof construction was known in the industry. Therefore the subject matter of V's claim derived in an obvious way from the state of the art and lacked any inventive step.

VERMUELEN-HOLLANDIA/VEHICLE OPEN ROOF (T43/98) [2001] E.P.O.R. 37, Alting van Geusau, European Patent Office (Technical Board of Appeal).

3934. Patents – European patents – lack of novelty – subject matter of amended claims – admissibility

[Council Directive 96/9 on the legal protection of database; European Patents Convention 1973 Art.76, Art.123 (2), r.86 (4).]

An application was made for a patent in respect of a compound comprising an oligo- or polynucleotide which comprised an entity which on hybridisation to a complementary polynucleotide was capable of generating a detectable change in property in the said hybrid, the said entity being covalently or non-covalently attached by means of a linker arm to the base moiety of a nucleotide in the said oligo- or polynucleotide. The Examining Division originally raised a unity objection in response to which the applicant elected to proceed on the basis of claims in group (c) which related to a compound comprising at least one moiety with a particular structure wherein the signal-generating entity was a phenanthridine. Groups (a) and (b) both required at least two entities. The Examining Division refused the group (c) claims for lack of novelty. The applicant appealed revising his claim to require at least one entity and made an auxiliary request requiring two entities.

Held, setting aside the decision and remitting the case to first instance for further prosecution on the basis of the auxiliary request, that (1) the subject matter in the main claim had not been searched and it did not combine with the originally claimed and searched groups of inventions to form a single general inventive concept because it was based on a different technical approach as, according to the present claim, one attached entity was enough for generating a detectable change on hybridisation with a target polynucleotide; (2) there was no need at this stage to investigate whether the application as filed provided support for such a claim, because under the European Patents Convention 1973 r.86 (4) the claim was not admissible; (3) the applicant might continue to pursue the subject matter of such a claim only in the form of a divisional application in accordance with Art.76. The first instance would have to deal with the question whether the subject-matter of the divisional application extended beyond the content of the earlier application as filed; (4) as regards the auxiliary request, the introduction of a proviso did not result in the creation of new subject matter. Thus no objection under Art.123(2) existed, and (5) as the subject-matter of the auxiliary application had not been examined by the Examining Division in respect of inventive step, it was appropriate to make use of the power granted to it under Art.111 (1) and to remit the case to the first instance for further prosecution.

ENZO/POLYNUCLEOTIDES (T442/95) [2001] E.P.O.R. 24, Kinkeldey, European Patent Office (Technical Board of Appeal).

3935. Patents – European patents – novelty – disclosure of claimed features prior to application filing date

L's European patent application in respect of a sealing complex for use in highway construction was revoked on the ground that the subject matter had become public knowledge before the filing date as a result of a technical publicity brochure issued in response to an invitation to tender. L appealed.

Held, allowing the appeal and remitting the matter with an order to maintain the patent as granted, that in France municipal authorities and government bodies were not permitted to disclose to the public any documents containing financial and technical information supplied by companies in the course of a public contract award procedure. Accordingly, the subject matter of the patent in the instant case could not have been made public by any confidential bid documents. With regard to the use of the sealing complex on actual roads, this could not constitute public disclosure since a laboratory analysis was necessary to determine its composition and it was illegal to take such samples from public structures.

LEFEBVRE/SEALING COMPLEX (T77/94) [2001] E.P.O.R. 52, Judge not specified, European Patent Office (Technical Board of Appeal).

3936. Patents – European patents – novelty – therapeutic treatments – testable criteria

E sought an European patent for the use of the drug (R)-fluoxetene to treat any condition which could be improved or prevented by its use. The application was refused for lack of clarity and inventive step. E appealed making an auxiliary request specifying various neurological disorders and conditions that could be treated by the drug.

Held, remitting the case for further examination, that (1) where a patent application was expressed in functional terms it would only satisfy the requirements for clarity if a skilled person could understand the functional definition and be able to implement the invention; (2) in the present case, the invention was based on a discovery as to a pharmacological effect of the drug (R)-fluoxetine; that in itself did not amount to a therapeutic application of the drug; there had to be a defined and real treatment of a pathological condition in order to make a technical contribution to the art and qualify for patent protection. E's application did not enable a skilled person to determine whether or not a particular condition fell within the scope of E's claim but; (3) by naming specific conditions in its auxiliary request E had not simply limited the scope of the original claim but had radically altered the nature of the invention. For this reason the case had to be remitted to the Examination Division for further consideration

ELI LILLY/SEROTONIN RECEPTOR (T241/95) [2001] E.P.O.R. 38, Lancon, European Patent Office (Technical Board of Appeal).

3937. Patents – European patents – novelty – unity of inventions – unpaid search fees – authority of Examination Division

[European Patent Convention 1973 Art 46.]

T's European patent application for the manufacture of a semiconductor was initially found to lack unity of invention and a partial search report was issued. T was required to pay additional search fees but failed to do so. The Examination Division reviewed the finding of lack of unity of invention and the application was refused instead for lack of novelty. T appealed and lodged amended claims. The question arose whether the Examination Division had the authority to review the entire application for lack of unity of invention or whether it was required to limit its review only to inventions for which search fees had been paid.

Held, remitting the case for further examination, that (1) the European Patent Convention 1973 Art 46 dealt only with the situation where further search fees had been paid and did not prohibit the Examination Division from reviewing the Search Division's opinion on lack of unity of invention where further search fees had not been paid; (2) since the subject matter of the amended claims differed substantially from the patent as originally claimed then it was appropriate to remit the case for further examination.

TOSHIBA/DOPED REGIONS (T631/97) [2001] E.P.O.R. 41, Shukla, European Patent Office (Technical Board of Appeal).

3938. **Patents – European patents – prior art – differentiation and evaluation**

A held a European patent relating to a canine vaccine against a viral gastric infection. The patent was revoked for lack of novelty on the grounds that other vaccines which were publicly available fell within the scope of the patent as claimed. A appealed filing an amended claim.

Held, allowing the appeal and ordering reinstatement of the patent, that a product was not considered to be publicly available if it was not possible for a person skilled in the art to discern the composition or internal structure of the product in order to be able to reproduce it *Availability to the public (G01/92)* [1993] E.P.O.R. 241 applied. Despite the public availability of the other vaccines, the intrinsic and extrinsic features of A's vaccine remained concealed from the skilled person who would be unable to determine its composition or internal structure and therefore unable to reproduce it.

AMERICAN HOME PRODUCTS/CANINE CORONAVIRUS (T977/93) [2001] E.P.O.R. 36, UM Kinkeldey, European Patent Office (Technical Board of Appeal).

3939. **Patents – European patents – prior art – identification – assessing novelty**

A obtained a European patent for a spray-drying process for granules. The patent was opposed for lack of inventive step but was maintained and the opponent appealed.

Held, allowing the appeal and revoking the patent, that (1) when assessing novelty an expression in a claim should be given its broadest technically sensible meaning; (2) where there were several prior art documents disclosing subject matter similar to the disputed patent, the most recent document should be regarded as the closest prior art and used for the purposes of evaluating whether the patent involved an inventive step; (3) on the facts of the present case the process lacked any inventive step and the patent could not be maintained.

APV ANHYDRO/GRANULATION BY SPRAY DRYING (T79/96) [2001] E.P.O.R. 40, Judge not specified, European Patent Office (Technical Board of Appeal).

3940. **Patents – European patents – prior art – identification – correct approach**

The Examining Division refused P a European patent for lack of inventive step. P appealed.

Held, allowing the appeal, that the correct application of the "problem and solution" approach in patent applications was to identify a "bridgehead" in the sense of the closest prior art which a person skilled in the relevant discipline would be likely to have examined when considering the circumstances to which the invention under consideration related. In general, it was appropriate to give greater weight to the designation of the invention's subject matter, the exposition of the problem it was invented to address, and its intended use and effects, rather than to the greatest number of identical technical features.

PHILIPS/ IMAGE PROJECTION APPARATUS (T870/96) [2001] E.P.O.R. 43, Judge not specified, European Patent Office (Technical Board of Appeal).

3941. Patents – European patents – prior art – inventive step – technical assessment

D appealed against the failure to grant its application for a patent for lack of an inventive step. The application concerned a process for incorporating fibrous filler into an elastometric polymer. The documents cited as constituting the state of the prior art showed that, hitherto, uniform dispersion of the fibres had been achieved by manufacturing a pre dispersion which, after further processing, was then mechanically mixed with the polymer. The process under application dispensed with the need to manufacture a pre dispersion, mixing the relevant substances directly in an extruder.

Held, setting aside the decision and remitting the application for necessary adaptation, that the examination division had erred in defining the technical problem as simply the provision of a further process for the incorporation of fibrous filler into an elastomer. The correct view was that the problem was the provision of a simpler, less expensive and more efficient process. On this view the process was inventive, since the modifications necessary to the prior process in order to arrive at D's process would require, at best, a totally redundant use of expensive equipment, and at worst, would entirely vitiate the D3 process itself. The teaching contained in other cited documents would not have led a skilled person to solve the technical problem, nor did the cited documentation support the examination division's finding that it was common knowledge that fibre-containing masses could be processed in an extruder.

DU PONT/FIBRE FILLED ELASTOMER (T345/96); *sub nom.* EI DU PONT DE NEMOURS EUROPEAN PATENT APPLICATION (NO.90120556.7) [2001] E.P.O.R. 15, Judge not specified, European Patent Office (Technical Board of Appeal).

3942. Patents – European patents – re-establishment of rights – failure to observe – time limits – need to show due care

[European Patent Convention 1973 Art.122.]

A patent application was refused by the Examining Division on the grounds of a lack of inventive step on January 16, 1998. That refusal had been promptly reported by S's representative to the Japanese patent attorney on January 21, together with notification of the deadline for filing an appeal. After the due date for appeal, the representative applied for re-establishment of rights on March 30. He claimed that he had "just" received instructions to file an appeal and that the applicant appeared to be still studying the case.

Held, refusing the application, that (1) the re-establishment of rights under the European Patent Convention Art.122 could only be granted if S was unable to observe a time limit in spite of all due care required by the circumstances; (2) both S and its representative must have taken all due care and here there were no reasons given for S's failure to give instructions in due time, and (3) the statement that S was apparently still studying the case could not be considered as a sufficient reason for re-establishment.

SUMITOMO/H-SHAPED STEELS (T366/98) [2000] E.P.O.R. 512, Gumbel, European Patent Office (Technical Board of Appeal).

3943. Patents – European patents – re-establishment of rights – time limits – non compliance due to administrative error

[European Patent Convention 1973 Art 122; European Patent Convention 1973 r.69(1).]

The third year renewal fee for a European patent application was not paid by the due date of May 2, 1989. The EPO informed K's European representative, A, that the renewal fee could still be paid within six months of the due date, subject to a surcharge. The fee was not paid by that date and A was advised that the application was deemed to have been withdrawn under the European Patent Convention 1973 Art.86(3). A subsequently filed a request for re-establishment pursuant to Art.122, together with payment of the renewal fee and surcharge. The

Receiving Section rejected the request as inadmissible and A appealed. He argued that on November 15, 1989 he had advised K of the deemed withdrawal, but that the application could be renewed. However, due to an administrative error, A had not received K's re-establishment instruction. On December 18, 1989 A received the r.69(1) notification of deemed withdrawal from the EPO and informed K that the time for re-establishment was February 18, 1990, due to the administrative error.

Held, dismissing the appeal, that (1) the removal of the cause of non compliance was a matter of fact to be determined on the facts of each case; (2) where the receipt of a r.69(1) notice was regarded as the removal of the cause of non compliance, it had to be clearly established that neither the representative nor the applicant was aware that the application had been deemed to have been withdrawn prior to receipt of that notification. That was not so in the instant case, and (3) A's argument could not be accepted as it contravened Art.122(5) because the Art.122(2) time limit had not been complied with.

KITABAYASHI/SPRAY HEAD (T900/90) [2000] E.P.O.R. 500, Judge not specified, European Patent Office (Technical Board of Appeal).

3944. **Patents – European patents – re-establishment of rights following transfer of files – requisite standard of care**

[European Patent Convention 1973 Art.86(3).]

A European patent application was filed by representative A, who was asked to transfer all L's files to representative B. Those files were collected by L's assistant shortly before the renewal fee was due, but the relevant file was apparently not passed on to B. A notified B that the renewal fee could still be paid within six months, but it was unclear whether A had agreed to make the necessary payments. In the event, no payments were made and the EPO advised that the application was deemed to have been withdrawn under the European Patent Convention 1973 Art.86(3). L applied for re-establishment on the basis that, since neither A nor B had possession of the relevant file, the assistant had acted without due care. The Examining Division determined that L was responsible, because it had delegated responsibility for the transfer to an assistant. L appealed against the decision and further requested that the Enlarged Board of Appeal determine the duties of an assistant and representatives involved in a changeover.

Held, dismissing the appeal, that (1) the exchange of precise information was an indispensable prerequisite for a transfer of a patent portfolio; (2) the failure to give clear information about cases to be transferred was not an isolated mistake in a special situation and the change of representation did not amount to an extraordinary situation for professional representatives; (3) L had not exercised all due care since it had delegated the relevant tasks to an assistant; (4) those involved in the transfer had not act with all due care required in the circumstances, and (5) no important point of law arose that justified referral to the Enlarged Board of Appeal.

LINDBERG/RE-ESTABLISHMENT OF RIGHTS (T338/98) [2000] E.P.O.R. 505, Turrini, European Patent Office (Technical Board of Appeal).

3945. **Patents – European patents – refusal – infringement of fundamental right**

[European Patent Convention 1973 Art.97(1).]

A divisional patent application was made in respect of data storage devices comprising a substrate and a zirconia-containing dielectric layer. The Examining Division refused the application on the ground that subject matter of the application overlapped with the parent application and the same subject matter was claimed twice. K appealed arguing that the divisional claim was wider than the parent claim which had been granted. The parent claim was in respect of A plus B whereas the divisional claim was in respect of A, implicitly with or without B.

Held, setting aside the decision and remitting the case for further prosecution that (1) there were no provisions in the European Patent Convention 1973 which prohibited the presence in a divisional application of an independent claim, explicitly or as a notional claim arrived at by partitioning of an actual claim into notional claims reciting explicit alternatives, which was related to an independent claim in the parent application (or patent if it had already been granted as here) in such a way that the "parent" claim included all the features of the "divisional" claim combined with an additional feature; and (2) the application had been refused under Art.97(1) for non-compliance with a non-existent requirement of the Convention. The refusal therefore infringed K's fundamental right that there should be a legal basis for any requirement relied on to invoke Art.97(1). Since the applicant was obliged to file the present appeal to overcome that refusal, it was equitable that the appeal fee should be reimbursed.

KOMAG/CONFLICTING DIVISIONAL CLAIM (T587/98) [2001] E.P.O.R. 19, Wheeler, European Patent Office (Technical Board of Appeal).

3946. Patents – European patents – refusal of application on procedural grounds a substantial violation justifying appeal and refund of fee

In an application for a patent relating to modified yeast, the applicant had responded substantively to objections over lack of clarity raised in 1994 and 1995 by the Examining Division, but had subsequently failed (even though a two month extension was granted) to reply substantively to a communication from the Examining Division in 1996. The applicant was therefore informed that the application was deemed withdrawn. The applicant sought further consideration of the application and paid the requisite fee. The Examining Division resumed consideration of the application, and refused it on the grounds that the applicant had failed to deal substantively with the Examining Division's communication of 1994. The applicant appealed, and filed revised claims following the delivery of observations on the application by the Appeal Board.

Held, allowing the appeal, remitting the application for further consideration by the Examining Division and refunding the appeal fee: 1) the Examining Division had erred in refusing the application since the applicant had answered the 1994 communication, and had successfully obtained further consideration of the application following the failure to deal with the 1996 communication; 2) in any event, the true reason for the Examining Division's rejection of the application was a divergence of views on the technical features in the relevant prior art, the Examining Division having incorrectly held that the patent in suit did not contain technical features distinguishing it from the prior art; 3) the Notice of Appeal was admissible even though it did not deal with the main reason for the Examining Division's decision; 4) the applicant had not been given an opportunity to comment on the propositions on which the Examining Division's decision had been based, which constituted a serious procedural defect, and justified the refund of the applicant's appeal fee.

ELSWORTH/MODIFIED YEAST (T484/98) [2001] E.P.O.R. 27, Kinkeldy, European Patent Office (Technical Board of Appeal).

3947. Patents – European patents – revocation – abandonment of amendments – reliance on original claim

[European Patent Convention 1973 Art.123(2).]

Opposition by reason of lack of inventive step had been raised to the patentee's request. The patentee had propounded amendments to its claims, in response to which the Opposition Division held that amendments were in breach of the European Patent Convention 1973 Art.123(2). The patent was accordingly revoked, and the patentee appealed to the Board, relying on his unamended claim as granted as constituting his main request.

Held, setting aside the decision, that Art.123(2) was of no application, since the impugned amendments had been abandoned and the applicant had reverted to the granted format. The application would be remitted to the Opposition Division for consideration of the questions of novelty and inventive step.

THAMES WATER/SLOW SAND FILTER CLEANING DEVICE (T443/95); *sub nom.* THAMES WATER UTILITIES LTD'S EUROPEAN PATENT (NO.0310221)

[2001] E.P.O.R. 10, Judge not specified, European Patent Office (Technical Board of Appeal).

3948. Patents – European patents – revocation – absence of reasoned decision – fee refund

[European Patent Convention 1973.]

U appealed against a decision of the Opposition Division to revoke its European patent for an optical memory system. The reason for the revocation was that U had failed to produce the required documents.

Held, allowing the appeal, that where the Opposition Division revoked a patent on the sole ground that there were no documents meeting all the requirements of the European Patent Convention 1973 without dealing with the substance of the application, that amounted to a failure to comply with the minimum requirements for a reasoned decision. U had not, however, requested reimbursement of the appeal fee, apparently tacitly recognising the need to amend its application further; therefore it would be inequitable to order a refund of the appeal fee.

UNISYS/OPTICAL MEMORY SYSTEM (T167/96); *sub nom.* UNISYS CORP'S EUROPEAN PATENT (NO.0088538) [2001] E.P.O.R. 11, Judge not specified, European Patent Office (Technical Board of Appeal).

3949. Patents – European patents – revocation – admissibility of amendments

[European Patent Convention 1973 Art.113(2), Art.123(2).]

The Office had revoked a patent relating to an internal mold release composition on the ground of lack of inventive step and breach of the European Patent Convention 1973 Art.123(2) by reason of amendments introduced into the patent claims. The patentee appealed, seeking to have amended claims included, two of which were introduced at the oral hearing of the appeal, the Board and the respondent having objected to previous amendments. The patentee also sought permission to bring forward further amendments in the event that his current request for amendments was refused.

Held, dismissing the appeal, that the claims in their amended form as put forward at the oral hearing were not allowable and would not be admitted. Further, the request for leave to file a further set of claims was improper and would be refused. The effect of the amendments requested by the patentee was that there was no text agreed by the patentee before the Board, and that prejudiced the maintenance of the patent, in the light of the provisions of Art.113(2) of the Convention.

DOW/MOLD-RELEASE (T206/93) [2001] E.P.O.R. 9, Judge not specified, European Patent Office (Technical Board of Appeal).

3950. Patents – European patents – revocation – appeals – res judicata

The patent related to a treatment for improving milk yield in dairy cows without a consequent decrease in milk fat content. The Opposition Division revoked the patent for want of inventive step but on appeal the Board, although upholding the Opposition Division's finding on the main request, remitted the matter to the Opposition Division for further consideration of the auxiliary request. The Opposition Division held that the latter point had, in fact, already been dealt with by the Board in its consideration of the main request. The auxiliary request was therefore rejected. The patentee appealed, and filed a more restricted main request, together with a fresh auxiliary request. Opposition was maintained, but the opponents took no further part in the appeal. Observations were submitted by a third party.

Held, allowing the appeal and remitting the matter to the Opposition Division, that (1) the patent would remain pending consideration at first instance of the newly amended claims as put forward at the appeal hearing; (2) the new main request raised issues sufficiently distinct from the earlier request so as not to be barred under the doctrine of res judicata; (3) observations from a third party out of time could only be admitted in appeal proceedings with the consent of the patentee. That had not been forthcoming in the instant case, and accordingly such observations would be disregarded, and (4) there was an inventive step in the main request, in that a person skilled in the relevant field would not have expected the increased milk yield achieved by the patented process to arise without a corresponding decrease in milk fat content.

ELI LILLY/RUMINANT LACTATION IMPROVEMENT (T667/92); *sub nom.* ELI LILLY'S EUROPEAN PATENT (NO.063491) (T667/92) [2001] E.P.O.R. 12, Judge not specified, European Patent Office (Technical Board of Appeal).

3951. **Patents – European patents – revocation – revocation based on experimental data – burden of proof**

[European Patents Convention 1973 Art.83.]

O was granted a European patent relating to a mouse monoclonal antibody. The application had been opposed on the grounds of lack of novelty, inventive step and sufficiency. The parties had adduced conflicting experimental data, but no clear reason for the divergence had been forthcoming. The Opposition Division had therefore given the benefit of the doubt to the applicant and had allowed the patent in substantially the form of the application. The fourth opponent appealed.

Held, dismissing the appeal, that the experimental data relied upon by the opponents could not be accorded significance, in the light of the considerable body of literature relating to use of the antibody in the first two years of its availability. It was for the opponents to prove that the provisions of the European Patents Convention 1973 Art.83 had not been met, and there was no converse burden on the patentee to show that the requirements of Art.83 had been met. There was therefore no need to discuss the patentee's experimental data.

ORTHO/ MONOCLONAL ANTIBODY (OKT 5) (T510/94) [2001] E.P.O.R. 49, Judge not specified, European Patent Office (Technical Board of Appeal).

3952. **Patents – European patents – software – computers – patentability**

[European Patent Convention 1973 Art.52.]

A's application for a European patent for a computer system to generate software programs was refused on the grounds that it was not an invention within the meaning of the European Patent Convention 1973 Art.52. A appealed claiming that its invention had a technical effect in improving the performance of the computer as a machine.

Held, dismissing the appeal, that Art.52 specifically excluded computer programs from patentability. A combination of hardware and software might be patentable if it improved the performance of the computer. A's invention would improve the efficiency of the programmer using it but it had not been shown that it would result in any technical improvement of the efficiency of the computer as a machine.

AT&T/COMPUTER SYSTEM (T204/93) [2001] E.P.O.R. 39, Judge not specified, European Patent Office (Technical Board of Appeal).

3953. **Patents – European patents – special factors determining patentabilty of distributed inventions**

[European Patents Convention Art.52(2), Art.52(3).]

P lodged two claims for patents. The first was in respect of a system for the retrieval of pictures, consisting of two elements (each of which might be sold separately), namely a record carrier and a read device. The second claim related solely to the record carrier, and was rejected by the Examining Division on the grounds of lack of clarity and want of novelty, which, the Examining Division, held took the claim outside the requirements of the European Patents Convention Art.52(2)(d) and Art.52(3). P appealed.

Held, allowing the appeal and remitting the application in respect of the record carrier to first instance with a direction to grant a patent on a specified basis, that (1) the fact that the claim in respect of the record carrier stated that it was "for use" with the system the subject of the first claim reflected a description of the aspects of the record carrier in functional terms, and was not devoid of clarity by reason of being framed in very general terms. The claim accordingly met the requirements of Art.84 of the European Patents Convention, and (2) the Examining Division had placed an incorrect construction on the phrase "for use". The record carrier had technical features which had clear functions, and these features did not (as the Examining Division had held) constitute nothing more than a presentation of information. It was essential to distinguish between data encoding cognitive content and functional data which constituted inherent features of the system in which the record carrier was to operate. The statement at C-IV, 2.3 of the Guidelines for Examination at the EPO did not make this distinction, and as a consequence, unduly extended the breadth of exclusion from patentability.

PHILIPS/RECORD CARRIER (T1194/97); *sub nom.* KONINKLIJKE PHILIPS ELECTRONICS NV'S EUROPEAN PATENT APPLICATION (T1194/97) [2001] E.P.O.R. 25, WJ Wheeler, EPO (Technical Bd App).

3954. Patents – European patents – surgical treatment methods – patentability

[European Patents Convention Art.52(4).]

A patent application was made in respect of a method for transvenously accessing the pericardial space between the heart and its pericardium in preparation for a medical procedure. The method involved catheter guiding and penetration steps. The application was refused by the Examining Division on the ground that the method was of a surgical character and was therefore excluded from patentability under the European Patents Convention Art.52(4). G appealed and requested a reference on the interpretation of Art.52(4) to the Enlarged Board if the Board was unwilling to allow the appeal.

Held, dismissing the appeal and refusing to make the reference sought, that (1) the excluded methods in Art.52(4) were to ensure that persons carrying out such methods as part of the medical treatment of humans or the veterinary treatment of animals should not be inhibited by patents; (2) a claim would not be allowed under Art.52(4) where it included at least one feature defining a physical activity or action which was a method for treatment of the human body by surgery or therapy. It was not relevant whether the method in question could be carried out in isolation or only in conjunction with other methods to achieve the intended medical effect, and (3) it was not appropriate to make a reference to the Enlarged Board as the case did not raise any new point of law which could not be decided in conformity with the comprehensive and uniform jurisprudence which already existed.

GEORGETOWN UNIVERSITY/PERICARDIAL ACCESS (T35/99) [2001] E.P.O.R. 21, Weiss, European Patent Office (Technical Board of Appeal).

3955. Patents – European patents – technical problem defined by specification – novelty and inventive steps

[European Patents Convention 1973 Art.84.]

A patent application was made in respect of a relatively simple gel-forming composition but it contained 191 claims. The application was refused by the Examining Division for lack of unity and inventive step. X appealed and the Board indicated that 191 claims was excessive and contrary to the European Patents Convention 1973 Art.84. X then reduced the number of claims to 157. It also filed a new claim to counter a novelty objection which the Board had raised.

Held, setting aside the decision and remitting the case to the Examining Division for further prosecution on the basis of the new claim; that (1) the new claim overcame the novelty objection and complied with the requirements of Art.123(2) as it did not contain subject-matter extending beyond the content of the application as filed; (2) as regards inventive step, the starting point when considering an objective definition of the technical problem, was the problem as described in the specification; (3) the Board should only investigate whether an alternative problem existed objectively, if it found that the incorrect state of the art was used to define the problem or the problem defined was not solved; (4) there was no reason to doubt that the technical problem was adequately defined and solved by the composition in the specification. The technical problem described in the specification was the correct basis on which inventive should be evaluated; (5) the documents relied on by the Examining Division for refusing the application did not relate to solving the technical problem and accordingly did not constitute a valid starting point from which to evaluate inventive step; (6) the closest prior art did not suggest the patented solution to the problem with the result that the application was inventive and did not lack unity; (7) an applicant was entitled to make a reasonable number of claims. What was reasonable in relation to each application depended on the facts of the particular case, and (8) in the present case the number of claims made imposed a severe and undue burden on the public and therefore was unreasonable.

OXY/GEL FORMING COMPOSITION (T246/91) [2001] E.P.O.R. 22, Judge not specified, European Patent Office (Technical Board of Appeal).

3956. Patents – European patents – time limits – abusive disclosure – interpretation of six month time limit

[European Patent Convention 1973 Art.55(1).]

The Technical Board of Appeal referred to the Enlarged Board of Appeal the question whether, for the purposes of the European Patent Convention 1973 Art.55(1), if priority is given to a European patent application, the term of six months' before filing of the European patent application takes into account the priority period or whether the relevant date is the date of actual filing of the application.

Held, answering the point of law, that the six month period runs from the date of filing of the patent application, not from the date of priority.

UNIVERSITY PATENTS/SIX-MONTH PERIOD (G03/98) [2001] E.P.O.R. 33, Messerli, European Patent Office (Enlarged Board of Appeal).

3957. Patents – European patents – time limits – re establishment of rights – error by assistant to patent agent – otherwise satisfactory system

[Patent Cooperation Treaty 1970 Art.22(1); European Patent Convention 1973 Art.122.]

A's patent agent, a sole practitioner, omitted to file the English translation of an international application with the European Patent Office within the time limit prescribed by the Patent Cooperation Treaty 1970 Art.22(1). A was subsequently informed that its European patent application had been withdrawn. A's application for re-establishment of rights under the European Patent Convention 1973 Art.122 was rejected on the grounds that the representative had not taken due care having apparently delegated the preparation of the documentation to her secretary. A appealed.

Held, allowing the appeal, that (1) the purpose of Art.122 of the Convention was to ensure that substantive rights were not lost because of isolated mistakes occurring in otherwise satisfactory systems; (2) A's representative had established and operated, together with her secretary, a satisfactory system for observing time limits. The secretary's failure to file the translation was the first time in 10 years that she had made such an error. However, the absence of simple procedural checks meant that due care could be found lacking in future cases, and (3) the strict standards of care required of a representative were not expected of a representative's assistant. Routine tasks could be delegated to an assistant, provided that the representative exercised the necessary care in choosing, training and supervising the assistant, SOCIETE PARISIENNE/ Restitutio in integrum (J05/80) [1979-85] E.P.O.R. A31 applied. In the instant case, the secretary was a suitable person to carry out the work and had been properly instructed and supervised and the failure was due to an error on her part. At the time of the mistake she had been under severe stress due to illness. The facts showed that this was an isolated mistake in a satisfactory system.

Furthermore, similar mistakes that had occurred in two other cases during the same period were taken to form one isolated mistake.

SECRETARIAL ERROR (J32/90) [2001] E.P.O.R. 6, Judge not specified, European Patent Office (Technical Board of Appeal).

3958. Patents – herbicides – definition of terminology used in patent

RH was the registered proprietor of an agrochemical patent concerned with the manufacture of water dispersible granules containing herbicide. RH brought an action for patent infringement against C in respect of two processes used by C, Process A and Process B. C applied for the determination of two preliminary issues, arguing that (1) the definition of "surfactant" as used in the patent included only amphiphiles, those being surface acting agents which only acted at the surface of a liquid, and (2) that Process B did not infringe the patent as it did not involve the use of amphiphiles.

Held, giving judgment on the preliminary issue for C, that (1) the definition put forward by C was to be preferred for a number of reasons, including the fact that the term "surfactant" was described in the patent as a dispersing and wetting agent and that the expert evidence supported C's definition, and (2) Process B did not therefore infringe the patent since it did not employ amphiphiles.

ROHM & HAAS CO v. COLLAG LTD (NO.1) [2001] F.S.R. 28, Neuberger, J., Pat Ct.

3959. Patents – infringement – claim not evident in priority document – claim not entitled to priority date of first application

B was the proprietor of a patent relating to the support for a buoyancy element around a subsea pipe. B commenced proceedings against C for the infringement of its patent. C denied infringement and counterclaimed for revocation, contending that the patent was invalid for obviousness and lack of novelty. The judge dismissed B's claim and held that the invention of the external clamping band in claim 1 was not supported by matters disclosed in the first application and therefore claim 1 was not entitled to the priority date of the first application. Consequently, the first claim was invalid and the patent was ordered to be revoked unless amended. B appealed, contending that the judge had erred in failing to accept the expert's evidence of a clamping band in the first application, which had established support for the argument that it was the same clamping mechanism as that contained within claim 1 of the patent in suit.

Held, dismissing the appeal, that there was no support in the first application for the concept in claim 1 of the clamping mechanism. The feature of an external clamping band had not been disclosed in the first application and was materially different from the patent granted. It would be unjust to permit B to obtain a monopoly and as a result, the clamping feature in claim 1 was not entitled to the priority date of the first application. B would be afforded an opportunity to seek an amendment of the patent in suit and accordingly the action would be stayed pending the outcome of any amendment application.

BALMORAL GROUP LTD v. CRP MARINE LTD [2000] F.S.R. 860, Aldous, L.J., CA.

3960. Patents – infringement – inventive step – vacuum cleaners – development of cyclone technology

D sought damages and an injunction against H for the alleged infringement of a patent concerned with the manufacture of a bagless vacuum cleaner which incorporated the use of D's cyclone technology. H contended that the patent in suit was void for lack of novelty, obviousness and insufficiency and relied upon various items of prior art.

Held, giving judgment for D, that H's product had infringed the patent in suit, that the prior art did not demonstrate that the development of bagless cyclone driven vacuum technology was a logical progression to the notional skilled addressee, and that the presence of a certain industry "mindset" which had been committed to the use of bags only served to reinforce such a conclusion.

DYSON APPLIANCES LTD v. HOOVER LTD (NO.1) [2001] R.P.C. 26, Michael Fysh Q.C., Pat Ct.

3961. Patents – injunctions – grant of "springboard" relief

[Patents Act 1977 s.61 (1); Supreme Court Act 1981 s.37 (1).]

D, the successful claimant in proceedings for infringement of a patent concerned with a cyclone device in vacuum cleaners, sought "springboard" injunctive relief to prevent H from manufacturing or selling the infringing appliances for a specified period following the expiration of the patent in suit. D contended that such relief was a valid secondary loss on the basis that, unless so restrained, H would be able to take advantage of their previous wrongdoing to D's disadvantage. H submitted that the relief sought had not been pleaded and in any event was outside the scope of relief available under the Patents Act 1977 s.61 (1).

Held, granting the application for an injunction for a 12 month period following expiration of the patent in suit, that s.61 (1) made specific reference to the preservation of "any other jurisdiction of the court". This phrase was apt to include the Supreme Court Act 1981 s.37(1) pursuant to which the court was entitled to grant the type of post expiry relief sought by D where it was just and convenient to do so, *Smith v. Peters* (1875) L.R. 20 Eq. 511 applied. On the facts, H had gained a 12 month advantage from its wrongful development of the infringing appliance as a direct result of which it would be able to make a swift re-entry into the market upon expiration of the patent in suit. It was both just and convenient to make the order sought in relation to the infringing appliance but not in relation to H's trademark for the "Hoover Triple Vortex" or in relation to any new appliance which H might seek to develop and market, *Generics BV v. Smith Kline & French Laboratories Ltd (C316/95)* [1997] E.C.R. I-3929, [1998] C.L.Y. 728 applied.

DYSON APPLIANCES LTD v. HOOVER LTD (NO.2) [2001] R.P.C. 27, Michael Fysh Q.C., Pat Ct.

3962. Patents – international patent application – combined manufacturing process and product – additional fees requested

An international patent application made both process and product claims. The EPO, acting as the international preliminary examining authority, considered that four independent claims were being made, as the sole common feature of the product claims arose from the process claim and the claimed process did not necessarily lead to the manufacture of the three product claims. NN paid the requested additional fees under protest and claimed that the special properties of the products were merely advantages resulting from the application of the new process.

Held, upholding the protest, that (1) corresponding special technical features were usually assumed to be present when a manufacturing process and products were being claimed in the same application where the process was new and actually suited to making the claimed products; (2) a manufacturing process and its product did not lack unity simply because the process was not confined to the manufacture of the claimed product, and (3) the grounds given in the invitation to pay did not justify the payment of three further application fees and those additional fees and the protest fee would be reimbursed.

NN/PERCARBONATE (W11/99) [2000] E.P.O.R. 515, Spangenberg, European Patent Office (Technical Board of Appeal).

3963. Patents – inventive step – self adhesive labels for curved surfaces – judge's approach

I appealed against the dismissal ((2000) 23(7) I.P.D. 23053) of his claim against D alleging infringement of patents relating to self-adhesive labels which could be attached to curved surfaces. The judge had found that the patent was invalid for obviousness and that anyone in the art who saw the label illustrated would immediately understand how it could work. I argued that the judge had erred in principle in not adopting the structured approach to deciding obviousness set out in *Windsurfing International Inc v. Tabur Marine (Great Britain) Ltd* [1985] R.P.C. 59.

Held, dismissing the appeal, that the test formulated in *Windsurfing* was useful but not essential. The court was required to decide whether an invention was obvious and a judge could not be faulted for going straight to that question provided he adopted the mantle of the skilled person and asked the correct question. The judge in the instant case had correctly assessed the common general knowledge at the priority date, the alleged inventive concept and the prior art relied on by I, which was one of its own labels. The difference between the prior art and the invention was an offset base label, which the judge had found to be a step which would have been obvious to a skilled person. The decision that the patent was invalid for obviousness should accordingly be upheld, *Windsurfing* considered.

INSTANCE v. DENNY BROS PRINTING LTD (PATENT ACTION); *sub nom.* DAVID J INSTANCE LTD v. DENNY BROS PRINTING LTD (PATENT ACTION), [2001] EWCA Civ 939, [2002] R.P.C. 14, Aldous, L.J., CA.

3964. **Patents – inventive step – silicone breast implants – manufacture of covering**

M, the proprietor of a patent relating to a silicone foam covering for prostheses used for implantation in the human body, instituted infringement proceedings against N. M contended that the silicone breast implants manufactured by N infringed its method claim in that the foam was produced by embedding salt crystals within a fluid silicone layer. N denied infringement and contended that the patent should be revoked for lack of novelty, obviousness or added matter.

Held, giving judgment for N on the infringement claim and dismissing the counterclaim, that the patent in suit had not been infringed as the salt crystals used by N were not embedded in the fluid silicone layer but were sprayed onto the outer layer of the implant to produce a textured surface. Further, the patent was not invalid for lack of novelty or an inventive step.

McGHAN MEDICAL UK LTD v. NAGOR LTD (2001) 24(7) I.P.D. 24043, RM Fysh Q.C., Pat Ct.

3965. **Patents – medical treatment – recognition of Swiss type claims – New Zealand**

[Statute of Monopolies 1623 s.6; Patents Act 1953 (New Zealand); European Patent Convention 1973.]

PMC sought judicial review of a practice note issued by the Commissioner allowing the use of Swiss type claims for the new pharmaceutical use of compounds with a known pharmaceutical use. The judge at first instance ([1999] R.P.C. 752), declared that it was legitimate in principle to allow Swiss type claims. PMC appealed and the question arose as to whether the Patents Act 1953 permitted the Commissioner to recognise as an invention and grant a patent to protect the discovery of a new pharmaceutical use where the substance or composition already had a known medical use.

Held, dismissing the appeal, that (1) it was unclear how much of the Statute of Monopolies 1623 s.6 was incorporated into the definition of "invention" in the 1953 Act; (2) a method of treating humans was now accepted as an invention, *Wellcome Foundation Ltd (Hitchings') Application* [1983] F.S.R. 593, [1983] C.L.Y. 2785 considered; (3) the necessary step in finding Swiss type claims acceptable was to recognise that novelty and inventiveness existed in the newly discovered purpose. The question under consideration was essentially an issue of interpretation of the novelty requirement in the light of international developments; (4) there was nothing in the 1953 Act nor the authorities that directly precluded a similar process of reasoning to that adopted in *EISAI/ Second medical indication (G05/83)* [1979-85] E.P.O.R. B241. The law on patentability in New Zealand differed little to that in the European Patent

Convention 1973. New methods of treating humans could be claimed as inventions, except for the areas of diagnosis and therapy, and product claims for inventions arising from the discovery of a first pharmaceutical use for known substances were allowed. The difference lay in where novelty was seen to lie, *EISAI* referred to; (5) if the courts recognised inventiveness in newly discovered properties in substances of a class previously disclosed, a doctrine could be formulated to recognise the inventiveness in new advantageous properties identified in known compounds, *El Du Pont de Nemours & Co (Witsiepe's) Application* [1982] F.S.R. 303, [1982] C.L.Y. 2284 referred to; (6) a Swiss type claim was a use claim not a product claim as a combination of the active compound and the carrier not made for the relevant purpose would not infringe. Novelty existed as carrying out the prior disclosure did not involve doing anything within the claim, and (7) once it was accepted that there could be new invention in the discovery of a chemical compound's previously unrecognised advantageous properties, the obligation to make patent protection available applied and the 1953 Act was to be construed to give that effect in Swiss type claims. If the subject matter and novelty of the new use could not be the subject of a method claim, a purpose designation would suffice.

PHARMACEUTICAL MANAGEMENT AGENCY LTD v. COMMISSIONER OF PATENTS [2000] R.P.C. 857, Gault, J., CA (NZ).

3966. Patents – negotiation – actionable threats – extent of "without prejudice" protection

K sought a declaration that X had made actionable threats of infringement proceedings and further claimed damages for losses sustained as a result of the threats. X had entered into an agreement with AIC which purported to grant X exclusive rights within the UK in respect of the distribution of children's three wheel buggies. K subsequently entered into an arrangement with API to import and distribute similar buggies. X wrote to K claiming infringement of its exclusive distribution rights and sent a copy of the letter to T, a major UK retailer whom K had undertaken to supply with the buggies. Both letters were headed "without prejudice". X later wrote a second letter to T contending that T's marketing of the buggy amounted to an infringement of patent and design rights. K argued that X in fact had no such exclusive rights but also indicated that they intended to cease distribution of the product when its existing stocks had been used. K sought an apology from X but no such apology was received and K instituted proceedings. X contended that the letters were protected by privilege. K argued that the "without prejudice" rule did not prevent the letters being admitted into evidence as X had abused the rules in respect of privilege.

Held, granting the declaration, that there were no patent or design rights in respect of the buggy and, whilst the first letter from X did not contain an actionable threat of infringement of a patent, the second letter did. The label "without prejudice" could not be used generally and accordingly would not preclude an action from its legal repercussions in circumstances where there was not an actual dispute or negotiations, *Unilever Plc v. Procter & Gamble Co* [2000] F.S.R. 344, [1999] C.L.Y. 349 considered. The threat or claim made by X was not so serious as to amount to abuse of privilege. In any event, the claims had not been made within the course of relevant privileged negotiations as X had not responded to replies from K but had written instead to K's principal customer, T. X had not withdrawn its claims to infringement of patent even when it had become aware that the claim was unfounded and had made no response to K's request that X notify T that the allegations had been withdrawn. T had ceased to order more buggies from K as a result of the letters from X and therefore K had established a prima facie loss and an enquiry into damages was justified, *Brain v. Ingledew Brown Bennison & Garrett (No.3)* [1997] F.S.R. 511, [1997] C.L.Y. 3917 followed.

KOOLTRADE LTD v. XTS LTD [2001] E.C.D.R. 11, Pumfrey, J., Pat Ct.

3967. Patents – revocation – application to amend specification – New Zealand

A, holders of a patent relating to a veterinary liquid anthelmintic composition containing praziquantel used as a sheep drench, appealed against a decision to allow N's application for revocation on the basis that (1) the patent was invalid for obviousness and lack of novelty, and (2) the refusal to allow its proposed amendments, the trial judge having found that the amendments would not overcome the revocation on the ground of obviousness and that they included material not substantially disclosed in the original specification. A contended that the patent, in its proposed amended form, satisfied the requirement of novelty and that the amendments simply provided clarification of matters which skilled addressees would have appreciated in any event. Further, A submitted that praziquantel was known as a difficult substance with which to work and that its inclusion in the composition was not an obvious step. A claimed novelty in that it had shown that scientific teaching that the tapeworm did not affect the growth rate of lambs was incorrect.

Held, dismissing the appeal, that (1) it was necessary for the invention to be clearly defined and for competitors to know the extent of the monopoly which they were barred from infringing. Amendments having the effect of propounding alternative versions of a patent were not consistent with this requirement, *Windsurfing International Inc v. Tabur Marine (Great Britain) Ltd* [1985] R.P.C. 59 followed; (2) the test for obviousness was whether the propounded inventive step would, to the skilled person, have been obvious as something that was either possible or worth attempting, but not inventive. The test for obviousness required reference to what was known and used, including practice within the market, and was not restricted to scientific literature; (3) a test which was obvious for one purpose did not become inventive by virtue of its use for another purpose, *Hallen Co v. Brabantia (UK) Ltd (No.1)* [1991] R.P.C. 195, [1992] C.L.Y. 3318 followed, and (4) in the instant case, the question to be asked was not whether persons skilled in the field would have thought of producing a combination sheep drench, which was already on the market prior to the product in suit but whether they would have specifically considered how to combine praziquantel with other substances so as to achieve a broad spectrum of activity.

ANCARE NEW ZEALAND LTD'S PATENT, *Re* [2001] R.P.C. 20, Gault, J., CA (NZ).

3968. Patents – revocation – lack of inventive step

N sought the revocation of a patent registered by D on the grounds that it was invalid for obviousness and insufficiency. D contended that the patent had comprised a valid inventive step concerned with the production of phytase, an enzyme facilitating the metabolism of phosphorus, beyond the general knowledge and research of the time.

Held, granting the application and revoking the patent in suit, that the invention had been obvious over both common general knowledge and skilled research conducted prior to the priority date. It was also insufficient given the breadth of the claim.

NOVO NORDISK A/S v. DSM NV; *sub nom.* DSM NV'S PATENT [2001] R.P.C. 35, Neuberger, J., Pat Ct.

3969. Patents – revocation – locus standi of applicant

[Patents Act 1977 s.72; Civil Procedure Rules 1998 (SI 1998 3132); European Patent Convention 1973 Art.99(1).]

AH, the patentee of drugs used in the treatment of duodenal ulcers, sought an order striking out an application made by C, a company which had no commercial interest in the pharmaceutical industry, to revoke its patents. AH argued that C was acting on behalf of a third party with a true commercial interest in the matter, that C's application was an abuse of process and that, were it to continue, the court would be precluded from exercising its powers in accordance with the overriding objective of the Civil Procedure Rules 1998.

Held, refusing AH's application, that the Patents Act 1977 s.72, which reflected the European Patent Convention 1973 Art.99(1), permitted "any person" to apply to revoke a patent. There was no requirement for that person to have any interest in the invalidation of the patent, and the use by a third party of a "straw man" was, save in exceptional circumstances, of no importance. Furthermore, the continuation of the claim would not be inconsistent with the overriding objective of the 1998 Rules.

CAIRNSTORES LTD v. AKTIEBOLAGET HASSLE (2001) 24(8) I.P.D. 24052, Pumfrey, J., Pat Ct.

3970. Plant breeders rights – fees

PLANT BREEDERS' RIGHTS (FEES) (AMENDMENT) REGULATIONS 2001, SI 2001 3630; made under the Plant Varieties Act 1997 s.29, s.48. In force: December 1, 2001; £1.75.

These Regulations, which amend the Plant Breeders' Rights (Fees) Regulations 1998 (SI 1998 1021), prescribe revised fees in respect of various matters relating to plant breeders' rights arising under the Plant Varieties Act 1997.

3971. Practice directions – practice note on hearings before Registrar of Trade Marks

The Registrar of Trade Marks has issued a Practice Note replacing that published in Trade Mark Journal number 6196 on October 8, 1997 which will take effect from January 2, 2001, concerning the notification and conduct of hearings.

Held, that (1) at the conclusion of the evidence rounds, a hearing officer will review each case and consider whether the case could be determined on the papers alone without a hearing; (2) either party can request a hearing, in which case parties will be given at least one month's notice of the hearing date; (3) If the parties consider that the hearing will take more than half a day, they must inform the hearings clerk at the earliest opportunity, and (4) where parties are professionally represented at substantive and preliminary hearings, skeleton arguments are to be submitted at least 24 hours before the hearing with copies supplied to the other side.

TRIBUNAL PRACTICE NOTICE TPN 05/2000 (TMR: CHANGE IN PRACTICE OF APPOINTMENT AND CONDUCT OF HEARINGS) [2001] R.P.C. 15, Judge not specified, TMR.

3972. Practice directions – trade marks – registration of retail services

The Registrar of Trade Marks issued a Practice Direction detailing a change of practice in allowing applications to register trade marks for certain types of retail services.

Held, that (1) in view of the confirmation by the ECJ that the essential function of a trade mark is to guarantee to the consumer that the goods or services offered under a mark are controlled by a single undertaking responsible for quality; (2) the UK retailers that have substantial goodwill in their names, so that they function as a trade mark for services comprising the range, display and selection of goods, and (3) the decision of the Office for the Harmonisation of the Internal Market, Second Board of Appeal that "retail services" can be registered as a Community trade mark, there will be no objection to specifications describing the bringing together of goods for the purposes of convenient viewing and selection by customers, provided that the nature of the retail service and market sector, where applicable, are indicated. Although it is doubtful whether a company promoting its own goods via a catalogue or website could provide a registrable service, applications would be accepted from services that bring together other traders' goods, provided some indication is given of the relevant field of activity. A provisional view suggests that there will only be a likelihood of confusion between the retailer's mark and a mark for related goods if the retail service specialises in bringing together goods for which a conflicting mark is registered in a goods class or where it is common trade practice for retail businesses to produce their own brand goods.

PRACTICE DIRECTION (TMR: CHANGE OF PRACTICE ON RETAIL SERVICES) [2001] R.P.C. 2, Allan James, TMR.

3973. Public lending right – scheme variations

PUBLIC LENDING RIGHT SCHEME 1982 (COMMENCEMENT OF VARIATIONS) ORDER 2001, SI 2001 3984; made under the Public Lending Right Act 1979 s.3. In force: January 4, 2002; £1.50.

This Order brings into force on January 4, 2002 a variation to the Public Lending Right Scheme 1982 made by the Secretary of State on December 11, 2001, so that the sum attributable to each qualifying loan for the purposes of calculating the amount payable in respect of loans of a particular book is increased from £2.49 to £2.67.

3974. Registered designs – Isle of Man

REGISTERED DESIGNS (ISLE OF MAN) ORDER 2001, SI 2001 3678; made under the Registered Designs Act 1949 s.37; the Designs Act 1949 s.47; and the Copyright, Designs and Patents Act 1988 s.304. In force: December 9, 2001; £3.50.

This Order, which amends the Registered Designs Act 1949, the Copyright, Designs and Patents Act 1988, the Copyright, Designs and Patents Act 1988 (Isle of Man) (No.2) Order 1989 (SI 1989 1292) and the Copyright, Designs and Patents Act 1988 (Isle of Man) Order 1990 (SI 1990 1505), revokes the Registered Designs Act 1949 (Isle of Man) Order 1989 (SI 1989 982). It extends to the Isle of Man provisions of the Registered Designs Act 1949 and the Copyright, Designs and Patents Act 1988.

3975. Registered designs – legal protection

REGISTERED DESIGNS REGULATIONS 2001, SI 2001 3949; made under the European Communities Act 1972 s.2. In force: December 9, 2001; £3.50.

These Regulations amend the Chartered Associations (Protection of Names and Uniforms) Act 1926, the Registered Designs Act 1949, the Copyright, Designs and Patents Act 1988, the Merchant Shipping Act 1995 and the Olympic Symbol etc. (Protection) Act 1995. They implement Directive 98/71 ([1998] OJ L289/28) on the protection of designs which provide for harmonisation in the EC of the matters of registered design protection which most closely affect the functioning of the internal market. The Directive extends the definition of "design", to allow the designer to apply for protection up to a year after he first discloses a design without his own disclosures counting against the registration, amends the period of protection to a maximum of 25 years from the filing date of the application, provides that the use of the design of a component part used for the purpose of the repair of a complex product so as to restore its original appearance shall not be an infringement of the rights in the design and makes explicit the principle of "exhaustion of rights", whereby a right-holder cannot continue to use these rights to control movement or use of a product after it has been put on the market in the EEA by him or with his consent.

3976. Registered designs – legal protection

REGISTERED DESIGNS (AMENDMENT) RULES 2001, SI 2001 3950; made under the Registered Designs Act 1949 s.3, s.3B, s.5, s.11, s.18, s.22, s.30, s.36, s.39, s.44. In force: December 9, 2001; £2.50.

These Rules amend the Registered Designs Rules 1995 (SI 1995 2912 as amended by SI 1999 3196), consequent upon amendments made to the Registered Designs Act 1949 by the Registered Designs Regulations 2001 (SI

2001 3949). Those regulations implement Directive 98/71 ([1998] OJ L289/28) on the legal protection of designs.

3977. Registered designs – legal protection – fees

REGISTERED DESIGNS (FEES) (AMENDMENT) RULES 2001, SI 2001 3951; made under the Registered Designs Act 1949 s.36, s.40, s.44; and the Department of Trade and Industry (Fees) Order 1988 (SI 1988 93). In force: December 9, 2001; £1.50.

These Rules amend the Registered Designs (Fees) Rules 1998 (SI 1998 1777) consequent upon amendments made to the Registered Designs Act 1949 and the Registered Designs Rules 1995 (SI 1995 2912 as amended by SI 1999 3196) in order to implement Directive 98/71 ([1998] OJ L289/28) on the legal protection of designs.

3978. Restraint of trade – dispute resolution – reasonableness of restraints in settlement agreement – injurious association

[EC Treaty Art.85 (now Art.81 EC).]

W1 applied for summary judgment in proceedings concerned with the enforcement of a contract with W2, made in settlement of actual and prospective litigation, which imposed restrictions upon the ability of W2 to use the initials "WWF" during the course of its business. Whilst W2 had initially complied with the terms of the contract, from 1997 it had effectively ignored the agreed terms of restraint. W2 maintained that such infringement as there had been was justified since the relevant contract terms were void at common law as either an unreasonable restraint of trade or, in the alternative, under the EC Treaty Art.85 (now Art.81 EC).

Held, granting the application, that (1) whilst the restraints imposed an actual fetter on W2's business activities, the imposition of the restraint had been reasonable since W1 had been entitled to have reservations concerning any injurious association with W2 and, in many ways, the image of W1 was entirely at odds with that of W2, and (2) W2's contention that Art.85 of the Treaty applied as the restraint had become more onerous since the agreement had been entered into as a result of its increasing use of the initials W1 and its establishment of a website using those initials, could not be maintained since a party could not rely upon its own contractual breach in order to escape from the terms of that contract.

WORLD WIDE FUND FOR NATURE (FORMERLY WORLD WILDLIFE FUND) v. WORLD WRESTLING FEDERATION ENTERTAINMENT INC; *sub nom.* WWF v. WORLD WRESTLING FEDERATION ENTERTAINMENT INC *The Times*, November 13, 2001, Jacob, J., Ch D.

3979. Trade marks – advertisements – websites – intention to address localised clientele – criteria for infringement

[Trade Marks Act 1994 s.9(1), s.11 (2) (a).]

P, the owner of a shop in Dublin called "Crate & Barrel" advertised in a magazine circulating in Ireland and the UK, and operated a website. ED, an American company operating a chain of stores in the United States, sought summary judgment, contending that the advertisement and website infringed its UK registered trade mark of the same name. P contended that the advertisement did not constitute use of the mark in the UK or alternatively that the advertisement was not in the course of business, since the website was aimed at local clientele and not the whole world. It was further submitted that the own name defence under the Trade Marks Act 1994 s.11 (2) (a) applied. ED contended that the intended audience for the advertisement was irrelevant and any advertisement which appeared in the UK, and similarly the website which was accessible to the whole world, constituted an infringement of s.9(1) of the Act.

Held, refusing the application, that there was a realistic prospect of a successful defence. The relevant test was whether the reasonable trader would regard the use concerned as "in the course of trade in relation to goods" within the Member State concerned. In the instant case there was no infringement because (1) the advertisement was intended to address only clientele local to the shop premises; (2) anyone visiting the website from anywhere other than Ireland would understand that the site was not directed at them; (3) P had not acted dishonestly, and (4) the own name defence could apply to company names.

EUROMARKET DESIGNS INC v. PETERS [2000] E.T.M.R. 1025, Jacob, J., Ch D.

3980. Trade marks – application to register words "TINY PENIS" – refusal on moral grounds

[Trade Marks Act 1994 s.3(3)(a).]

G requested a hearing following an objection to his application to register the words "TINY PENIS" in Class 25 for use on clothing, footwear and headgear, on the ground that it would be contrary to accepted moral principles under the Trade Marks Act 1994 s.3(3)(a).

Held, refusing to register the trade mark, that the issue of morality was to be determined in light of contemporary standards and susceptibilities. Refusal under s.3(3)(a) was warranted if the mark was liable to offend a sizeable minority, *HALLELUJAH Trade Mark* [1976] R.P.C. 605, [1976] C.L.Y. 2798 followed and was not to be reserved only for the most outrageous expletives. As the goods intended to carry the mark would be displayed for sale in public, consumers would be exposed to the mark without having any choice in the matter and it was such that offence could be caused to a substantial percentage.

GHAZILIAN'S TRADE MARK APPLICATION; *sub nom.* TINY PENIS TRADE MARK [2001] R.P.C. 33, Janet Folwell, TMR.

3981. Trade marks – applications – priority claimed on basis of earlier US application – bad faith in choice of class

[Trade Marks Act 1994 s.3(1), s.35; Council Directive 89/104 on trade marks Art.4(4)(g).]

FNX applied to register the mark FSS in Class 9 for personal computers and software for use in the financial services field and in Class 36 for financial services consultancy services in the UK on June 25, 1995, based on a UK use dating from 1989 and priority based on a US application of January 1995. The application was assigned to A on June 5, 1996, and A took over from FNX in resisting opposition proceedings brought by B on the grounds that the sign was incapable of distinguishing the goods of A and B and that the application had been made in bad faith and conflicted with B's earlier rights consisting of two trade mark applications for FSS and FSS-device in Class 9 and Class 42. A argued, however, that its FSS mark had been used in the UK since December 1988, thereby pre dating B's use by at least three years. B claimed that the convention priority date under the Trade Marks Act 1994 s.35 should be disallowed as the US trade mark application was not a "regular national filing" within the meaning of the s.35(3). Further, that a three letter mark could not distinguish between the goods from different undertakings, contrary to s.3(1)(a). The hearing officer upheld the objection against the Class 36 application but rejected that against the Class 9 application. A appealed against the rejection of its Class 36 application and B cross appealed on the acceptance of the Class 9 application.

Held, dismissing the appeal and the cross appeal, that (1) Parliament had not provided a ground for objection based on conflict with an earlier right under Council Directive 89/104 Art.4(4)(g); (2) a regular filing date for the purposes of s.35(3) meant one that could determine the date of filing and it was satisfied by evidence of a regular filing in a convention country; (3) two and three letter marks were acceptable if there was no reason to believe they would not be viewed as a trade mark by the average consumer; (4) s.3(6) provided that a sign could be registered as a trade mark where the application had not been made in bad faith and was free from objections; it did not require an open ended assessment of commercial morality and the proper status of applications was assumed in the absence of contrary evidence; (5) A had used the trade mark FSS in connection with Class 9 goods since 1989, and (6) the Class 36 registration application was made in bad faith as FNX knew that Class 42 was the most appropriate for consultancy services.

FSS TRADE MARK [2001] R.P.C. 40, Geoffrey Hobbs Q.C., Appointed Person.

3982. **Trade marks – assignment of application – applicant dissolved at date of assignment – ownership**

[Trade Marks Act 1994 s.27(3), s.32; Trade Mark Rules 1994 (SI 1994 2583) r.13(3), r.60.]

JC applied to register the mark PELLE PELLE MARC BUCHANAN in Class 25 in 1995. In 1997, P filed notice of opposition, submitting supporting evidence under the Trade Mark Rules 1994 r.13(3) in the form of a statutory declaration by N. However, N subsequently applied to withdraw his evidence and the Trade Mark Registry acceded to this request. P argued that N could not withdraw his evidence as he was not a party to the proceedings. In June 1999, JC purported to assign the application to another company with the same name. The Registrar recorded this assignment. P informed the Registrar that JC had been dissolved in December 1998 and contended that the assignment was therefore invalid so that any property remaining at the date of dissolution vested with the Crown. As the Crown could not have the requisite intention to use the trade mark, the application should be deemed withdrawn. The application should therefore be deemed to be abandoned at the date that the property vested in the Crown.

Held, continuing the opposition, that (1) property belonging to JC at the dissolution date was bona vacantia so that the assignment June 1, 1999 was a nullity; (2) a distinction was to be drawn between the recording of details against an application and an entry on the register. Details of an assignment were simply recorded against an application and as the assignment was a nullity it should not have been recorded in that way. This was an irregularity in procedure and the details of the assignment should be removed from the record so that the application would revert back to JC under the Trade Mark Rules 1994 r.60, *DUCATI Trade Mark* [1998] R.P.C. 227, [1998] C.L.Y. 3536 distinguished; (3) P's submissions regarding lack of necessary intention on the Crown's part could not be accepted as the Act required that intention must be lacking at the date of the application for s.32(3) to apply; (4) there was no evidence to show that JC held the trade mark at the date of dissolution. Therefore, the most appropriate course of action was to return the record against the application to show that JC was the applicant, and (5) as a witness N could not withdraw his evidence and P was directed to re file it.

JOE COOL (MANCHESTER) LTD'S TRADE MARK APPLICATION [2000] R.P.C. 926, SP Rowan, TMR.

3983. **Trade marks – character merchandising – distinctive character – name of well known historical literary figure**

[Trade Marks Act 1994 s.3(1)(b), s.3(3)(a), s.3(3)(b), s.3(6).]

C applied to register the as yet unused mark JANE AUSTEN for use in relation to toiletries, soaps and perfume. The application was opposed byT, the trustees of the Jane Austen MemorialTrust. Towned JaneAusten's house and ran a museum selling Jane Austen related souvenirs. Topposed the application on a number of grounds, including lack of distinctive character under theTrade Marks Act1994 s.3(1)(b); that such use would be likely to deceive the public as to the nature of the goods in terms of s.3(3)(b) and the application was in bad faith under s.3(6), given the damage it would do to Jane Austen's reputation. C contended that Jane Austen had not reached the point where a purchaser would buy the name, rather that a product, and as such would be distinguishable in terms of A's goods.

Held, refusing the application, that (1) factors to consider in determining how a literary or artistic person's name was perceived and whether it amounted to trade origin, included: the extent of the reputation concerned; whether there was a trade in associated souvenirs; established rights in the name; extent of media and public interest and the type of goods for which registration was sought, *ELVIS PRESLEY Trade Marks* [1999] R.P.C. 567, [1999] C.L.Y. 3574 and *TARZAN Trade Mark* [1970] F.S.R. 245, [1970] C.L.Y. 2859 referred to; (2) well known literary figures were likely to generate a high level of demand for merchandise, due to their fame and geographical associations. Lesser figures could, however, fulfil the functions of a trade mark. In the instant case, however, Jane Austen's name enjoyed high standing in literature; (3) T had developed a trade in Jane Austen related souvenirs which was the only use the public were familiar with. Unless educated to see the name differently, it would not amount to a badge of origin. Therefore, T's objection under s.3(1)(b) succeeded; (4) the objections under s.3(3)(a) and s.3(3)(b) failed. There was no discernible public policy interest exceeding the rights that could be built up and protected through other areas of law. The public would not be deceived into thinking that C's goods had T's approval or were connected with Jane Austen's literary works, and (5) the objection under s.3(6) also failed. There was no general presumption against registering a historic literary figure's name and registration would not be detrimental to Jane Austen's standing or literary reputation.

JANE AUSTEN TRADE MARK [2000] R.P.C. 879, M Reynolds, TMR.

3984. Trade marks – Community trade marks – applications – mistaken non payment of fee – reestablishment of rights

[Council Regulation 40/94 on the Community trade mark Art.27, Art.78; International Convention for the Protection of Industrial Property (Paris Convention); Munich Convention on the Grant of European Patents; Washington Patent Cooperation Treaty.]

R applied to annul the decision of the First Board of Appeal of the Office for Harmonisation in the Internal Market upholding the dismissal of his application under Council Regulation 40/94 Art.78 for re-establishment of rights in relation to the award of a filing date for his application for registration of a figurative patent. When filing the application, R had stated on the form that he would pay the application fee later. The fee had not, however, been paid within the one month limit established under Art.27 due to an alleged oversight by one of his staff members. It was submitted that (1) Art.27 was not compatible with a number of international conventions on the protection of industrial property; (2) R should have been informed of the one month time limit, and (3) all due care had been taken for the purposes of Art.78(1) and therefore there had not been grounds for refusing to reestablish R's rights.

Held, dismissing the application, that (1) the International Convention for the Protection of Industrial Property (Paris Convention), the Munich Convention on the Grant of European Patents and the Washington Patent Cooperation Treaty did not establish any principle relating to filing dates with which Art.27 could be said to be incompatible; (2) given that R's staff had general instructions aimed at ensuring that the one month time limited was observed, it was irrelevant that R had not been informed of that time limit, and (3) the failure to pay the fee within the one month limit being a result of one of R's staff members not following the office policy, it could not be said that non-observance with that limit had occurred "in spite of all due care" as required under Art.78.

RUF v. OFFICE FOR HARMONISATION IN THE INTERNAL MARKET (TRADE MARKS AND DESIGNS) (OHIM) (T146/00) [2001] C.E.C. 209, AWH Meij (President), CFI.

3985. Trade marks – Community trade marks – confusion – footwear – similarity of shoe imprint

M applied to register a trademark consisting of a shoe imprint for goods in Class 14 (horological and chronometric instruments), Class 16 (stationery and office requisites, other than furniture), Class 18 (leather and imitation leather goods) and Class 25 (clothing, in particular sports and leisure wear, knitwear, headgear; clothing accessories, namely headkerchiefs, neckerchiefs (scarves), shawls, hoods, sweatbands, gloves, panty hoses, socks and belts). L opposed the application in all classes, citing its earlier registration of a shoe imprint as a Community and German trade mark for men's shoes in Class 25.

Held, rejecting the opposition, that there was no similarity between men's shoes in Class 25 and M's goods in Classes 14, 16, and 18. As to the Class 25 application, confusion was unlikely between men's shoes and clothing, despite the similarity of purpose. A shoe imprint was only a weak distinctive element as it only represented part of the goods and protection would only be granted where a later design was extremely similar or identical to the earlier sign.

DR MARTENS INTERNATIONAL TRADING GmbH'S TRADE MARK APPLICATION [2000] E.T.M.R. 1151, Panayotis Geroulakos, Office for Harmonization in the Internal Market (Opposition Division).

3986. **Trade marks – Community trade marks – confusion – identical goods – no similarity between marks**

IPC applied to register the word GRANDEE as a Community trade mark for stationery products and teaching materials in Class 16. L opposed the application on the basis of its earlier German registration of LANDRE for the same class of products. The opposition was dismissed on the grounds that there was no visual, conceptual or phonetic similarity between the marks. L appealed.

Held, dismissing the appeal, that (1) there was no likelihood of confusion, despite the identical nature of the products, due to the difference between the marks, and (2) although a low level of similarity could justify an opposition in the case of identical goods, in the instant case IPC's mark differed sufficiently from L's so that no confusion would occur.

LANDRE GmbH v. INTERNATIONAL PAPER CO [2001] E.T.M.R. 73, K Sundstrom (Chairman), Office for Harmonization in the Internal Market (First Board of Appeal).

3987. **Trade marks – Community trade marks – confusion – medicines – prescription only and over the counter goods**

BI applied to register the word EVASIL as a Community trade mark for pharmaceutical preparations in Class 5 for a product made up of plant extracts for the treatment of pre menstrual and climacterial disorders. C opposed the application on the basis of its earlier registrations of the word EXACYL as a trade mark in France and Portugal for a prescription only drug in the same class for the treatment of hemorrhages. The opposition was refused as the Opposition Division decided that, although the marks were to be used for similar goods, the marks themselves were not similar. Although they bore some visual similarity, they lacked conceptual similarity and were not pronounced similarly in French or Portuguese. C appealed.

Held, dismissing the appeal, that (1) likelihood of confusion had to be decided appraising visual, phonetic and conceptual similarities, based on the overall impression given by the marks and keeping their distinctive and dominant components in mind, *Sabel BV v. Puma AG (C251/95)* [1997] E.C.R. I-6191, [1998] C.L.Y. 3512 referred to; (2) the similarity of the marks and the goods were interdependent criteria so that a reduction in the degree of similarity between goods could be offset by greater similarity between the marks, *Canon Kabushiki Kaisha v. Metro Goldwyn Mayer Inc (C39/97)* [1998] All E.R. (EC) 934, [1998] C.L.Y. 3526 applied; (3) the marks were phonetically and visually similar but did not have any conceptual similarities as they were both made up words and the likelihood of confusion did not arise merely because they were devoid of meaning; (4) the goods were not similar as they had different functions, and (5) no special considerations arose in connection with the risk of confusion regarding pharmaceutical products, although arguments could be made out in cases where adverse consequences could occur if a patient was confused by marks. This did not arise in the instant case, however, as EXACYL was prescription only and there was little likelihood that a person would purchase EVASIL over the counter after being prescribed EXACYL.

CHOAY SA v. BOEHRINGER INGELHEIM INTERNATIONAL GmbH [2001] E.T.M.R. 64, H Preglau (Chairman), Office for Harmonization in the Internal Market (First Board of Appeal).

3988. Trade marks – Community trade marks – confusion – phonetic similarities

[Council Regulation 40/94 on the Community trade mark Art.8(1)(b).]

S applied to register the words BLACK BULL as a Community trade mark for goods in Classes 25, 32 and 33 (clothing, headgear and footwear, non alcoholic and alcoholic drinks) and Class 42 (various hospitality services). RB opposed the application on the basis of its prior national registrations of the trademark RED BULL. R argued that the mark BLACK BULL was similar to its marks, and related to the same goods, in terms of Council Regulation 40/94 on the Community trade mark Art.8(1)(b).

Held, allowing the opposition in part, but allowing registration for use in Classes 33 and 42, that the two marks shared close phonetic similarities and the word BULL was not usually found in relation to Classes 25 and 32. The dominant nature of the word meant that the marks were similar. Of the national registrations relied on by RB, only Irish marks for goods in Classes 25 and 32 were relevant and these showed that the public would be likely to believe the goods had a shared source, giving rise to the risk of confusion.

SCOTTISH & NEWCASTLE PLC'S TRADE MARK APPLICATION [2000] E.T.M.R. 1143, Tomas de las Heras, Office for Harmonization in the Internal Market (Opposition Division).

3989. Trade marks – Community trade marks – confusion – similarity of marks featuring same surname – identical nature of goods

L applied to register the words LINDA JACKSON in script form as a Community trade mark for clothing in Class 25. D opposed the application on the basis of its prior Austrian registration of a heraldic device bearing the words DAVID JACKSON, also registered for clothing in Class 25, on the basis of a likelihood of confusion between the two marks in the Austrian market.

Held, refusing the opposition, that there was a weak similarity between the two marks in that the Austrian public would appreciate that both marks featured a foreign name with a shared surname between the marks. However, in spite of this, and the similarity of the goods involved, the similarity was not sufficient to give rise to a likelihood of confusion. The marks also differed in their visual appearance, although they shared a common surname.

LINDA JACKSON PTY LTD COMMUNITY TRADE MARK APPLICATION (520/2000) [2001] E.T.M.R. 35, Panayotis Geroulakos, Office for Harmonization in the Internal Market (Opposition Division).

3990. Trade marks – Community trade marks – confusion – word marks "DAVINA" and "BABINA"

B sought registration of the mark DAVINA for goods including baby food in Classes 5, 30 and 32. SM opposed the application on the basis of its international trade mark BABINA, covering Spain and Germany, relating to baby food in Classes 5 and 29, contending that the similarity between the marks was such that confusion was likely. B gave an oral indication that he would withdraw the application, but formal notification was not received prior to the decision date.

Held, upholding the opposition in relation to baby food, that as the application had not been formally withdrawn the Opposition Division was obliged to treat it as still being on foot and to determine SM's opposition to it. The marks had the same number of letters with the same vowels appearing in identical order. Moreover, there was no phonetic distinction in Spanish between the letters "B" and "V", with the effect that the only difference in pronunciation between the marks was there respective initial consonant.

BRACKENBROUGH'S COMMUNITY TRADE MARK APPLICATION [2001] E.T.M.R. 39, Benoit Lory, Office for Harmonization in the Internal Market (Opposition Division).

3991. **Trade marks – Community trade marks – distinctiveness**

[Council regulation 40/94 on the Community trade mark Art.7 (1), Art.51 (1) (a).]

B registered the words POUDRE LIBRE NATURELLE as a Community trade mark for cosmetics in Class 3. L sought a declaration under Council Regulation 40/94 Art.51 (1) (a) that the trade mark was invalid as it lacked the distinctive character to designate cosmetics required by Art.7 (1).

Held, allowing the application and cancelling the registration, that the trade mark was descriptive and not distinctive. The words "poudre libre" in common French usage referred to a loose powder used to prevent the skin from shining when make up was applied. The addition of "naturelle" was also descriptive and did not make the trade mark distinctive. Furthermore, the trade mark would be deceptive or misleading if used for cosmetics other than powder products; therefore, B's use of the general heading "cosmetics" and its failure to limit the trade mark to specific goods to which grounds of invalidity would not apply, meant that the trade mark was rejected in its entirety.

BEIERSDORF AG'S COMMUNITY TRADE MARK [2001] E.T.M.R. 19, H Meister (Chairman), Office for Harmonization in the Internal Market (Cancellation Div).

3992. **Trade marks – Community trade marks – distinctiveness – acquisition through use of figurative mark**

[Council Regulation 40/94 on the Community trade mark Art.7 (1) (b).]

D applied to register a figurative mark consisting of an outline hexagon shape for a range of goods for use in stables in Classes 6, 7 and 27. The application was refused on the ground that the hexagon shape lacked distinctive character. D appealed, contending that basic shapes were not excluded from registration under Council Regulation 40/94 Art.7 (1) (b), and that the mark, which was customarily used for honey but not stable equipment, had acquired distinctiveness through use in Germany and the Benelux countries.

Held, dismissing the appeal, that the mark was a basic shape that did not indicate the source of the goods for which registration was sought. The fact that it was not customarily used for stable equipment was not sufficient to confer distinctiveness. The evidence did not show that the mark had acquired distinctiveness through use, but rather that it had been used as a trade mark other than as the mark in suit.

DE BOER STALINRICHTINGEN BV'S APPLICATION [2001] E.T.M.R. 79, C Hoffrichter-Daunicht, Office for Harmonization in the Internal Market (Fourth Board of Appeal).

3993. **Trade marks – Community trade marks – distinctiveness – application to register "electronica" for use in relation to electronic trade fairs**

[Council Regulation 40/94 on the Community trade mark Art.4, Art.7 (1) (b), Art.7 (1) (c).]

MM applied to register the word "electronica" as a Community trade mark for use in connection with electronic trade fairs. The application was refused by the examiner on the grounds that the mark lacked distinctive character and because the word was descriptive of the goods and services involved. The Board of Appeal dismissed an appeal against that decision and MM appealed to the CFI, arguing that the mark satisfied the registration requirements of Council Regulation 40/94 Art.7 (1) (b) and Art.7 (1) (c).

Held, dismissing the appeal, that (1) for a mark to be eligible for registration Art.4 of the Regulation required that it had to be capable of distinguishing goods of different undertakings; (2) distinctive character could only be assessed by reference to the goods or services for which registration was sought, and (3) Art.7(1)(b) prevented registration of a mark that did not have any distinctive character. In the instant case, the word "electronica" in several European languages described an essential characteristic of the goods in question and the mark had no feature capable of differentiating it from its meaning that actually described goods and services.

MESSE MUNCHEN GmbH v. OFFICE FOR HARMONISATION IN THE INTERNAL MARKET (TRADE MARKS AND DESIGNS) (OHIM) (T32/00) [2001] C.E.C. 3, V Tiili (President), CFI.

3994. Trade marks – Community trade marks – distinctiveness – composite word not capable of allowing single meaning

[Council Regulation 40/94 on the Community trade mark Art.4, Art.7.]

W's application to register the word "DOUBLEMINT" for various goods including chewing gum in Classes 3, 5 and 30 was refused on the ground that it was purely descriptive and therefore unregistrable under Council Regulation 40/94 Art.7(1)(c). W appealed, arguing that, taken as a whole, DOUBLEMINT was a new word that would not be understood by consumers as having a single meaning and that a final meaning would require several stages of mental effort. The Board of Appeal concluded that the word was descriptive as it combined two English words without an extra fanciful or imaginative element. W appealed to the CFI.

Held, allowing the appeal and annulling the Board's decision, that (1) the decisive factor in favour of recognition under Art.4 was the ability to distinguish between goods of different undertakings; (2) absolute grounds for refusal under Art.7(1) could only be assessed in relation to goods for which registration was sought, *Procter & Gamble Co v. Office for Harmonisation in the Internal Market (Trade Marks and Designs) (T163/98)* [2000] 1 W.L.R. 91, [1999] C.L.Y. 3533 referred to; (3) the legislature intended that the signs listed in Art.7(1)(c) would not be capable of distinguishing between the goods of different undertakings and would therefore be unregistrable, subject to the exception in Art.7(3); (4) the Board of Appeal had been wrong to find that DOUBLEMINT was purely descriptive. When used in praise of a certain product, "double" was unusual when compared with more commonplace adjectives such as "much", "strong" or "extra". This was especially true in the instant case as "double" did not allude to the single state of either W's or a competing product; (5) the many meanings of the term DOUBLEMINT, although made up of two common English words, would be obvious to English speaking consumers and would be accorded a fanciful meaning by those not proficient in the language, and (6) therefore the sign was not descriptive in nature as it did not allow a characteristic description of goods to be detected immediately.

WM WRIGLEY JR CO v. OFFICE FOR HARMONISATION IN THE INTERNAL MARKET (TRADE MARKS AND DESIGNS) (OHIM) (T193/99) [2001] E.T.M.R. 58, J Pirrung (President), CFI.

3995. Trade marks – Community trade marks – distinctiveness – figurative mark

[Council Regulation 40/94 on the Community trade mark Art.7(1).]

A sought to register the figurative mark EURO followed by the symbol of the European currency in respect of its business consultancy and financial services. The examiner determined that the combination was devoid of distinctive character for the specified services. A appealed against that decision, claiming that its limitation of the symbol and the word to a particular colour made it distinctive.

Held, dismissing the appeal, that (1) the particular presentation of the word and symbol was not eligible for registration because it did not distinguish the goods and services of one undertaking from those of other undertakings; (2) the European currency symbol fell within Council Regulation 40/94 on the Community trade mark Art.7(1)(i) which excluded from registration badges, emblems or escutcheons "which are of particular public interest". The shadow and the slanted shape in which the European currency symbol was represented in the trade mark was not sufficient to overcome the application of that provision, and (3) the fact that the mark had been registered in Benelux was not conclusive of its entitlement to be registered under the Community Trade Mark Regulation.

ABN AMRO HOLDING NV'S APPLICATION (R 190/1999-3) [2001] E.T.M.R. 8, S Sandri (Chairman), Office for Harmonization in the Internal Market (Third Board of Appeal).

3996. **Trade marks – Community trade marks – distinctiveness – figurative mark made up of "THE" – additions needed for grammatical sense**

T's application to register a figurative mark made up of the word "THE" for screws, nuts, bolts etc in Class 6 was refused. The examiner held that the mark lacked distinctiveness even taking into account its figurative makeup. T appealed, arguing that the mark had acquired distinctiveness through use within the EU. T did not contest the examiner's finding of lack of distinctiveness, but adduced evidence of use, including sales details and advertising material.

Held, annulling the examiner's decision and remitting the application for further consideration, that the Board could consider the question of distinctiveness of its own motion. T's mark did not inherently lack distinctiveness, even if it did lack any meaning in isolation, including any indication of merit in T's products. Simplicity on its own was not a ground for objection due to lack of distinctiveness, and the mark was fanciful since it required additions to make grammatical sense.

TONG HWEI ENTERPRISE CO LTD'S COMMUNITY TRADE MARK APPLICATION [2001] E.T.M.R. 86, K Sundstrom (Chairman), Office for Harmonization in the Internal Market (First Board of Appeal).

3997. **Trade marks – Community trade marks – distinctiveness – grammatically incorrect composite word**

Registration of the word INVESTORWORLD as a Community trade mark in respect of financial services in Class 36 was refused on the ground that the word was devoid of distinctive character. C appealed to the CFI having unsuccessfully appealed to the Board of Appeal.

Held, dismissing the appeal, that the term INVESTORWORLD was a composite of the words "investor" and "world". The former indicated that C's services were aimed at investors and relevant to Class 36. The addition of "world" did not add a further characteristic capable of distinguishing C's services from those of other companies. The fact that the composite word was intentionally grammatically incorrect did not invest it with a distinctive character.

COMMUNITY CONCEPTS AG v. OFFICE FOR HARMONISATION IN THE INTERNAL MARKET (TRADE MARKS AND DESIGNS) (OHIM) (T360/99) [2001] E.T.M.R. 17,V Tiili (President), CFI.

3998. **Trade marks – Community trade marks – distinctiveness – industrial goods – technical and functional aspects**

[Council Regulation 40/94 on the Community trade mark Art.7(1)(b).]

W applied to register a three dimensional trade mark in Class 7 (pumps, agitators, cyclones, thickeners, apron feeders and machinery of all kinds of chemical metallurgical and refining processes). The examiner refused the application on the grounds that it lacked the distinctive character required by Council Regulation 40/94 Art.7(1)(b), as it amounted to a three dimensional representation of W's goods. Further, that the particular shape was due to the nature of the goods being necessary to attain a given technical result. W argued that the mark had acquired distinctiveness by use, but the examiner held that evidence of use was merely evidence of use in a functional capacity. W appealed.

Held, allowing the appeal, that the shape had a striking appearance and was more attractive than usually found in industrial goods with a functional purpose.

The specialised nature of the goods meant that there were few alternative suppliers, so that purchasers would probably recognise the shape of W's goods. Although some features might be necessary for technical or functional purposes, other producers would not need to embody the same features for their goods to function. Therefore the shape was not due to the nature of W's goods and was unnecessary to achieve a technical result.

WARMAN INTERNATIONAL LTD'S THREE DIMENSIONAL TRADE MARK APPLICATION [2000] E.T.M.R. 1159, H Preglau, Office for Harmonization in the Internal Market (First Board of Appeal).

3999. Trade marks – Community trade marks – distinctiveness – three dimensional mark applied to optical lenses

C applied to register a three dimensional mark in Class 9 in the form of three ribs projecting from the circumference of optical lens blanks. The ribs were referred to in the application as being discernible when a finger was applied to the surface. The examiner found that the mark was devoid of distinctive character as it was incapable of distinguishing C's goods from those of its competitors. Further, that it was excessively simple. C appealed, arguing that (1) the mark functioned as an indication of origin; (2) three dimensional marks containing other elements should be registered where those elements were sufficient, either alone or in combination with the three dimensional shape, to permit registration; (3) lens products were not usually ribbed, and (4) excessive simplicity was not a sufficient ground for refusing registration as it was necessary to consider how intended consumers would perceive the mark.

Held, allowing the appeal and remitting the application for further consideration, that: (1) the examiner had erred in treating the application as relating both to the shape of the lens and the ribs when it related only to the three ribs. Therefore, lens shape should not to have been considered in relation to distinctiveness; (2) the three ribs were an unusual design feature and it was hard to argue that they were bereft of any distinctive character, and (3) since the products were provided only to specialist lens finishers, who would realise that the ribs were not functional and served only to identify C's products, the ribs were sufficiently distinctive as they would mark C's goods out from those of C's competitors.

CORNING INC'S THREE DIMENSIONAL TRADE MARK APPLICATION [2001] E.T.M.R. 83, K Sundstrom (Chairman), Office for Harmonization in the Internal Market (Second Board of Appeal).

4000. Trade marks – Community trade marks – distinctiveness – three dimensional mark used in conjunction with other marks

C's application to register a three dimensional mark in the form of a package shape was refused on the grounds that it lacked distinctiveness. C argued that it had used the shape exclusively throughout the Community since 1974 and that it had used the packaging since 1974. The package was an arbitrary design that was not intended to achieve a technical purpose. The examiner maintained his objection, stating that the mark was not distinctive as it was always used in conjunction with other marks. C appealed, contending that the combined use of two or more trade marks together did not mean that one could not be distinctive merely because it was generally used with the other marks.

Held, dismissing the appeal, that there were instances in which consumers could recognise a product by its shape even though they were accustomed to seeing it used in conjunction with other marks or logos. However, in the instant case, the mere shape of C's packaging was not such that consumers would recognise it as signifying specific goods from a particular source.

CABOT SAFETY INTERMEDIATE CORP'S THREE DIMENSIONAL TRADE MARK APPLICATION [2001] E.T.M.R. 85, K Sundstrom (Chairman), Office for Harmonization in the Internal Market (First Board of Appeal).

4001. Trade marks – Community trade marks – distinctiveness – three dimensional shape of detergent product

[Council Regulation 40/94 on the Community trade mark Art.7(1)(b).]

P sought to register as a Class 3 Community trade mark a white three dimensional square shape with blue and green speckles for a domestic detergent product. The examiner decided that the trade mark was not eligible for registration, finding that the trade mark represented the goods themselves, namely detergent in tablet form, and was devoid of any distinctive character, as required by Council Regulation 40/94 Art.7(1)(b). P appealed.

Held, dismissing the appeal, that (1) P should not have an exclusive entitlement to sell Class 3 detergent products in solid form, as other traders should be allowed to use geometric shapes for their products. Such shapes were the most obvious for detergent manufacturers and P's choice of a square was therefore not distinctive. Similarly, the colours chosen by P were obvious in this context. White suggested cleanliness and blue and green were commonly associated with clean water and environmental protection respectively, while speckling was used to denote active ingredients, and (2) registration of similar marks in individual Member States was not binding on the Office. Neither did it show that the Office was out of step with practices in the Member States.

PROCTER & GAMBLE FRANCE'S COMMUNITY TRADE MARK APPLICATION (R 529/1999-1) [2001] E.T.M.R. 22, H Preglau, Office for Harmonization in the Internal Market (First Board of Appeal).

4002. Trade marks – Community trade marks – distinctiveness – web page design software – descriptive nature of term used

[Council Regulation 40/94 on the Community trade mark Art.7(1)(b).]

N applied to register the wordmark "SITEPRODUCER" under class 9 in respect of computer software, development and authoring tools. The examiner decided that the trade mark was not eligible for registration because it lacked distinctiveness in terms of Council Regulation 40/94 Art.7(1)(b). N appealed, and sought to amend the specification to show that the product was a graphic design tool for creating web pages.

Held, dismissing the appeal, that the examiner had correctly determined that the amendment only served to clarify the product. Differences in the means of technical production were not relevant for the purposes of establishing distinctiveness. The name itself was insufficiently distinctive as a means of enabling consumers to make decisions about products sharing similar characteristics.

NETOBJECTS TRADE MARK APPLICATION; *sub nom* SITEPRODUCER TRADE MARK [1998-99] Info. T.L.R. 265, S Sandri (Chairman), Office for Harmonization in the Internal Market (Third Board of Appeal).

4003. Trade marks – Community trade marks – distinctiveness – word combination mark "BABY-DRY"

[Council Regulation 40/94 on the Community trade mark Art.7(1)(c).]

PG, which sought to register under Council Regulation 40/94 the name "Baby-Dry" as a Community trade mark in relation to babies nappies, applied to annul the decision of the Court of First Instance ([2000] 1 W.L.R. 91, [1999] C.L.Y. 3533) that OHIM and the examiner had been correct in finding that the name was not capable of amounting to a Community trade mark by virtue of Art.7(1)(c) of the Regulation. The CFI had found that since the purpose of nappies was to keep a baby dry and the combination of the words "Baby-Dry" only served to identify such a purpose, the term was not sufficiently distinctive.

Held, allowing the application, that the prohibition contained within Art.7(1)(c) of the Regulation was intended to preclude the registration of marks which were purely descriptive signs or indications and did not serve to identify the undertaking from which the goods emanated. Where a trade mark was formulated from a word combination, its distinctiveness was to be judged not only on the basis of the separate words used but also on the basis of the resultant whole. It was accordingly necessary to ascertain whether any particular combination of words amounted to a standard way of referring to the goods from the point of view of an English speaking consumer. In the instant case, whilst the relevant words were each normal everyday expressions used to describe the function of babies nappies, their unusual juxtaposition was not a familiar way in which to describe babies nappies or their functions.

PROCTER & GAMBLE CO v. OFFICE FOR HARMONISATION IN THE INTERNAL MARKET (TRADE MARKS AND DESIGNS) (OHIM) (C383/99 P) [2002] Ch. 82, GC Rodriguez Iglesias (President), ECJ.

4004. Trade marks – Community trade marks – distinctiveness – word mark "Giroform" – descriptive meaning of two common words

[Council Regulation 40/94 Art.7(1)(c).]

Application was made for registration of the word mark Giroform as a Community trade mark in class 16 (paper, cardboard, and goods made from these materials not included in other classes, and printed matter). Registration was granted as asked, save in respect of "cardboard and goods made from cardboard", in respect of which the mark was held to lack distinctiveness, and to be exclusively descriptive. The Board of Appeal dismissed the applicant's appeal on this point, and in a further appeal, the applicant argued that Council Regulation 40/94 Art.7(1)(c) only prohibited registration of signs or marks whose descriptive nature was unambiguously apparent, and that the Board had made an error of law in finding that the mark in suit was incapable of distinguishing the applicant's goods from those of other undertakings.

Held, dismissing the appeal, that (1) the mark consisted of two elements, "giro" and "form" which both had a customary meaning in English speaking countries ("giro" indicating printed matter). Consequently, the Board was correct to find that the mark informed customers of the product's use, and (2) writing "Giroform" as one word with an initial capital letter was not a significant departure from the normal English writing of the elements as two words in lower case letters, and was not therefore evidence of creativity capable of distinguishing the applicant's products from those of third parties, *Procter & Gamble Co v. Office for Harmonisation in the Internal Market (Trade Marks and Designs) (T163/98)* [2000] 1 W.L.R. 91, [1999] C.L.Y. 3533 and *Procter & Gamble Co v. Office for Harmonisation in the Internal Market (Trade Marks and Designs) (T122/99)* [2000] 2 C.M.L.R. 303, [2000] 6 C.L. 452 applied).

MITSUBISHI HITEC PAPER BIELEFELD GmbH (FORMERLY STORA CARBONLESS PAPER GmbH) v. OFFICE FOR HARMONISATION IN THE INTERNAL MARKET (TRADE MARKS AND DESIGNS) (OHIM) (T331/99) [2001] E.T.M.R. 57,V Tiili, CFI (4th Chamber).

4005. Trade marks – Community trade marks – distinctiveness – words with different meanings in different countries

[Council Directive 89/104 on trade marks; Council Regulation 40/94 on the Community trade mark Art.7(1).]

S applied for registration of the word VITALITE as a Community trade mark, in relation to a wide range of goods in classes 5, 29 and 32. The application was initially refused in its entirety, but was successfully appealed in part, although the Board of Appeal excluded many goods from each of the three classes from registration. The Board found that the word VITALITE might be read in France as "vitalit" (English "vitality"), since in French, capital letters do not generally bear accents. This reading would render the sign descriptive, and lacking in distinctive character for many of the goods in the three relevant classes, within the meaning of Council Regulation 40/94 on the Community trade mark Art.7(1)(b) and 7(1)(c). S appealed further, arguing that since VITALITE had already been registered in several EU member states (including French speaking states), a refusal to register ran counter to Council Directive 89/104 on trade marks which sought to bring together national trade mark laws and to further the aim of free movement of goods within Europe.

Held, allowing the appeal solely in respect of "food for babies" and "mineral and aerated waters", that VITALITE, even when read as "vitalite", did not directly and immediately describe any of the characteristics of those products, and was not therefore precluded by the provisions of Art.7(1)(b) or (c) of the Regulation. The registration of the mark in other EU countries was in different form from that in respect of which Community registration was sought, and accordingly S's contention in relation to the Directive failed.

SUNRIDER CORP v. OFFICE FOR HARMONISATION IN THE INTERNAL MARKET (TRADE MARKS AND DESIGNS) (OHIM) (T24/00) [2001] E.T.M.R. 56, J Pirrung (President), CFI.

4006. Trade marks – Community trade marks – distinctiveness of word mark "EUROHEALTH" for financial affairs services

[Council Regulation 40/94 on the Community trade mark Art.7.]

DKV appealed against a decision of the appeal board of the OHIM upholding the refusal of its application for registration of the word "EuroHealth" as a Community trade mark in respect of insurance and financial affairs under Council Regulation 40/94. The appeal board had found that the word was both devoid of distinctive character under Art.7(1)(b) and was purely descriptive thus precluding its registration under Art.7(1)(c).

Held, allowing the appeal in part, that although the board of appeal had been justified in refusing registration of "EuroHealth" on account of its purely descriptive character in relation to health insurance services, the term was not purely descriptive in relation to financial affairs services. OHIM had not established a sufficient association between the content of the term and financial affairs such as to enable target consumers to make a definite and direct association with those services, therefore the connection between "EuroHealth" and the financial services concerned was too indeterminate to be precluded by Art.7(1)(c). Further, the board of appeal had concluded that the sign was devoid of distinctive character because it was purely descriptive in relation to the services referred to, however, as the sign was not purely descriptive in relation to financial services, it could not be considered to be indistinct. It followed therefore that OHIM's decision refusing registration should be annulled in so far as it referred to financial services.

DEUTSCHE KRANKENVERSICHERUNG AG (DKV) v. OFFICE FOR HARMONISATION IN THE INTERNAL MARKET (TRADE MARKS AND DESIGNS) (OHIM) (T359/99) [2001] E.T.M.R. 81, Judge not specified, CFI.

4007. Trade marks – Community trade marks – "EASYBANK" for on-line banking – distinctiveness

[Council Regulation 94/40 on Community trade mark Art.7(1)(b), Art.7(1)(c).]

A applied to register 'EASYBANK' as a Community trade mark for on-line banking services. The application and subsequent appeal were unsuccessful on the grounds that the word was descriptive and devoid of distinctive character. A appealed.

Held, allowing the appeal, that (1) in finding that the term 'EASYBANK' was exclusively descriptive of the services of an on-line bank the Board of Appeal had erred in its interpretation of Council Regulation 94/40 Art.7(1)(c). When combined with the word 'bank' the word 'easy' was intended to give potential customers the impression that in general the bank itself was accessible and using its services would be free from difficulty or effort. The term did not designate either objectively or specifically any of the banking services actually on offer. The link between the meaning of the term 'EASYBANK' and the services capable of being provided by an on-line bank was too vague and indeterminate to confer a descriptive character on the term in relation to such services. Accordingly, the term could not be said to be exclusively descriptive within the meaning of Art.7(1)(c), and; (2) the Board of Appeal had further erred in law in basing its finding as to lack of distinctive character under Council Regulation 94/40 Reg.7(1)(b) on its finding that the term was descriptive under Reg.7(1)(c). A lack of distinctive character could not be demonstrated simply through the absence of an additional element of imagination or through a sign not looking unusual or striking. Art.7(1)(b) required an examination of whether the sign in question made it impossible for the public at whom was aimed to distinguish the goods or services to which it related from other goods or services. The Board had not addressed that question in the present case and therefore its decision would be annulled.

BANK FUR ARBEIT UND WIRTSCHAFT AG v. OFFICE FOR HARMONISATION IN THE INTERNAL MARKET (TRADE MARKS AND DESIGNS) (OHIM) (T87/00) [2001] C.E.C. 73, AWH Meij (President), CFI.

4008. Trade marks – Community trade marks – exclusively descriptive of goods and service

[Council Regulation 40/94 on the Community trade mark Art.7(1)(b), Art.7(1)(c).]

T applied for the annulment of the decisions refusing registration of the words "Universaltelfonbuch" and "Universalkommunikationsverzeichnis" as Community trade marks in respect of goods and services. Registration had been refused on the basis that the words were devoid of distinctive character and purely descriptive pursuant to Council Regulation 40/94 Art.7(1)(b) and Art.7(1)(c). It was submitted that the words were not exclusively descriptive as consumers would have to make a considerable intellectual effort in order to understand the message contained therein and further, that the disputed words were composed of a combination of words and constituted new words which were devoid of any obvious meaning.

Held, refusing the application, that in the German speaking parts of the Community, the words were exclusively descriptive in nature with regard to the goods and services in respect of which registration was refused under the Regulation. The words were correctly constructed in accordance with German grammar and when translated, they meant "universal telephone directory" and "universal communications directory" respectively. The combination of the words was not unusual and there was no doubt that the average German speaking consumer would immediately establish a direct association between those goods and services covered by the applications for registration of the marks.

TELEFON & BUCH VERLAGS GmbH v. OFFICE FOR HARMONISATION IN THE INTERNAL MARKET (TRADE MARKS AND DESIGNS) (OHIM) (T357/99) [2001] 3 C.M.L.R. 3, P Mengozzi (President), CFI.

4009. Trade marks – Community trade marks – infringement – revocation of mark for non-use

[Trade Marks Act 1994 s.10(1), s.10(2), s.46(5); Council Regulation 40/94 on the Community trade mark Art.50(1)(a), Art.50(1).]

DL, the holder of two registered trade marks for cleaning products with essentially a non-domestic use, brought an action for infringement against FB. DL maintained that FB had used a sign identical to the registered marks contrary to the Trade Marks Act 1994 s.10(1). FB counterclaimed, seeking the revocation of the trade marks for non-use under s.46(1)(a) of the Act and Council Regulation 40/94 Art.50(1)(a). FB contended that the registration should be limited to use for the decontamination of certain substances only, with the result that there would be no infringement of the resulting registration, and that the mark was in any event liable to revocation under s.46(1)(a) of the Act and Art.51(1) of the Regulation as DL had been acting in bad faith when applying to register it in that it had had no bona fide intention to use it.

Held, giving judgment for DL and allowing the counterclaim, that (1) FB had infringed the marks under s.10(1) and s.10(2) of the Act. The marks could not be revoked due to non-use within the first five years of registration. However, partial revocation could take place where non-use had not been total pursuant to s.46(5), *MINERVA Trade Mark* [2000] F.S.R. 734, [2000] 11 C.L. 364 applied and *Premier Brands UK Ltd v. Typhoon Europe Ltd* [2000] E.T.M.R. 1071, [2000] 3 C.L. 417 not applied. Revocation in part was only justified if the proprietor was able to demonstrate actual confusion. It was not expedient to give the proprietor of a mark greater protection than his use of it warranted by widening the specification of goods, each case depending on its own facts. The marks in the instant case should accordingly be revoked to the extent of the present specification subject to the qualification "all for non-domestic use", and (2) the objection of bad faith was only available in limited circumstances, *Trillium Digital Systems Inc's Trade Mark* [2000] E.T.M.R. 1054 (Note)) applied. It was unlikely, but not impossible, that a decision in relation to the width of the specification of goods would be made in bad faith.

DECON LABORATORIES LTD v. FRED BAKER SCIENTIFIC LTD [2001] E.T.M.R. 46, Pumfrey, J., Ch D.

4010. Trade marks – Community trade marks – medicines – evidence of risk of confusion – opponent's duty to adduce

[Council Regulation 40/94 on the Community trade mark Art.43(2), Art.73, Art.74(1); Commission Regulation 2868/95 implementing Council Regulation 40/94 on the Community trade mark r.22.]

L applied to register the sign ENANTYUM as a Community trade mark for "a non steroidal anti-inflammatory drug (NSAID) indicated for the treatment of pain of mild to moderate intensity, of different aetiology, such as dysmenorrhea, dental pain, surgical procedures, traumas, sprains and pain associated with inflammatory conditions" in Class 5. TC opposed the application on the ground that the opponent had already registered the trade marks ENANTON and ENANTONE in Denmark, Finland, France and Sweden for a variety of similar pharmaceutical products and that granting the application would create the risk of confusion. The Opposition Division found in favour of T. L appealed, arguing that there was no risk of confusion in relation to the goods covered by its trade mark application, given the difference in use, cost and administration methods between the two products. Further, that the Opposition Division had not considered an implicit request for T to produce evidence of use and had failed to take into account only those goods for which T had used its marks, not all the goods for which the mark was registered, as required by Council Regulation 40/94 Art.43(2).

Held, allowing the appeal and dismissing the opposition, that (1) it was a principle of adversarial opposition proceedings that a fact was taken to be admitted if it was not denied; (2) T had not availed itself of the opportunity to deny L's assertion as to use of the trade mark on an individual product, even thought the necessary information was within its knowledge; (3) Commission Regulation 2868/95 r.22 provided that an opponent had to show use or reason for non use under Regulation 40/94 Art.43(2) or (3) within a specified time period, with the opposition liable to rejection for non compliance; (5) Art.43(2) placed an opponent under a duty to provide evidence of use when asked. The emphasis being on provision, rather than the method or form of the request; (6) the Opposition Division had breached of Art.73 of Regulation 40/94 as part of its decision was based on a reason that L had not been allowed to address, and (7) Regulation 40/94 Art.74(1) had also been breached because the decision to allow the opposition was not restricted to an examination of the facts, evidence and arguments provided by the parties.

LABORATORIOS MENARINI SA v. TAKEDA CHEMICAL INDUSTRIES LTD [2001] E.T.M.R. 65, K Sundstrom (Chairman), Office for Harmonization in the Internal Market (Second Board of Appeal).

4011. Trade marks – Community trade marks – opposition based on similarity to earlier German mark – risk of confusion

[Council Regulation 40/94 on the Community trade mark Art.8(1)(b).]

DU applied for the registration of a Community trade mark in respect of the words DUCKS UNLIMITED. The mark was sought for outer clothing for children and adults, caps, sports wear and footwear in class 25. R opposed the application under Council Regulation 40/94 Art.8(1)(b), on the grounds of similarity to an earlier mark in that R had prior ownership of a figurative mark that included the words "ducks unlimited" in relation to duck-down-filled clothing.

Held, allowing the opposition, that the goods covered by DU's application were similar to those covered by R's mark. They were of the same essential nature and were often sold in the same outlets to the same end users. The words "ducks unlimited" were the dominant feature of R's mark so that the two marks shared phonetic and conceptual similarities that were likely to lead to confusion.

DUCKS UNLIMITED'S TRADE MARK APPLICATION (849/1999) [2000] E.T.M.R. 820, P Geroulakos, Office for Harmonization in the Internal Market (Opposition Division).

4012. Trade marks – Community trade marks – pharmaceutical preparations – colours applied to inhalers – likelihood of confusion

[Trade Marks Act 1994 s.3(1).]

R applied for invalidation of Glaxo's trade mark (coloured maroon and pink) in respect of inhalers. R claimed that the mark was registered in breach of the Trade Marks Act 1994 s.3(1), as it was (1) devoid of any distinctive character; (2) consisted exclusively of signs which served in the pharmaceutical trade to designate the intended purpose of the goods, and (3) consisted exclusively of a sign which had become customary within the pharmaceutical trade to designate intended purpose and strength of the product. For R it was further suggested that the colour pink, as used in the trade mark, was, when applied to inhalers, an indication that the product was stronger than the usual dosage and registration was contrary to public policy because it was said to be of particular concern to asthma sufferers that the colour of inhalers be used to describe the strength of the product therein, no matter who the manufacturer might be.

Held, allowing the application for invalidation, that (1) R had not identified any public policy regarding the use of colours on inhalers and, given that the Department of Health had no such policy, it was not for the Registrar to introduce one via the Trade Marks Act; (2) the fact that the choice of colours had not been used before in relation to inhalers did not mean that those colours were inherently distinctive; (3) the registered trade mark was not readily capable of distinguishing the goods of one undertaking and was, therefore devoid of any distinctive character and excluded from registration by s.3(1)(b) of the 1994 Act, and (4) there was no evidence of continuing use such as to give the mark an acquired distinction.

GLAXO GROUP LTD'S TRADE MARK [2001] E.T.M.R. 9, A James, TMR.

4013. Trade marks – Community trade marks – prior registration for use in same class – evidence of risk of confusion

P applied to register a sign containing a figurative element and the words PAYLESS CAR RENTAL as a trade mark in Class 39. C, a company resident in the Canary Islands, opposed the application on the grounds of its 1985 Spanish registration of the word mark PAYLESS for car rental services in Class 39 and claimed a likelihood of confusion because of similarity between the marks and the identical nature of the services. As evidence of use, C submitted photographs of signs at its branches, stickers, stationery, a picture of a car with the mark on its side, advertising material and letters in Spanish expressing an interest in buying the mark.

Held, allowing the application, that evidence proving use of a mark had to show the location, purpose and extent of the use of the opposing mark. The material submitted did not meet those requirements. Further, the letters were not evidence of use as they could have been motivated by the fact of registration.

PAYLESS CAR RENTAL SYSTEM INC'S TRADE MARK APPLICATION [2000] E.T.M.R. 1136, Panayotis Geroulakos, Office for Harmonization in the Internal Market (Opposition Division).

4014. **Trade marks – Community trade marks – procedure – mark surrendered following cancellation application – entitlement to determination of validity**

D was the proprietor of the word mark AROME TONIQUE, registered in Class 3 for cosmetic products. In January 1999, L obtained registration of the word mark AROMATONIC in the same class and D sought cancellation of L's registration on the grounds that it lacked distinctive character and consisted solely of indications that described the makeup or characteristics of the goods covered by the mark. D also argued that L had acted in bad faith in seeking registration, and that D was entitled to restrain L's use of mark in the United Kingdom by an action for passing off. L surrendered its Community registration of the AROMATONIC mark and sought the conversion into applications for national trade marks in each Member State. Following the surrender, D requested a that proceedings be continued before the Cancellation Division to obtain the Division's finding on the existence of grounds for invalidity of L's mark prior to the date it was surrendered.

Held, allowing the application, that (1) L's surrender of the Community registration of AROMATONIC and its request for conversion gave D a legitimate interest in seeking resumption of the original cancellation proceedings; (2) AROMATONIC did not lack distinctiveness and the combination of the elements constituting the mark had no particular meaning when applied to the goods for which it was registered, and (3) there was no bad faith on L's part in obtaining registration of AROMATONIC and it had tried to reach an arrangement with D for the co-existence of the two marks before proceeding with its registration application.

LANCOME PARFUMS ET BEAUTE & CIE'S COMMUNITY TRADE MARK APPLICATION [2001] E.T.M.R. 89, Herbert E Meister (Chairman), Office for Harmonization in the Internal Market (Cancellation Div).

4015. **Trade marks – Community trade marks – registration – descriptive or generic nature of word mark**

P applied to register the word mark K GLASS as a Community trade mark for sheet glass not including glass fibre or optic fibre products in Classes 19 an 21. The examiner rejected the application on the grounds that the words were a generic trade term for glass fibres, as evidenced by four US patents, and that they were indicative of a special type of glass used for glass fibre and optical fibre production. P appealed, contending that the glass referred to in its application differed from that in the US patents and that K GLASS was not a generic term for sheet glass.

Held, allowing the appeal, that K GLASS was not generic for glass in sheet form. Further, the words had already been accepted for registration in several Community Member States, and this was a fact from which the Board could take reassurance as to their eligibility for registration as a Community trademark, *POLY COLOR Trade Mark* (Unreported, September 21, 1999) applied. National decisions could also be relevant where, as in the instant case, the mark had been examined according to the language of the Member State of registration.

PILKINGTON PLC'S TRADE MARK APPLICATION (K GLASS) [2000] E.T.M.R. 1130, S Sandri (Chairman), Office for Harmonization in the Internal Market (Third Board of Appeal).

4016. Trade marks – Community trade marks – registration – distinctiveness – word mark "Cine action"

[Council Regulation 40/94 on the Community trade mark Art.7 (1).]

T applied for registration of the words CINE ACTION as a Community trade mark. Registration was sought for a wide range of goods in classes 9 and 16, and a wide variety of services in classes 38, 41 and 42. The Examiner rejected the application under Council Regulation 40/94 on the Community trade mark Art.7 (1) (b) and 7 (1) (c) for lack of distinctive character, and on the ground that the mark consisted solely of words relating to the character and quality of the relevant goods or services. The applicant appealed to the Third Board of Appeal, which held that CINE was understood in several European languages as pertaining to film and cinema, and that in modern colloquial German, ACTION was an abbreviation for "action film". Germans would therefore interpret CINE ACTION as meaning "action films". The Board reinstated the application in respect of goods in classes 9 and 16, and certain services in classes 38, 41 and 42, remitting the application to the Examiner for fresh consideration. The Board dismissed T's appeal in relation to the remaining services within classes 38, 41 and 42 as well as T's application for the costs of the appeal on the basis that insufficient reasons had been advanced for the rejection of the application. T pursued a further appeal.

Held, allowing the appeal in part, that (1) grounds for a refusal of registration under Arts.7 (1) (b) and 7 (1) (c) of the Regulation could only be assessed in relation the goods and services for which registration of the relevant sign was sought, *Procter & Gamble Co v. Office for Harmonisation in the Internal Market (Trade Marks and Designs) (T163/98)* [2000] 1 W.L.R. 91, [1999] C.L.Y. 3533 applied; (2) the appeal would be allowed in respect of allocation and transfer of rights of access for users of various communication networks within class 38, along with cultural activities, quizzes and musical events, and various services connected with broadcasting and entertainment within class 41, and dealings in copyright, industrial rights and media technology within class 42. This was on the basis that, in respect of these services, CINE ACTION as a mark could not be said to be merely descriptive, or devoid of even a "minimum of imagination", and (3) since the Third Board of Appeal had not fallen into substantial procedural error in the delivery of its decision, there were no grounds for ordering reimbursement of appeal fees to T.

TAURUS FILM GmbH & CO v. OFFICE FOR HARMONISATION IN THE INTERNAL MARKET (TRADE MARKS AND DESIGNS) (OHIM) (T135/99) [2001] E.T.M.R. 55, Judge J Pirrung, CFI (2nd Chamber).

4017. Trade marks – Community trade marks – registration – word mark "BLOOD PRESSURE WATCH" – lack of distinctiveness

[Council Regulation 40/94 on the Community trade mark Art.7 (1) (c).]

M sought to register the words "BLOOD PRESSURE WATCH" as a Community trade mark for Class 10 goods (sphygmomanometers). The examiner objected on the basis that those words were commonly used in English to describe goods so that the mark lacked distinctive character. M contended that the mark was not descriptive and had already been registered in France, Germany and Italy. The application was refused and M appealed to the First Board of Appeal.

Held, dismissing the appeal, that the phrase "blood pressure watch" would immediately cause people to think of a watch like device used to monitor blood pressure. Although "watch" was a commonly used English word with different meanings, it did not confer any special status on the term "blood pressure watch". In allowing registration in Germany, the national court had found that foreign language word marks were only excluded in Germany if they were easily recognised as a technical term or used descriptively for imported or exported goods and domestic products. Therefore the fact of German registration did not amount to a guiding principle for defining descriptive character under Council Regulation 40/94 Art.7(1)(c).

MATSUSHITA ELECTRIC WORKS LTD'S TRADE MARK APPLICATION [2000] E.T.M.R. 962, H Preglau (Chairman), Office for Harmonization in the Internal Market (First Board of Appeal).

4018. Trade marks – Community trade marks – registration of mark "SENSO DI DONNA" – likelihood of confusion

A Community trade mark SENSO DI DONNA was registered for a variety of classes of goods, including footwear. M was the owner of earlier SENSO trade mark registrations in respect of footwear and applied for a declaration of invalidity in respect of the registration as it applied to footwear claiming that it had been registered in bad faith. M claimed that the use of the mark would deceive the public into believing that it was connected with the SENSO mark and that its use would take unfair advantage of, or be detrimental to, the distinctive character of the SENSO mark. The proprietor of the Community trade mark argued that the marks were different enough to prevent any likelihood of confusion. It further contended that the Community trade mark had a definitive meaning as a whole, namely "the sense of a woman" as opposed to "sense" alone.

Held, declaring the registration invalid, that (1) bad faith was to be interpreted as unfair practices involving a dishonest intent on the part of the applicant of the Community trade mark at the time of filing. In the instant case there was no evidence that the applicant had acted dishonestly or was involved in unfair practices or the like, but (2) the products in question, namely footwear, were identical and the dominant element of the sign "SENSO" was visually and phonetically similar. There was also a conceptual similarity between the marks.

SENSO DI DONNA'S TRADE MARK [2001] E.T.M.R. 5, Herbert E Meister (Chairman), Office for Harmonization in the Internal Market (Cancellation Div).

4019. Trade marks – Community trade marks – registration of word "TRUSTEDLINK" – lack of distinctiveness

[Council Regulation 40/94 on the Community trade mark Art.7(1).]

H applied for a Community trade mark for the term "TRUSTEDLINK" in respect of various computer and internet products and services. The term was already registered as a trade mark in the United States. H's application was refused on the ground that the sign "TRUSTEDLINK" was devoid of any distinctive character and that refusal was upheld by the Board of Appeal. H appealed contending that the term was not devoid of any distinctive character since it had not been shown to be cumulatively devoid of distinctive character under all the grounds of absolute unregistrability. H further claimed that the Board had failed to give reasons for its analysis with regard to each class of goods and services for which protection was sought.

Held, dismissing the appeal, that (1) for a sign to be ineligible for registration as a Community trade mark under Council Regulation 40/94 Art.7(1), it was sufficient that one of the absolute grounds for refusal applied. Joining the words "trusted" and "link" did not give them any additional characteristic which, taken as a whole, rendered them capable of distinguishing the applicant's goods and services from those of other undertakings; (2) it was clear from the Board's decision that the facts and legal considerations that it relied on to justify the lack of distinctiveness of the sign applied to all the classes of goods and services in respect of which registration was requested, and (3) the United States trade mark registration was not binding on the office.

HARBINGER CORP v. OFFICE FOR HARMONISATION IN THE INTERNAL MARKET (TRADE MARKS AND DESIGNS) (OHIM) (T345/99) [2001] E.T.M.R. 2, V Tiili (President), CFI.

4020. Trade marks – Community trade marks – risk of confusion with earlier unregistered mark – disputed mark not completely descriptive

[Council Regulation 40/94 on the Community trade mark.]

MSI obtained a Community trade mark in the form of a representation of a mortar and pestle for pharmaceutical products in class 5 and related services in class 42. CMR sought a declaration of invalidity on the grounds that the mark should not have been registered, since it was descriptive of MSI's products and services in terms of Art.7(1). Further, that CMR had an earlier trade mark right in a similar sign, by virtue of Art.8(4) and Art.52(1)(c), because of its use in Ireland for identical goods. In the alternative, should validity be upheld, CMR applied for an order for a disclaimer to show that the protection was limited only to MSI's specific representation.

Held, refusing the application, that the two marks were dissimilar. The Examination Division was responsible for permitting registration of MSI's mark, and enjoyed a certain discretion in that regard. The mark itself did not completely describe MSI's goods and services, but in any event, the Cancellation Division was of equal status with the Examination Division and did not have the power to substitute its own discretion for that of the Examination Division on an application for an invalidity declaration. The Cancellation Division did not have the power to order a disclaimer, although the Office could do so when appropriate on an application for a Community trade mark under Art.38(2).

CAHILL MAY ROBERTS LTD'S APPLICATION FOR A DECLARATION OF INVALIDITY; *sub nom.* MEDICINE SHOPPE INTERNATIONAL'S COMMUNITY TRADE MARK [2000] E.T.M.R. 794, Herbert E Meister (Chairman), Office for Harmonization in the Internal Market (Cancellation Div).

4021. Trade marks – Community trade marks – similarity to existing registered mark but entirely different goods – likelihood of confusion

[Council Regulation 40/94 on the Community trade mark.]

L applied to register as a Community trade mark the words, "LONG JOHN SILVER'S" for foods and confections and restaurant and franchising services. The application was opposed by S, the owner of an earlier trade mark "JOHN SILVER" registered in Sweden and applying to cigarettes. S claimed that there was a likelihood of confusion because its earlier mark had a reputation and that using the contested mark would take advantage of, or be detrimental to, the distinctive character or the repute of the earlier mark. L claimed that there was no likelihood of confusion and that the use of the contested mark would not take an unfair advantage, or be detrimental to, the distinctive nature or the repute of the earlier mark.

Held, dismissing the opposition, that (1) the earlier Swedish registration had not been clearly identified within the opposition period. There had been no indication of the earlier right's registration or application number, and (2) considering, in relation to the goods in issue, their nature, their end user and their method of use and whether they were in competition with, or complementary to, each other, it could not be considered that "cigarettes" and "restaurants" were either identical or similar in terms of Council Regulation 40/94.

LONG JOHN SILVER'S, INC'S APPLICATION [2001] E.T.M.R. 11, Tomas de las Heras, Office for Harmonization in the Internal Market (Opposition Division).

4022. Trade marks – Community trade marks – University with intellectual property rights in Einstein's name and likeness – unregistered trade name

[Council Regulation 40/94 on the Community trade mark Art.8(4).]

ESH applied to register the word "EinStein" for food and beverages in Classes 30, 32 and 33. HUJ opposed the application under Council Regulation 40/94 Art.8(4), on the grounds of a prior unregistered mark used within the Community and ownership of Einstein's intellectual property rights, including use of his name and likeness for all goods and services. HUJ filed copies of Einstein's will in support, together with an agreement ceding the intellectual property rights of all beneficiaries to a trust set up by the will in HUJ.

Held, dismissing the opposition, that the rights invoked by HUJ were not indicative of unregistered marks or trade usage in terms of Art.8(4). The documents filed in support only showed that Einstein's name and likeness had been licensed for use for goods and services outside the Community and it could not be determined that the unregistered mark HUJ contended for had indeed ever been used within the Community.

EINSTEIN STADTCAFE VERWALTUNGS-UND BETRIEBSGESELLSCHAFT MBH'S TRADE MARK APPLICATION [2000] E.T.M.R. 952, P Geroulakos, Office for Harmonization in the Internal Market (Opposition Division).

4023. Trade marks – comparative advertising – infringement – malicious falsehood

[Trade Marks Act 1994 s.10(1), s.10(6), s.11(2)(b); Council Directive 97/55 concerning misleading advertising so as to include comparative advertising.]

BA brought an action against R, a rival airline, alleging trade mark infringement and malicious falsehood arising from two advertisements. The advertisements, which made comparisons of the fares offered on specified routes, were headed "EXPENSIVE BA − − DS"and "EXPENSIVE BA" respectively. BA submitted that (1) the use by R of the exact registered trade mark "BA" fell within the Trade Marks Act 1994 s.10(1), and (2) the "BA − − DS" headline was offensive and the price comparisons within the adverts unfair.

Held, giving judgment for R, that (1) the references to BA's trade mark constituted honest comparative advertising for the purposes of s.10(6) and s.11(2)(b) of the Act. The Comparative Advertising Directive 97/55 did not qualify s.10(6) *Cable & Wireless Plc v. British Telecommunications Plc* [1998] F.S.R. 383, [1998] C.L.Y. 3507 applied, and (2) in an action concerning comparative advertising, a claim for trade mark infringement was not generally aided by the addition of the tort of malicious falsehood. The claim for malicious falsehood itself failed since the advertisements could not be considered as false. The "average consumer" would not be misled by the price comparisons, which in any case were sufficiently accurate. Moreover, the slogan "EXPENSIVE BA − − DS" amounted to no more than vulgar abuse.

BRITISH AIRWAYS PLC v. RYANAIR LTD [2001] E.T.M.R. 24, Jacob, J., Ch D.

4024. Trade marks – confusion – dual branding

[Trade Marks Act 1994 s.3(6), s.5(2)(b).]

G, the makers of Coronation Street, applied to register the mark BETTY'S KITCHEN CORONATION STREET for goods in Classes 29 and 30, including eggs and dairy products, preserves, snack foods, pies, hot pots, biscuits, cakes, pastry and puddings and deserts. B owned a number of restaurants and tea rooms in Yorkshire and also operated a food and drink mail order business. B had a number of earlier trade mark registrations for the mark BETTYS and opposed G's application under the Trade Marks Act 1994 s.3(6) and 5(2)(b).

Held, refusing the application, that (1) G's use of the mark applied for was neither normal nor fair. The mark as it appeared on G's product packaging was not such that customers would regard BETTY'S KITCHEN and CORONATION STREET as elements of a composite mark. There was no real intention to use the mark in the form applied for so that G's dealings were below the accepted standards of commercial behaviour, *Gromax Plasticulture Ltd v. Don & Low Nonwovens Ltd* [1999] R.P.C. 367, [1999] C.L.Y. 3592 referred to, and (2) G could only show actual use in relation to pies and hot pots and had not adduced evidence of preparations for its use in relation to other goods in the specification. The opposition succeeded under s.3(6) and s.5(2)(b). B had shown that there was a likelihood of confusion in that use of its marks broadly matched the coverage of its registrations and the distinctiveness of its marks was enhanced by their public reputation. B had produced persuasive evidence of public awareness of dual branding and there was a real risk that a significant number of people would believe that the mark was a further example of this, indicating a connection between BETTYS and the Coronation Street programme, *Sabel BV v. Puma AG (C251/95)* [1997] E.C.R. I-6191, [1998] C.L.Y. 3512 and *Canon Kabushiki Kaisha v. Metro Goldwyn Mayer Inc (C39/97)* [1998] All E.R. (EC) 934, [1998] C.L.Y. 3526 referred to.

BETTY'S KITCHEN CORONATION STREET TRADE MARK [2000] R.P.C. 825, M Reynolds, TMR.

4025. Trade marks – confusion – word mark "UNITED" – prior registration of "Manchester United"

R's application to register the mark UNITED for bottled beer and non alcoholic drinks in Class 32 was opposed by MU, a football club, on the ground of its prior registration of the mark RED TRIBE for beers in Class 32 and word and badge marks consisting of "MANCHESTER UNITED" for non alcoholic drinks in Class 32. MU contended that it had acquired a close association with the word UNITED because of its football tradition and that there was a likelihood of confusion with its own marks if R's registration was allowed, especially if R were to use the mark on a red background.

Held, dismissing the opposition, that (1) the RED TRIBE mark had no bearing on the opposition; (2) the distinctiveness of the MANCHESTER UNITED mark subsisted in the entire mark, and not simply in the word UNITED, which MU shared with other clubs; (3) it was unlikely that the marks would be confused looking at the matter globally in terms of the perception of an average consumer, based on an assessment of the similarities between the marks and the degree of possible association in the public mind, *Sabel BV v. Puma AG (C251/95)* [1997] E.C.R. I-6191 and *Canon Kabushiki Kaisha v. Metro Goldwyn Mayer Inc (C39/97)* [1998] All E.R. (EC) 934 applied; (4) MU had no trade mark registration for the colour red, which was also used by other football clubs. Further, the likelihood that R would print UNITED on a red background was not a point to be considered, and (5) there was no evidence to show that MU could succeed in an action for passing off should R use the UNITED mark.

RYGRANGE LTD'S TRADE MARK APPLICATIONS [2001] E.T.M.R. 78, M Reynolds, TMR.

4026. Trade marks – distinctiveness – antibiotic tablet shape – evidence of pharmaceutical industry practice – South Africa

[Trade Marks Act 1993 (South Africa) s.10(1); Trade Marks Act 1994.]

T sought an order to expunge B's trade mark 95/13154 in Class 5 from the Register of Trade Marks. The trade mark was registered in respect of antibiotics and consisted of the curved shape of a tablet. T and B were trade competitors with T importing and selling Augmaxcil, the generic equivalent of B's product, Augmentin. The shape of T's product was the same as B's product and expungement was sought on the ground that the registered shape lacked distinctiveness. B counterclaimed for an injunction to restrain T's alleged infringing behaviour and for unfair competition.

Held, allowing the application and dismissing the counterclaim, that (1) a mark was incapable of distinguishing a product unless the public knew that it was a trade mark; (2) recognition of an article could not be equated with that article's capacity to fulfil the purposes of a trade mark; (3) T's evidence showed that the same shape was commonly used by pharmaceutical producers; (4) when dealing with the Trade Marks Act No. 194 of 1993 s.10(1), decisions on the corresponding provisions of the United Kingdom Trade Marks Act 1994 were applicable and, in the case of a shape mark, that shape had to be of a distinctive character, *Philips Electronics NV v. Remington Consumer Products Ltd (No.1)* [1999] E.T.M.R. 816, [1999] C.L.Y. 3564 referred to, and (5) a balance had to be struck between a manufacturer's right to identify its products and the right of free competition and public policy prevented a functional feature from being protected by an action for passing off or trade mark infringement.

TRIOMED (PROPRIETARY) LTD v. BEECHAM GROUP [2001] F.S.R. 34, Smit, J., Prov Div (SA).

4027. Trade marks – distinctiveness – applicable test

[Trade Marks Act 1994 s.3(1)(b).]

K, who sold a cultured milk drink under the brand name "Yakult", appealed against a decision of the Registrar of Trade Marks refusing to register as a mark the shape of the bottle in which Yakult was sold. The Registrar had concluded that the shape was devoid of distinctive character and that it had not become distinctive through use.

Held, dismissing the appeal, that (1) when considering the question of distinctive character under the Trade Marks Act 1994 s.3(1)(b), the test to be applied was whether the mark had a meaning which denoted the origin of the goods even before the public had been educated that the mark was to be used for that purpose. K had been unable to demonstrate that the public would realise that the bottle was intended as an indication of origin, and (2) the sales, marketing and survey evidence adduced by K was insufficient to show that the shape of the bottle had become distinctive through use.

KABUSHIKI KAISHA YAKULT HONSHA'S TRADE MARK APPLICATION (NOS.1260017 AND 1560018); *sub nom.* YAKULT HONSHA KK'S TRADE MARK APPLICATION (NOS.1260017 AND 1560018) [2001] R.P.C. 39, Laddie, J., Ch D.

4028. Trade marks – distinctiveness – evidence of "genuine use" – alternative form to that of registered mark

[Trade Marks Act 1994 s.46(1)(a), s.46(1)(b), s.46(2).]

M had registered the trade mark SECOND SKIN in Class 5 for "medical and surgical bandages; plasters and dressings, all for medical or surgical use; material prepared for bandaging". S sought revocation of the registration on the ground that it had not been in "genuine use" for five years, as required by the Trade Marks Act 1994 s.46(1)(a) and (b). Although M could not show a "genuine use", it contended that it had used the mark 2ND SKIN for wound dressings and claimed that the two marks were indistinguishable as they shared common pronunciation and were identical if used in telephone sales.

Held, allowing the application in part and ordering revocation for all uses except surgical and medical dressings, that (1) M had failed to show use on "medical and surgical bandages; plasters; material prepared for bandaging". Oral use by customers would not satisfy the requirements of s.46(1)(a), and (2) the public seeing 2ND SKIN would translate it into SECOND SKIN. The marks represented alternatives to each other in everyday use and were interchangeable without loss of meaning. Therefore 2ND SKIN came within s.46(2) as it was a use of the trade mark in different form that did not affect the mark's distinctive character in its registered form, *ELLE Trade Marks (Revocation)* [1997] E.T.M.R. 552, [1997] C.L.Y. 4903 applied.

SECOND SKIN TRADE MARK [2001] R.P.C. 30, Stephen Rowan, TMR.

4029. Trade marks – distinctiveness – likelihood of confusion – similarity with goods and services included in earlier mark

[Trade Marks Act 1994 s.5(2), s.5(4); Council Directive 89/104 on trade marks Art.13.]

R, a charity with the object of furthering education amongst young people through the exploration of undeveloped regions, applied to register the mark RALEIGH INTERNATIONAL and a globe device as a trade mark in September 1995 for use in relation to goods and services in Classes 16, 21, 25, 26, 36 and 41. In May 1997, D, the proprietor of the famous mark RALEIGH, used mainly for bicycles, filed notice of opposition, contending that registration should be refused under Trade Marks Act 1994 s.5(2) and s.5(4). D claimed that different products in addition to bicycles were manufactured under licence. However, the evidence was not sufficient to establish that such licensing took place prior to September 1995. The hearing officer allowed the R's application with amendments excluding use for clothing for cyclists and cycling related badges. D appealed.

Held, dismissing the appeal, that (1) there was no objection to registration under s.5(2) where it was not shown that the public would believe goods and services came from the same producer or a linked undertaking, including licensed or joint venture arrangements, *Canon Kabushiki Kaisha v. Metro Goldwyn Mayer Inc (C39/97)* [1998] All E.R. (EC) 934, [1998] C.L.Y. 3526, *IHT Internationale Heiztechnik GmbH v. Ideal Standard GmbH (C9/93)* [1994] E.C.R. I-2789, [1994] C.L.Y. 4870 and *Bayerische Motorenwerke AG v. Deenik (C63/97)* [1999] All E.R. (EC) 235, [1999] C.L.Y. 3550 followed; (2) an earlier mark's distinctive character had to be taken into account when determining if the similarity between goods and services covered by two trade marks was sufficient to cause confusion, therefore an objection under s.5(2) could succeed based on the distinctiveness and reputation of the earlier mark, even if people would not expect the same producer or a linked undertaking to supply those types of goods or services; (3) a highly distinctive earlier trade mark could be afforded wider protection than less distinctive marks. However, merely increased use was not proof of distinctiveness; (4) trade marks used under licence had to be examined in the context of that use and whether it increased the mark's distinctiveness and reputation, which was a question of fact; (5) objections under s.5(2) had to be based on the likelihood of confusion that would exist even if the earlier trade mark had not been used for goods or services beyond those for which it was registered. Evidence of such use could only go to the question of whether the goods or services featured in the opposed application and those in the earlier registration could be seen as similar; (6) Council Directive 89/104 Art.13 envisaged that a trade mark application could be restricted if necessary to confine use to that for which the mark was fully registrable. Therefore, a mark had to be assessed in terms of its normal and whether this would impinge on the earlier mark's distinctiveness leading to confusion; (7) the word RALEIGH was the primary distinguishing feature of R's application. Since D's earlier mark was international in context, the word INTERNATIONAL and the globe in R's application would not prevent the likelihood of confusion if used in a cycling related context; (8) D's evidence did not show that the distinctiveness of its earlier mark had been increased by licensed use, and (9) the amended specification of R's mark did not include items covered by D's mark.

RALEIGH INTERNATIONAL TRADE MARK [2001] R.P.C. 11, Geoffrey Hobbs Q.C., Appointed Person.

4030. **Trade marks – distinctiveness – three dimensional mark – obligation to refer to ECJ**

[Trade Marks Act 1994 s.3, s.76(3); Trade Mark Rules 1994 (SI 1994 2583) r.38.]

M's application to register a three dimensional trade mark relating to the shape of a tine for agricultural and horticultural use in Class 7 was rejected by the hearing officer under the Trade Marks Act 1994 s.3(1)(a) and (b) and s.3(2)(b) and (c). He determined that the bulbous end of the tine and the configuration of the fixing end were used to achieve a technical effect and were features amounting to minor embellishments. People would think that they made the tine easier to fit and prolonged its working life. The evidence did not show a sufficient degree of recognition of the tine's shape as a trade mark. He therefore concluded that the shape was incapable of distinguishing M's goods so that it was excluded from registration by s.3(1)(a). Further, he did not think that the shape possessed a distinctive character through use so that it was also excluded by s.3(1)(b). M appealed but then applied to adjourn the appeal pending the ECJ's ruling in *Philips Electronics NV v. Remington Consumer Products Ltd (No.1)* [1999] E.T.M.R. 816, [1999] C.L.Y. 3564, and that if the adjournment was not granted, it would seek its own reference to the ECJ on the interpretation of s.3(2)(b), and that if that order was not made it would seek an order under s.76(3) for an appeal to the High Court. The Appointed Person decided that the Registrar's objections under s.3(1) should be considered at a substantive hearing. If the shape was excluded by s.3(1) the matter would end there. If not, the hearing would be adjourned to await the ECJ's decision in *Philips Electronics*. M then sought an adjournment of the appeal pending a reference to the ECJ.

Held, refusing the adjournment but referring the appeal to the High Court under s.76(3), that (1) the obligation to request a preliminary ruling from the ECJ applied to courts of last resort, not those whose decisions could be appealed or were susceptible to judicial review, *Chiron Corp v. Murex Diagnostics Ltd (No.8)* [1995] All E.R. (E.C.) 88, [1995] C.L.Y. 4201 referred to. As the Registrar's decisions were susceptible to judicial review it was therefore within his discretion to make a reference to the ECJ, bearing in mind that s.76(3) and the Trade Mark Rules 1994 r.58 allowed appeals to the High Court on points of general legal importance; (2) the presence of functional or technical features in a three dimensional shape was to be considered when assessing distinctive character for registration purposes. Such features could designate intended purpose or other characteristics of the goods to the extent that the shape as a whole was unregistrable under s.3(1)(a) to (d); (3) "exclusivity" under s.3(2) had to be considered and guidance could be needed from the ECJ. However, it was likely that this would be given in *Philips Electronics*, but in the meantime there was no bar to the court considering the effect of s.3(1) on the application, *Dualit Ltd's Trade Mark Application (No.2023846)* [1999] R.P.C. 890, [1999] C.L.Y. 3583 and *Procter & Gamble Ltd's Trade Mark Applications (Detergent Bottles)* [1999] E.T.M.R. 375, [1999] C.L.Y. 3567 referred to, and (4) therefore it was unnecessary to adjourn the consideration of the application of s.3(1) pending the decision in *Philips Electronics*, nor was there a need for a referral to the ECJ on the questions raised by M.

MAASLAND NV'S APPLICATION FOR A THREE DIMENSIONAL TRADE MARK; *sub nom.* MAASLAND NV'S TRADE MARK APPLICATION (NO.2000360), *Re* [2000] R.P.C. 893, G Hobbs Q.C., Appointed Person.

4031. Trade marks – distinctiveness – use of initials

Financial Systems Software, who had applied to register the letters "FSS" as a trade mark in respect of computer programming services, appealed against a decision of the judge that the mark had not become distinctive through use.

Held, dismissing the appeal, that the judge had been entitled to conclude (1) that others in the field of computer programming would be likely to want to use the initials "FSS" as an abbreviation of their own and that the three letter mark was therefore inherently incapable of distinguishing the services of one provider from those of another, *W&G du Cros Ltd's Application, Re* (1913) 30 R.P.C. 660 applied, and (2) that use of the mark other than as an abbreviation had been insignificant.

FINANCIAL SYSTEMS SOFTWARE (UK) LTD v. FINANCIAL SOFTWARE SYSTEMS INC; *sub nom.* FINANCIAL SYSTEMS SOFTWARE (UK) LTD'S TRADE MARK APPLICATION [2001] EWCA Civ 386,[2001] R.P.C. 41, Chadwick, L.J., CA.

4032. Trade marks – European Economic Area – proprietorial consent to marketing of goods obtained outside EEA – European Community

[First Council Directive 89/104 on Trade Marks Art.7(1).]

A number of questions relating to the interpretation of the Trade Marks Directive 89/104 Art.7 were referred to the ECJ for a preliminary ruling. Z had an exclusive distribution contract with a third party based in Singapore whereby Z's products were only to be sold to retailers or sub-distributors located in specified territory outside the European Economic Area, EEA. A condition was imposed prohibiting further resale outside the specified territory. A acquired a stock of Z's products which had originally been placed on the market in Singapore and began to sell them in the United Kingdom. Z brought proceedings in the UK alleging that A was acting in breach of its trade mark rights. The national court sought guidance on the interpretation to be given to consent in the context of Art.7 and asked whether (1) the consent of a trade mark proprietor to marketing in the EEA could be implied; (2) implied consent could be inferred from the mere silence of a trade mark proprietor, and (3) the consequence of ignorance, on the part of the trader importing the marked goods into the EEA, of the proprietor's expressed opposition to such imports.

Held, giving a preliminary ruling, that (1) the consent of a trade mark proprietor to the marketing within the EEA of products bearing its mark, such products having previously been placed on the market outside the EEA by that proprietor or with his consent, could be implied where the facts and circumstances prior to, simultaneous with, or subsequent to the placing of the goods on the market outside the EEA, unequivocally demonstrated that the proprietor had renounced his right to oppose the placing of the goods on the market within the EEA; (2) implied consent could not be inferred from the fact that; (a) the trade mark proprietor had not communicated to all subsequent purchasers outside the EEA his continued opposition to marketing within the EEA; (b) the goods carried no warning of the prohibition; (c) ownership was transferred without a contractual reservation prohibiting resale within the EEA, and (3) with regard to the exhaustion of the proprietor's exclusive right, it was not relevant that the importer was ignorant of the objections to resale in the EEA or that the authorised retailers had failed to impose a contractual reservation on subsequent purchasers setting out such opposition.

ZINO DAVIDOFF SA v. A&G IMPORTS LTD (C414/99); LEVI STRAUSS & CO v. TESCO STORES LTD (C415/99); LEVI STRAUSS & CO v. COSTCO WHOLESALE UK LTD (C416/99); *sub nom.* LEVI STRAUSS & CO v. TESCO PLC (C415/99) [2002] Ch. 109, GC Rodriguez Iglesias (President), ECJ.

4033. **Trade marks – infringement – interim injunctions – time limit for commencing substantive proceedings – applicability of TRIPS Agreement Art.50(6) – European Union**

[Agreement on Trade-Related Aspects of Intellectual Property Rights 1994 Art.50(6).]

S appealed to the Dutch Supreme Court against an order for interim relief in trade mark infringement proceedings brought by G, arguing that the order had expired as substantive proceedings had not been commenced within the time limits of the Agreement on Trade-Related Aspects of Intellectual Property Rights 1994 Art.50(6). The court referred to the ECJ for a preliminary ruling on the interpretation of Art.50 and the AG gave his opinion.

Held, giving a preliminary ruling, that (1) in areas covered by both Community law and the Agreement, Member States were required to apply their domestic law pertaining to provisional measures in keeping with Art.50 of the Agreement; (2) Community law did not require Member States to allow individuals to rely directly on Art.50(6) or for their courts to apply it on their own motion; (3) under Art.50(6) a party against whom provisional measures had been ordered had to request revocation and where a decision ordering such measures did not stipulate a commencement date for proceedings on the merits the relevant time limit was a matter for the national law. It was consistent with Art.50(6) for time either to run from the date provisional measures were ordered or the date that decision was served, and (4) national law determined whether an appellate court could set time limits for the commencement of proceedings on the merits.

SCHIEVING-NIJSTAD VOF v. GROENEVELD (C89/99); *sub nom.* VOF SCHIEVING-NIJSTAD v. GROENEVELD (C89/99) [2001] E.T.M.R. 59, Advocate General Jacobs, AGO.

4034. **Trade marks – infringement – passing off – manufacture in accordance with owner's specification – requirement for adoption of goods by owner**

[Trade Marks Act 1994 s.10(1).]

P applied for summary judgment on its claim against L of trade mark infringement and passing off. L had supplied to a retailer clothing which was apparently identical to clothing sold by P bearing the labels of "Primark" and "Denim Co". P asserted that it only ever sold its clothing in its own retail outlets. L submitted that the goods had been manufactured by P's own supplier and could have been P's actual clothing.

Held, granting the application, that L had no arguable defence. The goods labelled "Primark" were identical to P's clothing and were clearly an infringement of P's trade mark pursuant to the Trade Marks Act 1994 s.10(1). The labelling "Denim Co" was so closely similar to P's labelling of "Denim Company" as to be capable of causing confusion in the minds of the public as to the origin of the clothes contrary to s.10(2). Even if the clothes had been manufactured to P's specification, the purpose of the trade mark encompassed not only that the goods would be of a particular origin, but also that P would stand by their quality. P had not had the opportunity to assess the quality of the "Primark" clothes, and therefore the clothes could not be said to be P's property, *Glaxo Group Ltd v. Dowelhurst Ltd (Infringement Action)* [2000] 2 C.M.L.R. 571, [2000] 4 C.L. 416 applied. Similarly the fact that P did not allow its clothes to be sold in other outlets as a matter of course meant that the suppliers did not have consent to supply the clothes to L, and L therefore had no defence to the passing off action, *Vokes v. Evans* (1932) 49 R.P.C. 140 applied.

PRIMARK STORES LTD v. LOLLYPOP CLOTHING LTD [2001] E.T.M.R. 30, John Martin Q.C., Ch D.

4035. **Trade marks – infringement – use of "MERC" by clothing retailer – likelihood of confusion with "MERCEDES"**

[Trade Marks Act 1994 s.10(3).]

DC, the proprietor of the registered marks "Mercedes" and "Mercedes-Benz", brought an action against A, the owner of a shop called "Merc" selling clothing and shoes, alleging trade mark infringement and passing off. DC argued that the sign "Merc" was likely to be confused with its registered marks and that A's use of the sign would damage the reputation of its marks since A's business was targeted at mods, skinheads and casuals, none of which groups it wished to be associated with.

Held, giving judgment for A, that while evidence existed that the word "Merc" was used as an abbreviation for the name of the car, there was no evidence either that A's sign was likely to be confused with DC's marks or that the reputation of DC's marks had been damaged by A's use of the sign. DC had failed to meet the requirements of the Trade Marks Act 1994 s.10(3) whereby the claimant had to show either that the association between its mark and the defendant's sign had caused the defendant to gain an unfair advantage from the association or that the association had resulted in the reputation of its mark being damaged.

DAIMLER CHRYSLER AG v. ALAVI (T/A MERC); *sub nom.* DAIMLERCHRYSLER AG v. ALAVI [2001] E.T.M.R. 98, Pumfrey, J., Ch D.

4036. **Trade marks – infringement – VIAGRA anti-impotence product – proposed VIAGRENE aphrodisiac drink – likelihood of confusion**

[Trade Marks Act 1994 s.10(2); Council Directive 89/104 on trade marks Art.5(1)(b).]

P was the owner of the UK trade mark and Community trade mark VIAGRA and marketed Viagra as a prescription-only pharmaceutical treatment for male impotence. P became aware that E was seeking to launch VIAGRENE, a drink intended to be promoted as an aphrodisiac. P commenced actions against E for infringement of trade marks under the Trade Marks Act 1994 s.10(2) and Council Directive 89/104 Art.5(1)(b).

Held, giving judgment for P, that (1) for the purposes of s.10(2) the likelihood of confusion in a case where neither the trade marks nor the goods were identical had to be assessed as a matter of global appreciation taking all the relevant factors into account, *Sabel BV v. Puma AG (C251/95)* [1997] E.C.R. I-6191, [1998] C.L.Y. 3512 applied. In order to be able to make a global assessment of the likelihood of confusion there had to be some interdependence between the relevant factors; specifically there needed to be some similarity between the trade marks and between the goods, *Canon Kabushiki Kaisha v. Metro Goldwyn Mayer Inc (C39/97)* [1998] All E.R. (EC) 934, [1998] C.L.Y. 3526 applied. There was no automatic bar to a finding of infringement under s.10(2) merely because the goods were in some respects dissimilar, and (2) on the facts, there was a substantial similarity between the trade marks which were inherently likely to be confused if used in relation to similar goods. Although the goods were superficially different, they were similar in that they were both designed to appeal to men suffering from impotence. There was a real likelihood that members of the public seeing the trade mark VIAGRENE would assume a connection with the manufacturer of VIAGRA and accordingly, P's trade marks in the United Kingdom and in the Community had been infringed.

PFIZER LTD v. EUROFOOD LINK (UNITED KINGDOM) LTD [2000] E.T.M.R. 896, SimonThorley Q.C., Ch D.

4037. Trade marks – infringement – websites – appropriate measure of damages

[Civil Procedure Rules 1998 (SI 1998 3132) Part 3 r.3.4(2).]

R applied for judgment on admissions for trademark infringement and for summary judgment for passing off against M. The claims had arisen after R alleged that M had used meta-tags to re-direct users away from R's website to its own. RCS sought damages for use of its website, corrective advertising, diversion of trade and general damages for goodwill. M subsequently applied for the claims to be struck out under the Civil Procedure Rules 1998 Part 3 r.3.4(2), contending that it had no prospects of success and that resources would be wasted on both sides. M further argued that it had given an undertaking to remove the meta-tags and that RCS had suffered no damage. R countered that it was reasonable to pursue the claim and that it had received no proper undertaking from M.

Held, giving judgment for the claimant, that (1) the jurisdiction of r.3.4 was a narrow one that should not be readily invoked and that R had done nothing which amounted to an abuse of process; (2) there had been a clear infringement of trade mark; (3) all of the ingredients in respect of the passing off claim had been made out and M had put forward no defence, and (4) a trade mark was a property right for the purpose of the user principle and that R was entitled to an award of £15,000 under that head of claim. However, R was not entitled to the costs of corrective advertising to counteract the effect of the infringement as the advertisements had not been published promptly and there was insufficient evidence that there had been a significant diversion of trade as little access to MMDS's website had occurred as a result of its actions. Similarly there had been insufficient impact upon R to justify any award under the goodwill head of claim.

ROADTECH COMPUTER SYSTEMS LTD v. MANDATA (MANAGEMENT AND DATA SERVICES) LTD [2000] E.T.M.R. 970, Master Bowman, Ch D.

4038. Trade marks – licences – grant of bare exclusive licence – likelihood of misleading customers

[Trade Marks Act 1994 s.11(2), s.46(1)(d); Trade Marks Directive 89/104 Art.12(2)(b).]

SD, proprietor of the trade mark "SCANDECOR" and a related logo mark, appealed against an order ([1999] F.S.R. 26, [1998] C.L.Y. 3519) that the marks should be revoked. SD and SM had been formed as a result of a split in founding company, S. SM had been entitled to use the marks on its own goods pursuant to the grant of a licence by SD. Following termination of the licence, SM continued to carry on business as Scandecor and SD carried on a competing business using the trade marks. SD brought infringement proceedings and SM counterclaimed for revocation of the marks on the basis that they had ceased to be distinctive. The trial judge ([1998] F.S.R. 500) did not revoke the registration of the marks but held that SM was entitled to continue trading as Scandecor. On appeal, the marks were revoked. SD contended that the marks were valid whilst SM maintained that use of the marks by SM with consent of SD as the registered proprietor was "liable to mislead" retailers such as to justify revocation under the Trade Marks Act 1994 s.46(1)(d). SM maintained that grant of a bare licence to use a trade mark necessarily resulted in a trademark losing its distinctiveness and that accordingly such bare licences were inherently objectionable as being liable to deceive, *McGregor Clothing Co Ltd's Trade Mark* [1979] R.P.C. 36, [1978] C.L.Y. 2970 cited.

Held, adjourning the appeal and making a reference to the ECJ, that the question of whether the use of a trademark by a bare exclusive licencee could lead to the mark being liable to mislead for the purposes of s.46(1) and the Trade Marks Directive 89/104 Art.12(2)(b), was of fundamental importance and accordingly required a reference to the ECJ.

Observed, that the approach to be preferred was that the "business source" of the goods in question was the proprietor or licencee for the time being of the relevant trade mark. Such an approach accorded with current business practice and customer perceptions. The potential for would be reduced by the fact that if a trade mark owner did not take an interest in the quality of the goods produced by a particular licencee, the value of his brand would diminish. Accordingly during the period that the marks were operated by SM as a duly authorised licencee they would not have been liable to mislead.

SCANDECOR DEVELOPMENT AB v. SCANDECOR MARKETING AB [2001] UKHL 21, [2001] 2 C.M.L.R. 30, Lord Nicholls of Birkenhead, HL.

4039. Trade marks – origin marking – "PARFUMS DE PARIS" – goods manufactured in UK – risk of confusion

[Trade Marks Act 1994 s.3(3)(b), s.5(4).]

M applied to register the words "MCL PARFUMS DE PARIS" in class 3 for goods, including soaps, toiletries, perfumes, suntanning preparations and dentifrices. FIP, an association of French parfumiers, opposed the application on the grounds, inter alia, that the mark indicated that the goods concerned were manufactured in Paris or France, and thus likely to mislead the public as to their nature or geographical origin under the Trade Marks Act 1994 s.3(3)(b). Further, that the application should be refused as the use constituted passing off, contrary to s.5(4).

Held, upholding the opposition in part, that (1) judicial notice would be taken of the international reputation for perfume enjoyed by France, and Paris in particular; (2) although M had evidenced an intention to obtain perfume oils from France, the goods were to be manufactured in the UK. Use of the words "Parfums de Paris" created an expectation that the products would be manufactured there. If the actual specification of the goods did not reflect that expectation, then it would be likely to mislead the public as to the origin, nature and quality of M's goods; (3) FIP's opposition under s.3(3)(b) would be upheld, except for dentifrices, which were not expected to be perfumed; (4) the objection could be overcome, however, by limiting the scope of the mark to those goods that were either produced in Paris or scented with perfume produced there, and (5) FIP's objection under s.5(4) could not be upheld in the absence of evidence on an industry-wide basis that the reputation of Paris parfumiers would be harmed by M's use of the mark.

MADGECOURT LTD'S TRADE MARK APPLICATION (NO.2104616) [2000] E.T.M.R. 825, M Knight, TMR.

4040. Trade marks – origin marking – "WARSTEINER" used for beer brewed elsewhere – European Union

[Council Regulation 2081/92 on the protection of geographical indications and designations of origin for agricultural products and foodstuffs Art.1(1), Art.2(2)(b).]

W, a brewery located in Warstein, Germany, owned the German trade mark "WARSTEINER" for Pilsener style beer. W acquired another brewery in Paderborn, where it produced two types of beer, each of which bore the mark WARSTEINER as part of its label description. The labels clearly stated that the beers were brewed in Paderborn. Warsteiner was the adjectival form of the place name "Warstein" and that beer brewed in Warstein had no qualities peculiar to that particular locality. The reputation of Warsteiner branded beer was therefore due to the quality of the product and the marketing of its brand name. S, a German association with a statutory duty to counter unfair competition, brought proceedings in the national court contending that W's labels were misleading and that beer brewed in Paderborn should not be described as "Warsteiner". W responded that customers did not consider "Warsteiner" to be a reference to geographical origin, but that even if some did, appreciation of the beer was not dependent on local factors. S succeeded in its application for an injunction at first instance, but this was quashed on appeal. On a further appeal on a point of law, the court stayed the proceedings and referred to the ECJ for a preliminary ruling as to whether Council Regulation 2081/92 precluded national legislation prohibiting the misleading use of a geographic source designation where there was no link between a product's characteristics and its place of origin.

Held, giving a preliminary ruling, that Member States were required to regulate product marketing in the absence of relevant Community rules and by Art.1 (1) and Art.2(2)(b) the Regulation was restricted to origin designations and geographical indications provided for by the Regulation where quality, reputation or other characteristics were linked. The Regulation did not apply to mere geographical source indicators not linked to the product's characteristics or its geographical origin. Geographical indications could be protected by national law intended to prevent misleading used of such indicators, but these were restricted to the territory of the Member State concerned.

SCHUTZVERBAND GEGEN UNWESEN IN DER WIRTSCHAFT EV v. WARSTEINER BRAUEREI HAUS CRAMER GmbH & CO KG (C312/98) [2001] 2 C.M.L.R. 11, GC Rodriguez Iglesias (President), ECJ.

4041. Trade marks – passing off – football souvenirs and memorabilia – trade mark use as pre requisite to infringement

[Trade Marks Act 1994 s.10.]

A, a football club which had registered the words "Arsenal" and "Gunners" as well as the club emblem as trade marks in relation to sports clothing and footwear, brought an action against R, who sold souvenirs and memorabilia, alleging trade mark infringement and passing off. In relation to the allegation of passing off, A contended that the sale by R of various unlicensed souvenirs or memorabilia might mislead individuals into the belief that they were the "official" products of A, or goods associated with them. The allegation of infringement related to scarves bearing A's registered words and emblems. R denied passing off, maintaining that the registered words merely amounted to badges of allegiance and argued that for the purposes of the Trade Marks Act 1994 s.10, a sign had to be used as a trade mark.

Held, giving judgment for the defendant, that (1) on the balance of probabilities, A had not discharged the onus upon it to demonstrate that actual confusion had occurred as a result of R selling his souvenirs and memorabilia. It was apparent that some customers purchased such items merely because the signs they displayed indicated an allegiance to the football club. Given that R had carried on his business for over thirty years, the court could have regard to what had actually occurred. A had not produced any evidence to suggest that purchasers had ever complained of being confused. Moreover, R's products did not state a trade origin. A had not shown that R's method of trading suggested to a potential customer that his goods came from them, and (2) the question of whether a sign had to be used as a trade mark before it constituted infringement required resolution by the ECJ, *Philips Electronics NV v. Remington Consumer Products Ltd (No.1)* [1999] E.T.M.R. 816, [1999] C.L.Y. 3564 considered.

ARSENAL FOOTBALL CLUB PLC v. REED [2001] 2 C.M.L.R. 23, Laddie, J., Ch D.

4042. Trade marks – Registrar of Trade Marks – rectification – discretion of Registrar

[Trade Marks Act 1994 s.38, s.40, s.64, s.76 (3); Trade Marks Rules 1994 (SI 1994 2583) r.60.]

In December 1994, S applied to register a trade mark in Class 7 for, inter alia, power saws, mechanical cutting devices and domestic vacuum cleaners. The Trade Marks Registry objected to registration in that form and a revised specification was agreed. The revised speculation was then advertised in the Trade Marks Journal. However, due to an error, the advertisement failed to mention industrial vacuum and high pressure cleaners and also contained a typographical mistake. The application was accepted for registration, but when A's agents received the registration certificate it was noticed that the mark had been advertised and registered with an incorrect specification of goods. S sought rectification of the register so as to conform with the agreed specification. The hearing officer allowed rectification for the typographical mistake, but refused it in respect of the specification, on the ground that the scope of the registration would be extended from that which had been advertised. S appealed.

Held, referring the matter to the High Court under the Trade Marks Act 1994 s.76(3), that (1) allowing rectification would extend the registration to include matters that had not been advertised, which was precluded by s.64; (2) the registration was irregular under s.38 to s.40 as it contained a discrepancy between the application for registration and the registration as granted; (3) the registrar only had the statutory power to make a singular determination in the course of proceedings, so that a decision could only be revoked or modified once, *R. v. Cripps, ex p. Muldoon* [1984] Q.B. 686, [1984] C.L.Y. 2606 considered. Whilst there was a power to correct errors, which had been correctly exercised in the case of the typographical mistake, s.64 prescribed a wider power to correct errors of the kind in the instant case, *DUCATI Trade Mark* [1998] R.P.C. 227, [1998] C.L.Y. 3536 not followed, and (4) although S could have applied for the registration to be withdrawn under the registrar's discretionary powers and for the application to be re-advertised correctly, this would be contrary to the practice under the Trade Marks Rules 1994 r.60. Accordingly, the matter would be referred to the High Court.

ANDREAS STIHL AG & CO'S TRADE MARK APPLICATION [2001] R.P.C. 12, Geoffrey Hobbs Q.C., TMR.

4043. Trade marks – Registrar of Trade Marks – security for costs – discretion to order

[Trade Marks Act 1994 s.68(3); Civil Procedure Rules 1998 (SI 1998 3132); Trade Marks Rules 2000 (SI 2000 136) r.61.]

V opposed S's application to register the trade mark "JINI" and applied for security for costs on the grounds that S, a US company, was outside the jurisdiction. S opposed the security for costs application, arguing that it was in the same situation as a defendant, against whom costs could not be ordered, and as a multinational company with nine English subsidiaries it would in any event be able to meet a costs order against it. V was not represented at the hearing of the costs application and S sought a wasted costs order against V on an indemnity basis.

Held, refusing V's application for security for costs and S's application for a wasted costs order but ordering V to pay a contribution of £200 toward S's costs, that (1) the Civil Procedure Rules 1998 did not apply to proceedings before the Trade Marks Registrar but could be relied upon as a guide to the exercise of discretion, *ST TRUDO Trade Mark* [1995] F.S.R. 345 referred to; (2) the Registrar had power to order security for costs under the Trade Marks Act 1994 s.68(3) and the Trade Mark Rules 2000 r.61, but this did not apply in the instant case as S had assets within the jurisdiction, *Apollinaris Co's Trade Marks (No.1)* [1891] 1 Ch. 1 referred to; (3) V's conduct did not justify the making of a wasted costs order and it had genuinely believed that there was a valid issue to be decided, therefore the normal order for costs would apply, *Rizla Ltd's Trade Mark Application* [1993] R.P.C. 365 applied.

SUN MICROSYSTEMS INC'S TRADE MARK APPLICATION [2001] R.P.C. 25, Stephen Rowan, TMR.

4044. Trade marks – registration – alphanumeric telephone name

[Trade Marks Act 1938 s.10(2)(a), s.17(1).]

F, a United States company, appealed against the refusal ([2000] E.T.M.R. 369, [2000] C.L.Y. 3759) of its application to register under the Trade Marks Act 1938 s.17(1) the trade mark "800-FLOWERS" in respect of services consisting of the receipt and transfer of orders for flowers and floral products. P, who had opposed the application, cross appealed against the summary assessment of its costs. F had the right to use in the US the toll free telephone number 1-800-356-9377 which on an alphanumeric telephone keypad translated to 1-800-FLOWERS. P had the right to use the United Kingdom telephone number 0800-365-9377. The judge had found that, inter alia, the mark did not have the requisite inherent capacity to distinguish F's services for the purposes of s.10(2)(a) of the Act since it was no more than an encoded telephone number.

Held, dismissing the appeal and allowing the cross appeal, that the judge had been correct to refuse the application. The mark had been adopted as a result of its telephonic significance, F having been aware at the time of applying to register it that the use of alphanumeric phone names in the UK was on the increase. Further, as the mark was no more than an encoded telephone number and F did not have the right to use it in the UK, it would inevitably cause confusion. F had not been able to prove actual use of the mark in the UK, and any future use was dependent on it acquiring the corresponding UK number. In relation to the cross appeal, the judge had erred in failing to examine the costs P had actually incurred and applying his own tariff. It was observed that the jurisdiction to summarily assess costs should not be used as a means of introducing a range of judicial tariffs for different categories of case.

1-800 FLOWERS INC v. PHONENAMES LTD; *sub nom.* 800-FLOWERS TRADE MARK, [2001] EWCA Civ 721, [2001] 2 Costs L.R. 286, Jonathan Parker, L.J., CA.

4045. Trade marks – registration – amendment of classification – ultra vires

[Trade Marks Act 1994 s.32, s.34, s.39.]

A, the applicant in a trade mark application, appealed against a decision that an amendment to the classification of its mark was ultra vires. The registrar had held that the original erroneous classification was not an obvious mistake within the terms of the Trade Marks Act 1994 s.39(2)(c) and thus could not be amended.

Held, allowing the appeal, that there had been no need to show that the erroneous classification had been an obvious mistake as the application to change class was not an application to amend under s.39. The amendment had been a permissible exercise of the registrar's powers under s.34. The classification of a trademark, for the purposes of registration, was for administrative convenience and was not a critical requirement. It followed that the failure to state such a class did not constitute a breach of s.32. Moreover, final classification lay with the registrar.

ALTECNIC LTD'S TRADE MARK APPLICATION (NO.2126884); *sub nom.* ALTECNIC LTD v. RELIANCE WATER CONTROLS LTD [2001] R.P.C. 37, Laddie, J., Ch D.

4047. Trade marks – registration – application by unconnected party – bad faith

[Trade Marks Act 1994 s.5(4).]

K, had applied to register the mark NONOGRAM in classes 9 and 28 for, inter alia, coin operated game machines, computer games, video games, toys and playthings, and electronic games. K claimed to have made the application in order to protect the interests of N who had invented a numerical puzzle. N had, in fact, entered into an agreement with D, whereby D was to be her agent in the UK in relation to the publication of her puzzles in UK newspapers. D suggested publication under the name NONOGRAM. K agreed to transfer the application to N, but D argued that the application had been made in bad faith because K had no connection to the mark for which application was made, and that defect would not be cured by the subsequent assignment of the application to N. Further, D contended that he was the true owner of the mark because he had devised it, and that use by K of the mark on goods unconnected with either D or N would have been actionable as passing off at the suit of either the opponent or N under the Trade Marks Act 1994 s.5(4).

Held, refusing registration, that since K was not the owner of the mark at the date of the original application then notwithstanding the assignment, the application was fatally flawed. It was not in conformity with acceptable commercial behaviour and therefore lodged in bad faith, making refusal mandatory (*Gromax Plasticulture Ltd v. Don & Low Nonwovens Ltd* [1999] R.P.C. 367, [1999] C.L.Y. 3592 followed).

NONOGRAM TRADE MARK [2001] R.P.C. 21, Judge not applicable, TMR.

4048. Trade marks – registration – classification

TRADE MARKS (AMENDMENT) RULES 2001, SI 2001 3832; made under the Trade Marks Act 1994 s.34, s.65, s.78. In force: January 1, 2002; £1.75.

These Rules amend the Trade Marks Rules 2000 (SI 2000 136) to reflect the reclassification which has taken place of trade mark registrations dated before July 27, 1938, and to allow for classification under the Eighth Edition of the International Classification of Goods and Services on or after January 1, 2002. The Rules also revoke the classification system in force before July 27, 1938 and allow applications made before January 1, 2002 to proceed under Sch.3.

4049. Trade marks – registration – distinctiveness – three headed rotary shaver

[Council Directive 89/104 on trade marks Art.3.]

P had marketed an electric shaver comprising three rotary heads configured as an equilateral triangle since 1966. P filed a trade mark application in 1985 in relation to a picture of an electric shaver possessing the said characteristics. Registration was granted. P marketed its shavers extensively in the UK, and became well known there in respect thereof. R began to manufacture and market a three headed rotary shaver in the UK in 1995. The configuration of the shaving heads was similar to that of P's product. P commenced proceedings against R claiming inter alia infringement of its trademark. R counterclaimed, seeking revocation of P's trade mark. At first instance, R's counterclaim was upheld on the basis that it was not capable of distinguishing the goods concerned and lacked distinctive character. It was also held that P's trade mark consisted exclusively of a sign intended to designate the intended purpose of the goods, and of a configuration necessary to achieve a technical result. The sign also gave substantial value to the goods. P appealed. The Court of Appeal stayed the appeal and referred a number of questions to the Court of Justice in relation to the operation of Council Directive 89/104 on trade marks Art.3.

Held, giving an opinion, that the Court of Appeal had presented a number of questions of which only one (the fourth) required an answer in order to determine the present case. That question was in three parts: (1) given Art.3(1)(e)(ii) provided that a mark might not be registered where "...it consists exclusively of the shape of goods which is necessary to achieve a technical result", is this restriction overcome if it is shown that the same technical result could be achieved by other shapes? (2) is the shape unregisterable by virtue thereof if it is shown that the essential features of the shape are attributable only to the technical result? (3) is some other, and if so what, test appropriate for determining whether the restriction applies? The answer was that Art.3(1)(e) must be interpreted as meaning that any shape the essential features of which serve the achievement of a technical result must be regarded as a sign which consists exclusively of the shape of goods which is necessary to obtain such result, irrespective of whether it is possible to achieve that result using other shapes. If a sign meets those conditions, there is no need to consider whether it has any distinctive character.

PHILIPS ELECTRONICS NV v. REMINGTON CONSUMER PRODUCTS LTD (C299/99) [2001] E.T.M.R. 48, Advocate General Ruiz-Jarabo Colomer, AGO.

4050. **Trade marks – registration – distinctiveness of trade mark "Diana, Princess of Wales"**

[Trade Marks Act 1994 s.3(1)(b).]

S and M, the executrices of the estate of Diana, Princess of Wales, applied to register the words DIANA, PRINCESS OF WALES as a trade mark to control the trade in memorabilia and commemorative items bearing Diana's name. They contended that, following her death, use of the name in connection with any product would be taken by the public to be authorised by the memorial fund or the estate.

Held, refusing the application, that (1) as a living person could not own the rights to their own name, Diana, Princess of Wales, had no exclusive right to use her name for commercial purposes when she was alive, *ELVIS PRESLEY Trade Marks* [1999] R.P.C. 567, [1999] C.L.Y. 3574 followed; (2) a name unique to a particular person did not of itself have distinctive character as a trade mark. The essential function of a trade mark was to guarantee that the items bearing it had originated under the control of a single undertaking responsible for their quality. Unless, therefore, such control could be shown, the use of a famous name to endorse a product was not a trade mark use. In the instant case, the average consumer would not have expected all commemorative items bearing Diana's name to be marketed under the control of a single undertaking. The fact that the estate had resorted to additional means of denoting official authorisation, namely the use of a logo and hallmark suggested that it was not confident that the use of her name alone would guarantee a trade connection between the goods and the estate. Accordingly, at the date of the application the words DIANA, PRINCESS OF WALES did not have the distinctive character required for a trade mark and were excluded from registration by the Trade Marks Act 1994 s.3(1)(b).

DIANA, PRINCESS OF WALES TRADE MARK [2001] E.T.M.R. 25, Judge not specified, TMR.

4051. **Trade marks – registration – distinctiveness of "VISION DIRECT" – descriptive nature of mark**

R unsuccessfully sought to register the word mark VISION DIRECT for software designed to manage travel expense information. In the light of the dictionary definitions of the words "vision" and "direct", the examiner considered that the mark lacked distinctiveness and was descriptive of R's product. R appealed.

Held, allowing the appeal and remitting the case for further examination, that (1) a mark may be distinctive if it merely hints at but does not describe some characteristic of the goods, and (2) the relevant consumer would not regard VISION DIRECT as being descriptive of R's computer software without an effort of the imagination, *Easyplan (R 109/1998-2), Re* (Unreported, February 11, 1999) distinguished.

ROSENBLUTH INTERNATIONAL INC'S TRADE MARK APPLICATION [2000] E.T.M.R. 934, K Sundstrom (Chairman), Office for Harmonization in the Internal Market (Second Board of Appeal).

4052. **Trade marks – registration – French phrase descriptive of product in English translation**

[Trade Marks Act 1994 s.3(1).]

L applied to register the French words TONALITE HENNE, meaning "henna hue" in Class 3 for henna hair colouring, hair dyes, hair waving preparations, hair cosmetics, hair lotions and shampoos. W successfully opposed the application on the ground that the mark consisted solely of a sign that served in the trade to designate the quality, type or other characteristics of the goods, pursuant to the Trade Marks Act 1994 s.3(1)(b) or (c). L appealed, contending that, although the English translation of the word would not be registrable, the burden moved to W in the case of a foreign language to show that consumers would understand the mark to have a descriptive meaning in English. Further, that insufficient weight had been accorded to the fact that the mark had been registered in France.

Held, dismissing the appeal, that (1) foreign words did not have to be examined for registrability by reference to their translated meaning. Translations ensured that foreign words were not registered where their meaning was unknown. The less obscure a foreign word was, the greater the weight to be given to its meaning in translation, *EL CANAL DE LAS ESTRELLAS Trade Mark* [2000] R.P.C. 291, [2000] C.L.Y. 3766 followed; (2) although the burden of proof was on W to show that the words had a descriptive meaning when translated, the evidence in the instant case was sufficient to transfer the burden to L to show that the actual meaning would be lost on the average consumer, and L had not done so; (3) even if the average consumer did not translate TONALITE as "hue", this meaning would occur in the context of beauty products, once the language was recognised as French. Caution should therefore be exercised in respect of applications for marks in a foreign language that were descriptive in English, and (4) although harmonisation was important, registration in other countries had to be considered in the light of cultural, social and factual differences.

TONALITE HENNE TRADE MARK [2001] R.P.C. 36, Simon Thorley Q.C., Appointed Person.

4053. Trade marks – registration – honest concurrent use – likelihood of confusion

[Trade Marks Act 1994 s.5(2)(b), s.7.]

CDS applied to register the mark CODAS in Classes 9, 37, 41 and 42 in respect of computers, software and related services for use in the oil distribution industry, having used the mark continuously since 1975 for computer applications in that industry. C opposed the application on the basis of its existing trade mark registrations for CODA and similar marks, which it had used continuously in the UK since 1981 for various financial, accounting and sales computer software and associated design, consultancy and training purposes. Many of C's customers were in the oil industry, however, there were no instances of confusion between the respective marks. CDS therefore claimed that the application should be allowed on the basis of honest concurrent use under the Trade Marks Act 1994 s.7.

Held, allowing the application subject to restriction in respect of Class 9, that (1) where an application had been opposed under s.5(2)(b) by the owner of an earlier trade mark s.7(2) did not make refusal mandatory. If an opposition was filed, then it had to be determined whether the grounds for refusal were made out. In relation to s.5(2), the fact that there had been actual concurrent use would be relevant in determining whether there was a likelihood of confusion. Honest concurrent use was therefore not a defence capable of saving an application, but it was one of the relevant factors to be taken into account when deciding the likelihood of confusion; (2) C's marks for CODA were nearly identical to CODAS, particularly when used in the plural. Similarly, C's marks for CODA-IAS and CODA OAS had a high degree of similarity; (3) limiting the scope of the application to the oil distribution industry would have no effect given the range of goods and services that could be used in an industry. The restriction did not affect the similarity between CDS's goods and services and those of C, and (4) CDS had only used the CODAS mark for certain goods in Class 9 and there was a likelihood of confusion if the application proceeded as applied for. However, since no instances of confusion had arisen to date, limiting the application to the goods for which there had been concurrent use would obviate this likelihood.

CODAS TRADE MARK [2001] R.P.C. 14, M Foley, TMR.

4054. Trade marks – registration – inclusion of "OLYMPIC" in mark – opposition by International Olympic Committee

B applied to register a word-and-device sign "Family Club Belmont Olympic" in relation to business management services and the distribution, transport and storage of goods. The application was opposed by IOC, the International Olympic Committee, based on IOC's prior international registration of the word OLYMPIC and the registration in France of the trade name COMITE INTERNATIONAL OLYMPIQUE.

Held, rejecting B's application for all goods and services, that given the high profile of IOC's mark in France, B's use without due cause of a mark which included the sign OLYMPIC was likely take unfair advantage of, or be detrimental to, the distinctiveness and reputation of IOC's mark, even though B's goods and services were different from those for which IOC had gained its reputation.

BELMONT OLYMPIC SA'S TRADE MARK APPLICATION [2000] E.T.M.R. 919, Benoit Lory, Office for Harmonization in the Internal Market (Opposition Division).

4055. Trade marks – registration – likelihood of confusion – word mark "Momentum"

[Council Regulation 40/94 on the Community trade mark Art.8(4).]

ME applied to register the word mark MOMENTUM for services in classes 35,36 and 42 (advertising, sports sponsorship, design consultancy etc) in January 1997. M opposed the application claiming to have used the trade mark "Momentum" for some years prior to the application in respect of similar services. M contended that it was entitled to restrain ME's use of the mark in suit by an action for passing off.

Held, dismissing ME's application, that the parties' marks were identical, that the opponent had used its mark for some years prior to the application, and the use by M of the mark (which was unregistered) was more than of "merely local significance" under Council Regulation 40/94 on the Community trade mark Art.8(4).

McCANN ERICKSON ADVERTISING LTD'S TRADE MARK APPLICATION [2001] E.T.M.R. 52, Mauro Buffolo, OHIM (Opposition Div).

4056. Trade marks – registration – likelihood of confusion with existing mark – relevant considerations

[Trade Marks Act 1994 s.5(2).]

R appealed against the refusal to grant its application for registration of the mark "10 Royal Berkshire POLO CLUB" for perfumery, cosmetic and toiletry products. The application had been opposed by P, the owner of an earlier mark, "POLO", which was registered in the same class and for similar products. P had successfully argued that registration should be refused pursuant to the Trade Marks Act 1994 s.5(2), the hearing officer finding, inter alia, that the use of the word "POLO" in R's mark was likely to cause confusion amongst the general public. R submitted that the hearing officer had overestimated the significance that consumers would attach to the word "POLO" in its mark.

Held, allowing the appeal, that the issue to be determined when considering an objection under s.5(2) of the Act was whether there were similarities between the marks which would create a likelihood of confusion amongst the general public, and such objections were to be considered in the light of commercial reality and from the perspective of "the average consumer" in the ordinary course of trade. An objection under s.5(2) could not be upheld if there was no possibility that consumers could form the opinion that the goods had originated from a common or financially linked supplier. In general, the more distinctive a mark, the more protection it would be given; however mere use of a mark did not in itself establish its distinctiveness. In the instant case, the two marks were distinguishable because of the use of the numeral 10 in R's mark and since R's mark used the word "POLO" as an adjective rather than as a noun, *Lloyd Schuhfabrik Meyer & Co GmbH v. Klijsen Handel BV (C342/97)* [1999]

All E.R. (EC) 587, [1999] C.L.Y. 3538 and *European Ltd v. Economist Newspaper Ltd* [1998] E.T.M.R. 307, [1998] C.L.Y. 3509 applied.

POLO LAUREN CO'S TRADE MARK APPLICATION; *sub nom*. 10 ROYAL BERKSHIRE POLO CLUB TRADE MARK [2001] R.P.C. 32, Geoffrey Hobbs Q.C., TMR.

4057. Trade marks – registration – mark "REEF BRAZIL" – likelihood of confusion

[Trade Marks Act 1994 s.5(2)(b).]

SC, which had registered the mark "REEF BRAZIL", appealed against the decision of a hearing officer dismissing its opposition to the registration of the mark "REEF" in relation to goods such as T shirts and jackets. Registration of the mark had been sought by the members of a pop group called "Reef", which had a strong association with surfing. SC argued, inter alia, that the mark could not be registered by virtue of the Trade Marks Act 1994 s.5(2)(b). The hearing officer had found that SC had significant goodwill in footwear and, in particular, sandals but that there was not sufficient evidence to extend such goodwill to products such as clothing. SC submitted that insufficient regard had been had to the channels of trade and the users of the relevant goods.

Held, allowing the appeal, that the hearing officer had erred in reaching his conclusion under s.5(2)(b) of the Act and accordingly it was appropriate for the court to carry out its own appraisal. It was apparent that SC's footwear was directed primarily at surfers and that the pop group was also strongly oriented toward surfers. It followed therefore that the group's goods were likely to be sold in shops aiming for the surfer market and there was accordingly a significant overlap in the potential customers for the products in question. Moreover, the mark "REEF" was a prominent part of SC's mark and there was a likelihood of confusion. Accordingly, the mark was not registrable.

REEF TRADE MARK; *sub nom*. SOUTH CONE INC v. BESSANT (T/A REEF) [2002] R.P.C. 19, Pumfrey, J., Ch D.

4058. Trade marks – registration – opposition by owner of earlier lapsed marks

[Trade Marks Act 1994 s.5(2)(b), s.6, s.37, s.40.]

BB applied to register the word TRANSPAY in Classes 16 and 36 for money orders, cheques, cheque books, bankers drafts, plastic cards, banking and financial services in November 1994 and in February 1995 it applied to register another version of the device in the same classes. Both applications were accepted and published. In November 1995, CE filed notice of opposition under the Trade Marks Act 1994 s.5(2)(b). CE owned two earlier trade marks for TRANSCHEQ in the same classes, but these had expired following non renewal in February 1997 and the question arose as to whether a valid objection could be taken under s.5(2)(b) in respect of lapsed earlier marks. CE argued that, as the earlier trade marks were on the register when BB made its applications, they were earlier marks in terms of s.6 and their status was not affected by the subsequent lapse.

Held, dismissing the opposition and allowing registration, that (1) s.6 provided that a registered trade mark with an application date that preceded a trade mark application for similar goods or services was a bar to the later application's acceptance. However, this was not absolute and account had to be taken of matters that occurred after the application date and prior to the final decision on registration for the later mark, otherwise unfairness could result. If consideration was restricted to matters that existed at the application date, it would be impossible for part cancellation of goods or services to be taken into account that could allow the later mark to be registered. Further, the effect of cancellation or assignment of a mark could not be considered; (2) the construction of the Act showed that acceptance for registration and actual registration were two separate events. Section 37 dealt with the examination of a registration application and s.40 made provision for the actual registration and required registration to proceed, unless it had been accepted in error. Therefore, acceptance of an application was not the same as registration, so that a trade mark that otherwise would have been refused, on the basis of a pre-existing mark, could be accepted where information on the earlier mark was unavailable at the application date, and (3) CE's earlier marks no longer existed as registered trade marks under s.6 so CE could not rely on s.5(2) as the basis for its opposition in the instant case.

TRANSPAY TRADE MARK [2001] R.P.C. 10, M Knight, TMR.

4059. **Trade marks – registration – smell mark – inadequacy of graphical representation**

[Trade Marks Act 1994 s.32.]

JL's application to register the "smell, aroma or essence of cinnamon" for use in respect of furniture, including parts and fittings, in Class 20 was refused ([2001] E.T.M.R. 36, [2001] 6 C.L. 426) on the ground that it lacked precise definition by way of a graphic representation, as required by the Trade Marks Act 1994 s.32(2)(d). Further, that the examiners could not compare it to other signs without the use of samples. JL appealed.

Held, dismissing the appeal, that (1) the requirement for something other than the graphic representation to show an immediate and non subjective perception of a sign did not necessarily mean that the representation was inadequate for the purposes of s.32(1) and (2). In the instant case, the use of electronic sensory analysis had not given an adequate representation of the smell for registration purposes; (2) a smell mark's identity had to be clearly shown in the graphic representation filed under s.32(1)(d), *Ty Nant Spring Water Ltd's Trade Mark Application (No.2162950)* [1999] E.T.M.R. 981, [2000] C.L.Y. 3789 referred to, so that the sign could be distinguished from those use by other suppliers, and (3) the words used in JL's application were not precise enough to allow people to know how closely a smell matched that shown in the graphic representation.

JOHN LEWIS OF HUNGERFORD LTD'S TRADE MARK APPLICATION [2001] E.T.M.R. 104, Geoffrey Hobbs Q.C., Appointed Person.

4060. **Trade marks – registration – time limit in which to adduce evidence in support of opposition**

S applied to register a device consisting of a symbol, words in the Arabic alphabet and the English words "The Muslim Parliament of Great Britain" in Classes 9, 16, 38, 41 and 42. The application was lodged in June 1999. K, as nominee of the Muslim Parliament of Great Britain, filed notice of opposition. S filed a counter statement, and K was given until March 3, 2000 to file evidence supporting his opposition. K applied for a three month extension in which to file this evidence, claiming that S held material relating to one of the opposition grounds and was unwilling to release it to K. K also claimed a general difficulty in obtaining documentation owing to another ongoing dispute as to who was the rightful representative of the Parliament. S objected to K's request for a time extension, denying that K had made any requests for documentation since August 1999, when K had asked S for confidential financial information. S also stated that he did not know of any other.

Held, refusing the request for an extension of time and withdrawing the opposition, that an application for further time to file evidence in support of an opposition should not be granted in the absence of an explanation of the failure to apply for disclosure of documentation.

SIDDIQUI'S TRADE MARK APPLICATION [2001] E.T.M.R. 38, Lynda Adams, TMR.

4062. **Trade marks – registration – use of deceptive words – bad faith**

[Trade Marks Act 1994, ss3(3)(b), 3(6).]

K sought registration of the phrase 'KENCO, THE REAL COFFEE EXPERTS' as a word mark relating to coffee and related goods in class 30. N had a greater UK market share in freeze dried coffee (the technology for which it had pioneered), and it opposed the application contending that the use of the mark was deceptive and that the application was lodged in bad faith.

Held, granting the application and awarding costs against N. There was no evidence of actual deception, and for the application to have been made in bad faith required deliberate action by K which it knew to be wrong or commercially unacceptable behaviour. There was no evidence of such behaviour in the instant case (*Gromax Plasticulture Ltd v. Don & Low Nonwovens Ltd* [1999] R.P.C 367, [1999] C.L.Y. 3592 and *DEMON ALE Trade Mark* [2000] R.P.C 345, [2000] 6 C.L. 443 applied).

KRAFT JACOBS SUCHARD LTD'S TRADE MARK APPLICATION [2001] E.T.M.R. 54, Judge not applicable, TMR.

4063. **Trade marks – revocation – non-use of mark – burden of proof**

[Trade Marks Act 1994 s.46.]

"Floris" was registered as a mark in class 24 for "towels (textiles), face cloths, pillowcases, bed linen and bed covers." I had sought revocation of the mark for non use and the registrar had allowed revocation in respect of pillowcases, bed linen and bed covers, but had refused it in respect of towels (textiles) and face cloths, holding that the registered proprietor of the mark had established use of the mark for the latter goods during the relevant five year period. The registered proprietor had adduced two sample invoices of low value in relation to those goods, only one of which related to the relevant five year period. The registered proprietor, whose main business was the sale of toiletries, also adduced evidence in the form of advertisements for toiletries featuring face cloths and towels, although the advertisements did not refer to the latter goods being for sale or supply. I appealed.

Held, allowing the appeal and revoking the registration in its entirety, that the registered proprietor was required under the Trade Marks Act 1994 to show a genuine use of the mark, judged against commercial criteria (*BON MATIN Trade Mark* [1989] R.P.C. 537 and *NODOZ Trade Mark* [1962] R.P.C. 1, [1962] C.L.Y. 3046 referred to). In the absence of actual evidence of sales during the relevant five year period, use could nonetheless be shown where there was evidence that the mark had been used in relation to goods offered for sale during the relevant five year period. It was for the registered proprietor to prove genuine use of the mark in a commercial sense for the duration of the relevant period, and the registered proprietor had not discharged that burden in the instant case (*HERMES Trade Mark* [1982] Com. L.R. 98, [1982] C.L.Y. 3265 referred to).

FLORIS TRADE MARK [2001] R.P.C. 19, Michael Clarke Q.C., Appointed Person.

4064. **Trade secrets – confidentiality – general knowledge acquired by employees**

P, a firm of electroplaters, produced nickel silicon carbide plated internal combustion engines. The production process involved the use of an electrolytic cell that used out of tank plating and a central, insoluble anode. H was employed by P as a sales engineer but was at no time regularly involved in the plating process. H subsequently set up his own electroplating business and used equipment similar to P's. P brought an action claiming that H had wrongfully taken and used confidential information relating to the design of their electrolytic apparatus. The judge upheld P's claim and granted injunctions restraining H from using the apparatus. H appealed, contending that the judge had erred in finding for P and, in the alternative, that the injunctive relief granted to P was inappropriate.

Held, allowing the appeal, that there was no express term in H's contract of employment relating to trade secrets and confidential information, nor was H made aware of a need for secrecy. It was doubtful that the design of P's electroplating cell was such that it gave rise to a trade secret, as the concept of out of tank plating and the related design features, were clearly in the public domain. If, however, it was assumed that the design was capable of being a trade secret, it was not a secret of the type that attained such a degree of confidentiality that H could not lawfully use it for the benefit of a party other than P, *Faccenda Chicken Ltd v. Fowler* [1987] Ch. 117, [1986] C.L.Y. 1167 followed. The information relating to the process and apparatus used by P could not easily be isolated from the general knowledge that he had gained during the course of his employment and he was not in breach of an implied term of confidentiality.

AT POETON (GLOUCESTER PLATING) LTD v. HORTON; *sub nom.* POETON INDUSTRIES LTD v. HORTON [2000] I.C.R. 1208, Morritt, L.J., CA.

4065. Works of art – resale rights – Council Directive

European Parliament and Council Directive 2001/84 of 27 September 2001 on the resale right for the benefit of the author of an original work of art. [2001] OJ L272/32.

4066. Books

Barendt, Eric; Firth, Alison – Yearbook of Copyright and Media Law: 5. Hardback: £95.00. ISBN 0-19-829919-2. Oxford University Press.

Baumer, David; Poindexter, J. Carl – Cyberlaw and E-commerce. Paperback: £31.99. ISBN 0-07-112300-8. McGraw-Hill Publishing Company.

Blakeney, Michael – Border Control of Intellectual Property Rights. Looseleaf/ring bound: £250.00. ISBN 0-421-71000-4. Sweet & Maxwell.

Brown, Travis – Popular Patents. Paperback: £15.20. ISBN 1-57886-010-5. Scarecrow Press.

Cornish, Graham P. – Copyright: Interpreting the Law for Libraries and Information Services 3rd Rev Ed. The Library Association Copyright Guides. Paperback: £19.95. ISBN 1-85604-409-2. Library Association Publishing.

C.I.P.A Guide to the Patents Acts 5th Ed. Intellectual Property Library. Hardback: £240.00. ISBN 0-421-74950-4. Sweet & Maxwell.

C.I.P.A Guide to the Patents Acts: 1st Supplement. 5th Ed. Intellectual Property Library. Paperback. ISBN 0-421-74940-7. Sweet & Maxwell.

Drahos, Peter; Blakeney, Michael – IP in Biodiversity and Agriculture: Regulating the Biosphere. Perspectives on Intellectual Property, 9. Paperback: £45.00. ISBN 0-421-76630-1. Sweet & Maxwell.

Dreyfuss, Rochelle; Zimmerman, Diane L.; First, Harry – Expanding the Boundaries of Intellectual Property. Hardback: £40.00. ISBN 0-19-829857-9. Oxford University Press.

Evans, Judith; Templeman, Lord – Intellectual Property: Textbook. 1st Ed. Old Bailey Press Textbooks. Paperback: £14.95. ISBN 1-85836-355-1. Old Bailey Press.

Flint, Michael F. – User's Guide to Copyright. 5th Ed. Paperback: £55.00. ISBN 0-406-91498-2. Butterworths Law.

Gastinel, Eric; Milford, Mark – Legal Aspects of the Community Trade Mark. Hardback: £77.50. ISBN 90-411-9831-8. Kluwer Law International.

Heines, M. Henry – Patent Empowerment for Small Corporations. Hardback: £53.95. ISBN 1-56720-452-X. Quorum Books.

Holyoak; Torremans – Holyoak and Torremans: Intellectual Property Law. 3rd Ed. Butterworths Student Statutes. Paperback: £24.95. ISBN 0-406-93400-2. Butterworths Law.

Kitchen, David; Mellor, James; Meade, Richard – Kerly's Law of Trade Marks and Trade Names. 13th Ed. Hardback: £185.00. ISBN 0-421-45610-8. Sweet & Maxwell.

Miele, Anthony L. – Patent Strategy. Hardback: £42.95. ISBN 0-471-39075-5. John Wiley and Sons.

Moore, Adam D. – Intellectual Property and Information Control. Hardback: £24.95. ISBN 0-7658-0070-5. Hardback: £24.95. ISBN 0-7658-0070-5. Transaction Publishers.

Munzer, Stephen – New Essays in the Legal and Political Theory of Property. Cambridge Studies in Philosophy and Law. Hardback: £37.50. ISBN 0-521-64001-6. Cambridge University Press.

Owen, Lynette – Selling Rights. Hardback: £40.00. ISBN 0-415-23508-1. Routledge, an imprint of Taylor & Francis Books Ltd.

Parr, Russell. L. – Intellectual Property Infringement Damages. 2nd Ed. Paperback: £46.50. ISBN 0-471-39050-X. John Wiley and Sons.

Paterson, Gerald – European Patent System. 2nd Ed. Hardback: £150.00. ISBN 0-421-58600-1. Hardback: £170.00. ISBN 0-421-58600-1. Sweet & Maxwell.

Pierce, Jennifer; Purvis, Ian – Working with Technology: Funding, Protection and Exploitation. Hardback: £95.00. ISBN 0-421-59810-7. Sweet & Maxwell.

Sherman, Brad; Bently, Lionel – Intellectual Property Law-Reissue. Paperback: £32.99. ISBN 0-19-876343-3. Oxford University Press.

Sykes, John and Wright, Patrick – Valuation and Commercial Assessment of Intellectual Property Assets. Hardback: £70.00. ISBN 0-421-57920-X. Sweet & Maxwell.

Towse, Ruth – Creativity, Incentive and Reward-An Economic Analysis of Copyright and Culture in the Information Age. Hardback: £55.00. ISBN 1-84064-254-8. Edward Elgar.

von Lewinski, Silke; Reinbothe, Jong – WIPO Treaties 1996. 2nd Ed. Paperback: £75.00. ISBN 0-406-89669-0. Butterworths Law.

Wilson, Lee – Copyright Guide. Paperback: £14.95. ISBN 1-58115-067-9. Allworth Press.

Zoellick, Bill – CyberRegs. AW Information Technology Series. Paperback: £30.99. ISBN 0-201-72230-5. Addison Wesley.

INTERNATIONAL LAW

4067. Child abduction – custody – parties to Luxembourg Convention

CHILD ABDUCTION AND CUSTODY (PARTIES TO CONVENTIONS) (AMENDMENT) ORDER 2001, SI 2001 3923; made under the Child Abduction and Custody Act 1985 s.2, s.13. In force: December 11, 2001; £1.75.

This Order amends the Child Abduction and Custody (Parties to Conventions) Order 1986 (SI 1986 1159) in order to add Malta, Slovakia and Turkey to the list of Contracting States to the Convention on the Civil Aspects of International Child Abduction and to add the Czech Republic and Turkey to the list of Contracting States to the European Convention on Recognition and Enforcement of Decisions concerning Custody of Children and on Restoration of Custody of Children, signed at Luxembourg on May 20, 1980.

4068. Continental shelf – UK rights to natural resources

CONTINENTAL SHELF (DESIGNATION OF AREAS) ORDER 2001, SI 2001 3670; made under the Continental Shelf Act 1964 s.1. In force: December 6, 2001; £1.50.

This Order designates a further area of continental shelf in the Irish Sea as an area in which the rights of the UK with respect to the sea bed and subsoil and their natural resources are exercisable. The Order also corrects an error in the Schedule to the Continental Shelf (Designation of Areas) (Consolidation) Order 2000 (SI 2000 3062).

4069. Embargoes – Iraq – part performance of contracts prior to Gulf War – permanent prohibition of claims

[Council Regulation 3541/92 prohibiting the satisfying of Iraqi claims with regard to contracts and transactions Art.2.]

R appealed against a decision ([2000] Lloyd's Rep. Bank. 215, [2000] C.L.Y. 3808) that Council Regulation 3541/92 operated to permanently prohibit claims made by Iraqi parties to contracts formed prior to the imposition of the embargo which arose owing to the Gulf War. R, an Iraqi bank, had agreed to guarantee its customer's payment obligations to S incurred under a supply contract. The guarantee was subject to English law. L had granted a counter guarantee to R, for which it was indemnified by S. The obligations of the contract had been nearly completed at the time that war was declared and the embargo was imposed. The Court of Appeal had upheld the judge's decision that Art.2 of the Regulation prohibited R's claim against L and L's claim against S.

Held, dismissing the appeal, that to allow the claims to proceed would defeat the obvious intent and effect of the Regulation which had been imposed to halt the performance of contracts in place at the time of the unrest. The embargo had prevented the completion of contractual duties, thereby exposing non-Iraqi parties to claims for non-performance. It would not be in the interests of justice to allow those claims to proceed. The Regulation had not expressly provided for the discharge of contracts, as that would leave restitutional remedies available to the Iraqi parties, and it was therefore preferable to prohibit the claims permanently.

SHANNING INTERNATIONAL LTD (IN LIQUIDATION) v. LLOYDS TSB BANK PLC (FORMERLY LLOYDS BANK PLC); *sub nom.* LLOYDS TSB BANK PLC (FORMERLY LLOYDS BANK PLC) v. RASHEED BANK; SHANNING INTERNATIONAL LTD (IN LIQUIDATION) v. RASHEED BANK, [2001] UKHL 31, [2001] 1 W.L.R. 1462, Lord Bingham of Cornhill, HL.

4070. European Community – immunities and privileges – North Atlantic Salmon Conservation Organization

EUROPEAN COMMUNITIES (IMMUNITIES AND PRIVILEGES OF THE NORTH ATLANTIC SALMON CONSERVATION ORGANIZATION) ORDER 2001, SI 2001 3673; made under the European Communities Act 1972 s.2. In force: November 15, 2001; £1.50.

This Order confers relief by way of refund from payment of insurance premium tax and air passenger duty. The Order enables the UK to give effect to an Exchange of Notes dated December 20, 2000 and January 4, 2001 between Her Majesty's Government and the North Atlantic Salmon Conservation Organization (Cm. 5093).

4071. Explosives – landmines – prohibited conduct – Jersey

LANDMINES ACT 1998 (JERSEY) ORDER 2001, SI 2001 3930; made under the Landmines Act 1998 s.3, s.29. In force: January 2, 2002; £1.75.

This Order applies the Landmines Act 1998 s.21 which has effect in the UK in respect of conduct outside the UK, to bodies incorporated under the law of the Bailiwick of Jersey. The Order also extends that Act to the Bailiwick of Jersey with the exceptions and modifications specified.

4072. Explosives – landmines – prohibited conduct – overseas territories

LANDMINES ACT 1998 (OVERSEAS TERRITORIES) ORDER 2001, SI 2001 3499; made under the Landmines Act 1998 s.29. In force: November 14, 2001; £3.50.

This Order amends the Landmines Act 1998 by extending certain provisions, adaptions and modifications to the territories listed in Schedule 2.

4073. Extradition – parties to European Convention

EUROPEAN CONVENTION ON EXTRADITION ORDER 2001, SI 2001 962; made under the Extradition Act 1989 s.4, s.37. In force: April 17, 2001; £6.50.

This Order revokes, with savings, the Order in Council directing that the Extradition Acts shall apply in the case of Serbia (SR & O 1901 586), and the Order in Council directing that Extradition Acts shall apply in the cases of Cuba, Italy, Luxembourg, Switzerland and Yugoslavia in accordance with existing Treaties as supplemented by Convention of May 4, 1910, for the suppression of the White Slave Traffic (SR & O 1931 718), and revokes the European Convention on Extradition Order 1990 (SI 1990 1507), European Convention on Extradition (Czech and Slovak Federal Republic) (Amendment) Order 1992 (SI 1992 2663), the European Convention on Extradition (Hungary and Poland) (Amendment)

Order 1993 (SI 1993 2667), the European Convention on Extradition (Bulgaria) (Amendment) Order 1994 (SI 1994 2796), the European Convention on Extradition (Amendment) Order 1994 (SI 1994 3203), the European Convention on Extradition Order 1990 (Amendment) (No.2) Order 1995 (SI 1995 1962), the European Convention on Extradition Order 1990 (Amendment) (No.3) Order 1995 (SI 1995 2703), European Convention on Extradition Order 1990 (Amendment) Order 1997 (SI 1997 1759), the European Convention on Extradition Order 1990 (Amendment) (No.2) Order 1997 (SI 1997 2596), the European Convention on Extradition Order 1990 (Amendment) Order 1998 (SI 1998 259) and the European Convention on Extradition Order 1990 (Amendment) Order 1999 (SI 1999 2035). The main amendments are the addition of Andorra, the Former Yugoslav Republic of Macedonia and the Russian Federation to the list of States parties to the European Convention on Extradition together with the declarations and reservations made by those States, and the addition of certain reservations or declarations made by Austria, Germany, the Netherlands, Portugal, Hungary, Turkey, Slovakia and Israel.

4074. Extradition – parties to European Convention – fiscal offences

EUROPEAN CONVENTION ON EXTRADITION (FISCAL OFFENCES) ORDER 2001, SI 2001 1453; made under the Extradition Act 1989 s.4. In force: May 16, 2001; £2.00.

This Order, which revokes the European Convention on Extradition (Fiscal Offences) Order 1993 (SI 1993 2663) so as to take account of the revocation and replacement of the European Convention on Extradition Order 1990 (SI 1990 1507), updates the references to the European Convention on Extradition, and the States parties to it. It takes into account the additional States which have become parties to the Protocol and accepted Chapter II, namely Albania, Belgium, Bulgaria, Croatia, Czech Republic, Estonia, Latvia, Lithuania, Former Yugoslav Republic of Macedonia, Malta, Romania, the Russian Federation, Slovakia, Slovenia and the Ukraine, together with any reservations and declarations made by those States.

4075. Food aid – developing countries – special operations – Council Regulation

European Parliament and Council Regulation 1726/2001 of 23 July 2001 amending Art.21 of Council Regulation 1292/96 on food-aid policy and food-aid management and special operations in support of food security. [2001] OJ L234/10.

4076. International Criminal Court Act 2001 (c.17)

This Act gives effect to the Statute of the International Criminal Court and provides for offences under the law of England and Wales and Northern Ireland corresponding to offences within the jurisdiction of that Court.

This Act received Royal Assent on May 11, 2001.

4077. International Criminal Court Act 2001 (c.17) – Commencement Order

INTERNATIONAL CRIMINAL COURT ACT 2001 (COMMENCEMENT) ORDER 2001, SI 2001 2161 (C.69); made under the International Criminal Court Act 2001 s.82. Commencement details: bringing into force various provisions of the Act on September 1, 2001; £1.50.

This Order brings into force the International Criminal Court Act 2001 on September 1, 2001 to the extent necessary for the making of any Order in Council, Order and Regulations.

4078. International Criminal Court Act 2001 (c.17) – Commencement Order – Amendment

INTERNATIONAL CRIMINAL COURT ACT 2001 (COMMENCEMENT) (AMENDMENT) ORDER 2001, SI 2001 2304 (C.77); made under the International Criminal Court Act 2001 s.82. In force: June 25, 2001; £1.50.

This Order amends the International Criminal Court Act 2001 (Commencement) Order 2001 (SI 2001 2161) to bring into force the power in Sch.1 of the 2001 Act to make an Order in Council to confer legal capacity, privileges and immunities on the International Criminal Court.

4079. International criminal law – elements of crime

INTERNATIONAL CRIMINAL COURT ACT 2001 (ELEMENTS OF CRIMES) REGULATIONS 2001, SI 2001 2505; made under the International Criminal Court Act 2001 s.50. In force: September 1, 2001; £6.00.

These Regulations set out the Elements of Crimes contained in the Report of the Preparatory Commission for the International Criminal Court adopted on June 30, 2000. In accordance with the International Criminal Court Act 2001 these shall be taken into account by a court considering offences under domestic law.

4080. International criminal law – fines – forfeiture – reparation orders

INTERNATIONAL CRIMINAL COURT ACT 2001 (ENFORCEMENT OF FINES, FORFEITURE AND REPARATION ORDERS) REGULATIONS 2001, SI 2001 2379; made under the International Criminal Court Act 2001 s.49. In force: August 1, 2001; £1.50.

These Regulations make provision for the enforcement in England, Wales and Northern Ireland of fines and forfeitures ordered by the International Criminal Court and of orders by that court against convicted persons specifying reparations to, or in respect of, victims.

4081. International criminal law – reservations and declarations

INTERNATIONAL CRIMINAL COURT ACT 2001 (RESERVATIONS AND DECLARATIONS) ORDER 2001, SI 2001 2559; made under the International Criminal Court Act 2001 s.50. In force: September 1, 2001; £2.00.

This Order sets out the relevant reservations and declarations made by the UK when ratifying various treaties. The International Criminal Court Act 2001 s.50(4)(a) provides that in relation to criminal offences created under Part V of the Act certain articles of the Statute of the International Criminal Court shall be construed subject to and in accordance with such reservations and declarations.

4082. International organisations – Organisation for the Prohibition of Chemical Weapons – immunities

ORGANISATION FOR THE PROHIBITION OF CHEMICAL WEAPONS (IMMUNITIES AND PRIVILEGES) ORDER 2001, SI 2001 3921; made under the International Organisations Act 1968 s.1. In force: in accordance with Art.1; £2.00.

This Order confers privileges and immunities upon the Organisation for the Prohibition of Chemical Weapons, on representatives of its Members, its officials and experts. These privileges and immunities are conferred in accordance with the Agreement of October 26, 2000 between the Organisation for the Prohibition of Chemical Weapons and the Government of the UK of Great Britain and Northern Ireland on the Privileges and Immunities of the OPCW (Cm. 5099). The Order will enable Her Majesty's Government to give effect to that Convention and will come into force on the date on which that Convention enters into force.

4083. Letters of request – enforcement of letters rogatory – request for international judicial assistance – Canada

[British Columbia Evidence Act 1996 s.53(1)(a), s.53(1)(c).]

P, a Canadian lawyer, had advised G on Canadian aspects of a transaction in the United States. G subsequently issued proceedings in NewYork in connection with the transaction against other lawyers who had advised G in connection therewith. P was not a party to those proceedings, but G believed that P could give relevant testimony in the New York proceedings. Letters rogatory were sent for an enforcement order to the court in British Columbia encompassing a very wide request for deposition of testimony and discovery. P resisted the application on the ground that the letters rogatory were unduly burdensome to him and the named commissioner was not independent.

Held, allowing the letters rogatory to be enforced subject to limitations, that (1) the British Columbia Evidence Act 1996 s.53(1)(a) gave the court discretion, when faced with a wide ranging request for assistance, to modify the contents of the request where the same were unduly burdensome. In particular, the court would consider issues of privilege, confidentiality, examination and cross examination, monetary compensation, access to legal advice, and the imposition of terms that the evidence obtained could be used only for the purpose of the proceedings in respect of which the request was made and; (2) the British Columbia Evidence Act 1996 s.53(1)(c) gave the court power to substitute the named commissioner.

GST TELECOMMUNICATIONS v. PROVENZANO [2001] I.L.Pr. 32, B.M. Davies, J., Sup Ct (BC).

4084. Local authorities – overseas assistance – London Pensions Fund Authority

LOCAL GOVERNMENT OVERSEAS ASSISTANCE (LONDON PENSIONS FUND AUTHORITY) ORDER 2001, SI 2001 3618; made under the Local Government (Overseas Assistance) Act 1993 s.1. In force: December 5, 2001; £1.50.

This Order amends the Local Government (Overseas Assistance Act) 1993 to provide that the London Pensions Fund Authority is a local authority for the purposes of that Act.

4085. Magistrates courts – forms – delivery proceedings – International Criminal Court

MAGISTRATES' COURTS (INTERNATIONAL CRIMINAL COURT) (FORMS) RULES 2001, SI 2001 2600 (L.27); made under the Magistrates' Courts Act 1980 s.144. In force: September 1, 2001; £1.75.

These Rules prescribe forms in relation to delivery proceedings under the International Criminal Court Act 2001.

4086. Offences – freezing of funds – Yugoslavia

FEDERAL REPUBLIC OF YUGOSLAVIA (FREEZING OF FUNDS) REGULATIONS 2001, SI 2001 59; made under the European Communities Act 1972 s.2. In force: February 5, 2001; £1.75.

These Regulations provide that breaches of certain provisions of Council Regulation 2488/2000 maintaining a freeze of funds in relation to Mr Milosevic and those persons associated with him, are to be criminal offences. They provide for the freezing of funds belonging to Mr Milosevic and persons associated with him, and prohibit the making of funds available to or for the benefit of those persons, prohibit the knowing and intentional participation in activities the object or effect of which is to circumvent the provisions of the EC Regulation and require banks, insurance companies and others to provide to the Treasury or the Bank of England and to the European Commission information which would facilitate compliance with the EC Regulation, but require such information to be used only for the purposes for which it was provided or received. In addition, the Regulations make provision for information to be requested by or on behalf of the Treasury or the Bank of England for the purpose of ensuring compliance with the EC Regulation.

Failure to provide such information, the provision of false information or the suppression of information is made a criminal offence. Unauthorised disclosure of information acquired under the Schedule is also made a criminal offence. The Federal Republic of Yugoslavia (Freezing of Funds and Prohibition on Investment) Regulations 1999 (SI 1999 1786) are revoked.

4087. Telecommunications – EUTELSAT – customs duty – exemption

EUTELSAT (IMMUNITIES AND PRIVILEGES) (AMENDMENT) ORDER 2001, SI 2001 963; made under the International Organisations Act 1968 s.1. In force: in accordance with Art.1; £1.50.

This Order amends the EUTELSAT (Immunities and Privileges) Order 1988 (SI 1988 1299) by exempting EUTELSAT from all customs duties within the scope of its official activities to give effect to Amendments to the Convention and the Operating Agreement relating to the European Telecommunication Satellites Organisation which extend EUTELSAT's exemption from customs duties.

4088. Terrorism – enforcement of external orders

TERRORISM ACT 2000 (ENFORCEMENT OF EXTERNAL ORDERS) ORDER 2001, SI 2001 3927; made under the Terrorism Act 2000 Sch.4 para.14, para.28, para.44. In force: December 13, 2001; £2.50.

This Order, which revokes the Prevention of Terrorism (Temporary Provisions) Act 1989 (Enforcement of External Orders) Order 1995 (SI 1995 760), makes provision for the purpose of enabling the enforcement in the UK of certain types of order made by a court in a designated country or territory. The types of order in question are orders which provide for the forfeiture of terrorist property, or orders which make provision prohibiting dealing with property which is subject to an external forfeiture order or in respect of which such an order could be made in proceedings which have been or are to be instituted in the designated country or territory.

4089. Terrorism – United Nations measures – powers and prohibitions

TERRORISM (UNITED NATIONS MEASURES) ORDER 2001, SI 2001 3365; made under the United Nations Act 1946 s.1. In force: October 10, 2001; £2.00.

This Order restricts the making available of funds and financial services to terrorists, and provides powers to freeze accounts of suspected terrorists, pursuant to a decision of the Security Council of the United Nations in its resolution 1373 of September 28, 2001.

4090. Terrorism – United Nations measures – powers and prohibitions – Channel Islands

TERRORISM (UNITED NATIONS MEASURES) (CHANNEL ISLANDS) ORDER 2001, SI 2001 3363; made under the United Nations Act 1946 s.1. In force: October 10, 2001; £2.00.

This Order imposes measures in the Channel Islands against terrorism pursuant to a decision of the Security Council of the United Nations in its Resolution 1373 of September 28, 2001. It prohibits fundraising for, and restricts the making available of funds to or the provision of financial services to terrorists. It also provides powers to freeze accounts of suspected terrorists.

4091. Terrorism – United Nations measures – powers and prohibitions – Isle of Man

TERRORISM (UNITED NATIONS MEASURES) (ISLE OF MAN) ORDER 2001, SI 2001 3364; made under the United Nations Act 1946 s.1. In force: October 10, 2001; £2.00.

This Order imposes measures in the Isle of Man against terrorism pursuant to a decision of the Security Council of the United Nations in its Resolution 1373 of September 28, 2001. It prohibits fundraising for, and restricts the making available of funds to, or the provision of financial services to terrorists. It also provides powers to freeze accounts of suspected terrorists.

4092. Terrorism – United Nations measures – powers and prohibitions – overseas territories

TERRORISM (UNITED NATIONS MEASURES) (OVERSEAS TERRITORIES) ORDER 2001, SI 2001 3366; made under the United Nations Act 1946 s.1. In force: October 10, 2001; £2.50.

This Order, which applies to each of the specified territories, prohibits fundraising for terrorism purposes and restricts the making available of funds and financial services to terrorists. In addition, it provides powers to freeze accounts of suspected terrorists, pursuant to a decision of the Security Council of the United Nations in its resolution 1373 of September 28, 2001.

4093. Treaties – agreements – African, Caribbean and Pacific Group of States

EUROPEAN COMMUNITIES (DEFINITION OF TREATIES) (PARTNERSHIP AGREEMENT BETWEEN THE MEMBERS OF THE AFRICAN, CARIBBEAN AND PACIFIC GROUP OF STATES AND THE EUROPEAN COMMUNITY AND ITS MEMBER STATES (THE COTONOU AGREEMENT)) ORDER 2001, SI 2001 3935; made under the European Communities Act 1972 s.1. In force: in accordance with Art.1; £1.50.

This Order declares the Partnership and Co-operation Agreement between the European Communities and their Member States and the Members of the African, Caribbean and Pacific Group of States signed on June 23, 2000 and the related Internal Financing Agreement, to be Community Treaties as defined in European Communities Act 1972 s.1 (2).

4094. United Nations – immunities and priveleges – specialized agencies

SPECIALIZED AGENCIES OF THE UNITED NATIONS (IMMUNITIES AND PRIVILEGES OF UNESCO) ORDER 2001, SI 2001 2560; made under the International Organisations Act 1968 s.1, s.10. In force: in accordance with Art.1; £1.50.

Although the Specialized Agencies of the United Nations (Immunities and Privileges) Order 1974 (SI 1974 1260) applied to and in relation to UNESCO, that application lapsed when the UK withdrew from the organisation on December 31, 1985. The UK rejoined UNESCO on July 1, 1997. This Order restores the privileges and immunities previously enjoyed by UNESCO and persons connected with it by reapplying the 1974 Order to them.

4095. United Nations – international tribunals – Rwanda

UNITED NATIONS (INTERNATIONAL TRIBUNAL) (RWANDA) (AMENDMENT) ORDER 2001, SI 2001 3920; made under the United Nations Act 1946 s.1. In force: December 14, 2001; £2.00.

This Order amends the United Nations (International Tribunal) (Rwanda) Order 1996 (SI 1996 1296) so as to provide that an application to a court for the registration of a Tribunal freezing or restitution order is to be made by a person appointed by the Secretary of State or authorised by the Scottish Ministers, to provide for orders for production of, or access to, evidence to be made at the request of the Tribunal, and to provide for the transmission of documents to be made by facsimile.

4096. United Nations – international tribunals – Yugoslavia

UNITED NATIONS (INTERNATIONAL TRIBUNAL) (FORMER YUGOSLAVIA) (AMENDMENT) ORDER 2001, SI 2001 2563; made under the United Nations Act 1946 s.1. In force: September 1, 2001; £2.00.

This Order amends the United Nations (International Tribunal) (Former Yugoslavia) Order 1996 (SI 1996 716) to provide that an application to a court for the registration of a Tribunal freezing or restitution order is to be made by a person appointed by the Secretary of State or authorised by the Scottish Ministers. It also provides for orders for production of, or access to, evidence to be made at the request of the Tribunal, and for the transmission of documents to be made by facsimile.

4097. United Nations – international tribunals – Yugoslavia and Rwanda

UNITED NATIONS (INTERNATIONAL TRIBUNALS) (FORMER YUGOSLAVIA AND RWANDA) (AMENDMENT) ORDER 2001, SI 2001 412; made under the United Nations Act 1946 s.1. In force: March 12, 2001; £2.00.

This Order makes provision to implement a resolution of the Security Council of the United Nations which established a pool of ad litem judges in the International Tribunal for the Former Yugoslavia and increased the number of judges in the Appeals Chambers of the two International Tribunals. It amends the United Nations (International Tribunal) (Former Yugoslavia) Order 1996 (SI 1996 716) to reflect the decision of the Security Council of the United Nations in Resolution 1329 (2000) to amend the Statute of the International Tribunal for the Prosecution of Persons Responsible for Serious Violations of International Humanitarian Law Committed in the Territory of the Former Yugoslavia since 1991. It also amends the the United Nations (International Tribunal) (Rwanda) (Order) 1996 (SI 1996 1296) to reflect the decision of the Security Council of the United Nations in Resolution 1329 (2000) to amend the Statute of the International Tribunal for the Prosecution of Persons Responsible for Genocide and Other Serious Violations of International Humanitarian Law Committed in the Territory of Rwanda and Rwandan citizens responsible for genocide and other such violations committed in the territory of neighbouring states, between January 1, 1994 and December 31, 1994.

4098. United Nations – sanctions – Afghanistan

AFGHANISTAN (UNITED NATIONS SANCTIONS) ORDER 2001, SI 2001 396; made under the United Nations Act 1946 s.1. In force: February 16, 2001; £3.00.

This Order, which makes provision to give effect to a decision of the Security Council of the United Nations in Resolution 1333 of December 19, 2000, prohibits the making of funds available to Usama bin Laden and his associates and prohibits the establishment or maintenance of Taliban offices or the carrying on of any business by Ariana Afghan Airlines. In addition, it imposes restrictions on flights taking off from, landing in or flying over the UK if they are destined for or originate in Afghanistan. The Afghanistan (United Nations Sanctions) Order 1999 (SI 1999 3133) is revoked.

4099. United Nations – sanctions – Afghanistan

AFGHANISTAN (UNITED NATIONS SANCTIONS) (AMENDMENT) ORDER 2001, SI 2001 2557; made under the United Nations Act 1946 s.1. In force: July 20, 2001; £1.75.

This Order amends the Afghanistan (United Nations Sanctions) Order 2001 (SI 2001 396) to enhance the financial sanctions regime imposed against the Taliban.

4100. United Nations – sanctions – Afghanistan – Channel Islands

AFGHANISTAN (UNITED NATIONS SANCTIONS) (CHANNEL ISLANDS) ORDER 2001, SI 2001 393; made under the United Nations Act 1946 s.1. In force: February 16, 2001; £3.50.

This Order, which revokes the Afghanistan (United Nations Sanctions) (Channel Islands) Order 1999 (SI 1999 3134) and the Afghanistan (United Nations Sanctions) (Channel Islands) (Amendment) Order 1999 (SI 1999 3317), imposes in the Channel Islands restrictions pursuant to a decision of the Security Council of the United Nations in Resolution 1333 of December 19, 2000. It restricts the delivery or supply of arms and related materiel and the provision of related technical assistance and training to Afghanistan and restricts the delivery and supply of acetic anhydride to Afghanistan. It prohibits the making of funds available to Usama bin Laden and his associates, imposes restrictions on flights destined for or originating from Afghanistan to take off from, land in, or fly over the Channel Islands and prohibits the establishment or maintenance of Taliban offices or the carrying on of any business by Ariana Afghan Airlines. The Order imposes restrictions pursuant to a decision of the Security Council of the United Nations in its Resolution 1267 of October 15, 1999 by prohibiting any aircraft from taking off from or landing in the Channel Islands if it is owned, leased, or operated by or on behalf of the Taliban and freezes assets of the Taliban or any undertaking owned or controlled by them.

4101. United Nations – sanctions – Afghanistan – Channel Islands

AFGHANISTAN (UNITED NATIONS SANCTIONS) (CHANNEL ISLANDS) (AMENDMENT) ORDER 2001, SI 2001 2562; made under the United Nations Act 1946 s.1. In force: July 20, 2001; £1.50.

This Order amends the Afghanistan (United Nations Sanctions) (Channel Islands) Order 2001 (SI 2001 393) to enhance the financial sanctions regime imposed against the Taliban.

4102. United Nations – sanctions – Afghanistan – Isle of Man

AFGHANISTAN (UNITED NATIONS SANCTIONS) (ISLE OF MAN) ORDER 2001, SI 2001 394; made under the United Nations Act 1946 s.1. In force: February 16, 2001; £3.00.

This Order, which revokes the Afghanistan (United Nations Sanctions) (Isle of Man) Order 1999 (SI 1999 3135) and the Afghanistan (United Nations Sanctions) (Isle of Man) (Amendment) Order 1999 (SI 1999 3318) imposes in the Isle of Man restrictions pursuant to a decision of the Security Council of the United Nations in Resolution 1333 of December 19, 2000. It restricts the delivery or supply of arms and related materiel and the provision of related technical assistance and training to Afghanistan and restricts the delivery and supply of acetic anhydride to Afghanistan. It prohibits the making of funds available to Usama bin Laden and his associates, imposes restrictions on flights destined for or originating from Afghanistan to take off from, land in, or fly over the Channel Islands and prohibits the establishment or maintenance of Taliban offices or the carrying on of any business by Ariana Afghan Airlines. The Order imposes restrictions pursuant to a decision of the Security Council of the United Nations in its Resolution 1267 of October 15, 1999 by prohibiting any aircraft from taking off from or landing in the Channel Islands if it is owned, leased, or operated by or on behalf of the Taliban and freezes assets of the Taliban or any undertaking owned or controlled by them.

4103. United Nations – sanctions – Afghanistan – Isle of Man

AFGHANISTAN (UNITED NATIONS SANCTIONS) (ISLE OF MAN) (AMENDMENT) ORDER 2001, SI 2001 2566; made under the United Nations Act 1946 s.1. In force: July 20, 2001; £1.50.

This Order amends the Afghanistan (United Nations Sanctions) (Isle of Man) Order 2001 (SI 2001 394) to enhance the financial sanctions regime imposed against the Taliban.

4104. United Nations – sanctions – Afghanistan – overseas territories

AFGHANISTAN (UNITED NATIONS SANCTIONS) (OVERSEAS TERRITORIES) ORDER 2001, SI 2001 392; made under the United Nations Act 1946 s.1. In force: February 16, 2001; £3.00.

This Order, which applies to specified territories, imposes restrictions pursuant to a decision of the Security Council of the United Nations in its Resolution 1333 of December 19, 2000 on the delivery or supply of arms and related materiel, the provision of technical assistance and training, and the supply of acetic anhydride to Afghanistan. It restricts the taking off from, landing in or flying over any of the specified territories of flights destined for or originating from Afghanistan, prohibits the making available of funds to Usama bin Laden and his associates, prohibits the establishment or maintenance of Taliban offices or the carrying on of any business by Ariana Afghan Airlines and freezes assets of the Taliban or any undertaking owned or controlled by them. In addition, the Order revokes the Afghanistan (United Nations Sanctions) (Overseas Territories) Order 1999 (SI 1999 3218).

4105. United Nations – sanctions – Afghanistan – overseas territories

AFGHANISTAN (UNITED NATIONS SANCTIONS) (OVERSEAS TERRITORIES) (AMENDMENT) ORDER 2001, SI 2001 2558; made under the United Nations Act 1946 s.1. In force: July 20, 2001; £1.75.

This Order amends the Afghanistan (United Nations Sanctions) (Overseas Territories) Order 2001 (SI 2001 392) to enhance the financial sanctions regime imposed against the Taliban.

4106. United Nations – sanctions – Iraq – overseas territories

IRAQ (UNITED NATIONS SANCTIONS) (OVERSEAS TERRITORIES) (AMENDMENT) ORDER 2001, SI 2001 395; made under the United Nations Act 1946 s.1. In force: February 16, 2001; £1.50.

This Order amends the Iraq (United Nations Sanctions) (Overseas Territories) Order 2000 (SI 2000 3242) to correct an error.

4108. United Nations – sanctions – Liberia

LIBERIA (UNITED NATIONS SANCTIONS) ORDER 2001, SI 2001 947; made under the United Nations Act 1946 s.1. In force: March 16, 2001; £2.50.

This Order, which revokes the United Nations Arms Embargoes (Liberia, Somalia and the former Yugoslavia) Order 1993 (SI 1993 1787) in so far as it applies to Liberia, imposes restrictions on the delivery or supply of arms and related materiel and the provision of related technical assistance and training to Liberia pursuant to a decision of the Security Council of the United Nations in its resolution 1343 of March 7, 2001.

4109. United Nations – sanctions – Liberia – Channel Islands

LIBERIA (UNITED NATIONS SANCTIONS) (CHANNEL ISLANDS) ORDER 2001, SI 2001 949; made under the United Nations Act 1946 s.1. In force: March 16, 2001; £3.00.

This Order, which amends the United Nations Arms Embargoes (Somalia, Liberia and Rwanda) (Channel Islands) Order 1996 (SI 1996 3154), imposes in the Channel Islands restrictions pursuant to a decision of the Security Council of the

United Nations in its resolution 1344 of March 7, 2001, on the delivery and supply of arms and related materiel, and on the provision of related technical assistance and training, to Liberia.

4110. United Nations – sanctions – Liberia – Isle of Man

LIBERIA (UNITED NATIONS SANCTIONS) (ISLE OF MAN) ORDER 2001, SI 2001 948; made under the United Nations Act 1946 s.1. In force: March 16, 2001; £2.50.

This Order, which amends the United Nations Arms Embargoes (Somalia, Liberia and Rwanda) (Isle of Man) Order 1996 (SI 1996 3153), imposes, in the Isle of Man, restrictions pursuant to a decision of the Security Council of the United Nations in its Resolution 1344 of March 7, 2001 on the delivery or supply of arms and related materiel, and on the provision of technical assistance and training to Liberia.

4111. United Nations – sanctions – Liberia – overseas territories

LIBERIA (UNITED NATIONS SANCTIONS) (OVERSEAS TERRITORIES) ORDER 2001, SI 2001 946; made under the United Nations Act 1946 s.1. In force: March 16, 2001; £2.50.

This Order, which revokes the United Nations Arms Embargoes (Dependent Territories) Order 1995 (SI 1995 1032), applies to specified territories. It imposes restrictions on the delivery or supply of arms and related materiel and the provision of related technical assistance and training to Liberia pursuant to a decision of the Security Council of the United Nations in its resolution 1343 of March 7, 2001.

4112. United Nations – sanctions – Liberia – overseas territories

LIBERIA (UNITED NATIONS SANCTIONS) (OVERSEAS TERRITORIES) (NO.2) ORDER 2001, SI 2001 1867; made under the United Nations Act 1946 s.1. In force: May 15, 2001; £2.00.

This Order, which amends the Liberia (United Nations Sanctions) (Overseas Territories) Order 1991 (SI 1991 946), imposes restrictions on the import of rough diamonds from Liberia.

4113. Weapons – anti-personnel landmines – elimination of use – Council Regulation

Council Regulation 1725/2001 of 23 July 2001 concerning action against anti-personnel landmines in third world countries other than developing countries. [2001] OJ L234/6.

4114. Weapons – landmines – elimination of use – Council Regulation

European Parliament and Council Regulation 1724/2001 of 23 July 2001 concerning action against anti-personnel landmines in developing countries. [2001] OJ L234/1.

4115. World Trade Organisation – legal advice – Advisory Centre for WTO Law

ADVISORY CENTRE ON WTO LAW (IMMUNITIES AND PRIVILEGES) ORDER 2001, SI 2001 1868; made under the International Organisations Act 1968 s.1. In force: in accordance with Art.1; £1.50.

This Order confers the legal capacities of a body corporate on the Advisory Centre for WTO Law. The legal capacity is conferred in accordance with the Agreement establishing the Advisory Centre on WTO Law (Cm. 4721) Art.10(1). The Order will enable the government to give effect to Art.10(1) of the agreement, and will come into force on the date on which the agreement enters into force in respect of the UK.

4116. Books

Allott, Philip – Eunomia. Paperback: £16.99. ISBN 0-19-924493-6. Oxford University Press.

Askin, Kelly D.; Koenig, Dorean – Women and International Human Rights Law. Hardback: £257.50. ISBN 1-57105-094-9. Transnational Publishers, Inc.

Barker, Craig – International Law and International Relations. IR for the 21st Century. Hardback: £45.00. ISBN 0-8264-5029-6. Paperback: £14.99. ISBN 0-8264-5028-8. Continuum Publishing Group.

Beck, Robert A.; Ambrosio, Thomas – International Law and the Rise of Nations. Paperback: £28.95. ISBN 1-889119-30-X. Chatham House Publishers of Seven Bridges Press, LLC.

Bederman, David J. – An International Law in Antiquity. Cambridge Studies in International and Comparative Law, 16. Hardback: £45.00. ISBN 0-521-79197-9. Cambridge University Press.

Bermann, George; Herdegen, Matthias; Lindseth, Peter – Transatlantic Regulatory Co-operation: Legal Problems and Political Prospects. Hardback: £60.00. ISBN 0-19-829892-7. Oxford University Press.

Bloxham, Donald – Genocide on Trial-War Crimes Trials and the Formation of Holocaust History and Memory. Hardback: £35.00. ISBN 0-19-820872-3. Oxford University Press.

Bouchet-Saulnier, Francois – Practical Guide to Humanitarian Law. First English Language Edition. Paperback: £27.00. ISBN 0-7425-1063-8. Rowman & Littlefield Publishers.

Brownlie, Ian; Crawford, James; Lowe, Vaughan – British Year Book of International Law: Vol 70. 1999. Hardback: £110.00. ISBN 0-19-829914-1. Hardback: £110.00. ISBN 0-19-829914-1. Oxford University Press.

Brunnee, Jutta; Hey, Ellen – Yearbook of International Environmental Law: Vol 11. 2000. Yearbook of International Environmental Law. Hardback: £115.00. ISBN 0-19-924708-0. Oxford University Press.

Cassese, Antonio – International Law. 2nd Ed. Paperback: £21.99. ISBN 0-19-829998-2. Oxford University Press.

Castellino, Joshua – International Law of Self-determination: the Interplay of the Politics of Territorial Possession with Formulations of Post-colonial "national" Identity. Developments in International Law, 38. Hardback: £57.50. ISBN 90-411-1409-2. Martinus Nijhoff Publishers.

Chen, Lung-chu – An Introduction to Contemporary International Law. Hardback: £40.00. ISBN 0-300-08454-4. Paperback: £20.00. ISBN 0-300-08477-3. Yale University Press.

Crawford, James; Lowe, Vaughan – British Year Book of International Law: Vol 71. 2000. Hardback: £115.00. ISBN 0-19-924692-0. Oxford University Press Inc, USA.

Dinstein, Yoram – War, Aggression and Self-defence. Hardback: £70.00. ISBN 0-521-79344-0. Paperback: £24.95. ISBN 0-521-79758-6. Cambridge University Press.

Everall, Mark; Hamilton, Carolyn; Lowe, Nigel – International Child Abduction-law and Practice. Paperback (C format): £39.95. ISBN 0-406-00541-9. Butterworths Law.

Jazbec, Milan – Diplomacies of New Small States: the Case of Slovenia with Some Comparison from the Baltics. Hardback: £42.50. ISBN 0-7546-1706-8. Ashgate Publishing Limited.

Kaczorowska, Alina – Public International Law Textbook. 2nd Ed. Old Bailey Press Textbooks. Paperback: £14.95. ISBN 1-85836-416-7. Old Bailey Press.

Kemp, Walter A. – Quiet Diplomacy in Action: the OSCE High Commissioner on National Minorities. Hardback: £28.00. ISBN 90-411-1651-6. Kluwer Law International.

Kjonstad, Asbjorn; Robson, Peter – Poverty and the Law. Onati International Series in Law and Society. Hardback: £35.00. ISBN 1-84113-190-3. Paperback: £20.00. ISBN 1-84113-191-1. Hart Publishing.

Koskenniemi, Martti – Sources of International Law. The Library of Essays in International Law, No 5. Hardback: £90.00. ISBN 1-84014-097-6. Dartmouth.

Krieger, Heike – Kosovo Conflict and International Law: An Analytical Documentation 1974-1999. Cambridge International Documents Series, 11. Hardback: £80.00. ISBN 0-521-80071-4. Cambridge University Press.

Lauterpacht, E.; Greenwood, C. J. – International Law Reports. International Law Reports. Hardback: £95.00. ISBN 0-521-66120-X. Cambridge University Press.

Lauterpacht, E.; Greenwood, C.J. – International Law Reports. International Law Reports. Hardback: £110.00. ISBN 0-521-66121-8. Cambridge University Press.

Letterman, G. Gregory – Basics of International Intellectual Property Law. The Basics of International Law. Hardback: £116.99. ISBN 1-57105-207-0. Transnational Publishers, Inc.

Lorenz, Edward C. – Defining Global Justice. Hardback: £45.95. ISBN 0-268-02550-9. Paperback: £23.50. ISBN 0-268-02551-7. University of Notre Dame Press.

Malanczuk, Peter – Key Documents in International Law. Hardback: £50.00. ISBN 0-415-24687-3. Routledge, an imprint of Taylor & Francis Books Ltd.

Malanczuk, Peter – Akehurst's Modern Introduction to International Law. Hardback: £60.00. ISBN 0-415-24355-6. Routledge, an imprint of Taylor & Francis Books Ltd.

Malanczuk, Peter – Key Documents in International Law. Paperback: £17.99. ISBN 0-415-24688-1. Routledge, an imprint of Taylor & Francis Books Ltd.

Malanczuk, Peter – Akehurst's Modern Introduction to International Law. Paperback: £19.99. ISBN 0-415-24356-4. Routledge, an imprint of Taylor & Francis Books Ltd.

Meyer, Howard N. – World Court in Action-Judging Among the Nations. Hardback: £57.00. ISBN 0-74250-923-0. Paperback: £20.95. ISBN 0-74250-924-9. Rowman & Littlefield Publishers.

O'Brien, John – International Law. Paperback: £36.95. ISBN 1-85941-630-6. Cavendish Publishing Ltd.

Sands, Philippe; Klein, Pierre – Bowett: Law of International Institutions. 5th Ed. Paperback: £30.00. ISBN 0-421-53690-X. Sweet & Maxwell.

Sarooshi, Danesh – United Nations and the Development of Collective Security. Oxford Monographs in International Law. Paperback: £22.50. ISBN 0-19-829934-6. Oxford University Press.

Sienho Yee; Wang Tieya – International Law in the Post-cold War World. Routledge Studies in International Law, 1. Hardback: £95.00. ISBN 0-415-23608-8. Routledge, an imprint of Taylor & Francis Books Ltd.

Sims, Nicholas – Evolution of Biological Disarmament. SIPRI Chemical & Biological Warfare Studies. Paperback: £25.00. ISBN 0-19-829578-2. Oxford University Press.

Smith, Karen E.; Light, Margot – Ethics and Foreign Policy. LSE Monographs in International Studies. Hardback: £40.00. ISBN 0-521-80415-9. Cambridge University Press.

Stokke, Olav Schram – Governing High-seas Fisheries. Hardback: £65.00. ISBN 0-19-829949-4. Oxford University Press.

Treverton, Gregory W. – Reshaping Intelligence for the 21st Century. Hardback: £24.95. ISBN 0-521-58096-X. Cambridge University Press.

Zedalis, Rex J. – International Energy Law: Rules Governing Future Exploration, Exploitation and Use of Renewable Resources. Hardback: £60.00. ISBN 0-7546-2164-2. Ashgate Publishing Limited.

INTERNATIONAL TRADE

4117. Common customs tariff duty – garlic – Council Regulation

Council Regulation 2241/2001 of 15 November 2001 amending the autonomous common customs tariff duty for garlic falling within CN code 0703 20 00. [2001] OJ L303/8.

4118. Community trade – statistics – Council Decision

European Parliament and Council Decision 507/2001 of 12 March 2001 concerning a set of actions relating to the trans-European network for the collection, production and dissemination of statistics on the trading of goods within the Community and between the Community and non member countries (Edicom). [2001] OJ L76/1.

4119. Customs – tariff duties – suspension – Council Regulation

Council Regulation 1159/2001 of 11 June 2001 amending Regulation 1255/96 temporarily suspending the autonomous common customs tariff duties on certain industrial, agricultural and fishery products. [2001] OJ L169/1.

4120. Customs duty – community transit – entitlement to raise import duty – compliance with relevant time limits

[Council Regulation 2913/92 establishing the Community Customs Code Art.215; Commission Regulation 2454/93 laying down provisions for the implementation of Council Regulation 2913/92 establishing the Community Customs Code Art.378, Art.379.]

PSL appealed against a ruling of the Vat and duties tribunal and disputed liability for a customs debt which CE contended had arisen in the United Kingdom pursuant to the Community Customs Code as established by Council Regulation 2913/92. PSL carried on business as a freight forwarder and had despatched a cargo of cigarettes from the UK to Spain in accordance with the External Community Transit Procedure, ECTP. The cargo disappeared in transit, giving rise to a customs debt for the import duty which would have been payable but for the ECTP. PSL maintained that CE were not entitled to recover import duty having failed to comply with the time limits for the service of relevant notices specified in Commission Regulation 2454/93 Art.379.

Held, allowing the appeal, that Commission Regulation 2454/93 Art.379 supplemented Council Regulation 2913/92 Art.215. Commission Regulation 2454/93 Art.378 required that the procedure stipulated under Art.379(2) had to be observed and if it was not then the member state departing from the procedure was not permitted to levy import charges. On the facts the failure by Customs to seek proof of regularity or confirmation of the place of irregularity within the relevant time limits precluded it from recovering the outstanding duty, *Hauptzollant Neubrandenberg v. Lensing and Brockhausen GmbH (C233/98)* [1999] E.C.R. I-7349 applied.

PSL FREIGHT LTD v. CUSTOMS AND EXCISE COMMISSIONERS [2001] B.T.C. 5437, Sir Andrew Morritt V.C., Ch D.

4121. Customs duty – remission – fraud – liability of principal – facts constituting a "special situation"

[Council Regulation 2913/92 establishing the Community Customs Code Art.239; Commission Regulation 2454/93 laying down provision for the implementation of Community Customs Codes Art.905.]

S, a German customs agent liable for import duty arising from the improper transport of goods within the European Community, sought the annulment of a decision of the European Commission which found that the remission of those duties sought was not justified. The goods in question were to have been transported from Germany to Spain in accordance with the ECT procedure, under which goods could travel through the Community without duty until they reached there final destination, but in the event, the declared recipient produced the required Spanish documentation fraudulently and distributed the goods in Germany. Whilst S conceded that it was liable to pay the duties arising from the improper completion of the ECT procedure, it claimed that such duties should be remitted on the basis that there was a "special situation" within the terms of Council Regulation 2913/92 Art. 239(1) and Commission Regulation 2454/93 Art. 905(1). S maintained that the facts of the case constituted a "special situation" since it had acted in good faith and at least one Spanish customs official must have been involved in the commission of the fraud. Moreover, that the Commission had misapplied the Regulations and had erred in concluding that in the absence of a formal finding by the Spanish authority of fraud involving customs officials, there had been insufficient evidence to conclude that a "special situation" existed.

Held, granting the application and allowing remission of duties, that having regard to the relevant authorities, Art. 905 contained an equitable provision intended to deal with exceptional situations faced by an operator and was intended to apply, inter alia, where the circumstances of the relationship between a trader and administrator was such that it would be inequitable to require the trader to bear a loss which, in normal circumstances, it would not have incurred, *Woltmann (t/a Trans-ex-Import) v. Hauptzollamt Potsdam (C86/97)* [1999] E.C.R. I-1041 and *Eyckeler & Malt AG v. Commission of the European Communities (T42/96)* [1998] E.C.R. II-401 applied. The Commission in deciding whether a "special situation" existed, must balance the Community interest against the interests of a trader who had acted in good faith. In the instant case, the facts relating to the fraud could only be reasonably explained by the active compliance of a Spanish customs official or a failure by that office that permitted a third party to use its equipment to produce fraudulent documents. S could not monitor or influence such matters with the result that those were circumstances beyond the normal risk and constituted a "special situation". Further, the Commission had been wrong to restrict its consideration to the possibility of active fraudulent involvement by a customs officer and had erred in requiring S to produce formal and definitive proof of such complicity.

SPEDITION WILHELM ROTERMUND GmbH v. COMMISSION OF THE EUROPEAN COMMUNITIES (T330/99) [2001] 3 C.M.L.R. 32, AWH Meij (President), CFI.

4122. Dumping – anti-subsidy matters – Council Regulation

Council Regulation 1515/2001 of 23 July 2001 on the measures that may be taken by the Community following a report adopted by the WTO Dispute Settlement Body concerning anti-dumping and anti-subsidy matters. [2001] OJ L201/10.

4123. Embargoes – Iraq – illegality of contract – bar to recovery – effect on peaceful enjoyment of property

[Human Rights Act1998 Sch.1 Part II Art.1; Control of Gold, Securities, Payments and Credits (Republic of Iraq) Directions 1990 (SI 1990 1616) Art.2.]

A and S, both of whom originated from Iraq and were parties to a contract under which S advanced certain monies to A, appealed against a decision (Times, June 16, 1999, [1999] C.L.Y. 3644) that S was entitled to recover those monies. The judge had concluded that the monies had not been advanced in contravention of the Control of Gold, Securities, Payments and Credits (Republic of Iraq) Directions 1990 Art.2 which prohibited any trading with Iraqi residents and were therefore recoverable. A maintained that (1) S should be prevented from recovery as the monies had been advanced illegally and the judge had erred in his conclusion that the Directions did not apply to A since he no longer resided in Iraq, and (2) a bar to recovery on the basis of illegality would amount to a depravation of A's right to possession of the monies in contravention of the Human Rights Act1998 Sch.1 Part II Art.1, which provided for the peaceful enjoyment of property.

Held, allowing the appeal, that (1) the judge had erred in his interpretation of the Directions. On a proper interpretation the trade embargo applied to persons who were resident in Iraq at the time the Directions came into force. To allow a more limited interpretation based on an absurd literal approach would be to create a situation whereby the Treasury's control over transactions affected by the sanctions could easily be avoided by Iraqi residents simply moving their de facto residence to a different country after the Directions came into force, *Boissevain v. Weil* [1950] A.C. 327 applied. Accordingly, the monies were irrecoverable since S's claim was founded on illegality, *Soleimany v. Soleimany*

[1999] Q.B. 785, [1998] C.L.Y. 236 applied, and (2) assuming that Art.1 was engaged, the matter clearly fell within the public interest exception to the right and the illegality defence was compatible with the right to possession.

AL-KISHTAINI v. SHANSHAL; *sub nom.* SHANSHAL v. AL-KISHTAINI, [2001] EWCA Civ 264, [2001] 2 All E.R. (Comm) 601, Mummery, L.J., CA.

4124. Export controls – dual use goods

DUAL-USE ITEMS (EXPORT CONTROL) (AMENDMENT) REGULATIONS 2001, SI 2001 1344; made under the European Communities Act 1972 s.2. In force: April 26, 2001; £1.75.

These Regulations amend the Dual-Use Items (Export Control) Regulations 2000 (SI 2000 2620) by extending the definition of "the Regulation" to include Council Regulation 2889/2000 ([2000] OJ L336/14) and Council Regulation 458/2001 ([2001] OJ L65/19), by removing the general prohibition on exports of all items that relate to marine, aircraft, space vehicles, propulsion systems and related equipment to Iran and Iraq and by extending the items in relation to which the notification requirements are not applicable.

4125. Export controls – export prohibitions

EXPORT OF GOODS (CONTROL) (AMENDMENT NO.2) ORDER 2001, SI 2001 3166; made under the Import, Export and Customs Powers (Defence) Act 1939 s.1. In force: September 19, 2001; £1.50.

This Order makes changes to the formulation used to express export prohibitions in the Export of Goods (Control) Order 1994 (SI 1994 1191).

4126. Export controls – petroleum – Yugoslavia

FEDERAL REPUBLIC OF YUGOSLAVIA (SUPPLY, SALE AND EXPORT OF PETROLEUM AND PETROLEUM PRODUCTS) (REVOCATION) REGULATIONS 2001, SI 2001 17; made under the European Communities Act 1972 s.2. In force: January 31, 2001; £1.50.

These Regulations revoke the Federal Republic of Yugoslavia (Supply, Sale and Export of Petroleum and Petroleum Products) (Penalties and Licences) Regulations 1999 (SI 1999 1516) and the Federal Republic of Yugoslavia (Supply, Sale and export of Petroleum and Petroleum Products) (Penalties and Licences) (No.3) Regulations 1999 (SI 1999 2821) in consequence of the repeal of Council Regulations 900/1999 ([1999] OJ L114/1) and 2111/99 ([1999] OJ L258/12) which prohibited the supply, sale and export of specified petroleum and petroleum products to certain parts of the Federal Republic of Yugoslavia.

4127. Export controls – weapons – Yugoslavia

EXPORT OF GOODS (CONTROL) (AMENDMENT) ORDER 2001, SI 2001 729; made under the Import, Export and Customs Powers (Defence) Act 1939 s.1. In force: March 26, 2001; £1.75.

This Order amends the Export of Goods (Control) Order 1994 (SI 1994 1191) by applying the 1994 Order to dual use goods that have been imported into the UK for transit or transhipment. It makes amendments to prohibit the exportation through transit or transhipment of any dual use goods which are or may be intended to be used in the production of weapons of mass destruction, to remove such dual use goods from the existing broad exception of most goods in transit from the requirement for licensing and to remove the prohibition on the export of specified electronic equipment used for television broadcasting or television news gathering to the Federal Republic of Yugoslavia. In addition, the Order makes amendments to provide a further exception in respect of down-hole oil field applications to the controls that are in place on equipment and devices for use with explosives or dealing with "improvised explosive devices" and makes technical amendments to the Military List to reflect changes agreed at the Wassenaar Plenary in December 2000.

4128. Exports – dual use goods – Council Regulation

Council Regulation 458/2001 of 6 March 2001 amending Regulation 1334/2000 with regard to the list of controlled dual use items and technology when exported. [2001] OJ L65/19.

4129. Import controls – European Union – direct effect of restrictions contained in Council regulations

[European Communities Act 1972 s.2(1); Customs and Excise Management Act 1979 s.170(2)(b); EC Treaty Art.189 (now Art.249 EC); Council Regulation 3626/82 on the implementation in the Community of the Convention on international trade in endangered species of wild fauna and flora; Council Regulation 338/97 on the protection of species of wild fauna and flora by regulating trade therein.]

S, who had imported a number of endangered parrots into Austria and subsequently brought them into the United Kingdom, appealed against his conviction of four counts of being knowingly concerned in the fraudulent evasion of a restriction on the importation of goods contrary to the Customs and Excise Management Act 1979 s.170(2)(b). S contended that Council Regulation 3626/82 Art.5(1) and Council Regulation 338/97 Art.4(1), both of which restricted the entry of certain goods into the European Union and were applicable to the species of parrot imported by S, did not have direct effect in the UK. He submitted in the alternative that if those provisions did have direct effect in the UK, they only restricted the introduction of the parrots at the point of entry, and since that was not the UK, he had not committed an offence within the UK.

Held, dismissing the appeal, that (1) S had attempted to apply to the regulations tests which were relevant only to the direct effect of Treaty provisions. It was expressly provided by the EC Treaty Art.189 (now Art.249 EC) that Council regulations were directly applicable within Member States, and the European Communities Act 1972 s.2(1) ensured that regulations became part of domestic law without any requirement for national legislation; (2) for the purposes of s.170(2)(b) of the 1979 Act, both regulations were "enactments" containing restrictions within the scope of the 1979 Act, with the result that it was an offence to be knowingly concerned in the fraudulent evasion of those restrictions, and (3) the 1979 Act applied where restrictions were evaded in any country within the European Union. For the purpose of s.170(2), therefore, it did not matter which country had been the point of entry.

R. v. SISSEN (HENRY THOMAS) [2001] 1 W.L.R. 902, Ouseley, J., CA (Crim Div).

4130. Imports – textile products – Taiwan

Council Regulation 2279/2001 of 16 November 2001 amending Regulation 47/1999 on the arrangements for imports of certain textile products originating in Taiwan. [2001] OJ L307/1.

4131. Infectious disease control – foot and mouth disease – import and export restrictions

IMPORT AND EXPORT RESTRICTIONS (FOOT-AND-MOUTH DISEASE) (NO.14) REGULATIONS 2001, SI 2001 4046; made under the European Communities Act 1972 s.2. In force: December 20, 2001 at 8 pm; £4.00.

These Regulations, which revoke the Import and Export Restrictions (Foot-and-Mouth Disease) (No.13) Regulations 2001 (SI 2001 3861), implement Commission Decision 2001/911 ([2001] OJ L337/39) amending for the fourth time Decision 2001/740 concerning certain protection measures with regard to foot and mouth disease in the UK. They regulate the importation of live animals, the export of live animals, the export of fresh meat, the export of meat products, milk,

milk preparations, the export of semen, ova or embryos of animals of the bovine, ovine, caprine and porcine species and other biungulates and also the export of equidae.

4132. Infectious disease control – foot and mouth disease – import and export restrictions – fees

IMPORT AND EXPORT RESTRICTIONS (FOOT-AND-MOUTH DISEASE) (NO.10) (FEES) REGULATIONS 2001, SI 2001 3509; made under the European Communities Act 1972 s.2. In force: October 30, 2001 at 10 am; £1.50.

These Regulations permit the Food Standards Agency to charge a reasonable fee for supervision or inspections carried out by them for the purposes of establishing eligibility for the dispatch of products under the Import and Export Restrictions (Foot-and-Mouth Disease) (No.10) Regulations 2001 (SI 2001 3451).

4133. Tariffs – imports – soluble coffee – Council Regulation

Council Regulation 2165/2001 of 5 November 2001 opening and providing for the administration of a tariff quota for imports of soluble coffee covered by CN code 2101 11 11. [2001] OJ L292/1.

4134. Tariffs – quotas – agricultural and industrial products – Council Regulation

Council Regulation 1142/2001 of 7 June 2001 amending Regulation 2505/96 opening and providing for the administration of autonomous Community tariff quotas for certain agricultural and industrial products. [2001] OJ L155/1.

4135. Taxation – duty free – quantitative restrictions limitation – Council Regulation

Council Regulation 416/2001 of 28 February 2001 amending Regulation 2820/ 98 applying a multi-annual scheme of generalised tariff preferences for the period 1 July 1999 to 31 December 2001 so as to extend duty free access without any quantitative restrictions to products originating in the least developed countries. [2001] OJ L60/43.

4136. Trade policy – preferential trade – Council Regulation

Council Regulation 1207/2001 of 11 June 2001 on procedures to facilitate the issue of movement certificates EUR.1, the making-out of invoice declarations and forms EUR.2 and the issue of certain approved exporter authorisations under the provisions governing preferential trade between the European Community and certain countries and repealing Regulation 3351/83. [2001] OJ L165/1.

4137. Trade policy – preferential trade concessions – Bulgaria, Hugary and Romania – Council Regulation

Council Regulation 678/2001 ([2001] OJ L94/1) of February 26 2001 concerning the conclusion of Agreements in the form of Exchanges of Letters between the European Community and the Republic of Bulgaria, the Republic of Hungary and Romania on reciprocal preferential trade concessions for certain wines and spirits, and amending Regulation 933/95. [2001] OJ L94/1.

4138. Books

Appelbaum, Richard; Felstiner, William; Gessner, Volkmar – Rules and Networks. Hardback: £45.00. ISBN 1-84113-295-0. Paperback: £20.00. ISBN 1-84113-296-9. Hart Publishing.

Chuah, Jason – Law of International Trade. 2nd Ed. Paperback: £22.95. ISBN 0-421-74650-5. Sweet & Maxwell.

D'arcy, Leo; Murray, Carol and Cleave, Barbara – Schmitthoff's Export Trade: the Law and Practice of International Trade. 10th Ed. International Student Edition. Paperback: £14.95. ISBN 0-421-60690-8. Sweet & Maxwell.

D'arcy, Leo; Murray, Carol; Cleave, Barbara – Schmitthoff: Export Trade: the Law and Practice of International Trade. 10th Ed. Paperback: £40.00. ISBN 0-421-54680-8. Sweet & Maxwell.

de Burca, Grainne; Scott, Joanne – EU and the WTO. Hardback: £35.00. ISBN 1-84113-199-7. Hart Publishing.

Dillon, Sara – International Trade and Economic Law and the European Union. Paperback: £25.00. ISBN 1-84113-113-X. Hart Publishing.

Dispute Settlement Reports 1998: Vol IX. World Trade Organization Dispute Settlement Reports. Hardback: £75.00. ISBN 0-521-80100-1. Paperback: £30.00. ISBN 0-521-80505-8. Cambridge University Press.

Dispute Settlement Reports 1998: Vol VII. World Trade Organization Dispute Settlement Reports. Paperback: £30.00. ISBN 0-521-80503-1. Cambridge University Press.

Dispute Settlement Reports 1998: Vol VIII. World Trade Organization Dispute Settlement Reports. Paperback: £30.00. ISBN 0-521-80504-X. Cambridge University Press.

Dispute Settlement Reports 1999. World Trade Organization Dispute Settlement Reports. Paperback: £30.00. ISBN 0-521-00565-5. Cambridge University Press.

Dispute Settlement Reports 1999: Volume I. World Trade Organization Dispute Settlement Reports. Hardback: £75.00. ISBN 0-521-80320-9. Paperback: £30.00. ISBN 0-521-00562-0. Cambridge University Press.

Dispute Settlement Reports 1999: Volume II. World Trade Organization Dispute Settlement Reports. Hardback: £75.00. ISBN 0-521-80321-7. Paperback: £30.00. ISBN 0-521-00564-7. Cambridge University Press.

Dispute Settlement Reports 1999: Volume III. World Trade Organization Dispute Settlement Reports. Hardback: £75.00. ISBN 0-521-80322-5. Cambridge University Press.

Evans, Judith – Law of International Trade Textbook . 3rd Ed. Old Bailey Press Textbooks. Paperback: £14.95. ISBN 1-85836-411-6. Old Bailey Press.

Fletcher, Ian F.; Mistelis, Loukas; Cremona, Marise – Foundations and Perspectives of International Trade Law. Paperback: £40.00. ISBN 0-421-74100-7. Sweet & Maxwell.

Hoda, Anwarul – Tariff Negotiations and Renegotiations Under the GATT and the WTO-Procedures and Practices. Hardback: £45.00. ISBN 0-521-80449-3. Cambridge University Press.

Purcell, Oliver Ryan – Milk Quotas. Paperback. ISBN 1-899738-73-8. Round Hall Ltd.

Rowley, J. William – Business Law International: Volume 1. Hardback: £120.00. ISBN 0-521-80100-1. Sweet & Maxwell.

Sellman, Pamela; Evans, Judith – Law of International Trade. 1st Ed. Old Bailey Press 150 Leading Cases Series. Paperback: £9.95. ISBN 1-85836-364-0. Old Bailey Press.

Snyder, Francis – Regional and Global Regulation of International Trade. Hardback: £35.00. ISBN 1-84113-218-7. Hart Publishing.

Todd – International Trade Law. Paperback: £45.00. ISBN 1-85978-573-5. LLP Professional Publishing.

World Trade Organization – World Trade Organization Agreements. World Trade Organization Schedules. Audio CD: £250.00. ISBN 0-521-79645-8. Cambridge University Press.

World Trade Organization – Dispute Settlement Reports 1998. World Trade Organization Dispute Settlement Reports. Hardback: £65.00. ISBN 0-521-78329-1. Hardback: £75.00. ISBN 0-521-80099-4. Cambridge University Press.

World Trade Organization – Dispute Settlement Reports 1998: Vol IV. World Trade Organization Dispute Settlement Reports. Paperback: £30.00. ISBN 0-521-78896-X. Cambridge University Press.

WTO Dispute Settlement Procedures. Hardback: £60.00. ISBN 0-521-80448-5. Paperback: £20.00. ISBN 0-521-01077-2. Cambridge University Press.

JURISPRUDENCE

4139. Books

Ahdar, Rex J. – Law and Religion. Issues in Law and Society. Hardback: £55.00. ISBN 1-84014-745-8. Dartmouth. Paperback: £19.50. ISBN 1-84014-757-1. Ashgate Publishing Limited.

Bederman, David J. – Classical Canons. Applied Legal Philosophy. Hardback: £55.00. ISBN 0-7546-2161-8. Dartmouth.

Cane, Peter; Gardner, John – Relating to Responsibility. Hardback: £35.00. ISBN 1-84113-210-1. Hart Publishing.

Cane, Peter; Gardner, John Professor of Jurisprudence and Fellow of University College, Oxford) – Relating to Responsibility. Hardback: £40.00. ISBN 1-84113-210-1. Hart Publishing.

Christodoulidis, Emilios; Veitch, Scott – Lethe's Law. Hardback: £25.00. ISBN 1-84113-109-1. Hart Publishing.

Coleman, Jules – Practice of Principle. Hardback: £25.00. ISBN 0-19-829814-5. Oxford University Press.

Coleman, Jules L. – Hart's Postscript: Essays on the Postscript to "The Concept of Law". 2nd Ed. Hardback: £40.00. ISBN 0-19-829908-7. Paperback: £14.99. ISBN 0-19-924362-X. Oxford University Press.

Cotterrell, Roger – Sociological Perspectives on Law: Vols 1&2, Classical Foundations / Contemporary Debates. International Library of Essays in Law and Legal Theory (Second Series). Hardback: £195.00. ISBN 0-7546-2128-6. Dartmouth.

Cracknell, D.G. – English Legal System. 3rd Ed. Cracknell's Statutes Series. Paperback: £9.95. ISBN 1-85836-378-0. Old Bailey Press.

Curzon, L.B. – Q&A Jurisprudence. Questions and Answers. Paperback: £9.95. ISBN 1-85941-623-3. Cavendish Publishing Ltd.

Davies, Margaret; Naffine, Ngaire – Are Persons Property? Applied Legal Philosophy. Hardback: £50.00. ISBN 0-7546-2032-8. Ashgate Publishing Limited.

Dickson, Julie – Evaluation and Legal Theory. Hardback: £22.00. ISBN 1-84113-184-9. Paperback: £10.00. ISBN 1-84113-081-8. Hart Publishing.

Doherty, Michael – Jurisprudence. 2nd Ed. Old Bailey Press Textbooks. Paperback: £14.95. ISBN 1-85836-409-4. Old Bailey Press.

Dorsen, Norman; Gifford, Prosser – Democracy and the Rule of Law. Hardback: £50.50. ISBN 1-56802-599-8. Congressional Quarterly Inc.

Duxbury, Neil – Jurists and Judges. Paperback: £15.00. ISBN 1-84113-204-7. Hart Publishing.

Economides, Kim; Betten, Lammy; Bridge, John; Tettenborn, Andrew; Shrubsall, Vivien – Fundamental Values. Hardback: £35.00. ISBN 1-84113-118-0. Hart Publishing.

Ehrlich, Eugen – Fundamental Principles of the Sociology of Law. Paperback: £30.50. ISBN 0-7658-0701-7. Transaction Publishers.

Endicott, Timothy – Vagueness in Law. Hardback: £40.00. ISBN 0-19-826840-8. Oxford University Press.

Evans, J. – English Legal System. Suggested Solutions. £6.95. ISBN 1-85836-392-6. Old Bailey Press.

Fitzpatrick, Peter – Modernism and the Grounds of Law. Cambridge Studies in Law and Society. Hardback: £37.50. ISBN 0-521-80222-9. Paperback: £13.95. ISBN 0-521-00253-2. Cambridge University Press.

Freeman, M.D.A. – Current Legal Problems: Vol 53. 2000. Hardback: £60.00. ISBN 0-19-829940-0. Oxford University Press.

George, Robert – Natural Law, Liberalism, and Morality. Paperback: £12.99. ISBN 0-19-924300-X. Oxford University Press.

Gray,W. Robert – Four Faces of Affirmative Action. Contributions in Legal Studies, No 99. Hardback: £51.95. ISBN 0-313-31559-0. Greenwood Press.

Hohfeld,W.N.; Campbell, David;Thomas, Philip – Fundamental Legal Conceptions As Applied in Judicial Reasoning by Wesley Newcomb Hohfeld. New Ed. Classical Jurisprudence Series. Hardback: £40.00. ISBN 1-85521-668-X. Dartmouth.

Jackson, Emily – Regulating Reproduction-Law, Technology and Autonomy. Paperback: £16.99. ISBN 1-84113-301-9. Hart Publishing.

Kamali – Dignity of Man-an Islamic Perspective. Hardback: £24.95. ISBN 1-903682-03-7. Paperback: £11.95. ISBN 1-903682-00-2. The Islamic Texts Society.

Kamali – Freedom, Equality and Justice in Islam. Paperback: £15.95. ISBN 1-903682-01-0. The Islamic Texts Society.

Kramer, Matthew H. – Rights, Wrongs and Responsibilities. Hardback: £42.50. ISBN 0-333-96329-6. Palgrave, formerly Macmillan Press.

Kutz, Christopher – Complicity: Ethics and Law for a Collective Age. Cambridge Studies in Philosophy and Law. Hardback: £37.50. ISBN 0-521-59452-9. Cambridge University Press.

Law Update 2001. £9.95. ISBN 1-85836-385-3. Old Bailey Press.

Maine, Henry Sumner – Ancient Law. Paperback: £29.50. ISBN 0-7658-0795-5. Transaction Publishers.

Marmor, Andrei – Positive Law and Objective Values. Hardback: £30.00. ISBN 0-19-826897-1. Oxford University Press.

Mayes, David G.; Berghman, Jos; Salais, Robert – Social Exclusion and European Policy. Hardback: £65.00. ISBN 1-84064-688-8. Edward Elgar.

Musson, Anthony – Expectations of the Law in the Middle Ages. Hardback: £50.00. ISBN 0-85115-842-0. The Boydell Press.

Narain,Vrinda – Gender and Community. Hardback: £32.00. ISBN 0-8020-4869-2. University of Toronto Press Inc.

Niemeyer, Gerhart – Law Without Force: the Function of Politics in International Law. Paperback: £19.50. ISBN 0-7658-0640-1. Transaction Publishers.

Nonet, Philippe; Selznick, Philip – Law and Society in Transition: Toward Responsive Law. Paperback: £20.00. ISBN 0-7658-0642-8. Transaction Publishers.

Norrie, Alan – Norrie: Crime, Reason and History. 2nd Ed. Law in Context. Paperback: £21.95. ISBN 0-406-93246-8. Butterworths Law.

Obeng, M. – Jurisprudence and Legal Theory. Suggested Solutions. £6.95. ISBN 1-85836-393-4. Old Bailey Press.

Priban, Jiri; Nelken, David – Law's New Boundaries-the Consequences of Legal Autopiesis. Applied Legal Philosophy. Hardback: £50.00. ISBN 0-7546-2202-9. Ashgate Publishing Limited.

Quinney, Richard – Critique of the Legal Order. Law and Society Series. Paperback: £20.95. ISBN 0-7658-0797-1. Transaction Publishers.

Raz, Joseph – Value, Respect and Attachment. The Seeley Lectures, 4. Hardback: £37.50. ISBN 0-521-80180-X. Paperback (C format): £12.95. ISBN 0-521-00022-X. Cambridge University Press.

Ross, Hamish – Law As a Social Institution. Legal Theory Today. Hardback: £22.00. ISBN 1-84113-230-6. Paperback: £10.00. ISBN 1-84113-231-4. Hart Publishing.

Roznovschi, Mirela – Toward the Cyberlegal Culture. Hardback: £76.99. ISBN 1-57105-168-6. Transnational Publishers, Inc.

Rubenfeld, Jed – Freedom and Time. Hardback: £27.50. ISBN 0-300-08048-4. Yale University Press.

Russell, Peter H.; O'Brien, David M. – Judicial Independence in the Age of Democracy. Constitutionalism and Democracy Series. Hardback: £58.95. ISBN 0-8139-2015-9. Paperback: £18.95. ISBN 0-8139-2016-7. University Press of Virginia.

Sadurski, Wojciech – Justice. International Library of Essays in Law and Legal Theory, Second Series. Hardback: £95.00. ISBN 0-7546-2088-3. Ashgate Publishing Limited.

Seiter, Richard P. – Correctional Administration-Integrating Theory and Practice. Paperback: £29.99. ISBN 0-13-087147-8. Prentice Hall.

Serajuddin, Alamgir Muhammad – Shari'a Law and Society. Hardback: £13.95. ISBN 0-19-579666-7. OUP Pakistan.

Stacy, Helen M. – Postmodernism and Law-Jurisprudence in a Fragmenting World. Applied Legal Philosophy. Hardback: £50.00. ISBN 1-84014-749-0. Dartmouth.

Stinchcombe, Arthur L. – When Formality Works-Authority and Abstraction in Law and Organizations. Hardback: £30.00. ISBN 0-226-77495-3. Paperback: £10.50. ISBN 0-226-77496-1. University of Chicago Press.

Strang, Heather; Braithwaite, John – Restorative Justice and Civil Society. Hardback: £47.50. ISBN 0-521-80599-6. Paperback: £17.95. ISBN 0-521-00053-X. Cambridge University Press.

Tamanaha, Brian Z. – General Jurisprudence of Law and Society. Oxford Socio-Legal Studies. Hardback: £40.00. ISBN 0-19-924466-9. Paperback: £15.99. ISBN 0-19-924467-7. Oxford University Press.

Tigar, Michael – Law and the Rise of Capitalism 2nd Ed. Paperback: £15.00. ISBN 1-58367-030-0. New York University Press.

Tunick, Mark – Practices and Principles. Paperback: £12.95. ISBN 0-691-07079-2. Princeton University Press.

Wickham, Gary; Pavlich, George – Rethinking Law Society and Governance. Onati International Series in Law and Society. Hardback: £45.00. ISBN 1-84113-293-4. Paperback: £20.00. ISBN 1-84113-294-2. Hart Publishing.

Widner, Jennifer A. – Building the Rule of Law. Hardback: £24.00. ISBN 0-393-05037-8. W.W. Norton.

Winston, Kenneth – Fuller's Principles of Social Order. Paperback: £25.00. ISBN 1-84113-234-9. Hart Publishing.

Zucker, Ross – Democratic Distributive Justice. Hardback: £42.50. ISBN 0-521-79033-6. Cambridge University Press.

LANDLORD AND TENANT

4140. Agricultural holdings – units of production – net annual income

AGRICULTURAL HOLDINGS (UNITS OF PRODUCTION) (ENGLAND) ORDER 2001, SI 2001 2751; made under the Agricultural Holdings Act 1986 Sch.6 para.4. In force: September 12, 2001; £2.00.

This Order, which revokes the Agricultural Holdings (Units of Production) (England) Order 2000 (SI 2000 1984), prescribes units of production for the assessment of the productive capacity of agricultural land situated in England and the amount to be regarded as the net annual income from each such unit for the year September 12, 2001 to September 11, 2002 inclusive.

4141. Agricultural holdings – units of production – net annual income – Wales

AGRICULTURAL HOLDINGS (UNITS OF PRODUCTION) (WALES) ORDER 2001, SI 2001 2982 (W.249); made under the Agricultural Holdings Act 1986 Sch.6 para.4. In force: August 31, 2001; £3.00.

This Order, which revokes the Agricultural Holdings (Units of Production) Order 1998 (SI 1998 2025), prescribes units of production for the assessment of the productive capacity of agricultural land in Wales and sets out the amount to be regarded as the net annual income from each such unit for the year September 12, 1999 to September 11, 2000 inclusive.

4142. Agricultural holdings – units of production – net annual income – Wales

AGRICULTURAL HOLDINGS (UNITS OF PRODUCTION) (WALES) (NO.2) ORDER 2001, SI 2001 2983 (W.250); made under the Agricultural Holdings Act 1986 Sch.6 para.4. In force: August 31, 2001; £3.00.

This Order prescribes units of production for the assessment of the productive capacity of agricultural land in Wales and sets out the amount to be regarded as the net annual income from each such unit for the year September 12, 2000 to September 11, 2001 inclusive.

4143. Agricultural holdings – units of production – net annual income – Wales

AGRICULTURAL HOLDINGS (UNITS OF PRODUCTION) (WALES) (NO.3) ORDER 2001, SI 2001 3064 (W.253); made under the Agricultural Holdings Act 1986 Sch.6 para.4. In force: September 12, 2001; £3.00.

This Order prescribes units of production for the assessment of the productive capacity of agricultural land situated in Wales and sets out the amount to be regarded as the net annual income from each such unit for the year September 12, 2001 to September 11, 2002.

4144. Assured shorthold tenancies – notices – service on agent

[Housing Act 1988 s.20; Civil Procedure Rules 1998 (SI 1998 3132) Part 8; The Access to Justice Act 1999 (Destination of Appeals) Order 2000 (SI 2000 1071) Art.4.]

In proceedings brought by Y, the lessor, for a declaration that a tenancy created by an agreement for a lease was an assured shorthold tenancy, Y appealed against a decision that a notice served pursuant to the Housing Act 1988 s.20 on M, a licensed conveyancer engaged by N, the lessee, was invalid. The court below had ruled that a notice issued under s.20 could not be served on an agent and, in any event, M had no authority to accept service.

Held, allowing the appeal and granting the declaration, that service on an agent for a tenant of a s.20 notice was valid service under the Act provided that acceptance of the notice was within the scope of the agent's authority. M had the necessary authority to accept service so that the s.20 notice was validly served. It was observed that where, as in the instant case, a claimant had issued proceedings under the Civil Procedure Rules 1998 Part 8 in the mistaken belief that there was no substantial dispute of fact and the court made no order allocating the claim to the multi track, the claim was deemed to have been so allocated with the result that there could be no appeal from the eventual judgment under The Access to Justice Act 1999 (Destination of Appeals) Order 2000 Art.4.

YENULA PROPERTIES LTD v. NAIDU *The Times*, August 1, 2001, Lloyd, J., Ch D.

4145. Assured shorthold tenancies – possession orders – declaration of incompatibility – public status of housing association – right to family life

[Housing Act 1988 s.21; Human Rights Act 1998 Sch.1 Part I Art.6, Art.8.]

D, a tenant, appealed against a possession order under the Housing Act 1988 s.21 granted in favour of her landlord, P, a housing association, which had been created by the local authority to take over part of its housing stock. D contended that the hearing should have been adjourned so that she could adduce fresh evidence as to whether P was a public body for the purposes of a declaration of incompatibility and whether the mandatory nature of s.21 of the 1988 Act constituted a breach of her right to family life under the Human Rights Act 1998 Sch.1 Part I Art.8 and her right to a fair trial under Art.6.

Held, dismissing the appeal, that the judge had been correct not to adjourn the hearing as otherwise he would have contravened the clear terms of s.21 (4) of the 1988 Act. Although it was not necessarily the case that a body performing a duty that otherwise would be required of a local authority was performing a public function, in the instant case P was so closely identified with the local authority that it was performing public functions. Section 21 (4) was not incompatible with D's right to family life nor with Art.6. The lack of judicial discretion under s.21 (4) was necessary in the public interest to provide a certain procedure to recover possession of property following termination of a shorthold tenancy. The question of whether it was legitimate and proportional was one for Parliament to decide. The correct procedure on an application for a declaration of incompatibility was to give as much informal notice to the Crown as practicable and also to send a copy of the informal notice to the relevant court and to the other party.

POPLAR HOUSING & REGENERATION COMMUNITY ASSOCIATION LTD v. DONOGHUE; *sub nom.* POPLAR HOUSING & REGENERATION COMMUNITY ASSOCIATION LTD v. DONAGHUE; DONOGHUE v. POPLAR HOUSING & REGENERATION COMMUNITY ASSOCIATION LTD, [2001] EWCA Civ 595, [2002] Q.B. 48, Lord Woolf of Barnes, L.C.J., CA.

4146. **Assured tenancies – agreements – determined by court order – discharge of rent arrears – creation of new tenancy**

S, whose assured tenancy had been brought to an end by an order for possession obtained in reliance on a mandatory ground for possession, appealed against a finding that a new tenancy had not been entered into when, shortly before the order for possession was made, the landlord's agent had agreed in writing that he could discharge the outstanding rent arrears by paying a fixed sum each month.

Held, dismissing the appeal, that it was necessary to decide whether the parties had by their actions intended to alter the legal relations that had subsisted between them as governed by the order for possession. In the instant case, the parties had not reached new or different terms as to S's occupation of the property. S would continue to pay for his occupation of the property at the contractual rate, and the only point dealt with expressly by the parties had been the rate at which S would discharge the rent arrears. It would be artificial to distinguish the circumstances of the instant case from a case where the landlord did nothing more than accept payments from a former tenant by way of mesne profits, at the rate set out in a court order and towards the arrears, and refrained from enforcing the order for possession. The relevant letter from the landlord's agent had not been intended to and had not affected the legal relations between the parties as governed by the terms of the order for possession, *Street v. Mountford* [1985] A.C. 809, [1985] C.L.Y. 1893 applied and *Burrows v. Brent LBC* [1996] 1 W.L.R. 1448, [1996] C.L.Y. 3829 distinguished.

LEADENHALL RESIDENTIAL 2 LTD v. STIRLING; *sub nom.* STIRLING v. LEADENHALL RESIDENTIAL 2 LTD, [2001] EWCA Civ 1011, [2002] 1 W.L.R. 499, Lloyd, J., CA.

4147. **Assured tenancies – assured shorthold tenancies – prior tenancy an assured tenancy – secondary declaration unnecessary**

[Housing Act 1988 s.20(3).]

A, the second defendant, appealed against a declaration made during the course of possession proceedings that, based upon an agreement dated June 12, 1996, he was an assured shorthold tenant of property held by GI and their predecessors in title. A submitted that the original tenancy was an assured tenancy agreement and accordingly that the tenancy with GI could not be an assured shorthold tenancy pursuant to the Housing Act 1988 s.20(3).

Held, allowing the appeal, that it was unfortunate that the declaration had been made because the issue was secondary and not essential for the determination of the action, possession proceedings having been dismissed for invalid service, and that the position was incomplete. The court therefore set aside the judge's finding of fact and the declaration and ordered that any subsequent possession proceedings should be heard by a different judge.

GRACECHURCH INTERNATIONAL SA v. TRIBHOVAN (2001) 33 H.L.R. 28, Simon Brown, L.J., CA.

4148. Assured tenancies – hotels – long term occupancy of room – absence of cooking facilities – meaning of "dwelling"

[Housing Act 1998 s.1 (1).]

C appealed against a decision ((2001) 33 H.L.R. 4) to allow U's appeal against the dismissal of a claim for possession of a hotel room which C had occupied as a long term resident. C challenged the finding that in the absence of cooking facilities, the room could not constitute a "dwelling" for the purposes of the Housing Act 1998 s.1 (1) and that C was therefore not an assured tenant under the Act.

Held, allowing the appeal, that a person's home was a dwelling and was no less so just because the person did not cook there. There was no legislation stating that there had to be cooking facilities in order for premises to qualify as a dwelling, nor was there any case law to the effect that the existence of cooking facilities was an essential precondition for security of tenure. The essential feature of a dwelling was that it contained living accommodation, which included a kitchen if there was one. Having identified the subject matter of the tenancy agreement, the issue for consideration was whether at the date of proceedings the premises, or the part of the premises the tenant occupied, was his home. If it was, then it was his dwelling. The absence of cooking facilities was irrelevant.

URATEMP VENTURES LTD v. COLLINS; URATEMP VENTURES LTD v. CARRELL, [2001] UKHL 43, [2002] 1 A.C. 301, Lord Millett, HL.

4149. Assured tenancies – possession orders – application for housing benefit delayed – discretion to adjourn proceedings

[Housing Act 1988 s.9(1), s.9(8).]

O appealed against a decision refusing his application for an adjournment of possession proceedings. The basis of O's application was not that there was any substantive defence but that, with the benefit of a short adjournment, he would be able to resolve problems with his application for housing benefit. A letter from the local authority acknowledged that it had been slow to process the application. The district judge had originally indicated a willingness to adjourn and had so ordered but, on discovering that the court could not re-list the hearing for 10 weeks, revisited his own decision. He stated that he was unwilling to adjourn for so long a period and that, by virtue of the Housing Act 1988 s.9(6), he did not have jurisdiction to adjourn at all; therefore he made an order for possession.

Held, dismissing the appeal, that (1) it was important to distinguish between an adjournment made on procedural grounds where the court was unable to make an immediate determination of the parties' substantive rights and accordingly could not be satisfied that the claim was truly founded upon a mandatory ground, and an adjournment simply to permit a party time to remedy a situation where the parties' respective rights were not in doubt; (2) the power conferred by s.9(1) of the Act related to the latter situation and provided the court with a statutory power to adjourn in a situation where its inherent procedural power to adjourn could not properly be exercised in the applicant's favour; (3) s.9(6) expressly provided that the power conferred by s.9(1) was not exercisable in situations where the court was satisfied that the claimant was entitled to possession on a mandatory ground. Therefore the power could not be exercised in the instant case, with the result that the district judge would have been wrong to adjourn even for a short period, and (4) it made no difference whether the evidence had been heard or not since such a distinction was artificial and impractical in a busy possession list. In a case where the landlord relied on a mandatory ground and the tenant's application to adjourn was based on facts which tended to affirm the landlord's application for possession, the adjournment must be refused and the case decided there and then.

RAZACK v. OSMAN, March 6, 2001, Recorder Adrienne Page Q.C., MCLC. [*Ex rel.* Andrew Butler, Barrister, Francis Taylor Building, Temple, London].

4150. **Assured tenancies – rent reviews – device to circumvent statutory protection**

[Housing Act 1988.]

D appealed against a possession order and judgment for outstanding rent in respect of an assured tenancy which had been granted by B's predecessor pursuant to the Housing Act 1988. The agreement contained a rent review clause under which the rent was increased from £4,680 per annum to £25,000 per annum. D failed to pay the increased amount and contended that, since the landlord had been aware that they were in receipt of housing benefit when they entered into the tenancy, and ought therefore to have known that they had no prospect of meeting the increased rent liability, the rent review clause was a mere device inserted in order to gain possession, or circumvent the protection conferred by the assured tenancy.

Held, allowing the appeal, that the clause was inconsistent with the intention of the parties to grant an assured tenancy when the substance and reality of the transaction was considered in the light of all the relevant circumstances, *AG Securities v. Vaughan* [1990] 1 A.C. 417, [1989] C.L.Y. 2145 considered. The clause in effect amounted to an unlawful contracting out of the statutory scheme for assured tenancies and was not therefore enforceable.

BANKWAY PROPERTIES LTD v. DUNSFORD; *sub nom.* BANKWAY PROPERTIES LTD v. PENFOLD-DUNSFORD; DUNSFORD v. BANKWAY PROPERTIES LTD, [2001] EWCA Civ 528, [2001] 26 E.G. 164, Arden, L.J., CA.

4151. **Business tenancies – compensation – entitlement**

[Landlord and Tenant Act 1954 Part II s.23, s.25, s.37, s.38.]

LB applied for compensation under the Landlord and Tenant Act 1954 Part II s.37 following a ruling that it had been a tenant at will of a unit on R's station concourse after it had failed to give a tenant's notice in response to a landlord's notice issued by R under s.25 of the 1954 Act. LB had been a protected tenant for four years prior to the issue of the notice but the total period of occupancy exceeded five years. LB contended that (1) a clause in the lease excluding compensation where the "period" of occupancy was less than five years was a reference to the whole of the period of occupation and not simply to the length of the protected tenancy, and (2) in the alternative, s.37(1) afforded a right to compensation regardless of the terms of the lease.

Held, refusing the application, that (1) on a proper construction of the lease, "the date upon which the tenant [was] to quit the premises" was the date upon which LB was obliged to leave the premises under the terms of the lease. Accordingly, it followed that the lease excluded compensation if the period of the protected tenancy was less than five years, and (2) the provisions of the 1954 Act did not apply to a tenancy at will by virtue of the effect of s.23 and s.38. Accordingly, the clause in the lease precluding compensation could only take effect in relation to the duration of the protected tenancy.

LONDON BAGGAGE CO (CHARING CROSS) LTD v. RAILTRACK PLC (NO.2) [2001] L.&.T.R. 19, Pumfrey, J., Ch D.

4152. **Business tenancies – derogation from grant – increase in tenant's profits – landlord's right of set off – arrears of rent**

P, a retail trader operating two kiosks inside a London Underground station, instituted proceedings for derogation of grant against his landlord, LU, following the closure to passengers of an exit adjacent to one of the kiosks. P maintained that in consequence he was prevented from trading effectively. LU contended that any detrimental impact upon P's trade at the first kiosk was more than adequately compensated for by the increase in trade at the second kiosk which had resulted directly from passengers who would normally have departed from the station via the exit which was now closed.

Held, giving judgment for P and judgement for U on the counterclaim, that LU had been guilty of a derogation from grant. However, LU was nevertheless entitled to take into account any increased profits made at the second kiosk by way of set off, *Hussey v. Eels* [1990] 2 Q.B. 227, [1990] C.L.Y. 1565 considered. The arrears of rent were due to LU and were to be set off against damages for derogation which were to be assessed if not agreed.

PLATT v. LONDON UNDERGROUND LTD *The Times*, March 13, 2001, Neuberger, J., Ch D.

4153. **Business tenancies – distress – set off – tenant's rights – need for demand for return of overpayment**

In proceedings commenced by F, a business tenant under a lease with HS, the court was asked to determine a number of preliminary issues. The premises let to F had been subject to severe storm damage in 1994 and repairs were not carried out until August 1996. In September 1995 F ceased paying rent and in February 1997 HS instructed bailiffs to levy distress. F contended that pursuant to the terms of the lease a proportion of the rent due should have been suspended and that accordingly he had a right to recover the overpayments that he had made in the period prior to distress being levied. F maintained, furthermore, that he had a right to legal set off. HS contended that F would only become entitled to repayment following a demand for repayment.

Held, granting a declaration in favour of F, that (1) a right of restitution arose immediately following overpayment. There was no requirement for the service of a demand for repayment other than in cases involving rescission, *Freeman v. Jefferies* (1868-69) L.R. 4 Ex. 189 and *Baker v. Courage & Co* [1910] 1 K.B. 56 applied, and (2) legal set off was confined to judicial proceedings, but F was entitled to rely on the principle of equitable set off in view of the close link between the claim and the cross claim, *Eller v. Grovecrest Investments Ltd* [1995] Q.B. 272, [1995] C.L.Y. 3052 considered. A landlord intending to levy distress should ensure that a tenant had no claims which could be offset against the outstanding rent by way of equitable set off.

FULLER v. HAPPY SHOPPER MARKETS LTD [2001] 1 W.L.R. 1681, Lightman, J., Ch D.

4154. **Business tenancies – forfeiture – landlord's re-entry of premises – relief**

[Insolvency Act 1986 s.11 (3).]

E, the subject of an administration order, sought a summary order and summary relief against N, who had forfeited E's lease on commercial premises by taking possession of the premises. E had applied for N's consent to assign the premises. E submitted that N's purported re-entry of the premises contravened the Insolvency Act 1986 s.11 (3), that the proposals put forward to recompense for the breach of covenant were sufficient and that it was wrong to consider other breaches of covenant when deciding on relief against forfeiture.

Held, granting the application until the trial of the action, that (1) there was no basis for saying that the purported re-entry contravened s.11 (3) of the Act, *Razzaq v. Pala* [1997] 1 W.L.R. 1336, [1997] C.L.Y. 3291 applied, and (2) with regard to the breach of covenant, all the circumstances had to be considered including the fact that there could be an unreasonable refusal to assign the licence to the premises, which could only be considered on a formal application.

ESSEX FURNITURE PLC v. NATIONAL PROVIDENT INSTITUTION [2001] L. & T.R. 3, Ferris, J., Ch D.

4155. **Business tenancies – land registration – meaning of competent landlord for purposes of s.25 notice**

[Land Registration Act 1925 s.9, s.69; Landlord and Tenant Act 1954 s.25, s.44.]

PA served a notice on ER, the tenant of premises used as a sandwich bar and restaurant, pursuant to the Landlord and Tenant Act 1954 s.25. ER challenged the validity of the notice on the basis that PA was not the competent landlord within the meaning of s.44 of the Act. ER contended that the freehold title to part of the premises remained vested in a third party notwithstanding the fact that it had purportedly been demised to PA. ER appealed against a declaration that PA was the competent landlord.

Held, dismissing the appeal, that since PA was shown to be the registered proprietor of the leases relating to the whole of the premises, it was, by virtue of the Land Registration Act 1925 s.9 and s.69, deemed to have vested in it the legal interest in the whole of the premises. Furthermore, ER, as lessee in possession, was estopped from arguing as against PA, the lessee of the reversion, that the disputed part of the premises had not been demised to PA. PA was therefore the competent landlord for the purpose of s.44 of the 1954 Act.

PRUDENTIAL ASSURANCE CO LTD v. EDEN RESTAURANTS (HOLBORN) LTD [2000] L. & T.R. 480, Mummery, L.J., CA.

4156. Business tenancies – notices – mistake – service of two inconsistent notices – effect on validity

[Landlord and Tenant Act 1954 s.25.]

BB, tenants, appealed against a decision to allow an appeal by B, the landlord, against a decision that a notice served on BB opposing the grant of a new tenancy pursuant to the Landlord and Tenant Act 1954 s.25 was valid. B had previously sent two notices to BB in error, one of which opposed the tenancy without stating the grounds, and one which stated that the tenancy would not be opposed. Realising their error, B had then sent another notice to BB opposing the tenancy and stating the grounds for that opposition. BB contended that the first notice in which the tenancy was not opposed remained valid since the opposing notice was rendered invalid through the failure to state the grounds for opposition.

Held, dismissing the appeal, that B was entitled to rely on the notice opposing the grant of a new business tenancy since neither of the first two notices were valid. The notice opposing the tenancy was not valid because it failed to state the grounds for opposition but because the notice agreeing to the tenancy was inconsistent with the opposing notice, that too was invalid since it would have been impossible for the recipients to ascertain the landlord's intentions, *Mannai Investment Co Ltd v. Eagle Star Life Assurance Co Ltd* [1997] A.C. 749, [1997] C.L.Y. 3256 applied and *Lewis v. MTC Cars Ltd* [1974] 1 W.L.R. 1499, [1974] C.L.Y. 2084 considered.

BARCLAYS BANK PLC v. BEE, [2001] EWCA Civ 1126, [2002] 1 W.L.R. 332, Aldous, L.J., CA.

4157. Business tenancies – possession of land – car parks – exclusive possession – agreement to manage premises

[Landlord and Tenant Act 1954 Part 2.]

NCP, the managers and operators of a car park pursuant to an agreement with TD and its predecessors in title, sought to establish that the notice given by TD to determine the agreement was ineffective because the agreement amounted to a tenancy rather than a licence and, as such, was afforded the protection of the Landlord and Tenant Act 1954 Part 2. NCP submitted that the substance of the agreement as a whole granted it exclusive possession, notwithstanding that the words of the agreement, when literally construed, merely implied a right to exclude TD and in fact imposed certain obligations on NCP, including the provision of a car park for use by TD's servants..

Held, giving judgment for the defendant, that the agreement did not afford NCP exclusive possession of the premises. There was nothing in the agreement to show that NCP's implied rights included a right to exclude TD. The express intention of the agreement was to grant a licence and, in particular, the obligation imposed upon NCP by a clause in the agreement to provide free car parking for TD's servants and agents was not inconsistent with TD exercising rights of entry over the car park, *Shell-Mex and BP Ltd v. Manchester Garages*

[1971] 1 W.L.R. 612, [1971] C.L.Y. 6651 and *Street v. Mountford* [1985] A.C. 809, [1985] C.L.Y. 1893 applied.
NATIONAL CAR PARKS LTD v. TRINITY DEVELOPMENT CO (BANBURY) LTD [2001] L. & T.R. 33, Judge Rich Q.C., Ch D.

4158. **Business tenancies – renewal – tenant's intention irrelevant – statutory compensation**

[Landlord and Tenant Act 1954 s.26, s.37.]
T, the tenant of commercial premises of which S was the landlord, appealed against a finding ([2000] 1 E.G.L.R. 138, [2000] C.L.Y. 3887) that, owing to lack of intention, it was not entitled to statutory compensation under the Landlord and Tenant Act 1954 s.37. T had served a request for a new tenancy pursuant to s.26 of the Act despite the fact that it had exchanged contracts for the purchase of an alternative site and had no intention of renewing the lease. On the termination of the lease, S had commenced proceedings for damages for dilapidations and T had counterclaimed maintaining that notwithstanding the lack of intention to take up a new tenancy at the time of making the request, it was nonetheless entitled to compensation by virtue of s.37.
Held, allowing the appeal, that s.26 of the Act was a statutory formality and intention was not a precondition to compensation. The words "proposal" and "request" contained in s.26 were to be given their natural meaning and determined objectively, the intention of the tenant who was making the proposal or request was legally irrelevant, *Viscount Chelsea v. Morris* [1999] 31 H.L.R. 732, [1998] C.L.Y. 3657 considered. Further, the Act specifically mentioned intention where one was required and neither s.26 nor s.37 made any reference to the tenant's intentions or motives.
SUN LIFE ASSURANCE PLC v. THALES TRACS LTD (FORMERLY RACAL TRACS LTD); *sub nom.* SUN LIFE ASSURANCE PLC v. RACAL TRACS LTD, [2001] EWCA Civ 704, [2001] 1 W.L.R. 1562, Dyson, L.J., CA.

4159. **Business tenancies – rent reviews – meaning of direction to value property in parts – terms of hypothetical lease**

WN, the head lessee, sought the determination of two issues arising from the construction of a rent review clause in an underlease granted to BMBC by WN's predecessor in title. At the date of the grant of the lease of the premises, it had been anticipated that the ground floor would be sublet in two parts, however, only part of the ground floor had been sublet with the remainder under the occupation of BMBC. The issues to be determined were (1) the correct interpretation of a direction to value the property in parts. WN contended that a reasonable organisation of the demised premises was a sufficient way by which to value the parts and not, as argued by BMBC, with regard to the way in which the division of the building had been contemplated at the time of the granting of the lease, and (2) assuming the building was to be valued in parts, what would be the term of each hypothetical lease. WN argued that the terms of each lease would be the expected term for that part of the building at the review date in an open market, as opposed to a term equivalent to the unexpired part of the actual lease as maintained by BMBC.
Held, granting the declaration in favour of WN, that (1) the language of the rent review clause, which suggested a flexible approach should be taken as to what amounted to "parts", and the consistency of the authorities indicated that the valuation was not confined to assessing the "parts" on the basis of how the parties originally contemplated the divisions, and (2) the purpose of a rent review clause was to ensure that the rent paid was consistent with current property prices and such an aim would be hampered by the adoption of the approach argued for by BMBC requiring, as it did, an unrealistic and difficult valuation exercise and carrying the possibility of an undeserved and unanticipated windfall to one party, *Brown v. Gloucester City Council* [1998] 1 E.G.L.R. 95, [1998] C.L.Y. 3674 applied.
WESTSIDE NOMINEES LTD v. BOLTON MBC (2001) 81 P. & C.R. 11, Neuberger, J., Ch D.

4160. Business tenancies – repair covenants – extent of obligations – entitlement to damages

HB leased a high street property to HH on a 21 year lease, which contained repair covenants. HH defaulted on the rent and HB brought an action for recovery of the arrears. HH entered a counterclaim by way of set off alleging that HB was in breach of its repairing covenant. At a preliminary hearing, the court held that HB was obliged to keep in repair the roof, foundations and exterior of the building, whilst HH was responsible for the interior. HH sought (1) reimbursement by HB for works to the roof which HH had carried out; (2) damages for HB's alleged failure to put a damp proof course into the basement and to carry out repairs to the walls and floor of the basement and to a hole in the ceiling of one of the rooms, and (3) an injunction requiring HB to carry out the work.

Held, giving judgment for HB and dismissing the counterclaim, that HB was entitled to recover the rent in full and HH was not entitled to any damages as (1) although the roof was the responsibility of HB, HH had not shown that it had informed HB of the disrepair prior to it carrying out the work, and therefore HB's repair obligation had not been triggered; (2) on the facts of the instant case, insertion of a damp proof course did not constitute repair, *Elmcroft Developments Ltd v. Tankersley-Sawyer* (1984) 15 H.L.R. 63, [1984] C.L.Y. 1958 distinguished. As HH was responsible for repairing the internal walls and floors of the basement, it should bear the cost of the damp proof course. Equally, since damage in the basement had been caused by rising damp in the walls, repair of that damage was the responsibility of HH. The hole in the ceiling and some other minor repairs were the responsibility of HB. Further, HH was not entitled to damages as it had suffered no loss. It had been able to carry on its business in the property and had apparently left the property because of lack of customers in the area, rather than because of the state of the building, and (3) an injunction was not appropriate as HB had conceded that repairs needed to be carried out to the exterior of the building, HH was no longer in occupation, and in light of the pending appeal from the preliminary decision.

HOLDING & BARNES PLC v. HILL HOUSE HAMMOND LTD CH 1998 H 6870, Neuberger, J., Ch D.

4161. Business tenancies – repairs – consent orders – relief from forfeiture – breaches of repairing obligations – jurisdiction to interfere with consent order

F, the landlord of a hotel, began proceedings against a tenant, JR, alleging that JR had breached its obligations to repair a hotel. JR responded to an application for summary judgment by seeking relief from forfeiture which resulted in a consent order being entered into providing that certain works would be carried out within a specified time. F alleged that JR had carried out only limited work pursuant to the consent order and a second consent order was entered into which imposed on JR additional obligations as to the performance of works. JR failed to fully and properly carry out the relevant works and the master made a possession order. JR appealed, asking the court to grant them relief by extending for a period of two years the time by which the works were to be carried out. JR argued that (1) the court had jurisdiction to decline to enforce a consent order when to do so would be inequitable; (2) they were entitled to rely on the "liberty to apply" provisions which had been incorporated into the consent orders, and (3) it having transpired that work of a different nature from that initially envisaged had to be carried out and that the work had taken much longer to complete than had been expected, this was an exceptional case which justified the court interfering with the consent order by granting the extension of time requested.

Held, dismissing the appeal, that (1) the court had the power to interfere with a consent order of the type that the parties had entered into, but only in exceptional circumstances and in the instant case, it would not be appropriate to take that step; (2) the liberty to apply provisions could only be used to implement the terms of the order not to alter the parties' substantive rights, and (3) JR's breaches of the consent orders had been numerous and serious. They did not appear to have the resources to fund the works, and furthermore, they had failed to specify what work remained to be carried out, when it was to be carried out and how it was to be financed, *Ropac Ltd v. Inntrepreneur Pub Co (CPC) Ltd* Times, June 21, 2000, [2000] 8 C.L. 70 applied.

FIVECOURTS LTD v. JR LEISURE DEVELOPMENT CO LTD (2001) 81 P. & C.R. 22, Gray, J., QBD.

4162. Business tenancies – termination – continued acceptance of rent – existence of periodic tenancy

[Landlord and Tenant Act 1954 s.25, Part II, s.30(1)(f).]

A company, LB, ran the left luggage office at Charing Cross Station. LB's premises at the station were occupied pursuant to a periodic tenancy granted by R. R served a notice on LB pursuant to the Landlord and Tenant Act 1954 s.25 stating that the grant of any further tenancy would be opposed on the basis of s.30(1)(f), namely that R intended to carry out demolition or construction works such that it was not reasonable for LB to remain in occupation. Upon the expiry of the yearly periodic tenancy, rent was submitted to R's agents, HP, on five occasions. All the rent paid was retained by HP, apart from one payment which was returned to LB. LB remained in the premises and was served with a notice to quit, in response to which LB instituted proceedings seeking a declaration that it occupied the premises under a periodic tenancy subject to the provisions of the Landlord and Tenant Act 1954 Part II. LB asserted that the existence of a tenancy was evidenced by the payment and acceptance of rent. LB also sought an injunction to prevent any attempt by R at eviction. R contended that LB was no longer a periodic tenant, but was merely a tenant at will.

Held, dismissing the application, that it was necessary to assess objectively the intention of the parties in accordance with the guidance expressed in Chitty on Contracts vol.1 Chap.2 para 2.105 et.seq. The fact that R had accepted the proffered rent without explanation to LB was not inconsistent with R's stated aim that no new tenancy should be created. LB had been aware that there were plans for redevelopment during part of the period that he continued to submit rent and therefore acceptance of the rent during this period was equivocal since LB was still at the time potentially a tenant for the new left luggage office. For the remainder of the period that LB continued to pay rent, LB was aware that a new tenant was to run the left luggage office following LB's failure to tender for the contract. In the circumstances, there was no evidence of any intention to create a new tenancy, *Longrigg Burrough & Trounson v. Smith* [1979] 2 E.G.L.R. 42, [1979] C.L.Y. 1582, *Javad v. Aqil* [1991] 1 W.L.R. 1007, [1991] C.L.Y. 2218 and *Land v. Sykes* [1992] 1 E.G.L.R. 1, [1992] C.L.Y. 110 considered.

Observed, that if it were correct to consider subjective intention, in particular R's subjective and undisclosed intention to retain the rent as mesne profits in the anticipation that subsequent recovery might prove difficult, such subjective evidence would not alter the conclusion reached.

LONDON BAGGAGE CO (CHARING CROSS) LTD v. RAILTRACK PLC (NO.1) [2000] L. & T.R. 439, Pumfrey, J., Ch D.

4163. Defective premises – landlords powers and duties – extent of landlord's duty in absence of knowledge

[Defective Premises Act 1972 s.4; Landlord and Tenant Act 1985 s.11.]

S appealed against the dismissal of his claim for personal injuries which he had brought against his landlord, H. Having been injured as a result of gas and fumes coming from a gas fire, S had brought proceedings against H, relying both on the Defective Premises Act 1972 s.4 and on the Landlord and Tenant Act 1985 s.11, which imposed on H an implied obligation to keep the gas fire in repair and proper working order. The judge had ruled that the facts, including the absence of knowledge of the relevant defect on the part of H, were insufficient to establish liability against him.

Held, allowing the appeal, that the judge had erred in concluding that for the purpose of establishing liability under s.4 of the 1972 Act, S had to show that H had had actual or constructive notice of the relevant defect in the gas fire. While notice on the part of the landlord had to be established for the purpose of s.11 of the 1985 Act, s.4 imposed no such requirement. Under s.4 it merely had to be shown that the landlord had failed to take such care as was reasonable in the circumstances to ensure that the tenant was reasonably safe from injury. Had the judge approached the matter correctly, he would have found H liable under s.4.

SYKES v. HARRY; *sub nom.* SYKES v. TRUSTEE OF HARRY'S ESTATE (A BANKRUPT), [2001] EWCA Civ 167, [2001] Q.B. 1014, Potter, L.J., CA.

4164. Eviction – assured shorthold tenancies – psychological trauma – aggravated damages

[Housing Act 1988 s.27, s.28.]

F was a tenant of G under an assured shorthold tenancy. When rent arrears arose due to difficulties with housing benefit, G changed the locks, permanently excluding F from the property and from her belongings that she had left there. Those possessions included some relating to her son who had died at a young age. After the eviction, F suffered an anxiety/depression reaction. Although she had certain premorbid tendencies that accounted, on a psychologist's view, for 50 to 60 per cent of her post-eviction difficulties, the trauma stemming directly from the eviction caused her psychological problems for 18 months to two years after the eviction.

Held, giving judgment for the claimant, that F should be awarded (1) statutory damages of £3,300 under the Housing Act 1988 s.27 and s.28; (2) damages of £300 for the possessions that she had not been able to recover from the premises, and (3) the return of her deposit. Aggravated damages were also awarded given G's conduct in converting F's personal belongings and for the further facts that he had denied liability and given untruthful evidence, *Francis v. Brown* (1998) 30 H.L.R. 143, [1997] C.L.Y. 3286 followed.

FAIRWEATHER v. GHAFOOR, September 14, 2000, District Judge Geddes, CC (Rawtenstall). [*Ex rel.* James Fryer-Spedding, Barrister, St James's Chambers, 68 Quay Street, Manchester].

4165. Eviction – possession orders – secure tenancies – oppression in execution of warrant for possession

R had been H's secure tenant for 16 months until an outright possession order took effect. Thereafter, H agreed not to enforce the warrant on condition that R paid both the current rent and instalments of arrears by agreement. R failed to make any payments and housing benefit lapsed. The warrant was executed when the arrears stood at £2,798. R applied to set aside the warrant on grounds of oppression.

Held, granting the application, that there had been oppression on two grounds, namely (1) H had served a notice to quit on R containing the prescribed information that the landlord had to obtain a posession order from the court before the tenant could be evicted. R had telephoned a solicitor, who had advised her to make an appointment when she had been notified of a court hearing date. Accordingly, the notice had misled R into believing she would be notified of a court hearing before being evicted. After receipt of the notice to quit, H had advised in writing that it was applying for an eviction warrant. Neither the letter nor subsequent telephone advice from the housing officer had indicated that eviction could occur without a court hearing; hence the misleading impression given by the statement in the notice to quit had never been corrected, and (2) R had renewed her housing benefit application and H was at fault for not having processed it.

HACKNEY LBC v. REDFORD, January 31, 2001, Recorder Powles Q.C., CC (Shoreditch). [*Ex rel.* Jon Holbrook, Barrister, 2 Garden Court, London].

4166. Eviction – possession orders – setting aside warrant for possession – oppressive conduct

[Housing Act 1985 s.85(2).]

H occupied a property let to him by LLBC under a secure tenancy. He fell into arrears with the rent, and following his failure to comply with a suspended possession order, LLBC wrote to him informing him that an eviction date had been set. The letter stated that the eviction could only be prevented if the rent arrears were paid in full. H then went to see LLBC's housing officer who repeated the message given in the letter and told him to seek legal advice. Having been unable to obtain assistance from two advice centres, H contacted the county court. He was informed that no warrant for possession had been issued and that he should make an application to stay or suspend the warrant when he received a warning letter from the court. Six days before the eviction was due to take place, the court sent H a letter by second class post informing him of the eviction date and stating that an application to suspend the warrant would have to be made no less than two days prior to the date of the eviction. H did not see the letter until the day of the eviction and was duly evicted. An application to set aside the execution of the warrant was dismissed and H appealed, arguing that the conduct of LLBC and the county court had amounted to oppression.

Held, allowing the appeal, that both LLBC and the county court had acted oppressively. LLBC's letter had suggested that H had had no alternative but to pay the rent arrears in full whereas he had the right under the Housing Act 1985 s.85(2) to stay or suspend the execution of the possession order. LLBC's housing officer had given him the same message and the officer's suggestion that he should obtain legal advice did not alter that fact. In addition, the county court had incorrectly told him that no warrant for possession had been issued and that he should wait for a letter from the court before making an application under s.85(2). Furthermore, the court's letter had been despatched too late to enable him to make such an application in time. Accordingly, the execution of the warrant would be set aside so as to allow H the opportunity to suspend or stay the warrant of possession, *Hammersmith and Fulham LBC v. Lemeh* (2000) 80 P. & C.R. D25 applied, *Camden LBC v. Akanni* (1997) 29 H.L.R. 845, [1998] C.L.Y. 3046 distinguished, and *Hammersmith and Fulham LBC v. Hill* (1995) 27 H.L.R. 368, [1995] C.L.Y. 3042, *Barking and Dagenham LBC v. Saint* (1999) 31 H.L.R. 620, [1998] C.L.Y. 3045 and *Southwark LBC v. Sarfo* (2000) 32 H.L.R. 602, [1999] C.L.Y. 3705 considered.

LAMBETH LBC v. HUGHES (2001) 33 H.L.R. 33, Waller, L.J., CA.

4167. Eviction – possession orders – warrant issued without notice – right to fair trial – right to family life

[Housing Act 1985 s.82, s.85; Human Rights Act 1998 Sch.1 Part I Art.6, Art.8, Art.14; Rules of Supreme Court 1965 (SI 1965 1776); County Court Rules 1981 (SI 1981 1687).]

S, a secure tenant against whom an order for possession had been obtained under the Housing Act 1985 s.82, appealed against the dismissal of his application to set aside a warrant of possession. The county court had previously issued a possession order against S which, on three separate occasions, had been suspended upon certain terms. Upon S's failure to comply with the most recent terms, SLBC had applied for a warrant of possession without notice and evicted S. S submitted that (1) by applying for the warrant without notice, SLBC had infringed his right to a fair trial and right to respect for family life under the Human Rights Act 1998 Sch.1 Part I Art.6 and Art. 8 respectively. S maintained that the issue of a warrant was judicial as opposed to administrative, and that a tenant should receive formal notice of such hearing and should be entitled to make representations, and (2) he had been discriminated against by proceedings having been initiated in the county court as opposed to the High Court since the

County Court Rules, unlike the Supreme Court Rules, did not require that a tenant be notified of an application of warrant for possession.

Held, dismissing the appeal, that (1) SLBC had not contravened the 1998 Act by evicting S without notice under a warrant for possession. The issue of a warrant of possession was an administrative process required to give effect to a possession order which, it was accepted in the instant case, had been determined in accordance with Art.6. Following S's failure to comply with the terms of the suspended possession order, it could not be said that SLBC had acted in a disproportionate manner in applying for the warrant following since S had been informed of the warrant and had been entitled to apply for the suspension of its execution under s.85(2) of the 1985 Act, *Schuler-Zgraggen v. Switzerland (A/263)* [1994] 1 F.C.R. 453, [1995] C.L.Y. 2667 considered, and (2) SLBC's choice, in initiating proceedings in the county court, had not been based on any personal characteristic of S and therefore was not capable of establishing a claim of discrimination under Art 14.

ST BRICE v. SOUTHWARK LBC; *sub nom.* SOUTHWARK LBC v. ST BRICE, [2001] EWCA Civ 1138, [2002] 1 P. & C.R. 27, Kennedy, L.J., CA.

4168. Eviction – setting aside – oppression in execution of warrant – tenant's misapprehension

[Housing Act 1985 s.85(2).]

M appealed against the dismissal of her application to set aside a warrant of possession which had resulted in her eviction from the home in which she had resided as a secure tenant since 1977. M maintained that she had held a genuine belief that she had taken all necessary steps in order to ensure that the warrant was not executed and, in consequence, did not lodge an application pursuant to the Housing Act 1985 s.85(2). M submitted, inter alia, that she was entitled to rely upon the third limb of the test in *Leicester City Council v. Aldwinckle* (1992) 24 H.L.R. 40, [1992] C.L.Y. 2705, namely that there had been oppression in the execution of the warrant arising from her misapprehension.

Held, dismissing the appeal, that in order to succeed on grounds of oppression, a tenant would have to establish some wrongdoing on the part of the court or the landlord such that the tenant was misled or obstructed in the pursuance of his rights. In the instant case neither was present and accordingly relief was not available, *Aldwinckle* and *London Borough of Hammersmith and Fulham LBC v. Hill* (1995) 27 H.L.R. 368, [1995] C.L.Y. 3042 applied, *Camden LBC v. Akanni* (1997) 29 H.L.R. 845, [1998] C.L.Y. 3046 and *Hammersmith and Fulham LBC v. Lemeh* [2000] L. & T.R. 423, [2001] 1 C.L. 398 considered.

JEPHSON HOMES HOUSING ASSOCIATION LTD v. MOISEJEVS; *sub nom.* MOISJEVS v. JEPHSON HOMES HOUSING ASSOCIATION [2001] 2 All E.R. 901, Simon Brown, L.J., CA.

4169. Eviction – stay of execution – loss of opportunity by tenant to apply following error by court official

L, a tenant of HFLBC, called in at the West London County Court office on 29th September 1999, saying that he believed that he was due to be evicted the following day. A court official looked through the records and found a case relating to L that had no warrant, not realising that there were other matters outstanding against L. She informed L of her finding and suggested that he contact HFLBC directly. L went to their offices but they were closed, and the warrant was executed on 30th September. L applied for the warrant to be set aside and the District Judge found that there had been oppression in that L had been prevented from applying for a stay of execution by the advice of the court official. The decision was upheld on appeal and HFLBC appealed to the Court of Appeal, arguing that the decision was not one which the district judge could have reached on the facts.

Held, dismissing the appeal, that the judge was entitled to reach the decision that he did. Execution of the warrant was a matter for the court in which the landlord played no part, and therefore it was appropriate that the definition of oppression in this context should include oppressive acts by the court and not just by the landlord. It was open to the judge to find that without the wrong advice L would have made an application for a stay on 29th September, and that this was not a finding which no reasonable tribunal of fact would have made.

HAMMERSMITH AND FULHAM LBC v. LEMEH (2001) 33 H.L.R. 23, Nourse, L.J., CA.

4170. **Introductory tenancies – possession orders – compatibility of introductory tenant evictions with right to fair trial and right to respect for private and family life**

[Housing Act 1996 s.124, s.127(2), s.128; Human Rights Act 1998 Sch.1 Part I Art.6, Art.8, Art.14.]

M, a local authority tenant, appealed against a decision that an order for possession issued by the local authority under the introductory tenancy scheme did not contravene the Human Rights Act 1998 Sch.1 Part I Art.6, Art.8 or Art.14. The local authority had elected under the Housing Act 1996 s.124(1) to adopt an introductory tenancy regime which enabled it to deal more effectively with those tenants who were in rent arrears or exhibited anti-social tendencies. Where such circumstances arose, a local authority was entitled to obtain an order for possession under s.127(2) of the 1996 Act provided the procedures given in s.128 were followed. M contended that (1) the review panel which decided to seek the order for possession was not sufficiently independent and therefore he had been denied his right to a fair hearing under Art.6 of the Convention, and (2) enforcement of the order would infringe his right to respect for private and family life under Art.8(1).

Held, dismissing the appeal, that (1) whilst accepting that the review panel did not exhibit the degree of independence required by Art.6 of the Convention, in considering the decision-making procedure as a whole, the court could find no reason why the review process could not be conducted fairly. Furthermore, the remedy of judicial review provided an adequate safeguard for those tenants who wished to challenge a decision on the grounds of unfairness or contravention of Convention rights, and (2) eviction of a tenant under the scheme was justifiable under Art.8(2) of the Convention as such a course of action was necessary in a democratic society so as to ensure the protection of the rights and freedoms of others. Moreover, where a possession order was sought, the county court judge had the power to adjourn the hearing to allow for a judicial review application where the reasons given by a local authority were challengeable or where the tenant felt that the Art.8(2) exceptions did not apply.

R. (ON THE APPLICATION OF McLELLAN) v. BRACKNELL FOREST BC; REIGATE AND BANSTEAD BC v. BENFIELD; *sub nom.* McLELLAN v. BRACKNELL FOREST BC; FORREST v. REIGATE AND BANSTEAD BC, [2001] EWCA Civ 1510, [2002] 1 All E.R. 899, Waller, L.J., CA.

4171. **Introductory tenancies – possession orders – conduct of review board hearing – compatibility of review procedure with Convention rights**

[Housing Act 1996 s.128, s.129; Human Rights Act 1998 Sch.1 Part I Art.6.]

M sought to challenge a decision by SDC to terminate her introductory tenancy of a property owned by the council. Following various alleged incidents, SDC issued a notice pursuant to the Housing Act 1996 s.128 indicating its intention to seek possession of the property. M sought a review of that decision in accordance with s.129(1) of the 1996 Act. The review board upheld the decision to initiate proceedings and subsequently an order for possession was granted subject to a temporary stay. M applied for judicial review and following the grant of permission a second review hearing was held by SDC which upheld the decision of the initial review board. M contended that (1) neither review hearing had complied with the requirements of s.129, and (2) the review procedure as contained in s.128 and s.129 was incompatible with the Human Rights Act 1998 Sch.1 Part I Art.6.

Held, granting the application in part, that (1) the initial review board had not complied with the requirements of s.129 of the 1996 Act in that it had considered whether the decision of the housing officer to initiate possession proceedings had been unreasonable in the *Wednesbury* sense, rather than considering afresh whether it had been appropriate to initiate proceedings; (2) there had been no procedural flaws in the conduct of the second review hearing and the correct standard of proof had been applied, and (3) the review procedure was not incompatible with Art.6, *R. (on the application of Johns) v. Bracknell Forest BC* (2001) 33 H.L.R. 45, [2001] 8 C.L. 354 applied.

R. (ON THE APPLICATION OF McDONAGH) v. SALISBURY DC; *sub nom.* McDONAGH v. SALISBURY DC, [2001] EWHC Admin 567, *The Times*, August 15, 2001, Jackson, J., QBD (Admin Ct).

4172. **Joint tenancies – trusts of land – unilateral notice to quit – duty to consult with other joint tenant**

[Trusts of Land and Appointment of Trustees Act 1996 s.11.]

B, who was joint tenant with his wife of a property let to them on a monthly periodic tenancy, appealed against an order for possession following separation from his wife, W. W had moved out of the property and had, without consulting B, served a notice to quit on N, the landlord. When the tenancy had determined in accordance with the notice, N had sought and gained a possession order. B maintained that since the joint tenancy had been held under a trust for land within the meaning of the Trusts of Land and Appointment of Trustees Act 1996 s.11, W had acted in breach of trust by failing to consult with him, as joint beneficiary, before terminating the tenancy, that being the execution of a relevant "function" for the purposes of s.11 of the Act.

Held, dismissing the appeal, that the giving of a notice to quit was not the exercise of a "function" within the meaning of the word in s.11 of the Act; it was merely an indication by one joint tenant of an unwillingness for the tenancy to continue. The Act had affected neither the operation of a periodic tenancy, nor the consequences of the giving of a notice to quit, *Hammersmith and Fulham LBC v. Monk* [1992] 1 A.C. 478, [1992] C.L.Y. 2684 and *Crawley BC v. Ure* [1996] Q.B. 13, [1995] C.L.Y. 2997 applied.

NOTTING HILL HOUSING TRUST v. BRACKLEY, [2001] EWCA Civ 601, [2002] H.L.R. 10, Peter Gibson, L.J., CA.

4173. **Landlords powers and duties – covenants – liability upon transfer of freehold reversion**

[Landlord and Tenant (Covenants) Act 1995 s.28.]

A tenant, BHP, applied for summary judgment on its claim for a declaration that its landlord, C, remained liable for remedying defects in office premises forming the subject of the lease, notwithstanding the transfer of the freehold reversion from C to CN. Upon the transfer C had served a notice on BHP regarding release of all of its covenants under the lease, in consequence of which, C maintained that it was no longer under any liability to BHP. BHP maintained that the transfer was ineffective to enable C to evade its liability under a personal covenant to repair that had been imposed under the terms of a collateral agreement between the parties.

Held, granting the application, that C remained liable on the personal covenants contained in the agreement since these were not transmissible. In order to determine whether the notice served by C was effective to secure C's release from the personal covenant, the court had to have regard to the definition of a landlord covenant in the Landlord and Tenant (Covenants) Act 1995 s.28. Having regard to the reference to the landlord as the person "for the time being entitled to the reversion", it was clear that such a covenant, whether by landlord or tenant, had to be complied with on an ongoing basis and therefore had to be transmissible. Therefore, in the instant case service of the notice would have been effective to secure C's release had the covenants not been personal in nature.

BHP PETROLEUM GREAT BRITAIN LTD v. CHESTERFIELD PROPERTIES LTD [2002] Ch. 12, Lightman, J., Ch D.

4174. Landlords powers and duties – leases – validity of landlord's counter notice

[Leasehold Reform, Housing and Urban Development Act 1993 s.42, s.45, s.49.]

B appealed against a decision refusing her application pursuant to the Leasehold Reform, Housing and Urban Development Act 1993 s.49, for the determination of the terms upon which she was entitled to acquire a new lease of her flat from her landlord, M. B leased a flat from M under a long lease at low rent and had served a notice under s.42 of the Act, asserting her right to acquire a new lease. In the notice she set out her proposals in respect of the premium she would be prepared to pay, the terms of the new lease and the date by which M was to serve any counter-notice. M served a document which purported to be a counter-notice which B deemed to be invalid. The judge had found that the counter notice was valid.

Held, allowing the appeal, that where a qualifying tenant had served a notice under s.42 of the Act, any counter-notice served by the landlord had to comply with the requirements of s.45. In the instant case the landlord's counter-notice was invalid as it did not contain the requisite statements specified in s.45(2) and s.45(3), namely whether or not the landlord admitted that the tenant had a right to acquire a new lease and, if he did, which of the tenant's proposals were acceptable or what his counter-proposals were.

BURMAN v. MOUNT COOK LAND LTD, [2001] EWCA Civ 1712, [2002] 1 All E.R. 144, Chadwick, L.J., CA.

4175. Landlords powers and duties – set off – charge on rent deposit

[Companies Act 1985 s.396(1)(c).]

O, the liquidator of G, appealed against a decision that GL, G's landlord, was entitled to exercise a right of set off in relation to G's rent deposit. Under a contractual clause, clause 3, contained in a deed executed by the parties, the deposit was to be released to G "after first being applied by payment to the landlord in satisfaction of all claims made by the landlord against the tenant arising out of default by the tenant". A separate clause, clause 4, charged G with a number of obligations with the deposit forming security for their performance. O contended that the charge was void in view of the fact that (1) it had not been registered as required by the terms of the deed, and (2) GL held the deposit monies on trust for G and therefore no right of set off could arise in relation to a personal claim such as a claim for arrears of rent.

Held, dismissing the appeal, that clause 3 of the deed, relating to the release of the deposit, in effect created a charge with an independent effect from the charge specifically created by clause 4, which was subject to the requirement of registration. The charge in clause 3 took effect over G's beneficial interest in the deposit but did not constitute a "charge on book debts of the company" for the purposes of the Companies Act 1985 s.396(1)(c) and was not therefore registrable. It followed that GL was entitled to exercise a right of set off on the basis of its contractual rights.

OBARAY v. GATEWAY (LONDON) LTD [2001] L.& T.R. 20, Hazel Williamson Q.C., Ch D (Companies Court).

4176. Lands Tribunal – costs – enforceability of order for costs – tribunal's power to adjudicate on costs of appeal from leasehold valuation tribunal

[Lands Tribunal Act 1949 s.3(5); Leasehold Reform, Housing and Urban Development Act 1993 s.90(2), s.91(8); Arbitration Act 1996 s.66; Lands Tribunal Rules 1996 (SI 1996 1022) r.32(d).]

C, the tenant of a flat, appealed against a decision of the High Court that it had the power to enforce an order of the Lands Tribunal ([1999] 1 E.G.L.R. 95) giving effect to an agreement between C and his landlord, G, whereby C would pay G's costs, including the costs of proceedings before the leasehold valuation tribunal.

Held, dismissing the appeal, that (1) the effect of the Lands Tribunal Rules 1996 r.32(d), as amended, was to apply the Arbitration Act 1996 s.66 to all proceedings before the Lands Tribunal, including those in which the tribunal did not act as arbitrator. Accordingly, an order of the tribunal could be enforced in the same way as an arbitration award; (2) the Lands Tribunal had the jurisdiction to adjudicate on the costs of proceedings before it under the Lands Tribunal Act 1949 s.3(5). While the Leasehold Reform, Housing and Urban Development Act 1993 s.91(8) provided that the tenant was not to be liable for the landlord's costs in proceedings before the leasehold valuation tribunal, it did not make the costs of and incidental to an appeal before the Lands Tribunal irrecoverable, *Wright v. Bennett (No.1)* [1948] 1 K.B. 601 applied. It had therefore been open to the parties to agree, as they had done, that the costs of the proceedings before the Lands Tribunal should follow the event, and (3) for the purpose of s.90(2) of the 1993 Act, the proceedings were not "proceedings for determining any question arising under or by virtue of any provision" of the Act which had to be brought in the county court. Accordingly, the High Court had been empowered to determine the case.

GOLDSTEIN v. CONLEY, [2001] EWCA Civ 637, [2002] 1 W.L.R. 281, Clarke, L.J., CA.

4177. Lands Tribunal – jurisdiction to award costs

[Lands Tribunal Act 1949 s.3(2).]

BC applied to the leasehold valuation tribunal to determine various property issues. The tribunal refused to order the landlord's costs of the tribunal proceedings to be recoverable as service charge. Permission to appeal was refused by both the leasehold valuation tribunal and the Lands Tribunal. BC challenged the Lands Tribunal's jurisdiction to determine costs.

Held, allowing the application in part, that (1) the Lands Tribunal did have jurisdiction to determine costs because an application for permission was a "case" within the meaning of the Lands Tribunal Act 1949 s.3(a) and (2) in the instant case, the costs itemised were excessive and should be assessed by a robust approach to decide a reasonable lump sum.

BARRINGTON COURT DEVELOPMENTS LTD v. BARRINGTON COURT RESIDENTS ASSOCIATION [2001] 29 E.G. 128, NJ Rose FRICS, Lands Tr.

4178. Leaseholds – compensation payable to intermediate leaseholder – gross rent calculation method

[Leasehold Reform, Housing and Urban Development Act 1993 Sch.13 para.8(6).]

V appealed against a leasehold valuation tribunal determination that compensation of £184 was payable to it on the application for a new lease by W, the tenant of a flat of which V was intermediate leaseholder. V argued that the calculation of compensation should have been done on a gross rent, rather than a profit rent basis.

Held, allowing the appeal, that the correct figure for compensation, based on the loss to V of gross rental income, was £256. The tribunal had been wrong to treat V's interest as a minor leasehold interest under the Leasehold Reform, Housing and Urban Development Act 1993 Sch.13 para.8(6). The tribunal should have taken into account the fact that the flat was one of a number of which V was intermediate leaseholder on a single lease, which meant that the gross calculation under Sch.13 para.7(1) was appropriate.

VISIBLE INFORMATION PACKAGED SYSTEMS LTD v. SQUAREPOINT (LONDON) LTD [2000] 2 E.G.L.R. 93, Paul R Francis, Lands Tr.

4179. Leaseholds – enfranchisement – disputed valuation – offer to settle not inclusive of costs – landlord's obligation

[Leasehold Reform, Housing and Urban Development Act 1993.]

L, the nominee purchaser of P's freehold interest in a block of flats under the Leasehold Reform, Housing and Urban Development Act 1993, appealed against a decision of the lands tribunal awarding P the costs of its appeal from a determination of a leasehold valuation tribunal on the valuation of the premises. After P had given notice to appeal against the leasehold valuation tribunal's award, L had made a *Calderbank* offer to settle the disputed valuation of the freehold interest. P had rejected the offer on the basis that it had not included the costs of the appeal and the lands tribunal concurred, the offer having been regarded as incapable of acceptance in view of the lack of inclusion of costs.

Held, allowing the appeal, that the lands tribunal had erred in finding that L's offer was incapable of acceptance simply because it did not contain a provision as to costs. A landlord was under an obligation to give a purchaser's offer proper consideration and should not be afforded the opportunity to threaten the costs of appeal as a way of obliging tenants to pay more for the freehold. Further, the lands tribunal should have taken into account the reasonableness of P's rejection of the offer to settle regardless of whether costs were included particularly as the power to award costs should be exercised with a view to encouraging not discouraging settlements.

PHILLIS TRADING LTD v. 86 LORDSHIP ROAD LTD *The Times*, March 16, 2001, Chadwick, L.J., CA.

4180. Leaseholds – enfranchisement – meaning of "house" – material parts

[Leasehold Reform Act 1967 s.2(1), s.2(2).]

M appealed against a preliminary ruling ([2000] E.G.C.S. 37) that premises in relation to which M was the owner of the head lease, did not constitute a single house for the purposes of the Leasehold Reform Act 1967 s.2(1). The headlease related to a house together with a mews house at the rear. The main house comprised flats including a basement flat which extended underneath the mews house and included two storerooms. In 1960 an underlease of the mews house was granted which included the two storerooms forming part of the basement flat of the house. Following the expiration of the underlease, M served notices on the freeholder pursuant to the 1967 Act seeking to acquire the freehold. The judge at first instance held that (1) there were two houses and that the two together could not reasonably be called a single house for the purposes of s.2(1), and (2) neither property could itself separately constitute a house for the purposes of s.2(2) because of the undershoot of the basement which amounted to a material part.

Held, allowing the appeal in part, that (1) the correct test to pose under s.2(1) of the Act was whether the premises could reasonably be called a house even in circumstances where the premises in question could reasonably be called two houses, *Tandon v. Trustees of Spurgeons Homes* [1982] A.C. 755, [1982] C.L.Y. 1767 applied. On the facts of the instant case, the entire area was occupied by a built structure and there was always a means of access as between the two parts. Accordingly, the whole structure was reasonably capable of being described as a house, and (2) the issue of what matters were material for the purposes of s.2(2) did not depend upon a comparison of floor areas but rather upon whether the overhang or undershoot would, following enfranchisement, significantly prejudice the adjoining owners enjoyment of their respective properties, *Parsons v. Viscount Gage (Trustees of Henry Smith's Charity)* [1974] 1 W.L.R. 435, [1974] C.L.Y. 2099 and *Duke of Westminster v. Birrane* [1995] Q.B. 262, [1995] C.L.Y. 3022 applied. The judge had been correct in his conclusion that the freeholder's enjoyment of the mews house would be prejudiced were the freehold of the main house to be owned separately.

MALEKSHAD v. HOWARD DE WALDEN ESTATES LTD, [2001] EWCA Civ 761, [2002] Q.B. 364, Robert Walker, L.J., CA.

4181. Leaseholds – enfranchisement – notices – landlord's counter notice for premium – tenant's right to new lease not admitted

[Leasehold Reform, Housing and Urban Development Act 1993 s.45(2)(a), s.45(2)(b).]

The tenant, B, issued a notice for a new lease under the Leasehold Reform, Housing and Urban Development Act 1993 s.42 and served a notice of claim with a proposed premium of £110,000. M, the landlord, served a counter notice for a premium of £175,000. B claimed that the counter notice was invalid under s.45(2)(a) and (b) because it did not state that M admitted B's right to a new lease.

Held, dismissing the application, that M's counter proposal regarding the premium did not amount to a non admission of the right to a tenancy. A reasonable tenant would have understood that the combination of the counter proposal and the lack of reasons denying the right to a new tenancy did not invalidate M's counter notice under s.45(2)(a).

BURMAN v. MOUNT COOK LAND LTD [2001] 1 E.G.L.R. 62, Judge Brian Knight Q.C., CC (Central London).

4182. Leaseholds – enfranchisement – tenant's notices – procedural requirements

[Leasehold Reform Act 1967 s.9(1), s.9(1A), Sch.3 Part II para.6(1), Sch.3 Part II para.6(3).]

Three tenants occupying properties under long leases appealed against a decision that the notices served on their landlords seeking to acquire the freeholds of their respective properties pursuant to the Leasehold Reform Act 1967 were invalid. The tenants conceded that their notices had not been correctly completed but argued that since the landlords had been aware of the facts required to be specified in the notices, the notices had conveyed all the information that they needed to.

Held, dismissing the appeals, that Sch.3 Part II para.6(1) of the Act, which provided that a tenant's notice should be in the prescribed form and that it should contain specified particulars, was mandatory and had to be complied with. Accordingly, the adequacy of the particulars to be set out in the prescribed form was not to be assessed by reference to the landlord's knowledge of the facts. Although the dates of the relevant leases had not been supplied and the parties to the leases had not been correctly named, the information that had been supplied concerning the leases had been sufficient to enable the landlords to identify them, *Mannai Investment Co Ltd v. Eagle Star Life Assurance Co Ltd* [1997] A.C. 749, [1997] C.L.Y. 3256 applied. Furthermore, the tenants had been guilty of no more than an "inaccuracy" within the meaning of Sch.3 Part II para.6(3) in giving the apportioned rent payable without also identifying the rateable value of their properties on the appropriate day. The tenants' failure, however, to specify the periods during which they had occupied their properties during the previous 10 years, to state that the value of the properties did not exceed the applicable financial limit, and to state whether the properties were to be valued in accordance with s.9(1) or s.9(1A) were material omissions which rendered the notices invalid, *Cresswell v. Duke of Westminster* [1985] 2 E.G.L.R. 151, [1985] C.L.Y. 1889 considered.

SPEEDWELL ESTATES LTD v. DALZIEL, [2001] EWCA Civ 1277, [2002] L. & T.R. 12, Rimer, J., CA.

4183. Leaseholds – enfranchisement – valuation – effect of survivorship clause on operation of Law of Property Act s.149(6)

[Law of Property Act 1925 s.149(6).]

B appealed against the valuation of its freehold property by the leasehold valuation tribunal at £47,684. The tenant, L, who had been granted a 70 year lease of the property in 1962, had died in 1995. The lease then took effect as a 90 year term under the Law of Property Act 1925 s.149(6). L's widow, P, applied to acquire the freehold interest. B argued on appeal that the valuation should have been £180,000 on the ground that s.149(6) allowed B to give one month's notice to determine the lease, alternatively, if the term of the lease that it was determinable on P's death was still applicable, the valuation should be £159,000.

Held, allowing the appeal, that £159,000 was the correct figure. On a proper interpretation of s.149(6) its effect was not to turn on its head the intention of the parties to the original lease. Section 149(6)(c) allowed the survivorship clause in the lease to take effect so that the lease determined on P's death. Using Parry's Valuation Tables, P had a life expectancy of 10 years, so that the lease had no sale value. The marriage value was the value of the freehold in possession after subtracting the value of the encumbered freehold which amounted to £84,037. B was entitled to a sum equivalent to 75 per cent of the marriage value.

BISTERN ESTATE TRUST'S APPEAL, *Re* [2000] 2 E.G.L.R. 91, George Bartlett Q.C. (President), LandsTr.

4184. Leaseholds – enfranchisement – valuation – lack of mutual enforceability clause

[Leasehold Reform, Housing and Urban Development Act 1993.]

Three of the four tenants of a detached block of four purpose built maisonettes qualified under the Leasehold Reform, Housing and Urban Development Act 1993 under which they applied to acquire the freehold. The valuation tribunal fixed the freehold price at £14,000. The landlord appealed.

Held, raising the enfranchisement freehold price to £29,816, that (1) The value of the leases in the "no-1993 Act world" would be £62,400 with 60.75 years unexpired on those leases, being 78 per cent of the long leasehold value; (2) there was no evidence to suggest that the lack of a mutual enforceability clause would have the effect of depressing the value; (3) the appropriate yield for valuing the freehold was 10 per cent; (4) the value should be increased by 15 per cent to account for the possible marriage value of the non-participating, and (5) legal costs, including counsel's fees, would also be included.

SHULEM B ASSOCIATION LTD v. LEASEHOLD VALUATION TRIBUNAL; *sub nom.* SHULEM B ASSOCIATION LTD'S APPEAL, *Re* [2001] 1 E.G.L.R. 105, NJ Rose, FRICS, LandsTr.

4185. Leases – assignment – reasonableness of refusal of consent – likely breach of user covenant

G, a landlord, appealed against a decision ([2000] 80 P. & C.R. 11) that it had no right to refuse consent to the assignment of a lease on the sole basis of a potential breach of user covenant by the prospective assignee. A, the tenant, cross appealed against a finding that the covenant in question was a restrictive user covenant. The lease contained a term that the demised premises could not be assigned without the landlord's consent, such consent not to be unreasonably withheld. A contended, in reliance on *Killick v. Second Covent Garden Property Co* [1973] 1 W.L.R. 658, [1973] C.L.Y. 1890, that it would be unreasonable to refuse consent even if it appeared likely that the proposed assignee would breach the terms of the lease.

Held, allowing the appeal and cross appeal (Lord Bingham and Lord Rodger dissenting in respect of the cross appeal), that there was no principle of law which stated that it was unreasonable for a landlord to withhold consent on the sole basis that the proposed assignee would breach a user covenant. Conversely, there was no rule of law to the effect that it would always be reasonable for a landlord to refuse consent on the sole basis that the proposed assignee's likely use of the demised premises would breach the user covenant. Whether a landlord had acted unreasonably in withholding consent was a question of fact to be determined in each case and it was not appropriate for the courts to lay down rigid rules about how a landlord should exercise his power of refusal nor should a court treat one decision as a binding precedent containing a rule of law which had to be applied in each case irrespective of the particular circumstances, *Bickel v. Duke of Westminster* [1977] Q.B. 517, [1978]

C.L.Y. 1763 applied and *Killick* overruled. In the instant case the proposed use by the assignee would not constitute a breach of the user covenant.

ASHWORTH FRAZER LTD v. GLOUCESTER CITY COUNCIL (CONSENT TO ASSIGNMENT), [2001] UKHL 59, [2001] 1 W.L.R. 2180, Lord Rodger of Earlsferry, HL.

4186. **Leases – forfeiture – relief – application by equitable chargee of former lease**

Following the decision ([2001] 2 W.L.R. 1638) that B, the equitable chargee of a former lease, could seek relief from forfeiture by joining the former tenants as defendants in circumstances where the former tenants had not sought such relief themselves, the Court adjourned to consider the terms of the relief to which B and the former tenants were entitled in the particular circumstances of the case, which included an existing second lease entered into precipitately with notice of the relief proceedings.

Held, granting relief, that it was settled law that a right of re-entry was regarded as an equitable security for rent and the object for the court when granting relief was, as far as possible, to put the lessor and lessee in the position in which they would have been if there had been no forfeiture, which normally required the lessee to pay the rent arrears and the costs associated with peaceful re-entry. An order granting relief from forfeiture also had the effect of restoring the lease. In the instant case, the existing tenants, U and F, were interposed as landlords between the freeholder owner, I, and the former tenants since they were the persons entitled in reversion upon the determination of the earlier lease and they, rather than I, were entitled to any payment of rent and arrears which B and the former tenants were required to make as a condition of relief from forfeiture. The entitlement to relief from forfeiture was equivalent to the sum of the arrears of rent, I's costs in the instant proceedings and interest. However, U and F had been in actual possession of the premises and equity required that account be taken of the benefits associated with that occupation, *Wilson v. Burne* (1888) L.R. 24 Ir. 14 applied. Further, the former tenants could not bring an action against U and F in trespass after restoration of the 1994 lease because U and F's occupation of the premises had been lawful during the period of "inchoate forfeiture"; therefore any mesne profits which the former tenants were entitled to recover were also to be taken into account in determining the level of relief.

BLAND v. INGRAMS ESTATES LTD (NO.2); *sub nom.* BLAND v. INGRAM'S ESTATES LTD (NO.2), [2001] EWCA Civ 1088, [2002] 2 W.L.R. 361, Chadwick, L.J., CA.

4187. **Leases – forfeiture – relief – entitlement of equitable chargee**

B, the holder of charging orders registered against a lease of business premises, appealed against an order ([1999] 2 E.G.L.R. 49, [1999] C.L.Y. 3678) dismissing her claim for relief from forfeiture of the lease. IE, the landlord, had forfeited the lease on the ground of non payment of rent, but the tenants had not sought relief from forfeiture themselves. B argued that she was entitled to seek relief by effectively standing in the shoes of the tenants.

Held, allowing the appeal, that since an equitable chargee did not have a legal estate or an equitable interest in land and was not entitled to possession of it, the court could not entertain a claim on his part for direct relief. It did, however, have jurisdiction to entertain a claim for indirect relief. Such jurisdiction was based on the implied obligation of a chargor to take reasonable steps to protect the chargee's security. A tenant would be expected to seek relief from forfeiture himself to prevent the security from being destroyed, and if he failed to do so, the chargee could join him as a defendant and claim relief in his place. The position of the chargee was comparable with that of the beneficiary in a trust case where the trustee neglected his duty to protect the trust property. Since B's claim for indirect relief had not been raised until the appeal hearing, the court was not in a position to determine whether relief should be granted.

Subject to B being required to discharge the outstanding rent and costs, however, her claim ought in principle to succeed.

BLAND v. INGRAMS ESTATES LTD (NO.1) [2001] Ch. 767, Nourse, L.J., CA.

4188. **Leases – improvements – transfer of freehold land – meaning of "improvement" – calculation of amount payable**

[Leasehold Reform Act 1967 s.2(3), s.9(1A), s.9(1A)(d).]

R appealed against a decision of the Lands Tribunal concerning the price payable by him to C for the transfer of a freehold under the provisions of the Leasehold Reform Act 1967. The amount payable was calculated under s.9(1A) as being the price the house would fetch on the open market, with a reduction for any increase in value caused by any improvement carried out by the tenant or his predecessors at their own expense. In 1850, C had auctioned the site of a workhouse. The successful bidder entered into an agreement with C whereby he would construct a number of houses on the site and, upon their completion, be granted a 99-year lease. One of the houses, which had been constructed before the lease was granted, was later leased to G, and R was the successor in title. R submitted that the house was "an improvement" within the meaning of s.9(1A)(d).

Held, dismissing the appeal, that under s.2(3), "house and premises" were not independent of each other. Accordingly, the construction of a house on open land, even on land on which a previous building had been demolished, was not an "improvement" for the purposes of s.9(1A)(d) of the "house and premises", but rather the provision of the house. There was no reason to distinguish between the treatment of a tenant on a long tenancy who had paid a premium and a tenant who had expended money equivalent to a premium in building a house on the land.

ROSEN v. CAMPDEN CHARITIES TRUSTEES; *sub nom.* ROSEN v. CAMDEN CHARITIES TRUSTEES [2002] Ch. 69, Evans-Lombe, J., CA.

4189. **Leases – notice to quit – validity of notice to terminate tenancy – right to tenancy as spouse**

[Protection from Eviction Act 1977 s.5(1); Matrimonial Homes Act 1983 s.1.]

S appealed against an order for possession of leasehold premises occupied by him. The premises had been let to S's wife, as the sole tenant, who had given notice to quit following domestic violence inflicted on her by S, and who was subsequently re-housed by H elsewhere. S contended that (1) there had been no surrender of the tenancy by operation of law because the notice of termination of tenancy given by his wife was invalid under the Protection from Eviction Act 1977 s.5(1); (2) his wife's tenancy had not come to an end as H had never acted on that notice, and (3) he was entitled under the Matrimonial Homes Act 1983 s.1 to occupy the matrimonial home and, in any event, H had created a new tenancy in favour of S by allowing him to remain in occupation of the premises.

Held, dismissing the appeal, that (1) it was open to a landlord and tenant to agree to waive the requirement for notice under s.5 of the 1977 Act and that in the instant case, both parties had, in the light of the issues of domestic violence, clearly agreed to terminate the tenancy before the conclusion of the requisite four week notice period, *Elsden v. Pick* [1980] 1 W.L.R. 898, [1980] C.L.Y. 30 considered; (2) the judge was entitled to conclude from the actions of H that the tenancy was determined and that the notice to quit had been accepted, and (3) s.1 of the 1983 Act related only to the rights of spouses against each other, it did not establish an entitlement against the landlord. Moreover, the Housing Acts did not not restrict the tenant's right, as opposed to that of the landlord, to bring a tenancy to an end, *Sanctuary Housing Association v. Campbell* [1999] 1 W.L.R. 1279, [1999] C.L.Y. 3740 followed.

HACKNEY LBC v. SNOWDEN (2001) 33 H.L.R. 49, Peter Gibson, L.J., CA.

LANDLORD AND TENANT

4190. Leases – repair covenants – interpretation – overlapping obligations to repair

PPE, a landlord, appealed against a finding that it was responsible for the repair of P's roof terrace, the trial judge concluding that upon true construction of both P and PPE's repair covenants, both parties were mutually liable for the repair and maintenance of the roof terraces. PPE contended that the repair covenants should be construed so as to avoid the creation of overlapping obligations. PPE further submitted that its repair covenant could reasonably be construed so as to exclude the roof terraces from its obligation to repair.

Held, allowing the appeal, that if it was reasonably possible to interpret a clause so as to avoid the effect of overlapping obligations, the court should adopt that construction notwithstanding that might not be the most obvious sense given to the clause, *Toff v. McDowell* (1993) 25 H.L.R. 650, [1994] C.L.Y. 3409 considered. In the instant case, it was found that PPE's repair covenant could be construed so that PPE was not liable for the repair of the roof terrace, so avoiding any overlap of obligations.

PETERSSON v. PITT PLACE (EPSOM) LTD, [2001] EWCA Civ 86, [2001] L.& T.R. 21, Laws, L.J., CA.

4191. Leases – repair covenants – reversions – required repairs did not affect value of property

U claimed damages for breach of repair covenants contained in a lease, subsequently between U and G, U having obtained the freehold interest in the property. U contended that the property could have been sold at the end of the lease for greater consideration if the property had been in the state of repair as required by the covenants.

Held, giving judgment for the defendant, that the property could not be valued at more than it had been sold for, even if in a state of required repair, U had suffered no loss by way of diminution in the value of the reversion.

ULTRAWORTH LTD v. GENERAL ACCIDENT FIRE & LIFE ASSURANCE CORP PLC [2000] L. & T.R. 495, Judge Havery Q.C., QBD (T&CC).

4192. Leases – repairs – roof terrace of flat – part of "main structure" of building

D, a landlord, appealed against a declaration that it was responsible for the repair of a roof terrace which formed part of the roof of a flat of which I was the tenant. The roof terrace was also used by the tenants of two other flats located immediately above I's flat. I had issued proceedings against D seeking to compel D to carry out its repairing obligations as water had percolated into his flat from the roof terrace. D submitted that it was not obliged to carry out the repairs since its repair obligations under the lease only extended to the "main structure" of the building which, as far as the terrace was concerned, included only the wooden joists forming its foundation. Therefore, all layers of the roof terrace other than the joists, formed part of each flat's demise and any repairs were the responsibility of the respective lessees.

Held, dismissing the appeal that, only the surface layer of the terrace was included in the demise whereas all the other layers above the joists formed part of the main structure since the terrace made a material contribution to the "essential appearance, stability and shape" of the building and served the vital function of a roof for the top floor flats, *Irvine v. Moran* (1992) 24 H.L.R. 1, [1992] C.L.Y. 2670 and *Hallisey v. Petmoor Developments Ltd* Times, November 7, 2000, [2000] C.L.Y. 3915 applied. Accordingly, the repair was D's obligation.

IBRAHIM v. DOVECORN REVERSIONS LTD [2001] 30 E.G. 116, Rimer, J., Ch D.

4193. Leases – service charges – construction of lease

B owned land with frontages on Marylebone Street and Marylebone High Street comprising shops with residential flats above. There were six flats on the Marylebone High Street frontage and three on the Marylebone Street side. B granted underleases of five flats on the Marylebone High Street frontage to S and others which included covenants by B to repair and maintain "the building".

The building was defined merely as "the building of which the demised premises form part". There were covenants by the lessees to pay one sixth or one quarter of this expenditure by way of service charges. B issued service charge demands amounting to £115,000 for the cost of works to both frontages. The lessees applied for a declaration that "the building" meant only the Marylebone High Street parts. At first instance, the judge found for S. B appealed.

Held, dismissing the appeal, that (1) a material consideration was the obvious disproportion if the lessees were to be asked to pay for one quarter or one sixth of a structure which contained nine flats, and (2) the lessee's definition was supported by the disproportion factor. It would be surprising if they had to contribute their respective shares of the whole property and such a reading would have to be justified by clear words.

STAPEL v. BELLSHORE PROPERTY INVESTMENTS LTD (NO.2) [2001] 20 E.G. 231, Lloyd, J., Ch D.

4194. Leases – service charges – inclusion of caretaker's rent – reasonableness – leasehold valuation tribunal jurisdiction

[Landlord and Tenant Act 1985 s.19(2A), s.19(2B), s.19(2C).]

G appealed against a leasehold valuation tribunal decision that the sum included in a service charge levied by CS as G's landlord for the services of a caretaker was reasonable, and applied to the county court for a declaration that CS was not entitled to recover the cost of the flat provided to the caretaker by way of service charge. The caretaker was originally paid wages of £125 per week and charged no rent, but in 1995 CS increased her wages to £275, deducting £150 per week at source as a notional rent. CS passed on these costs to G through the service charge. G's county court application was heard at the same time as the appeal by a circuit judge who was also a member of the Lands Tribunal.

Held, allowing the appeal, that the tribunal had no jurisdiction to consider whether the sums were recoverable, its jurisdiction being limited by the Landlord and Tenant Act 1985 s.19(2A) to s.19(2C) to a consideration of whether the sums were reasonably incurred. The tribunal had been wrong to find that the sums were reasonably incurred as on a proper construction of the underlease it did not permit the caretaker's housing to be passed on to G by way of service charge, *Lloyds Bank Plc v. Bowker Orford* [1992] 2 E.G.L.R. 44, [1993] C.L.Y. 2542 applied.

GILJE v. CHARLEGROVE SECURITIES LTD [2001] L.&.T.R. 17, Judge Michael Rich Q.C., Lands Tr.

4195. Leases – underleases – absence of consent – waiver of forfeiture – rectification

C, the landlord, applied for an order that the grant by its tenant, Y, of two underleases comprising the whole of the demised premises, without the consent of C, constituted a breach of covenant entitling it to forfeiture. Y contended that, even if C were able to succeed in showing grounds for forfeiture, it had waived its right to forfeit by the subsequent service of an insurance demand, through its agents, since this was in effect a demand for rent. C further applied for rectification of the lease to the effect that any underlease was to be at a full rack rent and that any rent review under an underlease was to take place on February 25 in each year to tie in with the rent review provisions contained in the headlease, or alternatively that there was an implied term to such effect.

Held, granting judgment for C in part, that the grant of the two underleases without C's consent was a breach of covenant since Y had acted outside the proviso which permitted underletting of a part of the premises, as the effect of the two underleases was a subletting of the whole, *Chatterton v. Terrell* [1923] A.C. 578 applied. The insurance demand by C's agents did not constitute a waiver of the right to forfeiture since insurance demands were not to be treated in the same way as rent demands, notwithstanding that C had a contractual right to distrain in respect of the charge. The demand was not so unequivocal so as to be regarded as being consistent with the lease continuing and was more consistent with a routine administrative act, *Expert Clothing Service & Sales Ltd v. Hillgate House Ltd* [1986] Ch. 340, [1985] C.L.Y. 1875 considered. C had failed to show a common intention between the parties that underleases were to be granted at a full rack rent, since the evidence indicated that Y was to be granted a considerable degree of latitude in respect of its management of the demised premises, and the court would not therefore imply such a term. C had however, proved a common intention that rent reviews were to take place on February 25 in each year.

YORKSHIRE METROPOLITAN PROPERTIES LTD v. COOPERATIVE RETAIL SERVICES LTD [2001] L. & T.R. 26, Neuberger, J., Ch D.

4196. Leases – underleases – companies – "sham" lessee – corporate tax advantage

O appealed against an order requiring him to give up possession of a property on the expiry of an underlease which had been executed by a company controlled by him. O argued that he was entitled to statutory protection since it had been the intention of the parties that he, rather than his company, would be the underlessee and that the company had only executed the underlease in order to secure a tax advantage accruing from the set off of the costs of refurbishing the property as against the company's liability to corporation tax.

Held, dismissing the appeal, that there had been no intention to create a "sham" lease. The lease had been taken out in the company's name in order to achieve a particular purpose. The fact that the reason was to secure a legitimate tax advantage did not render the lease a sham since the deemed intention had been to give the company the beneficial effect of the lease, *Hilton v. Plustitle* [1989] 1 W.L.R. 149, [1989] C.L.Y. 2113 considered.

EATON SQUARE PROPERTIES LTD v. O'HIGGINS (2001) 33 H.L.R. 68, Evans-Lombe, J., CA.

4197. Nuisance – negligence – landlord's liability to third party for acts of tenant

M appealed against the striking out of her claim in nuisance against WLBC, in which she had made various allegations concerning the actions of her neighbour, A, who suffered from a mental disorder and was a secure tenant of WLBC. M submitted that (1) WLBC had failed to take effective steps to prevent A from continuing to cause a nuisance to M despite there being ample information available to WLBC upon which to act, and (2) in the alternative WLBC was in breach of a duty of care to M in negligence.

Held, dismissing the appeal, that (1) it was settled law that a landlord had no liability to third parties for acts of nuisance committed by a tenant except where those acts had been authorised and that A's acts had not been authorised by WLBC, *Smith v. Scott* [1973] Ch. 314, [1972] C.L.Y. 2532 applied, and (2) the allegation in negligence mirrored the allegation in nuisance and was governed by the same authorities, *Hussain v. Lancaster City Council* [2000] Q.B. 1, [1998] C.L.Y. 4047 applied.

MOWAN v. WANDSWORTH LBC (2001) 33 H.L.R. 56, Sir Christopher Staughton, CA.

4198. Possession orders – discretion – criteria for stay or suspension of warrant for possession

[Housing Act 1985 s.85(2), Part IV; Human Rights Act 1998 Sch.1 Part I Art.8.]

SCC appealed against a ruling that it was not permitted to adduce evidence of a tenant's acts of nuisance on the hearing of the tenant's application for a suspension of a warrant for possession. SCC had initiated proceedings solely on the basis of rent arrears and the district judge had concluded that in exercising his discretion to stay, suspend or postpone the warrant pursuant to the Housing Act 1985 s.85(2), he was restricted to a consideration of those matters relied upon by the landlord in the grounds for possession.

Held, allowing the appeal and remitting the case, that the court was not restricted to a consideration of the grounds relied upon by a landlord in the notice of his intention to seek possession or in the proceedings themselves. In seeking an order for possession there were dual requirements of a ground for possession and the need for it to be reasonable to make an order. Since the discretion of the court with regard to reasonableness was not limited to circumstances connected with the ground relied on for seeking possession, it was difficult to see how the same was not true in respect of the discretion given to the court under s.85(2), *Cumming v. Danson* [1942] 2 All E.R. 653 applied and *Darlington BC v. Sterling* (1997) 29 H.L.R. 309, [1997] C.L.Y. 2717 considered. However, the matters to be taken into account had to be relevant and in order to ensure consistency of decision-making it was important for the court to have regard to the aim of Part IV of the 1985 Act, as emphasised by the Human Rights Act 1998 Sch.1 Part I Art.8, namely that a tenant should only be evicted in circumstances where it was reasonable to do so following a serious breach of his obligations as a tenant and where a breach of any condition under which the warrant had been suspended had been established. All allegations made against a tenant should be clearly notified to him.

SHEFFIELD CITY COUNCIL v. HOPKINS, [2001] EWCA Civ 1023, [2002] H.L.R. 12, Lord Woolf of Barnes, L.C.J., CA.

4199. Possession orders – protected tenancies – change in nature of premises occupied – protected status

[Rent Act 1977; Housing Act 1988 s.34(1)(b).]

R appealed against a possession order granted in respect of premises which R had occupied as a tenant since 1972 when the premises were owned by his father. R had initially occupied the whole of the lower ground floor. Following his father's death, and for a period of eight years from 1982, R occupied a single room in the lower ground floor with his mother's permission, and paid a correspondingly reduced rent. During that period the remainder of the lower ground floor was occupied by other tenants. When the tenants vacated the premises in 1990, R resumed his occupation of the whole of the lower ground floor. The property was subsequently purchased in 1995 at auction by A. The court at first instance held that R's tenancy was not protected under the Rent Act 1977 nor was it an assured tenancy under the Housing Act 1988. The court found that R had surrendered his protected tenancy of the single room when he moved to occupy the whole ground floor in 1990, and that the new tenancy was excluded from the protection of the 1988 Act as a tenancy at a low rent. R contended that s.34(1)(b) of the 1988 Act was applicable and that to qualify for the protection therein, the identity of the landlord and tenant, rather than the premises themselves, were the crucial factors.

Held, allowing the appeal, that (1) the identity of the premises was irrelevant to a determination of the applicability of s.34(1)(b), *Laimond Properties Ltd v. Al-Shakarchi (No.2)* (1998) 30 H.L.R. 1099, [1998] C.L.Y. 3682 applied; (2) as at the date of the grant of the new tenancy the landlord had been R's mother, and accordingly there had been the necessary continuity of parties for the purposes of s.34(1)(b), and (3) there had been no evidence to support the conclusion that the new tenancy commenced as of April 1, 1990 so as to render the low rent regime under the 1988 Act applicable.

RAJAH v. AROGOL CO LTD; *sub nom.* AROGOL CO LTD v. RAJAH, [2001] EWCA Civ 454, *The Times,* April 13, 2001, Hale, L.J., CA.

4200. Possession orders – suspension – right to private life – harassment of neighbour – proportionality

[Human Rights Act 1998 Sch.1 Part I Art.8.]

H appealed against a decision not to suspend the terms of a possession order in respect of his council flat following a history of harassment against his female neighbour and her daughter. H contended that following his arrest and charge he had demonstrated for 11 months that he could behave properly towards his victim and that consequently the possession order should have been suspended.

Held, dismissing the appeal, that the judge had correctly weighed up the fact that during the period pending trial only one minor incident had occurred against the fear and tension that would be caused to his victim by H's return to his flat under a suspended order. The response was proportionate and did not breach H's rights under the Human Rights Act 1998 Sch.1 Part I Art.8.

LAMBETH LBC v. HOWARD, [2001] EWCA Civ 468, (2001) 33 H.L.R. 58, Sedley, L.J., CA.

4201. Possession orders – variation – power of court to review unexecuted order

[Civil Procedure Rules 1998 (SI 1998 3132) Sch.1 RSC Ord.59 r.10(1).]

A, a tenant of premises owned by T, applied for the variation and suspension of a possession order. T had brought an action for possession against A as substantial rent arrears had accrued since 1992. The premises had been in a poor state of repair for some years and A compromised T's claim by setting off an amount of damages for lack of repair against the arrears, the sum of £14,500 being the balance payable by A to T by way of set off. The possession order had been suspended on terms that A should repay this sum at the rate of £5 per week, the judge having found that higher repayments were beyond A's means. Repayment would therefore have taken 55 years. T appealed and an order was made for almost immediate possession. A sought variation and suspension of the order on terms that he paid the arrears at £242 per month over a period of five years given that his personal circumstances had changed and submitted that the court had a residual power to review an unexecuted order.

Held, dismissing the application, that the Court of Appeal retained the powers of the lower court in respect of unexecuted orders for possession if there had been a significant and unexpected change in the circumstances. However, on the facts in the instant case, there had been no such change.

TAJ v. ALI (VARIATION OF ORDER) (2001) 33 H.L.R. 27, Robert Walker, L.J., CA.

4202. Public sector tenancies – possession orders – relevance of rehousing proposals

[County Courts Act 1984; Housing Act 1985 Part VII.]

In the course of possession proceedings against S, the local authority, WBC, appealed against an order that it should submit to S a note of its proposals to rehouse her and her family, in default of which there would be a costs penalty. S was a tenant of WBC, one of the conditions of her tenancy being to cause no nuisance to neighbours. After numerous complaints about the behaviour of S and her children, and repeated warnings to her without abatement of the nuisance, WBC had sought possession. At the hearing, S had applied for an adjournment to consider fresh allegations. The judge vacated the hearing and made the order which became the subject of the instant appeal. WBC contended that it was beyond the judge's power to make such an order, since what was before the court was a possession application and not a question of the exercise of its statutory duty to rehouse.

Held, allowing the appeal, and setting aside part of the order, that the judge had proceeded from a fundamental misunderstanding of (1) the law relating to the possession application, and (2) his powers under the County Courts Act 1984. Whilst the order had been made with the best of intentions, it was not the role of the judge to seek a solution to the problem which would arise if he granted a possession order against S. The judge had erred in assuming that an automatic statutory duty would lie upon WBC to rehouse S and her children in the event of such a possession order being made. Properly construed, the Housing Act 1985 Part VII did not impose such a duty.

WATFORD BC v. SIMPSON (2000) 32 H.L.R. 901, Beldam, L.J., CA.

4203. Public sector tenancies – repairs – design faults – duties of local authority

[Defective Premises Act 1972 s.4; Landlord and Tenant Act 1985 s.11; Human Rights Act 1998.]

R brought a claim under the Defective Premises Act 1972 s.4 for damages for personal injury, allegedly caused by breach of a repairing obligation owed to their mother by SMBC as her landlord. The personal injury alleged was exacerbation of asthma by dampness at the property. It was agreed by the parties that the asthma had been aggravated and that the source of the dampness was condensation and that this was due to design faults in the building. The parties agreed that the court should, as a preliminary issue, decide whether a landlord had an obligation to rectify the design faults causing the condensation.

Held, deciding in favour of the defendant as a preliminary issue, that (1) the obligation upon the tenant not to part with possession of the premises, to give notice of any damage or defect to the premises, to keep the interior of the premises in a clean and proper condition and in a reasonable state of decorative repair did not require the implication of a term to rectify design faults as a matter of business efficacy; (2) the Landlord and Tenant Act 1985 s.11 did not apply to design faults where there was no evidence of physical damage or want of repair to the structure or exterior, *Quick v. Taff Ely BC* [1986] Q.B. 809, [1985] C.L.Y. 1610 followed, and (3) there had been no interference with R's rights by a public body directly or by that body failing to act against a third party. The condensation had arisen because of design defects in the building. Accordingly, there was no need to construe s.11 so as to require SMBC to rectify design faults as a result of the implementation of the Human Rights Act 1998.

RATCLIFFE v. SANDWELL MBC, November 2, 2000, Judge Geddes, CC (Birmingham). [*Ex rel.* Tracy Lakin, Barrister, Victoria Chambers, 177 Corporation Street, Birmingham].

4204. Rent – distress for rent – closure of county courts

DISTRESS FOR RENT (AMENDMENT) RULES 2001, SI 2001 4026 (L.34); made under the Law of Distress Amendment Act 1888 s.8; and the Law of Distress Amendment Act 1895 s.3. In force: April 1, 2002; £1.50.

These Rules, which make provisions consequential on the closure of the county courts at Chepstow and Monmouth, amend the Distress for Rent Rules 1988 (SI 1988 2050) by removing references to such courts from the list in Appendix 3.

4205. Rent – fair rent – redetermination following repair – change in condition of property

[Rent Act 1977 s.67(3)(a), s.75.]

H appealed against the refusal of its application for judicial review ((2001) 81 P. & C.R. D5) of a decision not to review the registered fair rent of a property of which it was the landlord. The earlier registration had been reduced by the rent assessment panel which had notified H that it could reapply for registration after it had complied with a repair notice issued by the local authority. After H had carried out the required repairs and submitted a further application, the rent officer had refused to consider it since it had been made within two years of the date upon which the previous fair rent registration had taken effect. H contended that the repairs that it had carried out to the property constituted a "change in condition" for the purposes of the Rent Act 1977 s.67(3)(a), permitting the rent officer to consider the application and redetermine the fair rent.

Held, allowing the appeal, that repairs which had rendered fit for human habitation a house which had previously been unfit constituted a "change in condition" for the purposes of s.67(3)(a), notwithstanding that the repairs had been carried out in accordance with the landlord's repairing obligations, and the fact that the repairs did not amount to an improvement for the purposes of s.75. Accordingly, the rent officer had either misdirected himself in law or his decision had been perverse and H was entitled to a redetermination of a fair rent.

R. (ON THE APPLICATION OF HAYSPORT PROPERTIES LTD) v.WEST SUSSEX REGISTRATION AREA RENT OFFICER; *sub nom.* R. v. WEST SUSSEX REGISTRATION AREA RENT OFFICER, *ex p.* HAYSPORT PROPERTIES LTD; R. v. WEST SUSSEX REGISTRATION AREA, *ex p.* HAYSPORT PROPERTIES LTD; R. v. WEST SUSSEX RENT OFFICER, *ex p.* HAYSPORT PROPERTIES LTD, [2001] EWCA Civ 237, (2001) 33 H.L.R. 71, Chadwick, L.J., CA.

4206. Rent – fair rent – scope of ministerial discretion to restrict rent increases – statutory interpretation

[Housing Rents and Subsidies Act 1975 s.11; Landlord and Tenant Act 1985 s.31 (1); Rent Acts (Maximum Fair Rent) Order 1999 (SI 1999 6).]

The Secretary of State appealed against a ruling ([2000] 3 W.L.R. 141) that ministers had possessed no power to make the Rent Acts (Maximum Fair Rent) Order 1999 pursuant to the discretion conferred by the Landlord and Tenant Act 1985 s.31 (1). SH, a landlord who had challenged the Order, argued that (1) s.31 was ambiguous, and by reference to the Housing Rents and Subsidies Act 1975 s.11, from which the 1985 Act had been derived, it was possible to discern an intention that the power to restrict rent increases should be exercised solely for the purposes of restricting general inflation in the national economy, and (2) in the alternative, the court was entitled to have regard to Hansard, from which it was apparent that the scope of s.31 had been intended to be limited in that way.

Held, allowing the appeal, that (1) while countering inflation had been part of the mischief at which s.31 had been aimed, it had not been the sole mischief. The provision could also be used to alleviate the hardship caused to tenants by increased or excessive rents. If it had been intended to restrict the power in the manner suggested, far more specific wording would have been required, *Maunsell v. Olins* [1975] A.C. 373, [1975] C.L.Y. 2857 applied, and (2) in order to counter the risks of questioning proceedings in Parliament, incurring disproportionate cost and wasting court time, it was essential when interpreting legislation that the courts should adhere strictly to the principles set out in *Pepper (Inspector of Taxes) v. Hart* [1993] A.C. 593, [1993] C.L.Y. 459. Since the wording of s.31 was clear and unambiguous, the first limb of the test in *Pepper* had not been satisfied.

R. (ON THE APPLICATION OF SPATH HOLME LTD) v. SECRETARY OF STATE FOR THE ENVIRONMENT, TRANSPORT AND THE REGIONS; *sub nom.* R. v. SECRETARY OF STATE FOR THE ENVIRONMENT, TRANSPORT AND THE REGIONS, *ex p.* SPATH HOLME LTD [2001] 2 A.C. 349, Lord Bingham of Cornhill, HL.

4207. Rent reviews – notices – review clause specifying time limit for service of counter notice – presumption time not of the essence

S appealed against a ruling ([2000] 3 E.G.L.R. 37, [2000] C.L.Y. 3914) that a counter notice served in response to a landlord's rent review notice was valid. The lease enabled the tenant to serve a counter notice within a specified time limit in response to a rent review notice served by the landlord but provided that the proposed new rent would be deemed to be the rent if the counter notice was served outside the time limit. S had served a rent review notice on CPL, which had responded with a counter notice outside the specified time limit.

Held, allowing the appeal, that the presumption that time was not of the essence in a rent review clause did not apply in relation to rent review clauses containing specific time-limiting deeming provisions, *United Scientific Holdings v. Burnley BC* [1978] A.C. 904, [1977] C.L.Y. 1758, *Bickenhall Engineering Co Ltd v. Grandmet Restaurants Ltd* [1995] 1 E.G.L.R. 110, [1995] C.L.Y. 3068 and *Trustees of Henry Smith's Charity v. AWADA Trading & Promotion Services Ltd* (1984) 47 P. & C.R. 607, [1984] C.L.Y. 1952 followed and *Mecca Leisure Ltd v. Renown Investments (Holdings) Ltd* (1985) 49 P. & C.R. 12, [1985] C.L.Y. 1935 overruled. The court would not apply the general principle that it would follow the latter of two conflicting decisions where it was apparent that the latter case had been wrongly decided.

STARMARK ENTERPRISES LTD v. CPL DISTRIBUTION LTD, [2001] EWCA Civ 1252, [2002] L. & T.R. 13, Kay, L.J., CA.

4208. Rent reviews – time limits – effect of late service of rent review notice

The lessee under a 21 year lease sought a declaration regarding the rent payable under the lease. The lessor had failed to serve a rent review notice in accordance with the time limit specified in the lease but maintained that the notice was nevertheless valid since time was not of the essence in rent review clauses. The lessee argued that the comments in *United Scientific Holdings v. Burnley BC* [1978] A.C. 904, [1977] C.L.Y. 1758 to the effect that time was not of the essence in such clauses were obiter.

Held, ruling in favour of the lessor, that whilst the comments made in *United Scientific* were strictly obiter, they were nevertheless authoritative in the instant case where the clause in question was virtually indistinguishable from the one in *United Scientific*. A rebuttable presumption that time was not of the essence in a rent review clause was a principle of general application and accordingly late service did not render the lessor's notice invalid, *United Scientific* applied.

McDONALD'S PROPERTY CO LTD v. HSBC BANK PLC [2002] 1 P. & C.R. 25, Peter Leaver Q.C., Ch D.

4209. Repair covenants – defective premises – dangerous structure notice – lessee's right to indemnity

[London Building Acts (Amendment) Act 1939.]

R was the head lessee of a building comprising a retail shop and residential upper parts. M and A were contractual licensees of the retail shop. Under the terms of the licence, M and A agreed to keep the shop in good repair and condition. The premises were in poor condition and in 1994 the local authority, W, served a dangerous structure notice. In 1995, R commenced proceedings for possession as a result of arrears of licence fees and M and A quit the premises. W carried out works in default under the London Building Acts (Amendment) Act 1939 and demanded payment from R. R then amended his claim against M and A to include a claim for an indemnity against the costs demanded by W. The trial judge gave judgment for R and ordered M and A to indemnify R for his liability to W. M appealed.

Held, allowing the appeal, that (1) the effect of the repairing covenant was clear. If there was a breach, there arose a claim for damages normally assessed by the damage suffered to the reversion as a result of the disrepair; (2) the covenant in the instant case could not be interpreted as a covenant to indemnify R against his liability resulting from a dangerous structure notice; (3) the amount of damages under (1) could coincide with the amount of R's liability to W. However, this was dependent on there being evidence of the work carried out by W and there was no such evidence, and (4) the judge was wrong to hold that there was a contractual obligation to indemnify R for the work carried out by W.

RIAZ v. MASAKU [2001] L. & T.R. 22, Chadwick, L.J., CA.

4210. Repair covenants – landlords powers and duties – liability of tenants for cost

F, the sub-underlessee of a property of which S was the landlord, claimed against the recovery by S of the cost of repairs carried out on the property pursuant to a covenant in the lease. F contended that (1) it was not for S to decide on the mode of performance of the repairs, and (2) the standard of work carried out at F's expense was restricted by F's limited interest as a tenant.

Held, giving judgment for F in part, that (1) the mode of conducting the repairs was for S as covenantor to decide, provided that it acted reasonably, *Plough Investments v. Manchester City Council* [1989] 1 E.G.L.R. 244 considered. The primary purpose of the repairs in the instant case was to benefit F, but S nevertheless retained a separate interest in ensuring that the high commercial rental value of the property was retained and this right could not be released by the tenant, and (2) the cost of the work, however, was restricted to that which was reasonable in view of F's limited interest in the property and any further costs should be borne by S.

FLUOR DANIEL PROPERTIES LTD v. SHORTLANDS INVESTMENTS LTD *The Times*, February 21, 2001, Blackburne, J., Ch D.

4211. Repair covenants – subsidence and flooding – repair obligations not extending to outbuildings

[Landlord and Tenant Act 1985 s.11.]

C claimed damages under the Landlord and Tenant Act 1985 s.11 for disrepair to outbuildings at her home which she rented from SMBC. The outbuildings were separate from the house itself and contained a garden shed, coal store and WC. They were affected by subsidence and were cracked and occasionally flooded. SMBC applied to strike out C's claim as disclosing no cause of action.

Held, granting the application, that the repairing obligations relating to the "structure and exterior" of the premises imposed by s.11 did not extend to the outbuildings. They were an entirely separate structure, even though there was a WC in one of the outbuildings, *Irvine v. Moran* (1992) 24 H.L.R. 1, [1992] C.L.Y. 2670 applied.

CRESSWELL v. SANDWELL MBC, October 26, 2000, Deputy District Judge Evans, CC (Birmingham). [*Ex rel.* C Rowlands, Barrister, Victoria Chambers, 177 Corporation Street, Birmingham].

4212. Repairs – measure of damages – landlords powers and duties – disrepair – subsidence – loss of enjoyment of property

[Landlord and Tenant Act 1985 s.11.]

P, a tenant of CW for 25 years, sought damages in respect of disrepair pursuant to the Landlord and Tenant Act 1985 S.11. P had suffered the effects of subsidence to the property for a period of ten years, the effect of which had been to cause cracks to appear in the walls and ceilings of her rooms. The worst cracks had grown to a width of 12mm, plaster was falling down, making decoration impossible, and the property was unable to retain heat due to the many draughts.

Held, giving judgment for the claimant and awarding damages in the sum of £5,450, reflecting a multiplier of 7.25 and a multiplicand of between £500 and £1,000, that the interference with P's comfort and enjoyment of the property was towards the lower end of the scale. The property had not been rendered uninhabitable, but there had been a real disruption to her life.

PEIRCE v. CITY OF WESTMINSTER, January 18, 2001, Judge Sich, CC (Willesden). [*Ex rel.* Jon Holbrook, Barrister, 2 Garden Court, London].

4213. Residential tenancies – termination – division of demised premises – validity of notices

[Landlord and Tenant Act 1954 s.3(1), s.4, s.4(1), s.4(3).]

P appealed against a decision that two notices served pursuant to the Landlord and Tenant Act 1954 s.4 purporting to terminate the tenancies of two maisonettes and proposing statutory tenancies, were valid and effective. The premises in question were originally demised for a term of 99 years from 1894 by a lease made in 1896 and in 1981, when E acquired the freehold reversion, the house had been divided into two maisonettes. In 1993 when the lease expired by the effluxion of time, E served on the tenants two s.4 notices and then applied for the settlement of the terms of statutory tenancies of the two maisonettes. The Recorder had held that the tenants qualified for protection under the Act at the expiry of the long lease in respect of the whole house and that the s.4 notices were valid and effective notwithstanding that they had not been served in respect of the whole of the premises which formed the subject of the original lease.

Held, allowing the appeal, that the effect of s.3(1) and s.4(1) of the Act was that, irrespective of whether the tenants would have been entitled to statutory protection in respect of the whole or part of the premises, the landlord ought to have given a single notice terminating the tenancy of the whole. In any event the Recorder found as a fact that the tenants qualified for protection under the Act in respect of the whole premises. Therefore the continuation tenancy could only have been and could only be terminated by a single notice given in respect of the whole premises. The two notices were therefore ineffective and the tenancy of the premises continued. That conclusion could not be affected by any belief of the landlord under s 4(3) that the two maisonettes qualified for protection separately. Section 4(3) could not confer validity on an otherwise invalid notice, but merely prevented any notice which did not so specify the premises from having effect.

ST ERMINS PROPERTY CO LTD v. PATEL (NO.2), [2001] EWCA Civ 804, [2002] H.L.R. 11, Sir Martin Nourse, CA.

4214. Residential tenancies – termination – validity of notices

[Landlord and Tenant Act 1954 Part I; Housing Act 1988 Sch.1; Local Government and Housing Act 1989.]

M, the tenant of residential premises, applied for judicial review of a decision of LRAC that (1) a notice served by the landlord under the Landlord and Tenant Act 1954 Part I, which had proposed a statutory tenancy and had been addressed to a previous tenant, was invalid, and (2) a notice under the Local Government and Housing Act 1989 terminating M's long residential tenancy and proposing an assured tenancy at a rent of £3,900 per month was valid, notwithstanding that it specified a rent in excess of £25,000. LRAC had concluded that it could determine the market rent for M's flat without reference to the £25,000 limit under the Housing Act 1988 Sch.1.

Held, refusing the application, that (1) the notice served under the 1954 Act was not valid as it had been addressed to the wrong person. The landlord had addressed the notice to a person he had wrongly thought was the tenant, rather than merely making a spelling or typographical error, and (2) LRAC had been correct in determining that the notice under the 1989 Act was valid. The 1989 Act should be construed purposively, and not in such a way as to require a long residential tenancy to become an assured tenancy, upon termination, subject to a maximum rent of £25,000, *R. v. London Rent Assessment Panel, ex p. Cadogan Estates Ltd* [1998] Q.B. 398, [1997] C.L.Y. 3253 applied.

R. (ON THE APPLICATION OF MORRIS) v. LONDON RENT ASSESSMENT COMMITTEE, [2001] EWHC Admin 309, [2001] L. & T.R. 36, Hooper, J., QBD (Admin Ct).

4215. Right to buy – green belt – inconsistent legislative provisions – implied repeal

[Green Belt (London and Home Counties) Act 1938; Housing Act 1985 s.138.]

O, the secure tenant of a flat owned by the local authority, appealed against the dismissal of her application for judicial review (Independent, June 13, 2000) of the Secretary of State's refusal to grant his consent for her to exercise her right to buy under the Housing Act 1985 s.138. The flat was located on property situated within the Green Belt, which the council had purchased under the Green Belt (London and Home Counties) Act 1938. The 1938 Act required the consent of the Secretary of State before any of the land could be sold and O contended that the discretionary veto contained within the Green Belt legislation was wholly inconsistent with the right to buy legislation, the purpose of which was to afford secure tenants a settled right to purchase their homes. It was thus submitted that the 1938 Act had been impliedly repealed by the 1985 Act.

Held, allowing the appeal, that the 1938 Act and the 1985 Act were sufficiently contradictory to be unable to stand together. While the mere existence of an irregularity between two statutes did not automatically lead to the earlier being repealed, O had successfully demonstrated that the right to buy provisions of the 1985 Act were inconsistent with the provisions of the 1938 Act, with the result that the latter was impliedly repealed.

R. (ON THE APPLICATION OF O'BYRNE) v. SECRETARY OF STATE FOR THE ENVIRONMENT, TRANSPORT AND THE REGIONS; *sub nom.* O'BYRNE v. SECRETARY OF STATE FOR THE ENVIRONMENT, TRANSPORT AND THE REGIONS, R. v. SECRETARY OF STATE FOR THE ENVIRONMENT, TRANSPORT AND THE REGIONS, *ex p.* O'BYRNE, [2001] EWCA Civ 499, *The Times*, April 17, 2001, Laws, L.J., CA.

4216. Secure tenancies – occupancy – failure to reside at rented premises – right to buy scheme – intention of tenant

D1 and D2 were jointly granted a secure tenancy of local authority premises in 1986. Ten years later, D1 won the National Lottery and D1 and D2 together purchased another property of which they became joint registered owners. At the same time ILBC issued an offer notice of right to buy in respect of their rented property and the defendants accepted the right to buy terms. ILBC subsequently refused to sell the property, alleging that D1 and D2 had ceased to reside at the rented premises as their only or principal home. A caretaker employed by ILBC gave evidence that there was nobody living at the premises and that lights were hardly ever turned on at night and rubbish was not put out for collection. Other investigations revealed that the defendants' motor vehicles were registered from the property of which they were joint registered owners. ILBC served a notice to quit 13 months after the right to buy offer, on the basis that secure status had been lost and the tenancy was, by then, contractual. D1 and D2 counterclaimed for an injunction to complete the right to buy contract. D2 contended that she had not ceased to reside at the rented premises and merely stayed with D1 at the new property on occasions. She maintained that she had retained her furniture at the rented premises and gave evidence that she and D1 had separated and that she was engaged in domestic violence proceedings against him.

Held, giving judgment for the claimant, that upon disclosure of documents relating to the domestic violence proceedings, it was clear that D2 did not use the address of the rented premises as her home address; she repeatedly stated that she had moved to the new property as the family home. Although it was possible to occupy two residences at the same time, the intention of the tenant was a crucial factor, *Crawley BC v. Sawyer* (1988) 20 H.L.R. 98, [1988] C.L.Y. 2078 applied. D2's intention during the previous two years had not, on the evidence, been to retain her interest in the rented premises so that she could ultimately return there as her only or principal home, but rather to purchase the premises at a substantial discount so that she could profit from the transaction. While it would have been possible for D2 to have retrieved her secure status, the notice to quit had already been served, which had had the effect of terminating the tenancy.

ISLINGTON LBC v. DEMETRIOU, February 28, 2001, Judge Reynolds, CC (Clerkenwell). [*Ex rel.* Maurice Rifat, Barrister, Verulam Chambers, 8 -14 Verulam Street, London].

4217. Service charges – leasehold valuation tribunals – jurisdiction to consider reasonableness

[Limitation Act 1980; Landlord and Tenant Act 1985 s.19(2A).]

D appealed against the refusal of its application for judicial review of a decision that a leasehold valuation tribunal had jurisdiction to determine, under the Landlord and Tenant Act 1985 s.19(2A), whether service charges already paid by lessees of flats owned by D, were reasonably incurred. The tribunal had further held that the Limitation Act 1980 was not applicable to applications under s.19(2A) of the 1985 Act.

Held, allowing the appeal, that when determining the reasonableness of service charges, the jurisdiction of the leasehold valuation tribunal was limited to service charges that remained unpaid, including the position where payments were made under an interim contractual arrangement for repayment if the charge was found to be excessive. A decision to the contrary would necessitate a number of proceedings investigating past charges and, in the event that the lessees were successful, proceedings in the county court for the repayment of any service charges which had been overpaid. Furthermore, if there was an overlap between the jurisdiction of the tribunal and that of the county court, any inquiry before the tribunal into the reasonableness of previous service charge payments could involve a waste of both time and money. If the 1980 Act did not apply, there was the possibility of the tribunal being able to examine the reasonableness of past service charges over an indefinite period, and if it did apply there was still the chance of the tribunal being able to investigate charges which had been accrued over a considerable period of time. However, if the jurisdiction of the tribunal was limited to unpaid charges, no issue of limitation arose.

R. (ON THE APPLICATION OF DAEJAN PROPERTIES LTD) v. LONDON LEASEHOLD VALUATION TRIBUNAL; *sub nom.* DAEJAN PROPERTIES LTD v. LONDON LEASEHOLD VALUATION TRIBUNAL; R. v. LONDON LEASEHOLD VALUATION TRIBUNAL, *ex p.* DAEJAN PROPERTIES LTD, [2001] EWCA Civ 1095, [2002] L. & T.R. 5, Simon Brown, L.J., CA.

4218. Books

Colbey, Richard – Practice Notes on Residential Tenancies. Practice Notes. Paperback: £15.95. ISBN 1-85941-452-4. Cavendish Publishing Ltd.

Morgan, Jill; Brand, Clive – Practice Notes on Business Tenancies. 4th Ed. Practice Notes. Paperback: £15.95. ISBN 1-85941-458-3. Cavendish Publishing Ltd.

Radevsky, Anthony; Clark, Wayne – Radevsky and Clark: Tenant's Right of First Refusal. Hardback: £55.00. ISBN 0-406-91104-5. Butterworths Law.

Rent Review and Lease Renewal. Hardback: £60.00. ISBN 1-85978-964-1. LLP Professional Publishing.

Residential Letting Kit. Looseleaf/ring bound: £6.99. ISBN 1-902646-73-8. Law Pack Publishing.

Tessa, Shepperson – Residential Lettings. CD-ROM (software). ISBN 1-902646-82-7. Law Pack Publishing.

LEGAL AID

4219. Care proceedings – limitation of amount – meaning of "limitations"

[Legal Aid Act 1988 s.15(4); Children Act 1989 s.31.]

B, who had acted for the mother of a child in connection with an application for a care order under the Children Act 1989 s.31, appealed against the refusal of his application for judicial review ((2000) 150 N.L.J. 1263) of the decision of the Legal Aid Board to limit the costs payable to him to the sum of £5,000, that being the costs limitation set under the relevant legal aid certificate. B argued that (1) properly construed, the word "limitations" under the Legal Aid Act 1988 s.15(4) did not include financial limitations, and (2) the granting of legal aid in care proceedings being mandatory rather than discretionary, it would be irrational to make legal aid in such cases subject to financial limitations since that would have the effect of reintroducing the merits test that Parliament had intended should not apply to such cases.

Held, dismissing the appeal, that (1) the word "limitations" under s.15(4) of the 1988 Act was wide enough to cover financial as well as "scope" limitations. There were no provisions in the Act which indicated that the word should be given the restrictive meaning argued for by B, and (2) the imposition of financial limitations on legal aid certificates ensured that no more than was reasonable and proportionate was spent on publicly funded civil litigation and could not therefore be described as irrational.

R. (ON THE APPLICATION OF BURROWS (T/A DAVID BURROWS (A FIRM))) v. LEGAL SERVICES COMMISSION (FORMERLY LEGAL AID BOARD); *sub nom.* R.

v. LEGAL AID BOARD, *ex p.* BURROWS; R. v. LEGAL SERVICES COMMISSION (FORMERLY LEGAL AID BOARD), *ex p.* BURROWS (T/A DAVID BURROWS (A FIRM)), [2001] EWCA Civ 205, [2001] 2 F.L.R. 998, Dyson, L.J., CA.

4220. Civil procedure – care proceedings – transfer of functions – justices' clerks to justices' chief executives

CIVIL LEGAL AID (GENERAL) (AMENDMENT) REGULATIONS 2001, SI 2001 617; made under the Legal Aid Act 1988 s.34. In force: April 1, 2001; £1.50.

These Regulations amend the Civil Legal Aid (General) Regulations 1989 (SI 1989 339) to transfer the administrative functions of justices' clerks under the Regulations to justices' chief executives in line with the Access to Justice Act 1999 s.90, s.91 and Sch.13, which make corresponding transfers in primary legislation.

4221. Civil procedure – interlocutory proceedings – successful applications funded by third party – appropriate order for costs

[Civil Legal Aid (General) Regulations 1989 (SI 1989 339) Reg.64.]

In proceedings brought by S against P the court was asked to rule on the costs of interlocutory applications which had been decided in S's favour. S had been granted legal aid for the proceedings, but the Legal Services Commission had withdrawn funding in respect of the interlocutory applications after a third party had offered to pay the costs of those applications.

Held, making no order for costs, that the case was an exception to the usual rule that the loser should pay the winner's costs. S's legal aid certificate for the proceedings had covered the interlocutory applications since all such applications formed part of the proceedings for which legal aid had been granted. The Civil Legal Aid (General) Regulations 1989 Reg.64, however, provided that where a legal aid certificate had been issued, the assisted person's legal representatives could only receive payment for work done during the currency of the certificate from the Legal Aid fund. Were costs to be awarded in S's favour, it would result in his solicitors and counsel being paid from another source. Accordingly, it would be appropriate to make no order for costs.

STACEY v. PLAYER *The Times*, February 23, 2001, Peter Leaver Q.C., Ch D.

4222. Contempt of court – magistrates – refusal to grant aid

[Legal Aid Act 1988 s.29(9).]

D applied for judicial review of a decision of the justices refusing to grant him legal aid. D had attended court to support a friend and, on leaving, had uttered a trivial remark which the clerk had referred to the justices as possibly amounting to contempt of court. D had been called into court, where he instructed his solicitor to apologise on his behalf. The justices had found that there had been no contempt but had withheld legal aid. D submitted that since he had been liable to be punished by way of committal or fine, he had been eligible for legal aid and it was immaterial that no finding of contempt had actually been made.

Held, granting the application, that whilst the grant of legal aid was not mandatory, potential liability for contempt of court was sufficiently serious to justify legal representation and the justices had been wrong to refuse to grant legal aid for the representations made by D's solicitor. Under the Legal Aid Act 1988 s.29(9), the court could grant legal aid in proceedings for contempt of court where it was "desirable to do so in the interests of justice". The clerk's advice to the justices that there was no entitlement to legal aid due to the fact that contempt had not been found, had been wrong in law.

R. (ON THE APPLICATION OF DALTRY) v. SELBY MAGISTRATES COURT; *sub nom.* R. v. SELBY JUSTICES, *ex p.* DALTRY; R. v. SELBY MAGISTRATES COURT, *ex p.* DALTRY (2001) 165 J.P. 89, Rose, L.J., QBD.

4223. Criminal Defence Service

CRIMINAL DEFENCE SERVICE (GENERAL) (NO.2) REGULATIONS 2001, SI 2001 1437; made under the Access to Justice Act 1999 s.12, s.13, s.15, s.20, Sch.3; and the Criminal Defence Service (Advice and Assistance) Act 2001 s.1. In force: April 2, 2001; £4.00.

These Regulations, which revoke the Criminal Defence Service (General) Regulations 2001 (SI 2001 1144), govern the provision of advice and assistance and representation by the Criminal Defence Service under the Access to Justice Act 1999 Part I. They provide for, inter alia, the proceedings which are prescribed as criminal proceedings for the purposes of s.12(2)(g) of the Act; the circumstances in which an individual may receive advice and assistance, including with regard to his financial eligibility; the manner in which applications for the grant of a representation order are to be made; the representatives who may provide legal services; and the withdrawal of representation.

4224. Criminal Defence Service – recovery of costs

CRIMINAL DEFENCE SERVICE (RECOVERY OF DEFENCE COSTS ORDERS) REGULATIONS 2001, SI 2001 856; made under the Access to Justice Act 1999 s.17. In force: April 2, 2001; £1.75.

These Regulations provide for the Recovery of Defence Costs Orders to be made against, primarily, funded defendants convicted other than in the magistrates' court. The purpose of the Order is to recover such part of the costs of the representation provided as part of the Criminal Defence Service as is reasonable in all the circumstances of the case, including the financial resources of the defendant. In addition, they provide for the provision of information so that the judge may make the Order, and for the freezing of assets where such information is required.

4225. Criminal Defence Service (Advice and Assistance) Act 2001 (c.4)

This Act clarifies the extent of the duty of the Legal Services Commission under the Access to Justice Act 1999 s.13(1).

This Act received Royal Assent on April 10, 2001 and comes into force on April 10, 2001.

4226. Criminal procedure – care proceedings – costs

LEGAL AID IN CRIMINAL AND CARE PROCEEDINGS (COSTS) (AMENDMENT) REGULATIONS 2001, SI 2001 1180; made under the Legal Aid Act 1988 s.25, s.34, s.43. In force: April 2, 2001; £1.75.

These Regulations, which amend the Legal Aid in Criminal and Care Proceedings (Costs) Regulations 1989 (SI 1989 343), provide increased rates of remuneration for solicitors who hold general criminal contracts under the Access to Justice Act 1999.

4227. Criminal procedure – care proceedings – costs

LEGAL AID IN CRIMINAL AND CARE PROCEEDINGS (COSTS) (AMENDMENT NO.2) REGULATIONS 2001, SI 2001 3425; made under the Legal Aid Act 1988 s.25, s.34, s.43. In force: November 15, 2001; £1.50.

These Regulations amend the Legal Aid in Criminal and Care Proceedings (Costs) Regulations 1989 (SI 1989 343) to correct two defective references inserted by the Legal Aid in Criminal and Care Proceedings (Costs) (Amendment) Regulations 2001 (SI 2001 1180), which increased rates of remuneration for solicitors who hold general criminal contracts under the Access to Justice Act 1999.

4228. Criminal procedure – care proceedings – transfer of functions – justices' clerks to justices' chief executives

LEGAL AID IN CRIMINAL AND CARE PROCEEDINGS (GENERAL) (AMENDMENT) REGULATIONS 2001, SI 2001 616; made under the Legal Aid Act 1988 s.23, s.24, s.34. In force: April 1, 2001; £1.50.

These Regulations amend the Legal Aid in Criminal and Care Proceedings (General) Regulations 1989 (SI 1989 344) to transfer the administrative functions of justices' clerks under the Regulations to justices' chief executives in line with the Access to Justice Act 1999 s.90 and Sch.13 which make corresponding transfers in primary legislation.

4229. Criminal procedure – duty solicitors – maladministration – failure to reselect – tortious liability required bad faith

[Legal Advice and Assistance Regulations 1989 (SI 1989 340).]

A appealed against the dismissal of her claim for damages for misfeasance in public office. The local and national duty solicitor committees had refused to reselect her to the local duty solicitor schemes run under the Legal Advice and Assistance Regulations 1989 and, although she was subsequently reinstated, the judge below found that there had been no malice or reckless disregard for her interests notwithstanding that the committees might have acted unlawfully.

Held, dismissing the appeal, that although it was apparent that maladministration had occurred, the statutory purpose of the schemes was to offer free legal advice to the public rather than to provide solicitors with an income. Provided that the decisions had been made with an honest belief in their legality and they had not been made arbitrarily or in bad faith, then there could be no misfeasance even if the committees' actions had subsequently proved to be unlawful.

AMOO-GOTTFRIED v. LEGAL AID BOARD *The Independent*, December 8, 2000, Hale, L.J., CA.

4230. Criminal procedure – fees – costs regulations – exceptional uplift confined to cases involving serious fraud – scope of Lord Chancellor's powers

[Legal Aid in Criminal and Care Proceedings (Costs) Regulations 1989 (SI 1989 343) Reg.3.]

L was tried and found guilty of murder. L's solicitors sought an enhancement of their fees by 200% contending that Legal Aid in Criminal and Care Proceedings (Costs) Regulations 1989 Reg.3 should be extended from cases involving fraud to murder. The determining officer rejected their claim and they appealed. On appeal it was argued that the Regulation was ultra vires.

Held, dismissing the appeal, that the Regulation was not ultra vires and was within the scope of the Lord Chancellor's power.

R. v. LAWRENCE [2000] 2 Costs L.R. 334, Master PR Rogers, Supreme Court Costs Office.

4231. Criminal procedure – fees – Queen's Counsel acting without authority under legal aid certificate

Following an advice from junior counsel in a criminal case D's legal aid order was extended to allow him to be represented by two junior counsel. The order was sent by mistake to D's codefendant and, in a later conversation with the listing office D's solicitor was told that the legal aid order allowed for Queens Counsel. At the trial D was represented by leading and junior counsel but at taxation the determining officer allowed only the fees of junior counsel. Leading counsel's fees were not disallowed in full. D appealed.

Held, allowing the appeal, that although it was the responsibility of counsel or his clerk to ascertain the terms of any legal aid order and no argument on estoppel could be raised to go behind the terms of the order, the rules did not expressly prevent leading counsel from claiming payment as junior counsel.

R. v. DUZGUN (SELIM) [2000] 2 Costs L.R. 316, Judge Rogers, Supreme Court Costs Office.

4232. Family proceedings – remuneration

LEGAL AID IN FAMILY PROCEEDINGS (REMUNERATION) (AMENDMENT) REGULATIONS 2001, SI 2001 830; made under the Legal Aid Act 1988 s.34, s.43. In force: April 2, 2001; £2.00.

These Regulations, which amend the Legal Aid in Family Proceedings (Remuneration) Regulations 1991 (SI 1991 2038), introduce new rates of remuneration for representation in family proceedings which is still being provided by suppliers with a family contract with the Legal Services Commission under the Legal Aid Act 1988 Part IV. In addition, they introduce an uplift of 15 per cent in cases where the supplier is a member of the Solicitors' Family Law Association Panel or, in relation to proceedings relating to children, the Law Society's Children Act Panel and make some amendments reflecting changes in terminology brought about by the Civil Procedure Rules 1998.

4233. Family proceedings – remuneration

LEGAL AID IN FAMILY PROCEEDINGS (REMUNERATION) (AMENDMENT NO.2) REGULATIONS 2001, SI 2001 1255; made under the Legal Aid Act 1988 s.34, s.43. In force: April 2, 2001; £1.50.

These Regulations, which amend the Legal Aid in Family Proceedings (Remuneration) Regulations 1991 (SI 1991 2038), make a correction to the amendments made by the Legal Aid in Family Proceedings (Remuneration) (Amendment) Regulations 2001 (SI 2001 830). The rate of remuneration for attending without counsel at the trial or hearing of any cause or the hearing of any summons or other application at court or other appointment, in a county court or magistrates' court, is amended to £71.50 per hour.

4234. Family proceedings – remuneration

LEGAL AID IN FAMILY PROCEEDINGS (REMUNERATION) (AMENDMENT NO.3) REGULATIONS 2001, SI 2001 2417; made under the Legal Aid Act 1988 s.34, s.43. In force: July 26, 2001; £1.50.

These Regulations, which amend the Legal Aid in Family Proceedings (Remuneration) Regulations 1991 (SI 1991 2038), make corrections to the amendments made by the Legal Aid in Family Proceedings (Remuneration) (Amendment) Regulations 2001 (SI 2001 830) by removing the words "per hour" in the rates for preparing a bill and completing a detailed assessment in relation to care proceedings and prescribed family proceedings.

4235. Legal Aid Board – dissolution

LEGAL AID BOARD (ABOLITION) REGULATIONS 2001, SI 2001 779; made under the Access to Justice Act 1999 Sch.14 para.7. In force: April 2, 2001; £1.50.

This Order provides for the abolition of the Legal Aid Board, which was established under the Legal Aid Act 1988.

4236. Legal services – advice and assistance

LEGAL ADVICE AND ASSISTANCE (AMENDMENT) REGULATIONS 2001, SI 2001 191; made under the Legal Aid Act 1988 s.9, s.34, s.43. In force: February 19, 2001; £1.50.

These Regulations, which are consequential on the Legal Advice and Assistance (Scope) Regulations 2001 (SI 2001 179), amend the Legal Advice and Assistance Regulations 1989 (SI 1989 340) so that the normal provisions relating to applications for advice and assistance do not apply. They also amend the 1989

Regulations so that assistance by way of representation is available without regard to the applicant's financial resources and so that assistance by way of representation does not require the approval of the Legal Services Commission.

4237. Legal services – advice and assistance

LEGAL ADVICE AND ASSISTANCE (AMENDMENT NO.2) REGULATIONS 2001, SI 2001 829; made under the Legal Aid Act 1988 s.34, s.43. In force: Regs.1: April 1, 2001, Reg.3: April 1, 2001; Remainder: April 2, 2001; £1.75.

These Regulations, which amend the Legal Advice and Assistance Regulations 1989 (SI 1989 340), alter the rates of remuneration paid to suppliers with a General Civil Contract with the Legal Services Commission. Special enhanced rates are introduced in respect of advice and assistance in relation to immigration, mental health, education, public law, community care or actions against the police etc. and family, housing or employment where the relevant work category is specifically authorised by the supplier's contract. In addition, these Regulations make amendments to references to justices' clerks to reflect the transfer of functions to justices' chief executives effected by the Access to Justice Act 1999 s.90.

4238. Legal services – advice and assistance

LEGAL ADVICE AND ASSISTANCE (AMENDMENT NO.3) REGULATIONS 2001, SI 2001 1182; made under the Legal Aid Act 1988 s.34, s.43. In force: April 2, 2001; £1.75.

These Regulations, which amend the Legal Advice and Assistance Regulations 1989 (SI 1989 340), provide for revised rates of remuneration for advice and assistance in criminal matters provided by persons holding general criminal contracts under the Access to Justice Act 1999.

4239. Legal services – advice and assistance – terrorism

LEGAL ADVICE AND ASSISTANCE (SCOPE) (AMENDMENT) REGULATIONS 2001, SI 2001 179; made under the Legal Aid Act 1988 s.8. In force: February 19, 2001; £1.50.

These Regulations, which amend the Legal Advice and Assistance (Scope) Regulations 1989 (SI 1989 550), make assistance by way of representation available to a person in respect of whom an application is made for a warrant of further detention under the Terrorism Act 2000 Sch.8.

4240. Legal services – Community Legal Service – assessment of financial resources

COMMUNITY LEGAL SERVICE (FINANCIAL) (AMENDMENT) REGULATIONS 2001, SI 2001 950; made under the Access to Justice Act 1999 s.7, s.10. In force: April 9, 2001; £1.50.

These Regulations amend the Legal Services Commission (Financial) Regulations 2000 (SI 2000 516) so as to increase the income limits for the purposes of determining eligibility for services provided by the Legal Services Commission as part of the Community Legal Service. This is in line with the relevant uprating of social security benefits.

4241. Legal services – Community Legal Service – assessment of financial resources

COMMUNITY LEGAL SERVICE (FINANCIAL) (AMENDMENT NO.2) REGULATIONS 2001, SI 2001 2997; made under the Access to Justice Act 1999 s.7, s.10. In force: October 1, 2001; £1.50.

These Regulations amend the Community Legal Service (Financial) Regulations 2000 (SI 2000 516) so as to extend the areas in which funded services are available irrespective of the financial resources of the client, and make various further minor changes regarding financial eligibility.

4242. Legal services – Community Legal Service – assessment of financial resources

COMMUNITY LEGAL SERVICE (FINANCIAL) (AMENDMENT NO.3) REGULATIONS 2001, SI 2001 3663; made under the Access to Justice Act 1999 s.7, s.10. In force: December 3, 2001; £2.00.

These Regulations, which amend the Community Legal Service (Financial) Regulations 2000 (SI 2000 516), further align the financial eligibility limits applied in respect of the various levels of service and introduce a new means test which applies to all levels of service. They also extend the discretion of the Legal Services Commission in respect of financial eligibility and contributions payable in cases of wider public interest, change the manner in which interest on the statutory charge is calculated and make various further changes regarding financial eligibility, contributions and the statutory charge.

4243. Legal services – Community Legal Service – costs

COMMUNITY LEGAL SERVICE (COSTS) (AMENDMENT) REGULATIONS 2001, SI 2001 822; made under the Access to Justice Act 1999 s.11, s.22. In force: April 2, 2001; £1.50.

These Regulations make changes to the Community Legal Service (Costs) Regulations 2000 (SI 2000 441) Part II, which contains provisions about costs orders against parties funded by the Legal Services Commission and costs orders against the Commission. Amendments are made to clarify the effect of Reg.9, which deals with the procedure for quantifying a costs order against a funded party, and new provisions are inserted which enable the court to order a funded party to pay an amount on account of costs, before the court has finally determined the amount of costs which he should have to pay.

4244. Legal services – Community Legal Service – enforcement of order for costs

COMMUNITY LEGAL SERVICE (COST PROTECTION) (AMENDMENT) REGULATIONS 2001, SI 2001 823; made under the Access to Justice Act 1999 s.11. In force: April 2, 2001; £1.50.

These Regulations, which amend the Community Legal Service (Cost Protection) Regulations 2000 (SI 2000 824), insert provisions about costs orders against the Legal Services Commission in proceedings in relation to which a party has been funded by the Commission, a new provision which specifies, in relation to different types of proceedings, which court, tribunal or person may make such costs orders.

4245. Legal services – Community Legal Service – enforcement of order for costs

COMMUNITY LEGAL SERVICE (COST PROTECTION) (AMENDMENT NO.2) REGULATIONS 2001, SI 2001 3812; made under the Access to Justice Act 1999 s.11. In force: December 3, 2001; £1.50.

These Regulations make changes to the Community Legal Service (Cost Protection) Regulations 2000 (SI 2000 824) so as to amend the conditions which must be satisfied in order for an order to be made against the Legal Services Commission for the payment of costs incurred by a party who has not received funded services.

4246. Legal services – Community Legal Service – funding

COMMUNITY LEGAL SERVICE (FUNDING) (AMENDMENT) ORDER 2001, SI 2001 831; made under the Access to Justice Act 1999 s.6. In force: April 2, 2001; £1.75.

This Order, which amends the Community Legal Service (Funding) Order 2000 (SI 2000 627), sets out amended maximum figures for remuneration payable under contracts for the following types of work: Legal Help and Help at Court relating to immigration, mental health, education, public law, actions against the police etc. and community care; Legal Help and Help at Court relating to family, housing and employment; other Legal Help and Help at Court carried out under contracts; Help with Mediation; and Legal Representation before a Mental Health Review Tribunal or before the Immigration Appeal Tribunal or an immigration adjudicator. The maximum relating to Legal Representation before the Immigration Appeal Tribunal or an immigration adjudicator is disapplied if the case raises an exceptionally novel or complex point of law, or has significant potential to produce real benefits for individuals other than the client.

4247. **Legal services – Community Legal Service – funding**

COMMUNITY LEGAL SERVICE (FUNDING) (AMENDMENT NO.2) ORDER 2001, SI 2001 2996; made under the Access to Justice Act 1999 s.6. In force: October 1, 2001; £1.50.

This Order amends the Community Legal Service (Funding) Order 2000 (SI 2000 627) so as to disapply contracts which are awarded as part of the housing possession court duty scheme pilot or the alternative methods of delivery pilot from the limits as to rates of payment.

4248. **Legal services – Community Legal Service – funding – counsel in family proceedings**

COMMUNITY LEGAL SERVICE (FUNDING) (COUNSEL IN FAMILY PROCEEDINGS) ORDER 2001, SI 2001 1077; made under the Access to Justice Act 1999 s.6. In force: May 1, 2001; £3.00.

This Order introduces a new system for the payment of graduated fees for counsel for work in family proceedings in the High Court, County Court and magistrates' courts. The graduated fees vary with the nature of the proceedings and a number of factors designed to reflect their complexity. Provision is also made for an additional fee to be payable in proceedings involving an exceptional amount of preparation. In addition, the Order covers how and when claims for payment are to be made, and appeals and reviews of payments.

4249. **Legal services – police stations – duty solicitors**

LEGAL ADVICE AND ASSISTANCE AT POLICE STATIONS (REMUNERATION) (AMENDMENT) REGULATIONS 2001, SI 2001 1181; made under the Legal Aid Act 1988 s.34, s.43. In force: April 2, 2001; £1.75.

These Regulations, which amend the Legal Advice and Assistance at Police Stations (Remunerations) Regulations 1989 (SI 1989 342), provide increased remuneration for solicitors who hold general criminal contracts with the Legal Services Commission. The provisions relating to increased remuneration for December 31, 1999 and January 1, 2000 are omitted as spent.

4250. **Legal Services Commission – costs – jurisdiction to make costs order for unsuccessful judicial review proceedings**

See CIVIL PROCEDURE: R. (on the application of Gunn) v. Secretary of State for the Home Department (Recovery of Costs). §491

4251. **Revocation – costs – retrospective effect of revocation – meaning of "circumstances"**

[Legal Aid Act 1988 s.17 (1), s.17 (2); Civil Legal Aid (General) Regulations 1989 (SI 1989 339) Reg.74 (2), Reg.130 (a), Reg.130 (b).]

D appealed against a limited order for costs made against K, who had been legally assisted under emergency legal aid when the order was made, and against the dismissal, on the ground of lack of jurisdiction, of its subsequent application to vary the costs order. The order limited K's costs liability pending a determination under the Legal Aid Act 1988 s.17 (2). K's emergency legal aid certificate was revoked, and D applied to have the costs order varied to take account of the retrospective effect of the revocation. The judge below held that the revocation meant that K was deemed never to have been an assisted person and therefore any change in his circumstances was irrelevant for the purposes of Reg.130(b). D submitted that in a situation where a legal aid certificate was revoked, the purpose of the Civil Legal Aid (General) Regulations 1989 Reg.74(2) was that the person losing his certificate also lost the protection of s.17(1) for the future and for the time during which the certificate had been valid. Furthermore an assisted person's "circumstances" in Reg.130(b) had a wider interpretation than "means" used in Reg.130(a).

Held, allowing the appeal, that Reg.74(2) withdrew the protection afforded to persons whose legal aid certificates had been revoked. The judge's interpretation of Reg.130 had frustrated its legislative purpose in that it had maintained K's protection, notwithstanding the fact that "circumstances" in Reg.130(b) was not restricted to financial circumstances, and the revocation of legal aid with retrospective effect was a significant change in circumstances. The costs order was therefore varied to direct K to pay the costs of both applications.

DEUTSCHE INVESTITIONS UND ENTWICKLUNGSGESELLSCHAFT MBH (DEG) v. KOSHY; *sub nom.* DEG-DEUTSCHE INVESTITIONS UND ENTWICKLUNGSGESELLSCHAFT MBH v. KOSHY, [2001] EWCA Civ 79, [2001] 3 All E.R. 878, Robert Walker, L.J., CA.

4252. Statutory charge – calculation of interest – civil legal aid

CIVIL LEGAL AID (GENERAL) (AMENDMENT NO.2) REGULATIONS 2001, SI 2001 3735; made under the Legal Aid Act 1988 s.16, s.34, s.43. In force: December 3, 2001; £1.50.

These Regulations amend the Civil Legal Aid (General) Regulations 1989 (SI 1989 339) in order to change the method of calculation of interest on the statutory charge created by the Legal Aid Act 1988 s.16. They make amendments consequential on amendments to the Civil Procedure Rules 1998 governing appeals.

4253. Taxation – Crown Court – costs for sitting behind counsel for sentencing – requirement for likelihood of custodial sentence

See CRIMINAL PROCEDURE: R. v. Crocker. §1117

LEGAL METHODOLOGY

4254. Books

Butler, William E. – Russian-English Legal Dictionary. Hardback. ISBN 1-57105-194-5. Hardback: £116.99. ISBN 1-57105-194-5. Transnational Publishers, Inc.

Chatterjee, Charles – Methods of Research in Law. 2nd Ed. Paperback: £9.95. ISBN 1-85836-386-1. Old Bailey Press.

Gerlis, Stephen; Blackford, Robert – Civil Practitioner's Handbook: 2001. Practitioner Series. Paperback: £50.00. ISBN 0-421-82640-1. Sweet & Maxwell.

Holborn, Guy – Butterworths Legal Research Guide. 2nd Ed. Paperback: £19.95. ISBN 0-406-93023-6. Butterworths Law.

Words and Phrases Supplement 2001. Paperback: £47.00. ISBN 0-406-94819-4. Butterworths Law.

LEGAL PROFESSION

4255. **Access to Justice Act 1999 (c.22) – Commencement No.8 Order**

ACCESS TO JUSTICE ACT 1999 (COMMENCEMENT NO.8) ORDER 2001, SI 2001 1655 (C.58); made under the Access to Justice Act 1999 s.108. Commencement details: bringing into force various provisions of the Act on May 25, 2001; £1.75.

This Order brings the Access to Justice Act 1999 s.47 relating to fees for solicitors' practising certificates into force on May 25, 2001.

4256. **Barristers – costs – imposition of personal liability – dereliction of duty – pursuit of hopeless case – New Zealand**

H, a New Zealand barrister, appealed against an order that she should personally bear a proportion of her client, M's, costs liability to his opponent on the ground that in pursuing and losing a hopeless case she had been negligent. The order arose from H's conduct of a negligence claim against M's former solicitors. The judge had found that, having been advised by the court to reconsider the merit of M's case and the wisdom of continuing it, H ought to have made a more realistic assessment of the case and advised M accordingly.

Held, allowing the appeal, that the pursuit of a hopeless case by a barrister was, of itself, insufficient to demonstrate a failure to achieve the appropriate level of competence and care, *Myers v. Elman* [1940] A.C. 282 applied. In order to justify the imposition of a personal costs order it was not enough for there to have been a mistake or error of judgment. The relevant test was whether the conduct amounted to a serious dereliction of the duty owed to the court. The courts in New Zealand had inherent jurisdiction to make a costs order against a client's solicitor in order to maintain an appropriate level of competence and ensure public confidence. Given that there was no difference between the duties owed to the court by solicitors and those owed by barristers, together with the similarities in their route to qualification and manner of practice, there was no distinction capable of justifying differential treatment so far as personal costs liability was concerned. Furthermore, it was desirable in the public interest that the High Court should have authority in appropriate circumstances to award punitive costs against a barrister.

HARLEY v. McDONALD; GLASGOW HARLEY (A FIRM) v. McDONALD; *sub nom.* HARLEY v. McDONALD GLASGOW HARLEY; HARLEY v. GLASGOW HARLEY, [2001] UKPC 18, [2001] 2 A.C. 678, Lord Hope of Craighead, Privy Council (New Zealand).

4257. **Barristers – practising certificates**

ACCESS TO JUSTICE ACT 1999 (BAR PRACTISING CERTIFICATES) ORDER 2001, SI 2001 135; made under the Access to Justice Act 1999 s.46. In force: January 31, 2001; £1.50.

This Order amends the Access to Justice Act 1999 s.46 by adding to the existing purposes referred to in that section for which the General Council of the Bar may raise fees for the issuing of practising certificates.

4258. **Licensed conveyancers – disciplinary procedures**

COUNCIL FOR LICENSED CONVEYANCERS (DISCIPLINARY POWERS) ORDER 2001, SI 2001 48; made under the Courts and Legal Services Act 1990 s.53, s.120, Sch.19 para.15. In force: February 1, 2001; £1.50.

This Order specifies February 1, 2001 as the date on which the disciplinary powers, specified in the Courts and Legal Services Act 1990 Sch.19 para.15(2), become exercisable by the Council for Licensed Conveyancers.

4259. Licensed conveyancers – Discipline and Appeals Committee – procedure

LICENSED CONVEYANCERS' DISCIPLINE AND APPEALS COMMITTEE (PROCEDURE) RULES APPROVAL ORDER 2001, SI 2001 2797; made under the Administration of Justice Act 1985 Sch.4 para.1. In force: September 30, 2001; £3.00.

This Order contains the Lord Chancellor's approval of the Licensed Conveyancers' Discipline and Appeals Committee (Procedure) Rules 2001 which form the Schedule to the Order.

4260. Solicitors – barristers – legal executives – free movement of services

EUROPEAN COMMUNITIES (LAWYER'S PRACTICE) (AMENDMENT) REGULATIONS 2001, SI 2001 644; made under the European Communities Act 1972 s.2. In force: April 6, 2001; £1.50.

These Regulations amend the European Communities (Lawyer's Practice) Regulations 2000 (SI 2000 1119) which give effect to European Communities Council Directive 98/5 ([1998] OJ L77/36) of February 16, 1998, which facilitates the practice of the profession of lawyer on a permanent basis in a Member State of the European Community other than the State in which the qualification was obtained.

4261. Solicitors – clients – ascertainment of retainer

JF appealed against the dismissal (Unreported, February 26, 1999) of its action for breach of retainer against LM, a firm of solicitors, the judge having found that LM had not been retained by JF to advise in connection with the grant to it of a debenture by an associated company.

Held, dismissing the appeal, that the relevant enquiry was not on whose behalf had JF intended to instruct LM, but rather on whose behalf was LM reasonably entitled to conclude that it had been retained, given all that had been said to LM and the context in which it had been said, *McCutcheon v. David MacBrayne Ltd* [1962] 1 Lloyd's Rep 303, [1964] C.L.Y. 4455 applied. In the present case, the judge had clearly taken the view that the solicitor was careful and competent. If that solicitor had concluded that he was retained by a different company to JF, then JF faced a difficult task in seeking to assert that it was not reasonable for the solicitor to have reached that conclusion, *Owners of the SS Hontestroom v. Owners of the SS Sogaporak* [1927] A.C. 37 applied. Generally, a powerful indication as to whom a solicitor regarded as their client was to be found in the fee note they rendered at the completion of the transaction. In the instant case, the solicitor's explanation as to why the fee note was addressed to JF was accepted by the judge, who was entitled to conclude that this was not inconsistent with the solicitor's belief that he was not retained by them.

JEWO FERROUS BV v. LEWIS MOORE (A FIRM) [2001] Lloyd's Rep. P.N. 6, Chadwick, L.J., CA.

4262. Solicitors – conveyancing – acting for borrower and lender – extent of duty to disclose

See NEGLIGENCE: Bristol and West Building Society v. Baden Barnes Groves & Co. §4523

4263. Solicitors – conveyancing – reliance on undertaking – common conveyancing practice – potential breach of duty

P, the sole shareholders and directors of a company, VL, retained D, a firm of solicitors, to act for them in relation to the purchase of a sports club. On completion, the vendor's solicitor failed to honour its undertaking to redeem a pre-existing charge on the property, and P subsequently brought proceedings against D alleging negligence. Two preliminary issues arose: (1) whether D had breached its duty of care in failing to ensure that charges attached to the property had been discharged and in relying on the vendor's solicitor's undertaking, and (2) whether the right to recovery was restricted to the amount required to redeem the charge. D submitted that it had dealt with the conveyance in accordance with general practice.

Held, determining the preliminary issues, that (1) solicitors acting for a purchaser could potentially act in breach of duty if they completed a purchase in reliance on a promise by the vendor's solicitor to discharge an unsettled charge on the property to be transferred, notwithstanding that a solicitor in so acting was following a common conveyancing practice, *Edward Wong Finance Co Ltd v. Johnson Stokes & Master* [1984] A.C. 296, [1984] C.L.Y. 3624, *Bolitho (Deceased) v. City and Hackney HA* [1998] A.C. 232, [1997] C.L.Y. 3789 and *National Home Loans Corp Plc v. Kaufmann* (Unreported, June 21, 1995) applied. However, given the facts of the instant case, particularly the time constraints and difficulty in ascertaining the value of the charge, it had not been feasible for D to adopt the approach laid out in *Wong*. It followed that D had not acted in breach of its duty, and (2) it was not appropriate to restrict P's claim to the amount required to redeem the charge since there had been a diminution of value of the property as a result of the existence of the charge. Accordingly, P would be, if able to prove so, entitled to recover any loss stemming from their inability to sell the property following the breach, *South Australia Asset Management Corp v. York Montague Ltd* [1997] A.C. 191, [1996] C.L.Y. 4519 considered and *Gregory v. Shepherds (A Firm)* Times, June 28, 2000, [2000] 8 C.L. 529 followed.

PATEL v. DAYBELLS [2000] Lloyd's Rep. P.N. 844, Gray, J., QBD.

4264. **Solicitors – disciplinary procedures – second set of proceedings arising from same facts – abuse of process**

L appealed against a finding of the Solicitors' Disciplinary Tribunal that a second set of disciplinary proceedings against G relating to matters arising out of the same facts was an abuse of process. G had been suspended from practice for three years having confessed to conduct unbefitting of a solicitor in relation to the keeping of accounts and the misappropriation of funds from client accounts. He was later convicted of theft on the basis primarily of the same facts and L brought a second set of proceedings on account of that conviction.

Held, allowing the appeal, that in the light of G's criminal conviction it had not been appropriate to describe the bringing of the second set of proceedings as an abuse of process. It was important to bear in mind the public interest in maintaining the integrity of the legal profession. The situation that was before the first tribunal was significantly different from that which was before the second; the first tribunal was not able to take into account the fact of G's conviction, although they were able to deal with the underlying facts. It was accordingly perfectly in order for L to decide that the situation had changed as a result of the conviction to the extent that the position was sufficiently different to justify the commencement of the second disciplinary proceedings, *Manson v. Vooght (No.1)* [1999] C.P.L.R. 133, [1998] C.L.Y. 367 considered.

LAW SOCIETY v. GILBERT; *sub nom.* SOLICITOR (CO/2504/2000), *Re The Times*, January 12, 2001, Lord Woolf of Barnes, L.C.J., QBD.

4265. **Solicitors – fiduciary duty – conveyancing – termination of retainer – confidential information**

S instituted proceedings against P, a firm of solicitors, seeking to recover losses arising from an alleged breach of duty by P. S contended that (1) P had acted in breach of fiduciary duty to S when P had terminated its retainer with S and exchanged contracts for the purchase of an industrial estate. S maintained that P had wrongly caused the purchase to be made in the name of the subsidiary of another company, L, which had introduced S to the transaction and for whom P had acted in respect of the same transaction, rather than in the name of S's subsidiary as instructed by S, and (2) P was accordingly liable to S for the loss of profit that would have been made upon the re-sale of the land had the property been owned by S.

Held, giving judgment for P, that (1) P had acted in breach of its duty to S in accepting instructions to act on behalf of L and terminating its retainer with S, and (2) despite the breach of duty, S was unable to recover damages from P since the transaction had been confidential as between L, S and the vendor, and S was not entitled to use the information without L's consent. Since L had not agreed to the terms of a revised profit share with S, S could not have used that information to complete the transaction without being liable to account to L for the whole of any profit made because of the law relating to confidentiality, *Seager v. Copydex Ltd (No.1)* [1967] 1 W.L.R. 923, [1967] C.L.Y. 1486 applied.

SUMMIT PROPERTY LTD v. PITMANS [2001] Lloyd's Rep. P.N. 164, Park, J., Ch D.

4266. Solicitors – incorporated practices

SOLICITORS' INCORPORATED PRACTICES (AMENDMENT) ORDER 2001, SI 2001 645; made under the Administration of Justice Act 1985 s.9. In force: April 6, 2001; £1.50.

This Order, which amends the Solicitors' Incorporated Practices Order 1991 (SI 1991 2684), allows the enactments referred to in that Order to apply to limited liability partnerships, which are recognised bodies, and to their members.

4267. Solicitors – partners liabilities – money belonging to third party deposited in client account – solicitor's duties

A brought an action against HA and K, who had been partners in a solicitors' practice, for the recovery of approximately £30,000. Following the sale of various properties owned by M, a company effectively run by A's husband but of which she was a director, the sum of £100,000 had been deposited in an account under A's control. That sum had subsequently been used, at the recommendation of G, a friend and business acquaintance of A, to support a banker's draft made out to the solicitors' practice. Thereafter, HA had paid out sums from the £100,000 on the instructions of G. He had continued to do so after being instructed by A that the money should be held to her order alone. After A had issued proceedings, HA paid her approximately £70,000.

Held, giving judgment for K, that (1) a sum of £19,511 had been paid out by HA at a time when he reasonably believed that G was the owner of the money. It followed that A only had a claim for £10,489; (2) the sum of £100,000 had been received by A at a time when she had been aware, or ought to have been aware, that M was in serious financial difficulties. Accordingly, she had received the money in breach of trust and was liable to M's liquidators. K had believed, but had not been notified, that A might not be the beneficial owner of the money. He could not rely on the defence of jus tertii, whereby the defendant was unable to plead that the claimant was not entitled to possession as against him because a third party was the true owner of the money. It was not, except in unusual circumstances, the duty of a bona fide recipient of money who suspected that a third party might have a claim to it to make efforts to verify his suspicions. Such a person should, however, subject to the question of confidentiality, contemplate informing that third party, and (3) in receiving the sum of £100,000, HA had not been acting within the scope of his authority. Furthermore, the money had not been received in the "normal course of business of a solicitor", with the result that K incurred no liability, *Hirst v. Etherington* [1999] Lloyd's Rep. P.N. 938, [1999] C.L.Y. 3814, *Dubai Aluminium Co Ltd v. Salaam* [2001] Q.B. 113, [2000] C.L.Y. 4316 and *United Bank of Kuwait v. Hammoud* [1988] 1 W.L.R. 1051, [1989] C.L.Y. 3491 applied.

ANTONELLI v. ALLEN [2001] Lloyd's Rep. P.N. 487, Neuberger, J., Ch D.

4268. Solicitors – privilege – disclosure – mortgage fraud – degree of solicitor's participation in client's iniquitous conduct

M applied to AN for a mortgage stating that he intended to build a detached home for his own personal occupation. His actual intention was to build three terraced houses for sale on an adjoining plot of land already subject to a mortgage that was in considerable arrears with another mortgagee. A brought a claim alleging professional negligence against DP, M's solicitors, and sought disclosure of the conveyancing file.

Held, allowing the application, that M, as DP's client, was entitled to legal professional privilege in respect of all communications between M and DP. That privilege could only be removed by the court in very exceptional circumstances, including where the client had acted iniquitously, *Nationwide Anglia Building Society v. Various Solicitors (No.1)* [1999] P.N.L.R. 52, [1998] C.L.Y. 356 applied. There was prima facie evidence that M had made a fraudulent statement in support of his mortgage application and that amounted to iniquitous conduct for the purposes of the instant case. Furthermore, in order to override the privilege it was sufficient that there had been some participation by DP; it was not necessary for DP to have been knowingly involved in the fraud.

ABBEY NATIONAL PLC v. DAVID PROSSER & CO [2001] P.N.L.R. 15, Judge Moseley Q.C., Ch D.

4269. Solicitors – professional negligence – terminally ill client – delay in carrying out instructions

See NEGLIGENCE: X (A Child) v. Woollcombe Yonge (A Firm). §4534

4270. Solicitors – Solicitors Disciplinary Tribunal – tribunal's power to refer case to Office for Supervision of Solicitors – tribunal's duties

[Solicitors Act 1974; Solicitors (Disciplinary Proceedings) Rules 1994 (SI 1994 288) Part II r.4, Part III r.28.]

T, who had alleged that a solicitor had misled the court and otherwise acted improperly, applied for judicial review of the decision of the Solicitors Disciplinary Tribunal whereby it declined to determine whether he had a prima facie case in relation to his complaint made pursuant to the Solicitors (Disciplinary Proceedings) Rules 1994 Part II r.4. The tribunal had concluded that the matters raised in T's complaint should be investigated but that as it did not have any powers of investigation, the appropriate body to carry them out was the Office for the Supervision of Solicitors, OSS. T submitted that (1) Part III r.28 of the Rules, which provided that the tribunal could "at any stage of the proceedings against a solicitor" refer the case to the OSS, applied only upon it being found that a prima facie case existed, and (2) Part III r.28 did not allow for a reference to the OSS, and the consequent adjournment of a case, in order to facilitate an investigation into the matters raised by a complaint.

Held, granting the application in part, that (1) the powers provided under Part III r.28 to refer a case to the OSS applied both prior to and after certification under r.4(4)(i) as to whether a prima facie case existed. The word "proceedings" within r.28 had a wide meaning. The power to refer an application to the OSS had to be exercised for the purpose of enabling the OSS to determine whether to lodge a further application against the solicitor or whether the prosecution of the solicitor should be carried out on the complainant's behalf, and (2) the tribunal could not delegate to any other body the performance of duties established pursuant to the Solicitors Act 1974. In the instant case, the tribunal had not been justified in declining to reach a conclusion as to whether a prima facie case had been established. If the evidence established such a case, the tribunal should not without good reason postpone certification in order to refer a case to the OSS.

R. (ON THE APPLICATION OF TOTH) v. SOLICITORS DISCIPLINARY TRIBUNAL; *sub nom.* R. v. SOLICITORS DISCIPLINARY TRIBUNAL, *ex p.* TOTH,

[2001] EWHC Admin 240, [2001] 3 All E.R. 180, Stanley Burnton, J., QBD (Admin Ct).

4271. Solicitors – undertakings – supervisory jurisdiction of court

R applied for an order to enforce undertakings given by D, relying on the court's inherent supervisory jurisdiction over the conduct of solicitors. A and D had been partners in a firm of solicitors.

Held, refusing the application, that the evidence showed that D had not given the undertakings in her capacity as a solicitor with the result that they could not be enforced under the court's inherent jurisdiction. D had had no ostensible authority to bind the partnership when giving the undertakings so that A could not be liable thereunder, *United Bank of Kuwait v. Hammoud* [1988] 1 W.L.R. 1051, [1989] C.L.Y. 3491 considered.

RUPAREL v. AWAN [2001] Lloyd's Rep. P.N. 258, David Donaldson Q.C., Ch D.

4272. Solicitors – undertakings – surrounding circumstances fundamental to interpretation

R appealed against a finding that a letter from L, a solicitor, had not contained an undertaking. L had acted for G, a company director, who had been interested in purchasing from R his majority shareholding in a football club. G had sent instructions to L for the transfer of monies which were copied to R and which included a request that L provide an undertaking to R. L had then written to R stating that he was confirming G's instructions that the monies would be forwarded, and asking for R's bank details. G subsequently changed his instructions and the money was not paid. L contended that his letter was not an undertaking but merely confirmation of his instructions.

Held, allowing the appeal, that it was entirely reasonable that R should take L's statement that he was complying with G's instructions as an assertion that he was giving the undertaking requested by G in his copy letter. L's letter could not be taken in isolation, but had to be viewed in the context of the copy letter from G which R had already received, *Investors Compensation Scheme Ltd v. West Bromwich Building Society (No.1)* [1998] 1 W.L.R. 896, [1997] C.L.Y. 2537 applied.

REDDY v. LACHLAN [2000] Lloyd's Rep. P.N. 858, Simon Brown, L.J., CA.

4273. Books

Biehl, Kathy; Calishain, Tara – Lawyer's Guide to Internet Legal Research. Paperback: £28.00. ISBN 0-8108-3885-0. Scarecrow Press.

Boyle, Fiona; Capps, Deveral; Plowden, Philip; Sandford, Claire – Practical Guide to Lawyering Skills. Paperback: £17.95. ISBN 1-85941-420-6. Cavendish Publishing Ltd.

Boyle, Fiona; Capps, Deveral; Plowden, Philip; Sandford, Clare – Practical Guide to Lawyering Skills. Paperback: £20.95. ISBN 1-85941-420-6. Cavendish Publishing Ltd.

Brambley, S. – Pervasive and Core Topics. 9th Ed. Legal Practice Course. Paperback: £23.50. ISBN 0-85308-720-2. Jordans.

Brockman, Joan – Gender in the Legal Profession: Fitting or Breaking the Mould. Law and Society. Hardback: £71.50. ISBN 0-7748-0834-9. University of British Columbia Press.

Butt, Peter; Castle, Richard – Modern Legal Drafting. Hardback: £40.00. ISBN 0-521-80217-2. Paperback: £15.95. ISBN 0-521-00186-2. Cambridge University Press.

Chapman, Michael D. – Waterlow's Solicitors' & Barristers' Directory: 2001. Hardback: £59.00. ISBN 1-85783-906-4. Waterlow Professional Publishing.

Christian, Charles – Virtual Lawyer-marketing, Selling and Delivering Legal Services Online. Paperback: £45.00. ISBN 0-406-92401-5. Butterworths.

Curzon, L. – Dictionary of Law. 6th Ed. Paperback: £26.99. ISBN 0-582-43809-8. Longman.

De Wilde, Robin – Facts and Figures 2000. 5th Ed. Paperback: £28.00. ISBN 0-421-73760-3. Sweet & Maxwell.

Delaney, Patrick; Hopkins, Debra – Wiley CPA Examination Review 2001: Business Law and Professional Responsibilities. Paperback: £29.50. ISBN 0-471-39791-1. John Wiley and Sons.

Doonan, Elmer – Drafting. Legal Skills. Paperback: £12.95. ISBN 1-85941-486-9. Cavendish Publishing Ltd.

Garner, Bryan A. – Legal Writing in Plain English. Chicago Guides to Writing, Editing, and Publishing. Hardback: £25.50. ISBN 0-226-28417-4. University of Chicago Press.

Garner, Bryan A. – Dictionary of Modern Legal Usage. 2nd Ed. Paperback: £14.99. ISBN 0-19-514236-5. Oxford University Press Inc, USA.

Garner, Bryan A. – Legal Writing in Plain English. Chicago Guides to Writing, Editing, and Publishing. Paperback: £9.50. ISBN 0-226-28418-2. University of Chicago Press.

Green, D. – Skills for Lawyers. Legal Practice Course. Paperback: £23.50. ISBN 0-85308-721-0. Jordans.

Home and Family Solicitor. £19.99. ISBN 1-902646-30-4. Law Pack Publishing.

Kaczorowska, Alina – EU Law for Today's Lawyers. Paperback: £16.95. ISBN 1-85836-356-X. Old Bailey Press.

King, L. – Accounts for Solicitors. Legal Practice Course. Paperback: £23.95. ISBN 0-85308-715-6. Jordans.

Klami, Hannu Tapani; Grans, Minna; Sorvettula, Johanna – Law and Truth: A theory of Evidence. Paperback: £25.00. ISBN 951-653-306-X. The Finnish Academy of Science and Letters.

Langum, David J. – William M. Kunstler-The Most Hated Lawyer in America. Paperback: £18.95. ISBN 0-8147-5151-2. New York University Press.

Lazega, Emmanuel – Collegial Phenomenon. Hardback: £50.00. ISBN 0-19-924272-0. Oxford University Press.

Nemeth, Charles P. – Aquinas in the Courtroom. Contributions in Philosophy, 82. Hardback: £58.50. ISBN 0-313-31929-4. Paperback: £19.95. ISBN 0-275-97290-9. Greenwood Press.

O'Malley, Thomas – Round Hall Guide to the Sources of Law. 2nd Ed. Paperback: £40.00. ISBN 1-85800-185-4. Round Hall Ltd.

Porter, David S.; Openshaw, Vanessa – Business Management for Solicitors-Turning Your Practice Into a Business-New Ed. Paperback: £38.00. ISBN 1-85811-274-5. EMIS Professional Publishing.

Resumes for Law Careers-with Sample Cover Letters. 2nd Ed. VGM Professional Resumes. Book (details unknown): £7.99. ISBN 0-658-01723-3. McGraw-Hill Publishing Company.

Rutherford, L.; et al – Osborn's Concise Law Dictionary 9th Ed. Paperback: £9.95. ISBN 0-421-75340-4. Sweet & Maxwell.

Stewart, William – Collins Dictionary of Law. 2nd Ed. Paperback: £9.99. ISBN 0-00-710294-1. Collins.

Warren, Chief Justice Earl – Memoirs of Chief Justice Earl Warren. Paperback: £14.50. ISBN 1-56833-234-3. Cooper Square Press.

LEGAL SYSTEMS

4274. Books

Abrams, Roger I. – Legal Bases. Paperback: £15.95. ISBN 1-56639-890-8. Temple University Press.

Ahdar, Rex J. – Worlds Colliding. Hardback: £50.00. ISBN 0-7546-2200-2. Dartmouth.

Anthony and Berryman's Magistrates Court Guide 2002. Paperback: £35.00. ISBN 0-406-94598-5. Butterworths Law.

Asouzu, Amazu A. – International Commercial Arbitration and African States. Cambridge Studies in International and Comparative Law. Hardback: £70.00. ISBN 0-521-64132-2. Cambridge University Press.

Bellamy, Richard; Warleigh, Alex – Citizenship and Governance in the EU. Hardback: £50.00. ISBN 0-8264-5348-1. Paperback: £16.99. ISBN 0-8264-5347-3. Continuum International Publishing Group-Academic and Professional.

Bennion, F.A.R. – Understanding Common Law Legislation-Drafting and Interpretation. Hardback: £30.00. ISBN 0-19-924777-3. Oxford University Press.

Blackstone, Sir William; Morrison, Wayne J. – Blackstone Commentaries on Laws of England: Vols 1-4. Cavendish Commentaries. Hardback: £250.00. ISBN 1-85941-482-6. Cavendish Publishing Ltd.

Burton, William C. – Burton's Legal Thesaurus. £21.99. ISBN 0-07-137309-8. McGraw-Hill Publishing Company.

Byrne, Raymond; Binchy, William – Annual Review of Irish Law: 1998. Hardback: £115.00. ISBN 1-85800-124-2. Round Hall Ltd.

Chanock, Martin – Making of South African Legal Culture 1902-1936. Hardback: £60.00. ISBN 0-521-79156-1. Cambridge University Press.

Cook, Michael – Cook on Costs 2001-a Guide to Legal Remuneration in Civil Contentious and Non-contentious Business. Paperback: £58.00. ISBN 0-406-94454-7. Butterworths Law.

Darbyshire, Penny – Nutshells-English Legal System. Nutshells. Paperback: £5.50. ISBN 0-421-74280-1. Sweet & Maxwell.

Douglas-Lewis, N. – Law and Governance. Paperback: £38.95. ISBN 1-85941-547-4. Cavendish Publishing Ltd.

Egan, Michelle – Constructing a European Market-Standards, Regulation, and Governance. Hardback: £40.00. ISBN 0-19-924405-7. Oxford University Press.

Evans, Judith – English and European Legal Systems: Textbook. 2nd Ed. Old Bailey Press Textbooks. Paperback: £14.95. ISBN 1-85836-405-1. Old Bailey Press.

Fordham, Michael – Judicial Review Handbook: 2001. 3rd Ed. Hardback: £75.00. ISBN 1-84113-238-1. Hart Publishing.

Gibson, Bryan – Introduction to the Magistrate's Court. 4th Ed. Paperback: £17.00. ISBN 1-872870-99-6. Waterside Press.

Greenberg, Janelle – Radical Face of the Ancient Constitution. Hardback: £45.00. ISBN 0-521-79131-6. Cambridge University Press.

Hart, C. – Civil Litigation. Hardback: £23.95. ISBN 0-85308-709-1. Jordans.

Henham, Ralph J. – Sentence Discounts and the Criminal Process. Hardback: £45.00. ISBN 0-7546-2018-2. Dartmouth.

Herrup, Cynthia – House in Gross Disorder. Paperback: £8.99. ISBN 0-19-513925-9. Oxford University Press Inc, USA.

Holtam, J. – Criminal Litigation. Hardback: £23.95. ISBN 0-85308-719-9. Jordans.

Kahn, Paul W. – Cultural Study of Law. Paperback: £9.00. ISBN 0-226-42255-0. University of Chicago Press.

Keenan, Denis – Smith and Keenan's English Law. Paperback: £26.99. ISBN 0-582-43816-0. Longman Higher Education.

Kressel, Neil; Kressel, Dorit – Stack and Sway. Hardback: £19.99. ISBN 0-8133-9772-3. Westview Press.

Leubsdorf, John – Man in His Original Dignity. Hardback: £40.00. ISBN 0-7546-2110-3. Ashgate Publishing Limited.

Lorton, Roger – A-Z of Policing Law. 2nd Ed. Paperback: £20.00. ISBN 0-11-702812-6. The Stationery Office Books.

Matthews, John F. – Laying Down the Law. Hardback: £27.50. ISBN 0-300-07900-1. Yale University Press.

Miller, Richard Lawrence – Whittaker-Struggles of a Supreme Court Justice. Contributions in Legal Studies, No 102. Hardback: £54.50. ISBN 0-313-31250-8. Greenwood Press.

Moddelmog, William E. – Reconstituting Authority. Hardback: £27.95. ISBN 0-87745-736-0. University of Iowa Press.

Mohammad Hashim Kamali – Islamic Commercial Law. Hardback: £45.00. ISBN 0-946621-79-9. The IslamicTexts Society.

Moore, Sally Falk – Law As Process: an Anthropological Approach. 2nd Ed. Classics in African Anthropology. Paperback (C format): £14.95. ISBN 0-85255-910-0. James Currey Publishers.

Phillips, Jim; Chapman, Bruce; Stevens, David – Between State and Market. Hardback: £52.50. ISBN 0-7735-2096-1. Paperback: £24.95. ISBN 0-7735-2112-7. McGill-Queen's University Press.

Reilly, Ben – Democracy in Divided Societies-electoral Engineering for Conflict Management. Theories of Institutional Design. Hardback: £40.00. ISBN 0-521-79323-8. Paperback: £14.95. ISBN 0-521-79730-6. Cambridge University Press.

Riles, Annelise – Rethinking the Masters of Comparative Law. Hardback: £40.00. ISBN 1-84113-289-6. Paperback: £25.00. ISBN 1-84113-290-X. Hart Publishing.

Robert, Henry M. – Robert's Rules of Order. Paperback: £12.99. ISBN 0-7382-0307-6. Perseus Books.

Simmons, A. John – Justification and Legitimacy. Hardback: £35.00. ISBN 0-521-79016-6. Paperback: £12.95. ISBN 0-521-79365-3. Cambridge University Press.

Slapper, Gary – Organisational Proscecutions. Hardback: £40.00. ISBN 0-7546-2059-X. Dartmouth.

Slapper, Gary; Kelly, David – English Legal System 5th Ed. Paperback: £25.95. ISBN 1-85941-657-8. Cavendish Publishing Ltd.

Slapper, Gary; Kelly, David – Sourcebook on the English Legal System. 2nd Ed. Sourcebook Series. Paperback: £32.95. ISBN 1-85941-553-9. Cavendish Publishing Ltd.

Whisenhunt, William Benton – In Search of Legality-Mikhail M. Speranskii and the Codification of Russian Law. Hardback: £19.00. ISBN 0-88033-468-1. Columbia University Press.

Whitehead, Laurence – International Dimensions of Democratization-Europe and the Americas. 2nd Ed. Oxford Studies in Democratization. Paperback: £16.99. ISBN 0-19-924375-1. Oxford University Press.

Wormald, Patrick – Making of English Law: King Alfred to the 12th Century: Vol 1. Paperback: £29.99. ISBN 0-631-22740-7. Blackwell Publishers.

Zimmermann, Reinhard – Roman Law, Contemporary Law, European Law. Clarendon Law Lectures. Hardback: £25.00. ISBN 0-19-829913-3. Oxford University Press.

LEISURE INDUSTRY

4275. **Holidays – accommodation – holiday property bond companies – property exchanges – failure to provide suitable alternative apartment – award for distress and inconvenience**

T claimed accommodation costs and also sought to recover damages for disappointment, distress and inconvenience. T had paid a fee to RCI to exchange the use of an apartment which she owned in Portugal for an apartment in the US for the duration of a holiday for herself and members of her family. T alleged that the accommodation in the US was totally unacceptable, principally because the apartment could only be reached by climbing 87 open wooded steps. The steps were covered in leaves and, as such, were totally inappropriate for the party, which included a two year old child and T herself, aged 69. T immediately made it clear to RCI that the apartment was unsatisfactory and unsuitable and she was informed that no alternative accommodation was available. T initially found a motel for three nights and, thereafter, a house where the party stayed for the remainder of their holiday. RCI submitted, inter alia, that it merely offered an accommodation exchange service and that the case was not analogous to a package holiday claim.

Held, giving judgment for the claimant, that the case was analogous to a package holiday claim. T was awarded £1,030 for the cost of the alternative accommodation and £1,000 by way of general damages for upset, distress and inconvenience, *Jarvis v. Swans Tours Ltd* [1973] Q.B. 233, [1973] C.L.Y. 723 and *Jackson v. Horizon Holidays Ltd* [1975] 1 W.L.R. 1468, [1975] C.L.Y. 393 applied.

THOMSON v. RCI EUROPE, February 14, 2001, Deputy District Judge Hugman, CC (Manchester). [*Ex rel.* Nicholls & Co, Solicitors, 671 Manchester Road, Denton, Manchester].

4276. **Holidays – package holidays – breach of contract – delay – technical transport difficulties – foreseeability – award for disappointment**

[PackageTravel, Package Holidays and PackageTours Regulations 1992 (SI 1992 3288) Reg.15(2)(c).]

C sought to recover damages for breach of contract and loss of enjoyment. C and his wife booked a 14 day "gold" package holiday in Majorca with T for a total cost of £1,320. The outward flight was delayed by more than 23 hours due to severe problems with air traffic control and technical problems with the aircraft, as a result of which the crew ran out of flight hours. C was not informed until 11.45 pm, some 10 and a half hours after their flight had been due to depart, that there would be no available flight that night. C was offered a hotel for the night which involved a wait for a taxi, a one hour drive and a return to the airport by 7.30 am the next morning. C refused the hotel and was offered blankets which never materialised; accordingly C and his wife spent the night in freezing and uncomfortable conditions and the first two days of the holiday were ruined. T denied liability and argued that (1) liability for loss caused by technical problems with aircraft was expressly excluded under the contract by virtue of the section entitled "events beyond our control"; (2) the technical fault could not reasonably have been foreseen or guarded against and hence there was no liability under the Package Travel, Package Holidays and Package Tours Regulations 1992 Reg.15(2)(c), and (3) any loss was not a consequence of a significant failure on its part, T having made satisfactory arrangements for the period of delay.

Held, giving judgment for the claimant, that there was no evidence that the brochure relied upon by T was applicable. It was implied that a "gold" holiday must have been of a quality above the ordinary and therefore T should have given prompt assistance to C. The circumstances of the delay were foreseeable and C did not unreasonably refuse the offer of a hotel. Accordingly, C was awarded a total of £550 for a three day period of frustration, disappointment, tiredness and irritability, the sum of £40 which was paid from a separate insurance policy having been taken into account.

COUGHLAN v. THOMSON HOLIDAYS LTD, March 20, 2001, District Judge White, CC (Romford). [*Ex rel.* Martina Murphy, Barrister, Tanfield Chambers, Francis Taylor Building, Temple, London].

4277. **Holidays – package holidays – breach of contract – foreseeability – exclusion of liability under contract**

[PackageTravel, Package Holidays and PackageTours Regulations 1992 (SI 1992 3288) Reg.15.]

B, a couple, booked two consecutive seven night cruises with A. Each cruise was to depart from Montego Bay, Jamaica. B paid an upgrade fee for a "premiair service", which secured priority luggage collection and better in-flight catering and seats. Difficulties occurred with the outbound flight; there was delay due to a number of factors, namely delay of the incoming flight, prolonged safety checks, a damaged runway and strong headwinds. The flight was diverted for re-fuelling and a new crew had to be obtained for the last part of the journey. During the flight B were given the same meal as standard passengers and they found the crew unhelpful during the onboard delay. At all times B had been reassured that their cruise ship would wait for them. Upon arrival at Montego Bay, B were advised that the cruise ship had left. B were offered a choice of either returning home and receiving a full refund and additional compensation or accepting a week at an all-inclusive four star resort, catching the second cruise and receiving £100 compensation per person. B chose the latter option and sought damages against A under the Package Travel, Package Holidays and Package Tours Regulations 1992 Reg. 15(1) for failure to perform the first part of the holiday contract. In particular, B contended that the cruise ship should have waited for them and that the initial delay and strong headwinds had been foreseeable. A relied upon a clause in its Fair Trading Agreement, which excluded A from liability where delay or change to the holiday arose out of unforeseeable circumstances. A further relied upon Reg.15(2) of the Regulations conceding that, as Reg.15(2)(c)(i) had not been specifically pleaded, A would have to rely upon Reg.15(2)(ii), namely that there was no liability for failure to perform the contract, properly or at all, when that failure was due to, "an event which the other party...even with all due care, could not foresee or forestall."

Held, giving judgment for the defendant, that by virtue of Reg.15(5), A could not exclude liability under the 1992 Regulations by a contractual term, no matter how close that contractual term follows the wording within the Regulations. There had been a failure to perform the contract properly and some of the delay had been foreseeable. However, the combination of all the incidents contributing to the delay could not have been foreseen, even with all due care. The cruise ship could not have waited, as a duty was also owed to other passengers. The departure of the ship was an event that could not be forestalled; consequently A was not in breach of the Regulations. There had been a breach of the "premiair service" on the outbound journey and B were each entitled to recover the fee they had paid for that service.

BENSUSAN v. AIRTOURS HOLIDAYS LTD, January 25, 2001, District Judge Jenkins, CC (Brentford). [*Ex rel.* Sarah Tozzi, Barrister, Farrar's Building, Temple, London].

4278. Holidays – package holidays – breach of contract – tour operator unable to comply with special request – measure of damages

[Package Travel, Package Holidays and Package Tours Regulations 1992 (SI 1992 3288).]

C, a couple, booked a two week holiday in Spain at a cost of £894 each. The hotel was rated as "platinum" in M's brochure and was described as being of a high standard and quality. At the time of booking, C specifically requested a quiet room, although they were aware that M would only endeavour to fulfil the request. In fact, their room was above the kitchen and was adjacent to the restaurant. The noise carried on until 12.30 am and started again at 6.00 am. After the first night, C requested to be moved, but that was not possible because M did not have the use of any other rooms at the hotel. They were offered a room in another hotel over 10 km away, but were told they would have to pay additional costs. C decided to pay to fly home immediately. Relying on the Package Travel, Package Holidays and Package Tours Regulations 1992, C sought to recover the entire cost of the holiday together with damages for loss of enjoyment of the holiday.

Held, giving judgment for the claimants, that the room could not be described as "quiet" however subjective that test was. M had made no endeavour to fulfil the special request and, indeed, it appeared that it was impossible for M to fulfil the request at that hotel. M had not discharged its obligations under the Regulations and C had been entitled to act as they did. They were entitled to a refund of the total cost of the holiday, the cost of the flight home and £225 each for the loss of enjoyment.

CURRIE v. MAGIC TRAVEL GROUP (HOLIDAYS) LTD, January 2, 2001, District Judge Vincent, CC (Worcester). [*Ex rel.* James Morgan, Barrister, St. Philip's Chambers, Fountain Court, Steelhouse Lane, Birmingham].

4279. Holidays – package holidays – implied terms – duty of reasonable care and skill in provision of contractual services – mitigation of loss

[PackageTravel, Package Holidays and PackageTours Regulations 1992 (SI 1992 3288) Reg.6, Reg.14, Reg.15.]

B brought a claim against a tour operator, C, with whom he had booked a two week holiday in Sardinia promised by C in its brochure to be "opulent luxury in a dramatic landscape and a beautiful villa with private garden and swimming pool". On arrival, B and his family found that the villa was infested with rats. B complained to C, who eventually offered smaller alternative accommodation with only a communal pool and no private garden. No compensation was offered. B declined the alternative accommodation and returned home. B contended that C was in breach of (1) an implied contractual term to exercise reasonable care and skill in the provision of holiday services, and (2) the terms of the PackageTravel, Package Holidays and PackageTours Regulations 1992. C argued that the rodent infestation was mice rather than rats and was unavoidable in that area. Further, that B, by declining the alternative accommodation, had failed to mitigate his loss.

Held, finding in favour of B, that (1) Reg.6, Reg.14, and Reg.15 of the 1992 Regulations applied to the holiday contract; (2) C had failed to provide luxury, rat-free accommodation in breach of the implied warranties in the descriptive material in its brochure and had failed to comply with its duties under Reg.14(2) and Reg.14(3); (3) C had failed to exercise reasonable care and skill in the provision of contractual services, and (4) B's refusal of the alternative accommodation had to be judged by reference to the luxury holiday that he had booked. In the circumstances, he had acted reasonably and mitigated his loss, particularly as C's offer had not included an offer of compensation. B was awarded a sum representing the whole of the holiday lost and consequential losses, together with the sum of £2,000 for loss of enjoyment.

BUHUS-ORWIN v. COSTA SMERALDA HOLIDAYS LTD, August 16, 2001, District Judge Trent, MCLC. [*Ex rel.* Matthew Chapman, Barrister, No.1 Serjeant's Inn, Fleet Street, London].

4280. Holidays – package holidays – personal injuries – alleged negligence of tutor – liability of tour operator

[PackageTravel, Package Holidays and PackageTour Regulations 1992 (SI 1992 3288) Reg.2, Reg.15.]

G brought an action in negligence against a tour operator, A, with which she had booked a skiing holiday. The booking made and paid for by G was for the provision of international flights, chalet accommodation, coach transfers to and from the airport and the services of a local representative. On the transfer coach journey between the airport and resort, G purchased a "ski-pack" from A's representative, which included the hire of skis and boots, lift passes and a course of lessons with a ski school, ESF. In the course of a lesson, G was attempting to follow the ESF tutor, a probationer, in executing a tricky, off-piste manoeuvre. She lost control of her trajectory and skied over a 40 foot cliff sustaining serious multiple orthopaedic injuries. G claimed that the tuition was negligent in quality and in choice of skiing location and sued A for breach of the package holiday contract and under the Package Travel, Package Holidays and Package Tours Regulations 1992 Reg.15 alleging that A was responsible for the ski tutor's negligence.

Held, giving judgment for the defendant, that (1) on the facts, and in the absence of any expert evidence from G as to the standard to be expected of ESF in providing tutors and choosing teaching locations, it had not been proved that the tutor or ESF had been negligent in any of the respects alleged; (2) even if negligence had been established, A was not liable for such negligence; (3) A's fair trading charter was plain. Liability was accepted in the contract for "the holiday sold to you". A's brochure made it clear that the "holiday sold" to G comprised only those items confirmed in A's invoice and that ski-packs were not included in the holiday sold to consumers, and (4) the Regulations did not apply to the ski-pack because the ski-pack had been sold separately at extra cost and therefore could not fall within the meaning of a "pre-arranged combination" of holiday components; neither could it be said that it had been sold at an "inclusive price" as part of a regulated package within the meaning of Reg.2.

GALLAGHER v. AIRTOURS HOLIDAYS LTD, October 23, 2000, Judge Appleton, CC (Preston). [*Ex rel.* Alan Saggerson, Barrister, No. 1 Serjeants' Inn, London].

4281. Holidays – package holidays – personal injuries – compliance with foreign standards – liability of tour operator

[Package Travel, Package Holidays and Package Tour Regulations 1992 (SI 1992 3288) Reg.15(2).]

L, who was staying at a hotel in Ibiza whilst on holiday, lost his balance and fell. He put out his right hand to arrest his fall and it went through the glass patio window of his bedroom. L sustained serious injuries when the window shattered into large pieces which lacerated his arm and brachial artery. The glass was found to be 5 mm thick and was annealed, rather than toughened glass. Expert evidence was that there were no regulations in Spain, or more locally in Ibiza, specifying the thickness of glass to be used in patio windows and that there had been no breach of generally accepted standards in Spain despite the fact that the thickness of the glass would not have complied with standards in the United Kingdom. L contended that (1) the Package Travel, Package Holidays and Package Tour Regulations 1992 Reg.15(2) imposed strict liability upon F for personal injuries, subject to the exceptions stated within that provision, and (2) the Directive which led to the implementation of the Regulations was intended to create a common standard throughout the European Community and that standard required the provision of safety glass in hotel balcony and patio doors. F argued that Reg.15 was concerned with the proper performance of the holiday contract and that there could be no failure to perform, or an improper performance, when the supplier had complied with applicable local standards, whether those standards were to be found in local regulations or were the generally expected standards of accommodation locally.

Held, giving judgment for the defendant, that Reg.15 of the 1992 Regulations imposed liability on a tour operator only if the holiday contract was breached by a commission or omission on the part of the tour operator or a supplier. The meaning of Reg.15 was clear and there had been no improper performance of the holiday contract because local standards had been complied with, *Wilson v. Best Travel Ltd* [1993] 1 All E.R. 353, [1993] C.L.Y. 494 followed. Had liability been established, L's contributory fault would have been assessed at 75 per cent as he was considerably affected by alcohol at the time of the accident.

LOGUE v. FLYING COLOURS LTD, March 7, 2001, Judge Zucker Q.C., CC (Central London). [*Ex rel.* Alan Saggerson, Barrister, No. 1 Serjeants Inn, Fleet Street, London].

4282. Holidays – package holidays – personal injuries – organised excursions – level of care and skill expected of tour operator

[Package Travel, Package Holidays and Package Tours Regulations 1992 (SI 1992 3288) Reg.15(2).]

W booked a package holiday in Corfu with a division of FC that specialised in holidays for young adults aged 17 to 29 years. FC's advertising emphasised the hedonistic aspects of the holidays sold, with references to wild and exciting fun. Upon arrival in Corfu, W booked a number of excursions which were arranged by FC and sold to her by FC's local representatives. One of the excursions purchased by W was a trip to a taverna which was advertised as a "Greek Night". Participants were told that the evening would involve the supervised smashing of plaster plates. Guests were warned during both the journey to the taverna and upon arrival, of the need to use the special plaster plates. Free wine was provided during the meal, at the end of which, all china plates were removed from the tables, save for those used for the dessert course. Guests were led to a special area, provided with plaster plates and told where to smash them. W, who accepted that she was slightly intoxicated when the plate smashing commenced, was injured when a fellow guest smashed a china dessert plate and a shard of it entered her foot, severing the achilles tendon. W submitted that FC's representatives had incited wild and drunken behaviour, had negligently failed to ensure that all china plates had been removed before the plate smashing commenced and that FC was liable to her for her injuries and losses by virtue of the Package Travel, Package Holidays and Package Tours Regulations 1992 Reg. 15(2).

Held, giving judgment for the defendant, that the question of reasonable care and skill had to be approached by reference to the type of holiday purchased by W, which was a wild, exciting youth-orientated holiday. The fact that warnings had been given by FC's representatives, that soft drinks were freely available and that special plates were to be used in a designated area meant that FC had exercised reasonable care and skill in the organisation of the Greek Night. The removal of all china or the use of paper plates would have placed too onerous a burden on FC and its suppliers. While the person who threw the china plate might be personally liable to W, it was unfair to transfer that burden to FC, *Brannan v. Airtours Plc* Times, February 1, 1999, [1999] C.L.Y. 3945 distinguished. The injury sustained by W had been unforeseeable; an accident of that type had not previously occurred.

WILLIAMS v. FIRST CHOICE HOLIDAYS AND FLIGHTS LTD, April 2, 2001, Judge Hughes, CC (Warrington). [*Ex rel.* Matthew Chapman, Barrister, No.1 Serjeants' Inn, London].

4283. **Holidays – package holidays – poor weather conditions – duty to warn – foreseeability**

[Package Travel, Package Holidays and Package Tours Regulations 1992 (SI 1992 3288) Reg.12, Reg.15(2).]

H booked a 14-day package holiday in the Dominican Republic through A, a tour operator. Two days after their arrival at the resort, it was struck by a severe hurricane with the consequence that the resort was wrecked and H had to be moved to another resort in the north of the island. H brought an action for damages contending that A (1) had withheld hurricane forecast information on the predicted path of the hurricane and had thus put its commercial interest above the lives and safety of customers; (2) had failed in its duty of care to warn H of the risk of the hurricane striking the island, and (3) was in breach of contract with particular reference to the Package Travel, Package Holidays and Package Tours Regulations 1992 Reg.15(2) because it had failed to perform the contract to provide the holiday advertised in its brochure. A contended that at the time H flew to the Dominican Republic there was only at most a 20 per cent chance that the hurricane would come within 75 nautical miles of the eastern tip of the island. Accordingly, A was unable to justify cancellation of the holiday, as provided for in Reg.12 because it was not clearly forced or constrained to alter a significant term of or cancel the holiday contract. A could avail itself of the defence in Reg.15(2)(ii)(c) that the hurricane was an event that, even with all due care, it could neither foresee nor forestall.

Held, giving judgment for A, that A did not know or could not reasonably have known that before or at the time of H's departure from the UK, the hurricane was likely to strike the Dominican Republic. It was possible for hurricanes to change course and in any event the best prediction was that it would miss the island. It could not be said that A had been forced pursuant to Reg.12 to cancel holidays or the flight. The damage sustained by H could not have been forestalled even with the exercise of all due care even though hurricanes in the Caribbean were foreseeable. There had not been a duty to warn about poor weather conditions, and the courts should be slow to find a tour operator in breach of contract as a result of poor or extreme weather conditions.

HAYES v. AIRTOURS HOLIDAYS LTD, September 26, 2000, District Judge Birchall, CC (Norwich). [*Ex rel.* David Thomson, Barrister, No.1 Sergeants Inn, London, EC4Y 1LH].

4284. Holidays – package holidays – travel agents – contractual liability – strict liability – use of parliamentary material

[PackageTravel, Package Holidays and PackageTours Regulations 1992 (SI 1992 3288) Reg.15; Council Directive 90/314 on package travel, package holidays and package tours.]

H appealed against the dismissal of his claim against a travel agent, G, brought under the Package Travel, Package Holidays and Package Tour Regulations 1992 Reg.15 for damages for personal injuries sustained whilst descending from an aircraft via the emergency chute following a crash landing on the return flight from a package holiday. The judge concluded that H had failed to show that there had been improper performance of the contract agreed for the package tour in that he had failed to establish that his injuries were attributable to the fault of a party supplying services in relation to the tour. H submitted that (1) the liability imposed under Reg.15 was strict or absolute, subject to defences which G could not show were available, and (2) the judge had erred in refusing to have regard to evidence of ministerial statements contained in Hansard which related to the intended nature of the liability imposed under Reg.15.

Held, dismissing the appeal, that (1) liability under Reg.15 was not strict. Reg. 15(2) imposed a liability upon G for any damage caused to H by improper performance of a contractual obligation and it was necessary to refer to the terms of the contract in order to determine what constituted improper performance. There was no express obligation to execute safe air carriage and in the absence of such a term, the implication was that the air carriage would be performed with reasonable skill and care, and (2) in those cases where resort to Hansard was permissible, it was important to have regard to the context of such statements. In the instant case, no assistance was to be gained from the ministerial statement recorded to the effect that liability imposed under Reg.15 was strict since, having regard to the full text of the speech, the relevant minister had not been purporting to construe the terms of Council Directive 90/314 requiring the Regulations to be enacted, *Pepper (Inspector of Taxes) v. Hart* [1993] A.C. 593, [1993] C.L.Y. 459 distinguished.

HONE v. GOING PLACES LEISURE TRAVEL LTD, [2001] EWCA Civ 947, *The Times*, August 6, 2001, Longmore, L.J., CA.

4285. Occupiers liability – sports – bowling alleys – sufficiency of warnings

[Occupiers Liability Act 1957 s.2(4).]

T had suffered injury when she slipped, fell and slid along the bowling lane at O's Superbowl premises. T, who had only been bowling once before and who was visiting O's premises for the first time, issued proceedings against O, contending that the premises were unsafe because there were no sufficiently obvious warnings of the dangerous nature of the slippery oiled lanes. O maintained that the written signs instructing bowlers not to cross the "foul line", together with audible announcements requesting bowlers not to cross those lines "in the interests of safety" were sufficient to discharge its duty under the Occupiers Liability Act 1957 s.2(4).

Held, giving judgment for the claimant, that as far as the written notices were concerned, the wording used was inadequate to convey the potential hazards of the game. The signs could easily be interpreted as indicating a rule of the game, since there was no mention of inherent danger such as the possibility of slipping. The audible announcements alone were insufficient to constitute a warning, especially as, on the evidence, there was uncertainty as to their regularity and their efficiency was entirely dependent on visitors listening to and concentrating upon them.

THOMAS v. OSPREY LEISURE LTD, December 8, 2000, District Judge James, CC (Whitehaven). [*Ex rel.* John Baldwin, Barrister, Oriel Chambers, 14 Water Street, Liverpool].

4286. Package holidays – tour operators and travel agents – non discriminatory pricing

FOREIGN PACKAGE HOLIDAYS (TOUR OPERATORS AND TRAVEL AGENTS) ORDER 2001, SI 2001 2581; made under the FairTrading Act 1973 s.56, s.90, Sch.8 para.1, Sch.8 para.4, Sch.8 para.6. In force: August 20, 2001; £1.75.

This Order, which revokes the Foreign Package Holidays (Tour Operators and Travel Agents) Order 1998 (SI 1998 1945), prohibits travel agents from discriminating in the price charged for a foreign package holiday, or by imposing an additional charge, against a person who does not buy travel insurance in respect of that holiday from the agent or tour operator. It prohibits tour operators from entering into or carrying out an agreement which requires the travel agent to comply with a most favoured customer requirement except where the tour operator is required to compensate the travel agent for the value of the inducements required to be offered by the travel agent as a result of such a requirement and also prohibits tour operators from withholding supplies or threatening to withhold supplies of foreign package holidays from, or discriminating in respect of the supply of foreign package holidays to, a travel agent as a result of the failure of the travel agent to enter into or comply with an agreement which is or would be unlawful.

4287. Sporting organisations – boxing – negligence – duty of care of British Boxing Board of Control

See NEGLIGENCE: Watson v. British Boxing Board of Control Ltd. §4468

4288. Sports – football – football grounds – seating

FOOTBALL SPECTATORS (SEATING) ORDER 2001, SI 2001 2373; made under the Football Spectators Act 1989 s.11. In force: July 23, 2001; £1.50.

This Order directs the Football Licensing Authority to include in any licence to admit spectators to Southampton Football Club and Stockport County Football Club a condition imposing specified requirements for the seating of spectators at designated football matches at those premises.

4289. Sports – sports grounds – safety certificates

SAFETY OF SPORTS GROUNDS (DESIGNATION) ORDER 2001, SI 2001 2372; made under the Safety of Sports Grounds Act 1989 s.1, s.18. In force: July 23, 2001; £1.50.

This Order amends the Safety of Sports Grounds (Designation) Order 1986 (SI 1986 1296) by omitting Borough Sports Ground, Sutton, which is no longer a sports ground requiring a safety certificate under the Safety of Sports Grounds Act 1975 and designating other sports grounds as sports grounds requiring a safety certificate.

4290. Tour operators – joinder – separate claims in contract and tort – claims arising out of same facts

[PackageTravel, Package Holidays and PackageTours Regulations 1992 (SI 1992 3288); Council Directive 90/314 on package travel, package holidays and package tours; Brussels Convention on Jurisdiction and Enforcement of Judgments in Civil and Commercial Matters 1968 Art.6(1).]

W appealed against a decision that A could not be joined as a defendant to proceedings brought against F. W had purchased a package holiday in Spain from F, a tour operator. Whilst on holiday W had visited an accommodation block owned and managed by A and had been chased away by a security guard. During the chase W had jumped over a wall and sustained serious injuries as a result. W had subsequently sued F for breach of contract and A in tort and A had challenged the jurisdiction of the English courts. The court below had held that A could not be joined as a defendant to the proceedings against F under the Brussels

Convention 1968 Art.6(1) because the legal basis of the claims differed, one being contractual, the other tortious.

Held, referring the matter to the ECJ, that joinder was precluded where the legal basis of the two claims were contractual and tortious respectively *Reunion Europeenne SA v. Spliethoffs Bevrachtingskantoor BV (C51/97)* [2000] Q.B. 690, [1998] C.L.Y. 769 followed. However, there was a substantial connection between the two claims since the facts to be investigated were the same, the alleged liability of F arose from the fault of A and, as a result of the Package Travel, Package Holidays and Package Tours Regulations 1992 implementing Council Directive 90/314, the contractual liability of a tour operator was bound to extend to cover the consequences of events giving rise to tortious liability on the part of another. Consequently the ECJ should consider the implications of *Reunion Europeenne* since too rigid an application of the principle established by that case could give rise to a situation where there was no single jurisdiction in which a claimant could bring proceedings against two defendants domiciled in different jurisdictions notwithstanding a clear connection between the two claims, which could produce inconsistent results. Accordingly, the question of whether Art.6(1) prevented joinder of contract and tort claims where there was a clear connection between the claims and of whether an allegedly negligent supplier could be joined in proceedings against a tour operator for breach of contract was referred to the ECJ.

WATSON v. FIRST CHOICE HOLIDAYS & FLIGHTS LTD; APARTA HOTELS CALEDONIA SA v. WATSON, [2001] EWCA Civ 972, [2001] 2 Lloyd's Rep. 339, Lloyd, J., CA.

4291. Tour operators – standard of care – personal injuries – defective furniture

[Package Travel, Package Holidays and Package Tours Regulations 1992 (SI 1992 3288) Reg.15.]

M had booked a two week holiday to Gran Canaria through TH. His accommodation was in an apartment complex. Seven days into the holiday, M suffered an accident when one of the legs on a plastic poolside sunbed upon which he was lying face down, bent, causing him to "jolt". M did not fall from the bed, nor did he experience immediate pain. He got off the sunbed, straightened the leg by hand and continued to use the bed for a further hour. When he subsequently attempted to get off, he was unable to move. M contended that the incident had caused him to suffer a slipped disc. TH admitted the accident, but denied causation. Proceedings were issued, in which M pleaded breach of contract and breach of the Package Travel, Package Holidays and Package Tours Regulations 1992 Reg.15. TH maintained that (1) as a matter of contract, the imposition of liability for personal injury depended upon proof of fault, and (2) the standard of care applicable by contract was not an absolute guarantee of safety, but a duty to ensure that the consumer was reasonably safe, and, by extension, to keep furniture in a reasonable condition.

Held, dismissing the claim, that (1) strict liability was not applicable. TH had a duty to exercise reasonable care and skill; (2) as there had been no visible defect in the sunbed, it was difficult to accept that any non-scientific inspection prior to the accident could have detected the fault. Therefore, it could not be said that the sunbed had been unsafe at that time or that enforcement of a reasonable system of inspection would have avoided the accident, and (3) M had not established that the incident was causative of his injuries.

McRAE v. THOMSON HOLIDAYS LTD, October 26, 2000, Judge Hill Q.C., CC (Epsom). [*Ex rel.* Matthew Chapman, Barrister, No 1 Serjeants' Inn, Fleet Street, London].

4292. Books

A-Z Essentials: Licensed Premises Management. Paperback: £27.50. ISBN 1-85524-611-2. Croner Publications.

Greenfield, Steve; Osborn Guy – Law and Sport in Contemporary Society. Sport in the Global Society, No. 22. Hardback: £45.00. ISBN 0-7146-5048-X. Paperback: £18.50. ISBN 0-7146-8124-5. Frank Cass Publishers.

Weiler, Paul – Leveling the Playing Field. Paperback: £12.50. ISBN 0-674-00687-9. Harvard University Press.

LIBRARIES

4293. Books

Thomas, P.A.; Knowles, John – Dane & Thomas: How to Use a Law Library. 4th Ed. Paperback: £14.95. ISBN 0-421-74410-3. Sweet & Maxwell.

LICENSING

4294. Alcohol – licensed premises – permitted hours – New Year's Eve 2001

REGULATORY REFORM (SPECIAL OCCASIONS LICENSING) ORDER 2001, SI 2001 3937; made under the Regulatory Reform Act 2001 s.1. In force: December 7, 2001; £2.00.

This Order reforms the law relating to licensing hours which has the effect of imposing burdens on people carrying out certain activities with a view to reducing those burdens in respect of New Year's Eve 2001. It does so by amending the Licensing Act 1964 to relax the licensing hours on New Year's Eve 2001. The Order allows the sale of intoxicating liquor in licensed premises other than off-licences, in registered clubs and in licensed canteens in the period between what would otherwise be the end of the permitted hours on New Year's Eve 2001 and the beginning of the permitted hours on New Year's Day 2002.

4295. Alcohol – transfer of functions – justices' clerks to justices chief executives – Isles of Scilly

ISLES OF SCILLY (SALE OF INTOXICATING LIQUOR) (AMENDMENT) ORDER 2001, SI 2001 1099; made under the Licensing Act 1964 s.198, s.202. In force: April 1, 2001; £1.50.

This Order amends the Isles of Scilly (Sale of Intoxicating Liquor) Order 1973 (SI 1973 1958) to transfer the administrative functions of justices' clerks to justices' chief executives in accordance with the Access to Justice Act 1999 s.90, s.91 and Sch.13.

4296. Excise duty – repayment of duty

EXCISE DUTY (PAYMENTS IN CASE OF ERROR OR DELAY) REGULATIONS 2001, SI 2001 3299; made under the Finance Act 2001 Sch.3 para.3, para.12, para.22. In force: November 1, 2001; £1.50.

These Regulations describe the provisions that need to be met by any person making a claim for repayment of duty or interest under the Finance Act 2001 Sch.3. They also describe what must be included in any claim made for the repayment of duty where the Commissioners have incorrectly refused authorisation or approval to obtain goods relieved of excise duty and what must be included in any claim made for the payment of interest on excise duty which has been overpaid or underclaimed as a result of the Commissioners' error.

4297. Gambling – amusement machines – medium-prize machines – maximum pay out

AMUSEMENT MACHINE LICENCE DUTY (MEDIUM-PRIZE MACHINES) ORDER 2001, SI 2001 4028; made under the Betting, Gaming and Duties Act 1981 s.22. In force: January 14, 2002; £1.50.

This Order, which amends the Betting and Gaming Duties Act 1981, increases, from £15 to £25, the maximum amount that an amusement machine may pay out for a single game before it ceases to be a medium-prize machine for the purposes of the amusement machine licence duty.

4298. Gambling – bingo – fees

GAMING (BINGO) ACT (FEES) (AMENDMENT) ORDER 2001, SI 2001 727; made under the Gaming (Bingo) Act 1985 Sch.para.5. In force: April 1, 2001; £1.50.

This Order amends the Gaming (Bingo) Act (Fees) (Order) 1986 (SI 1986 833) so as to reduce the fee payable to the Gaming Board for Great Britain for the issue of a certificate issued by the Board to an organiser of games of multiple bingo from £165,020 to £150,168. It also reduces the fee payable to the Gaming Board for Great Britain for the continuing in force, for a period of three years, of such a certificate from £158,875 to £144,576 and revokes the Gaming (Bingo) Act (Fees) (Amendment) Order 2000 (SI 2000 1211).

4299. Gambling – bingo – variation of monetary limits

GAMING ACT (VARIATION OF MONETARY LIMITS) (NO.2) ORDER 2001, SI 2001 4035; made under the Gaming Act 1968 s.21, s.51. In force: January 14, 2002; £1.50.

This Order increases the maximum cash prize that may be offered in a prize bingo game played in a bingo club from £15 to £25.

4300. Gambling – bookmakers – general betting duty

GENERAL BETTING DUTY REGULATIONS 2001, SI 2001 3088; made under the Betting and Gaming Duties Act 1981 s.5D, s.12, Sch.1 para.2. In force: October 6, 2001; £2.00.

These Regulations, which revoke the General Betting Duty Regulations 1987 (SI 1987 1963) and the General Betting Duty (Amendment) Regulations 2000 (SI 2000 1726), provide the machinery for administering the general betting duty charged by the Betting and Gaming Duties Act 1981 and also amend the Betting and Gaming Duties (Payment) Regulations 1995 (SI 1995 1555).

4301. Gambling – gaming machines – cash-only – variation of monetary limits

GAMING ACT (VARIATION OF MONETARY LIMITS) ORDER 2001, SI 2001 3971; made under the Gaming Act 1968 s.34, s.51. In force: January 1, 2002; £1.50.

This Order increases the maximum amount that may be offered as a prize in a game played on a cash-only gaming machine from £15 to £25.

4302. Gambling – gaming machines – maximum prizes – increase

GAMING MACHINES (MAXIMUM PRIZES) REGULATIONS 2001, SI 2001 3970; made under the Gaming Act 1968 s.31, s.51. In force: January 1, 2002; £1.50.

These Regulations increase the maximum amount which may be paid in respect of any one game by a gaming machine on premises licensed under the Gaming Act 1968, other than a bingo club, from £1,000 to £2,000.

4303. Gambling – licences and certificates – fees

GAMING ACT (VARIATION OF FEES) (ENGLAND AND WALES AND SCOTLAND) ORDER 2001, SI 2001 726; made under the Gaming Act 1968 s.48, s.51. In force: April 1, 2001; £1.75.

This Order, which amends the Gaming Act (Variation of Fees) Order 2000 (SI 2000 1212), amends the fees to be charged in England and Wales and Scotland under the Gaming Act 1968 for the registration of a club or institute, the renewal of registration, the issuing of a certificate of approval, the issuing of a machine certificate, the renewal of a certificate, the application for a certificate consenting to the making of an application for the grant of a licence and the application for a certificate consenting to the making of an application for the transfer of a licence.

4304. Gambling – prizes – variation of monetary limits

AMUSEMENTS WITH PRIZES (VARIATION OF MONETARY LIMITS) ORDER 2001, SI 2001 4034; made under the Lotteries and Amusements Act 1976 s.18, s.24. In force: January 14, 2002; £1.50.

This Order, which amends the Amusements with Prizes (Variation of Monetary Limits) Order 1999 (SI 1999 1259), increases the monetary limits specified in the Lotteries and Amusements Act 1976 s.16 and revokes previous provisions which are superseded. It increases the maximum aggregate amount that may be taken by way of the sale of chances in any one determination of winners in a prize bingo game played at certain commercial entertainments from £60 to £90, and increases the maximum money prize that may be distributed or offered at those entertainments from £15 to £25.

4305. Gambling – prizes – variation of monetary limits

GAMING ACT (VARIATION OF MONETARY LIMITS) ORDER 2001, SI 2001 757; made under the Gaming Act 1968 s.20, s.51. In force: May 1, 2001; £1.50.

The maximum permitted aggregate amount of winnings in respect of games of bingo played in one week simultaneously on different club premises is specified in the Gaming Act 1968 s.20 as £50,000. This Order, which amends the Gaming Act (Variation of Monetary Limits) Order 1999 (SI 1999 1260) and the Gaming Act (Variation of Monetary Limits) Order 2000 (SI 2000 1213) increases the maximum permitted aggregate amount of winnings in respect of games of bingo played in one week simultaneously on different club premises to £55,000.

4306. Gambling – renewal of licences – fees

GAMING ACT (VARIATION OF FEES) (ENGLAND AND WALES) ORDER 2001, SI 2001 725; made under the Gaming Act 1968 s.48, s.51. In force: April 1, 2001; £1.75.

This Order, which amends the Gaming Act (Variation of Fees) Order 2000 (SI 2000 1212), amends the fees to be charged in England and Wales under the Gaming Act 1968 in relation to the granting of, renewing of and transference of gaming licences.

4307. Lotteries – Gaming Board fees

LOTTERIES (GAMING BOARD FEES) ORDER 2001, SI 2001 728; made under the Lotteries and Amusements Act 1976 s.18, s.24, Sch.1A para.6, Sch.2 para.7. In force: April 1, 2001; £1.75.

This Order, which revokes the Lotteries (Gaming Board Fees) Order 2000 (SI 2000 1210), makes provision as to the fees payable to the Gaming Board for Great Britain by societies under the Lotteries and Amusements Act 1976 and by local authorities. A society or local authority wishing to promote a lottery is required to pay a fee of £3,840 to register itself or a scheme with the Board. A fee of £142 is payable every 3 years in respect of continued registration with the Board. The fee payable by members of the public inspecting returns made in respect of societies and local authorities remains at £5.00 and the fee payable under the Act on an application for certification as a lottery manager is £5,470.

4308. Magistrates courts – transfer of functions – justices' clerks to justices' chief executives

LICENSING (AMENDMENT OF VARIOUS RULES) RULES 2001, SI 2001 1096; made under the Licensing Act 1964 s.61, s.91, s.198. In force: April 1, 2001; £1.50.

These Rules amend the Licensing Rules 1961 (SI 1961 2477), the Licensing (Extended Hours Orders) Rules 1962 (SI 1962 75) and the Licensing (Special Hours Certificates) Rules 1982 (SI 1982 1384) to transfer the administrative functions of justices' clerks to justices' chief executives. They provide that the administrative functions of justices' clerks are all of their functions apart from those which are legal functions within the meaning given by the Justices of the Peace Act 1997 s.48.

4309. Magistrates courts – transfer of functions – justices' clerks to justices' chief executives

ORDER PRESCRIBING FORMS UNDER THE LICENSING ACT 1902 (AMENDMENT) ORDER 2001, SI 2001 1098; made under the Licensing Act 1964 s.31, s.198. In force: April 1, 2001; £1.50.

This Order amends the Order of the Secretary of State dated October 28, 1902, (SR & O 1902 831) prescribing forms under the Licensing Act 1902 to transfer the functions of the justices' clerks under the Order to justices' chief executives and is consequential on an amendment to the Licensing Act 1964 s.31 by the Access to Justice Act 1999 Sch.13.

4310. National Lottery – distributing bodies – New Opportunities Fund

NEW OPPORTUNITIES FUND (SPECIFICATION OF INITIATIVES) ORDER 2001, SI 2001 1404; made under the National Lottery etc. Act 1993 s.43B. In force: April 6, 2001; £1.75.

The New Opportunities Fund is a distributor of funds derived from the National Lottery. It may make grants to fund or assist in the funding of projects, or make or enter into arrangements, which are designed to give effect to initiatives specified by the Secretary of State that are concerned or connected with health, education or the environment. This Order, which amends the New Opportunities Fund (Specification of Initiatives) Order 1999 (SI 1999 966), specifies a number of such initiatives applying throughout the UK.

4311. National Lottery – licence fees – prescibed sum

NATIONAL LOTTERY (LICENCE FEES) ORDER 2001, SI 2001 2506; made under the National Lottery etc. Act 1993 s.7, s.60. In force: August 9, 2001; £1.50.

This Order, which revokes the National Lottery (Licence Fees) Order 1994 (SI 1994 1200), prescribes the sums payable by the licensee to the National Lottery Commission by way of fees on the granting of licences under the National Lottery etc. Act 1993 s.5 and s.6.

4312. Private hire vehicles – appeals – conditions – locus standi of prospective licence holder

[Local Government (Miscellaneous Provisions) Act 1976 s.52 (2).]

P appealed against the dismissal of his appeal against the attaching of conditions to a licence to drive private hire vehicles. P, who held a Hackney carriage licence which had been successfully renewed, had made enquiries regarding the terms and conditions upon which a private hire licence could be issued and had been told that a police check was required every three years, and that in the event of a delay in the police checks, the whole application procedure would have to be recommenced. The renewal of P's Hackney carriage licence had previously been delayed by police checks and he sought to bring a complaint as a prospective private licence holder against the council under the Local Government (Miscellaneous Provisions) Act 1976 s.52(2).

Held, dismissing the appeal, that the council only had the power to impose conditions on the licence following an actual application for one. Since P had not made a licence application and had not therefore been refused one, nor had conditions been attached to the licence already granted to him, he was not a person aggrieved within the meaning of s.52 of the Act.

PEDDUBRIWNY v. CAMBRIDGE CITY COUNCIL, [2001] EWHC Admin 200, [2001] R.T.R. 31, Silber, J., QBD (Admin Ct).

4313. **Public entertainments – licences – registration scheme for club doormen – local authorities powers and duties**

[Local Government (Miscellaneous Provisions) Act 1982 Sch.1.]

B appealed against the refusal of his application for permission to seek judicial review of a decision of the local authority to impose a compulsory precondition for the grant of a public entertainment licence, namely that all door staff should be registered with the authority. A fee was charged for the registration. B contended that such a scheme was not authorised by the Local Government (Miscellaneous Provisions) Act 1982, since the Act was concerned with the regulation of those who were responsible for management rather than those individuals actually employed to work in the public entertainment sector.

Held, allowing the appeal in part, (the Master of the Rolls and Lord Justice Dyson dissenting as to the statutory basis for the power), that the local authority had acted within its statutory powers under Sch.1 of the 1982 Act. The underlying purpose of the statute was the improvement of public health and safety at entertainment venues and the reduction in disruption to neighbours. Such a purpose was served by the scheme as formulated. However, the local authority was not entitled to charge a fee to applicants. A fee could only be charged where there was express or implied statutory authority to do so.

R. (ON THE APPLICATION OF BARRY) v. LIVERPOOL CITY COUNCIL; *sub nom.* R. v. LIVERPOOL CITY COUNCIL, *ex p.* BARRY, [2001] EWCA Civ 384, (2001) 3 L.G.L.R. 40, Kennedy, L.J., CA.

4314. **Restaurants – opening hours – operating premises contrary to condition in licence**

Held, allowing the appeal and quashing the decision, that the magistrates had erred in dismissing an information alleging that a night cafe owner was operating his premises contrary to a condition in his licence which specified that the premises had to close by midnight; it was clear that customers had been permitted to enter the premises and place food orders after midnight.

CAMDEN LBC v. SONKOR, [2001] EWHC Admin 41, [2001] E.H.L.R. 21, Morison, J., QBD (Admin Ct).

4315. **Sex establishments – licences – licence of premises for exhibition comprising individual stalls – need for individual licences**

[Local Government (Miscellaneous Provisions) Act 1982 Sch.3 para.4, Sch.3 para.6(1), Sch.3 para.20(1) (c).]

CI challenged a decision of the local authority, N, to grant a licence to X to use premises as a sex establishment for the purpose of holding a three-day exhibition of sexual paraphernalia. The licence was granted subject to a number of conditions. CI contended that (1) pursuant to the Local Government (Miscellaneous Provisions) Act 1982 Sch.3 para.4 and para.6(1), the use of the premises as a "sex establishment" was by the individual stall holders rather than X as licensee of the premises and accordingly the individual stall holders required licences, and (2) it was an inappropriate delegation of responsibility for N to leave it to X to decide who should be allowed to run stalls in the exhibition and it could not have been the intention of the 1982 Act that a licence should be given to an organiser who had no direct control over the activities of the individual stall holders.

Held, dismissing the application, that (1) in the ordinary meaning of the terms, X was proposing to use the premises as a "sex establishment". The individual stall holders did not require any separate licence, as they were covered by the licence granted to X, and (2) it was clear from Sch.3 that N had a wide discretion on each licensing application and the fact that it had imposed conditions demonstrated that it had had regard to the need to ensure that proper control was kept. Furthermore, para.20(1)(c) of the Schedule rendered the licensee guilty of an offence where there was any breach of a licence condition by a stall holder with the knowledge of the licensee. It followed that the granting of the licence had been lawful.

R. v. NEWCASTLE UPON TYNE CITY COUNCIL, *ex p.* CHRISTIAN INSTITUTE [2001] B.L.G.R. 165, Collins, J., QBD.

4316. Sporting rights – licences – powers of local authority to refuse renewal of shooting licence

[Local Government Act 1972 s.120(1)(b); Conservation (Natural Habitats etc.) Regulations 1994 (SI 1994 2716).]

BASC challenged the legality of a decision by the local authority, SMBC, to cancel a wildfowling licence previously in force on Council land, contending that (1) the Council committee had been misdirected that the source of its powers was the Local Government Act 1972 s.120(1)(b) since s.120(1)(b) related to the power to acquire land and was not concerned with land management; (2) the committee had also been misinformed as to the relevance of the Conservation (Natural Habitats etc.) Regulations 1994 Reg.48, and (3) the decision to revoke the licence had been irrational.

Held, dismissing the application, that (1) although s.120(1)(b) did not explicitly refer to the authority of a Council to manage its land, it was nevertheless logical, in the absence of a more specific provision, to assume that the Council had authority to manage the land for the purposes for which it was acquired, following the reasoning of the Court of Appeal in *R. v. Somerset CC, ex p. Fewings* [1995] 1 W.L.R. 1037, [1995] C.L.Y. 3253; (2) Reg.48 had no relevance to the issue of cancellation of a shooting licence and therefore if SMBC had considered it in reaching its decision it would have been in error. However, in the minutes, there was no evidence to support the conclusion that Reg.48 had been discussed, therefore the challenge could not be sustained on that basis, and (3) there had been a rational basis for the decision to refuse a renewal, namely SMBC's desire to promote green tourism in the area.

R. v. SEFTON MBC, *ex p.* BRITISH ASSOCIATION OF SHOOTING & CONSERVATION LTD [2001] Env. L.R. 10, Moses, J., QBD.

4317. Street trading – exemptions – ice cream vans – meaning of "roundsman"

[Local Government (Miscellaneous Provisions) Act 1982 Sch.4 para.1 (2), Sch.4 para.10(1), Sch.4 para.10(4).]

K appealed against his conviction for two offences of street trading without a licence in a consent street contrary to the Local Government (Miscellaneous Provisions) Act 1982 Sch.4 para.10(1) and (4), submitting that the district judge had misinterpreted the Act's provisions. K contended that the selling of ice creams and snacks from his fleet of mobile vans fell within the definition of "roundsman", being one of the exemptions under Sch.4 para.1 (2) of the Act, since the van operators followed a regular route, making regular stops and serving regular customers.

Held, dismissing the appeal, that the district judge had been correct in her view that a "roundsman" was a person who followed the round of his customers to take orders and deliver the pre ordered goods of his customers. Therefore

K's activities were not exempt under Sch.4 para.1 (2) (f), and as he was a street trader a licence to trade was required.

KEMPIN (T/A BRITISH BULLDOG ICE CREAM) v. BRIGHTON AND HOVE COUNCIL, [2001] EWHC Admin 140, [2001] E.H.L.R. 19, Potts, J., QBD.

4318. Sunday trading – deregulation

DEREGULATION (SUNDAY LICENSING) ORDER 2001, SI 2001 920; made under the Deregulation and Contracting Out Act 1994 s.1. In force: March 19, 2001; £2.00.

This Order reduces burdens on business by amending the provisions of the Licensing Act 1964 relating to extended hours in restaurants to apply them to Sundays, and those relating to special hours certificates to permit such certificates to apply on Sundays where the licensing authority consider it appropriate to do so.

4319. Books

McGrath, Michael – Liquor Licensing Law. Butterworth Irish Annotated Statutes. £85.00. ISBN 1-85475-365-7. Butterworths Law.

Monkcom, Stephen – Law of Betting, Gaming and Lotteries. 2nd Ed. Hardback: £160.00. ISBN 0-406-90313-1. Butterworths Law.

Patersons Licensing Acts 2002. Hardback: £190.00. ISBN 0-406-94566-7. Butterworths Law.

LOCAL GOVERNMENT

4320. Accounts – statement of accounts – Wales

ACCOUNTS AND AUDIT (AMENDMENT) (WALES) REGULATIONS 2001, SI 2001 3760 (W.309); made under the Audit Commission Act 1998 s.27. In force: January 18, 2002; £1.75.

These Regulations amend the Accounts and Audit Regulations 1996 (SI 1996 590) to omit the reference to a "probation committee". The Regulations also increase the financial threshold above which community councils in Wales are required to prepare income and expenditure accounts from £5,000 to £50,000 and insert a new requirement for relevant bodies to publish the annual audit letter they receive from their auditor.

4321. Administration – standards investigations – local commissioner – Wales

LOCAL COMMISSIONER IN WALES (STANDARDS INVESTIGATIONS) ORDER 2001, SI 2001 2286 (W.174); made under the Local Government Act 2000 s.70. In force: July 28, 2001; £2.00.

The National Assembly for Wales may make provision with respect to standards investigations by a Local Commissioner in Wales under the Local Government 2000 s.70. These investigations concern the conduct of members or co-opted members of a relevant authority in Wales where an allegation has been made or there may be a case of a failure to deal with an authority's code of conduct. This Order makes provision for the application s.60, which relates to the conduct of investigations, s.61, which relates to the procedure in respect of investigations, s.62, which provides further provisions in relation to investigations and s.63, which relates to restrictions on the disclosure of information, to standards investigations.

4322. Best value – local authorities powers and duties – non commercial matters – contract workers

LOCAL GOVERNMENT BEST VALUE (EXCLUSION OF NON-COMMERCIAL CONSIDERATIONS) ORDER 2001, SI 2001 909; made under the Local Government Act 1999 s.19. In force: March 13, 2001; £1.75.

The Local Government Act 1988 s.17 contains a list of matters by reference to which public authorities may not exercise certain functions in relation to proposed public supply or works contracts with the authority. This Order provides for certain matters, relating to the terms and conditions of employment etc. of a contractor's workforce and the conduct of contractors or their workers in industrial disputes, to be non-commercial matters for the purposes of s.17 of the 1988 Act. But, under the Order, those matters cease to be non-commercial matters only so far as necessary or expedient to permit or facilitate compliance with the best value requirements of the Local Government Act 1999 Part I or where there is a transfer of staff to which the Transfer of Undertakings (Protection of Employment) Regulations 1981 (SI 1981 1794) may apply.

4323. Best value – local authorities powers and duties – performance indicators – Wales

LOCAL GOVERNMENT (BEST VALUE PERFORMANCE INDICATORS) (WALES) ORDER 2001, SI 2001 1337 (W.83); made under the Local Government Act 1999 s.4, s.29. In force: April 1, 2001; £10.50.

This Order prescribes performance indicators by reference to which the performance of county councils, county borough councils and National Park Authorities in Wales, in exercising their functions as best value authorities, will be measured from April 1, 2001. The Local Government (Best Value Performance Indicators) (Wales) Order 2000 (SI 2000 1030) is revoked.

4324. Best value – local authorities powers and duties – performance indicators and standards

LOCAL GOVERNMENT (BEST VALUE) PERFORMANCE INDICATORS AND PERFORMANCE STANDARDS ORDER 2001, SI 2001 724; made under the Local Government Act 1999 s.4, s.28. In force: April 1, 2001; £4.00.

The Local Government Act 1999 Part I imposes requirements on local authorities and other authorities relating to economy, efficiency and effectiveness in exercise of their functions. This Order specifies performance indicators by reference to which a best value authority's performance in exercising functions can be measured and specifies standards in respect of particular functions and particular best value authorities. The Local Government (Best Value) Performance Indicators Order 2000 (SI 2000 896) is revoked.

4325. Capital finance – rate of discount

LOCAL AUTHORITIES (CAPITAL FINANCE) (RATE OF DISCOUNT FOR 2001/ 02) (ENGLAND) REGULATIONS 2001, SI 2001 384; made under the Local Government and Housing Act 1989 s.49. In force: April 1, 2001; £1.50.

These Regulations prescribe 7.5 per cent as the percentage rate of discount for the financial year beginning on April 1, 2001 for determining the value of the consideration falling to be given by a local authority under a credit arrangement.

4326. Capital finance – rate of discount – Wales

LOCAL AUTHORITIES (CAPITAL FINANCE) (RATE OF DISCOUNT FOR 2001/ 2002) (WALES) REGULATIONS 2001, SI 2001 1287 (W.75); made under the Local Government and Housing Act 1989 s.49. In force: April 1, 2001; £1.75.

The Local Government and Housing Act 1989 Part IV makes provision for the capital finance of local authorities and s.49 of that Act sets out a formula for determining the value of the consideration falling to be given by an authority under a credit arrangement in any financial year after the year in which the arrangement comes into being. The percentage rate of discount prescribed for a financial year is one of the key elements which make up the formula. For the financial year beginning on April 1, 2001 these Regulations prescribe a rate of discount of 7 per cent which is 0.5 per cent less than the rate of discount prescribed for 2000/ 2001.

4327. Care – children – local authorities duties

CHILDREN (LEAVING CARE) (ENGLAND) REGULATIONS 2001, SI 2001 2874; made under the Children Act 1989 s.23A, s.23B, s.23D, s.23E, s.24B, s.24D, s.104, Sch.2 para.19B. In force: October 1, 2001; £2.00.

These Regulations, which amend the Representation Procedure (Children) Regulations 1991 (SI 1991 894), make provision about support for children and young people aged 16 and over who are, or have been, looked after by a local authority. They prescribe further categories of children to whom local authorities will, or as the case may be, will not, owe additional duties as provided for in the Children Act 1989 and make provision about the assessment of needs, the preparation and review of pathway plans, and the keeping of records.

4328. Care – children – local authorities duties – Wales

CHILDREN (LEAVING CARE) (WALES) REGULATIONS 2001, SI 2001 2189 (W.151); made under the Children Act 1989 s.23A, s.23B, s.23D, s.23E, s.24B, s.24D, s.104, Sch.2 para.19B. In force: October 1, 2001; £2.50.

These Regulations, which amend the Representations Procedure (Children) Regulations 1991 (SI 1991 879), make provision about support for children and young people aged 16 and over, who are, or have been, looked after by a local authority. They prescribe further categories of children to whom local authorities will, or as the case may be, will not, owe additional duties as provided for in the Children Act 1989 Part III.

4329. Children (Leaving Care) Act 2000 (c.35) – Commencement No.1 Order – England

CHILDREN (LEAVING CARE) ACT 2000 (COMMENCEMENT NO.1) (ENGLAND) ORDER 2001, SI 2001 2878 (C.96); made under the Children (Leaving Care) Act 2000 s.8. Commencement details: bringing into force various provisions of the Act on October 1, 2001; £1.50.

This Order brings into force certain provisions of the Children (Leaving Care) Act 2000 which amend the Children Act 1989 as respects the arrangements to be made for the care and support of children who are, or have been looked after by local authorities.

4330. Children (Leaving Care) Act 2000 (c.35) – Commencement No.2 and Consequential Provisions Order

CHILDREN (LEAVING CARE) ACT 2000 (COMMENCEMENT NO.2 AND CONSEQUENTIAL PROVISIONS) ORDER 2001, SI 2001 3070 (C.98); made under the Children (Leaving Care) Act 2000 s.8. Commencement details: bringing into force various provisions of the Act on September 10, 2001 and October 1, 2001; £1.75.

This Order amends the Income Support (General) Regulations 1987 (SI 1987 1967), the Housing Benefit (General) Regulations 1987 (SI 1987 1971), the Council Tax Benefit (General) Regulations 1992 (SI 1992 1814) and the Jobseeker's Allowance Regulations 1996. It provides that the Children (Leaving Care) Act 2000 s.6 shall come into force on September 10, 2001 for the purpose of making regulations and on October 1, 2001 for all other purposes.

4331. Children (Leaving Care) Act 2000 (c.35) – Commencement Order – Wales

CHILDREN (LEAVING CARE) ACT 2000 (COMMENCEMENT) (WALES) ORDER 2001, SI 2001 2191 (W.153; C.71); made under the Children (Leaving Care) Act 2000 s.8. Commencement details: bringing into force various provisions of the 2000 Act on October 1, 2001; £1.75.

This Order brings into force in relation to Wales, the Children (Leaving Care) Act 2000 sections 1 to 5, which provide new powers and duties for social services authorities.

4332. Colchester Borough Council Act 2001 (c.ii)

This Act makes provision for the closure of certain commercial harbour facilities and to enable the Colchester Borough Council to cease to be a harbour authority for the harbour of Colchester.

This Act received Royal Assent on March 22, 2001 and comes into force on March 22, 2001.

4333. Councillors – misconduct – status of standards committee proceedings

L, a councillor, appealed against a decision ((2000) 2 L.G.L.R. 933) refusing her application for judicial review of a decision of the standards committee of her local council, BDC, to the effect that her conduct had fallen short of the highest standards expected of councillors but that no further action would be taken against her. L, who had been accused of losing her temper with one of BDC's employees, argued that the proceedings before the standards committee had been ultra vires the powers of BDC since they had amounted to disciplinary proceedings aimed at enforcing the National Code of Local Government Conduct, which councils had no power to enforce.

Held, dismissing the appeal, that the proceedings before BDC's standards committee had been aimed at facilitating BDC's functions in maintaining its administration and internal workings in an efficient state and in furthering the welfare of its employees. The proceedings were therefore intra vires BDC's powers. If a local government officer complained about the way in which a councillor had behaved towards him, that complaint had to be investigated, and it was sensible for the investigating officer to report to a committee. Although the committee's powers were limited, it did have the power to recommend the removal of a councillor from a committee, to suggest changes to working practices and, in extreme cases, to report matters to the police or the council's auditors.

R. (ON THE APPLICATION OF LASHLEY) v. BROADLAND DC; *sub nom.* R. v. BROAD DC, *ex p.* LASHLEY; R. v. BROADLAND DC, *ex p.* LASHLEY, [2001] EWCA Civ 179, (2001) 3 L.G.L.R. 25, Kennedy, L.J., CA.

4334. Councillors – procedure – requirement for proposer and seconder – consideration of democratic implications

[Local Government Act 1972 Sch.12 para.42.]

A, who was an elected member of his local council, FCC, and the sole council representative belonging to the Green Party, appealed against the refusal of his application for judicial review of the passing by FCC of an amendment to a standing order whereby before any resolution would be included on the agenda at a council meeting it had to be seconded by another council member. The judge had found that since the standing order complied with the Local Government Act 1972, it could not be criticised.

Held, allowing the appeal, that a local council should, following receipt of proper advice, give careful consideration to the potential damage that such an order might cause to local democracy. Under the order an individual council member who was not affiliated to one of the main political parties or groups would be precluded from raising matters unless he gained the support of another council member. The order having related to the "regulation of the council's proceedings and business" for the purposes of Sch.12 para.42 of the

Act, it was apparent that no consideration had been given to the democratic implications. The order would accordingly be quashed.

R. (ON THE APPLICATION OF ARMSTRONG-BRAUN) v. FLINTSHIRE CC; *sub nom.* R. v. FLINTSHIRE CC, *ex p.* ARMSTRONG-BRAUN, [2001] EWCA Civ 345, (2001) 3 L.G.L.R. 34, Schiemann, L.J., CA.

4335. Grants – charities – opportunity to make representations before reduction in grant

H, a voluntary organisation providing services to the disabled, challenged a decision of the local authority, HLBC, to cut its statutory grant. H submitted that the local authority had failed to follow a fair procedure in reaching its decision since there had been minimal opportunity to make representations to the council before the decision was taken, relevant matters had been excluded from consideration and irrelevant matters taken into account.

Held, granting the application, that H had not been given an adequate opportunity to make representations against the cuts in their grant. Before any decision was made, H should have been provided with a written notice from HLBC containing reasons for the decision together with the opportunity to make representations, which should then have been given consideration, *R. v. Somerset CC, ex p. Fewings* [1995] 1 All E.R. 513, [1995] C.L.Y. 5406 applied.

R. (ON THE APPLICATION OF HARINGEY CONSORTIUM OF DISABLED PEOPLE AND CARERS ASSOCIATION) v. HARINGEY LBC; *sub nom.* R. v. HARINGEY LBC, *ex p.* HARINGEY CONSORTIUM OF DISABLED PEOPLE AND CARERS ASSOCIATION (2001) 58 B.M.L.R. 160, Scott Baker, J., QBD (Admin Ct).

4336. Greater London – Greater London Authority – legal proceedings – representation

GREATER LONDON AUTHORITY (MISCELLANEOUS AMENDMENTS) (NO.2) ORDER 2001, SI 2001 3719; made under the Greater London Authority Act 1999 s.405, s.406, s.420. In force: November 20, 2001; £1.75.

This Order makes incidental, consequential, and supplementary provision for the general or particular purposes of the Greater London Authority Act 1999, and for giving full effect to that Act. It amends the Local Government Act 1972 in relation to the Greater London Authority's ability to be represented in legal proceedings, and its procedure for making byelaws. It also amends the European Communities (Amendment) Act 1993 so that the Mayor of London and members of the London Assembly may become members of the European Community's Committee of the Regions. The Order amends the Environment Act 1995 by giving the Mayor of London power to issue directions to local authorities in Greater London regarding their obligations in relation to air quality, and by making a consequential amendment in respect of that power. In addition, it amends the Greater London Authority Act 1999 by confirming the Greater London Authority's power to enforce byelaws made by the Authority in respect of Trafalgar Square and Parliament Square Garden.

4337. Greater London Authority Act 1999 (c.29) – Commencement No.10 Order

GREATER LONDON AUTHORITY ACT 1999 (COMMENCEMENT NO.10) ORDER 2001, SI 2001 3603 (C.116); made under the Greater London Authority Act 1999 s.425. Commencement details: bringing into force various provisions of the 1999 Act on November 7, 2001; £2.00.

This Order brings into force those provisions of the Greater London Authority Act 1999 not already in force which relate to the Private Hire Vehicles (London) Act 1998.

4338. Kent County Council Act 2001 (c.iii)

This Act provides for the regulation of dealers in secondhand goods and the regulation of occasional sales and certain other trading in the County of Kent.
This Act received Royal Assent on April 10, 2001.

4339. Licensing – private hire vehicles – conditions – locus standi of prospective licence holder

See LICENSING: Peddubriwny v. Cambridge City Council. §4312

4340. Local authorities – approved investments – Wales

LOCAL AUTHORITIES (APPROVED INVESTMENTS) (AMENDMENT) (WALES) REGULATIONS 2001, SI 2001 3731 (W.308); made under the Local Government and Housing Act 1989 s.66. In force: December 1, 2001; £1.75.

The Local Authorities (Capital Finance) (Approved Investments) Regulations 1990 (SI 1990 426) contain a list of investments which are approved for the purposes of the Local Government and Housing Act 1989 Part IV. These Regulations amend the 1990 Regulations in consequence of the coming into force of the Financial Services and Markets Act 2000.

4341. Local authorities – armorial bearings – Crickhowell Town – Wales

LOCAL AUTHORITIES (ARMORIAL BEARINGS) (WALES) ORDER 2001, SI 2001 1869; made under the Local Government Act 1972 s.247. In force: May 17, 2001; £1.50.

This Order authorises Crickhowell Town Council to bear and use the armorial bearings of the former Crickhowell Rural District Council and the Vale of Glamorgan County Borough Council to bear and use the armorial bearings of the former Vale of Glamorgan Borough Council.

4342. Local authorities – armorial bearings – Pickering Town Council – Sudbury Town Council

LOCAL AUTHORITIES (ARMORIAL BEARINGS) ORDER 2001, SI 2001 1454; made under the Local Government Act 1972 s.247. In force: April 12, 2001; £1.50.

This Order authorises Pickering Town Council and Sudbury Town Council to bear and use the armorial bearings formerly borne and used by the Pickering Urban District Council and the corporation of the Borough of Sudbury respectively.

4343. Local authorities – code of conduct – grant of dispensations – Wales

STANDARDS COMMITTEES (GRANT OF DISPENSATIONS) (WALES) REGULATIONS 2001, SI 2001 2279 (W.169); made under the Local Government Act 2000 s.81. In force: July 28, 2001; £2.00.

County and county borough councils, community councils, fire authorities and National Park Authorities in Wales are required by the Local Government Act 2000 s.51 to adopt a code of conduct for members and co-opted members which must incorporate any mandatory provisions of any model code of conduct issued by the National Assembly for Wales. Section 81 of the Act provides that any participation by a member or co-opted member of a relevant authority in any business which is prohibited by the mandatory provisions is not a failure to comply with the authority's code of conduct if the member or co-opted member has acted in accordance with a dispensation from the prohibition granted by the authority's standards committee. These Regulations prescribe the circumstances in which standards committees of relevant authorities may grant such dispensations.

4344. Local authorities – codes of conduct – investigations – Wales

LOCAL GOVERNMENT INVESTIGATIONS (FUNCTIONS OF MONITORING OFFICERS AND STANDARDS COMMITTEES) (WALES) REGULATIONS 2001,

SI 2001 2281 (W.171); made under the Local Government Act 2000 s.73. In force: July 28, 2001; £2.50.

The Local Government Act 2000 s.51 imposes a duty upon local authorities to adopt codes of the conduct expected of their members and co-opted members. A Local Commissioner in Wales may investigate any alleged breach by members or co-opted members the code of conduct of a local authority in Wales. Where a Local Commissioner in Wales ceases such an investigation before it is completed, he or she may refer the matter subject to the investigation to the monitoring officer of the relevant local authority. Section 73 of the Act enables the National Assembly for Wales to make regulations specifying how such referred matters are to be dealt with. These Regulations provide that the monitoring officer of the relevant authority will investigate matters before reporting and, if appropriate, making recommendations, to the relevant authority's Standards Committee or where a matter has been referred, he or she will consider the report of the Local Commissioner in Wales, before, if appropriate, making recommendations to the relevant authority's Standards Committee.

4345. Local authorities – companies

LOCAL AUTHORITIES (COMPANIES) (AMENDMENT) (ENGLAND) ORDER 2001, SI 2001 722; made under the Local Government and Housing Act 1989 s.39. In force: April 1, 2001; £1.75.

This Order amends the Local Authorities (Companies) Order 1995 (SI 1995 849) Art.14, which requires an authority to have available an amount of credit cover for the liabilities of companies, which for the purposes of the Local Government and Housing Act 1989 Part IV, are treated as companies regulated by the authority. It allows an authority to designate as credit cover provision, and treat as credit cover, any amount treated as added to the authority's basic credit approval in respect of which no determination has been made by an authority. In addition, it makes amendments which allow an authority to disregard, as respects a company which becomes a regulated company in relation to the authority, expenditure defrayed by the company, after it becomes a regulated company, from monies accumulated before it became a regulated company, and liabilities of a regulated company under a credit transaction, whether entered into before or after the company became a regulated company.

4346. Local authorities – companies – revenue accounts and capital finance

LOCAL AUTHORITIES (COMPANIES) (AMENDMENT NO.2) (ENGLAND) ORDER 2001, SI 2001 3042; made under the Local Government and Housing Act 1989 s.39. In force: October 1, 2001; £1.50.

The Local Authorities (Companies) Order 1995 (SI 1995 849) Art.14 requires an authority to have available an amount of credit cover for the liabilities of companies which are treated as companies regulated by the authority. Article 15 of the 1995 Order modifies the Local Government and Housing Act 1989 Part IV by permitting an authority to treat a basic credit approval as increased by the amount by which its regulated companies reduce their liabilities. This Order amends the Local Authorities (Companies) Order 1995 (SI 1995 849) to make it clear that the specified Articles do not apply the whole of Part IV of the 1989 Act to such companies.

4347. Local authorities – conduct – model codes of practice

LOCAL AUTHORITIES (MODEL CODE OF CONDUCT) (ENGLAND) ORDER 2001, SI 2001 3575; made under the Local Government Act 2000 s.50, s.81, s.105. In force: November 27, 2001; £3.00.

This Order contains a model code of conduct as regards the conduct which is expected of members and co-opted members of local authorities in England. Under the Local Government Act 2000 s.51, each relevant authority must adopt a code of conduct applying to its members which must incorporate any mandatory provisions of the model code and where an authority does not adopt such a code within six months of the Order coming into force, the mandatory provisions of the model code will apply to the members of the authority until it does.

4348. Local authorities – conduct – model codes of practice – Wales

CONDUCT OF MEMBERS (MODEL CODE OF CONDUCT) (WALES) ORDER 2001, SI 2001 2289 (W.177); made under the Local Government Act 2000 s.50, s.81. In force: July 28, 2001; £2.50.

The Local Government Act 2000 Part III establishes a new ethical framework for local government in Wales. Section 50 of the Act provides that the National Assembly for Wales may by order issue a model code as regards the conduct which is expected of members and co-opted members of relevant authorities in Wales. The relevant authorities are county, community and county borough councils, fire authorities and National Park authorities but not police authorities. This Order issues a model code of conduct for members and co-opted members of relevant authorities in Wales.

4349. Local authorities – conduct – standards committees – Wales

STANDARDS COMMITTEES (WALES) REGULATIONS 2001, SI 2001 2283 (W.172); made under the Local Government Act 2000 s.53, s.56, s.105. In force: July 28, 2001; £3.00.

The Local Government Act 2000 Part III makes provision with respect to the conduct of local government members and employers. It requires every relevant authority, which in Wales includes county and county borough councils, fire authorities, National Park authorities and police authorities but not community councils, to establish a standards committee to have the functions conferred on it by or under the Act. Under s.53 of the Act, the National Assembly for Wales may by regulations make provision as to the size, composition and proceedings of standards committees of relevant authorities in Wales, other than police authorities, and of any sub-committees. These Regulations make provision with respect to the size and composition of standards committees and sub-committees, make provision with respect to the term of office and re-appointment of members of standards committees and sub-committees and make provision with respect to the office of chairperson and vice-chairperson of a standards committee or sub-committee and with respect to voting at meetings. In addition, these Regulations make provision with respect to a Quorum at meetings of standards committees and sub-committees, the frequency of meetings and the attendance of the authority's monitoring officer or a representative of the monitoring officer.

4350. Local authorities – conduct principles – model codes of practice – Wales

CONDUCT OF MEMBERS (PRINCIPLES) (WALES) ORDER 2001, SI 2001 2276 (W.166); made under the Local Government Act 2000 s.49, s.105. In force: July 28, 2001; £2.00.

The Local Government Act 2000 Part III establishes a new ethical framework for local government in Wales and provides that the New Assembly for Wales may by order specify the principles to govern the conduct of members and co-opted members of relevant authorities. This Order specifies the relevant principles.

4351. Local authorities – contracting out – highway functions

LOCAL AUTHORITIES (CONTRACTING OUT OF HIGHWAY FUNCTIONS) (ENGLAND) ORDER 2001, SI 2001 4061; made under the Deregulation and Contracting Out Act 1994 s.70. In force: December 21, 2001; £1.75.

This Order enables local highway authorities to authorise another person, or that person's employees, to exercise certain of their functions in relation to street works in highways in respect of which they are the highway authority. Those functions relate to fees to be paid by undertakers to a highway authority on the registration of specified information on a street works register; to the sharing of costs of works required to divert undertakers' apparatus where these are occasioned by major highway, bridge or transport works; and to charges payable to a highway authority by an undertaker whose street works are unreasonably prolonged.

4352. Local authorities – council meetings – modification of enactments

LOCAL AUTHORITIES (EXECUTIVE ARRANGEMENTS) (MODIFICATION OF ENACTMENTS AND FURTHER PROVISIONS) (ENGLAND) ORDER 2001, SI 2001 1517; made under the Local Government Act 2000 s.47, s.105. In force: May 18, 2001; £2.00.

These Regulations, which amend the Local Government Act 1972, the Local Government and Housing Act 1989 and the Local Government Act 2000, prevent local authorities from making arrangements for the discharge of functions by another local authority to the extent that the function in question is the responsibility of the executive of that other local authority. They provide that the arrangements for the discharge of a local authority's functions, by either another local authority or a joint committee, existing at the time when any of the participating local authorities begin to operate executive arrangements, shall cease to the extent that the function in question becomes the responsibility of the executive of any of those authorities; enable local authorities to appoint advisory committees to advise the executive of the local authority and any committee or individual member of that executive; and introduces a requirement for local authorities who are or will be operating executive arrangements to make standing orders in respect of local authority contracts and specify the provisions to be included in the standing orders, including the procedure to be followed in the making of such contracts.

4353. Local authorities – councillors – attendance allowance

LOCAL AUTHORITIES (MEMBERS' ALLOWANCES) (ENGLAND) REGULATIONS 2001, SI 2001 1280; made under the Local Government Act 1972 s.177; and the Local Government and Housing Act 1989 s.18, s.190. In force: May 4, 2001; £2.00.

These Regulations, which amend the Local Authorities (Members'Allowances) Regulations 1991 (SI 1991 351), apply to district, county and London borough councils and provide that they must have regard to the recommendations of independent remuneration panels in relation to allowance schemes. They provide that authorities must have regard to the recommendations of an independent remuneration panel, enable authorities to revoke or amend an existing allowance scheme in order to give effect to any changes necessary as a consequence of the coming into force of Local Government and Housing Act 1989 s.18 and provide that an allowance scheme may include provision for the payment to members of allowances in respect of expenses of arranging for the care of children or dependents in order to conduct the duties specified in that regulation. In addition, the Regulations require authorities to publicise the allowance schemes.

4354. Local authorities – councillors – attendance allowance – Wales

LOCAL AUTHORITIES (MEMBERS' ALLOWANCES) (AMENDMENT) (WALES) REGULATIONS 2001, SI 2001 2781 (W.234); made under the Local Government Act 1972 s.173, s.175. In force: August 1, 2001; £1.75.

The Local Government Act 1972 s.173 makes provisions for a member of, in England, a parish or, in Wales, a community council who is a councillor to receive a payment by way of attendance allowance which does not exceed the amount prescribed by regulations and for a member of such a council who is not entitled to receive such a payment to receive a payment by way of financial loss allowance which does not exceed the amount prescribed by regulations. These Regulations, which revoke the Local Authorities (Members'Allowances) (Amendment) (Wales) Regulations 2000 (SI 2000 2492), amend the Local Authorities (Members' Allowances) Regulations 1991 (SI 1991 351) by increasing the amount paid to a member of a local authority.

4355. **Local authorities – designated public places – alcohol – police powers**

LOCAL AUTHORITIES (ALCOHOL CONSUMPTION IN DESIGNATED PUBLIC PLACES) REGULATIONS 2001, SI 2001 2831; made under the Local Government Act 2000.13; and the Criminal Justice and Police Act 2001 s.13, s.105. In force: September 1, 2001; £1.75.

These Regulations, which amend the Local Authorities (Functions and Responsibilities) (England) Regulations 2000 (SI 2000 2853), set out the procedure to be followed by local authorities in connection with orders designating a public place under the Criminal Justice and Police Act 2001 s.13. Once an order is made under that section in relation to a public place in their area, police powers to require a person not to consume intoxicating liquor and to surrender opened containers of such liquor will be available.

4356. **Local authorities – education overview and scrutiny committees – alternative arrangements**

LOCAL AUTHORITIES (ALTERNATIVE ARRANGEMENTS) (ENGLAND) REGULATIONS 2001, SI 2001 1299; made under the Local Government Act 2000 s.32, s.105. In force: April 2, 2001; £2.50.

The Local Government Act 2000 s.32 provides for the Secretary of State to make Regulations setting out a regime which is an alternative to the three forms of executive detailed in the Act. These Regulations set out the main features of alternative arrangements and deal with church and parent governor representation on education overview and scrutiny committees within alternative arrangements. They set out which functions must be carried out by the authority, make provision for the appointment of committees by an authority which are operating alternative arrangements for the purpose of discharging the authority's functions, provide for overview and scrutiny within the arrangements and provide for the representation of church nominees on education overview and scrutiny committees. In addition, the Regulations provide for the representation of parent governors on education overview and scrutiny committees, set out the the election procedures for election as a parent governor representative, deal with the eligibility for voting in elections, set out circumstances which may disqualify a person from being elected as, or continuing to act as a parent governor, provide the term of office of a parent governor representative to be between two and four years, unless the office is vacated mid-term, set out what happens when the office is vacated and deal with the voting rights of a parent governor representative.

4357. **Local authorities – executive arrangements – discharge of functions**

LOCAL AUTHORITIES (ARRANGEMENTS FOR THE DISCHARGE OF FUNCTIONS) (ENGLAND) (AMENDMENT) REGULATIONS 2001, SI 2001 3961; made under the Local Government Act 2000 s.20, s.105. In force: January 1, 2002; £2.00.

These Regulations amend the Local Authorities (Arrangements for the Discharge of Functions) (England) Regulations 2000 (SI 2000 2851). They enable joint arrangements to provide for one joint committee to discharge a number of functions where the functions are the subject of different arrangements under the Local Government Act 1972 s.101(5) and those arrangements have been made at the same time; joint arrangements to provide for the discharge of functions by a new joint committee or an existing joint committee; provide for the situation where a function becomes the responsibility of an executive of a local authority after the authority made joint arrangements in relation to the function in accordance with the 2000 Regulations; make provision regarding who, in relation to an authority, may appoint the joint committee and may fix the number of members to be appointed, their term of office, or the area (if restricted) within which the committee is to exercise its authority, under the Local Government Act 1972 s.102(1)(b)(2); provides that where a joint committee is discharging a function in relation to five or more local authorities or a function required by statute to be discharged by a joint committee, and an executive, executive member or executive committee makes appointments to the joint committee, non-executive members of the authority as well as members of the executive may be appointed; enables a local authority, which makes appointments to a joint committee, to appoint persons who are not members of the authority; provides that where a local authority makes appointments to a joint committee with the agreement of the executive, if only one member of the authority is a member of the joint committee, that person need not be a member of the executive and if more than one member of the authority is a member of the joint committee, at least one member of the executive must be a member of the joint committee; and provide that where an executive takes over the role of appointment of members of a joint committee from a local authority, any members of the joint committee who, if the executive had made the appointments, the executive would not have been able to appoint, will cease to be members of the joint committee. Any other members appointed by the local authority will be treated as if they had been appointed by the executive.

4358. Local authorities – executive arrangements – discharge of functions – Wales

LOCAL AUTHORITIES (EXECUTIVE ARRANGEMENTS) (DISCHARGE OF FUNCTIONS) (WALES) REGULATIONS 2001, SI 2001 2287 (W.175); made under the Local Government Act 2000 s.18, s.19, s.20, s.105, s.106. In force: July 28, 2001; £2.50.

The Local Government Act 2000 Part II provides for local authorities to make arrangements for the creation and operation of an executive of the authority under which certain functions of the authority are the responsibility of the executive. The National Assembly for Wales may by regulations make provision which enables an executive of a local authority in Wales, or a committee or a specified member of such an executive, to make arrangements for the discharge by an area committee of the authority or by another local authority of any functions which, under executive arrangements, are the responsibility of the authority. The National Assembly for Wales may by regulations make provision which enables a local authority in Wales to make arrangements for the discharge by that authority and one or more other local authorities jointly of any functions which, under the executive arrangements, are the responsibility of the executive of the authority. These Regulations specify the persons who have the power to make such arrangements in the case of a mayor and cabinet executive, a leader and cabinet executive and a mayor and council manager executive respectively and provide for the making of arrangements for the discharge of functions, which are the responsibility of the executive of a local authority in Wales by an area committee of that authority. They provide for the making of arrangements for the discharge of functions which are the responsibility of the executive of a local authority in Wales by another local authority and also for the making, in specified circumstances, of arrangements for the discharge of functions which are not the responsibility of the executive of a local authority in Wales by the executive of another local authority.

4359. Local authorities – executive arrangements – functions and responsibilities – Wales

LOCAL AUTHORITIES EXECUTIVE ARRANGEMENTS (FUNCTIONS AND RESPONSIBILITIES) (WALES) REGULATIONS 2001, SI 2001 2291 (W.179); made under the Local Government Act 2000 s.13, s.105, s.106. In force: July 28, 2001; £6.50.

The Local Government Act 2000 Part II provides for the discharge of a local authority's functions by an executive of the authority unless those functions are specified as functions that are not to be the responsibility of the authority's executive. These Regulations specify functions that are not to be the responsibility of an authority's executive or are to be the responsibility of such an executive only to a limited extent or only in specified circumstances.

4360. Local authorities – executive arrangements – modification of enactments

LOCAL AUTHORITIES (EXECUTIVE AND ALTERNATIVE ARRANGEMENTS) (MODIFICATION OF ENACTMENTS AND OTHER PROVISIONS) (ENGLAND) ORDER 2001, SI 2001 2237; made under the Local Government Act 2000 s.47, s.105. In force: July 11, 2001; £4.00.

This Order modifies primary and secondary legislation and makes other provisions for the purposes of, in consequence of, or for giving full effect to provisions in the Local Government Act 2000 Part II. This Order and the modifications made by it apply to England only.

4361. Local authorities – executive arrangements – powers and duties

LOCAL AUTHORITIES (CHANGING EXECUTIVE ARRANGEMENTS AND ALTERNATIVE ARRANGEMENTS) (ENGLAND) REGULATIONS 2001, SI 2001 1003; made under the Local Government Act 2000 s.30, s.33, s.105. In force: April 12, 2001; £2.00.

The Local Government Act 2000 Part II provides for local authorities to draw up proposals for the operation of executive arrangements or, in the case of certain authorities, for the operation of alternative arrangements. These Regulations enable a local authority operating executive arrangements to draw up proposals to change those executive arrangements or, in the case of certain local authorities, to replace them with alternative arrangements. The Regulations also enable a local authority operating alternative arrangements to draw up proposals to change those alternative arrangements or to replace them with executive arrangements. They make provision in relation to certain proposals, for consultation and for what must be included in the proposals, set out when a referendum is required before a local authority can take steps to implement its proposals, require a resolution of the local authority in order for that authority to operate different arrangements, provide for certain information to be sent to the Secretary of State and provide certain proposals, which do not require a referendum, to be implemented in accordance with the timetable included in the proposals.

4362. Local authorities – executive arrangements – powers and duties – Wales

LOCAL AUTHORITIES (EXECUTIVE ARRANGEMENTS) (DECISIONS, DOCUMENTS AND MEETINGS) (WALES) REGULATIONS 2001, SI 2001 2290 (W.178); made under the Local Government Act 2000 s.22, s.105, s.106. In force: July 28, 2001; £3.50.

These Regulations, which apply to county councils and county borough officials in Wales which are operating executive arrangements under the Local Government Act 2000 Part II, make provision relating to public access to meetings, decisions and documents of local authority executives and their committees. They also deal with access to information relating to decisions made by joint committees of local authorities where these are solely comprised of executive members and are discharging an executive function.

4363. Local authorities – executive arrangements – standing orders

LOCAL AUTHORITIES (STANDING ORDERS) (ENGLAND) REGULATIONS 2001, SI 2001 3384; made under the Local Government and Housing Act 1989 s.8, s.20, s.190; and the Local Government Act 1992 s.19, s.26. In force: November 7, 2001; £3.00.

These Regulations, which amend the Local Authorities (Standing Orders) Regulations 1993 (SI 1993 202) and the Local Government Changes for England Regulations 1994 (SI 1994 867), require certain local authorities in England to make or modify standing orders so that a county council, district council or London borough council which is operating executive arrangements must have standing orders relating to its staff which include the specified provisions.

4364. Local authorities – executives – functions

LOCAL AUTHORITIES (FUNCTIONS AND RESPONSIBILITIES) (ENGLAND) (AMENDMENT) REGULATIONS 2001, SI 2001 2212; made under the Local Government Act 2000 s.13, s.105. In force: July 10, 2001; £2.00.

These Regulations amend the Local Authorities (Functions and Responsibilities) (England) Regulations 2000 (SI 2000 2853) with the effect of securing that approval of issues papers and draft policies and proposals associated with the preparation of an altered or replacement development plan, prior to public consultation is not the function of the executive of a local authority. The Regulations make amendments with the effect of limiting the responsibility of an authority's executive to the making of applications and to restrict the authority's executive to authorising the contracting out of functions that are the responsibility of the executive, and to revoking only those authorisations that relate to functions that are the executive's responsibility.

4365. Local authorities – executives – referendums – Wales

LOCAL AUTHORITIES (REFERENDUMS) (PETITIONS AND DIRECTIONS) (WALES) REGULATIONS 2001, SI 2001 2292 (W.180); made under the Local Government Act 2000 s.34, s.35, s.105, s.106. In force: July 28, 2001; £6.50.

Under the Local Government Act 2000 Part II, every county and county borough council in Wales is able to make arrangements for the discharge of its functions by executives. Where an authority's proposals for an executive involve an elected mayor, they are required to hold a referendum before taking steps to implement the proposals. These Regulations provide for circumstances in which an authority must hold a referendum other than where required to do so.

4366. Local authorities – executives functions – alternative arrangements – Wales

LOCAL AUTHORITIES (PROPOSALS FOR ALTERNATIVE ARRANGEMENTS) (WALES) REGULATIONS 2001, SI 2001 2293 (W.181); made under the Local Government Act 2000 s.31, s.105, s.106. In force: July 28, 2001; £2.00.

Under the Local Government Act 2000 Part II, local authorities are required to make arrangements for the discharge of their functions by executives which must take one of the forms specified in s.11 of the Act. Section 25 of the Act requires local authorities to draw up proposals for executive arrangements and s.31 permits a local authority to draw up proposals for alternative arrangements of a particular type permitted. These regulations contain requirements as to those proposals for alternative arrangement.

4367. Local authorities – functions and expenses – local commissioner – Wales

COMMISSION FOR LOCAL ADMINISTRATION IN WALES AND LOCAL COMMISSIONER IN WALES (FUNCTIONS AND EXPENSES) REGULATIONS 2001, SI 2001 2275 (W.165); made under the Local Government Act 2000 s.68. In force: July 28, 2001; £1.75.

The National Assembly for Wales makes regulations with respect to the treatment of functions of a Local Commissioner in Wales and the Commission for Local Administration in Wales under the Local Government Act 1974 Part III. These Regulations make provision for the application of specified sections to include the expenses of a Local Commissioner in Wales.

4368. Local authorities – Greater London Authority – miscellaneous amendments

GREATER LONDON AUTHORITY (MISCELLANEOUS AMENDMENTS) ORDER 2001, SI 2001 2620; made under the Greater London Authority Act 1999 s.405, s.406, s.408, s.420. In force: August 14, 2001; £1.50.

This Order, which amends the GLA Roads Designation Order 2000 (SI 2000 1117) and the GLA Roads and Side Roads (Transfer of Property etc.) Order 2000 (SI 2001 1552), makes provision for the general or particular purposes of the Greater London Authority Act 1999 and for giving full effect to that Act.

4369. Local authorities – Parish Councils – conduct – model codes of practice

PARISH COUNCILS (MODEL CODE OF CONDUCT) ORDER 2001, SI 2001 3576; made under the Local Government Act 2000 s.50, s.81, s.105. In force: November 27, 2001; £2.00.

This Order contains a model code of conduct as regards the conduct expected of members and co-opted members of parish councils in England. Under the Local Government Act 2000 s.51, each relevant authority must adopt a code of conduct applying to its members which must incorporate any mandatory provisions of the model code and where an authority does not adopt such a code within six months of the Order coming into force, the mandatory provisions of the model code will apply to the members of the authority until it does.

4370. Local authorities – pensions – illegal bonus payments – impact of prior settlement

G, a district council executive, challenged the Secretary of State's decision that his pension had been correctly calculated by the district auditor and that it had been within the county council's powers to reduce his pension on the basis that illegal bonus payments paid to G in addition to his salary should not have formed part of his remuneration. It was submitted, following a successful challenge to that determination by two of G's colleagues and the acknowledgement by the Secretary of State that his determination was flawed, that G should be granted relief from the determination notwithstanding a settlement agreement reached with the district auditor, as part of which G had agreed that he would not pursue any application to challenge the Secretary of State's decision, because (1) he had been incapable of bringing proceedings earlier because of illness; (2) the agreement did not form a contract, and (3) it was unfair to treat him differently from his colleagues.

Held, refusing the application for judicial review, that (1) G could have joined the proceedings initiated by his colleagues, despite his illness, because the basis of the challenge was almost identical; (2) G had never established a contractual right to a particular pension amount and the issue as to whether bonus payments were to be taken into account when calculating pension entitlement had always been in dispute, and (3) G's position was different from that of his colleagues, primarily because he was the architect of the scheme. G had effectively surrendered his right to challenge the Secretary of State's decision as part of the compromise reached with the District Auditor and it was not now open to him to go behind that agreement.

R. (ON THE APPLICATION OF GARLAND) v. SECRETARY OF STATE FOR THE ENVIRONMENT, TRANSPORT AND THE REGIONS (2001) 3 L.G.L.R. 26, Turner, J., QBD (Admin Ct).

4371. Local authorities – powers and duties – alternative arrangements – Wales

LOCAL AUTHORITIES (ALTERNATIVE ARRANGEMENTS) (WALES) REGULATIONS 2001, SI 2001 2284 (W.173); made under the Local Government Act 2000 s.31, s.32. In force: July 28, 2001; £7.50.

The Local Government Act 2000 Part II provides for the National Assembly for Wales to specify which local authorities may operate "alternative arrangements" and what form those arrangements should take. These Regulations permit all county councils and county borough councils in Wales to operate alternative arrangements provided that those arrangements are in the form required by these Regulations.

4372. Local authorities – proposals – executive arrangements – Wales

LOCAL AUTHORITIES (PROPOSALS FOR EXECUTIVE ARRANGEMENTS) (WALES) ORDER 2001, SI 2001 2277 (W.167); made under the Local Government Act 2000 s.25, s.105, s.106. In force: July 28, 2001; £1.75.

Subject to the exception below, every county and county borough council in Wales is required to draw up proposals for the operation of executive arrangements under the Local Government Act 2000 s.25. The exception is where s.31 of the Act applies to the local authority and it decides to draw up proposals for the operation of alternative arrangements. In drawing up proposals, a local authority must decide what form its executive is to take and a copy of the proposals must be sent to the National Assembly for Wales accompanied by a statement describing the steps taken by the local authority to consult the local government electors for, and other interested persons in, its area. This Order specifies January 31, 2002 as the date by which a local authority must comply with the requirements.

4373. Local authorities powers and duties – childminders – cancellation of registration – duty of care

See NEGLIGENCE: Bowden v. Lancashire CC. §4470

4374. Local authorities powers and duties – childrens welfare – meaning of "within their area" in context of duty to assess under Children Act 1989 s.17(1)

[Children Act 1989 s.17(1), s.27; Housing Act 1996 s.190.]

S sought judicial review of decisions by three local authorities whereby each had refused her application for assessment of the needs of her children under the Children Act 1989 s.17(1). S and her children, who attended school in Wandsworth, were temporarily accommodated at a hostel owned and managed by Hammersmith and Fulham LBC, but situated in Lambeth. In seeking a determination as to which of the three local authorities was under a duty to provide a needs assessment the contentions revolved around interpretation of the phrase "within their area" given in s.17(1).

Held, granting the application for judicial review, that there was no justification for ascribing a different meaning to the words "within their area" in s.17(1) to that given to the phrase where it appeared in other sections of the 1989 Act. Consequently, the sole determinant factor in deciding whether a person was "within their area" was simple physical presence, *R. v. Lambeth LBC, ex p. Caddell* [1998] 1 F.L.R. 253, [1997] C.L.Y. 361 and *R. v. Kent CC, ex p. S* [2000] 1 F.L.R. 155, [1999] C.L.Y. 4629 followed. Thus, as the duties of Hammersmith and Fulham arising under the Housing Act 1996 s.190 had ceased, it was under no further duty towards S. However, the physical presence test imposed a duty on both Wandsworth and Lambeth to provide an assessment of the children's needs. Such a circumstance provided a manifest case for the co-operation of the two authorities pursuant to s.27 of the 1989 Act.

R. (ON THE APPLICATION OF S) v. WANDSWORTH LBC, [2001] EWHC Admin 709, [2002] 1 F.L.R. 469, Jack Beatson Q.C., QBD (Admin Ct).

4375. Local authorities powers and duties – contract for sale of land – completion constituted "disposal"

[Local Government Act 1972 s.123, s.128(2).]

S, a property company that had put forward the highest bid upon the offer for sale of certain properties, applied for judicial review of a decision of HLBC to enter into a contract for the sale of those properties to third parties. Whilst conceding that they had acted in breach of the Local Government Act 1972 s.123 by failing to obtain the best price for the properties, and furthermore, had not gained the consent of the Secretary of State for a sale of the properties at a price lower than had been reasonably obtainable, HLBC argued that the buyers were entitled to rely on s.128(2) of the Act which provided that a disposal of land would not be invalidated as against the buyer by reason of the fact that the consent of the Secretary of State had not been obtained.

Held, granting the application, that (1) for the purpose of s.128(2) of the Act a "disposal" of land took place at the time of completion rather than when contracts were entered into. In the context of a sale of land, the moment of disposal was best described as at the time of the transfer of the legal interest as opposed to the establishing of an equitable interest through a contract. Moreover, in entering into the contract HLBC had not disposed of its rights as owners of the properties; the buyers equitable interest was limited in nature, *Wilkins v. Horrowitz* [1990] 2 E.G.L.R. 217 applied, and (2) s.128(2) only applied where there had been a failure to obtain the requisite consent and could not be relied on in cases where the local authority's decision to dispose of land was unlawful for other reasons.

R. (ON THE APPLICATION OF STRUCTADENE LTD) v. HACKNEY LBC; *sub nom.* R. v. HACKNEY LBC, *ex p.* STRUCTADENE LTD; STRUCTADENE v. HACKNEY LBC [2001] 2 All E.R. 225, Elias, J., QBD (Admin Ct).

4376. Local authorities powers and duties – data protection – supply of electoral register to commercial organisations – refusal of right to request exclusion

[Data Protection Act 1998 s.11; Human Rights Act 1998 Sch.1 Part I Art.8, Part II Art.3; Representation of the People Regulations 1986 (SI 1986 1081) Reg.54(4); Representation of the People (England and Wales) Regulations 2001 (SI 2001 341); Council Directive 95/46 on the protection of individuals with regard to the processing of personal data and on the free movement of such data Art.14(b).]

R sought judicial review of the refusal of an electoral registration officer, ERO, to assent to his request to have his name and address removed from copies of the electoral register supplied to commercial organisations. By virtue of the Representation of the People Regulations 1986 Reg.54(4), as amended, the ERO was obliged to supply copies of the register to any person who paid the prescribed fee. R wrote to the ERO stating that he did not intend to complete the application form for inclusion as he objected to to the practice of selling copies to commercial interests. In response, the ERO maintained that the process of electoral registration was a separate issue to the sale of the registers and therefore, as R met the qualifying criteria, he would be included on the register. R contended that (1) the 1986 Regulations did not allow for "the data subject's right to object"as provided by the Data Protection Directive 95/46 Art.14(b); (2) his right to family and private life under the Human Rights Act 1998 Sch.1 Part I Art.8 had been breached, and (3) his right to free elections under Sch.1 Part II Art.3 of the 1998 Act had been infringed. *Held*, granting the application, that (1) Art.14(b) of the Directive, which had direct effect, had been successfully implemented into national law by the Data Protection Act 1998 s.11. However, the right to object under s.11 had not been transposed into the 1986 Regulations or the superseding Representation of the People (England and Wales) Regulations 2001 and consequently, ERO's had administered the register unlawfully; (2) the disclosure of personal details exposed electors to invasive marketing strategies and accordingly, prima facie, Art.8 had been engaged. Moreover, the failure to afford electors a right of objection was disproportionate to the legitimate economic aim of maintaining a commercially available register and hence, R's Art.8 rights had been breached, and (3) in the absence of an individual right to exclusion, the 1986 and 2001 Regulations made the right to vote conditional upon consent to, or acquiescence in, the supply of personal details to commercial organisations and therefore, they operated in contravention of the right to free elections.

R. (ON THE APPLICATION OF ROBERTSON) v. WAKEFIELD MDC; *sub nom.* R. (ON THE APPLICATION OF ROBERTSON) v. ELECTORAL REGISTRATION OFFICER, [2001] EWHC Admin 915, [2002] 2 W.L.R. 889, Maurice Kay, J., QBD (Admin Ct).

4377. Local authorities powers and duties – footpaths – maintenance – personal injury – requirement for immediate repair

See NEGLIGENCE: Dee v. Durham County Council. §4497

4378. Local authorities powers and duties – local authority housing – foreign national with child "in need" – duty to make provision

[Children Act 1989 s.17, s.20, s.23.]

BLBC, a local authority, appealed against a decision ([2001] EWHC Admin 5, [2001] 5 C.L. 585) to allow an application by G, a Dutch national, for judicial review of BLBC's decision to refuse to provide her with accommodation, income support or housing benefit. G was eligible for neither housing nor financial assistance as she had failed the requisite habitual residence test. However, the judge had concluded that as her child was "in need" within the meaning of the Children Act 1989 s.17(10) and it was in the child's best interests that he be placed with his mother, BLBC should have exercised its duty under s.23 to accommodate them together. BLBC contended that (1) pursuant to s.17(3), it had a power but not a duty to provide accommodation and subsistence to both G and her child together, and (2) its duty under s.20(1) to provide accommodation was a duty to the child only.

Held, allowing the appeal, that (1) s.17 of the Act did not impose a duty upon BLBC to provide accommodation for both G and her child together. BLBC had acted lawfully in refusing to provide accommodation for G and its decision had been within the range of powers available to it. Moreover, BLBC had made a lawful decision to offer G her fare to return to Holland where the child could be adequately cared for, but that offer had been refused, and (2) BLBC had fulfilled its duty under s.20 by offering accommodation to the child alone. Further, BLBC was not obliged under s.23(6) to provide accommodation for both G and her child.

R. (ON THE APPLICATION OF G) v. BARNET LBC, [2001] EWCA Civ 540, [2001] 2 F.L.R. 877, Ward, L.J., CA.

4379. Local authorities powers and duties – race discrimination – gypsies

See HUMAN RIGHTS: Hallam v. Avery. §3492

4380. Local authorities powers and duties – sex establishments – service of closure notice – additional occupants

[City of Westminster Act 1996 s.3, s.4(1), s.4(5)(a).]

M appealed against a ruling allowing WCC's appeal following the dismissal of proceedings commenced by WCC under the City of Westminster Act 1996 s.3 for the closure of an unlicensed sex establishment. Following service of a closure notice upon M, the proceedings had been adjourned when it became apparent that the basement of the building in question was occupied by others, O. Immediately thereafter WCC served O with notice of the proceedings. M contended that WCC's complaint to the justices was invalid as (1) s.4(1) which required proceedings to be commenced no earlier than 14 days after service of a closure notice and no later than six months after service, related to the service of a closure notice upon both the principal of the sex establishment and also, under s.3(2)(a)(ii), upon the other occupiers, and (2) s.4(5)(a) which required there to be consideration by the justices of whether there had been proper service, also related to service upon both the principal and other occupiers.

Held, dismissing the appeal, that (1) section 4(1) referred solely to s.3(2)(a)(i), namely service upon the principal of the establishment in question, prior to the issue of any complaint. Any other interpretation would render the operation of s.4(1) problematic in practice and was also contradicted by the other provisions of s.4, and (2) in determining whether a closure notice had been properly served for the purposes of s.4(5)(a), the position of both the principal and other occupiers was relevant but that did not result in any strict requirement that the other occupiers be served with a notice prior to issue of the complaint. It was necessary to consider the intention behind the legislation, specifically to ensure that such other occupiers had an opportunity to be heard. On the facts, O had become aware of the proceedings by virtue of the notice served upon M and had subsequently attended the initial hearing which had then been adjourned in order that a further notice might be served. Accordingly the requirements for service had been met, *R. v. Secretary of State for the Home*

Department, ex p. Jeyeanthan [2000] 1 W.L.R. 354, [1999] C.L.Y. 3162 applied.

WESTMINSTER CITY COUNCIL v. MENDOZA, [2001] EWCA Civ 216, [2001] E.H.L.R. 16, Lord Woolf of Barnes, L.C.J., CA.

4381. Local elections – electoral process – transfer of functions

LOCAL GOVERNMENT COMMISSION FOR ENGLAND (TRANSFER OF FUNCTIONS) ORDER 2001, SI 2001 3962; made under the Political Parties, Elections and Referendums Act 2000 s.18, s.156. In force: April 1, 2002; £2.50.

This Order, which amends the Local Government Act 1972, the Local Government Act 1992, the Local Government and Rating Act 1997 and the Greater London Authority Act 1999, makes provision for the transfer to the Electoral Commission of all the functions of the Local Government Commission for England and of the functions of the Secretary of State in relation to local government and London Assembly electoral changes.

4382. Local elections – Forest of Dean

DISTRICT OF FOREST OF DEAN (ELECTORAL CHANGES) ORDER 2001, SI 2001 3880; made under the Local Government Act 1992 s.17, s.26. In force: in accordance with Art.1 (2); £2.00.

This Order, which revokes the Forest of Dean (Electoral Arrangements) Order 1980 (SI 1980 43), gives effect to recommendations by the Local Government Commission for England for electoral changes in the district of Forest of Dean. It abolishes the existing wards of the district and provides for the creation of 27 new wards, provides for the election of all councillors of the district of Forest of Dean to take place in 2003 and every four years after that year and makes electoral changes in the parishes of Coleford, Cinderford, Drybrook, Lydney, Newent and West Dean. The changes have effect in relation to local government elections to be held on and after May 1, 2003.

4383. Local elections – postponement provisions – local authority meetings

ELECTIONS ACT 2001 (SUPPLEMENTAL PROVISIONS) ORDER 2001, SI 2001 1630; made under the Elections Act 2001 s.7. In force: May 25, 2001; £1.50.

The Elections Act 2001 postponed certain local government elections from May 3, 2001 to June 7, 2001. This postponement also has an impact on the dates by which annual meeting must be held by joint authorities and certain parish and community councils. This Order amends the Local Government Act 1972 in relation to such meetings. The date by which a joint authority or police authority must hold its annual meeting in 2001 is extended to August 31, and the date by which a parish or community council which is not holding ordinary elections in 2001 must hold its annual meeting is extended to the end of June.

4384. Local Government Act 2000 (c.22) – Commencement No.2 Order – Wales

LOCAL GOVERNMENT ACT 2000 (COMMENCEMENT) (NO.2) (WALES) ORDER 2001, SI 2001 1471 (W.97; C.51); made under the Local Government Act 2000 s.108. Commencement details: bringing into force various provsions of the Act on April 9, 2001; £2.00.

This Order brings into force those provisions of the Local Government Act 2000 Part I which are not yet in force on April 9, 2001.

4385. Local Government Act 2000 (c.22) – Commencement No.6 Order

LOCAL GOVERNMENT ACT 2000 (COMMENCEMENT NO.6) ORDER 2001, SI 2001 415 (C.19); made under the Local Government Act 2000 s.108.

Commencement details: bringing into force various provisions of the Act on February 19, 2001; £1.75.

This Order brings the remaining provisions of the Local Government Act 2000 s.45 and all the provisions relating to allowances and pensions for local authority members contained in s.99 and s.100 of the Act, with the exception of the abolition of the attendance allowance which is currently payable under the Local Government and Housing Act 1989 s.18 on February 19, 2001 into force on February 19, 2001.

4386. Local Government Act 2000 (c.22) – Commencement No.7 Order – England

LOCAL GOVERNMENT ACT 2000 (COMMENCEMENT NO.7) ORDER 2001, SI 2001 2684 (C.89); made under the Local Government Act 2000 s.108. Commencement details: bringing into force various provisions of the Act on August 1, 2001; £1.75.

This Order brings into force specified provisions of the Local Government Act 2000 relating to the supply of information about welfare benefits to certain local authorities and providers of welfare services in connection with grants paid on August 1, 2001.

4387. Local government finance – allocation of grants – council tax calculations

GREATER LONDON AUTHORITY (ALLOCATION OF GRANTS FOR PRECEPT CALCULATIONS) REGULATIONS 2001, SI 2001 320; made under the Greater London Authority Act 1999 s.88, s.89. In force: February 10, 2001; £1.50.

These Regulations prescribe the amounts of redistributed non-domestic rates and specified grants, which the Secretary of State considers relate to the police and non-police expenditure of the Greater London Authority and functional bodies, which the Greater London Authority must take into account when carrying out the calculations of the amounts of council tax for the two parts of Greater London for the financial year beginning on April 1, 2001.

4388. Local government finance – budget requirements – amendment to calculations

LOCAL AUTHORITIES (ALTERATIONS OF REQUISITE CALCULATIONS) (ENGLAND) REGULATIONS 2001, SI 2001 216; made under the Local Government Finance Act 1992 s.32, s.33, s.43, s.44; and the Greater London Authority Act 1999 s.86, s.89. In force: February 2, 2001; £1.75.

These Regulations, which apply for the financial year beginning on April 1, 2001, modify various provisions of the Local Government Act 1992 and the Greater London Authority Act 1999, which set out how billing authorities and major precepting authorities are to calculate their budget requirements and the basic amount of their council tax, to provide for the limitation of council tax benefit subsidy.

4389. Local government finance – budget requirements – amendment to calculations – Wales

LOCAL AUTHORITIES (ALTERATION OF REQUISITE CALCULATIONS) (WALES) REGULATIONS 2001, SI 2001 559 (W.24); made under the Local Government Finance Act 1992 s.32, s.33. In force: February 28, 2001; £1.75.

The Local Government Finance Act 1992 s.32 and s.33 set out how a billing authority is to calculate its budget requirement and the basic amount of its council tax for a financial year. These Regulations amend the definition of "relevant special grant" in s.32(12) for the financial year beginning on April 1, 2001 in relation to Wales only.

4390. **Local government finance – budget requirements – calculation of payments**

MAJOR PRECEPTING AUTHORITIES (EXCESSIVE BUDGET REQUIREMENTS - PAYMENTS) (ENGLAND) REGULATIONS 2001, SI 2001 219; made under the Local Government Act 1999 s.31. In force: February 22, 2001; £2.00.

These Regulations contain provisions for the calculation and timing of payments which must be made by a major precepting authority whose budget requirement is excessive to each billing authority to which the precepting authority may issue a precept.

4391. **Local government finance – capital finance – investments and contracts**

LOCAL AUTHORITIES (CAPITAL FINANCE, APPROVED INVESTMENTS AND CONTRACTS -AMENDMENT) (ENGLAND) REGULATIONS 2001, SI 2001 723; made under the Local Government and Housing Act 1989 s.48, s.49, s.66, Sch.3 para.10, Sch.3 para.15; and the Local Government (Contracts) Act 1997 s.3. In force: April 1, 2001; £1.75.

These Regulations amend the Local Authorities (Capital Finance) Regulations 1997 (SI 1997 2862), the Local Authorities (Capital Finance) (Approved Investments) Regulations 1990 (SI 1990 426) and the Local Authorities (Capital Finance) Regulations 1997 (SI 1997 319) to make a number of amendments to the capital finance system resulting from the implementation of the Access to Justice Act 1999 which establishes the Greater London Magistrates' Courts Authority.

4392. **Local government finance – housing revenue account – electronic notification of decisions – Wales**

LOCAL GOVERNMENT AND HOUSING ACT 1989 (ELECTRONIC COMMUNICATIONS) (WALES) ORDER 2001, SI 2001 605 (W.28); made under the Electronic Communications Act 2000 s.8, s.10. In force: April 1, 2001; £2.00.

This Order allows the National Assembly for Wales, to use electronic communications to notify a local housing authority of its final decision, under the Local Government and Housing Act 1989 s.80A, as to the amount of housing revenue account subsidy payable to that authority for the year, or to publish the decision on a website and notify the authority that it has done so, where the decision may be found and how it may be accessed, if it has agreed to do so with the authority. In addition, it amends the 1989 Act to allow the Assembly to use electronic communications to send to a local housing authority a copy of any determination made under Part VI of that Act and to discharge the Assembly's obligation to send a copy of a determination to an authority by publishing the determination on a website and notifying the authority that it may be found there, and how it may be accessed there, if the Assembly has so agreed with the authority.

4393. **Medway Council Act 2001 (c.iv)**

This Act provides for the regulation of dealers in secondhand goods and the regulation of occasional sales and certain other trading in the borough of Medway.

This Act received Royal Assent on April 10, 2001 and comes into force on April 10, 2001.

4394. **National Assembly for Wales – South Wales Sea Fisheries Committtee – substituted levies – Wales**

SOUTH WALES SEA FISHERIES COMMITTEE (LEVIES) REGULATIONS 2001, SI 2001 3811 (W.316); made under the Local Government Finance Act 1988 s.74, s.143. In force: November 30, 2001; £1.75.

The Local Government Finance Act 1988 gives the National Assembly for Wales power to make Regulations in relation to levying bodies including the Committee of the South Wales Sea Fisheries District. These Regulations permit the South Wales

Sea Fisheries Committee to issue substituted levies to its Constituent Councils and to Rhondda CynonTaff County Borough Council for the financial year 2001-2002. These new levies will replace those previously issued. In the case of Rhondda Cynon Taff the substituted levy will be nil whilst for the other councils the figures will be adjusted in line with the Order.

4395. National parks – Broads Authorities – conduct – model codes of practice

NATIONAL PARK AND BROADS AUTHORITIES (MODEL CODE OF CONDUCT) (ENGLAND) ORDER 2001, SI 2001 3577; made under the Local Government Act 2000 s.50, s.81, s.105. In force: November 27, 2001; £2.00.

This Order contains a model code of conduct as regards the conduct expected of members and co-opted members of National Park authorities in England, and the Broads authority. Under the Local Government Act 2000 s.51, each relevant authority must adopt a code of conduct applying to its members which must incorporate any mandatory provisions of the model code and where an authority does not adopt such a code within six months of the Order coming into force, the mandatory provisions of the model code will apply to the members of the authority until it does.

4396. National parks – national park authorities – levies – Wales

NATIONAL PARK AUTHORITIES LEVIES (WALES) (AMENDMENT) REGULATIONS 2001, SI 2001 429 (W.19); made under the Local Government Finance Act 1988 s.74, s.140, s.143. In force: February 16, 2001; £2.00.

The National Park Authorities (Levies) (Wales) Regulations 1995 (SI 1995 3019) provide for the issue of levies by National Park Authorities to Welsh county or county borough councils as billing authorities for National Parks in Wales. These Regulations, which revoke the National Park Authorities Levies (Wales) (Amendment) Regulations 2000 (SI 2000 244), reinstate provisions of the 1995 Regulations which were revoked by the 2000 Regulations but without affecting the provisions for the financial year which began in 2000.

4397. Police authorities – conduct – model codes of practice

POLICE AUTHORITIES (MODEL CODE OF CONDUCT) ORDER 2001, SI 2001 3578; made under the Local Government Act 2000 s.50, s.81, s.105. In force: November 27, 2001; £2.00.

This Order contains a model code of conduct as regards the conduct expected of members and co-opted members of police authorities in England and Wales and the Metropolitan Police Authority. Under the Local Government Act 2000 s.51, each relevant authority must adopt a code of conduct applying to its members which must incorporate any mandatory provisions of the model code and where an authority does not adopt such a code within six months of the Order coming into force, the mandatory provisions of the model code will apply to the members of the authority until it does.

4398. Public authorities – conduct of members – code of practice

RELEVANT AUTHORITIES (GENERAL PRINCIPLES) ORDER 2001, SI 2001 1401; made under the Local Government Act 2000 s.49, s.105. In force: April 6, 2001; £1.75.

This Order specifies the principles to govern the conduct of members and co-opted members of relevant authorities in England and police authorities in Wales, in accordance with the Local Government Act 2000 s.49(1). It specifies the principles, and provides that the principles are expected to govern only the official conduct of members and co-opted members, apart from honesty and integrity and a duty to uphold the law, which have effect on all occasions.

4399. Public authorities – standards committees – code of practice

RELEVANT AUTHORITIES (STANDARDS COMMITTEE) REGULATIONS 2001, SI 2001 2812; made under the Local Government Act 2000 s.53, s.55, s.105. In force: August 28, 2001; £1.75.

These Regulations which apply to relevant authorities in England, other than parish councils, and to police authorities in Wales, set out additional compositional and procedural requirements on standards committees established under the Local Government Act 2000, make provision for the composition of standards committees and prescribe a minimum number of independent members and a maximum number of executive members. They also prescribe a procedure for the appointment of independent members, make transitional provision enabling authorities to retain certain standards committees already in existence before the commencement of the Act and require meetings of standards committees to have a quorum.

4400. Public nuisance – interim injunctions – injunctions in aid of criminal law

[Local Government Act 1972 s.222; Highways Act 1980 s.130, s.130(5).]

NCC appealed against a decision striking out its claim for injunctive relief sought under the Local Government Act 1972 s.222 in order to exclude a known drug dealer, Z, from a certain housing estate. The judge held that s.222 did not empower a local authority to commence proceedings unless it was under a duty to protect the inhabitants of the area, concluding that the NCC was under no obligation to enforce the criminal regime against drugs, and that such matters were for the police. NCC submitted that it was entitled to institute proceedings in its own name pursuant to s.222 since (1) drug dealing amounted a public nuisance, or (2) under the Highways Act 1980 s.130 it had a duty to protect the use and enjoyment of the highway, and Z's activities interfered with that use. Z argued that s.130(5) of the 1980 Act indicated that s.222 of the 1972 Act was not to be used in such highway cases.

Held, allowing the appeal, that (1) a local authority could bring proceedings in its own name for injunctive relief in order to restrain a public nuisance provided that it considered it "expedient to do so for the promotion and protection of the interests of the inhabitants" of its area pursuant to s.222 of the 1972 Act. It was arguable that local authorities could apply for injunctions to enforce the criminal law in all such cases. However, the courts should be cautious to allow such an exercise of power, *Stoke on Trent City Council v. B&Q (Retail) Ltd* [1984] A.C. 754, [1984] C.L.Y. 3231 considered. In the instant case, it was unnecessary to find whether drug dealing was a relevant public nuisance as NCC's claim succeeded on the basis of the 1980 Act, and (2) s.130(5) of the 1980 Act did not impinge on the powers of NCC under s.222 of the 1972 Act, and nothing within the provisions of s.130(5) indicated that s.222 could not be used in Highway Act cases.

NOTTINGHAM CITY COUNCIL v. Z (A CHILD), [2001] EWCA Civ 1248, [2002] 1 W.L.R. 607, Schiemann, L.J., CA.

4401. Supply of services – designation of public bodies

LOCAL AUTHORITIES (GOODS AND SERVICES) (PUBLIC BODIES) (ENGLAND) ORDER 2001, SI 2001 243; made under the Local Authorities (Goods and Services) Act 1970 s.1. In force: March 1, 2001; £1.50.

This Order designates persons of a specified description as public bodies for the purposes of the Local Authorities (Goods and Services) Act 1970. The effect of designation is to allow a local authority in England to provide goods and services to a designated body. The Order limits the agreements that English local authorities may make with persons who contract with a local education authority to carry out certain local education authority functions in consequence of a direction made by the Secretary of State under the Education Act 1996 s.497A.

4402. Supply of services – designation of public bodies

LOCAL AUTHORITIES (GOODS AND SERVICES) (PUBLIC BODIES) (ENGLAND) (NO.2) ORDER 2001, SI 2001 691; made under the Local Authorities (Goods and Services) Act 1970 s.1. In force: March 31, 2001; £1.75.

This Order designates New Schools (Cornwall) Ltd and the United Waste Services (South Gloucestershire) Ltd as public bodies under the Local Authorities (Goods and Services) Act 1970 s.1. The effect of designation is to allow local authorities to provide goods and services to the designated public bodies by way of an agreement for any of the purposes prescribed by that section. The Order imposes restrictions on the agreements that can be made by the bodies designated, in particular that only the named local authorities may provide services for the specified purposes to the appropriate designated public body within the area of that local authority.

4403. Supply of services – designation of public bodies

LOCAL AUTHORITIES (GOODS AND SERVICES) (PUBLIC BODIES) (ENGLAND) (NO.3) ORDER 2001, SI 2001 1823; made under the Local Authorities (Goods and Services) Act 1970 s.1. In force: May 31, 2001; £1.75.

This Order designates Thurrock Community Leisure Ltd, Care Plus Trust Ltd, and Paddington Development Trust as public bodies under the Local Authorities (Goods and Services) Act 1970 s.1 (5). The effect of designation is to allow local authorities to provide services and goods to the designated public bodies by way of an agreement for any of the purposes prescribed by s.1 (1) of that Act. The Order imposes restrictions on the agreements that can be made by the bodies designated, in particular that only the named local authorities may provide services for the specified purposes to the appropriate designated public body within the area of that local authority.

4404. Supply of services – designation of public bodies

LOCAL AUTHORITIES (GOODS AND SERVICES) (PUBLIC BODIES) (ENGLAND) (NO.4) ORDER 2001, SI 2001 3347; made under the Local Authorities (Goods and Services) Act 1970 s.1. In force: October 25, 2001; £1.50.

This Order designates Liverpool Direct Ltd, Schools PBS Ltd and Tynedale Housing Ltd as public bodies under the Local Authorities (Goods and Services) Act 1970 s.1 to allow local authorities to provide goods and services to the designated bodies by way of an agreement for any of the specified purposes. In addition, the Order provides that only the named local authorities may provide services for the specified purposes to the appropriate designated public body within the area of that local authority.

4405. Tenders – local authorities powers and duties – building contractors – removal from tender list – amenability to review

[Local Government Act 1988 s.20.]

DLB, building contractors, applied for judicial review of BCC's decision to remove DLB's name from all its housing services' approved lists of contractors. The decision had been taken following disputes arising from work commenced by DLB under contract with BCC in which BCC had alleged defects existed and had refused to settle the final account. DLB contended that BCC had failed to give valid and sufficient reasons for its decision under the Local Government Act 1988 s.20 and it was therefore unlawful. BCC resisted those contentions, submitting that (1) the decision was not of a type which was amenable to review, and (2) the decision had been taken on proper commercial grounds and the reasons given were sound.

Held, granting the application, that (1) BCC's decision was susceptible to review. The provision of reasons did not exclude review as DLB was entitled to a legitimate expectation of fair treatment, *R. v. Enfield LBC, ex p. TF Unwin (Roydon)* 46 B.L.R. 1, [1990] C.L.Y. 59 followed, and (2) as BCC's reasons for its decision did not stand up to critical scrutiny, it had no justification for striking

DLB off the list of approved tenderers. The problem had arisen owing to the chaotic manner in which BCC had administered the contract and to its failure to deal with any defects during the correct liability period. The decision was therefore quashed and DLB restored to the list.

R. v. BRISTOL CITY COUNCIL, *ex p.* DL BARRETT & SONS (2001) 3 L.G.L.R. 11, Jackson, J., QBD.

4406. Tenders – service contracts – contract for online recruitment service – classification

[Public Services Contracts Regulations 1993 (SI 1993 3228).]

D appealed against a decision that it had breached the Public Services Contracts Regulations 1993 in the tendering process it had used. D had issued a briefing document inviting tenders for the "development and management of an online recruitment service for the National Health Service", but had not shortlisted J following the submission of its tender. J claimed that D had wrongly categorised the service as a contract for recruitment services rather than for computer services and had followed the wrong procedure. The judge had found for J, extending time for its application on the basis that the cause of action had arisen when J was informed that its tender had failed. D argued that the tender was correct for recruitment services and that the cause of action had arisen when the briefing document was issued.

Held, allowing the appeal, that the application had been made out of time and the judge had erred by extending it, although he had been right to find that the tender was for computer services. The contract would be to provide the means by which D could recruit staff over the internet, with all the actual procedure of recruitment being undertaken by D. It would be nonsensical and against the spirit of the Regulations if computer services were only ever seen as the vehicle for the provision of other services. As the tender was for computer services, the procedure from the outset was in breach of the Regulations and therefore the cause of action had arisen when the briefing document was issued.

JOBSIN CO UK PLC (T/A INTERNET RECRUITMENT SOLUTIONS) v. DEPARTMENT OF HEALTH; *sub nom.* JOBSIN.CO.UK PLC v. DEPARTMENT OF HEALTH, [2001] EWCA Civ 1241, [2002] 1 C.M.L.R. 44, Dyson, L.J., CA.

4407. Transport policy – public transport – duty of government bodies to act in accordance with Mayor of London's policy

See TRANSPORT: R. (on the application of Transport for London) v. London Underground Ltd. §5448

4408. Books

Collins, Scott; Colville, Iain; Pengelly, Sarah – Guide to the Greater London Authority Act. Hardback: £48.00. ISBN 0-421-72700-4. Sweet & Maxwell.

Federal Regulatory Directory 10th Ed. Hardback: £130.50. ISBN 1-56802-503-3. CQ Press.

Selman, Andy; Hunter, Caroline – Best Value in Housing Management: Law and Practice in the Management of Social Housing. Arden's Housing Library. Paperback: £18.95. ISBN 1-898001-70-7. Lemos & Crane.

MEDIA

4409. **Advertising – Advertising Standards Authority – adjudications – freedom of expression – adjudications "prescribed by law"**

[Control of Misleading Advertisements Regulations 1988 (SI 1988 915); European Convention on Human Rights 1950 Art.10, Art.10(2).]

MR applied for permission to move for judicial review of the decision of the ASA to publish an adjudication of a complaint made against MR and the subsequent refusal of the Independent Reviewer of the ASA to reconsider that adjudication. A local health authority had made a complaint about an advertising leaflet published by MR marketing various health products. The ASA having made its adjudication pursuant to the British Codes of Advertising and Sales Promotion (10th edition 1999), MR sought to halt publication of the adjudication on the grounds that its publication would be contrary to their right to freedom of expression under the European Convention on Human Rights 1950 Art.10 and would damage their standing. MR submitted that the adjudication did not fall within the exceptions contained in Art.10(2) since it was not "prescribed by law".

Held, refusing the application, that the adjudications of the ASA published under the Codes were "prescribed by law" for the purposes of Art.10(2). The Control of Misleading Advertisements Regulations 1988 provided statutory recognition of accepted methods for handling complaints. It was therefore apparent that the Codes were recognised within subordinate legislation. They also satisfied the requirements of accessibility and precision set out in *Barthold v. Germany (A/90)* (1985) 7 E.H.R.R. 383. Accordingly, whilst not having direct statutory effect, the Codes fell within the meaning of Art.10(2). Furthermore, in the instant case the adjudications were, for the purpose of Art.10(2), "necessary for the protection of health".

R. (ON THE APPLICATION OF MATTHIAS RATH BV) v. ADVERTISING STANDARDS AUTHORITY LTD; *sub nom.* R. v. ADVERTISING STANDARDS AUTHORITY LTD, *ex p.* MATTHIAS RATH BV [2001] E.M.L.R. 22, Turner, J., QBD (Admin Ct).

4410. **Broadcasting – digital television – limit on multiplex services**

BROADCASTING (LIMIT ON THE HOLDING OF LICENCES TO PROVIDE TELEVISION MULTIPLEX SERVICES) ORDER 2001, SI 2001 223; made under the Broadcasting Act 1990 Sch.2 Part III. In force: January 31, 2001; £1.50.

This Order changes the limit on the number of licences to provide television multiplex services which a person may at any time hold, from three to six.

4411. **Broadcasting – digital television – subtitling**

BROADCASTING (SUBTITLING) ORDER 2001, SI 2001 2378; made under the Broadcasting Act 1996 s.21. In force: July 4, 2001; £1.50.

This Order amends the Broadcasting Act 1996 s.20(3)(a) to increase from 50 to 80 the specified percentage in relation to subtitling for the deaf on digital programme services. This means the the relevant code published by the Independent Television Commission must require that, as from the 10th anniversary of the date of commencement of the provision of any digital programme service, at least 80 per cent of that service's non-excluded programmes in each week must be accompanied by such subtitling. Excluded programmes consist of those in relation to which the Commission considers it to be inappropriate for the requirement to apply.

4412. Broadcasting – football – events of national interest – exclusive broadcast to Member State – refusal of consent by ITC – European Community

[Broadcasting Act 1996 s.101B; Council Directive 97/36 amending Council Directive 89/552 Art.3a; Council Directive 89/552 concerning the pursuit of television broadcasting activities.]

ITC appealed against an order ([2000] 1 W.L.R. 74, [2000] C.L.Y. 4150) allowing an appeal by T, a UK broadcaster, against the refusal of its application for judicial review of the refusal of ITC to give consent to T to televise in Denmark live football matches involving the Danish national team. The matches had been designated by the Danish government as events of national interest, pursuant to Council Directive 97/36 Art.3(a)(1). T had acquired the rights to broadcast the matches live but, because it was only able to transmit the matches to 60 per cent of the Danish public, it required the consent of ITC to the broadcast pursuant to the Broadcasting Act 1996 s.101B. The Danish Ministry of Culture indicated that, because T had not made an offer to share the rights with other broadcasters in accordance with the Danish regulatory system, the broadcast by T would contravene Art.3a(3) of the Directive. ITC refused consent. The Court of Appeal accepted T's submission that, since there had been a fair auction in which public broadcasters had been entitled to participate in accordance with the ITC Code, the refusal of consent by ITC had been unreasonable.

Held, allowing the appeal, that the purpose of Art.3(a)(3) of the Directive was to protect the public interest by preventing broadcasters from exercising exclusive rights in a manner which deprived a substantial part of the public of another Member State of the opportunity to watch an event of national interest. When determining whether to grant consent to the broadcast of the live matches into Denmark pursuant to s.101B(1) of the Act, the ITC Code did not require ITC to give consent to the highest bidder in a free and open competition, nor did any legitimate expectation arise that consent would be granted in such circumstances. Art.3(a)(3) envisaged the harmonisation of regulations between states so far as possible so that T was obliged to take account of the Danish system of regulation and ITC had paid proper regard to T's failure to offer to share the transmission rights with other broadcasters.

R. (ON THE APPLICATION OF TVDANMARK 1 LTD) v. INDEPENDENT TELEVISION COMMISSION; *sub nom.* R. v. INDEPENDENT TELEVISION COMMISSION, *ex p.* TVDANMARK 1 LTD; R. (ON THE APPLICATION OF TV DANMARK 1 LTD) v. INDEPENDENT TELEVISION COMMISSION; TVDANMARK 1 LTD v. INDEPENDENT TELEVISION COMMISSION, [2001] UKHL 42, [2001] 1 W.L.R. 1604, Lord Hoffmann, HL.

4413. Confidential information – medical records – disclosure of source's identity – court's jurisdiction in equity and tort

[Contempt of Court Act 1981 s.10; European Convention on Human Rights 1950 Art.10.]

MGN, a newspaper group, appealed against an order that it disclose the identity of an intermediary who had supplied information relating to a well known offender from the database of A, a special security hospital. MGN contended that (1) the court lacked the requisite tortious jurisdiction to make such an order, *Norwich Pharmacal Co v. Customs and Excise Commissioners* [1974] A.C. 133, [1973] C.L.Y. 2643 and *Broadmoor Special Hospital Authority v. R* [2000] Q.B. 775, [2000] 2 C.L. 423 referred to, and (2) the order infringed both the Contempt of Court Act 1981 s.10 and the European Convention on Human Rights 1950 Art.10. A countered that, following the principle in *Norwich Pharmacal*, where a person became involved in the tortious acts of others there was a duty upon that person to disclose the identity of the wrongdoer.

Held, dismissing the appeal, that (1) jurisdiction to order the disclosure of the identity of a wrongdoer did not have to be confined to cases involving tort but should be of general application, *Norwich Pharmacal* applied, and (2) the exercise of the court's jurisdiction was not precluded by the provisions of the 1981 Act or the Convention. In interpreting s.10 of the Act the court should, where possible, (a) equate the specific purposes for which disclosure of the source was permitted under s.10 with "legitimate aims" under Art.10 of the Convention, and (b) apply the same test of necessity as that applied by the European court. Applying that test to the instant case, it was found that the disclosure of confidential medical records to the press was misconduct which was contrary to the public interest.

ASHWORTH HOSPITAL AUTHORITY v. MGN LTD; *sub nom.* ASHWORTH SECURITY HOSPITAL v. MGN LTD [2001] 1 W.L.R. 515, Lord Phillips of Worth Matravers, M.R., CA.

4414. Confidential information – newspapers – variation of undertaking – publication of information already in public domain

The Attorney General appealed against a decision to allow an application by TN and two of its journalists to vary their undertaking not to publish confidential information provided by RT, a former officer of the Special Intelligence Service, after he published a book in English which was available in Europe, the United States and on the internet. The variation allowed TN to republish previously published information which was considered to be in the public domain. The Attorney General submitted that the variation should contain a proviso that TN obtain clearance from the court or the Attorney General before publishing the information.

Held, dismissing the appeal, that it was not just to impose on TN the need to obtain confirmation from the Attorney General or the court that information it wanted to republish was in the public domain so that the cloak of confidentiality had been lifted. It was for the newspaper's editor to judge whether the information should be republished and the existing variation imposed a duty to comply with the law of confidentiality. Anything beyond that was a fetter on TN's freedom of expression.

ATTORNEY GENERAL v. TIMES NEWSPAPERS LTD; *sub nom.* ATTORNEY GENERAL v. KELSEY; ATTORNEY GENERAL v. LEPPARD, [2001] EWCA Civ 97, [2001] 1 W.L.R. 885, Lord Phillips of Worth Matravers, M.R., CA.

4415. Confidential information – privacy – sexual relationships – right of participants to confidentiality

A, a married sportsman, sought an injunction to prevent a newspaper from printing details of his sexual encounters with two women. A contended that a duty of confidentiality existed between the parties to a sexual relationship, even in the absence of any agreement to keep the fact of the relationship, or details of the sexual activity within it, confidential.

Held, granting the application, that in the absence of any agreement between the participants to keep the facts or detail of their relationship secret, the law could nevertheless recognise an obligation of confidentiality preventing disclosure. That duty arose in circumstances where the information was of a confidential nature, arising in circumstances importing an obligation of confidentiality, of which there had been unauthorised use, *Coco v. AN Clark (Engineers) Ltd* [1968] F.S.R. 415, [1968] C.L.Y. 1458 applied. It was appropriate to afford protection to relationships both within and outside marriage and the precise scope of such a duty would depend on the facts of each particular case. It was clear that the information in question had no possible public interest justification and was not in the public domain. It was also likely that A would succeed in establishing that his right to privacy should outweigh the newspaper's right to freedom of expression. Accordingly injunctive relief was granted as against the newspaper and also against the women concerned, preventing them from making any disclosure with a view to publication.

A v. B PLC; *sub nom.* A v. B (A FIRM) [2001] 1 W.L.R. 2341, Jack, J., QBD.

4416. Films – cinematic co-production agreements – additional countries – Malta and France

EUROPEAN CONVENTION ON CINEMATOGRAPHIC CO-PRODUCTION (AMENDMENT) (NO.2) ORDER 2001, SI 2001 3931; made under the Films Act 1985 Sch.1 para.4. In force: Art.4: March 1, 2002; remainder: January 1, 2002; £1.50.

This Order amends the European Convention on Cinematographic Co-production Order 1994 (SI 1994 1065) by adding Malta and France to the list of countries set out in the Schedule.

4417. Films – cinematic co-production agreements – additional county – Cyprus

EUROPEAN CONVENTION ON CINEMATOGRAPHIC CO-PRODUCTION (AMENDMENT) ORDER 2001, SI 2001 411; made under the Films Act 1985 Sch.1 para.4. In force: March 1, 2001; £1.50.

This Order amends the the European Convention on Cinematographic Co-production Order 1994 (SI 1994 1065) by adding Cyprus to the list of countries set out in the Schedule.

4418. Harassment – newspapers – foreseeability that publication of articles would provoke racist reaction

[Protection from Harassment Act 1997 s.1.(1).]

N, the publisher of "The Sun" newspaper, appealed against the dismissal of its application to strike out T's claim for harassment in respect of the publication of a series of newspaper articles. N contended that T's claim disclosed no reasonable prospects of success on the ground that the newspaper articles had not constituted the requisite course of conduct for the purposes of the Protection from Harassment Act 1997 s.1 (1). T argued that the articles had unnecessarily referred to her as "a black clerk" and, further, had suggested that, had it not been for her race, two police officers would not have been subject to disciplinary proceedings over remarks made about a third party in T's presence.

Held, dismissing the appeal, that the publication of a series of articles in a newspaper could constitute a course of conduct amounting to harassment for the purposes of s.1 (1) of the Act. On the facts of the instant case, it was foreseeable that the articles in question would have been likely to provoke a racist reaction and that as a result, T would have been caused distress.

THOMAS v. NEWS GROUP NEWSPAPERS LTD; *sub nom*. THOMAS v. HUGHES; THOMAS v. NEWS GROUP INTERNATIONAL LTD, [2001] EWCA Civ 1233, [2002] E.M.L.R. 4, Lord Phillips of Worth Matravers, M.R., CA.

4419. Newspapers – celebrities – injunction restraining publication of address – compatibility with right to freedom of expression

See HUMAN RIGHTS: Mills v. News Group Newspapers Ltd. §3577

4420. Satellite television – broadcasts – transmission of pornography – direct effect – European Community

[Foreign Satellite Service Proscription Order 1998 (SI 1998 1865); EC Treaty Art.173 (now, after amendment, Art.230).]

DSTV, a Danish satellite broadcasting company engaged in the transmission of pornography via its service "Eurotica Rendez-Vous", sought the annulment under EC Treaty Art.173 (now, after amendment, Art.230) of a decision of the Commission to the effect that steps taken by the UK government to prevent transmission to the UK were not discriminatory, were appropriate given the need to protect minors, and were compatible with Community law. The UK government had passed the Foreign Satellite Service Proscription Order 1998 which had the effect of making it an offence to supply equipment or goods relating to "Eurotica Rendez-Vous", or to advertise the service or publish the times of its programmes. DSTV contended that for the purposes of Art.173 of the Treaty it was directly affected by the decision having regard to the fact that as a result of the decision the 1998 Order was thereby validated.

Held, dismissing the application, that DSTV was not directly affected by the decision for the purposes of Art.173 of the Treaty since in order to be so affected, the measure in question had to directly affect the legal situation of the applicant and its implementation had to be the automatic result of the implementation of Community rules alone without the application of other intermediate rules. On the facts of the instant case, the Order was effective as a matter of law independently of the decision under challenge and accordingly DSTV was unable to establish that it had been directly affected for the purposes of Art.173, *Societe Louis Dreyfus & Cie v. Commission of the European Communities (C386/96)* [1996] E.C.R. II-1101 applied.

DANISH SATELLITE TV A/S (EUROTICA RENDEZ VOUS TELEVISION) v. COMMISSION OF THE EUROPEAN COMMUNITIES (T69/99) [2001] All E.R. (EC) 577, Judge Pirrung (President), CFI.

4421. Books

Fosbrook, Deborah and Laing, Adrian C – Media Contracts Handbook. 2nd Ed. Hardback: £210.00. ISBN 0-421-66130-5. Sweet & Maxwell.

Gallant, Simon; Epworth, Jennifer – Media Law and Risk Management: a Practical Guide. Hardback: £85.00. ISBN 0-421-59820-4. Sweet & Maxwell.

Greenfield, Steve; Robson, Peter; Osborn, Guy – Film and the Law. Paperback: £49.50. ISBN 1-85941-639-X. Cavendish Publishing Ltd.

Price, Monroe E.; Verhulst, Stefaan – Parental Control of Television Broadcasting. LEA'S Communication Series. Hardback: £63.95. ISBN 0-8058-2978-4. Paperback: £31.95. ISBN 0-8058-3902-X. Lawrence Erlbaum Associates, Inc.

Sadler, Pauline – National Security and the D-Notice System. Hardback: £50.00. ISBN 0-7546-2170-7. Dartmouth.

Stamatoudi, Irina – Copyright and Multimedia Products. Cambridge Studies in Intellectual Property Rights. Hardback: £55.00. ISBN 0-521-80819-7. Cambridge University Press.

MENTAL HEALTH

4423. Mental health review tribunals – adjournments – restricted patients – tribunal's power to make recommendations

[Mental Health Act 1983 s.72, s.78(2)(j); Mental Health Review Tribunal Rules 1983 (SI 1983 942) r.16(1).]

The Secretary of State sought judicial review of a decision of the Mental Health Review Tribunal to adjourn a case involving a restricted patient in order to consider making a recommendation that the patient be transferred to a less secure hospital. The Secretary of State submitted that the tribunal had no express power under the Mental Health Act 1983 to make such a recommendation, the general powers of the tribunal, contained in s.72 of the Act, being disapplied in relation to restricted patients. It was argued that the tribunal accordingly had no power to adjourn a case in order to consider making a recommendation. The tribunal maintained that it did have power to adjourn pursuant to s.78(2)(j) of the Act and under the Mental Health Review Tribunal Rules 1983 r.16(1).

Held, granting the application, that the tribunal had no express statutory power to make a recommendation in the case of a restricted patient. However, there was no provision which specifically prohibited the tribunal from making recommendations and it should not be inhibited from so doing in appropriate cases. The power of the tribunal to adjourn under r.16(1) of the Rules was to be construed in the context of the 1983 Act. Accordingly, the tribunal could only adjourn to enable it to carry out its statutory powers and it had therefore fallen into error in adjourning for the purpose of considering a recommendation, *R. v. Oxford Regional Mental Health Review Tribunal, ex p. Secretary of State for the*

Home Department [1986] 1 W.L.R. 1180, [1986] C.L.Y. 2139 and *R. v. Nottingham Mental Health Review Tribunal, ex p. Secretary of State for the Home Department* [1989] C.O.D. 221, [1988] C.L.Y. 2270 applied.

R. (ON THE APPLICATION OF SECRETARY OF STATE FOR THE HOME DEPARTMENT) v. MENTAL HEALTH REVIEW TRIBUNAL; *sub nom.* R. v. MENTAL HEALTH REVIEW TRIBUNAL FOR NORTH EAST THAMES REGION, *ex p.* SECRETARY OF STATE FOR THE HOME DEPARTMENT (2002) 63 B.M.L.R. 181, Collins, J., QBD (Admin Ct).

4424. Mental health review tribunals – hearings – delay in hearing patient's application for discharge – right to liberty and security

[Mental Health Act 1983 s.3; Human Rights Act 1998 Sch.1 Part I Art.5(4).]

C, who suffered from schizophrenia and had been detained in hospital under the Mental Health Act 1983 s.3, appealed against the refusal ([2001] A.C.D. 63) of his application for judicial review of the practice of the Mental Health Appeal Tribunal of listing hearings of applications for discharge eight weeks after the application had been made. C submitted that the practice was both arbitrary and did not satisfy the Human Rights Act 1998 Sch.1 Part I Art.5(4) which specified that the lawfulness of a detention should be determined "speedily".

Held, allowing the appeal, that in cases such as the instant case, where a patient was represented by a solicitor experienced in mental health who requested an early hearing date of an application for discharge, there was no reason to refuse that request. The practice of listing hearings eight weeks after an application stemmed from convenience rather than necessity. A target date of eight weeks was not inconsistent with the 1998 Act, given that some cases required such time for preparation. However, the policy of having an eight week lead time for applications made by patients detained under s.3 of the 1983 Act made no attempt to ensure that individual applications were heard as soon as reasonably practicable. Such an approach was not compatible with the approach adopted by the European Court of Human Rights and would result in some applications not being resolved speedily thereby, as in the instant case, breaching Art.5(4), *Sanchez-Reisse v. Switzerland (A/107)* (1987) 9 E.H.R.R. 71, [1986] C.L.Y. 1651 and *Bezicheri v. Italy (A/164)* (1990) 12 E.H.R.R. 210 applied.

R. (ON THE APPLICATION OF C) v. MENTAL HEALTH REVIEW TRIBUNAL; *sub nom.* R. (ON THE APPLICATION OF C) v. LONDON SOUTH AND SOUTH WEST REGION MENTAL HEALTH REVIEW TRIBUNAL, [2001] EWCA Civ 1110, [2002] 1 W.L.R. 176, Lord Phillips of Worth Matravers, M.R., CA.

4425. Mental health review tribunals – mental patients – discharge followed by fresh detention – natural justice

[Mental Health Act 1983 s.3, s.37.]

DE, a convicted mental patient, appealed against a decision of the High Court ([2001] EWHC Admin 312) quashing an order of the Mental Health Review Tribunal. The order discharged DE under the Mental Health Act 1983 s.37 and detained him afresh pursuant to the provisions of s.3 of that Act. DE submitted that the High Court's decision amounted to a breach of natural justice because it effectively quashed an acquittal.

Held, dismissing the appeal, that there had been no breach of natural justice since the effect of the High Court's decision was to invalidate an unlawful decision of an inferior tribunal, *F Hoffmann La Roche & Co AG v. Secretary of State for Trade and Industry* [1975] A.C. 295, [1974] C.L.Y. 3801 applied. The effect of quashing the order was to retrospectively invalidate an unlawful act since it was a well established principle of public law that although there existed a presumption that an administrative act would be presumed lawful until it was pronounced unlawful, once the act was impugned it would then be recognised as never having any legal effect at all, *Boddington v. British Transport Police* [1999] 2 A.C.143, [1998] C.L.Y. 89 applied.

R. (ON THE APPLICATION OF WIRRAL HA) v. MENTAL HEALTH REVIEW TRIBUNAL; R. (ON THE APPLICATION OF WIRRAL HA) v. FINNEGAN, [2001] EWCA Civ 1901,*The Times*, November 26, 2001, Dyson, L.J., CA.

4426. **Mental hospitals – hospital authority – abolition – Broadmoor**

BROADMOOR HOSPITAL AUTHORITY (ABOLITION) ORDER 2001, SI 2001 834; made under the National Health Service Act 1977 s.11, s.126. In force: April 1, 2001; £1.75.

This Order abolishes, on April 1, 2001, the Broadmoor Hospital Authority, a special health authority established under the National Health Service Act 1977 s.11 by the Authorities for the Ashworth, Broadmoor and Rampton Hospital Authorities (Establishment and Constitution) Order 1996 (SI 1996 488). In addition, it makes provision for the transfer of officers, property, rights and liabilities of the Authority and for the winding up of its affairs.

4427. **Mental hospitals – hospital authority – abolition – Rampton**

RAMPTON HOSPITAL AUTHORITY (ABOLITION) ORDER 2001, SI 2001 714; made under the National Health Service Act 1977 s.11, s.126. In force: April 1, 2001; £1.75.

This Order abolishes, on April 1, 2001, the Rampton Hospital Authority, a Special Health Authority established under the National Health Service Act 1977 s.11 by the Authorities for the Ashworth, Broadmoor and Rampton Hospital Authorities (Establishment and Constitution) Order 1996 (SI 1996 488). It makes provision for the transfer of officers, property, rights and liabilities of the Authority and for the winding-up of its affairs. In addition, it makes amendments to the Ashworth, Broadmoor and Rampton Hospital Authorities (Functions and Membership) Regulations 1996 (SI 1996 489) by omitting "Rampton" from the definition of "the hospitals".

4428. **Mental patients – classification – mental health review tribunal decision – purported reclassification by responsible medical officer**

[Mental Health Act 1983 s.3, s.16.]

W applied for judicial review of a decision of a doctor, O, to classify him under the Mental Health Act 1983 as suffering from "mental illness and psychopathic disorder". W was detained in 1996 under s.3 and classified as having a mental illness. In October 1997, O reclassified him as having a psychopathic disorder and W appealed to the Mental Health Tribunal. His appeal was successful, but shortly afterwards O, purportedly relying on his powers as responsible medical officer under s.16, reclassified W as having a psychopathic disorder for a second time.

Held, allowing the application, that O had no power to reclassify following the tribunal's decision. The right of appeal to the tribunal was an important protection of the patient's rights, which could not be randomly overridden by doctors unless new circumstances came to light, which had not occurred in the instant case.

R. v. PATHFINDER NHS TRUST, *ex p.* W (2000) 3 C.C.L. Rep. 271, Kay, J., QBD.

4429. **Mental patients – compulsory admissions – requirement for change in circumstances for readmission following discharge**

[Mental Health Act 1983 s.2, s.3, s.13; Human Rights Act 1998 Sch.1 Part I Art.5(1), Art.5(4).]

B, a mental patient, appealed against a refusal to grant judicial review of a decision made pursuant to the Mental Health Act 1983 s.3 to detain him in hospital after a mental health review tribunal had ordered his discharge. B submitted that (1) properly construed, the Act implied an obligation to demonstrate a relevant change of circumstances before an application for compulsory re-admission could be made in respect of a patient who had been discharged by a tribunal, and that in the absence of such an obligation, the tribunal would be deprived of its status as a court, and (2) it would constitute a violation of the Human Rights Act 1998 Sch.1 Part I Art.5(1) if the relevant professionals could override a tribunal's decision to discharge.

Held, dismissing the appeal, that (1) the professionals concerned in an application under s.2 or s.3 of the Act were not bound by an earlier tribunal decision as the nature of mental illness made fluctuations in the need for treatment inevitable, *R. v. Managers of South Western Hospital, ex p. M* [1993] Q.B. 683, [1994] C.L.Y. 3062 followed. As a general rule it was sufficient for the relevant professionals to act objectively and bona fide, and there was no requirement to prove a change of circumstances. Where, however, an application was made only days after a tribunal's decision to discharge a patient, particularly if the patient's environmental circumstances had not changed, it suggested a conflict of opinion between the patient's professional team and the tribunal as to whether or not the criteria justifying detention had been satisfied. In those circumstances, the opinion of the tribunal prevailed and unless there were facts which the tribunal had not been made aware of and which, once drawn to its attention, would invalidate its decision, an application under s.13 of the Act should be held unlawful on the ground of irrationality, and (2) the tribunal was sufficiently similar to a court for the purposes of Art.5(4) and there was no incompatibility between the sections of the Act addressing the compulsory detention of a patient to a hospital and Art.5(1).

R. (ON THE APPLICATION OF B) v. EAST LONDON AND THE CITY MENTAL HEALTH NHS TRUST; *sub nom.* R. v. EAST LONDON AND THE CITY MENTAL HEALTH NHS TRUST, *ex p.* B; R. v. TOWER HAMLETS HEALTHCARE NHS TRUST, *ex p.* V; R. v. TOWER HAMLETS HEALTHCARE NHS TRUST, *ex p.* B, [2001] EWCA Civ 239, [2002] Q.B. 235, Lord Phillips of Worth Matravers, M.R., CA.

4430. **Mental patients – health authorities – conditions of discharge – obligation to comply**

[Mental Health Act 1983 s.37, s.41, s.117; Human Rights Act 1998 Sch.1 Part I Art.5.]

K, a restricted patient under the Mental Health Act 1983 s.37 and s.41, appealed against the refusal ((2000) 3 C.C.L. Rep. 256) of her application for judicial review. K had challenged the health authority's failure to provide her with supervision by a consultant forensic psychiatrist following a decision by a mental health review tribunal that she should be conditionally discharged to reside at her parent's home. K contended that (1) s.117 of the 1983 Act imposed an absolute obligation upon the health authority to comply with the requirements set by the tribunal as a condition of discharge, and (2) a failure to comply with the conditions would result in a breach of her right to liberty pursuant to the Human Rights Act 1998 Sch.1 Part I Art.5.

Held, dismissing the appeal, that (1) an absolute obligation was not expressly imposed by s.117 and could not reasonably be inferred. Whilst the section did impose an obligation to provide services for patients post discharge, the ambit of such services had to be a matter of discretion and would also necessarily be limited by budget constraints, and (2) where a health authority had used all reasonable endeavours to comply with the requirements imposed as a condition of discharge and had been unable to do so, the continued detention of a patient would not constitute a breach of Art.5.

R. (ON THE APPLICATION OF K) v. CAMDEN AND ISLINGTON HA; *sub nom.* R. v. CAMDEN AND ISLINGTON HA, *ex p.* K, [2001] EWCA Civ 240, [2002] Q.B. 198, Lord Phillips of Worth Matravers, M.R., CA.

4431. Mental patients – medical treatment – challenge to forcibly administered treatment – attendance of medical witnesses

[Human Rights Act 1998 s.7; European Convention on Human Rights 1950 Art.2, Art.3, Art.6, Art.8.]

W, a mental patient, appealed against the refusal of his application for medical witnesses to attend for cross-examination in judicial review proceedings brought by him concerning a decision to administer treatment without his consent and under restraint. In those proceedings, W sought to argue that the forcible administration of treatment infringed his rights under the European Convention on Human Rights 1950 Art.2, Art.3 and Art.8. W submitted that for the purposes of Art.6 of the Convention, the court would be required to reach its own conclusions as to the disputed issues of fact and that it was therefore essential that the medical witnesses attend and be cross-examined.

Held, allowing the appeal, that where a mental patient challenged the forcible administration of medical treatment, the court was entitled to reach its own view as to the merits of the medical decision and whether it infringed the patient's human rights. Accordingly, it was appropriate that medical witnesses attend and be cross-examined. In so requiring, the provisions of Art.6 of the Convention would be met. A mental patient was not entitled by virtue of Art.6 to challenge a treatment plan in advance to his being subjected to it; a medically justifiable decision to administer forcible treatment to a patient without prior warning was not, of itself, contrary to Art.6. In the opinion of Hale, L.J., whether the proceedings in relation to forcible treatment were brought in tort, under the Human Rights Act 1998 s.7(1), or by way of judicial review, if there were disputed issues of fact they needed to be determined, by cross-examination where necessary. Simon Brown, L.J. observed that the approach in *R. v. Collins, ex p. Brady* [2000] Lloyd's Rep. Med. 355, [2000] C.L.Y. 4172, a decision made prior to the 1998 Act coming into force, was no longer appropriate in the case of the forcible treatment of detained patients, *Herczegfalvy v. Austria (A/ 242B)* (1993) 15 E.H.R.R. 437, [1993] C.L.Y. 2154 and *Brady* considered.

R. (ON THE APPLICATION OF WILKINSON) v. BROADMOOR HOSPITAL; *sub nom.* R. (ON THE APPLICATION OF WILKINSON) v. BROADMOOR SPECIAL HOSPITAL AUTHORITY, [2001] EWCA Civ 1545, [2002] 1 W.L.R. 419, Simon Brown, L.J., CA.

4432. Mental patients rights – discharge – burden of proof on patient – incompatibility with right to liberty

[Mental Health Act 1983 s.72, s.73; Human Rights Act 1998 Sch.1 Part I Art.5.]

H, a restricted patient, appealed against the dismissal of his application for judicial review of a decision of a Mental Health Review Tribunal refusing to discharge him from detention. H had been detained in a secure hospital following his conviction for manslaughter and had applied to the tribunal for a discharge pursuant to the Mental Health Act 1983 s.73. It was submitted that the test contained in s.73, which a tribunal applied for the purpose of determining a restricted patient's entitlement to release, was incompatible with the right to liberty enshrined in the Human Rights Act 1998 Sch.1 Part I Art.5.

Held, allowing the appeal and making a declaration of incompatibility, that s.73 of the 1983 Act did contravene Art.5 as the burden of proof rested on the patient to show that he no longer suffered from a mental disorder which warranted his detention. As the requirements of the 1998 Act could only be fulfilled if a tribunal was obliged to order a patient's discharge unless it could be shown that all three of the conditions for his continued detention had been met, both s.72 and s.73 of the 1983 Act were incompatible. The concept of burden of proof and the applicable test for discharge were inseparable and the failure of the 1983 Act to require a tribunal to discharge a patient where it could not be shown that he suffered from a mental disorder warranting detention amounted to unlawful detention and infringed a person's right to liberty.

R. (ON THE APPLICATION OF H) v. MENTAL HEALTH REVIEW TRIBUNAL FOR NORTH AND EAST LONDON REGION; *sub nom.* R. (ON THE APPLICATION OF

H) v. NORTH AND EAST LONDON REGIONAL MENTAL HEALTH REVIEW TRIBUNAL; R. (ON THE APPLICATION OF H) v. LONDON NORTH AND EAST REGION MENTAL HEALTH REVIEW TRIBUNAL, [2001] EWCA Civ 415, [2002] Q.B.1, Lord Phillips of Worth Matravers, M.R., CA.

4433. **Mental patients rights – telephone tapping – random recording of patient's calls – right to private life**

[Human Rights Act 1998 Sch.1 Part I Art.8; National Health Service Act 1977 s.4(1).]

N applied for judicial review of a provision in the Safety and Security in Ashworth, Broadmoor and Rampton Hospitals Directions 2000, issued by the Secretary of State under the National Health Service Act 1977, which conferred on a high security hospital a discretionary power to record, and subsequently listen to, a random ten per cent of outgoing and incoming patient telephone calls. N contended that the provision breached his right to a private life under the Human Rights Act 1998 Sch.1 Part I Art.8 since the interference involved was disproportionate and not necessary to achieve a legitimate aim, particularly since he had not been classified as high risk. N maintained that the extent of the risk posed by individual patients should be assessed and the monitoring tailored accordingly.

Held, refusing the application, that the random recording and listening in to ten per cent of calls was a justified infringement of Art.8 since it was a proportionate measure which was necessary to achieve the legitimate aim of providing and maintaining high security conditions for persons of dangerous, violent or criminal propensities as required under s.4(1) of the 1977 Act. Notwithstanding that N had not been assessed as high risk, he had the status and was in the category of persons defined by s.4, despite the fact that other patients posed a significantly higher risk, *R. v. Secretary of State for the Home Department, ex p. Isiko* [2001] 1 F.L.R. 930, [2001] 3 C.L.Y. 436 applied. Furthermore, when assessing the degree of interference it was necessary to have regard to the actual level of monitoring undertaken. On the facts, there was a real distinction between the treatment of N as a lower risk patient in that he was only subject to random monitoring and the treatment of high risk patients, all of whose calls were subject to monitoring. Accordingly, the measures taken had been properly tailored to reflect the degree of risk posed.

R. (ON THE APPLICATION OF N) v. ASHWORTH SPECIAL HOSPITAL AUTHORITY; *sub nom.* R. v. ASHWORTH SPECIAL HOSPITAL AUTHORITY, *ex p.* N, [2001] EWHC Admin 339, [2001] H.R.L.R. 46, Newman, J., QBD (Admin Ct).

4434. **NHS trusts – change of name – Avon and Western Wiltshire Mental Health Care**

See HEALTH. §2996

4435. **NHS trusts – dissolution – Ealing, Hammersmith and Fulham Mental Health**

See HEALTH. §3008

4436. **NHS trusts – dissolution – Essex and Herts Community, the Mid Essex Community and Mental Health, and the North East Essex Mental Health**

See HEALTH. §3010

4437. **NHS trusts – dissolution – Northumberland Mental Health**

See HEALTH. §3018

4438. **NHS trusts – establishment – Barnet, Enfield and Haringey Mental Health**

See HEALTH. §3033

4439. NHS trusts – establishment – Buckinghamshire

See HEALTH. §3035

4440. NHS trusts – establishment – Camden and Islington Mental Health

See HEALTH. §3037

4441. NHS trusts – establishment – Newcastle, North Tyneside and Northumberland Mental Health

See HEALTH. §3043

4442. NHS trusts – establishment – North Cumbria Mental Health and Learning Disabilities

See HEALTH. §3047

4443. NHS trusts – establishment – North Essex Mental Health Partnership

See HEALTH. §3048

4444. NHS trusts – establishment and change of name – Southern Derbyshire Mental Health Services

See HEALTH. §3067

4445. Powers of attorney – enduring powers of attorney – disclosure of accountant's report prepared for court of protection

C executed an enduring power of attorney in 1998 in favour of J, with whom he had cohabited for many years, and M, a long standing friend and business partner. C's children, including D, objected to the registration of the power on the grounds of lack of capacity and undue pressure, and sought disclosure of an accountant's report into the affairs of C that had been prepared at the request of the Court of Protection. The judge ordered the power to be registered and refused to permit the report to be disclosed to the children ((2001) W.T.L.R. 33). D appealed.

Held, dismissing the appeal, that the judge could properly find on a summary hearing that the allegation that C was not mentally competent when he executed the power failed, and that accordingly it was not necessary to cause inquiries to be made. This was particularly so given the extent of the court's powers to regulate the attorneys, and the judge was entitled to find that the accountant's report should not be disclosed to the children. However, the matter was remitted to the Court of Protection with a direction that consideration should be given to the question whether M was suitable to remain C's attorney.

C (ENDURING POWER OF ATTORNEY), *Re* [2001] W.T.L.R. 39, Waller, L.J., CA.

4446. Books

Bullis, Ronald – Sacred Calling, Secular Accountability. Hardback: £35.95. ISBN 1-58391-061-1. Paperback: £14.95. ISBN 1-58391-062-X. Brunner-Routledge.

Parsons, Andrew – Mental Health Law Compendium. Spiral/comb bound: £95.00. ISBN 1-85978-932-3. Monitor Press.

Ramsey, Rosalind; Szmuckler, George; Gerada, Clare; Mars, Sara – Mental Illness- A Handbook for Carers. 2nd Ed. Paperback: £15.95. ISBN 1-85302-934-3. Jessica Kingsley Publishers.

NEGLIGENCE

4447. Apportionment – accidents – road traffic – child carried in vehicle without adequate restraint

[Civil Liability (Contribution) Act 1978.]

W, who had caused a road accident in which J, a two year old child, had sustained multiple injuries, appealed against the decision apportioning liability. J had been travelling on her mother's knee in the front passenger seat of a vehicle being driven by her mother's sister, restrained only by the lap belt part of the seat belt on her mother's knee. Having considered the report of an expert, the judge had found that had J been wearing an approved child restraint, the risk of serious injury would have been entirely, or almost entirely, eliminated. Apportioning liability under the Civil Liability (Contribution) Act 1978, the judge held that W was 75 per cent to blame and J's mother and aunt 25 per cent to blame for J's injuries. W argued that the judge's decision failed to reflect the seriousness of the risk to which J had been subjected by her mother and aunt.

Held, dismissing the appeal, that the judge had been entitled to apportion liability in the manner in which he had done because (1) there was no prohibition on a child travelling in the front of a vehicle; (2) while J had not been secured with an appropriate restraint, she had not been entirely unrestrained; (3) while the expert had stressed that the use of a lap belt on its own could have devastating consequences where a child was being carried, there was no evidence that J's mother or her aunt had realised that that was the case or had deliberately taken a risk, and (4) the accident had been caused by the gross inattention of W. The principles adopted in assessing fault under the 1978 Act were similar to those adopted in assessing contributory negligence. Accordingly, the judge had been entitled to rely on the guidelines set in *Froom v. Butcher* [1976] Q.B. 286, [1975] C.L.Y. 2295, which would apply unless there were exceptional circumstances, for example where an adult had deliberately carried someone, especially a child, in the front seat of a vehicle without using any seat belt or other restraint at all.

J (A CHILD) v. WILKINS [2001] P.I.Q.R. P12, Keene, L.J., CA.

4448. Apportionment – personal injuries – damages – limitation

A appealed against a decision of the trial judge to apportion his damages for personal injury, awarding him £4,000 from a total of £11,000. A had developed vibration white finger, VWF, during the course of his employment with B from the 1950s until 1987. The judge had found that B should have been aware of the risk of contracting the disease from early 1973 and should have taken steps to ameliorate it between 1973 and 1976. She had deducted from the total damages award sums attributable to the period prior to 1976, and the period after 1987 when A was no longer an employee of B. She had then reduced the remaining figure by 50 per cent to reflect the fact that A would have developed VWF even if B had not been negligent. A argued that, having been found to have made a material contribution to his injury, B were liable for the entirety of the injury suffered between 1973 and 1987, save where it could be proven to have been exacerbated by non negligent exposure.

Held, dismissing the appeal, that the degree of liability was limited to the extent to which the tort had contributed to the disability. Apportionment, which by its nature could not be an exact science, was appropriate in the instant case, given that VWF was a cumulative condition and that it was not possible to prove conclusively how much damage had been caused by B's negligence, *Thompson v. Smiths Shiprepairers (North Shields) Ltd* [1984] Q.B. 405, [1984] C.L.Y. 2307, *Bonnington Castings Ltd v. Wardlaw* [1956] A.C. 613, [1956] C.L.Y. 3489 and *Holtby v. Brigham & Cowan (Hull) Ltd* [2000] 3 All E.R. 421, [2000] 5 C.L. 624 applied.

ALLEN v. BRITISH RAIL ENGINEERING LTD (BREL), [2001] EWCA Civ 242, [2001] I.C.R. 942, Schiemann, L.J., CA.

4449. Causation – accidents – motorcycles – use of vehicle on road – meaning of "road"

[Road Traffic Act 1988 Part VI s.145; Motor Vehicles (Compulsory Insurance) Regulations 2000 (SI 2000 726).]

I sought permission to appeal against a finding that the personal injuries she sustained when a motorcycle driven by K collided with her as she sat in a park did not arise from the use of a vehicle on a road for the purposes of the Road Traffic Act 1988 Part VI s.145. K had driven along a metalled path in the park before climbing a grassy bank, temporarily leaving the ground at top of the bank and then colliding with I. I contended that (1) since K had used the metalled path which was a road for the purposes of s.145, in order to build up enough speed he had been committed to a course of action whereby he used the grassy bank as a ramp in order to "take off" and that there was, accordingly, a sufficient causal connection for the purposes of s.145, and (2) the finding that the grassy bank was not a road was incorrect since the insertion of the words "or public place" into the 1988 Act by the Motor Vehicles (Compulsory Insurance) Regulations 2000 which had been implemented to comply with EC law, meant that the word "road" had to construed more widely.

Held, dismissing the application, that (1) having built up speed on the metalled path, it was not correct to state that K was committed to the course of action that he had subsequently taken. K had not lost control of the motorcycle and could have driven straight over the bank rather than "taking off", braked or taken an alternative route up the bank, *Clarke v. Kato* [1998] 1 W.L.R. 1647, [1998] C.L.Y. 3395 applied, and (2) there was no obligation on the court to construe the word "road" more widely since the 2000 Regulations came into force after the accident, the explanatory notes accompanying them did not have binding effect and the EC Directives which the Regulations were intended to implement, did not require such a construction.

INMAN v. KENNY, [2001] EWCA Civ 35, [2001] P.I.Q.R. P18, Peter Gibson, L.J., CA.

4450. Causation – fire – use of polystyrene sandwich panels – likelihood of responding to advice – contributory negligence

[Law Reform (Contributory Negligence) Act 1945 s.1.]

PV, whose factory had been destroyed by fire, appealed against, inter alia, the decision of the judge that (1) R, PV's managing director, would not have accepted the advice of H, the project managers for the construction of the factory, relating to the danger of using highly combustible polystyrene sandwich panels in the building, and (2) the assessment under the Law Reform (Contributory Negligence) Act 1945 s.1 that even if such advice had been accepted PV had been 50 per cent responsible for the damage. H cross appealed against the judge's finding that it had not provided advice to PV in relation to, inter alia, the danger of using the panels in the building. The factory, which was purpose built, was used for the manufacture of speciality breads.

Held, allowing the appeal in part and dismissing the cross appeal, that (1) it was apparent that the basis for the judge's finding that R would not have accepted H's advice if given was R's preference for using the panels due to his concerns about conforming to high standards of hygiene and his desire that the factory should be built as cheaply as possible. Such a finding relied considerably on the judge's assessment of R as a person and it was not appropriate for the court to substitute its own views for those of the judge, *Piglowska v. Piglowski* [1999] 1 W.L.R. 1360 considered. However, it was unlikely that if R had been advised that the problem with using the panels could be remedied cheaply, he would have rejected such advice. The judge had failed to give reasons as to why he considered R would still reject such advice which was suggestive that he had overlooked the fact that a cheap solution had existed. Accordingly, the judge had erred in his finding; (2) the assessment of the judge under s.1 of the Act was within the acceptable range, *Kerry v. Carter* [1969] 1 W.L.R. 1372 considered. Sedley, L.J. observed, in relation to a submission that contributory negligence should be approached on the same footing as contribution between joint tortfeasors, that whilst the principles for assessing contributory negligence could in some cases form the basis for the apportionment of liability between joint tortfeasors, it did not follow that the reverse was true, *J (A Child) v. Wilkins* [2001] R.T.R. 19 considered, and (3) it was not appropriate to interfere with the judge's conclusion that H had not provided advice in relation to the dangers of using the panels.

PRIDE VALLEY FOODS LTD v. HALL & PARTNERS (CONTRACT MANAGEMENT) LTD, [2001] EWCA Civ 1001, 76 Con. L.R. 1„ Dyson, L.J., CA.

4451. Causation – personal injuries – development of multiple sclerosis following accident trauma

N instituted proceedings against M following a road traffic accident in which a lamp standard had fallen onto his vehicle. After the accident N had developed sensations of dizziness and unsteadiness and was diagnosed as suffering from multiple sclerosis two years later. N contended that his condition had resulted from the accident trauma.

Held, giving judgment for M, that in a rare or exceptional case it was potentially possible to make a finding that a causal connection existed between trauma and the subsequent development of multiple sclerosis, where the trauma in question consisted of an injury to the brain, or more usually, to the cervical spinal cord. On the facts of the instant case it was not possible to make a causal connection given that N had not sustained any injury to the cervical spinal cord.

NIXON v. FJ MORRIS CONTRACTING LTD *The Times*, February 6, 2001, Garland, J., QBD.

4452. Causation – psychiatric illness – onset of schizophrenia following road traffic accident

In a claim for damages for personal injuries following a road traffic accident, it fell to the court to determine as preliminary issues (1) the extent of W's contributory negligence in failing to wear a seat belt and travelling in the vehicle when he was aware that the driver had been drinking alcohol, and (2) whether the head injury suffered by W had been sufficiently serious to have caused him to develop schizophrenia.

Held, giving judgment for the claimant in part, that (1) W was 15 per cent to blame for his injuries, and (2) on the balance of probabilities, the accident was causative of W's schizophrenia. A complicating factor was that, when W started to show symptoms of psychosis, he was at an age for those predisposed to develop schizophrenia, to display symptoms, namely between the ages of 16 and 22. On the evidence there was no indication of any pre-morbid condition that was likely to have led to development of the disease in the absence of the accident. Although W sustained only minor physical injuries, and although he had failed to seek medical help until 15 months after the accident, it was evident that he had talked to family about troubled thoughts and dreams that he was having within seven to 10 days of the accident. Within six months of the accident, he had withdrawn from social contact and had developed florid symptoms, such as delusions. The judge found that the severity of the head injury was measured partly by the extent of post traumatic amnesia and accepted that, in W's case, that had lasted for six to eight hours after the accident.

W v. HARDMAN, January 19, 2001, Judge Lightfoot, CC (Leeds). [*Ex rel.* Hartley & Worstenholme, Solicitors, 20 Bank Street, Castleford].

4453. Causation – tour operators – children – hotel pool safety – apportionment of liability

[Ministerial Order of 31 May 1960 (Spain) Art.22.]

R, a six year old boy who had suffered catastrophic brain damage following an incident in a swimming pool in a hotel complex in Majorca, brought a claim for damages against I, the holiday company with whom the package holiday had been booked. R, who could not swim, had been left, momentarily, in the company of his nine year old brother in the shallow end of the pool without arm bands. As a result of an unexpectedly steep gradient of the pool of approximately 15 per cent, R had become immersed. In the absence of lifeguards, resuscitation had been delayed. The holiday contract had specified that I was liable for the acts and omissions of the Majorcan suppliers. I contended that it was entitled to a full indemnity from the hotel on the ground that the hotel had breached its contractual warranty, or alternatively that the hotel was a joint tortfeasor. I also sought contribution from R's parents, contending that their failure to take reasonable care of him had contributed to his accident.

Held, apportioning liability and assessing causation at 50 per cent, 17 per cent and 33 per cent for the hotel, parents and the defendant respectively, that (1) Spanish legislation specifying a maximum gradient of 10 per cent for children's pools did not apply since the pool in question was not intended for use exclusively by children, and no reliance could be placed on the provisions of English regulations, *Wilson v. Best Travel Ltd* [1993] 1 All E.R. 353, [1993] C.L.Y. 494 and *C (A Child) v. Thomson Tour Operations Ltd* Times, October 20, 2000, [2000] C.L.Y. 4041 followed. In accordance with its own standards, I were under a duty to ensure that the hotel provided comprehensive depth markings around the pool, notices advising that it was unsuitable for children and non-swimmers, and a hotel information booklet outlining the layout and depth of the pool, and in the absence of such provision, I's failure to warn its customers of the risks of using the pool was negligent and, on the facts, in breach of contract; (2) I's duty to take reasonable steps to ensure that the facilities offered by the hotel were of an acceptable standard could be reduced but could not be discharged by way of the indemnity and warranty in the contract with the hotel. I had known about the lack of lifeguards and had failed to check resuscitation facilities; thus on a contra proferentum construction of the contract, I was not entitled to a full indemnity from the hotel; (3) the Ministerial Order of 31 May 1960 Art.22, which provided for the presence of trained lifesaver pool attendants and their active supervision at the pool side, had been breached and I was contractually liable for that breach, and (4) in reliance upon the English law of tort, and in the absence of contrary evidence of Spanish law, the hotel was in breach of its duty of care to take reasonable steps to ensure that the pool was safe for visitors to use. Responsibility for the extent of R's injuries was apportioned equally between his original immersion and the failure to resuscitate.

R (A CHILD) v. IBEROTRAVEL LTD (T/A SUNWORLD LTD), March 9, 2000, Gibbs, J., QBD. [*Ex rel.* Pannone & Partners, Solicitors, 123 Deansgate, Manchester].

4454. Clinical negligence – causation – birth defects – conflicting expert evidence

S, a child born in the defendant's hospital, was diagnosed shortly after birth as having both a fractured clavicle and an Erb's palsy, a disorder arising from damage to the nerves of the brachial plexus. S contended that (1) the Erb's palsy occurred in the course of delivery, the obstetrician having failed to notice difficulty when S's shoulder became caught on the rim of the mother's pelvis, and (2) excessive traction had been applied in the absence of recognising the difficulty, rather than the agreed appropriate measures. The NHS Trust submitted that S's injury and palsy were explicable by reason of damage other than excessive traction during the course of delivery.

Held, giving judgment for the claimant on liability, that the evidence of the claimant's expert was cogent and sound and was therefore to be preferred to that of the defendant's expert. On the balance of probabilities, the cause of S's

Erb's palsy was excessive traction resulting from shoulder dystocia or difficulty in delivering the shoulders. Such an explanation was straightforward and did not rely upon hypotheses unsupported by proper empirical evidence. The literature relied upon by the defendant could not be given substantial weight, *Loveday v. Renton* Times, March 31, 1988, [1988] C.L.Y. 1599 applied.

S (A CHILD) v. COUNTESS OF CHESTER HOSPITALS NHS TRUST, May 24, 2001, Thomas, J., HC. [*Ex rel.* Christopher Limb, Barrister, Young Street Chambers, 38 Young Street, Manchester].

4455. Clinical negligence – causation – birth of brain damaged child – long term psychological condition of mother

F issued proceedings against MSW, the local health authority, claiming damages arising out of their negligence in the delivery of her son, K, who had been born in 1990 with severe and irreversible brain damage. MSW admitted liability, but a dispute arose concerning the scope of F's damages. In addition to damages for physical pain and suffering arising out of an emergency caesarean section, F claimed for the psychological consequences of the trauma of the birth, which comprised the shock of having to undergo a caesarean operation, the shock upon learning of K's condition, long term depression and anxiety. F also sought damages in respect of loss of amenity and the onset of a back injury caused by having to lift and move K. F contended that although she had not been permitted to see K or told about his condition until he was one day old, there had been no break in the chain of causation between his birth and her first sight of him with the result that she was liable to be compensated as a primary victim in respect of psychological complaints which were still ongoing. MSW submitted that the cause of F's psychiatric illness was not the events surrounding the birth, but F's gradual realisation of K's condition. They maintained that such realisation was wholly unrelated to their breach of duty to K with the result that F was only eligible for compensation as a secondary victim.

Held, giving judgment for F, that (1) the "trauma of the birth" included the Caesarean section, the first sight of K and the conversation with the doctor, who had broken the news to F about K's disabilities and accordingly F was to be treated as a primary victim. The court was satisfied on the balance of probabilities that F had suffered from a recognised psychiatric illness which had been a direct result of the "trauma of the birth" such that the whole of her psychiatric illness attracted damages from MSW; (2) although the back injury was associated directly with K's condition, it could not be directly attributed to the trauma of his birth, and (3) a separate award for loss of amenity was not appropriate, but there was an element included in the general damages award of £75,000 to reflect the fact that F had had to suffer a complete change of lifestyle, tantamount to loss of a private life far beyond the usual constraints imposed by rearing offspring.

FARRELL v. MERTON SUTTON AND WANDSWORTH HA; *sub nom.* F v. RICHMOND TWICKENHAM AND ROEHAMPTON HA (2001) 57 B.M.L.R. 158, Judge Elizabeth Steel DL, QBD.

4456. Clinical negligence – causation – severe brain damage suffered in post operative state

G claimed damages for clinical negligence contending that an operation some sixteen years previously had left her brain damaged. S contended that the injury had resulted from status epilepticus.

Held, giving judgment for the defendant, that G was unable to satisfy the court that her injury had been caused by the negligence of S.

G v. SOUTHAMPTON AND SOUTH WEST HAMPSHIRE HA (2001) 57 B.M.L.R. 148, Toulson, J., QBD.

4457. **Clinical negligence – diagnosis – babies – neonatal tests – breach of duty of care**

S, who was born with a congenitally displaced hip, CDH, claimed damages from the NHS at the age of 23, for personal injuries arising from its negligence. S contended that her condition should have been diagnosed within a few days of her birth with the likelihood that the condition would have been cured with little difficulty. S submitted that the NHS's failure to conduct Ortolani-Barlow tests, designed to identify CDH, in the early neo-natal period and six weeks after the birth, had resulted in her suffering the trauma of a great deal of complex surgery throughout her life. NHS submitted that, owing to the lapse of time, there was insufficient evidence to prove that the test had not been carried out at either of the two stages, and the claim had not been brought within the limitation period.

Held, granting judgment for the NHS, that, while failure to ensure that a test took place at birth would not have amounted to a breach of duty, failure to carry out a test at six weeks would have constituted such a breach. However, taking into account the evidence and the fact that S had been born at home, the general practitioner had, on the balance of probabilities, observed the recommended practice and carried out the examination both at birth and at six weeks old. The fact that CDH had not been detected did not suggest otherwise, in view of the inherently unreliable nature of the test. Accordingly, the NHS had not been negligent. On the limitation issue, the claimant could not reasonably be expected to have had the requisite knowledge prior to her consultation with a specialist two years before commencing the action, particularly since the alleged negligence was due to an omission.

SMITH (CAROLINE) v. NATIONAL HEALTH SERVICE LITIGATION AUTHORITY [2001] Lloyd's Rep. Med. 90, Andrew Smith, J., QBD.

4458. **Clinical negligence – diagnosis – failure to diagnose and treat deep vein thrombosis**

S appealed against a finding that W had not been negligent in its failure to diagnose and treat a deep vein thrombosis suffered by her husband, and from which he had died, whilst undergoing medical treatment for a leg injury. S submitted that the judge had failed to make findings of fact in respect of her allegations that her husband had complained of the swelling and pain in his leg to the occupational therapist, E, and that the staff nurse, N, taking him to theatre had commented on the fact that his foot was discoloured.

Held, allowing the appeal, that the judge had failed to directly address the conflicts in evidence, particularly as S's evidence was to be preferred as she had detailed her assertions within weeks of her husband's death, and the evidence of E and N had not served to contradict her. Accordingly, damages of £175,000 were agreed and approved.

STARCEVIC v. WEST HERTFORDSHIRE HA, [2001] EWCA Civ 192, (2001) 60 B.M.L.R. 221, Mantell, L.J., CA.

4459. **Clinical negligence – diagnosis – pregnancy – brain damage – failure to diagnose condition**

FR, the mother, and PR, her 12 year old son, alleged negligence against T and J, two doctors who attended FR during her pregnancy (1) in relation to FR's pain, suffering and psychiatric illness as a result of their failure to diagnose pre-eclampsia, and (2) for PR's post-natal brain damage as a result of the failure to admit FR to hospital earlier. It was contended that FR's condition should have been diagnosed and that she should have been admitted to hospital earlier due to the abdominal pain from which she was suffering.

Held, giving judgment for T and J, that on the evidence, there had been no breach of duty by J. Notwithstanding T's admission of breach of his duty, the claims failed on causation as the overwhelming probability was that, even if FR had been admitted to hospital earlier, the birth would have occurred around the same time and brain damage could have resulted.

R v. TILSLEY (2001) 60 B.M.L.R. 202, Goldring, J., QBD.

4460. Clinical negligence – limitations – date of knowledge

[Limitation Act 1980 s.14.]

A preliminary issue arose in an action brought by H, an aircraftsman in the Royal Air Force who sought damages for clinical negligence after suffering a heart attack during his admission to hospital, as to whether the action was barred by virtue of the Limitation Act 1980. H had been suffering from acute chest pain and it was submitted that the MOD's failure to carry out basic medical diagnostic tests on his admission to hospital, such as an electrocardiogram, had resulted in a condition which could have been avoided. The MOD contended that the date of H's knowledge was the date of the cause of action, which was outside the limitation period.

Held, determining the preliminary issue in favour of H, that whilst H had had knowledge of the significance of his injury at the time of the cause of action for the purposes of s.14(1)(a) of the Act, he had not known that his heart attack was actually attributable to an act or omission alleged to constitute negligence for the purposes of s.14(1)(b). It was not until sometime later when H had consulted his sister, a cardiac nurse, about his condition that he had acquired the requisite actual knowledge, *Ali v. Courtaulds Textiles Ltd* [1999] Lloyd's Rep. Med. 301, [1999] C.L.Y. 465 applied. Further, having regard to H's state of mind and the circumstances, it would be unreasonable to consider him to have had constructive knowledge that his condition was attributable to the omissions of the MOD prior to his sister having confirmed his suspicions.

HARRILD v. MINISTRY OF DEFENCE [2001] Lloyd's Rep. Med. 117, Toulson, J., QBD.

4461. Clinical negligence – limitations – omissions – date of claimant's actual knowledge – delay in obtaining expert's report

[Limitation Act 1980 s.14, s.33.]

H, who was born with dwarfism, appealed against a decision that her claim in negligence against S, a surgeon, arising from an alleged failure to notice a fracture revealed by X-ray following an operation in October 1986 to lengthen H's right leg was time barred. A similar operation was performed on her left leg in October 1987. However, there were problems following both operations and in January 1989 S carried out a further operation to H's left leg. In September 1990, H was told that the bones in her legs could be dying and she then sought legal advice. Her solicitors requested a medical report but this was not supplied until May 1992 and was unfavourable to H. Another report from a different expert was produced in November 1994, which supported H's claim, and proceedings were issued in May 1995. Limitation was decided as a preliminary issue and the judge found that H had had the requisite knowledge to commence her claim in September 1990.

Held, dismissing the appeal, that H had had sufficient knowledge to put her on notice in 1990 that her medical problems could be attributed to negligence, which was enough to satisfy the test of actual knowledge in the Limitation Act 1980 s.14, *Spargo v. North Essex DHA* [1997] P.I.Q.R. P235, [1997] C.L.Y. 663 applied. Matters highlighted in the 1994 report were additional to those she could have relied on earlier. Further, it could also be said that H had constructive knowledge prior to 1992. The judge had therefore been entitled to decline to exercise his discretion under s.33 and had given due weight to all relevant factors.

HAYWARD v. SHARRARD (2000) 56 B.M.L.R. 155, Hutchison, L.J., CA.

4462. Clinical negligence – wrongful birth – failure to diagnose pregnancy – birth of disabled child – measure of damages

[Human Rights Act 1998 Sch.1 Part I Art.6, Art.8.]

In negligence proceedings commenced by G against S, a GP, following the birth of G's disabled daughter, M, it fell to the court to determine as preliminary issues whether M suffered from congenital abnormalities which necessitated additional care, and whether G was entitled to claim damages for all or part of the costs of M's care and upbringing and. G had undergone a sterilisation procedure but due to the admitted negligence of S, no pregnancy test had been carried out prior to the operation. G had, in fact, conceived by the date upon which the sterilisation was performed and would have terminated the pregnancy had it been diagnosed when she visited S. M was born three weeks prematurely and, whilst initially healthy, developed salmonella meningitis. M's condition was complicated by brain abscesses and she suffered from septicaemia, convulsions and an immune deficiency which ultimately resolved. S contended that clear causal proximity was required between the negligent act and the risk of disability, a factor which was absent in the instant case. G maintained that causal proximity was not required but that it was sufficient if the consequence fell within the scope of the risk of negligence

Held, determining the preliminary issues in favour of the claimant in part, that (1) whilst it was necessary to establish proximity in the relationship between the claimant and defendant, it was not necessary to establish a causally proximate link between the negligence complained of and the pure economic loss suffered. On the facts of the instant case there was a sufficiently proximate relationship between G and S and it was fair, just and reasonable that liability should be imposed upon S for the consequences of the birth of an unwanted disabled child, *Caparo Industries Plc v. Dickman* [1990] 2 A.C. 605, [1990] C.L.Y. 3266, *McFarlane v. Tayside Health Board* [2000] 2 A.C. 59, [2000] 1 C.L. 481, *Hardman v. Amin* [2000] Lloyd's Rep. Med. 498, [2001] 3 C.L. 554 and *Rand v. East Dorset HA* [2000] Lloyd's Rep. Med. 181, [2000] 8 C.L. 521 applied, and (2) the medical evidence demonstrated that M was not a healthy child. M did not suffer from a congenital birth defect but was disabled. Limiting the recoverable losses to the additional expenses arising from M's disability was proportionate as between the parties and consistent with the Human Rights Act 1998 Sch.1 Part I Art.6 and Art.8, *Frost v. Chief Constable of South Yorkshire* [1999] 2 A.C. 455, [1999] C.L.Y. 4059 applied.

GROOM v. SELBY [2001] Lloyd's Rep. Med. 39, Judge Peter Clark, QBD.

4463. Clinical negligence – wrongful birth – failure to diagnose pregnancy – damages for loss of employment

[Human Rights Act 1998 Sch.1 Part I Art.8.]

G appealed against a declaration that were she successful at trial in showing that a nurse, when prescribing a contraceptive injection, had negligently given the implied advice that she was not pregnant, she would not be able to claim compensatory damages for the loss of her employment arising from the need to care for the child. Had she been correctly diagnosed, G maintained that she would have terminated the pregnancy, and would therefore have continued to work outside the home. G argued that all the costs of the child's upbringing should be recoverable as they were consequential to the physical injury of the pregnancy, rather than as a result of negligent advice.

Held, dismissing the appeal, that the distinction between advice and physical harm was irrelevant, *McFarlane v. Tayside Health Board* [2000] 2 A.C. 59, [2000] 1 C.L. 481 considered. As a healthy child was an incalculable benefit, any compensation for lost employment was beyond the duty of care. Furthermore, right to family life set out in the Human Rights Act 1998 Sch.1 Part I Art.8 did not require the court to provide a remedy for G.

GREENFIELD v. IRWIN (A FIRM); *sub nom.* GREENFIELD v. FLATHER, [2001] EWCA Civ 113, [2001] 1 W.L.R. 1279, Buxton, L.J., CA.

4464. Clinical negligence – wrongful birth – misdiagnosis during pregnancy – pure economic loss – recoverable heads of damage

H sought damages from her GP, A, following the birth of her severely disabled son, D. A had admitted negligence in respect of a failure to diagnose that H was suffering from rubella during her pregnancy and had conceded that H would have chosen to terminate the pregnancy had she received appropriate counselling in relation to the likelihood of damage to the foetus. D, who was likely to survive well into adulthood, required constant care and would never be able to live or work independently. It fell to the court to determine the recoverable heads of damage and the appropriate basis for calculation of the awards.

Held, giving judgment for the claimant on the preliminary issues, that (1) the continuation of a pregnancy that was likely to result in the birth of a disabled child could amount to a personal injury and therefore H could claim special damages for losses and expenses incurred as a result of the pregnancy and the birth, including an award for loss of earnings, subject to set off if applicable; (2) H's claim for damages for D's past and future care amounted to a claim for pure economic loss. However, the birth of a disabled child was a foreseeable consequence of A's negligence and the relationship between A and H was sufficiently proximate for liability to be established, *McFarlane v. Tayside Health Board* [2000] 2 A.C. 59, [2000] 1 C.L. 481 distinguished and *Caparo Industries Plc v. Dickman* [1990] 2 A.C. 605, [1990] C.L.Y. 3266 applied; (3) the award for D's care was not limited to the sum that H would have been capable of expending towards such costs in the absence of an award, *Rand v. East Dorset HA* [2000] Lloyd's Rep. Med. 181, [2000] 8 C.L. 521 not followed, and (4) H was further entitled to an award for her personal contribution to D's care to be calculated either by way of damages for loss of amenity or on a commercial basis with a discount of 25 per cent, *Housecroft v. Burnett* [1986] 1 All E.R. 332, [1986] C.L.Y. 989 and *Allen v. Bloomsbury HA* [1993] 1 All E.R. 651, [1993] C.L.Y. 1416 applied.

HARDMAN v. AMIN [2000] Lloyd's Rep. Med. 498, Henriques, J., QBD.

4465. Contributory negligence – accidents – road traffic – apportionment of liability

H appealed against a decision that she was 100 per cent to blame for a road traffic accident in which she and C had been injured. There had been no witnesses to the accident and no other cars had been involved. The judge found that one party or the other must have been on the wrong side of the road and that the evidence pointed to the collision taking place on C's side of the road. H had admitted 50 per cent liability and contended that blame should be apportioned equally.

Held, allowing the appeal (Lord Justice Pill dissenting), that the judge had been wrong to rely on evidence from C's employer on C's driving ability given that it was not an accident in which character evidence was of assistance. Furthermore, there was no adequate evidential basis on which to conclude that H was solely to blame for the accident. The judge had erred in finding that blame rested on either C or H, and it was only reasonable to conclude that each was partly responsible for the accident and that they were equally responsible, *Baker v. Market Harborough Industrial Cooperative Society* [1953] 1 W.L.R. 1472, [1953] C.L.Y. 2473 followed.

COOPER v. HATTON; *sub nom.* HATTON v. COOPER, [2001] EWCA Civ 623, [2001] R.T.R. 36, Pill, L.J., CA.

4466. Contributory negligence – accidents – road traffic – cyclist emerging into path of oncoming vehicle

A, aged 14 at the date of the accident, was injured whilst riding his brother's cycle, with which he was familiar, on his way from his home to his part time job as a paper delivery boy at about 6am. He came out of a pedestrian shopping area, through one of three arches, across the pavement, and on to the road at a speed of approximately

10 to 15 mph into the path of S, a serving police officer, who was driving his camper van home from work after having completed a 12 hour shift.

Held, giving judgment for the defendant, that the cycle was so close to the camper van when it emerged on to the road that S had no opportunity to brake, steer or avoid an impact. S had been driving at a speed between 20 mph and 25 mph and the distance between the two vehicles was 20 feet. There was a defect in the steering of the camper van, although this had no relevance to the accident. There was no evidence that S was unduly tired after his shift or that his reactions were dulled by fatigue and, in any event, not even the most alert and quickest at reacting could have stopped in time. If the judge had found for A on liability, A would have been held 50 per cent to blame on the basis that he was familiar with the layout of the roads having followed that route for over a year, and he rode out on to the road without stopping at the kerb or checking to see if the road was clear. He would not however have found contributory negligence based upon A's failure to wear a safety helmet as there was no statutory requirement for him to do so, and he was not engaged in any particularly hazardous kind of driving during which it might be thought prudent to wear a helmet.

A (A CHILD) v. SHORROCK, March 19, 2001, Judge Brown, QBD. [*Ex rel.* Sinton & Co Solicitors, 5 Osborne Terrace, Newcastle Upon Tyne].

4467. Contributory negligence – hazardous substances – child injured whilst deliberately starting fire – apportionment of blame

[Environmental Protection Act 1990 s.73(6).]

C, a child who, at the age of 13, had suffered severe burns as a result of an accident involving flammable liquid that I had negligently left outside its factory premises, appealed against a finding of contributory negligence to the extent of 70 per cent. The judge had concluded that C had been aware that his actions were dangerous and had been warned of the dangers by his companions. C contended that the apportionment was too high given that I had blatantly failed to guard against the occurrence of danger which was emphasised by its breach of a statutory duty under the Environmental Protection Act 1990 s.73(6). Further, when assessing the degree of contributory negligence, the judge had failed to take into account the fact that the liquid also carried a risk of explosion of which C was ignorant. I cross appealed, arguing that C had not proved that the container had emanated from its premises and that the judge had been wrong to find otherwise.

Held, allowing the appeal and dismissing the cross appeal, that I had utterly failed to demonstrate any compliance with the statutory duty. Further, although C had taken a deliberate risk, he had not been aware of the danger of explosion owing to the chemicals in the container, but, as a child, was only aware that fire carried risks. Accordingly, C's liability was reduced from 75 percent to 50 per cent. In respect of I's cross appeal, the trial judge had been entitled to conclude that the container had originated from I's premises.

C (A CHILD) v. IMPERIAL DESIGN LTD [2001] Env. L.R. 33, Potter, L.J., CA.

4468. Duty of care – boxing – British Boxing Board of Control – failure to ensure immediate medical treatment

B appealed against a decision ([2000] E.C.C.141, [1999] C.L.Y. 3954) that it had breached its duty of care towards W, a boxer, by failing to ensure that he received immediate ringside medical attention. B contended that (1) there was insufficient proximity to establish the existence of a duty of care since (a) it exercised a broad public function to support boxing and not a function to determine the appropriate nature of medical facilities and assistance to be provided in boxing contests; (b) the duty alleged was to an indeterminate number of persons, and (c) given that B did not create the danger of injury or the requirement for medical assistance it owed no greater duty than that imposed on a rescuer; (2) W had not relied on the alleged duty of care, and (3) it was not fair just and reasonable to impose a duty of care in the instant case.

Held, dismissing the appeal, that (1) sufficient proximity was established since (a) B assumed responsibility for determining the nature of medical facilities and assistance to be provided to restrict the foreseeable injuries to boxers, by making regulations setting out details of the medical care which should be available; (b) the duty owed was to B's members which was a determinate class of persons, and (c) there was a distinction to be drawn between B and a rescuer, as the injuries sustained by professional boxers were almost inevitable and foreseeable and a result of the activities of which B controlled; (2) it had been within the reasonable contemplation of B, having special knowledge and acting as the sole controlling body regulating professional boxing, that W, belonging to a defined class of persons, would rely on its skill and expertise to take reasonable care in providing for his safety, and (3) there were no policy reasons why a duty should not be imposed on B since such a duty would not necessarily extend to other sporting organisations and the fact that B was a non profit making body should not provide an immunity in negligence. W had adequately proved that had the correct procedures been implemented and followed his injuries could have been mitigated.

WATSON v. BRITISH BOXING BOARD OF CONTROL LTD [2001] Q.B. 1134, Lord Phillips of Worth Matravers, M.R., CA.

4469. Duty of care – building and engineering contracts – extension of duty to subcontractors – New Zealand

T, a contractor, appealed against the dismissal of its action in negligence against K, an engineering firm. The court had found that an engineer who had prepared a mechanical services specification to be incorporated into a contract for the construction of a building owed no duty of care to the contractor who had carried out those mechanical services as a component of the entire construction. K had been engaged by G, a firm of architects, to prepare a mechanical services specification and the related subcontract for the construction of a new hospital. T, which had won the head contract, was responsible for undertaking the work, including the installation of a heating system in accordance with the mechanical services specification. Subsequent to the installation of the system by T's subcontractor, it was found to perform below the minimum specified output and T carried out remedial work. T sought to recover the cost of undertaking that remedial work from K, basing its claim on the tort of negligent misstatement.

Held, dismissing the appeal (Thomas, J. dissenting), that (1) given the contractual relationship between the parties, it would not be fair, just or reasonable to impose a duty of care. The relationship between each of the relevant parties was specified in separate contracts, which set out the parties' rights and obligations. T had owed a contractual obligation in respect of defects to the hospital owner. Such an obligation had been owed to T by its subcontractor, but not by K. Moreover, T had relied on the expertise of the subcontractor. Accordingly, K had not assumed any responsibility to T. It was appropriate to consider each case in its own context. K had not indicated that it was providing advice to T or the subcontractor, *British Telecommunications Plc v. James Thomson & Sons (Engineers) Ltd* [1999] 1 W.L.R. 9, [1999] C.L.Y. 5783 applied and *Edgeworth Construction Ltd v. ND Lea & Associates Ltd* 66 B.L.R. 56 distinguished. Thomas, J., however, found that the contractual structure did not preclude K from being liable to T since the principle of concurrent liability in contract and tort applied. Moreover, the case of *Edgeworth* could not be distinguished and provided persuasive authority that a duty of care had existed.

RM TURTON & CO LTD (IN LIQUIDATION) v. KERSLAKE & PARTNERS [2000] Lloyd's Rep. P.N. 967, Henry, J., CA (NZ).

4470. Duty of care – childminders – local authority's application to cancel registration

[Children Act 1989 s.75(3).]

B, who ran a day nursery, brought an action against the local authority, LCC, who had successfully applied without notice under the Children Act 1989 s.75(3), to cancel her registration as a day care provider. B claimed that, although the order had been overturned on appeal, her reputation and business had been damaged beyond repair, such that she had been forced to sell the nursery. B contended that the local authority owed her a common law duty to act with reasonable care so as to not cause her economic loss and that LCC had a discretion under s.75(3) of the Act whether or not to proceed without notice and that its decision to do so had been *Wednesbury* unreasonable and unlawful. Furthermore, that the damage caused by LCC's decision was foreseeable, there was a relationship of proximity, and it was just and reasonable for LCC to owe a duty of care to a registered childminder.

Held, giving judgment for LCC, that it was not just and reasonable to impose a common law duty of care on the local authority in relation to the performance of its statutory duties, because of the interdisciplinary nature of the system of child protection involving the joint decisions of many interrelated bodies. To impose such a duty would lead to impossible problems disentangling these bodies to determine their respective liabilities. Furthermore, it was not appropriate to extend the categories of negligence to include childminders as such a category represented a wholly novel duty with no previous analogies, *Caparo Industries Plc v. Dickman* [1990] 2 A.C. 605, [1990] C.L.Y. 3266 followed. The purpose of the 1989 Act was to protect children and in the exercise of that duty, a child did not have a cause of action under common law and it was therefore difficult to comprehend the idea that a third party would have such a cause of action, *X (Minors) v. Bedfordshire CC* [1995] 2 A.C. 633, [1995] C.L.Y. 3452 applied.

BOWDEN v. LANCASHIRE CC [2001] B.L.G.R. 409, Judge David Wilcox, QBD.

4471. Duty of care – employers – stiff neck caused by draught – extent of duty

W, an employee of ES, sought damages for personal injury, loss and damage arising out of a faulty air conditioning system on ES's premises. She testified that a vent above her desk had been defective for a period of three and a half days, such that she was subjected to a cold draught during that period, which resulted in her developing a chronic myo facial pain syndrome. She contended that ES had been negligent in failing to take reasonable care not to expose her to conditions which might foreseeably cause her such injury.

Held, granting judgment for the defendant, that (1) common sense and medical opinion were agreed that prolonged exposure to a substantial cold draft could result in discomfort, and a stiff neck was capable of constituting a personal injury, but (2) having suggested to W that she sit elsewhere, and there being two vacant desks in the vicinity, ES had discharged its obligation to W, it being unnecessary, since W was a mature adult, to order her out of the draught.

WINGROVE v. EMPLOYMENT SERVICE, April 5, 2000, Judge Charles Harris Q.C., CC (Northampton). [*Ex rel.* DLA & Partners Solicitors, Fountain Precinct, Balm Green, Sheffield].

4472. Duty of care – hospitals – employees – extent of duty to use warning signs

P, who was employed as a porter in the operating theatre of the defendant's hospital, slipped on the floor surface in the course of his duties, suffering a twisting injury to his lumbar spine. He alleged that the hospital was negligent and in breach of statutory duty for failing to provide a safe workplace. P stated that he fell due to the existence of a puddle even though that had not been stated in the accident reports at the time. He also claimed that he had not been warned of the residual wetness on the floor after it had been cleaned following an operation. In his submission, P's expert claimed that a verbal warning should have been given to the employees or signs placed on the theatre door or floor informing them of any hazards. The Trust stated that no member of staff had any recollection of the existence of a puddle following the accident. Furthermore, evidence from its expert stated that it was universal practice to place a sign in the operating theatre at the end of the operating list following the cleaning of the whole of the theatre and not in between operations on the list where only spot mopping took place.

Held, granting judgment for the defendant, that the Trust had provided a safe system and place of work. There was no real evidence that a puddle had existed at the time of the accident. Furthermore, placing a sign on the door or in the theatre was time consuming in light of the theatre's tight schedule and unnecessary in light of the specialist team working there. It also presented another hazard to the work area. It was routine between operations to clean the area around the operating table and everyone was aware of that in light of the close knit working environment in the theatre. The matter would be different and a sign necessary should the area be, for example, a public area in a supermarket. The hospital in the instant case had fulfilled its duty by taking all reasonable steps to protect the safety of its employees.

PROSHO v. ROYAL DEVON & EXETER HEALTHCARE TRUST, April 20, 2001, Judge not specified, QBD) Queens Bench Division. [*Ex rel.* Bevan Ashford, Solicitors, 35 Colston Avenue, Bristol].

4473. Duty of care – misrepresentation – liability of professional agent to contractor

See CONSTRUCTION LAW: J Jarvis & Sons Ltd v. Castle Wharf Developments Ltd. §871

4474. Duty of care – mortgagees powers and duties – repossession – sale of land – alleged transaction at an undervalue

M, a guarantor of the liabilities of S to L, sought damages against L for the alleged sale at an undervalue of a drag racing site owned by S. L was mortgagee of the site and following S's failure to discharge its debts, L appointed administrative receivers of S with instructions that the site be sold in time for Easter racing to take place. The site was valued at about £1 million, and was eventually sold for £965, 000 by the bank as mortgagee. M submitted that L could not choose to sell by a date which would result in the sale being for a lower price than would have been achieved had a proper period for marketing been allowed, and therefore by selling in time for an Easter race meeting, L should have commenced marketing earlier or left it as close to Easter as possible before agreeing to the sale. Furthermore, had the site been marketed properly, in particular by impressing upon prospective purchasers the urgency of a quick sale, it could have been sold at a higher price, particularly to MP, a prospective purchaser who had expressed interest in acquiring the site for a greater consideration.

Held, giving judgment for L, that the duty of a mortgagee was to achieve the best price reasonably obtainable and L had not acted in breach of such duty. The mortgagee was entitled to choose the most convenient time for sale and notwithstanding that with more time the sale may have achieved a better price, L and the administrative receivers had taken all reasonable steps to achieve the best price reasonably obtainable in the time scale which they had been entitled to set. Although there was no reference in advertisements to the urgency of the sale, there was nothing to indicate that had it been included there would have been any greater interest. The evidence that MP would have been willing to pay a higher price was false and had been concocted in order for it to appear that there had been a sale at an undervalue.

MEFTAH v. LLOYDS TSB BANK PLC (NO.2) [2001] 2 All E.R. (Comm) 741, Lawrence Collins, J., Ch D.

4475. Duty of care – personal injuries – animals – liability for dangerous animals

[Animals Act 1971 s.2 (2); Management of Health and Safety at Work Regulations 1992 (SI 1992 2051); Manual Handling Operations Regulations 1992 (SI 1992 2793.]

G, a trainee jockey and stable lad, sought damages for, inter alia, personal injuries following an incident in which his leg became crushed between a horse which he was, at the time, attempting to mount and a steel girder at SJB's premises. G contended that SJB was aware that the horse was of a vicious and mischievous propensity for the purposes of the Animals Act 1971 s.2 (2) and maintained that the accident was caused by SJB's negligence in failing to heed the horse's characteristics and failing to devise a suitable and safe system of handling the horse. G maintained in the alternative that the accident was caused by SJB's breach of statutory duty in failing to undertake a risk assessment pursuant to the Management of Health and Safety at Work Regulations 1992.

Held, giving judgment for the defendant, that the horse had not exhibited unusual behaviour on the day of G's accident and, while it was a lively and exuberant animal, it could not be described as difficult or dangerous and had no unusual characteristics for the purposes of s.2(2) of the Act. It was difficult to assess the health and safety aspects of the case given that no two horses could be considered to be the same. However, G had 15 years' experience with horses and it was reasonable to expect him to have used his judgment and abandoned the mounting exercise should he have felt that to be prudent. SJB's failure to carry out a risk assessment as required by the 1992 Regulations did not give rise to civil liability and would not have made any difference to the accident circumstances. The accident would not have happened had the horse not been in close proximity to the steel girder. The positioning of the horse was determined by G alone and, accordingly, SJB had not been negligent.

GREGORY v. SIR JOHN BARLOW (A FIRM), December 15, 2000, District Judge Gosnell, CC (Manchester). [*Ex rel.* Weightmans, Solicitors, 41 Spring Gardens, Manchester].

4476. Duty of care – personal injuries – courses – training – outdoor pursuits group activity courses – weather conditions – safety precautions

P attended with work colleagues and at the instigation of their employer, a character building outdoor pursuits training course run by S. As part of an exercise to encourage teamwork, the group participated in an activity in which one person had to place his trust in two colleagues to prevent him from falling while he swayed backwards and forwards. During the course of the exercise, P slipped and his colleague fell on him, as a result of which P sustained a fracture to the leg and dislocation of the right knee. P contended that there had been rainfall on the day which had left the ground wet and slippery and that he had informed the instructor that he had a weak knee and that he had already slipped on wet leaves on the uneven ground. It was alleged that the area was unsuitable, that the exercise should have been carried out indoors, or that non-slip matting ought to have been laid on the ground where the exercise was to take place. S argued that it had taken adequate precautions to ensure P's safety, that the area was suitable in all of the circumstances and that P had been negligent for failing to opt out of the exercise.

Held, giving judgment for the defendant, that although S may not have given adequate instructions as to the maximum extent of the sway to be performed by P, there was no evidence before the court that a sway greater than the six inches contended for by S was dangerous. P had participated in several parts of the exercise by way of demonstration prior to taking an active part. None of P's witnesses thought that the weather conditions or conditions underfoot were reasons not to take part in the exercises. S had been carrying out these exercises for a long period of time and had no history of any other accidents. On the balance of probabilities it had been acceptable for the activity to proceed and for it to do so out of doors.

PATEL v. SHAYLOR PARTNERS, March 8, 2001, District Judge Jackson, CC (Romford). [*Ex rel.* Royal & Sun Alliance UK, Legal Department, PO Box 8470, Birmingham].

4477. Duty of care – personal injuries – pedestrians – illegally parked vehicle – liability

An ambulance owned by D, the second defendants, was parked outside a convenience store to allow one of its personnel to do some shopping. It was parked illegally on double yellow lines. The ambulance obscured the vision of pedestrians crossing the road in front of it, and also the visibility of the pedestrians to motorists approaching from the rear. E was driving his car within the speed limit of 30 mph and he approached the scene from the rear of the ambulance. An elderly woman, M, walked from the convenience store and proceeded to cross the road in front of the ambulance. She could not see around it and did not stop to look before she stepped out beyond it into the road. She continued walking at an angle facing away from F's car. E was about 10 meters away from her when she stepped into his path. He braked and swerved but there was a collision as a result of which M suffered serious injury.

Held, giving judgment for the claimant in part, that the primary cause of the accident was the wrongful parking of the ambulance. Accordingly, D were two thirds to blame for parking the ambulance in a position whereby it caused a hazard. M was one third to blame for failing to look before crossing the road.

MARKOWSKI v. ELSON, November 3, 2000, Judge Thompson Q.C., CC (Weymouth). [*Ex rel.* Lamport Bassitt Solicitors, 46 The Avenue, Southampton].

4478. Duty of care – police – arrested person attempting to escape – no duty owed to prevent injuries

[Law Reform (Contributory Negligence) Act 1945.]

V, who had sustained serious injuries while attempting to escape from police custody, appealed against a decision that the police did not owe a duty of care to an arrested person to ensure that he did not injure himself in a foreseeable attempt to escape from custody. V had a history of being arrested at his flat and of seeking to evade arrest by jumping from the windows of the flat. He maintained that two police officers who had attended at his flat to arrest him had taken no action to prevent him from jumping from a window. The judge, whilst finding that it had been foreseeable that in jumping V would be likely to sustain injury and that if a duty existed the police officers had been in breach thereof, concluded that escaping from custody was a sufficiently serious criminal offence to attract the principle of ex turpi causa non oritur actio and in such circumstances no duty existed.

Held, dismissing the appeal (Sedley, L.J. dissenting), that a police officer carrying out an arrest did not owe the person being arrested a duty of care to prevent him from injuring himself in a foreseeable attempt to escape from custody. It followed that in the circumstances of the instant case the two officers had not owed V a duty to prevent him from heading towards the window in an attempt to escape, *Sacco v. Chief Constable of South Wales* (Unreported, May 15, 1998) applied. The act of escaping from custody was a criminal offence at common law but did not give rise to any liability in tort, *National Coal Board v. England* [1954] A.C. 403, [1954] C.L.Y. 2076 considered. Moreover, the Law Reform (Contributory Negligence) Act 1945 did not apply in circumstances where a claimant's action constituted a common law crime which did not give rise to tortious liability. V's criminal conduct had been sufficiently serious to merit the application of the principle of ex turpi causa. In the opinion of Sedley, L.J., a duty was owed by police officers not to afford the temptation or opportunity for a person in custody to escape where there was a known risk that he would do himself serious harm in so doing.

VELLINO v. CHIEF CONSTABLE OF GREATER MANCHESTER, [2001] EWCA Civ 1249, [2002] 1 W.L.R. 218, Schiemann, L.J., CA.

4479. Duty of care – police – assured tenant threatened with eviction – failure to prevent commission of offence

[Protection from Eviction Act 1977 s.1.]

C appealed against the dismissal of his claim for damages in negligence against the Chief Constable. C had been threatened by letter with eviction from a property which he occupied under an assured tenancy. He contacted the police, but the officers who responded to the call were unaware that, in the absence of a court order ending the tenancy, C's eviction would have constituted an offence under the Protection from Eviction Act 1977 s.1. In the event, the officers remained at the scene only to prevent any breach of the peace. C claimed that the officers owed him a duty of care to prevent the commission of a crime under s.1.

Held, dismissing the appeal, that no general duty was owed by the police to individual members of the public for their activities in the investigation and suppression of crime, *Hill v. Chief Constable of West Yorkshire* [1989] A.C. 53, [1988] C.L.Y. 2435 followed. C's case could not be excepted from this general principle as, in the absence of any indication of an assumption of responsibility to prevent the commission of the s.1 offence, the police presence at the scene did not in itself create a relationship of sufficient proximity, *Costello v. Chief Constable of Northumbria* [1999] 1 All E.R. 550, [1999] C.L.Y. 3970 and *Swinney v. Chief Constable of Northumbria (No.1)* [1997] Q.B. 464 followed. Moreover, it would not be in the public interest to impose of duty of care in such circumstances as responses to urgent calls would be delayed were the police required to analyse relevant legal information before acting. The primary role of the police was not to offer legal advice, but to prevent crime.

COWAN v. CHIEF CONSTABLE OF AVON AND SOMERSET *The Times*, December 11, 2001, Keene, L.J., CA.

4480. Duty of care – police – death in police custody – extent of duty

O appealed against the dismissal of her claim in negligence for damages following her husband's suicide, the deceased having hanged himself whilst in the Chief Constable's custody. She alleged that the police were negligent in failing to remove the deceased's belt, failing to monitor him properly and by placing him in a cell, the gate to which provided a suspension point. The judge had dismissed the claims on the ground that the police officers had no reason to believe that he presented a risk of suicide. O contended that the judge (1) was wrong to hold that a duty to take reasonable care to prevent the deceased from taking his life only arose if the risk of suicide was foreseeable; (2) failed to deal with the failure of the police to ensure that the cell did not contain a suspension point, and (3) was wrong to conclude that the deceased was not a person with a foreseeability of enhanced risk of killing himself whilst in police custody.

Held, dismissing the appeal, that (1) the police were under a duty to take reasonable steps to identify whether or not a prisoner presented a suicide risk. The obligation to take reasonable care to prevent a prisoner from taking his own life only arose where the police knew or ought to have known that the individual prisoner presented a suicide risk, *Reeves v. Commissioner of Police of the Metropolis* [2000] 1 A.C. 360, [1999] C.L.Y. 4022 applied. In the instant case, the police officers took reasonable steps to assess whether or not the deceased was a suicide risk; (2) since the deceased was not a person whom the officers knew or ought to have known was a suicide risk, there was no breach of duty in placing him in a cell with a suspension point, and (3) there was no evidence that those arrested for being drunk and disorderly formed a category of prisoner in respect of which there was any significantly increased risk of suicide.

ORANGE v. CHIEF CONSTABLE OF WEST YORKSHIRE, [2001] EWCA Civ 611, [2002] Q.B. 347, Latham, L.J., CA.

4481. Duty of care – police – social workers – investigation into sexual abuse of child – duty owed to child and accused

L, a child, and her father, F, brought an action against the police and social services claiming damages for psychological harm suffered as a result of an investigation into allegations, subsequently found to be groundless, that L had been sexually abused by F. L and F appealed against the findings of the judge, who had ruled that (1) L could pursue a claim in negligence; (2) there was no proximity between F, as a suspect, and the police, with the result that he could not sue the police for negligence, and (3) although both L and F had arguable claims based on misfeasance and conspiracy, the police were entitled to witness immunity in respect of the conduct of the interviewing officer.

Held, allowing the appeal, that (1) L could pursue a claim in negligence against the police since there had been an assumption of responsibility by the interviewing officer and a special relationship between her and the interviewing officer; (2) once the police had decided that there was a risk of further abuse, there existed an assumption of responsibility, a special relationship and a duty of care to take reasonable steps not to damage F by subsequent actions, and (3) given that they had caused proceedings to be initiated on the basis of unfounded allegations, the police were not entitled to immunity.

L (A CHILD) v. READING BC, [2001] EWCA Civ 346, [2001] 1 W.L.R. 1575, Otton, L.J., CA.

4482. Duty of care – right of support – demolition – withdrawal of support

R appealed against a decision that S, a former owner of demolished property adjoining R's terraced house, was not liable in negligence or nuisance in respect of damage caused to the flank wall. The judge had held that R was entitled to a right of support from the former property but had accepted expert evidence that damage by cracking was suffered because the wall had become subject to wind load from which it would have been sheltered previously but that was not attributable to the withdrawal of support. Further, the judge had held that notwithstanding that the flank wall had suffered considerable damp penetration since the demolition of the adjoining house which was directly attributable to the inadequate precautions taken at the time of demolition, R could not rely on any easement of protection.

Held, allowing the appeal, that the judge had erred in finding that wind support was not within the scope of the right of support. The wall was unstable as a result of weight pressure because of the weight of the wall itself. The effect of wind suction, to which the wall was not previously exposed, was to manifest the instability by cracking. The type of damage suffered in this case as a result of wind suction was within the scope of the right to support, *Phipps v. Pears* [1965] 1 Q.B. 76, [1964] C.L.Y. 1199 distinguished. Further, given that S owed a common law duty of care in negligence or nuisance and that it was foreseeable that when one of two adjoining owners demolished his property that the exposed wall if not properly weatherproofed would suffer damage, a duty was owed to the neighbour to take reasonable steps to protect the wall, *Leakey v. National Trust for Places of Historic Interest or Natural Beauty* [1980] Q.B. 485, [1980] C.L.Y. 2006 applied. In the instant case, S knew or should have known of the risk of damage likely to result from his demolition works in the absence of proper weatherproofing and the damage which resulted would have been prevented by such works as it would have been reasonable for S to have carried out.

REES v. SKERRETT; *sub nom.* REES v. SKERET; REES v. SKERRET, [2001] EWCA Civ 760, [2001] 1 W.L.R. 1541, Lloyd, J., CA.

4483. Duty of care – road traffic – accidents – existence of common law duty

[Road Traffic Act 1988 s.39.]

L appealed against the dismissal of her claim for damages against S following a road traffic accident as a result of which she had sustained serious injuries. L had driven across the junction of two roads. In emerging into the junction, she had passed "Give Way" signs situated at either side of the mouth of the junction. She maintained that S should have provided additional advance warning that she had to give way. She contended that a common law duty of care should be superimposed upon the statutory duty under the Road Traffic Act 1988 s.39.

Held, dismissing the appeal, that (1) the statutory duty imposed under the 1988 Act to promote road safety and to take action to prevent accidents allowed a considerable degree of discretion to local authorities and required SMBC to exercise its powers in a manner that it considered was appropriate; (2) the fact that a power was discretionary did not mean, however, that a common law duty of care could not exist. If in exercising that discretion it acted unreasonably, it could be liable in negligence to a driver injured owing to a road traffic accident, *Stovin v. Wise and Norfolk CC* [1996] A.C. 923, [1996] C.L.Y. 4058 applied, and (3) the judge had fully investigated the facts and he had not erred in finding that there was no breach of duty.

LARNER v. SOLIHULL MBC [2001] R.T.R. 32, Lord Woolf of Barnes, L.C.J., CA.

4484. Duty of care – service stations – sale of petrol to person under age – duty of supplier

[Petroleum (Consolidation) Act 1928 s.1.]

E claimed damages against S for personal injuries sustained as a result of the accidental ignition of petrol that S had sold to E. At the time E bought the petrol he was aged 13, which made the sale illegal under the provisions of the Petroleum (Consolidation) Act 1928 s.1 to which S was subject. It was contended that S also owed E a common law duty of care to prevent him from being in control of the the petrol and that that duty continued until the time of the accident in which E sustained serious burn injuries.

Held, giving judgment for E, that in addition to the statutory duty imposed on S by the Act, a common law duty of care was also owed to E. In light of the fact that the mishandling, resulting spillage and ignition of the petrol causing the accident was reasonably foreseeable, S was liable in negligence for the damage sustained by E. This was in spite of E's blameworthy conduct in inhaling the petrol fumes, given that S the supplier of petrol, should have been aware of the potential for such established misconduct and guarded against it, *R. v. HM Coroner for Southwark, ex p. Kendall* [1988] 1 W.L.R. 1186, [1989] C.L.Y. 523 applied. The defence of volenti non fit injuria was inapplicable since E had not assented to the foolish behaviour of his friend which had caused the spillage, although he had been contributorily negligence to the extent of one third of the claim.

E (A CHILD) v. SOULS GARAGES LTD *The Times*, January 23, 2001, John Leighton Williams Q.C., QBD.

4485. Duty of care – teachers – psychiatric injury caused by stress

S, a former teacher at K's school for children with special educational needs, sought to recover in the region of £150,000 by way of damages for psychiatric injury which she alleged had been caused by stress at work. S contended that K should have been on notice of the fact that she was not a person of ordinary fortitude because (1) she had been subject to a number of assaults and injuries perpetrated by children, and (2) an incident had arisen as a result of which S was chastised by the headteacher following a formal complaint from another member of staff. After a subsequent meeting with the headteacher relating to a further and separate dispute, S complained that the headteacher had been insensitive to her as he should have been aware that she was not of ordinary fortitude. S subsequently developed a psychiatric condition as a result of which she was retired on the grounds of ill health.

Held, giving judgment for the defendant, that stress and personality conflicts were part of most jobs and could not be avoided. Furthermore, although S had presented subjective evidence of her own perception and feelings about her job, there was no evidence that K had been put on notice of the risk that she might have sustained, or was likely to sustain, a psychiatric injury as a result of any aspect of her employment. There had therefore been no breach of duty on the part of K.

SALISBURY v. KIRKLEES MBC, June 21, 2001, Judge Hawksworth Q.C., CC (Huddersfield). [*Ex rel.* Halliwell Landau, Solicitors, City Plaza, 2 Pinfold Street, Sheffield].

4486. Duty of care – tour operators – personal injuries sustained during organised excursion – appropriate level of reasonable care and skill

See LEISURE INDUSTRY: Williams v. First Choice Holidays and Flights Ltd. §4282

4487. Economic loss – carriage by road – loss of utility or amenity – assumption of responsibility

EG brought an action against M and H concerning possible damage to EG's generator, which EG alleged had occurred during its transportation. EG's claim was for economic loss based upon a reasonable belief that damage might have occurred to the generator since it had been transported upon a conventional trailer as opposed to the "air ride" system contracted for. The legitimacy of the cause of action was dealt with by the court as a preliminary issue and EG submitted that (1) the fact that the generator could not be used until after detailed inspection amounted to a loss of utility or amenity such as to constitute actual "damage" regardless of whether there was any actual physical damage, and (2) H, subcontracted by M to transport the generator, had assumed responsibility to EG for the goods and was therefore liable in damages in respect of economic loss.

Held, giving judgment on the preliminary issues, that (1) loss of utility did not constitute physical damage such as to give rise to a claim in negligence and loss of amenity could not be classified as a separate head of damage, and (2) the correct test to determine assumption of responsibility was whether there was a conscious assumption of responsibility to perform the relevant task rather than a conscious assumption of legal responsibility, *White v. Jones* [1995] 2 A.C. 207, [1995] C.L.Y. 3701 considered. If this governing principle applied, it was irrelevant whether recovery of the loss was fair, just and reasonable. In the instant case, it was clear that H and M had not sought to contend that they were not responsible to EG for the carriage of goods and on the facts of the case H was responsible to EG for carriage and EG had a valid claim for economic loss, *Henderson v. Merrett Syndicates Ltd* [1995] 2 A.C. 145, [1994] C.L.Y. 3362 applied.

EUROPEAN GAS TURBINES LTD (FORMERLY RUSTON GAS TURBINES LTD) v. MSAS CARGO INTERNATIONAL INC [2001] C.L.C. 880, Sir Oliver Popplewell, QBD.

4488. Economic loss – exclusion clauses – propriety rights – insurance claim arising from negligence and public nuisance

See INSURANCE: Jan De Nul (UK) Ltd v. Royale Belge NV. §3800

4489. Economic loss – exclusion of liability – scope of "supply of power"

[Electricity Act 1989 s.21.]

B, a freeholder, appealed against a finding that M's liability for economic loss was excluded by a term of the conditions under which M supplied electricity to S and P, poultry and egg businesses, when structures belonging to S and P were badly damaged by a fire held to be electrical in origin. B contended that the Electricity Act 1989 s.21 permitted a supplier to exclude liability for economic loss caused by negligence in relation to the provision of the power itself, but not in relation to the installation of equipment to enable the provision of power to take place, thus s.21 envisaged economic loss arising from negligence affecting the supply of power. M contended that, when s.21 was considered as a whole, it was clear that "the supply" had to be given a meaning which included the installation of equipment in order to provide the supply of electricity.

Held, allowing the appeal, that various passages of parliamentary debate admitted pursuant to *Pepper (Inspector of Taxes) v. Hart* [1993] A.C. 593, [1993] C.L.Y. 459 led to the conclusion that s.21 was introduced to permit exclusion of negligent liability for economic loss, resulting from the interruption or variation of the supply of electricity. Liability for economic loss arising from the negligent installation of the equipment to provide for the supply of electricity could not be excluded under s.21.

AE BECKETT & SONS (LYNDONS) LTD v. MIDLAND ELECTRICITY PLC [2001] 1 W.L.R. 281, Lord Phillips of Worth Matravers, M.R., CA.

4490. Economic loss – insurance policies – failure of insurer to implement direct debit mandate – nature of duty to insured

W, the executrix of the estate of her son, TW, appealed against the summary dismissal of her claim against G with whom TW had attempted to take out a life assurance policy as collateral security for his home which was mortgaged to P's predecessors, N. TW completed a deed of assignment in favour of N and provided a correctly completed direct debit mandate form to enable G to collect the premiums payable under the terms of the policy. G presented the form to the wrong branch of the bank with the result that no premiums were paid and the policy was treated by G as lapsed and void. TW completed a second mandate form which, again, was not implemented by G. Following TW's death, his home was repossessed by P and the property was sold for substantially less than its market value, leaving TW's estate with an indebtedness of £120,000. W sought to recover the loss, contending that, by virtue of its failure to collect the premiums, G had been in breach of the terms of the policy or the underlying agreement and, in the alternative, that G had been negligent.

Held, allowing the appeal, that W's claim had a real prospect of success. The correct completion of a direct debit instruction amounted to payment, or tender of payment, of the premiums. G had been under a duty, either as a matter of construction of the policy terms or by implication, to implement TW's direct debit mandate. Therefore, G could not rely upon its own failure to collect the premiums in order to treat the policy as lapsed or void. The assignment of the benefit but not the burden of the policy left W a party to the contract and therefore able to sue upon it. Further, the existence of an insurance contract did not necessarily prevent the existence of a duty of care in tort arising, unless specifically precluded by the contract terms. In the instant case, it was reasonably foreseeable that TW and his successors would suffer loss as a consequence of G's failure to implement the direct debit instruction. G and TW, as insurer and insured, were in sufficient proximity to make it just and reasonable for a duty of care to arise in relation to the collection of premiums. No such duty was precluded by the terms of the insurance contract and G had, in fact, voluntarily assumed responsibility for the collection of the premiums, *Banque Financiere de la Cite SA (formerly Banque Keyser Ullmann SA) v. Westgate Insurance Co (formerly Hodge General & Mercantile Co Ltd)* [1991] 2 A.C. 249, [1990] C.L.Y. 2696 considered, *Henderson v. Merrett Syndicates Ltd* [1995] 2 A.C. 145, [1994] C.L.Y. 3362 applied.

WELDON v. GRE LINKED LIFE ASSURANCE LTD [2000] 2 All E.R. (Comm) 914, Nelson, J., QBD.

4491. Foreseeability – accidents – employee climbing onto roof for legitimate purpose

PFC appealed against a finding upholding a claim in negligence brought by P, its sales director, arising from an incident in which P had gone on to the roof of PFC's premises to investigate the presence of a wire thought to have been attached by burglars or vandals. Having climbed on to the roof using a ladder, P had taken a couple of steps before slipping and falling through a skylight, sustaining serious injury. PFC argued, inter alia, that the accident had not been reasonably foreseeable and that it was not reasonable to require the erection of signs warning employees not to go on to the roof since the dangers of doing so were self-evident.

Held, dismissing the appeal, that the judge had been correct to conclude that the accident had been reasonably foreseeable and that PFC had breached its duty of care to take reasonable steps to prevent employees from going on to the roof. An employer owed a duty to take reasonable steps to guard against risks that were reasonably foreseeable as being likely to occur in the course of the employee's employment. The nature of those risks depended on the nature, functions, restrictions and parameters of the employee's job and the broad areas of activity in which he was likely to be engaged. P's job had been of a general nature, had involved his being responsible for security, and might reasonably have led him to go on to the roof for a legitimate purpose. Since the accident had been foreseeable, PFC should have issued a specific warning that access was not permitted to the roof. On the issue of contributory negligence the judge had been entitled to find that P was 50 per cent to blame for the accident.

PARKER v. PFC FLOORING SUPPLIES LTD [2001] EWCA Civ 1533, Potter, L.J., CA.

4492. Foreseeability – asbestos – respiratory diseases

[Factory and Workshop Act 1901 s.79; Asbestos Industry Regulations 1931 (SI 1931 1140) Reg.2.]

S appealed against a finding that it was liable in negligence for the deaths of two former employees, J and D, who had contracted mesothelioma following prolonged exposure to asbestos. C, who had employed D for a period of four years prior to his employment with S, appealed against a finding that it was in breach of its statutory duty, pursuant to the Asbestos Industry Regulations 1931 Reg.2, to provide an exhaust draught to suppress asbestos dust. It was submitted that (1) S had not acted negligently in failing to take precautions to protect J and D against exposure to asbestos, given the limited knowledge then available as to the risk of harm arising from the limited level of exposure experienced by J and D, and (2) C was not in breach of the Regulations since they applied only to the "asbestos industry" and C's use of asbestos had been merely incidental to its business.

Held, dismissing the appeals, that (1) the trial judge had been entitled to conclude that the risks flowing from exposure to asbestos had been sufficiently foreseeable at the relevant time, such that S should have taken appropriate precautions, and (2) it was clear from the Factory and Workshop Act 1901 s.79, under which the Regulations were made, that the Regulations were intended to apply to any factory or workshop where a process involving the manipulation of asbestos was used, and there was no reason not to attribute a natural and ordinary meaning to the words used in that section, *Banks v. Woodhall Duckham Ltd (No.1)* (Unreported, November 30, 1995), [1996] C.L.Y. 2990 considered. Further, C was not exempt from the Regulations, as D's involvement in the manipulation of the asbestos could not be described as "occasional". Correctly construed, "occasional" was something which occurred casually or intermittently and regular work could not be described as such.

SHELL TANKERS UK LTD v. JEROMSON; CHERRY TREE MACHINE CO LTD v. DAWSON; SHELL TANKERS UK LTD v. DAWSON; *sub nom.* JEROMSON v. SHELL TANKERS (UK) LTD; DAWSON v. CHERRY TREE MACHINE CO LTD, [2001] EWCA Civ 101, [2001] I.C.R. 1223, Hale, L.J., CA.

4493. Health and safety at work – personal injuries – suitability of vacuuming machine for specific user – employer's duty

See HEALTH AND SAFETY AT WORK: Watson v. Warwickshire CC. §3302

4494. Health and safety at work – stress – settlement of constructive dismissal claim – effect on personal injury action arising from same contract

T applied for summary judgment in relation to H's claim for damages for personal injuries sustained in the course of his employment. Two years after resigning from his position as storeman with T, H brought the proceedings contending that because T had been unhappy with the time H had taken off work to assist his wife following the birth of their child, it had undermined his position which resulted in H suffering a stress related disorder. H relied upon a psychiatrist's report which opined that his problems were work related. However, H's medical records revealed other personal difficulties which could have added to his stress. T contended that the claim had no reasonable prospect of success because of difficulties with both causation and foreseeability and that in any event, H had compromised his claim as a result of a settlement agreement reached in a constructive dismissal action against T arising from the same employment contract.

Held, granting summary judgment for T, that (1) it was not clear on the balance of probabilities that employment difficulties were the cause of H's depression; (2) there was no medical evidence capable of satisfying a court that psychiatric illness was a reasonably foreseeable consequence of T's alleged conduct, and (3) H had compromised his claim because the terms of the settlement agreement reached in the constructive dismissal action provided for T to pay a sum in full and final settlement of all claims H may have "arising out of his contract of employment or its termination" and the instant action arose from the contract of employment or its termination, *Sheriff v. Klyne Tugs (Lowestoft) Ltd* [1999] I.C.R. 1170, [1999] C.L.Y. 2056 applied.

HARRISON v. TEX INDUSTRIAL PLASTICS LTD, April 3, 2001, Judge Orrell, CC (Derby). [*Ex rel.* Buller Jeffries, Solicitors, 36 Bennetts Hill, Birmingham].

4495. Local authorities – footpaths – dangerous exit onto main road – liability for injuries suffered by pedestrian

K appealed against a decision that his claim against NFDC for breach of duty, which had arisen following an incident in which he was injured by a car after emerging from a footpath onto a main road, had no real prospect of success. Before granting planning permission for a residential development, NFDC had entered into an agreement with the developer for the construction of the footpath, the exit of which was on the inside of a bend on the main road. A further agreement dedicated a strip of land to be used by the highway authority to improve sight lines at the footpaths exit. However, the footpath had been opened and K subsequently injured before the improvements had taken place.

Held, allowing the appeal, that far from having no real prospect of success, K had a strong case against NFDC. NFDC owed a duty to those who might have wanted to use the footpath, to ensure that it was not opened until the sight line dangers were removed. It was clear that NFDC had been aware of the danger but that only preliminary steps had been taken to remove it. The fact that NFDC was exercising a statutory function under planning legislation did not make it immune from a negligence claim, *Stovin v. Wise and Norfolk CC* [1996] A.C. 923, [1996] C.L.Y. 4058 distinguished and *Chung Tak Lam v. Brennan (t/a Namesakes of Torbay)* [1998] E.H.L.R. 111, [1997] C.L.Y. 4087 considered.

KANE v. NEW FOREST DC (NO.1), [2001] EWCA Civ 878, [2002] 1 W.L.R. 312, Simon Brown, L.J., CA.

4496. Local authorities – footpaths – extent of duty to maintain

[Occupiers' Liability Act 1957 s.2.]

RBC was the occupier of a stretch of coast, including the cliffs and the foreshore beneath. Along the top of the cliffs was a coastal path for use by the general public. There were various beaches and coves beneath the cliffs along that stretch of coast. A number of unofficial paths, which had not been created by RBC and were not public footpaths nor highways, but which to RBC's knowledge were habitually used by members of the public, had been created by people taking short cuts down from the cliffs to the shore beneath. On one such path two pieces of wood had been vertically inserted into the slope by RBC's predecessor, and had the appearance of steps. As V climbed down the steps she tripped on the second step and fell. V brought an action against RBC on the grounds of negligence and claiming a breach of the Occupiers' Liability Act 1957 s.2 by failing to warn her of the danger created by the step, and in failing to inspect and maintain the path adequately RBC conceded that V was a visitor to that stretch of coast.

Held, dismissing the claim, that (1) the nature of the path and the risks inherent in climbing down it were clearly visible to and were seen by V, and she had needed no warning in relation to them, further, that those visible risks placed a heavy burden on her to take great care for her own safety, *Cotton v. Derbyshire Dales DC* Times, June 20, 1994, [1994] C.L.Y. 4286 and *Staples v. West Dorset DC* [1995] P.I.Q.R. P439, [1995] C.L.Y. 4731 considered; (2) it would be in excess of what RBC ought reasonably to be expected to do, to provide periodic inspection and maintenance such a path and to take steps to prevent access thereto. There was no evidence of negligence or breach prior to V's accident.

VINCENT v. RESTORMEL BC, July 27, 2000, District Judge Vincent, CC (Truro). [*Ex rel.* Veitch Penny Solicitors, 1 Manor Court, Dix's Field, Exeter, Devon].

4497. **Local authorities – footpaths – maintenance – dangerous defects – requirement for immediate repair**

D sustained personal injuries when leaving her home. She crossed the pavement to go to her parked car, when she caught her right heel in a depression caused by chipped kerbstones. She lost her balance and fell against the bonnet of her car. She suffered serious consequences eventually having to have her kneecap removed. The accident happened in a busy cul-de-sac. D alleged that the triangular depression over which she fell was 50 mm deep. DCC, as highway authority, alleged that the depression was 90 mm long and 30 mm deep at the worst point of the depression. The evidence suggested that the defect in the pavement was of long standing. The pavement had been regularly inspected by DCC and the inspection records did not mention a defect at the locus of the accident. No defect had been reported by D or anyone else prior to the accident. The defect was inspected after the accident and was brought to DCC's attention, and it was not considered to be dangerous by the highways inspector and not repaired.

Held, giving judgment for the defendant, that the triangular defect was 90 mm long and 30 mm deep at the worst point. The fact that the depression was 90mm long did not in itself make the defect dangerous. The relevant test was to ask if the defect was one that would cause a danger to road users. In the instant case, there was nothing remarkable about the area of pavement at all. It was necessary to balance private and public interests, and the public must expect that there will be defects in pavements. Having looked at the pavement and in light of the views of experienced road engineers and the fact that no complaint had been made about the defect prior to the accident, D had not proved that the pavement was dangerous such as required immediate repair, *Mills v. Barnsley MBC* [1992] P.I.Q.R. P291, [1993] C.L.Y. 2967, and *James v. Preseli Pembrokeshire DC* [1993] P.I.Q.R. P114, [1993] C.L.Y.2966 applied.

DEE v. DURHAM COUNTY COUNCIL, February 12, 2001, Recorder Bullock, CC (Newcastle). [*Ex rel.* Dickinson Dees Solicitors, St Ann's Wharf, 112 Quayside, Newcastle upon Tyne].

4498. **Local authorities – footpaths – no duty to maintain footpath established as public right of way**

[Highways Act 1980 s.31.]

B, a housing association, owned a large housing development in respect of which they retained ownership and control of some 10 per cent of the roads and footpaths not adopted by the Highway Authority. As a consequence of missing paving blocks removed by vandals, G tripped and fell in a former play area within a footpath crossing B's land. The public had regularly used the footpath and play area and B had taken no steps to restrict that use since 1977. On G's evidence, the play area had been block paved approximately five years earlier and the paving blocks had been missing for two months.

Held, dismissing the claim, that (1) if a duty was owed, B's inspection system was reasonable and in the absence of any reported defects, to have expected

B to have discovered the hole within two months would place too high a duty on them; (2) there had been at least 20 years uninterrupted use by the public of the footpath, resulting in a presumed dedication of a highway in accordance with the Highways Act 1980 s.31; (3) there had been free access and use of the play area and once it had been paved and therefore removed, that area became part of the footpath and therefore part of the right of way; (4) there was no "presumed" obligation on B to continue to maintain the footpath once the public right of way was established and, (5) no duty was owed by landowners to persons using a public right of way *McGeown v. Northern Ireland Housing Executive* [1995] 1 A.C. 233, [1994] C.L.Y. 4285 followed.

GARSIDE v. BRADFORD & NORTHERN HOUSING ASSOCIATION LTD, July 17, 2001, District Judge Gee, CC (Blackpool). [*Ex rel.* Langleys Solicitors, Queens House, Micklegate, York].

4499. Local authorities – roads – road maintenance – intermittent salting of icy roads

H was driving on a frosty morning when she skidded on a patch of ice and collided with a central reservation. In her claim for personal injuries against SHBC, the local highway authority, H stated in evidence that she had relied on the fact that the roads had been salted and drove accordingly. The road had indeed been salted by SHBC prior to the accident. H contended that (1) the careless salting of the road had created a dangerous trap, as a reasonable driver would not expect a properly salted road surface to carry areas of ice, and that "intermittent salting" carried a higher risk than if the road had not been salted at all, and (2) SHBC had also to cater for the less attentive driver, who would be more likely to suffer a mishap. H conceded that no statutory duty arose, *Goodes v. East Sussex CC* [2000] 1 W.L.R. 1356, [2000] 7 C.L. 394 followed. It was also accepted that there was no primary duty of care to salt the road in question. The duty was alleged to arise once the decision had been made to salt the road. It was that duty which, H contended, had to be discharged properly.

Held, dismissing the claim, that (1) a highway authority was under no duty to exercise its statutory power to salt icy roads, *Stovin v. Wise and Norfolk CC* [1996] A.C. 923, [1996] C.L.Y. 4058 applied. An authority could not be liable for the negligent exercise of that statutory power unless it made the roads less safe than where no salting had occurred at all; (2) intermittent salting was not worse than no salt being on the roads, and (3) the presence of ice on a salted road was no evidence of negligence, as there were many reasons why a patch of ice might remain after the proper salting of a road. The primary duty remained on the driver to take reasonable care.

HOLT v. SURREY HEATH BC, January 9, 2000, Judge Hull Q.C., CC (Kingston on Thames). [*Ex rel.* David Platt, Barrister, Crown Office Chambers, 1 Paper Buildings, Temple, London].

4500. Measure of damages – personal injuries – assessment – relevant governing law

[Private International Law (Miscellaneous Provisions) Act 1995 s.11, s.14 (3) (b).]

A preliminary issue arose in an action in negligence brought by H against C following a road accident in Greece, as to what law should apply to the assessment of damages. C had admitted liability for causing personal injuries to H while driving in a hire car whilst on holiday in Greece. It was common ground that pursuant to the Private International Law (Miscellaneous Provisions) Act 1995 s.11, the applicable law was Greek law. In accordance with Greek law, a right of action supported the suing of the Greek insurance company which, in any event, had admitted liability to indemnify the defendant. H had prepared a schedule of damages and contended that since the assessment of damages was a procedural matter English law applied. C argued that not only the head of damage but its assessment was the subject of the substantive applicable law.

Held, determining the preliminary issue in favour of H, that the assessment of damages was subject to the procedural law governing the English court. The assessment of damages was a procedural matter for the English court, falling within s.14(3)(b) of the Act. Accordingly, damages would be assessed in accordance with English law irrespective of the provisions of the local law. The assessment of damages was a "jury question" albeit one that was usually taken over by the judge. To impose a Greek bracket would inevitably take that assessment away from the judge as jury.

H (A CHILD) v. C [2001] 1 W.L.R. 2386, Holland, J., QBD.

4501. Measure of damages – restitution – destruction of chattels – reasonableness of ordering cost of replacement

[Civil Procedure Rules 1998 (SI 1998 3132) Part 36 r.36.1 (2).]

S appealed against the measure of the damages awarded ([1999] 2 Lloyd's Rep. 491, [2000] C.L.Y. 4729) against H for the damage caused to its quayside crane as a result of H's negligent manoeuvering of its container vessel. S further challenged as being wrong in principle the decision to order it to pay costs accrued after its rejection of H's written offer to settle. S submitted that on authority, it should have been awarded the replacement value of the crane as opposed to its resale value. There was a significant difference between the two figures because a replacement crane bought in the United States would have had to have been modified and then shipped to Britain at an extra cost of £1.7 million.

Held, dismissing the appeal, that given that S had already ordered two cranes and had never contemplated replacing the crane with a secondhand modified crane from the United States, it was unreasonable to order H to pay the replacement value rather than the resale value of the crane. Some inconvenience had been caused by the loss of the crane but S had not lost any capacity nor been subject to any serious financial loss, *Ruxley Electronics and Construction Ltd v. Forsyth* [1996] A.C. 344, [1995] C.L.Y. 1561 applied. The judge's decision as to costs was within his discretion under the Civil Procedure Rules 1998 Part 36 r.36.1 (2) and was not wrong in principle, notwithstanding the fact that no payment into court had been made, *Amber v. Stacey* [2001] 2 All E.R. 88 distinguished on its facts.

SOUTHAMPTON CONTAINER TERMINALS LTD v. HANSA SCHIFFAHRTS GmbH (THE MAERSK COLOMBO); *sub nom.* SOUTHAMPTON CONTAINER TERMINALS LTD v. SCHIFFAHRISGESELLSCH "HANSA AUSTRALIA" MGH & CO; SOUTHAMPTON CONTAINER TERMINALS LTD v. HANSA SCHIFFAHRTSGESELLSCHAFT MBH, [2001] EWCA Civ 717, [2001] 2 Lloyd's Rep. 275, Clarke, L.J., CA.

4502. Occupiers liability – defective premises – duty of care – injury to child from central heating pipework – expectation of parental vigilance

[Defective Premises Act 1972 s.4.]

B, a nine month old baby, claimed damages for severe burns which occurred when he became trapped against hot central heating pipes. B alleged that C, the local authority landlord, had been negligent or in breach of the Defective Premises Act 1972 s.4 in that the central heating system had been defectively operating 24 hours a day at higher temperatures than those at which it was set and, regardless of any defects, that the pipe work should have been encased given the temperature at which the heating system operated. C maintained that its actions in not encasing the pipework had been reasonable given the excessive costs of encasing pipework in all its properties and that it had been entitled to expect B's parents to protect him from such risks.

Held, dismissing the claim, that it had not been negligent to allow the heating system to run constantly. While the system's controls had probably allowed temperatures in excess of those set, that had not been causative of the accident. Although local authorities must be taken to be aware of the risk, *Ryan v. Camden LBC* (1983) 13 Fam. Law 81, [1983] C.L.Y. 2545 followed, a reasonable local authority could have concluded that the risk was slight and, on the assumption that the parents of children of crawling age would guard against the slight risk of a child becoming trapped against pipework, was entitled to weigh that risk against the costs of encasing pipework in all its properties, *Walker v. Northumberland CC* [1995] 1 All E.R. 737, [1995] C.L.Y. 3659 and *Bull v. Devon AHA* [1993] 4 Med. L.R. 117 considered.

B (A CHILD) v. CAMDEN LBC [2001] P.I.Q.R. P9, Nelson, J., QBD.

4503. Occupiers liability – rights of way – dominant tenement owner's duty to repair

[Occupiers' Liability Act 1984.]

V sustained injuries caused by a fall from her moped on a field track owned by G. V had a private right of way over the track. She brought a claim under the Occupiers' Liability Act 1984, contending that the accident was due to the condition of the track. V stated that her husband had offered to repair the track prior to the accident, but that his offer had been refused by G. G asserted that the track's condition was reasonable given the circumstances and its location, and denied that he had refused V permission to repair it.

Held, refusing the claim, that the relationship between V and G was that of owners of a dominant tenement and servient tenement. As the resident owner, G exercised extensive control over the track and was an occupier in terms of the Act, even though V also had a degree of control over it, such that she owed a duty to her own visitors, *Wheat v. E Lacon & Co Ltd* [1966] A.C. 552, [1966] C.L.Y. 8132 applied. On the facts, however, the track had not deteriorated to such an extent that a reasonable person would have found repairs to be necessary. Occupiers would be faced with an excessive burden if they owed a duty to visitors to fill in potholes similar to those in the track at the time of V's accident.

VODDEN v. GAYTON [2001] P.I.Q.R. P4, Toulson, J., QBD.

4504. Occupiers liability – visitors – warning notices – obvious risk – variety of risks

[Occupiers' Liability Act 1957 s.2.]

N appealed against a finding that it had been negligent and in breach of its duty of care owed under the Occupiers' Liability Act 1957 s.2 to KD, who had drowned whilst swimming in a pond in the grounds of a stately home under the control of N. It was found that N had failed to prevent visitors from swimming in the pond and had failed to erect adequate warning notices. N submitted that it was under no duty to warn against the obvious danger of swimming given that the relevant pond was no more hazardous than any other. D, the widow of KD, submitted that (1) the risk of drowning was reasonably foreseeable as the pond was often used by bathers. Further, that bathers might have failed to appreciate the less obvious risk that a normally competent swimmer might experience difficulties in cold water, and (2) given that evidence showed there was a danger of contracting Weils disease from swimming in the pond, had there been a notice warning of that danger D would not have swum in the pond.

Held, allowing the appeal, that (1) in the absence of a relative causative risk that was not obvious, there was no duty on the occupier of land to warn against an obvious danger, *Staples v. West Dorset DC* [1995] P.I.Q.R. P439, [1995] C.L.Y. 4731 applied. In the instant case, the risk of drowning was clearly obvious, and (2) the risk of contracting Weils disease and the risk of drowning were fundamentally different. A breach of duty to protect against Weils disease could not support a claim for damages attributable to a different cause, *South Australia Asset Management Corp v. York Montague Ltd* [1997] A.C. 191, [1996] C.L.Y. 4519 applied. Since the risks were intrinsically different, so were any dependent duties.

DARBY v. NATIONAL TRUST FOR PLACES OF HISTORIC INTEREST OR NATURAL BEAUTY, [2001] EWCA Civ 189, (2001) 3 L.G.L.R. 29, May, L.J., CA.

4505. Personal injuries – package holidays – alleged negligence of tutor – liability of tour operator

See LEISURE INDUSTRY: Gallagher v. Airtours Holidays Ltd. §4280

4506. Personal injuries – tour operators – standard of care – defective furniture

See LEISURE INDUSTRY: McRae v. Thomson Holidays Ltd. §4291

4507. Professional negligence – accountants – liability to third party for negligent share valuation

[Unfair Contract Terms Act 1977.]

The executors of H's estate, K, sought summary judgment in an action against a firm of accountants, PWC, for professional negligence. H had owned a substantial shareholding in a company, BGG, and following his death BGG, in accordance with a "buy back" provision in its Articles of Association, requested that PWC prepare a valuation of H's shareholding. PWC duly produced a valuation of £2.1 per share. The bulk of the shareholding was subsequently sold at that price pursuant to a deemed notice given by K. Following the sale, a report was prepared by a second firm of accountants at K's request which valued the shares at £4 each. Proceedings were thereafter issued against PWC in negligence seeking damages in excess of £30 million. Two issues arose, namely (1) whether an accountant assigned by the director of a company to carry out a valuation of that company's shares and in so doing establishing the price at which shares in the ownership of specific shareholders would be compulsorily acquired in accordance with the company's Articles of Association, owed the specific shareholders a duty of care when carrying out the valuation, and (2) whether such liability, if established, could be subject to a clause in the contract between the company and accountant limiting liability and, if so, whether such a clause fulfilled the requirements of reasonableness within the Unfair Contract Terms Act 1977.

Held, granting the application in part, that (1) a duty of care was owed by PWC to K despite the absence of any contractual relationship between the parties. Such a conclusion was justified in the light of the fact that (a) PWC was appointed for a particular purpose of which it was well aware, namely the sale of the shares by K; (b) K could have no means of protecting themselves as against a negligent valuation whilst PWC always had the option of obtaining additional indemnity insurance, a larger fee or simply refusing to act; (c) the imposition of a duty would not result in an "indeterminate risk to an indeterminate number of people"; (d) K had not participated in agreeing the terms and conditions on the basis of which PWC were retained and which furthermore did not exclude the possibility of liability for negligence to third parties, and (e) K was the only party with any claim if the valuation proved to be negligent and therefore if no duty of care existed PWC would be free to act with impunity, *White v. Jones* [1995] 2 A.C. 207, [1995] C.L.Y. 3701 applied, and (2) it was not appropriate to determine whether PWC could rely on the limitation clause or whether such clause was unfair under the 1977 Act prior to the full trial. A decision on such issues would not result in the action being concluded, and, furthermore, might produce further delays given the likelihood of an appeal.

KILLICK v. PRICEWATERHOUSECOOPERS (NO.1) [2001] 1 B.C.L.C. 65, Neuberger, J., Ch D.

4508. Professional negligence – accountants – tax avoidance schemes – measure of damages

[Finance Act 1985 Sch.19 Part III para.9(1).]

GS, a firm of accountants, appealed against the assessment of damages in proceedings for professional negligence commenced by L. L carried on business with F under the auspices of a limited company. GS were instructed to devise a scheme to avoid the personal liability of L and F to CGT. The scheme proposed involved the sale of F's shares to L and their subsequent buy back by the company. It was envisaged that this would create capital losses whilst the company's resultant liability to ACT could be offset against its liability to mainstream corporation tax. GS overlooked the impact of the Finance Act 1985 Sch.19 Part III para.9(1), as a result of which a much reduced allowable loss would have arisen on the company purchase of the shares. F's shares were purchased by L but the remainder of the scheme was not implemented. The judge had found that GS had been negligent and, in particular, that if only enough shares were purchased before the end of the 1989/1990 tax year as was necessary to extinguish the liability to CGT, the resulting ACT liability would have been reduced to £34,000. The measure of damages was assessed as the CGT liability of L less the income tax payable by L arising out of the company purchase of the shares. The judge concluded that if ACT of £34,000 had been payable in 1990 the company would have paid it but that if it had been decided to postpone the payment until 1991, the company would not have had the necessary funds and L would have been obliged to contribute. Assuming that the company would have paid the ACT of £34,000 in 1990, L did not have to give credit for that amount as going to reduce their tax saving. GS contended that L were entitled to nominal damages only as they would have been obliged to make a personal contribution to the ACT liability at some stage even if the company had been able to meet its liability at the relevant time, thus eliminating any tax saving.

Held, dismissing the appeal, that the suggestion that L would have been obliged to make a personal contribution to the company's ACT liability at some stage even if the company was able to meet its liability at the relevant time, was unsupported by the relevant findings of the judge.

LITTLE v. GEORGE LITTLE SEBIRE & CO, [2001] EWCA Civ 894, [2001] S.T.C. 1065, Peter Gibson, L.J., CA.

4509. Professional negligence – architects – flood damage – liability to ultimate occupier

B, the occupier of an industrial unit which had been damaged by flooding, instituted proceedings against SW, a firm of architects, who had been responsible for the design of the premises. B contended that whilst there had been no contract between the parties, an architect could nevertheless be liable to the ultimate occupier of the premises.

Held, giving judgment for B, that SW could reasonably have foreseen that a future occupier of the premises would ultimately suffer damage as a result of the defective drainage system. Accordingly an architect could be held liable and owe a duty of care in appropriate circumstances, *Murphy v. Brentwood DC* [1991] 1 A.C. 398, [1991] C.L.Y. 2661 and *Donoghue v. Stevenson* [1932] A.C. 562 applied. B had had a reasonable opportunity to discover the absence of overflows in the drainage system on a professional inspection of the premises before taking the lease and it followed that, as the first flood was caused by the absence of overflows, SW could not be held liable for the damage caused as a result. The second flood had, however, resulted from a combination of the absence of overflows and the under design of the system, the latter of which B could not reasonably have been expected to discover and for which SW were thus liable.

BAXALL SECURITIES LTD v. SHEARD WALSHAW PARTNERSHIP; *sub nom.* BLAXHALL SECURITIES LTD v. SHEARD WALSHAW PARTNERSHIP [2001] C.L.C. 188, Judge Peter Bowsher Q.C., QBD (T&CC).

4510. Professional negligence – architects – set off by way of counterclaim – measure of damages – improper specification supplied

CG, a firm of architects, were retained by CM on a building project. CG subsequently claimed for its fees, with CM eventually admitting CG's entitlement but claiming set off by way of a counterclaim. CM complained that the rake angle of a roof terrace was incorrect, an underground car park access ramp had been wrongly designed, the specification for a swimming pool was negligent and the access to a room was incorrect. CG's claim was agreed in the sum of £85,000 and the case proceeded on the counterclaim alone.

Held, giving judgment on the counterclaim in the sum of £9,978, that CG had specified the rake incorrectly and the measure of damages was the cost of achieving a satisfactory terrace. The ramp design accorded with best practice but CM had requested alterations that meant it was not constructed to that standard. Given the scope of CG's skills and instructions and its advice that CM should engage pool consultant there was no evidence of any lack of skill on CG's part. The room access problem was not CG's fault and was attributable to the engineers. It was only a minor problem that was easily remedied and was typical of the difficulties that occurred in projects of this type in the absence of any actionable form of negligence.

CHRISTOPHER MORAN HOLDINGS LTD v. CARDEN & GODFREY (A FIRM) 73 Con. L.R. 28, Judge David Wilcox, QBD (T&CC).

4511. Professional negligence – architects – soundproofing – latent damage – accrual of cause of action

[Limitation Act 1980 s.14A(6).]

N sought damages for breach of contract and negligence following the discovery of inadequate soundproofing at a number of properties that had been designed by P, a firm of architects. N contended that (1) the defect resulted from P's negligence and that P had been under a continuing duty to review its design until final certificates of completion had been issued. In particular it was argued that, following receipt of N's letter concerning the quality of the soundproofing, P had been under a contractual obligation to investigate the matter and remedy any defect, and (2) P's liability in negligence had accrued only when the tenants had discovered the problems after a period in residence. P denied liability and argued that both causes of action were time barred.

Held, giving judgment for the defendant, that (1) the RIBA standard terms and conditions upon which P had been engaged contained no express terms specifying an ongoing duty to review the design following practical completion. The letter sent to P had not operated to give notice to P that it ought to review the design nor investigate the soundproofing problem or its cause, and (2) the cause of action in negligence had accrued no later than the date of practical completion. The relevant date upon which the cause of action accrued was not the date when N had knowledge or ought to have had knowledge of the damage suffered, but rather the date upon which the fault existed. It followed that the cause of action in negligence had accrued when the properties were handed over, *Pirelli General Cable Works Ltd v. Oscar Faber & Partners* [1983] 2 A.C. 1, [1983] C.L.Y. 2216 and *Tozer Kemsley & Millbourn Holdings Ltd v. J Jarvis & Sons Ltd* (1984) 1 Const. L.J. 79, [1985] C.L.Y. 209 applied. N had acquired the requisite knowledge for the purposes of the Limitation Act 1980 s.14A(6) earlier than it had contended and accordingly the actions had been brought out of time.

NEW ISLINGTON AND HACKNEY HOUSING ASSOCIATION LTD v. POLLARD THOMAS & EDWARDS LTD [2001] B.L.R. 74, Dyson, J., QBD (T&CC).

4512. Professional negligence – architects – standard of care – duties of expert witnesses

C's hospital, underwent major building works between 1987 and 1990 out of which arose numerous disputes. The main contract was between C and TW. The contractor made claims against C amounting to £22 million for delay, variations and disruption. Arbitration proceedings between C and TW were eventually compromised by C paying £6.2 million to TW. C then brought proceedings against its professional advisers, including the architects, WG. The allegations against WG was that they were negligent in relation to the extensions of time granted to TW in that, either no extensions should have been granted or that shorter extensions should have been granted. The court at first instance rejected C's expert evidence as inadequate and determined the issues on the basis of the contemporaneous documents. It was held that C had to prove (1) the standards of the ordinarily competent architect at the time of the act complained of, and (2) what was actually done and that the actions taken fell below the required standard. Both parties applied to the Court of Appeal for permission to appeal.

Held, dismissing the applications, that there was no reasonable prospect of the Court of Appeal interfering with the judge's decision. Furthermore it would not be possible to deal with the issues raised on appeal without reopening or revisiting the evidence on other issues decided by the judge, which were not the subject of appeal. Such an approach would not be a proper use of the appeal process.

ROYAL BROMPTON HOSPITAL NHS TRUST v. HAMMOND (NO.7), [2001] EWCA Civ 206, 76 Con. L.R. 148, Sir Anthony Evans, CA.

4513. Professional negligence – architects – standards of care – duties of expert witnesses

R instituted professional negligence claims against a number of contractors, including P, its project managers and W, its architects, in connection with the construction of a new hospital. R contended that W had negligently, and in breach of their retainer, granted extensions of time for completion, and that P, in failing to ensure that W performed their contractual duties to a proper standard, had also been negligent and in breach of their contract. At trial, the experts appearing for R had been recently retained and had not contributed to the formulation of the claim or the drafting of proceedings.

Held, giving judgment for the claimant in part only, that (1) in relation to the grant of an extension of time by an architect or project manager, it was virtually impossible to reach a finding of professional negligence in the absence of plain factual error since there was ample scope for a genuine divergence of opinion as between such professionals, *Bolam v. Friern Hospital Management Committee* [1957] 1 W.L.R. 582, [1957] C.L.Y. 2431, applied, and (2) the expert evidence adduced in favour of R was unacceptable. The retained experts had failed to recognise that their task was not to judge others by their own personal professional standards, but to consider the standard of the ordinarily competent member of their respective professions. Neither was fully familiar with the documentation relevant to the opinions about the professional performance of W and P and one expert had been overly partial to R's case at the expense of his actual beliefs and duty to assist the court. There were occasions when the court could substitute its own common sense for sub standard expert evidence, but it was not permitted to do so in circumstances, such as the instant case, where an informed conclusion could not be achieved without the application of particular skill, training or expertise, *JD Williams & Co Ltd v. Michael Hyde & Associates Ltd* [2000] Lloyd's Rep. P.N. 823, [2000] 9 C.L. 519 applied. Accordingly, in the main, R had failed to discharge the onus upon it to prove that the extensions had been granted negligently.

ROYAL BROMPTON HOSPITAL NHS TRUST v. HAMMOND (NO.6) 76 Con. L.R. 131, Judge Richard Seymour Q.C., QBD (T&CC).

4514. Professional negligence – banks – duty of care – borrower led to believe that insurers should be changed – bank's duties

F brought a claim in negligence against a bank, J. In order to refurbish a property which she owned with a view to sale, F had borrowed £250,000 from J. The property had been valued by surveyors acting for the bank. F had also insured the property with EIG through a broker which was a subsidiary of the bank. In 1991 builders working on the property reported cracking and that was reported to EIG, which appointed loss adjusters. In 1994 the bank demanded repayment and in 1995 it obtained an order for possession. In 1996 F issued proceedings against EIG which were compromised on terms that EIG would complete remedial works to the property and pay F damages and costs. The bank sold the property in 1999 for less than the amount of F's indebtedness. F contended that her losses were a direct result of J having advised or required her to insure with EIG. F maintained that J had been negligent in advising or requiring her to change insurers because at the material time J had been in possession of a 1989 report from the surveyors which referred to cracking.

Held, giving judgment for F, that whilst J had not expressly advised F to change her insurers and it was not a term of the proposed lending that that she should do so, its actions had led her reasonably to believe that she was required to do so as a condition of the facility. The actual advice to change had emanated from her broker and solicitor. If a bank advised a customer to change his insurers, it could potentially owe the customer a duty to draw to his attention any fact bearing upon the prudence of such a change, but if it was simply a condition of the facility that such a change was made, then on ordinary principles the bank would be under no obligation to consider the advisability of such a course of action. On the particular facts of the instant case, although the bank had not acted formally as F's broker, it had held the broker out as its "insurance division" and F had been entitled to assume that the services that she was being offered were services provided by J. Accordingly, J had assumed the responsibilities of an insurance broker and had been in breach of a duty owed to F in accepting instructions from her to change insurers whilst in possession of the knowledge of the cracking revealed in the 1989 report. A broker in possession of the 1989 report would have been obliged to advise F of the need to disclose its contents to the new insurance company. Even if the view was taken that no disclosure was necessary, there would be an obvious risk that any new insurer would take the view that its liability was restricted.

FROST v. JAMES FINLAY BANK LTD [2001] Lloyd's Rep. Bank. 302, Hart, J., Ch D.

4515. Professional negligence – barristers – advice given concerning settlement

H appealed against a decision upholding a determination to strike out his claim for negligence against a barrister, B. H contended that he had been negligently or dishonestly advised by B to settle a claim against an insurance company in order to pursue a second claim and had suffered substantial loss as a result. H submitted that the sum offered did not cover his losses and that B had acted negligently in advising him to accept the settlement.

Held, dismissing the appeal, that H had no real prospect of showing that the estimate of loss had been wrong to the extent of being negligent. Further, H had no real prospect of showing that no competent barrister could reasonably have advised, on the basis of the material available to him, as B had done, *Arthur JS Hall & Co v. Simons* [2000] 3 W.L.R. 543, [2000] 8 C.L. 533 considered.

HUSSAIN v. CUDDY WOODS & COCHRANE [2001] Lloyd's Rep. P.N.134, Pill, L.J., CA.

4516. Professional negligence – barristers – client advised to compromise claim in best interests – standard of informed and competent counsel

M brought an action in negligence against solicitors, BLJ, and counsel, G, in respect of advice given to him in the course of a conference in G's chambers that M had no defence to a personal injury claim brought against him in a personal capacity as the former managing director of a liquidated company. He was advised to settle the claim on the best available terms. M argued that if he had been properly advised he could have successfully defended the personal injury claim.

Held, dismissing the claim, that if the facts were such that a significant proportion of informed and competent barristers would have advised as G had, then M could not succeed in a professional negligence claim, *Ridehalgh v. Horsefield* [1994] Ch. 205, [1994] C.L.Y. 3623 applied. The facts of the instant case were such that G was entitled to come to the opinion that it would be in M's best interests to settle the claim. Although this view was unpalatable to M, G had a clear duty to give advice that was in his client's best interest.

McILGORM v. BELL LAMB & JOYNSON [2001] P.N.L.R. 28, Gibbs, J., QBD.

4517. Professional negligence – barristers – striking out – summary judgment

[Civil Procedure Rules 1998 (SI 1988 3132) Part 24 r.24(2).]

H appealed against the dismissal of its application for either summary judgment under the Civil Procedure Rules 1998 Part 24 r.24(2) or the striking out of G's negligence action. G had been the majority shareholder of a company, DD, which had owned land which it sought to develop. DD was unable to obtain planning permission and was ultimately wound up. The land was compulsorily purchased by the local authority which subsequently granted itself planning permission for development and sold the land at a substantial profit. G took advice from H as to whether he could bring an action against the local authority. A barrister, A, instructed by H, advised that G could make a claim in his own right despite the fact that DD was no longer in existence. G's claim against the local authority was struck out, and G then brought the claim against H and A, arguing that the advice given was negligent as it failed to take account of G's lack of locus standi. In its appeal, H argued that the judge was wrong not to strike out or give summary judgment on G's action as the advice had not been negligent according to the law as it then stood.

Held, dismissing the appeal, that the judge's decision had been right and he had taken the right approach in that he decided that if there were to be a trial in any event, it was more satisfactory that all the matters should be considered by the judge at that trial. It was arguable that the advice given had failed to properly identify all the possible avenues open to G and to address the potential blocks to his claim. It was not possible to say with certainty that G would not have found a way to proceed if he had been properly advised.

GREEN v. HANCOCKS (A FIRM) [2001] Lloyd's Rep. P.N. 212, Chadwick, L.J., CA.

4518. Professional negligence – building contractors – defective building work – liability for failure to warn of safety aspects – Part 20 proceedings

X, an investment company, brought an action against Y for faulty construction work, and Y joined Z as a Part 20 defendant. Y had agreed with X to construct building works and in order to safeguard the flank wall of a neighbouring property had decided to underpin it, being advised on the matter by a structural engineering company, K. Z had been hired to carry out the underpinning, which it completed successfully and backfilled. Y started excavating the basement but the underpinning moved laterally and the central section alongside the flank wall collapsed. The lateral movement could have been prevented by the provision of temporary lateral support. Y was unaware of the necessity to provide such support and contended that Z had a duty to warn it of the danger. Although Z did not know how the excavation work would be carried out, it knew of the danger, and so should not have assumed that the work would be done safely.

Held, giving judgment for Y, that Z was not under a duty to warn Y of the potential danger of excavation of the underpinning. Z was aware of the involvement of K, and it did not know that Y would excavate in a way which would compromise the safety of the underpinning, it would be unreasonable to expect Z to warn Y of the possible danger.

AURUM INVESTMENTS LTD v. AVONFORCE LTD (IN LIQUIDATION) (2001) 3 T.C.L.R. 21, Dyson, J., QBD (T&CC).

4519. Professional negligence – consultants – computer contracts – consultancy services

SB, a company carrying on various manufacturing and trading activities, brought proceedings against SH, who had been retained by SB to provide information technology consultancy services, alleging that SH had acted negligently and in breach of contract in recommending O, a supplier of computer systems, in connection with the acquisition of a computerised accounting system.

Held, giving judgment for SB, that SH had or should have known that the software provided by O was not well proven and that the hardware that O had supplied would be inadequate for SB's purposes. The court defined SH's responsibilities, described the breaches of those responsibilities, set out the principles by which damages would be assessed and dealt with SH's allegations that SB had contributed to and failed to mitigate its losses.

STEPHENSON BLAKE (HOLDINGS) LTD v. STREETS HEAVER LTD [2001] Lloyd's Rep. P.N. 44, Judge Hicks Q.C., QBD (OR).

4520. Professional negligence – financial advisers – limitations – deliberate concealment of negligent advice concerning transfer of pension

[Limitation Act 1980 s.32(1)(b).]

In a negligence action brought by L against F, her former financial adviser, the parties agreed that the question of limitation should be tried as a preliminary issue. L alleged that in 1988, relying on the advice of F, she had opted out of her occupational pension scheme and taken out a personal pension plan, thereby incurring a financial loss.

Held, determining the preliminary issue in favour of L, that the advice that F had given in 1988, which had been negligent, was deliberate in that it was intended to be given. Accordingly, L could rely on the Limitation Act 1980 s.32(1)(b) which extended the limitation period where any fact relevant to the claimant's right of action had been deliberately concealed. The facts relevant to L's right of action which were to be treated as concealed were F's failure to compare the respective benefits of the occupational and personal pension schemes, its failure to satisfy itself that L understood the risk that she was undertaking and the financial loss which L had incurred as a result of such omissions. Since L had commenced proceedings within six years of the date when she had discovered that she had been negligently advised, her action was not barred by limitation, *Brocklesby v. Armitage & Guest* [2001] 1 All E.R. 172, [2000] 3 C.L. 485 and *Liverpool Roman Catholic Archdiocesan Trustees Inc v. Goldberg (No.1)* [2001] 1 All E.R. 182, [2000] 8 C.L. 60 applied and *Foreman v. O'Driscoll & Partners* [2000] Lloyd's Rep. P.N. 720, [2000] 12 C.L. 389 not followed.

LOOSEMORE v. FINANCIAL CONCEPTS (A FIRM) [2001] Lloyd's Rep. P.N. 235, Judge Raymond Jack Q.C., QBD (Merc Ct).

4521. Professional negligence – financial advisers – misselling of personal pensions – date of knowledge of loss

[Limitation Act 1980 s.14A.]

The claimant, C, brought an action in negligence against the defendant, D, a financial adviser, who had advised him to transfer his accrued early leaver benefits from an occupational pension scheme into a personal pension plan. Two years later C had become aware of a pensions misselling scandal and had sought reassurance from his plan provider that he had not suffered loss as a result of the transfer of his pension. He was advised to contact D and was subsequently provided with a fact sheet prepared by the Securities and Investments Board in which it was stated that those who suspected or knew that advice given to them had been bad should take prompt steps to avoid potential claims being time barred. C did not instigate proceedings until after the primary six year limitation period had expired but C contended that, by virtue of the Limitation Act 1980 s.14A, he was not time barred in that he had not known about the loss he had suffered by acting upon D's negligent advice until later actuarial advice confirmed that a loss had arisen.

Held, determining the preliminary issue in favour of C, that, whilst C had suspected that he had been improperly advised, actual knowledge of the alleged damage suffered only arose upon receipt of the actuary's calculations of the purported loss. The fact sheet produced by the Securities and Investments Board had been aimed at calming fears and had not resulted in imputed knowledge. A reasonable person reading the fact sheet would have concluded that automatic redress would have been provided to victims of pension misselling from within the financial services industry.

GLAISTER v. GREENWOOD [2001] Lloyd's Rep. P.N. 412, Lawrence Collins, J., Ch D.

4522. Professional negligence – solicitors – choice of forum – comparative awards for personal injuries – duty to investigate

W, who had sustained serious injuries in a road traffic accident in Austria, brought a claim against a firm of solicitors, AB, alleging that AB had been negligent in that it had failed to commence proceedings against the defendant driver, H, in the UK. C, a solicitor employed by AB, had issued proceedings in Austria notwithstanding that H was an English national. The Austrian claim realised only a small fraction of the damages that would have been awarded to W by a UK court. Three preliminary issues relating to liability fell to be determined by the court, namely (1) whether AB had investigated sufficiently, or at all, the merits of commencing proceedings in the UK; (2) whether AB had ascertained whether any award made by a UK court was enforceable against H's Austrian insurers, and (3) whether it had been reasonable for AB to conclude that any award made against H would not have been satisfied in full by the insurers.

Held, giving judgment for W on preliminary issues, that C had failed to ascertain the comparative values of likely awards in Austria and the UK. He had been naive to accept the insurer's view that the claim should be brought under Austrian law and had failed to discover whether it would be possible to enforce a judgment obtained in the UK against an Austria insurance company. C had failed to obtain the advice of counsel and had taken only limited advice from an Austrian lawyer and it had not been reasonable for him to reach the conclusions that he did.

WALLER v. AB (A FIRM), July 19, 2000, Recorder Goddard Q.C., QBD (Queens Bench Division). [*Ex rel.* Hugh Potter & Co Solicitors, 14-32 Hewitt Street, Manchester].

4523. Professional negligence – solicitors – conveyancing – extent of duty to disclose when acting for lender and borrower

B, solicitors facing allegations of professional negligence, applied to strike out the claim against them on the grounds that it disclosed no reasonable cause of action, that it was scandalous, frivolous or vexatious, or that it was an abuse of process. The claimant, BW, had advanced a loan to B's client, A who had subsequently defaulted on the repayments. B had been retained by both parties. The advance had been subject to a special condition that "existing mortgages in the name of the applicants" had to be redeemed prior to completion. BW submitted that B's failure to draw to its attention the existence of A's two other mortgages and the fact that A's declared investment income was already committed to discharging those loans, had induced it to make an advance which it would not otherwise have made. B maintained that the claim had no legal basis.

Held, giving the claimant 14 days in which to amend its statement of claim, failing which it be struck out, that (1) it would be an absurd construction of the special condition if mortgages on other properties with other lenders had to be discharged before completion, *Birmingham Midshires Mortgage Services Ltd v. David Parry & Co* 51 Con. L.R. 1, [1996] C.L.Y. 3914 applied, and (2) a solicitor acting for both parties had a qualified duty of disclosure; he was required to disclose information of which he became aware while carrying out the lender's instructions, but he was not obliged to impart his entire knowledge of the borrower's circumstances to the lender, such as information arising out of previous dealings with the borrower, therefore failure to disclose the latter did not create a conflict of interest.

BRISTOL AND WEST BUILDING SOCIETY v. BADEN BARNES GROVES & CO [2000] Lloyd's Rep. P.N. 788, Chadwick, J., Ch D.

4524. Professional negligence – solicitors – duty of care – elderly client in hospital – cancellation of appointment relating to execution of will

F, a firm of solicitors, appealed against a decision that it had acted negligently in failing to monitor the state of health of an elderly client, C, who had recently been taken into hospital, and in failing to make an appointment to execute his will. Prior to falling ill, C had contacted one of the solicitors in the firm stating that he wanted to make a will and to execute an enduring power of attorney. The will was drawn up but was not executed. The solicitor was informed of C's illness by H, a relation of C, but understood his condition not to be serious, following a message left by a friend of C. No further action was taken regarding the matter until the hospital arranged an appointment which the solicitor cancelled for personal reasons. F contended that the judge had overlooked, or not fully taken into account, the effect which the message from the friend would have had upon a reasonable solicitor, armed with the knowledge possessed by the solicitor in the instant case.

Held, dismissing the appeal, that a solicitor owed a duty of care to a beneficiary under a will that was similar to that owed to the testator. Such duty was not altered by the circumstances of the intended beneficiary or the amount intended to be given under the will to that beneficiary, *White v. Jones* [1995] 2 A.C. 207, [1995] C.L.Y. 3701 applied. In the instant case, the solicitor had had a duty to satisfy himself that the delay in executing the will owing to the cancellation of the appointment would not be disadvantageous to C, and if necessary a substitute should have been appointed. It was observed that an appointment with an elderly client in hospital should not to be cancelled unless the client was agreeable to it.

HOOPER v. FYNMORES (A FIRM) [2001] W.T.L.R. 1019, Pumfrey, J., Ch D.

4525. **Professional negligence – solicitors – duty of care owed to beneficiary – testator's intention as to size of bequest**

T claimed damages against CC, a firm of solicitors, and B, a former partner, for alleged negligence on the part of B in acting for T's great uncle, E. T alleged that, but for B's negligence, E would have executed a new will under which T would have been entitled to greater benefits than those he actually received under a 1984 will as varied by a Deed of Family Arrangement. To succeed in his claim it was necessary for T to establish that B owed him a duty of care which B had breached thereby causing loss to T.

Held, dismissing the claim, that the evidence showed that E had not decided to confer the particular testamentary benefit that T claimed. On the contrary, until his death E had evidenced a continuing intention that T's entitlement under the new will should be limited to the legacy under the Family Arrangement. Further, E had not reached the position where he could give B definite instructions as to the dispositions to be effected under his proposed new will with the result that no duty of care was owed by B to T, *White v. Jones* [1995] 2 A.C. 207, [1995] C.L.Y. 3701 considered.

TRUSTED v. CLIFFORD CHANCE [2000] W.T.L.R. 1219, Jonathan Parker, J., Ch D.

4526. **Professional negligence – solicitors – failure to advise client to obtain coal mining report – accrual of cause of action for limitation purposes**

GJ, a firm of solicitors, appealed against a finding, determined as a preliminary issue, that the action in negligence commenced against it in February 1996 by H had been begun within the relevant limitation period of six years. It had been assumed for the purpose of the judge's finding that GJ had been negligent in failing to advise H to obtain a mining engineer's report prior to its purchase, in 1987, of a property intended to be converted into a nursing home. In August 1990 significant cracks in the property became apparent, and a surveyor's report revealed that they had been caused by underground mining activities. GJ argued that, for limitation purposes, H had suffered actual loss either at the date of the purchase of the property or, at the latest, when cracks first appeared, both events having occurred outside the limitation period.

Held, allowing the appeal (Sir Anthony Evans dissenting), that the action had been commenced outside the limitation period. According to Buxton, L.J., damage had been sustained for limitation purposes at the date of the purchase of the property. It was at that stage that H had committed itself to a purchase which proved to be totally unsuitable for its purposes, *Knapp v. Ecclesiastical*

Insurance Group Plc [1998] Lloyd's Rep. I.R. 390, [1997] C.L.Y. 645, *DW Moore v. Ferrier* [1988] 1 W.L.R. 267, [1988] C.L.Y. 2154, *Forster v. Outred & Co* [1982] 1 W.L.R. 86, [1982] C.L.Y. 1849 and *Byrne v. Hall Pain & Foster* [1999] 1 W.L.R. 1849, [1999] C.L.Y. 477 applied. Pill, L.J., on the other hand, found that there had been no recoverable loss at the time of the purchase since the property had been bought at its market value. Instead, H had sustained actionable loss when significant sums were spent on redeveloping and converting the property, which took place prior to February 1990, thus completing the cause of action before that date.

HAVENLEDGE LTD v. GRAEME JOHN & PARTNERS [2001] Lloyd's Rep. P.N. 223, Sir Anthony Evans, CA.

4527. Professional negligence – solicitors – failure to advise on liability clause in partnership loan documents – limitations

[Limitation Act 1980 s.14A, s.32.]

Following a decision ([2000] 2 All E.R. (Comm) 686, [2000] C.L.Y. 2606) that G was liable to AIB, a bank, for certain borrowings incurred in relation to a property investment and dealing partnership, G sought an indemnity from M, his former solicitors. G had been found to be liable under a liability clause for all the liabilities, both personal and partnership-related, of his former partner. M had advised G concerning AIB's mortgage agreements, all of which had included the clause, and admitted liability for negligence. M maintained, however, that the action should be dismissed on the ground that G's claim was barred by virtue of the Limitation Act 1980.

Held, giving judgment for G, that (1) given that when signing the earlier mortgage agreements G had been worse off and had therefore suffered damage, time started to run for the purposes of the Act from the dates when those agreements were signed, *Forster v. Outred & Co* [1982] 1 W.L.R. 86, [1982] C.L.Y. 1849 and *UBAF Ltd v. European American Banking Corp (The Pacific Colocotronis)* [1984] Q.B. 713, [1984] C.L.Y. 1579 applied and *Nykredit Mortgage Bank Plc v. Edward Erdman Group Ltd (No.2)* [1997] 1 W.L.R. 1627, [1998] C.L.Y. 1432 distinguished. On that basis, G's claim was prima facie statute barred; (2) for the purposes of s.14A of the Act, time would start to run when a claimant knew such facts as, if pleaded, would constitute a valid claim, *Johnson v. Chief Constable of Surrey* Times, November 23, 1992, [1992] C.L.Y. 2817 applied. In the instant case, it was necessary to ascertain when G had known that he was liable under the earlier mortgage agreements for a greater amount than he had understood or intended. It was apparent that G had only acquired such knowledge within the primary limitation period; (3) G was also entitled to rely on s.32 of the Act. It was appropriate to give s.32(2) a wide meaning. In the instant case, it could be said that the liability clause had been effectively concealed from G until AIB had raised it, *Liverpool Roman Catholic Archdiocesan Trustees Inc v. Goldberg (No.1)* [2001] 1 All E.R. 182, [2000] C.L.Y. 534 followed, and (4) even if G could not rely on s.14A and s.32(2), a fresh cause of action had arisen through M's failure when advising on the latest mortgage agreement to bring its earlier negligence to his attention.

GOLD v. MINCOFF SCIENCE & GOLD [2001] Lloyd's Rep. P.N. 423, Neuberger, J., Ch D.

4529. Professional negligence – solicitors – failure to inform lender of restrictive covenants – date of lender's knowledge for limitation purposes – measure of damages

[Limitation Act 1980 s.14A.]

CC, a firm of solicitors and the second defendant in an action brought by L, appealed against the awarding of damages ([2000] P.N.L.R. 71, [2000] C.L.Y. 4272) against them following a finding that they had been negligent in failing to advise L of the existence of certain restrictive covenants affecting a plot of land. L had lent money for the purchase of the plot and had requested that CC enquire into any matter that might affect the plot's value or saleability. In a subsequent transaction concerning the same plot, L had instructed BP, another firm of solicitors, on more limited terms. The judge in reaching his conclusions and awarding damages had not made any findings on the expert valuation evidence before him. The issues before the court related to (1) whether L could rely on the Limitation Act 1980 s.14A, and (2) the correct measure of damage.

Held, allowing the appeal in part, that (1) L could rely on s.14A of the 1980 Act. The relevant "starting date" for the purposes of the Act had been when L discovered the terms of the restrictive covenants. L and BP had not been under a duty to make their own enquiries regarding the existence of the covenants. Moreover, since it was not appropriate to view BP as an agent who had been authorised to receive such information, there was no basis for imputing any knowledge that BP had of the covenants to L, *El Ajou v. Dollar Land Holdings Plc (No.1)* [1994] 2 All E.R. 685, [1994] C.L.Y. 416 applied, and (2) having regard to the nature of CC's duty to L, it could not be said that had L known of the covenants, the transaction would not have occurred. The existence of the covenants had not meant that the plot had no value. Moreover, L had been willing in the past to lend to the purchaser. The position of CC was akin to that of a valuer; the breach in its duty had caused L to take a security which was worth less than it had believed. Accordingly, it was necessary to remit the case for a finding to be made concerning the valuation of the plot, *Bristol and West Building Society v. Fancy & Jackson* [1997] 4 All E.R. 582, [1998] C.L.Y. 4027 considered and *South Australia Asset Management Corp v. York Montague Ltd* [1997] A.C. 191, [1996] C.L.Y. 4519 applied.

LLOYDS BANK PLC v. BURD PEARSE; *sub nom* CROSSE & CROSSE v. LLOYD'S BANK PLC, [2001] EWCA Civ 366, [2001] Lloyd's Rep. P.N. 452, Potter, L.J., CA.

4530. Professional negligence – solicitors – failure to progress case proactively

H claimed in negligence against E, his former solicitor, contending that E had failed to take sufficient action in prosecuting H's claim for personal injuries sustained in a road traffic accident with the result that the claim had been struck out for want of prosecution. The insurers in the case had been willing to reach a settlement but E had failed to notify H of any applications relating to his case and as a result of the successful application to strike out, H had been ordered to repay monies that had been paid into court and had lost the chance of effective negotiation. E disputed that he had been negligent and argued that (1) H had been contributorily negligent by his failure to provide adequate instructions and notify E of his changes of address, and (2) in any event, damages awarded to H would not have exceeded the amount which had been paid into court.

Held, giving judgment for H, that (1) knowing that H had difficulty with short term memory loss and concentration as a result of his head injury, K should have been much more proactive and had failed to act with reasonable competence. Despite H's failure to remain in contact, E would have been able to obtain instructions had the appropriate steps been taken, and (2) given H's lasting and serious head injuries and his loss of future earnings as an engineer, an industry which he was now unlikely to enter, damages paid to H would have clearly exceeded the payment into court.

HUNTER v. EARNSHAW [2001] P.N.L.R. 42, Garland, J., QBD.

4531. Professional negligence – solicitors – failure to renew business lease – measure of damages

[Landlord and Tenant Act 1954 Part II.]

M brought an action for damages against P, a firm of solicitors, for negligence and breach of contract in relation to P's alleged breach of duty when acting for M with regard to the renewal of a lease of premises used for a garage business. As a result of the alleged breach, M lost the protection of the Landlord and Tenant Act 1954 Part II and the lease was determined. Thereafter, M ceased trading on the lease sites and closed down all of its other business activities. P having conceded liability, the issue before the court related to the extent of the losses that had resulted from the breach of duty.

Held, giving judgment for M, that (1) the appropriate method for assessing the loss was to establish (a) the extent to which M's profit earning capacity had been curtailed as a result of the breach of duty; (b) the profits that M would have been likely to earn on the basis of that capacity each year, having regard to its business practices prior to losing the lease, and (c) the length of time such profits could reasonably have been expected to be made. Having reached a figure via that method, allowance would be made, inter alia, for losses incurred or benefits achieved through the unforeseen closure of the business and the sale of its assets, and (2) having regard to the evidence, M was only entitled to recover a sum equating to the profits that it could reasonably have been expected to make. It was apparent that upon the lease being determined M had sold off its other businesses, with the exception of an accessory shop, as going concerns. None had been forced to cease trading. In relation to the accessory shop, the business had been allowed to run down and no effort had been made to mitigate any losses.

MATLOCK GREEN GARAGE LTD v. POTTER BROOKE-TAYLOR & WILDGOOSE [2000] Lloyd's Rep. P.N. 935, Wright, J., QBD.

4532. Professional negligence – solicitors – failure to search commons register – measure of damages

D brought an action against DBF, a firm of solicitors, alleging professional negligence arising in relation to D's purchase of a property. No search of the commons register had been carried out by DBF prior or subsequent to the purchase. After D had built a substantial new property on the land, it emerged that part of the land was registered as common land. D secured partial deregistration of the common land and intended to continue residing at the property. DBF having admitted negligence, the issue before the court related to the assessment of damages.

Held, giving judgment for D, that (1) it was necessary to ascertain the loss attributable to the inaccurate information supplied, that loss having been been suffered by reason of D having entered into the transaction on the understanding that the information was accurate. Whilst DBF had been under a duty to supply information concerning the commons register, the measure of D's loss could not be calculated simply on the basis that if there had been no breach of duty the transaction would not have been entered into, *South Australia Asset Management Corp v. York Montague Ltd* [1997] A.C. 191, [1996] C.L.Y. 4519 and *Nykredit Mortgage Bank Plc v. Edward Erdman Group Ltd (No.2)* [1997] 1 W.L.R. 1627, [1998] C.L.Y. 1432 applied. The principles set out in those two cases applied to claims brought by purchasers against their solicitors; (2) DBF had been under a duty to carry out a search of the commons register and inform D of the result of the search. There had been no duty to provide advice as to whether D should purchase the land. DBF's breach of duty had occurred, at the latest, when D had committed himself to the purchase of the property, and (3) the appropriate approach to the assessment of damages was the "diminution in value" rule. The assessment of D's loss should include the cost of achieving partial deregistration of the common land.

DENT v. DAVIS BLANK FURNISS [2001] Lloyd's Rep. P.N. 534, Blackburne, J., Ch D.

4533. Professional negligence – solicitors – financial provision – variation of lump sum payments – foreseeability

[Matrimonial Causes Act 1973 s.31.]

W appealed against the dismissal of his claim in negligence against S, his former solicitor, following the latter's admitted failure to advise W of the court's jurisdiction to vary a lump sum order by instalments pursuant to the Matrimonial Causes Act 1973 s.31. The order had been payable to W by his former wife when it was anticipated that she would retain the matrimonial home and raise the capital to purchaseW's interest in the property, however, the situation changed and the equity available on the sale of the property was substantially less than envisaged. W contended that the loss from which he had suffered as a result of his wife's successful variation application had been reasonably foreseeable and that it had been directly attributable to S's failure to advise him on s.31.

Held, dismissing the appeal, that although S could have advised W to avoid an instalment option in the settlement which would have taken the order out of s.31, W would not have been able to achieve an order with true finality because of the possibility of his wife being granted leave to appeal out of time in the light of the changed circumstances. Therefore, W had failed to establish that his loss had either been foreseeable or caused by S's admitted failure to proffer advice on s.31.

WESTBURY v. SAMPSON, [2001] EWCA Civ 407, [2002] 1 F.L.R. 166, Bodey, J., CA.

4534. **Professional negligence – solicitors – instructions to change will by terminally ill client – promptness in carrying out instructions**

X brought an action against W, the solicitors instructed by her late great aunt, H, to change her will so as to make X the principal beneficiary, alleging that W had acted negligently by failing to carry out their instructions within a reasonable time. H had died five days after conveying her instructions to W in hospital and, according to the evidence, one or two days before W intended to present a new will to her for execution.

Held, giving judgment for the defendant, that X, as an intended beneficiary, had a prima facie claim for damages against W, *White v. Jones* [1995] 2 A.C. 207, [1995] C.L.Y. 3701 followed and *Worby v. Rosser* [1999] Lloyd's Rep. P.N. 972, [1999] C.L.Y. 4050 considered. Whilst W had owed a duty to H to prepare a new will promptly, the appropriate time frame in which to do so would depend on the circumstances of each case. In the instant case, W had not acted negligently by failing to advise H as to the possibility of making a codicil on the day she was visited in hospital or by failing to ensure that a new will was presented to her for execution before her death. H's mental state when visited, the comments that she had made to W and her medical notes supported the view that she would live for at least another six weeks. A solicitor would only be required to act urgently where there was a real prospect that his client was about to die. Moreover, the expert evidence which had been given by solicitors experienced in the drafting of wills had, given that neither expert had relied on textbooks or practitioners' books to establish any particular practice, been of minimal value and amounted to no more than evidence as to what each of them would have done in the same situation.

X (A CHILD) v. WOOLLCOMBE YONGE (A FIRM); *sub nom.* X (AN INFANT) v. WOOLLCOMBE YONGE (A FIRM) [2001] Lloyd's Rep. P.N. 274, Neuberger, J., Ch D.

4535. **Professional negligence – solicitors – limitations – failure to advise on absence of right of way – deliberate concealment**

[Limitation Act 1980 s.32(1)(b).]

T claimed damages against A, their former solicitors, in respect of A's alleged negligence when acting for them on the purchase of two neighbouring properties. T contended that A had failed to advise that there was no right of way between a cottage and a nearby paddock, both of which T were acquiring. After purchasing the properties, T were notified by the owner of the adjoining land that they had no rights of access to the paddock from the cottage. T sought advice from A, who advised that T had either a prescriptive right or an easement of necessity to the paddock and recommended that proceedings be brought for a declaration that they had a right of way over the land, which proceedings were subsequently struck out for want of prosecution. T contended that A had been negligent both in respect of the initial conveyance and later by failing to advise them that they had an actionable claim in negligence against A. A submitted that T's claim was time barred.

Held, granting judgment for T, that A had been negligent in its handling of the conveyancing transaction. A should have been aware that T had no formal right of access to the paddock and that it had not considered the issues of prescription or an easement of necessity. A had deliberately concealed such actionable failings from A. As a consequence, the Limitation Act 1980 s.32(1)(b) applied so that the claim was not time barred, *Brocklesby v. Armitage & Guest* [2001] 1 All E.R. 172, [2000] 3 C.L. 485 and *Liverpool Roman Catholic Archdiocesan Trustees Inc v. Goldberg (No.1)* [2001] 1 All E.R. 182, [2000] 8 C.L. 60 applied and *Foreman v. O'Driscoll & Partners* [2000] Lloyd's Rep. P.N. 720, [2000] 12 C.L. 389 distinguished. The failure to advise T that they had a cause of action against A when the problem was later brought to A's attention had also constituted a deliberate commission of a breach of duty.

TUCKER v. ALLEN [2001] P.N.L.R. 37, Michael Supperstone Q.C., QBD.

4536. Professional negligence – solicitors – negligent conduct of client's counterclaim – prospects of success – appropriate measure of damages

M, a firm of solicitors, appealed against a finding that the measure of damages arising from their negligent handling of H's counterclaim against insurers following fire damage at a nightclub owned by H, could be quantified at 25 per cent. H's counterclaim had been struck out for want of prosecution but previously the insurers had defended the claim on the basis that (1) H had failed to pay an instalment of the premium; (2) H had misrepresented the opening hours of the nightclub, and (3) that H's partner had deliberately started the fire. M contended that the judge, having made a finding that the fire had been the result of arson on the part of H's partner, had been wrong to attempt to assess H's prospects of establishing the contrary. M further argued that the judge had erred in taking the lowest percentage chances of success on the three discrete issues to achieve an overall figure of 25 per cent rather than 12 per cent if the various percentages were multiplied together, a percentage which was so small that it should be discounted.

Held, allowing the appeal in part, that the judge could not have made findings of fact as he had not had the opportunity to hear all of the relevant evidence in respect of the allegation of arson. The judge had been correct to consider the three issues raised in the defence to the counterclaim and, accordingly, make a finding as to H's prospects of success. Having assessed H's chances of refuting the three issues raised in the insurer's defence as 80 per cent, 60 per cent and 25 per cent respectively, the judge had then erred in quantifying H's overall chance of success at 25 per cent. Whilst the judge should not have simply multiplied the various percentages together having concluded that H had a 25 per cent chance of succeeding against the insurers on the main issue, he should have reduced the quantum of damages to 20 per cent to take account of the likelihood of H's success in respect of the two remaining matters, *Inter-Leisure Ltd v. Lamberts* [1997] N.P.C. 49 considered.

HANIF v. MIDDLEWEEKS (A FIRM) [2000] Lloyd's Rep. P.N. 920, Mance, L.J., CA.

4537. Professional negligence – solicitors – negligently executed will – liability for litigation costs of solemn form action

B, a firm of solicitors, appealed against a decision ([2000] Lloyd's Rep. P.N. 805) that it was liable to repay to an estate the £15,000 costs of its successful action (*Corbett v. Newey* [1998] Ch. 57, [1996] C.L.Y. 5558) to declare a will invalid. B contended that in a settlement of professional negligence proceedings it had fully compensated the disappointed beneficiaries for what they would have received as residuary legatees under the later will without any allowance for the diminution of the estate by litigation costs and that if the estate were also compensated it would thus be receiving a windfall.

Held, allowing the appeal, that the disappointed beneficiaries had rightfully been compensated in full, but B should not have to incur a double liability to both the specific legatee and to C, the personal representative, since, at least if the estate was solvent, any such recovery by C would enure for the benefit of the residuary beneficiary rather than the intended specific legatee, *White v. Jones* [1995] 2 A.C. 207, [1995] C.L.Y. 3701 followed and *Carr-Glynn v. Frearsons* [1999] Ch. 326, [1998] C.L.Y. 4595 applied. B's duty to procure the execution of a valid will was owed to the testatrix and to the intended beneficiaries under the later invalid will, and not to her personal representatives or the residuary beneficiaries under the earlier will. It was clear from *Carr-Glynn* that any loss suffered by the beneficiaries under the earlier will was not within the scope of B's duty. In the instant case, the sums paid to the disappointed beneficiaries and those sought to be recovered represented the same monetary loss. Therefore C was not able to recover the costs of the will action.

CORBETT v. BOND PEARCE (A FIRM), [2001] EWCA Civ 531, [2001] 3 All E.R. 769, Sir Christopher Slade, CA.

4538. Professional negligence – solicitors – solicitors retained by borrower on grant of charge to lender – duty of care to lender

[Law of Property (Miscellaneous Provisions) Act 1989 s.2.]

D, who had made a loan to B secured by a charge over property, appealed against a decision ([2000] Lloyd's Rep. P.N. 469) that B's solicitors, AW, did not owe him a duty of care to ensure that the charge represented valid security. D had not been legally represented in the transaction, but it had been agreed between the parties that effective security for the loan was fundamental to the loan agreement. AW had been aware of that and also of the fact that D was unrepresented. D submitted that there was an implied retainer giving rise to a contractual duty of care on the part of AW towards D.

Held, allowing the appeal, that on the facts, although an implied retainer had not arisen, AW had owed a duty of care both to their client and to D, *Searles v. Cann & Hallett* [1999] P.N.L.R. 494, [1999] C.L.Y. 4029 approved. In a situation where, to the knowledge of both parties, a solicitor was retained by one party and there was an identity of interest between the client and the other party, the court should be slow to find that the solicitor had assumed a duty of care to the other party. Nevertheless, such an assumption of responsibility was possible in special circumstances and, in the instant case, AW should have known that D was relying upon them to obtain effective security; hence the imposition of a duty was fair and reasonable even though D ought to have obtained independent advice, *White v. Jones* [1995] 2 A.C. 207, [1995] C.L.Y. 3701 and *Bank of Credit and Commerce International (Overseas) Ltd (In Liquidation) v. Price Waterhouse (No.2)* [1998] Lloyd's Rep. Bank. 85, [1998] C.L.Y. 3921 applied. The finding of negligence on the part of AW was upheld.

DEAN v. ALLIN & WATTS [2001] EWCA Civ 758, [2001] 2 Lloyd's Rep. 249, Lightman, J., CA.

4539. Professional negligence – surveyors – failure to warn of aircraft noise – damages for "discomfort"

F appealed against the decision of the Court of Appeal (73 Con. L.R. 70, [2000] C.L.Y. 1485) allowing the appeal of S, a surveyor, against the award of £10,000 made to F by way of damages for the interference with the enjoyment of his property caused by aircraft noise. S, who had been instructed by F to survey the property prior to his purchase of it, and to specifically investigate the likelihood of aircraft noise from a nearby major airport, had negligently concluded that the house was unlikely to be affected.

Held, allowing the appeal, that S's obligation to investigate aircraft noise had been an important part of the contract, and S's failure to properly investigate that aspect had prevented F from making an informed choice as to whether or not to buy the property. That had, in turn, led to mental distress and disappoinment for which damages had been sought. The guidance in *Watts v. Morrow* [1991] 1 W.L.R. 1421, [1992] C.L.Y. 1548 was still valuable in the context of determining whether damages were available for breach of contract, but there was no reason in principle and policy why the scope of recovery in the exceptional category should be dependent on the object of the contract as ascertained from all its constituent parts. It was enough that an important object of the contract had been to give "pleasure, relaxation or peace of mind" and that it had been breached, *Watts* considered, *Knott v. Bolton* 45 Con. L.R. 127, [1996] C.L.Y. 1211 overruled. F had not forfeited his right to damages by remaining at the property, given that he had acted reasonably in making the best of the situation, and that his decision not to move had prevented a larger claim against S.

FARLEY v. SKINNER (NO.2); *sub nom.* SKINNER v. FARLEY, [2001] UKHL 49, [2001] 3 W.L.R. 899, Lord Steyn, HL.

4540. Professional negligence – surveyors – mortgage valuation – personal duty of care – reliance

B, a surveyor, appealed against a decision that he was personally liable to M in respect of losses caused as a result of a negligent valuation of a property. B had been employed by a firm of surveyors and valuers which had ceased business following a bankruptcy order against the firm's principal. Prior to this, B had been instructed by a building society to prepare a valuation report in respect of the property, for the purpose of M's mortgage application. M claimed against B in his personal capacity since the firm's professional indemnity insurance had been cancelled by the trustee in bankruptcy and B was not covered by personal insurance. B contended that he owed no personal duty of care to M and his only duty was owed to the firm.

Held, dismissing the appeal, that a professional valuer owed a personal duty of care to a mortgagor to exercise reasonable skill and care when carrying out a valuation on the instructions of the potential mortgagee, if he knew that the mortgagor would rely on that valuation when deciding whether to purchase the property and did not intend to have an independent survey, *Smith v. Eric S Bush* [1990] 1 A.C. 831, [1989] C.L.Y. 2566 and *Phelps v. Hillingdon LBC* [2000] 3 W.L.R. 776, [2000] 9 C.L. 252 applied. In the instant case, B knew that M would be relying on his report and moreover, because he had signed it in his personal capacity, he had assumed personal responsibility for it.

MERRETT v. BABB, [2001] EWCA Civ 214, [2001] Q.B. 1174, May, L.J., CA.

4541. Professional negligence – surveyors – mortgagees powers and duties – bankruptcy – extent of duty of care owed to mortgagor

C sought summary judgment in its favour on N's claim in negligence. N had applied to C for a mortgage for the purchase of a flat. C instructed a surveyor, W, to value the property. N did not obtain any survey report of his own and relied on W's valuation to C. Just before exchange of contracts, C became aware that W had been adjudged bankrupt, but did not check whether W had reported on any pending transactions and did not inform N of W's bankruptcy. N completed the purchase with the aid of the mortgage from C and thereafter, on discovering a damp problem, sought to sue W for negligence. It subsequently transpired that W's professional indemnity insurance had lapsed and N issued proceedings against C, alleging that C owed a duty of care to inform N if it became aware of any matter which meant that N's reliance on the valuation report was prejudiced.

Held, granting summary judgment for the defendant, that a prospective mortgagee owed no such duty to its customer. Mortgagee's duties were closely confined and in the exercise of its powers no general duty of care to the mortgagor was owed, *Downsview Nominees Ltd v. First City Corp Ltd (No.1)* [1993] A.C. 295, [1993] C.L.Y. 2881 considered. A mortgagee owed a duty simply to take reasonable care in the selection of a reasonably competent valuer, *Smith v. Eric S Bush* [1990] 1 A.C. 831, [1989] C.L.Y. 2566 applied, and (2) fairness, justice and reasonableness did not require the expansion of the scope of this duty as proposed by N, *Caparo Industries Plc v. Dickman* [1990] 2 A.C. 605, [1990] C.L.Y. 3266, applied. The imposition of such a duty would create a paradox in that the borrower who does not obtain his own survey would have more protection than the prudent borrower who does obtain his own survey and who would be unlikely to discover a subsequent insolvency.

NOBLE v. COUTTS & CO, October 24, 2000, Master Price, Ch D. [*Ex rel.* Philip Rainey, Barrister, 2nd Floor, Francis Taylor Building, Temple, London].

4542. Professional negligence – veterinary surgeons – expert witnesses – preference of one body of opinion

W appealed against an order granting judgment for C after a finding that the death of C's horse from an infection eight months after it had aborted its foal, was caused by H's negligent treatment in his capacity as a vet employed by W. Experts instructed by both parties disagreed as to whether H's decision not to conduct an internal examination and administer antibiotics on treating the horse after it had aborted, had been negligent.

Held, allowing the appeal, that the judge had reached his decision by preferring the opinion of one body of experts to another, yet there was nothing in the evidence to conclude that the opinion of H and his expert witness was illogical, *Bolitho (Deceased) v. City and Hackney HA* [1998] A.C. 232, [1997] C.L.Y. 3789 applied.

CALVER v. WESTWOOD VETERINARY GROUP [2001] P.I.Q.R. P11, Simon Brown, L.J., CA.

4543. Vicarious liability – employers – accidents – road traffic – vehicle driven by subcontractor

E claimed damages for personal injuries arising out of an accident which occurred when he was driving J's vehicle. A ladder fell from C's truck and crashed into J's vehicle. The driver of C's truck, I, was not employed by C but was a sub contractor. I contended that the ladder had been attached to the vehicle by a third party, X, and that X was primarily responsible for the accident. Further I argued that, in any event, C was vicariously liable as to all intents and purposes C was his employer. C submitted that it was not liable for the actions of either I or X as neither were its employees and, although the vehicle belonged to C, it was effectively hired to I for the day. E and J contended that, (1) I, as the driver, had a duty to ensure that the vehicle was safe for other road users and that he had been negligent in failing to check whether or not the ladder was securely tied to the truck, and (2) whether or not I was an "employee" for the purposes of establishing employer's liability, C was liable as the owner of the motor vehicle, *Launchbury v. Morgans* [1973] A.C.127, [1972] C.L.Y. 2376 referred to.

Held, giving judgment for the claimants, that X was not the employee of I, and probably not the employee of C. However I had a duty as the driver to ensure that the ladder was secure. He had not done this and was therefore liable. There was no evidence that I had hired the vehicle from C; the only evidence was that he had been instructed by C to use the vehicle to perform a job for C. Therefore C was liable as I was its agent.

JOHN LAING CONSTRUCTION v. INCE, April 2, 2001, District Judge Collier, CC (Southend). [*Ex rel.* Katya Melluish, Barrister, 3 Paper Buildings, Temple].

4544. Vicarious liability – sporting events – injuries sustained in football match – illegal tackle

L brought an action against the MOD in respect of personal injuries suffered while playing in a football tournament organised by the Royal Navy. L represented his ship and was playing a team from another ship. During the course of the game, L sustained a serious injury to his leg following an allegedly negligent tackle by a member of the opposing team. The referee took no action and it was left to the senior officer present to forfeit the game. L subsequently brought a claim for personal injury against the MOD contending that it was vicariously liable for the negligent tackle of the opposing player.

Held, granting judgment for L, that the offending player went to tackle L from behind with both legs and that the tackle was deliberately aimed at the man and not the ball which was two to three yards ahead of L. The tackle was illegal, outside the rules of Association Football and dangerous in all the circumstances, *Condon v. Basi* [1985] 1 W.L.R. 866, [1985] C.L.Y. 2329 followed.

LEEBODY v. MINISTRY OF DEFENCE, July 9, 2001, Judge Burcell, CC (Bristol). [*Ex rel.* Nash & Co, Solicitors, Beaumont House, Beaumont Park, Plymouth].

4545. Vicarious liability – taxis – passengers – driver responsible for negligent actions of passenger

E, the owner of a black cab driven by his agent, R, brought an action in negligence against H, another black cab driver, claiming the costs of repair to his vehicle arising from damage caused when a passenger of H opened a rear door of the cab into R's path. H counterclaimed, alleging that R should have avoided the collision. The collision occurred in the "drop off" area outside busy train station where in order to drop passengers, a cab needed to pull up to the kerb on its offside. A rear passenger opened her nearside door into R's path but left the scene without leaving any details. Evidence was given that the area outside the station was badly designed for dropping passengers off, and that a driver of a black cab had some degree of control over unlocking the rear doors.

Held, giving judgment for the claimant, that the passenger was clearly negligent in opening the rear door when it was unsafe to do so. However, there were circumstances when a cab driver was responsible for the actions of his passengers but such liability only arose if there was negligence on the part of the driver. As H had acknowledged that the area was unsafe, he should have taken steps to prevent the passenger opening the door into a line of traffic by either keeping the doors locked or by telling the passenger not to get out on the nearside of the cab; accordingly H was negligent.

EDELMAN v. HARCOTT, February 21, 2001, Deputy District Judge Joslin, CC (Ilford). [*Ex rel.* Jamas Hodivala, Barrister, Trinity Chambers, 140 New London Road, Chelmsford, Essex].

4546. Books

Bhat, Vasanthakumar N. – Medical Malpractice. Hardback: £53.95. ISBN 0-86569-279-3. Auburn House.

Burton, Frank; Nelson-Jones, Rodney – Clinical Negligence Case Law. Hardback: £120.00. ISBN 0-406-91959-3. Butterworths Law.

Rodway, Susan; Levene, Simon – Medical Negligence: Managing Medical Disputes. Hardback: £60.00. ISBN 1-902558-05-7. Palladian Law Publishing Ltd.

Simpson, Mark; Hoffman, Lord – Professional Negligence and Liability. Looseleaf/ring bound: £250.00. ISBN 1-85978-673-1. LLP Professional Publishing.

Walton, Christopher; Percy, R.A. – Charlesworth and Percy on Negligence. 10th Ed. Common Law Library. Hardback: £225.00. ISBN 0-421-82590-1. Sweet & Maxwell.

NUISANCE

4547. Private nuisance – floods – occupier's duty to abate

B, the owner of premises damaged by floodwater, appealed against the dismissal of its claim against KCC, the relevant highway authority, for nuisance. B contended that (1) the judge at first instance had made a finding of fact that a culvert, originally constructed by KCC's predecessors, impeded the flow of a natural stream, and that as a result of that finding KCC was liable in nuisance for any resultant flooding, even if the culvert had been fit for its purpose as at the date of construction and the flooding had been unforeseeable at that time and the result of unusual factors, and (2) in the alternative, an occupier owed a general duty of care to his neighbour to minimise the risk of injury or damage which he knew, or should have known, would emanate from hazards on his land. KCC maintained that since the culvert did not constitute a nuisance or potential nuisance when it was made, it could not become a nuisance merely with the effluxion of time.

Held, allowing the appeal, that if a nuisance had not been created by the occupier, or had not constituted a nuisance when constructed, the occupier would nevertheless be liable if he permitted it to continue unabated. The occupier's liability was to be measured by reference to that which it was reasonable for him to do. Accordingly, although KCC did not have strict liability for all eventualities resulting from construction of the culvert, it was subject to a high degree of responsibility to ensure that the stream could continue to flow, *Leakey v. National Trust for Places of Historic Interest or Natural Beauty* [1980] Q.B. 485, [1980] C.L.Y. 2006 applied, *Radstock Cooperative & Industrial Society v. Norton-Radstock Urban DC* [1968] Ch. 605, [1968] C.L.Y. 2880 doubted and *Greenock Corp v. Caledonian Railway Co* [1917] A.C. 556 considered.

BYBROOK BARN GARDEN CENTRE LTD v. KENT CC; *sub nom.* BYBROOK BARN CENTRE LTD v. KENT CC [2001] B.L.R. 55, Waller, L.J., CA.

4548. **Private nuisance – trees – land heave resulting from tree root encroachment prior to acquisition – freeholder's entitlement to recover remedial expenditure**

WCC appealed against a decision of the Court of Appeal ([2000] B.L.R. 1, [1999] C.L.Y. 4067) allowing F's appeal against the dismissal (88 B.L.R. 99) of a claim for damages for nuisance. F was a wholly owned subsidiary of D, the management company for a group of mansion blocks, three of which had been damaged by tree root encroachment. The judge at first instance had concluded that while the remedial works carried out had been reasonably and properly incurred, F had not established that any new damage to the foundations had occurred during its ownership of the properties. The Court of Appeal had determined that F was able to sustain a claim for damages on the basis that there had been a continuing nuisance. WCC maintained that all of the damage to the premises had been caused before F acquired the freehold and that only the former owners could litigate in respect of it.

Held, dismissing the appeal, that the common law was concerned to impose a fair and just duty as between neighbours as opposed to applying a label of nuisance or negligence and drawing inferences as to the consequential extent of the duty, *Overseas Tankship (UK) Ltd v. Miller Steamship Co Pty Ltd (The Wagon Mound) (No.2)* [1967] 1 A.C. 617, [1966] C.L.Y. 3445 and *Goldman v. Hargrave* [1967] 1 A.C. 645, [1966] C.L.Y. 8145 considered. In circumstances where a continuing nuisance existed which the defendant knew or ought to have been aware of, a property owner was entitled to recover expenditure reasonably incurred in order to abate that nuisance. It was, however, important not to place too onerous a financial duty on tree owners and they had to be given an opportunity to consider removal of the tree before being faced with a bill for remedial works. In the instant case, while there had been no new structural "cracking" following F's acquisition of the properties, the tree root encroachment had continued to cause desiccation of the soil underlying the foundations such as to constitute a continuing nuisance. Since the damage incurred was foreseeable, WCC was obliged to reimburse F for the costs incurred in piling and underpinning the foundations.

DELAWARE MANSIONS LTD v. WESTMINSTER CITY COUNCIL; *sub nom.* FLECKSUN LTD v. WESTMINSTER CITY COUNCIL, [2001] UKHL 55, [2002] 1 A.C. 321, Lord Cooke of Thorndon, HL.

4549. Public nuisance – birds – interference with public use of footpath – liability for failure to remedy

[Public Health Act 1961 s.74.]

R appealed against the decision ([2001] 1 W.L.R. 368, [2000] C.L.Y. 4292) that it was liable in public nuisance for the fouling of a public footpath caused by a pigeon infestation under one of its railway bridges. R submitted that the pigeons proliferated because local people provided food for them, and therefore the local authority, as representatives of the local people, should have solved the problem by exercising its powers under the Public Health Act 1961 s.74, and by exercising its contractual and statutory street cleaning duties.

Held, dismissing the appeal, that the infestation of a bridge by pigeons which interfered with the comfort and convenience of pedestrians constituted a public nuisance which was the responsibility of the owner and it was immaterial that the pigeons were wild and that the local authority possessed the power to abate the nuisance, *Attorney General v. Tod Heatley* [1897] 1 Ch. 560 and *Slater v. Worthington's Cash Stores (1930)* [1941] 1 K.B. 488 applied. R's failure to tackle the nuisance after it became aware of the problem, when there were reasonable steps it could have taken to prevent or abate it, left it liable in public nuisance.

WANDSWORTH LBC v. RAILTRACK PLC; *sub nom.* RAILTRACK PLC v. WANDSWORTH LBC, [2001] EWCA Civ 1236, [2002] 2 W.L.R. 512, Kennedy, L.J., CA.

4550. Statutory nuisance – noise – requirement for injury to health – calculation of noise levels – validity of abatement notice

[Environmental Protection Act 1990 s.80.]

G appealed by way of case stated against a decision that he had committed a statutory nuisance by playing drums and amplified music in a building in a rural setting. G contended that in order for such a nuisance to arise the precise noise level in terms of decibels had to have been calibrated and it also had to have caused injury to health. Further, the failure to specify in the abatement notice exactly what had to be done to abate the nuisance rendered the notice invalid.

Held, dismissing the appeal, that measurement of noise levels was not a prerequisite to a finding of statutory nuisance. The appropriate test was identical to that used to establish private nuisance at common law, namely whether the noise constituted an unreasonable interference with the use and enjoyment of the complainant's land, *Murdoch v. Glacier Metal Co Ltd* [1998] Env. L.R. 732, [1998] C.L.Y. 4045 applied. Neither was it necessary to establish any injury to health, *Bishop Auckland Local Board v. Bishop Auckland Iron and Steel Co* (1882) L.R. 10 Q.B.D. 138 considered. Further, to be valid, an abatement notice served under the Environmental Protection Act 1990 s.80 did not have to specify the acts or omissions which would result in criminal liability, *R. v. Falmouth and Truro Port HA, ex p. South West Water Ltd* [2000] 3 W.L.R. 1464, [2000] 6 C.L. 254 applied.

GODFREY v. CONWY CBC [2001] Env. L.R. 38, Rose, L.J., QBD.

4551. Statutory nuisance – sanitation – local authority housing – design and layout of premises

[Environmental Protection Act 1990 s.79(1)(a).]

BCC appealed against a finding ([1999] E.H.L.R. 209, [1999] C.L.Y. 4072) that the layout of a council house constituted a statutory nuisance under the Environmental Protection Act 1990 s.79(1)(a). The only lavatory in the house was too small to contain a wash basin consequently requiring the use of the kitchen sink or the basin in a bathroom on the other side of the kitchen for the washing of hands. The justices had found that the arrangement contained a risk of cross infection in the kitchen.

Held, allowing the appeal (Lord Steyn and Lord Clyde dissenting), that for premises to be "prejudicial to health" within the meaning of s.79, there had to be something in the feature of them, such as the condition of the lavatory or a defective drain that was, of itself, prejudicial to health. The fact that there was no wash basin in the lavatory and that it was only possible to access wash facilities in or through the kitchen was a design and layout problem and was not in itself prejudicial to health. Any confusion about the meaning and scope of s.79 could be avoided if its background and purpose was borne in mind. The purpose of the section was to deal with foul and filthy conditions that posed a risk of disease and germs or were the source of unpleasant smells. The words "in such a state" in s.79 referred to the condition of the premises, such as dampness, excessive dirt or rat infestation. These conditions could be regarded as being prejudicial to health. However, on the facts of the instant case, there was nothing wrong with the lavatory or with the wash facilities.

OAKLEY v. BIRMINGHAM CITY COUNCIL; *sub nom.* BIRMINGHAM CITY COUNCIL v. OAKLEY [2001] 1 A.C. 617, Lord Slynn of Hadley, HL.

OIL AND GAS INDUSTRY

4552. Contract terms – pipelines – commencement date of contract

A, which had contracted with T to allow the latter to use part of A's pipeline capacity for the transportation of gas, appealed against a finding that notification to T in April 1993 that conditions which were a prerequisite to the commencement of the contract, had been satisfied, had not been effective as such. A contended that the Court of Appeal had erred in finding that on the notified commencement date, A's transportation facilities had not been "available" to perform the transportation service as on that date T could not have tied into A's pipeline because of leaking valves at the entry point.

Held, allowing the appeal, that the stipulation that the commencement date would take effect when, inter alia, A notified T that its transportation facilities were "available", was not intended to be descriptive of a state of affairs but was rather in the nature of a declaration which, assuming the other conditions were satisfied and the declaration was given bona fide, triggered the commencement date. Thus a commencement date notification could be validly given by A, even though owing to a hidden defect or some other unknown reason, A had in fact been incapable of providing the transportation service on that date.

AMOCO (UK) EXPLORATION CO v. TEESSIDE GAS TRANSPORTATION LTD; AMOCO (UK) EXPLORATION CO v. IMPERIAL CHEMICAL INDUSTRIES PLC (ICI), [2001] UKHL 18, [2001] 1 All E.R. (Comm) 865, Lord Hoffmann, HL.

4553. Offshore installations – safety zones

OFFSHORE INSTALLATIONS (SAFETY ZONES) ORDER 2001, SI 2001 1914; made under the Petroleum Act 1987 s.22. In force: May 25, 2001; £1.50.

This Order establishes safety zones having a radius of 500 metres from the specified point, around specified installations stationed in waters to which the Petroleum Act 1987 s.21(7) applies. Vessels, which for this purpose include hovercraft, submersible apparatus and installations in transit, are prohibited from entering or remaining in a safety zone except with the consent of the Health and Safety Executive or in accordance with the Offshore Installations (Safety Zones) Regulations (SI 1987 1331).

4554. Offshore installations – safety zones

OFFSHORE INSTALLATIONS (SAFETY ZONES) (NO.2) ORDER 2001, SI 2001 2528; made under the Petroleum Act 1987 s.22. In force: August 1, 2001; £1.50.

This Order establishes safety zones having a radius of 500 metres from a specified point, around specified installations stationed in waters to which the Petroleum Act 1987 s.21(7) applies. Vessels, which for this purpose include hovercraft, submersible apparatus and installations in transit, are prohibited from entering or remaining in a safety zone except with the consent of the Health and Safety Executive or in accordance with the Offshore Installations (Safety Zones) Regulations (SI 1987 1331).

4555. Offshore installations – safety zones

OFFSHORE INSTALLATIONS (SAFETY ZONES) (NO.3) ORDER 2001, SI 2001 2978; made under the Petroleum Act 1987 s.22, s.24. In force: September 14, 2001; £1.50.

This Order establishes safety zones having a radius of 500 metres from the specified point around each specified installation and station in waters to which the Petroleum Act 1987 s.21 applies. Vessels, which for this purpose include hovercraft, submersible apparatus and installations in transit, are prohibited from entering or remaining in a safety zone except with the consent of the Health and Safety Executive.

4556. Offshore installations – safety zones

OFFSHORE INSTALLATIONS (SAFETY ZONES) (NO.4) ORDER 2001, SI 2001 3790; made under the Petroleum Act 1987 s.22. In force: December 18, 2001; £1.50.

This Order establishes a safety zone having a radius of 500m from the specified point, around the installation specified in the Schedule to this order and stationed in waters to which the Petroleum Act 1987 s.21 (7) applies. Vessels, which for this purpose include hovercraft, submersible apparatus and installations in transit, are prohibited from entering or remaining in the safety zone except with the consent of the Health and Safety Executive or in accordance with regulations made under the 1987 Act.

PARTNERSHIPS

4557. Partners – Limited Liability Partnerships

LIMITED LIABILITY PARTNERSHIPS REGULATIONS 2001, SI 2001 1090; made under the Limited Liability Partnerships Act 2000 s.14, s.15, s.16, s.17. In force: April 6, 2001; £7.50.

These Regulations, which regulate limited liability partnerships, amend the relevant primary legislation by way of general modifications which provide that references to a company include references to a member of a limited liability partnership.

4558. Partners – Limited Liability Partnerships – fees

LIMITED LIABILITY PARTNERSHIPS (FEES) (NO.2) REGULATIONS 2001, SI 2001 969; made under the Companies Act 1985 s.708. In force: April 6, 2001; £1.75.

These Regulations, which revoke the Limited Liability Partnerships (Fees) Regulations 2001 (SI 2001 529), provide for the introduction of specified fees which apply to limited liability partnerships.

4559. Partners – Limited Liability Partnerships – forms

LIMITED LIABILITY PARTNERSHIPS (FORMS) REGULATIONS 2001, SI 2001 927; made under the Companies Act 1985 s.190, s.225, s.244, s.363, s.391, s.395, s.397, s.398, s.400, s.401, s.403, s.405, s.410, s.413, s.416, s.417, s.419, s.466, s.652A, s.652D. In force: April 6, 2001; £7.50.

These Regulations set out the forms to be used by limited liability partnerships.

4560. Partners – Limited Liability Partnerships – forms – Wales

LIMITED LIABILITY PARTNERSHIPS (WELSH LANGUAGE FORMS) REGULATIONS 2001, SI 2001 2917; made under the Companies Act 1985 s.225, s.363, s.652A, s.652D; and the Welsh Language Act 1993 s.26. In force: September 17, 2001; £3.00.

These Regulations prescribe new specified forms which correspond to forms prescribed by the Limited Liability Partnerships (Forms) Regulations 2001 (SI 2001 927) and have been prescribed in addition to those forms.

4561. Partners – restricted size of partnership – exemptions – investment business

PARTNERSHIPS (UNRESTRICTED SIZE) NO.16 REGULATIONS 2001, SI 2001 1389; made under the Companies Act 1985 s.716, s.744. In force: May 10, 2001; £1.50.

The Companies Act 1985 s.716 prohibits the formation of partnerships consisting of more than 20 persons. These Regulations exempt from that prohibition partnerships formed for the purpose of carrying on investment business which are authorised to carry on that business under the Financial Services Act 1986 or "European investment firms" carrying on "home-regulated business" in the UK.

4562. Partners – trusts of land – dissolution of partnership – prohibited sale of goodwill

[National Health Service Act 1977 s.54(1), Sch.10 para.2(1); Trusts of Land and Appointment of Trustees Act 1996 s.13.]

R appealed against a decision that he could not buy a property of which he was a trustee and beneficiary, the property having been owned by R and L during their time as doctors and partners. The judge held that the property could not be sold to R, but should be divided into two separate units with each party having exclusive occupation of one unit, as any sale would be contrary to the National Health Service Act 1977 s.54(1), amounting to a purchase of goodwill in the medical practice. R contended that the judge had erred both in his finding that the sale would fall within Sch.10 para.2(1) of the 1977 Act, and in the exercise of his discretion regarding the future use of the property.

Held, dismissing the appeal, that the judge had been correct in his interpretation of the statutory provisions. A sale to R would have been a sale of premises for the purposes of medical practice. As the value of the property was less than the loan originally obtained to purchase the premises, any sale would involve a purchase of goodwill and, therefore, was prohibited by the Act. Further, the judge had been entitled to make an order under the Trusts of Land and Appointment of Trustees Act 1996 s.13 directing that the partnership premises should be divided into two units, with each party being given exclusive occupation of one of those units.

RODWAY v. LANDY, [2001] EWCA Civ 471, [2001] Ch. 703, Peter Gibson, L.J., CA.

4563. Partners – unrestricted size of partnership – exemptions – insolvency practitioners

PARTNERSHIPS (UNRESTRICTED SIZE) NO.17 REGULATIONS 2001, SI 2001 2422; made under the Companies Act 1985 s.716, s.744. In force: July 9, 2001; £1.50.

The Companies Act 1985 s.716 prohibits the formation of partnerships consisting of more than 20 persons. These Regulations exempt from that prohibition partnerships formed for the purpose of carrying on practice as insolvency practitioners and consisting of persons the majority of whom are authorised to act as insolvency practitioners under the Insolvency Act 1986 or have an equivalent authorisation under the law of a Member State of the European Economic Area.

4564. Partners liabilities – guarantees – authority to bind partnership – waiver – duty to disclose misuse of account to guarantor

[Partnership Act 1890 s.6.]

An auctioneer, H, entered into an arrangement with a partnership, HB, whereby HB agreed to guarantee his borrowing in return for a share of fee income. A guarantee was executed bearing the signature of four of the partners. The bank, B, subsequently called on the guarantee. HB sought to defend the claim under the guarantee on the basis that (1) the partners who had entered into the guarantee had possessed no authority to do so, and (2) the guarantee had been discharged since B had permitted H to use his account for purposes other than his business interests, a fact which should have been disclosed to HB by B.

Held, giving judgment for the claimant, that (1) the signing of the guarantee was an act relating to the partnership business and bound the partnership pursuant to the Partnership Act 1890 s.6. The fact that the partners had not been authorised to execute the guarantee was immaterial having regard to the fact that there had been no subsequent dissent by the other partners, nor had the bank been informed that the signatories lacked authority. Accordingly, the partnership had affirmed the transaction and waived any right to rely upon the absence of authority, *Sandilands v. Marsh* (1819) 2 B. & Ald. 673 considered. Further, the individual partners of the firm were bound, even if they lacked intent, and (2) exceptional circumstances were required before a bank was required to disclose to a guarantor that an account was being used other than in accordance with the terms of the guarantee. On the facts of the instant case, none of the payments made by H were capable of supporting the contention that a duty of disclosure should have been imposed, *Hamilton v. Watson* (1845) 12 Cl. & F. 109, *National Provincial Bank of England Ltd v. Glanusk* [1913] 3 K.B. 335 and *Commercial Bank of Australia v. Amadio* (1983) 46 A.L.R. 402 considered.

BANK OF SCOTLAND v. HENRY BUTCHER & CO [2001] 2 All E.R. (Comm) 691, M Kallipetis Q.C., Ch D.

PENOLOGY

4565. Community service orders – electronic monitoring – responsible officer

COMMUNITY ORDER (ELECTRONIC MONITORING OF REQUIREMENTS) (RESPONSIBLE OFFICER) ORDER 2001, SI 2001 2233; made under the Powers of Criminal Courts (Sentencing) Act 2000 s.36B. In force: July 2, 2001; £1.75.

This Order specifies the descriptions of persons to be made responsible, by a community order in any part of England and Wales, for the electronic monitoring of an offender's compliance with the requirements of that community order.

4566. Community service orders – electronic monitoring – responsible officer

COMMUNITY ORDER (ELECTRONIC MONITORING OF REQUIREMENTS) (RESPONSIBLE OFFICER) (AMENDMENT) ORDER 2001, SI 2001 3346; made under the Powers of Criminal Courts (Sentencing) Act 2000 s.36B. In force: October 1, 2001 at 7 pm; £1.50.

This Order amends the Community Order (Electronic Monitoring of Requirements) (Responsible Officer) Order 2001 (SI 2001 2233) by modifying the descriptions of persons who are to be made responsible for the electronic monitoring of an offender's compliance with the requirements of that community order. Employees of GSSC of Europe Limited are replaced by employees of Reliance Secure Task Management Limited in the areas in which GSSC of Europe Limited formerly operated.

4567. Curfew orders – curfew requirements – responsible officer

CURFEW ORDER AND CURFEW REQUIREMENT (RESPONSIBLE OFFICER) ORDER 2001, SI 2001 2234; made under the Powers of Criminal Courts (Sentencing) Act 2000 s.37, Sch.2 para.7. In force: July 2, 2001; £1.75.

This Order, which revokes the Curfew Order (Responsible Officer) Order 1999 (SI 1999 3155), specifies the descriptions of persons to be made responsible, by a curfew order or a curfew requirement included in a community rehabilitation order in any part of England and Wales, for monitoring an offender's whereabouts during the curfew periods. This monitoring may be carried out electronically or not, as the curfew order or the curfew requirement specifies.

4568. Curfew orders – curfew requirements – responsible officer

CURFEW ORDER AND CURFEW REQUIREMENT (RESPONSIBLE OFFICER) (AMENDMENT) ORDER 2001, SI 2001 3344; made under the Powers of Criminal Courts (Sentencing) Act 2000 s.37, Sch.2 para.7. In force: October 1, 2001 at 7 pm; £1.50.

This Order amends the Curfew Order and Curfew Requirement (Responsible Officer) Order 2001 (SI 2001 2234) by modifying the descriptions of persons who are to be made responsible for monitoring an offender's whereabouts during the curfew periods. Employees of GSSC of Europe Limited are replaced by employees of Reliance Secure Task Management Limited in the areas in which GSSC of Europe Limited formerly operated.

4569. Curfew orders – responsible officers

CURFEW CONDITION (RESPONSIBLE OFFICER) (AMENDMENT) ORDER 2001, SI 2001 3345; made under the Criminal Justice Act 1991 s.37A. In force: October 1, 2001 at 7 pm; £1.50.

This Order amends the Curfew Condition (Responsible Officer) Order 1999 (SI 1999 9) by modifying the descriptions of persons who are to be made responsible for monitoring a released person's whereabouts during the curfew periods. Employees of GSSC of Europe Limited are replaced by employees of Reliance Secure Task Management Limited in the areas in which GSSC of Europe Limited formerly operated.

4570. Parole – revocation under emergency powers – duty to follow recommendation of Parole Board

[Crime (Sentences) Act 1997 s.32(2).]

C appealed against the dismissal of his application for a writ of habeus corpus. C had been released on licence from a life sentence for murder and he subsequently married a woman with four children and had two further children by her. Following the death of C's wife, the local authority applied for the six children to be taken into care. As a result of the concerns that led to the grant of an emergency protection order, the Secretary of State revoked C's licence and referred the matter to the Parole Board under his usual informal policy. The Board recommended that C be allowed to continue under licence conditions but the Secretary of State informed C that he did not intend to follow the Board's advice. C argued that, having chosen to consult the Board, the Secretary of State was bound to follow its recommendation and that his decision was irrational.

Held, dismissing the appeal, that the decision was not irrational. Under the Crime (Sentences) Act 1997 s.32(2), the Secretary of State had the power in an emergency situation where the public were perceived to be at risk to revoke C's licence without reference to the Board. His policy of nevertheless asking the Board's advice in such situations did not override that statutory provision, and he was therefore not bound to follow the Board's recommendation, *R. v. Parole Board, ex p. Watson* [1996] 1 W.L.R. 906, [1996] C.L.Y. 4576 applied.

R. v. SECRETARY OF STATE FOR THE HOME DEPARTMENT, *ex p.* CUMMINGS; *sub nom.* CUMMINGS, *Re* [2001] EWCA Civ 45, Lord Phillips of Worth Matravers, M.R., CA.

4571. **Prison discipline – breach of prison rules – imposition of additional days – applicability of right to fair trial**

[Criminal Justice Act 1991 s.42; Human Rights Act 1998 Sch.1 Part I Art.6; Prison Rules 1999 (SI 1999 728).]

A and C appealed against the refusal of their application for judicial review of the Secretary of State's decision to uphold a disciplinary decision that they had disobeyed lawful orders in refusing to participate in a squat search, contrary to the Prison Rules 1999. G, a prisoner at a different prison, appealed against the refusal of his application for declarations that the Secretary of State had acted unlawfully in not providing him with an independent tribunal hearing with legal representation in accordance with the Human Rights Act 1998 Sch.1 Part I Art.6 in relation to a charge of breaching the Rules for administering a controlled drug to himself or failing to prevent the administration of a controlled drug by another person. A submitted that the fact that additional days of imprisonment had been imposed as a penalty for the breach meant that he fell to be treated as charged with a criminal offence for the purposes of Art.6, and that the reasons behind the order that they be subjected to a squat search should have been given before the search.

Held, dismissing the appeals, that under the Criminal Justice Act 1991 s.42, the imposition of additional days to a sentence were aggregated with the period which would have originally had to have been served before a release on licence, and therefore only served to postpone the release on licence. The fact that disciplinary proceedings could postpone a release on licence did not make them criminal proceedings within the remit of Art.6. To require reasons to be given for ordering a squat search, was impractical, and although a search should not be carried out without there being good reason, there was nothing requiring reasons to be given. It was appropriate to describe the drug offence in relating to G as a disciplinary offence, given the potential consequences the taking of drugs could have on the control of prisoners, and the fact that the offence did not replicate any in criminal law and did not result in a criminal record. Furthermore, the power of punishment was not disproportionate for a disciplinary offence and was within the discretion afforded to prison authorities.

R. (ON THE APPLICATION OF CARROLL) v. SECRETARY OF STATE FOR THE HOME DEPARTMENT; R. (ON THE APPLICATION OF GREENFIELD) v. SECRETARY OF STATE FOR THE HOME DEPARTMENT; R. (ON THE APPLICATION OF AL-HASAN) v. SECRETARY OF STATE FOR THE HOME DEPARTMENT; *sub nom.* R. v. SECRETARY OF STATE FOR THE HOME DEPARTMENT, *ex p.* CARROLL, [2001] EWCA Civ 1224, [2002] 1 W.L.R. 545, Lord Woolf of Barnes, L.C.J., CA.

4572. **Prison discipline – drugs – extension of sentence – right to fair trial**

[Criminal Justice Act 1991 s.33, s.42; Human Rights Act 1998 Sch.1 Part I Art.5(1), Art.5(4), Art.6; Prison Rules 1999 (SI 1999 728) r.51(9).]

G, a serving prisoner, applied for judicial review of the award of 21 additional days to his sentence following the finding at an adjudication that he had taken a controlled drug, contrary to the Prison Rules 1999 r.51(9). G contended that since the charge he faced was a criminal charge for the purposes of the Human Rights Act 1998 Sch.1 Part I Art.6, he had been entitled to legal representation and to a fair hearing before an independent and impartial tribunal. G submitted, furthermore, that as he had been deprived of his liberty he was entitled pursuant to Art.5(4) to bring proceedings whereby the lawfulness of the additional detention could be decided.

Held, refusing the application, that (1) the disciplinary proceedings in the instant case did not amount to a criminal charge and did not therefore gain the protection afforded under Art.6 of the Convention. As a serving prisoner, G was already deprived of his liberty at the time of the imposition of the additional days to his sentence. It was appropriate, when considering an offence that could be considered as either criminal or disciplinary in nature, to take into account the degree to which the punishment imposed equated to an offence against discipline rather than crime. In the instant case, the award of 21 additional days to G's sentence equated to a disciplinary sanction. Were such procedures viewed otherwise, the prison service would be hindered in carrying out a fast and efficient disciplinary system, and (2) all serving prisoners faced the risk of an extension to their sentence by virtue of the Criminal Justice Act 1991 s.33 and s.42 which provided a mechanism to enforce prison discipline by administrative means. The extension of G's sentence had arisen from drug testing procedures which were considered necessary for the maintenance of prison discipline. His extended detention did not therefore contravene Art.5(1) because he had already been deprived of his liberty pursuant to the original sentence of the court.

R. (ON THE APPLICATION OF GREENFIELD) v. SECRETARY OF STATE FOR THE HOME DEPARTMENT; *sub nom.* GREENFIELD v. SECRETARY OF STATE FOR THE HOME DEPARTMENT, [2001] EWHC Admin 129, [2001] 1 W.L.R. 1731, Latham, L.J., QBD (Admin Ct).

4573. Prisoners rights – discretionary life imprisonment – excessive delay between review board hearings – right to liberty

[European Convention on Human Rights 1950 Art.5(4).]

H, a discretionary life sentence prisoner, challenged the lawfulness of Parole Board review hearings conducted at 21 and 24 month intervals. He contended that the delay between reviews violated his right to an expeditious determination under the European Convention on Human Rights 1950 Art.5(4). The United Kingdom government maintained that (1) the problems which H had to confront and the progress that he needed to make could not be achieved in a lesser period; (2) discretionary life sentence prisoners could not be compared to prisoners detained on grounds of mental instability, and (3) it was possible for the Secretary of State to request an earlier review where it became apparent that an individual prisoner was making particularly rapid progress.

Held, allowing the application, that (1) the periods of time which had passed in between review board hearings could not be justified on the basis of rehabilitation and monitoring. Whilst it was clear that H did have problems that he needed to confront, it was also clear from the findings of the two previous panels that H had improved and that the gradual introduction of a less restrictive regime was appropriate. Having regard to the improvement thus far and the potential for further improvement, it could not be said that delays of 21 and 24 months between review hearings had been reasonable; (2) Art.5(4) was applicable to discretionary life sentence prisoners having regard to the fact that the reason for the imposition of such a sentence, namely mental instability and danger to the public, was subject to alteration with time, *Thynne v. United Kingdom (A/190)* (1991) 13 E.H.R.R. 666, [1990] C.L.Y. 2529 considered, and (3) there was some flexibility in the system which ameliorated the impact of the two year review system but whilst the Secretary of State could request an earlier review and the panel recommend it, there was no possibility of the applicant himself applying for a review within the two year period.

HIRST v. UNITED KINGDOM (40787/98) *The Times*, August 3, 2001, J-P Costa (President), ECHR.

4574. Prisoners rights – mothers – babies – policy of separating mother and child – right to family life

[Human Rights Act 1998 Sch.1 Part I Art.8(2).]

P and Q, who were both serving prison sentences, appealed against the dismissal ([2001] EWHC Admin 357) of their application for judicial review of the policy contained in Prison Service Order No 4801 which only allowed babies to remain with their mothers in prison until they had reached the age of 18 months.

Held, dismissing P's appeal and allowing Q's appeal, that although such a policy was legitimate, it was to be applied flexibly, bearing in mind the effect of the separation on the mother and child in each case and the alternative placement available for the child. In all but the most exceptional cases it was preferable for the separation to take place before the child reached the age of 18 months. The aim of the policy was to promote the child's welfare but that had to be read against the purpose and aims behind prison, and furthermore any interference with the family life of a child had to be justified under the Human Rights Act 1998 Sch.1 Part I Art.8(2). In P's case, she was serving a lengthy sentence in a closed prison, and without her being given parole, her child would have been five years' old at the time of her release, after which it was likely they would both be deported. Therefore it could not be concluded that the harm done by separation outweighed other considerations. However, Q's case was exceptional. She was in an open prison, serving a shorter sentence, and there was no suitable placement for the child outside the prison, therefore the potential harm to her child from separation was considerable, *R. (on the application of Daly) v. Secretary of State for the Home Department* [2001] UKHL 26, [2001] 2 W.L.R.1622, [2001] 6 C.L. 485 considered.

R. (ON THE APPLICATION OF P) v. SECRETARY OF STATE FOR THE HOME DEPARTMENT; R. (ON THE APPLICATION OF Q) v. SECRETARY OF STATE FOR THE HOME DEPARTMENT; *sub nom.* R. v. SECRETARY OF STATE FOR THE HOME DEPARTMENT, *ex p.* Q, [2001] EWCA Civ 1151, [2001] 1 W.L.R. 2002, Lord Phillips of Worth Matravers, M.R., CA.

4575. Prisoners rights – mothers – legality of prison policy separating mothers from babies after 18 months

[Prison Act1952; Children Act1989; Human Rights Act1998 Sch.1 Part I Art.8.]

P and Q, female prisoners, applied for judicial review of the policy of the Prison Service, contained in Prison Service Order No. 4801, whereby babies were allowed to remain with their mothers only until they reached the age of 18 months. They argued that the policy contravened both the Children Act 1989 and the Human Rights Act 1998 Sch.1 Part I Art.8.

Held, refusing the applications, that (1) the Prison Act 1952, which gave the Secretary of State wide managerial powers in relation to prisoners and prisons, impliedly authorised the Secretary of State or the Prison Service to adopt the policy; (2) the provisions of the 1989 Act had no direct application to the Secretary of State or the Prison Service in the present context; (3) the policy was not incompatible with Art.8 because the qualifications under Art.8(2) applied. The impairment of the right to family life was a consequence of the deprivation of liberty that prison involved, and promoting the welfare of prisoners' children was constrained by considerations of punishment and the need for the efficient running of, and the maintenance of good order and discipline within prisons, *R. (on the application of Mellor) v. Secretary of State for the Home Department* [2001] EWCA Civ 472, Times, May 1, 2001, [2001] 5 C.L. 452 considered, and (4) while each case should be assessed individually, assessment should take place against the background of the basic policy.

R. (ON THE APPLICATION OF P) v. SECRETARY OF STATE FOR THE HOME DEPARTMENT; R. (ON THE APPLICATION OF Q) v. SECRETARY OF STATE FOR THE HOME DEPARTMENT; *sub nom.* R. v. SECRETARY OF STATE FOR THE HOME DEPARTMENT, *ex p.* Q, [2001] EWHC Admin 357, [2001] 2 F.L.R. 383, Lord Woolf of Barnes, L.C.J., QBD (Admin Ct).

4576. Prisoners rights – natural justice – re categorisation – opportunity to make representations

H, a prisoner who had completed the tariff element of a discretionary life sentence, appealed against the dismissal of his application for judicial review of a decision to regrade his category status from C to B. H maintained that, as a matter of natural justice, he had been entitled to be informed of any intention to alter his status, together with an opportunity to make representations.

Held, allowing the appeal, that since most life sentence prisoners were only released once they had achieved category D status, the decision to re-categorise in H's case had significantly affected his prospects for release on licence. Whilst it was important that the prison service had the ability to make necessary operational decisions, the requirements of natural justice were capable of adapting to meet such requirements. In the instant case, given the importance of the decision, H should have been informed of any prospective re-categorisation, the reasons behind the proposal and afforded a reasonable opportunity in which to make representations.

R. v. SECRETARY OF STATE FOR THE HOME DEPARTMENT, *ex p.* HIRST; *sub nom.* HIRST v. SECRETARY OF STATE FOR THE HOME DEPARTMENT; R. (ON THE APPLICATION OF HIRST) v. SECRETARY OF STATE FOR THE HOME DEPARTMENT (CATEGORY STATUS), [2001] EWCA Civ 378, *The Times*, March 22, 2001, Lord Woolf of Barnes, L.C.J., CA.

4577. Prisoners rights – parole – delay in review – right to liberty and security

[Human Rights Act 1998 Sch.1 Part I Art.5(4).]

M, a convicted murderer who had been released on licence but then recalled to prison following his conviction of a further offence, appealed against the dismissal of his application for judicial review of the decision of the parole board that he should be detained in open conditions for a period of two years before a review was carried out. He argued that the decision to delay the review for two years breached his right under the Human Rights Act 1998 Sch.1 Part I Art.5(4) to have the lawfulness of his detention decided speedily by the court.

Held, dismissing the appeal, that while a review should take place at reasonable intervals, the unreasonableness of any delay would depend on the facts of the case. The decision to delay the review in M's case for a period of two years was not unreasonable and did not contravene Art.5(4), *Oldham v. United Kingdom* [2000] Crim. L.R. 1011, [2000] 11 C.L. 430 considered.

R. (ON THE APPLICATION OF MacNEIL) v. HMP LIFER PANEL; *sub nom.* R. v. HMP LIFER PANEL, *ex p.* MACNEIL, R. (ON THE APPLICATION OF MacNEIL) v. HMP DISCRETIONARY LIFER PANEL; R. v. PAROLE BOARD, *ex p.* MACNEIL, [2001] EWCA Civ 448, *The Times*, April 18, 2001, Lord Phillips of Worth Matravers, M.R., CA.

4578. Prisoners rights – privilege – examination of legal correspondence in prisoner's absence – right to private life

[Prison Act 1952 s.47(1); Human Rights Act 1998 Sch 1 Part I Art.8(1).]

D, a long term prisoner, appealed against the refusal by the Court of Appeal ([1999] C.O.D. 388) of his application for judicial review of the blanket policy introduced by the Home Secretary which authorised cell searches in prisons and in particular, required correspondence between a prisoner and his legal advisers to be examined in the prisoner's absence. It was submitted that the examination of legal correspondence in a prisoner's absence was not authorised by the Prison Act 1952 s.47(1) and constituted a breach of the Human Rights Act 1998 Sch.1 Part I Art.8(1).

Held, allowing the appeal, that the blanket policy infringed D's common law right to legal professional privilege, *R. v. Secretary of State for the Home Department, ex p. Simms* [1999] Q.B. 349, [1998] C.L.Y. 4084 considered. The only way in which a prisoner's right of access to legal advice and to communicate confidentially with a legal adviser could reasonably be curtailed would be by express words to that effect and that curtailment had to be justified. In the instant case, the infringement was greater than could be shown to be justified and no support for the intrusion could be found in either s.47(1) of the 1952 Act or in the 1998 Act. Lord Steyn observed that the comments of Lord Phillips of Worth Matravers, M.R. made in *R. (on the application of Mahmood (Amjad)) v. Secretary of State for the Home Department* [2001] 1 W.L.R. 840, [2001] 2 C.L. 342 concerning the review of executive decisions that interfered with human rights required clarification. The intensity of review was greater under the proportionality approach. Whilst not exhaustive, he set out three concrete differences in approach.

R. (ON THE APPLICATION OF DALY) v. SECRETARY OF STATE FOR THE HOME DEPARTMENT; *sub nom.* R. v. SECRETARY OF STATE FOR THE HOME

DEPARTMENT, *ex p.* DALY, [2001] UKHL 26, [2001] 2 A.C. 532, Lord Bingham of Cornhill, HL.

4579. Prisoners rights – right to family life – right to conceive child via artificial insemination

[Human Rights Act 1998 Sch.1 Part I Art.8, Art.12.]

M, a prisoner serving a life sentence for murder, appealed against the dismissal of his application for judicial review ([2000] 2 F.L.R. 951) of the refusal by the Secretary of State to grant him the opportunity to conceive a child with his wife via the aid of artificial insemination. The request had been refused on the basis that no exceptional circumstances existed to justify the grant of such facilities. M contended that the refusal infringed his right to respect for his private and family life and his right to found a family, contrary to the Human Rights Act 1998 Sch.1 Part I Art.8 and Art.12. M maintained that such a refusal could not be justified on the basis of prison security.

Held, dismissing the appeal, that the Secretary of State had not acted in breach of M's right to respect for his family life or his right to marry and found a family in refusing him access to the facilities he had requested. One aspect of the punishment meted out to M was the denial of precisely those rights which he now sought to avail himself of. No interference with those rights would amount to a breach of his fundamental rights, provided that it was proportionate to the aim of operating a penal system designed for both punishment and deterrence. Nevertheless, in certain exceptional circumstances, having regard to the principle of proportionality, it might not be appropriate to deny a prisoner the opportunity to conceive a child, whether by natural or artificial means.

R. (ON THE APPLICATION OF MELLOR) v. SECRETARY OF STATE FOR THE HOME DEPARTMENT; *sub nom.* R. v. SECRETARY OF STATE FOR THE HOME DEPARTMENT, *ex p.* MELLOR, [2001] EWCA Civ 472, [2002] Q.B. 13, Lord Phillips of Worth Matravers, M.R., CA.

4580. Prisoners rights – right to have wife artificially seminated

See PENOLOGY: R. (on the application of Mellor) v. Secretary of State for the Home Department. §4579

4581. Prisoners rights – spent convictions – disclosure of offences against children to social services

[Children and Young Persons Act 1933 Sch.1; Rehabilitation of Offenders Act 1974 s.4(1); Human Rights Act 1998 Sch.1 Part I Art.8.]

N applied for judicial review of a decision of the Governor, G, to disclose to social services the fact that he had a spent conviction for gross indecency with a child. After N had been convicted and imprisoned on drug offences, G implemented the procedure under IG 54/1994 to inform social services that he was an offender under the Children and Young Persons Act 1933 Sch.1 and was likely to be a risk to children on release. N argued that (1) the Rehabilitation of Offenders Act 1974 s.4(1) prevented G from making the disclosure as he had to be treated "for all purposes" as if he had not been convicted of the offence; (2) disclosure was a discretionary not a mandatory power, and (3) disclosure breached N's right to privacy under the Human Rights Act 1998 Sch.1 Part I Art.8.

Held, refusing the application, that G had been acting legitimately within his powers in making the disclosure since (1) N's interpretation of s.4(1) was incorrect. The phrase "for all purposes in law", in the context of the Act as a whole, had to be interpreted as meaning "for all legal purposes". Disclosure to social services was not a legal purpose and to hold otherwise would lead to an unworkable and inappropriate result in which social services were prevented from fulfilling their duty to protect children. Furthermore, s.9(2) expressly allowed disclosure unless made for an extraneous purpose, *X v. Commissioner of Police of the Metropolis* [1985] 1 W.L.R. 420, [1985] C.L.Y. 2564 considered; (2) IG 54/94 placed a mandatory not a discretionary duty on G to disclose the information, and (3) an invasion of N's privacy was not inevitable but remained at the discretion of social services. Given the internationally recognised obligation to protect children from harm, any balancing exercise conducted with N's right to privacy necessarily resulted in child protection being afforded priority.

R. (ON THE APPLICATION OF N) v. GOVERNOR OF DARTMOOR PRISON; *sub nom.* N v. GOVERNOR OF DARTMOOR PRISON; R. v. GOVERNOR OF DARTMOOR PRISON, *ex p.* N [2001] EWHC Admin 93, Turner, J., QBD (Admin Ct).

4582. Prisoners rights – voting rights – life prisoners – entitlement to vote

[Representation of the People Act 1983 s.3(1); Human Rights Act 1998 Sch.1 Part I Art.14, Part II Art.3.]

P and M, convicted prisoners, sought judicial review of a refusal by the electoral registration officer to register their names on the electoral register. H, a convicted prisoner serving a discretionary life sentence of which the tariff term had expired, sought a declaration that the Representation of the People Act 1983 s.3(1) was incompatible with the Human Rights Act 1998 Sch.1 Part I Art.14 and Sch.1 Part II Art.3. P and M maintained that in relation to discretionary life sentence prisoners who had served their tariff term, the continued denial of voting rights could not be justified since their continued detention was a preventative rather than a punitive measure.

Held, refusing the applications, that although a convicted prisoner still retained his civil rights, Sch.1 Part II Art.3 of the 1998 Act did not provide an absolute right to vote, *Raymond v. Honey* [1983] 1 A.C. 1, [1982] C.L.Y. 2613 considered and *Mathieu-Mohin v. Belgium (A/113)* (1988) 10 E.H.R.R. 1 applied. Contracting states had a discretion to impose restrictions upon voting rights, but such restrictions had to accord with a legitimate aim and the means employed were not to be disproportionate. The loss of voting rights pursuant to s.3(1) of the 1983 Act, was not incompatible with Sch.1 Part II Art.3. Although disenfranchisement did impair the right to vote, it accorded with a legitimate aim of the legislature, albeit an aim that was difficult to define with precision. The question of proportionality was a matter upon which the courts should defer to the legislature. The position in relation to life sentence prisoners who had served their tariff term was also justifiable and there was no violation of Sch.1 Part I Art.14 of the 1998 Act. If released on licence such individuals would be entitled to vote, but if there was reasonable justification for their continued detention, then the same considerations as those arising out of Art.3 were applicable, *Belgian Linguistic Case (No.1) (A/5)* (1979-80) 1 E.H.R.R. 241, [1981] C.L.Y. 1087 applied.

R. (ON THE APPLICATION OF PEARSON) v. SECRETARY OF STATE FOR THE HOME DEPARTMENT; R. (ON THE APPLICATION OF MARTINEZ) v. SECRETARY OF STATE FOR THE HOME DEPARTMENT; HIRST v. ATTORNEY GENERAL, [2001] EWHC Admin 239, [2001] H.R.L.R. 39, Kennedy, L.J., QBD (Admin Ct).

4583. Probation – approved premises

CRIMINAL JUSTICE AND COURT SERVICES ACT 2000 (APPROVED PREMISES) REGULATIONS 2001, SI 2001 850; made under the Criminal Justice and Court Services Act 2000 s.9. In force: April 1, 2001; £2.00.

These Regulations make provision for the regulation, management and inspection of premises approved under Criminal Justice and Court Services Act 2000 s.9. The Regulations, which revoke the Approved Probation and Bail Hostel Rules 1995 (SI 1995 302), lay down particular requirements for the management of approved premises by organisations other than local probation boards and for those boards to approve the constitutions and, together with a representative of the Secretary of State, to attend the meetings of the managing bodies of such premises and also lay down requirements that apply to the management of all approved premises. In addition, they require the management bodies of all approved premises to adopt admissions policies and place restrictions on the circumstances in which certain residents may be asked to leave.

4584. Probation – local probation boards – appointments and miscellaneous provisions

LOCAL PROBATION BOARDS (APPOINTMENTS AND MISCELLANEOUS PROVISIONS) REGULATIONS 2001, SI 2001 1035; made under the Criminal Justice and Court Services Act 2000 s.4, s.25, Sch.1 para.2, Sch.1 para.6. In force: April 10, 2001; £1.75.

These Regulations, which amend the Local Probation Boards (Miscellaneous Provisions) Regulations 2001 (SI 2001 85), make provision for appointments to local probation boards. They provide for the application to be made to the Secretary of State or a person providing services to him, establish the functions of selection panels, provide that a quorum of the audit committee is three or more and that the chairman of the committee is to be appointed by the local probation board.

4585. Probation – local probation boards – miscellaneous provisions

LOCAL PROBATION BOARDS (MISCELLANEOUS PROVISIONS) REGULATIONS 2001, SI 2001 786; made under the Criminal Justice and Court Services Act 2000 s.1, s.5, Sch.1 para.6, Sch.1 para.7, Sch.1 para.10, Sch.1 para.18. In force: April 1, 2001; £1.75.

These Regulations, which make miscellaneous provision in connection with local probation boards, extend the purposes of the National Probation Service to include the giving of information to victims of offenders and alleged offenders. They prescribe the functions of boards which are to be exercised by chief officers on behalf of local probation boards, prescribe the persons eligible to make complaints in relation to things done under arrangements made by local boards under the Criminal Justice and Court Services Act 2000 s.5 and provide for the establishment and functions of audit committees and for the procedure of local and audit committees. In addition, the Regulations provide for the appointment of secretaries and treasurers to local probation boards and for their tenure of office and amend the Local Probation Boards (Appointment) Regulations 2000 (SI 2000 3342) so as to substitute a period of six months instead of two months as the period after which the Secretary of State can suspend or remove from office a member of the board who has failed to attend board meetings without consent during that period.

4586. Sentencing – repatriation of prisoners – extension to Isle of Man

REPATRIATION OF PRISONERS ACT 1984 (ISLE OF MAN) ORDER 2001, SI 2001 3936; made under the Repatriation of Prisoners Act 1984 s.9. In force: January 2, 2002; £1.75.

This Order, which revokes the Repatriation of Prisoners Act 1984 (Isle of Man) Order 1986 (SI 1986 598), extends to the Isle of Man the Repatriation of Prisoners Act 1984 with the exceptions, adaptations and modifications specified in the Schedule to this Order.

4587. Young offender institutions – prison governors – safety of inmates – liability in negligence

The Home Office appealed against a decision that it was liable to T for personal injuries he had sustained in a razor attack by another inmate whilst he was serving a custodial sentence in a young offenders institution. The institution had operated a system whereby an inmate would keep a razor until it was necessary to change it. When changing a razor, an inmate had to show it to an officer on duty who would check that the blade remained in place. The judge had found that there had been a breach in the duty to take reasonable care of T's safety and that at little cost or disruption to the lifestyle of inmates, action could have been taken to reduce the risk inherent in razors being available.

Held, allowing the appeal, that the governor of the institution had not been negligent in adopting a system of providing inmates with razors. That system had been implemented in accordance with Home Office guidelines, which provided that inmates should be allowed to keep razors unless there were good reasons for withholding them. In exercising his discretion, the governor had made a balanced judgment, taking into account both the need for tight security and the desirability of establishing a regime aimed at rehabilitation, in which inmates were required to exercise responsibility.

THOMPSON v. HOME OFFICE [2001] EWCA Civ 331, May, L.J., CA.

4588. Books

Tarde, Gabriel – Penal Philosophy. Paperback: £33.50. ISBN 0-7658-0705-X. Transaction Publishers.

PENSIONS

4589. Armed forces – disablement or death in service

NAVAL, MILITARY AND AIR FORCES ETC. (DISABLEMENT AND DEATH) SERVICE PENSIONS AMENDMENT ORDER 2001, SI 2001 409; made under the Naval and Marine Pay and Pensions Act 1865 s.3; the Pensions and Yeomanry Pay Act 1884 s.2; the Air Force (Constitution) Act 1917 s.2; the Social Security (Miscellaneous Provisions) Act 1977 s.12; and the Naval and Marine Pay and Pensions Act 1865 s.24. In force: April 9, 2001; £3.50.

This Order amends the Naval, Military and Air Forces Etc. (Disablement and Death) Service Pensions Order 1983 (SI 1983 883) which makes provisions for pensions and other awards in respect of disablement or death due to service in the naval, military and air forces. The Order provides for four rates of constant attendance allowance, the meaning of therapeutic earnings for the purposes of unemployability allowance is clarified, ages are equalised for unemployability allowance, invalidity allowance and allowance for lowered standard of occupation, and the conditions for award of treatment allowance are clarified as is disablement for the purposes of mobility supplement. The Order also increases the amount of a widow's pension payable, makes amendments in relation to awards in respect of children, funeral expenses, varies the rates of retired pay, pensions, gratuities and allowances in respect of disablement or death due to service in the armed forces, and enables the Secretary of State to review an assessment or decision of the Pensions Appeal Tribunal where there is a change of circumstances and to review any assessment where there is an improvement in the disablement.

4590. Employees – remuneration – European Commission – Council Regulation

Council Regulation 1986/2001 (EC, ECSC, EURATOM) of 8 October 2001 correcting with effect from 1 July 2000 the remuneration and pensions of officials and other servants of the European Communities. [2001] OJ L271/1.

4591. Financial advisers – professional negligence – misselling of personal pensions – date of knowledge

See NEGLIGENCE: Glaister v. Greenwood. §4521

4592. Fire services – firemens pension scheme – divorce – pension sharing

FIREMEN'S PENSION SCHEME (PENSION SHARING) ORDER 2001, SI 2001 3691; made under the Fire Services Act 1947 s.26; and the Superannuation Act 1972 s.12. In force: December 1, 2001; £2.00.

This Order amends the Firemen's Pension Scheme, as set out in the Firemen's Pension Scheme Order 1992 (SI 1992 129) Sch.2, as it applies in England and Wales. The amendments make provision for the implementation of pension sharing on divorce and nullity in accordance with the Welfare and Pensions Reform Act 1999 and subordinate legislation made under that Act. In particular, they implement the overriding reduction of benefits made by s.31 of that Act. The amendments are set out in the Schedule to this Order.

4593. Misselling – measure of damages – calculation of damages for negligent financial advice – effect of demutualisation benefits

N, who had provided negligent financial advice to T, a pensioner, in connection with his pension fund, sought to determine a question of law concerning the calculation of the compensation payable to T. N had offered to make an award of compensation on condition that the value of shares allocated to him when the pension company had demutualised were taken into account so as to minimise its liability. N maintained, citing *Livingstone v. Rawyards Coal Co* (1879-80) L.R. 5 App. Cas. 25, that in accordance with the basic rule established in that case, the demutualisation benefit had to be included in the calculation in order to place T in the same position as he would have been in had he not been negligently advised.

Held, giving judgment for the defendant, that the source of T's loss was entirely separate to the source of his demutualisation benefit and it could not be said that the two were part of the same continuous transaction. The loss resulted from the negligent advice, yet the benefits resulted from the introduction of a new corporate structure to the company and, therefore, did not flow from the company's breach of duty. Whether the demutualisation benefits took the form of a cash payment, allocation of shares or a policy bonus, N could not use them to minimise its liability and their value had to be deducted before calculation of the loss could begin.

NEEDLER FINANCIAL SERVICES v. TABER [2001] Pens. L.R. 253, Sir Andrew Morritt V.C., Ch D.

4594. Occupational pensions – airlines – disposable surplus

Within proceedings originally concerned with the proposed merger of two British Airways pension schemes, the court was asked to resolve a number of questions of construction concerning the terms of the Airways Pension Scheme.

Held, granting declaratory relief, that in the context of an actuarial valuation of the pension fund, "disposable surplus" was not the sum by which assets exceeded liabilities, but rather the surplus after the actuary had made allowance by way of reserve against either general contingencies or more specific factors. In calculating the disposable surplus, the actuary could not take into account the way in which the management trustees of the fund might wish to use the disposable surplus, but was entitled to forecast how they were likely to dispose of it and to allow that forecast to influence his calculations.

STEVENS v. BELL; *sub nom*. AIRWAYS PENSION SCHEME, *Re* [2001] Pens. L.R. 99, Lloyd, J., Ch D.

4595. Occupational pensions – amendments – accidental benefits increase – rectification to reflect intention

In proceedings commenced by AMP against the trustees of its non contributory pension scheme, AMP sought rectification of certain amendments which had previously been made to the rules of the scheme or, alternatively, a declaration that the amendments had been vitiated by error or by the trustees' failure to take into account material considerations. The amendments had the effect of increasing the benefits payable to those employees retiring as a result of incapacity, and AMP maintained that the trustees had failed to appreciate the fact that owing to the link, under the rules of the scheme between early leavers' benefit and incapacity benefit, the benefits payable to "early leavers" would increase dramatically as those people were also treated as if they were retiring on the ground of incapacity.

Held, granting an order for rectification, that AMP had sufficiently demonstrated that it had been the continuing intention of the trustees and of NPI, as the principal employer at the requisite time, to affect only incapacity benefits and no other, particularly given the overwhelming increased cost involved in the accidental inclusion of early leavers' benefits. Rectification in order to express true intention was available where, as in the instant case, the wording used in the instrument had been as intended but where it had had a different impact to that which had been contemplated, *Butlin's Settlement Trusts (Rectification), Re* [1976] Ch. 251, [1976] C.L.Y. 2508 followed. Further, as the beneficiaries of the scheme had not given additional consideration for the pension rights accruing to them as the result of the error, they were not bona fide purchasers of the amended scheme for the purpose of resisting rectification.

AMP (UK) PLC v. BARKER [2001] Pens. L.R. 77, Lawrence Collins, J., Ch D.

4596. Occupational pensions – benefits – revaluation percentages

OCCUPATIONAL PENSIONS (REVALUATION) ORDER 2001, SI 2001 3690; made under the Pension Schemes Act 1993 Sch.3 para.2. In force: January 1, 2002; £1.50.

This Order is made, as required by the Pension Schemes Act 1993 Sch.3 para.2(1), in the year beginning January 1, 2001 and specifies revaluation percentages for the purpose of the revaluation on or after January 1, 2002 of benefits under occupational pension schemes, as required by s.84 of, and Sch.3 to, that Act.

4597. Occupational pensions – Civil Aviation Authority pension scheme

TRANSPORT ACT 2000 (CIVIL AVIATION AUTHORITY PENSION SCHEME) ORDER 2001, SI 2001 853; made under the Transport Act 2000 s.96, s.103. In force: March 31, 2001; £10.50.

This Order amends the Civil Aviation Authority Pension Scheme and provides for the allocation of assets, rights, liabilities and obligations between different sections of the Scheme.

4598. Occupational pensions – civil servants

PENSIONS INCREASE (REVIEW) ORDER 2001, SI 2001 664; made under the Social Security Pensions Act 1975 s.59. In force: April 9, 2001; £2.00.

This Order prescribes the increase in the rate of public service pensions, deferred lump sums, and reductions in respect of guaranteed minimum pension.

4599. Occupational pensions – compensation provision

OCCUPATIONAL PENSION SCHEMES (PENSIONS COMPENSATION PROVISIONS) AMENDMENT REGULATIONS 2001, SI 2001 1218; made under the Pensions Act 1995 s.56, s.81, s.83, s.84, s.86, s.119, s.124, s.125, s.174. In force: April 23, 2001; £1.75.

These Regulations amend the Occupational Pension Schemes (Pensions Compensation Provisions) Regulations 1997 (SI 1997 665) which make provision in relation to the payment, by the Pensions Compensation Board under the Pensions Act 1995 s.81 to s.85, of compensation to occupational pension schemes whose assets have been reduced in value as a result of certain acts or omissions. These amendments are made in consequence of changes made to the compensation provisions by the Welfare Reform and Pensions Act 1999 s.17 in connection with the criteria which must be met when an occupational pension scheme seeks compensation from the Board, and with the maximum amount of compensation payable. The 1997 Regulations are amended to specify the class of members in respect of whom liabilities of the scheme are included among the liabilities by reference to which "the protection level" is calculated under s.81 (2A) of the 1995 Act, and to remove the 90 per cent. limit by reference to which the maximum amount of compensation, and the amount of interest and of payments made in anticipation, are calculated. Equivalent amendments are also made in Reg.10 of the 1997 Regulations, which modifies s.81 and s.83 of the 1995 Act, and other provisions of those Regulations, in their application to money purchase schemes and "ear-marked schemes" where money purchase benefits may be provided.

4600. Occupational pensions – compulsory pensions – compatibility with EC competition law provisions

See COMPETITION LAW: Pavlov v. Stichting Pensioenfonds Medische Specialisten (C180-C184/98). §763

4601. Occupational pensions – death in service benefits – exercise of trustees' discretionary powers

K died in 1994 while still in pensionable service. In that year he had made a will which, according to a letter from his solicitor, made provision for the three children from his first marriage, in the belief that the death benefit payable under his pension would go to his second wife. Since 1981, decisions on death in service benefit had been made by two trustees and the pension manager had sent a memorandum outlining the facts of the instant case and notice of K's election to two trustees, who recommended payment in accordance with K's wishes. The children of K's first marriage complained to the Pensions Ombudsman on the grounds that the trustees should have paid more regard to their needs. The Ombudsman decided that no proper decision had been made regarding the payment, although he did not suggest that the trustees could not have come to exactly the same conclusion. The trustees appealed.

Held, allowing the appeal, that the 1981 decision was an effective exercise of the trustees' power of delegation. The signatures of the two trustees showed that they had agreed with the pension manager's recommendation. Further, a full meeting of the trustees had been informed of the decision and effectively ratified it. Accordingly, the death benefit had gone to the person nominated by K.

LIBBY v. KENNEDY [1998] O.P.L.R. 213, Jacob, J., Ch D.

4602. Occupational pensions – deferred pensions – entitlement dependent on scheme being funded

[Pension Schemes Act 1993 Chapter 1 Part IV.]

RMH, which had established a pension scheme in 1949, appealed against a decision that Z, a member of the scheme, was entitled to a deferred pension pursuant to the Pension Schemes Act 1993 Chapter 1 Part IV. Under the provisions of Chapter 1 Part IV, a deferred right to receive a pension upon attaining pensionable age was established in certain circumstances. RMH's scheme did not require it or any employee member to make contributions.

Held, allowing the appeal, that Chapter 1 Part IV applied only to occupational schemes that were funded. Given that pension payments under the scheme would derive from RMH's general assets rather than from contributions, the scheme could not be said to be funded. It followed that Z was not entitled to deferred pension rights.

ROYAL MASONIC HOSPITAL v. PENSIONS OMBUDSMAN [2001] 3 All E.R. 408, Rimer, J., Ch D.

4603.   Occupational pensions – early retirement – ill health – binding nature of decision by Pensions Ombudsman

[Pension Schemes Act 1993 s.151.]

K commenced employment with C in 1979 and joined the company pension scheme in 1988. In 1986 she began to suffer from pains in her neck, shoulders and arms. The condition worsened and, because of its severity, she ceased work in April 1992, aged 44. She was seen by C's medical adviser, D, who stated that it was possible that K would return to work at a future date. K saw a consultant neurologist in October 1992 and was seen by D again in December 1992. She had not returned to work when in February 1993 D wrote to C having obtained a report from K's GP that referred to the consultant's findings. D stated that K would be unlikely to return to work in the short term. Following that letter, C terminated K's employment on the basis that she could not perform her job. Rule 19 of the pension scheme allowed an employee retiring on incapacity grounds to elect to receive an immediate pension, whereas rule 17 allowed a person to be awarded a pension with C's consent on reaching age 50 if they left before that date with two years' service. K was awarded a pension on the basis of rule 17 and complained to the Pensions Ombudsman as she considered that she was eligible for an immediate pension under rule 19. The Ombudsman found that K had not been dismissed on ill health grounds and K appealed.

Held, dismissing the appeal, that the Ombudsman's decision on findings of fact was final under the Pension Schemes Act 1993 s.151, so that his determination was binding unless it could be shown that he had erred on a point of law. There was material before the Ombudsman supporting his conclusion that K had been dismissed due to ill health. Although the Ombudsman could have further investigated K's medical condition that was a matter for the Ombudsman to decide. K's objection was not based on a point of law, but arose from her disagreement with the Ombudsman's factual conclusions.

KEY v. COURTAULDS TEXTILES PLC [1999] O.P.L.R. 27, Sir Richard Scott V.C., Ch D.

4604.   Occupational pensions – equal treatment – calculation method – different pensionable age for men and women

[Council Directive 79/7 on equal treatment for men and women in matters of social security Art.4(1), Art.7(1)(a).]

Prior to 1991, Belgium fixed the normal retirement age for men at 65 and 60 for women. This changed in 1991, so that both sexes could benefit from a flexible retirement age between 60 and 65. However, pension calculation was still carried out as before, with different denominators used for men and women. Council Directive 79/7 Art.4(1) prohibited all discrimination on gender grounds in the calculation of benefits and pensions. However, under Art.7(1)(a) Member States could exclude the fixing of pensionable age for retirement pension calculation purposes. W applied to the national court for annulment of ONP's decision to calculate his pension using the method applicable to males, as the denominator used for females would have given a higher figure. The ECJ was asked to decide whether a retirement scheme that retained a calculation method based on sex, while allowing both sexes to retire at age 60 came within the Art.7(1)(a) derogation.

Held, giving a preliminary ruling, that Art.7(1)(a) had to be interpreted strictly where national legislation prescribed different pensionable ages for male and female workers. In the instant case, a 1996 retrospective amendment to the 1991 legislation provided that the age at which workers became unfit for work on age grounds was 65 for males and 60 for females, so that Art.7(1)(a) permitted a different calculation depending on gender, *Secretary of State for Social Security v. Thomas (C328/91)* [1993] Q.B. 747, [1993] C.L.Y. 4386 and *Van Cant (Remi) v. Rijksdienst voor Pensioenen (C154/92)* [1993] E.C.R. I-3811, [1993] C.L.Y. 4385 followed.

WOLFS v. OFFICE NATIONAL DES PENSIONS (ONP) (C154/96) [2000] 3 C.M.L.R. 1414, PJG Kapteyn (President), ECJ.

4605. Occupational pensions – equal treatment – guaranteed minimum pension – Pensions Ombudsman – jurisdiction

[Pensions Act 1995 s.62; Council Directive 75/117 relating to the application of the principle of equal pay for men and women.]

M, employers and trustees of a contracted out pension scheme, appealed against a determination of the Pensions Ombudsman that the scheme discriminated improperly between men and women in respect of guaranteed minimum pensions, with the result that the scheme contravened the equal treatment rule in the Pensions Act 1995 s.62 and should be amended. It had been argued by W, a former employee of M, that the scheme failed to equalise the GMP element of the pension because the accrual rate for women who left the scheme before reaching pensionable age was higher than the corresponding rate for male members. M contended that the Ombudsman had no jurisdiction to deal with the issue except in relation to W's original complaint, which related to the transfer value of his own pension and that, in any event, the Ombudsman's ruling was wrong in law.

Held, allowing the appeal, that the Ombudsman's approach was flawed in that he had determined a general question and had given a general direction in respect of the rewriting of the scheme which would effect all members of the scheme. No opportunity had been given to other members to argue against a general equalisation direction. The correct approach was to decide the issue as between M and W, *Edge v. Pensions Ombudsman* [1998] Ch. 512, [1998] C.L.Y. 4144 followed. Obiter, GMPs were not pensions, nor discrete elements of a pension, rather they were a factor to be taken into account when calculating a pension. However, they could not be ignored when considering equal pay requirements under the Equal Pay Directive 75/117 and potentially discriminatory features of GMPs could be raised by members before that discrimination became a reality, *Barber v. Guardian Royal Exchange Assurance Group (C262/88)* [1991] 1 Q.B. 344, [1990] C.L.Y. 1915 and *Birds Eye Walls Ltd v. Roberts (C132/92)* [1993] E.C.R. I-5579, [1994] C.L.Y. 4823 considered.

MARSH & McLENNAN COMPANIES UK LTD v. PENSIONS OMBUDSMAN [2001] I.R.L.R. 505, Rimer, J., Ch D.

4606. Occupational pensions – guaranteed minimum pensions – increase

GUARANTEED MINIMUM PENSIONS INCREASE (NO.2) ORDER 2001, SI 2001 160; made under the Pension Schemes Act 1993 s.109. In force: April 6, 2001; £1.50.

This Order, which is made in consequence of a review under the Pension Schemes Act 1993 s.109, specifies 3 per cent as the percentage by which that part of any guaranteed minimum pension attributable to earnings factors for the tax years 1988-89 to 1996-97 and payable by occupational pension schemes is to be increased.

4607. Occupational pensions – Inner London court staff

INNER LONDON COURT STAFF PENSIONS ORDER 2001, SI 2001 733; made under the Access to Justice Act 1999 Sch.14 para.36. In force: April 1, 2001; £1.50.

This Order provides for people employed as Inner London court staff immediately before April 1, 2001, to continue to be eligible to be members of the Metropolitan Civil Staffs Superannuation Scheme after the transfer of their employment to the Greater London Magistrates' Courts Authority under the Access to Justice Act 1999 Sch.14 para.33. The Order also provides for that Authority to bear the cost of payments under the Scheme to or in respect of current or former Inner London court staff.

4608. Occupational pensions – Inner London court staff

INNER LONDON COURT STAFF PENSIONS (AMENDMENT) ORDER 2001, SI 2001 1425; made under the Access to Justice Act 1999 Sch.14 para.36. In force: April 11, 2001; £1.50.

This Order corrects an error in the Inner London Court Staff Pensions Order 2001 (SI 2001 733) by providing that the reference in Art.2 of the Order, were regarded as members of the metropolitan civil staffs superannuation scheme is to be replaced by a reference to people who, before the commencement of the Order, were so regarded.

4609. Occupational pensions – local government pension scheme

LOCAL GOVERNMENT PENSION SCHEME (MISCELLANEOUS) REGULATIONS 2001, SI 2001 770; made under the Superannuation Act 1972 s.7, s.12. In force: April 2, 2001; £2.50.

These Regulations, which amend the Local Government Pension Scheme Regulations 1997 (SI 1997 1612) which comprise the Local Government Pension Scheme, make certain amendments to enable employees of a wider category of bodies, who are not Scheme employers and who provide services or assets in connection with the exercise of a function of a Scheme employer, to become members of the Scheme. The Regulations amend the 1997 Regulations by removing the provision allowing entry to the Scheme after age 65, clarify the provisions in connection with the normal retirement age under the Scheme, clarify the treatment of aggregated and non-aggregated periods of membership, provide a new method of calculating membership where one of two concurrent employments terminates and the member elects to keep the periods of service aggregated for the purposes of calculating benefits and removes the requirement for a member to be 50 before he can exercise the right to elect for pension in lieu of retirement grant. They allow a longer period after retirement before the value of the additional voluntary contributions must be used to pay for a pension, allow the actuary to provide that where an outgoing admission body cannot pay revised contributions to a fund, that liability is borne by the Scheme employer who is a party to the admission agreement and replace provisions in connection with former members of the Metropolitan Civil Staffs Superannuation Scheme. In addition, they amend the Local Government Pension Scheme (Transitional Provisions) Regulations 1997 (SI 1997 1613) by adding a provision allowing a person who was a deferred member of the Scheme on March 31, 1998 to elect for a pension in lieu of his retirement grant or to elect for a lump sum in lieu of part of his pension and revoke the Local Government Pension Scheme (Miscellaneous Provisions) Regulations 1999 (SI 1999 1212) Reg.14, the Local Government Pension Scheme (Amendment etc.) Regulations 1999 (SI 1999 3438) Reg.6 and the Local Government Pension Scheme (Greater London Authority etc.) Regulations 2000 (SI 2000 1164) Reg.7.

4610. Occupational pensions – local government pension scheme – employment

LOCAL GOVERNMENT PENSION SCHEME (HER MAJESTY'S CHIEF INSPECTOR OF SCHOOLS IN ENGLAND) (TRANSFERS) REGULATIONS 2001, SI 2001 2866; made under the Superannuation Act 1972 s.7. In force: August 31, 2001; £1.75.

These Regulations make provision for the calculation and payment of transfer payments for active members of the Local Government Pension Scheme who transfer from local government employment to employment with Her Majesty's Chief Inspector of Schools in England on or before September 1, 2001 as a consequence of provision of the Care Standards Act 2000 Part VI.

4611. Occupational pensions – local government pension scheme – membership

LOCAL GOVERNMENT PENSION SCHEME (AMENDMENT) REGULATIONS 2001, SI 2001 1481; made under the Superannuation Act 1972 s.7, s.12. In force: Reg.17(f): September 1, 2001; remainder: May 1, 2001; £2.00.

These Regulations, which amend the Local Government Pension Scheme Regulations 1997 (SI 1997 1612), add the Greater London Magistrates' Courts Authority and the Children and Family Court Advisory and Support Service as resolution bodies and the National College for School Leadership, the Standards Board for England and city academies as Scheme employers. They ensure that periods of membership before and after unpaid periods of maternity absence or parental leave are treated as continuous and provide that a member who leaves employment with an admission body is entitled to count the additional period of membership even where he does not immediately become entitled to a pension on leaving the employment.

4612. Occupational pensions – local government pension scheme – membership

LOCAL GOVERNMENT PENSION SCHEME (AMENDMENT NO.2) REGULATIONS 2001, SI 2001 3401; made under the Superannuation Act 1972 s.7, s.12. In force: Reg 6(b): April 1, 2002; remainder: November 13, 2001; £1.75.

These Regulations amend the Local Government Pension Scheme Regulations 1997 (SI 1997 1612) which comprise the Local Government Pension Scheme. They ensure that certain members of the Scheme who were members before April 1, 1998 continue to have a normal retirement date between age 60 and 65 and substitute a new Regulation only allowing the use of the accumulated value of the additional voluntary contributions to provide a scheme benefit when a member ceases to be an active member of the Scheme with immediate entitlement to a pension.

4613. Occupational pensions – maladministration – advice to scheme beneficiaries – assumption of duty of care

[Pension Schemes Act 1993 s.146(1); Local Government Superannuation Regulations 1986 (1986 24).]

WBC, the administrators of a scheme constituted under the Local Government Superannuation Regulations 1986, appealed against a decision of the Pensions Ombudsman that they had been guilty of maladministration under the Pension Schemes Act 1993 s.146(1) which had caused loss to E. E maintained that, on leaving his previous employment and being invited to join the statutory scheme, he had sought clarification over the telephone from WBC about the impact of transferring his accrued pension benefits into the new scheme and that WBC had failed to advise him that the transfer would result in the devaluation of those rights. Upholding his complaint, the Ombudsman had found that, had WBC adequately explained to E the distinction between "reckonable" and "qualifying" service, he would not have transferred his accrued rights.

Held, allowing the appeal, that there had been no duty on the administrators to advise E, *Outram v. Academy Plastics Ltd* [2000] I.R.L.R. 499, [2000] 6 C.L. 504 followed. However, if specific advice had been given to E, WBC might have assumed a duty of care to exercise reasonable care and skill when providing such advice. The Ombudsman had failed to make any findings in relation to the alleged telephone conversation so the question of whether a conversation had occurred in which E had been wrongly advised, and whether WBC was accordingly guilty of maladministration, was remitted for a rehearing.

WIRRAL BC v. EVANS (2001) 3 L.G.L.R. 30, Evans-Lombe, J., Ch D.

4614. Occupational pensions – maladministration – causation – delay in providing accurate transfer value

[Pension Schemes Act 1993 s.146(1); Occupational Pension Schemes (Disclosure of Information) Regulations 1986 (SI 1986 1046) Reg.6(7), Sch.2.]

D was made redundant from his employment with D in October 1993. He was a member of D's pension scheme, a funded scheme established by a trust deed. The trustees had delegated the scheme's administration to H, a professional management company. B had the right to transfer the value of his pension into a personal pension scheme. However, the sum available for transfer was found to be incorrect and a final figure was not supplied by H until after the expiry of a three month guaranteed payment period. B contended that the incorrect initial figure and the delay were due to maladministration by H and the trustees. His complaint was upheld by the Ombudsman, who directed H to make up the transfer value to the sum B would have received but for the maladministration. H and the trustees appealed.

Held, allowing the appeal in part, that the Pension Schemes Act 1993 s.146(1) required the Ombudsman to determine the existence of maladministration by reference to a three part test. Applying that test to the facts, H was guilty of maladministration in failing to give an accurate transfer, contrary to the Occupational Pension Schemes (Disclosure of Information) Regulations 1986 Reg.6(7) and Sch.2. However, it was not maladministration on H's part to refuse to extend the guarantee period, as maladministration could only exist in the procedures followed, not the way a decision was reached. Similarly, the trustees were not guilty of maladministration for not providing H with guidelines as to their duty to protect the members' interests. The question of the effect of the delay and whether it resulted from maladministration would be remitted to the Ombudsman for a decision as to causation.

HOGG ROBINSON FINANCIAL SERVICES LTD v. PENSIONS OMBUDSMAN [1998] O.P.L.R. 131, Park, J., Ch D.

4615. **Occupational pensions – maladministration – liability of council employees**

See INSURANCE: Redbridge LBC v. Municipal Mutual Insurance Ltd. §3813

4616. **Occupational pensions – maladministration – misinformation relating to entitlement – employment choices affected**

B, a local authority employee, appealed against a decision of the Pensions Ombudsman which had held that, although the local authority pension administrator, BCC, had been guilty of maladministration, B had not suffered any injustice as a result. BCC had misinformed B as to the effects of other public sector employment on his pension entitlement. B contended that but for this advice he would have taken a better paid position in the private sector rather than accepting a position in the public sector, and submitted that the decision of the Ombudsman was perverse and breached the rules of natural justice.

Held, dismissing the appeal, that the decision had not been procedurally unfair because the Ombudsman had fulfilled his obligations, and that there was evidence to support the Ombudsman's decision.

BLAKE v. PENSIONS OMBUDSMAN [2000] O.P.L.R. 341, Lightman, J., Ch D.

4617. **Occupational pensions – maladministration – Pensions Ombudsman – awards – entitlement to interest**

MPS appealed against a decision of the Pensions Ombudsman, PO, that it was liable to account to H, a former employee for interest after MPS had wrongly failed to pay H an injury award following his retirement from the police service. MPS contended that, in the absence of an express finding of maladministration, PO was not entitled to award interest on the arrears of H's injury pension notwithstanding the general principle that PO's determinations were to be upheld wherever possible.

Held, allowing the appeal and quashing the decision, that there had been no express finding of maladministration on the part of MPS throughout a significant period between H's retirement on the grounds of ill health and the award of his injury pension, *R. v. Local Commissioner for Administration for the North and East Area of England, ex p. Bradford City Council* [1979] Q.B. 287, [1979] C.L.Y. 1693 applied. However, it could be inferred from the terms of PO's determination in this case, that he considered there to be culpability on the part of MPS in some respects and therefore it was appropriate for the matter to be remitted to PO for the award of interest on the delayed pension payments to be re-calculated.

METROPOLITAN POLICE SERVICE v. HOAR [2000] O.P.L.R. 267, Neuberger, J., Ch D.

4618. **Occupational pensions – maladministration – repayment of employer contributions made on account and in excess of funding requirements**

MH was an employer and trustee of a retirement benefit scheme. Between 1992 to 1993, it made contributions to the Scheme at the same rate as it had in the previous scheme year. A preliminary valuation in October 1992 disclosed a substantial surplus. MH stopped paying contributions, and the trustees of the scheme later agreed a one year retroactive contributions holiday. In addition, contributions made in 1992 and 1993 amounting to some £600,000 paid by MH were refunded. The Pension Ombudsman received a complaint from B, a pensioner, to the effect that the repayment of the contributions was a refund of surplus contrary to the rules of the scheme. The Ombudsman found that the repayment of contributions was, effectively, a return of the scheme's surplus, and thus constituted maladministration and breach of trust. He ordered MH to repay the contributions to the scheme.

Held, allowing the appeal, that (1) if there was no evidence to support the Ombudsman's finding of fact, then that was a question of law and an appeal lay to the High Court; (2) all the documents before the court showed that the contributions made to the scheme had been payments on account, and not deliberate attempts to put the scheme into greater surplus; (3) it followed that there was no evidence to support the Ombudsman's finding that the refunding of contributions to MH was in effect a return to MH of a surplus; (4) the repayment was a return to MH of money paid on account which turned out to be unnecessary, and (5) the order as to costs on the appeal would include, inter alia, an order that the Ombudsman pay MH's costs including costs which MH was liable to pay to the scheme's professional trustee, to the extent that the Ombudsman's opposition to the appeal had increased those costs.

MERRETT HOLDINGS PLC v. PENSIONS OMBUDSMAN [1998] O.P.L.R. 161, Jacob, J., Ch D.

4619. **Occupational pensions – National Health Service – additional voluntary contributions**

NATIONAL HEALTH SERVICE (PENSION SCHEME AND ADDITIONAL VOLUNTARY CONTRIBUTIONS) (PENSION SHARING) AMENDMENT REGULATIONS 2001, SI 2001 1428; made under the Superannuation Act 1972 s.10, Sch.3; and the Welfare Reform and Pensions Act 1999 s.42. In force: May 1, 2001; £3.00.

These Regulations, which amend the National Health Service Pension Scheme Regulations 1995 (SI 1995 300) and the National Health Service Pension Scheme (Additional Voluntary Contributions) Regulations 2000 (SI 2000 619), make provision in relation to rights resulting in the payment of pensions credit benefit to or in respect of those entitled to pension credits as a result of the sharing of pensions following divorce or nullity of marriage.

4620. **Occupational pensions – Parliament – pension sharing**

PARLIAMENTARY PENSIONS (AMENDMENT) (PENSION SHARING) REGULATIONS 2001, SI 2001 2649; made under the Parliamentary and other Pensions Act 1987 s.2. In force: August 21, 2001; £2.50.

These Regulations amend the Parliamentary Pensions (Additional Voluntary Contributions Scheme) Regulations 1993 (SI 1993 3252), the Parliamentary Pension (Consolidation and Amendment) Regulations 1993 (SI 1993 3253) and the Parliamentary Pensions (Amendment) Regulations 1995 (SI 1995 2867). They amend the main pension scheme and the AVC scheme for Members of the House of Commons, and certain office holders specified in the Pensions Act 1987, to enable pension sharing orders and similar provisions to be implemented in respect of those schemes pursuant to the Welfare Reform and Pensions Act 1999.

4621. Occupational pensions – Parliament – trustees

PARLIAMENTARY PENSIONS (AMENDMENT) REGULATIONS 2001, SI 2001 835; made under the Parliamentary and other Pensions Act 1987 s.2. In force: April 1, 2001; £1.75.

These Regulations, which amend the Parliamentary Pensions (Consolidation and Amendment) Regulations 1993 (SI 1993 3253), remove the requirement for a Custodian Trustee, leaving the Trustees with responsibility for the Parliamentary Contributory Pension Fund. Trustees may place the assets of the Fund under the control of a nominee, are required to appoint a fund manager and prepare a statement of investment principles.

4622. Occupational pensions – pension sharing – excepted public service schemes

PENSION SHARING (EXCEPTED SCHEMES) ORDER 2001, SI 2001 358; made under the Welfare Reform and Pensions Act 1999 s.27. In force: March 5, 2001; £1.50.

This Order, which revokes the Pension Sharing (Excepted Schemes) Order 2000 (SI 2000 3088), excepts the public service pension schemes relating to the office of the Prime Minister and First Lord of the Treasury, Lord Chancellor and Speaker of the House of Commons for the purposes of the Welfare Reform and Pensions Act 1999 s.27(1).

4623. Occupational pensions – personal pensions – perpetuities and contracting out

OCCUPATIONAL AND PERSONAL PENSION SCHEMES (PERPETUITIES AND CONTRACTING-OUT) AMENDMENT REGULATIONS 2001, SI 2001 943; made under the Pension Schemes Act 1993 s.9, s.163, s.181, s.182. In force: April 6, 2001; £1.75.

These Regulations amend the Personal and Occupational Pension Schemes (Perpetuities) Regulations 1990 (SI 1990 1143) to take account of changes made by the Finance Act 2000 Sch.13 under which certain occupational pension schemes may from April 6, 2001 receive approval for tax relief purposes under the Income and Corporation Taxes Act 1988 Part XIV Ch. IV. An amendment is also made to the Occupational Pension Schemes (Contracting Out) Regulations 1996 (SI 1996 1172) for the same purpose and the Personal Pensions Schemes (Appropriate Schemes) Regulations 1997 (SI 1997 470) are amended to include, among the personal pension schemes which may be appropriate schemes, stakeholder pension schemes which are not self invested personal pension schemes.

4624. Occupational pensions – railway pension scheme – railway workers

RAILWAY PENSIONS (DESIGNATION, SUBSTITUTION AND MISCELLANEOUS PROVISIONS) ORDER 2001, SI 2001 2264; made under the Transport Act 1980 s.52B, s.52D; and the Railways Act 1993 Sch.11 para.10. In force: July 13, 2001; £4.00.

This Order, which amends the Railway Pensions (Substitution) Order 1994 (SI 1994 2388) and the Railway Pensions (Substitution and Miscellaneous Provisions) Order 1995 (SI 1995 430) terminates the liability of the Secretary of State to make payments under the Transport Act 1980 s.52(1) in respect of two sections of the Railways Pension Scheme, designated for that purpose by the Order, and makes provision for payments to be made in substitution for that liability. It specifies August 13, 2001 as the termination date in respect of each such section, specifies the capital value of the unfunded obligations in respect of each of the sections as at the termination date, requires the Secretary of State to make payments in respect of the capital values of the unfunded obligations and provide for the accrual and payment of interest on the outstanding balances of those capital values, and provides for the liability of the Secretary of State to make payments to be discharged in the event of the winding up of both sections.

4625. Occupational pensions – surplus final salary and money purchase schemes funded from same source – use of surplus

[Pensions Act 1995 s.67.]

B operated a non contributory pension fund. Until June 1997, the fund provided pensions solely on a final salary basis. However, B decided to provide benefits for future recruits on a money purchase basis. The pension fund deed was amended to introduce the money purchase scheme from July 1, 1997 and to close the final salary scheme to new starters, with existing employees having the right to transfer into the money purchase scheme. B used a pre conversion surplus to meet its money purchase contributions. H, a final salary scheme member, complained to the Ombudsman that B's use of the surplus in this was constituted maladministration. The Ombudsman concluded that the money purchase scheme was separate from the final salary scheme with the result that the surplus in the latter scheme could not be used to fund the former. B appealed and also sought a determination as to whether a further amendment to the deed would ensure that, if the appeal failed, it would be entitled to fund its contributions to the money purchase scheme out of surplus.

Held, allowing the appeal, that the final salary scheme rules, as amended, supported the conclusion that the two schemes were funded from one source. As there was only one fund, B's final salary scheme contributions could be paid from the surplus. The fact that new and transferring employees' pensions would be funded out of the final salary scheme did not mean that B's acts in drawing on the surplus amounted to an alteration. Further, although it was unnecessary to consider the effect of the post transfer amendment, it did not operate to the detriment of the entitlement of members of the money purchase scheme, as "entitlement" in the Pensions Act 1995 s.67 referred to pensions already being paid and did not include increases to a future pension expected on the basis of continuing employment and salary increases.

BARCLAYS BANK PLC v. HOLMES [2000] Pens. L.R. 339, Neuberger, J., Ch D.

4626. Occupational pensions – surplus pension funds – discharge of debt from actuarial surplus

IP appealed against a ruling ([2000] I.C.R. 174, [1999] C.L.Y. 4142) that arrangements it had made to dispose of an actuarial surplus in its occupational pension scheme, were unlawful. IP had sought to dispose of the surplus by discharging its accrued liabilities to the scheme, thereby reducing the amount of its contributions. Scheme members objected to the proposals, contending that the satisfaction of a debt constituted a payment to IP as employer and was accordingly precluded by clauses included in the scheme. The Court of Appeal concluded that, while the discharge of a debt did not amount to a payment to the employer for the purposes of the scheme, there was no power within the scheme as formulated to discharge a debt and, accordingly, an amendment would be required. Following the ruling IP executed a deed of amendment, contending that its proposals were thereafter duly authorised. The scheme members maintained that it would be contrary to the underlying purposes of the scheme to permit IP as employer to reduce the fund in the manner proposed.

Held, allowing the appeal, that having regard to the underlying fiscal purpose of the clauses, the arrangements made by IP to discharge its accrued liabilities out of actuarial surpluses did not constitute a payment to the employer for the purposes of the scheme. Further, it would not be inconsistent with the purposes of the scheme to permit the proposals to proceed, having regard to the fact that a surplus was, by definition, something additional to that which was required to meet the objectives of the scheme, *Mettoy Pension Trustees Ltd v. Evans* [1990] 1 W.L.R. 1587, [1991] C.L.Y. 2726 and *Landau (A Bankrupt), Re*

[1998] Ch. 223, [1997] C.L.Y. 3018 considered, and *British Coal Corp v. British Coal Staff Superannuation Fund Scheme Trustees* [1995] 1 All E.R. 912, [1995] C.L.Y. 3805 distinguished.

NATIONAL GRID CO PLC v. MAYES; JEFFERIES v. MAYES; NATIONAL POWER PLC v. FELDON; LAWS v. NATIONAL GRID CO PLC; NATIONAL GRID CO PLC v. LEWIS; INTERNATIONAL POWER PLC (FORMERLY NATIONAL POWER PLC) v. HEALY; *sub nom.* NATIONAL GRID CO PLC v. LAWS, [2001] UKHL 20, [2001] 1 W.L.R. 864, Lord Hoffmann, HL.

4627. Occupational pensions – teachers

TEACHERS' PENSIONS (AMENDMENT) REGULATIONS 2001, SI 2001 871; made under the Superannuation Act 1972 s.9, s.12, Sch.3. In force: March 31, 2001; £1.50.

These Regulations, which amend the Teachers' Pensions Regulations 1997 (SI 1997 3001), provide for payments under the School Achievement Award Scheme to be non-contributable for the purposes of teachers' pensions, notwithstanding the general rule that performance-related pay measures should be contributable. In addition, the 1997 Regulations are amended to include City Academies within the Teachers' Pension Scheme.

4628. Occupational pensions – trustees powers and duties – transfer scheme – requirement for certification

[Pension Scheme Act 1993 s.67; Occupational Pension Schemes (Preservation of Benefit) Regulations 1991 (SI 1991 167) Reg.12(2)(a).]

M, the trustees of an occupational pension scheme, sought certification of a proposed scheme whereby accrued benefits from one scheme would be transferred to another in order to secure the future of the fund, which was in danger of being wound up due to a substantial fund deficiency. The proposal was challenged by the pensioners who would receive their full pension entitlement if the scheme were wound up. It was contended that, in order to make the proposal workable, the trustees would have to introduce a compulsory transfer of the beneficiaries' pension rights without their consent, which was in breach of the Pension Scheme Act 1993 s.67.

Held, granting the application for sanction of the proposed scheme, that where the transferring scheme and the receiving scheme concerned employment with the same withdrawing employer, the restrictions imposed by the Occupational Pension Schemes (Preservation of Benefit) Regulations 1991 Reg.12(2)(a) were fulfilled, regardless of whether an individual beneficiary had been employed at any time with the employer in question, *Courage Group's Pension Schemes, Re* [1987] 1 W.L.R. 495, [1987] C.L.Y. 2822 distinguished. The object of the transfer was identical to the objects of the scheme, namely to ensure the provision of benefits which the scheme had been formulated to provide; however the fact that an accrued entitlement was being transferred did not dispense with the requirement for certification.

MERCHANT NAVY RATINGS PENSION FUND TRUSTEES LTD v. CHAMBERS [2002] I.C.R. 359, Blackburne, J., Ch D.

4629. Pension funds – surplus – partial dissolution – reasonableness of decision not to allocate share of actuarial surplus to new scheme – New Zealand

W, a company that had withdrawn from a group superannuation scheme, appealed against a decision of the Court of Appeal of New Zealand ([1999] Pens. L.R. 355, [2000] C.L.Y. 4392), that the decision of the trustee of the plan not to allocate to a new scheme set up by W a share of the actuarial surplus, was a proper exercise of his discretion. Under the terms of the trust deed, the withdrawal of W amounted to a partial dissolution of the plan. W maintained that, in accordance with the trust deed, the trustee should have made a pro rata allocation of the assets of the plan at the time of its withdrawal so that the new scheme would receive the share of the actuarial surplus that was attributable to W's members.

Held, dismissing the appeal, that the trustee had been entitled to determine that no part of the surplus should be allocated to W's new scheme. Having regard to the trust deed and to the diversity of circumstances attendant upon a partial dissolution, it was not appropriate to restrict the discretion provided to the trustee of the plan to choose between different approaches, even to the extent of suggesting a presumptive "starting point". As a "defined benefits scheme", the plan had two common features to which importance should be attached. Firstly, the members did not have proprietary interests in the scheme funds, those funds being security for the payment of benefits to them. Secondly, whilst the scheme was continuing, any surplus formed an actuarial valuation that could be falsified by events. It was necessary for such a surplus to remain as continuing security until such time as the scheme was wound up. Since the discretion given to the trustee was a wide one and the surplus was relatively small, the trustee had not erred.

WRIGHTSON LTD v. FLETCHER CHALLENGE NOMINEES LTD; *sub nom.* FLETCHER CHALLENGE NOMINEES LTD v. WRIGHTSON LTD, [2001] UKPC 23, [2001] Pens. L.R. 207, Lord Millett, PC.

4630. **Pension funds – surplus – transfer of pension funds surplus – distribution by reference to rules – South Africa**

T set up two "balance-of-cost" pension schemes: a final salary scheme (the pension fund) and a money-purchase scheme (the provident fund). Rule 19.5.2 of the pension fund provided that if a valuation disclosed a substantial surplus, the trustees were to make recommendations as to how it should be dealt with, with the principal employer's decision being final. Most of the active members of the pension fund eventually transferred to the provident fund, together with the actuarially assessed value of their interest in the pension fund. The employer decided to take a contributions holiday from the provident fund, expecting to be funded by the transfer of surplus from the pension fund, but the transfer did not take place. In 1994 a division of T was sold to M and a large number of members of the provident fund transferred to the M pension scheme. Some of the transferred members said that part of the surplus in the pension fund should have followed them into the provident fund and then to the M fund. One of those members instituted proceedings in court seeking declaratory orders as to the correct position. The court at first instance declared that the trustees of the pension fund were not entitled to use the surplus in the pension fund to enable the employer to avoid paying contributions to the provident fund or otherwise for the benefit of the employer, and that the appropriate portion of the surplus should be transferred to the provident fund. On appeal it was argued that while there was a surplus in the pension fund, the employer was under no obligation to contribute to the fund. Members had no right to demand that the surplus be used to increase benefits on retirement or its transfer to another fund. Furthermore the pension fund rules did not permit the trustees to comply with the orders made by the court at first instance.

Held, allowing the appeal in part, that (1) in a situation concerning balance-of-cost pension schemes, a surplus did not belong to the employer. Once a surplus arose it was an integral component of the fund. Unless the employer could point to a relevant rule of the fund, or statutory enactment, or principle of common law which conferred such entitlement, or empowered the trustees to use the surplus for its benefit, the employer had no right in law to the surplus; (2) under the pension fund rules, during the continuance of the fund, the employer was accorded a good deal of say in what happened to any surplus by r.19.5.2, but limitations were imposed which were designed to ensure that the objects of the fund were realised. That did not mean that the employer could derive no benefit whatsoever from the existence of a surplus. For example, a recommendation by trustees that a surplus be retained to counter a perceived risk of future adverse investment performance, would benefit the employer in as much as it would not be liable to make contributions to the fund for so long as the surplus existed; (3) where there was a surplus there was no liability to contribute, and the source of the surplus was not relevant; (4) The fact, however, that there was a rule allowing trustees to increase pensions in payment, was an indication that the employer was not entitled to insist upon the trustees preserving the surplus, and (5) the trustees and the employer were wrong to insist that the employer alone was entitled to decide what would be done with the surplus. The employer should have negotiated with the trustees and the employees as to the application of the surplus.

TEK CORPORATION PROVIDENT FUND v. LORENTZ [2001] O.P.L.R. 137, Marais, J., Sup Ct (SA).

4631. Pension schemes – group personal pensions – collective bargaining

[Trade Union Recognition (Method of Collective Bargaining) Order 2000 (SI 2000 1300).]

B provided a non contributory group personal pension scheme for all its permanent staff which also allowed employees to pay additional voluntary contributions. The money purchase scheme was administered by an independent financial advisor, who received payments from B for payment on to the scheme provider. Issues arose as to the method by which B and U should conduct collective bargaining and the Central Arbitration Committee was asked to decide whether the obligation to take part in pay negotiations included pensions provided under the group scheme for the purposes of the Trade Union Recognition (Method of Collective Bargaining) Order 2000.

Held, finding that B was obliged to negotiate with U on pension matters, that (1) rights under the group personal pension scheme were derived from the contract of employment and the contributions paid on the employees' behalf and their pensions had the status of deferred pay, *Air Jamaica Ltd v. Charlton* [1999] 1 W.L.R. 1399, [1999] C.L.Y. 4958 applied; (2) "pay" for the purposes of the Employment Relations Act 1999 had a wider meaning than "remuneration" or "wages", as used in previous employment legislation; (3) B had an obligation to fund the promised benefits and make good any deficit, as well as the right to benefit from any surplus, *National Grid Co Plc v. Mayes* [2001] UKHL 20, [2001] 1 W.L.R. 864, [2001] 5 C.L. 624 considered, and (4) negotiation on pension matters was on a par with wage negotiations, *Young v. Carr Fasteners Ltd* [1979] I.C.R. 844, [1980] C.L.Y. 987 and *STC Submarine Systems v. Piper* [1993] Pens. L.R. 185 considered.

UNIFI v. UNION BANK OF NIGERIA PLC [2001] I.R.L.R. 712, Mary Stacey (Chairperson), Arbitration.

4632. Pensions Appeal Tribunals

PENSIONS APPEAL TRIBUNALS (ENGLAND AND WALES) (AMENDMENT) RULES 2001, SI 2001 257 (L.8); made under the Pensions Appeal Tribunals Act 1943 Sch. In force: April 9, 2001; £0.75.

These Rules, which amend the Pensions Appeal Tribunals (England and Wales) Rules 1980 (SI 1980 1120) to reflect the amendments to the Pensions Appeal Tribunals Acts 1945 made by the Child Support, Pensions and Social Security Act 2000, provide for appeal against "specified decisions" under Pensions Appeal Tribunals Act 1943 s.5A. They provide for the position and powers of the Deputy President of Pensions Appeal Tribunals for England and Wales, for the power to strike out an appeal for want of prosecution, for the omission of some unnecessary words in defining what persons may represent an appellant, for the statement of reasons for a decision of a Tribunal, including a decision to adjourn an appeal and for the power to extend time limits to be confined to the President.

4633. Pensions Appeal Tribunals

PENSIONS APPEAL TRIBUNALS (ENGLAND AND WALES) (AMENDMENT NO.2) RULES 2001, SI 2001 1183 (L.19); made under the Pensions Appeal Tribunals Act 1943 Sch para.5. In force: April 9, 2001; £1.75.

These Rules, which amend the Pensions Appeal Tribunals (England and Wales) Rules 1980 (SI 1980 1120) and replace the Pensions Appeal Tribunals (England and Wales) (Amendment) Rules 2001 (SI 2001 257), reflect the amendments to the Pensions Appeal Tribunals Acts made by the Child Support, Pensions and Social Security Act 2000. They provide for appeals against "specified decisions" under the Pensions Appeal Tribunals Act 1943 s.5A, the position and powers of the Deputy President of Pensions Appeal Tribunals for England and Wales, the omission of some unnecessary words in defining what persons may represent an appellant and for the statement of reasons for a decision of a Tribunal, including a decision to adjourn an appeal.

4634. Pensions Appeal Tribunals – late appeals

PENSIONS APPEAL TRIBUNALS (LATE APPEALS) REGULATIONS 2001, SI 2001 1032; made under the Pensions Appeal Tribunals Act 1943 s.8. In force: April 9, 2001; £1.75.

These Regulations, which relate to war pensions and the circumstances in which a Pensions Appeal Tribunal may, under the Pensions Appeal Tribunals Act 1943, hear a late appeal against a decision by the Secretary of State, provide that a late appeal may be brought within a year of the expiry of the statutory time limit in certain circumstances. These are where the delay has been caused by serious illness of the claimant or a member of the claimant's family, postal disruption, failure of the Secretary of State to notify the decision or where a claimant has suffered exceptional circumstances which prevented the bringing of an appeal within the time limit.

4635. Pensions Appeal Tribunals – posthumous appeals

PENSIONS APPEAL TRIBUNALS (POSTHUMOUS APPEALS) AMENDMENT ORDER 2001, SI 2001 408; made under the Social Security Act 1980 s.16. In force: April 9, 2001; £1.75.

This Order amends the Pensions Appeal Tribunals (Posthumous Appeals) Order 1980 (SI 1980 1082) to reflect amendments made to the Pensions Appeal Tribunals Act 1943 s.8 by the Child Support, Pensions and Social Security Act 2000 s.58.

4636. Pensions Appeal Tribunals – rights of appeal

PENSIONS APPEAL TRIBUNALS (ADDITIONAL RIGHTS OF APPEAL) REGULATIONS 2001, SI 2001 1031; made under the Pensions Appeal Tribunals Act 1943 s.5A. In force: April 9, 2001; £2.00.

These Regulations, which apply where the Secretary of State notifies a decision on certain war pension matters, extend the scope of appeal rights so that further war pension decisions may be the subject of an appeal. They confer these rights in relation to the Naval, Military and Air Forces Etc. (Disablement and Death) Service Pensions Order 1983 (SI 1983 883) and the Personal Injuries (Civilians) Order 1983 (SI 1983 686).

4637. Personal pensions – free standing AVC's – reviews

FINANCIAL SERVICES AND MARKETS ACT 2000 (TRANSITIONAL PROVISIONS) (REVIEWS OF PENSIONS BUSINESS) ORDER 2001, SI 2001 2512; made under the Financial Services and Markets Act 2000 s.426, s.427, s.428. In force: August 6, 2001; £2.00.

This Order makes transitional provisions with respect to the reviews of pension selling being conducted under the Financial Services Act 1986. The reviews concern the selling of personal pension schemes between April 29, 1988 and June 30, 1994. The reviews also concern the selling of free standing additional voluntary contribution schemes between April 29, 1988 and August 15, 1999. The Order provides for the reviews to be treated as if they constituted a scheme under the Financial Services and Markets Act 2000 s.404 which means that the Financial Services Authority will be able to continue to conduct the reviews using its powers under the 2000 Act.

4638. Personal pensions – permitted investments – restriction on discretion to approve

PERSONAL PENSION SCHEMES (RESTRICTION ON DISCRETION TO APPROVE) (PERMITTED INVESTMENTS) REGULATIONS 2001, SI 2001 117; made under the Income and Corporation Taxes Act 1988 s.638A. In force: April 6, 2001; £2.50.

These Regulations, which impose restrictions on the Board of Inland Revenue's discretion to approve a personal pension scheme by restricting the investments in which the scheme may invest, provide that a self-invested personal pension scheme may only invest in specified investments, and stipulate restrictions on a self-invested personal pension scheme's borrowing powers. They prohibit personal pension schemes other than self-invested personal pension schemes from investing in personal chattels or residential property, from lending to any person, and personal pension schemes that are not self-invested personal pension schemes from lending to members of the scheme or persons connected with members, from purchasing, selling or leasing assets from or to members of the scheme or persons connected with members and from setting up borrowing arrangements for a member, or issuing further instalments of an existing serialised loan, after an annuity first becomes payable to the member under the scheme or the member elects to defer the purchase of an annuity. The acquisition of commercial property for a member after the member's pension date or he attains 65, whichever is the later, is also prohibited.

4639. SERPS – succession – rate increase

SOCIAL SECURITY (INHERITED SERPS) REGULATIONS 2001, SI 2001 1085; made under the Welfare Reform and Pensions Act 1999 s.52, s.83. In force: October 6, 2002; £1.75.

These Regulations provide for an increase in the rate of the additional pension under the State Earnings Related Pension Scheme (SERPS) to which persons of a specified description would otherwise be entitled under or by virtue of certain provisions of the Social Security Contributions and Benefits Act 1992 Part II in the event that they are widowed on or after October 6, 2002 which is the date on which the maximum amount of the additional pension which may be inherited by a surviving spouse under SERPS is reduced from 100 per cent to 50 per cent. They increase the rate of the additional pension, or of any constituent element of an increase in that pension, which would otherwise be payable to persons of a specified description under or by virtue of those provisions in the event that they are widowed on or after October 6, 2002.

4640. Stakeholder pensions – restriction of membership

STAKEHOLDER PENSION SCHEMES (AMENDMENT) REGULATIONS 2001, SI 2001 104; made under the Welfare Reform and Pensions Act 1999 s.1, s.8, s.83. In force: February 14, 2001; £1.75.

These Regulations, which amend the Stakeholder Pension Schemes Regulations 2000 (SI 2000 1403), permit stakeholder schemes established otherwise than under a trust to restrict membership of the scheme by reference to employment or to membership of a particular organisation, clarify that, for both non trust and trust schemes, restrictions may be imposed on payment of contributions by cash or credit card, include the authorised corporate director of an open-ended investment company among the categories of person who may be the manager of a non-trust scheme and to clarify the reference to "pension credits".

4641. Stakeholder pensions – restriction of membership

STAKEHOLDER PENSION SCHEMES (AMENDMENT) (NO.2) REGULATIONS 2001, SI 2001 934; made under the Pensions Act 1995 s.3, s.10, s.41, s.124, s.174; the Welfare Reform and Pensions Act 1999 s.1; and the Pensions Act 1995 s.3, s.8, s.83. In force: April 5, 2001; £3.50.

These Regulations, which amend the Stakeholder Pension Schemes Regulations 2000 (SI 2000 1403), provide that those who are not employees of the employer on the date of commencement of consultation do not have to be consulted; make different provision as to means of payment of contributions; include provisions which the trust instruments are not allowed to enable to be modified or disapplied; expand on the requirements relating to investments and investment options; clarify that a reporting accountant must be appointed for a scheme established under a trust; impose additional requirements for eligibility for appointment as the reporting accountant; and change the required content of the trustees' or manager's annual declaration. In addition, they provide for an additional ground of refusal of contributions, to allow different statement years to be chosen for different persons; revise the existing provisions as to the start date for a statement year to change and clarify provisions governing deductions of contributions from remuneration; and ensure that there remains a time limit for appointment of a replacement reporting accountant in relation to removal, resignation or death.

4642. Superannuation – civil service pension scheme – additional employments

SUPERANNUATION (ADMISSION TO SCHEDULE 1 TO THE SUPERANNUATION ACT 1972) ORDER 2001, SI 2001 1587; made under the Superannuation Act 1972 s.1. In force: May 17, 2001; £1.75.

The Superannuation Act 1972 s.1, under which the Principal Civil Service Pension Scheme, the Civil Service Additional Voluntary Contribution Scheme and the Civil Service Compensation Scheme have been made, applies to employment and offices listed in Sch.1 to that Act. This Order adds the offices of the First Civil Service Commissioner and the Immigration Services Commissioner and Deputy Immigration Services Commissioner and employment by the Immigration Services Commissioner and the Human Fertilisation and Embryology Authority to those listed in the Schedule.

4643. Trustees powers and duties – ill health retirement – disqualifying conduct – meaning of "total and permanent invalidity" – Australia

G was a member of a company pension scheme and wished to retire on the grounds of ill-health. To take advantage of benefits under the pension scheme, the member must have ceased to be an employee due to "total and permanent invalidity". There was an exception to the granting of the benefit in relation to a disability, the existence or continuation of which was attributable to deliberate action or inaction for the purpose of causing benefit to become or continue to be payable "including without limitation what the trustee considered to be unreasonable refusal to submit to treatment". G's ceased to be an employee before attaining the age of 60. She claimed that that was because of total and permanent invalidity and that, accordingly she was entitled to a lump sum benefit under the pension scheme. Her claim was rejected both by a committee of the employer and by its board of directors. The court was asked to consider the meaning of "total and permanent invalidity" and "unreasonable refusal to submit to treatment" and the way in which the trustee should act in considering its powers if the matter was remitted to it.

Held, remitting the case back to the trustee to reconsider the member's claim, that (1) the disqualifying conduct included without limitation what the trustee considered to be an unreasonable refusal to submit to treatment; (2) it was not necessary for the trustee to be of the opinion, in the case of an unreasonable refusal to submit to treatment, that that refusal was also for the purpose of causing a benefit to become or to continue to be payable from the fund. It would be sufficient to bring the member's claim or a like claim within the exception of the definition of "total and permanent invalidity" that the trustee considered that there had been an unreasonable refusal to submit to treatment; (3) a trustee considering whether there had been an unreasonable refusal to submit to treatment must act in good faith and upon real and genuine consideration of that question and not for an extraneous purpose, *Karger v. Paul* [1984] V.R. 161 applied; (4) it would be unwise to give hypothetical examples of the ways in which the requirements of good faith, real and genuine consideration and proper purpose might be instantiated. It was sufficient to concentrate on the gravamen of the complaint; (5) in this case the member was concerned that the reason the trustee had denied her claim was a view on its part that she had unreasonably refused to submit to treatment. She desired to correct what she believed to be misinformation in the possession of the trustee or information wrongly interpreted by it and to place material before it to allay its concern, and (6) one could not ordinarily decide a question of fact in good faith and give it real and genuine consideration without conducting some investigation and in some cases that would entail making an inquiry of a person who was willing to provide information and was in the best position to do so. It was not a matter of natural justice but bona fide inquiry and genuine decision making.

TELSTRA SUPER PTY LTD v. FLEGELTAUB [2001] Pens. L.R. 7, Ormiston, J.A., Sup Ct (Vic).

4644. War pensions – merchant navy – commencing dates of awards

WAR PENSIONS (MERCANTILE MARINE) (AMENDMENT) SCHEME 2001, SI 2001 419; made under the Pensions (Navy, Army, Air Force and Mercantile Marine) Act 1939 s.3, s.4, s.7. In force: April 9, 2001; £2.50.

This Scheme amends the War Pensions (Mercantile Marine) Scheme 1964 (SI 1964 2058) as regards commencing dates for awards. References to appeals are removed to reflect changes to other war pension instruments following amendments to the Pensions Appeal Tribunals Act 1943 s.8 by the Child Support, Pensions and Social Security Act 2000 s.58.

4645. War pensions – payments to civilians

PERSONAL INJURIES (CIVILIANS) AMENDMENT SCHEME 2001, SI 2001 420; made under the Personal Injuries (Emergency Provisions) Act 1939 s.1, s.2. In force: April 9, 2001; 2.50.

This Scheme amends the Personal Injuries (Civilians) Scheme 1983 (SI 1983 686), which makes provision for the payment of pensions and allowances to or in respect of civilians who were killed or injured during the 1939-45 World War, with the effect that new definitions of "adopted" and "dependent child" are introduced, four rates of constant attendance allowance are provided for, the meaning of therapeutic earnings for the purposes of unemployability allowances is clarified, ages are equalised for unemployability allowances, invalidity allowance and allowance for lowered standard of occupation and the conditions of award of treatment allowance are clarified as is disablement for the purposes of mobility supplement. It clarifies the funeral expenses which may be claimed, makes amendments as regards awards in respect of children and relating to deductions. It enables the Secretary of State to review an assessment or decision of the Pensions Appeal Tribunal where there is a change of circumstances and to review any assessment where there is an improvement in the disablement. In addition, the Scheme increase the amounts of allowances, pensions and awards payable under the principal Scheme and the amounts of income to be disregarded for the purposes of certain parts of the Scheme.

4646. Books

Greenstreet, Ian – Stakeholder Pensions and Pooled Pension Investments. Special Reports. Hardback: £150.00. ISBN 0-421-73970-3. Sweet & Maxwell.

Hall, Brendan; Burman, Ian; Everill, Lindsey – Planning and Surviving Your Retirement. Paperback: £48.00. ISBN 1-902558-23-5. Palladian Law Publishing Ltd.

Quarrel, John – Law of Pension Fund Investment. £49.95. ISBN 0-7545-0803-X. Tolley Publishing.

Salter, David; Bamber, Roger; Bird, Roger; Salter, David – Pensions and Insurance on Family Breakdown. Paperback: CD-ROM: £45.00. ISBN 0-85308-698-2. Family Law.

PERSONAL PROPERTY

4647. Books

Johnston, David; Zimmermann, Reinhard – Comparative Law of Unjust Enrichment. Hardback: £50.00. ISBN 0-521-80820-0. Cambridge University Press.

Pejovich, Svetozar – Economics of Property Rights. International Library of Critical Writings in Economics, 129. Hardback: £280.00. ISBN1-84064-232-7. Edward Elgar.

PLANNING

4648. Advertisements – consent – requirements under regulations

[Town and Country Planning Act 1990 s.224; Town and Country Planning (Control of Advertisements) Regulations 1992 (SI 1992 666) Sch.1 para.1, Sch.3 Class 14.]

HBC, a local authority, appealed by way of case stated against the justices' finding that R enjoyed deemed consent to display an advertisement, contending that the sign was in contravention of the Town and Country Planning (Control of Advertisements) Regulations 1992 Sch.1 para. 1 and the Town and Country Planning Act 1990 s.224. R submitted that consent was deemed to be granted by virtue of Sch. 3, Class 14 of the 1992 Regulations.

Held, allowing the appeal, that the justices' decision was flawed as it focused on the reasonableness of the steps taken by R to clean the advertisement, rather than the requirement that the advertisement be clean to the satisfaction of HBC. This was the crucial requirement of Sch. 1 Para. 1 of the 1992 Regulations in order to establish deemed consent. The case was remitted to the justices for conviction.

HERTSMERE BC v. REID ESTATES LTD (2001) 81 P. & C.R. 16, Rose, L.J., QBD.

4649. Ancient monuments – consent – forms – Wales

ANCIENT MONUMENTS (APPLICATIONS FOR SCHEDULED MONUMENT CONSENT) (WELSH FORMS AND PARTICULARS) REGULATIONS 2001, SI 2001 1438 (W.100); made under the Ancient Monuments and Archeological Areas Act 1979 Sch.1 para.1, para.2. In force: May 1, 2001; £2.00.

The Ancient Monuments and Archaeological Areas Act 1979 Sch.1 confers a power to make regulations to prescribe the forms for use in applications for scheduled monument consent. This power is now exercisable, in relation to Wales, by the National Assembly for Wales. The Secretary of State for Wales, in conjunction with the Secretary of State for the Environment, prescribed an English version of the forms by the Ancient Monuments (Applications for Scheduled Monument Consent) Regulations 1981 (SI 1981 1301). These Regulations prescribe the Welsh version of the relevant forms which may be used in Wales instead of the English version of the forms prescribed by the 1981 Regulations.

4650. **Appeals – costs – unreasonable conduct of local authority**

B applied for judicial review of the inspector's refusal to award costs in a planning case. B had lost the substantive appeal but contended that LDC and the Secretary of State, the local authority and second respondent, had acted unreasonably by taking an intransigent stance, without which at least part of the appeal could have been avoided. The inspector had refused to make a finding as to the nature of LDC's behaviour and had held that an inquiry would have been necessary in any event and that any additional costs were a matter of speculation. B submitted that the inspector's approach was flawed, as findings on whether misconduct was proved, and in what respects, should have been given. In addition, B submitted that the inspector had applied the wrong standard of proof in assessing whether the issue of the incurring of increased costs had been established.

Held, refusing the application, that the inspector's report was not wrong in law purely because of the lack of findings on misconduct, there was no reason to conclude that he had applied the wrong standard of proof and he had given clear reasons for his decision.

R. (ON THE APPLICATION OF BRANDVIK KINTON LTD) v. SECRETARY OF STATE FOR THE ENVIRONMENT, TRANSPORT AND THE REGIONS; *sub nom*. R. v. SECRETARY OF STATE FOR THE ENVIRONMENT, TRANSPORT AND THE REGIONS, *ex p*. BRANDVIK KINTON LTD [2001] P.L.C.R. 19, Gibbs, J., QBD (Admin Ct).

4651. **Change of use – compensation – assumed planning permission – original use of site – change of use and enlarged development**

[Land Compensation Act 1961 s.15(3)(a); Town and Country Planning Act 1990 s.137, Sch.3 para.1.]

O purchased the site of a demolished railway station for which it unsuccessfully applied to T for outline planning permission for residential development. O served a purchase notice on T under the Town and Country Planning Act 1990 s.137. That was confirmed on appeal by the Secretary of State for the Environment, Transport and the Regions. It was agreed that the basis for compensation under the Land Compensation Act 1961 s.15(3)(a) should be determined as a preliminary issue. O argued that, under Sch.3 para.1 of the 1990 Act, assumed planning permission permitted rebuilding as one large building, or four houses if "hope value" was taken into account. T argued that the original buildings had to be assumed to have been rebuilt on their original sites for their former use.

Held, giving judgment for T, that (1) although planning permission under s.15(3)(a) was an assumed permission, it could not be totally removed from reality, as would be the case if it was taken to be for the building of up to four houses; (2) the original residential use had only occupied a small part of the site and there had never been a house in existence for which rebuilding could be assumed for the purposes of s.15(3)(a), and (3) planning assumption was intended to compensate an owner for the loss of the existing use right to rebuild and did not allow an owner to assume the right to carry out development unrelated to the original use. O's position could not, therefore, be supported as T was to acquire the land on the basis that it could not be used for a beneficial purpose in its present state, whereas O's claim was based on the building of up to four houses.

OLD ENGLAND PROPERTIES LTD v. TELFORD AND WREKIN COUNCIL [2000] 3 E.G.L.R. 153, PH Clarke FRICS, Lands Tr.

4652. **Change of use – development plan policies**

[Town and Country Planning (Use Classes) Order 1987 (SI 1987 764).]

W, a local planning authority, appealed against an inspector's decision to uphold an appeal by AB, a firm of developers, who had sought planning permission to demolish an existing office building and replace it with a new building and a car park. AB had been granted planning permission on appeal for the change of use of the ground floor to Class A2 within the Town and Country Planning (Use Classes) Order 1987. A dispute arose as to whether subsequent occupation by a company, C, constituted A2 use. W submitted that the inspector had (1) erred in his approach to whether the proposed redevelopment contravened development plan policies, and (2) made no finding as to the possibility that AB would implement a fall-back use if the permission sought was not granted.

Held, dismissing the appeal, that it was clear that AB had intended lawful use of the premises through its lease to C and the fact that W disputed whether the use by C was A2 use was not a basis for disputing AB's intention. Furthermore, the inspector had given adequate reasons, dealing with "the principal controversial issues", for his decision, *Save Britain's Heritage v. Number 1 Poultry Ltd* [1991] 1 W.L.R. 153, [1991] C.L.Y. 3494 applied.

R. (ON THE APPLICATION OF WINDSOR AND MAIDENHEAD RBC) v. SECRETARY OF STATE FOR THE ENVIRONMENT, TRANSPORT AND THE REGIONS; *sub nom.* R. (ON THE APPLICATION OF WINDSOR AND MAIDENHEAD RLBC) v. SECRETARY OF STATE FOR THE ENVIRONMENT, TRANSPORT AND THE REGIONS; WINDSOR AND MAIDENHEAD RBC v. SECRETARY OF STATE FOR THE ENVIRONMENT, TRANSPORT AND THE REGIONS, [2001] EWHC Admin 84, [2001] P.L.C.R. 30, Elias, J., QBD (Admin Ct).

4653. **Change of use – enforcement notices – immunity – meaning of "continuous use"**

[Town and Country Planning Act 1990 s.171 (B) (3), s.174 (2) (d).]

TBC appealed against the Secretary of State's decision to allow H's appeal against an enforcement notice which alleged an unlawful change of use. The inspector had allowed H's appeal on the basis that he had satisfied the ground of appeal contained in the Town and Country Planning Act 1990 s.174 (2) (d) which provided that if the unlawful use had begun more than 10 years prior to the issue of the notice, no enforcement action could be taken by virtue of s.171 (B) (3) of the Act.

Held, allowing the appeal, that a material change of use amounting to a breach of planning control could be considered to have existed for a period of 10 years if the use had been continuous throughout that period, *Panton v. Secretary of State for the Environment, Transport and the Regions* (1999) 78 P. & C.R. 186, [1999] C.L.Y. 4219 considered. Whilst short periods of inactivity could not amount to a cessation of the unlawful activity, longer periods could and cessation of the unlawful use merely constituted compliance with the law. In the instant case, the inspector had fallen into error because he had deemed the unlawful change of use to be a once and for all event. There had been times during the 10 year period when TBC could not have taken enforcement action against H because there was no breach of planning control. Those periods did not count towards the rolling period of 10 years which gave rise to immunity under s.174 (2) (d) of the Act.

THURROCK BC v. SECRETARY OF STATE FOR THE ENVIRONMENT, TRANSPORT AND THE REGIONS (NO.2); THURROCK BC v. HOLDING, [2001] EWHC Admin 128, [2001] 3 P.L.R. 14, Newman, J., QBD (Admin Ct).

4654. **Change of use – golf courses – meaning of "waste materials" – power of inspector to vary enforcement notice**

[Town and Country Planning Act 1990 s.176 (1) (b).]

W appealed against a decision of the planning inspector to uphold three enforcement notices served upon them requiring the discontinuation of the importation of waste materials onto their land, which was used as a golf course. W argued that (1) the materials in question were not waste, as they were to be used in the construction of golf holes, an activity permitted by the original planning permission, and (2) the steps required to be taken under the notices exceeded those necessary to remedy any injury to amenity caused by the alleged breach.

Held, allowing the appeal in part, that the inspector had applied the right test to determine whether material brought on to the land was waste, namely asking whether, at the time it was deposited, the intention of the depositer was that it would be reused. He had been entitled to find that some of the material was legitimately to be used for golf hole development, but that the remainder of it was waste, for the deposit of which W had received payment. The inspector, therefore, had been justified in drawing the conclusion that these activities amounted to a material change of use and that the original planning permission, for clay extraction and irrigation purposes, did not extend to works on a scale necessary to utilise all of the material on W's land. However, the inspector had erred in his limited view of his powers to vary the notices pursuant to the Town and Country Planning Act 1990 s.176(1)(b) in order to avoid an unsatisfactory situation arising as a result of a technical defect in the notices, subject to such a variation not causing injustice to either the planning authority or the other parties.

WYATT BROS (OXFORD) LTD v. SECRETARY OF STATE FOR THE ENVIRONMENT, TRANSPORT AND THE REGIONS [2001] P.L.C.R. 10, Judge Rich Q.C., QBD.

4655. **Change of use – land use – certificates of lawful development – intensification as material change of use – limits on generalised descriptions of proposed use**

[Town and Country Planning Act 1990 s.192.]

T sought to quash two certificates of lawful development issued by the local planning authority, TDC, to the Ministry of Defence, MOD, who proposed to sell the airfield, to which the certificates related, to a third party, K. TDC had granted certificates in respect of the proposed use of existing airfield buildings and of the development of the airfield and buildings for commercial and civilian use, pursuant to the Town and Country Planning Act 1990 s.192. T had previously issued three certificates under s.192 of the Act authorising the continuation of existing civilian use and the retention of certain buildings in connection with that use. T submitted that TDC had erred in that (1) they had failed to take into account the fact that the increase in civilian air traffic might constitute a material change of use; (2) the description of the proposed use contained in the certificates was so general that TDC would be unable to bring enforcement proceedings against intensification in the future, and (3) TDC should have imposed limits on the otherwise generalised descriptions of proposed use to prevent uncontrolled intensification of user.

Held, refusing the application, that while a local authority did not have an implied power to modify generalised descriptions of proposed use in relation to applications made under s.192, they could request the applicant to make amendments in appropriate circumstances and refuse to grant a certificate if an amendment was not made. In the instant case, even if it had been practical to devise a limitation to the proposed use, it could not have had any realistic impact because the prior certificates of proposed use issued under s.192 meant that a significant intensification of civilian use of the airfield would be lawful in any event.

R. (ON THE APPLICATION OF TAPP) v. THANET DC; *sub nom*. R. v. THANET DC, *ex p.* TAPP (2001) 81 P. & C.R. 37, Sullivan, J., QBD.

4656. **Change of use – mixed use – criteria for determining use for limitation purposes**

[Town and Country Planning Act 1990 s.171B(2), s.171B(3).]

S appealed against the decision of an inspector to dismiss her appeal against an enforcement notice which had alleged a breach of planning control by the change of the use of land to a mixed use involving both the stabling of horses and residential use. The inspector had rejected S's argument that the four year limitation period under the Town and Country Planning Act 1990 s.171B(2), which applied where the change of use had been "to use as a single dwellinghouse", was relevant, concluding instead that the 10 year limitation period provided for by s.171B(3), which referred to "any other breach of planning control", was applicable.

Held, allowing the appeal, that while the inspector seemed to have found sufficient physical and functional links between the living accommodation and the remainder of S's stabling block to justify his conclusion that there had been a mixed use rendering s.171B(3) applicable, he had also confusingly referred to the links as being "tenuous". Accordingly, he had failed to give clear or sufficient reasons for concluding that the development constituted a change to a mixed use, *Gravesham BC v. Secretary of State for the Environment* (1984) 47 P. & C.R. 142, [1984] C.L.Y. 3421 and *Burdle v. Secretary of State for the Environment* [1972] 1 W.L.R. 1207, [1972] C.L.Y. 3335 considered and the decision was remitted for reconsideration.

STANWAY v. SECRETARY OF STATE FOR THE ENVIRONMENT, TRANSPORT AND THE REGIONS [2001] J.P.L. 1063, Nigel MacLeod Q.C., QBD (Admin Ct).

4657. Change of use – ordinarily incidental usage – formulation of appropriate test

[Town and Country Planning Act 1990 s.288; Use Classes Order 1987 (SI 1987 764) Art.3(3).]

H applied for a lawful use certificate in relation to the use of the roof of its premises in London for the landing of the chairman's helicopter. The local authority refused the application on the basis that the proposed use was not ordinarily incidental to the keeping and running of H's department store. An appeal to the Secretary of State was dismissed. H challenged the dismissal pursuant to the Town and Country Planning Act 1990 s.288, contending that a consideration of whether the proposed use was "ordinarily incidental" to the retail use of H's premises was the wrong test and that the correct test should be whether the use was "incidental and ancillary".

Held, refusing the application, that when seeking to determine whether a proposed use was ancillary to another proposed use, the correct test to pose was whether such a use was "ordinarily incidental", *Millington v. Secretary of State for the Environment, Transport and the Regions* [1999] 3 P.L.R. 118, [1999] C.L.Y. 4172 applied. That concept was consistent with the Use Classes Order 1987 Art.3(3), which formed part of the framework upon which the 1990 Act had been built.

HARRODS LTD v. SECRETARY OF STATE FOR THE ENVIRONMENT, TRANSPORT AND THE REGIONS, [2001] EWHC Admin 600, *The Times*, November 15, 2001, Sullivan, J., QBD (Admin Ct).

4658. Change of use – planning units – protection of existing rights

K appealed against the inspector's dismissal of its appeal against the issue of an enforcement notice requiring the cessation of storage and manufacturing activities in buildings formerly used for agricultural purposes. K contended, inter alia, that the inspector's conclusions were inconsistent in that she had found that the alleged use had been both sporadic, occasional, and yet significant and had failed to take steps to protect existing rights of use. K further contended that confusion existed in the findings that, although the sites were separate planning units, they were used for purposes ancillary to one another.

Held, allowing the appeal, and remitting the matter for reconsideration, that the decision letter, when read as a whole, reflected K's evidence given at the inquiry but that the inspector had misunderstood and overlooked some of the evidence and had not given adequate reasons for her decision on the principal issues, in particular failing to make explicit which rights were to be protected in the future.

KINNERSLEY ENGINEERING LTD v. SECRETARY OF STATE FOR THE ENVIRONMENT, TRANSPORT AND THE REGIONS [2001] J.P.L. 1082, Duncan Ousley Q.C., QBD (Admin Ct).

4659. Change of use – waste disposal – burning of fuel recovered from waste solvents

L appealed against the dismissal of an application for judicial review ([2001] Env. L.R. 18) of the decision of DCC's planning sub-committee that the burning of a substance known as "secondary liquid fuel", SLF, which had been recovered from waste solvents and was used to heat kilns, did not amount to waste disposal requiring planning permission. LR, the owner of a quarry, had switched from using petcoke to using SLF to heat the kilns in which lime was produced. The sub-committee's decision had been based on an opinion of senior planning counsel that the use of SLF was waste recovery rather than waste disposal and that its use was so integral to the manufacturing process that it could not be characterised as a separate use. L maintained that the burning of SLF amounted, for planning purposes, to a separate land use.

Held, dismissing the appeal, that burning waste on a significant scale did not necessarily constitute a separate use of land for planning purposes if it was an integral part of some other process, *West Bowers Farm Products v. Essex CC* (1985) 50 P. & C.R. 368, [1986] C.L.Y. 3326 considered. The objective in burning the SLF was not simply to dispose of it but to improve LR's manufacturing process. Although SLF was made from waste solvent, it was being used as fuel and there was no waste disposal in addition to the permitted use of the land, nor did the substitution of SLF for part of the petcoke so alter the process as to result in a change in the use of the land. An alteration in the source of power or fuel was capable of constituting a material change of use, but as a matter of fact and degree it did not do so in the instant case. Accordingly, the judge had correctly concluded that the sub-committee had not erred in its conclusion.

R. (ON THE APPLICATION OF LOWTHER) v. DURHAM CC; *sub nom.* R. v. DURHAM CC, *ex p.* LOWTHER, [2001] EWCA Civ 781, [2002] Env. L.R. 13, Lord Phillips of Worth Matravers, M.R., CA.

4660. Compensation – business cessation – discontinuance orders – entitlement to interest

[Arbitration Act1950 s.19A; Town and Country Planning Act1971 s.170(2); Town and Country Planning Act 1990 s.115(2), s.118; Planning and Compensation Act 1991 s.80(1).]

A appealed against a determination of the lands tribunal ([2000] R.V.R.121), on a reference under the Town and Country Planning Act 1990 s.118, of his claim for compensation under the Town and Country Planning Act 1971 s.170(2) following the making of a discontinuance order in relation to an abattoir of which he was the tenant. A challenged the decision not to award interest on the amount of compensation beginning at the effective date of loss to the date on which payment was made, nearly 10 years later.

Held, allowing the appeal, that the Planning and Compensation Act 1991 s.80(1) which allowed the recovery of interest, previously unrecoverable on compensation payable under s.115 of the 1990 Act, was inapplicable in the instant case. Furthermore, proceedings brought under s.118 were not for "the recovery of any debt or damage" which would have allowed the tribunal to award interest, but were for the tribunal to determine the issue of disputed compensation, the obligation to make payment arising from s.115(2) of the 1990 Act, *Knibb v. National Coal Board* [1987] Q.B. 906, [1987] C.L.Y. 2429 considered. However, the tribunal should have exercised the discretionary power available at the time of the determination to award interest under the Arbitration Act 1950 s.19A, notwithstanding its subsequent repeal, to provide adequate compensation for the damage incurred as a result of the discontinuance order, thus fulfilling the objective of s.115(2).

ASLAM v. SOUTH BEDFORDSHIRE DC [2001] R.V.R. 65, Chadwick, L.J., CA.

4661. Compulsory purchase – compensation – business relocation – consequential loss of profit and disturbance

[Land Compensation Act 1961 s.5 r.(5).]

E sought the determination of a preliminary issue as to the extent of compensation available to it under the Land Compensation Act 1961 s.5 r.(5). E operated a nursing home. Following highway development, E had served a blight notice on the Secretary of State and the property was effectively compulsorily purchased and the home relocated. E argued that compensation under s.5 r.(5) should include the loss of profit and disturbance consequent on relocation.

Held, allowing the application, that there was nothing in the Act nor its predecessor to suggest that s.5 r.(5) should be limited to actual reinstatement costs. Indeed, it would be contrary to the principal of equivalence for E to be denied compensation for consequential losses simply because the matter fell within the provision of reinstatement under s.5 r.(5), when such losses were recoverable in the case of market value compensation under s.5 r.(2) for land that was not devoted to a particular purpose, *Birmingham Corp v. West Midland Baptist (Trust) Association Inc* [1970] A.C. 874, [1969] C.L.Y. 433 followed.

ERON PARK LTD v. SECRETARY OF STATE FOR THE ENVIRONMENT, TRANSPORT AND THE REGIONS (NO.1); *sub nom.* ERONPARK LTD v. SECRETARY OF STATE FOR TRANSPORT [2000] 2 E.G.L.R. 165, Judge Marder Q.C. (President), LandsTr.

4662. Compulsory purchase – compensation – claim for holding costs

[Land Compensation Act 1961 s.5.]

R built forty-one retirement homes and a wardens bungalow which were difficult to sell because of threatened compulsory purchase. They were compulsorily acquired in 1997. R claimed compensation under the Land Compensation Act 1961 s.5 for holding costs (interest less rents received) from 1993 to 1997. The issue as to whether holding costs could be compensated under the statute was heard by the tribunal as a preliminary issue.

Held, determining the preliminary issue, that holding costs were a valid head of claim under the Land Compensation Act 1961 s.5. The threat of compulsory purchase was a sufficient causal connection to satisfy one of the three required conditions *Director of Buildings and Lands v. Shun Fung Ironworks Ltd* (1995) 2 A.C. 111, [1995] C.L.Y. 664 disapproved, and the other two conditions against remoteness and avoidability were satisfied.

RYDE INTERNATIONAL PLC v. LONDON REGIONAL TRANSPORT [2001] 1 E.G.L.R. 101, Judge Rich Q.C., LandsTr.

4663. Compulsory purchase – compensation – disturbance payment – licensee displaced by development corporation acquiring land

[Land Compensation Act 1961 s.39(1); Land Compensation Act 1973 s.37; Local Government Planning and Land Act 1980 s.142.]

M claimed a disturbance payment under the Land Compensation Act 1973 s.37 in respect of an advertising hoarding occupied under a licence from B. The land was subsequently acquired by T, a development corporation. CNT, T's successor, contended that no payment was due as M did not have an interest in the land and had only been displaced under a clause in the licence agreement. Further, that M had not been in lawful possession when the displacement occurred and there was no compulsory purchase order in force for the land when M was displaced.

Held, giving judgment for M, that s.37 of the 1973 Act provided for compensation to be paid to parties that did not have an interest in compulsorily purchased land. T's acquisition of the land from B ended M's right to occupy. M did not have to be in lawful possession when it was displaced for the purposes of s.37, only at the time of the agreement between B and T. T possessed compulsory purchase powers under the Land Compensation Act 1961 s.39(1) as it was authorised to acquire interests in land under the Local Government Planning and Land Act 1980 s.142 and there was no basis for contending that s.37 of the 1973 Act was to be interpreted as requiring actual authorisation to acquire the land concerned.

MILLS & ALLEN LTD v. COMMISSIONERS FOR NEW TOWNS [2001] R.V.R. 114, Judge not specified, LandsTr.

4664. Compulsory purchase – compensation – freehold business premises in redevelopment scheme area – effect of vandalism

[Land Compensation Act 1961 s.5 r.6.]

G sought compensation following the compulsory purchase of his freehold comprising a shop of 370 square feet, office of 115 square feet and store 80 square feet used by his insurance broking business and three bedsits located in an area covered by an urban regeneration scheme. The premises had had to be demolished due to fire damage. Prior to the fire, they had also suffered extensive vandalism. Net income for the bedsits was agreed at £3,900 with £32,541 for trade disturbance under the Land Compensation Act 1961 s.5 r.6 subject to liability being determined. G sought a reference as issues remained outstanding as to the nature of the development scheme to be disregarded for compensation purposes and whether the vandalism was due to the scheme and its effect on the property's market value.

Held, finding DMBC liable to pay compensation of £42,500, comprising £3,000 for site value and £39,625 as to 60 per cent of the land's additional value in its pre fire condition, that (1) the redevelopment scheme for the street on which the premises were located was to be disregarded as it formed part of DMBC's plans for environmental improvement; (2) responsibility for the diminution in value of the property was attributed at 60 per cent to DMBC and 40 per cent to G. The rationale for this approach being that G was responsible for the reduction in value due to vandalism on his own property. However, G had taken necessary steps to reduce the effects of vandalism which had increased following the demolition of other properties in the area and the way DMBC had implemented the scheme had exacerbated the problem, and (3) DMBC were responsible for 60 per cent of the business compensation because G had given up occupation of the property in May 1994 due to the vandalism and from January 1994 the destruction of his business records by vandals had made it very difficult for him to use the premises.

GREEN v. DONCASTER MBC [2001] R.V.R. 117, AP Musto FRICS, Lands Tr.

4665. Compulsory purchase – compensation – grade two listed dwelling in rural location – open market valuation

The question arose as to the amount of compensation payable in relation to the compulsory acquisition of a grade 2 listed dwelling with equestrian use and an 11 acre field comprising part of a road scheme. Comparisons were made with two other properties acquired as part of the road scheme and three open market transactions all in the same neighbourhood varying between £300,000 and £475,000, the lowest of the valuations being based on a non agreed sale. L contended that the property should be valued at £450,000, whereas ECC valued it at £330,000, based on its location close to a scrap yard

Held, that the value would be based on an open market valuation, as opposed to negotiated settlements because these would embody factors differentiating them from open market valuation. The property, although attractive and set in a rural location, offered limited accommodation and needed repairs and modernisation work. ECC had placed too much reliance on the scrap yard. Taking an overall view of the closest comparables, the open market value of the property was £375,000, along with a previously agreed home loss payment of £15,000.

LEPLEY v. ESSEX CC [2001] R.V.R. 147, PR Francis FRICS, Lands Tr.

4666. Compulsory purchase – compensation – land required for replacement nature reserve – change in value due to purpose of acquisition

[Land Compensation Act 1961 s.5 r.3.]

W sought compensation for the compulsory purchase of his land by WDA for a nature reserve. As a result of the building of the Cardiff Bay Barrage a large area of wetlands was to be inundated, and W's land was required for the formation of a compensatory nature reserve. W argued that the land should be valued as more than just agricultural land because it was the only suitable land for the reserve so that a ransom value applied.

Held, dismissing the application, that the land was to be given only its normal agricultural value. Other sites had been available for the reserve and it was not intended that the replacement would be identical to the site lost because of the scheme. W's land was not therefore special in terms of its suitability or adaptability for use as a reserve so that the Land Compensation Act 1961 s.5 r.3 did not apply. Compensation was intended to put W into the position he would have been in if his land had not been compulsorily purchased and any change in value to W's land due to the barrage scheme was to be ignored, *Pointe Gourde Quarrying & Transport Co v. Sub-Intendent of Crown Lands* [1947] A.C. 565 applied.

WALTERS v. WELSH DEVELOPMENT AGENCY [2001] R.V.R. 93, George Bartlett Q.C. (President), Lands Tr.

4667. **Compulsory purchase – compensation – land use – valuation assumptions**

[Land Compensation Act 1961 s.17.]

S owned a market garden near Manchester. In 1993 planning permission was granted for development of part of the land with other land bordering the proposed route of the M66. In 1996 a notice to treat was served on S for part of its land. A certificate under the Land Compensation Act s.17 was issued in respect of the acquired land. In assessing compensation it was ordered that the following preliminary issues be determined namely (1) what development would have been permitted in a no-scheme world, and (2) what development could be anticipated after the valuation date.

Held, that (1) since the 1993 planning permission did not apply to the acquired land it was not to be taken into account; (2) s.17 certificate related only to the acquired land and bore little weight in determining the development for a no-scheme world; (3) the likely development for the acquired land was frontage development, and (4) no development could be expected on the retained land.

STAYLEY DEVELOPMENTS v. SECRETARY OF STATE FOR THE ENVIRONMENT, TRANSPORT AND THE REGIONS [2001] 1 E.G.L.R. 167, George Bartlett Q.C. (President), Lands Tr.

4668. **Compulsory purchase – compensation – limitations – negotiation – estoppel**

SCC acquired land from S in 1992 pursuant to a compulsory purchase order. The time limit of six years for referring the issue of compensation to the Lands Tribunal expired on December 25, 1998. Following protracted and unsuccessful negotiations S lodged notice of reference on September 20, 1999. The Tribunal was asked to decide the preliminary issue whether the reference was statute barred. S argued that because negotiations had continued after December 1998 there had been an election and SCC was estopped from relying on the limitation defence.

Held, determining the preliminary issue, that the reference to the tribunal was time barred. All parties were aware of the limitation period at all material times and SCC did nothing to waive the limitation defence.

SITA (FORMERLY EBENEZER MEARS (SAND PRODUCERS) LTD) v. SURREY CC [2001] R.V.R. 56, George Bartlett Q.C. (President), Lands Tr.

4669. **Compulsory purchase – compensation – motor repairs garage – total cessation of trade**

Held, determining preliminary issues, that the compensation payable on the compulsory purchase of a motor repairs garage in Warrington leading to total cessation of trade would not include any figure for profit rents since the lease was not assignable, and the nature and quality of the evidence would determine whether the compensation should include a deduction for head office costs and the method of calculating the permanent loss of profits.

BUD AND JET LTD v. WARRINGTON BC [2001] R.V.R. 22, NJ Rose FRICS, Lands Tr.

4670. **Compulsory purchase – compensation – nature reserves – underlying purpose of scheme**

The construction of the Cardiff Bay barrage involved the loss of part of the Taff/ Ely Site of Special Scientific Interest and therefore the Land Authority for Wales was authorised to acquire land for the construction of a wetlands nature reserve. The owners of agricultural land which had been compulsorily bought under the scheme contended their land had special suitability or adaptability for the purposes of providing a nature reserve which ought to be taken into account when valuing their compensation. The tribunal was asked to determine two preliminary issues namely (1) did the subject lands have a special suitability for the nature reserve?, and (2) was the underlying scheme the Cardiff Bay barrage or the nature reserve?

Held, rejecting the claims of the applicants, that (1) the subject lands had no special suitability or adaptability for the purposes of providing a nature reserve to compensate for the loss of the Taff/Ely Site of Special Scientific Interest, and (2) the underlying scheme was the Cardiff Bay Barrage.

WATERS v. WELSH DEVELOPMENT AGENCY [2001] 1 E.G.L.R. 185, George Bartlett Q.C. (President), Lands Tr.

4671. **Compulsory purchase – compensation – registered nursing home – loss of actual profits and inability to proceed with expansion**

Held, that compensation of £488,569 was payable on the compulsory purchase of a 30 bed registered nursing home in Staffordshire, which included payments for actual loss of profit while the property was blighted giving a reduced occupancy, and for future loss of profit resulting from the inability to proceed with an expansion scheme. Interest was also awarded for loss of profit over the relevant time scale at LIBOR plus two per cent.

ERON PARK LTD v. SECRETARY OF STATE FOR THE ENVIRONMENT, TRANSPORT AND THE REGIONS (NO.2) [2001] R.V.R. 5, PR Francis FRICS, Lands Tr.

4672. **Compulsory purchase – compensation – total extinguishment of hairdressing business – basis for valuation and net profit determination**

[Landlord and Tenant Act 1954 Pt II.]

H, aged over 60, sought compensation for the compulsory acquisition and total extinguishment of his hairdressing business, on the basis that he was a protected tenant under the Landlord and Tenant Act 1954 Pt II. Disagreements arose between H and L as to the treatment of H's wife's earnings, the depreciation of capital assets and the appropriate multiplier to be applied to the net profit. H sought a multiplier of three, as this within the middle range of earlier Lands Tribunal decisions, whereas L argued for 1.25, determined on a prospective purchaser basis.

Held, finding for H and awarding compensation of £73,176, that (1) H's wife's services had to be taken into account when determining the appropriate level of profit, with no deduction from net profits for her earnings; (2) H's protected tenancy meant that compensation should be based on total extinguishment of his business in terms of its secure occupation of the premises; (3) no depreciation could be allowed for the shop equipment as its age was such that it would have been written off previously; (4) the business was of more value to H, given his age and the length of time he had spent in the trade in that area, than it would have achieved on the open market, and (5) a multiplier of three was appropriate due to the uncertainties surrounding H's actual retirement age and future business levels.

HALIL v. LAMBETH LBC [2001] R.V.R. 181, PR Francis FRICS, Lands Tr.

4673. Compulsory purchase – compensation – valuation factors – large warehouse – contaminated land

P claimed compensation for the compulsory purchase of its warehouse property by LCC. The value of one of the warehouses on the site was in dispute. The building was approximately 130,000 square feet in size with an asbestos roof, internal loading platform and subject to below ground methane and carbon dioxide contamination. P argued that it should be valued at £18 per square foot, comparing it with other properties sold in the area, and making no deduction for contamination. LCC contended that the value should be £12 per square foot.

Held, that the value should be £13 per square foot, that the most effective way to assess comparable properties was by using experience based judgment, rather than imposing percentage reductions for items such as distance from the city centre, as had been done by P. The comparables suggested by LCC were closer in size to P's building, which was an important factor. Its value would be below the band of values evident from the comparables, however, because of its relatively large size, contamination and the internal loading platform.

PREMIER WAREHOUSING AND DISTRIBUTION CO LTD v. LEICESTER CITY COUNCIL [2000] R.V.R. 351, George Bartlett Q.C., LandsTr.

4674. Compulsory purchase – compensation – valuation of land forming area of comprehensive development in relevant development plan

[Land Compensation Act 1961 s.16(3).]

H sought compensation of £455,000 for three acres of land near Swansea, whereas SCC valued the site at £70,000. H contended that planning permission would have been granted for 15 detached houses if the land had not been included on the development plan as an area of comprehensive development on the basis of the Land Compensation Act 1961 s.16(3). SCC argued that s.16(3) did not apply in the instant case because the land was not allocated for a particular use on the plan.

Held, awarding compensation of £138,250, that s.16(3) did not apply because the land was not part of the residential development area in the current development plan, although it was assumed that planning permission would have been granted as it came within the plan's general policy and had been granted to comparable land. However, H had failed to restrict its valuation to the date agreed between the parties and was based on a one year period commencing on that date. SCC's residential valuation was accepted, based on a valuation of property in the same area for which planning permission had been granted.

HOOPER v. SWANSEA CITY AND COUNTY [2001] R.V.R. 153, NJ Rose FRICS, LandsTr.

4675. Compulsory purchase – compensation – valuation of service station site – choice of comparables – use of capital value system

T claimed compensation of £2,937,000 for the compulsory purchase by TBC of its petrol filling station. TBC argued that the figure should be £1,035,572, using only comparables in the north west of England rather than across the UK, as contended for by T.

Held, granting compensation in the sum of £1,753,375, that the core volume figure had to be calculated by looking at the average throughput since 1991, disregarding 1994 when profits were affected by adjacent roadworks, and making adjustments for improvements to the station made in 1991. The figure would be reduced by 30 per cent to reflect T's competitive pricing policy, and by 7.5 per cent to take into account future risk of competition. The appropriate comparables were in the north west, as values in the south east were markedly different. Based on this, the capital value was £1.225 per gallon of the core volume. The capital value system was to be preferred over investment basis analysis because of problems in verifying the latter. Factors such as the value of the improvements made in 1991 and the likelihood of the station being bought by a major oil company had also to be taken into account.

TELEGRAPH SERVICE STATIONS LTD v. TRAFFORD BC [2000] 3 E.G.L.R.145, Judge not applicable, Lands Tr.

4676. **Compulsory purchase – delay – jurisdiction to allow premature application**

[Acquisition of Land Act 1981 s.15, s.23 (4) (b); European Convention on Human Rights 1950 Art.6 (1).]

Liverpool City Council, LCC, sought to redevelop part of a conservation area in the centre of Liverpool. Pursuant to this goal LCC promulgated a compulsory purchase order under the Acquisition of Land Act 1981. Following an inquiry an inspector recommended that the order be confirmed, and by a letter dated June 21, 1999 the Secretary of State accepted the inspectors recommendation. On July 30, 1999 E, the owner of a pub subject to the compulsory purchase order, applied under s.23 to challenge the order. Notice of Confirmation was subsequently published on August 2, 1999. During the hearing a preliminary point arose as to whether the court had jurisdiction to hear the application following the submission of LCC that it had been made outside the time limit established under s.23 (4) (b). LCC argued that the court did not have jurisdiction to hear a claim made before publication of the Notice of Confirmation. E contended, inter alia, that (1) the court had a discretion to allow a premature application, and (2) the delay in the publication of the Notice of Confirmation from the date of the Secretary of State's confirmation had been contrary to s.15 which required publication "as soon as may be".

Held, dismissing the application, that (1) s.23 (4) was not ambiguous and did not allow for applications outside the statutory six week window. Parliament had expressly established a trigger point from which applications could be made and accordingly the court had not been conferred with a discretion to allow premature applications, *R. v. Cornwall CC, ex p. Huntington* [1994] 1 All E.R. 694, [1994] C.L.Y. 65 applied. Given that the statute was unambiguous, the European Convention on Human Rights 1950 Art.6 (1) did not assist E. Article 6 (1) was not an absolute right. A time limit for challenges was justified by the interests of certainty and good public administration, and (2) the words contained within s.15 that the Notice of Confirmation be published "as soon as may be" were not to be read as requiring publication as soon as possible. It followed that despite the delay, publication had been in accordance with the Act.

ENTERPRISE INNS PLC v. SECRETARY OF STATE FOR THE ENVIRONMENT, TRANSPORT AND THE REGIONS (2001) 81 P. & C.R. 18, Maurice Kay, J., QBD.

4677. **Compulsory purchase – development plans – requirement for precedent fact**

[Town and Country Planning Act 1990 s.226, s.247.]

G applied to quash the Secretary of State's decision to confirm a compulsory purchase order, relating to a proposed city centre redevelopment scheme. The scheme necessitated the closure of some of the city's roads by means of an application under the Town and Country Planning Act 1990 s.247. G contended that the Secretary of State's conclusion that the development had a reasonable prospect of proceeding was flawed, given the absence of all the relevant facts and matters concerning alternative options. It followed, G submitted, that the Secretary of State was unable to conclude that the order was in the public interest.

Held, dismissing the application, that there was no requirement for a precedent fact before the Secretary of State could confirm a compulsory purchase order and accordingly it was not necessary for him to conclude that the development would probably take place in order to find a substantial public interest. The lawfulness of the decision depended upon a proper consideration of the whole of the circumstances of the case rather than focusing on a single issue, *Chesterfield Properties Plc v. Secretary of State for the Environment, Transport and the Regions* (1998) 76 P. & C.R. 117, [1997] C.L.Y. 4042 followed. The Secretary of State had considered fully the difficulties regarding planning permission for the scheme, as required by s.226 of the 1990 Act, and resolution of those difficulties was not required by that section.

GALA LEISURE LTD v. SECRETARY OF STATE FOR THE ENVIRONMENT, TRANSPORT AND THE REGIONS (2001) 82 P. & C.R. 11, Nigel MacLeod Q.C., QBD (Admin Ct).

4678. **Compulsory purchase – Lands Tribunal – valuation – option to obtain planning permission**

P appealed, by way of case stated, against the decision of the Lands Tribunal awarding S the value of a piece of land as determined by the tribunal. P owned industrial and residential development land adjoining a ransom strip, which as part of a planning agreement was to be developed into a link road for P's land, and which P was to purchase. P had challenged the valuation of the ransom strip by the Lands Tribunal in the Court of Appeal, which had remitted the decision on the single issue of whether the tribunal had omitted to consider the option that P had of obtaining fresh planning permissions, free from conditions to develop the link road, thus causing less delay than renegotiating the agreement. The tribunal amended its valuation by reducing the percentage share of the released development value of the residential land. P submitted that the tribunal erred in deciding the compensation on that basis and contended that the tribunal should have conducted a complete review of its valuation.

Held, dismissing the appeal, that the reduction was within the judgment and expertise of the tribunal, which was entitled to determine the award by confining itself to the valuation of the land affected by the error, and that furthermore, P was not permitted to relitigate the issues, *Henderson v. Henderson* [1843-60] All E.R. Rep. 378 and *Barrow v. Bankside Members Agency Ltd* [1996] 1 W.L.R. 257, [1995] C.L.Y. 3894 applied.

JA PYE (OXFORD) LTD v. SOUTH GLOUCESTERSHIRE DC (COMPULSORY PURCHASE: VALUATION) (2001) 81 P. & C.R. 31, Otton, L.J., CA.

4679. **Compulsory purchase – supermarkets – town centre redevelopment – balance of private and public interests**

[Acquisition of Land Act 1981 s.23.]

T applied under the Acquisition of Land Act 1981 s.23 to quash the Secretary of State's confirmation of a compulsory purchase order made in respect of a supermarket owned by T, to enable the local authority to carry out redevelopment of a town centre. T contended that the Secretary of State had failed to perform a balancing exercise between the public interest and its private property interest and had failed to consider an alternative redevelopment scheme in which the existing supermarket would be modified and remain in the town centre.

Held, refusing the application, that the alternative scheme had been considered by the inspector and he was entitled to conclude that the supermarket could not be accommodated in the redevelopment scheme together with a departmental store. T's interest had been considered and the conclusion that there was a compelling case in the public interest for the order was justified.

TESCO STORES LTD v. SECRETARY OF STATE FOR ENVIRONMENT, TRANSPORT AND THE REGIONS (COMPULSORY PURCHASE) (2000) 80 P. & C.R. 427, Sullivan, J., QBD.

4680. **Development – business parks – lawfulness of outline planning permission where environmental impact assessment necessary**

[Town and Country Planning (Assessment of Environmental Effects) Regulations 1988 (SI 1988 1199) Sch.3 para.2(a); Council Directive 97/11 on the assessment of the effects of certain public and private projects on the environment Art.5.2.]

M sought judicial review of a redesigned application for outline planning permission for a business park development. M contended that (1) the revised plans failed to incorporate a description of the proposed development detailed enough to comply with the Town and Country Planning (Assessment of Environmental Effects) Regulations 1988 Sch.3 para.2(a), and (2) outline planning permission was precluded in any case where an environmental impact assessment would be required since it could not be said with confidence that none of the reserved matters would result in any significant environmental impact.

Held, dismissing the application, that (1) where a project was not predetermined from the start but anticipated to evolve depending upon the requirements of potential occupants, there was good reason for the project description to recognise that fact and allow for a degree of flexibility. Such an approach was not contrary to Environmental Impact Assessment Directive 97/11 Art.5.2 or the Regulations, and (2) the grant of outline planning permission in such projects was not inconsistent with the aims of the Directive provided that the outline application clearly stated the developing nature of the project and included specific parameters, the environmental impact assessment took account of the potential significant effects flowing from such a flexible approach, and the local authority imposed stringent conditions to ensure that the project remained within the anticipated boundaries of the original application. The local authority were fully entitled, in any given case, to declare themselves satisfied that none of the reserved matters were likely to result in any significant environmental impact.

R. v. ROCHDALE MBC, *ex p.* MILNE (NO.2) [2001] Env. L.R. 22, Sullivan, J., QBD.

4681. **Development – compensation – alterations to airport – impact on local residents – considerations affecting compensatory award**

[Land Compensation Act 1973 s.15(2).]

PCA, the lessee of an airport, appealed against the refusal of its challenge to a certificate issued by the Secretary of State pursuant to the Land Compensation Act 1973 s.15(2). The certificate established conclusively that alterations to the airport amounted to works within the meaning of s.9 of the Act, rendering PCA liable to pay compensation for any qualifying depreciation in the value of neighbouring land. T, a local resident, claimed that he had been adversely affected by noise and that the value of his home had fallen following alterations to the airport apron to facilitate its use by Royal Navy helicopters. PCA submitted that (1) the alterations were not works within the meaning of s.9 as they had not been "substantial" and had not increased airport capacity, and (2) the Secretary of State had misinterpreted the information available to him and had overlooked material factors.

Held, dismissing the appeal, that (1) the court was required to consider the purpose for which the works had been undertaken and the Secretary of State had been entitled to conclude that the MOD had carried out the works for the purpose of enabling a greater number of its helicopters to operate from the airport, and (2) the fact that a standing area had been available for use prior to the carrying out of the works was not a relevant consideration.

R. (ON THE APPLICATION OF PLYMOUTH CITY AIRPORT LTD) v. SECRETARY OF STATE FOR THE ENVIRONMENT, TRANSPORT AND THE REGIONS; *sub nom.* R. v. PLYMOUTH CITY AIRPORT LTD; R. v. SECRETARY OF STATE FOR THE ENVIRONMENT, TRANSPORT AND THE REGIONS, *ex p.* PLYMOUTH CITY AIRPORT LTD, [2001] EWCA Civ 144, (2001) 82 P. & C.R. 20, Jonathan Parker, L.J., CA.

4682. **Development – planning agreements – conditions accompanying grant of permission – absence of connection between road scheme and industrial development – reasonableness**

[Town and Country Planning Act 1971 s.52.]

P appealed against a refusal ([2000] E.G.C.S. 116) to grant a declaration that it was not liable to pay in excess of £400 000 to a number of local authorities, who were the successors to ACC, and with whom it had entered into two agreements relating to the construction of a road. The first agreement had been made pursuant to the Town and Country Planning Act 1971 s.52 and was conditional on P being granted planning permission for a proposed industrial development. P submitted that there was no connection between the building of the road and the proposed development and, therefore, the exercise of ACC's powers under s.52 had been unlawful. Moreover, given that the second agreement was not connected with the development, P argued that it was purely an agreement whereby it bought its planning permission, and was therefore *Wednesbury* unreasonable, as ACC must have taken into account an irrelevant consideration.

Held, dismissing the appeal, that there was no precondition that an agreement under s.52 had to relate to a specific development, it was merely dependent on whether or not its purpose was for restricting or regulating the development or use of the land, *Tesco Stores Ltd v. Secretary of State for the Environment* [1995] 1 W.L.R. 759, [1995] C.L.Y. 4784 applied. The agreement was for the relevant purpose, and therefore the issue was one of reasonableness. There was nothing to indicate that ACC had, in entering into the s.52 agreement, taken into account anything other than highway or planning considerations, and therefore the agreement was not rendered invalid by the absence of a connection between the development and the road.

JA PYE (OXFORD) LTD v. SOUTH GLOUCESTERSHIRE DC (NO.1); *sub nom.* JA PYE (OXFORD) LTD v. SOUTH GLOUCESTER DC, [2001] EWCA Civ 450, [2001] 2 P.L.R. 66, Latham, L.J., CA.

4683. **Development plans – agricultural land – agricultural workers – personal needs as material considerations justifying departure from development plan**

[Town and Country Planning Act 1990 s.54A.]

T sought to challenge the grant of outline planning permission for the construction of an agricultural worker's dwelling upon farm land. T contended that (1) MBC had breached the Town and Country Planning Act 1990 s.54A on the basis that the grant of permission contravened the requirements of the development plan, and had wrongly taken into account the personal wishes of the planned occupant as a material consideration when, on the facts, no proven agricultural need could be identified, and (2) the decision had been irrational in a *Wednesbury* sense.

Held, refusing the application for judicial review, that MBC were fully entitled to depart from the development plan if there were material considerations capable of justifying that view. On the facts of the instant case the accommodation, which the worker responsible for the care of the livestock at the farm occupied, was unsuitable for his personal needs. MBC had been entitled to treat those needs as material considerations, *Westminster City Council v. Great Portland Estates Plc* [1985] A.C. 661, [1984] C.L.Y. 3413 and *Fowler v. Secretary of State for the Environment and Berwick Trust* [1992] 3 P.L.R. 140, [1993] C.L.Y. 3947 applied, and (2) MBC had not taken any irrelevant considerations into account and their conclusions could not be described as either irrational or perverse.

R. v. MAIDSTONE BC, *ex p.* TAIT AND CHURCHILL [2001] J.P.L. 704, Maurice Kay, J., QBD (Admin Ct).

4684. **Development plans – green belt – planning inquiries – material considerations – correction of typographical errors**

[Town and Country Planning Act 1990 s.54A, s.70; Town and Country Planning (Development Plan) Regulations 1991 (SI 1991 2794) Reg.33.]

S applied for judicial review of the Secretary of State's decision to refuse it planning permission for a housing development on the recommendation of an Inspector following a public inquiry. The Inspector had found that the area set aside for housing had been wrongly set out in the local unitary development plan, UDP, owing to a typing error which meant that the land in S's application included an area of Green Belt and was therefore unacceptable. S argued that the decision was flawed as the Secretary of State had (1) ignored relevant policy; (2) had no power to substitute a figure into the UDP to "correct" the typing error, and (3) had failed to give S an adequate opportunity to deal with the typing error issue.

Held, allowing the application, that (1) under the Town and Country Planning Act 1990 s.54A and s.70, the Secretary of State was obliged to give consideration to all the policies under the UDP, including a policy proposing a reduction of Green Belt land and one defining Green Belt land according to the proposals map, rather than the text, *Bolton MDC v. Secretary of State for the Environment* 94 L.G.R. 387, [1996] C.L.Y. 4834 applied. Given the importance of the Green Belt issue to the final decision, the Secretary of State should have taken those policies into account even though they had not been raised specifically at the Inquiry; (2) the Secretary of State had wrongly applied the Town and Country Planning (Development Plan) Regulations 1991 Reg.33, by virtue of which the proposals map had to take precedence where there were discrepancies in a UDP. Therefore, the Secretary of State had erred by "correcting" the typing error, and (3) S had been given an adequate opportunity in the totality of the Inquiry to counter the typing error issue.

R. (ON THE APPLICATION OF ST JAMES HOMES LTD) v. SECRETARY OF STATE FOR THE ENVIRONMENT, TRANSPORT AND THE REGIONS; *sub nom.* ST JAMES HOMES LTD v. SECRETARY OF STATE FOR THE ENVIRONMENT, TRANSPORT AND THE REGIONS, [2001] EWHC Admin 30, [2001] P.L.C.R. 27, Ouseley, J., QBD (Admin Ct).

4685. Development plans – planning blight – review of council policy – accrual of relief sought

[Highways Act 1980 s.246(2A).]

S sought to challenge LCC's decision not to exercise its discretionary power pursuant to the Highways Act 1980 s.246(2A) to purchase property affected by planning blight and sought a ruling that LCC's policy regarding the acquisition of blighted land was unreasonable and should be reviewed. S had applied to LCC to purchase their property following the approval of planning permission for the construction of a bypass on neighbouring land. LCC refused on the basis that the criterion that the property had to be rendered virtually inhabitable by the proposed scheme had not been satisfied. Following a review of the council policy, S made a further application to LCC which was likewise refused. LCC then adopted a new policy which promised to give proper consideration to requests to purchase property under s.246(2A) and invited S to make another application for purchase. No further application was made by S and LCC subsequently determined not to proceed with their plans for the bypass.

Held, dismissing the application, that LCC had now decided not to proceed with the proposed development plans and the policy originally challenged by S had since been replaced by a more flexible policy under which S had been invited to make a new application. The sense of injustice felt by S was an insufficient basis for relief and, in any event, the relief sought had accrued by the passage of time.

R. v. LANCASHIRE CC, *ex p.* SMITH [2000] J.P.L. 1305 (Note), Lightman, J., QBD.

4686. Development plans – planning permission – application for supermarket development – extent of Secretary of State's duty

[Town and Country Planning Act 1990 s.70(1).]

WM appealed against the Secretary of State's decision to follow the inspector's recommendation at a public inquiry to uphold SBC's refusal to grant planning permission for a superstore to be built on the site of a college, which was then to relocate. The inspector had recommended that the refusal be upheld, because the harm to the town outweighed the benefit. WM sought to quash the Secretary of State's decision on the basis that he had failed to make explicit reference to two material advantages of the development to which the inspector had referred.

Held, allowing the appeal and quashing the decision, that as a matter of law, and in accordance with the Town and Country Planning Act 1990 s.70(1), the

Secretary of State's primary duty was to balance all of the advantages against all of the disadvantages in order to determine the acceptability of a development application. Upon reading the Secretary of State's decision letter, it did not appear that a full balancing exercise had been carried out. It was clear that WM had suffered severe prejudice as a result, because in order to assess the likelihood of success of a future application, it had to be aware of the Secretary of State's views on the advantages already identified.

WM MORRISON SUPERMARKETS PLC v. SECRETARY OF STATE FOR THE ENVIRONMENT, TRANSPORT AND THE REGIONS; *sub nom.* WILLIAM MORRISON SUPERMARKETS PLC v. SECRETARY OF STATE FOR THE ENVIRONMENT, TRANSPORT AND THE REGIONS [2000] J.P.L. 1139, Lightman, J., QBD.

4687. Development plans – planning procedures – wind farms – validity of Secretary of State's approval

[Town and Country Planning (Inquiries Procedure) Rules 1992 (SI 1992 2038) r.16.]

C applied to quash a decision of the Secretary of State which approved planning permission for six wind turbine generators. The approval had been granted following a public inquiry conducted by an inspector. C contended that the Secretary of State had (1) acted in breach of the Town and Country Planning (Inquiries Procedure) Rules 1992 r.16 by differing from the inspector's findings and yet providing no opportunity for further submissions; (2) acted perversely in not conducting a site visit but rather had relied upon visualisation and photomontage evidence which had been criticised during the inquiry, and (3) failed to take the development plan into account.

Held, dismissing the application, that (1) r.16 was not applicable as the difference between the findings was one of judgment not fact; (2) appropriate material had been available to the Secretary of State. It was important to have regard to the fact that the development was not yet in place, there were no significant differences between the expert evidence in relation to the issue of visibility, the relevant technical advice note recommended precisely the material utilised by the Secretary of State and the inspector himself had not been critical of the evidence upon which the Secretary of State had relied, and (3) the relevant plan policies had been carefully considered and the Secretary of State had made a finding that there was no unacceptable impact.

CAMPAIGN FOR THE PROTECTION OF RURAL WALES v. SECRETARY OF STATE FOR WALES [2000] J.P.L. 1304 (Note), Nigel MacLeod Q.C., QBD.

4688. Development plans – schools – development of primary school in accordance with plan – plan construed broadly and purposively – absence of bias

[Town and Country Planning General Development Order 1988 (SI 1988 1813) s.74(1)(a).]

P challenged the decision of his local authority to grant planning permission for the development of a primary school on green belt land to replace an existing village school. P contended that (1) the application was one which departed from the relevant development plan and that that the planning authority had erred in law in failing to notify the Secretary of State of the application, as was required under DoE Circular 19/92, issued under the Town and Country Planning General Development Order 1988 s.74(1)(a); (2) the committee had been misled on a number of material considerations, in that the planning officer failed to advise the planning committee of green belt issues and had misinterpreted the local plan to such an extent that the decision was tainted with illegality, and (3) there had been a real danger of bias because a member of the local education committee had been permitted to adjudicate on the application.

Held, refusing the application, that (1) the local development plan should be construed broadly and purposively and, although not expressly mentioned, the plan had allowed for the relaxation of the green belt policy in granting permission on the site, which had been identified within the plan as required for educational purposes. The application was in accordance with the development plan, *Main v. Swansea City Council* (1985) 49 P. & C.R. 26, [1985] C.L.Y. 3463 and *R. v. Doncaster MDC, ex p. British Railways Board* [1987] J.P.L. 444, [1987] C.L.Y. 3700 considered; (2) the committee had taken into account all material considerations, having considered other possible sites, and their decision was not defective in law. *Trusthouse Forte Hotels Ltd v. Secretary of State for the Environment* (1987) 53 P. & C.R. 293, [1987] C.L.Y. 3711 considered, and (3) the decision had not been tainted with bias.

R. v. DERBYSHIRE CC, *ex p.* POOLE [2001] P.L.C.R. 3, Gibbs, J., QBD.

4689. **Enforcement notices – agricultural land – development orders – infill of valley to provide agricultural hardstanding**

[Town and Country Planning (General Permitted Development) Order 1995 (SI 1995 418) Part 6.]

A farmer, S, appealed against the issue of an enforcement notice following the infill of a small valley on his farm with 24,000 cubic metres of inert waste in order to produce a 0.67 hectare area of hardstanding. S contended that, under the Town and Country Planning (General Permitted Development) Order 1995 Part 6, he was permitted to erect a hardstanding area of less than half a hectare and that the inspector dealing with the appeal had accepted that the construction of a hardstanding area was reasonably necessary. Further, if the inspector had compared what had actually been constructed with what S could have lawfully constructed under the Order without obtaining planning permission, the difference was negligible and should have prompted the inspector to consider quashing the enforcement notice.

Held, dismissing the appeal, that those arguments had not been suggested to the inspector and he was not to be expected to have raised them himself. In any event, even if the inspector had concluded that a hardstanding of less than half of one hectare was required for agricultural purposes, there was no reason why the infill of a valley should have been necessary to achieve the desired result.

SCOTT v. SECRETARY OF STATE FOR THE ENVIRONMENT, TRANSPORT AND THE REGIONS (ENFORCEMENT NOTICE); SCOTT v. CHESHIRE CC C/2000/0202, C/2000/0203, Schiemann, L.J., CA.

4690. **Enforcement notices – agricultural land – validity unaffected by technical deficiency**

[Town and Country Planning Act 1990 s.179(2).]

A local authority, EHDC, served an enforcement notice on a builder, B, requiring the removal of building materials and waste from land to the rear of B's home. B failed to comply and was subsequently charged and convicted of an offence of failing to comply with an enforcement notice contrary to the Town and Country Planning Act 1990 s.179(2). B appealed, contending that (1) the justices had erred in rejecting his submission that the enforcement notice had been rendered void by the inclusion of B's dwelling house on an attached plan and the failure to specify the precise boundaries of the land which comprised the subject matter of the notice, and (2) the justices were not entitled on the basis of the available evidence to conclude that the items on site amounted to building materials or waste.

Held, dismissing the appeal, that (1) it was a nonsense to suggest that an error in drawing a red line on the notice meant that the notice was null and void. Such an approach was contrary to the modern view that minor technical deficiencies should not defeat an otherwise clearly legitimate notice, particularly in view of the fact that B was in no doubt as to the nature of the complaint and the remedy required, *Eldon Garages Ltd v. Kingston upon Hull CBC* [1974] 1 W.L.R. 276, [1974] C.L.Y. 3740 and *West Oxfordshire DC v. Secretary of State for the Environment* (1988) 56 P. & C.R. 434, [1989] C.L.Y. 3553 considered, and (2) to be satisfied that the offence charged had been committed, the justices were concerned to ascertain that on at least one of the dates specified, building materials and waste had been deposited on the land at the rear of B's property.

The evidence in support of such a conclusion, including photographic evidence, had been compelling and had established the offence to the requisite standard of proof.

BRACKEN v. EAST HERTFORDSHIRE DC [2000] P.L.C.R. 434, Roch, L.J., QBD.

4691. Enforcement notices – change of use – inspector's findings of fact – maintaining status of gypsy site after development

[Town and Country Planning Act 1990 s.289.]

H, who had been brought up as a gypsy, sited a residential caravan on land and undertook associated works. Housing needs of gypsies were a special consideration in planning in the relevant area. Council served enforcement notices on H. The inspector determined that at the time that H moved on to the land he had given up his gypsy status, intending to settle on the land and to cease altogether his nomadic lifestyle. The inspector therefore determined that for change of use purposes the application was to be considered as though H was not a gypsy. H appealed pursuant to Town and Country Planning Act 1990 s.289.

Held, dismissing the appeal, that (1) to change status from gypsy, a person must intend not only to settle, but to give up nomadic life altogether. It was insufficient that the person intended to settle somewhere permanently, as having a permanent base was inconsistent with a nomadic lifestyle, *Greenwich LBC v. Powell* [1989] A.C. 995, [1989] C.L.Y. 2293 considered, and (2) in assessing planning applications for gypsy sites, the question was whether the development was for someone who was going to retain his gypsy status, and not whether an applicant was a gypsy at the time of the application, *Runnymede BC v. Secretary of State for the Environment* [1992] J.P.L. 178, [1992] C.L.Y. 4247 not followed.

HEARNE v. NATIONAL ASSEMBLY FOR WALES; *sub nom.* HEARNE v. SECRETARY OF STATE FOR WALES [2000] J.P.L. 161, Collins, J., QBD.

4692. Enforcement notices – change of use – previous lawful use as residential accommodation

[Town and Country Planning Act 1990 s.171B.]

B appealed against the dismissal of his appeal against an enforcement notice relating to an alleged breach of planning law over the change of use of the whole of an agricultural storage building into a residential dwelling. B submitted that having lived in part of the building longer than the period of four years required under the Town and Country Planning Act 1990 s.171B, the initial change of use of part of the building had become lawful and the inspector had erred in thinking that such part use was insufficient to establish change of use to a residential dwelling.

Held, allowing the appeal, that the enforcement notice was too wide and was more than was necessary to prevent the breach of planning control in that it prevented reversion to the lawful use of part of the building for residential purposes. The decision was referred back to the Secretary of State.

BAKER v. SECRETARY OF STATE FOR THE ENVIRONMENT, TRANSPORT AND THE REGIONS, [2001] EWHC Admin 39, (2001) 82 P. & C.R. 24, Elias, J., QBD (Admin Ct).

4693. Enforcement notices – change of use – right to family life – retrospective legislation

[Human Rights Act 1998 s.22(4), Sch.1 Part I Art.8.]

M appealed against the dismissal of his appeal against an enforcement notice served by the local planning authority alleging a change in use of a building, previously used as a workshop, to use for residential purposes. M submitted that (1) the inspector had failed to apply the correct test when determining whether a material change of use had taken place, having focused on the actual use of the building by M but not on the conversion work that had been carried out, and (2) since the Human Rights Act 1998 s.22(4) gave that Act retrospective effect, the issue of whether the infringement of M's right to family life under the Human Rights Act 1998 Sch.1 Part I Art.8 should be considered, such consideration only to be undertaken by the inspector who had the relevant information.

Held, dismissing the appeal, that (1) the inspector had proceeded on the basis of M's stated case and had not been required to consider conversion work, and (2) the instant proceedings had not been brought by the local authority and accordingly fell outside the parameters of s.22(4) of the 1998 Act. The enforcement process could not be viewed as a continuing process and therefore it did not constitute "proceedings brought by ... a public authority" under s.22(4). However, M would be entitled to raise arguments under Art.8 of the Convention in the event that the local authority decided to take action in the magistrates' court to ensure compliance with the enforcement notice

MABEY v. SECRETARY OF STATE FOR THE ENVIRONMENT, TRANSPORT AND THE REGIONS [2001] P.L.C.R. 26, Harrison, J., QBD (Admin Ct).

4694. Enforcement notices – defences – validity of notice – appropriateness of judicial review

See ADMINISTRATION OF JUSTICE: Palacegate Properties Ltd v. Camden LBC. §81

4695. Enforcement notices – green belt – construction of ancillary buildings – material considerations

[Town and Country Planning Act 1990 s.72(1)(a), s.177(3).]

RBC sought judicial review of a planning inspector's decision allowing an appeal against an enforcement notice requiring the demolition of ancillary buildings constructed along with a dwellinghouse on green belt land in breach of planning control. RBC submitted that the decision to quash the enforcement notice on the basis that there were special circumstances, notwithstanding that the ancillary buildings constituted inappropriate development, had been incorrect, and that the planning inspector could have achieved the same result by upholding the enforcement notice in part and imposing a condition removing GPDO rights preventing any further development. RBC relied on the Town and Country Planning Act 1990 s.177(3) and s.72(1)(a) in support of the principle that a condition might be imposed which had the effect of modifying the development, provided that it did not constitute a fundamental alteration to the proposal. The Secretary of State contended that (1) it was unclear whether the inspector was being asked to vary the notice so as to seek partial removal of the structures, or was being asked to consider total removal and then to grant permission for a varied or reduced structure, and (2) the case now being advanced by RBC contradicted evidence which it had put to the inquiry.

Held, granting the application for judicial review, that the inspector had failed to take a material consideration into account in that he had omitted to consider the option of upholding the enforcement notice in part. This failure, together with the failure to give sufficient reasons for his decision, constituted an error of law justifying the quashing of the inspector's decision.

RUNNYMEDE BC v. SECRETARY OF STATE FOR THE ENVIRONMENT, TRANSPORT AND THE REGIONS [2001] P.L.C.R. 24, Nigel MacLeod Q.C., QBD (Admin Ct).

4696. Enforcement notices – permitted development – safeguard of rights

[Town and Country Planning Act 1990 s.179; Town and Country Planning (General Permitted Development) Order 1995 (SI 1995 418) Sch.2 Part 4 Class B.]

D challenged the dismissal of his appeal ([2000] J.P.L. 704) against an enforcement notice prohibiting him from using an area of land for mixed agricultural use, car parking and Sunday markets. D had been using the land for agricultural purposes in accordance with planning controls but had subsequently, and additionally, used part of the site for car parking, markets and car boot sales despite the absence of planning permission for these activities. Pursuant to the

Town and Country Planning (General Permitted Development) Order 1995 Sch.2 Part 4 Class B, which authorised a temporary change of use for up to 28 days per annum, it was permissible to use the land for the purposes of holding car boot sales and markets for not more than 14 days in any calendar year. D contended that the inspector had erred in refusing his appeal as the enforcement notice should have been amended to safeguard his rights under the General Permitted Development Order and that, in the absence of such an amendment, he would be at risk of prosecution under the Town and Country Planning Act 1990 s.179 for non compliance with the notice.

Held, dismissing the appeal, that no enforcement notice could take away legally permitted rights of use. It had not been necessary for the enforcement notice to specify that D's rights under the General Permitted Development Order were unaffected because those rights were clearly defined by the Order itself. D was not at risk of prosecution in the absence of an amendment to the notice as, upon a proper construction of s.179, the only activities that were required to cease were those in breach of the planning permission which, in the instant case, was the use of the land for permanent markets and/or car boot sales, *R. v. Harfield* [1993] 2 P.L.R. 23, [1994] C.L.Y. 4364 and *Mansi v. Elstree Rural DC* 62 L.G.R. 172, [1964] C.L.Y. 3580 applied.

DUGUID v. SECRETARY OF STATE FOR THE ENVIRONMENT, TRANSPORT AND THE REGIONS (2001) 82 P. & C.R. 6, Ward, L.J., CA.

4697. **Enforcement notices – planning authorities – revocation of established use of certificate – reasonableness**

[Town and Country Planning Act 1990 s.191.]

W applied for a certificate of lawfulness of existing use for its activities on a site that had formerly been used as a treatment works. The application was supported by statutory declarations and an aerial photograph. The certificate was granted and issued by SCC. Subsequently an expert considered the aerial photograph and expressed doubts as to the photograph. This prompted SCC to obtain its own expert report on the aerial photograph which again case doubt on the photograph and statutory declarations. A subsequent transfer of land left W with no fixed assets and the shares in W and the site were bought by B. The council decided to revoke the certificates and sent notice to W's agents. B later informed SCC that it owned the site and had not been served with the revocation notice. SCC served enforcement notices on W. B and R, an occupier of part of the site, sought judicial review to quash the enforcement notices and challenged the decision to revoke the certificate.

Held, granting the applications, that B was the owner of the site and that notice of the proposed revocation ought to have been given to B and R. B had suffered no prejudice as it had knowledge of the material facts but R had been prejudiced as he had not been in a position to make representations against the proposed revocation of the certificate. The decision to revoke the certificate was unreasonable given the need for further investigations that had been identified by SCC's officers. Those investigations and further evidence had not been sought by SCC before its decision to revoke the certificate. As the decision to revoke the certificate had to be quashed it followed that the enforcement notices, which were predicated on the revocation of the certificate, were also liable to be quashed and set aside.

R. v. SURREY CC, *ex p.* BRIDGE COURT HOLDINGS LTD [2000] 4 P.L.R. 30, Potts, J., QBD.

4698. **Enforcement notices – time limits – incomplete interior works – effect on "substantial completion" of building operations**

[Town and Country Planning Act 1990 s.55(1), s.55(2)(a), s.171B.]

MBC, a local authority, appealed against a decision ([2001] J.P.L. 732 (Note)) allowing S's appeal against an enforcement notice in respect of the "partial erection of a dwelling house". S's appeal had been allowed on the basis that the four year limitation period under the Town and Country Planning Act 1990 s.171B had elapsed since the building operations had been "substantially completed" more than four years before the issue of proceedings. MBC contended that the limitation period had not begun to run, since when assessing whether the "building operations" had been substantially completed, the meaning of "operations" was not confined to operations which amounted to development. It argued that on such basis, the internal works which had not been completed should have been included when assessing whether or not there had been substantial completion.

Held, dismissing the appeal, that operations and works which did not amount to development within the meaning of s.55(1) and s.55(2)(a) of the Act were not to be taken into account when deciding whether there had been substantial completion for the purposes of s.171B, *Ewen Developments v. Secretary of State for the Environment* [1980] J.P.L. 404, [1980] C.L.Y. 2645 distinguished. Accordingly, incomplete internal works which, when completed, would not materially affect the external appearance of the building, did not delay the start of the four year limitation period.

SAGE v. MAIDSTONE BC; *sub nom.* SAGE v. SECRETARY OF STATE FOR THE ENVIRONMENT, TRANSPORT AND THE REGIONS, [2001] EWCA Civ 1100, [2001] 3 P.L.R. 107, Keene, L.J., CA.

4699. Enforcement notices – waste management – continued use of land without planning permission

[Town and Country Planning Act 1990 s.57.]

W appealed against the upholding of an enforcement notice which alleged that land W had used for its concrete crushing operations was used without planning permission and that all work had to be stopped, buildings removed and the land returned to agricultural use. W submitted that the inspector had failed to give adequate consideration to the area's inclusion in the waste local plan and therefore its finding that additional sites were not needed was flawed, and that further, the Town and Country Planning Act 1990 s.57 did not apply, there being no development, merely a continued use of the land throughout.

Held, dismissing the appeal, that the inspector's consideration of the need for an additional site had been sufficient, and that planning permission was necessary for the continued use of the site, *Newbury DC v. Secretary of State for the Environment* [1981] A.C. 578, [1980] C.L.Y. 2667 distinguished. Furthermore, any breach of conditions to the permission could be dealt with by enforcement action.

WIGGINS v. SECRETARY OF STATE FOR THE ENVIRONMENT, TRANSPORT AND THE REGIONS [2001] P.L.C.R. 22, Collins, J., QBD (Admin Ct).

4700. Environmental impact assessments – EC law – transposition of Directive into national law

[Town and Country Planning (Environmental Impact Assessment) (England and Wales) Regulations 1999 (SI 1999 293) Reg.4(8), Reg.9(2), Sch.2; Council Directive 85/337 on the assessment of the effects of certain public and private projects on the environment; Council Directive 97/11 on the assessment of the effects of certain public and private projects on the environment.]

B, who had objected to a development containing 30 flats, appealed against a decision ([2001] Env. L.R. 32) that the development did not require an environmental impact assessment to be carried out. B argued that (1) properly construed, the Town and Country Planning (Environmental Impact Assessment) (England and Wales) Regulations 1999 Reg.9(2) imposed a duty on an inspector to refer to the Secretary of State every application for planning permission in respect of which a plausible submission had been made that the Secretary of State might make a direction under Reg.4(8) of the Regulations. Regulation 4(8) empowered the Secretary of State to direct that a development required an environmental impact assessment despite the fact that the development did not satisfy the conditions set out in Sch.2 to the Regulations, one of which was that an urban development project had to exceed one half of a hectare in area, and (2) since the situation could arise in which it could plausibly be argued that a certain development would have serious environmental consequences without an environmental impact assessment being required under the Regulations, the Regulations had not properly transposed Council Directive 85/337, as amended by Council Directive 97/11, into national law.

Held, dismissing the appeal, that (1) the Secretary of State was not obliged to make a direction under Reg.4(8). Furthermore, a planning authority or an inspector could grant planning permission without an environmental impact assessment having been carried out even if a plausible submission had been made that the development was one in respect of which the Secretary of State could make a direction under Reg.4(8), and (2) the aim of the amended Directive was not to prevent all development likely to have a significant effect on the environment, but rather to improve the quality of decision-making in a group of cases. Annex III to the Directive set out the selection criteria to be applied by Member States in specifying the relevant parameters, and if Member States failed to apply those criteria, the relevant legislation would not comply with Community law. While the Directive did not permit the setting of criteria solely by reference to size, it did not follow that the criteria had to be expressed as referring to all of the relevant considerations. Member States were obliged to ensure that projects "likely to have significant effects on the environment" were subject to an environmental impact assessment. There was, however, no justification for concluding that the Secretary of State had failed to do that. In the instant case, the inspector had had no reason to conclude that the development would require an environmental impact assessment, and it could not be said that the decision-making process would have been significantly improved by the carrying out of such an assessment. Insofar as they concerned urban development projects, the Regulations had properly transposed the Directive, *Aannamaersbedrijf PK Kraaijveld BV v. Gedeputeerde Staten Van Zuid-Holland (C72/95)* [1997] All E.R. (EC) 134, [1997] C.L.Y. 2319 and *World Wildlife Fund (WWF) v. Autonome Provinz Bozen (C435/97)* [1999] E.C.R. I-5613, [1999] C.L.Y. 2162 applied.

BERKELEY v. SECRETARY OF STATE FOR THE ENVIRONMENT, TRANSPORT AND THE REGIONS (NO.3), [2001] EWCA Civ 1012, [2001] 3 C.M.L.R. 11, Schiemann, L.J., CA.

4701. **Environmental impact assessments – reserved matters – consideration – relationship between grant of outline permission and approval of reserved matters**

In March 1998 BLBC granted outline planning permission for the construction of leisure and recreational facilities in Crystal Palace Park. Detailed proposals submitted by the applicant under the "reserved matters" procedure were approved by BLBC in May 1999. In June 1999 B applied for judicial review referring to both decisions in her application notice. She argued that BLBC had failed to (1) give proper consideration to the need for an environmental assessment; (2) realise that it could control the scale of the development at the "reserved matters" stage, and (3) have regard to a ministerial statement and Government White Paper which had been published after the grant of outline permission, when considering the matters which had been reserved. Permission to move for judicial review having been granted, BLBC applied to set aside that permission. BLBC argued that B had been out of time in challenging the grant of outline permission, that she had failed to explain the reasons for her delay in applying, and that she had failed to disclose the extent of her knowledge of the grant of outline permission.

Held, setting aside the permission to move for judicial review in so far as it related to the grant of outline permission and refusing the application for judicial review, that (1) concerning the grant of outline permission, B had failed in her application notice to deal adequately with the question of delay, to request an extension of time, and to set out the reasons why an extension of time should be granted. Furthermore, it would not be appropriate to allow B to challenge the grant of outline permission since (a) the delay had been lengthy, (b) no good reason had been given for extending time, (c) having incurred substantial expenditure in reliance on the grant of outline permission, the applicant would be significantly prejudiced, and (d) the grant of outline permission had been challenged, albeit on different grounds, in separate judicial review proceedings, (2) in the case of an urban development project, the necessity for an environmental assessment fell to be considered at the stage when outline permission was under consideration and did not arise when reserved matters came to be considered, *R. v. Hammersmith and Fulham LBC, ex p. CPRE London Branch (Costs Order)* [2000] Env. L.R. 544 followed. BLBC had decided when outline permission was being considered that an environmental assessment was not necessary, and (3) once outline permission had been granted, the applicant had established his right to carry out the development and was entitled to expect that he would secure approval for a scheme which accorded with the permission, any changes in government policy occurring after the grant of permission would not justify a departure from the matters which had been approved by virtue of that permission. In any event, the Parliamentary statement was not relevant to the matters which had been reserved, and the Government White Paper had not been contravened by BLBC.

R. (ON THE APPLICATION OF BARKER) v. BROMLEY LBC; *sub nom.* R. v. BROMLEY LBC, *ex p.* BARKER; R. v. BROMLEY LBC, *ex p.* BAKER [2001] Env. L.R. 1, Jackson, J., QBD.

4702. **Environmental protection – criminal conduct – issue of certificate of lawful use – public policy considerations**

[Town and Country Planning Act 1990 s.191; Environmental Protection Act 1990 s.33.]

P appealed against the dismissal of his application for judicial review ([2000] Env. L.R. 745) of EF's decision to grant a certificate of lawful use pursuant to the Town and Country Planning Act 1990 s.191 in relation to land used for the breaking of vehicles. The certificate had been granted notwithstanding the fact that the operation had been carried out without a waste management licence in contravention of the Environmental Protection Act 1990 s.33. P contended that s.191 could not certify criminal acts as lawful and that to permit it to do so would be in breach of the fundamental principle that the law should not operate so as to enable an individual to profit from his own crime.

Held, dismissing the appeal, that the general principle of public policy relied upon was not applicable to an instance where Parliament had clearly stipulated which activities were lawful. The meaning of s.191(2) was clear and had been intended to render lawful those acts which would otherwise have been criminal under the Environmental Protection Act in order to remove the anomaly that had previously existed of acts which were unlawful but immune from enforcement owing to the passage of time, *R. v. Chief National Insurance Commissioner, ex p. Connor* [1981] Q.B. 758, [1981] C.L.Y. 2619 and *Glamorgan CC v. Carter* [1963] 1 W.L.R. 1, [1962] C.L.Y. 3002 considered.

R. (ON THE APPLICATION OF PHILCOX) v. EPPING FOREST DC; *sub nom.* R. v. EPPING FOREST DC, *ex p.* PHILCOX (CERTIFICATE: UNLAWFUL GRANTING); EPPING FOREST DC v. PHILCOX [2002] Env. L.R. 2, Pill, L.J., CA.

4703. **Footpaths – extinguishment – lack of use owing to sea erosion**

A local authority, GCC, challenged a decision of the planning inspector that a riverside footpath, which was so badly eroded as to have disappeared in parts, should not be extinguished. GCC argued that (1) the cost of reinstatement was disproportionate to the possible advantage to a small section of the public, who, on the evidence, were likely to use the path, and was thus an unreasonable use of public funds; (2) it was under a duty only to repair the highway and not to prevent erosion; (3) members of the public were not entitled to deviate onto adjacent land along the riverbank as a consequence of the footpath being eroded, there being no such thing in law as a moving right of way. A right to deviate only existed where the adjoining landowner was at fault in failing to repair a footpath.

Held, granting the application for judicial review, that (1) the public right over part of a highway had a defined route which could not be lost by lack of use, but could be by physical destruction; (2) there was no authority to support the proposition that a right to deviate arose upon the destruction, rather than obstruction, of a right of way, therefore the public had no right to deviate onto the nearest path; (3) there was no evidence that a moving right of way existed in law, and for one to arise there would have to be some new factor of usage or dedication, and the inspector had been wrong to find that the path still existed on a different alignment and was likely to be used by the public.

R. (ON THE APPLICATION OF GLOUCESTER CC) v. SECRETARY OF STATE FOR THE ENVIRONMENT, TRANSPORT AND THE REGIONS; *sub nom.* R. (ON THE APPLICATION OF GLOUCESTERSHIRE CC) v. SECRETARY OF STATE FOR THE ENVIRONMENT, TRANSPORT AND THE REGIONS; R. v. SECRETARY OF STATE FOR THE ENVIRONMENT, TRANSPORT AND THE REGIONS, *ex p.* GLOUCESTERSHIRE CC (2001) 82 P. & C.R. 15, Hallett, J., QBD (Admin Ct).

4704. Footpaths – local authorities powers and duties – extinguishment – lack of use owing to sea erosion

See PLANNING: R. (on the application of Gloucester CC) v. Secretary of State for the Environment, Transport and the Regions. §4703

4705. Green belt – agricultural land – construction of equestrian centre – characteristics of "agricultural use"

SS sought judicial review of the grant of planning permission for the construction of an equestrian centre in an area of green belt land. SS contended that SDC erred in granting permission in that (1) the development constituted inappropriate development in a green belt area justifiable only on the basis that very special circumstances existed, but the planning officer had wrongly advised the relevant committee that the absence of any highway objection on two previous occasions could amount to a very special circumstance, and (2) the planning officer had erred in advising the planning committee that the proposed use of the centre was a use related to agriculture for the purposes of PPG2 para.1.6.

Held, granting the application, that (1) the proposals clearly amounted to inappropriate development in a green belt area requiring the existence of very special circumstances to justify the grant of permission. Very special circumstances had been established but not on the basis that there had been no prior highway objections. When the previous proposals had been submitted, the only objections had concerned highways and there had, significantly, been no objection on green belt grounds. The highway objection had since been resolved and, therefore, the relevant criteria had been satisfied, and (2) the proposed use, involving as it did the all round training and stabling of thoroughbred horses, could not be viewed as related to an agricultural use so as to fall with PPG2 para.1.6.

R. v. SELBY DC, *ex p.* SAMUEL SMITH OLD BREWERY LTD [2001] P.L.C.R. 6, Harrison, J., QBD.

4706. Green belt – gypsies – injunctive relief available for breach

[Town and Country Planning Act 1990 s.187B.]

C, owners of a designated green belt site, sought to challenge the dismissal of their application for judicial review of a decision of RBBC to seek injunctive relief under the Town and Country Planning Act 1990 s.187B. The injunction sought to prevent the development of the land in accordance with local planning policy implemented to protect the area from urban sprawl and C had received a previous written warning with respect to the limitations on development. C contended that (1) RBBC's decision was premature in the light of their application for planning consent which, if approved, would have made their action lawful, (2) on the authority of *City of London Corp v. Bovis Construction Ltd* [1992] 3 All E.R. 697, [1989] C.L.Y. 3133 cited, an injunction should have been granted only where there was a grave risk of irreparable harm and not for a mere infringement of planning law, and (3) RBBC gave insufficient consideration to humanitarian factors such as the size and age range of the family.

Held, dismissing the appeal that the only condition imposed upon RBBC by Parliament was that it had to consider the restraint of the breach to be necessary in its application for an injunction and the humanitarian factors were taken into account by RBBC's planning officer before a decision was made.

CONNORS v. REIGATE AND BANSTEAD BC [2000] J.P.L. 1178 (Note), Beldam, L.J., CA.

4707. Green belt – gypsies – planning permission for caravan site – right to family life

[European Convention on Human Rights 1950 Art.8.]

A case concerning Mr and Mrs V, who were gypsies by birth, was referred to the European Court of Human Rights following the refusal of the Secretary of State to grant planning permission for a gypsy caravan site. The planning inspector had repeatedly recommended that permission be granted, but the Secretary of State had dismissed all appeals on public policy grounds, fearing an increase in applications. The proposed site was within a green belt and it had been decided that V's needs did not override the stringent policy controls in the area. The inspector had recommended that permission be granted, as the site was well maintained and the impact of the site would be lessened by the construction of a prison and roads nearby. The Secretary of State had, however, maintained that the area would be damaged by the development. The former European Commission of Human Rights had declared the refusal to be in breach of the European Convention on Human Rights 1950 Art.8, the right to family life.

Held, striking the case from the list, that a settlement agreement reached between the United Kingdom and V had resolved the matter and continuing examination of the application was not necessary. The Court was satisfied that the agreement reflected a respect for human rights.

VAREY v. UNITED KINGDOM (26662/95) *The Times*, January 30, 2001, L Wildhaber (President), ECHR.

4708. Green belt – gypsies – relevance of personal circumstances – material considerations

BDC appealed against a decision of the Secretary of State to allow an appeal by gypsies, A, S and B, against a refusal of planning permission for residential caravans in a green belt area. BDC contended that (1) the personal circumstances of the families concerned were irrelevant; (2) the decision had been irrational since the caravans constituted inappropriate development, and (3) even if relevant, the personal circumstances of the families concerned could not outweigh the inevitable and substantial harm to the green belt.

Held, dismissing the appeal, that (1) the personal circumstances and educational needs of the families concerned were material considerations; (2) there was no requirement in law that the circumstances of the applicants had to be exceptional amongst the general gypsy population, *Westminster City Council v. Great Portland Estates Plc* [1985] A.C. 661, [1984] C.L.Y. 3413 considered, and (3) the weight to be attached to such considerations was a matter for the Secretary of State and depended upon the circumstances of each individual case.

BASILDON DC v. SECRETARY OF STATE FOR THE ENVIRONMENT, TRANSPORT AND THE REGIONS [2001] J.P.L. 1184, Ouseley, J., QBD (Admin Ct).

4709. Green belt – motorways – policy for development of motorway service stations on Green Belt land

G appealed against the refusal of the Secretary of State to grant planning permission for the proposed extension to two Travelodges at a motorway service station in an area of green belt. G contended that the Secretary of States's reliance on the inspector's finding that there was no unusually high incidence of driver fatigue on that section of motorway was unfair, inconsistent and represented a change of policy.

Held, dismissing the appeal, that it had not been unlawful for the Secretary of State to accept the inspector's conclusion in relation to driver fatigue, that point having been raised by G at the inquiry, nor to find that there were no special factors that justified development within the green belt.

GRANADA HOSPITALITY LTD v. SECRETARY OF STATE FOR THE ENVIRONMENT, TRANSPORT AND THE REGIONS (2001) 81 P. & C.R. 36, Collins, J., QBD.

4710. Land drainage – Internal Drainage Boards – reorganisation – Buckingham and River Ouzel

AMALGAMATION OF THE BUCKINGHAM AND RIVER OUZEL INTERNAL DRAINAGE DISTRICTS ORDER 2001, SI 2001 2886; made under the Land Drainage Act 1991 s.3, Sch.3. In force: August 8, 2001; £1.75.

This Order confirms a Scheme submitted by the Environment Agency for the abolition of the Buckingham and River Ouzel Internal Drainage Boards. These Boards are replaced by a new "Buckingham and River Ouzel Inernal Drainage Board" and two former internal drainage districts are amalgamated together to form the corresponding new internal drainage district.

4711. Land drainage – Internal Drainage Boards – reorganisation – Denge and Southbrooks, Pett, Romney Marsh Levels, Rother and Walland Marsh

AMALGAMATION OF THE DENGE AND SOUTHBROOKS, PETT, ROMNEY MARSH LEVELS, ROTHER AND WALLAND MARSH INTERNAL DRAINAGE DISTRICTS ORDER 2000 2001, SI 2001 646; made under the Land Drainage Act 1991 s.3, Sch.3. In force: March 1, 2001; £2.00.

This Order confirms a Scheme submitted by the Environment Agency for the abolition of the Denge and Southbrooks, Pett, Romney Marsh Levels, Rother and Walland Marsh Internal Drainage Boards and replaces these boards with a new "Romney Marshes Area Internal Drainage Board". The five former internal drainage districts are amalgamated to form the corresponding new internal drainage district.

4712. Land drainage – Internal Drainage Boards – reorganisation – South Gloucestershire and West Gloucestershire

AMALGAMATION OF THE SOUTH GLOUCESTERSHIRE AND WEST GLOUCESTERSHIRE INTERNAL DRAINAGE DISTRICTS ORDER 2000 2001, SI 2001 647; made under the Land Drainage Act 1991 s.3, Sch.3. In force: March 1, 2001; £1.75.

This Order confirms a Scheme submitted by the Environment Agency for the abolition of the South Gloucestershire and West Gloucestershire Internal Drainage Boards and replaces these boards with a new "Lower Severn Internal Drainage Board". The two former internal drainage districts are amalgamated to form the corresponding new internal drainage district.

4713. Land use – lawful use certificates – entitlement to certificate where planning approval outstanding

[Town and Country Planning Act 1990 s.191, s.192.]

BA, a local authority applied to quash the Secretary of State's decision to grant a certificate of lawful use following the construction by DP of a dyke used to moor boats at the site of a holiday village. BA had previously refused to issue a certificate, which decision was initially upheld on appeal by the Secretary of State, on the grounds that the dyke had been unlawfully constructed, because outline permission was insufficient; alternatively, even if full permission was to be implied, then the cutting of the dyke had still infringed a condition of it. BA had maintained that if the permission to be considered was valid, then construction of the dyke was to be viewed as severable from the remainder of the development, outline permission relating to the latter having lapsed, since approval had not been sought from the planning authority for reserved matters before the deadline specified for doing so. Following a re-determination, which resulted in a finding that the combination of two permissions rendered the construction of the dyke lawful, and that the remainder of the development was ancillary to such construction, the certificate had been granted under the Town and Country Planning Act 1990 s.192. BA contended that (1) s.192 of the Act was not intended to legalise a development when, by virtue of the permission itself, planning authority approval was required before the proposed uses could commence; (2) the certificate was invalid because it purported to have been issued under s.191 of the Act, not s.192, which was the correct section on the facts, and (3) there was no basis in law for a "hybrid" permission which could validate ancillary development.

Held, refusing the application, that (1) it was intended that s.192 would avoid the need to apply to the court to establish planning permission, and given that the certificate did not suggest that development could take place without the permission conditions being satisfied, there was no justification for construing the Act as precluding a certificate of lawfulness on the ground that an outstanding approval had yet to be sought; (2) the reference to s.191 of the Act, although repeated, was a procedural error, which had not resulted in prejudice to BA. The ensuing certificate communicated the essential point, and did not have to be in any specific form *R. v. Secretary of State for the Home Department, ex p. Jeyeanthan* [2000] 1 W.L.R. 354, [1999] C.L.Y. 3162 referred to, and (3) the Secretary of State's decision that the dyke and the rest of the development were linked was merely a common sense conclusion, which he was entitled to reach, and which was not to be interpreted as a technical judgment *Salisbury DC v. Secretary of State for the Environment* [1982] J.P.L. 702, [1982] C.L.Y. 3201 referred to.

BROADS AUTHORITY v. SECRETARY OF STATE FOR THE ENVIRONMENT, TRANSPORT AND THE REGIONS (2001) 81 P. & C.R. 3, Nigel MacLeod Q.C., QBD.

4714. **Land use – purchase notices – land capable of reasonably beneficial use – works required prior to use – alternative uses for land**

[Town and Country Planning Act 1990 s.137, s.138, Sch.3.]

H appealed against a decision of the Secretary of State refusing to confirm a purchase notice which had been served on WDC pursuant to the Town and Country Planning Act 1990 s.137 and s.138 and which related to a plot of land which H owned. H contended that the Secretary of State, in concluding that the land was capable of reasonably beneficial use in its existing state if used in conjunction with intervening land for horse grazing purposes, had erred in (1) considering the state of the land after the carrying out of potential works, rather than in its current state which was unsuitable for grazing purposes, and (2) failing to take into account the existing right under s.138 to rebuild houses on the land.

Held, dismissing the appeal, that (1) the Act envisaged the decision maker considering not merely the present state but also the potential state of the land, taking any necessary work into consideration. Even if that interpretation was incorrect, the decision of the Secretary of State could not be impugned as having been *Wednesbury* unreasonable, *Adams & Wade Ltd v. Minister of Housing and Local Government* (1967) 18 P. & C.R. 60, [1967] C.L.Y. 3850 applied, and (2) the right to rebuild houses under Sch.3 of the Act was not relevant. As the land was capable of one form of beneficial use, it was unnecessary to consider other possible uses, and even if it were necessary, consideration of the right to rebuild only served to fortify the decision reached.

HUDSCOTT ESTATES (EAST) LTD v. SECRETARY OF STATE FOR THE ENVIRONMENT, TRANSPORT AND THE REGIONS (2001) 82 P. & C.R. 8, Silber, J., QBD (Admin Ct).

4715. Listed buildings – consent void for mistake – injunction of unauthorised works – competence

[Planning (Listed Buildings and Conservation Areas) Act 1990; Town and Country Planning Act 1990 s.44A(1).]

In 1988 planning permission and listed building consent were granted by FDC in respect of properties owned by RR. In 1993 consent was given to applications for revised planning permission and listed building consent. FDC omitted to advise the Secretary of State of the 1993 application for listed building consent pursuant to the Planning (Listed Buildings and Conservation Areas) Act 1990. After discovering its mistake FDC wrote to RR advising them that the purported grant of listed building consent in 1993 was in fact void and threatening prosecution if work did not cease immediately. RR refused to accede to this request and FDC obtained an interlocutory injunction. RR appealed, contending that in accordance with the dicta in *O'Reilly v. Mackman* [1983] 2 A.C. 237, [1982] C.L.Y. 2603, FDC were constrained to seek judicial review of the 1993 consent rather than pursue an injunction application under the Town and Country Planning Act 1990 s.44A(1).

Held, dismissing the appeal, that (1) there was nothing to prevent a local authority from seeking an injunction under s.44A(1) based upon the fact that damage to a listed building was imminent, simply because the unauthorised works or damage resulted from a mistake by the planning authority, and (2) an application for judicial review would not have been an appropriate form of remedy since FDC had not been seeking to challenge their 1993 decision but rather to stop any further unauthorised works, *O'Reilly* considered.

FENLAND DC v. RUEBEN ROSE (PROPERTIES) LTD; *sub nom.* FENLAND DC v. REUBEN ROSE (PROPERTIES) LTD [2000] P.L.C.R. 376, Judge, L.J., CA.

4716. Listed buildings – demolition – authorisation of works

AUTHORISATION OF WORKS (LISTED BUILDINGS) (ENGLAND) ORDER 2001, SI 2001 24; made under the Planning (Listed Buildings and Conservation Areas) Act 1990 s.8, s.93. In force: February 19, 2001; £1.50.

This Order, which applies to works for the demolition of a listed building executed on or after February 19, 2001, substitutes "the Commission" for each of the references in the Planning (Listed Buildings and Conservation Areas) Act 1990 s.8(2) to "the Royal Commission". Any proposal to execute works for the demolition of a listed building under s.8(2)(b) has to be given to English Heritage instead of the Royal Commission. Also, after such notice is given, members or officers of English Heritage have to be given access to the building for at least one month after listed building consent is granted but before works commence for the purpose of recording it. Alternatively, English Heritage have to state in writing that they have completed their recording of the building or do not wish to record it.

4717. Listed buildings – garages – failure to advertise application for requisite period

[Planning (Listed Buildings and Conservation Areas) Act 1990 s.66(1), s.67(2); Town and Country Planning (General Development Procedure) Order 1995 (SI 1995 419) Art.8(5).]

P, who lived in a grade II listed building in the grounds of a historic country hall which was also a listed building, sought to quash a decision of BDC, the local planning authority, to grant permission to the owner of the hall for the construction of a new brick garage next to P's home, the original wooden garage having been demolished. P contended that (1) BDC had failed to display a notice on or near to the site for a period of not less than 21 days as required by the Town and Country Planning (General Development Procedure) Order 1995 Art.8(5) and had failed to place a notice in a local newspaper in accordance with the Planning (Listed Buildings and Conservation Areas) Act 1990 s.67(2) with the result that he had been unable to table objections to the proposals at an early stage, and (2) BDC were under a duty, arising from s.66(1) of the Act, to consider the impact of the garage on P's home as a listed building but had, in fact, only considered the impact upon the hall. BDC argued that, whilst they had been unable to show that the requisite notice had been given, the court should exercise its discretion not to quash the grant of planning permission as P had suffered no prejudice and the same decision would have been taken had P been able to make objections to the proposals.

Held, granting the application for judicial review and quashing the grant of planning permission, that the evidence indicated that BDC must have considered the impact of the proposed development on P's property and that the decision may have been unaffected by P's objections. Nonetheless, the failure of BDC to notify P and their refusal to adjourn the matter, following P's request for more time in order to take expert advice, meant that P had been denied the opportunity to present his case.

R. v. BOLSOVER DC, *ex p.* PATERSON [2001] J.P.L. 211, Collins, J., QBD.

4718. Local plans – local authorities powers and duties – power to withdraw prior to consultation

[Town and Country Planning Act 1990 s.34; The Town and Country Planning (Development Plan) (England) Regulations 1999 (SI 1999 3280) Reg.25(1).]

P applied for judicial review of NHDC's decision to withdraw its local plan proposals, notice of which had been given under The Town and Country Planning (Development Plan) (England) Regulations 1999 Reg.25(1). P argued that no power existed under which the plan could be withdrawn or abandoned and that Reg.25(1), which established the procedure following the decision to withdraw, had been erroneously enacted. It was submitted that, as express powers existed under the Town and Country Planning Act 1990 s.34 to withdraw structure plans, in contrast to the lack of powers regarding local plans, such a power should not be implied, but only arose prior to adoption following consultation.

Held, refusing the application, that it was absurd that a local plan should undergo lengthy and expensive consideration when the local authority knew that it was going to be abandoned. The establishment of notice procedures within the regulations suggested that it was expected that the local authority would be able to withdraw plans prior to the consultation stage and therefore it was appropriate to imply terms rendering the authority's actions lawful.

R. (ON THE APPLICATION OF PERSIMMON HOMES (THAMES VALLEY) LTD) v. NORTH HERTFORDSHIRE DC; *sub nom.* PERSIMMON HOMES (THAMES VALLEY) LTD v. NORTH HERTFORDSHIRE DC, [2001] EWHC Admin 565, [2001] 1 W.L.R. 2393, Collins, J., QBD (Admin Ct).

4719. Local plans – planning policy guidance – size thresholds for social housing – Secretary of State's discretion

S sought to quash a decision of the Secretary of State directing S to modify its local plan so as to increase the size threshold of land on which affordable housing was to be developed, to reflect the guidance given in a Government Circular 6/98. S submitted that the decision was perverse and ran contrary to planning policy guidance contained in PPG3, which required the housing needs of the whole community to be met, since S would be prevented from supplying the amount of affordable housing needed. It was further argued that the Secretary of State had unlawfully fettered his discretion by failing to have regard to local circumstances ascertainable from the material evidence, when contending that a threshold of less that 0.5 of a hectare would deter developers from developing sites. It was contended that in placing reliance on the flawed findings of a planning inspector the Secretary of State's decision had been based on speculation and guesswork

Held, refusing the application, that the Secretary of State had not unlawfully fettered his discretion by following a predetermined rule of policy, since when deciding whether to depart from the guidance he had considered whether the local circumstances justified the imposition of a lower threshold and concluded that they did not and the reasons given could not be criticised as ambiguous or unintelligible. Neither had the decision been perverse since prediction for the future necessarily involved speculative judgments based on experience. The Secretary of State had been entitled to consider wider planning issues when exercising his wide discretion as to site size thresholds, such considerations not being limited to individual counties.

R. (ON THE APPLICATION OF SPELTHORNE BC) v. SECRETARY OF STATE FOR THE ENVIRONMENT, TRANSPORT AND THE REGIONS (2001) 82 P. & C.R. 10, Harrison, J., QBD (Admin Ct).

4720. **Local plans – planning procedures – failure to adopt recommendations of public enquiry**

[Town and Country Planning Act 1990 s.287.]

FC, which wanted to expand its port and entrepot operation, appealed against the refusal ([2001] EWHC Admin 19) of its application made under the Town and Country Planning Act 1990 s.287 to quash sections of the local plan adopted by the local authority following the requisite public enquiry. FC submitted that the judge had erred in law in deciding that the local authority was neither *Wednesbury* unreasonable nor perverse in holding that a further enquiry into the provisions of the local plan was unnecessary.

Held, dismissing the appeal, that the decision of the local authority not to hold a further enquiry following its decision to disregard the recommendations of the inspector appointed to administer the local enquiry, was neither perverse nor irrational and, given the mistaken basis on which the inspector had compiled his report, it was not *Wednesbury* unreasonable. It was also noted, obiter, that for an application under s.287 of the Act, the parts of the local plan that an applicant wanted quashed had to be specified and although quashing might be the logical remedy in instances where the error complained of related to the adopted proposals, if the complaint was an error in procedure, as in the instant case, it was an inappropriate remedy. Had there been a public law error, a declaration by the court or a remission to the local authority might have been an appropriate remedy, however neither was available under s.287.

FIRST CORPORATE SHIPPING LTD (T/A BRISTOL PORT CO) v. NORTH SOMERSET COUNCIL, [2001] EWCA Civ 693, [2002] P.L.C.R. 7, Buxton, L.J., CA.

4721. **Permitted development – agricultural land – accommodation of livestock**

[Town and Country Planning (General Permitted Development) Order 1995 (SI 1995 418).]

The Secretary of State appealed against the decision (Times, January 30, 2001) allowing T's appeal against enforcement notices issued in respect of his land. T, a sheep farmer, had brought waste materials onto his land and built areas of hardstanding and a roadway. The notices were issued on the basis that the works and the importation of waste materials were unauthorised. T had appealed to a planning inspector on the ground that the development was "reasonably necessary for the purposes of agriculture" and therefore permitted by the Town and Country Planning (General Permitted Development) Order 1995. The inspector had, however, upheld the enforcement notices. In allowing his appeal from that decision, the judge had found that the inspector had wrongly held that part of the works were used for the accommodation of livestock and that she should have allowed T to keep such of the materials that had been used for reasonable agricultural purposes and remove the rest.

Held, allowing the appeal, that the judge had erred in finding that the inspector should have made amendments to the notices. T had not made specific submissions to the inspector as to which areas of the works he would wish to keep in order to bring them within the permitted size limit of 465 square meters set by the Order. The judge had given too narrow an interpretation to the word "accommodate" which could mean "suitable for". The limitations on the size of land used for the "accommodation of livestock" under the Order were not confined to works for habitation and included all provisions of work suitable for livestock use. The inspector had therefore been right to hold that use of the hardstanding for the feeding of sheep amounted to accommodation of livestock.

TAYLOR & SONS (FARMS) v. SECRETARY OF STATE FOR THE ENVIRONMENT, TRANSPORT AND THE REGIONS; *sub nom.* R. (ON THE APPLICATION OF TAYLOR (T/A DAVID TAYLOR & SONS (FARMS))) v. SECRETARY OF STATE FOR THE ENVIRONMENT, TRANSPORT AND THE REGIONS, [2001] EWCA Civ 1254, [2002] P.L.C.R. 11, Schiemann, L.J., CA.

4722. **Permitted development – engineering operation – invalid determination by inspector – unfair to rely on alternative basis for decision**

[Town and Country Planning Act 1990 s.55(2)(g), s.191(2); Town and Country Planning (General Permitted Development) Order 1995 (SI 1995 418) Sch.2 Part 31 Class B.]

CDC applied for a review of the decision of the Secretary of State that the removal of a Cornish hedge bank to enable a cottage extension was lawful for the purposes of the Town and Country Planning Act 1990 s.191(2) (as amended), as it constituted permitted development. The inspector had erred in finding that the Town and Country Planning (General Permitted Development) Order 1995 Sch.2 Part 31 Class B applied to the works which constituted a permitted development as he had identified the works as an "engineering operation" rather than a "building operation" to which the order applied. However, the Secretary of State contended that this did not invalidate the decision as there was an independent basis that could be relied upon as the works constituted the demolition of an enclosure for the purposes of s.55(2)(g) of the 1990 Act and therefore planning permission was not required. CDC submitted that as the ground relied upon had not been put to the planning inspector they had not been allowed to address that contention, and the inspector had not given reasons to justify his decision based on the alternative ground.

Held, granting the application, that it would be wrong to uphold the decision of the inspector on the alternative basis argued for by the Secretary State and the decision was therefore quashed and the matter remitted to the Secretary of State for further consideration.

CARADON DC v. SECRETARY OF STATE FOR THE ENVIRONMENT, TRANSPORT AND THE REGIONS [2001] P.L.C.R. 18, David Pannick Q.C., QBD.

4723. **Permitted development – land use – intermittent use – permanent physical changes to landscape**

[Town and Country Planning Act 1990 s.192(1); Town and Country Planning (General Permitted Development) Order 1995 (SI 1995 418) Sch.2 Part 4 Art.3, Class B.]

R appealed against a decision to uphold the refusal of his application for the grant of a lawful development certificate under the Town and Country Planning Act 1990 s.192(1) in relation to the use of agricultural land as a motorcycle scramble track for 28 days per year. R maintained that he was not required to seek planning permission since the proposed temporary use fell within the remit of the Town and Country Planning (General Permitted Development) Order 1995 Sch.2 Part 4 Art.3 and Sch.2 Part 4 Class B. The local authority argued that the proposal involved a permanent change of use from single to mixed user, albeit that one use was seasonal in nature, and that permanent physical changes to the landscape were involved.

Held, dismissing the appeal, that the usage proposed by R did not fall within the scope of the 1995 Order. Despite the fact that the change of use involved a period of limited duration, such a consideration was not conclusive. The inspector had been entitled to take into account the fact that the layout of the land, following works undertaken by R resulting in permanent physical changes, made it particularly suited to the proposed use. The Order did not carry the right to carry out physical works to the land and the proposed change would amount to a permanent, though intermittent use in relation to which an express grant of planning permission was required, *Tidswell v. Secretary of State for the Environment* (1976) 34 P. & C.R. 152, [1978] C.L.Y. 2877 considered..

RAMSEY v. SECRETARY OF STATE FOR THE ENVIRONMENT, TRANSPORT AND THE REGIONS; *sub nom.* RAMSAY v. SECRETARY OF STATE FOR THE ENVIRONMENT, TRANSPORT AND THE REGIONS, [2001] EWHC Admin 277, *The Times*, May 15, 2001, Scott Baker, J., QBD (Admin Ct).

4724. Planning appeals – claim forms – permission sought unnecessarily – discretion to allow amendment

See CIVIL PROCEDURE: Thurrock BC v. Secretary of State for the Environment, Transport and the Regions (No.1). §415

4725. Planning applications – Secretary of State for Transport – power to withdraw or revoke "call in" direction

[Town and Country Planning Act 1990 s.77.]

T sought judicial review of a decision by the Secretary of State to withdraw a "call in" direction made pursuant to the Town and Country Planning Act 1990 s.77 following an application by B to conduct quarrying operations in the Lake District. T contended that the purported withdrawal was ultra vires in the absence of any express statutory power of withdrawal.

Held, refusing the application, that it was implicit within s.77 that the Secretary of State possessed the power to revoke or withdraw a "call in" direction. Sound practical reasons existed for such a conclusion. The absence of such a power would mean that following such a direction the Secretary of State was obliged to determine the application even if there had been a change in circumstances and to do so would be contrary to his own departmental policy. The Secretary of State would also be obliged to conduct a public inquiry in circumstances where there was no need for an inquiry. Such an outcome could not be an accurate reflection of Parliamentary intention. Furthermore, the power was a procedural power which only determined the decision maker and not the outcome of the application itself. Accordingly the very nature of the power indicated that it should not be irrevocable.

R. (ON THE APPLICATION OF TRUSTEES OF THE FRIENDS OF THE LAKE DISTRICT) v. SECRETARY OF STATE FOR THE ENVIRONMENT, TRANSPORT AND THE REGIONS; *sub nom.* TRUSTEES OF THE FRIENDS OF THE LAKE DISTRICT v. SECRETARY OF STATE FOR THE ENVIRONMENT, TRANSPORT AND THE REGIONS, [2001] EWHC Admin 281, [2002] 1 P. & C.R. 23, Harrison, J., QBD (Admin Ct).

4726. Planning applications – ultra vires acts – refusal to quash unlawful planning decision – compensation

C, a councillor, appealed against a refusal ([2001] J.P.L. 445) to quash a planning permission granted by RBC in 1997. The permission had been granted in breach of RBC's obligation to refer a proposed departure from the Development Plan to the Secretary of State, and to order the substitution of a modified permission. C contended that the unlawful planning decision should have been quashed unless the party resisting such an order could establish some detriment resulting from it, and that since the owners of the land in question had never had the benefit of any lawfully granted permission they should not be entitled to compensation from RBC.

Held, dismissing the appeal, that the court was entitled to exercise its discretion afresh, but since the dispute was essentially about compensation and none of the facts relied upon by the judge at first instance had been the subject of challenge, the decision not to declare the 1997 grant of permission a nullity could not be impugned, *Berkeley v. Secretary of State for the Environment, Transport and the Regions (No.1)* [2000] 3 W.L.R. 420, [2000] 8 C.L. 552 considered. Such a result also accorded with the justice of the situation whereby the innocent owners of the property in question stood to incur a far greater loss than RBC if the permission were to be quashed.

R. (ON THE APPLICATION OF PARKYN) v. RESTORMEL BC; R. (ON THE APPLICATION OF CORBETT) v. RESTORMEL BC; *sub nom.* CORBETT v. RESTORMEL BC; R. v. RESTORMEL BC, *ex p.* PARKYN; R. v. RESTORMEL BC, *ex p.* CORBETT, [2001] EWCA Civ 330, [2001] 1 P.L.R. 108, Schiemann, L.J., CA.

4727. **Planning control – advertisements – extent of deemed consent – unauthorised hoarding placed on hotel – strict liability**

[Interpretation Act 1978 s.7; Town and Country Planning Act 1990 s.224(3); Town and Country Planning (Control of Advertisements) Regulations 1992 (SI 1992 666) Reg.5, Reg.27, Sch.3 Part 1 Class 8.]

In or around May 1998 P placed a hoarding on a hotel. In doing so, it relied on the Town and Country Planning (Control of Advertisements) Regulations 1992 Sch.3 Part 1 Class 8 by which deemed consent was to be granted in respect of "an advertisement on a hoarding which [enclosed] ... land on which building operations ... [were] about to take place" subject to conditions which, inter alia, prohibited the displaying of advertisements earlier than three months before the commencement of the building operations and required the person displaying the advertisement to give the local planning authority at least 14 days' written notification of his intention to do so. Planning permission for the carrying out of certain works at the hotel had been granted in March 1998. In September 1998 P placed a different hoarding on the hotel. A charge was brought against P alleging that in October 1998 it had displayed an advertisement on the hotel contrary to Reg.5 and Reg.27 of the 1992 Regulations and the Town and Country Planning Act 1990 s.224(3). The magistrates convicted P having found, inter alia, that no building works had been commenced pursuant to the permission by October 1998, and that a letter sent by P to the council in August 1998 stating that the first hoarding was to be replaced had not been received. P appealed arguing that (1) on the date when the offence was allegedly committed, it had reasonably believed that building operations would begin within three months with the result that the deemed consent remained effective; (2) the council had been given appropriate notice by means of the letter sent in August 1998 of its intention to replace the initial hoarding. In this connection, P relied on the Interpretation Act 1978 s.7 which provided that a properly addressed letter sent by post should be deemed to have been served, and (3) provided that a notice of an intention to display an advertisement was properly served under Class 8, the advertiser could display successive advertisements on the same hoarding.

Held, dismissing the appeal, that (1) for the purpose of Class 8, the onus was on the advertiser to ensure that building operations were commenced within three months of the date on which the advertisement was first displayed. If building operations were not begun within that period, the deemed consent would no longer apply and an offence would be committed by the presence of the advertisement. As regards the commencement of building operations, there was no justification for introducing the concept of reasonable belief on the part of the advertiser; (2) as the relevant condition in Class 8 did not provide for the service of an intention to display by post, s.7 of the 1978 Act did not apply. The condition provided that the council "[should] be notified in writing" of an intention to display. Given that the magistrates had found that the council had not received P's letter, service of that letter had not been effected, and (3) although the point had now been rendered academic, Class 8, properly construed, limited the grant of a deemed consent to a single advertisement at a particular site.

POSTERMOBILE PLC v. KENSINGTON AND CHELSEA RLBC (2000) 80 P. & C.R. 524, Pill, L.J., QBD.

4728. **Planning control – advertisements – refusal of consent – factual error in decision letter – court's discretion to quash decision letter**

[Town and Country Planning Act 1990 s.79.]

HLI sought to quash an advertisement control officer's refusal to allow an appeal to grant consent for the replacement of a large illuminated sign by a similar sign on the external elevations of a building. The inspector admitted that the decision letter incorrectly stated that the sign was in place when it was not. HLI submitted that the officer had failed to discharge his duty under the Town and Country Planning Act 1990 s.79 in that he had not considered the proposed sign but had based his decision upon the sign to be replaced that was in situ, and that the decision letter was rendered invalid because of the factual error.

Held, granting the application, that the officer could not be criticised for failing to consider the proposed sign since HLI had omitted to send him the relevant details. However, the decision letter did reveal a factual error and it was not certain that, in the absence of the error, the officer would have reached the same conclusion as he did, *GE Simplex (Holdings) v. Secretary of State for the Environment* (1989) 57 P. & C.R. 306, [1989] C.L.Y. 3578 applied.

HARPERS LEISURE INTERNATIONAL LTD v. SECRETARY OF STATE FOR THE ENVIRONMENT, TRANSPORT AND THE REGIONS (2001) 82 P. & C.R. 7, Christopher Lockhart-Mummery Q.C., QBD.

4729. **Planning control – gypsies – injunctions – necessary interference with right to family and private life**

[Town and Country Planning Act 1990 s.187B; Human Rights Act 1998 Sch.1 Part I Art.8.]

In four joined appeals the Court of Appeal was concerned with the appropriate approach of a court when exercising its power under the Town and Country Planning Act 1990 s.187B to grant injunctive relief to restrain a breach of planning control. The appellants in the four cases were gypsies who were occupying land in breach of planning control. Injunctions had been granted against them requiring that they move from the relevant land. The issue before the court related to whether, having regard to the right to family and private life under the Human Rights Act 1998 Sch.1 Part I Art.8, any interference with that right was "necessary in a democratic society" and, in particular, was proportionate.

Held, allowing the appeals of P, S and B and dismissing the appeal of H, that in considering whether to grant injunctive relief under s.187B of the Act, the court had a duty to act proportionately; it was necessary that an injunction not only fulfill the public interest objective but also that the private interests of the individual affected not be subject to an excessive burden. It was not the role of a judge to independently determine the planning merits of a case. Injunctive relief should not be granted unless a judge was prepared, where necessary, to consider committing a defendant to prison for its breach. In reaching such a conclusion, it would be necessary to have regard to the hardship caused to the defendant's family by requiring it to move and to the availability of alternative sites. Relevant considerations included the consequences to the family's health and education, the extent of the alleged breach of planning control and prior planning decisions, *Mole Valley DC v. Smith* (1992) 24 H.L.R. 442, [1992] C.L.Y. 4263 and *Hambleton DC v. Bird* [1995] 3 P.L.R. 8, [1996] C.L.Y. 4743 not applied. The approach in *Hambleton* was not consistent with the court's duty to act in accordance with Convention rights.

SOUTH BUCKINGHAMSHIRE DC v. PORTER; CHICHESTER DC v. SEARLE; WREXHAM CBC v. BERRY; HERTSMERE BC v. HARTY; *sub nom.* SOUTH

BUCKS DC v. PORTER, [2001] EWCA Civ 1549, [2002] 1 W.L.R. 1359, Simon Brown, L.J., CA.

4730. Planning inquiries – planning inspectors – illness resulting in delay – fairness of proceedings

B, which sought to develop existing riding facilities on green belt land, appealed against the refusal of planning permission for the construction of an indoor arena and related facilities. The planning inspector had suffered a stroke during the planning inquiry causing a period of delay. Following his recovery the inquiry resumed and each party was given opportunity to make submissions as to the evidential position at the time of the adjournment. The inspector having completed his report, the Secretary of State accepted his findings and refused the planning permission. B submitted that owing to the lack of a generally usable record from the initial part of the inquiry, the inspector's subsequent decision had been unfair, or had the appearance of unfairness.

Held, dismissing the appeal, that there was no duty on an inspector to make notes of inquiry proceedings that might be usable by others. Such notes did not comprise, and were not destined to comprise, an element of the public record. Disclosure of such notes would only be granted in very rare instances of which the instant case was not one, *Warwick Rural DC v. Miller-Mead (No.1)* [1961] Ch. 590 considered. To impose such a duty would be of limited use and result in longer inquiries. In the circumstances there was no evidence that the delay had resulted in unfairness or impeded the inspector's reasoning.

BELMONT RIDING CENTRE v. SECRETARY OF STATE FOR THE ENVIRONMENT, TRANSPORT AND THE REGIONS [2001] P.L.C.R. 12, Sullivan, J., QBD (Admin Ct).

4731. Planning obligations – retail trade – supermarket development on brown field site

[Town and Country Planning Act 1990 s.106.]

L applied for judicial review of SHDC's decision to grant planning permission to W for a supermarket development on a brown field site. The proposed development had been rejected by SHDC in 1998 on the ground that it would have an adverse effect on the vitality and viability of the nearby town centre. W reapplied in 1999 and included an offer to pay £100,000 to SHDC under the Town and Country Planning Act 1990 s.106, stating that the sum could be used to provide a rural bus service to both the supermarket and the town centre and to make other improvements to the town centre. SHDC granted planning permission for the development. L argued that the s.106 obligation was not sufficiently linked to the development to make it a material consideration and that the proposals for its use were so vague that the decision was *Wednesbury* unreasonable.

Held, allowing the application, that although the s.106 obligation did pass the test for materiality as its connection to the development was more than de minimis, SHDC's decision had been one which no reasonable local planning authority could have reached, *Tesco Stores Ltd v. Secretary of State for the Environment* [1995] 1 W.L.R. 759, [1995] C.L.Y. 4784 applied. W's application had not changed in any respect apart from the addition of the s.106 obligation and therefore all the reasons for refusing the first application were still relevant. The suggestions as to how the money could be applied were ill thought out and had not been backed up by costings. There was no evidence to support a finding that the application of the money would outweigh the adverse effect of the development to a degree sufficient to justify the grant of planning permission.

R. (ON THE APPLICATION OF LINCOLN COOPERATIVE SOCIETY LTD) v. SOUTH HOLLAND DC; *sub nom.* R. v. SOUTH HOLLAND DC, *ex p.* LINCOLN COOPERATIVE SOCIETY LTD [2001] J.P.L. 675, Smith, J., QBD (Admin Ct).

4732. Planning permission – advertisements – amenity protection – assessment of amenity – consistency

[Town and Country Planning (Control of Advertisements) Regulations 1992 (SI 1992 666) Reg.4.]

R challenged S's dismissal of its appeal against a local authority's refusal to grant it planning permission for an illuminated advertising panel. R argued that S had erred in not properly taking into account the fact that there were already similar panels on a bus shelter close to the proposed site.

Held, allowing the appeal, that S had not given adequate reasons to show how he had considered the amenity of the site under the Town and Country Planning (Control of Advertisements) Regulations 1992 Reg.4. It was not possible to ascertain from the decision letter whether the bus shelter had been ignored altogether or whether S considered that it was not relevant to compare it with the proposed advertising panel. R was prejudiced by this omission as it prevented a proper analysis of whether S had been acting within his powers when he reached his decision.

RETAIL MEDIA LTD v. SECRETARY OF STATE FOR THE ENVIRONMENT, TRANSPORT AND THE REGIONS [2001] J.P.L. 1050, Duncan Ousley Q.C., QBD (Admin Ct).

4733. Planning permission – agricultural holdings – conversion for residential use – personal circumstances of occupier material consideration

A, a tenant dairy farmer, challenged a decision of the district council to grant planning permission to T, the freehold owner of the land farmed by A, for the conversion of three barns for residential use. A contended that the loss of those barns would prevent him from farming and that this fact had not been properly considered by the council members as they had been given erroneous advice by planning officers. As a result, submitted A, the council members had been given the impression that his personal circumstances would not, as a matter of law, amount to a sufficient reason for refusing planning permission.

Held, allowing the application and quashing the planning permission, that the personal circumstances of the occupier of premises could exceptionally be taken into account as material considerations when considering planning applications. The council members had been misdirected by the planning officers in respect of this and had not fully understood the policy framework within which they had made their decision, *Westminster City Council v. Great Portland Estates Plc* [1985] A.C. 661, [1984] C.L.Y. 3413 followed.

R. v. VALE OF GLAMORGAN DC, *ex p.* ADAMS [2001] J.P.L. 93, Richards, J., QBD.

4734. Planning permission – agricultural land – retrospective planning permission

[Town and Country Planning Act 1990 s.176 (2) (b).]

D appealed against the grant of retrospective planning permission by a planning inspector for a swimming pool and ancillary development on agricultural land. D contended that, although not specifically mentioned, a timber fence enclosing the pool was also subject to the enforcement notice relating to the development or, alternatively, the notice should have been varied under the Town and Country Planning Act 1990 s.176 (2) (b) to require removal of the fence.

Held, allowing the application and quashing the decision, that the failure to specify the removal of the fence meant that it did not have to be removed; however, as the requirement to return the land to open pasture was inconsistent with the retention of the fence, the notice should have been varied to include its removal.

DACORUM BC v. SECRETARY OF STATE FOR THE ENVIRONMENT, TRANSPORT AND THE REGIONS AND WALSH [2001] J.P.L. 420, George Bartlett Q.C., QBD.

4735. Planning permission – applications and certificates – fees

TOWN AND COUNTRY PLANNING (FEES FOR APPLICATIONS AND DEEMED APPLICATIONS) (AMENDMENT) (ENGLAND) REGULATIONS 2001, SI 2001 2719; made under the Town and Country Planning Act 1990 s.303. In force: August 22, 2001; £1.50.

These Regulations, which amend the Town and Country Planning (Fees for Applications and Deemed Applications) Regulations 1989 (SI 1989 193), provide for an increase in the fee payable for an application to the local planning authority for a determination as to whether prior approval will be required for proposed telecommunication development. The fee is increased from £35 to £190 and reflects the notification and consultation requirements imposed on local planning authorities.

4736. Planning permission – areas of outstanding beauty – precedent and cumulative effect

R challenged the dismissal by the Secretary of State's inspector of his appeal against WBC's refusal to grant planning permission for an upper floor extension to his bungalow which stood in an area classed as possessing outstanding natural beauty and great landscape value. R contended that the inspector had (1) erred in finding that, although the development itself would not be harmful, it would set a precedent for similar extensions culminating in an effect that would be harmful to the general character and appearance of the area, *Poundstretcher v. Secretary of State for the Environment* [1988] 3 P.L.R 69, [1989] C.L.Y. 3560 cited, and (2) failed to give adequate reasons for his decision.

Held, dismissing the application, that (1) the inspector had found that the effect of the proposed extension would be adverse in isolation but that the adverse impact would be insufficient to justify a refusal to grant planning permission. His further finding that consequential accumulation would be harmful could not be impugned. *Poundstretcher* did not provide a precise test as to the circumstances which must exist before a finding of cumulative effect could be made. The reasoning in *Poundstretcher* to the effect that mere fear or generalised concern was insufficient was merely an expression of the view that an inspector must have some cogent material upon which to base a finding of precedent effect which would vary according to the circumstances of each case, *Poundstretcher* considered, and (2) the reasons given were sufficient when read in context with the decision letter.

RUMSEY v. SECRETARY OF STATE FOR THE ENVIRONMENT, TRANSPORT AND THE REGIONS (2001) 81 P. & C.R. 32, Duncan Ouseley Q.C., QBD (Admin Ct).

4737. Planning permission – conditions – noise – adequacy of reasons

W, who had sought planning permission to enable a mansion to be used for various social functions, challenged the inspector's decision that a proposed noise level condition would be insufficient to prevent a noise nuisance affecting nearby residents. W contended that the inspector had not given W the opportunity of making representations concerning the level of potential noise emissions and had failed to provide adequate reasons for his decision.

Held, granting the application and quashing the decision, that the inspector's decision should be quashed for its lack of reasoning since the inspector had failed to explain why he had rejected part of the expert evidence supporting the adequacy of the noise level condition suggested by W.

WOOD v. SECRETARY OF STATE FOR THE ENVIRONMENT, TRANSPORT AND THE REGIONS, [2001] EWHC Admin 35, [2001] J.P.L. 1111 (Note), Turner, J., QBD (Admin Ct).

4738. Planning permission – conditions – variation of conditions attached to planning permission – inconsistencies between original permission and varied conditions

[Town and Country Planning Act 1990 s.73.]

A sought judicial review of C's resolution to approve an application submitted under the Town and Country Planning Act 1990 s.73. C had granted planning permission for the redevelopment of a gas works site subject to conditions which, essentially, limited the aggregate size of the buildings in the site plan. An application under s.73 of the Act to vary the conditions of the planning permission by substituting six separate non food variety stores for the single variety superstore permitted by the original development had been granted, which amounted to a new planning permission. In its application for judicial review, A contended that C had no power to grant that new permission, as the variation had the effect of creating a fundamental inconsistency between the conditions and the description of the development contained in the original permission. It was submitted on behalf of the interested parties that the aim of s.73 of the Act was to enable planning conditions to be varied in such a way as to create a substantially different planning permission.

Held, granting the application, that while a successful application under s.73 of the Act would result in a new planning permission, any new conditions imposed had to be ones which could lawfully have been imposed under the original planning permission, *Powergen UK Plc v. Leicester City Council* (2001) 81 P. & C.R. 5, [2001] 1 C.L. 475 considered. The new conditions failed to satisfy that test in that the proposal to construct six non food retail units was fundamentally different from the initial proposal relating to a single variety superstore.

R. v. COVENTRY CITY COUNCIL, *ex p.* ARROWCROFT GROUP PLC [2001] P.L.C.R. 7, Sullivan, J., QBD.

4739. Planning permission – conservation areas – additional accommodation in green belt area

F applied to quash a decision by the inspector to dismiss an appeal against a refusal to grant planning permission for a two bedroom dwelling within Green Belt and a designated conservation area. F contended that the decision of the inspector was not one that could have been reasonably arrived at and that the reasons given for the decision were inadequate.

Held, dismissing the application, that whilst the decision was harsh, F had not shown that it was so absurd as to be unreasonable in the legal sense. The reasoning given was adequate and the inspector was entitled to form his conclusions.

FENTON v. SECRETARY OF STATE FOR THE ENVIRONMENT, TRANSPORT AND THE REGIONS [2000] J.P.L. 1179 (Note), Lockhart-Mummery Q.C., QBD.

4740. Planning permission – costs – publication of planning applications – degree of prejudice

[Town and Country Planning Act 1990 s.54A; Town and Country Planning (General Development Procedure) Order (SI 1995 419) Art.8, Sch.3.]

B sought to recover his costs following proceedings against HDC, a local planning authority. B had objected to R's proposals for redevelopment of a site adjacent to his property on the basis that the land was in an area of open countryside close to a site of special scientific interest, and that the proposals constituted a departure from the development plans. HDC granted planning consent and B instituted proceedings, contending that the proposals had not been adequately publicised and that HDC had failed to have due regard to the Town and Country Planning Act 1990 s.54A. R made a second, identical, application and HDC again granted planning consent but, on that occasion, with more stringent conditions attached. A dispute remained as to whether or not the first permission could still be used and considerable costs had been incurred. HDC resisted B's assertion that he was entitled to his costs and argued that it should have its costs throughout, as B's application to quash the first planning permission was bound to fail.

Held, awarding costs in favour of HDC, that, although determination of the original application had become academic, in order to determine liability for costs alone, the substantive merits of the application fell to be considered, *R. v. Holderness BC, ex p. James Robert Developments Ltd* (1993) 5 Admin. L.R. 470, [1993] C.L.Y. 3933 followed. Pursuant to the Town and Country Planning (General Development Procedure) Order 1995 Art.8 and Sch.3, HDC had been obliged to provide requisite notice of R's application for planning consent. HDC had published a block of applications in a local newspaper which did not comply with the statutory requirements as the notices did not contain all of the necessary information. However, B had not suffered any prejudice as a result of the defective notice as he had been aware of R's application and had the opportunity to make objections. HDC was under a duty by virtue of s.54A to grant planning consent in accordance with the development plan. While the proposed development in the instant case was contrary to one policy, HDC's approach had not been inconsistent with s.54A as they had considered all relevant factors and explained why a departure from the policy was acceptable. B's case would not have succeeded and HDC was, therefore, entitled to its costs from the commencement of proceedings.

R. v. HORSHAM DC, *ex p.* BAYLEY [2001] P.L.C.R. 11, Collins, J., QBD.

4741. Planning permission – delay – lack of environmental statement – prejudice resulting from delay

[Town and Country Planning (Environmental Impact Assessment) (England and Wales) Regulations 1999 (SI 1999 293).]

B sought judicial review of WDC's resolution to grant conditional planning permission for the construction of a printing works. B contended that the grant was in breach of the mandatory requirements of the Town and Country Planning (Environmental Impact Assessment) (England and Wales) Regulations 1999 because of the absence of a valid environmental statement. The document which purported to be the statement contained no information about the design of the development. WDC conceded that the regulations had been breached but contended that the court should not exercise its discretion to quash because of undue delay in challenging the resolution which had resulted in prejudice to good administration.

Held, granting the application, that the breach was blatant and serious. Further, WDC had resolved to grant the permission notwithstanding the clearest possible warning that such action would be unlawful. The discretion of the court in the face of such breaches was exercisable on a narrow basis. There was no evidence that good administration had been prejudiced or of any specific prejudice in the form of the reliance by any third parties upon the permission and it was therefore quashed.

R. v. WAVENEY DC, *ex p.* BELL [2001] Env. L.R. 24, Sullivan, J., QBD.

4742. Planning permission – environmental impact assessments – port development – consent given prior to Council Directive 85/337 implementation date

[Council Directive 85/337 on the assessment of the effects of certain public and private projects on the environment Art.2(1); Council Directive 85/337 on the assessment of the effects of certain public and private projects on the environment Annex I.]

In the course of a challenge to the decision of the North Holland municipal authorities to approve a plan for the development of a port and industrial zone without an environmental impact assessment, the question was referred to the ECJ for a preliminary ruling as to whether an assessment was required under

Council Directive 84/337 Art.2(1), where approval was given in May 1993 for the development that had featured in regional plans dating from 1968.

Held, giving a preliminary ruling, that (1) the Directive did not exempt projects from the requirements of Art.2(1) in respect of which the consent procedures were initiated after the deadline for transposition on July 3 1988; (2) in the case of such projects Art.2(1) required an assessment in respect of projects that were likely to have significant effects on the environment, as listed in Annex I to the Directive, and (3) Member States were not permitted to waive the obligation to carry out environmental assessments for projects listed in Annex I where consent had been granted prior to the transposition date, or where the consent did not follow an environmental impact assessment carried out in accordance with the Directive but which had not been used, or where a fresh consent procedure was formally commenced after July 3 1988.

BURGEMEESTER EN WETHOUDERS VAN HAARLEMMERLIEDE EN SPAARNWOUDE v. GEDEPUTEERDE STATEN VAN NOORD-HOLLAND (C81/96) [1998] E.C.R. I-3923, H Ragnemalm (President), ECJ.

4743. Planning permission – gypsies – grant of permission perverse and irrational

PCC appealed against H's successful appeal against PCC's refusal to grant planning permission to site two caravans on PCC's land. H, a gypsy, had appealed against PCC's earlier refusal and been granted personal permission by the inspector for a period limited to two years, to allow H's daughter to complete her primary education and for the family to find suitable alternative accommodation, which was not then available. The inspector had concluded that those exceptional personal circumstances outweighed the considerable planning factors against granting permission. H's subsequent application to PCC for full planning permission was refused, but allowed on appeal by the inspector. Upon challenging that order, PCC submitted that (1) the inspector had erred in his finding that H was a gypsy; (2) strong planning objections could not be overridden by H's personal circumstances; (3) the inspector had failed to consider material planning considerations, including the fact that H had made no effort to find alternative living arrangements and there was a suitable gypsy site nearby, and (4) in the presence of evidence which showed that H's daughter could be educated at another school without suffering disruption, there was no substance to his finding that that factor outweighed strong and convincing planning considerations.

Held, allowing the appeal, that the inspector had reached a conclusion which was perverse and irrational on the facts. Although he had a wide discretion, and the court's power to intervene was limited, it was clear from contradictory statements in his decision letter that he had largely misunderstood the evidence, overlooked important considerations and failed to give reasons for his decision. His finding in relation to H's gypsy status was an issue of fact, and was not amenable to challenge. However the remainder of PCC's submissions were justified, *Edinburgh City Council v. Secretary of State for Scotland* [1997] 1 W.L.R. 1447, [1997] C.L.Y. 6350 considered.

POWYS CC v. NATIONAL ASSEMBLY FOR WALES [2000] P.L.C.R. 385,Turner, J., QBD.

4744. Planning permission – gypsies – right to family life – gypsy landowners – enforcement of planning restrictions – environmental preservation

[Human Rights Act 1998 Sch.1 Part I Art.8, Art.14, Part II Art.1.]

C, a gypsy, challenged a refusal to allow her planning permission to station her caravan on a plot of green belt land which she owned. C submitted that (1) the enforcement of planning restrictions pertaining to the land violated a number of rights guaranteed by the Human Rights Act 1998, namely the right to respect for private and family life under Sch.1 Part I Art.8 and the right to the peaceful enjoyment of her land under Sch.1 Part II Art.1, and (2) the decision constituted discrimination against gypsies as an ethnic group and was consequently in breach of Sch.1 Part I Art.14.

Held, refusing the application, that notwithstanding that the planning decisions hindered C in her enjoyment of the lifestyle common to her ethnic group, her individual desires had to be weighed against the environmental objections to her proposed use of her land. The existence of authorised gypsy sites, even though there was an insufficient number of them to satisfy demand, was indicative of the fact that occupation of her own land was not C's only alternative to conventional housing. Furthermore, Art.8 could not be construed as obliging contracting states to supply the demand for gypsy sites. The interference with C's enjoyment of her property was therefore proportional and fairly weighed against the requirements of Protocol 1 Art.1, and (2) since C's interests had been balanced against those of society at large, Art.14 had not been breached.

CHAPMAN v. UNITED KINGDOM (27238/95) (2001) 33 E.H.R.R. 18, L Wildhaber (President), ECHR.

4745. Planning permission – gypsies – right to private life – residential use of caravan – existence of alternative conventional housing – relevant considerations

[Human Rights Act 1998 Sch.1 Part I Art.8, Art.14.]

C, a Romany gypsy, appealed against a decision of the inspector to uphold the local authority's refusal to grant planning permission for the residential use of a caravan in a special landscape area. C contended, inter alia, that the fact that the inspector had taken into account C's refusal to accept an earlier offer of alternative conventional housing had resulted in (1) a breach of his right to respect for private and family life as guaranteed by the Human Rights Act 1998 Sch.1 Part I Art.8, and (2) a breach of the anti-discriminatory provisions of Art.14 of the Convention. The Secretary of State submitted that the inspector had been entitled to take C's refusal into account in the balancing exercise when determining if a refusal of planning permission would render C homeless and that it was inappropriate for the court to review the weighing exercise carried out by a planning specialist.

Held, allowing the appeal, that in certain circumstances it would be a breach of Art.8 and Art.14 to penalise a gypsy applying for planning permission, or resisting eviction, for refusing an offer of conventional housing on the ground that it was contrary to his gypsy culture and beliefs. Such circumstances were limited and the onus was on the gypsy in each individual case to satisfy the inspector of his status as a gypsy and to show that his refusal of conventional accommodation was based on his cultural values. However, it did not necessarily follow that planning permission must be granted in every case. In the instant case, the inspector's conclusions in relation to C's refusal of conventional housing was unclear and the factors which had been taken into account and the weight attached to them was not easily discernible. Accordingly, the decision was quashed and the matter remitted for consideration afresh.

CLARKE v. SECRETARY OF STATE FOR THE ENVIRONMENT, TRANSPORT AND THE REGIONS, [2001] EWHC Admin 800, *The Times*, November 9, 2001, Burton, J., QBD (Admin Ct).

4746. Planning permission – judicial review – guidelines for challenging planning permission where permission referred to Secretary of State for approval

[Town and Country Planning Act 1990 s.106.]

On December 1, 1999 CCC granted planning permission for a development subject to the satisfactory implementation of an agreement under the Town and Country Planning Act 1990 s.106 and, given that CCC owned the relevant site, the approval of the Secretary of State. In the early part of February 2000 the Secretary of State declined to call in the application, and on February 9 CCC decided that the development could proceed. On February 29, shortly after notifying CCC of its intention to challenge the decision to grant planning permission,W, an interested party, applied for permission to move for judicial review of that decision. W explained its delay in making the application by referring to the decision in *R. v. Samuel Smith Old Brewery* (Unreported, November 29, 1999) wherein it was held that it would be premature to challenge an indication that planning permission was to be granted where the permission would have to be approved by the Secretary of State or where the grant of permission was dependent on conditions precedent.

Held, granting W permission to move for judicial review, that (1) case law made it clear that, in the area of planning, an application for permission to move for judicial review should be made within six weeks of the date of the relevant decision; that approach resulted from the fact that under planning legislation an applicant was obliged to appeal against a refusal to grant planning permission within that period; (2) in a case where the approval of the Secretary of State was required, any person wishing to challenge a decision to grant permission should within six weeks of a referral notify all relevant parties of the grounds of his challenge and his intention to pursue his challenge immediately in the event of the Secretary of State granting approval. Such notification could take the form of a letter. If the Secretary of State decided to approve the relevant decision, any delay in the filing of an application beyond that decision would not be tolerated; (3) where a planning permission was subject to the fulfilment of conditions precedent, it would be appropriate within six weeks of the planning authority's decision to file an application for permission to move for judicial review. The Secretary of State was obliged to reach a decision within 21 days and there was no substantial delay to the applicant. Conditions precedent might take longer to fulfil, and delays and uncertainty as to the legality of the planning permission until they were fulfilled could cause significant prejudice to the applicant, and (4) although W should have informed CCC at an earlier stage that it intended to challenge the decision to grant planning permission, it was not to be penalised for having relied on the authority which it had cited. Accordingly, permission to proceed with its application would be granted.

R. v. CAMBRIDGE CITY COUNCIL, *ex p.* WARNER VILLAGE CINEMAS LTD (PERMISSION TO MOVE FOR JUDICIAL REVIEW) [2001] 1 P.L.R. 7, Collins, J., QBD.

4747. Planning permission – land use – inadequate reasons for refusal – long use without complaint

D applied to quash the decision of an inspector refusing to grant permanent planning permission to enable him to repair motor vehicles from home. D contended that the ruling that his business would cause unacceptable noise and disturbance to adjacent residents did not take into account the difference between the perceived impact and the actual impact of the use of D's garage.

Held, granting the application, that the inspector had failed to give adequate reasons for his decision, considering that the use had continued for six and a half years with no evidence of detrimental noise impact or complaints from local residents, *Save Britain's Heritage v. Number 1 Poultry Ltd* [1991] 1 W.L.R. 153, [1991] C.L.Y. 3494 applied.

DHOKIA v. SECRETARY OF STATE FOR THE ENVIRONMENT, TRANSPORT AND THE REGIONS [2001] P.L.C.R. 9, Judge Christopher Lockhart-Mummery, QBD.

4748. Planning permission – legitimate expectation – permission for development of site granted prior to receipt of inspector's recommendations

P sought to quash S's decision to grant outline planning permission for the development of a site of which S was a joint owner, the site being in close proximity to potential development land owned by P. P contended that in granting the permission prior to the inspector's report S had failed to take into

PLANNING

account all material considerations, had acted unreasonably and had thwarted P's legitimate expectation that S would act in accordance with the usual procedure.

Held, dismissing the application, that S had acted fairly and that P had no legitimate expectation other than that S would act in accordance with the law.

R. v. SOUTH NORFOLK CC, *ex p.* PELHAM HOMES LTD [2001] P.L.C.R. 8, Munby, J., QBD.

4749. Planning permission – local plans – impact of non-conformity upon existing local plan – relevance of proposed local plan

TDC appealed against a planning inspector's decision to allow an appeal against its refusal to grant planning permission to G. It was contended that (1) the inspector should have disregarded a Local Plan in force that did not conform to the Structure Plan; (2) the inspector had erred in taking the proposed Local Plan into account, and (3) a decision that the proposals were consistent with the objective of sustainable development had been flawed.

Held, dismissing the appeal, that (1) whilst the non conforming Local Plan had lost its precedence over the Structure Plan, there were no statutory provisions to support TDC's submission that the non-conforming Local Plan should be disregarded; (2) the inspector had been entitled to attach limited weight only to the proposed Local Plan having properly considered the issue of prematurity, and (3) there was material to support the inspector's conclusion that there was no prejudice to sustainable development.

R. (ON THE APPLICATION OF TORRIDGE DC) v. SECRETARY OF STATE FOR THE ENVIRONMENT, TRANSPORT AND THE REGIONS [2001] J.P.L. 1195, Newman, J., QBD (Admin Ct).

4750. Planning permission – motorways – service stations – impact of fresh policy statements

HI appealed against decisions to quash its grant by the Secretary of State of outline planning permission for a motorway service area on land adjoining the A1(M) in North Yorkshire and to quash the Secretary of State's refusal of planning permission for M, another developer, to build a similar facility on an alternative site close to the same motorway. M contended that fresh government policy documents issued between the dates of the inspector's report and the Secretary of State's decisions disentitled him from simply accepting the inspector's conclusions, since they had become inappropriate in the light of the new policy.

Held, dismissing the appeals, that the Secretary of State's decisions had been flawed. He had given no reasons for concluding that the policy changes which had taken place since the hearing before the inspector should not be taken into account when making his decision. Those policy changes had removed the uncertainty which was the chief barrier to the acceptance of M's proposed development site, with the result that the Secretary of State had not been entitled merely to adopt his inspector's conclusions, which were no longer valid, *Save Britain's Heritage v. Number 1 Poultry Ltd* [1991] 1 W.L.R. 153, [1991] C.L.Y. 3494 followed.

MacGAY LTD v. SECRETARY OF STATE FOR THE ENVIRONMENT, TRANSPORT AND THE REGIONS; HARROGATE BC v. SECRETARY OF STATE FOR THE ENVIRONMENT, TRANSPORT AND THE REGIONS [2001] P.L.C.R. 21, Pill, L.J., CA.

4751. Planning permission – permitted development – telecommunications development

TOWN AND COUNTRY PLANNING (GENERAL PERMITTED DEVELOPMENT) (AMENDMENT) (ENGLAND) ORDER 2001, SI 2001 2718; made under the Town and Country Planning Act 1990 s.59, s.60, s.61, s.333. In force: August 22, 2001; £2.50.

This Order amends the Town and Country Planning (General Permitted Development) Order 1995 (SI 1995 418 as amended by SI 1998 462 and SI 1999 1661) in relation to permitted development rights for certain telecommunications development. Where such rights apply, no specific application for planning permission is needed. The Order introduces a revised prior approval procedure and a requirement for the developer to notify the owner, or agricultural tenant, of the land to which the proposed development relates, before making an application to the local planning authority for a determination as to whether prior approval is required.

4752. Planning permission – residential developments – material considerations – alternative sites

[Town and Country Planning Act 1990 s.70.]

NWBC appealed against a decision to quash planning permission granted for the purpose of building bungalows intended for the elderly. J had raised an objection to the permission on the basis that children used the land as a playing area. The judge had found that the availability of an alternative site was a material consideration which, under the Town and Country Planning Act 1990 s.70, NWBC had been obliged to take into account, or at least consider whether to take into account, and that they had not done so. NWBC argued that the fact that there was an alternative site was not a material consideration which they were required to take into account.

Held, allowing the appeal, that the fact that an alternative site existed was not a good enough reason to refuse planning permission and that an alternative site would only be a material consideration where the proposed development would have conspicuous adverse effects. Permission would only be refused where the objections and adverse effects of a proposal outweighed its benefits. This was not so in the instant case.

R. (ON THE APPLICATION OF J (A CHILD)) v. NORTH WARWICKSHIRE BC; *sub nom*. R. v. NORTH WARWICKSHIRE BC, *ex p*. J (A CHILD), [2001] EWCA Civ 315, [2001] 2 P.L.R. 59, Laws, L.J., CA.

4753. Planning permission – telecommunications – local plans – requirement that development be essential for operation of telecommunications service

T, a telecommunications company, challenged a decision to refuse planning permission for the erection of a telecommunications development near a village situated in a National Park, close to an existing telecommunications structure used by other operators. T contended that (1) the inspector had come to an irrational decision in finding that the proposed development was not essential for the operation of the relevant licensed service and therefore contrary to the Local Plan Policy PU10, since he had already accepted that there was a gap in T's transmission and reception coverage in the locality, and (2) the policy requirement that the development be "essential for their operation" referred to a need in the relevant locality, not for the business as a whole.

Held, granting the application for judicial review, that it was clear that the inspector had found that the proposed development contravened Policy PU10 as not being "essential for their operation" but he appeared to accept that T could not share the existing structure with the other operator and that there were no satisfactory alternative means of providing for the facility. The correct interpretation of Policy PU10 was that the development to which it referred must be essential for the operation of the service within the relevant locality, rather than essential for the success of the business as a whole. Consequently, the inspector's approach to Policy PU10 was flawed and if it had not been for that error he might have found the development to be in accordance with the Policy, given his earlier finding that there was a gap in coverage.

TELECOM SECURICOR CELLULAR RADIO LTD v. NATIONAL ASSEMBLY FOR WALES [2001] P.L.C.R. 23, Richards, J., QBD (Admin Ct).

4754. Planning permission – unitary development plans – recommendations of inspector – decision of planning authority to ignore recommendations

[Town and Country Planning Act 1990 s.78, s.287.]

S, developers, applied, pursuant to the Town and Country Planning Act 1990 s.287, to quash the decision of G, a local planning authority, to adopt two planning policies as parts of the unitary development plan, UDP. S owned a site which had been allocated for employment purposes, but wished to develop the land for housing. A second site located within the Green Belt, not owned by S, had been allocated by G for residential purposes. Following the public inquiry held in relation to G's proposed implementation of the UDP, the inspector made recommendations to G that the two relevant planning policies be modified, having found that the site owned by S could be viably utilised for housing, thus avoiding development on the Green Belt site. Following a separate inquiry under s.78 of the 1990 Act, arising from G's refusal to grant outline planning permission to S for their site, the s.78 inspector had reported that G should review its policy in relation to employment allocation, as it was not feasible. S had subsequently requested that G take the s.78 inspector's report into account when considering the adoption of the two planning policies and the implementation of the UDP. G refused, arguing that there was no requirement for them to do so. S appealed, contending that G had (1) been wrong to ignore the conclusions of the s.78 inspector; (2) failed to take into account the findings of the UDP inspector, and (3) failed to reconsider the allocation of the two sites in question following the successful outcome of S's s.78 appeal.

Held, allowing the application, that G had (1) failed to take into account material matters arising from the s.78 process before reaching its decision to adopt the UDP; (2) failed to provide any reasoned response to the inspector's conclusion that there were no exceptional circumstances subsisting such as to justify revision of the existing green belt boundaries, and to respond to the conclusions reached in relation to urban regeneration and commuting, and (3) failed to exercise its discretion to consider holding a further inquiry.

ST PAUL'S DEVELOPMENTS LTD v. GATESHEAD MBC [2001] P.L.C.R.1, Nigel MacLeod Q.C., QBD.

4755. Planning permission – use classes – sports facilities – proposed use of sports stadium as concert venue

[Town and Country Planning Act 1990 s.192(2), s.288; Town and Country Planning (Use Classes) 1987 (S1 1987 764) Sch.1 Part 4 para.2.]

R, the owners of a rugby football stadium, applied under the Town and Country Planning Act 1990 s.288 to quash a decision by the Secretary of State not to grant a certificate of lawfulness of proposed use under s.192(2) of the Act. R proposed using the stadium for musical concerts.

Held, dismissing the application, that the use of a rugby football stadium as a concert hall did not fall within the Town and Country Planning (Use Classes) Order 1987 Sch.1 Part 4 para.2 Class D2. Since it did not have a roof it lacked the necessary degree of enclosure for the purposes of Class D2(b). Concert going was not a sport and thus did not constitute recreation within the meaning of Class D2(e), *Millington v. Secretary of State for the Environment, Transport and the Regions* [1999] 3 P.L.R. 118, [1999] C.L.Y. 4172 applied.

RUGBY FOOTBALL UNION v. SECRETARY OF STATE FOR LOCAL GOVERNMENT, TRANSPORT AND THE REGIONS; *sub nom.* RUGBY FOOTBALL UNION v. SECRETARY OF STATE FOR THE ENVIRONMENT, TRANSPORT AND THE REGIONS, [2001] EWHC Admin 927, *The Times*, November 8, 2001, Ouseley, J., QBD (Admin Ct).

4756. Planning permission – variation of reserved matters – approval prior to commencement – change of planning policy

[Town and Country Planning Act 1990 s.73, s.92.]

LCC granted P outline planning permission for development of a site for retail, business, petrol station, public house and restaurant uses in January 1995. The permission was subject to conditions: (1) that approval of reserved matters was to be made within three years and that development was to begin within five years of the date of the permission or two years from final approval of all reserved matters, and (2) that detailed plans of the reserved matters were to be approved before development began. The permission also imposed conditions envisaged by the Town and Country Planning Act 1990 s.92. With matters taking longer than anticipated, on January 8, 1998, P applied for approval of reserved matters for the retail and petrol station part and gave an indicative layout for the remainder. On January 12, 1998, P applied under the s.73 to amend condition (1) to extend the time limit for submitting reserved matters. LCC refused that application but approved the plans for the retail part. P then applied under s.73 to vary condition (2) so that the reserved matters in condition (1) related only to the part of the site P was proceeding with at the time. This was refused on the basis that it would be contrary to the local plan for work to commence on a food superstore in that location. P's application for judicial review was refused at first instance ((2000) 80 P. & C.R. 176, [2000] C.L.Y. 4502) and it appealed.

Held, dismissing the appeal, that it was plain from s.92 that "reserved matters" referred to all matters reserved by the outline planning permission and "development" referred to the entire development. LCC's permission expressly or impliedly imposed those conditions and so P could not treat "the development" in condition (2) as referring only to the parts it wanted to proceed with. Granting P's application would allow development to proceed after the expiry date in the original permission. Given that P had accepted LCC's decision not to extend the time permitted in condition (1) as correct, to allow P to achieve the same result by altering condition (2) would be contrary to the policy behind the statutory time limits. In any event, current planning policy had to be considered when reaching a decision in the instant case and it was not irrational to refuse permission on the basis of a change of policy.

POWERGEN UK PLC v. LEICESTER CITY COUNCIL; *sub nom.* R. v. LEICESTER CITY COUNCIL, *ex p.* POWERGEN UK PLC (2001) 81 P. & C.R. 5, Schiemann, L.J., CA.

4757. Planning policy – change of use – permission refused for proposed housing development on industrial site

FM applied for an order quashing a decision of the inspector to uphold the refusal of planning permission to develop housing on an industrial site. FM contended that the inspector failed to give full consideration to the development policy, to seek further submissions as to the likelihood of continued industrial use and to inspect the site fully.

Held, dismissing the application, that the inspector, having considered the evidence before him, was entitled to conclude that permission was inappropriate.

FEDERAL MOGUL CORP v. SECRETARY OF STATE FOR THE ENVIRONMENT, TRANSPORT AND THE REGIONS [2000] J.P.L. 1181 (Note), Judge Christopher Lockhart-Mummery Q.C., QBD.

4758. Planning policy – conditions – requirement to provide "low cost affordable housing" – developer's obligations

[Town and Country Planning Act 1990 s.106.]

W purchased land with attached planning permission to erect 70 residential houses subject to a condition pursuant to the Town and Country Planning Act 1990 s.106 that 10 per cent of the houses be "low cost affordable housing" as required by the local planning policy. W sought confirmation from WDC that the condition could be fulfilled by its provision of smaller houses suitable for first time buyers at affordable prices and that the involvement of a housing association was not a prerequisite. WDC replied that affordable housing was required for the rental sector, thus W's proposal was unacceptable. The housing estate was completed but W failed to secure a contract with a housing association in respect of seven low cost houses which it had identified and WDC sought a declaration that W had not discharged its obligation by performance. W argued that there was no requirement for it to provide subsidised housing and that 10 per cent of the houses on the development were being sold at a price which was substantially less than the average selling price of the remaining 90 per cent, thus the condition had been complied with.

Held, granting the declaration, that "low cost affordable housing" was a well known planning term and the requirement could be met in different ways depending on the circumstances. Although the obligation to provide low cost housing did not render the developer itself responsible for any subsidy, in the context of the development in question, there was a need for properties to rent and provision of such was necessary to satisfy the condition. It was up to W to decide how that would be achieved but it was under an obligation to provide social housing, which obligation had not been met.

WYCHAVON DC v. WESTBURY HOMES (HOLDINGS) LTD [2001] P.L.C.R. 13, Judge Boggis Q.C., Ch D.

4759. Planning policy – green belt – inappropriate development

S appealed against a refusal, on Green Belt grounds, to grant him planning permission for a first floor residential extension to a house and the retention of a detached garage block, which did not qualify as permitted development under the General Permitted Development Order. Following the refusal, S had made a new application which was granted subject to the garage being altered, and contended that as the development was now permitted it could not be inappropriate development within the meaning of the planning policy.

Held, allowing the appeal and remitting the case, that the judge's conclusion that the fact that the development which would occur would be almost identical regardless of whether the appeal was allowed or not, did not amount to a very special circumstance, which was logically unjustifiable, and the decision was quashed.

SAPRA v. SECRETARY OF STATE FOR THE ENVIRONMENT, TRANSPORT AND THE REGIONS [2001] J.P.L. 1205, Judge Rich Q.C., QBD (Admin Ct).

4760. Planning policy – hotels – use of proposed development site for local policy purposes

F applied to quash the decision of an inspector to dismiss F's planning appeal. F's application for permission to construct a 40 bedroom Travelodge and associated facilities had been refused by the local borough council, RBC, on the basis that the proposed development site had been designated as "land for business, industry and warehousing use" in two local plan policies. The inspector, appointed following F's appeal to the Secretary of State, held a public inquiry into the matter and concluded that the proposed use of the land would result in a loss of land for policy purposes that could not be justified by the need for hotel accommodation. F submitted that (1) the development site did not fall within the terms of policy, as it did not have a history of business or industrial use or permission for such use and it had not been allocated for such use in either the Structure Plan or the Local Plan, and (2) the inspector had failed to provide adequate, cogent reasons for the decision.

Held, dismissing the application, that (1) the inspector's interpretation of both local plan policies had been reasonable and he had been entitled to conclude that the proposed construction of a hotel on the development site would not have been a use in accordance with local policy, and (2) the inspector's explanation of his decision had been adequate and clear.

FORTE (UK) LTD v. SECRETARY OF STATE FOR THE ENVIRONMENT, TRANSPORT AND THE REGIONS; FORTE (UK) LTD v. RESTORMEL BC; *sub nom.* R. v. SECRETARY OF STATE FOR THE ENVIRONMENT, TRANSPORT AND THE REGIONS, *ex p.* FORTE (UK) LTD [2000] J.P.L. 1303 (Note), Nigel MacLeod Q.C., QBD.

4761. Planning policy – right to fair trial – bias – policy maker also acting as adjudicator

[Human Rights Act 1998 Sch.1 Part I Art.6(1).]

The Secretary of State appealed against a declaration ([2001] H.R.L.R. 2) that his powers to determine planning applications were incompatible with the Human Rights Act 1998 Sch.1 Part I Art.6.1, given his involvement in the formulation of planning policy. HB contended that whilst there had been no actual bias, the dual role of the Secretary of State in formulating policy and taking decisions on applications received inevitably resulted in a situation whereby there had not been a disposal before an independent and impartial tribunal. The Secretary of State conceded that his role in the process could not be described as independent and impartial but maintained that there was adequate judicial control to safeguard the overall fairness of the process.

Held, allowing the appeal, that the courts were able to exercise sufficient control over the decision making portion of the Secretary of State's role by means of judicial review as a result of which it was possible to set aside a particular decision for a multiplicity of reasons. The courts were only obliged to exercise control over that portion of the role that was concerned with the lawfulness of the decision and the adequacy of the procedural steps involved. The court had no function to review the policy making portion of the Secretary of State's role, *Zumtobel v. Austria (A/268-A)* (1994) 17 E.H.R.R. 116, [1994] C.L.Y. 2393, *Iskcon v. United Kingdom* (Unreported, March 8, 1994) and *Bryan v. United Kingdom (A/335-A)*(1996) 21 E.H.R.R. 342, [1996] C.L.Y. 4707 applied. It had often been suggested that the reference to "full jurisdiction" in *Albert v. Belgium (A/58)* (1983) 5 E.H.R.R. 533 required that an underlying policy decision taken by an administrator who did not comply with Art.6 had to be capable of review on its merits. To subsume the Secretary of State's role in policy making in such a fashion would be undemocratic and contrary to established European jurisprudence. Accordingly there were sufficient procedural safeguards in the form of judicial review available to render the adoption of the dual role lawful, *Albert* explained.

R. (ON THE APPLICATION OF HOLDING & BARNES PLC) v. SECRETARY OF STATE FOR THE ENVIRONMENT, TRANSPORT AND THE REGIONS; R. (ON THE APPLICATION OF PREMIER LEISURE UK LTD) v. SECRETARY OF STATE FOR THE ENVIRONMENT, TRANSPORT AND THE REGIONS; R. (ON THE APPLICATION OF ALCONBURY DEVELOPMENTS LTD) v. SECRETARY OF STATE FOR THE ENVIRONMENT, TRANSPORT AND THE REGIONS; SECRETARY OF STATE FOR THE ENVIRONMENT, TRANSPORT AND THE REGIONS v. LEGAL AND GENERAL ASSURANCE SOCIETY LTD; *sub nom.* R. v. SECRETARY OF STATE FOR THE ENVIRONMENT, TRANSPORT AND THE REGIONS, *ex p.* HOLDINGS & BARNES PLC, [2001] UKHL 23, [2001] 2 W.L.R. 1389, Lord Slynn of Hadley, HL.

4762. Planning policy – structure plans – statement of general development policy – erroneous inclusion in memorandum to plan

[Town and Country Planning Act 1990 s.31(2), s.287; Town and Country Planning (Development Plan) Regulations 1991 (SI 1991 2794) Reg.16.]

K challenged the adoption of the Cheshire Replacement Structure Plan under the Town and Country Planning Act 1990 s.287. He contended that (1) he had been prejudiced by the failure of the local authority to comply with the Town and Country Planning (Development Plan) Regulations 1991 Reg.16 in that no adequate reasons had been given for the decision to adopt the replacement plan in the light of the panel recommendations following an examination in public of the draft plan, and (2) the replacement plan did not meet the requirements of the Town and Country Planning Act 1990 s.31 (2) because it did not contain a statement of general development policy, such policy being wrongly included instead within the explanatory memorandum. Alternatively, K sought judicial review in relation to quashing the memorandum in part, since it contained policies themselves rather than reasons justifying policies.

Held, giving judgment for the claimant in part, that (1) the main thrust of the panel's recommendations was that it was opposed to the strategic release of Green Belt for housing provision, favouring local Green Belt release as the alternative should a release prove necessary. The local authority had clearly adopted this approach and, in so doing, had given sufficient reasons for that decision, and (2) the explanatory memorandum contained policy which did not appear within the body of the plan, thereby giving rise to a breach of s.31 (2) of the 1990 Act, *Westminster City Council v. Great Portland Estates Plc* [1985] A.C. 661, [1984] C.L.Y. 3413 applied. However, it was not possible to challenge the memorandum directly under s.287 of the Act and the quashing of the entire plan would result in disproportionate administrative difficulties for the planning authority. Therefore, K's alternative application for judicial review would be granted, allowing the appropriate amendments to be made to the replacement plan.

KINGSLEY v. SECRETARY OF STATE FOR THE ENVIRONMENT, TRANSPORT AND THE REGIONS (2001) 82 P. & C.R. 9, Ouseley, J., QBD (Admin Ct).

4763. Planning policy guidance – retail development – district centre location – demonstration of "need"

T, a supermarket chain, challenged the Secretary of State's decision to refuse its application for permission to extend the floor space and storage area of one of its stores. The store was located in a district centre situated 2.5 km from a town centre. T contended that the Secretary of State had erred in accepting the inspector's interpretation of PPG 6 that town centre sites were to be preferred over district centres by virtue of the sequential approach to site selection and thus "need" had to be demonstrated for all retail development located outside a town centre. T maintained that the words "town centre" contained in the policy were intended to be interpreted broadly so as to include a district centre.

Held, allowing the application, that the interpretation of planning policy should only be interfered with if it could be shown to be legally erroneous, *R. v. Derbyshire CC, ex p. Woods* [1998] Env. L.R. 277, [1997] C.L.Y. 4106 applied. PPG 6, when read together with the relevant Ministerial Policy Statement, indicated that district centres and the sites contained therein did not have to show need. The objective of planning policies was to ensure the sustainability of district and town centres which a retail development could fulfil without demonstrating a specific need. It followed that the inspector had erred in her interpretation of the policies as had the Secretary of State by upholding it.

R. (ON THE APPLICATION OF TESCO STORES LTD) v. SECRETARY OF STATE FOR THE ENVIRONMENT, TRANSPORT AND THE REGIONS; *sub nom.* TESCO STORES LTD v. SECRETARY OF STATE FOR THE ENVIRONMENT, TRANSPORT AND THE REGIONS; R. v. SECRETARY OF STATE FOR THE ENVIRONMENT, TRANSPORT AND THE REGIONS, *ex p.* TESCO STORES LTD [2001] J.P.L. 686, Keene, J., QBD (Admin Ct).

4764. Rights of way – bridleways – deletion from definitive map – extent of inspector's powers – standard of proof

See REAL PROPERTY: Trevelyan v. Secretary of State for the Environment, Transport and the Regions. §4887

4765. Roads – improvements – intention to create – right to compensation

[Highways Act 1980 s.73(9).]

C sought compensation under the Highways Act 1980 s.73(9) for the injurious effect on its land of an improvement line that it maintained had been set by B, the local authority, under s.73. C asserted that B had passed a resolution in 1995 setting an improvement line for highway expansion beyond which no new building was permitted, or, alternatively, that such a decision could be established from the facts so that B was estopped from claiming otherwise. B argued that no improvement line had been drawn for s.73 purposes and that there was no intention to do so. The matter fell to be determined as a preliminary issue

Held, giving judgment for B, that the 1995 resolution was not intended to set an improvement line. No mention had been made of the Act in the resolution and the procedures required for such a decision were not present. Even if the resolution had been ambiguous, the facts did not show that there was any intention to invoke the Act. The estoppel argument was ill founded as it was an attempt to achieve the positive result of compensation rather than to protect C from an injustice.

CITYPARK PROPERTIES LTD v. BOLTON MBC [2000] R.V.R. 343, George Bartlett Q.C., Lands Tr.

4766. Rural areas – countryside access – local access forum – Wales

See ENVIRONMENT. §2404

4767. Rural areas – countryside access – maps

ACCESS TO THE COUNTRYSIDE (MAPS IN DRAFT FORM) (ENGLAND) REGULATIONS 2001, SI 2001 3301; made under the Countryside and Rights of Way Act 2000 s.5, s.11, s.44, s.45. In force: November 1, 2001; £2.00.

The Countryside and Rights of Way Act 2000 Part I establishes a new regime for access to the countryside. Under Part I maps prepared by the Countryside Agency will show registered common land and open country. These Regulations, which extend to England only, make provision for the preparation of and consultation on maps in draft form.

4768. Rural areas – countryside access – maps – Wales

See ENVIRONMENT. §2405

4769. Tree preservation orders – certificates – issue of special amenity certificates

[Town and Country Planning Act 1990 s.288; The Town and Country Planning (Tree Preservation Order) Regulations 1969 (SI 1969 17).]

B applied pursuant to the Town and Country Planning Act 1990 s.288 to challenge the decision of the Secretary of State to uphold (1) the refusal of the local planning authority to grant its consent to the felling of an oak tree which was covered by a tree preservation order, in turn governed by the Town and Country Planning (Tree Preservation Order) Regulations 1969, and (2) the issue of a special amenity certificate under Art.5 of the tree preservation order. The tree, a mature oak of 120 years age, was located outside B's house and had caused structural damage due to the action of its roots resulting in subsidence and ground heave. B contended that the certificate was a nullity as it had not been issued at the same time as the decision to refuse consent. B maintained that a mere decision to issue a certificate, albeit made at the same time as the decision to refuse consent, was insufficient for the purposes of Art.5.

Held, granting the application, that there was no jurisdiction to issue a special amenity certificate other than at the time of the decision on the application to fell. It followed that given a certificate had been omitted from the decision letter, a later formal communication had been insufficient to regularise matters. For the purposes of Art.5, "certify" meant the formal and communicated act of affirming an authority's contentment pursuant to the Article. It was required that some form of public or communicated act of certification take place.

BEYERS v. SECRETARY OF STATE FOR THE ENVIRONMENT,TRANSPORT AND THE REGIONS (2001) 82 P. & C.R. 5, Robin Purchas Q.C., QBD.

4770. Urban areas – Commission for the NewTowns – transfer of functions – Tees Barrage

COMMISSION FOR THE NEW TOWNS (TRANSFER OF UNDERTAKING AND FUNCTIONS) (TEES BARRAGE) ORDER 2001, SI 2001 361; made under the RiverTees Barrage and Crossing Act 1990 s.69. In force: February 20, 2001; £1.50.

This Order, which revokes the Teesside Development Corporation (Transfer of Undertaking and Functions) Order 1998 (SI 1998 570), transfers from the Commission for the New Towns to the British Waterways Board, all the undertaking of the former Teesside Development Corporation authorised by the River Tees Barrage and Crossing Act 1990 and all the functions conferred on the Corporation by that Act.

4771. Books

Curran, Susan – Land Use and Planning and Your Business. And Your Business. Paperback: £17.99. ISBN 0-11-702705-7. The Stationery Office Books.

Stallworthy, Mark – Sustainability, Land Use and Environment. Paperback: £48.40. ISBN 1-85941-647-0. Cavendish Publishing Ltd.

POLICE

4772. Grant – budget statement – National Crime Squad

NCS SERVICE AUTHORITY (BUDGET STATEMENT) ORDER 2001, SI 2001 2427; made under the Police Act 1997 s.61A. In force: August 1, 2001; £1.50.

This Order prescribes additional matters which the NCS (National Crime Squad) Service Authority must take into account in preparing a budget statement of the amount of grant it estimates it will require for the next financial year for submission to the Secretary of State under the Police Act 1997 s.61A. It also prescribes the information which the budget statement must contain.

4773. Grant – budget statement – National Criminal Intelligence Service

NCIS SERVICE AUTHORITY (BUDGET STATEMENT) ORDER 2001, SI 2001 2428; made under the Police Act 1997 s.16A. In force: August 1, 2001; £1.50.

This Order prescribes additional matters which the NCIS (National Criminal Intelligence Service) Service Authority must take into account in preparing a budget statement of the amount of grant it estimates it will require for the next financial year for submission to the Secretary of State under the Police Act 1997 s.61A. It also prescribes the information which the budget statement must contain.

4774. Informers – remuneration – existence of contract – criteria for appointment – jurisdiction to strike out claim

[Civil Procedure Rules 1998 (SI 1998 3132) Part 3 r.3.4, Part 24 r.24.2.]

R, a police inspector, appealed against the dismissal of his application to strike out a claim brought by C, a police informer, who sought remuneration pursuant to an alleged agreement. C maintained that he had entered into an agreement whereby he was to be remunerated according to such factors as the seriousness of the criminal activity and the risk he had been under. R had argued that no contractual obligation had existed and that, in any event, C had not earned any remuneration. It was submitted that the alleged agreement was too uncertain to be enforceable or that it could not be enforced without risking the disclosure by the police of information which they were entitled to protect on public immunity grounds.

Held, allowing the appeal (Waller, L.J. dissenting), that (1) it could not be said without the aid of evidence that the alleged agreement was too uncertain to be enforced, and (2) given that the court could not predict the extent to which sensitive issues relating to police operations and informers would have to be investigated, it was appropriate to strike out the action as embarrassing or abusive under the Civil Procedure Rules 1998 Part 3 r.3.4. The disclosure of such information if a trial took place was contrary to the public interest. In the opinion of Waller, L.J., the court did not have clear jurisdiction under Part 3 r.3.4 or Part 24 r.24.2 of the Rules to strike out the action. Accordingly, assuming that C was able to show that the police had entered into a binding contract, it was appropriate to allow him to pursue the action at least as far as the trial of a preliminary issue, notwithstanding that the police might be forced to disclose sensitive information.

CARNDUFF v. ROCK, [2001] EWCA Civ 680, [2001] 1 W.L.R. 1786, Laws, L.J., CA.

4775. **Negligence – police officers – duty of care to prevent arrested person's escape – forseeability**

See NEGLIGENCE: Vellino v. Chief Constable of Greater Manchester. §4478

4776. **Police Act 1997 (c.50) – Commencement No.7 Order**

POLICE ACT 1997 (COMMENCEMENT NO.7) ORDER 2001, SI 2001 1097 (C.36); made under the Police Act 1997 s.135. Commencement details: bringing into force various provisions of the Act on March 19, 2001 and May 1, 2001; £1.75.

This Order, which extends to England and Wales, brings into force The Police Act 1997 s.120, which relates to the register to be maintained by the Secretary of State under Part V of the Act, into force in part on March 19, 2001 and the remaining provisions on May 1, 2001. It also brings s.122(1)(2), which relates to the code of practice to be published in connection with the use of information provided to registered persons, and s.125 which relates regulations made under Part V of the 1997 Act into force, on March 19, 2001.

4777. **Police officers – disciplinary proceedings – fixed term contracts – applicability where contract expired**

[Police Regulations 1995 (SI 1995 215) Reg.16(1).]

S, a police authority, appealed against the dismissal (Times, July 5, 2001) of its claim for a declaration that it was entitled to continue disciplinary proceedings against B, its Senior Assistant Chief Constable, beyond the date on which his fixed term contract expired. B had been suspended following complaints of sexual harassment against him, and disciplinary proceedings had been instigated. It subsequently became apparent that the internal proceedings would not be resolved until after the expiry of B's contract. SPA submitted that under the Police Regulations 1995 Reg.16(1), a police officer could not just allow his fixed term contract to expire, but had also to give written notice to the effect that he intended to retire on the expiry date.

Held, dismissing the appeal, that a police officer could not be subject to disciplinary proceedings after the expiry of his fixed term contract. S's submission as to written notice was inconsistent with both the terms of the fixed term contract and with the 1995 Regulations. Had the proceedings been able to continue, no financial penalty could have been imposed on B. As it was, SPA had been saved from having to pay B's salary for any further period of suspension.

SURREY POLICE AUTHORITY v. BECKETT, [2001] EWCA Civ 1253, [2002] I.C.R. 257, Simon Brown, L.J., CA.

4778. Police officers – disciplinary proceedings – psychiatric illness – entitlement to gratuity and injury pension

[Police Pensions Regulations 1987 (SI 1987 257).]

The Police Commissioner appealed against the quashing of a decision made by an independent medical referee, who had found that a permanently disabling psychiatric injury suffered by a police constable, S, was not an injury received in the execution of his duty as a constable for the purposes of the Police Pensions Regulations 1987. S had suffered a stress related depressive illness after being subjected to internal disciplinary proceedings as a result of a complaint by a member of the public whom he had arrested whilst on duty. The Police Commissioner contended that the strict wording of the Regulations did not apply to a case of developing illness. Further, that a causal test was involved such that the injury had to have been caused in the execution of duty. Accordingly the stress related illness suffered by S was as a result of the allegations made against him, not by his work as a police officer, and his involvement in the complaints procedure did not constitute the execution of his duty.

Held, allowing the appeal, that the Regulations should not be afforded the strict interpretation contended for by the Police Commissioner in that an officer suffering a permanent disability as a result of an injury received whilst on duty would be entitled to a gratuity and injury pension. However, an injury resulting from subjection to disciplinary proceedings could not be said to have been incurred in the execution of duty, as that injury resulted from the police officer's status as such, *R. v. Kellam, ex p. South Wales Police Authority* [2000] I.C.R. 632, [1999] C.L.Y. 4299 followed.

R. (ON THE APPLICATION OF STUNT) v. MALLETT; *sub nom.* COMMISSIONER OF POLICE v. STUNT; R. v. METROPOLITAN POLICE SERVICE, *ex p.* STUNT; R. v. MALLETT, *ex p.* STUNT, [2001] EWCA Civ 265, [2001] I.C.R. 989, Simon Brown, L.J., CA.

4779. Police officers – senior police ranks – consequential amendments

CRIMINAL JUSTICE AND POLICE ACT 2001 (CONSEQUENTIAL AMENDMENTS) (POLICE RANKS) REGULATIONS 2001, SI 2001 3888; made under the Police Pensions Act 1976 s.1; and the Police Act 1996 s.50. In force: January 1, 2002; £1.75.

These Regulations make amendments to the Police Pensions Regulations 1987 (SI 1987 257), the Police Regulations 1995 (SI 1995 215), the Police (Efficiency) Regulations 1999 (SI 1999 732), the Police (Conduct) Regulations 1999 (SI 1999 730) and the Police (Conduct) (Senior Officers) Regulations 1999 (SI 1999 731) consequential on provisions in the Criminal Justice and Police Act 2001 s.122 to s.125 relating to senior police ranks.

4780. Police officers – wrongful arrest – false entries in police national computer – sufficiency of honest belief

The Chief Constable appealed against an award of damages made in favour of H in proceedings for wrongful arrest, assault and false imprisonment. H had been a passenger in a car stopped by traffic officers. A routine check on the police national computer had purportedly revealed that H might be armed with a firearm and as a result an armed response unit was summoned and he was arrested and detained. The computer entry was subsequently determined by the trial judge to have been false and he further determined that no objective grounds for arrest had accordingly existed despite the honestly held belief of the arresting officer that H was likely to be in possession of a firearm. The Chief Constable contended that the only issue of relevance was the belief held by the officer at the time of arrest and that it was of no importance whether the officer who made the computer entry had had reasonable grounds for placing the information.

Held, allowing the appeal, that an entry in the police national computer was likely to constitute sufficient objective justification for an arrest and the facts of the instant case had provided such justification. This was necessarily the case in view of the fact that an officer was clearly entitled to base the grounds for his suspicion upon information received via a police informer or from the public. However, in certain other circumstances, such as where the situation was not so urgent, the arresting officer was likely to be subject to a duty to make additional enquiries before a reasonable suspicion could be founded, *O'Hara v. Chief Constable of the Royal Ulster Constabulary* [1997] A.C. 286 applied and *Millington v. Commissioner of Police of the Metropolis* Times, May 28, 1983, [1983] C.L.Y. 1076 doubted.

HOUGH v. CHIEF CONSTABLE OF STAFFORDSHIRE *The Times*, February 14, 2001, Simon Brown, L.J., CA.

4781. Police powers – codes of practice – drug testing provisions

POLICE AND CRIMINAL EVIDENCE ACT 1984 (CODES OF PRACTICE) (MODIFICATION) ORDER 2001, SI 2001 2254; made under the Police and Criminal Evidence Act 1984 s.67. In force: July 16, 2001; £1.75.

The Police and Criminal Evidence Act 1984 s.63B gives police officers a new power to undertake tests for the presence of specified Class A drugs in relation to certain persons in police detention and s.66(2) of the Act provides that codes in connection with these powers must be in place before the powers are exercised. This Order puts in place modifications to the Police and Criminal Evidence Act 1984 codes of practice to provide for drug testing within police detention. The modifications are to have effect only for two years and extend only to named police areas where the drug testing provisions are to be piloted.

4782. Police powers – detention – death in custody – level of care and supervision required for alcoholic

M, an alcoholic aged 32, was arrested by police and detained in the police station overnight, officers believing he was too drunk to be interviewed immediately. M's sister spoke to the custody sergeant by telephone, telling him that M was likely to have the "shakes", to which the custody sergeant replied that medical attention would be sought if necessary. The conversation was not noted on the custody record. The following morning, despite M showing symptoms of alcohol withdrawal manifested by badly shaking hands, no medical attention was sought and M was released alone into the exercise yard. A short time later he was found lying on the ground suffering convulsions and with a wound to his head. Upon reaching hospital he suffered two further serious fits and died. A scan taken whilst he was in hospital showed that he had a very large inter cerebral blood clot, a fractured skull and two pre-existing congenital lesions of the brain. The inquest jury returned a verdict of accidental death aggravated by neglect. The Chief Constable sought judicial review of the verdict contending that there was no basis on which to invite the jury to make such a finding, since there was no evidence of a causal link between the acts of the police officers and the death. Furthermore that neglect could only be said to contribute to a death which was already in train at the time of the neglect.

Held, refusing the application for judicial review, that there was sufficient evidence to support the verdict. It amounted to a finding that, given M's condition and the knowledge imparted to the officers by M's sister, he should not have been left alone in the exercise yard. Such a finding could not be regarded as unsafe. In relation to causation, the test was not the same as in civil negligence and there was no need to establish that death was already in train. As it was possible to extrapolate from the facts of the instant case that a greater level of care could have prevented M's death, the causal link was made out.

R. v. HM CORONER FOR COVENTRY, *ex p*. CHIEF CONSTABLE OF STAFFORDSHIRE (2000) 164 J.P. 665, Tomlinson, J, QBD.

4783. Police powers – driving licences – disclosure of information

MOTOR VEHICLES (ACCESS TO DRIVER LICENSING RECORDS) REGULATIONS 2001, SI 2001 3343; made under the Criminal Justice and Court Services Act 2000 s.71. In force: October 29, 2001; £1.50.

These Regulations determine the purposes for which information contained in the Driver Licensing Register and made available to the Police Information Technology Organisation may be passed on to constables. They also provide for such information to be further disclosed to civilian employees of police authorities to facilitate the use of the information by constables.

4784. Police powers – duty solicitor scheme – objections to legal representative – blanket ban

[Police and Criminal Evidence Act 1984 Code C para.6.12.]

T, a former police officer who had been dismissed for misconduct and whose appeal against dismissal was pending, appealed against the refusal of his application for judicial review of a decision of the Chief Constable prohibiting him from attending at any police station within the area of the force in his capacity as a probationary police station representative, PSR. T submitted that under the Police and Criminal Evidence Act 1984 Code C para.6.12, the only justifiable ground for excluding a PSR from a police station was if "his visit would hinder the investigation of crime" and that the capacity of a PSR to provide legal advice was not a direct concern of the police.

Held, allowing the appeal, that the Chief Constable was not entitled to impose a blanket ban on a PSR attending at police stations to perform his duty as the role of the police was limited to a consideration of whether the investigation of a specific crime would be hindered by a PSR, and this could only be undertaken on a case by case basis, *R. v. Chief Constable of Avon and Somerset, ex p. Robinson* [1989] 1 W.L.R. 793, [1989] C.L.Y. 764 applied. The Chief Constable could advise that the character of a PSR was likely to hinder an investigation and an officer could reach a decision, in the light of that advice, as to whether the attendance of a PSR at a station might hinder a particular investigation. The police had a duty to ensure that arrested persons detained at a police station had access to legal advice but were not required to concern themselves with the quality of that advice. It was important that the advice should be independent and the responsibility for ensuring that this was so was that of the solicitor rather than the police. Recourse in the event of dissatisfaction was to the Law Society.

R. (ON THE APPLICATION OF THOMPSON) v. CHIEF CONSTABLE OF NORTHUMBRIA; *sub nom.* R. v. CHIEF CONSTABLE OF NORTHUMBRIA, *ex p.* THOMPSON, [2001] EWCA Civ 321, [2001] 1 W.L.R. 1342, Lord Woolf of Barnes, L.C.J., CA.

4785. Police powers – motor vehicles – removal when abandoned

[Road Traffic Regulation Act 1984 s.99(1); Removal and Disposal of Vehicles Regulations 1986 (SI 1986 183) Reg.4.]

C appealed against the dismissal of his application for the return of a vehicle. C had reported the theft of the vehicle, which belonged to a friend, to the police. The vehicle had subsequently been found by a police officer and towed away in accordance with usual police procedure under the Road Traffic Regulation Act 1984 s.99(1) and the Removal and Disposal of Vehicles Regulations 1986 Reg.4, which empowered an officer to remove a vehicle if it "appear[ed] to have been abandoned without lawful authority". C maintained that the term "abandoned" within Reg.4 meant given up by the owner and that accordingly, as the officer had or should have known the vehicle to be stolen, there had been no power to remove it without the owner's consent.

Held, dismissing the appeal, that the relevant question for the purposes of Reg.4 was not whether the vehicle had been abandoned but whether it appeared to the police officer to have been abandoned. Since in the instant case there was no evidence to suggest that it did not appear to the police officer who found the vehicle that it had been abandoned, the officer had acted both reasonably and lawfully in having the vehicle removed. Furthermore, as the judge had correctly concluded, C had not had the right to bring the instant proceedings without evidence from the vehicle owner.

CLARKE v. CHIEF CONSTABLE OF WEST MIDLANDS; *sub nom.* CLARKE v. RYLEY, [2001] EWCA Civ 1169, [2002] R.T.R. 5, Longmore, L.J., CA.

4786. Police powers – police authorities – balance of representatives according to political party

[Police Act 1996 Sch.2 para.4(1)(b).]

E applied for judicial review of a decision by J appointing members to the Humberside Police Authority, H. E, which was one of four local authorities included in the H area, argued that J should have taken into account the numbers of independent councillors in each authority for the purposes of calculating how many councillors should be appointed to the H in order to reflect "the balance of parties" among the relevant councils, as required by the Police Act 1996 Sch.2 para.4(1)(b). J contended that "balance of parties" referred only to the balance of numbers of seats held by councillors as representatives of political parties, and independents were therefore excluded.

Held, dismissing the application, that the wording of para.4 of the Act clearly referred to "parties" and it had to be assumed that it was Parliament's intention that only representatives of political parties were to be included in the calculation. Reference to Hansard only served to confirm that assumption. The wording had to be given its natural meaning, and independent councillors who by definition did not belong to any party could not be taken into account. Any apparent unfairness which resulted could only be remedied by Parliament.

R. (ON THE APPLICATION OF EAST RIDING OF YORKSHIRE COUNCIL) v. JOINT COMMITTEE FOR THE PURPOSE OF MAKING APPOINTMENTS TO THE HUMBERSIDE POLICE AUTHORITY; *sub nom.* R. v. JOINT COMMITTEE FOR THE PURPOSE OF MAKING APPOINTMENTS TO THE HUMBERSIDE POLICE AUTHORITY, *ex p.* EAST RIDING OF YORKSHIRE COUNCIL (2001) 3 L.G.L.R. 46, Rafferty, J., QBD (Admin Ct).

4787. Police powers – powers of entry – failure to fulfil search requirements

[Police and Criminal Evidence Act 1984 s.18.]

PL had been arrested on suspicion of burglary and subsequently the arresting police officers visited his home address with a search warrant with the intention of searching the premises for the proceeds of the burglary. On arrival at the house, PL's father, L, the appellant, requested that the officers slide the search warrant under the door, which they refused to do requesting L to come to the window to view the warrant. Upon his refusal, the officers forced entry and arrested L after he had assaulted them. L appealed by case stated against his conviction for assaulting a constable in the exercise of his duty, contending that since the officers had not complied with the requirements of the Police and Criminal Evidence Act 1984 s.18 in stating their purpose for the search, the grounds for undertaking it or showing the search warrant, then the search was conducted without authority and the officers were not acting in the execution of their duty.

Held, allowing the appeal and quashing the convictions, that the officers had failed to give a proper explanation for the search and there was insufficient evidence on which to found an inference that L knew the reason for the search, accordingly the magistrates were not entitled to find that the officers were acting in the execution of their duty. The evidence presented in the case stated was defective in that it did not provide enough material on which to ascertain the answers to the crucial questions of fact necessary to determine the key issues.

LINEHAN v. DPP [2000] Crim. L.R. 861, Laws, L.J., QBD.

4788. Police powers – search and seizure – request to demonstrator to remove mask

[Police and Criminal Evidence Act 1984 s.2; Criminal Justice and Public Order Act 1994 s.60.]

The DPP appealed against a decision of the magistrates dismissing charges against A of assault on a police officer in the execution of his duty and criminal damage to a pair of spectacles belonging to that officer. The officer had requested A, who had been taking part in a demonstration, to remove a mask she was wearing. Upon her refusing to do so, the officer took hold of the mask in order to remove it. The officer did not provide A with details of his name, the station at which he was based or the reason he wished her to remove the mask. A hit the officer and his spectacles fell to the ground. At the time of the incident, authorisation had been given by a senior police officer that the powers conferred by the Criminal Justice and Public Order Act 1994 s.60, as amended, were exercisable. The magistrates had concluded that the officer's powers under s.60(4A) of the 1994 Act had to be exercised pursuant to the provisions relating to searches within the Police and Criminal Evidence Act 1984 s.2(2)(b) and s.2(3), failing which the seizure of the mask was unlawful and the officer had not been acting in the execution of his duty.

Held, allowing the appeal, that a police officer was not required to comply with s.2 of the 1984 Act when exercising a power conferred by s.60(4A) of the 1994 Act. Section 60(4A) of the 1994 Act was not concerned with powers to search. It was apparent that the reason for an officer to request that an individual remove a mask was self explanatory, namely, it was a request to such person to reveal his identity. In such circumstances there was nothing gained by an officer explaining to such person that he believed they were concealing their identity. Moreover, the fact that an officer was required to have a subjective belief amounted to a legislative restraint on the exercise of the power either oppressively or arbitrarily, *Brazil v. Chief Constable of Surrey* [1983] 3 All E.R. 537, [1983] C.L.Y. 2841 considered.

DPP v. AVERY, [2001] EWHC Admin 748, [2002] 1 Cr. App. R. 31, Newman, J., QBD (Admin Ct).

4789. Police powers – search and seizure – title to stolen motor vehicle – obligation to return property seized to wrongdoer

C appealed against the refusal of his claim for the return of a car and for damages for wrongful detention following its seizure by the police. The owner of the car was unknown. The judge had found that as C had known the car to be stolen, he was precluded from maintaining his claim to it. C argued that as a result of the Court of Appeals's judgment in *Webb v. Chief Constable of Merseyside* [2000] Q.B. 427, [2000] C.L.Y. 4546 in which it had been held that following the cessation of the right of the police to retain property, the person from whom it was seized was entitled to its return and the court was required to uphold his claim. CCD argued that as the car was stolen, the police became its possessory owners and had no obligation to restore it to C.

Held, allowing the appeal, that although the judge had been entitled to conclude that C was aware that the car was stolen, a person with possessory title was entitled to the same legal protection whether or not that title had been obtained by legal means and that a moral disinclination or public policy were not sufficient grounds to remove that protection, *Webb* followed.

COSTELLO v. CHIEF CONSTABLE OF DERBYSHIRE, [2001] EWCA Civ 381, [2001] 1 W.L.R. 1437, Lightman, J., CA.

4790. Police powers – warrants – execution of default warrant – police discretion as to timing of execution

H, who had brought proceedings against the Chief Constable for wrongful detention, appealed against a decision upholding a preliminary determination that the police had a lawful discretion as to when to execute a default warrant issued in respect of the non payment of a fine, provided that the exercise of that discretion was not *Wednesbury* unreasonable. H submitted that having regard to the statutory background and wording of the warrant, the warrant had to be executed as soon as was reasonably practicable and that such obligation applied to both the arrest and taking before the court. In the alternative, H argued that it was an unreasonable exercise of that discretion to delay the execution of the warrant until the conclusion of a criminal investigation with the result that he was arrested at a time when it meant that he would not appear before the court for 40 hours because the magistrates court was closed.

Held, dismissing the appeal, that (1) a default warrant issued by the magistrates' court in respect of unpaid fines was to be executed at the discretion of the police but such discretion had to be exercised in accordance with *Wednesbury* principles. As to the interpretation of the warrant, the word "immediately" governed when a defaulter had to be taken before the court but did not govern when the arrest had to take place, *Hoye v. Bush* (1840) 1 Man. & G. 775 distinguished, and (2) it might, dependent upon the circumstances and particular facts of a case, be a reasonable and lawful exercise of their discretion, for the police to delay the execution of the default warrant until the conclusion of a criminal investigation. The exercise of such discretion was reviewable on *Wednesbury* grounds but could also have private law consequences, *Holgate-Mohammed v. Duke* [1984] A.C. 437, [1984] C.L.Y. 147 considered. However, the circumstances in which an action for damages would be appropriate would be limited.

HENDERSON v. CHIEF CONSTABLE OF CLEVELAND, [2001] EWCA Civ 335, [2001] 1 W.L.R. 1103, Lord Woolf of Barnes, L.C.J., CA.

4791. Police service – conditions of employment – allowances

POLICE (AMENDMENT) REGULATIONS 2001, SI 2001 3293; made under the Police Act 1996 s.50. In force: in accordance with Reg.1 (2); £2.00.

These Regulations, which amend the Police Regulations 1995 (SI 1995 215), make provision for part-time workers, including those taking part in job share arrangements. They provide that the pay of a chief inspector who for 14 days in any year performs the duties of a superintendent will be determined in respect of any further days in that year in which the chief inspector performs those duties by reference to the pay Range applicable to superintendents. In addition, the Regulations increase the amount of the London weighting, provide for a higher rate on pay on promotion, increase removal allowances, abolish detecting expenses allowances, provide additional allowances for members serving in forces in London and the south east of England and increases a single dog handler's allowance.

4792. Books

Walker, Neil – Policing in a Changing Constitutional Order. Modern Legal Studies. Paperback: £19.95. ISBN 0-421-63370-0. Sweet & Maxwell.

POSTAL SERVICES

4793. Dominant position – postal rates – interception by public postal authorities of ABA remail taking advantage of lower postal rates – European Union

[EC Treaty Art.86 (now Art.82 EC), Art.173 (now, after amendment, Art.230 EC); Universal Postal Union Convention 1964 Art.23.]

IE represented the interests of express mail service providers. Its members offered "remail" services, which involved transporting mail from its country of origin to another State where it was placed with a public postal operator for final delivery. IE complained, inter alia, that certain public postal operators were operating a market allocation scheme under the Universal Postal Union

Convention 1964 Art.23, in breach of the EC Treaty Art.86 (now Art.82 EC), which involved declining deliveries of mail posted by customers with public postal operators in countries other than their states of residence. The Commission rejected the complaint but the CFI annulled that decision ([1998] E.C.R. II-3645, [1998] C.L.Y. 4294) on the ground that, contrary to the Commission's view, the existence of the postal monopoly and the necessity for the public postal operators to defend their monopoly could not remove the interceptions from the scope of Art.86. The operators appealed to the ECJ, seeking the annulment of the CFI's decision.

Held, dismissing the appeal, that the CFI had correctly confined itself to determining whether the Commission's reasoning was valid, as it was required to do in an action for annulment based on EC Treaty Art.173 (now, after amendment, Art.230 EC). The subsequent annulment of the Commission's decision was not equivalent to a finding of abuse. Further, it was not for the CFI in an action for the annulment of a decision to establish the existence of abuse of a dominant position. As the CFI's jurisdiction was not unlimited, it could not substitute another decision for the contested decision or amend that decision.

DEUTSCHE POST AG v. INTERNATIONAL EXPRESS CARRIERS CONFERENCE (C428/98) [2001] 4 C.M.L.R. 3, Edward (President), ECJ.

4794. Postal service – post offices – subsidies

SUB-POST OFFICE START-UP CAPITAL SUBSIDY SCHEME ORDER 2001, SI 2001 2664; made under the Postal Services Act 2000 s.103, s.122. In force: July 19, 2001; £1.75.

This Order sets out the Sub-Post Office Start-Up Capital Subsidy Scheme which provides for the payment of subsidy by the Secretary of State in respect of the costs of establishing a sub-post office or to secure the continued operation of a sub-post office in a settlement of fewer than 10,000 inhabitants where an existing sub-post office has closed or is likely to close. The functions of the Secretary of State under the Scheme are exercisable by Post Office Counters Ltd. The maximum amount of grant payable in respect of an application is £20,000 and the total maximum amount of subsidy available is £2,000,000.

4795. Postal Services Act 2000 (c.26) – Commencement No.2 Order

POSTAL SERVICES ACT 2000 (COMMENCEMENT NO.2) ORDER 2001, SI 2001 534 (C.22); made under the Postal Services Act 2000 s.130. Commencement details: bringing into force various provisions of the Act on February 26, 2001; £1.75.

This Order brings into force certain provisions of the Postal Services Act 2000 on February 26, 2001.

4796. Postal Services Act 2000 (c.26) – Commencement No.3 and Transitional and Saving Provisions Order

POSTAL SERVICES ACT 2000 (COMMENCEMENT NO.3 AND TRANSITIONAL AND SAVING PROVISIONS) ORDER 2001, SI 2001 878 (C.31); made under the Postal Services Act 2000 s.129, s.130. Commencement details: bringing into force various provisions of Act on March 26, 2001; £2.00.

This Order brings into force various provisions of the Postal Services Act 2000 on March 26, 2001.

4797. Postal Services Act 2000 (c.26) – Commencement No.4 and Transitional and Saving Provisions Order

POSTAL SERVICES ACT 2000 (COMMENCEMENT NO.4 AND TRANSITIONAL AND SAVING PROVISIONS) ORDER 2001, SI 2001 1148 (C.37); made under the

Postal Services Act 2000 s.122, s.129, s.130. Commencement details: bringing into force various provisions of Act on March 25, 2001 and March 26, 2001; £3.00.

This Order, which amends the Postal Services Act 2000 (Commencement No. 1 and Transitional Provisions) Order 2000 (SI 2000 2957), brings into force the Postal Services Act 2000 s.116 on March 25, 2001 and provisions specified in the Schedule to the Order, on March 26, 2001.

4798. Postal Services Commission – register – public access

POSTAL SERVICES COMMISSION (REGISTER) ORDER 2001, SI 2001 620; made under the Postal Service Act 2000 s.38. In force: March 26, 2001; £1.50.

This Order specifies the hours during which the register maintained by the Postal Services Commission under the Postal Services Act 2000 s.38 is to be kept open for the public.

4799. Supply of services – disclosure of information

POSTAL SERVICES ACT 2000 (DISCLOSURE OF INFORMATION) ORDER 2001, SI 2001 3617; made under the Postal Services Act 2000 Sch.7 para.4. In force: December 1, 2001; £1.75.

This Order, which amends the Postal Services Act 2000, prohibits the disclosure of certain information obtained under the Act.

4800. Supply of services – licences – penalties – determination of turnover

POSTAL SERVICES ACT 2000 (DETERMINATION OF TURNOVER FOR PENALTIES) ORDER 2001, SI 2001 1135; made under the Postal Services Act 2000 s.30. In force: March 26, 2001; £1.50.

This Order specifies the way to determine the turnover of a licence holder for the purposes of the Postal Services Act 2000 s.30. Where the Postal Services Commission is satisfied that a licence holder has contravened or is contravening any condition of his licence, the Commission may impose on the licence holder a penalty of up to 10 per cent of its turnover determined in accordance with the provisions specified in this Order.

4801. Supply of services – modifications

POSTAL SERVICES ACT 2000 (CONSEQUENTIAL MODIFICATIONS NO.1) ORDER 2001, SI 2001 1149; made under the Postal Services Act 2000 s.122, s.127. In force: March 26, 2001; £6.50.

This Order makes consequential and supplementary provisions in connection with the commencement of the provisions of the Postal Services Act 2000.

4802. Supply of services – universal service provider – local enactments

POSTAL SERVICES ACT 2000 (CONSEQUENTIAL MODIFICATIONS TO LOCAL ENACTMENTS NO.1) ORDER 2001, SI 2001 648; made under the Postal Services Act 2000 s.122, s.128. In force: March 26, 2001; £2.00.

This Order, which makes supplemental, incidental and consequential provision in relation to local enactments in connection with the commencement of the provisions of the Postal Services Act 2000, confers on universal service providers the benefit of certain compulsory powers in relation to land originally conferred by local enactments on the Postmaster-General and transferred to the Post Office by the Postal Services Act 1969 Sch.4 para.100 which is repealed by the Order. The Order requires references in any such orders to a Post Office vehicle or a vehicle bearing the Royal Mail livery to be construed as a reference to a vehicle that bears a livery that is used by a universal service provider in connection with the provision of a universal postal service and requires references to a statutory duty of the Post Office to be construed as references to the duty of the universal service provider to provide a universal postal service. It also makes amendments to various local enactments.

RATES

4803. Central rating list – designated persons and hereditaments

CENTRAL RATING LISTS (ENGLAND) (AMENDMENT) REGULATIONS 2001, SI 2001 737; made under the Local Government Finance Act 1988 s.53, s.64, s.65. In force: April 1, 2001; £1.75.

These Regulations amend the Central Rating Lists (England) Regulations 2000 (SI 2000 525) by designating a group of gas transporting companies and securing that the prescribed premises each of them uses for the purposes of acting as a public gas transporter are rated as a single hereditament and by substituting Ineos Chlor Ltd for Imperial Chemical Industries Plc.

4804. Community charge – council tax – non domestic rates

COMMUNITY CHARGES, COUNCIL TAX AND NON-DOMESTIC RATING (ENFORCEMENT) (MAGISTRATES' COURTS) (ENGLAND) REGULATIONS 2001, SI 2001 362; made under the Local Government Finance Act 1988 s.143, Sch.4 para.1, Sch.4 para.8, Sch.9 para.1, Sch.9 para.3; the Local Government Act 1992 s.113; and the Local Government Act Sch.4 para.1, para.8. In force: April 1, 2001; £1.50.

These Regulations, which amend the Community Charges (Administration and Enforcement) Regulations 1989 (SI 1989 438), Non-Domestic Rating (Collection and Enforcement) (Local Lists) Regulations 1989 (SI 1989 1058) and the Council Tax (Administration and Enforcement) Regulations 1992 (SI 1992 613) in relation to England only, transfer the administrative functions of justices' clerks under them to justices' chief executives.

4805. Community charge – council tax – non domestic rates – Wales

COMMUNITY CHARGES, COUNCIL TAX AND NON-DOMESTIC RATING (ENFORCEMENT) (MAGISTRATES' COURTS) (WALES) REGULATIONS 2001, SI 2001 1076 (W.52); made under the Local Government Finance Act 1988 Sch.4 para.1, para.13, Sch.9 para.1; and the Local Government Finance Act 1992 Sch.4 para.1, para.13. In force: In accordance with Reg.1; £2.00.

These Regulations, which amend the Community Charges (Administration and Enforcement) Regulations 1989 (SI 1989 438), the Non-Domestic Rating (Collection and Enforcement) (Local Lists) Regulations 1989 (SI 1989 1058) and the Council Tax (Administration and Enforcement) Regulations 1992 (SI 1992 613), take account of the Access to Justice Act 1999 which unifies and renames the stipendiary magistrates' bench and provides for the transfer of the administrative functions of justices' clerks to justices' chief executives.

4806. Council tax – caravans – meaning of "rateable hereditament"

B, a former council officer with Copeland Borough Council, CPC, made a formal complaint to the district auditor that the finance director, W, had been guilty of wilful misconduct in failing to pay council tax for a period of two weeks in which he had been living in a caravan prior to moving in to his new house. B alleged that this had resulted in a loss to CPC of some £13. The district auditor rejected B's complaint, and B appealed, arguing that the auditor's decision was wrong in law.

Held, dismissing the appeal, that there had been no liability on W to pay council tax for the period in the caravan, and therefore there had been no loss to CPC. A caravan, being a chattel, could only be a rateable hereditament where it occupied a specific site for more than a transient period, *Field Place Caravan Park Ltd v. Harding (Valuation Officer)* [1966] 2 Q.B. 484, [1966] C.L.Y. 10227 applied. The two weeks in which W was resident in the caravan was not sufficient to bring it within that definition.

BOARDMAN v. PORTMAN (2001) 3 L.G.L.R. 7, Elias, J., QBD.

4807. Council tax – demand notices

COUNCIL TAX AND NON-DOMESTIC RATING (DEMAND NOTICES) (ENGLAND) (AMENDMENT) REGULATIONS 2001, SI 2001 3554; made under the Local Government Finance Act 1992 s.113, Sch.2 para.1, Sch.2 para.2. In force: November 29, 2001; £1.75.

These Regulations amend the Council Tax and Non-Domestic Rating (Demand Notices) (England) Regulations 1993 (SI 1993 191) in relation to the information to be included on council tax demand notices. They insert a new paragraph which requires billing authorities to include information on their demand notices as to the annual percentage changes in council tax between the previous year and the relevant year.

4808. Council tax – licences – occupants not tenants – no exclusive possession or liability for rent

[Council Tax (Liability for Owners) Regulations 1992 (SI 1992 551) Class C(b)(i), Class C(b)(ii).]

N owned a property which was occupied by W and M under an agreement which granted each occupier exclusive possession of a room. M later left and a series of co-occupiers shared the property with W thereafter. The subsequent agreements entered into for occupation of the premises did not contain any provision for exclusive possession of any part of the dwelling. A valuation tribunal concluded that the Council Tax (Liability for Owners) Regulations 1992 Class C(b)(i) did not apply, on the basis that the occupants did not have exclusive possession of any part of the dwelling and did not therefore fulfil the definition of a tenancy. The tribunal went on to conclude that the arrangements constituted a licence to occupy under Class C(b)(ii). N appealed, contending that (1) the occupants were joint tenants of the whole dwelling, and (2) alternatively, any individual sharing with W was a sub tenant or lodger of W.

Held, dismissing the appeal, that the tribunal had been correct to conclude that the "tenants" only had a licence to occupy since (1) the occupants never had exclusive possession of any part of the premises despite the assertions made in the original agreements with W and M; (2) if one occupant left then the remaining occupant was not then liable for their share of the rent and therefore it could not be argued that each individual occupied the dwelling as a whole. Furthermore, in the case of W, the agreement specifically stated that she was only entitled to occupy the premises if sharing with another, *AG Securities v. Vaughan* [1990] 1 A.C. 417, [1989] C.L.Y. 2145 applied, and (3) the fact that W was able to choose the individual that shared the property with her was not indicative of any illegal sub agreement since that choice was always subject to the approval of N.

NORRIS v. BIRMINGHAM CITY COUNCIL [2001] R.V.R. 89, Newman, J., QBD.

4809. Council tax – multiple occupation – bedsitting accommodation – shared bathroom and toilet facilities

M sought permission to appeal against the refusal of his application for permission to apply for judicial review of the decision of the tribunal upholding the designation by a listing officer of M's accommodation as a separate dwelling in council tax band A. M lived in a bed sitting room with a kitchen but shared bathroom and toilet facilities with up to 13 other people. M argued that his accommodation did not constitute a separate dwelling for council tax purposes as it had no sale value as a separate unit.

Held, dismissing the application, that the tribunal's decision was based on a correct application of the principles of law that such dwellings could be "separate" dwellings, *James v. Williams* [1973] J.P.L. 658, [1973] C.L.Y. 2766.12 applied. There was no merit in M's application, and in any event he should have appealed against the tribunal's decision rather than proceeding by way of a judicial review application.

R. v. LONDON SOUTH EAST VALUATION TRIBUNAL, *ex p.* MOORE [2001] R.V.R. 92, Simon Brown, L.J., CA.

4810. Non domestic rates – agricultural property

NON-DOMESTIC RATING (FORMER AGRICULTURAL PREMISES) (ENGLAND) ORDER 2001, SI 2001 2585; made under the Local Government Finance Act 1988 s.43. In force: August 15, 2001; £1.50.

The Rating (Former Agricultural Premises and Rural Shops) Act 2001 inserts subsections (6F) to (6L) into the Local Government Finance Act 1988 s.43, thus providing for mandatory rate relief for certain former agricultural premises. This Order provides that £6,000 is the maximum rateable value of a hereditament which can be eligible for such relief.

4811. Non domestic rates – alteration of lists – appeals

NON-DOMESTIC RATING (ALTERATION OF LISTS AND APPEALS) (AMENDMENT) (ENGLAND) REGULATIONS 2001, SI 2001 1271; made under the Local Government Finance Act 1988 s.55, s.143. In force: April 1, 2001; £2.00.

These Regulations amend the Non-Domestic Rating (Alteration of Lists and Appeals) Regulations 1993 (SI 1993 291) to extend in the cases specified, the time from which an alteration to the list will have effect. The cases are in relation to local rating lists compiled in 2000 where the alteration is made pursuant to a proposal served after March 31 and before July 1, 2001, where the grounds of the proposal arose before April 1, 2001 and where the relevant hereditament is in an area listed in Sch.3 to the Regulations.

4812. Non domestic rates – alteration of lists – appeals – Wales

NON-DOMESTIC RATING (ALTERATION OF LISTS AND APPEALS) (AMENDMENT) (WALES) REGULATIONS 2001, SI 2001 1203 (W.64); made under the Local Government Finance Act 1988 s.55, s.140, s.143. In force: April 1, 2001; £1.75.

These Regulations, which amend the Non-Domestic Rating (Alteration of Lists and Appeals) Regulations 1993 (SI 1993 291) in relation to Wales, concern the alteration of non-domestic rating lists compiled under the Local Government Finance Act 1988. They include provision for an alteration to a list compiled on or after April 1, 2000 which is made on the grounds of a material change of circumstances to have effect from the day on which the circumstances giving rise to the alteration first arose or from the first day of the financial year in which the proposal is served, whichever is the later. Consequently, the alteration in the list will only take effect from the day on which the change of circumstances first arose if the proposal is served before the end of the financial year in which the change first occurred. The effect of these Regulation is that, where the list compiled on April 1, 2000 is altered following a proposal on the grounds of a material change of circumstances which first arose on a day after December 31, 2000 but before April 1, 2001, the alteration will have effect from that day if the proposal is served before July 1, 2001.

4813. Non domestic rates – calculation of contributions – amendment of rules

NON-DOMESTIC RATING CONTRIBUTIONS (ENGLAND) (AMENDMENT) REGULATIONS 2001, SI 2001 3944; made under the Local Government Finance 1988 s.143, Sch.8 para.4, Sch.8 para.6. In force: December 31, 2001; £1.75.

Under the Local Government Finance Act 1988 billing authorities are required to pay amounts to the Secretary of State. Payments in respect of a provisional amount of the contributions are made during the financial year, final calculations and any adjustments of payments being made after the year ends. These Regulations amend the rules for calculation of contributions contained in the Non-Domestic Rating Contributions (England) Regulations 1992 (SI 1992 3082) by altering certain figures used in the calculations.

4814. Non domestic rates – calculation of contributions – amendment of rules – Wales

NON-DOMESTIC RATING CONTRIBUTIONS (WALES) (AMENDMENT) REGULATIONS 2001, SI 2001 3910 (W.322); made under the Local Government Finance Act 1988 s.140, s.143, Sch.8 para.4, Sch.8 para.5, Sch.8 para.6. In force: December 31, 2001; £1.75.

Under the Local Government Finance Act 1988 Part II billing authorities in Wales are required to pay amounts to the National Assembly for Wales. These Regulations amend the Non-Domestic Rating Contributions (Wales) Regulations 1992 (SI 1992 3238) by substituting a new percentage for the calculation of those amounts.

4815. Non domestic rates – designation of rural areas

NON-DOMESTIC RATING (DESIGNATION OF RURAL AREAS) (ENGLAND) ORDER 2001, SI 2001 3916; made under the Local Government Finance Act 1988 s.42A. In force: December 31, 2001; £1.75.

The Local Government Finance Act 1988 provides for mandatory relief from non-domestic rates for public houses, petrol filling stations, general stores, food stores and post offices, and discretionary relief for hereditaments used for purposes beneficial to the local community, in certain rural settlements in areas designated as rural areas by order of the Secretary of State. This Order designates further areas in England only and provides for all of England outside of the local authority areas specified to be designated as a rural area.

4816. Non domestic rates – double taxation – electricity power stations – intention to permit double assessment

[Local Government Finance Act 1988 Sch.6 para.3(2); Electricity Supply Industry (Rateable Values) Order 1994 (SI 1994 3282).]

E, an electricity generating company, appealed against a decision ([2001] R.A.1) refusing its application for judicial review of a refusal to amend the central rating list for the year 1999/2000 in respect of two power stations acquired by E from P. As a result of the acquisition, E had become liable to not only local non-domestic rates but also, pursuant to the Electricity Supply Industry (Rateable Values) Order 1994, to central non domestic rates. E contended that by providing for annual rather than daily revisions of liability, the scheme for providing for liability to central non domestic rates offended the principle against double taxation and was ultra vires the Local Government Finance Act 1988 Sch.6 para.3(2).

Held, dismissing the appeal (Dyson L.J. dissenting), that the 1994 Order concerned the method of valuation rather than liability to rates so that an intention on the part of Parliament to allow for double assessment could be more readily inferred. Accordingly, the scheme for determining central list non domestic rateable values was not ultra vires, *Milford Haven Conservancy Board v. Inland Revenue Commissioners* [1976] 1 W.L.R. 817, [1976] C.L.Y. 2273 applied.

R. (ON THE APPLICATION OF EDISON FIRST POWER LTD) v. SECRETARY OF STATE FOR THE ENVIRONMENT, TRANSPORT AND THE REGIONS; R. (ON THE APPLICATION OF EDISON FIRST POWER LTD) v. CENTRAL VALUATION OFFICER; *sub nom.* EDISON FIRST POWER LTD v. SECRETARY OF STATE FOR THE ENVIRONMENT, TRANSPORT AND THE REGIONS [2001] EWCA Civ 1096, Simon Brown, L.J., CA.

4817. Non domestic rates – double taxation – statutory schemes for power stations – power to amend central rating list for designated persons

[Electricity Supply Industry (Rateable Values) Order 1994 (SI 1994 3282).]

E, an electricity generating company, challenged a refusal by the central valuation officer to amend the central rating list in respect of two power stations acquired by E from P. E contended that it constituted unlawful double taxation to take into account the generating capacity of the power stations in the central list rateable value, pursuant to the status of P as a designated person, in addition to the rateable value in the local list, applicable to E as an occupier. Further, the decision was irrational and the Secretary of State could correct the unlawfulness by refunding one element of the double taxation or by altering the list pursuant to his duty to maintain an accurate list.

Held, refusing the application, that whilst there had undoubtedly been double taxation, it was implicit in the Electricity Supply Industry (Rateable Values) Order 1994 that no account was to be taken of changes in occupation during the rating year, so long as the designated person remained on the list, thus the presumption against double taxation had been rebutted, *Milford Haven Conservancy Board v. Inland Revenue Commissioners* [1976] 1 W.L.R. 817, [1976] C.L.Y. 2273 and *R. v. Secretary of State for the Environment, ex p. British Telecommunications Plc* [1991] R.A. 307, [1992] C.L.Y. 3679 applied. The system was not unfair or absurd given the extensive consultation exercise performed prior to its introduction, nor was there any evidence that the Secretary of State had acted in bad faith or from an improper motive, notwithstanding that the scheme worked to the disadvantage of E, *R. v. Secretary of State, ex p. Nottinghamshire CC* [1986] A.C. 240, [1986] C.L.Y. 27 applied. Since P's liability arose from its status as a designated person and not its occupation of the hereditament, there was no power for the valuation officer to alter the effect of the statutory scheme and the demand for rates was accordingly not ultra vires.

R. (ON THE APPLICATION OF EDISON FIRST POWER LTD) v. SECRETARY OF STATE FOR THE ENVIRONMENT, TRANSPORT AND THE REGIONS; R. (ON THE APPLICATION OF EDISON FIRST POWER LTD) v. CENTRAL VALUATION OFFICER; *sub nom.* R. v. SECRETARY OF STATE FOR THE ENVIRONMENT, TRANSPORT AND THE REGIONS, *ex p.* EDISON FIRST POWER LTD; R. v. CENTRAL VALUATION OFFICER, *ex p.* EDISON FIRST POWER LTD [2001] R.A. 1, Carnwath, J., QBD (Admin Ct).

4818. Non domestic rates – factory premises – revaluation – failure to provide evidence regarding comparables

D owned factory premises in Birmingham, built originally in or about 1910. Following a revaluation in 1995, the premises were entered in the relevant non domestic rating list at a rateable value of £51,000. In April 1997, approximately a third of the premises were destroyed by fire, and the rateable value was reduced to £37,750. Following reconstruction of the premises in 1998, the rateable value was revised to £90,000. D challenged this before the Birmingham Valuation Tribunal, which confirmed a rateable value of £85,400. D appealed, on the grounds that (1) the increase in rateable value was unfair, unintelligible and bordering on the farcical; (2) the reconstruction was a replacement of an old building; (3) the new building was smaller than the old, and (4) the new building was unfinished and had maintenance expenses. D adduced no evidence and did not challenge the valuation officers comparables. The valuation officer argued that the building should be valued as a whole in line with comparables which he adduced in evidence.

Held, dismissing the appeal, that the valuation was in line with the rating list and took into account the nature of the building. D had failed to discharge the burden of proof to show that the tribunal's decision was wrong.

DUNNETTS (BIRMINGHAM) LTD v. GUTT (VALUATION OFFICER) [2000] R.V.R. 310, PR Francis FRICS, LandsTr.

4819. Non domestic rates – maximum rateable values – public houses and petrol filling stations

NON-DOMESTIC RATING (PUBLIC HOUSES AND PETROL FILLING STATIONS) (ENGLAND) ORDER 2001, SI 2001 1345; made under the Local Government Finance Act 1988 s.43. In force: April 5, 2001; £1.50.

The Local Government Finance Act 1988 s.43 contains provisions for mandatory relief from non domestic rates for certain properties in rural settlements. This order adds public houses and petrol filling stations to the properties that qualify.

4820. Non domestic rates – occupancy – liability of leaseholder

M was the leaseholder of ground floor premises, parts of which were occupied under licence by different businesses for storage purposes. The justices, making findings on the basis of two incomplete written licence documents, a sketch plan by BDLB's taxation officer and no oral evidence from M, found that M was in occupation of the property and therefore liable for rates. M applied for judicial review of the decision arguing that it was flawed as (1) the presumption on which it was based, namely that ownership of a hereditament was evidence of occupation, was not a sound one; (2) there was adequate evidence to prove that M was not in occupation, and (3) in order for M to be in rateable occupation she would have had to have been in physical occupation of at least part of the premises.

Held, refusing the application, that the justices were entitled to reach the conclusion that they did as (1) the presumption was a sound one in law and was well established by authority, *Westminster City Council v. Tomlin* [1989] 1 W.L.R. 1287, [1990] C.L.Y. 3913 applied; (2) the evidence put to the justices was unsatisfactory and not sufficient to rebut the presumption, and (3) there was no such principle as argued for by M. It was only necessary to show that an owner had comprehensive control of the premises, and there was no secondary requirement that they be in physical occupation of at least part of it, *Westminster City Council v. Southern Railway Co Ltd* [1936] A.C. 511 applied. M retained control in that she was running a business of allowing storage at the premises.

MAGON v. BARKING AND DAGENHAM LBC [2000] R.A. 459, Burton, J., QBD.

4821. Non domestic rates – occupancy – liability of licensee

J, a plant hire company, appealed against a finding of the justices that it was liable to pay non domestic rates to B in respect of the ground floor of a property and a storage yard. The storage yard had been subdivided into a number of units which J had licensed out separately. J contended that it was not in rateable occupation of the units because it did not benefit from physical, non-transient occupation of the premises, *John Laing & Son v. Kingswood Assessment Committee* [1949] 1 K.B. 344 cited. B contended that since the tenants had no security of tenure J retained regulation and control and thus liability for the rates, *Holywell Union v. Halkyn District Mines Drainage Co* [1895] A.C. 117 cited.

Held, dismissing the appeal, that the justices' finding was a reasonable one given the restrictive nature of the licence agreements. The principles governing rateable occupation were set out in *John Laing* and it was clear that physical occupation was not required. J was in actual occupation for the purpose of rateable liability on the basis that (1) their business was to allow third parties to use the premises, which constituted actual occupation, and (2) given that the licensees shared a common access, it was clear that J retained for themselves general control over the parts occupied by the licensees, otherwise they could not perform their own obligation under the licences.

JDE PLANT HIRE LTD v. BARKING AND DAGENHAM LBC; *sub nom.* R. v. BARKING AND DAGENHAM LBC, *ex p.* JDE PLANT HIRE LTD [2000] R.A. 471, Tomlinson, J, QBD.

4822. Non domestic rates – retrospective legislation – alteration to rating list – meaning of "hereditament"

[Non Domestic Rating (Alteration of Lists and Appeals) Regulations 1993 (SI 1993 291) Reg.13(8A).]

L appealed against a decision of the Lands Tribunal ([1999] R.A. 373, [2000] C.L.Y. 4614) that a retrospective charge in respect of non domestic rates had been lawfully imposed. Premises formerly occupied as two separate units were converted and occupied as a single unit by L from 1986. In the 1990 non domestic rating list the property was wrongly described as two separate units and each was allocated a rateable value. In 1995 the list was altered to reflect the fact that the property was in fact a single unit. The rateable value was reassessed and L was informed that the revised rate would be backdated to 1990. L contended that the alteration fell with the Non Domestic Rating (Alteration of Lists and Appeals) Regulations 1993 Reg.13(8A) with the result that the increase in rateable value would only have effect from the day on which the alteration had been made.

Held, dismissing the appeal, that an alteration to remedy an inaccurate reference in the rating list would not fall within the ambit of Reg.13(8A) in circumstances where there was no rateable value for the premises in question included in the rating list prior to the alteration, since the reference to "hereditament" in Reg.13(8A) was a reference to the hereditament as shown after the alteration.

BLISS (VALUATION OFFICER) v. LAMB & SHIRLEY LTD; *sub nom.* LAMB & SHIRLEY LTD v. BLISS (VALUATION OFFICER), [2001] EWCA Civ 562, [2001] R.A. 99, Jonathan Parker, L.J., CA.

4823.   Non domestic rates – rural rate relief – maximum rateable values

NON-DOMESTIC RATING (RURAL SETTLEMENTS) (ENGLAND) (AMENDMENT) ORDER 2001, SI 2001 1346; made under the Local Government Finance Act 1988 s.43, s.143. In force: April 5, 2001; £1.50.

The Local Government Act 1988 s.43(6A)(6B) contains provisions for mandatory relief from non-domestic rates for certain hereditaments in rural settlements and the Non-Domestic Rating (Public Houses and Petrol Filling Stations) (England) Order 2001 (SI 2001 1345) added public houses and petrol filling stations to the hereditaments that qualify. This Order amends the Non-Domestic Rating (Rural Settlements) (England) Order 1997 (SI 1997 2792) to prescribe the maximum rateable values above which hereditament which include a public house or a petrol filling station will not be eligible for relief. For both types of hereditaments the maximum will be 9,000.

4824.   Non domestic rates – stud farms

NON-DOMESTIC RATING (STUD FARMS) (ENGLAND) ORDER 2001, SI 2001 2586; made under the Local Government Finance Act 1988 Sch.6 para.2A. In force: August 15, 2001; £1.50.

The Local Government Finance Act 1988 Sch.6 para.2A provides for deductions from the amount which would otherwise be the rateable value of hereditaments comprising buildings used in whole or in part for the breeding and rearing of horses and ponies, or for either purpose, and which are occupied together with agricultural land or buildings. The deduction is to be the smaller of a specified amount and the amount which would otherwise be the rent that a hypothetical tenant would pay for so much of the hereditaments as consists of buildings used for such purposes. This Order, which revokes the Non-Domestic Rating (Stud Farms) Order 1989 (SI 1989 2331), prescribes £3,000 as the specified amount in question, replacing £2,500 which was the amount specified in 1989.

4825.   Non domestic rates – valuation – composite hereditaments – shop premises with living accommodation above

S appealed against the decision of a local valuation tribunal to enter two composite hereditaments, shops with living accommodation above, in Maidenhead on the 1995 rating list at rateable values of £1,600 and £6,100, respectively.

Held, allowing the appeal in part, that the valuations would be reduced from £1,600 to £1,440 and from £6,100 to £5,390 by deducting an end user allowance to reflect road layout and parking restrictions.

SHEA v. DRURY (VALUATION OFFICER) [2001] R.A. 263, PH Clarke, FRICS, Lands Tr.

4826. Non domestic rates – valuation – failure to provide evidence regarding comparables

C was the owner of premises which consisted partly of domestic accommodation which was not self-contained, and partly of business accommodation. The premises had originally been assessed for rating purposes jointly with an adjoining residential property. In 1973, that joint assessment had produced a rateable value of £347. In 1983, the adjoining property and the premises were divided for rating purposes. The adjoining property was listed with a rateable value of £132, and the premises were listed with a rateable value of £326. Thus, the total rateable value attributable to both properties after the split was £458, as against the original figure of £347. C argued that this had been a fundamental error on the part of the valuation officer which had tainted each succeeding revaluation of the premises. The effect of this, C argued, was that the domestic element of the premises (on which C now paid council tax under band A) had still not been severed from the non domestic area, and that consequently C was effectively paying twice for the residential part of the Premises.

Held, dismissing the appeal, that (1) the valuation officer's evidence in relation to the original rating division between the premises and the adjoining property showed that the apparent disparity in figures arose because of amendments and alterations which had taken place in the intervening years; (2) the valuation officer had demonstrated in a comprehensive and convincing manner that he had valued only the business portion of the premises, and had done so with the aid of comparables which provided conclusive evidence in support of the levels of rent attributed to the shop and stores at the premises, and (3) there was a history of appeals lodged by C against various assessments in respect of the premises. Some had been lodged by rating surveyors instructed by C, and then withdrawn, suggesting that in many instances, the surveyors had been unable to sustain arguments against the valuation officer's assessments.

CHRISTIE v. HUDSON (VALUATION OFFICER) [2000] R.V.R. 313, PR Francis, FRICS, Lands Tr.

4827. Non domestic rates – valuation – members' clubs

Issues arose as to the proper method of valuation for two members' clubs in south west London. The clubs contended that the valuation method should be based on turnover, as shown in their annual accounts, and the fact that the properties were not let. T, the valuation officer, defended valuations of £19,150 and £38,500, respectively, based on rental evidence from other members' clubs in the same area.

Held, confirming the assessment of £19,150 and reducing that of £38,500 to £29,000 due to its location and lack of car parking, that three of the four clubs offered as comparators by T were relied upon as they were in the same location with valuations based on rental value. Similar properties cited by the clubs were not accepted as they were not located in London and the valuations of public houses were not appropriate as such premises were operated on profit making lines, which was not the case with members' clubs.

UNITED SERVICES & SERVICES RENDERED CLUB (TOOTING AND BALHAM) LTD v. THORNELEY (VALUATION OFFICER) [2001] R.A. 145, NJ Rose FRICS, Lands Tr.

4828. Non domestic rates – valuation – plant and machinery

VALUATION FOR RATING (PLANT AND MACHINERY) (ENGLAND) (AMENDMENT) REGULATIONS 2001, SI 2001 846; made under the Local Government Finance Act 1988 s.143, Sch.6 para.2. In force: April 1, 2001; £1.50.

These Regulations amend the Valuation for Rating (Plant and Machinery) (England) Regulation 2000 (SI 2000 540) by conferring exemption from rating on an additional class of plant and machinery, namely specified plant and machinery comprised in a combined heat and power station fully or partly exempt from climate change levy and which produces electrical power.

4829. Non domestic rates – valuation – plant and machinery – Wales

VALUATION FOR RATING (PLANT AND MACHINERY) (WALES) (AMENDMENT) REGULATIONS 2001, SI 2001 2357 (W.195); made under the Local Government Finance Act 1988 s.143, Sch.6 para.2. In force: June 27, 2001; £1.75.

These Regulations amend the Valuation for Rating (Plant and Machinery) (Wales) Regulations 2001 (SI 2000 1097) by conferring exemption from rating on an additional class of plant and machinery, namely specified plant and machinery comprised in a combined heat and power station fully or partly exempt from climate change levy and which produces electrical power.

4830. Non domestic rates – valuation – rateable value of cricket clubhouse – exemptions

G occupied a field of about 10.95 acres containing two football pitches, a bowling green, an all-weather pitch, a cricket ground, a changing room for footballers, a bowling clubhouse, an unused tennis clubhouse, a cricket pavilion, stores for ground keeping machinery and a cricket clubhouse. The rateable value was entered in the rating list as £4,100. G was an unincorporated members cricket club which proposed a reduction of the rateable value to £1. The valuation officer accepted that the cricket ground and the pavilion were exempt but took the view that the clubhouse was rateable. The valuation tribunal accepted that argument and reduced the rateable value to £3,200 to reflect the amounts attributable to the ground and the pavilion. G appealed contending that the clubhouse was exempt, or alternatively, if it was not, the rateable value should be reduced to £2,100.

Held, allowing the appeal and amending the rateable value to £2,100, that (1) the tribunal had jurisdiction to consider whether the clubhouse was exempt. The words in the proposal "the assessment(s) of the hereditaments(s) is/are bad in law" were wide enough to encompass the question of rateability and there was no reason to limit their scope so as to prevent the ratepayer from advancing a legitimate argument, or the tribunal from ordering the list to be corrected if it found it to be inaccurate in that respect; (2) although the clubhouse was used from time to time for local community purposes, it was a separate hereditament in the occupation of the cricket club and did not form part of the recreation ground as a public park and was, therefore, not exempt from rates, and (3) the clubhouse, which was described in an agreed statement as being in poor condition, was properly to be assessed at £10 psm, including heating. The entry in the rating list should be amended to read a rateable value of £2,100.

GALGATE CRICKET CLUB v. DOYLE (VALUATION OFFICER) [2001] R.A. 21, George Bartlett Q.C. (President), Lands Tr.

4831. Non domestic rates – valuation – rateable value of retail unit at out of town shopping centre

[Local Government Finance Act 1988 Sch.6; Lands Tribunal Rules 1996 (SI 1996 1022) r.28.]

This appeal was heard under the simplified procedure in the Lands Tribunal Rules 1996 r.28. It concerned the rateable value of a purpose built retail unit at a major out of town shopping centre, fixed pursuant to a determination of a valuation tribunal, which reduced the valuation officer's proposed assessment in the 1995 rating list from £21,700 to £20,700. M, the ratepayer appealed.

Held, dismissing the appeal, that (1) the burden of proof was on the ratepayer to show that the assessment was wrong; (2) no such evidence was forthcoming prior to the Lands Tribunal hearing and, by failing to appear, M had failed to make out his case, and (3) the valuation officer produced evidence that set out the background to the appeal, the basis of his initial approach to the assessments, a comprehensive list of comparables and a revised valuation in accordance with the provisions of the Local Government Finance Act 1988 Sch.6. Although costs were not awarded, except in exceptional circumstances, bearing in mind the taxpayer's failure to attend the hearing or to communicate his intentions to the court office beforehand, the valuation officer was offered an opportunity to seek his costs.

WARREN v. CARSON (VALUATION OFFICER) [2001] R.V.R. 35, Judge not applicable, Lands Tr.

4832. Non domestic rates – valuation – retail premises – effect of temporary closure of lane running past side entrance

L appealed against a Valuation Tribunal decision confirming J's refusal to allow a temporary rating assessment reduction for L's shop premises due to the closure of a lane running past the shop's side entrance. J argued that the temporary closure had not affected the shop's rental value as a prospective purchaser would not have reduced his bid owing the affect of the work on his trading opportunities.

Held, dismissing the appeal, that (1) L had the burden of showing that the tribunal had been wrong to decide that a hypothetical landlord would not have accepted a lower bid because of the lane closure; (2) evidence of L's turnover did not show that trade had been solely reduced by the closure, *Berrill (t/a Cobweb Antiques) v. Hill (Valuation Officer)* [2000] R.A. 194, [2000] C.L.Y. 4600 considered, and (3) L had not adduced evidence to show that the side entrance was actually used by more than the occasional passing customer.

LA BOULANGERIE LTD v. JACOBS (VALUATION OFFICER) [2001] R.V.R. 167, PR Francis FRICS, Lands Tr.

4833. Non domestic rates – valuation – shops – relevance of existing use of property

[Local Government Finance Act 1988 Sch.6 para.2(7).]

The valuation officer appealed against a decision of the Lands Tribunal allowing ratepayers' appeals against a decision to alter the rating valuations of their premises. The ratepayers occupied units in a shopping centre which had a license to serve food and alcoholic drinks, whereas other similar units in the centre were let as shops. It was submitted that the Lands Tribunal had erred in determining that the units should be valued in accordance with their actual user as opposed to their more lucrative potential as shops.

Held, dismissing the appeal, that the valuation was to be based on the existing use of the property. The correct interpretation of the words "mode or category of occupation" in the Local Government Finance Act 1988 Sch.6 para.2(7) was to recognise the importance of user and to reinforce the second limb of the doctrine at the heart of the modern law of rating known as "rebus sic stantibus" or "as things stand". It was contradictory to take into account the alternative uses of a property when making a valuation on its existing use, *Fir Mill v. Royton Urban DC* (1960) 175 E.G. 1029, [1960] C.L.Y. 2669.75 applied and *Midland Bank Plc v. Lanham (Valuation Officer)* (1977) 246 E.G. 1117, [1979] C.L.Y. 2229.22 not applied.

WILLIAMS (VALUATION OFFICER) v. SCOTTISH & NEWCASTLE RETAIL LTD; ALLIED DOMECQ RETAILING LTD v. WILLIAMS (VALUATION OFFICER); *sub nom*. SCOTTISH & NEWCASTLE RETAIL LTD v. WILLIAMS (VALUATION OFFICER), [2001] EWCA Civ 185, [2001] 1 E.G.L.R. 157, Robert Walker, L.J., CA.

4834. Non domestic rates – valuation – shops – use classes – existing use of property on material day

H appealed against a decision of the North Wales Valuation Tribunal setting the rateable value of his shop at £2,550. H argued that there should be a 10 per cent end allowance because of problems with cooking smells and drains caused by a kebab shop next door, and the fact that the shop had a shared outside toilet. He also argued that the shop should be compared to two other A1 shops in the area and that W had wrongly relied on comparables with A3 use.

Held, allowing the appeal in part, that an end allowance of five per cent was appropriate because of the shared toilet, but that none of the other issues raised by H were relevant. The comparison to other A1 shops was legitimate and led to a conclusion that the original valuation had been correct. However, W's argument that comparison could be made to A3 shops was incorrect, as an assumption had to be made that the shop would only be used for a purpose in the same category as that which pertained on the material day, *Williams (Valuation Officer) v. Scottish & Newcastle Retail Ltd* [2001] EWCA Civ 185, [2001] R.A. 41, [2001] 3 C.L. 607 applied.

HUMPHREYS-JONES (T/A CATHEDRAL FRAMES) v. WELSBY [2001] R.A. 67, PR Francis FRICS, Lands Tr.

4835. **Rateable value – development sites – determination of rent payable on land leased from Government – Hong Kong**

[Basic Law (Hong Kong) Art.121; Rating Ordinance (Hong Kong) s.7, s.7A; Government Rent (Assessment and Collection) Ordinance (Hong Kong) s.8, s.34; Government Rent (Assessment and Collection) Regulations (Hong Kong) Reg.2.]

A, the lessee of Hong Kong Government land in the course of redevelopment, received a rent demand based on three per cent of the property's rateable value. The assessment was based upon valuation assumptions given in the Rating Ordinance although the site was not rateable under that Ordinance. A and the Commissioner appealed against a Court of Appeal decision ([2000] R.A. 21, [2000] C.L.Y. 4613) allowing A's appeal from a lands tribunal decision upholding the Commissioner's assessment. A argued that rent was not payable where the site was not liable for rates. The Commissioner contested that claim. The dispute concerned two main issues (1) whether it was permissible to ascertain a rateable value for the purposes of assessing Government rent under the Rent Ordinance for land that was not liable for rates under the Rating Ordinance, and (2) whether, in deciding rateable value for rent purposes, account could be taken of the development potential of vacant land where construction was pending or in progress.

Held, allowing the Commissioner's appeal and dismissing A's appeal, that (1) when determining the amount of Government rent payable, Reg.2 of the Rent Regulations treated the leased land as being liable for rate assessment under s.7 and s.7A of the Rating Ordinance; (2) the Chief Executive in Council could determine the rateable value of the leased land prior to or during development under s.34 of the Rent Ordinance by means that included the aggregate of the last ascertained rateable values for all interests in the land before demolition, as opposed to rateable values decided under the Rating Ordinance; (3) s.8 of the Rent Ordinance and Reg.2, Reg.4 and Reg.5 complied with the Basic Law Art.121 which was not to be interpreted as applying to rateable value as defined in the Rating Ordinance, and (4) the hypothetical tenancy terms in s.7(2) of the Rating Ordinance applied to a valuation made under s.8 of the Rent Ordinance, with the state of the site being that as on the relevant date and taking all relevant characteristics into account, along with the form of occupation.

RATING AND VALUATION COMMISSIONER v. AGRILA LTD; *sub nom.* AGRILA LTD v. RATING AND VALUATION COMMISSIONER [2001] R.A. 189, Sir Anthony Mason N.P.J., CFA (HK).

4836. **Rating (Former Agricultural Premises and Rural Shops) Act 2001 (c.14)**

This Act makes provision about non domestic rating in respect of hereditaments including land or buildings which were formerly agricultural and in respect of food stores in rural settlements.

This Act received Royal Assent on May 11, 2001.

4837. **Rating (Former Agricultural Premises and Rural Shops) Act 2001 (c.14) – Commencement No.1 Order – England**

RATING (FORMER AGRICULTURAL PREMISES AND RURAL SHOPS) ACT 2001 (COMMENCEMENT NO.1) ORDER 2001, SI 2001 2580 (C.84); made under the Rating (Former Agricultural Premises and Rural Shops) Act 2001 s.6.

Commencement details: bringing into force various provisions of the Act on July 17, 2001 and August 15, 2001; £1.50.

This Order brings into force the remaining provisions of the Rating (Former Agricultural Premises and Rural Shops) Act 2001 on July 17, 2001 and August 15, 2001.

4838. **Valuation – central rating lists – industry hereditaments – Wales**

CENTRAL RATING LIST (WALES) (AMENDMENT) REGULATIONS 2001, SI 2001 2222 (W.160); made under the Local Government Finance Act 1988 s.53, s.64, s.65. In force: August 1, 2001; £1.75.

The Local Government Finance Act 1988 s.53, which designates a person and prescribes in relation to that person one or more descriptions of non-domestic hereditament, enables regulations to be made with a view to securing the central rating en bloc of certain hereditaments. These Regulations amend the Rating List (Wales) Regulations 1999 (SI 1999 3453) by designating a group of gas transporting companies and providing that the prescribed hereditaments which each of them uses for the purposes of acting as a public gas transporter are rated as a single hereditament.

REAL PROPERTY

4839. **Abuse of process – mortgages – arrears – pursuit of money judgment following dismissal of possession proceedings**

A appealed against the dismissal of its application for leave to pursue a money judgment against H. In 1991 A had commenced possession proceedings against H after he fell into arrears with repayments of a loan secured against his home. W, his wife, was joined as a party and successfully argued that as she had put capital into the property and had signed a consent form without advice her interest was overriding. The possession proceedings against her were dismissed and those against H adjourned. In 1998 A applied for leave to amend the pleadings to allow it to pursue a money judgment against H. The judge refused the application on the ground that it was an abuse of process and an attempt to circumvent W's equity in the property.

Held, allowing the appeal, that A was not prevented from pursuing a different remedy following its failure to realise its security through possession proceedings, even where such proceedings might result in an application by the trustee in bankruptcy for sale of the property. It had not been an abuse of process for A to apply for a money judgment as an unsecured creditor, *Zandfarid v. Bank of Credit and Commerce International SA (In Liquidation)* [1996] 1 W.L.R. 1420, [1996] C.L.Y. 3448 followed. Although H was elderly and W suffered from epilepsy, those factors had to be weighed against the size of the arrears, which together with interest were in excess of £60,000, and the fact that H and W had had the benefit of living in the property for a long period without paying towards the arrears.

ALLIANCE & LEICESTER PLC v. SLAYFORD [2001] 1 All E.R. (Comm) 1, Peter Gibson, L.J., CA.

4840. **Adverse possession – intention – proof of state of mind – interference with owner's right to peaceful enjoyment**

[Limitation Act 1980 s.15; Human Rights Act 1998 s.3.]

P appealed against the dismissal ([2000] Ch. 676, [2000] C.L.Y. 4615) of its claim for possession of 57 acres of grazing land which had been licensed to G in 1983 for one year. After the expiration of the initial term P had declined to renew the licence but G had continued to use the land for grazing purposes. The judge had found that P's claim was statute barred pursuant to the Limitation Act 1980 s.15 and that G had obtained adverse possession, having formed the intention to occupy upon the expiry of the initial licence term in 1984. P contended that (1) whilst G had continued to use the land, the judge's finding with regard to his intention had been unsupported by the evidence, and (2) the provisions of the 1980 Act were incompatible with the Human Rights Act 1998 s.3, which required legislation to be interpreted as far as possible so as to comply with the Convention rights.

Held, allowing the appeal, that (1) the judge had been wrong to infer G's state of mind from circumstantial evidence and ignore the direct evidence from him. A subjective state of mind required proof. An intention to possess was not necessarily justified on the basis of the objective fact that there had been a restricted use of the land for grazing purposes. G's unchallenged evidence had been to the effect that his intention had been to continue to occupy the land solely for grazing purposes in the hope that he would be granted a further licence. Accordingly, P had not been dispossessed and the limitation period had never commenced, *Buckinghamshire CC v. Moran* [1990] Ch. 623, [1989] C.L.Y. 449 applied; (2) s.3 of the 1998 Act had no relevance since the provisions of the 1980 Act did not operate to deprive an individual of his property but rather his access to the courts after he had delayed the institution of legal proceedings. The fact that title to property was extinguished in such cases was a rational consequence of the time limits imposed, and (3) it was observed that s.3 of the 1998 Act could be relied on irrespective of when the decision appealed against occurred.

JA PYE (OXFORD) LTD v. GRAHAM, [2001] EWCA Civ 117, [2001] Ch. 804, Mummery, L.J., CA.

4841. Adverse possession – intention – provision of keys to other persons – animus possidendi

B appealed against a decision that it had not established adverse possession of an area of land that was registered in WLBC's name. B had purchased the freehold of of an adjoining house, the tenant of which, S, had used the land at issue for growing flowers and vegetables for at least twelve years without payment of rent or licence fee. WLBC argued that the land had been divided into six allotments for tenants of its own flats which also adjoined the land who had originally paid to WLBC a nominal annual charge. WLBC argued that S had used the land by arrangement with WLBC's tenants to whom he had provided keys and S had no intention to exclude the world from the land.

Held, dismissing the appeal, that the there was insufficient evidence to support the finding of the judge below that WLBC's tenants had allowed S to take over their licences. However, by giving the keys to others, it could not be said that S had shown sufficient intention to exclude the world at large and it followed that B was precluded from claiming a right to adverse possession, *Powell v. McFarlane* (1979) P. & C.R. 452, [1979] C.L.Y. 2248 applied. The position had not altered when subsequently S had stopped providing keys to others.

BATTERSEA FREEHOLD & LEASEHOLD PROPERTY CO LTD v. WANDSWORTH LBC (2001) 82 P. & C.R. 12, Rimer, J., Ch D.

4842. Adverse possession – limitations – issue of proceedings

[Limitation Act 1980 s.15.]

M appealed against an order that E's claim to adverse possession of a piece of land, in respect of which M held the title and E was in exclusive occupation, was not interrupted by the issue and subsequent dismissal for want of prosecution of proceedings by M's predecessor in title. M contended that the issue of a claim for possession was in itself sufficient to stop time running in favour of E's claim for adverse possession, since such an action amounted to a re-entry onto the land constituting a form of constructive possession by the owner, which defeated the fact of adverse possession.

Held, dismissing the appeal, that if proceedings were commenced within the twelve year period, any subsequent order in the owners favour granted after the expiration of the twelve year period was not time barred by virtue of the

Limitation Act 1980 s.15, if, however, those proceedings were never progressed to a conclusion, the very fact that a writ had been issued was irrelevant to any subsequent proceedings and did not "stop time running" so as to prevent the accrual of the twelve years' possession necessary to establish adverse possession, *BP Properties Ltd v. Buckler* (1988) 55 P.& C.R. 337, [1988] C.L.Y. 2155 followed. The issue of a writ in earlier proceedings amounted to no more than a demand for possession and did not, in itself, start time running afresh, *Mount Carmel Investments Ltd v. Thurlow* [1988] 1 W.L.R. 1078, [1989] C.L.Y. 2278 applied.

MARKFIELD INVESTMENTS LTD v. EVANS [2001] 1 W.L.R. 1321, Simon Brown, L.J., CA.

4843. Adverse possession – squatting – intention to remain in possession of property – willingness to pay rent

[Land Registration Act 1925 s.75(1); Limitation Act 1980 s.15(1).]

B appealed against an order that he relinquish possession of a property, owned by the local authority, that he had occupied as a home for 12 years. B had initially gained entry to the property by breaking the padlock on the front door and he had then installed his own yale lock. Over the years he had improved the property and made it habitable. He had had no intention of vacating it unless evicted but he would have readily stayed on as a tenant had he been offered the chance to do so. B contended that the local authority's claim to the property was statute barred by virtue of the Limitation Act 1980 s.15(1) and that the property was held on trust for him pursuant to the Land Registration Act 1925 s.75(1). The local authority maintained that B had not shown the necessary intention to possess the property such as to establish a claim of adverse possession.

Held, allowing the appeal, that a squatter claiming adverse possession only had to have the intention to possess the property "for the time being". The fact that he expected to be evicted at any moment did not prevent him from having that intention, *Powell v. McFarlane* (1979) 38 P. & C.R. 452, [1979] C.L.Y. 2248 applied. Active and passive occupation could not be distinguished unless passive occupation meant occupation without the intention to possess. While a squatter's expression of willingness to pay rent, assessed in its context, might negate an intention to possess a property, ordinarily such an admission was one which any candid squatter who hoped in time to acquire possessory title would be very likely to make and therefore should not be considered as indicating an absence of the necessary intention to possess. In the instant case, B had shown the necessary intention to remain in the property for the time being throughout the twelve years or more that he had in fact been in possession, *R. v. Secretary of State for the Environment, ex p. Davies* (1991) 61 P. & C.R. 487, [1991] C.L.Y. 546 considered.

LAMBETH LBC v. BLACKBURN; *sub nom.* LAMBETH LBC (MAYOR & BURGESSES) v. BLACKBURN, [2001] EWCA Civ 912, (2001) 33 H.L.R. 74, Clarke, L.J., CA.

4844. Adverse possession – title to land – landlord and tenant – intention to possess – accretion of title to benefit of landlord – power to bind third party

[Land Registration Act 1925 s.82(1)(g).]

B appealed against an order of the deputy solicitor to the Land Registry that a filed plan be rectified pursuant to the Land Registration Act 1925 s.82(1)(g) and that A be registered as proprietor of an area of agricultural land. The deputy solicitor found that A's tenant, H, had exercised more than 12 years' adverse possession and that the benefit passed to A when the tenancy determined. B contended that (1) H had not been in adverse possession for the necessary period; (2) H had not had the necessary intention to exclude all others from the disputed land; (3) the presumption that title acquired by a tenant in adverse possession accrues to the landlord was not binding upon a third party, and (4) if the presumption was binding on a third party, A's son was the landlord when the tenancy determined and he had made no claim to the land.

Held, allowing the appeal, that even though H had not used the land for farming purposes for the necessary continuous period, he had exercised control over it for more than 12 years. However, H had been unaware that the title to the land was owned by anybody other than A. H believed that he could use the land at will but he did not intentionally exclude a person with title. Therefore, A had failed to prove H's unequivocal intention to possess the land and his claim to title by adverse possession failed, *Powell v. McFarlane* (1979) 38 P. & C.R. 452, [1979] C.L.Y. 2248 followed. The presumption that a landlord could advance a claim to a title claimed by his tenant in adverse possession applied to third party land but that presumption was rebuttable. Title to the land passed to the landlord at the end of the tenancy. In the instant case, A was not the landlord when the tenancy determined; accordingly, if there had been acquisition of title to the disputed land by H's adverse possession, that title would have passed to A's son who was the landlord at the relevant time, *Kingsmill v. Millard* (1855) 11 Ex. 313 and *Whitmore v. Humphries* (1871-72) L.R. 7 C.P. 1 applied.

BATT v. ADAMS; *sub nom.* ADAMS v. TRUSTEES OF THE MICHAEL BATT CHARITABLE TRUST [2001] 32 E.G. 90, Laddie, J., Ch D.

4845.   Adverse possession – title to land – squatting – acknowledgement of title within relevant period

A appealed against a possession order made in favour of LLBC, a local authority, the judge having rejected A's defence of adverse possession on the basis that A had acknowledged LLBC's title within the 12 year period relied upon for the acquisition of a squatter's title. A contended that the judge was wrong to conclude that a letter written by A to a council officer referring to the property as "Lambeth's property" amounted to an acknowledgement of LLBC's title.

Held, dismissing the appeal, that the letter plainly acknowledged the local authority's title and it followed that LLBC's claim for possession was not statute barred.

LAMBETH LBC v. ARCHANGEL; *sub nom.* ARCHANGEL v. LAMBETH LBC (2001) 33 H.L.R. 44, Mummery, L.J., CA.

4846.   Agreements – estoppel – oral agreement for transfer of land

B, who had brought proceedings against their neighbour, M, appealed against an order rectifying the land register following a finding ([1999] E.G.C.S. 84) that they should be estopped from denying the enforceability of a tripartite oral agreement concerning the transfer of two plots of land. Under that agreement B's predecessor in title, T, had transferred one plot of land, "the red land", then registered as belonging to him, to M, and G, another neighbour, had transferred the other plot of land, "the brown land", then registered as belonging to her, to T. The judge had held that although the red land was not protected by an entry in the register and M did not have an overriding interest in it, B should be estopped from denying the enforceability of the agreement since by acquiring the benefit conferred by the transfer of the brown land to T, they should not be allowed to escape the burden imposed by the transfer of the red land to M.

Held, allowing the appeal, that while the judge had probably been right to conclude that the agreement had created indivisible obligations, he had erred in determining the issue of estoppel without G having been made a party to the proceedings. As G had not been involved in the proceedings, there had been no consideration of the effect of any estoppel as between her and B. Were the order for rectification of the register to stand, there would be a risk of injustice to B in the event of a claim by G, who might or might not be estopped from asserting title to the brown land. Furthermore, orders rectifying the register should not be made without all relevant parties being given the right to make representations.

BHULLAR v. McARDLE, [2001] EWCA Civ 510, (2001) 82 P. & C.R. 38, Mummery, L.J., CA.

4847. Boundaries – oral evidence – agreement as to boundary line

C and O were parties to a boundary dispute. The boundary was shown as a pecked line on a 1977 Ordnance Survey plan of 1:2500 attached to the contract of sale. After exchange of contracts and prior to the transfer, the vendor, P, and C had agreed the boundary, marking it with stakes, and confirmed that they had done so in correspondence and had subsequently shown it on a larger scale plan attached to the transfer. O later contended that the boundary followed a ridge, which she maintained was shown on the map. C contended for another line. C succeeded, the judge at first instance admitting C's oral evidence as to the line of the agreed boundary. O appealed on the basis that such evidence ought not to have been admitted, given the existence of the OS plan attached to the sale.

Held, dismissing the appeal, that the OS plan showed the boundary as an imprecise pecked line, and the Ordnance Survey had indicated by letter that the line indicated the edge of vegetation, which was not necessarily the same as the ridge. Therefore extrinsic evidence of what P and C had actually agreed was admissible given the uncertainty over the line.

CLARKE v. O'KEEFE (2000) 80 P. & C.R. 126, Peter Gibson, L.J., CA.

4848. Commons – established use – defeat of claim to use "as of right" by implied permission

[Commons Registration Act 1965 s.13, s.22(1).]

B appealed against the dismissal ([2001] 1 W.L.R. 1327) of her application for judicial review of a refusal by SCC to register certain land as a town green under the Commons Registration Act 1965 s.13. SCC's licensing committee had refused the application on the basis that despite the land being used by local residents for more than 20 years, there had been an implied permission to use the land thereby defeating the claim of use "as of right" within the meaning of s.22(1) of the Act. B submitted that a claim to use "as of right" could only be defeated on the grounds that the use had been permissive if there was an overt and contemporaneous oral or written expression of such permission.

Held, dismissing the appeal, that in principle there was no reason why an implied permission could not defeat a claim to use as of right since a legal distinction existed between an owner's acquiescence in the use of his land and the giving of a licence for such use. Furthermore, although permission for the use of land required a positive act from the owner, an implied permission could be inferred from a variety of acts by the owner and evidence of written permission or an oral grant of consent was not essential. Accordingly, the committee had not erred in finding that the claim had been defeated.

R. (ON THE APPLICATION OF BERESFORD) v. SUNDERLAND CITY COUNCIL; *sub nom.* R. v. SUNDERLAND CITY COUNCIL, *ex p.* BERESFORD, [2001] EWCA Civ 1218, [2002] 2 W.L.R. 693, Dyson, L.J., CA.

4849. Commons – grazing – profits a prendre – appurtenant right limited to specific number of animals – severance

[Law of Property Act 1925 s.187; Commons Registration Act 1965 s.15.]

P, the owners of a farm on the edge of land registered as a common under the Commons Registration Act 1965 appealed against a decision ([2000] Ch. 54) that an appurtenant right of pasturage for a fixed number of animals could be severed from the land to which it was appurtenant. L, the previous owners of P's farm, had sold the right of pasturage which had been registered under s.15(3) of the 1965 Act thereby fixing the number of animals to 10 cattle and 30 sheep, to B. It was argued that it was not possible in law for L to have severed the right of pasturage from the land with the result that the right had continued to vest in L and subsequently passed on to P.

Held, dismissing the appeal (Lord Nicholls of Birkenhead dissenting), that the appurtenant right of pasturage for a fixed number of animals was severable transforming it from a right appurtenant to a right in gross and that position was not altered by the Law of Property Act 1925 s.187. Severance of such a right restricted to a certain number of animals could not increase the burden on the servient tenement. The effect of registration of the right under s.15 of the 1965 Act was that rights formally determined by levancy and couchancy, that is, the right to graze on the land the number of cattle which could be maintained thereon, became rights to graze a fixed number of animals. The section did not operate to restrict the common law rule that the right to pasture a fixed number of animals on common land could be severed from the dominant land, since this was in accordance with the general principle of keeping land freely alienable.

BETTISON v. LANGTON; *sub nom.* BETTISON v. PENTON, [2001] UKHL 24, [2002] 1 A.C. 27, Lord Scott of Foscote, HL.

4850. Compensation – closing orders – valuation evidence – lack of comparables

[Housing Act 1985 s.584A.]

P sought compensation under the Housing Act 1985 s.584A as the result of a closing order made by CBC over a flat in Cheltenham located in a dilapidated building. P contended that there was a market for the property based on sales of flats in that building dating back to 1994. P claimed that such sales were in the region of £30,000, with a discount of 60 per cent applying in the instant case due to the condition of the building. CBC contended that the property had no value.

Held, refusing the application, that P had not shown that any loss had been suffered because of the closing order. The valuations P sought to rely on were not acceptable as they had not been made by reference to comparables. Further, there was no allowance for borrowing or management costs or insurance.

POWELL v. CHELTENHAM BC [2001] R.V.R. 144, PR Francis FRICS, LandsTr.

4851. Compensation – footpaths – footpath creation order – limitation period

[Highways Act 1980 s.28; Limitation Act 1980 s.9; Public Path Orders and Extinguishment of Public Right of Way Orders Regulations 1983 (SI 1983 23) Reg.16.]

OCC applied for determination of a preliminary issue as to whether a claim by R for compensation under the Highways Act 1980 s.28 was statute barred. R made the claim in June 1989 following the making by OCC of a footpath creation order over R's land in December 1988. Negotiations failed to reach a resolution, and in April 1999 R referred the matter to the tribunal.

Held, that the claim was statute barred. Although the Public Path Orders and Extinguishment of Public Right of Way Orders Regulations 1983 Reg.16 provided that compensation claims should be made within six months of the order coming into force, this did not disapply the Limitation Act 1980 s.9 as it was not a limitation prescription. The right of action arose when the footpath creation order gave rise to entitlement to compensation, not when the claim was made, *Hillingdon LBC v. ARC Ltd (No.1)* [1999] Ch. 139, [1998] C.L.Y. 4179 applied. Given the delays in the case, no issue of estoppel arose in relation to OCC's reliance on the limitation point.

ROTHERWICK'S EXECUTORS v. OXFORDSHIRE CC [2000] 2 E.G.L.R. 84, George Bartlett Q.C. (President), LandsTr.

4852. Contract for sale of land – contract terms – agreement to discharge third party debt – existence of collateral contract

[Law of Property (Miscellaneous Provisions) Act 1989 s.2.]

H, who had been married to G, appealed against a judgment in favour of G for the specific performance of an agreement to sell to G a property of which he was the sole legal owner. H had contended that the agreement contained in a letter signed by both parties did not comply with the Law of Property (Miscellaneous Provisions) Act 1989 s.2 because it did not have as an express term the discharge of a debt owed to a third party in respect of a loan to reduce earlier mortgage arrears on the property, although that was a part of the agreement. The judge relying on *Tootal Clothing Ltd v. Guinea Properties Management Ltd* (1992) 64 P. & C.R. 452, [1993] C.L.Y. 2491 had found that the agreement to discharge the debt was a collateral contract "hived off" from the main contract and was not required to be in writing.

Held, dismissing the appeal, that the issue was whether the contract for sale was irrelevant or conditional upon the agreement to discharge the loan. The contract was valid given the finding that G had never disputed liability for the debt and although the discharge of the loan had been contained in earlier drafts of the agreement, it had been deliberately omitted from the final version. The discharge of the debt had not been in issue at the time of making the contract and was therefore not a term of the bargain. The question of the existence of a collateral contract was not helpful, *Tootal* doubted.

GROSSMAN v. HOOPER, [2001] EWCA Civ 615, [2001] 3 F.C.R. 662, Chadwick, L.J., CA.

4853. Contract for sale of land – contract terms – completion conditional on obtaining planning permission

C contracted to buy a property owned by J in August 1998. It was a condition of the contract that completion was conditional on C obtaining planning permission for a residential development. In October 1998, C submitted an application for planning permission and made an amended application by a different architect in June 1999. Planning permission was refused. J commenced an action for breach of contract, alleging that C was in breach of an implied term to obtain planning permission within a reasonable time. C counterclaimed on the basis that a letter sent by J to the local planning authority in August 1999, stating that C's application should be refused as C was no longer in a contractual relationship with J, was itself a breach of contract

Held, dismissing the claim and allowing the counterclaim, that the term contended for by J would be implied into the contract, but as it was innominate in nature, breach of it would only be repudiatory if it were sufficiently serious. C could not be said to have been in breach as it was continuing to make reasonable efforts to obtain permission, and any delays had been due to factors beyond C's control. If a date had to be put on compliance, a period of 20 months from the making of the application would be appropriate. The contract was thus still in force. Nominal damages of £2 would allowed on the counterclaim as J's actions were obviously intended to lead to a refusal in breach of the implied term not to hinder the planning process.

JOLLEY v. CARMEL LTD [2000] 2 E.G.L.R. 153, Kim Lewison Q.C., Ch D.

4854. Contract for sale of land – deposits – failure to complete

[Law of Property Act 1925 s.49(2).]

O appealed against the decision that he was not entitled to the return of his deposit on the purchase of a house from W. The action had arisen from two agreements, one a business transfer agreement and the other relating to the sale of a property. The judge had found that the deposit, which amounted to approximately 30 per cent of the purchase price of the relevant property, had not been paid. The issue arose as to whether, if, contrary to the judge's finding, a deposit had been paid, the court should exercise its discretion under the Law of Property Act 1925 s.49(2) and order its return.

Held, dismissing the appeal, that (1) the judge had erred in finding that O had not paid the deposit, and (2) where a purchaser was unable himself to perform, it would only be appropriate for the court to exercise its discretion under s.49(2) of the Act in exceptional circumstances, *Universal Corp v. Five Ways Properties* [1979] 1 All E.R. 552, [1979] C.L.Y. 2775 considered. The inability to complete was the very risk which the deposit was intended to guard against. In the instant case it was not appropriate to exercise such discretion given that O should have known, or been advised, of the consequences to him of failing to complete the contract.

OMAR v. EL-WAKIL; *sub nom.* OMAR v. WAKIL, [2001] EWCA Civ 1090, *The Times*, November 2, 2001, Arden, L.J., CA.

4855. **Contract for sale of land – receivers – breach of duty – extent and nature of duty of good faith**

Y, the receiver appointed by a mortgagee of two properties owned by H, sought summary judgment against H in respect of H's claim that the properties had been sold at an undervalue. Y contended that since the only duty of care that arose in relation to the exercise of his powers as receiver was that of good faith, H had failed to establish any breach of duty. Furthermore, as H had failed to serve a particularised statement of claim timeously, failing to allow Y the opportunity to reply, the claim should not be allowed to proceed to trial. H, who had refused to cooperate since the commencement of possession proceedings, argued that the properties had been in perfect condition when she had vacated them and that the reduced price which Y had accepted as a result of the valuation, had been unreasonable.

Held, giving judgment for Y, that H had no realistic prospect of establishing that Y had breached his duty of good faith, as there was no evidence of any dishonesty, improper motive or bad faith, *Medforth v. Blake* [2000] Ch. 86, [1999] C.L.Y. 3286 applied. Neither was Y guilty of any failure to act properly in any way, were such a duty capable of subsisting, given that the sale of the properties did not involve a sale of business as a going concern, which arguably gave rise to a higher duty of care, *AIB Finance Ltd v. Alsop* [1998] 2 All E.R. 929, [1998] C.L.Y. 3342 considered. None of the grounds on which she had based her claim had a real prospect of success, *Swain v. Hillman* [2001] 1 All E.R. 91, [1999] C.L.Y. 561 applied, and many were unsupported by the evidence.

HADJIPANAYI v. YELDON [2001] B.P.I.R. 487, Nicholas Warren Q.C., Ch D.

4856. **Easements – right of support – withdrawal of support upon demolition of adjoining property**

See NEGLIGENCE: Rees v. Skerrett. §4482

4857. **Easements – right to light – proposed development impinging on covenant for quiet enjoyment – right of tenant as against third parties**

P, the underlessee of office premises demised by freeholder M, applied for summary judgment of its claim against C and sought, inter alia, a declaration that the premises enjoyed an easement of light over neighbouring property, formerly a public highway, which C sought to develop. It was agreed between the parties that the right to light was included in the demised premises as defined in the underlease. The proposed development would interfere with the light to the building occupied by P. C sought to rely on a clause in the lease whereby nothing "contained or implied" in the lease would "operate to prevent or restrict in any way the development of any land not comprised in the lease". P contended that that clause was stated to be "without prejudice to" the covenant as to quiet enjoyment.

Held, giving summary judgment for P, that on construing the lease, M had reserved a right to develop land that was not the subject matter of the demise, notwithstanding that such development would impinge on P's right to quiet enjoyment. However, that right was to be construed restrictively and against M. Therefore the right of the landlord only extended to land owned by him and no similar right was afforded to third party landowners to develop adjacent sites. Accordingly, P was entitled to assert its right to an easement of light against CLRP, *Overcom Properties v. Stockleigh Hall Residents Management Ltd* (1989)

58 P. & C.R. 1, [1989] C.L.Y. 2097 and *William Hill (Southern) Ltd v. Cabras Ltd* (1987) 54 P. & C.R. 42, [1987] C.L.Y. 1231 applied.
PARAGON FINANCE PLC v. CITY OF LONDON REAL PROPERTY CO LTD [2002] L. & T.R. 9, Judge Rich Q.C., Ch D.

4858.   Equitable interests in land – pre emption rights – non fulfilment of condition precedent – contractual right

[Law of Property (Miscellaneous Provisions) Act 1989 s.2.]
B, trustees and also the lessor of a long lease held by W, appealed against a decision refusing to grant specific performance in respect of a right of pre emption contained in the lease. W had informed B that it had received an acceptable offer for the leasehold interest and had asked B if it intended to exercise the right to pre emption. B had purported to accept the offer to acquire the leasehold interest by fax. Shortly afterwards the shares in W were sold to the prospective purchaser of the property and W asserted that there was no binding contract for the sale of the leasehold interest to B, because there was no proper offer and acceptance. In any event, W submitted, the Law of Property (Miscellaneous Provisions) Act 1989 s.2 had not been complied with. B contended that there was a proper contract and even if that were wrong, it had an equitable interest in the lease which could be enforced without the subsequent requirement for a contract.
Held, dismissing the appeal, that the right of pre emption did not impose on W an obligation to make an offer to sell to the lessor at any time earlier than immediately before entering a binding contract to sell to a third party. Therefore, such offer could be withdrawn at any time before it had been converted into a binding contract by acceptance, *Tuck v. Baker* [1990] 32 E.G. 46, [1990] C.L.Y. 713 applied. A right of pre emption did not create an interest in land but was merely a contractual right which created no right to call for a conveyance until certain conditions had been fulfilled, namely contracting to sell to a third party, which had not happened in the present case, *Pritchard v. Briggs* [1980] Ch. 338, [1980] C.L.Y. 1563 and *Kling v. Keston Properties Ltd* (1985) 49 P. & C.R. 212, [1985] C.L.Y. 3607 applied. If an offer was made which would remain open for a specific period of time, an equitable interest would be created, indistinguishable from the interest under an option. However, in the present case, no such interest arose since the offer was made on terms that it could be withdrawn at any time before acceptance in circumstances where the lessee no longer wished to dispose of the lease. Furthermore, the requirements of s.2 of the Act had not been satisfied.
BIRCHAM & CO NOMINEES (NO.2) LTD v. WORRELL HOLDINGS LTD, [2001] EWCA Civ 775, (2001) 82 P. & C.R. 34, Chadwick, L.J., CA.

4859.   Equitable remedies – proprietary estoppel – lodger acted as carer – lodger's reliance on assurances of life interest to his detriment

C appealed against an order granting possession of a house to G, the executors of the property. C had been a lodger in the house for over 20 years. For a number of those years he had taken increasingly greater care of the elderly couple he was lodging with as they became more and more infirm. He had developed a close relationship with the couple and they had assured him that he would have a home for life. The husband executed a codicil to his will leaving C a life interest in the house, however, as the house was held by the couple as a joint tenancy, and the wife had lost her testamentary capacity by that stage and had not added a corresponding codicil to her will, the gift failed by survivorship. C had made his claim based on the doctrine of proprietary estoppel and the judge had found that although assurances about C's life interest in the house had been given, C had not relied on them to his detriment because he had taken care of the couple out of friendship and a sense of responsibility.
Held, allowing the appeal, that C had acted to his detriment in taking care of the couple and he should accordingly be given a charge over the property. He had been doing much more than would have been ascribed to even the most

friendly lodger and a live in carer would have expected payment for undertaking such duties. It was highly probable that his conduct had been influenced by the assurances given by the couple, *Wayling v. Jones* [1995] 2 F.L.R. 1029, [1994] C.L.Y. 2108 considered. A broad enquiry into all the circumstances was necessary as opposed to a mere assessment of any financial loss incurred, *Gillett v. Holt* [2001] Ch. 210, [2000] 4 C.L. 243 considered.

CAMPBELL v. GRIFFIN, [2001] EWCA Civ 990, [2001] W.T.L.R. 981, Robert Walker, L.J., CA.

4860. Human rights – property rights – expropriation of land by Italian local authority – violation of peaceful enjoyment of possessions

[European Convention on Human Rights First Protocol Art.1.]

B owned a hotel and adjoining land giving its guests direct access to the sea. The local municipal authority approved the construction of a new road, which involved the compulsory acquisition of B's land. The acquisition was carried into effect, and the road building commenced. When the road was virtually complete, the Tuscany Regional Administrative Court quashed the original approval of the scheme, since insufficient technical surveys had been carried out beforehand. This rendered the scheme unlawful, and not in the public interest. B therefore applied to the Consiglio di Stato for an order for the return of the land. The order was refused, on the basis of a doctrine developed by Italian judges of "constructive expropriation", whereby where works had been substantially completed, title to the relevant land was deemed transferred, with no possibility of restitution to the original owner. B applied to the European Court of Human Rights, claiming a breach of the European Convention on Human Rights First Protocol Art.1, with regard to right to peaceful enjoyment of possessions, and deprivation thereof only in the public interest, and subject to the conditions provided by law and by the general principles of international law.

Held, upholding the complaint, that (1) the court was required to investigate the realities of the case before it, and to see if there had been a de facto appropriation; (2) the judgment of the Consiglio di Stato had been to deprive B of its property within the meaning of Art.1; (3) the evolution of Italian case law on "constructive appropriation" had led to inconsistency in the application of the doctrine, and might result in arbitrary outcomes thus depriving litigants of their rights. It was therefore inconsistent with the requirement of lawfulness in Art.1, and (4) the effect of the appropriation was to confer a benefit arising from an unlawful situation and to present B with a situation about which it could do nothing. This was incompatible with Art.1

BELVEDERE ALBERGHIERA SRL v. ITALY [2000] R.V.R. 303, CL Rozakis (President), ECHR.

4861. Land registers – rectification – possession of land – exercise of discretion

[Land Registration Act 1925s.3(ii), s.5, s.20(1), s.82(1), s.82(3).]

T, a property development company, appealed against a decision to order rectification of the land register so as to give effect to declarations made in favour of K in relation to the boundary of its registered land and that of T. It was submitted that the judge was wrong in exercising his discretion to order rectification against T as registered proprietor in possession. T argued that the judge had misdirected himself in law, as (1) he need not have considered the application of the Land Registration Act 1925 s.82(3) as the issues raised under that subsection did not arise where rectification of the register had been made, as in the instant case, pursuant to an order of the court, and (2) he had considered the exercise of his discretion under s.82(1) on the mistaken basis that T had not acquired "possession" of the disputed land.

Held, allowing the appeal and setting aside the rectification of the land register, that (1) the instant case fell within the exception in s.82(3) so that the section was inapplicable. Parliament had intended to infer an unfettered discretion solely on the High Court when ordering rectification pursuant to s.3(ii) of the Act. However, the court should have regard to the policy of the Act which placed special weight on a proprietor in possession of registered land being permitted to keep his title, and (2) given the combined effect of s.5 and s.20(1), T must, on registration of the land, be taken to have acquired possession on which basis discretion should have been exercised pursuant to s.82(1). It followed that the court could consider the exercise of the issue of rectification afresh, concluding that on the balance of interests rectification should not be allowed.

KINGSALTON LTD v. THAMES WATER DEVELOPMENTS LTD; *sub nom.* THAMES WATER DEVELOPMENTS LTD v. KINGSALTON LTD, [2001] EWCA Civ 20, [2002] 1 P. & C.R. 15, Peter Gibson, L.J., CA.

4862. **Land registration – district registries**

LAND REGISTRATION (DISTRICT REGISTRIES) ORDER 2001, SI 2001 3424; made under the Land Registration Act 1925 s.132. In force: January 2, 2002; £2.00.

This Order, which amends the Land Registration (District Registries) Order 2000 (SI 2000 430), transfers responsibility for the registration of titles in Corby, East Northamptonshire, Kettering and Wellingborough from the Peterborough District Land Registry to the Leicester District Registry.

4863. **Land registration – fees**

LAND REGISTRATION FEES ORDER 2001, SI 2001 1179; made under the Land Registration Act 1925 s.145; the Public Offices Fees Act 1879 s.2; the Land Registration Act 1925 s.3; and the Finance Act 1990 c.128. In force: May 1, 2001; £3.00.

This Order, which revokes the Land Registration Fees Order 1999 (SI 1999 2254), makes amendments to Scale 1 which sets out the fees for applications for first registration of title to land and for transfers of registered land for monetary consideration by reducing the fee for applications within the £40,001 to £70,000 value band. It makes changes by introducing fees of £2 and £4 for outline applications to secure priority for certain dealings with registered land where made by means of a remote terminal communicating with the Registrar's computer system or by other means, introduces a fee of £2 for an official search of the register by a mortgagee and a fee of £1 for an application for day list information made by means of a remote terminal communicating with the Registrar's computer system.

4864. **Land registration – rules – electronic communication**

LAND REGISTRATION RULES 2001, SI 2001 619; made under the Land Registration Act 1925 s.54, s.94, s.123A, s.144. In force: May 28, 2001; £2.00.

These Rules amend the Land Registration Rules 1925 (SR & O 1925 1093) to allow applications to register dealings with registered land to be lodged electronically following the issue of a notice by the Registrar, which can be issued once the Registrar is satisfied that appropriate arrangements are in place in relation to specified types of application. They also amend the Land Registration (Matrimonial Home Rights) Rules 1997 (SI 1997 1964) to allow applications to register or renew matrimonial home rights to be submitted electronically following the issue of a notice by the Registrar, which can be issued once the Registrar is satisfied that appropriate arrangements are in place in relation to these types of application and amend the application forms to include a warning that notice of the application will be given to the registered owner.

4865. **Land registry – loss prevention – fraud – appropriate test for seeking indemnity**

[Land Registration Act 1925 s.83, s.83(5).]

D purchased an investment property in 1981, which was registered at the Land Registry. D's wife fraudulently effected a transfer of the property to the third defendant without D's knowledge and in 1994 the property was sold to innocent third parties. D commenced proceedings in 1996 seeking damages against the first four defendants and seeking rectification of the land register, or an indemnity under the Land Registration Act 1925 s.83 against CLR. In 1999 D's claim against CLR was struck out on the basis that D had no prospect of successfully claiming an indemnity (rectification being inappropriate), it having been held that such a claim would fail under s.83(5), the court having found that "but for" D's failure to take proper care, the problem would never have occurred. D appealed, contending that the judge had erred in (1) applying a "but for" test to s.83; (2) his subsequent conclusion that the fraud could not have occurred "but for" D's lack of proper care, and (3) his evaluation of the evidence of D's supposed lack of care in attending to matters concerning the property.

Held, allowing the appeal, that (1) the "but for " test was not the applicable test for the purposes of s.83 as, even if satisfied, it did not exclude the possibility that there were other causes of D's loss. Section 83 was clear in stating that the loss had to be wholly as a result of a claimants lack of proper care for an indemnity claim to fail, and in the present case it was apparent that D's loss was, at least in part, a result of the actions of fraudsters, and (2) the judge had misdirected himself on a number of factual issues concerning D's actions and his entitlement to assume that all was in order after delegating responsibilities to his wife and a property management company.

DEAN v. DEAN (APPEAL AGAINST STRIKING OUT) (2000) 80 P. & C.R. 457, Peter Gibson, L.J., CA.

4866. **Leases – overriding interests – evidence of occupation**

[Land Registration Act 1925 s.22(2)(a).]

M appealed against a decision requiring him to give possession of a flat to L. The issue before the court related to the priority of the respective parties' interests in the flat. M claimed possession pursuant to an assignment of a leasehold interest whereas L claimed by way of an underlease. M contended that (1) the fact that the transfer to him had not been registered was irrelevant; (2) the lease taken by L had not been properly executed and was consequently invalid, and (3) the judge at first instance had been wrong in his conclusion that M did not have an overriding interest since he was not in actual occupation of the flat.

Held, dismissing the appeal, that (1) whilst the contract assigning a leasehold interest to M had been valid and effective in conferring an equitable interest in the lease upon him which was capable of amounting to an overriding interest, the consequential transfer had not been registered and therefore the assignor had remained the proprietor and had been capable of granting interests with priority over that of M, *Bridges v. Mees* [1957] Ch. 475, [1957] C.L.Y. 1906 applied; (2) the lease granted to L, which provided an option for two further leases, fell within the Land Registration Act 1925 s.22(2)(a) being a lease granted for 21 years or less and thereby conferring a legal estate upon L as if it were a registered disposition subject solely to any overriding interests in existence, and (3) since the available evidence did not suggest that M was in actual occupation, he had not had an overriding interest on the date when the lease had been executed.

LEEMAN v. MOHAMMED, [2001] EWCA Civ 198, (2001) 82 P. & C.R. 14, Mance, L.J., CA.

4867. Leases – rights of way – express and implied reservation – overriding interests – effect of transfer of headlease subject to Law Society's Conditions of Sale

[Land Registration Act 1925 s.70(1)(g).]

H applied for rectification of a transfer deed relating to his land, A, to include the express reservation of a right of way over adjoining land, B, claiming that the right already existed by virtue of an earlier contractual condition. The headleases of the two properties had previously been assigned to a company, CIS, which created various underleases to different parties, one of which had included the right of way. However, in 1989 the headlease relating to B was transferred subject to the Law Society's Conditions of Sale with no express reservation of the right of way in favour of A. The headlease of B was then transferred to S, and H contended that (1) in view of the condition to which the 1989 transfer was subject, the reservation of the right of way had survived by implication notwithstanding the transfer to S, and (2) in any event, the right to rectify was an overriding interest binding on S by virtue of the Land Registration Act 1925 s.70(1)(g).

Held, dismissing the application for rectification, that (1) H had no basis for a claim of rectification against S. The 1989 transfer had reserved no rights in favour of A, and there had not been any form of agreement between the parties concerning the express or implied reservation of the right of way. In the absence of necessity, the fact that CIS's tenant had been using the way as a means of obtaining access to the car park on A was insufficient basis upon which to justify an implied reservation of the right of way *Webb's Lease, Re* [1951] Ch. 808 applied, and (2) the use of a right of way could not amount to actual occupation of the way for the purpose of s.70(1)(g) of the 1925 Act, *Abbey National Building Society v. Cann* [1991] 1 A.C. 56, [1990] C.L.Y. 707 applied. The right to rectify arose at the execution of the transfer, by which time CIS had been freed of any interest in B and the receipt of any rent therefrom. Further, S had enquired as to any rights which affected B prior to the completion of the transfer, which precluded reliance on s.70(1)(g) of the 1925 Act.

HOLAW (470) LTD v. STOCKTON ESTATES LTD (2001) 81 P. & C.R. 29, Neuberger, J., Ch D.

4868. Licences – proprietary estoppel – agreement for lease – without prejudice negotiations

E applied for a mandatory injunction to compel its landlord, W, to allow it back into possession of premises of which it claimed to be the tenant. E had previously been a tenant of adjoining premises prior to entering an agreement with W to enter into a lease of the premises in question. E was to occupy initially as a licensee on payment of a licence fee until the lease was granted, with rent to be payable from a certain date. The parties entered into protracted correspondence, largely expressed to be "subject to contract". The lease was never granted, nor the licence fee nor any rent paid by E, and W subsequently repossessed the premises. E argued that W had agreed to allow it rent free periods in return for E carrying out works to the premises and that W was therefore estopped from enforcing the agreement.

Held, refusing the application, that E had not met the necessary threshold for a mandatory injunction as there was no serious issue to be tried because E did not have an arguable case on the issue of proprietary estoppel. The negotiations between the parties had clearly been "subject to contract" on a without prejudice basis, with the effect that any assurances purportedly given by W were not binding and E could not argue that it had acted in reliance on them. E had no defence to the contention that the licence fee had been due in any event.

EDWIN SHIRLEY PRODUCTIONS LTD v. WORKSPACE MANAGEMENT LTD [2001] 23 E.G. 158, Lawrence Collins, J., Ch D.

4869. Mortgagees powers and duties – negligence – insolvency of surveyor – extent of duty owed to mortgagor

See NEGLIGENCE: Noble v. Coutts & Co. §4541

4870. Mortgages – charges – equitable interests in land – order for sale of property – material considerations

[Trusts of Land and Appointment of Trustees Act 1996 s.14, s.15.]

BI, a bank and mortgagee of a property co-owned by B and her former husband, appealed against an order allowing B's appeal against an order for possession. The judge had ordered rectification of the charges register in order to delete the charge on the property in favour of BI, and held that the charge was to operate on an equitable basis only over the property because of doubts as to the validity of B's signature on the mortgage documents. BI contended that (1) the judge should have found as a fact that B had signed the relevant documents, and (2) a sale of the property should have been ordered.

Held, allowing the appeal in part and substituting an order for sale, that (1) on the overall evidence, it was impossible to say that the judge had erred in his findings of fact, and (2) the judge had erred in the exercise of his discretion by refusing to order the sale of the property pursuant to the Trusts of Land and Appointment of Trustees Act 1996 s.14 as he had failed to take into account certain material considerations referred to in s.15. The judge had not taken into account the fact that BI would take all the proceeds on the sale of the property given B's minimal beneficial interest or the subsequent injustice to BI resulting from an indefinite postponement of any sale. Neither had the judge drawn accurate conclusions with regard to occupation of the property or the intention concerning its use at the time of purchase.

BANK OF IRELAND HOME MORTGAGES LTD v. BELL [2001] 2 All E.R. (Comm) 920, Peter Gibson, L.J., CA.

4871. Mortgages – equitable interests – payment of interest where charge silent as to payment

I, the owner of property occupied by its associated company, IP, appealed against a finding that an equitable charge on the property granted to A to secure loans that he had made to IP should carry interest from the date specified in a memorandum prepared by IP as the date when the charge would be redeemed. I argued that there was no evidence that IP had agreed that the loans provided by A would carry interest and that no such term should be implied into a loan contract.

Held, dismissing the appeal, that the judge had been correct to award interest from the date specified in the memorandum. I, IP and A had been parties to a tripartite contract whose purpose was to secure IP's indebtedness to A. While I had not received the benefit of the loans, it must have considered that it was to its advantage that the loans should be made by A to IP. The authorities showed that, when it was equitable to do so, the obligation to pay interest would be imposed on the security rather than on the surety personally. The fact that the debtor was under no personal or legal obligation to pay interest because the loan contract did not deal with the point did not preclude interest from being awarded. It therefore followed that the fact that I, as surety, was under no personal or legal obligation to pay interest did not prevent interest from being awarded in respect of the property which it had made security for the loans.

AL-WAZIR v. ISLAMIC PRESS AGENCY INC (INTEREST); *sub nom.* ISLAMIC PRESS AGENCY v. AL-WAZIR, [2001] EWCA Civ 1276, [2002] 1 Lloyd's Rep. 410, Robert Walker, L.J., CA.

4872. Mortgages – guarantees – conditional guarantee set aside

P, a director of a company, signed a legal mortgage on her home in favour of N to ensure N's continued financial backing of the company, supposedly committing herself to the extent of £30,000, being the value of a guarantee over the company's debts to the bank allegedly signed at the same time. N had no documentary evidence to prove the existence or extent of that guarantee. Subsequently, G and L joined P on the board of directors. N required an increase in P's guarantee to £100,000, a guarantee secured by a legal mortgage from G in the sum of £50,000 and a £50,000 cash injection from L. All three directors alleged that their understanding was that each of their contributions was dependent upon the others being in place to be enforceable. L provided the cash injection. P eventually signed a guarantee for £120,000. Later G executed her guarantee, but it was never secured by a mortgage and she was eventually released from it. N sought possession of P's home, calling on the guarantee. The only documentary evidence of conditionality was a postscript in a letter purportedly sent by L to N's investments department, informing N that his understanding was that each contribution would be dependent upon the other being in place. N did not respond to this point and did not produce the letter on disclosure.

Held, giving judgment for the defendant and setting aside the guarantee, that little short of an express mention to N's officers that the guarantee was conditional would be sufficient to demonstrate a breach of contract in failing to take a secured guarantee from G. The court was satisfied on the evidence that L's letter had been sent and would have come to the attention of N's officers. No objection was raised by N, which went ahead and took the security from P. Any inconsistent term in the standard form of the guarantee was overridden by N's inferred agreement to the matters raised in the postscript. It was contemplated that there would be a guarantee from G backed by a charge. The failure to obtain the charge amounted to a breach of contract, entitling P to have the guarantee set aside. Possession was refused, *Greer v. Kettle* [1938] A.C. 156 and *Byblos Bank SAL v. Rushingdale SA* [1987] B.C.L.C. 232, [1986] C.L.Y. 323 applied.

NATWEST BANK PLC v. PICKERING, October 10, 2000, Recorder Vosper, CC (Chester). [*Ex rel.* John Baldwin, Barrister, Oriel Chambers, 14 Water Street, Liverpool].

4873. Mortgages – implied terms – equitable duty to sell at fair price – applicable limitation period

[Limitation Act 1980 s.8.]

R appealed against a ruling ([2000] Lloyd's Rep. Bank. 377, [2000] C.L.Y. 4657) that his action against L, the mortgagee in possession, for breach of its duty to obtain the best price for the property and incur only reasonable expenses, was time barred pursuant to the Limitation Act 1980. R contended that the duties of a mortgagee in possession were implied terms under the charge and that pursuant to s.8, his claim, being founded upon the legal charge, was an action upon a speciality, whereby the relevant limitation period was twelve years.

Held, dismissing the appeal, that the relevant duties did not arise from any implied contractual obligation, since the same duty was also owed by L to any subsequent mortgagee and such a duty would also be owed by receivers, being a general obligation in equity to take reasonable care to obtain a proper price, *Cuckmere Brick Co v. Mutual Finance* [1971] Ch. 949, [1971] C.L.Y. 7479 applied and *Bishop v. Bonham* [1988] 1 W.L.R. 742, [1988] C.L.Y. 2388 explained. Therefore the claim was not based upon a specialty and, as the relevant limitation period was six years, the action was time barred.

RAJA v. LLOYDS TSB BANK PLC, [2001] EWCA Civ 210, [2001] Lloyd s Rep. Bank. 113, Judge, L.J., CA.

4874. Mortgages – interest rates – variation – implied term to vary rates fairly – extortionate credit bargains

[Consumer Credit Act 1974 s.138, s.139; Unfair Contract Terms Act 1977 s.3(2)(b).]

N appealed against the striking out of a defence and counterclaim to a possession action brought by the mortgagee, PF, after N had fallen into mortgage interest arrears. N contended that the mortgage agreement, which contained a variable interest clause, became an extortionate credit bargain under the Consumer Credit Act 1974 s.138 following the failure by PF to bring its interest rates in line with the Bank of England or prevailing market rates. N sought to have the loan agreements reopened under s.139 of the 1974 Act, and to plead an implied term that PF was bound to exercise its discretion in varying interest rates fairly, honestly, in good faith, and not arbitrarily, capriciously or unreasonably, having regard to all relevant matters and ignoring the irrelevant.

Held, dismissing the appeal, that the discretion to vary interest rates was not completely unfettered and was subject to the implied term contended for by N, *Lombard Tricity Finance v. Paton* [1989] 1 All E.R. 918, [1989] C.L.Y. 402 not followed. However, the fact that PF had set interest rates without reference to those of other market lenders did not place PF in breach of the implied term. PF had been attempting to alleviate serious financial difficulties by passing its increasing costs onto its borrowers. Therefore it could not be said that its discretion to set interest rates was being exercised capriciously, arbitrarily, unreasonably or for an improper purpose. The argument that the rates of interest were exorbitant so as to bring the agreement within s.138 of the 1974 Act had no real prospect of success, given that only charges existing at the time of the agreement could be taken into account in determining whether a credit bargain was extortionate. Furthermore, it was not open to N to establish a breach of the Unfair Contract Terms Act 1977 s.3(2)(b) by arguing that PF had defeated their reasonable expectations, given that the setting of interest rates was not "contractual performance". The court could only intervene if a credit bargain had been grossly unfair to a borrower by requiring grossly exorbitant payments or if it had grossly contravened principles of fair dealing.

PARAGON FINANCE PLC (FORMERLY NATIONAL HOME LOANS CORP) v. NASH; PARAGON FINANCE PLC v. STAUNTON; *sub nom.* NASH v. PARAGON FINANCE PLC; STAUNTON v. PARAGON FINANCE PLC, [2001] EWCA Civ 1466, [2002] 1 W.L.R. 685, Dyson, L.J., CA.

4875. **Mortgages – possession orders – reasonable time for payment – point in time used to assess status of property as dwelling**

[Administration of Justice Act 1970 s.36(1); Administration of Justice Act 1973 s.8(1).]

M appealed against a decision dismissing her appeal against a possession order issued in respect of premises which she owned subject to a legal charge in favour of RBS. M contended that the judge at first instance had erred in his conclusion that the premises, comprising a nightclub with a flat above in which M had lived at various times, were not used as a dwelling for the purposes of the Administration of Justice Act 1970 s.36(1), at the time the charge was entered into. M was therefore not entitled to a reasonable period in which to pay the sums due. RBS opposed the application contending that the relevant time was the date at which the mortgage was taken out and, further, that M was not entitled to defer repayment under the Administration of Justice Act 1973 s.8(1), since payment under the terms of the agreement was not to be made by way of regular instalments but on a specified future date out of the proceeds of certain investment policies.

Held, allowing the appeal, that (1) the relevant time for determining whether the property was a dwelling for the purposes of s.36(1), was the date on which the action for possession had been commenced, *Birmingham Citizens Permanent Building Society v. Caunt* [1962] Ch. 883, [1962] C.L.Y. 1938 considered. Accordingly M was entitled to the protection granted under the 1970 Act thereby fulfilling the social objectives of the statute, and (2) M was entitled to defer repayment under the Administration of Justice Act 1973 s.8(1), since her agreement with RBS did amount to a form of deferred payment in accordance with the reasoning in *Bank of Scotland v. Grimes* [1985] Q.B. 1179, [1985] C.L.Y. 2266.

ROYAL BANK OF SCOTLAND PLC v. MILLER, [2001] EWCA Civ 344, [2002] Q.B. 255, Dyson, L.J., CA.

4876. **Mortgages – redemption – agreement to transfer interest in property to mortgagee – clog on equity of redemption**

J appealed against the dismissal of his application to enforce an agreement between J and M whereby M and his brother had agreed to transfer to J one half of their interest in certain property. The parties initially entered into an agreement in 1994 whereby J advanced £105,000 secured by way of legal charge over M's property, to fund the development of the property for use as a nursing home. When the development did not take place, in order to raise further funds for an alternative development, M entered into an agreement for the sale of 40 acres of the charged land, to a third party. In order to effect this transaction, J's consent was required so that the land could be sold free of the 1994 encumbrance. Accordingly, an agreement was entered into in 1997 under which J agreed to release the land in question for sale in return for a half share in the remaining property. The land was duly sold and the proceeds remitted to J by way of partial discharge of the sum outstanding under the 1994 charge. J subsequently commenced proceedings for specific performance of the agreement to transfer a 50 per cent interest in the property to him. J submitted that the judge had been wrong to find that the 1997 agreement was void on grounds that it was unconscionable and harsh.

Held, dismissing the appeal (Pill, L.J. dissenting), that (1) the 1997 agreement had not been unconscionable since J had not acted in any morally reprehensible manner in failing to draw to W's attention the failure in the agreement to include a promise by J to advance further monies, *Alec Lobb Garages Ltd v. Total Oil Great Britain Ltd* [1983] 1 W.L.R. 87, [1983] C.L.Y. 453 applied. Whilst M may have been naive and trusting, the transaction was not so absurd that a solicitor would have been obliged to advise his client not to enter into it and withdraw from acting had he insisted upon doing so. Accordingly the judge was not entitled to infer that M had not received adequate advice, and (2) the agreement was nevertheless void as a clog on the equity of redemption. Had it been part of the original transaction in 1994, the agreement to transfer a share of the property would have been an integral part of that mortgage and not a separate collateral contract. It was irrelevant that the stipulation was included in the 1997 agreement since in effect the 1997 agreement converted a single indivisible mortgage loan into two distinct mortgage loans which were not independent, *G&C Kreglinger v. New Patagonia Meat & Cold Storage Co Ltd* [1914] A.C. 25 and *Lewis v. Frank Love Ltd* [1961] 1 W.L.R. 261, [1961] C.L.Y. 5596 applied.

JONES v. MORGAN, [2001] EWCA Civ 995, [2001] Lloyd's Rep. Bank 323, Chadwick, L.J., CA.

4877. **Mortgages – subrogation – increase in borrowing without notification to co-surety – entitlement to subrogate**

A bank, L, appealed against a decision dismissing its claim for an order for sale in respect of a property owned by H and W. The property in question had originally been mortgaged by H and W in order to secure H's business debts under a guarantee to a limit of £150,000. Subsequently, and without W's knowledge, H had increased his borrowing from the bank by means of further guarantees. On default, L initiated possession proceedings and monies belonging to W were used to discharge the mortgage. The court, reversing a first instance decision, had held that (1) W had redeemed the mortgage and was entitled to be subrogated to the bank's interest as against H, and (2) L was precluded from relying upon a term in the mortgage deed which would otherwise have operated to preclude W from obtaining rights of subrogation having regard to the fact that W had never been notified of the increases in H's borrowing. L contended that the terms of the mortgage were not limited to H's borrowing under the initial guarantee and the fact that W had not been notified of any increase was immaterial.

Held, dismissing the appeal, that the mortgage had been entered into in order to support a guarantee for £150,000 which related to company facilities for which H would otherwise have had no liability to the bank, having sold his interest in the company. It was not comparable to the situation where facilities were granted on a running account and where further increases might have been expected. Accordingly it was not within the norm to expect further increases to be granted without notification to W, as to do so would undoubtedly prejudice her position as co-surety. Further, there was nothing within the terms of the mortgage which permitted L to place W in a position contrary to that which had been in her reasonable contemplation when entering into the mortgage, *Rees v. Berrington* (1795) 2 Ves. Jr. 540, *Egbert v. National Crown Bank* [1918] A.C. 903 and *Far Eastern Shipping Plc v. Scales Trading Ltd* [2001] 1 All E.R. (Comm.) 319, [2001] 3 C.L. 72 applied.

LLOYDS TSB BANK PLC v. SHORNEY, [2001] EWCA Civ 1161, [2002] 1 F.L.R. 81, Waller, L.J., CA.

4878. Mortgages – undue influence – conflict of interest of solicitor advising

B, who had executed a second mortgage following misrepresentations and coercion on the part of her husband, appealed against a finding that N, the mortgagee, had taken reasonable steps to ensure that she had entered into the transaction of her own free will and with knowledge of the consequences. The judge had found that the fact that the solicitor advising B was also the company secretary of B's husband's company, which would benefit from the mortgage, did not justify the conclusion that N should have decided that he should not advise her. B had not been involved in the management of her husband's business and had not held any shares in the company.

Held, allowing the appeal, that N had been aware that B had no direct financial interest in her husband's company and had therefore been put on enquiry, *Barclays Bank Plc v. O'Brien* [1994] 1 A.C. 180, [1994] C.L.Y. 3300 applied and *Royal Bank of Scotland Plc v. Etridge (No.2)* [1998] 4 All E.R. 705, [1998] C.L.Y. 4358 considered, and (2) given that N had known that the company was seeking funds urgently, that B's husband and business partner were unreliable, and that the solicitor providing advice to B was also company secretary and played an integral part in the company, the circumstances had been suggestive of a real conflict of interest. In such circumstances, it had not been reasonable for N to rely on the solicitor to dispel that conflict of interest, *Credit Lyonnais Bank Nederland NV v. Burch* [1997] 1 All E.R. 144, [1996] C.L.Y. 2784 considered and *Bank of Baroda v. Rayarel* [1996] E.C.C. 157, [1996] C.L.Y. 4967 distinguished.

NATIONAL WESTMINSTER BANK PLC v. BREEDS [2001] Lloyd's Rep. Bank. 98, Lawrence Collins, J., Ch D.

4879. Mortgages – undue influence – duty to ensure independent legal advice taken by spouse

B, a bank, appealed against a finding that it had not discharged its duty to ensure that G had taken independent legal advice before agreeing to an all monies charge over her house as security against the businesses of her husband and son, and that it had had constructive notice of undue influence on the part of the husband prior to the agreement being signed. G had been given the impression by her husband that the charge was limited to £10,000, and although the bank had advised G to take independent legal advice, which she had done, unbeknown to the bank the husband had attended the meeting with her, and she had remained under the misapprehension that her liability was limited. The bank had later agreed to accept payment of a lesser sum from the husband to be paid in instalments, but that was not paid and B had sought repossession of the house.

Held, allowing the appeal, that in an ordinary case a bank would relieve itself of constructive notice by instructing a solicitor to give G independent legal advice and then confirming that had been done, *Royal Bank of Scotland plc v. Etridge (No.2)* [1998] 4 All E.R. 705, [1998] C.L.Y. 4358 applied. The judge had erred in holding that the case was exceptional as there was nothing out of the ordinary in a wife agreeing to provide security for a company in which her husband had an interest and in which she did not. The later agreement had affirmed the charge which was to G's advantage, and there was no misrepresentation or undue influence. Both Mantell, L.J. and Pill, L.J. expressed unease with aspects of the test set out in para 49 of *Royal Bank of Scotland Plc v. Etridge*. It was observed that it was preferable to regard the exception to the general rule as arising in circumstances where any competent solicitor would advise against the wife entering into the transaction.

BARCLAYS BANK PLC v. GOFF, [2001] EWCA Civ 635, [2001] 2 All E.R. (Comm) 847, Mantell, L.J., CA.

4880. Mortgages – undue influence – wife's requirement for independent advice – extent of lenders' duty

The court was required to determine eight appeals in cases where a wife's interest in her home had stood as security for her husband's indebtedness.

Held, dismissing E, G and C's appeals and allowing appeals by H, W, M, DB and B, that (1) a lender was placed on enquiry whenever one party to a cohabiting couple offered to stand surety for the debts of the other party. That included married couples and unmarried couples, whether heterosexual or homosexual, if the bank knew about the relationship. Where a wife became surety for the debts of a company in which she held shares with her husband, the bank was similarly placed on enquiry, even in circumstances where the wife was a director or company secretary; (2) in future a bank would be required to insist that a wife attend a private meeting in order that it might explain the nature of the risk and urge her to seek independent advice. The most that a bank could be expected to do, was to take reasonable steps to satisfy itself that the practical consequences of the proposed transaction had been clearly explained; (3) the decision whether to proceed with the transaction or not had to rest with the wife and it was not a solicitor's role to intervene and attempt to prevent the transaction even if it was thought not to be in her best interests. Guidance was given as to the minimum extent of a solicitor's advice to such a client. In an exceptional case where the transaction was clearly seriously adverse to the interests of the wife, a solicitor should decline to act further; (4) as well as being retained by the wife, a solicitor was entitled to act for the bank or for the husband so long as such an arrangement did not give rise to a conflict of interest. A solicitor was not in the position of agent for the bank and accordingly could not be held liable to the bank for any deficiencies in the advice given, and (5) in order to ensure that a wife had been provided with independent advice a bank should communicate directly with her regarding the nature of the advice that she was to receive and ensure that the confirmation required by the bank from her nominated solicitor was fully explained to her. The following cases were considered, *Bainbrigge v. Browne* (1880-81) L.R. 18 Ch. D. 188, *Barclays Bank Plc v. O'Brien* [1994] 1 A.C. 180, [1994] C.L.Y. 3300, *Credit Lyonnais Bank Nederland NV v. Burch* [1997] 1 All E.R. 144 and *Allcard and Skinner* (1887) L.R. 36 Ch. D. 145 was applied.

ROYAL BANK OF SCOTLAND PLC v. ETRIDGE (NO.2); BARCLAYS BANK PLC v. COLEMAN; BARCLAYS BANK PLC v. HARRIS; MIDLAND BANK PLC v. WALLACE; NATIONAL WESTMINSTER BANK PLC v. GILL; UCB HOME LOANS CORP LTD v. MOORE; BANK OF SCOTLAND v. BENNETT; KENYON-BROWN v. DESMOND BANKS & CO (UNDUE INFLUENCE), [2001] UKHL 44, [2001] 3 W.L.R. 1021, Lord Nicholls of Birkenhead, HL.

4881. Party walls – repairs – surveyors – entitlement to make ex parte award

[London Building Acts (Amendment) Act 1939 s.55(e).]

W and WA, a married couple, were statutory tenants of a property. Extensive works were required to the adjoining property. The appointed surveyor for W and WA, made an ex parte award under the London Building Acts (Amendment) Act 1939 s.55(e). The court determined within the meaning of the Act two preliminary issues namely (1) statutory tenants were not owners, and (2) the ex parte award was defective on the face and therefore invalid. The adjoining owner appealed.

Held, allowing the appeal, that the ex parte award was defective because it did not refer correctly to the appropriate head of s.55(e) of the 1939 Act under which the award was sought, and (2) the respondent was not an owner of adjoining property for the purposes of the Act and did not hold a legal interest in land being only entitled to a statutory tenancy.

FRANCES HOLLAND SCHOOL v. WASSEF [2001] 29 E.G. 123, District Judge Crawford Lindsay Q.C., CC (Central London).

4882. Possession orders – charging orders – estoppel – validity of trust created in breach of solicitor's professional duty

M and her son, trustees of an off shore trust company, appealed against decisions that a declaration of trust by M's husband, H, was ineffective so that H retained the legal and beneficial interest in the matrimonial home and S cross appealed claiming that M was estopped from claiming otherwise. The decisions had been made on the basis that it was improbable that the firm of solicitors that drew up the declaration of trust would have created a valid trust in breach of their professional duty to one of their clients, the mortgagee, and that the declaration was really a sham created for tax avoidance purposes. Therefore under a charging order to S against H, orders of possession and sale could be made in respect of the house. M submitted that either the trust was effective in which case the beneficial interest belonged to the trust rather than H, or that the beneficial interest belonged in full or in part to her.

Held, allowing the appeal and dismissing the cross appeal, that the declaration of trust was effective even if that involved a breach of professional duty by the solicitors, and therefore H held the house as a nominee on the trust. Although H had a beneficial life interest in a half share under the trust on which the charging order could bite, it was a discretionary and therefore a defeasible interest which could not serve as a basis for orders for possession and sale. The financial interests of M either as a trustee or in person were not identical to those of H and the decision of the judge below on the estoppel issue was flawed, *House of Spring Gardens Ltd v. Waite (No.2)* [1991] 1 Q.B. 241, [1990] 2 C.L.Y. 3686 distinguished.

SKYPARKS GROUP PLC v. MARKS, [2001] EWCA Civ 319, [2001] B.P.I.R. 683, Robert Walker, L.J., CA.

4883. Premises management – residential developments – amenity protection

[Leasehold Reform, Housing and Urban Development Act 1993.]

P appealed against a decision that W was entitled to prevent the erection of gates in the wall of their property which was within the boundaries of a management scheme operated by W, and pursuant to the Leasehold Reform, Housing and Urban Development Act 1993. W cross appealed against the judge's decision to award it only three quarters of its costs in the action. P submitted that (1) the gates would have only been an alteration to the external appearance of the wall and therefore W should only have considered the external appearance of the gates, whereas it had refused consent on other grounds, and (2) the management scheme should have been read in light of the 1993 Act, so that the guardian was precluded from considering the interests of those outside the area covered by the scheme, and had therefore acted incorrectly by considering the effect of the gates on other properties beyond the scheme.

Held dismissing the appeal and allowing the cross appeal, that (1) the double gates constituted a new structure or building within the management scheme rather than a mere alteration and the judge had been entitled to refuse consent on grounds unrelated to appearance, and (2) the rules and rationale of the scheme provided for a consideration of the wider locality beyond the boundaries of the scheme. Furthermore, the fact that the case was a test case, the outcome of which could benefit the successful party in future actions, did not necessarily justify depriving that successful party of its costs.

PEXTON v. WELLCOME TRUST LTD (2001) 82 P. & C.R. 4, Simon Brown, L.J., CA.

4884. Property rights – customary law – rights of servitude – Jersey

S appealed against a decision of the Channel Islands Court of Appeal to allow B's appeal against an order enforcing an agreement between B and S whereby B had given S permission to exercise a right of way across her property. B and S had originally entered into an amicable written agreement but B had failed to sign the final contract on the advice of her solicitors who had argued that the consideration paid by S was derisory and that a greater sum could be gained by a sale of the freehold. S contended that the court had erred in its conclusion that under the principle in Jersey law of "deception d'outre moitie du juste prix", whereby a contract would be rescinded if less than half of the market value or "juste prix" were paid, that B was not additionally required to establish some form of fraud, deceit or other misrepresentation.

Held, allowing the appeal, (Lord Cooke and Lord Hutton dissenting), that (1) the essential elements of "deception d'outre moitie du juste prix", under the customary law of Jersey, whereby a free standing remedy was provided on proof that less than half of the "juste prix" had been paid without further evidence being required, had not altered over time and accordingly the court had been correct in their conclusion that no additional element of deceit was required to be proven, and (2) nevertheless as the transaction between S and B had been for the grant of a servitude right, as opposed to a sale of land, it did not fall within the scope of the remedy which was confined to contracts for the sale of land as evidenced by the customary law and its commentators. Further support for such a conclusion lay in the fact that such a contract had no ascertainable market value.

SNELL v. BEADLE (OTHERWISE SILCOCK), [2001] UKPC 5, [2001] 2 A.C. 304, Lord Hope of Craighead, PC.

4885. Restrictive covenants – discharge – Lands Tribunal procedure – addition of second covenant – commencement of proceedings

[Law of Property Act 1925 s.84(1); Lands Tribunal Rules 1996 (SI 1996 1022) r.36.]

D sought the discharge or modification of a restrictive covenant under the Law of Property Act 1925 s.84(1). The covenant limited building on D's property to either a detached or semi detached dwelling whereas D wished to build five properties. After commencing the proceedings, D applied for a direction at an interlocutory hearing that he could include a second restrictive covenant in the s.84(1) application, on the basis that this prevent the need for a further substantive application. O objected to the application, contending that the addition was contrary to the Land Tribunal Rules 1996 r.36.

Held, refusing the application for a direction, that r.36 did not permit the addition of a second covenant after proceedings had commenced. Rule 36 only allowed additional grounds to be relied on in the course of an existing application and the word "grounds" did not include the addition of another restrictive covenant.

DIGGENS APPLICATION, *Re; sub nom.* DIGGEN'S APPLICATION, *Re* [2000] 3 E.G.L.R. 87, George Bartlett Q.C., Lands Tr.

4886. Restrictive covenants – variation – obsolescence – commercial value

[Law of Property Act 1925 s.84(1)(a).]

In 1986 the Forestry Commission, FC, sold a house and stables subject to restrictive covenants not to alter existing buildings or erect new ones. The stables were gifted away and in 1994 planning permission was granted to convert the stables into a dwelling house. D applied to have the covenants discharged or modified on the grounds of obsolescence and that the proposed change would not injure FC. FC objected on the grounds that the covenants protected its adjoining forest and had commercial value.

Held, granting the application in part, that whilst the covenants should not be discharged, they should be varied so as to permit the proposed development in accordance with the planning permission. The covenant was not obsolete within the Law of Property Act 1925 s.84(1)(a) because it provided FC with a means of safeguarding its adjoining forest. The commercial value of the covenant, by virtue of the bargaining power it gave, was not a valid consideration and the purpose of the covenant could be achieved by a limited modification. FC should be awarded compensation equal to the increased value of the land without the covenant at the time of sale indexed to the present day.

DAVIES APPLICATION, *Re* [2001] 1 E.G. 111, Norman J Rose, FRICS, Lands Tr.

4887. **Rights of way – bridleways – deletion from definitive map – extent of inspector's powers – standard of proof**

[Wildlife and Countryside Act 1981 Sch.15.]

T, who represented the Ramblers' Association, appealed against the refusal of his application for judicial review ([2000] 2 P.L.R. 49, [2000] C.L.Y. 4637) of the decision of a planning inspector to confirm an order of the Secretary of State deleting part of a bridleway from the definitive map, it having been found that the relevant route had never been a right of way. T argued that the inspector had erred by (1) concluding that it had not been open to him to confirm the order subject to a modification whereby a footpath was substituted for the bridleway that had been shown on the definitive map, and (2) giving insufficient weight to the fact that the route had been shown as a bridleway on the definitive map.

Held, dismissing the appeal, that (1) when new facts arose during an inquiry, an inspector had wide powers for the purpose of confirming an order subject to modifications under the Wildlife and Countryside Act 1981 Sch.15. If satisfied that the definitive map should depart from the proposed order, the inspector should, subject to hearing representations and objections, make the necessary modifications. In the instant case, the inspector had erred when considering the extent of his powers, and (2) the inspector had, however, correctly concluded that clear and cogent evidence was required to displace the presumption whereby the presence on the definitive map of a right of way showed that the right of way in fact existed. The inspector's conclusion that such evidence had been available in the instant case was a finding of fact that was not open to challenge.

TREVELYAN v. SECRETARY OF STATE FOR THE ENVIRONMENT, TRANSPORT AND THE REGIONS, [2001] EWCA Civ 266, [2001] 1 W.L.R. 1264, Lord Phillips of Worth Matravers, M.R., CA.

4888. **Riparian rights – moorings – right of local authority to grant licence or impose fee – overriding power of port authority**

[Ipswich Dock Act 1950.]

IBC, owners of the foreshore and bed of the River Orwell, appealed against a ruling (Times, July 4, 2000, [2000] C.L.Y. 111) to the effect that it had no power to require M, the holder of a mooring licence issued by the Port Authority pursuant to the Ipswich Dock Act 1950, to pay an additional licence fee to that paid to the port authority. The judge had found that IBC was not entitled to require its separate consent prior to the laying and use of the same mooring. IBC contended that the various Ipswich Dock Acts merely created a regulatory scheme which could not be interpreted as expropriating without compensation any pre-existing private right or entitlement which it held as the freehold owner of the river bed and foreshore. IBC maintained that in consequence, it was entitled to require its consent at a fee for use made by vessels for mooring in the river.

Held, dismissing the appeal, that the Act vested control over moorings in a Commission, in terms which made it apparent that the rights of IBC as owner of the bed and foreshore were subject to the powers conferred on the Commission. The regulatory scheme introduced by the Act was accordingly superimposed upon IBC's rights which took effect subject to those rights granted under licence pursuant to the statutory scheme.

IPSWICH BC v. MOORE; IPSWICH BC v. DUKE, [2001] EWCA Civ 1273, *The Times* October 25, 2001, Chadwick, L.J., CA.

4889. Sale of land – mortgagees powers and duties – extent of duty to obtain best price

See NEGLIGENCE: Meftah v. LloydsTSB Bank Plc (No.2). §4474

4890. Squatting – interim orders – discretion as to making of interim possession orders – violation of Convention rights

[Criminal Law Act 1977 s.6; Civil Procedure Rules 1998 (SI 1998 3132) Sch.2 CCR Ord.24 r.12(5).]

C was the owner of a block of flats which were due for demolition. It had secured vacant possession of one of the flats in July 2000 but subsequently learnt in July 2001 that squatters had entered the premises. C accordingly issued an application for an interim possession order against the squatters. One of the squatters attended the hearing and gave evidence that one of C's housing officers had told her that as a squatter she could reside at the property until the court decided otherwise. The judge refused to make an interim possession order on the ground that C had given its consent to the squatters being at the premises, therefore the condition under the Civil Procedure Rules 1998 Sch.2 CCR Ord.24 r.9(c) had not been met. Further, that in any event he had a discretion whether or not to make an interim possession order. Instead, the judge proceeded to grant a forthwith order for possession under Sch.2 CCR Ord.24 of the 1998 Rules. C appealed.

Held, allowing the appeal, that the judge had been wrong in treating the housing officer's comment as amounting to consent for the squatters to enter or continue to enter the premises. In the light of the Criminal Law Act 1977 s.6, the statement could only sensibly be construed as one to the effect that C would have to obtain a court order to evict them. Further, as all the conditions for the making of an order were satisfied, under the terms of Sch.2 CCR Ord.24 r.12(5) the judge had no discretion whether or not to make the order but was bound to do so. There was no conceivable violation of any Convention right of the squatters by the making of an interim possession order.

CANALSIDE HOUSING PARTNERSHIP v. ALI, August 16, 2001, Park, J., Ch D. [*Ex rel.* Edward Francis, Barrister, Enterprise Chambers, Gold Square, Lincoln's Inn, London].

4891. Tenancies in common – trusts for sale – transfer for no value

DL sought a declaration that a residential property, owned by his father and his brother, UL, jointly as tenants in common prior to his father's death and subsequent intestacy, was held on trust for sale for himself and UL in equal shares. UL contended that a transfer, purported to have been signed by him, of his half share in the property to his father for no consideration was a forgery and that since the other half share had passed on intestacy to UL and his brother DL as tenants in common he had a three quarter share in the property. UL further contended that, even if the court were to find that there had been a transfer, there had been no change in the beneficial interest, as a resulting trust had been established by the transfer for no value.

Held, granting judgment for DL, that (1) UL had transferred his original half share of the property; (2) the voluntary transfer had not created a resulting trust in UL's favour, and (3) accordingly the property was owned by DL and UL as tenants in common in equal shares.

LOHIA v. LOHIA [2001] W.T.L.R. 101, Nicholas Strauss Q.C., Ch D.

4892. Title to land – tenancies at will – adverse possession – Trinidad and Tobago

[Real Property Limitation Ordinance 1940 (Trinidad and Tobago) s.3, s.8.]

R appealed against a decision of the Court of Appeal of Trinidad and Tobago that she had not acquired title to L's land through adverse possession. L's parents, who were R's aunt and uncle, had given R permission to live on the land until such time as she could afford to buy it. The uncle died in 1977, the aunt in 1988 and, in October 1990, R enclosed part of the land with a fence. R served proceedings against L in November 1991 claiming possessory title. At first instance the judge found that R had been a tenant at will in 1974 and that the tenancy had expired in 1975 in accordance with the Real Property Limitation Ordinance 1940 (Trinidad and Tobago) s.8. L had thereafter remained in possession for the 16 years necessary under s.3 of the Ordinance to claim title. The Court of Appeal held that L had been a licensee and had not therefore been in adverse possession.

Held, allowing the appeal, that the judge had been entitled to find that there had been a tenancy at will, as there was evidence sufficient to show that R and her aunt and uncle intended to create legal relations, and that R had been in exclusive possession. The Court of Appeal had given insufficient weight to these factors. Since R had entered the land as a tenant at will and as an intending purchaser in 1974, her tenancy had determined in 1975 and she was subsequently in adverse possession. The service of notices to quit did not stop time running in R's favour and L's title was extinguished 16 years later in 1991 prior to L lodging his counterclaim to recover the land.

RAMNARACE v. LUTCHMAN, [2001] UKPC 25, [2001] 1 W.L.R. 1651, Lord Millett, PC (Trin).

4893. Books

Bell, Cedric D. – Land: the Law of Real Property Textbook. 3rd Ed. Old Bailey Press Textbooks. Paperback: £14.95. ISBN 1-85836-410-8. Old Bailey Press.

Bradshaw, Joseph – House Buying, Selling and Conveyancing. CD-ROM (software). ISBN 1-902646-84-3. Law Pack Publishing.

Buck, A.R.; McLaren, John; Wright, Nancy E. – Land and Freedom-Law, Property Rights and the British Diaspora. Hardback: £45.00. ISBN 0-7546-2209-6. Ashgate Publishing Limited.

Butt, P. – Conveyancing. Hardback: £23.95. ISBN 0-85308-718-0. Jordans.

Campbell, Gordon – Heritage Law and Policy. Paperback: £55.00. ISBN 1-902558-27-8. Palladian Law Publishing Ltd.

Cannon – Irish Nutshells: Land Law. Paperback: £11.95. ISBN 1-85800-170-6. Round Hall Ltd.

Cartwright, A.L. – Return of the Peasant. Hardback: £50.00. ISBN 0-7546-2166-9. Ashgate Publishing Limited.

Chappelle, Diane – Land Law 5th Ed. Foundation Studies in Law Series. Paperback: £26.99. ISBN 0-582-43818-7. Longman Higher Education.

Coates, Ross; Attwell, Nicholas – Practice Notes on Conveyancing. Practice Notes. Paperback: £15.95. ISBN 1-85941-453-2. Cavendish Publishing Ltd.

Cook, Louise; Stilton, Ruth – Commercial Conveyancing. Legal Support Practitioner Series-the Law Society's NVQ in Legal Practice. Paperback: £25.00. ISBN 1-85941-447-8. Cavendish Publishing Ltd.

Coombes, A – Land Law. Suggested Solutions. £6.95. ISBN 1-85836-394-2. Old Bailey Press.

Cousins, Edward; Clarke, Ian – Law of Mortgages. 2nd Ed. Property and Conveyancing Library. Hardback: £165.00. ISBN 0-421-52950-4. Sweet & Maxwell.

Cracknell, D.G. – Land: the Law of Real Property. 4th Ed. Cracknell's Statutes Series. Paperback: £9.95. ISBN 1-85836-381-0. Old Bailey Press.

Gray, K.J.; Gray, Susan Francis – Butterworths Core Text: Land Law. 2nd Ed. Butterworths Core Text. Paperback: £12.95. ISBN 0-406-94685-X. Butterworths Law.

Harker, Stephen – Matrimonial Conveyancing. 7th Ed. Paperback: £59.00. ISBN 0-421-82360-7. Sweet & Maxwell.

Hepburn, Samantha – Principles of Property Law 2nd Ed. Principles of Law. Paperback: £32.95. ISBN 1-87690-508-5. Cavendish Publishing (Australia) Pty Ltd.

Hopkins, Nicholas – Informal Acquisition of Rights in Land. Modern Legal Studies. Paperback: £23.95. ISBN 0-421-68100-4. Sweet & Maxwell.

House Buying, Selling and Conveyancing. £9.99. ISBN 1-902646-70-3. Law Pack Publishing.

Hughes, Theodore E.; Klein, David – Executor's Handbook 2nd Ed. Hardback: £29.50. ISBN 0-8160-4426-0. Facts on File Inc.

Jessel, Christopher – Development Land-overage and Clawback. Hardback: £80.00. ISBN 0-85308-669-9. Jordans.

Magnus, Alan – Property Joint Ventures: Structures and Precedents. 2nd Ed. Hardback: Floppy disk: £195.00. ISBN 0-421-82500-6. Sweet & Maxwell.

Panesar, Sukhinder – General Principles of Property Law. Paperback: £19.99. ISBN 0-582-42332-5. Longman Higher Education.

Pascoe, Susan – Land Law-A Student Friendly Introduction and Revision Guide. Law. Paperback: £9.95. ISBN 1-84285-003-2. Studymates Limited.

Peaple, Sheree – Storey: Conveyancing. 5th Ed. Paperback: £21.95. ISBN 0-406-93760-5. Butterworths Law.

Robertson, Douglas; Rosenberry, Katharine – Home Ownership with Responsibility. Paperback: £12.95. ISBN 1-84263-057-1. York Publishing Services-Joseph Rowntree Foundation.

Rodger, Richard – Transformation of Edinburgh-Land, Property and Trust in the 19th Century. Hardback: £55.00. ISBN 0-521-78024-1. Cambridge University Press.

Rostron, J. – Dictionary of Property and Construction Law. Hardback: £50.00. ISBN 0-419-26100-1. Spon Press.

Rotherham, Craig – Proprietary Remedies in Context. Hardback: £27.50. ISBN 1-84113-165-2. Hart Publishing.

Siegan, Bernard H. – Rights of Englishmen. New Studies in Social Policy. Hardback: £37.95. ISBN 0-7658-0057-8. Paperback: £24.95. ISBN 0-7658-0755-6. Transaction Publishers.

Stevens, John and Pearce, Professor Robert – Land Law. 2nd Ed. Textbook Series. Paperback: £23.95. ISBN 0-421-69000-3. Sweet & Maxwell.

Tessa, Shepperson – Residential Lettings. CD-ROM (software). ISBN 1-902646-82-7. Law Pack Publishing.

Walker, Andrew – Conveyancing Textbook. 3rd Ed. Old Bailey Press Textbooks. Paperback: £14.95. ISBN 1-85836-402-7. Old Bailey Press.

Walker, Andrew – Conveyancing. Old Bailey Press Leading Cases. Paperback: £9.95. ISBN 1-85836-421-3. Old Bailey Press.

SALE OF GOODS

4894. **Books**

McKendrick, Ewan – Sale of Goods. Hardback: £185.00. ISBN 1-85978-305-8. LLP Professional Publishing.

SCIENCE

4895. **Human Reproductive Cloning Act 2001 (c.23)**

This Act prohibits the placing in a woman of a human embryo which has been created otherwise than by fertilisation.

This Act received Royal Assent on December 4, 2001.

4896. **Medical research – Human Fertilisation and Embryology – research**

HUMAN FERTILISATION AND EMBRYOLOGY (RESEARCH PURPOSES) REGULATIONS 2001, SI 2001 188; made under the Human Fertilisation and Embryology Act 1990 s.45, Sch.2 para.3. In force: January 31, 2001; £1.50.

These Regulations specify additional purposes for which the Human Fertilisation and Embryology Authority may grant licences for research involving embryos under the Human Fertilisation and Embryology Act 1990, for the purposes of increasing knowledge about the development of embryos, or about serious disease, and enabling such knowledge to be applied.

4897. Books

Sheridan, Brian – EU Bio-technology Law & Practice. Paperback: £65.00. ISBN 1-902558-30-8. Palladian Law Publishing Ltd.

SHIPPING

4898. Bills of lading – negotiable instruments – direct consignment bills – misdelivery – Hong Kong

The claimants, G, instituted proceedings for breach of contract and in tort against W, shipowners and carriers, for misdelivery of clothing manufactured in Hong Kong and exported to South America. W was in the practice of issuing bills of lading naming G as both the shipper and the consignee to order, and A, the agent for the buyer, as the notify party and G obtained payment from the buyer using those bills. Without G's knowledge, agents for C, the vessels operators, separately issued its own bills of lading to W naming the shipper as W and the consignee as A. The goods were delivered to the Venezuelan Customs which released them to A as consignee under the C bills but A's principal did not pay. G contended that (1) it was a party to the contract with W and C under the C bills of lading on the basis that W was acting in the capacity of agent, and (2) the C bills of lading were ordinary negotiable bills of lading capable of transfer to a third party by endorsement and which required production of the original bills on delivery. W maintained that G had never been a party to the contract and that the bills of lading were non negotiable direct consignment bills.

Held, giving judgment for W, that (1) it was clear that W had contracted with C as principal in view of the financial arrangements between the parties and the fact that G was entirely unaware of the existence of the C bills, and (2) the bills were non negotiable direct consignment bills. From the evidence it was clear that the C bills were not regarded as documents of title and there was no intention to negotiate with them. Further W had treated the C bills as obliging them to make delivery to the named consignee, A, and no other.

BRIJ, THE [2001] 1 Lloyd's Rep. 431, Waung, J., CFI (HK).

4899. Breach of contract – cargo – contamination – effect of decision to load on chain of causation

V brought a claim against T for contamination of cargo belonging to V which had been carried in T's ship. V had bought a cargo of ethylene from P under a contract by which title would pass to V "at ship's flange connection at loadport". Prior to loading, the ship's Master, M, attempted to make the vessel ready for the cargo by "gassing up" the tanks to remove residues of previous chemical cargoes. The tanks were tested and found to be below the required specification. This information was passed to P and to V, who authorised the continuation of loading up to "first foot level". Tests revealed that there were still contaminants in the tank. V was told by P that loading would continue in the hope that the proportion of contaminants would thereby lessen. V agreed on condition that if the problem was not resolved it would not accept the cargo. When 50 per cent of the cargo had been loaded, further tests showed a slight improvement and V agreed to the loading being completed. The test figures were not used to extrapolate possible final contaminant levels and no attempt was made to find out the nature of the contaminant. On arrival at the destination port, the cargo was found to be highly contaminated to the extent that it was unusable. T admitted that the ship had not been in a fit state to carry the cargo, but contended that the chain of causation had been broken by V's decision to allow the loading to be completed.

Held, allowing the application, that T was responsible for the contamination of the cargo and the chain of causation had not been broken. T had failed to provide a vessel capable of carrying the cargo properly in that, through M, it had failed to make proper checks to ensure that the cargo would not be contaminated. M, as a responsible master, should have been more proactive in the process of decision making about whether the loading should have continued. V's decisions to both allow the loading to continue and to be completed, whilst unwise in hindsight, were not unreasonable in the prevailing situation in which V had limited options because of T's breach of duty. The decisions therefore were "not sufficiently aberrant as wholly to supplant the unfitness of the vessel as the effective cause of the contamination".

VINMAR INTERNATIONAL LTD v. THERESA NAVIGATION SA [2001] 2 All E.R. (Comm) 243, Tomlinson, J., QBD (Comm Ct).

4900. Bulk carriers – safe loading and unloading – draft Council Directive

Proposal for a European Parliament and Council Directive establishing requirements and harmonised procedures for the safe loading and unloading of bulk carriers. [2000] OJ C311E/240.

4901. Bulk carriers – safe loading and unloading – draft Council Directive

Proposal for a European Parliament and Council Directive establishing requirements and harmonised procedures for the safe loading and unloading of bulk carriers. [2000] OJ C311E/240.

4902. Carriage by sea – bills of lading – application of tests for determining competing claims for jurisdiction – Canada

A dispute concerning the carriage of goods by sea had connections with many jurisdictions including Canada. The bill of lading conferred jurisdiction on the courts of South Korea, although on the facts the applicable law was likely to be that of the US. A issued proceedings in Canada. On the application of H those proceedings were stayed in favour of the South Korean courts. The stay was granted in reliance on *Owners of Cargo Lately Laden on Board the Eleftheria v. Owners of the Eleftheria (The Eleftheria)* [1970] P. 94, [1969] C.L.Y. 3293 which held that where a bill of lading contained a jurisdiction clause, a "strong cause" was required to displace the presumption that the issue should be litigated in the nominated jurisdiction. A appealed.

Held, allowing the appeal, that in applying the test in *The Eleftheria* it was relevant not only to consider whether the evidence on the issues of fact was situated in the forum state, but also (1) whether such evidence was more readily available in that state, and (2) in which state would the pursuit of the litigation be least expensive. The tests in *The Eleftheria* were satisfied by permitting the action to proceed in the Canadian courts.

ANRAJ FISH PRODUCTS INDUSTRIES LTD v. HYUNDAI MERCHANT MARINE CO LTD [2000] I.L.Pr. 717, Reed, J., Fed Ct (Can).

4903. Carriage by sea – locus standi – entitlement to sue under contract of carriage – Indonesian law – New Zealand

[Admiralty Act 1973.]

SN, a company registered in Hong Kong and carrying on business in New Zealand, sought compensation for damage to a cargo of cement which had occurred during a voyage from Indonesia to Western Samoa on the vessel "Seven Pioneer". SN had concluded a contract for the purchase and shipping of the cement with I. A voyage charterparty had been entered into between SN and charterers, SS. The bills of lading issued by the agent for the vessel's owner confirmed I as the shipper and SN as the consignee and were expressed to be governed by Indonesian law. During the voyage the cargo incurred damage which SN attributed to poor stowage. SN contended that SS were in breach of its charter agreement with SN in that the contract contained an implied term that the cement would be loaded in accordance with proper and good stevedoring practice. In the alternative, SN maintained that SS were liable in negligence. SS maintained that whilst SN had based its pleaded claim upon breach of the charterparty, pursuant to the Admiralty Act 1973, an action in rem could only be brought against a party being the beneficial owner of all the shares in the vessel or a demise charterer of the vessel. Since SS did not meet those criteria, it was submitted that SN could only maintain a claim against the vessel itself under the bills of lading. SS maintained that SN had no entitlement to sue since it had never been a party to the contract of carriage and had not acquired a sufficient proprietary or possessory interest in the cargo to found a claim in tort.

Held, giving judgment for the defendant, that (1) under Indonesian law a third party could not acquire rights under the contract of carriage unless they became a lawful holder of the bill of lading. Having regard to the fact that SN had never been an indorsee or holder of the bills of lading, SN had no locus standi to sue under the contract of carriage, and (2) a tort committed in a foreign jurisdiction was actionable in New Zealand only in circumstances where it was also demonstrated to be actionable in the relevant foreign jurisdiction, *Phillips v. Eyre* (1870-71) L.R. 6 Q.B. 1 applied. SN had failed to establish any right to sue in tort independently of the contract of carriage under either New Zealand or Indonesian law. Under New Zealand law, SN was required to establish legal ownership or possessory title to the cargo and a contractual interest in the cargo was insufficient, *Leigh and Sillivan Ltd v. Aliakmon Shipping Co Ltd (The Aliakmon)* [1986] A.C. 785, [1986] C.L.Y. 2252 applied. Under Indonesian law, SN had failed to establish that the ability to sue could arise other than in the context of the lawful holder of the relevant bill of lading.

SEVEN PIONEER, THE [2001] 2 Lloyd's Rep. 57, Rodney Hansen, J., HC (NZ).

4904. Carriage by sea – safety at sea – ferries – high speed passenger craft

MERCHANT SHIPPING (MANDATORY SURVEYS FOR RO-RO FERRY AND HIGH SPEED PASSENGER CRAFT) REGULATIONS 2001, SI 2001 152; made under the European Communities Act 1972 s.2. In force: February 16, 2001; £2.00.

These Regulations, which implement Council Directive 1999/35 ([1999] OJ L138/1) on a system of mandatory surveys for the safe operation of regular ro-ro ferry and high speed passenger craft services, require the Maritime and Coastguard Agency to carry out verifications in relation to the vessel, including checks of documentation and a check for the presence of a voyage data recorder. They require the Agency to carry out verifications in relation to the company operating the vessel, and the flag State of the vessel, to carry out an initial specific survey before the vessel begins operating on a regular service to or from a UK port, to carry out further surveys every year, or where the circumstances of the vessel change, to issue reports of prevention of operation notices preventing a vessel which does not meet the requirements of the Directive from operating, or reports of inspection and improvement notices requiring defects to be remedied and to operate a shore-based navigational guidance system. In addition, the Regulations require the Chief Inspector of Marine Accidents to allow substantially interested Member States or EEA States to be involved with a marine accident investigation.

4905. Charterparties – arbitral jurisdiction – fishing vessels arrested by charterer – security provided by owners – New Zealand

[Arbitration Act 1996 (New Zealand) s.10, Sch.1, cl.8(1).]

RMF entered into charters with FV and S for the fishing vessels IZ and KZ. On conclusion of the charters, however, both vessels were subject to investigation and charges were laid against RMF for fishing offences allegedly committed during the charters. RMF sought an indemnity from FV and S to cover any penalties for breach of the fishing legislation. RMF commenced claims in rem against both vessels and under threat of arrest FV and S gave security. FV and S subsequently applied for the proceedings to be stayed and repayment of the security, whereupon RMF arrested the vessels and obtained an ex parte Mareva injunction. FV and S applied for the release of the vessels and the discharge of the injunction, contending that the charters contained arbitration clauses with the result that an arbitral award would preclude a judgment in rem.

Held, allowing the release of the vessels but refusing to discharge the injunction, that (1) an arbitrator could not give an in rem judgment under the

Arbitration Act 1996 (New Zealand) s.10 and a judgment in rem would bind parties that were not subject to the arbitration. The arbitration clause was also incapable of being performed under Sch.1 cl.8(1) of the Act due to the existence of the in rem claim, and (2) if RMF was successful in the arbitration, it could have difficulty obtaining payment from FV and S as they had no assets in the jurisdiction and it was unlikely that they would voluntarily meet n award against them.

IRINA ZHARKIKH,THE AND KSENIA ZHARKIKH,THE [2001] 2 Lloyd's Rep. 319, Young, J., HC (NZ).

4906. Charterparties – bills of lading – applicability of NYPE Inter Club agreement – requirement to prove bill issued in accordance with charterparty

[Hague Visby Rules.]

TD, shipowners, appealed against a decision that the NYPE Inter Club agreement, ICA, applied to TD's claim against charterers, C. TD had chartered a bulk carrier to C on an amended New York Produce Exchange Form for a single trip charter. During the voyage a fire, resulting from the unseaworthiness of the vessel, damaged the cargo of cotton bales. TD settled claims made by the cargo owners and instituted proceedings against C who defended the claims on the basis that, under the ICA, cargo damage which resulted from unseaworthiness was the responsibility of shipowners. The arbitrator concluded that the alleged defects in the bills of lading had no bearing upon the claims and that the ICA was accordingly applicable. TD contended that the ICA did not apply since the bills of lading had been ante dated and not claused in accordance with the mate's receipts and that accordingly they had not been properly issued under the charterparty.

Held, dismissing the appeal, that if the goods were shipped but the bills of lading were not issued in accordance with the charterparty, the ICA was nevertheless applicable if the cargo claim was a claim under the bills and subject to the Hague Visby Rules or their equivalent. The ICA only ceased to apply if the cargo claim was not made under the bills or, in the alternative, the protections and limits in the rules were lost. The requirement for charterers to prove that the bill of lading was authorised should be confined to shortage claims since such a requirement would otherwise defeat the purpose of the ICA, *Iverans Rederei A/S v. MS Holstencruiser Seeschiffahrts GmbH & Co KG (The Holstencruiser)* [1992] 2 Lloyd's Rep. 378, [1993] C.L.Y. 3591 considered and *Oceanfocus Shipping Ltd v. Hyundai Merchant Marine Co Ltd (The Hawk)* [1999] 1 Lloyd's Rep. 176, [1999] C.L.Y. 4453 applied.

TRANSPACIFIC DISCOVERY SA v. CARGILL INTERNATIONAL SA (THE ELPA) [2001] 1 All E.R. (Comm) 937, Morison, J., QBD (Comm Ct).

4907. Charterparties – bills of lading – negligent stowage of cargo – liability of carrier prior to acquisition of title

Shipowners, O, appealed against a ruling that O could be sued in tort by cargo owners, C, for negligent stowage of cargo at shipment and that O's protection under Himalaya clauses in the bills of lading was limited to the same extent afforded to the carrier. O contended that (1) it was not possible to impose any liability upon O to C for damage to the cargo since C had not acquired title to the goods in question until after the negligent act had occurred, albeit whilst the cargo was still afloat, and (2) the limitation upon the carrier's liability was without prejudice to the general blanket exemption from all liability in both contract and tort granted to third parties under the bills of lading. C cross appealed against a finding that bills of lading concerned with the transport of the cargo of timber and plywood were charterer's bills, a decision which had been reached on the basis that the word "carrier" had been appended in some form or another to the bills after the signature which otherwise appeared to be in the owner's standard form. C contended that the normal presumption that written words would supersede printed words on a form had been effectively displaced by clause 35 within the bills of lading which stipulated that the contract of carriage was with the owners "notwithstanding anything that appear[ed] to the contrary".

Held, allowing the appeal in part and the cross appeal in part (Rix L.J. dissenting in part), that (1) the condensation damage caused to the cargo had been progressive and had arisen prior to the acquisition of title. Such progressive damage resulting from a single act or omission gave rise to a single cause of action, which had accrued to the previous cargo owners, *Pirelli General Cable Works Ltd v. Oscar Faber & Partners* [1983] 2 A.C. 1, [1983] C.L.Y. 2216 applied; (2) the Himalaya clauses would not have operated to provide a blanket exclusion of liability to third parties had the bills been charterer's bills, and (3) the bills had to be construed as a whole and the weight to be attached to the words within the signature boxes qualified to the extent stipulated by clause 35, *Sunrise Maritime Inc v. Uvisco Ltd (The Hector)* [1998] 2 Lloyd's Rep. 287, [1998] C.L.Y. 4397 and *Fetim BV v. Oceanspeed Shipping Ltd (The Flecha)* [1999] 1 Lloyd's Rep. 612, [1998] C.L.Y. 4394 considered.

HOMBURG HOUTIMPORT BV v. AGROSIN PRIVATE LTD (THE STARSIN); OWNERS OF THE CARGO LATELY LADEN ON BOARD THE STARSIN v. OWNERS OF THE STARSIN; HUNTER TIMBER LTD v. AGROSIN PRIVATE LTD [2001] EWCA Civ 56, Rix, L.J., CA.

4908. Charterparties – cargo – duty to load complete cargo – duty to receive cargo

C, who had chartered a vessel from G, appealed against the dismissal of its counterclaim for damages arising from G's failure to load the full and complete cargo contrary to the terms of the charterparty. The arbitrator had held that loading of the cargo, which had taken place on a floating terminal, had been terminated because of poor weather and had not resumed because of C's instruction that G proceed to the discharge port. C submitted that the arbitrator had been obliged to conclude that G was in breach of the charterparty as the agreement imposed a strict obligation on C to deliver a complete load.

Held, dismissing the appeal, that the charterparty imposed a mutual obligation on the parties, requiring C to tender a full load and G to receive it. There was no absolute obligation upon G to load a complete cargo as the fulfilment of its obligation had been dependent upon C tendering a complete load. The arbitrator had been entitled to conclude that the reason the vessel had not loaded a full cargo had been C's instruction to G to continue to port. It followed that as C had failed to tender a complete load, G was not in breach of the charterparty.

CHINA OFFSHORE OIL (SINGAPORE) INTERNATIONAL PTE LTD v. GIANT SHIPPING LTD [2001] 1 All E.R. (Comm) 429, Tomlinson, J., QBD (Comm Ct).

4909. Charterparties – contract terms – arbitration clauses

See ARBITRATION: Owners of Cargo Lately Laden on Board the MV Delos v. Delos Shipping Ltd. §344

4910. Charterparties – contract terms – redelivery window – illegitimate voyage – paramount clauses

M, the charterers of a vessel, applied for summary judgment against the owners of that vessel, C, in proceedings commenced by M for alleged breach of a time charterparty on the Shelltime 4 form. C applied for the claim to be struck out or dismissed. The charterparty had a duration of 12 months with an option to extend for a further six months. M had given voyage orders that would have resulted in the vessel being redelivered to C well outside the redelivery window. C had declined to accept the orders and instructed the master to decline them. The vessel had been duly redelivered to C. M submitted that the clear wording of clause 19 of the charterparty overrode the redelivery obligations set out in clause 4 such as to permit the charterers to give orders in relation to a voyage that would be likely to, or inevitably would, conclude after the redelivery window had expired. C maintained that clause 19 was not paramount and that the orders were for an illegitimate last voyage such as to entitle it to refuse to comply.

Held, allowing the application of C and dismissing the claim, that in the absence of clear words indicating that clause 19 was to have effect "notwithstanding clause 4", the charterers were subject to the redelivery obligations in clause 4 and were not permitted to order a vessel on an illegitimate voyage, *Chiswell Shipping and Liberian Jaguar Transports Inc v. National Iranian Tankers Co (The World Symphony and The World Renown)* [1992] 2 Lloyd's Rep. 115, [1992] C.L.Y. 3941 considered. Clause 19 was restricted to the protection of a charterer from the repercussions of late redelivery.

MARIMPEX MINERALOEL HANDELSGESELLSCHAFT MBH & CO KB v. COMPAGNIE DE GESTION ET D'EXPLOITATION LTD (THE AMBOR AND THE ONCE) [2001] 1 All E.R. (Comm) 182, Peter Gross Q.C., QBD (Comm Ct).

4911. Charterparties – laytime – effect of clause narrowing laycan – precondition to obligation to nominate vessel – repudiatory breach

U appealed against a decision ([2000] 1 Lloyd's Rep. 459) that in the absence of wording to the contrary, compliance with a clause obliging the charterer to narrow laycan spread was not a precondition to the owner's contractual obligation to nominate a vessel. A, the charterer, had chartered from U a vessel to be nominated for the carriage of a cargo from the USA to West Malaysia. The charterparty was on an amended Baltimore berth grain form C of 1913. The agreement contained a clause that laycan in the first half of December 1996 was to be narrowed to a 10 days spread following service of a notice 32 days prior to the first layday. A failed to give the laycan narrowing notice within the required period. As a result P claimed that it was no longer required to nominate a vessel since A's failure amounted to a repudiatory breach of contract, which it purported to accept. Following arbitration, an award was made in favour of A on the basis that the narrowing clause conferred an option on A to narrow the laycan spread rather than an obligation. A's appeal was dismissed and it was given leave to appeal.

Held, dismissing the appeal, that the clause, as drafted, imposed an obligation on A to serve a notice within the specified time frame to narrow the laycan spread. However, A's failure to comply with its obligation did not constitute a repudiatory breach of contract justifying U's refusal to nominate a vessel. The effect of the clause was that if A failed to serve a notice, the laycan spread would be fixed as the first half of December with the result that the charterparty could still be performed in accordance with its terms. Since the contract could be performed irrespective of A's breach, and there were no interdependent contractual obligations, it was unlikely that the clause had been intended as a precondition, *Bunge Corp v. Tradax Export SA* [1981] 1 W.L.R. 711, [1981] C.L.Y. 2433 considered, *Hyundai Merchant Marine Co Ltd v. Karander Maritime Inc (The Nizuru)* [1996] 2 Lloyd's Rep. 66, [1996] C.L.Y. 5308 distinguished on the ground that it involved a time charterparty wherein the charterer's failure to narrow the laycan was of importance to the owners.

UNIVERSAL BULK CARRIERS PTE LTD v. ANDRE ET CIE SA; *sub nom.* ANDRE ET CIE SA v. UNIVERSAL BULK CARRIERS LTD, [2001] EWCA Civ 588, [2001] 2 Lloyd's Rep. 65, Clarke, L.J., CA.

4912. Charterparties – laytime – validity of notice of readiness – commencement of laytime

G, charterers of a vessel pursuant to a berth charter, appealed against an arbitral finding that an invalid notice of readiness was nevertheless effective to commence laytime. The charterparty provided that a notice was required at the port of discharge in order to trigger laytime but the relevant notice had been served outside the port at a time when the vessel was prevented from entering the port having missed the tide. G contended that there was no authority for a finding that an invalid notice could be held to be effective in order to commence laytime or that the notice requirement could effectively be dispensed with and that accordingly laytime had never commenced so G was not liable for demurrage, and conversely the shipowners, F, were liable for despatch.

Held, allowing the appeal, that the notice had never been accepted by G but had merely been acknowledged as received, that acknowledgment having been given on the implied assurance that the ship was at the berth or ready for discharge. The fact that it had not been specifically rejected, and discharge had commenced as planned, did not remedy the lack of a valid notice. To hold otherwise would be to rewrite the parties' contract, *Transgrain Shipping BV v. Global Transporte Oceanico SA (The Mexico 1)* [1990] 1 Lloyd's Rep. 507, [1991] C.L.Y. 3234 applied.

GLENCORE GRAIN LTD v. FLACKER SHIPPING LTD (THE HAPPY DAY) [2001] 1 All E.R. (Comm) 659, Langley, J., QBD (Comm Ct).

4913. Charterparties – repudiation – classification of contract term – conditions

B, charterers of a vessel owned by M, appealed against a ruling that a term within the charterparty requiring M to obtain approval of the vessel by an oil company, Exxon, within 60 days, was an intermediate term, breach of which by M did not entitle B to terminate the charterparty. B maintained that the clause in question was a condition of the charterparty, breach of which amounted to repudiatory conduct. M maintained that the breach had been of an intermediate term and that B's sole remedy was by way of damages unless the consequences of the breach were such as to justify an entitlement to terminate the charterparty.

Held, allowing the appeal, that in order to achieve consistency with the requirement to obtain approval from other major oil companies and ensure commercial certainty the term was to be classed as a condition. The only reason that the Exxon approval had been treated differently had been the fact that it had not been obtained as at the date of the charterparty, *Bunge Corp v. Tradax Export SA* [1981] 1 W.L.R. 711, [1981] C.L.Y. 2433 applied.

BS&N LTD (BVI) v. MICADO SHIPPING LTD (MALTA) (THE SEAFLOWER) (NO.1) [2001] 1 All E.R. (Comm) 240, Waller, L.J., CA.

4914. Charterparties – termination – meaning of cancellation clause

Following the purported termination by MNS of its drill rig contract with RBF and the consequent giving by MNS of notice of termination to M, the provider of a tug supply vessel, pursuant to a cancellation clause in the charterparty between MNS and M, issues arose as to whether MNS could rely on the clause and, if so, whether compensation was payable to M. The clause provided that MNS could terminate the charter immediately by providing prior written notice in the event that the drill rig contract was terminated. The drill rig contract had been terminated because MNS believed the rig to be unfit for its purpose.

Held, determining the preliminary issues, that (1) a repudiatory breach of the drill rig contract by one party that was accepted by the other did amount to a termination for the purposes of the clause. The word "immediately" within the clause showed that the notice of termination would have immediate effect and did not require MNS to provide immediate notification of termination. However, any right to cancel following the termination of the drill rig contract had to be exercised within a reasonable time, and (2) having regard to the terms of the original charterparty and an amendment thereto, compensation was payable to M from the time that the supply vessel had come on hire.

AKTIESELSKABET DAMPSKIBSSELSKABET SVENDBORG v. MOBIL NORTH SEA LTD; *sub nom.* AKTIELSELKABET DAMPSKIBSSELSKABEL SVENDBORG v. MOBIL NORTH SEA LTD; AKTIESELSKABET DAMPSKIBSSELSKABET SVENDORG v. MOBIL NORTH SEA LTD [2001] 2 All E.R. (Comm) 553, David Steel, J., QBD (Comm Ct).

4915. Charterparties – time charterparties – choice of route

A dispute arose between KK, the time charterer of a vessel, and WI, the owner of the vessel, resulting from the master's failure to follow KK's instructions as to the route to be taken by the vessel in respect of two journeys from Canada to Japan. Having previously encountered adverse weather on the route chosen by KK, the master took a longer route, causing the two voyages to be delayed. In arbitration proceedings, it was held that WI had breached obligations forming part of the time charter requiring it to ensure firstly that the master should proceed with the voyages with the utmost dispatch and secondly that he should follow KK's orders and directions as to the employment of the vessel. WI appealed to the judge, who, allowing the appeal, held ([1999] Q.B. 72, [1998] C.L.Y. 4413) that the dispute concerned matters of navigation rather than the employment of the vessel. The judge's finding having been upheld by the Court of Appeal ([2000] Q.B. 241), KK appealed.

Held, allowing the appeal, that the arbitrators had been correct to conclude that WI had breached its contractual obligation to ensure that the master complied with the utmost dispatch clause in the charter by taking the shorter route chosen by KK. The master's previous experience of adverse weather conditions on that route did not justify his decision to follow the longer route. What was more, the charter contained, in addition to an utmost dispatch clause, a provision whereby WI undertook that the vessel would be fit to sail in the waters falling within the ambit of the charter. Accordingly, WI was precluded from arguing that the vessel was not fit to sail in those waters. The judge had been wrong to conclude that all questions involving the route to be taken were matters of navigation. The choice of route was, in the absence of some overriding consideration, a matter relating to the employment of a vessel, her scheduling and her trading. Whereas the employment of a vessel involved the economic aspect of its operation, navigation involved matters of seamanship.

WHISTLER INTERNATIONAL LTD v. KAWASAKI KISEN KAISHA LTD (THE HILL HARMONY); KAWASAKI KISEN KAISHA LTD v. TOKAI SHIPPING CO LTD OF TOKYO [2001] 1 A.C. 638, Lord Hobhouse of Woodborough, HL.

4916. Charterparties – voyage charterparties – demurrage – claim submitted without proof of shipowner's claim – time limits

M, sellers of a cargo of fuel oil, claimed monies representing discharge port demurrage from EP, buyers, pursuant to a voyage charterparty. A clause within the charterparty provided in respect of demurrage that "any claim barred if not duly notified duly supported by relevant documents (whereof copy of c/p and copy of owner's demurrage claim and invoice) within 90 days from b/l date". EP maintained that the absence of a formal demurrage claim by the shipowners meant that the claim was time barred despite submission of the claim by M within the applicable time limit.

Held, giving judgment for EP, that the clause was by way of indemnity ensuring that M was limited to recovering from EP only that sum claimed by the owners. A written claim from the owners within the specified time limit, including demurrage calculations and an invoice, was therefore an essential prerequisite to the success of M's claim, *Mira Oil Resources of Tortola v. Bocimar NV* [1999] 1 All E.R. (Comm) 732, [1999] C.L.Y. 4429 and *Babanaft International Co SA v. Avanti Petroleum Inc (The Oltenia)* [1982] 1 W.L.R. 871, [1982] C.L.Y. 138 applied.

MABANAFT INTERNATIONAL LTD v. ERG PETROLI SpA (THE YELLOW STAR) [2000] 2 Lloyd's Rep. 637, Judge Hallgarten Q.C., CC (Central London).

4917. Charterparties – warranties – vessel fuel consumption stated "without guarantee" – status of term

L, shipowners, appealed against a ruling by arbitrators that a charterparty contained a warranty as to the vessel's fuel consumption. V, the charterers, had sought a reference to arbitration on the basis that the vessel consumed excessive quantities of fuel oil. The charterparty contained a section entitled "Vessel's Description" incorporating details of gas oil consumption at various speeds which were qualified by the description "about". A further statement underneath provided "All details "about" -all details given in good faith but without guarantee". The arbitrators concluded that whilst the words "without guarantee" necessarily qualified the owner's liabilities, they could not remove all liability and that whereas a five per cent margin above the figures specified would have been appropriate in the absence of any additional wording, with that wording in place the appropriate margin was in the order of ten per cent. L contended that in the light of relevant authority the effect of the wording "without guarantee" was to preclude a warranty.

Held, allowing the appeal, that the wording "without guarantee" was directed to those details qualified by "about" and had the effect that the charterparty did not contain any warranty as to the vessel's consumption of fuel oil, *Tor Line A/B v. Alltrans Group of Canada Ltd (The TFL Prosperity)* [1984] 1 W.L.R. 48, [1984] C.L.Y. 3166, *Japy Freres & Co v. RWJ Sutherland & Co* (1921) 6 Ll. L. Rep. 381 and *Continental Pacific Shipping Ltd v. Deemand Shipping Co Ltd (The Lendoudis Evangelos II)* [1997] 1 Lloyd's Rep. 404, [1997] C.L.Y. 4594 applied.

LOSINJSKA PLOVIDBA BRODARSTOVO DD v. VALFRACHT MARITIME CO LTD (THE LIPA) [2001] 2 Lloyd's Rep. 17, Andrew Smith, J., QBD (Comm Ct).

4918. Collisions at sea – apportionment – failure to comply with traffic regulations

Following a collision between two ships, SI and SP, travelling west and east respectively, the issue of apportionment fell to be decided by the court. The ships were travelling through straits which were subject to traffic regulations requiring westbound vessels to keep to the north side of the fairway. The collision occurred on the southern side of the fairway with SP making a substantial alteration to port in the last four or five minutes prior to impact.

Held, giving judgment for the owners of SP, that SI had crossed to the wrong side of the fairway two miles short of the collision in breach of the traffic regulations thereby causing the collision. The vessels had been sufficiently close for there to have been a risk of collision and under the regulations SI was obliged to give way to SP. Notwithstanding that SP had been put in a difficult position by SI, the correct course of action would have been to steam on with a view to crossing ahead rather than making an alteration to port. Accordingly, the responsibility for the collision would be apportioned 75 per cent to SI and 25 per cent to SP.

OWNERS OF THE SITAREM v. OWNERS AND/OR DEMISE CHARTERERS OF THE SPIRIT [2001] 2 All E.R. (Comm) 837, David Steel, J., QBD (Adm Ct).

4919. Collisions at sea – limit of liability – loss of cargo

[Merchant Shipping Act 1995.]

The defendant, L, appealed against a decree of limitation granted to the claimant, M. In 1998 a ship, ZP, belonging to M, had collided with a ship containing cargo belonging to L, causing the cargo to be lost. M applied under the Merchant Shipping Act 1995 for a decree limiting its liability. L challenged the application, arguing that there should be discovery to enable it to investigate whether the loss was caused by M's "personal act or omission, committed with the intent to cause such loss, or recklessly and with knowledge that such loss would probably result" as required by the Act. The judge in the court below held that M was entitled to the decree as L's challenge was no more than a fishing exercise which was highly unlikely to produce evidence capable of shifting the substantial burden of proof upon it. On appeal, L argued that the judge had taken the wrong approach and should not have made the decision on the basis only of the material before him.

Held, dismissing the appeal, that the judge's decision was correct. The provisions for limitation of liability under the Act were narrowly and very clearly defined. The burden on a party seeking to bar the right to limit was very high and involved showing that a shipowner had had knowledge of the actual loss that would result. It was highly unlikely that L would be able to prove any such knowledge in this case, even with further discovery, and its speculative theorising was "totally absurd". In making its application L had misjudged the purpose and effect of the limitation provisions of the Act.

SCHIFFAHRTSGESELLSCHAFT MS MERKUR SKY MBH & CO KG v. MS LEERORT NTH SCHIFFAHRTS GmbH & CO KG, [2001] EWCA Civ 1055, [2001] 2 Lloyd's Rep. 291, Lord Phillips of Worth Matravers, M.R., CA.

4920. **Harbours – harbour development – Portsmouth**

PORTSMOUTH HARBOUR (GUNWHARF QUAYS) (MILLENNIUM TOWER) ORDER 2001, SI 2001 1086; made under the Transport and Works Act 1992 s.3, s.5, Sch.1 para.1, Sch.1 para.2, Sch.1 para.4, Sch.1 para.5, Sch.1 para.7, Sch.1 para.8, Sch.1 para.10, Sch.1 para.15, Sch.1 para.16, Sch.1 para.17. In force: March 19, 2001; £2.00.

This Order authorises the Berkeley Festival Waterfront Company Ltd to construct works which interfere with navigation, namely a fixed observation structure for viewing events, objects and the surrounding region, in Portsmouth Harbour at Gunwharf Quays.

4921. **Harbours – revision – constitution – Cowes**

COWES HARBOUR (CONSTITUTION) REVISION ORDER 2001, SI 2001 2183; made under the Harbours Act 1964 s.14. In force: June 18, 2001; £2.50.

This Order renames and reconstitutes the Cowes Harbour Commissioners as from July 1, 2001. It provides for the Commissioners to consist of a body of 10 Commissioners with experience in relevant matters. Nine persons will be appointed by the Commissioners, the Chief Executive will also hold office as a Commissioner and under the terms of the Order the appointed Commissioners will retire in rotation. The Order also includes other provisions with respect to the Commissioners' constitution including provisions for the co-option of up to two additional Commissioners and for the protection of the Commissioners from personal liability in the discharge of their functions. In addition the Commissioners' borrowing powers are increased, existing statutory requirements as to the Commissioners' accounts are amended and certain statutory provisions are repealed or revoked.

4922. **Harbours – revision – constitution – King's Lynn Conservancy Board**

KING'S LYNN CONSERVANCY BOARD (CONSTITUTION) HARBOUR REVISION ORDER 2001, SI 2001 2675; made under the Harbours Act 1964 s.14. In force: August 1, 2001; £2.50.

This Order, which amends the King's Lynn Conservancy Act 1897, the King's Lynn Conservancy Board (Constitution) Revision Order 1983 (SI 1983 1345) and revokes the King's Lynn Conservancy Board Revision Order 1968 (SI 1968 1976), reconstitutes the King's Lynn Conservancy Board as from February 1, 2002. It provides for the Board to consist of a body of twelve members with experience in relevant matters, includes other provisions with respect to the Board's constitution including provisions for the protection of the members from personal liability in the discharge of their functions and also increases the Board's borrowing powers.

4923. **Harbours – revision – constitution – Yarmouth**

YARMOUTH (ISLE OF WIGHT) HARBOUR REVISION (CONSTITUTION) ORDER 2001, SI 2001 2185; made under the Harbours Act 1964 s.14. In force: June 18, 2001; £2.50.

This Order reconstitutes the Yarmouth (Isle of Wight) Harbour Commissioners as from July 1, 2001. It provides for the Commissioners to consist of a body of nine Commissioners with experience in relevant matters. Four persons will be appointed by the Commissioners and four persons will be appointed jointly by the Isle of Wight Council, Yarmouth Town Council, Freshwater Parish Council and Totland Parish Council. The Chief Executive will also hold office as a Commissioner and under the terms of the Order the appointed Commissioners will retire in rotation. The Order also includes other provisions with respect to the Commissioners' constitution including transitional provision for the co-option of five additional Commissioners and provisions for the protection of the Commissioners from personal liability in the discharge of their functions. In addition existing statutory requirements as to the Commissioners' accounts are amended and certain statutory provisions are repealed or revoked.

4924. Harbours – revision – Fowey

FOWEY HARBOUR REVISION ORDER 2001, SI 2001 2184; made under the Harbours Act 1964 s.14. In force: June 18, 2001; £2.50.

This Order reconstitutes the Fowey Harbour Commissioners as from September 1, 2001. It provides for the Commissioners to consist of a body of 10 Commissioners with experience in relevant matters. Six persons will be appointed by the Commissioners and three by the Restormel Borough Council, the Chief Executive will also hold office as a Commissioner and under the terms of the Order the appointed Commissioners will retire in rotation. The Order also includes other provisions with respect to the Commissioners' constitution including provisions for the protection of the Commissioners from personal liability in the discharge of their functions. In addition the Commissioners' borrowing powers are increased, existing statutory requirements as to the Commissioners' accounts are amended and certain statutory provisions are repealed or revoked.

4925. Harbours – revision – Poole

POOLE HARBOUR REVISION ORDER 2001, SI 2001 2820; made under the Harbours Act 1964 s.14. In force: August 25, 2001; £2.50.

This Order, which amends the Poole Harbour Act 1895, the Poole Harbour Act 1914 and the Poole Harbour Act 1925 and revokes the Poole Harbour Order 1981 (SI 1981 1097), reconstitutes the Poole Harbour Commissioners as from November 1, 2001. It provides for the Commissioners to consist of a body with experience in relevant matters. One Commissioner will be appointed by the Transport and General Workers Union and three jointly by Dorset County Council, Poole Borough Council and Purbeck District Council. Six Commissioners will be appointed by a selection panel constituted under the Order. The Chief Executive and one other officer will also hold office as Commissioners while provision is also made for the co-operation of up to two additional Commissioners. The Commissioners as so reconstituted will thus consist of a body of between 12 and 14 members. The Order also includes other provisions with respect to the Commissioners' constitution, amends existing statutory requirements as to the Commissioners' accounts and repeals or revokes certain statutory provisions.

4926. Harbours – revision – Port of Tyne

PORT OF TYNE HARBOUR REVISION ORDER 2001, SI 2001 416; made under the Harbours Act 1964 s.14. In force: March 1, 2001; £1.75.

This Order enables the closure of Northumberland Dock by the Port of Tyne Authority. It also provides powers to allow the Authority to regulate dredging in the Port.

4927. Harbours – revision – Swanage

SWANAGE HARBOUR REVISION ORDER 2001, SI 2001 2984; made under the Harbours Act 1964 s.14. In force: October 1, 2001; £1.50.

This Order makes amendments to the Swanage Pier Order 1895 and the Swanage Pier Order 1948, which govern the functions of the Swanage Pier Company, to extend the Company's powers to construct certain facilities by enabling it to permit other persons to construct such facilities, by enabling it to let the site on which the facilities are to be constructed, and by extending from seven years to 21 years the period for which the Company may grant a lease of such a site or facilities. In addition, the Order repeals a provision requiring the Board of Trade (now the Secretary of State for Trade and Industry) to be sent a copy of the Company's annual account.

4928. Health and safety at work – ships

MERCHANT SHIPPING AND FISHING VESSELS (HEALTH AND SAFETY AT WORK) (AMENDMENT) REGULATIONS 2001, SI 2001 54; made under the European Communities Act 1972 s.2; and the Merchant Shipping Act 1995 s.85. In force: February 12, 2001; £1.50.

These Regulations amend the Merchant Shipping and Fishing Vessels (Health and Safety at Work) Regulations 1997 (SI 1997 2962) to implement recommendations made by Lord Justice Clarke in his Interim Report on the Thames Safety Inquiry (Cm 4530). They provide for the application of merchant shipping health and safety legislation to non-seagoing ships thereby allowing effective enforcement by the Maritime and Coastguard Agency and align the duties under merchant shipping legislation with those under the Health and Safety at Work Act 1974.

4929. Health and safety at work – ships – safety signs and signals

MERCHANT SHIPPING AND FISHING VESSELS (SAFETY SIGNS AND SIGNALS) REGULATIONS 2001, SI 2001 3444; made under the European Communities Act 1972 s.2; and the Merchant Shipping Act 1995 s.85, s.86. In force: February 15, 2002; £2.00.

These Regulations, which amend the Merchant Shipping (Safe Movement on Board Ship) Regulations 1988 (SI 1988 1641), implement Council Directive 92/58 ([1992] OJ L245/23) on the minimum requirements for the provision of safety and/or health signs at work. They specify the persons on whom duties are imposed, require safety signs to comply with the descriptions in the Annexes to the Directive and require that workers receive adequate instruction and training in the meaning of safety signs and the measures to be taken in connection with safety signs.

4930. Industrial action – interim injunctions – strike action by Danish dock workers – exercise of discretion to grant relief

W sought an interim injunction against ITF. Following the arrival of two of W's vessels in Denmark industrial action by dock workers had prevented discharge operations from proceeding. W maintained that ITF's Danish coordinator was responsible for instigating the industrial action, an allegation which was strenuously denied, and sought relief preventing ITF from instigating or instructing dock workers from breaching their contracts of employment in the future.

Held, refusing the application, that (1) there was insufficient evidence to found a conclusion that ITF had been responsible for instigating the industrial action and accordingly W had no good arguable case such as to justify the grant of interim relief, and (2) whilst the court possessed jurisdiction to grant interlocutory relief it would be inappropriate to do so in circumstances where the action was in essence a domestic Danish dispute and the Danish courts also possessed jurisdiction.

WHITE SEA & ONEGA SHIPPING CO LTD v. INTERNATIONAL TRANSPORT WORKERS FEDERATION (THE AMUR-2528 AND THE PYALMA) [2001] 1 Lloyd's Rep. 421, Tomlinson, J., QBD (Comm Ct).

4931. Limitations – counterclaims – cargo – claim for losses caused by delay

[Hague Rules Art. III r.1.]

A applied for a declaration that its counterclaim for damages for losses caused by the delay in loading cargo on to L's barge was not time barred under the Hague

Rules Art. III r.1. L had agreed with A to ship two cranes from Venezuela to Trinidad on L's barge. The barge was damaged by the cranes during the voyage and L sought compensation from A. A counterclaimed, asserting that its specialised personnel and loading equipment had had to wait seven days because the barge had not been seaworthy and had had to undergo repairs before the cranes could be loaded. L argued that the claim related to the goods to be shipped and therefore came within the 12 month time limit in Art. III, and that A's claim had not been made in time.

Held, dismissing the application, that the application was time barred. A's claim did have a "sufficiently close association with the cargo" as it consisted of losses caused by specialised personnel and equipment having to "stand idle", such personnel and equipment only being required because of the nature of the cargo to be loaded, *Interbulk Ltd v. Ponte Dei Sospiri Shipping Co (The Standard Ardour)* [1988] 2 Lloyd's Rep. 159, [1989] C.L.Y. 3400 applied. Although there had been discussion between the parties about extension of any time limits that might arise in the course of the litigation, L had only granted an extension in relation to a potential indemnity claim by A if it were to be sued by the owners of the cranes.

LINEA NAVIERA PARAMACONI SA v. ABNORMAL LOAD ENGINEERING LTD [2001] 1 All E.R. (Comm) 946, Tomlinson, J, QBD (Comm Ct).

4932. **Marine insurance – general average – "Bigham" clause limiting cargo owners' liability – effect of clause on hull underwriters' liability**

[Marine Insurance Act 1906 s.66(4); York-Antwerp Rules 1974; York-Antwerp Rules 1994.]

C, the owner of a ship who had entered into a non separation agreement with a cargo owner, after suffering a loss as a result of an insured peril, appealed against a ruling that it was not entitled to claim from the hull underwriters the shortfall between the amount of its loss and the cargo owner's contribution. The non separation agreement incorporated a Bigham clause, the effect of which was to cap the cargo owner's contribution to the loss. C had sought to recover the excess Bigham amount from the underwriters, whose policy of insurance was subject to the terms of the Institute Time Clauses-Hulls. Its submissions that it was entitled to do so by virtue of the Marine Insurance Act 1906 s.66(4), were rejected by the court of first instance, ([1999] 2 All E.R. (Comm) 1002). In its appeal, C contended that the proportion of the loss which fell upon it, within the meaning of s.66(4) of the Act, included the Bigham excess, and that since the underwriters had agreed to be bound by loss calculations and formulas set out in part of the separation agreement, then by reason of the fact that the agreement was indivisible, they were bound by all the clauses of the agreement, including the Bigham clause. The underwriters, maintaining that rateable proportion was appropriate, argued that, although the York-Antwerp Rules 1994 had introduced provisions practically identical to the Bigham clause, the instant separation agreement was subject to the York-Antwerp Rules 1974, which did not include such a clause, and there was no principle upon which agreements made between ship owners and cargo owners could be binding upon them.

Held, allowing the appeal, that C was entitled to claim its share of the general average in full, to include the Bigham excess. To order otherwise would be to treat only part of an indivisible agreement as defining the underwriter's liability, but not the whole. There was no reason to construe s.66(4) of the 1906 Act as referring to rateable proportion, when there was no express direction to do so, *Green Star Shipping Co Ltd v. London Assurance (No.1)* [1933] 1 K.B. 378 applied. Their inclusion in the 1994 Rules indicated that Bigham clauses were considered to be reasonable agreements when entered into as a consequence of an insured peril, and a vessel's proportion of general average for the purposes of clause 11.1 of the Institute Clauses was therefore the proportion calculated in accordance with the non separation agreement applied as a whole.

COMATRA LTD v. VARIOUS UNDERWRITERS (THE ABT RASHA); *sub nom.* COMATRA LTD v. LLOYD'S UNDERWRITERS [2000] 2 All E.R. (Comm) 609, Clarke, L.J., CA.

4933. Maritime and Coastguard Agency – fees

MERCHANT SHIPPING (FEES) (AMENDMENT) REGULATIONS 2001, SI 2001 3340; made under the Merchant Shipping Act 1995 s.302. In force: November 1, 2001; £1.75.

These Regulations, which amend the Merchant Shipping (Fees) Regulations 1996 (SI 1996 3243), increase the hourly rates applicable to work involved in the issue of a certificate where a survey was performed abroad by a locally appointed surveyor from £23 for fishing vessels and from £26 for other ships to £32 in each case. They make increases in the hourly rates charged for services in relation to the Radio Rules by increasing the hourly survey rates of £24.60 in respect of fishing vessels and £27.90 in respect of other ships, to £32 in each case. The Regulations, which also increase the flat rate charged for administrative and other work from £32 to £50, substitute a reference to the Maritime and Coastguard Agency which was created by the merger of the Marine Safety Agency and the Coastguard Agency.

4934. Maritime and Coastguard Agency – fees

MERCHANT SHIPPING (FEES) (AMENDMENT NO.2) REGULATIONS 2001, SI 2001 3628; made under the Merchant Shipping Act 1995 s.302. In force: December 3, 2001; £2.00.

These Regulations, which amend the Merchant Shipping (Fees) Regulations 1996 (SI 1996 3243), prescribe changes in some of the fees charged and introduce new fees. In particular the hourly rate for fees relating to services listed in Part I of the Schedule have been increased from £72 to £74 and fees in connection with tonnage measurements are to be charged at the hourly rate for services in Part I of the Schedule.

4935. Maritime liens – assignment   preferential creditor – priority as against mortgagee – Hong Kong

MTB, the mortgagee of a vessel, Sparti, and the purported assignee of crew wages, AMC, sought to clarify the priority of their respective claims. AMC had voluntarily met the crew's wages claim but had not obtained sanction from the Admiralty Court to do so and now sought to pursue a claim against the vessel's owners. MTB submitted that (1) it was not possible to make a valid assignment of a maritime lien of wages and accordingly AMC had no greater priority than MTB, and (2) even if assignment were possible it would be prohibited by reason of the Merchant Shipping (Seafarers) Ordinance s.93(1).

Held, giving judgment for MTB, that (1) it was not possible to make any effective transfer of a maritime lien whether by contractual assignment or otherwise. It would be contrary to settled principles of English law to find that a volunteer making a payment to a privileged creditor accrued the rights of the said creditor as against the debtor, *Petone, The* [1917] P. 198 applied, and (2) observed, obiter, that the intent of s.93(1) had been to prohibit the loss of entitlement to wages under an inequitable agreement rather than the transfer of the wages lien to another, *Rosario, The* (1876) 3 Asp. 334 considered.

SPARTI, THE [2000] 2 Lloyd's Rep. 618, Waung, J., HC (HK).

4936. Measure of damages – cargo loss – limit of liability – special drawing rights – appropriate currency

K, who had successfully settled liability against C arising from the loss of cargo, sought to argue matters arising relating to quantum. It was not disputed that C was entitled to limit liability, but argument concerning the correct currency of the limit, the gross rate of interest and any amendment to that rate to reflect the conversion from special drawing rights fell to be decided by the court. K argued that the appropriate currency was United State's dollars, that the US prime rate of interest should be used, running from the date of loss, and that no adjustments were required. K maintained that although it was an Italian company, it was part of a US group and that the contract had arisen from US dealings. C argued that the limitation should be calculated in Italian lira, using the Italian prime rate, and calculated from the date of payment for the replacements, as the replacement cargoes had been manufactured in Italy and paid for in lira, and that it should be discounted to reflect inflation only, as K was protected against the loss in the value of money through the special drawing rights.

Held, giving judgment for K, that the appropriate currency which most justly expressed the loss sustained by K was US dollars and that the US prime rate of interest would be used, *Kuwait Airways Corp v. Kuwait Insurance Co (No.3)* [2000] 1 All E.R. (Comm) 972, [2000] 9 C.L. 440 applied. Further, there was no justification for depriving K of the interest through any reduction, which should be calculated from the date of loss, in accordance with conventional practice. However, although K had succeeded in obtaining monies slightly in excess of the payment into court, their continuance of the action was found to have been unsatisfactory and costs were awarded accordingly.

KINETICS TECHNOLOGY INTERNATIONAL SpA v. CROSS SEAS SHIPPING CORP (THE MOSCONICI) [2001] 2 Lloyd's Rep. 313, David Steel, J., QBD (Comm Ct).

4937. Merchant navy – miscellaneous amendments

MERCHANT SHIPPING (MISCELLANEOUS AMENDMENTS) REGULATIONS 2001, SI 2001 1638; made under the Merchant Shipping Act 1995 s.85, s.86. In force: June 11, 2001; £1.75.

These Regulations amend the Merchant Shipping (Reporting Requirements for Ships Carrying Dangerous or Polluting Goods) Regulations 1995 (SI 1995 2498), the Merchant Shipping (Fire Protection: Large Ships) Regulations 1998 (SI 1998 1012), the Merchant Shipping (Radio Installations) Regulations 1998 (SI 1998 2070), the Merchant Shipping (Passenger Ship Construction: Ships of Classes I, II and II(A)) Regulations 1998 (SI 1998 2514), the Merchant Shipping (Passenger Ship Construction: Ships of Classes III to VI(A)) Regulations 1998 (SI 1998 2515), the Merchant Shipping (Fire Protection) (Amendment) Regulations 1999 (SI 1999 992) and the Merchant Shipping (Marine Equipment) Regulations 1999 (SI 1999 1957) to correct specified mistakes in each instrument.

4938. Merchant navy – war pensions

See PENSIONS. §4644

4939. Oil pollution – claims against limitation fund – time bar – amendment of claim

See PRESCRIPTION: Assuranceforeningen Skuld v. International Oil Pollution Compensation Fund (No.2). §6869

4940. Oil pollution – Conventions – preparedness, response and cooperation

MERCHANT SHIPPING (OIL POLLUTION PREPAREDNESS, RESPONSE AND COOPERATION CONVENTION) (AMENDMENT) REGULATIONS 2001, SI 2001 1639; made under the Merchant Shipping (Oil Pollution Preparedness, Response and Cooperation Convention) Order 1997 (SI 1997 2567) Art.2. In force: June 11, 2001; £1.50.

These Regulations, which amend the Merchant Shipping (Oil Pollution Preparedness, Response and Cooperation Convention) Regulations 1998 (SI 1998 1056), are made in consequence of a defect in the 1998 Regulations.

4941. Port state control – marine safety

MERCHANT SHIPPING (PORT STATE CONTROL) (AMENDMENT) REGULATIONS 2001, SI 2001 2349; made under the European Communities Act 1972 s.2. In force: July 31, 2001; £1.50.

These Regulations amend the Merchant Shipping (Port State Control) Regulations 1995 (SI 1995 3128) to implement Commission Directive 1999/97

([1999] OJ L331/67) and to implement a requirement of Council Directive 1999/35 ([1999] OJ L138/1) on a system of mandatory surveys for the safe operation of regular ro-ro ferry and high-speed craft services to avoid duplication of inspections. The Regulations require the Maritime and Coastguard Agency, in accordance with the Directive, to ensure that publication takes place each month, as a minimum, of information listed in Annex IX Part I of Merchant Shipping Notice MSN No.1725 in respect of ships which have been detained or have been subject to a refusal of access to ports in the UK in the previous month.

4942. Risk allocation – seaworthiness – "knock for knock" agreements – limitation of liability

[Merchant Shipping Act 1995 s.185; Convention on Limitation of Liability for Maritime Claims 1976 Art.2.1.]

M, the hirer of a tug from S under a contract concluded on the "Bimco Towhire" conditions and containing a "knock for knock" agreement, sought to set aside a default judgment obtained by S for losses and outstanding hire charges. During the period of hire a collision had occurred between the tow and a third party. A subsequent claim by the third party had been settled by S who had claimed indemnity from M. Clause 18(2)(b) of the towhire conditions provided that loss or damage caused to, or sustained by, the tow was the sole responsibility of the hirer. M contended that it had a good arguable defence to the claim on the basis that (1) the tug had been unseaworthy in breach of towhire condition 13, and (2) the claim by S under clause 18(2)(b) had amounted to a claim under the Convention on Limitation of Liability for Maritime Claims 1976 Art.2.1, which had been incorporated into United Kingdom law by virtue of the Merchant Shipping Act 1995 s.185, since it was concerned with damage to property, namely the dredger owned by the third party, arising out of the operation of a ship, namely the tug, entitling M to limit any liability by reference to the tonnage of the tug.

Held, refusing the application, that (1) M was not entitled to introduce arguments concerning the seaworthiness of the vessel in question since the "knock for knock" agreement was a basic, but nevertheless, workable allocation of risk and responsibility. To permit M to rely upon the condition of the vessel would undermine the effectiveness of such an agreement, and (2) the claim did not arise as a result of a direct connection with the operation of the tow, but rather by reason of the existence of the "knock for knock" agreement and accordingly Art.2.1 of the Convention was not applicable to the claim under clause 18(2)(b).

SMIT INTERNATIONAL (DEUTSCHLAND) GmbH v. JOSEF MOBIUS BAUGESELLSCHAFT GmbH & CO [2001] 2 All E.R. (Comm) 265, Morison, J., QBD (Comm Ct).

4943. Safety at sea – domestic passenger ships – safety management code

MERCHANT SHIPPING (DOMESTIC PASSENGER SHIPS) (SAFETY MANAGEMENT CODE) REGULATIONS 2001, SI 2001 3209; made under the European Communities Act 1972 s.2; the Merchant Shipping Act 1995 s.85, s.86; and the Merchant Shipping (Control of Pollution) (SOLAS) Order 1998 (SI 1998 1500). In force: November 1, 2001; £2.00.

These Regulations, which amend the Merchant Shipping (ISM Code) (Ro-Ro Passenger Ferries) Regulations 1997 (SI 1997 3022) and the Merchant Shipping (International Safety Management (ISM) Code) Regulations 1998 (SI 1998 1561), require passenger ships of Classes III to VI operating within domestic waters, to develop and implement a Safety Management Code. They also provide for the issue of Domestic Ship Safety Management Certificates by the Maritime and Coastguard Agency, for the ship to be operated in accordance with the requirements of the Code by its owner, master and operator, for enforcement and for offences and penalties.

4944. Safety at sea – life saving appliances

MERCHANT SHIPPING (LIFE-SAVING APPLIANCES) (AMENDMENT) REGULATIONS 2001, SI 2001 2642; made under the Merchant Shipping Act 1995 s.85; and the the Merchant Shipping Act 1995 s.86. In force: August 14, 2001; £1.75.

These Regulations, which amend the Merchant Shipping (Life-Saving Appliances for Ships Other Than Ships of Classes III to VI(A)) Regulations 1999 (SI 1999 2721) and the Merchant Shipping (Life Saving Appliances for Passenger Ships of Classes III to VI(A)) Regulations 1999 (SI 1999 2723), implement recommendations of Lord Justice Clark's report on the Thames Safety Inquiry to ensure that all passenger ships carry life-saving appliances. The Regulations provide certain Class V ships shall carry emergency communications equipment which can make contact with the emergency services for the area in which the ship is operating and provide for ships of Classes IV, V, VI and VI(A) to broadcast emergency alarms over a suitable public address system rather than a general emergency alarm system.

4945. Seafarers – supply of services – provision of crew – meaning of "goods or materials"

[Supreme Court Act 1981 s.20(2)(m).]

LL, the owner of the vessels the "Nore Challenger" and the "Nore Commander", applied to strike out proceedings brought by LI in respect of unpaid invoices relating to the supply of crew and crew services on the ground that LI's claims fell outwith the ambit of the Supreme Court Act 1981 s.20. LI maintained that the court did have admiralty jurisdiction to entertain the claims on the basis that they were "in respect of goods or materials supplied to a ship for her operation or maintenance" and were thus within s.20(2)(m) of the Act.

Held, refusing the application, that despite the use of the words "goods or materials" in s.20(2)(m) which might suggest the supply of purely physical items, a claim for goods or materials supplied to a ship for her operation and maintenance was akin to the former "claim for necessaries". The supply of necessaries had traditionally been given a broad construction and was inclusive of the provision of crew services. It followed that the court had jurisdiction to hear LI's claims, *River Rima, The* [1988] 1 W.L.R. 758, [1988] C.L.Y. 3183 and *Edinburgh Castle, The* [1999] 2 Lloyd's Rep. 362, [2000] C.L.Y. 4740 considered.

LAVINGTON INTERNATIONAL LTD v. BAREBOAT CHARTERERS OF NORE CHALLENGER AND NORE COMMANDER [2001] 2 All E.R. (Comm) 667, David Steel, J., QBD (Adm Ct).

4946. Service of process – limitations – requirements for mandatory extension

[Merchant Shipping Act 1995 s.190; Civil Procedure Rules 1998 (SI 1998 3132) Part 7 r.7.6(3)(b), r.7.6(3)(c).]

P, a Phillipino seaman, sought an extension of time to bring a second action against F, the owners of the vessel, "Flinterdam", pursuant to the Merchant Shipping Act 1995 s.190. P had previously issued proceedings against F on June 8, 1999, following a collision between two vessels as a result of which P had sustained personal injuries. Following the issue of proceedings, service had not been effected upon F within the 12 months prescribed for service and the limitation period had expired on March 16, 2000, without P's representatives appreciating that fact. A second claim form was issued and served when the vessel "Flinterdam" arrived in the UK in July 2000. F contended that (1) P had not taken reasonable steps to serve the claim form within the period of its validity and in particular had erred in failing to place the vessel, "Flinterdam," on world wide watch and effect service upon the vessel in August 1999 upon its arrival at a UK port, and (2) P had not applied promptly to extend the validity of the claim form.

Held, granting the application, that (1) the requirements for a mandatory extension under s.190 were not satisfied but a discretion remained under s.190(5) which fell to be exercised in line with the rules of court as a result of which the Civil Procedure Rules 1998 Part 7 r.7.6, were applicable, *Asianac International Panama SA and Transocean Transport Corp v. Transocean Ro-Ro-Corp (The Seaspeed America)* [1990] 1 Lloyd's Rep. 150, [1991] C.L.Y. 2345 and *Kleinwort Benson Ltd v. Barbrak Ltd (The Myrto)* [1987] A.C. 597, [1987] C.L.Y. 3125 applied. Accordingly there was an unfettered discretion to extend time, in circumstances where the application was made after the expiration of the time prescribed for service and the expiration of the primary limitation period, *Bua International Ltd v. Hai Hing Shipping Co Ltd (The Hai Hing)* [2000] 1 Lloyd's Rep. 300, [2000] 6 C.L.Y. 93 applied. On the facts even if a world wide watch had been maintained it was unlikely that information concerning the arrival of the vessel in August 1999 would have been communicated to P's representatives in time for service to have been effected. That had been the only time that the vessel had visited the UK within the currency of the limitation period and therefore the failure to effect service at that time had not been due to any default on the part of P's representatives, and (2) despite the failure of P's representatives to appreciate that the limitation period had expired it was clear that Part 7 r.7.6(3)(b) and r.7.6(3)(c) were only intended to be of application in circumstances where the limitation period had expired. Accordingly in all cases where reliance was sought to be placed upon Part 7 r.7.6(3)(b) and r.7.6(3)(c), a period of time would have passed following the expiration of the limitation period. Having regard to the fact that if an application to renew the first claim had been made, instead of issuing a second claim, the application would have been held to satisfy the requirement for promptness, together with the fact that the time prescribed for service of the first claim form had expired only three weeks prior to the making of the application, P had satisfied the threshold criteria for promptness in Part 7 r.7.6(3)(c).

SANTOS v. OWNERS OF THE BALTIC CARRIER [2001] 1 Lloyd's Rep. 689, David Steel, J., QBD (Comm Ct).

4947. Shipbuilding – contract terms – possession of vessel in unfinished state – liability to make final payment upon completion

[Arbitration Act 1996 s.69(7)(c), s.70(4).]

H, the builder of a deep water drill ship under a shipbuilding contract with B, appealed against a decision ([2001] C.L.C. 559) that upon termination of the contract for its alleged default, it was neither entitled to payment of the final instalment nor was B obliged to complete the vessel. A contractual clause provided, inter alia, that on H's default B could take possession of the vessel in its unfinished state and complete it at H's yard or elsewhere and that in such circumstances, if the cost of completing the vessel amounted to more than the sum outstanding to H, H would be liable for the difference with interest. The judge had found that it would be extraordinary and uncommercial to construe, as the arbitrators had done, the contractual clause as requiring B, upon taking the vessel, to complete it in accordance with the contract thus requiring payment of the final instalment less the cost of completion. B submitted that the arbitrators' award should be remitted on the basis that the costs of completion had been greater than the arbitrators' estimate when making their interim award.

Held, allowing the appeal, that (1) having regard to the clause, the arbitrators had been correct in finding that it required, if B took possession of the vessel instead of cancelling the contract, B to complete the vessel in accordance with the contract. Such a construction could not be said to be unusual or uncommercial. Further, it was appropriate to imply a term, if it was needed, allowing B to deduct from the final instalment any cost incurred in completing the vessel not in excess of that amount, and (2) where subsequent events or a change of circumstances allegedly rendered an arbitrators' award unduly advantageous to one party, neither the power to remit under the Arbitration Act

1996 s.69(7)(c) nor the court's power under s.70(4) could be used. The arbitrators' award was provisional rather than final.

BMBF (NO.12) LTD v. HARLAND & WOLFF SHIPBUILDING & HEAVY INDUSTRIES LTD, [2001] EWCA Civ 862, [2001] 2 All E.R. (Comm) 385, Potter, L.J., CA.

4948. Shipping contracts – carriers liabilities – bills of lading – liability for contaminated cargo – meaning of "demand"

[Carriage of Goods by Sea Act 1992 s.3.]

BDY, shipowners, appealed against a decision ([1999] Q.B. 868, [1998] C.L.Y. 4395) that its contractual claim against BAB, the purchasers of a cargo of contaminated propane, was bad in law with the consequence that its claim against SA, the supplier of the cargo, also failed. BDY contended that (1) BAB had become liable under the Carriage of Goods by Sea Act 1992 s.3 when it received the bills of lading, despite the fact that it had clearly rejected the contaminated cargo and had sold it on to DE at a much reduced price, and (2) BAB's liability survived its subsequent endorsement of the bills of lading to DE.

Held, dismissing the appeal, that (1) BAB's rejection of the cargo could not be considered a "demand" for the purposes of the Act and therefore it was under no liability to BDY, and (2) although the facts would be preeminent in each case, the principle of mutuality required that where a party passed on his rights to another then his liability was extinguished, *Smurthwaite v. Wilkins* (1862) 11 C.B. N.S. 842 applied.

BOREALIS AB (FORMERLY BOREALIS PETROKEMI AB AND STATOIL PETROKEMI AB) v. STARGAS LTD (THE BERGE SISAR), [2001] UKHL 17, [2001] 2 W.L.R. 1118, Lord Hobhouse of Woodborough, HL.

4949. Shipping contracts – demurrage – exercise of due diligence – accrual of interest on demurrage

B appealed against a finding that it was liable under the terms of its contract with GE to pay GE demurrage. GE cross appealed against a decision that interest was payable on demurrage from the date on which B had been found not to have exercised due diligence. Under a clause in the contract between the parties, demurrage was recoverable "to the extent that [it could] be recovered" by B from a third party. The judge at first instance had found that B had not exercised due diligence in effecting recovery of the demurrage, in particular that there had been no reason preventing B from bringing proceedings against the third party.

Held, dismissing the appeal and allowing the cross appeal, that (1) having regard to the contractual clause, B had been under an obligation to exercise due diligence to recover the demurrage. The words within the clause "[could] be recovered" should be construed as meaning "[could] with the exercise of due diligence be recovered". An implication between the parties to act with due diligence was both expedient and reasonable. It could not be said that the implication to make reasonable efforts to recover the demurrage constituted simply the presentation by B of a claim and the request for payment. Given the contractual implications, it was implausible that the parties would have agreed that there was no need for B to bring proceedings against the third party, and (2) in principle interest accrued on the demurrage from the date at which the demurrage had been incurred or the date when the claim to demurrage could be calculated. It was apparent that the judge had not considered GE's primary submission to that effect.

GALAXY ENERGY INTERNATIONAL LTD v. BAYOIL SA (THE AMA ULGEN) [2001] 1 All E.R. (Comm) 289, Rix, L.J., CA.

4950. Shipping contracts – novation – replacement of original slot charterer

[Supreme Court Act 1981 s.21(4).]

POL appealed against a judgment ([2001] 1 Lloyd's Rep.10) in favour of MSC for sums outstanding by way of slot charter hire in respect of various vessels. By agreements made in 1993, POL had agreed to purchase space in various vessels owned or operated by MSC. MSC had subsequently issued proceedings against POL for slot hire charges which were allegedly outstanding. POL maintained that prior to the sums claimed falling due, there had been a novation whereby POL was replaced as slot charterer by its subsidiary POL-A. POL argued that it would not therefore be liable on an action in personam within the Supreme Court Act 1981 s.21 (4) (b) and did not satisfy the definition of a slot charterer within s.21 (4) (i). MSC denied that any novation had taken place and contended that even if it had, it had been reversed by a 1999 addendum. Moreover, MSC maintained that POL had submitted to the in personam jurisdiction of the court. The judge had found that there had been no novation and that POL had been slot charterers throughout.

Held, allowing the appeal and remitting the case, that (1) having regard to the admissible evidence relating to events occurring prior to 1996, it was apparent that there had been an agreement to a novation with POL-A replacing POL as slot charterer. In circumstances where it was alleged that an agreement had been reached in the course of dealings which had not culminated in the drawing up of a formal contract, it was necessary to ascertain whether, and if so which, terms proposed in the negotiations had become the subject of a joint agreement, *Reardon Smith Line Ltd v. Hansen-Tangen (The Diana Prosperity)* [1976] 1 W.L.R. 989, [1977] C.L.Y. 2816 and *Investors Compensation Scheme Ltd v. West Bromwich Building Society (No.1)* [1998] 1 W.L.R. 896, [1997] C.L.Y. 2537 applied, and (2) the 1999 addendum did not result in a re-novation of POL as slot charterer. Any obligations on the part of POL to MSC under the addendum were free-standing in the nature of a guarantee. It followed that MSC's claims did not fall within the jurisdiction of s.21 (4) (b) of the Act. It was necessary to remit the case in order for it to be determined whether the court had in personam jurisdiction as a result of POL submitting to the jurisdiction.

MSC MEDITERRANEAN SHIPPING CO SA v. POLISH OCEAN LINES (THE TYCHY) (NO.2); *sub nom.* MSC MEDITERRANEAN SHIPPING CO SA v. OWNERS OF THE TYCHY; POLISH OCEAN LINES JOINT STOCK CO (FORMERLY POLISH OCEAN LINES) v. MSC MEDITERRANEAN SHIPPING CO SA, [2001] EWCA Civ 1198, [2001] 2 Lloyd s Rep. 403, Lord Phillips of Worth Matravers, M.R., CA.

4951. Ships – arrest – wrongful detention of vessel – grounds for arrest – duress

I, the alter ego of a company, L, appealed against the grant of summary judgment in proceedings commenced by GA for damages for wrongful detention of a vessel, the Dubai Valour. The vessel had been detained in port by L upon the discovery that part of L's cargo was missing. L had subsequently issued proceedings in Nigeria seeking damages for the lost cargo and claiming a sum of $17 million. The vessel and certain crew members were detained for a period in excess of 21 months until GA entered into a settlement agreement with regard to L's claim under which GA agreed to pay $3 million. No monies were subsequently paid to L as GA successfully obtained a freezing injunction preventing payment by a relevant bank. I contended that (1) the vessel and its crew had not been detained by, or on behalf of him; (2) there was no evidence that he had acted without serious regard as to the existence of any adequate grounds for the arrest, and (3) the detention of the vessel did not amount to duress such as to entitle GA to avoid the settlement agreement.

Held, dismissing the appeal, that (1) the fact that the vessel had been detained pursuant to an order of the Nigerian court was irrelevant since the court's process had been invoked by L and I. Moreover, the courts had not issued any order preventing the crew from leaving. Accordingly, their lengthy detention could only have resulted from the actions of L and I; (2) having regard to the fact that I had not sought to appeal against an earlier ruling to the effect that the maximum sustainable claim for the lost cargo was in the order of $1 million, together with I's decision to arrest the vessel for a lengthy period, it was clear that no objective justification had existed for the sum originally claimed at the time of arrest, and (3) having regard to the conclusion that no objective justification had existed for the original decision to arrest the vessel, there had undoubtedly been duress of the vessel and even more clearly, duress of the individual crew members. Accordingly, GA were entitled to avoid the settlement agreement and return of the $3 million.

GULF AZOV SHIPPING CO LTD v. CHIEF IDISI (NO.2); UNITED KINGDOM MUTUAL STEAMSHIP ASSURANCE ASSOCIATION (BERMUDA) LTD v. LONESTAR DRILLING NIGERIA LTD; GULF AZOV SHIPPING CO LTD v. LONESTAR DRILLING NIGERIA LTD; UNITED KINGDOM MUTUAL STEAMSHIP ASSURANCE ASSOCIATION (BERMUDA) LTD v. LONESTAR OVERSEAS LTD; *sub nom.* GULF AZOV SHIPPING CO LTD v. IDISI, [2001] EWCA Civ 505, [2001] 2 All E.R. (Comm) 673, Longmore, L.J., CA.

4952. Ships – fishing vessels – small vessels – code of practice

FISHING VESSELS (CODE OF PRACTICE FOR THE SAFETY OF SMALL FISHING VESSELS) REGULATIONS 2001, SI 2001 9; made under the Merchant Shipping Act 1995 s.85, s.86. In force: April 1, 2001; £1.75.

These Regulations, which provide for fishing vessels of less than 12 metres in length to comply with the requirements of the "Code of Practice for the Safety of Small Fishing Vessels" published by the MCA, amend the Fishing Vessels (Safety Provisions) Rules 1975 (SI 1975 330) and the Fishing Vessels (Life-Saving Appliances) Regulations 1988 (SI 1988 38) so that those instruments no longer apply to fishing vessels of less than 12 metres in length. The Regulations provide that it is an offence on the part of the owner and the skipper if a vessel proceeds on any voyage without complying with the Code of Practice and the vessel is liable to be detained.

4953. Ships – seaworthiness – damage – grounded vessel – irresponsible act of crew member – causation

D, shipowners, sought to recover from the defendant cargo owners and insurers the sum indicated by the average adjusters following an incident at sea in which its vessel had sustained serious damage. The vessel had suffered a complete electrical failure which had caused the main engine to stop. The crew had dropped anchor but the vessel grounded. The power failure had occurred because a member of the crew had deliberately moved the control lever of the fuel tank's emergency shut off system closing the outlet valve of the generator's service tank. It was common ground that the crew member could not have activated the shut off system accidentally and that the person concerned probably did not intend to cause damage to the ship. The defendants denied liability for general average, contending that (1) the damage had been caused by D's actionable breach of its obligations to make the vessel seaworthy because the glass panel in front of the control box which housed the shut off device was missing at the commencement of the voyage, and (2) if the panel had been in place the casualty would not have occurred.

Held, giving judgment for D, that (1) there was no class requirement for any form of guard against unauthorised operation of such a safety device. The primary requirements were accessibility and ease of use in the event of an emergency and those had been fulfilled. Moreover, there was evidence that the glass panel had not originally been designed to prevent unauthorised operation. Further, other essential pieces of equipment on board were not, in practice, protected from a grossly irresponsible act by a member of the crew. A prudent shipowner weighing comparative risks would not have insisted upon replacement of the panel. Accordingly, the vessel was seaworthy at the material time, and (2) the operation of the shut off device was an irresponsible act by an unknown crew member, whose motive was a matter of speculation, and the defendants had not shown that he would have been deterred and the casualty prevented by a pane of glass on the device housing.

DEMAND SHIPPING CO LTD v. MINISTRY OF FOOD (BANGLADESH) (THE LENDOUDIS EVANGELOS II) [2001] 2 Lloyd's Rep. 304, Cresswell, J., QBD (Comm Ct).

4954. Wrecks – protection – restricted area designation

PROTECTION OF WRECKS (DESIGNATION) ORDER 2001, SI 2001 2403; made under the Protection of Wrecks Act 1973 s.1. In force: July 5, 2001; £1.50.

This Order designates as a restricted area for the purposes of the Protection of Wrecks Act 1973 the area within a distance of 300 metres from the site of the wreck of part of HMS Colossus, which the Secretary of State is satisfied ought to be protected from unauthorised interference on account of its historical, archaeological and artistic importance.

4955. Books

Bowtle, Graeme; McGuinness, Kevin – Law of Ship Mortgages. Llyod's Shipping Law Library. Hardback: £175.00. ISBN 1-85978-997-8. LLP Professional Publishing.

Caminos, Hugo – Law of the Sea. The Library of Essays in International Law, No. 3. Hardback: £110.00. ISBN 1-84014-090-9. Hardback: £94.50. ISBN 1-84014-090-9. Ashgate Publishing Limited.

Cooke, Julian; Young, Timothy; et al – Voyage Charters. 2nd Ed. Lloyd's Shipping Law Library. Hardback: £275.00. ISBN 1-85978-599-9. LLP Professional Publishing.

Hodges, Susan; Hill, Christopher – Principles of Maritime Law: Case and Comment. Hardback: £120.00. ISBN 1-85978-998-6. LLP Professional Publishing.

Jackson, David – Enforcement of Maritime Claims. 3rd Ed. Lloyds Shipping Law Library. Hardback: £180.00. ISBN 1-85978-583-2. LLP Professional Publishing.

Mandaraka-Sheppard, Aleka – Modern Admiralty Law. Paperback: £80.00. ISBN 1-85941-531-8. Cavendish Publishing Ltd.

Philips, Nevil; Craig, Nicholas – Merchant Shipping Act 1995. 2nd Ed. Paperback: £88.00. ISBN 1-85978-563-8. LLP Professional Publishing.

Treitel, Guenter H.; Reynolds, Francis M.B. – Carver: Bills of Lading. New Ed. Hardback: £210.00. ISBN 0-421-56470-9. Sweet & Maxwell.

SOCIAL SECURITY

4956. Benefits – capital disregards

SOCIAL SECURITY AMENDMENT (CAPITAL DISREGARDS) REGULATIONS 2001, SI 2001 22; made under the Social Security Contributions and Benefits Act 1992 s.123, s.136, s.137, s.175; and the Jobseekers Act 1995 s.12, s.35, s.36. In force: February 1, 2001; £1.50.

These Regulations, which amend the Income Support (General) Regulations 1987 (SI 1987 1967), the Jobseeker's Allowance Regulations 1996 (SI 1996 207), the Housing Benefit (General) Regulations 1987 (SI 1987 1971 and the Council Tax Benefit (General) Regulations 1992 (SI 1992 1814), provide that ex-gratia payments of £10,000 made on or after February 1, 2001 by the Secretary of State in consequence of a person's imprisonment or internment by the Japanese during the Second World War, shall be disregarded as capital when ascertaining entitlement to those benefits.

4957. Benefits – capital disregards

SOCIAL SECURITY AMENDMENT (CAPITAL DISREGARDS) (NO.2) REGULATIONS 2001, SI 2001 3481; made under the Social Security Contributions and Benefits Act 1992 s.123, s.136, s.137, s.175; and the Jobseekers Act 1995 s.12, s.35, s.36. In force: November 19, 2001; £1.50.

These Regulations amend the Income Support (General) Regulations 1987 (SI 1987 1967), the Housing Benefit (General) Regulations 1987 (SI 1987 1971), the Council Tax Benefit (General) Regulations 1992 (SI 1992 1814) and the Jobseeker's

Allowance Regulations 1996 (SI 1996 207). They provide that payments made to compensate for a person being a slave labourer or a forced labourer, suffering property loss or personal injury or being the parent of a child who had died, during the Second World War, shall be disregarded as capital when ascertaining the entitlement of the recipient of that payment to those benefits.

4958. Benefits – capital disregards – recovery of benefits

SOCIAL SECURITY AMENDMENT (CAPITAL DISREGARDS AND RECOVERY OF BENEFITS) REGULATIONS 2001, SI 2001 1118; made under the Social Security Administration 1992 s.189; the Social Security Contributions and Benefits Act 1992 s.123, s.136, s.137, s.138, s.175; the Jobseekers Act 1995 s.12, s.35, s.36; and the Social Security (Recovery of Benefits) Act 1997 s.29, s.30, Sch.1 para.4. In force: April 12, 2001; £2.00.

These Regulations amend the Social Fund Maternity and Funeral Expenses (General) Regulations 1987 (SI 1987 481), the Income Support (General) Regulations 1987 (SI 1987 1967), the Housing Benefit (General) Regulations 1987 (SI 1987 1971), the Council Tax Benefit (General) Regulations 1992 (SI 1992 1814), Jobseeker's Allowance Regulations 1996 (SI 1996 207) and the Social Security (Recovery of Benefits) Regulations 1997 (SI 1997 2205). In particular, they provide that payments under a trust established out of funds provided by the Secretary of State in respect of persons who suffered, or who are suffering, from variant Creutzfeldt-Jakob disease which are made to certain persons and payments made by, or out of the estate of, persons receiving such payments which are made to certain persons, shall be disregarded in council tax benefit, housing benefit, income support and jobseeker's allowance and provide that any payment from such a trust shall be disregarded for the purpose of any deduction to be made from a social fund funeral payment.

4959. Benefits – children and young persons – personal allowances

SOCIAL SECURITY AMENDMENT (PERSONAL ALLOWANCES FOR CHILDREN AND YOUNG PERSONS) REGULATIONS 2001, SI 2001 2980; made under the Social Security Contributions and Benefits Act 1992 s.123, s.135, s.137, s.175; and the Jobseekers Act 1995 s.4, s.35, s.36. In force: October 22, 2001; £1.75.

These Regulations amend the Income Support (General) Regulations 1987 (SI 1987 1967), the Housing Benefit (General) Regulations 1987 (SI 1987 1971), the Council Tax Benefit (General) Regulations 1992 (SI 1992 1814) and the Jobseeker's Allowance Regulations 1996 (SI 1996 207). They increase by £1.50 from October 22, 2001, the amounts of the weekly personal allowance applicable in respect of children and young persons in income support, jobseeker's allowance, housing benefit and council tax benefit.

4960. Benefits – claims and information – work focused interviews for lone parents

SOCIAL SECURITY (CLAIMS AND INFORMATION AND WORK-FOCUSED INTERVIEWS FOR LONE PARENTS) AMENDMENT REGULATIONS 2001, SI 2001 1189; made under the Welfare Reform and Pensions Act 1999 s.72, s.83; and the Social Security Administration Act 1992 s.2A, s.189, s.191. In force: April 23, 2001; £1.50.

These Regulations amend the Social Security (Claims and Information) Regulations 1999 (SI 1999 3108) which enable social security information to be supplied by a relevant authority to the partner of a claimant for a qualifying benefit. They provide that for the information to be supplied under that regulation, a qualifying benefit must have been payable to the claimant for at least six months; invalid care allowance is added to the list of qualifying benefits; and restriction is removed that the benefit payable must include an increase for the partner and that the partner of the person entitled to benefit must be aged 50 or over. The Social Security (Work-focused Interviews for Lone Parents) and Miscellaneous Amendments Regulations 2000 (SI 2000 1926) are amended by clarifying the date until which the requirement to take part in a work-focused interview may be deferred.

4961. Benefits – EC law – migrant workers – equal treatment – provision restricting benefit to those with full residence permits

[Protocol Association Agreement between the EEC and Turkey 1963; Decision 3/80 EC-Turkey Association Council on the application of social security schemes of Member States to Turkish workers and members of their family Art.3(1).]

The ECJ was asked to rule on the interpretation of Decision 3/80 Art.3(1), adopted pursuant to the Protocol to the Association Agreement between the EEC and Turkey 1963, which provided that Turkish workers and their families resident in a Member State were to enjoy the same social security benefits as nationals of that State. S, a Turkish national resident in Germany, had her benefit entitlement suspended following a change in the national law that only conferred the right to benefits on persons with full rights of residence or a permanent residence permit. S, who held a temporary permit that precluded the acquisition of permanent authorisation, argued that she should be treated in the same way as German nationals, irrespective of her resident status.

Held, finding the measures discriminatory, that Art.3(1) prohibited discrimination on nationality grounds against a person covered by the Decision. Turkish nationals, therefore, had to be treated in the same way as German nationals when deciding their entitlement to benefits and the host State could not impose stricter conditions on S than those that pertained to its own nationals.

SURUL v. BUNDESANSTALT FUR ARBEIT (C262/96) [1999] E.C.R. I-2685, GC Rodriguez Iglesias (President), ECJ.

4962. Benefits – employment programmes – New Deal Scheme

SOCIAL SECURITY AMENDMENT (NEW DEAL) REGULATIONS 2001, SI 2001 1029; made under the Social Security Contributions and Benefits Act 1992 s.123, s.135, s.136, s.137, s.175; and the Jobseekers Act 1995 s.4, s.12, s.19, s.20, s.20B, s.21, s.35, s.36, Sch.1 para.3. In force: April 9, 2001; £2.50.

These Regulations amend the Income Support (General) Regulations 1987 (SI 1987 1967), the Housing Benefit (General) Regulations 1987 (SI 1987 1971), the Council Tax Benefit (General) Regulations 1992 (SI 1992 1814), the Jobseekers Act 1995 and the Jobseeker's Allowance Regulations 1996 (SI 1996 207). They define the Intensive Activity Period (IAP) for 50 plus, provide that individuals between 25 and 49 participating in the IAP are considered to be participating in an employment programme, provide a different period for a sanction that is applied in relation to the IAP, allow claims for jobseeker's allowance separated by periods on the IAP or IAP for 50 plus to link and allow certain periods of participation in the IAP or IAP for 50 plus to be treated as periods of entitlement to those benefits for the purpose of applying the rules on payment of housing costs in those benefits.

4963. Benefits – exemptions – discretionary financial assistance

DISCRETIONARY FINANCIAL ASSISTANCE REGULATIONS 2001, SI 2001 1167; made under the Social Security Administration Act 1992 s.189; and the Child Support, Pensions and Social Security Act 2000 s.69. In force: July 2, 2001; £1.75.

These Regulations are exempt from the requirement in the Social Security Administration Act 1992 s.172(2) to refer proposals to make Regulations to the Social Security Advisory Committee. They provides relevant authorities with a power to make discretionary payments by way of financial assistance, provide the circumstances in which discretionary housing payments may be made, a limit on the amount and the period for which discretionary housing payments are made, the procedure for claims, and provides relevant authorities with discretion to review any decision it has made in respect of discretionary housing payments.

4964. Benefits – fraud

SOCIAL SECURITY (LOSS OF BENEFIT) REGULATIONS 2001, SI 2001 4022; made under the Pensions Appeal Tribunals Act 1943 s.5A; the Social Security Administration Act 1992 s.189; the Social Security Act 1998 s.79, s.84, Sch.2 para.9; and the Social Security Fraud Act 2001 s.7, s.8, s.9, s.10, s.11. In force: April 1, 2002; £3.00.

These Regulations are made by virtue of, or in consequence of, s.7 to s.13 of the Social Security Fraud Act 2001 and relate to restrictions in payment of certain benefits which apply where a person has been convicted of one or more benefit offences in each of two separate proceedings and one offence is committed within three years of the conviction for another such offence. The Social Security and Child Support (Decisions and Appeals) Regulations 1999 (SI 1999 991) and the Pensions Appeal Tribunals (Additional Rights of Appeal) Regulations 2001 (SI 2001 1031) are amended.

4965. Benefits – home responsibilities

SOCIAL SECURITY PENSIONS (HOME RESPONSIBILITIES) (AMENDMENT) REGULATIONS 2001, SI 2001 1265; made under the Social Security Contributions and Benefits Act 1992 s.122, s.175, Sch.3 para.5. In force: April 6, 2002; £1.50.

These Regulations amend the Social Security Pensions (Home Responsibilities) Regulations 1994 (SI 1994 704) by applying where child benefit first becomes payable to a person in respect of a child on the first Monday of a tax year and would have been so payable for the part of that year falling before that first Monday but for the provisions of the Social Security Contributions and Benefits Act 1992 s.147 (2). Where it applies, the Regulations provide that such a person shall be treated as if he were entitled to child benefit and as if child benefit had been payable to him for that part of that year, in order to be treated for the purpose of the 1994 Regulations as precluded from regular employment in that year due to responsibilities at home.

4966. Benefits – hospital in-patients

SOCIAL SECURITY (HOSPITAL IN-PATIENTS) AMENDMENT REGULATIONS 2001, SI 2001 944; made under the Social Security Administration Act 1992 s.73, s.189, s.191. In force: April 9, 2001; £1.50.

These Regulations amend the Social Security (Hospital In-Patients) Regulations 1975 (SI 1975 555). A person who receives free in-patient treatment in a hospital or similar institution for between six and 53 weeks, has his entitlement to receive incapacity benefit, widow's or widowed mother's allowance, widow's or widower's pension, age addition, severe disablement allowance, retirement pension, unemployability supplement, bereavement allowance or widowed parent's allowance, reduced. These Regulations decrease the reduction which would otherwise apply in certain circumstances, from 40 per cent to 39 per cent of the basic retirement pension.

4967. Benefits – joint claims

SOCIAL SECURITY AMENDMENT (JOINT CLAIMS) REGULATIONS 2001, SI 2001 518; made under the Social Security Administration Act 1992 s.5, s.189, s.191; the Social Security Contributions and Benefits Act 1992 s.22, s.122, s.136, s.137, s.175; the Jobseekers Act 1995 s.1, s.4, s.5, s.21, s.35, s.36, Sch.1 para.8A; and the Social Security Act 1998 s.8, s.10, s.12, s.39, s.79, Sch.3 para.9. In force: March 19, 2001; £2.00.

These Regulations amend the Jobseeker's Allowance Regulations 1996 (SI 1996 207) by clarifying the definition of a joint-claim couple so that it includes a couple where at least one member must be aged 18 or over, clarifying the position as to when a joint-claim couple may be entitled to a joint-claim jobseeker's allowance whilst one member is not required to satisfy the conditions in the Jobseekers Act 1995 s.1 and ensuring that joint claims do not have to be made in certain circumstances where one member of the couple is working 16 hours per week. They provide that days where a member of a joint-claim couple satisfies the conditions for entitlement to a contribution-based jobseeker's allowance and a joint-claim jobseeker's allowance is not payable or is reduced because he is subject to sanctions for the purposes of the Jobseekers Act 1995 s.20A shall be treated as a day of entitlement to a contribution-based jobseeker's allowance. The Regulations also make an amendment which clarifies the rule as to when those receiving full-time education or those who are full-time students may be exempt from having to comply with the jobseeking conditions. They amend the Social Security (Credits) Regulations 1975 (SI 1975 556) by preventing credits from being awarded where a joint-claim jobseeker's allowance is not payable or is reduced because a person is subject to sanctions, amend the Social Security and Child Support (Decisions and Appeals) Regulations 1999 (SI 1999 991) providing a new right of appeal against a decision that a couple are required to make a joint claim and the reason for that decision is that one member of the couple who is working is not engaged in remunerative work and amend the Social Security (Claims and Payments) Regulations 1987 (SI 1987 1968) by providing that where a member of a joint-claim couple to whom a joint-claim jobseeker's allowance is payable disappears, that allowance shall be payable to the other member of that couple. In addition, they amend the Housing Benefit (General) Regulations 1987 (SI 1987 1971) and the Council Tax Benefit (General) Regulations 1992 (SI 1992 1814) by ensuring that where a claimant for those benefits is a member of a joint-claim couple and his partner is getting income-based jobseeker's allowance, the whole of his income and capital will nevertheless be disregarded.

4968. Benefits – maternity expenses – entitlement

SOCIAL FUND MATERNITY AND FUNERAL EXPENSES (GENERAL) AMENDMENT REGULATIONS 2001, SI 2001 3023; made under the Social Security Contributions and Benefits Act 1992 s.138, s.175. In force: October 8, 2001; £1.50.

These Regulations, which apply to claims made on or after October 8, 2001, amend the Social Fund Maternity and Funeral Expenses (General) Regulations 1987 (SI 1987 418) in relation to the "immediate family" and "close relative" conditions of entitlement to a funeral payment and by abolishing the capital rules in relation to claims for Sure Start Maternity Grants and funeral payments.

4969. Benefits – miscellaneous amendments

SOCIAL SECURITY (MISCELLANEOUS AMENDMENTS) REGULATIONS 2001, SI 2001 488; made under the Social Security Administration Act 1992 s.1, s.15A, s.189, s.191; the Social Security Contributions and Benefits Act 1992 s.123, s.124, s.135, s.136, s.137, s.175; and the Jobseekers Act 1995 s.4, s.21, s.26, s.35, s.36, Sch.1 para.1. In force: April 9, 2001; £2.00.

These Regulations amend the Income Support (General) Regulations 1987 (SI 1987 1967), the Social Security (Claims and Payments) Regulations 1987 (SI 1987 1968), the Jobseeker's Allowance Regulations 1996 (SI 1996 207) and the Social Security (Back to Work Bonus) (No.2) Regulations 1996 (SI 1996 2570). They provide that for the purposes of entitlement to income support, a person may be treated as not engaged in remunerative work for the first two weeks, or as the case may be, four weeks, after commencing such work following a period of entitlement to income support or income-based jobseeker's allowance of at least 26 weeks. They also provide that such persons shall not be required to make a claim for income support in order to be entitled to it, that any relevant benefit payable to such persons shall not be paid to a qualifying lender, during the two week or four week period, any earnings from the employment which caused the person to be treated as not engaged in remunerative work shall be disregarded, as is the whole of their income and their capital, and income support paid to such persons does not qualify for the purpose of entitlement to, or claiming, a back to work bonus. The Regulations omit provisions whereby, in income support and jobseeker's allowance, a lone parent who was previously treated as not engaged in remunerative work, was so treated for a specified period if he ceases to be so engaged in such work within five weeks of commencing it. In addition, they extend to 52 weeks certain maximum periods which link, for the purpose of the applicability of housing costs, separate periods of benefit entitlement where a claimant has ceased to be entitled to income support or jobseeker's allowance because he or his partner has commenced work.

4970. Benefits – miscellaneous amendments

SOCIAL SECURITY (MISCELLANEOUS AMENDMENTS) (NO.2) REGULATIONS 2001, SI 2001 652; made under the Social Security Contributions and Benefits Act 1992 s.123, s.124, s.136, s.137, s.175; the Social Security Administration Act 1992 s.2A, s.189, s.191; and the Jobseekers Act 1995 s.3, s.3A, s.17, s.19, s.20A, s.21, s.35, s.36, Sch.1 para.8, Sch.1 para.8A. In force: in accordance with Reg.1; £2.00.

These Regulations, which amend the Council Tax Benefit (General) Regulations 1992 (SI 1992 1814), the Housing Benefit (General) Regulations 1987 (SI 1987 1971), the Income Support (General) Regulations 1987 (SI 1987 1967), the Jobseeker's Allowance Regulations 1996 (SI 1996 207) and the Social Security (Work-focused Interviews) Regulations 2000 (SI 2000 897), make necessary changes to those regulations to reflect the establishment of the Learning and Skills Council and the National Council for Education and Training for Wales. They amend regulations to reflect that certain training allowances are payable by the Learning and Skills Council and by the National Assembly for Wales and amend the definition of the "self-employment route" in those regulations to include assistance in pursuing self-employed earner's employment whilst participating in a course of training or instruction funded by or on behalf of the Secretary of State for Education and Employment, the National Assembly for Wales, the Scottish Enterprise or Highlands and Islands Enterprise.

4971. Benefits – miscellaneous amendments

SOCIAL SECURITY (MISCELLANEOUS AMENDMENTS) (NO.3) REGULATIONS 2001, SI 2001 859; made under the Social Security Contributions and Benefits Act 1992 s.123, s.124, s.135, s.136, s.137, s.138, s.175; and the Jobseekers Act 1995 s.12, s.35, s.36. In force: in accordance with Reg.1; £2.00.

These Regulations amend the Social Fund Maternity and Funeral Expenses (General) Regulations 1987 (SI 1987 481), the Income Support (General) Regulations 1987 (SI 1987 1967), the Housing Benefit (General) Regulations 1987 (SI 1987 1971), the Council Tax Benefit (General) Regulations 1992 (SI 1992 1814), and the Jobseeker's Allowance Regulations 1996 (SI 1996 207). They create a new disregard in housing benefit and council tax benefit in respect of training grants payable under the New Deal 50 Plus Employment Credit Scheme, update the legislative references in the definition of "attendance allowance" applying in council tax benefit and housing benefit, amend references in the rules relating to the treatment of child care charges in housing benefit and council tax benefit, clarify the links between the sub-paragraphs prescribing when a carer is entitled to income support, allow employment credits to be disregarded if paid to a lone parent whilst she is entitled to income support during a "run-on" period, allow a bereavement payment to be disregarded for the purpose of ascertaining entitlement to Sure Start Maternity Grants and funeral payments, change the commencement date of the Social Security Amendment (Enhanced Disability Premium) Regulations 2000 (SI 2000 2629) in relation to income support and jobseeker's allowance so as to take into account benefit weeks and allow the disregard in all the benefits in respect of payments made in respect of persons in the temporary care of another person to apply to payments made by primary care trusts.

4972. Benefits – prisoners – quashed convictions

SOCIAL SECURITY (CREDITS AND INCAPACITY BENEFIT) AMENDMENT REGULATIONS 2001, SI 2001 573; made under the Social Security Contributions and Benefits Act 1992 s.22, s.122, s.175, Sch.3 para.2. In force: Reg.3: April 6, 2001; remainder: March 26, 2001; £1.75.

These Regulations amend the Social Security (Credits) Regulations 1975 (SI 1975 556) and the Social Security (Incapacity Benefit) Regulations 1994 (SI 1994 2946). Reg.2 amends the 1975 Regulations by inserting a new Reg.9D to provide that, for the purposes of entitlement to any contributory benefit, certain prisoners who have had their conviction of a single offence or convictions of two or more offences quashed shall be entitled to be credited with such earnings of a reckonable year for the purposes of entitlement to any benefit. Reg.3 amends the 1994 Regulations to extend the relaxation of the first contribution condition for incapacity benefit to prisoners to which Reg.2 of these Regulations apply.

4973. Benefits – social security – change of circumstances – failure to notify

SOCIAL SECURITY (NOTIFICATION OF CHANGE OF CIRCUMSTANCES) REGULATIONS 2001, SI 2001 3252; made under the Social Security Admininstration Act 1992 s.111A, s.112, s.189, s.191. In force: October 18, 2001; £1.75.

The Social Security Fraud Act 2001 s.16 amends the Social Security Administration Act 1992 s. 111A and 112 by substituting new offences relating to failure to notify a change of circumstances affecting entitlement to any benefit, payment or other advantage. For each offence there must be a failure to give prompt notification "in the prescribed manner to the prescribed person". These matters are prescribed in relation to jobseeker's allowance, in relation to housing benefit and council tax benefit and in relation to any other benefit, payment or advantage. As these Regulations are made within six months of the commencement of the Fraud Act s.16, they are exempt from the requirement to refer them to the Social Security Advisory Committee.

4974. Benefits – statutory maternity pay – medical evidence

SOCIAL SECURITY (MEDICAL EVIDENCE) AND STATUTORY MATERNITY PAY (MEDICAL EVIDENCE) (AMENDMENT) REGULATIONS 2001, SI 2001 2931; made under the Social Security Administration Act 1992 s.5, s.15, s.189, s.191. In force: September 28, 2001; £1.50.

These Regulations amend the Social Security (Medical Evidence) Regulations 1976 (SI 1976 615) and the Statutory Maternity Pay (Medical Evidence) Regulations 1987 (SI 1987 235) which are concerned with the evidence to be provided in connection with claims for maternity allowance and statutory maternity pay. They provide that a maternity certificate from a doctor or a registered midwife is to be given not more than 20 weeks before the week the baby is expected.

4975. Benefits – up rating

SOCIAL SECURITY BENEFITS UP-RATING (NO.2) ORDER 2001, SI 2001 207; made under the Social Security Administration Act 1992 s.150, s.189. In force: in accordance with Art.1 (2); £7.50.

This Order, which is made as a consequence of a review of the Social Security Administration Act 1992, increases the rates and amounts of certain pensions and allowances under the Social Security Contributions and Benefits Act 1992. It increases the rates of certain workmen's compensation and industrial injuries benefits in respect of employment before July 5, 1948, specifies earnings limits for child dependency increases, increases the weekly rates of statutory sick and maternity pay, increases the rate of graduated retirement benefit, increases the weekly rates of age addition to long-term incapacity benefit and increases the age-related amounts of contribution based jobseeker's allowance. In addition, the Order revokes the Social Security Benefits Up-rating Order 2000 (SI 2000 440).

4976. Benefits – up rating – appeals

SOCIAL SECURITY BENEFITS UP-RATING REGULATIONS 2001, SI 2001 910; made under the Social Security Contributions and Benefits Act 1992 s.30E, s.90, s.113, s.122, s.171D, s.171G, s.175, Sch.7 para.2; and the Social Security Administration Act 1992 s.155, s.189, s.191. In force: April 9, 2001; £1.75.

These Regulations, which contain only provisions in consequence of an order under the Social Security Administration Act 1992 s.150, provide that where a question has arisen about the effect of the Social Security Benefits Up-rating (No. 2) Order 2000 (SI 2001 207) on a benefit already in payment, the altered rates will not apply until that question is determined by the Secretary of State, an appeal tribunal or a commissioner. The Regulations apply the provisions of the Social Security Benefit (Persons Abroad) Regulations 1975 (SI 1975 563) so as to restrict the application of the increase specified in the Up-rating Order in cases where the beneficiary lives abroad, raise from £3,094 to £3,146 per year the earnings limit which applies to unemployability supplement and raise from £59.50 to £60.50 per week the limit of earnings from a councillor's allowance in relation to incapacity benefit. In addition, the Social Security Benefit (Dependency) Regulations 1977 (SI 1977 343), the Social Security (General Benefit) Regulations 1982 (SI 1982 1408), the Social Security (Incapacity Benefit) Regulations 1994 (SI 1994 2946) and the Social Security (Incapacity for Work) (General) Regulations 1995 (SI 1995 311) are amended and the Social Security Benefits Up-rating Regulations 1999 (SI 1999 858), the Social Security Benefits Up-rating Regulations 2000 (SI 2000 256), the Social Security Benefits Up-rating and Miscellaneous Increases Regulations 2000 (SI 2000 527) and the Social Security (Therapeutic Earnings Limits) Amendments Regulations 2000 (SI 2000 2028) are revoked.

4977. Benefits – voluntary workers

SOCIAL SECURITY AMENDMENT (VOLUNTEERS) REGULATIONS 2001, SI 2001 2296; made under the Social Security Contributions and Benefits Act 1992 s.123, s.136, s.137, s.175; and the Jobseekers Act 1995 s.12, s.35, s.36. In force: September 24, 2001; £1.50.

These Regulations amend the Income Support (General) Regulations 1987 (SI 1987 1967), the Jobseeker's Allowance Regulations 1996 (SI 1996 207), the Housing Benefit (General) Regulations 1987 (SI 1987 1971) and the Council Tax Benefit (General) Regulations 1992 (SI 1992 1814) to allow payments in respect of expenses to be incurred by a claimant for those benefits to be disregarded where he is engaged by a charitable or voluntary organisation or is a volunteer.

4978. Benefits – widow's benefit – retirement pensions

SOCIAL SECURITY (WIDOW'S BENEFIT AND RETIREMENT PENSIONS) AMENDMENT REGULATIONS 2001, SI 2001 1235; made under the Social Security Contributions and Benefits Act 1992 s.122, s.175; and the Social Security Administration Act 1992 s.1, s.189, s.191. In force: April 9, 2001; £1.50.

These Regulations, made by virtue of amendments made to the Social Security Contributions and Benefits Act 1992 by the Welfare Reform and Pensions Act 1999 s.55, make amendments to the Social Security (Widow's Benefit and Retirement Pensions) Regulations 1979 (SI 1979 642) in relation to the introduction of widowed parent's allowance by virtue of s.55(2) of the 1999 Act, which inserted s.39A (widowed parent's allowance) into the Social Security Contributions and Benefits Act 1992. A new regulation is inserted to provide for a person to be treated as entitled to child benefit in certain circumstances where eligibility for a widowed parent's allowance is dependent on such entitlement, and an amendment is made to disapply to claims for widowed parent's allowance certain requirements as to the claimant's national insurance number.

4979. Benefits – widows and widowers – expatriates

WELFARE REFORM AND PENSIONS (PERSONS ABROAD: BENEFITS FOR WIDOWS AND WIDOWERS) (CONSEQUENTIAL AMENDMENTS) REGULATIONS 2001, SI 2001 2618; made under the Welfare Reform and Pensions Act 1999 s.85. In force: August 20, 2001; £1.50.

These Regulations amend the Social Security Benefit (Persons Abroad) Regulations 1975 (SI 1975 563) by inserting a definition of "bereavement payment" and so that a person is not to be disqualified for receiving a bereavement payment by reason of being absent from Great Britain where, at the date of the deceased spouse's death, either the deceased spouse or the surviving spouse was in Great Britain.

4980. Benefits – work focused interviews – lone parents

SOCIAL SECURITY (JOBCENTRE PLUS INTERVIEWS) REGULATIONS 2001, SI 2001 3210; made under the Social Security Administration Act 1992 s.2A, s.2B, s.5, s.189, s.191. In force: October 22, 2001; £2.50.

These Regulations amend the Social Security (Claims and Payments) Regulations 1987 (SI 1987 1968), the Social Security (Work focused Interviews) Regulations 2000 (SI 2000 897) and the Social Security (Work-focused Interviews for Lone Parents) and Miscellaneous Amendments Regulations 2000 (SI 2000 1926). They impose a requirement on persons who live in certain areas who claim, or are entitled to, certain benefits to take part in a work focused interview.

4981. Care – children – local authorities duties – benefits

CHILDREN (LEAVING CARE) SOCIAL SECURITY BENEFITS REGULATIONS 2001, SI 2001 3074; made under the Children (Leaving Care) Act 2000 s.6. In force: October 1, 2001; £1.75.

These Regulations prescribe the categories of cases where the Children (Leaving Care) Act 2000 s.6 does not apply in England and Wales.

4982. Child support – collection and enforcement

CHILD SUPPORT (MISCELLANEOUS AMENDMENTS) REGULATIONS 2001, SI 2001 1775; made under the Child Support, Pensions and Social Security Act 2000 s.29. In force: May 31, 2001; £1.50.

These Regulations amend the Child Support (Collection and Enforcement and Miscellaneous Amendments) Regulations 2001 (SI 2001 162) to provide for the coming into force on May 31, 2001 of Reg.2(6)(b).

4983. Child Support, Pensions and Social Security Act 2000 (c.19) – Commencement No.8 Order

CHILD SUPPORT, PENSIONS AND SOCIAL SECURITY ACT 2000 (COMMENCEMENT NO.8) ORDER 2001, SI 2001 1252 (C.45); made under the Child Support; and the Pensions and Social Security Act 2000 s.86. Commencement details: bringing into force various provisions of the Act on April 2, 2001 and July 2, 2001; £2.00.

This Order brings into force further provisions of the Child Support, Pensions and Social Security Act 2000 which amend the provisions governing powers of investigation for social security purposes and concern the payment to an employer of any surplus out of the funds of an occupational pension scheme on April 2, 2001. Further provisions for revisions and appeals in connection with housing benefit and council tax benefit are brought into force on July 2, 2001. The Child Support, Pensions and Social Security Act 2000 (Commencement No.4) Order 2000 (SI 2000 3166) is amended to revoke the day previously appointed for the coming fully into force of Sch.5 Part II.

4984. **Child Support, Pensions and Social Security Act 2000 (c.19) – Commencement No.9 Order**

CHILD SUPPORT, PENSIONS AND SOCIAL SECURITY ACT 2000 (COMMENCEMENT NO.9) ORDER 2001, SI 2001 2295 (C.76); made under the Child Support; and the Pensions and Social Security Act 2000 s.86. Commencement details: bringing into force various provisions of the Act on June 26, 2001, July 2, 2001, July 23, 2001 and April 6, 2002; £2.00.

This Order brings the Child Support, Pensions and Social Security Act 2000 s.55, regarding prohibition on occupational pension schemes having different rules for overseas residents, into force on July 23, 2001. Schedule 5 Part II to the Act, which provides for an alternative to the anti-franking rules relating to salary related contracted-out occupational pension schemes is brought fully into force on April 6, 2002. The Order also brings s.70, relating to grants towards cost of discretionary housing payments, into force on June 26, 2001 for the purpose of making an order and on July 2, 2001 for all other purposes, and s.71, relating to recovery of housing benefit, is brought fully into force on October 1, 2001.

4985. **Claims – payments**

SOCIAL SECURITY (CLAIMS AND PAYMENTS) AMENDMENT REGULATIONS 2001, SI 2001 18; made under the Social Security Administration Act 1992 s.5, s.189, s.191; and the Child Support Act 1991 s.43. In force: January 31, 2001; £1.75.

These Regulations, which amend the Social Security (Claims and Payments) Regulations 1987 (SI 1987 1968), provide for the Secretary of State to deduct an amount in respect of certain child support maintenance liabilities from certain social security benefits or war pensions awarded to a beneficiary who is a non-resident parent, or in some cases his partner, and pay it to the person with care.

4986. **Community service orders – breach**

SOCIAL SECURITY (BREACH OF COMMUNITY ORDER) REGULATIONS 2001, SI 2001 1395; made under the Social Security Administration Act 1992 s.189; and the Child Support, Pensions and Social Security Act 2000 s.62, s.63, s.64, s.65. In force: October 15, 2001; £2.50.

These Regulations, which relate to restrictions in payment of certain benefits where a person has been found by a court to have breached a community service order, are made before the end of the period of six months beginning with the coming into force of the relevant provisions in the Child Support, Pensions and Social Security Act 2000. The Regulations prescribe what payment is to be a relevant benefit, the period of the loss or reduction of benefit by reference to whether the offender was entitled to benefit on the day on which the Secretary of State examines his records, what are to be the reduced amounts of income support of joint-claim jobseeker's allowance when the restrictions apply and make provision for jobseeker's allowance to be paid where the offender is a person in hardship. In addition they make provision in relation to exchanges of information necessary to enable the system to operate and for evaluation and monitoring purposes.

4987. **Community service orders – breach**

SOCIAL SECURITY (BREACH OF COMMUNITY ORDER) (CONSEQUENTIAL AMENDMENTS) REGULATIONS 2001, SI 2001 1711; made under the Social Security Contributions and Benefits Act 1992 s.22, s.122, s.123, s.137, s.175; the Jobseekers Act 1995 s.5, s.21, s.26, s.35, s.36, Sch.1 para.8; the Social Security Act 1998 s.9, s.10, s.79, s.84; and the Child Support, Pensions and Social Security Act 2000 s.69. In force: October 15, 2001; £1.75.

These Regulations amend the Social Security (Credits) Regulations 1975 (SI 1975 556), the Housing Benefit (General) Regulations 1987 (SI 1987 1971), the Council Tax Benefit (General) Regulations 1992 (SI 1992 1814), the Jobseeker's Allowance Regulations 1996 (SI 1996 207), the Social Security (Back to Work Bonus) (No.2) Regulations 1996 (SI 1996 2570), the Social Security and Child

Support (Decisions and Appeals) Regulations 1999 (SI 1999 991) and the Discretionary Financial Assistance Regulations 2001 (SI 2001 1167) in consequence of the Child Support, Pensions and Social Security Act 2000 s.62 to s.65 which relate to restrictions in payment of certain benefits where a person has been found by a court to have breached a community service order.

4988. Contributions

SOCIAL SECURITY (CONTRIBUTIONS) REGULATIONS 2001, SI 2001 1004; made under the Social Security Contributions and Benefits Act 1992 s.1, s.3, s.4, s.5, s.6, s.6A, s.10, s.10A, s.11, s.12, s.13, s.14, s.17, s.18, s.19, s.19A, s.116, s.117, s.118, s.119, s.120, s.122, s.175, Sch.1 para.1, Sch.1 para.2, Sch.1 para.3, Sch.1 para.3B, Sch.1 para.4, Sch.1 para.5, Sch.1 para.5A, Sch.1 para.6, Sch.1 para.7A, Sch.1 para.7B, Sch.1 para.7BA, Sch.1 para.8, Sch.1 para.11; the Social Security Administration Act 1992 s.113, s.162, s.191; the Social Security Contributions and Benefits (Northern Ireland) Act 1992 s.1, s.3, s.4, s.5, s.6, s.6A, s.10, s.10A, s.11, s.12, s.13, s.14, s.17, s.18, s.19, s.116, s.117, s.118, s.119, s.121, s.171, Sch.1 para.1, Sch.1 para.2, Sch.1 para.3, Sch.1 para.3B, Sch.1 para.4, Sch.1 para.5, Sch.1 para.5A, Sch.1 para.6, Sch.1 para.7A, Sch.1 para.7B, Sch.1 para.7BA, Sch.1 para.8, Sch.1 para.10; the Social Security Administration (Northern Ireland) Act 1992 s.107, s.142, s.167; and the Finance Act 1999 s.133. In force: in accordance with Reg.1; £12.00.

These Regulations consolidate the Social Security (Contributions) Regulations 1979 (SI 1979 591) and the Social Security (Contributions) Regulations (Northern Ireland) 1979 (SR 1979 186).

4989. Contributions

SOCIAL SECURITY (CONTRIBUTIONS) (AMENDMENT NO.5) REGULATIONS 2001, SI 2001 2412; made under the Social Security Contributions and Benefits Act 1992 s.3, s.10, s.175; the Social Security Contributions and Benefits (Northern Ireland) Act 1992 s.1, s.3, s.4, s.10, s.13, s.171, Sch.1 para.6; and the Child Support Pensions and Social Security Act 2000 s.78. In force: July 26, 2001; £1.75.

These Regulations amend the Social Security (Contributions) Regulations 2001 (SI 2001 1004) and revoke the Social Security (Contributions) (Amendment No.3) Regulations (Northern Ireland) 1989 (SR 1989 112), the Social Security (Contributions) (Amendment No.6) Regulations (Northern Ireland) 1992 (SR 1992 280) and the Social Security (Contributions) (Amendment No.3) (Northern Ireland) Regulations 2001 (SI 2001 597). They introduce a disregard for a non cash voucher which can be used only to obtain a meal subject to a maximum of £0.15 per voucher and £1.05 per week, introduce a disregard for share options granted on or after April 6, 1999 and a disregard in respect of payments of rewards by issuers of charge, cheque, credit and debit cards for the provision of assistance in respect of the recovery or identification of such a card which has been lost or stolen.

4990. Contributions – bereavement benefits

SOCIAL SECURITY (CONTRIBUTIONS) (AMENDMENT NO.6) REGULATIONS 2001, SI 2001 3728; made under the Social Security Contributions and Benefits Act 1992 s.13; and the Social Security Contributions and Benefits (Northern Ireland) Act 1992 s.13. In force: December 12, 2001; £1.50.

These Regulations amend the Social Security (Contributions) Regulations 2001 (SI 2001 1004) to permit a person who wishes to do so to pay a Class 3 contribution for the purpose of satisfying the contribution conditions for the new bereavement benefits introduced by the Welfare Reform and Pensions Act 1999 and the Welfare Reform and Pensions (Northern Ireland) Order 1999 (SI 1999 3147 (NI.11)).

4991. Contributions – calculation of earnings

SOCIAL SECURITY (CONTRIBUTIONS) (AMENDMENT NO.3) REGULATIONS 2001, SI 2001 596; made under the Social Security Contributions and Benefits Act 1992 s.3, s.4, s.10, s.175; and the Child Support, Pensions and Social Security Act 2000 s.74. In force: April 6, 2001; £4.00.

These Regulations, which amend the Social Security (Contributions) Regulations 1979 (SI 1979 591), make amendments by inserting a definition for "cash voucher" and make amendments consequential on the restructuring of the provisions dealing with the calculation of earnings and payments to be disregarded in their calculation. They provide that the amount of a contribution paid through ignorance or error is to be calculated by reference to the rate applicable at the start of the period within which the payment should have been made.

4992. Contributions – Class 1 – money purchase contracted-out schemes

SOCIAL SECURITY (REDUCED RATES OF CLASS 1 CONTRIBUTIONS AND REBATES) (MONEY PURCHASE CONTRACTED-OUT SCHEMES) ORDER 2001, SI 2001 1355; made under the Pension Schemes Act 1993 s.42B; and the Pension Schemes (Northern Ireland) Act 1993 s.38B, s.181. In force: April 6, 2002; £1.75.

This Order is made as a consequence of a review by the Secretary of State of the Pension Schemes Act 1993 following a report by the Government Actuary in relation to the contracted-out percentages. It specifies the appropriate flat rate percentage and the appropriate age related percentages in respect of earners who are members of money purchase contracted out pension schemes for the purposes of the Pension Schemes Act 1993 s.42A and the Pension Schemes (Northern Ireland) Act 1993 s.38A with effect from April 6, 2002.

4993. Contributions – Class 1 – salary related contracted-out schemes

SOCIAL SECURITY (REDUCED RATES OF CLASS 1 CONTRIBUTIONS) (SALARY RELATED CONTRACTED-OUT SCHEMES) ORDER 2001, SI 2001 1356; made under the Pension Schemes Act 1993 s.42; and the Pension Schemes (Northern Ireland) Act 1993 s.38, s.181. In force: April 6, 2002; £1.75.

This Order is made as a consequence of a review by the Secretary of State of the Pension Schemes Act 1993 following a report by the Government Actuary in relation to the contracted-out percentages. It alters the contracted-out percentage to be deducted from secondary Class 1 contributions in respect of members of salary related contracted out pension schemes for the purposes of the Pension Schemes Act 1993 s.41 and the Pension Schemes (Northern Ireland) Act 1993 s.37 with effect from April 6, 2002.

4994. Contributions – Class 1, 1A, 1B contributions – deferred payments

SOCIAL SECURITY (CONTRIBUTIONS) (DEFERRED PAYMENTS AND INTEREST) REGULATIONS 2001, SI 2001 1818; made under the Social Security Contributions and Benefits Act 1992 Sch.1 para.6; and the Social Security Contributions and Benefits (Northern Ireland) Act 1992 Sch.1 para.6. In force: May 12, 2001; £1.50.

These Regulations apply the provisions of the Finance Act 2001 s.107 for the purposes of Class 1, Class 1A and Class 1B social security contributions, s.107 provides for interest not to be charged where, in the exercise of their powers of care and management, the Commissioners of Inland Revenue agree that, by reason of circumstances arising as a result of the outbreak of foot and mouth disease, the payment of tax may be deferred.

4995. Contributions – Class 1A – electronic communications – identity

SOCIAL SECURITY (CONTRIBUTIONS) (AMENDMENT NO.4) REGULATIONS 2001, SI 2001 2187; made under the Social Security Contributions and Benefits Act 1992 Sch.1 para.7B; the Social Security Contributions and Benefits (Northern

Ireland) Act 1992 Sch.1 para.7B; and the Finance Act 1999 s.133. In force: July 6, 2001; £1.75.

These Regulations amend the Social Security (Contributions) Regulations 2001 (SI 2001 1004) by inserting a new Reg.80A which provides that a return rendered, by electronic means, on a person's behalf, is deemed to be rendered by that person unless he proves that it was rendered without his knowledge or connivance. The Regulations are also amended to permit a return of Class 1A contributions to be rendered by delivering it to the inspector; transmitting the particulars required by the return to a computer system maintained by or on behalf of the inspector; or delivering the return by an approved means of electronic communications to an official computer system. It also makes provision about proving what has been delivered to an official computer system or transmitted to a computer system maintained by or on behalf of an inspector or by or on behalf of the Board and the time at which it has been delivered or transmitted.

4996. Contributions – Class 1A – modification

SOCIAL SECURITY CONTRIBUTIONS AND BENEFITS ACT 1992 (MODIFICATION OF SECTION 10(7)) REGULATIONS 2001, SI 2001 966; made under the Social Security Contributions and Benefits Act 1992 s.10; and the Child Support, Pensions and Social Security Act 2000 s.74. In force: April 6, 2001; £1.50.

These Regulations, which modify the list of provisions contained in the Social Security Contributions and Benefits Act 1992 s.10, have effect in relation to any time in the tax year in which they are made. They provide for a deduction from the total amount of an employee's emoluments in respect of which Class 1A contributions are payable if the employee is entitled to a corresponding deduction at least equal to the whole amount which would otherwise be brought into charge to Class 1A contributions.

4997. Contributions – Class 2 contributions

SOCIAL SECURITY (CONTRIBUTIONS) (AMENDMENT) REGULATIONS 2001, SI 2001 45; made under the Social Security Contributions and Benefits Act 1992 s.175, Sch.1 para.8; and the Social Security Administration Act 1992 s.113. In force: January 31, 2001; £1.50.

These Regulations, which amend the Social Security (Contributions) Regulations 1979 (SI 1979 591) Reg.53A, provide for a penalty of £100 in respect of the failure by a person becoming liable to pay a Class 2 contribution to notify the Inland Revenue.

4998. Contributions – Class 3 contributions

SOCIAL SECURITY (CREDITING AND TREATMENT OF CONTRIBUTIONS, AND NATIONAL INSURANCE NUMBERS) REGULATIONS 2001, SI 2001 769; made under the Social Security Contributions and Benefits Act 1992 s.13, s.22, s.122, s.175, Sch.1 para.8, Sch.1 para.10; and the Social Security Administration Act 1992 s.182C, s.189. In force: April 6, 2001; £2.50.

These Regulations consolidate certain regulations in the Social Security (Contributions) Regulations 1979 (SI 1979 591) relating to the appropriation and crediting of Class 3 contributions and the late treatment of late paid social security contributions for the purposes of entitlement to contributory benefit and the application for the allocation of a national insurance number, which are hereby revoked. They provide for the appropriation of Class 3 contributions to the earnings factor of another year, for the crediting of a Class 3 contributions where a person's earnings factor falls short of a figure equal to 52 times the lower earnings limit for Class 1 contributions for the relevant year, for the treatment of late paid contributions for contributory benefit purposes, for an application to be made to the Secretary of State or the Inland Revenue for the allocation of a national insurance number and specify the enactments and instruments in respect of which the Secretary of State has the power to deduct contributions from certain pensions or allowances. In addition, the Regulations revoke the Social Security

(Contributions) Amendment Regulations 1980 (SI 1980 1975) Reg.4, the Social Security (Contributions) Amendment Regulations 1984 (SI 1984 77) Reg.13, the Social Security (Contributions) Amendment (No.2) Regulations 1987 (SI 1987 413) Reg.8 and Reg.9, the Social Security (Contributions) Amendment (No.5) Regulations 1992 (SI 1992 669) Reg.2 and Reg.4, the Social Security (Contributions) Amendment (No.6) Regulations 1993 (SI 1993 2094) Reg.3 to Reg.5, the Social Security (Contributions) Amendment (No.2) Regulations 1994 (SI 1994 1553) Reg.3, the Social Security (Incapacity Benefit) (Consequential and Transitional Amendments and Savings) Regulations 1995 (SI 1995 829) Reg.13 (in part), the Social Security (Credits and Contributions) (Jobseeker's Allowance Consequential and Miscellaneous Amendments) Regulations 1996 (SI 1996 2367) Reg.3 (in part), the Social Security Contributions, Statutory Maternity Pay and Statutory Sick Pay (Miscellaneous Amendments) Regulations 1999 (SI 1999 567) Reg.7, the Social Security (Contributions and Credits) (Miscellaneous Amendments) Regulations 1999 (SI 1999 568) Reg.13 and the Social Security (Contributions) (Amendment No.8) Regulations 2000 (SI 2000 2207) Reg.6.

4999. Contributions – earnings limits and tax thresholds

SOCIAL SECURITY (CONTRIBUTIONS) (AMENDMENT NO.2) REGULATIONS 2001, SI 2001 313; made under the Social Security Contributions and Benefits Act 1992 s.5, s.175, Sch.1 para.6. In force: April 6, 2001; £1.75.

These Regulations, which amend the Social Security (Contributions) Regulations 1979 (SI 1979 591), specify the lower earnings limit, upper earnings limit, primary threshold and secondary threshold for the tax year beginning April 6, 2001. In addition, they provide for the equivalents of the primary threshold and secondary threshold where an employed earner's earnings period is other than a week.

5000. Contributions – employers liability – firm carrying out activities primarily in another Member State

[Council Regulation 1408/71 on the application of social security schemes to employed persons and their families moving within the Community Art.13(2)(a), Art.14(1)(a).]

In proceedings between P and A, the local health insurance fund, concerning the liability of P to pay social security contributions for a specified period, two questions concerning the interpretation of Council Regulation 1408/71 Art.13(2)(a) and Art.14(1)(a) were referred to the ECJ. P had established a company in the Netherlands which had carried out building projects exclusively in Germany. The national court sought determination as to whether, inter alia, a person who was employed by a company that had been established and maintained an office in one Member State, but carried out its activities essentially in the territory of another Member State, was a person employed in the territory of the first Member State.

Held, giving a preliminary ruling, that Art.14(1)(a) did not apply to workers of a company established in one Member State who were sent to undertake work in another Member State in which, save for the carrying out of internal management, the company performed all of its activities. Such workers fell under the social security legislation of the Member State in which they actually worked pursuant to Art.13(2)(a), *Fitzwilliam Executive Search Ltd (t/a Fitzwilliam Technical Services) v. Bestuur van het Landelijk Instituut Sociale Verzekeringen (C202/97)* [2000] Q.B. 906, [2000] 4 C.L. 217 applied.

PLUM v. ALLGEMEINE ORTSKRANKENKASSE RHEINLAND (REGIONALDIREKTION KOLN) (C404/98) [2001] All E.R. (EC) 240, C Gulmann (President), ECJ.

5001. Contributions – personal pensions – contributions

SOCIAL SECURITY (MINIMUM CONTRIBUTIONS TO APPROPRIATE PERSONAL PENSION SCHEMES) ORDER 2001, SI 2001 1354; made under the

Pension Schemes Act 1993 s.45A, s.182; and the Pension Schemes (Northern Ireland) Act 1993 s.41A, s.181. In force: April 6, 2002; £2.00.

This Order is made as a consequence of a review by the Secretary of State of the Pension Schemes Act 1993 following a report by the Government Actuary in relation to minimum contributions. It specifies the appropriate age related percentages of earnings payable as minimum contributions in respect of members of appropriate personal pension schemes for the purposes of the Pension Schemes Act 1993 s.45 and the Pension Schemes (Northern Ireland) Act 1993 s.41 with effect from April 6, 2002.

5002. Contributions – share option schemes

SOCIAL SECURITY CONTRIBUTIONS (SHARE OPTIONS) REGULATIONS 2001, SI 2001 1817; made under the Social Security Contributions and Benefits Act 1992 s.175, Sch.1 para.6, Sch.1 para.7B, Sch.1 para.8; the Social Security Contributions and Benefits (Northern Ireland) Act 1992 s.171, Sch.1 para.7B, Sch.1 para.8; and the Social Security Contributions (Share Options) Act 2001 s.1, s.5. In force: May 12, 2001; £2.00.

The Social Security Contributions (Share Options) Act 2001 contains provisions for the limitation of liability to pay social security contributions in respect of gains arising on the exercise, assignment or release of certain share options. In order for these provisions to be used, a notice must be given to the Inland Revenue within 92 days of the day on which the Act is passed. Where such a notice is given, a special contribution is payable in respect of the gain, if any, which would have arisen had the share option been exercised, assigned or released on November 7, 2000. These Regulations set out the matters to be contained in the notice to be given to the Inland Revenue, provide for the payment of special contributions, provide for interest on overdue special contributions and provide for the records which a person who has given a notice to the Inland Revenue must maintain and for the period for which such records must be retained.

5003. Contributions – statutory sick pay and statutory maternity pay – appeals

SOCIAL SECURITY CONTRIBUTIONS (DECISIONS AND APPEALS) (AMENDMENT) REGULATIONS 2001, SI 2001 4023; made under the Social Security Contributions (Transfer of Functions, etc.) Act 1999 s.13, s.25; the Social Security Contributions (Transfer of Functions, etc.) (Northern Ireland) Order 1999 (SI 1999 671) Art.12; and the Social Security Contributions (Transfer of Functions, etc.) (Northern Ireland) Order (SI 1999 671) Art.23. In force: January 31, 2002; £1.75.

These Regulations amend the Social Security Contributions (Decisions and Appeals) Regulations 1999 (SI 1999 1027) in consequence of the provisions of the Social Security Contributions (Transfer of Functions, etc.) Act 1999 and the Social Security (Transfer of Functions, etc.) (Northern Ireland) Order 1999 (SI 1999 671) and concern appeals against decisions in relation to social security contributions and entitlements to statutory sick pay and statutory maternity pay.

5004. Council tax benefit – permitted totals

COUNCIL TAX BENEFIT (PERMITTED TOTALS) (AMENDMENT) ORDER 2001, SI 2001 1130; made under the Social Security Administration Act 1992 s.139, s.189. In force: April 1, 2001; £1.50.

This Order, which amends the Council Tax Benefit (Permitted Totals) Order 1996 (SI 1996 678), limits the amount by which council benefit may be increased on the exercise of the discretion provided by the Council Tax Benefit (General) Regulations 1992 (SI 1992 1814).

5005. Disability living allowance – aliens – transitional provisions – new and repeat claims

[Social Security (Persons from Abroad) Miscellaneous Amendments Regulations 1996 (SI 1996 30) Reg.12(3).]

M, a nine year old, severely disabled child, appealed against the dismissal of her appeal following a ruling that she was not entitled to disability living allowance. M had been born in Pakistan and had been brought to the United Kingdom by her parents at the age of one. In 1992 M was awarded Disability Living Allowance for a three year period. In 1996 the Social Security (Persons from Abroad) Miscellaneous Amendments Regulations 1996 introduced a requirement that in order to claim the allowance, the potential recipient's right to remain in the UK had not to be subject to any limitation or condition. In 1996 M did not satisfy that requirement because she had overstayed her leave to enter, and accordingly her claim to a further award was refused. M contended that pursuant to Reg.12(3), there existed a right to receive not only those benefits due under an existing award in accordance with the unamended regulations, but also any repeat claim.

Held, dismissing the appeal, that the aim and effect of Reg.12(3) was to safeguard accrued rights to benefits to which an individual claimant was entitled immediately prior to the commencement of the Regulations and the words "where, before coming into force of these Regulations" were not be given the literal meaning of "any time before". It was necessary to consider the context and object of the Regulations such that they would not be applied to every case which fell within their literal scope, *International Tin Council, Re* [1989] Ch. 309, [1989] C.L.Y. 274 considered. The extent of M's accrued rights to benefit consisted of the three year award of disability living allowance. Reg.12(3) did not have the effect of extending the right to benefit beyond the term originally awarded and, consequently, did not apply to new or repeat claims, *R. v. Chief Adjudication Officer, ex p. B* [1999] 1 W.L.R. 1695, [1999] C.L.Y. 4544 applied.

M (A CHILD) v. SECRETARY OF STATE FOR SOCIAL SECURITY, [2001] UKHL 35, [2001] 1 W.L.R. 1453, Lord Millett, HL.

5006. Disability living allowance – attendance allowance – residential care homes and nursing homes

SOCIAL SECURITY AMENDMENT (RESIDENTIAL CARE AND NURSING HOMES) REGULATIONS 2001, SI 2001 3767; made under the Social Security Contributions and Benefits Act 1992 s.67, s.72, s.123, s.124, s.135, s.136, s.137, s.175; the Jobseekers Act 1995 s.4, s.12, s.13, s.35, s.36, Sch.1 para.1; and the Health and Social Care Act 2001 s.52. In force: April 8, 2002; £2.50.

These Regulations amend the Income Support (General) Regulations 1987 (SI 1987 1967) and the Jobseeker's Allowance Regulations 1996 (SI 1996 207) so as to provide that the special amounts which are applicable to those persons in residential care homes and nursing homes who have preserved rights, shall no longer be applicable from April 8, 2002. The Regulations also amend the Social Security (Attendance Allowance) Regulations 1991 (SI 1991 2740) and the Social Security (Disability Living Allowance) Regulations 1991 (SI 1991 2890) so as to remove the separate provision in respect of payment of attendance allowance and the care component of disability living allowance for those persons in residential care homes and nursing homes with preserved rights.

5007. Earnings factors – calculation of additional pension

SOCIAL SECURITY REVALUATION OF EARNINGS FACTORS ORDER 2001, SI 2001 631; made under the Social Security Administration Act 1992 s.148, s.189. In force: April 6, 2001; £1.75.

This Order, consequent upon a review under the Social Security Administration Act 1992 s.148, directs that the earnings factors relevant to the calculation of the additional pension in the rate of any long term benefit or of any guaranteed minimum pension, or to any other calculation required under Pension Schemes Act 1993, are to be increased for the tax years specified in the Schedule to the Order by the percentage of their amount specified in that Schedule. In addition, this Order provides for the rounding of fractional amounts for earnings factors relevant to the calculation of the additional pension in the rate of any long term benefit.

5008. Educational institutions – teachers – national insurance contributions – relationship between college and self employed music teachers

[Social Security (Categorisation of Earners) Regulations 1978 (SI 1978 1689) Reg.2(2), Sch.1 Part 1 para.4.]

SJ appealed a decision of the Secretary of State for Social Security that for the purposes of the Social Security (Categorisation of Earners) Regulations 1978 Reg.2(2), visiting instrumental teachers, VIT's, were to be categorised as employed by SJ notwithstanding the fact that no contract of service subsisted between SJ and the VIT's. SJ found suitable VIT's to provide musical tuition to pupils on its premises but the VIT's were treated by all parties as self employed with a contract existing only between the parents of each child and the individual VIT. SJ submitted that (1) the Secretary of State had erred in his conclusion that SJ was an "educational establishment" for the purposes of Sch.1 Part 1 para.4 of the Regulations. SJ maintained that in the particular context of the Regulations the definition provided was exhaustive and SJ did not satisfy the criteria therein, and (2) the Secretary of State's conclusion that the VIT's were employed by SJ was *Wednesbury* unreasonable.

Held, dismissing the appeal, that (1) the word "includes" in the definition of "educational establishment" necessarily indicated that the definition was not exhaustive, and accordingly the Secretary of State had been entitled to conclude that SJ was an educational establishment for the purposes of the Regulations, and (2) having regard to all the primary findings of fact made by the Secretary of State concerning the nature of the relationship between the VIT's and SJ and the information provided in the school guide, which listed all the full time music staff and all the VIT's, without distinction, the impression created was that the VIT's were very much part of the school and therefore their "employment" had properly been held to be with SJ.

ST JOHN'S COLLEGE SCHOOL (CAMBRIDGE) v. SECRETARY OF STATE FOR SOCIAL SECURITY [2001] E.L.R. 103, Munby, J., QBD.

5009. Housing benefit – burden of proof – liability for rent

[Social Security Contributions and Benefits Act 1992 s.130; Housing Benefit (General) Regulations 1987 (SI 1987 1971) Reg.7(1)(b).]

D's application for housing benefit in respect of a property which he occupied and which was owned by his son was refused by GLBC. Purporting to rely on the Housing Benefit (General) Regulations 1987 Reg.7(1)(b), GLBC justified its decision by referring to various matters, which included the fact that D had not received housing benefit when he had previously occupied the property for a period of two years, the son's failure to take action to recover what were substantial rent arrears, and its finding that the letting to D had not been at arm's length. D sought judicial review of GLBC's decision.

Held, granting the application, that (1) GLBC had misdirected itself as to the relevant statutory provisions. Whereas it had purported to rely on Reg.7(1)(b) of the Regulations which concerned individuals who intended to take advantage of the housing benefit scheme, the reasons for its decision had been directed to the issue of whether D had a genuine liability to pay rent. That issue fell within the Social Security Contributions and Benefits Act 1992 s.130, and (2) although GLBC had correctly stated that, for the purpose of establishing that D did not have a genuine liability to pay rent the burden of proof lay on the housing benefits officer, doubt existed as to whether it had reached its decision by approaching the burden of proof in that way. Such a conclusion was supported by various considerations which favoured D's case and which GLBC had failed to adequately address. They included his undisputed assertion that he had had legitimate reasons for returning to live at his son's property, the fact that he had produced a tenancy agreement and rent book, and the fact that he had paid rent for a period of 10 weeks.

R. v. GREENWICH LBC, *ex p.* DHADLY (2000) 32 H.L.R. 829, Richards, J., QBD.

5010. Housing benefit – council tax benefit – childcare charges

HOUSING BENEFIT AND COUNCIL TAX BENEFIT (GENERAL) AMENDMENT REGULATIONS 2001, SI 2001 1864; made under the Social Security Contributions and Benefits Act 1992 s.123, s.136, s.137, s.175. In force: August 13, 2001; £1.75.

These Regulations, which amend the Housing Benefit (General) Regulations 1987 (SI 1987 1971) and the Council Tax Benefit (General) Regulations 1992 (SI 1992 1814), increase the maximum deduction which may be made from a claimant's weekly income in respect of relevant child care charges for the purpose of assessing entitlement to housing benefit or council tax benefit. They provide for a woman on maternity leave to be treated as if she were engaged in remunerative work so enabling relevant child care charges to be deducted from her weekly income for the purpose of assessing entitlement to either benefit. Any child care charges incurred in respect of the child to whom the maternity leave relates are not treated as relevant child care charges.

5011. Housing benefit – council tax benefit – decisions and appeals

HOUSING BENEFIT AND COUNCIL TAX BENEFIT (DECISIONS AND APPEALS) REGULATIONS 2001, SI 2001 1002; made under the Social Security Administration Act 1992 s.5, s.6; the Social Security Act 1998 s.7; the Social Security Act 1992 s.79; and the Child Support Pensions and Social Security Act 2000 s.68, Sch.7 para.3, Sch.7 para.4, Sch.7 para.6, Sch.7 para.8, Sch.7 para.10, Sch.7 para.12, Sch.7 para.13, Sch.7 para.14, Sch.7 para.15, Sch.7 para.16, Sch.7 para.19, Sch.7 para.20, Sch.7 para.23. In force: July 2, 2001; £3.50.

These Regulations, which supplement changes introduced by the Child Support, Pensions and Social Security Act 2000 to the decision-making process for housing benefit and council tax benefit and to the new appeals system, are made before the end of the period of six months beginning with the coming into force of the relevant provisions in the Act and are therefore exempt from the requirement in the Social Security Administration Act 1992 s.172 to refer proposals to make these Regulations to the Social Security Advisory Committee. They make provision as to the circumstances in which a relevant authority may revise or supersede decisions, when such decisions take effect and related procedural matters, and for the suspension and termination of housing benefit and council tax benefit and decisions involving issues that arise in appeals in other cases. In addition, the Regulations make provision in respect of rights of appeal and procedure for bringing appeals and make provision in respect of appeal tribunal composition and procedure.

5012. Housing benefit – council tax benefit – decisions and appeals

HOUSING BENEFIT AND COUNCIL TAX BENEFIT (DECISIONS AND APPEALS) (TRANSITIONAL AND SAVINGS) REGULATIONS 2001, SI 2001 1264; made under the Pensions Act 1995 s.174; and the Child Support, Pensions and Social Security Act 2000 s.86. In force: July 2, 2001; £2.00.

These Regulations make transitional and saving provisions in consequence of the coming into force of Child Support, Pensions and Social Security Act 2000 Sch.7 which introduces new arrangements for decision making in relation to housing benefit and council tax benefit. In particular, they provide for the manner in which matters are to be dealt with on or after July 2, 2001, which are awaiting determination under the existing arrangements for decision making immediately before that date.

5013. Housing benefit – council tax benefit – decisions and appeals

HOUSING BENEFIT AND COUNCIL TAX BENEFIT (DECISIONS AND APPEALS AND DISCRETIONARY FINANCIAL ASSISTANCE) (CONSEQUENTIAL AMENDMENTS AND REVOCATIONS) REGULATIONS 2001, SI 2001 1605; made under the Social Security Administration Act 1992 s.5, s.6, s.189, s.191; the Social Security Act 1998 s.79; and the Child Support, Pensions and Social Security Act 2000 s.68, s.69, Sch.7 para.20. In force: July 2, 2001; £3.00.

These Regulations amend the Housing Benefit (General) Regulations 1987 (SI 1987 1971) and the Council Tax Benefit (General) Regulations 1992 (SI 1992 1814) in consequence of the coming into force of the Child Support, Pensions and Social Security Act 2000 s.68 which introduces new arrangements for decision-making in relation to housing benefit and council tax benefit.

5014. Housing benefit – council tax benefit – extended claims – entitlement

HOUSING BENEFIT AND COUNCIL TAX BENEFIT (EXTENDED PAYMENTS) REGULATIONS 2001, SI 2001 537; made under the Social Security Administration Act 1992 s.5, s.6, s.128, s.189, s.191; the Social Security Contributions and Benefits Act 1992 s.123, s.130, s.131, s.137, s.175; and the Social Security Act 1998 s.34, s.39, s.79. In force: April 9, 2001; £2.00.

These Regulations, which amend the Housing Benefit (General) Regulations 1987 (SI 1987 1971), the Council Tax Benefit (General) Regulations 1992 (SI 1992 1814) and the Housing Benefit (Supply of Information) Regulations 1988 (SI 1988 662), make changes to the rules relating to entitlement to, and claims for, extended payments of those benefits and also provide that extended payments of those benefits shall not be payable to a person entitled to income support by virtue of the Income Support (General) Regulations 1987 (SI 1987 1967).

5015. Housing benefit – determination of single room rent

HOUSING BENEFIT (GENERAL) AMENDMENT (NO.3) REGULATIONS 2001, SI 2001 1324; made under the Social Security Contributions and Benefits Act 1992 s.123, s.130, s.137, s.175; the Housing Act 1996 s.122; and the Child Support, Pensions and Social Security Act 2000 Sch.7 para.4. In force: July 2, 2001; £1.75.

These Regulations, which amend the Housing Benefit (General) Regulations 1987 (SI 1987 1971), are consequential upon amendments in the criteria applying to determinations of the single room rent in the Rent Officers (Housing Benefit Functions) Order 1997 (SI 1997 1984) and the Rent Officers (Housing Benefit Functions) (Scotland) Order 1997 (SI 1997 1995).

5016. Housing benefit – discretion – reduction in eligible rent – relevance of applicant's personal circumstances

[Housing Benefit (General) Regulations 1987 (SI 1987 1971) Reg.11 (2).]

W appealed against a decision that it was entitled to take the personal circumstances of an applicant for housing benefit into account when determining the extent to which the eligible rent should be reduced, following a finding that the rent payable was unreasonably high by comparison with that of other suitable alternative accommodation. W maintained that in satisfying its obligation under the Housing Benefit (General) Regulations 1987 Reg.11 (2) to reduce the eligible rent and in exercising its discretion to reduce it "by such amount as it considers appropriate", personal factors, such as the pregnancy of the applicant's wife, the reduced amount of income support payable to the applicant by virtue of his status as an asylum seeker, and the impact of accommodating the applicant and his family as homeless persons, were irrelevant.

Held, dismissing the appeal, that the wording of the statute whereby suitable alternative accommodation was to be considered "in particular", indicated that in exercising its discretion W was entitled to have regard to other factors, and that the factors identified by the applicant were all properly to be regarded as relevant to the applicant's housing situation. Such an interpretation also served the underlying policy objective of the legislation, namely to ensure that the housing needs of society's most disadvantaged sector were met.

R. (ON THE APPLICATION OF MEHANNE) v. WESTMINSTER HOUSING BENEFIT REVIEW BOARD; *sub nom.* MEHANNE v. WESTMINSTER HOUSING BENEFIT REVIEW BOARD; R. v. WESTMINSTER HOUSING BENEFIT REVIEW BOARD, *ex p.* MEHANNE, [2001] UKHL 11, [2001] 1 W.L.R. 539, Lord Bingham of Cornhill, HL.

5017. Housing benefit – discretionary payments

DISCRETIONARY HOUSING PAYMENTS (GRANTS) ORDER 2001, SI 2001 2340; made under the Social Security Administration Act 1992 s.140B, s.140C, s.189; and the Child Support, Pensions and Social Security Act 2000 s.70. In force: July 2, 2001; £1.75.

This Order sets out the procedure by which the Secretary of State will make payments towards the cost of discretionary housing payments in accordance with the Child Support, Pensions and Social Security Act 2000 s.70. It provides for the determination of the amount of grant the Secretary of State makes to a relevant authority, the procedure for making claims, the requirement to keep records and provision of information, audit requirements, payment of the grant and imposes a limit on the total amount of expenditure that may be incurred in any year by a relevant authority in making discretionary housing payments.

5018. Housing benefit – discretionary payments

SOCIAL SECURITY AMENDMENT (DISCRETIONARY HOUSING PAYMENTS) REGULATIONS 2001, SI 2001 2333; made under the Social Security Contributions and Benefits Act 1992 s.123, s.130, s.136, s.137, s.175; the Jobseekers Act 1995 s.12, s.35, s.36; and the Housing Act 1996 s.122. In force: July 2, 2001; £1.75.

These Regulations amend the Income Support (General) Regulations 1987 (SI 1987 1967), the Jobseeker's Allowance Regulations 1996 (SI 1996 207), the Housing Benefit (General) Regulations 1987 (SI 1987 1971) and the Council Tax Benefit (General) Regulations 1992 (SI 1992 1814) to provide that discretionary housing payments paid pursuant to the Discretionary Financial Assistance Regulations 2001 (SI 2001 1167) shall be disregarded as income in those benefits and that arrears of such payments shall be disregarded as capital for up to 52 weeks.

5019. Housing benefit – entitlement – dwelling occupied with ex partner

[Human Rights Act 1998 Sch.1 Part I Art.8, Art.14; Housing Benefit General Regulations 1987 (SI 1987 1971) Reg.7 (1) (c) (i).]

P sought judicial review of a decision of the review board refusing his claim for housing benefit following a determination by the local authority that the Housing Benefit General Regulations 1987 Reg.7 (1) (c) (i) applied. P had originally been a lodger in residential accommodation where he rented a bedroom and had the right to use the common parts. P had subsequently formed a relationship with his landlady and moved into her room and jointly occupied the accommodation. However, he had reverted back to a tenant at the end of the relationship and was liable to make payments of rent. It was argued that (1) Reg. 7 (1) (c) (i) only applied if the dwelling in respect of which the payments were due was the same dwelling which had been occupied during the relationship. P submitted that the dwelling was in fact different as it no longer included the landlady's room, and (2) if the regulation was applicable, it was incompatible with the Human Rights Act 1998 Sch. 1 Part I Art.8 and Art.14.

Held, refusing the applications, that (1) the regulation applied. The informal arrangements to occupy separate rooms did not affect the reality of the situation that the dwelling remained the same, *Neale v. Del Soto* [1945] K.B. 144 applied, and (2) there had been no breach of the Convention rights. Any discrimination was justifiable as a precaution against potential abuse of the housing benefit system, *R. v. Secretary of State for the Home Department, ex p. Isiko* [2001] 1 F.L.R. 930, [2001] 3 C.L. 436 applied.

R. (ON THE APPLICATION OF PAINTER) v. CARMARTHENSHIRE CC HOUSING BENEFIT REVIEW BOARD; R. (ON THE APPLICATION OF MURPHY) v. WESTMINSTER CITY COUNCIL, [2001] EWHC Admin 308, *The Times*, May 16, 2001, Lightman, J., QBD (Admin Ct).

5020. Housing benefit – entitlement – home owneship

HOUSING BENEFIT (GENERAL) AMENDMENT REGULATIONS 2001, SI 2001 487; made under the Social Security Contributions and Benefits Act 1992 s.123, s.130, s.137, s.175; and the Housing Act 1996 s.122. In force: May 21, 2001; £1.75.

These Regulations amend the Housing Benefit (General) Regulations 1987 (SI 1987 1971) by providing that a person who is liable to make payments in respect of a dwelling shall be treated as not being so liable for housing benefit purposes where the claimant or his partner owned that dwelling before they rented it unless, where the claimant demonstrates that he could not have continued to live there without selling the property, more than five years elapses between the date on which the claimant or his partner relinquished ownership of the property and the date on which housing benefit is claimed. They specify how a claimant's eligible rent is established for housing benefit purposes, how a claimant's maximum rent is established for housing benefit purposes, that a claimant's maximum housing benefit may be increased if a maximum rent has been determined in respect of him and he, or a member of his family, would suffer exceptional hardship. In determining such an increase an authority is bound by any determination made by a rent officer as to the amount of any service charges which remain, in any event, ineligible. They also provide that an authority must apply for a fresh rent officer determination in respect of a continuous claim which has lasted 52 weeks or more when the previous determination has ceased to be applicable.

5021. Housing benefit – families – meaning of "residing with" – approach to precedent involving assumed proposition of law

[Housing Benefit (General) Regulations 1987 (SI 1987 1971) Reg.3(4), Reg.7(1).]

K appealed against a finding ([2000] C.O.D. 472) upholding a decision of the Housing Benefit Review Board to reject his claim for housing benefit. The board had concluded that K was caught by the Housing Benefit (General) Regulations 1987 Reg.7(1), which provided that a person residing with a close relative to whom he was liable to make payments would be ineligible for housing benefit. Declaring himself to be bound by the decision in *Thamesdown BC v. Goonery* (Unreported, February 13, 1995), [1995] C.L.Y. 2600, the judge had found that the issue of residence was to be determined solely by reference to Reg.3(4), which provided that a person resided with another only if the two of them shared "accommodation except a bathroom, a lavatory or a communal area". K argued that (1) while a finding that a person resided with another entailed the requirements of Reg.3(4) being met, Reg.3(4) was not determinative of that question, and (2) the judge need not have followed *Goonery* since the ratio decidendi of that case had been assumed to be correct without the benefit of argument.

Held, allowing the appeal, that (1) a proposition of law which had not been the subject of argument before the court or consideration by it, and which had been assumed by the court to be correct, did not bind subsequent courts, *Baker v. Queen, The* [1975] A.C. 774, [1975] C.L.Y. 220, *National Enterprises Ltd v. Racal Communications Ltd* [1975] Ch. 397, [1975] C.L.Y. 105, *Barrs v. Bethell* [1982] Ch. 294, [1981] C.L.Y. 1626 and *Hetherington (Deceased), Re* [1990] Ch. 1, [1989] C.L.Y. 262 considered. It appeared that the court in *Goonery* had incorrectly assumed that Reg.3(4) was determinative in deciding the issue of residence. Accordingly, the judge need not have followed that decision, and (2) the question of residence was not to be determined solely by reference to

Reg.3(4) and the words "reside with" were to be given their natural and obvious meaning, *Goonery* not followed.

R. (ON THE APPLICATION OF KADHIM) v. BRENT LBC HOUSING BENEFIT REVIEW BOARD; *sub nom.* KADHIM v. BRENT LBC HOUSING BENEFIT BOARD; R. (ON THE APPLICATION OF KHADIM) v. BRENT LBC HOUSING BENEFIT REVIEW BOARD; R. v. BRENT LBC HOUSING BENEFIT REVIEW BOARD, *ex p.* KHADIM; R. v. BRENT LBC HOUSING BENEFIT REVIEW BOARD, *ex p.* KADHIM [2001] Q.B. 955, Buxton, L.J., CA.

5022. Housing benefit – ill health – restriction of benefit to tenant with AIDS – power to set aside decision of Housing Benefit Review Board

[Housing Benefit (General) Regulations 1987 (SI 1987 1971) Reg.86(1)(c).]

W, who was suffering from an AIDS related virus appealed against the dismissal of his application for judicial review, in which he had sought to reverse the decision of the clerk to a Housing Review Board. W had claimed housing benefit in respect of a two bedroom flat, which he occupied alone after his joint tenant moved out. Following a substantial rent increase on the property, the Benefits Division decided to restrict the amount of housing benefit payable to W, and he appealed to the Housing Benefit Review Board, which upheld the decision of the Benefits Division on the basis that the rent was unreasonably high in comparison with other properties in the area. W requested the Review Board to set aside its decision, but the clerk refused, concluding that there was no justification for a review. W sought to challenge that decision by judicial review, contending that (1) the Review Board had not adequately considered either the reasonableness of expecting W to move, in view of his medical condition, nor his submissions of landlords' prejudice against victims of HIV and AIDS related illnesses, and (2) that the Housing Benefit (General) Regulations 1987 Reg.86(1)(c) should be interpreted widely, so as to enable a decision of the Review Board to be set aside whenever the interests of justice so required.

Held, dismissing the appeal, that (1) the court had no power to adjudicate on issues of fact, and the Board's decision that W was fit to move for the purposes of the Regulations was an issue of fact and would not be overturned, unless irrational, and (2) Reg.86(1)(c) did not have the wide application argued for by N. Although there could be no definitive guidance as to all of the circumstances in which a decision of the Review Board could be set aside, it was likely to be confined to procedural mishaps, or cases where a decision had been undermined by supervening events.

R. v. CAMDEN LBC HOUSING BENEFIT REVIEW BOARD, *ex p.* W (2000) 32 H.L.R. 879, Kennedy, L.J., CA.

5023. Housing benefit – local authority housing – right to buy – use of trust deed to improve housing benefit claim

[Housing Benefit (General) Regulations 1987 (SI 1987 1971) Reg.43 para.1.]

J and her late husband were secure tenants of a council house valued at £25,000 and became entitled under the right to buy provisions to purchase it for £10,000. They could not raise this amount themselves, so their son agreed to raise the purchase money provided that it was secured. The property was conveyed to J subject to a trust deed executed on the same date, which provided that the house was to be held on trust for their son and daughter in law and which gave a licence to J and her husband to live there for life, or until they wished to move. Subsequently, J's husband became ill and they moved into a ground floor council flat. Following her husband's death, J remained in the flat and the son moved into the house. Some two years later, J applied for housing benefit for the flat and was refused on the ground that a significant reason for the trust deed had been to improve her position to claim housing benefit. The disbursement of capital was therefore to be ignored pursuant to the Housing Benefit (General) Regulations 1987 Reg.43 para.1, with the effect that J was not eligible for the benefit. J applied for judicial review of the decision of the Housing Benefit Review Board, claiming that her husband had become ill only after the transfer of the property and it was on the advice of a doctor that they had moved.

Held, allowing the application, that there could be no dispute that the execution of the trust deed in preference to the granting of a charge had established an element of gift because the son would be able to realise the full value of the house, but it was the purpose of the gift that was in question. It was necessary to show that the deed was intended to reduce J's capital in order to assist a claim for housing benefit. The Board had accepted the unsupported evidence of the local authority that J knew that a move was inevitable before the purchase of the property. The Board also appeared to have ignored contemporary evidence from the conveyancing solicitor to the effect that a trust deed was chosen to protect the son and make sure that the property became his in any event. In addition, it did not appear to have considered the period of over two years before J left the house and made the claim for benefit. It was also unsatisfactory that a delay of over three months took place between the hearing and the decision and that the key findings of fact were not stated in it. Although courts are usually reluctant to examine the merits of an application for judicial review, two reasons led to the court to do so in the instant case. Firstly, as J was legally aided, there was a danger that the Law Society would have first claim on any housing benefit if she was not awarded costs, and, secondly, the merits had been examined in the judge's pre-reading, which had saved court time, but led him to consider the merits in his judgment.

R. v. CAERPHILLY CBC HOUSING BENEFIT REVIEW BOARD, *ex p.* JONES (2000) 32 H.L.R. 82, Jowitt, J., QBD.

5024. Housing benefit – overpayment – restitution – demand for repayment – procedural failure by local authority

[Housing Benefit (General) Regulations 1987 (SI 1987 1971) Reg.77(1).]

A landlord, S, appealed against the dismissal of his counterclaim following an overpayment of housing benefit by NCC. S received housing benefit directly in respect of his tenant and had received a demand from NCC to repay housing benefit which had been overpaid at a time when the tenant had already vacated the property. S voluntarily paid part of the sum demanded, contending that he should not be liable to pay the whole amount since he had not been aware that the tenant had left the property. He conceded that he was liable for the period after which he became aware of the tenant's departure. NCC did not accept that arrangement and sued S for the whole amount. S issued a counterclaim for reimbursement of the amount he had voluntarily paid, contending that he was not in fact liable for that amount since the local authority had failed to comply with the requirements for notification as provided for in the Housing Benefit (General) Regulations 1987 reg.77(1) and that owing to that failure NCC could not sustain an action for recovery in the county court. S was successful at first instance but an appeal by NCC was subsequently allowed. S appealed, relying on the principle of restitution outlined in *Woolwich Building Society (formerly Woolwich Equitable Building Society) v. Inland Revenue Commissioners* [1993] A.C. 70, [1992] C.L.Y. 2508, to contend that he was entitled as of right to recover the amount paid pursuant to an ultra vires demand. NCC cross appealed, arguing that S had never been entitled to housing benefit in respect of the period in question and he was precluded from recovering that amount merely because NCC had failed to follow a particular procedure. There was no question of NCC being unjustly enriched by S's payment and thus he should not be able to recover the payment.

Held, dismissing the appeal, that there had been no demand backed by coercive power of the state putting the citizen at a disadvantage, in the way that a demand for tax would have operated, as the demand was in any event unenforceable, *Woolwich* distinguished. Restitution was not available in such circumstances merely on the basis that if S had not repaid the money NCC would have been unable to recover it.

NORWICH CITY COUNCIL v. STRINGER (2001) 33 H.L.R. 15, Buxton, L.J., CA.

5025. Housing benefit – overpayment of benefits – notice of recovery of benefits – procedural requirements

[Housing Benefit (General) Regulations 1987 (SI 1987 1971) Sch.6, s.79.]

TDC maintained a policy of invoicing accommodation providers where an overpayment of housing benefit had occurred and then setting off the sums due against benefit otherwise payable. After receiving multiple invoices following reassessment of individual entitlements, a hotel chain, WCH, brought proceedings for judicial review challenging the lawfulness of the procedure. WCH contended that (1) in each case the notice issued by TDC giving details of its determination to recover an overpayment, had been invalid since there had been no statement of the recipient's right to request a statement of reasons or information as to why an overpayment had occurred, as prescribed by the Housing Benefit (General) Regulations 1987 Sch.6 para.2 and Sch.6 para.14(1)(b); (2) TDC had unlawfully fettered its discretion in making the decision to recoup in the case of each and every tenant, and (3) a refusal to refer to a review board WCH's objections to the individual determinations, had been unlawful.

Held, granting the application, that (1) TDC had failed to comply with Sch.6 para.2 and Sch.6 para.14(1)(b) of the Regulations, resulting in significant prejudice to WCH; (2) TDC had not fettered the exercise of its discretion to recover overpayments either as a matter of policy or in the application of the policy, and (3) although there had been 56 instances in which TDC had sought to recover overpayments from WCH, only nine cases were the subject of the application before the court and in none of those cases had WCH sought to exercise its right to demand a review under s.79 of the Regulations.

R. v. THANET DC, *ex p.* WARREN COURT HOTELS LTD (2001) 33 H.L.R. 32, Jackson, J., QBD.

5026. Housing benefit – permitted totals

HOUSING BENEFIT (PERMITTED TOTALS) (AMENDMENT) ORDER 2001, SI 2001 1129; made under the Social Security Administration Act 1992 s.134, s.189. In force: April 1, 2001; £3.00.

This Order, which amends the Housing Benefit (Permitted Totals) Order 1996 (SI 1996 677), limits the amount by which housing benefit may be increased on the exercise of the discretion provided by the Housing Benefit (General) Regulations 1987 (SI 1987 1971).

5027. Housing benefit – recovery of benefits

HOUSING BENEFIT (GENERAL) AMENDMENT (NO.2) REGULATIONS 2001, SI 2001 1190; made under the Social Security Administration Act 1992 s.75, s.189, s.191. In force: October 1, 2001; £1.50.

These Regulations, which amend the Housing Benefit (General) Regulations 1987 (SI 1987 1971) in consequence of the coming into force of the Child Support, Pensions and Social Security Act 2000 s.71, prescribe circumstances when overpaid housing benefit need not be recovered from the person to whom such benefit was paid and prescribe persons from whom such benefit may be recovered in addition to, or instead of, the person to whom it was paid.

5028. Housing benefit – religious groups – communal occupation – payment of rent made from common fund – entitlement

[Housing Benefit (General) Regulations 1987 (SI 1987 1971) Reg.10(1)(b).]

M appealed against a decision that S, an elder in the Jesus Fellowship Church, who lived communally in a property owned by the Jesus Fellowship Community Trust could claim housing benefit on behalf of himself and the other residents. Under the terms of a written agreement, the elders, as licensees, were responsible for and liable to pay rent to the Trust by means of contributions from themselves and other residents. A further clause stipulated that elders and residents were obliged to contribute to a common fund. M contended that the Housing Benefit (General) Regulations 1987 Reg.10(1)(b) did not apply to S as his responsibility to pay rent on behalf of all members was an administrative responsibility in his capacity as an elder, but that his obligation to pay to the common fund was a payment in respect of a licence for which housing benefit was claimable. S contended that his liability to pay to the Trust was a legal liability in respect of the whole dwelling

Held, dismissing the appeal, that the payments made by the elders to the Trust were in respect of a licence to occupy the communal property and so S was entitled to claim housing benefit for the whole of the sum payable to the Trust in respect of all the residents' occupation. Further, the payments to the Trust had to be met irrespective of whether the other residents met their own individual payments, *R. v. Sheffield Housing Benefit Review Board, ex p. Smith* (1996) 28 H.L.R. 36, [1995] C.L.Y. 2597 considered.

R. (ON THE APPLICATION OF SAXBY) v. MILTON KEYNES HOUSING BENEFIT REVIEW BOARD; *sub nom.* R. v. MILTON KEYNES HOUSING BENEFIT REVIEW BOARD, *ex p.* SAXBY, [2001] EWCA Civ 456, (2001) 33 H.L.R. 82, Hale, L.J., CA.

5029. Housing benefit – rent – local reference rent – meaning of "locality"

[Rent Officers (Housing Benefit Functions) Order 1997 (SI 1997 1984) Sch.1 Part 1 para.4.]

S, an assured shorthold tenant, appealed against a decision ([2001] EWHC Admin 65) refusing her application for judicial review of a rent officer's determination, pursuant to the Rent Officers (Housing Benefit Functions) Order 1997 Sch.1 Part 1 para.4, of the local reference rent and her consequent entitlement to housing benefit. S contended that the rent officer had determined the local reference rent by having regard to too wide a geographical area which had adversely affected her entitlement to housing benefit. S submitted that the rent officer should have taken a more limited area as the basis for assessment.

Held, allowing the appeal, that the rent officer had ascertained the local reference rent by having regard to too wide an area. In determining the local reference rent, "locality" for the purposes of para.4(2)(a)(i) of the Order was an area no larger than was necessary to enable the relevant rent officer to properly arrive at the required judgments and calculations based on the character of the area in which the dwelling was situated. Selecting too wide an area would result in an unfairly high local reference rent applying in poorer areas which offended the purpose of the scheme, that being to ensure that those under-occupying property and not over-paying rent were not rendered homeless through an inability to pay.

R. (ON THE APPLICATION OF DINSDALE) v. RENT SERVICE; R. (ON THE APPLICATION OF WILSON) v. RENT SERVICE; R. (ON THE APPLICATION OF SHAW) v. RENT SERVICE; R. (ON THE APPLICATION OF SAADAT) v. RENT SERVICE, [2001] EWCA Civ 1559, *The Times*, November 6, 2001, Sedley, L.J., CA.

5030. Incapacity benefit – allowances

SOCIAL SECURITY (INCAPACITY) (MISCELLANEOUS AMENDMENTS) REGULATIONS 2001, SI 2001 2979; made under the Social Security Contributions and Benefits Act 1992 s.30E, s.122, s.171D, s.171G, s.175, Sch.3 para.2, Sch.7 para.2. In force: October 1, 2001; £1.75.

These Regulations amend the Social Security (General Benefit) Regulations 1982 (SI 1982 1408), the Social Security (Incapacity Benefit) Regulations 1994 (SI 1994 2946) and the Social Security (Incapacity for Work) (General) Regulations 1995 (SI 1995 311) to raise the earnings limit which applies to industrial injuries unemployability supplement from £3,146 to £3,432. The Regulations also raise from £60.50 to £66.00 per week the earnings limit for exempt work, generally known as the "therapeutic earnings limit", which applies to incapacity for work.

5031. Incapacity benefit – allowances

SOCIAL SECURITY (INCAPACITY BENEFIT) AMENDMENT REGULATIONS 2001, SI 2001 1305; made under the Social Security Contributions and Benefits Act 1992 s.30A, s.122, s.175, Sch.3 para.2. In force: April 25, 2001; £1.50.

These Regulations, which amend the Social Security (Incapacity Benefit) Regulations 1994 (SI 1994 2946), clarify the position relating to the relaxation of the first contribution condition for incapacity benefit, and the circumstances where a person may be entitled to incapacity benefit when he is aged between 20 and 25, or where he has previously been so entitled.

5032. Income – capital – assessment

NATIONAL ASSISTANCE (ASSESSMENT OF RESOURCES) (AMENDMENT) (ENGLAND) REGULATIONS 2001, SI 2001 58; made under the National Assistance Act 1948 s.22. In force: February 1, 2001; £1.50.

These Regulations make further amendments to the National Assistance (Assessment of Resources) Regulations 1992 (SI 1992 2977), which concern the assessment of the ability of a person to pay for accommodation arranged by local authorities under the National Assistance Act 1948 Part III, so that, for the purpose of calculating a resident's capital, any ex-gratia payment of £10,000 made on or after February 1, 2001 by the Secretary of State in consequence of a person's imprisonment or internment by the Japanese during the Second World War shall be disregarded as capital.

5033. Income – capital – assessment

NATIONAL ASSISTANCE (ASSESSMENT OF RESOURCES) (AMENDMENT) (NO.2) (ENGLAND) REGULATIONS 2001, SI 2001 1066; made under the National Assistance Act 1948 s.22. In force: April 9, 2001; £1.75.

These Regulations amend the National Assistance (Assessment of Resources) Regulations 1992 (SI 1992 2977) concerning the assessment of the ability of a person to pay for accommodation arranged by local authorities so that the capital limit set out in Reg.20 of the 1992 Regulations becomes £18,500. They also make amendments so that the capital limits set out in Reg.28 become £11,500 and £18,500. In addition, these Regulations make amendments so as to introduce a further category of capital to be disregarded under Sch.4 namely property which the resident would normally occupy as his only or main residence.

5034. Income – capital – assessment

NATIONAL ASSISTANCE (ASSESSMENT OF RESOURCES) (AMENDMENT) (NO.3) (ENGLAND) REGULATIONS 2001, SI 2001 1124; made under the National Assistance Act 1948 s.22. In force: April 12, 2001; £1.50.

These Regulations amend the National Assistance (Assessment of Resources) Regulations 1992 (SI 1992 2977) concerning the assessment of the ability of a person to pay for accommodation arranged by local authorities so as to disregard payments made under a trust established out of funds provided by the Secretary of State in respect of persons suffering from variant Creutzfeldt-Jakob disease.

5035. Income – capital – assessment – Wales

NATIONAL ASSISTANCE (ASSESSMENT OF RESOURCES) (AMENDMENT) (WALES) REGULATIONS 2001, SI 2001 276 (W.12); made under the National Assistance Act 1948 s.22. In force: February 1, 2001; £1.75.

These Regulations make further amendments to the National Assistance (Assessment of Resources) Regulations 1992 (SI 1992 2977), which concern the assessment of the ability of a person to pay for accommodation arranged by local authorities under the National Assistance Act 1948 Part III, so that, for the purpose of calculating a resident's capital, any ex-gratia payment of £10,000 made on or after February 1, 2001 by the Department of Social Security in consequence of a person's imprisonment or internment by the Japanese during the Second World War shall be disregarded as capital.

5036. Income – capital – assessment – Wales

NATIONAL ASSISTANCE (ASSESSMENT OF RESOURCES) (AMENDMENT NO.2) (WALES) REGULATIONS 2001, SI 2001 1409 (W.95); made under the National Assistance Act 1948 s.22. In force: Reg.2(6): April 12, 2001; remainder: April 9, 2001; £2.00.

These Regulations amend the National Assistance (Assessment of Resources) Regulations 1992 (SI 1992 2977) which concern the assessment of the ability of a person to pay for accommodation arranged by local authorities and provide that no resident shall be assessed as unable to pay for accommodation at the standard rate if that resident's capital exceeds £16,000. These Regulations make amendments by increasing the capital limit from £16,000 to £18,500. The principal Regulations also provide for the calculation of a resident's income to take account of capital treated as equivalent to income. These Regulations amend the upper and lower limits of such capital between which each complete £250 is treated as equivalent to a weekly income of £1. In addition, these Regulations introduce further categories of capital to be disregarded in the assessment of a resident's resources.

5037. Income related benefits – subsidy to authorities

INCOME-RELATED BENEFITS (SUBSIDY TO AUTHORITIES) AMENDMENT ORDER 2001, SI 2001 2350; made under the Social Security Administration Act 1992 s.140B, s.140F, s.189. In force: July 25, 2001; £3.50.

This Order amends the Income-related Benefits (Subsidy to Authorities) Order 1998 (SI 1998 562) to provide that the additional subsidy payable to Scottish Homes is not to exceed £773,042 and substitutes new schedules of figures to be used in calculating subsidy and thresholds for subsidy on rent allowances respectively.

5038. Income support – asylum seekers – effect of period of employment

[Social Security (Persons From Abroad) Miscellaneous Amendments Regulations 1996 (SI 1996 30) Reg.12.]

Y, an asylum seeker who had arrived in the United Kingdom in 1994, appealed against a decision of the Social Security Commissioner that he had lost his entitlement to income support by virtue of having secured employment for a period of three weeks in 1998. The Commissioner had held that the Social Security (Persons From Abroad) Miscellaneous Amendments Regulations 1996 Reg.12, which contained transitional provisions providing for an asylum seeker already in receipt of income support to retain his entitlement to that benefit until the next decision on his asylum claim, only applied to claims that were in existence as at February 5, 1996, and that the purpose of the Regulation was to bring to an end at the earliest possible opportunity rights existing on February 4, 1996.

Held, allowing the appeal, that Reg.12, properly construed, entitled an asylum seeker to renew a claim for income support following a period of employment. Had the Secretary of State really intended to introduce the policy adopted by the Commissioner, very clear words to that effect would have to have been used.

YILDIZ v. SECRETARY OF STATE FOR SOCIAL SECURITY *The Independent*, March 9, 2001, Henry, L.J., CA.

5039. Income support – definitions – students

INCOME SUPPORT (GENERAL) AMENDMENT REGULATIONS 2001, SI 2001 721; made under the Social Security Contributions and Benefits Act 1992 s.123, s.136, s.137, s.175. In force: March 29, 2001; £1.50.

These Regulations amend the Income Support (General Regulations) 1987 (SI 1987 1967) so as to change certain references in those Regulations to "full-time students" to references to "students".

5040. Income support – employees – special needs assistant – benefit entitlement during school holidays

[Income Support (General) Regulations 1987 (SI 1987 1967) Part II Reg.5(2)(b)(i), Reg.5(3B).]

B, a special needs assistant employed by a junior school, appealed against a decision ([2000] 1 All E.R. 686, [1999] C.L.Y. 4562) to allow an appeal by the Chief Adjudication Officer against a ruling that he was entitled to claim income support and job seeker's allowance during the school holidays. B was paid solely for the work that he carried out in term time, which amounted to 20 hours per week. He did not work during school holidays. B had lodged a claim, initially for income support and latterly for job seekers allowance, in respect of the school holidays.

Held, dismissing the appeal (Lord Scott and Lord Cooke dissenting), that since B's hours of work fluctuated, the Income Support (General) Regulations 1987 Part II Reg.5(2)(b)(i) applied and it was accordingly necessary to calculate B's average hours of work. B's recognisable cycle of work was one year at school and since he was not obliged to work during the school holidays those periods were to be ignored when calculating his average weekly hours by virtue of Reg.5(3B). On that basis, B's weekly average exceeded the 16 hour cut off point for benefit eligibility. The fact that he had made a claim for benefits in relation to a week in which no work had been done made no difference to his position. The same result under the Regulations would have accrued if the claim had been made in relation to a week in which he had been working. Lord Scott observed that as a result of the decision B, and others in a similar position to him, would be earning an income below the poverty level. Accordingly, it was necessary for the Secretary of State to remedy such a situation by introducing new legislation as soon as possible.

STAFFORD v. CHIEF ADJUDICATION OFFICER; BANKS v. CHIEF ADJUDICATION OFFICER; *sub nom.* CHIEF ADJUDICATION OFFICER v. STAFFORD, [2001] UKHL 33, [2001] 1 W.L.R. 1411, Lord Slynn of Hadley, HL.

5041. Income support – jobseekers allowance – entitlement – housing costs

INCOME SUPPORT (GENERAL) AND JOBSEEKER'S ALLOWANCE AMENDMENT REGULATIONS 2001, SI 2001 3651; made under the Social Security Contributions and Benefits Act 1992 s.123, s.135, s.137, s.175; and the Jobseekers Act 1995 s.4, s.35, s.36. In force: December 10, 2001; £1.50.

These Regulations amend the Income Support (General) Regulations 1987 (SI 1987 1967) and the Jobseeker's Allowance Regulations 1996 (SI 1996 207) so as to amend the formula for the calculation of the weekly amount of a person's housing costs to take account of the abolition of mortgage interest payable under deduction of tax.

5042. Income support – jobseekers allowance – entitlement – persons in residential care and nursing homes

INCOME SUPPORT AND JOBSEEKER'S ALLOWANCE (AMOUNTS FOR PERSONS IN RESIDENTIAL CARE AND NURSING HOMES) REGULATIONS 2001, SI 2001 1785; made under the Social Security Contributions and Benefits Act 1992 s.123, s.135, s.137, s.175; and the Jobseekers Act 1995 s.4, s.35, s.36. In force: July 2, 2001; £1.75.

These Regulations amend the Income Support (General) Regulations 1987 (SI 1987 1967) and the Jobseeker's Allowance Regulations 1996 (SI 1996 207) by increasing the applicable amounts in those benefits in respect of those in residential care and nursing homes.

5043. Income support – loans – interest rate

INCOME SUPPORT (GENERAL) (STANDARD INTEREST RATE AMENDMENT) REGULATIONS 2001, SI 2001 1831; made under the Social Security Contributions and Benefits Act 1992 s.123, s.135, s.137, s.175. In force: June 17, 2001; £1.50.

These Regulations amend the Income Support (General) Regulations 1987 (SI 1987 1967) and the Social Security (Claims and Payments) Regulations 1987 (SI 1987 1968) by lowering the standard rate of interest applicable to a loan which qualifies for income support to 6.94 per cent. In addition, the Regulations revoke the Income Support (General) (Standard Interest Rate Amendment) (No.2) Regulations 2000 (SI 2000 1402).

5044. Income support – loans – interest rate

INCOME SUPPORT (GENERAL) (STANDARD INTEREST RATE AMENDMENT) (NO.2) REGULATIONS 2001, SI 2001 2676; made under the Social Security Contributions and Benefits Act 1992 s.123, s.135, s.137, s.175. In force: August 19, 2001; £1.50.

These Regulations amend the Income Support (General) Regulations 1987 (SI 1987 1967) with respect to the standard rate of interest applicable to a loan which qualifies for income support. The new rate is 6.65 per cent. In addition, these Regulations revoke the Income Support (General) (Standard Interest Rate Amendment) Regulations 2001 (SI 2001 1831). The Income Support (General) (Standard Interest Rate Amendment) Regulations 2001 (SI 2001 1831) are revoked.

5045. Income support – loans – interest rate

INCOME SUPPORT (GENERAL) (STANDARD INTEREST RATE AMENDMENT) (NO.3) REGULATIONS 2001, SI 2001 3721; made under the Social Security Contributions and Benefits Act 1992 s.123, s.135, s.137, s.175. In force: December 16, 2001; £1.50.

These Regulations, which revoke with savings the Income Support (General) (Standard Interest Rate Amendment) (No.2) Regulations 2001 (SI 2001 2676), amend the Income Support (General) Regulations 1987 (SI 1987 1967) with respect to the standard rate of interest applicable to a loan which qualifies for income support. The new rate is set at 6.19 per cent.

5046. Income support – mortgages – interest payments – move to larger property

[Income Support (General) Regulations 1987 Sch.3 para.5A(9)(b).]

S appealed against the dismissal by a Social Security Commissioner of his appeal against the Secretary of State's decision not to take into account, for the purposes of his income support calculation, the full amount of his increased mortgage interest payments. S had eight children, four boys and four girls, and had purchased a larger property in order to accommodate them, thereby increasing his mortgage. However, each property had three bedrooms and the Commissioner held that the Social Security Appeal Tribunal had been right to find that S had not moved "solely by reason of the need to provide separate sleeping accommodation for children of different sexes aged 10 or over" as set out in the Income Support (General) Regulations 1987 Sch.3 para.5A(9)(b). S argued that the Commissioner had erred in giving that provision a subjective construction, or, alternatively, that the provision was ultra vires for irrationality or because it did not comply with the enabling statute.

Held, dismissing the appeal, that the Commissioner had been right to hold that the correct test was to ask what was the "operative reason" for the move according to the circumstances of the case. In the instant case, the reason for the move had been to provide more roomy accommodation generally, rather than to provide separate sleeping accommodation for the children. The provision was not irrational as there would undoubtedly be cases in which it would apply. The argument that it did not comply with the enabling statute amounted to an argument that Parliament had been misled, which was not sustainable.

SALEEM v. SECRETARY OF STATE FOR SOCIAL SECURITY [2001] EWCA Civ 69, Cresswell, J., CA.

5047. Income support – structured settlements – annuities – capital treated as income – role of Court of Protection receiver

[Social Security Contributions and Benefits Act 1992 s.124(1)(b); Income Support (General) Regulations 1987 (SI 1987 459) Reg.41(2).]

B, a child patient who had been awarded damages in excess of £1.5 million following a road traffic accident as a result of which he had been rendered quadriplegic, appealed against a decision that he was not entitled to income support. B's damages were administered by means of a structured settlement and the Social Security Commissioner had found that payments falling to be treated as income from that settlement exceeded the applicable amount for the purposes of the Social Security Contributions and Benefits Act 1992 s.124(1)(b) and the Income Support (General) Regulations 1987 Reg.41(2). B contended for a broad view of the effect of the settlement, submitting that it was under the supervision of the Court of Protection; hence payments should be treated as being made to the receiver, with the result that they came within the scope of Reg.42(4)(a)(ii).

Held, dismissing the appeal, that the present arrangement was a typical example of an annuity and payments received under an annuity came within the category of capital treated as income under Reg.41(2). The payments were made for the benefit of B and the continuing role of the Court of Protection was immaterial as far as the operation of Reg.41 was concerned.

B (A CHILD) v. SECRETARY OF STATE FOR SOCIAL SECURITY, [2001] EWCA Civ 498, [2001] 1 W.L.R. 1404, Pill, L.J., CA.

5048. Industrial injuries – compensation – adjustments to lower rate of incapacity allowance

WORKMEN'S COMPENSATION (SUPPLEMENTATION) (AMENDMENT) SCHEME 2001, SI 2001 1001; made under the Social Security Contributions and Benefits Act 1992 Sch.8 para.2; and the Social Security Administration Act 1992 Sch.9 para.1. In force: April 11, 2001; £1.75.

This Scheme amends the Workmen's Compensation (Supplementation) Scheme 1982 (SI 1982 1489) by making adjustments to the rate of lesser incapacity allowance consequential upon the increase in the maximum rate of that allowance made by the Social Security Benefits Up-rating (No.2) Order 2000 (SI 2000 207).

5049. Industrial injuries – compensation – payment of claims

PNEUMOCONIOSIS ETC. (WORKERS' COMPENSATION) (PAYMENT OF CLAIMS) (AMENDMENT) REGULATIONS 2001, SI 2001 3525; made under the Pneumoconiosis etc. (Workers' Compensation) Act 1979 s.1, s.7. In force: December 1, 2001; £2.00.

Under the Pneumoconiosis etc. (Workers' Compensation) Act 1979, lump sum payments may be made to certain persons disabled by a disease to which the Act applies, or to dependants of persons who were so disabled immediately before they died. These Regulations amend the Pneumoconiosis etc. (Workers' Compensation) (Payment of Claims) Regulations 1988 (SI 1998 668) so as to increase the amount payable under the Act. The increase in each case is 3.8 per cent. The diseases to which the Act applies are pneumoconiosis, byssinosis, diffuse mesothelioma, primary carcinoma of the lung and diffuse pleural thickening.

5050. Industrial injuries – dependants – permitted earnings limits

SOCIAL SECURITY (INDUSTRIAL INJURIES) (DEPENDENCY) (PERMITTED EARNINGS LIMITS) ORDER 2001, SI 2001 911; made under the Social Security Contributions and Benefits Act 1992 s.175, Sch.7 para.4. In force: April 9, 2001; £1.50.

Where a disablement pension with unemployability supplement is increased in respect of a child or children, and the beneficiary is one of two persons who are spouses residing together or an unmarried couple, the Social Security Contributions and Benefits Act 1992 Sch.7 para.4 is amended to provide that the increase shall not be payable in respect of the first child if the other person's earnings are £145 a week or more and in respect of a further child for each complete £19 by which the earnings exceed £145. This Order revokes the Social Security (Industrial Injuries) (Dependency) (Permitted Earnings Limits) Order 1999 (SI 1999 529).

5051. Industrial injuries disablement benefit – industrial diseases – hand held vibrating tools

[Social Security (Industrial Injuries) (Prescribed Diseases) Regulations 1985 (SI 1985 967) Sch.1 Part I A12.]

J appealed against the refusal of her application for industrial injuries benefit after developing carpal tunnel syndrome whilst employed as a machinist. As part of her job, J used an industrial sewing machine which vibrated, together with wire cutters and scissors which were so heavy that they had to be used in situ on the machine with the consequence that they too vibrated. It was submitted that the Commissioner had erred in finding that J's employment did not involve the "use of hand held vibrating tools" for the purposes of the Social Security (Industrial Injuries) (Prescribed Diseases) Regulations 1985 Sch.1 Part I A12.

Held, allowing the appeal, that since the source of the vibration was not essential where a hand held tool that vibrated was used, the "use of hand held vibrating tools" incorporated the use of a hand held tool that did not itself vibrate but was used whilst resting on a machine which, due to its own vibration, caused the tool to vibrate. It followed that J was entitled to industrial injuries benefit.

JANICKI v. SECRETARY OF STATE FOR SOCIAL SECURITY; *sub nom.* JANICKI v. SECRETARY OF STATE FOR THE HOME DEPARTMENT [2001] I.C.R. 1220, Jacob, J., CA.

5052. Invalid care allowance – gainful employment

SOCIAL SECURITY (INVALID CARE ALLOWANCE) AMENDMENT REGULATIONS 2001, SI 2001 538; made under the Social Security Contributions and Benefits Act 1992 s.70. In force: April 6, 2001; £1.50.

These Regulations amend the Social Security (Invalid Care Allowance) Regulations 1976 (SI 1976 409). Under s.70 of the Social Security Contributions and Benefits Act 1992, a person is entitled to an invalid care allowance for any day on which he is engaged in caring for a severely disabled person if, among other things, he is not gainfully employed. These Regulations amend Reg.8, which provides that a person is not to be treated as gainfully employed on any day in a week unless his earnings in the immediately preceding week have exceeded a specified sum, by replacing that specified sum with an amount to be ascertained by reference to the lower earnings limit.

5053. Invalidity benefits – residence – former frontier worker precluded from claiming child and maternity benefits – European Union

[EC Treaty Art.48 (now, after amendment, Art.39 EC) Council Regulation 1408/71 on the application of social security schemes to employed persons and their families moving within the Community; Council Regulation 1612/68 on freedom of movement for workers within the Community Art.7.]

GL and DL, a married couple who were nationals of and resident in Belgium, appealed against a refusal by C, the Luxembourg family benefits fund, to pay maternity, childbirth and child raising allowances in respect of their son, born in 1995, on the basis that they were not resident in Luxembourg. GL had been employed in Luxembourg until 1981, when he was awarded an invalidity pension following an industrial accident. GL was liable to pay Luxembourg compulsory sickness insurance on his pension payments. The appeal to the Social Insurance Arbitration Board was unsuccessful and L appealed to the Appeals Board, which stayed the proceedings and referred the matter to the ECJ for a preliminary ruling as to (1) the validity of Council Regulation 1408/71 Art.4 which permitted a residence condition to be imposed in respect of childbirth and maternity allowances; (2) whether the child raising allowance was a family allowance payable to pensioners under Regulation 1408/71 Art.71, irrespective of their state of residence; (3) whether a person in receipt of invalidity pension could claim family allowances other than those referred to in Art.77 of Regulation 1408/71 and (4) whether a person in receipt of an invalidity pension residing in a Member State other than the State paying the pension had the rights of a worker under Council Regulation 1612/68 Art.7.

Held, giving a preliminary ruling that (1) the residence requirements for the grant of antenatal and childbirth allowances were valid under Regulation 1408/71 Art.1 (u) (i) and Annex II as other conditions also applied to them. However, the maternity allowance was payable solely on condition of Luxembourg residence and it was not a special allowance covered by the derogation in Regulation 1408/71 Art.4(1); (2) the child raising allowance was not a family allowance in terms of Regulation 1408/71 Art.77, as these were periodical payments dependent on the number and age of persons in a family, whereas child raising allowance was intended to make up for lost income when a parent was primarily engaged in raising children under two and was not payable to pensioners irrespective of their Member State of residence under Regulation 1408/71 Art.77; (3) the fact that a pension was subject to compulsory insurance scheme deductions did not mean that its recipient was employed or self employed in terms of Art.73, and (4) in the context of EC Treaty Art.48 (now, after amendment, Art.39 EC), a person was no longer a worker once their employment ceased. When a former worker ceased to pursue an occupation he could retain an entitlement to advantages due to that employment, however this did not mean that a person in receipt of invalidity pension retained the status of a worker in terms of Regulation 1612/68 Art.7. Any rights attached to their former status remained due to their previous professional activities.

LECLERE v. CAISSE NATIONALE DES PRESTATIONS FAMILIALES (C43/99) [2001] 2 C.M.L.R. 49, GC Rodriguez Iglesias (President), ECJ.

5054. **Jobseekers allowance – child benefit – linking of additional amount of jobseekers allowance with entitlement to child benefit – possible discrimination**

[Jobseeker's Allowance Regulations 1996 (SI 1996 207) Reg.77, Reg.83(b); Council Regulation 79/7 on the progressive implementation of the principle of equal treatment for men and women in matters of social security Art.3.]

H appealed against a decision of the Social Security Commissioner, upholding an initial decision of an adjudication officer, that whilst he was entitled to income based jobseeker's allowance, he was not so entitled to an additional amount in respect of his children. H, who was estranged from his wife, had two children, the subject of a joint residence order, who resided with their mother and H for different but approximately equal parts of the week. The adjudication officer had found that, applying the Jobseeker's Allowance Regulations 1996 Reg.77 and Reg.83(b), H's entitlement to the allowance should not include the additional amount because of the fact that the mother was a recipient of child benefit. On appeal, H contended that the way in which the statutory provisions for calculating the amount of jobseeker's allowance was linked to child benefit, favoured mothers over fathers and therefore contravened Council Directive 79/7 which was intended to implement the principle of equal treatment for men and women in matters of social security.

Held, allowing the appeal, that income-based jobseeker's allowance was directly and effectively linked to the protection against risk of unemployment provided by Art.3 of the Directive. It was irrelevant that the allowance was means tested as was the fact that it incorporated many features of income support, those simply being features incorporated into a comprehensive statutory code which provided protection against unemployment. It could be discriminatory to connect entitlement to the additional amount of jobseeker's allowance with entitlement to child benefit, and the case would be remitted to a commissioner to look at the question of discrimination against the background of the facts.

HOCKENJOS v. SECRETARY OF STATE FOR SOCIAL SECURITY, [2001] EWCA Civ 624, [2001] 2 C.M.L.R. 51, Aldous, L.J., CA.

5055. Jobseekers allowance – detention – effect of detention in police custody

[Jobseeker's Allowance Regulations 1996 (SI 1996 207) Reg.13(3).]

The Secretary of State appealed against a decision of the Social Security Commissioner that D was not to be treated as unavailable for work for the purpose of his entitlement to jobseeker's allowance because he had been detained in police custody for a period of 42 hours. The Commissioner had concluded that D was entitled to rely on the Jobseeker's Allowance Regulations 1996 Reg.13(3), which provided that a person could "restrict his availability in any way provided the restrictions [were] reasonable in the light of his physical or mental condition".

Held, allowing the appeal, that the Commissioner had erred in concluding that D could rely on Reg.13(3). The words "physical or mental condition" were limited to an applicant's physical disability. Furthermore, Reg.13(3) required an applicant to specify in advance any restrictions on his future unavailability. The court observed that the Regulations failed to deal with unforeseen circumstances causing an applicant to be unavailable for work, and recommended that the Secretary of State should consider amending the jobseeker's allowance scheme so as to give adjudication officers a degree of discretion where such circumstances applied.

SECRETARY OF STATE FOR SOCIAL SECURITY v. DAVID *The Times*, January 30, 2001, Simon Brown, L.J., CA.

5056. Jobseekers allowance – pilot scheme – literacy skills training programme

SOCIAL SECURITY (LITERACY ETC. SKILLS TRAINING PILOT) REGULATIONS 2001, SI 2001 2710; made under the Jobseekers Act 1995 s.19, s.29, s.35, s.36. In force: September 17, 2001; £1.75.

These Regulations establish a pilot scheme relating to persons who claim a jobseeker's allowance and who fulfil specified criteria as to age, period over which they have been receiving benefit and the location of appropriate offices at which they are claiming benefit. They have the effect that if such a person without good cause refuses or fails to participate in the training programme known as literacy and numeracy skills training, or loses his place on such a programme due to misconduct, he will receive a sanction under the Jobseekers Act 1995 and the Jobseeker's Allowance Regulations 1996 (SI 1996 207). The effect of this will be a loss or reduction of his jobseeker's allowance for a period of two weeks or four weeks.

5057. Jobseekers allowance – training – funding

JOBSEEKER'S ALLOWANCE (AMENDMENT) REGULATIONS 2001, SI 2001 1434; made under the Jobseekers Act 1995 s.4, s.6, s.7, s.12, s.19, s.20, s.20A, s.20B, s.21, s.36, Sch.1 para.8A, Sch.1 para.14. In force: Reg.1: March 26, 2001; Reg.2(1)(3): March 26, 2001; Reg.2(2): April 1, 2001; £1.75.

These Regulations amend the Jobseeker's Allowance Regulations 1996 (SI 1996 207) to reflect the establishment of the Learning and Skills Council for England and the National Council for Education and Training for Wales by the Learning and Skills Act 2000. The amendments reflect that training is provided and funded by Councils, by substituting references to the Further Education and Funding Councils for both England and Wales and to a Training or Enterprise Council with references to the Councils.

5058. National insurance – contributions

SOCIAL SECURITY (CONTRIBUTIONS) (RE-RATING AND NATIONAL INSURANCE FUNDS PAYMENTS) ORDER 2001, SI 2001 477; made under the Social Security Administration Act 1992 s.141, s.142, s.143, s.144, s.189; the Social Security Administration (Northern Ireland) Act 1992 s.129, s.165; and the Social Security Act 1993 s.2. In force: April 6, 2001; £1.75.

This Order, which reduces the rate of secondary Class 1 contributions specified in the Social Security Contributions and Benefits Act 1992 s.9 from 12.2 per cent to 11.9 per cent, increases the amount of earnings below which an earner may be excepted from liability for Class 2 contributions from £3,825 to £3,955. It amends the lower and upper limits of profits or gains specified in s.15 and s.18 of the 1992 Act from £4,385 to £4,535 and from £27,820 to £29,900. In addition, it provides for s.2 of the Social Security Act 1993 to have effect for the tax year 2001 to 2002 and provides that the amount of any money that may be provided by Parliament to be paid into the National Insurance Fund in that year shall not exceed in aggregate two per cent of the estimated benefit expenditure for the financial year ending March 31, 2002.

5059. Reciprocity – agreements

SOCIAL SECURITY (RECIPROCAL AGREEMENTS) ORDER 2001, SI 2001 407; made under the Social Security Administration Act 1992 s.179. In force: April 9, 2001; £2.00.

This Order provides for social security legislation to be modified or adapted to take account of changes made by the Welfare Reform and Pensions Act 1999 which replaces widows benefit with bereavement benefit in relation to the National Insurance and Industrial Injuries (Reciprocal Agreement with Italy) Order 1953 (SI 1953 884), the National Insurance and Industrial Injuries (Luxembourg) Order 1955 (SI 1955 420), the National Insurance and Industrial Injuries (Netherlands) Order 1955 (SI 1955 874), the National Insurance and Industrial Injuries (Israel) Order 1957 (SI 1957 1879), the National Insurance and Industrial Injuries (France) Order 1958 (SI 1958 597), the Family Allowances, National Insurance and Industrial Injuries (Belgium) Order 1958 (SI 1958 771), the Family Allowances, National Insurance and Industrial Injuries (Yugoslavia) Order 1958 (SI 1958 1263), the Family Allowances, National Insurance and Industrial Injuries (Denmark) Order 1960 (SI 1960 211), the National Insurance and Industrial Injuries (Republic of Ireland) Order 1960 (SI 1960 707), the National Insurance and Industrial Injuries (Turkey) Order 1961 (SI 1961 584), the Family Allowances, National Insurance and Industrial Injuries (Germany) Order 1961 (SI 1961 1202), the National Insurance (Republic of Ireland) Order 1966 (SI 1966 270), the Family Allowances, National Insurance and Industrial Injuries (Switzerland) Order 1969 (SI 1969 384), the National Insurance and Industrial Injuries (Bermuda) Order 1969 (SI 1969 1686), the National Insurance (Republic of Ireland) Order 1971 (SI 1971 1742), the Family Allowances, National Insurance and Industrial Injuries (Spain) Order 1975 (SI 1975 415), the Social Security (Portugal) Order 1979 (SI 1979 921), the Social Security (Austria) Order 1981 (SI 1981 605), the Social Security (Mauritius) Order 1981 (SI 1981 1542), the Social Security (Cyprus) Order 1983 S (1983 1698), the Social Security (New Zealand) Order 1983 (SI 1983 1894), the Social Security (Finland) Order 1984 (SI 1984 125), the Social Security (United States of America) Order 1984 (SI 1984 1817), the Social Security (Iceland) Order

1985 (SI 1985 1202), the Social Security (Sweden) Order 1988 (SI 1988 590), the Social Security (Philippines) Order 1989 (SI 1989 2002), the Social Security (Norway) Order 1991 (SI 1991 767), the Social Security (Barbados) Order 1992 (SI 1992 812), the Social Security (Jersey and Guernsey) Order 1994 (SI 1994 2802), the Social Security (Canada) Order 1995 (SI 1995 2699), the Social Security (Malta) Order 1996 (SI 1996 1927), the Social Security (Jamaica) Order 1997 (SI 1997 871), and the Social Security (United States of America) Order 1997 (SI 1997 1778) which give effect to agreements made between the Governments of the United Kingdom and other countries providing for reciprocity in certain social security matters.

5060. Recovery of benefits – payment into court – refusal to allow amendment

[Social Security (Recovery of Benefits) Act 1997 s.6, s.8; Social Security (Recovery of Benefits) Regulations 1997 (SI 1997 2205) Reg.11.]

H, in an action brought against them by S for personal injuries to his back, appealed against the refusal to allow it to amend its notice of payment into court. S had pre-existing back problems and a medical report obtained by H attributed almost none of his back problems to the accident. The CRU certificate obtained by H four and a half years post accident certified past accident benefits of £40,124 as having been paid. H made the payment into court consisting of £6,000 plus £40,124 withheld under the Social Security (Recovery of Benefits) Act 1997 s.8, the gross compensation payment stated to be £46,124. S accepted the sum of £46,124 paid into court, the matter was stayed, S took the £6,000 out of court and H paid the £40,124 to the Secretary of State under s.6. Thereafter, both parties appealed against the certificate and a fresh certificate was issued certifying the sum as nil, and H was reimbursed the sums it had paid under the original certificate. S demanded this sum, and on H refusing to pay, applied to the court for an order that he be paid the £40,124. H cross applied for permission to amend the notice of payment in to delete any reference to the certified sum and thus retrospectively change the gross value of the payment in to £6,000. It was ordered that under the Social Security (Recovery of Benefits) Regulations 1997 Reg.11, H should pay the monies reimbursed to it by the Secretary of State to S, and H's application was dismissed. H appealed, contending that there could be no doubt as to what it intended by its payment in, that that intention been frustrated by the operation of Reg. 11, and that it would be unjust if, as a result, S should take advantage of an unexpected windfall.

Held, dismissing the appeal, that in order to achieve the object they were pursuing, H could either have identified the gross compensation payment as nil, or such lesser sum than £40,124 as they assessed; or it could have served a Calderbank letter making its intentions clear. As it was, H told S the gross compensation payment was £46,124 without reservation of any kind, and the result had been that S had received a windfall of between approximately £6,700 and £40,000, depending on what conclusions a court would have reached when assessing damages. The judge had applied the test that he should only grant H's application if the circumstances were exceptional, which meant that S had taken unfair advantage of H. The judge's findings that S could not be fixed with knowledge that the notice of payment in meant anything other than it appeared to, and that no exceptional circumstances therefore existed, could not be impugned.

HILTON INTERNATIONAL HOTELS (UK) LTD v. SMITH; *sub nom.* SMITH v. BASS PLC; SMITH v. HILTON INTERNATIONAL HOTELS (UK) LTD [2001] P.I.Q.R. P14, Pitchford, J., QBD.

5061. Residential accommodation – local authorities – additional payments

NATIONAL ASSISTANCE (RESIDENTIAL ACCOMMODATION) (ADDITIONAL PAYMENTS) (ENGLAND) REGULATIONS 2001, SI 2001 3068; made under the Health and Social Care Act 2001 s.54, s.64. In force: October 1, 2001; £1.50.

These Regulations make provision for additional payments to be made so that a person who has been assessed as needing residential accommodation can choose to live in accommodation more expensive than the local authority would usually pay for someone with that person's assessed needs. Under these Regulations the additional payments may be made by a third party, including a liable relative who is not making payments to maintain the resident. In certain circumstances, that is when the 12 weeks' property disregard applies or when a deferred payment agreement is in place, the resident himself may also contribute any or all of the additional payments.

5062. Residential accommodation – local authorities – additional payments and assessment of resources

NATIONAL ASSISTANCE (RESIDENTIAL ACCOMMODATION) (ADDITIONAL PAYMENTS AND ASSESSMENT OF RESOURCES) (AMENDMENT) (ENGLAND) REGULATIONS 2001, SI 2001 3441; made under the National Assistance Act 1948 s.22; and the Health and Social Care Act 2001 s.54, s.64. In force: October 24, 2001; £1.75.

These Regulations, which amend the National Assistance (Assessment of Resources) Regulations 1992 (SI 1992 2977) and revoke the National Assistance (Residential Accommodation) (Additional Payments) (England) Regulations 2001 (SI 2001 3068), make provision for additional payments to be made so that a person who has been assessed as needing residential accommodation can choose to live in accommodation which is more expensive than the local authority would usually pay for someone with that person's assessed needs. They provide that the additional payments may be made by a third party, including a liable relative who is not making payments to maintain the resident.

5063. Residential accommodation – local authorities – disregarding of resources

NATIONAL ASSISTANCE (RESIDENTIAL ACCOMMODATION) (DISREGARDING OF RESOURCES) (ENGLAND) REGULATIONS 2001, SI 2001 3067; made under the National Assistance Act 1948 s.21. In force: October 1, 2001; £1.50.

The Health and Social Care Act 2001 provides that regulations may specify certain of the person's resources, which the local authority shall disregard when deciding whether or not the person needs care and attention which is not otherwise available to him. These Regulations specify the resources which are to be disregarded for that purpose.

5064. Residential accommodation – local authorities – relevant contributions – deferred payments

NATIONAL ASSISTANCE (RESIDENTIAL ACCOMMODATION) (RELEVANT CONTRIBUTIONS) (ENGLAND) REGULATIONS 2001, SI 2001 3069; made under the Health and Social Care Act 2001 s.55. In force: October 1, 2001; £1.50.

The Health and Social Care Act 2001 makes provision for local authorities and residents in residential accommodation provided for or arranged by the local authority to enter into a deferred payment agreement. The agreement allows a resident to defer part of the payment which he is liable to pay to the local authority and in return the resident will allow the local authority to secure payment of the total amount of relevant contributions by granting the local authority a charge in their favour on his home. These Regulations set out how the relevant contributions are to be determined.

5065. Residential accommodation – sums for personal requirements – Wales

NATIONAL ASSISTANCE (SUMS FOR PERSONAL REQUIREMENTS) (WALES) REGULATIONS 2001, SI 2001 1408 (W.94); made under the National Assistance Act 1948 s.22. In force: April 9, 2001; £1.75.

These Regulations, which revoke the National Assistance (Sums for Personal Requirements) (Wales) Regulations 2000 (SI 2000 1145), set out the weekly sum which local authorities in Wales are to assume, in the absence of special circumstances, that residents in accommodation arranged under the National Assistance Act 1948 Part III will need for their personal requirements. From April 9, 2001 all such residents will be assumed to need £16.05 per week for their personal requirements.

5066. Social fund – cold weather payments – weather stations and postcode districts

SOCIAL FUND COLD WEATHER PAYMENTS (GENERAL) AMENDMENT REGULATIONS 2001, SI 2001 3368; made under the Social Security Contributions and Benefits Act 1992 s.138, s.175. In force: November 1, 2001; £1.75.

These Regulations amend the Social Fund Cold Weather Payments (General) Regulations 1988 (SI 1988 1724) in relation to the list of weather stations and applicable postcode districts to take account of an additional weather station and changes to postcodes.

5067. Social fund – winter fuel payments – increase

SOCIAL FUND WINTER FUEL PAYMENT (AMENDMENT) REGULATIONS 2001, SI 2001 3375; made under the Social Security Contributions and Benefits Act 1992 s.138, s.175. In force: November 2, 2001; £1.50.

These Regulations amend the Social Fund Winter Fuel Payment Regulations 2000 (SI 2000 729) by increasing the amount of the winter fuel payment and by making some clarificatory drafting amendments.

5068. Social Security Act 1998 (c.14) – Commencement No.13 Order

SOCIAL SECURITY ACT 1998 (COMMENCEMENT NO.13) ORDER 2001, SI 2001 2316 (C.78); made under the Social Security Act 1998 s.79, s.87. Commencement details: bringing into force various provisions of the Act on July 2, 2001; £2.00.

This Order provides for the coming into force on July 2, 2001, of further provisions of the Social Security Act 1998 in respect of repeals relating to Housing Benefit and Council Tax Benefit.

5069. Social Security Commissioners – unified appeals tribunals – procedure

SOCIAL SECURITY COMMISSIONERS (PROCEDURE) (AMENDMENT) REGULATIONS 2001, SI 2001 1095; made under the Forfeiture Act 1982 s.4; the Social Security Act 1998 s.14, s.15, s.16, s.28, s.79, s.84, Sch.4, Sch.5; and the Child Support, Pensions and Social Security Act 2000 Sch.7 para.8, para.9, para.10, para.19, para.20, para.23. In force: July 2, 2001; £1.75.

These Regulations amend the Social Security Commissioners (Procedure) Regulations 1999 (SI 1999 1495) in consequence of the Child Support, Pensions and Social Security Act 2000 Sch.7 which makes provision for appeals against decisions made in connection with claims for housing benefit and council tax benefit.

5070. Social Security Contributions (Share Options) Act 2001 (c.20)

This Act makes provision about the payment of National Insurance Contributions in respect of share options and similar rights obtained by persons as directors or employees during the period beginning April 6, 1999 and ending with May 19, 2000.

This Act received Royal Assent on May 11, 2001 and comes into force on May 11, 2001.

5071. Social Security Fraud Act 2001 (c.11)

This Act to makes provision, for the purposes of the law relating to social security, about the obtaining and disclosure of information; and to make provision for restricting the payment of social security benefits and war pensions in the case of persons convicted of offences relating to such benefits or pensions and about the institution of proceedings for such offences.

This Act received Royal Assent on May 11, 2001.

5072. Social Security Fraud Act 2001 (c.11) – Commencement No.1 Order

SOCIAL SECURITY FRAUD ACT 2001 (COMMENCEMENT NO.1) ORDER 2001, SI 2001 3251 (C.105); made under the Social Security Fraud Act 2001 s.20. Commencement details: bringing into force various provisions of the 2001 Act on September 26, 2001 and October 18, 2001; £1.50.

This Order provides for the coming into force of the Social Security Fraud Act 2001 s.16 which provides for offences in relation to the failure to notify a change of circumstances) for the purposes of making regulations.

5073. Social Security Fraud Act 2001 (c.11) – Commencement No.2 Order

SOCIAL SECURITY FRAUD ACT 2001 (COMMENCEMENT NO.2) ORDER 2001, SI 2001 3689 (C.119); made under the Social Security Fraud Act 2001 s.20. Commencement details: bringing into force various provisions of the 2001 Act on November 17, 2001 and April 1, 2002; £1.50.

This Order provides for the coming into force of specified sections of the Social Security Fraud Act 2001.

5074. State retirement pensions – first appointed year – 2002-03

ADDITIONAL PENSION (FIRST APPOINTED YEAR) ORDER 2001, SI 2001 208; made under the Social Security Contributions and Benefits Act 1992 s.122. In force: January 28, 2001; £1.50.

This Order appoints the tax year 2002-03 as the "first appointed year" for the purposes of the definition of that expression in the Social Security Contributions and Benefits Act 1992 s.122 and is therefore the first tax year in which the provisions governing the State Second Pension, which reform the current State Earnings Related Pension Scheme, will be in force.

5075. State retirement pensions – free movement of persons – periods devoted to child rearing – credits for frontier workers

[EC Treaty Art.8A (now, after amendment, Art.18 EC), Art.48 (now, after amendment, Art.39 EC), Art.51 (now, after amendment, Art.42 EC).]

A German court referred to the ECJ questions regarding whether the competent institution of a Member State was required to give pension credits in respect of periods devoted to child rearing completed in another Member State by a person who, at the time when the child was born, was a frontier worker employed in the territory of the first Member State and residing in the territory of the second Member State.

Held, giving a preliminary ruling, that the EC Treaty Arts.8A, 48 and 51 (now, after amendment, Arts.18 EC, 39 EC and 42 EC) required pension credits to be given in respect of such periods. Although it was up to individual Member States to organise their own social security schemes, they were under an obligation to comply with Community law when doing so. A national law which had the effect of causing an EC national to automatically lose pension rights as a consequence of residing in another Member State, whilst continuing to work in the Member State in which he had previously resided, infringed the principle of free movement of workers and was incompatible with Community law.

ELSEN v. BUNDESVERSICHERUNGSANSTALT FUR ANGESTELLTE (C135/99) *The Times*, February 14, 2001, AM La Pergola, ECJ.

5076. State retirement pensions – free movement of persons – Spanish national working in both Spain and Germany – method of calculating Spanish pension – validity under EC law

[EC Treaty Art.48 (now, after amendment, Art.39 EC), Art.51 (now, after amendment, Art.42 EC); Council Regulation 1408/71 on the application of social security schemes to employed persons and their families moving within the Community Annex VI, para.4, Heading D; Convention on Social Security concluded between Spain and Germany 1973.]

G, a Spanish national, spent periods working in both Spain and Germany from 1953 until his retirement in 1993, when he was awarded a Spanish retirement pension calculated on the basis of the pension contributions he had made in Spain prior to 1969, with a revalorisation using a calculation method that conformed with Council Regulation 1408/71 Annex VI, para.4, Heading D. G disputed the amount, claiming that the appropriate reference period should be the eight years before his retirement. This was accepted at first instance, where the court ordered that he be paid a pension calculated in accordance with the ceilings for contributions applicable to manual workers in Spain during that period. However, that decision was overturned on appeal, where it was held that G's pension should be calculated on the basis of contributions he had made in the eight years before 1969, the last year he had paid Spanish social security contributions, with revalorisations from then until his retirement. G appealed and the national court sought a preliminary ruling as to whether the calculation method under the Annex was compatible with the EC Treaty Art.48 and Art.51 (now, after amendment, Art.39 and Art.42 EC), and whether G's pension should be determined on the basis of the contributions he would have made had he remained in Spain during the period prior to his retirement.

Held, giving a preliminary ruling, that Art.51 provided that migrant workers were not to be disadvantaged in terms of social security benefits because they had exercised their right of freedom of movement, so that such benefits were to be the same as if the right had not been exercised. Accordingly, the contributions made had to be updated and revalorised to correspond with the amount that G would have been paid if he had remained in Spain. Heading D was consistent with that interpretation and clarified the rules under the Regulation by which the average contribution was to be determined. Contributions made in another Member State did not have to be taken into account, provided that the basis of calculation was the same as if the worker had not exercised the right to freedom of movement. It was for the national court to determine whether the benefit had been calculated on that basis. Further, as G had worked in Germany before the Regulation came into force, the national court had to determine if G would have received more advantageous treatment under the Convention on Social Security concluded between Spain and Germany 1973 and apply those provisions if that was the case, *Ronfeldt v. Bundesversicherungsanstalt fur Angestellte (C227/89)* [1991] E.C.R. I-323 followed.

RODRIGUEZ v. INSTITUTO NACIONAL DE LA SEGURIDAD SOCIAL (INSS) (C153/97) [2001] 1 C.M.L.R. 42, J-P Puissochet (President), ECJ.

5077. State retirement pensions – home responsibilities

ADDITIONAL PENSION AND SOCIAL SECURITY PENSIONS (HOME RESPONSIBILITIES) (AMENDMENT) REGULATIONS 2001, SI 2001 1323; made under the Social Security Contributions and Benefits Act 1992 s.44A, s.122, s.175, Sch.3 para.5, Sch.4A para.9. In force: April 6, 2002; £2.00.

These Regulations, which amend the Social Security Pensions (Home Responsibilities) Regulations 1994 (SI 1994 704) to specify a time limit for providing the Secretary of State with information where a person is to be treated as precluded from regular employment after April 5, 2002 due to responsibilities at home, are made before the end of the period of six months beginning with the coming into force of the Child Support, Pensions and Social Security Act 2000 s.30, s.40 and Sch.4. They make additional provision for the calculation of the state second pension and for conditions to be satisfied, in certain circumstances, in order for a person to be treated as precluded from regular employment due to responsibilities at home and therefore entitled to additional pension.

5078. Students – income related benefits

SOCIAL SECURITY AMENDMENT (STUDENTS AND INCOME-RELATED BENEFITS) REGULATIONS 2001, SI 2001 2319; made under the Social Security Contributions and Benefits Act 1992 s.123, s.136, s.137, s.175; and the Jobseekers Act 1995 s.12, s.35, s.36. In force: in accordance with Reg.1; £2.00.

These Regulations amend the Council Tax Benefit (General) Regulations 1992 (SI 1992 1814), the Housing Benefit (General) Regulations 1987 (SI 1987 1971), the Income Support (General) Regulations 1987 (SI 1987 1967) and the Jobseeker's Allowance Regulations 1996 (SI 1996 207) in so far as those Regulations apply to students and former students. They insert a definition of "academic year", remove the definition of "year" and amend the definitions of "access funds", "contribution", "standard maintenance grant", "student loan", "full-time course of study", "full-time course of advanced education" and "full-time student". They increase the amounts of grant and loan income to be disregarded in respect of books and equipment and for travel costs and allow the former to be disregarded even if a student's grant income includes an amount for books and equipment; add new exclusions for grants paid to certain students who are lone parents, for child care costs and for certain course-related expenditure and increase the amount deducted from rent for calculating eligible rent; provide rules as to the apportionment of student loans where the academic year starts other than on September 1; provide a formula for calculating the income of a former student who has received a student loan or an amount intended for the maintenance of dependants and who abandons, or is dismissed from, his course before the end of the penultimate term of the academic year; ensure that grants paid to students receiving instruction as officers of hospital authorities are taken into account over 12 months and not 10; and disregard school meal grants paid in Scotland as income in housing benefit and council tax benefit.

5079. Tax credits – disabled persons tax credit – working families tax credit

TAX CREDITS (MISCELLANEOUS AMENDMENTS NO.3) REGULATIONS 2001, SI 2001 892; made under the Social Security Contributions and Benefits Act 1992 s.128, s.129, s.136, s.137, s.175; the Social Security Administration Act 1992 s.5, s.189; and the Tax Credits Act 1999 s.2, s.6, Sch.2 para.1, Sch.2 para.7, Sch.2 para.20. In force: in accordance with Reg.1 (2) (3); £2.50.

These Regulations amend the Disability Working Allowance (General) Regulations 1991 (SI 1991 2887), the Social Security (Claims and Payments) Regulations 1987 (SI 1987 1968), the Family Credit (General) Regulations 1987 (SI 1987 1973) and the Tax Credits (Payment by Employers) Regulations 1999 (SI 1999 3219) to enable a person to claim, with effect from April 4, 2001, working families' tax credit or disabled person's tax credit in respect of a newly born or adopted child, or a surrogate child.

5080. Tax credits – disabled persons tax credit – working families tax credit

TAX CREDITS (MISCELLANEOUS AMENDMENTS NO.4) REGULATIONS 2001, SI 2001 1082; made under the Social Security Contributions and Benefits Act 1992 s.128, s.129, s.136, s.137, s.175; and the Tax Credits Act 1999 s.2, Sch.2 para.1, Sch.2 para.20. In force: April 10, 2001; £1.75.

These Regulations amend the Family Credit (General) Regulations 1987 (SI 1987 1973) and the Disability Working Allowance (General) Regulations 1991 (SI 1991 2887) in relation to award periods of working families' tax credit and disabled person's tax credit commencing on or after April 10, 2001.

5081. Tax credits – disabled persons tax credit – working families tax credit

TAX CREDITS (MISCELLANEOUS AMENDMENTS NO.5) REGULATIONS 2001, SI 2001 1351; made under the Social Security Contributions and Benefits Act 1992 s.128, s.129, s.175; and the Tax Credits Act 1999 s.2, Sch.2 para.1, Sch.2 para.20. In force: June 5, 2001; £1.50.

These Regulations, which amend the Family Credit (General) Regulations 1987 (SI 1987 1973) and the Disability Working Allowance (General) Regulations 1991 (SI 1991 2887), provide for increases of certain of the credits by reference to which the appropriate maximum disabled person's tax credit are calculated. The amendments have effect in relation to award periods of both tax credits commencing on or after June 5, 2001.

5082. Tax credits – disabled persons tax credit – working families tax credit

TAX CREDITS (MISCELLANEOUS AMENDMENTS NO.6) REGULATIONS 2001, SI 2001 2220; made under the Social Security Contributions and Benefits Act 1992 s.136, s.137, s.175; and the Tax Credits Act 1999 s.2, Sch.2 para.1, Sch.2 para.20. In force: July 3, 2001; £1.50.

These Regulations amend the Family Credit (General) Regulations 1987 (SI 1987 1973) and the Disability Working Allowance (General) Regulations 1991 (SI 1991 2887), to add to the lists of income and capital to be disregarded in calculating a claimant's gross income, or capital, discretionary housing payments or capital discretionary payments made pursuant to the Discretionary Financial Assistance Regulations 2001 (SI 2001 1167) Reg.2(1).

5083. Tax credits – disabled persons tax credit – working families tax credit

TAX CREDITS (MISCELLANEOUS AMENDMENTS NO.7) REGULATIONS 2001, SI 2001 2539; made under the Social Security Contributions and Benefits Act 1992 s.128, s.129, s.136, s.137, s.175; and the Tax Credits Act 1999 s.2, Sch.2 para.1, Sch.2 para.20. In force: August 7, 2001; £1.75.

These Regulations make various amendments to the provisions relating to students in the Family Credit (General) Regulations 1987 (SI 1987 1973) and the Disability Working Allowance (General) Regulations 1991 (SI 1991 2887).

5084. Tax credits – disabled persons tax credit – working families tax credit

TAX CREDITS (MISCELLANEOUS AMENDMENTS NO.8) REGULATIONS 2001, SI 2001 3085; made under the Social Security Contributions and Benefits Act 1992 s.136, s.137, s.175; and the Tax Credits Act 1999 s.2, Sch.2 para.1, Sch.2 para.20. In force: October 9, 2001; £1.75.

These Regulations amend the Family Credit (General) Regulations 1987 (SI 1987 1973) and the Disability Working Allowance Regulations 1991 (SI 1991 2887) to add to the list of capital to be disregarded in calculating a claimant's capital for the purposes of working families' tax credit and disabled person's tax credit a dwelling which the claimant intends in due course to occupy as his home but which he currently does not occupy due to living in job-related accommodation.

5085. Tax credits – disabled persons tax credit – working families tax credit – claims and payments

TAX CREDITS (CLAIMS AND PAYMENTS) (AMENDMENT) REGULATIONS 2001, SI 2001 567; made under the Social Security Administration Act 1992 s.5, s.189; and the Tax Credits Act 1999 s.2, Sch.2 para.7, Sch.2 para.20. In force: April 10, 2001; £1.50.

These Regulations, which amend the Social Security (Claims and Payments) Regulations 1987 (SI 1987 1968) with respect only to working families' tax credit and disabled person's tax credit, provide for the date on which certain claims for working families' tax credit or disabled person's tax credit are treated as being made. In addition, the Regulations are amended in consequence of recent amendments to the Income Support (General) Regulations 1987 (SI 1987

1967) by extending the circumstances in which claims for working families' tax credit and disabled person's tax credit may be backdated.

5086. Tax credits – disabled persons tax credit – working families tax credit – prisoners of Japan

TAX CREDITS SCHEMES (MISCELLANEOUS AMENDMENTS) REGULATIONS 2001, SI 2001 19; made under the Social Security Contributions and Benefits Act 1992 s.136, s.137, s.175; and the Tax Credits Act 1999 s.2, Sch.2 para.1, Sch.2 para.20. In force: January 30, 2001; £1.50.

These Regulations amend the Family Credit (General) Regulations 1987 (1987 1973) Sch.2 and the Disability Working Allowance (General) Regulation 1991 (SI 1991 2887) Sch.3 to add the sum of £15 of any widowed mother's allowance or widowed parent's allowance to the categories of income to be disregarded. In addition, they amend Sch.3 to the Family Credit Regulations and Sch.4 to the Disability Working Allowance Regulations to add payments of £10,000 made by the Secretary of State for Social Security to persons who were held prisoner by the Japanese during World War Two or to the spouses of such persons.

5087. Tax credits – employment schemes – disabled persons tax credit – working families tax credit

TAX CREDITS (NEW DEAL CONSEQUENTIAL AMENDMENTS) REGULATIONS 2001, SI 2001 1334; made under the Social Security Contributions and Benefits Act 1992 s.123, s.136, s.137, s.175. In force: April 24, 2001; £1.75.

These Regulations amend the Family Credit (General) Regulations 1987 (SI 1987 1973) and the Disability Working Allowance (General) Regulations 1991 (SI 1991 2887) in consequence of the introduction of two new employment programmes known as the "Intensive Activity Period" and the "Intensive Activity Period for 50 plus".

5088. Tax credits – up rating

TAX CREDITS UP-RATING ORDER 2001, SI 2001 1141; made under the Social Security Administration Act 1992 s.150, s.189; the Social Security Administration (Northern Ireland) Act 1992 s.132; and the Tax Credits Act 1999 s.2, Sch.2 para.2, Sch.2 para.4, Sch.2 para.20. In force: April 10, 2001; £2.00.

This Order, a consequence of a review of the Social Security Administration Act 1992 s.150 in relation to working families' tax credit and disabled person's tax credit, specifies the applicable amount for working families' tax credit and the amount of credits for an adult, child or young person which determines a family's maximum working families' tax credit. In addition, it specifies the applicable amount for disabled person's tax credit and the amount of credit for an adult, child or young person which determines the appropriate maximum disabled person's tax credit. The Family Credit (General) Regulations (Northern Ireland) 1987 (SR 1987 463), the Family Credit (General) Regulations 1987 (SI 1987 1973), the Disability Working Allowance (General) Regulations 1991 (SI 1991 2887), and the Disability Working Allowance (General) Regulations (Northern Ireland) 1992 (SR 1992 78) are amended.

5089. Unemployment – New Deal – miscellaneous provisions

NEW DEAL (LONE PARENTS) (MISCELLANEOUS PROVISIONS) ORDER 2001, SI 2001 2915; made under the Employment Act 1988 s.26. In force: September 13, 2001; £1.75.

This Order provides that a person using facilities provided in pursuance of the employment programme known as "the New Deal for Lone Parents self-employment route" and receiving or entitled to receive in connection with the use of those facilities a top up payment or assistance with the expenses of participation or both shall be treated as being in receipt of a training allowance for the purposes of the remunerative work rule in income support and as in receipt of a training premium for all other purposes. The Order has the effect that receipt of the top up payment and expenses by a person using those facilities does not affect his entitlement to income support or the amount of income support to which he is entitled.

5090. Unemployment – New Deal – miscellaneous provisions

NEW DEAL (MISCELLANEOUS PROVISIONS) ORDER 2001, SI 2001 970; made under the Employment Act 1988 s.26. In force: April 9, 2001; £1.75.

This Order provides that, for the purposes of the Social Security Contributions and Benefits Act 1992 Part I and the Jobseekers Act 1995 and of specified subordinate legislation, a person using facilities provided in pursuance of the employment programme known as "the Intensive Activity Period" or "the Intensive Activity Period for 50 plus" and receiving or entitled to receive from the Secretary of State a training allowance in connection with the use of those facilities shall be treated not as being employed but as participating in arrangements for training under the Employment and Training Act 1973 s.2. Any payment made to such a person in connection with his use of those facilities, other than a trading payment made to a person receiving assistance in pursuing self-employed earner's employment, shall be treated as a payment of training allowance made in respect of such training.

5091. War – disablement during auxiliary service – compensation – increase in weekly allowance

INJURIES IN WAR (SHORE EMPLOYMENTS) COMPENSATION (AMENDMENT) SCHEME 2001, SI 2001 1015; made under the Injuries in War Compensation Act 1914 s.1. In force: April 9, 2001; £1.50.

The Injuries in War (Shore Employments) Compensation Schemes 1914 to 2000 provide for the payment of weekly allowances to ex-members of the women's auxiliary forces who suffered disablement from their service overseas during the 1914 to 1918 war. This amending Scheme provides that the maximum weekly allowance shall be increased from £116.00 to £119.80 on April 9, 2001.

5092. Welfare Reform and Pensions Act 1999 (c.30) – Commencement No.10, and Transitional Provisions Order

WELFARE REFORM AND PENSIONS ACT 1999 (COMMENCEMENT NO.10, AND TRANSITIONAL PROVISIONS) ORDER 2001, SI 2001 933 (C.34); made under the Welfare Reform and Pensions Act 1999 s.83, s.89. Commencement details: bringing into force various provisions of the Act on March 19, 2001, April 6, 2001 and October 8, 2001; £2.00.

This Order, which brings into force provisions of the Welfare Reform and Pensions Act 1999, amends the Welfare Reform and Pensions Act 1999 (Commencement No. 9, and Transitional and Savings Provisions) Order 2000 (SI 2000 2958) and the Welfare Reform and Pensions Act 1999 (Commencement No.4) Order 2000 (SI 2000 1047).

5093. Welfare Reform and Pensions Act 1999 (c.30) – Commencement No.11 Order

WELFARE REFORM AND PENSIONS ACT 1999 (COMMENCEMENT NO.11) ORDER 2001, SI 2001 1219 (C.44); made under the Welfare Reform and Pensions Act 1999 s.89. Commencement details: bringing into force various provisions of the Act on April 23, 2001; £2.00.

This Order brings into force the Welfare Reform and Pensions Act 1999 s.17 which amends the Pensions Act 1995 to make further provision for the compensation payable by the Pensions Compensation Board to schemes whose assets have been reduced in value as a result of certain acts or omissions.

5094. Welfare Reform and Pensions Act 1999 (c.30) – Commencement No.12 Order

WELFARE REFORM AND PENSIONS ACT 1999 (COMMENCEMENT NO.12) ORDER 2001, SI 2001 4049 (C.130); made under the Welfare Reform and Pensions Act 1999 s.89. Commencement details: bringing into force various provisions of the 1999 Act in accordance with Art.2; £2.00.

This Order brings into force specified provisions of the Welfare Reform and Pensions Act 1999.

5095. Books

Bonner, David; Hooker, Ian; White, Robin – Social Security: Legislation 2001: Vol 1, Non-means Tested Benefits. Paperback: £59.00. ISBN 0-421-82610-X. Sweet & Maxwell.

Rowland, Mark; White, Robin – Social Security Tribunals: the Legislation 2000: Vol 3. Administration, Adjudication and the European Dimension. £55.00. ISBN 0-421-82480-8. Sweet & Maxwell.

Rowland, Mark; White, Robin – Social Security: Legislation 2001: Vol III, Administration, Adjudication and the European Dimension. Paperback: £59.00. ISBN 0-421-82630-4. Sweet & Maxwell.

Wood, Penny; Wikeley, Nick; Poynter, Richard; Bonn – Social Security Tribunals: the Legislation 2000: Vol 2. Income Support, Jobseeker's Allowance, Tax Credits and the Social Fund. £55.00. ISBN 0-421-82470-0. Sweet & Maxwell.

SOCIAL WELFARE

5096. Appointments – care – standards

GENERAL SOCIAL CARE COUNCIL (APPOINTMENTS AND PROCEDURE) REGULATIONS 2001, SI 2001 1744; made under the Care Standards Act 2000 s.54, s.118, Sch.1 para.6. In force: June 10, 2001; £2.50.

These Regulations make provision concerning the membership and procedure of the General Social Care Council established under the Care Standards Act 2000 Part IV. They make provision for the appointment and tenure of office of the chairman and members of the Council; for disqualification of appointment; for resignations; for the termination of appointments by the Secretary of State and for the appointment of a deputy chairman. In addition, provision is made for the establishment of committees and sub committees, the conduct of meetings and the exclusion from meeting of those with a pecuniary interest in matters under discussion.

5097. Assessment – children – "child in need" – local authority's duty to carry out core assessment – provision of services

[Local Authority Social Services Act 1970 s.7(1); Children Act 1989 s.17.]

AB applied for judicial review of NCC's alleged failure to assess and provide for both her needs as a carer and those of her 14 year old son, SB, who was a "child in need" under the Children Act 1989 s.17. It was contended that the council had unjustifiably departed from the relevant guidance which had been issued pursuant to the Local Authority Social Services Act 1970 s.7(1) in relation to the duty of a local authority to carry out a full and proper assessment of children in need and their families.

Held, granting the application, that whilst the council's approach in addressing the possibility that SB could be at risk from significant harm was permissible, the outcome had not been akin to a core assessment of the child's needs which had amounted to an impermissible departure from the guidance. There was no evidence to support the existence of a systematic assessment with regard to SB, the purpose of which was to identify his needs, to produce a care plan in order to meet those needs and to provide the identified services, nor was there any evidence to support the adequacy of the assessments with regard to housing and educational needs. Any difficulties experienced by NCC in obtaining cooperation from AB or SB could not diminish NCC's responsibilities and, further, the fact that SB was the subject of anti social behaviour order proceedings could not excuse NCC's failure to comply with its duty under s.17 of the 1989 Act.

R. (ON THE APPLICATION OF AB) v. NOTTINGHAM CITY COUNCIL, [2001] EWHC Admin 235, [2001] 3 F.C.R. 350, Richards, J., QBD (Admin Ct).

5098. Care plans – assessment – reduction in care provision – failure to consider impact of reduction

K, aged 40, had multiple sclerosis and her condition was deteriorating. She was blind, had deep vein thrombosis, epilepsy and was incontinent. Her husband had hip and back problems and was registered disabled. K had 12 hours continuous care per day, seven days per week. BCC undertook a "manual handling risk assessment" and decided that manual handling of K required two carers. New care plans were produced, the latest of which provided for six hours care per day by two carers to assist with toileting. K sought judicial review of the assessment.

Held, allowing the application and quashing the care plans, that the reassessment was based on the need for two carers for lifting purposes, but failed, contrary to policy guidance, to assess why 12-hour care was no longer needed. In particular it failed to address K's needs in an emergency if no carers were present. Although it was open to BCC to find that continuous supervision should not be provided, that decision could only be made following an examination of K's medical records and taking her GP's opinion into account, neither of which had been done when formulating the care plans.

R. v. BIRMINGHAM CITY COUNCIL, *ex p.* KILLIGREW; *sub nom.* R. v. BIRMINGHAM CC, *ex p.* KILLIGREW (2000) 3 C.C.L. Rep. 109, Hooper, J., QBD.

5099. Care plans – disabled persons – assessment of needs in view of redevelopment

[National Health Service and Community Care Act 1990 s.47.]

L, a severely disabled woman living in residential care accommodation, appealed against the refusal ([2001] B.L.G.R. 86) of her application for judicial review of the local authority's decision to redevelop her home. L feared that her needs would not be met in the new accommodation, particularly relating to her reliance on social interaction through communal dining. It was argued that the local authority had breached earlier undertakings made to the court and had failed to produce a lawful assessment of her needs under the National Health Service and Community Care Act 1990 s.47 as the current plan lacked sufficient detail and had not been properly prepared due to a lack of consultation with L and her family. It was further contended that L had a legitimate expectation that her previous care routine would continue under the new regime, which was no longer the case.

Held, dismissing the appeal, that the local authority had not acted unlawfully. The proposed redevelopment did not inhibit communal dining and, through the support of her care workers, L's needs could be met. Any legitimate expectation had therefore not been breached. Further, the court was not the appropriate body to prescribe the degree of detail to be included in a care plan, or the appropriate degree of consultation. Such were matters for the local authority and where necessary its complaints procedure. Where the local authority had arguably breached the guidance provided by the Secretary of State, it was appropriate to turn to him first.

R. (ON THE APPLICATION OF L) v. BARKING AND DAGENHAM LBC; *sub nom.* R. v. BARKING AND DAGENHAM LBC, *ex p.* L; R. v. L, [2001] EWCA Civ 533, [2001] 2 F.L.R. 763, Schiemann, L.J., CA.

5100. Care plans – local authorities power and duties – judicial review application – liability for costs

[National Health Service and Community Care Act 1990.]

H applied for a costs order following the withdrawal of her application for judicial review of CMBC's care plan which had been made for her under the National Health Service and Community Care Act 1990. H had multiple sclerosis and other disabilities and claimed that the care plan was inadequate. At the first hearing of the matter CMBC agreed to file a new plan, with which H was ultimately satisfied.

Held, allowing the application, that H's judicial review application would arguably have succeeded as the original care plan had inadequately addressed CMBC's assessment of H's needs. H was therefore entitled to her costs.

R. v. CALDERDALE MBC, *ex p.* HOUGHTON (2000) 3 C.C.L. Rep. 228, Smith, J., QBD.

5101. Care Standards Act 2000 (c.14) – Commencement No.2 and Transitional Provisions Order – England

CARE STANDARDS ACT 2000 (COMMENCEMENT NO.2) (ENGLAND) AND TRANSITIONAL PROVISIONS) ORDER 2001, SI 2001 290 (C.17); made under the Care Standards Act 2000 s.118, s.122. Commencement details: bringing into force various provisions of the Act on February 19, 2001 and March 19, 2001; £1.75.

This Order brings into force the Care Standards Act 2000 s.39 in relation to England only, which amends the Registered Homes Act 1984 s.21 so as to extend the meaning of "nursing home". The effect of the amendment is to require a dentist who uses premises for the purpose of treating patients under general anaesthesia to be registered in respect of those premises. Dentist who are already registered under Part II of the 1984 Act must notify the Health Authority by March 19, 2001, bringing into force various provisions of the 2000 Act on February 19, 2001 and March 19, 2001.

5102. Care standards Act 2000 (c.14) – Commencement No.2 and Transitional Provisions Order – Wales

CARE STANDARDS ACT 2000 (COMMENCEMENT NO.2 AND TRANSITIONAL PROVISIONS) (WALES) ORDER 2001, SI 2001 139 (W.5; C.7); made under the Care Standards Act 2000 s.118, s.122. Commencement details: bringing into force various provisions of the Act on February 1, 2001 and February 28, 2001; £2.00.

This Order, brings into force the Care Standards Act 2000 s.40 in Wales, which amends the Children Act 1989 so as to require privately operated children's homes accommodating and caring for less than four children to be registered with the local authority in whose area they are located on February 1, 2001, for the purpose of enabling applications for registration to be made, and on February 28, 2001 for all other purposes. It makes transitional provision so that a small children's home in respect of which an application for registration has been duly made by February 28, 2001 is not to be treated as an unregistered children's home until the registration process for it has been completed. The Care Standards Act 2000 s.41 is brought into force in Wales on February 28, 2001, which amends the Children Act 1989 to provide that the registration of a children's home of any description may be cancelled even if the home has ceased to exist, such as where the proprietor closes it before the conclusion of any enforcement action, bringing into force various provisions of the 2000 act on February 1, 2001 and February 28, 2001.

5103. Care Standards Act 2000 (c.14) – Commencement No.3 Order – England

CARE STANDARDS ACT 2000 (COMMENCEMENT NO.3) (ENGLAND) ORDER 2001, SI 2001 731 (C.26); made under the Care Standards Act 2000 s.122. Commencement details: bringing into force various provisions of the Act on March 2, 2001; £1.75.

This Order brings into force, on March 2, 2001, the Care Standards Act 2000 s.23. This section enables the appropriate Minister to prepare and publish statements of national minimum standards applicable to establishments or agencies to which the Act relates, requires the appropriate Minister to keep the standards set out in the statements under review, and provides for the publication of amended statements. In addition it makes provision for consultation before a statement is issued.

5104. Care Standards Act 2000 (c.14) – Commencement No.3 Order – Wales

CARE STANDARDS ACT 2000 (COMMENCEMENT NO.3) (WALES) ORDER 2001, SI 2001 2190 (W.152; C.70); made under the Care Standards Act 2000 s.122. Commencement details: bringing into force various provisions of the Act on July 1, 2001; £2.00.

This Order, which appoints a day for certain provisions of the Care Standards Act 2000 to come into force, brings into force all powers to make subordinate legislation and to prepare and publish national minimum standards. The Order also brings into force specified sections which will facilitate activities that prepare for the coming into force of those provisions of the Act that require the Assembly to register the provision of social care in Wales and to allow the Assembly to issue guidance and directions to local authorities in Wales in relation to their power to levy charges for welfare services they provide.

5105. Care Standards Act 2000 (c.14) – Commencement No.4 Order – England

CARE STANDARDS ACT 2000 (COMMENCEMENT NO.4) (ENGLAND) ORDER 2001, SI 2001 1193 (C.39); made under the Care Standards Act 2000 s.122. Commencement details: bringing into force various provisions of the on March 16, 2001, April 1, 2001 and April 9, 2001; £1.75.

This Order brings into force certain provisions of the Care Standards Act 2000 which relate to the National Care Standards Commission to enable regulations to be made concerning the membership and procedure of the Commission and its committees on March 16, 2001. It brings into force the remainder of s.6 and Sch.1 of the 2000 Act which establish the Commission as a corporate body on April 9, 2001. In addition, the Order brings into force s.98 which relates to the circumstances in which a local authority may refer an individual employed to provide care to a child funded by direct payments for inclusion in the list kept by the Secretary of State on April 1, 2001.

5106. Care Standards Act 2000 (c.14) – Commencement No.4 Order – Wales

CARE STANDARDS ACT 2000 (COMMENCEMENT NO.4) (WALES) ORDER 2001, SI 2001 2354 (W.192; C.80); made under the Care Standards Act 2000 s.122. Commencement details: bringing into force various provisions of the Act on July 1, 2001; £2.00.

This Order appoints July 1, 2001 as the day on which the Care Standards Act 2000 s.98 is to come into force in relation to Wales.

5107. Care Standards Act 2000 (c.14) – Commencement No.5 Order – England

CARE STANDARDS ACT 2000 (COMMENCEMENT NO.5) (ENGLAND) ORDER 2001, SI 2001 1210 (C.41); made under the Care Standards Act 2000 s.122. Commencement details: bringing into force various provisions of the Act on March 16, 2001; £1.75.

This Order brings into force certain provisions of the Care Standards Act 2000 on March 16, 2001.

5108. Care Standards Act 2000 (c.14) – Commencement No.5 Order – Wales

CARE STANDARDS ACT 2000 (COMMENCEMENT NO.5 AND TRANSITIONAL PROVISIONS) (WALES) ORDER 2001, SI 2001 2504 (W.205; C.82); made under the Care Standards Act 2000 s.118, s.122. Commencement details: bringing into force various provisions of the Act on July 31, 2001 and August 31, 2001; £2.00.

This Order brings into force the Care Standards Act 2000 s.39 in relation to Wales which extends the meaning of "nursing home" with the effect to require a person carrying on premises used or intended to be used by a dental practitioner for the purposes of treating patients under general anaesthesia to register those premises as a 'nursing home' under the Registered Homes Act 1984 unless the exemption applies. The exemption applies if the premises are used by a dental practitioner for the purposes of treating patients under general anaesthesia for the National Health Service. Section 39 comes into force on July 31, 2001 only for the purpose of enabling applications for registration to be made in respect of newly registerable premises and for all other purposes on August 31, 2001

5109. Care Standards Act 2000 (c.14) – Commencement No.6 Order – England

CARE STANDARDS ACT 2000 (COMMENCEMENT NO.6) (ENGLAND) ORDER 2001, SI 2001 1536 (C.55); made under the Care Standards Act 2000 s.118, s.122. Commencement details: bringing into force various provisions of the Act on April 10, 2001 and May 7, 2001; £1.75.

This Order provides for the coming into force of certain sections of the Care Standards Act 2000 in so far as they relate to the General Social Care Council on April 10, 2001 and May 7, 2001.

5110. Care Standards Act 2000 (c.14) – Commencement No.6 Order – Wales

CARE STANDARDS ACT 2000 (COMMENCEMENT NO.6) (WALES) ORDER 2001, SI 2001 2538 (W.213; C.83); made under the Care Standards Act 2000 s.122. Commencement details: bringing into force various provisions of the Act on July 31, 2001 and October 1, 2001; £2.00.

This Order appoints days for certain provisions of the Care Standards Act 2000 Part IV, relating to the training of social care workers in Wales, to come into force.

5111. Care Standards Act 2000 (c.14) – Commencement No.7 Order – Wales

CARE STANDARDS ACT 2000 (COMMENCEMENT NO.7) (WALES) ORDER 2001, SI 2001 2782 (W.235; C.92); made under the Care Standards Act 2000 s.122. In force: bringing in to force various provisions of the Act on August 26, 2001; £2.00.

This Order appoints a day for certain provisions of the Care Standards Act 2000 to come into force concerning the Children's Commissioner for Wales.

5112. Care Standards Act 2000 (c.14) – Commencement No.7 Order, England

CARE STANDARDS ACT 2000 (COMMENCEMENT NO.7 (ENGLAND) AND TRANSITIONAL, TRANSITORY AND SAVINGS PROVISIONS) ORDER 2001, SI 2001 2041 (C.68); made under the Care Standards Act 2000 s.118, s.122. Commencement details: bringing into force various provisions of the Act on July 2, 2001; £3.00.

This Order brings into force certain provisions of the Care Standards Act 2000 on July 2, 2001. It sets September 2, 2002 as the date on which s.79(1) comes into force for the purpose of giving effect to the Children Act 1989 s.79P(1)(2) and s.79Q(2)(3) and makes certain transitional, transitory and savings provisions in relation to Part X of that Act.

5113. Care Standards Act 2000 (c.14) – Commencement No.8 Order – England

CARE STANDARDS ACT 2000 (COMMENCEMENT NO.8) (ENGLAND) ORDER 2001, SI 2001 3331 (C.109); made under the Care Standards Act 2000 s.122. Commencement details: bringing into force various provisions of the 2000 Act on October 4, 2001; £1.75.

This Order brings into force specified provisions of the Care Standards Act 2000 in relation to England only. It provides for the amendment of the 2000 Act so that the powers of local authorities to charge for certain non residential services are to be treated as social services functions as defined in the Local Authority Social Services Act 1970. It also brings into force provisions which provide for local authorities to supply to the Secretary of State information as to residential accommodation which is provided under the National Assistance Act 1948.

5114. Care Standards Act 2000 (c.14) – Commencement No.9 (England) and Transitional and Savings Provisions Order

CARE STANDARDS ACT 2000 (COMMENCEMENT NO.9 (ENGLAND) AND TRANSITIONAL AND SAVINGS PROVISIONS) ORDER 2001, SI 2001 3852 (C.125); made under the Care Standards Act 2000 s.118, s.122. Commencement details: bringing into force various provisions of the 2000 Act in accordance with Art.3; £6.00.

This Order brings various provisions of the Care Standards Act 2000, in relation to England only, into force on November 20, 2001, January 1, 2002, April 1, 2002, and July 1, 2002.

5115. Care Standards Act 2000 (c.14) – Commencement No.10 Order – England

CARE STANDARDS ACT 2000 (COMMENCEMENT NO.10 (ENGLAND) AND TRANSITIONAL, SAVINGS AND AMENDMENT PROVISIONS) ORDER 2001, SI 2001 4150 (C.134); made under the Care Standards Act 2000 s.118, s.122. Commencement details: bringing into force various provisions of the 2000 Act on April 1, 2002 and July 1, 2002; £2.50.

This Order, which amends the Care Standards Act 2000 (Commencement No.9 (England) and Transitional and Savings Provisions) Order 2001 (SI 2001 3852), brings into force provisions of the Care Standards Act 2000 which amend or repeal other statutory provisions.

5116. Carers and Disabled Children Act 2000 (c.16) – Commencement No.1 Order – England

CARERS AND DISABLED CHILDREN ACT 2000 (COMMENCEMENT NO.1) (ENGLAND) ORDER 2001, SI 2001 510 (C.20); made under the Carers and Disabled Children Act 2000 s.12. Commencement details: bringing into force various provisions of the Act on April 1, 2001; £1.75.

This Order brings into force certain provisions of the Carers and Disabled Children Act 2000 on April 1, 2001.

5117. Carers and Disabled Children Act 2000 (c.16) – Commencement No.1 Order – Wales

CARERS AND DISABLED CHILDREN ACT 2000 (COMMENCEMENT NO.1) (WALES) ORDER 2001, SI 2001 2196 (W.156; C.72); made under the Carers and Disabled Children Act 2000 s.12. Commencement details: bringing into force various provisions of the Act on July 1, 2001; £1.75.

This Order brings into force certain provisions of the Carers and Disabled Children Act 2000 on July 1, 2001 in relation to Wales.

5118. Child Support, Pensions and Social Security Act 2000 (c.19) – Commencement No.6 Order

CHILD SUPPORT, PENSIONS AND SOCIAL SECURITY ACT 2000 (COMMENCEMENT NO.6) ORDER 2001, SI 2001 153 (C.8); made under the Child Support; and the Pensions and Social Security Act 2000 s.86.

SOCIAL WELFARE

Commencement details: bringing into force various provisions of the Act on January 25, 2001, April 6, 2001 and April 9, 2001; £1.75.

This Order, which makes provision for the coming into force of provisions of the Child Support, Pensions and Social Security Act 2000, provides for the state second pension which is brought into force January 25, 2001 for the purposes of making reports and orders in relation to the review, determination and alteration of rebate and rates of contributions and minimum contributions under the Pension Schemes Act 1993 Part III. The provisions of the Order also relate to the revaluation of earning threshold and earnings factors and the calculations of Category B retirement pension which are brought into force on April 9, 2001, bringing into force various provisions of the 2000 Act on January 25, 2001 and April 9, 2001.

5119. Child Support, Pensions and Social Security Act 2000 (c.19) – Commencement No.10 Order

CHILD SUPPORT, PENSIONS AND SOCIAL SECURITY ACT 2000 (COMMENCEMENT NO.10) ORDER 2001, SI 2001 2619 (C.86); made under the Child Support; the Pensions; and the Social Security Act 2000 s.86. Commencement details: bringing into force various provisions of the Act on October 15, 2001; £1.75.

This Order brings into force the Child Support, Pensions and Social Security Act 2000 s.62 to s.66, which relate to loss of benefit for breach of community order, on October 15, 2001 for the purposes of their application to persons in relation to whom specified community orders are made, and who fall to be supervised in the probation areas of Derbyshire, Hertfordshire, Teesside or West Midlands.

5120. Community care – direct payments – eligibility

CARERS (SERVICES) AND DIRECT PAYMENTS (AMENDMENT) (ENGLAND) REGULATIONS 2001, SI 2001 441; made under the Community Care (Direct Payments) Act 1996 s.1; and the Carers and Disabled Children Act 2000 s.2, s.11. In force: April 1, 2001; £1.75.

The Carers and Disabled Children Act 2000 imposes a duty on local authorities to assess the needs of carers in certain circumstances, gives local authorities the power to then offer services to carers to support them in their caring role and enables local authorities to make direct payments to carers in lieu of carers' services they have been assessed as needing. These Regulations, which amend the Community Care (Direct Payments) Regulations 1997 (SI 1997 734), specify who may not be the recipient of a direct payment in lieu of carers' services.

5121. Community care – direct payments – eligibility – Wales

CARERS (SERVICES) AND DIRECT PAYMENTS (AMENDMENT) (WALES) REGULATIONS 2001, SI 2001 2186 (W.150); made under the Community Care (Direct Payments) Act 1996 s.1; and the Carers and Disabled Children Act 2000 s.2, s.11. In force: July 1, 2001; £2.00.

The Carers and Disabled Children Act 2000 imposes a duty on local authorities to assess the needs of carers in certain circumstances, and gives local authorities the power to support them in their caring role. It enables local authorities to make direct payments to carers in lieu of the carers services they have been assessed as needing. Under s.2 of the Act, a service provided to a carer may be delivered to the person cared for with the agreement of the carer and the person cared for. A service so delivered may not include anything of an intimate nature, except in prescribed circumstances. These Regulations provide for what is of an intimate nature, further prescribe the circumstances in which a service of an intimate nature may be delivered to the person cared for, specify who may not be the recipient of a direct payment in lieu of carers services and make a minor amendment to the Community Care (Direct Payments) Regulations 1997 (SI 1997 734).

5122. Disability discrimination – service providers – adjustment of premises

DISABILITY DISCRIMINATION (PROVIDERS OF SERVICES) (ADJUSTMENT OF PREMISES) REGULATIONS 2001, SI 2001 3253; made under the Disability Discrimination Act 1995 s.21, s.27, s.67, Sch.4 para.8, Sch.4 para.9. In force: October 1, 2004; £2.00.

These Regulations, which amend the Disability Discrimination Act 1995 Part III, prescribe particular circumstances in which it is reasonable or not reasonable for a service provider to have to take steps in relation to alterations to his premises.

5123. Disability Discrimination Act 1995 (c.50) – Commencement No.9 Order

DISABILITY DISCRIMINATION ACT 1995 (COMMENCEMENT NO.9) ORDER 2001, SI 2001 2030 (C.67); made under the Disability Discrimination Act 1995 s.70. In force: brings into force various provisions of the Act on May 9, 2001; £2.00.

This Order brings into force certain Regulation making powers in the Disability Discrimination Act 1995 s.27 and Sch.4 on May 9, 2001. The remaining provisions of s.21, relating to the duty of providers of services to make reasonable adjustments for disabled persons, and provisions in Sch.4 relating to obtaining the consent of a lessor to alterations to premises occupied under a lease; failure of a service provider to obtain such consent; referring a refusal by a lessor to grant unconditional consent to such an alteration to court; joining a lessor in proceedings under s.25 come into force on October 1, 2004.

5124. Disabled persons – children – direct payments – Wales

DISABLED CHILDREN (DIRECT PAYMENTS) (WALES) REGULATIONS 2001, SI 2001 2192 (W.154); made under the Children Act 1989 s.17A, s.104. In force: July 1, 2001; £2.00.

The Carers and Disabled Children Act 2000 inserts into the Children Act 1989 a new s.17A enabling local authorities to make direct payments to persons with parental responsibility for a disabled child or to a disabled child aged 16 or 17, in lieu of services which would have otherwise been provided for them by the local authority. These Regulations specify those persons from whom services may not be secured by means of a direct payment and specify the maximum periods of residential accommodation which may be secured by means of a direct payment.

5125. Executive agencies – National Care Standards Commission – fees and frequency of inspections

NATIONAL CARE STANDARDS COMMISSION (FEES AND FREQUENCY OF INSPECTIONS) REGULATIONS 2001, SI 2001 3980; made under the Care Standards Act 2000 s.12, s.15, s.16, s.31, s.45, s.51, s.118; and the Children Act 1989 s.87D. In force: January 1, 2002; £3.00.

These Regulations prescribe the fees to be paid by establishments and agencies under the Care Standards Act 2000 Part II on an application for registration and on an application for the variation or removal of any condition in force in relation to registration. In addition, the Regulations prescribe the annual fee to be paid by certain establishments and agencies, the annual fee that is to be paid by a local authority fostering service and the annual fee that is to be paid by schools, residential special schools and further education colleges under the Children Act 1989 s.87D. The Regulations also prescribe the frequency of inspections of premises used for the purposes of certain establishments and agencies pursuant to the Care Standards Act 2000 s.31 (7) and of premises used for the purposes of a local authority fostering service.

5126. Executive agencies – National Care Standards Commission – membership and procedure

NATIONAL CARE STANDARDS COMMISSION (MEMBERSHIP AND PROCEDURE) REGULATIONS 2001, SI 2001 1042; made under the Care Standards Act 2000 Sch.1 para.6. In force: April 9, 2001; £2.00.

These Regulations make provision concerning the membership and procedure of the National Care Standards Commission established by the Care Standards Act 2000 s.6. They provide for the numbers of members, the appointment and tenure of office of members; the appointment of a deputy-chairman; the disqualification for appointment; the removal from office; the appointment of committees and sub-committees; and for meetings and proceedings and include a provision for disability for participation in proceedings on account of pecuniary interest.

5127. Executive agencies – National Care Standards Commission – registration

NATIONAL CARE STANDARDS COMMISSION (REGISTRATION) REGULATIONS 2001, SI 2001 3969; made under the Care Standards Act 2000 s.11, s.12, s.14, s.15, s.16, s.25, s.118. In force: January 1, 2002; £3.50.

These Regulations make provision in relation to the registration of the establishments and agencies specified in the Care Standards Act 2000 Part II, except for voluntary adoption agencies. They specify the information and documents to be provided by an applicant for registration, require the responsible person to attend an interview, require the Commission to keep a register in respect of each description of establishment or agency and require the registered person to report the relevant circumstances to the Commission if it appears that the establishment or agency is likely to cease to be financially viable.

5128. Food – milk – price increase

WELFARE FOOD (AMENDMENT) REGULATIONS 2001, SI 2001 758; made under the Social Security Act 1988 s.13; and the Social Security Contributions and Benefits Act 1992 s.175. In force: April 1, 2001; £1.50.

These Regulations, which amend the Welfare Food Regulations 1996 (SI 1996 1434), remove references to family credit as family credit is no longer in existence and increase the price payable for dried milk by a person entitled to purchase it at a reduced price from £3.90 to £4.05 for 900 grammes.

5129. Freedom to provide services – benefits – self employed artists and journalists – liability to make payments to benefit scheme – European Union

[EC Treaty Art.51 (now, after amendment, Art.42), Art.52 (now, after amendment, Art.43), Art.59 (now, after amendment, Art.49); Council Regulation 1408/71 on the application of social security schemes to employed persons and their families moving within the Community.]

The Commission sought a declaration that a scheme under the Law on Social Security for Artists and Journalists, whereby a charge was levied in proportion to the payments made by German organisations marketing the work of non resident self employed artists and journalists was contrary to the EC Treaty Art.51, Art.52 and Art.59 (now, after amendment, Art.42, Art.43 and Art.49 EC) and Council Regulation 1408/71

Held, refusing the application, that (1) the scheme treated self employed artists and journalists equally, irrespective of the Member State in which they lived and was compatible with Regulation 1408/71 Art.13 as it did not affect their liability to make comparable payments in their own Member States, and (2) non resident self employed artists and journalists were not placed in a worse position than German residents under the scheme as the liability to make payments was the same in both cases and did not reduce the amounts they received for their work.

COMMISSION OF THE EUROPEAN COMMUNITIES v. GERMANY (C68/99) [2001] 2 C.M.L.R. 35, C Gulmann (President), ECJ.

5130. Health care – private and voluntary health care

PRIVATE AND VOLUNTARY HEALTH CARE (ENGLAND) REGULATIONS 2001, SI 2001 3968; made under the Care Standards Act 2000 s.2, s.22, s.25, s.34, s.35, s.118. In force: April 1, 2002; £4.50.

These Regulations provide that "listed services" includes treatment using the prescribed techniques and technology specified and exclude certain techniques and technology from being listed services. They also exclude certain establishments from the definition of an independent hospital and include establishments providing medical or psychiatric treatment but which have no overnight beds for patients plus establishments which are service hospitals under the Armed Forces Act 1981, or which cater for offenders under the Prison Act 1952. The Regulations modify the definition of cosmetic surgery, define the meaning of the term "independent clinic" and exempt certain establishments from being an independent medical agency. In addition, they make provision about the fitness of the persons carrying on and managing an establishment or agency and require satisfactory information to be obtained and make provision about the conduct of establishments or agencies, in particular about the quality of the services to be provided in an establishment or agency, including matters relating to privacy, dignity and religious observance, the staffing of the establishment or agency and the fitness of workers and about complaints and record keeping.

5131. Local authorities powers and duties – childrens welfare – power to communicate feared risk of sexual abuse to other organisations

[Children Act 1989 s.17, s.27, s.47, Sch.2 para.4.]

A, a former head teacher, appealed against the refusal of his application for judicial review following his dismissal for gross misconduct. A contended that the social services department, following an investigation pursuant to the Children Act 1989 s.47, was not empowered to communicate to the local education authority and to the Chairman of the school governors, its belief that A posed a risk to children . A maintained that if Parliament had intended to grant such a power, then it would have been expressly conferred.

Held, dismissing the appeal, that a local authority had power to communicate its conclusions resulting from an investigation where it genuinely and reasonably believed that such a step was required in order to protect children from a risk of sexual abuse. Such a power arose by way of implication from the general duties conferred upon a local authority with regard to child protection under s.17 of the 1989 Act together with s.27, s.47 and Sch.2 para.4., *R. v. Devon CC, ex p. L* [1991] 2 F.L.R. 541, [1992] C.L.Y. 3058 considered, and *L (Minors) (Sexual Abuse: Disclosure), Re* [1999] 1 W.L.R. 299, [1998] C.L.Y. 2386 distinguished.

R. (ON THE APPLICATION OF A) v. HERTFORDSHIRE CC; *sub nom.* R. v. HERTFORDSHIRE CC, *ex p.* A, [2001] EWHC Admin 211, [2001] B.L.G.R. 435, Keene, L.J., CA.

5132. Local authorities powers and duties – community care – elderly persons – extent of duty to provide preferred accommodation type

[National Assistance Act 1948 s.21; National Health Service and Community Care Act 1990 s.47.]

K, a 91 year old Iraqi Kurd suffering from, inter alia, paranoid schizophrenia and severely impaired mobility, appealed against the refusal of her application for judicial review of S's decision to make her an offer of full time residential care. K and her husband had been granted permission to enter the United Kingdom on condition that they did not have recourse to public funds; hence they were entitled to community care services pursuant to the National Assistance Act 1948 and the National Health Service and Community Care Act 1990 s.47 but not to income support or housing benefit. K, her husband and daughter lived in a one bedroom second floor flat. Following an assessment of K's needs, S offered a joint placement in a residential home for K and her husband, the primary carer. It was K's contention that her needs would be best met by the provision of a two bedroom ground floor flat so that her daughter could continue to live with them. At first instance, the court held that S's offer of joint residential accommodation was the only reasonable offer and that K's refusal to accept that offer was objectively unreasonable. K appealed, contending that S had acted in a way which no reasonable local authority could and had behaved unlawfully in failing to take her wishes into account.

Held, dismissing the appeal, that whilst S was under a duty to consider K's preferences and beliefs, the assessment of K's accommodation needs and how those needs were best met were ultimately matters for S. S had made an offer of accommodation of the only type which it considered would meet K's assessed needs. S was required to take K's wishes into account but was under no obligation pursuant to s.21 of the 1948 Act to provide an alternative that would satisfy K's preference if that alternative would not meet all of the assessed needs, *R. v. Kensington and Chelsea RLBC, ex p. Kujtim* [1999] 4 All E.R. 161, [1999] C.L.Y. 3052 applied.

R. (ON THE APPLICATION OF K) v. SOUTHWARK LBC; *sub nom.* K v. SOUTHWARK LBC, [2001] EWCA Civ 999, [2002] B.L.G.R. 15, Mance, L.J., CA.

5133.   Medical treatment – sickness insurance – conditions for reimbursement – compatibility with freedom to provide services – European Community

[EC Treaty Art.59 (now, after amendment, Art.49 EC), Art.60 (now Art.50 EC).]

The Netherlands court referred questions to the ECJ as to the compatibility of certain legislation with the freedom to provide services. The questions had arisen in proceedings brought by G and P, both of whom were Dutch nationals, challenging the refusal of their sickness insurance funds to reimburse the costs incurred receiving treatment. G, who suffered from Parkinson's disease, had been treated in a specialist clinic in Germany without obtaining prior authorisation from her sickness insurance fund. P had fallen into a coma following an accident and had received special intensive therapy in an Austrian clinic which was only available in the Netherlands on an experimental basis. Under the relevant Dutch law, the ZFW treatment abroad was only authorised if it was "normal" and "necessary".

Held, giving a preliminary ruling, that in the absence of harmonisation at Community level, Member States were free to determine the conditions concerning the right or duty to be insured with a social security scheme, and the conditions for entitlements to benefits as long as they conformed with Community law. Notwithstanding the fact that hospital medical treatment was financed directly by sickness insurance funds, hospital services fell within the EC Treaty Art.59 (now, after amendment, Art.49 EC) and Art.60 (now Art.50 EC). In requiring prior authorisation for the reimbursement of the costs incurred in another Member State whereas treatment provided in contracted hospitals situated in the Netherlands was paid for by the sickness insurance funds without prior authorisation and in providing for such reimbursement to be refused where certain requirements were not met, the ZFW constituted a barrier to the freedom to provide services. That restriction might, however, be justified by the objective of maintaining a balanced medical and hospital service open to all, and by the risk of seriously undermining the social security system's financial balance. In deciding whether treatment was "normal", the national authorities had to take into consideration all the relevant reliable scientific information and in deciding whether it was "necessity", treatment could only be refused on the grounds that the same or equally effective treatment could be obtained without undue delay from an establishment with which the insured person's sickness insurance fund had contractual arrangements.

GERAETS-SMITS v. STICHTING ZIEKENFONDS VGZ (C157/99); PEERBOOMS v. STICHTING CZ GROEP ZORGVERZEKERINGEN [2002] Q.B. 409, GC Rodriguez Iglesias (President), ECJ.

5134. Medical treatment – sickness insurance – reimbursement of costs incurred in another Member State – applicable rules – European Community

[EC Treaty Art.59 (now, after amendment, Art.49 EC); Council Regulation 1408/71.]

The Belgian court referred questions to the ECJ concerning whether, once it had been established that hospital treatment in another Member State should have been authorised, reimbursement of the costs of hospital treatment had to be made in accordance with the scheme of the state of the competent institution or in accordance with that organised by the State on whose territory the hospital treatment has taken place. The ECJ was also asked about the rules on assumption of costs to be followed when the authorisation provided for in the Community rules to obtain hospital treatment in another Member State had been obtained, by declaration of a court where appropriate. D, a Belgian national, was refused authorisation from her sickness insurance fund to undergo orthopaedic surgery in France because her request was deemed insufficiently supported in the absence of the opinion of a doctor from a Belgian university. D went ahead with the operation and brought an action against her sickness insurance fund before the Belgian courts for reimbursement of the costs incurred on the basis of the tariffs applied in Belgium and not those applied in France. A subsequent report by a medical expert confirmed that the surgery was not currently performed in Belgium and that the restoration of D's health did indeed necessitate hospital treatment abroad.

Held, giving a preliminary ruling, that Council Regulation 1408/71 established a system which ensured that a person covered by social insurance who was authorised to receive medical benefits in kind in a Member State other than the state in which he was insured enjoyed in the Member State in which the treatment was provided conditions as favourable as those enjoyed by insured persons covered by the legislation of that state. Therefore the applicable rules on assumption of costs were those applied in the state in which treatment was provided. The costs of benefits in kind were borne, in principle, by the institutions of the state in which the treatment was provided and were subsequently refunded by the institution with which the person concerned was insured. Where the costs were not assumed owing to an unjustified refusal to grant authorisation by the institution with which the person concerned was insured, the latter institution had to guarantee directly to the person concerned reimbursement of an amount equivalent to that which it would ordinarily have assumed if authorisation had been properly granted. As medical activities fell within the EC Treaty Art. 59 (now, after amendment, Art.49 EC), national legislation had to guarantee that an insured person who had been authorised to receive hospital treatment abroad received a level of payment comparable to that which he would have received if he had received hospital treatment in his own Member State. Article 59 precluded rules which prevented additional reimbursement corresponding to the difference between the lower tariff of reimbursement of the state in which the hospital treatment was carried out and the more favourable tariff laid down in the social insurance scheme of the state of registration. Although the risk of seriously undermining the financial balance of the social security system could constitute an overriding reason in the general interest capable of justifying a barrier to the principle of freedom to provide services, there was no reason to consider that payment of the additional reimbursement in question would entail an additional financial burden for the sickness insurance scheme of the state in which the person concerned was originally insured capable of preventing the maintenance of treatment capacity or medical competence on national territory.

VANBRAEKEL v. ALLIANCE NATIONALE DES MUTUALITIES CHRETIENNES (ANMC) (C368/98) *The Times*, September 4, 2001, GC Rodriguez Iglesias (President), ECJ.

5135. Nursing homes – registration – availability of premises

[Registered Homes Act 1984 s.21 (1) (a), s.28, s.30.]

S appealed against a decision of the Registered Homes Tribunal that her appeal against a decision to close the nursing home which she ran should be dismissed on the basis that she no longer had the use of, or intended to use, the home. Following an emergency closure order issued pursuant to the Registered Homes Act 1984 s.30 the home had been closed with immediate effect. Subsequently a further application by the local authority to cancel S's registration to run the home had been filed pursuant to s.28. Thereafter the home had been repossessed and sold by the mortgagee. S contended that for the purposes of s.21 (1) (a), which contained the definition of "nursing home", the individual concerned was not required to establish that they were using, or intending to use, any premises.

Held, dismissing the appeal, that registration of the person was inextricably linked with the availability of premises, with the result that it would be appropriate for the registration to be cancelled and any pending appeal dismissed if the premises ceased to be available, *Woodard v. North Somerset DC* [1998] 1 F.L.R. 950, [1998] C.L.Y. 2390 applied.

SANJIVI v. EAST KENT HA (2001) 59 B.M.L.R. 115, Hallett, J., QBD (Admin Ct).

5136. Residential accommodation – local authorities

RESIDENTIAL ACCOMMODATION (RELEVANT PREMISES, ORDINARY RESIDENCE AND EXEMPTIONS) (AMENDMENT) (ENGLAND) REGULATIONS 2001, SI 2001 1859; made under the National Assistance Act 1948 s.26A. In force: June 1, 2001; £1.50.

These Regulations amend the Residential Accommodation (Relevant Premises, Ordinary Residence and Exemptions) Regulations 1993 (SI 1993 477) which enable local authorities to make residential accommodation arrangements for certain categories of people who were in or temporarily absent from independent sector residential care and nursing homes on March 1993. These categories include people under pensionable age and, in certain circumstances, people over pensionable age. Both categories of people are subject to the restriction that if they are evicted from a residential care home or nursing home, served with a notice to quit or temporarily absent from a home to which they will not be allowed to return, no accommodation may be provided for them in that home, or any other premises owned or managed by the person who owned or managed that home, unless it is ceasing to operate as a home. These Regulations remove this restriction.

5137. Residential accommodation – sums for personal requirements

NATIONAL ASSISTANCE (SUMS FOR PERSONAL REQUIREMENTS) (ENGLAND) REGULATIONS 2001, SI 2001 1005; made under the National Assistance Act 1948 s.22. In force: April 9, 2001; £1.75.

These Regulations, which revoke the National Assistance (Sums for Personal Requirements) Regulations 2000 (SI 2000 798), set out the weekly sum which local authorities in England are to assume, in the absence of special circumstances, that residents in accommodation arranged under the National Assistance Act 1948 Part III will need for their personal requirements. From April 9, 2001 all residents will be assumed to need £16.05 per week for their personal requirements.

5138. Residential care – care homes and nursing homes

CARE HOMES REGULATIONS 2001, SI 2001 3965; made under the Care Standards Act 2000 s.3, s.22, s.25, s.34, s.35, s.118. In force: April 1, 2002; £4.50.

These Regulations, which replace the regulatory system provided for in relation to residential care homes and nursing homes by the Registered Homes Act 1984, exclude from the definition of a care home under the Care Standards Act 2000 certain NHS hospitals and establishments providing nursing, universities, schools and certain further education institutions. Under the Regulations, each home must have a statement of purpose and supply a guide to the home to each service user. The Regulations make provision about the fitness of the persons carrying on and managing the home, and require satisfactory information to be available in relation to certain specified matters. In addition, they prescribe the circumstances where a manager must be appointed for the home, impose general requirements in relation to the proper conduct of the home, make provision about the conduct of care homes and about the suitability of premises and fire precautions to be taken.

5139. Residential care – children – sexual abuse – vicarious liability of employer

See TORTS: L v. Hesley Hall Ltd. §5359

5140. Residential care – elderly persons – placement in private home – susceptibility to review

[National Assistance Act 1948 s.26; National Health Service and Community Care Act 1990 s.47.]

G, aged 91, had been assessed by Wandsworth London Borough Council, WLBC, as in need of residential accommodation under the National Health Service and Community Care Act 1990 s.47. WLBC chose to discharge its duty to G by placing her in a residential home run by S, a charity, as it was entitled to do under the National Assistance Act 1948 s.26. G was told by S that they would provide her with a "home for life", unless her health deteriorated to the extent that she would require specialist nursing care which the home could not provide. G lived in the home for four years, until in 1999 S decided to close it for financial reasons. G brought an application for judicial review, contending that G had moved into the home in reliance on S's promise that it would be a "home for life" and that although S was a private body it owed G a public law duty that was open to scrutiny by judicial review, or alternatively that S and WLBC were bound together by WLBC's statutory duty. S and WLBC argued that there was no such public duty as WLBC was not empowered to force S to keep the home open, having discharged its duty by placing G there.

Held, dismissing the application, that G had been given only a qualified assurance that she would be able to remain at the home for the rest of her life. S had not acted as WLBC's agent. Although S could be said to be carrying out a public function, it was not the case that if S did not provide the services the state would be obliged to intervene, as WLBC were authorised to place G in another private institution instead, *R. v. Advertising Standards Authority, ex p. Insurance Services* (1990) 2 Admin. L.R. 77, [1991] C.L.Y. 8 considered. S.26 of the 1948 Act did no more than allow WLBC to tender out its residential accommodation duties. It did not establish a statutory public duty on S over and above its private contractual duties. Thus the relationship between S and WLBC was a purely commercial one to which the court could not affix a public law duty, *R. v. Panel on Take-overs and Mergers, ex p. Datafin Plc* (1987) Q.B. 815, [1987] C.L.Y. 21 and *R. v. Disciplinary Committee of the Jockey Club, ex p. The Aga Khan* [1993] 1 W.L.R. 909, [1993] C.L.Y. 33 applied. WLBC's duty remained only to reassess G's needs and ensure that they were met, in alternative accommodation if necessary, and there had been no breach of that duty.

R. v. SERVITE HOUSES, *ex p.* GOLDSMITH (2001) 33 H.L.R. 35, Moses, J., QBD.

5141. Residential care – nursing homes – cancellation of registration – impact of surrender and cesser of use

[Registered Homes Act 1984 Part II.]

K appealed against a decision upholding the cancellation of their registration to operate a nursing home under the Registered Homes Act 1984 Part II. K maintained that (1) they had voluntarily surrendered their registration in response to a notice of proposal of cancellation issued by SHA. Accordingly a subsequent decision by the Registered Homes Tribunal to dismiss K's appeal against the confirmation of cancellation had been wrong in law since there was no longer any registration in existence capable of being cancelled, and (2) the decision to cancel did not take effect until the tribunal had made its decision and by that date use of the premises as a nursing home had ceased. SHA maintained that despite the correspondence passing between the parties with regard to the issue of surrender, SHA had never waived its right to adopt the notice of proposal, and that if a registered person were able to surrender their registration at will they would be able to evade the consequence of cancellation, namely the inclusion of their name upon a list maintained by the Department of Health of those persons deemed unfit to run a nursing home.

Held, dismissing the appeal, that (1) there had been no agreement to surrender. The authority had simply raised no objection to the suggestion made by K, and .(2) the tribunal had been entitled to have regard to the facts in existence as at the date of SHA's decision to adopt the proposal to cancel the registration at which time K was still using the premises as nursing home. The fact that the premises had subsequently ceased to be used as a nursing home by the time that the appeal hearing before the tribunal took place did not nullify the decision to cancel. There was nothing within the Act to suggest such a conclusion was justified and to allow it would enable otherwise unfit persons to avoid inclusion on the list maintained by the Department of Health.

R. v. SUFFOLK HA, *ex p.* KOWLESSUR; *sub nom.* KOWLESSUR v. SUFFOLK HA *The Independent*, December 15, 2000, Jonathan Parker, L.J., CA.

5142. Social security – appointments – members – Wales

CARE COUNCIL FOR WALES (APPOINTMENT, MEMBERSHIP AND PROCEDURE) REGULATIONS 2001, SI 2001 2136 (W.149); made under the Care Standards Act 2000 s.118, Sch.1 para.6. In force: in accordance with Reg.1; £3.50.

These Regulations make provision about the appointment, membership and procedure of the Care Council for Wales by setting a maximum number of members for the Council, all of whom are to be appointed by the National Assembly, and require a majority of members of the Council, including its Chair, to be lay persons.

5143. Social services – community care – accommodation

PRESERVED RIGHTS (TRANSFER OF RESPONSIBILITIES TO LOCAL AUTHORITIES) REGULATIONS 2001, SI 2001 3776; made under the Health and Social Care Act 2001 s.50. In force: December 19, 2001; £1.75.

These Regulations provide exceptions to the duties, imposed by the Health and Social Care Act 2001 on certain authorities to ensure the provision of community care services for people who were preserved rights cases before the appointed day. The exceptions are cases where a person, in respect of the day before the appointed day, is not entitled to income support, or is so entitled but not at the preserved rights rate, or is being provided with after care services under the Mental Health Act 1983. They provide for the amount that can be recovered where certain authorities are responsible for payments under arrangements which existed before the appointed day which continue until community care services are provided.

5144. Social services – community care – accommodation – Wales

PRESERVED RIGHTS (TRANSFER OF RESPONSIBILITIES TO LOCAL AUTHORITIES) (WALES) REGULATIONS 2001, SI 2001 3985 (W.326); made under the Health and Social Care Act 2001 s.50. In force: December 19, 2001; £2.00.

These Regulations are made under the Health and Social Care Act 2001 s.50 which relates to the removal of prohibitions against local authorities providing accommodation to persons who were in such accommodation on March 31, 1993. They provide for exceptions to the duties imposed by s.50(3) to (7) of the 2001 Act on local authorities to ensure the provision of community care services for people who were preserved rights cases before the day appointed for the coming into force of s.50(1); for the amount that can be recovered where, under s.50(6) of the 2001 Act, certain authorities are responsible for payments under arrangements which existed before the appointed day and which will continue until community care services are provided; and makes provision for the circumstances in which a person is to be treated as ordinarily resident for the purposes of s.50 of the 2001 Act.

5145. Social services – direct payments – disabled children

DISABLED CHILDREN (DIRECT PAYMENTS) (ENGLAND) REGULATIONS 2001, SI 2001 442; made under the Children Act 1989 s.17A, s.104. In force: April 1, 2001; £1.75.

The Carers and Disabled Children Act 2000 inserts a new s.17A into the Children Act 1989 enabling local authorities to make direct payments to persons with parental responsibility for a disabled child or a disabled child aged 16 or 17, in lieu of services which would have otherwise been provided for them by the local authority under the Children Act 1989 s.17. These Regulations specify those persons from whom services may not be secured by means of a direct payment and the maximum periods of residential accommodation which may be secured by means of a direct payment.

5146. Social work – education and training – transfer scheme

CENTRAL COUNCIL FOR EDUCATION AND TRAINING IN SOCIAL WORK (TRANSFER SCHEME) ORDER 2001, SI 2001 2561; made under the Care Standards Act 2000 s.70, s.118. In force: September 1, 2001; £1.75.

This Order contains provisions consequential upon the Central Council for Education and Training in Social Work (CCETSW) ceasing to exercise functions conferred upon the Council by the Health and Social Services and Adjudications Act 1983 s.10. It relates to the transfer of staff from CCETSW to new bodies established in England, Wales, Scotland and Northern Ireland, to the transfer of property to those new bodies, provides for the transfer of the liabilities and obligations of CCETSW and provides for the transfer to the English Council of CCETSW's function relating to the issue of replacement certificates.

5147. Tax credits – disabled persons tax credit – working families tax credit

TAX CREDITS (MISCELLANEOUS AMENDMENTS NO.9) REGULATIONS 2001, SI 2001 3454; made under the Social Security Contributions and Benefits (Northern Ireland) Act 1992 s.136, s.137, s.175; and the Tax Credits Act 1999 s.2, Sch.2 para.1, Sch.2 para.20. In force: November 13, 2001; £1.50.

These Regulations amend the Family Credit (General) Regulations 1987 (SI 1987 1973) and the Disability Working Allowance (General) Regulations 1991 (SI 1991 2887) which provide that subject to certain exceptions, income derived from capital shall be treated as capital for the purposes of calculating a claimant's entitlement to disabled person's tax credit or working families' tax credit. The amendment adds to the list of exceptions income derived from a dwelling which the claimant intends in due course to occupy as his home but which he currently does not occupy due to living in job-related accommodation. In addition, the Regulations add to the list of capital to be disregarded in calculating a claimant's capital for the purposes of ascertaining his entitlement to disabled person's tax credit or working families' tax credit payments made for victims of National Socialism during the Second World War.

5148. Books

Cull, Lesley-Ann; Roche, Jeremy – Law and Social Work: Contemporary Issues for Practice. Paperback: £14.50. ISBN 0-333-94587-5. Palgrave, formerly Macmillan Press.

Penton, John – Widening the Eye of the Needle. 2nd Ed. Conservation and Mission. Paperback: £10.95. ISBN 0-7151-7589-0. Church House Publishing.
Ramsey, Rosalind; Szmuckler, George; Gerada, Clare; Mars, Sara – Mental Illness. Paperback: £14.95. ISBN 1-85302-934-3. Jessica Kingsley Publishers.
Tingle, John; Garwood-Gowers, Austen – Healthcare Law: the Impact of the Human Rights Act 1998. Paperback: £48.40. ISBN 1-85941-670-5. Cavendish Publishing Ltd.
Williams, Brian – Reparation and Victim-focused Social Work. Paperback: £15.95. ISBN 1-84310-023-1. Jessica Kingsley Publishers.
Wilson, Kate; James, Adrian – Child Protection Handbook. 2nd Ed. Hardback: £34.95. ISBN 0-7020-2584-4. Bailliere Tindall.

SUCCESSION

5149. Administration of estates – caveats – claim to interest in stepmother's estate arising from father's intestacy

S applied by way of a summons for directions to maintain the caveat she had issued in respect of her late stepmother's estate. R, a proposed executor under the stepmother's will, sought to have the summons dismissed and a direction that the caveat should cease. S claimed an interest in the estate arising from her late father's intestacy and also alleged fraud by the solicitor who administered her father's estate.

Held, dismissing S's summons and ordering cessation of the caveat, that any right of action that S might have could not proceed by way of a probate action but would lie instead against either the administrator of her father's estate or the executor of her stepmother's estate. Any such action would not be advanced by maintaining the caveat in being as this would effectively prevent administration of the stepmother's estate.

STOKER v. ROSE; *sub nom.* KRZYSZTOFOWICZ (DECEASED), *Re* [2001] W.T.L.R. 883, District Judge Kenworthy-Browne, Fam Div.

5150. Administration of estates – costs – payment of trustee's indemnity from trust funds

See CIVIL PROCEDURE: D'Abo v. Paget (No.2). §455

5151. Administration of estates – intestacy – discriminatory treatment accorded to black intestates – South Africa

[Black Administration Act 1927 (South Africa) Reg.3(1); Black Administration Act 1927 s.23(7); Constitution of South Africa 1996.]

M, a widow, brought an application contending that the Black Administration Act 1927 (South Africa) was in breach of the Constitution of South Africa 1996. M's husband, H, who was black, had died intestate. Regulation 3(1) of the Act required that the estate of a black intestate could only be administered by a magistrate, and s.23(7) prohibited its administration by the Master of the High Court, who was responsible for the administration of the estates of white intestates. The High Court made an order declaring Reg.3(1) invalid, but leaving s.23(7) in place, with the effect that neither a magistrate nor the Master could administer H's estate.

Held, allowing the application, that the Act was a reminder both of South Africa's racist past and also that transition was a continuing process. The Act was entirely contrary to the Constitution's purpose of ensuring a democratic society based on fairness and in breach of the right to dignity. The administration of estates required a complete overhaul, but this was a process that could not be hurried. Although s.23(7) and Reg.3(1) were both invalid, Reg.3(1) would be retained for a period of two years, allowing the estates of black intestates to be administered during the period that Parliament could address the matter.

MOSENEKE v. MASTER OF THE HIGH COURT 10 B.H.R.C. 117, Sachs, J., Const Ct (SA).

5152. Beneficiaries – advancement – inter vivos gift of house and testamentary gifts by parent – rule against double portions

L and his wife lived with their daughter, S, from 1972, initially in S's rented flat. In 1981, S's mother was paralysed by a stroke and in 1984 L was hospitalised with a heart condition. On his return home, S, L and S's children decided that L would purchase a property in S's name where she, L and her daughter and son in law could live together. By his will of June 1985, L appointed S as his executor. He also gave S all his furniture, with the residue of the estate being shared in various proportions between S, her two brothers, C and T, and any grandchildren living at his death. Following L's death in 1990, C became concerned that the purchase of the house in S's name had been undertaken as the result of undue influence. Further, that if the purchase had been a gift, the presumption against double portions applied, so that the purchase price should be brought into account against S's division of the residuary estate.

Held, dismissing C's claim, that the evidence showed that L had intended that S should hold the property beneficially so that it was not held on a resulting trust for L's estate. The presumption of advancement in S's favour was not rebutted. The gift of the house to S differed from the testamentary gift to S so that the presumption against double portions did not arise. It was clear that the house was recognition of the care S had given to her parents. Further, it would have been surprising if L had failed to mention to his solicitor that the gift of the house was intended to form part of his residuary estate when giving instructions for his will.

CASIMIR v. ALEXANDER [2001] W.T.L.R. 939, Michael Hart Q.C., Ch D.

5153. Beneficiaries – disclaimers – effectiveness of beneficiaries – disclaimer before testator's death

FS applied for a declaration that a voluntary disclaimer made in 1979 by his brother, RS, was binding. RS had renounced all benefit to which he might, in the future, become entitled upon the death of their mother, LS. LS subsequently died, having specified in her will that the residue of her estate be divided equally between her sons.

Held, refusing the declaration, that the disclaimer was ineffective because, at the date upon which it was made, RS had had no interest to accept or disclaim; he had had a mere expectation of an interest, *Stratton's Disclaimer, Re* [1958] Ch. 42, [1957] C.L.Y. 981 and *Paradise Motor Co, Re* [1968] 1 W.L.R. 1125, [1968] C.L.Y. 447 considered. Furthermore, FS could not rely upon the disclaimer as an enforceable agreement because he had provided no consideration for it.

SMITH v. SMITH (DISCLAIMER OF INTEREST UNDER WILL); *sub nom.* SMITH (DECEASED), *Re* [2001] 1 W.L.R. 1937, Anthony Mann Q.C., Ch D.

5154. Beneficiaries – fiduciary duty – partnership agreement – termination of onerous tenancy

R was tenant of his father N's farm. R had three children J, S and H. R died in 1980 leaving his farm to his three children equally. His children entered into a partnership agreement to run the farm with S actually it. The farm ran at a loss and in 1990 J commenced proceedings against S and H to dissolve the partnership alleging that S had not acted in good faith. H sold her interest in the farm to S for £14,000. Subsequently, knowing these facts, N made a will granting S an option to purchase the freehold of the farm. Following his death, S confirmed her wish to exercise her option. A declaration was later made by consent, pursuant to the proceedings issued by J, that the partnership was dissolved from that time. In

1993 S and R's executors sold part of the farm's milk quota. In 1996 S completed the purchase of the farm from N's executors. In 1997 S, as one of the joint tenants of the continuing tenancy of herself and J, gave notice to J to terminate the tenancy. S and J were entitled to compensation from their landlord, S, in respect of milk quota. J sought a declaration from the Court that S had acted in breach of her fiduciary duty in selling part of the milk quota and in terminating the tenancy.

Held, granting a declaration in favour of S, that S had taken no profit from her fiduciary position. She had been entitled to acquire the freehold as a beneficiary under the reversioner's will and not as a partner. Therefore, no liability to account arose in this context. On these facts the service of the notice to quit was not a breach of fiduciary duty because the tenancy itself was a liability to the partnership. In any event, there was no loss occasioned on these facts. In relation to the milk quota, the partnership had lost its opportunity to claim under the milk quota because it had allowed the statutory deadline to pass.

WARD v. BRUNT [2000] W.T.L.R. 731, Peter Leaver Q.C., Ch D.

5155. **Family provision – divorcees – challenge to will of former spouse – existence of special circumstances**

[Matrimonial Proceedings and Property Act 1970; Inheritance (Provision for Family and Dependants) Act 1975 s.2.]

B was the principal beneficiary under the will of her brother in law, D. D's ex wife, H, whom he divorced in 1964, was awarded £30,000 under the Inheritance (Provision for Family and Dependants) Act 1975 s.2. The judge at first instance held that there were special circumstances justifying an order under s.2, namely the capital value of the estate, which was in excess of £200,000, the poor state of H's finances, and the rapprochement between D and his adopted son from his first marriage immediately prior to D's death. B appealed, contending that the judge had erred in finding that any special circumstances existed. H maintained that, because she and D were divorced prior to the widening of the relief available on divorce under the Matrimonial Proceedings and Property Act 1970, her situation should be treated differently from post 1970 cases for the purposes of the 1975 Act and that justified the order made.

Held, allowing the appeal, that the court was obliged to answer two questions, namely whether the disposition on divorce had been reasonable, and, if not, what provision should have been made. H's submission about divorces pre 1970 and post 1970 was flawed. The divorce between D and H had been a clean break and D had assumed no continuing responsibility towards H. D had no continuing moral obligation towards H and entitlement could only be established on the basis that special circumstances existed. The judge had erred in finding the existence of any special circumstances. The capital sum involved was not significant by the today's standards and the limited reconciliation between father and son could not justify extending relief to the former spouse, *Cameron v. Treasury Solicitor* [1996] 2 F.L.R. 716, [1996] C.L.Y. 5551 and *Fullard (Deceased), Re* [1982] Fam. 42, [1982] C.L.Y. 3385 applied.

BARRASS v. HARDING [2001] 1 F.L.R. 138, Dame Elizabeth Butler-Sloss (President), CA.

5156. **Family provision – spouses – reasonable provision determined by reference to situation on divorce**

[Inheritance (Provision for Family and Dependants) Act 1975 s.2, s.3.]

A married couple had had 12 children during their 54 year marriage. The wife, W, had never worked and been dependent on H throughout. By his will, H, who was sole owner of the matrimonial home, left all his household goods to W along with a legacy of £10,000. The residue of his estate was to be divided equally between his children, with a power to his executors to provide W with a home. W sought an order under the Inheritance (Provision for Family and Dependants) Act 1975 s.2 that she was entitled to half the estate, on the basis that was the amount she would have received had the marriage ended in divorce.

Held, allowing the application, that the matrimonial home would be transferred into W's name and the legacy reduced to £5,000 to give W half the value of H's estate. Reasonable provision in terms of s.3 of the Act called for a two stage inquiry as to the extent of the provision made by the will before going on to decide how the powers under the Act should be applied in relation to it. In the instant case, s.3(2) required a consideration of the provision W could have expected to receive on divorce. Both spouses had made an equal contribution to the marriage for this purpose, *White (Pamela) v. White (Martin)* [2001] 1 A.C. 596 applied. On the facts, therefore, an equal division of assets would have been possible in the context of a clean break divorce and that would be followed in determining the claim under the Act.

ADAMS v. LEWIS; *sub nom*. ADAMS (FRANCIS CHRISTOPHER) (DECEASED), *Re* [2001] W.T.L.R. 493, Judge Behrens, Ch D.

5157. Family provision – spouses – separation – conclusive financial arrangements

[Inheritance (Provision for Family and Dependants) Act 1975.]

P appealed against the dismissal of her claim under the Inheritance (Provision for Family and Dependants) Act 1975 for reasonable financial provision, from the estate of her deceased husband. P had separated from her husband, and in his will, save for a legacy of his business assets to a friend, the deceased had left his entire estate to S with whom he had been cohabiting at the time of his death. P contended that the judge had erred in concluding that (1) P and the deceased had arranged their affairs conclusively following their separation, and (2) P had allowed the deceased to labour under the misapprehension that they were divorced, there having been no evidence before the judge to support such findings.

Held, dismissing the appeal, that the judge had conducted a careful review of all the circumstances and had properly directed herself as to the applicable law. Accordingly, her decision could not be impugned.

PARISH v. SHARMAN [2001] W.T.L.R. 593, Jonathan Parker, L.J., CA.

5158. Intestacy – breach of promise – promises made to gardener and handyman – non payment for work carried out – proprietary estoppel – quantifying equity

[Inheritance (Provision for Family and Dependants) Act 1975.]

R, a childless widow who had no contact with her remaining family, died wholly intestate in 1997 aged 93. Her net estate, after inheritance tax and other debts, consisted of her home, valued at £420,000, possessions worth about £15,000 and £583,615 on deposit. J had started to work for R as a part time gardener in 1970 but later did other jobs for her as well. Originally he was paid per hour, but R stopped paying him in the late 1980s. Although J asked her for money, she told him he would "be all right" and intimated that she would leave the house to him when she died. However, no written agreement was made. R did provide J with the deposit to buy a house so that he could remain close by and lent him money to buy a car, which he repaid. As R became more infirm, J cared for her and toward the end of her life he stayed the night at her house and helped to feed and dress her and with toiletting. On R's death intestate, J claimed under the Inheritance (Provision for Family and Dependants) Act 1975 and on the basis of a proprietary estoppel.

Held, allowing the proprietary estoppel claim, that J had no claim under the 1975 Act as R had not maintained him and the fact that he had stayed in her house had been a benefit to R. However, the evidence showed that R had led J to believe that he would receive some, or even all, of her estate and he had acted to his detriment in reliance on her assurances. It was therefore unconscionable for R to fail to fulfil her assurances when she had enjoyed the benefit provided by J. The problem lay in quantifying the equity to which J was entitled. The size of the estate exceeded his needs and reasonable expectations. Taking the cost of full time nursing care of R over the last eight years of her life

at £25,000 per annum, the equity would be satisfied by a payment of
£200,000 to J, *Gillett v. Holt* [2001] Ch. 210, [2000] C.L.Y. 2321 followed.
JENNINGS v. RICE [2001] W.T.L.R. 871, Judge Weeks Q.C., Ch D.

5159. Intestacy – cohabitation – future intention to give survivor beneficial interest

See EQUITY: Otway v. Gibbs. §2431

5160. Intestacy – fatal accidents – provision for family and dependants

[Inheritance (Provision for Family and Dependants) Act 1975.]

In 1982 R married D by whom he had two children A and J, aged fifteen and
twelve at the time of trial. They were divorced and in 1990 R married A by whom he
had one child, P, aged seven at the time of trial. In 1991 R died intestate as a result of
car accident. Under the intestacy his net estate of £91,000 was divided £75,000 to
A, and a life interest in half the remainder £8,000 with the other half remainder
divided equally between the three children £2,666 each. As a result of R's death
A also received £272,000 and the mortgage on the house which she inherited by
survivorship was repaid. At the time of trial she had the house worth £104,000 and
other assets of £184,000. D had remarried and was living with her second husband
and the children A and J in a former council house with negative equity. They had
little money. As a result of claims against the other motorist A received £29,900 and
J received £34,500. These sums were set aside to establish themselves later in life.
A and J applied to the court for reasonable financial provision from R's estate under
the Inheritance (Provision for Family and Dependants) Act 1975.

Held, allowing the application and awarding A and J each a lump sum of
£30,000 from R's estate that (1) there was no requirement for the children to
show special circumstances; (2) the sums received by way of settlement against
the motorist were not to be taken as reasonable provision, and (3) there was
inadequate provision under the intestacy.

ROBINSON (DECEASED), *Re*; ROBINSON (ANNE) v. ROBINSON (ANGELA)
[2001] W.T.L.R. 267, John Martin Q.C., Ch D.

5161. Intestacy – illegitimacy – exclusion from inheritance – right to family life

See HUMAN RIGHTS: Camp v. Netherlands (28369/95). §3555

5162. Powers of attorney – capacity – mental health of donor – burden of proof

[Enduring Powers of Attorney Act 1985 s.6(5)(a).]

Y and Z appealed against the allowing of X's appeal ([2000] Ch. 343, [2000]
C.L.Y. 4904) against the refusal of an application to register an enduring power of
attorney over the estate of the donor, W. The power of attorney had been granted in
favour of X, W's child, but Y and Z, W's other children, objected to the registration
contending that W had lacked the mental capacity to understand the nature and
effect of the power when she had granted it. Y and Z submitted that the judge had
erred in holding that where objection was raised under the Enduring Powers of
Attorney Act 1985 s.6(5)(a) on the basis of invalidity due to the donor's
incapacity, the burden of proof was on the objectors throughout to show the
lack of necessary understanding on the part of the donor. They argued that the
judge should have held that once evidence of a lack of understanding had been
established, the burden was reversed and fell on the attorney to prove that the
donor had the necessary understanding when the power was granted.

Held, dismissing the appeal, that there was no authority to the effect that the
burden of proof fell on the attorney to show that the donor had the necessary
understanding upon granting the power, *K (Enduring Powers of Attorney), Re*
[1988] Ch. 310, [1988] C.L.Y. 59 considered. The correct approach in cases
where there was only one issue to be determined was to hear all the evidence
before reaching a decision rather than to alter the burden of proof after evidence
had been adduced. Accordingly, the judge had been entitled to conclude that

the burden of proof had remained on Y and Z throughout and that they had failed to discharge that burden.

W (ENDURING POWER OF ATTORNEY), Re [2001] Ch. 609, Sir Christopher Staughton, CA.

5163. Property – valuation – option to purchase – value at time of death – subsequent events

L sought a declaration regarding the valuation of an option to purchase flats gifted by the deceased, B, in her will. The trustees were responsible for the valuation of the two flats, one of which had been occupied by B's husband until her death. The will, as amended by codicil, stated that L could exercise their option at a price of 80 per cent of the full market price, as assessed by a valuer appointed by the trustees.

Held, granting the declaration, that the flat had to be valued at the time of B's death, irrespective of the probate valuation. The valuation should take into account the facts which were known about the property at the time of death and could not be amended in light of subsequent events, *Mackay v. McSparran* [1974] N.I. 136, [1976] C.L.Y. 1998 followed. The valuation should consider the husband's occupation and the development potential of the property at the time. B's husband's subsequent vacation of the flat, the planning policy changes and the money expended by L, were to be disregarded. There was no requirement to impute the knowledge of those developments to the valuer, *Talbot v. Talbot* [1968] Ch. 1, [1967] C.L.Y. 4121 distinguished.

BLISS (DECEASED), Re [2001] 1 W.L.R. 1973, Ferris, J., Ch D.

5164. Valuation – chartered surveyors – option to purchase granted by testator to son with existing interest in portion of estate – correct basis for valuation

A testator, M, left his estate on trust for his three sons, A, J and N in equal shares. An option was granted in M's will to A to purchase M's home and adjoining land at a price to be determined by a chartered surveyor to be appointed by the trustees. A deed of gift executed prior to M's death resulted in a portion of the estate known as the "red land" being held on trust by M and A as tenants in common in equal shares. Following M's death the executors took counsel's advice as to the effect of the option and instructed a chartered surveyor to value the house and land on the basis of an arm's length transaction between willing vendor and willing purchaser. For the purposes of the valuation the surveyor sought to value the property on an open market basis and split the property into three portions, making a deduction of 15 per cent representing A's half share in the red land. J and N contended that it had been inappropriate to seek to value the property on an open market basis since that was a term of art and there had been no confirmation by the valuer that he had taken due account of A's status as a "special purchaser". J and N further maintained that a term should be implied that the price was one that was fair and reasonable and that M's property should have been valued as a single unit with a deduction representing A's interest in the red land made on the basis that he was willing to sell.

Held, giving judgment for J and N and directing that a further valuation be commissioned, that M had intended to grant an option over the whole of his interest in the home and land despite the fact that A owned a portion of it. The valuer was required to ascertain the price for M's interest excluding A's interest in the red land. The reference to price in the option clause had not been intended as a reference to open market value since that was a term of art and if M had been aware of it and its significance it was likely that he would have made specific reference to it. On that basis his intention was that the price should be a fair and reasonable one, *Mulder, Re* [1943] 2 All E.R. 150 distinguished and *Sudbrook Trading Estate Ltd v. Eggleton* [1983] 1 A.C. 444, [1982] C.L.Y. 1776 applied. The method for valuation would be left to the valuer to be determined in accordance with objective criteria and the property should be divided into plots only in circumstances where such division would assist the valuer in determining a fair and reasonable price.

DUTTON v. DUTTON [2001] W.T.L.R. 553, Arden, J., Ch D.

5165. Wills – capacity, knowledge and approval – implied revocation by destruction in hands of third party

X, the deceased suffered a massive stroke in 1986. In 1987 he was placed in the care of the Court of Protection because he was unable to manage his own affairs though not specifically by reason of mental disorder but because he was incapable of making himself understood verbally or otherwise. In 1988 X was taken to the offices of a bank by D, his former dancing partner. The bank accepted instructions for a will leaving everything to D with substitution in favour of the RSPB. The instructions were given entirely by D and the deceased's only action was to point to D during the interview. On a second visit to the bank with D the deceased executed the will which was not read over to him. The original of the will was retained and lost by the bank. D applied to prove a copy of the will in solemn form and the defendants, the statutory next-of-kin of the deceased who stood to inherit in default, opposed the application.

Held, refusing to grant probate of the will, that (1) the will was executed by X; (2) the presumption of revocation did not apply to the lost will since X was never in possession of it; (3) on balance the deceased was just of testamentary capacity *Banks v. Goodfellow* (1870) L.R. 5 Q.B. 549 applied, but (4) X did not fully understand the dispositions he was making and accordingly he lacked knowledge and approval, *Tyrrell v. Painton (No.1)* [1894] P. 151 applied.

D'EYE v. AVERY [2001] 2 W.T.L.R. 227, Judge Colyer Q.C., Ch D.

5166. Wills – execution – capacity – knowledge and approval – burden and standard of proof

X, the deceased, gave instructions for the making of a will on October 29, 1992 at a meeting with her solicitor in his office. X was an elderly lady who was very deaf and forgetful. She instructed the solicitor to prepare a will leaving everything to her daughter E, to the exclusion of her other daughter, B, because she had loaned money to B over the years which had not been repaid. On the advice of the solicitor she agreed to leave B a legacy of £5,000 to avoid any difficulty after her death. The solicitor asked her to sign his instructions by way of confirmation. He then discussed a draft of the will at a second meeting on November 11, 1992 and the engrossed will was executed on November 18, 1992 at the solicitor's office before two secretaries. The solicitor was not present. In October 1992 X made an application for attendance allowance and the assessing doctor found communication difficult because of severe deafness and there were early signs of senile dementia. By Christmas 1992 she was incontinent and wandering around her daughter's house semi-naked. In January she was found by a psychiatric nurse to have serious memory impairment. B challenged the will on the grounds of due execution, capacity and knowledge and approval. The challenge was rejected and B appealed on the issues of capacity, knowledge and approval.

Held, dismissing the appeal, that the judge had directed himself correctly on the burden and standard of proof and his findings of fact were unchallengeable.

EWING v. BENNETT [2001] W.T.L.R. 249, Chadwick, L.J., CA.

5167. Wills – intoxication – effect on capacity – implied revocation by destruction in hands of third party.

H, the deceased, remarried and made a will in favour of his new wife. One or more of his sons by his first marriage tried to persuade him to pass property to them and subsequently assaulted him when he declined to do so. He asked a friend, B, to draw a new will for him specifically saying that he did not want to leave anything to his sons because of the assault and verbal abuse by the sons. One of the sons was severely physically disabled. B tried to persuade H to leave something to the sons but he was determined not to do so. B was not a solicitor but was a respectable businessman and local councillor who had drafted wills for friends before. The new will was executed by H and witnessed by B and another friend, S, in the hallway of the block of flats where H lived. Both H and S had been drinking but were not apparently drunk. H gave the new will to his wife for safekeeping and subsequently gave it back to H who then gave it to his sister for safekeeping. H, an alcoholic, died of his alcoholism 10 months after the will was executed. On his death, the original could not be found although copies were available. The three issues for determination were (1) whether there was a presumption of revocation of the last will because the original could not be produced by the person seeking to propound it; (2) whether the deceased lacked testamentary capacity because of his intoxication or lack of ability in English; (3) whether the deceased knew or approved the contents of the will.

Held, pronouncing the last will in solemn form, that as to the first issue, the presumption of revocation could only arise if the will was in the custody of H because it was a presumption that he had destroyed it. In the instant case the reverse was the position since the will had deliberately been given to another specifically for safekeeping. Accordingly the presumption did not arise, *Allan v. Morrison* [1900] A.C. 604, *Sykes, Re* (1907) 23 T.L.R. 747 considered. With regard to the second issue, it was clear that at the time when he gave instructions the deceased was clear in his own mind what he wanted and why and that he had capacity. He had adequate English as was evidenced by his success in business as a carpenter and builder. The fact that he had been drinking when he signed it was not sufficient to demonstrate that he was not of testamentary capacity, *Banks v. Goodfellow* (1870) L.R. 5 Q.B. 549 applied, *Battan Singh v. Amirchand* [1948] A.C. 161 distinguished, *Brunt v. Brunt* (1872-75) 3 P. & D. 37 considered. As to the third issue, on the facts it was clear that the deceased did know and approve the contents of the will however hard that might be particularly on the disabled son. There were no circumstances to rebut the presumption of knowledge and approval, *Guardhouse v. Blackburn* (1866) L.R. 1 P. & D. 109 and *Atter v. Atkinson* (1869) L.R. 1 P. & D. 665 disapproved, *Morris, Re* [1971] P. 62, [1970] C.L.Y. 2935 applied.

CHANA (GRAVINDER) v. CHANA (HARJIT KAUR) [2001] W.T.L.R. 205, John Jarvis Q.C., Ch D.

5168. Wills – probate – foreign jurisdiction – validity of subsequent will – creation of trust – Singapore

[Evidence Act (Singapore) s.46; Rules of Court (Singapore) Ord.14 r.12.]

MH, made a will in Hong Kong in 1986 with HA as the executor. He died in Singapore in 1994. The will was admitted to probate in Hong Kong. MH's daughter in law, H, contended that MH had made a later will in California in 1988, however, this had not been witnessed, but H submitted that it was sufficient to evidence a trust in favour of her husband and she sought determination of this question as a preliminary issue. The matter was decided against her by the registrar and on appeal. H appealed.

Held, dismissing the appeal and finding the 1986 will valid, that (1) the issue was suitable for summary disposal under the Rules of Court Ord.14 r.12; (2) the 1988 document relied on by H was intended only to take effect after MH's death and therefore it could not create a trust; (3) there was no secret or half secret trust as there was no evidence of acceptance by either a beneficiary or trustee, and (4) the Hong Kong probate could in principle be impeached in the courts of Singapore under the Evidence Act s.46 and further evidence of its proper execution had validly been sought in the court below.

HIRANAND v. HARILELA (2000-01) 3 I.T.E.L.R. 297, LP Thean, J.A., CA (Sing).

5169. Wills – probate – validity of will prepared by major beneficiary – testator's knowledge at time signature witnessed

LD destroyed his former will in 1995 with the full intention of revoking it. On August 19, 1996 he signed three identical copies of a new will which had been prepared on a computer by H, who was to be a major beneficiary under it, and his signatures were witnessed by R and M. On August 24 LD was admitted to hospital. He discharged himself six days later but was found in a coma later that evening and re-admitted to hospital. He was discharged on September 13 and later that day was found dead in his garage with pipes leading from the exhaust pipe into the car. Initially the coroner returned a suicide verdict but that was later amended to a verdict of unlawful killing after the police had become suspicious of the death. H was interviewed, along with others, in connection with the death but the CPS eventually decided not to charge H with LD's murder. H produced the will signed on August 19 to LD's family as though he had had no knowledge of it and sought to have it admitted to probate. TD, LD's brother, challenged the validity of the will, contending that LD did not know that the document executed on August 19 was a will or had no knowledge of its contents and the will's validity fell to be determined by way of a preliminary issue. H did not give evidence on his own behalf.

Held, giving judgment for H on the preliminary issue, that the will was valid and should be admitted to probate. The evidence of R and M showed that LD both knew that the document was a will and had notice of its contents at the time they witnessed his signature. The burden of proof rested with H to show that LD knew and approved the will and extreme vigilance was required in the highly contentious circumstances when determining the validity of the will, *Wintle v. Nye (No.2)* [1959] 1 W.L.R. 284 followed.

HART v. DABBS; *sub nom.* DABBS (LAWRENCE STANLEY) (DECEASED), *Re* [2001] W.T.L.R. 527, Lloyd, J., Ch D.

5170. Wills – residuary gifts – UK situated assets – directions as to proceeds of Jersey bank account – Jersey

EL died in January 1995 in Morocco, leaving an illegitimate son, A, in Scotland and an estranged wife and six legitimate children in the Lebanon, where he was born. EL had made a will in Aberdeen, naming M as his executor. EL had come to the UK in 1972 and was naturalised as a British citizen in 1987. Although he visited his family in the Lebanon twice after coming to Scotland, he remained resident in the UK during the last 23 years of his life and in his will stipulated that he should be buried in the Muslim cemetery in Aberdeen. His will also stated that his flat in Aberdeen and his other UK situated assets were to go to A. However, EL's only bank account was held in Jersey and MBT sought directions as to whether the proceeds of that account should be paid to A.

Held, directing that the money was to be paid to A, that the evidence showed that EL had established himself in Scotland and wanted to remain there permanently, as shown by his burial instructions. It was also clear that he intended both his flat and other assets to go to A. As the only bank account was in Jersey, and there was evidence to show that EL regarded Jersey as being part of the UK, clearly the account proceeds formed part of his UK estate.

MIDLAND BANK TRUSTEE (JERSEY) LTD v. MacLEOD; *sub nom.* EL-KAISI (DECEASED), *Re* [2001] W.T.L.R. 817, Sir Philip Bailhache, Royal Ct (Jer).

5171. Wills – solicitors – cancellation of appointment with elderly hospitalised client – duty of care to beneficiary

See NEGLIGENCE: Hooper v. Fynmores (A Firm). §4524

5172. Books

Chatterton, David – Practice Notes on Wills. Practice Notes. Paperback: £15.95. ISBN 1-85941-663-2. Cavendish Publishing Ltd.

Cracknell, D.G. – Equity and Trusts. 3rd Ed. Cracknell's Statutes Series. Paperback: £9.95. ISBN 1-85836-379-9. Old Bailey Press.

Cracknell, D.G. – Succession: the Law of Wills and Estates. 4th Ed. Cracknell's Statutes Series. Paperback: £9.95. ISBN 1-85836-382-9. Old Bailey Press.

D'Costa, Roland – Executorship and Administration of Estates. Practice Notes. Paperback: £15.95. ISBN 1-85941-459-1. Cavendish Publishing Ltd.

Hickman, David – Lincoln Wills, 1532-1534. Publications of the Lincoln Record Society, 89. Hardback: £50.00. ISBN 0-90150-366-5. The Lincoln Record Society.

Hughes,Theodore E.; Klein, David – Family Guide toWills, Funerals & Probate 2nd Ed. Hardback: £29.50. ISBN 0-8160-4550-X. Facts on File Inc.

Iwobi, Andrew – Essential Succession. 2nd Ed. Essential Law Series. Paperback: £5.50. ISBN 1-85941-617-9. Cavendish Publishing Ltd.

Kanda-Rovati,Veena – Succession: the Law ofWills and EstatesTextbook. 3rd Ed. Old Bailey Press Textbooks. Paperback: £14.95. ISBN 1-85836-418-3. Old Bailey Press.

Kanda-Rovati,Veena – Succession: the Law of Wills and Estates Casebook. Old Bailey Press Leading Cases. Paperback: £9.95. ISBN 1-85836-423-X. Old Bailey Press.

Last Will and Testament 3rd Ed. Paperback: £9.99. ISBN 1-902646-85-1. Law Pack Publishing.

Last Will and Testament Kit. New Ed. Book: £9.99. ISBN 1-902646-22-3. Law Pack Publishing.

Last Will and Testament. 2nd Ed. CD-ROM: £17.01. ISBN 1-902646-21-5. Law Pack Publishing.

Ross, Jamie – LastWill andTestament Guide. £9.99. ISBN 1-902646-70-3. Law Pack Publishing.

Sunnucks, James H.G. – Williams, Mortimer & Sunnucks-executors, Administrators and Probate. 18th Ed. Property and Conveyancing Library. Hardback: £235.00. ISBN 0-421-65330-2. Sweet & Maxwell.

Whitehouse, Chris; Hassall, Nicholas – Principles of Trust and Will Drafting. Paperback: £50.00. ISBN 0-406-91444-3. Butterworths Law.

TAXATION

5173. **Advance corporation tax – freedom of establishment – liability of subsidiary companies of non resident parent company**

[EC TreatyArt.52 (now, after amendment, Art.43).]

The question of whether a system whereby resident UK companies could avoid liability to advance corporation tax, ACT, on dividends paid to its UK resident parent company by making a group income election, was contrary to Community law was referred to the ECJ for a preliminary ruling. The system operated by the UK was challenged by a number of other UK companies whose parent companies were established in another Member State. It was contended that the system infringed the principle of freedom of establishment since these companies were being discriminated against on the basis of nationality because they were not entitled to elect group income and thus had to payACT.

Held, giving a preliminary ruling, that the system infringed the EC Treaty Art 52 (now, after amendment, Art.43) as it afforded companies resident in the UK a benefit by allowing them to pay dividends to parent companies, without having to pay ACT where the parent company was also resident in the UK. The same benefit was denied to other companies merely because the parent company's residence was in another Member State. The argument that the system could objectively be justified in order to preserve the cohesion of the UK tax system on the basis that subsidiaries which had parent companies in another Member State were in a different position from subsidiaries of resident parent companies, was rejected. Furthermore, Art.52 required that these companies should have an effective legal remedy in order to obtain reimbursement of the financial loss which they had sustained and from which the UK authorities had benefited as a result of the ACT paid by non qualifying subsidiaries. Accordingly, the fact that the sole objective of the claims was the payment of interest equivalent to the financial loss suffered as a result of the loss of the use of sums paid prematurely did not in itself constitute a ground for dismissing the action.

METALLGESELLSCHAFT LTD v. INLAND REVENUE COMMISSIONERS (C397/ 98); HOECHST AG v. INLAND REVENUE COMMISSIONERS (C410/98) [2001] Ch. 620, La Pergola (President), ECJ.

5174. Advance corporation tax – tax planning – payment of dividends following acquisition – meaning of "transaction in securities"

[Finance Act 1960; Income and Corporation Taxes Act 1988 s.703(1)(b).]

The Revenue appealed against a decision ([2000] S.T.C. (S.C.D.) 75, [2000] C.L.Y. 4943) that the declaration and payment of a dividend was not a "transaction in securities" for the purposes of the Income and Corporation Taxes Act 1988 s.703(1)(b). L had acquired the issued share capital of a private company, S. Following the acquisition, S had paid out a large dividend which was subject to advance corporation tax. L had subsequently set the figure paid by S to the Revenue against its own corporation tax payments, both past and present, and S had received a repayment of "mainstream" corporation tax. L, having received S's dividend as franked investment income, set off the advance corporation tax paid by S against its own liability.

Held, dismissing the appeal, that (1) given that the declaration and payment of a dividend did not involve any dealing with securities or a modification of rights deriving from such securities, it could not be said that such a transaction amounted to a "transaction in securities", and (2) in considering the term "transaction in securities", it was not appropriate to refer to Parliamentary commentary in Hansard relating to the Finance Act 1960 when interpreting the 1988 Act, which was consolidated legislation, since the relevant provisions had been judicially considered prior to consolidation, *Pepper (Inspector of Taxes) v. Hart* [1993] A.C. 593, [1993] C.L.Y. 459 considered.

INLAND REVENUE COMMISSIONERS v. LAIRD GROUP PLC; *sub nom.* LAIRD GROUP PLC v. INLAND REVENUE COMMISSIONERS [2001] S.T.C. 689, Lightman, J., Ch D.

5175. Air passenger duty – amendment

AIR PASSENGER DUTY (AMENDMENT) REGULATIONS 2001, SI 2001 836; made under the Finance Act 1994 s.38. In force: April 1, 2001; £1.75.

These Regulations amend the Air Passenger Duty Regulations 1994 (SI 1994 1738) by substituting the prescribed form of return which an operator of an aircraft, who is liable to be registered for Air Passenger Duty, is required to make following changes to the rates of duty applicable to standard and other classes of travel made by the Finance Act 2000 s.18.

5176. Air passenger duty – connected flights – Isle of Man

AIR PASSENGER DUTY (CONNECTED FLIGHTS) (AMENDMENT) ORDER 2001, SI 2001 809; made under the Finance Act 1994 s.30. In force: April 1, 2001; £1.50.

This Order amends the Air Passenger Duty (Connected Flights) Order 1994 (SI 1994 1821) which determines whether successive flights are treated as connected for the purposes of the Finance Act 1994 s.30 and s.31. The Order amends the notes of interpretation by omitting the reference to an airport in the Isle of Man being treated as within the UK for air passenger duty purposes where duty equivalent to air passenger duty is charged in the Isle of Man by virtue of an Act of Tynwald.

5177. Air passenger duty – designated region – Highlands and Islands Enterprise

AIR PASSENGER DUTY (DESIGNATED REGION OF THE UNITED KINGDOM) ORDER 2001, SI 2001 808; made under the Finance Act 1994 s.31. In force: April 1, 2001; £1.50.

This Order designates a region comprising certain areas for the purposes of the Finance Act 1994 s.31 so that an air passenger whose flight departs from an airport in the region will not be treated as a chargeable passenger for the purposes of Air Passenger Duty. The areas described comprise the area within or in relation to which the functions of the body known as the Highlands and Islands Enterprise are exercisable by virtue of the Enterprise and New Towns (Scotland) Act 1990.

5178. Assessment – inheritance tax – inheritance from Italy – dispute with Italian authorities – confirmation of determination

W, a taxpayer, appealed against a notice of determination issued in relation to a chargeable transfer which had occurred when he had inherited a substantial sum upon the death of his Italian aunt. W contended that he should not be obliged to pay the sum assessed since (1) he was in dispute with the Italian authorities concerning a tax liability which he maintained that he should not be obliged to pay and which could take some considerable time to resolve, and (2) he was unable to pay the sum requested because exchange rate fluctuations had operated to his disadvantage.

Held, dismissing the appeal, that there were no valid grounds for appeal. Any adjustment required to the United Kingdom tax liability as determined would take place in due course upon the conclusion of the Italian proceedings but should be confirmed in the interim. The Revenue had adopted the exchange rate suggested by W notwithstanding that the rate adopted had not been in force as at the date of death and had operated to W's advantage. The fault for any inability to pay the sums demanded lay entirely with W given that he had clearly inherited a substantial sum.

WHITTAKER v. INLAND REVENUE COMMISSIONERS [2001] S.T.C. (S.C.D.) 61 (Note), TG Coutts Q.C. (Chairman), Sp Comm.

5179. Assessment – Inland Revenue – negligent conduct – extended time assessment – appeals to Special Commissioners by way of case stated

[Taxes Management Act 1970 s.36.]

L appealed to the General Commissioners against a number of extended time assessments raised by the Revenue under Taxes Management Act 1970 s.36 alleging negligent conduct and further estimated assessments. The appeals were dismissed. L appealed against the extended time assessments, by way of case stated.

Held, dismissing the appeals, that on the facts which could not be challenged the Commissioners were amply justified in arriving at the conclusion which they did.

LAST VICEROY RESTAURANT v. JACKSON (INSPECTOR OF TAXES) [2000] S.T.C. 1093, Evans-Lombe, J., Ch D.

5180. Capital allowances – energy conservation – machinery

CAPITAL ALLOWANCES (ENERGY SAVING PLANT AND MACHINERY) ORDER 2001, SI 2001 2541; made under the Capital Allowances Act 2001 s.45A, s.45B, s.45C, s.180A. In force: August 7, 2001; £1.75.

The Finance Act 2001 amends the Capital Allowances Act 2001 to introduce a scheme for 100 per cent first year allowances to encourage businesses to invest in energy saving plant and machinery. The 2001 Act defines energy saving plant or machinery and provides for the plant and machinery to be specified in an order made by the Treasury which can refer to any technology list, or product list, issued by the Secretary of State. This Order specifies plant or machinery falling within the Energy Technology Criteria and Product Lists published by the Department of the Environment, Transport and the Regions on April 1, 2001 and meeting the energy saving criteria set out in those Lists. The Order provides that no first year allowance may be made in the case of plant or machinery falling within the technology class "Combined Heat and Power" set out in the Energy Technology Criteria List unless a certificate of energy efficiency is in force with respect to that plant or machinery.

5181. Capital Allowances Act 2001 (c.2)

This Act restates, with minor changes, certain enactments relating to capital allowances.

This Act received Royal Assent on March 22, 2001 and comes into force on March 22, 2001.

5182. Capital gains tax – allowances – legal expenses incurred in defending title to goodwill

[Taxation of Chargeable Gains Act 1992 s.38(1)(b).]

L was a partner in an accountancy firm. Three new partners joined, and paid £150,000 between them for what was at the time described as a 20 per cent share in the goodwill of the partnership. A new partnership agreement was drawn up in which there was a reference to goodwill. The partnership subsequently broke down, and the three new partners sought to dissolve the partnership. They also brought High Court proceedings against L for recovery of £75,000, being L's share of the GPB 150,000 they had originally paid. They argued that the goodwill was actually valueless at the date of the new partnership agreement. Accordingly, the payment of GPB 150,000 had been a premium for entry into the partnership, and as such was returnable on a dissolution of the partnership. The High Court action was settled on terms which did not require L to pay the £75,000 claimed (the judge having given his opinion that the payment was not a premium), and L later disposed of the goodwill elsewhere. He was assessed to capital gains tax for his gain on the disposal. The Revenue refused an allowance for legal costs argued that L's valuation of the goodwill, rather than his title to it, had been the issue, and that his costs were not therefore deductible. L appealed the assessment on the grounds that in computing the gain, the legal costs incurred by him in defending the High Court action should be deducted, as having been wholly and exclusively incurred in establishing, preserving or defending his title to the goodwill, pursuant to the Taxation of Chargeable Gains Act 1992 s.38(1)(b).

Held, allowing L's appeal that the evidence was overwhelmingly in favour of L who incurred the costs in defending his title to goodwill.

LEE v. JEWITT (INSPECTOR OF TAXES) [2000] S.T.C. (S.C.D.) 517, Judge not applicable, Sp Comm.

5183. Capital gains tax – disposals – shares – company divided into two – meaning of "reconstruction"

[Capital Gains Tax Act 1979 s.86.]

F, the executor of M, appealed against a capital gains tax assessment of £448,020, payable from M's estate. M had owned shares in a company, X, which had two areas of business, locks and enamelling. In 1979, X's business was split into two companies and its shares were divided into A and B shares. X was then put into liquidation and two new companies, L and R, were created. Holders of A shares, which included M, were transferred to L, and holders of B shares to R. M subsequently disposed of his shares and the Revenue raised an assessment on chargeable gains of £1.5 million, contending that the division of X and re-issue of shares was a reconstruction in terms of the Capital Gains Tax Act 1979 s.86. F argued that there had not been a reconstruction within the meaning of s.86.

Held, dismissing the appeal, that the transaction was within s.86 of the Act. The fact that X had been divided into two new companies was no different for the purposes of s.86 from one company becoming a new company. The term "reconstruction" had no clear legal or business meaning, *South African Supply and Cold Storage Co, Re* [1904] 2 Ch. 268 applied, and had to be looked at within its statutory context. On the facts, L was run by the same people as had run X's lock business so that s.86 applied.

FALLON (MORGAN'S EXECUTORS) v. FELLOWS (INSPECTOR OF TAXES) [2001] S.T.C. (S.C.D.) 45, AN Brice, Sp Comm.

5184. Capital gains tax – exempt amount – 2001-02

CAPITAL GAINS TAX (ANNUAL EXEMPT AMOUNT) ORDER 2001, SI 2001 636; made under the Taxation of Chargeable Gains Act 1992 s.3. In force: March 7, 2001; £1.50.

This Order specifies £7,500 as the amount which, under the Taxation of Chargeable Gains Act 1992 s.3, is the exempt amount for the year 2001-02 and above which an individual's capital gains for a year of assessment are chargeable to capital gains tax.

5185. Capital gains tax – gilt edged securities – exemptions

CAPITAL GAINS TAX (GILT-EDGED SECURITIES) ORDER 2001, SI 2001 1122; made under the Taxation of Chargeable Gains Act 1992 Sch.9 para.1. In force: March 23, 2001; £2.00.

This Order specifies gilt-edged securities disposals of which are exempt from tax on chargeable gains in accordance with the Taxation of Chargeable Gains Act 1992 s.115.

5186. Capital gains tax – offshore trusts – interest free loans repayable on demand – liability of beneficiary

[Taxation of Chargeable Gains Act 1992 s.97(2).]

C, the taxpayer, appealed against a decision ([2000] S.T.C. 122, [2000] 4 C.L. 587) that by making him an interest free loan repayable on demand but not in fact called in, the overseas trustees of a UK trust were making to a beneficiary capital payments on which he was liable to capital gains tax. C was entitled to interest on the loan as he had a life interest in possession but contended that the making of the loan conferred no or a negligible benefit on him because it was repayable on demand, and that the failure to call it in was mere inaction on the part of the trustees so that it did not constitute the conferring of a benefit for the purposes of the Taxation of Chargeable Gains Act 1992 s.97(2).

Held, dismissing the appeal, that the interest free loan had amounted to a "capital payment" for the purposes of s.97 of the Act. Whilst there was some difficulty, having regard to the language of the provision, in treating the initial grant of the loan by the trustees as falling within s.97 and its continuance as conferring a benefit, to view the trustees' decisions not to seek repayment as a series of omissions would unjustifiably assume that they were not undertaking their fiduciary duties. It was apparent that Parliament had introduced strong measures to combat the avoidance of capital gains tax through offshore trusts. The scheme of the legislation required the court to determine what benefit a beneficiary actually received other than as income or under an "arms length" transaction.

COOPER v. BILLINGHAM (INSPECTOR OF TAXES); EDWARDS (INSPECTOR OF TAXES) v. FISHER; *sub nom.* BILLINGHAM (INSPECTOR OF TAXES) v. COOPER; FISHER v. EDWARDS (INSPECTOR OF TAXES), [2001] EWCA Civ 1041, [2001] S.T.C. 1177, Robert Walker, L.J., CA.

5187. Capital gains tax – reliefs – main residence – area required for reasonable enjoyment

[Taxation of Chargeable Gains Act 1992 s.222.]

L appealed against a determination for the purposes of capital gains tax relief of the additional area of land above the permitted area that was required for the reasonable enjoyment of a dwelling. L owned a farmhouse with outbuildings and land on which he grazed horses. On sale of the property at a price which reflected its development potential, the Revenue determined the relevant permitted area of land to be a fraction of the entirety and assessed L to capital gains tax. L contended that the whole of the land was required to accompany the stabling for the horses which the Revenue had accepted as part of the house.

Held, dismissing the appeal, that objectively it was not essential for the reasonable enjoyment of the property that the stables were used for horses. The permitted area defined in accordance with the Taxation of Chargeable Gains Act 1992 s.222 was not affected by the subjective preferences of the landowner which would not be allowed to defeat the statutory purpose.

LONGSON v. BAKER (INSPECTOR OF TAXES) [2001] S.T.C. 6, Evans-Lombe, J., Ch D.

5188. Capital gains tax – valuation – unquoted company shares – out of time assessment to tax

[Taxes Management Act 1970 s.36.]

B made two gifts of unquoted company shares to his children in 1986. The first, in April 1986, was for 20 shares, of which details were disclosed in his 1986-87 tax return. In December 1986, B made a further gift of 678 shares, but no transfer of chargeable assets was shown on his 1987-88 return. B was assessed to capital gains tax under an out of time assessment in 1994 pursuant to the Taxes Management Act 1970 s.36, on the basis that it was necessary to recover tax lost due to B's negligent conduct. April 1986 valuation negotiations had valued the company at £100,000, however the Revenue asserted that it was worth £365,000 in December 1986, with the shares being valued at £310.25 each. B appealed.

Held, allowing the appeal, that the increase contended for by the Revenue was not sustained by the evidence. B's company was faced with a downturn in its market at the time. The s.36 assessment was justified on the basis of B's conduct, but the share valuation for December 1986 would be reduced to £1.95.

BILLOWS v. HAMMOND (INSPECTOR OF TAXES) [2000] S.T.C. (S.C.D.) 430, THK Everett, Sp Comm.

5189. Capital taxation – notaries – notarial fees on instruments recording increase in share capital – indirect taxation – European Community

[Council Directive 69/335 concerning indirect taxes on the raising of capital Art.10(c), Art.12(1)(e); Council Directive 85/303 amending Directive 69/335 concerning indirect taxes on the raising of capital.]

In proceedings concerning the payment of a charge for the notarial certification of deeds recording an increase in the share capital of M, a Portuguese company, a reference was made to the ECJ for a ruling on the interpretation of Council Directive 69/335 as amended by Council Directive 85/303. The ECJ was asked to determine whether the notarial charges required by Portuguese law on the drawing up of public instruments to record changes to a company's share capital and constitutional documentation amounted to a tax for the purpose of the Directive and, if so, whether it was permissible by virtue of the derogation contained in Art.12(1)(e) of the Directive for duties paid by way of fees or dues. The amount of the notarial charge reflected the amount of the company's capital involved and was in part used by the government to subsidise public expenditure.

Held, giving a preliminary ruling, that a notarial charge payable for the drawing up of a notarial instrument recording an increase in a company's share capital or change in its name or registered office amounted to a tax for the purposes of the Directive in circumstances where notaries were employed by the state and the charges were used by the state for funding public expenditure and was prohibited by Art.10(c). Having regard to the purpose of the Directive, a charge calculated by reference to the company's share capital must be regarded as having the characteristics of capital duty. The amount of the charge did not reflect the cost of the notarial service provided and was not subject to an upper limit and accordingly fell outside the ambit of the derogation contained in Art.12(1)(e).

MODELO SGPS SA v. DIRECTOR-GERAL DOS REGISTROS E NOTARIADO (C56/98); *sub nom.* MODELO SGPS SA v. DIRECTOR-GENERAL DOS REGISTROS E NOTARIADO (C56/98) [2001] S.T.C. 1043, PJG Kapteyn (President), ECJ.

5190. Car tax – discrimination – second hand imported vehicles – valuation method laid down in domestic law – European Union

[EC Treaty Art.95 (now, after amendment, Art.90 EC), Art.169 (now Art.226 EC); Decree Law 40/93 of 18 February 1993 (Portugal) Art.1.]

GV purchased a second hand car first registered in France in 1991 and imported it into Portugal in 1996. GV appealed against a car tax assessment made under Decree Law 40/93 Art.1, contending that it was contrary to the EC Treaty Art.95 (now, after amendment, Art.90 EC), on the ground that it was not based on a fixed percentage formula, as opposed to the car's commercial value. His appeal was dismissed at first instance and on appeal the matter was stayed pending a reference to the ECJ for a preliminary ruling as to the compatibility of the Decree Law with Art.90. Decree Law 40/93 had previously been subject to proceedings initiated by the European Commission under Art.169 (now Art.226 EC). These were discontinued following changes to the Decree Law in 1994, but new proceedings were commenced after the reference in the instant case.

Held, giving a preliminary ruling, that the Decree Law breached Art.90 EC, that (1) the discontinued Commission proceedings had no effect on the appeal court's obligation to refer the matter in the instant case; (2) Art.90(1) EC was infringed as car tax was imposed at a higher level on imported vehicles, *Commission of the European Communities v. Greece (C375/95)* [1997] E.C.R. I-5981, [1998] C.L.Y. 4663 applied; (3) fixed scales could be used to determine a vehicle's value for car tax purposes as long that method did not discriminate against imported vehicles, which had occurred in the instant case as the tax was levied on a value exceeding that which would have applied to a domestic used vehicle.

MINISTERIO PUBLICO v. FAZENDA PUBLICA (C393/98); *sub nom.* VALENTE v. FAZENDA PUBLICA [2001] 2 C.M.L.R. 29, La Pergola (President), ECJ.

5191. Climate change levy

CLIMATE CHANGE LEVY (GENERAL) REGULATIONS 2001, SI 2001 838; made under the Finance Act 1997 s.51; the Finance Act 2000 s.30; and the Finance Act 1997 Sch.6 para.19, para.21, para.22, para.23, para.27, para.29, para.41, para.43, para.44, para.62, para.63, para.65, para.73, para.74, para.100, para.118, para.119, para.120, para.125, para.146. In force: April 1, 2001; £6.00.

These Regulations, which make provision for climate change levy following the Climate Change Levy (Registration and Miscellaneous Provisions) Regulations 2001 (SI 2001 7), require relevant traders to make returns and pay the CCL due from them in accordance with their allocated accounting periods, require the traders to keep proper records for up to six years and provide mechanisms for adjusting, correcting or properly establishing the amount of CCL paid or due. The Regulations provide for the administration of CCL exclusions, exemptions and lower rates, enable solid fuel to be delivered for storage away from a facility covered by a climate change agreement without loss of the reduced-rate of CCL, prescribe the initial generation and certification requirements on which the exemption for renewable source electricity depends, ensure that producers of electricity in large scale hydro generating stations or nuclear power stations do not escape CCL if they consume any of that electricity themselves and prescribe limits above which a person is not a small-scale user of electricity or gas. In addition, they make provision for the early termination of a special utility scheme and echo older provisions in force for other taxes and duties.

5192. Climate change levy – electricity and gas industries

CLIMATE CHANGE LEVY (ELECTRICITY AND GAS) REGULATIONS 2001, SI 2001 1136; made under the Finance Act 2000 s.30, Sch.6 para.14, Sch.6 para.146, Sch.6 para.151, Sch.6 para.152. In force: April 1, 2001; £1.75.

These Regulations make provision for the proper application of climate change levy in sectors of the electricity and gas industries. They treat supplies of electricity unlawfully made for not holding a supply licence as those of an electricity utility, supplies of electricity received by an electricity utility in the course of acting outside the scope of its supply licence as nevertheless received by an electricity utility, keep a supply of electricity from a fully exempt combined heat and power station outside the charge to CCL when the supplier is an electricity utility and prevent CCL being charged under more than one provision when an electricity utility supplies electricity from a partly exempt combined heat and power station or burns electricity it has produced from taxable commodities. In addition, they treat supplies of gas unlawfully made for not holding a supply licence as those of a gas utility.

5193. Climate change levy – exemptions – combined heat and power stations

CLIMATE CHANGE LEVY (COMBINED HEAT AND POWER STATIONS) EXEMPTIONS CERTIFICATE REGULATIONS 2001, SI 2001 486; made under the Finance Act 2000 Sch.6 para.148. In force: March 19, 2001; £1.75.

These Regulations relate to certificates to be issued by the Secretary of State relating to the exemption, under certain circumstances, of combined heat and power stations from climate change levy contained in the Finance Act 2000 Sch.6. The Regulations provide for the content, validity, variation and revocation of certificates.

5194. Climate change levy – exemptions – combined heat and power stations

CLIMATE CHANGE LEVY (COMBINED HEAT AND POWER STATIONS) PRESCRIBED CONDITIONS AND EFFICIENCY PERCENTAGES REGULATIONS 2001, SI 2001 1140; made under the Finance Act 2000 s.30, Sch.6 para.15, Sch.6 para.16, Sch.6 para.146, Sch.6 para.148, Sch.6 para.149. In force: in accordance with Reg.1; £1.75.

These Regulations, which relate to the exemption of combined heat and power stations from climate change levy, prescribe two conditions before a combined heat and power station is entitled to a full-exemption certificate. The first requires a station to have been assessed against the Combined Heat and Power Quality Assurance Standard, the second relates to the station's efficiency. The second condition can be met in two ways, the second of which only applies to small stations which have been assessed in accordance with the simplified arrangements under the Standard, and are therefore not required to calculate the quantifying power output. The Regulations define the threshold efficiency percentage for combined heat and power stations, provide the method of calculating a station's efficiency percentage and specify the limit for levy exemption of a partly-exempt combined heat and power station, and what supplies are to be included or excluded when calculating whether the limit has been exceeded.

5195. Climate change levy – exemptions – solid fuel

CLIMATE CHANGE LEVY (SOLID FUEL) REGULATIONS 2001, SI 2001 1137; made under the Finance Act 2000 s.30, Sch.6 para.3, Sch.6 para.146. In force: April 1, 2001; £1.50.

These Regulations provide that solid fuel with an open market value not exceeding £15 per tonne at the time it is supplied is not a taxable commodity for the purposes of climate change levy.

5196. Climate change levy – exemptions – use as fuel

CLIMATE CHANGE LEVY (USE AS FUEL) REGULATIONS 2001, SI 2001 1138; made under the Finance Act 2000 s.30, Sch.6 para.18, Sch.6 para.146. In force: April 1, 2001; £1.75.

A supply of a taxable commodity may be exempt from climate change levy if it is received by a person who does not intend to use the commodity as fuel. The Treasury may specify by regulations uses of a commodity that are or are not to be taken as being uses as fuel. These Regulations specify the non fuel uses.

5197. Climate change levy – registration

CLIMATE CHANGE LEVY (REGISTRATION AND MISCELLANEOUS PROVISIONS) REGULATIONS 2001, SI 2001 7; made under the Finance Act 2000 s.30, Sch.6 para.59, Sch.6 para.60, Sch.6 para.114, Sch.6 para.115, Sch.6 para.116, Sch.6 para.117, Sch.6 para.146. In force: January 29, 2001; £3.50.

These regulations make provision about registration for climate change levy. They regulate the notification process for the registration of climate change levy to Customs and Excise, provide for Customs and Excise to allow companies to form climate change levy groups, provide for who is responsible for certain climate change levy requirements in the case of partnerships and unincorporated associations, and provide a penalty for breaching the provisions

5198. Company registration – fees – annual administrative charge deemed contrary to Council Directive 69/335 Art.10 – repayment under national law

[Council Directive 69/335 concerning indirect taxes on the raising of capital Art.10.]

Following a decision of the ECJ ([1993] E.C.R. I-1915, [1993] C.L.Y. 4405) that the annual administrative charge for company registrations was contrary to Council Directive 69/335 Art.10, IN obtained an order for repayment of charges paid prior to that decision. The Ministry challenged the orders and the national court made a reference to the ECJ for a preliminary ruling as to whether the incompatibility of Art.10 with the national law meant that national provisions had to be set aside in their entirety. The court also asked whether the non application of the national law retrospectively deprived the charge of its legal character, so that the national court should not take it into account when determining repayment eligibility.

Held, giving a preliminary ruling, that (1) the obligation to disapply national legislation that established a charge contrary to Community law gave rise to a right to a repayment, to be decided in accordance with national law, as long as those rules did not hinder or prevent the exercise of Community rights, and (2) any reclassification of the legal relationship between the tax authorities of a Member State and resident companies, following a finding that a charge levied under national law was contrary to Community law, was to be determined on the basis of national law.

MINISTERO DELLE FINANZE v. IN.CO.GE.'90 SRL (C10/97) [2001] 1 C.M.L.R. 31, GC Rodriguez Iglesias (President), ECJ.

5199. Corporation tax – allowances – charges on income – payment by tax exempt lender – meaning of "paid" by the company

[Income and Corporation Taxes Act 1988 s.338.]

The Revenue appealed against a ruling ([1998] S.T.C. 1131, [1998] C.L.Y. 4631) that payments made by W to the sole shareholders of its parent company, pension scheme trustees, in satisfaction of an interest debt amounted to charges on income "paid" by the company for the purposes of the Income and Corporation Taxes Act 1988 s.338. The monies used to pay the interest debt had themselves been advanced by the pension scheme trustees. W had then paid the interest net of tax and accounted to the Revenue for the tax due. The pension scheme was, however, exempt from income tax and the trustees were therefore entitled to reclaim the tax paid. The Revenue contended that the transaction was a preordained circular one whose sole purpose was the avoidance of taxation and that, applying the principle in *WT Ramsay Ltd v. Inland Revenue Commissioners* [1982] A.C. 300, [1981] C.L.Y. 1385, the payments should not be capable of being set off against future profits since they had no commercial purpose.

Held, dismissing the appeal, that having regard to the language of the statute it was clear that the word "paid" had to have the same meaning whatever the status of the source of the funds. The Revenue had not sought to submit that payment had to involve a negative cash flow which was not compensated by a cash flow in the opposite direction and there was nothing within s.338 to suggest that such an interpretation might be valid. The fact that the source of the funds in the instant case was an exempt lender was accordingly immaterial and the payments made by W therefore fell within the ambit of s.338(3) so that they constituted charges on income and were capable of set off, *Furniss (Inspector of Taxes) v. Dawson* [1984] A.C. 474, [1984] C.L.Y. 270 and *Ramsay* considered.

MacNIVEN (INSPECTOR OF TAXES) v. WESTMORELAND INVESTMENTS LTD; *sub nom.* WESTMORELAND INVESTMENTS LTD v. MacNIVEN (INSPECTOR OF TAXES) [2001] UKHL 6, [2001] 2 W.L.R. 377, Lord Nicholls of Birkenhead, HL.

5200. Corporation tax – assessment – computation of profits – mistake by taxpayer – basis of appeal

[Taxes Management Act 1970 s.33(4).]

EL appealed against a decision of the Special Commissioner ([1999] S.T.C. 771, [1999] C.L.Y. 4663) dismissing its appeal against the refusal by the Board of the Inland Revenue of its claim for relief under the Taxes Management Act 1970 s.33. EL had sought relief on the basis that it had made an error or mistake in the computation of its accounts. The judge had found that the appeal was not permitted pursuant to s.33(4), since it did not relate to "a point of law arising in connection with the computation of profits".

Held, dismissing the appeal, that (1) the words "in connection with the computation of profits" should be given their natural meaning; (2) the correctness of a decision of a Special Commissioner was generally a question of law but decisions made "in connection with the computation of profits" could not be viewed as such, *Carrimore Six Wheelers Ltd v. Inland Revenue Commissioners* 26 T.C. 301 and *Arranmore Investment Co Ltd v. Inland Revenue Commissioners* [1973] S.T.C. 195, [1973] C.L.Y. 1642 applied. It was not sufficient that the outcome of an appeal might affect the amount of profits, rather it was necessary that the issue relate to the method used for the computation of profits, and (3) if the Special Commissioners failed to properly consider an appeal under s.33(4) of the Act then the decision would be susceptible to judicial review.

EAGERPATH LTD v. EDWARDS (INSPECTOR OF TAXES) [2001] S.T.C. 26, Robert Walker, L.J., CA.

5201. Corporation tax – assets – leave surrender payment – capital nature of payment

B surrendered a rack rent lease for a payment of £550,000. The Revenue refused to allow the payment as a deduction from B's annual profits on the grounds that the lease was a capital asset. B appealed, contending that the payment was revenue in character as it had been made in the course of changes to its business structure and did not form part of its profit making operations. Further, that a rack rent lease could not be a capital asset.

Held, dismissing the appeal, that dealing in leases did not form part of B's trade, so that the lease had been acquired for the purposes of conducting trade, *Mallett (Inspector of Taxes) v. Staveley Coal & Iron Co Ltd* [1928] 2 K.B. 405 applied. The payment was made to terminate the onerous effect of the lease and was capital in nature even though the lease was for a rack rent, no premium had been paid for it and it did not form part of B's profit making operation, *Tucker v. Granada Motorway Services Ltd* [1979] 1 W.L.R. 683, [1979] C.L.Y. 374 applied.

BULLRUN INC v. INSPECTOR OF TAXES [2000] S.T.C. (S.C.D.) 384, AN Brice, Sp Comm.

5202. Corporation tax – capital gains – reorganisation of share capital under scheme of arrangement

[Taxation of Chargeable Gains Act 1992 s.126, s.128.]

U disposed of ordinary stock it held in B in 1992. The stock had been acquired prior to April 6, 1965 as the result of a scheme of arrangement. Under the scheme, U obtained sole control of B and the effect of the scheme was to reduce B's issued share capital and increase its authorised capital to the same value by the creation of ordinary shares with a nominal £1 value. U appealed against its 1998 corporation tax assessment and sought to set the loss made on the 1992 disposal against the 1998 chargeable gain.

Held, refusing the appeal, that the effect of the scheme of arrangement did not amount to a "reorganisation" in terms of the Taxation of Chargeable Gains Act 1992 s.126, as it had not resulted in a change in B's ownership, nor a reduction in its share capital. To qualify as a reduction for the purposes of s.126(1) the holder of the original shares had to obtain a new holding as the result of a transaction, with the company remaining in the same common ownership throughout. In the instant case, however, B's preference stock had been cancelled and the fact that ownership had remained with U, an ordinary stock holder, meant that its ownership had not changed for the purposes of s.126. Even if that analysis was incorrect, U's stock holding still had to be "concerned in" the reorganisation, and this could not be determined merely from the fact of U's involvement in the reorganisation as s.126 was concerned with the shares and whether there had been a "disposal" for tax purposes. The facts showed that U's holding had remained the same throughout and the payments it had made to the preference stock holders was not consideration for new stock, as required by s.128.

UNILEVER (UK) HOLDINGS LTD v. SMITH (INSPECTOR OF TAXES) [2001] S.T.C. (S.C.D.) 6, Judge not applicable, Sp Comm.

5203. Corporation tax – friendly societies – insurance business

FRIENDLY SOCIETIES (MODIFICATION OF THE CORPORATION TAX ACTS) (AMENDMENT) REGULATIONS 2001, SI 2001 3975; made under the Income and Corporation Taxes Act 1988 s.463. In force: January 1, 2002; £1.75.

These Regulations amend the Friendly Societies (Modification of the Corporation Tax Acts) Regulations 1997 (SI 1997 473) by inserting two new regulations which secure that as not all of a friendly society's income or chargeable gains arising from basic life assurance or general annuity business is taxable, such income and chargeable gains are treated as referable to the society's taxable basic life assurance or general annuity business. The second new regulation provides a method for computing the proportion of the assets of a friendly society held for the purposes of long-term business where the society does not have a long-term insurance fund. The Regulations also limit capital allowances on management assets of the life assurance business of friendly societies to that part of their basic life assurance and general annuity business which is taxable.

5204. Corporation tax – insolvency – minimum charge levied – compatibility with Council Directive 69/335 Art.10 – European Union

[Council Directive 69/335 concerning indirect taxes on the raising of capital Art.4, Art.10 Corporation Tax Act 1993 (Austria).]

S, the insolvency administrator of an Austrian company, P, complained against the imposition of an assessment to the minimum amount of corporation tax under the Corporation Tax Act 1988. S contended that such a charge, levied on the basis of P's unlimited corporation tax liability at a time when the company was not receiving any income was incompatible with Council Directive 69/335 Art.10.

Held, giving a preliminary ruling, that the minimum charge under the 1988 Act was not precluded by Art.10, that (1) Art.4 and Art.10 applied to the movement of capital or assets whereas the domestic legislation provided for a minimum corporation tax charge to be levied for each quarter that a company had an unlimited corporation tax liability, regardless of any capital movement, and (2) the Directive only applied to indirect taxes, whereas corporation tax was a direct tax reserved to the Member States.

SCHMID v. FINANZLANDESDIREKTION FUR WIEN, NIEDEROSTERREICH UND BURGENLAND (C113/99) [2001] 2 C.M.L.R. 13, V Skouris (President), ECJ.

5205. Corporation tax – real property – rent – assignment of right to future rental income – categorisation of lump sum receipt in hands of taxpayer – interests in land

The Commissioners appealed against the decision of a Special Commissioner ([2000] S.T.C. (S.C.D.) 494) allowing in principle the appeal of JLP, the property holding company of JL, against an assessment for corporation tax. A number of properties were rented by JLP to JL. JLP subsequently assigned its rights to future rental income over a five year period to R, a bank, in return for a lump sum calculated by discounting the rent payable over the relevant term at a commercial rate of interest. A swap transaction was entered into by JLP and R on the same day. Under it, JLP would pay to, or receive from, R the amount by which a notional commercial floating rate of interest on an amount equal to the consideration for the rental assignment exceeded, or was less than, the discount rate applied in determining the consideration for the assignment. The court was concerned to determine (1) whether the assignment constituted an assignment of an interest in land; (2) whether the lump sum was to be treated as capital or income in the hands of the taxpayer, and (3) if the payment was to be treated as a capital payment, whether it amounted to a partial disposal of JLP's interest in the relevant property.

Held, dismissing the appeal, that (1) the right to a reserved rent was an interest in land; (2) the proceeds from a sale of the right to receive future rental income constituted capital rather than income in the hands of the taxpayer, *Inland Revenue Commissioners v. Paget* [1938] 2 K.B. 25, *Inland Revenue Commissioners v. McGuckian* [1997] 1 W.L.R. 991, [1997] C.L.Y. 2979 and *Macniven (Inspector of Taxes) v. Westmoreland Investments Ltd* [2001] UKHL 6, [2001] 2 W.L.R. 377, [2001] 3 C.L. 645 applied. It was observed that such a decision was reached with reluctance. There was merit in the Commissioners' approach that the price obtained for a temporary disposal should be taxed as income. The decision in *Westmoreland* suggested, however, that any change in approach would have to come through legislation, and (3) the transaction constituted a partial disposal of JLP's interest in the relevant land since following assignment JLP's interest was no longer unencumbered.

JOHN LEWIS PROPERTIES PLC v. INLAND REVENUE COMMISSIONERS; *sub nom.* INLAND REVENUE COMMISSIONERS v. JOHN LEWIS PROPERTIES PLC [2002] 1 W.L.R. 35, Lightman, J., Ch D.

5206. Corporation tax – reliefs – associated companies – power to attribute rights and powers

[Finance Act 1972; Income and Corporation Taxes Act 1988 s.416(6).]

The Revenue appealed against a decision, ([2000] S.T.C. 52) that the rights and powers of N's associates were not attributed to the person who controlled N, thereby giving N an entitlement to claim small companies relief under the Finance Act 1972. N's share capital was held by trustees of a will trust in which the testator's widow, A, held a life interest. A was also the widow of the settlor of a discretionary trust, whose trustees controlled an associate company, thereby rendering A the associate of the trustees of both trusts. The Revenue contended that under the Income and Corporation Taxes Act 1988 s.416(6) they were obliged to exercise the power to attribute the rights and powers of the trustees to A as her associates, for the purpose of ascertaining whether the two companies were under the control of the same person. N contended that the word "may" in the first part of s.416(6) gave the Revenue a discretionary power when assessing the degree of control exercised by a single person or their associates.

Held, allowing the appeal, that (1) the Revenue did not have a discretion when deciding whether to attribute the rights and powers of associates to A since s.416 did not identify a person in whom such a discretion was vested. Furthermore, there was in the instant case, an absence of grounds upon which a discretion should be exercised. The definition of "control" within s.416 was wide and could apply to people who had no real control over the company's affairs, thus making it difficult to apply the reality of control as a criterion for exercising discretion. The question of whether rights and powers should be attributed depended upon whether the necessary conditions had been satisfied, which in effect amounted to whether a person who controlled a company applying for relief also controlled one or more other companies, and (2) the concluding words of s.416(6) which stated that attributions should only be made as would result in a company being treated as under the control of five or fewer participants, did not form part of the definition of "control" to be applied by the 1972 Act.

R. (ON THE APPLICATION OF NEWFIELDS DEVELOPMENTS LTD) v. INLAND REVENUE COMMISSIONERS; *sub nom.* R. v. INLAND REVENUE COMMISSIONERS, *ex p.* NEWFIELDS DEVELOPMENT LTD; R. v. INLAND REVENUE COMMISSIONERS, *ex p.* NEWFIELDS DEVELOPMENTS LTD, [2001] UKHL 27, [2001] 1 W.L.R. 1111, Lord Hoffmann, HL.

5207. Corporation tax – reliefs – determination of company profits – statutory interpretation of gains, losses and allowances

[Income and Corporation Taxes Act 1988 s.403 (7), s.403(8); Taxation of Chargeable Gains Act 1992 s.8(1).]

M was a member of a group relief group for corporation tax. In the relevant accounting period, M had made profits of £300,000, incurred charges on income of £48,644,400, and made chargeable gains of £6,040,284. Allowable losses brought forward from past accounting periods exceeded the chargeable gains. The Revenue refused to permit M to set the brought forward allowable losses against the chargeable gains so as to reduce them to nil, arguing that since the Income and Corporation Taxes Act 1988 s.403(8) prohibited the deduction of "losses or allowances" for any period other than the accounting period within which the relevant chargeable gains were realised, it followed that M could not avail itself of allowable losses brought forward from previous accounting periods to reduce profits accruing in the period under review.

Held, allowing the appeal, that in interpreting s.403(7) and (8) of the 1988 Act on the basis that words should be given their normal meaning and that nothing should be implied, (1) "profits" meant income and chargeable gains. "Chargeable gains" meant realised gains less allowable losses for current and previous years; (2) "losses" meant trading losses and "allowances" meant capital allowances; (3) "losses or allowances" meant trading losses or capital allowances, and not "allowable losses", and (4) "allowable losses" meant capital losses deductible from capital gains.

MEPC HOLDINGS LTD v. TAYLOR (INSPECTOR OF TAXES) [2000] S.T.C. (S.C.D.) 504, Judge not applicable, Sp Comm.

5208. Corporation tax – reliefs – group relief – deductions in respect of allowable losses

[Income and Corporation Taxes Act 1988 s.403(7), s.403(8).]

The Revenue appealed against a determination of the Special Commissioners ([2000] S.T.C. (S.C.D.) 504) upholding a group relief claim by MEPC, an investment company, regarding the amount available for surrender by way of group relief under the Income and Corporation Taxes Act 1988 s.403(7) and s.403(8) for the accounting period to September 1994. The allowable losses brought forward from past accounting periods had substantially exceeded the realised chargeable gains for the instant accounting period. The Commissioners had upheld MEPC's contention that the amount eligible for surrender for group relief should not be reduced by realised chargeable gains which were more than set off by the brought forward allowable losses.

Held, allowing the appeal, that the amount of a company's losses eligible for surrender for group relief was to be assessed without deducting from the realised capital gains allowable losses of preceding accounting periods. The Commissioners had erred in their finding that "losses or allowances" within s.403(8) referred to trading losses or capital allowances and not to allowable losses, as the normal and ordinary meaning of the words indicated that no regard should be had to any deduction for any loss. Therefore no deduction could be made in respect of the allowable losses of a previous period.

TAYLOR (INSPECTOR OF TAXES) v. MEPC HOLDINGS LTD; *sub nom.* MEPC HOLDINGS LTD v. TAYLOR (INSPECTOR OF TAXES) [2002] S.T.C. 430, Sir Donald Rattee, Ch D.

5209. Customs and Excise – statistics of trade

STATISTICS OF TRADE (CUSTOMS AND EXCISE) (AMENDMENT) REGULATIONS 2001, SI 2001 3887; made under the European Communities Act 1972 s.2. In force: January 1, 2002; £1.50.

These Regulations amend the Statistics of Trade (Customs and Excise) Regulations 1992 (SI 1992 2790) so as to establish a single time limit for furnishing supplementary declarations irrespective of the means by which they are furnished. The Regulations also raise the monetary limit to £13,500,000. A person whose annual value of goods arriving from, or dispatched to other Member States does not exceed that monetary limit is not required to include particulars relating to delivery terms in his supplementary declarations.

5210. Customs duty – free movement of goods – duty levied on goods imported from another Member State

[EC Treaty Art.9 (now, after amendment, Art.23 EC), Art.10(1) (now, after amendment, Art.24(1) EC), Art.12 (now, after amendment, Art.25 EC), Art.13 (repealed by the Treaty of Amsterdam); Act of Accession of Norway, Austria, Finland and Sweden to the European Communities 1994 Art.99.]

K, a Finnish company, imported into Finland from Sweden textile and clothing products that had originated from a non Member State. Customs duty had been levied on the goods when they entered Sweden, where they were in free circulation. On importation into Finland, K was required to pay the difference between the duty imposed under domestic law and that charged on entry into Sweden. K appealed against that decision, arguing that, as a provision introducing a derogation from the fundamental principle of the free movement of goods, the Act of Accession of Norway, Austria, Finland and Sweden to the European Communities 1994 Art.99 was to be narrowly interpreted, and that the imposition of customs duty for goods imported from Sweden was contrary to the EC Treaty Art.9 and Art.12 (now, after amendment, Art.23 and Art.25 EC) and Art.13 (repealed by the Treaty of Amsterdam). Finland accepted that the wording of Art.99 was unclear, but contended that customs duties did not apply to countries but to goods, and that Art.99 of the Act referred both to goods imported from non Member States and to goods originating there. The ECJ was asked for a preliminary ruling on the interpretation of Art.99.

Held, giving a preliminary ruling, that the prohibition on customs duties between Member States and charges having equivalent effect, applied both to products originating from Member States and to products originating from third countries that were in free circulation there. Article 99 permitted only a temporary derogation from the Commons Customs Tariff in trade between the Member States covered by the Act and third countries. That only applied for three years from their accession to the Community. However, Art.99 did not allow a derogation from the prohibition on customs duties between Member States. Therefore, the levy of such duties on imports from another Member State of goods that had been in free circulation there, was not permitted under Art.99 and a finding to the contrary would breach Art.9 and Art.10(1) (now, after amendment, Art.24(1) EC).

KAPPAHL OY (C233/97), *Re* [1998] E.C.R. I-8069, DAO Edward (President), ECJ.

5211. Customs duty – tobacco products – extent to which repayment could be refused on unjust enrichment grounds

[EC Treaty Art.9 (now, after amendment, Art.23 EC), Art.12 (now, after amendment, Art.25 EC), Art.16 (repealed by the Treaty of Amsterdam).]

KM, a tobacco trader, brought an action in the administrative court for the annulment of two decisions refusing recovery of certain charges paid to a tobacco workers' insurance fund and the general social security fund on tobacco exports. The administrative court referred the question to the ECJ for a preliminary ruling as to whether a Greek tax levied on tobacco exports was a charge with an effect equivalent to a customs duty contrary to the EC Treaty Art.9, Art.12 (now, after amendment, Art.23 and Art.25 EC) and Art.16 (repealed by the Treaty of Amsterdam) and, if so, whether reimbursement of the improperly levied tax could be refused on the ground of unjust enrichment.

Held, giving a preliminary ruling, that the charge was equivalent to a customs duty in breach of the Treaty, that (1) the fact that the charge was levied for social security purposes did not prevent it being equivalent to a customs duty; (2) the essential feature of an equivalent charge that distinguished it from internally levied taxes was that it was only payable on products that crossed a frontier, while internal taxes were levied on imported, exported and domestic goods; (3) the charge in the instant case was a charge having an equivalent effect to a customs duty as there was no comparable charge on similar domestic goods; (4) a Member State could refuse to repay a charge that breached Community law only if it was shown that the charge has been borne entirely by a party other than the trader, so that reimbursement would unjustly enrich the trader. However, partial repayment could be made if the burden had not passed entirely to the third party, and (5) the burden of proving that the charge had been passed to a third party did not shift to the trader under Community law, so that KM could adduce evidence to refute allegations that the charge had been passed on.

KAPNIKI MIKHAILIDIS AE v. IDRIMA KINONIKON ASPHALISEON (IKA) (C441/98) [2001] 1 C.M.L.R. 13, DAO Edward (President), ECJ.

5212. Double taxation – freedom of establishment – concession under agreement with non Member State not accorded to non resident with permanent establishment – European Union

[EC Treaty Art.52 (now, after amendment, Art.43 EC), Art.58 (now Art.48 EC).]

SG, the German branch of a French resident company, was refused a corporation tax exemption on foreign dividends paid under a profit transfer agreement on the basis of double taxation agreements concluded between Germany and certain non Member States. The German court referred to the ECJ for a preliminary ruling as to whether the exclusion of non resident with a permanent establishment in Germany was contrary to the EC Treaty Art.52 (now, after amendment, Art.43 EC) and Art.58 (now Art.48 EC). Germany contended that SG could be refused the concessions available to residents as this was necessary to prevent a reduction of tax revenues and that double taxation agreements concluded with non Member States were beyond the scope of Community law.

Held, that the exclusion was contrary to Art.52 and Art.58, *ICI Plc v. Colmer (Inspector of Taxes) (C264/96)* [1999] 1 W.L.R. 108, [1998] C.L.Y. 4620 considered. A difference in taxation treatment between resident and non resident companies could not be justified by reference to the reduction in revenues that would result if the concession was granted to non residents with a permanent establishment. Although direct taxation was a matter for individual Member States when concluding double taxation agreements with non Member States, benefits under such agreements had to be accorded to non residents with a permanent establishment on the same basis as they were granted to residents if the Member State was to comply with the national treatment principle.

COMPAGNIE DE SAINT-GOBAIN, ZWEIGNIEDERLASSUNG DEUTSCHLAND v. FINANZAMT AACHEN-INNENSTADT (C307/97); *sub nom.* SAINT-GOBAIN ZN

v. FINANZAMT AACHEN-INNENSTADT (C307/97); COMPAGNIE DE SAINT-GOBAIN, ZWEIGNIEDERLASSUNG, GERMANY v. TAX OFFICE AACHEN-INNENSTADT [2000] S.T.C. 854, GC Rodriguez Iglesias (President), ECJ.

5213. Double taxation – reliefs – dividends – dual resident companies

DOUBLE TAXATION RELIEF (TAXES ON INCOME) (UNDERLYING TAX ON DIVIDENDS AND DUAL RESIDENT COMPANIES) REGULATIONS 2001, SI 2001 1156; made under the Income and Corporation Taxes Act 1988 s.801. In force: March 31, 2001; £1.50.

These Regulations prescribe additional cases in which the restriction on relief from UK tax to the underlying rate of tax applies in respect of dividends paid to the UK by overseas companies. In addition, they prescribe additional cases in which the cap on relief in respect of foreign taxation on dividends paid by overseas companies is to apply. The additional cases are those in which either the overseas company paying the dividend to the UK, or the third company which has paid a dividend over to an overseas company which it in turn pays to the UK, is a dual resident company resident in the same overseas territory as the other company but treated as resident in a different territory.

5214. Double taxation – reliefs – dual resident company

DOUBLE TAXATION RELIEF (SURRENDER OF RELIEVABLE TAX WITHIN A GROUP) (AMENDMENT) REGULATIONS 2001, SI 2001 3873; made under the Income and Corporation Taxes Act 1988 s.806H. In force: December 5, 2001; £1.50.

These Regulations amend the Double Taxation Relief (Surrender of Relievable Tax Within A Group) Regulations 2001 (SI 2001 1163) by removing the rule that prevents a dual resident company from surrendering eligible unrelieved foreign tax. A dual resident company is one that in any accounting period is both resident in the UK and also within a charge to tax under the laws of a territory outside the UK.

5215. Double taxation – reliefs – groups of companies

DOUBLE TAXATION RELIEF (SURRENDER OF RELIEVABLE TAX WITHIN A GROUP) REGULATIONS 2001, SI 2001 1163; made under the Income and Corporation Taxes Act 1988 s.806H. In force: March 31, 2001; £1.75.

These Regulations, which provide for the surrender of eligible unrelieved foreign tax (EUFT) by one company in a group to another, provide for the amount of EUFT that may be surrendered. They provide for the claiming and utilisation of EUFT by the claimant company, that the surrendering company and the claimant company must be members of the same group throughout the accounting period of the surrendering company in which the EUFT available for surrender arises, and also provide for the case where the accounting periods of the surrendering company and the claimant company are not coterminous.

5216. Double taxation – reliefs – Jordan

DOUBLE TAXATION RELIEF (TAXES ON INCOME) (THE HASHEMITE KINGDOM OF JORDAN) ORDER 2001, SI 2001 3924; made under the Income and Corporation Taxes Act 1988 s.788. In force: to be published in the London, Edinburgh and Belfast Gazettes; £3.50.

The Convention with the Hashemite Kingdom of Jordan, which is set out in this Order, provides for business profits not arising through a permanent establishment to be taxed only in the country of the taxpayer's residence; profits attributable to a permanent establishment may be taxed in the country in which the permanent establishment is situated; income from immovable property and gains derived from the alienation of such property may be taxed in the country in which the property is situated; and international shipping and air transport profits are generally to be taxed only in the country of residence of the operator.

5217. Double taxation – reliefs – Lithuania

DOUBLE TAXATION RELIEF (TAXES ON INCOME) (LITHUANIA) ORDER 2001, SI 2001 3925; made under the Income and Corporation Taxes Act 1988 s.788. In force: to be published in the London, Edinburgh and Belfast Gazettes; £3.50.

The Convention with Lithuania, which is set out in this Order, provides for business profits not arising through a permanent establishment to be taxed only in the country of the taxpayer's residence; profits attributable to a permanent establishment may be taxed in the country in which the permanent establishment is situated; income from immovable property and gains derived from the alienation of such property may be taxed in the country in which the property is situated; and international shipping and air transport profits are generally to be taxed only in the country of residence of the operator.

5218. Enterprise investment scheme – reliefs – supply of accountancy services

[Income and Corporation Taxes Act 1988 Part VII Chapter III, s.297 (2) (f).]

C, a company whose main business consisted of making employees available to an accountancy firm, appealed against the refusal by an inspector to issue the certificates required in order for five individuals to make Enterprise Investment Scheme, EIS, claims in relation to shares issued in the company. C maintained that it had satisfied the conditions for EIS relief set out in the Income and Corporation Taxes Act 1988 Part VII Chapter III.

Held, dismissing the appeal, that since the activity of C had to be viewed as supplying accountancy services, it was not carrying on a qualifying trade by virtue of s.297 (2) (f) of the Act.

CASTLETON MANAGEMENT SERVICES LTD v. KIRKWOOD (INSPECTOR OF TAXES); *sub nom*. CASTLETON MANAGEMENT SERVICE LTD v. KIRKWOOD (INSPECTOR OF TAXES) [2001] S.T.C. (S.C.D.) 95, THK Everett, Sp Comm.

5219. Environmental protection – climate change agreements – energy-intensive installations

CLIMATE CHANGE AGREEMENTS (ENERGY-INTENSIVE INSTALLATIONS) REGULATIONS 2001, SI 2001 1139; made under the Finance Act 2000 Sch.6 para.52. In force: in accordance with Reg.1; £1.75.

These Regulations, which vary the installations covered by the Finance Act 2000 Sch.6 para.51, substitute various specified descriptions of installation for the entries in the Table.

5220. Excise duty – aircraft operators – information – air passenger duty

AIRCRAFT OPERATORS (ACCOUNTS AND RECORDS) (AMENDMENT) REGULATIONS 2001, SI 2001 837; made under the Customs and Excise Act 1979 s.118A; and the Finance Act 1994 Sch.6 para.1. In force: April 1, 2001; £1.50.

These Regulations amend the Aircraft Operators (Accounts and Records) Regulations 1994 (SI 1994 1737) which list the information which should be kept in an air passenger duty account for each accounting period. They require aircraft operators to keep a record of the number of passengers chargeable at the rates of air passenger duty applicable to standard and other classes of travel in respect of journeys ending in the UK, EEA, or a territory for whose external relations the UK or another member State, is responsible.

5221. Excise duty – cider – perry

CIDER AND PERRY (AMENDMENT) REGULATIONS 2001, SI 2001 2449; made under the Alcoholic Liquor Duties Act 1979 s.62. In force: August 1, 2001; £1.50.

These Regulations, which amend the Cider and Perry Regulations 1989 (SI 1989 1355), prohibit operations after the excise duty point, such as dilution of cider, that if carried out before the duty point would have increased the duty payable.

5222. Excise duty – excise duty points – movement of excise goods

EXCISE DUTY POINTS (DUTY SUSPENDED MOVEMENTS OF EXCISE GOODS) REGULATIONS 2001, SI 2001 3022; made under the European Communities Act 1972 s.2, s.100H; the Customs and Excise Management Act 1979 s.100G; and the Finance (No.2) Act 1992 s.1. In force: September 28, 2001; £2.00.

These Regulations, which amend the Excise Goods (Holding, Movement, Warehousing and REDS) Regulations 1992 (SI 1992 3135) and the Finance Act 1994, provide for the creation of excise duty points, and identify the persons liable to pay, where an irregularity occurs during the course of an intra-EU movement of duty suspended excise goods. In addition, the Regulations implement Council Directive 92/12 ([1992] OJ L176/1) on the general arrangements for products subject to excise duty and on the holding, movement and monitoring of such products.

5223. Excise duty – gambling – gaming duty rates

GAMING DUTY (AMENDMENT) REGULATIONS 2001, SI 2001 3021; made under the Finance Act 1997 s.12, s.14. In force: October 1, 2001; £1.50.

These Regulations, which amend the Gaming Duty Regulations 1997 (SI 1997 2196) and revoke the Gaming Duty (Amendment) Regulations 1999 (SI 1999 2489), substitute a new table reflecting changes to gaming duty made by the Finance Act 2001 s.7 and will apply in the case of payments on account of gaming duty for any quarter that ends on or after October 31, 2001.

5224. Excise duty – tobacco products

TOBACCO PRODUCTS REGULATIONS 2001, SI 2001 1712; made under the Customs and Excise Management Act 1979 s.93, s.100G, s.100H, s.118A, s.127A; the Tobacco Products Duty Act 1979 s.2, s.7, s.8B, s.8C, s.8G; and the Finance (No.2) Act 1992 s.1, s.2. In force: June 1, 2001; £3.00.

These Regulations, which amend the Excise Warehousing (Etc.) Regulations 1988 (SI 1988 809) and the Excise Goods (Holding, Movement, Warehousing and REDS) Regulations 1992 (SI 1992 3135), revoke the Tobacco Products Regulations 1979 (SI 1979 904), the Excise Warehousing Regulations 1979, etc. (Amendment) Regulations 1980 (SI 1980 992), the Tobacco Products (Amendment) Regulations 1982 (SI 1982 964), the Tobacco Products Regulations 1979 (Amendment) Regulations 1990 (SI 1990 544), the Tobacco Products (Amendment) Regulations 1992 (SI 1992 3154) and the Tobacco Products (Amendment) Regulations 1993 (SI 1993 2167). They provide the machinery for administering the excise duty on tobacco products and regulate the circumstances in which tobacco products are required to carry fiscal marks and related matters. In addition, the Regulations implement Council Directive 92/12 ([1992] OJ L76/4) on the general arrangements for products subject to excise duty and Council Directive 95/59 ([1995] OJ L291/40) on taxes other than turnover taxes which affect the consumption of manufactured tobacco.

5225. Finance Act 1989 (c.26) – Appointed Day Order – s.178(1)

FINANCE ACT 1989, SECTION 178(1), (APPOINTED DAY) ORDER 2001, SI 2001 253 (C.14); made under the Finance Act 1989 s.178. Commencement details: bringing into force various provisions of the Act on March 7, 2001; £1.50.

This Order appoints March 7, 2001, as the day for periods beginning on or after which the Finance Act 1989 s.178(1) has effect in relation to the rate of interest on recoverable amounts of working families' tax credit or disabled person's tax credit, and the rate of interest on penalties for fraudulently or negligently making any incorrect statement or declaration in connection with a claim for tax credit.

5226. Finance Act 1996 (c.8) – Appointed Day Order – s.167

FINANCE ACT 1996, SECTION 167, (APPOINTED DAY) ORDER 2001, SI 2001 3643 (C.118); made under the Finance Act 1996 s.167; and the Income and

Corporation Taxes Act 1988 Sch.14 para.8, Sch.15 para.8A, Sch.15 para.18. Commencement details: bringing into force various provisions of the 1996 Act on December 1, 2001; £1.50.

This order appoints December 1, 2001 as the day on which certain amendments under the Finance Act 1996 s.167, which makes various amendments to provisions of the Tax Acts relating to the tax treatment of industrial assurance business, take effect.

5227. Finance Act 2001 (c.9)

This Act grants certain duties, alters other duties, and amends the law relating to the national debt and the public revenue, and makes further provision in connection with finance.

This Act received Royal Assent on May 11, 2001.

5228. Finance Act 2001 (c.9) – Appointed Day Order – s.24 and Sch.4

FINANCE ACT 2001, SECTION 24 AND SCHEDULE 4, (APPOINTED DAY) ORDER 2001, SI 2001 4033 (C.129); made under the Finance Act 2001 s.24. Commencement details: bringing into force various provisions of the 2001 Act on December 20, 2001 and January 11, 2002; £1.50.

This Order brings into force provisions of the Finance Act 2001 that empower Customs and Excise to make regulations in respect of the registration process for aggregates levy.

5229. Finance Act 2001 (c.9) – Commencement No.2 Order

FINANCE ACT 2001 (COMMENCEMENT NO.2 AND SAVING PROVISION) ORDER 2001, SI 2001 3300 (C.108); made under the Finance Act 2001 Sch.3 para.21, para.22. Commencement details: bringing into force various provisions of the 2001 Act on November 1, 2001; £1.50.

This Order brings into force the Finance Act 2001 Sch.3 which provides for the Commissioners of Customs and Excise to pay interest on excise duty overpaid or underclaimed as a result of their error or undue delay and to repay, with interest, certain excise duties to persons to whom they have incorrectly denied certain authorisations or approvals, and who as a result have paid duty when they need not have done so.

5230. Finance Act 2001 (c.9) – Commencement Order

FINANCE ACT 2001 (COMMENCEMENT) ORDER 2001, SI 2001 3089 (C.97); made under the Finance Act 2001 s.6. Commencement details: bringing into force various provisions of the Act on October 6, 2001; £1.50.

This Order brings into force the Finance Act 2001 s.6, giving effect to Schedule 1 of that Act which makes provisions concerning general betting duty.

5231. Finance Act 2001 (c.9) – Specified Day Order – s.92(8)

FINANCE ACT 2001, SECTION 92(8), (SPECIFIED DAY) ORDER 2001, SI 2001 3748 (C.123); made under the Finance Act 2001 s.92. Commencement details: bringing into force various provisions of the 2001 Act on November 30, 2001; £1.50.

The Finance Act 2001 provides for an exemption from the stamp duty chargeable on a conveyance or transfer on sale of an estate or interest in land or a lease of land if the land in question is situated in a disadvantaged area. It also makes similar provision in relation to cases where land is partly in a disadvantaged area. In addition, the 2001 Act has effect in relation to instruments executed on or after such date as may be specified by order made by the Treasury. This Order specifies November 30, 2001 as the day in question.

5232. Free zones – designation – Liverpool

FREE ZONE (LIVERPOOL) DESIGNATION ORDER 2001, SI 2001 2881; made under the Customs and Excise Managment Act 1979 s.100A. In force: August 10, 2001; £1.50.

This Order, which replaces the Free Zone (Liverpool) Designation Order1991 (SI 1991 1738), designates an area of 383.28 hectares, in the County of Merseyside, comprising 269.56 hectares in the Metropolitan Borough of Sefton, 77.87 hectares in the Metropolitan Borough of Wirral and 35.85 hectares within the City of Liverpool as a free zone, appoints the responsible authority and imposes obligations upon that authority relating to the operation of the zone.

5233. Free zones – designation – Prestwick Airport

FREE ZONE (PRESTWICK AIRPORT) DESIGNATION ORDER 2001, SI 2001 2882; made under the Customs and Excise Managment Act 1979 s.100A. In force: August 10, 2001; £1.50.

This Order, which replaces the Free Zone (Prestwick Airport) Designation Order 1991 (SI 1991 1739) designates an area of 7.0359 acres at Prestwick Airport as a free zone, appoints the responsible authority and imposes obligations upon that authority relating to the operation of the zone.

5234. Free zones – designation – Southampton

FREE ZONE (SOUTHAMPTON) DESIGNATION ORDER 2001, SI 2001 2880; made under the Customs and Excise Management Act 1979 s.100A. In force: August 10, 2001; £1.50.

This Order, which replaces the Free Zone (Southampton) Designation Order 1991 (SI 1991 1740), designates an area of 3.2436 hectares at Southampton as a free zone, appoints the responsible authority and imposes obligations upon that authority relating to the operation of the zone.

5235. House of Lords – hereditary peers – local government electors register

HOLDERS OF HEREDITARY PEERAGES (OVERSEAS ELECTORS) (TRANSITIONAL PROVISIONS) ORDER 2001, SI 2001 84; made under the House of Lords Act 1999 s.5. In force: February 16, 2001; £1.50.

This Order, which revokes and replaces the Holders of Hereditary Peerages (Extension of the Franchise) (Transitional Provisions) Order 1999 (SI 1999 3322), allows a peer to whom the House of Lords Act 1999 s.3 applies to rely on his registration as a local Government elector in respect of any register prior to the date when such peers were entitled to be included in a register of parliamentary electors for the purposes of the Representation of the People Act 1985 s.1 and amends the reference to a register of parliamentary electors in s.1 of that Act to a reference to a register of local electors.

5236. Income tax – appeals – application of non statutory practice – mode of challenge

M, a director of two companies, sought to appeal against the assessment of his remuneration on an earnings basis as opposed to assessment on the basis of the sums shown in the company's accounts for the periods ending in the tax year in question. M maintained that he was entitled to be assessed on an "accounts" basis given that the Revenue had previously accepted claims made on that basis by other directors for the same year.

Held, dismissing the appeal, that having regard to the relevant authorities, judicial review was the appropriate remedy where a taxpayer sought to challenge the application by the Revenue of a non statutory practice. Accordingly, the Special Commissioners had no jurisdiction to determine the appeal. In any event, it was clear in the instant case that there had been no agreement with M that the account basis of assessment would be used to determine his tax liability.

MALONE v. QUINN (INSPECTOR OF TAXES) [2001] S.T.C. (S.C.D.) 63, AN Brice, Sp Comm.

5237. **Income tax – bonus payments – tax avoidance scheme designed to avoid PAYE**

[Income and Corporation Taxes Act 1988 s.203(1), s.203F.]

DTE, which had paid a bonus of £40,000 to each one of its directors by means of a series of transactions involving two offshore companies, appealed against a decision ([1999] S.T.C. 1061, [1999] C.L.Y. 4709) upholding a finding of the special commissioner that it was liable to account for income tax on the bonuses under the PAYE system. DTE contended that as the scheme effectively provided the directors with a contingent reversionary interest and not with a cash payment, the PAYE system was inapplicable.

Held, dismissing the appeal, that whilst the reversionary interest could not amount to a "tradeable asset" for the purposes of the Income and Corporation Taxes Act 1988 s.203F, the reality of the transaction simply involved DTE paying a bonus to each director which amounted to a payment of assessable income within the meaning of s.203(1) with the result that DTE was liable, *WT Ramsay Ltd v. Inland Revenue Commissioners* [1982] A.C. 300, [1981] C.L.Y. 1385 applied.

DTE FINANCIAL SERVICES LTD v. WILSON (INSPECTOR OF TAXES); *sub nom.* DTE FINANCIAL SERVICES LTD v. INSPECTOR OF TAXES, [2001] EWCA Civ 455, [2001] S.T.C. 777, Jonathan Parker, L.J., CA.

5238. **Income tax – building societies – dividends and interest**

INCOME TAX (BUILDING SOCIETIES) (DIVIDENDS AND INTEREST) (AMENDMENT) REGULATIONS 2001, SI 2001 404; made under the Income and Corporation Taxes Act 1988 s.477A. In force: March 9, 2001; £2.00.

These Regulations amend the Income Tax (Building Societies) (Dividends and Interest) Regulations 1990 (SI 1990 2231) in relation to payments of dividends and interest by building societies made on or after April 6, 2001, and certificates, notifications and declarations given or made for the purposes of the 1990 Regulations on or after that date. They insert definitions of "electronic communication" and "electronic signature", add a category of gross payment, make provision for cases where certificates of non-liability to tax are given otherwise than in writing, and provide for the procedure for building societies to make a return to the Inland Revenue, the information to be included and the inspection of documents.

5239. **Income tax – car fuel benefits**

INCOME TAX (CAR BENEFITS) (REDUCTION OF VALUE OF APPROPRIATE PERCENTAGE) REGULATIONS 2001, SI 2001 1123; made under the Income and Corporation Taxes Act 1988 Sch.6 para.5, para.8. In force: April 12, 2001; £1.75.

The Income and Corporation Taxes Act 1988 Sch.6 is amended by the Finance Act 2000 Sch.11 to provide for a new system for taxing car benefits from April 6, 2002. Under the new system the income tax charge on the benefit of a car will be calculated by reference to a percentage for the year of the price of the car as regards that year. These Regulations, which amend the Income Tax (Replacement Cars) Regulations 1994 (SI 1994 778), prescribe various reductions of the value of the appropriate percentage in relation to cars propelled solely by diesel and electrically propelled cars which meet a European Community standard for cleaner cars.

5240. Income tax – car fuel benefits

INCOME TAX (CASH EQUIVALENTS OF CAR FUEL BENEFITS) ORDER 2001, SI 2001 635; made under the Income and Corporation Taxes Act 1988 s.158. In force: April 6, 2001; £1.50.

This Order substitutes new tables of flat rate cash equivalents in the Income and Corporation Taxes Act 1988 s.158(2) which provides that directors and employees earning £8,500 or more a year for whom fuel is provided for private use in a company car are chargeable to income tax on an amount equal to the appropriate cash equivalent of the benefit.

5241. Income tax – construction industry – subcontractors

INCOME TAX (SUB-CONTRACTORS IN THE CONSTRUCTION INDUSTRY) (AMENDMENT) REGULATIONS 2001, SI 2001 1531; made under the Income and Corporation Taxes Act 1988 s.566. In force: May 1, 2001; £1.75.

These Regulations amend the Income Tax (Sub-contractors in the Construction Industry) Regulations 1993 (SI 1993 743) to allow a subcontractor's tax certificate in the form CIS5 (Partner), equivalent to the CIS5 for companies, to be issued to certain partners in firms of subcontractors.

5242. Income tax – deductions – expenditure on dietary supplements – performance of employment duties

[Income and Corporation Taxes Act 1988 s.198(1).]

The Revenue appealed against a finding of the Commissioners that B, a professional rugby player, could lawfully claim a deduction against Schedule E income tax in respect of the expenditure he incurred on dietary supplements. B maintained that as his profession required him to maintain certain levels of fitness and weight, he was entitled to relief on the basis that the expense of the supplements had been incurred wholly and exclusively in the performance of his duties of employment within the meaning of the Income and Corporation Taxes Act 1988 s.198(1).

Held, allowing the appeal, that the Commissioners had misdirected themselves in law as B's expenditure had not been incurred in the performance of his duties of employment but had simply been of a preparatory nature. It was necessary for an employee to be obliged to incur the expenditure in the performance of the duties of his employment, the test being an objective one. In the instant case the expenditure had merely enabled B to perform his duties and that was insufficient to warrant relief as the expenditure had not strictly been incurred "in the performance of the duties" of his employment.

ANSELL (INSPECTOR OF TAXES) v. BROWN [2001] S.T.C. 1166, Lightman, J., Ch D.

5243. Income tax – deposit takers – interest payments

INCOME TAX (DEPOSIT-TAKERS) (INTEREST PAYMENTS) (AMENDMENT) REGULATIONS 2001, SI 2001 406; made under the Taxes and Corporation Taxes Act 1988 s.480B, s.482; and the Finance Act 1999 s.132, s.133. In force: March 9, 2001; £0.75.

These Regulations, which amend the Income Tax (Deposit takers) (Interest Payments) Regulations 1990 (SI 1990 2232) in relation to payments by deposit takers made or received on or after April 6, 2001 and declarations made on or after that date to the effect that the person beneficially entitled to a payment of interest is not ordinarily resident in the UK, inserts definitions of "electronic communication" and "electronic signature". They amend the Regulations in relation to cases where certificates of non liability to tax under that regulation are made otherwise than in writing and provide that declarations that the person beneficially entitled to the payment of deposit interest is not ordinarily resident in the UK may be made by means of electronic communication.

5244. Income tax – discrimination – free movement of persons – spouses resident in different Member States – validity under EC law

[EC Treaty Art.48(2) (now, after amendment, Art.39(2) EC); Council Regulation 1612/68 on freedom of movement for workers within the Community Art.7(2).]

Z, a Belgian national, worked in Luxembourg, where he earned 98 per cent of his income. His wife, from whom he was not separated or divorced, lived in Belgium, where Z spent his weekends. Spouses residing in Luxembourg were assessed to tax jointly which was levied at a lower rate than for single persons. Z was assessed to tax at the single person's rate on the basis that he did not live with his spouse in Luxembourg. He appealed, arguing that the assessment was discriminatory as it placed Z and his wife in a less advantageous position to couples that were resident in Luxembourg. The national court stayed the proceedings pending a reference to the ECJ for a preliminary ruling as to whether the EC Treaty Art.48(2) (now, after amendment Art.39(2) EC), and Council Regulation 1612/68 Art.7(2) precluded income tax rules which stipulated that the applicable tax rate was conditional on both spouses being residents of the same Member State and which denied a tax advantage to a worker resident in the Member State where he earned virtually all his income on the basis that his spouse was resident in another Member State.

Held, giving a preliminary ruling, that (1) the residence condition was contrary to Art.48(2) EC as it favoured Luxembourg nationals over nationals of other Member States who worked in Luxembourg, and (2) Art.48(2) EC and Art.7(2) of the Regulation precluded an income tax assessment that was conditional on both spouses residing in the same Member State where this meant that an advantageous tax rate was denied to a resident worker because his spouse resided in another Member State.

ZURSTRASSEN v. ADMINISTRATION DES CONTRIBUTIONS DIRECTES (C87/99) [2001] S.T.C. 1102, JC Moitinho de Almeida (President), ECJ.

5245. Income tax – discrimination – frontier worker precluded from spousal income splitting provision – European Union

[EC Treaty Art.48(2) (now, after amendment, Art.39(2) EC).]

G, a married Dutch resident, worked in Germany during 1991 and 1992 and was assessed to income tax there as a single person. His wife was resident in the Netherlands throughout and earned all her income there. G contended that he and his wife should have been accorded the benefit of a German provision that would have allowed their joint income to be aggregated and attributed to each of them on a 50 per cent basis. The German court stayed the proceedings and referred the question to the ECJ for a preliminary ruling as to whether it was contrary to the EC Treaty Art.48(2) (now, after amendment, Art.39(2) EC) to allow resident couples to benefit from the income splitting provision, when non residents could do so only if they either earned 90 per cent of their income in Germany or their foreign income did not exceed a certain level.

Held, that the disputed provision was not contrary to Art.48(2). The status of residents and non residents was not comparable for direct taxation purposes, as non residents' incomes usually fell to be determined in their state of residence, *Finanzamt Koln-Altstadt v. Schumacker (C279/93)* [1996] Q.B. 28, [1995] C.L.Y. 2773 followed. For discrimination to exist, a non resident would have to earn the majority of his income in the state where he was employed so that his state of residence would be unable to take his personal circumstances into account when deciding his eligibility for income tax benefits.

GSCHWIND v. FINANZAMT AACHEN-AUSSENSTADT (C391/97) [2001] S.T.C. 331, GC Rodriguez Iglesias (President), ECJ.

5246. Income tax – emoluments – deductibility at source – income tax on bonuses paid as unit trusts

[Income and Corporation Taxes Act 1988 s.203(1).]

G, a company, paid bonuses to four employees, E, in the form of unit trusts. The Revenue assessed them to income tax on the bonuses. E appealed, contending that under Income and Corporation Taxes Act 1988 s.203(1) tax should have been deducted by the company on the issue of the units.

Held, allowing the appeal, that E had a pre-existing entitlement to the bonuses and accordingly the company should have deducted the tax on payment.

BLACK v. INSPECTOR OF TAXES [2000] S.T.C. (S.C.D.) 540, Judge not applicable, Sp Comm.

5247. **Income tax – emoluments – occupational pensions – retired medical practitioner voluntarily paying GMC registration fee**

[Income and Corporation Taxes Act 1988 s.131 (1), s.198, s.201.]

S was a retired medical practitioner in receipt of a civil service pension. As he wished to remain on the register of medical practitioners, he paid an annual fee to the General Medical Council which he sought to deduct as an allowable expense against his taxable income. The Revenue disallowed the deduction and S appealed, contending that his pension was a deferred emolument in terms of the Income and Corporation Taxes Act 1988 s.131 (1). The Revenue argued that pensions were not emoluments and that the payment was made voluntarily and not for the necessary performance of duties, as required by s.198.

Held, dismissing the appeal, that S's pension was not an emolument or payment made as the result of an office of employment, *Tilley v. Wales (Inspector of Taxes)* [1943] A.C. 386 applied. Section 198 applied only to expenses necessarily incurred and not payments made voluntarily. Although s.201 allowed the deduction of fees paid to "professional bodies and learned societies", these had to be deducted from emoluments or earnings from an employment, so it did not apply in the instant case.

SINGH v. WILLIAMS (INSPECTOR OF TAXES) [2000] S.T.C. (S.C.D.) 404, THK Everett, Sp Comm.

5248. **Income tax – emoluments – payment inducing employee to enter into employment with purchaser of business**

[Income and Corporation Taxes Act 1988 s.19(1).]

G sold a chemical plant to S. T had been G's operations manager and S was keen to retain his services. T accepted a three year contract with S on substantially the same terms he had enjoyed with G. As part of the negotiations, T obtained a payment of £24,103, grossed up to 40 per cent, from S to compensate him for losing benefits under G's share option schemes. T was subsequently assessed to income tax on that payment and he appealed, contending that it was compensatory in nature and not an emolument of his employment under the Income and Corporation Taxes Act 1988 s.19(1).

Held, dismissing the appeal, that (1) although the payment was not part of T's contract of employment with S it acted as an inducement for him to enter into that contract, and (2) the sum had been paid "grossed up" on the basis that it would be liable to tax, therefore it was an emolument of T's employment with S.

TEWARD v. INLAND REVENUE COMMISSIONERS [2001] S.T.C. (S.C.D.) 36, Judge not applicable, Sp Comm.

5249. **Income tax – emoluments – payments made to sportspersons under promotional and consultation agreements**

[Income and Corporation Taxes Act 1988 s.19, s.154.]

SC appealed against a determination that it was liable to income tax in respect of certain payments made to J and E, two sporting celebrities. J and E had entered into service and promotional and consultation agreements with SC and issues arose as to whether payments made under the latter were emoluments of employment for the purposes of the Income and Corporation Taxes Act 1988 s.19 or benefits under s.154.

Held, allowing the appeal, that the agreements were concluded for genuine commercial purposes and had not been used to hide remuneration payments so that no liability arose under s.19. Further, the payments were not made in connection with any employment so s.154 did not apply as no benefit had passed to J and E. Although E had referred to certain payments made under the agreements as being for his retirement fund, they had been paid by SC so that it could obtain the rights under the agreement and their final destination was irrelevant.

SPORTS CLUB v. INSPECTOR OF TAXES [2000] S.T.C. (S.C.D.) 443, AN Brice, Sp Comm.

5250. Income tax – friendly societies – provisional repayments for exempt business

FRIENDLY SOCIETIES (PROVISIONAL REPAYMENTS FOR EXEMPT BUSINESS) (AMENDMENT) REGULATIONS 2001, SI 2001 3973; made under the Finance Act 1993 s.121; and the Finance Act 2001 s.87. In force: January 1, 2002; £2.50.

These Regulations, which amend the Income and Corporation Taxes Act 1988 and the Friendly Societies (Provisional Repayments for Exempt Business) Regulations 1999 (SI 1999 622), make provision in relation to the tax exempt life or endowment business of friendly societies whose profits are not wholly exempt from tax. In addition, the Regulations introduce a simplified method of estimating the provisional repayments of tax credits which are referable to tax exempt life or endowment business.

5251. Income tax – general commissioners – costs

GENERAL COMMISSIONERS OF INCOME TAX (COSTS) REGULATIONS 2001, SI 2001 1304; made under the Taxes Management Act 1970 s.2A. In force: April 1, 2001; £1.75.

These Regulations, which apply where a court makes an order under the Taxes Management Act 1970 s.2A (3) that the Lord Chancellor make a payment in respect of the costs of a person in the proceedings, provide for when such an order cannot be made, and when such an order is made, how the costs shall be determined.

5252. Income tax – indexation

INCOME TAX (INDEXATION) ORDER 2001, SI 2001 638; made under the Income and Corporation Taxes Act 1988 s.1, s.257C. In force: March 7, 2001; £1.50.

The Income and Corporation Taxes Act 1988 s.1 and s.257C (3) provides that the Treasury shall, by order made by statutory instrument before April 6, 2001, specify the amounts which by virtue of those sections shall, unless Parliament otherwise determines, be treated as specified for the year 2001-02. This Order specifies the relevant amounts for the purposes of the Income and Corporation Taxes Act 1988 s.1 (2), starting rate and basic rate limits, s.257 (2), s.257 (3) and s.257 (5), personal allowances for persons of 65 or more, s.257A, married couple's allowances for those born before April 6, 1935, and s.265(1), blind persons allowance for the year 2000/2001.

5253. Income tax – indexation

INCOME TAX (INDEXATION) (NO.2) ORDER 2001, SI 2001 3773; made under the Income and Corporation Taxes Act 1988 s.257C. In force: 2001; £1.50.

The Income and Corporation Taxes Act 1988 s.257C operates to provide that the Treasury shall by order made by statutory instrument before April 6, 2002 specify the amounts which by virtue of that section shall, unless Parliament otherwise determines, be treated as specified for the purposes of s.257 (personal allowances) and s.257A (married couple's allowances for those born before April 6, 1935) of the Act for the year of assessment 2002/03. This Order increases the amounts of basic personal allowance, age-related personal allowances and income limit for age-related personal allowances in accordance with the percentage increase in the retail prices index for September 2001 over that for September 2000.

5254. Income tax – information – interest payments

INCOME TAX (INTEREST PAYMENTS) (INFORMATION POWERS) (AMENDMENT) REGULATIONS 2001, SI 2001 405; made under the Taxes Management Act 1970 s.17, s.18. In force: March 9, 2001; £2.00.

These Regulations, which amend the Income Tax (Interest Payments) (Information Powers) Regulations 1992 (SI 1992 15) in relation to payments of interest by banks and other persons made, credited or received on or after April 6, 2001, insert a definition of "Building Societies Regulations", and amend the definition of "payment". They list payments information on which is not required to be contained in a return under the Taxes Management Act 1970 s.17, amend the principal Regulations by adding to the list of further information required to be contained in a return, insert a new section providing for the form in which a return is to be delivered and add regulations dealing with information that the Board of Inland Revenue may require, and inspection and retention of documents, to ensure that a return or information furnished to the inspector is correct and complete.

5255. Income tax – insurance companies – overseas insurers

OVERSEAS INSURERS (TAX REPRESENTATIVES) (AMENDMENT) REGULATIONS 2001, SI 2001 2726; made under the Income and Corporation Taxes Act 1988 s.552A. In force: August 17, 2001; £1.50.

These Regulations amend the definition of "gain" used in the Schedule to the Overseas Insurers (Tax Representatives) Regulations 1999 (SI 1999 881) so as to include reference to a gain treated as arising under the Income and Corporation Taxes Act 1988 s.546C.

5256. Income tax – interest rates

TAXES (INTEREST RATE) (AMENDMENT NO.1) REGULATIONS 2001, SI 2001 204; made under the Finance Act 1989 s.178. In force: March 6, 2001; £1.50.

These Regulations amend the Taxes (Interest Rate) Regulations 1989 (SI 1989 1297) Reg.3 and 3A to ensure those Regulations specify the rate of interest applicable under the Finance Act 1989 s.178 for the purposes of the Taxes Management Act 1970 s.86.

5257. Income tax – interest rates

TAXES (INTEREST RATE) (AMENDMENT NO.3) REGULATIONS 2001, SI 2001 3860; made under the Finance Act 1989 s.178. In force: January 6, 2002; £1.50.

These Regulations amend the Taxes (Interest Rate) Regulations 1989 (SI 1989 1297) which provide for the official rate of interest for the purposes of Income and Corporation Taxes Act 1988 s.160 by first specifying an official rate of interest generally and then specifying, by way of exception, different official rates of interest for certain beneficial loans in the currencies of countries. The Regulations specify a new general official rate of interest of 5 per cent per annum.

5258. Income tax – liability – Iranian domicile – intention to return

The executors of F, a former Iranian national who had died in 1993, appealed against the determination of the Revenue that he had been domiciled in the United Kingdom for the years of assessment 1986/87 to 1992/93 inclusive. F had operated an accountancy business in Iran. He had bought land with a view to developing it, owned three houses and had constructed a large family home. At the time of the Iranian revolution he had sent his wife and children to live in the UK while remaining himself in Iran. At the time of the United States hostage crisis F had decided to remain outside Iran and at the same time he had been placed on an exit barred list due to alleged outstanding tax liabilities. In 1980 he had been granted indefinite leave to remain in the UK. He had subsequently applied for naturalisation, falsely claiming that he had left Iran to escape religious persecution. Up until the time of his death, F had made efforts at getting the exit bar removed. He had continued to consider Iran as his home.

Held, allowing the appeal, that the Revenue had not discharged the burden of proof to demonstrate that F had not abandoned his Iranian domicile. Having regard to the evidence, it had always been F's intention to return to Iran permanently during the relevant years for assessment. His acquisition of British citizenship and a British passport had not effected his domicile of origin in Iran, *Wahl v. Attorney General* (1932) 147 L.T. 382 applied. He had been keen to gain the necessary documentation that would enable him to continue to travel freely in the furtherance of his business interests and had been willing to lie in order to gain such documentation. His return to Iran had been precluded by the exit bar. Such external pressures had prevented F from forming a free intention to acquire another domicile.

F v. INLAND REVENUE COMMISSIONERS [2000] W.T.L.R. 505, Judge not applicable, Sp Comm.

5259. **Income tax – lump sum payments – termination of employment – agreement not to institute further proceedings**

[Income and Corporation Taxes Act 1988 s.148, s.313.]

As part of an ACAS negotiated agreement, A agreed to leave his employment on voluntary redundancy grounds and withdraw a racial discrimination complaint to the employment tribunal in return for an immediate pension, a lump sum payment under the terms of a benefit scheme and an additional sum of £65,684, bringing the total payment to £180,000. The Revenue decided that the additional payment was taxable under the Income and Corporation Taxes Act 1988 s.148 and issued an amendment to A's self assessment return to include the sum of £65,684 as income from his employment. Alternatively, the Revenue asserted that the additional payment had been paid in return for A giving restrictive undertakings in connection with his employment and was, therefore, taxable under s.313. A appealed, contending that the additional payment was consideration for his entering into a confidentiality agreement and agreeing not to take further proceedings against his former employer.

Held, dismissing the appeal, that the agreement showed that the additional amount was paid for the voluntary termination of A's employment and was, therefore, taxable under s.148. In the alternative, if the additional payment had been paid as consideration for A's agreement not to institute further proceedings, that would have meant that a value had been placed on the agreement which would have been liable to tax under s.313.

APPELLANT v. INSPECTOR OF TAXES [2001] S.T.C. (S.C.D.) 21, Judge not applicable, Sp Comm.

5260. **Income tax – manufactured overseas dividends**

INCOME TAX (MANUFACTURED OVERSEAS DIVIDENDS) (AMENDMENT) REGULATIONS 2001, SI 2001 403; made under the Income and Corporation Taxes Act 1988 Sch.23A para.1, para.8. In force: March 9, 2001; £1.50.

These Regulations amend the Income Tax (Manufactured Overseas Dividends) Regulations 1993 (SI 1993 2004) by substituting a new definition of "collecting agent" in relation to manufactured overseas dividends paid or received on or after April 1, 2001. The former definition is rendered obsolete by the repeal from that date of the Income and Corporation Taxes Act 1988 Part IV Ch.VIIA.

5261. Income tax – partnerships – business expansion scheme – reliefs – connected individuals – statutory interpretation

[Income and Corporation Taxes Act 1988 s.289, s.291 (1) (c), s.291 (8).]

The Revenue appealed against a decision ([1999] S.T.C. 661, [1999] C.L.Y. 4748) that B and his business partners, who collectively owned all of the shares in a company, FH, were entitled to tax relief in accordance with the Income and Corporation Taxes Act 1988 s.289. Each owned less than 30 per cent of the issued share capital and claimed tax relief under the provisions governing business expansion schemes. The Revenue contended that B and his partners were all "connected with" FH and therefore did not satisfy the requirements of s.291 (1) (c) of the Act, in that they were classed as associates of one another, with the result that each was treated as directly possessing more than 30 per cent of the issued share capital and therefore did not qualify for relief.

Held, allowing the appeal, that s.291 (8) comprised two distinct and separate provisions as opposed to a single provision made up of two interrelated clauses. The true construction of s.291 (8) was that the opening words: "For the purposes of this section", governed the whole of the subsection. Accordingly, although the first part of s.291 (8) was, on the facts, inapplicable to B, the latter part stood alone and was governed by the opening words. It was therefore available for the construction of other parts of s.291, including subsection 4. It followed that there was to be attributed to each individual in the instant case the rights of "any other person who is an associate of his" and therefore all should be treated as possessing more than 30 per cent and failed to qualify for relief.

COOK (INSPECTOR OF TAXES) v. BILLINGS [2001] S.T.C. 16, Mummery, L.J., CA.

5262. Income tax – PAYE – director's bonus paid in form of tradeable asset – time limit for paying tax

[Income and Corporation Taxes Act 1988 s.144A (1).]

F, a company director, appealed against an assessment to Sch. E income tax under the Income and Corporation Taxes Act 1988 s.144A (1). The company had arranged for a bonus payment to F in the form of rhodium metal, a tradeable asset in terms of s.144A (1). The metal was transferred to F's ownership on September 25, 1995 and sold the following day, with the proceeds paid to F and a sum equal to the PAYE liability transferred to his loan account. Under s.144A (1) (c) tax was due by the end of the month after the bonus was paid, but due to erroneous advice and accounting errors, it was not paid until April 16, 1996. F contended that the tax liability had been available from September 26, 1996 and he believed that the PAYE would be paid, although, in reality, the full amount had wrongly been credited to his loan account. The Revenue asserted that F's failure to deduct the tax due until the following tax year meant that s.144A (1) had not been complied with and raised the assessment for the PAYE due on the bonus in the sum of £19,948.

Held, allowing the appeal, that F's evidence as to the nature of the accounting mistake was accepted. Although he could have shown the amount paid into his loan account as a tax liability due to the Revenue, he knew that this was the case and that it was only being held there pending the due payment date, which he wrongly believed to be April 1996.

FERGUSON v. INLAND REVENUE COMMISSIONERS (BONUS PAYMENTS) [2001] S.T.C. (S.C.D.) 1, TG Coutts Q.C., Sp Comm.

5263. Income tax – pension schemes – meaning of "retirement" – tax status of payments made in breach of pension trust deed

[Income and Corporation Taxes Act 1988 s.600 (2).]

V, the 53 year old former executive director and chairman of a company, V, appealed against a decision of the Special Commissioner ([2001] Pens. L.R. 17) that he had "retired" on the ground of ill health and that payments made to him under the company retirement benefit scheme were not expressly authorised by the scheme and were accordingly chargeable to tax pursuant to the Income and Corporation Taxes Act 1988 s.600(2). The Revenue cross appealed against the finding that he had retired for the purposes of the pension scheme. The trustees of the scheme had authority to award an immediate pension to a member retiring "in normal health on or after the age of 50". Following concerns about his health V, who had been working close to 50 hour weeks, had given up his employment but was still consulted on some aspects of the business. At the time of his giving up, V was overweight and suffering from high blood pressure and mild diabetes.

Held, allowing V's appeal and dismissing the cross appeal, that the phrase "in normal health" could not be construed in a vacuum; it had to be linked, in this case, to V's fitness to do his job. There was no evidence to indicate that, at the time of making his decision, he was unfit to perform his role in the company and, furthermore, there was no indication that he was not in "normal" health, since high blood pressure and mild diabetes were common conditions for a male of his age and constitution. Moreover, whether or not a person had "retired" was a matter of fact and degree. A reduction in workload alone was insufficient to constitute retirement, but there was no principle that a person who relinquished a managerial role, but retained an executive role, could not "retire" and, on the facts, the finding that V had retired was justified. It was observed that if the payments to V had not been authorised by the terms of the trust, then so long as V was accountable to the trustees as an actual or constructive trustee and was able and prepared to account to those trustees, then the payment would not be taxable under s.600 of the Act, *Hillsdown Holdings Plc v. Inland Revenue Commissioners* [1999] S.T.C. 561, [1999] C.L.Y. 4679 considered.

VENABLES v. HORNBY (INSPECTOR OF TAXES); *sub nom* TRUSTEES OF THE FUSSELL PENSION SCHEME v. HORNBY (INSPECTOR OF TAXES) [2001] S.T.C. 1221, Lawrence Collins, J., Ch D.

5264. Income tax – personal portfolio bonds

PERSONAL PORTFOLIO BONDS (TAX) (AMENDMENT) REGULATIONS 2001, SI 2001 2724; made under the Income and Corporation Taxes Act 1988 s.553C. In force: August 17, 2001; £1.50.

These Regulations amend the Personal Portfolio Bonds (Tax) Regulations 1999 (SI 1999 1029) to reflect changes made to the taxation of personal portfolio bonds by the Finance Act 2001 Sch.28.

5265. Income tax – reliefs – double taxation agreements – interpretation of conflicting statutory provisions

[Income and Corporation Taxes Act 1970 s.497(1); Finance (No.2) Act 1987 s.62(1); Income and Corporation Taxes Act 1988 s.112(4), s.788(3); Double Taxation Relief (Taxes on Income) (Jersey) Order 1952 (SI 1952 1216) para.3.]

P appealed against a decision in principle of the special commissioners upholding the Revenue's refusal of his claim for income tax relief in respect of his share of profits of a partnership resident in Jersey. The claim for relief had been made under the Income and Corporation Taxes Act 1970 s.497(1) and the Income and Corporation Taxes Act 1988 s.788(3), in each case in reliance upon the Double Taxation Relief (Taxes on Income) (Jersey) Order 1952 para.3. It was common ground between the parties that the provisions relied on by P conflicted with the Finance (No.2) Act 1987 s.62(1) and s.112(4) of the 1988 Act, which limited the effect of double taxation agreements. P relied on s.788(3) of the 1988 Act whereby double taxation arrangements were to have effect "notwithstanding anything in any enactment".

Held, dismissing the appeal, that s.62(1) of the 1987 Act and s.112(4) of the 1988 Act overrode the general provisions of s.497(1) of the 1970 Act and s.788(3) of the 1988 Act so that P was not entitled to the relief claimed. The interpretation of the conflicting provisions in the manner contended for by P would have rendered s.62(1) and s.112(4) wholly ineffective, which was a construction of last resort, *Associated Newspapers Group v. Fleming (Inspector of Taxes)* [1973] A.C. 628, [1972] C.L.Y. 1753 applied. Instead, applying a purposive construction to the legislation, s.62(1) and 112(4) were specific exceptions to the general rule governing double taxation arrangements set out under s.497(1) and s.788(3).

PADMORE v. INLAND REVENUE COMMISSIONERS (NO.2) [2001] S.T.C. 280, Lightman, J., Ch D.

5266. Income tax – reliefs – foreign earnings – impact of residence abroad upon qualifying period of absence

[Income and Corporation Taxes Act 1988 s.193(1).]

C appealed against the General Commissioners' decision to discharge an assessment to Schedule E income tax served upon S, a taxpayer. S had lived and worked in Asia for a period of approximately six years, after which time he had returned to the UK. C contended that the six-year period could not be included to aggregate a qualifying period of absence for the purpose of tax relief for foreign earnings pursuant to the Income and Corporation Taxes Act 1988 s.193(1) as absence for tax relief was not intended to include residence abroad.

Held, allowing the appeal, that to make sense of the qualifying period of absence, the periods of time in which the taxpayer was neither physically present nor ordinarily resident in the UK had to be disregarded.

CARSTAIRS (INSPECTOR OF TAXES) v. SYKES [2000] S.T.C. 1103, Hart, J., Ch D.

5267. Income tax – reliefs – medical insurance – taxpayer not privy to contract that also included other employees

[Finance Act 1989 s.54.]

W appealed against the refusal of medical insurance relief under the Finance Act 1989 s.54 in respect of premiums paid under a contract of private medical insurance.

Held, dismissing the appeal, that W did not within s.54(1) (a), (b) or (c) as he was not a party to the contract, which was made by his former employer. Other persons were also covered by the contract, some of whom were under 60 years of age. Further, lack of certification by the Inland Revenue Board meant that the contract was ineligible.

WILLIAMS v. INLAND REVENUE COMMISSIONERS [2001] S.T.C. (S.C.D.) 35 (Note), Judge not applicable, Sp Comm.

5268. Income tax – retirement benefits scheme – indexation of earnings cap

RETIREMENT BENEFITS SCHEMES (INDEXATION OF EARNINGS CAP) ORDER 2001, SI 2001 637; made under the Income and Corporation Taxes Act 1988 s.590C. In force: March 7, 2001; £1.50.

The Income and Corporation Taxes Act 1988 s.590C(1) provides that in arriving at an employee's final remuneration for the purposes of s.590(3)(a) or (d) of that Act any excess over the permitted maximum figure for the year of assessment in which the employee's participation in the scheme ceases shall be disregarded. This Order specifies £95,400 as the earnings cap for the year of assessment 2000/02.

5269. Income tax – seafarers – tax treatment of oil rig crew – meaning of "ship"

[Merchant Shipping Act 1894; Income and Corporation Taxes Act 1988.]

P, taxpayers, appealed against a decision ([2000] S.T.C. 428, [2000] C.L.Y. 5007) that the "jack-up" oil drilling rig on which they were employed was not a ship and that they were therefore not employed as "seafarers" for the purposes of the Income and Corporation Taxes Act 1988 and were consequently unable to claim foreign earnings reductions. The Commissioners had held that the rigs were capable of being used in navigation and were therefore ships within the definition of the Merchant Shipping Act 1894. P contended that the judge at first instance had erred in finding that the definition of ships for tax purposes was a question of law, and maintained that the finding of the Commissioners should not have been interfered with. The Revenue resisted the appeal, arguing that it was necessary to ascertain the real use and purpose of the rig and that since any movement was incidental to their "real work" as stationary drilling platforms, they could not be categorised as ships.

Held, allowing the appeal, that the finding had been a question of fact with which the court should not have interfered. The Commissioners had not erred by failing to apply the "real work" test as formulated in *Polpen Shipping Co Ltd v. Commercial Union Assurance Co Ltd* [1943] K.B. 161, but had correctly found that as navigation was a function of the rig, it fell within the definition of a ship, *Merchants Marine Insurance Co Ltd v. North of England Protecting and Indemnity Association* (1926) 26 Ll. L. Rep 201 considered. P was therefore entitled to more favourable tax treatment, *Polpen* not followed.

CLARK (INSPECTOR OF TAXES) v. PERKS; MacLEOD (INSPECTOR OF TAXES) v. PERKS; GUILD (INSPECTOR OF TAXES) v. NEWRICK; *sub nom.* CLARK v. PERKS (INSPECTOR OF TAXES); PERKS v. CLARK (INSPECTOR OF TAXES), [2001] EWCA Civ 1228, [2001] 2 Lloyd's Rep. 431, Carnwath, J., CA.

5270. Income tax – securities – calculation of dividends received by taxpayer

[Income and Corporation Taxes Act 1988 s.704A.]

Held, allowing the appeal, that when determining whether a person had received "an abnormal amount by way of dividend" within the meaning of the Income and Corporation Taxes Act 1988 s.704A, it was necessary to take into account the amount of the distribution actually received by the taxpayer, not including the amount of any tax credit, and also the length of time for which the securities were held.

TRUSTEES OF THE OMEGA GROUP PENSION SCHEME v. INLAND REVENUE COMMISSIONERS [2001] Pens. L.R. 305, Judge not applicable, Sp Comm.

5271. Income tax – shadow directors – living accommodation and benefits in kind

[Taxes Management Act 1970 s.20(1); Income and Corporation Taxes Act 1988 s.168(8); Human Rights Act 1998.]

A, the shadow director of various off-shore businesses, appealed against the decision of the Court of Appeal ([2000] Q.B. 744, [1999] C.L.Y. 4704) upholding his conviction for offences of cheating the public revenue. In his capacity as shadow director, A received living accommodation and other benefits, but had failed to disclose such benefits to the Inland Revenue. He contended that (1) as a shadow director he was not liable to tax in respect of living accommodation and benefits in kind; (2) there had been a breach of his rights under the Human Rights 1998, and (3) compelling him to provide a schedule of his assets was a violation of his right against self-incrimination.

Held, dismissing the appeal, that (1) in enacting the Income and Corporation Taxes Act 1988 s.168(8), Parliament had intended that accommodation and benefits in kind received by shadow directors would be taxed in the same way as those received by directors; (2) a conviction entered before October 2, 2000 which, at that date, was safe under English law was not rendered unsafe by virtue of the 1998 Act, *R. v. Lambert (Steven)* [2001] UKHL 37, [2001] 3 W.L.R. 206, [2001] 8 C.L. 360 followed, and (3) a notice under the Taxes Management Act 1970 s.20(1) did not violate the right against self-incrimination.

R. v. ALLEN (BRIAN ROGER), [2001] UKHL 45, [2001] 3 W.L.R. 843, Lord Hutton, HL.

5272. Income tax – tax returns – electronic communication – incentive payments

INCOME TAX (ELECTRONIC COMMUNICATIONS) (INCENTIVE PAYMENTS) REGULATIONS 2001, SI 2001 56; made under the Finance Act 2000 s.143, Sch.38. In force: February 1, 2001; £2.00.

These Regulations, which provide for incentive payments to be made to individuals and employers who submit returns to the Inland Revenue using electronic communications, provide that an incentive payment of £10 shall be made to an individual who submits a personal return under the Taxes Management Act 1970 s.8 and an incentive payment of £50 shall be made to an employer who submits an end of year PAYE return using electronic communications.

5273. **Income tax – termination of employment – lump sum payments – breach of statutory duty – status of payment**

[Income and Corporation Taxes Act 1988 s.19; Trade Union and Labour Relations (Consolidation) Act 1992 s.188; Income Tax (Employments) Regulations 1993 (SI 1993 744) Reg.49.]

M appealed against a determination made pursuant to the Income Tax (Employments) Regulations 1993 Reg.49 that it was liable to pay income tax in the sum of £34,500 in relation to emoluments of £150,000. The issue before the Special Commissioners related to whether payments made to redundant employees as compensation for M's failure to consult trade union representatives over the redundancy proposals constituted emoluments within the meaning of the Income and Corporation Taxes Act 1988 s.19.

Held, allowing the appeal, that a "protective award" for an employer's failure to consult with trade union representatives concerning redundancies in accordance with the Trade Union and Labour Relations (Consolidation) Act 1992 s.188 arose from the breach of a statutory duty rather than from the employment relationship as such. Accordingly, it was not an emolument within s.19 of the 1988 Act. The fact that the employment legislation referred to a payment for a failure to consult as "remuneration" did not affect such a conclusion.

MIMTEC LTD v. INLAND REVENUE COMMISSIONERS [2001] S.T.C. (S.C.D.) 101, Stephen Oliver Q.C., Sp Comm.

5274. **Income tax – termination of employment – lump sum payments – emolument from employment – liability to tax**

[Income and Corporation Taxes Act 1988 s.19, s.148.]

The Revenue appealed against a determination allowing an appeal by D against an assessment to tax under Schedule E in respect of a lump sum payment of £75,000 which he had received upon the termination of his employment. The Commissioners had concluded that the payment had been by way of compensation for breach of contract and that it fell within the Income and Corporation Taxes Act 1988 s.148, with the result that the first £30,000 of the payment was tax free. The Revenue submitted that there had been no breach of contract by the employer and that the payment was simply an "emolument" derived from D's employment and it was thus taxable in its entirety under s.19 of the Act.

Held, allowing the appeal, that the lump sum payment was an emolument from employment, taxable under s.19 of the Act. The whole sum was chargeable to tax. There was no evidential basis for the Commissioners' finding that D's employer had acted in breach of contract and, therefore, his decision had been fundamentally flawed. The lump sum had been part of a negotiated agreement to terminate D's employment and that was not sufficient for it to attract the relief provided by s.148 of the Act; s.148 was only applicable if the payment was not otherwise chargeable to tax under alternative provisions of the Act, *Dale v. de Soissons* [1950] 2 All E.R. 460, *EMI Group Electronics Ltd v. Coldicott (Inspector of Taxes)* [2000] 1 W.L.R. 540, [1999] C.L.Y. 4729 and *Delaney v. RJ Staples (t/a De Montfort Recruitment)* [1992] 1 A.C. 687, [1992] C.L.Y. 2028 considered.

RICHARDSON (INSPECTOR OF TAXES) v. DELANEY [2001] S.T.C. 1328, Lloyd, J., Ch D.

5275. Income tax – transfer of assets – lack of consideration – availability of base price adjustment – New Zealand

[IncomeTax Act 1976 (New Zealand).]

A transferred local government and Government stock for no consideration to two trusts that it had established prior to its abolition as part of local government reform. The transfer amounted to a "financial arrangement" in terms of the Income Tax Act 1976 s.64B and was liable to tax on an accrual basis under s.64B to s.64M, so that the entire yield was taxable, irrespective of whether it was capital or income in nature. A sought to deduct the base price adjustment from its income tax liability under s.64F, on the basis that it had disposed of the stock prior to maturity. The deduction was refused under s.64J(1) as the Commissioner deemed the consideration for the transfer to be that which would have been realised on an arm's length transfer by unrelated parties because the transfers had been used to prevent the application of s.64B to s.64M. A's appeal against this decision was dismissed at first instance, but succeeded on appeal to the New Zealand Court of Appeal. The Commissioner appealed.

Held, dismissing the appeal, that the transfers had been made for no consideration, but A remained eligible to deduct the base price adjustment by virtue of s.64F. However, s.64J(1) did not confer a discretion on the Commissioner to interpret the statute in such a way that he could deem a market value consideration to apply in the instant case. The accrual regime rules were such that no power could be inferred, *Inland Revenue Commissioners v. Challenge Corp* [1987] A.C.155, [1987] C.L.Y. 2036 considered.

INLAND REVENUE COMMISSIONER v. AUCKLAND HARBOUR BOARD [2001] UKPC 21, Lord Hoffmann, PC NZ.

5276. Indirect taxes – beverages – prohibition upon indirect tax possessing characteristics of VAT – specific purpose of duty

[Sixth Council Directive 77/388 on a common system of VAT Art.33(1); Council Directive 92/12 on the general arrangements for products subject to excise duty and on the holding, movement and monitoring of such products Art.3.]

EKW operated a hospital cafeteria in Vienna and was made subject to a recovery assessment by the relevant tax recovery authority. Under the assessment a sum was levied on the sale of non alcoholic drinks and ice cream over a specified period. An appeal against the decision was dismissed by the Vienna Tax Appeals Commission. EKW initiated proceedings before the Verwaltungsgerichtshof, maintaining that the imposition of the duty was contrary to the Sixth Council Directive 77/388 Art.33(1) and Council Directive 92/12 Art.3. W, a wine trading company, was subjected to a similar assessment in respect of its sales of wine. An administrative appeal against the decision was unsuccessful and W also initiated proceedings before the Verwaltungsgerichtshof during which similar arguments were raised. The issue was referred to the European Court of Justice for a preliminary ruling.

Held, giving a preliminary ruling, that (1) Art.33 of Council Directive 77/388 prohibited any kind of tax or charge possessing the essential characteristics of VAT. The duty imposed in the instant case did not fall within the prohibition since it was not intended to apply to all economic transactions in the relevant Member State, *Fazenda Publica v. Solisnor-Estaleiros Navais SA (C130/96)* [1998] S.T.C. 191, [1998] C.L.Y. 4944 and *Beaulande v. Directeur des Services Fiscaux de Nantes (C208/91)* [1996] S.T.C. 1111, [1993] C.L.Y. 4407 applied, and (2) pursuant to Council Directive 92/12 Art 3(3), a tax levied against products other than those listed in para (1) of the Directive or which was levied on a supply of services and could not be classed as a turnover tax, was permissible if it did not give rise to border-crossing formalities in trade between member states. The duty on non alcoholic drinks and ice cream satisfied that condition and was accordingly compatible with Art.3(3). However, alcoholic drinks did fall within the scope of para (1) whereby indirect taxes were permitted if such a tax pursued one or more specific purposes in the manner contemplated by the provision and was also compliant with the tax rules applicable for excise duty and VAT purposes as far as determination of the tax base, calculation of the tax and chargeability and monitoring of the tax were concerned. The underlying purposes argued for by the Austrian government, namely reinforcement of the municipalities' tax autonomy, the offsetting of substantial costs incurred by municipalities as a result of tourism and the protection of public health could not be sustained. Furthermore the duty did not comply with the VAT rules on calculation and chargeability. Therefore, in the instant case, maintenance of the tax charged on alcoholic beverages was precluded under Art. 3(2).

EVANGELISCHER KRANKENHAUSVEREIN WIEN v. ABGABENBERUFUNGSKOMMISSION WIEN (C437/97); WEIN & CO HANDELSGES MBH v. OBEROSTERREICHISCHE LANDESREGIERUNG (C437/97) [2001] All E.R. (EC) 735, DAO Edward (President), ECJ.

5277. Indirect taxes – interest rates

AIR PASSENGER DUTY AND OTHER INDIRECT TAXES (INTEREST RATE) (AMENDMENT) REGULATIONS 2001, SI 2001 3337; made under the Finance Act 1996 s.197. In force: November 1, 2001; £1.50.

These Regulations, which come into force on November 1, 2001, amend the Air Passenger Duty and Other Indirect Taxes (Interest Rate) Regulations 1998 (SI 1998 1461, as amended by SI 2000 631). The primary purpose of this amendment is to extend the existing provisions for setting interest rates on payments to and by the Commissioners on certain indirect taxes to include excise duties generally, and climate change levy. The Regulations also extend those provisions for setting interest rates so as to cover cases where the Commissioners assess to recover excessive repayments of excise duty, or climate change levy.

5278. Inheritance tax – business property – reliefs – group memberships

[Inheritance Tax Act 1984 s.103(2), s.104, s.105.]

M owned shares in four companies, two of which were resident in England, one in Jersey and the fourth in Ireland. Following M's death, the Revenue served notice on GT, M's personal representative, that the shareholdings did not qualify for business property relief under the Inheritance Tax Act 1984. GT appealed, contending that M's shareholdings were liable for relief under s.104 as the companies formed part of a group, and that, although the Irish resident company held land in the UK, this was used by another group member for farming purposes that qualified for business property relief under s.105.

Held, dismissing the appeal, that the companies were not part of a group for the purposes of s.103(2) and M's shareholdings did not make the companies a group of companies. Furthermore, the companies acquired land for occupation by members of M's family and the fact that they made losses did not prevent them from being engaged in investment business for the purposes of the Act, so that they did not qualify for business property relief.

GRIMWOOD-TAYLOR v. INLAND REVENUE COMMISSIONERS [2000] W.T.L.R. 321, Judge not applicable, Sp Comm.

5279. Inheritance tax – business property – voting rights of deceased – extent of "control"

[Inheritance Tax Act 1984 s.269.]

The executors of W appealed against a decision that her estate was not entitled to 100 per cent business property relief in respect of the shares she had held in a company of which she had been chairman of directors. W had held 50 per cent of the shares in the company and, as chairman, she had been entitled to a casting vote at general meetings.

Held, allowing the appeal, that since W had had "control of the company" by virtue of having had the casting vote at general meetings, her estate was entitled to 100 per cent business relief in respect of the shares. Control, for the purposes of the Inheritance Tax Act 1984 s.269, was dependent on the voting power in general meetings prior to an individuals death. Notwithstanding that some constraints might have existed on the exercise of W's casting vote, these had not been sufficient to prevent such a vote giving W control.

WALKER'S EXECUTORS v. INLAND REVENUE COMMISSIONERS [2001] S.T.C. (S.C.D.) 86, Wallace (Chairman), Sp Comm.

5280. **Inheritance tax – disposals – valuation based on site divided into plots – hope value of obtaining planning permission**

P, the executor of J's estate, appealed against a Revenue decision valuing J's home at £115,000 on a deemed disposal for inheritance tax purposes. P initially contended for a market value of £65,000, which was later raised to £85,000 on the basis of a second valuation that did not take comparable local transactions into account. The Revenue based its valuation on the division of the site into two separate lots. The first comprising the house and a reduced garden and the second being a potential building site sold without planning permission. P argued that hope value could not be taken into account for the second plot as the local planning authority had refused permission for other homes in the area.

Held, allowing the appeal in part and giving a market value of £85,000, that (1) the Revenue's value for the first plot of £72,500 was accepted as P had not adduced evidence to support a lower figure; (2) the value of the building plot would be reduced to reflect P's evidence relating to a similar site sold in 1993, giving a value of £50,000 to reflect 1995 prices, as opposed to the Revenue's figure of £55,000; (3) the prospect of obtaining planning permission could be assessed by reference to the policy on frontage developments being allowed where the curtilage was similar to those existing in the same vicinity; (4) the value of the property could be determined on that basis of its existing use with the added hope element. A minimal use value would be considered as neither P nor the Revenue had referred to it in evidence, and (5) a speculative purchaser would probably have paid 25 per cent of the development value of the building plot in view of the chance of obtaining planning permission, giving a market value of £12,500 for the second plot.

PROSSER v. INLAND REVENUE COMMISSIONERS [2001] R.V.R. 170, NJ Rose FRICS, Lands Tr.

5281. **Inheritance tax – indexation**

INHERITANCE TAX (INDEXATION) ORDER 2001, SI 2001 639; made under the Inheritance Tax Act 1984 s.8. In force: April 6, 2001; £1.50.

This Order substitutes a new table of rate bands and rates in the Inheritance Act 1984 Sch.1 for the table which was substituted by the Inheritance Tax (Indexation) Order 2000 (SI 2000 803) in relation to chargeable transfers made in the year beginning April 6, 2000. The new table will apply in relation to chargeable transfers on or after April 6, 2001 unless Parliament otherwise determines.

5282. **Inheritance tax – life interests – beneficial entitlement to interest in property**

[Inheritance Tax Act 1984 s.49.]

W, was the personal representative of his brother. Under the will of their father, W, his brother and a sister were entitled to reside in a house. W and the sister ceased to reside there and the sister died. The brother lived in it until his death. The Revenue determined that under Inheritance Tax Act 1984 s.49 the brother was entitled to an interest in possession in the whole house. W appealed.

Held, allowing the appeal in part, that W and the brother each had an interest in possession in one half of the house, *Pearson v. Inland Revenue Commissioners* [1981] A.C. 753, [1980] C.L.Y. 228 applied.

WOODHALL v. INLAND REVENUE COMMISSIONERS [2000] S.T.C. (S.C.D.) 558, Judge not applicable, Sp Comm.

5283. Inheritance tax – reliefs – business property – caravan site

[InheritanceTax Act 1984 s.105(3).]

W appealed against the decision of a special commissioner that shares owned by his late mother in a company which ran a residential caravan site did not qualify for relief from inheritance tax by virtue of the InheritanceTax Act 1984 s.105(3) which exempted from relief a business that consisted "wholly or mainly of ... making or holding investments". The commissioner had found that the occupiers of the site had been required to purchase their caravans and to pay pitch fees to the company. W argued that the business of the company amounted to one single business and that the company's receipt of pitch fees was ancillary to the sale of the caravans.

Held, dismissing the appeal, that the commissioner had been correct to find that the business fell within the exemption from relief under s.105(3). Having taken into account the limited amount of caravan sales and the company accounts, which revealed that the profit received from pitch fees exceeded that received from sales and that the caravan site represented a significant proportion of the company's capital, the commissioner had rightly rejected W's contention that the company's receipt of pitch fees was ancillary to its caravan sales; if anything, the reverse was true.

WESTON v. INLAND REVENUE COMMISSIONERS [2000] S.T.C. 1064, Lawrence Collins, J., Ch D.

5284. Inheritance tax – reliefs – business property – liability incurred in day to day running of business

[InheritanceTax Act 1984 s.110(b).]

H was the executor of V, a Lloyd's underwriter. The Revenue determined thatV's debt under an estate protection policy should be deducted from the value of his business assets. H appealed, contending that the debt should be deducted from his general assets.

Held, allowing the appeal, that for the purposes of Inheritance Tax Act 1984 s.110(b) the policy was an ordinary liability incurred in the day to day running of the business and not a liability incurred "for the purposes of the business", *Van den Berghs Ltd v. Clark* [1935] A.C. 431 applied.

HARDCASTLE v. INLAND REVENUE COMMISSIONERS [2000] S.T.C. (S.C.D.) 532, Judge not applicable, Sp Comm.

5285. Inheritance tax – reliefs – underwriting business – meaning of "relevant business property"

[InheritanceTax Act 1984 s.105(1)(a), s.110.]

The Revenue appealed against a decision of a special commissioner that the value of a piece of land, the freehold owner of which was deceased, was to be included in the net value of the assets used in the deceased's business for the purposes of the InheritanceTax Act 1984 s.110. The deceased had been a Lloyd's underwriter, in support of which, he had committed assets to Lloyds. The Lloyd's funds had included the piece of land for which the bank had given a guarantee in return for a charge over the land. The Revenue contended that as the land itself had not been used in the underwriting business and had merely been used as security for a bank guarantee, it did not constitute "relevant business property" within the meaning of s.105(1)(a) of the Act and thus the executors of the deceased's estate were not entitled to relief in respect of it.

Held, allowing the appeal, that it was the guarantee that was relevant with regard to the business and not the associated property which had been used to secure it. In the provision of Lloyd's funds, the bank was not concerned with the security behind a guarantee, however, where shares and securities had been committed in support of the business, the bank would assess the value. In the absence of a link between the charge and the land, the land could not be considered as "property consisting of a business" nor could it be considered as an "asset used" in the underwriting business for the purposes of the Act.

MALLENDER v. INLAND REVENUE COMMISSIONERS; *sub nom.* INLAND REVENUE COMMISSIONERS v. MALLENDER [2001] S.T.C. 514, Jacob, J., Ch D.

5286. Inheritance tax – settlements – value of general power of appointment

[Inheritance Tax Act 1984 s.3, s.5.]

The Revenue appealed against a decision ([2000] S.T.C. 628, [2000] C.L.Y. 5029) upholding a challenge by M in respect of notices of determination made by the Revenue to the effect that a general power of appointment exercisable by M enabling him to require the trustees to exercise their powers of appointment in such manner as he might direct was not "property" forming part of M's estate for the purposes of the Inheritance Tax Act 1984. The issue before the court related to whether, by virtue of s.5 of the Act, a general power of appointment relating to settled property was to be taken into account when valuing an estate for inheritance tax purposes.

Held, dismissing the appeal, that the general power of appointment was part of M's estate for the purposes of inheritance tax. Having regard to s.3 of the Act, a general power of appointment, being a power exercisable by the holder, was a valuable right and was to be taken into account when valuing an estate.

MELVILLE v. INLAND REVENUE COMMISSIONERS, [2001] EWCA Civ 1247, [2002] 1 W.L.R. 407, Peter Gibson, L.J., CA.

5287. Inheritance tax – trustees powers and duties – nature of proprietary interest

[Inheritance Tax Act 1984 s.49(1).]

F, a trustee, appealed against a notice of determination issued by the Revenue by which he was rendered liable for inheritance tax following the transfer of property of the deceased, A. A's will had directed the trustees that H and his wife were to be allowed to live in the house for as long as they wished. Following their deaths, the Revenue had held that H had an interest in possession of settled property under the Inheritance Tax Act 1984 s.49(1) and that F, as the surviving trustee, was liable. F argued that H had occupied the property as a mere licensee and, in the alternative, that any interest was divided between H and the residuary beneficiaries.

Held, dismissing the appeal, that the will did not empower the trustees to allow the occupation, but rather it directed them to. H's occupation of the property was not dependent upon the actions of the trustees but existed in its own right. H had, at the time of his death, a present right to present enjoyment and therefore an interest in possession. The residuary beneficiaries had no interest during H's lifetime. Moreover, although the will was phrased as directions for the trustees, the purpose and effect was to allow H's occupation, *Inland Revenue Commissioners v. Lloyds Private Banking Ltd* [1998] S.T.C. 559, [1998] C.L.Y. 4689 considered.

FAULKNER v. INLAND REVENUE COMMISSIONERS [2001] S.T.C. (S.C.D.) 112, Nuala Brice, Sp Comm.

5288. Insurance companies – individual savings accounts – tax credits

INDIVIDUAL SAVINGS ACCOUNT (INSURANCE COMPANIES) (AMENDMENT) REGULATIONS 2001, SI 2001 3974; made under the Income and Corporation Taxes Act 1988 s.333B; and the Finance Act 2001 s.87. In force: January 1, 2002; £2.00.

These Regulations, which amend the Income and Corporation Taxes Act 1988 and the Individual Savings Account (Insurance Companies) Regulations 1998 (SI 1998 1871), make provision in relation to the individual savings account business of life assurance companies and introduce a simplified method of estimating the provisional repayments of tax credits which are referable to the individual savings account business of life assurance companies.

5289. Insurance premium tax – customs and excise – rights of appeal

[Finance Act 1994 s.59(1)(b), s.59(1)(l), s.59(2).]

CH appealed against the striking out of its appeal ([2001] S.T.I. 152) against a decision by the Commissioners to confirm a decision as to the level of insurance premium tax payable following a review. The judge had found that the Commissioners' decision was not a decision on review for the purposes of the Finance Act 1994 s.59(1)(b) and gave no rights of appeal because the tax had been challenged only after the sum demanded had been paid. He further held that the only avenue of challenge available once the tax had been paid was pursuant to s.59(1)(l), a regime that was distinct and mutually exclusive of s.59(1)(b), and which could only be pursued by the tax payer.

Held, allowing the appeal, that s.59(1)(b) was not to be interpreted as restrictively as the judge at first instance had determined. Such a conclusion was justified by analogy with the historical treatment of VAT by the VAT Tribunal, whereby appeals could be brought not only by the supplier but also by the recipient of supplies, and in circumstances where the tax under consideration had already been paid, *Processed Vegetable Growers Association v. Customs and Excise Commissioners (Decision LEE/73/4)* [1974] 1 C.M.L.R. 113, [1974] C.L.Y. 1395 and *Williams & Glyn's Bank v. Customs and Excise Commissioners* [1974] V.A.T.T.R. 262, [1975] C.L.Y. 3504.14 considered. Accordingly those affected by a ruling of the Commissioners as to the amount of tax payable were entitled to pursue an appeal under s.59(1)(b) regardless of whether they had also brought, or were entitled to bring, a claim under s.59(1)(l). Whilst it was clear from the plain wording of the statute that only the taxpayer could pursue a claim for repayment, once such a claim had been rejected there was no sound reason to prevent those affected by the decision from pursuing an appeal as a person "affected" for the purposes of s.59(2).

CUSTOMS AND EXCISE COMMISSIONERS v. CRESTA HOLIDAYS LTD [2001] EWCA Civ 215, Simon Brown, L.J., CA.

5290. Lottery duty – national lottery – electronic communication

LOTTERY DUTY (AMENDMENT) REGULATIONS 2001, SI 2001 4021; made under the Finance Act 1993 s.26, s.28, s.38; and the Finance Act 1999 s.132. In force: January 27, 2002; £1.75.

These Regulations amend the Lottery Duty Regulations 1993 (SI 1993 3212) to require payment of lottery duty by specified means of electronic communication; to amend the date by which a return must be furnished to the Commissioners; and to provide for the furnishing of a return by electronic communication. They also provide that payment of lottery duty be made using either the Bankers' Automated Clearing Services (BACS) or the Clearing House Automated Payment System (CHAPS) and that payment must be credited to the required bank account on or before the day by which the return is required to be furnished. They provide that a registered lottery promoter is to furnish a return to the Commissioners by no later than the thirteenth day following the end of every accounting period; specify where returns must be furnished; and make provision for a registered promoter who applies to and is authorised by the Commissioners to furnish returns using approved forms of electronic communication. Certain formalities are provided for to take account of the special characteristics of electronic communication.

5291. Penalties – assessment – power of findings on prior assessment to bind subsequent assessment – applicability of Human Rights Act 1998

[Taxes Management Act 1970 s.46(2); Human Rights Act 1998 Sch.1 Part I Art.6(2).]

K appealed against interest assessments and penalty determinations imposed by the Revenue which had held that he was liable for tax having obtained profits through the acquisition of properties ([2000] S.T.C. (S.C.D.) 179, [2000] C.L.Y. 4989). K contended that (1) in relation to the interest assessments, the Revenue had erred in concluding that it was, by virtue of the Taxes Management Act 1970 s.46(2), bound by a finding of wilful neglect arising from an assessment in 1991, and (2) that the Human Rights Act 1998 Sch.1 Part I Art.6(2) applied to the penalty determinations and had been breached by a reversal of the presumption of innocence.

Held, dismissing the appeal, that (1) the Revenue had erred in concluding that it was bound by the previous findings of wilful neglect. Assessments were independent of each other and an issue heard and determined in relation to a particular assessment was not binding on future and consequential assessments. The Revenue had in fact been bound only by the assessment of the amount of tax owing, *Caffoor (Trustees of the Abdul Gaffoor Trust) v. Income Tax Commissioner (Colombo)* [1961] A.C. 584, [1961] C.L.Y. 4092 applied. However, there was ample evidence to support the conclusion that K had been guilty of wilful neglect, and (2) the 1998 Act applied by virtue of s.22(4) which afforded retrospective effect to actions instigated by a public authority. Since an appeal against assessment constituted a defensive rather than offensive step it would be wrong to categorise the proceedings as having been instigated by the taxpayer, *R. v. DPP, ex p. Kebilene* [2000] 2 A.C. 326, [1999] C.L.Y. 1045 applied. Article 6(2) was applicable since the imposition of a penalty constituted proceedings of a criminal character having regard, inter alia, to the potential size of the penalty, the punitive and deterrent nature of the proceedings and the consideration given to mitigation, *Georgiou (t/a Marios Chippery) v. United Kingdom (40042/98)* [2001] S.T.C. 80, [2001] 4 C.L. 407 applied. On the facts of the instant case there had been no breach of Art.6(2). The fact that the Revenue had taken account of the primary facts determined by the Revenue in 1991 merely constituted part of the evidence against K and could not amount to a reversal of the burden of proof which ultimately still rested with the Revenue, *Brown (Margaret) v. Stott* [2001] 2 W.L.R. 817, [2001] 1 C.L. 639 considered.

KING v. WALDEN (INSPECTOR OF TAXES) [2001] S.T.C. 822, Jacob, J., Ch D.

5292. Personal pensions – conversion of retirement benefits

PERSONAL PENSION SCHEMES (CONVERSION OF RETIREMENT BENEFITS SCHEMES) REGULATIONS 2001, SI 2001 118; made under the Income and Corporation Taxes Act 1988 Sch.23 para.2, para.4. In force: April 6, 2001; £2.00.

These Regulations, which prescribe the way in which retirement benefits schemes which are money purchase schemes may apply to the Inland Revenue for approval as personal pensions schemes, introduce the possibility of conversion of occupational money purchase schemes into personal pension schemes.

5293. Personal pensions – transfer payments

PERSONAL PENSION SCHEMES (TRANSFER PAYMENTS) REGULATIONS 2001, SI 2001 119; made under the Income and Corporation Taxes Act 1988 s.638. In force: in accordance with Reg.1; £2.50.

These Regulations, which amend the Personal Pension Schemes (Transfer Payments) Regulations 1988 (SI 1988 1014), amend and consolidate the requirements in the Income and Corporation Taxes Act 1988 s.638 providing that the Commissioners of Inland Revenue shall not approve a personal pension scheme unless it makes such provision for the making, acceptance and application of transfer payments as satisfies any requirements imposed by or under regulations made by the Board. The Personal Pension Schemes (Transfer Payments) (Amendment) Regulations 1989 (SI 1989 115) and the Personal Pension Schemes (Transfer Payments) (Amendment) Regulations 1997 (SI 1997 480) are revoked.

5294. Petroleum revenue tax – deductions – offshore exploration – drilling outside taxable field

[Oil Taxation Act 1975 s.3(1)(a).]

The Commissioners appealed against a decision that the cost of abortive oil drilling incurred by A was tax deductible. The drilling had taken place within 5000 metres of a field which remained subject to a liability to petroleum revenue tax. The Commissioners submitted that the expenditure was not allowable against receipts from the taxable field, since the abortive drilling was not for a purpose related to the taxable field and, applying a purposive construction to the Oil Taxation Act 1975 s.3(1)(a), there was required to be a relationship, beyond one of geography, between the particular field and the exploratory drilling.

Held, dismissing the appeal, that the relevant qualification to render exploration costs allowable against receipts from a taxable field was simply a geographical one, namely whether or not the drilling had taken place within 5000 metres of the field and s.3(1)(a) could not be interpreted as requiring exploration costs to be incurred exclusively in relation to the field in question.

AMERADA HESS LTD v. INLAND REVENUE COMMISSIONERS; *sub nom.* INLAND REVENUE COMMISSIONERS v. AMERADA HESS LTD [2001] S.T.C. 420, Lloyd, J., Ch D.

5295. Petroleum revenue tax – oil terminals – relief for expenditure on vapour recovery system at separate oil installations

[Petroleum (Production) Act 1934; Oil Taxation Act 1975 s.1, s.5B, s.12; Oil Taxation Act 1983 s.3.]

BP spent just under £60 million in designing and installing a Marine Vapour Recovery (MVR) system, which was co-located at two of BP's North Sea facilities (the Facilities). The purpose of the MVR was to recover volatile organic compounds (VOCs) emitted during the process of loading crude oil on to tankers, and to liquefy and reinject the VOCs into the crude oil. Hitherto, the practice had been to vent the VOCs into the atmosphere. This had generated complaints from the local community, and BP also expected that international regulations would be in place in any event by 2004-2006, which would oblige them to introduce VOC emission controls. BP claimed relief in respect of its charge to petroleum revenue tax, under Oil Taxation Act 1983 s. 3(1) and (8) and the Oil Taxation Act 1975 ss.1 (1), (2), 5B, 12(1) and 12(2), on the basis that the MVR was a long term non mobile asset, and the expenditure on it had enhanced the Facilities, which BP contended were in fact a single asset used (as required under the legislation) in connection with an oilfield. Further, in order to qualify for relief, the expenditure had to be for one or more of the purposes set out in s.3(1) of the 1975 Act. The claims were disallowed on the grounds that: (1) the MVR was not located at a single facility, and was therefore not a single asset; (2) s.12(1) of the 1975 Act provided for relief in respect of expenditure on "initial treatment" (as therein defined) the sole purpose of which was to facilitate safe loading of oil onto a tanker. BP were found to have had wider collateral purposes, including the preemption of potentially onerous legislation; (3) for the purposes of the Petroleum (Production) Act 1934 Act the VOCs were not oil won from the oil field, since they were recovered at the point of delivery and then reinjected into the crude oil. Nor were the VOCs recovered from the oil's natural condition in the strata; (4) for the purposes of s.3(1)(h) of the 1975 Act, the MVR was not used in order to dispose of oil in arm's length sales, and (5) for the purpose of s.3(1)(f) of the 1975 Act, the VOCs arose and were recovered after delivery, and hence after the point at which the charge to petroleum revenue tax was deemed to arise. Thus, the expenditure incurred in their recovery and reinjection was not for the purpose of transportation of oil. BP appealed.

Held, allowing BP's appeal, that (1) the Facilities were properly regarded as a single asset, and had been enhanced by the expenditure on the MVR; (2) it was proper to regard the sole purpose of the MVR as safe loading. Safety was a broad concept, and what was considered safe might vary from generation to generation. Expenditure reducing or removing the risk of harm on a broad scale was properly to be seen as having the purpose of the safe loading of oil. On the facts, the point in the operation at which the MVR functioned brought it within the statutory definition of "initial treatment"; (3) BP had not shown that the expenditure on the MVR was incurred for the disposal of the oil in arm's length transactions, and BP's case under s.3.1 (h) of the 1975 Act accordingly failed, but (4) the expenditure on the MVR was properly regarded as incurred for the purpose of transporting oil to a location in the UK where the seller in an arm's length transaction could reasonably be expected to deliver it, and BP's case under s.3(1)(f) of the 1975 Act accordingly succeeded.

BP EXPLORATION OPERATING CO LTD v. INLAND REVENUE COMMISSIONERS [2000] S.T.C. (S.C.D.) 466, Judge not applicable, Sp Comm.

5296. Procedure – inheritance tax – variation of notice of determination by consent

[Special Commissioners (Jurisdiction and Procedure) Regulations 1994 (SI 1994 1811) Reg.16.]

A determination was issued by the Revenue to trustees, who appealed but did not appear at the hearing. The Commissioner proceeded to hear and determine the appeal under the Special Commissioners (Jurisdiction and Procedure) Regulations 1994 Reg.16, which detailed the procedure to be followed where a party failed to attend or was unrepresented at a hearing. Further information had been provided by the trustees, relating to the value of the property at issue.

Held, varying the notice of determination, that having regard to the further information provided by the trustees, the notice of determination would be varied by consent.

HENDERSON v. INLAND REVENUE COMMISSIONERS [2000] S.T.C. (S.C.D.) 572, AN Brice, Sp Comm.

5297. Registration – aggregates levy

AGGREGATES LEVY (REGISTRATION AND MISCELLANEOUS PROVISIONS) REGULATIONS 2001, SI 2001 4027; made under the Finance Act 1999; the s.132; and the Finance Act 2001 s.24, s.33, s.34, s.35, s.36, s.45, Sch.4 para.5, Sch.4 para.6, Sch.9 para.7. In force: January 11, 2002; £4.50.

These Regulations make provision about registration for aggregates levy (AL) and certain related matters. They provide that people who carry out or intend to carry out activities that make them registrable for AL must notify Customs and Excise accordingly; a person has 30 days to notify Customs using Form AL 1; site details must be notified on Form AL 1A; partnership details must be notified individually using Form AL 2; and customs may require further details in particular cases. Provision is also made for notifying Customs about errors and changes in circumstances. Group members are to be registered in the name of the group's representative member who is to account for levy due from all the members of the group on a joint return. Provision is made in relation to a number of applications and notifications, including applications and notifications relating to changes in the composition of the group, the identity of the representative member and the ending of group treatment; about who is responsible for certain AL requirements in the case of partnerships and unincorporated associations. It also makes provision for the voluntary or compulsory appointment of tax representatives for taxpayers not resident in the UK; and a breach of these regulations may lead to a penalty under Part V, or, in certain cases where so specified, under the Finance Act 2001 s.16 to s.49 and Sch.4 to Sch.10.

5298. Right to fair trial – delay – proceedings to challenge tax assessments – overriding interest of states in tax matters

[European Convention on Human Rights 1950 Art.6(1), Protocol 1 Art.1.]

F applied for supplementary tax assessments raised against himself and a company in which he was the majority shareholder following a land and property transfer to be set aside in January 1988. In March 1998, F was informed that a hearing had been set for May 1998. However, the proceedings were adjourned to allow him to instruct a lawyer. The company's application was dismissed in May 1999 and it appealed. In the meantime, F complained that the length of time taken in the proceedings was in breach of the European Convention on Human Rights 1950 Art.6(1)

Held, dismissing the application, that Art.6(1) did not cover tax disputes, notwithstanding the pecuniary effects they had on the taxpayer. The Convention had to be applied in its entirety and Protocol 1 Art.1 preserved the rights of States to enact legislation necessary for the imposition and collection of taxes.

FERRAZZINI v. ITALY (44759/98) [2001] S.T.C. 1314, Judge Wildhaber (President), ECHR.

5299. Self assessment – profits – entitlement of Special Commissioners to hear new evidence on rehearing

S, an accountant, deducted interest and bank charges on various loans in computing professional profits. The Revenue disallowed the deductions because the loans had been used to fund private expenditure. On appeal the commissioner held that an add back of £55,276 should be reduced by the excess of debtors over creditors to be agreed with the Revenue. No agreement was reached and S applied for a further hearing.

Held, determining the amount, that no new argument could be heard.

SILK v. FLETCHER (INSPECTOR OF TAXES) (NO.2) [2000] S.T.C. (S.C.D.) 565, Judge not applicable, Sp Comm.

5300. Share option schemes – gross asset requirement – enterprise management incentives

ENTERPRISE MANAGEMENT INCENTIVES (GROSS ASSET REQUIREMENT) ORDER 2001, SI 2001 3799; made under the Finance Act 2000 s.62, Sch.14 para.69. In force: January 1, 2002; £1.50.

This Order amends the Finance Act 2000 Sch.14 para.16 to increase the gross asset requirement of a qualifying company granting a right to acquire shares under the enterprise management incentives provisions. The Order has effect in relation to rights to acquire shares granted on or after January 1, 2002. In the case of a single company the requirement that the value of the company's gross assets does not exceed £15 million is increased to not exceeding £30 million. In the case of a parent company the requirement that the consolidated value of the group assets does not exceed £15 million is increased to not exceeding £30 million.

5301. Shipping – tonnage tax companies – training commitment

TONNAGE TAX (TRAINING REQUIREMENT) (AMENDMENT) REGULATIONS 2001, SI 2001 3999; made under the Finance Act 2000 Sch.22 para.29, para.31, para.36. In force: February 1, 2002; £1.50.

These Regulations amend the Tonnage Tax (Training Requirement) Regulations 2000 (SI 2000 2129) by increasing the amount of the payments in lieu of training. In respect of a relevant four month period falling on or after February 1, 2002, the figure by which the number of months is to be multiplied is increased from £550 to £562 and in the case of the higher rate of payment where there has been failure to meet the training requirement, the basic rate to be used in the calculations is increased from £500 to £512.

5302. Special Commissioners – appeals – referrals

REFERRALS TO THE SPECIAL COMMISSIONERS REGULATIONS 2001, SI 2001 4024; made under the Taxes Management Act 1970 s.28ZC. In force: January 31, 2002; £1.75.

The Taxes Management Act 1970 provides for the subject-matter of an enquiry in progress to be referred to the Special Commissioners for their determination. These Regulations apply specified sections of the 1970 Act to ensure that there are similar rights of appeal from the Special Commissioners in relation to a determination on a referral as there are in relation to the determination of an appeal.

5303. Stamp duties – sale of land

STAMP DUTY (DISADVANTAGED AREAS) REGULATIONS 2001, SI 2001 3747; made under the Finance Act 2001 s.92. In force: November 30, 2001; £6.50.

The Finance Act 2001 s.92 provides for an exemption from the stamp duty chargeable on a conveyance or transfer on sale of an estate or interest in land or a lease of land if the land in question is situated in a disadvantaged area. Sch.30 to the Act makes similar provision in relation to cases where land is partly in a disadvantaged area. Section 92(4) of the 2001 Act provides that a disadvantaged area is an area designated as such by regulations made by the Treasury. These Regulations designate the areas as disadvantaged areas for the purposes of the 2001 Act.

5304. Stamp duties – stamp duty reserve tax – unit trust schemes and open-ended investment company – definition

STAMP DUTY AND STAMP DUTY RESERVE TAX (DEFINITION OF UNIT TRUST SCHEME AND OPEN-ENDED INVESTMENT COMPANY) REGULATIONS 2001, SI 2001 964; made under the Finance Act 1986 s.98; the Finance Act 1995 s.152; and the Finance Act 1999 s.121, Sch.19 para.17. In force: April 6, 2001; £1.75.

These Regulations, which amend the Stamp Duty Reserve Tax Regulations 1986 (SI 1986 1711) and the Stamp Duty and Stamp Duty Reserve Tax (Open-ended Investment Companies) Regulations 1997 (SI 1997 1156), provide for unit trust schemes of a specified description, and open-ended investment companies of a specified description, to be treated as not being unit trust schemes, or, as the case may be, open-ended investment companies, for the purposes of the enactments relating to stamp duty and the enactments relating to stamp duty reserve tax.

5305. Stamp duties – variation

VARIATION OF STAMP DUTIES REGULATIONS 2001, SI 2001 3746; made under the Finance Act 2000 Sch.33 para.1. In force: November 28, 2001; £1.75.

These Regulations are made under the Finance Act 2000 Sch.33 para.1 which confers upon the Treasury a power to vary existing stamp duties. They provide that certain stamp duty reliefs for land in disadvantaged areas, contained in the Finance Act 2001 s.92(1) and Sch.30 para.1, shall not apply to certain instruments and otherwise restrict those reliefs.

5306. Stamp duty reserve tax – amalgamations – unit trusts – schemes of arrangement

[Finance Act 1986 s.87(1); Financial Services Act 1986; Financial Services (Regulated Schemes) Regulations 1991 Reg.11.05.]

S appealed against a determination that the amalgamation of two unit trusts it managed was liable to stamp duty reserve tax under the Finance Act 1986 s.87(1), on the grounds that it was based on an agreement between unit holders and S for a consideration based transfer of securities. The agreement provided that units held in a trust to be discontinued would be exchanged for units in a continuing trust.

Held, allowing the appeal, that the transfer involved changes to both trusts, as equitable rights were given up in both the discontinuing and continuing schemes in return for new rights. The overall scheme was subject to the Financial Services Act 1986 and the Financial Services (Regulated Schemes) Regulations 1991 Reg.11.05, under which it was characterised as a "scheme of arrangement". The various changes under the scheme did not therefore amount to an "arrangement" for the purposes of s.87(1) of the 1986 Finance Act.

SAVE & PROSPER SECURITIES LTD v. INLAND REVENUE COMMISSIONERS [2000] S.T.C. (S.C.D.) 408, Dr AN Brice, Sp Comm.

5307. Stamp duty reserve tax – foreign securities

STAMP DUTY RESERVE TAX (UK DEPOSITARY INTERESTS IN FOREIGN SECURITIES) (AMENDMENT) REGULATIONS 2001, SI 2001 3779; made under the Finance Act 1999 s.119. In force: December 19, 2001; £1.50.

These Regulations amend the Stamp Duty Reserve Tax (UK Depositary Interests in Foreign Securities) Regulations 1999 (SI 1999 2383) following the Inland Revenue's adoption of a revised interpretation of the term "listed on a recognised stock exchange" and other similar phrases. In consequence of that revised interpretation, certain investments would cease to fall within the definition "foreign securities" for the purposes of the principal Regulations and, accordingly, UK depositary interests in those investments would fall outside the scope of those Regulations.

5308. Stamp duty reserve tax – investment exchanges – London stock exchange

STAMP DUTY RESERVE TAX (INVESTMENT EXCHANGES AND CLEARING HOUSES) (THE LONDON STOCK EXCHANGE) REGULATIONS 2001, SI 2001 255; made under the Finance Act 1991 s.116, s.117. In force: February 26, 2001; £1.75.

These Regulations provide for certain agreements to transfer equity securities made in the course of trading in those securities on The London Stock Exchange to be exempt from stamp duty reserve tax (SDRT). They prescribe, for the purposes of the exemption from SDRT, The London Clearing House as a recognised clearing house and London Stock Exchange Plc as a recognised investment exchange; the circumstances in which SDRT will not be charged; and make consequential provision to the effect that equity securities which are the subject of a prescribed agreement shall be dealt with by a clearing participant in a separate designated account.

5309. Stamp duty reserve tax – transfer of business – Tradepoint Financial Networks plc

STAMP DUTY RESERVE TAX (TRADEPOINT) (AMENDMENT) REGULATIONS 2001, SI 2001 2267; made under the Finance Act 1991 s.116, s.117. In force: June 25, 2001; £1.50.

These Regulations amend the Stamp Duty Reserve Tax (Tradepoint) Regulations 1995 (SI 1995 2051) to reflect the transfer of all the business of Tradepoint Financial Networks Plc (now known as virt-x Plc) as a recognised investment exchange to a wholly owned subsidiary, virt-x Exchange Ltd.

5310. Tax – general insurance – administration

GENERAL INSURANCE RESERVES (TAX) REGULATIONS 2001, SI 2001 1757; made under the Finance Act 2000 s.107. In force: May 29, 2001; £2.50.

These Regulations supplement the Finance Act 2000 s.107 which provides that where it becomes apparent in a period of account that technical provisions made by a general insurer for an earlier period were excessive, or insufficient, an amount is to be treated as added as a receipt or expense, respectively, of the general insurer's trade in the later period, for tax purposes. These Regulations provide the method of calculating whether the technical provisions were excessive or insufficient, provide for the currencies in which the calculations, including the discount rate, are to be carried out, and provide for modifications of those rules where they apply to underwriting members.

5311. Tax credits – disabled persons tax credit – working families tax credit

TAX CREDITS SCHEMES (MISCELLANEOUS AMENDMENTS NO.2) REGULATIONS 2001, SI 2001 367; made under the Social Security

Contributions and Benefits Act 1992 s.128, s.129, s.175; and the Tax Credits Act 1999 s.2, Sch.2 para.1, Sch.2 para.20. In force: April 10, 2001; £2.00.

These Regulations, which amend the Family Credit (General) Regulations 1987 (SI 1987 1973) and the Disability Working Allowance (General) Regulations 1991 (SI 1991 2887), add new credits in respect of severely disabled adults, children and young persons to the computation of both working families' tax credit and disabled person's tax credit.

5312. Tax evasion – free movement of capital – Eurobonds – prohibition on acquisition by Belgian residents – European Union

[EC Treaty Art.73b (now Art.56 EC), Art.73d(1)(d) (now Art.58 EC).]

The Commission sought a declaration that B had failed to fulfil its obligations under the EC Treaty Art.73b (now Art.56 EC) by enacting a provision that prohibited Belgian residents from acquiring Belgian Eurobond securities on which Belgian withholding tax had been waived. B accepted that the prohibition could affect the free movement of capital, but contended that it was necessary to prevent tax evasion by Belgian residents, so that it was permitted under EC Treaty Art.73d(1)(b) (now Art.58 EC).

Held, allowing the application, that the prohibition breached the principle of proportionality as it was based on a presumption of tax evasion that affected the exercise of basic Treaty freedom. Further, it did not prevent residents from acquiring Eurobond securities from other issuers that were themselves not subject to withholding tax.

COMMISSION OF THE EUROPEAN COMMUNITIES v. BELGIUM (C478/98) [2000] S.T.C. 830, GC Rodriguez Iglesias (President), ECJ.

5313. Tax inspectors – disclosure – applicability of legal professional privilege

[Taxes Management Act 1970 s.20(1).]

MG, a taxpayer, appealed against the refusal of their application for judicial review ([2001] 1 All E.R. 535) of a decision of a Special Commissioner to consent to the issuing by a tax inspector of a notice, served pursuant to the Taxes Management Act 1970 s.20(1), requiring them to disclose documents which included documents that they contended were protected by legal professional privilege. MG had argued that (1) s.20(1) was by "necessary implication" subject to the rule relating to legal professional privilege, and (2) given that the Special Commissioner had been asked to decide a matter of substantial importance, he should have given them the right to make representations at a hearing before deciding whether to consent to the issuing of the notice.

Held, dismissing the appeal, that (1) a tax inspector had the power under s.20(1) to require a taxpayer to disclose documents that were subject to the rule of legal professional privilege. The rule was impliedly excluded by the 1970 Act save where it was expressly retained. The public interest in the speedy, fair and complete collection of public revenue had to be taken into account as well as the right of an individual to keep from disclosure documents that were protected by the rule, and (2) the nature of the relevant process excluded the possibility of the taxpayer having the right to make oral representations at a hearing against the issuing of a notice under s.20(1).

R. (ON THE APPLICATION OF MORGAN GRENFELL & CO LTD) v. SPECIAL COMMISSIONER OF INCOME TAX; *sub nom.* R. v. INLAND REVENUE COMMISSIONERS, *ex p.* MORGAN GRENFELL & CO LTD; R. v. SPECIAL COMMISSIONERS OF INCOME TAX, *ex p.* MORGAN GRENFELL & CO LTD, [2001] EWCA Civ 329, [2002] 2 W.L.R. 255, Blackburne, J., CA.

5314. Tax inspectors – notices – request that tax payer produce documents relating to accounts and tax affairs – reasonableness

[Taxes Management Act 1970 s.19A(2)(a), s.19A(2)(b), s.12B.]

A was an accountant in practice on his own account. He maintained an undesignated clients' current and general deposit account. He had no personal bank account. In respect of the general deposit account, he received an annual certificate of deduction of income tax. The Inspector gave notice to A under the Taxes Management Act 1970 s.19A requiring him to produce all interest bearing bank and building society accounts for the year ended April 5, 1997, and all statements, cheque books and paying in books for all bank and building society accounts "used by"A from September 1, 1994 to August 31, 1996 inclusive. A was also required to prepare and furnish a balance sheet for his practice. A appealed against the Inspector's notice, arguing (inter alia) that (1) he could not be required to prepare and furnish a balance sheet, since s.19A of the 1970 Act was limited to production of existing documents used to prepare a return; (2) the certificates of deduction of income tax were sufficient to check the accuracy of his return, and (3) the notice was unreasonable, since A did not have a personal bank account, and compliance with the notice with respect to the accounts which he did operate would involve the disclosure of confidential information about his clients.

Held, dismissing the appeal, that (1) A could be required to produce the requested balance sheet under s.19A(2)(b) of the Act, which did not contain words restricting such a request to existing documents (unlike s.19A(2)(a), which did contain such a restriction); (2) it appeared reasonable for the Inspector's inquiries not to be limited to existing documents in the course of his inquiry into a return; (3) neither s.12B nor s.19A limited an Inspector to requiring production only of those documents mentioned in s.12B, and it would not necessarily be unreasonable for an Inspector to require production of other documents; (4) in order to check the accuracy or completeness of a return, it might well be necessary to consult documents not used in the preparation of the return; (5) s.19A was not limited in scope to those documents which the taxpayer thought were appropriate. The certificate of income tax deduction was not, in this case, sufficient to check the accuracy of the return under review, and (6) the Inspector's request for documents relating to A's two accounts was reasonable, as A was liable for tax on interest paid under the general deposit account, and had been asked to supply information in his capacity as a taxpayer. Although the designated clients' account was not interest bearing, it was "used by"A within the terms of the notice, and, on the facts of this case, the Inspector's requirements in relation to it were reasonable dicta of Bingham L.J. in *R. v. Inland Revenue Commissioners, ex p. Taylor (No.2)* [1990] 2 All E.R. 409, [1990] C.L.Y. 2642 and *Mother v. Inspector of Taxes* [1999] S.T.C. (S.C.D.) 278 applied.

ACCOUNTANT v. INSPECTOR OF TAXES [2000] S.T.C. (S.C.D.) 522, Judge not applicable, Sp Comm.

5315. Tax planning – accountants – liability for professional negligence
See NEGLIGENCE: Little v. George Little Sebire & Co. §4508

5316. Tax planning – contract workers – computer industry – lawfulness of anti avoidance scheme
[Human Rights Act 1998 Sch.1 Part II Art.1; Welfare Reform and Pensions Act 1999 s.75, s.76; Finance Act 2000 s.60; Social Security Contributions (Intermediaries) Regulations 2000 (SI 2000 727); EC Treaty.]
PCG, an organisation representing individuals who provided knowledge based skills via one man service companies, particularly in the computer industry, sought judicial review of composite legislation known as IR35, contained in the Finance Act 2000 s.60, Welfare Reform and Pensions Act 1999 s.75 and s.76, and Social Security Contributions (Intermediaries) Regulations 2000. The legislation had been introduced as an anti avoidance measure with the effect that fees paid to contractors would be treated as deemed salary liable to income tax, rather than company revenue liable to corporation tax. PCG contended that (1) the impact of the legislation was to render the right to possess a shareholding in such a service company more costly and uncertain, amounting to an unlawful interference with the right to peaceful enjoyment of property, pursuant to the Human Rights Act 1998 Sch.1 Part II Art.1, and (2) IR35 breached a number of provisions under the EC

Treaty, in that it amounted to an unnotifed state aid, impeded the free movement of workers, freedom of establishment and freedom to provide services.

Held, refusing the application, that (1) IR35 was not harsh enough to amount to confiscation of an individual's property or an interference with his financial position. Neither did it amount to an abuse of the UK's right to impose taxes, and (2) IR35 as a general anti avoidance measure did not constitute a state aid, *R. v. Customs and Excise Commissioners, ex p. Lunn Poly Ltd* [1999] S.T.C. 350, [1999] C.L.Y. 4743 applied. Despite the apparent existence of an obstacle to the provision of services in the UK by individuals in other Member States, the impediment presented by IR35 was not discriminatory or dislocating and, consequently, did not offend any of the freedoms under the Treaty.

R. (ON THE APPLICATION OF PROFESSIONAL CONTRACTORS GROUP LTD) v. INLAND REVENUE COMMISSIONERS; *sub nom.* R. v. INLAND REVENUE COMMISSIONERS, *ex p.* PROFESSIONAL CONTRACTORS GROUP LTD, [2001] EWHC Admin 236, [2001] S.T.C. 629, Burton, J., QBD (Admin Ct).

5317. Tax planning – life insurance – certification of qualifying policy – discretion – tax avoidance

[Income and Corporation Taxes Act 1988 Sch.15 Part I, Part II.]

M, a company providing life assurance, appealed against a decision ([2001] S.T.C. 92) that the Revenue's refusal to issue a certificate certifying a draft policy as a "qualifying policy" under the Income and Corporation Taxes Act 1988 Sch.15 Part II had not been irrational or otherwise improper. The Revenue cross appealed against the decision that M's policy did meet the statutory test for a qualifying policy. The judge had concluded that in relation to the certification of policies, the Revenue had a discretion and not a mandatory duty. M's managing director was a solicitor who specialised in tax avoidance schemes.

Held, dismissing the appeal and allowing the cross appeal, that having regard to para.21 of Sch.15 Part II, the Revenue did not have an unqualified and mandatory duty to certify a draft form of policy even in circumstances where the policy appeared to meet the statutory requirements of Sch.15 Part I of the Act. It was not, however, appropriate to reach a conclusion as to whether a refusal to certify could be justified on the ground that there was reason to believe that a policy which met the statutory requirements was, or might be, part of a tax avoidance scheme. In the instant case the judge had erred in his conclusion that the draft policy did meet the statutory requirements.

R. (ON THE APPLICATION OF MONARCH ASSURANCE PLC) v. INLAND REVENUE COMMISSIONERS; *sub nom.* MONARCH ASSURANCE PLC v. INLAND REVENUE COMMISSIONERS, [2001] EWCA Civ 1681, [2001] S.T.C. 1639, Robert Walker, L.J., CA.

5318. Tax planning – offshore companies – impact of deeming provision on income received by transferee – double taxation

[Income and Corporation Taxes Act 1988 s.739(2), Part XVII Chapter III; European Convention on Human Rights 1950 Protocol 1 Art.1.]

D appealed against the decision of the Court of Appeal ([2000] Q.B. 744, [1999] C.L.Y. 4704) upholding his conviction for conspiracy to cheat the public revenue of corporation tax by allegedly concealing profits made by three offshore companies. The companies had been established by D, a financial services adviser, for C, a United Kingdom resident. D maintained that a finding that the monies were company income would be inconsistent with the right to property guaranteed by the Human Rights Act 1998 Sch.1 Part II Art.1.

Held, dismissing the appeal, that the legislative history of the Income and Corporation Taxes Act 1988 s.739(2), coupled with the other provisions in Part XVII Chapter III of the Act, and a comparison of s.739(2) with other tax avoidance provisions and the underlying purpose of s.739, made it impossible to attribute to Parliament any intention that there should be a distinction between the impact of the deeming provision on the liability to tax of a company transferee and an individual transferee. Neither was it Parliament's intention, by imposing liability on tax avoiders, to relieve a transferee of tax liability on the income received from the tax avoider. On its true construction, the operation of s.739(2) fell well within the scope of the discretion permitted to Member States and there was nothing within Art.1 of the First Protocol that would require a different construction in order to render the provision Convention compliant.

R. v. DIMSEY (DERMOT JEREMY), [2001] UKHL 46, [2001] 3 W.L.R. 843, Lord Scott of Foscote, HL.

5319. **Tax planning – real property – sham transactions**

S appealed against a ruling ([1999] S.T.C. 431, [1999] C.L.Y. 4764) that an agreement entered into in 1984 by H was not a sham entered into for the purposes of tax avoidance. H had entered into an agreement whereby land owned by him was leased for 999 years to a company in Singapore. Pursuant to the agreement, the company was obliged to pay a basic rent related to the agricultural value of the land together with an annuity related to any increase in the value of the land payable when 70 per cent of the land had become capable of development. The benefit of the lease in relation to part of the land was assigned by the company to the developer. The commissioners had concluded that the arrangement was part of a larger scheme designed for the purposes of tax avoidance, details of which had not been disclosed by the parties.

Held, allowing the appeal, that whilst the conclusion reached by the commissioners that the agreement was a sham had been fully justified it had been insufficient to merit disallowing H's appeal. In order to substantiate such a ruling the commissioners should also have proceeded to consider the validity of the deed whereby the transaction was put into effect. On the facts, parts of the 1984 deed whereby the agreement was put into effect also constituted a sham, *Snook v. London & West Riding Investments Ltd* [1967] 2 Q.B. 786, [1967] C.L.Y. 1836 applied.

HITCH v. STONE (INSPECTOR OF TAXES); *sub nom.* STONE (INSPECTOR OF TAXES) v. HITCH [2001] EWCA Civ 63, Arden, L.J., CA.

5320. **Tax returns – disclosure – privilege – notice of enquiry – interference with right to family life**

[Taxes Management Act 1970 s.19A; Human Rights Act 1998 Sch.1 Part I Art.8; Data Protection Act 1998.]

G, a solicitor, appealed against a notice of enquiry and a further notice requiring disclosure of documentation relating to his practice, including client ledgers and cash books, issued by the Revenue pursuant to the Taxes Management Act 1970 s.19A following the submission of his self-assessment return. The issues before the court were whether (1) the requested documents were reasonably required for the purpose of determining if G's tax return was incorrect or incomplete; (2) the duty of client confidentiality precluded G from the requirement to disclose the documents; (3) the documents were covered by legal professional privilege; (4) disclosure of the documents would contravene the Human Rights Act 1998 Sch.1 Part I Art.8, and (5) disclosure would infringe the Data Protection Act 1988.

Held, dismissing the appeal, that (1) the documents were "reasonably required" by the Revenue to help reconcile discrepancies in the return; (2) the duty of confidentiality was overriden by s.19A of the 1970 Act. It was apparent that statutory provisions could override the duty of confidentiality, *Parry-Jones v. Law Society* [1969] 1 Ch. 1, [1968] C.L.Y. 3703 considered; (3) it was not clear that the documents were covered by legal professional privilege but, in any event, the relevant case law established that the 1970 Act excluded the rule of legal professional privilege save where it was expressly preserved, *R. v. Inland Revenue Commissioners, ex p. Lorimer* [2000] S.T.C. 751 and *R. (on the application of Morgan Grenfell & Co Ltd) v. Special Commissioner of Income Tax* [2001] 1 All E.R. 535, [2000] 12 C.L. 471 considered; (4) although the requirements of the notice interfered with the right to family life, that interference was justified on public interest grounds, namely the prompt, fair and complete collection of tax, and (5) the protection afforded by the 1998 Act did not apply where it was overriden by another statute as it was in the instant case by s.19A of the 1970 Act.

GUYER v. WALTON (INSPECTOR OF TAXES) [2001] S.T.C. (S.C.D.) 75, AN Brice, Sp Comm.

5321. Vehicle excise duty – fuel types

GRADUATED VEHICLE EXCISE DUTY (PRESCRIBED TYPES OF FUEL) REGULATIONS 2001, SI 2001 93; made under the Vehicle Excise and Registration Act 1994 Sch.1 para.1C, para.1F. In force: February 15, 2001; £1.50.

These Regulations prescribe the types of fuel by which vehicles must be propelled in order to qualify for the reduced rate of vehicle excise duty prescribed for certain light passenger vehicles first registered on or after March 1, 2001 by the Vehicle Excise and Registration Act 1994. The effect of the Regulations is that vehicles propelled solely by road fuel gas and those capable of being propelled both by petrol and road fuel gas, or by electricity and either petrol or diesel, qualify for the reduced rate.

5322. Vehicle excise duty – unlicensed vehicles – removal from public roads

VEHICLE EXCISE DUTY (IMMOBILISATION, REMOVAL AND DISPOSAL OF VEHICLES) (AMENDMENT) REGULATIONS 2001, SI 2001 936; made under the Vehicle Excise and Registration Act 1994 s.57, Sch.2A. In force: April 9, 2001; £1.75.

These Regulations, which amend the Vehicle Excise Duty (Immobilisation, Removal and Disposal of Vehicles) Regulations 1997 (SI 1997 2439) to increase the amounts of specified charges, provide for increases in the prescribed charges for the release, removal and storage of specified vehicles.

5323. Books

Baker, Philip – Double Taxation Conventions and International Tax Law. 3rd Ed. Looseleaf/ringbound: £250.00. ISBN 0-421-67360-5. Sweet & Maxwell.

BDO Stoy Hayward's Orange Tax Guide 2001-02. Paperback: £45.00. ISBN 0-406-93911-X. Butterworths Tolley.

BDO Stoy Hayward's Yellow Tax Guide 2001-02. Paperback: £65.00. ISBN 0-406-93910-1. Butterworths Tolley.

Beveridge, Fiona C. – Treatment and Taxation of Foreign Investment Under International Law. Melland Schill Studies in International Law. Hardback: £45.00. ISBN 0-7190-4309-3. Manchester University Press.

CCH Tax Handbook 2001-2002: Vol 2. Paperback: £40.00. ISBN 0-86325-562-0. Croner CCH Group Ltd.

Chapman, Alison – Tolley's Tax and the Business Car 2001-02. 5th Ed. Floppy disk: £44.95. ISBN 0-7545-1191-X. Tolley Publishing.

Clarke, Giles – Clarke: Offshore Tax Planning. 8th Ed. Paperback: £89.95. ISBN 0-406-93909-8. Butterworths Tolley.

Deeks, Sarah – Tax Practice Management. Paperback: £61.95. ISBN 0-7545-0470-0. Tolley Publishing.

Dolton, Alan; Saunders, Glyn – Tolley's Tax Cases: 2001. Paperback: £59.95. ISBN 0-7545-1161-8. Tolley Publishing.

Dolton, Alan; Wareham, Robert – Tolley's Vat Cases: 2001. Paperback: £89.95. ISBN 0-7545-1159-6. Tolley Publishing.

Hart, Gerry; Rayney, Peter – Tolley's Tax Planning for Family Companies and Owner-managed Businesses. 4th Ed. Paperback: £48.95. ISBN 0-7545-0713-0. Tolley Publishing.

Hoffman, Anthony – Civil Costs Cases: a Civil Guide. 2nd Ed. Paperback: £62.00. ISBN 0-421-72650-4. Sweet & Maxwell.

Homer, Arnold; Burrows, Rita – Tolley's Taxwise 2001-2002: II. Paperback: £38.95. ISBN 0-7545-1218-5. Tolley Publishing.

Jordan, Ronald R.; Quynn, Katelyn – Planned Giving: Management, Marketing and Law. 2nd Ed. Paperback: £46.50. ISBN 0-471-39027-5. John Wiley and Sons.

Kirkbride; Olowofoyeku – Law and Theory of Income Tax. Paperback: £24.95. ISBN 1-90349-900-3. Liverpool Academic Press.

Lasser – Profit from the New Tax Law. Paperback: £7.95. ISBN 0-471-09280-0. John Wiley and Sons.

Lawrence, Nick; Homer, Arnold; Burrows, Rita – Tolley's VATwise 2001-02. Paperback: £38.95. ISBN 0-7545-1292-4. Tolley Publishing.

McKie, Simon; Ansley, Sharan – Tolley's Estate Planning 2000-01. Paperback: £57.95. ISBN 0-7545-0724-6. Tolley Publishing.

McKie, Simon; Anstey, Sharon – Tolley's Estate Planning 2001-02. Paperback: £64.95. ISBN 0-7545-1196-0. Tolley Publishing.

Picciotto, Sol – International Business Taxation. Law in Context. Paperback: £224.95. ISBN 0-406-93404-5. Butterworths Law.

Revenue Law. ISBN 1-85800-132-3. Round Hall Ltd.

Sanders, Michael – Joint Ventures Involving Tax-exempt Organizations: 2001 Cumulative Supplement. Paperback: £42.95. ISBN 0-471-39034-8. John Wiley and Sons.

Smith, David – IR35 Defence Strategies: from Contracts to Commissioners. Paperback: £45.00. ISBN 0-7545-1426-9. Tolley Publishing.

Southern, David – Taxation of Corporate Debt and Financial Instruments. 4th Ed. Paperback: £62.95. ISBN 0-7545-0861-7. Tolley Publishing.

Steward, Clive – Taxation Simplified: 2001. Paperback: £9.99. ISBN 1-85252-368-9. Management Books 2000.

Tax Statutes and Statutory Instruments 2001-2002. Paperback: £73.00. ISBN 0-86325-559-0. Croner CCH Group Ltd.

Tiley, John; Collison, David – Simon's Tiley and Collison: UK Tax Guide 2001-2002. 19th Ed. Paperback: £75.00. ISBN 0-406-94058-4. Butterworths Tolley.

Tolley's National Insurance Contributions 2001-02. Tolley's Tax Annuals. Paperback: CD-ROM: £54.95. ISBN 0-7545-1392-0. Tolley Publishing.

Tolley's Tax Computations: 2000-2001. Paperback: £54.95. ISBN 0-7545-0712-2. Tolley Publishing.

Tolley's Tax Planning: 2000-2001. Paperback: £125.00. ISBN 0-7545-0721-1. Tolley Publishing.

Transfer Pricing: a UK Perspective. 2nd Ed. £65.00. ISBN 0-406-91901-1. Butterworths Law.

Voller, Mike – Tolley's Taxation of Lloyd's Underwriters. 9th Ed. Hardback: £92.95. ISBN 0-7545-0705-X. Tolley Publishing.

Walton, Keith – Tolley's Capital Allowances 2000-01. Paperback: £49.95. ISBN 0-7545-0718-1. Tolley Publishing.

Wareham, Robert; Dolton, Alan – Tolley's Value Added Tax 2001-02. Paperback: £60.00. ISBN 0-7545-1517-6. Tolley Publishing.

Wareham, Robert; Dolton, Alan – Value Added Tax 2001-2002 2nd Ed. Paperback: £95.00. ISBN 0-7545-1071-9. Tolley Publishing.

Whiteman, Peter; Gammie, Malcolm; Herbert, Mark – Whiteman on Capital Gains Tax: 11th Supplement to the 4th Edition. British Tax Library. Paperback: £90.00. ISBN 0-421-68190-X. Sweet & Maxwell.

Whiteman, Peter; Goy, David; Sandison, Francis and; Sherry, Michael – Whiteman on Income Tax: 11th Supplement to the 3rd Edition. British Tax Library. Paperback: £90.00. ISBN 0-421-68180-2. Sweet & Maxwell.

TELECOMMUNICATIONS

5324. Broadcasting – television licences – increase in fees

WIRELESS TELEGRAPHY (TELEVISION LICENCE FEES) (AMENDMENT) REGULATIONS 2001, SI 2001 772; made under the Wireless Telegraphy Act 1949 s.2. In force: April 1, 2001; £2.00.

These Regulations amend the Wireless Telegraphy (Television Licence Fees) Regulations 1997 (SI 1997 290) by increasing the amount of basic fee for television licences from £34.50 to £36.50 in the case of black and white and from £104.00 to £109.00 in the case of colour. They also make provision to abolish the fee payable for the replacement of a lost or destroyed licence in a case where the lost or destroyed licence was issued or renewed free of charge. In addition, they amend (except in the Channel Islands and the Isle of Man) the provision made for calculating the fee for an Accommodation for Residential Care Composite Form television licence, such that no account is taken of any unit of accommodation or dwelling that is the sole or main residence of a resident aged 75 years or more.

5325. Broadcasting – wireless telegraphy – equipment – exemptions

WIRELESS TELEGRAPHY (EXEMPTION) (AMENDMENT) REGULATIONS 2001, SI 2001 730; made under the Wireless Telegraphy Act 1949 s.1, s.3. In force: March 28, 2001; £1.75.

These Regulations amend the Wireless Telegraphy (Exemption) Regulations 1999 (SI 1999 930) in order to exempt additional wireless telegraphy equipment from the requirement to be licensed under the Wireless Telegraphy Act 1949 s.1.

5326. Broadcasting – wireless telegraphy – licence fees

WIRELESS TELEGRAPHY (LICENCE CHARGES) (AMENDMENT) REGULATIONS 2001, SI 2001 2265; made under the Wireless Telegraphy Act 1998 s.1. In force: Reg.2(d)(vii), Sch.2: October 30, 2001; remainder: July 19, 2001; £2.00.

These Regulations amend the Wireless Telegraphy (Licence Charges) Regulations 1999 (SI 1999 1774) by altering fees to be paid in relation to certain wireless telegraphy licences granted under the Wireless Telegraphy Act 1949. Amends SI 1999 1774.

5327. Broadcasting – wireless telegraphy – licences

WIRELESS TELEGRAPHY (BROADBAND FIXED WIRELESS ACCESS LICENCES) REGULATIONS 2001, SI 2001 3193; made under the Wireless Telegraphy Act 1998 s.3, s.6. In force: October 11, 2001; £1.75.

These Regulations make provision for a procedure for the grant of wireless telegraphy licences authorising the use of apparatus at specified frequencies for the provision by means of a wireless communications system of Broadband Fixed Wireless Access, two-way wireless communications links over which data may be transmitted and received at rates of at least 2Mbits/second on demand and whereby end users gain access to other telecommunication systems.

5328. Licences – Alpha Telecom Communications Limited

PUBLIC TELECOMMUNICATION SYSTEM DESIGNATION (ALPHA TELECOM COMMUNICATIONS LIMITED) ORDER 2001, SI 2001 3869; made under the Telecommunications Act 1984 s.9. In force: January 4, 2002; £1.50.

The Secretary of State has granted a licence to Alpha Telecom Communications Ltd to run specified telecommunication systems. This Order designates those telecommunication systems as public telecommunication systems; consequently

AlphaTelecom Communications Ltd will be a public telecommunications operator when the Order comes into force.

5329. Licences – Broadnet UK Ltd

PUBLIC TELECOMMUNICATION SYSTEM DESIGNATION (BROADNET UK LIMITED) ORDER 2001, SI 2001 2609; made under the Telecommunications Act 1984 s.9. In force: August 17, 2001; £1.50.

The Secretary of State has granted a licence to Broadnet UK Ltd to run specified telecommunication systems. This Order designates those telecommunication systems as public telecommunication systems and consequently, Broadnet UK Ltd will be a public telecommunications operator when the Order comes into force.

5330. Licences – Carrier 1 UK Ltd

PUBLIC TELECOMMUNICATION SYSTEM DESIGNATION (CARRIER 1 UK LIMITED) ORDER 2001, SI 2001 2608; made under the Telecommunications Act 1984 s.9. In force: August 17, 2001; £1.50.

The Secretary of State has granted a licence to Carrier 1 UK Ltd to run specified telecommunication systems. This Order designates those telecommunication systems as public telecommunication systems and consequently, Carrier 1 UK Ltd will be a public telecommunications operator when the Order comes into force.

5331. Licences – Eigernet Ltd

PUBLIC TELECOMMUNICATION SYSTEM DESIGNATION (EIGERNET LIMITED) ORDER 2001, SI 2001 3870; made under the Telecommunications Act 1984 s.9. In force: January 4, 2002; £1.50.

The Secretary of State has granted a licence to Eigernet Ltd to run specified telecommunication systems. This Order designates those telecommunication systems as public telecommunication systems; consequently Eigernet Ltd will be a public telecommunications operator when the Order comes into force.

5332. Licences – Energis Local Access Ltd

PUBLIC TELECOMMUNICATION SYSTEM DESIGNATION (ENERGIS LOCAL ACCESS LIMITED) ORDER 2001, SI 2001 2605; made under the Telecommunications Act 1984 s.9. In force: August 17, 2001; £1.50.

The Secretary of State has granted a licence to Energis Local Access Ltd to run specified telecommunication systems. This Order designates those telecommunication systems as public telecommunication systems and consequently, Energis Local Access Ltd will be a public telecommunications operator when the Order comes into force.

5333. Licences – Fibreway Ltd

PUBLIC TELECOMMUNICATION SYSTEM DESIGNATION (FIBREWAY LIMITED) ORDER 2001, SI 2001 2603; made under the Telecommunications Act 1984 s.9. In force: August 17, 2001; £1.50.

The Secretary of State has granted a licence to Fibreway Ltd to run specified telecommunication systems. This Order designates those telecommunication systems as public telecommunication systems and consequently, Fibreway Ltd will be a public telecommunications operator when the Order comes into force.

5334. Licences – FirstMark Carrier Services (UK) Ltd

PUBLIC TELECOMMUNICATION SYSTEM DESIGNATION (FIRSTMARK CARRIER SERVICES (UK) LIMITED) ORDER 2001, SI 2001 2582; made under the Telecommunications Act 1984 s.9. In force: August 16, 2001; £1.50.

The Secretary of State granted a licence to FirstMark Carrier Services (UK) Limited on January 8, 2001, under the Telecommunications Act 1984 s.7, to run the telecommunications systems specified in the licence. This Order designates those telecommunication systems as public telecommunication systems and consequently FirstMark Carrier Services (UK) Limited will be a public telecommunications operator when the Order comes into force on August 16, 2001.

5335. Licences – Isle of Wight Cable & Telephone Company Ltd

PUBLIC TELECOMMUNICATION SYSTEM DESIGNATION (ISLE OF WIGHT CABLE & TELEPHONE COMPANY LIMITED) ORDER 2001, SI 2001 2602; made under the Telecommunications Act 1984 s.9. In force: August 17, 2001; £1.50.

The Secretary of State has granted a licence to Isle of Wight Cable & Telephone Co Ltd to run the specified telecommunication systems. This Order designates those telecommunication systems as public telecommunication systems and consequently, the Isle of Wight Cable & Telephone Co Ltd will be a public telecommunications operator when the Order comes into force.

5336. Licences – LETel Ltd

PUBLIC TELECOMMUNICATION SYSTEM DESIGNATION (LETEL LIMITED) ORDER 2001, SI 2001 3871; made under the Telecommunications Act 1984 s.9. In force: January 4, 2002; £1.50.

The Secretary of State has granted a licence to LETel Ltd to run specified telecommunication systems. This Order designates those telecommunication systems as public telecommunication systems; consequently LETel Ltd will be a public telecommunications operator when the Order comes into force.

5337. Licences – Midlands Electricity PLC

PUBLIC TELECOMMUNICATION SYSTEM DESIGNATION (MIDLANDS ELECTRICITY PLC) ORDER 2001, SI 2001 3868; made under the Telecommunications Act 1984 s.9. In force: January 4, 2002; £1.50.

The Secretary of State has granted a licence to Midlands Electricity Plc to run specified telecommunication systems. This Order designates those telecommunication systems as public telecommunication systems; consequently Midlands Electricity Plc will be a public telecommunications operator when the Order comes into force.

5338. Licences – Nextlink UK Ltd

PUBLIC TELECOMMUNICATION SYSTEM DESIGNATION (NEXTLINK UK LIMITED) ORDER 2001, SI 2001 2583; made under the Telecommunication Act 1984 s.9. In force: August 16, 2001; £1.50.

The Secretary of State granted a licence to Nextlink UK Limited on January 5, 2001, under the Telecommunications Act 1984 s.7, to run the telecommunications systems specified in the licence. This Order designates those telecommunication systems as public telecommunication systems and consequently Nextlink UK Limited will be a public telecommunications operator when the Order comes into force on August 16, 2001.

5339. Licences – ntl Group Ltd

PUBLIC TELECOMMUNICATION SYSTEM DESIGNATION (NTL GROUP LTD) ORDER 2001, SI 2001 2604; made under the Telecommunications Act 1984 s.9. In force: August 17, 2001; £1.50.

The Secretary of State has granted a licence to ntl Group Ltd to run specified telecommunication systems. This Order designates those telecommunication systems as public telecommunication systems and consequently, ntl Group Ltd will be a public telecommunications operator when the Order comes into force.

5340. Licences – public telecommunications operators – charges

TELECOMMUNICATIONS (LICENCE MODIFICATIONS) (AMENDMENT) REGULATIONS 2001, SI 2001 2495; made under the European Communities Act 1972 s.2. In force: August 13, 2001; £1.50.

These Regulations amend minor errors in conditions relating to number portability contained in the Telecommunications (Interconnection) (Number Portability, etc.) Regulations 1999 (SI 1999 2450) and the Telecommunications (Licence Modification) (Satellite Operator Licences) Regulations 2000 (SI 2000 1711). The essential change is that when a subscriber transfers from one operator to another while keeping the same number, the operator from whom the number is transferred may not charge "Additional Conveyance Costs" as defined in the licence conditions.

5341. Licences – Sprintlink UK Limited

PUBLIC TELECOMMUNICATION SYSTEM DESIGNATION (SPRINTLINK UK LIMITED) ORDER 2001, SI 2001 3866; made under the Telecommunications Act 1984 s.9. In force: January 4, 2002; £1.50.

The Secretary of State has granted a licence to Sprintlink UK Ltd to run specified telecommunication systems. This Order designates those telecommunication systems as public telecommunication systems; consequently Sprintlink UK Ltd will be a public telecommunications operator when the Order comes into force.

5342. Licences – SSE Telecommunications Ltd

PUBLIC TELECOMMUNICATION SYSTEM DESIGNATION (SSE TELECOMMUNICATIONS LIMITED) ORDER 2001, SI 2001 3867; made under the Telecommunications Act 1984 s.9. In force: January 4, 2002; £1.50.

The Secretary of State has granted a licence to SSE Telecommunications Ltd to run specified telecommunication systems. This Order designates those telecommunication systems as public telecommunication systems; consequently SSE Telecommunications Ltd will be a public telecommunications operator when the Order comes into force.

5343. Licences – Universal Access UK Ltd

PUBLIC TELECOMMUNICATION SYSTEM DESIGNATION (UNIVERSAL ACCESS UK LIMITED) ORDER 2001, SI 2001 2610; made under the Telecommunications Act 1984 s.9. In force: August 17, 2001; £1.50.

The Secretary of State has granted a licence to Universal Access UK Ltd to run specified telecommunication systems. This Order designates those telecommunication systems as public telecommunication systems and consequently, Universal Access UK Ltd will be a public telecommunications operator when the Order comes into force.

5344. Licences – Verizon Global Solutions U.K. Ltd

PUBLIC TELECOMMUNICATION SYSTEM DESIGNATION (VERIZON GLOBAL SOLUTIONS U.K. LIMITED) ORDER 2001, SI 2001 2611; made under the Telecommunications Act 1984 s.9. In force: August 17, 2001; £1.50.

The Secretary of State has granted a licence to Verizon Global Solutions UK Ltd to run the telecommunication systems specified in the licence. This Order designates those telecommunication systems as public telecommunication systems and consequently, Verizon Global Solutions UK Ltd will be a public telecommunications operator when the Order comes into force.

5345. Licences – Williams Communications UK Ltd

PUBLIC TELECOMMUNICATION SYSTEM DESIGNATION (WILLIAMS COMMUNICATIONS UK LIMITED) ORDER 2001, SI 2001 2607; made under the Telecommunications Act 1984 s.9. In force: August 17, 2001; £1.50.

The Secretary of State has granted a licence to Williams Communications UK Ltd to run specified telecommunication systems. This Order designates those telecommunication systems as public telecommunication systems and consequently, Williams Communications UK Ltd will be a public telecommunications operator when the Order comes into force.

5346. Mobile telephones – competition – auction rules for grant of licences – deferred payment by associated bidders – grant of state aid

[Wireless Telegraph (Third Generation) Licences Regulations 1999 (SI 1999 3162).]

O sought permission to apply for judicial review of the conduct of an auction conducted by the Secretary of State for the sale of licences for the "third generation" of mobile telephone networks carried out in accordance with the rules issued pursuant to the Wireless Telegraph (Third Generation Licences) Regulations 1999. The rules required that payment for a licence be made when granted and also contained a condition that a licence could not be granted to a bidder associated with another prospective bidder. O contended that the fact that two competitors who had also been awarded a licence had been able to defer payment for their licences until they had complied with the condition to sever the association between them meant that it had effectively paid a higher price for its licence because of the interest lost as a result of the earlier payment. O contended that the Secretary of State's failure to ensure that all bidders paid for the grant of their respective licences at the same time was unfair, discriminatory and contrary to the rules on state aid.

Held, granting the application for permission to move for judicial review and refusing the application for judicial review, that the Secretary of State had been fully entitled not to require all of the applicants to make payment for their licences at the same time. There was a sound objective justification for withholding a licence until all of the relevant conditions had been met. Whilst the benefit in not having to pay for the licences until the satisfaction of the preconditions was capable of amounting to the grant of state aid, there was no basis for a finding that the delayed payment constituted state aid, particularly since the delay had resulted from a decision designed to avoid anti competitive activity and since the auction rules had been transparent from the outset, *R. v. Customs and Excise Commissioners, ex p. Lunn Poly Ltd* [1999] S.T.C. 350, [1999] C.L.Y. 4743 and *Demenagements-Manutention Transport SA (DMT) (C256/97), Re* [1999] All E.R. [EC] 601, [1999] C.L.Y. 706 applied and *R. v. Secretary of State for National Heritage, ex p. J Paul Getty Trust* [1997] Eu. L.R. 407 considered. The auction rules were proportionate and the Secretary of State had acted in a manner which had been within the range of options open to him and which was neither unfair nor discriminatory.

R. (ON THE APPLICATION OF ONE 2 ONE PERSONAL COMMUNICATIONS LTD) v. SECRETARY OF STATE FOR TRADE AND INDUSTRY; R. (ON THE APPLICATION OF BT3G LTD) v. SECRETARY OF STATE FOR TRADE AND INDUSTRY [2001] Eu. L.R. 325, Silber, J., QBD (Admin Ct).

5347. Telecommunications systems – meters – approval fees

TELECOMMUNICATION METERS (APPROVAL FEES) (BABT) (AMENDMENT) ORDER 2001, SI 2001 2606; made under the Telecommunications Act 1984 s.24. In force: August 13, 2001; £1.50.

This Order, which amends the Telecommunication Meters (Approval Fees) (British Approvals Board for Telecommunications) Order 1992 (SI 1992 712) and the Telecommunication Meters (Approval Fees) (BABT) (Amendment) Order 1994 (SI 1994 3163), increases the fees payable for the approval and monitoring of telecommunication meters from £50.68 per man hour to £83.33 per man hour.

5348. Books

Akdeniz, Yaman; Walker, Clive – Internet, Law and Society. Paperback: £29.99. ISBN 0-582-35656-3. Prentice Hall.

Black, Sharon – Telecommunications Law in the Internet Age. Hardback: £36.95. ISBN 1-55860-546-0. Hardback: £36.95. ISBN 1-55860-546-0. Morgan Kaufmann.

Gantzias, George – Dynamics of Regulation: Global Control, Local Resistance. Hardback: £49.95. ISBN 1-84014-085-2. Ashgate Publishing Limited.

Long, Colin – Global Telecommunications Law and Practice. 3rd Ed. Looseleaf/ring bound: £195.00. ISBN 0-421-65360-4. Sweet & Maxwell.

Mecklenberg, Keith – Telecommunications-law and Policy. Paperback: £24.95. ISBN 0-406-90580-0. Butterworths Law.

Salin, Patrick-Andre – Satellite Communications Regulations in the Early 21st Century. Utrecht Studies in Air and Space Law, 19. Hardback: £123.00. ISBN 90-411-1238-3. Martinus Nijhoff Publishers.

TORTS

5349. Accidents – road traffic – claimant driving without insurance – illegality no bar to recovery

R appealed against an award of £10,400 made in favour of E by way of damages for personal injuries and damage to a motorcycle with associated losses following a road traffic accident. E had not been insured at the time of the accident and there was no evidence to suggest that he would have arranged insurance for the motorcycle in the period following the accident. R contended, inter alia, that E should not recover in tort because illegality acted as a bar to recovery.

Held, dismissing the appeal, that (1) the appropriate test was to ask whether E had to plead or rely upon the illegality in order to establish his case, *Tinsley v. Milligan* [1994] 1 A.C. 340, [1993] C.L.Y. 1839 and *Revill v. Newberry* [1996] Q.B. 567, [1995] C.L.Y. 3660 followed; (2) it was clear that the direct loss, namely the personal injury and the value of the motorcycle, were not tainted by the illegality and as such E could recover these heads of loss, and (3) E's hire of an alternative vehicle could also be recovered because the hire car itself was provided with insurance and hence the agreement was not tainted by illegality. In addition, the purpose of motor insurance was to provide protection against claims brought by injured third parties. The law only required a person to have third party insurance which would protect a tortfeasor from claims brought by third parties as a result of his negligence. Hence, even if E had been riding legally with third party insurance, R would still have been required to compensate him.

EDGAR v. RAYSON, October 23, 2000, Judge Tetlow, CC (Altrincham). [*Ex rel.* NDH Edwards, Barrister 8, King Street, Manchester].

5350. Deceit – letters of credit – fraudulent endorsements

K sought to recover losses arising under letters of credit issued by I to K from two separate banks. Upon presentation, the letters of credit had been rejected by the banks on the basis that they did not comply with the terms and conditions of the credit. K contended that a beneficiary's certificate included with the documentation had been fraudulently endorsed to the effect that one complete set of non negotiable documents had been despatched to a purchaser within 10 working days of the shipment forming the basis of the contract between the parties, whereas on the basis of the known facts, the documents in question could not have been despatched within the time limit prescribed.

Held, giving judgment for K, that H, the individual responsible for the despatch of the non negotiable set of documents, had been fully aware that the beneficiary's certificate contained a false statement, and accordingly I were liable in deceit, *Standard Chartered Bank v. Pakistan National Shipping Corp (No.2)* [2000] 1 All E.R. (Comm) 1, [2000] 1 C.L. 354 applied.

KBC BANK v. INDUSTRIAL STEELS (UK) LTD [2001] 1 All E.R. (Comm) 409, David Steel, J., QBD (Comm Ct).

5351. Deceit – paternity – actionable tort between cohabitees – duty to promote honesty

A question arose as to whether the tort of deceit applied between a cohabiting couple as a preliminary issue in circumstances in which P contended that he had been deceived by his cohabitee, B, into believing that he was the father of her child.

Held, giving judgment for P on the preliminary issue, that actionable deceit could arise between cohabitees. However, the law should promote honesty between couples and actions for deceit would only be commenced when a relationship had already broken down.

P v. B (PATERNITY: DAMAGES FOR DECEIT) [2001] 1 F.L.R. 1041, Stanley Burnton, J., QBD.

5352. Foreseeability – psychiatric harm – post traumatic stress disorder – eyewitness to fatal accident involving work colleagues – ties of love and affection

R sought to recover damages for post traumatic stress disorder suffered as a result of witnessing a fatal accident involving H, his work colleague and friend, that occurred whilst both men were acting in the course of their employment with SV. It fell to the court to determine as a preliminary issue whether there were such close ties of love and affection between R and H that SV should reasonably have foreseen that R might suffer psychiatric injury as a result of witnessing H's accident or its immediate aftermath, and whether a duty of care was owed by SV to R in this respect.

Held, determining the preliminary issue in favour of the claimant, that whilst R had many other friends and mixed in a variety of circles, R and H had worked in a close knit environment. They had worked together on the night shift for 10 hours at a stretch, sharing their breaks. Their relationship had not been confined to the work place but extended to social activities including fishing, spending whole days and evenings in each others' company and spending the night at each others' homes. The relationship between R and H was therefore of such a quality as to amount to a genuine tie of love and affection. It was eminently foreseeable that a person such as R was at risk of suffering psychiatric harm as a result of witnessing the death of or injury to a work colleague. In the circumstances of the case, SV should reasonably have foreseen that R might suffer a psychiatric injury as a result of witnessing H's accident or its immediate aftermath, *Alcock v. Chief Constable of South Yorkshire* [1992] 1 A.C. 310, [1992] C.L.Y. 3250 applied, *McFarlane v. EE Caledonia Ltd* [1994] 2 All E.R. 1, [1994] C.L.Y. 3353 considered and *Robertson v. Forth Road Bridge Joint Board (No.2)* [1995] S.C. 364, [1995] C.L.Y. 6157 distinguished.

RENWICK v. STANLEY VICKERS LTD, February 6, 2001, Recorder Bowerman, CC (Middlesbrough). [*Ex rel.* Jeremy Freedman, Barrister, Plowden Buildings, Temple, London].

5353. Harassment – psychiatric harm – intention to inflict harm – recognition of tort of harassment at common law

[Offences Against the Person Act 1861 s.45; Protection from Harassment Act 1997.]

W appealed against the striking out of her claim against M, a fellow employee with the NHS trust. As a result of an alleged campaign of harassment against W carried out by M and two other employees, W suffered physical and psychiatric injuries. She successfully brought a private prosecution against M for assault and subsequently brought a negligence claim against the trust on the basis of its vicariously liability for the torts of its employees. W also brought a claim of "intentional harassment" against M which was struck out on the basis that there was no tort of harassment at common law before the Protection from Harassment Act 1997. Furthermore, because having already been the subject of a prosecution, the assault was excluded from consideration under the Offences Against the Person Act 1861 s.45 the remaining complaints against M could not amount to the tort of intentional infliction of harm.

Held, dismissing the appeal, that the issue was whether M's behaviour was such that it was likely to result in such harm that an intention of harm could be imputed from it. Once the assault had been excluded from consideration by virtue of the 1861 Act, all that remained were W's allegations that M had been rude and unfriendly, from which an intention to cause harm could not be imputed. Furthermore, before the coming into force of the 1997 Act, the common law did not recognise the tort of intentional harassment and there had been no right to damages for behaviour not constituting a tort.

WONG v. PARKSIDE HEALTH NHS TRUST, [2001] EWCA Civ 1721, *The Times*, December 7, 2001, Hale, L.J., CA.

5354. Malicious falsehood – limitations – causes of action – guidance concerning pleadings containing allegations of fraud

[Limitation Act 1980 s.4A, s.32A.]

CG, a property development company which had purchased office premises that were to be converted into a hotel, appealed against orders that (1) its claim against ROG, a neighbouring land owner, and C, surveyors, in respect of malicious falsehood was time barred under the Limitation Act 1980 s.4A (2) its claim against ROG and C for unlawful interference with rights was also time barred under the principle in *Letang v. Cooper* [1965] 1 Q.B. 232, [1964] C.L.Y. 3499, and (3) it was not appropriate to grant an extension of time under s.32A of the Act. C had written a letter to the local planning authority in which it asserted that ROG enjoyed a right of way over the car park of the development land which would render it impossible for CG to satisfy certain planning conditions without ROG's consent. CG maintained that the statement was false and that it had been made maliciously.

Held, dismissing the appeal, that (1) it was possible that facts which formed the basis of a claim for "wrongful interference with rights" were capable of amounting to a cause of action that was distinguishable from an action for malicious falsehood. However, in the instant case, the facts as pleaded by CG fell squarely within the description of "other malicious falsehood" in s.4A of the Act. Accordingly, a time limit of 12 months applied, *Letang* considered; (2) the judge had made no error of law in exercising his discretion under s.32A of the Act not to allow an extension of the time limit for bringing the claim. CG had failed to establish that ROG had no right of way over the car park; moreover, CG had not proved that ROG and C knew or were recklessly indifferent to the fact that they had no arguable defence to the claim, and (3) it was not appropriate to give permission to CG to amend its statement of case. The court endorsed the guidance of the Bar Council that in the absence of clear instructions and reasonably credible admissible evidence that established a prima facie case, counsel should not draft any pleading containing an allegation of fraud. It was observed that such guidance applied equally to an allegation of malicious falsehood, *Medcalf v. Mardell (Wasted Costs Order)* [2001] Lloyd's Rep. P.N. 146, [2001] 2 C.L. 53 applied.

CORNWALL GARDENS PTE LTD v. RO GARRARD & CO LTD, [2001] EWCA Civ 699, *The Times*, June 19, 2001, Lord Phillips of Worth Matravers, M.R., CA.

5355. Misfeasance in public office – Bank of England – prospects of success

T and various other depositors who had lost money following the collapse of the Bank of Credit and Commerce International, appealed against a decision ([2000] 2 W.L.R. 15, [1999] C.L.Y. 4854) upholding an order striking out their action against the Bank of England alleging misfeasance in public office. The Bank argued that the claim should be struck out due to the inadequacy of the pleadings and as an abuse of process.

Held, allowing the appeal (Lord Hobhouse and Lord Millett dissenting), that (1) the pleadings leaving no doubt as to the case alleged, it was apparent that the argument in relation to them was directed toward the state of the evidence. However, the question of whether that evidence indicated negligence rather than misfeasance in public office was a matter for the trial judge to determine, and (2) there was a risk of pre-judging the claim if the court in determining its prospects of success prior to the hearing of evidence, took into account the plausibility or improbability of the case against the bank as regulator. Having regard to the principle that each case was to be dealt with justly, the court, when considering if it had a reasonable prospect of success, should not be swayed by the possible length or cost of the litigation. In the opinion of Lord Hobhouse, the available material did not support a prima facie case that the allegations were made out. Lord Millett found that the claim had no real prospect of success.

THREE RIVERS DC v. BANK OF ENGLAND (NO.3) (SUMMARY JUDGMENT), [2001] UKHL 16, [2001] 2 All E.R. 513, Lord Hope of Craighead, HL.

5356. **Misrepresentation – deceit – joint venture with fraudster – nature and scope of fiduciary relationship**

G entered into a joint enterprise with B, whereby they agreed to purchase agricultural land in France. It was agreed between the parties that the purchase price for the land would be paid in Swiss francs and that G's land would be charged as security together with a collection of gemstones owned by B. B retained a firm of chartered accountants, WS, to act on behalf of himself and G in connection with the venture. B subsequently misappropriated monies raised by G against his property and G instituted proceedings against WS, contending that WS had made various fraudulent or negligent representations to the effect that the gemstones were owned by B and comprised available security for the project. G also pursued alternative allegations of breach of contract and breach of fiduciary duty. The court at first instance dismissed the claim, on the basis that WS were not liable in negligence for the representation that the gemstones were available security, as WS had not intended to induce G to enter into the transaction and that, in any event, G had not relied upon anything said or done by WS. The court also held that there was no fiduciary duty between G and B capable of giving rise to any claim for knowing assistance on the part of WS. G appealed, contending that the judge (1) had confused the concept of motive with that of intention; (2) had paid insufficient attention to the presumption of intention following the making of a dishonest representation; (3) had wrongly limited the concept of intention to induce to act, and (4) had wrongly restricted the scope of the relationship and duties giving rise to a fiduciary relationship and, in consequence, wrongly rejected G's contention that WS had been guilty of knowing assistance in breach of a fiduciary duty owed to G by B.

Held, dismissing the appeal, that (1) the judge's conclusions were clearly related to the issue of intention rather than motive. Despite the fact that W's reference to the stones as being owned by B was a dishonest representation, the third requirement in establishing the tort of deceit, namely that the representation be made with the intention that it should be acted upon, was missing, *Bradford Third Equitable Benefit Building Society v. Borders* [1941] 2 All E.R. 205 applied; (2) the judge's words clearly indicated that he recognised the existence of the presumption concerning intention, despite the absence of any reference to authorities dealing with the issue; (3) there was no evidence that the judge had wrongly restricted the principle that the maker of the statement should have intended the recipient to act on it in the manner which actually resulted in damage to him, and (4) while B had been under a fiduciary duty to G to apply B's funds in the agreed furtherance of the joint venture and also to use the gemstones in the agreed manner, a fiduciary duty did not arise until the loan had been secured and there was no basis for any suggestion that WS had participated in any subsequent misappropriation or misuse of those funds, *United Dominions Corp Ltd v. Brian Pty Ltd* (1985) 60 A.L.R. 741 considered.

GOOSE v. WILSON SANDFORD & CO (NO.2) [2001] Lloyd's Rep. P.N. 189, Morritt, L.J., CA.

5357. **Passing off – domain names – damage to reputation – New Zealand**

[Fair Trading Act 1986 (New Zealand) s.9.]

NZ provided postal services in New Zealand and had electronic media interests. NZ had registered the internet domain names "nzpost.co.nz" and "nzpost.co" in 1995. L, a New Zealand resident, registered the domain name "nzpost.com" in 1996. This was hosted in California and contained subdirectories relating to pornography and the sex industry. NZ contended that it owned a common law trade mark, claimed for passing off and misleading and deceptive conduct under the Fair Trading Act 1986 s.9, seeking an interim injunction to prevent L from using "nzpost" as a domain name component.

Held, allowing the application, that NZ had goodwill in its name that was recognised both nationally and internationally. The evidence showed that there was a likelihood of confusion amongst internet users, including those using search engines, and the risk of association between the names was such to constitute passing off, *British Telecommunications Plc v. One in a Million Ltd* [1999] 1 W.L.R. 903, [1998] C.L.Y. 3520 considered. The balance of convenience lay in favour of granting the injunction because of the risk of damage to NZ's established reputation. Delay on NZ's part in seeking the remedy did not preclude the grant, as the application was based on a recent change in the law. Jurisdiction lay with the court as L was a New Zealand resident and had used the name for business purposes within the jurisdiction.

NEW ZEALAND POST LTD v. LENG [1998-99] Info. T.L.R. 233, Williams, J., HC (NZ).

5358. **Vicarious liability – Home Office – liability for acts of detention centre employee – ability to delegate operation of centres**

[Immigration Act 1971 Sch.2 para.18(1).]

In proceedings brought by Q seeking damages from G, which operated a detention centre in which he had been detained, and the Home Office, the preliminary issue arose as to whether the Home Office was liable to Q for the tortious acts of a detention officer employed by G. Q had been detained at the centre pursuant to an authority signed by an immigration officer under the Immigration Act 1971. The centre was operated and managed by G under a contract with the Home Office. Following a disturbance at the centre, Q had been charged with violent disorder but was subsequently acquitted on the direction of the trial judge. Q contended that the exercise of an immigration officer's powers under the Act imposed a duty on the Home Office to have regard to the safety of persons detained in such centres so that the tortious acts of an employee against a detainee constituted a breach of that duty for which the Home Office was liable. The Home Office maintained that given the ability of the Secretary of State to delegate the running of such centres to other bodies, the case fell within the principle that it was not liable for the tortious acts of an independent contractor.

Held, determining the preliminary issue in favour of the Home Office, that it was necessary to have regard to the statutory provisions which governed Q's detention. At the relevant time, the Immigration (Places of Detention) Direction 1996 made by the Secretary of State pursuant to Sch.2 para.18(1) of the Act specified a number of places at which persons could be detained and whilst that included the centre at which Q was detained, the Direction also identified, inter alia, any police station, hospital or prison. As a result, once the immigration officer had exercised his powers of detention under the Act, the physical detention then became the responsibility of persons not directly employed by the Secretary of State nor in relation to whom, vicarious liability arose. Accordingly, at the relevant time the Secretary of State had been empowered to delegate the operation and management of the centre to an independent contractor. Further, owing to the fact that all reasonable care had been taken in the selection of the independent contractor, no liability arose for the torts of G's servants or agents. It followed that Q's claim against the Home Office had no reasonable prospect of success, it should be struck out.

QUAQUAH v. GROUP 4 SECURITIES LTD (NO.2); *sub nom.* QUAQUAH v. GROUP FOUR (TOTAL SECURITY) LTD *The Times*, June 27, 2001, Wright, J., QBD.

5359. Vicarious liability – sexual abuse – children – residential care – employer's liability for acts of sexual abuse by employee

T, who had been subjected to sexual abuse by D, the warden of a residential home, appealed against a decision (Times, October 13, 1999, [1999] C.L.Y. 2147) that the owner of the home, HH, was not vicariously liable for the tortious acts of D, its employee and the home's warden, in sexually abusing children in his care. The matter had proceeded before the Court of Appeal, upon the basis that HH was liable for D's failure to report the risk of or actual harm caused to the children since, bound by the decision in *T v. North Yorkshire CC* [1999] I.R.L.R. 98, [1998] C.L.Y. 2243, it had not been open to the court to consider whether HH had been vicariously liable for the actual abuse. T challenged the validity of the decision in *T v. North Yorkshire CC* submitting that employers might be vicariously liable for the sexual torts of an employee even though the sexual abuse could not be considered as an unauthorised mode of carrying out an authorised act.

Held, allowing the appeal, that the line of authority relating to vicarious liability for intentional torts as exemplified by *Morris v. CW Martin & Sons Ltd* [1966] 1 Q.B. 716, [1965] C.L.Y. 178 was of general application and was not restricted to bailment cases, *T v. North Yorkshire CC* overruled. When applying the test laid down in Salmond and Heutson on Torts, 21st edition (1996) p.443 in respect of whether a wrongful act was outside the scope of employment, the Court of Appeal in *T v. North Yorkshire CC* had wrongly categorised the sexual assaults which took place as far removed from an unauthorised mode of carrying out a teacher's duty and failed to acknowledge the close connection between the employment and the tort, *Bazley v. Curry* (1999) 174 D.L.R. (4th) 45 and *Jacobi v. Griffiths* (1999) 174 D.L.R. (4th) 71 considered. In applying the *Salmond* test it was crucial to focus on the right act of the employee and its connection with the tortious act *Rose v. Plenty* [1976] 1 W.L.R. 141, [1976] C.L.Y. 1876 considered. The court must not simply consider whether the acts of sexual abuse were modes of doing an authorised act but must also consider whether there existed a close connection between the tort and the employee's duties. In the instant case, HH had undertaken to care for the resident children and had entrusted that obligation to D. D's torts were so closely connected with his employment that it would be fair and just to hold HH vicariously liable.

L v. HESLEY HALL LTD, [2001] UKHL 22, [2002] 1 A.C. 215, Lord Steyn, HL.

5360. Books

Bagshaw, Roderick; McBride, Nicholas – Tort Law. Longman Law Series. Paperback: £28.99. ISBN 0-582-35701-2. Longman.

Campbell, Euan; Rowe, Bernie – Practical Guide to Motor Accident Claims. Paperback: £85.00. ISBN 0-406-91780-9. Butterworths Law.

Coates, S. – Law of Tort. Suggested Solutions. £6.95. ISBN 1-85836-395-0. Old Bailey Press.

Cooke, John – Law of Tort 5th Ed. Foundation Studies in Law Series. Paperback: £25.99. ISBN 0-582-43819-5. Longman.

Cracknell, D.G. – Obligations: the Law of Tort Textbook. 3rd Ed. Old Bailey Press Textbooks. Paperback: £14.95. ISBN 1-85836-415-9. Old Bailey Press.

Dugdale, Anthony – Clerk & Lindsell on Torts. 18th Ed. Common Law Library. Hardback: £220.00. ISBN 0-421-69340-1. Sweet & Maxwell.

Elliott, Catherine; Quinn, Frances – Tort Law 3rd Ed. Paperback: £15.99. ISBN 0-582-43811-X. Longman Higher Education.

Grubb, Andrew – Law of Tort. Butterworths Common Law. Hardback: £195.00. ISBN 0-406-89672-0. Butterworths Law.

Hartley, Hazel – Exploring Sport and Leisure Disasters Law: a Socio-legal Perspective. Paperback: £48.40. ISBN 1-85941-650-0. Cavendish Publishing Ltd.

Martin, Jacqueline; Turner, Chris – Key Facts: Tort. Key Facts. Paperback: £4.99. ISBN 0-340-80182-4. Hodder & Stoughton Educational.

Porat, Ariel; Stein, Alex – Liability Under Uncertainty. Hardback: £50.00. ISBN 0-19-826797-5. Oxford University Press.

Wright, Jane – Tort Law and Human Rights. Hardback: £25.00. ISBN 1-84113-035-4. Hart Publishing.

Wright, Jane – Tort Law and Human Rights-The Impact of the ECHR on English Law. Hardback: £30.00. ISBN 1-84113-035-4. Hart Publishing.

TRANSPORT

5361. Air traffic – provision of air traffic services – exemption

AIR TRAFFIC SERVICES (EXEMPTION) ORDER 2001, SI 2001 287; made under the Transport Act 2000 s.4. In force: April 1, 2001; £1.50.

The Transport Act 2000 s.3 states that a person commits an offence if he provides air traffic services in respect of a managed area unless he is authorised to do so by an exemption granted under s.4 or by a licence granted under s.5 of the Act. This Order authorises the provision of air traffic services, other than area control and information services provided from an area control centre. The authorisation does not extend to services provided by the holder of a licence granted under Transport Act 2000 s.5. The authorisation is to last for 10 years.

5362. Air transport – air navigation – air traffic central approval

AIR NAVIGATION (AMENDMENT) ORDER 2001, SI 2001 397; made under the Civil Aviation Act 1982 s.60, s.61, s.102, Sch.13. In force: March 20, 2001; £2.00.

This Order makes amendments to the Air Navigation Order 2000 (SI 2000 1562) by requiring the Civil Aviation Authority (CAA) to grant air traffic control approval in respect of UK airspace and outside the UK for which the UK provides air navigation services which shall remain in force for the period specified on it. The Order provides that the CAA or an authorised person may require production of any documents and records relating to approved air traffic service equipment, specifies that the CAA may direct the holder of a licence to provide air traffic services granted under the Transport Act 2000 Part I to provide such air traffic control service, flight information service or means of two way radiocommunication as the CAA considers appropriate and specifies that the CAA may, in the interests of ensuring the efficient use of airspace so as to require that air traffic services are provided to a standard appropriate for the airspace classification, direct any person in charge of the provision of air traffic services to provide such services as the CAA considers appropriate. In addition, the definition of air traffic service equipment is amended to mean ground based equipment including an aeronautical radio station, gives the CAA and authorised persons right of access to any building or place from which an air traffic control service is being provided or where any approved air traffic service equipment is situated and specifies that co-pilots of helicopters flying on scheduled journeys for public transport in instrument meteorological conditions must hold an instrument rating.

5363. Air transport – air navigation – carriage by air – dangerous goods

AIR NAVIGATION (DANGEROUS GOODS) (AMENDMENT) REGULATIONS 2001, SI 2001 918; made under the Air Navigation Order 2000 (SI 2000 1562) Art.60, Art.129. In force: March 30, 2001; £1.50.

These Regulations, which amend the Air Navigation (Dangerous Goods) Regulations 1994 (SI 1994 3187), amend the definition of "Technical Instructions" so as to include an addendum to the 1999-2000 edition of the International Civil Aviation Organisation's Technical Instructions for the Safe Transport of Goods by Air.

5364. Air transport – air navigation – Civil Aviation Authority – publication of directions

CIVIL AVIATION (PUBLICATION OF DIRECTIONS) REGULATIONS 2001, SI 2001 353; made under the Transport Act 2000 s.69. In force: April 1, 2001; £1.50.

These Regulations prescribe the manner of publication of directions to the Civil Aviation Authority by the Secretary of State under the Transport Act 2000 s.66(1) in relation to air navigation in managed areas.

5365. Air transport – chargeable air services

TRANSPORT ACT 2000 (AMENDMENT) ORDER 2001, SI 2001 492; made under the Transport Act 2000 s.77. In force: April 1, 2001; £1.50.

This Order amends the Transport Act 2000 s.77 to extend the meaning of "chargeable air services". The effect of these amendments is that air traffic services which are provided by the owner or manager of an aerodrome or by his employee, are chargeable air services if they are services for which Euro control is to collect charges under the multilateral agreement relating to route charges signed at Brussels on February 12, 1981. They are also chargeable air services if they are provided under contract or any other arrangement made by the owner or manager and the Civil Aviation Authority where, in making that contract or other arrangement, the Civil Aviation Authority is acting in the performance of functions with regard to air navigation which it is directed to perform.

5366. Air transport – chargeable air services – aircraft – confiscation and detention

CIVIL AVIATION (CHARGEABLE AIR SERVICES) (DETENTION AND SALE OF AIRCRAFT) REGULATIONS 2001, SI 2001 493; made under the Transport Act 2000 s.83, s.103. In force: April 1, 2001; £2.00.

These Regulations provide for the detention and sale of aircraft where default is made in the payment of charges for air services specified by the Civil Aviation Authority by virtue of the Transport Act 2000 s.73 other than charges payable to Eurocontrol.

5367. Air transport – chargeable air services – aircraft – confiscation and detention

CIVIL AVIATION (CHARGEABLE AIR SERVICES) (DETENTION AND SALE OF AIRCRAFT FOR EUROCONTROL) REGULATIONS 2001, SI 2001 494; made under the Transport Act 2000 s.83, s.103. In force: April 1, 2001; £2.00.

These Regulations provide for the detention and sale of aircraft on behalf of Eurocontrol where default is made in the payment to Eurocontrol of charges for air services specified by the Civil Aviation Authority by virtue of the Transport Act 2000 s.73.

5368. Air transport – chargeable air services – designation

AERODROMES (DESIGNATION) (CHARGEABLE AIR SERVICES) ORDER 2001, SI 2001 354; made under the Transport Act 2000 s.77. In force: April 1, 2001; £1.50.

This Order designates London Heathrow, London Gatwick, London Stansted, Aberdeen (Dyce), Edinburgh and Glasgow as aerodromes for the purpose of the Transport Act 2000 s.73 which specifies charges in respect of chargeable air services as defined in s.77 of the Act.

5369. Air transport – chargeable air services – records

CIVIL AVIATION (CHARGEABLE AIR SERVICES) (RECORDS) REGULATIONS 2001, SI 2001 399; made under the Transport Act 2000 s.81, s.103. In force: April 1, 2001; £1.50.

The Regulations require the manager of every aerodrome to which Civil Aviation Act 1982 s.88 applies together with Belfast International Airport, Belfast City Airport and Eglinton Airport, Northern Ireland, to keep an aircraft movement log which records particulars of the type and registration mark of each aircraft taking off from or landing at the aerodrome, the date and time of each such take off and landing and the origin or destination of each aircraft in order to facilitate the assessment and collection of charges payable by virtue of the Transport Act 2000 s.73. The log has to be preserved to the extent that it comprises particulars recorded for a period of two years or less and those particulars have to be capable of being reproduced; and produced in a legible form within seven days of request by an officer of the CAA or an officer of a person to whom the CAA has specified that charges are to be paid.

5370. Air transport – Civil Aviation Authority – electronic publication

CIVIL AVIATION AUTHORITY (AMENDMENT) REGULATIONS 2001, SI 2001 2448; made under the Civil Aviation Act 1982 s.7, s.102, Sch.1 para.15; and the Transport Act 2000 s.7. In force: July 31, 2001; £2.00.

These Regulations amend the Civil Aviation Authority's Regulations 1991 (SI 1991 1672) to permit electronic publication by and service on the Authority and to entitle persons requesting a review to an oral hearing. They provide a provisional air traffic direction is not subject to Reg.6 review and make provision for an appeal to the Secretary of State against a determination by the Authority.

5371. Air transport – navigation – nuclear power – restriction of flying

AIR NAVIGATION (RESTRICTION OF FLYING) (NUCLEAR INSTALLATIONS) REGULATIONS 2001, SI 2001 1607; made under the Air Navigation Order 2000 (SI 2000 1562) Art.85. In force: May 11, 2001; £1.75.

These Regulations revoke the Air Navigation (Restriction of Flying) (Nuclear Installations) Regulations 1988 (SI 1988 1138), the Air Navigation (Restriction of Flying) (Nuclear Installations) (Amendment) Regulations 1992 and the Air Navigation (Restriction of Flying) (Nuclear Installations) (Amendment No.2) Regulations 1992 (SI 1992 2085). They reduce the restricted area in respect of Winfrith to a radius of one nautical mile and a height of 1,000 feet above mean sea level.

5372. Air transport – navigation – nuclear power – restriction of flying

AIR NAVIGATION (RESTRICTION OF FLYING) (NUCLEAR INSTALLATIONS) (REVOCATION) REGULATIONS 2001, SI 2001 2904; made under the Air Navigation Order 2000 (SI 2000 1562) Art.85. In force: August 10, 2001; £1.50.

These Regulations revoke the Air Navigation (Restriction of Flying) (Nuclear Installations) Regulations 1998 (SI 1998 2425).

5373. Air transport – navigation – overseas territories

AIR NAVIGATION (OVERSEAS TERRITORIES) ORDER 2001, SI 2001 2128; made under the Civil Aviation Act 1949 s.8, s.41, s.57, s.58, s.59, s.61. In force: July 16, 2001; £16.50.

This Order revokes the Air Navigation (Overseas Territories) Order 1989 (SI 1989 2395), the Air Navigation (Overseas Territories) (Amendment) Order 1991 (SI 1991 189), the Air Navigation (Overseas Territories) (Amendment) (No.2) Order 1991 (SI 1991 1697), the Air Navigation (Overseas Territories) (Amendment) Order 1992 (SI 1992 3198), the Air Navigation (Overseas Territories) (Amendment) Order 1995 (SI 1995 2701) and the Air Navigation (Overseas Territories) (Amendment) Order 1997 (SI 1997 1746). The Order is based closely on the Air Navigation Order 2000 (SI 2000 1562) but the main difference between this Order and the 2000 Order is that some of the provisions of the Air Navigation Order which reflect obligations of the UK as a member of the European Union and as a member of the Joint Aviation Authorities (JAA) are not reproduced in this Order.

5374. Air transport – navigation – overseas territories

CIVIL AVIATION ACT 1982 (OVERSEAS TERRITORIES) ORDER 2001, SI 2001 1452; made under the Civil Aviation Act 1949 s.66; the Civil Aviation Act 1971 s.66; and the Civil Aviation Act 1982 s.108. In force: May 16, 2001; £1.75.

This Order, which revokes in part the Civil Aviation Act 1971 (Overseas Territories) Order 1976 (SI 1976 1912), amends the Civil Aviation Act 1949 (Overseas Territories) Order 1969 (SI 1969 592) and extends the Civil Aviation Act 1982 s.61 and s.75 to specified territories.

5375. Air transport – navigation – prisons – restriction of flying

AIR NAVIGATION (RESTRICTION OF FLYING) (PRISONS) REGULATIONS 2001, SI 2001 1657; made under the Air Navigation Order 2000 (SI 2000 1562) Art.85. In force: May 11, 2001; £1.75.

These Regulations, which revoke and replace the Air Navigation (Restriction of Flying) (High Security Prisons) Regulations 1989 (SI 1989 2118 as amended by SI 1991 1679, SI 1992 1876 and SI 1993 2123), do not apply to HMP Parkhurst. They introduce restrictions in respect of Her Majesty's Prisons at Altcourse, Bristol, Doncaster, High Down, Manchester, Wakefield and Woodhill and the area within which restrictions apply in respect of HMP Frankland is extended to encompass HMP Durham.

5376. Air transport – navigation – transfer of owners liability – overseas territories

CIVIL AVIATION ACT 1982 (OVERSEAS TERRITORIES) (NO.2) ORDER 2001, SI 2001 3367; made under the Civil Aviation Act 1982 s.108. In force: October 10, 2001; £1.75.

This Order extends the Civil Aviation Act 1982 s.76(4) to the territories listed in Sch.2 to the Order. The liability of the owner as extended to those territories, for loss or damage caused by an aircraft in flight or by a person in, or an article, animal or person falling from such an aircraft, is transferred to the person to whom the owner has demised, let or hired out the aircraft if the demise, let or hire is for a period of more than 14 days and no crew member is employed by the owner.

5377. Air transport – rules – conformity with notified instrument departure procedures

RULES OF THE AIR (AMENDMENT) REGULATIONS 2001, SI 2001 917; made under the Air Navigation Order 2000 (SI 2000 1562) Art.84. In force: April 1, 2001; £1.50.

These Regulations amend the Rules of the Air Regulations 1996 (SI 1996 1393) by requiring an aircraft commander to fly in conformity with any notified instrument departure procedures.

5378. **Aircraft – noise – night time flying at Heathrow airport – right to respect for private and family life**

[European Convention on Human Rights 1950 Art.8, Art.13.]

H and other residents of properties surrounding Heathrow airport complained to the European Court of Human Rights alleging that the introduction in October 1993 of a noise quota system as a means of controlling night time flying at the airport infringed their right to respect for private and family life conferred by the European Convention on Human Rights 1950 Art.8 and their right to an effective remedy under Art.13. Until October 1993 the noise caused by night time flying had been controlled by restrictions placed on the number of take offs and landings at the airport. However, the noise quota system had introduced a new system whereby aircraft operators could select fewer noisier aircraft or a greater number of quieter aircraft as long as neither exceeded the quota. The residents contended that the new system had resulted in an increase in the level of noise at their homes caused by the aircraft using the Heathrow flight path.

Held, granting the applications (Sir Brian Kerr dissenting and Judge Greve dissenting in part), that although the United Kingdom could not be deemed to have interfered in the residents' right to respect for private and family life because neither the airport or aircraft were owned or controlled by the government, the state did have a duty to take reasonable and appropriate steps to uphold the residents' rights. A balance had to be struck between the interests of the residents and the interests of the community in general, and notwithstanding concerns for the economic well being of the country, the state had to take measures to try and protect an applicant's right, *Lopez Ostra v. Spain (A/303-C)* (1995) 20 E.H.R.R. 277, [1996] C.L.Y. 3118 considered. In the instant case, the UK Government had failed to strike a balance between the competing interests, and had done little to research the contribution night time flying made to the economy, or the impact the increase in night flights had had on the applicants, and as such had violated their rights under Art.8 of the Convention. Moreover, review by the domestic courts had been limited and had not allowed consideration of whether the increase in night flights under the new scheme had represented a justifiable limitation of the right to respect for the private and family lives of those living near to Heathrow airport. It followed that such review had not complied with Art.13. The applicants were each awarded £4,000 for non-pecuniary damages.

HATTON v. UNITED KINGDOM (36022/97) [2002] 1 F.C.R. 732, J-P Costa (President), ECHR.

5379. **Airports – business tenancies – contract terms – restrictions on use of airport**

BLBC appealed against a declaration (Times, January 9, 2001) entitling BH to use the airport it leased from BLBC for scheduled and chartered air services. BLBC submitted that such use was not within the meaning of the terms "business aviation" and "other airport and aviation related uses" included in the permitted user covenant of the airport's lease.

Held, allowing the appeal, that the phrase "business aviation" had to be interpreted objectively and in view of the factual background. A reasonable observer would have known that the phrase did not have a generally accepted meaning, and would have known that the main use of BH was for the operation of aircraft owned and chartered by businesses for its own use. This was a separate category of airport business to that involving transport for the public. The phrase "other airport and aviation related uses" only permitted additional uses which were aviation related, such as aircraft maintenance facilities. Accordingly, the use of BH was restricted to the operation of aircraft by companies for business purposes, providing that fare paying passengers were not accepted.

BIGGIN HILL AIRPORT LTD v. BROMLEY LBC, [2001] EWCA Civ 1089, *The Times*, August 13, 2001, Arden, L.J., CA.

5380. Bridges – Castlefield

CITY OF SALFORD (CASTLEFIELD BRIDGE) SCHEME 2000 CONFIRMATION INSTRUMENT 2001, SI 2001 2932; made under the Highways Act 1980 s.106. In force: in accordance with Art.1; £3.00.

This Instrument confirms the City of Salford (Castlefield Bridge) Scheme 2000.

5381. Bridges – River Thames – Hungerford footbridges

RIVER THAMES (HUNGERFORD FOOTBRIDGES) (VARIATION) ORDER 2001, SI 2001 4038; made under the Transport and Works Act 1992 s.3, s.5, Sch.1 para.1, Sch.1 para.2, Sch.1 para.4, Sch.1 para.8; and the Transport and Works (Descriptions of Works Interfering with Navigation) Order 1992 (SI 1992 3230). In force: December 11, 2001; £2.00.

This Order which authorises the variation of certain provisions of the River Thames (Hungerford Footbridges) Order 1999 (SI 1999 2981), authorises the relocation and redesign of the supporting pylons of the footbridges from the Middlesex Pier of the Railway Bridge to Victoria Embankment and an increase in the height of the pylons. It also makes provision for changes to the layout of streets and stopping-up of streets consequent upon the redesign of the pylons.

5382. British waterways – British Waterways Board – limit on borrowing

BRITISH WATERWAYS BOARD (LIMIT FOR BORROWING) ORDER 2001, SI 2001 1054; made under the Transport Act 1962 s.19. In force: March 20, 2001; £1.50.

This Order, which revokes the British Waterways Board (Limit for Borrowing) Order 1983 (SI 1983 1957), increases the borrowing limit of the British Waterways Board from £30m to £35m.

5383. Bus lanes – London

TRANSPORT FOR LONDON (BUS LANES) ORDER 2001, SI 2001 690; made under the Greater London Authority Act 1999 s.405, s.406. In force: April 1, 2001; £2.00.

This Order amends various provisions of the London Local Authorities Act 1996 and repeals certain provisions of the London Local Authorities Act 2000 consequential upon the status of Transport for London as the traffic authority for GLA roads and GLA side roads to enable Transport for London to serve and enforce penalty charge notices with respect to vehicles which contravene or fail to comply with provisions for the reservation of all or part of the carriageway of a GLA road or a GLA side road as a bus lane.

5384. Bus services – penalties – traffic commissioner's powers

R, a bus operator, appealed against a decision of the Transport Tribunal that a traffic commissioner had correctly exercised his powers when attaching a condition to R's public service vehicle licences and ordering R to forfeit part of its fuel duty rebate for the previous three months. During a monitoring exercise it had been found that there had been an overall failure on R's part to meet its timetabling requirements.

Held, dismissing the appeal, that (1) while the commissioner had had to satisfy himself that the sample of journeys monitored was sufficient and a fair reflection of R's operation as a whole, the question of whether R had complied with its timetabling requirements during the monitoring exercise was a matter of fact and degree, and the commissioner had been entitled to assess R's performance generally rather than by reference to individual specific services; (2) it would be for the operator to prove, on the balance of probabilities, that it had had a reasonable excuse for failing to meet its timetabling requirements, and (3) when taking into account excuses which he had described as "ordinary everyday occurrences", the commissioner had been justified in setting a benchmark of 95 per cent. Furthermore, when setting such a benchmark, the commissioner had been entitled to take into account such general experience as could be ascertained from the experience and decisions of other commissioners as well as the information that he himself had gained from previous inquiries.

RIBBLE MOTOR SERVICES LTD v. TRAFFIC COMMISSIONER FOR THE NORTH WEST TRAFFIC AREA; *sub nom.* RIBBLE MOTOR SERVICES LTD v. TRAFFIC COMMISSION FOR THE NORTH WESTERN TRAFFIC AREA, [2001] EWCA Civ 267, [2001] R.T.R. 37, Simon Brown, L.J., CA.

5385. Carriage by air – personal injuries – liability of airline to compensate for psychiatric illness – meaning of "bodily injury"

[Warsaw Convention on International Carriage by Air 1929 Art.17.]

K, an airline, appealed against the entry of summary judgment against it in a claim brought by M, a child who had travelled unaccompanied on one of K's flights, and who claimed that she had suffered from clinical depression following an indecent assault by a male passenger. M's claim was founded upon the Warsaw Convention on International Carriage by Air 1929 Art.17, which provided that a carrier was liable for "bodily injury" suffered by a passenger in an accident occurring either on board the aircraft or during the process of embarking or disembarking. K submitted that (1) the incident which M claimed had caused her depressive illness was not an "accident" within the meaning of Art.17, and (2) psychiatric illness did not constitute "bodily injury" for the purposes of Art.17.

Held, allowing the appeal, that (1) liability under Art.17 of the Convention would arise if a passenger's injury was brought about by the air travel and was caused by an unexpected or unusual event or happening that was external to the passenger, *Air France v. Saks* 470 U.S. 392 applied and *Wallace v. Korean Air* (Unreported) considered. That included torts committed by fellow passengers. Accordingly, M had sustained an "accident" for the purpose of Art.17, and (2) the natural meaning of the words "bodily injury" was an injury to the body not extending to mental injury. The purpose of the Convention was to compensate those who suffered damage in the sense of legally recognised harm, and that harm had to be interpreted in a manner consistent with the intention of the Convention. Accordingly, "bodily injury" did not extend to psychiatric illness, *Eastern Airlines Inc v. Floyd* 499 U.S. 530 followed and *King v. Bristow Helicopters Ltd* [2001] 1 Lloyd's Rep. 95, [2000] 11 C.L. 671 not followed.

M (A CHILD) v. KLM ROYAL DUTCH AIRLINES; *sub nom.* KLM ROYAL DUTCH AIRLINES v. M (A CHILD), [2001] EWCA Civ 790, [2002] Q.B. 100, Lord Phillips of Worth Matravers, M.R., CA.

5386. Carriage by air – sports – claimant injured on paragliding course – meaning of "aircraft", "carriage", "for reward" and "passenger"

[Carriage by Air Acts (Application of Provisions) Order 1967 (SI 1967 480); Warsaw Convention 1929.]

L, who provided paragliding courses, appealed against a decision ([2001] P.I.Q.R. P10) in relation to preliminary issues arising from a claim brought by D, who had been injured during a course, that (1) a tandem paraglider was not an "aircraft" for the purposes of the Carriage by Air Acts (Application of Provisions) Order 1967; (2) the carriage of D had not amounted to carriage "for reward" for the purposes of the Order, and (3) D had not been a "passenger" for the purposes of the Order.

Held, dismissing the appeal, that (1) having regard to the regulatory system relating to commercial and recreational flying and to the intention of Parliament when enacting the Order, a paraglider could not be said to amount to an "aircraft", *Holmes (Keiko) v. Bangladesh Biman Corp* [1989] A.C. 1112, [1989] C.L.Y. 253 applied. In the opinion of Buxton, L.J., the Warsaw Convention 1929, which when it had been applied by the Order had not been altered in its meaning, should be read by having regard to the context of the industry that it had been formulated to regulate. Applying such an approach, those formulating the Convention would not have considered that it would apply to a machine such as a paraglider, *M (A Child) v. KLM Royal Dutch Airlines* [2001] EWCA Civ 790, [2001] 3 W.L.R. 351, [2001] 6 C.L. 559 considered; (2) the purpose of the flight in which D had been injured was one of instruction. It followed that there had been no carriage "for reward", and (3) D was on the paraglider flight as a pilot under instruction rather than as a passenger. She had as her principal objective the wish to learn how to fly a paraglider, *Fellowes v. Clyde Helicopters Ltd* [1997] A.C. 534, [1997] C.L.Y. 5595 applied.

DISLEY v. LEVINE (T/A AIRTRAK LEVINE PARAGLIDING), [2001] EWCA Civ 1087, [2002] 1 W.L.R. 785, Henry, L.J., CA.

5387. Carriage by rail – dangerous goods – Commission Directive

Commission Directive 2001/6 of January 29, 2001 adapting for the third time to technical progress Council Directive 96/49 on the approximation of the laws of the Member States with regard to the transports of dangerous goods by rail. [2001] OJ L30/42.

5388. Carriage by road – dangerous goods – Commission Directive

Commission Directive 2001/7 of January 29, 2001 adapting for the third time to technical progress Council Directive 94/55 on the approximation of the laws of the Member States with regard to the transport of dangerous goods by road. [2001] OJ L30/43.

5389. Carriage by road – dangerous goods – transport checks – Council Directive

European Parliament and Council Directive 2001/26 of May 7, 2001 amending Council Directive 95/50 on uniform procedures for checks on the transport of dangerous goods by road. [2001] OJ L168/23.

5390. Carriage of goods – motor vehicles – type approval – fees

INTERNATIONAL TRANSPORT OF GOODS UNDER COVER OF TIR CARNETS (FEES) (AMENDMENT) REGULATIONS 2001, SI 2001 1811; made under the Finance Act 1973 s.56; and the Department of Transport (Fees) Order (SI 1988 643). In force: June 1, 2001; £1.50.

These Regulations, which amend the International Transport of Goods under Cover of TIR Carnets (Fees) Regulations 1988 (SI 1988 371), increase the fee for an inspection of a vehicle design type in connection with the grant of TIR design-type approval from £68 to £70 where the inspection of a design-type which is a variation of a design-type for which a TIR design-type approval has been granted and from £420 to £433 in any other case. The fee for the issue of a TIR vehicle approval certificate for a vehicle which is of a design-type for which TIR design-type approval has been granted is increased to £10.50 and the fee for an inspection of a vehicle in connection with the issue of a TIR vehicle approval certificate is increased to £47 where the inspection is carried out following refusal of such a certificate for the vehicle to £68 in any other case.

5391. Carriage of goods – theft – compensation

[Warsaw Convention 1929; Convention for the International Carriage of Goods by Road 1956.]

Q, which had entered into a contract with AF, an airline, for the carriage of a consignment of hard drives from Singapore to Dublin, applied for summary judgment in relation to its claim for compensation following the theft of the consignment. The consignment had been flown by AF from Singapore to Paris, from where AF had engaged a subcontractor, P, to carry it by road to Dublin. The theft had occurred during the course of that journey. AF, whilst admitting liability, had claimed a limit to its liability pursuant to the general conditions of carriage. Q argued that the Convention for the International Carriage of Goods by Road 1956 applied, or, alternatively, that the Warsaw Convention 1929, as amended, applied and that AF could not rely on the limits of liability contained within those Conventions due to the wilful misconduct of P.

Held, refusing the application but assessing damages against AF as to an interim payment, that (1) the 1956 Convention did not apply since the contract was not one for the carriage of goods by road and liability for the goods had already been assumed prior to their carriage by road. Having regard to the way in which the waybill had been made out, it was apparent that the parties had proceeded on the assumption that the consignment would be carried by road between Paris and Dublin. However, AF had not been obliged under the contract to carry the consignment in such a way and could have continued their carriage between Paris and Dublin by air, and (2) the 1929 Convention, as amended, did not apply as it imposed liability only during carriage by air and the claim related to the theft of the goods during their carriage by road. The admission of liability by AF did not result in the Convention applying by virtue of the extended definition of air carriage in the general conditions of carriage.

QUANTUM CORP LTD v. PLANE TRUCKING LTD [2001] 1 All E.R. (Comm) 916, Tomlinson, J, QBD (Comm Ct).

5392. Channel Tunnel – security – government directions – requirements of consultation and assent

C, which operated the Channel Tunnel together with a French company, appealed against a judgment ([2000] N.P.C. 137) that directions made by the Secretary of State imposing requirements upon it for the defence and security of the tunnel were enforceable. The directions, which required C to instal a new X-ray system and to increase the proportion of vehicles searched, were made without the prior approval of the French government. The Treaty and Concession entered into by the French and United Kingdom governments regulating the operation of the tunnel contained a requirement for the two governments to consult one another and to "act jointly" before requiring C to take measures concerning the defence and security of the tunnel, save in exceptional circumstances. C contended that the absence of consultation and prior agreement as to the subject matter of the directions meant that the directions had been made in contravention of the provisions of the Treaty.

Held, allowing the appeal, that the directions were unlawful. The Secretary of State had no power to unilaterally impose requirements for the defence and security of the tunnel. The mere absence of objections from the French government to the directions proposed was insufficient to denote agreement and, although there was no obligation for each government to give the directions, there was a requirement for positive assent from the French government which had been lacking in the instant case.

R. (ON THE APPLICATION OF CHANNEL TUNNEL GROUP LTD) v. SECRETARY OF STATE FOR THE ENVIRONMENT, TRANSPORT AND THE REGIONS; R. (ON THE APPLICATION OF FRANCE MANCHE SA) v. SECRETARY OF STATE FOR THE ENVIRONMENT, TRANSPORT AND THE REGIONS, [2001] EWCA Civ 1185, *The Times*, August 7, 2001, Peter Gibson, L.J., CA.

5393. Civil Aviation Authority – extinguishment of loans

TRANSPORT ACT 2000 (EXTINGUISHMENT OF LOANS) (CIVIL AVIATION AUTHORITY) ORDER 2001, SI 2001 755; made under the Transport Act 2000 s.57. In force: March 31, 2001; £1.75.

This Order extinguishes, on March 31, 2001, all of the Civil Aviation Authority's liabilities in respect of the principal of the loans set out in the Schedule to the Order. The sum of those liabilities is £247,696,842.57.

5394. Companies – designation – National Air Traffic Services Ltd

TRANSPORT ACT 2000 (DESIGNATION OF COMPANIES) ORDER 2001, SI 2001 321; made under the Transport Act 2000 s.56. In force: March 31, 2001; £1.50.

The Transport Act 2000 s.56 provides that, for the purposes of specified provisions of the Companies Act 1985 and of the Companies (Northern Ireland) Order 1986 (SI 1986 1032 (NI.6)), Ministers of the Crown, Northern Ireland Ministers, their nominees and Northern Ireland Departments are not to be regarded as shadow directors of any transferee under a transfer scheme or of any company associated with a transferee under a transfer scheme. This Order designates National Air Traffic Services Ltd, NATS (Services) Ltd and NATS (En Route) Ltd for the purposes of the Transport Act 2000 s.56 (11). These companies are all wholly owned subsidiaries of National Air Traffic Services (No. 2) Ltd. Provided that that company is a transferee under a transfer scheme and that the other conditions of the section are satisfied, s.56 will apply in relation to the three designated companies.

5395. Companies – designation – National Air Traffic Services (No.2) Ltd

TRANSPORT ACT 2000 (DESIGNATION OF TRANSFEREE) ORDER 2001, SI 2001 1292; made under the Transport Act 2000 s.51. In force: March 31, 2001; £1.50.

This Order, which designates National Air Traffic Services (No.2) Ltd for the purposes of the Transport Act 2000 s.51, which applies when a transfer to a specified company in relation to a company which is designated for the purposes of s.51 of the Act, the Secretary of State is under the duty to ensure that the Crown does not dispose of shares in the company unless satisfied that a scheme to complete the development of major facilities connected with air traffic services is in place and to ensure that the Crown does not dispose of shares in the company unless the Crown holds at least 49 per cent of the issued ordinary share capital before disposal and will continue to do so immediately after disposal. It ensures that at any given time the Crown holds at least 25 per cent of the company's issued ordinary share capital, ensures that the Crown continues to hold any special share in the company and disallows the Secretary of State from consenting to any alteration of the company's articles of association which requires his consent on behalf of the Crown as special shareholder without the approval of parliament.

5396. Driving licences

MOTOR VEHICLES (DRIVING LICENCES) (AMENDMENT) REGULATIONS 2001, SI 2001 53; made under the Road Traffic Act 1988 s.89, s.97, s.99, s.105. In force: February 1, 2001; £2.00.

These Regulations, which amend the Motor Vehicles (Driving Licences) Regulations 1999 (SI 1999 2864), provide for a generally applicable definition of "certified direct access instructor", revoke Reg.13 which requires the Secretary of State to refuse to grant a provisional licence to drive a motor bicycle to a person who has been the holder of a previous licence in certain circumstances, and Reg.15 to allow a provisional licence to be granted for the same period as a provisional car licence. They amend the 1999 Regulations so as to make it a condition of a provisional licence to drive a moped or learner motor bicycle that, when receiving professional tuition on a road after compulsory basic training, the holder of the licence cannot have with him more than three other such learners, to remove some of the exemptions from the requirement to pass a theory test for the purpose of obtaining a licence in category A or B, in relation to a person passing the test of competence to drive a vehicle in category B on or after February 1, 2001, a licence to drive vehicles in category B does not confer entitlement to drive vehicles in category P unless the licence holder has successfully completed an approved training course for motor cyclists and insert a new regulation to provide for the grant of a licence restricted to three-wheeled vehicles in category P.

5397. Driving licences – catergories of entitlement

MOTOR VEHICLES (DRIVING LICENCES) (AMENDMENT) (NO.2) REGULATIONS 2001, SI 2001 236; made under the Road Traffic Act 1988 s.89, s.105. In force: February 1, 2001; £1.50.

These Regulations, which amend the Motor Vehicles (Driving Licences) Regulations 1999 (SI 1999 2864), insert a new paragraph whereby a person who passes a test of competence to drive vehicles in Category A will no longer have full entitlement also to drive vehicles in sub-category B1, unless they passed the test before February 1, 2001. In addition, they remedy an omission from the Motor Vehicles (Driving Licences) (Amendment) Regulations 2001 (SI 2001 53) which make other amendments to the 1999 Regulations and come into force on February 1, 2001.

5398. Driving licences – diseases and disorders – diabetes

MOTOR VEHICLES (DRIVING LICENCES) (AMENDMENT) (NO.3) REGULATIONS 2001, SI 2001 937; made under the Road Traffic Act 1988 s.92, s.105. In force: April 5, 2001; £1.50.

These Regulations, which amend the provisions of the Motor Vehicles (Driving Licences) Regulations 1999 (SI 1999 2864) enabling diabetics requiring insulin treatment to obtain certain Group 2 licences, remove the limitation of the present provisions to persons who suffered from diabetes before 1998 and held a relevant licence at the end of 1996. The conditions for the granting of licences are amended with a view to ensuring that the applicant obtains proper treatment for his condition, abides by the treatment plan drawn up by his doctor and monitors his condition appropriately.

5399. Driving licences – disqualification until test passed – prescribed offences

DRIVING LICENCES (DISQUALIFICATION UNTIL TEST PASSED) (PRESCRIBED OFFENCE) ORDER 2001, SI 2001 4051; made under the Road Traffic Offenders Act 1988 s.36. In force: January 31, 2002; £1.50.

The Road Traffic Offenders Act 1988 s.36 requires the court to disqualify a person until he has passed "the appropriate driving test". This is either a test of competence to drive, or an extended driving test, depending upon the offence committed. The 1988 Act enables the Secretary of State to prescribe other offences involving obligatory endorsement to which the subsection applies. This Order prescribes the offence of causing death by careless driving whilst under the influence of drink or drugs for that purpose if the offence is committed on or after January 31, 2002. The court is thereby required to disqualify a person convicted of such an offence until he has passed the appropriate driving test.

5400. Driving licences – renewal application fees – non driving related matters

MOTOR VEHICLES (DRIVING LICENCES) (AMENDMENT) (NO.5) REGULATIONS 2001, SI 2001 3486; made under the Road Traffic Act 1988 s.97, s.105, s.108. In force: November 15, 2001; £1.75.

These Regulations, which amend the Motor Vehicles (Driving Licences) Regulations 1999 (SI 1999 2864) substitute a new Sch.3 Part I specifying revised fees payable upon an application for a driving licence made on or after November 15, 2001. A fee for the renewal of a licence following a period of disqualification ordered by a court as a result of a non-driving related matter is introduced for the first time. This fee will apply to applications for a licence following a period of disqualification ordered by a court under the Crime Sentences Act 1977 and the Child Support, Pensions and Social Security Act 2000.

5401. Employers liability – drivers – rest periods – adequacy of weekly tachograph checks

YT appealed against a finding that it was guilty of permitting failures by its bus drivers to observe statutory rest periods. The alleged offences occurred over a three week period during which YT had operated its normal system of weekly checks of driver tachograph records. The justices had concluded that despite the fact that YT had been genuinely unaware of the breaches, its system of checks had been sufficiently inadequate so as to give rise to a finding that YT had permitted the breaches to occur. YT contended that since the offence was not one involving strict liability, it had to be shown that the employer had been reckless in its failure to take reasonable steps to prevent such breaches from occurring.

Held, allowing the appeal, that a system of weekly checks of driver tachograph records could not be said to be inadequate in itself, particularly having regard to the fact that drivers were required to retain tachograph records for the entire current driving week and the last driving day of the previous week, and could retain those records lawfully for up to 21 days. Further, the justices had made no finding as to YT's knowledge of the incidents during the relevant period. In order to found a guilty verdict, the justices had to be satisfied that YT had the requisite degree of knowledge that breaches were likely to occur and had failed to take adequate steps in order to prevent their occurrence.

YORKSHIRE TRACTION CO LTD v. VEHICLE INSPECTORATE, [2001] EWHC Admin 190, [2001] R.T.R. 34, Rose, L.J., QBD.

5402. Equipment – transportable pressure equipment – Commission Directive

Commission Directive 2001/2 of January 4, 2001 adapting to technical progress Council Directive 1999/36 on transportable pressure equipment. [2001] OJ L5/4.

5403. Flights – licences – brokers' functions – requirements for licensing

[Civil Aviation (Air Travel Organisers' Licensing) Regulations 1995 (SI 1995 1054).]

CAA appealed against a finding at judicial review that J, a broker, was not providing flight accommodation and therefore did not require a licence under the Civil Aviation (Air Travel Organisers' Licensing) Regulations 1995. J acted for ATOL holders seeking to purchase flight accommodation from airlines and other ATOL holders. The contracts were between the ATOL holders themselves, J dealing with the purchase monies and receiving a commission.

Held, dismissing the appeal, that the purpose of the Regulations was to protect passengers who had paid for flight accommodation and therefore required the licensing of those who provided the accommodation but not of those in an intermediary position who handled the customer's money. Although J made the provision of accommodation possible through its negotiations with the airlines, it did not have the right to provide it directly, acting only between airlines and its principal, which was typically a tour operator. It was the principal which made the accommodation available to the end users, J's function being merely ministerial and facilitative.

R. (ON THE APPLICATION OF JET SERVICES LTD) v. CIVIL AVIATION AUTHORITY; *sub nom.* R. v. CIVIL AVIATION AUTHORITY, *ex p.* JET SERVICES LTD, [2001] EWCA Civ 610, [2001] 2 All E.R. (Comm) 769, Peter Gibson, L.J., CA.

5404. Fuel – composition and content

MOTOR FUEL (COMPOSITION AND CONTENT) (AMENDMENT) REGULATIONS 2001, SI 2001 3896; made under the European Communities Act 1972 s.2; and the Clean Air Act 1993 s.30. In force: December 31, 2001; £1.75.

These Regulations amend the Motor Fuel (Composition and Content) Regulations 1999 (SI 1999 3107) which implement Council Directive 98/70 ([1998] OJ L350/58) relating to the quality of petrol and diesel fuels. These

TRANSPORT

Regulations implement Commission Directive 2000/71 ([2000] OJ L287/46) adapting the measuring methods as laid down in Annexes I, II, III and IV to Directive 98/70 to technical progress as foreseen in Art.10 of that Directive and remove the requirements to provide details of the expected monthly distribution of leaded petrol to the proposed nominated filling stations and to express that expected distribution as a percentage of the total tonnage of leaded petrol which the applicant proposes to sell. The Regulations also make amendments so that it is no longer mandatory for a permit to require the holder to ensure that the amount of leaded petrol distributed to the nominated filling stations each month remains within a percentage or to prepare monthly statements of the amount of leaded petrol sold from the nominated filling stations and from each individual station. In addition, the Regulations make amendments to ensure that conditions relating to the amount of leaded petrol distributed to nominated filling stations can continue to be varied.

5405. Heavy goods vehicles – drivers hours – exemptions – foot and mouth disease
COMMUNITY DRIVERS' HOURS (FOOT-AND-MOUTH DISEASE) (TEMPORARY EXCEPTION) REGULATIONS 2001, SI 2001 628; made under the European Communities Act 1972 s.2. In force: March 6, 2001; £1.75.
Council Regulation 3820/85 ([1985] OJ L370/1), of December 20, 1985 on harmonisation of certain social legislation relating to road transport, provides that Member States may in urgent cases grant a temporary exception for a period not exceeding 30 days to transport operations carried out in exceptional circumstances. These Regulations provide that until April 4, 2001, any time spent driving vehicles, for the purposes of collecting or delivering to or from a farm of agricultural products, of moving livestock and transporting feeding stuff and grain, to meet the exceptional circumstances occasioned by the outbreak of foot and mouth disease in Great Britain shall not be taken into account for the purposes of the application of the Regulation.

5406. Heavy goods vehicles – drivers hours – exemptions – foot and mouth disease
COMMUNITY DRIVERS' HOURS (FOOT-AND-MOUTH DISEASE) (TEMPORARY EXCEPTION) (NO.2) REGULATIONS 2001, SI 2001 1293; made under the European Communities Act 1972 s.2. In force: April 5, 2001; £1.75.
Council Regulation 3820/85 ([1985] OJ L370/1) relating to road transport, provides that Member States may in urgent cases grant a temporary exception for a period not exceeding 30 days to transport operations carried out in exceptional circumstances. These Regulations provide that until June 3, 2001, any time spent driving vehicles, for the purposes of collecting or delivering to or from a farm of agricultural products, of moving livestock and transporting feeding stuff and grain, to meet the exceptional circumstances occasioned by the outbreak of foot and mouth disease in Great Britain shall not be taken into account for the purposes of the application of the Regulation.

5407. Heavy goods vehicles – drivers hours – exemptions – foot and mouth disease
COMMUNITY DRIVERS' HOURS (FOOT-AND-MOUTH DISEASE) (TEMPORARY EXCEPTION) (NO.2) (AMENDMENT) REGULATIONS 2001, SI 2001 1822; made under the European Communities Act 1972 s.2. In force: June 2, 2001; £1.50.
These Regulations amend the Community Drivers' Hours (Foot-and-Mouth Disease) (Temporary Exception) (No.2) Regulations 2001 (SI 2001 1293), so as to extend the expiry date of the exceptions provided for in those Regulations for a further period of 30 days until July 3, 2001.

5408. Heavy goods vehicles – drivers hours – exemptions – foot and mouth disease
COMMUNITY DRIVERS' HOURS (FOOT-AND-MOUTH DISEASE) (TEMPORARY EXCEPTION) (NO.2) (AMENDMENT NO.2) REGULATIONS

2001, SI 2001 2358; made under the European Communities Act 1972 s.2. In force: July 3, 2001; £1.50.

These Regulations amend the Community Drivers' Hours (Foot-and-Mouth Disease) (Temporary Exception) (No.2) Regulations 2001 (SI 2001 1293) to extend the expiry date of the exceptions provided for in those Regulations for a further period of 30 days until August 2, 2001.

5409. Heavy goods vehicles – drivers hours – exemptions – foot and mouth disease

COMMUNITY DRIVERS' HOURS (FOOT-AND-MOUTH DISEASE) (TEMPORARY EXCEPTION) (NO.2) (AMENDMENT NO.3) REGULATIONS 2001, SI 2001 2741; made under the European Communities Act 1972 s.2. In force: August 1, 2001; £1.50.

Council Regulation 3820/85 ([1985] OJ L370/1) on harmonisation of certain social legislation relating to road transport provides that Member States may, after authorisation by the Commission, grant exceptions from the application of the provisions of that Regulation to transport operations carried out in exceptional circumstances. These Regulations further extend the Community Drivers' Hours (Foot-and-Mouth Disease) (Temporary Exception) (No.2) Regulations 2001 so as to extend the expiry date of the exceptions provided for in those Regulations for a further period of 30 days until September 1, 2001.

5410. Heavy goods vehicles – drivers hours – exemptions – foot and mouth disease

COMMUNITY DRIVERS' HOURS (FOOT-AND-MOUTH DISEASE) (TEMPORARY EXCEPTION) (NO.2) (AMENDMENT NO.4) REGULATIONS 2001, SI 2001 2959; made under the European Communities Act 1972 s.2. In force: August 31, 2001; £1.50.

Council Regulation 3820/85 ([1985] OJ L370/1) on the harmonisation of certain social legislation relating to road transport provides that Member States may, after authorisation by the Commission, grant exceptions from the application of the provisions of that Regulation to transport operations carried out in exceptional circumstances. These Regulations amend the Community Drivers' Hours (Foot-and-Mouth Disease) (Temporary Exception) (No.2) Regulations 2001 (SI 2001 1293) so as to extend the expiry date of the exceptions provided for in those Regulations for a further period of 30 days until October 1, 2001.

5411. Heavy goods vehicles – drivers hours – exemptions – foot and mouth disease

COMMUNITY DRIVERS' HOURS (FOOT-AND-MOUTH DISEASE) (TEMPORARY EXCEPTION) (NO.2) (AMENDMENT NO.5) REGULATIONS 2001, SI 2001 3260; made under the European Communities Act 1972 s.2. In force: September 30, 2001; £1.50.

Council Regulation 3820/85 ([1985] OJ L370/1) relating to road transport provides that Member States may in urgent cases grant a temporary exception for a period not exceeding 30 days to transport operations carried out in exceptional circumstances. These Regulations, which amend the Community Drivers' Hours (Foot-and-Mouth Disease) (Temporary Exception) (No.2) Regulations 2001 (SI 2001 1293), provide that until October 31, 2001, any time spent driving vehicles for a specified purpose shall not be taken into account for the purposes of the application of Art.6 of the Council Regulation.

5412. Heavy goods vehicles – drivers hours – exemptions – foot and mouth disease

COMMUNITY DRIVERS' HOURS (FOOT-AND-MOUTH DISEASE) (TEMPORARY EXCEPTION) (NO.2) (AMENDMENT NO.6) REGULATIONS 2001, SI 2001 3508; made under the European Communities Act 1972 s.2. In force: October 31, 2001; £1.50.

Council Regulation 3820/85 ([1985] OJ L370/1) on harmonisation of certain social legislation relating to road transport provides that Member States may grant a temporary exception for a period not exceeding 30 days to transport operations carried out in exceptional circumstances. These Regulations, which amend the Community Drivers' Hours (Foot-and-Mouth Disease) (Temporary Exception) (No.2) Regulations 2001 (SI 2001 1293), provide that until October 31, 2001, any time spent driving vehicles for a specified purpose shall not be taken into account for the purposes of the application of Art.6 of the Council Regulation.

5413. Heavy goods vehicles – drivers hours – exemptions – milk collection

DRIVERS' HOURS (GOODS VEHICLES) (MILK COLLECTION) (TEMPORARY EXEMPTION) REGULATIONS 2001, SI 2001 629; made under the Transport Act 1968 s.96. In force: March 6, 2001; £1.50.

These Regulations, which amend the Transport Act 1968, extend the permissible maximum working day of a driver engaged in the collection and transportation of milk, from a maximum of eleven to thirteen hours, to meet the special needs occasioned by the outbreak of foot and mouth disease in Great Britain, or the effects or consequences of such outbreak.

5414. Heavy goods vehicles – drivers hours – exemptions – milk collection

DRIVERS' HOURS (GOODS VEHICLES) (MILK COLLECTION) (TEMPORARY EXEMPTION) (REVOCATION) REGULATIONS 2001, SI 2001 3908; made under the Transport Act 1968 s.96. In force: December 31, 2001; £1.50.

These Regulations revoke the Drivers' Hours (Goods Vehicles) (Milk Collection) (Temporary Exemption) Regulations 2001 (SI 2001 629) which extended the permissible maximum working day of a driver engaged in the collection and transportation of milk to meet the special needs occasioned by the outbreak of foot and mouth disease in Great Britain, or the effects or consequences of such outbreak. These Regulations restore the maximum working day as prescribed by the Transport Act 1968.

5415. Heavy goods vehicles – enforcement

GOODS VEHICLES (ENFORCEMENT POWERS) REGULATIONS 2001, SI 2001 3981; made under the Goods Vehicles (Licensing of Operators) Act 1995 Sch.1A. In force: January 4, 2002; £2.50.

The Goods Vehicles (Licensing of Operators) Act 1995 Sch.1A enables regulations to be made permitting an authorised person to detain a heavy goods vehicle and its contents in circumstances where the person using the vehicle did not hold an operator's licence for that or any other vehicle. These Regulations are made pursuant to that Schedule and empower an authorised person to detain a vehicle and its contents where he has reason to believe it is being operated without a licence; provide for the release of a detained vehicle to an owner in circumstances where at the time the vehicle was detained, the person using the vehicle held an operator's licence or the vehicle was not being, and had not been, used in contravention of s.2 of the 1995 Act; for the immobilisation of vehicles, criminal offences arising from the unlawful removal of, or interference with, immobilisation notices or devices, and the release of immobilised vehicles; for the removal and delivery of vehicles and contents detained and the giving of notice of detention; for the owner of a vehicle to make an application to a traffic commissioner for the return of the vehicle. There is provision for a hearing to be held if a party to an application requests one or the traffic commissioner so decides; for appeals from a traffic commissioner to the Transport Tribunal; for the return of a vehicle detained where the traffic commissioner determines that one or more of the grounds specified in Reg.10(4) is made out; empower authorised persons to sell or destroy vehicles in other cases and requires an authorised person to serve a notice of disposal of a vehicle on specified persons after the vehicle has been disposed of; provide for the return of contents of detained vehicles and the disposal of such contents; for the application of proceeds of sale of any property sold by an authorised person; deal with disputes about the return or disposal of contents of a vehicle or the application of the proceeds of sale of a vehicle or its contents. Such applications are to be made to the Secretary of State. There is provision for an appeal to be made from the Secretary of State's determination to a magistrates' court (in England and Wales) or to a sheriff court (in Scotland); and create a criminal offence to obstruct an authorised person in the exercise of his powers.

5416. Heavy goods vehicles – fees – international journeys

GOODS VEHICLES (AUTHORISATION OF INTERNATIONAL JOURNEYS) (FEES) REGULATIONS 2001, SI 2001 3606; made under the Finance Act 1973 s.56. In force: December 1, 2001; £2.00.

These Regulations, which revoke the Goods Vehicles (Authorisation of International Journeys) (Fees) Regulations 2000 (SI 2000 3207) and the Goods Vehicles (Authorisation of International Journeys) (Fees) (Amendment) Regulations 2001 (SI 2001 309), prescribe the fees to be paid to the Department for Transport, Local Government and the Regions, as from December 1, 2001, for the issue of documents authorising the operation of goods vehicles on journeys between the UK and other member countries of the European Conference of Ministers of Transport. They also prescribe the fees to be paid to the Department for Transport, Local Government and the Regions for the issue of documents authorising the operation of goods vehicles on journeys between the UK and certain states with whom bilateral agreements or arrangements have been concluded, in transit through Austria and in Switzerland. In addition, the Regulations prescribe fees higher than those previously charged.

5417. Heavy goods vehicles – fees – Swiss permits

GOODS VEHICLES (AUTHORISATION OF INTERNATIONAL JOURNEYS) (FEES) (AMENDMENT) REGULATIONS 2001, SI 2001 309; made under the Finance Act 1973 s.56. In force: March 12, 2001; £1.50.

These Regulations, which amend the Goods Vehicles (Authorisation of International Journeys) (Fees) Regulations 2000 (SI 2000 3207), prescribe the fee to be paid for the issue of a Swiss permit in order to gain access to Switzerland for Community heavy goods vehicles because from January 1, 2001 to December 31, 2004 access to Switzerland is controlled by means of quotas of Swiss permits, as allocated to the Community by Switzerland. European Parliament and Council Regulation 2888/2000 ([2000] OJ L336/9).

5418. International carriage by road – dangerous goods – fees

INTERNATIONAL CARRIAGE OF DANGEROUS GOODS BY ROAD (FEES) (AMENDMENT) REGULATIONS 2001, SI 2001 1812; made under the Finance Act 1973 s.56; and the Department of Transport (Fees) Order (SI 1988 643). In force: June 1, 2001; £1.75.

These Regulations, which amend the International Carriage of Dangerous Goods by Road (Fees) Regulations 1988 (SI 1988 370), increase the fee payable where a first inspection in relation to an application for an ADR certificate is carried out on the same day as an examination under the Goods Vehicles (Plating and Testing) Regulations 1988 (SI 1988 370) from £64 to £66. The additional fee payable where a vehicle fails to pass an inspection and arrangements are made for a further inspection to be carried out not more than 14 days after the first inspection is increased to £33, and fees are also increased for the issue of a copy of an ADR certificate which has been lost or destroyed and for an application for an ADR certificate.

5419. International carriage by road – jurisdiction – impact of "pending" proceedings upon later proceedings

[Convention for the International Carriage of Goods by Road 1956 Art.31 (2).] ISL appealed against a decision that its action against AM for a declaration of non liability did not bar AM's application against ISL for an indemnity payment. AM had entered into a contract of carriage for the transport of whisky from Scotland to Austria. AM had made a subcontract with ISL who had made a further subcontract with a Scottish company. The whisky had been stolen whilst still in the UK. AM had paid out compensation under the main contract, and sought an indemnity from ISL by way of proceedings commenced in the English court on October 15, 1999 and served on ISL on 21 October. ISL had issued its proceedings for the declaration in the Austrian court in July 1999, but did not serve AM until December 1999. AM argued that ISL's proceedings were not proceedings that were already "pending" so as to operate as a bar to AM's proceedings under the Convention for the International Carriage of Goods by Road 1956 Art.31 (2).

Held, dismissing the appeal, that in order to give sensible and meaningful effect to international law it was necessary to look at both English and Austrian law in order to interpret the phrase "pending". In Austrian law an action was only "pending" once served, and therefore ISL's application would not have been taken by an Austrian court to have been "pending" at the time of issue and service of AM's application. The language of Art.31 (2), which differentiated between a case that was "pending" and a case that had been "started", pointed towards a similar interpretation. Equally, international law generally suggested that service was a requirement for establishing "pendency", *Zelger v. Salinitri (129/83)* [1984] E.C.R. 2397, [1985] C.L.Y. 1380 applied. Art.31 (2) therefore should be taken as requiring service before a case could be "pending" so as to bar a later application. It followed that ISL's application did not come within the terms of Art.31 (2). It was observed that an application for a declaration of non liability should not be capable of barring a substantive application for relief whenever the former was issued and served, *Frans Maas Logistics (UK) Ltd v. CDR Trucking BV* [1999] 1 All E.R. (Comm) 737, [1999] C.L.Y. 732 approved.

ANDREA MERZARIO LTD v. INTERNATIONALE SPEDITION LEITNER GESELLSCHAFT GmbH, [2001] EWCA Civ 61, [2001] 1 All E.R. (Comm) 883, Rix, L.J., CA.

5420. Motor vehicles – driving tests – fees

MOTOR VEHICLES (DRIVING LICENCES) (AMENDMENT) (NO.4) REGULATIONS 2001, SI 2001 2779; made under the Road Traffic Act 1988 s.89, s.105. In force: August 27, 2001; £1.50.

These Regulations amend the Motor Vehicles (Driving Licences) Regulations 1999 (SI 1999 2864) by increasing the fees payable upon an application for a practical or for a unitary driving test where the test is to be conducted on or after the coming into force of these Regulations.

5421. Motor vehicles – EC type approval

MOTOR VEHICLES (EC TYPE APPROVAL) (AMENDMENT) REGULATIONS 2001, SI 2001 2809; made under the European Communities Act 1972 s.2. In force: August 31, 2001; £1.50.

These Regulations amend the Motor Vehicles (EC Type Approval) Regulations 1998 (SI 1998 2051) by inserting references to certain recent EC Directives.

5422. Motor vehicles – goods vehicles – construction and use

ROAD VEHICLES (CONSTRUCTION AND USE) (AMENDMENT) REGULATIONS 2001, SI 2001 306; made under the Road Traffic Act 1988 s.41. In force: March 1, 2001; £1.50.

These Regulations amend the Road Vehicles (Construction and Use) Regulations 1986 (SI 1986 1078) to provide for certain goods vehicles which are designed or adapted to operate at a weight of between 3,500 kg and 5,500 kg when laden, and for which the most recent Minister's approval certificate was one issued by virtue of the Motor Vehicles (Approval) Regulations 2001 (SI 2001 25), to bear a plate showing a weight of 3,500 kg. The Goods Vehicles (Plating and Testing) (Amendment) Regulations 2001 (SI 2001 307), made at the same time as these Regulations, excludes such vehicles from the provisions of the Goods Vehicles (Plating and Testing) Regulations 1988 (SI 1988 1478).

5423. Motor vehicles – goods vehicles – plating and testing

GOODS VEHICLES (PLATING AND TESTING) (AMENDMENT) REGULATIONS 2001, SI 2001 307; made under the Road Traffic Act 1988 s.49, s.50, s.63A. In force: March 1, 2001; £1.50.

These Regulations amend the Goods Vehicles (Plating and Testing) Regulations 1988 (SI 1988 1478) by excluding from the application of those Regulations certain goods vehicles which are designed or adapted to operate at a weight of between 3,500 kg and 5,500 kg when laden and for which the most recent Minister's approval certificate was one issued under the Motor Vehicles (Approval) Regulations 2001 (SI 2001 25). In consequence, such vehicles cannot be plated in accordance with the 1988 Regulations until approved under the Motor Vehicles (Type Approval for Goods Vehicles) (Great Britain) Regulations 1988 (SI 1982 1271). The Road Vehicles (Construction and Use) (Amendment) Regulations 2001 (SI 2001 306) made at the same time as these Regulations, provides for the vehicles to bear a plate showing a weight of 3,500 kg.

5424. Motor vehicles – goods vehicles – plating and testing – fees

GOODS VEHICLES (PLATING AND TESTING) (AMENDMENT) REGULATIONS 2001, SI 2001 1650; made under the Road Traffic Act 1988 s.49, s.51, s.53. In force: May 28, 2001; £1.75.

These Regulations, which amend the Goods Vehicles (Plating and Testing) Regulations 1988 (SI 1988 1478), amend the fees payable for first examinations, periodical tests or retests, alterations of plated weights and plating certificates.

5425. Motor vehicles – MOT certificates – withdrawal of authorisation to test – efficacy of prior written warning

H, together with his company, JH, sought judicial review of the Secretary of State's decision to withdraw their respective authorisations as nominated MOT vehicle tester and MOT examiner. Previously when operating as a partnership, H and the business had received numerous notices of contemplated withdrawal of authorisation in respect of alleged shortcomings in vehicle testing including a final written warning requiring an assurance of future good conduct. The partnership had been dissolved and the business had continued under H's control in the form of a limited company. Two further notices were then served upon H and JH containing allegations of the improper testing of vehicles and they were notified that the prior written warning would be taken into account. The authorisations were subsequently withdrawn under the MOT Testing Guide paragraphs 42 and 48. On appeal the notices were held to be justified under paragraphs 45 and 49 of the Guide. It was contended that (1) as the final determination had placed reliance on different paragraphs of the Guide to those given in the initial notice of withdrawal, there should have been an opportunity to make further representations; (2) the Secretary of State had not been entitled to take the written warning into account as it had been issued to the partnership before JH came into existence, and (3) they should have been entitled to see the case summary and recommendations prepared prior to the final decision.

Held, dismissing the application, that (1) the Guide should not be treated as a penal code creating specific offences but should be seen as giving guidance on the general approach to be taken. Moreover, the applicants had not been prejudiced by not being afforded the opportunity to give further representations; (2) the partnership had been authorised as an examiner on the basis of H's capacity as an authorised vehicle tester. It would be unreasonable if a written warning could be disregarded following transfer of the business in which H was the active partner to a company under H's control, and (3) although full disclosure was desirable, on the facts of the case, no unfairness had been caused.

R. v. VEHICLE INSPECTORATE, *ex p.* HEALY [2001] R.T.R. 17, Smith, J., QBD.

5426. Motor vehicles – M.O.T. standardisation – Commission Directive

Commission Directive 2001/11 of 14 February 2001 adapting to technical progress Council Directive 96/96 on the approximation of the laws of the Member States relating to roadworthiness tests for motor vehicles and their trailers -functional testing of commercial vehicles' speed limitation device. [2001] OJ L48/20.

5427. Motor vehicles – M.O.T. standardisation – Commission Directive

Commission Directive 2001/9 of 12 February 2001 adapting to technical progress Council Directive 96/96 on the approximation of the laws of the Member States relating to roadworthiness tests for motor vehicles and their trailers. [2001] OJ L48/18.

5428. Motor vehicles – registration marks

ROAD VEHICLES (DISPLAY OF REGISTRATION MARKS) REGULATIONS 2001, SI 2001 561; made under the Vehicle Excise and Registration Act 1994 s.23, s.57. In force: Reg.1 (1) (a): March 21, 2001; Reg.17: March 21, 2001; remainder: September 1, 2001; £4.50.

These Regulations revoke and replace Reg.17 to Reg.22 of the Road Vehicles (Registration and Licensing) Regulations 1971 (SI 1971 450) and Reg.18 to Reg.23 of the Road Vehicles (Registration and Licensing) Regulations (Northern Ireland) 1973 (SR&O (NI) 1973 490) by introducing a mandatory requirement for the use of registration plates conforming to a British Standard specification or an equivalent standard laid down by an EEA State on all vehicles first registered on or after September 1, 2001 and on other vehicles registered on or after January 1, 1973 if an existing plate is replaced. They introduce a provision making it lawful for rear plates to be fixed in the space provided on vehicles constructed in accordance with the requirements of relevant EC type-approval directives and to be lit in a manner provided for in those directives, provide for the introduction of a new registration mark format, introduce new mandatory character sizes, a standard character font and prohibit plates being fitted in a manner so as to obscure or disguise the mark.

5429. Motor vehicles – registration marks

ROAD VEHICLES (DISPLAY OF REGISTRATION MARKS) (AMENDMENT) REGULATIONS 2001, SI 2001 1079; made under the Vehicle Excise and Registration Act 1994 s.23, s.57. In force: Reg.1 (1) (a): March 21, 2001; Reg.17: March 21, 2001; Remainder: September 1, 2001; £1.50.

These Regulations make minor amendments to the Road Vehicles (Display of Registration Marks) Regulations 2001 (SI 2001 561) to correct errors in the original text.

5430. Motor vehicles – road safety – lighting

ROAD VEHICLES LIGHTING (AMENDMENT) REGULATIONS 2001, SI 2001 560; made under the Road Traffic Act 1988 s.41. In force: March 21, 2001; £1.50.

These Regulations, which amend the Road Vehicles Lighting Regulations 1989 (SI 1989 1796) by permitting on the rear of a vehicle a plate displaying the international distinguishing sign of the UK in accordance with Council Regulation 2411/98, have been made in consequence of the making of the Road Vehicles (Display of Registration Marks) Regulations 2001 (SI 2001 561).

5431. Motor vehicles – testing – fees

MOTOR VEHICLES (TESTS) (AMENDMENT) (NO.2) REGULATIONS 2001, SI 2001 3330; made under the RoadTraffic Act 1988 s.45, s.46. In force: November 1, 2001; £1.75.

These Regulations amend the MotorVehicles (Tests) Regulations 1981 (SI 1981 1694) which make provision for certain motor vehicles to be examined by persons authorised by the Secretary of State and for test certificates to be issued for vehicles that are found to meet certain requirements. They increase, from November 1, 2001, the fees payable for test examinations of vehicles except those in classVI orVIa.

5432. Motor vehicles – trailers – heating sytems – Council Directive

European Parliament and Council Directive 2001/56 of 27 September 2001 relating to heating systems for motor vehicles and their trailers, amending Council Directive 70/156 and repealing Council Directive 78/548. [2001] OJ L292/21.

5433. Motor vehicles – trailers – safety glazing – Commission Directive

Commission Directive 2001/92 of 30 October 2001 adapting to technical progress Council Directive 92/22 on safety glazing and glazing materials on motor vehicles and their trailers and Council Directive 70/156 relating to the type-approval of motor vehicles and their trailers. [2001] OJ L291/24.

5434. Motor vehicles – type approval – standards – construction

MOTOR VEHICLES (APPROVAL) REGULATIONS 2001, SI 2001 25; made under the Road Traffic Act 1988 s.54, s.61, s.63, s.66. In force: February 1, 2001; £7.50.

These Regulations, which replace the Motor Vehicles (Approval) Regulations 1996 (SI 1996 3013 as amended), establish a revised system for approving the construction of single vehicles before they enter into service. They apply to passenger vehicles and dual-purpose vehicles constructed to carry no more than eight passengers excluding the driver, certain three wheeled vehicles having a maximum unladen weight of more than 410 kg, light goods vehicles and certain other goods vehicles with a design gross weight not exceeding 5,500 kg. They specify the dates appointed for the purposes of the Road Traffic Act 1988 s.63(1), on or after which it is an offence to use a vehicle of a relevant class without the appropriate certificate and specify February 1, 2001 as the day appointed for all other vehicles to which these Regulations apply which are not of a class for which a day had previously been appointed and provide that a licence under the Vehicles Excise and Registration Act 1994 is not to be granted unless, in the first application made for it after the relevant appointed day, there is produced evidence that a certificate is in force for the vehicle.

5435. Motor vehicles – type approval – standards – fees

MOTOR VEHICLES (APPROVAL) (FEES) REGULATIONS 2001, SI 2001 2486; made under the Road Traffic Act 1988 s.61; the Department of Transport (Fees) Order 1988; and the Finance Act 1990 s.128. In force: August 1, 2001; £2.00.

The Motor Vehicles (Approval) Regulations 2001 (SI 2001 25) established a revised statutory system for approving the construction of single vehicles before they enter into service. These Regulations, which revoke and replace the Motor Vehicles (Approval) (Fees) Regulation 1997 (SI 1997 1459), prescribe the fees payable in connection with applications and appeals made in accordance with the 2001 Regulations and prescribe the fee payable for the replacement of a Minister's approval certificate which has been lost or defaced and make provision for the repayment of fees in certain circumstances.

5436. Motor vehicles – tyres – fitting requirements – Council Directive

European Parliament and Council Directive 2001/43 of 27 June 2001 amending Council Directive 92/33 relating to tyres for motor vehicles and their trailers and to their fitting. [2001] OJ L211/25.

5437. Motor vehicles – vehicle tests

MOTOR VEHICLES (TESTS) (AMENDMENT) REGULATIONS 2001, SI 2001 1648; made under the Road Traffic Act 1988 s.45, s.46; and the Department of Transport (Fees) Order (SI 1988 643). In force: May 28, 2001; £1.75.

These Regulations amend the Motor Vehicles (Tests) Regulations 1981 (SI 1981 1694) to make provision for certain motor vehicles to be examined by persons authorised by the Secretary of State and for test certificates to be issued for vehicles found to meet certain requirements and amend the fees for examinations.

5438. Motor vehicles – weight limits

ROAD VEHICLES (AUTHORISED WEIGHT) (AMENDMENT) REGULATIONS 2001, SI 2001 1125; made under the Road Traffic Act 1988 s.41. In force: April 17, 2001; £1.50.

These Regulations correct a number of errors in the drafting of the Road Traffic (Authorised Weight) (Amendment) Regulations 2000 (SI 2000 3234) which amend the the Road Traffic (Authorised Weight) Regulations 1998 (SI 1998 3111).

5439. Motorcycles – EC type approval

MOTOR CYCLES ETC. (EC TYPE APPROVAL) (AMENDMENT) REGULATIONS 2001, SI 2001 368; made under the European Communities Act 1972 s.2. In force: March 15, 2001; £1.50.

These Regulations, which amend the Motor Cycles Etc. (EC Type Approval) Regulations 1999 (SI 1999 2920), extend the meaning of the expression "separate Directive" by inserting a reference to Directive 2000/7 [2000] OJ L106/3 as a new item in Sch.1 to the 1999 Regulations.

5440. Motorcycles – EC type approval

MOTOR CYCLES ETC. (EC TYPE APPROVAL) (AMENDMENT) (NO.2) REGULATIONS 2001, SI 2001 1547; made under the European Communities Act 1972 s.2. In force: May 24, 2001; £1.50.

These Regulations, which amend the Motor Cycles Etc. (EC Type Approval) Regulations 1999 (SI 1999 2920), insert references to recent EC Directives in Sch.1 of the 1999 Regulations.

5441. Passenger transport – driving periods – rest breaks – effect of rest before driving period commenced

[Transport Act 1968 s.96(11A); Council Regulation 3820/85 on social legislation relating to road transport Art.6(1), Art.8(3), Art.8(4).]

VI appealed against a ruling allowing YP's appeal against 12 convictions for breach of the Transport Act 1968 s.96(11A) by failing to ensure that the driver of a passenger coach took the required amount of rest between journeys. The Crown Court had allowed the appeal on the basis that the amount of rest taken prior to the driving undertaken in the relevant period could be taken into account when determining whether the mandatory weekly rest period under Council Regulation 3820/85 Art.6(1) had been observed. VI contended that the object of the Regulation was to ensure that the weekly rest period was taken after driving and that this was a separate and distinct obligation from the requirement in Art.8(3) of the Regulation. YP contended that Art.8(4) of the Regulation entitled the company to take into account a period of rest before driving began and which spanned from the end of one week into the beginning of another.

Held, allowing the appeal, that if the argument raised by YP in relation to Art.8(4) were permitted to succeed it would undermine and frustrate the purpose of the Regulation. Art.6(1) was a distinct and paramount obligation which required a driver to take a weekly rest period after driving in the same way that breaks for rest were required within each 24 hour period, *Criminal Proceedings against Hume (Graeme Edgar) (C193/99)* [2000] All E.R. (E.C.) 852, [2000] 11 C.L. 527 applied.

VEHICLE INSPECTORATE v. YORK PULLMAN LTD [2001] EWHC Admin 113, Newman, J., QBD.

5442. Passenger vehicles – construction and use – braking systems

ROAD VEHICLES (CONSTRUCTION AND USE) (AMENDMENT) (NO.4) REGULATIONS 2001, SI 2001 3208; made under the Road Traffic Act 1988 s.41. In force: Reg.1: October 16, 2001; Reg.2: October 16, 2001; Reg.8: October 16, 2001; Reg.10: October 16, 2001; remainder: May 1, 2002; £2.00.

These Regulations, which amend the Road Vehicles (Construction and Use) Regulations 1986 (SI 1986 1078) in relation to brakes, insert a number of new definitions and introduce two new exemptions from the requirements concerning anti-lock braking systems.

5443. Passenger vehicles – construction and use – emissions

ROAD VEHICLES (CONSTRUCTION AND USE) (AMENDMENT) (NO.3) REGULATIONS 2001, SI 2001 1825; made under the Road Traffic Act 1988 s.41. In force: August 1, 2001; £1.50.

These Regulations, which amend the Road Vehicles (Construction and Use) Regulations 1986 (SI 1986 1078), add a reference to Directive 2001/1 ([2001] OJ L35/34) amending Directive 70/220 concerning measures to be taken against air pollution be emissions from motor vehicles and adds the Directive to the list of Community Directives specified in Sch.2. They also amend the definition of "the emissions publication" to refer to the most recent edition of the publication entitled "In-Service Exhaust Emission Standards for Road Vehicles". The publication specifies, with respect to vehicles with spark ignition engines, the maximum permitted carbon monoxide content of exhaust emissions at idling speed and the limits for the ratio of air to petrol vapour entering the combustion chamber, in relation to each of the vehicle models named in the publication.

5444. Passenger vehicles – construction and use – seat belts

ROAD VEHICLES (CONSTRUCTION AND USE) (AMENDMENT) (NO.2) REGULATIONS 2001, SI 2001 1043; made under the Road Traffic Act 1988 s.41. In force: October 1, 2001; £2.00.

These Regulations, which amend the Road Vehicles (Construction and Use) Regulations 1986 (SI 1986 1078) in relation to seat belts and their anchorage points in light of Directive 96/36, Directive 96/38 and Directive 2000/3, substitute a new regulation which specifies what anchorage points are to be fitted to which vehicles and the technical requirements for anchorage points. In addition, they make amendments so as to enable rearward-facing seats meeting specified requirements to count towards the minimum number of forward-facing seats with seat belts that must be provided on minibuses and coaches used to carry groups of children on organised trips.

5445. Passenger vehicles – goods vehicles – tachographs – fees

PASSENGER AND GOODS VEHICLES (RECORDING EQUIPMENT) (APPROVAL OF FITTERS AND WORKSHOPS) (FEES) (AMENDMENT) REGULATIONS 2001,

SI 2001 1810; made under the Finance Act 1973 s.56; and the Department of Transport (Fees) Order (SI 1988 643). In force: June 1, 2001; £1.50.

These Regulations, which amend the Passenger and Goods Vehicles (Recording Equipment) (Approval of Fitters and Workshops) (Fees) Regulations 1986 (SI 1986 2128), increase the fees for the approval of fitters or workshops for the installation or repair of recording equipment. The fee for the issue of an approval is increased by 2.9 per cent from £244 to £251.

5446. Passenger vehicles – roadworthiness – fees

PUBLIC SERVICE VEHICLES (CONDITIONS OF FITNESS, EQUIPMENT, USE AND CERTIFICATION) (AMENDMENT) REGULATIONS 2001, SI 2001 1649; made under the Public Passenger Vehicles Act 1981 s.10, s.52, s.60. In force: May 28, 2001; £1.50.

These Regulations, which amend the Public Service Vehicles (Conditions of Fitness, Equipment, Use and Certification) Regulations 1981 (SI 1981 257), increase the fee payable for a certificate of initial fitness from £164 to £169 in respect of a public service vehicle which, when equipped with seat belts, is not of a type of vehicle in respect of which the Secretary of State is satisfied that the vehicle manufacturer holds certain approvals relating to seat belt anchorage points. The fee payable for a certificate of initial fitness is increased from £131 to £135 on the first application in any other case and from £131 to £135 on any subsequent application when the test which that application will require includes a test of stability. Fees payable for type approvals are also increased.

5447. Public transport – rapid transit system

SOUTH HAMPSHIRE RAPID TRANSIT ORDER 2001, SI 2001 3627; made under the Transport and Works Act 1992 s.1, s.3, s.5, Sch.1 para.1, Sch.1 para.2, Sch.1 para.3, Sch.1 para.4, Sch.1 para.5, Sch.1 para.7, Sch.1 para.8, Sch.1 para.9, Sch.1 para.10, Sch.1 para.11, Sch.1 para.12, Sch.1 para.13, Sch.1 para.14, Sch.1 para.15, Sch.1 para.16, Sch.1 para.17. In force: July 24, 2001; £9.00.

This Order authorises Hampshire County Council and Portsmouth City Council to construct and operate a rapid transit system between Fareham, Gosport and Portsmouth and, for that purpose compulsorily or by agreement to acquire land and rights in land. It contains a number of protective provisions for the benefit of affected undertakings.

5448. Public transport – transport policy – public private partnerships – mayor's responsibility to provide safe and efficient transport in London

[Greater London Authority Act 1999 s.173(1).]

TFL, which had been established under the Greater London Authority Act 1999 and of which the Mayor of London was chairman, applied for judicial review of the decision of LUL, a company formed with the aim of providing public transport services in Greater London, and LRT, a statutory body corporate with responsibility for London's transport, to enter into 30 year contracts for the private provision, construction, renewal, improvement and maintenance of the London Underground, with responsibility for management of the system remaining the responsibility of LUL. TFL, which was empowered under s.173(1) of the Act to "provide or secure the provision of public passenger transport services to, from or within Greater London", argued that the decision would prevent the Mayor of London from developing and implementing his own policies for a safe and efficient transport system, and that if LUL or LRT were to enter into contracts inconsistent with the Mayor's transport strategy they would be usurping his powers.

Held, refusing the application, that there was no implied duty requiring LRT or LUL to act in accordance with the Mayor of London's transport strategy made under the Act; the Act merely required the bodies in question to have regard to the strategy. It followed that LUL and LRT did have the power to enter into contracts inconsistent with the Mayor's strategy. It was apparent that the

Secretary of State rather than the Mayor could approve the way in which LRT would operate the Underground and could direct the passing of "public private sector" contracts to bidders who were successful. It was the Secretary of State alone who could refuse such agreements by refusing to designate them. The Mayor only gained such power when the transition period specified under the Act for the transfer of transport responsibility had ended.

R. (ON THE APPLICATION OF TRANSPORT FOR LONDON) v. LONDON UNDERGROUND LTD, [2001] EWHC Admin 637, *The Times*, August 2, 2001, Sullivan, J., QBD (Admin Ct).

5449. Public transport – travel concessions – elderly and disabled passengers – Wales

MANDATORY TRAVEL CONCESSIONS (REIMBURSEMENT ARRANGEMENTS) (WALES) REGULATIONS 2001, SI 2001 3764 (W.312); made under the Transport Act 2000 s.149, s.150. In force: November 30, 2001; £3.50.

The Transport Act 2000 s.145 provides for mandatory travel concessions to be provided by operators of eligible services to certain classes of passenger, including those who are elderly or disabled. Section 149 of the Act requires travel concession authorities to reimburse operators for providing the concessions in accordance with arrangements agreed with the operators or determined by the authorities. These Regulations set out the overall objective for reimbursement arrangements, require that reimbursement payments must meet the costs incurred by operators in providing mandatory travel concessions and make provision for the periods in respect of which payments are to be calculated and the dates when they must be made. The Regulations require authorities to adopt a standard method for determining the total number of journeys made by those entitled to the concessions and the fares values to be attributed to those journeys and permit authorities to establish criteria for exempting operators.

5450. Railways – accessibility – disabled persons – exemptions

RAIL VEHICLE ACCESSIBILITY (C2C CLASS 357/0 VEHICLES) EXEMPTION ORDER 2001, SI 2001 3955; made under the Discrimination Act 1995 s.47. In force: January 1, 2002; £1.75.

This Order, which revokes the Rail Vehicle Accessibility (LTS Rail Class 357 Vehicles) Exemption Order 2000 (SI 2000 182), authorises the use of specified rail vehicles forming Class 357/0 multiple-units although they do not conform with provisions of the Rail Vehicle Accessibility Regulations 1998 (SI 1998 2456). This is because the passenger operation of some doors is by means of non-compliant beam-operated sensors; the door control devices for doors in the sides of the vehicles are positioned above the maximum permissible height; and the vehicles have neither the required minimum number of priority seats nor any tables at those priority seats they do have. The Order sets time limits on the exemptions from those provisions and imposes a condition.

5451. Railways – accessibility – disabled persons – exemptions

RAIL VEHICLE ACCESSIBILITY (CONNEX SOUTH EASTERN CLASS 375 VEHICLES) EXEMPTION (AMENDMENT) ORDER 2001, SI 2001 250; made under the Disability Discrimination Act 1995 s.47. In force: April 1, 2001; £1.50.

This Order, which amends the Rail Vehicle Accessibility (Connex South Eastern Class 375 Vehicles) Exemption Order 2000 (SI 2000 2050), extends the date on which one of the exemptions in that Order expires to September 30, 2001.

5452. Railways – accessibility – disabled persons – exemptions

RAIL VEHICLE ACCESSIBILITY (CROYDON TRAMLINK CLASS CR4000 VEHICLES) EXEMPTION ORDER 2001, SI 2001 3952; made under the Disability Discrimination Act 1995 s.47. In force: January 1, 2002; £1.75.

This Order, which revokes the Rail Vehicle Accessibility (Croydon Tramlink Class CR4000 Vehicles) Exemption Order 2000 (SI 2000 6), authorises the use of specified rail vehicles of Bombardier Class CR4000 although they do not conform with certain provisions of the Rail Vehicle Accessibility Regulations 1998 (SI 1998 2456). This is because the request-stop controls on handrails beside priority seats are below the minimum required height above the floor; the next stop is not announced while the tram is travelling to that stop; the wheelchair space does not have a structure or fitting to prevent a wheelchair moving or tipping; and the floor adjacent to the wheelchair compatible doorway has a slope exceeding that specified. The Order sets a time limit of one year on one exemption from those provisions and imposes conditions, the most significant of which is to require notification to the Secretary of State of a relevant injury in any part of a rail vehicle to which this Order applies.

5453. Railways – accessibility – disabled persons – exemptions

RAIL VEHICLE ACCESSIBILITY (GATWICK EXPRESS CLASS 460 VEHICLES) EXEMPTION ORDER 2001, SI 2001 847; made under the Disability Discrimination Act 1995 s.47. In force: March 31, 2001; £2.00.

This Order authorises the use of specified rail vehicles forming Class 460 electrical multiple-units although they do not conform with the Rail Vehicle Accessibility Regulations 1998 (SI 1998 2546) and sets time limits on the authorisation. In addition, it consolidates and replaces the provisions of the Rail Vehicle Accessibility (Gatwick Express Class 460 Vehicles) Exemption Order 2000 (SI 2000 770), the Rail Vehicle Accessibility (Gatwick Express Class 460 Vehicles) Exemption (Amendment) Order 2000 (SI 2000 2327) and the Rail Vehicle Accessibility (Gatwick Express Class 460 Vehicles) Exemption (Amendment No. 2) Order 2000 (SI 2000 3187).

5454. Railways – accessibility – disabled persons – exemptions

RAIL VEHICLE ACCESSIBILITY (GATWICK EXPRESS CLASS 460 VEHICLES) EXEMPTION (AMENDMENT) ORDER 2001, SI 2001 3954; made under the Disability Discrimination Act 1995 s.47. In force: January 1, 2002; £1.50.

This Order amends The Rail Vehicle Accessibility (Gatwick Express Class 460 Vehicles) Exemption Order 2001 (SI 2001 847) by extending the expiry date for the exemption granted from the Rail Vehicle Accessibility Regulations 1998 (SI 1998 2456, as amended by SI 2000 3215) in respect of audible warning devices on passenger doors from December 31, 2001 to April 28, 2011. It makes it a condition of the exemption that the operator must, so far as is practicable, make staff available on the platform to assist blind or partially sighted persons.

5455. Railways – accessibility – disabled persons – exemptions

RAIL VEHICLE ACCESSIBILITY (GREAT WESTERN TRAINS COMPANY CLASS 180 VEHICLES) EXEMPTION ORDER 2001, SI 2001 1747; made under the Disability Discrimination Act 1995 s.47. In force: June 1, 2001; £1.50.

This Order authorises the use of specified rail vehicles forming Class 180 diesel multiple-units trains, although they do not conform with certain requirements of the Rail Vehicle Accessibility Regulations 1998 (SI 1998 2546) because there is not the required headroom above the priority seats and the passageway between some wheelchair spaces and the toilet for disabled persons is narrower than permitted.

5456. Railways – accessibility – disabled persons – exemptions

RAIL VEHICLE ACCESSIBILITY (MIDLAND MAINLINE CLASS 170/1 VEHICLES) EXEMPTION ORDER 2001, SI 2001 499; made under the Disability Discrimination Act 1995 s.47. In force: March 15, 2001; £1.75.

This Order authorises the use of specified rail vehicles which form part of Class 170/1 diesel multiple-units trains, although they do not confirm with certain requirements of the Rail Vehicle Accessibility Regulations 1998 (SI 1998 2456) because there is not the required exterior visual passenger information system, and there are not enough wheelchair spaces.

5457. Railways – accessibility – disabled persons – exemptions

RAIL VEHICLE ACCESSIBILITY (MIDLAND METRO T69 VEHICLES) EXEMPTION ORDER 2001, SI 2001 785; made under the Disability Discrimination Act 1995 s.47. In force: March 30, 2001; £1.75.

This Order authorises the use of T69 vehicles numbers 1 to 16 on Line 1 of the Midland Metro System, although they do not conform with the Rail Vehicle Accessibility Regulations 1998 (SI 1998 2546) and sets time limits on the authorisation. In addition, it consolidates and replaces the provisions of the Rail Vehicle Accessibility (Midland Metro T69 Vehicles) Exemption Order 1999 (SI 1999 520), the Rail Vehicle Accessibility (Midland Metro T69 Vehicles) Exemption (Amendment) Order 1999 (SI 1999 586) and the Rail Vehicle Accessibility (Midland Metro T69 Vehicles) (Exemption No.2) Order 1999 (SI 1999 1256).

5458. Railways – accessibility – disabled persons – exemptions

RAIL VEHICLE ACCESSIBILITY (NORTH WESTERN TRAINS CLASS 175/0 AND CLASS 175/1 VEHICLES) EXEMPTION ORDER 2001, SI 2001 3434; made under the Disability Discrimination Act 1995 s.47. In force: November 9, 2001; £1.50.

This Order authorises, until the end of April 30, 2011, the use of specified rail vehicles forming Class 175/0 and Class 175/1, although they do not comply with a requirement of the Rail Vehicle Accessibility Regulations 1998 because there is not the required headroom above some priority seats.

5459. Railways – accessibility – disabled persons – exemptions

RAIL VEHICLE ACCESSIBILITY (SCOTRAIL CLASS 170/4 VEHICLES) EXEMPTION ORDER 2001, SI 2001 3953; made under the Disability Discrimination Act 1995 s.47. In force: January 1, 2002; £1.75.

This Order, which revokes the Rail Vehicle Accessibility (ScotRail Class 170/4 Vehicles) Exemption Order 2000 (SI 2000 1769), authorises the use of specified rail vehicles forming Class 170/4 diesel multiple-units, although they do not conform with certain provisions of the Rail Vehicle Accessibility Regulations 1998 (SI 1998 2456). It sets time limits on the exemption from those provisions and imposes conditions.

5460. Railways – accessibility – disabled persons – exemptions

RAIL VEHICLE ACCESSIBILITY (SCOTRAIL CLASS 334 VEHICLES) EXEMPTION ORDER 2001, SI 2001 277; made under the Disability Discrimination Act 1995 s.47. In force: February 26, 2001; £1.50.

This Order authorises the use of specified rail vehicles forming Class 334 electric multiple units, although they do not conform with certain requirements of the Rail Vehicle Accessibility Regulations 1998 (SI 1998 2456), because audible warning sounds are not made on the outside of the vehicle, some door control devices are not illuminated, steps in the vehicles are not illuminated and some handrails are not fitted at the required height.

5461. Railways – accessibility – disabled persons – exemptions

RAIL VEHICLE ACCESSIBILITY (SOUTH WEST TRAINS CLASS 458 VEHICLES) EXEMPTION ORDER 2001, SI 2001 848; made under the Disability Discrimination Act 1995 s.47. In force: April 1, 2001; £1.75.

This Order authorises the use of specified rail vehicles forming Class 458 electrical multiple-units, although they do not conform with certain requirements of the Rail Vehicle Accessibility Regulations 1998 (SI 1998 2546) and sets time limits on the authorisation. In addition, it consolidates and replaces the Rail Vehicle Accessibility (South West Trains Class 458 Vehicles) Exemption Order 1999 (SI 1999 2404) and the Rail Vehicle Accessibility (South West Trains Class 458 Vehicles) Exemption (Amendment) Order 2000 (SI 2000 2398).

5462. Railways – accidents – prohibition notice following suspension of activities – legality

See HEALTH AND SAFETY AT WORK: Railtrack Plc v. Smallwood. §3317

5463. Railways – British Railways Board – membership

BRITISH RAILWAYS BOARD (REDUCTION OF MEMBERSHIP) ORDER 2001, SI 2001 217; made under the Transport Act 2000 s.241. In force: February 1, 2001; £1.50.

This Order reduces the membership of the British Railways Board to a chairman and one or more other persons appointed by the Secretary of State.

5464. Railways – Channel Tunnel Rail Link – Stratford station

CHANNEL TUNNEL RAIL LINK (STRATFORD STATION AND SUBSIDIARY WORKS) ORDER 2001, SI 2001 1451; made under the Transport and Works Act 1992 s.1, s.3, s.5, Sch.1 para.1, Sch.1 para.2, Sch.1 para.3, Sch.1 para.4, Sch.1 para.5, Sch.1 para.7, Sch.1 para.8, Sch.1 para.9, Sch.1 para.10, Sch.1 para.11, Sch.1 para.12, Sch.1 para.15, Sch.1 para.16, Sch.1 para.17. In force: March 22, 2001; £3.00.

This Order, which provides for certain works supplementary to the works provided for in the Channel Tunnel Rail Link Act 1996, makes provision for a station at Stratford in London for use in connection with the rail link, for a connection from the rail link to the North London Line to provide access to the West Coast Main Line, and for certain ancillary works, including a pedestrian link from the proposed new station at Stratford to the existing Stratford suburban station.

5465. Railways – closure of operational passenger networks – St. Pancras station

RAILWAYS (CLOSURE PROVISIONS) (EXEMPTIONS) (ST. PANCRAS) ORDER 2001, SI 2001 1768; made under the Railways Act 1993 s.49, s.143. In force: June 1, 2001 as regards Art.1 (a); remainder: July 1, 2001; £1.50.

This Order, which provides that the Railways Act 1993 s.41 is not to apply to St. Pancras railway station in London, also provides that s.39 of that Act is not apply to certain of the railway lines running into that station.

5466. Railways – insolvency – administration – protected companies

RAILWAY ADMINISTRATION ORDER RULES 2001, SI 2001 3352; made under the Insolvency Act 1986 s.411; and the Railways Act 1993 s.59. In force: October 7, 2001; £7.50.

These Rules, which set out the procedure for the conduct of railway administration proceedings for protected railway companies under the Insolvency Act 1986 and the Railways Act 1993, apply the relevant rules contained in the 1986 Rules with modifications.

5467. Railways – light railways – Greater Manchester – Ashton Moss variation

GREATER MANCHESTER (LIGHT RAPID TRANSIT SYSTEM) (ASHTON MOSS VARIATION) ORDER 2001, SI 2001 224; made under the Transport and Works Act 1992 s.1, s.5, Sch.1 para.1, Sch.1 para.2, Sch.1 para.3, Sch.1 para.4, Sch.1 para.6, Sch.1 para.7, Sch.1 para.8, Sch.1 para.9, Sch.1 para.10, Sch.1 para.11, Sch.1 para.12, Sch.1 para.13, Sch.1 para.15, Sch.1 para.16, Sch.1 para.17. In force: January 24, 2001; £1.75.

This Order amends the Greater Manchester (Light Rapid Transit System) (Ashton-under-Lyne Extension) Order 1998 (SI 1998 1936) so as to authorise Greater Manchester Passenger Transport Executive to construct works intended to form part of the proposed Piccadilly to Ashton-under-Lyne extension of its Metrolink rapid transit system on an alternative alignment across Ashton Moss to that originally authorised by the 1998 Order. Powers including compulsory purchase, contained in the 1998 Order, apply in relation to the works for the alternative alignment as now authorised.

5468. Railways – light railways – Greater Manchester – compulsory acquisition of land

GREATER MANCHESTER (LIGHT RAPID TRANSIT SYSTEM) (LAND ACQUISITION) ORDER 2001, SI 2001 1369; made under the Transport and Works Act 1992 s.1, s.5, Sch.1 para.3, Sch.1 para.4, Sch.1 para.5, Sch.1 para.7, Sch.1 para.11. In force: March 2, 2001; £2.50.

This Order confers fresh powers of compulsory acquisition on Greater Manchester Passenger Transport Executive for the purposes of the Greater Manchester (Light Rapid Transit System) Act 1994. The land affected was subject to powers of compulsory acquisition under that Act which are now time expired.

5469. Railways – light railways – Greater Manchester – Mumps surface crossing

GREATER MANCHESTER (LIGHT RAPID TRANSIT SYSTEM) (MUMPS SURFACE CROSSING) ORDER 2001, SI 2001 1368; made under the Transport and Works Act 1992 s.1, s.5, Sch.1 para.1, Sch.1 para.2, Sch.1 para.3, Sch.1 para.4, Sch.1 para.6, Sch.1 para.7, Sch.1 para.8, Sch.1 para.11, Sch.1 para.12, Sch.1 para.13, Sch.1 para.15, Sch.1 para.16, Sch.1 para.17. In force: March 2, 2001; £3.00.

This Order authorises Greater Manchester Passenger Transport Executive to construct works and compulsorily to acquire land and rights in land for the purpose of those works comprising an alternative arrangement (including a surface level tramway) for part of the works authorised by the Greater Manchester (Light Rapid Transit System) Act 1994 at and in the vicinity of the Mumps roundabout in Oldham.

5470. Railways – light railways – Greater Manchester – Trafford Park

GREATER MANCHESTER (LIGHT RAPID TRANSIT SYSTEM) (TRAFFORD PARK) ORDER 2001, SI 2001 1367; made under the Transport and Works Act 1992 s.1, s.5, Sch.1 para.1, Sch.1 para.2, Sch.1 para.3, Sch.1 para.4, Sch.1 para.6, Sch.1 para.7, Sch.1 para.8, Sch.1 para.11, Sch.1 para.12, Sch.1 para.13, Sch.1 para.15, Sch.1 para.16, Sch.1 para.17. In force: March 2, 2001; £3.00.

This Order authorises Greater Manchester Passenger Transport Executive to construct works comprising a modification of a tramroad authorised by the Greater Manchester (Light Rapid Transit System) Act 1992 in the vicinity of the Bridgewater Canal and confers on the Executive new compulsory purchase powers for the works authorised by the 1992 Act to replace powers which are now time expired.

5471. **Railways – light railways – Leeds Supertram – compulsory acquisition of land**

LEEDS SUPERTRAM (LAND ACQUISITION AND ROAD WORKS) ORDER 2001, SI 2001 1348; made under the Transport and Works Act 1992 s.1, s.5, Sch.1 para.1, Sch.1 para.2, Sch.1 para.3, Sch.1 para.4, Sch.1 para.5, Sch.1 para.7, Sch.1 para.8, Sch.1 para.10, Sch.1 para.11, Sch.1 para.13, Sch.1 para.15, Sch.1 para.16. In force: March 29, 2001; £4.00.

This Order, which confers fresh powers of compulsory acquisition on West Yorkshire Passenger Transport Executive and Leeds City Council for the purposes of the works authorised by the Leeds Supertram Act 1993, authorises a realignment of Chadwick Street and Waterloo Street in the City of Leeds, and makes other ancillary provision for the tramway authorised by the 1993 Act, including provision continuing the effect of certain agreements made between the Executive and petitioners against the Bill for the 1993 Act.

5472. **Railways – light railways – Leeds Supertram – extension**

LEEDS SUPERTRAM (EXTENSION) ORDER 2001, SI 2001 1347; made under the Transport and Works Act 1992 s.1, s.5, Sch.1 para.1, Sch.1 para.2, Sch.1 para.3, Sch.1 para.4, Sch.1 para.5, Sch.1 para.6, Sch.1 para.7, Sch.1 para.8, Sch.1 para.9, Sch.1 para.10, Sch.1 para.11, Sch.1 para.12, Sch.1 para.13, Sch.1 para.15, Sch.1 para.16, Sch.1 para.17. In force: March 29, 2001; £7.50.

This Order, which amends the Compulsory Purchase Act 1965 and the Land Compensation Act 1973, authorises the West Yorkshire Passenger Transport Executive to construct works and compulsorily to acquire land for the purpose of extending the tramway system authorised by the Leeds Supertram Act 1993 between Leeds City Centre and Seacroft in the City of Leeds.

5473. **Railways – London Underground – construction and maintenance**

LONDON UNDERGROUND (EAST LONDON LINE EXTENSION) (NO.2) ORDER 2001, SI 2001 3682; made under the Transport and Works Act 1992 s.1, s.5, Sch.1 para.1, Sch.1 para.2, Sch.1 para.3, Sch.1 para.4, Sch.1 para.5, Sch.1 para.6, Sch.1 para.7, Sch.1 para.8, Sch.1 para.10, Sch.1 para.11, Sch.1 para.15, Sch.1 para.16, Sch.1 para.17. In force: November 9, 2001; £6.50.

This Order authorises the construction and maintenance of railway and other works in the London boroughs of Southwark and Lewisham in connection with the construction of an extension to the existing East London Line railway from a point south of Surrey Quays station to a point south of South Bermondsey station on the South London Line railway of Railtrack Plc including the construction of a new railway station spanning Surrey Canal Road; and in the London borough of Lewisham in connection with the construction of an extension to the existing East London Line railway from a point south of Surrey Canal Road to a point south of New Cross Gate station on the London Bridge to Brockley railway of Railtrack Plc including the construction of a train servicing facility with sidings on land off Cold Blow Lane.

5474. **Railways – Norfolk – transfer of rights and liabilities**

MID-NORFOLK RAILWAY ORDER 2001, SI 2001 3413; made under the Transport and Works Act 1992 s.1, s.5, Sch.1 para.1, Sch.1 para.15. In force: October 15, 2001; £2.00.

This Order, which authorises the transfer to the Mid-Norfolk Railway Preservation Trust of the railway line between Dereham and North Elmham, Norfolk, together with certain statutory and other rights and liabilities, makes provision for the safety of works and equipment and for the safe operation of level crossings.

5475. Railways – passengers – delayed train – abortive journey – contract terms

H claimed damages in respect of the cost of a train ticket. H had bought a ticket to London Euston at about 9 am on the day of travel. A short time into the journey he was informed that the train would be delayed by up to three hours. H, therefore, caught a train back home but, as a consequence of not travelling to London on that day, he had to send goods to Europe by air mail and he sought to recover the associated costs. H contended that V, by its agents or servants at Runcorn station, was in fundamental breach of contract for having sold him a ticket to Euston when it was known by V at 8 am that day that Euston station was closed. V, which had paid £51 in vouchers to H as compensation and £63 by way of refund for the cost of the ticket, argued that the parties were bound only by the National Rail Conditions of Carriage, incorporated into the contract by virtue of a notice to that effect on the face of the ticket. V therefore submitted that it had no liability in respect of consequential loss and that it had already fulfilled its obligations to H.

Held, giving judgment for the defendant, that V was protected by the Conditions which were incorporated into the contract. It was not a term of the contract that V would carry a passenger to a destination within a given time, only that it would carry him to that destination. Accordingly V was not in breach of contract even if it had known that Euston station was closed at the time that it sold the ticket to H. V had already exceeded its contractual obligations to compensate H and section 43 of the Conditions excluded V from liability for any consequential losses.

HILL v. VIRGIN TRAINS LTD, January 17, 2001, District Judge Ewing, CC (Chester). [*Ex rel.* Katya Melluish, Barrister, 3 Paper Buildings, Temple, London].

5476. Railways – railway infrastructure – charges and safety – Council Directive

European Parliament and Council Directive 2001/14 of 26 February 2001 on the allocation of railway infrastructure capacity and the levying of charges for the use of railway infrastructure and safety certification. [2001] OJ L75/29.

5477. Railways – railway infrastructure – charges and safety – Council Directive

European Parliament and Council Directive 2001/14 of 26 February 2001 on the allocation of railway infrastructure capacity and the levying of charges for the use of railway infrastructure and safety certification. [2001] OJ L75/29.

5478. Railways – railway infrastructure – trans-European network – Council Directive

European Parliament and Council Directive 2001/16 of 19 March 2001 on the interoperability of the trans-European conventional rail system. [2001] OJ L110/1.

5479. Railways – safety

RAILWAY SAFETY (MISCELLANEOUS AMENDMENTS) REGULATIONS 2001, SI 2001 3291; made under the Health and Safety at Work etc. Act 1974 s.15, s.43, s.82, Sch.3 para.1, Sch.3 para.8, Sch.3 para.9, Sch.3 para.15, Sch.3 para.16. In force: October 24, 2001; £1.75.

These Regulations amend the Railways Regulations 1998 (SI 1998 1340), the Railway Safety Regulations 1999 (SI 1999 2244) and the Railways (Safety Case) Regulations 2000 (SI 2000 2688) so as to require a revision to a safety case to be submitted to the relevant infrastructure controller at the same time that it is submitted to the Health and Safety Executive. The Regulations extend the duty on infrastructure controllers to procure 12 monthly audits by an assessment body to cover, additionally, their train operations and include a requirement on railway operators who operate trains to include in their railway safety case particulars of the arrangements which they have established for the provision of equipment and arrangements for escape of persons in an emergency from trains operated by them.

5480. Railways – Shortlands Junction

RAILTRACK (SHORTLANDS JUNCTION) ORDER 2001, SI 2001 2870; made under the Transport and Works Act 1992 s.1, s.5, Sch.1 para.1, Sch.1 para.2, Sch.1 para.3, Sch.1 para.4, Sch.1 para.5, Sch.1 para.7, Sch.1 para.8, Sch.1 para.10, Sch.1 para.11, Sch.1 para.16, Sch.1 para.17. In force: July 18, 2001; £4.50.

This Order makes provision for the construction of railways and other works, and acquisition of land and rights, in connection with the Shortlands Junction Separation scheme in the London Borough of Bromley.

5481. Railways – Strategic Rail Authority – capital allowances

STRATEGIC RAIL AUTHORITY (CAPITAL ALLOWANCES) ORDER 2001, SI 2001 262; made under the Transport Act 2000 Sch.26 para.5, para.13. In force: February 1, 2001; £1.75.

This Order makes provision relating to the expenditure which the Strategic Rail Authority is to be taken as having incurred, for the purposes of capital allowances under the Corporation Tax Acts, on certain plant and machinery which is transferred to it under provisions of the Transport Act 2000 Part IV. It also prescribes the amount of expenditure incurred on the transfer of the plant and machinery from the Franchising Director by virtue of the Transport Act 2000 s.215 and provides a mechanism for the determination of the amount of expenditure incurred on the transfer of the plant and machinery from the British Railways Board by virtue of the Transport Act 2000 Sch.18 para.11. The amount will be that determined by the Secretary of State to be equivalent to the plant and machinery capital allowances "pool" attributable to the British Transport Police activities in the British Railways Board immediately prior to the transfer.

5482. Railways – Strategic Rail Authority – licence exemption

STRATEGIC RAIL AUTHORITY (LICENCE EXEMPTION) ORDER 2001, SI 2001 218; made under the Railways Act 1993 s.7, s.143. In force: March 1, 2001; £1.50.

This Order provides for the grant of exemptions to the Strategic Rail Authority and its wholly owned subsidiaries from the requirements of the Railways Act 1993 s.6 to be authorised by licence to be the operator of any railway asset. The exemptions may be revoked by not less than one month's notice given by the Secretary of State to that Authority.

5483. Road traffic – parking levy – classes of motor vehicle

ROAD USER CHARGING AND WORKPLACE PARKING LEVY (CLASSES OF MOTOR VEHICLES) (ENGLAND) REGULATIONS 2001, SI 2001 2793; made under the Transport Act 2000 s.197, s.198. In force: August 28, 2001; £2.00.

These Regulations relate to the Transport Act 2000 Part III which enable road user charging or workplace parking levy schemes to be made, inter alia, by a non-metropolitan local traffic authority, jointly by more than one non-metropolitan local traffic authority or jointly by one or more non-metropolitan local traffic authorities and one or more London traffic authorities. Section 186(3)(d) of the Act provides that charges that may be imposed by a licensing scheme include different charges for different classes of motor vehicles. These Regulations provide for specified classes of motor vehicles to be classes of motor vehicles for the purposes of Part III of the Act and ensure that a charging or licensing scheme cannot impose charges for classes of motor vehicles by reference to their maximum mass as well as the number of their axles.

5484. Road Traffic (Vehicle Testing) Act 1999 (c.12) – Commencement No.1 Order

ROAD TRAFFIC (VEHICLE TESTING) ACT 1999 (COMMENCEMENT NO.1) ORDER 2001, SI 2001 1896 (C.63); made under the Road Traffic (Vehicle

Testing) Act 1999 s.9. Commencement details: bringing into force various provisions of the Act on June 1, 2001; £1.50.

This Order brings into force s.1 (3) of the Road Traffic (Vehicle Testing) Act 1999 in so far as it relates to the insertion of a new subsection (6B), relating to the maintenance of records of vehicles submitted for examination and the carrying out of and the result of examinations, in s.45 of the Road Traffic Act 1988 on June 1, 2001. It also brings into force s.3 which inserts a new s.46A in the Road Traffic Act 1988 relating to the use of records maintained by the Secretary of State, or caused by him to be maintained, under the new s.45(6B) and of records maintained by the Secretary of State in connection with the functions exercisable by him under or by virtue of the Vehicle Excise and Registration Act 1994 on June 1, 2001.

5485. Road transport – tachographs – driving periods – EC law – time spent travelling to pick up points

[Transport Act 1968 s.67; Council Regulation 3821/85 on recording equipment in road transport.]

The question of whether time spent by coach drivers travelling to a pick up point for a vehicle which was subject to tachograph requirements, had to be recorded on that vehicle's tachograph in order to comply with Council Regulation 3821/85 Art.15, was referred to the ECJ for a preliminary ruling. D and two other drivers who were required by their employer to travel to pick up points away from their home or the company base, had been charged under the Transport Act 1968 s.97 with infringements of the Regulation. It was contended that since the company did not specify how the drivers were to reach the pick up points, the drivers could dispose of their time freely and the travelling periods therefore constituted rest time.

Held, giving a preliminary ruling, that the periods during which the drivers spent travelling to the pick up points in vehicles to which the tachograph regulations did not apply, had to be recorded on the pick up vehicle's tachograph pursuant to Art.15(3)(b) which referred to "other periods of work". The drivers were under an obligation to the employer to travel to the pick up points and the time could not therefore be regarded as rest time. One of the objectives of the Regulation was to ensure that drivers had rest periods in between periods of work so that tiredness caused by long periods at the wheel would not jeopardise road safety. Since the time spent by the driver travelling to the pick up point was likely to have a bearing on his driving once he reached the pick up point, it would go against the objective of the Regulation if that time were not recorded.

SKILLS MOTOR COACHES LTD v. DENMAN (C297/99); *sub nom.* CRIMINAL PROCEEDINGS AGAINST SKILLS MOTOR COACHES LTD (C297/99), *Re* [2001] All E.R. (EC) 289, La Pergola (President), ECJ.

5486. Road works – penalties – unreasonably prolonged occupation of the highway

STREET WORKS (CHARGES FOR UNREASONABLY PROLONGED OCCUPATION OF THE HIGHWAY) (ENGLAND) REGULATIONS 2001, SI 2001 1281; made under the New Roads and Street Works Act 1991 s.74, s.104. In force: April 1, 2001; £2.00.

These Regulations, which prescribe the charges payable to highway authorities by undertakers for the occupation of the highway where street works executed in a maintainable highway are unreasonably prolonged, make provision for the giving of notices relating to works to which they apply, create an offence of failing without reasonable cause to give a prescribed notice and make provision for the application by local highway authorities of charges received and the keeping of accounts.

5487. Roads – road user charging – charges

ROAD USER CHARGING (CHARGES AND PENALTY CHARGES) (LONDON) REGULATIONS 2001, SI 2001 2285; made under the Greater London Authority

Act 1999 s.420, Sch.23 para.12, Sch.23 para.13, Sch.23 para.26, Sch.23 para.27. In force: July 16, 2001; £2.00.

These Regulations deal with the procedures relating to the imposition of charges and penalty charges for road user charging in Greater London under the Greater London Authority Act 1999 Sch.23. They cover requirements about the imposition, setting and liability for charges and penalty charges, examination of, and entry to vehicles, powers of seizure, powers of immobilisation, removal and disposal of vehicles, recovery of penalty charges in relation to removed vehicles, taking possession of vehicles and claims by owners of vehicles after their disposal.

5488. Roads – road user charging – enforcement and adjudication

ROAD USER CHARGING (ENFORCEMENT AND ADJUDICATION) (LONDON) REGULATIONS 2001, SI 2001 2313; made under the Greater London Authority Act 1999 s.420, Sch.23 para.12, Sch.23 para.28, Sch.23 para.30. In force: July 30, 2001; £3.00.

These Regulations set out the procedures for the enforcement and adjudication of road user charging schemes in Greater London under the Greater London Authority Act 1999 Sch.23. They cover requirements relating to the notification, adjudication and enforcement of penalty charges, the determination of disputes, appeals against determinations, the appointment of persons to hear any such appeals and the admissibility of evidence in proceedings under Sch.23.

5489. Tachographs – passenger vehicles – coach operator – inspection and copying of records

[Transport Act 1968 s.4(a), s.99(1)(bb); Council Regulation 3821/85 on recording equipment in road transport Art.14(2), Art.15(7).]

C, a coach operator, appealed against the upholding of its conviction ((2000) 164 J.P. 593, [2000] C.L.Y. 5241) for failure to hand over to an authorised officer of the Vehicle Inspectorate, contrary to the Transport Act 1968 s.99(1)(bb) and s.4)(a), tachograph records which it was required to keep or be able to produce by Council Regulation 3821/85 Art.14(2) and Art.15(7). C had offered to let the officer inspect the records at its premises but refused him permission to physically remove them. *Held*, dismissing the appeal, that C had failed in its duty to allow the officer to inspect and copy the tachograph records. A statutory removal power had been granted for this purpose and whether removal of the records was necessary and, if so, the length of time for which the documents could be removed, would depend on what was reasonable in terms of the number of documents involved and the copying facilities available at the premises. Although the instant case was a test case in relation to tachograph records, the officer's entitlement to request production was also applicable to other documents. C had not contended that the removal request had been unreasonable and on the facts the court had been entitled to convict.

VEHICLE INSPECTORATE v. CANTABRICA COACH HOLDINGS LTD; *sub nom.* CANTABRICA COACH HOLDINGS LTD v. VEHICLE INSPECTORATE, [2001] UKHL 60, [2001] 1 W.L.R. 2288, Lord Slynn of Hadley, HL.

5490. Tachographs – strict liability – failure to use tachograph – statutory defence – standard of proof

[Transport Act 1968 s.97; Council Regulation 3821/85 on recording equipment in road transport.]

The Vehicle Inspectorate appealed against the dismissal of an information laid against S for its use of a heavy goods vehicle in which the tachograph was being used improperly contrary to Council Regulation 3821/85 Art.13 to Art.15 and contrary to the Transport Act 1968 s.97(1)(a)(iii). Upon a vehicle belonging to S being stopped, an examiner from the Inspectorate had formed the impression that the seal to the plastic cover over the dil switches had been tampered with. S having sought to rely on the statutory defence in s.97(4) of the 1968 Act, the issue before the court concerned the standard of proof required to enable a defendant to rely on that defence.

Held, allowing the appeal, that (1) the statutory defence could not be invoked simply by a defendant proving that the breaking or removal of the tachograph seal could not have been avoided; (2) the term "avoid" within s.97(4)(a) of the 1968 Act did not mean the same as "prevent" so that a defendant could not escape liability by claiming that he could not prevent that of which he had no knowledge, and (3) the defendant had to prove that the breaking or removal of the seal could not have been avoided in itself.

VEHICLE INSPECTORATE v. SAM ANDERSON (NEWHOUSE) LTD, [2001] EWHC Admin 893, [2002] R.T.R. 13, Poole, J., QBD (Admin Ct).

5491. Transport Act 2000 (c.38) – Commencement No.1 Order – Wales

TRANSPORT ACT 2000 (COMMENCEMENT NO.1) (WALES) ORDER 2001, SI 2001 2788 (W.238; C.94); made under the Transport Act 2000 s.275, s.276. Commencement details: bringing into force various provisions of the 2000 Act on August 1, 2001 and April 1, 2002; £2.00.

This Order brings into force in Wales specified provisions of the Transport Act 2000 which include placing a duty on local authorities to prepare local transport plans and bus strategies and provide for local transport authorities to make bus service quality partnership schemes. The provision also includes enabling local authorities to make a scheme for joint and through bus ticketing, providing for mandatory concessionary travel on local buses for the elderly or disabled, providing for road user charging schemes and relating to grants for local public transport and competition tests relating to the exercise of functions relating to bus services.

5492. Transport Act 2000 (c.38) – Commencement No.3 Order

TRANSPORT ACT 2000 (COMMENCEMENT NO.3) ORDER 2001, SI 2001 57 (C.3); made under the Transport Act 2000 s.275, s.276. Commencement details: bringing into force various provisions of the Act on January 30, 2001 and February 1, 2001; £2.00.

This Order brings certain provisions of the Transport Act 2000 into force on January 30, 2001, and February 1, 2001.

5493. Transport Act 2000 (c.38) – Commencement No.3 Order – Amendment Order

TRANSPORT ACT 2000 (COMMENCEMENT NO.3) (AMENDMENT) ORDER 2001, SI 2001 115 (C.5); made under the Transport Act 2000 s.275, s.276. In force: January 22, 2001; £2.00.

This Order amends the Transport Act 2000 (Commencement No.3) Order 2001 (SI 2000 57) by omitting s.253, ss.257 to 260, s.265 and s.267 from the provisions specified in Sch.2 Part I to that Order. It contains provisions relating to driver training and driving instructors and the licensing of private hire vehicle and amends the transitional provisions in Sch.3 Part II relating to the commencement of s.158 and Sch.11 para.22, which amend provisions relating to the repayment of fuel grant duty for unregistered and unreliable local services.

5494. Transport Act 2000 (c.38) – Commencement No.4 Order

TRANSPORT ACT 2000 (COMMENCEMENT NO.4) ORDER 2001, SI 2001 242 (C.13); made under the Transport Act 2000 s.275. Commencement details: bringing into force various provisions of the Act on February 20, 2001; £1.75.

This Order, which brings into force most of the Transport Act 1985 s.111, empowers a traffic commissioner to make a determination that the operation of a local service has operated a service in contravention of a registration.

5495. Transport Act 2000 (c.38) – Commencement No.5 Order

TRANSPORT ACT 2000 (COMMENCEMENT NO.5) ORDER 2001, SI 2001 869 (C.30); made under the Transport Act 2000 s.275. Commencement details: bringing into force various provisions of the Act on April 1, 2001; £2.00.

This Order brings into force all the remaining provisions of the Transport Act 2000 Part I on April 1, 2001.

5496. Transport Act 2000 (c.38) – Commencement No.6 Order

TRANSPORT ACT 2000 (COMMENCEMENT NO.6) ORDER 2001, SI 20011498 (C.53); made under the Transport Act 2000 s.275. Commencement details: bringing into force various provisions of the Act on May 1, 2001 and July 1, 2001; £2.00.

This Order brings into force the Transport Act 2000 s.3, which makes it a criminal offence if a person provides air traffic services in respect of a managed area save where those services are excepted, on May 1, 2001. It also brings s.265 of the Act into force on July 1, 2001, which amends the Public Passenger Vehicles Act 1981 to provide that a vehicle with no more than eight passenger seats provided for hire with the services of a driver which carries passengers otherwise than at separate fares must, with certain exceptions, be licensed as a private hire vehicle.

5497. Transport Act 2000 (c.38) – Commencement No.7 Order – England

TRANSPORT ACT 2000 (COMMENCEMENT NO.7) ORDER 2001, SI 2001 3342 (C.110); made under the Transport Act 2000 s.275. Commencement details: bringing into force various provisions of the 2000 Act on October 26, 2001; £2.00.

This Order brings into force as respects England, the provision of the Transport Act 2000 relating to quality partnerships and quality contract schemes.

5498. Transport policy – consequential amendments

TRANSPORT ACT 2000 (CONSEQUENTIAL AMENDMENTS) ORDER 2001, SI 2001 4050; made under the Transport Act 2000 s.277. In force: December 21, 2001; £2.50.

This Order amends the Consumer Credit Act 1974, the Welsh Development Agency Act 1975, the Local Government (Miscellaneous Provisions) Act 1976, the Estate Agents Act 1979, the Highways Act 1980, the Acquisition of Land Act 1981, the Civil Aviation Act 1982, the Aviation Security Act 1982, the Building Act 1984, the Telecommunications Act 1984, the Airports Act 1986, the Consumer Protection Act 1987, the Water Act 1989, the Town and Country Planning Act 1990, the Water Industry Act 1991, the Water Resources Act 1991, the Town and Country Planning (Control of Advertisements) Regulations 1992 (SI 1992 666), the Railways Act 1993, the Coal Industry Act 1994, the Town and Country Planning (General Permitted Development) Order 1995 (SI 1995 418), the Town and Country Planning (Trees) Regulations 1999 (SI 1999 1892), the Utilities Act 2000, the Countryside and Rights of Way Act 2000 and the Transport and Works (Applications and Objections Procedure) (England and Wales) Rules 2000 (SI 2000 2190). This Order amends the enactments, which relate to aviation security, statutory undertakers, town and country planning, disclosure and civil aviation, in consequence of the provisions of the Transport Act 2000 Part I.

5499. Transport policy – quality partnership schemes

QUALITY PARTNERSHIP SCHEMES (EXISTING FACILITIES) REGULATIONS 2001, SI 2001 3317; made under the Transport Act 2000 s.119. In force: October 26, 2001; £1.50.

These Regulations, which make provision for existing facilities to form part of a quality partnership scheme, provide that existing facilities may not form part of a quality partnership scheme where they were first provided more than 10 years before notice of the proposed scheme is given. However, where an existing facility was provided more than 5 years but less than 10 years before notice of the proposed scheme is given, it may form part of a quality partnership scheme providing no objection is made and not withdrawn by any person relying upon that facility in the provision of local services. In addition, they provide that an authority must, in the course of consultation in respect of a proposed scheme, specify the date on which it believes each relevant existing facility was first provided.

5500. Books

Abeyratne, Ruwantissa – Aviation Trends in the New Millennium. Hardback: £69.95. ISBN 0-7546-1299-6. Ashgate Publishing Limited.

Hannibal, Martin; Hardy, Stephen – Road Traffic. Practice Notes. Paperback: £15.95. ISBN 1-85941-456-7. Cavendish Publishing Ltd.

Orlik, Michael – Introduction to Highway Law. 2nd Ed. Paperback: £21.95. ISBN 0-7219-1331-8. Shaw & Sons.

Professional Driver's Guide 2002. Paperback: £25.00. ISBN 1-85524-617-1. Croner Publications.

Spence, Charles F. – AIM/FAR 2002. "Aviation Week". Paperback: Internet resource: £13.99. ISBN 0-07-137737-9. McGraw-Hill Publishing Company.

Your Rights on the Road. CD-ROM: £19.99. ISBN 1-902646-49-5. Law Pack Publishing.

TRUSTS

5501. Charitable trusts – advancement of religion – Serbian Orthodox community – rules providing for lay management of trust property – Australia

The trustees of a Serbian Orthodox church school sought a declaration to show that they were entitled to hold the property on trust for the local Serbian Church community without being subject to the authority of the Bishop of the Serbian Orthodox Diocese of Australia and New Zealand and the Belgrade Patriarchate. The community had been founded by anti communist Serb emigres and was mistrustful of the Patriarchate during Communist rule in the former Yugoslavia.

Held, granting the declaration sought, that a trust in favour of an unincorporated association was only valid if it was for the members' benefit and did not offend the rule against perpetuities, *Denley's Trust Deed, Re* [1969] 1 Ch. 373, [1968] C.L.Y. 3586 applied. In the instant case, the community's rules showed that its members were precluded from dividing up the property and if the community ceased the property had to be transferred to the Diocese, accordingly the trust was not covered by the *Denley* principle. The trust would therefore fail, unless it was concerned with the advancement of religion, which required the promotion of spiritual or doctrinal matters, *Craigdallie v. Aikman* (1813) 1 Dow 1. The facts showed that the property belonged to the Orthodox Church and was subject to its constitution. The rules of the community, which formed part of the trust's scheme of management, provided for considerable lay involvement in the management of the trust property, so that the declaration of trust had to include lay involvement to the detriment of the Church's hierarchy.

RADMANOVICH v. NEDELLKOVIC (2000-01) 3 I.T.E.L.R. 802, Young, C.J., Sup Ct (NSW).

5502. Charitable trusts – legacies – closure of church named in bequest – general purposes of gift

I, a charity, appealed against a decision that a bequest made by B to the vicar and churchwardens of a named church did not fail despite the church's closure. B had left her residuary estate on trust for three charities in equal shares. In relation to her bequest to the named church, she requested that the money be used "primarily for the upkeep of the fabric of the church". The church had been established under a trust deed which permitted the trustees to sell the land and buildings and hold the proceeds on trust for the purchase of another plot or building, or for other religious or charitable purposes. The judge had found that the relevant share of the residue should be paid to the trustees of the deed to be held on the trusts of that deed.

Held, dismissing the appeal, that as a charity still existed for the general purposes of the church the bequest did not fail, notwithstanding that the precatory request of B could not be complied with. The closure and sale of the church building did not result in the failure of the charity established under the original deed. The fact that there were no vicar and churchwardens did not matter; a trust for charitable purposes would not fail due to the misdescription of the trustees. B's primary wishes concerning the division of her estate were clear. Her precatory words relating to the upkeep of the fabric of the church were indicative that the gift was intended for the general purposes of the church.

BROADBENT (DECEASED), *Re*; *sub nom.* IMPERIAL CANCER RESEARCH FUND v. BRADLEY, [2001] EWCA Civ 714, [2001] W.T.L.R. 967, Mummery, L.J., CA.

5503. **Constructive trusts – equitable interests in land – communication of intention between parties**

Following the sale of a house whose legal title was vested in the defendant, C, her former husband, A, and the couple's sons, AM and NM, claimed a share of the sale proceeds on the basis that they were beneficial owners of the property. It was contended that the proceeds of sale were held on constructive trust by C, operating in favour of the sons. In the alternative, it was argued that A and C were the joint beneficial owners of the property

Held, giving judgment for the claimants, that a common intention that AM and NM were to enjoy a beneficial interest in the property could not be inferred from the evidence. However, C held part of the sale proceeds as constructive trustee for A, in respect of his contribution to the purchase price which included quantification of his contributions in terms of labour, time and money spent in refurbishment of the property. The intention that there should be shared beneficial ownership had been clearly communicated between A and C, as evidenced by their actions. Therefore, it followed that A was entitled to 25 per cent of the proceeds of sale, reflecting his contribution to the purchase, *Gissing v. Gissing* [1971] A.C. 886, [1970] C.L.Y. 1243 applied, *Grant v. Edwards* [1986] Ch. 638, [1986] C.L.Y. 3034 applied, *Lloyds Bank Plc v. Rosset* [1991] 1 A.C. 107, [1990] C.L.Y. 706 applied.

MOLLO v. MOLLO; *sub nom* MOLLO v. DIEZ [2000] W.T.L.R. 227, Ian Hunter Q.C., Ch D.

5504. **Constructive trusts – gifts – loans to family members – sums repaid by controlling director – no breach of fiduciary duty – Australia**

HFM, a private family company, and HP, another member of the same family group, sought to recover real property and a motor car bought with funds supplied by HP to H, the group founder and person with total control. Between 1989 and 1991, H sold his shares in HP to HFM, with the sale value being credited to his loan account. H used this balance to credit his own loan account and those of his family members. In 1983, H's first wife died and he subsequently married P, his former housekeeper, to whom he transferred several properties and a Bentley car, which were held by companies operated in her name. H's daughter, G, assumed control of the group on H's death and the two companies, contending that the share sale was a sham, sought recovery on the basis of either resulting or constructive trusts, or alternatively, by invoking the equitable doctrine of tracing.

Held, refusing the applications, that although HP had been used as a family treasury, with the payments termed loans to family members being more in the nature of gifts that H repaid by debiting his own loan account, the share sale was not a sham. HP was effectively HFM's creditor. Therefore, no constructive or resulting trust could arise between them unless or until a breach of fiduciary duty occurred. Tracing was also denied as it had not been shown that P had received any property belonging to HP or HFM, given the fact that all sums had been repaid by H.

HANCOCK FAMILY MEMORIAL FOUNDATION LTD v. PORTEOUS; HANCOCK PROSPECTING PTY LTD v. BELLE ROSA HOLDINGS PTY LTD; HANCOCK PROSPECTING PTY LTD v. PORTEOUS; HANCOCK FAMILY MEMORIAL FOUNDATION LTD v. BELLE ROSA HOLDINGS PTY LTD; HANCOCK MEMORIAL FOUNDATION LTD v. JOHANNA LACSON NOMINEES PTY LTD [2000] W.T.L.R. 1113, Anderson, J., Sup Ct (WA) (Sgl judge).

5505. Constructive trusts – works of art – existence of fiduciary duty between broker and artist – undue influence – nature of trust

[Limitation Act 1980 s.36(1) (f).]

C, the executor of the will of a celebrated artist, B, sought permission to amend his particulars of claim in an action for breach of fiduciary duty against M, so as to allege that M had failed to disclose or otherwise obtain B's consent to the profits made on the sale of B's paintings to third parties. The relationship between M and B had been governed by an agreement made in 1958 whereby M was entitled to purchase B's paintings at a price governed by an agreed formula. C maintained that by 1964 a relationship of trust and confidence had been created such as to give rise to a presumption of undue influence and that in consequence subsequent sales were to be dealt with on a commission basis. M opposed the application contending that (1) there was no valid basis to the claim and it was accordingly entitled to summary judgment and, (2) it was in any event time barred pursuant to the Limitation Act 1980 s.36(1) (f).

Held, granting the application in part, that (1) the evidence from M to the effect that B had provided informed consent to the arrangements between the parties did not merit the strike out of C's claim at the present time; (2) the issue of limitation would have to be reserved until trial. For limitation purposes the crucial issue was whether M was a true trustee or not. If not the claim would be prima facie statute barred. The essential constituent of true trusteeship was trust property but it was unclear on the facts of the instant case whether a remedial constructive trust or true constructive trust was involved, *Paragon Finance Plc v. Thakerar & Co* [1999] 1 All E.R. 400, [1998] C.L.Y. 536 considered. Where it was apparent that a relationship of trust had always existed in respect to property, it was not necessary to establish the existence of an obligation to keep monies or other property separate, normally a prerequisite to the conversion of a contractual obligation to account into a constructive trust.

CLARKE v. MARLBOROUGH FINE ART (LONDON) LTD (CONSTRUCTIVE TRUSTS) *The Times*, July 5, 2001, Patten, J., Ch D.

5506. Disclosure – trust documents – object of dispositive power – Isle of Man

V was a member of a class of potential beneficiaries of two trusts of which R was corporate trustee. Following V's death, his son, S, acting as V's personal representative, sought disclosure of information relating to R's management of the trusts and bank account details. An order was made at first instance granting access to information that would allow the tracing of transfers relating to the trusts. R appealed and leave was granted to amend the petition of appeal to argue that V was the object of a mere power and not therefore entitled to the disclosure sought.

Held, allowing the appeal, that the judge below had erred in finding that V as a potential object of the trust had the same rights as a beneficiary. V's rights as an object were limited to requiring R to consider the exercise of the power in his favour. Only a person to whom a trust resulted in default of the exercise of such a power could obtain discovery.

ROSEWOOD TRUST LTD v. SCHMIDT; *sub nom.* ANGORA TRUST, RE; EVEREST TRUST, *Re* [2001] W.T.L.R. 1081, Kerruish, J.A., HC (IoM).

5507. **Discretionary trusts – Advancement – distribution contrary to beneficiary's wishes – benefit accruing to creditor – Jersey**

The trustee of two Jersey discretionary trusts established by AS, of which he and his family were the beneficiaries, sought an order having surrendered discretion for a distribution of trust funds to GT. AS owed approximately $687 million to GT as the result of fraud and the order would allow the trustee to pay the total value of the two trusts of approximately $18 million to GT. AS opposed the distribution but did not appear in the instant case.

Held, refusing the application, that there was no bar to the trustee distributing property against AS's wishes. However, a distinction was made between distributions that conferred a direct benefit on AS, which he could refuse, and those amounting to an indirect benefit, which he could not, *Pilkington v. Inland Revenue Commissioners* [1964] A.C. 612, [1962] C.L.Y. 2800 considered. On the facts, a payment to GT would not benefit AS, given his present financial status and the only benefit would accrue to GT. It was not sufficient that the debt owed to GT arose from fraud and the trustee was not expected to decide on the morality of AS's actions, *Clore's Settlement Trusts, Re* [1966] 1 W.L.R. 955, [1966] C.L.Y. 11045 applied. Further, the trustee had to balance the needs of the other beneficiaries in the exercise of a power of advancement and the distribution would not have been to their benefit either.

GRUPO TORRAS SA v. AL-SABAH (NO.6); *sub nom.* ESTEEM SETTLEMENT, RE; ABACUS (CI) LTD v. AL-SABAH [2001] W.T.L.R. 641, MC St J Birt, Deputy Bailiff, Royal Ct (Jer).

5508. **Discretionary trusts – appointment – power of appointment exercised out of time – disappointed beneficiary's entitlement to relief**

B, a trustee of a discretionary settlement established in 1973, sought a declaration as to whether the trust fund was held entirely for GG, the adopted son of the settlor, or on trust for GG and his three cousins in equal shares. Under a 1976 appointment, the trustees were provided with a power of appointment, inter alia, to reappoint the trust fund for the sole benefit of GG. That power had to be exercised before a closing date, which was defined as the day before the day on which the first principal beneficiary reached the age of 25. The trustees purported to exercise the power on the eve of the principal beneficiary's 25th birthday. It was submitted that (1) the clause stipulating that the power was to be exercised "before the closing date" should be read so as to render the power exercisable "on or before" that date, with the result that the reappointment in favour of GG had been valid; (2) an equitable principle existed whereby the trustees should be directed to hold the fund on the trusts that would have applied had the 1976 power been correctly exercised, and (3) under an ancient doctrine, equity would relieve against the defective execution of powers.

Held, granting a declaration in favour of the cousins, that (1) the words "before the closing date" should be given their natural and ordinary meaning. Read in such a way, the 1976 appointment achieved the purpose for which it was intended, *Investors Compensation Scheme Ltd v. West Bromwich Building Society (No.1)* [1998] 1 W.L.R. 896, [1997] C.L.Y. 2537 applied. Accordingly, the 1976 power had not been validly exercised; (2) while the trustees had been under a duty to consider exercising the 1976 power and while they would, had they considered it in time, have exercised it in favour of GG, redress for GG existed against the trustees rather than in removing the rights of the cousins. The cousins benefited from the trust in reliance on the 1976 appointment and not as a result of a breach of the trustees' duty. It was not appropriate to extend the principle established in *Hastings-Bass (Deceased), Re* [1975] Ch. 25, [1974] C.L.Y. 993 to cover something which the trustees did not do but which they would have done had all proper considerations been made, and (3) the trustees had not exercised their power defectively, but rather had sought to exercise a power that no longer existed. There were no grounds for applying a doctrine that had fallen into disuse, *Cooper v. Martin* (1867) L.R. 3 Ch. App. 47 considered.

BREADNER v. GRANVILLE-GROSSMAN [2001] Ch. 523, Park, J., Ch D.

5509. Discretionary trusts – employee beneficiaries – right of former employee to examine trust records – Australia

GA died in 1904, leaving one tenth of his estate in trust for the benefit of his employees. M had received benefits from the trust when employed by GA's company, and on leaving his employment he sought access to trust records by way of an originating summons.

Held, granting the access sought, that the parties were bound by the decision in *Barry v. Adams* (Unreported, October 15, 1907) relating to the same will which held that the relevant relationship was one of trustee and beneficiary. Discretionary trust beneficiaries had the right to examine trust records, subject to the equitable jurisdiction of the court, dependent on the circumstances of the case. As a former beneficiary, H had the same right in respect of the period when he had been a beneficiary, *Barry v. Adams* and *Blair v. Curran* (1939) 62 C.L.R. 464, considered.

MILLAR v. HORNSBY (2000-01) 3 I.T.E.L.R. 81, Mandie, J., Sup Ct (Vic).

5510. Discretionary trusts – rectification – "children" to include both legitimate and illegitimate issue – Bahamas

A trust was set up for the benefit of B whose beneficiaries included his wife and their children, including adopted children. After B's death, the trustees made payments to the beneficiaries including an illegitimate child born to B's estranged wife after B died and an illegitimate son of B discovered after his death. The trust deed was drafted under English law, which included both legitimate and illegitimate children in the word "children". However, the trust was governed by Bahamian law under which the word "children", on its own, meant only legitimate children. The settlor, AF, sought rectification of the trust deed to reflect B's intention to include illegitimate children as beneficiaries.

Held, ordering retrospective rectification of the trust deed, that rectification was available where the purposive meaning of a trust deed meant that it carried a different meaning from that intended by a true construction. Where this occurred it was the settlor's own intention in making the voluntary gift that was crucial, if the settlement was not founded on a contract with the trustees. Therefore, the trustees' understanding of the terms used to describe the donee/ beneficiaries was not determinative of the matter, *Butlin's Settlement Trusts (Rectification), Re* [1976] Ch. 251, [1976] C.L.Y. 2508 applied. The civil standard of proof applied when establishing common intention, but where this contradicted the trust deed, evidence of such intention had to be strong enough to counteract that displayed on the face of the deed, *Thomas Bates & Son Ltd v. Wyndham's (Lingerie) Ltd* [1981] 1 W.L.R. 505, [1981] C.L.Y. 1584 applied. On the facts of the instant case, both AF and B had intended that "children" should include legitimate and illegitimate issue.

FREY v. ROYAL BANK OF SCOTLAND (NASSAU) LTD [2001] W.T.L.R. 1009, Hayton, A.J., Sup Ct (Bah).

5511. Discretionary trusts – settlors – validity of appointment of trustees – Isle of Man

In 1990 two trusts were executed by M, who no longer had a beneficial interest, as discretionary settlements for his wife and children. The original trustee, A Ltd. was replaced by C Ltd in May 1997. A disputed that it had resigned as trustee and claimed a lien on certain assets of the trustees for costs, charges and disbursements. It also retained substantial cash assets of the trusts. In October 1997 C resigned as trustee and D Ltd., a company incorporated in the Isle of Man, was appointed trustee, the trusts being moved to the Isle of Man. In July 1999, M, as settlor, under powers granted under the trusts, appointed O Ltd., a Jersey company, and G Ltd., an Isle of Man company, as additional trustees to act jointly with D. Both C and D took the view that M interfered excessively with the management of the trusts which prompted O and G to seek the opinion and/or direction of the court whether their appointment as an additional trustee was valid.

Held, declaring that the appointment of O and G was valid, that (1) the power to appoint additional trustees, vested in M as settlor, by the express provisions of the settlements the power was "fiduciary" and limited in scope so as to be exercised only in good faith and in the interests of the beneficiaries; (2) the appointment by M, as settlor, of additional trustees was not the exercise of an equitable power by a trustee, but the exercise of a legal power by a person who was not a trustee. The effect of the appointment of a trustee was to vest the legal estate in the trust assets in the trustee, and in accordance with the principles set out in the case of *Cloutte v. Storey* [1911] 1 Ch. 18, such an appointment was voidable only, if there had been a fraudulent exercise of the power of appointment; (3) as the fiduciary nature of the power of appointment was limited to acting in good faith in the interests of the beneficiaries, the appointment of additional trustees was voidable only at the instance of the beneficiaries and not the continuing trustee; (4) on the evidence it had not been established that M appointed the additional trustees on July 12, 1999 for improper reasons. They were appointed with the full support of his wife and children, the principal beneficiaries in good faith in their best interests, and (5) finally, the correct interpretation of cl.10(4) of the trusts was that the minimum number of trustees should be two individuals or one corporation so that two or more corporations might be appointed.

OSIRIS TRUSTEES LTD, *Re* [2000] W.T.L.R. 933, Deemster Cain, HC (IoM).

5512. Discretionary trusts – trustees powers and duties – disclosure of trust accounts to beneficiary – Jersey

The applicants were trustees of four settlements, two governed by Jersey law and two by British Virgin Islands law and administered in Jersey. The discretionary beneficiaries were J and others. J and his wife subsequently separated and divorce proceedings were commenced in the English High Court where a dispute arose as to the financial provision which J should make for his wife. In relation to the trusts, J was ordered to disclose six categories of accounting documents and all letters of wishes current and past. The trustees of all but the L trust were granted leave to intervene in the matrimonial proceedings. J asked the trustees for the documents he was ordered to disclose but the trustees were not satisfied that this would be in the interests of the beneficiaries as a whole and applied to the court for directions as to whether they should disclose all or any of the relevant documents to J and whether they should intervene in the English proceedings.

Held, granting the application for directions, that (1) a beneficiary was normally entitled to inspect trust documents such as the trust deed and documents which showed the nature and value of the trust property, the trust income and how the trustees had been investing and distributing the trust property. However there was a discretion in the court to refuse disclosure to a beneficiary where it was satisfied that that would not be in the best interests of beneficiaries as a whole; (2) a beneficiary was not normally entitled to see a letter of wishes both because it was covered by the principles laid down in *Londonderry's Settlement, Re* [1965] Ch. 918 and because it was a document which was confidential to the trustees. However, there was a discretion in the court to allow disclosure where it was satisfied that there was good reason to do so in any particular case; (3) on the facts of this case, the court was satisfied that there were no good grounds for holding that the trust documents in question should not be disclosed to J. It was also satisfied that there were good grounds for holding that, on the particular facts of this case, the letter of wishes in relation to each settlement should be disclosed to J; (4) however the court did not think it would be in the best interests of the beneficiaries as a whole for the trustees to intervene in the English matrimonial proceedings, and (5) the court could only speak authoritatively on the law of Jersey, which was the proper law of two of the settlements. However it seemed that the general principles also reflected the law of the British Virgin Islands.

RABAIOTTI 1989 SETTLEMENT, *Re*; *sub nom.* LATOUR TRUST CO LTD AND LATOUR TRUSTEES (JERSEY) LTDS' REPRESENTATION, *Re* [2000] W.T.L.R. 953, MC St J Birt, Deputy Bailiff, Royal Ct (Jer).

5513. Equitable interests in land – resulting trusts – company property purchase funded by debtor – beneficial interest

N and other casino owners had obtained charging orders nisi against a property owned by a company, O, which was connected with M, a gambler who had incurred substantial debts by drawing cheques at various casinos which were subsequently dishonoured. The proceedings prompted an inquiry to establish if M was in fact the beneficial owner of the property within a complex underlying offshore trust structure. At the hearing of the inquiry, N contended that (1) M had provided the purchase price and that O had been no more than a bare trustee holding legal title for M, or, in the alternative, that O held the property on a resulting trust for M.

Held, giving judgment for M, that notwithstanding the fact that M had provided the purchase monies from his own funds, the degree of M's control over the trust resulting from the transfer to I and F suggested that for the purpose of tax avoidance, M clearly intended to relinquish both legal and beneficial interests in the property. It was not appropriate for the corporate veil to be lifted, or for the court to conclude that the agreement was a sham, simply because the chosen method of ownership through the offshore trust structure possessed an artificial quality.

NIGHTINGALE MAYFAIR LTD v. MEHTA [2000] W.T.L.R. 901, Blackburne, J., Ch D.

5514. Gifts – trusts – vesting – gift completed before vested

TCI appealed against the decision of the Court of Appeal of the British Virgin Islands upholding a finding that the actions of P prior to his death had not been enough to amount to a completed gift to the charitable foundation which he had established and of which he was a trustee, and that the foundation had no right in equity to enforce the completion of the gift. Having signed the trust deed, P spoke from his death bed of having given his wealth to the trust. However, whilst still alive no share transfers had been undertaken by him. It had been found that (1) P had made or tried to make an immediate and unconditional gift to the charitable foundation but that such a gift had not been meant to be irrecoverable, and (2) the gifted property had not been vested in all the trustees, as there had been an imperfect gift which, notwithstanding P's intentions, could not be enforced.

Held, allowing the appeal, that (1) it was apparent that P had intended to make an immediate unconditional gift to the charitable foundation. The judge had erred in his conclusion that P had meant the gift to be recoverable. The transaction had been undertaken by P's declaration that those assets he already held were thereafter vested in him as a trustee of the charitable foundation, and (2) whilst P's words had been indicative of an outright gift, given the context in which they had been spoken there had been no breach of the principle established in *Milroy v. Lord* (1862) 4 De G.F. & J. 264. The sole legal basis for the charitable foundation derived from the trust declared through the foundation trust deed. Accordingly, in stating that he had given his wealth to the charitable foundation, P could only be understood to mean that he had given "to the trustees of the foundation trust deed to be held by them on the trusts of the foundation trust deed". P, as one of the trustees, having declared his intention and subsequently given his wealth to the trust, his conscience was affected and it would be improper and against equitable principles for him to be authorised to go back on that gift.

T CHOITHRAM INTERNATIONAL SA v. PAGARANI [2001] 1 W.L.R. 1, Lord Browne-Wilkinson, PC.

5515. Offshore trusts – trustees powers and duties – appointment of funds – failure to have regard to capital gains tax consequences

G, trustees of an offshore will trust, sought a declaration that a deed appointing funds to an accumulation and maintenance settlement in favour of the testator's sixteen year old granddaughter was void. G contended that the deed amounted to an invalid exercise of the previous trustees' discretionary power of appointment, submitting that their failure to have regard to the capital gains tax consequences of the deed had led to an appointment of funds with a significant risk that the will trust might become a UK resident trust for capital gains tax purposes.

Held, granting a declaration in favour of the claimant, that it was clear that the trustees would not have proceeded to make the appointment had they paid proper regard to the likely capital gains tax outcome, *Hastings-Bass (Deceased), Re* [1975] Ch. 25, [1974] C.L.Y. 993 applied. The deed was consequently invalid.

GREEN v. COBHAM [2000] W.T.L.R. 1101, Jonathan Parker, J., Ch D.

5516. Public trustee – notices affecting land – title on death

PUBLIC TRUSTEE (NOTICES AFFECTING LAND) (TITLE ON DEATH) (AMENDMENT) REGULATIONS 2001, SI 2001 3902; made under the Law of Property (Miscellaneous Provisions) Act 1994 s.19. In force: January 1, 2002; £1.50.

These Regulations amend references to the Public Trust Office in the forms prescribed by the Public Trustee (Notices Affecting Land) (Title on Death) Regulations 1995 (SI 1995 1330) as a consequence of the Public Trust Office ceasing to exist.

5517. Resulting trusts – Joint accounts – evidence of donor's intention

A, the son of X, claimed that a joint investment account held at the bank, C, in the names of X and Y, a distant relative, was in the sole beneficial ownership of X, that C had wrongly transferred assets at the direction of Y, and that it was therefore guilty of the wrongful distribution of trust assets. A argued that the account had been opened in joint names purely for convenience and that it had not been the intention of X to give Y a beneficial interest. A submitted that Y had provided no consideration for the establishment of the joint account and as the relationship between X and Y was not such as to create a presumption of advancement, the contents of the account were held subject to a resulting trust in favour of X's estate. C maintained that the effect of the mandate was to hold X and Y as joint tenants in equity, and that on the death of one, the survivor would become the sole beneficiary.

Held, giving judgment for C, that the bank had adduced sufficient evidence to displace the presumption in favour of the creation of a resulting trust for the benefit of X's estate, *Young v. Sealey* [1949] Ch. 278 considered. There was evidence that X had intended Y to take a beneficial interest. The terms of the mandate were clear, and the effects of the transfer had been explained to X. There was also clear and unchallenged evidence from a representative of C that X had understood his actions in establishing the account.

AROSO v. COUTTS & CO [2002] 1 All E.R. (Comm) 241, Lawrence Collins, J., Ch D.

5518. Secret trusts – fiduciary duty – requirements to be met before secret trust implied

SM appealed against the striking out of his action to establish the existence of a secret trust in his favour with respect to his father's complex and substantial estate, which had been bequeathed entirely to MM, his older brother. The action had been the latest in a series of inheritance disputes within the family, in which SM and MM had been opponents. The father had made MM the sole beneficiary, but written numerous letters to him, some expressing the hope that MM would ensure that SM was financially secure in the future, others clearly stating that MM was to have absolute discretion in the disposal of the estate. The court at first instance had concluded that there was no obvious reason for secrecy, and that SM had failed to show an arguable case for a legally binding trust, as opposed to a mere moral obligation. On appeal, SM contended that tax evasion was the reason for the secrecy.

Held, dismissing the appeal, that on the evidence there was nothing to support the existence of a trust, or a fiduciary obligation on MM to dispose of one third of the estate in SM's favour. Of the three requirements for a secret trust laid down by *Kasperbauer v. Griffith* (Unreported, November 21, 1997), even accepting that SM had shown an arguable case regarding certainty of beneficiaries, none of the written communication between the father and MM was expressed in certain language in imperative form, nor was there any certainty that the subject matter of the alleged trust was one third of the estate, *Kasperbauer* considered.

MARGULIES v. MARGULIES (1999-2000) 2 I.T.E.L.R. 641, Nourse, L.J., CA.

5519. Secret trusts – intention – use of lump sum from occupational pension scheme

H, knowing that he was seriously ill, instructed his solicitor to prepare a will in favour of W, whom he wished to marry, and his two adopted children from a former marriage, S and R. Although there were subsequently some alterations to his instructions, the will reflected H's intention to use the inheritance tax nil rate band by way of gifts to S and R, with the house and a lump sum from his pension going to W, so that she could discharge the mortgage. This was communicated to W, S and R at a family meeting called by H, at which he also said that the house should be sold to W with the proceeds going to S and R. None of this was committed to writing, as H was of the opinion that W would carry out his wishes. By the time H died, however, he had not instructed the pension scheme trustees to pay the lump sum to his estate, so that W received the payment and the residue of his estate was insufficient to discharge the mortgage or pay pecuniary legacies to S and R. S and R failed at first instance in their claim that the house and lump sum were held by W on a secret trust for their benefit and they appealed.

Held, dismissing the appeal, that the evidence did not show that H had intended to impose a secret trust at the meeting convened to discuss his will. Rather, his reference to W "knowing what she had to do" indicated only a moral obligation, not a legally enforceable duty. Further, the fact that H had changed his mind in relation to certain matters showed that he did not have the settled intention necessary to create a secret trust.

KASPERBAUER v. GRIFFITH [2000] W.T.L.R. 333, Peter Gibson, L.J., CA.

5520. Trust instruments – amendments – requirement for notarisation – meaning of notarisation under Cayman Islands law

A trust instrument provided that an amendment could only be made by a written instrument that had been signed, witnessed and notarised. T, the settlor, executed an amendment in 1996, but it was not notarised until 1999 by which time he had lost his mental capacity. The notarisation in the form of a proof of execution by a witness to the amendment, took place in Texas, but it was unclear whether it was carried out at the request of B, the trustee, or the attorney who had drafted it. The meaning of notarisation under Cayman law and whether the 1999 amendment could be retrospectively validated fell to be determined as preliminary issues.

Held, that under Cayman law notarisation included both the acknowledgement of an act witnessed by a notary and certifying proof of execution by a witness to that act. Accordingly, the amendment had been notarised by the actions of the witness before the notary. However, the requirement that the amendment be signed, witnessed and notarised meant that to be valid, notarisation had to have been carried out by T, who had lost his capacity before the notarisation was in fact carried out, so that the 1999 notarisation could not retrospectively validate the amendment.

AL-IBRAHEEM v. BANK OF BUTTERFIELD INTERNATIONAL (CAYMAN) LTD (2000-01) 3 I.T.E.L.R. 1, Murphy, J., Grand Court (Cayman Islands).

5521. Trustee Act 2000 (c.29) – Commencement Order

TRUSTEE ACT 2000 (COMMENCEMENT) ORDER 2001, SI 2001 29 (C.2); made under the Trustee Act 2000 s.42. Commencement details: bringing into force the Act on February 1, 2001; £1.50.

This Order brings the remaining provisions of the Trustee Act 2000 into force on February 1, 2001.

5522. Trustees – removal – costs – participation of trustee in proceedings – Cayman Islands

The trust protector sought to replace the trustee of an existing trust in the face of objection by the principal beneficiary. The trustee wished to voice concerns to the court about the protector's motives, but did not intend to formally oppose the action. The trustee applied to the court for an order for costs in any event from the trust funds.

Held, granting the application, that the costs should be paid from the trust fund on an indemnity basis. The court should seek to ensure the fullest ventilation of matters concerning the trust. The expenses of a trustee constituted a possible exception to the general rule that an unsuccessful litigant should bear all the costs, *Buckton, Re* [1907] 2 Ch. 406 considered. The question of the removal of a trustee could not be properly addressed without the participation of the trustee, particularly where impropriety had been alleged by that trustee.

DANIAL AND ROYWEST TRUST CORP (CAYMAN) LTD'S DEED OF SETTLEMENT, *Re* [2000] W.T.L.R. 713, Chief Justice Harre, Grand Court (Cayman Islands).

5523. Trustees – sole trustee – breach of duty – failure to properly administer trust – removal by court – Australia

[Trustee Act 1925-1942 New South Wales (Australia).]

The testator died in 1990 appointing a trust company and his daughter T as trustees, leaving one third of his estate to T and the remaining two-thirds between his other two children, A, the claimant, and S upon discretionary trusts. S was intellectually disabled. The trust company ceased to be trustee in 1993 and T remained sole trustee. From 1993 to 1996 there were delays and difficulties with the administration of the trust the beneficiaries were left in a position where they were liable to pay tax on moneys that they had not in fact received. T failed to respond to communications for several years. A applied to the court for T's removal as trustee.

Held, allowing the application, that T ought to be removed as trustee with a public trustee appointed in her stead. The power to remove a trustee did not derive from statute but from the inherent power of the court, *Miller v. Cameron* (1936) 54 C.L.R. 572 followed. The primary considerations were at all times the interests of all the beneficiaries, the security of the trust property, the efficient and satisfactory execution of the trusts and a faithful and sound exercise of the powers conferred on the trustee.

TITTERTON v. OATES [2001] W.T.L.R. 319, Crispin, J., Sup Ct (ACT) (Full Ct).

5524. Trustees powers and duties – appointment – former husband made beneficiary – use of trust assets to meet financial provision liability

[Matrimonial Causes Act 1973 s.25(2)(c).]

In family proceedings it was determined how much H should pay W out of his own assets. Following that determination, the trustees of a trust fund under which H was potentially a beneficiary appointed him a beneficiary so that funds could be transferred to him so that he could pay W. The trustees sought a declaration as to whether the proposed appointment was valid or whether it would be a fraud on the power.

Held, allowing the application and making the declaration sought, that the appointment would benefit H as it would replenish the assets he would deplete in discharging his liability to W. The possibility that a valid appointment could be made was something that the court would have considered in the family proceedings when determining H's future assets in terms of the Matrimonial Causes Act 1973 s.25(2)(c).

NETHERTON v. NETHERTON [2000] W.T.L.R. 1171, Charles, J., Ch D.

5525. Trustees powers and duties – charitable trusts – discretionary power to allow investment management by group companies – Hong Kong

HSBC acted as corporate trustee of a charitable trust and sought approval for a scheme of investment that would allow the power to delegate investment functions to other HSBC subsidiary companies. The Secretary for Justice objected to the terms of the scheme, contending that it would permit the HSBC group as a whole to profit from its position as trustee. Therefore, she applied for a condition to be added to the scheme to prevent the trustees from employing wholly owned HSBC subsidiaries in a fund management or advisory role.

Held, approving the scheme but refusing the application for the added condition, that (1) major changes to investment practice in recent years required extended discretionary powers for trustees, including the right to employ professional investment managers, subject to the trustees' monitoring and control; (2) in the instant case, the scheme embodied sufficient restrictions to ensure that the investment business would remain subject to the trustees' management and control, and (3) the risk of a conflict of interest had to be determined by asking whether a reasonable man, taking all of the relevant facts and circumstances into account, would find that it was a real possibility, *Boardman v. Phipps* [1967] 2 A.C. 46, [1966] C.L.Y. 11052 and *Queensland Mines Ltd v. Hudson* (1978) 18 A.L.R. 1 applied. On the facts, however, no such risk arose so that there was no need for the condition to be imposed.

HSBC (HK) LTD v. SECRETARY OF JUSTICE (2000-01) 3 I.T.E.L.R. 763, Hartmann, J., CFI (HK).

5526. Trustees powers and duties – costs – litigation against beneficiary to determine ownership of fund – liability for costs

[Civil Procedure Rules 1998 (SI 1998 3132) Part 44 r.44.3(2).]

A mistake by the trustees' predecessor led to the trustees, B, bringing litigation against a beneficiary, J, to establish who owned the beneficial title to a fund ([2001] 2 W.L.R. 593) and the question arose as to whether the costs should be borne by B, J or the other beneficiaries.

Held, finding B liable for costs, that the Civil Procedure Rules 1998 Part 44 r.44.3(2) provided that the unsuccessful party was liable for costs. B was the unsuccessful party in the instant case, and, although it was undesirable that B were required to pay costs from their personal resources, they were professionals and had insurance against the effects of this action. Further, the exclusion of liability clause did not protect B from liability for the costs of the litigation. On the other hand, the beneficiaries were defendants in this action and as such were not responsible for its commencement.

BREADNER v. GRANVILLE-GROSSMAN (COSTS) [2001] W.T.L.R. 377, Park, J., Ch D.

5527. Trustees powers and duties – discretion – sale of shares in special circumstances – contention application for approval tantamount to surrender of discretion

PT, the trustees of a provident fund settlement sought court approval for a decision to sell their shareholding. The settlor, S, had been mentally incapacitated from birth and the trust had been set up in order to protect his substantial fortune in the family brewery business, MB. The trust consisted of (1) a personal fund for S, which came to an end on his death in January 1997; (2) a charitable fund, and (3) the provident fund which was for the benefit of MB's employees and their dependants. The charitable fund held 30 per cent of the shares in MB, and the provident fund 18 per cent, both being governed by a provision which prohibited the trustees from disposing of the shares unless there were "special circumstances which make it desirable to do so". There were trustees common to both funds. A question arose as to the long term viability of MB's business because of changes in the brewing industry. PT, together with the trustees of the charitable fund, CT, took advice as to whether special circumstances existed to justify selling their shares in MB in order to protect the funds. A purchaser was identified and CT took the decision to sell. PT separately decided that it was in the interests of their fund to sell as the offer was attractive and they did not want to be left in the position of minority shareholders. PT applied to the court for a declaration that their decision was the appropriate one. C, as representative of the employee beneficiaries, argued that in approaching the court PT were wrongly surrendering their discretion, that the provident fund had to operate to preserve the interests of MB and that a conflict of interests had arisen because some of the trustees were common to both funds.

Held, granting the declaration, that this was a case where PT, who were clear about their powers and their view of the right course to take, were seeking the court's approval for a pivotal decision. They were not surrendering their discretion. The inclusion in the funds of the provision allowing for sale showed that there had been an intention when the funds were set up to allow for diversification, and the funds could not be given the purposive aim argued for by C. There was no evidence to show that PT's decision that special circumstances existed was irrational or unreasonable. They were right to bear in mind the position already reached by CT and its consequences. Although there was potential for conflicts of interest, none had been shown. Thus PT reached a decision they were entitled to reach, based on appropriate advice and taking into account all relevant factors and ignoring irrelevant ones.

PUBLIC TRUSTEE v. COOPER [2001] W.T.L.R. 901, Hart, J., Ch D.

5528. Trustees powers and duties – discretionary powers – adjustment to equalise benefits – irrelevant considerations – New Zealand

B, a beneficiary of his father's discretionary trust, applied for an injunction restraining the trustees from making further capital distribution or adjustment other than in a way that was consistent to the advice of a report, and, more specifically, restraining the trustees from debiting him a sum for an alleged loss. Shortly before winding up the trust, the trustees had attempted to equalise the benefits received by the various beneficiaries over the years. In so doing they had debited B with intangible benefits including an amount that he was perceived to have received from re-selling trust assets, albeit those bought at market value.

Held, granting the injunction, that the trustees had not acted reasonably in seeking to calculate "intangible asset adjustments" in order to justify paying less to some beneficiaries than others. The trustees could not justify their methodology in calculating intangible benefits so as to equal benefits already paid to other beneficiaries.

BLAIR v. VALLELY [2000] W.T.L.R. 615, Wild, J., HC (NZ).

5529. Trustees powers and duties – guardianship – purchase of family home by guardian – express trust not created by statute – ownership of property at time of conveyance – Australia

[Limitation Act 1935 (Western Australia); Guardianship of Children Act 1972 (Western Australia) s.10.]

JC, stepmother of MC and his three siblings, was the widow of their father, C. On C's death, JC became the children's guardian pursuant to the Guardianship of Children Act 1972 s.10. Subsequently, the family home was conveyed to JC in

1973 for AUD45,000 by C's executors. MC contended that JC's status as guardian meant that she was trustee of the family home in favour of the step children. The claim was refused at first instance but partially succeeded on appeal, where it was decided that JC held the home on an undivided fourth share for the children as an express trustee because the acquisition was in breach of her fiduciary duty as the children's guardian under s.10 of the 1972 Act, which was not subject to a limitation period under the Limitation Act 1935. JC appealed.

Held, allowing the appeal, that JC had not breached her fiduciary duties as guardian by purchasing the family home. She had not bought property belonging to the children or a beneficial interest that had accrued to them because they had no interest in the property at that time so that neither the rule against self dealing nor the fair dealing rule applied in the instant case. The 1935 Act did not apply to JC as she was not a trustee by virtue of s.10 of the 1972 Act, as guardianship was not sufficient to constitute JC an express trustee, given that none of the children's property was vested in her as their guardian when the property was conveyed to her.

CLAY v. CLAY [2001] W.T.L.R. 393, Gleeson, C.J., HC (Aus).

5530. Trustees powers and duties – investments – entitlement to make profit from trust funds

[Trustee Investments Act 1961.]

The defendant bank, M, was the sole administrator of the estate of B acted outside its powers of investment under the Trustee Investments Act 1961 and applied to have its investments of estate funds in its own deposits approved. The application was refused and the following order made (1) that the investment of estate funds with M and in Government registered stocks be approved, but there was insufficient evidence for this to be retroactive; (2) that M could place funds in banks other than itself yielding a higher rate of interest than ordinary trustee investments; (3) that M make quarterly returns to the beneficiaries, and (4) that costs be paid out of the estate. The beneficiaries appealed unsuccessfully to the Jamaican Court of Appeal on the grounds that M should account for all profits made from estate funds placed on deposit. Records of meetings between B and the beneficiaries was conclusive evidence of their agreement to M investing in its own deposits. The deposits already made were sanctioned and permitted in the future. The case came before the Privy Council.

Held, allowing the appeal, that trustees were not entitled to make a profit from trust funds. The judge at first instance was correct in refusing to approve M investing in its own deposits. Three of the beneficiaries had not been represented at meetings with M but, ultimately, infant beneficiaries could not be bound by an agreement against their best interests. The order of the judge was to be restored, except for paragraph three dealing with the submission of quarterly returns. M to pay the appellants' costs of appeal and cross appeal and costs of summons and order to be paid out of the estate.

MARLEY v. MUTUAL SECURITY MERCHANT BANK AND TRUST CO LTD [2001] W.T.L.R. 483, Lord Griffiths, PC.

5531. Trustees powers and duties – investments – failure to keep pace with ordinary share index – prevailing investment orthodoxies

NW, a bank, acted as sole trustee of the will of N, who died in 1922. It managed the investments firstly for N's widow and two sons to provide annuities as expressly required by the will and then for the two sons. From time to time the investment strategy was changed to provide the sons with more income to meet their particular tax requirements. In 1986 G, the granddaughter of N and the sole remaining beneficiary, became absolutely entitled. At that time the fund was worth £269,203. If it had kept pace with the ordinary share index since 1922 it would have been worth £1,800,000. G issued proceedings for negligence against NW.

Held, giving judgment for NW, that NW had not been negligent. It had adhered to the standards of prudent investment management and was entitled to be judged by the prevailing investment orthodoxies of the time, *Learoyd v.*

Whiteley (1886) L.R. 33 Ch. D. 347 applied. The standard to be borne by a trustee was to act with the care of an ordinary, prudent individual acting for someone for whom he felt morally bound to provide. A trustee's duties towards investments were extremely flexible. If the trustee had acted prudently in the interests of the beneficiaries from time to time it was not negligent if the investments failed to keep pace with market indices.

NESTLE v. NATIONAL WESTMINSTER BANK PLC [2000] W.T.L.R. 795, Hoffmann, J., Ch D.

5532. **Trustees powers and duties – settlements – deeds of appointment – financial consequences – failure to follow advice of counsel**

A, the trustee of a settlement made by O, sought a declaration that a deed of appointment in favour of NSPCC was void ab initio. The deed was to be executed as a means of avoiding capital gains tax liabilities. A submitted that in executing the deed on April 3, 1998 it had failed to have regard to the advice of counsel that the deed should not be executed before the 6th April, the consequence of which gave rise to a deemed disposal of the entire trust and created a liability to capital gains tax for O. A contended that as trustee, it had been under a duty to consider the financial consequences of its actions, and had the tax implications of the deed been considered the deed would not have been executed before the April 6. Therefore, A argued, the deed of appointment should be treated as void ab initio since it was an invalid exercise of the trustee's power.

Held, giving judgment for A, that the trustees had a duty to consider the fiscal consequences of a proposed deed of appointment before executing it, including any consequent liability by the trust or its beneficiaries to tax, therefore their failure to follow the advice of counsel when it was evident that had it been followed the deed would not have been executed before the April 6, vitiated the exercise of the trustees' power and rendered the deed void ab initio, *Green v. Cobham* [2000] 1 W.T.L.R. 1101, [2001] 3 C.L. 694 followed.

ABACUS TRUST CO (ISLE OF MAN) LTD v. NATIONAL SOCIETY FOR THE PREVENTION OF CRUELTY TO CHILDREN; *sub nom.* ABACUS TRUST CO (ISLE OF MAN) LTD v. NSPCC [2001] S.T.C. 1344, Patten, J., Ch D.

5533. **Trustees powers and duties – variation – narrow power of investment – convenience**

[Trustee Act 1925 s.57; Variation of Trusts Act 1958.]

AK, a life tenant subject to a power over to other beneficiaries in remainder, applied to the court for the approval of an extension of the power of investment and other associated powers pursuant to the Trustee Act 1925 s.57, or alternatively, pursuant to the Variation of Trusts Act 1958. The trustees wished to invest beyond their very limited powers of investment.

Held, granting the application, that the requested powers should be allowed. Jurisdiction existed under s.57 of the 1925 Act to enlarge the investment clause. The procedure under s.57 would lead to the granting of the powers in most instances on the basis of convenience. Such an application taken in chambers would normally be cheaper and more convenient. The trustees would be the normal applicants under s.57. Only exceptionally would such an application need to be made under the 1958 Act. The interests of the beneficiaries would generally be considered collectively.

ANKER-PETERSEN v. ANKER-PETERSEN [2000] W.T.L.R. 581, Judge Paul Baker Q.C., Ch D.

5534. **Trusts of land – reversions – land conveyed for educational purposes – cessation of use**

[School Sites Act 1841 s.2.]

F, assignees of a claim by a beneficiary to the estate of L, who had conveyed a parcel of land on trust for the education of poor children in 1872 by the Church of England, appealed against a ruling (Times, February 22, 2000) that their claim was statute barred pursuant to the School Sites Act 1841. F contended that (1) there had been no cessation of use when the school changed status from private to provided, as it had not ceased to be used for the education of "poor persons", a purpose referred to in s.2 of the Act, and (2) the judge had erred in his conclusion that the beneficiaries of L's estate had no locus standi to pursue a claim in any event, any reversion having been to the owners of neighbouring land out of which the original parcel of land had been formed and conveyed.

Held, dismissing the appeal, that (1) it was necessary to have regard to the specific objects chosen by the grantor when considering the issue of cessation rather than the various uses which might fall within the scope of s.2 of the Act, *Habermehl v. Attorney General* [1996] E.G.C.S. 148 applied. On the facts of the instant case there had been a cessation of use when the school lost its Church of England status because the site was no longer being used for the express purpose for which it had originally been placed in trust, the result of which was the automatic invocation of s.2 of the Act and reversion to the grantor or to his successors in title. Accordingly the present proceedings were statute barred, and (2) it was observed that the judge had erred in his decision that had the claim not been statute barred the site would have reverted to the owner of the land from which the site had originally been carved. Under s.2 of the Act the reference to "estate" was a reference to the holding of interests in land of differing duration rather than a reference to the physical extent of land, *Marchant v. Onslow* [1995] Ch. 1, [1994] C.L.Y. 607 overruled.

FRASER v. CANTERBURY DIOCESAN BOARD OF FINANCE [2001] Ch. 669, Mummery, L.J., CA.

5535. **Variation – beneficiaries – outright payment on attaining twentieth birthday – substitution – powers of advancement – Jersey**

[Trusts (Jersey) Law 1984 Art.43.]

The trustee of a Jersey trust, established in conformity with Swiss inheritance laws, sought an order under the Trusts (Jersey) Law 1984 Art.43 to vary the terms of the trust. In its original form, the trustee was required to pay the entire fund of $44 million to the beneficiary, S, a US resident, on her twentieth birthday. The trustee, supported by S, argued that it would be undesirable for S to obtain access to a fund of that size. Further, that the payment carried a potential US tax liability in respect of 55 per cent of the fund. In reliance upon these points, the trustee therefore sought the substitution of the payment with discretionary powers to pay income and capital, which carried a reduced tax liability.

Held, allowing the application, that the size of the fund meant that it would be undesirable for S to have full access to it at such a young age. The attendant tax consequences were sufficient for the outright payment to be substituted for discretionary powers of advancement in favour of the trustee.

ARTICLE 43 OF TRUSTS (JERSEY) LAW 1984, *Re* [2001] W.T.L.R. 571, Sir Philip Bailhache, Royal Ct (Jer).

5536. **Books**

Halliwell, Maragret – Equity and Trusts Textbook. 3rd Ed. Old Bailey Press Textbooks. Paperback: £14.95. ISBN 1-85836-406-X. Old Bailey Press.

Hartley, William M. – Declarations of Trust. Paperback: £49.00. ISBN 0-7520-0605-3. Sweet & Maxwell.

Lupoi, Maurizio – Trusts. Cambridge Studies in International and Comparative Law, 12. Hardback: £65.00. ISBN 0-521-62329-4. Cambridge University Press.

Mowbray, John; Tucker, Lynton; Poidevin, Nicholas le; Simpson, Edwin – Lewin on Trusts. 17th Ed. Property and Conveyancing Library. Hardback: £195.00. ISBN 0-421-23390-7. Sweet & Maxwell.

Pettit, Philip – Equity and the Law of Trusts. 9th Ed. Paperback: £29.95. ISBN 0-406-93761-3. Butterworths Law.

Scott-Hunt, Susan; Lim, Hilary – Feminist Perspectives on Equity and Trusts. Feminist Perspectives. Paperback: £19.95. ISBN 1-85941-606-3. Cavendish Publishing Ltd.

Soares, Patrick – Non-resident Trusts. 6th Ed. Hardback: £175.00. ISBN 0-421-75970-4. Sweet & Maxwell.

UTILITIES

5537. Contracts

UTILITIES CONTRACTS (AMENDMENT) REGULATIONS 2001, SI 2001 2418; made under the European Communities Act 1972 s.2. In force: July 26, 2001; £4.00.

These Regulations, which amend the Utilities Contracts Regulations 1996 (SI 1996 2911), implement European Parliament and Council Directive 98/4 ([1998] OJ L101/1) amending Directive 93/38 ([1993] OJ L199/84) coordinating the procurement procedures of entities operating in the water, energy, transport and telecommunications sectors. In addition, these Regulations make provision for utilities whose contract award procedures and practices have been attested as being in conformity with Community law and national legislation under an attestation system established in accordance with Council Directive 92/13 ([1992] OJ L76/14) concerning the co-ordination of laws, regulations and administrative provisions relating to the application of Community rules to the procurement of entities operating in the water, energy, transport and telecommunications sector.

5538. Electricity supply industry – energy efficiency

ELECTRICITY AND GAS (ENERGY EFFICIENCY OBLIGATIONS) ORDER 2001, SI 2001 4011; made under the Gas Act 1986 s.33BC; the Electricity Act 1989 s.41A; and the Utilities Act 2000 s.103. In force: December 15, 2001; £2.50.

This Order imposes on each electricity and gas supplier which, on December 31, 2001, supplies in any part of Great Britain at least 15,000 domestic consumers, an obligation to achieve improvements in energy efficiency over the period beginning on April 1, 2002 and ending immediately before April 1, 2005. It makes corresponding provision for those suppliers whose domestic consumers in Great Britain are fewer than 15,000 on December 31, 2001 but are at least 15,000 on December 31, 2002 and corresponding provision for those suppliers whose domestic consumers in Great Britain are fewer than 15,000 both on December 31, 2001 and on December 31, 2002, but are at least 15,000 on December 31, 2003. The Order requires the Gas and Electricity Markets Authority (the Authority) to determine the target of individual electricity and gas suppliers with a view to achieving an overall improvement in energy efficiency in Great Britain of 62 fuel-standardised terawatt hours during the period beginning on April 1, 2002 and ending immediately before April 1, 2005 and requires the Authority to alter a supplier's target to reflect certain changes in the number of the supplier's domestic consumers. It also provides that efficiency in the use by consumers of coal, liquid petroleum gas or oil is to be regarded as energy efficiency for the purposes of the term "energy efficiency target" used in the Gas Act 1986 s.33 and in the Electricity Act 1989 s.41A; provides that any improvement in energy efficiency is qualifying action contributing to the satisfaction of a supplier's target; enables the Authority to require information from suppliers as to the steps to be taken by them to comply with their obligations under the Order; requires the Authority to make determinations as to whether particular action that a supplier intends to take will qualify for the purpose of achieving the whole or any part of its energy efficiency target; makes provision for the case where a domestic consumer changes his supplier; enables the Authority to obtain information from suppliers about the steps they have taken towards satisfaction of their targets; allows suppliers, with the Authority's agreement, to "trade" qualifying action, to transfer the whole or part of their target, and to treat action taken before April 1, 2002 as contributing to the achievement of their target under the Order; requires the Authority to make annual reports to the Secretary of State on the progress made by suppliers in meeting their targets under the Order; and makes provision for enforcement.

5539. Electricity supply industry – exemptions – licences
UTILITIES ACT 2000 (TRANSITIONAL PROVISIONS) (NO.2) REGULATIONS 2001, SI 2001 3264; made under the Utilities Act 2000 s.109. In force: October 1, 2001; £1.75.
These Regulations amend the Electricity Act 1989 by replacing the existing order-making powers which relate to the granting of exemptions from the prohibitions in s.4 of the Act. The Regulations ensure continuity in relation to the provision of electric lines and electrical plants and provide that specified obligations in the 1989 Act apply to all those who may, by virtue of the substitution from the appointed day, be authorised by an exemption to generate, transmit, distribute or supply electricity without holding a licence.

5540. Electricity supply industry – licence holders – statutory consultation
UTILITIES ACT 2000 (TRANSITIONAL PROVISIONS) REGULATIONS 2001, SI 2001 1782; made under the Utilities Act 2000 s.109. In force: May 16, 2001; £1.75.
The Electricity Act 1989 s.32 allows the Secretary of State to make orders requiring electricity suppliers to produce to the Gas and Electricity Markets Authority evidence showing that they have supplied to customers in Great Britain a specified amount of electricity generated by using renewable sources. These Regulations enable the Secretary of State to begin the statutory consultation on an order and provide that consultation of those persons who hold electricity supply licences granted under the Electricity Act will be regarded as consultation falling within new s.32 of the Electricity Act.

5541. Leicestershire – recovery of expenses
LEICESTERSHIRE (RECOVERY OF EXPENSES) ORDER 2001, SI 2001 595; made under the Leicestershire Act 1985 s.35. In force: April 1, 2001; £1.50.
This Order specifies the maximum sum that a district council in the county of Leicestershire may recover from the owner of premises for any necessary repair, renewal or provision of apparatus urgently required to restore a sufficient supply of water, gas or electricity to the premises for domestic purposes.

5542. Utilities Act 2000 (c.27) – Commencement No.4 Order and Transitional Provisions Order
UTILITIES ACT 2000 (COMMENCEMENT NO.4 AND TRANSITIONAL PROVISIONS) (AMENDMENT) ORDER 2001, SI 2001 1780 (C.60); made under the Utilities Act 2000 s.110. Commencement details: bringing into force various provisions of the Act on May 14, 2001; £1.50.
This Order amends the Utilities Act 2000 (Commencement No.4 and Transitional Provisions) Order 2000 (SI 2000 3343) by providing a definition of "electricity supplier" in relation to certain provisions of the Utilities Act 2000 Sch.4.

5543. Utilities Act 2000 (c.27) – Commencement No.5 Order and Transitional Provisions Order
UTILITIES ACT 2000 (COMMENCEMENT NO.5 AND TRANSITIONAL PROVISIONS) ORDER 2001, SI 2001 1781 (C.61); made under the Utilities Act 2000 s.110. Commencement details: bringing into force various provisions of the Act on May 16, 2001; £2.50.
This Order, which amends the House of Commons Disqualification Act 1975, the Gas Act 1986, the Electricity Act 1989 and the Utilities Act 2000, brings into force those provisions of the Act listed in the Schedule to the Order for the purposes specified therein. These are principally enabling provisions to facilitate certain actions which need to be taken by the Secretary of State or the Gas and

Electricity Markets Authority prior to the commencement of other provisions of the Act which make changes to the licensing regimes for gas and electricity.

5544. Utilities Act 2000 (c.27) – Commencement No.6 and Transitional Provisions Order

UTILITIES ACT 2000 (COMMENCEMENT NO.6 AND TRANSITIONAL PROVISIONS) ORDER 2001, SI 2001 3266 (C.106); made under the Utilities Act 2000 s.110. Commencement details: bringing into force various provisions of the 2000 Act on October 1, 2001; £3.00.

This Order brings into force specified provisions of the Utilities Act 2000 which makes amendments to the House of Commons Disqualification Act 1975, the Northern Ireland Assembly Disqualification Act 1975, the Gas Act 1986, the Insolvency Act 1986, the Electricity Act 1989, the Offshore Safety Act 1992, the Environment Act 1995, the Gas Act 1995 and the Competition Act 1998. The Act also revokes the Fossil Fuel Levy Act 1998.

VAT

5545. Accounts – limits

VALUE ADDED TAX (AMENDMENT) (NO.2) REGULATIONS 2001, SI 2001 677; made under the Value Added Tax Act 1994 s.25, Sch.11 para.2. In force: April 1, 2001; £1.50.

These Regulations, which amend the Value Added Tax Regulations 1995 (SI 1995 2518) Part VII and Part VIII, increase the maximum turnover limit for entrants to the annual accounting scheme from £300,000 to £600,000. In addition, they increase the maximum turnover limit for entrants to the cash accounting scheme from £350,000 to £600,000. The maximum turnover limit for those already operating the scheme is also increased from £437,500 to £750,000.

5546. Assessment – estoppel – withdrawal of first assessment following adjudication – power to issue fresh assessment

[Value Added Tax Act 1994 s.73(9); Human Rights Act 1998 Sch.1 Part I Art.6.]

B appealed against a decision of the VAT and Duties Tribunal ([2000] B.V.C. 2334) refusing his application for directions that a statement of case and an assessment to VAT be struck out. Customs had withdrawn an initial assessment following a decision that the assessment had not been made to best judgment, and had then raised a second assessment in respect of the same period. B contended that (1) the statement of case had been served out of time; (2) the Value Added Tax Act 1994 s.73(9) prevented Customs from raising a new assessment in respect of a period for which an assessment had already been raised and adjudicated upon, and that Customs had acted ultra vires by raising the new assessment; (3) the statement of case was an attempt to re-litigate an issue already determined, and (4) the raising of a new assessment amounted to an infringement of the Human Rights Act 1998 Sch.1 Part I Art.6.

Held, dismissing the appeal, that (1) the tribunal had no jurisdiction to strike out for delayed service; (2) s.73(9) of the 1994 Act did not prevent the issuing of a new assessment in respect of a period for which an earlier assessment had already been made and subsequently withdrawn following an adjudication, provided that the later assessment did not attempt to reopen issues which had already been determined; (3) the tribunal had not determined the amount of the liability to taxation that was due but had simply found that the first assessment had not been made to best judgment so that the issues covered by the statement of case and assessment had not already been determined. Customs could not therefore be estopped from raising the second assessment which was not res judicata or an abuse of process, and (4) the raising of the new assessment did not contravene Art.6. [B sought to appeal against this decision and a date was set for a hearing before the Court of Appeal. One week before the hearing Customs withdrew the new assessment for reasons, unconnected with the issues in the appeal, which they had been asked to accept in 1999. The Court of Appeal held that (1) the appeal was moot and they would not hear it, and (2) they had no jurisdiction to overturn the costs order of Patten, J. but B was awarded the costs of the appeal.]

BENNETT v. CUSTOMS AND EXCISE COMMISSIONERS (NO.2) [2001] S.T.C. 137, Patten, J., Ch D.

5547. **Assessment – time limits – date of assessment as basis of notification that tax due**

[Value Added Tax Act 1994 s.73(6).]

In March, June and September 1995, a customs officer, S, completed three separate VAT Forms 641 following visits to C's premises. However, only the latter form was signed by a check officer. On September 11, 1996 the notice of assessment was given on VAT Form 655. C contended that the notice of assessment referred to assessments made in September 1996, so that 15 of the 17 total assessments were out of time by virtue of the two year time limit in the Value Added Tax Act 1994 s.73(6). Customs asserted that the assessments had been made in March 1996 when the determination of tax due had first been made. The VAT and Duties Tribunal agreed that the assessments were made in March 1996 and were not time barred. C appealed.

Held, allowing the appeal, that the notice of assessment was based on the VAT Form 641 dated September 1995. Notification was necessary so that a taxpayer should know whether an assessment had been made, *Customs and Excise Commissioners v. Le Rififi Ltd* [1995] S.T.C. 103, [1995] C.L.Y. 5027 applied. On the facts, the notification of September 1996 was based on the September 1995 assessment. The tribunal had therefore erred in finding that the March 1995 assessment formed the basis for the notification.

CHEESEMAN (T/A WELL IN TUNE) v. CUSTOMS AND EXCISE COMMISSIONERS; *sub nom.* CHEESMAN (T/A WELL IN TUNE) v. CUSTOMS AND EXCISE COMMISSIONERS [2000] S.T.C. 1119, Lawrence Collins, J., Ch D.

5548. **Assets – EC directives – mixed private and business use – accountability on sale – European Community**

[Sixth Council Directive 77/388 on a common system of VAT Art.2(1), Art.11A(1)(a).]

The Federal Finance Court in Germany referred a question to the ECJ relating to the interpretation of the Sixth Council Directive 77/388 on a common system of VAT, in respect of goods acquired for both business and private purposes. The court questioned whether a taxable person who had acquired a capital item from a private non taxable individual whereby input VAT could not be deducted, later had to account for VAT on a sale of the item if it had been used partly for business purposes.

Held, giving a preliminary ruling, that a taxable person who acquired a capital item in order to use it for both business and private purposes was entitled to retain it wholly within his private assets and thereby exclude it entirely from the system of VAT. The sale of the item in these circumstances would be conducted by the person in his private capacity. If the taxable person had chosen to wholly incorporate the item into his business assets, the sale of the item would be subject to VAT in full in accordance with Art.2(1) and Art.11A(1)(a) of the Directive. There was also the option of incorporating only part of the item into business assets, in which case, VAT would only be payable in respect of that part.

BAKCSI v. FINANZAMT FURSTENFELDBRUCK (C415/98) *The Times*, March 22, 2001, DAO Edward (President), ECJ.

5549. Buildings – change of use

VALUE ADDED TAX (CONVERSION OF BUILDINGS) ORDER 2001, SI 2001 2305; made under the Value Added Tax Act 1994 s.30, s.35, s.96. In force: August 1, 2001; £1.50.

This Order amends the Value Added Tax Act 1994 Sch.8 Group 5 by replacing Note 7 and introducing a new Note 7A which contain a change in the definition of a "non residential" building or part of a building which will now include buildings used as a dwelling or number of dwellings or for a relevant residential purpose for a period of 10 years or more.

5550. Business tenancies – supply of services – lease and lease back arrangement

L, who had converted a barn for use as a nursery, appealed against a decision that a lease and lease back arrangement entered into for the purpose of recovering the VAT on the conversion of the barn was not a supply in the course or furtherance of the nursery business. In regard to the lease and lease back agreement, the consideration under the lease was a small tin of beans, if demanded.

Held, dismissing the appeal, that notwithstanding that the transactions entered into were real transactions, they had not been effected in the course or furtherance of the business, *Halifax Plc v. Customs and Excise Commissioners (Input Tax on Building Works)* [2001] B.V.C. 2240, [2001] 9 C.L. 582 applied.

LAURIE (T/A PEACOCK MONTESSORI NURSERY) v. CUSTOMS AND EXCISE COMMISSIONERS [2001] B.V.C. 2317, PH Lawson (Chairman), V&DTr.

5551. Cars – sale of goods – commission

VALUE ADDED TAX (CARS) (AMENDMENT) ORDER 2001, SI 2001 3754; made under the Value Added Tax Act 1994 s.50A. In force: January 2, 2002; £1.50.

This Order, which amends the Value Added Tax (Cars) Order 1992 (SI 1992 3122), provides that, for the purposes of calculating the price at which a motor car was obtained, only the commission charged to the vendor under the contract for the sale of the motor car may be deducted from the successful bid.

5552. Companies – business gifts – amount increase

VALUE ADDED TAX (BUSINESS GIFTS OF SMALL VALUE) ORDER 2001, SI 2001 735; made under the Value Added Tax Act 1994 Sch.4 para.5. In force: March 8, 2001; £1.50.

This Order amends the Value Added Tax Act 1994 Sch.4 para.5(2)(a) by increasing the amount allowable for the gift of goods in the course or furtherance of a business for VAT purposes from £15 to £50.

5553. Company cars – employee benefits – fuel

VALUE ADDED TAX (CONSIDERATION FOR FUEL PROVIDED FOR PRIVATE USE) ORDER 2001, SI 2001 736; made under the Value Added Tax Act 1994 s.57. In force: April 6, 2001; £1.50.

This Order, which amends the Value Added Tax Act 1994 s.57, reduces the flat rate values used for calculating VAT relating to engine type and size if road fuel of a business is used for private motoring by 3 per cent for diesel vehicles and 5 per cent for those using other fuels with effect from April 6, 2001.

5554. Consideration – gifts – voucher based customer loyalty scheme – value of gifts liable to VAT under Sixth Directive Art.5(6)

[Sixth Council Directive 77/388 on a common system for VAT Art.5(6).]

KP appealed against a VAT and Duties Tribunal decision ([2000] B.V.C. 2300) which held, following a reference to the ECJ as to the applicability of the Sixth Council Directive 77/388 Art.5(6) ([1999] All E.R. (EC) 450, [1999] C.L.Y. 4967), that KP was liable to account for the VAT on goods supplied free to customers under a voucher based loyalty scheme. KP contended that the tribunal had wrongly decided the case because of an erroneous finding of fact and that the value of the goods should have been deducted from the price of the fuel supplied and excluded from the fuel output tax calculation by virtue of Art.11C(1).

Held, dismissing the appeal, that the tribunal had correctly determined by reference to the facts and statements made by KP that the goods were not supplied for consideration. Customers paid the same price for the fuel supplied whether or not they accepted KP's vouchers or selected goods in exchange for the vouchers. Article 5(6) provided an exception to the principle of fiscal neutrality in that goods freely given away by a business as part of its trading activities were deemed liable to VAT, notwithstanding the lack of consideration. This provision could not be evaded by seeking to rely on Art.11C(1) as a means of using the goods to reduce the price of the fuel.

KUWAIT PETROLEUM (GB) LTD v. CUSTOMS AND EXCISE COMMISSIONERS [2001] S.T.C. 62, Laddie, J., Ch D.

5555. **Consumer credit – retail trade – provision of finance by third party – deduction of commission – taxable sum – European Community**

[Sixth Council Directive 77/388 on a common system for VAT Art.11A(1)(a).]

In an action commenced by the Commissioners of Customs and Excise against P, a furniture retailer, ([1996] S.T.C. 757, [1996] C.L.Y. 5891), three questions concerning the interpretation of the Sixth Council Directive 77/388 Art.11A(1)(a) were referred to the ECJ for a preliminary ruling. P operated a system whereby customers had the option of purchasing its goods by obtaining interest free credit from a finance house which deducted commission by way of consideration for the provision of such credit, from the sums paid to P. The questions for determination concerned whether, pursuant to Art.11A(1)(a) of the Directive, the taxable sum for VAT purposes on the sale transaction consisted of the sum received by P or the full amount paid by the individual purchaser.

Held, giving a preliminary ruling, that for VAT purposes the taxable amount was the total sum payable by the purchaser. When ascertaining the value of consideration provided for the purposes of the Directive, the determining factor was the existence of an agreement between the parties for reciprocal performance; the payment received by the one being the counter value for the goods provided to the other. P and its customers had agreed that the consideration for the goods would be the price as advertised which was not varied according to whether the customer took advantage of the credit option. For the purposes of charging VAT, payments made by credit card and payments made by way of interest free credit, offered by the seller and provided by a third party, should be treated as equivalent, *Chaussures Bally SA v. Belgium (C18/92)* [1997] S.T.C. 209, [1993] C.L.Y. 4408 applied.

CUSTOMS AND EXCISE COMMISSIONERS v. PRIMBACK LTD (C34/99); *sub nom.* PRIMBACK LTD v. CUSTOMS AND EXCISE COMMISSIONERS (C34/99) [2001] 1 W.L.R. 1693, GC Rodriguez Iglesias (President), ECJ.

5556. **Discounts – consideration – value of non monetary consideration for VAT purposes**

[Sixth Council Directive 77/388 on a common system for VAT Art.11 (C)(1); Value Added Tax Tribunals Rules 1986 (SI 1986 590).]

Four cases concerned with the determination for VAT purposes of the monetary equivalent of non monetary consideration in respect of a supply of goods were heard together. (1) L, a mail order company, appealed against a decision ([2000] S.T.C. 588, [2000] C.L.Y. 5345) that commission paid to its agents was to be treated, for VAT purposes, as consideration for the agent's services and was therefore to be included in determining the taxable amount. L contended that enhanced commission, which was available to the agent if she took it in the form of catalogue goods, was to be treated as a price discount on those goods; (2) LS, a car supplier, appealed against a decision ([2000] S.T.C. 697, [2000] C.L.Y. 5319) that the value of a customer's car taken in part exchange was the price agreed between L and the customer not the invariably lower trade value of the vehicle; (3) Customs appealed against the dismissal of its appeal ([2000] S.T.C. 1, [2000] C.L.Y. 5339) against a ruling on the sum liable to tax in circumstances where a video cassette was part exchanged for a another video cassette together with a sum of money. B, the retailer, sold marked video cassettes for £20 and was prepared to accept a marked video cassette by way of part exchange together with the sum of £10 on any subsequent purchase. The Value Added Tax Tribunal determined that the sum liable to tax on the latter transaction was £10 whereas Customs maintained that the sum liable to should be £20, and (4) K appealed against a decision ([2001] S.T.C. 62, [2001] 4 C.L. 684) made following a reference to the ECJ ((1999) All E.R. (EC) 450, [1999] C.L.Y. 4967) that it was liable to account for the VAT on goods supplied free to customers under a voucher based loyalty scheme. K relied on *Elida Gibbs Ltd v. Customs and Excise Commissioners (C317/94)* [1996] S.T.C. 1387, [1996] C.L.Y. 5908 to raise a new point that the provision of the free goods was a reduction in the price of the fuel made post supply within the Sixth Council Directive 77/388 Art.11 (C) (1).

Held, allowing L's appeal, dismissing the appeals of LS and K and allowing the appeal of Customs in the case of B, that (1) in the case of L, the commission in goods had to be treated as a rebate allowed to the agent at the time of the supply of secondary goods and could not be included in the taxable amount. There was no direct link between the agent's sales to third parties and her right to take commission in goods at an increased rate. Consequently there was no justification for treating the provision of services as a non monetary element in the consideration for the supply of goods to the agent; (2) with regard to the case of LS, it was apparent that where the parties to a transaction had ascertained the value of the non monetary consideration, then that was the amount on which VAT was payable; (3) with respect to the case of B, it was necessary to establish the monetary value of the non monetary element of the transaction. On that basis the true sum liable to tax was £20 since the consideration for the video cassette comprised the sum of £10 together with the return of a video previously sold by B. The only difference between the transaction and a standard part exchange was that B had agreed in advance to accept any video cassette which he had previously sold by way of part exchange, *Customs and Excise Commissioners v. Westmorland Motorway Services Ltd* [1998] S.T.C. 431, [1998] C.L.Y. 4936, *Rosgill Group Ltd v. Customs and Excise Commissioners* [1997] 3 All E.R. 1012, [1997] C.L.Y. 4975 and *Naturally Yours Cosmetics Ltd v. Customs and Excise Commissioners (C230/87)* [1988] S.T.C. 879, [1989] C.L.Y. 1683 considered, and (4) there existed no statutory power under the Value Added Tax Tribunals Rules 1986 for an appeal to be heard on a point that had not been raised before the tribunal, *Elida Gibbs* considered.

LITTLEWOODS ORGANISATION PLC v. CUSTOMS AND EXCISE COMMISSIONERS; LEX SERVICES PLC v. CUSTOMS AND EXCISE COMMISSIONERS; BUGEJA v. CUSTOMS AND EXCISE COMMISSIONERS (NO.2); KUWAIT PETROLEUM (GB) LTD v. CUSTOMS AND EXCISE COMMISSIONERS; *sub nom.* CUSTOMS AND EXCISE COMMISSIONERS v. LITTLEWOODS ORGANISATION PLC; CUSTOMS AND EXCISE COMMISSIONERS v. BUGEJA (NO.2), [2001] EWCA Civ 1542, [2001] S.T.C. 1568, Chadwick, L.J., CA.

5557. **Excise duty – evasion – right to fair trial – status of civil penalties as "criminal charges" for purposes of Human Rights Act**

[Value Added Tax Act 1994 s.60(1); Finance Act 1994 s.8(1); Human Rights Act 1998 Sch.1 Part I Art.6(1).]

The Commissioners appealed against a decision ([2001] B.V.C. 2163) of the VAT and Duties Tribunal that "civil" penalties imposed against H, and others, pursuant to the Value Added Tax Act 1994 s.60(1) and the Finance Act 1994 s.8(1) for the dishonest evasion of tax were, in fact, "criminal charges" for the purposes of the Human Rights Act 1998 Sch.1 Part I Art.6(1).

Held, dismissing the appeal (Sir Martin Nourse dissenting), that the tribunal had been correct in its decision. When determining whether a "criminal charge" had been imposed within the meaning of Art.6(1), three criteria had to be applied, namely (1) the classification of the proceedings in domestic law; (2) the nature of the offence, and (3) the severity of the possible penalty. Under s.60(1) of the 1994 VAT Act, the classification of the penalties as civil was only a starting point, given that the purpose of the penalties was to punish and deter dishonest acts. The classification was not designed to decriminalise dishonest evasion of VAT. The Commissioners had a discretion as to whether they applied a civil penalty or prosecuted, and their decision was not meant to reflect the level of criminality of the offence in question. The differences between the two options was procedural and the European Court of Human Rights would not permit procedural features to define the nature of an offence. In applying the third criterion it was not necessary, in order for a penalty to be classified as "criminal" to show that the penalty to which the taxpayer was subject might involve imprisonment. All that had to be demonstrated was that the penalty was substantial and that its purpose was punitive. Accordingly, the civil penalties were criminal charges for the purposes of Art.6(1).

HAN (T/A MURDISHAW SUPPER BAR) v. CUSTOMS AND EXCISE COMMISSIONERS; MARTINS v. CUSTOMS AND EXCISE COMMISSIONERS; MORRIS v. CUSTOMS AND EXCISE COMMISSIONERS; YAU v. CUSTOMS AND EXCISE COMMISSIONERS, [2001] EWCA Civ 1048, [2001] 1 W.L.R. 2253, Potter, L.J., CA.

5558. Exemptions – advertising – supply of services – supply made through advertising agency in contract with advertiser

[Sixth Council Directive 77/388 on a common system for VAT Art.9(2) (3).]

In line with the Sixth Council Directive 77/388 Art.9(2)(e) second indent, French law exempted from VAT supplies of advertising made to other Member States or outside the EU. However, the exemption was subject to a Ministry of Economics, Finance and Industry administrative instruction which restricted it to supplies made directly to advertisers, so that supplies made through advertising agencies were precluded. SPI contended that the restriction was contrary to Art.9(2) and the Conseil d'Etat referred the matter to the ECJ for a preliminary ruling as to the scope of the exemption under Art.9(2)(e).

Held, upholding the complaint, that Art.9(2)(e) applied to situations where services were included in the price of goods. The nature of such services determined where the supply was actually made and included a supply of advertising services made by an advertising agency under a contract with the advertiser, *Commission of the European Communities v. France (C68/92)* [1997] S.T.C. 684, [1997] C.L.Y. 5015 and *Commission of the European Communities v. Luxembourg (C69/92)* [1997] S.T.C. 712, [1997] C.L.Y. 5016 applied.

SYNDICAT DES PRODUCTEURS INDEPENDANTS (SPI) v. MINISTERE DE L'ECONOMIE, DES FINANCES ET DE L'INDUSTRIE (C108/00) [2001] All E.R. (EC) 564, La Pergola (President), ECJ.

5559. Exemptions – alterations – conversion of listed building – meaning of "protected building"

[Planning (Listed Buildings and Conservation Areas) Act 1990 s.1 (5)(b); Value Added Tax Act 1994 Sch.8 Group 6.]

Customs appealed against a decision of the VAT and duties tribunal ([2001] B.V.C. 2059) that alterations to the outbuilding of a "listed building" amounted to alterations to a "protected building" within the meaning of the Value Added Tax Act 1994 Sch.8 Group 6 and, therefore, qualified for zero rating. The outbuilding, which constituted a "listed building" for the purposes of the Planning (Listed Buildings and Conservation Areas) Act 1990 s.1 (5)(b), had been converted for use as a games room and to provide changing facilities for an adjoining swimming pool. Customs contended that the outbuilding did not fall within the ambit of Group 6 since it had not been "designed to remain as or become a dwelling", and did not amount to self contained living accommodation.

Held, allowing the appeal, that upon the correct interpretation of Sch.8 Group 6 of the 1994 Act, a "protected building" was limited to a single building made up of one or more dwellings, each of which constituted self contained accommodation. Moreover, the social purpose behind Group 6 did not provide assistance when determining the degree to which the relief that it afforded was intended to extend, *Commission of the European Communities v. United Kingdom (C416/85)* [1990] 2 Q.B. 130, [1989] C.L.Y. 1685 considered.

CUSTOMS AND EXCISE COMMISSIONERS v. ZIELINSKI BAKER & PARTNERS LTD; *sub nom*. ZIELINSKI BAKER & PARTNERS LTD v. CUSTOMS AND EXCISE COMMISSIONERS [2001] S.T.C. 585, Etherton, J., Ch D.

5560. **Exemptions – analysis – medical samples – transmission fee paid by laboratory related to analysis under Sixth Council Directive – European Community**

[Sixth Council Directive 77/388 on a common system for VAT Art.13A(1)(b).]

Under French law the biological analysis of medical samples was exempt from VAT under the Sixth Council Directive 77/388 Art.13A(1)(b). However, where specialised analysis was performed by officially designated laboratories, fixed transmission fees were payable by the analysing laboratories to the laboratory that obtained the sample from the patient and these fees were subject to VAT. The Commission took the view that the transmission of a medical sample was related to hospital and medical care in terms of Art.13A(1)(b) and sought a declaration that France had failed to fulfil its obligations under Art.13A(1)(b).

Held, granting the declaration, that Art.13A(1)(b) did not include any definition of the concept of activities related to hospital and medical care. However, the exemption of such activities was intended to ensure that medical care was not subject to the increased costs of VAT levied on related activities. It followed that the transmission that was necessary between the taking of the sample and its analysis was related to the analysis and therefore exempt from VAT by virtue of Art.13A(1)(b).

COMMISSION OF THE EUROPEAN COMMUNITIES v. FRANCE (C76/99) [2001] 1 C.M.L.R. 48, Skouris (President), ECJ.

5561. **Exemptions – car parking fees – local authority acts coming under Sixth Directive 77/388 Art.4(5) – European Union**

[Sixth Council Directive 77/388 on a common system for VAT Art.4(5), Art.13B(b); Sixth Council Directive 77/388 on a common system for VAT Annex D.]

C, a local authority which levied payments in return for letting car parking spaces, objected to the imposition of VAT on those receipts. C contended that it was not liable to VAT as it was acting as a public authority under the Sixth Council Directive 77/388 Art.4(5). This argument was upheld in part at first instance and C and P, the Portuguese Treasury, appealed and questions as to the applicability of Art.4(5) were referred to the ECJ for a preliminary ruling.

Held, giving a preliminary ruling, that, (1) the letting of car parking spaces by CMP came within Art.4(5) where it was not carrying those activities under the same rules that applied to private undertakings; (2) public law bodies did not necessarily become liable to VAT because of the extent that they engaged in such activities. The scale of the activities was only to be considered in respect of the matters detailed in Annex D to the Directive where domestic law allowed an exemption for negligible activities under Art. 4(5); (3) Member States could define both "significant distortions" and "negligible activities" for the purposes of Art.4(5), as long as those definitions were susceptible to judicial review by the national courts, and (4) Art.4(5) was to be interpreted as meaning that the lack of an exemption for letting parking spaces in terms of Art.13B(b) did not prevent CMP from being as not liable to VAT if it otherwise complied with Art.4(5).

FAZENDA PUBLICA v. CAMARA MUNICIPAL DO PORTO (C446/98) [2001] S.T.C. 560, La Pergola (President), ECJ.

5562. **Exemptions – education – supplies made by students' union – determination of status by reference to university constitution**

[Value Added Tax Act 1994 Sch.9 Group 6 Item 4.]

U was established by royal charter which laid out its constitution and provided for a students' union, L. One of L's functions was the sale of soft drinks to students from a shop on U's premises. L accounted for VAT on those sales, but subsequently claimed that the supplies were exempt as supplies related to the provision of education by an eligible body for the purposes of the Value Added Tax Act 1994 Sch.9 Group 6 Item 4. This was denied by Customs, and L appealed. The VAT and Duties Tribunal ([2001] B.V.C. 2102) held that L formed an integral part of U and was therefore involved in the supply of education in terms of item 4(a). Customs appealed.

Held, allowing the appeal, that the question of whether L was an integral part of U had to be decided by reference to U's constitution. On a proper construction, this showed that L was not a constituent body, and although L was dependent on U, this did not suffice to make it an integral part. L's separate VAT registration pointed away from such a conclusion in any event. On the facts, therefore, L's soft drink sales were not supplies made by a body concerned in the main supply of education so that the exemption did not apply.

CUSTOMS AND EXCISE COMMISSIONERS v. LEICESTER UNIVERSITY STUDENTS UNION; *sub nom.* CUSTOMS AND EXCISE COMMISSIONERS v. UNIVERSITY OF LEICESTER STUDENTS UNION [2001] S.T.C. 550, Rimer, J., Ch D.

5563. **Exemptions – gardens – status as museum – effect of cultural activities – exemption under Sixth Council Directive**

[Value Added Tax Act 1994 Sch.9 Group 13 item 2; Sixth Council Directive 77/388 on a common system for VAT Art.13A(1)(n).]

T was a registered charity whose object was the preservation of a garden for the purposes of public education. T appealed against a decision that the garden did not come within the exemption for museums under the Value Added Tax Act 1994 Sch.9 Group 13 item 2, arguing that the Sixth Council Directive 77/388 Art.13A(1)(n) provided an exemption for cultural activities capable of including the garden. Customs asserted that it was for Member States to determine the relevant exempt cultural activities and under the 1994 Act the garden did not qualify as a museum. Further, that T did not qualify for exemption as a museum because it did not satisfy the conditions of an eligible body. H, who had set up the trust and donated the house and garden to it, remained actively involved in its day to day management. He lived in part of the house rent free and was entitled to repayment of an interest free loan which meant that he had a financial interest in T's activities.

Held, dismissing the appeal, that although a "museum" was not to be defined too literally, in terms of being restricted to items displayed in a building, *Dean and Canons of Windsor v. Customs and Excise Commissioners* [1999] B.V.C. 2010, [1999] C.L.Y. 4974 considered. Taken objectively, however, the average visitor would not regard the garden as a museum. Accordingly, it did not qualify for the exemption. However, T was an eligible body for the purposes of the exemption as H's occupation of the accommodation was a requirement of the duties he carried out for T. His right to repayment of the loan was largely theoretical, as it would be impracticable given the present state of T's income. On the facts, therefore, H did not have a financial interest in T's operation,

Glastonbury Abbey v. Customs and Excise Commissioners [1996] V. & D.R. 307, [1997] C.L.Y. 4984.
TREBAH GARDEN TRUST v. CUSTOMS AND EXCISE COMMISSIONERS [2000] B.V.C. 2345, RK Miller, CB (Chairman), V&DTr.

5564. Exemptions – insurance transactions – contractual relationship between insurer and insured required under Sixth Directive – European Community

[Sixth Council Directive 77/388 on a common system for VAT Art.2(1), Art.13(B)(a).]
The Swedish Supreme Court referred a question to the ECJ on the interpretation of Sixth Council Directive 77/388 on a common system for VAT Art.13(B)(a). S, an insurance company, and L, one of its subsidiaries, had been contemplating an arrangement whereby their insurance activities would be merged and S would conduct all of L's business in return for which, it would receive remuneration at market rates. L, however, would continue to be an insurer for the purposes of Swedish civil law for which S would assume no liability. S had sought an opinion from the Supreme Court on whether the assumption of a commitment to conduct L's business activities could be regarded as an insurance transaction for the purposes of Art.13(B)(a) and thus be exempt from VAT.
Held, giving a preliminary ruling, that an arrangement whereby an insurance company ran the business activities of a wholly owned subsidiary company in return for remuneration at market rates without assuming the related liabilities of the subsidiary continuing to act as an insurer, could not be included in the exemption provision of Art.13(B)(a). An insurance transaction within Art.13(B)(a) implied the existence of a contractual relationship between the insurance service provider and the insured and it was clear in the instant case that there would be no legal relationship between S and L's clients under the agreement, *Card Protection Plan Ltd v. Customs and Excise Commissioners (C349/96)* [1999] 2 A.C. 601, [1999] C.L.Y. 4972 distinguished. The arrangement between the companies amounted to a service effected for consideration within Art.2(1) of the Directive and was thus subject to VAT.
FORSAKRINGSAKTIEBOLAGET SKANDIA (C240/99), *Re; sub nom.* PROCEEDINGS BROUGHT BY FORSAKRINGSAKTIEBOLAGET SKANDIA (C240/99) [2001] 1 W.L.R. 1617, Wathelet (President), ECJ.

5565. Exemptions – licences – sale of cigarettes through vending machines – letting of immovable property

[Value Added Tax Act 1994 s.31, Sch.9 Part II Group 1; Sixth Council Directive 77/388 on a common system for VAT Art.13(B)(b).]
SC appealed against a decision ([1999] S.T.C. 701) that an agreement to provide, operate and maintain vending machines for the sale of cigarettes in public houses, clubs and hotels constituted the grant of a licence to occupy land and accordingly was an exempt supply for the purposes of the Value Added Tax 1994 s.31 and Sch.9 Part II Group 1. The vending machines were supplied on an exclusive basis for a two year term in consideration of the owner of the premises receiving a part of the sale proceeds from the machines.
Held, adjourning the appeal, that the agreement constituted one composite supply rather than two separate supplies and the grant of the right to sell cigarettes was ancillary and consequential to the grant of the right to install the machines. The question for determination was therefore whether the grant of the right to install the machines constituted the leasing or letting of immovable property within the Sixth Council Directive 77/388 Art.13(B)(b). It was, however, appropriate to refer determination on that issue to the European Court of Justice.
SINCLAIR COLLIS LTD v. CUSTOMS AND EXCISE COMMISSIONERS; *sub nom.* CUSTOMS AND EXCISE COMMISSIONERS v. SINCLAIR COLLIS LTD, [2001] UKHL 30, [2001] S.T.C. 989, Lord Slynn of Hadley, HL.

5566. Exemptions – professional bodies – organisation with aims of civic nature

[Value Added Tax Act 1994 Sch.9 Group 9 para (e); Sixth Council Directive 77/388 on a common system for VAT Art.13A(1) (l).]

E, an organisation established to ensure the provision of unbiased advice as part of the administration of justice, appealed against a decision of the VAT and Duties Tribunal ([2001] B.V.C. 2125) that it was liable to VAT on supplies to its members.

Held, allowing the appeal, that the aims of the Institute could properly be described as being for the promotion of the proper administration of justice and the early resolution of disputes. Accordingly, it was exempt from VAT as an organisation with aims of a civic nature within the Sixth Council Directive 77/388 Art.13A(1)(l) and as a body which had objects that were in the public domain and were of a civic nature within the Value Added Tax Act 1994 Sch.9 Group 9 para (e).

EXPERT WITNESS INSTITUTE v. CUSTOMS AND EXCISE COMMISSIONERS [2001] 1 W.L.R. 1658, Lloyd, J., Ch D.

5567. Exemptions – sale of land – election to waive – intention to change to residential use – seller's knowledge at time of sale

[Value Added Tax Act 1994 Sch.10 para.2(2) (a).]

F, a member of SEH's VAT group, appealed against a decision that the supply of a public house which F sold to G and T for conversion into residential dwellings was not, on the date of purchase, an exempt supply under the Value Added Tax Act 1994 Sch.10 para. 2(2) (a). The seller had elected to waive the VAT exemption on the sale to F and the contract stipulated that the sale was subject to VAT. However, F contended that the exemption for residential use in Sch.10 para.2(2) (a) was not restricted to the intended use of the purchaser and applied as long as the seller was aware of the ultimate intention at the time of the sale.

Held, dismissing the appeal, that the exemption had to be construed strictly and therefore did not apply in the instant case where F had sold the property on to G and T. The seller must know of the purchaser's intended use, and although G and T had told the seller that it wanted to apply for planning permission in respect of the property, that had been 12 months before the sale to F and F had not shown that the seller was aware of the intention to change to residential use at the time of the sale.

SEH HOLDINGS LTD v. CUSTOMS AND EXCISE COMMISSIONERS [2001] B.V.C. 2093, AN Brice (Chairman), V&DTr.

5568. Exemptions – state security – import and acquisition of arms for exclusive use by military

[EC Treaty Art.223 (now, after amendment, Art.296); Sixth Council Directive 77/388 on a common system for VAT.]

The Commission sought a declaration that Spain had infringed the Sixth Council Directive 77/388 by exempting from VAT intra-Community imports and acquisitions of arms, ammunition and equipment exclusively for military use. The Spanish Government relied on the derogation in respect of national security provided by the EC Treaty Art.223 (now, after amendment, Art.296).

Held, granting the declaration, that Art.296 applied only in exceptional and clearly defined cases. Therefore it was for the Member State seeking to rely on the derogation to provide evidence that the exemption in question fell within Art.296. In the present case, it was clear that the law enacting the VAT exemptions had a fiscal purpose and accordingly Spain had not demonstrated that the VAT exemptions were necessary for the protection of the essential interests of its national security.

COMMISSION OF THE EUROPEAN COMMUNITIES v. SPAIN (C414/97) [2001] 2 C.M.L.R. 4, Kapteyn (President), ECJ.

5569. Exemptions – supply of services – composite services – stabling and livery services

[Value Added Tax Act 1994 Sch.9 Group 1 Item 1.]

W, who supplied stabling for horses with an optional livery service, appealed against Customs' decision that whilst the supply of stabling was exempt from VAT for the purposes of the Value Added Tax Act 1994 Sch.9 Group 1 Item 1, the supply of stabling together with the livery service constituted a composite standard-rated supply and was subject to VAT. W charged for the two services separately, consisting of a fixed stable rent fee and livery fees dependent upon the services required which could include general grooming and schooling. The services were paid for by a single combined payment and some 58 per cent of those horses stabled made use of livery services. At issue was whether the supply of stabling together with other livery services constituted a composite standard-rated supply subject to VAT, or whether the two services constituted a composite exempt supply, the exempt part of the supply, namely the stabling service, being the principal service.

Held, allowing the appeal, that whilst the supply of a livery service on its own was a standard-rated supply, the supply of stabling with the optional livery service amounted to a single exempt supply since the livery service was ancillary to and dependent on the principal and exempt service of stabling. Whilst the rent for stables was a separate matter from any livery services agreed, it was apparent that the principal reason horse owners paid for livery and stabling together was to secure stabling.

WINDOW v. CUSTOMS AND EXCISE COMMISSIONERS [2001] B.V.C. 2299, Cornwell-Kelly (Chairman), V&DTr.

5570. Exemptions – trade unions – definition of union function – lack of defence and representational role

[Sixth Council Directive 77/388 on a common system for VAT Art.13A(1)(1).]

M was a voluntary association of workers and employers associated with the motor industry. Its aims were to advance the standing and training of its members and to enhance the industry's standing in the eyes of the public. To achieve these aims, M sponsored courses and offered a range of services to its members. M appealed against a decision that its activities did not qualify for the trade union exemption in the Sixth Council Directive 77/388 Art.13A(1)(1) and the tribunal referred the question of the definition of "trade union" for a preliminary ruling to the ECJ ([1996] V. & D. R. 370). The ECJ held ([1998] S.T.C. 1219, [1998] C.L.Y. 4901) that the essential aim of a trade union was the collective defence of its members' interests and their representation before third parties.

Held, dismissing the appeal, that although membership of M conferred quantifiable benefits, these did not include the defence and representational services associated with a trade union. Therefore M did not qualify for the exemption under Art.13A(1)(1).

INSTITUTE OF THE MOTOR INDUSTRY v. CUSTOMS AND EXCISE COMMISSIONERS [2000] B.V.C. 2307, Stephen Oliver Q.C. (Chairman), V&DTr.

5571. Fiscal policy – France – reduced rate for medicinal products – compatibility with Sixth Council Directive – European Community

[Sixth Council Directive 77/388 on a common system of VAT Art.12, Art.17.]

The Commission sought a declaration that France was in breach of its obligations under the Sixth Council Directive 77/388 Art.12 by its introduction and maintenance of legislation which provided for a reduced VAT rate of 2.1 per cent to be charged on medicinal products reimbursable under the social security system, whereas other medicinal products were to be charged at the reduced rate of 5.5 per cent. France argued that the system of two different reduced rates of VAT for medicinal products was consistent with Community law, in particular the principle of fiscal neutrality and further, that the reduced rate had been introduced for social reasons and for the benefit of the final consumer thus fulfilling the criteria set out in Art.17 of the Directive.

Held, refusing the application, that as reimbursable and non reimbursable medicinal products were sufficiently dissimilar so as not to be in competition with each other, the principle of fiscal neutrality which was inherent in the common system of VAT had remained intact. On the classification of a medicinal product as reimbursable, it would become distinct from a non reimbursable medicinal product for the purpose of competition in spite of a similar curative or preventive effect and it would also be preferred by the consumer. Further, the reduced rate of VAT for medicinal products had clearly been introduced by France for a social reason and not an economic reason as maintained by the Commission.

COMMISSION OF THE EUROPEAN COMMUNITIES v. FRANCE (C481/98), [2001] S.T.C. 919,, C Gulmann (President), ECJ.

5572. Implied terms – supply of services – duty to maintain accounting records – inclusion of implied contractual term requiring the issue of VAT invoices

[Value Added Tax Regulations (SI 1995 2518) Reg.13(1).]

E applied for an order of specific performance that F provide it with VAT invoices relating to the supply of telecommunications services as required by an implied term of the contract between the parties for telecommunications services. F applied to have the application struck out. E's argument was that under the implied term F was to supply E with a number of monthly VAT invoices that it required to meet its obligation to account for VAT. Additionally, E contended that the Value Added Tax Regulations 1995 Reg.13(1) provided that a registered person making a taxable supply to another taxable person should produce to that person a taxable invoice.

Held, granting the application to strike out, that the duty of a trader to maintain proper accounting records did not justify the inclusion in commercial contracts of an implied term concerning the speedy and regular issuing of VAT invoices, otherwise such a term would have to be implied into every contract for goods and services, *Hughes v. Greenwich LBC* [1994] 1 A.C. 170, [1994] C.L.Y. 2367 and *Society of Lloyd's v. Clementson* [1995] C.L.C. 117, [1994] C.L.Y. 2684 considered.

EUROPHONE INTERNATIONAL LTD v. FRONTEL COMMUNICATIONS LTD (T/A FRONTIER COMMUNICATIONS INTERNATIONAL); *sub nom.* EUROPHONE INTERNATIONAL LTD v. FRONTEL COMMUNICATIONS LTD; EUROPHONE INTERNATIONAL LTD v. FRONTIER COMMUNICATIONS INTERNATIONAL [2001] S.T.C. 1399, Ferris, J., Ch D.

5573. Imports – non Member States – payable as customs duty

VALUE ADDED TAX (AMENDMENT) REGULATIONS 2001, SI 2001 630; made under the Value Added Tax Act 1994 s.16, s.25, Sch.11 para.2. In force: April 1, 2001; £1.75.

These Regulations, which amend the Value Added Tax Regulations 1995 (SI 1995 2518), remove the Community legislation associated with processing under customs control from the existing lists of Community customs provisions excepted from applying to import VAT with the result that the import VAT on goods under processing for customs control becomes due at the same time as customs duty, thus implementing the UK's obligations. They ensure that goods on which VAT has been charged before April 1, 2001 are not chargeable to VAT again on release for free circulation and add the Community legislation that charges are compensatory interest on customs debts to the lists of excepted customs legislation.

5574. Indirect taxes – tourism – charges lacking characteristics of turnover tax – European Union

[Sixth Council Directive 77/388 on a common system for VAT Art.33(1).]

The ECJ was asked to determine whether charges levied in three areas of Austria intended to promote tourism amounted to turnover taxes that adversely affected the common system of VAT and as such prohibited by the Sixth Council Directive 77/388 Art.33(1). The charges were payable by traders with an interest in tourism. They was levied at different rates, depending upon the benefit that the trader derived from tourism, based on the annual taxable turnover achieved.

Held, finding that the charges did not have the characteristics of VAT, that for a charge to constitute a turnover tax for the purposes of Art.33 it was necessary to determine whether it affected the functioning of the VAT system. On the facts, the charges did not permit the deduction of input tax and they were not passed on to the final consumer, as was the case with VAT. Further, it was not possible to determine the precise amount of the charge passed on to the final consumer when a sale was made or a service was supplied. Accordingly, the charges were not a tax on consumption resting on the final consumer but were levied on traders engaged in tourism related activities.

PELZL v. STEIERMARKISCHE LANDESREGIERUNG (C338/97); WIENER STADTISCHE ALLGEMEINE VERSICHERUNGS AG v. TIROLER LANDESREGIERUNG (C344/97); STUAG BAUAKTIENGESELLSCHAFT v. KARNTNER LANDESREGIERUNG (C390/97) [1999] E.C.R. I-3319, J-P Puissochet (President), ECJ.

5575. Input tax – cars – high value sports car acquired solely for business use – availability for private use

[Value Added Tax (Input Tax) Order 1992 (SI 1992 3222) Art.7.]

Customs appealed against a VAT and duties tribunal decision ([2001] B.V.C. 2099) allowing U's appeal against a decision to refuse his claim for input tax of £19,517.85 incurred on the acquisition of a Lamborghini Diabolo. U's business involved the servicing and supply of cigarette machines in licensed premises. Although the car was insured for private and domestic use, U contended that it was only acquired to impress business clients and to give him an edge over the competition. The car was kept garaged near to his home during the day and used only in the evenings, when it was parked outside clubs while he serviced cigarette machines and emptied the cash boxes. The tribunal found that input tax could be reclaimed as the car was not "made available" for private use in terms of the Value Added Tax (Input Order) 1992 Art.7(2G)(b) where U had no intention that it would ever be used for private purposes.

Held, allowing the appeal, that the tribunal had applied the wrong test when finding that U did not intend to use the car for private purposes in terms of Art.7(2G)(b). The intention that a car was available for private use would be satisfied under Art.7(2G)(b) if the person acquiring it did not take steps to exclude such use. As the tribunal had gone on to recognise that the car was available for private use in theory, with no steps being taken to exclude it, then U was precluded from reclaiming input tax by Art.7(1).

CUSTOMS AND EXCISE COMMISSIONERS v. UPTON (T/A FAGOMATIC) [2001] S.T.C. 912, Sir Andrew Morritt V.C., Ch D.

5576. Input tax – colleges – distribution of prospectuses – taxable supplies

[Value Added Tax Act 1994 Sch.4 para.5(1).]

The Commissioners appealed against a decision of the VAT and Duties Tribunal that the distribution of prospectuses by W came within the Value Added Tax Act 1994 Sch.4 para.5(1) and therefore constituted taxable supplies to which the input tax, which W sought to reclaim, was directly attributable. The Commissioners submitted that (1) para.5(1) was not applicable unless the taxable person already had the right to credit for input tax in respect of goods and services made to him, and (2) the input tax which W sought to deduct was input tax on goods and services which were used by the college to make its exempt supply of education and that the prospectuses should not be regarded as the subject of a separate supply.

Held, dismissing the appeal, that (1) given that the Commissioners had never before challenged W's right to deduct part of the input tax in respect of goods and supplies, it was not open for them to do so in the appeal, and (2) the transfer of goods, such as prospectuses, for promotional purposes was not excluded from Sch.4 para.5(1) of the Act.

CUSTOMS AND EXCISE COMMISSIONERS v. WEST HERTS COLLEGE; *sub nom.* WEST HERTS COLLEGE v. CUSTOMS AND EXCISE COMMISSIONERS [2001] S.T.C.1245, Hart, J., Ch D.

5577. Input tax – deductions – right to deduct – sale of land and buildings – intention to commence economic activity never realised

[Sixth Council Directive 77/388 on a common system for VAT Art.4, Art.17.]

B intended to operate a motor vehicle dealership. However, due to increased building costs, she could not complete the building work and sold the uncompleted works to a third party for a price including VAT. She later sold the land to the same person. B declared the sale of the land in her VAT return and deducted the VAT incurred on the building works. The deduction was refused, but B successfully appealed against the refusal and the court held that B's trading activity, giving rise to a right to deduct VAT, began when she commenced acts preparatory to trade. The tax authorities appealed and the matter was stayed pending a reference to the ECJ for a preliminary ruling as to whether (1) the right to deduct under the Sixth Council Directive 77/388 Art.17 existed when there was only an intention to start an economic activity, even though no taxable transactions were ever made, and (2) if (1) was answered in the affirmative, whether the option to tax under Art.4(3) could be limited to only parts of buildings or extended over the entire site.

Held, that (1) Art.4 and Art.17 allowed the deduction of input tax on transactions carried out with a view to conducting an economic activity, even where the tax authorities knew that the activity would not actually commence. The right to deduct input tax arose when investment expenditure was made and could only be precluded in cases of fraud or abuse, *Belgium v. Ghent Coal Terminal NV (C37/95)* [1998] All E.R. (EC) 223 and *Gabalfrisa SL v. Agencia Estatal de Administracion Tributaria (C147/98)* [2000] S.T.I. 502 applied, and (2) the option to tax under Art.4(3)(a) exercised at the time of the supply of buildings and land was inseparable from those supplies, so that a supply of buildings, and the land on which they stood, could be subject either to a VAT exemption for the entire supply, or taxed as a whole, in which case the person making the supply could deduct VAT incurred on the building work where the sale of the land itself was subject to VAT.

FINANZAMT GOSLAR v. BREITSOHL (C400/98) [2001] S.T.C. 355, JC Moitinho de Almeida (President), ECJ.

5578. Input tax – EC law – partial deduction – dividend and interest payments made to holding company by subsidiaries

[Sixth Council Directive 77/388 on a common system for VAT Art.4(2), Art.19(1).]

The national court referred to the ECJ for a preliminary ruling the question whether the Sixth Council Directive 77/388 Art.19 was to be interpreted as precluding dividends and loan interest paid to a holding company, F, by its subsidiaries, to which F supplied management and administrative services, when calculating the amount of deductible input tax in respect of supplies made to F. The tax authorities contended that the input tax could not be deducted be deducted in its entirety and that F should have included the loan interest and the dividends when calculating the proportion eligible for deduction.

Held, giving a preliminary ruling, that loan transactions were only subject to VAT if they formed part of F's economic activities, in terms of Art.4(2), or were directly attributable to its taxable activities. Capital made available to a subsidiary could be included in the deductible proportion if it was done so regularly and was not restricted to managing investments in the same way as a private investor. Loans made to subsidiaries receiving management and other services from F were not liable to VAT and they did not have the necessary link to supplies made to it. Similarly, dividends paid to F which were then reinvested in the subsidiaries as loans were not liable to VAT and could not be included when calculating input tax deductions.

FLORIDIENNE SA v. BELGIUM (C142/99) [2001] All E.R. (EC) 37, M Wathelet (President), ECJ.

5579. Input tax – exemptions – meaning of "business activity"

[Value Added Taxes Act 1994 s.33; Sixth Council Directive 77/388 Art.4(5).]

WD appealed against a VAT assessment imposed in relation to conversion work carried out by building contractors. The funds for the work had been made available from WD's own reserves, from grant monies and from a limited company. WD had entered into an agreement with the company whereby in return for payment of £130,000, the company agreed to enter into an underlease of the premises 14 days following practical completion at a peppercorn rent and operate an arts centre on a non profit making basis. The Commissioners disallowed various deductions to input tax charged by the building contractors on their invoices and concluded that the grant of the underlease had been undertaken in return for a premium of £130,000 which therefore constituted a business activity for the purposes of the Value Added Taxes Act 1994 s.33, with the result that the exemption in s.33(1)(b) was not available. WD contended that the grant of the underlease was not an activity undertaken in the course or furtherance of a business and that accordingly input tax was recoverable.

Held, dismissing the appeal, that when interpreting the concept of "business", it was necessary to have regard to the Sixth Council Directive 77/ 388 Art.4(5). The critical factor was whether the transaction in question was governed by ordinary private law rules or whether it took effect under a special legal regime applicable to local authorities, *Ufficio Distrettuale delle Imposte Dirette di Fiorenzuola d'Arda v. Comune di Carpaneto Piacentino (C231/87)* [1991] S.T.C. 205, [1991] C.L.Y. 3661 considered. On the facts, the arrangements between the company and WD were standard private law terms and not governed by any particular regime. Whilst the arts centre run from the premises in question was non profit making and the arrangements made by WD in relation to the project had lacked commerciality, it was clear that the relevant supply, namely the grant of the underlease, could constitute a business. Furthermore, all the relevant criteria for the existence of a business had been met, namely the creation of a legal relationship in exchange for a monetary consideration upon terms which included full repairing covenants, *Customs and Excise Commissioners v. Morrison's Academy Boarding Houses Association* [1978] S.T.C. 1, [1977] C.L.Y. 3812 considered.

WEST DEVON BC v. CUSTOMS AND EXCISE COMMISSIONERS; *sub nom.* WEST DEVON DC v. CUSTOMS AND EXCISE COMMISSIONERS [2001] S.T.C. 1282, Patten, J., Ch D.

5580. Input tax – exemptions – police authorities – refund of input tax for new motor vehicles

[Value Added Tax Act 1994 s.25(7), s.33; Value Added Tax (Input Tax) Order 1992 (SI 1992 3222) Art.7; Sixth Council Directive 77/388 on a common system for VAT Art.4(5).]

GMPA, a public body which also undertook business activities for remuneration, appealed against the refusal of its application ([2000] S.T.C. 620, [2000] C.L.Y. 5307) for judicial review of the Commissioner's refusal of a claim for the refund of VAT under the Value Added Tax Act 1994 s.33. The claim, amounting to about £500,000, related to the VAT paid on the purchase of motor vehicles destined for use for public duties. Under s.33(6) a scheme to refund public bodies was subject to any exclusion set out in an order made pursuant to s.25(7). The judge had found that a refund was barred due to the Value Added Tax (Input Tax) Order 1992 Art.7, which excluded the recovery of VAT charged on the purchase of motor vehicles. It was common ground that the purpose of the Act was to provide a refund scheme to prevent the burden of VAT falling on public bodies and that that purpose accorded with the Sixth Council Directive 77/388 Art.4(5). GMPA contended that the use of the particular wording "VAT chargeable" in s.33(6) indicated that it applied only to s.33(2) which dealt with mixed business and private use and not to s.33(1) which covered solely non business use. Furthermore, it was argued that a refund under s.33(1) was of VAT incurred in a non business activity to which s.25(7) did not apply and which could never be VAT "excluded from credit under that section".

Held, dismissing the appeal, that VAT on motor cars was excluded from credit under s.25 by Art.7 of the 1992 Order, as amended. The intention of s.33(6) was to apply, with the necessary changes, that provision to the refund scheme. The 1992 Order was a "blunt instrument" designed to prevent tax evasion from the use of company cars for private purposes but it also had the effect of limiting the refund scheme in relation to motor cars supplied to public bodies which were not taxable persons, *Royscot Leasing Ltd v. Customs and Excise Commissioners (C305/97)* [2000] 1 W.L.R. 1151, [1999] C.L.Y. 4992 considered.

R. v. CUSTOMS AND EXCISE COMMISSIONERS, *ex p.* GREATER MANCHESTER POLICE AUTHORITY, [2001] EWCA Civ 213, [2001] S.T.C. 406, Aldous, L.J., CA.

5581. **Input tax – exemptions – sporting facilities – compatibility with Sixth Directive 77/388 in respect of profit making operations – European Community**

[Sixth Council Directive 77/388 on a common system for VAT Art.13A, Art.13B.]

SL operated a golf course as a profit making business. It claimed damages in the national court against S, on the grounds that a general VAT exemption for sporting activities featured in national legislation from January 1, 1995 to January 1, 1997, meant that SL had lost the opportunity to reclaim SKR 500,000 in input tax incurred in the course of its business activities. SL's claim was upheld at first instance and SL and S appealed. The appeal court referred to the ECJ for a preliminary ruling as to whether the general exemption was permitted under the Sixth Council Directive 77/388 Art.13A and Art.13B, and, if not, whether the breach was sufficiently serious to allow SL to bring a claim for damages.

Held, giving a preliminary ruling, that a total exemption for sporting activities was contrary to Art.13A(1)(m) and Art.13B(b) as the exemption therein was restricted to non profit making operations. The relevant provisions of the Sixth Directive were sufficiently precise for SL to be able to rely on them before the national court. Further, the breach was of sufficient gravity to render S liable to SL in damages, *Brasserie du Pecheur SA v. Germany (C46/93)* [1996] Q.B. 404, [1996] C.L.Y. 2803, *Dillenkofer v. Germany (C178/94)* [1997] Q.B. 259, [1996] C.L.Y. 2802 and *Rechberger v. Austria (C140/97)* [1999] E.C.R. I-3499, [2000] 10 C.L. 398 applied.

SWEDEN v. STOCKHOLM LINDOPARK AB (C150/99); STOCKHOLM LINDOPARK AB v. SWEDEN (C150/99) [2001] S.T.C. 103, DAO Edward (President), ECJ.

5582. **Input tax – harmonisation of laws – apportionment of residual input tax – value-based or use-based apportionment – compatibility with EC law**

[Value Added Tax (General) Regulations 1985 (SI 1985 886) Reg.30, Reg.32; Sixth Council Directive 77/388 on a common system for VAT Art.17(5), Art.19.]

L, which had supplied educational services in the field of performing arts, such services being an exempt supply for the purposes of VAT, appealed against a decision ([1999] S.T.C. 424, [1999] C.L.Y. 4991) that "taxable supplies" within the meaning of the Value Added Tax (General) Regulations 1985 Reg.30 did not include supplies to countries outside the United Kingdom, the latter being covered by the regime laid down in Reg.32 of the Regulations. L submitted that (1) the operation of the Sixth Council Directive 77/388 Art.17(5) and Art.19 required a value-based approach to the apportionment of residual input tax as between supplies in respect of which input tax could be recovered, and supplies in respect of which input tax could not be deducted. L maintained that Reg.30(2)(d) provided that apportionment, while Reg.32, although limited to determining the amount of input tax to be attributed to out-of-country supplies, did not prevent the out-of-country supplies, which would have been taxable had they been made in-country, from being "taxable supplies" for the purposes of Reg.30, alternatively (2) if Regs.30 and 32 were two separate and self-contained regimes, then Reg.32 was inconsistent with, and had to give way to, Arts.17(5) and 19 of the Directive.

Held, dismissing the appeal, that (1) the combined effect of Arts.17(5) and 19 of the Directive did, indeed, contemplate a value-based approach to the apportionment of residual input tax, but they did not insist upon such an approach. Article 17(5)(c) also allowed apportionment on the basis of use and there was no restriction upon the exercise of a use-based apportionment in respect of the input tax on a portion of the goods and services and the exercise of the value-based apportionment prescribed by Reg.30(2)(d) for the remainder, and (2) Reg.32, which was an entirely separate regime for out-of-country supplies from that provided by Reg.30 for taxable supplies and exempt supplies, required a use-based apportionment, but that was not inconsistent with the Directive, as Art.17(5) envisaged more than one basis of apportionment. Furthermore "all supplies" in Reg.30(2)(d) did not include out-of-country supplies that would, if made in the UK, have been taxable.

CUSTOMS AND EXCISE COMMISSIONERS v. LIVERPOOL INSTITUTE FOR PERFORMING ARTS; *sub nom.* CUSTOMS AND EXCISE COMMISSIONERS v. LIVERPOOL SCHOOL OF PERFORMING ARTS, [2001] UKHL 28, [2001] 1 W.L.R. 1187, Lord Scott of Foscote, HL.

5583. **Input tax – repayments – goods and services purchased by French branch used in making taxable transactions in Italy – European Union**

[Sixth Council Directive 77/388 on a common system for VAT Art.17; Eighth Council Directive 79/1072 on arrangements for the refund of value added tax to taxable persons not established in the territory of the country Art.2, Art.5.]

MPS, an Italian bank with an office in France, applied for the refund of VAT paid on goods and services purchased in France but used in the course of both taxable and exempt transactions in Italy. This was refused by the French tax authorities and MPS unsuccessfully appealed to the administrative court. That decision was itself overturned on appeal, where MPS was allowed a VAT refund, based on a percentage of its Italian taxable turnover. The French Ministry of the Economy and Finance appealed to the Conseil d'Etat, which stayed the proceedings and sought a preliminary ruling from the ECJ as to whether MPS was entitled to a VAT refund in France under the Sixth Council Directive 77/388 Art.17 and the Eighth Council Directive 79/1072 Art.2 and Art.5

Held, giving a preliminary ruling, that (1) Art. 17 of the Sixth Directive gave rise to right to deduct VAT incurred on goods and services used in the course of making taxable transactions. Under Art.2 of the Eighth Directive, MPS had the right to claim a partial refund in France of VAT charged there in respect of goods and services used to make taxable transactions in Italy, and (2) the refund was calculated by first identifying which transactions carried a right of deduction under Art.17 of the Sixth Directive in Italy and then focusing on those transactions and expenses that also qualified for a deduction in France if undertaken there.

MINISTRE DU BUDGET v. SOCIETE MONTE DEI PASCHI DI SIENA (C136/99) [2001] S.T.C. 1029, DAO Edward (President), ECJ.

5584. Input tax – repayments – three year cap – claim made subsequent to original repayment claim

[Value Added Tax Act 1994 s.77, s.80.]

U appealed against a decision that claims to recover residual input tax, made in 1996 as a result of errors discovered following a change of accountants, were precluded where they related to periods going back more than three years. U's original accountants, C, had submitted claims for overpaid input tax for the period from August 1973 to July 1993. However, when K took over as U's accountants, further claims relating to those periods were submitted in 1996. U contended that the 1996 claim was an amendment in terms of the Value Added Tax Act 1994 s.80 and, as such, was not liable to the three year repayment cap. Further, that as the cap was intended to give parity to both taxpayers and Customs, additional claims should be allowed outside the cap on the same basis that Customs could make a supplementary assessment more than three years after an original assessment under s.77.

Held, dismissing the appeal, that (1) although Customs had paid some of the 1996 claim relating to periods less than three years old, that did not mean that the 1996 claim was an amendment to the claim originally made by C. As that claim was complete when the 1996 claim was made, the latter claim did not qualify as a new claim for the purposes of s.80, and (2) the power to make a supplementary assessment under s.77 only ran until the final day that the original assessment could have been made. By contrast U claimed that the time limit for a repayment claim was the date of its final determination, irrespective of when the three year cap actually expired.

UNIVERSITY OF LIVERPOOL v. CUSTOMS AND EXCISE COMMISSIONERS [2001] B.V.C. 2088, JD Demack (Chairman), V&DTr.

5585. Input tax – sale of land – exempt supply of land – provision of housing – apportionment

[Value Added Tax Act 1994.]

Customs appealed against a decision of the VAT and Duties Tribunal ([2001] B.V.C. 2159) allowing W's appeal against its assessment of the input tax payable by W. W, a land developing business, had purchased land and agreed to sell it on to a housing association, A, as part of a package in which W were to build flats for A on the land. Customs had assessed the transaction in relation to the sale element only, that being an exempt supply under the Value Added Tax Act 1994. The tribunal found that W had only ever intended to sell the land as part of a development package and therefore the assessment should be apportioned to take into account the taxable element of the provision of housing. Customs argued that the tribunal had applied the wrong test.

Held, dismissing the appeal, that the tribunal had applied the right test. It had considered whether the input was "objectively linked" in a "direct and immediate" way to the taxable transaction, *BLP Group Plc v. Customs and Excise Commissioners (C4/94)* [1996] 1 W.L.R. 174, [1995] C.L.Y. 5059 applied. Later authorities had not significantly altered that test and therefore it remained the appropriate one, which the tribunal had properly applied by looking at all the relevant factors, such as W's overall business and the nature of the package that formed the deal between W and A, *Midland Bank Plc v. Customs and Excise Commissioners (C98/98)* [2000] 1 W.L.R. 2080, [2000] 7 C.L. 514 and *Abbey National Plc v. Customs and Excise Commissioners (C408/98)* [2001] 1 W.L.R. 769, [2001] 4 C.L. 688 considered. The court would only interfere with the tribunal's findings where, in applying the correct test, its conclusions could not properly have been reached on the material before it.

WIGGETT CONSTRUCTION LTD v. CUSTOMS AND EXCISE COMMISSIONERS; *sub nom.* CUSTOMS AND EXCISE COMMISSIONERS v. WIGGETT CONSTRUCTION LTD [2001] S.T.C. 933, Lightman, J., Ch D.

5586. Input tax – transfer of going concern – right to deduct on services acquired to effect transfer

[Sixth Council Directive 77/388 on a common system for VAT Art.5(8), Art.17(2), Art.17(5).]

The question of whether on a correct interpretation of the Sixth Council Directive 77/388 Arts.5(8),17(2)(a) and (5),VAT could be deducted as input tax where there had been a transfer of a business or part of one, was referred to the ECJ for a preliminary ruling. The United Kingdom had exercised its option under Art.5(8) so that in the event of a transfer of a totality of assets or a part thereof as a going concern, it was considered that no supply of goods or services had taken place and accordingly no VAT would become due on the transaction. SM, a life assurance company and a subsidiary of AN, carried on business leasing premises for commercial or professional use and sought to recover the VAT paid in respect of various services involved in effecting the transfer of a lease to another company. The VAT Commissioners rejected its claim maintaining that the transfer of the lease constituted a transfer of a going concern under UK legislation on which no VAT was due.

Held, giving a preliminary ruling, that in order to give rise to the right to deduct, the Directive had to be interpreted as meaning that the existence of a direct and immediate link between the particular input transaction and a particular output transaction or transactions giving rise to the right to deduct, was a necessary requirement. Consequently, a taxable person could deduct only the VAT on the goods and services used for the purposes of his own taxable transactions, *Midland Bank Plc v. Customs and Excise Commissioners (C98/98)* [2000] 1 W.L.R. 2080, [2000] 7 C.L. 514 applied. In the instant case, the various services acquired by the transferor in order to effect the transfer of the lease did not have a direct and immediate link with one or more output transactions giving rise to the right to deduct, such that the expenditure was not part of the costs components of the company's taxable transactions.

ABBEY NATIONAL PLC v. CUSTOMS AND EXCISE COMMISSIONERS (C408/98) [2001] 1 W.L.R. 769, DAO Edward (President), ECJ.

5587. Mail order – discounts – credits held on account for agents – deductibility in calculating taxable amount – European Community

[Sixth Council Directive 77/388 on a common system for VAT Art.11 (A).]

A reference was made to the ECJ concerning the correct taxable amount for value added purposes on payments received by F, a catalogue supplier. F sold goods to customers via agents, who then paid for the goods in instalments. For each instalment received, F credited an account with the equivalent of 10 per cent of the purchase price. The agents could then withdraw the amount, set it off against their existing balance, or use it for new purchases. In the event that the credit was not claimed, it was retained by F. F argued that the taxable amount was the catalogue price minus the discount as it was never in a contractual position to receive the full amount. Customs submitted that the taxable amount was the full catalogue price which the agents were obliged to pay in the first instance and which formed the consideration under the Sixth Council Directive 77/388 on a common system for VAT Art.11 (A).

Held, giving a preliminary ruling, that at the time of transfer, which was the time of adoption of the goods by the agent, the consideration due from the agents was the full catalogue price. This formed the taxable amount, subject to any deductions made when the credits were actually drawn down. The credits were not discounts within Art.11 (A)(3)(b) as the agents obtained only the legal entitlement to a discount, not the discount itself. If the credits were discounted from the calculations of VAT and the credits were not claimed, F would retain that deduction without tax which would breach Art.11 (A)(1)(a).

FREEMANS PLC v. CUSTOMS AND EXCISE COMMISSIONERS (C86/99); *sub nom.* FREEMANS PLC v. CUSTOMS AND EXCISE COMMISSIONERS (NO.1) [2001] 1 W.L.R. 1713, C Gulmann (President), ECJ (6th Chamber).

5588. Place of supply – groups of companies – establishments outside Community – creation for intentional financial advantage

[Sixth Council Directive 77/388 on a common system for VAT Art.9(2)(e).]

BUPA appealed against an assessment for VAT arising from the determination that the BUPA VAT Group, of which it was a representative member, had received advertising services at a United Kingdom establishment, WW, from a company which the Group had set up in Guernsey. The transactions giving rise to the assessment consisted of the Guernsey company supplying advertising services to WW, which in turn made supplies to BUPA. The Guernsey company had itself been supplied with advertising services from a third party. Such supply was, however, outside the scope of VAT. WW operated an office in Guernsey which consisted of a single part-time employee at an office which was supplied with communication and computer equipment. The issue before the tribunal was whether the supply of advertising services by the Guernsey company to WW fell within the scope of the Sixth Council Directive 77/388 Art.9(2)(e).

Held, allowing the appeal, that it was apparent that WW fell within the requirements of Art.9(2)(e), namely that it was both a customer "established outside the Community" and that it had "established [its] business" outside the Community. WW was involved in genuine economic activity in Guernsey notwithstanding that the way in which it undertook its work had been created intentionally for financial advantage. The fact that WW's registered office was in the UK did not alter such a conclusion. Moreover, WW met the requirements of the test established in *Berkholz v. Finanzampt Hamburg Mitte-Altstadt (C168/84)* [1985] E.C.R. 2251, [1986] C.L.Y. 1495 in that it had "the permanent presence of both the human and technical resources necessary for the provision of the services", *Berkholz* applied.

BUPA LTD v. CUSTOMS AND EXCISE COMMISSIONERS; *sub nom.* BRITISH UNITED PROVIDENT ASSOCIATION LTD v. CUSTOMS AND EXCISE COMMISSIONERS [2001] B.V.C. 2353, Paul Heim CMG (Chairman), V&DTr.

5589. Place of supply – waste management – composite supplies – French sub contractors carrying out work for non resident main contractors – European Community

[Sixth Council Directive 77/388 on a common system for VAT Art.9(1); Eighth Council Directive 79/1072 on arrangements for the refund of value added tax to taxable persons not established in the territory of the country Art.2.]

The Commission sought a declaration that France had failed to fulfil its obligations under the Eighth Council Directive 79/1072 Art.2 by refusing to refund VAT to waste disposal and recycling contractors established in other Member States for those parts of a composite supply that were performed in France by resident sub contractors. France contended that it was the place of supply for those operations, as they were carried out on "moveable tangible property" for the purposes of the Sixth Council Directive 77/388 Art.9(2)(c).

Held, granting the declaration, that the composite supply fell within the scope of Art.9(1) of the Sixth Directive, so that the place of supply was deemed to be the Member State where the contractor was established. This was not affected by the fact that certain parts of the composite supply were performed in France by French resident sub contractors. The main contractors could therefore rely on Art.2 of the Eighth Directive to obtain a refund of the VAT paid for those parts of the supply performed in France.

COMMISSION OF THE EUROPEAN COMMUNITIES v. FRANCE (C429/97) [2001] S.T.C. 156, C Gulmann (President), ECJ.

5590. Registration – partnership details forms

VALUE ADDED TAX (AMENDMENT) (NO.3) REGULATIONS 2001, SI 2001 3828; made under the Value Added Tax Act 1994 s.3, Sch.1 para.17. In force: January 1, 2002; £2.50.

These Regulations amend theValueAddedTax Regulations1995 (SI1995 2518) by substituting revised Forms1 and 2, theApplication forVAT Registration and the Partnership Details forms respectively.

5591. Registration – partnerships – spouses operating separate businesses from same premises – validity of global assessment

L were spouses who ran a seaside cafe.The husband sold food and drink on the premises and the wife sold ice cream to passers by. They believed that they were each sole proprietors of separate businesses. However, Customs decided that they should have registered for VAT as a partnership. Although there was no formal partnership agreement, there was no separation of the respective business activities, with a common till being used by both and their respective takings being paid into the same bank account. L appealed against a VAT assessment and late payment penalty.

Held, allowing the appeal in part, that allowing for the fact that L were married, they had failed to show there were two separate businesses operating at arm's length. However, the partnership was not obvious either to L or their accountants. In the circumstances, therefore, L had a reasonable belief that they were not in partnership. Customs had failed to show precisely what L's obligations were in relation to the assessment and L had been presented with a series of ambiguous dates when they should have received a clear indication of their liability. As they had not been properly informed of their obligations there was no effective direction specifying the relevant accounting period. The assessment was therefore global in nature and invalid as part of it was out of time.

LEONIDAS v. CUSTOMS AND EXCISE COMMISSIONERS [2000] B.V.C. 2316, JC Gort (Chairman),V&DTr.

5592. Registration – shops – compulsory registration – validity of best judgment assessment

[Value AddedTax Act 1994 s.73(1), Sch.1 para.5.]

H appealed against an adverse decision by theVATand duties tribunal upholding Customs' decision to compulsorily register his fish and chip shop business from October 1, 1991. The decision was taken following an investigation on March 1, 1996 which established an average price per transaction, based on sales over a single lunchtime period. H appealed, contending that the registration should have commenced from September 30,1991, as required by theValueAddedTax Act1994 Sch.1 para.5, and that the average transaction price had not been determined on the basis of best judgment under s.73(1).

Held, dismissing the appeal, that the registration date was correct as Sch.1 para.5 established that liability commenced at the end of the month after "the relevant month", which Customs had determined was August 1991 in the instant case. A registration starting at the end of September would therefore commence on October 1. The validity of a best judgment assessment was a question of fact for the tribunal and it had correctly approached the issue by reference to the reasonableness of Customs' methods, particularly from the point of view of available resources and the amount at stake, *Van Boeckel v. Customs and Excise Commissioners* [1981] 2 All E.R. 505 and *Rahman (t/a Khayam Restaurant) v. Customs and Excise Commissioners* [1998] S.T.C. 826 applied.

HENDERSON (T/A TONY'S FISH & CHIP SHOP) v. CUSTOMS AND EXCISE COMMISSIONERS [2001] S.T.C. 47, Park, J., Ch D.

5593. Registration – supplies and acquisitions – limits

VALUE ADDED TAX (INCREASE OF REGISTRATION LIMITS) ORDER 2001, SI 2001 640; made under the Value Added Tax Act 1994 Sch.1 para.15, Sch.3 para.9. In force: April 1, 2001; £1.50.

This Order amends the Value Added Tax Act 1994 by increasing the VAT registration limits for taxable supplies and for acquisitions from other Member States from £52,000 to £54,000, the limit for cancellation of registration in the case of taxable supplies from £50,000 to £52,000, and in the case of acquisitions from other Member States from £52,000 to £54,000 with effect from April 1, 2001.

5594. Registration – VAT planning – capital assets – cars sold by motor dealer registered for VAT in Ireland – disposals as part of turnover

[Sixth Council Directive 77/388 on a common system for VAT Art.24(4).]

H, a company registered for VAT in Ireland, obtained cars purchased from UK dealers by its parent company, L, also an Irish VAT registered company. The cars were leased to a UK subsidiary under a buy back agreement concluded between L and the dealers, and transferred to H as an agreed transfer of a going concern when there was only a short period of the lease left to run. On expiry, the cars were sold back to the dealers by H. L reclaimed VAT on the purchase price but no output tax was accounted for on the disposal, as H was not registered for VAT in the UK. H, while conceding that the scheme was intended to save VAT, contended that the cars were capital assets that did not count towards the calculation of turnover or for VAT registration purposes. Customs refused H's claim that the cars were capital assets on the basis that H was a motor dealer incorporated solely to dispose of cars under the buy back agreements, and that the short term nature of the scheme militated against the cars being capital assets in terms of the Sixth Council Directive 77/388 Art.24(4). H appealed.

Held, dismissing the appeal, that the short time H held the cars showed that they were not intended to be durable business assets or used on a daily basis for business purposes, as required by Art.24(4), *Verbond Van Nederlandse Ondernemingen v. Inspecteur der Invoerrechten en Accijnzen (C51/76)* [1977] E.C.R. 113, [1977] C.L.Y. 1359 applied.

HARBIG LEASING TWO LTD v. CUSTOMS AND EXCISE COMMISSIONERS [2001] B.V.C. 2134, AN Brice (Chairman), V&DTr.

5595. Repayments – Greater London Magistrates' Courts Authority

VALUE ADDED TAX (REFUND OF TAX) ORDER 2001, SI 2001 3453; made under the Value Added Tax Act 1994 s.33. In force: December 1, 2001; £1.50.

This Order specifies the Greater London Magistrates' Courts Authority for the purposes of the Value Added Tax Act 1994 s.33. This gives the body the right to claim refunds of VAT on supplies to, or acquisitions or importations by, the body provided the supplies, acquisitions or importations are not for the purpose of any business carried on by it.

5596. Sale of goods – commission – special provisions

VALUE ADDED TAX (SPECIAL PROVISIONS) (AMENDMENT) ORDER 2001, SI 2001 3753; made under the Value Added Tax Act 1994 s.50A. In force: January 2, 2002; £1.50.

This Order, which amends the Value Added Tax (Special Provisions) Order 1995 (SI 1995 1268), provides that, for the purpose of calculating the price at which goods were obtained, only the commission charged to the vendor under the contract for the sale of the goods may be deducted from the successful bid.

5597. Supplies – consideration – sports – value of surrendered golf club

The Commissioners appealed against a decision of the VAT and duties tribunal ([2001] S.T.I. 743) that the monetary value attributable to the surrender of a certain golf club sold by P was nil. The club had been found by the Royal and Ancient Golf Club, the sport's ruling body, to be illegal on the basis that it did not comply with its rules. As a consequence, P had offered every person owning the club the right to purchase a new club for £22 upon their surrendering the old club. The wholesale price of the new club was £49.99 and the recommended retail price £72.

Held, dismissing the appeal, that the tribunal had not erred in finding that the value of the surrendered club was nil. It could not be said that the transaction either expressly or impliedly attributed a value to the surrendered club. Rather, the transaction had been necessitated by the ruling of the Royal and Ancient Golf Club which had resulted in the old club becoming illegal for the purposes of the sport. The price which the owner of the illegal club might have gained in a different transaction was irrelevant; it was apparent that the owner of such a club would prefer to own a version that complied with the sport's rules, *Naturally Yours Cosmetics Ltd v. Customs and Excise Commissioners (C230/87)* [1988] S.T.C. 879, [1989] C.L.Y. 1683 applied.

CUSTOMS AND EXCISE COMMISSIONERS v. PING (EUROPE) LTD; *sub nom.* PING (EUROPE) LTD v. CUSTOMS AND EXCISE COMMISSIONERS [2001] S.T.C. 1144, Hart, J., Ch D.

5598. Supplies – discounts – vouchers – tripartite agreements – tax payable on sale of vouchers

[Value Added Tax Act 1994 Sch.6 para.5, Sch.9 Group 5 Item 1; Council Directive 77/388 on the law relating to turnover taxes Art.13B(d).]

F & I, which had devised a scheme whereby vouchers could be purchased by car dealers to sell to their customers offering them discounts on the purchase of goods and services offered by certain retailers, appealed against the refusal of judicial review ([2000] S.T.C. 364) of the decision of Customs to reverse its original finding that there was no chargeable VAT on the supply of the vouchers to customers and against the dismissal of its statutory appeal. It was accepted that VAT applied to the supply to the dealers, but F & I contended that no liability arose at the stage of supply to the customers as (1) it was exempted by the Value Added Tax Act 1994 Sch.6 para.5; (2) the end retailer received non monetary consideration by the issue of the vouchers in the form of marketing services; (3) the vouchers should be treated as a form of prepayment to the end retailer; (4) F & I was exempted by Sch. 9 Group 5 Item 1 of the 1994 Act and Council Directive 77/388 Art.13B(d), and (5) F & I had a valid basis for judicial review arising from the change in the decision of Customs which had unfairly breached their legitimate expectation.

Held, dismissing the appeal, that (1) Sch.6 para.5 of the 1994 Act did not operate to exempt the vouchers, *Customs and Excise Commissioners v. Granton Marketing Ltd* [1996] S.T.C. 1049 applied; (2) there was no direct link between the end retailer and F & I and therefore no consideration existed, *Naturally Yours Cosmetics Ltd v. Customs and Excise Commissioners (C230/87)* [1988] S.T.C. 879, [1989] C.L.Y. 1683 considered; (3) the end retailer did not receive the monies paid by the customer to the dealer and therefore the vouchers could not be regarded as a form of prepayment; (4) the supply was not exempted by the Directive or under Sch.9, *Kingfisher Plc v. Customs and Excise Commissioners* [2000] S.T.C. 992, [2001] 3 C.L. 703 distinguished, and (5) there was no valid basis for the application as Customs were entitled to resile from their previous decision which had been wrong in law.

F&I SERVICES LTD v. CUSTOMS AND EXCISE COMMISSIONERS; *sub nom.* R. v. CUSTOMS AND EXCISE COMMISSIONERS, *ex p.* F & I SERVICES, [2001] EWCA Civ 762, [2001] S.T.C. 939, Robert Walker, L.J., CA.

5599. Supply of services – bonuses in kind – Sixth VAT Directive – meaning of "consideration"

[Sixth Council Directive 77/388 on a common system of VAT Art.11A(1)(a).]

A German court referred a question to the ECJ on the meaning of the word "consideration" in the Sixth VAT Directive 77/388 Art. 11A(1)(a). A number of companies in the B group ran book and record clubs, which operated schemes whereby members were given bonuses in kind (books, records, bicycles, etc.) in return for the introduction of new members. The companies bought the bonuses in kind from third party suppliers and bore the cost of delivering them to the recipient members. In assessing the VAT due on the bonuses in kind, F calculated the taxable amount by including the cost of delivery. B disputed the inclusion of the cost of delivery, and challenged the assessments.

Held, giving a preliminary ruling, that the consideration for a supply of goods could consist of a supply of services, and so constitute the taxable amount within the meaning of Art.11A(1)(a), if there was a direct link between the two and the value of the services could be expressed in monetary terms, *Naturally Yours Cosmetics Ltd v. Customs and Excise Commissioners (C230/87)* [1988] S.T.C. 879, [1989] C.L.Y. 1683 and *Empire Stores Ltd v. Customs and Excise Commissioners (C 33/93)* [1994] 3 All E.R. 90, [1994] C.L.Y. 4964 considered. In the present case, a supply of goods was made in consideration for a supply of services consisting of the introduction of new customers. There was a direct link between the supply of the bonuses in kind and the introduction of new customers and, since the services rendered to B were remunerated by supplies of goods, their value could be expressed in monetary terms. A supply would be regarded as incidental to a principal supply if it did not constitute for the customer an end in itself but a means of better enjoying the principal supply, *Card Protection Plan Ltd v. Customs and Excise Commissioners (C349/96)* [1999] 2 A.C. 601, [1999] C.L.Y. 4972 considered. In the present case, the delivery of the bonuses in kind constituted a service incidental to the principal supply, which was the supply of the bonuses. The customers who had introduced new customers were entitled to the supply of the bonus in kind and its delivery. Therefore the supply and the delivery of the bonus together formed a single transaction, remunerated by consideration which consisted of the introduction of new customers. All expenses borne by the recipient to obtain that supply had to be taken into account in determining the taxable amount, including the delivery costs.

BERTELSMANN AG v. FINANZAMT WIEDENBRUCK (C380/99) [2001] S.T.C. 1153, C Gulman (President), ECJ.

5600. Supply of services – credit cards – card registration and insurance services – dominant purpose

[Value Added Tax Act 1983 Sch.6 Group 2; Sixth Council Directive 77/388 on a common system for VAT Art.13(B)(a).]

CPP appealed against a finding ([1994] S.T.C 199, [1994] C.L.Y. 4608) that the card protection scheme that it operated amounted to a single supply of a card registration service to which the supply of insurance was incidental and that the premiums paid by its customers were accordingly wholly liable to VAT at the standard rate. In return for a yearly premium CPP maintained a register of credit and other cards held by its members and maintained a policy of insurance with an insurance company to meet any liabilities accruing to individual card holders as a result of the misuse of lost or stolen cards. CPP contended that the "package of services" was such that it amounted to an arrangement for the provision of insurance services or, in the alternative, that the services should be subdivided, one into a VAT exempt supply of insurance and the other non exempt supply consisting of the additional services arising from the maintenance of the register.

Held, allowing the appeal and following the reference of questions to the ECJ, *Card Protection Plan Ltd v. Customs and Excise Commissioners (C349/96)* [1999] 2 A.C. 601, [1999] C.L.Y. 4972, that the dominant purpose of the scheme was to provide insurance cover. The other aspects of the scheme which could not be categorised as insurance were ancillary to the main purpose but could not be disassociated from the insurance cover. Accordingly for the purposes of the Value Added Tax Act 1983 Sch.6 Group 2 and the Sixth Council Directive 77/388 Art.13(B)(a), the individual arrangements with cardholders consisted of a principal exempt insurance supply with the other services supplied also being afforded VAT exempt status due to their ancillary nature

within the transaction as a whole, *Commission of the European Communities v. United Kingdom (C353/85)* [1988] 2 All E.R. 557, [1988] C.L.Y. 1574 applied.
   CARD PROTECTION PLAN LTD v. CUSTOMS AND EXCISE COMMISSIONERS, [2001] UKHL 4, [2002] 1 A.C. 202, Lord Slynn of Hadley, HL.

5601. Supply of services – educational institutions – meaning of "college of" for VAT purposes

[Value Added Tax Act 1994 Sch.9 Group 6.]
   S, a body providing degree level education to fee paying overseas students, appealed against a decision of the Commissioners that it was not an "eligible body" within the Value Added Tax Act 1994 Sch.9 Group 6. S's courses were exclusively validated by the University of Lincolnshire and Humberside, ULH. The arrangements between S and ULH were governed by a memorandum of cooperation, which, whilst not signed, was adhered to. Under its terms, S was referred to as an associated college of ULH and the principles on which the agreement was based were set out. Those included the fact that S would act as an approved centre for the delivery of ULH's courses, that students who enrolled for those courses would be accorded the same rights and responsibilities as ULH's students and further, contained a statement of ULH's responsibilities including the requirement to appoint course managers and liaison officers. S contended that it was an "eligible body" and thus exempt from VAT on its supplies by virtue of being "any college, institution, school or hall of such a university" within Note (1)(b) of Group 6 to Sch.9 of the Act.
   Held, allowing the appeal, that although S was not a "college of" ULH in the traditional sense, the system of further and higher education had undergone such change in the last decade that notwithstanding its status, the "always speaking" doctrine should prevail. As the fundamental purpose of S's business was the provision of educational services leading to the award of a university degree, it could fairly be regarded as a "college of a university". It followed that at all material times, S was a "college of" ULH and therefore supplies made by S were exempt from VAT.
   SCHOOL OF FINANCE AND MANAGEMENT (LONDON) LTD v. CUSTOMS AND EXCISE COMMISSIONERS [2001] B.V.C. 2284, PH Lawson, V&DTr.

5602. Supply of services – exemptions – lease option with payment held in escrow – compatibility with Sixth VAT Directive

The High court asked the ECJ for a preliminary ruling on whether the Sixth Council Directive 77/388 Art.13(B)(b) provided VAT exemption for a person who had no initial interest in immovable property where that person (1) is paid consideration by a landlord for entering into an option agreement relating to leases of that immovable property, payment being held on security in an escrow account, and/or (2) then accepts grant of leases under the option agreement in return for the release of payments from the escrow account. M had agreed to take a lease of five floors in a building and, in return, received payment from the landlord. It also had an option (exercisable in parts) to take leases of up to four more floors. Money was paid into an escrow account and released to M as and when it exercised the option. M contended that these transactions should be exempt from VAT as they involved "the leasing or letting of immovable property" within Art.13B(b) of the Directive.
   Held, giving a preliminary ruling, that (1) a future tenant made a supply of services for consideration if the landlord, taking the view that the presence of an "anchor tenant" in the building containing the leased premises would attract other tenants, made a payment by way of consideration for the future tenant's undertaking to transfer its business to the building concerned. In those circumstances, the undertaking of such a tenant could be qualified as a taxable supply of advertising services. It followed that such a transaction was not exempt from VAT as it did not fall within the ambit of the term "letting or leasing of immovable property" given by Art.13(B)(b) as no right of occupation had been surrendered, *Lubbock Fine & Co v. Customs and Excise Commissioners*

(C63/92) [1994] Q.B. 571, [1994] C.L.Y. 4961 distinguished, and (2) following the same line of reasoning, the ECJ held that whilst entry into an option agreement without mutual exchange of supplies would not qualify as a supply of services under Art.2(1) of the Directive, exercising the option agreement and thus accepting the grant of the leases and any concomitant payment from the escrow account amounted to a supply of services that remained outside the scope of the exemption contained in Art.13(B)(b).

CUSTOMS AND EXCISE COMMISSIONERS v. MIRROR GROUP PLC (C409/98); CUSTOMS AND EXCISE COMMISSIONERS v. CANTOR FITZGERALD INTERNATIONAL (C108/99) [2002] Q.B. 546, F Macken (President), ECJ.

5603. Supply of services – exemptions – place of supply – status of intercountry adoption services

[Value Added Tax Act 1994 Sch.8 Group 7 Item 2(c), Sch.9 Group 7 Note (6); Sixth Council Directive 77/388 on a common system for VAT Art.13A(1)(i).]

PACT, an approved voluntary adoption agency which provided advice to and assessed people wishing to adopt children from overseas, appealed against a decision that the services which it supplied were standard rated for VAT purposes. PACT argued that (1) it was providing an exempt supply within the meaning of the Value Added Tax Act 1994 Sch.9 Group 7 Note (6) since it was providing services which were "directly connected with ... the protection of children". Similarly, its services were exempt within the meaning of the Sixth Council Directive 77/388 Art.13A(1)(i) because they were "closely linked to the protection of children", and (2) its supplies were zero rated within the meaning of Sch.8 Group 7 Item 2(c) of the 1994 Act since they consisted of the making of arrangements for the supply of services outside the Member States.

Held, dismissing the appeal, that (1) the contractual services which PACT provided were neither "directly connected with" nor "closely linked to" the protection of children. The services were provided to the prospective adopters and were aimed at assessing the suitability of those individuals and, if applicable, enabling them to obtain certificates of eligibility from the Department of Health. The fact that PACT's services might ultimately play a part in securing the protection of a particular child was insufficient to bring those services within Sch.9 Group 7 Note (6) or Art.13A(1)(i), and (2) PACT's services were provided solely in the UK. Its obligation to provide those services was based on its agreement with the prospective adopters, who were based in the UK. Furthermore, the services were supplied prior to the stage when the overseas child was adopted.

PARENTS AND CHILDREN TOGETHER (PACT) v. CUSTOMS AND EXCISE COMMISSIONERS [2001] 3 C.M.L.R. 30, Stephen Oliver Q.C. (Chairman), V&DTr.

5604. Supply of services – promotional services – determination of single or separate supplies

[Value Added Tax Act 1994 s.30, Sch.8 Group 3 Item 1.]

AB supplied promotional services, including printed marketing material to C, an insurance consultancy. C paid an annual fee of £10,000 in monthly instalments for AB's promotional services, but was invoiced in two separate stages for printed brochures, which it ordered as and when required. Customs decided that AB was making a single supply of standard rated services. AB contended that it made separate supplies and that the supply of brochures should be zero rated under the Value Added Tax Act 1994 s.30 and Sch.8 Group 3, Item 1. Customs' view was upheld by a VAT and duties tribunal ([2000] S.T.I. 1500) and AB appealed.

Held, allowing the appeal, that it was a question of law as to whether a number of elements comprised a single supply, and the determination of the matter depended on the incidental or ancillary nature of one or more of the elements concerned. In the instant case, the fact that C ordered, and paid for, the brochures separately from the other supplies was indicative of a separate supply that was not ancillary to the supply of promotional services. Although the tribunal had begun by considering the matter by reference to the type of supplies involved, it had erred by going on to decide whether one element was ancillary to the whole, when it should have decided whether one part of the transaction was ancillary to any other, which it was necessary to do when faced with the question whether a transaction formed a single or multiple supply, *Cooperative Wholesale Society Ltd v. Customs and Excise Commissioners* [2000] S.T.C. 727, [2000] 9 C.L. 648 and *Customs and Excise Commissioners v. Wellington Private Hospital Ltd* [1997] S.T.C. 445, [1997] C.L.Y. 5057 applied.

APPLEBY BOWERS v. CUSTOMS AND EXCISE COMMISSIONERS [2001] S.T.C. 185, Neuberger, J., Ch D.

5605. **Supply of services – satellite television – supply of listings magazines**

B sought judicial review of a decision concerning its VAT liability. In 1994 Customs had ruled that B did not have to pay VAT on the supply of a television listings magazine to its customers, the cost of which was included in the subscription fee. In 1997 it changed its view, deciding that the magazine was integral to the supply of satellite services and that VAT was payable on the whole subscription fee. The new rate became payable from June 1998. B argued that Customs should, at the same time, have required all companies supplying listings magazines with their cable television services to pay the same rate of VAT on their magazines. B contended that it had been treated unfairly by Customs and it claimed compensation for the 14 month period prior to June 1998, during which it had been required to pay the revised rate when other companies had not been so required.

Held, dismissing the application, that Customs had not acted unfairly. The threshold of unfairness in order to show abuse of process was high. Customs' decision could not be judged in the light of what was known now about the positions of the various companies, but had to be considered in the light of information known to it at the time of the decision. On the evidence, Customs had not viewed the companies as being in identical positions, and could therefore not be said to have treated them differently in a way that was unfair, *R. v. Inland Revenue Commissioners, ex p. Unilever Plc* [1996] S.T.C. 681 considered.

BRITISH SKY BROADCASTING GROUP PLC v. CUSTOMS AND EXCISE COMMISSIONERS; *sub nom.* R. v. CUSTOMS AND EXCISE COMMISSIONERS, *ex p.* BRITISH SKY BROADCASTING GROUP, [2001] EWHC Admin 127, [2001] S.T.C. 437, Elias, J., QBD (Admin Ct).

5606. **Supply of services – share issues – exemptions – recovery of input tax on professional fees**

[Sixth Council Directive 77/388 on a common system for VAT Art.17 (2).]

TM appealed against a decision ([2000] S.T.C. 156, [2000] C.L.Y. 5337) dismissing its appeal against a VAT tribunal ruling that part of the input tax on the fees of its legal and financial advisors was irrecoverable. The fees had been incurred in connection with an issue of TM's own shares, issued in order to raise finance to expand its business. The court below had determined that such a share issue was a supply of services and therefore input tax was irrecoverable under the Sixth Council Directive 77/338 Art.17 (2) except in relation to those shares taken up by individuals outside the European Union. TM contended that (1) VAT was a turnover tax and in order to constitute a supply of services, the consideration received must have affected turnover, and (2) that the raising of finance by means of a share issue was comparable with the raising of a loan which was not a supply of services for the borrower.

Held, dismissing the appeal, that (1) for the purposes of VAT legislation "turnover" had a wider meaning than its normal accounting usage and whether a transaction affected turnover was not determinative of whether it was a supply of goods, *Sofitam SA (formerly Satam SA) v. Ministre Charge du Budget (C333/91)* [1997] S.T.C. 226, [1997] C.L.Y. 5002 considered, and (2) the judge below had been correct to find that an issue of its own shares by a VAT rated individual was a supply of services for VAT purposes and there was clear authority that such a supply was exempt and therefore not deductible, *BLP Group Plc v. Customs and Excise Commissioners (C4/94)* [1996] 1 W.L.R. 174, [1995] C.L.Y. 5059 followed.

TRINITY MIRROR PLC (FORMERLY MIRROR GROUP NEWSPAPERS LTD) v. CUSTOMS AND EXCISE COMMISSIONERS; *sub nom.* MIRROR GROUP NEWSPAPERS LTD v. CUSTOMS AND EXCISE COMMISSIONERS, [2001] EWCA Civ 65, [2001] S.T.C. 192, Chadwick, L.J., CA.

5607. Supply of services – unincorporated associations – taxable supplies – private hire drivers association

[Interpretation Act 1978 Sch.1; Value Added Tax Act 1994 s.4(1), Sch.1 para.13(2).]

E, an unincorporated club which provided various services for its members, local private hire taxi drivers, appealed against a decision ([1998] S.T.C. 669) that, for the purposes of the Value Added Tax Act 1994, it was making taxable supplies to its members in excess of the registration threshold, as a result of which it would be inappropriate for its registration to be cancelled under Sch.1 para.13(2) of the Act. E submitted that since it was a non profit making organisation, whose costs were reimbursed by the members by way of a joining fee and a periodical contribution towards expenses, and since the club's employees were, according to the statement of conditions of service provided to them, employed by "each of the members [of the association] for the time being", then that was sufficient to remove VAT liability from E.

Held, dismissing the appeal, that according to the definition provided in the Interpretation Act 1978 Sch.1 an association, whether incorporated or not, was a "person" within the meaning of s.4(1) of the 1994 Act. In the provision of advantages to its members for consideration, E was clearly carrying on a business and would be liable for VAT if it was making taxable supplies. Taxable supplies would be found to occur where (1) the individuals constituting the club or employed by it, were governed by a set of rules or bye laws rather than merely sharing a contractual arrangement, and (2) in return for a member's entitlement to the services of the club, there was, under the rules, a requirement to contribute to the funds of the club. The fact that the members' contributions were calculated by merely dividing the club's expenses between them was immaterial. Each case had to be considered on its facts and it was not necessary, for the determination of the instant case, to consider what arrangements might have been necessary in order to escape VAT liability.

EASTBOURNE TOWN RADIO CARS ASSOCIATION v. CUSTOMS AND EXCISE COMMISSIONERS, [2001] UKHL 19, [2001] 1 W.L.R. 794, Lord Slynn of Hadley, HL.

5608. Tax planning – supplies – recovery of input tax on building works – use of subsidiary companies

[Sixth Council Directive 77/388 on a common system for VAT Art.2, Art.4.]

H, a bank, applied for a declaration that a proposed scheme relating to the recovery of input tax on building works was effective. As a bank the majority of H's supplies were exempt with the result that it was unable to recover much of its input tax. H needed, for the furtherance of its business, to construct "call centres" but was concerned that it would be unable to recover the input tax arising out of the building works. It therefore devised a scheme using three subsidiary companies. The first company would agree to take an interest in the sites from H and would then engage the second company to carry out the construction works. Payment to the second company would take place in a prescribed accounting period falling shortly before the end of the first company's partial exemption year. During such accounting period the first company would make a relatively low value standard rated supply so that when the period ended it would be able to recover the excess of input tax over output tax for such period. The second company would discharge its contractual obligations by engaging professional builders on arms length terms and would account for the VAT charged on the invoice issued to the first company and in due course recover the VAT charged by the builders. In the next partial exemption year of the first company it would transfer its interest in the sites to a third company, thereby making exempt supplies, and would lease them back to H.

Held, refusing the declaration, that the proposed scheme was ineffective for recovering the input tax on the building works. For the purposes of the Sixth Council Directive 77/388 Art.2 and Art.4 the transactions would be construed as a supply of construction works by the builders direct to H.

HALIFAX PLC v. CUSTOMS AND EXCISE COMMISSIONERS (INPUT TAX ON BUILDING WORKS) [2001] B.V.C. 2240, Stephen Oliver Q.C. (Chairman), V&DTr.

5609. Tax rates – EC law – imposition of VAT by Member State at rate below that stipulated in Sixth Council Directive 77/388 Art.12(3) and Art.28(2)

[Sixth Council Directive 77/388 on a common system for VAT Art.4(5), Art.12(3), Art.28(2).]

Portugal applied a rate of five per cent to various transactions, including wine, agricultural equipment, alternative energy machinery and bridge tolls, compared to a normal rate of 17 per cent. The Commission sought a declaration that the reduced rate meant that Portugal was in breach of its obligations under the Sixth Council Directive 77/388 Art.12(3) and Art.28(2).

Held, allowing the application in part, that (1) as the reduced rate in respect of wine and machinery supplies had applied since January 1, 1991, Portugal could apply a reduced rate of 12 per cent, as provided for by Art.12(3) and Art.28(2). Although Portugal accepted that the five per cent rate was in breach of those provisions, and had expressed an intention to increase the rate to 12 per cent, the proceedings could not be suspended pending that increase, and (2) the bridge toll charging authority was a public law body and as such was not a taxable person under Art.4(5), *Ufficio Distrettuale delle Imposte Dirette di Fiorenzuola d'Arda v. Comune di Carpaneto Piacentino (C231/87)* [1991] S.T.C. 205, [1991] C.L.Y. 3361 considered, so that the reduced rate for the bridge tolls was not in breach of Art.12(3) and Art.28(2).

COMMISSION OF THE EUROPEAN COMMUNITIES v. PORTUGAL (C276/98) [2001] B.T.C. 5135, V Skouris (President), ECJ.

5610. VAT – common system – minimum standard rate – Council Directive

Council Directive 2001/41 of January 19, 2001 amending the sixth Directive (77/388) on the common system of value added tax, with regard to the length of time during which the minimum standard rate it to be applied. [2001] OJ L22/17.

5611. VAT – refunds – museums and galleries

VALUE ADDED TAX (REFUND OF TAX TO MUSEUMS AND GALLERIES) ORDER 2001, SI 2001 2879; made under the Value Added Tax Act 1994 s.33A. In force: September 1, 2001; £2.00.

This Order names the bodies entitled to claim refunds of VAT under the Value Added Tax 1994 s.33A.

5612. VAT and duties tribunals – appeals – new submissions on appeal – public interest

The Commissioners appealed against a decision of the VAT and duties tribunal allowing G's appeal against a refusal by the Commissioners to permit G to make a recovery of input tax in connection with G's business. G's original claim to recover input tax had been refused on the basis that it arose in the context of a fraudulent scheme. The allegation of fraud was subsequently withdrawn but the Commissioners had failed to comply with a direction from the VAT and duties tribunal to plead an arguable case by way of answer to the claim. The appeal was accordingly allowed as of right and without any substantive hearing taking place. The Commissioners contended that the supplies were not taxable supplies or, in the alternative, that they were not supplies of goods to be used by the taxpayer in the course of its business.

Held, dismissing the appeal, that none of the submissions made on appeal had been advanced by the Commissioners before the tribunal. The fact that a different decision would promote justice or the public interest by protecting the Revenue from unmeritorious claims could not justify an appellate court interfering with a determination of the tribunal in circumstances where the submissions on appeal had not been advanced at the substantive hearing, *Customs and Excise Commissioners v. Young* [1993] S.T.C. 394, [1996] C.L.Y. 7393 applied.

CUSTOMS AND EXCISE COMMISSIONERS v. A&D GODDARD (A FIRM) [2001] S.T.C. 725, Lightman, J., Ch D.

5613. VAT and Duties Tribunals – jurisdiction – appeals

VALUE ADDED TAX TRIBUNALS (AMENDMENT) RULES 2001, SI 2001 3073; made under the Value Added Tax 1994 Sch.12 para.9. In force: October 1, 2001; £1.50.

These Rules amend the Value Added Tax Tribunals Rules 1986 (SI 1986 590) to provide for a new jurisdiction, covering appeals relating to the climate change levy, to be given to the VAT and Duties Tribunals by the Finance Act 2000.

5614. VAT groups – retail schemes – vouchers – assessment of output tax

[Value Added Tax Act 1994 Sch.9 Group 5 Item 1.]

W, a retailer within K's VAT group, participated in a voucher scheme operated by P. Under the scheme, customers bought vouchers from P on credit, the vouchers then being used to purchase goods at W's stores. Goods were purchased at their shelf price and vouchers accepted at their face value. W then submitted the vouchers to P which paid out the face value minus an agreed percentage. K asserted that (1) VAT should have been accounted for on the basis of the shelf price less P's percentage deduction, or alternatively (2) P's deductions from its payments to W were consideration for standard rated services supplied by P to W, which W was entitled to deduct as input tax. The tribunal held against K and appealed.

Held, dismissing the appeal, that (1) the scheme was similar to the relationship between customer, retailer and credit card company. On that basis, the amount on which output tax should be assessed was the price which the customer effectively agreed to pay, namely the shelf price, and not the amount actually transmitted by P to W, namely the shelf price less commission, *Chaussures Bally SA v. Belgium (C18/92)* [1997] S.T.C. 209, [1993] C.L.Y. 4408 followed, *Boots Co Plc v. Customs and Excise Commissioners (C126/88)* [1990] S.T.C. 387, [1991] C.L.Y. 3668, *Argos Distributors Ltd v. Customs and Excise Commissioners (C288/94)* [1997] Q.B. 499, [1996] C.L.Y. 5909 and *Elida Gibbs Ltd v. Customs and Excise Commissioners (C317/94)* [1996] S.T.C. 1387, [1996] C.L.Y. 5908 distinguished. W received numerous benefits through participation in the scheme, and (2) the service provided by P to W fell within Value Added Tax Act 1994 Sch.9 Group 5 Item 1 and therefore was an exempt supply.

KINGFISHER PLC v. CUSTOMS AND EXCISE COMMISSIONERS [2000] S.T.C. 992, Neuberger, J., Ch D.

5615. VAT groups – subsidiary companies – effective date of cessation of membership of group for VAT purposes

[Value Added Tax Act 1994 s.43; Sixth Council Directive 77/388 on a common system of VAT Art.4.4.]

Customs appealed against a ruling that for VAT purposes, TDL, a wholly owned subsidiary of BB, whose shareholding had been transferred to a charitable trust, was no longer a member of BB's group from the date of its transfer rather than commencement of the next accounting period. Customs relied upon the Value Added Tax Act 1994 s.43, in particular s.43(4) through to s.43(6), whereby exit from a group required an application by the company or a notice from Customs. B contended that it was necessary to ignore s.43(6) which entitled the commissioners to specify the date upon which a body corporate ceased to be treated for VAT purposes as a member of the group, since it was inconsistent with the Sixth Council Directive 77/388 Art.4.4, to the effect that group treatment should only be extended to persons "eligible" for it, namely those closely bound by financial, economic or organisational links. B maintained that on that basis once membership of the group ceased, group treatment also automatically ceased and Customs had no discretion to extend that time pursuant to s.43(6).

Held, allowing the appeal, that the subsidiary ceased to be part of the group for VAT purposes not on the date of its transfer to the charitable trust but at the beginning of the next accounting period following the transfer. Automatic termination of group treatment could lead to significant administrative difficulties, whereas by utilising s.43(6) Customs could determine a date suitable to the particular facts. Whilst single taxable person status would as a result be conferred for a short period on persons no longer members of the group in question, that would be limited to part of a prescribed accounting period and was justified by the underlying aim of the Directive, namely the efficient administration of VAT.

CUSTOMS AND EXCISE COMMISSIONERS v. BARCLAYS BANK PLC, [2001] EWCA Civ 1513, [2001] S.T.C. 1558, Sir Robert Andrew Morritt V.C., CA.

5616. VAT returns – electronic communications – incentives

VALUE ADDED TAX (ELECTRONIC COMMUNICATIONS) (INCENTIVES) REGULATIONS 2001, SI 2001 759; made under the Finance Act 2000 Sch.38. In force: April 1, 2001; £1.75.

These Regulations, which provide for incentive payments to be made to taxable persons who make VAT returns to the Commissioners of Customs and Excise electronically, provide for a taxable incentive payment of £50.00 for the first return he makes electronically after these Regulations come into force provided that he satisfies certain conditions specified in a direction given by the Commissioners of Customs and Excise. In addition, they provide for the withdrawal of an incentive payment where not all of the conditions are satisfied and, where a payment has already been made, for its recovery and provide rights of appeal to a VAT and duties tribunal against an assessment and a decision that the conditions of entitlement to an incentive payment are not met.

5617. Zero rating – charities – administrative office – public law status – supplies in course of business

[Value Added Tax Act 1994 Sch.8 Group 5 Item 2; Sixth Council Directive 77/388 on a common system for VAT Art.4(5); Council Directive 93/36 coordinating procedures for the award of public supply contracts.]

C, a charity reliant on public funding to provide housing and welfare services to the homeless, appealed against a decision that a new office constructed for housing management and maintenance services was not eligible for zero rating under the Value Added Tax Act 1994 Sch.8 Group 5 Item 2.

Held, allowing the appeal, that C was not carrying on a business, since it had no autonomy in the way it functioned given the extent of its statutory functions. Further, C was not a taxable person as its public law status satisfied the requirements of the Sixth Council Directive 77/388 Art.4(5) and Council Directive 93/36. Customs Notices relating to the VAT treatment of other buildings used for administrative purposes by C and similar bodies were not relevant as they gave Customs' views on matters unrelated to the instant case.

CARDIFF COMMUNITY HOUSING ASSOCIATION v. CUSTOMS AND EXCISE COMMISSIONERS [2001] B.V.C. 2112, JC Gort (Chairman), V&DTr.

5618. Zero rating – concessions – hiring out of university accommodation – via third party

[Value Added Tax Act 1994 Sch.8.]

G challenged the Commissioners' decision that it was not entitled to the benefit of a concession which would have allowed it to treat the construction of student halls of residence, hired out in the university vacations, as zero rated for VAT purposes pursuant to the Value Added Tax Act 1994 Sch.8. The hiring out of the accommodation during vacations was licensed to A, the construction company behind the accommodation, and the Commissioners contended that the concession was only applicable where the university itself hired out the rooms during holiday time.

Held, granting the application for judicial review, that there was nothing in the wording of the concession to prevent taking advantage of the concession by way of a third party.

R. (ON THE APPLICATION OF GREENWICH PROPERTY LTD) v. CUSTOMS AND EXCISE COMMISSIONERS; *sub nom.* GREENWICH PROPERTY LTD v. CUSTOMS AND EXCISE COMMISSIONERS, [2001] EWHC Admin 230, [2001] S.T.C. 618, Collins, J., QBD (Admin Ct).

5619. Zero rating – conversion – former bedsit accommodation converted to self contained flats

[Value Added Tax Act 1994 Sch.8 Group 5 Note (2), Sch.8 Group 5 Note (7).]

L appealed against a decision refusing zero rating for the conversion of two houses from bedsitting accommodation into self contained flats. L contended that the bedsits did not provide "dwellings" as defined by the Value Added Tax Act 1994 Sch.8 Group 5 Note (2) due to shared bathroom and kitchen facilities. Customs argued that the exemption was restricted to the provision of new accommodation, so that zero rating was not available on a conversion from one type of dwelling to another.

Held, allowing the appeal, that zero rating applied as the bedsits were not dwellings in terms of Note (7), which fell to be construed separately from the conditions in Note (2), *University of Bath v. Customs and Excise Commissioners* [1996] B.V.C. 2909 applied and *Temple House Developments Ltd v. Customs and Excise Commissioners* [1998] B.V.C. 2302 considered.

LOOK AHEAD HOUSING ASSOCIATION v. CUSTOMS AND EXCISE COMMISSIONERS [2001] B.V.C. 2107, RK Miller (Chairman), V&DTr.

5620. Zero rating – frozen yoghurt – product supplied at minus 5 degrees celsius – meaning of "frozen products"

[Value Added Tax Act 1994 Sch.8 Group 1 item 1.]

M imported frozen yoghurt at a temperature of between minus 18 and minus 22 degrees celsius, which was then heated and whipped prior to sale to the consumer as "soft frozen yoghurt" at a temperature of minus 5 degrees. Customs decided that the product was liable to VAT at the standard rate as it was excluded from zero rating by virtue of the Value Added Tax Act 1994 Sch.8 Group 1 item 1. M's appeal to the VAT and duties tribunal ([2000] S.T.I. 824) on the ground that the product was not liable to VAT as it was not sold in a frozen state was dismissed and M appealed.

Held, dismissing the appeal, that in the absence of a commonly accepted definition of "frozen yoghurt", the phrase "similar frozen products" in Sch.8 Group 1 item 1, taken in the context of the preceding items, referred to goods supplied to the consumer at a temperature below the freezing point of water. The fact that M supplied its product in a semi viscous state did not alter the fact that it was sold to the consumer below zero degrees celsius.

MESCHIA'S FROZEN FOODS v. CUSTOMS AND EXCISE COMMISSIONERS [2001] S.T.C. 1, Hart, J., Ch D.

5621. Zero rating – motorcycles – protective helmets

VALUE ADDED TAX (PROTECTIVE HELMETS) ORDER 2001, SI 2001 732; made under the Value Added Tax 1994 s.30, s.96. In force: April 1, 2001; £1.50.

This Order amends the Value Added Tax Act 1994 Sch.8 Group 16 which makes provision for the supply of certain goods at the zero rate with the effect to zero rate the supply of pedal cycle helmets and bring up to date the manufacturing standards with which the goods contained within the Group have to comply if they are to be zero rated. In addition, it brings pedal cycle helmets into the scope of the relief available for the supply of protective helmets for wear by persons driving or riding motor bicycles.

5622. Zero rating – passenger vehicles – seating capacity

VALUE ADDED TAX (PASSENGER VEHICLES) ORDER 2001, SI 2001753; made under the Value Added Tax Act 1994 s.30, s.96. In force: April 1, 2001; £1.50.

This Order, which amends the Value Added Tax 1994, reduces the minimum number of seats for passenger transport on vehicles, ships or aircraft for which fares are zero rated from 12 to 10. It also allows zero rating to apply where passengers transported in vehicles which, but for the fact that they have been designed or adapted for wheelchair users, would have been capable of carrying 10 or more passengers.

5623. Zero rating – passenger vehicles – seating capacity

VALUE ADDED TAX (VEHICLES DESIGNATED OR ADAPTED FOR HANDICAPPED PERSONS) ORDER 2001, SI 2001 754; made under the Value Added Tax Act 1994 s.30, s.96. In force: April 1, 2001; £1.50.

This Order, which amends the Value Added Tax Act 1994, increases the size of the vehicles eligible for the zero rate from those carrying a total of six persons, to those carrying a total of 12 persons. It makes provision for the zero-rating of supplies of vehicles carrying up to 12 persons and designed, or substantially and permanently adapted, to enable a wheelchair or stretcher user to travel in the vehicle without the need to be in a wheelchair or on a stretcher. In addition it makes provision for the zero-rating of repair and maintenance services for these vehicles and applies the zero rate where the vehicles are let out on hire.

5624. Zero rating – supplies – goods "accessory" to medical equipment

[Value Added Tax Act 1994 Sch.8 Part II Group 15 Item 5, Part II Group 15 Note 3(c).]

R, a registered charity which provided residential medical care to the seriously ill, appealed against a decision of the VAT and duties tribunal ([2001] S.T.I. 745) that the purchase of an electricity generator was not a zero rated supply for the purposes of the Value Added Tax Act 1994 Sch.8 Part II Group 15 Item 5. The generator had been purchased on the advice of the local authority to provide a back up facility in the event of a power failure. Customs maintained that the fact that the generator would be used to power items other than medical equipment prevented it from being described as an "accessory" to such equipment and therefore that it fell outside the ambit of Note 3(c) to Group 15. The tribunal had held that the supply was not zero rated on the basis that to constitute an "accessory" for the purposes of Note 3(c) the goods in question were required to be in the nature of an optional extra rather than, as in the instant case, a replacement for existing equipment. R submitted that the tribunal had erred by applying an objective test to the reasons for the purchase.

Held, allowing the appeal, that the supply fell within Note 3(c) to Group 15 and was accordingly zero rated. The correct test was to consider, subjectively, to what use the purchaser intended to put the goods. Further, if the generator was capable of falling within Note 3(c), the fact that it could also be used for purposes other than as an accessory to medical equipment was not necessarily fatal to the supply being zero rated. The fact that the generator was regarded by R as essential did not necessarily preclude it from being an accessory as inessentiality was not a necessary component of an accessory.

ROYAL MIDLAND COUNTIES HOME FOR DISABLED PEOPLE v. CUSTOMS AND EXCISE COMMISSIONERS [2002] S.T.C. 395, Neuberger, J., Ch D.

5625. Zero rating – supply of animals – bait for fishing purposes

[Value Added Tax Act 1994 Sch.8 Group 1.]

F appealed against the decision that the sale of live maggots from vending machines for use as fishing bait by coarse fishermen was not zero rated. It was contended that the tribunal had erred in concluding that the supply could not be categorised as the supply of animal feeding stuffs which was exempt from VAT under the Value Added Tax Act 1994 Sch.8 Group 1.

Held, dismissing the appeal, that the tribunal had been correct in their conclusion that the supply was a supply of bait rather than animal feeding stuff since the maggots were not being used to feed the fish but to entice them onto the hooks. To find otherwise would result in the absurd conclusion that any edible product would fall into the exempt category.

FLUFF LTD (T/A MAG-IT) v. CUSTOMS AND EXCISE COMMISSIONERS [2001] S.T.C. 674, Laddie, J., QBD.

5626. Zero rating – supply of services – electronic mail

[VAT Act 1994 Sch.8 Group 3.]

F appealed against a decision of the Commissioners that the publication and distribution of a regular news digest by fax, web site and email was subject to the standard rate of VAT when supplied in the United Kingdom. The Commissioners had concluded that when a supply was made by fax, email or through a web-site, the information being supplied was not a leaflet or a periodical, but material which the recipient then transformed into a periodical or leaflet using his or her own equipment and paper. F contended that that amounted to a supply of services rather than a supply of goods which would have been zero-rated. If the document had been delivered by post, courier or by hand then the supply would have been zero-rated under the VAT Act 1994 Sch.8 Group 3.

Held, dismissing the appeal, that the Commissioners' conclusion was correct. Exemptions and zero-ratings were to be strictly construed. Sch.8 Group 3 clearly refers to goods and the transfer of the right to dispose of goods, as owner, constitutes a supply. F had been supplying information in the form of electrical impulses.

FOREXIA (UK) LTD v. CUSTOMS AND EXCISE COMMISSIONERS [2001] E.B.L.R. 30, Judge not specified, V&DTr.

5627. Books

Wareham, Robert; Dolton, Alan – Tolley's VAT Planning: 2000-2001. Paperback: £68.95. ISBN 0-7545-0725-4. Tolley Publishing.

WATER INDUSTRY

5628. Land drainage – Internal Drainage Boards – reorganisation – Holmewood and Stilton and Yaxley

AMALGAMATION OF THE HOLMEWOOD AND STILTON AND YAXLEY INTERNAL DRAINAGE DISTRICTS ORDER 2001, SI 2001 4114; made under the Land Drainage Act 1991 s.3, Sch.3. In force: January 7, 2002; £1.75.

This Order confirms a Scheme submitted by the Environment Agency for the abolition of the Holmewood and Stilton and Yaxley Internal Drainage Boards which are to be replaced by a new "Holmewood and District Internal Drainage

Board". The two former internal drainage districts are amalgamated to form the corresponding new internal drainage district.

5629. Land drainage – Internal Drainage Boards – reorganisation – Whittlesey and Whittlesey Fifth

AMALGAMATION OF THE WHITTLESEY AND WHITTLESEY FIFTH INTERNAL DRAINAGE DISTRICTS ORDER 2001, SI 2001 4115; made under the Land Drainage Act 1991 s.3, Sch.3. In force: January 7, 2002; £1.75.

This Order confirms a Scheme submitted by the Environment Agency for the abolition of the Whittlesey and Whittlesey Fifth Internal Drainage Boards which are replaced by a new "Whittlesey Internal Drainage Board". The two former internal drainage districts are amalgamated to form the corresponding new internal drainage district.

5630. Sewerage – compulsory purchase – bathing water regulations

[Water Industry Act 1981 s.23; Bathing Waters (Classification) Regulations 1991 (SI 1991 1597); Council Directive 76/160 concerning the quality of bathing water.]

M appealed against the dismissal of his application challenging the Secretary of State's decision to approve the compulsory purchase of land, C, for the construction of a sewage treatment works. S, a water authority, had applied for confirmation of a compulsory purchase order made to acquire land at site C. At the public inquiry, M and others had argued that the proposed development and operation of a sewerage treatment works at C would pollute the sea water at nearby locations and that an alternative site, N, was more suitable. The inspector concluded that site C was to be preferred and the order was confirmed by the Secretary of State. M applied, pursuant to the Water Industry Act 1981 s.23, to quash the Secretary of State's decision and further applied to adduce new evidence that, according to M's contention, showed that the policy of the Environment Agency could not guarantee compliance with mandatory standards for bathing water laid down in Council Directive 76/160. The judge at first instance rejected M's submissions ([2000] Env.L.R. 266) and held that the affected waters were not bathing waters for the purposes of the directive as they did not qualify as such under the Bathing Waters (Classification) Regulations 1991 and that the inspector had been satisfied that the terms of the Environment Agency's consent to discharge sewage from an outfall pipe would ensure that the relevant standards would be met. M appealed, contending that (1) the fresh evidence should have been admitted by the judge; (2) the inspector should have considered the minimum mandatory requirements notwithstanding that the point had not been raised by M at the inquiry, and (3) the judge had an independent duty to determine if the mandatory minimum requirements had been met.

Held, dismissing the appeal, that (1) it would have been unfair to S to allow evidence to be adduced that related to a point that had not been raised at the inquiry; (2) in considering whether to confirm a compulsory purchase order, the inspector had been entitled to presume that compliance would result from the implementation of the Environment Agency's policy and the terms of consent unless proved otherwise, *Hobday v. Secretary of State for the Environment* (1991) 61 P. & C.R. 225, [1991] C.L.Y. 3514 applied, and (3) there had been no evidence of illegality and thus the court had not been obliged to take the point of its own motion.

MOASE v. SECRETARY OF STATE FOR THE ENVIRONMENT, TRANSPORT AND THE REGIONS; LOMAS v. SECRETARY OF STATE FOR THE ENVIRONMENT, TRANSPORT AND THE REGIONS [2001] Env. L.R. 13, Swinton Thomas, L.J., CA.

5631. Sewerage – sewerage inspectors – duty of sewerage undertakers to provide public sewerage services – viability of private sewerage options

[Water Industry Act 1991.]

AW, a water and sewerage undertaker, applied for judicial review of EA's decision, made pursuant to the Water Industry Act 1991, that it was required to provide public sewerage services to four villages. AW argued that EA had (1) unlawfully imposed a blanket policy rejecting cesspools as an option; (2) wrongly taken the view that the practicability test in s.101A(3)(e) of the Act could not be met where residents refused to cooperate between themselves in the provision of a private treatment plant, and (3) wrongly assumed that if public sewerage was required to supply certain residences, then it had to be supplied to the entire locality and that its discretion in identifying a "locality" was not amenable to challenge.

Held, granting the application, that (1) while EA was justified in discouraging the building of cesspools for environmental reasons, it had acted unlawfully in failing to give any consideration to cesspools as an option that might be appropriate in some circumstances. Furthermore, EA had assumed an incorrect interpretation of government guidance on the Act, namely that s.101A required that inadequate private sewerage options had to be replaced on a "like for like" basis, regardless of cost; it was consequently not clear whether the private option had been disregarded on merit or as a result of that error in approach; (2) lack of cooperation by residents did not impose a duty on AW to provide a public sewer service. EA had authority under the Act to coerce residents to contribute to a private system, which Parliament clearly intended as a means of giving effect to the Act, and (3) EA's mechanistic conclusion that sewerage had to be supplied to the entire locality was unlawful as it had the effect of bypassing the criteria set out in the Act for assessing sewerage need. There was no "parasitic entitlement" to public services; the criteria had to be applied to premises on an individual basis, taking into account all factors including cost and appropriateness.

R. (ON THE APPLICATION OF ANGLIAN WATER SERVICES LTD) v. ENVIRONMENT AGENCY; *sub nom.* R. v. ENVIRONMENT AGENCY, *ex p.* ANGLIAN WATER SERVICES LTD [2001] E.H.L.R. 22, Tomlinson, J, QBD (Admin Ct).

5632. Sewerage undertakers – British Waterways – implied power to discharge water from sewers – requirement of consent

[Water Industry Act 1991 s.94(1)(b), s.159, s.165.]

The British Waterways Board, B, appealed against a finding ([2001] Ch. 32, [1999] C.L.Y. 5036) that S, a sewerage undertaker, had an implied power under the Water Industry Act 1991 s.159 to discharge surface water into a canal without gaining consent. B had entered into a licence agreement with S's statutory predecessor which had provided for the discharge of surface water into the Stourbridge canal subject to an annual charge. Upon S's failure to make a similar agreement with B, B had terminated the licence and had sought a declaration that a sewerage authority had no power under the Act to make such a discharge into a canal or waterway without an owner's consent. The judge had found that as S had a statutory pipe laying power pursuant to s.159, it had a discharge power by implication.

Held, allowing the appeal, that having regard to the Act as a whole, a power to discharge without the gaining of a canal owners consent could not be implied. In so determining, there was no need to look at the legislation that had preceded the Act, which was one of consolidation, *R. v. Secretary of State for the Environment, Transport and the Regions, ex p. Spath Holme Ltd* [2001] 2 W.L.R. 15, [2001] 1 C.L. 399 applied. The judge had erred by finding support for her conclusion that a discharge power was implied in previous legislation and in the decision of *Durrant v. Branksome Urban DC* [1897] 2 Ch. 291 which was irrelevant to the present position under the Act, *Durrant* distinguished. The express power of discharge provided by virtue of s.165 was limited to water undertakers. Further, far from providing an implied power, s.94(1)(b) expressly imposed a duty on sewerage undertakers to provide for the disposal of the contents of sewers. In the absence of an implied statutory authority, the discharge of water without consent amounted to trespass and the intention of Parliament could not be construed as implying a right to interfere with private rights.

BRITISH WATERWAYS BOARD v. SEVERN TRENT WATER LTD, [2001] EWCA Civ 276, [2002] Ch. 25, Peter Gibson, L.J., CA.

5633.   Sewerage undertakers – sewers and drains – drainage from private premises – meaning of "sewer"

[Public Health Act 1875 s.4; Environmental Protection Act 1990 s.80.]

B appealed against the allowing of an appeal by Y, a sewerage undertaker with a statutory responsibility to maintain public sewers in its area, against an abatement notice issued by B pursuant to the Environmental Protection Act 1990 s.80. The abatement notice concerned the deposit of sewage emanating from the drainage system in private premises, "the farmhouse". The court below found that the drainage pipe in question did not serve more than one building or premises within the same curtilage and was therefore not a public sewer within the meaning of the Public Health Act 1875 s.4. B contended that the drainage system from which the sewage emanated was a public sewer within the meaning of s.4 since the word "sewer" should be given a wide meaning and since the pipe in question drained water from the highway as well as the farmhouse. Y maintained that the pipe did not constitute a public sewer and therefore it had no responsibility for it.

Held, dismissing the appeal, that the fact that the pipe took water from the farmhouse and the surface of the highway did not mean that it was a public sewer. In considering whether the pipe was a drain or sewer for the purposes of s.4 of the 1875 Act, the court should consider the purpose for which the pipe was constructed. The actual purpose of the pipe was to protect the farmhouse rather than the highway, and consequently had been constructed to serve only one building or premises. The pipe was therefore a drain, *Wincanton Rural DC v. Parsons* [1905] 2 K.B. 34 applied. It was possible that an unadopted street could constitute "premises" within the meaning of s.4, but that issue did not apply on the facts of the instant case.

BRADFORD MDC v. YORKSHIRE WATER SERVICES LTD, [2001] EWHC Admin 687, [2002] Env. L.R.16, Brooke, L.J., QBD (Admin Ct).

5634.   Water charges – contractual liability – charges levied upon estate – discharge of charging agreement

[Water Industry Act 1991 s.142.]

T appealed against a decision that it could not charge, pursuant to the Water Industry Act 1991 s.142, for water supplied to R's house. R contended that T had not supplied him with a water service since T had agreed to supply water to the estate on which R's house was situated, rather than R personally, and that T had agreed to charge the estate rather than its occupants.

Held, allowing the appeal, that the evidence showed that the agreement between B, T's predecessor as statutory water undertaker, and the estate, by which B was precluded from charging for the water supplied to residents of the estate, had been discharged by agreement so that T could now charge the residents directly.

THAMES WATER UTILITIES LTD v. RICHARDSON [2001] E.H.L.R. 15, Potter, L.J., CA.

5635. Water companies – competitive tendering – provision of services

[Utilities Contracts Regulations 1996 (SI 1996 2911); Council Directive 93/38 coordinating the procurement procedures of entities operating in the water, energy, transport and telecommunications sectors.]

ST, a provider of water and sewage services in parts of England and Wales, sought to prevent DCC, a Welsh water and sewerage supplier, from contracting with a third party, U, for the provision of operation and maintenance services. ST contended that the services comprising the subject matter of the agreement should be put out to tender in order to comply with Council Directive 93/38 and the Utilities Contracts Regulations 1996. DCC argued that the agreement was an incidental part of a share sale agreement pursuant to which services would be relocated in company NC and then sold on to U.

Held, giving judgment for the claimant, that the underlying purpose of the Regulations would be undermined if a utility company were able to marshal assets and services into a single corporate entity and then sell them on to a chosen purchaser. The agreement did not comprise the simple sale of a business, nor could it be described as the incidental sale of assets as contended for by DCC.

SEVERN TRENT PLC v. DWR CYMRU CYFYNGEDIG (WELSH WATER LTD) [2001] C.L.C. 107, Langley, J., QBD (Comm Ct).

5636. Water quality – water supply

WATER SUPPLY (WATER QUALITY) (AMENDMENT) REGULATIONS 2001, SI 2001 2885; made under the Water Industry Act 1991 s.67, s.69, s.213. In force: September 5, 2001; £1.75.

These Regulations amend the Water Supply (Water Quality) Regulations 2000 (SI 2000 3184) to enable proceedings to be taken in respect of contraventions of those Regulations and to commence the revocation of provisions relating to the functions of English local authorities under the Water Supply (Water Quality) Regulations 1989 (SI 1989 1147).

5637. Water quality – water supply – Wales

WATER SUPPLY (WATER QUALITY) REGULATIONS 2001, SI 2001 3911 (W.323); made under the Water Industry Act 1991 s.67, s.69, s.77, s.213. In force: in accordance with Reg.1 (2) - (5); £7.50.

These Regulations supplement the Water Industry Act 1991 Ch. III and amend, for a limited period, the Water Supply (Water Quality) (Amendment) Regulations 1989 (SI 1989 1384) and, on January 1, 2004, revoke and replace those Regulations. They are primarily concerned with the quality of water supplied by water undertakers whose areas are wholly or mainly in Wales for drinking, washing, cooking and food preparation, and for food production, and with arrangements for the publication of information about water quality. The Regulations are directed at the achievement of the objective set out in Council Directive 98/83 ([1998] OJ L330/32) Art.2, to protect human health from the adverse effects of any contamination of water intended for human consumption by ensuring that it is wholesome and clean.

NORTHERN IRELAND

ADMINISTRATION OF JUSTICE

5638. County courts – financial limits

COUNTY COURTS (FINANCIAL LIMITS) ORDER (NORTHERN IRELAND) 2001, SR 2001 67; made under the County Courts (Northern Ireland) Order 1980 (SI 1980 397 (NI.3)) Art.22. In force: in accordance with Art.1; £1.50.

This Order, which amends the County Courts (Northern Ireland) Order 1980 (SI 1980 397 (NI.3)), the County Courts (Financial Limits) Order (Northern Ireland) 1993 (SR 1993 282) and the County Courts (Financial Limits) Order (Northern Ireland) 1992 (SR 1992 372), increases the jurisdiction of district judges in the county courts in Northern Ireland from £3,000 to £5,000 in respect of defended actions and from £1,000 to £2,000 in respect of arbitrations.

5639. Criminal appeals – human rights compatibility – notice of issues

CRIMINAL APPEAL (AMENDMENT) (NORTHERN IRELAND) RULES 2001, SR 2001 250; made under the Judicature (Northern Ireland) Act 1978 s.55. In force: July 16, 2001; £1.75.

These Rules amend the Criminal Appeal (Northern Ireland) Rules 1968 (SR & O 1968 218) to make corrections to the provisions which apply where issues under the Human Rights Act 1998 arise in criminal appeal proceedings in the Court of Appeal.

5640. Crown courts – rules – cross examination – sexual offences

CROWN COURT (AMENDMENT) RULES (NORTHERN IRELAND) 2001, SR 2001 253; made under the Judicature (Northern Ireland) Act 1978 s.52; and the Criminal Evidence (Northern Ireland) Order 1999 (SI 1999 2789 (NI.8)) Art.26, Art.39. In force: in accordance with r.1; £2.00.

These Rules amend the Crown Court Rules (Northern Ireland) 1979 (SR 1979 90) to prescribe the time when, and the manner in which, a legal representative is to be appointed to act for the defendant for the purpose of cross examining any witness which the defendant is prevented from cross examining in person by virtue of the Criminal Evidence (Northern Ireland) Order 1999 (SI 1999 2789 (NI.8)). They provide for the appointment by the Court of a qualified legal representative where the defendant fails to appoint a legal representative and make a minor amendment to take account of the additional powers conferred on financial investigators by the Financial Investigations (Northern Ireland) Order 2001 (SI 2001 1866 (NI.1)).

5641. High Court – judges – increase in numbers

MAXIMUM NUMBER OF JUDGES (NORTHERN IRELAND) ORDER 2001, SI 2001 958; made under the Judicature (Northern Ireland) Act 1978 s.2. In force: April 2, 2001; £1.50.

This Order amends the Judicature (Northern Ireland) Act 1978 to increase from seven to nine the maximum number of puisne judges in Her Majesty's High Court of Justice in Northern Ireland.

5642. Human rights – intervention – power of Human Rights Commission to intervene in legal proceedings and appear as amicus curiae

[Northern Ireland Act 1998 s.69(5).]

The Northern Ireland Human Rights Commission appealed against the refusal of its application for judicial review of a coroner's ruling that it had no power to intervene in legal proceedings or appear as amicus curiae. The Commission had sought to make submissions to the coroner regarding the scope of the inquest into deaths resulting from a bomb attack in the town of Omagh and contended that pursuant to the Northern Ireland Act 1998, it had the power to make submissions on all matters concerning the observance of human rights and human rights law.

Held, dismissing the appeal (Kerr, Justice dissenting), that the Commission could only exercise such powers as had been conferred upon it by the 1998 Act, together with those powers that might be derived by reasonable implication from its provisions, *Attorney General v. Great Eastern Railway Co* (1879-80) L.R. 5 App. Cas. 473 and *Baroness Wenlock v. River Dee Co (No.3)* (1887) L.R. 36 Ch. D. 674 applied. Under s.69(5) of the 1998 Act, the Commission was empowered to "bring" proceedings but the plain meaning of that word could not accommodate intervention in other proceedings in order to promote the interests or arguments of a party to those proceedings. Whilst it might initially appear sensible to enable the Commission to appear as a party in legal proceedings, such a role might not prove to be helpful. The Commission was not sufficiently dispassionate to act effectively as an amicus curiae and the independence of the judiciary might be subject to doubt in the minds of the public if the outcome of proceedings could be seen to be affected by a public body who was not a party to proceedings. The involvement of the Commission might also increase the costs of proceedings and would threaten the principle of equality of arms.

R. (ON THE APPLICATION OF NORTHERN IRELAND HUMAN RIGHTS COMMISSION) v. GREATER BELFAST CORONER; *sub nom.* NORTHERN IRELAND HUMAN RIGHTS COMMISSION'S APPLICATION FOR JUDICIAL REVIEW, *Re* [2001] N.I. 271, McCollum, L.J., CA (NI).

5643. Lands tribunal – salaries

LANDS TRIBUNAL (SALARIES) ORDER (NORTHERN IRELAND) 2001, SR 2001 293; made under the Administrative and Financial Provisions Act (Northern Ireland) 1962 s.18; and the Lands Tribunal and Compensation Act (Northern Ireland) 1964 s.2. In force: July 18, 2001; £1.50.

This Order, which revokes the Lands Tribunal (Salaries) Order (Northern Ireland) 1999 (SR 1999 236), provides for changes in the annual salaries payable to members of the Lands Tribunal for Northern Ireland following recommendations made in the Report of the Review Body on Senior Salaries in 2000 and the Report of the Review Body on Senior Salaries in 2001. The Order increases the annual salary of the President of the Lands Tribunal and all members of the Tribunal.

5644. Magistrates courts – proceedings – costs

RESIDENT MAGISTRATE, JUSTICE OF THE PEACE AND CLERK OF PETTY SESSIONS (COSTS) REGULATIONS (NORTHERN IRELAND) 2001, SR 2001 185; made under the Magistrates Courts (Northern Ireland) Order 1981 (SI 1981 1675 (NI.26)) Art.6A. In force: June 1, 2001; £1.75.

These Regulations apply in relation to orders under the Magistrates' Courts (Northern Ireland) Order 1981 (SI 1981 1675 (NI.26)) Art.6A(3) that the Lord Chancellor make a payment in respect of the costs of a person in the proceedings. They provide for when such an order cannot be made and how the costs shall be determined. Article 6A(3) of the 1981 Order applies where a court is prevented by Art.6A(1) of that Order from ordering a resident magistrate, a justice of the peace, or a clerk of petty sessions to pay costs in any proceedings in respect of any act or omission in the execution (or purported execution) of his duty as such a magistrate or justice or as such a clerk exercising, by virtue of any statutory provision, any of the functions of a magistrates' court.

5645. Magistrates courts – terrorist organisations – seizure, detention and forfeiture of assets

MAGISTRATES' COURTS (TERRORISM ACT 2000) RULES (NORTHERN IRELAND) 2001, SR 2001 65; made under the Terrorism Act 2000 s.31; and the Magistrates' Courts (Northern Ireland) Order 1980 (SI 1980 1675 (NI.26)) Art.13. In force: February 19, 2001; £3.50.

These Rules make provision for various applications under the Terrorism Act 2000 Part III in respect of the seizure, detention and forfeiture of cash suspected to form the whole or part of the resources of a proscribed organisation, suspected to be terrorist property, or intended to be used for the purposes of terrorism. In addition, they set out the procedure to be followed where an appeal is to be made and provides for the procedure to be followed where an application is made for the release of cash to meet an appellant's legal expenses.

5646. Magistrates courts – warrants in proceedings

MAGISTRATES' COURTS (AMENDMENT) RULES (NORTHERN IRELAND) 2001, SR 2001 432; made under the Magistrates' Courts (Northern Ireland) Order 1981 (SI 1981 1675 (NI.26)) Art.13. In force: January 11, 2002; £1.50.

These Rules amend the Magistrates' Courts Rules (Northern Ireland) 1984 (SR 1984 225) to substitute a new r.143 which provides for warrants in proceedings upon complaint to be sent for execution to the district commander for the police district in which the warrant is issued.

5647. Miscarriage of justice – convictions – compensation for time in custody – basis for determining award

F's conviction for murder was quashed after he had served eight years and eight months of a life sentence. The Secretary of State determined that H was entitled to compensation for the time spent in custody, and appointed NH to assess the compensation. There was a delay in the submission of H's claim documentation, with the result that H's compensation assessment did not take place until three years after that of his two co-accused, A and B. When assessing H's non pecuniary compensation, NH applied the same scale that he had used for A, rather than the scale that applied at the time, on the basis that H ought not to gain an advantage over A because of the delay. H sought judicial review of the decision, contending that the assessment should have been conducted on the same basis as the quantification of damages in ordinary civil proceedings, using values applicable at the time of assessment. NH accepted that quantification should have followed that used in civil cases, but stated that he had departed from that principle for good reasons.

Held, allowing the application, that (1) using the same method employed to assess A's damages meant that NH had not used a similar method to that used in assessing civil damages at the time when H's assessment was made; (2) NH had failed to pay proper regard to the principles governing the assessment exercise merely by recalling and then ignoring them. He was required to decide whether or not to apply those principles, and he had not done that by believing he had followed a similar course when in reality had had not done so, and (3) NH had taken account of irrelevant matters when setting H's assessment at a comparable level to A's and by considering the delay in producing the relevant material.

HEGAN'S APPLICATION FOR JUDICIAL REVIEW, *Re* [2000] N.I. 461, Kerr, J., QBD (NI).

5648. Reporting restrictions – retrials – power of court to order restriction pending appeal or retrial

[Contempt of Court Act 1981 s.4(2).]

The BBC renewed an application for permission to appeal against an order under the Contempt of Court Act 1981 s.4(2) prohibiting the reporting of criminal proceedings involving L, or any sentences passed on him until the time for giving notice of appeal had expired or the appeal or any retrial ordered on appeal had been heard. The judge below had held that the fact that L had indicated that he could appeal was sufficient to bring the matter within the meaning of "imminent" or "pending" proceedings for the purposes of s.4(2).

Held, refusing the reapplication, that (1) the order to postpone publication of the report of proceedings could be made in the interests of the administration of justice even though an ordered retrial was not usually regarded as pending proceedings, and (2) the court of appeal could only review the exercise of judicial discretion to make such an order if the judge below had made an error of law, which had not occurred in the instant case.

R. v. LEES (WILLIAM JOHN); *sub nom.* BBC'S APPLICATION, RE; BRITISH BROADCASTING CORP'S APPLICATION, *Re* [2001] N.I. 233, Carswell, L.C.J., CA (NI).

5649. Supreme Court – rules – mortgage actions

RULES OF THE SUPREME COURT (NORTHERN IRELAND) (AMENDMENT) 2001, SR 2001 254; made under the Judicature (Northern Ireland) Act 1978 s.55. In force: September 5, 2001; £3.00.

These Rules, which amend the Rules of the Supreme Court (Northern Ireland) 1980 (SR 1980 346), implement certain recommendations of the Final Report of the Civil Justice Reform Group and ensure that all persons in occupation of mortgaged properties are afforded adequate notice of proceedings for possession or made parties to such proceedings. The Rules also make amendments to the 1980 Rules to take account of the Civil Evidence (Northern Ireland) Order 1997 (SI 1997 2983 (NI.21)), to take account of the Family Homes and Domestic Violence (Northern Ireland) Order 1998 (SI 1998 1071 (NI.6)) in the context of applications relating to mortgaged properties, to ensure that copies of exhibits to the plaintiff's grounding affidavits in mortgage actions for possession are served on defendants who do not enter appearances and to ensure that sufficient particulars of mortgage interest are available.

5650. Warrants – false imprisonment – mistake – innocent party named in warrant – meaning of "person charged with an offence"

[Criminal Law Act 1977 s.38(3).]

The Chief Constable appealed against a decision of the Court of Appeal of Northern Ireland ([2000] N.I. 56, [2000] C.L.Y. 5663) to allow M's appeal against the dismissal of his claim for damages for false arrest and false imprisonment. A third party had falsely given M's name to police upon arrest in Scotland and, following the failure of the third party to answer bail, a warrant was issued by the court in M's name. M was arrested by police in Northern Ireland and taken to Scotland but was later released when it was discovered that he was not the person who had committed the offence. The Court of Appeal held that M was not a "person charged with an offence" within the meaning of the Criminal Law Act 1977 s.38(3) and that his arrest had therefore been unlawful.

Held, allowing the appeal, that in the absence of malice or bad faith, the police in Northern Ireland were not liable for false arrest and imprisonment, since s.38(3) did not require that the person named in the warrant be the person who had in fact been charged with an offence. The purpose of s.38(3) was to enable a warrant issued in one part of the United Kingdom to be enforced in another part of the UK. If M had been in Scotland and the warrant had been executed in Scotland, the arrest in conformity with the warrant would have been lawful because its issue had been within the jurisdiction of the judge. That position was still the same despite the fact that M was arrested in Northern

Ireland since s.38 simply gave the power to execute the warrant in another jurisdiction. The act of executing a warrant was purely ministerial and as such the arresting police officer was entitled to rely on the face of the warrant, *Hoye v. Bush* (1840) 1 Man. & G. 775 applied. In any event, if s.38(3) was to be read so that the person named in the warrant was to be the person who had actually committed the offence, M could still be considered as "a person charged with an offence", albeit that he had been charged by mistake.

McGRATH v. CHIEF CONSTABLE OF THE ROYAL ULSTER CONSTABULARY, [2001] UKHL 39, [2001] 2 A.C. 731, Lord Clyde, HL (NI).

ADMINISTRATIVE LAW

5651. Administrative decision making – appointments – Parades Commission – departure from advertised procedure – validity

[Public Processions (Northern Ireland) Act 1998 Sch.1 para.2(3).]

W, a Garvaghy Road resident, sought judicial review of a decision by the Secretary of State for Northern Ireland on the selection and appointment of the chair and members of the Parades Commission. Advertisements inviting applications had stated that no application received after November 5, 1999 would be considered. However, three applications submitted after that date were considered and an individual was asked by the Secretary of State to accept an appointment when he had not taken part in the application process. W also contended that the final composition of the Commission was not representative of the community, as required by the Public Processions (Northern Ireland) Act 1998 Sch.1 para. 2(3), and that an assurance by the Minister of State to the Garvaghy Road residents regarding appointment to the Commission had created a legitimate expectation that the application and selection procedures would be in accordance with guidance published by the Commissioner for Public Appointments.

Held, refusing the application, that Sch.1 para.2(3) required the Commission's composition to reflect that of the community "as far as practicable" and in the circumstances all reasonable steps had been taken to make the Commission representative. Practicable in the instant case was equated to "feasible", *Brookes v. JP Coates (UK) Ltd* [1984] 1 All E.R. 702, [1984] C.L.Y. 1012. Appointment procedures did not have to be followed slavishly and the failure to do so would not make the procedure void. The guidance had been followed in spirit and the departures had been justified given the task the Commission was charged with, its size and the need to make appointments on merit. There was no evidence of less favourable treatment on the basis of political opinion in the way that the appointments had been made and balance had been achieved in terms of both religious and political affiliations.

WHITE'S APPLICATION FOR JUDICIAL REVIEW, *Re* [2000] N.I. 432, Carswell, L.C.J., QBD (NI).

5652. Administrative decision making – investigations – Equality Commission for Northern Ireland to investigate employer

[Sex Discrimination (Northern Ireland) Order 1976 (SI 1976 1042 (NI.15)) Art.57; European Convention on Human Rights 1950 Art.6.]

The Equality Commission for Northern Ireland, EC, investigated BT following complaints of discrimination from BT's employees. BT sought judicial review of EC's subsequent decision to conduct a further investigation under the Sex Discrimination (Northern Ireland) Order 1976 Art.57 on the basis that EC's staff members, as opposed to the named commissioners, had wrongly been allowed to participate in the initial investigation and their opinions had influenced the commissioners' decision making process. A commissioner, C, gave evidence that the decision to launch the further investigation had not been delegated to EC's staff. EC appealed against an order for discovery of documents detailing advice or assistance given by EC's staff in the investigation and BT contended that the rules governing discovery in judicial review were contrary to the European Convention on Human Rights 1950 Art.6.

Held, allowing the appeal, that (1) EC's staff could be entrusted with aspects of an investigation by the decision making commissioners, in the course of which they could express views and opinions, as long as the commissioners reached their own decision. C had shown that the decision to carry out the investigation under Art.57 was taken only by the two nominated commissioners and had not been delegated to anyone else so that BT had not passed the threshold of showing that EC's decision was incorrect, *R. v. Secretary of State for Education and Science, ex p. J* [1993] C.O.D. 146, [1993] C.L.Y. 3214 applied, and (2) the decision to carry out the investigation under Art.57 determined only that the investigation should proceed so that Art.6 of the Convention did not apply in the instant case, *Al-Fayed v. United Kingdom (A/294-B)* (1994) 18 E.H.R.R. 393, [1995] C.L.Y. 2622 and *Rooney's Application, Re* [1995] N.I. 398 applied.

BELFAST TELEGRAPH NEWSPAPERS LTD'S APPLICATION FOR JUDICIAL REVIEW, *Re* [2001] N.I. 178, Carswell, L.C.J., CA (NI).

5653.   Legal aid – applications – criteria

[Legal Aid (General) Regulations (Northern Ireland) 1965 (SR 1965 217) Reg.5(11); Legal Aid, Advice and Assistance (Northern Ireland) Order 1981 (SI 1981 228) Art.10.]

H, a Sinn Fein member of Belfast City Council, BCC, applied for legal aid to challenge what he and other members of his party perceived was a policy of deliberately excluding Sinn Fein members from certain key council posts. The papers in support of H's application focused on Sinn Fein's wider complaint, as opposed to H's own exclusion. The Law Society's certifying committee refused H's application, as it found he had failed to show reasonable grounds for bringing the claim or taking part in the proceedings. This decision was upheld on appeal to the Society's Legal Aid Committee, LAC, on the grounds that it would be unreasonable for H to receive legal aid. The LAC had taken as a guideline, rather than directly applying, the Legal Aid (General) Regulations (Northern Ireland) 1965 Reg.5(11), which provided that where an individual's legal aid application included matters that affected others, who could also have a cause of action, then the application could be refused by the "appropriate committee", unless to do so would be prejudicial to the applicant or if it was reasonable for others to pay the costs. The decision to refuse legal aid was quashed at judicial review ([2000] N.I.J.B. 50), on the basis that Reg.5(11) was limited to civil matters in private law and did not include public law matters, and, accordingly, the Committee should not have used Reg.5(11) as a guideline. The Law Society appealed.

Held, allowing the appeal, that although the substantive matter had been determined, the subject matter of the appeal would be heard as it raised points of interest in future cases. The Committee had found that H had reasonable grounds for taking proceedings against BCC, in terms of the Legal Aid, Advice and Assistance (Northern Ireland) Order 1981 Art.10(4), but had gone on to find that it would be unreasonable to grant legal aid. That was a finding open to the Committee under Art.10 of the 1981 Order. Regulation 5 of the 1965 Regulations applied to judicial review proceedings and the Committee had actually applied the Reg.5(11) criteria, even though it had not felt it had to do so. Even if that construction of Reg.5(11) was incorrect, it could still be used as a guideline. As a result, the Committee was entitled to reach the decision it had in the instant case, *McLaughlin's Application, Re* (Unreported, 1990) distinguished as decided in curiam. As a legal aid certificate operated only from the date it was issued, and only applied to work done after that point, then the judge below should have refused to make the order, as by that stage the substantive matter had been decided, *Lacey v. Silk (W) & Son* [1951] 2 All E.R. 128 and *R&T Thew Ltd v. Reeves (No.1)* [1982] Q.B. 172, [1981] C.L.Y. 1604 approved.

HARTLEY'S APPLICATION FOR JUDICIAL REVIEW, *Re* [2000] N.I. 376, Carswell, L.C.J., CA (NI).

5654. Ombudsmen – salaries

SALARIES (ASSEMBLY OMBUDSMAN AND COMMISSIONER FOR COMPLAINTS) ORDER (NORTHERN IRELAND) 2001, SR 2001 302; made under the Ombudsman (Northern Ireland) Order 1996 (SI 1996 1298 (NI.8)) Art.5; and the Commissioner for Complaints (Northern Ireland) Order 1996 (SI 1996 1297 (NI.7)) Art.4. In force: September 27, 2001; £1.50.

This Order, which revokes the Salaries (Assembly Ombudsman and Commissioner for Complaints) Order (Northern Ireland) 2000 (SR 2000 292), provides for an increase in the annual salaries payable to the Assembly Ombudsman for Northern Ireland and the Northern Ireland Commissioner for Complaints.

5655. Public processions – accounts and audit

PUBLIC PROCESSIONS (NORTHERN IRELAND) ACT 1998 (ACCOUNTS AND AUDIT) ORDER 2001, SI 2001 852; made under the Public Processions (Northern Ireland) Act 1998 Sch.1 para.12. In force: March 30, 2001; £1.50.

This Order, which amends the Public Procession (Northern Ireland) Act 1998 and revokes the Public Processions (Northern Ireland) Act 1998 (Accounts and Audit) Order 2000 (SI 2000 655), makes amendments so as to make it clear that the financial year which commenced on January 1, 2000 shall end on March 31, 2001.

5656. Public processions – accounts and audit

PUBLIC PROCESSIONS (NORTHERN IRELAND) ACT 1998 (ACCOUNTS AND AUDIT) ORDER (NO.2) 2001, SI 2001 999; made under the Public Processions (Northern Ireland) Act 1998 Sch.1 para.12. In force: May 26, 2001; £1.50.

This Order revokes the Public Processions (Northern Ireland) Act 1998 (Accounts and Audit) Order 2001 (SI 2001 852) which amended the financial year of the Parades Commission for Northern Ireland in the Public Processions (Northern Ireland) Act 1998 Sch.1 para.12 (5).

5657. Public processions – public order

PUBLIC ORDER, NORTHERN IRELAND THE PUBLIC PROCESSIONS (NORTHERN IRELAND) ACT 1998 (ACCOUNTS AND AUDIT) ORDER 2001, SI 2001 851; made under the Public Processions (Northern Ireland) Act 1998 s.16, Sch.1 para.12. In force: December 29, 2001; £1.50.

This Order amends the Public Processions (Northern Ireland) Act 1998

AGRICULTURE

5658. Agricultural policy – wine

See AGRICULTURE. §123

5659. Agricultural produce – milk – quota arrangements

DAIRY PRODUCE QUOTAS (AMENDMENT) REGULATIONS (NORTHERN IRELAND) 2001, SR 2001 27; made under the European Communities Act 1972 s.2. In force: February 23, 2001; £2.50.

These Regulations, which come into operation on February 23, 2001, amend the Dairy Produce Quotas Regulations 1997 (SI 1997 733) in so far as they apply to Northern Ireland. The principal change introduced by these Regulations is provision for the award of quota being the specific quota increases for allocation to Northern Ireland pursuant to Council Regulation 3950/92 ([1992] OJ L405/1).

5660. Animal products – beef – premiums

BEEF SPECIAL PREMIUM REGULATIONS (NORTHERN IRELAND) 2001, SR 2001 363; made under the European Communities Act 1972 s.2. In force: October 16, 2001; £3.00.

These Regulations, which revoke the provisions of the Beef Special Premium (Protection of Payments) Regulations (Northern Ireland) 1996 (SR 1996 611), lay down implementing measures for the beef special premium scheme provided for in Council Regulation 1254/1999 ([1999] OJ L160/21) on the common organisation of the market in beef and veal. The Regulations provide for the administration of the scheme in relation to applicants and their holdings where those holdings are situated wholly in Northern Ireland, and also holdings situated partly in Northern Ireland and partly elsewhere in the UK, where the Department of Agriculture and Rural Development is responsible for processing the farmer's claim for beef special premium. In addition, they lay down enforcement provisions.

5661. Animal products – diseases and disorders – BSE – monitoring

BOVINE SPONGIFORM ENCEPHALOPATHY MONITORING REGULATIONS (NORTHERN IRELAND) 2001, SR 2001 292; made under the European Communities Act 1972 s.2. In force: August 27, 2001; £2.00.

These Regulations, which amend the Cattle Passport Regulations (Northern Ireland) 1999 (SR 1999 324), make provision for the purpose of dealing in Northern Ireland with the obligations in Council Regulation 999/2001 ([2001] OJ L147/1) laying down rules for the prevention, control and eradication of certain transmissible spongiform encephalopathies. This Council Regulation requires Member States to ensure that certain categories of bovine animals over 24 months of age are examined in accordance with prescribed minimum requirements for monitoring bovine spongiform encephalopathy. These Regulations require the person in possession of a notifiable bovine animal which dies on any farm or in transport or which has been killed otherwise than for human consumption, to notify the death to a Divisional Veterinary Officer of the Department of Agriculture and Rural Development and provide powers of entry, examination and search, offences and penalties.

5662. Animal products – diseases and disorders – specified risk material

SPECIFIED RISK MATERIAL (AMENDMENT) ORDER (NORTHERN IRELAND) 2001, SR 2001 1; made under the Diseases of Animals (Northern Ireland) Order 1981 (SI 1981 1115 (NI.22)) Art.2, Art.5, Art.19, Art.24, Art.29, Art.32, Art.44, Art.46, Art.60. In force: January 3, 2001; £2.00.

This Order implements in Northern Ireland the requirements of Article 3.1 of Commission Decision 2000/418/EC regulating the use of material presenting risks as regards transmissible spongiform encephalopathies, as amended by Article 1 of the Commission Decision adopted on December 27, 2000. It does so by amending the Specified Risk Material Order (Northern Ireland) 1997 (SR 1997 551).

5663. Animal products – diseases and disorders – specified risk material

SPECIFIED RISK MATERIAL (AMENDMENT) REGULATIONS (NORTHERN IRELAND) 2001, SR 2001 48; made under the Food Safety (Northern Ireland) Order 1991 (SI 1991 762 (NI.7)) Art.15, Art.16, Art.18, Art.25, Art.47, Sch.1 para.2, Sch.1 para.3, Sch.1 para.5, Sch.1 para.6. In force: February 8, 2001; £1.75.

These Regulations, which amend the Specified Risk Material Regulations (Northern Ireland) 1997 (SR 1997 552), give effect to Art.1 of Commission Decision 2001/2 ([2001] OJ L1/21), adopted on December 27, 2000, which amends Commission Decision 2000/418 ([2000] OJ L158/76) regulating the use of material presenting risk as regards transmissible spongiform encephalopathies. It brings the definition of specified risk material into line with that contained within the Commission Decision.

5664. Animal products – food hygiene – slaughtering

POULTRY MEAT, FARMED GAME BIRD MEAT AND RABBIT MEAT (HYGIENE AND INSPECTION) (AMENDMENT) REGULATIONS (NORTHERN IRELAND) 2001, SR 2001 429; made under the European Communities Act 1972 s.2. In force: Reg.2(2)(3)(4): December 1, 2002; remainder: February 1, 2002; £2.00.

These Regulations amend the Poultry Meat, Farmed Game Bird Meat and Rabbit Meat (Hygiene and Inspection) Regulations (Northern Ireland) 1995 (SR 1995 396) and the Products of Animal Origin (Import and Export) Regulations (Northern Ireland) 1998 (SR 1998 45). The amendments have effect to disapply the Regulations in so far as farmers and producers with a limited annual production of birds or rabbits make certain sales, primarily of a retail nature and prohibit a person from operating a licensed low throughput slaughterhouse unless he has notified the Food Standards Agency of the number and origin of the birds and rabbits to be slaughtered there. In addition, these Regulations implement in part the provisions of Council Directive 91/495 ([1991] OJ L268/41) concerning public health and animal health problems affecting the production and placing on the market of rabbit meat and farmed game meat and Council Directive 71/118 on health problems affecting the production and placing on the market of fresh poultry meat.

5665. Animal products – infectious disease control – ruminant related fluid – waste disposal

RENDERING (FLUID TREATMENT) ORDER (NORTHERN IRELAND) 2001, SR 2001 378; made under the Diseases of Animals (Northern Ireland) Order 1981 (SI 1981 1115 (NI.22)) Art.5, Art.44, Art.60. In force: November 6, 2001; £2.00.

This Order, which prohibits the spreading of untreated ruminant condensate on land, defines ruminant related fluid and makes provision in relation to the rendering of animal products and the treatment and discharge of ruminant related fluid. It makes provision in relation to the testing of treated ruminant related fluid, imposes record keeping requirements and makes provision in relation to powers of inspectors.

5666. Animal products – waste disposal – animal feed

CATERING WASTE (FEEDING TO LIVESTOCK) ORDER (NORTHERN IRELAND) 2001, SR 2001 286; made under the Diseases of Animals (Northern Ireland) Order 1981 (SI 1981 1115 (NI.22)) Art.2, Art.5, Art.19, Art.29, Art.44, Art.60. In force: August 20, 2001; £2.00.

This Order, which amends the Diseases of Animals (Animal Protein) (No.2) Order (Northern Ireland) 1989 (SR 1989 347), revokes the Diseases of Animals (Landing of Waste Foods) Order (Northern Ireland) 1971 (SR & O (NI) 1971 353), the Waste Food (Feeding to Livestock and Poultry) Order (Northern Ireland) 1974 (SR & O (NI) 1974 12) and the Waste Food (Feeding to Livestock and Poultry) (Amendment) Order (Northern Ireland) 1976 (SR 1976 400). The Order prohibits the feeding to livestock of certain categories of catering waste, regulates the landing of catering waste in Northern Ireland from a means of transport from outside Northern Ireland, regulates the disposal of catering waste and makes provision for an inspector to serve a notice on any person in possession of catering waste to dispose of it as may be specified in the notice.

5667. Animals – feedingstuffs

FEEDING STUFFS REGULATIONS (NORTHERN IRELAND) 2001, SR 2001 47; made under the Agriculture Act 1970 s.66, s.68, s.69, s.70, s.73, s.74, s.74A, s.77, s.78, s.84, s.86; and the European Communities Act 1972 s.2. In force: April 2, 2001; £15.00.

These Regulations, which revoke and replace the Feeding Stuffs Regulations (Northern Ireland) 1995 (SR 1995 451 as amended by SR 1996 259, SR 1998 124, SR 1998 373 and SR 1999 287), implement specified European Community Directives and Decisions. They prescribe permitted limits of variation in mis-statements in statutory statements; prescribe the manner in which compound feedingstuffs, additives and premixtures are to be packaged and sealed; regulate the putting into circulation of feed materials; regulate the putting into circulation and use of feedingstuffs containing additives and additives to be incorporated in feeding stuffs, and their incorporation therein; restrict the marketing and use of feedingstuffs containing certain undesirable products and the putting into circulation and mixing of ingredients containing such substances; prohibit the marketing of compound feedingstuffs containing certain materials; control the marketing of feedingstuffs intended for particular nutritional purposes; and make consequential amendments to the Agriculture Act 1970, the Feeding Stuffs (Sampling and Analysis) Regulations (Northern Ireland) 1999 (SR 1999 296), the Feeding Stuffs (Establishments and Intermediaries) Regulations 1999 (SI 1999 1872) and the Feeding Stuffs (Enforcement) Regulations 1999 (SI 1999 2325).

5668. Animals – feedingstuffs – additives

FEEDING STUFFS (AMENDMENT) REGULATIONS (NORTHERN IRELAND) 2001, SR 2001 428; made under the Agriculture Act 1970 s.66, s.68, s.69, s.70, s.73, s.74, s.74A, s.77, s.78, s.84, s.86; and the European Communities Act 1972 s.2. In force: February 1, 2002; £2.50.

These Regulations, which amend the Feeding Stuffs (Enforcement) Regulations 1999 and the Feeding Stuffs Regulations (Northern Ireland) 2001 (SI 2001 47), implement European Parliament and Council Directive 2000/16 ([2000] OJ L105/36) amending Council Directive 79/393 on the marketing of compound feedingstuffs and Council Directive 96/25 on the circulation of feed materials. The Regulations also implement Commission Decision 2000/285 ([2000] OJ L94/43) amending Decision 91/516 establishing a list of ingredients whose use is prohibited in compound feedingstuffs. They also provide enforcement for Commission Regulation 2437/2000 ([2000] OJ L280/28) concerning the permanent authorisation of an additive and the provisional authorisation of new additives in feedingstuffs, Commission Regulation 418/2001 ([2001] OJ L62/3) concerning the authorisation of new additives and uses of additives in feeding stuffs and Commission Regulation 937/2001 ([2001] OJ L130/25) concerning authorisation of new additive uses, new additive preparation, the prolongation of provisional authorisations, and the ten year authorisation of an additive in feeding stuffs. The Regulations extend the controls on sale and possession with a view to sale of compound feeding stuffs to cover supply other than sale, and possession with a view to such supply, prohibit the importation, supply, possession with a view to such supply and use of feed materials harmful to animals, to humans consuming products of such animals or to the environment, prohibit the sale for use as a compound feeding stuff, or use as such a feeding stuff, of "sludge from sewage plants treating waste water", is replaced by one on the sale or use of "waste obtained from the treatment of waste water", prescribe labelling requirements for feed materials and compound feeding stuffs and extend the scope of certain provisions to cover all States which are signatories to the Agreement on the European Economic Area.

5669. Animals – feedingstuffs – animal protein

PROCESSED ANIMAL PROTEIN REGULATIONS (NORTHERN IRELAND) 2001, SR 2001 405; made under the European Communities Act 1972 s.2. In force: December 10, 2001; £4.50.

These Regulations, which amend the Bovine Spongiform Encephalopathy (Feedingstuffs and Surveillance) Regulations (Northern Ireland) 1999 (SR 1999 323), give effect in Northern Ireland to Council Decision 2000/766 ([2000] OJ L307/32) concerning certain protection measures with regard to transmissible spongiform encephalopathies and the feeding of animal protein. The Regulations prohibit the feeding of processed animal protein to farmed animals, make provision for approval of premises, suspension and withdrawal of approval, make provision for the manufacture of feedingstuffs and impose requirements in respect of records relating to processed animal protein.

5670. **Animals – feedingstuffs – sampling and analysis**

FEEDING STUFFS (SAMPLING AND ANALYSIS) (AMENDMENT) REGULATIONS (NORTHERN IRELAND) 2001, SR 2001 209; made under the Agriculture Act 1970 s.66, s.74A, s.75, s.76, s.77, s.78, s.79, s.84, s.86; and the European Communities Act 1972 s.2. In force: July 2, 2001; £1.75.

These Regulations, which amend the Feeding Stuffs (Establishments and Intermediaries) Regulations 1999 (SI 1999 1872), the Feeding Stuffs (Enforcement) Regulations 1999 (SI 1999 2325), the Feeding Stuffs (Sampling and Analysis) Regulations (Northern Ireland) 1999 (SR 1999 296) and the Feeding Stuffs Regulations (Northern Ireland) 2001 (SR 2001 47), implement Commission Directive 2001/45 ([2001] OJ L174/32) establishing Community methods of analysis for the determination of vitamin A, vitamin E and trytophan in feedingstuffs.

5671. **Cattle – suckler cow premiums – administration**

SUCKLER COW PREMIUM REGULATIONS (NORTHERN IRELAND) 2001, SR 2001 362; made under the European Communities Act 1972 s.2. In force: October 16, 2001; £2.50.

These Regulations, which revoke the Suckler Cow Premium Regulations (Northern Ireland) 1987 (SR 1987 85 as amended by SR 1994 211, SR 1993 280, SR 1995 246, SR 1996 229 and SR 1997 53), lay down implementing measures for the suckler cow premium scheme provided for in Council Regulation 1254/1999 ([1999] OJ L160/21) on the common organisation of the market in beef and veal. They provide for the administration of the scheme in relation to applicants and their holdings where those holdings are situated wholly in Northern Ireland, and also holdings situated partly in Northern Ireland and partly elsewhere in the UK, where the Department of Agriculture and Rural Development is responsible for processing the farmer's claim for suckler cow premium.

5672. **Environmentally sensitive areas – designation**

ENVIRONMENTALLY SENSITIVE AREAS DESIGNATION ORDER (NORTHERN IRELAND) 2001, SR 2001 269; made under the Agriculture (Environmental Areas) (Northern Ireland) Order 1987 (SI 1987 458 (NI.3)) Art.3. In force: September 10, 2001; £4.00.

This Order revokes the Environmentally Sensitive Areas (Mourne Mountains and Slieve Croob) Designation Order (Northern Ireland) 1993 (SR 1993 178), the Environmentally Sensitive Areas (Antrim Coast, Glens and Rathlin) Designation Order (Northern Ireland) 1993 (SR 1993 179), the Environmentally Sensitive Areas (West Fermanagh and Erne Lakeland) Designation Order (Northern Ireland) 1993 (SR 1993 180), the Environmentally Sensitive Areas (Slieve Gullion) Designation Order (Northern Ireland) 1994 (SR 1994 212), the Environmentally Sensitive Areas (Sperrins) Designation Order (Northern Ireland) 1994 (SR 1994 213), the Environmentally Sensitive Areas (Mourne Mountains and Slieve Croob) Designation (Amendment) Order (Northern Ireland) 1994 (SR 1994 375), the Environmentally Sensitive Areas (Antrim Coast, Glens and Rathlin) Designation (Amendment) Order (Northern Ireland) 1994 (SR 1994 376), the Environmentally Sensitive Areas (West Fermanagh and Erne Lakeland) Designation (Amendment) Order (Northern Ireland) 1994 (SR 1994 377), the Environmentally Sensitive Areas (Sperrins) Designation (Amendment) Order (Northern Ireland) 1995 (SR 1995 179), the Environmentally Sensitive Areas (Antrim Coast, Glens and Rathlin) Designation (Amendment) Order (Northern Ireland) 1997 (SR 1997 297), the Environmentally Sensitive Areas (Slieve Gullion) Designation (Amendment) Order (Northern Ireland) 1997 (SR 1997 298), the Environmentally Sensitive Areas (Mourne Mountains and Slieve Croob) Designation (Amendment) Order (Northern Ireland) 1997 (SR 1997 299), the Environmentally Sensitive Areas (West Fermanagh and Erne Lakeland) Designation (Amendment) Order (Northern Ireland) 1997 (SR 1997 300) and the Environmentally Sensitive Areas (Sperrins) Designation (Amendment) Order (Northern Ireland) 1997 (SR 1997

301). The Agriculture (Environmental Areas) (Northern Ireland) Order 1987 (SI 1987 458) gives the Department of Agriculture and Rural Development power to designate areas as environmentally sensitive areas where it appears to it particularly desirable to conserve, protect or enhance environmental features in those areas by the maintenance or adoption of particular agricultural methods. This Order designates certain areas of land as environmentally sensitive areas and gives effect in part to the agri-environment element of the programming document based on the rural development plan for Northern Ireland submitted by the UK to the European Commission pursuant to Council Regulation 1257/1999 ([1999] OJ L160/80) on support for rural development from the European Agricultural Guidance and Guarantee Fund (EAGGF).

5673. Environmentally sensitive areas – enforcement

ENVIRONMENTALLY SENSITIVE AREAS (ENFORCEMENT) REGULATIONS (NORTHERN IRELAND) 2001, SR 2001 270; made under the European Communities Act 1972 s.2. In force: September 10, 2001; £2.00.

These Regulations, which revoke the Environmentally Sensitive Areas Designation Orders (Amendment) Regulations (Northern Ireland) 1996 (SR 1996 606) with savings, supplement the Environmentally Sensitive Areas Designation Order (Northern Ireland) 2001 (SR 2001 269) which gives effect in part to the agri-environment element of the programming document based on the rural development plan for Northern Ireland submitted by the UK to the European Commission pursuant to Council Regulation 1257/1999 ([1999] OJ L160/80). These Regulations provide for the withholding and recovery of payments payable under an agreement made after the coming into operation of these Regulations under the Agriculture (Environmental Areas) (Northern Ireland) Order 1987 (SI 1987 458). They also provide for the recovery of interest and the imposition of penalties.

5674. Farms – farm subsidies – review of decisions

FARM SUBSIDIES (REVIEW OF DECISIONS) REGULATIONS (NORTHERN IRELAND) 2001, SR 2001 391; made under the European Communities Act 1972 s.2. In force: November 14, 2001; £2.50.

These Regulations, which amend the Less Favoured Areas Compensatory Allowances Regulations (Northern Ireland) 2001 (SR 2001 71) and the Slaughter Premium Regulations (Northern Ireland) 2001 (SR 2001 199), have effect in relation to holdings administered by the Department of Agriculture and Rural Development in accordance with the Integrated Administration and Control System Regulations 1993 (SI 1993 1317). They introduce legal rights to seek a review of certain decisions of the Department in relation to payment of certain farm subsidies.

5675. Food safety – BSE – EC law – emergency powers of Member States

[Specified Risk Material (Northern Ireland) Order 1997 (SR 1997 551); EC Treaty Art.30 (now, after amendment, Art.28 EC); Council Directive 89/662 concerning veterinary checks in intra-community trade with a view to the completion of the internal market Art.9(1); Commission Decision 97/534.]

E, the owner of a slaughterhouse in Northern Ireland engaged in the deboning of bovine heads imported from the Republic of Ireland, from which the cheek meat was extracted and then exported to the UK and France. The remaining skull material was treated as specified risk material under Commission Decision 97/534 which prohibited the use of material carrying the risk of transmission of spongiform encephalopathies. The coming into force of the Decision was postponed, but during the period of postponement, the UK enacted the Specified Risk Material (Northern Ireland) Order 1997, relying on Council Directive 89/662 on veterinary checks Art.9(1), which authorised Member States to take emergency measures to deal with an epidemic, pending the introduction of measures at Community level, and provided that notification of any such emergency measure was given to the

Commission. A consignment of bovine heads was seized from E under the provisions of the Order, and condemned, without prior inspection, on the ground that it contained contaminated material, despite the consignment having been certified fit for human consumption. E claimed that the Order was unlawful, being a fetter on the free movement of goods contrary to EC Treaty Art.30 (now, after amendment, Art.28 EC). The High Court in Northern Ireland held the Order to be unlawful under Art.9(1) of the Directive, and the Department of Agriculture for Northern Ireland appealed to the Court of Appeal in Northern Ireland, which posed questions to the European Court of Justice as to the extent of the powers of Member States under Art.9(1) of the Directive to take short term protective action to halt the spread of an epidemic.

Held, giving a ruling on the preliminary issues raised, that (1) Member States were authorised, under Art.9(1) of the Directive, to take interim protective measures in order to combat serious risks, pending the promulgation of Community wide provisions, unless the postponement of Community wide provisions had been decided upon because no such provisions were needed at all, at either national or Community level; (2) the Decision promulgated minimum measures, and did not prevent Member States from taking or maintaining protective measures. The postponement of the coming into force of the Decision was prompted by the need for further assessment of its implications, and did not suggest that the risk had lessened. Member States therefore remained entitled to take interim protective action under Art.9(1) of the Directive. In the light of available scientific evidence at the time of the enactment of the Order, which regarded BSE as a grave risk to public health and recommended the removal of risk material from the food chain, together with the banning of tissues likely to bear BSE agents from entering the food chain, the Order was proportional when judged against the possible transmission of BSE, and justified by reason of the possibility of leakage of highly infective material on to healthy tissue.

EUROSTOCK MEAT MARKETING LTD v. DEPARTMENT OF AGRICULTURE FOR NORTHERN IRELAND (C477/98) [2001] 1 C.M.L.R. 32, GC Rodriguez Iglesias (President), ECJ.

5676. Infectious disease control – foot and mouth disease – controlled areas

FOOT-AND-MOUTH DISEASE (AMENDMENT) ORDER (NORTHERN IRELAND) 2001, SR 2001 82; made under the Diseases of Animals (Northern Ireland) Order 1981 (SI 1981 1115 (NI.22)) Art.12, Art.14, Art.19, Art.60. In force: February 27, 2001; £1.75.

This Order amends the Foot-and-Mouth Disease Order (Northern Ireland) 1962 (SR & O 1962 209) so as to make provision for the isolation of animals placed or kept on commons or unenclosed lands within an infected area or controlled area in the event of an outbreak of foot and mouth disease in such an area.

5677. Infectious disease control – foot and mouth disease – controlled areas

FOOT-AND-MOUTH DISEASE (CONTROLLED AREA) (NO.2) ORDER (NORTHERN IRELAND) 2001, SR 2001 93; made under the Diseases of Animals (Northern Ireland) Order 1981 (SI 1981 1115 (NI.22)) Art.5, Art.10, Art.12, Art.14, Art.19, Art.20, Art.60; and the Foot-and-Mouth Disease Order (Northern Ireland) 1962 (SI 1962 209) Art.29. In force: March 5, 2001; £1.75.

This Order imposes, with variations, the restrictions contained in the Foot-and-Mouth Disease Order (Northern Ireland) 1962 (SR & O 1962 209) Part III within a specified infected area in Northern Ireland. The controls on the movement of animals and carcasses and on the holding of markets and sales are replaced by the provisions set out in the Schedule and new provisions on the movement of horses and stalking of deer are added.

5678. Infectious disease control – foot and mouth disease – controlled areas

FOOT-AND-MOUTH DISEASE (CONTROLLED AREA) (NO.3) ORDER (NORTHERN IRELAND) 2001, SR 2001 212; made under the Foot-and-Mouth Disease Order (Northern Ireland) 1962 (SR & O 1962 209) Art.29; and the Diseases of Animals (Northern Ireland) Order 1981 (SI 1981 1115 (NI.22)) Art.5, Art.10, Art.12, Art.14, Art.19, Art.20, Art.60. In force: May 18, 2001; £1.75.

This Order repeals and replaces the Foot-and-Mouth Disease (Controlled Area) (No.2) Order (Northern Ireland) 2001 (SR 2001 93) which imposed, with variations and exceptions, the restrictions contained in the Foot-and-Mouth Disease Order (Northern Ireland) 1962 (SR & O 1962 209) Part III in Northern Ireland. The only change of substance is that the prohibition on horse racing and jumping competitions and pigeon racing set out in Sch.5 para.A(5) to the 1962 Order is revoked. Any person who contravenes any provision of this Order shall be guilty of an offence against the Diseases of Animals (Northern Ireland) Order 1981 (SI 1981 1115 (NI.22)) and shall be liable, on summary conviction, either to imprisonment for a term not exceeding one month or to a fine not exceeding level 5 on the standard scale or in the case of an offence committed with respect to more than five animals, not exceeding level 3 on the standard scale for each animal.

5679. Infectious disease control – foot and mouth disease – controlled areas

FOOT-AND-MOUTH DISEASE (CONTROLLED AREA) (NO.4) ORDER (NORTHERN IRELAND) 2001, SR 2001 303; made under the Foot-and-Mouth Disease Order (Northern Ireland) 1962 (SR & O 1962 209) Art.29; and the Diseases of Animals (Northern Ireland) Order 1981 (SI 1981 1115 (NI.22)) Art.5, Art.10, Art.12, Art.14, Art.19, Art.20, Art.60. In force: August 20, 2001; £1.75.

This Order revokes the Foot and Mouth Disease (Controlled Area) (No.3) Order (Northern Ireland) 2001 (SR 2001 212) which imposed, with variations and exceptions, the restrictions contained in the Foot and Mouth Disease Order (Northern Ireland) 1962 (SR & O (NI) 1962 209). The only change in substance is that the prohibition on deer stalking is revoked.

5680. Infectious disease control – foot and mouth disease – controlled areas

FOOT-AND-MOUTH DISEASE (CONTROLLED AREA) (NO.5) ORDER (NORTHERN IRELAND) 2001, SR 2001 336; made under the Foot-and-Mouth Disease Order (Northern Ireland) 1962 (SR & O 1962 209) Art.29; and the Diseases of Animals (Northern Ireland) Order 1981 (SI 1981 1115 (NI.22)) Art.5, Art.10, Art.12, Art.14, Art.19, Art.20, Art.60. In force: October 1, 2001; £1.75.

This Order revokes and replaces the Foot-and-Mouth Disease (Controlled Area) (No.4) Order (Northern Ireland) 2001 (SR 2001 303) which imposed in Northern Ireland the restrictions contained in the Foot-and-Mouth Disease Order (Northern Ireland) 1962 (SR & O 1962 209) Part III. It revokes the prohibition on polo and the racing or coursing or training for racing or coursing of any dogs or hounds and the pursuit of game and rabbits but continues to prohibit hunting with horses and/or dogs.

5681. Infectious disease control – foot and mouth disease – controlled areas

FOOT-AND-MOUTH DISEASE (CONTROLLED AREA) (NO.6) ORDER (NORTHERN IRELAND) 2001, SR 2001 424; made under the Foot-and-Mouth Disease Order (Northern Ireland) 1962 (SR & O 1962 209) Art.29; and the Diseases of Animals (Northern Ireland) Order 1981 (SI 1981 1115 (NI.22)) Art.5, Art.10, Art.12, Art.14, Art.19, Art.20, Art.60. In force: December 8, 2001; £1.75.

This Order revokes the Foot-and-Mouth Disease (Controlled Area) (No.5) Order (Northern Ireland) 2001 (SI 2001 336) which imposed the restrictions contained in the Foot-and-Mouth Disease Order (Northern Ireland) 1962 (SR & O 1962 209) Part III, in Northern Ireland. It varies the controls set out in the fifth Schedule to the 1962 Order and removes the prohibition on the hunting of animals with horses and/or dogs and the prohibition on the movement of horses except under the authority of a licence.

5682. Infectious disease control – foot and mouth disease – import and export restrictions

IMPORT AND EXPORT RESTRICTIONS (FOOT-AND-MOUTH DISEASE) REGULATIONS (NORTHERN IRELAND) 2001, SR 2001 183; made under the European Communities Act 1972 s.2. In force: April 27, 2001; £3.00.

These Regulations, which implement in Northern Ireland restrictions on imports and exports of certain animals and animal products in accordance with Commission Decision 2001/318 ([2001] OJ L109/75), regulate the export of biungulates, fresh meat, meat products, milk, milk products and other animal products. In addition, they contain powers of inspectors, and provisions relating to illegal consignments.

5683. Infectious disease control – foot and mouth disease – import and export restrictions

IMPORT AND EXPORT RESTRICTIONS (FOOT-AND-MOUTH DISEASE) (NO.2) REGULATIONS (NORTHERN IRELAND) 2001, SR 2001 204; made under the European Communities Act 1972 s.2. In force: May 11, 2001; £3.00.

These Regulations, which revoke the Import and Export Restrictions (Foot-and-Mouth Disease) Regulations (Northern Ireland) 2001 (SR 2001 183), implement in Northern Ireland certain changes in the restrictions on imports and exports of certain animals and animal products in accordance with Commission Decision 2001/356 ([2001] OJ L125/40) concerning certain protection measures with regard to foot and mouth disease in the UK. The Regulations continue to control the export of biungulates, fresh meat, meat products, milk, milk products and other animal products. They contain powers of inspectors, and provisions relating to illegal consignments.

5684. Infectious disease control – foot and mouth disease – import and export restrictions

IMPORT AND EXPORT RESTRICTIONS (FOOT-AND-MOUTH DISEASE) (NO.2) (REVOCATION) REGULATIONS (NORTHERN IRELAND) 2001, SR 2001 239; made under the European Communities Act 1972 s.2. In force: June 8, 2001; £1.50.

These Regulations, which revoke the Import and Export Restrictions (Foot-and-Mouth Disease) (No.2) Regulations (Northern Ireland) 2001 (SR 2001 204), implement in Northern Ireland Commission Decision 2001/430 ([2001] OJ L153/33) amending for the third time Commission Decision 2001/356 ([2001] OJ L125/46) concerning certain protection measures with regard to foot and mouth disease in the UK. They remove protection measures which restrict the import and export of certain animal and animal products with regard to the control of foot and mouth disease.

5685. Infectious disease control – foot and mouth disease – infected areas

FOOT-AND-MOUTH DISEASE (INFECTED AREA) ORDER (NORTHERN IRELAND) 2001, SR 2001 83; made under the Diseases of Animals (Northern Ireland) Order 1981 (SI 1981 1115 (NI.22)) Art.12, Art.60. In force: February 27, 2001; £1.75.

This Order provides that where the Department of Agriculture and Rural Development has grounds for suspecting that foot and mouth disease exists in Northern Ireland or in such part of the Republic of Ireland as may entail the risk of its spread into Northern Ireland it may by notice in writing declare any area in Northern Ireland to be an infected area. Such a notice must be published and must specify the date on which it comes into operation. Where an area is declared to be an infected area then the provisions of the Foot-and-Mouth Disease Order (Northern Ireland) 1962 (SR & O 1962 209) shall have effect in relation to that area. The main restrictions imposed are prohibitions on the movement of animals out of, into or within an infected area except under the authority of and in accordance with the conditions of a licence.

5686. Infectious disease control – foot and mouth disease – movement of animals

FOOT-AND-MOUTH DISEASE (CONTROLLED AREA) ORDER (NORTHERN IRELAND) 2001, SR 2001 87; made under the Diseases of Animals (Northern Ireland) Order 1981 (SI 1981 1115 (NI.22)) Art.5, Art.10, Art.12, Art.14, Art.19, Art.20, Art.60; and the Foot-and-Mouth Disease Order (Northern Ireland) 1962 (SI 1962 209) Art.29. In force: March 1, 2001; £1.75.

This Order imposes, with variations, the restrictions contained in the Foot-and-Mouth Disease Order (Northern Ireland) 1962 (SR & O 1962 209) Part III within a specified infected area in Northern Ireland. The controls on the movement of animals and carcasses and on the holding of markets and sales are replaced by the provisions set out in the Schedule and a new provision on the stalking of deer is added.

5687. Livestock – extensification payment

EXTENSIFICATION PAYMENT REGULATIONS (NORTHERN IRELAND) 2001, SR 2001 127; made under the European Communities Act 1972 s.2. In force: April 27, 2001; £2.50.

These Regulations lay down implementing measures for the extensification payment scheme introduced by Council Regulation 1254/1999 ([1999] OJ L160/21) on the common organisation of the market in beef and veal for beef producers who comply with certain stocking density requirements. They prescribe the rules for the administration of the scheme in relation to holdings in Northern Ireland and also holdings situated partly in Northern Ireland and partly elsewhere in the UK, where the Department of Agriculture and Rural Development is responsible for processing the farmer's claim for extensification payments.

5688. Livestock – slaughter premiums

SLAUGHTER PREMIUM REGULATIONS (NORTHERN IRELAND) 2001, SR 2001 199; made under the European Communities Act 1972 s.2. In force: June 6, 2001; £3.00.

These Regulations, which lay down implementing measures for the slaughter premium scheme for bovine animals introduced by Council Regulation 1254/1999 ([1999] OJ L160/21) on the common organisation of the market in beef and veal, provide for the administration of the scheme in relation to holdings in Northern Ireland and also holding situated partly in Northern Ireland and partly elsewhere in the UK where the Department of Agriculture and Rural Development is responsible for processing the farmer's claim for slaughter premium. In addition, the Regulations lay down enforcement provisions in relation to holdings or parts of holdings in Northern Ireland. They establish the procedure for submitting claims for premium, impose sanctions for overgrazing and the use of supplementary feeding methods and provide for the witholding or or recovery of slaughter premium where there is a breach of the rules of the scheme.

5689. Milk – pupils in educational establishments

MILK AND MILK PRODUCTS (PUPILS IN EDUCATIONAL ESTABLISHMENTS) REGULATIONS (NORTHERN IRELAND) 2001, SR 2001 129; made under the European Communities Act 1972 s.2. In force: April 24, 2001; £1.75.

These Regulations provide that, in the making of any national "top-up" aid payments as permitted by Council Regulation 1255/1999 ([1999] OJ L193/10) Art.14 on the common organisation of the market in milk and milk products and for the supply of milk and milk products to pupils in educational establishments, such payments shall be subject to the same rules, requirements and conditions as apply to Community aid which are contained in Commission Regulation 2707/2000 ([2000] OJ L311/37) laying down the rules for supplying milk and certain milk products to pupils in educational establishments. They provide for the withholding or recovery of any Community aid or national payments to which an applicant is reasonably believed not to be entitled or where he is in breach of any of his commitments given as a condition of such aid or payment.

5690. Organic farming – subsidies

ORGANIC FARMING REGULATIONS (NORTHERN IRELAND) 2001, SR 2001 5; made under the European Communities Act 1972 s.2. In force: March 1, 2001; £3.50.

These Regulations, which revoke and replace, with savings, the Organic Farming Regulations (Northern Ireland) 1999 (SR 1999 237), provide for the payment of aid to farmers who undertake to introduce organic farming methods and comply with certain environmental management conditions, pursuant to Art.22 of Council Regulation 1257/1999 ([1999] OJ L160/80). They implement certain provisions of Commission Regulation 1750/1999 ([1999] OJ L214/31) laying down detailed rules for the application of the of the Rural Development Regulation. In addition, they enable the Department of Agriculture and Rural Development to make payments of aid, specify the conditions of eligibility to be satisfied by applicants for aid, preconditions for the acceptance of applications of aid, restrictions on payment and allow the refusal of applications in certain circumstances. They provide for the payment of aid to a new occupant where there has been a change in the occupation of an organic unit or part of an organic unit due to the death of a beneficiary or otherwise, impose obligations in respect of the keeping of records and confer powers of entry and inspection, provide for the withholding or recovery of aid and the recovery of interest, provide for an offence of making a false statement, and change the period for which an applicant must undertake to ensure that no livestock other than organic livestock or livestock undergoing organic conversion are grazed on his organic unit without the prior written agreement of the Department is extended from 62 days to 120 days in each grazing year, introduce an arbitration procedure and a requirement that a beneficiary must undertake to abide by the Code of Good Farming Practice for the Environment.

5691. Pigs – pig industry – capital grants

PIG INDUSTRY RESTRUCTURING (CAPITAL GRANT) SCHEME (NORTHERN IRELAND) 2001, SR 2001 90; made under the Agriculture and Fisheries (Financial Assistance) (Northern Ireland) Order 1987 (SI 1987 166 (NI.1)) Art.16. In force: March 30, 2001; £1.75.

This Scheme makes provision for the payment of grants towards the cost of loans obtained in order to pay for expenditure incurred in the restructuring of a pig production business.

5692. Pigs – pig industry – non-capital grants

PIG INDUSTRY RESTRUCTURING (NON-CAPITAL GRANT) SCHEME ORDER (NORTHERN IRELAND) 2001, SR 2001 91; made under the Farm Businesses (Northern Ireland) Order 1988 (SI 1988 1302 (NI.12)) Art.3. In force: March 30, 2001; £2.00.

The Scheme made by this Order makes provision for the payment of grants towards the cost of loans incurred in connection with the establishment or promotion of farm businesses ancillary to pig production businesses and relate to the products of pig production as part of the restructuring of a pig production business. It describes those eligible for a grant, provides that claims for a grant shall be made in such form as the Minister may reasonably require and enables monies to be withheld or recovered in certain circumstances.

5693. Plant varieties – marketing and examination – beet seeds

BEET SEEDS (AMENDMENT) REGULATIONS (NORTHERN IRELAND) 2001, SR 2001 331; made under the Seeds Act (Northern Ireland) 1965 s.1, s.2. In force: November 2, 2001; £2.00.

These Regulations amend the Beet Seeds Regulations (Northern Ireland) 1994 (SR 1994 251) to give effect to Council Directive 98/95 ([1999] OJ L25/1) in respect of the consolidation of the internal market, genetically modified plant resources and plant genetic resources and Council Directive 98/96 ([1999] OJ L25/27) amending, as regards unofficial field inspections, directives in respect of the marketing of seeds and the common catalogue of varieties of agricultural plant species. In particular, they amend certain definitions, including "marketing" and "official examination", make provision in relation to marketing and marketing authorisations, tests and trials, seed as grown, selection work and other scientific purposes, provide for the marketing of genetically modified fodder plant seeds, clear indications for genetically modified varieties, and the supply of information about imported seeds and remove provisions in respect of small packages.

5694. Plant varieties – marketing and examination – cereal seeds

CEREAL SEEDS (AMENDMENT) REGULATIONS (NORTHERN IRELAND) 2001, SR 2001 330; made under the Seeds Act (Northern Ireland) 1965 s.1, s.2. In force: November 2, 2001; £2.00.

These Regulations amend the Cereal Seeds Regulations (Northern Ireland) 1994 (SR 1994 254) to give effect to Council Directive 98/95 ([1999] OJ L25/1) in respect of the consolidation of the internal market, genetically modified plant resources and plant genetic resources and Council Directive 98/96 ([1999] OJ L25/27) amending, as regards unofficial field inspections, directives in respect of the marketing of seeds and the common catalogue of varieties of agricultural plant species. In particular, they amend certain definitions, including "marketing" and "official examination", make provision in relation to marketing and marketing authorisations, tests and trials, seed as grown, selection work and other scientific purposes, provide for the marketing of genetically modified fodder plant seeds, clear indications for genetically modified varieties, and the supply of information about imported seeds and remove provisions in respect of small packages.

5695. Plant varieties – marketing and examination – fodder plant seeds

FODDER PLANT SEEDS (AMENDMENT) REGULATIONS (NORTHERN IRELAND) 2001, SR 2001 329; made under the Seeds Act (Northern Ireland) 1965 s.1, s.2. In force: November 2, 2001; £2.50.

These Regulations amend the Plant Seeds Regulations (Northern Ireland) 1994 (SR 1994 252) to give effect to Council Directive 98/95 ([1999] OJ L25/1) in respect of the consolidation of the internal market, genetically modified plant resources and plant genetic resources and Council Directive 98/96 ([1999] OJ L25/27) amending, as regards unofficial field inspections, directives in respect of the marketing of seeds and the common catalogue of varieties of agricultural plant species. In particular, they amend certain definitions, including "marketing" and "official examination", make provision in relation to marketing and marketing authorisations, tests and trials, seed as grown, selection work and other scientific purposes, provide for the marketing of genetically modified fodder plant seeds, clear indications for genetically modified varieties, and the supply of information about imported seeds and remove provisions in respect of small packages.

5696. Plant varieties – marketing and examination – oil and fibre plant seeds

OIL AND FIBRE PLANT SEEDS (AMENDMENT) REGULATIONS (NORTHERN IRELAND) 2001, SR 2001 328; made under the Seeds Act (Northern Ireland) 1965 s.1, s.2. In force: November 2, 2001; £2.00.

These Regulations amend the Oil and Fibre Plant Seeds Regulations (Northern Ireland) 1994 (SR 1994 255) to give effect to Council Directive 98/95 ([1999] OJ L25/1) in respect of the consolidation of the internal market, genetically modified plant resources and plant genetic resources and Council Directive 98/96 ([1999] OJ L25/27) amending, as regards unofficial field inspections, directives in respect of the marketing of seeds and the common catalogue of varieties of agricultural plant species. In particular, they amend certain definitions including "marketing"and "official examination", make provision in relation to marketing and marketing authorisations, tests and trials, seed as grown, selection work and other scientific purposes, provide for the marketing of genetically modified oil and fibre plant seeds, clear indications for genetically modified varieties and the supply of information about imported seeds and amend provisions in respect of small packages.

5697. Plant varieties – marketing and examination – vegetable seeds

VEGETABLE SEEDS (AMENDMENT) REGULATIONS (NORTHERN IRELAND) 2001, SR 2001 327; made under the Seeds Act (Northern Ireland) 1965 s.1, s.2. In force: November 2, 2001; £2.00.

These Regulations amend the Vegetable Seeds Regulations (Northern Ireland) 1994 (SR 1994 250) to give effect to Council Directive 98/95 ([1999] OJ L25/1) in respect of the consolidation of the internal market, genetically modified plant resources and plant genetic resources. In particular, they amend certain definitions including "marketing" and "official examination", make provision in relation to marketing and marketing authorisations, tests and trials, seed as grown, selection work and other scientific purposes, provide for the marketing of genetically modified vegetable seeds, clear indications for genetically modified varieties and the supply of information about imported seeds.

5698. Plants – plant health – protected zones

PLANT HEALTH (AMENDMENT) ORDER (NORTHERN IRELAND) 2001, SR 2001 437; made under the Plant Health Act (Northern Ireland) 1967 s.2, s.3, s.3A, s.3B, s.4. In force: January 21, 2002; £2.00.

This Order, which amends the Plant Health Order (Northern Ireland) 1993 (SR 1993 256), implements Commission Directive 2001/32 ([2001] OJ L127/38) which recognises protected zones exposed to particular plant health risks in the Community, and Commission Directive 2001/33 ([2001] OJ L127/42) which amends certain annexes to Council Directive 2000/29 ([2000] OJ L169/1) on protective measures against the introduction into the Community of organisms harmful to plants or plant products and against their spread within the Community.

5699. Plants – plant health – wood packing

PLANT HEALTH (WOOD AND BARK) (AMENDMENT) ORDER (NORTHERN IRELAND) 2001, SR 2001 401; made under the Plant Health Act (Northern Ireland) 1967 s.2, s.3, s.3A, s.3B, s.4. In force: December 31, 2001; £2.00.

This Order, which amends the Plant Health (Wood and Bark) Order (Northern Ireland) 1993 (SR 1993 460) by creating additional items and conditions of landing, implements Commission Decision 2001/219 ([2001] OJ L81/39) on temporary emergency measures in respect of wood packing comprised in whole or in part of non-manufactured coniferous wood originating in Canada, China, Japan and the US. The Decision requires measures to be taken to protect the European Community against the pest Bursaphelenchus xylophilus Nickle et al., the pine wood nematode. The Order prohibits the landing in Northern Ireland of certain wood packing material originating in Canada, China, Japan and the US and despatched to the European Community after September 30, 2001 which does not comply with certain treatment and stamping requirements. In addition, the Order imposes a requirement on importers landing wood packing material from any part of China to retain the phytosanitary certificate accompanying the material for a period of one year after the date of landing, and to produce the certificate to an inspector authorised by the Department of Agriculture and Rural Development immediately on request.

5700. Plants – plant protection products – marketing

PLANT PROTECTION PRODUCTS (AMENDMENT) REGULATIONS (NORTHERN IRELAND) 2001, SR 2001 280; made under the European Communities Act 1972 s.2. In force: August 23, 2001; £1.75.

These Regulations, which revoke the Plant Protection Products (Amendment) Regulations (Northern Ireland) 2000 (SR 2000 24), amend the Plant Protection Products Regulations (Northern Ireland) 1995 (SR 1995 371) which implement Council Directive 91/414 ([1991] OJ L230/1) concerning the placing of plant protection products on the market. They amend the definition of the Directive provided in consequence of Commission Directive 2000/10 ([2000] OJ L57/28), Commission Directive 2000/49 ([2000] OJ L197/32) and Commission Directive 2000/50 ([2000] OJ L198/39).

5701. Potatoes – imports – infectious disease control – Egypt

POTATOES ORIGINATING IN EGYPT (AMENDMENT) REGULATIONS (NORTHERN IRELAND) 2001, SR 2001 32; made under the European Communities Act 1972 s.2. In force: March 5, 2001; £1.75.

These Regulations, which implement in Northern Ireland Commission Decision 2000/568 ([2000] OJ L238/59) amending Commission Decision 96/301 authorising Member States temporarily to take emergency measures against the dissemination of Pseudomonas solanacearum (Smith) as regards Egypt, amend the definition of "the Decision" in the Potatoes Originating in Egypt Regulations (Northern Ireland) 1998 (SR 1998 107).

5702. Potatoes – seed potatoes – certification of crops – fees

SEED POTATOES (CROP FEES) REGULATIONS (NORTHERN IRELAND) 2001, SR 2001 228; made under the Seeds Act (Northern Ireland) 1965 s.1. In force: May 30, 2001; £1.75.

These Regulations, which revoke the Seed Potatoes (Crop Fees) Regulations (Northern Ireland) 2000 (SR 2000 138) increase the fees payable to the Department of Agriculture and Rural Development in respect of the certification of seed potato crops arising under the Seed Potatoes Regulations (Northern Ireland) 2001 (SR 2001 188).

5703. Potatoes – seed potatoes – marketing, labelling and classification

SEED POTATOES REGULATIONS (NORTHERN IRELAND) 2001, SR 2001 188; made under the Seeds Act (Northern Ireland) 1965 s.1, s.2, s.12; the European Communities Act 1972 s.2; and the Agriculture (Miscellaneous Provisions) (Northern Ireland) Order 1984 (SI 1984 702 (NI.2)) Art.3. In force: Reg.22: December 31, 2001; remainder: May 25, 2001; £6.00.

These Regulations amend the Seeds Act (Northern Ireland) 1965 c.22 and the Plant Health Order (Northern Ireland) 1993 (SR 1993 256) and revoke the Seed Potatoes Regulations (Northern Ireland) 1981 (SR 1981 243 as amended by SR 1983 244, SR 1985 2, SR 1991 397, SR 1993 372, SR 1994 459, SR 1996 242 and SR 1997 402). The Regulations regulate the production with a view to the classification and marketing of seed potatoes and give effect to Directive 66/403 ([1966] OJ L125/154). They also give effect to Commission Decision 93/231 ([1993] OJ L106/13) authorising in respect of the marketing of seed potatoes in all or part of the territory of certain Member States more stringent measures against certain diseases. The Regulations introduce provisions recognising generations of seed potatoes earlier than basic seed potatoes referred to as pre-basic seed potatoes, introduce an amended definition of marketing, introduce provisions in relation to the marketing of small quantities for scientific purposes or selection work of seed potatoes which contain genetically modified material, introduce a provision in respect of production methods in the interests of plant health and introduce a prohibition on the planting in Northern Ireland of any potatoes other than potatoes which may be marketed in Northern Ireland under these Regulations or one year's progeny of such potatoes.

5704. Rural areas – less favoured areas – compensatory allowances

LESS FAVOURED AREA COMPENSATORY ALLOWANCES REGULATIONS (NORTHERN IRELAND) 2001, SR 2001 71; made under the European Communities Act 1972 s.2. In force: March 6, 2001; £2.50.

These Regulations implement Commission Regulation 1750/1999 ([1999] OJ L214/31) laying down detailed rules for the application of Council Regulation 1257/1999 ([1999] OJ L160/80) on support for rural development from the European Agricultural Guidance and Guarantee Fund. In addition, they implement Measure 2 of the Northern Ireland Rural Development Programme. They implement Articles which deal with support for less favoured areas by defining the conditions of eligibility for less favoured area compensatory allowance and the rates at which it is to be paid. They provide for the exclusion of forage area in respect of claimants who held milk quota at March 31, 2000, confer powers of entry and inspection on persons authorised by the Department of Agriculture and Rural Development, provide for the recovery of interest on sums recovered and create offences of making false or misleading statements and of obstructing persons authorised by the Department.

5705. Rural areas – rural development – financial assistance – obligations

RURAL DEVELOPMENT (FINANCIAL ASSISTANCE) REGULATIONS (NORTHERN IRELAND) 2001, SR 2001 332; made under the European Communities Act 1972 s.2. In force: October 29, 2001; £2.50.

These Regulations supplement Community legislation which provides for assistance to be paid from the Guidance Section of the European Agricultural Guidance and Guarantee Fund and the European Regional Development Fund towards operations which promote rural development by facilitating the development and structural adjustment of rural areas. The Community legislation also provides for assistance to be paid from the Guidance Section of the European Agricultural Guidance and Guarantee Fund towards operations which fall within Community initiatives to promote rural development. The Regulations operate within the scope of the Community legislation by enabling financial assistance to be paid by the Department of Agriculture and Rural Development or its agents in respect of operations which it or they have approved. They also provide for the making of claims for, and the payment of, financial assistance following approval and also impose obligations concerning the provision of information on those in receipt of financial assistance. In addition they introduce a system of penalties to be imposed in the event of a breach of obligations by granting the Department various powers to take action, up to and including termination of the approval in the event of breaches of the conditions of an approval and in a number of other cases.

5706. Sheep – premiums

SHEEP ANNUAL PREMIUM (AMENDMENT) REGULATIONS (NORTHERN IRELAND) 2001, SR 2001 411; made under the European Communities Act 1972 s.2. In force: December 4, 2001; £1.75.

These Regulations further amend the Sheep Annual Premium Regulations (Northern Ireland) 1992 (SR 1992 476) to provide for a shorter period in which to apply for sheep annual premium in respect of any marketing year as defined by Council Regulation 2467/98 ([1998] OJ L312/98) Art.3(3) on the common organisation of the market in sheepmeat and goatmeat Art.3(3). A producer shall deliver his application on or after December 4, in the preceding calendar year and not later than January 4 in the marketing year. Previously the producer was requested to deliver his application in the period from November 27, 2000 to December 29, 2000.

ANIMALS

5707. Animal welfare – slaughter

WELFARE OF ANIMALS (SLAUGHTER OR KILLING) (AMENDMENT) REGULATIONS (NORTHERN IRELAND) 2001, SR 2001 66; made under the European Communities Act 1972 s.2. In force: March 30, 2001; £1.50.

These Regulations, which amend the Welfare of Animals (Slaughter or Killing) Regulations (Northern Ireland) 1996 (SR 1996 558), substitute a new paragraph so as to permit a new gas mixture for killing surplus chicks.

5708. Dogs – licensing – identification

DOGS (LICENSING AND IDENTIFICATION) (AMENDMENT) REGULATIONS (NORTHERN IRELAND) 2001, SR 2001 393; made under the Dogs (Northern Ireland) Order 1983 (SI 1983 764 (NI.8)) Art.31. In force: January 1, 2002; £1.75.

These Regulations, which revoke Dogs (Licensing and Identification) (Amendment) Regulations (Northern Ireland) 1985 (SR 1985 142), the Dogs (Licensing and Identification) (Amendment No.2) Regulations (Northern Ireland) 1985 (SR 1985 338) and the Dogs (Licensing and Identification) (Amendment) Regulations (Northern Ireland) 1997 (SR 1997 462), amend the Dogs (Licensing and Identification) Regulations (Northern Ireland) 1983 (SR 1983 378) by setting out, for the period January 1, 2002 up to and including December 31, 2005, the shape, dimensions and colour of licence identification discs issued by district councils.

5709. Dogs (Amendment) Act (Northern Ireland) 2001 (c.1)

This Act makes provision regarding the destruction of dogs under the Dogs (Northern Ireland) Order 1983 (SI 1983 764 (NI 8)).

This Act received Royal Assent on January 29, 2001.

CIVIL PROCEDURE

5710. Abuse of process – personal injuries – spouse bringing action in own name after action on behalf of late husband settled on terms

[Fatal Accidents (Northern Ireland) Order 1977.]

DM was injured and her husband, CM, killed when their car collided with one driven by M, who brought an action in negligence against C's estate claiming damages for personal injuries, loss and damage. D, as C's personal representative, brought an action against M seeking damages for her alleged negligence and under the Fatal Accidents (Northern Ireland) Order 1977. M's action was compromised on terms and D's was settled on payment of £75,000. D subsequently brought proceedings for her own personal injuries and consequential loss against M and C's estate, which M and C's estate sought to have stayed on the ground that it was an abuse of process.

Held, refusing the application for a stay, that D did not acknowledge that C had been to blame for the accident and in the circumstances it was not unreasonable for her to wait for the outcome of the first two actions before bringing her own claim for personal injuries. M had not shown that this action was an abuse of process and there was no res judicata where an action was settled on terms *Johnson v. Gore Wood & Co (No.1)* [2001] 2 W.L.R. 72, [2001] 1 C.L. 49 and *Ulster Bank Ltd v. Fisher & Fisher (A Firm)* [1999] N.I. 68, [1995] C.L.Y. 5146 considered.

McNALLY v. McWILLIAMS [2001] N.I. 106, Sheil, J., QBD (NI).

5711. Costs – security – right to fair trial – justification for order following incorporation of ECHR

[Human Rights Act 1998 Sch.1 Part I Art.6; Companies (Northern Ireland) Order 1986 (SI 1986 1032) Art.674.]

B sought a declaration that it held a valid lease granted by M's widow, S. M died in 1993 and his estate was declared insolvent in 1995. B claimed that the lease was granted when neither it nor S knew that M's estate was insolvent. L, the trustee of M's estate, resisted B's claim and sought security for costs under the Companies (Northern Ireland) Order 1986 Art.674, which allowed the court to make an order for security if the company bringing proceedings lacked the financial resources to pay the defendant's costs. B was a dormant company with no income or assets, apart from the alleged lease. The authorities showed that the court had to exercise judicial discretion in deciding whether to order security and the question arose as to the proper approach to be followed after the coming into force of the Human Rights Act 1998 Sch.1 Part I Art.6.

Held, allowing the application and ordering security for costs, that Art.6 required effective access to the court, subject only to limitations that embodied a legitimate aim and were proportionate in terms of their intended aims and the means by which they were to be achieved. The power to order security meant that the court could control its own procedure in a way that avoided injustice. In certain circumstances, however, this could mean that an order would be justified even if it prevented a claimant proceeding with a claim. An order for security was reasonable on the facts of the instant case as the person behind B would provide security if the order was made. Although the situation would be different if there was no appropriate backer, the court could then be justified in piercing the corporate veil to determine the financial reality of the situation, *Sir Lindsay Parkinson & Co v. Triplan Ltd* [1973] Q.B. 609, [1973] C.L.Y. 2632, *Bremer Vulkan Schiffbau und Maschinenfabrik v. South India Shipping Corp Ltd* [1981] A.C. 909, [1981] C.L.Y. 119 and *R. v. Lord Chancellor, ex p. Witham* [1998] Q.B. 575 considered.

McATEER v. LISMORE (TRUSTEE OF THE ESTATE OF JAMES KEVIN McATEER) (NO.2) [2000] N.I. 477, Girvan, J., Ch D (NI).

5712. Costs – third parties – representation provided by Commission for Racial Equality – exercise of statutory function

[Judicature (Northern Ireland) Act 1978 s.59; County Courts (Northern Ireland) Order 1980 (SI 1980 397) Art.34 (1); Race Relations (Northern Ireland) Order 1997 (SI 1997/869).]

W, a member of the Irish Traveller Community, obtained the backing of the Commission for Racial Equality to bring a discrimination action against S under the Race Relations (NI) Order 1997. The Commission agreed to lodge papers and provide representation in the county court, but stated that it was under no obligation to satisfy any order for costs made against W and would consider a request to do so only in exceptional circumstances. W's claims were dismissed with costs in the county court. The county court had jurisdiction to make an award of costs against a non party under the Judicature (Northern Ireland) Act 1978 s.59 and the County Courts (Northern Ireland) Order 1980 Art.34 (1) but S did not know at that stage how W had funded the action and did not apply for an order that the Commission pay W's costs. Notices of appeal were lodged on W's behalf as a protective measure, but the Commission declined to give further assistance and the appeals were withdrawn. S subsequently applied for an order for the Commission to pay the costs of the action and the appeal, on the grounds that the Commission had directed the litigation, was interested in its outcome and had appointed W's solicitors. The Commission argued that such an order would frustrate the intention behind the legislation, in that the Commission had only limited funds with which to carry on its work.

Held, allowing the application in part, that the Commission was a statutory body charged with working to end racial discrimination and promoting equality. To make an order against it for the costs of the county court action could hinder it in its work. Moreover, the Commission had clearly stated to W that it did not accept liability for S's costs. S had not applied for its costs against the Commission to the trial judge and it was undesirable that the High Court should be asked on appeal to exercise a discretion available to the trial judge. Since the appeals had been withdrawn, the decrees of the county court remained undisturbed, and those decrees included orders for costs which the High Court could not reopen in the absence of a cross appeal. However, the costs of the withdrawn appeal were different. The Commission had told W's solicitors to lodge the notices of appeal and S had not been told whether W was intending to prosecute the appeals, with the result that it had incurred costs on the basis that the appeals would run. Further, W's counsel had delayed in providing advice on the merits of the appeal. In those circumstances, it was right that the Commission should pay the costs that S had incurred on the appeal, *Murphy v. Young & Co's Brewery Plc* [1997] 1 W.L.R. 1591, [1997] C.L.Y. 3113 considered.

WARD v. SABHERWAL (T/A NATH BROS, FASHION WHOLESALE & RETAIL) [2000] N.I. 551, Girvan, J., QBD (NI).

COMMERCIAL LAW

5713. Weights and measures – equipment

NON-AUTOMATIC WEIGHING INSTRUMENTS (USE FOR TRADE) REGULATIONS (NORTHERN IRELAND) 2001, SR 2001 202; made under the Weights and Measures (Northern Ireland) Order 1981 (SI 1981 231 (NI.10)) Art.13. In force: June 15, 2001; £2.00.

These Regulations, which revoke and replace the Non automatic Weighing Instruments (EEC Requirements) (Use for Trade) Regulations (Northern Ireland) 1992 (SR 1992 32), allow a Class IIII instrument to be used for trade for the purposes of weighing any material the disposal of which constitutes a landfill disposal and any commercial, household or industrial waste.

COMPANY LAW

5714. Small businesses – audits – exemptions

COMPANIES (1986 ORDER) (AUDIT EXEMPTION) (AMENDMENT) REGULATIONS (NORTHERN IRELAND) 2001, SR 2001 153; made under the Companies (Northern Ireland) Order 1986 (SI 1986 1032 (NI.6)) Art.265. In force: April 13, 2001; £2.00.

These Regulations, which amend provisions of the Companies (Northern Ireland) Order 1986 (SI 1986 1032 (NI.6)) concerning the exemption of certain small companies from the requirement to have their annual accounts audited and the conditions a company must satisfy in order to qualify as dormant, apply to annual accounts and reports in respect of financial years ending on or after June 13, 2001. They increase the turnover limit which a small company other than a small charitable company must not exceed in respect of a financial year if it is to be exempt from audit from £350,000 to £1 million and impose new requirements for companies claiming dormancy status.

CONSTITUTIONAL LAW

5715. Northern Ireland Assembly – restoration of devolved government

NORTHERN IRELAND ACT 2000 (RESTORATION OF DEVOLVED GOVERNMENT) ORDER 2001, SI 2001 2895; made under the Northern Ireland Act 2000 s.2. In force: August 12, 2001; £1.50.

This Order, which revokes the Northern Ireland Act 2000 (Suspension of Devolved Government) Order 2001 (SI 2001 2884), provides that the Northern Ireland Act 2000 s.1 is to cease to have effect on August 12, 2001 with the effect that the devolved government in Northern Ireland is restored.

5716. Northern Ireland Assembly – restoration of devolved government

NORTHERN IRELAND ACT 2000 (RESTORATION OF DEVOLVED GOVERNMENT) (NO.2) ORDER 2001, SI 2001 3231; made under the Northern Ireland Act 2000 s.2. In force: September 23, 2001; £1.50.

This Order, which revokes the Northern Ireland Act 2000 (Suspension of Devolved Government) (No.2) Order 2001 (SI 2001 3230), provides that the Northern Ireland Act 2000 s.1 is to cease to have effect on September 23, 2001 and restores devolved government in Northern Ireland.

5717. Northern Ireland Assembly – suspension of devolved government

NORTHERN IRELAND ACT 2000 (SUSPENSION OF DEVOLVED GOVERNMENT) ORDER 2001, SI 2001 2884; made under the Northern Ireland Act 2000 s.2. In force: August 11, 2001; £1.50.

This Order revokes the Northern Ireland Act 2000 (Restoration of Devolved Government) Order 2000 (SI 2000 1445) which restored devolved government in Northern Ireland on May 30, 2000.

5718. Northern Ireland Assembly – suspension of devolved government

NORTHERN IRELAND ACT 2000 (SUSPENSION OF DEVOLVED GOVERNMENT) (NO.2) ORDER 2001, SI 2001 3230; made under the Northern Ireland Act 2000 s.2. In force: September 22, 2001; £1.50.

This Order revokes the Northern Ireland Act 2000 (Restoration of Devolved Government) Order 2001 (SI 2001 2895) which restored devolved government in Northern Ireland on August 12, 2001. The effect of this Order is to bring into force the Northern Ireland Act 2000 s.1 which suspends devolved government.

5719. Public authorities – designation

NORTHERN IRELAND ACT 1998 (DESIGNATION OF PUBLIC AUTHORITIES) ORDER 2001, SI 2001 1294; made under the Northern Ireland Act 1998 s.75. In force: April 5, 2001; £1.75.

This Order designates bodies as "public authorities" for the purposes of the Northern Ireland Act 1998 s.75. Such a public authority is subject to the statutory duties to have regard in carrying out its functions relating to Northern Ireland to the need to promote equality of opportunity and to the desirability of promoting good relations between people of different religious belief, political opinion or racial group.

5720. Weapons – decommissioning scheme – amnesty period

NORTHERN IRELAND ARMS DECOMMISSIONING ACT 1997 (AMNESTY PERIOD) ORDER 2001, SI 2001 1622; made under the Northern Ireland Arms Decommissioning Act 1997 s.2. In force: April 14, 2001; £1.50.

Under the Northern Ireland Arms Decommissioning Act 1997 s.2(1) a decommissioning scheme must identify a period during which firearms, ammunition and explosives may be dealt with in accordance with the scheme and the amnesty period must end before the first anniversary of the day on which the Act was passed or such later day as the Secretary of State may by order from time to time appoint. This Order, which repeals the Northern Ireland Arms Decommissioning Act 1997 (Amnesty Period) (No.2) Order 2000 (SI 2000 1409), appoints February 27, 2002 as the day before which the amnesty period identified in a decommissioning scheme must end.

CONSTRUCTION LAW

5721. Construction industry – Construction Industry Training Board – levy on employers

INDUSTRIAL TRAINING LEVY (CONSTRUCTION INDUSTRY) ORDER (NORTHERN IRELAND) 2001, SR 2001 281; made under the Industrial Training (Northern Ireland) Order 1984 (SI 1984 1159 (NI.9)) Art.23, Art.24. In force: August 31, 2001; £2.00.

This Order gives effect to proposals submitted by the Construction Industry Training Board to the Department of Higher and Further Education, Training and Employment for the imposition of a further levy upon employers in the construction industry for the purpose of raising money towards the expenses of the Board. The levy is to be imposed in respect of the 37th levy period, commencing on September 1, 2001 and ending on August 31, 2002.

CONSUMER LAW

5722. Consumer protection – hazardous substances – packaging and labelling

CHEMICALS (HAZARD INFORMATION AND PACKAGING FOR SUPPLY) (AMENDMENT) REGULATIONS (NORTHERN IRELAND) 2001, SR 2001 168; made under the European Communities Act 1972 s.2; and the Health and Safety at Work (Northern Ireland) Order 1978 (SI 1978 1039 (NI.9)) Art.17, Art.55, Sch.3 para.1, Sch.3 para.2, Sch.3 para.14, Sch.3 para.15. In force: May 15, 2001; £15.50.

These Regulations, which amend the Chemicals (Hazard Information and Packaging for Supply) Regulations (Northern Ireland) 1995 (SR 1995 60), implement Commission Directive 98/98 ([1998] OJ L335/1) adapting to technical progress for the 25th time, Commission Directive 2000/32 ([2000] OJ L136/1) adapting to technical progress for the 26th time and Council Directive 67/548 ([1967] OJ L196/1) relating to the classification, packaging and labelling of dangerous substances.

5723. Product Liability (Amendment) Act (Northern Ireland) 2001 (c.13)

This Act amends the Consumer Protection (Northern Ireland) Order 1987 (SI 1987 2049 (NI. 20)) PartII.

CRIMINAL EVIDENCE

5724. Confessions – admissibility – statement made to Gardai by suspect when not under caution

[Police and Criminal Evidence (Northern Ireland) Order 1989 (SI 1989 1341 (NI.12)) Code C para.10.1.]

M appealed by way of case stated against conviction by a resident magistrate of five road traffic offences. A van owned by M was involved in an accident in Northern Ireland, close to the border with the Republic. Acting on a request from the RUC, two Gardai spoke to M and he admitted driving the van at the time of the accident. However, the admission was not made under caution as none was required under the law of the Irish Republic. M later attended an RUC station for interview where he admitted being the vehicle's owner but denied driving it when it was involved in the accident. M submitted that the statements of the Gardai should not have been admitted in evidence as they had been obtained in breach of the Police and Criminal Evidence (Northern Ireland Order) 1989 Code C para.10.1.

Held, dismissing the appeal, that the statements of the Gardai had been properly admitted as they had been correctly obtained under the law of the Irish Republic. There was no evidence that M had been pressured into making the admission and the Gardai could not have been expected to observe the requirements of the 1989 Order when asking M about the accident, *R. v. Quinn* [1990] Crim. L.R. 581, [1990] C.L.Y. 809 and *R. v. Konscol* [1993] Crim. L.R. 950, [1994] C.L.Y. 953 approved.

RUSSELL v. McADAMS [2001] N.I. 157, Carswell, L.C.J., CA (NI).

5725. Supply of drugs – forfeiture orders – burden of proof – money obtained from drug dealing or used to purchase supplies

[Misuse of Drugs Act 1971 s.27(1); Criminal Justice (Northern Ireland) Order 1994 (SI 1994 2795) Art.11.]

Following F conviction on a guilty plea to supplying and possessing controlled drugs with intent to supply, the Crown requested variation of his sentence by way of a forfeiture order in respect of F's car under the Criminal Justice (Northern Ireland) Order 1994 Art.11 and £6,000 under the Misuse of Drugs Act 1971 s.27(1). The judge agreed on the ground that he was satisfied on the balance of probabilities that the money had been obtained from drug dealing. F sought leave to appeal against the forfeiture of the money, arguing that the wrong standard of proof had been applied and that the facts proved were not sufficient for an application under the 1971 Act.

Held, allowing the application and the appeal, that criminal penalties required proof to the criminal standard. For a forfeiture application under s.27(1) of the 1971 Act it had to be shown that the money was related to the offence, and even if the sums found in F's possession were part of his working capital for drug dealing it would not have been needed to commit the offence to which the judge stated it was related, ie the possession with intent to supply. Neither was the probability that the money could have been used to buy further supplies sufficient for a forfeiture order, as it was possible that it could have been used for other things, *R. v. Morgan* [1977] Crim. L.R. 488, [1977] C.L.Y. 643.25 and *R. v. O'Neill* [1998] N.I.J.B. 1 applied.

R. v. FENTON (WILLIAM DENIS) [2001] N.I. 65, Carswell, L.C.J., CA (Crim Div) (NI).

CRIMINAL LAW

5726. Conspiracy – grievous bodily harm – insufficient evidence for charge of conspiracy to murder

[Criminal Law Act (Northern Ireland) 1967 s.6(2).]

C appealed against conviction of conspiracy to cause grievous bodily harm, having been charged with conspiracy to murder police officers. C had armed and transported two blast bombs that he handed to two fellow members of a paramilitary group who threw them at police officers. The trial judge held that the evidence was not sufficient for a charge of conspiracy to murder, but found that it sufficed for a charge of conspiracy to cause grievous bodily harm, for which he sentenced C to 15 years' imprisonment. The Crown contended that the judge's decision was correct in view of the Criminal Law Act (Northern Ireland) 1967 s.6(2), which allowed a defendant found not guilty of the offence he had been charged with to be found guilty of another offence on the basis of allegations in the indictment.

Held, dismissing the appeal, that the judge had correctly inferred that the conspirators intended to cause grievous bodily harm by agreeing to throw the blast bombs even though there was no evidence of the consequences they intended to bring about. Therefore C had properly been convicted on the charge of conspiracy to cause grievous bodily harm, *R. v. Barnard* (1980) 70 Cr. App. R. 28, [1980] C.L.Y. 446 distinguished.

R. v. CROTHERS (FREDERICK IRVINE) [2001] N.I. 55, Carswell, L.C.J., CA (Crim Div) (NI).

5727. Drugs – controlled drugs – designation

MISUSE OF DRUGS (DESIGNATION) ORDER (NORTHERN IRELAND) 2001, SR 2001 431; made under the Misuse of Drugs Act 1971 s.7. In force: February 1, 2002; £2.00.

This Order revokes the Misuse of Drugs (Designation) (Northern Ireland) Order 1987 (SR 1987 66), the Misuse of Drugs (Designation) (Variation) Order (Northern Ireland) 1991 (SR 1991 2), the Misuse of Drugs (Designation) (Variation) Order (Northern Ireland) 1995 (SR 1995 306) and the Misuse of Drugs (Designation) (Variation) Order (Northern Ireland) 1998 (SR 1998 129). The Misuse of Drugs Act 1971 requires regulations to be made to allow the use for medical purposes of the drugs which are subject to control under the Act. This Order designates for this purpose the drugs specified in Part I of the Schedule to the Order.

5728. Firearms offences – duress of circumstances – possession of unlicensed firearm – availability of defence

[Firearms (Northern Ireland) Order 1981 (SI 1981 155) Art.3, Art.23; Human Rights Act 1998 s.3; European Convention on Human Rights 1950 Art.2.]

C appealed against conviction and concurrent sentences of two years' imprisonment, suspended for three years, imposed for possessing a firearm and ammunition without a licence, contrary to the Firearms (Northern Ireland) Order 1981 Art.3. C had been found not guilty of possessing the firearm and ammunition in suspicious circumstances under Art.23, on the basis that he had acquired the weapon and ammunition to protect himself and his family. C argued that the defence of duress of circumstances applied and that this should have been allowed under the Human Rights Act 1998 s.3 so as to preclude his liability under the 1981 Order in reliance upon the right to life under the European Convention on Human Rights 1950 Art.2.

Held, dismissing the appeal against conviction and allowing that against sentence by substituting the concurrent sentences with a fine of £100 on each count, that (1) the defence of duress of circumstances was only available in circumstances where the criminal conduct ceased as soon as possible. However, in the instant case, C's conduct was continuing so that duress of circumstances did not apply, even though C came within the statutory defence in Art.23. In any event, C had not shown there was any immediate threat to himself or his family when he acquired the firearm and ammunition, *R. v. Pommell (Fitzroy Derek)* [1995] 2 Cr. App. R. 607, [1995] C.L.Y. 1258 followed, and (2) firearms licensing was a discretionary State function that did not impinge upon the individual's right to life under the convention so that Art.2 did not apply.

R. v. CLINTON (JAMES PATRICK) [2001] N.I. 207, Carswell, L.C.J., CA (Crim Div) (NI).

5729. Murder – provocation – jury directions – personal characteristics of defendant to include self control

[Criminal Evidence Act (Northern Ireland) 1923 s.1 (f).]

M was convicted of murdering his wife after a jury trial, in the course of which the Crown was allowed to put evidence of a spent conviction to a defence expert witness to discredit his evidence as to M's previous good character. M's guilt was not in issue, but he sought to rely on the defence of provocation. The judge directed the jury that they could return a manslaughter verdict either on the basis of lack of intention or diminished responsibility or both diminished responsibility and provocation. M appealed, contending that the spent conviction had been wrongly admitted and that the jury had been misdirected as to extent that his personal characteristics were relevant to the question of self control. Further, that a manslaughter verdict could be returned even if the jury did not agree as to the basis on which the charge was reduced from murder.

Held, allowing the appeal and ordering a retrial, that (1) although it was generally contrary to common law and the Criminal Evidence Act (Northern Ireland) 1923 s.1 (f) to allow evidence of bad character, a judge had discretion in certain circumstances, and in the instant case the judge had been concerned that the witness's evidence could mislead the jury, given his knowledge of M's record. The disclosure was limited as to its effect on the jury when determining the issue of provocation or diminished responsibility and they had been warned as to the extent they could take the matter into account; (2) however, the conviction was unsafe as the judge had restricted the consideration of M's personal characteristics so as to exclude self control, *R. v. Smith (Morgan James)* [2001] 1 A.C. 146, [2000] C.L.Y. 986 followed, and (3) (Nicholson L.J. dissenting) a jury had to be agreed on the basis on which it decided on a manslaughter verdict. The direction was correct on that point and it was not sufficient to allow the verdict on the basis that the jury had agreed on the ingredients of the offence where the trial judge could not determine whether the jury were agreed on the applicability of provocation or diminished responsibility.

R. v. McCANDLESS (TREVOR) [2001] N.I. 86, Carswell, L.C.J., CA (Crim Div) (NI).

5730. Road traffic offences – unlicensed vehicles – prescribed devices

ROAD TRAFFIC OFFENDERS (ADDITIONAL OFFENCES AND PRESCRIBED DEVICES) ORDER (NORTHERN IRELAND) 2001, SR 2001 375; made under the Road Traffic Offenders (Northern Ireland) Order 1996 (SI 1996 1320 (NI.10)) Art.23. In force: December 1, 2001; £1.75.

This Order amends the Road Traffic Offenders (Northern Ireland) Order 1996 (SI 1996 1320) to add the offence of using, or keeping, an unlicensed vehicle other than an exempt vehicle on a public road to the offences to which Article 23 of the 1996 Order applies. It also prescribes as devices which may be used to produce evidence under that Article, automatic number plate recognition systems designed or adapted to record the presence of such a vehicle on a public road.

5731. Terrorism – police interviews – video tape recordings – code of practice

TERRORISM ACT 2000 (CODE OF PRACTICE ON VIDEO RECORDING OF INTERVIEWS) (NORTHERN IRELAND) ORDER 2001, SI 2001 402; made under the Terrorism Act 2000 Sch.8 para.4. In force: February 19, 2001; £1.50.

This Order appoints February 19, 2001, as the date on which the code of practice on the video recording with sound of interviews by police officers of persons detained in a police station under the Terrorism Act 2000 comes into operation. "Police station" includes any place which the Secretary of State has designated under the Terrorism Act 2000 Sch.8 para.1 (1) as a place where a person may be detained under s.41 of that Act.

5732. Terrorism – police powers – code of practice

TERRORISM ACT 2000 (CODE OF PRACTICE ON THE EXERCISE OF POLICE POWERS) (NORTHERN IRELAND) ORDER 2001, SI 2001 401; made under the Terrorism Act 2000 s.101. In force: February 19, 2001; £1.50.

This order appoints February 19, 2001, as the date upon which the code of practice on the exercise by police officers of the powers of detention and identification conferred by the Terrorism Act 2000 shall come into operation in Northern Ireland.

CRIMINAL PROCEDURE

5733. Appeals – abuse of process – defendant's guilt not in issue – sentence length under accelerated release provisions

[Treatment of Offenders Act (Northern Ireland) 1968 s.26(2); Criminal Appeal (Northern Ireland) Act 1980 s.2(1); Criminal Appeal Act 1995 s.2; Northern Ireland (Sentences) Act 1998; Human Rights Act 1998 Sch.1 Part I Art.6.]

M was arrested in Northern Ireland in April 1997 along with four others in relation to an arms find, three of whom were then charged and remanded in custody. M was convicted in England in June 1998 of conspiracy to murder and sentenced to 25 years' imprisonment, becoming a sentenced prisoner in England. M was transferred to prison in Northern Ireland in September 1998. It was then decided to prosecute him in connection with the 1997 arms find, and, following an unsuccessful application for the prosecution to be halted on the grounds of abuse of process, M was convicted in March 1999 and sentenced to 20 years' imprisonment. Under the Treatment of Offenders Act (Northern Ireland) 1968 s.26(2) M, as a sentenced prisoner, was not entitled to have any remand period taken into account in relation to the sentence imposed for the arms find. The effect of this was that, whilst his three co-accused could rely on time remanded in custody for the purposes of accelerated release under the Northern Ireland (Sentences) Act 1998, making them eligible for release in July 2000, M would not be eligible for release under the 1998 Act until March 2001. M appealed against conviction and sentence, contending that the delay in the prosecution was an abuse of process and that a shorter sentence should have been passed, allowing for his release at the same time as his co-accused. Further, on a preliminary issue, whether, given that M's guilt was not in issue, the court could entertain the appeal under the Criminal Appeal (Northern Ireland) Act 1980 s.2(1), as amended by the Criminal Appeal Act 1995 s.2, pursuant to which an appeal against conviction could be allowed if it was found to be unsafe when conviction followed an abuse of process.

Held, dismissing the appeal, that (1) abuse of process could be a ground for finding a conviction to be unsafe and the term was broad enough to allow the quashing of a conviction because of an abuse of process prior to trial. Moreover, this interpretation accorded with the Human Rights Act 1998 Sch.1 Part I Art.6, so that there was jurisdiction to hear the appeal, *R. v. Mullen (Nicholas Robert) (No.2)* [2000] Q.B. 520, [1999] C.L.Y. 972 applied; (2) the Director of Public Prosecutions had no duty to take account of the sentence that an accused could receive if convicted. Neither was it appropriate for a judge dealing with an application to stay proceedings on the grounds of abuse of process to consider the length of sentence an accused could receive on conviction, and (3) the accelerated release provisions of the 1998 Act were irrelevant where the court was passing a custodial sentence, other than one fixed by law. Sentences were fixed by reference to what was appropriate, given the seriousness of the offence. The judge would have been wrong to take the 1998 Act into account when deciding the length of M's sentence, by ensuring that M's sentence would not exceed that of his co-accused.

R. v. McARDLE [2000] N.I. 390, Nicholson, L.J., Campbell, L.J., McLaughlin, L.J., CA (NI).

5734. Disclosure – discretion – third party disclosure – court's need to balance right of privacy and right of fair trial

[Judicature (Northern Ireland) Act 1978 s.51A to s.51H; Crown Court (Amendment) Rules 2000 (SR 2000 227).]

P and M were charged with sexual offences and physical assaults on P's stepdaughters. They obtained orders for disclosure against a social services board, the girls' school and the Compensation Agency. The papers concerned were delivered to court on the morning of the trial and the judge, having examined them, ordered an adjournment and the disclosure of the material to P and M. P and M then sought a direction for the disclosure of the family GP's records and the disclosure of social services records held by a Health and Social Services Trust. In deciding the application, the judge had to interpret the Judicature (Northern Ireland) Act 1978 s.51A to s.51H, dealing with third party disclosure and witness attendance at trial.

Held, allowing the application as an exercise of the court's inherent discretion and issuing summonses to the GP and the Trust, that (1) although S.51A to s.51H and the Crown Court (Amendment) Rules 2000 provided an exhaustive code for third party disclosure in criminal proceedings, the court retained the power to order disclosure of its own motion in the interests of justice and of ensuring a fair trial, exercisable on the application of the parties, and (2) the statutory code provided that the court could issue a witness summons, requiring a third party to attend the trial or on a given date to produce material that was admissible in evidence and likely to assist the defence. Where disclosure could affect the right to privacy of the third party or complainant, such rights had to be balanced against the defendant's right to a fair trial. The need for the court's sanction in respect of such material precluded voluntary disclosure.

R. v. O'N [2001] N.I. 136, Girvan, J., Crown Ct (Belfast).

5735. Magistrates courts – pleadings – change of plea – discussion between judge and counsel in chambers – change not on basis of informed consent

M was accused of indecent assault. He initially pleaded guilty, but later changed his plea to not guilty. During the course of the substantive hearing in the magistrates' court, however, M's counsel discussed the case with the resident magistrate in chambers following which M asserted that his counsel prevailed upon him to change his plea, which he did and was sentenced to eight months' imprisonment on conviction. M contended that, following the consultation with the resident magistrate, his counsel had advised him that he would receive six months' imprisonment on a guilty plea, but that if he contested the case and was found guilty, the matter would be referred to the Crown Court for sentence, where he would receive at least 18 months' imprisonment. The magistrate did not in fact have jurisdiction to refer the case to the Crown Court for sentence: he was obliged either to commit M to the Crown Court for trial or to determine the case himself, where the maximum sentence was 12 months' imprisonment. M's appeal to the county court was refused and the sentence upheld, but the judge queried whether he had jurisdiction to determine an appeal following a guilty plea and suggested that M pursue the matter by way of judicial review. M sought judicial review of the resident magistrate's decision and the county court order affirming the sentence.

Held, allowing the application and quashing the conviction, that a conviction could be set aside on the ground of procedural unfairness. In the instant case, M had misunderstood the magistrate's comment about his power to refer the matter to the Crown Court for sentencing. This had the effect of vitiating his plea as it had not been made with his fully informed consent. If M known that the maximum sentence was 12 months, he could have assumed the risk of continuing to defend the case, whereas a sentence of at least 18 months could have presented too great a risk.

Observed, Although counsel should have ready access to trial judges in chambers, the facility should only be used when it was necessary to discuss issues pertaining to the client's interest that could not be ventilated in open court. Reticence in conducting such discussions should be especially observed in sentencing matters, as this could adversely affect the defendant's freedom of choice as to his course of action, dictum of Hutton, L.C.J. in, *R. v. McNeill (Stephen Victor)* [1993] N.I. 46 doubted.

McFARLAND'S APPLICATION FOR JUDICIAL REVIEW, Re [2000] N.I. 403, Carswell, L.C.J., Sir John MacDermott, QBD (NI).

5736. Magistrates courts – remand – accused remanded on Easter Sunday – lawfulness of remand

[Police and Criminal Evidence (Northern Ireland) Order 1989 (SI 1989 1341 (NI.12)) Art.47; European Convention on Human Rights 1950 Art.5(3).]

The DPP sought judicial review of a resident magistrate's decision to release S, who had been remanded to appear on charges of threatening to kill and intimidation. S had been charged with the offences on the Saturday before Easter, but was brought before the magistrate on Easter Sunday, when he was remanded in custody. S successfully contended before the resident magistrate that the decision to remand was unlawful as the Police and Criminal Evidence (Northern Ireland) Order 1989 Art.47(2) stipulated that an accused could not be brought before a court on a Sunday.

Held, allowing the application, that Part V of the 1989 Order containing Art.47 was concerned with the condition and length of detention. It was therefore inconsistent with the remainder of that Part to rely on Art.47 to prevent a court of sitting on a Sunday when that could conveniently be arranged. This interpretation accorded with the European Convention on Human Rights 1950 Art.5(3) which provided that an accused was to be brought promptly before a court.

DPP FOR NORTHERN IRELAND'S APPLICATION FOR JUDICIAL REVIEW, *Re* [2001] N.I. 60, Kerr, J., QBD (NI).

5737. Pleas – legal advice – requirement for judge to ensure change of plea made in absence of undue pressure

W was convicted of arson. His counsel had withdrawn at the initial trial following a disagreement with W over advice to change his plea to guilty. The judge had then discharged the jury and at a new hearing, where W was represented by different counsel, W changed his plea on advice. However, he subsequently denied his guilt during a pre sentencing report interview and his counsel withdrew as he felt unable to mitigate on the basis of the pre sentence report. W was represented by a third counsel at the sentencing hearing, who sought to have W re-arraigned so that he could enter a not guilty plea. The application was refused and the judge allowed counsel to withdraw before proceeding to pass sentence. W sought permission to appeal, contending that the sentencing judge had not exercised his discretion by making inquiries to satisfy himself that W was not pressured into changing his plea.

Held, refusing the application, that the judge had found that W was being obstructive but his reasoning did not show that he had exercised his discretion by satisfying himself that W had not been unduly pressured into changing his plea. However, the strength of the prosecution's case, which included the identification evidence of two police officers, and the fact that the plea was entered on the advice of experienced counsel meant that permission would not be given for the guilty plea to be withdrawn.

R. v. WHITE (LESLIE JAMES) [2001] N.I. 172, Carswell, L.C.J., CA (Crim Div) (NI).

5738. Sexual offences – sexual offenders – restraining orders

SEX OFFENDERS ACT 1997 (NORTHERN IRELAND) ORDER 2001, SI 2001 1853; made under the Sex Offenders Act 1997 s.10. In force: June 1, 2001; £1.50.

This Order amends the Sex Offenders Act 1997 s.5A to provide for a court to have the power to make a restraining order when sentencing a sex offender.

CRIMINAL SENTENCING

5739. Offenders – rehabilitation – exceptions – health services

REHABILITATION OF OFFENDERS (EXCEPTIONS) (AMENDMENT) ORDER (NORTHERN IRELAND) 2001, SR 2001 248; made under the Rehabilitation of

Offenders (Northern Ireland) Order 1978 (SI 1978 1908 (NI.27)) Art.5, Art.8. In force: August 14, 2001; £1.75.

This Order amends the Rehabilitation of Offenders (Exceptions) Order (Northern Ireland) 1979 (SR 1979 195) by excepting work which is concerned with the provision of health services and which is of such a kind as to enable the holder to have access to persons in receipt of such services in the course of his normal duties.

5740. Offenders – rehabilitation – exceptions – specified status

REHABILITATION OF OFFENDERS (EXCEPTIONS) (AMENDMENT) (NO.2) ORDER (NORTHERN IRELAND) 2001, SR 2001 400; made under the Rehabilitation of Offenders (Northern Ireland) Order 1978 (SI 1978 1908 (NI.27)) Art.5, Art.8. In force: December 1, 2001; £2.50.

This Order amends the Rehabilitation of Offenders (Exceptions) Order (Northern Ireland) 1979 (SR 1979 195) to provide for exceptions from the Rehabilitation of Offenders (Northern Ireland) Order 1978 (SI 1978 1908). The exceptions apply to questions asked by specified persons to asses the suitability of an individual to have a specified status.

5741. Prisoners – release – paramilitary organisations

NORTHERN IRELAND (SENTENCES) ACT 1998 (SPECIFIED ORGANISATIONS) ORDER 2001, SI 2001 3411; made under the Northern Ireland (Sentences) Act 1998 s.3. In force: October 13, 2001; £1.75.

Under the Northern Ireland (Sentences) Act 1998, the Secretary of State must specify an organisation if he believes that it is concerned with terrorism connected with the affairs of Northern Ireland, or in promoting or encouraging it, and that it has not established or is not maintaining a complete and unequivocal ceasefire. The Secretary of State is obliged to review the list of specified organisations from time to time. Following such a review, the Secretary of State has decided to specify the Ulster Defence Association, the Ulster Freedom Fighters and the Loyalist Volunteer Force in addition to the Continuity IRA, the "Real" IRA, the Red Hand Defenders and the Orange Volunteers which were specified by the Northern Ireland (Sentences) Act 1998 (Specified Organisations) Order 1999 (SI 1999 1152), which this Order revokes. The effect of specifying an organisation is that a prisoner who is, or who would be likely to become, a supporter of such an organisation, is ineligible for release under the 1998 Act or, if released, is liable to recall to prison.

5742. Road traffic offences – fixed penalties

ROAD TRAFFIC (FIXED PENALTY) ORDER (NORTHERN IRELAND) 2001, SR 2001 3; made under the Road Traffic Offenders (Northern Ireland) Order 1996 (SI 1996 1320 (NI.10)) Art.59. In force: March 1, 2001; £1.50.

This Order, which revokes and replaces the Road Traffic (Fixed Penalty) Order (Northern Ireland) 1997 (SR 1997 368), increases the fixed penalties for fixed penalty offences. The penalty for offences which do not involve obligatory endorsement is increased from £20 to £30 and the penalty for offences involving obligatory endorsement is increased from £40 to £60.

DAMAGES

5743. Dogs – statutory duty – liability of deemed keeper – dog on farmland with landowner's knowledge

[Dogs (Northern Ireland) Order 1983 (SI 1983 764).]

C, a three year old boy, was bitten on the face by a dog during a visit to CS's farm. CS's sister, J, lived in the farmhouse, but CS owned and worked the farm. He had bought the dog for J, who held the licence for it and looked after it. C commenced an action against CS and JS, claiming breach of the statutory duty under the Dogs (Northern Ireland) Order 1983 Art.53(1). Article 4(1) of the Order stipulated that the holder of the dog licence was the keeper of the dog, but Art.2(7) provided that the occupier of the land where the dog was found was deemed to be its keeper unless it was proved that the landowner was not the keeper and the dog was on the land without his knowledge. C obtained judgment by default against JS and proceeded with the action against S. The trial judge dismissed the claim and C appealed.

Held, allowing the appeal and giving judgment in C's favour in the sum of £15,000 (Campbell LJ dissenting), that the wording of Art.22(3)(a)(i) and Art.24(1)(a)(i) meant that a dog could have more than one keeper for the purposes of the Order. Article 2(7) provided that the occupier retained liability even though he was not the keeper, as long as he knew that the dog was on his land so that CS was the deemed keeper of the dog by virtue of Art.2(7). Therefore, CS was liable to C for the injury in addition to J as the dog's owner.

C (A CHILD) v. SCOTT [2001] N.I. 48, Carswell, L.C.J., CA (NI).

DEFAMATION

5744. **Libel – disclosure – source of leaked police report referred to in Parliament and press article – freedom of expression**

[Bill of Rights 1689 Art.9; Contempt of Court Act 1981 s.10; Human Rights Act 1998 s.3; European Convention on Human Rights 1950 Art.10.]

An article in C's newspaper written by O alleged that R's brothers, who had been murdered by loyalist terrorists, were themselves members of the IRA and were responsible for terrorist acts on the basis of a leaked police report. O also alleged, in the course of a telephone conversation with R, that he was an IRA member. Shortly after the article was published, P, an MP, named R and his brothers as IRA members in the House of Commons. R sought disclosure of the report and the name of the person who had supplied it to O and P by way of originating summons so that he could commence an action in libel or malicious falsehood. C relied on the Contempt of Court Act 1981 s.10 and the European Convention on Human Rights 1950 Art.10 to counter R's claim on the basis of freedom of expression. As to P, R contended that absolute privilege accorded to Parliamentary debates and proceedings by the Bill of Rights 1689 Art.9 was to be interpreted in a manner compatible with his right to life under Art.2 and right to family life under Art.8 by virtue of the Human Rights Act 1998 s.3.

Held, refusing the application, that R's interest in bringing an action in libel or malicious falsehood in the instant case was not sufficient to outweigh the public interest in the freedom of the press. Although the Bill of Rights was to be interpreted in a manner that was compatible with R's Convention rights, the fundamental importance of free and impartial Parliamentary debates was such that the absolute privilege accorded to such proceedings could not be set aside. Any abuse of that privilege was a matter for Parliament, not the courts.

REAVEY v. CENTURY NEWSPAPERS LTD [2001] N.I. 187, Sheil, J., QBD (NI).

EDUCATION

5745. **Examinations – dyslexia – 11 plus candidate – refusal of extra time – compatibility with right to education**

[European Convention on Human Rights 1950 Art.14, Protocol 1 Art.2.]

N, an 11 year old dyslexic, sat the transfer tests for admission to secondary school in November 2000. His parents were provided with guidance as to the special circumstances procedure so that they could submit a claim on N's behalf to the governors of the relevant school, notifying them of N's condition. In June 2000, N's mother wrote to the Minister of Education, requesting extra time for N in the test. She was informed, however, that such arrangements did not apply to the transfer tests and that N would have to rely on the notified procedure. N, acting by his mother, sought judicial review of the decision to refuse him extra time and a declaration that the Disability Discrimination Act 1995 s.19(5), disapplying the Act in relation to education, was incompatible with the European Convention on Human Rights 1950 Art.14 and Protocol 1 Art.2.

Held, refusing the applications, that (1) N could not claim that he had been treated less favourably than GCSE or A level candidates, as the transfer tests were subject to predetermined pass limits which did not apply in the case of the latter examinations so that there had been no breach of Art.14, *Belgian Linguistic Case (No.2) (A/6)* (1979-80) 1 E.H.R.R. 252, [1981] C.L.Y. 1088 applied; (2) account had been taken of both N's disability and the differences between the transfer tests and the GCSE and A level examinations, so that the decision to refuse extra time in favour of the special procedure was fair in the circumstances, and (3) as N had not been prevented from relying on any Convention rights no declaration of incompatibility would be issued.

N'S APPLICATION FOR JUDICIAL REVIEW, *Re* [2001] N.I. 115, Coghlin, J., QBD (NI).

5746. Grants – disabled students – additional expenditure

EDUCATION (GRANTS FOR DISABLED POSTGRADUATE STUDENTS) REGULATIONS (NORTHERN IRELAND) 2001, SR 2001 285; made under the Education (Student Support) (Northern Ireland) Order 1998 (SI 1998 1760 (NI.14)) Art.3. In force: September 1, 2001; £2.50.

These Regulations make provision for grants to disabled postgraduate students to meet additional expenditure incurred in undertaking their courses by reason of their disability. They provide for the method of application for grant, transfers between courses, termination of eligibility and the provision of information by students to the Department for the purpose of exercising its functions under the Regulations on a similar basis to those applying to undergraduate student support. In addition, the Regulations enable the Department to pay grant at such time and in such manner as it considers appropriate and make provision for the recovery of overpayments.

5747. Grants – students – eligibility

EDUCATION (STUDENT SUPPORT) REGULATIONS (NORTHERN IRELAND) 2001, SR 2001 277; made under the Education (Student Support) (Northern Ireland) Order 1998 (SI 1998 1760 (NI.14)) Art.3, Art.8. In force: August 2, 2001; £7.00.

These Regulations, which revoke the Education (Student Support) (Amendment) Regulations (Northern Ireland) 2000 (SR 2000 254), the Education (Student Support) (Amendment No.2) Regulations (Northern Ireland) 2000 (SR 2000 296) and the Education (Student Support) (Amendment No.3) Regulations (Northern Ireland) 2001 (SR 2001 77), provide for support for students attending higher education courses in respect of academic years beginning on or after September 1, 2001.

5748. Grants – students – eligibility

EDUCATION (STUDENT SUPPORT) (AMENDMENT NO.3) REGULATIONS (NORTHERN IRELAND) 2001, SR 2001 77; made under the Education (Student Support) (Northern Ireland) Order 1998 (SI 1998 1760 (NI.14)) Art.3, Art.8. In force: April 2, 2001; £2.00.

These Regulations, which amend the Education (Student Support) Regulations (Northern Ireland) 2000 (SR 2000 213), provide for support for students undertaking part time designated courses whether they attend the course or whether they pursue the course through open learning.

5749. Pupils – records

EDUCATION (PUPIL RECORDS) (AMENDMENT) REGULATIONS (NORTHERN IRELAND) 2001, SR 2001 236; made under the Education and Libraries (Northern Ireland) Order 1986 (SI 1986 594 (NI. 3)) Art.17A, Art.134. In force: July 6, 2001; £1.75.

These Regulations amend the Education (Pupil Records) Regulations (Northern Ireland) 1998 (SR 1998 11) to omit the provisions relating to the right of access by pupils to information contained in their educational records, which, with effect from March 1, 2000, is governed by the Data Protection Act 1998.

5750. Students – educational awards

STUDENTS AWARDS REGULATIONS (NORTHERN IRELAND) 2001, SR 2001 298; made under the Education and Libraries (Northern Ireland) Order 1986 (SI 1986 594 (NI.3)) Art.50, Art.134. In force: September 1, 2001; £7.00.

These Regulations, which revoke the Students Awards Regulations (Northern Ireland) 2000 (SR 2000 311), provide that where the student is attending a flexible postgraduate course for the initial training of teachers approved by the Teacher Training Agency, the board is not under a duty to make an award in respect of fees.

5751. Students – loans – mortgage style repayment loans

EDUCATION (STUDENT LOANS) (AMENDMENT) REGULATIONS (NORTHERN IRELAND) 2001, SR 2001 276; made under the Education (Student Loans) (Northern Ireland) Order 1990 (SI 1990 1506 (NI.11)) Art.3, Sch.2 para.1. In force: August 1, 2001; £1.50.

These Regulations amend the Education (Student Loans) Regulations (Northern Ireland) 1998 (SR 1998 58) which govern loans made under the Education (Student Loans) (Northern Ireland) Order 1990 (SI 1990 1506 (NI.11)), which are mortgage style repayment loans. They increase in line with inflation the maximum amounts which may be lent in relation to an academic year.

5752. Students – loans – repayments

EDUCATION (STUDENT LOANS) (REPAYMENT) (AMENDMENT) REGULATIONS (NORTHERN IRELAND) 2001, SR 2001 162; made under the Education (Student Support) (Northern Ireland) Order (SI 1998 1760 (NI.14)) Art.3, Art.8. In force: April 6, 2001; £2.00.

These Regulations amend the Education (Student Loans) (Repayment) Regulations (Northern Ireland) 2000 (SR 2000 121) to bring them more closely into line with the corresponding Income Tax (Employments) Regulations 1993 (SI 1993 744). They make amendments to permit notices given by the Board to an employer to cover more than one borrower and permit a tax collector to require a return of the amount in respect of student loans which an employer is required to pay for a specified period.

5753. Teachers – General Teaching Council for Northern Ireland – membership and constitiution

GENERAL TEACHING COUNCIL FOR NORTHERN IRELAND (CONSTITUTION) REGULATIONS (NORTHERN IRELAND) 2001, SR 2001 288; made under the Education (Northern Ireland) Order 1998 (SI 1998 1759 (NI.13)) Art.34, Sch.1 para.1. In force: October 1, 2001; £2.00.

These Regulations provide for the composition of the membership of the General Teaching Council for Northern Ireland and also make provision for the election of a chairman, the vacation of office by members and by the chairman in certain circumstances, and the filling of vacancies among members.

ELECTORAL PROCESS

5754. Elections – conduct of elections

REPRESENTATION OF THE PEOPLE (NORTHERN IRELAND) REGULATIONS 2001, SI 2001 400; made under the European Communities Act 1972 s.2; the European Parliamentary Elections Act 1978 Sch.1 para.2; the Representation of the People Act 1983 s.10A, s.13A, s.53, s.201, Sch.1 r.24, Sch.2; and the Representation of the People Act 1985 s.3. In force: February 16, 2001; £0.50.

These Regulations, which replace the Representation of the People (Northern Ireland) Regulations 1986 (SI 1986 1091 as amended by SI 1989 1304, SI 1990 561, SI 1991 1674, SI 1992 832, SI 1994 342, SI 1995 1948, SI 1997 967 and SI 1998 2870), are made in consequence of changes made by the Representation of the People Act 2000.

5755. Elections – conduct of elections – rolling registration

REPRESENTATION OF THE PEOPLE (NORTHERN IRELAND) (AMENDMENT) REGULATIONS 2001, SI 2001 1877; made under the Representation of the People Act 1983 s.53, s.201, Sch.2 para.10B. In force: May 11, 2001; £1.50.

These Regulations, which amend the Representation of the People (Northern Ireland) Regulations 2001 (SI 2001 400), ensure that the provisions empowering the supply of copies of the register extend to providing copies of any revised versions of the register in between the annual revision of the register. This is consequential on the introduction of the rolling register. In addition, they amend the definition of "data".

5756. Elections – date of next assembly poll

NORTHERN IRELAND (DATE OF NEXT ASSEMBLY POLL) ORDER 2001, SI 2001 3959; made under the Northern Ireland Act 1998 s.32. In force: March 20, 2003; £1.50.

Under the Northern Ireland Act 1998 s.32(3) the Secretary of State must propose a date for the next Assembly election if the period of six weeks specified in s.16(8) ends without a First and Deputy First Minister having been elected. The relevant period ended on November 3, 2001 without a successful election. But as a First and Deputy First Minister were elected on November 6, 2001 the Secretary of State, having consulted the parties in the Assembly, concluded that it would be in the best interests of Northern Ireland for the next Assembly election to be held on May 1, 2003, the date specified in s.31 of the Act. This Order accordingly directs that the election should be on that date and provides for the Assembly to be dissolved on March 21, 2003.

5757. Elections – Elections and Referendums Act 2000 Part IV – disapplication for Northern Ireland parties

See ELECTORAL PROCESS. §2095

5758. Elections – forms of canvass – registration

REPRESENTATION OF THE PEOPLE (FORM OF CANVASS) (NORTHERN IRELAND) REGULATIONS 2001, SI 2001 2725; made under the Representation of the People Act 1983 s.10, s.201. In force: August 9, 2001; £2.00.

Under the Representation of the People Act 1983 s.10, the Chief Electoral Officer as the registration officer is required to conduct an annual canvass in his registration area to ascertain the persons who are entitled to be or remain registered as parliamentary or local electors in that area. These Regulations specify a form for the purposes of that canvass.

5759. Elections – Northern Ireland Assembly

NORTHERN IRELAND ASSEMBLY (ELECTIONS) ORDER 2001, SI 2001 2599; made under the Northern Ireland Act 1998 s.34, s.35. In force: August 1, 2001; £6.50.

This Order, which revokes and replaces the New Northern Ireland Assembly (Elections) Order 1998 (SI 1998 1287) and amends the Representation of the People Act 1983, the Representation of the People Act 1985, the Elections (Northern Ireland) Act 1985, the Election Petition Rules 1964 (SR & O (NI) 1964 28), the Planning (Control of Advertisements) Regulations (Northern Ireland) 1992 (SR 1992 448) and the Representation of the People (Northern Ireland) Regulations 2001 (SR 2001 400) provides for the conduct of the election of members of the Northern Ireland Assembly.

5760. Elections – returning officers – expenses

PARLIAMENTARY ELECTIONS (RETURNING OFFICER'S CHARGES) (NORTHERN IRELAND) (AMENDMENT) ORDER 2001, SI 2001 1659; made under the Representation of the People Act 1983 s.29. In force: May 15, 2001; £1.50.

This Order, which amends the Parliamentary Elections (Returning Officer's Charges) (Northern Ireland) Order 1997 (SI 1997 774), increases the maximum recoverable amounts which the Chief Electoral Officer as the returning officer for each constituency at a parliamentary election in Northern Ireland is entitled to recover in respect of his expenses in connection with the election. He is also to be entitled to recover expenses for providing at polling stations the large version of the ballot paper and the prescribed device to assist voters with disabilities.

5761. Local elections – expenses and registration

LOCAL ELECTIONS (NORTHERN IRELAND) (AMENDMENT) ORDER 2001, SI 2001 417; made under the Northern Ireland Act 1998 s.84. In force: February 28, 2001; £2.50.

This Order, which makes provision with respect to local elections in Northern Ireland, amends the restrictions on the expenses which a third party may incur in respect of an election to bring the law in line with that under the Political Parties, Elections and Referendums Act 2000 and consequent on the changes to the method of registration made by the Representation of the People Act 2000 Sch.3. It makes changes to the law in respect of local election petitions, in respect of the incapacities following conviction for a corrupt or illegal practice at a local election, amends the local elections rules in the Electoral Law Act (Northern Ireland) 1962 Sch.5, amends the law on local elections to bring it into line with that on parliamentary elections.

EMPLOYMENT

5762. Benefits – statutory maternity pay – statutory sick pay

STATUTORY MATERNITY PAY (GENERAL) AND STATUTORY SICK PAY (GENERAL) (AMENDMENT) REGULATIONS (NORTHERN IRELAND) 2001, SR 2001 36; made under the Social Security Administration (Northern Ireland) Act 1992 s.107, s.122, s.124, s.165. In force: February 23, 2001; £1.75.

These Regulations provide that any person who contravenes or fails to comply with certain provisions of the Statutory Sick Pay (General) Regulations (Northern Ireland) 1982 (SR 1982 263) or of the Statutory Maternity Pay (General) Regulations (Northern Ireland) 1987 (SR 1987 30) is guilty of an offence. The Statutory Sick Pay (General) (Amendment) Regulations (Northern Ireland) 1986 (SR 1986 83) Reg.9, the Social Security (Miscellaneous Provisions) (Amendment) Regulations (Northern Ireland) 1991 (SR 1991 488) Reg.3, and the Social Security (Miscellaneous Provisions) (Amendment) Regulations (Northern Ireland) 1992 (SR 1992 83) Reg.4 are revoked.

5763. Codes of practice – trade union recognition – ballots

CODE OF PRACTICE (ACCESS TO WORKERS DURING RECOGNITION AND DERECOGNITION BALLOTS) (APPOINTED DAY) ORDER (NORTHERN IRELAND) 2001, SR 2001 208; made under the Industrial Relations (Northern Ireland) Order 1992 (SI 1992 807 (NI. 5)) Art.95. In force: June 17, 2001; £1.50.

This Order brings into operation the Code of Practice on Access to Workers during Recognition and Derecognition Ballots, which is issued by the Department of Higher and Further Education, Training and Employment under the Industrial Relations (Northern Ireland) Order 1992 (SI 1992 807 (NI. 5)). The Code of Practice shall be admissible in evidence in any proceedings before a Court or Industrial Tribunal or the Industrial Court and any provision of the Code which appears to the Court, Industrial Tribunal or Industrial Court to be relevant to any question arising in those proceedings shall be taken into account in determining that question.

5764. Discrimination – sex discrimination – burden of proof

SEX DISCRIMINATION (INDIRECT DISCRIMINATION AND BURDEN OF PROOF) REGULATIONS (NORTHERN IRELAND) 2001, SR 2001 282; made under the European Communities Act 1972 s.2. In force: August 20, 2001; £2.00.

These Regulations, which amend the Sex Discrimination (Northern Ireland) Order 1976 (SI 1976 1042 (NI.15)) and the Employment (Miscellaneous Provisions) (Northern Ireland) Order 1990 (SI 1990 246 (NI.2)), implement Council Directive 97/80 ([1998] OJ L14/6) concerning the burden of proof in cases of discrimination based on sex.

5765. Employees rights – increase of limits

EMPLOYMENT RIGHTS (INCREASE OF LIMITS) ORDER (NORTHERN IRELAND) 2001, SR 2001 54; made under the Employment Relations (Northern Ireland) Order 1999 (SI 1999 2790 (NI.9)) Art.33, Art.39. In force: March 11, 2001; £2.00.

This Order increases, from March 11, 2001, the limits applying to certain awards of industrial tribunals, and other amounts payable under the Trade Union and Labour Relations (Northern Ireland) Order 1995 (SI 1995 1980 (NI.12) and the Employment Rights (Northern Ireland) Order 1996 (SI 1996 1919 (NI.16). Orders under Art.33 are required to change the limits by the amount by which the retail prices index for the September immediately preceding the making of the Order is higher (or lower) than the index for the previous September.

5766. Equal opportunities – public bodies – specification

FAIR EMPLOYMENT (SPECIFICATION OF PUBLIC AUTHORITIES) (AMENDMENT) ORDER (NORTHERN IRELAND) 2001, SR 2001 421; made under the Fair Employment and Treatment (Northern Ireland) Order 1998 (SI 1998 3162 (NI.21)) Art.50, Art.51. In force: January 1, 2002; £2.00.

This Order amends the Fair Employment (Specification of Public Authorities) (No.2) Order (Northern Ireland) 2000 (SR 2000 371) which specifies a number of persons or bodies as public authorities for certain purposes under the Fair Employment and Treatment (Northern Ireland) Order 1998 (SI 1998 3162) and provides for the persons who are to be treated for such purposes as the employees of some of those authorities. The Order adds a number of persons or bodies as public authorities for certain purposes.

5767. Equal treatment – part time employees

PART-TIME WORKERS (PREVENTION OF LESS FAVOURABLE TREATMENT) REGULATIONS (NORTHERN IRELAND) 2001, SR 2001 319; made under the Employment Relations (Northern Ireland) Order 1999 (SI 1999 2790 (NI.9)) Art.21. In force: October 21, 2001; £1.75.

These Regulations make amendments to the Employment Rights (Northern Ireland) Order 1996 (SI 1996 1919) and the Industrial Tribunals (Northern Ireland) Order 1996 (SI 1996 1921) to secure that the powers that conciliation officers appointed by the Labour Relations Agency normally have to conciliate in relation to industrial tribunal claims apply to such claims brought under the Part-Time Workers (Prevention of Less Favourable Treatment) Regulations (Northern Ireland) 2000 (SR 2000 219) that a part-time worker has been treated less favourably than a worker who is not part-time. The amendments are also made in order to secure that the restrictions against contracting out of the rights in the Employment Order do not apply where a compromise agreement is made.

5768. Equality Commission for Northern Ireland – investigations – time limits

EQUALITY COMMISSION (TIME LIMITS) REGULATIONS (NORTHERN IRELAND) 2001, SR 2001 6; made under the Equality (Disability, etc.) (Northern Ireland) Order 2000 (SI 2000 1110 (NI.2)) Art.14, Sch.1 para.15, Sch.1 para.16, Sch.1 para.17, Sch.1 para.18, Sch.1 para.26. In force: February 26, 2001; £2.00.

These Regulations supplement the Equality (Disability, etc.) (Northern Ireland) Order 2000 (SI 2000 1110 (NI.2)) Sch.1 Part I by making provision for time limits in relation to the conduct of formal investigations by the Equality Commission for Northern Ireland and prescribe the periods at the end of which action plans become final under Sch.1 Part III of the 2000 Order.

5769. Freedom of movement – state security – Irish citizens denied appointment – public service posts

[British Nationality Act 1981 s.51 (4); EC Treaty Art.48 (now, after amendment, Art.39 EC).]

O and P were Irish citizens who had been rejected for positions they had applied for with the Northern Ireland Fire Authority and the Inland Revenue respectively. Both contended that the refusal infringed their right to freedom of movement under the EC Treaty Art.48 (now, after amendment, Art.39 EC). O and P sought judicial review of the decisions but this was refused on the ground that the positions had been correctly designated as public service posts under Art.48(4) and their contention that the requirement for allegiance to the State formed a separate condition for such appointments was also rejected. O and P appealed.

Held, dismissing the appeals, that in O's case the post of deputy chief fire officer was responsible for fighting fires at military bases and for liaison with the police, security services and government ministers so that amounted to employment in the public service of a particularly sensitive nature. As far as P was concerned, a revenue officer's duties included an element of safeguarding the general interests of the State, so that the Revenue properly regarded the post as also being in the public service for the purposes of Art.48(4). In both instances, post holders would be required to exercise decision-making powers that required allegiance to the state. Although Irish citizens were not aliens under the British Nationality Act 1981 s.51 (4) not every category of nationality was recognised or provided for under the Act and the Government could therefore bar Irish citizens from public service appointments. The decisions complained of were not *Wednesbury* unreasonable and the principle of proportionality did not apply to this type of administrative act, *R. v. Secretary of State for the Home Department, ex p. Brind* [1991] 1 A.C. 696, [1991] C.L.Y. 71 applied.

O'BOYLE'S APPLICATION, *Re*; PLUNKETT'S APPLICATION, *Re* [2000] Eu. L.R. 637, Carswell, L.C.J., CA (NI).

5770. Industrial tribunals – discrimination – procedure

INDUSTRIAL TRIBUNALS (1996 ORDER) (APPLICATION OF CONCILIATION PROVISIONS) ORDER (NORTHERN IRELAND) 2001, SR 2001 37; made under the Industrial Tribunals (Northern Ireland) Order 1996 (SI 1996 1921 (NI.18)) Art.20. In force: March 8, 2001; £1.75.

This Order directs the Employment Rights (Northern Ireland) Order 1996 (SI 1996 1919 (NI.16)) Art.112(1) be added to the list in the Industrial Tribunals (Northern Ireland) Order 1996 (SI 1996 1921) (NI.18) Art.20 with the effect of providing for the Labour Relations Agency to conciliate between the parties to proceedings before industrial tribunals are applied in relation to proceedings arising out of a contravention of the provision.

5771. Sex discrimination – police – female officer ordered not to carry out staff appraisals – meaning of "detriment"

[Sex Discrimination (Northern Ireland) Order 1976 (SI 1976 1042 (NI.15)) Art.8(2)(b).]

The Chief Constable appealed by way of case stated against an industrial tribunal decision that S, a Chief Inspector in the Traffic Branch, had been discriminated against on the grounds of her sex when she was instructed not to carry out staff appraisals by her superior. S claimed that she had been singled out, as the two male Chief Inspectors in the branch continued to carry out appraisals. The tribunal held that S had been less favourably treated than the two male officers. The Chief Constable challenged those findings on the ground that S was not discriminated against as she had not been subjected to a "detriment" in terms of the Sex Discrimination (Northern Ireland) Order 1976 Art.8(2)(b) as her removal had been the result of complaints raised with her superior by two officers and the Police Federation.

Held, allowing the appeal, that detriment for the purposes of Art.8(2)(b) required a substantial physical or financial loss that occurred as the result of discrimination, which the tribunal had failed to consider, *Lord Chancellor v. Coker* [2001] I.C.R. 507, [2001] 2 C.L. 227 and *Barclays Bank Plc v. Kapur (No.2)* [1995] I.R.L.R. 87, [1995] C.L.Y. 2028 followed. The carrying out of appraisals by Chief Inspectors was a practice in the traffic branch and S's removal had not caused a reduction in her rank or financial loss.

SHAMOON v. CHIEF CONSTABLE OF THE ROYAL ULSTER CONSTABULARY [2001] I.R.L.R. 520, Sir Robert Carswell, CA (NI).

5772. Trade unions – recognition – collective bargaining

TRADE UNION RECOGNITION (METHOD OF COLLECTIVE BARGAINING) ORDER (NORTHERN IRELAND) 2001, SR 2001 39; made under the Trade Union and Labour Relations (Northern Ireland) Order1995 (SI1995 1980 (NI.12)) Sch.1A para.168. In force: March 8, 2001; £2.50.

This Order specifies the method by which collective bargaining might be carried out for the purpose of certain provisions of the Trade Union and Labour Relations (Northern Ireland) Order 1995 (SI 1995 1980 (NI.12)). The specified method is required to be taken into account by the Industrial Court when, following an application for trade union recognition, it is required to specify a method by which the union and employer concerned are to conduct collective bargaining.

5773. Trade unions – recognition – collective bargaining – ballots

RECOGNITION AND DERECOGNITION BALLOTS (QUALIFIED PERSONS) ORDER (NORTHERN IRELAND) 2001, SR 2001 38; made under the Trade Union and Labour Relations (Northern Ireland) Order1995 (SI1995 1980 (NI.12)) Sch.1A para.25, para.117. In force: March 8, 2001; £1.75.

This Order specifies conditions which must be satisfied for an individual or partnership to be appointed as a "qualified independent person" to conduct a ballot where the Industrial Court arranges a ballot on the recognition or derecognition of a trade union for collective bargaining under the Trade Union and Labour Relations (Northern Ireland) Order 1995 (SI 1995 1980 (NI.12).

ENVIRONMENT

5774. Ancient monuments – conservation

HISTORIC MONUMENTS (CLASS CONTENTS) ORDER (NORTHERN IRELAND) 2001, SR 2001 101; made under the Historic Monuments and Archaeological Objects (Northern Ireland) Order 1995 (SR 1995 1625 (NI.9)) Art.5. In force: April 23, 2001; £2.00.

This Order grants scheduled monument consent under the Historic Monuments and Archaeological Objects (Northern Ireland) Order 1995 (SI 1995 1625 (NI.9)) for the execution of certain classes or descriptions of works. The works for which consent is granted comprise certain agricultural, horticultural and forestry works of the same kind as those carried out lawfully in the same location and on the same spot within that location during the previous three years; certain works for the repair or maintenance to a canal; certain works for the repair or maintenance of machinery; minimum works urgently necessary in the interests of safety or health subject to giving subsequent notice in writing as soon as reasonably practicable; and certain works carried out in accordance with agreements made between the occupier of a scheduled monument and the Department under Art.19 of the Order.

5775. Environmental impact assessments – uncultivated land and semi-natural areas

ENVIRONMENTAL IMPACT ASSESSMENT (UNCULTIVATED LAND AND SEMI-NATURAL AREAS) REGULATIONS (NORTHERN IRELAND) 2001, SR 2001 435; made under the European Communities Act 1972 s.2. In force: February 11, 2002; £5.50.

These Regulations implement, in relation to projects for the use of uncultivated land and semi-natural areas in Northern Ireland for intensive agricultural purposes, Council Directive 85/337 ([1985] OJ L175/40) on the assessment of the effects of certain public and private projects on the environment and Council Directive 1992/43 ([1992] OJ L1206/7) on the conservation of natural habitats and of wild fauna and flora insofar as it applies to such projects. The Regulations prohibit a relevant project from being carried out without consent first having been obtained from the Secretary of State, entitles the prospective applicant for consent to obtain an opinion from the Secretary of State as to the information which will be required as part of the environmental statement to accompany the application for consent and requires the specified environmental bodies referred to provide any relevant information in their possession to the applicant for consent.

5776. Environmental protection – countryside management

COUNTRYSIDE MANAGEMENT REGULATIONS (NORTHERN IRELAND) 2001, SR 2001 43; made under the European Communities Act 1972 s.2; and the Agriculture (Conservation Grants) (Northern Ireland) Order 1995 (SI 1995 3212 (NI.21)) Art.3. In force: March 20, 2001; £4.50.

These Regulations, which revoke, with savings, and replace the Countryside Management Regulations (Northern Ireland) 1999 (SR 1999 208), supplement certain provisions of Council Regulation 1257/1999 ([1999] OJ L160/80) on support for rural development from the European Agricultural Guidance and Guarantee Fund (EAGGF) and amending and repealing certain Regulations. They include provisions to meet the requirements of Commission Regulation 1750/1999 ([1999] OJ L214/31) which lays down detailed rules for the application of Council Regulation 1257/1999. They provide for payment of a grant in respect of an undertaking to follow certain general environmental conditions and to carry out at least one specified activity, specify the requirements in relation to applications, specify restrictions on the acceptance of applications, make provision for beneficiaries under the Habitat Improvement Regulations (Northern Ireland) 1995 SR 1995 134) and the Moorland (Livestock Extensification) Regulations (Northern Ireland) 1995 (SR 1995 239) to substitute for the unexpired period of an undertaking under any of those Regulations, an undertaking to which these Regulations apply, specify the maximum payment rate in respect of each activity which is the subject of an undertaking, permit the Department to refuse applications for grant in the event that the financial resources available for grant under the Regulations are insufficient, specify the conditions which apply where there is a change of occupation of the land to which an undertaking relates, impose an obligation on applicants to permit entry and inspection, and provide for the withholding and recovery of grant, recovery of interest and the imposition of penalties.

5777. Pollution control – registers – consent for discharges – application procedure

CONTROL OF POLLUTION (APPLICATIONS AND REGISTERS) REGULATIONS (NORTHERN IRELAND) 2001, SR 2001 284; made under the Water (Northern Ireland) Order 1999 (SI 1999 662 (NI.6)) Art.30, Art.61, Sch.1 para.1, Sch.1 para.2, Sch.1 para.4, Sch.1 para.7. In force: August 24, 2001; £2.00.

These Regulations prescribe the procedure to be followed in relation to applications for consents under the Water (Northern Ireland) Order 1999 (SI 1999 662 (NI.6)) Part II. They provide for the advertising of applications for discharge consents, or the variation of a consent in one or more newspapers circulating in the locality in which the consent is issued and the content of such advertisement, for the timing of the publication of such advertising and for the procedure to be followed when a discharge consent is granted. The Regulations also prescribe the particulars to be entered in water pollution control registers.

5778. Smoke control – authorisation of fireplaces – exemptions

SMOKE CONTROL AREAS (EXEMPTED FIREPLACES) (AMENDMENT) REGULATIONS (NORTHERN IRELAND) 2001, SR 2001 211; made under the Clean Air (Northern Ireland) Order 1981 (SI 1981 158 (NI. 4)) Art.17. In force: July 2, 2001; £1.75.

The Clean Air (Northern Ireland) Order 1981 (SI 1981 158 (NI. 4)) Art.17 generally prohibits the emission of smoke in smoke control areas. Under that Article, the Department may exempt certain classes of fireplace from the provision if it is satisfied they can be used for burning fuel other than authorised fuels without producing any smoke or a substantial quantity of smoke. These Regulations amend the Smoke Control Areas (Exempted Fireplaces) Regulations (Northern Ireland) 1999 (SR 1999 289), which prescribed those fireplaces exempted from the provisions, by exempting two additional classes of fireplace.

5779. Waste and Contaminated Land (Northern Ireland) Order 1997 (SI 1997 2778 (NI.19)) – Commencement No.5 Order

WASTE AND CONTAMINATED LAND (1997 ORDER) (COMMENCEMENT NO.5) ORDER (NORTHERN IRELAND) 2001, SR 2001 40 (C.2); made under the Waste and Contaminated Land (Northern Ireland) Order 1997 (SI 1997 2778 (NI.19)) Art.1. Commencement details: bringing into force various provisions of the Order on March 1, 2001; £1.75.

This Order brings certain provisions of the Waste and Contaminated Land (Northern Ireland) Order 1997 (SI 1997 2778 (NI.19) into force on March 1, 2001.

EQUITY

5780. Trustee Act (Northern Ireland) 2001 (c.14)

This Act amends the law relating to trustees and persons having the investment powers of trustees.

EUROPEAN UNION

5781. Northern Ireland – amendment of enactment

NORTHERN IRELAND ACT 1998 (AMENDMENT OF ENACTMENT) ORDER 2001, SI 2001 3675; made under the Northern Ireland Act 1998 s.86. In force: November 15, 2001 in accordance with Art.1; £1.50.

This Order amends the European Communities (Amendment) Act 1993 s.6 by adding members of the Northern Ireland Assembly to the list of persons who may be proposed for membership of the Committee of the Regions constituted under Art.198a of the EC Treaty.

5782. Northern Ireland – transfer of functions – Common Agricultural Policy

NORTHERN IRELAND ACT 1998 (TRANSFER OF FUNCTIONS) ORDER 2001, SI 2001 3676; made under the Northern Ireland Act 1998 s.86. In force: in accordance with Art.1; £1.50.

This Order transfers from the Secretary of State for Northern Ireland to the Department of Agriculture and Rural Development all the non-statutory functions with which the Intervention Board for Agricultural Produce was charged in relation to Northern Ireland prior to the abolition of that Board. The functions are mainly related to the Common Agricultural Policy of the European Union.

EXTRADITION

5783. Arrest – false imprisonment – accused facing charges other than those stated in extradition warrant

[Backing of Warrants (Republic of Ireland) Act 1965 s.2(2); Supression of Terrorism Act 1978 s.1 (1).]

M sought judicial review of a resident magistrate's decision that he should be delivered into the custody of the gardai. M had been brought before the court under the Backing of Warrants (Republic of Ireland) Act 1965 on the basis of three warrants issued in the Irish Republic concerned with alleged firearms offences. However, after the magistrate's decision it emerged that the gardai intended to arrest M on a charge of false imprisonment and M contended that this latter offence was of a political character. Section 2(2)(a) of the 1965 Act stipulated that an extradition order was not to be made for political offences and s.2(2)(b) provided that no order should be made if it was believed that an accused could be prosecuted for such an offence having been extradited. The Suppression of Terrorism Act 1978 s.1(1) restricted the number of political offences for which extradition could be denied, so that false imprisonment was no longer political in nature. M argued that this only applied where a warrant had actually been issued under s.2(2)(a) and not in respect of s.2(2)(b) of the 1965 Act.

Held, refusing the application, that the 1978 Act applied to both s.2(2)(a) and (b) of the 1965 Act, *Ismail, Re* [1999] 1 A.C. 320, [1998] C.L.Y. 2357 applied. A person was "accused" of an offence in terms of s.2(2)(b) of the 1965 Act where the court was satisfied that there were substantial grounds for believing that they could be prosecuted for another offence in the future. On the facts, therefore, M was accordingly an accused person under the 1978 Act *Belgium v. Postlethwaite* [1988] A.C. 924, [1987] C.L.Y. 1703 considered.

McCRORY'S APPLICATION FOR JUDICIAL REVIEW, *Re* [2000] N.I. 487, Carswell, L.C.J., QBD (NI).

FAMILY LAW

5784. Adoption (Intercountry Aspects) Act (Northern Ireland) 2001 (c.11)

This Act makes provision for giving effect to the Convention on Protection of Children and Co-operation in respect of Intercountry Adoption concluded at the Hague on May 29, 1993 and to make further provision in relation to adoptions with an international element.

5785. Adoption (Intercountry Aspects) Act (Northern Ireland) 2001 (c.11) – Commencement No.1 Order

ADOPTION (INTERCOUNTRY ASPECTS) ACT (NORTHERN IRELAND) 2001 (COMMENCEMENT NO.1) ORDER (NORTHERN IRELAND) 2001, SR 2001 322 (C.15); made under the Adoption (Intercountry Aspects) Act (Northern Ireland) 2001 s.16. In force: bringing into operation various provisions of the 2001 Act on October 1, 2001; £1.50.

This Order brings into force specified sections of the Adoption (Intercountry Aspects) Act (Northern Ireland) 2001.

5786. Child support – child maintenance – variation

CHILD SUPPORT (VARIATIONS) REGULATIONS (NORTHERN IRELAND) 2001, SR 2001 20; made under the Child Support (Northern Ireland) Order 1991 (SI 1991 2628 (NI.23)) Art.28A, Art.28B, Art.28C, Art.28E, Art.28F, Art.28G, Art.47, Art.48, Sch.4A para.1, Sch.4A para.2, Sch.4A para.4, Sch.4A para.5, Sch.4B para.2, Sch.4B para.3, Sch.4B para.4, Sch.4B para.5, Sch.4B para.6. In force: in accordance with Reg.1 (1); £6.00.

These Regulations provide for variations to the rate of child maintenance payable under the Child Support (Northern Ireland) Order 1991 (SI 1991 2628 (NI.23)) consequent upon the introduction of changes to the child support system made by the Child Support, Pensions and Social Security Act (Northern Ireland) 2000. Subject to savings for transitional purposes these Regulations revoke the Child Support Departure Direction and Consequential Amendments Regulations (Northern Ireland) 1996 (SR 1996 54). The Regulations set out the procedure for making and determining applications for variations, give details of what constitutes expenses for the purposes of the grounds for variations, provide for the effective date of maintenance calculations which take account of variations and prescribe the amount payable under the regular payments condition.

5787. Child support – collection and enforcement

CHILD SUPPORT (COLLECTION AND ENFORCEMENT AND MISCELLANEOUS AMENDMENTS) REGULATIONS (NORTHERN IRELAND) 2001, SR 2001 15; made under the Child Support (Northern Ireland) Order 1991 (SI 1991 2628 (NI.23)) Art.28J, Art.29, Art.30, Art.31, Art.32, Art.34, Art.36, Art.37, Art.37A, Art.38, Art.38A, Art.44, Art.47, Art.48. In force: in accordance with Reg.1 (2) (3); £3.00.

These Regulations amend the Child Support (Arrears, Interest and Adjustment of Maintenance Assessments) Regulations (Northern Ireland) 1992 (SR 1992 342), the Child Support (Collection and Enforcement) Regulations (Northern Ireland) 1992 (SR 1992 390), the Child Support (Collection and Enforcement of Other Forms of Maintenance) Regulations (Northern Ireland) 1992 (SR 1992 465), and revoke, with savings, the Child Support Fees Regulations (Northern Ireland)

1993 (SR 1993 73), to reflect amendments made to the Child Support (Northern Ireland) Order 1991 (SI 1991 2628 (NI.23)) by the Child Support, Pensions and Social Security Act (Northern Ireland) 2000.

5788. Child support – consequential amendments – transitional provisions

CHILD SUPPORT (CONSEQUENTIAL AMENDMENTS AND TRANSITIONAL PROVISIONS) REGULATIONS (NORTHERN IRELAND) 2001, SR 2001 29; made under the Child Support, Pensions and Social Security Act (Northern Ireland) 2000 s.28. In force: in accordance with Reg.1 (1) (2); £2.00.

These Regulations amend the Social Security (Guardian's Allowances) Regulations (Northern Ireland) 1975 (SR 1975 98), the Income Support (General) Regulations (Northern Ireland) 1987 (SR 1987 459), the Jobseeker's Allowance Regulations (Northern Ireland) 1996 (SR 1996 198), the the Social Security Benefits (Maintenance Payments and Consequential Amendments) Regulations (Northern Ireland) 1996 (SR 1996 202), the New Deal (Miscellaneous Provisions) Order (Northern Ireland) 1998 (SI 1998 127) and the Social Security and Child Support (Decisions and Appeals) Regulations (Northern Ireland) 1999 (SR 1999 278) to reflect changes in terminology in the Child Support (Northern Ireland) Order 1991 (SI 1991 2628 (NI.23)) in consequence of amendments to it by the Child Support, Pensions and Social Security Act (Northern Ireland) 2000.

5789. Child support – decisions and appeals

SOCIAL SECURITY AND CHILD SUPPORT (DECISIONS AND APPEALS) (AMENDMENT) REGULATIONS (NORTHERN IRELAND) 2001, SR 2001 23; made under the Child Support (Northern Ireland) Order 1991 (SI 1991 2628 (NI.23)) Art.18, Art.19, Art.28G, Art.47, Art.48; and the Child Support, Pensions and Social Security Act (Northern Ireland) 2000 s.28. In force: in accordance with Reg.1 (1); £4.00.

These Regulations, which amend the Social Security and Child Support (Decisions and Appeals) Regulations (Northern Ireland) 1999 (SR 1999 162), provide for the decision-making process under the Child Support (Northern Ireland) Order 1991 (SI 1991 2628 (NI.23)) consequent upon the introduction of changes to the child support system made by the Child Support, Pensions and Social Security Act (Northern Ireland) 2000. The Child Support (Arrears, Interest and Adjustment of Maintenance Assessments) Regulations (Northern Ireland) 1992 (SR 1992 342) Reg.10(2)(3) and Part IV, the Child Support and Income Support (Amendment) Regulations (Northern Ireland) 1995 (SR 1995 162) Reg.3(4) and the Social Security (1998 Order) (Commencement No.6 and Transitional Provisions) Order (Northern Ireland) 1999 (SR 1999 246) Art.10(4) (c) (d) (5) (6) are revoked.

5790. Child support – information, evidence and disclosure – maintenance arrangements – jurisdiction

CHILD SUPPORT (INFORMATION, EVIDENCE AND DISCLOSURE AND MAINTENANCE ARRANGEMENTS AND JURISDICTION) (AMENDMENT) REGULATIONS (NORTHERN IRELAND) 2001, SR 2001 16; made under the Child Support (Northern Ireland) Order 1991 (SI 1991 2628 (NI.23)) Art.7, Art.9, Art.12, Art.16, Art.41, Art.47, Art.48, Art.50. In force: in accordance with Reg.1 (1); £2.50.

These Regulations, which amend the Child Support (Information, Evidence and Disclosure) Regulations (Northern Ireland) 1992 (SR 1992 339) and the Child Support (Maintenance Arrangements and Jurisdiction) Regulations (Northern Ireland) 1992 (SR 1992 466) mainly consequent upon the introduction of the changes to the child support system made by the Child Support, Pensions and Social Security Act (Northern Ireland) 2000, come into operation at different times for different cases according to the dates on which provisions of the Act which are relevant to these Regulations are commenced for the different cases.

5791. Child support – maintenance arrears – voluntary payments

CHILD SUPPORT (VOLUNTARY PAYMENTS) REGULATIONS (NORTHERN IRELAND) 2001, SR 2001 21; made under the Child Support (Northern Ireland) Order 1991 (SI 1991 2628 (NI.23)) Art.28J, Art.48. In force: in accordance with Reg.1 (1); £1.75.

These Regulations, which are made pursuant to the Child Support (Northern Ireland) Order 1991 (SI 1991 2628 (NI.23)) Art.28J, provide for the Department for Social Development to offset against child support maintenance arrears, or to adjust a maintenance calculation to take account of, voluntary payments. The Regulations, define a "voluntary payment" by reference to Reg.3 and 4, provide that to be a voluntary payment, a payment must be made on or after the effective date of the maintenance calculation which is governed by the Child Support (Maintenance Calculation Procedure) Regulations (Northern Ireland) 2001 (SR 2001 18), define the types of payments which may count as voluntary payments and define the evidence or verification of such payments which the Department may require to be provided.

5792. Child support – maintenance assessments – transitional provisions

CHILD SUPPORT (TRANSITIONAL PROVISIONS) REGULATIONS (NORTHERN IRELAND) 2001, SR 2001 19; made under the Child Support, Pensions and Social Security Act (Northern Ireland) 2000 s.28; and the Child Support (Northern Ireland) Order 1991 (SI 1991 2628 (NI.23)) Art.18, Art.19, Art.47, Art.48. In force: in accordance with Reg.1; £5.50.

These Regulations make transitional provisions in consequence of the amendments made to the Child Support (Northern Ireland) Order 1991 (SI 1991 2628 (NI.23)) by the Child Support, Pensions and Social Security Act (Northern Ireland) 2000. They provide for decision making and appeals in relation to maintenance assessments made with effect before the date the new child support system comes into force for new cases, specify those cases where a transitional amount, instead of the new amount is payable during a transitional period beginning on the case conversion date, for a maximum transitional amount to be payable of 30 per cent of the non-resident parent's income and provide for the dispute of provisions of the Order to apply to the conversion decision when made.

5793. Child support – maintenance calculation – procedure

CHILD SUPPORT (MAINTENANCE CALCULATION PROCEDURE) REGULATIONS (NORTHERN IRELAND) 2001, SR 2001 17; made under the Child Support (Northern Ireland) Order 1991 (SI 1991 2628 (NI.23)) Art.3, Art.4, Art.8, Art.14, Art.43, Art.47, Art.48, Sch.1 para.11, Sch.1 para.14. In force: in accordance with Reg.1 (1); £5.50.

These Regulations, which revoke, with savings, the Child Support (Maintenance Assessment Procedure) Regulations (Northern Ireland) 1992 (SR 1992 340), provide for various procedural matters relating to an application for a maintenance calculation under the Child Support (Northern Ireland) Order 1991 (SI 1991 2628 (NI.23)), and make provision in respect of effective dates of calculations and of reduced benefit decisions, consequent upon the introduction of changes to the child support system made by the Child Support, Pensions and Social Security Act (Northern Ireland) 2000. They provide for multiple applications for a maintenance calculation, provide for notice to be given to the non resident parent and any other relevant person when an effective application for a maintenance calculation has been made or treated as made by the person with care, provide for the procedure on the death of a qualifying child, prescribe the default rate payable when a default maintenance decision is made and make provision as to the amount and duration of reduces benefit decisions.

5794. Child support – maintenance calculation – special cases

CHILD SUPPORT (MAINTENANCE CALCULATIONS AND SPECIAL CASES) REGULATIONS (NORTHERN IRELAND) 2001, SR 2001 18; made under the Child Support (Northern Ireland) Order 1991 (SI 1991 2628 (NI.23)) Art.16, Art.39, Art.47, Art.48, Sch.1 para.3, Sch.1 para.4, Sch.1 para.5, Sch.1 para.7, Sch.1 para.9, Sch.1 para.10, Sch.1 para.10C. In force: in accordance with Reg.1 (1); £5.50.

These Regulations provide for various matters relating to the calculation of child support maintenance under the Child Support (Northern Ireland) Order 1991 (SI 1991 2628 (NI.23)) and also make provision for special cases under the Order, consequent upon the introduction of changes to the child support system made by the Child Support, Pensions and Social Security Act (Northern Ireland) 2000. The Regulations revoke the Child Support (Maintenance Assessments and Special Cases) Regulations (Northern Ireland) 1992 (SI 1992 341), prescribe the method of calculating the reduced rate of child support maintenance, prescribe the circumstances for which the rate payable is nil, provide a general rule for adjusting the child support maintenance payable following apportionment and prescribe the circumstances in which cases are to be treated as special cases for the purposes of the Order.

5795. Child support – miscellaneous amendments

CHILD SUPPORT (MISCELLANEOUS AMENDMENTS) REGULATIONS (NORTHERN IRELAND) 2001, SR 2001 197; made under the Child Support, Pensions and Social Security Act (Northern Ireland) 2000 s.28. In force: May 31, 2001; £1.50.

These Regulations amend the Child Support (Collection and Enforcement and Miscellaneous Amendments) Regulations (Northern Ireland) 2001 (SR 2001 15) to provide for Reg.3 to come into operation on the date on which these Regulations come into operation.

5796. Child support – temporary compensation scheme – recovery of arrears

CHILD SUPPORT (TEMPORARY COMPENSATION PAYMENT SCHEME) REGULATIONS (NORTHERN IRELAND) 2001, SR 2001 12; made under the Child Support, Pensions and Social Security Act (Northern Ireland) 2000 s.26. In force: February 19, 2001; £2.00.

These Regulations, which provide for a temporary compensation scheme made under Child Support, Pensions and Social Security Act (Northern Ireland) 2000 s.26 in certain cases where there has been a delay in the making of a maintenance assessment under the Child Support (Northern Ireland) Order 1991 (SI 1991 2628 (NI.23)) leading to arrears of child support maintenance, provide the prescribed date for the purposes of s.26 of the Act. They set out additional cases to which the scheme will apply, prescribe the circumstances in which the Department for Social Development may agree that the absent parent will not be required to pay the whole of the arrears due under a maintenance assessment and in which the Department will not seek to recover any of the arrears, and prescribe the terms of the agreement when the scheme shall apply.

5797. Child support – variation applications

CHILD SUPPORT (VARIATIONS) (MODIFICATION OF STATUTORY PROVISIONS) REGULATIONS (NORTHERN IRELAND) 2001, SR 2001 24; made under the Child Support (Northern Ireland) Order 1991 (SI 1991 2628 (NI.23)) Art.28G. In force: January 31, 2001; £1.75.

These Regulations are made in connection with applications for variations to the rate of child support maintenance payable under the Child Support (Northern Ireland) Order 1991 (SI 1991 2628 (NI.23)) consequent upon the introduction of changes to the child support system made by the Child Support, Pensions and Social Security Act (Northern Ireland) 2000.

5798. Family Law Act (Northern Ireland) 2001 (c.12)

This Act makes further provision for the acquisition of parental responsibility under Children (Northern Ireland) Order 1995 (SI 1995 755 (NI. 2)) Art.7; and to provide for certain presumptions of parentage and for tests to determine parentage.

5799. Family proceedings – matrimonial jurisdiction and judgments

EUROPEAN COMMUNITIES (MATRIMONIAL JURISDICTION AND JUDGMENTS) (NORTHERN IRELAND) REGULATIONS 2001, SI 2001 660; made under the European Communities Act 1972 s.2. In force: March 30, 2001; £1.75.

These Regulations amend certain provisions of domestic law to clarify the relationship between those provisions and the provisions of Council Regulation 1347/2000 ([2000] OJ L160/19) on jurisdiction and the recognition and enforcement of judgments in matrimonial matters and in matters of parental responsibility for children of both spouses. The Regulations make amendments to the Matrimonial Causes (Northern Ireland) Order 1978 (SI 1978 1045 (NI.15)) concerning the jurisdiction in Northern Ireland to entertain proceedings for divorce, judicial separation and nullity of marriage, and the power of those courts to stay such proceedings. In addition, they make amendments to the Family Law Act 1986 concerning the jurisdiction of courts in Northern Ireland to make orders in or in connection with matrimonial proceedings with respect to children of both parties, and the rule as to recognition in Northern Ireland of divorces, annulments and judicial separations.

FINANCE

5800. Budget (No.2) Act (Northern Ireland) 2001 (c.16)

This Act authorises the issue out of the Consolidated Fund of certain sums for the service of the year ending March 31, 2002; to appropriate those sums for the specified purposes; to authorise the Department of Finance and Personnel to borrow on the credit of the appropriated sums; to authorise the use for the public service of certain resources (including accruing resources) for the year ending March 31, 2002; and to repeal spent enactments.

This Act comes into force on July 20, 2001.

5801. Mortgages – "all monies" mortgage – security for judgment debt – doctrine of merger disapplied

[Consumer Credit Act 1974 Part V.]

NB operated a current account and an "all monies" mortgage account for M. Although the mortgage included all continuing advances, it expressly excluded loans under a regulated consumer credit agreement covered by the Consumer Credit Act 1974 Part V. M defaulted on the mortgage and NB commenced possession proceedings by the way of originating summons which included a personal loan that was not secured by the mortgage but which was the subject of a judgment debt. NB accepted that the loan was unsecured and not covered by the mortgage, but argued that the "all monies" mortgage included judgment debts. This contention was not accepted at first instance, where a possession order was made in respect of the premises forming the subject of the mortgage charge. NB appealed and sought a declaration that the mortgage secured the judgment debt.

Held, dismissing the appeal, that the mortgage did not include debts due under an unsecured loan. An "all monies" mortgage did not provide security for a judgment debt under the doctrine of merger as this would be contrary to the intention of the 1974 Act, *Ealing LBC v. El Isaac* [1980] 1 W.L.R. 932, [1980] C.L.Y. 410 applied.

NORTHERN BANK LTD v. McKINSTRY [2001] N.I. 130, Girvan, J., Ch D (NI).

FINANCIAL SERVICES

5802. Financial Investigations (Northern Ireland) Order 2001 (SI 2001 1866 (NI.1))

This Order, which amends the Proceeds of Crime (Northern Ireland) Order 1996 (SI 1996 1299 (NI.9)), extends specified Articles to cover investigations into the extent or whereabouts of property held or transferred within the previous six years by or to a person who has benefited from conduct to which Art.49 applies. It also extends Art.49 to allow a senior customs officer to apply for a financial investigator to be appointed and to allow a senior police officer or a senior customs officer to apply for a police officer or customs officer to be authorised to exercise certain powers to require information from financial businesses and solicitors. In addition, they extend the power to require information to persons carrying on relevant financial business within the meaning of the Money Laundering Regulations 1993 (SI 1993 1933).

FISHERIES

5803. Fish farms – fish farming scheme – revocation

ASSISTANCE OF FISH FARMING SCHEME (REVOCATION) ORDER (NORTHERN IRELAND) 2001, SR 2001 145; made under the Fish Industry Act (Northern Ireland) 1972 s.6. In force: May 1, 2001; £1.50.

This Order revokes, with savings, the Assistance of Fish Farming Scheme (Northern Ireland) 1973 (SR & O 1973 500).

5804. Fisheries – conservation – lobster – revocation

LOBSTER (CONSERVATION OF STOCKS) (REVOCATION) REGULATIONS (NORTHERN IRELAND) 2001, SR 2001 144; made under the Fisheries Act (Northern Ireland) 1966 s.124. In force: May 7, 2001; £1.50.

These Regulations revoke the Lobster (Conservation of Stocks) Regulations (Northern Ireland) 1997 (SR 1997 154) which provided that all berried or sexually mature female lobsters marked with a V notch or mutilated to hide or obliterate a V notch are returned to the sea.

5805. Fisheries (Amendment) Act (Northern Ireland) 2001 (c.4)

This Act amends the Fisheries Act (Northern Ireland) 1966.

This Act received Royal Assent on March 20, 2001 and comes into force on March 20, 2001.

5806. Fishing – byelaws – amendments

FISHERIES (AMENDMENT) BYELAWS (NORTHERN IRELAND) 2001, SR 2001 433; made under the Fisheries Act (Northern Ireland) 1966 s.26, s.37, s.89, s.95. In force: January 1, 2002; £2.00.

These Byelaws amend the Fisheries Byelaws (Northern Ireland) 1997 (SR 1997 425) by reinserting Byelaw 72 concerning the annual close season for angling for salmon, trout, and rainbow trout which was previously revoked by the Fisheries (Amendment No.3) Byelaws (Northern Ireland) 2000 (SR 2000 364). In addition, they introduce new fishing rod licences, and the duties that apply to them, for disabled anglers.

5807. Fishing – close seasons – Foyle – Carlingford

FOYLE AREA AND CARLINGFORD AREA (CLOSE SEASONS FOR ANGLING) REGULATIONS 2001, SR 2001 160; made under the Foyle Fisheries Act 1952 s.13, s.28; and the Foyle Fisheries Act (Northern Ireland) 1952 s.13, s.27. In force: May 14, 2001; £1.75.

These Regulations, which revoke and replace the Foyle Area (Close Seasons for Angling) Regulations 1987 (SR 1987 344), specify the close seasons for angling for salmon and trout in the waters of the Foyle and Carlingford Areas.

5808. Fishing – controls – Foyle – Carlingford

FOYLE AREA AND CARLINGFORD AREA (ANGLING) REGULATIONS 2001, SR 2001 158; made under the Foyle Fisheries Act 1952 s.13; and the Foyle Fisheries Act (Northern Ireland) 1952 s.13. In force: May 14, 2001; £2.00.

These Regulations, which revoke and replace the Foyle Area (Angling) Regulations 1999 (SR 1999 182), specify the methods of angling which are permitted in certain waters in the Foyle Area. They prohibit the use of prawns or shrimps as bait, prohibit the use of certain vegetable based bait, maggots or worms while spinning, restrict the use of ground bait, the use of boats for angling on certain waters and restrict the number and length of fish which may be retained in any one day. In addition, the Regulations lift the prohibition on angling on the River Foyle between Islandmore in County Donegal and Magheramason in County Tyrone.

5809. Fishing – gill tags – export restrictions – byelaws

FISHERIES (TAGGING AND LOGBOOK) BYELAWS (NORTHERN IRELAND) 2001, SR 2001 291; made under the Fisheries Act (Northern Ireland) 1996 s.26, s.37. In force: September 3, 2001; £3.00.

These Byelaws require every person licensed pursuant to byelaws made under the Fisheries Act (Northern Ireland) 1966 to fish for wild salmon and sea trout to affix a gill tag to every wild salmon or sea trout captured and retained by him. They provide for the issue of gill tags to such persons, for the removal of a tag affixed to a wild salmon or sea trout only in specified circumstances and prohibit the affixing of a tag to any wild salmon or sea trout unlawfully captured. In addition, the Byelaws prohibit the sale, export or transhipment at sea of any wild salmon or sea trout which has not had a tag affixed to it, the possession of any captured and retained wild salmon or sea trout which does not have a tag affixed to it, the forging or alteration of tags, the sale of wild salmon or sea trout as being farmed salmon or sea trout and the giving of false information to obtain a tag.

5810. Fishing – licences – Foyle – Carlingford

FOYLE AREA AND CARLINGFORD AREA (LICENSING OF FISHING ENGINES) REGULATIONS 2001, SR 2001 397; made under the Foyle Fisheries Act 1952 s.13; and the Foyle Fisheries Act (Northern Ireland) 1952 s.13. In force: January 1, 2002; £2.00.

These Regulations revoke the Foyle Area (Licensing of Fishing Engines) Regulations 1976 (SI 1976 362), the Foyle Area (Licensing of Fishing Engines) (Amendment No.2) Regulations 1985 (SR 1985 341), the Foyle Area (Licensing of Fishing Engines) (Amendment No.2) Regulations 1989 (SR 1989 458), the Foyle Area (Licensing of Fishing Engines) (Amendment No.2) Regulations 1989 (SR 1989 461) and the Foyle Area (Licensing of Fishing Engines) (Amendment No.2) Regulations 1999 (SR 1999 485). They introduce coarse fishing licences in the Foyle and Carlingford Areas and prescribe fees both in sterling and euros to take account of the introduction of the euro in the Moville and Louth Areas.

5811. Fishing – tagging and logbook – Foyle – Carlingford

FOYLE AREA AND CARLINGFORD AREA (TAGGING AND LOGBOOK) REGULATIONS 2001, SR 2001 159; made under the Foyle Fisheries Act 1952 s.13; and the Foyle Fisheries Act (Northern Ireland) 1952 s.13. In force: May 14, 2001; £3.00.

These Regulations require every person who is licensed under the Foyle Fisheries Act 1952 or the Foyle Fisheries Act (Northern Ireland) 1952 to fish for wild salmon and sea trout to affix a gill tag to every wild salmon or sea trout captured and retained by him.

5812. Shellfish – emergency prohibitions – amnesic shellfish poisoning – scallops
See FOOD. §5831 - §5833
See FOOD. §5836

5813. Shellfish – emergency prohibitions – diarrhetic shellfish poisoning – scallops
See FOOD. §5834 - §5835
See FOOD. §5837

5814. Ships – fishing vessels – grants – decommissioning
FISHING VESSELS (DECOMMISSIONING) SCHEME (NORTHERN IRELAND) 2001, SR 2001 349; made under the Agriculture and Fisheries (Financial Assistance) (Northern Ireland) Order 1987 (SI 1987 166 (NI.1)) Art.17. In force: November 19, 2001; £2.50.

This Scheme provides for the making of grants by the Department of Agriculture and Rural Development, in respect of the decommissioning, by scrapping, of vessels.

FOOD

5815. Additives – colours
COLOURS IN FOOD (AMENDMENT) REGULATIONS (NORTHERN IRELAND) 2001, SR 2001 408; made under the Food Safety (Northern Ireland) Order 1991 (SI 1991 762 (NI.7)) Art.15, Art.16, Art.25, Art.26, Art.47, Sch.1 para.1. In force: January 15, 2002; £1.50.

These Regulations amend the Colours in Food Regulations (Northern Ireland) 1996 (SR 1996 49) by bringing up to date a reference to Commission Directive 95/45 ([1995] OJ L226/1) on specific purity criteria so as to cover its amendment, as regards the specifications for mixed carotenes and beta-carotene, by Commission Directive 2001/50 ([2001] OJ L190/14) amending Directive 95/45 laying down specific purity criteria concerning colours for use in foodstuffs.

5816. Animal products – bone in beef – despatch to domestic market
BOVINES AND BOVINE PRODUCTS (TRADE) (AMENDMENT) REGULATIONS (NORTHERN IRELAND) 2001, SR 2001 210; made under the European Communities Act 1972 s.2. In force: June 21, 2001; £2.00.

These Regulations amend the Bovines and Bovine Products (Trade) Regulations (Northern Ireland) 1999 (SR 1999 308) which implemented in respect of Northern Ireland the requirements of Commission Decision 98/692 ([1998] OJ L328/28) amending Council Decision 98/256 ([1998] OJ L113/32). The effect of the amendments is to permit the despatch of bone in beef from premises approved under the Date Based Export Scheme and the Export Certified Herds Scheme to the domestic market.

5817. Animal products – diseases and disorders – food safety
FRESH MEAT (BEEF CONTROLS) (AMENDMENT) REGULATIONS (NORTHERN IRELAND) 2001, SR 2001 155; made under the Food Safety (Northern Ireland) Order 1991 (SI 1991 762 (NI.7) Art.15, Art.16, Art.25, Art.26, Art.44, Art.47. In force: May 14, 2001; £1.75.

These Regulations, which amend the Fresh Meat (Beef Controls) Regulations (Northern Ireland) 1996 (SR 1996 404), provide for the enforcement of

Commission Regulation 2777/2000 ([2000] OJ L321/47) adopting exceptional support measures for the beef market.

5818. Animal products – diseases and disorders – specified risk material

RESTRICTION ON PITHING REGULATIONS (NORTHERN IRELAND) 2001, SR 2001 186; made under the European Communities Act 1972 s.2. In force: Reg.3: September 10, 2001; remainder: June 11, 2001; £2.00.

These Regulations, which give effect to Commission Decision 2000/418 ([2000] OJ L158/70) Art.5, prohibit the use of the technique known as "pithing" in the slaughter of bovine, ovine or caprine animals for sale for human or animal consumption. They provide that all parts of the carcass of an illegally pithed animal are deemed to be specified risk material for the purposes of the Specified Risk Material Regulations (Northern Ireland) 1997 (SR 1997 552) and the Specified Risk Material Order (Northern Ireland) 1997 (SR 1997 551), make a consequential amendment to the Welfare of Animals (Slaughter or Killing) Regulations (Northern Ireland) 1996 (SR 1996 558), give a power of entry to persons appointed as inspectors by the relevant enforcement authority, create offences and penalties and specify who is to enforce them.

5819. Animal products – diseases and disorders – specified risk material

SPECIFIED RISK MATERIAL (AMENDMENT) (NO.2) ORDER (NORTHERN IRELAND) 2001, SR 2001 377; made under the Diseases of Animals (Northern Ireland) Order 1981 (SI 1981 1115 (NI.22)) Art.2, Art.5, Art.19, Art.24, Art.29, Art.32, Art.44, Art.46, Art.60. In force: November 6, 2001; £2.00.

This Order makes amendments to the Specified Risk Material Order (Northern Ireland) 1997 (SR 1997 551) to reflect the provisions of Regulation 999/2001 ([2001] OJ L147/1) laying down rules for the prevention, control and eradication of certain transmissible spongiform encephalopathies.

5820. Animal products – diseases and disorders – specified risk material

SPECIFIED RISK MATERIAL (AMENDMENT) (NO.2) REGULATIONS (NORTHERN IRELAND) 2001, SR 2001 196; made under the European Communities Act 1972 s.2. In force: June 17, 2001; £1.75.

These Regulations, which amend the Specified Risk Material Regulations (Northern Ireland) 1997 (SR 1997 552), make provision for changes to the processing requirements at approved rendering plants in Northern Ireland. They give effect to Art.3.1 and Art.7 of Commission Decision 2000/418 ([2000] OJ L158/76) regulating the use of material presenting risks as regards transmissible spongiform encephalopathies. The changes mean specified risk material to be buried at licensed landfill sites must first have been processed at an approved rendering plant and allow mixing of specified risk material with other material at approved rendering plants providing all the material is dealt with a specified risk material.

5821. Animal products – diseases and disorders – specified risk material

SPECIFIED RISK MATERIAL (AMENDMENT NO.3) REGULATIONS (NORTHERN IRELAND) 2001, SR 2001 376; made under the Food Safety (Northern Ireland) Order 1991 (SI 1991 762 (NI.7)) Art.15, Art.16, Art.18, Art.25, Art.47, Sch.1 para.2, Sch.1 para.3, Sch.1 para.5, Sch.1 para.6. In force: November 6, 2001; £2.00.

These Regulations, which amend the Specified Risk Material Regulations (Northern Ireland) 1997 (SR 1997 552), reflect the provisions of Regulation 999/2001 ([2001] OJ L147/1) laying down rules for the prevention, control and eradication of certain transmissible spongiform encephalopathies.

5822. Animal products – food safety – intra-community trade – gelatine

GELATINE (INTRA-COMMUNITY TRADE) REGULATIONS (NORTHERN IRELAND) 2001, SR 2001 226; made under the European Communities Act 1972 s.2. In force: July 9, 2001; £2.00.

These Regulations, which amend the Products of Animal Origin (Import and Export) Regulations (Northern Ireland) 1998 (SR 1998 45), implement Commission Decision 99/724 ([1999] OJ L290/32) so far as it relates to trade between Member States of the European Community and imposes new or changed obligations on the UK. The Decision amends Annex II to Council Directive 92/118 ([1992] OJ L62/49) by imposing new requirements relating to gelatine intended for human consumption. The Regulations give power to district councils to issue, suspend, withdraw and cancel authorisations of collection centres and tanneries which supply raw materials for the manufacture of gelatine subject to the requirements of the Commission Decision.

5823. Animal products – import and export controls

ANIMALS AND ANIMAL PRODUCTS (IMPORT AND EXPORT) (AMENDMENT) REGULATIONS (NORTHERN IRELAND) 2001, SR 2001 312; made under the European Communities Act 1972 s.2. In force: October 1, 2001; £1.75.

These Regulations, which amend the Animals and Animal Products (Import and Export) Regulations (Northern Ireland) 2000 (SR 2000 253), insert a reference to Council Directive 2000/20 ([2000] OJ L163/35) of the European Parliament and Council amending Council Directive 64/432 ([1964] OJ L121/1977) on animal health problems affecting intra-Community trade in bovine animals and swine.

5824. Animal products – origin marking – imports and exports

PRODUCTS OF ANIMAL ORIGIN (IMPORT AND EXPORT) (AMENDMENT) REGULATIONS (NORTHERN IRELAND) 2001, SR 2001 242; made under the European Communities Act 1972 s.2. In force: July 16, 2001; £1.75.

These Regulations amend the Products of Animal Origin (Import and Export) Regulations (Northern Ireland) 1998 (SR 1998 45) to extend the powers of authorised officers as regards products of animal origin imported otherwise than in accordance with those Regulations or which constitute a risk to animal or human health. They confer on an authorised officer of the Department of Agriculture and Rural Development, the Food Standards Agency or a district council the power, in respect of intra-Community trade, to prohibit the movement of products of animal origin which he has reasonable grounds for believing do not comply with animal or public health conditions relating to import into Northern Ireland or the European Community and either order such products to be destroyed, re-exported or used for specified purposes; and, in respect of imports from third countries, to require the destruction or re-export of products of animal origin which he has reasonable grounds for believing do not comply with animal or public health conditions relating to import.

5825. Fishing – shellfish – prohibitions

STRANGFORD LOUGH (PROHIBITION OF FISHING FOR SHELLFISH) REGULATIONS (NORTHERN IRELAND) 2001, SR 2001 379; made under the Fisheries Act (Northern Ireland) 1966 s.124. In force: November 23, 2001; £1.75.

These Regulations prohibit the fishing for shellfish from the Northern Ireland inshore waters of Strangford Lough using any mechanically propelled vehicle except a fishing boat. However, this prohibition does not extend to any person operating under the authority of a fish culture licence.

5826. Food hygiene – butchers' shops – licensing

FOOD SAFETY (GENERAL FOOD HYGIENE) (AMENDMENT) REGULATIONS (NORTHERN IRELAND) 2001, SR 2001 85; made under the Food Safety (Northern Ireland) Order 1991 (SI 1991 762 (NI.7) Art.15, Art.18, Art.25, Art.44,

Art.47, Sch.1 para.5. In force: Reg.2 to Reg.4: October 1, 2001; Reg.1 and Reg.5: April 1, 2001; £2.00.

These Regulations amend the Food Safety (General Food Hygiene) Regulations (Northern Ireland) 1995 (SI 1995 360) by introducing a requirement for the premises of butchers' shops to be licensed by district councils. They insert provisions for the licensing of butchers' shops and make amendments so that using premises as a butcher's shop otherwise than in accordance with a licence is a criminal offence.

5827. Food safety – additives

MISCELLANEOUS FOOD ADDITIVES (AMENDMENT) REGULATIONS (NORTHERN IRELAND) 2001, SR 2001 46; made under the Food Safety (Northern Ireland) Order 1991 (SI 1991 762 (NI.7)) Art.15, Art.16, Art.25, Art.26, Art.47, Sch.1 para.1. In force: March 30, 2001; £2.00.

These Regulations, which amend the Miscellaneous Food Additives Regulations (Northern Ireland) 1996 (SR 1996 50), implement Commission Directive 2000/63 ([2000] OJ L277/1) amending Directive 96/77/EC laying down specific purity criteria on food additives other than colours and sweeteners. They amend the existing requirements in the 1996 Regulations as regards the purity criteria for butylated hydroxyanisole (BHA) and specify new purity criteria in relation to the additives specified in Annex II to Commission Directive 2000/63, subject to transitional provision. The Mineral Hydrocarbons in Food Regulations (Northern Ireland) 1966 (SR & O 1966 50), the Specified Sugar Products Regulations (Northern Ireland) 1976 (SR 1976 165), the Cocoa and Chocolate Products Regulations (Northern Ireland) 1976 (SR 1976 183), the Fruit Juices and Fruit Nectars Regulations (Northern Ireland) 1977 (SR 1977 182), the Condensed Milk and Dried Milk Regulations (Northern Ireland) 1977 (SR 1977 196), the Jam and Similar Products Regulations (Northern Ireland) 1982 (SR 1982 105), the Meat Products and Spreadable Fish Products Regulations (Northern Ireland) 1984 (SR 1984 408), the Food Additives Labelling Regulations (Northern Ireland) 1992 (SR 1992 417) and the Food Labelling Regulations (Northern Ireland) 1996 (SR 1996 383) are amended.

5828. Food safety – additives

MISCELLANEOUS FOOD ADDITIVES (AMENDMENT NO.2) REGULATIONS (NORTHERN IRELAND) 2001, SR 2001 419; made under the Food Safety (Northern Ireland) Order 1991 (SI 1991 762 (NI.7)) Art.15, Art.16, Art.25, Art.26, Art.47, Sch.1 para.1. In force: January 15, 2002; £1.75.

These Regulations, which amend the Miscellaneous Food Additives Regulations (Northern Ireland) 1996 (SR 1996 50), implement Commission Directive 2001/30 [2001] OJ L146/1) amending Directive 96/77 laying down specific purity criteria on food additives other than colours and sweeteners and Directive 2001/5 [2001] OJ L55) of the European Parliament and of the Council amending Directive 95/2 on food additives other than colours and sweeteners. The Regulations add a new additive to the list of miscellaneous food additives generally permitted for use in foods not referred to, modify the list by adding four new additives to that list and specifying additional foods in which Glycerol esters of wood rosins may be contained and also modify the list of permitted carriers and carrier solvents.

5829. Food safety – beef – labelling – enforcement of schemes

BEEF LABELLING (ENFORCEMENT) REGULATIONS (NORTHERN IRELAND) 2001, SR 2001 271; made under the European Communities Act 1972 s.2. In force: August 20, 2001; £2.00.

These Regulations provide for the enforcement in Northern Ireland of the compulsory and voluntary beef labelling schemes established by European Parliament and Council Regulation 1760/2000 ([2000] OJ L204/1) which establishes a system for the identification and registration of bovine animals and regarding the labelling of beef and beef products, Commission Regulation 1825/2000 ([2000] OJ L216/8) laying down detailed rules for the application of the 2000 Regulation, and Commission Regulation 1141/97 ([1997] OJ L165/7) laying down detailed rules for the implementation of Council Regulation 820/97 as regards the labelling of beef and beef products.

5830. Food safety – coffee and chicory extracts – labelling requirements

COFFEE EXTRACTS AND CHICORY EXTRACTS REGULATIONS (NORTHERN IRELAND) 2001, SR 2001 45; made under the Food Safety (Northern Ireland) Order 1991 (SI 1991 762 (NI.7)) Art.15, Art.16, Art.25, Art.26, Art.47. In force: March 19, 2001; £2.00.

These Regulations, which amend the Food (Revision of Penalties and Mode of Trial) Regulations (Northern Ireland) 1987 (SR 1987 38), the Food Safety (Northern Ireland) Order 1991 (Consequential Modifications) Order (Northern Ireland) 1991 (SR 1991 203), the Food Safety (Exports) Regulations (Northern Ireland) 1991 (SR 1991 344), the Food (Forces Exemptions) (Revocations) Regulations (Northern Ireland) 1992 (SR 1992 464), the Miscellaneous Food Additives Regulations (Northern Ireland) 1996 (SR 1996 50) and the Food Labelling Regulations (Northern Ireland) 1996 (SR 1996 383) and revoke and replace the Coffee and Coffee Products Regulations (Northern Ireland) 1979 (SR 1979 51), the Coffee and Coffee Products (Amendment) Regulations (Northern Ireland) 1982 (SR 1982 298) and the Coffee and Coffee Products (Amendment) Regulations (Northern Ireland) 1988 (SR 1988 23), implement Directive 1999/4 ([1999] OJ L66/26) of the European Parliament and the Council relating to coffee extracts and chicory extracts. They prescribe definitions and reserved descriptions for coffee extracts and chicory extracts, provide for the Regulations to apply to coffee extracts and chicory extracts ready for delivery to the ultimate consumer or to a catering establishment, except for the product known as cafe torrefacto soluble, restrict the sale of foods labelled with a reserved description, require reserved descriptions and specified declarations to be applied to designated products, and prescribe the manner of marking or labelling to be employed.

5831. Food safety – emergency prohibitions – amnesic shellfish poisoning – scallops

FOOD PROTECTION (EMERGENCY PROHIBITIONS) (REVOCATION) ORDER (NORTHERN IRELAND) 2001, SR 2001 342; made under the Food and Environment Protection Act 1985 s.1, s.24. In force: October 3, 2001; £1.75.

This Order revokes the Food Protection (Emergency Prohibitions) Order (Northern Ireland) 2001 (SR 2001 296) which contains emergency prohibitions restricting various activities in order to prevent human consumption of scallops or food which is derived from scallops originating in ICES Area VIA which are within British fishery limits and which are adjacent to Northern Ireland.

5832. Food safety – emergency prohibitions – amnesic shellfish poisoning – scallops

FOOD PROTECTION (EMERGENCY PROHIBITIONS NO.2) (REVOCATION) ORDER (NORTHERN IRELAND) 2001, SR 2001 399; made under the Food and Environment Protection Act 1985 s.1, s.24. In force: November 2, 2001; £1.50.

This Order revokes the Food Protection (Emergency Prohibitions No.2) Order (Northern Ireland) 2001 (SR 2001 341) which contains emergency prohibitions restricting various activities in order to prevent human consumption of scallops or food derived from scallops originating in waters in ICES Area VIIa which are within British fishery limits and adjacent to Northern Ireland.

5833. Food safety – emergency prohibitions – diarrhetic shellfish poisoning – scallops

FOOD PROTECTION (EMERGENCY PROHIBITIONS) ORDER (NORTHERN IRELAND) 2001, SR 2001 296; made under the Food and Environment Protection Act 1985 s.1, s.24. In force: August 8, 2001; £1.75.

This Order contains emergency prohibitions restricting various activities in order to prevent human consumption of scallops or food derived from scallops originating in the area described in the Schedule and which has been or may have been rendered unsuitable for human consumption in consequence of shellfish having been affected by the toxin which causes diarrhetic shellfish poisoning in human beings.

5834. Food safety – emergency prohibitions – diarrhetic shellfish poisoning – scallops

FOOD PROTECTION (EMERGENCY PROHIBITIONS) (REVOCATION NO.2) ORDER (NORTHERN IRELAND) 2001, SR 2001 407; made under the Food and Environment Protection Act 1985 s.1, s.24. In force: November 19, 2001; £1.50.

This Order revokes the Food Protection (Emergency Prohibitions No.3) Order (Northern Ireland) 2001 (SI 2001 368) and the Food Protection (Emergency Prohibitions No.4) Order (Northern Ireland) 2001 (SI 2001 389) which contain emergency prohibitions restricting various activities in order to prevent human consumption of scallops or food derived from scallops originating in waters in that part of ICES Area VIa within British fishery limits and adjacent to Northern Ireland.

5835. Food safety – emergency prohibitions – diarrhetic shellfish poisoning – scallops

FOOD PROTECTION (EMERGENCY PROHIBITIONS NO.2) ORDER (NORTHERN IRELAND) 2001, SR 2001 341; made under the Food and Environment Protection Act 1985 s.1, s.24. In force: October 3, 2001; £1.75.

This Order contains emergency prohibitions restricting various activities in order to prevent human consumption of scallops or food derived from scallops originating in the area described in the Schedule and which has been or may have been rendered unsuitable for human consumption in consequence of shellfish having been affected by the toxin which causes diarrhetic shellfish poisoning in human beings. The Order prohibits the fishing for or taking scallops and the movement of scallops out of the designated area. The preparation or processing of food or feeding stuffs derived from shellfish that were in the designated area on or after October 3, 2001 is also prohibited.

5836. Food safety – emergency prohibitions – diarrhetic shellfish poisoning – scallops

FOOD PROTECTION (EMERGENCY PROHIBITIONS NO.3) ORDER (NORTHERN IRELAND) 2001, SR 2001 368; made under the Food and Environment Protection Act 1985 s.1, s.24. In force: October 10, 2001; £1.75.

This Order contains emergency prohibitions restricting various activities in order to prevent human consumption of scallops or food derived from scallops originating in the area described in the Schedule and which has been or may have been rendered unsuitable for human consumption in consequence of shellfish affected by the toxin which causes diarrhetic shellfish poisoning in human beings. It prohibits the fishing for or taking scallops out of the designated area and also the preparation or processing of food or feeding stuffs derived from shellfish that were in the designated area on or after October 9, 2001.

5837. Food safety – emergency prohibitions – diarrhetic shellfish poisoning – scallops

FOOD PROTECTION (EMERGENCY PROHIBITIONS NO.4) ORDER (NORTHERN IRELAND) 2001, SR 2001 389; made under the Food and Environment Protection Act 1985 s.1, s.24. In force: October 19, 2001; £1.75.

This Order contains emergency prohibitions restricting various activities in order to prevent human consumption of scallops or food derived from scallops originating in the area described in the Schedule and which has been or may have been rendered unsuitable for human consumption in consequence of shellfish affected by the toxin which causes diarrhetic shellfish poisoning in human beings.

GOVERNMENT ADMINISTRATION

5838. Budget Act (Northern Ireland) 2001 (c.7)

This Act authorises the issue out of the Consolidated Fund of certain sums for the service of the years ending March 31, 2001 and 2002; to appropriate those sums for specified purposes and amend certain appropriations in aid for the year ending March 31, 2001; to authorise the Department of Finance and Personnel to borrow on the credit of the appropriated sums; and to authorise the use for the public service of certain resources for the year ending March 31, 2002.

This Act received Royal Assent on March 22, 2001 and comes into force on March 22, 2001.

5839. Department for Employment and Learning Act (Northern Ireland) 2001 (c.15)

This Act renames the Department of Higher and Further Education, Training and Employment as the Department for Employment and Learning.

This Act comes into force on July 20, 2001.

5840. Government Resources and Accounts Act (Northern Ireland) 2001 (c.6)

This Act makes provision about government resources and accounts.

This Act received Royal Assent on March 22, 2001.

5841. Ministerial functions – Northern Ireland departments – transfer of functions

DEPARTMENTS (TRANSFER OF FUNCTIONS) ORDER (NORTHERN IRELAND) 2001, SR 2001 229; made under the Departments (Northern Ireland) Order 1999 (SI 1999 283 (NI.1)) Art.8. In force: In accordance with Art.1 (2); £2.00.

This Order, which amends the Fisheries Act (Northern Ireland) 1966 and the Water and Sewerage Services (Northern Ireland) Order 1973 (SI 1973 70 (NI.2)), transfers certain functions of Northern Ireland departments and Ministers to other such departments and Ministers.

5842. Ministerial responsibility – confidentiality – failure to abide by collective responsibility on political grounds – refusal to provide committee papers

M and C, members of the DUP, a political party which held two ministries in the executive committee of the Northern Ireland Assembly, sought judicial review of a decision by the first minister, T, and his deputy, S, to withhold executive committee papers from them. As part of its campaign to have Sinn Fein excluded from the executive, the DUP had issued a press release which indicated that its ministers would not abide by the ministerial code of conduct or accept collective responsibility. T and S wrote to D, M's predecessor, stating that papers would not be supplied until they were satisfied that confidentiality would be observed by the DUP. Following M and C taking over as ministers, M assured T and S that the DUP ministers would respect the confidentiality of committee papers. However, T and S replied that M and C had taken up office on the same basis as their predecessors and that M's private assurance was not sufficient.

Held, refusing the application, that the advance supply of committee papers was not a statutory requirement and the failure to supply them before meetings had not affected M's ability to discharge his ministerial functions. The decision to withhold the papers was not susceptible to review on *Wednesbury* grounds as T and S had been entitled to reach their decision on confidentiality grounds on the basis that the threat contained in the press release had not been addressed by M's assurance.

MORROW'S APPLICATION, *Re* [2001] N.I. 261, Kerr, J., QBD (NI).

HEALTH

5843. Benefits – injury at work – Health and Personal Social Services

HEALTH AND PERSONAL SOCIAL SERVICES (INJURY BENEFITS) REGULATIONS (NORTHERN IRELAND) 2001, SR 2001 367; made under the Superannuation (Northern Ireland) Order 1973 (SI 1973 1073 (NI.10)) Art.12, Art.14, Sch.3. In force: December 1, 2001; £4.50.

These Regulations, which revoke the Health and Personal Social Services (Injury Benefits) Regulations (Northern Ireland) 1975 (SR 1975 85) and the Health and Personal Social Services (Injury Benefits) (Amendment) Regulations (Northern Ireland) 1986 (SR 1986 151), amend the Health and Personal Social Services (Superannuation, Premature Retirement and Injury Benefits) (Amendment) Regulations (Northern Ireland) 1991 (SI 1991 506). They provide for the payment, by the Department of Health, Social Services and Public Safety, of injury benefits to or in respect of any person engaged in the Health and Personal Social Services in Northern Ireland whose earning ability is reduced or who dies as a result of an injury suffered or disease contracted in the course of his or her duties.

5844. Dentistry – dental services – fees

DENTAL CHARGES (AMENDMENT) REGULATIONS (NORTHERN IRELAND) 2001, SR 2001 124; made under the Health and Personal Social Services (Northern Ireland) Order 1972 (SI 1972 1265 (NI.14)) Art.98, Art.106, Sch.15. In force: April 28, 2001; £1.50.

These Regulations amend the Dental Charges Regulations (Northern Ireland) 1989 (SR 1989 111) and the Dental Charges (Amendment) Regulations (Northern Ireland) 2000 (SR 2000 58) which relate to charges for dental treatment provided and dental appliances supplied as part of health service general dental services or under a pilot scheme by increasing from £354 to £360 the maximum charge which a patient may be required to pay towards the cost of his treatment or appliance under general dental services or under a pilot scheme. In addition, they provide that these new charges shall apply only where the arrangements for treatment or supply of a dental appliance is made on or after April 28, 2001.

5845. Dentistry – general dental services

GENERAL DENTAL SERVICES (AMENDMENT) REGULATIONS (NORTHERN IRELAND) 2001, SR 2001 2; made under the Health and Personal Social Services (Northern Ireland) Order 1972 (SI 1972 1265 (NI.14)) Art.61, Art.106, Art.107, Sch.11 Part I, Sch.11 para.8E. In force: Reg.6(3): April 2, 2001; remainder: February 5, 2001; £2.00.

These Regulations further amend the Health and Personal Social Services General Dental Services Regulations (Northern Ireland) 1993 (SR 1993 326) to require a Board to remove a name of a dentist from the dental list if he has been convicted of murder or a criminal offence in the United Kingdom and sentenced to at least six month's imprisonment; so that dentists who have undertaken to provide only Emergency Dental Services, are not required to have their name included in the dental list; to amend the circumstances in which records must be produced for inspection, inserts a new requirement for a dentist to ask to see evidence in support of a patient's claim that he is entitled to exemption from, or remission of, dental charges and to record in his claim for remuneration when he does not see such evidence, a requirement for separate claim forms to be completed for treatment given by assistants; and set out an additional declaration which requires the applicant to state any convictions or current proceedings for a criminal offence or action by a professional licensing or regulatory body.

5846. Dentistry – general dental services

GENERAL DENTAL SERVICES (AMENDMENT NO.2) REGULATIONS (NORTHERN IRELAND) 2001, SR 2001 89; made under the Health and Personal Social Services (Northern Ireland) Order 1972 (SI 1972 1265 (NI.14)) Art.61, Art.106, Art.107. In force: Reg.1 to Reg.7: April 1, 2001; remainder: April 30, 2001; £2.00.

These Regulations amend the Health and Personal Social Services General Dental Services Regulations (Northern Ireland) 1993 (SR 1993 326) by increasing the amount specified as the maximum cost of care and treatment which a dentist may undertake without seeking the prior approval of the Dental Practice Board from £230 to £260. In addition, they provide for the establishment of a list of those dentists providing treatment as part of their general dental services to patients under general anaesthesia and provide that treatment under general anaesthesia as part of general dental services cannot be provided unless the dentist is on the Board's general anaesthesia list, that general anaesthesia may not form part of treatment which mixes general dental services and private dentistry, and that dentists on the general anaesthesia list must permit inspections of their premises.

5847. Dentistry – general dental services

GENERAL DENTAL SERVICES (AMENDMENT NO.3) REGULATIONS (NORTHERN IRELAND) 2001, SR 2001 309; made under the Health and Personal Social Services (Northern Ireland) Order 1972 (SI 1972 1265 (NI.14)) Art.61, Art.106, Art.107. In force: October 1, 2001; £2.00.

These Regulations amend the Health and Personal Social Services General Dental Services Regulations (Northern Ireland) 1993 (SR 1993 326) which regulate the terms on which general dental services are provided under the Health and Personal Social Services (Northern Ireland) Order 1972 (SI 1972 1265). They impose three new terms of service applicable to dentists so that a dentist must undertake, over successive three year periods, 15 hours of activities involving clinical audit, establish and operate a practice based quality assurance system and make an annual return to the Health and Social Services Board in respect of that system.

5848. Health and Personal Social Services Act (Northern Ireland) 2001 (c.3)

This Act establishes a Northern Ireland Social Care Council and make provision for the registration, regulation and training of social care workers; it makes provision about the recovery of charges in connection with the treatment of road traffic casualties in health services hospitals; amends the law about the health and personal social services; and confers power to regulate the profession of pharmaceutical chemist.

This Act received Royal Assent on March 20, 2001.

5849. Health and Personal Social Services Act (Northern Ireland) 2001 (c.3) – Commencement No.1 Order

HEALTH AND PERSONAL SOCIAL SERVICES (2001 ACT) (COMMENCEMENT NO.1) ORDER 2001, SR 2001 128 (C.5); made under the Health and Personal

Social Services (Northern Ireland) Act 2001 s.61. Commencement details: bringing into force various provisions of the Act in accordance with Art.2; £2.00.

This Order brings into operation certain provisions of the Health and Personal Social Services Act (Northern Ireland) 2001 relating to social care workers.

5850. **Health and Personal Social Services Act (Northern Ireland) 2001 (c.3) – Commencement No.2 Order**

HEALTH AND PERSONAL SOCIAL SERVICES (2001 ACT) (COMMENCEMENT NO.2) ORDER (NORTHERN IRELAND) 2001, SR 2001 324 (C.16); made under the Health and Personal Social Services Act (Northern Ireland) 2001 s.61. In force: bringing into operation various provisions of the 2001 Act on October 1, 2001 and November 1, 2001, in accordance with Art. 2.; £1.75.

This Order brings into operation specified provisions of the Health and Personal Social Services Act (Northern Ireland) 2001 relating to social care workers.

5851. **Health services – drugs and appliances – fees**

CHARGES FOR DRUGS AND APPLIANCES (AMENDMENT) REGULATIONS (NORTHERN IRELAND) 2001, SR 2001 123; made under the Health and Personal Social Services (Northern Ireland) Order 1972 (SI 1972 1265 (NI.14)) Art.98, Art.106, Sch.15. In force: April 28, 2001; £2.00.

These Regulations, which amend the Charges for Drugs and Appliances Regulations (Northern Ireland) 1997 (SR 1997 382), increase the charge for each item on prescription from £6.00 to £6.10. The sums prescribed for the grant of pre-payment certificates of exemption from prescription charges are increased from £31.40 to £31.90 for a four month certificate and from £86.20 to £87.60 for a 12 month certificate. In addition, they increase charges for certain fabric supports and wigs.

5852. **Health services – general medical services – doctors – prescription of drugs**

GENERAL MEDICAL SERVICES (AMENDMENT) REGULATIONS (NORTHERN IRELAND) 2001, SR 2001 135; made under the Health and Personal Social Services (Northern Ireland) Order 1972 (SI 1972 1265 (NI.14)) Art.56, Art.106, Art.107. In force: April 17, 2001; £1.75.

These Regulations amend the General Medical Services Regulations (Northern Ireland) 1997 (SR 1997 380), which regulate the terms on which doctors provide general medical services under the Health and Personal Social Services (Northern Ireland) Order 1972 (SI 1972 1265 (NI.14)), by deleting specified nicotine replacement therapy products from the list in Sch.10 of drugs and other substances which may not be prescribed for supply under pharmaceutical services.

5853. **Health services – general medical services – issue of certificates**

GENERAL MEDICAL SERVICES (MISCELLANEOUS AMENDMENTS) REGULATIONS (NORTHERN IRELAND) 2001, SR 2001 218; made under the Health and Personal Social Services (Northern Ireland) Order 1972 (SI 1972 1265 (NI. 14)) Art.56, Art.95, Art.106, Art.107, Sch.3 para.7, Sch.10 para.2. In force: July 2, 2001; £1.75.

These Regulations, which amend the General Medical Services Regulations (Northern Ireland) 1997 (SR 1997 380), insert a new Reg.17A providing that a certificate issued under the Health and Personal Social Services (Northern Ireland) Order 1972 (SR 1972 1265 (NI.14)) Sch.10 para.2 should be in the form set out in the new Sch.7A. References to allowances for training doctors from the matters for which provision shall be made in a determination are removed and the Medical Committee is allowed, in the absence of the chairperson, to nominate a deputy chairperson from the four members who are doctors.

5854. Health services – general medical services – prescription of drugs – doctors

GENERAL MEDICAL SERVICES (AMENDMENT NO.4) REGULATIONS (NORTHERN IRELAND) 2001, SR 2001 374; made under the Health and Personal Social Services (Northern Ireland) Order 1972 (SI 1972 1265 (NI.14)) Art.56, Art.106, Art.107. In force: November 1, 2001; £1.75.

These Regulations amend the General Medical Services Regulations (Northern Ireland) 1997 (SR 1997 380) which regulate the terms on which doctors provide general medical services under the Health and Personal Social Services (Northern Ireland) Order 1972 (SI 1972 1265). They amend the list of drugs in the 1997 Regulations, which may be prescribed only in certain circumstances, by adding Uprima.

5855. Health services – general medical services – prescription of drugs – nurse prescribers

GENERAL MEDICAL SERVICES (AMENDMENT NO.2) REGULATIONS (NORTHERN IRELAND) 2001, SR 2001 167; made under the Health and Personal Social Services (Northern Ireland) Order 1972 (SI 1972 1265 (NI.14)) Art.56, Art.106, Art.107. In force: May 21, 2001; £1.75.

These Regulations amend the General Medical Services Regulations (Northern Ireland) 1997 (SR 1997 380) which regulate the terms on which doctors provide general medical services under the Health and Personal Social Services (Northern Ireland) Order 1972 (SI 1972 1265 (NI.14)). They add definitions of "nurse prescriber" and "professional register" and insert a new provision to impose an obligation on general practitioners to notify the relevant Health and Social Services Board when they employ, or ceases to employ, a nurse prescriber whose functions include prescribing in their practice, when the functions of a nurse prescriber whom they already employ are extended to include, or changed so as not to include, prescribing or when they become aware that a nurse prescriber in their practices have been removed or suspended from the professional register.

5856. Health services – travelling expenses – remission of charges

TRAVELLING EXPENSES AND REMISSION OF CHARGES (AMENDMENT) REGULATIONS (NORTHERN IRELAND) 2001, SR 2001 104; made under the Health and Personal Social Services (Northern Ireland) Order 1972 (SI 1972 1265 (NI.14)) Art.45, Art.98, Art.106, Art.107, Sch.15 para.1B. In force: April 10, 2001; £1.75.

These Regulations amend the Travelling Expenses and Remission of Charges Regulation (Northern Ireland) 1989 (SR 1989 348) which provide for remission and repayment of certain charges which would otherwise be payable under the Health and Personal Social Services (Northern Ireland) Order 1972 (SI 1972 1265) and for the payment by the Department of travelling expenses incurred in attending a hospital. They amend the definition of "capital limit" as it applies to people living permanently in a nursing or residential care home or in accommodation provided by Boards, increase the income level at which recipients of tax credits are entitled to remission from charges under the principal Regulations and provide, in relation to claims for repayment of relevant charges or travelling expenses, that the claimant's resources and requirements are to be calculated by reference to the date when the charges and expenses were paid in full.

5857. Medical and pharmaceutical services

PHARMACEUTICAL SERVICES (AMENDMENT) REGULATIONS (NORTHERN IRELAND) 2001, SR 2001 222; made under the Health and Personal Social Services (Northern Ireland) Order 1972 (SI 1972 1265 (NI. 14)) Art.63, Art.64, Art.106, Art.107. In force: July 2, 2001; £2.50.

These Regulations amend the Pharmaceutical Services Regulations (Northern Ireland) 1997 (SR 1997 381) by making provision for a Board to grant a temporary relocation for a designated period, and to allow a dispensing doctor to provide pharmaceutical services to his patients while performing personal medical services.

5858. Medical profession – nurses, midwives and health visitors – professional conduct

NURSES, MIDWIVES AND HEALTH VISITORS (PROFESSIONAL CONDUCT) (AMENDMENT) RULES 2001, APPROVAL ORDER (NORTHERN IRELAND) 2001, SR 2001 76; made under the Nurses, Midwives and Health Visitors Act 1997 s.19, s.22, Sch.3. In force: March 7, 2001; £1.75.

These Rules amend the professional conduct rules of the UKCC for nursing, midwifery and health visiting so as to reduce from three to two the quorum of each of the Preliminary Proceedings Committee, the Professional Conduct Committee and the health committee.

5859. Medical services – approved medical practices – conditions of residence

MEDICAL ACT 1983 (APPROVED MEDICAL PRACTICES AND CONDITIONS OF RESIDENCE) AND GENERAL MEDICAL SERVICES (AMENDMENT NO.3) REGULATIONS (NORTHERN IRELAND) 2001, SR 2001 217; made under the Health and Personal Social Services (Northern Ireland) Order 1972 (SI 1972 1265 (NI. 14)) Art.56, Art.95, Art.106, Art.107; and the Medical Act 1983 s.11. In force: July 2, 2001; £1.75.

These Regulations, which amend the General Medical Services Regulations (Northern Ireland) 1997 (SR 1997 380), prescribe the description of medical practice which may be approved for the purposes of employing a Pre-Registration House Officer pursuant to the Medical Act 1983, and also prescribe the conditions of residence with which a PRHO must comply throughout the period of such employment.

5860. Opticians – fees and payments

OPTICAL CHARGES AND PAYMENTS AND GENERAL OPHTHALMIC SERVICES (AMENDMENT) REGULATIONS (NORTHERN IRELAND) 2001, SR 2001 370; made under the Health and Personal Social Services (Northern Ireland) Order 1972 (SI 1972 1265 (NI.14)) Art.62, Art.98, Art.106, Art.107, Sch.15. In force: November 12, 2001; £2.00.

These Regulations amend the General Ophthalmic Services Regulations (Northern Ireland) 1986 (SR 1986 163) which provide for the arrangements under which ophthalmic medical practitioners and ophthalmic opticians provide General Ophthalmic Services. They also make amendments to the Optical Charges and Payments Regulations (Northern Ireland) 1997 (SR 1997 191) which provide for payments to be made, by means of a voucher system, in respect of costs incurred by certain categories of persons in connection with the supply, replacement and repair of optical appliances. The Regulations make amendments to require the supplier to ask the patient for satisfactory evidence that he is an eligible person when he presents a voucher to obtain an optical appliance and if he fails to do so, the supplier must record the fact on the voucher.

5861. Opticians – fees and payments

OPTICAL CHARGES AND PAYMENTS (AMENDMENT) REGULATIONS (NORTHERN IRELAND) 2001, SR 2001 133; made under the Health and Personal Social Services (Northern Ireland) Order 1972 (SI 1972 1265 (NI.14)) Art.62, Art.98, Art.106, Sch.15. In force: Reg.2: April 10, 2001; remainder: April 1, 2001; £2.00.

These Regulations, which amend the Optical Charges and Payments Regulations (Northern Ireland) 1997 (SR 1997 191), provide for an increase in the charges for glasses and contact lenses supplied by an HSS trust. They increase the income level at which recipients of tax credit are entitled to health service optical vouchers, increase the redemption value of two categories of vouchers, namely, vouchers for replacement and vouchers for repair, increase the value of vouchers issued towards the cost of the supply and replacement of glasses and contact lenses and the additional values for vouchers in respect of prisms, tints, and special categories of appliances.

5862. Opticians – provision of ophthalmic services

GENERAL OPHTHALMIC SERVICES (AMENDMENT) REGULATIONS (NORTHERN IRELAND) 2001, SR 2001 339; made under the Health and Personal Social Services (Northern Ireland) Order 1972 (SI 1972 1265 (NI.14)) Art.62, Art.106, Art.107. In force: October 12, 2001; £1.50.

These Regulations amend the General Ophthalmic Services Regulations (Northern Ireland) 1986 (SI 1986 163) which provide for the arrangements under which ophthalmic medical practitioners and ophthalmic opticians provide General Ophthalmic Services. The Regulations increase the income level applying to recipients of tax credits for the purposes of calculating whether a person's resources shall be treated as being less than, or equal to, his requirements in determining eligibility for Health Service sight tests from £70.00 to £71.00.

5863. Residential care – assessment of resources

HEALTH AND PERSONAL SOCIAL SERVICES (ASSESSMENT OF RESOURCES) (AMENDMENT) REGULATIONS (NORTHERN IRELAND) 2001, SR 2001 205; made under the Health and Personal Social Services (Northern Ireland) Order 1972 (SI 1972 1265 (NI.14)) Art.36, Art.99. In force: June 11, 2001; £1.75.

These Regulations amend the Health and Personal Social Services (Assessment of Resources) Regulations (Northern Ireland) 1993 (SR 1993 127) relating to the assessment by Health and Social Services Boards and HSS trusts of the resources of residents in accommodation arranged under the Health and Personal Social Services (Northern Ireland) Order 1972 (SI 1972 1265). They make amendments so that the capital limit above which a Resident is not entitled to be assessed as unable to pay for accommodation is increased from £16,000 to £18,500 and so the weekly tariff income is calculated on a Resident's capital between £11,500 and £18,500.

HEALTH AND SAFETY AT WORK

5864. Construction industry – design regulations

CONSTRUCTION (DESIGN AND MANAGEMENT) (AMENDMENT) REGULATIONS (NORTHERN IRELAND) 2001, SR 2001 142; made under the Health and Safety at Work (Northern Ireland) Order 1978 (SI 1978 1039 (NI.9)) Art.17, Art.20, Art.43, Art.55, Sch.3 para.1, Sch.3 para.5, Sch.3 para.13, Sch.3 para.14, Sch.3 para.15, Sch.3 para.19, Sch.3 para.20. In force: May 3, 2001; £1.75.

These Regulations amend the Construction (Design and Management) Regulations (Northern Ireland) 1995 (SR 1995 209) by substituting a new definition of "designer" and by providing that any reference in the 1995 Regulations to a person preparing a design shall include a reference to his employee or other person under his control preparing it for him thereby ensuring that the duty applies to a person where his employee or other such person prepares a design for him.

5865. Environmental protection – biocidal products

BIOCIDAL PRODUCTS REGULATIONS (NORTHERN IRELAND) 2001, SR 2001 422; made under the European Communities Act 1972 s.2; and the Health and Safety at Work (Northern Ireland) Order 1978 (SI 1978 1039 (NI.9)) Art.17,

Art.40, Art.55, Sch.3 para.1, Sch.3 para.3, Sch.3 para.12, Sch.3 para.14, Sch.3 para.15. In force: January 16, 2002; £7.00.

These Regulations, which amend the Control of Pesticides Regulations (Northern Ireland) 1987 (SR 1987 414), the Notification of New Substances Regulations (Northern Ireland) 1994 (SR 1994 6) and the Chemicals (Hazard Information and Packaging for Supply) Regulations (Northern Ireland) 1995 (SR 1995 60), enable applications to be made for agreement at Community level that an active substance can be used in a biocidal product and authorise the placing on the market and use of biocidal products to which these Regulations apply. They implement Directive 98/8 ([1998] OJ L123/1) concerning the placing of biocidal products on the market and Commission Directive 2000/21 ([2000] OJ L103/70) concerning the list of Community legislation referred to in the fifth indent of Art.13(1) of Council Directive 67/548. These Regulations do not apply to certain biocidal products nor to the carriage of biocidal products by rail, road, inland waterway, sea or air.

5866. Fire precautions – minimum safety requirements

FIRE PRECAUTIONS (WORKPLACE) REGULATIONS (NORTHERN IRELAND) 2001, SR 2001 348; made under the European Communities Act 1972 s.2; and the Fire Services (Northern Ireland) Order 1984 (SI 1984 1821 (NI.11)) Art.48, Art.49. In force: December 1, 2001; £3.50.

These Regulations amend the Health and Safety at Work (Northern Ireland) Order 1978 (SI 1978 1039), the Safety Representatives and Safety Committees Regulations (Northern Ireland) 1979 (SR 1979 437), the Fire Services (Northern Ireland) Order 1984 (SR 1984 1821), the Health and Safety (Consultation with Employees) Regulations (Northern Ireland) 1996 (SR 1996 511) and the Management of Health and Safety at Work Regulations (Northern Ireland) 2000 (SR 2000 388). They give effect in Northern Ireland to Council Directive 89/391 ([1989] OJ L183/1) on the introduction of measures to encourage improvements in the safety and health of workers at work and Council Directive 89/654 ([1989] OJ L393/1) concerning the minimum safety and health requirements for the workplace insofar as those provisions relate to fire precautions and insofar as more specific legislation does not make appropriate provision.

5867. Genetically modified organisms – contained use – health, safety and environmental protection

GENETICALLY MODIFIED ORGANISMS (CONTAINED USE) REGULATIONS (NORTHERN IRELAND) 2001, SR 2001 295; made under the European Communities Act 1972 s.2; and the Health and Safety at Work (Northern Ireland) Order 1978 (SI 1978 1039 (NI.9)) Art.2, Art.17, Art.40, Art.55, Sch.3 para.1, Sch.3 para.3, Sch.3 para.4, Sch.3 para.5, Sch.3 para.7, Sch.3 para.8, Sch.3 para.10, Sch.3 para.12, Sch.3 para.13, Sch.3 para.14, Sch.3 para.15, Sch.3 para.19. In force: September 25, 2001; £7.00.

These Regulations make amendments to the Genetically Modified Organisms (Deliberate Release) Regulations (Northern Ireland) 1994 (SR 1994 144), the Genetically Modified Organisms (Risk Assessment) (Records and Exemptions) Regulations (Northern Ireland) 1996 (SR 1996 442), the Health and Safety (Fees) Regulations (Northern Ireland) 1998 (SR 1998 125) and the Control of Substances Hazardous to Health Regulations (Northern Ireland) 2000 (SR 2000 120). They also revoke the Genetically Modified Organisms (Contained Use) Regulations (Northern Ireland) 1994 (SR 1994 143), the Genetically Modified Organisms (Contained Use) (Amendment) Regulations (Northern Ireland) 1996 (SR 1996 250) and the Genetically Modified Organisms (Contained Use) (Amendment) Regulations (Northern Ireland) 1999 (SR 1999 14). The Regulations aim to protect persons and the environment from risks arising from activities involving the contained use of genetically modified micro-organisms and protect persons from risks arising from activities involving the contained use of genetically modified organisms which are not micro-organisms.

5868. Radiation – employers duties

RADIATION (EMERGENCY PREPAREDNESS AND PUBLIC INFORMATION) REGULATIONS (NORTHERN IRELAND) 2001, SR 2001 436; made under the Health and Safety at Work (Northern Ireland) Order 1978 (SI 1978 1039 (NI.9)) Art.17, Art.40, Art.55, Sch.3 para.2, Sch.3 para.5, Sch.3 para.7, Sch.3 para.10, Sch.3 para.13, Sch.3 para.14, Sch.3 para.15. In force: February 4, 2002; £7.00.

These Regulations amend Ionising Radiations Regulations (Northern Ireland) 1985 (SR 1985 273), Fire Certificates (Special Premises) Regulations (Northern Ireland) 1991 (SR 1991 446), Reporting of Injuries, Diseases and Dangerous Occurrences Regulations (Northern Ireland) 1997 (SR 1997 455) and Ionising Radiations Regulations (Northern Ireland) 2000 (SR 2000 375) and revoke, with savings, the Public Information for Radiation Emergencies Regulations (Northern Ireland) (SR 1992 515). They implement as respects Northern Ireland Title IX, Section 1 (Intervention in cases of radiological emergency) of Council Directive 96/29 ([1991] OJ L159/1) laying down basic safety standards for the protection of the health of workers and the general public against the dangers arising from ionising radiation and impose requirements for that purpose on operators of premises where radioactive substances are present (in quantities exceeding specified thresholds). They also impose requirements on carriers transporting radioactive substances (in quantities exceeding specified thresholds) by rail or conveying them through public places, with the exception of carriers conveying radioactive substances by rail, road, inland waterway, sea or air or by means of a pipeline or similar means.

HIGHWAY CONTROL

5869. Road works – inspections – fees

STREET WORKS (INSPECTION FEES) REGULATIONS (NORTHERN IRELAND) 2001, SR 2001 409; made under the Street Works (Northern Ireland) Order 1995 (SI 1995 3210 (NI.19)) Art.35. In force: January 1, 2002; £1.75.

These Regulations prescribe a scheme for the payment by undertakers for inspections of their works by the Department in streets for which it is the street authority. A fee of £15.50 is prescribed for each chargeable inspection and where the undertaker holds a licence a chargeable inspection is every inspection of works or a phase of works subject to a maximum of 30 inspections where the undertaker's estimated number of units of inspection in a year is less than 100.

5870. Road works – inspections – maintenance

STREET WORKS (MAINTENANCE) REGULATIONS (NORTHERN IRELAND) 2001, SR 2001 413; made under the Street Works (Northern Ireland) Order 1995 (SI 1995 3210 (NI.19)) Art.41. In force: March 1, 2002; £1.75.

These Regulations define the circumstances in which a street authority, in cases where the undertaker has failed to afford to the authority facilities for inspecting its relevant apparatus in a street, may carry out works to enable it to inspect the apparatus where that authority has reasonable cause to believe that the apparatus has not been maintained as required by the Street Works (Northern Ireland) Order 1995 (SI 1995 3210 (NI.19)).

5871. Roads – private streets – construction requirements

PRIVATE STREETS (CONSTRUCTION) (AMENDMENT) REGULATIONS (NORTHERN IRELAND) 2001, SR 2001 73; made under the Private Streets (Northern Ireland) Order 1980 (SI 1980 1086 (NI.12) Art.5. In force: May 1, 2001; £6.00.

These Regulations, which amend the Private Streets (Construction) Regulations (Northern Ireland) 1994 (SR 1994 131), apply to the construction of streets in respect of which the Department for Regional Development has exercised street planning functions after the coming into operation of the Regulations. The Regulations prescribe standards and detailed requirements for the provision of street lighting in private streets and extend the specified expenses to include the cost of inspections and to provide for the bearing of such expenses by the person by whom or on whose behalf the plans were deposited.

5872. Street Works (Northen Ireland) Order 1995 (SI 1995 3210 (NI.19)) – Commencement No.5 Order

STREET WORKS (1995 ORDER) (COMMENCEMENT NO.5) ORDER (NORTHERN IRELAND) 2001, SR 2001 388 (C.18); made under the Street Works (Northern Ireland) Order 1995 (SI 1995 3210 (NI.19)) Art.1. Commencement details: bringing into force various provisions of the 1995 Order on November 18, 2001; £2.00.

This Order brings into force specified Articles of the Street Works (Northern Ireland) Order 1995 (SI 1995 3210).

HOUSING

5873. Grants – renovation grants – means test

HOUSING RENOVATION ETC. GRANTS (REDUCTION OF GRANT) (AMENDMENT) REGULATIONS (NORTHERN IRELAND) 2001, SR 2001 315; made under the Housing (Northern Ireland) Order 1992 (SI 1992 1725 (NI.15)) Art.47. In force: October 15, 2001; £3.00.

These Regulations amend the Housing Renovation etc. Grants (Reduction of Grant) Regulations (Northern Ireland) 1997 (SR 1997 456), which set out the means test determining the amount of renovation grant and disabled facilities grant which may be paid by the Housing Executive to owner-occupier and tenant, remove doubt as to whether persons with whom children or young persons have been placed for fostering may be treated as "responsible" for them for the purposes of grant applications, increase the "applicable amount" of income that can be received without reduction in grant and provide that working families' tax credit and disabled person's tax credit shall be taken into account in calculating the amount of allowable child care charges for the purposes of the means test. They provide that payments made to child care providers approved by organisations accredited by the Secretary of State for Education and Employment shall be allowable for the purposes of the means test and give the Housing Executive discretion to decide if it is reasonable for a person engaged by a charitable or voluntary organisation to provide his services free.

HUMAN RIGHTS

5874. Disability Discrimination Act 1995 (c.50) – Commencement No.8 Order

DISABILITY DISCRIMINATION ACT 1995 (COMMENCEMENT NO.8) ORDER (NORTHERN IRELAND) 2001, SR 2001 439 (C.22); made under the Disability Discrimination Act 1995 s.70. In force: bringing into operation various provisions of the 1995 Act on December 31, 2001 and October 1, 2004; £2.00.

This Order provides for the coming into operation of certain regulations making powers contained in the Disability Discrimination Act 1995.

5875. Freedom of association – pubic order – parades – grounds for prohibition on Orange Order parade from entering village

[Public Processions (Northern Ireland) Act 1998 s.8; European Convention on Human Rights 1950 Art.11 (2).]

T, the organiser of an Orange Order parade to be held in Dunloy on Reformation Sunday, gave notice to the police and the Parades Commission. The Commission prohibited the parade from entering the village under the Public Processions (Northern Ireland) Act 1998 s.8 and stated that the prohibition accorded with the restriction in the European Convention on Human Rights 1950 Art.11 (2) given the risk of public disorder. T sought judicial review of the Commission's decision, contending that the decision had been reached in reliance on the impact that the parade could have on community relations, which was not a ground contained in Art.11 (2) allowing restrictions to the right to freedom of assembly.

Held, refusing the application, that in reaching a decision under s.8(6) of the Act the Commission could take community relations into account, along with the threat to public order. The Convention was concerned with the substance of the Commission's decision, which included the effect of restrictions and their compatibility with Art.11 (2). The determination reached with regard to T's parade was a proper exercise of the Commission's powers under the Act and had not breached T's rights under Art.11.

TWEED'S APPLICATION FOR JUDICIAL REVIEW, *Re* [2001] N.I. 165, Carswell, L.C.J., CA (NI).

5876. Right to fair trial – civil service – issue of national security certificate

[Fair Employment (Northern Ireland) Act 1976 s.42; European Convention on Human Rights 1950 Art.6.]

D, an Irish national, complained to the European Court of Human Rights that the issue by the Secretary of State of a security certificate under the Fair Employment (Northern Ireland) Act 1976 s.42 certifying that the refusal to employ him as an administrative assistant in the Northern Ireland Civil Service was on national security grounds constituted a breach of the European Convention on Human Rights 1950 Art.6. D maintained that the refusal to employ him had been because he was a Catholic and a member of an association called the "Irish National Foresters". D had unsuccessfully applied for judicial review of the Secretary of State's decision to issue the certificate. The Government argued that Art.6 did not apply as the dispute related to the civil service to which special considerations applied.

Held, granting the application, that having regard to the fact that D was seeking employment at the lowest grade in the non-industrial Civil Service and would not be "wielding a portion of the State's sovereign power", Art.6 of the Convention was applicable, *Pellegrin v. France* (2001) 31 E.H.R.R. 26, [2001] 9 C.L. 343 considered. The court had previously in the decision of *Tinnelly & Sons Ltd v. United Kingdom* (1999) 27 E.H.R.R. 249, [1998] C.L.Y. 3147 found that the 1976 Act guaranteed a civil right for the purposes of Art.6(1) of the Convention. In the instant case there had been no independent analysis by any fact finding body of the facts upon which the Secretary of State had reached his determination. The issue by the Secretary of State of the certificate had been a disproportionate restriction on D's right of access to a court and accordingly constituted a breach of Art.6(1), *Tinnelly* applied.

DEVLIN v. UNITED KINGDOM (29545/95) [2002] I.R.L.R. 155, J-P Costa (President), ECHR.

5877. Right to fair trial – legal advice – denial of access to solicitor – safety of subsequent conviction in view of ECHR decision

[Northern Ireland (Emergency Provisions) Act 1987 s.15; Human Rights Act 1998; European Convention on Human Rights 1950 Art.6.]

M was convicted of serious terrorist offences for which he was sentenced to 20 years' imprisonment. The evidence against M consisted of oral admissions and a written statement he had made during police questioning. M contended that the statement was inadmissible as it was made after he had been ill treated and denied access to a solicitor under Northern Ireland (Emergency Provisions) Act 1987 s.15. The ill treatment allegations were rejected at trial and on appeal. M subsequently complained to the European Court of Human Rights, which held ((2001) 31 E.H.R.R. 35, [2000] C.L.Y. 3223) that the denial of access to a solicitor had breached the European Convention on Human Rights 1950 Art.6(1) and (3). Following the ECHR decision the matter was referred to the Court of Appeal by the Criminal Cases Review Commission and M submitted that the conviction was unsafe in view of the ECHR decision.

Held, allowing the appeal, that the decision of the ECHR that denying access to a solicitor was in breach of Art.6(1) meant that the conviction could not be regarded as safe. Any difference in approach that previously existed on that point had ended with the coming into force of the Human Rights Act 1998 and it would now be difficult for the domestic courts to reach a decision that differed from that of the ECHR, *R. v. Davis (Michael George) (No.3)* [2001] 1 Cr. App. R. 8, [2000] C.L.Y. 1056 and *R. v. Togher (Kenneth) (Appeal against Conviction)* [2001] 3 All E.R. 463, [2000] C.L.Y. 1026 followed.

R. v. MAGEE (MICHAEL GERARD) [2001] N.I. 217, Carswell, L.C.J., CA (Crim Div) (NI).

5878. **Right to liberty and security – personal injuries sustained following arrest – decision not to prosecute police officers – effectiveness of investigation**

[Human Rights Act 1998 s.6; European Convention on Human Rights 1950 Art.3, Art.7(1)(b).]

Following A's arrest for terrorist offences, for which he was later convicted, he was found to have a number of injuries and hospitalised for three weeks. A succeeded in an action against the RUC Chief Constable for damages for assault and battery, false imprisonment, breach of duty and misfeasance in public office by a number of officers. The DPP directed that no officers involved in A's arrest should be prosecuted and A sought judicial review of that decision. His application was dismissed at first instance and he appealed, contending that the DPP's decision was procedurally unfair and that the failure to give reasons for the decision amounted to continuing acts in terms of the Human Rights Act 1998. Further, that the refusal to allow A access to the investigation files was a breach of the State's duty to carry out an effective investigation into an alleged breach of the European Convention on Human Rights 1950 Art.3 and that the DPP had also failed to consider international human rights standards in reaching his decision.

Held, dismissing the appeal, that the DPP had to decide whether a prosecution should be brought in the public interest which meant that he was not subject to the rules of procedural fairness as he was not making an administrative decision. Similarly, he was not obliged to give reasons for his decisions and had no obligation to consult A or provide him with the investigation report. In any event, the public interest in keeping such details confidential outweighed A's desire to see the report, *R. v. DPP, ex p. Treadaway* Times, October 31, 1997, [1997] C.L.Y. 1371, approved. Although the DPP was a public authority in terms of s.6 of the 1998 Act he was not so bound when he made the decision in the instant case. As a result, there were no "continuing acts" that would allow A to invoke Art.7(1)(b) of the Convention to claim a breach of Art.3. A claimant could not demand access to the investigation report as a pre requisite for deeming the investigation effective as the effectiveness of a State investigation into its representatives' conduct was dependent on the facts of each case and could vary greatly from case to case. The DPP could resort to international human rights standards for guidance, but there was no obligation to do so where such standards had not been incorporated into domestic law, *R. v. Secretary of State for the Home Department, ex p. Brind* [1991] 1 A.C. 696, [1991] C.L.Y. 71 followed.

ADAMS'S APPLICATION FOR JUDICIAL REVIEW, Re [2001] N.I. 1, Carswell, L.C.J., CA (NI).

IMMIGRATION

5879. Deportation – right to life – suicide risk – effect of failure to take into account

[Human Rights Act 1998; Immigration (Control of Entry through the Republic of Ireland) Order 1972 (SI 1972 1610); European Convention on Human Rights 1950 Art.8; United Nations Convention on the Rights of the Child 1989; Treaty on European Union (Maastricht) 1992 Art.8(a).]

T, a US national, entered Northern Ireland legally from the Republic of Ireland. She stayed in Northern Ireland after the three months permitted under the Immigration (Control of Entry through the Republic of Ireland) Order 1972 and whilst illegally present in Northern Ireland she became pregnant and gave birth to a child. She afterwards contemplated suicide and a psychiatrist gave evidence that this would be a major concern if she was deported. The Secretary of State decided to deport T, and T sought judicial review of this decision, arguing that it was irrational on the grounds that the Secretary of State had merely paid "regard to" the European Convention on Human Rights 1950 Art.8. Further, that the Treaty on European Union (Maastricht) 1992 Art.8(a) created a right to move and settle freely within the EU, and if T were deported this right would be denied to her child. T also argued that she had a legitimate expectation that the UK would honour the terms of international agreements or treaties it had acceded to, including the 1950 Convention and the United Nations Convention on the Rights of the Child 1989. Additionally, that the Secretary of State had misdirected himself regarding the threat to her life if she was deported.

Held, allowing the application, that as the 1950 Convention did not yet have the force of law in the UK, it was not irrational only to pay regard to its provisions. A finding to the contrary would be to give effect to the Convention before the Human Rights Act 1998 entered into force. In any event, the facts showed there had been no breach of Art.8. *R. v. Ministry of Defence, ex p. Smith* [1996] Q.B. 517, [1996] C.L.Y. 383 applied. Article 8(a) of the 1992 Treaty did not create a free standing right to move or settle within the EU, so no rights had been denied to T's child, *R. v. Secretary of State for the Home Department, ex p. Phull* [1996] Imm. A.R. 72, [1996] C.L.Y. 3277 and *R. v. Secretary of State for the Home Department, ex p. Vitale* [1996] All E.R. (EC) 461, [1996] C.L.Y. 3164 applied. T's legitimate expectation extended only to the taking into account of the 1989 Convention and the UK's powers to exclude or deport those who were not entitled to remain when the Secretary of State was considering the position of T's child. This legitimate expectation had been fulfilled, *R. v. DPP, ex p. Kebilene* [2000] 2 A.C. 326, [1999] C.L.Y. 1045 and *R. v. North and East Devon HA, ex p. Coughlan* [2000] 2 W.L.R. 622, [1999] C.L.Y. 2643 applied. However, the Secretary of State had failed properly to assess the suicide risk and the effect it would have on T's child, so the decision would be quashed on that basis, *R. v. Ministry of Defence, ex p. Smith* and *R. v. Secretary of State for the Home Department, ex p. Turgut* [2001] 1 All E.R. 719, [2000] 3 C.L. 375 applied.

T'S APPLICATION FOR JUDICIAL REVIEW, Re [2000] N.I. 516, Coghlin, J., QBD (NI).

INSOLVENCY

5880. Administration of estates – disposition following death of insolvent – state of grantor's and grantee's knowledge

[Human Rights Act 1998 Sch.1 Part I Art.1, Art.6; Insolvency (Northern Ireland) Order 1989 (SI 1989 2405) Art.257; Administration of Insolvent Estates of Deceased Persons (Northern Ireland) Order 1991 (SR 1991 365) Sch.1 Pt.2

para.15; Rules of the Supreme Court (Northern Ireland) 1980 (SR 1980 346) Ord.18 r.19.]

B sought a declaration that it held a valid 25 year lease of premises granted to it by M's widow, S. M died in 1993 and his estate was declared insolvent in 1995. B claimed the lease was granted when neither it nor S knew M's estate was insolvent. L, the trustee of M's estate, contended that a disposition made between the date of death and the date when the estate vested in the trustee in bankruptcy was void by virtue of the Insolvency (Northern Ireland) Order 1989 Art.257, as amended by the Administration of Insolvent Estates of Deceased Persons (NI) Order 1991 Sch.1 Part 2 para.15. L therefore applied for B's claim to be struck out under the Rules of the Supreme Court (Northern Ireland) 1980 Ord.18 r.19 and under the court's inherent jurisdiction, on the grounds that it was an abuse of process and had no prospect of success. The application was refused at first instance and L appealed.

Held, dismissing the appeal, that Sch.1 Pt.2 para.15 was to be construed narrowly and in favour of the person whose interest was likely to be affected as it was a provision capable of expropriating property. The question was to be determined in line with common law principles and the Human Rights Act 1998 Sch.1 Part I Art.1, which prevented deprivation of property except where it was in the public interest and in accordance with domestic and international law. Article 1 required a balance to be observed between community rights and the rights of individuals, with the need for proportionality between the intended aim ·and the means used to achieve it. The deemed presentation of the petition on the date of death was not something that B had would have had notice of and neither B nor S knew of the insolvency when the lease was granted. Therefore there was a triable issue between B and L. Article 6 established the need for a fair trial in the circumstances and the court's inherent jurisdiction and its jurisdiction under RSC Ord.18 r.19 were compatible with Art.6.

McATEER v. LISMORE (TRUSTEE OF THE ESTATE OF JAMES KEVIN McATEER) (NO.1) [2000] N.I. 471, Girvan, J., Ch D (NI).

INTELLECTUAL PROPERTY

5881. Trade marks – distinctiveness – Pantone 348C used for service stations

[Trade Marks Act 1994.]

BP operated a chain of petrol stations in the Northern Ireland in a common livery of yellow and dark green (Pantone 348C) that were registered as a trade mark in Classes 4 and 37. JK operated a chain of petrol stations throughout Ireland under the name "TOP", using a darker green than BP (Pantone 341C) as the dominant colour. BP brought an action for trade mark infringement and passing off against JK, which counterclaimed for the revocation of BP's mark. Both the claim and counterclaim were refused at first instance ([2001] F.S.R. 21) and BP and JK appealed.

Held, allowing BP's appeal in respect of the infringement claim, that a colour or combination of colours could be registered as a trade mark under the Trade Marks Act 1994 s.1 (1) subject to refusal for lack of distinctiveness under s.3(1). BP had shown that consumers associated Pantone 348C with its stations by the time proceedings were commenced so that distinctiveness had been acquired through use for the purposes of s.47(1) and JK's appeal was dismissed, *Smith Kline & French Laboratories Ltd v. Sterling-Winthrop Group Ltd* [1975] 1 W.L.R. 914, [1976] C.L.Y. 2796 *Orange Personal Communications Services Ltd's Community Trade Mark Application (No.16139)* [1998] E.T.M.R. 337 and *Wm Wrigley Jr Co's Trade Mark Application* [1999] E.T.M.R. 214, [1999] C.L.Y. 3531 applied. Use of BP's registered mark precluded a defence based on the fact that the mark had been used with other material to distinguish it from BP's mark as this would deprive BP of the benefit of registration. The facts showed that confusion was likely so that the infringement claim was made out, *Lloyd Schuhfabrik Meyer & Co GmbH v. Klijsen Handel BV (C342/97)* [1999] All E.R.

(EC) 587, [1999] C.L.Y. 3538 applied; *Saville Perfumery v. June Perfect and FW Woolworth & Co Ltd* (1941) 58 R.P.C. 147, *Origins Natural Resources Inc v. Origin Clothing Ltd* [1995] F.S.R. 280, [1995] C.L.Y. 4940 followed. However, passing off was not established as consumers would notice when close enough to JK's stations that they were not selling BP's products.

BP AMOCO PLC v. JOHN KELLY LTD [2001] N.I. 25, Carswell, L.C.J., CA (NI).

LANDLORD AND TENANT

5882. Defective Premises (Landlord's Liability) Act (Northern Ireland) 2001 (c.10)

This Act amends the law as to the liability of landlords for injury or damage caused to persons through defects in the state of premises let under certain tenancies.

This Act comes into force on July 2, 2002.

5883. Registered rents – increase

REGISTERED RENTS (INCREASE) ORDER (NORTHERN IRELAND) 2001, SR 2001 57; made under the Rent (Northern Ireland) Order 1978 (SI 1978 1050 (NI.20)) Art.33. In force: March 5, 2001; £1.50.

This Order increases the rents registered with the Department for Social Development under the Rent (Northern Ireland) Order 1978 (SI 1978 1050 (NI.20)) Part.V, for dwelling houses let under regulated tenancies, by 3 per cent from March 5, 2001.

LEGAL AID

5884. Criminal procedure – costs

LEGAL AID IN CRIMINAL PROCEEDINGS (COSTS) (AMENDMENT) RULES (NORTHERN IRELAND) 2001, SR 2001 251; made under the Legal Aid, Advice and Assistance (Northern Ireland) Order 1981 (SI 1981 228 (NI.8)) Art.36. In force: June 29, 2001; £1.50.

These Rules amend the Legal Aid in Criminal Proceedings (Costs) Rules (Northern Ireland) 1992 (SR 1992 314) so as to alter the date after which certain work may be remunerated at discretionary instead of prescribed rates from June 30, 2001 to December 31, 2001.

5885. Criminal procedure – costs

LEGAL AID IN CRIMINAL PROCEEDINGS (COSTS) (AMENDMENT NO.2) RULES (NORTHERN IRELAND) 2001, SR 2001 426; made under the Legal Aid, Advice and Assistance (Northern Ireland) Order 1981 (SI 1981 228 (NI.8)) Art.36. In force: December 30, 2001; £1.50.

These Rules amend the Legal Aid in Criminal Proceedings (Costs) Rules (Northern Ireland) 1992 (SR 1992 314) to alter the date after which certain work may be remunerated at discretionary instead of prescribed rates from December 31, 2001 to December 31, 2002.

5886. Financial conditions – calculation of disposable income – limit increase

LEGAL AID (FINANCIAL CONDITIONS) REGULATIONS (NORTHERN IRELAND) 2001, SR 2001 111; made under the Legal Aid, Advice and Assistance (Northern Ireland) Order 1981 (SI 1981 228 (NI.8)) Art.9, Art.12, Art.22, Art.27. In force: April 9, 2001; £1.75.

These Regulations, which amend the Legal Aid, Advice and Assistance (Northern Ireland) Order 1981 (SI 1981 228 (NI.8)) and revoke, with savings, the Legal Aid (Financial Conditions) Regulations (Northern Ireland) 2000 (SR

2000 79), increase the upper income limit to make legal aid available to those with disposable incomes of not more than £8,196, or in connection with proceedings involving a personal injury £9,034. In addition, they increase the lower income limit below which legal aid is available without of a contribution to £2,767.

5887. Legal services – advice and assistance – contributions

LEGAL ADVICE AND ASSISTANCE (AMENDMENT NO.2) REGULATIONS (NORTHERN IRELAND) 2001, SR 2001 113; made under the Legal Aid, Advice and Assistance (Northern Ireland) Order 1981 (SI 1981 228 (NI.8)) Art.7(2), Art.22, Art.27. In force: April 9, 2001; £1.75.

These Regulations, which revoke the Legal Advice and Assistance (Amendment) Regulations (Northern Ireland) 2000 (SR 2000 81), amend the Legal Advice and Assistance Regulations (Northern Ireland) 1981 (SR 1981 366) to substitute a new scale of contributions payable for legal advice.

5888. Legal services – advice and assistance – income limits

LEGAL ADVICE AND ASSISTANCE (FINANCIAL CONDITIONS) REGULATIONS (NORTHERN IRELAND) 2001, SR 2001 112; made under the Legal Aid, Advice and Assistance (Northern Ireland) Order 1981 (SI 1981 228 (NI.8)) Art.3, Art.7, Art.22, Art.27. In force: April 9, 2001; £1.50.

These Regulations, which amend Legal Aid, Advice and Assistance (Northern Ireland) Order 1981 (SR 1981 228) and revoke the Legal Advice and Assistance (Financial Conditions) Regulations (Northern Ireland) 2000 (SR 2000 80), increase the upper income limit to make legal advice and assistance available to those with disposable income of not more than £186 a week. In addition, they increase the lower limit below which legal advice and assistance is available without payment of a contribution to £76.

5889. Legal services – advice and assistance – life sentence prisoners

LEGAL ADVICE AND ASSISTANCE (AMENDMENT NO.3) REGULATIONS (NORTHERN IRELAND) 2001, SR 2001 290; made under the Legal Aid, Advice and Assistance (Northern Ireland) Order 1981 (SI 1981 228 (NI.8)) Art.5, Art.22. In force: September 1, 2001; £1.50.

These Regulations amend the Legal Advice and Assistance Regulations (Northern Ireland) 1981 (SR 1981 366) to extend assistance by way of representation to life sentence prisoners at hearings before the Life Sentence Review Commissioners.

5890. Legal services – advice and assistance – warrant for detention

LEGAL ADVICE AND ASSISTANCE (AMENDMENT) REGULATIONS (NORTHERN IRELAND) 2001, SR 2001 9; made under the Legal Aid, Advice and Assistance (Northern Ireland) Order 1981 (SI 1981 228 (NI.8)) Art.5, Art.22, Art.27. In force: February 19, 2001; £1.50.

These Regulations, which amend the Legal Advice and Assistance Regulations (Northern Ireland) 1981 (SI 1981 228), provide that assistance by way of representation under the Legal Aid, Advice and Assistance (Northern Ireland) Order 1981 (SR 1981 366) Art.5 is extended to persons in respect of whom an application for a warrant of further detention or for an extension of such a warrant is made. They also provide that the means test and contributions test which would otherwise apply under the 1981 Order are removed in respect of applications for assistance by way of representation to proceedings under the Terrorism Act 2000 Sch.8 para.29 and Sch.8 para.36.

LEGAL SYSTEMS

5891. Books
> Byrne, Raymond; Mccutcheon, J.Paul – Byrne & Mccutcheon: the Irish Legal System. 4th Ed. Paperback: £60.00. ISBN 1-85475-286-3. Butterworths Law.

LICENSING

5892. Gambling – bingo – fees
> GAMING (BINGO) (AMENDMENT) REGULATIONS (NORTHERN IRELAND) 2001, SR 2001 415; made under the Betting, Gaming, Lotteries and Amusements (Northern Ireland) Order 1985 (SI 1985 1204 (NI.11)) Art.76. In force: January 16, 2002; £1.50.
>
> These Regulations amend the Gaming (Bingo) Regulations (Northern Ireland) 1987 (SR 1987 8) by increasing the maximum charge which may be made in respect of gaming by way of bingo on bingo club premises from £8.50 to £10. In addition, they revoke the Gaming (Bingo (Amendment) and Gaming Machine (Registered Clubs)) Regulations (Northern Ireland) 1999 (SR 1999 5)

5893. Gambling – prizes – variation of monetary limits
> GAMING (VARIATION OF MONETARY LIMITS) ORDER (NORTHERN IRELAND) 2001, SR 2001 414; made under the Betting, Gaming, Lotteries and Amusements (Northern Ireland) Order 1985 (SI 1985 1204 (NI.11)) Art.75, Art.76, Art.77, Art.126, Art.128. In force: in accordance with Art.1 (1); £2.00.
>
> This Order increases the maximum permitted aggregate amount of winnings in respect of games of bingo played in one week simultaneously on different bingo club premises from £30,000 to £55,000; increases the maximum amount by which weekly winnings on bingo club premises may exceed the stakes hazarded from £5,500 to £10,000; increases, in gaming for prizes on bingo club premises; increases, in gaming at entertainments not held for private gain; and increases the maximum daily charge for gaming in certain clubs from £0.50 to £0.60 and the maximum daily charge for gaming in such clubs from £6 to £15 when only bridge and/or whist are/is played.

LOCAL GOVERNMENT

5894. Grants – central funds – calculation of grant from Department of the Environment
> LOCAL GOVERNMENT (GENERAL GRANT) ORDER (NORTHERN IRELAND) 2001, SR 2001 395; made under the Local Government &c. (Northern Ireland) Order 1972 (SI 1972 1999 (NI.22)) Sch.1 para.3. In force: January 31, 2002; £1.75.
>
> This Order specifies those districts to be taken into account in calculating the standard penny rate products for the year ending March 31, 2002 for the purpose of computing the resources element of the grant made from central funds by the Department of the Environment to district councils. In addition, it revokes the Local Government (General Grant) Order (Northern Ireland) 1997 (SR 1997 242) and the Local Government (General Grant) Order (Northern Ireland) 1998 (SI 1998 185).

5895. Grants – central funds – specified bodies
> GENERAL GRANT (SPECIFIED BODIES) REGULATIONS (NORTHERN IRELAND) 2001, SR 2001 178; made under the Local Government &c.

(Northern Ireland) Order 1972 (SI 1972 1999 (NI.22)) Art.4. In force: June 4, 2001; £1.50.

These Regulations revoke and replace the General Grant (Specified Bodies) Regulations (Northern Ireland) 1994 (SR 1994 418). The bodies specified for the purposes of the Local Government etc. (Northern Ireland) Order 1972 (SI 1972 1999 (NI.22)) are amended to take account of the amalgamation of the National Joint Council for Local Authorities' Administrative, Professional Technical and Clerical Services with the National Joint Council for Local Authorities' Services (Manual Workers), which is now known as the National Joint Council for Local Government Services and the Northern Ireland Joint Council for Local Authorities' Administrative, Professional Technical and Clerical Services with the Northern Ireland Joint Industrial Council for Local Authorities' Services (Manual Workers), which is now known as the Northern Ireland Joint Council for Local Government Services.

5896. Street trading – form of licence

STREET TRADING (FORM OF LICENCE) REGULATIONS (NORTHERN IRELAND) 2001, SR 2001 166; made under the Street Trading Act (Northern Ireland) 2001 s.6. In force: October 1, 2001; £2.00.

These Regulations, which revoke the Street Trading Regulations 1929 (SR & O 1929 102), prescribe the form of a street trading licence, including its renewal and any variation in the conditions, which may be issued by a District Council authorising a person to trade as a stationary or mobile street trader.

5897. Street trading – penalties – notices and procedure

STREET TRADING (FIXED PENALTY) (NOTICE AND PROCEDURE) REGULATIONS (NORTHERN IRELAND) 2001, SR 2001 165; made under the Street Trading Act (Northern Ireland) 2001 s.22, Sch.1 para.2, Sch.1 para.3. In force: October 1, 2001; £2.00.

These Regulations prescribe the form of the fixed penalty notice which may be given by an authorised officer of a district council to a person under the Street Trading Act (Northern Ireland) 2001 Sch.1. The notice offers the opportunity of discharging any liability to conviction of the offence under s.21 (a) or (b) of the Act which relate to the contravention, without reasonable excuse, of certain conditions of a street trading licence by selling or supplying different articles, things or services to those specified; using receptacles of a different nature, size, type or number to those specified; failing to display prominently the name and licence number of the licence holder; failing to comply with the conditions governing the storage of articles, things or receptacles; and failing to comply with the conditions governing the deposit and removal of refuse, including any containers used and their location and failing, on demand, to produce a street trading licence or temporary licence to an authorised officer of the district council or a police constable. They also prescribe the information to be supplied to a clerk of petty sessions in relation to a fixed penalty notice.

5898. Street Trading Act (Northern Ireland) 2001 (c.8)

This Act makes provision for the regulation by district councils of street trading in their districts.

This Act received Royal Assent on April 5, 2001.

5899. Street Trading Act (Northern Ireland) 2001 (c.8) – Commencement Order

STREET TRADING (2001 ACT) (COMMENCEMENT) ORDER (NORTHERN IRELAND) 2001, SR 2001 164 (C.11); made under the Street Trading Act (Northern Ireland) 2001 s.29. Commencement details: bringing into force the 2001 Act on October 1, 2001; £1.50.

This Order provides for the coming into operation of the provisions of the Street Trading Act (Northern Ireland) 2001 on October 1, 2001.

NEGLIGENCE

5900. Professional negligence – solicitors – failure to take action as instructed by client – debts incurred due to borrowing – measure of damages

Following the purchase of freehold commercial premises, M instructed JD, a firm of solicitors, to pursue claims against the vendor and a subsequent tenant. JD failed to do so, although they informed M that the matters were in hand, however the claims eventually became statute barred. As M was relying on payment of sums due from the proceedings, he obtained an overdraft from the bank backed by assurances from JD that recovery was imminent. M also remortgaged his house to cover the overdraft and later sued JD for the value of the overdraft and the remortgage on the ground that he would not have had to borrow those amounts but for JD's negligence and/or breach of duty.

Held, giving judgment for M, that JD had a duty to inform M of the truth as they knew both the extent of his indebtedness and that no sums would be recovered from the proceedings, *Pearson v. Sanders Witherspoon (A Firm)* [2000] Lloyd's Rep. P.N. 151, [2000] C.L.Y. 4009 followed. JD's failure to reveal the true position led M to obtain the overdraft and the subsequent remortgage. On the facts, therefore, JD's breach of duty had caused M to take on the overdraft and remortgage his home in circumstances where JD had given assurances to the bank and mortgagee on the basis of the claims relating to the property purchase, *Galoo Ltd v. Bright Grahame Murray* [1994] 1 W.L.R. 1360, [1995] C.L.Y. 3691 considered.

MacMAHON v. JAMES DORAN & CO [2001] P.N.L.R. 35, Higgins, J., QBD (NI).

5901. Statutory duty – child injured playing on skateboard in alley – rights of way

[Roads (Northern Ireland) Order 1993 (SI 1993 3160) Art.8(1).]

S, a girl aged eight, sustained injury when the skateboard she was riding down an alley hit a piece of wood used as a temporary grate cover. The wood was not flush with the surrounding flags and the court at first instance awarded S damages of £5,000, holding that if S had been pedestrian who had tripped on the piece of wood, DENI would have been liable for failing to maintain the alley under the Roads (Northern Ireland) Order 1993 Art.8(1). DENI appealed, arguing that it had no duty to make footpaths safe for skateboarders, and that S was using the alley at the time of the incident for play, and not for passage.

Held, allowing the appeal, that DENI was under no duty to keep footpaths safe for anything other than pedestrian traffic, and the use of a skateboard did not fall within the definition of pedestrian traffic. However, DENI's submission that S was not entitled to recover because she was using the alley for play, as opposed to passage, was rejected. If she had simply been playing on foot in the alley and tripped on the piece of wood, she would have been entitled to recover damages against DENI for failing to maintain the alley, *Ingram v. Department of the Environment for Northern Ireland* (Unreported, September 6, 1993) followed.

S (A CHILD) v. DEPARTMENT OF THE ENVIRONMENT FOR NORTHERN IRELAND [2000] N.I. 512, Sheil, J., QBD (NI).

PENOLOGY

5902. Life imprisonment – consequential amendments

LIFE SENTENCES (NORTHERN IRELAND CONSEQUENTIAL AMENDMENTS) ORDER 2001, SI 2001 2565; made under the Northern Ireland Act 1998 s.84. In force: in accordance with Art.1 (2); £1.75.

This Order, which makes amendments to the Repatriation of Prisoners Act 1984, the Crime (Sentences) Act 1997, the Freedom of Information Act 2000 and the

International Criminal Court Act 2001, provides for the release and recall of persons serving a sentence of life imprisonment or detention during the pleasure of the Secretary of State.

5903. Life imprisonment – detention – prisoners – practice and procedure

LIFE SENTENCE REVIEW COMMISSIONERS' RULES 2001, SR 2001 317; made under the Life Sentences (Northern Ireland) Order 2001 (SI 2001 2564 (NI.2)) Art.4, Sch.2. In force: October 8, 2001; £3.00.

These Rules prescribe the practice and procedure to be followed by panels of Life Sentence Review Commissioners in dealing with the hearing of cases of life prisoners under the Life Sentences (Northern Ireland) Order 2001. They include provision for the appointment of, and procedures to be followed by, panels of Commissioners, the making of directions by the chairman of a panel for the conduct of a case, the appointment of a special advocate in cases involving confidential information and the reduction of time limits to permit the early hearing of cases involving recalled life prisoners. In addition, the Rules provide for the service of documents on the Secretary of State at Northern Ireland Prison Service Headquarters.

5904. Life Sentences (Northern Ireland) Order 2001 (SI 2001 2564 (NI.2))

This Order, which amends the Criminal Justice (Children) (Northern Ireland) Order 1998 (SI 1998 1504) (NI.9)), provides for the release and recall of persons serving a sentence of life imprisonment or detention during the pleasure of the Secretary of State.

5905. Life Sentences (Northern Ireland) Order 2001 (SI 2001/2564 (NI.2)) – Commencement Order

LIFE SENTENCES (NORTHERN IRELAND) ORDER 2001 (COMMENCEMENT) ORDER 2001, SR 2001 337 (C.17); made under the Life Sentences (Northern Ireland) Order 2001 Art.1. In force: bringing into operation the 2001 Order on October 8, 2001; £1.50.

This Order brings into operation the Life Sentences (Northern Ireland) Order 2001 (SI 2001 2564 (NI.2)) which provides for the release and recall of persons serving a sentence of life imprisonment or detention during the pleasure of the Secretary of State.

5906. Prisoners rights – freedom of association – segregation for own safety – transfer denied on policy grounds

[European Convention on Human Rights 1950 Art.3, Art.7, Art.8.]

F, a convicted prisoner, had been placed in the punishment and segregation unit, PSU, at M prison for his own protection. He applied for a transfer to another prison but this was refused and F sought to challenge the refusal by way of judicial review. The prison governor stated that the decision to refuse F's transfer was due to the policy of housing prisoners convicted of terrorist offences after April 10, 1998 at M prison. F contended that the conditions in which he was held, with association confined to one other inmate, were in breach of the European Convention on Human Rights 1950 Art.3, Art.7 and Art. 8.

Held, refusing the application, that (1) it was permissible to keep F in the PSU, provided that proper consideration was given to the length of his detention there and its potential effects. It was also relevant to take into account the Secretary of State's policy regarding the treatment of prisoners following the Good Friday Agreement and the ceasefires declared by certain terrorist groups. In the circumstances of the instant case, F's treatment was not in breach of Art.3; (2) since the court did not decide what conditions F should be held in after his conviction, such conditions were not a "penalty" in terms of Art.7, and (3) F's claim that the limitation on his right to association with other inmates infringed his rights under Art.8 could not succeed. Such limitations could be imposed for administrative or security purposes or for reasons of F's own safety. F's case amounted to a claim that he should be moved merely to allow him to associate. This would amount to a major breach in government policy on the accommodation of prisoners following the Good Friday Agreement and the factor on which the Agreement was based outweighed F's personal considerations.

FULTON'S APPLICATION FOR JUDICIAL REVIEW, Re [2000] N.I. 447, Kerr, J., QBD (NI).

PENSIONS

5907. Benefits – widows and widowers – expatriates

WELFARE REFORM AND PENSIONS (PERSONS ABROAD: BENEFITS FOR WIDOWS AND WIDOWERS) (CONSEQUENTIAL AMENDMENTS) REGULATIONS (NORTHERN IRELAND) 2001, SR 2001 287; made under the Welfare Reform and Pensions (Northern Ireland) Order 1999 (SI 1999 3147 (NI.11)) Art.75. In force: August 20, 2001; £1.75.

These Regulations amend the Social Security Benefit (Persons Abroad) Regulations (Northern Ireland) 1978 (SR 1978 114) by inserting a definition of "bereavement payment" and providing that a person is not to be disqualified for receiving a bereavement payment by reason of being absent from Northern Ireland where, at the time of the deceased spouse's death, either the deceased spouse or the surviving spouse was in Northern Ireland.

5908. Occupational pensions – benefits – revaluation percentages

OCCUPATIONAL PENSIONS (REVALUATION) ORDER (NORTHERN IRELAND) 2001, SR 2001 412; made under the Pension Schemes (Northern Ireland) Act 1993 Sch.2 para.2. In force: January 1, 2002; £1.50.

This Order specifies appropriate revaluation percentages relevant to the revaluation of benefits under occupational pension schemes, as required by the Pension Schemes (Northern Ireland) Act 1993.

5909. Occupational pensions – guaranteed minimum pensions – increase

GUARANTEED MINIMUM PENSIONS INCREASE ORDER (NORTHERN IRELAND) 2001, SR 2001 42; made under the Pension Schemes (Northern Ireland) Act 1993 s.105. In force: April 6, 2001; £1.75.

This Order specifies 3 per cent as the percentage by which that part of any guaranteed minimum pension attributable to earnings factors for the tax years 1988-89 to 1996-97 and payable by occupational pension schemes is to be increased.

5910. Occupational pensions – local government pension scheme

LOCAL GOVERNMENT PENSION SCHEME (AMENDMENT) REGULATIONS (NORTHERN IRELAND) 2001, SR 2001 63; made under the Superannuation (Northern Ireland) Order 1972 (SI 1972 1073 (NI.10)) Art.9, Art.14, Sch.3. In force: April 2, 2001; £1.75.

These Regulations, which amend the Local Government Pension Scheme Regulations (Northern Ireland) 2000 (SR 2000 177), remove an age restriction whereby a person aged 50 or more can be refused membership of the Scheme by his employer if he had been previously employed by that employer but despite being eligible had elected not to become or to cease being a member of the Scheme. Reg.E3 of the principal Regulations, which specified the death grant to be paid in respect of pensioners with 10 years' or more membership of the Scheme, is revoked and a new Reg.E4 is substituted which specifies that if any pensioner dies within five years of his retirement pension becoming payable a death grant equal to five years' pension less the pension already paid is payable.

5911. Occupational pensions – local government pension scheme – divorce – pension sharing

LOCAL GOVERNMENT PENSION SCHEME (PENSION SHARING ON DIVORCE) REGULATIONS (NORTHERN IRELAND) 2001, SR 2001 61; made under the Superannuation (Northern Ireland) Order 1972 (SI 1972 1073 (NI.10)) Art.9, Art.14, Sch.3. In force: April 2, 2001; £2.50.

These Regulations, which amend the Local Government Pension Scheme Regulations (Northern Ireland) 2000 (SR 2000 177) and the Local Government Pension Scheme (Investment and Management of Funds) Regulations (Northern Ireland) 2000 (SR 2000 178), make provision in connection with the pension rights of certain members of the Local Government Pension Scheme in relation to the sharing of pensions following divorce or nullity of a marriage, introduced by the Welfare Reform and Pensions (Northern Ireland) Order 1999 (SI 1999 3147 (NI.11)).

5912. Occupational pensions – local government pension scheme – management and investment of funds

LOCAL GOVERNMENT PENSION SCHEME (MANAGEMENT AND INVESTMENT OF FUNDS) (AMENDMENT) REGULATIONS (NORTHERN IRELAND) 2001, SR 2001 62; made under the Superannuation (Northern Ireland) Order 1972 (SI 1972 1073 (NI.10)) Art.9, Art.14, Sch.3. In force: April 2, 2001; £1.75.

These Regulations, which amend the Local Government Pension Scheme (Management and Investment of Funds) Regulations (Northern Ireland) 2000 (SR 2000 178), amend the description of an insurance company with whom an insurance contract, which counts as an investment for the purposes of the principal Regulations, may be made.

5913. Occupational pensions – local government pension scheme – membership

LOCAL GOVERNMENT PENSION SCHEME (AMENDMENT NO.2) REGULATIONS (NORTHERN IRELAND) 2001, SR 2001 64; made under the Superannuation (Northern Ireland) Order 1972 (SI 1972 1073 (NI.10)) Art.9, Sch.3. In force: April 2, 2001; £2.50.

These Regulations, which amend the Local Government Pension Scheme Regulations (Northern Ireland) 2000 (SR 2000 177) which comprise the Local Government Pension Scheme, allow employees of transferee admission bodies to become members.

5914. Occupational pensions – local government pension scheme – payments and injury benefits

LOCAL GOVERNMENT (DISCRETIONARY PAYMENTS) REGULATIONS (NORTHERN IRELAND) 2001, SR 2001 279; made under the Superannuation (Northern Ireland) Order 1972 (SI 1972 1073 (NI.10)) Art.9, Art.19. In force: August 28, 2001; £6.50.

These Regulations amend the Local Government (Superannuation and Compensation) (Amendment) Regulations (Northern Ireland) 1991 (SR 1991 19), the Local Government (Superannuation) Regulations (Northern Ireland) 1992 (SR 1992 547) and the Local Government (Superannuation and Compensation) (Institutions of Further Education) Regulations (Northern Ireland) 1998 (SR 1998 41). They revoke with savings the Local Government (Compensation for Premature Retirement) Regulations (Northern Ireland) 1983 (SR 1983 30), the Local Government (Compensation for Redundancy and Premature Retirement) Regulations (Northern Ireland 1986 (SR 1986 80) and the Local Government (Compensation for Premature Retirement) (Amendment)

Regulations (Northern Ireland) 1998 (SR 1998 286). These Regulations contain all the provisions relating to discretionary payments.

5915. Occupational pensions – mistaken payment – compensation for distressed caused

E was employed by SV for 27 years until her retirement in 1986, during which time she served as personnel manager and pension scheme trustee. In 1987 she agreed that a policy should be purchased on her behalf by the trustees in substitution for her rights under SV's pension scheme. In 1993, E was wrongly informed by the trustees agent that she was entitled to a pension of £5,712 per annum from the scheme, which she elected to receive as a tax free lump sum of £169,257 with annual payments of £3,875. The error was discovered in 1997 when the trustees requested their solicitor to reclaim the money from E with seven days notice. E complained to the Ombudsman, who found that the repayment demand amounted to maladministration for which E was liable to be compensated for the distress caused in the sum of £200 each from the trustees and their solicitor, even though E knew that the payments had been made under a mistake of fact. SV appealed.

Held, allowing the appeal, that the solicitor had not been concerned in the administration of the scheme so that the Ombudsman could not claim jurisdiction on that basis. The tone of the letter requesting the repayment was brusque but did not cause E any injustice, given her knowledge as to the nature of the mistake. However, it could not be determined that the Ombudsman was not entitled to find maladministration.

EWING v. STOCKHAM VALVE LTD STAFF RETIREMENT BENEFITS SCHEME TRUSTEES [2000] O.P.L.R. 257, Sir Robert Carswell, L.C.J., CA (NI).

5916. Occupational pensions – personal pensions – perpetuities and contracting out

OCCUPATIONAL AND PERSONAL PENSION SCHEMES (PERPETUITIES AND CONTRACTING-OUT) (AMENDMENT) REGULATIONS (NORTHERN IRELAND) 2001, SR 2001 118; made under the Pension Schemes (Northern Ireland) Act 1993 s.5, s.159, s.172. In force: April 6, 2001; £1.75.

These Regulations amend the Social Security (Hospital In-Patients) Regulations (Northern Ireland) 1975 (SR 1975 109) to provide for a decrease, from 40 per cent. to 39 per cent. of the basic retirement pension, in the percentage by which the personal rate of certain benefits is reduced in certain circumstances in respect of persons who receive continuous free in-patient treatment in a hospital or similar institution for more than 6 weeks but not more than 52 weeks.

5917. Pensions Appeal Tribunals

PENSIONS APPEAL TRIBUNALS (NORTHERN IRELAND) (AMENDMENT) RULES 2001, SR 2001 109; made under the Pensions Appeal Tribunals Act 1943 s.6, Sch.1 para.5, Sch.1 para.6. In force: April 9, 2001; £2.00.

These Rules amend the Pensions Appeal Tribunals (Northern Ireland) Rules 1981 (SR 1981 231) to reflect the amendments to the Pensions Appeal Tribunals Acts made by the Child Support, Pension and Social Security Act 2000.

5918. Police – Royal Ulster Constabulary – occupational pensions

ROYAL ULSTER CONSTABULARY PENSIONS (AMENDMENT) REGULATIONS 2001, SR 2001 263; made under the Police (Northern Ireland) Act 1998 s.25. In force: August 1, 2001; £2.50.

These Regulations apply the RUC Pensions Regulations 1988 (SR 1988 374) to auxiliary members in service from April 6, 1988 other than those who were permanent members of the Ulster Special Constabulary immediately before May 1, 1970.

5919. Public service – pensions – increase in rates

PENSIONS INCREASE (REVIEW) ORDER (NORTHERN IRELAND) 2001, SR 2001 94; made under the Social Security Pensions (Northern Ireland) Order 1975 (SI 1975 1503 (NI.19)) Art.69. In force: April 9, 2001; £2.00.

This Order provides for increases in the rates of public services pensions as required under the Social Security Pensions (Northern Ireland) Order 1975 (SI 1975 1503 (NI.15)) Art.69. The increase to be made in the rates of such pensions is the percentage (or in some circumstances a fraction of the percentage) by which the Department for Social Development has, by virtue of the provisions of s.132 of the Social Security Administration (Northern Ireland) Act 1992, increased the sums which are the additional pensions in long-term benefits, namely the additional pension entitlements accruing to employees in respect of their earnings after April 5, 1978.

5920. Stakeholder pensions – restriction of membership

STAKEHOLDER PENSION SCHEMES (AMENDMENT) REGULATIONS (NORTHERN IRELAND) 2001, SR 2001 13; made under the Welfare Reform and Pensions (Northern Ireland) Order 1999 (SI 1999 3147 (NI.11)) Art.3, Art.73. In force: February 14, 2001; £1.75.

These Regulations amend the Stakeholder Pension Schemes Regulations (Northern Ireland) 2000 (SR 2000 262) to permit stakeholder schemes established otherwise than under a trust to restrict membership of the scheme by reference to employment or to membership of a particular organisation. They clarify, for both non-trust and trust schemes, that restrictions may be imposed on payment of contributions by cash or a credit card and to include the authorised corporate director of an open-ended investment company among the categories of person who may be the manager of a non-trust scheme.

5921. Stakeholder pensions – restriction of membership

STAKEHOLDER PENSION SCHEMES (AMENDMENT NO.2) REGULATIONS (NORTHERN IRELAND) 2001, SR 2001 119; made under the Pensions (Northern Ireland) Order 1995 (SI 1995 3213 (NI.22)) Art.3, Art.10, Art.41, Art.50, Art.166; and the Welfare Reform and Pensions (Northern Ireland) Order 1999 3147 (NI.11)) Art.3, Art.5. In force: April 5, 2001; £4.00.

These Regulations, which amend the Stakeholder Pension Schemes Regulations (Northern Ireland) 2000 (SR 2000 262), provide that those who are not employees of the employer on the date of commencement of consultation do not have to be consulted. They make different provision as to means of payment of contributions, expand on the requirements relating to investments and investment options, clarify that a reporting accountant must be appointed for a scheme established under a trust, change the required content of the trustees' or manager's annual declaration, provide for an additional ground of refusal of contributions, allow different statement years to be chosen for different persons, prescribe additional exceptions to the definition of "relevant employees" and change and clarify provisions governing deductions of contributions from remuneration, including providing for additional grounds of non-compliance with requests as to such deductions. In addition, they ensure that there remains a time limit for appointment of a replacement reporting accountant in relation to removal, resignation or death.

5922. Superannuation – Chief Executive to the Mental Health Commission

SUPERANNUATION (CHIEF EXECUTIVE TO THE MENTAL HEALTH COMMISSION) ORDER (NORTHERN IRELAND) 2001, SR 2001 69; made under the Superannuation (Northern Ireland) Order 1972 (SI 1972 1073 (NI.10)) Art.3. In force: April 4, 2001; £1.50.

This Order adds the office of Chief Executive to the Mental Health Commission to the offices listed in the Superannunation (Northern Ireland) Order 1972 (SI 1972 1073 (NI.10)) for which the Department of Finance and Personnel may make pensions schemes. In addition, the Order revokes the Superannuation (Secretary toThe Mental Health Commission) Order (Northern Ireland) 1999 (SR 1999 438).

5923. Superannuation – teachers

TEACHER'S SUPERANNUATION (SHARING OF PENSIONS ON DIVORCE OR ANNULMENT) REGULATIONS (NORTHERN IRELAND) 2001, SR 2001 149; made under the Superannuation (Northern Ireland) Order 1972 (SI 1972 1073 (NI.10)) Art.11, Art.14, Sch.3 para.1, Sch.3 para.3, Sch.3 para.4, Sch.3 para.6, Sch.3 para.8, Sch.3 para.9, Sch.3 para.11, Sch.3 para.12, Sch.3 para.13. In force: May 1, 2001; £3.00.

These Regulations, which amend the Teachers' Superannuation (Additional Voluntary Contributions) Regulations (Northern Ireland) 1996 (SR 1996 260) and the Teachers' Superannuation Regulations (Northern Ireland) 1998 (SR 1998 333), make provision for pension benefits to a former spouse following the sharing of pensions on divorce or nullity of marriage.

5924. Welfare Reform and Pensions (Northern Ireland) Order 1999 (SI 1999 3147 (NI.11)) – Commencement No.8 Order

WELFARE REFORM AND PENSIONS (1999 ORDER) (COMMENCEMENT NO.8) ORDER (NORTHERN IRELAND) 2001, SR 2001 137 (C.7); made under the Welfare Reform and Pensions (Northern Ireland) Order 1999 (SI 1999 3147 (NI.11)) Art.1. Commencement details: bringing into force various provisions of the Order on April 23, 2001; £1.75.

This Order provides for the coming into operation on April 23, 2001 of the remaining provisions of the Welfare Reform and Pensions (Northern Ireland) Order 1999 (SI 1999 3147 (NI.11)) Art.16 to make further provision for the compensation payable by the Pensions Compensation Board to schemes whose assets have been reduced in value as a result of certain acts or omissions.

PLANNING

5925. Land drainage – environmental impact assessments

DRAINAGE (ENVIRONMENTAL IMPACT ASSESSMENT) REGULATIONS (NORTHERN IRELAND) 2001, SR 2001 394; made under the European Communities Act 1972 s.2. In force: November 26, 2001; £6.00.

These Regulations, which amend the Water and Sewerage Services (Northern Ireland) Order 1973 (SI 1973 69) and the Water (Northern Ireland) Order 1999 (SI 1999 662), revoke with savings the Drainage (Environmental Assessment) Regulations (Northern Ireland) 1991 (SI 1991 (SR 1991 376) and the Drainage (Environmental Assessment) (Amendment) Regulations (Northern Ireland) 1998 (SR 1998 446). They implement Council Directive 85/337 ([1985] OJ L175/40) on the assessment of the effects of certain public and private projects on the environment as amended by Council Directive 97/11 and prohibit the responsible Department carrying out drainage works or marina works, drainage schemes or canal schemes unless specified conditions are met.

5926. Planning permission – applications – fees

PLANNING (FEES) (AMENDMENT) REGULATIONS (NORTHERN IRELAND) 2001, SR 2001 225; made under the Planning (Northern Ireland) Order 1991 (SI 1991 1220 (NI. 11)) Art.127, Art.129. In force: July 9, 2001; £2.00.

These Regulations amend the Planning (Fees) Regulations (Northern Ireland) 1995 (SR 1995 78) which prescribe fees payable to the Department of the Environment in respect of applications made under the Planning (Northern Ireland) Order 1991 (SI 1991 1220) for planning permission for development of land and for approval of matters reserved in an outline planning permission, for consent for the display of advertisements and for listed building consent. In addition, they increase reduced fees, certain fees for deemed applications, fees for applications for determination as to the need for planning permission or listed building consent, fees for applications or deemed application by certain non-profit making organisations and for certain applications for approval of reserved matters and fees for applications for consent to display advertisements, by approximately 3 per cent.

5927. Planning (Compensation, etc.) Act (Northern Ireland) 2001 (c.2)

This Act abolishes the right to compensation in respect of certain planning decisions and amends Planning (Northern Ireland) Order 1991 Art.121 (1) (c) (iv).

This Act received Royal Assent on March 20, 2001 and comes into force on March 20, 2001.

POLICE

5928. Arrest – warrants – false imprisonment owing to mistake – liability of police in absence of bad faith

See ADMINISTRATION OF JUSTICE: McGrath v. Chief Constable of the Royal Ulster Constabulary. §5650

5929. Police – Northern Ireland Policing Board – nominations – prescribed period

NORTHERN IRELAND POLICING BOARD (PRESCRIBED PERIOD) REGULATIONS 2001, SR 2001 35; made under the Police (Northern Ireland) Act 2000 Sch.1 para.7. In force: February 2, 2001; £1.50.

These Regulations, which revoke the Northern Ireland Policing Board (Prescribed Period) Regulations 2000 (SR 2000 386), prescribe the period of 15 days as the period during which the process of appointing political members to the Northern Ireland Policing Board should be completed. They also provide for a period of three days during which a political party's nominating officer should make a nomination and the nominated person should take up office. The Regulations provide for a further period of three days during which the vacancy should be filled if the relevant nominating officer fails to nominate or the nominated person does not take up office.

5930. Police – Royal Ulster Constabulary – complaints

RUC (COMPLAINTS ETC) REGULATIONS 2001, SR 2001 184; made under the Police (Northern Ireland) Act 1998 s.64. In force: May 2, 2001; £2.00.

These Regulations amend the Royal Ulster Constabulary Reserve (Part-time) (Discipline and Disciplinary Appeals) Regulations 1988 (SR 1988 8), the Royal Ulster Constabulary (Discipline and Disciplinary) Appeals Regulations 1988 (SR 1988 10), the Royal Ulster Constabulary (Conduct) Regulations 2000 (SR 2000 315), the Royal Ulster Constabulary (Complaints etc.) Regulations 2000 (SR 2000 318) and the Royal Ulster Constabulary (Conduct) (Senior Officers) Regulations 2000 (SR 2000 320). They set out the circumstances in which the Ombudsman may investigate complaints depending on the date the police conduct in question took place and whether or not it has previously been dealt with.

5931. Police – Royal Ulster Constabulary Reserve – terms and conditions of service – full-time

ROYAL ULSTER CONSTABULARY RESERVE (FULL-TIME) (APPOINTMENT AND CONDITIONS OF SERVICE) (AMENDMENT) REGULATIONS 2001, SR

2001 80; made under the Police (Northern Ireland) Act 1998 s.26. In force: March 16, 2001; £2.50.

These Regulations, which amend the Royal Ulster Constabulary Reserve (Full-time) (Appointment and Conditions of Service) Regulations 1996 (SR 1996 564), authorise the chief constable to make part-time appointments and apply the regulations to part-time appointees. Part-time reserve constables may now be required to serve a further period of probation and part-time duty is to be performed in accordance with general arrangements made by the chief constable after consulting the Police Authority and the Police Association, an individual's normal period of duty during a duty roster period being a number of hours determined with his agreement by the chief constable.

5932. Police officers – recruitment – trainees

POLICE (RECRUITMENT) (NORTHERN IRELAND) REGULATIONS 2001, SR 2001 140; made under the Police (Northern Ireland) Act 1998 s.25, s.26; and the Police Act (Northern Ireland) 2000 s.43, s.44. In force: April 5, 2001; £3.00.

These Regulations set out the qualifications required for appointment to the police and prescribe functions to be exercised by a person appointed by the Chief Constable in connection with the recruitment of police trainees and police reserve trainees. They give effect to recommendations of the Independent Commission on Policing for Northern Ireland in its report "A New Beginning: Policing in Northern Ireland" published on September 9, 1999.

5933. Police officers – training

POLICE TRAINEE REGULATIONS (NORTHERN IRELAND) 2001, SR 2001 369; made under the Police (Northern Ireland) Act 2000 s.36, s.41. In force: November 2, 2001; £4.50.

These Regulations give effect to recommendations of the Independent Commission on Policing for Northern Ireland in its report A New Beginning: Policing in Northern Ireland published September 9, 1999. They make provision about the government, administration and conditions of service of police trainees. In addition, the Regulations prescribe the length of the period which police trainees must serve, and the other conditions with which police trainees must comply, before they can be appointed as constables.

5934. Police (Northern Ireland) Act 2000 (c.32) – Commencement No.2 Order

POLICE (NORTHERN IRELAND) ACT 2000 (COMMENCEMENT NO.2) ORDER 2001, SR 2001 132 (C.6); made under the Police (Northern Ireland) Act 2000 s.79. Commencement details: bringing into force various provisions of the Act on March 30, 2001; £1.75.

This Order brings into force specified provisions of the Police (Northern Ireland) Act 2000 on March 30, 2001.

5935. Police (Northern Ireland) Act 2000 (c.32) – Commencement No.3 and Transitional Provisions Order

POLICE (NORTHERN IRELAND) ACT 2000 (COMMENCEMENT NO.3 AND TRANSITIONAL PROVISIONS) ORDER 2001, SR 2001 396 (C.19); made under the Police (Northern Ireland) Act 2000 s.79. Commencement details: bringing into force various provisions of the 2000 Act on November 4, 2001; £1.75.

This Order brings into operation specified provisions of the Police (Northern Ireland) Act 2000.

5936. Police (Northern Ireland) Order 2001 (SI 2001 2513 (NI.3))

This Order amends the Police (Northern Ireland) Act 2000 s.41, which deals with trainees, so that before the Northern Ireland Policing Board is established, references to the Board are to be construed as references to the Police Authority for Northern Ireland. Section 76 is amended so that draft orders under s.47(3) and s.54 are subject to the affirmative resolution procedure rather than the procedure provided for in the Statutory Instruments Act 1946 s.6. In addition, this Order amends the Firearms (Northern Ireland) Order 1981 (SI 1981 155 (NI.2)) to include police trainees and police reserve trainees in the provision which exempts police officers from the need for a firearm certificate.

RATES

5937. Determination of rateable value

RATES (REGIONAL RATES) ORDER (NORTHERN IRELAND) 2001, SR 2001 55; made under the Rates (Northern Ireland) Order 1977 (SI 1977 2157 (NI.28)) Art.2, Art.7, Art.27. In force: May 14, 2001; £1.50.

This Order, which fixes the amounts of the regional rates for the year ending March 31, 2002, specifies the amount of the regional rate in respect of those hereditaments which are not dwelling houses, private garages or private storage premises and the amount of those hereditaments which are. It also fixes the amount by which the normal regional rate is reduced in respect of unspecified hereditaments and hereditaments which, though not unspecified hereditaments, are used partly for the purposes of unspecified hereditaments.

5938. Determination of rateable value

RATES (REGIONAL RATES) (NO.2) ORDER (NORTHERN IRELAND) 2001, SR 2001 84; made under the Rates (Northern Ireland) Order 1977 (SI 1977 2157 (NI.28)) Art.2, Art.7, Art.27. In force: April 1, 2001; £1.50.

This Order, which revokes the Rates (Regional Rates) Order (Northern Ireland) 2001 (SR 2001 55), fixes 30.42 pence in the pound as the amount of the regional rate in respect of those hereditaments which are not dwelling houses, private garages or private storage premises and 192.195 pence in the pound in respect of those hereditaments which are. In addition, it fixes 69.15 pence as the amount by which the normal regional rate is reduced in respect of unspecified hereditaments and hereditaments which, though not unspecified hereditaments, are used partly for the purposes of unspecified hereditaments.

5939. Exemptions – residential accommodation – student halls of residence – primary purpose of accommodation ·

[Rates (Northern Ireland) Order 1977 Art.41 (2).]

WMHC appealed against the commissioner's decision that a common room and three blocks of student accommodation in a hostel it provided were not exempt from rates because they were not used for a charitable purpose. WMHC contended that under the Rates (Northern Ireland) Order 1977 Art.41 (2), the hostel was exempt because it was (1) a building occupied by a charity and used for the advancement of religion within Art.41 (2) (c), or it was a building not established for profit whose main objectives were concerned with the advancement of religion and it was used mainly for those objectives within Art.41 (2) (d). WMHC maintained that the trust deed revealed that the purposes of the hostel were refuge, a Christian environment and a place for pleasant recreational and social activities, or (2) it constituted a church hall or similar building occupied by a religious body and used for religious purposes within Art.41 (2) (b) (ii).

Held, allowing the appeal in part, that (1) the trust deed was established in order to provide accommodation for young people from the Presbyterian faith and it did not establish a trust whose main purpose was the advancement of religion. Furthermore the use of the hostel did not qualify as wholly or mainly for a charitable purpose, given that on the evidence its main use was as student accommodation, and the students did not hold positions within the church and were not required to take part in charitable works relating to the advancement of religion. The promotion of religion within the building was incidental to its primary use as accommodation, and (2) the hostel building was not akin to a church hall, given that its main use was as student living accommodation, the facilities of which went beyond those which would be expected in a church hall. However, the common room was similar to a church hall, given the activities and facilities it provided to the students which were similar to those which a church hall would provide and accordingly exemption was available to the common room and the activity room under Art.41 (2) (b) (ii).

WAR MEMORIAL HOSTEL COMMITTEE OF THE PRESBYTERIAN CHURCH IN IRELAND v. COMMISSIONER OF VALUATION FOR NORTHERN IRELAND [2001] R.A. 166, Coghlin, J., LandsTr (NI).

5940. Non domestic rates – refunds of overpayment – sums paid under mistake of law – non exclusive nature of refund schemes

[Rates (Northern Ireland) Order 1977 (SI 1977 2157) Art.13, Art.15.]

M applied to the Department of the Environment for Northern Ireland, DENI, for a refund of part of the rates for his licensed premises under the Rates (Northern Ireland) Order 1977 Art.15. M had already been granted a reduction of net annual value of his premises under Art.13 of the Order, and DENI took the view that a refund under Art.15 was not applicable where Art.13 had already applied, arguing that the refund schemes under Art.13 and art.15 were mutually exclusive. M sought judicial review of that decision.

Held, allowing the application, that the purpose of Art.13 and Art.15 was to refund sums paid under a mistake of law. M had overpaid his rates because of such a mistake and was seeking to recover those sums under Art.15. The existence of a number of rates refund schemes did not mean that each was freestanding. Art.15 expressly stated that it applied without prejudice to Art.13(4)(a). A refund under Art.15 was therefore possible where there had already been a repayment under Art.13, and DENI's decision that a repayment under Art.13 precluded a refund under Art.15 was incorrect, *R. v. Tower Hamlets LBC, ex p. Chetnik Developments Ltd* [1988] A.C. 858, [1988] C.L.Y. 3020.1 applied)

McMULLAN'S APPLICATION FOR JUDICIAL REVIEW, *Re* [2000] N.I. 498, Kerr, J., QBD (NI).

5941. Non domestic rates – valuation – physical education centre of university

[Rates (Northern Ireland) Order 1977 (SI 1977 2157) Art.31.]

Q was established to provide education and had power to provide recreation. It occupied a building known as the Physical Education Centre, P. Q appealed against the decision of the Commissioner refusing to treat the P as a hereditament used for the purposes of recreation and entitled to a reduction in rates under the Rates (Northern Ireland) Order 1977 Art.31. Article 31 provided that a reduction could be granted where a hereditament was used solely for the purposes of a prescribed recreation and was occupied for the purposes of a "club, society or other organisation" that was not established or conducted for profit and did not employ any person to engage in any recreation for reward. The parties to the appeal agreed that the activities at P were those of a prescribed recreation but that the question was whether the University was a "club, society or organisation" that satisfied the tests laid down in Art.31.

Held, allowing the appeal but ordering that the parties address the tribunal further on the outstanding issue, that the word "organisation" in Art.31 did not refer to any organisation but following the ejusdem generis principle "organisation" had to be read in the context of the preceding words which restricted the meaning to be given to the words "other organisation". The organisation must be in the nature of a club or a society but it did not have to be one with a sporting or recreational character. It followed that Q satisfied that part of the test laid down by Art.31 and P was a hereditament occupied for the purposes of a club, society or other organisation that was not established for profit and did not employ any person to engage in any prescribed recreation for reward. However, the tribunal also found that the question put to it did not provide a complete test and invited the parties to address it on the issue of whether P was being used by Q to facilitate the advancement of education rather than being used solely for the purposes of a prescribed recreation.

QUEENS UNIVERSITY OF BELFAST v. COMMISSIONER OF VALUATION [2001] R.V.R. 112, Coghlin, J, LandsTr (NI).

5942. Valuation – access to prestigious building – disability to hypothetical tenant

N occupied a large prestigious building in the centre of Belfast. Access to the building was from three streets, W, D and H. The access from H was not used, the access from W was agreed to be poor. The access from D was imposing and impressive. The bank had arranged the building so that staff access was via the W entrance. The Commissioner rejected the bank's argument that the valuation of the premises for rating purposes ought to be reduced to take account of the poor quality of the W entrance. The Commissioner's approach was that, taken as a whole, for the entire building, the access arrangements did not present a distinct disability to a hypothetical tenant. N appealed.

Held, allowing the appeal in part, that the access arrangements were a distinct disability to a hypothetical tenant. The W entrance was poor and a hypothetical tenant would be unlikely to use the D entrance for staff access although the hypothetical tenant might also supplement that entrance by using the H entrance as well. That alternative entrance offset some of the disadvantage of the W entrance and a discount on the valuation of the upper floor offices of six per cent was appropriate.

NORTHERN BANK LTD v. COMMISSIONER OF VALUATION FOR NORTHERN IRELAND [2001] R.A. 83, Michael R Curry FRICS, LandsTr (NI).

REAL PROPERTY

5943. Ground Rents Act (Northern Ireland) 2001 (c.5)

This Act makes provision for the redemption of certain ground rents and other periodic payments.

This Act received Royal Assent on March 20, 2001.

5944. Land registration – compulsory registration areas

COMPULSORY REGISTRATION OF TITLE ORDER (NORTHERN IRELAND) 2001, SR 2001 237; made under the Land Registration Act (Northern Ireland) 1970 s.25. In force: September 7, 2001; £1.75.

This Order declares County Armagh to be a compulsory registration area under the Land Registration (Northern Ireland) Act 1970 upon the commencement of this Order. The type of property transaction which triggers a compulsory registration within that area is defined by entry 2 of Sch.2 to the 1970 Act.

5945. Licences – right of residence granted in return for transfer of farm to son – exclusive occupation

[Law Reform (Husband and Wife) Act (Northern Ireland) 1964.]

A and her late husband were farmers with six children but only one of them, W, wished to carry on in farming. In 1980, the farm and equipment was transferred to W and in 1983 he entered into an agreement with his parents, whereby they conveyed the land and building to him in return for a right to reside in the farmhouse for the remainder of their lives. The right was registered as a burden on the title. A remained in the house following her husband's death in 1997. Her own health deteriorated, however, and, following respite care in a nursing home, she returned to the farmhouse in spite of W's opposition, which included not allowing anyone to stay at the house with his mother overnight. As a result, A commenced proceedings to enforce her right of residence. Meanwhile, W had transferred the premises to his son, J, who moved into the farmhouse with his wife. A sought a declaration that she was entitled to remain in the house during her lifetime and an order restraining W from preventing access. W and J denied that A was entitled to an exclusive right of residence under the terms of the agreement.

Held, allowing the application, that the right of residence was a licence and a registered burden that formed part of the land transfer agreement that A could rely by virtue of the Law Reform (Husband and Wife) Act (Northern Ireland) 1964, *Federal Airports Corp v. Makucha Developments Pty Ltd* [1993] 115 A.L.R. 697 approved. Although the right did not have a clear meaning in law, the terms of the agreement showed that the farmhouse was intended to be used personally by A and her husband during their lifetimes so that neither W nor J could live their without A's consent, *National Bank v. Keegan* [1931] I.R. 344 considered.

JONES (AGNES) v. JONES (WILLIAM) [2001] N.I. 244, Girvan, J., Ch D (NI).

SOCIAL SECURITY

5946. Benefits – capital disregards

SOCIAL SECURITY (CAPITAL DISREGARDS AMENDMENT NO.2) REGULATIONS (NORTHERN IRELAND) 2001, SR 2001 157; made under the Social Security Contributions and Benefits (Northern Ireland) Act 1992 s.122, s.132, s.134, s.171; and the Jobseekers (Northern Ireland) Order (SI 1995 2705 (NI.15)) Art.14. In force: April 16, 2001; £1.75.

These Regulations amend the Income Support (General) Regulations (Northern Ireland) 1987 (SR 1987 459), the Housing Benefit (General) Regulations (Northern Ireland) 1987 (SR 1987 461), the Social Fund (Maternity and Funeral Expenses) (General) Regulations (Northern Ireland) 1987 (SR 1987 481), and the Jobseeker's Allowance Regulations (Northern Ireland) 1996 (SR 1996 198). They provide that ex-gratia payments made by the Secretary of State to members of the families of the disappeared shall be disregarded as capital when ascertaining the entitlement to those benefits, but only for 52 weeks from the date of receipt of those payments. In addition, the Regulations provide that any such payment shall be disregarded for the purpose of any deduction to be made from a social fund funeral payment.

5947. Benefits – capital disregards

SOCIAL SECURITY (CAPITAL DISREGARDS AMENDMENT NO.3) REGULATIONS (NORTHERN IRELAND) 2001, SR 2001 392; made under the Social Security Contributions and Benefits (Northern Ireland) Act 1992 s.122, s.132, s.171; and the Jobseekers (Northern Ireland) Order 1995 (SI 1995 2705 (NI.15)) Art.14. In force: November 19, 2001; £1.75.

These Regulations further amend the Income Support (General) Regulations (Northern Ireland) 1987 (SR 1987 459), the Housing Benefit (General) Regulations (Northern Ireland) 1987 (SR 1987 461) and the Jobseeker's Allowance Regulations (Northern Ireland) 1996 (SR 1997 198). They provide that payments made to compensate for a person being a slave labourer or a forced labourer, suffering property loss or personal injury or being the parent of a child who had died, during the Second World War, shall be disregarded as capital when ascertaining the entitlement of the recipient of that payment to those benefits.

5948. Benefits – capital disregards – ex gratia payments to Japanese prisoners of war

SOCIAL SECURITY (CAPITAL DISREGARDS AMENDMENT) REGULATIONS (NORTHERN IRELAND) 2001, SR 2001 4; made under the Social Security

Contributions and Benefits (Northern Ireland) Act 1992 s.122, s.132, s.171; and the Jobseekers (Northern Ireland) Order 1995 (SI 1995 2705 (NI.15))) Art.14. In force: February 1, 2001; £1.75.

These Regulations, which amend the the Income Support (General) Regulations (Northern Ireland) 1987 (SR 1987 459), the Housing Benefit (General) Regulations (Northern Ireland) 1987 (SR 1987 461) and the Jobseeker's Allowance Regulations (Northern Ireland) 1996 (SR 1996 198), provide that ex-gratia payments of £10,000 made on or after February 1, 2001 by the Secretary of State in consequence of a person's imprisonment or internment by the Japanese during the Second World War, shall be disregarded as capital when ascertaining the entitlement to those benefits.

5949. Benefits – capital disregards – recovery of benefits

SOCIAL SECURITY (CAPITAL DISREGARDS AND RECOVERY OF BENEFITS AMENDMENT) REGULATIONS (NORTHERN IRELAND) 2001, SR 2001 150; made under the Social Security Contributions and Benefits (Northern Ireland) Act 1992 s.122, s.132, s.134, s.171; the Social Security Administration (Northern Ireland) Act 1992 s.165; the Jobseekers (Northern Ireland) Order 1995 (SI 1995 2705 (NI.15)) Art.14; and the Social Security (Recovery of Benefits) (Northern Ireland) Order (SI 1997 1183 (NI.12)) Art.28, Sch.1 para.4. In force: April 12, 2001; £2.00.

These Regulations amend the Income Support (General) Regulations (Northern Ireland) 1987 (SR 1987 459), the Housing Benefit (General) Regulations (Northern Ireland) 1987 (SR 1987 461), the Social Fund (Maternity and Funeral Expenses) (General) Regulations (Northern Ireland) 1987 (SR 1987 481), the Jobseeker's Allowance Regulations (Northern Ireland) 1996 (SR 1996 198) and the Social Security (Recovery of Benefits) Regulations (Northern Ireland) 1997 (SR 1997 429). They provide that payments under a trust established out of funds provided by the Secretary of State in respect of persons who suffered, or who are suffering, from variant Creutzfeldt-Jakob disease which are made to certain persons and payments made by, or out of the estate of, persons receiving such payments which are made to certain persons, shall be disregarded in housing benefit, income support and jobseeker's allowance.

5950. Benefits – child maintenance premium

SOCIAL SECURITY (CHILD MAINTENANCE PREMIUM AND MISCELLANEOUS AMENDMENTS) REGULATIONS (NORTHERN IRELAND) 2001, SR 2001 25; made under the Social Security Contributions and Benefits (Northern Ireland) Act 1992 s.122, s.132, s.171; the Child Support (Northern Ireland) Order 1995 (SI 1995 2702 (NI.13)) Art.4, Art.19; the Jobseekers (Northern Ireland) Order 1995 (SI 1995 2705 (NI.15)) Art.14, Art.36; and the Northern Ireland Act 1998 s.87. In force: in accordance with Reg.1 (1); £2.00.

These Regulations, which amend the Income Support (General) Regulations (Northern Ireland) 1987 (SR 1987 459), the Jobseeker's Allowance Regulations (Northern Ireland) 1996 (SR 1996 198) and the Housing Benefit (General) Regulations (Northern Ireland) 1987 (SR 1987 461), provide that that for the purpose of ascertaining entitlement to income support and jobseeker's allowance, up to £10 of a payment of child maintenance shall be disregarded. They provide that, for the purpose of calculating the weekly amount of child support maintenance, payments by the Department in lieu of periodical payments of child maintenance shall, for the purpose of ascertaining entitlement to housing benefit, be treated as if they were payments of maintenance paid by a former partner of the claimant or his partner or by a parent of a child or young person. The Regulations revoke, with savings, the Child Maintenance Bonus (Great Britain Reciprocal Arrangements) Regulations (Northern Ireland) 1997 (SR 1997 126), the Social Security (Child Maintenance Bonus) Regulations (Northern Ireland) 1996 (SR 1996 198) Reg.2 to Reg.13, the Social Security (Miscellaneous Amendments) Regulations (Northern Ireland) 1997 (SR 1997 130) Reg.8 and the Social Security

(Miscellaneous Amendments No.2) Regulations (Northern Ireland) 1998 (SR 1998 81) Reg.2.

5951. Benefits – children and young persons – personal allowances

SOCIAL SECURITY (PERSONAL ALLOWANCES FOR CHILDREN AND YOUNG PERSONS AMENDMENT) REGULATIONS (NORTHERN IRELAND) 2001, SR 2001 314; made under the Social Security Administration (Northern Ireland) Act 1992 s.122, s.131, s.171; and the Jobseekers (Northern Ireland) Order 1995 (SI 1995 2705 (NI.15)) Art.6. In force: October 22, 2001; £1.75.

These Regulations, which amend the Housing Benefit (General) Regulations (Northern Ireland) 1987 (SR 1987 459), the Income Support (General) Regulations (Northern Ireland) 1987 (SR 1987 461) and the Jobseeker's Allowance Regulations (Northern Ireland) 1996 (SR 1996 198), increase by £1.50, from October 22, 2001, the amounts of the weekly personal allowance applicable in respect of children and young persons in housing benefit, income support and jobseeker's allowance.

5952. Benefits – claims – information – ONE service

SOCIAL SECURITY (CLAIMS AND INFORMATION) REGULATIONS (NORTHERN IRELAND) 2001, SR 2001 175; made under the Social Security Administration (Northern Ireland) Act 1992 s.5, s.5A, s.165; the Social Security Contributions and Benefits (Northern Ireland) Act 1992 s.122; and the Welfare Reform and Pensions (Northern Ireland) Order 1999 (SI 1999 3147 (NI.11)) Art.69, Art.73. In force: May 14, 2001; £3.00.

These Regulations, which amend the Housing Benefit (General) Regulations (Northern Ireland) 1987 (SR 1987 461), the Social Security (Claims and Payments) Regulations (Northern Ireland) 1987 (SR 1987 465) and the Jobseeker's Allowance Regulations (Northern Ireland) 1996 (SR 1996 198), introduce provisions to support the ONE service which will be introduced in specified postcode areas.

5953. Benefits – guardian contribution – child support maintenance

SOCIAL SECURITY (CLAIMS AND PAYMENT) (AMENDMENT) REGULATIONS (NORTHERN IRELAND) 2001, SR 2001 22; made under the Child Support (Northern Ireland) Order 1991 (SI 1991 2628 (NI.23)) Art.40; and the Social Security Administration (Northern Ireland) Act 1992 s.5, s.165. In force: January 31, 2001; £2.00.

These Regulations, which provide for the Department for Social Development to deduct an amount in respect of certain child support maintenance liabilities from certain social security benefits or war pensions awarded to a beneficiary who is a non-resident parent (or in some cases his partner) and pay it to the person with care, amend the Social Security (Claims and Payments) Regulations (Northern Ireland) 1987 (SR 1987 465) to give effect to the provisions set out in the Schedule.

5954. Benefits – hospital in-patients

SOCIAL SECURITY (HOSPITAL IN-PATIENTS) (AMENDMENT) REGULATIONS (NORTHERN IRELAND) 2001, SR 2001 115; made under the Social Security Administration (Northern Ireland) 1992 s.71, s.165. In force: April 9, 2001; £1.75.

These Regulations amend the Social Security (Hospital In-Patients) Regulations (Northern Ireland) 1975 (SR 1975 109) to provide for a decrease, from 40 per cent to 39 per cent, of the basic retirement pension, in the percentage by which the personal rate of certain benefits is reduced in certain circumstances in respect of persons who receive continuous free in-patient treatment in a hospital or similar institution for more than six weeks but not more than 52 weeks.

5955. Benefits – joint claims

SOCIAL SECURITY (JOINT CLAIMS AMENDMENTS) REGULATIONS (NORTHERN IRELAND) 2001, SR 2001 120; made under the Social Security Administration (Northern Ireland) Act 1992 s.5, s.165; the Social Security Contributions and Benefits (Northern Ireland) Act 1992 s.22, s.122, s.132, s.171; the Jobseekers (Northern Ireland) Order 1995 (SI 1995 2705 (NI.15)) Art.3, Art.6, Art.7, Art.36, Sch.1 para.8A; and the Social Security (Northern Ireland) Order 1998 (SI 1998 1506 (NI.10)) Art.9, Art.11, Art.13, Art.74, Sch.3 para.9. In force: March 19, 2001; £2.00.

These Regulations amend the Social Security (Credits) Regulations (Northern Ireland) 1975 (SR 1975 113), the Housing Benefit (General) Regulations (Northern Ireland) 1987 (SR 1987 461), the Social Security (Claims and Payments) Regulations (Northern Ireland) 1987 (SR 1987 465), the Jobseeker's Allowance Regulations (Northern Ireland) 1996 (SR 1996 198) and the Social Security and Child Support (Decisions and Appeals) Regulations (Northern Ireland) 1999 (SR 1999 162 to enable the effective introduction of the joint-claims regime.

5956. Benefits – maternity expenses – entitlement

SOCIAL FUND (MATERNITY AND FUNERAL EXPENSES) (GENERAL) (AMENDMENT) REGULATIONS (NORTHERN IRELAND) 2001, SR 2001 318; made under the Social Security Contributions and Benefits (Northern Ireland) Act 1992 s.134, s.171. In force: October 8, 2001; £1.75.

These Regulations amend the Social Fund (Maternity and Funeral Expenses) (General) Regulations (Northern Ireland) 1987 (SR 1987 150) in relation to the "immediate family" and "close relative" conditions of entitlement to a funeral payment and by abolishing the capital rules in relation to claims for Sure Start Maternity Grants and funeral payments.

5957. Benefits – miscellaneous amendments

SOCIAL SECURITY (MISCELLANEOUS AMENDMENTS) REGULATIONS (NORTHERN IRELAND) 2001, SR 2001 78; made under the Social Security Contributions and Benefits (Northern Ireland) Act 1992 s.122, s.123, s.131, s.132, s.133, s.171; the Social Security Administration (Northern Ireland) Act 1992 s.1, s.13A, s.165; and the Jobseekers (Northern Ireland) Order 1994 (SI 1995 2705 (NI.15)) Art.6, Art.23, Art.28, Art.36, Sch.1 para.1. In force: April 9, 2001; £2.50.

These Regulations, which amend the Income Support (General) Regulations (Northern Ireland) 1987 (SR 1987 459), the Social Security (Claims and Payments) Regulations (Northern Ireland) 1987 (SR 1987 465), the Jobseeker's Allowance Regulations (Northern Ireland) 1996 (SR 1996 198) and the Social Security (Back to Work Bonus) (No.2) Regulations (Northern Ireland) 1996 (SI 1996 519), provide that for the purposes of entitlement to income support, a person may be treated as not engaged in remunerative work for the first two weeks, or as the case may be, four weeks, after commencing such work following a period of entitlement to income support or income-based jobseeker's allowance of at least 26 weeks. Such persons are made a prescribed category of person for the purposes of income support entitlement and the applicable amount of such persons is limited to their housing costs. They provide that such persons shall not be required to make a claim for income support in order to be entitled to it, that any relevant benefit payable to such persons shall not be paid to a qualifying lender, during the two week or four week run on period, any earnings from the employment which caused the person to be treated as not engaged in remunerative work shall be disregarded as is the whole of their income and their capital and income support paid to such persons does not qualify for the purpose of entitlement to, or claiming, a back to work bonus. In addition, they omit provisions whereby, in income support and jobseeker's allowance, a lone parent who was previously treated as not engaged in remunerative work, was so treated for a specified period if he ceases to be so engaged in such work within five weeks of commencing it.

5958. Benefits – miscellaneous amendments

SOCIAL SECURITY (MISCELLANEOUS AMENDMENTS NO.2) REGULATIONS (NORTHERN IRELAND) 2001, SR 2001 134; made under the Social Security Contributions and Benefits (Northern Ireland) Act 1992 s.122, s.123, s.131, s.132, s.134, s.171. In force: in accordance with Reg.1; £2.00.

These Regulations amend the Social Fund (Maternity and Funeral Expenses) (General) Regulations (Northern Ireland) 1987 (SR 1987 150), the Income Support (General) Regulations (Northern Ireland) 1987 (SR 1987 459), the Housing Benefit (General) Regulations (Northern Ireland) 1987 (SR 1987 461) and the Social Security (Enhanced Disability Premium Amendment) Regulations (Northern Ireland) 2000 (SR 2000 367). They update legislative references in the definition of "attendance allowance" applying in housing benefit, amend the references in the rules relating to the treatment of childcare charges in housing benefit, amend the references relating to the notional income rule in income support, allow employment credits to be disregarded, if paid to a lone parent entitled to income support during a run-on period and allow a bereavement payment to be disregarded for the purpose of ascertaining entitlement to Sure Start Maternity Grants and funeral payments.

5959. Benefits – prisoners – quashed convictions

SOCIAL SECURITY (CREDITS AND INCAPACITY BENEFIT) (AMENDMENT) REGULATIONS (NORTHERN IRELAND) 2001, SR 2001 88; made under the Social Contributions and Benefits (Northern Ireland) Act 1992 s.22, s.171, Sch.3 para.2. In force: in accordance with Art.1; £2.00.

These Regulations, which amend the Social Security (Credits) Regulations (Northern Ireland) 1975 (SR 1975 113) and the Social Security (Incapacity Benefit) Regulations (Northern Ireland) 1994 (SR 1994 461), make amendments to provide that, for the purposes of entitlement to any contributory benefit, certain prisoners who have had their conviction of a single offence or convictions of two or more offences quashed shall, upon application in writing to the Department for Social Development, be entitled to be credited with such earnings or, as the case may be, contributions to make any tax year, in which there is a week during which such a prisoner was detained in legal custody, a reckonable year. They also provide for any such application to be made by electronic means and extend the relaxation of the first contribution condition for incapacity benefit to those prisoners to whom these Regulations apply.

5960. Benefits – social security – change of circumstances – failure to notify

SOCIAL SECURITY (NOTIFICATION OF CHANGE OF CIRCUMSTANCES) REGULATIONS (NORTHERN IRELAND) 2001, SR 2001 420; made under the Social Security Administration (Northern Ireland) Act 1992 s.105A, s.106, s.165. In force: January 7, 2002; £1.75.

The Social Security Fraud Act 2001 s.16 amends the Social Security Administration Act 1992 by substituting new offences relating to failure to notify a change of circumstances affecting entitlement to any benefit, payment or other advantage. These matters are prescribed in relation to jobseeker's allowance, in relation to housing benefit and council tax benefit and in relation to any other benefit, payment or advantage. As these Regulations are made within six months of the commencement of the Social Security Fraud Act s.16, they are exempt from the requirement to refer them to the Social Security Advisory Committee.

5961. Benefits – statutory maternity pay – medical evidence

SOCIAL SECURITY (MEDICAL EVIDENCE) AND STATUTORY MATERNITY PAY (MEDICAL EVIDENCE) (AMENDMENT) REGULATIONS (NORTHERN IRELAND)

2001, SR 2001 308; made under the Social Security Administration (Northern Ireland) Act 1992 s.5, s.13, s.165. In force: September 28, 2001; £1.75.

These Regulations amend the Social Security (Medical Evidence) Regulations (Northern Ireland) 1976 (SR 1976 175) and the Statutory Maternity Pay (Medical Evidence) Regulations (Northern Ireland) 1987 (SR 1987 99) to provide for a maternity certificate to be given not more than 20 weeks before the week the baby is expected.

5962. Benefits – up rating

SOCIAL SECURITY BENEFITS UP-RATING ORDER (NORTHERN IRELAND) 2001, SR 2001 41; made under the Social Security Administration (Northern Ireland) Act 1992 s.132, s.165. In force: in accordance with Art.1 (1); £7.00.

This Order, which increases the rates and amounts of certain social security benefits and other sums, relates to non income related benefits other than jobseeker's allowance. It increases the rates of benefits and increases of benefits specified in the Social Security Contributions and Benefits (Northern Ireland) Act 1992 and also increases the sums payable as part of a Category A or Category B retirement pension under the Pension Schemes (Northern Ireland) Act 1993. The Order specifies the dates from which the sums specified for rates or amounts of benefit under the Contributions and Benefits Act or the Pension Schemes Act are increased, increases the rate of certain workmen's compensation in respect of employment before July 5, 1948, specifies earnings limits for child dependency increases, increases the rate of statutory sick pay, increases the lower rate of statutory maternity pay, increases the rate of graduated retirement benefit, increases the rates of disability living allowance, increases the rates of child benefit, increases the rates of age addition to long-term incapacity benefit and increases the rates of transitional invalidity allowance in long-term incapacity benefit cases.

5963. Benefits – up rating

SOCIAL SECURITY BENEFITS UP-RATING REGULATIONS (NORTHERN IRELAND) 2001, SR 2001 106; made under the Social Security Contributions and Benefits (Northern Ireland) Act 1992 s.30E, s.90, s.113, s.167D, s.171, Sch.7 para.2; and the Social Security Administration (Northern Ireland) Act 1992 s.135, s.165. In force: April 9, 2001; £1.75.

These Regulations provide that where a question has arisen about the effect of the Social Security Benefits Up-rating Order (Northern Ireland) 2000 (SR 2000 38) on a benefit already in payment the altered rate will not apply until that question is determined. They apply the provisions of the Social Security Benefit (Persons Abroad) Regulations (Northern Ireland) 1978 (SR 1978 114) so as to restrict the application of the increases specified in the 2001 Order in cases where the beneficiary lives abroad. They raise from £3,094 to £3,146, the annual earnings limit which applies to unemployability supplement and raise from £59.50 to £60.50 the weekly earnings limit which must not be exceeded if work is to be treated as exempt for incapacity benefit purposes. They amend the Social Security Benefit (Dependency) Regulations (Northern Ireland) 1977 (SR 1977 74), the Social Security (General Benefit) Regulations (Northern Ireland) 1984 (SR 1984 92), the Social Security (Incapacity Benefit) Regulations (Northern Ireland) 1994 (SR 1994 461) and the Social Security (Incapacity for Work) (General) Regulations (Northern Ireland) 1995 (SR 1995 41) and revoke the The Social Security Benefits Up-rating Regulations (Northern Ireland) 1999 (SR 1999 139), the Social Security Benefits Up-rating Regulations (Northern Ireland) 2000 (SR 2000 47) and the Social Security (Therapeutic Earnings Limits) (Amendment) Regulations (Northern Ireland) 2000 (SR 2000 251).

5964. Benefits – volunteers amendments

SOCIAL SECURITY (VOLUNTEERS AMENDMENT) REGULATIONS (NORTHERN IRELAND) 2001, SR 2001 258; made under the Social Security

Contributions and Benefits (Northern Ireland) Act 1992 s.122, s.132, s.171; and the Jobseekers (Northern Ireland) Order 1995 (SI 1995 2705 (NI.15)) Art.14. In force: September 24, 2001; £1.75.

These Regulations, which amend the Income Support (General) Regulations (Northern Ireland) 1987 (SR 1987 459), the Housing Benefit (General) Regulations (Northern Ireland) 1987 (SR 1987 461) and the Jobseeker's Allowance Regulations (Northern Ireland) 1996 (SR 1996 198), allow payments in respect of expenses to be incurred by a claimant to be disregarded for those benefits where he is engaged by a charitable or voluntary organisation or is a volunteer.

5965. Benefits – widow's benefit – retirement pensions

SOCIAL SECURITY (WIDOW'S BENEFIT AND RETIREMENT PENSIONS) (AMENDMENT) REGULATIONS (NORTHERN IRELAND) 2001, SR 2001 148; made under the Social Security Contributions and Benefits (Northern Ireland) Act 1992 s.121, s.171; and the Social Security Administration (Northern Ireland) Act 1992 s.1, s.165. In force: April 9, 2001; £1.75.

These Regulations, which amend the Social Security (Widow's Benefit and Retirement Pensions) Regulations (Northern Ireland) 1979 (SR 1979 243), insert a new Regulation which provides for a person to be treated as entitled to child benefit in certain circumstances where eligibility to a widowed parent's allowance is dependent on such entitlement. In addition, the Regulations disapply for the purposes of a claim for widowed parent's allowance certain requirements in respect of the claimant's national insurance number.

5966. Benefits – widows and widowers

SOCIAL SECURITY (BENEFITS FOR WIDOWS AND WIDOWERS) (CONSEQUENTIAL AMENDMENTS) REGULATIONS (NORTHERN IRELAND) 2001, SR 2001 108; made under the Welfare Reform and Pensions (Northern Ireland) Order 1999 (SI 1999 3147 (NI.11)) Art.73, Art.75. In force: April 9, 2001; £3.00.

These Regulations amend the Social Security (Hospital In-Patients) Regulations (Northern Ireland) 1975 (SR 1975 109), the Social Security (Credits) Regulations (Northern Ireland) 1975 (SR 1975 113), the Child Benefit and Social Security (Fixing and Adjustment of Rates) Regulations (Northern Ireland) 1976 (SR 1976 223), the Social Security Benefit (Dependency) Regulations (Northern Ireland) 1977 (SR 1977 74), the Social Security Benefit (Persons Abroad) Regulations (Northern Ireland) 1978 (SR 1978 114), the Social Security (Overlapping Benefits) Regulations (Northern Ireland) 1979 (SR 1979 242), the Social Security (Widow's Benefit and Retirement Pensions) Regulations (Northern Ireland) 1979 (SR 1979 243), the Social Security (General Benefit) Regulations (Northern Ireland) 1984 (SR 1984 92), the Social Security (Claims and Payments) Regulations (Northern Ireland) 1987 (SR 1987 465), the Social Security (Payments on account, Overpayments and Recovery) Regulations (Northern Ireland) 1988 (SR 1988 142) and the Social Security and Child Support (Decisions and Appeals) Regulations (Northern Ireland) 1999 (SR 1999 162) to provide for the introduction of bereavement payment, bereavement allowance and widowed parent's allowance.

5967. Benefits – work focused interviews

SOCIAL SECURITY (WORK-FOCUSED INTERVIEWS) REGULATIONS (NORTHERN IRELAND) 2001, SR 2001 176; made under the Social Security Administration (Northern Ireland) Act 1992 s.2A, s.2B, s.5, s.165; the Social Security Contributions and Benefits (Northern Ireland) Act 1992 s.122; and the Welfare Reform and Pensions (Northern Ireland) Order 1999 (SI 1999 3147 (NI.11)) Art.73. In force: May 14, 2001; £4.00.

These Regulations, which amend the Housing Benefit (General) Regulations (Northern Ireland) 1987 (SR 1987 461), the Social Security (Claims and

Payments) Regulations (Northern Ireland) 1987 (SR 1987 465), the Child Support Departure Direction and Consequential Amendments Regulations (Northern Ireland) 1996 (SR 1996 541), the Social Security and Child Support (Decisions and Appeals) Regulations (Northern Ireland) 1999 (SR 1999 162) and the Social Security (Work-focused Interviews for Lone Parents) Regulations (Northern Ireland) 2001 (SR 2001 152), make provision for the introduction of work-focused interviews in specified postcode districts.

5968. Benefits – work focused interviews – lone parents

SOCIAL SECURITY (WORK-FOCUSED INTERVIEWS FOR LONE PARENTS) REGULATIONS (NORTHERN IRELAND) 2001, SR 2001 152; made under the Social Security Administration (Northern Ireland) Act 1992 s.2A, s.2B, s.165. In force: April 30, 2001; £2.00.

These Regulations, which impose a requirement on lone parents who claim, or are entitled to claim, income support to take part in a work-focused interview, prescribe circumstances as to when a lone parent is to be regarded as having taken part in an interview and specifies that an interview can be deferred. The Regulations provide that the requirement to take part in an interview can be waived where an interview would not be of assistance to the lone parent or it would not be appropriate in the circumstances of the case and set out the sanctions imposed on lone parents who fail to take part in an interview without good cause.

5969. Child Support, Pensions and Social Security Act (Northern Ireland) 2000 (c.4) – Commencement No.4 Order

CHILD SUPPORT, PENSIONS AND SOCIAL SECURITY (2000 ACT) (COMMENCEMENT NO.4) ORDER (NORTHERN IRELAND) 2001, SR 2001 34 (C.1); made under the Child Support, Pensions and Social Security Act (Northern Ireland) 2000 s.68. Commencement details: bringing into force various provisions of the Act on February 1, 2001, April 9, 2001 and April 6, 2002; £1.75.

This Order provides for the coming into operation of provisions of the Child Support, Pensions and Social Security Act (Northern Ireland) 2000 relating to state second pension on February 1, 2001, for the purposes of making orders and April 6, 2002 for all other purposes. It also provides for the coming into force of provisions relating to the revaluation of the low earnings threshold on February 1, 2001, and provisions relating to the calculation of Category B retirement pension on April 9, 2001.

5970. Child Support, Pensions and Social Security Act (Northern Ireland) 2000 (c.4) – Commencement No.5 Order

CHILD SUPPORT, PENSIONS AND SOCIAL SECURITY (2000 ACT) (COMMENCEMENT NO.5) ORDER (NORTHERN IRELAND) 2001, SR 2001 141 (C.8); made under the Child Support, Pensions and Social Security Act (Northern Ireland) 2000 s.68. In force: bringing in to force various provisions of the Act on April 2, 2001 and July 2, 2001; £2.00.

This Order, which amends the Child Support, Pensions and Social Security (Commencement No.2) Order (Northern Ireland) 2000 (SR 2000 374) to revoke the day previously appointed for the coming fully into operation of provision for an alternative to the anti-franking rules relating to salary related contracted-out pension schemes, provides for the coming into operation of provisions of the Child Support, Pensions and Social Security Act (Northern Ireland) 2000 relating to powers of investigation for social security purposes and the payment to an employer of any surplus out of the funds of an occupational pension scheme on April 2, 2001, and provisions relating to housing benefit revisions and appeals and discretionary financial assistance with housing on July 2, 2001.

5971. Contributions – calculation of earnings

SOCIAL SECURITY (CONTRIBUTIONS) (AMENDMENT NO.3) (NORTHERN IRELAND) REGULATIONS 2001, SI 2001 597; made under the Social Security Contributions and Benefits (Northern Ireland) Act 1992 s.3, s.4, s.10, s.171; and the Child Support, Pensions and Social Security Act 2000 s.78. In force: April 6, 2001; £4.00.

These Regulations, which amend the Social Security (Contributions) Regulations (Northern Ireland) 1979 (SR 1979 186), make amendments by inserting a definition for "cash voucher" and make amendments consequential on the restructuring of the provisions dealing with the calculation of earnings and payments to be disregarded in their calculation. In addition, they provide that the amount of a contribution paid through ignorance or error is to be calculated by reference to the rate applicable at the start of the period within which the payment should have been made.

5972. Contributions – Class 1 – money purchase contracted-out schemes

See SOCIAL SECURITY. §4992

5973. Contributions – Class 1 – salary related contracted-out schemes

See SOCIAL SECURITY. §4993

5974. Contributions – Class 1A – modification

SOCIAL SECURITY CONTRIBUTIONS AND BENEFITS (NORTHERN IRELAND) ACT 1992 (MODIFICATION OF SECTION 10(7)) REGULATIONS 2001, SI 2001 965; made under the Social Security Contributions and Benefits (Northern Ireland) Act 1992 s.10; and the Child Support, Pensions and Social Security Act 2000 s.78. In force: April 6, 2001; £1.50.

These Regulations, which modify the list of provisions contained in Social Security Contributions and Benefits (Northern Ireland) Act 1992 s.10, have effect in relation to any time in the tax year in which they are made. They provide for a deduction from the total amount of an employee's emoluments in respect of which Class 1A contributions are payable if the employee is entitled to a corresponding deduction at least equal to the whole amount which would otherwise be brought into charge to Class 1A contributions.

5975. Contributions – Class 2 contributions

SOCIAL SECURITY (CONTRIBUTIONS) (AMENDMENT) (NORTHERN IRELAND) REGULATIONS 2001, SI 2001 46; made under the Social Security Contributions and Benefits (Northern Ireland) Act 1992 s.171, Sch.1 para.8; and the Social Security Administration (Northern Ireland) Act 1992 s.107. In force: January 31, 2001; £1.50.

These Regulations, which amend the Social Security (Contributions) Regulations (Northern Ireland) 1979 (SR 1979 186) Reg.53A, provide for a penalty of £100 in respect of the failure by a person becoming liable to pay a Class 2 contribution to notify the Inland Revenue.

5976. Contributions – Class 3 contributions

SOCIAL SECURITY (CREDITING AND TREATMENT OF CONTRIBUTIONS, AND NATIONAL INSURANCE NUMBERS) REGULATIONS (NORTHERN IRELAND) 2001, SR 2001 102; made under the Social Security Contributions and Benefits (Northern Ireland) Act 1992 s.13, s.22, s.171, Sch.1 para.8; and the Social Security Administration (Northern Ireland) Act 1992 s.158C, s.165. In force: April 6, 2001; £2.50.

These Regulations amend the Social Security (Contributions) Regulations (Northern Ireland) 1979 (SR 1979 186), the Social Security (Contributions) (Amendment) Regulations (Northern Ireland) 1980 (SR 1980 463), the Social

Security (Contributions) (Amendment) Regulations (Northern Ireland) 1984 (SR 1984 43), the Social Security (Contributions) (Amendment No.2) Regulations (Northern Ireland) 1987 (SR 1987 143), the Social Security (Contributions) (Amendment No.5) Regulations (Northern Ireland) 1992 (SR 1992 138), the Social Security (Contributions) (Amendment No.6) Regulations (Northern Ireland) 1993, the Social Security (Contributions) (Amendment No.2) Regulations (Northern Ireland) 1994 (SR 1994 219), the Social Security (Incapacity Benefit) (Consequential and Transitional Amendments and Savings) Regulations (Northern Ireland) 1995 (SR 1995 150), the Social Security (Credits and Contributions) (Jobseeker's Allowance Consequential and Miscellaneous Amendments) Regulations (Northern Ireland) 1996 (SR 1996 430), Social Security (Contributions and Credits) (Miscellaneous Amendments) Regulations (Northern Ireland) 1999 (SR 1999 118) and the Social Security (Contributions) (Amendment No.2) Regulations (Northern Ireland) 1999 (SR 1999 151) in relation to the appropriation and crediting of Class 3 contributions, the treatment of late paid social security contributions for the purposes of entitlement to contributory benefit and the application for the allocation of a national insurance number.

5977. Contributions – earnings limits and tax thresholds

SOCIAL SECURITY (CONTRIBUTIONS) (AMENDMENT NO.2) (NORTHERN IRELAND) REGULATIONS 2001, SI 2001 314; made under the Social Security Contributions and Benefits (Northern Ireland) Act 1992 s.5, s.171, Sch.1 para.6. In force: April 6, 2001; £1.75.

These Regulations, which amend the Social Security (Contributions) Regulations (Northern Ireland) 1979 (SR 1979 186), specify the lower earnings limit, upper earnings limit, primary threshold and secondary threshold for the tax year beginning April 6, 2001. In addition, they provide for the equivalents of the primary threshold and secondary threshold where an employed earner's earnings period is other than a week.

5978. Contributions – personal pensions

See SOCIAL SECURITY. §5001

5979. Contributions

See SOCIAL SECURITY. §4988

5980. Housing benefit – decisions and appeals

HOUSING BENEFIT (DECISIONS AND APPEALS) REGULATIONS (NORTHERN IRELAND) 2001, SR 2001 213; made under the Social Security Administration (Northern Ireland) Act 1992 s.5; the Social Security (Northern Ireland) Order 1998 (SI 1998 1506 (NI.10)) Art.8, Art.74; and the Child Support, Pensions and Social Security Act (Northern Ireland) 2000 s.59, Sch.7 para.3, Sch.7 para.4, Sch.7 para.6, Sch.7 para.8, Sch.7 para.10, Sch.7 para.12, Sch.7 para.13, Sch.7 para.14, Sch.7 para.15, Sch.7 para.16, Sch.7 para.19, Sch.7 para.20, Sch.7 para.23. In force: July 2, 2001; £4.00.

These Regulations, which amend the Social Security and Child Support (Decisions and Appeals) (Amendment No.3) Regulations (Northern Ireland) 1999 (SR 1999 272), supplement the changes introduced by the Child Support, Pensions and Social Security Act (Northern Ireland) 2000 to the decision making process for housing benefit and to the new appeals system.

5981. Housing benefit – decisions and appeals

HOUSING BENEFIT (DECISIONS AND APPEALS) (TRANSITIONAL AND SAVINGS) REGULATIONS (NORTHERN IRELAND) 2001, SR 2001 214; made under the SI 1995 3213 (NI.22) Art.166; and the Child Support, Pensions and Social Security Act (Northern Ireland) 2000 s.68. In force: July 2, 2001; £2.00.

These Regulations make transitional and savings provisions in consequence of the coming into operation of the Child Support, Pensions and Social Security Act (Northern Ireland) 2000 Sch.7 which introduces new arrangements for decision making in relation to housing benefit. In particular, they provide for the manner in which matters are to be dealt with on or after July 2, 2001 which are awaiting determination under the existing arrangements for decision making immediately before that date.

5982. **Housing benefit – decisions and appeals – discretionary financial assistance**

HOUSING BENEFIT (DECISIONS AND APPEALS AND DISCRETIONARY FINANCIAL ASSISTANCE) (CONSEQUENTIAL AMENDMENTS AND REVOCATIONS) REGULATIONS (NORTHERN IRELAND) 2001, SR 2001 215; made under the Social Security Administration (Northern Ireland) Act 1992 s.5, s.165, s.167; the Social Security (Northern Ireland) Order 1998 (SI 1998 1506 (NI.10)) Art.74; and the Child Support, Pensions and Social Security Act (Northern Ireland) 2000 s.59, s.60, Sch.7 para.20. In force: July 2, 2001; £3.00.

These Regulations make consequential provision in the Housing Benefit (General) Regulations (Northern Ireland) 1987 (SR 1987 461) in consequence of the coming into operation of the Child Support, Pensions and Social Security Act (Northern Ireland) 2000 s.59 and Sch.7 which introduces new arrangements for decision making in relation to housing benefit and also upon s.60 of that Act which introduces a new scheme of discretionary financial assistance for those receiving housing benefit.

5983. **Housing benefit – deductions – child care**

HOUSING BENEFIT (GENERAL) (AMENDMENT NO.4) REGULATIONS (NORTHERN IRELAND) 2001, SR 2001 259; made under the Social Security Contributions and Benefits (Northern Ireland) Act 1992 s.122, s.132, s.133, s.171. In force: August 13, 2001; £1.75.

These Regulations, which amend the Housing Benefit (General) Regulations (Northern Ireland) 1987 (SR 1987 461), increase the maximum deduction which may be made from a claimant's weekly income in respect of relevant child care charges for the purpose of assessing entitlement to housing benefit. In addition, they provide for a woman on maternity leave to be treated as if she were engaged in remunerative work so enabling relevant child care charges to be deducted from her weekly income for the purpose of assessing entitlement to housing benefit. Any child care charges incurred in respect of the child to whom the maternity leave relates are not treated as relevant child care charges.

5984. **Housing benefit – determination of single room rent**

HOUSING BENEFIT (GENERAL) (AMENDMENT NO.3) REGULATIONS (NORTHERN IRELAND) 2001, SR 2001 238; made under the Social Security Contributions and Benefits (Northern Ireland) Act 1992 s.122, s.129, s.171. In force: July 2, 2001; £1.75.

These Regulations amend the Housing Benefit (General) Regulations (Northern Ireland) 1987 (SR 1987 461) by extending the criteria to which the Northern Ireland Housing Executive should have regard when deciding a single room rent from July 2, 2001.

5985. **Housing benefit – discretionary housing payments**

SOCIAL SECURITY (DISCRETIONARY HOUSING PAYMENTS AMENDMENT) REGULATIONS (NORTHERN IRELAND) 2001, SR 2001 261; made under the Social Security Contributions and Benefits (Northern Ireland) Act s.122, s.129, s.132, s.171; and the Jobseekers (Northern Ireland) Order 1995 (SI 1995 2705 (NI.15)) Art.14. In force: July 2, 2001; £1.75.

These Regulations, which amend the Income Support (General) Regulations (Northern Ireland) 1987 (SR 1987 459), the Housing Benefit (General) Regulations (Northern Ireland) 1987 (SR 1987 461), and the Jobseeker's Allowance Regulations (Northern Ireland) 1996 (SR 1996 198), provide that discretionary housing payments paid pursuant to the Discretionary Financial Assistance Regulations (Northern Ireland) 2001 (SR 2001 216) shall be disregarded as income in those benefits and that arrears of such payments shall be disregarded as capital for up to 52 weeks.

5986. Housing benefit – entitlement – home ownership

HOUSING BENEFIT (GENERAL) (AMENDMENT) REGULATIONS (NORTHERN IRELAND) 2001, SR 2001 79; made under the Social Security Contributions and Benefits (Northern Ireland) Act 1992 s.122, s.129, s.133, s.171; and the Social Security Administration (Northern Ireland) Act 1992 s.73, s.165. In force: May 21, 2001; £2.00.

These Regulations, which amend the Housing Benefit Regulation (Northern Ireland) 1987 (SR 1987 461), provide that a person who is liable to make payments in respect of a dwelling shall be treated as not being so liable for housing benefit purposes where the claimant or his partner owned that dwelling before they rented it unless, where the claimant demonstrates that he could not have continued to live there without selling the property, more than five years elapses between the date on which the claimant or his partner relinquished ownership of the property and the date on which housing benefit is claimed.

5987. Housing benefit – exemptions – discretionary financial assistance

DISCRETIONARY FINANCIAL ASSISTANCE REGULATIONS (NORTHERN IRELAND) 2001, SR 2001 216; made under the Social Security (Northern Ireland) Order 1998 (SI 1998 1506 (NI.10)) Art.74; and the Child Support, Pensions and Social Security Act (Northern Ireland) 2000 s.60. In force: July 2, 2001; £2.00.

These Regulations provide the Northern Ireland Housing Executive with a power to make discretionary payments by way of financial assistance, the circumstances in which discretionary payments may be made and the limit on the amount of discretionary housing payments that may be made. They provide the Executive with discretion as to the period for, or in which, discretionary housing payments may be made, make provision as to the form, manner and procedure for claims and provide that the total amount paid by way of discretionary housing payments by the Executive shall not exceed the amount allocated to it by the Department for Social Development.

5988. Housing benefit – extended payments

HOUSING BENEFIT (EXTENDED PAYMENTS) REGULATIONS (NORTHERN IRELAND) 2001, SR 2001 99; made under the Social Security Administration (Northern Ireland) Act 1992 s.5, s.165; the Social Security Contributions and Benefits (Northern Ireland) Act 1992 s.122, s.129, s.171; and the Social Security (Northern Ireland) Order 1998 (SI 1998 1506 (NI.10)) Art.34, Art.39, Art.74. In force: April 9, 2001; £2.00.

These Regulations amend the Housing Benefit (General) Regulations (Northern Ireland) 1987 (SR 1987 461) to make changes to the rules relating to entitlement to, and claims for, extended payments of Housing Benefit. They also provide that extended payments of housing benefit shall not be payable to a person who is entitled to income support.

5989. Housing benefit – recovery of benefits

HOUSING BENEFIT (GENERAL) (AMENDMENT NO.2) REGULATIONS (NORTHERN IRELAND) 2001, SR 2001 179; made under the Social Security Administration (Northern Ireland) Act 1992 s.73, s.165. In force: October 1, 2001; £1.75.

These Regulations, which amend the Housing Benefit (General) Regulations (Northern Ireland) 1987 (SR 1987 461), prescribe circumstances when overpaid housing benefit need not be recovered from the person to whom such benefit was paid and prescribes persons from whom such benefit may be recovered in addition to, or instead of, the person to whom it was paid.

5990. Incapacity benefit – allowances

SOCIAL SECURITY (INCAPACITY BENEFIT) (AMENDMENT) REGULATIONS (NORTHERN IRELAND) 2001, SR 2001 156; made under the Social Contributions and Benefit (Northern Ireland) Act 1992 s.30A, s.171, Sch.3 para.2. In force: April 25, 2001; £1.75.

These Regulations amend the Social Security (Incapacity Benefit) Regulations (Northern Ireland) 1994 (SR 1999 461) to clarify the position relating to the relaxation of the first contribution condition for incapacity benefit, and the circumstances where a person may be entitled to incapacity benefit when he is aged between 20 and 25, or where he has previously been so entitled.

5991. Incapacity benefit – allowances

SOCIAL SECURITY (INCAPACITY BENEFIT) (MISCELLANEOUS AMENDMENTS) REGULATIONS (NORTHERN IRELAND) 2001, SR 2001 316; made under the Social Security Contributions and Benefits (Northern Ireland) Act 1992 s.30E, s.167D, s.171, Sch.3 para.2, Sch.7 para.2. In force: October 1, 2001; £1.75.

These Regulations amend the Social Security (General Benefit) Regulations (Northern Ireland) 1984 (SR 1984 92), the Social Security (Incapacity Benefit) Regulations (Northern Ireland) 1994 (SR 1994 461), the Social Security (Incapacity for Work) (General) Regulations (Northern Ireland) 1995 (SR 1995 41) and the Social Security Benefits Up-rating Regulations (Northern Ireland) 2001 (SR 2001 106). They increase the annual unemployability supplement earnings level from £3,146 to £3,432, increase the weekly earnings limit for a councillor's allowance in relation to incapacity benefit from £60.50 to £66.00 and increase the weekly incapacity for work therapeutic earnings limit from £60.50 to £66.00.

5992. Income support – definitions – students

INCOME SUPPORT (GENERAL) (AMENDMENT) REGULATIONS (NORTHERN IRELAND) 2001, SR 2001 105; made under the Social Security Contributions and Benefits (Northern Ireland) Act 1992 s.122, s.132, s.171. In force: March 29, 2001; £1.75.

These Regulations amend the Income Support (General) Regulations (Northern Ireland) 1987 (SR 1987 459) to change certain references in those Regulations to "full-time students" to references to "students".

5993. Income support – jobseekers allowance – calculation of housing costs – amendment of formula

INCOME SUPPORT (GENERAL) AND JOBSEEKER'S ALLOWANCE (AMENDMENT) REGULATIONS (NORTHERN IRELAND) 2001, SR 2001 406; made under the Social Security Contributions and Benefits (Northern Ireland) Act 1992 s.122, s.131, s.171; and the Jobseekers (Northern Ireland) Order 1995 (SI 1995 2705 (NI.15)) Art.6, Art.36. In force: December 10, 2001; £1.75.

These Regulations amend the Income Support (General) Regulations (Northern Ireland) 1987 (SR 1987 459) and the Jobseeker's Allowance Regulations

(Northern Ireland) 1996 (SR 1996 198) so as to amend the formula for the calculation of the weekly amount of a person's housing costs to take account of the abolition of mortgage interest payable under deduction of tax. In addition, the Regulations make in relation to Northern Ireland only, provision corresponding to provision contained in Regulations made by the Secretary of State for Work and Pensions in relation to GB.

5994. Income support – jobseekers allowance – entitlement – persons in residential care and nursing homes

INCOME SUPPORT AND JOBSEEKER'S ALLOWANCE (AMOUNTS FOR PERSONS IN RESIDENTIAL CARE AND NURSING HOMES) REGULATIONS (NORTHERN IRELAND) 2001, SR 2001 227; made under the Social Security Contributions and Benefits (Northern Ireland) Act 1992 s.122, s.131, s.171; and the Jobseekers (Northern Ireland) Order (SI 1995 2705 (NI. 15)) Art.6. In force: in accordance with Reg.1; £1.75.

These Regulations amend the Income Support (General) Regulations (Northern Ireland) 1987 (SR 1987 459) and the Jobseeker's Allowance Regulations (Northern Ireland) 1996 (SR 1996 198) by increasing the applicable amounts in those benefits in respect of those in residential care and nursing homes.

5995. Income support – loans – interest rate

INCOME SUPPORT (GENERAL) (STANDARD INTEREST RATE AMENDMENT) REGULATIONS (NORTHERN IRELAND) 2001, SR 2001 219; made under the Social Security Contributions and Benefits (Northern Ireland) Act 1992 s.122, s.131, s.171. In force: June 17, 2001; £1.75.

These Regulations amend the Income Support (General) Regulations (Northern Ireland) 1987 (SR 1987 459) by decreasing the standard rate of interest applicable to a loan which qualifies for income support to 6.94 per cent. In addition, they revoke the Income Support (General) (Standard Interest Rate Amendment No.2) Regulations (Northern Ireland) 2000 (SR 2000 196) which made a previous amendment to the standard rate of interest.

5996. Income support – loans – interest rate

INCOME SUPPORT (GENERAL) (STANDARD INTEREST RATE AMENDMENT NO.2) REGULATIONS (NORTHERN IRELAND) 2001, SR 2001 289; made under the Social Security Contributions and Benefits (Northern Ireland) Act 1992 s.122, s.131, s.171. In force: August 19, 2001; £1.75.

These Regulations, which revoke the Income Support (General) (Standard Interest Rate Amendment) Regulations (Northern Ireland) 2001 (SR 2001 219), amend the Income Support (General) Regulations (Northern Ireland) 1987 (SR 1987 459) with respect to the standard rate of interest applicable to a loan which qualifies for income support. The rate is decreased from 6.94 per cent to 6.65 per cent.

5997. Income support – loans – interest rate

INCOME SUPPORT (GENERAL) (STANDARD INTEREST RATE AMENDMENT NO.3) REGULATIONS (NORTHERN IRELAND) 2001, SR 2001 410; made under the Social Security Contributions and Benefits (Northern Ireland) Act 1992 s.122, s.131, s.171. In force: December 16, 2001; £1.75.

These Regulations, which revoke the Income Support (General) (Standard Interest Rate Amendment No.2) Regulations (Northern Ireland) 2001 (SR 2001 289), amend the Income Support (General) Regulations (Northern Ireland) 1987 (SR 1987 459) with respect to the standard rate of interest applicable to a loan which qualifies for income support. The rate is decreased from 6.65 per cent to 6.19 per cent. In addition, these Regulations make in relation to Northern Ireland only, provision corresponding to provision contained in Regulations made by the Secretary of State for Work and Pensions in relation to GB.

5998. Industrial injuries – compensation – adjustments to lower rate of incapacity benefit

WORKMEN'S COMPENSATION (SUPPLEMENTATION) (AMENDMENT) REGULATIONS (NORTHERN IRELAND) 2001, SR 2001 116; made under the Social Security Contributions and Benefits (Northern Ireland) Act 1992 s.171, Sch.8 para.2; and the Social Security Administration (Northern Ireland) Act 1992 Sch.6 para.1. In force: April 11, 2001; £2.00.

These Regulations amend the Workmen's Compensation (Supplementation) Regulations (Northern Ireland) 1983 (SR 1983 101) by increasing the lower rates of lesser incapacity allowance consequential upon the increase in the maximum rate of that allowance made by the Social Security Benefits Up-rating Order (Northern Ireland) 2001 (SR 2001 41). In addition, they include transitional provisions and revoke the Workmen's Compensation (Supplementation) (Amendment) Regulations (Northern Ireland) 2000 (SR 2000 75).

5999. Industrial injuries – dependants – permitted earnings limits

SOCIAL SECURITY (INDUSTRIAL INJURIES) (DEPENDENCY) (PERMITTED EARNINGS LIMITS) ORDER (NORTHERN IRELAND) 2001, SR 2001 107; made under the Social Security Contributions and Benefits (Northern Ireland) Act 1992 s.171, Sch.7 para.4. In force: April 9, 2001; £1.50.

Where a disablement pension with unemployability supplement is increased in respect of a child or children, and the beneficiary is one of two persons who are spouses residing together or an unmarried couple, the Social Security Contributions and Benefits Act 1992 Sch.7 para.4 is amended to provide that the increase shall not be payable in respect of the first child if the other person's earnings are £145 a week or more and in respect of a further child for each complete £19 by which the earnings exceed £145. This Order revokes the Social Security (Industrial Injuries) (Dependency) (Permitted Earnings Limits) Order (Northern Ireland) 1999 (SR 1999 94).

6000. Invalid care allowance – gainful employment

SOCIAL SECURITY (INVALID CARE ALLOWANCE) (AMENDMENT) REGULATIONS (NORTHERN IRELAND) 2001, SR 2001 117; made under the Social Security Contributions and Benefits (Northern Ireland) Act 1992 s.70. In force: April 6, 2001; £1.50.

These Regulations amend the Social Security (Invalid Care Allowance) Regulations (Northern Ireland) 1976 (SR 1976 99) to increase the amount there specified so that a person shall not be treated as gainfully employed on any day in a week unless his earnings in the immediately preceding week have exceeded an amount equal to the lower earnings limit. In addition, they revoke the Social Security (Invalid Care Allowance) (Amendment) Regulations (Northern Ireland) 1993 (SR 1993 72).

6001. Jobseekers allowance – armed forces – entitlement

JOBSEEKER'S ALLOWANCE (MEMBERS OF THE FORCES) (JOINT CLAIMS: CONSEQUENTIAL AMENDMENTS) REGULATIONS (NORTHERN IRELAND) 2001, SI 2001 998; made under the Jobseekers (Northern Ireland) Order 1995 (SI 1995 2705 (NI.15)) Art.24. In force: March 19, 2001; £1.50.

These Regulations, which amend the Jobseeker's Allowance (Members of the Forces) (Northern Ireland) Regulations 1997 (SI 1997 932), provide that a member of a joint-claim couple shall be treated as though he had lost his job through misconduct where he is discharged, cashiered or otherwise dismissed as a consequence of being convicted on any proceedings under the Naval Discipline Act 1957, the Army Act 1955 or the Air Force Act 1955 or by any civil court and ensure that a member of a joint-claim couple is not disqualified from receiving joint-claim jobseeker's allowance where he is discharged from Her Majesty's Forces at his own request.

6002. Jobseekers allowance – joint claims

JOBSEEKER'S ALLOWANCE (JOINT CLAIMS: CONSEQUENTIAL AMENDMENTS) REGULATIONS (NORTHERN IRELAND) 2001, SR 2001 56; made under the Jobseekers (Northern Ireland) Order 1995 (SI 1995 2705 (NI.15)) Art.8, Art.9. In force: March 19, 2001; £1.75.

These Regulations, which amend the Jobseeker's Allowance Regulations (Northern Ireland) 1996 (SR 1996 198) consequent on the requirement for certain claimants to make a joint claim for a jobseeker's allowance, ensure that a joint claimant is treated in the same way as a single claimant for the purposes of the conditions of entitlement to a jobseeker's allowance. They amend the Regulations to ensure that the requirements for a young person to be available for and actively to seek employment are the same whether he is a member of a joint-claim couple or is a single claimant.

6003. Pensions – earnings factors – calculation of additional pension

SOCIAL SECURITY REVALUATION OF EARNINGS FACTORS ORDER (NORTHERN IRELAND) 2001, SR 2001 100; made under the Social Security Administration (Northern Ireland) Act 1992 s.130, s.165. In force: April 6, 2001; £1.75.

This Order directs that the earnings factors relevant to the calculation of the additional pension in the rate of any long term benefit or of any guaranteed minimum pension, or to any other calculation required under the Pension Schemes (Northern Ireland) Act 1993 Part III, are to be increased for the tax years specified in the Schedule to the Order by the percentage of their amount specified in that Schedule. In addition, this Order provides for the rounding of fractional amounts for earnings factors relevant to the calculation of the additional pension in the rate of any long term benefit.

6004. Reciprocity – agreements

SOCIAL SECURITY (RECIPROCAL AGREEMENTS) ORDER (NORTHERN IRELAND) 2001, SR 2001 86; made under the Social Security Administration (Northern Ireland) Act 1992 s.155. In force: April 9, 2001; £2.50.

This Order provides for social security legislation to be modified or adapted to take account of changes made by the Welfare Reform and Pensions Act 1999 which replaces widow's benefit with bereavement benefit in relation to the Orders in Council, and orders made by the Secretary of State, listed in Sch.2 to this order.

6005. SERPS – succession – rate increase

SOCIAL SECURITY (INHERITED SERPS) REGULATIONS (NORTHERN IRELAND) 2001, SR 2001 441; made under the Welfare Reform and Pensions (Northern Ireland) Order 1 (SI 1 3147 (NI.11)) Art.49, Art.73. In force: October 6, 2002; £2.00.

These Regulations provide for an increase in the rate of the additional pension under the State Earnings Related Pension Scheme (SERPS) to which persons of a specified description would otherwise be entitled under or by virtue of certain provisions of the Social Security Contributions and Benefits (Northern Ireland) Act 1992 Part II in the event that they are widowed on or after October 6, 2002 which is the date on which the maximum amount of the additional pension which may be inherited by a surviving spouse under SERPS is reduced from 100 per cent to 50 per cent. They increase the rate of the additional pension, or of any constituent element of an increase in that pension, which would otherwise be payable to persons of a specified description under or by virtue of those provisions in the event that they are widowed on or after October 6, 2002.

6006. Social fund – cold weather payments – weather stations and postcode districts

SOCIAL FUND (COLD WEATHER PAYMENTS) (GENERAL) (AMENDMENT) REGULATIONS (NORTHERN IRELAND) 2001, SR 2001 386; made under the Social Security Contributions and Benefits (Northern Ireland) Act 1992 s.134, s.171. In force: November 1, 2001; £1.75.

These Regulations amend the Social Fund (Cold Weather Payments) (General) Regulations (Northern Ireland) 1988 (SR 1988 368) to reflect changes to the list of weather stations and to also take account of minor changes to some postcode to weather station linkages.

6007. Social fund – widowed parent's allowance and bereavement allowance

SOCIAL FUND (RECOVERY BY DEDUCTIONS FROM BENEFITS) (AMENDMENT) REGULATIONS (NORTHERN IRELAND) 2001, SR 2001 52; made under the Social Security Administration (Northern Ireland) Act 1992 s.74, s.165. In force: April 9, 2001; £1.50.

These Regulations further amend the Social Fund (Recovery by Deductions from Benefits) Regulations (Northern Ireland) 1988 (SR 1988 21) to prescribe widowed parent's allowance and bereavement allowance as benefits from which awards from the social fund may be recovered by deduction.

6008. Social fund – winter fuel payments – increase

SOCIAL FUND WINTER FUEL PAYMENT (AMENDMENT) REGULATIONS (NORTHERN IRELAND) 2001, SR 2001 373; made under the Social Security Contributions and Benefits (Northern Ireland) Act 1992 s.134, s.171. In force: November 2, 2001; £1.75.

These Regulations amend the Social Fund Winter Fuel Payment Regulations (Northern Ireland) 2000 (SR 2000 91) by increasing the amount of winter fuel payment.

6009. Social Security Fraud Act (Northern Ireland) 2001 (c.17) – Commencement No.1 Order

SOCIAL SECURITY FRAUD (2001 ACT) (COMMENCEMENT NO.1) ORDER (NORTHERN IRELAND) 2001, SR 2001 416 (C.20); made under the Social Security Fraud Act (Northern Ireland) Act 2001 s.17. Commencement details: bringing into force various provisions of the 2001 Act on December 3, 2001 and January 7, 2002; £1.50.

This Order provides for the coming into operation of the Social Security Fraud Act (Northern Ireland) 2001 s.15 which provides for offences in relation to the failure to notify a change of circumstances.

6010. Social Security (Northern Ireland) Order 1998 (SI 1998 1506 (NI.10)) – Commencement No.12 Order

SOCIAL SECURITY (1998 ORDER) (COMMENCEMENT NO.12) ORDER (NORTHERN IRELAND) 2001, SR 2001 260 (C.13); made under the Social Security (Northern Ireland) Order 1998 (SI 1998 1506 (NI.10)) Art.1. Commencement details: bringing into force various provisions of the Order on July 2, 2001; £2.00.

This Order provides for the coming into operation of provisions of the Social Security (Northern Ireland) Order 1998 (SI 1998 1506 (NI.10)) in respect of repeals relating to housing benefit.

6011. State retirement pensions – first appointed year – 2002-03

ADDITIONAL PENSION (FIRST APPOINTED YEAR) ORDER (NORTHERN IRELAND) 2001, SR 2001 49; made under the Social Security Contributions and Benefits (Northern Ireland) Act 1992 s.121. In force: February 8, 2001; £1.50.

This Order appoints the tax year 2002-03 as the "first appointed year" for the purposes of the definition of that expression in the Social Security Contributions and Benefits (Northern Ireland) Act 1992 s.121 (1), making it the first tax year in which the provisions governing the State Second Pension, which reform the current State Earnings Related Pension Scheme will be in operation.

6012. State retirement pensions – home responsibilities

ADDITIONAL PENSION AND SOCIAL SECURITY PENSIONS (HOME RESPONSIBILITIES) (AMENDMENT) REGULATIONS (NORTHERN IRELAND) 2001, SR 2001 440; made under the Social Security Contributions and Benefits (Northern Ireland) Act 1992 s.44A, s.121, s.171, Sch.3 para.5, Sch.4A para.9. In force: April 6, 2002; £2.50.

These Regulations amend the Social Security Pensions (Home Responsibilities) Regulations (Northern Ireland) 1994 (SR 1994 89) to include certain persons who previously were not treated as precluded from regular employment by responsibilities at home in the first year of their child's life, and to specify a time limit for providing the Department for Social Development with information where a person is to be treated as precluded from regular employment after April 5, 2002 by responsibilities at home. They also make additional provision for the calculation of the state second pension (the additional pension element of a state retirement pension from April 6, 2002), and for conditions to be satisfied, in certain circumstances, in order for a person to be treated as precluded from regular employment by responsibilities at home and therefore entitled to additional pension by virtue of the Social Security Contributions and Benefits (Northern Ireland) Act 1992 s.44A.

6013. Students – income related benefits

SOCIAL SECURITY (STUDENTS AND INCOME-RELATED BENEFITS AMENDMENT) REGULATIONS (NORTHERN IRELAND) 2001, SR 2001 278; made under the Social Security Contributions and Benefits (Northern Ireland) Act 1992 s.122, s.132, s.171; and the Jobseekers (Northern Ireland) Order 1995 (SI 1995 2705 (NI.15)) Art.14. In force: in accordance with Reg.1; £2.50.

These Regulations amend the Income Support (General) Regulations (Northern Ireland) 1987 (SR 1987 459), the Income Support (General) Regulations (Northern Ireland) 1987 (SR 1987 461) and the Jobseeker's Allowance Regulations (Northern Ireland) 1996 (SR 1996 198) in so far as those Regulations apply to students and former students. They insert a definition of "academic year", increase the amounts of grant and loan income to be disregarded in respect of books and equipment and for travel costs and allow the former to be disregarded even if a student's grant income includes an amount for books and equipment, and add new exclusions for grants paid to certain students who are lone parents. In addition, the Regulations provide rules as to the apportionment of student loans where the academic year starts other than on September 1, provide a formula for calculating the income of a former student who has received a student loan or an amount intended for the maintenance of dependents and who abandons, or is dismissed from, his course before the end of the penultimate term of the academic year, ensure that grants paid to students receiving instruction as officers of hospital authorities are taken into account over 12 months and not 10 and disregard school meal grants paid in Scotland as income in housing benefit.

6014. Tax credits – disabled persons tax credit – working families tax credit

TAX CREDITS SCHEMES (MISCELLANEOUS AMENDMENTS) (NORTHERN IRELAND) REGULATIONS 2001, SI 2001 20; made under the Social Security

Contributions and Benefits (Northern Ireland) Act 1992 s.132, s.133, s.171; and the Tax Credits Act 1999 s.2, Sch.2 para.3, Sch.2 para.22. In force: January 30, 2001; £1.50.

These Regulations amend the Family Credit (General) Regulation (Northern Ireland) 1987 (SR 1987 463) Sch.2 and the Disability Working Allowance (General) Regulations (Northern Ireland) 1992 (SR 1992 78) Sch.3 to add the sum of £15 of of any widowed mother's allowance or widowed parent's allowance to the categories of income to be disregarded. In addition, they amend Sch.3 to the Family Credit Regulations and Sch.4 to the Disability Working Allowance Regulations so as to add payments of £10,000 made by the Secretary of State for Social Security to persons who were held prisoner by the Japanese during World War Two or to the spouses of such persons.

6015. Tax credits – disabled persons tax credit – working families tax credit

TAX CREDITS SCHEMES (MISCELLANEOUS AMENDMENTS NO.2) (NORTHERN IRELAND) REGULATIONS 2001, SI 2001 366; made under the Social Security Contributions and Benefits (Northern Ireland) Act 1992 s.127, s.128, s.171; and the Tax Credits Act 1999 s.2, Sch.2 para.3, Sch.2 para.22. In force: April 10, 2001; £2.00.

These Regulations, which amend the Family Credit (General) Regulations (Northern Ireland) 1987 (SR 1987 463) and the Disability Working Allowance (General) Regulations (Northern Ireland) 1992 (SR 1992 78), add new credits in respect of severely disabled adults, children and young persons to the computation of both working families' tax credit and disabled person's tax credit.

6016. Tax credits – disabled persons tax credit – working families tax credit

TAX CREDITS (MISCELLANEOUS AMENDMENTS NO.3) (NORTHERN IRELAND) REGULATIONS 2001, SI 2001 893; made under the Social Security Contributions and Benefits (Northern Ireland) Act 1992 s.127, s.128, s.132, s.133, s.171; the Social Security Administration (Northern Ireland) Act 1992 s.5, s.165; and the Tax Credits Act 1999 s.2, Sch.2 para.3, Sch.2 para.7, Sch.2 para.22. In force: in accordance with Reg.1 (2) (3); £2.00.

These Regulations amend the Disability Working Allowance (General) Regulations (Northern Ireland) 1992 (SR 1992 78), the Social Security (Claims and Payments) Regulations (Northern Ireland) 1987 (SR 1987 465) and the Family Credit (General) Regulations (Northern Ireland) 1987 (SR 1987 463) to enable a person to claim, with effect from April 4, 2001, working families' tax credit or disabled person's tax credit in respect of a newly born or adopted child, or a surrogate child.

6017. Tax credits – disabled persons tax credit – working families tax credit

TAX CREDITS (MISCELLANEOUS AMENDMENTS NO.4) (NORTHERN IRELAND) REGULATIONS 2001, SI 2001 1083; made under the Social Security Contributions and Benefits Act 1992 s.127, s.128, s.132, s.133, s.171; and the Tax Credits Act 1999 s.2, Sch.2 para.3, Sch.2 para.22. In force: April 10, 2001; £1.75.

These Regulations amend the Family Credit (General) Regulations (Northern Ireland) 1987 (SR 1987 463) and the Disability Working Allowance (General) Regulations (Northern Ireland) 1992 (SR 1992 78) in relation to award periods of working families' tax credit and disabled person's tax credit commencing on or after April 10, 2001.

6018. Tax credits – disabled persons tax credit – working families tax credit

TAX CREDITS (MISCELLANEOUS AMENDMENTS NO.5) (NORTHERN IRELAND) REGULATIONS 2001, SI 2001 1350; made under the Social Security

Contributions and Benefits (Northern Ireland) Act 1992 s.127, s.128, s.171; and the Tax Credits Act 1999 s.2, Sch.2 para.3, Sch.2 para.22. In force: June 5, 2001; £1.50.

These Regulations, which amend the Family Credit (General) Regulations (Northern Ireland) 1987 (SR 1987 463) and the Disability Working Allowance (General) Regulations (Northern Ireland) 1992 (SR 1992 78), provide for increases of certain of the credits by reference to which the appropriate maximum working families' tax credit and the appropriate maximum disabled person's tax credit are calculated. The amendments have effect in relation to award periods of both tax credits commencing on or after June 5, 2001.

6019. **Tax credits – disabled persons tax credit – working families tax credit**

TAX CREDITS (MISCELLANEOUS AMENDMENTS NO.6) (NORTHERN IRELAND) REGULATIONS 2001, SI 2001 2221; made under the Social Security Contributions and Benefits Act 1992 s.132, s.133, s.171; and the Tax Credits Act 1999 s.2, Sch.2 para.3, Sch.2 para.22. In force: July 3, 2001; £1.50.

These Regulations amend the Family Credit (General) Regulations (Northern Ireland) 1987 (SR 1987 463) and the Disability Working Allowance (General) Regulations (Northern Ireland) 1992 (SR 1992 78) to add to the lists of income and capital to be disregarded in calculating a claimant's gross income, or capital, discretionary housing payments or capital discretionary payments made pursuant to the Discretionary Financial Assistance Regulations (Northern Ireland) 2001 (SR 2001 216) Reg.2(1).

6020. **Tax credits – disabled persons tax credit – working families tax credit**

TAX CREDITS (MISCELLANEOUS AMENDMENTS NO.7) (NORTHERN IRELAND) REGULATIONS 2001, SI 2001 2540; made under the Social Security Contributions and Benefits Act (Northern Ireland) 1992 s.127, s.128, s.132, s.133, s.171; and the Tax Credits Act 1999 s.2, Sch.2 para.3, Sch.2 para.22. In force: August 7, 2001; £1.75.

These Regulations make various amendments to the provisions relating to students in the Family Credit (General) Regulations (Northern Ireland) 1987 (SR 1987 463) and the Disability Working Allowance (General) Regulations 1992 (SR 1992 78).

6021. **Tax credits – disabled persons tax credit – working families tax credit**

TAX CREDITS (MISCELLANEOUS AMENDMENTS NO.8) (NORTHERN IRELAND) REGULATIONS 2001, SI 2001 3086; made under the Social Security Contributions and Benefits Act 1992 s.132, s.133, s.171; and the Tax Credits Act 1999 s.2, Sch.2 para.3, Sch.2 para.22. In force: October 9, 2001; £1.75.

These Regulations amend the Family Credit (General) Regulations (Northern Ireland) 1987 (SI 1987 463) and the Disability Working Allowance Regulations (Northern Ireland) 1992 (SI 1992 78) so as to add to the list of capital to be disregarded in calculating a claimant's capital for the purposes of working families' tax credit and disabled person's tax credit a dwelling which the claimant intends in due course to occupy as his home but which he currently does not occupy due to living in job-related accommodation.

6022. **Tax credits – employment schemes – disabled persons tax credit – working families tax credit**

TAX CREDITS (NEW DEAL CONSEQUENTIAL AMENDMENTS) (NORTHERN IRELAND) REGULATIONS 2001, SI 2001 1333; made under the Social Security Contributions and Benefits (Northern Ireland) Act 1992 s.122, s.132, s.133, s.171. In force: April 24, 2001; £1.75.

These Regulations amend the Family Credit (General) Regulations (Northern Ireland) 1987 (SR 1987 463) and the Disability Working Allowance (General) Regulations (Northern Ireland) 1992 (SR 1992 78) in consequence of the introduction of two new employment programmes know as the "Preparation for

Employment Programme" and the "Preparation for Employment Programme for 50 plus".

6023. Tax credits – up rating
See SOCIAL SECURITY. §5088

6024. Unemployment – New Deal
SOCIAL SECURITY (NEW DEAL AMENDMENT) REGULATIONS (NORTHERN IRELAND) 2001, SR 2001 151; made under the Social Security Contributions and Benefits (Northern Ireland) Act 1992 s.122, s.131, s.132, s.171; and the Jobseekers (Northern Ireland) Order 1995 (SI 1995 2705 (NI.15)) Art.6, Art.14, Art.21, Art.22, Art.22B, Art.36, Sch.1 para.3. In force: April 9, 2001; £3.00.

These Regulations, which amend the Jobseeker's Allowance Regulations (Northern Ireland) 1996 (SR 1996 198), the Income Support (General) Regulations (Northern Ireland) 1987 (SR 1987 459) and the Housing Benefit (General) Regulations (Northern Ireland) 1987 (SR 1987 461), provide that individuals aged between 25 and 49 participating in the Preparation for Employment Programme with the effect that if such a person, without good cause, refuses or fails to participate in the PEP or loses his place on the PEP because of misconduct, he will receive a sanction. They allow claims for jobseeker's allowance separated by periods on the PEP and make various amendments to the rules on the treatment of income and capital.

6025. Unemployment – New Deal – miscellaneous provisions
NEW DEAL (LONE PARENTS) (MISCELLANEOUS PROVISIONS) ORDER (NORTHERN IRELAND) 2001, SR 2001 423; made under the Employment and Training (Amendment) (Northern Ireland) Order 1988 (SI 1988 1087 (NI.10)) Art.4. In force: January 14, 2002; £2.00.

This Order provides that a person using facilities provided in pursuance of the employment programme known as "the New Deal for Lone Parents self-employment route" and receiving or entitled to receive in connection with the use of those facilities a top-up payment or assistance with the expenses of participation or both shall be treated as being in receipt of a training allowance for the purposes of the remunerative work rule in income support and as in receipt of a training premium for all other purposes. The effect of the Order is that receipt of the top-up payment and expenses by a person using those facilities does not affect his entitlement to income support or the amount of income support to which he is entitled.

6026. Unemployment – New Deal – miscellaneous provisions
NEW DEAL (MISCELLANEOUS PROVISIONS) ORDER (NORTHERN IRELAND) 2001, SR 2001 110; made under the Employment and Training (Amendment) (Northern Ireland) Order 1988 (SI 1988 1087 (NI.10)) Art.4. In force: April 9, 2001; £2.00.

This Order provides that, for the purposes of the Social Security Contributions and Benefits (Northern Ireland) Act 1992 Part I and the Jobseekers (Northern Ireland) Order 1995 (SI 1995 2705 (NI.15)), a person using facilities provided in pursuance of the employment programme known as "the Preparation for Employment Programme" or "the Preparation for Employment Programme for 50 plus" and receiving or entitled to receive from the Department of Higher and Further Education, Training and Employment a training allowance in connection with the use of those facilities shall be treated not as being employed but as participating in arrangements for training under the Employment and Training Act (Northern Ireland) 1950 s.1. Any payment made to such a person in connection with his use of those facilities, other than a trading payment made to a person receiving assistance in pursuing self-employed earner's employment, shall be treated as a payment of training allowance made in respect of such training.

6027. Welfare Reform and Pensions (Northern Ireland) Order 1999 (SI 1999 3147 (NI.11)) – Commencement No.7 and Transitional Provisions Order

WELFARE REFORM AND PENSIONS (1999 ORDER) (COMMENCEMENT NO.7 AND TRANSITIONAL PROVISIONS) ORDER (NORTHERN IRELAND) 2001, SR 2001 114 (C.4); made under the Welfare Reform and Pensions (Northern Ireland) Order 1999 (SI 1999 3147 (NI.11)) Art.1, Art.73. Commencement details: bringing into force various provisions of the 1999 Order on March 19, 2001, April 6, 2001 and October 8, 2001; £2.00.

This Order, which amends the Welfare Reform and Pensions (1999 Order) (Commencement No.3) Order (Northern Ireland) 2000 (SR 2000 133) and the Welfare Reform and Pensions (1999 Order) (Commencement No.6 and Transitional and Savings Provisions) Order 2000 (SR 2000 332), provides for the coming into operation of certain provisions of the Welfare Reform and Pensions (Northern Ireland) Order 1999 (SI 1999 3147 (NI.11)). The commencement of parts of Art.5 which relates to stakeholder pension schemes is brought forward from October 8, 2001 to April 6, 2001 so that the requirement that an employer consult prior to designating a scheme is brought forward to allow valid designation of a scheme by an employer prior to October 8, 2001.

6028. Welfare Reform and Pensions (Northern Ireland) Order 1999 (SI 1999 3147 (NI.11)) – Commencement No.9 Order

WELFARE REFORM AND PENSIONS (1999 ORDER) (COMMENCEMENT NO.9) ORDER (NORTHERN IRELAND) 2001, SR 2001 438 (C.21); made under the Welfare Reform and Pensions (Northern Ireland) Order 1999 (SI 1999 3147 (NI.11)) Art.1. Commencement details: bringing into force various provisions of the 1999 Order on January 1, 2002 and February 1, 2002; £2.00.

This Order brings into force certain provisions of the Welfare Reform and Pensions (Northern Ireland) Order 1999 (SI 1999 3147 (NI.11)) on January 1, 2002, and February 1, 2002.

SOCIAL WELFARE

6029. Child Support, Pensions and Social Security Act (Northern Ireland) 2000 (c.4) – Commencement No.6 Order

CHILD SUPPORT, PENSIONS AND SOCIAL SECURITY (2000 ACT) (COMMENCEMENT NO.6) ORDER (NORTHERN IRELAND) 2001, SR 2001 249 (C.12); made under the Child Support, Pensions and Social Security Act (Northern Ireland) 2000 s.68. Commencement details: bringing into force various provisions of the 2000 Act in accordance with Art.2; £1.75.

This Order provides for the coming into operation provision of the Child Support, Pensions and Social Security Act (Northern Ireland) 2000 relating to grants towards the cost of discretionary housing payments, to the prohibition on occupational pension schemes having different rules for overseas residents, to the recovery of housing benefit and to an alternative to anti-franking rules.

6030. Food – milk

WELFARE FOODS (AMENDMENT) REGULATIONS (NORTHERN IRELAND) 2001, SR 2001 139; made under the Social Security (Northern Ireland) Order 1988 (SI 1988 594 (NI.2)) Art.13; and the Social Security Contributions and Benefits (Northern Ireland) Act 1992 s.171. In force: April 1, 2001; £1.75.

These Regulations, which amend the Welfare Foods Regulations (Northern Ireland) 1988 (SR 1988 137), remove references to family credit in the 1988 Regulations as family credit is no longer in existence. They increase the price payable for dried milk by a person entitled to purchase it at a reduced price, from £3.90 to £4.05 per 900 grams per week and increase from £70 to £71 the amount of any reduction in the appropriate maximum which may not be exceeded if a person is to be regarded as entitled to working families' tax credit.

6031. Social services – Social Care Council – appointments and procedure

NORTHERN IRELAND SOCIAL CARE COUNCIL (APPOINTMENTS AND PROCEDURE) REGULATIONS (NORTHERN IRELAND) 2001, SR 2001 313; made under the Health and Personal Social Services Act (Northern Ireland) 2001 s.1, s.57, Sch.1 para.5. In force: October 1, 2001; £2.50.

These Regulations make provision concerning the membership and procedure of the Northern Ireland Social Care Council established under the Health and Personal Social Services Act (Northern Ireland) 2001 Part I. They make provision for the appointment and tenure of office of the chairman and members of the Council, for resignations, for the termination of appointments by the Department and for the appointment of the deputy chairman. They also make provision for the establishment of committees and sub-committees, the conduct of meetings and the exclusion from meetings of those with a pecuniary interest in matters under discussion.

6032. Tax credits – disabled persons tax credit – working families tax credit

TAX CREDITS (MISCELLANEOUS AMENDMENTS NO.9) (NORTHERN IRELAND) REGULATIONS 2001, SI 2001 3456; made under the Social Security Contributions and Benefits (Northern Ireland) Act 1992 s.132, s.133, s.171; and the Tax Credits Act 1999 s.2, Sch.2 para.3, Sch.2 para.22. In force: November 13, 2001; £1.50.

These Regulations amend the Family Credit (General) Regulations (Northern Ireland) 1987 (SR 1987 463) and the Disability Working Allowance (General) Regulations (Northern Ireland) 1992 (SR 1992 78) which provide that subject to certain exceptions, income derived from capital shall be treated as capital for the purposes of calculating a claimant's entitlement to disabled person's tax credit or working families' tax credit. The amendment adds to the list of exceptions income derived from a dwelling which the claimant intends in due course to occupy as his home but which he currently does not occupy due to living in job-related accommodation. In addition, the Regulations add to the list of capital to be disregarded in calculating a claimant's capital for the purposes of ascertaining his entitlement to disabled person's tax credit or working families' tax credit payments made for victims of National Socialism during the Second World War.

SUCCESSION

6033. Administration of estates – intestacy – share of child of marriage between deceased's aunt and uncle

[Administration of Estates Act (Northern Ireland) 1955 s.11.]

Held, that on a true construction of the Administration of Estates Act (NI) 1955 s.11 (1) and s.11 (2), where on an intestacy there were children or remoter issue of the marriage of a paternal uncle and a maternal aunt of the deceased, the shares of the estate to which the issue were entitled would be calculated by reference to the two separate stirpes subsisting in relation to the deceased's uncle and the deceased's aunt. If, therefore, a beneficiary of the estate could trace descent from more than one uncle or aunt of the deceased, that beneficiary was entitled to participate in the share of the estate to which that uncle or aunt would have succeeded had he or she survived the deceased.

PATRICK'S ESTATE, *Re*; *sub nom*. PATRICK v. DE ZEEUW [2000] N.I. 506, Girvan, J., Ch D (NI).

6034. Intestacy – cohabitees – provision for reasonable maintenance – equitable interest in home

[Inheritance (Provision for Family and Dependants) (Northern Ireland) Order 1979 Art.3(1)(ba); European Convention on Human Rights 1950 Art.8, Art.12.]

G died intestate leaving an estranged widow, M, to whom he had paid weekly maintenance, and an adult son, D. Both M and D obtained benefits from G's former employers, with M receiving widow's pensions and D obtaining a lump sum of £29,000. For nine years prior to his death G had cohabited with B as man and wife. B applied under the Inheritance (Provision for Family and Dependants) (Northern Ireland) Order 1979 Art.3(1)(ba) for reasonable financial provision to be made for her maintenance on the ground that she had lived in the same household with G as man and wife for at least two years prior to his death.

Held, allowing the application and awarding the house to B, subject to an index linked charge of £25,000 in favour of M and D, realisable on sale, B's death, marriage or further cohabitation, that the different treatment accorded to spouses and cohabitees by the 1979 Order was recognition of the special status accorded to marriage and in keeping with the European Convention on Human Rights 1950 Art.8 and Art.12. On the facts of the instant case, B's contributions gave rise to an equitable interest in the property, whereas his marriage to M had been over for many years and both M and D had obtained benefits commensurate with their status outside G's estate.

GUIDERA'S ESTATE, *Re; sub nom.* BINGHAM v. GUIDERA [2001] N.I. 71, Girvan, J., Ch D (NI).

TAXATION

6035. Benefits – working families' and disabled person's tax credit – false claims – interest rates

TAXES (INTEREST RATE) (AMENDMENT NO.2) REGULATIONS 2001, SI 2001 254; made under the Finance Act 1989 s.178. In force: March 7, 2001; £0.50.

These Regulations amend the Taxes (Interest Rate) Regulations 1989 (SI 1989 1297) so as to provide for the rate of interest recoverable amounts of working families' tax credit and disabled person's tax credit, and for the rate of interest on penalties for fraudulently or negligently making any incorrect statement or declaration in connection with a claim for working families' tax credit or disabled person's tax credit and have effect in relation to periods beginning on or after March 7, 2001.

6036. Capital allowances – grants

CAPITAL ALLOWANCES (CORRESPONDING NORTHERN IRELAND GRANTS) ORDER 2001, SI 2001 810; made under the Capital Allowances Act 1990 s.153; and the Northern Ireland Act 1998 Sch.12 para.3. In force: April 1, 2001; £1.50.

This Order specifies certain grants made in Northern Ireland under the Industrial Development (Northern Ireland) Order 1982 (SI 1982 1083) as corresponding to grants made in Great Britain under Industrial Development Act 1982 Part II and is in succession to the Capital Allowances (Corresponding Northern Ireland Grants) Order 1999 (SI 1999 719), which applies to grants made under agreements entered into before April 1, 2001. The effect of the Order is that the amounts of the specified grants are not deducted from the recipient's capital expenditure when his capital allowances are calculated.

6037. Corporation tax – close companies – loans to participators – series of eight loans made over 14 year period did not constitute investment business for purposes of ICTA s.419(1)

[Income and Corporation Taxes Act 1988 s.419.]

The Revenue appealed against a special commissioner's decision ([2000] S.T.C. (S.C.D.) 172, [2000] C.L.Y. 5781) allowing D's appeal against an assessment made under the Income and Corporation Taxes Act 1988 s.419 resulting from a loan made by D, a close company, to M, who was an associate of a participator in D in terms of s.419(1). Between 1983 and 1997, D made eight loans to M, all at commercial interest rates. Those loans, with the exception of a loan of £30,000 made in September 1997, had been repaid. During the accounting period covering September 1997 other loans were made to two related close companies and to a separate company chaired by M. The commissioner held that the September 1997 loan was an investment made in the ordinary course of D's business.

Held, allowing the appeal, that making eight loans in 14 years did not constitute a business for the purposes of s.419(1). Although the commissioner had been entitled to find that the loans made to M were investments by D, he could not then merely assume that the act of making the loan satisfied the requirements of s.419(1) and should have gone on to consider what extra elements were necessary to bring the loan within the s.419(1) exception, *Steen v. Law* [1964] A.C. 287, [1963] C.L.Y. 413 considered.

BRENNAN (INSPECTOR OF TAXES) v. DEANBY INVESTMENT CO LTD [2001] S.T.C. 536, Carswell, L.C.J., CA (NI).

6038. Tax credits – disabled persons tax credit – working families tax credit – claims and payments

TAX CREDITS (CLAIMS AND PAYMENTS) (NORTHERN IRELAND) (AMENDMENT) REGULATIONS 2001, SI 2001 568; made under the Social Security Administration (Northern Ireland) Act 1992 s.5, s.165; and the Tax Credits Act 1999 s.21, Sch.2 para.7, Sch.2 para.22. In force: April 10, 2001; £1.50.

These Regulations, which amend the Social Security (Claims and Payments) Regulations (Northern Ireland) 1987 (SR 1987 465) with respect only to working families' tax credit and disabled persons' tax credit, provide for the date on which certain claims for working families' tax credit or disabled person's tax credit are treated as being made. In addition, the Regulations are amended in consequence of the recent amendments to the Income Support (General) Regulations (Northern Ireland) 1987 (SR 1987 459) by extending the circumstances in which claims for working families' tax credit and disabled person's tax credit may be backdated.

6039. Books

Ward, John – Judge: Irish Income Tax 2001-2002. Butterworth's Irish Tax Library. Paperback: £100.00. ISBN 1-85475-697-4. Butterworths Law.

TELECOMMUNICATIONS

6040. Electronic Communications Act (Northern Ireland) 2001 (c.9)

This Act makes provision to facilitate the use of electronic communications and electronic data storage.

This Act received Royal Assent on April 5, 2001 and comes into force on April 5, 2001.

6041. Licences – GTS Network (Ireland) Ltd

PUBLIC TELECOMMUNICATION SYSTEM DESIGNATION (GTS NETWORK (IRELAND) LTD) ORDER 2001, SI 2001 2584; made under the Telecommunications Act 1984 s.9. In force: August 16, 2001; £1.50.

The Secretary of State granted a licence to GTS Network (Ireland) Ltd on November 1, 2001, under the Telecommunications Act 1984 s.7, to run the telecommunications systems specified in the licence. This Order designates those telecommunication systems as public telecommunication systems and consequently GTS Network (Ireland) Ltd will be a public telecommunications operator when the Order comes into force on August 16, 2001.

TORTS

6042. Road traffic – health services charges

ROAD TRAFFIC (HEALTH SERVICES CHARGES) REGULATIONS (NORTHERN IRELAND) 2001, SR 2001 125; made under the Health and Personal Social Services Act (Northern Ireland) 2001 s.23, s.24, s.25, s.28, s.32, s.33, s.35, s.36, s.37, s.57. In force: April 2, 2001; £2.50.

These Regulations make provision for a scheme for the recovery from insurers and certain other persons of charges in connection with the health services treatment of road traffic casualties.

6043. Road traffic – health services charges

ROAD TRAFFIC (HEALTH SERVICES CHARGES) (AMENDMENT) REGULATIONS (NORTHERN IRELAND) 2001, SR 2001 434; made under the Health and Personal Social Services Act (Northern Ireland) 2001 s.23, s.25, s.32, s.37, s.57. In force: January 28, 2002; £1.75.

These Regulations amend the Road Traffic (Health Services Charges) Regulations (Northern Ireland) 2001 (SI 2001 125) which provide for a scheme for the recovery from insurers and certain other persons of charges in connection with the health services treatment of road traffic casualties. They increase the charge where the traffic casualty received NHS treatment but was not admitted to hospital from £354 to £402, increase the daily charge for NHS treatment where the traffic casualty is admitted to hospital from £435 to £494 and increase the maximum charge for treatment where the traffic casualty is admitted to hospital from £10,000 to £30,000.

6044. Road traffic – health services charges – appeals

ROAD TRAFFIC (HEALTH SERVICES CHARGES) (APPEALS) REGULATIONS (NORTHERN IRELAND) 2001, SR 2001 299; made under the Health and Personal Social Services Act (Northern Ireland) 2001 s.29, s.30, s.31, s.57. In force: September 10, 2001; £2.50.

These Regulations provide for the procedural rules and other requirements for bringing appeals against certificates of health services charges issued by virtue of provisions of the Health and Personal Social Services Act (Northern Ireland) 2001.

6045. Trespass to the person – contributory negligence – reduction in measure of damages

[Law Reform (Miscellaneous Provisions) Act (Northern Ireland) 1948.]

W claimed damages for assault, battery and trespass to the person, alleging that a police officer had pushed her over a low wall when she remonstrated with him during the arrest of her son. W suffered significant pain and bruising. The police officer denied pushing W over the wall, but admitted using reasonable force to push her away when she struck him. W's claim failed in the county court and she appealed, where the issue arose as to whether the Chief Constable could rely on

W's conduct under the Law Reform (Miscellaneous Provisions) Act (Northern Ireland) 1948 to establish the partial defence of contributory negligence.

Held, allowing the appeal, that an award of damages could be reduced where the damage had occurred partly due to the claimant's fault. In the instant case, a distinction had to be drawn between provocative but non tortious behaviour, and physical contact with the officer, which amounted to a tort. On the balance of probabilities, W had been pushed over the wall, having probably made some minor contact with the officer. Therefore, although excessive force had been used against W, she bore partial responsibility for the damage she had suffered, *Lane v. Holloway* [1968] 1 Q.B. 379, [1967] C.L.Y. 1047 and *Barnes v. Nayer* Times, December 19, 1986, [1987] C.L.Y. 3795 considered. As W would have been entitled to damages of £1,500 this would be reduced by a third to £1,000 to reflect her contributory negligence.

WARD v. CHIEF CONSTABLE OF THE ROYAL ULSTER CONSTABULARY [2000] N.I. 543, Girvan, J., QBD (NI).

TRANSPORT

6046. Carriage by rail – explosives – prohibitions

CARRIAGE OF EXPLOSIVES BY RAIL REGULATIONS (NORTHERN IRELAND) 2001, SR 2001 387; made under the Health and Safety at Work (Northern Ireland) Order 1978 (SI 1978 1039 (NI.9)) Art.17, Art.54, Art.55, Sch.3 para.1, Sch.3 para.2, Sch.3 para.6, Sch.3 para.11, Sch.3 para.13, Sch.3 para.14, Sch.3 para.15, Sch.3 para.19. In force: November 22, 2001; £6.00.

These Regulations, which amend the Explosives Act 1875, implement Commission Directive 96/87 ([1996] OJ L335/45) adapting to technical progress Council Directive 96/49 ([1996] OJ L235/25) on the approximation of the laws of the Member States with regard to the transport of explosives by rail and Commission Directive 99/48 ([1999] OJ L169/58) adapting to technical progress Council Directive 96/49 and Commission Directive 96/87 on the approximation of the laws of the Member States with regard to the transport of explosives by rail. The Regulations impose requirements and prohibitions in relation to the carriage of explosives by rail in a container, package or wagon. They prohibit the carriage of explosives in bulk, prohibit the carriage of explosives in small containers unless in each case certain requirements are complied with, require containers, packages and wagons used for the carriage of explosives to be suitable for such carriage and adequately maintained, prohibit the carriage of explosives in any container or wagon unless the operator has taken all reasonable steps to ensure that those explosives have been classified, packaged and labelled and require Carriage Information to be provided to operators of containers and wagons, train operators and infrastructure controllers prior to carriage and for that information to be kept. In addition, the Regulations prohibit the carriage of specified mixed or inadequately segregated loads, impose requirements in relation to the loading, stowage, unloading and cleaning of containers and wagons used for the carriage of explosives and permit the granting of exemptions by the Secretary of State or the Secretary of State for Defence in given circumstances.

6047. Carriage by road – explosives

CARRIAGE OF EXPLOSIVES (AMENDMENT) REGULATIONS (NORTHERN IRELAND) 2001, SR 2001 390; made under the Health and Safety at Work (Northern Ireland) Order 1978 (SI 1978 1039 (NI.9)) Art.17, Art.40, Art.43, Art.54, Art.55, Sch.3 para.1, Sch.3 para.2, Sch.3 para.3, Sch.3 para.5, Sch.3 para.6, Sch.3 para.11, Sch.3 para.13, Sch.3 para.14, Sch.3 para.15, Sch.3 para.19. In force: November 22, 2001; £3.50.

These Regulations amend the Classification and Labelling of Explosives Regulations (Northern Ireland) 1991 (SR 1991 516), the Packaging of Explosives for Carriage Regulations (Northern Ireland) 1993 (SR 1993 268), the Carriage of Explosives by Road Regulations (Northern Ireland) 1997 (SR 1997 474), the Carriage of Explosives by Road (Driver Training) Regulations (Northern Ireland) 1997 (SR 1997 475) and the Transport of Explosives (Safety Advisers) Regulations (Northern Ireland) 2000 (SR 2000 171). They implement Commission Directive 96/86 ([1996] OJ L335/43) adapting to technical progress Council Directive 94/55 ([1994] OJ L319/7) on the approximation of the laws of the Member States with regard to the transport of dangerous goods by road and Commission Directive 99/47 ([1999] OJ L169/1) adapting to technical progress Council Directive 94/55 and Commission Directive 96/86 on the approximation of the laws of the Member States with regard to the transport of dangerous goods by road. The amendments align the Regulations with the latest versions of the ADR agreement.

6048. Disability Discrimination Act 1995 (c.50) – Commencement No.7 Order

DISABILITY DISCRIMINATION ACT 1995 (COMMENCEMENT NO.7) ORDER (NORTHERN IRELAND) 2001, SR 2001 163 (C.10); made under the Disability Discrimination Act 1995 s.70. Commencement details: bringing into force various provisions of the 1995 Act on June 1, 2001 and August 1, 2001; £2.00.

This Order brings into operation the Disability Discrimination Act 1995 s.37, which imposes a duty on taxi drivers to carry in their taxis a guide dog, hearing dog or other prescribed category of dog when it accompanies the hirer, on June 1, 2001, for the purpose of enabling the Department to deal with applications for exemptions and the prescription by the Department of the notice of exemption and on August 1, 2001, for all other purposes. It also provides for a taxi driver to be exempted from that duty on medical grounds if a certificate of exemption has been issued to him by the Department of the Environment. It also brings s.38 of the Act, which provides for a right of appeal against the refusal of the Department to issue a certificate of exemption, into force on June 1, 2001.

6049. Disabled persons – taxis – carriage of guide dogs

DISABILITY DISCRIMINATION (TAXIS) (CARRYING OF GUIDE DOGS ETC.) REGULATIONS (NORTHERN IRELAND) 2001, SR 2001 169; made under the Disability Discrimination Act 1995 s.37. In force: Reg.2(1): June 1, 2001; remainder: August 1, 2001; £1.75.

The Disability Discrimination Act 1995 s.37 imposes a duty on taxi drivers to carry, without additional charge, a guide dog, hearing dog and other prescribed category of dog when it accompanies the hirer. It also provides that a taxi driver may be exempted from this obligation on medical grounds. These Regulations, which apply to taxis licensed for public hire, prescribe the form of the exemption notice which must be displayed by an exempted driver and the manner of its display in the taxi and also prescribe as an additional category of dog to which s.37 applies certain dogs helping people with epilepsy or certain general physical disabilities.

6050. Driving licences – diseases and disorders – diabetes

MOTOR VEHICLES (DRIVING LICENCES) (AMENDMENT) REGULATIONS (NORTHERN IRELAND) 2001, SR 2001 267; made under the Road Traffic (Northern Ireland) Order 1981 (SI 1981 154 (NI.1)) Art.9, Art.218. In force: August 20, 2001; £1.75.

These Regulations amend the Motor Vehicles (Driving Licences) Regulations (Northern Ireland) 1996 (SR 1996 542) in respect of the circumstances in which a person suffering from diabetes requiring insulin may hold certain Group 2 licences. They remove the limitation of the present provisions to persons who suffered from diabetes before 1998 and held a relevant licence at the end of 1996, and they extend the provisions to the C1 and E subcategory. The conditions for the granting of licences are amended with a view to ensuring that the applicant obtains proper treatment for his condition, abides by the treatment plan drawn up by his doctor and monitors his condition appropriately. In addition, these Regulations revoke the Motor Vehicles (Driving Licences) (Amendment) Regulations (Northern Ireland) 2000 (SR 2000 115).

6051. Driving licences – disqualification – fees

MOTOR VEHICLES (DRIVING LICENCES) (FEES) (AMENDMENT) REGULATIONS (NORTHERN IRELAND) 2001, SR 2001 240; made under the Road Traffic (Northern Ireland) Order 1981 (SI 1981 154 (NI. 1)) Art.13, Art.19C, Art.218. In force: July 23, 2001; £1.75.

The Child Support, Pensions and Social Security Act (Northern Ireland) 2000 inserted a new Art.37A into the Child Support (Northern Ireland) Order 1991 (SI 1991 2628 (NI. 23)) whereby a court may order a person to be disqualified from driving on the grounds of non-payment of child support maintenance. These Regulations amend the Motor Vehicles (Driving Licences) Regulations (Northern Ireland) 1996 (SR 1996 542) Sch.2 to extend the provision enabling the Department to charge a fee for a licence granted upon the expiry of a period of disqualification ordered by a court to include such a disqualification.

6052. Driving licences – refusal of renewal – medical grounds

MOTOR VEHICLES (DRIVING LICENCES) (AMENDMENT NO.2) REGULATIONS (NORTHERN IRELAND) 2001, SR 2001 402; made under the Road Traffic (Northern Ireland) Order 1981 (SI 1981/154 (NI.1)) Art.5, Art.13, Art.218. In force: January 14, 2002; £1.75.

These Regulations amend the Motor Vehicles (Driving Licences) Regulations (Northern Ireland) 1996 (SR 1996 542). Where an application has been made for a full driving licence following the revocation of such a licence, or the refusal of its renewal, on medical grounds, the Department may serve a notice requiring the applicant to take a driving test to assist in determining whether he is fit to regain his licence. The Regulations provide that a provisional licence granted for this purpose may be used only during such period up to and including the taking of a test as is specified by the Department when serving the notice. In addition, they also specify by whom the tests may be conducted.

6053. Heavy goods vehicles – drivers hours – exemptions – foot and mouth disease

COMMUNITY DRIVERS' HOURS (FOOT-AND-MOUTH DISEASE) (TEMPORARY EXCEPTION) REGULATIONS (NORTHERN IRELAND) 2001, SR 2001 103; made under the European Communities Act 1972 s.2. In force: March 10, 2001; £1.75.

Council Regulation 3820/85 ([1985] OJ L370/1) relating to road transport provides that Member States may in urgent cases grant a temporary exception for a period not exceeding 30 days to transport operations carried out in exceptional circumstances. These Regulations provide that until April 8, 2001, any time spent driving vehicles for a specified purpose shall not be taken into account for the purposes of the application of Art.6 of the Council Regulation. In addition, the Regulations provide that in relation to the driving of such vehicles Art.6 and Art.8 of the Council Regulation shall have effect subject to certain modifications.

6054. Heavy goods vehicles – drivers hours – exemptions – foot and mouth disease

COMMUNITY DRIVERS' HOURS (FOOT-AND-MOUTH DISEASE) (TEMPORARY EXCEPTION) (NO.2) REGULATIONS (NORTHERN IRELAND) 2001, SR 2001 154; made under the European Communities Act 1972 s.2. In force: April 9, 2001; £1.75.

Council Regulation 3820/85 ([1985] OJ L370/1) relating to road transport provides that Member States may, after authorisation by the Commission, grant exceptions from the application of the provisions of that Regulation to transport operations carried out in exceptional circumstances. The Community Drivers' Hours (Foot-and-Mouth Disease) (Temporary Exception) Regulations

(Northern Ireland) 2001 (SR 2001103) applied a temporary exception for 30 days from March 10, 2001 to April 8, 2001. These Regulations provide that until June 7, 2001 any time spent driving vehicles to meet the exceptional circumstances occasioned by the outbreak of foot-and-mouth disease in Northern Ireland, or the effects or consequences of such exceptional circumstances, shall not be taken into account for the purposes of the application of the Council Regulation.

6055. **Heavy goods vehicles – drivers hours – exemptions – foot and mouth disease**
COMMUNITY DRIVERS' HOURS (FOOT-AND-MOUTH DISEASE) (TEMPORARY EXCEPTION) (NO.2) (AMENDMENT) REGULATIONS (NORTHERN IRELAND) 2001, SR 2001 223; made under the European Communities Act 1972 s.2. In force: June 8, 2001; £1.50.
These Regulations amend the Community Drivers' Hours (Foot-and-Mouth Disease) (Temporary Exception) (No.2) Regulations (Northern Ireland) 2001 (SR 2001 154) to extend the expiry date of the exceptions provided for in those Regulations for a further period of 30 days until July 7, 2001.

6056. **Heavy goods vehicles – drivers hours – exemptions – foot and mouth disease**
COMMUNITY DRIVERS' HOURS (FOOT-AND-MOUTH DISEASE) (TEMPORARY EXCEPTION) (NO.2) (AMENDMENT NO.2) REGULATIONS (NORTHERN IRELAND) 2001, SR 2001 268; made under the European Communities Act 1972 s.2. In force: July 7, 2001; £1.75.
These Regulations, which amend the Community Drivers' Hours (Foot-and-Mouth Disease) (Temporary Exception) (No.2) Regulations (Northern Ireland) 2001 (SR 2001 154), extend the expiry date of the exceptions for a further period of 30 days from July 7, 2001 to August 5, 2001.

6057. **Heavy goods vehicles – drivers hours – exemptions – foot and mouth disease**
COMMUNITY DRIVERS' HOURS (FOOT-AND-MOUTH DISEASE) (TEMPORARY EXCEPTION) (NO.2) (AMENDMENT NO.3) REGULATIONS (NORTHERN IRELAND) 2001, SR 2001 294; made under the European Communities Act 1972 s.2. In force: August 6, 2001; £1.50.
These Regulations amend the Community Drivers' Hours (Foot-and-Mouth Disease) (Temporary Exception) (No.2) Regulations (Northern Ireland) 2001 (SR 2001 154) so as to extend the expiry date of the exception for a further period of 30 days from August 6, 2001 to September 4, 2001.

6058. **Heavy goods vehicles – drivers hours – exemptions – foot and mouth disease**
COMMUNITY DRIVERS' HOURS (FOOT-AND-MOUTH DISEASE) (TEMPORARY EXCEPTION) (NO.2) (AMENDMENT NO.4) REGULATIONS (NORTHERN IRELAND) 2001, SR 2001 311; made under the European Communities Act 1972 s.2. In force: September 5, 2001; £1.50.
These Regulations, which amend the Community Drivers' Hours (Foot-and-Mouth Disease) (Temporary Exception) (No.2) Regulations (Northern Ireland) 2001 (SR 2001 154), extend the expiry date of the exceptions for a further period of 30 days from September 5, 2001 to October 4, 2001.

6059. **Heavy goods vehicles – drivers hours – exemptions – foot and mouth disease**
COMMUNITY DRIVERS' HOURS (FOOT-AND-MOUTH DISEASE) (TEMPORARY EXCEPTION) (NO.2) (AMENDMENT NO.5) REGULATIONS (NORTHERN IRELAND) 2001, SR 2001 340; made under the European Communities Act 1972 s.2. In force: October 5, 2001; £1.75.
These Regulations, which amend the Community Drivers' Hours (Foot-and-Mouth Disease) (Temporary Exception) (No.2) Regulations (Northern Ireland) 2001 (SR 2001 154), extend the expiry date of the exceptions for a further period of 30 days from October 5, 2001 to November 3, 2001.

6060. Heavy goods vehicles – drivers hours – exemptions – foot and mouth disease

COMMUNITY DRIVERS' HOURS (FOOT-AND-MOUTH DISEASE) (TEMPORARY EXCEPTION) (NO.2) (AMENDMENT NO.6) REGULATIONS (NORTHERN IRELAND) 2001, SR 2001 398; made under the European Communities Act 1972 s.2. In force: November 4, 2001; £1.75.

These Regulations, which amend the Community Drivers' Hours (Foot and Mouth Disease) (Temporary Exception) (No.2) Regulations (Northern Ireland) 2001 (SR 2001 154), extend the expiry date of the exceptions for a further period of 56 days from November 4, 2001 to December 29, 2001. They provide for the removal of the temporary exception to the weekly rest requirement, except for vehicles driven for the purpose of the movement of livestock.

6061. Heavy goods vehicles – testing – fees

GOODS VEHICLES (TESTING) (FEES) (AMENDMENT) REGULATIONS (NORTHERN IRELAND) 2001, SR 2001 247; made under the Road Traffic (Northern Ireland) Order 1995 (SI 1995 2994 (NI.18)) Art.65, Art.67, Art.110. In force: August 1, 2001; £1.75.

These Regulations amend the Goods Vehicles (Testing) Regulations (Northern Ireland) 1995 (SR 1995 450) by increasing specified fees relating to the testing of goods vehicles.

6062. Heavy goods vehicles – testing – notice of refusal

GOODS VEHICLES (TESTING) (AMENDMENT) REGULATIONS (NORTHERN IRELAND) 2001, SR 2001 365; made under the Road Traffic (Northern Ireland) Order 1995 (SI 1995 2994 (NI.18)) Art.65, Art.66, Art.67, Art.110. In force: December 1, 2001; £2.00.

These Regulations amend the Goods Vehicles (Testing) Regulations (Northern Ireland) 1995 (SR 1995 450) by removing the requirement for a notice of refusal to be signed by a vehicle examiner and by reducing the notice required to one clear day for the repayment of goods vehicle test fees where notice of cancellation of a test appointment is given.

6063. Motor vehicles – construction and use – agricultural vehicles

MOTOR VEHICLES (CONSTRUCTION AND USE) (AMENDMENT) REGULATIONS (NORTHERN IRELAND) 2001, SR 2001 28; made under the Road Traffic (Northern Ireland) Order 1995 (SI 1995 2994 (NI.18)) Art.55, Art.110. In force: April 2, 2001; £1.75.

These Regulations amend the the Motor Vehicles (Construction and Use) Regulations (Northern Ireland) 1999 (SR 1999 454) to enable agricultural motor vehicles to comply with various Council Directives.

6064. Motor vehicles – construction and use – exemptions

MOTOR VEHICLES (CONSTRUCTION AND USE) (AMENDMENT NO.2) REGULATIONS (NORTHERN IRELAND) 2001, SR 2001 173; made under the Road Traffic (Northern Ireland) Order 1995 (SI 1995 2994 (NI.18)) Art.55, Art.110. In force: June 1, 2001; £2.00.

These Regulations amend the Motor Vehicles (Construction and Use) Regulations (Northern Ireland) 1999 (SR 1999 454) in relation to vehicles which are the subject of a Department's approval certificate issued under the Motor Vehicles (Approval) Regulations (Northern Ireland) 2001 (SR 2001 172). If they comply with the relevant requirements of the Approval Regulations, such vehicles are exempt from the requirements of specified sections of the 1999 Regulations with regard to glazing, mirrors, speedometers, fuel tanks, emissions and seat belts.

6065. Motor vehicles – construction and use – exhaust emissions

MOTOR VEHICLES (CONSTRUCTION AND USE) (AMENDMENT NO.3) REGULATIONS (NORTHERN IRELAND) 2001, SR 2001 241; made under the Road Traffic (Northern Ireland) Order 1995 (SI 1995 2994 (NI. 18)) Art.55, Art.110. In force: October 1, 2001; £1.75.

These Regulations amend the definition of "the emissions publication" in the Motor Vehicles (Construction and Use) Regulations (Northern Ireland) 1999 (SR 1999 454) Sch.10 so as to refer to the most recent edition of the publication entitled "In-Service Exhaust Emission Standards for Road Vehicles". The publication specifies, with respect to vehicles with spark ignition engines, the maximum permitted carbon monoxide content of exhaust emissions at idling speed and the limits for the ratio of air to petrol vapour entering the combustion chamber, in relation to each of the vehicle models named in the publication.

6066. Motor vehicles – driving tests – fees

MOTOR VEHICLES (DRIVING LICENCES) (AMENDMENT) (TEST FEES) REGULATIONS (NORTHERN IRELAND) 2001, SR 2001 245; made under the Road Traffic (Northern Ireland) Order 1981 (SI 1981 154 (NI.1)) Art.5, Art.218. In force: August 1, 2001; £1.75.

These Regulations, which revoke the Motor Vehicles (Driving Licences) (Amendment) (Test Fees) Regulations (Northern Ireland) 2000 (SR 2000 150), amend the Motor Vehicles (Driving Licences) Regulations (Northern Ireland) 1996 (SR 1996 542) by increasing the fees for specified types of driving tests.

6067. Motor vehicles – driving tests – fees

MOTOR VEHICLES (DRIVING LICENCES) (AMENDMENT NO.2) (TEST FEES) REGULATIONS (NORTHERN IRELAND) 2001, SR 2001 310; made under the Road Traffic (Northern Ireland) Order 1981 (SI 1981 154 (NI.1)) Art.5, Art.218. In force: October 8, 2001; £1.50.

These Regulations amend the Motor Vehicles (Driving Licences) Regulations (Northern Ireland) 1996 (SR 1996 542) by increasing the fee for a theory test from £16.50 to £17.00.

6068. Motor vehicles – road safety – lighting

ROAD VEHICLES LIGHTING (AMENDMENT) REGULATIONS (NORTHERN IRELAND) 2001, SR 2001 171; made under the Road Traffic (Northern Ireland) Order 1995 (SI 1995 2994 (NI.18)) Art.55, Art.110. In force: June 1, 2001; £1.75.

These Regulations amend the Road Vehicles Lighting Regulations (Northern Ireland) 2000 (SR 2000 169) in relation to certain passenger vehicles which are the subject of a Department's approval certificate given pursuant to the Motor Vehicles (Approval) Regulations (Northern Ireland) 2001 (SR 2001 172).

6069. Motor vehicles – road safety – lighting

ROAD VEHICLES LIGHTING (AMENDMENT NO.2) REGULATIONS (NORTHERN IRELAND) 2001, SR 2001 372; made under the Road Traffic (Northern Ireland) Order 1995 (SI 1995 2994 (NI.18)) Art.55, Art.110. In force: December 1, 2001; £1.50.

These Regulations amend the Road Vehicles Lighting Regulations (Northern Ireland) 2000 (SR 2000 169) by permitting, on the rear of the vehicle, a plate displaying the international distinguishing sign of the UK in accordance with Council Regulation 2411/98 ([1998] OJ L299/1) on the recognition in intra-Community traffic of the distinguishing sign of the Member State in which motor vehicles and their trailers are registered.

6070. Motor vehicles – testing – fees

MOTOR VEHICLES TESTING (AMENDMENT) (FEES) REGULATIONS (NORTHERN IRELAND) 2001, SR 2001 246; made under the Road Traffic (Northern Ireland) Order 1995 (SI 1995 2994 NI.18) Art.61; the Road Traffic (Northern Ireland) Order 1995 (SI 1995 2994 (NI.18)) Art.62; and the Road Traffic (Northern Ireland) Order 1995 (SI 1995 2994 NI.18) Art.75, Art.81, Art.110. In force: August 1, 2001; £1.75.

These Regulations amend the Motor Vehicle Testing Regulations (Northern Ireland) 1995 (SR 1995 448) by increasing the fees payable for most examinations, tests and inspections.

6071. Motor vehicles – testing – test certificate – notice of refusal

MOTOR VEHICLE TESTING (AMENDMENT) REGULATIONS (NORTHERN IRELAND) 2001, SR 2001 364; made under the Road Traffic (Northern Ireland) Order 1995 (SI 1995 2994 (NI.18)) Art.61, Art.62, Art.110. In force: December 1, 2001; £1.75.

These Regulations amend the Motor Vehicle Testing Regulations (Northern Ireland) 1995 (SR 1995 448) to remove the requirement for notices of refusal of a test certificate to be signed by a vehicle examiner. They also make amendments to the 1995 Regulations which provide for the repayment of test fees where notice of cancellation of a test appointment is given by reducing notice required to one clear day before the date of appointment.

6072. Motor vehicles – type approval – construction – single passenger vehicles

MOTOR VEHICLES (TYPE APPROVAL) (AMENDMENT) REGULATIONS (NORTHERN IRELAND) 2001, SR 2001 174; made under the Road Traffic (Northern Ireland) Order 1981 (SI 1981 154 (NI.1)) Art.31A, Art.31D, Art.31E, Art.218. In force: June 1, 2001; £1.75.

These Regulations amend the Motor Vehicles (Type Approval) Regulations (Northern Ireland) 1985 (SR 1985 294) and establish a statutory scheme for approving the construction of single passenger vehicles before such vehicles are brought into service together with the Motor Vehicles (Approval) Regulations (Northern Ireland) 2001 (SR 2001 172).

6073. Motor vehicles – type approval – standards – construction

MOTOR VEHICLES (APPROVAL) REGULATIONS (NORTHERN IRELAND) 2001, SR 2001 172; made under the Road Traffic (Northern Ireland) Order 1981 (SI 1981 154 (NI.1)) Art.31A, Art.31C, Art.31D, Art.31E, Art.218. In force: June 1, 2001; £7.00.

These Regulations, which establish a statutory system for approving the construction of single vehicles before they enter into service, apply to passenger vehicles and dual-purpose vehicles constructed to carry no more than eight passengers excluding the driver and certain three-wheeled vehicles having a maximum unladen weight of more than 410 kg.

6074. Motor vehicles – type approval – standards – fees

MOTOR VEHICLES (APPROVAL) (FEES) REGULATIONS (NORTHERN IRELAND) 2001, SR 2001 170; made under the Road Traffic (Northern Ireland) Order 1981 (SI 1981 154 (NI.1)) Art.31D, Art.218; and the Finance Act 1990 s.128. In force: June 1, 2001; £1.75.

The Motor Vehicles (Approval) Regulations (Northern Ireland) 2001 (SR 2001 172) establish a statutory system for approving the construction of single vehicles before they enter into service. These Regulations prescribe the fees payable in connection with applications made in accordance with the Approval Regulations, prescribe the fee payable for the replacement of a Department's approval certificate which has been lost or defaced and make provision for the repayment of fees in certain circumstances.

6075. Motorcycles – eye protectors

MOTOR CYCLES (EYE PROTECTORS) (AMENDMENT) REGULATIONS (NORTHERN IRELAND) 2001, SR 2001 146; made under the Road Traffic (Northern Ireland) Order 1995 (SI 1995 2994 (NI.18)) Art.29, Art.110. In force: May 14, 2001; £1.75.

These Regulations amend the Motor Cycles (Eye Protectors) Regulations (Northern Ireland) 2000 (SR 2000 161) by adding, as a new prescribed type of authorised eye protector, those protectors which conform with ECE Regulation 22.05 including the approval, marking and conformity of production requirements. Only these eye protectors and the other types of eye protector prescribed by the 2000 Regulations may be sold as being authorised for use by motorcyclists.

6076. Motorcycles – protective headgear

MOTOR CYCLES (PROTECTIVE HEADGEAR) (AMENDMENT) REGULATIONS (NORTHERN IRELAND) 2001, SR 2001 147; made under the Road Traffic (Northern Ireland) Order 1995 (SI 1995 2994 (NI.18)) Art.27, Art.28, Art.110. In force: May 14, 2001; £1.75.

These Regulations amend the Motor Cycles (Protective Headgear) Regulations (Northern Ireland) 1999 (SR 1999 170) by adding, as a new prescribed type of recommended helmet, those helmets which conform with ECE Regulation 22.05 including the approval, marking and conformity of production requirements. Only these helmets and the other types of helmet prescribed by the 1999 Regulations may be sold as affording protection from injury to motorcyclists.

6077. Passenger vehicles – buses and taxis – licensing – fees

PUBLIC SERVICE VEHICLES (LICENCE FEES) (AMENDMENT) REGULATIONS (NORTHERN IRELAND) 2001, SR 2001 244; made under the Road Traffic (Northern Ireland) Order 1981 (SI 1981 154 (NI.1)) Art.61, Art.66, Art.218. In force: August 1, 2001; £1.75.

These Regulations amend the Public Service Vehicles Regulations (Northern Ireland) 1985 (SR 1985 123) by increasing the fee payable for certain applications and re-applications for a licence for a taxi or a bus.

6078. Passenger vehicles – vehicle licences – discs – requirements

PUBLIC SERVICE VEHICLES (AMENDMENT) REGULATIONS (NORTHERN IRELAND) 2001, SR 2001 366; made under the Road Traffic (Northern Ireland) Order 1981 (SI 1981 154 (NI.1)) Art.61, Art.66, Art.80, Art.218. In force: December 1, 2001; £2.00.

These Regulations, which amend the Public Service Vehicles Regulations (Northern Ireland) 1985 (SI 1985 123), specify the details which are required to be contained in discs issued with a Public Service Vehicle Licence, remove the requirement for application for re-inspection to be on a form prescribed by the Department and specify unique identifying symbols which discs must contain for public hire taxis and buses. The provision for refund of fees is amended to reduce the notice required to one clear day before the date of appointment, enable an applicant to apply for a vehicle licence without completing a form issued by the Department, remove the requirement that the Department shall notify the applicant of the time and date of an inspection in writing and remove the requirement for the Department to notify an applicant about inspection of a vehicle in writing.

6079. Private Streets (Amendment) (Northern Ireland) Order 1992 (SI 1992 3203 (NI.18)) – Commencement Order

PRIVATE STREETS (AMENDMENT) (1992 ORDER) (COMMENCEMENT) ORDER (NORTHERN IRELAND) 2001, SR 2001 72 (C.3); made under the Northern Ireland Act 2000 Sch.para.4; and the Private Streets (Amendment)

(Northern Ireland) Order 1992 (SI 1992 3203 (NI.18)) Art.1. Commencement details: bringing into force various provisions of the Order on February 20, 2001; £1.50.

This Order, brings the Private Streets (Amendment) (Northern Ireland) Order 1992 (SI 1992 3203 (NI.18)) Art.3, which provides for the bringing of street lighting within the definition of "street works", the vesting and control of lighting equipment and makes a consequential amendment to the Private Streets (Northern Ireland) Order 1980 (SI 1980 1086 (NI.12)) on February 20, 2001.

6080. Railways – accessibility – disabled persons

RAIL VEHICLE ACCESSIBILITY REGULATIONS (NORTHERN IRELAND) 2001, SR 2001 264; made under the Disability Discrimination Act 1995 s.46. In force: October 19, 2001; £3.50.

These Regulations, which impose requirements for the benefit of disabled persons, apply to passenger carrying vehicles used on railways which were first brought into use after December 31, 1998.

6081. Railways – accessibility – disabled persons – exemption applications

RAIL VEHICLE (EXEMPTION APPLICATIONS) REGULATIONS (NORTHERN IRELAND) 2001, SR 2001 265; made under the Disability Discrimination Act 1995 s.47. In force: October 19, 2001; £1.75.

These Regulations specify the manner in which applications to the Department for exemption from the requirement of the Rail Vehicle Accessibility Regulations (Northern Ireland) 2001 (SR 2001 264) are to be made, and for the information which must be supplied with any such application. The Regulations also make provision for the period and revocation of exemptions.

6082. Taxis – motor Hackney Carriages – Belfast

MOTOR HACKNEY CARRIAGES (BELFAST) (AMENDMENT) BY-LAWS (NORTHERN IRELAND) 2001, SR 2001 198; made under the Road Traffic (Northern Ireland) Order 1981 (SI 1981 154 (NI.1)) Art.65. In force: June 18, 2001; £1.75.

These By Laws, which revoke the Motor Hackney Carriages (Belfast) (Amendment No.2) By-Laws (Northern Ireland) 1996 (SR 1996 523), amend the Motor Hackney Carriages (Belfast) By-Laws made by the Council of the County Borough of Belfast on June 4, 1951 by fixing the minimum and maximum fares payable.

WATER INDUSTRY

6083. Water (Northern Ireland) Order 1999 (1999 662 (NI.6)) – Commencement Order

WATER (1999 ORDER) (COMMENCEMENT AND TRANSITIONAL PROVISIONS) ORDER (NORTHERN IRELAND) 2001, SR 2001 283 (C.14); made under the Water (Northern Ireland) Order 1999 (SI 1999 662 (NI.6)) Art.1. Commencement details: bringing into force various provisions of the 1999 Order on August 24, 2001; £1.75.

This Order brings into operation the remaining provisions of the Water (Northern Ireland) Order 1999 (SI 1999 662 (NI.6)) which relate to functions of the Department of the Environment affecting water and certain other miscellaneous and general matters.

SCOTLAND

ADMINISTRATION OF JUSTICE

6084. Court of Session – district courts – tribunals

JUSTICES OF THE PEACE (TRIBUNAL) (SCOTLAND) REGULATIONS 2001, SSI 2001 217; made under the District Courts (Scotland) Act 1975 s.9A. In force: May 24, 2001; £1.75.

These Regulations make provision for the procedure to be followed by and before a tribunal constituted under the District Courts (Scotland) Act 1975 s.9A(3). Such a tribunal is constituted to carry out an investigation at the request of the Scottish Ministers in order to ascertain whether a justice is, by reason of inability, neglect of duty or misbehaviour unfit for office or unfit for performing functions of a judicial nature.

6085. Court of Session – judges – increase in numbers

NUMBER OF INNER HOUSE JUDGES (VARIATION) ORDER 2001, SSI 2001 41; made under the Court of Session Act 1988 s.2. In force: February 26, 2001; £1.50.

This Order amends the Court of Session Act 1988 s.2 so as to increase the number of senior judges in each of the two Divisions of the Inner House of the Court of Session from three to four. The total number of judges in the Inner House, including the Lord President and the Lord Justice Clerk, will therefore be increased from eight to 10.

6086. Judicial factors – title to sue

T's judicial factor raised an action against R in respect of alleged professional negligence. R was the remaining sole practitioner in a firm of solicitors, which had acted for T since its inception in 1878. T was an unregistered building society established as a joint venture by five individuals, the last of whom had died in 1936. Following R's retirement, his business was taken over by another firm of solicitors who decided to distribute the funds in T's client account. On examination of R's intromissions in the client account, allegations of professional negligence arose. An application was made to the court and a judicial factor was permanently appointed in 1994. R claimed that T's judicial factor had no title to sue as the joint venture had come to an end, at the latest, in 1936. R further claimed that a joint venture, when concluded, did not retain a legal persona and the only people with a title and interest to sue in respect of R's alleged actings in the 1980's were the descendants of the original joint venturers. T's judicial factor argued that, although the joint venture had come to an end in 1936, there remained a set of rights and obligations, which had arisen out of the joint venture which required management and administration. The losses incurred by R's actions had been losses to that estate and the judicial factor, in his appointment as manager and administrator of that estate, had title to sue in respect of those losses.

Held, allowing a proof, that (1) the court might appoint a judicial factor whenever a collection of property, rights and obligations required management or distribution by an independent factor supervised by the court, (2) a court could appoint a judicial factor on the estate of a partnership or joint venture where all the partners or joint venturers were dead, and (3) in appointing a judicial factor a court was granting that judicial factor title to sue in relational to all matters relevant to the management and administration of the estate to which he was appointed including the realisation of claims and collection of debts.

THURSO BUILDING SOCIETY'S JUDICIAL FACTOR v. ROBERTSON; *sub nom.* ROBERTSON v. ROBERTSON 2001 S.L.T. 797, Lady Paton, OH.

6087. Judiciary – sheriffs – request by accused that sheriff declare whether a freemason

See HUMAN RIGHTS: Stott v. Minogue. §6705

6088. Messengers at arms – fees

ACT OF SEDERUNT (FEES OF MESSENGERS-AT-ARMS) 2001, SSI 2001 440; made under the Execution of Diligence (Scotland) Act 1926 s.6; and the Court of Session Act 1988 s.5. In force: January 1, 2002; £2.00.

This Act of Sederunt amends the Act of Sederunt (Fees of Messengers-at-Arms) 1994 (SI 1994 391) by increasing the fees payable to Messengers-at-Arms by approximately 3.25 per cent.

6089. Sheriff courts – fees

ACT OF SEDERUNT (FEES OF SOLICITORS IN THE SHERIFF COURT) (AMENDMENT) 2001, SSI 2001 438; made under the Sheriff Courts (Scotland) Act 1907 s.40. In force: January 1, 2002; £2.00.

This Act of Sederunt amends the Table of Fees in the Act of Sederunt (Fees of Solicitors in the Sheriff Court) (Amendment and Further Provisions) 1993 (SI 1993 3080) in Sch.1 by increasing the fees payable to solicitors by approximately 3 per cent. The fee for work done before action commences is increased by approximately 6 per cent. It also introduces a block fee in defended actions for attending consultation with counsel to consider tender, extrajudicial settlement or with a view to settlement, whether or not settlement is agreed.

6090. Sheriff courts – rules – commercial actions

ACT OF SEDERUNT (ORDINARY CAUSE RULES) AMENDMENT (COMMERCIAL ACTIONS) 2001, SSI 2001 8; made under the Sheriff Courts (Scotland) Act 1971 s.32. In force: March 1, 2001; £2.00.

This Act of Sederunt inserts a new Chapter into the Ordinary Cause Rules 1993 (SI 1993 1956) to make provision for a new category of commercial actions and provides for various matters of procedure in commercial actions.

6091. Sheriff courts – rules – European Matrimonial and Parental Responsibility Jurisdiction and Judgments

ACT OF SEDERUNT (ORDINARY CAUSE RULES) AMENDMENT (EUROPEAN MATRIMONIAL AND PARENTAL RESPONSIBILITY JURISDICTION AND JUDGMENTS) 2001, SSI 2001 144; made under the Sheriff Courts (Scotland) Act 1971 s.32. In force: April 2, 2001; £2.00.

This Act of Sederunt amends the Act of Sederunt (Ordinary Cause Rules) 1993 (SI 1993 1956) by amending rules in connection with the provisions of Council Regulation 1347/2000 ([2000] OJ L160/19) on jurisdiction and the recognition and enforcement of judgments in matrimonial matters and in matters of parental responsibility for children of both spouses by providing a requirement that averments relevant to the issue of a list of proceedings under the Council Regulation be made. It also inserts a new rule in connection with the Council Regulation by providing for the issue of a certificate to an interested party by the sheriff in relation to an action of divorce or separation following on either the grant of decree of divorce or separation or the grant of an order in such proceedings relating to a child of both spouses.

6092. Sheriff courts – sheriff officers – fees

ACT OF SEDERUNT (FEES OF SHERIFF OFFICERS) 2001, SSI 2001 439; made under the Sheriff Courts (Scotland) Act 1907 s.40; and the Execution of Diligence (Scotland) Act 1926 s.6. In force: January 1, 2002; £2.00.

This Act of Sederunt amends the Act of Sederunt (Fees of Sheriff Officers) 1994 (SI 1994 392) by increasing the fees payable to Sheriff Officers by approximately 3.25 per cent.

6093. Sheriff courts – shorthand writers – fees

ACT OF SEDERUNT (FEES OF SHORTHAND WRITERS IN THE SHERIFF COURT) (AMENDMENT) 2001, SSI 2001 136; made under the Sheriff Courts (Scotland) Act 1907 s.40. In force: May 1, 2001; £1.75.

This Act of Sederunt, which amends the Act of Sederunt (Fees of Witnesses and Shorthand Writers in the Sheriff Court) 1992 (SI 1992 1878), increases the fees payable to shorthand writers in the Sheriff Court by 3.55 per cent.

6094. Sheriff officers – appointment in a number of sheriffdoms

M, a sheriff officer in North and South Strathclyde, Dumfries and Galloway, petitioned for a commission as a sheriff officer in all the districts of the sheriffdom of Grampian, Highlands and Islands. M's employers had successfully tendered for and won a contract with Highland Regional Council to execute around 9,000 warrants each year in connection with council tax collection. They had attempted to employ someone locally who already held an appropriate commission and failed. They had established an office in the area and begun employing other staff. M although resident in the Borders, if successful in his application, would relocate to Inverness. Existing sheriff officers within the sheriffdom objected on six grounds, that (1) M could not conduct his business effectively within the sheriffdom when he was still accepting and executing instructions in the other sheriffdoms in which he held commissions; (2) there would be no improvement in the current sheriff officer services by granting the application; (3) work available in the sheriffdom had decreased and was likely to decrease further when changes to poinding and warrant sales were implemented; (4) M's employers carried on business in Glasgow and the surrounding area and had no connection with Inverness; (5) there were enough sheriff officers operating in the Inverness area to provide a good level of service, and (6) a surplus of sheriff officers would affect the career prospects of trainee sheriff officers in the area. Additionally, the objectors argued that M's employers could fulfil their obligations under the contract with Highland Regional Council by using existing sheriff officers as agents and that their success in tendering for the contract had resulted in a local firm suffering financial difficulties.

Held, granting the petition, that (1) M had demonstrated a need for the commission as the use of agents would be unlikely to provide the quality of service that the council had anticipated in awarding the contract to M's employers, and (2) although it was acknowledged by the court that the level of work available was decreasing, the existence of only two firms with Inverness bases which were likely to merge had effectively created a monopoly which was contrary to public interest.

MOORE, PETITIONER 2001 S.L.T. (Sh Ct) 111, JC McInnes, Sheriff Principal, Sh Ct.

6095. Tribunals – part time sheriffs – removal from office

PART-TIME SHERIFFS (REMOVAL TRIBUNAL) REGULATIONS 2001, SSI 2001 205; made under the Sheriff Courts (Scotland) Act 1971 s.11C. In force: May 24, 2001; £1.75.

These Regulations make provision for the procedure to be followed by and before a tribunal constituted under the Sheriff Courts (Scotland) Act 1971 s.11C to carry out an investigation at the request of the Scottish Ministers in order to ascertain whether a part-time sheriff is unfit for office by reason of inability, neglect of duty or misbehaviour. Before any investigation by a tribunal commences, the Scottish Ministers must give the sheriff written notice of the investigation and of the reasons why the investigation has been requested. The Scottish Ministers are given the power to pay the members of the tribunal for carrying out their duties. Subject to the specific provisions made by the Regulations, the tribunal is free to regulate its own procedure. The Regulations make provision for the tribunal to receive oral or written evidence; for the sheriff to make written or oral representations; for such representations to be made personally by the sheriff or anyone acting on behalf of the sheriff, and for the confidentiality of proceedings before the tribunal. The Regulations also make provision for the procedure to be followed where there is a change in the membership of the tribunal after an investigation has commenced. They make provision allowing the tribunal to suspend the sheriff from office during the investigation. The tribunal may direct that a sheriff so suspended may remain in office for the limited purpose of continuing to deal with proceedings commenced before the suspension took effect. The tribunal must send a draft of its findings on the investigation to the sheriff and must give the sheriff the opportunity to make comments on the draft. On completion of the investigation, the tribunal must submit a written report to the Scottish Ministers and send a copy of it to the sheriff. The report must specify the tribunal's findings on the investigation and its decision on whether to order removal of the sheriff from office.

ADMINISTRATIVE LAW

6096. Judicial review – competency – adoption of way as public road – sufficiency of alternative available remedy

[Roads (Scotland) Act 1984 (c.54) s.16(1), s.16(3), s.151 (1), s.151 (3) (c); Local Government and Planning (Scotland) Act 1982 (c.43) s.14.]

M, owner of leisure facilities and a caravan park, sought judicial review of the decision of the local council (C) to add a way on the land to the list of public roads, and reduction of the entry of the way in the list. M owned part of the land, leased part from C and operated a part owned by C under a management contract. Following acts of vandalism, agreement was reached between M and C to erect a gate at the entrance to the area. There was local opposition and C decided to adopt the way as a public road and sent a letter to M intimating that and setting a time limit for objections. M objected and sent two letters to this effect, one by M's solicitor. C failed to respond and a third letter was written. C still did not reply and only after the road had been adopted did C deal with any of M's points, in a letter informing him of the adoption. M argued that (1) C's action was ultra vires: (a) the way was not a road under the Roads (Scotland) Act 1984 s.151 (1), and (b) s.151 (3) (c) excluded parts of land owned or managed by a local authority and used by them for leisure facilities in fulfilment of their duties under the Local Government and Planning (Scotland) Act 1982 s.14, and (2) the decision to adopt the road was (a) *Wednesbury* unreasonable; (b) for a purpose other than the legitimate purpose for which the power to adopt roads was conferred on C, and (c) a result of material procedural impropriety. C argued that (1) the petition was incompetent as s.16(3) of the 1984 Act provided for arbitration in disputes over road adoption, and (2) M had failed to make relevant averments of fact that the way was not a road under s.16(1).

Held, granting reduction, that (1) s.16(3) did not provide an adequate remedy in the context of the issues which had arisen as M was alleging an abuse of statutory power and material procedural impropriety which happened prior to the adoption; an arbiter appointed under s.16(3), though he could deal with disputes arising in relation to the requirements under s.16(1), could not declare an act of a roads authority invalid as was requested here and the petition was competent, *Tarmac Econowaste Ltd v. Assessor for Lothian Region* 1991 S.L.T. 77, [1991] C.L.Y. 5502 applied; (2) the word "right" in "public right of passage", used to define "road" in s.151 (1), did not connote a legal right in the ordinary sense, and a public right of passage was not the same as a public right of way and could not and need not be established by prescriptive possession; (3) M had sufficiently averred that there was no public right of passage over the way; (4) under s.16(1), C had a duty to add a private road to their list of public roads, if it achieved the specific standards and an application was made to them; in the absence of any discretion, *Wednesbury* could not apply; (5) the way fell within s.151 (3) (c) and the adoption of it under s.16(1) was ultra vires: the solum of the way ran between the two areas owned by C and C accepted that it was used for leisure facilities; the lease between M and C limited M to using that part of the land as a caravan site, and the management agreement made it clear that the area was to be used as a car park and amenity ground for the beach and slip road adjacent to it; (6) as there was no discretion under s.16(1) C's intention was simply irrelevant, and (7) M's objections were fundamental objections raising the issue of ultra vires and the shortcomings in C's response were such as to constitute a breach of natural justice, and on this ground also the decision should be quashed.

MacKINNON v. ARGYLL AND BUTE COUNCIL 2001 S.L.T. 1275, Lord Osborne, OH.

6097. **Judicial review – competency – damages claim**

See LICENSING: Stewart v. Perth and Kinross DC (No.2). §6781

6098. **Judicial review – competency – decision not yet taken**

See PLANNING: Bett Properties Ltd v. Scottish Ministers. §6855

6099. **Judicial review – competency – rent review before arbiter**

See LANDLORD AND TENANT: AGE Ltd v. Kwik Save Stores Ltd. §6751

6100. **Judicial review – natural justice – licensing – failure to give notice of factors affecting decision**

See LICENSING: Macdonald v. Western Isles Licensing Board. §6784

6101. **Judicial review – ultra vires – access over land compulsorily purchased for road building**

See HIGHWAY CONTROL: Elmford Ltd v. Glasgow City Council. §6681

6102. **Judicial review – ultra vires – reduction of compulsory purchase decision**

See PLANNING: Standard Commercial Property Securities Ltd v. Glasgow City Council. §6849

6103. **Local authorities – disposal of assets – duty to obtain best price – duty to consider late bid – meaning of "reasonably obtained"**

[Local Government (Scotland) Act 1973 (c.65) s.74.]

M (a development company) sought judicial review of E's (a local authority) refusal to consider M's late bid in a competitive tendering exercise for the sale of land. The final date for bids was specified as June 16, 2000. M, following an unsuccessful earlier bid, faxed a further offer on August 11, which was not considered by E. M averred that the offer E accepted was lower than M's August offer. M argued that "the best [consideration] that can reasonably be obtained" in terms of the Local Government (Scotland) Act 1973 s.74 was restricted to the amount of the consideration in an absolute sense, requiring E to evaluate all offers, including any made long after the closing date, in order to ascertain whether by accepting a late offer they might get a higher price, there being no technical legal obstruction in Scotland, notwithstanding the terms of the earlier particulars of sale.

Held, dismissing the petition, that while the setting of a closing date did not, as a matter of strict law, prevent a seller from accepting a higher offer from a potential purchaser made after the closing date, for understandable reasons the adoption of such a course was not well regarded, and in the present case would involve E departing from the clearly stated basis of the competitive tendering exercise which would rightly be seen by bidders before the closing date as an act of bad faith, putting in question the reliability of any future exercise by E. "Reasonably obtained" in the context of s.74 was not confined purely to the quantum of consideration and was directed in large measure to the method of obtaining best price.

MORSTON ASSETS LTD v. EDINBURGH CITY COUNCIL 2001 S.L.T. 613, Lord Eassie, OH.

AGENCY

6104. Estate agents – sole selling rights – missives concluded after agency terminated – purchaser not introduced by estate agents – entitlement to commission

[Estate Agents (Provision of Information) Regulations 1991 (SI 1991 859).]

G, an estate agent, raised an action against F, a former client for commission on the sale of F's house. F and G had entered into a "sole selling" rights agreement as defined in the Estate Agents (Provision of Information) Regulations 1991. F and G's agreement had been terminated prior to the conclusion of missives, but G argued that, contractually, they were due commission, the purchaser having been introduced during the period of agency. The sheriff assoilzied F after finding that the introduction had not been instigated by G, and G appealed to the Court of Session after their appeal to the sheriff principal had been refused. G argued that the sheriff had subtly altered the meaning of the clause by adding the words "by us" to the "introduction". G argued that the clause in the contract relating to sole selling rights should have been construed as the draftsman intended, not by a contractual approach to the intention of the parties.

Held, refusing the appeal, that the clause had to be construed in the ordinary contractual context and not by a statutory approach to construction. The clause did not give G any right to commission where the missives had been concluded after termination of the agency and the introduction had not been effected by them.

G&S PROPERTIES v. FRANCIS 2001 S.L.T. 934, Lord Coulsfield, Lord Cowie, Lord Kirkwood, Ex Div.

6105. Guarantees – cautionary obligations – actual or ostensible authority – sufficiency of averments

J sought payment of certain sums from F on the basis that F had guaranteed supplies by J to FES. F contended that J has failed to aver that FES's obligation that had been so guaranteed.

Held, sustaining F's plea of irrelevancy and dismissing the action, that (1) the authority granted by F to certain individuals to represent to third parties that F would stand behind the financial obligations of FES and that FES was part of F, fell short of the express terms required for a grant of actual authority to commit F to a legally binding guarantee in respect of FES's debts, *Freeman & Lockyer v. Buckhurst Park Properties (Mangal) Ltd* [1964] 2 Q.B. 480, [1964] C.L.Y. 444, followed, and (2) in determining whether a particular individual had ostensible authority to bind F, no reliance could be placed on representations made by W, *Freeman & Lockyer v. Buckhurst Park Properties (Mangal) Ltd*, followed, and the change of name to FES, use of F's logo, stationery and documentation and the sharing of premises, whilst consistent with the presumption that F held FES out as a subsidiary of F, fell short of any representation on the part of F that particular individuals had authority to bind F to guarantee FES's debts. Opinion of the Court as per Lord Macfadyen, Lord Ordinary.

JOHN DAVIDSON (PIPES) LTD v. FIRST ENGINEERING LTD 2001 S.C.L.R. 73, Lord Macfadyen, OH.

AGRICULTURE

6106. Agricultural policy – business development scheme

FARM BUSINESS DEVELOPMENT (SCOTLAND) SCHEME 2001, SSI 2001 259; made under the Agriculture Act 1970 s.28, s.29. In force: July 2, 2001; £2.00.

This instrument establishes the Farm Business Development (Scotland) Scheme for that part of Scotland outwith the Highlands and Islands area and enables the payment of financial assistance under the Scheme for certain measures. These are capital measures by creating new or improving existing diversified agricultural activities and diversification outwith agricultural activities to provide alternative sources of income. They include support for training and marketing. Any of these measures can also be undertaken as collaborative ventures. The instrument also provides for the procedure for applications for financial assistance.

6107. Agricultural produce – Intervention Board for Agricultural Produce – abolition

ABOLITION OF THE INTERVENTION BOARD FOR AGRICULTURAL PRODUCE (CONSEQUENTIAL PROVISIONS) (SCOTLAND) REGULATIONS 2001, SSI 2001 390; made under the European Communities Act 1972 s.2. In force: in accordance with Reg.1 (1); £2.00.

The Intervention Board for Agricultural Produce is to be abolished by virtue of the Intervention Board for Agricultural Produce (Abolition) Regulations 2001 (SI 2001 3686). These Regulations amend the Foot-and-Mouth Disease Order 1983 (SI 1983 1950), the Home-Grown Cereals Authority Levy Scheme (Approval) Order 1987 (SI 1987 671), the Agricultural Levies (Export Control) Regulations 1988 (SI 1988 2135), the Beef Special Premium (Protection of Payments) Order 1989 (SI 1989 574), the Beef Special Premium (Recovery Powers) Regulations 1989 (SI 1989 575), the Agricultural Levies (Terms of Payment) Regulations 1990 (SI 1990 1185), the Home-Grown Cereals Authority Oilseeds Levy Scheme (Approval) Order 1990 (SI 1990 1317), the Common Agricultural Policy (Protection of Community Arrangements) Regulations 1992 (SI 1992 314), the Surplus Foods Regulations 1995 (SI 1995 184), the Arable Area Payments Regulations 1996 (SI 1996 3142), the Dairy Produce Quotas Regulations 1997 (SI 1997 733), the Charges for Inspections and Controls (Amendment) Regulations 1998 (SI 1998 2880) and the Common Agricultural Policy Support Schemes (Modulation) (Scotland) Regulations 2000 (SSI 2000 429). The Regulations empower the Scottish Ministers to enter into agency arrangements with DEFRA for the exercise of those functions formerly carried out by the Board to be carried out by Rural Payments Agency on their behalf.

6108. Agricultural produce – marketing grants

AGRICULTURAL PROCESSING AND MARKETING GRANTS (SCOTLAND) REGULATIONS 2001, SSI 2001 220; made under the European Communities Act 1972 s.2. In force: July 2, 2001; £2.50.

These Regulations introduce measures to supplement Council Regulation 1257/ 1999 ([1999] OJ L160/80) of on support for rural development from the European Agricultural Guidance and Guarantee Fund (EAGGF) and amending and repealing certain Regulations, Council Regulation 1260/1999 ([1999] OJ L161/1) of laying down general provisions on the Structural Funds, and Commission Regulation

1750/1999 ([1999] OJ L214/31) of laying down detailed rules for the application of Council Regulation 1257/1999 on support for rural development from the European Agricultural Guidance and Guarantee Fund (EAGGF) which provides for payment of assistance from the Guidance Section of the European Agricultural Guidance and Guarantee Fund for measures which promote rural development falling within the scope of Council Regulation 1257/1999. These Regulations establish a framework for the payment in Scotland of grants for those and related purposes towards projects associated with the processing and marketing of agricultural products. They re-enact the Regulations establishing the Highland and Islands Agricultural Processing and Marketing Grants scheme and establish a similar scheme in relation to agricultural processing and marketing grants in the Lowlands area of Scotland.

6109. Agricultural produce – marketing grants – Highland and Islands

HIGHLAND AND ISLANDS AGRICULTURAL PROCESSING AND MARKETING GRANTS ETC. (SCOTLAND) REGULATIONS 2001, SSI 2001 40; made under the European Communities Act 1972 s.2. In force: in accordance with Reg.1 (2); £2.50.

These Regulations introduce measures to supplement Council Regulation 1257/ 1999 ([1999] OJ L214/31) of May 17, 1999 on support for rural development from the European Agricultural Guidance and Guarantee Fund, Council Regulation 1260/1999 ([1999 OJ L161/1) of June 21, 1999 laying down general provisions on the Structural Funds and Commission Regulation 1750/1999 ([1999] L160/ 80) of July 23, 1999 laying down detailed rules for the application of Council Regulation 1257/1999. The Regulations set up the Highlands and Islands Agricultural Processing and Marketing Grants scheme, enable the payment of grants under the Single Programming Document for the Highlands and Islands Special Transitional Programme and provide for the procedure for applications for grants. They make provision for the determination of applications by the Scottish Ministers, how grants may be claimed and for the Scottish Ministers to determine the manner and timing of payment of the approved grants, retention of information and records, confer powers of entry and inspection for authorised persons to enforce the Regulations, make provision for the revocation and variation of approval and the withholding or recovery of grants, for payment of interest on grants recovered and create offences of knowingly or recklessly making a false statement to obtain grants or of obstructing authorised persons. In addition, the Regulations make minor consequential amendments to the Scotland Act 1998 (Consequential Modifications) (No.2) Order 1999 (SI 1999 1820) and the Agricultural Business Development Scheme (Scotland) Regulations 2000 (SSI 2000 448) and revoke, with savings, the Agricultural Processing and Marketing Grant Regulations 1995 (SI 1995 362).

6110. Animal products – beef – premiums

BEEF SPECIAL PREMIUM (SCOTLAND) REGULATIONS 2001, SSI 2001 445; made under the European Communities Act 1972 s.2. In force: January 1, 2002; £3.00.

These Regulations, which revoke the provisions of the Cattle Identification Regulations 1998 (SI 1998 871) and the Integrated Administration and Control System (Amendment) Regulations 2000 (SI 2000 2573), lay down implementing measures for the beef special premium scheme provided for in Council Regulation 1254/1999 ([1999] OJ L160/21) on the common organisation of the market in beef and veal. The Regulations provide for the administration of the scheme in relation to holdings situated wholly in Scotland and holdings situated partly in Scotland and partly elsewhere in the UK, where the Scottish Ministers are the competent authority in respect of an application for beef special premium.

6111. Animal products – diseases and disorders – BSE

BSE MONITORING (SCOTLAND) REGULATIONS 2001, SSI 2001 231; made under the European Communities Act 1972 s.2. In force: July 1, 2001; £2.00.

These Regulations, which amend the Bovine Spongiform Encephalopathy (No.2) Order 1996 (SI 1996 3183), the Cattle Identification Regulations 1998 (SI 1998 871) and the Cattle (Identification of Older Animals) (Scotland) Regulations 2001 (SSI 2001 1), make provision for the purpose of dealing in Scotland with the obligations in Art.1.2 of Commission Decision 2000/764 ([2000] OJ L305/35) on the testing of bovine animals for the presence of bovine spongiform encephalopathy and amending Decision 98/272 ([1998] OJ L122/59) on epidemio-surveillance for transmissible encephalopathies. These require Member States to ensure that certain categories of bovine animals over 30 months of age are examined in accordance with prescribed minimum requirements for monitoring BSE. The Regulations require the person in possession or in charge of a notifiable bovine animal to notify the death to the Scottish Ministers or an agent appointed for that purpose and also provide powers of entry, examination and search, offences and penalties and enforcement.

6112. Animal products – diseases and disorders – specified risk material

SPECIFIED RISK MATERIAL AMENDMENT (SCOTLAND) REGULATIONS 2001, SSI 2001 3; made under the Food Safety Act 1990 s.16, s.17, s.19, s.26, s.48, Sch.1 para.2, Sch.1 para.3, Sch.1 para.5, Sch.1 para.6. In force: January 10, 2001; £1.75.

These Regulations, which amend the Specified Risk Material Regulations 1997 (SI 1997 2965) in relation to Scotland, give effect to Article 1.1 of Commission Decision 2001/2 ([2001] OJ L1/21) by bringing the definition of specified bovine material into line with the definition of specified risk material in the Commission Decision by including the intestines of any bovine animal which has died or was slaughtered elsewhere than in Australia or New Zealand as specified risk material.

6113. Animal products – diseases and disorders – specified risk material

SPECIFIED RISK MATERIAL ORDER AMENDMENT (SCOTLAND) REGULATIONS 2001, SSI 2001 4; made under the European Communities Act 1972 s.2. In force: January 10, 2001; £1.75.

These Regulations, which amend the Specified Risk Material Order 1997 (SI 1997 2964) in relation to Scotland, give effect to Article 1.1 of Commission Decision 2001/2 ([2001] OJ L1/21) by bringing the definition of specified bovine material into line with the definition of specified risk material in the Commission Decision by including the intestines of any bovine animal which has died or was slaughtered elsewhere than in Australia or New Zealand as specified risk material.

6114. Animal products – diseases and disorders – spongiform encephalopathy – compensation

SHEEP AND GOATS SPONGIFORM ENCEPHALOPATHY (COMPENSATION) AMENDMENT (SCOTLAND) ORDER 2001, SSI 2001 458; made under the Animal Health Act 1981 s.32, s.34. In force: January 19, 2002; £1.75.

This Order, which amends the Sheep and Goats Spongiform Encephalopathy (Compensation) Order 1998 (SI 1998 1647), provides that the amount of compensation payable for sheep and goats caused to be slaughtered by the Scottish Ministers under the Animal Health Act 1981 s.32 because they are affected with any transmissible spongiform encephalopathy shall be £30 in the case of a cull animal and £90 for any other affected animal.

6115. Animal products – infectious disease control – ruminant related fluid – waste disposal

RENDERING (FLUID TREATMENT) (SCOTLAND) ORDER 2001, SSI 2001189; made under the Animal Health Act 1981 s.1, s.7, s.8. In force: May 31, 2001; £2.00.

This Order defines ruminant related fluid and makes provision in relation to the rendering, treatment and discharge of ruminant related fluid. It makes provision in relation to the testing of treated fluid, imposes record keeping requirements and imposes requirements in relation to cleansing and disinfection.

6116. Animal products – waste disposal – animal feed

ANIMAL BY-PRODUCTS AMENDMENT (SCOTLAND) ORDER 2001, SSI 2001 171; made under the Animal Health Act 1981 s.1. In force: May 24, 2001; £1.75.

This Order, which amends the Animal By-Products Order 1999 (SI 1999 646), prohibits the feeding to livestock of certain categories of catering waste, whether processed or unprocessed. In addition, it removes the possibility of non-mammalian animal by products being rendered for the production of swill for feeding to pigs or poultry.

6117. Animals – feedingstuffs – additives

FEEDING STUFFS AND THE FEEDING STUFFS (ENFORCEMENT) AMENDMENT (SCOTLAND) REGULATIONS 2001, SSI 2001 334; made under the Agriculture Act 1970 s.66, s.68, s.69, s.74A, s.84; and the European Communites Act 1972 s.2. In force: November 3, 2001; £2.00.

These Regulations, which amend the Feeding Stuffs (Enforcement) Regulations 1999 (SI 1999 2325) and the Feeding Stuffs (Scotland) Regulations 2000 (SSI 2000 453), implement Commission Decision 2000/285 ([2000] OJ L94/43) amending Decision 91/516 establishing a list of ingredients whose use is prohibited in compound feeding stuffs. They also provide enforcement for Commission Regulation 418/2001 ([2001] OJ L62/3) concerning the authorisation of new additives and uses of additives in feeding stuffs and Commission Regulation 937/2001 ([2001] OJ L130/25) concerning authorisation of new additive uses, new additive preparation, the prolongation of provisional authorisations, and the ten year authorisation of an additive in feeding stuffs. The Regulations extend the controls on sale and possession with a view to sale of compound feeding stuffs to cover supply other than sale, and possession with a view to such supply by replacing the references to "marketing" and "sold" with "put into circulation" and add prohibitions on the importation, supply, possession with a view to such supply and use of feed materials harmful to animals, to humans consuming products of such animals, or are deleterious to the environment. In addition, these Regulations amend the list of materials prohibited for use in compound materials, and widen the definition of "sludge from sewage plants treating waste waters" to include waste from various phases of urban, domestic and industrial waste water treatment processes and require that compound foods be labelled to include the approval or registration number of the establishment manufacturing the food in the relevant statutory statement.

6118. Animals – feedingstuffs – animal protein

PROCESSED ANIMAL PROTEIN (SCOTLAND) AMENDMENT REGULATIONS 2001, SSI 2001383; made under the European Communities Act 1972 s.2. In force: November 12, 2001; £1.50.

These Regulations amend the Process Animal Protein (Scotland) Regulations 2001 (SSI 2001 276) which give effect in Scotland to Council Decision 2000/766 ([2000] OJ L306/32) concerning certain protection measures with regard to transmissible spongiform encephalopathies and the feeding of animal protein. The amendments delete the words "of the place of destination" where they appear in duplicate in error and correct an error, by making it clear that, subject to an exception, feedingstuffs containing processed animal protein may not be manufactured in premises which prepare food for farmed animals.

6119. Animals – feedingstuffs – animal protein

PROCESSED ANIMAL PROTEIN (SCOTLAND) REGULATIONS 2001, SSI 2001 276; made under the European Communities Act 1972 s.2. In force: August 1, 2001; £3.50.

These Regulations, which amend the Bovine Spongiform Encephalopathy (Feeding Stuffs and Surveillance) Regulations 1999 (SI 1999 882), give effect to Council Decision 2000/766 ([2000] OJ L306/32) concerning certain protection measures with regard to transmissible spongiform encephalopathies and the feeding of animal protein. They make provision in relation to the production of fishmeal for feeding to farmed animals other than ruminants, define a farmed animal as an animal kept, fattened or bred for the production of food, provide for the approval of premises, suspension and withdrawal of approval and make provision for sale or supply of processed animal protein intended for the feeding of farmed animals. In addition, the Regulations make provision for the manufacture of feedingstuffs and impose requirements in respect of records relating to processed animal protein.

6120. Animals – feedingstuffs – sampling and analysis

FEEDING STUFFS (SAMPLING AND ANALYSIS) AMENDMENT (SCOTLAND) REGULATIONS 2001, SSI 2001 104; made under the Agriculture Act 1970 s.66, s.77, s.78, s.84; and the European Communities Act 1972 s.2. In force: April 6, 2001; £1.75.

These Regulations amend the Feeding Stuffs (Sampling and Analysis) Regulations 1999 (SI 1999 1663) and the Feeding Stuffs (Enforcement) Regulations 1999 (SI 1999 3235) implementing Commission Directive 2000/45 ([2000] OJ L174/32) establishing Community methods of analysis for the determination of vitamin A, vitamin E and tryptophan in feedingstuffs. They prescribe a revised method of analysis for the determination of vitamin A, and new methods for the determination of vitamin E and tryptophan, in feeding stuffs and, in the cases of vitamin A and E, in premixtures.

6121. Cattle – artificial insemination – emergency licences

ARTIFICIAL INSEMINATION OF CATTLE (EMERGENCY LICENCES) (SCOTLAND) REGULATIONS 2001, SSI 2001 179; made under the Animal Health and Welfare Act 1984 s.10. In force: May 17, 2001; £1.75.

These Regulations empower the Scottish Ministers to issue emergency licences during outbreaks of foot and mouth disease and provide that these emergency licences may authorise the licensee to do things normally prohibited by the Artificial Insemination of Cattle (Animal Health) (Scotland) Regulations 1985 (SI 1985 1857) which controls a range of activities related to the artificial insemination of cattle.

6122. Cattle – identification and registration – movement control

CATTLE (IDENTIFICATION OF OLDER ANIMALS) (SCOTLAND) REGULATIONS 2001, SSI 2001 1; made under the European Communities Act 1972 s.2. In force: Reg.5: January 11, 2001; Reg.6: January 11, 2001, remainder: January 29, 2001; £2.00.

These Regulations, which implement in relation to Scotland the provisions of Council Regulation 1760/2000 ([2000] OJ L204/1) concerning older cattle, require cattle born before July 1, 1996 which are not already registered on a voluntary basis to be registered before January 29, 2001. They require notification of the location of all cattle with passports without movement cards not already registered and provide for the issue of movement cards. In relation to cattle born before September 28, 1998, these Regulations require notification to the Scottish Ministers when these animals are moved. They also provide for the use of electronic notification of movement as an alternative to notification using movement cards, for a register of approved users of electronic notification, for the notification of the death of cattle born before July 1, 1996, for powers of inspectors and provide for an officer of the Scottish Ministers to impose movement restrictions for cattle to which the Regulations relate where there has been a contravention of these Regulations.

6123. Cattle – suckler cow premiums – administration

SUCKLER COW PREMIUM (SCOTLAND) REGULATIONS 2001, SSI 2001 225; made under the European Communities Act 1972 s.2. In force: July 1, 2001; £2.50.

These Regulations, which revoke provisions of the Suckler Cow Premium Regulations 1993 (SI 1993 1441 as amended by SI 1994 1528, SI 1995 15, SI 1995 1446, SI 1996 1488 and SI 1997 249), lay down implementing measures for the suckler cow premium scheme provided for in Art.6 of Council Regulation 1254/1999 ([1999] OJ L160/21) on the common organisation of the market in beef and veal and provide for the administration of the scheme in relation to applicants and their holdings where those holdings are situated wholly in Scotland, and also holdings situated partly in Scotland and partly elsewhere in the UK, where the Scottish Ministers are responsible for processing the farmer's claim for suckler cow premium. In addition, they lay down enforcement provisions applicable where the Scottish Ministers have such responsibility.

6124. Farming – conservation – grants – time extensions

FARM AND CONSERVATION GRANT AMENDMENT (SCOTLAND) REGULATIONS 2001, SSI 2001 321; made under the European Communities Act 1972 s.2. In force: October 30, 2001; £1.50.

These Regulation make amendments to the Farm and Conservation Grant Regulations 1991 (SI 1991 1630) as a consequence of the necessary restrictions in place as a result of foot and mouth disease which has meant that certain farmers have not been able to complete projects assisted under the scheme in the time scales specified in the particular grant approval. The Scottish Ministers have agreed to delay the dates for completion of such projects in the south of Scotland in circumstances where they are satisfied that such projects were unable to be completed on time as a direct consequence of the restrictions.

6125. Infectious disease control – foot and mouth disease – animals – ascertainment of value

FOOT-AND-MOUTH DISEASE (ASCERTAINMENT OF VALUE) (SCOTLAND) ORDER 2001, SSI 2001 120; made under the Animal Health Act 1981 s.1, s.34. In force: March 22, 2001 at 2.30pm; £1.75.

This Order establishes the system for ascertaining the value of animals slaughtered because of foot and mouth disease.

6126. Infectious disease control – foot and mouth disease – animals – ascertainment of value

FOOT-AND-MOUTH DISEASE (ASCERTAINMENT OF VALUE) (SCOTLAND) (NO.2) ORDER 2001, SSI 2001 121; made under the Animal Health Act 1981 s.1, s.34. In force: March 23, 2001 at 7.00pm; £1.75.

This Order, which revokes and remakes the Foot-and-Mouth Mouth Disease (Ascertainment of Value) (Scotland) Order 2001 (SSI 2001 120) principally with amendments to the Schedule to provide a value for cull cattle, establishes the system for ascertaining the value of animals slaughtered because of foot and mouth disease.

6127. Infectious disease control – foot and mouth disease – animals – ascertainment of value

FOOT-AND-MOUTH DISEASE (ASCERTAINMENT OF VALUE) (SCOTLAND) (NO.3) ORDER 2001, SSI 2001 130; made under the Animal Health Act 1981 s.1, s.34. In force: March 30, 2001 at 5.00pm; £1.75.

This Order replaces the existing system for ascertaining the value of animals slaughtered because of foot and mouth disease. It replaces the Foot-and-Mouth Disease (Ascertainment of Value) (Scotland) (No.2) Order 2001 (SSI 2001 121) with amendments to the procedure for valuation and the Schedule of values to allow a standard value for calves.

6128. Infectious disease control – foot and mouth disease – animals – ascertainment of value

FOOT-AND-MOUTH DISEASE (ASCERTAINMENT OF VALUE) (SCOTLAND) (NO.4) ORDER 2001, SSI 2001 297; made under the Animal Health Act 1981 s.1, s.34. In force: August 31, 2001; £1.75.

This Order, which amends the Foot-and-Mouth Disease (Ascertainment of Value) (Scotland) (No.3) Order 2001 (SSI 2001 130), extends to Scotland only and replaces the existing system for ascertaining the value of animals slaughtered because of foot and mouth disease.

6129. Infectious disease control – foot and mouth disease – animals – meat products

FOOT-AND-MOUTH DISEASE (MARKING OF MEAT AND MEAT PRODUCTS) (SCOTLAND) REGULATIONS 2001, SSI 2001 160; made under the European Communities Act 1972 s.2. In force: April 23, 2001; £1.75.

These Regulations, which amend the Meat Products (Hygiene) Regulations 1994 (SI 1994 3082) and the Fresh Meat (Hygiene and Inspection) Regulations 1995 (SI 1995 539), implement Commission Decision 2001/304 on marking and use of certain animal products in relation to Decision 2001/172 ([2001] OJ L104/6) concerning certain protection measures with regard to foot and mouth disease in the UK. In addition, they introduce a new type of health mark (circular stamp) for marking meat from animals of the bovine, ovine, caprine and porcine species.

6130. Infectious disease control – foot and mouth disease – controlled areas

FOOT-AND-MOUTH DISEASE DECLARATORY (CONTROLLED AREA) (SCOTLAND) ORDER 2001, SSI 2001 49; made under the Foot-and-Mouth Disease Order 1983 (SI 1983 1950) Art.30. In force: February 23, 2001 at 6.15pm; £1.75.

This Order imposes, with variations, the restrictions contained in the Foot-and-Mouth Disease Order 1983 (SI 1983 1950) Part IV within Scotland.

6131. Infectious disease control – foot and mouth disease – controlled areas

FOOT-AND-MOUTH DISEASE DECLARATORY (CONTROLLED AREA) (SCOTLAND) (NO. 2) ORDER 2001, SSI 2001 60; made under the Foot-and-Mouth Disease Order 1983 (SI 1983 1950) Art.30. In force: March 2, 2001 at 12.00am; £2.50.

This Order imposes in relation to Scotland, the restrictions contained in the Foot-and-Mouth Disease Order 1983 (SI 1983 1950) Part IV.

6132. Infectious disease control – foot and mouth disease – controlled areas

FOOT-AND-MOUTH DISEASE DECLARATORY (CONTROLLED AREA) (SCOTLAND) (NO.3) AMENDMENT ORDER 2001, SSI 2001 131; made under the Foot-and-Mouth Disease Order 1983 (SI 1983 1950) Art.30. In force: March 30, 2001 at 7 pm; £1.75.

This Order amends the Foot-and-Mouth Disease Declaratory (Controlled Area) (Scotland) (No.3) Order 2001 (SSI 2001 111) in relation to the whole of Scotland to amend the ban on hunting and stalking for deer. This allows exceptions to the ban for certain types of deer in certain circumstances, while maintaining the complete ban on the hunting and stalking of other types of deer and of other animals.

6133. Infectious disease control – foot and mouth disease – controlled areas

FOOT-AND-MOUTH DISEASE DECLARATORY (CONTROLLED AREA) (SCOTLAND) (NO.3) AMENDMENT (NO.2) ORDER 2001, SSI 2001 150; made under the Foot-and-Mouth Disease Order 1983 (SI 1983 1950) Art.30. In force: Art.2: April 12, 2001 at 7.00pm; Art.3: April 16, 2001; £1.75.

This Order, which amends the Foot-and-Mouth Disease Declaratory (Controlled Area) (Scotland) (No.3) Order 2001 (SSI 2001 111), modifies the number of days within which licensed movement to slaughter must be completed from five days to seven. In addition, it amends the ban on hunting and stalking for deer, by adding the areas of the Edinburgh and Glasgow Councils to the permitted areas, where in certain circumstances, exceptions are allowed to the ban on hunting or stalking certain types of deer.

6134. Infectious disease control – foot and mouth disease – controlled areas

FOOT-AND-MOUTH DISEASE DECLARATORY (CONTROLLED AREA) (SCOTLAND) (NO.3) AMENDMENT (NO.3) ORDER 2001, SSI 2001 170; made under the Foot-and-Mouth Disease Order 1983 (SI 1983 1950) Art.30. In force: May 1, 2001 at 8.00pm; £1.75.

This Order, which amends the Foot-and-Mouth Disease Declaratory (Controlled Area) (Scotland) (No.3) Order 2001 (SSI 2001 111), requires the owner or person in charge of an animal in a Controlled Area not to allow it to stray and makes provision for stray or feral animals to be detained and, if the owner cannot be found, destroyed. It amends the ban on hunting and stalking deer by changing the permitted areas where in certain circumstances, exceptions are allowed to the ban on hunting or stalking certain types of deer. Permitted areas now will comprise all of Scotland except the Dumfries and Galloway and the Scottish Borders council areas and those parts of Scotland outwith those council areas. In addition, it allows for individual licences for movement to slaughter to permit scheduled stops to occur at specified collection centres.

6135. Infectious disease control – foot and mouth disease – controlled areas

FOOT-AND-MOUTH DISEASE DECLARATORY (CONTROLLED AREA) (SCOTLAND) (NO.3) AMENDMENT (NO.4) ORDER 2001, SSI 2001 181; made under the Foot-and-Mouth Disease Order 1983 Art.30. In force: May 16, 2001; £1.75.

This Order, which amends the Foot-and-Mouth Disease Declaratory (Controlled Area) (Scotland) (No.3) Order 2001 (SSI 2001 111) within the permitted areas, requires the written approval of the Divisional Veterinary Manager and notification to the Scottish Ministers to permit the use of the power of an inspector to prohibit entry by notice onto land or into agricultural buildings under the Controlled Area Order. Where such entry has been prohibited without such approval or notification, that prohibition shall cease to have effect.

6136. Infectious disease control – foot and mouth disease – controlled areas

FOOT-AND-MOUTH DISEASE DECLARATORY (CONTROLLED AREA) (SCOTLAND) (NO.3) AMENDMENT (NO.5) ORDER 2001, SSI 2001 290; made under the Foot-and-Mouth Disease Order 1983 (SI 1983 1950) Art.30. In force: August 16, 2001 at 12pm; £1.75.

This Order amends the Foot-and-Mouth Disease Declaratory (Controlled Area) (Scotland) (No.3) Order 2001 (SSI 2001 111) to allow the Scottish Ministers to authorise the use of places other than collecting centres for licensing onward movement of animals to slaughterhouses. In addition, it amends the restrictions in the Controlled Area Order on gatherings of animals to allow an inspector of a local authority, or the Scottish Ministers, to permit these by licence, and to specifically prohibit on farm sales of standing stock.

6137. Infectious disease control – foot and mouth disease – controlled areas

FOOT-AND-MOUTH DISEASE DECLARATORY (CONTROLLED AREA) (SCOTLAND) (NO.3) ORDER 2001, SSI 2001 111; made under the Foot-and-Mouth Disease Order 1983 (SI 1983 1950) Art.30. In force: Art.8(2): March 16, 2001; remainder: March 17, 2001; £2.50.

This Order imposes in relation to Scotland the restrictions contained in the Foot-and-Mouth Disease Order 1983 (SI 1983 1950) Part IV, subject to certain disapplications and variations, and amends the Foot-and-Mouth Disease (Scotland) (Declaratory and Controlled Area) Amendment Order 2001 (SSI 2001 66) and the Foot-and-Mouth Disease (Scotland) (Declaratory and Controlled Area) Amendment (No.2) Order 2001 (SSI 2001 90).

6138. Infectious disease control – foot and mouth disease – controlled areas

FOOT-AND-MOUTH DISEASE (SCOTLAND) DECLARATORY ORDER 2001, SSI 2001 56; made under the Foot-and-Mouth Disease Order 1983 (SI 1983 1950) Art.17. In force: March 1, 2001 at 8.00pm; £1.75.

This Order imposes, with variations, the restrictions contained in the Foot-and-Mouth Disease Order 1983 (SI 1983 1950) Part III within a specified infected area.

6139. Infectious disease control – foot and mouth disease – controlled areas

FOOT-AND-MOUTH DISEASE (SCOTLAND) DECLARATORY (AMENDMENT) (NO.3) ORDER 2001, SSI 2001 91; made under the Foot-and-Mouth Disease Order 1983 (SI 1983 1950) Art.17. In force: March 9, 2001 at 2.00pm; £1.75.

This Order, which amends the Foot-and-Mouth Disease (Scotland) Declaratory Order 2001 (SSI 2001 56) and the Foot-and-Mouth Disease (Scotland) (Declaratory and Controlled Area) Amendment Order 2001 (SSI 2001 66), extends the infected area declared by the Foot-and-Mouth Disease (Scotland) Declaratory Order 2001 (SSI 2001 65) and subject to the restrictions therein.

6140. Infectious disease control – foot and mouth disease – controlled areas

FOOT-AND-MOUTH DISEASE (SCOTLAND) DECLARATORY (AMENDMENT) (NO.4) ORDER 2001, SSI 2001 110; made under the Foot-and-Mouth Disease Order 1983 (SI 1983 1950) Art.17. In force: March 16, 2001 at 2.30pm; £1.75.

This Order extends the infected area declared by the Foot-and-Mouth Disease (Scotland) Declaratory Order 2001 (SSI 2001 56) and subject to the restrictions therein. The Foot-and-Mouth Disease (Scotland) Declaratory (Amendment) (No.3) Order 2001 (SSI 2001 91) is revoked.

6141. Infectious disease control – foot and mouth disease – controlled areas

FOOT-AND-MOUTH DISEASE (SCOTLAND) DECLARATORY (AMENDMENT) (NO.5) ORDER 2001, SSI 2001 122; made under the Foot-and-

Mouth Disease Order 1983 (SI 1983 1950) Art.17. In force: March 25, 2001 at 6.00pm; £1.75.

This Order amends the Foot-and-Mouth Disease (Scotland) Declaratory Order 2001 (SSI 2001 56) and revokes the Foot-and-Mouth Disease (Scotland) Declaratory (No.2) Order 2001 (SI 2001 59) and the Foot-and-Mouth Disease (Scotland) Declaratory (No.4) Order 2001 (SSI 2001 110) by extending the infected areas declared and combines them in one description.

6142. Infectious disease control – foot and mouth disease – controlled areas

FOOT-AND-MOUTH DISEASE (SCOTLAND) DECLARATORY (AMENDMENT) (NO.6) ORDER 2001, SSI 2001 148; made under the Foot-and-Mouth Disease Order 1983 (SI 1983 1950) Art.17. In force: April 10, 2001 at 2.00pm; £1.75.

This Order, which revokes the Foot-and-Mouth Disease (Scotland) Declaratory (Amendment) (No.5) Order 2001 (SSI 2001 122), extends the infected area declared by the Foot-and-Mouth Disease (Scotland) Declaratory Order (SSI 2001 56).

6143. Infectious disease control – foot and mouth disease – controlled areas

FOOT-AND-MOUTH DISEASE (SCOTLAND) DECLARATORY (AMENDMENT) (NO.7) ORDER 2001, SSI 2001 149; made under the Foot-and-Mouth Disease Order 1983 (SI 1983 1950) Art.17. In force: April 10, 2001 at 8.00pm; £1.75.

This Order, which revokes the Foot-and-Mouth Disease (Scotland) Declaratory (Amendment) (No.6) Order 2001 (SSI 2001 148), extends the infected area declared by the Foot-and-Mouth Disease (Scotland) Declaratory Order (SSI 2001 56).

6144. Infectious disease control – foot and mouth disease – controlled areas

FOOT-AND-MOUTH DISEASE (SCOTLAND) DECLARATORY (AMENDMENT NO.2) ORDER 2001, SSI 2001 65; made under the Foot-and-Mouth Disease Order 1983 (SI 1983 1950) Art.17. In force: March 6, 2001 at 12.30pm; £1.75.

This Order extends the infected area declared by the Foot-and-Mouth Disease (Scotland) Declaratory Order 2001 (SSI 2001 56).

6145. Infectious disease control – foot and mouth disease – controlled areas

FOOT-AND-MOUTH DISEASE (SCOTLAND) DECLARATORY (NO.2) ORDER 2001, SSI 2001 59; made under the Foot-and-Mouth Disease Order 1983 (SI 1983 1950) Art.17. In force: March 2, 2001 at 5.00pm; £1.75.

This Order imposes, with variations, the restrictions contained in the Foot-and-Mouth Disease Order 1983 (SI 1983 1950) Part III within a specified infected area.

6146. Infectious disease control – foot and mouth disease – controlled areas

FOOT-AND-MOUTH DISEASE (SCOTLAND) DECLARATORY (NO.3) ORDER 2001, SSI 2001 153; made under the Foot-and-Mouth Disease Order 1983 (SI 1983 1950) Art.17. In force: April 14, 2001 at 2.00pm; £1.75.

This Order imposes, with variations, the restrictions contained in the Foot-and-Mouth Disease Order 1983 (SI 1983 1950) Part III within a specified infected area.

6147. Infectious disease control – foot and mouth disease – controlled areas

FOOT-AND-MOUTH DISEASE (SCOTLAND) DECLARATORY (NO.4) ORDER 2001, SSI 2001 157; made under the Foot-and-Mouth Disease Order 1983 (SI 1983 1950) Art.17. In force: April 20, 2001 at 9.00pm; £2.00.

This Order, which amends the Foot-and-Mouth Disease (Scotland) (Declaratory and Controlled area) Amendment Order 2001 (SSI 2001 66 as amended by SSI 2001 90 and SSI 2001 146) and revokes the Foot-and-Mouth Disease (Scotland) Declaratory Order 2001 (SSI 2001 56 as amended by SSI 2001 63, SSI 2001 109 and SSI 2001 149), imposes, with variations, the restrictions contained in the Foot-and-Mouth Disease Order 1983 (SI 1983 1950) Part III within a specified infected area.

6148. Infectious disease control – foot and mouth disease – controlled areas

FOOT-AND-MOUTH DISEASE (SCOTLAND) DECLARATORY (NO.5) AMENDMENT ORDER 2001, SSI 2001 180; made under the Foot-and-Mouth Disease Order 1983 Art.17. In force: May 16, 2001 at 2.00pm; £1.75.

This Order amends the Foot-and-Mouth Disease (Scotland) Declaratory (No.5) Order 2001 (SSI 2001 165) by extending the declared infected area.

6149. Infectious disease control – foot and mouth disease – controlled areas

FOOT-AND-MOUTH DISEASE (SCOTLAND) DECLARATORY (NO.5) AMENDMENT (NO.2) ORDER 2001, SSI 2001 192; made under the Foot-and-Mouth Disease Order 1983 Art.17. In force: May 23, 2001 at 5.00pm; £1.75.

This Order amends the infected area declared by the Foot-and-Mouth Disease (Scotland) Declaratory (No.5) Order 2001 (SSI 2001 187) and subject to the restrictions therein.

6150. Infectious disease control – foot and mouth disease – controlled areas

FOOT-AND-MOUTH DISEASE (SCOTLAND) DECLARATORY (NO.5) AMENDMENT (NO.3) ORDER 2001, SSI 2001 203; made under the Foot-and-Mouth Disease Order 1983 Art.17. In force: June 1, 2001 at 5.00pm; £1.75.

This Order reduces the infected area declared by the Foot-and-Mouth Disease (Scotland) Declaratory (No.5) Order 2001 (SSI 2001 165) and subject to the restrictions therein.

6151. Infectious disease control – foot and mouth disease – controlled areas

FOOT-AND-MOUTH DISEASE (SCOTLAND) DECLARATORY (NO.5) AMENDMENT (NO.4) ORDER 2001, SSI 2001 247; made under the Foot-and-Mouth Disease Order 1983 Art.17. In force: June 22, 2001 at 5.00pm; £1.75.

This Order, which revokes the Foot-and-Mouth Disease (Scotland) Declaratory (No.3) Order 2001 (SSI 2001 203), amends the Foot-and-Mouth Disease (Scotland) Declaratory (No.5) Order 2001 (SSI 2001 165) by reducing the infected area declared in that Order subject to certain restrictions.

6152. Infectious disease control – foot and mouth disease – controlled areas

FOOT-AND-MOUTH DISEASE (SCOTLAND) DECLARATORY (NO.5) AMENDMENT (NO.5) ORDER 2001, SSI 2001 272; made under the Foot-and-Mouth Disease Order 1983 (SI 1983 1950) Art.17. In force: July 20, 2001 at 5 pm; £1.75.

This Order, which revokes the Foot-and-Mouth Disease (Scotland) Declaratory (No.5) Amendment (No.4) Order 2001 (SSI 2001 247), further reduces the infected area declared by the Foot-and-Mouth Disease (Scotland) Declaratory (No.5) Order 2001 (SSI 2001 165).

6153. Infectious disease control – foot and mouth disease – controlled areas

FOOT-AND-MOUTH DISEASE (SCOTLAND) DECLARATORY (NO.5) AMENDMENT (NO.6) ORDER 2001, SSI 2001 275; made under the Foot-and-Mouth Disease Order 1983 (SI 1983 1950) Art.17. In force: July 27, 2001 at 5 pm; £1.75.

This Order, which revokes the Foot-and-Mouth Disease (Scotland) Declaratory (No.5) Amendment (No.5) Order 2001 (SSI 2001 272), further reduces the infected area declared by the Foot-and-Mouth Disease (Scotland) Declaratory (No.5) Order 2001 (SSI 2001 165).

6154. Infectious disease control – foot and mouth disease – controlled areas

FOOT-AND-MOUTH DISEASE (SCOTLAND) DECLARATORY (NO.5) ORDER 2001, SSI 2001 165; made under the Foot-and-Mouth Disease Order 1983 (SI 1983 1950) Art.17. In force: April 25, 2001 at 5.00pm; £3.00.

This Order, which amends the Foot-and-Mouth Disease (Scotland) (Declaratory and Controlled Area) Amendment (No.4) Order 2001 (SSI 2001 159) and revokes the Foot-and-Mouth Disease (Scotland) Declaratory (No.3) Order 2001 (SSI 2001 153) and the Foot-and-Mouth Disease (Scotland) Declaratory (No.4) Order 2001 (SSI 2001 157), imposes the restrictions contained in the Foot-and-Mouth Disease Order 1983 (SI 1983 1950) Part III within a specified infected area.

6155. Infectious disease control – foot and mouth disease – controlled areas

FOOT-AND-MOUTH DISEASE (SCOTLAND) DECLARATORY (NO.5) REVOCATION ORDER 2001, SSI 2001 312; made under the Foot-and-Mouth Disease Order 1983 (SI 1983 1950) Art.17. In force: September 10, 2001 at 6pm; £1.75.

This Order amends the Foot-and-Mouth Disease (Scotland) (Declaratory and Controlled Area) Amendment (No.5) Order 2001 (SSI 2001 187), the Foot-and-Mouth Disease (Scotland) (Declaratory and Controlled Area) Amendment (No.6) Order 2001 (SSI 2001 204) and the Foot-and-Mouth Disease (Scotland) (Declaratory and Controlled Area) Amendment (No.7) Order 2001 (SSI 2001 246). It also revokes the Foot-and-Mouth Disease (Scotland) Declaratory (No.5) Order 2001 (SSI 2001 165), the Foot-and-Mouth Disease (Scotland) (Declaratory Orders) General Amendment (No.2) Order 2001 (SSI 2001 258) and the Foot-and-Mouth Disease (Scotland) Declaratory (No.5) Amendment (No.6) Order 2001 (SSI 2001 275).

6156. Infectious disease control – foot and mouth disease – controlled areas

FOOT-AND-MOUTH DISEASE (SCOTLAND) DECLARATORY (NO.6) AMENDMENT ORDER 2001, SSI 2001 194; made under the Foot-and-Mouth Disease Order 1983 Art.17. In force: May 25, 2001 at 5.00pm; £1.75.

This Order extends the infected area declared by the Foot-and-Mouth Disease (Scotland) Declaratory (No.6) Order 2001 (SSI 2001 168) and subject to the restrictions therein.

6157. Infectious disease control – foot and mouth disease – controlled areas

FOOT-AND-MOUTH DISEASE (SCOTLAND) DECLARATORY (NO.6) AMENDMENT (NO. 2) ORDER 2001, SSI 2001 196; made under the Foot-and-Mouth Disease Order 1983 Art.17. In force: May 29, 2001 at 5.00pm; £1.75.

This Order extends the infected area declared by the Foot-and-Mouth Disease (Scotland) Declaratory (No.6) Order 2001 (SI 2001 168) and subject to the restrictions therein.

6158. Infectious disease control – foot and mouth disease – controlled areas

FOOT-AND-MOUTH DISEASE (SCOTLAND) DECLARATORY (NO.6) ORDER 2001, SSI 2001 168; made under the Foot-and-Mouth Disease Order 1983 (SI 1983 1950) Art.17. In force: April 28, 2001 at 1.00pm; £2.50.

This Order imposes, with variations, the restrictions contained in the Foot-and-Mooth Disease Order 1983 (SI 1983 1950) Part III within a specified infected area.

6159. Infectious disease control – foot and mouth disease – controlled areas

FOOT-AND-MOUTH DISEASE (SCOTLAND) DECLARATORY (NO.7) ORDER 2001, SSI 2001 193; made under the Foot-and-Mouth Disease Order 1983 Art.17. In force: May 25, 2001 at 12.00pm; £2.00.

This Order imposes, with variations, the restrictions contained in the Foot-and-Mouth Disease Order 1983 (SI 1983 1950) Part III within the infected area described in Schedule 1.

6160. Infectious disease control – foot and mouth disease – controlled areas

FOOT-AND-MOUTH DISEASE (SCOTLAND) (DECLARATORY AND CONTROLLED AREA) AMENDMENT ORDER 2001, SSI 2001 66; made under the Foot-and-Mouth Disease Order 1983 (SI 1983 1950) Art.17, Art.30. In force: March 6, 2001 at 9.30pm; £1.75.

This Order amends the Foot-and-Mouth Disease Order 1983 (SI 1983 1950), the Foot-and-Mouth Disease (Scotland) Declaratory Order 2001 (SSI 2001 56) and the Foot-and-Mouth Disease (Scotland) Declaratory (No.2) Order 2001 (SSI 2001 59) which declare certain areas in Scotland as infected areas, in each case for the purpose of combating the foot and mouth outbreak, in their application to slaughterhouse or knackery products.

6161. Infectious disease control – foot and mouth disease – controlled areas

FOOT-AND-MOUTH DISEASE (SCOTLAND) (DECLARATORY AND CONTROLLED AREA) AMENDMENT (NO.2) ORDER 2001, SSI 2001 90; made under the Foot-and-Mouth Disease Order 1983 (SI 1983 1950) Art.17, Art.30. In force: March 9, 2001 at 9.30pm; £1.75.

This Order amends the Foot-and-Mouth Disease Declaratory (Controlled Area) (Scotland) (No.2) Order 2001 (SSI 2001 56), the Foot-and-Mouth Disease (Scotland) Declaratory Order 2001 (SSI 2001 60) and the Foot-and-Mouth Disease (Scotland) Declaratory (No.2) Order 2001 (SSI 2001 63) which declare Scotland to be a controlled area and declare certain areas in Scotland as infected areas for the purpose of combating the foot and mouth outbreak. It prohibits the movement of carcasses from premises other than slaughterhouses or knacker's yards except under a licence issued by the Scottish Ministers.

6162. Infectious disease control – foot and mouth disease – controlled areas

FOOT-AND-MOUTH DISEASE (SCOTLAND) (DECLARATORY AND CONTROLLED AREA) AMENDMENT (NO.3) ORDER 2001, SSI 2001 146; made under the Foot-and-Mouth Disease Order 1983 (SI 1983 1950) Art.17, Art.30. In force: April 7, 2001; £1.75.

This Order, which amends the Foot-and-Mouth Disease (Scotland) Declaratory Order 2001 (SI 2001 56) and the Foot-and-Mouth Disease Declaratory (Controlled Area) (Scotland) (No.3) Order 2001 (SSI 2001 111), permits the Scottish Ministers to allow movement for slaughter by way of a general licence if considered appropriate. It extends the categories of animals within a controlled area that can be moved to slaughter under licence and removes the requirement for movements of bovine semen into, out of or within an infected area to be authorised by a special movement licence.

6163. Infectious disease control – foot and mouth disease – controlled areas

FOOT-AND-MOUTH DISEASE (SCOTLAND) (DECLARATORY AND CONTROLLED AREA) AMENDMENT (NO.4) ORDER 2001, SSI 2001 159; made under the Foot-and-Mouth Disease Order 1983 (SI 1983 1950) Art.17, Art.30. In force: April 21, 2001; £2.50.

These Regulations amend the Foot-and-Mouth Disease Declaratory (Controlled Area) (Scotland) (No.3) Order 2001 (SSI 2001 111), the Foot-and-Mouth Disease (Scotland) Declaratory (No.3) Order 2001 (SSI 2001 153) and the Foot-and-Mouth Disease (Scotland) Declaratory (No.4) Order 2001 (SSI 2001

157). They amends the licence for movement to slaughter in connection with the maximum number of days within which movement must be completed and allow the licensing of movement from an infected area to slaughter, under a licence in the form prescribed, and make further provision in that regard. They also make provision in relation to stray or feral animals.

6164. Infectious disease control – foot and mouth disease – controlled areas

FOOT-AND-MOUTH DISEASE (SCOTLAND) (DECLARATORY AND CONTROLLED AREA) AMENDMENT (NO.5) ORDER 2001, SSI 2001 187; made under the Foot-and-Mouth Disease Order 1983 Art.17, Art.30. In force: May 19, 2001; £1.75.

This Order amends the Foot-and-Mouth Disease Declaratory (Controlled Area) (Scotland) (No.3) Order 2001 (SSI 2001 111), the Foot-and-Mouth Disease (Scotland) Declaratory (No.5) Order 2001 (SSI 2001 165) and the Foot-and-Mouth Disease (Scotland) Declaratory (No.6) Order 2001 (SSI 2001 168). It amends the ban on hunting and stalking deer by changing the permitted areas where in certain circumstances exceptions are allowed to the ban on hunting or stalking certain types of deer. Permitted areas now will comprise the whole of Scotland except those parts of Scotland where an order made by the Scottish Ministers is in force. In addition, the Order removes the prescribed form of the licence issued by an inspector for movement to slaughter under the Controlled Area Order and provides that such a licence shall be issued in a form to be prescribed by the Scottish Ministers in accordance with the advice of the Chief Veterinary Officer.

6165. Infectious disease control – foot and mouth disease – controlled areas

FOOT-AND-MOUTH DISEASE (SCOTLAND) (DECLARATORY AND CONTROLLED AREA) AMENDMENT (NO.6) ORDER 2001, SSI 2001 204; made under the Foot-and-Mouth Disease Order 1983 Art.17, Art.30. In force: June 1, 2001; £1.75.

This Order further amends the Foot-and-Mouth Disease Declaratory (Controlled Area) (Scotland) (No.3) Order 2001 (SSI 2001 111). It bans sheep shearing within Scotland, as a controlled area, except under the conditions of a licence issued by the Scottish Ministers. In certain restricted circumstances, the ban does not apply to an occupier of premises in relation to sheep on those premises, or in relation to an owner of sheep in common flocks. The Order also provides for similar restrictions in the infected areas under the Foot-and-Mouth Disease (Scotland) Declaratory (No.5) Order 2001 (SSI 2001 165), the Foot-and-Mouth Disease (Scotland) Declaratory (No.6) Order 2001 (SSI 2001 168), and the Foot-and-Mouth Disease (Scotland) Declaratory (No.7) Order 2001 (SSI 2001 193).

6166. Infectious disease control – foot and mouth disease – controlled areas

FOOT-AND-MOUTH DISEASE (SCOTLAND) (DECLARATORY AND CONTROLLED AREA) AMENDMENT (NO.7) ORDER 2001, SSI 2001 246; made under the Foot-and-Mouth Disease Order 1983 Art.17, Art.30. In force: June 18, 2001; £1.75.

This Order amends the Foot-and-Mouth Disease Declaratory (Controlled Area) (Scotland) (No.3) Order 2001 (SSI 2001 111), the Foot-and-Mouth Disease (Scotland) Declaratory (No.5) Order 2001 (SSI 2001 165), the Foot-and-Mouth Disease (Scotland) Declaratory (No.6) Order 2001 (SSI 2001 168) and the Foot-and-Mouth (Scotland) Declaratory (No.7) Order 2001 (SSI 2001 193). It bans sheep dipping within Scotland, as a controlled area, except under the conditions of a licence issued by the Scottish Ministers. In certain restricted circumstances, the ban does not apply to an occupier of premises in relation to sheep on those premises, or in relation to an owner of sheep in common flocks.

6167. Infectious disease control – foot and mouth disease – controlled areas

FOOT-AND-MOUTH DISEASE (SCOTLAND) (DECLARATORY ORDERS) GENERAL REVOCATION ORDER 2001, SSI 2001 264; made under the Foot-and-Mouth Disease Order 1983 (SI 1983 1950) Art.17. In force: July 13, 2001 at 2 pm; £1.50.

This Order revokes the infected areas designated by the Foot-and-Mouth Disease (Scotland) Declaratory (No.6) Order 2001 (SSI 2001 168) and the Foot-and-Mouth Disease (Scotland) Declaratory (No.7) Order 2001 (SSI 2001 193).

6168. Infectious disease control – foot and mouth disease – export restrictions

EXPORT RESTRICTIONS (FOOT-AND-MOUTH DISEASE) AMENDMENT (SCOTLAND) REGULATIONS 2001, SSI 2001 61; made under the European Communities Act 1972 s.2. In force: March 2, 2001 at 11.50pm; £2.00.

These Regulations continue the restrictions contained in the Export Restrictions (Foot-and-Mouth Disease) Regulations 2001 (SI 2001 498) and amend these restrictions in accordance with Commission Decision 2001/172 of March 1, 2001 concerning certain protection measures with regard to foot and mouth disease in the UK.

6169. Infectious disease control – foot and mouth disease – import and export restrictions

IMPORT AND EXPORT RESTRICTIONS (FOOT-AND-MOUTH DISEASE) (SCOTLAND) AMENDMENT REGULATIONS 2001, SSI 2001 112; made under the European Communities Act 1972 s.2. In force: March 17, 2001; £1.75.

These Regulations amend the restrictions on imports and exports of certain animals and animal products in the Import and Export Restrictions (Foot-and-Mouth Disease) (Scotland) Regulations 2001 (SSI 2001 95) to implement in Scotland restrictions on the export of certain animals and animal products in accordance with Commission Decision 2001/209 ([2001] OJ L76/35) amending Commission Decision 2001/172 ([2001] OJ L62/22) concerning certain protection measures with regard to foot and-mouth disease in the UK. These Regulations prohibit the export of equidae to other Member States unless the animals are accompanied by a certificate, which can only be issued if they have not been in an infected area during the 15 days prior to certification.

6170. Infectious disease control – foot and mouth disease – import and export restrictions

IMPORT AND EXPORT RESTRICTIONS (FOOT-AND-MOUTH DISEASE) (SCOTLAND) AMENDMENT (NO.2) REGULATIONS 2001, SSI 2001 127; made under the European Communities Act 1972 s.2. In force: March 27, 2001 at 8.00pm; £1.75.

These Regulations, which amend the Import and Export Restrictions (Foot-and-Mouth Disease) (Scotland) Regulations 2001 (SSI 2001 95) and the Import and Export Restrictions (Foot-and-Mouth Disease) (Scotland) Amendment Regulations 2001 (SSI 2001 112), implement in Scotland Commission Decision 2001/239 ([2001] OJ L86/33). They amend the restrictions on imports and exports of certain animals and animal products to continue the effect of those restrictions until midnight on April 4, 2001.

6171. Infectious disease control – foot and mouth disease – import and export restrictions

IMPORT AND EXPORT RESTRICTIONS (FOOT-AND-MOUTH DISEASE) (SCOTLAND) AMENDMENT (NO.3) REGULATIONS 2001, SSI 2001 141; made under the European Communities Act 1972 s.2. In force: April 4, 2001 at 8.00pm; £1.75.

These Regulations, which amend the Import and Export Restrictions (Foot-and-Mouth Disease) (Scotland) Regulations 2001 (SSI 2001 95), the Import and Export Restrictions (Foot-and-Mouth Disease) (Scotland) Amendment Regulations 2001 (SSI 2001 112) and the Import and Export Restrictions (Foot-and-Mouth Disease) (Scotland) Amendment (No.2) Regulations 2001 (SSI 2001 127), implement in Scotland Commission Decision 2001/268 ([2001] OJ L94/27). The amendments are made to continue the effect of restrictions contained in the Import and Export Restrictions (Foot-and-Mouth Disease) (Scotland) Regulations 2001 (SSI 2001 112) until midnight on April 19, 2001, and they make further changes to allow the export of certain meat products and milk if the meat and milk processed originated in Northern Ireland.

6172. Infectious disease control – foot and mouth disease – import and export restrictions

IMPORT AND EXPORT RESTRICTIONS (FOOT-AND-MOUTH DISEASE) (SCOTLAND) AMENDMENT (NO.4) REGULATIONS 2001, SSI 2001 158; made under the European Communities Act 1972 s.2. In force: April 19, 2001 at 9.00pm; £1.75.

These Regulations amend the Import and Export Restrictions (Foot-and-Mouth Disease) (Scotland) Regulations 2001 (SSI 2001 95 as amended by SSI 2001 112, SSI 2001 127 and SSI 2001 141). They amend the restrictions requiring certain certification to accompany meat products, milk, milk products and animal products and implement in Scotland Commission Decision 2001/316 ([2001] OJ L109/72) and Decision 2001/318 ([2001] OJ L109/75) concerning certain protective measures with regard to foot-and-mouth disease in the UK.

6173. Infectious disease control – foot and mouth disease – import and export restrictions

IMPORT AND EXPORT RESTRICTIONS (FOOT-AND-MOUTH DISEASE) (SCOTLAND) AMENDMENT (NO.5) REGULATIONS 2001, SSI 2001 178; made under the European Communities Act 1972 s.2. In force: May 9, 2001 at 6.00pm; £1.75.

These Regulations, which amend the Import and Export Restrictions (Foot-and-Mouth Disease) (Scotland) Regulations 2001 (SSI 2001 95), implement in Scotland a change in the restrictions on imports and exports of certain animals and animal products in accordance with Commission Decision 2001/356 ([2001] OJ L125/46) concerning certain protection measures with regard to foot and mouth disease in the UK and repealing Commission Decision 2001/172 ([2001] OJ L62/22). The Regulations continue to regulate the export of biungulates, equidae, fresh meat, meat products, milk, milk products and make alterations to the restrictions in relation to fresh meat exports, the sterilization of milk, the endorsement of commercial documents and the powers of inspectors.

6174. Infectious disease control – foot and mouth disease – import and export restrictions

IMPORT AND EXPORT RESTRICTIONS (FOOT-AND-MOUTH DISEASE) (SCOTLAND) REGULATIONS 2001, SSI 2001 95; made under the European Communities Act 1972 s.2. In force: March 9, 2001 at 11.50pm; £2.50.

These Regulations implement in Scotland restrictions on imports and exports of certain animals and animal products in accordance with Commission Decision 2001/190 ([2001] OJ L67/88) amending Decision 2001/172 ([2001] OJ L62/22) concerning certain protection measures with regard to foot and mouth disease in the UK. They revoke the Export Restrictions (Foot-and-Mouth Disease) Regulations 2001 (SI 2001 498), the Export Restrictions (Foot-and-Mouth Disease) (Amendment) Regulations 2001 (SI 2001 627), in so far as they apply in Scotland, and the Export Restrictions (Foot-and-Mouth Disease)

Amendment (Scotland) Regulations 2001 (SSI 2001 61). They prohibit the import and export of specified live animals and restrict the export of fresh meat, meat products, milk, milk products, semen and embryos from biungulate animals, hides and skins, and animal products. The restrictions differ from the previous Regulations in that the veterinary certificate required for the export of these products can in some circumstances be replaced by a commercial certificate. They also provide for certain products in transit, and products made from pre-processed products originating outside the UK; require a certification for exports to third countries as well as to other Member State; give inspectors appointed by the Scottish Ministers powers to enter premises and carry out examinations; empower the Scottish Ministers to stop and detain vehicles and vessels pending examination by an inspector; introduce a notice procedure whereby an inspector can prohibit export of a consignment if the inspector is not satisfied that products comply with these Regulations; provide that obstruction of a person carrying out duties under the Regulations is prohibited; and provide for the terms of punishment, by individuals and bodies corporate for breach of the Regulations.

6175. Infectious disease control – foot and mouth disease – import and export restrictions

IMPORT AND EXPORT RESTRICTIONS (FOOT-AND-MOUTH DISEASE) (SCOTLAND) (NO.2) AMENDMENT REGULATIONS 2001, SSI 2001 243; made under the European Communities Act 1972 s.2. In force: June 19, 2001 at 8.00pm; £1.75.

These Regulations, which amend the restriction on imports and exports of certain animals and animal products contained in the Import and Export Restrictions (Foot-and-Mouth Disease) (Scotland) (No.2) Regulations 2001 (SSI 2001 186), implement Commission Decision 2001/415 ([2001] OJ L149/38), Commission Decision 2001/430 ([2001] OJ L153/33) and Commission Decision 2001/356 ([2001] OJ L154/66). They make further changes in relation to the restrictions on import and export to the restrictions on the export of horses, allow for the export of certain animals and animal products if the meat and milk processed originated in Northern Ireland and the Isle of Man and otherwise enable the lifting of the restrictions in those territories, and lift certain restrictions on frozen bovine semen and embryos.

6176. Infectious disease control – foot and mouth disease – import and export restrictions

IMPORT AND EXPORT RESTRICTIONS (FOOT-AND-MOUTH DISEASE) (SCOTLAND) (NO.2) AMENDMENT (NO.2) REGULATIONS 2001, SSI 2001 271; made under the European Communities Act 1972 s.2. In force: July 20, 2001 at 8 pm; £1.75.

These Regulations, which amend the Import and Export Restrictions (Foot-and-Mouth Disease) (Scotland) (No.2) Regulations 2001 (SSI 2001 186) and the Import and Export Restrictions (Foot-and-Mouth Disease) (Scotland) (No.2) Amendment Regulations 2001 (SSI 2001 243), to continue the effect of those restrictions until midnight on September 30, 2001, implement Commission Decision 2001/518 ([2001] OJ L186/58) and Decision 2001/547 ([2001] OJ L195/61). The Regulations make further changes to clarify the application of those restrictions to consignments, to permit consolidated consignments in certain circumstances, to provide that restrictions on the export of horses apply from premises subject to Form D and to prohibit offering to dispatch or export, or accept orders to dispatch or export, in contravention of the principal Regulations.

6177. Infectious disease control – foot and mouth disease – import and export restrictions

IMPORT AND EXPORT RESTRICTIONS (FOOT-AND-MOUTH DISEASE) (SCOTLAND) (NO.2) AMENDMENT (NO.3) REGULATIONS 2001, SSI 2001

367; made under the European Communities Act 1972 s.2. In force: September 30, 2001 at 8 pm; £1.75.

These Regulations amend the Import and Export Restrictions (Foot-and-Mouth Disease) (Scotland) (No.2) Regulations 2001 (SSI 2001 186), the Import and Export Restrictions (Foot-and-Mouth Disease) (Scotland) (No.2) Amendment Regulations 2001 (SSI 2001 243) to continue the effect of those restrictions until November 30, 2001 and the Import and Export Restrictions (Foot-and-Mouth Disease) (Scotland) (No.2) Amendment (No.2) Regulations 2001 (SSI 2001 271). In addition, they permit the dispatch of frozen bovine semen produced after September 30, 2001 in accordance with specified conditions in a semen collection centre authorised by the Scottish Ministers to dispatch such semen and also require horses dispatched from Scotland to Northern Ireland or the Isle of Man to be accompanied by a health certificate.

6178. Infectious disease control – foot and mouth disease – import and export restrictions

IMPORT AND EXPORT RESTRICTIONS (FOOT-AND-MOUTH DISEASE) (SCOTLAND) (NO.2) AMENDMENT (NO.4) REGULATIONS 2001, SSI 2001 394; made under the European Communities Act 1972 s.2. In force: October 24, 2001 at 5 pm; £2.50.

These Regulations amend the Meat Products (Hygiene) Regulations 1994 (SI 1994 3082), the Fresh Meat (Hygiene and Inspection) Regulations 1995 (SI 1995 539), the Minced Meat and Meat Preparations (Hygiene) Regulations 1995 (SI 1995 3205), the Import and Export Restrictions (Foot-and-Mouth Disease) (Scotland) (No.2) Regulations 2001 (SSI 2001 186), the Import and Export Restrictions (Foot-and-Mouth Disease) (Scotland) (No.2) Amendment Regulations 2001 (SSI 2001 243), the Import and Export Restrictions (Foot-and-Mouth Disease) (Scotland) (No.2) Amendment (No.2) Regulations 2001 (SSI 2001 271), the Foot-and-Mouth Disease (Marking of Meat, Meat Products, Minced Meat and Meat Preparations) (Scotland) Regulations 2001 (SSI 2001 358) and the Import and Export Restrictions (Foot-and-Mouth Disease) (Scotland) (No.2) Amendment (No.3) Regulations 2001 (SSI 2001 367). The Regulations implement in Scotland, Commission Decision 2001/740 ([2001] OJ L227/30) concerning certain protection measures with regard to foot and mouth disease in the UK and repealing Commission Decision 2001/356. They amend the restrictions on imports and exports of certain animals and animal products to continue the effect of those restrictions until December 31, 2001. In addition, they make provision to amend the restrictions to permit the dispatch from Scotland of pig meat from certain areas, subject to compliance with certain restrictions, to permit the dispatch of certain milk products, and to permit the dispatch of frozen porcine semen produced after September 30, 2001 in accordance with specified conditions in a semen collection centre authorised by the Scottish Ministers to dispatch such semen.

6179. Infectious disease control – foot and mouth disease – import and export restrictions

IMPORT AND EXPORT RESTRICTIONS (FOOT-AND-MOUTH DISEASE) (SCOTLAND) (NO.2) AMENDMENT (NO.5) REGULATIONS 2001, SSI 2001 415; made under the European Communities Act 1972 s.2. In force: November 7, 2001 at 2 pm; £2.50.

These Regulations implement, in Scotland, Commission Decision 2001/763 amending Commission Decision 2001/740 concerning certain protection measures with regard to foot and mouth disease in the UK for the first time. They amend the restrictions on imports and exports of certain animals and animal products contained in the Import and Export Restrictions (Foot-and-Mouth Disease) (Scotland) (No.2) Regulations 2001 (SSI 2001 186) to permit the dispatch from Scotland of pig meat from those areas of Scotland from which such exports were prohibited, and to permit the dispatch of beef from certain areas of Scotland.

6180. Infectious disease control – foot and mouth disease – import and export restrictions

IMPORT AND EXPORT RESTRICTIONS (FOOT-AND-MOUTH DISEASE) (SCOTLAND) (NO.2) REGULATIONS 2001, SSI 2001 186; made under the European Communities Act 1972 s.2. In force: May 18, 2001 at 8.00pm; £2.50.

These Regulations revoke the Import and Export Restrictions (Foot-and-Mouth Disease) (Scotland) Regulations 2001 (SSI 2001 95), the Import and Export Restriction (Foot-and-Mouth Disease) (Scotland) Amendment Regulations 2001 (SSI 2001 112), the Import and Export Restrictions (Foot-and-Mouth Disease) (Scotland) Amendment (No.2) Regulations 2001 (SSI 2001 127), the Import and Export Restrictions (Foot-and-Mouth Disease) (Scotland) Amendment (No.3) Regulations 2001 (SSI 2001 141), the Import and Export Restrictions (Foot-and-Mouth Disease) (Scotland) Amendment (No.4) Regulations 2001 (SSI 2001 158) and the Import and Export Restrictions (Foot-and-Mouth Disease) (Scotland) Amendment (No.5) Regulations 2001 (SSI 2001 178). They implement the continuation of restrictions on imports and exports of certain animals and animal products in accordance with Commission Decision 2001/372 ([2001] OJ L125/46), prohibit the import and export of specified live animals and restrict the export of fresh meat, meat products, milk, milk products, semen and embryos from biungulate animals, hides and skins, and animal products.

6181. Infectious disease control – foot and mouth disease – import and export restrictions

IMPORT AND EXPORT RESTRICTIONS (FOOT-AND-MOUTH DISEASE) (SCOTLAND) (NO.3) REGULATIONS 2001, SSI 2001 429; made under the European Communities Act 1972 s.2. In force: November 20, 2001 at 1.30 pm; £4.50.

These Regulations implement the continuation of restrictions on imports and exports of certain animals and animal products in accordance with Commission Decision 2001/789 ([2001] OJ L295/25) amending for the second time Commission Decision 2001/740 concerning certain protection measures with regard to foot and mouth disease in the UK. They prohibit the import and export of specified live animals and restrict the export of fresh meat, meat products, milk, milk products, semen, ova and embryos from biungulate animals, hides and skins, and animal products.

6182. Infectious disease control – foot and mouth disease – import and export restrictions

IMPORT AND EXPORT RESTRICTIONS (FOOT-AND-MOUTH DISEASE) (SCOTLAND) (RECOVERY OF COSTS) REGULATIONS 2001, SSI 2001 401; made under the European Communities Act 1972 s.2. In force: October 30, 2001 at 3 pm; £1.50.

These Regulations permit the Scottish Ministers to recover reasonable costs for supervision or inspections carried out for the purposes of dispatch of products under the Import and Export Restrictions (Foot-and-Mouth Disease) (Scotland) (No.2) Regulations 2001 (SSI 2001 186), in implementation of Commission Decision 2001/740 ([2001] OJ L277/30).

6183. Infectious disease control – foot and mouth disease – marking of meat

FOOT-AND-MOUTH DISEASE (MARKING OF MEAT, MEAT PRODUCTS, MINCED MEAT AND MEAT PREPARATIONS) (SCOTLAND) REGULATIONS 2001, SSI 2001 358; made under the European Communities Act 1972 s.2. In force: November 12, 2001; £1.75.

These Regulations, which amend the Meat Products (Hygiene) Regulations 1994 (SI 1994 3082), the Fresh Meat (Hygiene and Inspection) Regulations 1995 (SI 1995 539), the Minced Meat and Meat Preparations (Hygiene) Regulations 1995 (SI 1995 3205) and the Foot-and-Mouth Disease (Marking of

Meat and Meal Products) (Scotland) Regulations 2001 (SSI 2001 16), implement Commission Decision 2001/345 ([2001] OJ L122/31) on marking and use of certain animal products relating to Commission Decision 2001/172 ([2001] OJ L125/46) concerning certain protection measures with regard to foot and mouth disease in the UK. The Regulations clarify the use of the round national health mark in relation to all meat products handled in GB made from meat from species susceptible to foot and mouth disease.

6184. Infectious disease control – foot and mouth disease – movement of animals
FOOT-AND-MOUTH DISEASE (AMENDMENT) (NO.3) (SCOTLAND) ORDER 2001, SSI 2001 101; made under the Animal Health Act 1981 s.1, s.2, s.8, s.23. In force: March 14, 2001 at 6.00pm; £1.75.

This Order amends the Foot-and-Mouth Disease Order 1983 (SI 1983 1950) to allow animals to be moved through areas where disease is suspected, notwithstanding that the area is under the restrictions of a Form C Notice, provided such movement is by motorway, trunk road or rail and that the animals are not unloaded in the area under restriction.

6185. Infectious disease control – foot and mouth disease – movement of animals
FOOT-AND-MOUTH DISEASE (SCOTLAND) DECLARATORY AMENDMENT ORDER 2001, SSI 2001 63; made under the Foot-and-Mouth Disease Order (SI 1983 1950) Art.17. In force: March 4, 2001 at 7.00pm; £1.50.

This Order amends the Foot-and-Mouth Disease (Scotland) Declaratory Order 2001 (SSI 2001 56) and the Foot-and-Mouth Disease (Scotland) Declaratory (No.2) Order 2001 (SSI 2001 59) which declare areas under the Foot-and-Mouth Disease Order 1983 (SI 1983 1950) Part III in order to permit the transit of animals through those infected areas by motorway, trunk road or railway. These amendments are in consequence of the Foot-and-Mouth Disease Declaratory (Controlled Area) (Scotland) (No.2) Order 2001 (SSI 2001 60).

6186. Infectious disease control – foot and mouth disease – movement of animals
FOOT-AND-MOUTH DISEASE (SCOTLAND) (DECLARATORY ORDERS) GENERAL AMENDMENT ORDER 2001, SSI 2001 109; made under the Foot-and-Mouth Disease Order 1983 (SI 1983 1950) Art.17. In force: March 16, 2001, at 9.00pm; £1.75.

This Order amends the Foot-and-Mouth Disease (Scotland) Declaratory Order 2001 (SSI 2001 56) and the Foot-and-Mouth Disease (Scotland) Declaratory (No.2) Order 2001 (SSI 2001 59) by removing requirements for certain movement licences to be in a form specified in the Foot-and-Mouth Disease Order 1983 (SI 1983 1950) Sch.3 Part I and substitutes a new requirement that no person shall seek to carry out the breeding of animals by artificial insemination except where the semen to be used is on the premises where the animals are kept or has been delivered to those premises under licence.

6187. Infectious disease control – foot and mouth disease – movement of animals
FOOT-AND-MOUTH DISEASE (SCOTLAND) (DECLARATORY ORDERS) GENERAL AMENDMENT (NO.2) ORDER 2001, SSI 2001 258; made under the Foot-and-Mouth Disease Order 1983 (SI 1983 1950) Art.17. In force: July 2, 2001 at 5 pm; £1.50.

This Order, which amends the Foot-and-Mouth Disease (Scotland) Declaratory (No.5) Order 2001 (SSI 2001 165), the Foot-and-Mouth Disease (Scotland) Declaratory (No.6) Order 2001 (SSI 2001 168) and the Foot-and-Mouth Disease (Scotland) Declaratory (No.7) Order 2001 (SSI 2001 193), provides that licences for movement of animals direct to approved slaughterhouses out of the infected areas which may be issued by a veterinary inspector, may also be issued by an inspector appointed by the Scottish Ministers or by a local authority.

6188. Infectious disease control – foot and mouth disease – prohibition of movement

FOOD-AND-MOUTH DISEASE (AMENDMENT) (SCOTLAND) ORDER 2001, SSI 2001 52; made under the Animal Health Act 1981 s.1, s.23, s.83. In force: February 27, 2001 at 3.00pm; £1.75.

This Order amends the Foot-and-Mouth Disease Order 1983 (SI 1983 1950) to allow inspectors to prohibit by notice the entry of any person onto any land or into any agricultural building in a controlled area, for the purposes of preventing the spreading of foot and mouth disease. The Order allows local authorities in areas where the foot and mouth disease has been confirmed to make declarations prohibiting the movement of persons into or out of specified areas except on public roads.

6189. Infectious disease control – foot and mouth disease – prohibition of movement

FOOT-AND-MOUTH DISEASE (AMENDMENT) (NO. 2) (SCOTLAND) ORDER 2001, SSI 2001 55; made under the Animal Health Act 1981 s.1, s.2, s.23. In force: March 1, 2001 at 8.00pm; £1.50.

This Order, which amends the Foot-and-Mouth Disease Order 1983 (SI 1983 1950), allows local authorities in areas where foot and mouth disease has been confirmed to make regulations prohibiting the movement of persons into or out of specified areas except on public roads. In areas where foot and mouth disease has not been confirmed the local authority may make such regulations with the consent of the Scottish Ministers.

6190. Infectious disease control – foot and mouth disease – vaccination control

FOOT-AND-MOUTH DISEASE (CONTROL OF VACCINATION) (SCOTLAND) REGULATIONS 2001, SSI 2001 261; made under the European Communities Act 1972 s.2. In force: July 10, 2001; £1.75.

These Regulations, which implement in Scotland Council Directive 85/511 ([1985] OJ L135/11) introducing Community measures for the control of foot and mouth disease, prohibit vaccination against foot and mouth disease in Scotland except in accordance with the conditions of a licence issued by the Scottish Ministers, but exempting vaccination licensed under the Specified Pathogens Order 1998 (SI 1998 463) by the Scottish Ministers. The Regulations make provisions for powers of inspectors and offences of obstruction in relation to the enforcement of these Regulations and make provision for offences by bodies corporate.

6191. Milk – pupils in educational establishments

MILK AND MILK PRODUCTS (PUPILS IN EDUCATIONAL ESTABLISHMENTS) (SCOTLAND) REGULATIONS 2001, SSI 2001 162; made under the European Communities Act 1972 s.2. In force: May 15, 2001; £1.75.

These Regulations provide that, in the making of national "top up" aid payments as permitted by Council Regulation 1255/1999 ([1999] OJ L160/48) on the common organisation of the market in milk and milk products, as amended, for the supply of milk and milk products to pupils in educational establishments, such payments shall be subject to the same rules, requirements and conditions as apply to Community aid. In addition, they provide for the withholding or recovery of any Community aid or any national payments to which an applicant is not entitled or where the applicant is in breach of any commitments given as a condition of such Community aid or payment.

6192. Pesticides – residue levels in crops – food and feedingstuffs

PESTICIDES (MAXIMUM RESIDUE LEVELS IN CROPS, FOOD AND FEEDING STUFFS) (SCOTLAND) AMENDMENT (NO.3) REGULATIONS 2001, SSI 2001

435; made under the European Communities Act 1972 s.2. In force: in accordance with Reg.1 (2) (3); £2.50.

These Regulations, which amend the Pesticides (Maximum Residue Levels in Crops, Food and Feeding Stuffs) (Scotland) Regulations 2000 (SSI 2000 22) and the Pesticides (Maximum Residue levels in Crops, Food and Feeding Stuffs) (Scotland) Amendment (No.2) Regulations 2001 (SSI 2001 221), specify maximum levels which crops, food and feedingstuffs may contain in implementation of Commission Directive 2001/39 ([2001] OJ L148/70), Commission Directive 2001/48 ([2001] OJ L180/26), and Commission Directive 2001/57 ([2001] OJ L208/36). The maximum level for iprodione on spring onions is amended to reflect Commission Directive 98/82 ([1998] OJ L290/25) and the maximum level for spiroxamine on liver and kidney is amended to reflect Commission Directive 2000/81 ([2000] OJ L326/56).

6193. **Pesticides – residue levels in crops, food and feedingstuffs**

PESTICIDES (MAXIMUM RESIDUE LEVELS IN CROPS, FOOD AND FEEDING STUFFS) (SCOTLAND) AMENDMENT REGULATIONS 2001, SSI 2001 84; made under the European Communities Act 1972 s.2. In force: April 1, 2001; £16.50.

These Regulations, which amend the provisions of the Pesticides (Maximum Residue Levels in Crops, Food and Feeding Stuffs) (Scotland) Regulations 2000 (SSI 2000 22), specify maximum levels of pesticide residues which crops, food and feedingstuffs may contain in implementation of Commission Directive 2000/24 ([2000] OJ L107/28), Commission Directive 2000/42 (([2000] OJ L158/51), Commission Directive 2000/48 ([2000] OJ L197/26), Commission Directive 2000/57 ([2000] OJ L244/76) and Commission Directive 2000/58 ([2000] OJ L244/78).

6194. **Pesticides – residue levels in crops, food and feedingstuffs**

PESTICIDES (MAXIMUM RESIDUE LEVELS IN CROPS, FOOD AND FEEDING STUFFS) (SCOTLAND) AMENDMENT (NO.2) REGULATIONS 2001, SSI 2001 221; made under the European Communities Act 1972 s.2. In force: July 2, 2001; £2.00.

These Regulations, which amend the Pesticides (Maximum Residue Levels in Crops, Food and Feeding Stuffs) (Scotland) Regulations 2000 (SSI 2000 22), specify maximum levels of pesticide residues which crops, food and feeding stuffs may contain in implementation of Commission Directive 2000/57 ([2000] OJ L244/76), Commission Directive 2000/81 ([2000] OJ L326/56), Commission Directive 2000/82 ([2001] OJ L3/18) and Commission Directive 2001/35 ([2001] OJ L136/42).

6195. **Pig Industry Development Scheme 2000**

See AGRICULTURE. §270

6196. **Plants – plant health – protected zones**

PLANT HEALTH (GREAT BRITAIN) (AMENDMENT) (SCOTLAND) ORDER 2001, SSI 2001 249; made under the European Communities Act 1972 s.2. In force: September 18, 2001; £1.75.

This Order, which amends the Plant Health (Great Britain) Order 1993 (SI 1993 1320), implements Commission Directive 2001/32 ([2001] OJ L127/38) which recognises protected zones exposed to particular plant health risks in the Community, and Commission Directive 2001/33 ([2001] OJ L127/42) which amends certain annexes to Council Directive 2000/29 ([2000] OJ L169/1) on protective measures against the introduction into the Community of organisms harmful to plants or plant products and against their spread within the Community.

6197. Plants – plant protection products – marketing

PLANT PROTECTION PRODUCTS AMENDMENT (NO.2) (SCOTLAND) REGULATIONS 2001, SSI 2001 202; made under the European Communities Act 1972 s.2; and the Finance Act 1973 s.56. In force: August 1, 2001; £1.75.

These Regulations further amend the Plant Protection Products Regulations 1995 (SI 1995 887), which implement Council Directive 91/414 ([1991] OJ L230/1) concerning the placing of plant protection products on the market. The Regulations amend the definition of "the Directive" in the 1995 Regulations so as to implement Commission Directive 2000/80 ([2000] OJ L309/14) from July 1, 2002, Commission Directive 2001/21 ([2001] OJ L69/17) from July 1, 2002 and Commission Directive 2001/28 ([2001] OJ L113/5) which add lambda-cyhalothrin, amitrole, diquat, pyridate, thiabendazote and fenhaxamid to Annex I to the Directive. The Regulations also make consequential amendments to the Plant Protection Products (Fees) Regulations 1995 (SI 1995 888) and revoke the Plant Protection Products Amendment (Scotland) Regulations 2001 (SI 2001 161) Reg.2(a).

6198. Plants – plant protection products – marketing

PLANT PROTECTION PRODUCTS AMENDMENT (NO.3) (SCOTLAND) REGULATIONS 2001, SSI 2001 454; made under the European Communities Act 1972 s.2. In force: in accordance with Reg.1 (2)(3); £1.75.

These Regulations amend the Plant Protection Products Regulations 1995 (SI 1995 887) by amending the definition of "the Directive" in the 1995 Regulations so as to implement Commission Directive 2000/80 ([2000] OJ L309/14) which revokes a number of Directives that amended Council Directive 1991/414 ([1991] OJ L230/1) and which amendments are consolidated in that Directive. They add amitrole, diquat, pyridate, thiabendazole, paecilomyces fumosoroseus and flupyrsulfuron-methyl to Annex I of the 1991 Directive; enable the Scottish Ministers to arrange, with the agreement of the UK Ministers, for any of their functions under or for the purposes of the 1995 Regulations or the 1991 Directive to be exercised on their behalf by a Minister of the Crown; and revoke the Plant Protection Products Amendment (No.2) (Scotland) Regulations 2001 (SSI 2001 161).

6199. Plants – plant protection products – marketing

PLANT PROTECTION PRODUCTS AMENDMENT (SCOTLAND) REGULATIONS 2001, SSI 2001 161; made under the European Communities Act 1972 s.2; and the Finance Act 1973 s.56. In force: May 14, 2001; £1.75.

These Regulations amend the Plant Protection Products Regulations 1995 (SI 1995 887) which implement Council Directive 91/414 ([1991] OJ L230/1) concerning the placing of plant protection products on the market. They amend the definition of "the Directive" in the 1995 Regulations to implement Commission Directive 2000/10 ([2000] OJ L57/28), Commission Directive 2000/49 ([2000] OJ L197/32), Commission Directive 2000/50 ([2000] OJ L198/39), Commission Directive 2000/66 ([2000] OJ L276/35), Commission Directive 2000/67 ([2000] OJ L276/38), and Commission Directive 2000/68 ([2000] OJ L276/41) which add fluroxypyr, metsulfuron-methyl, prohexadione-calcium, triasulfuron, esfenvalerate and bentazone respectively to Annex I to the Directive. The Regulations allow the Scottish Ministers to arrange with the Minister of Agriculture, Fisheries and Food and the Secretary of State acting jointly, for the discharge of any functions of the Scottish Ministers under the Regulations to be exercised on their behalf by a Minister of the Crown. In addition, they revoke the Plant Protection Products (Amendment) (No.2) Regulations 1999 (SI 1999 3430).

6200. Potatoes – import controls – notice – Germany

POTATOES ORIGINATING IN GERMANY (NOTIFICATION) (SCOTLAND) ORDER 2001, SSI 2001 333; made under the Plant Health Act 1967 s.2, s.3, s.4;

and the Agriculture (Miscellaneous Provisions) Act 1972. In force: October 15, 2001; £1.75.

This Order, which extends to Scotland only, places certain notification requirements upon persons who import potatoes from Germany which have been grown during 2001 or subsequently. The Order requires persons who import such potatoes into Scotland on or after October 18, 2001 to give at least 48 hours prior written notice to an inspector authorised by the Scottish Ministers, providing specified information as to, for example, the landing and intended use of the potatoes. Any person who has imported such potatoes on or after October 1, 2001 but prior to October 18, 2001 must provide specified information of a similar nature to an inspector by November 1, 2001.

6201. Potatoes – imports – infectious disease control – Egypt

POTATOES ORIGINATING IN EGYPT (SCOTLAND) REGULATIONS 2001, SSI 2001 421; made under the European Communities Act 1972 s.2. In force: December 3, 2001; £2.00.

These Regulations consolidate with amendments the Potatoes Originating in Egypt Regulations 1998 and implement Commission Decision 96/301 (as amended) authorising Member States temporarily to take additional measures against the dissemination of Pseudomonas solanacearum (Smith) Smith (now referred to as Ralstonia solanacearum (Smith) Yabuuchi et al.) as regards Egypt.

6202. Rural areas – grant assistance programmes – time extensions – Highlands and Islands

HIGHLANDS AND ISLANDS AGRICULTURAL PROGRAMME AND RURAL DIVERSIFICATION PROGRAMME (SCOTLAND) AMENDMENT REGULATIONS 2001, SSI 2001 319; made under the European Communities Act 1972 s.2. In force: October 30, 2001; £1.75.

These Regulations amend the Highlands and Islands Agricultural Programme and the Rural Diversification Programme as a consequence of the necessary restrictions in place as a result of foot and mouth disease, which has meant that many farmers have not been able to complete projects grant assisted under these programmes in the time scales specified in the particular grant approval. The Scottish Ministers have agreed to delay the dates for completion of such projects. In order to do so, these Regulations, which amend the Highlands and Islands Agricultural Programme Regulations 1994 (SI 1994 3096), extend the end dates for the making of claims for assistance under these programmes.

6203. Rural areas – Less Favoured Area Support Scheme

LESS FAVOURED AREA SUPPORT SCHEME (SCOTLAND) REGULATIONS 2001, SSI 2001 50; made under the European Communities Act 1972 s.2. In force: March 19, 2001; £3.50.

These Regulations, which make provision for the purposes of implementation of Council Regulation 1257/1999 ([1999] OJ L160/80) on support for rural development from the European Agricultural Guidance and Guarantee Fund and Commission Regulation 1750/1999 ([1999] OJ L214/31) laying down detailed rules for the application of Regulation 1257/1999, apply to holdings which are administered by the Scottish Ministers under the Integrated Administration and Control System Regulations 1993 (SI 1993 1317). The Agricultural Subsidies (Appeals) (Scotland) Regulations 2000 (SSI 2000 347) and the Hill Livestock (Compensatory Allowances) (Scotland) Regulations (SSI 1999 185) are revoked with savings.

6204. Rural areas – Rural Diversification Programme – time extensions

RURAL DIVERSIFICATION PROGRAMME (SCOTLAND) AMENDMENT REGULATIONS 2001, SSI 2001 484; made under the European Communities Act 1972 s.2. In force: December 31, 2001 at 8 pm; £1.75.

These Regulations make further amendments to the Rural Diversification Programme in relation to Dumfries and Galloway and the Scottish Borders as a consequence of the necessary restrictions in place as a result of foot and mouth disease, which have meant that many farmers in these areas have not been able to complete projects grant assisted under the Programme in the time scale specified in the particular grant approval. In addition, they amend the Rural Diversification Programme (Scotland) Regulations 1995 (SI 1995 3295) due to the need to allow for time for consideration of requests and for continuity.

6205. Rural areas – stewardship

RURAL STEWARDSHIP SCHEME (SCOTLAND) REGULATIONS 2001, SSI 2001 300; made under the European Communities Act 1972 s.2; and the Environment Act 1995 s.98. In force: September 28, 2001; £6.50.

These Regulations, which amend the Agricultural Subsidies (Appeals) (Scotland) Regulations 2000 (SSI 2000 347), implement Commission Decision 1750/1999 ([1999] OJ L214/31) which prescribes detailed rules for the application of Council Regulation 1257/1999 ([1999] OJ L160/80) on support for rural development from the European Agricultural Guidance and Guarantee Fund. The Regulations provide for payments of aid to be made to any person who enters into an undertaking with the Scottish Ministers to comply with specified environmental requirements and to carry out and maintain at least one of specified management or capital activities.

6206. Subsidies – appeals

AGRICULTURAL SUBSIDIES (APPEALS) (SCOTLAND) AMENDMENT REGULATIONS 2001, SSI 2001 226; made under the European Communities Act 1972 s.2. In force: Reg.5(4): June 9, 2001; remainder: June 29, 2001; £2.00.

These Regulations amend the Environmentally Sensitive Areas (Loch Lomond) Designation Order 1992 (SI 1992 1919), the Environmentally Sensitive Areas (Breadalbane) Designation Order 1992 (SI 1992 1920), the Environmentally Sensitive Areas (Central Southern Uplands) Designation Order 1993 (SI 1993 996), the Environmentally Sensitive Areas (Western Southern Uplands) Designation Order 1993 (SI 1993 997), the Environmentally Sensitive Areas (Cairngorms Straths) Designation Order 1993 (SI 1993 2354), the Environmentally Sensitive Areas (Central Borders) Designation Order 1993 (SI 1993 2767), the Environmentally Sensitive Areas (Stewartry) Designation Order 1993 (SI 1993 2768), the Environmentally Sensitive Areas (Argyll Islands) Designation Order 1993 (SI 1993 3136), the Environmentally Sensitive Areas (Machair of the Uists and Benbecula, Barra and Vatersay) Designation Order 1993 (SI 1993 3149), the Environmentally Sensitive Areas (Shetland Islands) Designation Order 1993 (SI 1993 3150) and the Agricultural Subsidies (Appeals) (Scotland) Regulations 2000 (SSI 2000 347) to add to certain decisions to the list of those amenable to review and appeal.

ANIMALS

6207. Animal welfare – slaughter

WELFARE OF ANIMALS (SLAUGHTER OR KILLING) AMENDMENT (SCOTLAND) REGULATIONS 2001, SSI 2001 145; made under the European Communities Act 1972 s.2. In force: May 15, 2001; £1.50.

These Regulations amend the Welfare of Animals (Slaughter or Killing) Regulations 1995 (SI 1995 731) which gave effect to Council Directive 93/119

([1993] OJ L340/21) on the protection of animals at the time of slaughter or killing to permit a new gas mixture for killing surplus chicks.

6208. Diseases and disorders – approved disinfectants

DISEASES OF ANIMALS (APPROVED DISINFECTANTS) AMENDMENT (SCOTLAND) ORDER 2001, SSI 2001 45; made under the Animal Health Act 1981 s.1, s.7, s.23. In force: February 22, 2001; £1.75.

This Order, which extends to Scotland only, amends the Diseases of Animals (Approved Disinfectants) Order 1978 (SI 1978 32) by deleting the entries for a number of disinfectants from Sch.1 to that Order, by substituting replacement entries for other disinfectants and by adding an entry for one other approved disinfectant to that Schedule. In addition, it deletes Sch.2 because there are no disinfectants approved on a transitional basis, the previous transitional period having expired.

6209. Infectious disease control – approved disinfectants

DISEASES OF ANIMALS (APPROVED DISINFECTANTS) AMENDMENT (NO.2) (SCOTLAND) ORDER 2001, SSI 2001 51; made under the Animal Health Act 1981 s.1, s.7, s.23. In force: March 1, 2001 at 8.00pm; £1.75.

This Order amends the Diseases of Animals (Approved Disinfectants) Order 1978 (SI 1978 32) by adding several entries for other approved disinfectants to Sch.1.

ARBITRATION

6210. Arbiter – dispute to be referred to arbiter chosen by both parties or Dean of Faculty of Arbiters – no faculty in existence – competency of court appointment

[Arbitration (Scotland) Act 1894 (57&58 Vict, c.13) s.2.]

B, a retiring partner in a firm of solicitors, raised an action against the remaining partners in the firm for payment of his entitlement on retirement and for an account of intromissions in the partnership fund. K enrolled a motion for the proceedings to be sisted for arbitration relying on cl.17 of the partnership agreement. Clause 17 purported to provide that disputes within the partnership be referred to arbitration with an arbiter to be appointed by "both the partners" or by the "Dean of the Faculty of Arbiters". B submitted that the clause was void due to the uncertainty created by the firm now consisting of five partners and there being no institution named the Faculty of Arbiters. K argued that the clause was clearly indicative of the parties' intent that disputes should be dealt with by way of arbitration, but that there had been error in expression. K submitted that both should be read as all and that the Faculty of Arbiters should be read as the Faculty of Advocates. Finally, K submitted that failing a reinterpretation, it was open to the court to appoint an arbiter through its powers under the Arbitration (Scotland) Act 1894 s.2.

Held, refusing the motion to sist, that (1) cl.17 as a whole was void from uncertainty as it was impossible to ascertain which of the partners within the five partner firm were entitled to exercise the choice of arbiter, or if all were to be included, whether a majority or unanimous decision was required. In addition, there was no way to identify the office, which the Dean referred to held, and (2) s.2 could not operate to allow the court to appoint an arbiter where there had been no agreement between the parties for such an appointment to be made or where a purported agreement had failed to adequately identify who was entitled to make the nomination.

BRUCE v. KORDULA 2001 S.L.T. 983, Lord Hamilton, OH.

6211. Books

Davidson, Fraser P. – Arbitration. Hardback: £180.00. ISBN 0-414-01104-X. W.Green & Son.

BANKING

6212. Abolition of Poindings and Warrant Sales Act 2001 (asp 1)

An Act of the Scottish Parliament to abolish poindings and warrant sales. This Act received Royal Assent on January 17, 2001.

6213. Cheques – arrestment of funds – cheque not cleared – no arrestable obligation to account prior to clearance

M raised an action of furthcoming against A, seeking payment of £15,000, awarded in a divorce action. The funds were deposited into her husband's bank account with A by his pension trustees. On the same day M arrested the funds on the basis that A had, from that point, an obligation to account to the husband with regard to the funds paid in. A appealed against grant of decree.

Held, allowing the appeal, that the obligation of a collecting bank (A, in the instant case) was to present a cheque for payment to the paying bank. A would not at that stage be liable for anything which related to the amount for which the cheque was drawn. A would not become the obligant with regard to the original debt due by the pension trustees, but would come under a new obligation to pay the husband once the cheque had cleared and the trustees obligation, had been discharged. Until that point there could be no obligation which would be capable of attachment. Opinion of the Court per Lord Prosser.

McLAUGHLIN v. ALLIED IRISH BANK 2001 S.C. 485, Lord Prosser, Lord Cowie, Lord McCluskey, Ex Div.

6214. Cheques – designation of payee with certainty – misappropriation of cheque – designation incomplete – drawer not responsible for misappropriation

[Bills of Exchange Act 1882 (45 & 46 Vict c.61) s.81A.]

A, a company in receivership, sought payment of £12,000 from its insurers C in respect of a claim. C had issued a crossed cheque payable to "Adam Associates" which had been received by the sole director. The director also acted as sole proprietor of two other firms with similar names. Despite knowing which company the cheque was intended for, the director paid it into another account. The sheriff rejected A's receivers' argument that it was not a valid discharge of the debt, on the basis that the cheque could have been paid into and cleared in the correct account. A's receivers appealed, arguing that under the Bills of Exchange Act 1882 s.81A the cheque was only valid between C and the party named on the cheque which did not in fact exist, therefore the sheriff had erred in finding that the payee had been designed with reasonable certainty. A also argued that C's actions, whilst knowing the correct designation for the cheque, had facilitated payment of the cheque into the wrong account and as such could not hold that it had discharged its debt.

Held, refusing the appeal, that the onus of deciding whether the payee was designed with certainty lay with A, and the sheriff, in finding that the cheque could have been paid into A's account and cleared, had in effect held that the designation was valid. C were entitled to rely upon the director's integrity and nothing they had done facilitated fraud to the extent of indicating that they could be held not to have settled the debt.

ADAM ASSOCIATES (STRATHCLYDE) LTD (IN RECEIVERSHIP) v. CGU INSURANCE PLC 2001 S.L.T. (Sh Ct) 18, EF Bowen Q.C., Sheriff Principal, Sh Ct.

6215. Overdrafts – action for payment – obligation not enforceable until action raised

See PRESCRIPTION: Royal Bank of Scotland Plc v. Home. §6867

6216. Books

Grier, Nicholas – Banking Law in Scotland. Greens Practice Library. Hardback: £80.00. ISBN 0-414-01309-3. W.Green & Son.

CIVIL EVIDENCE

6217. Admissibility – hearsay evidence – statement of child

[Civil Evidence (Scotland) Act 1988 (c.32) s.2(1)(b).]

T's application for a contact order in respect of his daughter E and an order depriving T of his parental responsibilities and rights was refused by the sheriff. T appealed and the appeal was remitted to a court of five judges to consider the proper interpretation of the Civil Evidence (Scotland) Act 1988 s.2(1)(b). A critical element of the sheriff's decision related to evidence led by a police officer, on behalf of E's mother (M), regarding answers given by E at an interview shortly after her fourth birthday. E's comments indicated that she had been sexually abused by T during a contact visit at the house of T's mother. E was called at the proof to allow the sheriff to assess whether or not she knew the difference between truth and falsehood. The sheriff found E to be a credible witness. Issues arose as to whether or not (1) the child was a competent witness, and (2) the question of competence fell to be determined by reference to E's competence at the time of the proof (as held by the sheriff and as argued by M, relying on *F (A Parent) v. Kennedy (Reporter to the Children's Panel) (No.1)* 1992 S.C. 28, [1992] C.L.Y. 5729, and *L v. L* 1996 S.L.T. 767, [1996] C.L.Y. 6627), or to her competence at the time of the police interview (as argued by T). T further argued that (1) if s.2(1)(b) was to be interpreted as not imposing any test of competency, then it would lead to the undesirable consequence that a judge or jury might have to hear evidence of the statement of a child who could not distinguish truth from falsehood, and (2) the sheriff's interlocutor depriving T of all rights and responsibilities had been unnecessarily sweeping.

Held, allowing the appeal and remitting the case to the sheriff to proceed as accords, that (1) it was clear from s.2(1)(b) that "admissible" referred to the content of statements and evidence and not to the competence of the parties making the statement or giving the evidence. The subsection performed a vital role in preventing the leading of hearsay evidence of a person making a statement about a matter as to which his direct oral evidence would not be admissible. There was nothing in its language which suggested that it should be given an extended meaning relating to the legal incapacity of witnesses. If Parliament had intended to incorporate a competency test it would have been expressly stated, *F v. Kennedy* and *L v. L* overruled; (2) a child might be unable to pass the test of competence to give evidence, but what he had to say might still be compelling. The res gestae and de recenti rules were not, as suggested by T, still applicable and available to counter that effect. Admissibility of hearsay depended on the 1988 Act, not common law; (3) the sheriff was correct to admit the evidence of what E had said to the police officer, but did so for the wrong reason. The correct reason was that it was hearsay evidence which was admissible in terms of s.2(1)(a), because there was no reason to exclude it, and it did not relate to a matter of which direct evidence, if given by E, would have been inadmissible; (4) the reasons given by the sheriff for his decision depriving T of all parental rights and responsibilities were not satisfactory and he had not taken proper advantage of having seen and heard the witnesses, *Clarke v. Edinburgh and District Tramways Co Ltd* 1919 1 S.L.T. 247 and *Thomas v. Thomas* [1947] A.C. 484 applied, and (5) as the court was in no position to reach a view on the matters in dispute between the parties, the case required to be remitted to a different sheriff.

MT v. DT; *sub nom*. T v. T 2001 S.C. 337, Lord Rodger L.P., Lord Allanbridge, Lord Bonomy, Lord Milligan, Lord Nimmo Smith, (IH) Ct of 5 judges.

6218. Expert evidence – medical negligence – proper procedure

Observed, that in medical negligence cases it would be desirable for the pursuer to call the allegedly negligent doctor as an early witness thereby giving the witnesses opportunity to comment. In the present case S was not led as a witness for M, nor was any other direct evidence led in connection to what S had done or why he had done it. Instead, expert witnesses gave opinion evidence based on M's records. That led to misunderstanding, the records being either misconstrued or incomplete and inaccurate. That clearly affected and could have invalidated, the opinions expressed by a doctor in his written reports and in his evidence-in-chief. S gave evidence that the records were not a complete account of his actions or his thoughts and that some of the records had been misconstrued by M's witnesses. The Lord Ordinary opined that the court should treat with caution submissions made on the basis that hospital records must be a complete record of events. Hospital records are not maintained by lawyers, for the use of lawyers, they are maintained for medical purposes and the courts should not give any encouragement to the development of "defensive" record keeping. The danger with regard to the use of records in this manner was pointed out in *Muir v. Grampian Health Board* 2000 G.W.D. 12-442 and *Loughran v. Lanarkshire Acute Hospitals NHS Trust* 2000 Rep. L.R. 58 (Note), [2000] C.L.Y. 6592. Calling the allegedly negligent doctor early would also lead to a more efficient disposal of cases, both parties would be in a better position to assess their prospects of success and public interest would be better served by reducing the days medical practitioners spend in court.

McCONNELL v. AYRSHIRE AND ARRAN HEALTH BOARD 2001 Rep. L.R. 85, Lord Reed, OH.

CIVIL PROCEDURE

6219. Actions – counterclaims – assignation of right – incompetent for assignee to pursue counterclaim while defender remained party to principal action

[Act of Sederunt (Rules of the Court of Session 1994) 1994 (SI 1994 1443) r.25.4(2); Court of Session Act 1988 (c.36) s.6.]

T raised an action for payment against A for sums they claimed were due. A counterclaimed in respect of loss or damage said to have been suffered through T's breach of contract or negligence, and a plea that they were entitled to retain any sum due pending resolution of the counterclaim. A assigned the right of action in the counterclaim and their assignees lodged a minute of sist in which they sought to be sisted as assignees in the counterclaim. The motion was refused and the assignees reclaimed, arguing that because they could pursue a claim that had been vested in their cedent, or might be sisted in place of A if T abandoned the present action, so that the counterclaim would continue in dependence "as if the counterclaim were a separate action" in terms of the Act of Sederunt (Rules of the Court of Session 1994) 1994 r.25.4(2) the Court should see the situation as analogous and should as an exercise of discretion grant the motion.

Held, refusing the reclaiming motion, that (1) the Rules of Court did not contemplate a counterclaim being brought by any party other than a defender and the introduction of counterclaim procedure was designed to allow a defender to make a counterclaim without bringing a separate action, not to allow a third party to maintain a claim against the pursuer, and (2) for a cedent to remain as defender in the principal action at the same time as the counterclaim was being pursued by the cedent's assignees was inconsistent with the purpose and provisions of the Court of Session Act 1988 s.6 and the Rules of the Court of Session.

Observed, that the refusal of the motion was a refusal of the specific procedure and did not touch upon the substantive rights which were said to have been assigned, which could be vindicated by competent procedures.

TODS MURRAY WS v. ARAKIN LTD 2001 S.C. 840, Lord Prosser, Lord Kingarth, Lord Mackay of Drumadoon, Ex Div.

6220. Arrestment – arrestment on dependence – prior floating charge – arrestments effective following liquidation

[Companies Act 1985 (c.6) s.463; Bankruptcy (Scotland) Act 1985 (c.66) s.37.]

In an action against R, a company in liquidation, for payment of VAT, R's liquidator (L) moved the court to recall arrestments on the dependence against R. R was wound up by the court in March 2000. L argued that the arrestments (served in November and December 1999) were ineffective because R had granted a floating charge over their entire assets to B, a bank, in 1994. Although receivers had not been appointed, the effect of the liquidation was to crystallise the floating charge, the arrestments then ceased to have effect and L was entitled to have them recalled (Companies Act 1985 s.463).

Held, refusing the motion, that s.463 conferred on B the rights and preference of a holder of a fixed security when R went into liquidation, but did not otherwise alter the effect of insolvency on diligence. The Bankruptcy (Scotland) Act 1985 s.37, as modified, precluded arrestment within 60 days prior to commencement of winding up from creating a preference and required the arrested estate to be handed over to the liquidator, but the arrestments predated the 60 day limit and L's rights were postponed, *Commercial Aluminium Windows Ltd v. Cumbernauld Development Corp* 1987 S.L.T. (Sh. Ct.) 91, [1987] C.L.Y. 4053, applied. The analogy with receivers was not well founded and significant distinctions had to be drawn with liquidations insofar as the vesting of property was concerned.

CUSTOMS AND EXCISE COMMISSIONERS v. JOHN D REID JOINERY LTD; *sub nom.* ADVOCATE GENERAL FOR SCOTLAND v. JOHN D REID JOINERY LTD 2001 S.L.T. 588, Lord Hardie, OH.

6221. Arrestment – arrestment on dependence – recall

In an action for payment of sums allegedly due in terms of a building subcontract, R sought recall of arrestments on the dependence. Previous arrestments against R in a sheriff court action by S had been recalled on the ground that there was no colourable or statable case. That action had then been dismissed on S's motion. A separate sheriff court action for rectification of the subcontract by substituting S's name for that of another company in the S's group was due for proof the following month. R argued that (1) the arrestments were nimious and oppressive, and (2) there was no colourable or statable case. S argued that the correct test was whether the averments disclosed an intelligible and discernible cause of action, which they did, and R was wrong to look at extraneous material like the terms of the contract.

Held, granting the motion, that (1) the arrestments were not nimious and oppressive. S was entitled to raise an action for payment in the sheriff court, seek dismissal of that action on payment of expenses and raise a similar or identical action in the Court of Session, and by adopting the current procedure they were not acting in mala fides or guilty of trickery, and (2) however, S had no colourable or statable case: where R contended that S had no title to sue, the court should look beyond the bare averments of the summons and adopt a prima facie approach to the whole circumstances before it, and S's title to sue was contingent on the outcome of the action of rectification.

STIELL FACILITIES LTD v. SIR ROBERT McALPINE LTD 2001 S.L.T. 1229, Lord Menzies, OH.

6222. Arrestment – arrestment on dependence – release of arrestment – amount of caution

T sought damages for breach of a management contract under which C had appointed T as manager of a drilling unit. Jurisdiction was founded on arrestment in security on the dependence. C sought release of the arrestment and caution was set at $15 million. T cross appealed arguing that there had been a mistake in the calculation because the market information had been misinterpreted and an inappropriate multiplier chosen.

Held, refusing the reclaiming motion, that (1) the Lord Ordinary had no sound justification for reducing the overall period during which T could have secured hire fees based on evidence of reliable industry forecast data from 4.25 years to three years, *Wells v. Wells* [1999] 1 A.C. 345, [1998] C.L.Y. 1446, distinguished, or for the stage of calculations at which he made deductions in respect of imponderables. However, the effect of reducing the period to three years had the same effect as using the 4.25 period and the deducting a percentage for imponderables at a later stage; (2) the Lord Ordinary was entitled to take account of the overall market position when deciding the utilisation percentage to be used in the calculations as the historical figures for the drilling unit were, by virtue of it having been stacked for over a year, no longer the most relevant indicator of future hiring and profitability; (3) the volatility in drilling operations caused by fluctuations in world oil prices entitled the Lord Ordinary to exercise his discretion in deciding which figures should be used as a basis for the calculations, and (4) it would be inappropriate for the court to take account, in deciding the appropriate level of caution to consider new material not available to the Lord Ordinary. Opinion of the Court as per Lord McCluskey.

TOR CORPORATE AS v. CHINA NATIONAL STAR PETROLEUM CORP 2001 S.C. 314, Lord Kirkwood, Lord Cowie, Lord McCluskey, Ex Div.

6223. Court of Session – dispensing power – competency – appropriateness

[Act of Sederunt (Rules of the Court of Session 1994) 1994 (SI 1994 1443) r.2.1, r.19.2.]

H enrolled a motion in terms of the Act of Sederunt (Rules of the Court of Session 1994) 1994 r.19.2, invoking the dispensing power in r.2.1 to overcome his failure to observe the seven day time limit. The action sought payment on the basis of unjust enrichment of a bonus received by H while a director of S, which sum S averred was based on earnings figures artificially increased by the directors deliberately not applying certain stated accounting policies. Service of the summons had been accepted by H's agent on May 15, 2001. On May 25 the agent wrote to S's agent, formally requesting to be told when the summons was to be lodged for calling. A trainee was subsequently informed by phone that it would be on the expiry of the induciae. That message was not passed on. H's agent, awaiting a response to his letter, did not enter appearance or lodge defences. S's agent twice enrolled for decree in absence without intimating the motion and obtained decree on June 29 on the second motion. The motion for recall was enrolled on July 16 following intimation of the decree. S argued that it was incompetent to invoke the dispensing power to overcome the time limit in r.19.2, which was itself a provision granting relief, that if it were competent it should only be done in very exceptional circumstances, that the defender had the remedy of reduction and further, that in averring that he had no knowledge of the relevant figures and had himself drawn the chairman's attention to the matter when it was disclosed to him, he had not pled a relevant defence.

Held, granting the motion, that (1) the motion was competent, there had been a failure within r.2.1 to comply with a provision in the rules due to mistake or oversight, and that failure was excusable in light of S's agents' failure to intimate the motions for decree, and (2) there was no requirement of exceptional circumstances, and justice required recalling the decree where it was known that the defender intended to defend, his alternative remedies were not certain of success and might take a long time, on recall the action would simply proceed without prejudice to either party, and where furthermore there was a real issue to try both on the relevancy of the pursuers' case and as to whether, given that an equitable remedy was sought, the equities lay with the defender.

SEMPLE COCHRANE PLC v. HUGHES 2001 S.L.T. 1121, Lord Carloway, OH.

6224. Court of Session – owner's offer – offer to settle action of damages – offer governed by law of contract – offer no longer open for acceptance when purportedly accepted by defenders

T sought damages from S in respect of personal injuries sustained while he was working. T lodged a minute on October 9, 2000 offering to settle the action for £15,000. S wrote to T on October 10 offering £12,000 and lodged a tender for that sum on October 19. T wrote to S on October 17 on other matters and observed "that something over £20,000 would be of interest", but that they could not confirm it. On January 30, 2001, S lodged a minute of acceptance of the £15,000 offer of October 9. T lodged a minute of withdrawal of that offer on January 31, 2001 and S sought decree in terms of their alleged acceptance of T's initial offer. S argued that it had been equivalent to judicial tender and would be open to acceptance at any time until decree was announced (unless expressedly or impliedly withdrawn). S also maintained that although their letter of October 10 refused the offer, that did not constitute a material change in circumstances and would not justify the implication that the offer was no longer available for acceptance.

Held, refusing the motion for decree, that T's offer was governed by the law of contract and not judicial tender. The refusal and counter offer of October 10 and the correspondence of November 17 demonstrated that the offer was no longer available for acceptance on January 30.

TENBEY v. STOLT COMEX SEAWAY LTD; *sub nom.* TENBY v. STOLT COMEX SEAWAY LTD 2001 S.C. 638, Lord Osborne, OH.

6225. Court of Session – pleadings – relevancy – matters within party's knowledge – treatment as admission

The bank raised an action for payment of sums due under standard securities and a personal bond and for declarators on the validity of those deeds. The standard securities and personal bond pertained to loan transactions in connection with business ventures in which F was involved. F and his wife, both party litigants, counterclaimed for production and reduction of the deeds and for payment of several million pounds sterling relating to losses F claimed to have incurred as a result of the bank's conduct in relation to the loan transactions. F's pleadings, particularly in relation to the counterclaim, were extensive, complex and very detailed making it difficult to determine the exact legal basis for his claims. In contrast, the bank's pleadings, particularly their defences to F's counterclaim, were brief containing mainly general denials with some short explanations and they did not answer all the points raised by F. At procedure roll debate, the bank argued that they should be assoilzied from the counterclaim without further inquiry. F argued that the principle action should be dismissed and decree de plano should be granted in terms of the counterclaim. Both submissions were rejected by the Lord Ordinary who granted an interlocutor allowing a preliminary proof on three issues central to the whole case, which he felt, if decided, would hasten a resolution to an already lengthy dispute. F appealed against the interlocutor arguing that the skeletal answers proffered by the bank to the counterclaim did not constitute a valid defence to the counterclaim as the bank had failed to expand on the general denials despite the opportunity to do so and the information being within their knowledge. Alternatively, F submitted that the case should proceed to a proof at large of the counterclaim.

Held, refusing the appeal except to the extent of varying the Lord Ordinary's interlocutor to make it clear that the option of further challenge to the relevancy of F's pleadings on the procedure roll was not foreclosed, that (1) there was no general rule in Scots law that a party's bare denials of averments made against them, where matters were within his knowledge, were equivalent to an admission of those averments, *Gray v. Boyd* 1996 S.L.T. 60, [1996] C.L.Y. 6662 followed; (2) although the bank's pleadings did not attempt to answer all the points raised by F, the bank's pleadings were not inconsistent, did not allow for any inference that the bank admitted the claims against it or the quantum of losses allegedly incurred by F, nor were there any admissions of fact within the bank's pleadings which could be used to infer liability, and (3) the Lord Ordinary's approach in granting a preliminary proof on three central issues in an attempt to hasten the resolution of the case was the correct approach.

Observed, that the bank's failure to fully answer the points raised in F's pleadings could have the effect, in the event of the case proceeding to proof, of restricting the evidence which the bank could adduce. Opinion of the Court per Lord Hamilton.

UNITY TRUST BANK PLC v. FROST (NO.1) 2001 S.C.L.R. 344, Lord Milligan, Lord Hamilton, Lord Marnoch, Ex Div.

6226. Court of Session – pleadings – relevancy and specification – personal injuries – valuation of services

See DAMAGES: Kendal v. Davies. §6418

6227. Court of Session – pleadings – relevancy plea – note of argument – failure to lodge timeously

[Act of Sederunt (Rules of the Court of Session 1994) 1994 (SI 1994 1443) r.22.4.]

F, who brought an action for damages against V following a road accident, sought the withdrawal of the case from procedure roll and the allowance of issues following V's failure to lodge a note in the terms of an interlocutor. An interlocutor had been pronounced on February 24, 2000 appointing the cause to procedure roll on V's general plea to relevancy and specification and appointing V to lodge a note of argument within 28 days. No note of argument was lodged until May 23. On March 7 an interlocutor was pronounced which allowed a minute of amendment for V to be received and appointed F to lodge answers, if so advised, within 14 days. A similar period was running in respect of a minute of amendment for F. On May 25 a jury trial was allowed in a separate action by F's wife. The case then came before the court on F's motion for withdrawal and V's motion that the note lodged on May 23 be allowed to be received late. F argued that there was no plea of special cause for withholding the case from a jury except in the minute of amendment, which was not yet part of the pleadings, that there was little merit in the points contained in V's note, that the delay in lodging the note was unacceptable, particularly as a procedure roll diet had been allocated for October and further, that his case should be dealt with in the same manner as his wife's. V submitted inter alia that another counsel had advised that the note should not be lodged until answers were provided to the earlier minute of amendment, which the pursuer had failed to do.

Held, allowing V's application, that (1) it would be illegitimate for the court to deprive V of the opportunity of having his preliminary plea debated at procedure roll; (2) while failure to lodge a note of argument could have repercussions, the purpose of the Act of Sederunt (Rules of the Court of Session 1994) 1994r.22.4 and Practice Note no.4 of 1997 did not extend beyond facilitating the efficient use of diets allocated for procedure roll discussions by giving advance notice of criticisms intended to be made of the pleadings, and (3) as acceptable reasons had been given for the delay and there would be no prejudice to F, the note of argument should be allowed to be received.

FAIRBAIRN v. VAYRO 2001 S.L.T. 1167, Lord Osborne, OH.

6228. Court of Session – proof or jury trial – compatibility of jury trial with right to fair hearing

[Court of Session Act 1988 (c.36) s.9(b); Human Rights Act 1998 (c.42) s.4(2), s.5(1); European Convention on Human Rights 1950 Art.6.]

G raised an action of damages for personal injuries suffered in a road traffic accident caused by N's negligent driving. N's liability was established by summary decree and G sought a jury trial on the quantification of damages. N contended that a jury trial, particularly on the quantum of damages in respect of solatium, was incompatible with her rights under the European Convention on Human Rights 1950 Art.6 in that a jury trial did not afford her a fair hearing. N further contended that to secure a fair hearing, the court should reinterpret the Court of Session Act 1988 s.9(b) to allow a proof where claims for solatium were to be assessed. The Lord Ordinary rejected the defender's argument for a reinterpretation of s.9(b) and allowed issues and N reclaimed. During the reclaiming motion, the question arose of whether N, if unsuccessful in persuading the court to reinterpret s.9(b), might seek a declaration under the Human Rights Act 1998 s.4(2) that s.9(b) was incompatible with the Convention as that would entitle the Crown to notice under the s.5(1) of the 1998 Act.

Held, ordering notice to be given under s.5(1), that (1) the interpretation or incompatibility of s.9(b) was one which would affect a large number of other cases in the future and it was essential that the matter was decided as soon as possible, (2) the Scottish Ministers should be given an opportunity to address the court on the object, purpose and interpretation of s.9(b), *R. v. A (Joinder of Appropriate Minister)* [2001] 1 W.L.R. 789, [2001] 4 C.L. 408, followed, and (3) it was appropriate to give notice at the stage when the possibility of N seeking a declaration had been identified rather than wait until after the question of reinterpretation had been decided would cause unnecessary delay in the case leading to a possible injustice. Opinion of the Court as per Lord Rodger, Lord President.

GUNN v. NEWMAN 2001 S.L.T. 776, Lord Rodger L.P., Lord Cameron of Lochbroom, Lord Osborne, 1 Div.

6229. Court of Session – proof or jury trial – special cause – pre-existing condition aggravated by accident – no infringement of Convention rights

S, a sales assistant, sought damages from her employer, G, after stepping on a box left on some stairs and falling whilst she was carrying a television set. S admitted that at the date of the accident she had pre-existing cervical spondylosis and maintained that the condition had been aggravated by the accident. S suffered back and neck pain and restricted shoulder movement as a result of which she could not continue her pre-accident sporting activities. S moved for issues and maintained that a clear inference could be drawn from the lack of pain she suffered as a result of cervical spondylosis prior to the accident. G argued that a jury trial would result in a breach of their Convention rights since a jury would be unable to give reasons for any award of loss of earnings and this would affect G's ability to appeal.

Held, that if S's pleadings had been clearly relevant and specific with regard to the medical issues there would be no reason why a jury could not be directed to address them and apply their conclusions. However that clarity was lacking and raised the possibility of S leading additional evidence that would complicate a jury trial such that special cause had been shown for withholding the case. However, none of G's arguments would justify the court holding that the allowance of issues would risk infringement of their Convention rights.

SANDISON v. GRAHAM BEGG LTD 2001 S.C. 821, Lord Mackay of Drumadoon, OH.

6230. Court of Session – proof or jury trial – special cause – pre-existing medical conditions

Held, that special cause making the matter unsuitable for jury trial had been shown in K's action for damages against his employers, F, in respect of a back injury allegedly sustained while working as a care assistant, where (1) there were many interlocking questions raised by K's pre-and post-accident physical and mental condition which could make directing a jury complicated, because K had pre-existing back problems, had a drink problem, which she maintained had been in abeyance some years before the accident, and suffered from depression prior to the accident; the impact on her back of the birth of a child subsequent to the accident would also need to be considered; and this was a matter on which calm reflection on many matters of detail was required which was more appropriately undertaken by a judge; and (2) the answers to a number of the factual questions concerning the likelihood of K returning to work and the cause of her inability to work could lead to a number of competing Ogden tables calculations.

KENNEDY v. FORREST-JONES 2001 S.L.T. 630, Judge TG Coutts Q.C., OH.

6231. Court of Session – rules – assistance to EU Commission

ACT OF SEDERUNT (RULES OF THE COURT OF SESSION AMENDMENT NO.2) (ASSISTANCE IN INVESTIGATIONS UNDERTAKEN BY EUROPEAN COMMISSION INTO CERTAIN PROHIBITED PRACTICES AND ABUSES) 2001, SSI 2001 92; made under the Court of Session Act 1988 s.5. In force: April 1, 2001; £1.75.

The Council of the European Communities Reg.14.6 requires Member States to afford assistance to officials authorised by The European Commission in any investigation necessary to bring to light an agreement, decision or concerted practice prohibited by Art.85(1) EC or an abuse of a dominant position prohibited by Art.86 EC. The assistance is to be given "where an undertaking opposes an investigation". This Act of Sederunt amends the Act of Sederunt (Rules of the Court of Session) 1994 (SI 1994 1443) to provide for applications by such officials for assistance to be made by petition and for warrant to be granted authorising messengers-at-arms to provide such assistance as is requisite.

6232. Court of Session – rules – miscellaneous amendments

ACT OF SEDERUNT (RULES OF THE COURT OF SESSION AMENDMENT NO.4) (MISCELLANEOUS) 2001, SSI 2001 305; made under the Court of Session Act 1988 s.5. In force: September 18, 2001; £2.00.

This Act of Sederunt, which amends the Rules of the Court of Session 1994 (SI 1994 1443), makes various miscellaneous amendments to the Rules of the Court of Session.

6233. Court of Session – rules – offers to make amends – procedure

ACT OF SEDERUNT (RULES OF THE COURT OF SESSION AMENDMENT NO.1) (PROCEDURE FOR OFFERS TO MAKE AMENDS) 2001, SSI 2001 93; made under the Court of Session Act 1988 s.5. In force: April 1, 2001; £1.75.

This Act of Sederunt replaces the Act of Sederunt (Rules of the Court of Session) (SI 1994 1443) Ch.54 to deal with the procedure relating to offers to make amends under the Defamation Act 1996 s.3.

6234. Court of Session – rules – terrorism

ACT OF SEDERUNT (RULES OF THE COURT OF SESSION AMENDMENT NO.6) (TERRORISM ACT 2000) 2001, SSI 2001 494; made under the Court of Session Act 1988 s.5; and the Terrorism Act 2000 Sch.4 para.17, para.27. In force: December 22, 2001; £1.75.

This Act of Sederunt makes various amendments to the Act of Sederunt (Rules of the Court of Session) 1994 (SI 1994 1443) in pursuance of the provisions of the Terrorism Act 2000 Sch.4 which makes provision in relation to forfeiture orders.

6235. Court of Session – shorthand writers – fees

ACT OF SEDERUNT (RULES OF THE COURT OF SESSION AMENDMENT NO.3) (FEES OF SHORTHAND WRITERS) 2001, SSI 2001 135; made under the Court of Session Act 1988 s.5. In force: May 1, 2001; £1.50.

This Act of Sederunt, which amends the Act of Sederunt (Rules of the Court of Session) 1994 (SI 1994 1443) increases the fees payable to shorthand writers in the Court of Session by 3.55 per cent.

6236. Court of Session – solicitors – fees

ACT OF SEDERUNT (RULES OF THE COURT OF SESSION AMENDMENT NO.5) (FEES OF SOLICITORS) 2001, SSI 2001 441; made under the Court of Session Act 1988 s.5. In force: January 1, 2002; £2.00.

This Act of Sederunt amends the Table of Fees in the Rules of the Court of Session 1994 (SI 1994 1443) in Ch.42 by increasing the fees payable to solicitors (and recoverable from opponents) by approximately 3 per cent. The fee for work done before action commences has been increased by approximately 6 per cent. It also introduces block fees in defended actions for arranging a commission to recover documents under a specification of documents and for attending consultation with counsel to consider tender, extra judicial settlement or with a view to settlement, whether or not settlement is agreed.

6237. Deduction from earnings orders – maintenance – deductible amount

DILIGENCE AGAINST EARNINGS (VARIATION) (SCOTLAND) REGULATIONS 2001, SSI 2001 408; made under the Debtors (Scotland) Act 1987 s.49, s.53, s.63. In force: December 3, 2001; £1.75.

These Regulations, which amend the Debtors (Scotland) Act 1987, vary a figure used in the calculation of deductions made from a person's pay when that pay is subject to a current maintenance or conjoined arrestment, and substitute new tables which set out the deductions made from a person's pay when that pay is subject to an earnings arrestment. The new figures reflect the increase in the Average Earnings Index since the tables were drawn up in 1985 and broadly restore the level of deductions in real terms to that applicable at the passing of the 1987 Act.

6238. Documents – service of judicial and extrajudicial documents

EUROPEAN COMMUNITIES (SERVICE OF JUDICIAL AND EXTRAJUDICIAL DOCUMENTS) (SCOTLAND) REGULATIONS 2001, SSI 2001 172; made under the European Communities Act 1972 s.2. In force: May 31, 2001; £1.75.

These Regulations designate certain persons for the purposes of Council Regulation 1348/2000 ([2000] OJ L160/37) on the service in the Member States of judicial and extrajudicial documents in civil or commercial matters.

6239. Expenses – abandonment of action at common law – conduct of both parties considered – award at discretion of sheriff

[Act of Sederunt (Sheriff Court Ordinary Cause Rules) 1993 (SI 1993 1956) r.23(1)(b).]

A father sought a contact order with regard to his child. After various child welfare hearings F intimated his intention to abandon the action. It was dismissed and award of expenses reserved. The mother argued that under the Act of Sederunt (Sheriff Court Ordinary Cause Rules) 1993 r. 23(1)(b) an automatic award in her favour should be made. M argued that the abandonment had been at common law and the sheriff should look at the conduct of the parties, including the lack of co-operation by M in previous contact arrangements and court appearances, in awarding expenses.

Held, that M was liable to the question of expenses. No minute of abandonment had been lodged, therefore the abandonment had not been effected under r.23(1), but abandoned at common law. Account was taken of M's conduct in making an award of expenses against her.

MASSON v. MASSON 2001 S.C.L.R. 501, Sheriff DJ Cusine, Sh Ct (Grampian, Highland and Islands).

6240. Expenses – action by company – caution for expenses – claimant on fund having status as pursuer

[Companies Act 1985 (c.6) s.726(2).]

S, salmon farmers, made a claim for compensation in respect of the Braer oil tanker grounding which prevented S from taking delivery of a contractual order of smolt. Objectors (O) moved that S be ordained to find caution for expenses. O sought caution of £40,000 after the Lord Ordinary had appointed a preliminary proof on the question of S's alleged fraud in the submission of the claim. S was no longer trading and it was accepted that as at June 30, 1999 shareholder funds were £142,305 subject to securities. In 1997 shareholder funds amounted to £1,000,000. S argued that (1) the Companies Act 1985 s.726(2) allowed the court to make an order for caution against a pursuer only, whereas they were defenders convened to a multiple poinding, and (2) S's financial position was a consequence of the incident for which compensation was claimed.

Held, granting the motions to the extent of £20,000 each, that (1) s.726(2) should be construed by reference to the reality of the situation. In the instant case S had begun as a pursuer against the Braer Corporation and S's status as such underpinned its claim in the instant action; (2) it was possible that the limitation funds available to meet valid claims would be insufficient and O's interests were therefore directly opposed to S's. These were "other legal proceedings" within s.726(2), *Star Fire and Burglary Insurance Co Ltd v. C Davidson & Sons Ltd* (1902) 10 S.L.T. 282 distinguished; (3) although the Braer incident might have caused S to cease to trade, that did not explain S's financial state because it seemed from the accounts that until 1998 S could have funded those proceedings and no information had been given to conclude that the post 1998 situation was attributable to Braer; (4) even if it was, that ought not to be a reason to refuse the motions where it was likely O would incur irrecoverable and substantial expenses if the claim should fail and S had not offered any alternative form of reassurance. That was a material consideration given that S was a wholly owned subsidiary of another company, and (5) as there was a realistic prospect that the preliminary proof would take less than the estimated two weeks and the cases of both objectors were virtually the same, caution would be restricted to £20,000 in each case.

ASSURANCEFORENINGEN SKULD v. INTERNATIONAL OIL POLLUTION COMPENSATION FUND (NO.3); *sub nom.* SHETLAND SEAFARMS LTD v. INTERNATIONAL OIL POLLUTION COMPENSATION FUND (NO.5) 2000 S.L.T. 1352, Lord Gill, OH.

6241. Expenses – caution for expenses – breach of Convention rights – award of caution limited to counterclaims

[Human Rights Act 1998 (c.42) Sch.1 Part I Art.6(1); Act of Sederunt (Sheriff Court Ordinary Cause Rules) 1993 (SI 1993 1956) r.19.4.]

W, a company, sought recovery of £12,693.87 allegedly misappropriated by D, who prior to his sequestration had been the company's manager and major shareholder. D counterclaimed, seeking £325,000 for wrongful dismissal and alleged that his ex wife, a current director of W had benefited personally from, and been guilty of, any misappropriation. D was ordained to find £10,000 caution for expenses and appealed to the sheriff principal arguing that the sheriff had misdirected himself by treating D as a pursuer on the basis of the size of the counterclaim where D had not admitted that W's claim was valid, and the counterclaim was not directed to the same contractual provisions nor the same factual basis. D maintained he was not in the position of a person with no statable defence and ordering caution would be a disproportionate restriction on his right of access to the court and contrary to the Human Rights Act 1998 Sch.1 Part I Art.6(1).

Held, allowing the appeal and ordaining D to find £5,000 in each counterclaim, that although D's defence amounted to little more than the denial of W's allegations, the sequestration award should not deprive him of the right to put W to proof with regard to their allegations. It was appropriate in this action, having regard to the Act of Sederunt (Sheriff Court Ordinary Cause Rules) 1993 r.19.4 to order caution for expenses in relation to the counterclaim alone. It was unclear whether Art.6(1) would be infringed by an order for caution but it was not unreasonable that W should have some reassurance in the event of success they would be able to recover some of their expenses, having regard to the competing claims, caution was restricted to the counterclaims only.

WILLIAM DOW (POTATOES) LTD v. DOW 2001 S.L.T. (Sh Ct) 37, JC McInnes Q.C., Sheriff Principal, Sh Ct.

6242. **Expenses – caution for expenses – insolvent Italian company pursuing retailer customer – no personal liability under Italian law**

[Companies Act 1985 (c.6) s.726; EC Treaty Art.6 (now, after amendment, Art.12 EC).]

F raised a commercial action against B for payment under, and damages for an alleged breach of a distribution agreement. During the preliminary stages of the proceedings, and at the instance of F's creditors, F entered a state of insolvent judicial administration under the law of Italy. Unlike a liquidator in the UK, an Italian curatore would not be personally liable for the expenses of any actions raised or defended by the insolvent company and, therefore, B enrolled a motion requiring F to obtain caution for the expenses of the action to the sum of £50,000 or to offer a similar alternative form of security. The action was raised under common law as companies incorporated outside Scotland, England and Wales did not fall subject to the provisions of the Companies Act 1985 s.726. F argued that their insolvency was as a direct result of B's default under the agreement and his refusal to pay for the goods supplied and that the value of the stock held, but not paid for, by B was higher than the sum required in caution for expenses. F further argued that Italian law had declared it unconstitutional for F, as a company in insolvent judicial administration, to find security for legal costs and for the court to make such an order was direct discrimination under the EC Treaty Art.6 (now, after amendment, Art.12 EC) as it would not make such an order against a native company.

Held, refusing the motion for caution, that (1) although there was no direct authority in Scotland for considering an application at common law to require a limited company to find caution for expenses, the court's jurisdiction involved discretion which required a number of factors, including the financial circumstances of the company, to be considered and accordingly such an order at common law would be competent, *DSQ Property Co Ltd v. Lotus Cars Ltd* [1987] 1 W.L.R. 127, [1987] C.L.Y. 2953, approved; (2) whilst the sum sued for was not necessarily sufficient to have caused F's insolvency, it was sufficiently large for the court to find that it had played a large part in F becoming insolvent and therefore that had to be taken into account in deciding whether caution should be ordered; (3) it was reasonable to expect that, if B was successful in the action, that the value of stock held by B and unpaid for, would be sufficient to meet the expenses of the action, and (4) as Italian law precluded F from finding caution, the result of a court order for caution would be F's withdrawal of the action and a motion for caution should not be used by parties to stifle claims.

Observed, that the court should have been fully informed of F's ability to find security and in particular, whether F's creditors or shareholders, who stood to benefit from any successful outcome in the action, would be prepared to offer caution if required. Opinion, that Community law did not exclude nor restrict the court's discretion to order caution for expenses as it was competent for the court make such an order against a native company.

FALLIMENTO LA PANTOFOLA D'ORO SpA v. BLANE LEISURE LTD (NO.2) 2000 S.L.T. 1264, Lord Hamilton, OH.

6243. Expenses – extrajudicial settlement – principal action and counterclaim – divided success – defender awarded expenses of principal action

G, contractors raised an action for payment of £8,734.41 in respect of works carried out on D's home. D counterclaimed for £30,000 in damages for injury and consequential loss resulting from alleged defects in the work. Proof was set for June 29, 2000. A week prior to the diet G lodged a minute of tender offering the sum of £10,000, with expenses, in satisfaction of the counterclaim, which D accepted. At around the same time D agreed informally to pay £6,500 in respect of the principal action. The sheriff awarded the expenses of the principal action in favour of D. G appealed, arguing there had been a miscarriage of justice: (1) the expenses in the principal action had to be considered separately and the general principle that expenses followed success should be applied; (2) G had been put to the expense of preparing for proof as D had denied liability and made no effort to pay even a part of the sum craved until the very last minute, and (3) a sentence in the sheriff's note demonstrated that he had wrongly regarded a right of retention as a complete defence.

Held, refusing the appeal, that (1) the principal action and the counterclaim were closely bound together and the sheriff had not erred in law in viewing the litigation as a whole when determining liability for expenses; (2) each party had an interest in the matter being resolved by proof if it was not settled extrajudicially, and it was incorrect to say that G had to prepare for proof simply due to D's intransigence; (3) the sentence in the sheriff's note relied on by G was an ambiguous narration of submissions and not the sheriff's own opinion, and the instant was a clear case where D was entitled to retain any money due under the contract until matters had been resolved, and (4) D having been left with a net gain of £3,500, it was open to the sheriff to conclude that she had been the net winner in the whole litigation, and in effect to award her the full expenses of process.

GRAHAM (PRESERVATION) LTD v. DOUGLAS 2001 S.L.T. (Sh Ct) 142, CGB Nicholson Q.C., Sheriff Principal, Sh Ct.

6244. Expenses – motion for expenses – competency

[Act of Sederunt (Rules of the Court of Session 1994) 1994 (SI 1994 1443) r.30(2), r.4.15(6).]

In an action for damages L, on the third day of the proof, lodged a minute of acceptance of tender and moved the court to grant decree for the principal sum, expenses to the date of the tender and to certify a skilled witness. The motions were granted by interlocutors dated June 17. Four days later, S enrolled a motion to find L liable for expenses from the date of tender but the motion did not ask for the interlocutors dated June 17 to be altered. The motion was opposed and, following submissions, the Lord Ordinary granted the motion and proceeded to alter the interlocutors of June 17 to include an award of expenses against L from the date of tender and insert a new interlocutor issued on November 16 but dated June 17. L reclaimed, arguing that the motion enrolled and the subsequent action by the Lord Ordinary in altering the interlocutors were incompetent as the interlocutors of June 17 were final and could only be amended where clerical or technical errors were identified. S contended that (1) there was a general power, at common law, to alter the substance of an interlocutor upon a de recenti application, (2) the interpretation of the Act of Sederunt (Rules of the Court of Session 1994) 1994 r.30(2) given in *Campbell v. James Walker Insulation Ltd* 1988 S.L.T. 263, [1988] C.L.Y. 4667, restricting any power to correct or alter an interlocutor to correction or alteration of expression and not the substance, was to be regarded as part of the obiter of the judgment and it was open to the court to reach a different conclusion regarding the interpretation of the r.4.15(6), and (3) that even if the Lord Ordinary was not permitted to correct or alter his original interlocutor, it was open to him to grant a new interlocutor on the matter of expenses from the date of tender.

Held, allowing the reclaiming motion, that (1) any power which might have existed at common law was superseded by the introduction of r.30(2) and subsequently r.4.15(6), (2) the interpretation given in *Campbell* was binding upon the court and clearly prohibited correction or alteration of the substance of an interlocutor, and as the purpose and function of the two rules was the same, the interpretation covered r.4.15(6), and (3) the rule applied that once the merits of a case had been exhausted, the case was at an end and the question of expenses was also exhausted, unless expressly reserved.

Observed, that inserting a new or additional interlocutor, to correct or alter a prior interlocutor, was inappropriate and undesirable and that, had the correction or alteration of the prior interlocutor been competent, it would have been more appropriate for the Lord Ordinary to have achieved the desired effect by alteration rather than the insertion of a new interlocutor.

LAING v. SCOTTISH ARTS COUNCIL 2001 S.C. 493, Lord Prosser, Lord Kirkwood, Lord Weir, Ex Div.

6245. Expenses – taxation – notice of objections – competency of challenge by notice

[Act of Sederunt (Rules of the Court of Session 1994) 1994 (SI 1994 1443) r.42.4.]

U raised an action of damages against A, which was settled by joint minute with expenses as taxed being awarded against A. U's account was submitted to the auditor for taxation and, despite writing to U objecting to several aspects of the account, A failed to lodge a note of objections with the auditor prior to the diet of taxation in accordance with the procedure set out in Practice Note 3 of 1993. A did, however, fax a copy of their letter to U to the auditor prior to the diet. As a result of A's failure to follow procedure, the auditor taxed the expenses at the figure requested by U, without abatements. A lodged a note of objections under the Act of Sederunt (Rules of the Court of Session 1994) 1994 r.42.4 to the auditor's report, which made no objections to any specific items contained in the report, nor did it require any specific amendment of the report. The note of objections made general criticisms of the procedure followed by the auditor and his strict adherence to the terms of the Practice Note and further criticised the auditor's failure to acknowledge the faxed copy letter as a competent intimation of objections when dealing with the account at the diet of taxation.

Held, repelling the note of objection, that the note of objection contained no issues which the court could competently deal with under the procedure set out in r.42.4, which clearly required objections to specific items in the report or specific amendments to be made.

URQUHART v. AYRSHIRE AND ARRAN HEALTH BOARD; *sub nom.* SPENCE v. AYRSHIRE AND ARRAN HEALTH BOARD 2000 S.L.T. 829, Lord Reed, OH.

6246. Expenses – tender – summary causes – appropriate scale

[Sheriff Courts (Scotland) Act 1971 (c.58) s.36B; Act of Sederunt (Fees of Solicitors in the Sheriff Court) (Amendment and Further Provisions) 1993 (SI 1993 3080) Sch.1 para.2.]

B raised a summary cause action against S for £1,150, liability for which was admitted but quantum disputed. A tender for £750 including expenses "as taxed of process" was lodged and accepted. S argued that expenses should be awarded on the small claims scale and be limited by the sum decerned for under the Act of Sederunt (Fees of Solicitors in the Sheriff Court) (Amendment and Further Provisions) 1993 Sch.1 para.2 and the Sheriff Courts (Scotland) Act 1971 s.36B. B argued that the tender had included "expenses as taxed" which had referred to the summary cause scale as small claims expenses could not be taxed. The sheriff awarded expenses on the summary cause scale on grounds that s.36B did not apply where a defender had stated a defence but not proceeded with it, *Glover v. Deighan* 1992 S.L.T. (Sh. Ct.) 88, [1992] C.L.Y. 5773, followed. S appealed to the sheriff principal arguing that the sheriff had incorrectly exercised his discretion.

Held, refusing the appeal, that a restriction of expenses under s.36B was not available to a defender who, having stated a defence, failed to proceed with it. It was at the discretion of the sheriff to determine, on the facts before him, whether a defence had been stated and not proceeded with where a tender had been accepted. It was also at the sheriff's absolute discretion to determine the scale of expenses which were appropriate in terms of a proviso to Sch.1 para.2.

Observed, that greater clarity in the formation of an agreement between the parties could have avoided the issue.

SEMPLE v. BLACK 2000 S.C.L.R.1098, John F Wheatley Q.C., Sheriff Principal, Sh Ct.

6247. Interdicts – interim interdict – disputed title to land – balance of convenience

[Prescription and Limitation (Scotland) Act 1973 (c.52) s.1 (1).]

M sought recall of interim interdicts preventing him from encroaching or entering land, the title of which was in dispute with P.

Held, refusing the motion that (1) it was impossible to predict the outcome of the dispute as to ownership in light of the apparent lack of clarity in the boundary descriptions and plans; (2) P had a prima facie case for claiming ownership and as P was opposed to the restoration work being carried out by M, it was appropriate in the circumstances to maintain the status quo until the question of ownership had been determined, and (3) continuation of the interim orders did not prevent him from complying with the planning permission on land undisputedly owned by him.

Observed, that the outcome of the title dispute might result in the land being owned by the Forestry Commission following the 1970 disposition in which case it could be appropriate for the Forestry Commission to be called as additional defenders.

PATTERSON v. MENZIES 2001 S.C.L.R. 266, Lord Nimmo Smith, OH.

6248. Judicial factors – title to sue

See ADMINISTRATION OF JUSTICE: Thurso Building Society's Judicial Factor v. Robertson. §6086

6249. Jurisdiction – declinature of jurisdiction – reclaiming motion – judge's prior involvement in procedural matters associated with the case

F, a party litigant, enrolled a motion to the effect that each member of the court should, or at least might, choose to decline jurisdiction to hear the reclaiming motion. The basis for the motion was the proposition that F had a legitimate apprehension that each judge, for varying reasons, would be unable to approach the issues of the case impartially. In respect of the first judge, F claimed that he had refused a motion in another case between the same parties, which was substantially the same as a motion introduced by F in this case. F further claimed that the judge had written a note refusing to hear a procedural roll debate in the other case. The judge had no recollection of such events and no copy of the note was produced to the court. In respect of the second judge, F claimed that the judge had the same surname as a witness to a will in 1982, which may become litigious at some stage due to an allegation that it was executed after the testator's death. F claimed that the judge was the witness, a fact denied by the judge, who also denied knowing the testator or the witness in question. The remaining judge was challenged on his attitude and behaviour on an occasion in 1996 when this case came before him in the Outer House. F alleged that the judge, in refusing to accept a faxed copy of an English order into process and continuing the case for one week to allow for authenticated documents to be produced, had in terms accused F of being a liar and the faxed copy of being a forgery. The judge could not recall the incident in question but accepted that he would have been firm with F regarding his need to demonstrate the authority of the order and the impossibility of accepting F's assertions before the bar as conclusive. Others present at the time could, similarly, not recall the judge acting improperly in any way.

Held, refusing the motion, that (1) the correct test for declinature of jurisdiction was whether there was a legitimate apprehension of partiality when judged objectively, *Hoekstra v. HM Advocate (No.3)* 2000 J.C. 391, [2000] C.L.Y. 6092 followed; (2) it would be entirely inappropriate for a judge to feel that jurisdiction should be declined on the basis of unfounded allegations made against him, and (3) F had failed to prove any basis for the allegations which he had made against the members of the court. Opinion of the Court per Lord Milligan.

UNITY TRUST BANK PLC v. FROST (NO.2) 2001 S.C.L.R. 350, Lord Milligan, Lord Hamilton, Lord Marnoch, Ex Div.

6250. **Jury trials – Court of Session – motion for new trial – excessive damages award – current test compatible with right to fair hearing – unnecessary judicial interference contrary to parliamentary intent**

[Court of Session Act 1988 (c.36) s.29(1); European Convention on Human Rights 1950 Art.6(1).]

M, who had suffered extensive electrical burns following an accident on a railway line owned by B, was awarded damages of £250,000 by a jury. B enrolled a motion for a new trial on the ground of excess of damages, arguing that the procedure for granting a new trial had to result in a fair hearing under the European Convention on Human Rights 1950 Art.6(1) and the Court of Session Act 1988 s.29(1) allowing an application for a new trial on the basis of "excess or inadequacy of damages" did not achieve that. B argued that the test did not give the court power to protect the rights of a party affected by a jury's decision, especially since that was given without explanation. B also argued that the lack of judicial control over the levels of awards created a system in which they lacked uniformity and created uncertainty for parties

Held, refusing the motion, that whilst accepting that no breach of Art.6(1) would arise if the jury performed their function properly, it was necessary for the court to be able to set aside the verdict if the award was inconsistent with one that would be reached by any reasonable jury. Any further interference would involve the award levels being set judicially and as such would run contrary to parliamentary intention. The unpredictability of jury awards was not a reason to infer that the trial had been unfair, the jury were in the best position to judge the effects of M's scars. It was impossible to say that no reasonable jury would have made the same award in the circumstances of the instant case.

McLEOD v. BRITISH RAILWAYS BOARD 2001 S.C. 534, Lord Rodger L.P., Lord Philip, Lord Weir, 1 Div.

6251. **Limitations – personal injuries – onus of proof of date from which time ran**

[Prescription and Limitation (Scotland) Act 1973 (c.52) s.17(2), s.19A.]

A raised an action for damages against his former employers in respect of injuries sustained in the course of his employment. His employment ceased in September 1995 and for the purposes of the action, the parties agreed to take September 30, 1995 as the effective date. The action was raised in June 1999 and S tabled a plea that the action was time barred under the provisions of the Prescription and Limitation (Scotland) Act 1973 s.17(2). A sought the court, on the basis of his averments, to exercise its discretion under s.19A to allow the action to proceed or to allow a proof before answer on the issue of time bar. In his pleadings, A averred that, during his employment, he had operated a vibrating plate machine. During the 1980s he had experienced intermittent symptoms which were not serious. In 1996 he became aware of successful claims for social security benefits in respect of similar symptoms and initiated a claim himself in 1997. In connection with that claim, he was medically examined in February 1998 and subsequently advised that his claim for benefits had been successful in respect of a prescribed disease known as vibration white finger. A then sought legal advice and his solicitors referred him to a vascular surgeon for additional tests which culminated in a medical report dated March 15, 1998 confirming the diagnosis. On the basis of the facts averred, A claimed that the date on which he was actually aware that he could claim damages from S was March 15, 1998 and the date on which he could first reasonably be said to have become aware of a claim was in February 1998, both dates being within the triennium. The circumstances, A claimed, fell within the provisions of s.17 (2) (b) and the case should be allowed to proceed. S argued that on the basis of the averments, the court should find that the date of constructive awareness of a claim should be set as the date in 1996 when A first became aware that his symptoms were similar to those which had resulted in successful claims for benefits, that date being outwith the triennium.

Held, allowing a proof before answer, that (1) the court had no discretion in the date from which the triennium began under s.17 (2) (b), the date of actual awareness of circumstances entitling an action was the effective date unless the court was satisfied that constructive awareness existed at an earlier date in which case, the date of constructive awareness was the effective date; (2) to invoke an extension of the triennium under s.17 (2) (b), A had to aver both the date of actual awareness and the date of constructive awareness; (3) the nature of the averments for actual awareness would differ from those for constructive awareness as actual awareness required a positive establishment of specific factual events and constructive awareness required a negative inference from the circumstances of the case, and (4) A's averments were sufficient on those respects to indicate that he had a possible case for an extension.

AGNEW v. SCOTT LITHGOW LTD (NO.1) 2001 S.C. 516, Lord Hamilton, OH.

6252. Limitations – personal injuries – psychiatric injury due to stress at work – commencement of limitation period – continuing course of conduct

[Prescription and Limitation (Scotland) Act 1973 (c.52) s.17 (2) (a).]

M raised an action of damages against BT for personal injuries in respect of psychiatric harm allegedly caused by stress at work. The case was raised against BT both as her employer and also in its capacity as employer of M's manager, for whose acts and omissions BT was vicariously liable. M stopped work due to illness on April 4, 1994 and tendered her resignation on September 1, 1994 which took effect on September 23, 1994. The action was raised on August 22, 1997 and served on BT on August 25, 1997. BT entered preliminary pleas that the action was time barred in terms of the Prescription and Limitation (Scotland) Act 1973 s.17 (2) (a) and that M's pleadings were irrelevant. M claimed to have been under considerable pressure at work prior to April 4, 1994 due to an excessive workload, lack of training and hostility and harassment at the hands of her manager, that BT ought to have realised that failure to monitor workloads, provide adequate training and supervise managerial staff to prevent harassment occurring were all liable to lead to stress amongst employees, and that her treatment by BT subsequent to April 4, 1994 materially contributed to her mental health injuries. M alleged that BT's formulation of her new duties and responsibilities, following an administrative reorganisation within the company in April 1994, took no account of the fact that she was unfit for work due to stress related illness and that resulted in her having to take redundancy in September 1994. BT argued that the acts or omissions which allegedly led to M's illness and caused her to leave work in April 1994 were distinct from the alleged acts or omissions occurring between April 4 and September 23, 1994 and could not, therefore, be considered to have been continuing beyond April 1994 making the action time barred.

Held, allowing a proof before answer and reserving all pleas, that (1) only one action had been raised against BT, albeit on two grounds of liability, and there was no support for BT's proposition that a separate triennium should apply to separate parts of the action; (2) whilst the content of the allegations relating to the period prior to April 4, 1994 differed from those for the period from April 4 to September 23, 1994, they shared the same basis that BT had failed to take reasonable care for M's safety, which if proved would result in the triennium, for the purposes of s.17 (2) (a), being calculated from September 23, 1994; (3) M had made averments, which if proved were capable of showing that the risk of psychiatric harm was foreseeable to BT, and (4) following *Jamieson v. Jamieson* [1952] A.C. 525, [1952] C.L.Y. 985, that an action should not be dismissed as irrelevant unless it would fail even if all the pursuers' averments were proved which did not appear to be the case in this instance.

MATHER v. BRITISH TELECOMMUNICATIONS PLC 2001 S.L.T. 325, Lord Osborne, OH.

6253. Personal injuries – optional procedure – medical witnesses – addition to list

[Act of Sederunt (Rules of the Court of Session 1994) 1994 (SI 1994 1443) r.43.26, r.43.27, r.43.27(3).]

P, a bus driver, raised an action under the optional procedure for damages in respect of an accident during the course of his employment with L. L conceded liability for the accident and a proof before answer was allowed and a diet of proof fixed. P lodged a minute of amendment to increase the damages sued for and to include details of his continuing ill health and treatment, to which L lodged defences. Before the court could consider the minute, P enrolled a motion to add further witnesses to his list who could provide evidence of his current medical treatment and the development of psychological problems related to the constant pain he was in. He submitted that the extent of his medical problems had not been apparent earlier and it would be in the interests of justice to allow the additional witnesses. L argued that the additions should not be permitted as the case was on the optional procedure role and in terms of the Act of Sederunt (Rules of the Court of Session 1994) 1994 r.43.26 and r.43.27, expert witnesses were to be kept to a minimum:

Held, granting the motion, that (1) there were no procedures contained in the rules for adding witness to the list under the optional procedure, but that in practice the court had allowed that where the court thought fit; (2) adequate notice had been given of the new witnesses prior to the proof, and (3) P had provided a reasonable explanation of why the witnesses had not been included on the original list.

Observed, that although the court was allowing the witnesses to be added, the use of additional medical witnesses at the proof had not been sanctioned under the optional procedure in terms of r.43.27(3) and no view had been expressed on whether the court would grant the sanction or whether the amendment in terms of the minute of amendment would be allowed.

PEDEN v. LOTHIAN REGION TRANSPORT 2001 S.L.T. 985, Lord Carloway, OH.

6254. Sheriff courts – appeals – competency – appeal taken without leave

[Sheriff Courts (Scotland) Act 1907 (7 Edw VII c.51) s.27.]

L appealed, without leave, against a sheriff's interlocutor of January 26, 2001 repelling L's objections to an auditor's report and reserving the question of expenses of the note of objections, in L's action of damages for defamation against T.

Held, dismissing the appeal, that (1) the sheriff's interlocutor could not be held to be a final judgment under the Sheriff Courts (Scotland) Act 1907 s.27, as for a judgment to be final there had to be some finding regarding expenses, and (2) that the interlocutor could not properly be described as disposing of the subject matter of the cause, and could not fall within any of the classes of appeal in s.27 which could competently be taken without leave.

LLOYD v. THOMPSON 2001 S.L.T. (Sh Ct) 127, CGB Nicholson Q.C., Sheriff Principal, Sh Ct.

6255. Sheriff courts – appeals – sheriff principal, to – without leave – interim decree in divorce proceedings – competency

[Matrimonial Homes (Family Protection) (Scotland) Act 1981 (c.59) s.2(4)(b); Sheriff Courts (Scotland) Act 1907 (7 Edw VII c.51) s.27(b).]

W raised an action of divorce. An interim order for aliment and an interim award for contributions to the mortgage and insurance of the matrimonial home were made by the sheriff under the Matrimonial Homes (Family Protection) (Scotland) Act 1981 s.2(4)(b). The former husband, H, appealed, without leave to the sheriff principal, against the interim orders. It was agreed that an appeal without leave against an interim order for aliment alone would not fall within the Sheriff Courts (Scotland) Act 1907 s.27(b) and as such would be incompetent.

Held, dismissing the appeal, that the interim order was so similar to an order for interim aliment that it would also be considered incompetent.

WILSON v. WILSON (APPEAL WITHOUT LEAVE) 2001 S.L.T. (Sh Ct) 55, BA Kerr Q.C., Sheriff Principal, Sh Ct.

6256. Sheriff courts – appeals – sheriff principal, to – without leave – interlocutor appointing debate – competency

[Sheriff Courts (Scotland) Act 1907 (7 Edw VII, c.51) s.27(d); Act of Sederunt (Sheriff Court Ordinary Cause Rules) 1993 (SI 1993 1956) r.9.12(3)(c).]

S raised an action for specific implement of missives to purchase heritable property. At a continued options hearing the sheriff appointed the cause for a debate on B's plea to the relevancy and specification of S's averments. S had moved for a proof before answer. S appealed without leave. The sheriff wrote a note questioning the competency of an appeal without leave, and S and B were invited to address the sheriff principal on that issue. S submitted that (1) where a motion for proof was made and refused, that interlocutor refused proof under the Sheriff Courts (Scotland) Act 1907 s.27(d); (2) a sheriff had three choices at an options hearing under the Act of Sederunt (Sheriff Court Ordinary Cause Rules) 1993 r.9.12(3) and where an order was made under paras.(a) or (b) of that rule, there was a right of appeal without leave and it would be strange if a decision under para.(c) could not also be appealed without leave, and (3) s.27 was not free from ambiguity and should be interpreted in light of r.9.12(3).

Held, refusing the appeal as incompetent, that the sheriff's interlocutor did not fall within s.27(d). An interlocutor refusing proof could only be pronounced once relevancy had been judicially determined. A debate was a procedural hearing where preliminary pleas were discussed. In appointing the cause to a debate, the sheriff might not have acceded to a motion to allow a proof, but that differed from refusing a proof.

SHARIF v. SINGH (T/A INDIA GATE TANDOORI RESTAURANT); *sub nom.* SHARIFF v. SINGH (T/A INDIA GATE TANDOORI RESTAURANT) 2000 S.L.T. (Sh Ct) 188, RA Dunlop Q.C., Sheriff Principal, Sh Ct (Tayside, Central and Fife).

6257. Sheriff courts – applications and appeals – adults with incapacity

ACT OF SEDERUNT (SUMMARY APPLICATIONS, STATUTORY APPLICATIONS AND APPEALS ETC. RULES) AMENDMENT (ADULTS WITH INCAPACITY) 2001, SSI 2001 142; made under the Sheriff Courts (Scotland) Act 1971 s.32; and the Adults with Incapacity (Scotland) Act 2000 s.2. In force: April 2, 2001; £2.50.

This Act of Sederunt amends the Act of Sederunt (Summary Applications, Statutory Applications and Appeals etc. Rules) 1999 (SI 1999 929) by inserting a new Part XVI containing specific provisions in relation to the Adults with Incapacity (Scotland) Act 2000.

6258. Sheriff courts – arbitration – plea to sist for arbitration – plea made out of time

[Act of Sederunt (Ordinary Cause Rules) 1993 (SI 1993 1956) r.18, r.22.]

Defenders J, S and O moved the sheriff to allow their minutes of amendment in the action of M, a firm of building contractors, for payment of £27,297.38 allegedly due under a contract entered into in 1995. The record lodged contained a plea by S and O that the action should be sisted pending arbitration and a general plea to the relevancy of M's averments, but no note made under the Act of Sederunt (Ordinary Cause Rules) 1993 r.22 was lodged. At the continued options hearing on May 20, 1999 S and O's preliminary pleas were repelled due to the lack of a note. M's motion for summary decree was continued to a debate at which leave was granted for J to lodge a minute of amendment. J's minute of amendment contained a plea in law seeking to have the action sisted for arbitration, though no r.18.8(1) note was lodged; the record was duly opened, amended and closed. At a further debate J, S and O sought to amend and lodged minutes including pleas seeking to sist the action pending arbitration, accompanied by r.18.8(1) notes, to which M objected. J, S and O argued that (1) the minute of amendment which sought to reintroduce the arbitration plea contained new matter, including averments referring to the arbitration provisions of the contract in greater detail than the original pleadings, and (2) the actings of J, S and O did not suggest that they had waived their contractual right to go to arbitration; the original arbitration plea, unsupported by a r.22 note, had been repelled through inadvertence.

Held, refusing reinstatement of arbitration pleas in terms of the minutes of amendment, that (1) S and O's failure to lodge a r.22 note in support of their arbitration plea prior to the options hearing might well have been inadvertence, but it was of considerable significance that they failed to lodge a note before the continued options hearing, and that no steps were taken once the plea was repelled to rectify the situation, the case being allowed to drift for some nine months after the record was closed. S and O's inactivity must be taken as meaning that they were to be presumed to have waived their contractual right to arbitration; (2) if a preliminary plea had been repelled at the options hearing it would be unjust to permit that party to reinstate his preliminary plea by amendment unless the other party had first by his amendment introduced new material which justified the preliminary plea of new. It was all the more important with an arbitration plea, where the ultimate resolution of the dispute might lie further in the future than an ordinary cause action, that the party who wished to send a case to arbitration should not be permitted to forgo his opportunity of doing so only to seek to grasp it again some time later, and (3) this reasoning applied equally to J, whose arbitration plea, inserted only once the record had closed, had not been not supported by a r.18 note.

GEORGE MARTIN (BUILDERS) LTD v. JAMAL; *sub nom*. MARTIN (GEORGE) BUILDERS LTD v. JAMAL 2001 S.L.T. (Sh Ct) 119, Sheriff AL Stewart Q.C., Sh Ct (Tayside, Central & Fife).

6259. Sheriff courts – citations – delivery – service of writ and warrant by special delivery letter – competency

[Act of Sederunt (Sheriff Court Ordinary Cause Rules) 1993 (SI 1993 1956) r.5.3(3), r.5.5(1).]

R, the pursuers in an ordinary cause action for payment moved for decree in absentia when no notice of intention to defend was lodged by H. R had served the writ and warrant on H by means of a Royal Mail special delivery letter and, in presenting a copy of the Royal Mail's "track and trace" document, it was argued that service had been properly effected in accordance with the Act of Sederunt (Sheriff Court Ordinary Cause Rules) 1993 r.5.5(1).

Held, refusing the decree, that the rules provided for service by way of registered letter or first class recorded delivery letter and service by Royal Mail special delivery could not be equiparated with those, the "track and trace" document only advising of delivery not of whether the requirement of endorsement on the letter in accordance with r.5.3(3) had actually been met.

ROSS & BONNYMAN LTD v. HAWSON GARNER LTD 2001 S.L.T. (Sh Ct) 134, K A Veal, Sh Ct (Tayside, Central and Fife).

6260. Sheriff courts – decree – interim decree – oral motion – in course of extra statutory consensual hearing – no written intimation – competency – appropriateness

[Act of Sederunt (Sheriff Court Ordinary Cause Rules) 1993 (SI 1993 1956) r.15.1(1)(a).]

In M's action against J, the sheriff granted a motion for interim decree against J for £19,965.53 in the course of a "preliminary hearing" which was an extra statutory consensual hearing designed to facilitate the progress of actions. J argued that it was incompetent for the sheriff to hear such a motion, because that was not a hearing within Act of Sederunt (Sheriff Court Ordinary Cause Rules) 1993 r.15.1 (1) (a) and in any event he had erred in his discretion in granting it.

Held, allowing the appeal and remitting the case to the sheriff, that (1) the sheriff failed to apply his mind to whether the motion should be granted orally and without notice, given that (a) the motion had not been intimated in writing in the ordinary way and the hearing was taking place by consent, and (b) the period for adjustment was still running, and (2) there were no circumstances which, as a matter of law, entitled the sheriff to grant the motion, and the sheriff's assertion that J's pleadings contained no substantive defence and that J had had plenty of time to adjust, whilst relevant to a motion for summary decree, was of no relevance to a motion for interim decree, especially where J's agent stated that there might be matters in respect of which he would wish to amplify the pleadings. There was no authority for an exception to the general rule that interim decrees would generally only be pronounced before the record closed, where a defender had made an unqualified admission of partial liability.

Observed, that the court was minded to the view that, since it was fixed by consent and was referred to in interlocutors, the hearing fell within r.15.1 (1) (a). Opinion of the Court per Lord Marnoch.

WILLIAM MILLER PLUMBING CONTRACTORS LTD v. JAMES LUMSDEN LTD 2000 S.L.T. 1425, Lord Prosser, Lord Clarke, Lord Marnoch, Ex Div.

6261. Sheriff courts – hearings – disposal of preliminary pleas

[Act of Sederunt (Sheriff Court Ordinary Cause Rules) 1993 (SI 1993 1956) r.9.12 (3) (c).]

In an action of accounting in which F sought to have Z account for transactions in respect of his bank account during a period in which they were cohabiting, F appealed against the decision of the sheriff to fix a proof before answer. The relationship was a distant one as Z remained in Scotland while F worked in Brazil. F, being the owner of their house in Scotland, granted Z a power of attorney to attend to his affairs while he was out of the country and he accepted that Z was entitled to use his bank account to meet "general costs attributable to the house", but contested the sufficiency of the averments of Z that she had spent £4,000 of her own funds on F's property. An issue had also arisen in relation to the use of a similar sum from F's funds for the purchase of a motor car for Z. F contended that a debate should be fixed because a greater specification of the circumstances in which the funds came to be removed from his account was required. Z argued that the decision of the sheriff to fix a proof before answer had been correct and that an appellate court should not readily interfere with the decision of the sheriff, *Gracey v. Sykes* 1994 S.C.L.R. 909, [1994] C.L.Y. 6290 cited.

Held, dismissing the appeal, that the sheriff had been correct to allow a proof before answer of the averments on record. It was unlikely that a debate could materially alter the extent of a proof and also unlikely that a sheriff would refuse to remit to proof any of Z's averments. The points at issue were matters within the knowledge of F and Z, rather than there being a substantial point of law in dispute and, until their agreement as regards the expenditure of funds had been clarified, it could not be said that F's complaints were irrelevant. Accordingly, a debate was not justified within the meaning of the Act of Sederunt (Sheriff Court Ordinary Cause Rules) 1993 r.9.12 (3) (c), *Tilcon (Scotland) Ltd v. Jarvis (Scotland) Ltd* 2000 S.L.T. (Sh Ct) 55, [2000] C.L.Y. 5945 not followed.

FERRARI v. ZUCCONI 2001 G.W.D. 16-587, JC McInnes Q.C., Sheriff Principal, Sh Ct (Grampian, Highland and Islands).

6262. Sheriff courts – pleadings – relevancy – discrimination by exclusion of gypsies from public house – knowledge of ethnic origin

See REPARATION: White v. Ferguson. §6878

6263. Sheriff courts – small claims – luggage rejected as defective – counterclaim not competent

J raised a small claim for payment of £669.57, the amount owed by N for luggage purchased. N lodged a defence and set out a counterclaim in which she sought $100 million. N argued that she had rejected the luggage as defective. The counterclaim claimed damages for "severe stress" and was dismissed by the sheriff as incompetent. A proof was heard in relation to the small claim and decree of absolvitor granted. Despite the decree in her favour N appealed and the Sheriff Principal directed the sheriff to state a case on the competency of the counterclaim.

Held, refusing the appeal, that the counterclaim was not competent as the absence of provision supporting a right to counterclaim can properly be interpreted as the exclusion of such a right.

JENNERS OF EDINBURGH v. NORRIS 2001 S.C.L.R. 516, RA Dunlop Q.C., Sheriff Principal, Sh Ct.

6264. Sheriff courts – small claims – whether note of appeal raised questions of law – whether sheriff bound to prepare stated case

[Act of Sederunt (Small Claim Rules) 1988 (SI 1988 1976) r.29(3).]

Following a decision in a small claims action to absolve S of liability and find no expenses due to or by either party, SR lodged a note of appeal. The sheriff considered the note of appeal and found that, as it contained no points of law on which the appeal could proceed, she was unable to draft a stated case. The note of appeal contained three paragraphs. It was accepted that the first paragraph contained no questions of law. The second paragraph claimed that the sheriff, on the basis of the facts proved, was not entitled to find that SR had failed to discharge the burden of proof, which rested upon them. It was followed by three subparagraphs: (1) subpara.2(a) stated that there was a difference between the defences put forward and the case at full hearing and contained no questions of law, (2) subpara.2(b) argued that the sheriff should have found that a contract existed between SR and Mrs S, for which SR were entitled to remuneration and (3) subpara.2(c), that there was no agreement as to price between the parties, and the sheriff should have found in favour of SR on the basis of quantum meruit or failing that, quantum lucratus. The third paragraph claimed that no sheriff acting reasonably could have reached the decision to assoilzie S.

Held, allowing the appeal, that as the Act of Sederunt (Small Claim Rules) 1988 r.29(3) required the sheriff to base the stated case on the points of law raised in the note of appeal, it was essential that the party wishing to appeal stated clearly the questions of law on which the appeal was to proceed. Paragraphs 1 and 2(a) of the note of appeal did not contain questions of law. Paragraphs 2(b) and 2(c) could lead to questions of law, but were worded in such a way that the basis for any questions of law had not been given. Paragraph 3 however, did potentially raise a question of law and the matter was referred back to the sheriff to prepare a stated case.

SEAMLESS ROOFING v. SMITH 2000 S.C.L.R. 1102, JC McInnes Q.C., Sheriff Principal, Sh Ct.

6265. Sheriff courts – summary causes – appeals – appeal after decree extracted – competency of use of dispensing power to hear appeal

[Housing (Scotland) Act 1987 s.48(4); Act of Sederunt (Summary Cause Rules) 1976 (SI 1976 476) r.89(1), r.19(1).]

ECC raised a summary cause action to recover possession of heritable property from their tenant S who owed rent. The sheriff granted decree for ejection after S failed to maintain a payment plan. S lodged an appeal, eight days after decree had been granted, along with an incidental application inviting the court to hear the appeal, although late, under the Act of Sederunt (Summary Cause Rules) Sheriff Court 1976. S argued that there were factors distinguishing the instant summary cause action from the general rule that a decree once extracted was no longer appealable. S maintained that under r.89(1) extract of decree was not as major a step in process as in ordinary cause procedure, and by virtue of r.19(1) the extract was open to recall even once issued. S also maintained that the decree had no practical effect until a date had been appointed under the Housing (Scotland) Act 1987 s.48(4), that being customarily four weeks after the date of decree.

Held, refusing the incidental application, that (1) there was no distinction between extracts under summary cause procedure and ordinary cause procedure except summary cause rules were expressed more briefly than the ordinary cause rules in order to keep them as simple as possible; (2) r.19(1) was of limited effect and did little more in summary cause actions than was achieved by reponing in ordinary cause procedure, and (3) s.48(4) did not prescribe a time that should elapse and as such did not effect the significance of the extract as properly issued. The existence of a dispensing power did not affect the general rule and any application inviting the court to hear an appeal which would otherwise be incompetent had itself to be incompetent.

EDINBURGH CITY COUNCIL v. SWANN 2001 S.L.T. (Sh Ct) 161, CGB Nicholson Q.C., Sheriff Principal, Sh Ct.

6266. Sheriff courts – summary causes – recall of decree – sist – no defence stated

[Act of Sederunt (Summary Cause Rules) 1976 (SI 1976 476) r.18(6), r.19(3).]
The local authority raised summary proceedings against R for recovery of possession of property tenanted by R. Decree was granted on June 30, 1998 when, after initial procedures, no defence had been stated. In November 1998 following a defence motion, the decree was recalled in terms of the Act of Sederunt (Summary Cause Rules) 1976 r.19(3). The cause was sisted to enable R to apply for legal aid although no defence was stated. R's agents withdrew in December 1998 and in January 2000, the local authority served an incidental application for the sist to be recalled and for expenses. At the hearing in March 2000, R failed to make an appearance and the sheriff granted decree in favour of the local authority under r.18(6) believing that the recalling of the sist under r.19(3) had the result of allowing the sheriff to consider the case at the hearing as falling into the category of a "first calling or a continuation thereof". R appealed by stated case questioning whether it was competent for the sheriff to grant decree under r.18(6) in those circumstances.

Held, recalling the decree and remitting the case back to the sheriff to be reheard on the motion to recall the sist, that (1) r.18 made it clear that there could only be one first calling in any summary cause action and that any continuation could not be for longer than 28 days; (2) it was a necessary implication of r.18(6) that where a defender intended to defend an action, he had to state a defence at the first calling or at a continuation of it and it followed that where a defender obtained a recall of decree under r.19(3) he had to state a defence; (3) failure to state a defence at the hearing for recall of a decree was not covered by the Rules, and (4) although R had succeeded in his appeal, the local authority could not be held liable for expenses caused by R's failure to state defences.

GLASGOW CITY COUNCIL v. RANKIN 2001 S.C.L.R. 876, EF Bowen Q.C., Sheriff Principal, Sh Ct.

6267. Sheriff courts – summary causes – repossession – competency of minute for recall

[Act of Sederunt (Summary Cause Rules) 1976 (SI 1976 476) r.18(6), r.18(9).]
C raised proceedings to recover possession of property from N who owed rent and had failed to stick to payment agreements. Decree was granted by the sheriff and the rule relied upon was not detailed. The rent owed was specified and N was unable to state a defence. N lodged minute of recall arguing that the decree had been pronounced in terms of the Act of Sederunt (Summary Cause Rules) Sheriff Court 1976 r.18(6). The sheriff held that decree had been pronounced in terms of r.18(9) and as such motion for recall was incompetent. N appealed arguing r.18(9)

was concerned with express admissions and a failure to state a defence could not be held as such.

Held, refusing the appeal that the proposition, that r.18(9) was only concerned with express or specific admissions could not be accepted. Situations could arise where the stance adopted by the parties and the procedural history of the case made their respective positions plain and lead to clear factual inferences which was far from suggesting that facts could be taken as admitted whenever a party failed to state a defence. It was sufficiently clear from the history of the case that substantial rent arrears were not in doubt and the sheriff had been entitled to act as he did.

CASTLEMILK EAST HOUSING COOPERATIVE LTD v. NIXON 2000 Hous. L.R. 133, EF Bowen Q.C., Sheriff Principal, Sh Ct (Glasgow and Strathkelvin).

6268. Summons – service of summons without citation – competence to grant relief

[Citation Act 1592 (c.59); Act of Sederunt (Rules of the Court of Session 1994) 1994 (SI 1994 1443) r.2.1, r.13.7(1) (a).]

C raised an action for damages for personal injury and served a summons on CP at its place of business in Hong Kong. By an oversight, C omitted to serve with the summons a citation as required by the Act of Sederunt (Rules of the Court of Session 1994) 1994 r.13.7(1) (a). The summons was lodged for calling. CP declined to enter an appearance and sought to have the summons withdrawn on the grounds of defective service. The Lord Ordinary decided that such a course of action was probably not competent, but that submissions should be heard on the matter. Although CP had failed to enter an appearance, it would be allowed to appear and make oral submissions. CP accepted that once a case had been called, it was not competent for the court to reverse that step. C sought relief under r.2.1 from the consequences of the failure to include the citation, but CP argued that the requirement to serve a citation could not be separated from the requirement to have the citation signed and that if C had failed to comply with the requirement to serve the citation, he had also failed to comply with the requirement under the Citation Act 1592 to have the citation signed, making r.2.1 inapplicable.

Held, granting relief in terms of r.2.1, that (1) whilst the requirement that a citation be signed rested in the 1592 Act to which r.2.1 was inapplicable, the requirement to serve a citation with the service copy summons rested in r.13.7(1) (a) and could therefore be cured by r.2.1, and (2) as there had been considerable correspondence between the solicitors acting for the parties regarding service in Hong Kong, CP was fully aware of the action which had been raised and was not, in any way, prejudiced by the failure to serve the citation with the summons, which was a genuine oversight on the part of an inexperienced solicitor.

COLLEY v. CELTIC PACIFIC SHIP MANAGEMENT (OVERSEAS) LTD 2001 S.L.T. 320, Lord Macfadyen, OH.

6269. Third party proceedings – appropriateness of arrestment on dependence

[Act of Sederunt (Rules of the Court of Session 1994) 1994 (SI 1994 1443) r.26.3.]

C had contracted with A to design and build a retail unit. C sought damages, averring breach of contract and breach of the duty of care on the basis of defective design and a problem with the fire protection. A maintained that all defects had been rectified and C had approved the final account. A obtained warrant for service against its subcontractor, N, as the party responsible for the design and fire protection, and raised a motion for warrant to arrest and inhibit on the dependence against N.

Held, refusing the motion, that the court had discretion, having regard to the Act of Sederunt (Rules of the Court of Session 1994) 1994 r.26.3, as to whether to grant warrant. A did not concede the possibility of liability on its part and in relation to N made no averments on the merits in respect of which it was conceivable that a situation could arise where they would actually seek relief, nor did they qualify any claim against N.

CHARTWELL LAND INVESTMENTS LTD v. AMEC CONSTRUCTION SCOTLAND LTD 2001 S.L.T. 732, Lord Bonomy, OH.

6270. Books

Genn, Hazel; Paterson, Alan – Paths of Justice in Scotland-What People in Scotland Think and Do about Going to Law. Paperback: £20.00. ISBN 1-841-13040-0. Hart Publishing.

Hennessy, C – Civil Court and Practice. Greens Concise Scots Law. Paperback: £32.00. ISBN 0-414-01283-6. W.Green & Son.

Jamieson, George – Summary Applications. Greens Practice Library. Hardback: £120.00. ISBN 0-414-01225-9. W.Green & Son.

COMMERCIAL LAW

6271. Advertising – national parks – commercial vehicles

HOLYROOD PARK AMENDMENT REGULATIONS 2001, SSI 2001 405; made under the Parks Regulations (Amendment) Act 1926 s.2. In force: November 6, 2001; £1.75.

These Regulations amend the Holyrood Park Regulations 1971 (SI 1971 593) which specifically ban commercial vehicles and the exhibition of advertising material in the Park. They permit commercial vehicles to use a specified route through the Park as an alternative to Holyrood Road which is scheduled for partial closure and permit the display of advertising material on such commercial vehicles.

6272. Books

Mercantile Statutes: 2001. Paperback: £44.00. ISBN 0-414-01425-1. Sweet & Maxwell.

COMPANY LAW

6273. Companies – registration – restoration of company to register – exercise of power – whether proper

[Prescription and Limitation (Scotland) Act 1973 (c.52) s.19A; Companies Act 1985 (c.6) s.651 (6).]

S, a limited company which had been removed from the Register of Companies in 1990 and restored to the register in April 1999, raised an action for reduction of part of the interlocutor effecting its restoration, so far as it purported to be an exercise of discretion under the Companies Act 1985 s.651 (6). The applicants for the restoration order wished to bring an action of damages in respect of the death, in February 1996, of B, a former employee, following his exposure to asbestos. S pled that the interlocutor had been pronounced without consideration of the Prescription and Limitation (Scotland) Act 1973 s.19A, namely the power of court to override the time limit, or the test therein, and as a result was incompetent.

Held, dismissing the action as irrelevant, that, in the absence of specific averments, it could not be assumed that the Lord Ordinary did not have sufficient material before him to exercise his discretion in the way he did, or that he did not have s.19A of the 1973 Act in mind.

SCOTTISH LION ENGINEERING LTD v. BENSON (RESTORATION TO REGISTER OF COMPANIES) 2001 S.L.T. 1037, Judge TG Coutts Q.C., OH.

6274. Directors – disqualification orders – summary application to dismiss – jurisdiction of sheriff court

[Company Directors Disqualification Act 1986 (c.46); Act of Sederunt (Sheriff Court Summary Application Rules) 1993 (SI 1993 3240) r.32.]

S sought disqualification of L as a director under the Company Directors Disqualification Act 1986. L's second plea in law sought to have the application dismissed relying on S's failure to deal with it expeditiously. S argued that L could not seek a dismissal, even if undue delay was established, there being no provision in the Act of Sederunt (Sheriff Court Summary Application Rules) 1993 for such an action. L argued that the only possible exception arose in r.32, which would allow the sheriff to make such order as he thought fit for the progress of a summary application.

Held, repelling L's second plea in law, that the sheriff had no power to dismiss the application on a substantive matter, either generally under the Rules or specifically under r.32, nor to go outwith the terms of the rules to dismiss the application.

SECRETARY OF STATE FOR TRADE AND INDUSTRY v. LOVAT (SUMMARY DISMISSAL) [2000] B.C.C. 485, Sheriff McIver, Sh Ct (Glasgow and Strathkelvin).

6275. Directors – payments in kind – payments for loss of office – benefits conferred on becoming honorary life president

[Companies Act 1985 (c.6) s.232, s.312, s.320.]

The former chairman of a football club sought declarator that he was honorary life president of the club, as conferred on him by the board of directors, and interdict against the club preventing him exercising privileges in connection with this position. The pursuer sought to rely on an exchange of letters dated June 10 and 12, 1994, following a meeting of the board on June 1. Under the terms of the letters, the word "honorary" indicated a position in perpetuity, and provided that the pursuer was entitled to two seats in the directors' box on match days, access for himself and a guest to the boardroom, and a pass for the car park. The club counterclaimed concluding for reduction of the relevant parts of the minutes of the board's meeting and of the purported agreement. The club submitted that the appointment was made "as consideration for or in connection with [the pursuer's] retirement" in terms of the Companies Act 1985 s.312, the motive being at least in part to mark his achievements while in office, that it was not disclosed to the members or approved by the club, contrary to s.312, and that "payment" under that section was capable of meaning payment in kind. The pursuer submitted inter alia that the benefits were subject only to the provisions in s.320 concerning property transactions by directors, but if falling under s.312, also fell under the requirement in s.232 of disclosure in the accounts, and approval of the accounts by the board constituted sufficient approval for the purpose of s.312.

Held, granting decree de plano and dismissing the counterclaim, that (1) there was no merit in the pursuer's subsidiary submissions: s.232 related only to payments made as compensation for loss of office, and the accounts were only laid before the members and reflected the payment ex post facto whereas s.312 contemplated disclosure of particulars to members and approval by the company in advance. It was wrong to construe s.312 in the light of s.320; (2) the documents made it clear that the privileges were essentially attached to the pursuer's future position as honorary president rather than in connection with his retirement; (3) while the primary meaning of "payment" under s.312 was transfer of money, the prevention of easy circumvention of s.312 required that a transfer of other property could constitute a "payment", but (4) although the privileges in question had a monetary value it was not obvious that it would cost the club money to enable the pursuer to enjoy them, and there were no relevant averments that they fell within s.312.

MERCER v. HEART OF MIDLOTHIAN PLC 2001 S.L.T. 945, Lord Macfadyen, OH.

6277. Dividends – payment – interim dividend – delay in payment of interest – competency

[Companies (Tables A to F) Regulations 1985 (SI 1985 805) Table A, Art.102, Art.103, Art.104, Art.107.]

D raised an action for payment of a dividend which company J, of which he was a shareholder, had declared but not paid. J appealed against the sheriff's decision to award interest at the judicial rate from the date of the raising of the action. J argued that D's averments had been irrelevant as, while D founded on Companies (Tables A to F) Regulations 1985 Table A, Art.102 and Art.104, which obliged J to pay dividends on declaration, only Art.103 applied to interim dividends which the dividend in question was averred to be. It was accepted that the sheriff had been wrong in his belief that the dividend had been paid. On 12 January 2000, J had consented to an interim decree for payment of the principal sum but this remained unpaid.

Held, refusing the appeal subject to amendment of the date from which interest became due, that (1) Art.102-108 of Table A were simply headed "Dividends" and there was nothing in Art.102 and 104 which expressly restricted them to final dividends. While a date for payment could be set down, in this case another shareholder had actually been paid; (2) that was also an attack on the relevancy of D's averments which was not made before the sheriff and which came far too late. The existence of the interim decrees granted of consent presented an insuperable obstacle to any further consideration of the submissions; (3) the sheriff was in error when he awarded interest from the date on which proceedings were commenced. The provisions of Art.107, which prohibited the payment of interest on any debt relating to a share, were clear and the raising of the action had no effect on this, and (4) interest would, however, be awarded from the date of the interim decrees. A sum awarded under judicial decree had a character of its own which was not restricted by the nature of the legal obligation leading to the granting of the decree, and Art.107 had no effect after the interim decrees were granted.

DOHERTY v. JAYMARKE DEVELOPMENTS (PROSPECTHILL) LTD (NO.2) 2001 S.L.T. (Sh Ct) 75, CGB Nicholson Q.C., Sheriff Principal, Sh Ct.

CONFLICT OF LAWS

6278. Choice of law – contracts – Scottish and Italian company providing service for work undertaken in Egypt – presumption under Rome Convention not rebutted

[Rome Convention on the law applicable to contractual obligations 1980.]

C, a diving contractor based in Scotland, entered into a contract with M, an Italian company, to carry out work in Egyptian waters. M was working under a contract with an Egyptian company that included an express choice of law clause naming the Arab Republic of Egypt. C brought an action in the Court of Session against M for sums allegedly due under the contract. A preliminary proof was heard on the issue of the law applicable to the contract. M conceded that if the Rome Convention presumption applied then Scots law would be the law applicable, but argued that the presumption did not apply because the contract was more closely connected to Egypt.

Held, that the applicable law was Scots. The Convention presumption was designed to establish the place of business, not performance, as the dominant factor. Although the place of performance could be a powerful factor in displacing the presumption, in the instant case it had been shown that there was a continuing and important connection with Scotland.

CALEDONIA SUBSEA LTD v. MICOPERI SRL; *sub nom.* CALEDONIA SUBSEA LTD v. MICROPERI SRL 2001 S.C. 716, Lord Hamilton, OH.

CONSTITUTIONAL LAW

6279. Devolution – road traffic enactments – consequential modifications

SCOTLAND ACT 1998 (CONSEQUENTIAL MODIFICATIONS) ORDER 2001, SI 2001 1400 (S.6); made under the Scotland Act 1998 s.105, s.112, s.113. In force: April 6, 2001; £1.75.

This Order, which amends the Road Traffic Regulation Act 1984 and the Roads (Scotland) Act 1984, makes modifications to pre-commencement enactments, within the meaning of the Scotland Act 1998, which appear to be necessary or expedient in consequence of the Act. The Order contains a saving provision which ensures that, in interpreting enactments which have not been textually amended because reliance is placed on the general modifications in the Act, no adverse implication can be drawn because of the presence in the Schedule of textual amendments to some enactments which replicate the effect of the general modifications.

6280. Ethical Standards in Public Life etc. (Scotland) Act 2000 (asp 7) – Commencement No.1 Order

ETHICAL STANDARDS IN PUBLIC LIFE ETC. (SCOTLAND) ACT 2000 (COMMENCEMENT NO.1) ORDER 2001, SSI 2001 113 (C.5); made under the Ethical Standards in Public Life etc. (Scotland) Act s.37. Commencement details: bringing into force various provisions of the Act on March 29, 2001; £1.50.

(Scotland) Act 2000 s.37(2). This Order brings into force provisions of the Ethical Standards in Public Life etc. (Scotland) Act 2000, on March 29, 2001, which allow the code of conduct for local authority councillors and the model code of conduct for members of certain public bodies to be laid before, and approved by resolution of, the Scottish Parliament; provisions which are about the Standards Commission for Scotland and about appointment of the Chief Investigating Officer and that Officer's staff and provisions which repeal the Local Government Act 1986 s.2A and impose new duties to children on local authorities.

6281. Ethical Standards in Public Life etc. (Scotland) Act 2000 (asp 7) – Commencement No.2 and Transitional Provisions Order

ETHICAL STANDARDS IN PUBLIC LIFE ETC. (SCOTLAND) ACT 2000 (COMMENCEMENT NO.2 AND TRANSITIONAL PROVISIONS) ORDER 2001, SSI 2001 474 (C.22); made under the Ethical Standards in Public Life etc. (Scotland) Act 2000 s.37. Commencement details: bringing into force various provisions of the 2000 Act on January 1, 2002; £1.50.

This Order brings into force provisions of the Ethical Standards in Public Life etc. (Scotland) Act 2000 s.33 which revises the special reports and hearings procedure by which the Accounts Commission for Scotland and the Controller of Audit investigate and respond to alleged failure, negligence or misconduct by individuals or local authorities in the management of public funds.

6282. Scottish devolution – legislative competence

SCOTLAND ACT 1998 (MODIFICATION OF SCHEDULE 5) ORDER 2001, SI 2001 1456; made under the Scotland Act 1998 s.30. In force: in accordance with Art.1; £1.75.

This Order amends the Scotland Act 1998 by adding a further exception to the insolvency reservation, bringing within the legislative competence of the Scottish Parliament certain matters relating to the insolvency of business associations which are social landlords as defined in the Order, in so far as relating to provision for a moratorium on the disposal of property held by a social landlord and the management and disposal of such property.

6283. Scottish devolution – Scottish Ministers – transfer of functions

SCOTLAND ACT 1998 (TRANSFER OF FUNCTIONS TO THE SCOTTISH MINISTERS ETC.) ORDER 2001, SI 2001 954; made under the Scotland Act 1998 s.63, s.113, s.124. In force: in accordance with Art.1 (1); £1.75.

This Order amends the Scotland Act 1998 by providing for certain specified functions of a Minister of the Crown, so far as they are exercisable by him in or as regards Scotland, to be exercisable by the Scottish Ministers instead of by the Minister of the Crown.

6284. Scottish devolution – Scottish Ministers – transfer of functions

SCOTLAND ACT 1998 (TRANSFER OF FUNCTIONS TO THE SCOTTISH MINISTERS ETC.) (NO.2) ORDER 2001, SI 2001 3504 (S.18); made under the Scotland Act1998 s.63, s.113, s.124. In force: in accordance with Art.1 (1) (2); £1.75.

This Order, which amends the Scotland Act 1998, provides for certain specified functions of a Minister of the Crown, so far as they are exercisable by that Minister in or as regards Scotland, to be exercisable by the Scottish Ministers instead of by the Minister of the Crown.

6285. Books

Convery, Jane – Constitutional Law Basics. 2nd Ed. Greens Law Basics. Paperback: £9.95. ISBN 0-414-01434-0. W.Green & Son.

CONSTRUCTION LAW

6286. Building and engineering contracts – adjudication – interpretation of contract – jurisdiction of adjudicator

[Housing Grants, Construction and Regeneration Act 1996 (c.53) s.108; Scheme for Construction Contracts (Scotland) Regulations 1988 (SI 1988 687).]

W, the main contractor in a construction contract, petitioned for judicial review and reduction of an adjudicator's decision that payment was due by W to their subcontractors on the ground that the adjudicator had no jurisdiction to hear the dispute. W admitted that the subcontract was a construction contract to which the Housing Grants, Construction and Regeneration Act 1996 s.108 applied. W also admitted that where the contract terms for adjudication did not comply with the requirements of s.108, the adjudication procedure would be governed by the Scheme for Construction Contracts (Scotland) Regulations 1988. W submitted, however, that the subcontract, by implied incorporation of the standard form of the Scottish Building Contract Contractors Designed Portion without Quantities (April 1998 revision), contained sufficient provisions to comply with s.108 and the 1988 Scheme should not apply. The terms of the subcontract, W submitted, listed the bodies authorised to appoint adjudicators. The Academy of Construction Adjudicators was not on the list and therefore any adjudicator appointed by them lacked jurisdiction. Finally, W submitted that it was not open to the adjudicator to determine his own jurisdiction, nor to determine that the subcontract did not comply with the 1996 Act thereby invoking the provisions of the 1988 Regulations. The adjudicator submitted that judicial review was inappropriate where the decision was open to challenge through arbitration or litigation. The adjudicator, together with the subcontractor, also submitted that W had, in their response to the referral, brought the issue of whether the subcontract contained sufficient terms to comply with the 1996 Act before the adjudicator making the question of compliance within the adjudicators jurisdiction.

Held, refusing the petition, that (1) in creating the provisions under the 1996 Act for adjudication, Parliament had intended that adjudicators would consider contract terms and make decisions on the meaning of those terms including terms relating to dispute resolution procedures, (2) the question of the proper construction of the subcontract terms as they related to provision for adjudication had been expressly placed before the adjudicator by W's response to the referral and the adjudicator was therefore entitled to make a determination on that issue, and (3) by cross referring the issue of jurisdiction to the adjudicator rather than following alternative courses of action open to W in challenging the adjudicator's jurisdiction, W had accepted that the adjudicator was competent to determine the issue and it was not open to W to challenge the adjudication by way of judicial review. Opinion, that the purported incorporation of the terms of the standard form into the subcontract had been effective as the terms of the standard form did not apply to the relationship between a main contractor and a subcontractor.

WATSON BUILDING SERVICES LTD v. HARRISON 2001 S.L.T. 846, Lady Paton, OH.

6287. Building and engineering contracts – adjudication – jurisdiction – excluded operations

[Housing Grants, Construction and Regeneration Act 1996 (c.53) s.105(2)(c).]

M, a construction company, sought judicial review of an adjudicator's decision that she did not have jurisdiction to adjudicate in its dispute with F, a supply company, as the relevant works were excluded from the adjudication scheme for construction contracts in terms of the Housing Grants, Construction and Regeneration Act 1996 s.105(2)(c)(ii) as involving "the production, transmission, processing or bulk storage...of chemicals [or] oil". F had contracted to supply M with equipment and piping to be used in the construction of two boilers. The boilers were being constructed on behalf of, and to be operated by, a company which had contracted to supply steam to a petrochemical company, and were to be located on land leased from the latter company, within its plant. M conceded that the ultimate use of the site was not irrelevant, but argued that the boilers would produce an identifiable commodity, steam, by a separate enterprise; the steam was to be delivered to the petrochemical company's plant, which was located outwith the boundaries of the construction site; the site was operated by a separate concern; and "site" was not defined by the Act and it was legally and contractually possible to distinguish between the construction site and the plant.

Held, refusing the application, that (1) M's concession was correct, *ABB Power Construction Ltd v. Norwest Holst Engineering Ltd* (2000) 2 T.C.L.R. 831, [2001] 1 C.L. 98 followed, and (2) the operations undertaken by M were exempt under s.105(2)(c)(ii) where the installation of the boilers was to further the primary activity of oil and chemical processing at the petrochemical plant, as the s.105(2)(c) exemption was directed to primary activity on site, not ownership or occupation.

MITSUI BABCOCK ENERGY SERVICES LTD v. FOSTER WHEELER ENERGIA OY 2001 S.L.T. 1158, Lord Hardie, OH.

6288. Building and engineering contracts – adjudication – jurisdiction of adjudicator

[Scheme for Construction Contracts (Scotland) Regulations 1998 (SI 1998 687).]

B, the contractors employed under a standard JCT form of management contract sought reduction of a purported decision of an adjudicator under the Scheme for Construction Contracts (Scotland) Regulations 1998, in a dispute with BC, their employers. The reference concerned a dispute over the sums due and payable under the contract. B alleged inter alia that BC had, in bad faith, prevented the issue of certificates relating to the contract work. The adjudicator refused to grant the redress sought, describing the referral as "not valid" on the ground that the parties had failed to abide strictly to the terms of the JCT contract in their dealings with each other and third parties, and concluded that the dispute could only be resolved through alternative dispute resolution. BC argued that the adjudicator had validly decided that B's claims did not arise under the contract and he therefore had no jurisdiction to reach a decision; in any event, if he was in error in equating "the contract" under the scheme with the JCT contract, that was an error within his jurisdiction with which the court could not interfere.

Held, reducing the decision, that (1) the scheme had to be interpreted as requiring the parties to comply with an adjudicator's decision, notwithstanding his failure to comply with the express or implied requirements of the scheme, unless the decision was a nullity, which it would be if the adjudicator had acted ultra vires in the broad sense of the term; (2) the adjudicator was bound to determine the dispute referred to him provided it fell within his jurisdiction, the limits of which could not be narrowed or extended by his misconstruing those limits, and (3) the adjudicator's approach to the validity of the referral was wrong in law and given the allegations of bad faith, that error was material and resulted in his failing to exercise his jurisdiction, which rendered his decision a nullity.

BALLAST PLC v. BURRELL CO (CONSTRUCTION MANAGEMENT) LTD 2001 S.L.T. 1039, Lord Reed, OH.

6289. Building and engineering contracts – adjudication – validity of decision

[Scheme for Construction Contracts (Scotland) Regulations 1998 (SI 1998 687) Pt II.]

K entered into a building subcontract agreement with S under which, S undertook to carry out certain construction works. S referred a dispute concerning an interim payment for works carried out by S to adjudication. K argued that under the subcontract, interim payments only became payable when the value of the equivalent works was included in the certificate from the architect or contract administrator of the main contract. K claimed that S had been paid to more than its certified entitlement and that, accordingly, no further sums were due. The referral to adjudication by S claimed that payment was due under the provisions of the Scheme for Construction Contracts (Scotland) Regulations 1998 Pt II, however K argued that the scheme did not apply as the mechanisms for interim payments contained in the subcontract were adequate. During the adjudication process, correspondence from S indicated that S was in agreement with K on that point. The adjudicator, having held a meeting with the parties to determine the exact value of work completed by S and the total of interim payments made, determined that, in terms of the Regulations, S was entitled to an immediate interim payment of £39,872.04 excluding VAT and with interest with K being liable for the adjudicator's fees. K petitioned for a judicial review arguing that, in determining that the subcontract did not contain adequate payment provisions and that Part II of the 1998 Regulations should, by default, apply; the adjudicator had based her decision on matters which were not included in the referral to adjudication and as such had acted ultra vires K sought reduction of her decision. K argued that both parties had ultimately agreed that the subcontract did contain adequate payment provisions and that, as that was not in dispute, the adjudicator had no remit to make a decision on it. S argued that the object of the referral was to settle the dispute regarding whether an immediate interim payment was due for work carried out by S.

Held, refusing the petition, that (1) the objective of the adjudication procedure was to get a practical provisional decision on the disputed matter in a situation where the parties were likely to have commercial interests in mind and unlikely to be concerned with an extensive legal analysis of the issues; (2) in determining the petition it was essential to establish what the matter in dispute between that parties at adjudication actually was; (3) although the adjudicator's reasons for finding that the subcontract did not adequately provide a mechanism for interim payments were not clearly given, she was within her remit in making that decision as the matter in dispute, which was whether S was entitled to payment for the work carried out, required an assessment of when the payment had fallen due, and (4) if the adjudicator had erred in deciding that the subcontract contained inadequate payment provisions, then that error was in respect of her treatment of the dispute and not any venture on her part beyond the jurisdiction afforded to her by the referral, *Bouygues UK Ltd v. Dahl-*

Jensen UK Ltd [2000] B.L.R. 49, [2000] 3 C.L. 21, followed. Opinion of the Court as per Lord Caplan, Lord Ordinary.

KARL CONSTRUCTION (SCOTLAND) LTD v. SWEENEY CIVIL ENGINEERING (SCOTLAND) LTD 2001 S.C.L.R. 95, Lord Caplan, OH.

6290. Building and engineering contracts – breach of contract – delay – loss assessment

B, a firm of house builders raised an action of damages against M, a land surveyor, for losses incurred through the delay in commencing a building project allegedly caused by M's erroneous plotting of a burn running across the land. B moved onto the site in accordance with the terms of the missives but was prevented from commencing work until a building warrant was granted following a revised grant of planning permission to accommodate the position of the burn. B averred inter alia that as a result of the delay they had suffered a reduction in turnover and loss of profit. B averred a formula by which that should be calculated, utilising the percentage of its turnover represented by overheads and profit, but at proof sought to advance a calculation based on average turnover of the preceding two financial years.

Held, granting decree, that (1) B's revised basis should be rejected as M had not had fair notice of it and it did not give a more reliable basis than the contract price, and (2) there was sufficient evidence from B's pattern of trading to allow an award for loss of turnover, and £31,007 was an appropriate award.

BEECHWOOD DEVELOPMENT CO (SCOTLAND) LTD v. MITCHELL (T/A DISCOVERY LAND SURVEYS) 2001 S.L.T. 1214, Lord Hamilton, OH.

6291. Building and engineering contracts – ICE conditions of contract – common law right of retention – interest continues to accrue

O entered into a contract with B to carry out construction work. The contract was subject to the ICE Conditions of Contract. Monies due to B, totalling £280,880 were withheld by O on the basis that B was insolvent. B subsequently became solvent. The dispute was taken to arbitration where the arbiter held that B was entitled to interest on the monies withheld. At O's request, the arbiter put forward a stated case for the opinion of the Court of Session as to whether he had erred in law in holding that interest would be due under cl.60(6) from the date of delivery of the statement until monies paid. O argued that they had been entitled to retain the sums on the principle of balancing the accounts in bankruptcy and as such there had not been a "failure" to make payment under cl.60(6). B argued that while O had a common law right of retention, that would not affect the running of interest.

Held, answering the stated case in the negative, that the question for determination was whether interest was due ex contractu for the period when O were exercising their common law right of retention. The right of O to withhold the sums due as security applied not only to the sums but also to the interest on those sums which would continue to accrue during the period of retention. Opinion of the Court per Lord Kirkwood.

CHARLES BRAND LTD v. ORKNEY ISLANDS COUNCIL 2001 S.C. 545, Lord Kirkwood, Lord Eassie, Lord Morison, Ex Div.

6292. Building and engineering contracts – interpretation – contractual time bar – generality of application

Following disputes between L, the subcontractors under a contract governed by the ICE General Conditions of Contract (June 1973), and J, the main contractors, J terminated L's employment in 1994. In 1995, J applied to the engineer to issue a completion certificate in respect of the main works in terms of cl.48 of the contract. The issuing of the certificate began a 12 month maintenance period following which a maintenance certificate was issued in 1996. In 1997, L intimated claims for payment arising out of the subcontract to J. J rejected the claims on the basis that they had been intimated too late in terms of cl.15(6) of the contract, which required that claims arising out of the contract should be intimated before the maintenance certificate has been issued. The matter proceeded to arbitration where L argued that cl.15(6) did not apply to claims of that type. The arbiter found in favour of L and J appealed by way of stated case on three questions. Only the first question was dealt with by the appeal court namely, whether the arbiter was correct in finding that cl.15(6) was limited in effect by its positioning in the contract as a subclause of cl.15.

Held, answering the question in the negative and remitting the case back to the arbiter, that the wording of cl.15(6) was deliberately wide and could not be construed as to be limited only to claims under cl.15(1) where no specific reference to cl.15(1) was made within cl.15(6). L had offered no explanation as to why the claims had not been intimated before the maintenance certificate was issued, and that, as the claims arose out of the subcontract, they were time expired under cl.15(6), *Blissgrange Ltd v. John G McGregor (Contractors) Ltd* 1987 G.W.D. 19-707 considered.

LOUDONHILL CONTRACTS LTD v. JOHN MOWLEM CONSTRUCTION LTD; *sub nom.* LOUNDONHILL CONTRACTS LTD v. JOHN MOWLEM CONSTRUCTION LTD 2000 S.C.L.R. 1111, Lord Rodger, L.P., Lord Cameron of Lochbroom, Lord Cowie, 1 Div.

6293. **Building and engineering contracts – right to payment – notice to withhold payment effective to give rise to arbitration**

[Housing Grants, Construction and Regeneration Act 1996 (c.53) s.111, s.115.]

S raised an action against G for payment under a contract for the construction of a showroom, office block and workshop. The construction contract was in the standard form of the Scottish Building Contract with Contractor's Design (July 1997 revision). G maintained that S had failed to complete the contract timeously and that, as a result of the delay, G had incurred costs. G wrote to S, intimating the cost incurred by S's delay and indicating G's intention to offset those sums against the £40,000 balance outstanding under the contract. S subsequently issued an invoice to G for the sum of £41,277.05 as an interim payment arising out of the contract in terms of cl.30.3.1 and cl.30.3.2. Upon receipt of the invoice, G telephoned S and left a verbal message with S's telephonist referring S to the terms of G's letter outlining costs to be offset against the balance. G claimed, in response to the action raised by S, that the letter and subsequent oral communication amounted to notice of intention to withhold payment in terms of the Housing Grants, Construction and Regeneration Act 1996 s.111 and that the action should be sisted for the matter to be referred to arbitration in terms of the contract.

Held, refusing the motion to sist the action and refer the matter to arbitration, that (1) there was binding authority in *Albyn Housing Society Ltd v. Taylor Woodrow Homes Ltd* 1985 S.C. 104, [1985] C.L.Y. 3689 that the court must, before sisting for arbitration, investigate the dispute between the parties and be satisfied that it amounted to an arbitral dispute; (2) the question of whether G's oral communication amounted to notice under the terms of cl.30.3.4 of the contract raised issues of agency which fell within the arbitration provisions, *Redpath Dorman Long Ltd v. Tarmac Construction Ltd* 1982 S.C. 14, [1982] C.L.Y. 3420, approved; (3) under s.111 and s.115, an effective notice of intention to withhold payment required to be in writing, and (4) s.111 created a procedure for issuing such notices which clearly required to notice to be given after an application for payment had been made and not before. Opinion reserved that a notice under s.111 issued after an application for payment had been made could refer for its terms to a written communication between the parties prior to the date of the application. Doubted, whether G's letter was sufficient in its terms, even if issued after the application for payment, to constitute an effective notice under s.111 as it was effectively only an offer to compromise on a restricted sum.

STRATHMORE BUILDING SERVICES LTD v. GREIG (T/A HESTIA FIRESIDE DESIGN) 2000 S.L.T. 815, Lord Hamilton, OH.

6294. Building and engineering contracts – standard forms of contract – obligation of employer to insure – no obligation to insure against contractor negligence

E contracted with M to have building work done. The form of contract used was the Scottish Minor Works Contract 1986 Edition (April 1987 Revision). M subcontracted some of the work to B, a fire broke out and E averred that the fire had been caused by B's faulty installation of a sauna heater. E sought reparation, jointly and severally, from M on the basis of breach of contract and indemnity under contract and from B, on the basis of negligence at common law. Under cl.8.3B of the contract P were obliged to insure, in joint names, against loss or damage. M argued that the losses fell within cl.8.3B and accordingly the action against them was irrelevant. P argued that they were not obliged to indemnify themselves against M's negligence.

Held, allowing proof before answer, that the standard form contract was identical to that in England and although not bound by English decisions it would be unfortunate if differing conclusions were reached. On proper construction of cl.8.3B the cover was not to extend to insuring the contractor against negligence or fault.

EUROPEAN AND INTERNATIONAL INVESTMENTS INC v. McLAREN BUILDING SERVICES LTD 2001 S.C. 745, Lord Hamilton, OH.

6295. Building regulations – fire precautions – energy conservation

BUILDING STANDARDS (SCOTLAND) AMENDMENT REGULATIONS 2001, SSI 2001 320; made under the Building (Scotland) Act 1959 s.3, s.6, s.11, s.24, s.29, Sch.4. In force: March 4, 2002; £2.00.

These Regulations make amendments to the Building Standards (Scotland) Regulations 1990 (SI 1990 2179) relating to structural fire precautions, means of escape from fire, facilities for fire fighting, conservation of fuel and power, drainage and sanitary facilities. The Regulations do not apply to any construction or change of use of a building where application for warrant was made before that date.

CONSUMER LAW

6296. Consumer credit agreements – credit cards – card payment for building work – excessive invoices – debtor's remedy against creditor

[Consumer Credit Act 1974 c.39) s.75.]

D raised an action on the basis of the Consumer Credit Act 1974 s.75, against N, a bank which had issued a credit card to him, in respect of domestic building work that he had paid for using the card. The contractors which had carried out the building work had ceased trading. D averred that the contractors' invoices were excessive for the work undertaken and in breach of a contract term that additional work would be carried out at a reasonable rate. N argued that as D's right of action against them was based not on breach of contract but on repetition of moneys paid in error, it was a remedy based on condictio indebiti and that the conditions in s.75 had thus not been satisfied.

Held, putting the case out by order for amendment in other respects, that (1) while D's claim would normally be based on the condictio indebiti, the dominant or real cause of the loss was the rendering of the invoices and it was clearly a breach of contract to render an invoice on a basis disconform to the contract, and D was entitled to invoke the remedies in cumulo, and (2) the breach and loss did not require to be contemporaneous, and D's loss should be treated as caused by the contractors' act disconform to contract and not by his actions in making payment of the invoices.

DALGLISH v. NATIONAL WESTMINSTER BANK PLC 2001 S.L.T. (Sh Ct) 124, Sheriff J A Taylor, Sh Ct (Glasgow and Strathkelvin).

6297. Consumer protection – product liability – primary agricultural products

CONSUMER PROTECTION ACT 1987 (PRODUCT LIABILITY) (MODIFICATION) (SCOTLAND) ORDER 2001, SSI 2001 265; made under the Consumer Protection Act 1987 s.8. In force: July 19, 2001; £1.50.

This Order, which amends the Consumer Protection Act 1987 Part I, implements European Parliament and Council Directive 1999/34 ([1999] OJ L141/20) which amends Council Directive 85/374 concerning liability for defective products. That Directive requires Member States to impose liability on producers for damage caused by defects in their products. This Order accordingly amends the scope of the provisions of Part I of the Consumer Protection Act to include primary agricultural products and game.

CONTRACTS

6298. Formation of contract – offer and acceptance – reply requested within two to three weeks – reply given nine months later – validity of time limit and acceptance

F and B, two fishermen, raised an action against I for declarator that I was liable for payment to them of sums agreed in two contracts between the parties relating to compensation for their inability to fish following the Braer oil tanker disaster. I sent letters, dated September 2 and 4 1997, to F and B's agents. The first letter offered £93,356.76 in full and final settlement of their claim in respect of the period from October 20, 1995 subject to any pro-rata adjustments which may have been made if the total value of all claims exceeded to value of the compensation fund. I indicated that they expected a reply to that letter within two to three weeks. The second letter offered £30,852.40 as compensation in respect of the period from June 27, 1995 to October 17, 1995 subject to the same pro-rata adjustments. F and B intimated acceptance of the offers by a letter dated June 18, 1998. I claimed that the acceptance was not timeous as the time delay between the offers and the acceptance was unreasonable and the action should therefor be dismissed as irrelevant. F and B argued that the first letter did not impose a valid time limit for acceptance. They maintained that the time between offer and acceptance had been used the time in an attempt to asses the effects of pro-rating on their claims and that they had not been aware of the existence of the second letter until June 1998 due it being improperly addressed and them changing agents. They admitted, however, that the reason for accepting the offer when they did was their financial inability to continue their action in pursuance of their claim.

Held, dismissing the action as irrelevant, that (1) the wording of the first offer was insufficiently precise to impose a valid time limit but was sufficiently indicative of the fact that I expected an early reply to the offer, (2) a period of nine months was unreasonably long for the acceptance of the offers made under a statutory scheme where the offers had been made following earlier negotiations and interim payments, *Glasgow and Newcastle and Middlesborough Steam Shipping Co v. Watson* (1873) 1 R. 189, followed, (3) the personal reasons given by F and B were not valid reasons for the delay, and (4) it was inappropriate to delay accepting the offers in an attempt to ascertain the pro-rated value of the claim as the offer only concerned the gross value of the claim and delays of that nature would unjustifiably prolong the limitation process.

FLAWS v. INTERNATIONAL OIL POLLUTION COMPENSATION FUND 2001 S.L.T. 897, Lord Gill, OH.

6299. Tenders – public works contracts – tender procedure

[Public Works Contracts Regulations 1991 (SI 1991 2680); Council Directive 93/ 37 concerning the coordination of procedures for the award of public works contracts.]

C, a consortium of local authorities formed to tender for a roads management and maintenance contract, reclaimed the dismissal of their petition seeking judicial review of the award of the contract to another.

Held, refusing the appeal and sustaining the Lord Ordinary's interlocutor dismissing the petition, that (1) it was possible to infer from the information provided by S in the tender documents, the range within which the base quantities would be expected to lie and that it was expressly stated in the tender documents that the tenderers were to use their own skill and judgment in determining this for the purpose of preparing the tender; (2) the base quantities were only an element in the machinery by which criteria fell to be taken into account in deciding whether a tender was the most economically advantageous; (3) there was nothing to indicate that S had treated the tenders unequally or that the procedures could be deemed to be arbitrary as all the tenderers had been given access to the same information and were all subject to the same assessment criteria; (4) there was no clear and unambiguous representation by S that the base quantities were to be assessed in any specific way other than by the application of good faith and with reference to the material available to each of the tenderers; (5) the Lord Ordinary's conclusion that the procedure was rational, that there had been no breach of the duties of transparency and objectivity as required by the Public Works Contracts Regulations 1991 or Council Directive 93/37 were well founded, and (6) the proceedings were not brought timeously as C had been aware of the grounds on which the petition was raised from the moment that they first considered preparing their tender, that being June 2000 and the petition was not lodged until January 2001. Opinion of the Court per Lord Cameron of Lochbroom.

CLYDE SOLWAY CONSORTIUM v. SCOTTISH MINISTERS; *sub nom.* CLYDE SOLWAY CONSORTIUM, PETITIONERS 2001 S.C. 553, Lord Cameron of Lochbroom, Lady Cosgrove, Lord Kingarth, Ex Div.

6300. Unincorporated associations – locus standi – club members suing club and third party

A, the members of F, an unincorporated association for persons holding timeshare rights in resort lodges, raised an action against F and B, the resort management company, alleging unlawful interference with the peaceful enjoyment of A's property rights at the resort. A sought declarator that F had neither right nor title in terms of F's constitution to charge A for refurbishment of the resort lodges and that the attempt to do so was ultra vires. The sheriff allowed proof before answer. F appealed to the sheriff principal, arguing that the sheriff had erred in reserving his opinion of the applicability of the rule in *Foss v. Harbottle* (1843) 2 Hare 461, until after inquiry; doing so defeated the whole purpose of the rule and sanctioned the very mischief it was designed to prevent. Only F as a whole had title to sue in the contractual relationship between it and B. Further, A's averments regarding two letters should have been excluded as they were using them to support an averment of F's view of what its constitution meant, contrary to the rules on construction of contracts.

Held, refusing the appeal, that (1) the court could interfere in the actings of an association where they affected the patrimonial interests or civil rights of its members, and in essence A were seeking to vindicate their personal rights as against F and B; (2) under the management agreement F had delegated its responsibilities to B, which stood in F's shoes in relation to those functions, and its actions were no less actionable than if carried out by F, and (3) A's averments concerning the letters could possibly justify the inference that the work that was being charged for was not within the constitution as a matter of fact.

Observed, that objection to any attempt to use the letters as an aid to construction would be well justified.

ABBOTT v. FOREST HILLS TROSSACHS CLUB; *sub nom.* ABOTT v. FOREST HILL TROSSACHS CLUB 2001 S.L.T. (Sh Ct) 155, RA Dunlop Q.C., Sheriff Principal, Sh Ct.

6301. Books

Huntley, John a K – Contract. Cases & Materials. Paperback: £45.00. ISBN 0-414-01281-X. W.Green & Son.

McBryde, William W. – Law of Contract in Scotland 2nd Ed. Hardback: £165.00. ISBN 0-414-01242-9. W.Green & Son.

CRIMINAL EVIDENCE

6302. Admissibility – accused detained by police on series of occasions – detention – meaning of "grounds arising out of same circumstances"

[Criminal Procedure (Scotland) Act 1995 (c.46) s.14(3).]

M was charged with murdering a man by striking him with a hammer. M was detained by the police on November 7, 1999 in connection with an alleged assault on another man and during the course of that inquiry M was also questioned in connection with the murder. M was again detained on December 7, 1999 in relation to drug offences and on December 17, 1999 in connection with the murder. M made a number of statements during his detentions and when they were led at trial, objection was taken on the basis that the final detention had been illegal under the Criminal Procedure (Scotland) Act 1995 s.14(3). A trial within a trial was held during which it was submitted that the man assaulted had been so because he had accused M of committing the murder. M maintained that demonstrated a connection between the first and last detentions.

Held, repelling the objection, that "the same ground" in s.14(3) must refer to the grounds for suspecting that M had committed the offence and it had not been contended here that the later detention involved the same grounds. The second basis for the s.14(3) prohibition, "or any ground arising out of the same circumstances", could not be said to have applied either, it highlighted only the possible motive for the assault. Neither would the forensic evidence gathered at any of the detentions be considered significant since it would not form part of the "circumstances" out of which the s.14(3) prohibition would apply.

HM ADVOCATE v. MAC MOWAT; *sub nom.* HM ADVOCATE v. MacMOWAT 2001 S.L.T. 738, Lord Osborne, HCJ.

6303. Admissibility – search in foreign jurisdiction under supervision of local police – evidence not irregularly obtained

An accused, F, charged with inter alia murder of the persons killed in the Lockerbie air disaster in 1988, objected to the Crown's attempts to introduce as evidence the contents of a diary belonging to him, on the grounds that the manner in which it was recovered rendered it inadmissible. A trial within a trial was held. Two Scottish police officers, an FBI special agent and a Maltese police officer had interviewed V, a business associate of F, in V's office in Malta under an agreement with the Maltese authorities which meant that Maltese criminal law and procedures applied. In the course of the interview the diary was found, apparently during a search. V did not object to the search or the removal of the diary. No warrant had been produced. There was evidence that under Maltese law a search was lawful if carried out in the presence of an inspector of police or under a warrant signed by him, although a warrant was normally required to take possession of property.

Held, repelling the objection, that (1) F was not properly a suspect at the material time as there was then only information to suggest a connection with F's coaccused, who was incriminated, and to indicate that his position in Malta might have provided an opportunity for him to be involved in placing the bomb, but given that that was a narrow question, the issue should be considered as if F was a suspect; (2) given that V, a director of the company that owned the office, had the power to consent to the search and did not object to the search, it was not unlawful; (3) the Crown had not proved that the taking of the diary, after it had been identified as F's personal property, was lawful on V's consent under Maltese law, and (4) applying *Lawrie (Jeanie) v. Muir* 1950 J.C. 19, the Crown would be permitted to lead the evidence given the public interest in the prosecution of a murder and as what occurred had been excusable. Even if F was a suspect, it was by association rather than directly; the interview and search were not unlawful up until the discovery of the diary; the Scottish police were acting with the agreement of the Maltese authorities and a police officer was present to ensure they acted in accordance with Maltese law; no device or trick had been employed; there was no evasion of the law; and the diary had been left there for about seven months.

HM ADVOCATE v. AL-MEGRAHI (NO.3); *sub nom.* MEGRAHI v. HM ADVOCATE (NO.3); HM ADVOCATE v. MEGRAHI (NO.3); AL-MEGRAHI v. HM ADVOCATE (NO.3) 2000 S.L.T. 1401, Lord Sutherland, Lord Coulsfield, Lord MacLean, HCJ.

6304. Admissibility – search of car for drugs without warrant – whether lack of statutory powers – power to search under s.23(2)(b) of the Misuse of Drugs Act 1971

[Misuse of Drugs Act 1971 (c.2) s.23(2)(b).]

N had been detained and convicted after the car he had been travelling in was removed to be searched on suspicion of containing controlled drugs. Drugs were found in the car and N was charged on indictment with being concerned in the supply of cocaine and diamorphine. N objected, arguing that the evidence from the searched car was inadmissible, since the search itself was unlawful, having been carried out without a warrant. The objection was repelled on the basis that the search had authority under the Misuse of Drugs Act 1971 s.23(2)(b). N appealed to the High Court against conviction and sentence arguing that with the inadmissibility of that evidence there would not have been sufficient evidence otherwise to sustain a conviction, and the trial judge should not have reached a decision on the matter without conducting a trial within a trial.

Held, refusing the appeal on conviction and continuing the appeal against sentence, that given the basis of the objection (that the police had acted without any statutory powers) there was no need for evidence to be led as to the matter of powers. There was no basis for criticism of the trial judge in deciding the matter without a trial within a trial since neither party had suggested such during debate before the judge. Given that the police officers had power to search the car under s.23(2)(b), there was nothing to suggest that they could not remove the car to a more convenient place in order to conduct that search efficiently. The underlying assumption of the appeal, that the police had had no statutory powers to conduct the search, was unfounded in law. Opinion of the Court per Lord Lochbroom.

NICOLSON (ALAN) v. HM ADVOCATE 2001 S.C.C.R. 13, Lord Cameron of Lochbroom, Lord Allanbridge, Lord Caplan, HCJ Appeal.

6305. Admissibility – statement before foreign magistrate – analogous to precognition on oath – no unfairness

[Criminal Procedure (Scotland) Act 1995 (c.46) s.263(4).]

Two accused, charged with inter alia murder of the persons killed in the Lockerbie air disaster in 1988, objected to the Crown's attempts to put to V, a witness, the transcript of evidence given before a magistrate in Malta for the purposes of the Criminal Procedure (Scotland) Act 1995 s.263(4), on the grounds that it was a precognition which did not constitute a precognition on oath because the transcript was not a verbatim record and was not signed by the witness.

Held, repelling the objection, that the transcript could validly be used as it would not be unfair to V to do so. It was a statement taken in a foreign jurisdiction under foreign rules of procedure; it was inappropriate to try to categorise that procedure as a precognition or not, but to consider whether the procedure possessed the necessary safeguards to prevent the use of the statement being regarded as unfair, which it was not: (a) the examination was conducted under oath in the presence of a legally qualified magistrate; (b) the wording used was dictated in the presence of the witness who had the opportunity of correcting anything said, and from the record, might have done so; and (c) though the transcript did not disclose whether the questioning was by way of leading questions, or whether the magistrate accurately narrated the exact meaning of the questions and answers, it was one of the features of Scottish procedure that at the investigative stage statements taken by police officers, which could be said to suffer from similar defects, were admissible. Such a position reinforced the view taken in *Coll, Petitioner* 1977 J.C. 29, [1977] C.L.Y. 3310, that the principal objection to precognitions was the risk of bias or partiality on the part of the taker of the statement, who was, by that stage of the proceedings, trying to build up a case against the accused, *Coll* and *Kerr (John) v. HM Advocate* 1958 J.C. 14, [1985] C.L.Y. 3660 referred to.

HM ADVOCATE v. AL-MEGRAHI (NO.2); *sub nom.* MEGRAHI v. HM ADVOCATE (NO.2); HM ADVOCATE v. MEGRAHI (NO.2); AL-MEGRAHI v. HM ADVOCATE (NO.2) 2000 S.L.T. 1399, Lord Sutherland, Lord Coulsfield, HCJ.

6306. Admissibility – statement by accused following s.172 admission

[Road Traffic Act 1988 (c.52) s.172; European Convention on Human Rights 1950 Art.6.]

M was named as the driver of a vehicle that had been involved in an accident and was subsequently tried on indictment on a number of road traffic offences. M had been identified as the driver by witnesses and police officers questioned him, requiring him to give information as to who the driver was under the Road Traffic Act 1988 s.172. M answered that he had been the driver and was arrested. He was then taken to a police station where he was interviewed under caution. The evidence of the interview was objected to on the ground that it immediately followed M's admission to being the driver and as such was inadmissible. Accordingly, to lead the evidence would be in breach of M's right to a fair trial under the European Convention on Human Rights 1950 Art.6.

Held, repelling the objection, that the police had correctly used their s.172 requirement power. The fact that the interview immediately followed an incriminating reply to a s.172 procedure would not inevitably result in the inadmissibility of that interview into evidence. However if the evidence could be led without any reference to the incriminating reply such evidence would be admissible.

HM ADVOCATE v. McLEAN 2001 S.L.T. 189, Lord Mackay of Drumadoon, HCJ.

6307. Appeals – fresh evidence – new medical evidence discrediting evidence heard at trial – murder conviction set aside – no substitution of culpable homicide verdict

[Criminal Procedure (Scotland) Act 1995 (c.46) s.118(1) (b).]

S was convicted of murder in 1977 by kicking the deceased on the head during a fight. S had always admitted being in the fight, but had pled self defence and denied the fatal kick on the head. New medical evidence showed that the deceased had died as a result of falling and hitting his head rather than being kicked, that rendered the evidence as led at the original trial as misconceived and without foundation. The Secretary of State referred the case back to the High Court and it was accepted that the conviction be set aside under the Criminal Procedure (Scotland) Act 1995 s.118(1)(b). The matter to be considered was whether an amended verdict of culpable homicide should be substituted.

Held, quashing the conviction, that in the absence of authority directly in point, the court would only substitute an amended verdict if it was satisfied that a reasonable jury, properly instructed, and on the basis of all the evidence, would have returned a verdict of culpable homicide. As the medical evidence in the previous trial had been so influential in reaching the verdict it would be unjust to take any other evidence in the form it had emerged at trial (as would usually be done). If the court could not say what the evidence would be, then a determination with regard to the verdict a jury may have returned would prove impossible and the test could not be met. Opinion of the court per Lord Rodger, Lord Justice General.

SMITH (ANDREW) v. HM ADVOCATE 2001 S.L.T. 438, Lord Rodger, L.J.G., Lord Marnoch, Lady Paton, HCJ Appeal.

6308. Assault – assault with intent to rape – sufficiency – jury deleted particular averments – entitlement to draw inference of intent to rape from circumstances

M was charged with assaulting a young woman by holding and punching her, forcing her to the ground, lifting her dress and attempting to remove her underwear, kneeling on top of her and pinning her to the ground with the intent of rape and did attempt to rape her. The assault took place in a darkened lane in the early hours of the morning. The jury convicted M, of assault with intent to rape, having deleted averments related to the lifting of her dress, removal of her underwear and attempt to rape. M appealed to the High Court arguing that in deleting those averments, the jury could no longer have legitimately reached the conclusion that there had been intent to commit rape.

Held, refusing the appeal, that the circumstances and evidence were such that the inference of assault with the intent to rape was one which any reasonable jury could be expected to have reached. Opinion of the Court per Lord Rodger, Lord Justice-General.

McGILL v. HM ADVOCATE (PROCEDURE) 2001 S.C.C.R. 28, Lord Rodger L.J.G., Lord Cameron of Lochbroom, Lord Weir, HCJ Appeal.

6309. Corroboration – assault – special knowledge of accused

C appealed against his conviction for assault. A man, S, was knocked unconscious in the street after being approached by three people. C had admitted to police that he had been in the vicinity with a woman and another man, and that after S had been punched in the face, C had run across and kicked him in the back. C argued that did not constitute a self corroborating confession because C's special knowledge could have come from him witnessing the assault, rather than him being a participant.

Held, refusing the appeal, that the sheriff had applied the correct test, namely whether the only reasonable explanation for C's special knowledge was that he was the perpetrator, and had properly applied that test to the material facts presented to him in finding C guilty. Opinion of the Court per Lord Cameron of Lochbroom.

CAIRNS v. HOWDLE 2000 S.C.C.R. 742, Lord Cameron of Lochbroom, Lord Cowie, Lord Nimmo Smith, HCJ Appeal.

6310. Corroboration – lewd, indecent and libidinous practices – evidence of distress – jury directions – misdirection

A was charged with abducting into his car and detaining in his house, X, a nine year old boy, and lewd, indecent and libidinous practices towards X. For corroboration of X's evidence that he had been detained against his will, the Crown relied on evidence of X's father that after the incident he had found X in the street, very distressed. The sheriff directed the jury to consider what the reason for the distress was, and whether it was due to his being detained rather than, for example, to his being out later than he was allowed. A was convicted of both charges and appealed, arguing that (1) since there was evidence in relation to charge 2 that A had appeared before X wearing only boxer shorts, which might in itself have been upsetting to X, the sheriff should have directed the jury in relation to charge 1 that they had to be satisfied that X's distress had not been caused by any indecent conduct covered by charge 2; and (2) on charge 2, given the jury had deleted an allegation that he had attempted to remove X's clothing, the remaining libel that he had removed his own clothing and exposed his partly naked body to X, could not constitute an offence of lewd, libidinous and indecent practices. The Crown submitted that where A had abducted and kept X in a strange house by himself and suddenly appeared in front of him wearing only his boxer shorts, the circumstances were sufficient to permit the necessary element of indecency to be inferred.

Held, allowing the appeal in respect of charge 2, that (1) even if the jury had thought that some incident during X's abduction and detention might have contributed to his distress, they must have been satisfied, applying the sheriff's directions, that it had indeed arisen because he had been abducted and detained against his will by A, and (2) even having regard to the circumstances, on the verdict A had not committed any lewd, indecent or libidinous act.

ANDERSON (JAMES STEWART) v. HM ADVOCATE 2001 S.L.T. 1265, Lord Rodger L.J.G., Lord Abernethy, Lord Sutherland, HCJ Appeal.

6311. Corroboration – Moorov doctrine – theft

W was charged on indictment libelling two charges of theft. In each case the complainer was in her 60s or 70s, and W had represented himself as a workman or local authority representative, thrust his way into her home and removed property. For corroboration the Crown sought to rely on the Moorov doctrine. W was convicted and appealed, contending that the evidence in relation to the second charge was not sufficient to establish the commission of a crime as the complainer was not able to state positively what items had been taken, having said that she saw him apparently wrapping something in a jacket and that she had since been unable to find her camera; and therefore that there was nothing to corroborate the evidence on the first charge.

Held, refusing the appeal, that (1) the Moorov doctrine was not confined to sexual or clandestine offences and there was no reason why witnesses speaking to different incidents of theft should not be held capable of corroborating one another, even if each of them was the only witness to the completed act on the occasion to which his or her evidence related; (2) there were sufficient similarities between the incidents to enable an inference of a course of conduct to be drawn; and (3) there was sufficient for the jury to accept that a camera had been stolen in the second incident and the precise identity of the item did not require separate corroboration in a Moorov case.

WILSON (ALEXANDER THOMAS) v. HM ADVOCATE 2001 S.L.T. 1203, Lord Coulsfield, Lord Cowie, Lord Marnoch, HCJ Appeal.

6312. Cross examination – cross examination of coaccused as to character – judicial discretion to refuse

[Criminal Procedure (Scotland) Act 1995 (c.46) s.266(4).]

B and a coaccused, McG, were charged with murder. During McG's cross examination B's counsel moved the court for leave to cross examine as to character, which was refused since McG had not given evidence against B and was protected against just such a cross examination by the Criminal Procedure (Scotland) Act 1995 s.266(4). McG subsequently did give evidence against B and counsel at that time renewed the motion arguing the court no longer had the discretion to deny it under s.266(4)(c). The trial judge refused the motion, B was convicted and appealed.

Held, refusing the appeal, that although a literal interpretation of s.266(4)(c) would allow the appeal, it would actually be undermining the parliamentary intention to protect McG from exposing previous criminal behaviour or bad character in front of a jury. Counsel who deliberately questioned coaccused with the intention of achieving just such a cross examination should not have that right conferred upon them. Opinion of the Court per Lord Rodger, Lord Justice-General.

BARNES (CRAIG BROWN) v. HM ADVOCATE 2001 J.C. 61, Lord Rodger L.J.G., Lord Philip, Lord Reed, HCJ Appeal.

6313. Cross examination – rape – sexual history of complainer

See CRIMINAL EVIDENCE: Thomson v. HM Advocate. §6318

6314. Disclosure – criminal records of witnesses – competency of recovery – public interest and accused's rights – proper purpose

M was charged with assault and petitioned for commission and diligence to recover parts of the criminal records of a number of the Crown's witnesses. M intended to plead self defence and attack the credibility of the witnesses, questioning them as to previous violent acts. The Crown opposed the application arguing that; (1) not only would it be incompetent based on the binding authority found in *HM Advocate v. Ashrif* 1988 S.L.T. 567, [1988] C.L.Y. 3944, and (2) it did not pass the test in *McLeod (Alastair) v. HM Advocate (No.2)* 1998 J.C. 67, [1998] C.L.Y. 5607, because making the order would not serve a proper purpose nor be in the interests of justice. The Crown also argued that the appropriate disclosure of that material would come during any false claims by a witness during cross examination.

Held, granting order for production, that the Crown had a duty to disclose information which might exonerate the accused. Included in that duty would be information indirectly bearing upon M's guilt or innocence such as the credibility of Crown witnesses. After considering the competing considerations as to disclosure, it was decided that the Crown's public interest considerations did not outweigh M's entitlement to disclosure. That entitlement was not absolute, but if the evidence as to previous convictions proved relevant and legitimate, M would be entitled to have it disclosed before trial to allow for preparation and proper presentation. The test in McLeod had been passed and it was unsatisfactory for M to rely upon the Crown to correct false evidence.

MAAN (HABIB) v. HM ADVOCATE; *sub nom.* MAAN (HABIB), PETITIONER 2001 S.L.T. 408, Lord Macfadyen, HCJ.

6315. Drug offences – intent to supply drugs – sufficiency of evidence

R appealed against conviction for possession of 93 ecstasy tablets with intent to supply, on the ground of insufficiency of evidence. R had been sentenced to 12 months' imprisonment. The police had approached R and B, his coaccused, as they exited B's car, and had apprehended R as he attempted to escape. The drugs were found in the car's glove compartment, directly in front of the seat occupied by R, and on top of documents belonging to R which R admitted taking into the car, although he said he put them somewhere else.

Held, refusing the appeal, that (1) the sheriff applied the proper test of knowledge and control, was entitled to consider the evidence noted, and no attack was made on his finding that the quantity involved was such as a dealer would possess, *Campbell (Duncan McNeil) v. HM Advocate* 1992 J.C. 6, [1992] C.L.Y. 5367 applied, and (2) sentence was not excessive against the background of R's lengthy, though non-analogous, record and the extreme seriousness of the offence for a summary complaint. Opinion of the Court per Lord Cameron of Lochbroom.

REID v. BUCHANAN 2000 S.C.C.R. 747, Lord Cameron of Lochbroom, Lord Cowie, Lord Nimmo Smith, HCJ Appeal.

6316. Drug offences – random sampling for drug – analysis as indicative of entire quantity

[Misuse of Drugs Act 1971 (c.38) s.53.]

S was charged with possession of heroin with the intention of supplying it to others, contrary to the Misuse of Drugs Act 1971 s.5 (3). S had 12 similarly sized and wrapped packages in her possession, three of which were randomly chosen and, after testing, were shown to contain heroin. S was convicted and appealed by stated case arguing that the evidence of the three packages shown to contain heroin was insufficient in quantity to uphold the notion of intent to supply.

Held, abandoning the stated case, that in the absence of alternative authority the court was entitled to infer that the three random samples tested were indicative of the nature of the 12 packages.

CARNEGIE v. FINDLAY 2000 S.C.C.R. 873, Sheriff Herald, Sh Ct (North Strathclyde).

6317. Electrical equipment – possession – pre-programmed scanning receiver – meaning of "wireless telegraphy apparatus"

[Wireless Telegraphy Act 1949 (c.54) s.5 (b), s.19.]

C appealed against his conviction for having a preprogrammed scanning receiver in his possession with intent to obtain information as to the content of messages without authorisation contrary to the Wireless Telegraphy Act 1949 s.5 (b) (i). Police officers had discovered the equipment at C's house when they heard a broadcast from their division control room on a radio other than their own personal radios. The magistrate found that the scanning receiver was "wireless telegraphy apparatus" within the meaning of s.19 of the Act, on the basis of the officers' evidence and that of a specialist officer in video and audio surveillance. C argued that the magistrate had not been entitled to make that finding.

Held, dismissing the appeal, that the definition in s.19 was concerned with apparatus adapted to receive wireless or radio signals not transmitted by a cable or other physical means, and the evidence had been sufficient to prove the essential elements of the charge.

COYLE v. HIGSON 2001 S.L.T. 1161, Lord Coulsfield, Lord Caplan, Lord Osborne, HCJ Appeal.

6318. Rape – cross examination of complainer – relevance of questioning to charge – previous allegations considered irrelevant

T was convicted of rape and appealed to the High Court arguing that there had been a miscarriage of justice. T maintained that the trial judge had erred in refusing to allow questioning of the complainer on particular points, that (1) with regard to allegations made in 1991 about consensual underage sex with D and B and an attempted rape by B, all of which were documented; (2) with regard to the complainers refusal on one occasion to attend hospital on the grounds that the medical staff had raped her; and (3) that she had made and withdrawn an allegation of sexual abuse against her stepfather.

Held, refusing the appeal, that D and B were not cited as witnesses and as such any evidence given by the complainer could not be refuted. The circumstances in that instance had been very different, dated and without conclusion so the judge had been justified in refusing to allow both that line of questioning and that related to the allegation of abuse. The trial judge, with regard to the hospital allegations, had applied the correct test, that of the interests of justice, and noted that such broad allegations at a time of stress were very different from a specific claim. It was held that other judges may have allowed the questioning, but with a lack of concrete rules the court could not hold that no other judge acting reasonably would have refused. Opinion of the Court per Lord McEwan.

THOMSON v. HM ADVOCATE 2001 S.C.C.R. 162, Lord McEwan, Lord Cowie, Lord Prosser, HCJ Appeal.

6319. Road traffic offences – identification of driver – statement by accused – self incrimination – right to fair and public hearing

[Road Traffic Act 1988 (c.52) s.172; European Convention on Human Rights 1950 Art.6.]

The procurator fiscal appealed against the decision of the High Court of Justiciary (2000 J.C. 328, [2000] C.L.Y. 6043) to grant a declarator that an admission by B obtained compulsorily under the Road Traffic Act 1988 s.172 that she had been the driver of a car when charged with drink driving was a breach of her right to a fair trial under the European Convention on Human Rights 1950 Art.6 and could not be relied on in court.

Held, allowing the appeal, that an admission obtained under s.172 did not breach Art.6 and could be relied on at trial, since the right against self incrimination was not an absolute right and had to be balanced against the clear public interest in the enforcement of road traffic legislation in order to address the high incidence of death and injury on the roads caused by the misuse of motor vehicles. The right to a fair trial could not be compromised, but the constituent rights within that overall right could be limited to the extent that it was necessary to fulfil a clear and proper public objective. Furthermore, s.172 did not sanction prolonged questioning but provided for the putting of a single question which could not, without other evidence, incriminate the suspect. The trial judge maintained the right to exclude admissions where there was a suggestion of improper coercion or oppression, *Saunders v. United Kingdom* [1998] 1 B.C.L.C. 362, [1997] C.L.Y. 2816 considered. The regulatory regime of which s.172 was part, was thus a proportionate response to the problem of maintaining road safety and anyone who owned or drove a car knowingly subjected themselves to that regime.

BROWN (MARGARET) v. STOTT; *sub nom.* STOTT (PROCURATOR FISCAL) v. BROWN; BROWN v. PROCURATOR FISCAL, DUNFERMLINE; PROCURATOR FISCAL, DUNFERMLINE v. BROWN [2001] 2 W.L.R. 817, Lord Bingham of Cornhill, Privy Council (Scotland).

6320. Stop and search – irregularly obtained evidence – detention without statutory power

[Wildlife and Countryside Act 1981 (c.69) s.19.]

Police suspected that M was setting traps to capture falcons They detained him under the Wildlife and Countryside Act 1981 s.19 and took M to a police station where a live pigeon was found in his rucksack. M was charged with, inter alia, the offences of possessing a live bird that could be used to commit another crime, possessing the bird, and causing the bird unnecessary suffering in the way it was transported. M objected to the evidence, arguing that the search had been executed whilst M was unlawfully detained. M argued that s.19 provided police with the power to stop and search and, only exceptionally, detain. M's objection was repelled, he was convicted and appealed to the High Court. The Crown conceded that the search had been irregular but sought excusal of the irregularity.

Held, allowing the appeal and quashing the conviction relating to the live pigeon, that the limits on the power of arrest in s.19 suggested that in the ordinary case, a person suspected of an offence should not be detained. In the instant case there was nothing to justify M's detention, and as such it could not be treated as an excusable irregularity. Accordingly, the finding of the live pigeon was inadmissible as evidence.

MORRISON v. O'DONNELL 2001 S.C.C.R. 272, Lord Coulsfield, Sir GH Gordon Q.C., Lord Hamilton, HCJ Appeal.

6321. Theft – sufficiency – possession of credit cards etc.

M was charged with the theft of a purse containing various credit cards and money etc. M, in statements to police, gave three different versions of how he came to have the cards in his jacket. M argued that there had been no evidence of theft libelled or proved and as such, there could be no case to answer. That submission was repelled and M convicted. M appealed by case stated to the

High Court, maintaining that the sheriff had erred in law in repelling the submission of no case to answer.

Held, refusing the appeal, that there had been sufficient evidence led to establish circumstances that were consistent with reset and thereby a conviction. Opinion of the Court per Lord Lochbroom.

MEARNS v. McFADYEN 2001 J.C. 51, Lord Cameron of Lochbroom, Lord Caplan, Lord Milligan, HCJ Appeal.

6322. Warrants – search warrants – Customs and Excise powers of search – warrant not validly executed – inadmissibility of evidence

[Value Added Tax Act 1983 (c.55) Sch.7.]

S, a husband and wife running two restaurant businesses in partnership, were convicted of fraudulently evading VAT. The evidence was gathered at their home during a search petitioned for by G, a senior Customs officer. In his petition G averred that there were reasonable grounds for suspicion that the offence had been committed and that only four persons authorised in terms of the Value Added Tax Act 1983 Sch.7 would carry out the search, with others attending to seize and remove documents under their direction. In the event, however, eight authorised officers attended and interviewed S during the execution of the warrant. S appealed against the conviction, arguing that the evidence gathered was inadmissible as result of the breach of the warrant. G argued that only four officers carried out the search in compliance with Sch.7 para.10(5)(a). S also argued that VAT books had been unlawfully removed from the office of his accountant, R, as the power to remove them under Sch.7 para.8 was no longer available following the search of his home and the interviews conducted there.

Held, allowing the appeal and quashing the conviction, that the search warrant had been unlawfully executed. It was unclear that only four officers had carried out the search and the presence of so many Customs officers at the house, coupled with the interviews they had conducted, had diverted S from the search which had been carried out in breach of Sch.7 para.10(5)(a). Further, the criminal investigation had already begun when the VAT books were removed from R's office so that the evidence obtained from them was inadmissible as it had been gathered illegally. Opinion of the Court per Lord Cameron of Lochbroom.

SINGH (MANJIT) v. HM ADVOCATE [2001] S.T.C. 790, Lord Cameron of Lochbroom, Lord Macfadyen, Lord Weir, HCJ Appeal.

6323. Witnesses – anonymity – no bar to a fair trial

[Misuse of Drugs Act 1971 (c.38) s.4(3)(b); European Convention on Human Rights 1950 Art.6.]

S was charged with supplying drugs in contravention of the Misuse of Drugs Act 1971 s.4(3)(b). The supply was to certain individuals who subsequently proved to be undercover policemen. The Crown lodged a minute of notice requesting that the undercover officers be allowed to give their evidence without revealing their identities as to do so would jeopardise their safety, and negate their continued usefulness as undercover police officers. The sheriff refused the minute, taking the view that the anonymity of the witnesses could not be balanced with the interests of S and the guarantees to a fair trial as set out in the European Convention on Human Rights 1950 Art.6. A conviction made solely on the basis of anonymous evidence simply could not be made. The Crown appealed stating that they would not be relying solely on the anonymous evidence and accepted that the true identities would be made known to the trial judge.

Held, allowing the appeal, that (1) in an application prior to trial, the correct test to be applied was whether the resulting arrangements would inevitably lead to an unfair trial. The considerations that would be given to the question of a fair trial after proceedings finished would be entirely different; (2) it was hard to see how the sheriff could have reached his conclusion before the trial that the interests of S and the Crown could not be balanced, and the sheriff had not in fact applied the correct test; (3) the question for the court was whether if the witnesses were permitted to conceal their identities it would not be possible for S to receive a fair trial, and (4) general principles were derived from the cases below in the following terms; (a) admissibility of evidence was a matter for national law, (b) evidence should normally be produced in the presence of the accused and be subjected to adversarial scrutiny; (c) although an accused should be given adequate and proper opportunity to challenge and question a witness, that the witness be anonymous was not per se incompatible with a fair trial; (d) police officers as anonymous witnesses should only be used in exceptional circumstances; (e) anonymity of police officers could be justified where strictly necessary to ensure operational effectiveness and defence rights are respected, *Kostovski v. Netherlands (A/166)* (1990) 12 E.H.R.R. 434, [1990] C.L.Y. 2539, *Ludi v. Switzerland (A/238)* (1993) 15 E.H.R.R. 173, [1993] C.L.Y. 2139, *Doorson v. Netherlands* (1996) 22 E.H.R.R. 330, [1996] C.L.Y. 3124, *Van Mechelen v. Netherlands (Art.6)* (1998) 25 E.H.R.R. 647, [1997] C.L.Y. 2815 applied, and (5) that the court was not satisfied that if the application for anonymity was granted S would not receive a fair trial or that the resulting restrictions imposed on the defence would necessarily result in a breach of Art. 6(3)(d). Opinion of the Court per Lord Kirkwood.

HM ADVOCATE v. SMITH (PETER THOMSON) 2000 S.C.C.R. 910, Lord Kirkwood, Lord Cowie, Lord Milligan, HCJ Appeal.

CRIMINAL LAW

6324. **Animals – injuries – dog biting child on neck – charge dependent on foreseeability**

[Civic Government (Scotland) Act 1982 (c.45) s.49(1).]

A, the owner of a mongrel collie, appealed against her conviction for an offence of permitting a creature in her charge to cause danger or injury to another person in a public place or give such person reasonable cause for alarm or annoyance contrary to the Civic Government (Scotland) Act 1982 s.49(1). The dog had broken free from a pole to which its lead had been tied and had bitten a nine year old boy on the neck. The sheriff found that the dog had attacked the boy on an earlier occasion, but not that A was aware of that, and that she had clearly accepted the need to secure the dog and her failure to do so had important consequences which she ought to have foreseen.

Held, allowing the appeal and quashing the conviction, that (1) while the charge alleged both alternatives in s.49(1) of the dog causing danger or injury, or giving reasonable cause for alarm or annoyance, the establishment of the charge depended on the foreseeability of the particular matter relied on, the dog causing danger or injury of the kind it did cause, and (2) there was insufficient material for a finding that A had the requisite knowledge that the dog might give reasonable cause for alarm, far less cause danger or injury if it was tied insecurely.

ANDERSON v. HIGSON 2001 S.L.T. 1035, Lord Prosser, Lord Bonomy, Lord Cowie, HCJ Appeal.

6325. **Anti-terrorism, Crime and Security Act 2001 (c.24) – Commencement No.2 Order**

ANTI-TERRORISM, CRIME AND SECURITY ACT 2001 (COMMENCEMENT NO.2) (SCOTLAND) ORDER 2001, SI 2001 4104 (C.132; S.22); made under the Anti-Terrorism, Crime and Security Act 2001 s.127. Commencement details: bringing into force various provisions of the 2001 Act on January 7, 2002; £1.75.

This Order brings into force the Anti-Terrorism, Crime and Security Act 2001 Part 10, Sch.7 and Sch.8 in respect of the Ministry of Defence Police and the British Transport Police.

6326. Assault – carrying offensive weapon – presenting a knife – conviction twice for same crime

[Criminal Law (Consolidation) (Scotland) Act 1995 (c.39) s.47(1).]

M was convicted of assault by presenting a knife at his victim, and of carrying an offensive weapon contrary to the Criminal Law (Consolidation) (Scotland) Act 1995 s.47(1). M appealed, arguing that he had essentially been convicted of the same offence twice.

Held, setting aside the conviction on the statutory offence with the Crown's consent, that the two crimes involved the same species facti.

McLEAN (FRASER) v. HIGSON 2000 S.C.C.R. 764, Lord Milligan, HCJ Appeal.

6327. Confiscation orders – right to fair trial – statutory confiscation provisions – compatibility with presumption of innocence

[Proceeds of Crime (Scotland) Act 1995 (c.43) s.3(2); Human Rights Act 1998 (c.42) Sch.1 Part I Art.1.]

HM Advocate appealed against a finding (2000 S.C.C.R. 1017, [2000] C.L.Y. 6074) that a prosecutor would be acting contrary to the presumption of a defendant's innocence under the Human Rights Act 1998 Sch.1 Part I Art.6(2) if, in applying for a confiscation order, he invited the court to rely on the assumptions within the Proceeds of Crime (Scotland) Act 1995 s.3(2). Under s.3(2) the court could, in relation to a person convicted of drug trafficking, assume that property held by or transferred to him had been a payment or reward for such trafficking.

Held, allowing the appeal, that (1) the making of a confiscation order did not of itself amount to a person being charged with a criminal offence. It followed that Art.6(2) did not apply, *Welch v. United Kingdom (A/307-A)* (1995) 20 E.H.R.R. 247, [1995] C.L.Y. 2650 and *R. v. Benjafield (Karl Robert)* Times, December 28, 2000, [2001] 1 C.L. 137 considered. The decision in *Benjafield* had not fully reflected the language of Art.6(2). It was clear that when, as in the instant case, Art.6(2) had no application, a defendant could still rely on the protection afforded by Art.6(1), and (2) if Art.6(2) did apply, the assumptions under s.3(2) of the 1995 Act, which only arose where a significant discrepancy existed between the property and expenditure of a defendant and his known income, were proportionate and in the public interest. Moreover, the procedures under the 1995 Act had been approved by Parliament and should not easily be rejected.

HM ADVOCATE v. McINTOSH (SENTENCING); *sub nom.* McINTOSH, PETITIONER; McINTOSH v. HM ADVOCATE; McINTOSH v. LORD ADVOCATE, [2001] UKPC D1, [2001] 3 W.L.R. 107, Lord Bingham of Cornhill, L.C.J., PC.

6328. Contempt of court – order postponing publication of court proceedings – purpose of order must be of limited nature

[Contempt of Court Act 1981 (c.49) s.4(2).]

G had been convicted of murdering her husband and appealed the conviction. The trial had been the subject of intense media interest and S moved the court to make an order under the Contempt of Court Act 1981 s.4(2) prohibiting reporting of the court proceedings until final determination of the appeal or completion of any retrial. G argued that the appeal, if successful, would probably result in a retrial and if the appeal was reported, as the initial case had been, in a manner hostile to G there would be a substantial risk of prejudice with regard to potential jurors for the retrial.

Held, refusing the motion, that (1) the court's powers under s.4(2) were not intended to be used to ward off prejudicial comment, and if a publication did create a substantial risk it would be in contempt of court under the strict liability rule; (2) the proposed order, postponing all reports of any aspect of the appeal was wider than was necessary to avoid the risk of prejudice and therefore could not be justified under the test in s.4(2), and (3) there was no reason to anticipate that a fair and accurate report of the proceedings would create a substantial risk of prejudice to the fairness of a possible retrial, and the court had no reason to believe that jurors who had read such reports would be unable to reach an impartial verdict. Opinion of the Court per Lord Rodger, Lord Justice-General.

GALBRAITH (KIM LOUISE) v. HM ADVOCATE (NO.1) 2001 S.L.T. 465, Lord Rodger, L.J.G., Lord Cameron of Lochbroom, Lord Kingarth, HCJ Appeal.

6329. **Defences – coercion – possession of drugs with intent to supply – threats of violence if failed to deliver or inform**

[European Convention on Human Rights 1950 Art.6(1).]

T visited his father in prison whilst carrying heroin. T was subsequently charged with possession with intent to supply. T maintained that he had been coerced into carrying the heroin to give to his father and had not told the authorities through fear for both his own and his father's life. The defence of coercion was removed from the jury by the sheriff, no notice having been made of it and the evidence not supporting it. T appealed on two grounds, that (1) the defence of coercion should have been allowed, and (2) his father being handcuffed whilst giving evidence was prejudicial and deprived T of a fair trial under the European Convention on Human Rights 1950 Art.6(1).

Held, refusing the appeal, that (1) T had had an opportunity to tell the authorities of the situation and had chosen not to because he was afraid, that could not amount to a complete defence, but, if accepted by the court could be taken into account in mitigation, and (2) the jury were aware before T's father appeared that he was a convicted prisoner and his evidence had not exonerated T. There was, accordingly, no ground on which it could be said that his being handcuffed had resulted in an unfair trial or a miscarriage of justice. Opinion of the Court per Lord Reed.

TROTTER (JAMES ALEXANDER) v. HM ADVOCATE 2001 S.L.T. 296, Lord Reed, Lord Philip, Lord Rodger, L.J.G., HCJ Appeal.

6330. **Drink driving offences – being in charge of vehicle while unfit through drink – defence of no likelihood of driving**

[Road Traffic Act 1988 (c.52) s.5(1)(b).]

C was convicted of a contravention of the Road Traffic Act 1988 s.5(1)(b) for being drunk in charge of a motor vehicle. He had been driven at 1 am to a point close to a friend's house where he normally stayed overnight, not driving again until the following afternoon. On the occasion in question, he had argued with his friend who had left him in the passenger seat of the car, which belonged to C, with the keys in the ignition. At 2 am he was found by police sleeping in the driver's seat of his car with the keys in his hand and when breathalysed was found to be over the prescribed limit for driving. He appealed against his conviction by stated case that (1) the sheriff was not entitled to find that C was in charge of the car, and (2) there were no grounds upon which the sheriff could hold that C had not made out his defence that there was no likelihood of his driving the car whilst still over the prescribed limit. C also appealed against his sentence.

Held, dismissing the appeal, that (1) as C was found sitting in the driver's seat of a car which belonged to him with the keys in his possession, the sheriff had been entitled to find that he was in charge of the vehicle, *Kelso (Alan) v. Brown* 1998 S.L.T. 921, [1998] C.L.Y. 5581, where that accused was found in the passenger seat of a car belonging to his wife, was distinguished, and (2) although C's normal pattern would be to sleep at his friend's house and only resume driving in the afternoon, that pattern had been broken by the argument and the sheriff had been entitled to find that there was a likelihood of C driving when he awoke, either to his own house or closer to his friend's house, when he would have been likely to be over the prescribed limit. The appeal against sentence was also rejected. Opinion of the Court per Lord Sutherland.

CARTMILL v. HEYWOOD 2000 S.L.T. 799, Lord McCluskey, Lord Sutherland, Lord Cowie, HCJ Appeal.

6331. Drink driving offences – failure to provide breath specimens – public access

[Road Traffic Act 1988 (c.52).]

MC appealed against his conviction for an offence of failing to provide specimens of breath without reasonable excuse to police officers investigating a complaint of drink driving. He had driven a motor car within the confines of a private driveway and had also travelled a short distance over an adjoining tarmac area which served as an access and parking area to a block of four flats and also gave access to two private driveways. The sheriff found that the lack of restriction on access to the tarmac area from the public road as well as the access it provided, supported the conclusion that it fell within the definition of "road or other public place" contained in the Road Traffic Act 1988.

Held, dismissing the appeal, that the Act was concerned with the protection of the public and while the instant case was marginal in view of the small number of properties served by the tarmac area, the sheriff was entitled to hold that it was a way to which the public had access.

McPHEE v. MAGUIRE 2002 J.C. 45, Lord Coulsfield, Lord Caplan, Lord Osborne, HCJ Appeal.

6332. Drug offences – supply of drugs – being concerned in the supply of drugs – evidence on single occasion sufficient to uphold conviction

[Misuse of Drugs Act 1971 (c.38) s.4(3)(b), s.5(3).]

K was charged under the Misuse of Drugs Act 1971 s.4(3)(b) with being concerned in the supply of drugs. K had been found to be in possession of an undisputed supply quantity of cocaine on one occasion. K submitted, at the conclusion of the Crown case, that there was no case to answer and maintained that the evidence was sufficient only to justify a conviction of possession with intent to supply contrary to the Misuse of Drugs Act 1971 s.5(3) and not a conviction of being concerned in the supply.

Held, repelling the submission, that the Crown had been entitled to choose the section under which to charge K since a person in possession of drugs with the intent to supply them to another, even as a courier, would be considered a supplier.

HM ADVOCATE v. KIERNAN (GORDON) 2001 S.C.C.R. 129, Sir GH Gordon Q.C., HCJ.

6333. Fatal accident inquiries – road traffic accident – extent of sheriff's powers to make recommendations

[Fatal Accident and Sudden Deaths Inquiry (Scotland) Act 1976 (c.14) s.6(1).]

D was killed in a road traffic accident after the car which he was driving collided with a van driven by W which was travelling the wrong way in a one-way traffic system. At the conclusion of the fatal accident inquiry, the representative of D's family asked the sheriff to make the following recommendations; (1) that a fatal accident inquiry should invariably be held following a death in a road traffic accident; (2) that a sheriff should be entitled to make a finding of fault in a fatal accident inquiry; (3) that road traffic legislation should be amended to increase penalties where a death resulted from a road traffic accident; (4) that the courts should decide whether driving should be regarded as dangerous or careless, and (5) that, in the particular circumstances, W should have been charged with causing death by dangerous driving, and not careless driving.

Held, refusing the application to make recommendations, that the sheriff was only empowered under the Fatal Accident and Sudden Deaths Inquiry (Scotland) Act 1976 s.6(1), to make recommendations which related to the circumstances of death. None of the proposals contributed to the accident nor could they, had they been in place at the time of the accident, have resulted in the accident being avoided. They were, therefore, beyond the sheriff's remit under s.6(1). Fatal accident inquiries were not the appropriate forum for determining matters of civil or criminal liability, nor were they the appropriate forum for criticising the decisions of the prosecuting authorities or courts, *Black v. Scott Lithgow Ltd* 1990 S.C. 322, [1990] C.L.Y. 5812 followed.

DEKKER (STEPHEN ALEXANDER), FATAL ACCIDENT INQUIRY 2000 S.C.L.R. 1087, Sheriff RH Dickson, Sh Ct (South Strathclyde, Dumfries and Galloway).

6334. Malicious damage – necessity – breach of international law – deployment of nuclear missiles – justification

[Criminal Procedure (Scotland) Act 1995 (c.46) s.123(1).]

The Lord Advocate referred, pursuant to the Criminal Procedure (Scotland) Act 1995 s.123(1), four questions of law to the court following the acquittal of Z, R and M of causing malicious damage to a vessel involved in the carrying of Trident nuclear missiles. Z, R and M maintained that causing the damage had been justified since the deployment of Trident was in breach of customary international law and therefore in breach of Scottish law.

Held, determining the issues arising, that (1) in a Scottish criminal trial, evidence could not be led as to the content of customary international law. A rule of customary international law was a rule of Scots law and the jury were not entitled to consider expert evidence but must be·directed thereon by the judge; (2) the conduct of the UK government had not been illegal because the peacetime deployment of Trident as a deterrent was not a threat. Furthermore there was no rule of customary international law justifying the commission of a crime in order to prevent the commission of another crime even in times of war; (3) the belief of Z, R and M that the deployment of Trident was in breach of customary international law did not provide a defence of justification to the charge of malicious damage, *Clark v. Syme* 1957 J.C. 1, [1957] C.L.Y. 3889 followed, and (4) save for the defence of necessity, it was not a defence to a criminal charge that the relevant actions had been taken to hinder the commission of an offence by another person. Although the defence of necessity could be employed where the malicious damage was remote from the threat to people or property, it was only available where the perceived threat was immediate and there was no alternative to a criminal act in order to avert the threat, *Moss v. Howdle* 1997 J.C. 123, [1997] C.L.Y. 6417 followed. In any event the defence of necessity was not available in the instant case where the actions of the Government had not been shown to be unlawful.

LORD ADVOCATE'S REFERENCE (NO.1 OF 2000), *Re* 2001 J.C. 143, Lord Prosser, HCJ Appeal.

6335. Murder – defences – diminished responsibility – applicable test

G appealed against her conviction for the murder of her husband on the ground of misdirection. During her trial, G claimed to have been subjected to abuse by the deceased for some years, and in support of a plea of diminished responsibility, she led evidence from two psychologists that she had been suffering from a form of post-traumatic stress disorder. The trial judge directed the jury that they had to be satisfied that all four elements of the test in *HM Advocate v. Savage (John Henry)* 1923 J.C. 49 were met and that the accused was suffering from some form of mental disorder. The directions were based on the interpretation of *Savage* in *Connelly v. HM Advocate* 1990 J.C. 349. G contended that *Connelly* had misinterpreted the relevant passage in *Savage* and in doing so had unduly narrowed the scope of the defence. Further, on a proper application of the law, the jury should have been directed that they could return a verdict of culpable homicide if they accepted her evidence of abuse and the psychologists' evidence as to its effect on her mental state, and *Savage* itself had been wrong to state that some form of mental disease was required. The case was remitted for a hearing before a bench of five judges in order that *Connelly* might be reconsidered. At the hearing, the Crown accepted that *Connelly* had misinterpreted *Savage*, that the cumulative approach derived from that misinterpretation was wrong and should not be followed, and that the requirement in *Savage* that there should be a mental disease was too restrictive.

Held, allowing the appeal and granting the Crown leave to bring a new prosecution, that (1) *Connelly* had misinterpreted *Savage* by requiring that all the criteria referred to in *Savage* had to be met. The test in *Savage* was intended to be a fluid one and the direction in the present case was accordingly unsound; (2) the term "mental disease" as used in *Savage* was not to be interpreted narrowly, later cases having interpreted the requirement more strictly than had originally been intended; (3) diminished responsibility required some form of abnormality of mind sufficient to have a substantial effect on a person's mind and in relation to his act, but it was not necessary to prove that the accused's mental state bordered on insanity and such a test should not be referred to except where a real question arose as to whether the accused was insane at the time of the killing; (4) the abnormality might take various forms; it had to be one that was recognised by the appropriate science, but it might be congenital or derive from an organic condition, from some psychotic illness or from the psychological effects of severe trauma, and could in principle include a recognised abnormality caused by sexual or other abuse. However, in every case there had to have been something far wrong with the accused which affected the way he acted, and (5) as diminished responsibility was a legal rather than a medical or psychological concept it was for the judge to decide whether sufficient evidence existed to support the plea; if, applying the appropriate tests, he concluded there was insufficient evidence, he should direct the jury that they could only convict of murder; if he considered the evidence sufficient, he should leave the plea for the jury to consider, but in that event, he should not simply recite the *Savage* formula but should tailor it, so far as possible, to the facts of the particular case.

GALBRAITH (KIM LOUISE) v. HM ADVOCATE (NO.3) 2002 J.C.1, Lord Rodger L.J.G., Lord Bonomy, Lady Cosgrove, Lord Nimmo Smith, Lord Penrose, HCJ.

6336. Murder – provocation – jury directions – requisite elements for charge

D appealed against his conviction for the murder of a woman with whom he had been in a relationship, on the ground of misdirection. At the trial he had given evidence that the fatal assault, namely an attack with a hammer, followed his discovery that the deceased was having intercourse with another man, and had pleaded provocation. The trial judge directed the jury as to the standard definition of murder, namely that culpable homicide occurred where there was no intention to kill and the circumstances fell short of the required degree of wicked recklessness for murder and that for provocation to succeed the violence used should not be disproportionate to the provocation offered.

Held, allowing the appeal and granting the Crown leave to bring a new prosecution, that (1) murder required a wicked intention to kill or wicked recklessness as to whether the victim lived or died, and a person who killed under provocation was to be convicted of culpable homicide rather than murder because, even if he intentionally killed his victim, he did not have the wicked intention required for murder; (2) while, as a matter of policy, Scots law admitted the plea of provocation only where the accused had been assaulted and there had been substantial provocation, it admitted an exception by recognising that violence due to a sudden and overwhelming indignation caused by the discovery of sexual infidelity, was not committed with the wicked state of mind required for murder; (3) that in such a case the sexual activity and the lethal attack were incommensurable, and where provocation was put in issue the jury should be directed to consider whether on the evidence the relationship between the accused and the deceased was such as to give rise to a bond of sexual fidelity, whether the accused had in fact lost his self control as a result of the provocation, and whether the ordinary man or woman would have been liable to react in the same way in the same circumstances, and (4) that there had accordingly been a material misdirection of the jury resulting in a miscarriage of justice.

DRURY v. HM ADVOCATE 2001 S.L.T. 1013, Lord Rodger L.J.G., HCJ Appeal.

6337. Sexual offences – sexual offenders – foreign travel – notice requirements

SEX OFFENDERS (NOTICE REQUIREMENTS) (FOREIGN TRAVEL) (SCOTLAND) REGULATIONS 2001, SSI 2001 188; made under the Sex Offenders Act 1997 s.2, s.10. In force: June 1, 2001; £1.75.

These Regulations extend to Scotland. The Sex Offenders Act 1997 specifies in Part I that certain sex offenders are subject to requirements to notify certain personal details to the police. The Criminal Justice and Court Services Act 2000 amended the Sex Offenders Act 1997 to provide for such offenders to be subject to additional requirements to give notices where they propose to leave, and return to, the United Kingdom. These Regulations impose such requirements.

6338. Sexual offences – shameless indecency – relevance of charge

G was charged with shameless indecency in that he encouraged men and women in his club to expose their private parts to the rest of the customers in return for free drinks. The disc jockey in the club had been instructed by G to announce this promotion and three individuals duly exposed, two women bared their breasts, and a man, his penis. G was convicted and appealed.

Held, allowing the appeal and quashing the conviction, that there was insufficient evidence. The test as laid down in *Watt (David Cuthbertson) v. Annan* 1978 J.C. 84, [1978] C.L.Y. 3235 required direction, intent and effect for the behaviour to be considered shamelessly indecent and in the instant case the complaint against G was lacking in specification as to the nature and extent of the conduct and its effect. Opinion of the Court per Lord Milligan.

GEDDES v. DICKSON 2001 J.C. 69, Lord Milligan, Lord Allanbridge, Lord Johnston, HCJ Appeal.

6339. Terrorism – legal representation – interviews

TERRORISM (INTERVIEWS) (SCOTLAND) ORDER 2001, SI 2001 428 (S.1); made under the Terrorism Act 2000 Sch.8 para.19. In force: February 19, 2001; £1.50.

This Order provides that where a person detained under Sch.7 to, or s.41 of, the Terrorism Act 2000 has been permitted to consult a solicitor, his solicitor shall be allowed to be present at any interview carried out in connection with a terrorist investigation or for the purposes of Sch.7 to the Terrorism Act 2000. The Order also specifies the condition subject to which the detained person's solicitor is allowed to be present at the interview.

6340. Theft – motor vehicles – fixing number plate to stolen vehicle

[Road Vehicles (Registration and Licensing) Regulations 1971 (SI 1971 1285) Reg.22.]

M was charged with the theft of a flat bed trailer. The stolen trailer was found in a parking space rented by M with registration plates attached which matched the registration plates of a van owned by M but registered in the name of one of his employees. The van was used for business purposes in connection with M's business. On inspection, M's fingerprints were found to be on the back of the registration plates. In response to the charge of theft, M pled no case to answer but the sheriff repelled the plea and found M guilty as charged, founding his decision on the fact that M, in changing the registration plates of the trailer had been attempting to conceal the true identity of the trailer. The sheriff held that this constituted criminitive behaviour which, when taken with other evidence, was sufficient to prove guilt. M appealed arguing that the sheriff had erred in concluding that there was sufficient evidence for a finding that the theft had been committed by M as changing the registration plates of a trailer to match those of the van being used to tow it was merely the act of any ordinary person in compliance with the Road Vehicles (Registration and Licensing) Regulations

1971 Reg. 22 and therefore did not constitute the criminitive behaviour required for a finding of guilt on a charge of theft.

Held, allowing the appeal, that (1) the act of changing the registration plates of the trailer did not constitute criminitive behaviour as it did not differ from the steps which would be taken by an entirely innocent van owner, and (2) the sheriff was not entitled to repel the plea of no case to answer, nor to find M guilty of theft on the evidence presented. Opinion of the Court per Lord Prosser.

MORGAN v. McFADYEN 2001 J.C. 58, Lord Prosser, Lord Allanbridge, Lord Coulsfield, HCJ Appeal.

6341. Books

Christie, Sarah – Inchoate Crimes. Greens Practice Library. Hardback: £65.00. ISBN 0-414-01390-5. W. Green & Son.

Criminal Statutes: 2001. Paperback: £33.00. ISBN 0-414-01426-X. W. Green & Son.

Gane, H W C and Stoddart, N C – Casebook on Scottish Criminal Law 3rd Ed. Paperback: £40.00. ISBN 0-414-01050-7. W. Green & Son.

McFadyen, Norman – Offences Against Justice. Scottish Criminal Law and Practice Series. Paperback: £40.00. ISBN 0-406-92322-1. Butterworths (Scotland).

CRIMINAL PROCEDURE

6342. 12 months elapsing after first appearance – accused in custody – retrospective extension granted

[Criminal Procedure (Scotland) Act 1995 (c.46) s.65(3).]

M was indicted for trial and since he was detained having been convicted previously, the 110 day period did not start to run. Upon expiration of M's detention the 110 days commenced and were extended as required. The Crown failed to apply for an extension to the 12 month time bar under the Criminal Procedure (Scotland) Act 1995 s.65(3) and it expired with M applying for an immediate discharge. The Crown then applied for a retrospective extension on the 12 month period arguing that their mistake had been in good faith, and if they had applied in time the extension would have been granted given the lack of objections to the 110 day extension. The trial judge granted the extension and M appealed.

Held, refusing the appeal, that it had not been shown that the trial judge had erred in law or exercised his discretion unreasonably when deciding to grant the time extension. Opinion of the Court per Lord Cameron of Lochbroom.

McGUIRE (JAMES) v. HM ADVOCATE 2000 S.C.C.R. 896, Lord Cameron of Lochbroom, Lord Allanbridge, Lord Caplan, HCJ Appeal.

6343. 12 months elapsing after first appearance – extension after abandonment – fault resulting in abandonment not bar to extension

[Criminal Procedure (Scotland) Act 1995 (c.46) s.264(3).]

M was tried on indictment for assault to severely injure and permanently disfigure. During the trial M's wife, whilst appearing as a witness for the Crown, declined to give evidence and this fact was alluded to during the Crown's address to the jury. This was a breach of the Criminal Procedure (Scotland) Act 1995 s.264(3) and the case was deserted pro loco et tempore. The Crown then applied for an extension of the 12 month period to allow a new indictment which was granted and M appealed to the High Court.

Held, refusing the appeal, that the commencement of the trial within the initial 12 month period and its subsequent abandonment would give rise to a right of extension. The fault of the Crown, resulting in the abandonment was not in itself a bar to the extension and the sheriff had correctly balanced that with the other relevant factors in considering the extension. Opinion of the Court per Lord Cameron of Lochbroom.

McCULLOCH (STEWART) v. HM ADVOCATE 2001 J.C. 100, Lord Cameron of Lochbroom, Lord Eassie, Lord Rodger L.J.G., HCJ Appeal.

6344. **12 months elapsing after first appearance – justification for extension**

[Criminal Procedure (Scotland) Act 1995 (c.46) s.65(3); Human Rights Act 1998 (c.42) Sch.1 Part I Art.6(1).]

W and another were charged on indictment with theft, reset and uttering of counterfeit cheques. At the first hearing the sheriff granted an unopposed motion for a three month extension of the 12 month time limit under the Criminal Procedure (Scotland) Act 1995 s.65(3). At the subsequent trial diet, the Crown applied for a further two month extension on the grounds of pressure of business and belief that the accused had intended to plead guilty. The extension was granted and the two accused appealed by note of appeal to the High Court arguing that the situation had arisen due to failure by the Crown to allocate sufficient priority to the case during the sitting and that there was no basis for the assumption that the accused would plead guilty.

Held, allowing the appeal, that pressure of business in a particular sitting was not sufficient justification for the sheriff to exercise her discretion to grant a further extension to the 12 month time limit, *HM Advocate v. Swift (James Aloysius)* 1984 J.C. 83, [1984] C.L.Y. 3906 and *McGinty v. HM Advocate* 1985 S.L.T. 25, [1985] C.L.Y. 3901 followed.

Observed, that there was an obligation on the Scottish Executive to organise the legal system in such a way as to allow cases to be brought within the time limits set by Parliament. Although the Human Rights Act 1998 Sch.1 Part I Art.6(1) required trials to be conducted within a reasonable time, temporary backlogs were allowed provided prompt action was taken to deal with them. Opinion of the Court as per Lord Philip.

WARNES (THOMAS ALFRED) v. HM ADVOCATE 2001 J.C. 110, Lord Rodger L.J.G., Lord Philip, Lord Reed, HCJ Appeal.

6345. **12 months elapsing after first appearance – justification for extension – error resulting in desertion of trial – entitlement to extension not precluded by fault of desertion**

E was tried for rape in October 2000. During the trial, the complainer was asked what she had said amidst the struggle and although reluctant to say, both counsel and the judge attributed her reluctance to an unwillingness to swear in court, and she was pressed for an answer. She answered "You bastard, you have done this before. I didn't believe it, but now I know you have done this before." The trial was deserted pro loco et tempore following her statements. The Crown applied for an extension to the 12 month period in order to place E on trial again. The extension was granted and E appealed to the High Court.

Held, refusing the appeal, that the Crown had shown sufficient cause for an extension and the Crown's actions which had resulted in the desertion did not constitute an error of sufficient magnitude to preclude an extension. Any discretion exercised by the Court should take account of the length of extension sought and any possible prejudice to E. In the instant case the extension sought was a short one and would not involve any prejudice. The desertion of the trial, pro loco et tempore had been appropriate in the circumstances and if the extension was denied the desertion would in effect be afforded the status of a desertion simpliciter. Opinion of the Court per Lord Rodger, Lord Justice-General.

E (JAMES) v. HM ADVOCATE 2001 J.C. 115, Lord Rodger, L.J.G., Lord Kirkwood, Lord Penrose, HCJ Appeal.

6346. 110 days elapsing after committal – justification for extension

[Criminal Procedure (Scotland) Act 1995 (c.46) s.65(7).]

S, having first appeared on December 1, 2000, was fully committed on December 8 in respect of two separate petitions containing charges of attempted murder. S was sentenced to four months' imprisonment on an unrelated matter on January 17, 2001. S's solicitor subsequently informed the Crown of that sentence, but when the Crown sought to confirm the matter with the prison authorities, they were told that S had been in custody on the sentence warrant from December 1, 2000 until March 16, 2001, and proceeded on the basis that the 110 day period would expire on July 3, 2001. On May 16, S's agents alerted the Crown to the discrepancy in the dates. The Crown did not have the matter properly checked until May 29, when it was discovered that the 110 days expired on May 26. The Crown's application to extend the 110 day period to May 30, 2001 was refused. The Crown appealed, arguing inter alia that the presiding judge had failed to recognise that the delay was attributable to a mistake on the part of the prison officials.

Held, refusing the appeal, that the Crown's application did not fall within the scope of the Criminal Procedure (Scotland) Act 1995 s.65(7), as their response to the information given was inadequate considering the effort that had been made to alert the Crown to the matter as well as the fact that the information from the prison concerning S's period in custody did not correspond to a typical period of custody under a four month sentence. While the prison authorities might have given inaccurate information to the Crown, had they checked prior to May 29, communication with S's agents would no doubt have revealed the true position allowing the Crown to take steps to avoid S being detained for more than 110 days before the commencement of his trial.

HM ADVOCATE v. SANDS (ANDREW) 2001 S.L.T. 1323, Lord Rodger L.J.G., Lord Abernethy, Lord Sutherland, HCJ Appeal.

6347. Appeals – fresh evidence – petition for recovery of documents – documentation not applicable to appeal

[Criminal Procedure (Scotland) Act 1995 (c.46) s.106(3A).]

H was charged, along with eight others, with illegally importing cannabis resin. It was alleged that H, the others and the cannabis resin had been aboard the ship Isolda and had rendezvoused with another vessel at sea and transferred the drug. H objected, at trial, to the leading of that evidence, arguing that the evidence relied upon in the Crown case had been supplied by a device placed on the Isolda unlawfully and as such was inadmissible. The objection was repelled and H appealed to the High Court petitioning for recovery of documents and records which related to the evidence. It was not disputed that counsel for H had had an opportunity to review the documentation and tracking device before trial. H criticised the approach in *McLeod (Alastair) v. HM Advocate (No.2)* 1998 J.C. 67, [1998] C.L.Y. 5607, arguing that there had been differences in the approaches of the judges and a larger court should convene to consider the question anew. H also contended that a general disclosure of documents should be ordered to enable a general investigation into the fairness of the trial's proceedings.

Held, refusing the application, that since it was not disputed that the tracking device had been placed on the Isolda unlawfully H would not require the recovery of any further documentation to advance the argument of inadmissibility. H was, essentially trying to introduce evidence that had not been led at trial, and under the Criminal Procedure (Scotland) Act 1995 s.106(3A), evidence not heard at trial could only found an appeal where a reasonable explanation was given as to why it was not heard. H had not achieved that. The approach by the judges in *McLeod* was held not to be inconsistent and H's criticism unfounded. An appeal court had statutory grounds under which it could allow an appeal and no power to enter into a general enquiry into the background of a case. The court was satisfied that H could advance his appeal without production of the requested documentation. Opinion of the Court per Lord Rodger, Lord Justice-General.

HOEKSTRA v. HM ADVOCATE (NO.6) 2001 J.C. 131, Lord Rodger, L.J.G., Lord Philip, Lord Weir, HCJ Appeal.

6348. **Bail – application for bail while already in custody – competency of application**

[Immigration Act 1971 (c.77); Criminal Procedure (Scotland) Act 1995 (c.46) s.23A; Scotland Act 1998 (c.46); European Convention on Human Rights 1950 Art.5(3), Art.6, Art.8(1), Art.14.]

G, a Guatemalan national while being detained under the Immigration Act 1971 was charged with importing drugs. He applied for and was granted bail by the sheriff but that was later denied due to the severity of the charge levied against him. G sought review of the adverse decision on the grounds that it adversely affected the preparation of his defence and the severity of the charge levied against him should not be a consideration in deciding the matter of bail. The Crown submitted that G's application was incompetent, he not being one of the class of persons under the Criminal Procedure (Scotland) Act 1995 s.23A. G also lodged three minutes intimating his intention to raise devolution issues. Minute I complained that G's bail had been refused as a result of his nationality and was a breach of his rights under the European Convention on Human Rights 1950 Art.5(3), Art.6(1) and Art.14. Minute II complained that the prison regime under which he was detained was in breach of Art.6(3)(b), Art.8(1) and Art.14. Minute III complained that the Crown's opposition to his application for bail was in contravention of his convention rights and that the subsequent actions of the Lord Advocate and Home Secretary had attempted to limit the legislative power of the Scottish Parliament and as such were in contravention of the Scotland Act 1998.

Held, refusing the petition and dismissing Minutes I, II and III, that (1) the gravity of the charge should be a factor when considering bail, since that would affect sentencing and, as such, the likelihood of G's reluctance to face trial; (2) G's application for bail was competent, the lack of reference in s.23A to the class of persons in custody under the Immigration Act 1971 did not imply incompetency and neither was the power to grant bail expressly excluded by G's custody under the 1971 Act; (3) Minute I was without foundation. The adequacy of time and facilities to prepare G's defence could not be properly assessed at that stage in proceedings and the court was not persuaded that the prison regime was in breach of any articles; (4) the alleged discrimination of G on the basis of his nationality was held not to be a factor in the proceedings, and (5) Minute III contained no relevant assertion of any devolution issue or breach of convention rights. Opinion of the Court per Lord Prosser.

MONTEROSSO v. SECRETARY OF STATE FOR THE HOME DEPARTMENT; *sub nom.* MONTEROSO v. HM ADVOCATE 2001 S.C. 291, Lord Prosser, Lord Allanbridge, Lord McEwan, OH.

6349. **Criminal appeals – legal representation – defective representation – expert evidence challenged under cross examination**

H was convicted of murdering C by shooting her. The Crown case relied heavily on spots of C's blood found on H's clothing. H asserted that he arrived on the scene shortly after the shooting and cradled the still breathing C, thereby getting blood on his clothing. The expert pathologist evidence led by the Crown indicated that as a result of the injuries sustained by C she would have stopped breathing almost immediately. The defence challenged at evidence in cross examination, but had not precognosced the Crown pathologist nor sought contrary opinion. After the conviction, a report from another pathologist indicated some findings contradictory to the Crown case. H appealed against the conviction arguing that his defence had been defective and there had been a miscarriage of justice.

Held, allowing the appeal, quashing the conviction and granting authority for a new prosecution, that the preparation of the defence case had been so fundamentally flawed that it had not provided H with a fair trial. An enquiry into the mechanics of C's death and precognition of the Crown experts would have highlighted the defence's need to instruct their own expert medical evidence which would have refuted the basis of the Crown case. The defence would not then have been reliant upon a theory of the mechanics of C's death that had no basis in expert testimony, *Garrow v. HM Advocate* 2000 S.C.C.R. 772, [2001] 1 C.L. 643 applied

HEMPHILL v. HM ADVOCATE 2001 S.C.C.R. 361, Lord Rodger L.J.G, Lord Cameron of Lochbroom, Lord McCluskey, HCJ Appeal.

6350. Criminal Justice and Court Service Act 2000 (c.8) – Commencement No.5 Order

CRIMINAL JUSTICE AND COURT SERVICES ACT 2000 (COMMENCEMENT NO.5) (SCOTLAND) ORDER 2001, SSI 2001 166 (C.8); made under the Criminal Justice and Court Service Act 2000 s.80. Commencement details: bringing into force various provisions of the Act on May 31, 2001; £1.50.

This Order brings into force the Criminal Justice and Court Services Act 2000 s.66 and Sch.5 which contain amendments to the Sex Offenders Act 1997. In particular, the amendments which are made to the 1997 Act include the reduction in the initial period during which offenders must register from 14 to three days; a requirement that initial notification to the police be in person; a new power for the police on initial notification to take fingerprints and photographs of the offender; provision enabling the Scottish Ministers to prescribe by Regulations those police stations at which notifications may be made; an increase in the maximum penalty for a failure to comply with the Act's requirements to 5 years imprisonment on indictment, or a fine, or both; and a new requirement that a relevant offender must notify the police of his or her intention to leave the UK and of his or her return.

6351. Devolution issues – charge of rape against 13 year olds – delay of 23 months considered unreasonable

[European Convention on Human Rights 1950 Art.6(1); United Nations Convention on the Rights of the Child 1989 Art.40; United Nations Standard Minimum Rules for the Administration of Juvenile Justice 1985 Art.20.]

DP and SM, aged 13 years, were indicted for the rape of a 14 year old girl with learning difficulties. The rape allegedly took place on March 11, 1999 and the accused were charged on March 16, 1999. The case was allocated for trial on February 19, 2001. DP and SM lodged a minute of notice of devolution issue in which they raised pleas in bar of trial on the grounds of unreasonable delay, relying on their rights as laid down in the European Convention on Human Rights 1950 Art.6(1), the United Nations Convention on the Rights of the Child 1989 Art.40 and the United Nations Standard Minimum Rules for the Administration of Juvenile Justice 1985 Art.20.

Held, sustaining the pleas in bar of trial and dismissing the indictment as incompetent, that the cumulative history of the case gave the impression that it was not dealt with as urgently as was required and there had been no priority afforded to the case given the involvement of children. The overall period of time lapsed was much longer than normal in a case like this, even where the complainer had learning difficulties. The delay was particularly unusual given the involvement of children and there had been no satisfactory explanation given for the delay.

HM ADVOCATE v. P; HM ADVOCATE v. SM; *sub nom.* HM ADVOCATE v. DP; DP v. SM 2001 S.L.T. 924, Lord Reed, HCJ.

6352. **Devolution issues – custody – time limits – jurisdiction of judicial committee**

[Criminal Procedure (Scotland) Act 1995 (c.46) s.65(4); Scotland Act 1998 (c.46) Sch.6 para.13; Human Rights Act 1998 (c.42) Sch.1 Part I Art.6.]

F sought special leave to appeal against the dismissal of his appeal by the High Court and its refusal of leave to appeal to the Judicial Committee. While out on licence from a sentence of six years' imprisonment for drug offences, F was caught with a large quantity of cannabis and his licence was revoked. F argued at first instance that he had been wrongly deprived of the protection of the Criminal Procedure (Scotland) Act 1995 s.65(4) which provided that he could not be held in custody for a period exceeding 110 days from the date of his committal until trial. The trial judge held that as F was being held for his earlier offence, he was not entitled to the protection of s.65(4) and in view of the complexity of the case the period of 10.5 months during which he had been detained was not excessive or in breach of his Convention rights. F sought to raise as a devolution issue the incompatibility of his continued prosecution with his right to a fair trial within a reasonable time under the Human Rights Act 1998 Sch.1 Part I Art.6.

Held, dismissing the petition, that the applicability of s.65(4) was a question of Scots criminal law and procedure and was not a devolution issue. The only devolution issue which could be raised in instant case was that of the compatibility of the prosecution with F's Convention rights. As F had failed to argue those points before the High Court, it had correctly refused leave to appeal to the Judicial Committee which, under the Scotland Act 1998 Sch.6 para.13 had a limited jurisdiction to hear only appeals against determinations by the High Court of Justiciary of devolution issues.

FOLLEN (GARY) v. HM ADVOCATE [2001] UKPC D2, [2001] 1 W.L.R. 1668, Lord Hope of Craighead, Lord Bingham of Cornhill, Lord Clyde, Privy Council (Scotland).

6353. **Indictments – assault – desertion pro loco et tempore – Crown wishing to bring more serious charge – oppressive and unfair**

G was charged on indictment with aggravated assault and pled guilty, under deletion of certain parts of the charge, after the Crown had indicted that they would accept such a plea. The Crown sought to desert the diet pro loco et tempore to bring a fresh indictment on a more serious charge relating to the same incident.

Held, continuing the case to the trial diet, that it would be oppressive to grant the Crown's motion, the informal agreement being analogous to the situation where the Crown had given an indication that no further proceedings would be taken, and the Crown having barred itself from proceeding as it had in the instant case sought to do; there was no suggestion that the Crown had discovered new evidence to justify that course.

Observed, that if the indictment were deserted and N successfully took a plea in bar of trial on the proposed fresh indictment, N would go unpunished despite his tendered guilty plea.

HM ADVOCATE v. NAIRN (MICHAEL ALEXANDER) 2000 S.L.T. (Sh Ct) 176, AL Stewart Q.C., Sh Ct (Tayside, Central and Fife).

6354. **Indictments – being concerned in supply of controlled drugs – specification**

[Misuse of Drugs Act 1971 (c.38) Sch.2 para.1 (c); Criminal Procedure (Scotland) Act 1995 (c.46) Sch.3 para.11.]

G was charged with possession of and being concerned with the supply of a controlled drug. The indictment described the drug as a compound of the type specified in the Misuse of Drugs Act 1971 Sch.2, para.1 (c), commonly known as ecstasy and also as a Class A drug in terms of the 1971 Act. G lodged a minute pleading to the relevancy of the indictment arguing that ecstasy was not a proscribed drug under Sch.2, para.1 (c). G argued that the use of a slang name for the drug which could vary within geographical locations did not afford him fair notice of the charges against him under the Criminal Procedure (Scotland)

Act 1995 Sch.3, para.11. G claimed that ecstasy came in two forms and the wording of the indictment left it open to the Crown to present arguments in relation to either without specifying to G which he was alleged to have been in possession of or been concerned with supplying. The prosecution admitted that the form of their indictments for ecstasy related offences had formerly specified the chemical names for the drugs, but that the indictment against G represented a new style being adopted to make the charges easier to read to juries.

Held, refusing the appeal, that (1) the charges were sufficiently specific to meet the requirements of Sch.3 to the 1995 Act, and (2) the inclusion of the reference to ecstasy was unnecessary but its inclusion provided the defence with additional notice to that required by statute.

GLENNIE (DEAN) v. HM ADVOCATE 2001 S.L.T. 903, Lord Cameron of Lochbroom, Judge Sir GH Gordon Q.C., Lord Mackay of Drumadoon, HCJ Appeal.

6355. Juries – verdicts – juror's knowledge of accused – inadequate directions

M appealed against his convictions for four charges comprising of assault, breach of the peace and police assault on the ground that the guilty verdict was tainted. M had been tried on indictment and before the jury had returned to deliver their verdict, the sheriff had been informed that a member of the jury had disclosed to other jurors that she knew the accused as a shoplifter. The sheriff had made an inquiry in open court and had been informed by the forewoman that the information was disclosed after the jury had reached their verdicts. The juror in question admitted her identity and, in response to a leading question by the sheriff, stated that the matter was a completely different one and had not affected her decision. The jury's verdict was then returned of guilty on all four charges, three by a majority. The Crown argued that the jury had been given proper directions and there was no evidence of personal partiality by the juror in question.

Held, allowing the appeal and quashing the convictions, with authority to the Crown to bring a new prosecution, that the allegation made was capable of causing the accused and any objective observer to hold legitimate doubts as to the impartiality of the court, which were objectively justified, and the action taken by the sheriff was insufficient as to give guarantees excluding such doubts.

McLEAN (RONALD) v. HM ADVOCATE 2001 S.C.C.R. 526, Lord Cameron of Lochbroom, Lord Rodger L.J.G., Lord Weir, HCJ Appeal.

6356. Jury directions – misdirection – corroboration

[Sexual Offences (Scotland) Act 1976 (c.67) s.2(2), s.3(1).]

W was tried on an indictment libelling charges of lewd, indecent and libidinous practices, rape and contraventions of the Sexual Offences (Scotland) Act 1976 s.2(2) and s.3(1) against A, the daughter of his cohabitee. The offences were allegedly committed between November 1983 and July 1989 when A was aged between nine and 15. For corroboration of A's evidence, the Crown sought to rely on an alleged admission made by W in 1997 in the presence of A and her husband during a confrontation in which W allegedly remarked that he was "sorry" and must have been "sick". The husband was not present throughout the entire conversation. W was convicted and appealed on the basis that the jury had been invited to use the same piece of evidence to establish a multiplicity of charges and it would have been preferable to bring a single charge of rape covering the whole period in question; and the judge had misdirected the jury in relation to whether the husband's evidence could corroborate A's evidence of W's admission. The Crown conceded that the advocate depute had erred in inviting the jury to have regard to all of W's responses to the confrontation and that there had been a misdirection as the judge had not corrected that error, nor explained that the husband's evidence was the only evidence which could afford the necessary corroboration, but argued that there had been no miscarriage of justice as he had referred to both A and her husband's evidence, and there was no real risk that the jury would convict if they believed A but not her husband.

Held, allowing the appeal and quashing the conviction, that (1) the Crown had adopted the correct approach to the indictment, as to follow the course proposed by W would risk circumventing the specific legislative provisions and fail to reflect Parliament's enacting that intercourse with a girl under 16 was unlawful whether or not she consented; (2) it was vital in the instant case that the jury understood the significance of A's husband's evidence and that they required to reach a view as to its credibility as a separate adminicle of evidence, and (3) the judge had failed to direct the jury that they could only convict if they accepted the husband's evidence that he heard both A's allegations and W's reply, and in the circumstances that omission constituted a miscarriage of justice.

WILKES v. HM ADVOCATE 2001 S.L.T. 1268, Lord Rodger L.J.G., Lord Carloway, Lady Cosgrove, HCJ Appeal.

6357. Jury trial – independent and impartial tribunal – reference in indictment to bail aggravation

[Bail Act 1980; Criminal Procedure (Scotland) Act 1995 (c.46); European Convention on Human Rights 1950 Art.6.]

B was charged with committing a number of offences while subject to various bail orders. B lodged a minute raising as a devolution issue that to make a jury aware that he was on bail at the time of the offences would prejudice their impartiality and would breach the presumption of innocence under the European Convention on Human Rights 1950 Art.6. The minute was repelled and B appealed.

Held, refusing the appeal, that the practice of libelling bail aggravations in indictments put before juries did not breach Art.6 given that there was nothing to suggest that a jury when properly directed was incapable of deciding the issues on the evidence before them, just because the jurors could work out from something contained in the indictment that the accused had previously been charged with some other offence, and that view was supported by experience of the system in operation both under the Bail Act 1980 and the Criminal Procedure (Scotland) Act 1995. The court referred to *X v. Austria (2742/66)* (Unreported), where the European Commission had rejected the view that reference to previous convictions during a trial before a court which included lay judges breached Art.6. Opinion of the Court per Lord Rodger, Lord Justice General.

BOYD (JOHN) v. HM ADVOCATE; MOFFAT (GRAEME WILLIAM) v. HM ADVOCATE 2001 J.C. 53, Lord Rodger L.J.G., Lord Philip, Lord Reed, HCJ Appeal.

6358. Nobile officium – refusal of legal aid – refusal a breach of human rights – finality of appeal court decision

[Criminal Procedure (Scotland) Act 1995 (c.46).]

G was convicted of perjury and sought, but was not granted, legal aid for an appeal where he appeared without counsel. The appeal was refused and G applied to the European Commission of Human Rights and ultimately the European Court of Human Rights held that the refusal of legal aid had been a breach of G's human rights under the Convention ([1990] 12 E.H.R.R. 469). G, in the absence of any other remedy, sought to have his conviction quashed by applying to the nobile officium of the High Court for an order for intimation and service.

Held, refusing the order, that G's petition was incompetent, given that its ultimate purpose was to have the High Court alter its appeal decision contrary to the Criminal Procedure (Scotland) Act 1995 s.124 (2).

GRANGER (JOSEPH), PETITIONER 2001 J.C. 183, Lord Hardie, HCJ.

6359. Rape – conduct of defence case – failure to obtain revised opinion from expert witness – miscarriage of justice

G appealed against his conviction for the rape of C, on the grounds of inadequate representation and preparation of his defence. After G's agents had obtained a report from a medical witness, X, agreeing with the Crown's evidence of penile penetration, G said he had penetrated C with his fingers. G's agents did not then obtain a further report from X commenting on that possibility; G had given instructions not to after hearing his solicitor advocate's advice that he considered the matter to be insignificant. At appeal, X provided a report indicating that digital penetration could have caused C's injuries.

Held, quashing the conviction, that (1) G's instructions not to call a medical witness X were vitiated because of the failure of his agents and solicitor advocate to discover X's views on the possibility that damage to C's vagina could have been caused by digital penetration; (2) the Crown's medical witness was not cross examined on that possibility, and therefore evidence to which the jury would have been likely to attach much weight had not been disclosed, and (3) the failure was fundamental and affected the defence to such an extent that there had been a miscarriage of justice, *Allan (Thomas Reid) v. HM Advocate* 2000 J.C. 75, [2000] 3 C.L. 645 distinguished. Opinion of the Court per Lord Rodger, Lord Justice General.

GARROW v. HM ADVOCATE 2000 S.C.C.R. 772, Lord Rodger, L.J.G., Lord Caplan, Lord Cowie, HCJ Appeal.

6360. Right to fair trial – adult witness at trial – boyfriend sitting nearby as "support" – allegation of improper communication – no breach of right to fair trial

M was tried on indictment for assault and committing lewd, indecent and libidinous practices against two sisters between 1983 and 1985, one of whom, D, was aged between 12 and 14. At trial the sheriff granted a motion allowing D's boyfriend to sit nearby for support while she gave evidence, relying on para.3(c) of the memorandum by the Lord Justice General with regard to child witnesses. M opposed the motion arguing that as D was aged 28 she should be able to give evidence without support. M was convicted and appealed arguing that the presence of D's boyfriend had prevented justice from being seen to be done, and that there had been improper communications between them including the exchange of glances and the mouthing of words.

Held, refusing the appeal, that the presence of persons in court to support adult witnesses did not give rise to material difficulties, and although it was unfortunate that D's support came from her boyfriend in front of whom she might have hesitated to speak frankly, the mere fact that he was present did not create a miscarriage of justice especially as D was subject to vigourous cross examination and the jury had been given clear direction that the matters of credibility and reliability were for them alone to decide. There was no basis for holding that improper communication, sufficient to justify quashing the conviction, had taken place especially given M's failure to move the court to desert the diet at the time of the trial or to ask for special jury directions.

McGINLEY v. HM ADVOCATE 2001 S.L.T. 198, Lord Rodger L.J.G., Lord Cameron of Lochbroom, Lord Weir, HCJ Appeal.

6361. Right to fair trial – delay – 17 months to investigate case not unreasonable

[European Convention on Human Rights 1950 Art.6(1).]

G was charged with stealing a trailer in December 1996 (charge 1) and between August and September 1998 (charge 2). The Crown spent 17 months investigating charge 1 and in May 2000 G was indicted for trial. G lodged a devolution minute on the ground of unreasonable delay with regard to charge 1. The sheriff accepted the Crown's explanation as to the delay, given the difficulties of investigating the ownership of the trailer and the minute was repelled. E appealed to the High

Court arguing that the explanation put forward by the Crown lacked detail and was insufficient in the circumstances.

Held, refusing the appeal, that the lapse of 17 months was unusual by general standards but a Crown investigation could be expected to take some time, and a period of inactivity prima facie would not bring about a finding of unreasonable delay. Delay implied a departure from the norm. The level of detail included in the explanation for the delay was irrelevant, the reasons for it were found in the broad circumstances of the instant case and the Crown was found not to have acted unreasonably. Opinion of the Court per Lord Prosser.

GIBSON (DAVID BLAIR) v. HM ADVOCATE 2001 J.C. 125, Lord Prosser, Lord Cowie, Lord Kirkwood, HCJ Appeal.

6362. Right to fair trial – delay – 23 months delay between charge and trial – attributability to underfunding – compatibility with Human Rights Act 1998

[Human Rights Act 1998 (c.42) Sch.1 Part 1 Art.6.]

O and another who were charged with assault to severe injury committed on February 7, 1999, took a plea in bar of trial that there had been a breach of their right to trial within a reasonable time contrary to the Human Rights Act 1998 Sch.1 Part 1 Art.6. Both had been cautioned and charged the following day but were not brought to trial until January 8, 2001. The Crown case depended on forensic evidence but a laboratory instructed to analyse certain bloodstains did not report until December 1999. The case was immediately marked for petition, but after the accuseds' appearance on petition on February 29, 2000, there was a further delay by the police until early October when precognition commenced. It was argued that while the Crown had not been at fault, the delays indicated a chronic underfunding of the system such as had been held by the European Court to amount to a failure on the part of a contracting state to allow compliance with Art.6 (1). The sheriff repelled the plea but granted leave to appeal.

Held, dismissing the appeal, that (1) if delays such as those in the present case occurred regularly and inevitably as a result of limited resources, there would be what could be described as systemic underfunding, and a failure to remedy that would properly be described as unreasonable in the context of a fair system of justice but whether, in any particular case, that produced a breach of Art.6 (1) would depend on the overall lapse of time; (2) it had not been shown, on either matter, that the defects which had occurred had passed from being temporary into being inherent and uncured elements in the system or that they demonstrated a persistent underfunding which had become unreasonable, and (3) as the accused had been charged almost immediately and the police delay alone would not result in a breach of the accuseds' rights under Art.6, the overall period did not amount to a breach of those rights.

O'BRIEN (ALAN) v. HM ADVOCATE 2001 S.L.T. 1101, Lord Prosser, Lord Cowie, Lord MacLean, HCJ Appeal.

6363. Right to fair trial – delay – continuing investigation – prioritisation as explanation

[European Convention on Human Rights 1950 Art.6 (1).]

M was charged with fraudulently obtaining payments from social security between 1991 and 1998, declaring that he was sick and unfit for work or not working. M was told he was being reported for prosecution in August 1998, but was not served with a petition warrant until a year later, the indictment was served in June 2000. M lodged a devolution minute claiming unreasonable delay under the right to trial within a reasonable time as provided in the European Convention on Human Rights 1950 Art.6 (1). The minute was repelled and M appealed to the High Court.

Held, refusing the appeal, that although not necessarily required, the nine month delay leading to petition was given a full and complete explanation, with regular activity between the parties in the investigation. The delay after service of the petition was attributed to matters of prioritisation and the Court found that there had been no unreasonableness in that regard. Opinion of the Court per Lord Prosser.

MITCHELL (ALEXANDER TODD) v. HM ADVOCATE 2001 S.C.C.R. 110, Lord Prosser, Lord Cowie, Lord McEwan, HCJ Appeal.

6364. Right to fair trial – delay – delay caused by police failure – total delay not unreasonable

[European Convention on Human Rights 1950 Art.6(1).]

H was charged with assault and breach of the peace on February 14, 1999. A petition warrant was issued two months later but H was not arrested until September 1999. The delay was attributed to police failure. Nine months later, H was due for trial and lodged a devolution minute on the ground of unreasonable delay in executing the warrant in contravention of the European Convention on Human Rights 1950 Art.6(1). The minute was repelled, but H, given leave, appealed to the High Court.

Held, refusing the appeal, that upon execution of the warrant it could not be said that there had been an overall delay that would be considered unreasonable, nor would it require accelerated procedure to avoid a consequent delay of unreasonableness. Opinion of the Court per Lord Prosser.

HENDRY (WILLIAM) v. HM ADVOCATE 2001 J.C. 122, Lord Prosser, Lord Cowie, Lord Kirkwood, HCJ Appeal.

6365. Right to fair trial – delay – devolution issues – appropriate remedy

[Human Rights Act 1998 (c.42) Sch.1 Part I Art.6, s.6, s.7; Scotland Act 1998 (c.46) s.57(2), s.100.]

R, charged on indictment with six offences of indecent behaviour towards children, raised an issue under the Human Rights Act 1998 Sch.1 Part I Art.6 as to whether he had been brought to trial within reasonable time. R was initially cautioned and charged in 1995 with indecent behaviour against the daughters of M with whom R resided. The procurator fiscal decided that there was then insufficient evidence. On October 30, 2000, following further allegations of indecent behaviour towards one daughter and two other children, R appeared on petition. R was thereafter indicted on charges involving all four children. R presented a minute stating that the proceedings insofar as they related to the charges concerning M's daughters were incompatible with Art.6, on the basis that (1) as the Lord Advocate was a public authority within the meaning of s.6 of the Human Rights Act 1998, it was unlawful for him to continue to prosecute R on those charges; (2) it was similarly unlawful for the court to allow those charges to be brought to trial, and (3) as the Lord Advocate had no power under the Scotland Act 1998 s.57(2) to do anything that was incompatible with the Convention, he had no power to continue to prosecute those charges. The Crown conceded that there was sufficient evidence in 1995 to have proceeded, and that there had been an unreasonable delay contrary to Art.6(1), but argued that R would not be treated as a "victim" under s.100 of the Scotland Act 1998 and s.7 of the Human Rights Act 1998 unless and until the proceedings against him were concluded and no effective redress given by way of a reduced sentence; and further that a breach of Art.6 was not necessarily a complete bar to further proceedings.

Held, refusing the plea, that (1) in every case it was essential to examine the specific nature and circumstances of the violation in order to determine its legal consequences and find an appropriate remedy; (2) a person affected directly by a violation of his Convention rights had to be regarded as a victim unless and until he was granted an effective remedy, it was his status as victim that entitled him to seek that remedy under the provisions in question; (3) it was plain from Convention jurisprudence that to proceed to trial would not be incompatible with R's rights merely by reason of the length of proceedings; (4) if a public authority had acted incompatibly with a Convention right, the court could grant such remedy, or make such order within its powers as it considered just and appropriate, and the court could reduce a sentence in recognition of the violation if the accused was convicted, or the Court of Session could grant a declarator or award damages; (5) the fact that the length of proceedings considered as a whole exceeded a reasonable time did not have the consequence that the acts undertaken by the prosecution in the course of the proceedings, whether considered individually or cumulatively, were in violation of the accused's Convention rights, and there was therefore no reason to conclude that they were rendered ultra vires by s.57(2), and s.57 of the Scotland Act 1998, and (6) there was accordingly no reason for Scottish courts to depart from their previous approach to pleas in bar of trial on the ground of delay, or their approach to delay as a mitigatory factor, although more explicit reasoning might be necessary, and following that approach, delay would only justify sustaining a plea in bar of trial in exceptional cases.

HM ADVOCATE v. R 2001 S.L.T. 1366, Lord Reed, HCJ Appeal.

6366. Right to fair trial – delay – devolution issues – children – age not a relevant factor in considering reasonableness of delay

[European Convention on Human Rights 1950 Art.6(1).]

C was charged with assault on November 9, 1999 and served with an indictment on July 5, 2000. C was 15 at the date of charge and 16 at indictment. C lodged a devolution minute arguing unreasonable delay under the European Convention on Human Rights 1950 Art. 6(1) which provided that everyone was entitled to a fair trial within a reasonable time; C relied particularly on the fact that he was a child at the date of the offence.

Held, refusing the minute, that the delay could not be considered unreasonable and C, although 15 was only four months from 16 and as such his age could not be considered a factor.

COOK (CRAIG GARRY) v. HM ADVOCATE; *sub nom.* HM ADVOCATE v. COOK (CRAIG GARRY) 2001 S.L.T. (Sh Ct) 53, Sheriff AL Stewart Q.C., Sh Ct (Tayside, Central and Fife).

6367. Right to fair trial – delay – devolution issues – total period of delay as measure of reasonableness – 15 months not unreasonable

[European Convention on Human Rights 1950 Art.6(1).]

S was charged with assault and appeared on petition on September 6, 1999. The case did not however come to precognition until March 3, 2000. S lodged a devolution minute arguing that under the European Convention on Human Rights 1950 Art.6(1) allowing everyone a fair and public trial within a reasonable time, the delay in the instant case was unreasonable. The minute was repelled by the sheriff and S appealed to the High Court.

Held, refusing the appeal, that when considering the words "within a reasonable time" it would be easy to find fault with a particular delay, it was however the reasonableness of the total delay that should be looked at and the six months in the instant case was not unreasonable when compared with normal experience, especially given the viable explanation for the particular delay. Opinion of the Court per Lord Prosser.

SMITH v. HM ADVOCATE (DELAY) 2000 S.C.C.R. 926, Lord Prosser, Lord Bonomy, Lord Penrose, HCJ Appeal.

6368. Right to fair trial – delay – right to fair trial within reasonable time

[European Convention on Human Rights 1950 Art.6(1).]

An accused person was charged on indictment with lewd and libidinous practices, rape and sodomy, committed on various occasions between January 1997 and October 1998, against four young children aged between five and eight. At the time of the alleged offences, the accused was aged between 12 and 13. The accused was charged on October 31, 1998 but no indictment was served until January 2001. The accused raised as a devolution issue that for the Lord Advocate to proceed with the indictment would be incompatible with his right to a hearing within a reasonable time under the European Convention on Human Rights 1950 Art.6(1). The Crown tendered an explanation for the delay covering a period of 17 months in which they submitted inter alia that there was a shortage of specialist fiscals to deal with the case, three of the children had failed to turn up for interview and had to be traced, a further delay arose from investigations regarding the fourth child and another possible complainer who had only come to light in 2000, the first three children then had to be re-precognosced but by then lived in a remote area; and consultation with the children's panel reporter was required before the investigation could begin and it was only on the emergence of the fourth child that the reporter conceded there was a case for trial. The trial judge repelled the minute and the accused appealed.

Held, allowing the appeal and dismissing the indictment, that (1) a delay of 27 months was substantially too long in a case involving children; the accused would be different in terms of physical development, maturity and understanding, as would the victims, and they would create a different impression before a jury than they might have done at an earlier time; furthermore harmful consequences could have arisen by leaving the accused uncertain about his fate; (2) the explanation tendered by the Crown lacked any indication that the lapse of time led the authorities, as it should have done, to treat the case with increasing urgency as time progressed, and (3) when the whole period of delay was considered, each individual explanation lost its force and the judge had erred in adopting a piecemeal approach.

K (A JUVENILE) v. HM ADVOCATE 2001 S.L.T. 1261, Lord Coulsfield, Judge Sir GH Gordon Q.C., Lord Nimmo Smith, HCJ Appeal.

6369. Right to fair trial – delay – right to fair trial within reasonable time

[Human Rights Act 1998 (c.42) Sch.1 Part I Art.6, s.6; Scotland Act 1998 (c.46) Sch.6 para 5.]

M, who had been convicted of assault by driving at a police officer and causing him to be thrown from the car, to his injury and danger of life, raised as a devolution issue that his rights under the Human Rights Act 1998 Sch.1 Part I Art.6 had been breached in relation to the subsequent appeal proceedings on the grounds that the proceedings had not been completed within a reasonable time. M initially appealed against a sentence of eight and a half years' detention in December 1996. In 1997 the appeal was continued to allow fresh evidence to be investigated. In January 1999 the court allowed the new evidence to be heard, and a hearing was fixed for May 6, 1999 when the Crown was granted a continuation. M was then released on bail. Transcripts of the evidence at trial were received at the Justiciary Office in August 1999, and the speeches in December, but no further hearing took place until May 9, 2001 when the fresh evidence was heard. The following day the appeal was refused. It was on that delay, for which no reason was given, that M founded the devolution minute. The Crown argued that as respects the period before October 2, 2000, when the court as a public authority became subject to the Convention, the accused could found only on delay by the Lord Advocate, but after conviction the Lord Advocate was no longer master of the instance and it was the court which bore responsibility for providing a decision within a reasonable time. The Advocate General appeared to obtain guidance on the proper manner of proceeding when an issue arose under the Convention and Human Rights Act now that the Act was fully in force, as questions had arisen whether an issue under s.6 of the Act could now be raised directly without the lodging of a devolution minute. The appeal on this issue was heard with that of C, who appealed against conviction of the assault and robbery of an elderly lady and sentence of two years' detention. The appeal called in June 1999 but was continued twice to enable further material to be obtained. The transcripts were obtained in December 1999 but the appeal was not heard until 2001.

Held, allowing the appeals, that (1) for M, there was an unexplained delay of over a year which, given the circumstances of the case, including the time which had already passed, was unreasonable; (2) while the Lord Advocate was no longer master of the instance after conviction, the Crown had obtained a discharge of a hearing for further preparation but had failed to intimate when its preparations were complete and to monitor the appeal's progress, and M had established a breach of Art.6 by the Lord Advocate; (3) where the Lord

Advocate had had the power to commence and continue the prosecution through to conviction, there was no sufficient reason why merely because of subsequent failure, the conviction needed be treated as invalid, and by the case law under the Convention such a breach of Art.6 could be compensated in various ways, including a shortening of the sentence; (4) considering the original appeal, although M's sentence was towards the upper end of the appropriate range, it was not excessive; but as his Convention rights had been breached, it was equitable to reduce the original sentence by nine months, leaving him six months to serve before becoming entitled to parole; (5) s.6 of the Human Rights Act 1998 did not affect the operation of the Scotland Act 1998 Sch.6 para.5, and if an issue was raised which fell within the definition of "devolution issue" in para.1 of Sch.6 to the Scotland Act, there had to be intimation to the Advocate General in accordance with that Schedule, and (6) for C, there had been undue delay for which some remedy should be provided, and in the instant case the appeal would be continued for a further year for C to prove himself of good behaviour before determining the appropriate sentence.

MILLS (KENNETH ANTHONY PATON) v. HM ADVOCATE (NO.2); COCHRANE (JOHN) v. HM ADVOCATE 2001 S.L.T.1359, Lord Coulsfield, Lord Rodger L.J.G., Lord Caplan, HCJ Appeal.

6370. **Right to fair trial – hearing within reasonable time of notification of charge**

[European Convention on Human Rights 1950 Art.6.]

Two policeman, W and B, were charged with perjuring themselves during a trial in April 1998. They pled in bar of trial that the European Convention on Human Rights 1950 Art.6 had been breached because their case had not come to trial within a reasonable time. The sheriff held that W and B had been charged for the purposes of Art.6(1) in July 1998 and that whether they had been charged then or in January 1999, as the Crown contended, the delay was unreasonable and dismissed the complaint. D appealed, arguing that 15 months was not an excessive period of time even with the relatively uncomplicated nature of the case and its prioritisation.

Held, refusing the appeal (Lord Hamilton dissenting in part), that a person could not be considered charged until officially notified that they had committed a criminal offence by a competent authority. In this respect the sheriff had erred. In deciding whether an unreasonable delay had occurred, it was relevant to take into account events prior to the official notification. The combination of the prospect of proceedings, as raised by the trial sheriffs comments in April 1998, and the simplicity of the case with regard to preparation made the delay unreasonable.

DYER v. WATSON 2001 S.L.T. 751, Lord Milligan, Sir GH Gordon Q.C., Lord Hamilton, HCJ Appeal.

6371. **Right to fair trial – pre trial publicity – prejudicial effect of pre trial publicity**

[Scotland Act 1998 (c.46) s.57(2); European Convention on Human Rights 1950 Art.6.]

M and C, who had been charged with murder, appealed against the decision of the High Court of Justiciary dismissing their appeal in relation to a minute raising a devolution issue. It was submitted that prejudicial publicity prior to the trial meant that the acts of the Lord Advocate in indicting them had been contrary to the Scotland Act 1998 s.57(2) given that their right to a fair trial under the European Convention on Human Rights 1950 Art.6 had been impinged. M and C were later acquitted of the murder charge.

Held, dismissing the appeal, that in deciding whether a defendant's right to a fair trial under Art.6 of the Convention would be affected by damaging publicity prior to their trial, it would be appropriate to adopt the test which was applied when considering whether such publicity would support a plea of oppression, namely that set out in *Stuurman v. HM Advocate* 1980 S.L.T. (Notes) 95, [1980] C.L.Y. 3011. However, the court would not be required to carry out a balancing exercise between the defendant's right to a fair trial and the public interest in the suppression of crime. In the instant case, the question of impartiality had to be considered objectively, *Pullar v. United Kingdom* 1996 S.C.C.R. 755, [1996] C.L.Y. 3169 considered. Consideration had to be given not just to the consequences of the publicity on the members of the jury, but also to the role of the judge in securing a fair trial so far as it was open to him to do so. There were no grounds to alter the findings of the High Court of Justiciary with regard to the consequences of the publicity and as to whether the jury would remain impartial.

MONTGOMERY (DAVID SHIELDS) v. HM ADVOCATE; COULTER v. HM ADVOCATE; *sub nom.* HM ADVOCATE v. MONTGOMERY (DAVID SHIELDS) [2001] 2 W.L.R. 779, Lord Hope of Craighead, PC.

6372. Right to fair trial – sheriffs – conduct of proceedings before temporary sheriff – waiver of right to fair trial

[Human Rights Act 1998 (c.42) Sch.1 Part I Art.6(1); Scotland Act 1998 (c.46) s.57(2).]

M and others appealed against a ruling (2000 S.L.T. 1111, [2000] C.L.Y. 6091) that they had waived their right to a hearing before an independent and impartial tribunal. The cases under appeal had been prosecuted before a temporary sheriff between May 20, 1999, and November 11, 1999, the first being the date on which the Scotland Act 1998 s. 57(2) came into force, and the latter, the date on which the High Court gave its decision in *Starrs v. Ruxton* 2000 J.C. 208, [1999] C.L.Y. 5884. M relied upon dicta in *Starrs* to the effect that temporary sheriffs were not an independent and impartial tribunal for the purposes of the Human Rights Act 1998 Sch.1 Part I Art.6(1). The Solicitor General maintained that (1) *Starrs* could be distinguished on the basis that the use of a temporary sheriff had been challenged at an early stage in the proceedings before the conclusion of the trial, and (2) although theoretical difficulties might exist in relation to the use of temporary sheriffs, in practice M had not been able to demonstrate any lack of impartiality and consequently had not been the victim of any injustice.

Held, allowing the appeal, that it was not possible to distinguish *Starrs* on the basis that the challenge would not have succeeded had it been made after the conclusion of the proceedings as opposed to at an early stage of the trial. Whilst there was no reason to doubt the impartiality of the proceedings it was nevertheless clear that the fundamental right of an accused to a fair trial before an independent and impartial tribunal could not be compromised in the absence of a valid waiver. It could not be suggested that the representatives for the individual accused had made a voluntary and unequivocal election to waive their rights under Art.6 since the defendants could only have made such a decision on an informed basis had they been fully aware of the judgment in *Starrs*. At the relevant time that judgment had not yet been pronounced and there was no basis for any suggestion that the defendant's representatives had appreciated that a judgment of that nature was likely to be forthcoming. Accordingly, there had been no effective waiver and the proceedings had been conducted in breach of Art.6(1), *Starrs* considered.

MILLAR v. DICKSON; STEWART v. HEYWOOD; PAYNE v. HEYWOOD; TRACEY v. HEYWOOD; MARSHALL v. RITCHIE; *sub nom.* MILLAR v. PROCURATOR FISCAL, ELGIN, [2001] UKPC D4, 2002 S.C. (P.C.) 30, Lord Bingham of Cornhill, PC (Sc).

6373. Rules – criminal procedure – Convention Rights

ACT OF ADJOURNAL (CRIMINAL PROCEDURAL RULES AMENDMENT) (CONVENTION RIGHTS (COMPLIANCE) (SCOTLAND) ACT 2001) 2001, SSI 2001 479; made under the Criminal Procedure (Scotland) Act 1995 s.305. In force: December 21, 2001; £1.75.

This Act of Adjournal amends the Criminal Procedure Rules 1996 (SI 1996 513) by adding new rules and a new form which make provision as to the intimation of punishment part hearings, as to disputing documents or lodging additional documents and as to procedural hearings.

6374. Scottish Criminal Cases Review Commission – access to documents – specification

[Criminal Procedure (Scotland) Act 1995 (c.46) s.194I.]

S sought an order in terms of the Criminal Procedure (Scotland) Act 1995 s.194I for production of documents and materials obtained and created by or on behalf of the Crown Office in a series of linked criminal cases. S claimed they were unable to give an exhaustive list of specific documents until all potentially relevant papers had been studied. S was also concerned at the time it took the Crown Office to produce documents and the fact that further relevant documents had repeatedly been found by the Crown Office, on being pressed by S, after assurances had been given that all relevant documents had been produced. The Crown argued that S's requirements were irrelevant and lacking in specification.

Held, putting the case out by order, that (1) given the recommendations of the committee which led to the creation of S and related sections in the 1985 Act, it was clear that Parliament intended S to have the fullest investigative powers and to be seen to act independently, and any restriction or directions of its powers could only be imposed by law; (2) nothing in the provisions made it irrelevant for S to seek the documents and the material to the extent which it did; (3) given the averments of S as to the history of the particular case and attempts made to recover documents, the requirements of s.194I were satisfied; it was for S to decide whether the material was of any use and it did not need to set out requirements as to why the documents were relevant. It was accepted by S that s.194I did not imply that the court would rubber stamp any such request and that the matter was one of the court's discretion, and (4) as the Crown had already indicated that special consideration might need to be accorded to certain categories of papers, they would be allowed, in the light of the decision on the application of s.194I, to make submissions on that point.

SCOTTISH CRIMINAL CASES REVIEW COMMISSION v. HM ADVOCATE 2001 J.C. 36, Lord Clarke, HCJ.

6375. Scottish Criminal Cases Review Commission – powers of investigation – contempt of court

[Contempt of Court Act 1981 (c.49) s.8; Criminal Procedure (Scotland) Act 1995 (c.46) s.194B, s.194D, s.194F.]

SCCRC petitioned the court under the Criminal Procedure (Scotland) Act 1995 s.194D(3) seeking an opinion on the effect of the Contempt of Court Act 1981 s.8 on its powers of investigation under s.194F of the 1995 Act. The commission were considering whether to refer the cases of two convicted murderers to the court under s.194B of the 1995 Act and the allegations under investigation concerned members of the jury which had convicted the accused. The commission ultimately accepted that it was bound by s.8 and could not exercise its powers in a manner which would constitute a contempt of court, but asked whether in that case it could ask the Lord Advocate or the court itself to carry out inquiries on its behalf under s.194F.

Held, giving an opinion, that (1) the "deliberations" covered by s.8 concerned only the time when the jurors were considering their verdict after having been directed to retire to do so by the judge; (2) the commission could therefore make inquiries and obtain statements from witnesses, including jurors, about matters which occurred before the jurors retired, provided however that it conducted its inquiries with a sufficient degree of discretion to prevent it from overstepping into the prohibited area; (3) s.8 did not expressly bind the Crown but it could be clearly implied from its terms, in particular, s.8(2)(b), that the Crown was bound by s.8, and any inquiries by the Lord Advocate would be limited in scope to the same extent as those of the commission itself, and (4) the commission had no express power in terms of the 1995 Act to ask the High Court to use its powers to undertake inquiries on their behalf, and no such power could be implied as this would affect the sensitive relationship between the court and the commission.

SCOTTISH CRIMINAL CASES REVIEW COMMISSION, PETITIONERS 2001 S.L.T. 1198, Lord Rodger L.J.G., Lord Marnoch, Lord Reed, HCJ.

6376. Sexual offences – notification requirements – prescribed police stations

SEX OFFENDERS (NOTIFICATION REQUIREMENTS) (PRESCRIBED POLICE STATIONS) (SCOTLAND) REGULATIONS 2001, SSI 2001 173; made under the Sex Offenders Act 1997 s.2, s.10. In force: June 1, 2001; £2.00.

The Sex Offenders Act 1997 Part I specifies that certain sex offenders are subject to requirements to notify certain personal details to the police and provides for such notifications to be given in some cases by attending at any police station in a person's local police area and in other cases by sending a written notice to any such police station. The Criminal Justice and Court Services Act 2000 also introduced a power for the Scottish Ministers to provide for the Sex Offenders Act 1997 s.2 to have effect such that instead of the required notification being at, or by writing to, any police station in a person's local police area, the police station would be one prescribed by regulations. These Regulations have the effect of requiring notifications to be made by attending at, or writing to, any police station in a person's local police area provided that station is mentioned in the list set out in the Schedule.

6377. Sexual offences – notification requirements – prescribed police stations

SEX OFFENDERS (NOTIFICATION REQUIREMENTS) (PRESCRIBED POLICE STATIONS) (SCOTLAND) (NO.2) REGULATIONS 2001, SSI 2001 190; made under the Sex Offenders Act 1997 s.2, s.10. In force: June 1, 2001; £2.00.

The Sex Offenders Act 1997 specifies in Part I that certain sex offenders are subject to requirements to notify certain personal details to the police. Section 2(5) of the 1997 Act (as amended by the Criminal Justice and Court Services Act 2000 provides for such notifications to be given in some cases by attending at any police station in a person's local police area and in other cases by sending a written notice to any such police station. "Local police area" is defined in s.2(7) of the 1997 Act. The 2000 Act also introduced a power for the Scottish Ministers to provide for s.2(5) of the 1997 Act to have effect such that instead of the required notification being at, or by writing to, any police station in a person's local police area, the police station would be one prescribed by regulations. These Regulations revoke and replace with amendments the Sex Offenders (Notification Requirements) (Prescribed Police Stations) (Scotland) Regulations 2001 (SSI 2001 173).

6378. Sheriff courts – jurisdiction – statutory offence committed abroad

[Criminal Law (Consolidation) (Scotland) Act 1995 (c.39) s.6; Criminal Procedure (Scotland) Act 1995 (c.46) s.11, s.16B.]

M was charged on indictment on two separate charges. The first charge was in respect of lewd, indecent and libidinous practices towards a 13 year old girl in Cowdenbeath in contravention of the Criminal Law (Consolidation) (Scotland) Act 1995 s.6 and the second charge was in respect of lewd, indecent and libidinous practices towards a 14 year old girl in Spain in contravention of the s.6 and s.16B of the 1995 Act. M challenged the jurisdiction of the sheriff court in respect of the second charge where the alleged offence took place in Spain. The sheriff repelled the plea but granted leave to appeal. On appeal, M submitted that the jurisdiction of the sheriff court was territorial and limited by the statutory provisions of the Criminal Procedure (Scotland) Act 1995 with exceptions to the territorial rule being specifically provided for in s.11. By Parliament's failure to include offences under s.16B in the specified exceptions to the territorial rule, M submitted that it was Parliament's intention that such offences when committed abroad could not be prosecuted in the sheriff court.

Held, allowing the appeal, that in the absence of any statutory provisions expressly conferring jurisdiction of s.16B offences on the sheriff court or excluding s.16B offences from the territorial rule affecting the sheriff court's jurisdiction, such offences must be considered as outwith the jurisdiction of the sheriff court.

Observed, that (1) s.16B clearly intended that such offences could be tried on indictment in Scotland and it would be open to the Lord Advocate to try such an offence on indictment in the high court, and (2) Parliament had failed to enact statutory provisions for the appropriate procedural machinery necessary to carry out the legislature's intention that such offences would be triable in the sheriff courts.

McCARRON (GEORGE WALLACE) v. HM ADVOCATE 2001 J.C. 199, Lord Rodger L.J.G., Lord Cameron of Lochbroom, Lady Paton, HCJ Appeal.

6379. Solemn procedure – adjournment – adjournment sought by defence for further preparation – judge entitled to deny

S was charged on indictment with several counts of shameless indecency with regard to his niece and nephew. S's counsel was changed a day and a half before trial began and an adjournment was applied for and granted. A further adjournment was sought to precognosce further witnesses, instruct expert witnesses and make further investigations. S's counsel also argued that the complexity and seriousness of the case coupled with his late instruction merited a further adjournment. The Crown opposed the motion on grounds of expense and inconvenience, giving as an example, the difficulty with which the male complainer would get additional time off work and travel from Canada. The motion was denied but the trial judge made it clear that he would be prepared to entertain a further application if serious difficulties arose. No motion was made. S was convicted and appealed to the High Court relying largely on the particular difficulties encountered by counsel.

Held, refusing the appeal, that the trial judge had given weight to all the factors laid before him, although other judges' approach might have differed. It was particularly important that the trial judge had made it clear that if there had been any further difficulty he would consider a further motion for adjournment and no such motion had been made. The trial judge's decision could not be said to have prejudiced S's case nor resulted in a miscarriage of justice; nor could it be said that S's case had not been fully presented.

S v. HM ADVOCATE (INDECENT CONDUCT) 2001 S.C.C.R. 276, Lord Coulsfield, Lord Cowie, Lord MacLean, HCJ Appeal.

6380. Summary procedure – adjournment – history of adjournments to be considered when granting others

[Criminal Procedure (Scotland) Act 1995 (c.46) s.146(7).]

L was charged on summary complaint with drunk driving. The case suffered five adjournments under the Criminal Procedure (Scotland) Act 1995 s.146(7). Four of the adjournments were as a result of inadequate equipment being available and pressures of other business. The fifth and final adjournment was granted by the sheriff when a police witness failed to attend, and a medical certificate was not made available. L appealed by bill of advocation to the High Court.

Held, passing the bill and quashing the decision, that a balance had to be struck between the wider interests of justice and the kind of considerations invoked in the bill. The sheriff had not had due regard to the history of adjournments and could not be said to have had a satisfactory explanation as to the absence of the Crown witness. Opinion of the Court per Lord Prosser.

LOVE (PHILIP ANDREW) v. BROWN 2000 S.C.C.R. 931, Lord Prosser, Lord Bonomy, Lord Penrose, HCJ Appeal.

6381. Terrorism

ACT OF ADJOURNAL (CRIMINAL PROCEDURAL RULES AMENDMENT NO.2) (TERRORISM ACT 2000 AND ANTI-TERRORISM, CRIME AND SECURITY ACT 2001) 2001, SSI 2001 486; made under the Criminal Procedure (Scotland) Act 1995 s.305; and the Terrorism Act 2000 Sch.5 para.27, Sch.6 para.4, Sch.6A para.5. In force: December 21, 2001; £1.75.

This Order amends the Act of Adjournment (Criminal Procedure Rules) 1996 (SI 1996 513) by adding new rules which deal with matters arising out of the Terrorism Act 2000 and the Anti-Terrorism, Crime and Security Act 2001.

6382. Trial – adjournment – devolution issues – reference to High Court – adjournment of diet competent – devolution reference falls with indictment

[Criminal Procedure Scotland Act 1995 (c.46); Act of Adjournal (Criminal Procedure Rules) 1996 (SI 1996 513) r.40.8; Scotland Act 1998 (c.46).]

T was charged with a breach of the peace, his trial date set for May 8, 2000. The diet was postponed until May 22 and T lodged a devolution minute on the ground that the charge was incompatible with his Convention rights. The sheriff referred the devolution issue to the High Court under the Scotland Act 1998 Sch.6, para 9 and adjourned the trial diet under the Act of Adjournal (Criminal Procedure Rules) 1996 r.40.8 initially to July 31 and then October 23. The indictment was not called and a further indictment was deserted pro loco et tempore in November and a third indictment was served for trial in February 2001, but adjourned. No devolution minutes were lodged in relation to the later indictments. The devolution reference had, in the meantime, gone to the High Court in June 2000 and had called at a procedural hearing in September 2000. In March 2001 the Crown sought a further procedural hearing after taking the view that the proceedings had fallen as a result of the adjournment between July and October 2000, longer than the two months provided in the Criminal Procedure Scotland Act 1995 s.80(1).

Held, that the Crown's view was misconceived, r.40.8 was deliberately flexible and the sheriff's order had been proper and competent. The devolution reference to the High Court should have been treated as a stage in the proceedings before the original court which would use the guidance to reach a decision. If the proceeding came to an end, as in the instant case, the original court would no longer need the decision and the reference would also come to an end.

HM ADVOCATE v. TOUATI 2001 S.L.T. 1195, Lord Rodger L.J.G., Lord Cameron of Lochbroom, Lady Paton, HCJ Appeal.

6383. Trial – adjournment – not stated in open court – compatibility with right to fair trial

[Human Rights Act 1998 (c.42) Sch.1 Part 1 Art.6.]

D, who had been charged on indictment with inter alia drugs offences, presented a bill of advocation arguing that the indictment had fallen. The case called for trial on August 3, 2001, when, D having moved for an adjournment, it was continued to August 7. On that day a renewed motion for adjournment was refused by the trial judge, who then left the court without calling on D to tender a plea. As the judge was engaged on another trial that day, a minute was signed which purported to adjourn the case as one of the remaining diets in the sitting until August 8. D argued that (1) the indictment had fallen as soon as the trial judge left the courtroom without having adjourned the case to a fixed date; the procedure approved in *Kiely (Anthony) v. HM Advocate* 1990 J.C. 264, [1990] C.L.Y. 4907, allowing an indictment to be continued from day to day by way of a minute, did not apply once any hearing had taken place in open court, in respect of that indictment, after the particular High Court or sheriff and jury sitting had commenced, and (2) the minute, having been written in private, infringed his rights to a "fair and public hearing" under the Human Rights Act 1998 Sch.1 Part 1 Art.6.

Held, refusing the bill, that (1) there was no reason in principle nor any practical consideration why the procedure in *Kiely* should not apply to D's case, notwithstanding the hearings that took place on August 3 and 7; accordingly it was competent to continue his case from day to day by a minute such as that signed, and (2) the European case law did not support the proposition that Art.6(1) required all substantive steps leading up to the determination of a criminal charge to be conducted in public.

DEGNAN v. HM ADVOCATE 2001 S.L.T.1233, Lord Mackay of Drumadoon, Lord Coulsfield, Lord Penrose, HCJ Appeal.

6384. Trial – criminal record laid mistakenly before sheriff – continuation of trial – justice not being seen to be done

[Road Traffic Act 1988 (c.52) s.6(1), s.7(6); Criminal Procedure (Scotland) Act 1995 (c.46) s.166(3).]

M was charged on summary complaint with failing to provide a breath specimen under the Road Traffic Act 1988 s.6(1) and s.7(6). During the course of the trial, a list of M's previous convictions were found to be amongst the sheriff's papers. The Criminal Procedure (Scotland) Act 1995 s.166(3) required that those should not be laid before the judge until the charge was proved. The sheriff brought the matter before the court and expressed "grave concerns" about the situation. Having adjourned to consider the matter and heard submissions, the sheriff decided to continue with the trial as there had been no breach of the statutory requirements. M was convicted and appealed to the High Court arguing that justice could not have been seen to be done in the circumstances of the case.

Held, allowing the appeal, that a reasonable bystander would, in light of the discussion in court, have the kind of suspicion or apprehension that would be interpreted as justice not being seen to be done, regardless of the knowledge that a sheriff would be able to, professionally, disregard the irrelevant material. Opinion of the Court per Lord Prosser.

McKEE v. BROWN 2001 S.C.C.R. 6, Lord Prosser, Lord Bonomy, Lord Penrose, HCJ Appeal.

6385. Trial – flawed search warrants – evidence ruled inadmissible – competency of subsequent argument for excusing irregularity

[Forgery and Counterfeiting Act 1981 (c.45).]

Four men, A, were convicted of various charges under the Forgery and Counterfeiting Act 1981. During the trial, A objected to evidence of a police search of premises, allegedly authorised by a search warrant. The warrant, signed by justices of the peace, contained a crave for a "Search Warrant under the Forgery and Counterfeiting Act 1989", an Act which did not exist. The trial judge sustained the objection and allowed the Crown an adjournment until the next day to consider the consequences of the decision. The next day, C argued that the irregularities in the warrants should be excused and the evidence deemed admissible. The trial judge ruled that, no proceedings of substance having taken place since the ruling, he could entertain the further submissions and that irregularities in the warrant could be excused in the interests of justice and evidence obtained on presentation of the warrant was admissible, *Lawrie (Jeanie) v. Muir* 1950 J.C. 19 referred to. A appealed, arguing that having sustained the defence objection, a decision duly minuted by the clerk, the trial judge could not subsequently hear further submissions from C and that his decision was incompetent.

Held, allowing the appeals and quashing the convictions, that (1) it was plain from the terms of the trial judge's first decision, and from the minute, that he had decided that the line of evidence relating to searches and related matters was inadmissible; his decision the following day to admit the evidence was a decision reversing his earlier decision; (2) there was no authority dealing with the competency of such a reversal of a ruling on a defence objection to a line of evidence, and since neither the members of the court nor counsel had ever heard of judges doing so in practice, the court was inclined to draw the inference that a defence objection once formulated and stated in open court was final and could not be reconsidered; exceptions to court practice should not readily be admitted; (3) whilst the defence, but not C, would be able to appeal an adverse decision, that was simply one aspect of the general scheme of the system whereby C had no right of appeal against an acquittal. It had therefore been incompetent for the judge to give effect to C's submissions, and (4) it was not material that the decision had been formally minuted. As such minutes were written by the clerk, so to hold would be to place the finality of the decision beyond the control of the trial judge who made it, introducing elements of chance which a well regulated criminal procedure system strove to avoid, *R. v. Cross (Patrick Vernon)* [1973] Q.B. 937, [1973] C.L.Y. 594 distinguished. Opinion of the Court per Lord Rodger, Lord Justice General.

McANEA (THOMAS) v. HM ADVOCATE; DEAN (RAYMOND) v. HM ADVOCATE; McGREGOR (JOHN JOSEPH) v. HM ADVOCATE; McGINNIS (DENNIS) v. HM ADVOCATE 2001 S.L.T. 12, Lord Rodger, L.J.G., Lord Allanbridge, Lord Prosser, HCJ Appeal.

6386. Trial – judge's charge – drug offences – supply of drugs – direction to jury on s.28 defence – direction amounted to misdirection

[Misuse of Drugs Act 1971 (c.38) s.4, s.28.]

G was charged with being concerned in the supply of drugs, contrary to the Misuse of Drugs Act 1971 s.4(3)(b). The police, with G's assistance, found quantities of drugs, including heroin, in G's flat. G denied being involved in the supply of drugs and claimed that the heroin found did not belong to him but to his brother, a known drug dealer. G admitted using certain articles in the flat to facilitate his personal drug use. The trial judge, in her direction, brought the s.28 defence to the jury's attention, although it had not been relied upon by G. G was convicted in July 2000, appealed to the High Court on the ground of misdirection and was released on bail in November 2000.

Held, allowing the appeal, quashing the convictions and denying a fresh prosecution, that there was a real risk that the judge's direction on s.28 might have materially misled the jury as to the question they had to answer; whether G had no knowledge of the drugs or whether, as G had defended, he knew of the drugs but had not been concerned in the supply. A fresh prosecution was not granted in light of the age of the charge and the four months G had already spent in custody.

GLANCY v. HM ADVOCATE 2001 S.C.C.R. 385, Lord Coulsfield, Lord Cowie, Lord Marnoch, HCJ Appeal.

6387. Trial – judge's charge – drug offences – supply of drugs – lack of specific jury direction – misdirection by sheriff

[Misuse of Drugs Act 1971 (c.38) s.4(3)(b).]

S was convicted of being concerned in the supply of drugs, contrary to the Misuse of Drugs Act 1971 s.4(3)(b), after a supply quantity was found in the house he occupied. S appealed arguing that the sheriff had misdirected the jury as to the necessary elements required for a conviction of that nature.

Held, allowing the appeal and quashing the conviction, that the sheriff had misdirected the jury. The sheriff had not concentrated on the important details of the charge and had failed to give directions defining the offence in terms detailed in, *Salmon (Donald) v. HM Advocate* 1999 J.C. 67, [1999] C.L.Y. 5832.

SHARKEY (JOHN JAMIESON) v. HM ADVOCATE 2001 S.C.C.R. 290, Lord Cameron of Lochbroom, Sir GH Gordon, Lord Mackay of Drumadoon, HCJ Appeal.

6388. Trial – judge's charge – failure to direct on dangers of identification evidence

F, was charged with two offences of assault and robbery. F had not been identified in an identification parade, only in court. F appealed on the ground of misdirection arguing that the sheriff had failed to highlight to the jury the level of care that should be exercised when considering the identification evidence, especially in the instant case where the only identification had been in court.

Held, refusing the appeal, that the sheriff could not be criticised for failing to give warning as to the evidence of identification given by the witness, the evidence had already been challenged by cross examination and criticised by F's solicitor in their speech to the jury. In the circumstances the jury was given all the guidance they needed in relation to the identification evidence. Opinion of the Court per Lord Reed.

FERGUSON (RAYMOND) v. HM ADVOCATE 2000 S.C.C.R. 954, Lord Reed, Lord Philip, Lord Rodger, L.J.G., HCJ Appeal.

6389. **Trial – judge's charge – misdirection – defence evidence**

In S's continued appeal against conviction for being concerned in the supply of diamorphine, S argued that (1) he had been prejudiced by the absence of a transcript of the judge's charge, in which, it was claimed, the judge had failed to give a specific direction in law as to how the jury should weigh the Crown evidence of the discovery of a large sum of cash in S's home against defence evidence suggesting an alternative explanation for the presence of the cash, and (2) the trial judge had not dealt with the highly speculative and prejudicial tone of the Crown's speech. Also, (3) the Crown conceded at an earlier hearing that S's conviction, instead of relating to the period from December 20, 1996 to June 26, 1997, should have been restricted to June 23 and 26, 1997. In the report prepared for the appeal, the trial judge had added that there was ample evidence to infer S's involvement over the longer period, and he was asked to prepare an additional report on this point.

Held, refusing the appeal, that (1) the lack of a proper transcript of the judge's charge had been partly made good by a transcription by the trial judge himself of the relevant passages, and the court was satisfied that there had been no prejudice to S. S had not suggested what directions the judge might have given relating to the cash, which revealed that the point taken was hollow. The question was one of fact and not law; (2) the judge had given a clear warning against speculation and S's criticism was unfounded, and (3) the court was not bound by the Crown's concession and, before substituting a conviction restricted to the reduced time period, the court had to be satisfied that this was justified in law. In the light of the trial judge's report and the evidence available to the jury, they were entitled to return the verdict in the terms they had. The alternative restricted verdict would have been inconsistent with S's own position at trial and entirely irrational given that neither the Crown nor S could suggest what involvement, in what was a huge drug trafficking operation, could have occurred on two days only. The court was not prepared to set aside the verdict and replace it with one which the jury were never asked to consider and which they would have been unlikely to return even if they had been. Opinion of the Court per Lord Rodger, Lord Justice General.

SANTINI v. HM ADVOCATE (MISDIRECTION) 2000 S.C.C.R. 726, Lord Rodger L.J.G., Lord Allanbridge, Lord Gill, HCJ Appeal.

6390. **Trial – judge's charge – misdirection – identification – miscarriage of justice**

[Criminal Procedure (Scotland) Act 1995 (c.46) s.106(3)(a).]

F appealed against conviction for assault and breach of the peace on the grounds that (1) the sheriff had misdirected the jury on the issue of identification of F by an eyewitness. F argued that identification had been of crucial importance and the sheriff should have directed the jury to take particular care in considering that evidence where three witnesses who had not identified F at an identification parade, had identified her in court, and (2) the significant evidence of witness X, which could exculpate F, had not been heard at the trial and there had been a miscarriage of justice which could be appealed under the Criminal Procedure (Scotland) Act 1995 s.106(3)(a).

Held, refusing the appeal, that (1) there was no misdirection. The sheriff had reminded the jury that a considerable amount had been said about identification, had referred to factors they might wish to take into account in assessing the quality of such evidence, and was under no obligation to repeat F's closing speech criticisms, and (2) there was a reasonable explanation why X's evidence was not known to F. X had only come forward after the trial and was unknown to anyone involved. However, because X's evidence did not contradict the Crown's position but did appear to contradict F's evidence of her movements, it was not evidence which was of such significance that the verdict of the jury had to be regarded as a miscarriage of justice. Opinion of the Court per Lord Kirkwood.

FRASER v. HM ADVOCATE; *sub nom.* 6 2000 S.C.C.R. 755, Lord Kirkwood, Lord Cowie, Lord Milligan, HCJ Appeal.

6391. Trial – judge's charge – video evidence – misdirection leading to miscarriage of justice

[Criminal Procedure (Scotland) Act 1995 (c.46) s.106(3)(b).]

D was charged with murdering a prostitute and subsequently convicted. D appealed against the conviction on a number of grounds. Firstly, that the evidence which led to his conviction was insufficient to justify it; secondly, that the jury's verdict was unreasonable, giving rise to review under the Criminal Procedure (Scotland) Act 1995 s.106(3)(b) and finally, that the judge misdirected the jury with regard to the video evidence purporting to identify the accused.

Held, allowing the appeal and quashing the conviction, that (1) court did not accept that there had been insufficient evidence to convict nor that the jury had been unreasonable in its verdict, and (2) the jury had been misdirected by the trial judge with regard to the video evidence given at trial and may have convicted D unjustly. Opinion of the Court per Lord Allanbridge.

DONNELLY (BRIAN) v. HM ADVOCATE 2000 S.C.C.R. 861, Lord Allanbridge, Lord Caplan, Lord Cameron of Lochbroom, HCJ Appeal.

6392. Trial – jury directions – miscarriage of justice – concert – not guilty and not proven verdicts

Two accused persons went on trial on a charge that, along with others, they had inflicted severe injury on the complainer. The accused were convicted and appealed on the ground of misdirection. They contended that the sheriff ought to have directed the jury that if they were not satisfied concert was established, they were entitled only to consider the evidence relating to the particular actings of each accused; and that the sheriff had further misdirected the jury in stating that the not proven verdict was appropriate where the jury felt the Crown had not established guilt and not guilty where the accused had exculpated themselves from the charge.

Held, quashing the convictions, and distinguishing *Fay (Edmund Louis) v. HM Advocate* 1989 S.L.T. 758, [1989] C.L.Y. 4077, that (1) in a case of alleged concert the jury had to be directed first to consider what evidence they accepted against each accused separately, then if there was sufficient evidence, to consider whether they were acting in furtherance of a common criminal purpose, and lastly on what to do if they did not find such a purpose established, and where the sheriff had failed to direct the jury on the last element there had been a misdirection amounting to a miscarriage of justice, and (2) where the sheriff had departed from the normal directions on the not guilty and not proven verdicts and described not guilty in terms of the accused having exculpated themselves, which was capable of being linked to defence pleas of self defence and incrimination, there had been a further misdirection amounting to a miscarriage of justice.

CUSSICK (BARRY) v. HM ADVOCATE 2001 S.L.T. 1316, Lord MacLean, Lady Cosgrove, Lord Kirkwood, HCJ Appeal.

CRIMINAL SENTENCING

6393. Adjournment – form of order – accused pleading guilty but subsequently raising devolution minutes

[Criminal Procedure (Scotland) Act 1995 (c.46) s.201.]

Two accused persons brought bills of advocation, arguing that proceedings against them for theft of mobile phones had lapsed to the extent that no sentence could competently be pronounced. The accused had raised devolution issues after they lodged guilty pleas. The sheriff continued the case for a diet of debate but failed to make an order deferring sentence. The accused argued that a subsequent attempt by the Crown to amend the minutes of proceedings to include an order deferring sentence was incompetent.

Held, refusing the bills, that there was nothing in the Criminal Procedure (Scotland) Act 1995 s.201 or at common law requiring particular words to be used in such circumstances; the words used were sufficient to make it clear there was a decision to adjourn the case, and there was no sufficient basis for suggesting that the sentencing process had been interrupted or brought to an end.

NAPIER v. DYER 2001 S.L.T. 1298, Lord Coulsfield, Lord Caplan, Lord Osborne, HCJ Appeal.

6394. Backdating – refusal to backdate attributed to inadequacy of sentence – sentence without backdate not considered excessive

[Criminal Procedure (Scotland) Act 1995 (c.46) s.210(1).]

H, having spent four months in custody awaiting trial, pleaded guilty to the charge of assault to severe injury and the danger of life. H was sentenced to four years' imprisonment and no account was taken of time already served. The trial judge had considered the four year sentence inadequate on its own, given the nature of the offence and its committal whilst H was on bail. H appealed to the High Court against the refusal to backdate.

Held, refusing the appeal, that the Court would only allow the appeal if the trial judge's explanation and choice of sentence demonstrated excess having been satisfied that the judge had taken account of the time H had already spent in custody. On the facts, H had used a pick axe handle to hit the victim repeatedly on the head, fracturing his skull and causing a haematoma which required an emergency operation, the sentence was not excessive. Opinion of the Court per Lord Rodger, Lord Justice-General.

HUTCHESON v. HM ADVOCATE (SENTENCING) 2001 S.C.C.R. 43, Lord Rodger L.J.G., Lord Cameron of Lochbroom, Lord Weir, HCJ Appeal.

6395. Bail – breach of bail – three charges of assault – one month of sentence attributed to bail aggravation – totality of sentence

[Criminal Procedure (Scotland) Act 1995 (c.46) s.27.]

J pleaded guilty to three charges of assault, all of which were committed whilst he was on bail. J was sentenced to eight months in custody, five relating to the first two charges, one month of that being attributed to the commission of the offence whilst on bail and three months in respect of the third charge. J appealed against the totality of the sentence, arguing that it was not competent in terms of the Criminal Procedure (Scotland) Act 1995 s.27

Held, allowing the appeal, that apart from bail, the sheriff was limited to a total of six months and since only one month was attributed to bail aggravation she had effectively limited her sentencing powers to seven months in total, therefore the third charge was beyond her powers and that sentence should be reduced to one of two months.

JACKSON (MATTHEW) v. McFADYEN (PROCURATOR FISCAL) 2001 S.C.C.R. 224, Lord Prosser, Lord Bonomy, Lord Cowie, HCJ Appeal.

6396. Breach of the peace – threats – imprisonment excessive

M was convicted for a road traffic offence, and for breach of the peace for producing a knife and drawing it across his face and neck in a slashing manner while driving alongside the occupants of another car, following an incident between the two vehicles. M appealed against a sentence of three months' imprisonment.

Held, substituting a fine of £1,500, that three months' imprisonment was excessive where M, who was also fined £150 with nine penalty points in respect of the road traffic offence had admitted that he had been foolish, had only one minor conviction, a social inquiry report recommended probation or community service. M had behaved well since the offence and was in a position to pay a substantial fine. Opinion of the Court per Lord Kirkwood.

MONSON v. HIGSON (SENTENCING); *sub nom.* MONSON v. HM ADVOCATE (SENTENCING) 2000 S.C.C.R. 751, Lord Kirkwood, Lord Allanbridge, HCJ Appeal.

6397. Compensation orders – competency – assault with no allegation of injury

[Criminal Procedure (Scotland) Act 1995 (c.46) s.249(1).]

Having found C guilty of assault, the sheriff imposed a compensation order on him for £100 in respect of the pain and suffering experienced by his victim. C appealed, arguing that (1) it was incompetent for the sentencing judge to award compensation on the basis of pain and suffering where no allegation of actual injury was specified in the complaint against him; (2) even if there was no requirement for allegations of injury to be made in the complaint, the information provided by the procurator fiscal, in the narrative, lacked sufficient specification to enable the sentencing judge to accurately determine compensation, and (3) the compensation awarded was excessive.

Held, refusing the appeal on all three grounds, that (1) under the terms of the Criminal Procedure (Scotland) Act 1995 s.249(1), there was no requirement for the complaint to libel actual injury caused provided that the narrative placed before the sentencing judge by the procurator fiscal contained details of the injuries; (2) sufficient specification had been given to the sentencing judge to enable him to make a compensation order, and (3) on the information supplied, the award was not excessive. Opinion of the Court per Lord Milligan.

CAMPBELL v. STOTT (COMPENSATION ORDER) 2001 S.L.T. 112, Lord Milligan, Lord Weir, HCJ Appeal.

6398. Consecutive sentences – competency – revocation of licence

[Prisoners and Criminal Proceedings (Scotland) Act 1993 (c.9) s.1 (2), s.17, s.27(5); Prison (Scotland) Rules (SI 1956 671).]

W sought declarator that (1) he had been entitled to release from prison unconditionally since May 20, 1998, and an order ordaining the Scottish Ministers to liberate him from prison (interim liberation having been granted on June 9, 1998), or (2) alternatively, he had been entitled to release on licence since May 30, 1998. W had been sentenced to four years' detention on May 30, 1994, backdated to January 17, 1994, and released on licence on November 8, 1996, by which point he had served both two thirds of his sentence and 52 additional days imposed by the Prison Governors under the Prison (Scotland) Rules. W's licence was revoked on April 22, 1997 and W was apprehended and returned to prison on August 24, 1997. On March 30, 1998 W was sentenced to six months' imprisonment for making false representations, backdated to February 16. W argued that (1) the sentences imposed in 1994 and 1998 respectively should not be aggregated and treated as one single term of imprisonment, because the Prisoners and Criminal Proceedings (Scotland) Act 1993 s.27(5) only required sentences to be aggregated if the second was imposed before a short term prisoner was released unconditionally or a long term prisoner was released on licence, and (2) if they fell to be treated as a single term, he should have been released on licence having served two thirds of the term under s.1 (2).

Held, dismissing the action and recalling an order for interim liberation, that (1) under s.27(5) the two sentences fell to be aggregated. W had put forward no justification for departing from the interpretation in *Duffy v. Secretary of State for Scotland* 1999 S.L.T 1372, [2000] 1 C.L. 474, which was supported by other authorities, and there was no logical basis for applying a variable interpretation depending on the particular circumstances of different prisoners, and (2) the right to be released under licence was only available to a prisoner who was in prison when the two thirds date was reached. A prisoner such as W, returned to prison after that date, whose licence had been revoked, was not entitled to release under s.1 (2), but was entitled to challenge the revocation under the procedure in s.17 and seek his release on licence.

WILLIAMS v. SCOTTISH MINISTERS (SENTENCING) 2001 S.C. 153, Lord Mackay of Drumadoon, OH.

6399. Drug offences – possession with intent to supply – supply not commercial – custodial sentence excessive

P pleaded guilty to possessing about £735 worth of cannabis resin. P was acting as one of a group of friends who pooled their monies which P would use to buy the drug at a lower price and distribute back amongst the friends on a non-commercial basis. P was sentenced to six months' imprisonment and appealed to the High Court arguing that the sentence was excessive given that the supply had not been commercial.

Held, allowing the appeal, that in the circumstances an alternative to custody was justified. The sentence was quashed and a £2,000 fine substituted.

PERKINS v. McFADYEN (SENTENCING) 2001 S.C.C.R. 264, Lord Prosser, Lord Cameron of Lochbroom, HCJ Appeal.

6400. Indecent assault – extended sentence

[Criminal Procedure (Scotland) Act 1995 (c.46) s.210A.]

K was convicted for masturbating and exposing his private parts to a woman, and assaulting another on the same day by placing his hands over her mouth, pulling her to the ground, lifting up her clothing, handling her buttocks, seizing hold of her and compelling her to take him to a particular house and going in there with her, all to her injury. K had a substantial record for sexual offences, and committed those offences while he was on licence from a four-year sentence for assault and robbery. The judge imposed a life sentence and designated three years and six months as the minimum period which should elapse before K could be considered for parole. K appealed, arguing that extended sentences under the Criminal Procedure (Scotland) Act 1995 s.210A were tailor made for his situation.

Held, substituting an extended sentence consisting of a custodial period of seven years and the maximum extension period of 10 years, that a life sentence was excessive given the existence of extended sentences, but in view of K's record and the serious risk of his reoffending as highlighted in a social inquiry report, the custodial period had to be substantial and the extended period should be 10 years. Opinion of the Court per Lord Rodger, Lord Justice General.

KELLY (FRANCIS KEVIN) v. HM ADVOCATE (SENTENCING) 2001 J.C. 12, Lord Rodger, L.J.G., Lord Allanbridge, Lord Caplan, HCJ Appeal.

6401. Murder – murder inflicted by "horrendous" violence – limited violence in criminal record – life imprisonment – minimum recommendation not required

[Criminal Procedure (Scotland) Act 1995 (c.46) s.205(4).]

M was convicted of murdering a young man by inflicting repeated blows with a pogo stick. The violence used was characterised by the trial judge as "truly horrendous" and a minimum recommendation order for 14 years under the

Criminal Procedure (Scotland) Act 1995 s.205(4) was imposed. Despite the lack of substantial violence in M's lengthy criminal record, the trial judge had taken the view that the level of violence in the case could only have been inflicted by a truly dangerous person and it would be difficult not to feel uneasy about the future. M appealed against the order.

Held, allowing the appeal and quashing the order for the minimum recommendation, that it could not be said that the violence was so remarkable as to automatically require a minimum recommendation.

McKAY (RONALD) v. HM ADVOCATE (SENTENCING) 2001 S.C.C.R. 341, Lord Rodger L.J.G., Lord Cameron of Lochbroom, Lady Paton, HCJ Appeal.

6402. Pornography – downloading indecent photographs of children from the internet

[Civic Government (Scotland) Act 1982 (c.45) s.52(1)(a), s.52A(1).]

O appealed against his sentence of two years' imprisonment in respect two contraventions of the Civic Government (Scotland) Act 1982 s.52(1)(a) and one of s.52A(1). O had downloaded 12,000 obscene photographs of young boys from the internet between October 1997 and April 1999 and a further 10,000 were found in December 1999.

Held, allowing the appeal and substituting concurrent sentences of three months and six months' imprisonment for the s.52(1)(a) offences and four months under s.52A(1), that (1) the sheriff had taken the correct sentencing approach in that each of the photographs represented a serious abuse of a child and were it not for the existence of consumers like O, those photographs would not be taken, and (2) the quantity of images made the instant a fairly serious case and O had immediately bought a second computer and downloaded further images after his first one had been confiscated, but that sentence was excessive where the accused was being disposed of as a first offender.

OGILVIE (ALAN JOSEPH) v. HM ADVOCATE (SENTENCING) 2002 J.C. 74, Lord Sutherland, Lord Abernethy, Lord Rodger L.J.G., HCJ Appeal.

6403. Pornography – downloading indecent photographs of children from the internet – ignorance of illegality – custodial sentence excessive

[Civic Government (Scotland) Act 1982 (c.33) s.52(1)(a).]

K pleaded guilty to the charge, on summary complaint, of making indecent photographs and psuedo-photographs, contrary to the Civic Government (Scotland) Act 1982 s.52(1)(a), by downloading indecent photographs of children from the internet in September 1998. K had not reproduced any of the images and argued that he was unaware of his actions being illegal. It had been held in *Longmuir (Derek) v. HM Advocate* 2000 J.C. 378, [2000] 8 C.L. 693 that using a computer to store pornographic images of children from the internet constituted an offence under s.52(1)(a). The sheriff considered the offence "a very serious one indeed" and indicated that there would be little incentive to place the photographs on the internet were there not persons such as K who downloaded them. K was sentenced to three months' imprisonment and placed on the Sex Offenders Register. K appealed against the sentence as excessive to the High Court.

Held, allowing the appeal, quashing the sentence and substituting the admonition, that the sheriff had exaggerated in categorising the offence "a very serious one indeed", the crime was victimless, many countries would not consider possession of the material illegal, and there was no basis for comparing the instant type of case with reset. The illegality of K's actions was not widely known in September 1998, the Longmuir case not being decided until February 2000. Ignorance, although irrelevant to conviction, could be relevant in considering sentencing. It was also relevant that in Longmuir, L did not receive a custodial sentence. Opinion of the Court per Lord McCluskey.

KIRK v. KENNEDY (SENTENCING) 2001 S.C.C.R. 31, Lord McCluskey, Lord Weir, HCJ Appeal.

6404. Prisoners – status of prisoners – addition to sentence affectory category

See PENOLOGY: Stewart (John) v. Scottish Ministers. §6835

6405. Road traffic offences – causing death by driving with excess alcohol

[Road Traffic Act 1988 (c.52).]

K pleaded and was found guilty of a contravention of the Road Traffic Act 1988. K had been driving at around 11pm in an area with no street lighting and had come round a bend, crossed into the wrong carriageway and struck and killed a motorcyclist. K was found to have a blood alcohol level of 94mg per 100ml of blood and had one previous drink driving conviction. K was sentenced to four years imprisonment and appealed to the High Court against the sentence as excessive.

Held, refusing the appeal, that a custodial sentence was appropriate and the length of sentence was not excessive.

KELLOCK v. HM ADVOCATE (SENTENCING) 2001 S.C.C.R. 267, Lord Kirkwood, Lord Morison, HCJ Appeal.

6406. Road traffic offences – DVLA printout – accused had no licence – sheriff entitled to consider information in printout

[Road Traffic Offenders Act 1988 (c.53) s.32.]

H was convicted of driving whilst disqualified and the case was continued for the purpose of obtaining a DVLA printout under the Road Traffic Offenders Act 1988 s.32. H appealed to the High Court after receiving leave from the sheriff, arguing that the sheriff was not in a position to call for a DVLA printout since H did not have a driving licence as a result of his disqualification.

Held, refusing the appeal, that where no licence was produced, regardless of reason for non-production, the Court could competently consider the convictions and other information contained in a DVLA printout. Opinion of the Court per Lord Sutherland.

HAMILTON v. RUXTON (PROCURATOR FISCAL) 2001 S.L.T. 351, Lord Sutherland, HCJ Appeal.

6407. Road traffic offences – speeding – new driver – fixed penalty offered but not taken up – relevancy to sentencing

[Road Traffic (New Drivers) Act 1995 (c.13) s.1, s.2, s.3.]

L, a new driver, was stopped by the police for driving at 89mph in a 70mph area. L was offered a fixed penalty including three penalty points on his driving licence, L tried to accept the offer but was not yet in possession of a full driving licence and could not. L was prosecuted, fined and given six penalty points resulting in the revocation of his driving licence under the Road Traffic (New Drivers) Act 1995 s.1, s.2 to s.3. L appealed arguing that account should have been taken of the offer of a fixed penalty, and revocation of his licence should not have been issued without an opportunity for him to appear before the court.

Held, refusing the appeal, that the court considered the history of the offer of a fixed penalty not in principle irrelevant, but could not envisage its significance either. In the instant case fixed penalty offer and the circumstances preventing its uptake could be seen to have been taken into account given the justices' statement that they had taken full account of L's comments. The ordering of six points would not automatically amount to disqualification; the revocation of the licence meant that the driver could drive using a provisional licence if accompanied by a licensed driver. Opinion of the Court per Lord Bonomy.

LAPPIN v. O'DONNELL (PROCURATOR FISCAL) 2001 J.C. 137, Lord Bonomy, Lord Cowie, Lord Prosser, HCJ Appeal.

6408. Sexual offences – indecency – teacher's indecent conduct towards female pupil – common law offence – relevance of statutory equivalent

[Sexual Offences (Scotland) Act 1976 (c.67) s.4(1).]

C, a teacher at a liberal private boarding school, appealed against a sentence of six years' imprisonment imposed for shamelessly indecent conduct between 1980 and 1982, inter alia by having unlawful sexual intercourse with a female pupil aged between 13 and 16 to which he had pled guilty under the accelerated procedure. C and the pupil had remained friendly for some years after their sexual relationship had ceased, and the matter had not been reported until 1999. The sentencing judge had found that a combination of the pupil's age, the gross abuse of a position of trust and the repetitive, persistent nature of the conduct warranted a sentence of six years' imprisonment. C appealed, declining to take a plea to the competency of bringing a charge at common law, although the equivalent statutory offence, under the Sexual Offences (Scotland) Act 1976 s.4(1), had become time barred after one year.

Held, allowing the appeal and substituting two years' imprisonment, that if the conduct as libelled had been reported within a year of its occurrence, the Crown would have prosecuted under the 1976 Act, in which case a maximum sentence of two years' imprisonment would have been competent in terms of s.4 and to exceed that term because of a failure to report the conduct for 17 years amounted to a miscarriage of justice.

CARTWRIGHT (NIGEL MARK) v. HM ADVOCATE (SENTENCING) 2001 S.L.T. 1163, Lord McCluskey, Lord Prosser, HCJ Appeal.

6409. Supervised attendance orders – imprisonment on breach – reports required prior to imprisonment – meaning of "sentence"

[Criminal Procedure (Scotland) Act 1995 (c.46) s.204(2), s.204(2A).]

W had been convicted of a road traffic offence. He failed to make any payment towards his fine of £500; he then failed to attend as required by a supervised attendance order imposed on him for not paying. Having considered a breach report before him which was nearly a year out of date but having called for no other reports, the sheriff revoked the order and sentenced W to imprisonment, stating that the imprisonment imposed was not as a "sentence passed on such conviction". W, who had carried out 23.5 hours of the attendance order, had spent 14 days in prison, had financial obligations to a partner and a child of his, and had lost his job due to being imprisoned, sought suspension of the sentence, arguing that the sheriff had failed to consider that the attendance order was a sentence of imprisonment for the purposes of the Criminal Procedure (Scotland) Act 1995 s.204.

Held, quashing the sentence and substituting a supervised release order of 48.5 hours, that (1) Parliament had envisaged that when an order for imprisonment was made on a failure to comply with supervised attendance, it was to be regarded as a new sentence, in contradistinction to an order for committal to imprisonment in default of payment of the fine. The statutory scheme in the 1995 Act which provided for the making of such an order, empowered the court to vary or to revoke it and impose a period of imprisonment by use of a separate and distinct power to penalise the breach. Such an order was to be regarded as a sentence in terms of s.204(2), and (2) the sheriff had failed to take into account the matters he required to take account of in terms of s.204(2A), in particular information obtained from an officer of the local authority or otherwise about W's circumstances, as W had never been imprisoned or detained before. That duty was not fulfilled by obtaining information from the prosecution or defence, and the information had to be pertinent to the circumstances at the time when the court was dealing with the breach, and the options for disposal. It was appropriate therefore to entertain the appeal, to treat it as if it had been made by the correct mechanism (petition to the nobile officium), and to look at the matter de novo. Opinion of the Court per Lord Cameron of Lochbroom.

WARD v. BROWN (SENTENCING) 2000 S.L.T. 1355, Lord Cameron of Lochbroom, Lord Caplan, Lord Milligan, HCJ Appeal.

6410. Theft – breach of the peace – racial aggravation

[Crime and Disorder Act 1998 (c.37) s.96.]

B appealed against sentences of six months' detention for theft and seven months concurrent for malicious damage on the same occasion. X appealed against concurrent sentences of nine months for each of breach of the peace and malicious mischief, and 12 months (two months attributable to bail contravention) for a further breach of the peace. On two occasions, the first involving only X, a takeaway was attacked, considerable damage caused, and racial abuse shouted. In the first attack, baseball bats were brandished.

Held, refusing the appeals, that the sentences were not excessive where both attacks were extremely serious and racially aggravated, and although the appellants were first offenders who maintained they were not ideologically racist, the Crime and Disorder Act 1998 s.96 simply dealt with whether or not there was racist behaviour on the occasion in question. Opinion of the Court per Lord Prosser.

BROWN v. HM ADVOCATE (SENTENCING) 2000 S.C.C.R. 736, Lord Prosser, Lady Cosgrove, HCJ Appeal.

6411. Books

Morrison, Nigel – Sentencing Practice: Cases and Materials. Looseleaf/ring bound: £245.00. ISBN 0-414-01339-5. W.Green & Son.

DAMAGES

6412. Clinical negligence – birth of disabled child – eligibility for ordinary maintenance costs

M, mother and F, father of a Down's syndrome child raised an action of damages against G in respect of their negligence in not carrying out an amniocentesis test during the mother's pregnancy. M maintained that the pregnancy would have been terminated, had they known their child was handicapped. G admitted negligence and decree was granted in respect of all the heads of loss sought. G reclaimed with regard to the damages awarded under (1) solatium for the child's father arguing he was a secondary victim of the injury done to the mother; (2) a layette and the basic maintenance costs of the child up to age 19 arguing the principle in *McFarlane v. Tayside Health Board* [2000] 2 A.C. 59, [2000] 1 C.L. 481 applied; (3) the child's care and maintenance beyond the age of 40 arguing that state funding would be available and the parents had not expressed interest in residential care, and (4) the mother's past and future wage loss arguing that the mother had had a second child and it had not been shown that she would actually have returned to work full time.

Held, allowing the reclaiming motion in part, that (1) it would have been reasonably foreseeable to the staff at G that if they failed in their duty of care the harmful effects would impact both the mother and father, accordingly the father was entitled to solatium. When the child reached 40 there might not be sufficient support available and since an award of damages in Scotland was traditionally a matter of broad judgment the Lord Ordinary had been entitled to reach the award he did; (2) in light of the evidence the Lord Ordinary was also correct to conclude that the mother, with two healthy children, would have been able to work full time, (Lord Morison dissenting). M were not entitled to the basic maintenance costs of the child, and (3) G had no responsibility to prevent an unwanted birth and on the evidence could not be held that the child was not unwanted. M were in the same position as the parents in *McFarlane* and not entitled to ordinary maintenance costs.

McLELLAND v. GREATER GLASGOW HEALTH BOARD 2001 S.L.T. 446, Lord Prosser, Lord Marnoch, Lord Morison, Ex Div.

6413. Criminal injuries compensation – pensions – deduction of ill health pension benefits on assessment

[Administration of Justice Act 1982 (c.53) s.10(a); Police Pensions Regulations 1987 (SI 1987 257).]

CICB appealed against a decision, (2000 S.C. 407, [2000] C.L.Y. 5816) that it had taken the wrong approach in assessing C's compensation claim. C had sustained personal injuries during an assault committed whilst he was carrying out his duties as a police officer, resulting in his early retirement from the force on medical grounds. Thereupon C became entitled to an ill health pension under the Police Pensions Regulations 1987 but lost the right to claim an ordinary retirement pension under the scheme on reaching his normal retirement age. CICB had deducted one half of C's ill health pension up to retirement age from the loss of earnings claim, and the whole of it after retirement age from his loss of pension claim. C claimed that under the Administration of Justice Act 1982 s.10(a) payments to an injured person under a pension scheme fell to be ignored in assessing common law damages and part of his claim to CICB represented the denial of opportunity to increase his pension entitlement by continuing to work until he reached normal retirement age.

Held, allowing the appeal, that s.10(a) of the Act did not apply when the head of damages claimed related to a loss of contractual pension. Therefore the assessment of loss of retirement pension had to take into account the amount of ill health pension received by the claimant. Damages for personal injury under Scots law were intended to be compensatory in nature such that the injured party would as far as possible be placed back in the same position as that which existed before the wrong had been committed. That approach required a like with like comparison of any benefits received with that which had been lost, in order to prevent the injured party from being placed in a better position than he had been before the injury was sustained. The correct approach in such cases was that periods before and after the normal retirement age had to be considered separately. The period before retirement age represented a claim for loss of earnings whereby pension benefits received during that period could not be set off against a claim for loss of earnings, but the period after retirement age represented a claim for loss of pension and in order to compare like with like, pension benefits received after that date must be brought into account, *Parry v. Cleaver* [1970] A.C. 1, [1969] C.L.Y. 906 applied.

CANTWELL v. CRIMINAL INJURIES COMPENSATION BOARD, [2001] UKHL 36, 2002 S.C. (H.L.) 1, Lord Hope of Craighead, HL.

6414. Defamation – measure of damages – excessive award

B, husband and wife, owned a nursing home together with their three children who were partners or worked there. B sought damages for defamatory statements made in a BBC documentary by two ex employees regarding the running of the home. The husband and wife had been awarded £50,000 and £60,000 respectively and each of their children £20,000. The BBC appealed, maintaining the awards were excessive in relation to other defamation awards in Scotland; that the award was compensatory and as such should be compared with awards for physical injury, and that the children's awards should be much less as they were not named in the documentary.

Held, refusing the reclaiming motion, that when considering damages awarded by a judge the appeal court had to consider what their assessment would have been in order to decide whether the award was excessive. In a defamation case that assessment was a free standing exercise and given the gravity of the accusations and their impact, the court considered that the awards could be described as conservative. Having conceded that the children were entitled to damages, the BBC had made no statable case for reduction and although not named in the documentary, as partners in a family firm the award made would have to reflect the impact on their reputations and social lives.

Observed, that comparators with personal injuries were not useful in defamation cases as each was unique, and personal injuries awards by be described as too low.

BAIGENT v. BBC; BAIGENT v. McCULLOCH (DAMAGES); BAIGENT v. O'HARE (DAMAGES) 2001 S.C. 281, Lord Johnston, Lord Milligan, Lord Prosser, Ex Div.

6415. Interim payments – admission of liability – contributory negligence not substantial

[Act of Sederunt (Rules of the Court of Session 1994) 1994 (SI 1994 1443) r.43.9 para. (3) (b).]

H was seriously injured in a road accident when a car crossed the central reservation of a dual carriageway and collided with his own. The accident was caused by the negligence of C, and H sought damages from C. H had been thrown from the car, causing his injuries, and admitted not wearing a seat belt. H moved for interim damages which C opposed arguing that although there had been an admission of fault there had not been an admission of liability to make reparation within the Act of Sederunt (Rules of the Court of Session 1994) 1994 r.43.9 para.3(a). C also argued that there was likely to be a "substantial finding of contributory negligence" as a result of H not wearing a seat belt, and that finding would preclude the award of interim damages under para.(3) (b).

Held, granting the motion, that the court was satisfied that H had admitted liability and a finding of contributory negligence even as high as 50 per cent would not, in the instant case, constitute a "substantial finding". H was bound to obtain damages, the only question to be answered was the amount and as such the proportion to be awarded at the interim stage.

HOGG v. CARRIGAN'S EXECUTRIX; *sub nom.* HOGG v. CARRIGAN 2001 S.C. 542, Judge TG Coutts Q.C., OH.

6416. Local authorities – planning certificate – negligent misstatement as to planning zone – measure of damages – reliance on certificate on purchase of land

A purchased a piece of land on which he proposed to develop an environmental centre. If the centre failed, A intended to use the land for residential development. During the purchase, A applied to P for confirmation of the planning position of the piece of land and was informed that outline planning permission existed for three houses and that the land was zoned for residential development. After receiving contrary information from the seller's solicitors that the land was zoned for industrial use, A asked P to confirm the position. P confirmed the outline planning permission and stated that the information being used by the sellers related to a different site. On that basis, A concluded the purchase. The outline planning permission lapsed four weeks after A took entry to the property and A made no efforts to renew it. The environmental centre failed and a year later A applied to P for planning permission for three houses. It was refused as the land was zoned for industrial purposes. A claimed damages from P for losses incurred in selling the site as industrial land, for improvements made to the site and for legal and professional expenses. The sheriff found that, although P had been negligent in issuing the planning certificate based on residential zoning, the losses were wholly incurred by A's failure to renew the outline planning permission. A appealed arguing that he would not have proceeded with the purchase if the correct information regarding industrial zoning had been given prior to the purchase or that if he had proceeded, he would have taken steps to ensure that the outline planning consent was renewed.

Held, allowing the appeal, that (1) A's losses were a direct result of P's negligence in stating that the land was zoned for residential use and that, on the balance of probabilities, A would not have proceeded with the purchase in the same manner had the correct facts been known. Damages, assessed as the difference between the value of the land with residential zoning and that with industrial zoning, of £28,000 were awarded; (2) interest would run from the date of refusal of A's application for planning permission following the failure of his environmental centre at a rate of 15 per cent per annum until the date of citation and 8 per cent per annum thereafter, *Boots the Chemist Ltd v. GA Estates Ltd* 1993 S.L.T. 136, [1993] C.L.Y. 5153 followed; (3) road improvements made to the site were made primarily for the benefit of the environmental centre, the cost of which would have been represented in the sale price of the land for industrial use, and (4) legal and professional expenses incurred in the purchase and development of the site were not recoverable as those would also have been incurred had A purchased the property for the correct valuation as industrial land.

ANDERSON v. PERTH AND KINROSS COUNCIL 2000 S.C.L.R. 987, Graham Cox Q.C., Sheriff Principal, Sh Ct.

6417. Pensions – loss – private pension scheme – precise specification of nature of loss

In T's action of damages for personal injuries, he averred inter alia that he had lost pension rights and benefits in respect of a personal pension he could no longer maintain. F argued that specification as to the precise nature of the loss was required, while conceding that had T's averments related to an occupational pension scheme, they would have been sufficient to entitle him to a proof before answer.

Held, allowing proof, that the test for relevancy of a claim for loss of rights from a private pension scheme was not necessarily different from that for an occupational one and by averring the nature of his pension arrangement, the company involved and the premium payable the pursuer had given sufficient information to enable F to investigate and answer his claim.

THAIN v. FISHERS SERVICES (ABERFELDY) LTD 2001 S.L.T. 1237, Lord Philip, OH.

6418. Personal injuries – necessary services by relative – valuation – relevancy

K raised an action for damages against D in respect of a road traffic accident in which K sustained a severe head injury. D accepted liability but argued that K's averments concerning services and paid care in the future, and services rendered to date, were lacking in specification and should be excluded from proof. K sought a total of £1.5 million. K averred inter alia that (1) his fiancee, N, who had also been hurt in the accident, provided substantial daily support for K, who required to live in a quiet rural area, and if she was not providing care for K, N would have been earning £17,000 per annum as a scientist, and (2) his mother, G, had had to give up employment to care for him during an 11 month period between the accident and his marriage to N.

Held, allowing proof before answer under deletion of disputed averments relating to N's services, that (1) the primary measure of damages should be the value of the services and the cost of paid care. In failing to aver certain basic elements concerning services and paid care, K had failed to give fair notice. It was insufficient simply to aver earnings lost by N, and in a case involving such large sums there needed to be specification of the nature of services rendered, the time period involved and the value placed on those services. Earnings lost by a relative providing services did not provide the true measure, though they could in some cases provide a cross check, and (2) given that the major part of G's services was rendered in a finite period and the averments did not imply that the services rendered were necessarily to be valued by the means of earnings foregone, and as there was just sufficient information to allow for an assessment of damages, proof before answer on services by G would be allowed.

KENDAL v. DAVIES 2001 S.C.L.R. 140, Lady Paton, OH.

6419. Professional negligence – property searches – measure of damages – loss of expected profits – inaccurate property inquiry certificate – sale of property at value lower than expected

[Housing (Scotland) Act 1987 (c.26) s.108.]

M bought a property on the strength of an inquiry certificate provided to the seller by S. The certificate proved inaccurate, the property was subject to a local authority notice and needed work on defective chimneys. When selling the property M argued that prospective buyers were put off by the scaffolding and sold the property for less than expected. Damages and cost of the repair were awarded to M. S appealed, arguing that they had not been in sufficient proximity to M to owe a duty of care, and that if they did owe a duty of care there was no evidence to show they had breached it.

Held, allowing the appeal, that S did owe a duty of care to M since S knew the identity of the prospective purchasers and as such were an identifiable class. In a situation where information was provided as part of a service and was in the nature of information collated rather than expert advice, the exercise of a skill to a particular standard was not central and it was sufficient for the sheriff to be satisfied that S had failed to exercise reasonable care. In giving inaccurate information S had been negligent. The law did not permit claims for loss of profits, and damages should be assessed at the time of the negligent act or as soon as M became aware of it, the relevant measure was the difference between the market value and the price actually paid.

MAYPARK PROPERTIES LTD v. STIRRAT; *sub nom.* MAYPARK PROPERTIES LTD v. STIRRIT 2001 S.L.T. (Sh Ct) 171, EF Bowen Q.C., Sheriff Principal, Sh Ct.

6420. Professional negligence – solicitors – measure of damages – loss of agricultural tenancy – effect on farming business

[Succession (Scotland) Act 1964 (c.41) s.16.]

P, partners in a farming business sought damages from O, their solicitor arguing that O had failed to advise them of their right, under the Succession (Scotland) Act 1964 s.16 to transfer their deceased father's interest in the farm to themselves. As a result of that failure the leases on both the agricultural holding and smallholding were terminated. Damages of £25,000 were agreed with regard to the loss of housing and the smallholding, but not with regard to the loss of a share in a potential development and other aspects of the secure tenancy and arable loss. An independent expert had determined the likelihood of planning permission being granted for the development was less than 50/50 in the next 10 years. P argued that there had been developments since the expert's report which should be taken into account. O argued that the loss should be assessed at the date upon which it happened and only nominal damages should be awarded for the development potential. O argued that even if planning permission had been awarded, P could have been required to give up the land under a resumptive clause in the lease.

Held, granting decree, that (1) P could not introduce new evidence relating to matters agreed to be the subject of the expert report. Any material change could have been assessed by remitting back to the expert; (2) the report detailed the likelihood of the granting of planning permission at 30 per cent at the five year point, and (3) damages should be assessed in light of the circumstances as known at the time of the assessment and with regard to the development potential, and thus P were entitled to more than nominal damages. P would have been in a strong position to resist any resumptive clause in the lease given the agricultural nature of the land. Award for loss of development potential: £181,000. Award for loss of other aspects of secure tenancy: £41,300. Award for arable loss: £39,300. Award for housing loss (as agreed): £15,000. Award for loss of West Millchen (as agreed): £10,000.

PAUL v. OGILVY 2001 S.L.T. 171, Lord Hamilton, OH.

Personal Injuries or Death–Quantum

Details have been received of the following cases in which damages for personal injuries or death were awarded. The classification and sequence of the classified awards follows that adopted in Kemp and Kemp. *The Quantum of Damages,* Vol. 2. Unless there is some statement to the contrary, the age of the applicant is his age at the time of the court hearing. Unless specified the damages are stated on the basis of full liability, *ie.* ignoring any deduction made for contributory negligence. The sum is the total amount of the damages awarded unless otherwise stated. For a cumulative guide to *quantum* of damages cases reported in Current Law during 2001, see the *Quantum* of Damages table. We must stress that we are entirely dependent on the contributor of an unreported case for the accuracy of his or her report; it is impracticable for us independently to check the facts stated to us. We welcome contributions and are most grateful for all the reports received. We would appreciate reports of any alterations to awards noted here, either in, or in anticipation of, appeal.

Severe brain damage

6421.   W raised an action for damages in respect of personal injuries sustained in a road traffic accident. She suffered brain damage resulting in severe impairment of her physical, mental and emotional functioning and retained an insight into her condition and the significant restrictions imposed on her life. W argued that damages in respect of solatium should be calculated according to the principles in *Heil v. Rankin* [2001] Q.B. 272, [2000] C.L.Y. 1478. She also claimed damages in respect of loss of earnings and the costs of a personal trainer. P argued that *Heil* being an English case, did not represent the appropriate principle to be applied in a Scottish court and that the damages awarded in that case had been increased for London weighting. P further argued that the amount of damages in respect of future earnings should be restricted due to the likelihood that W would, in the normal course of events, have had children and therefore had a period without working. On the claim for costs of a personal trainer, P argued that W would have been likely to incur fitness costs in the form of gym fees and that W would be unlikely to continue in the long term with a personal trainer. Held, awarding damages of £95,000 in respect of solatium, £233, 205 (multiplicand of £10,500; multiplier of 22.21), in respect of loss of earnings and £36,400 (multiplicand £3,640; multiplier of 10) for the costs of a personal trainer, that (1) the principles contained in *Heil* were of assistance to Scottish and English courts alike and damages were based on the injuries sustained and not on the physical location of the injured person, it being inappropriate to suggest that someone in London should be entitled to greater damages than someone in Scotland who had suffered the same injuries, (2) no reduction should be made in respect of W's potential to have children prior to the accident as the adoption of the multiplier of 22.21 already took account of uncertainties and imponderables, and (3) damages for the use of a personal trainer were appropriate as the benefit was therapeutic rather than for fitness purposes and the multiplier of 10 reflected the fact that this may not be required indefinitely.

Held, awarding Damages of £95,000 in respect of solatium, £233,205 (multiplicand of £10,500; multiplier of 22.21), in respect of loss of earnings and £36,400 (multiplicand £3,640; multiplier of 10) for the costs of a personal trainer, that (1) the principles contained in *Heil* were of assistance to Scottish and English courts alike and damages were based on the injuries sustained and not on the physical location of the injured person, it being inappropriate to suggest that someone in London should be entitled to greater damages than someone in Scotland who had suffered the same injuries; (2) no reduction should be made in respect of W's potential to have children prior to the accident as the adoption of the multiplier of 22.21 already took account of uncertainties and imponderables, and (3) damages for the use of a personal trainer were appropriate as the benefit was therapeutic rather than for fitness purposes and the multiplier of 10 reflected the fact that such use might not be required indefinitely.

WALLACE v. PATERSON 2001 S.C.L.R. 521, Lady Paton, OH.

Head

6422. S, a male, aged 21 at death, had always lived at home with his parents and was completing an electrical apprenticeship at the time of his death. He was killed in a head on car crash and his parents sought damages for loss of society in respect of their son's death. Jury award for loss of society: £30,000 for each parent.

STRANG v. LE BRUSQ 2001 Rep. L.R. 52, Judge not specified, CS.

Head

6423. Y sought damages for serious injuries when the car in which he was travelling, driven by his mother was struck from behind by M's vehicle. Y's mother was killed. Her parents also sought damages in respect of her death.

Held, M was granted assoilzie in respect of the claims by the parents and granting decree against M for payment to Y of the principal sum of £5,000 with interest thereon at the agreed sum of £401, both in terms of the joint minute and granting decree for payment by M to Y for the sum of £363,250 inclusive of interest in respect of personal injuries, that (1) the medical evidence clearly showed permanent and severe brain damage which could account for the memory impairment, learning difficulties and changes to Y's personality which had occurred following the head injury and the panic attacks were rightly attributable to his inability to perform more than one function at a time. It was the combination of those factors which severely affected Y's future employment prospects rather than any residual effects of the industrial accident, (2) the damages for personal injuries represented £50,000 for solatium as agreed, £37,250 for loss of earnings to date, £261,000 for future loss of earnings, a multiplier of 23 being applied, £10,000 for necessary services to date as agreed and £5,000 for future necessary services, all sums being inclusive of interest.

YOUNG v. McDOWALL 2001 S.C.L.R. 155, Lord Macfadyen, OH.

Facial scars

6424. W, male, aged 16 at the time of the accident, sustained facial scarring from under his jaw to below ear level. He was travelling, without wearing a seat belt, in the back of a car, which went out of control. Jury award of £25,000 in respect of solatium.

WALKER v. MONCUR 2001 Rep. L.R. 67, Judge not specified, OH.

Neck – whiplash type injury

6425. B suffered a whiplash injury in a road traffic accident and maintained that he had continuing neck pain throughout the period of four years from the date of the accident to the jury trial. He further claimed that he had developed loss of muscle power in his left arm and severe depression, both resulting directly from the accident. In addition to a claim for solatium in respect of pain and suffering, B also claimed for loss of earnings, both past and future. Jury award of £21,000 in respect of solatium, but no award for loss of earnings.

BUCHANAN v. MASON 2001 Rep. L.R. 67, Judge not specified, OH.

Wrist

6426. M, male, aged 44 at the time of the accident and 48 at proof fractured his wrist at work whilst securing the load on his lorry. One of the ropes broke and he fell to the ground. The complex fracture required open reduction and stabilisation with surgical wires. M underwent physiotherapy and returned to work earlier than expected but suffered increased pain and restricted movement. A medical expert suggested that surgical fusion could cure the pain but doubted whether M could continue working as an HGV driver. M also sought damages for loss of services under Administration of Justice Act 1982 s.8 and s.9 as he was no longer able to do basic DIY, decorating or gardening and required help from his wife both during and after his wrist was wired and plastered. Solatium: £12,500. Award for loss of past earnings: £4,750. Award for loss of future earnings: £45,000. Award for services: £1,250.

MacKENZIE v. HD FRASER & SONS 2001 S.L.T. 116, TG Coutts Q.C., OH.

Wrist

6427. M, aged 44 at proof, sought damages for a wrist injury sustained after being struck by a piece of falling timber at a football stadium. He suffered a bad, painful and disabling permanent ligamentous injury resulting in weakness and loss of grip and he suffered complete loss of flexion following arthodesis procedure in 1997. M continued to work as a designer in the construction industry despite the pain but claimed that it was likely that he would have to give up work when he was 50, and that as the nature of his work involved breaks in employment, he would have found work as a joiner, which he was previously trained to do, during periods of unemployment in 1991 and 1999, had it not been for his injuries. Solatium was properly assessed at £20,000, two thirds relating to the past; (2) past loss of earnings was assessed at £7,500; (3) £42,000 was a suitable award for loss of employability being £40,000 (after discounting at 3 per cent) to reflect the likely loss of salary if the pursuer chose to retire early and £2,000 for likely expenses to enable the pursuer to adapt his working practices, and (4) service claims were properly assessed at £2,000.

McDYER v. CELTIC FOOTBALL & ATHLETIC CO LTD (NO.2) 2001 S.L.T. 1387, Lord McCluskey, OH.

Claims for death of parent

6428. M, a child, claimed damages for loss of society in respect of the death of its father who was killed in a road traffic accident seven days before the child was born. Jury award of £37,500 in respect of loss of society.

McINTOSH v. FINDLAY 2001 Rep. L.R. 66, Judge not specified, OH.

DEFAMATION

6429. Defamation Act 1996 (c.31) – Commencement No.3 and Transitional Provision Order

DEFAMATION ACT 1996 (COMMENCEMENT NO.3 AND TRANSITIONAL PROVISION) (SCOTLAND) ORDER 2001, SSI 2001 98 (C.3); made under the Defamation Act 1996 s.19. Commencement details: bringing into force various provisions of the Act on March 31, 2001; £1.50.

This Order brings the remaining provisions of the Defamation Act 1996 in relation to Scotland which are not already in force on March 31, 2001 and provides that the Defamation Act 1952 s.4 continues to apply to offers of amends made before March 31, 2001.

6430. Reputation – newspaper article – no implication of involvement in crime

M sued a newspaper company, S, and a journalist, N, in respect of an article which M claimed was defamatory in implying that he had been directly involved in, or had at least connived at, a serious crime. The article stated that police had seized counterfeit banknotes and drugs at a pub run by M. The raid actually took place at premises being set up as sunbed premises in which M claimed to be one of six partners, though his actual relationship with the premises was uncertain. The accuracy of those details was not checked by S and N until M's action was raised. M did not rely on any particular circumstances affecting him as giving the article a defamatory meaning, and the question of whether the article was defamatory fell to be determined by a consideration of the words themselves. M argued that, at the least, the article implied that he had turned a blind eye to criminal activity at his premises.

Held, granting absolvitor, that M had read the article in an unduly sensitive way. It would not be read by an ordinary person as implicating M in dealings with counterfeit money or drugs; it did not refer to the licensee or tenant and there was no suggestion that M was one of the people arrested. The only reference to drugs was that a quantity was recovered, and without any indication of where the banknotes were found, it was not reasonable to infer from the expression "stash" of counterfeit money, read in the context of the whole article, a link between the money and the licensee of the premises. Furthermore, affidavits presented by M and sworn by a wide variety of people, showed that he had remained in high regard and no useful purpose would be served by reviewing the other issues raised.

McCUE v. SCOTTISH DAILY RECORD & SUNDAY MAIL LTD (NO.4) 2000 Rep. L.R. 133, Lord Bonomy, OH.

EDUCATION

6431. Colleges – Northern College of Education – closure

NORTHERN COLLEGE OF EDUCATION (CLOSURE) (SCOTLAND) ORDER 2001, SSI 2001 407; made under the Further and Higher Education (Scotland) Act 1992 s.47. In force: December 1, 2001; £2.00.

This Order amends the Colleges of Education (Scotland) Regulations 1987 (SI 1987 309), the Teachers Superannuation (Scotland) Regulations 1992 (SI 1992 280) and the Teachers (Compensation for Premature Retirement and Redundancy) (Scotland) Regulations 1996 (SI 1996 2317). This Order closes the Northern College of Education, which will cease to be a separate institution and becomes part of the University of Aberdeen or the University of Dundee, and provides for its governing body to be wound up. It transfers the whole property, rights, liabilities, obligations and contracts of the governing body of the College to the governing bodies of the Universities of Aberdeen and Dundee, makes provision regarding property provided with the aid of grant and provides for the transfer of staff of the College to the governing body of the University of Aberdeen or the University of Dundee without a break in their employment.

6432. Education (Graduate Endowment and Student Support) (Scotland) Act 2001 (asp 6) – Commencement Order

EDUCATION (GRADUATE ENDOWMENT AND STUDENT SUPPORT) (SCOTLAND) ACT 2001 (COMMENCEMENT) ORDER 2001, SSI 2001 191 (C.10); made under the Education (Graduate Endowment and Student Support) (Scotland) Act 2001 s.5. In force: brings into force various provisions of the Act on June 1, 2001; £1.50.

This Order brings into force on June 1, 2001 those provisions of the Education (Graduate Endowment and Student Support) (Scotland) Act 2001 which are not already in force. Section 4 of the Act is brought into force which provides for the amendment of the Local Government Finance Act 1992 s.75 and s.77 to exempt students from liability to pay the council tax.

6433. Education (Graduate Endowment and Student Support) (Scotland) Act 2001 (asp 6)

This Act of the Scottish Parliament makes provision for the payment by certain persons of the graduate endowment; makes provision in relation to the use of income arising from the graduate endowment for the purposes of the financial support of students; it make further provision as respects financial support for students and provision exempting students from liability for council tax.

This Act received Royal Assent on May 3, 2001.

6434. Further education – Bell College of Technology – designation

DESIGNATION OF BELL COLLEGE OF TECHNOLOGY (SCOTLAND) ORDER 2001, SSI 2001 199; made under the Further and Higher Education (Scotland) Act 1992 s.25, s.44, s.60. In force: August 1, 2001; £1.75.

This Order has the effect that on August 1, 2001 Bell College of Technology, a further education college under the management of a Board of Management established under the Further and Higher Education (Scotland) Act 1992 s.11 (2), becomes a designated institution within the meaning of Part II of that Act. The Order designates the college as eligible to receive funds from the Scottish Higher Education Funding Council and transfers the whole property, rights, liabilities and obligations of the Board of Management to the governing body of the designated institution which is established as a body corporate by virtue of s.45(2) of that Act.

6435. Further education – Bell College of Technology – discharge of functions

BELL COLLEGE OF TECHNOLOGY (SCOTLAND) ORDER OF COUNCIL 2001, SI 2001 2005 (S.13); made under the Further and Higher Education (Scotland) Act 1992 s.45, s.60. In force: August 1, 2001; £3.00.

This Order makes provision regarding the constitution, functions and powers of the Board of Governors of Bell College of Technology, as governing body of that college, and the arrangements to be adopted by it for discharging its functions and also designates Bell College of Technology as eligible to receive support from the Scottish Higher Education Funding Council.

6436. Further education – Bell College of Technology – governance

BELL COLLEGE OF TECHNOLOGY (SCOTLAND) ORDER OF COUNCIL 2001, SSI 2001 234; made under the Further and Higher Education (Scotland) Act 1992 s.45, s.60. In force: August 1, 2001; £3.00.

This Order makes provision regarding the constitution, functions and powers of the Board of Governors of Bell College of Technology, as governing body of that College, and the arrangements to be adopted by it for discharging its functions.

6437. Grants – graduate endowment

GRADUATE ENDOWMENT (SCOTLAND) REGULATIONS 2001, SSI 2001 280; made under the Education (Graduate Endowment and Student Support) (Scotland) Act 2001 s.1; the Education (Scotland) Act 1980 s.73; and the Education (Graduate Endowment and Student Support) (Scotland) Act 2001 s.73B. In force: August 1, 2001; £3.00.

These Regulations, the first made under the Education (Graduate Endowment and Student Support) (Scotland) Act 2001 with respect to the graduate endowment, specify which graduates are liable to pay the graduate endowment, the amount of the graduate endowment and when it is to be paid, and make provision for loans to be made available to graduates for the purposes of paying the graduate endowment.

6438. Grants – individual learning accounts

EDUCATION AND TRAINING (SCOTLAND) AMENDMENT REGULATIONS 2001, SSI 2001 329; made under the Education and Training (Scotland) Act 2000 s.1, s.3. In force: October 31, 2001; £1.50.

These Regulations, which amend the Education and Training (Scotland) Regulations 2000 (SSI 2000 292) providing for the payment of Individual Learning Accounts, remove the limit on the number of the £150 grants payable under the 2000 Regulations.

6439. Higher education – Scottish Higher Education Funding Council – designation – UHI Millennium Institute

DESIGNATION OF UHI MILLENNIUM INSTITUTE (SCOTLAND) ORDER 2001, SSI 2001 39; made under the Further and Higher Education (Scotland) Act 1992 s.44, s.60. In force: April 1, 2001; £1.50.

This Order designates UHI Millennium Institute as an institution which may be funded by the Scottish Higher Education Funding Council and makes provision for the designation to continue in the event of a change of name of UHI Millennium Institute.

6440. School attendance – failure to attend – sanction against parent

[Education (Scotland) Act 1980 (c.44) s.35, s.35(1), s.42(1)(c); Human Rights Act 1998 (c.42) s.3; European Convention on Human Rights 1950 Art.6(1).]

R was charged with an offence under the Education (Scotland) Act 1980 s.35 for failing to ensure that her child attended school regularly. R moved the court to desert simpliciter arguing (1) that prosecutions under s.35 of the 1980 Act arose from the actings of a child, but criminal responsibility was attached to the parent and a fair trial was impossible where no criminal acting could be attached to the accused, which was contrary to the European Convention on Human Rights 1950 Art.6(1), and (2) it was not open to the court to use re-interpretation as a tool to redraft flawed provisions within the legislation, that evidence could not be led on a flawed charge and the court was not entitled to convict in the circumstances. The education authority opposed the motion and argued that it was open to the judge to re-interpret domestic legislation so as to make it compatible with Convention rights and it would, therefore, be open to the trial judge to extend the powers under s.35(1) of the 1980 Act to consider circumstances relating to the parent which may afford a reasonable excuse for the child's non attendance, thus allowing the trial to continue.

Held, refusing the motion, that (1) Art.6(1) did not concern the subject matter of a trial, but was principally concerned with ensuring that procedures were fair; (2) s.35(1) of the 1980 Act was incompatible with Convention rights as those liable to be found guilty would include those parents who could do nothing to prevent the actions which, under s.35(1) would give rise to strict liability, and (3) the Human Rights Act 1998 s.3 imposed a duty on the court to interpret domestic legislation to make it compatible with Convention rights and by re-interpreting s.42(1)(c) of the 1980 Act to include any reasonable excuse afforded by a parent as well as a child, it would enable s.35(1) to be re-interpreted to provide parents with the opportunity to defend themselves against criminal liability, thus making it compatible with Convention rights.

Observed, that even if re-interpretation was not available, the motion would still have been refused as domestic legislation remained valid, despite its incompatibility with Convention rights, until repealed or amended.

O'HAGAN v. REA 2001 S.L.T. (Sh Ct) 30, Sheriff IC Simpson, Sh Ct (South Strathclyde, Dumfries and Galloway).

6441. Schools – aided places – St Mary's Music School

ST MARY'S MUSIC SCHOOL (AIDED PLACES) (SCOTLAND) REGULATIONS 2001, SSI 2001 223; made under the Education (Scotland) Act 1980 s.73, s.74. In force: August 1, 2001; £4.00.

These Regulations, which revoke and replace the St Mary's Music School (Aided Places) Regulations 1995 (SI 1995 1712 as amended by SI 1996 1807, SI 1997 1640, SI 1998 1498, SI 1999 1060, SSI 2000 196), provide for the payment of allowances to St Mary's Music School, Edinburgh, to reimburse them for their expenditure in respect of fees and charges remitted and grants made in operating the aided pupil scheme.

6442. Schools – assisted places scheme – elibility – incidental expenses

EDUCATION (ASSISTED PLACES) (SCOTLAND) REGULATIONS 2001, SSI 2001 222; made under the Education (Scotland) Act 1980 s.75A, s.75B. In force: August 1, 2001; £4.00.

These Regulations revoke and replace the Education (Assisted Places) (Scotland) Regulations 1995 (SI 1995 1713 as amended by SI 1996 1808, SI 1997 1641, SI 1997 2773, SI 1998 1497, SI 1998 1994, SI 1999 1059, and SSI 2000 195). They relate to the scheme for assisted places at independent schools which was required to be established under of the Education (Scotland) Act 1980 s.75A and deal with eligibility for assisted places, remission of fees, incidental expenses of pupils holding assisted places, reimbursement claims and conditions of payment and provides for the Scottish Ministers to authorise a replacement school to provide an assisted place for an existing pupil when a participating school merges with another school, closes or no longer wishes to participate in the scheme.

6443. Standards in Scotland's Schools etc. Act 2000 (asp 6) – Commencement No.3 and Transitional Provisions Amendment Order

STANDARDS IN SCOTLAND'S SCHOOLS ETC. ACT 2000 (COMMENCEMENT NO.3 AND TRANSITIONAL PROVISIONS) AMENDMENT ORDER 2001, SSI 2001 400 (C.19); made under the Standards in Scotland's Schools etc. Act 2000 s.61. Commencement details: bringing into force various provisions of the 2000 Act on October 31, 2001; £1.50.

This Order amends the Standards in Scotland's Schools etc. Act 2000 (Commencement No.3 and Transitional Provisions) Order 2000. It inserts into the Commencement Order further transitional and savings provisions. It provides for the current procedures under the Teaching Council (Scotland) Act 1965 s.10, s.11 and Sch.2 to continue to apply to cases where consideration by the Investigating and Disciplinary Committees has commenced prior to November 1, 2001.

6444. Standards in Scotland's Schools etc. Act 2000 (asp 6) – Commencement No.4 Order

STANDARDS IN SCOTLAND'S SCHOOLS ETC. ACT 2000 (COMMENCEMENT NO.4) ORDER 2001, SSI 2001 102 (C.4); made under the Standards in Scotland's Schools etc. Act s.61. Commencement details: bringing into force various provisions of the Act on March 23, 2001; £1.50.

Act 2000 s.61 (2). This Order brings the Standards in Scotland's Schools etc. Act 2000 s.55, which abolishes the Scottish Joint Negotiating Committee for School Education, the statutory collective bargaining forum for Scottish teachers' pay and conditions, on March 23, 2001.

6445. Students – allowances – eligibility – conditions and requirements

STUDENTS' ALLOWANCES (SCOTLAND) AMENDMENT REGULATIONS 2001, SSI 2001 229; made under the Education (Scotland) Act 1980 s.73, s.74. In force: August 1, 2001; £1.75.

These Regulations, which amend the Students' Allowances (Scotland) Regulations 1999 (SI 1999 1131), allow the Scottish Ministers to pay allowances to students on distance learning courses as well as students attending courses of education and remove the requirement for an application for an allowance to be made in writing and replaces it with a requirement for the application to be made in such form as the Scottish Ministers may require. This is to enable applications to be made electronically when electronic signatures are recognised as being legally binding by virtue of delegated legislation made under the Electronic Communications Act 2000.

6446. Students – loans

EDUCATION (STUDENT LOANS) AMENDMENT (SCOTLAND) REGULATIONS 2001, SSI 2001 210; made under the Education (Student Loans) Act 1990 s.1, Sch.2 para.1. In force: August 1, 2001; £1.75.

These Regulations, which amend the Education (Student Loans) Regulations 1998 (SI 1998 211), increase the maximum amounts, in line with inflation, which may be lent in relation to an academic year.

6447. Students – loans

EDUCATION (STUDENT LOANS) (SCOTLAND) REGULATIONS 2000 AMENDMENT REGULATIONS 2001, SSI 2001 228; made under the Education (Scotland) Act 1980 s.73, s.73B, s.74. In force: August 1, 2001; £1.75.

These Regulations, which amend the Education (Student Loans) (Scotland) Regulations 2000 (SSI 2000 200), allow the Scottish Ministers to pay loans to students on distance learning courses as well as students actually attending courses of education. They also amend the conditions which a part-time student must meet to be eligible for a loan by clarifying the date on which the relevant conditions must be satisfied and removing the requirement that married students must have been married for a period of two years.

6448. Students – loans – repayments

REPAYMENT OF STUDENT LOANS (SCOTLAND) AMENDMENT REGULATIONS 2001, SSI 2001 227; made under the Education (Scotland) Act 1980 s.73, s.73B, s.74. In force: August 1, 2001; £1.75.

These Regulations amend the Repayment of Student Loans (Scotland) Regulations 2000 (SSI 2000 110) which govern the repayment of income contingent student loans by students living and working abroad. These Regulations update the 2000 Regulations to take account of regulations which confer loan making functions on the Scottish Ministers since the 2000 Regulations were enacted.

6449. Students – loans – sandwich courses – full time study

EDUCATION (STUDENT LOANS) (SCOTLAND) REGULATIONS 2000 AMENDMENT (NO.2) REGULATIONS 2001, SSI 2001 311; made under the Education (Scotland) Act 1980 s.73, s.73B, s.74. In force: October 4, 2001; £1.50.

These Regulations amend the Education (Student Loans) (Scotland) Regulations 2000 (SSI 2000 200) so that a sandwich course is a designated course for the purposes of those Regulations if a student undertaking that course is required to attend periods of full time study of at least 18 weeks in each year. In addition, the Regulations add a new paragraph to provide that where periods of full time study and work experience occur within any week of a sandwich course, the days of full time study shall be aggregated with any weeks of full time study in determining the number of weeks of full time study in each year.

6450. Teachers – General Teaching Council for Scotland – elections

GENERAL TEACHING COUNCIL (SCOTLAND) ELECTION SCHEME 2001 APPROVAL ORDER 2001, SSI 2001 18; made under the Teaching Council (Scotland) Act 1965 s.14, Sch.1 para.1. In force: February 28, 2001; £2.50.

This Order, which approves the General Teaching Council for Scotland Election Scheme 2001, revokes the Teaching Council (Scotland) Election Scheme 1989 Approval Order 1989 (SI 1989 2308) and the General Teaching Council (Scotland) Election Amendment Scheme 1994 Approval Order 1994 (SI 1994 1702), details new rules in connection with the elections for members of the General Teaching Council for Scotland.

6451. Books

A-Z of Scots Education Law. Paperback: £9.99. ISBN 0-11-497288-5. The Stationery Office Agencies.

Gilchrist, Ian – Green's Scottish Early Years Manual. Greens Professional Publishing. Looseleaf/ring bound: £135.00. ISBN 0-414-01379-4. W.Green & Son.

ELECTORAL PROCESS

6452. Elections – forms of canvass – registration

REPRESENTATION OF THE PEOPLE (FORM OF CANVASS) (SCOTLAND) REGULATIONS 2001, SI 2001 2817 (S.15); made under the Representation of the People Act 1983 s.10, s.201. In force: August 16, 2001; £2.00.

Under the Representation of the People Act 1983 s.10 each registration officer is required to conduct an annual canvass in his registration area to ascertain the persons who are entitled to be or remain registered as parliamentary or local government electors in that area. These Regulations specify a form for the purposes of that canvass.

6453. Elections – registration officer – duties

REPRESENTATION OF THE PEOPLE (SCOTLAND) REGULATIONS 2001, SI 2001 497 (S.2); made under the European Parliamentary Elections Act 1978 Sch.1 para.2; the Representation of the People Act 1983 s.10A, s.13A, s.53, s.201, Sch.1 r.24, Sch.2; and the Representation of the People Act 1985 s.3. In force: February 16, 2001; £7.50.

These Regulations revoke (in part) the Representation of the People (Scotland) Regulations 1986 (SI 1986 1111), the Representation of the People (Scotland) Amendment Regulations 1990 (SI 1990 629), the Representation of the People (Scotland) Amendment Regulations 1992 (SI 1992 834), the Representation of the People (Scotland) Amendment Regulations 1997 (SI 1997 979) and amend the European Parliamentary Elections (Changes to the Franchise and Qualification of Representatives) Regulations 1994 (SI 1994 342) and the Local Government Elections (Changes to the Franchise and Qualification of Members) Regulations 1995 (SI 1995 1948). The Regulations are made in consequence of changes made by the Representation of the People Act 2000 and apply to elections for membership of the House of Commons and the European Parliament and to local government elections in Scotland. They no longer include provision about electors' lists and enable the registration officer to inspect the records listed in Reg.35 for electoral registration purposes.

6454. Elections – registration officer – duties

REPRESENTATION OF THE PEOPLE (SCOTLAND) (AMENDMENT) REGULATIONS 2001, SI 2001 1749 (S.11); made under the Representation of the People Act 1983 s.53, s.201, s.202, Sch.2 para.10B. In force: May 4, 2001 in accordance with Art.1 (1); £1.75.

These Regulations, which amend the Representation of the People (Scotland) Regulations 2001 (SI 2001 497), ensure the provisions of empowering the supply copies of any revised versions of the register and of notices published by registration officers in between the annual revision of the register.

6455. Elections – Scottish Parliament – conduct of elections

SCOTTISH PARLIAMENT (ELECTIONS ETC.) (AMENDMENT) ORDER 2001, SI 2001 1399 (S.5); made under the Scotland Act 1998 s.12, s.113. In force: April 6, 2001; £3.50.

This Order amends the Scottish Parliament (Elections etc.) Order 1999 (SI 1999 787) as a consequence of changes made by the Representation of the People Act 2000, the Political Parties, Elections and Referendums Act 2000, the Postal Services Act 2000 and the Representation of the People (Scotland) Regulations 2001 (SI 2001 497 (s.2)). The main changes to the 1999 Order result from the introduction by the Representation of the People Act 2000 of a new system of "rolling registration". Under this system the register of local government electors continues in force indefinitely. As eligibility to vote at elections for membership of the Scottish Parliament depends on registration in the register of local government electors, amendment of the 1999 Order is necessary to reflect, and take account of, the changes made by recent primary and subordinate legislation.

6456. Elections – Scottish Parliament – conduct of elections

SCOTTISH PARLIAMENT (ELECTIONS ETC.) (AMENDMENT) (NO.2) ORDER 2001, SI 2001 1748 (S.10); made under the Scotland Act 1998 s.12, s.113. In force: May 4, 2001 in accordance with Art.1; £1.75.

This Order amends the Scottish Parliament (Elections etc.) Order 1999 (SI 1999 787). This Order, which amends the timetable in the case of an election to fill a vacancy in a constituency seat, provides that the time for the publication of the notice of election to fill that vacancy is not to be earlier that 28 days before the date of the poll and not later than 14 days before the date of the poll. In addition, it provides that the time when constituency nomination papers are to be delivered is to be not later than 4 pm on any day after the date when the notice of election is published, but not later than the 11th day before the date of the poll.

6457. Elections – Scottish Parliament – conduct of elections

SCOTTISH PARLIAMENT (ELECTIONS ETC.) (AMENDMENT) (NO.3) ORDER 2001, SI 2001 1750 (S.12); made under the Scotland Act 1998 s.12, s.113. In force: May 4, 2001 in accordance with Art.1; £1.75.

This Order amends the Scottish Parliament (Elections etc.) Order 1999 (SI 1999 787), which contains provisions about electors lists and registers, and, in particular concerning the supply of free copies of the register, to ensure that the provisions empowering the supply of copies of the register extend to providing copies of any revised versions of the register and of notices published by registration officers in between the annual revision of the register. It also provides that applications to be removed from the record of absent voters or to vote by proxy need to be received by the registration officer on the 11th (working) day before the date of the poll at an election.

ELECTRICITY INDUSTRY

6458. Electricity generation – non fossil fuel sources

ELECTRICITY FROM NON-FOSSIL FUEL SOURCES (SCOTLAND) SAVING ARRANGEMENTS ORDER 2001, SI 2001 3269 (S.17); made under the Utilities Act 2000 s.67. In force: October 1, 2001; £2.00.

This Order makes provision for the saving and modification of arrangements made by public electricity suppliers in compliance with the Electricity Act 1989 s.32. It obliges the supply successor companies in Scotland to make arrangements which replace arrangements made in the past by public electricity suppliers and imposes agreements on operators of non-fossil fuel generating stations who had an arrangement making electricity available to public electricity suppliers. In addition, the Order makes various amendments to the Electricity Act which are largely to enable payments of fossil fuel levy to be paid to the supply successor companies instead of to public electricity suppliers.

EMPLOYMENT

6459. Contract of employment – compromise agreements – statutory prohibition on contracting out

[Employment Rights Act 1996 (c.18) s.203(1).]

S appealed a finding that a prior agreement with his former employer, NA, precluded pursuit of his claim to the employment tribunal. S had entered into a written agreement with his employer, NA, which provided that he would receive certain compensation "in full and final settlement of any claims [which he might have] arising out of [his] employment or its termination". S subsequently brought a claim against NA alleging, inter alia, unfair dismissal and various breaches of contract. The tribunal gave a preliminary ruling that the agreement which S had entered into prevented it from entertaining his contractual claims. S contended that his statutory and contractual rights could not be severed and, since the agreement had contravened the Employment Rights Act 1996 s.203(1), which prohibited agreements which purported to prevent statutory claims being pursued, the agreement was void in its entirety thereby entitling him to proceed with the contractual claims.

Held, dismissing the appeal, that, properly construed, s.203 provided that agreements were to be avoided only to the extent that they offended its provisions. The inclusion in the section of the words "in so far as" supported such a conclusion. Accordingly, the agreement was void only in so far as it precluded S from pursuing statutory claims. Had Parliament intended that contractual claims be given the protection afforded to statutory claims by s.203, it would have made express statutory provision, both in respect of claims in the employment tribunal and claims in the ordinary civil courts.

SUTHERLAND v. NETWORK APPLIANCE LTD [2001] I.R.L.R. 12, Lindsay, J. (President), EAT.

6460. Contract of employment – implied terms – custom and practice – collective agreement – interpretation

R, joint receivers of M's employer, made M redundant in April 1994. M received a redundancy payment calculated on a statutory basis, and argued that he should have received an enhanced payment based on his actual wage. In 1985, a collective agreement had been entered into whereby where fewer than 15 employees were being made redundant, redundancy payments would be calculated on actual earnings; if there were more than 15, payments would be "negotiated". The agreement was validly incorporated into M's contract of employment. In M's case there were more than 15 redundancies. M argued that (1) on the basis of custom and practice prior to 1985, there was an implied term of contract that redundancy would be calculated on the basis of a basic sum plus an enhanced negotiated payment, and (2) the collective agreement had to be interpreted in light of that custom and practice as allowing negotiation of a figure higher than that provided by the calculation on actual wages, but not lower. R argued that (1) custom and practice prior to 1985 had no contractual status, and (2) the 1985 agreement allowed for negotiation to any figure, but not one lower than the statutory minimum.

Held, rejecting M's claim, that (1) there was no implied term of contract arising from custom and practice. There was no evidence from which to infer that regular payment of an enhancement had been accepted by the management as a contractual obligation, *Quinn v. Calder Industrial Materials Ltd* [1996] I.R.L.R. 126 followed, and (2) prima facie, the natural interpretation of payments relative to 15 or more redundancies being "negotiated" meant negotiation of any figure not falling below the statutory minimum. There was no extrinsic evidence to displace that interpretation.

McGOWAN v. READMAN; *sub nom.* McGOWAN v. JOINT RECEIVERS OF CLYDE SHAW LTD 2000 S.C.L.R. 898, Lord Macfadyen, OH.

6461. Disability discrimination – depression – selection of suitable comparator

[Disability Discrimination Act 1995 (c.50) s.5(1)(a), s.6.]

C, a legal secretary formerly employed by CH, appealed against the dismissal of her complaint of disability discrimination. C, who had been suffering from depression, had been absent from work for one year and CH had given her 12 weeks notice of dismissal. At the hearing before the tribunal, C contended that she had been treated less favourably because of her disability, namely depression, and that CH had failed to take steps to obtain medical advice as to her prognosis. In determining whether C had been treated less favourably by reason of her disability contrary to the Disability Discrimination Act 1995 s.5(1)(a), the tribunal chose to compare CH's treatment of C to the likely treatment of an employee who had been absent from work for the same period.

Held, allowing the appeal in part, that the tribunal had erred in law as it had chosen to compare CH's treatment of C, who had a genuine reason for absence, to the likely treatment of an employee who had been absent for the same period for no good reason. The material reason for C's dismissal was her prolonged absence from work and that reason was related to her depression. CH would not have dismissed some other person to whom the material reason did not apply unless there was some other good reason for the dismissal, *Clark v. TDG Ltd (t/a Novacold Ltd)* [1999] 2 All E.R. 977, [1999] C.L.Y. 2022 applied. Further, the decision to dismiss C could not be justified since CH had failed to comply with its duty under s.6 to consider any adjustments that could have been made to C's working conditions; in fact CH had not considered depression to be a disability within the meaning of the Act. Accordingly, the decision of the tribunal was quashed and a finding that D had been discriminated against was substituted.

COSGROVE v. CAESAR & HOWIE [2001] I.R.L.R. 653, Lindsay, J. (President), EAT.

6462. Disability discrimination – justification – employer unaware of disability at time of dismissal

[Disability Discrimination Act 1995(c.50) s.5, s.6.]

Q appealed against the dismissal of his claim brought under the Disability Discrimination Act 1995 against his employers, S who had dismissed him. Q had been on long term sick leave for almost eight years when he was dismissed in 1998. He was diagnosed as having rheumatoid arthritis, a fact of which S had been unaware. The employment tribunal found that, although Q had been disabled and S had failed to make reasonable adjustments in contravention of s.6, under s.5 the failure to do so had been justified.

Held, allowing the appeal, that the tribunal had erred in considering the defence of justification at all when S's case was that they had no knowledge of Q's disability. Whilst Q was employed S had given no consideration as to what reasonable adjustments could be made, and could not thereafter seek to rely on justification with hindsight. Q had been discriminated against, contrary to s.5(1).

QUINN v. SCHWARZKOPF LTD [2001] I.R.L.R. 67, Lord Johnston, EAT.

6463. **Disability discrimination – justification – material and substantial reasons for discrimination**

[Disability Discrimination Act 1995 (c.50) s.5(3), s.6.]

C appealed against the refusal of his application under the Disability Discrimination Act 1995. C, who suffered from stress and depression, had been dismissed from his employment as a residential childcare worker with GCC following repeated absences from work. The tribunal found that, although C had been discriminated against by reason of his disability, and at the time of dismissal was unfit for work, his dismissal was justified in accordance with s.5(3) of the 1995 Act. C contended that GCC's failure to offer him part time work amounted to a failure to make reasonable adjustments for the purposes of s.6 of the Act.

Held, dismissing the appeal, that reasons for the discriminatory act being justified must be both material and substantial in the circumstances, meaning that there must be a causal connection between the act and the circumstances which was relevant and more than de minimis, *Jones v. Post Office* [2001] EWCA Civ 558, [2001] 5 C.L. 288 applied. GCC's lack of knowledge as to C's disability was not fatal to the issue of justification, *Quinn v. Schwarzkopf Ltd* [2001] I.R.L.R. 67, [2001] 5 C.L. 905 not followed. In the circumstances, given that C was unfit for work at the time of dismissal, the reasons for C's dismissal were material and substantial, therefore the requirements of justification were satisfied. Further, there was no duty on GCC to consider the question of "reasonable adjustment" within the meaning of s.6 of the 1995 Act, namely to offer part time work, in view of C's poor sickness and attendance record and that C had failed to cooperate with GCC's procedures in relation to sickness absence.

CALLAGHAN v. GLASGOW CITY COUNCIL; *sub nom.* CALLAGAN v. GLASGOW CITY COUNCIL [2001] I.R.L.R. 724, Lord Johnston, EAT.

6464. **Education – time off work – training**

RIGHT TO TIME OFF FOR STUDY OR TRAINING (SCOTLAND) AMENDMENT REGULATIONS 2001, SSI 2001 211; made under the Employment Rights Act 1996 s.63A, s.236. In force: September 1, 2001; £1.75.

These Regulations amend the Right to Time Off for Study or Training (Scotland) Regulations 1999 (SI 1999 1058) which set out the standard of achievement and the qualification awarding bodies as prescribed for in the Employment Rights Act 1996. An employee who has not attained the relevant standard of achievement has the right to take time off for study or training leading to a relevant qualification, as awarded or authenticated by the specified qualification awarding bodies. These Regulations amend the 1999 Regulations to reflect qualifications developments and changes in the list of awarding bodies.

6465. **Education – time off work – training**

RIGHT TO TIME OFF FOR STUDY OR TRAINING (SCOTLAND) AMENDMENT (NO.2) REGULATIONS 2001, SSI 2001 298; made under the Employment Rights Act 1996 s.63A, s.236. In force: October 1, 2001; £1.75.

These Regulations amend the Right to Time Off for Study or Training (Scotland) Regulations 1999 (SI 1999 1058) which set out the standard of achievement and the qualification awarding bodies as prescribed for in the Employment Rights Act

1996. They add definitions of the ASVCE, AVCE and Key Skills qualifications, amend the standard of achievement for the Key Skills qualifications, add the standard of achievement for ASVCE and AVCE qualifications, omit the Leather Producing Industry Vocational Qualifications Board from the SVQ list of awarding bodies and adds a further body which may award or authenticate a relevant qualification.

6466. Employment Appeal Tribunal – appeals – faxing documents not considered appropriate service

[Employment Appeal Tribunal Rules 1993 (SI 1993 2854) r.3.]

Z appealed to the Employment Appeal Tribunal, the lodging of which had to be completed by December 27, 1999. Z faxed a completed form of the appeal to the registrar on December 24, but failed to attach the extended reasoning. The registrar's office was subsequently closed until December 29, at which time Z faxed the additional material. Z's appeal was time barred, but an extension of time could still be sought. Z applied and the extension was refused without reasons. Z appealed to the Court of Session for a reduction of that decision.

Held, putting the case out by order to hear further submissions, that the only method of serving a notice or delivering a document to the EAT required under the Employment Tribunal Rules 1993 r.3 was by post or delivery to the registrar. Sending documents by fax would not constitute proper serving.

ZAFAR (RASHID), PETITIONER; *sub nom.* ZAFAR v. GLASGOW CITY COUNCIL 2001 S.C.L.R. 474, Lord McCluskey, OH.

6467. Employment status – employment agencies – casual workers – practical degree of control gave rise to employment relationship

M appealed against a finding that D, who had been employed under a contract for services through MC, an employment agency, was an employee because M, in reality, had sufficient practical control over D to give rise to the requisite employment relationship and that his claim of unfair dismissal should proceed. M contended that reality of control or its exercise was irrelevant and that the tribunal should have looked at the legal right or power to control D, which lay with MC, which was under no legal obligation to M and that MC could at any stage have removed D and assigned him elsewhere.

Held, dismissing the appeal, that the tribunal had been entitled to conclude that the requisite employment relationship existed given the practical degree of control exercised by M over D, and from the fact that M had conducted disciplinary proceedings culminating in D's dismissal without MC's knowledge, *Ready Mixed Concrete (South East) Ltd v. Minister of Pensions and National Insurance* [1968] 2 Q.B. 497, [1968] C.L.Y. 2550 considered and *Serco Ltd v. Blair* (Unreported, August 31, 1998) distinguished. The tribunal had correctly concluded that it was unreal to ignore the existence of the practical degree of control simply because direct control of D lay with MC, which was under a contractual obligation to M.

MOTOROLA LTD v. DAVIDSON [2001] I.R.L.R. 4, Lindsay, J. (President), EAT.

6468. Employment status – locus standi – gymnastics instructor – limited power to use substitute

M worked as a gymnastics instructor at premises owned and operated by GCC. Initially M worked on a casual basis and was paid per session. Subsequently, M began to work a greater number of hours and tax and national insurance were deducted from M's wages by GCC. If, for any reason, M was unable to take a gymnastic class she would appoint a replacement from GCC's approved list of instructors. GCC sought to regularise its relationship with M and provided her with a form of contract. M refused to sign the contract contending that she was an employee of GCC and the effect of the proposed contract would be to render her self employed. M instituted proceedings for unfair dismissal and constructive dismissal. The tribunal at first instance followed the decision in *Express & Echo*

Publications Ltd v. Tanton [1999] I.C.R. 693, [1999] C.L.Y. 2045 and held that M was not an employee since there was no obligation upon M to provide her services personally and that she therefore lacked the locus standi necessary to mount a claim for unfair dismissal. M appealed, contending that the tribunal had erred in its concentration upon the circumstances in which a substitute could take a class for M.

Held, allowing the appeal and remitting the matter for redetermination, that the tribunal had erred in concluding that the consequence of the decision in *Tanton* was that, for an employee relationship to exist, the individual concerned had to provide his services personally at all times. It was recognised that a limited power of delegation was not inconsistent with a contract of service, *Ready Mixed Concrete (South East) Ltd v. Minister of Pensions and National Insurance* [1968] 2 Q.B. 497, [1968] C.L.Y. 2550 considered. Whilst it was not necessarily the case that M fulfilled the criteria for an employee, the case required reconsideration in view of the very different factual situation prevailing compared with the facts in *Tanton*, namely (1) in *Tanton* the individual concerned could nominate anybody as a substitute at any time, whereas M was restricted to nominating substitutes from GCC's approved list and only at times when she was unable to take a class; (2) GCC occasionally organised the substitute, and (3) substitutes were paid direct contrary to the arrangement in *Tanton* where the individual still received payment in respect of all work performed by the replacement, *Tanton* distinguished.

MacFARLANE v. GLASGOW CITY COUNCIL [2001] I.R.L.R. 7, Lindsay, J., EAT.

6469. Employment tribunals – procedure – disclosure of information

EMPLOYMENT TRIBUNALS (CONSTITUTION AND RULES OF PROCEDURE) (SCOTLAND) REGULATIONS 2001, SI 2001 1170 (S.7); made under the Health and Safety at Work etc. Act s10; the Health and Safety at Work etc. Act s.24; the Employment Tribunals Act 1996 s.1, s.4, s.7, s.9, s.10A, s.11, s.12, s.13, s.19, s.41; and the Scotland Act 1998 Sch.6 para.37. In force: April 18, 2001; £7.50.

These Regulations revoke the Employment Tribunals (Constitution and Procedure) (Scotland) Regulations 1993 (SI 1993 2688) as amended by (SI 2000 1988). They contain new provisions setting out how time limits in the Regulations and in documents issued under them are to be calculated, enable the President of the Employment Tribunals (Scotland) and the panel of tribunal chairmen to be persons legally qualified not only in Scotland but in England and Wales or Northern Ireland, provide for the selection of panels of tribunal chairmen and members to hear national security cases, contain rules of procedure which apply to all employment tribunal proceedings in the absence of other provision, increase the maximum amount of costs which a tribunal may award without taxation from £500 to £10,000, provide for the Secretary of the Office of Tribunals to give notice to the Advocate General for Scotland and the Lord Advocate in any proceedings in which a devolution issue arises and provide for the Advocate General for Scotland to appoint a special advocate to represent the applicant's interests in the event of his, or his representative's exclusion.

6470. Employment tribunals – procedure – disclosure of information

EMPLOYMENT TRIBUNALS (CONSTITUTION AND RULES OF PROCEDURE) (SCOTLAND) (AMENDMENT) REGULATIONS 2001, SI 2001 1460 (S.8); made under the Employment Tribunals Act 1996 s.1; the Health and Safety at Work etc. Act 1974 s.4, s.7, s.9, s.10, s.10A, s.11, s.12, s.13, s.19, s.41; and the Scotland Act 1998 Sch.6 para.37. In force: April 16, 2001; £1.50.

These Regulations amend the Employment Tribunals (Constitution and Rules of Procedure) (Scotland) Regulations 2001 (SI 2001 1170) by changing the coming into force date of those Regulations from April 18, 2001 to July 16, 2001.

6471. Minimum wage – deductions – reduction of bonus payments – calculation of minimum wage

[Employment Rights Act 1996 (c.18) s.13(1); National Minimum Wage Act 1998 (c.39) s.1(1).]

L appealed against the finding of an employment tribunal that his employer's decision to increase his basic hourly rate but to reduce his hourly attendance bonus rate by a corresponding amount following the implementation of the National Minimum Wage Act 1998, was neither in breach of s.1(1) of the 1998 Act, nor an unlawful deduction which contravened the Employment Rights Act 1996 s.13(1). L submitted that the reduction of his bonus payment was synonymous with a deduction and that it was not permissible for an employer to unilaterally alter an employee's remuneration package.

Held, allowing the appeal in part and remitting the matter, that the calculation required by s.1(1) of the 1998 Act excluded bonus allowances, but such payments were included when calculating wages for the purposes of s.13 of the 1996 Act. The principle of reducing bonus payments to supplement the rate of pay in the absence of consent could not be distinguished from the act of funding holiday pay from wages and amounted to an unlawful deduction, *Davies v. MJ Wyatt (Decorators) Ltd* [2000] I.R.L.R. 759, [2000] C.L.Y. 2198 followed. However, the issue of consent in the present case could not be determined in respect of the whole period, therefore the case would be remitted for a determination on that issue.

LAIRD v. AK STODDART LTD [2001] I.R.L.R. 591, Lord Johnston, EAT.

6472. Minimum wage – workers – requirement to pay hourly minimum where employee permitted to sleep during shift

[National Minimum Wage Regulations 1999 (SI 1999 584) Reg.15.]

W, a night watchman employed by SC, appealed against the dismissal of his claim under the National Minimum Wage Regulations 1999. Under the terms of his employment, W was required to be present at SC's premises for seven days per week from 5 pm to 7 am. His duties were limited and sleeping facilities were provided. At first instance having regard to Reg.15 the employment tribunal held that W was engaged in "work" for no more than four hours per night and that accordingly his weekly wage of £210 did not fall below the prescribed hourly minimum.

Held, allowing the appeal, that Reg.15(1) was not applicable to W's situation, but was concerned with a specific time allocation for sleeping pursuant to a grant of permission from an employer. In the instant case where the employer required W to be present on the premises for a specific number of hours, the employee was entitled to be paid for all of the hours so specified.

WRIGHT v. SCOTTBRIDGE CONSTRUCTION LTD [2001] I.R.L.R. 589, Lord Johnston, EAT.

6473. Race discrimination – discrimination by employer on basis of national origin – English and Scottish ethnicity

[Race Relations Act 1976 (c.74).]

Between 1995 and 1997, B employed an English journalist, S to present "Rugby Special". S's employment took the form of successive contracts, but was not renewed in 1997. The BBC employed a Scottish woman to take his place and S complained of racial discrimination, maintaining that the major factor in his contract not being renewed was his "national origins". The employment tribunal and Employment Appeal Tribunal considered themselves bound by the decision in *Northern Joint Police Board v. Power* [1997] I.R.L.R. 610, [1998] C.L.Y. 5811. B appealed, arguing that "English" and "Scottish" were not distinct racial groups for the purpose of the Act and as such could not be relied upon by S. B also argued that the phrase "national origins" meant no more than the nationality acquired by S upon his birth.

Held, refusing the appeal, that the employment tribunal and Employment Appeal Tribunal were correct in holding that S could claim racial discrimination on the grounds that he was English under the phrase "national origins", it being much more than "nationality" in the legal sense. There could be racial discrimination within Great Britain on the basis of a person being of Scottish or English national origin, but S could not bring his claim on the basis of his ethnic origins, neither English nor Scottish being an ethnic group in the terms of the Act.

BBC SCOTLAND v. SOUSTER 2001 S.C. 458, Lord Cameron of Lochbroom, Lord Marnoch, Lord Nimmo Smith, Ex Div.

6474. Race discrimination – discrimination by potential employer – tribunal procedure – res judicata and its application

[Race Relations Act 1976 (c.74).]

B, after being refused a position with BA, brought a complaint of race discrimination under the Race Relations Act 1976. B maintained that he had been subject to discrimination as a result of his English "ethnic origins". B's complaint was dismissed on the basis that the English were not an ethnic group within the meaning of the Act. B lodged an identical complaint two years later alleging discrimination on the basis of his "national origins". BA resisted that complaint on the plea of res judicata, but that was rejected by the employment tribunal and the Employment Appeal Tribunal, although both on different grounds. BA appealed arguing that proceedings in employment tribunals were covered by the ruling in *Henderson v. Henderson* [1843-60] All E.R. Rep. 378, and as such, res judicata applied, subject to particular exceptions, to all points upon which the court has formed an opinion and pronounced a judgment and every point which the parties, exercising reasonable diligence might have brought forward at the time. B argued that in Scotland res judicata did not extend as far as the rule in *Henderson* and could not be applied in employment tribunal proceedings.

Held, allowing the appeal and dismissing the application, that the tribunals had erred in their rejection of BA's plea of res judicata. All legal arguments relating to a complaint should be raised in a single application and revised legal thinking, new understanding of the law or a fresh approach to the case could never be relevant to the test of what was res judicata. There was no reason why the principle of res judicata should not in some way be applied to proceedings before employment tribunals in Scotland.

BRITISH AIRWAYS PLC v. BOYCE 2001 S.C. 510, Lord Cameron of Lochbroom, Lord Marnoch, Lord Nimmo Smith, Ex Div.

6475. Sex discrimination – homosexuality – forced resignation of RAF officer – appropriate comparator

[Sex Discrimination Act 1975 (c.65); Human Rights Act 1998 s.3, s.5(3), s.7(1)(b); European Convention on Human Rights 1950 Art.8, Art.14.]

M, a former officer in the RAF, was forced to resign in 1997 following his admission of homosexuality. He brought an action against the RAF to an employment tribunal alleging that he had been discriminated against contrary to the Sex Discrimination Act 1975. In addition, M claimed that his forced resignation had breached his rights under the European Convention on Human Rights 1950 Art.8 and Art.14. The regulations governing homosexuality in the RAF would have required the same forced resignation of a homosexual woman. The employment tribunal, which heard the case before the Human Rights Act 1998 came into force, dismissed the application. M appealed to the employment appeal tribunal which, although making its decision before the 1998 Act came into force, took its provisions into account when determining that the word "sex" in the provisions of the 1975 Act should be interpreted as including sexual orientation. The Advocate General, on behalf of the Ministry of Defence, appealed conceding that M was entitled to compensation for a breach of his Convention rights, but argued that the meaning of sex under the 1975 Act should not be interpreted to include sexual orientation. The Advocate-General submitted that since the 1998 Act had not been in force at the time of the employment tribunal's decision, it would involve inconsistency for an appeal court to apply the s.3 of 1998 Act when interpreting the same provisions on appeal. M argued that even if the meaning of "sex" in the 1975 Act was confined to gender, the s.5(3) of the 1998 Act required the court to compare M's circumstances with those of a woman to determine whether she would have been treated in the same way. M contended that a woman admitting to having a sexual attraction to a man would have been treated differently to the manner in which he had been treated following such an admission.

Held, allowing the appeal, that (1) it was competent for a court to consider the compatibility of primary or secondary legislation with the European Convention on Human Rights 1950 under s.3 of the 1998 Act despite on appeal s.3 not being in force when the case had been heard before lower courts or tribunals even where the application of s.3 would lead to an alternative interpretation; (2) the 1975 Act intended the word sex to mean gender and the application of s.3 of the 1998 Act could not extend that interpretation to incorporate sexual orientation, *Smith v. Gardner Merchant Ltd* [1998] 3 All E.R. 852, [1998] C.L.Y. 2197 followed, and (3) (Lord Prosser dissenting) the appropriate comparator under s.5(3) of the 1975 Act was the treatment by the RAF of a homosexual woman. Per Lord Prosser, an appeal against a decision of a court or tribunal, when appealed by a public authority, could be deemed as an action at the instigation of a public authority under the 1998 Act thereby allowing the retrospective effect of s.7(1)(b) of the 1998 Act to take effect. Per Lord Prosser (dissenting), the correct comparator under s.5(3) of the 1975 Act for a man wanting a relationship with a man was a woman wanting a relationship with a man.

Observed, per Lord Kirkwood, that if the meaning of sex under the 1975 Act had included sexual orientation, the appropriate comparator would have been a heterosexual woman.

ADVOCATE GENERAL FOR SCOTLAND v. MacDONALD; *sub nom.* SECRETARY OF STATE FOR DEFENCE v. MacDONALD; MacDONALD v. MINISTRY OF DEFENCE 2002 S.C. 1, Lord Prosser, Lord Caplan, Lord Kirkwood, Ex Div.

6476. Transfer of undertakings – failure to consult – liability to pay compensation

[Transfer of Undertakings (Protection of Employment) Regulations 1981 (SI 1981 1794) Reg.5(2)(a), Reg.5(2)(b), Reg.10, Reg.11.]

TGWU, representing a number of employees of M, appealed against a decision that on M's transfer of its business to JM and B, and its subsequent failure to comply with the Transfer of Undertakings (Protection of Employment) Regulations 1981 Reg.10 with regard to consultation, the liability to pay compensation under Reg.11 for the failure to consult, did not transfer to JM and B. TGWU submitted that the liability to pay compensation under Reg.11 was controlled by Reg.5(2)(a) or (b) thereby passing the liability to JM and B as the relevant transferees.

Held, dismissing the appeal, that having regard to the need to maintain an incentive on the part of a transferor to comply with his obligations under the transfer process, the liability to pay compensation under Reg.11 for the failure of M to comply with Reg.10 did not transfer to the transferees, *Kerry Foods Ltd v. Creber* [2000] I.C.R. 556, [2000] C.L.Y. 2223 considered.

TRANSPORT & GENERAL WORKERS UNION v. McKINNON; TRANSPORT & GENERAL WORKERS UNION v. JR (HAULAGE) LTD [2001] I.C.R. 1281, Lord Johnston, EAT.

6477. Unfair dismissal – disclosure – protection for disclosure predating Public Interest Disclosure Act 1998

[Employment Rights Act 1996 (c.18) s.47B, s.103A; Public Interest Disclosure Act 1998 (c.23).]

M appealed against the dismissal of his claim for unfair dismissal. M had been dismissed by S in 1993 after he made a disclosure to the Inland Revenue that was detrimental to S. He subsequently became an employee of S again in 1999 following a transfer of undertakings, and in 2000 S dismissed him, allegedly on the ground of redundancy. M brought his claim arguing that the dismissal had been due to his disclosure, which following the introduction of the Public Interest Disclosure Act 1998 was protected under the Employment Rights Act 1996 s.47B and s.103A. The employment tribunal found that it had no jurisdiction to consider the claim as the disclosure had been made before the coming into force of the 1998 Act, which was not retrospective. On appeal, M argued that the actual date of the disclosure was irrelevant.

Held, allowing the appeal and remitting the case, that the dismissal was the relevant event and that had occurred after the coming into force of the 1998 Act which had inserted the relevant sections into the 1996 Act. The circumstances were analogous to claims of race and sex discrimination where the gender or ethnic status of the individual were established at birth and only the discriminatory conduct had to post date the relevant legislation. The dismissal had activated the right to protection of the disclosure and accordingly the issue of whether the 1998 Act had any retrospective effect was irrelevant.

MIKLASZEWICZ v. STOLT OFFSHORE LTD; *sub nom.* STOLT OFFSHORE LTD v. MIKLASZEWICZ; STOLT OFFSHORE v. MIKLASEWICZ [2001] I.R.L.R. 656, Lord Johnston, EAT.

6478. Wages – holidays – declaration of additional bank holiday – entitlement to additional day's wages

An employer, C, appealed against a decision that its failure to pay one day's wages to take account of the millennium holiday on December 31, 1999 amounted to an illegal deduction of wages. The contractual arrangements between C and its employees provided that employees were entitled to paid holiday for that day. C submitted that the declaration by the government of an extra bank holiday did not affect C which was a construction company and that in the absence of any contractual obligation to pay employees for any additional bank holidays declared, C was not required to pay additional wages for the millennium holiday.

Held, allowing the appeal, that, in the absence of a contractual provision covering variations to holiday entitlement to reflect additional matters, the declaration of the bank holiday did not create an additional entitlement to paid holiday. As the employees had actually been paid for the day in question there had been no unlawful deduction of wages by C.

CAMPBELL & SMITH CONSTRUCTION GROUP LTD v. GREENWOOD [2001] I.R.L.R. 588, Lord Johnston, EAT.

6479. Books

Craig, Victor; Miller, Kenneth – Employment Law: a Student Guide. Paperback: £23.95. ISBN 0-414-01450-2. W.Green & Son.

ENVIRONMENT

6480. Air pollution – air quality reviews

AIR QUALITY LIMIT VALUES (SCOTLAND) REGULATIONS 2001, SSI 2001 224; made under the European Communities Act 1972 s.2. In force: July 19, 2001; £3.50.

These Regulations, which amend the Air Quality Standards Regulations 1989 (SI 1989 317) are made in the implementation in Scotland of Council Directive 96/62 ([1996] OJ L296/55) on ambient air quality assessment and management, and Council Directive 99/30 ([1999] OJ L163/41) relating to limit values for sulphur dioxide, nitrogen dioxide and oxides of nitrogen, particulate matter and lead in ambient air. They require the Scottish Ministers to take the measures necessary to ensure that in each zone in Scotland concentrations of relevant pollutants do not exceed limit values; ensure that ambient air is assessed for each zone; classify each zone in relation to each of the relevant pollutants; review the classification of zones every five years or in the event of significant changes affecting levels of any of the relevant pollutants; ensure that specified methods are used for assessing air quality for each pollutant in each zone; draw up lists of zones where the levels of one or more of the relevant pollutants are above the limit value, or between the limit value and any specified margin of tolerance; list zones where levels of the relevant pollutants are below limit values; and ensure that up-to-date information on ambient concentrations of each of the relevant pollutants is routinely made available to the public. The Regulations provide for the determination of upper and lower assessment thresholds for each relevant pollutant and set out the requirements for measurement or other assessment of air quality depending on pollution levels in relation to these thresholds.

6481. Conservation – birds – protected species

WILDLIFE AND COUNTRYSIDE ACT 1981 (AMENDMENT) (SCOTLAND) REGULATIONS 2001, SSI 2001 337; made under the European Communities Act 1972 s.2. In force: November 4, 2001; £1.50.

These Regulations amend the Wildlife and Countryside Act 1981 by removing the capercaillie from the list of species which may be hunted in Scotland and placing it in Part I of Schedule 1 to the 1981 Act which provides greater legal protection to the species by making offences involving the bird punishable by special penalties.

6482. Energy conservation – grants

HOME ENERGY EFFICIENCY SCHEME AMENDMENT (SCOTLAND) REGULATIONS 2001, SSI 2001 267; made under the Social Security Act 1990 s.15. In force: August 10, 2001; £1.75.

These Regulations make amendments to the Home Energy Efficiency Scheme Regulations 1997 (SI 1997 790), which provide for the making of grants for the improvement of energy efficiency in dwellings occupied by persons on low income or elderly persons, to provide for a central heating programme under which grant may be paid to elderly persons.

6483. Environmental protection – genetically modified organisms

ENVIRONMENTAL PROTECTION ACT 1990 (AMENDMENT) (SCOTLAND) REGULATIONS 2001, SSI 2001 99; made under the European Communities Act 1972 s.2. In force: April 5, 2001; £1.50.

These Regulations amend the Environmental Protection Act 1990 s.113, which confers power to make and from time to time revise a scheme of fees payable in respect of applications for consents under Part VI of the 1990 Act and charges in respect of the subsistence of such consents, to provide that in making a scheme under that section Scottish Ministers may, with the consent of the Secretary of State, provide for any functions under the scheme to be performed by a Minister of the Crown or government department where Scottish Ministers consider it expedient to do so in relation to the implementation of Council Directive 90/220 ([1990] OJ L117/15) on the deliberate release into the environment of genetically modified organisms.

6484. Environmentally sensitive areas – designation – Argyll Islands

ENVIRONMENTALLY SENSITIVE AREAS (ARGYLL ISLANDS) DESIGNATION AMENDMENT ORDER 2001, SSI 2001 27; made under the Agriculture Act 1986 s.18. In force: March 8, 2001; £1.75.

This Order amends the Environmentally Sensitive Areas (Argyll Islands) Designation Order 1993 (SI 1993 3136) by allowing the creation of additional areas providing early and late cover for birds. It also allows for the creation and restoration of dykes.

6485. Environmentally sensitive areas – designation – Breadalbane

ENVIRONMENTALLY SENSITIVE AREAS (BREADALBANE) DESIGNATION AMENDMENT ORDER 2001, SSI 2001 30; made under the Agriculture Act 1986 s.18. In force: March 8, 2001; £1.75.

This Order, which amends the Environmentally Sensitive Areas (Breadalbane) Designation Order 1992 (SI 1992 1920), increases the ceiling on payments made to persons in respect of each five year conservation plan contained in an agreement from £25,000 to £30,000 and by allowing for the creation and restoration of dykes, hedges, stone fanks and ponds.

6486. Environmentally sensitive areas – designation – Cairngorms Straths

ENVIRONMENTALLY SENSITIVE AREAS (CAIRNGORMS STRATHS) DESIGNATION AMENDMENT ORDER 2001, SSI 2001 33; made under the Agriculture Act 1986 s.18. In force: March 8, 2001; £1.50.

This Order amends the Environmentally Sensitive Areas (Cairngorms Straths) Designation Order 1993 (SI 1993 2345) by allowing the farmer to take measures to create dykes and ponds.

6487. Environmentally sensitive areas – designation – Central Borders

ENVIRONMENTALLY SENSITIVE AREAS (CENTRAL BORDERS) DESIGNATION AMENDMENT ORDER 2001, SSI 2001 25; made under the Agriculture Act 1986 s.18. In force: March 8, 2001; £1.75.

This Order, which amends the Environmentally Sensitive Areas (Central Borders) Designation Order 1993 (SI 1993 2767), increases the ceiling for operations other than specially identified wetlands from £25,000 to £30,000 and allows the farmer to take measures to create and restore dykes, hedges, ponds, stone fanks, hedges, hedgerow and trees.

6488. Environmentally sensitive areas – designation – Central Southern Uplands

ENVIRONMENTALLY SENSITIVE AREAS (CENTRAL SOUTHERN UPLANDS) DESIGNATION AMENDMENT ORDER 2001, SSI 2001 32; made under the Agriculture Act 1986 s.18. In force: March 8, 2001; £1.50.

This Order amends the Environmentally Sensitive Areas (Central Southern Uplands) Designation Order 1993 (SI 1993 996) by allowing the farmer to take measures to create or restore dykes and hedges.

6489. Environmentally sensitive areas – designation – Loch Lomond

ENVIRONMENTALLY SENSITIVE AREAS (LOCH LOMOND) DESIGNATION AMENDMENT ORDER 2001, SSI 2001 34; made under the Agriculture Act 1986 s.18. In force: March 8, 2001; £1.75.

This Order, which amends the Environmentally Sensitive Areas (Loch Lomond) Designation Order 1992 (SI 1992 1919), increases the ceiling on payments made to persons from £25,000 to £30,000 in respect of each five year conservation plan contained in an agreement and by allowing the farmer to take measures for the creation of hedges and ponds and to conserve, enhance or extend water margins.

6490. Environmentally sensitive areas – designation – Machair of the Uists and Benbecula, Barra and Vatersay

ENVIRONMENTALLY SENSITIVE AREAS (MACHAIR OF THE UISTS AND BENBECULA, BARRA AND VATERSAY) DESIGNATION AMENDMENT ORDER 2001, SSI 2001 28; made under the Agriculture Act 1986 s.18. In force: March 8, 2001; £1.75.

This Order amends the Environmentally Sensitive Areas (Machair of the Uists and Benbecula, Barra and Vatersay) Designation Order 1993 (SI 1993 3149) by increasing the ceiling for farmer and crofters within the meaning of the 1993 Order to £30,000 and the ceiling for common grazing committees within the meaning of the 1993 Order to £75,000. It also allows the creation of additional areas of early and late cover for birds and makes minor amendments relating to the measures in the principal Order relating to the creation, as well as restoration of dykes.

6491. Environmentally sensitive areas – designation – Shetland Islands

ENVIRONMENTALLY SENSITIVE AREAS (SHETLAND ISLANDS) DESIGNATION AMENDMENT ORDER 2001, SSI 2001 29; made under the Agriculture Act 1986 s.18. In force: March 8, 2001; £1.75.

This Order amends the Environmentally Sensitive Areas (Shetland Islands) Designation Order 1993 (SI 1993 3150) by introducing a ceiling for payments for stock reduction of £52,500 and increasing the ceiling for payments for operations from £20,000 to £30,000. It also introduces a ceiling of £52,500 for payments for stock reductions made to common grazings committees and allows the inclusion of measures to restore or create dykes with respect to agreements with farmers or crofters and common grazings committees and for the creation of additional areas of early and late cover for birds.

6492. Environmentally sensitive areas – designation – Stewartry

ENVIRONMENTALLY SENSITIVE AREAS (STEWARTRY) DESIGNATION AMENDMENT ORDER 2001, SSI 2001 26; made under the Agriculture Act 1986 s.18. In force: March 8, 2001; £1.50.

This Order amends the Environmentally Sensitive Areas (Stewartry) Designation Order 1993 (SI 1993 2768) by allowing the farmer within the meaning of that Order to take measures to create as well as restore existing dykes, hedges and ponds.

6493. Environmentally sensitive areas – designation – Western Southern Uplands

ENVIRONMENTALLY SENSITIVE AREAS (WESTERN SOUTHERN UPLANDS) DESIGNATION AMENDMENT ORDER 2001, SSI 2001 31; made under the Agriculture Act 1986 s.18. In force: March 8, 2001; £1.50.

This Order amends the Environmentally Sensitive Areas (Western Southern Uplands) Designation Order 1993 (SI 1993 997) by allowing the farmer to take measures to create and restore dykes, hedges, stone buchts and fanks.

6494. Oil pollution – claims against limitation fund – amendment of claim

See PRESCRIPTION: Assuranceforeningen Skuld v. International Oil Pollution Compensation Fund (No.2). §6869

6495. Pollution control – water pollution – fuel

CONTROL OF POLLUTION (SILAGE, SLURRY AND AGRICULTURAL FUEL OIL) (SCOTLAND) AMENDMENT REGULATIONS 2001, SSI 2001 248; made under the Control of Pollution Act 1974 s.31A, s.104, s.105. In force: July 1, 2001; £1.50.

These Regulations amend the Control of Pollution (Silage, Slurry and Agricultural Fuel Oil) (Scotland) Regulations 2001 (SSI 2001 206) by correcting a numerical reference to the Control of Pollution (Silage, Slurry and Agricultural Fuel Oil) (Scotland) Regulations 1991 (SI 1991 346) Reg.9.

6496. Pollution control – water pollution – fuel

CONTROL OF POLLUTION (SILAGE, SLURRY AND AGRICULTURAL FUEL OIL) (SCOTLAND) REGULATIONS 2001, SSI 2001 206; made under the Control of Pollution Act 1974 s.31A, s.104, s.105. In force: July 1, 2001; £2.50.

These Regulations re-enact, with changes the Control of Pollution (Silage, Slurry and Agricultural Fuel Oil) (Scotland) Regulations 1991 (SI 1991 346), which require persons with custody or control of a crop being made into silage, of livestock slurry or of certain fuel oil to carry out works and take precautions and other steps for preventing pollution of inland or coastal waters. The principal changes are to clarify the meaning of the term "silage"; to make provision to ensure that places where silage is proposed to be stored are at least 10 metres from inland or coastal waters; to allow persons making bulk bagged silage on farms to do so without restrictions where bags in which that silage is kept incorporate a facility which allows for the safe removal of excess effluent; to remove the 30 days notice provision in the 1991 Regulations where bulk bagged silage is made in an acceptable manner since that provision is now considered to be unnecessary; to allow for substantial reconstruction of an exempt structure with the agreement of SEPA, where the risk of pollution will be reduced; to extend the powers available to SEPA to serve notices in respect of all structures used for purposes covered by the 1991 Regulations rather than being restricted to exempt structures where there is a significant risk of pollution identified; and to allow SEPA in cases where a notice requiring works is necessary to require the drawing up and implementation of a Farm Waste Management Plan in accordance with methods identified for the collection, storage and land application of slurry and manure contained within the Code of Good Practice for the Prevention of Environmental Pollution From Agricultural Activity.

6497. Smoke control – authorisation of fuel

SMOKE CONTROL AREAS (AUTHORISED FUELS) (SCOTLAND) REGULATIONS 2001, SSI 2001 433; made under the Clean Air Act 1993 s.20, s.63. In force: December 17, 2001; £2.50.

These Regulations, which extend to Scotland only, provide that Bord na Mona Firelogs, Bord na Mona Firepak, Bryant and May Firelogs and Charglow briquettes are authorised fuels for the purposes of the Clean Air Act 1993 s.20 which provides that where smoke is emitted from a chimney in a smoke control area and that chimney is either a chimney of a building or a chimney serving the furnace of a fixed boiler or industrial plant, the occupier of the building, or the person having possession of the boiler or plant, is guilty of an offence. It is a defence to show that the alleged emission was caused solely by the use of an authorised fuel. They also consolidate the nine sets of regulations which have previously declared fuels to be authorised fuels for the purposes of the Clean Air Act 1993. The Smoke Control Areas (Authorised Fuels) Regulations 1991 (SI 1991 1282 as amended by SI 1992 72, SI 1992 3148, SI 1993 2499, SI 1996 1145, SI 1997 2658, SI 1998 2154, SI 1998 3096, and SSI 2001 129) are revoked in relation to Scotland.

6498. Smoke control – exempt fireplaces

SMOKE CONTROL AREAS (EXEMPT FIREPLACES) (SCOTLAND) ORDER 2001, SSI 2001 16; made under the Clean Air Act 1993 s.21. In force: February 16, 2001; £1.75.

This Order exempts certain classes of fireplace from the provisions of the Clean Air Act 1993 s.20, subject to specified conditions.

6499. Water pollution – codes of practice

WATER (PREVENTION OF POLLUTION) (CODE OF PRACTICE) (SCOTLAND) AMENDMENT ORDER 2001, SSI 2001 175; made under the Control of Pollution Act 1974 s.51. In force: June 1, 2001; £1.75.

This Order, which amends the Water (Prevention of Pollution) (Code of Practice) (Scotland) Order 1997 (SI 1997 1584), approves the Nitrogen and Phosphorus Supplement to the Code of Good Practice for the Prevention of Environmental Pollution from Agricultural Activity which is to be issued by the Scottish Ministers on June 1, 2001 in so far as it relates to pollution of water.

ENVIRONMENTAL HEALTH

6500. Burials and cremation – disinterment – title to sue

P was holder of a lair certificate issued in 1961 by the Cemetery Board of the Roman Catholic Diocese of Motherwell which granted him exclusive right of burial in the lair for a period of 60 years from the date of issue of the certificate. Responsibility of the management of the cemetery passed to North Lanarkshire Council who authorised two burials in the lair without reference to P as lair holder. P petitioned the court to compel the council to disinter the remains from the unauthorised burials and to re-inter them in accordance with their relatives' wishes. The council and relatives of one of the deceased answered the petition and argued that P, not being a relative of the deceased or the manager of the cemetery, had no title to sue. The matter went to debate.

Held, repelling the pleas of no title to sue and putting the case out by order for discussion of further procedure, that (1) title to sue did not depend on P being a relative or the manager of the cemetery and nor did it depend on P having a special relationship with the deceased; (2) there was no basis in authority for a definitive list of persons entitled to raise an action for disinterment, *Commonwealth War Graves Commission, Petitioners* (Unreported, May 6, 1961) and *Kilpatrick, Petitioner* (Unreported), applied, *Black v. McCallum* (1924) 40 Sh. Ct. Rep. 108, disapproved, and (3) P's title to sue was based on the council's alleged infringement of his contractual rights under the granting of the lair certificate.

PATERSON, PETITIONER 2001 S.L.T. 869, Lord Penrose, OH.

EUROPEAN UNION

6501. European Court of Justice – reference to – failure properly to implement Directive

[Diseases of Fish (Control) Regulations 1994 (SI 1994 1447) Reg.7; European Convention on Human Rights 1950 Protocol 1; Council Directive 93/53 introducing minimum Community measures for the control of certain fish diseases Art.9.]

S served a notice on B's predecessors under the Diseases of Fish (Control) Regulations 1994 Reg. 7 requiring the destruction of the fish on a fish farm. S rejected a claim for compensation for the fish which had been destroyed and B sought judicial review of that decision and of the 1994 Regulations. The Lord

Ordinary pronounced declarator that S had acted illegally in failing to provide legislative or administrative measures for the payment of compensation. S reclaimed and B argued that (1) the 1994 Regulations amounted to a measure which the UK had adopted but which went further than the minimum required by Council Directive 93/53 introducing minimum Community measures for the control of certain fish diseases Art.9; (2) the absence of any possibility of the owner recovering compensation meant that Reg.7 was in breach of the right to property as enshrined in the European Convention on Human Rights 1950 Protocol 1 as that right was understood in EC law, and (3) the question of S's duty to provide for compensation fell to be answered by reference to EC law and in particular to the fundamental right to property which it recognised.

Held, making a reference to the ECJ, after considering a range of authorities, that (1) the interpretation of Art.9 was difficult, but given B's pursuit of the right to property argument it was unnecessary to deal with Art.9 more fully. In implementing the 1993 Directive the UK had been subject to the general principles of EC law, including the fundamental rights enshrined therein; (2) the availability of compensation was relevant to any consideration of whether the fundamental right to property had been respected. The right fell to be taken into account by Member States when implementing a directive; (3) the fundamental question was whether the 1994 Regulations and the matter of compensation were governed by EC or national law, and that fundamental question was a matter of EC law and a reference to the ECJ was required; it was expected that the ECJ would provide criteria to allow determination at national level whether the 1994 Regulations were compatible with EC law. The matter was put out to a by order hearing at which it was held that the reference would include a question specifically dealing with the criteria to be applied by the national courts if it were held that Community law governed the issue, the parties having requested that so as to leave nothing to chance, although the court saw no real need because in previous cases the ECJ had made it clear that they would give such criteria as a matter of course.

BOOKER AQUACULTURE LTD (T/A MARINE HARVEST McCONNELL) v. SECRETARY OF STATE FOR SCOTLAND (REFERENCE TO ECJ) [2000] Eu. L.R. 449, Lord Rodger, L.P., Lord McCluskey, Lord Sutherland, 1 Div.

FAMILY LAW

6502. Adoption – intercountry adoption – rules

ADOPTION OF CHILDREN FROM OVERSEAS (SCOTLAND) REGULATIONS 2001, SSI 2001 236; made under the Adoption (Scotland) Act 1978 s.9, s.50A. In force: July 2, 2001; £1.75.

These Regulations impose requirements with which a person who is habitually resident in the British Islands must comply before and after bringing a child who is habitually resident outside those Islands into the UK for the purpose of adoption. The prospective adopter is required to undergo assessment by an adoption agency, be approved as suitable to be an adoptive parent and have received notification from the Secretary of State that he is willing to issue a certificate confirming that the prospective adopter has been assessed and approved and that the child will be authorised to reside permanently in the British Islands if entry clearance is granted and an adoption order is made. In addition, the Regulations specify the procedure to be followed by an adoption agency and adoption panel in relation to assessment and approval of a person wishing to adopt a child from overseas, and require the provision of certain information to the Scottish Ministers.

6503. Adoption (Intercountry Aspects) Act 1999 (c.18) – Commencement No.6 Order

ADOPTION (INTERCOUNTRY ASPECTS) ACT 1999 (COMMENCEMENT NO.6) ORDER 2001, SSI 2001 235 (C.11); made under the Adoption (Intercountry

Aspects) Act 1999 s.18. Commencement details: bringing into force various provisions of the Act on July 2, 2001; £1.50.

This Order brings into force the Adoption (Intercountry Aspects) Act 1999 s.9, which inserts a new subsection into the Adoption (Scotland) Act 1978 which provides that references to adoption in Part I of that Act are to the adoption of children, wherever they may be habitually resident, whether effected within or outside the British Islands, and s.14, which inserts a new section into the 1978 Act which provides that a person habitually resident in the British Islands is guilty of an offence if he brings a child who is habitually resident elsewhere into the UK for the purposes of adoption, without complying with such requirements as may be prescribed by the Scottish Ministers, on July 2, 2001.

6504. Children – childminders – registration – fees

CHILD MINDING AND DAY CARE (REGISTRATION AND INSPECTION FEES) AMENDMENT (SCOTLAND) REGULATIONS 2001, SSI 2001 214; made under the Children Act 1989 s.71, s.104, Sch.9 para.1, Sch.9 para.7. In force: August 1, 2001; £1.75.

These Regulations, which amend the Child Minding and Day Care (Registration and Inspection Fees) Regulations 1991 (SI 1991 2076) and revoke the Child Minding and Day Care (Registration and Inspection of Fees) (Amendment) Regulations 1996 (SI 1996 3180), increase the registration fees for providers of full day care on non-domestic premises from £110 to £121 and for providers of sessional day care and child minders from £12.50 to £14.00. Annual inspection fees for such providers are increased from £85 to £94 and from £10 to £11 respectively.

6505. Children – childrens hearings – appeals – computation of time – decision date not included in computation

[Children (Scotland) Act 1995 (c.36) s.51 (1).]

A decision to vary a supervision requirement was made at a children's hearing on January 19, 2001. Under the Children (Scotland) Act 1995 s.51 (1) an appeal must be lodged within three weeks of the decision. The child's parents lodged an appeal on February 9, but that was challenged as incompetent by the reporter who argued it had been lodged late, the three week period having lapsed on February 8.

Held, finding the appeal competent but refusing it for reasons given verbally, that an interpretation of the three week period that did not include the decision day was in line with the general rule of computation of time. There was no compelling reason as to why the day of the decision should be included in the period and any distinction between "beginning with", as used in s.51 (1), and "from" should be rejected as too subtle.

J v. CALDWELL 2001 S.L.T. (Sh Ct) 164, Sheriff KA Ross, Sh Ct (South Strathclyde, Dumfries and Galloway).

6506. Children – childrens hearings – grounds for referral – offence committed by child – compatibility of proceedings with Human Rights Convention

[Scotland Act 1998 (c.42) Sch.6; Children (Scotland) Act 1995 (c.36) s.52 (2) (i); Act of Sederunt (Rules of the Court of Session 1994) 1994 (SI 1994 1443) r.82.3; Human Rights 1998 (c.42) Sch.1 Part I Art.5, Art.6.]

A child (S), aged 15, was alleged to have been involved in an assault along with his father, which resulted in the serious injury of an individual and the death of S's father. The procurator fiscal advised the reporter to the children's panel that criminal charges would not be brought against S. A children's hearing was arranged to consider grounds for referral in terms of the Children Scotland Act 1995 s.52 (2) (i), that S had committed an offence. The grounds not having been accepted by S or his mother, the case was referred to the sheriff. Before the sheriff, S lodged a minute contending that his rights in terms of the Human Rights Act 1998 Sch.1 Part I Art.5 and Art.6 were being infringed and that a devolution issue arose from the failure of the Scottish Ministers to take action to remedy structural deficiencies in the children's hearing system. The sheriff remitted the case to the Court of Session in terms of the Scotland Act 1998 Sch.6. and para.7. The minute was answered by the Principal Reporter and the Lord Advocate. The Lord Advocate, on his own behalf and on behalf of the Scottish Ministers, accepted that Art.6 applied to the children's hearing as it was determining S's civil rights and obligations. S argued inter alia that (1) in respect of the ground for referral the hearing was determining a criminal charge against S, thus the specific guarantees of Art.6(3) applied, and the proceedings themselves, without any appeal to the sheriff, required to meet the requirements of Art.6; (2) the structure of the hearing system infringed the right to an "independent and impartial tribunal", since children's panel members could be removed from office by the Scottish Ministers at any time; (3) the absence of provision requiring the reporter to provide S with copies of reports and documents furnished for the use of the hearing was incompatible with Art.6(1), and (4) the non-availability of legal aid for proceedings before a children's hearing breached Art.6.

Held, declaring that notice was to be given to the Advocate General prior to consideration of a declaration of incompatibility, but only as respects the legal aid question, and thereafter the case was to be put out by order, that (1) a child who was notified of grounds for referral under s.52(2)(i) of the 1995 Act, setting out the offence in question, was not thereby "charged with a criminal offence" in terms of Art.6, given the absence of any penal sanction. Since the proceedings were not criminal, the specific guarantees in Art.6(2) and (3) did not apply; however, it was trite that the specific guarantees in Art.6(3) related to aspects of a fair trial which were also embraced by the lex generalis in Art.6(1), which did apply, the extent of such application requiring consideration of the nature of the proceedings and the balancing of the general interest of the community and the personal rights of the children and others involved in the hearing; (2) children's hearings constituted an independent tribunal in terms of Art.6(1). The mere fact that members of that body did not enjoy the kind of tenure which the Convention required in a court of law of the classic kind, did not in itself show that the body concerned was not an independent tribunal for the purposes of Art.6; (3) the children's hearing system was not incompatible with Art.6(1) given the Principal Reporter's change of policy and decision to issue guidance to all reporters that, in future, reports and other papers provided to chairmen and members of the hearing would also be provided to the child, with certain exceptions, and (4) under Art.6, where deprivation of liberty was at stake, in principle the interests of justice called for legal representation and might require that a child be given free legal representation, the key consideration being whether the person involved in the litigation could effectively conduct his or her own case; the lack of free legal representation could significantly impair S's ability to affect the outcome of the hearing.

S v. MILLER (NO.1); *sub nom.* S v. PRINCIPAL REPORTER 2001 S.C. 977, Lord Rodger L.P., Lord Macfadyen, Lord Penrose, 1 Div.

6507. **Children – childrens hearings – grounds for referral – offence committed by child – non-availability of legal aid – compatibility with right to a fair hearing under the European Convention**

[Legal Aid (Scotland) Act 1986 (c.47) s.29; Human Rights Act 1998 (c.42) s.4(2), Sch.1 Part I Art.6.]

The court having reserved its opinion in (S v. Miller (No.1) 2001 S.L.T. 531) on whether or not the children's hearing system complied with the Human Rights Act 1998 Sch.1 Part I Art. 6 when legal aid in the form of legal representation could not be made available to a child, as the court was contemplating making a declaration of incompatibility under the Human Rights Act1998 s.4(2) in respect of the Legal Aid (Scotland) Act1986 s.29, the Advocate General indicated that she did not intend to enter the process. At the by order hearing all parties indicated their acceptance that the Scottish Ministers had power under the legislation in force to make regulations providing for representation before a children's hearing, although it had not been exercised, and no question of a declaration of incompatibility arose. The court then answered the question relating to the hearing system.

Held, that in all matters except legal aid the structure of the children's hearing system complied with the requirements of Art.6 in its application to civil proceedings; it did not comply when legal aid, in a form which allowed legal representation, could not be made available to a child, where the child was unable to represent himself properly and satisfactorily at the hearing.

S v. MILLER (NO.2); *sub nom.* S v. PRINCIPAL REPORTER 2001 S.L.T. 1304, Lord Rodger L.P., Lord Macfadyen, Lord Penrose, 1 Div.

6508. Children – childrens hearings – legal representation

CHILDREN'S HEARINGS (LEGAL REPRESENTATION) (SCOTLAND) RULES 2001, SSI 2001 478; made under the Children (Scotland) Act 1995 s.42, s.64. In force: February 23, 2002; £1.75.

These Rules, which permit legal representatives to attend children's hearings, specify when the business meeting and the children's hearing may consider the appointment of a legal representative, and the circumstances in which an appointment may be made. They authorise the Principal Reporter to make copies of the relevant documentation available to legal representatives and specify groups of persons from whom a legal representative may be appointed.

6509. Children – childrens hearings – panels – curators ad litem and reporting officers

CURATORS AD LITEM AND REPORTING OFFICERS (PANELS) (SCOTLAND) REGULATIONS 2001, SSI 2001 477; made under the Children (Scotland) Act 1995 s.101, s.103. In force: January 23, 2002; £1.75.

These Regulations, which revoke the Curators ad Litem and Reporting Officers (Panels) (Scotland) Regulations 1984 (SI 1984 566) and the Curators ad Litem and Reporting Officers (Panels) (Scotland) Amendment Regulations 1985 (SI 1985 1556), make provision for the establishment in the area of each local authority of panels of persons to act as curators ad litem and reporting officers. They provide that the local authority may establish more than one panel in its area, empower the local authority to consult with the Sheriff Principal as to the standard of qualification or experience which should be attained by persons nominated to serve on any panel and set out the procedure to be followed by the local authority in seeking nominations and making appointments to panels to be established in its area.

6510. Children – parental contact – presumption in favour of contact between child and parent – welfare principle in conformity with right to family life

[Children (Scotland) Act 1995 (c.36) s.1, s.11 (7) (a); Human Rights Act 1998 (c.42) Sch.1 Part I Art.8.]

F and M divorced in 1997 with residence relating to their children being awarded to M. At that time no order in respect of contact was requested or made. In 1998, F minuted for a variation to allow direct contact with the children on a regular basis. The eldest child, then 13 years old, expressed a desire not to have contact with F and with the agreement of F, the action was dismissed in respect of that child. F opposed the minute, but after a proof, the sheriff found in favour of F and varied the 1997 interlocutor to allow direct contact at fixed times between F and the younger child. The sheriff, in reaching his decision applied the general principle contained in the Children (Scotland) Act 1995 s.1 that it was the responsibility of an absent parent to maintain personal relations and direct contact with his/her child subject to s.11 (7) (a) which required the court to have regard to what was in the best interests of the child. No evidence had been led that F had ever acted in any way that could be construed as harmful to the child, indeed he had made considerable efforts to maintain contact with her. There had been evidence that the child suffered asthma attacks linked to the proceedings and that these were likely to worsen if contact resumed. It was, however, felt that they would subside once the child became more familiar with F. M successfully appealed to the sheriff principal who found that F had not discharged the onus upon him to prove that contact was in the best interests of the child. F appealed arguing that under the Human Rights Act 1998 Sch.1 Part I Art.8, a parent always had a right of access to his/her child unless it could be proved that it was not in the child's best interests. M argued that the sheriff had erred in applying a presumption in favour of contact, that an onus rested on the parent applying for contact and that if the appeal was going to be allowed, the court should intimate that to the child and afford the opportunity to be heard on the matter.

Held, allowing the appeal and restoring the order of the sheriff, that (1) in applying the general principle set out in s.1 and in *Sanderson v. McManus* 1997 S.C. (H.L.) 55, [1997] C.L.Y. 5631, that it was conducive to a child's welfare to maintain personal relations and direct contact with an absent parent, the court had to consider all the relevant material before it and then decide what would be in the best interests of the child; (2) s.11 (7) (a) of the 1995 Act did not impose any legal onus in a case where a court made a contact order spontaneously and therefore the section could not be read as imposing such an onus where a party had applied for such a contact order to be made; (3) if having considered the material before it the court decided that direct contact would benefit the child, the court then had to decided whether the granting of a contact order was in the best interests of the child or whether the parties should be left to agree contact, and (4) there was no requirement to intimate the intended decision to the child as she was already aware of, and had sought legal advice on, the proceedings and had not requested to be heard.

Observed, per the Lord President, that the time which had elapsed between lodging the appeal and the appeal being heard was unacceptable; if necessary, the rules of court should be amended to allow cases of this type involving the welfare of children to be heard without delay. Opinion, per Lord McCluskey, that it was inconceivable that a court, in deciding what was in the best interests and welfare of a child, and having heard all the evidence, should base its judgment on the failure of a party to discharge an onus of proof.

WHITE v. WHITE; *sub nom.* GRANT (OTHERWISE WHITE) v. WHITE 2001 S.C. 689, Lord Rodger L.P., Lord Kirkwood, Lord McCluskey, 1 Div.

6511. Children – parental responsibility orders – jurisdiction of hearing – local authority location determining jurisdiction

[Sheriff Courts (Scotland) Act 1907 (7 Edw VII c.51) s.6; Family Law Act 1986 (c.55) s.1; Children (Scotland) Act 1995 (c.36) s.86.]

GCC applied for a parental responsibilities order under the Children (Scotland) Act 1995 s.86 relating to a child under their care. The child had been placed with foster carers in Airdrie and as such was outwith GCC's sheriffdom. M, the child's mother, objected to the application and, ex proprio motu, the sheriff raised the issue of jurisdiction. GCC's application was dismissed as incompetent on the basis that jurisdiction followed the child in all family law matters. GCC appealed to the Court of Session. M argued that there needed to be a statutory basis for the sheriff's jurisdiction and since the order being sought was a Part I order in terms of the Family Law Act 1986 s.1 (1) jurisdiction would be related to the habitual residence of the child.

Held, allowing the appeal, that it would be possible, but not satisfactory, to find the statutory basis for jurisdiction in the Sheriff Courts (Scotland) Act 1907 s.6. The order being sought was a "public law " order and not a Part I order, and accordingly, its jurisdiction would not be related to the habitual residence of the child. Consistent with the statutory scheme regulating the intervention of third parties in the care of children the term "the sheriff" in Part II of the 1995 Act should be taken as the sheriff in whose sheriffdom the public authority lay. Opinion of the Court per Lord Milligan.

GLASGOW CITY COUNCIL v. M (TRANSFER OF PARENTAL RIGHTS: JURISDICTION) 2001 S.C. 415, Lord Milligan, Lord Kingarth, Lord Macfadyen, Ex Div.

6512. Children – parental rights – vesting in local authority – mother mentally ill – best interests of the child

[Social Work (Scotland) Act 1968 (c.49) s.15, s.16(8).]

G, a local authority, sought an order confirming a resolution vesting them with the parental rights and power with respect to a child, J. J's mother, B, opposed the order. The child had been in the care of G for three years under the Social Work (Scotland) Act 1968 s.15 and it was agreed that B suffered from a mental illness which rendered her unfit to care of J, thus establishing the terms of s.16(8) (b) of the Act. The matter at issue was whether the order was in the best interests of the child in terms of s.16(8) (a).

Held, granting the order, that the order was clearly in J's interests because (1) J's subjective perceptions, and not the objective state of affairs was the correct issue and there was evidence that J would feel more secure if the order was granted; (2) J had expressed a wish that the order be granted, and (3) B was unable to exercise her parental rights in an appropriate and proper manner. These factors outweighed the detrimental effect of the order on B's mental health, and that that would make it harder for J to maintain contact with B.

GLASGOW CITY COUNCIL v. B 2000 S.L.T. (Sh Ct) 167, IAS Peebles Q.C., Sh Ct (Glasgow and Strathkelvin).

6513. Children – residence – removal of child from Switzerland to Scotland – habitual residence

M, the mother of S, a five year old boy from her marriage to F, appealed against an order that he should be returned to Switzerland. M had removed S to Scotland and F had petitioned for his return. The family had moved from Germany to Switzerland, though remaining in the same locality, on September 1, 2000 but did not register with a doctor, dentist or kindergarten and M did not obtain a residence permit. The marriage was troubled and on September 22, F moved in with a girlfriend in Germany, returning occasionally to visit S. On October 11, F found that M had removed S. On December 19, F contacted the British Embassy in Berne expressing concern for S's welfare set against M's mental state, where she had attempted suicide several times previously, and requested that they locate S and ensure his welfare was satisfactory. Swiss authorities applied for the return of S on February 11. The Lord Ordinary ordered the return of S, holding that he had acquired habitual residence in Switzerland when removed, that F's initial inactivity did not demonstrate acceptance of S's removal, that M had not demonstrated that an order for S's return posed any risk to her mental health or that the resultant situation would be intolerable for him, and that, where there was a conflict between affidavits, if the court wished clarification or expansion on certain points there was no prohibition in the rules of court preventing it from taking into account ex parte statements, albeit it might have to take some care in assessing the content of what was said where unsupported by other evidence and even more care if contradicted by such evidence.

Held, allowing the appeal and dismissing the petition, that (1) where there were contradictions between the parties' affidavits and no other evidence to support a conclusion one way or another, it was impossible to arrive at any conclusion as to any shared intention in relation to S's residence, and there was nothing on which to base any inference as to habitual residence apart from the objective facts relating to the move, and (2) that the period spent in Switzerland was substantially too short, and the circumstances of the parties' living there too uncertain, to justify an inference that S had acquired a habitual residence there.

D v. D (PARENT AND CHILD: RESIDENCE) 2002 S.C. 33, Lord Coulsfield, Lord Cowie, Lord Rodger L.P., 1 Div.

6514. Children – residence orders – local authority title to oppose

[Children (Scotland) Act 1995 (c.36) Part I, Part II, s.11, s.17, s.17 (1) (a); Act of Sederunt (Ordinary Cause Rules) 1993 (SI 1993 1956).]

M sought an order for residence and parental rights and responsibilities in respect of her grandchild AP. The action was undefended by D, the child's mother, however the sheriff granted the local authority leave to enter the process and lodge defences. Following a debate on the local authority's entitlement to enter the process, the sheriff repelled the defences and allowed the cause to proceed undefended. In repelling the defences, the sheriff had based his decision on the fact that the action had been raised under the Children (Scotland) Act 1995 Part I which dealt specifically with the private rights of natural persons and more particularly under s.11. Following the reasoning in *Edinburgh City Council v. M* 1996 S.L.T. (Sh Ct) 112, [1996] C.L.Y. 6603, the sheriff had accepted that whilst the local authority had an interest in the case but they had no title to enter it. The local authority appealed arguing that they had duties in respect of AP and were required under s.17 (1) (a) to safeguard and promote the welfare of a child whom it looks after. AP was subject to a supervision order and resided with foster parents. AP was also subject to an application to free the child for adoption. The local authority accepted that they could not enter the proceedings in order to seek an order but argued that they were entitled to be given the opportunity to put material information before the court. M conceded that the local authority had an interest in the action but argued that the correct course of action for the local authority would have been to lodge a report in terms of the Ordinary Cause Rules 1993 and then to have used their powers under the 1995 Act Part II to apply for a parental rights order in their own right.

Held, allowing the appeal, that (1) although a local authority could not apply for a s.11 order in its own right, a court should take the views of the local authority into account when determining whether a s.11 order should be granted in respect of a child for whom the local authority had responsibilities; (2) the local authority had a responsibility under s.17 to safeguard the interests of a child under a supervision order; (3) without the intervention of the local authority, the action would proceed undefended and the court would be deprived of full knowledge of the facts of the case when determining what was in the best interest of the child, and (4) neither the 1995 Act nor the Ordinary Cause Rules 1993 contained any provisions which would render the procedure adopted by the local authority in requesting to enter the process as a party minuter incompetent.

Observed, that it might be appropriate for clarification of the rules by amendment to allow local authorities in such circumstances to lodge a minute in the process.

McLEAN v. DORNAN; *sub nom.* McLEAN v. DORMAN 2001 S.L.T. (Sh Ct) 97, JC McInnes Q.C., Sheriff Principal, Sh Ct.

6515. Children (Scotland) Act 1995 (c.36) – Commencement No.4 Order

CHILDREN (SCOTLAND) ACT 1995 (COMMENCEMENT NO.4) ORDER 2001, SSI 2001 475 (C.23); made under the Children (Scotland) Act 1995 s.105. Commencement details: bringing into force various provisions of the 1995 Act on January 22, 2002; £1.75.

This Order brings into force the Children (Scotland) Act 1995 s.101 which provides for the establishment of a panel of persons from whom curators ad litem, reporting officers and safeguarders may be appointed.

6516. Divorce – financial provision – capital sum – suspension of decree – relevancy

H, a party litigant, reclaimed against the Lord Ordinary's decision to dismiss his petition seeking suspension of the sheriff's award of a capital sum of £70,000 and expenses against H in granting divorce to W in January 1996. During the divorce action the sheriff ordered H, a farmer, to obtain a valuation report on heritable property and farm machinery. H failed to lodge the report. The sheriff held H in default for failing to obtemper the order, repelled H's defences and allowed the action to proceed as undefended, allowing W a proof of her averments by way of affidavit evidence. The Lord Ordinary held that H's averments failed to disclose exceptional circumstances justifying suspension, the relevant decree being a decree in foro and the correct test of relevancy being that in respect of reduction. H submitted that it was competent to impugn a sheriff court decree by petition for suspension, and that an action for reduction would be incompetent. The court having invited submissions on whether the sheriff had been entitled to grant decree for the capital sum without affidavit evidence on that matter, W argued that as she had set out details of her financial position in averments, to have repeated them in an affidavit would have been an empty exercise, and where a divorce action became undefended a pursuer was entitled to decree for the amount claimed, without evidence on the matter.

Held, allowing the reclaiming motion and a proof under exclusion of certain averments of both parties, that (1) the test for relevancy was effectively the same as in an action for reduction of the decree; (2) H's averments disclosed a larger basis for reviewing the sheriff's award than a mere claim that the amount awarded was not justified by the true financial position of the parties. Even if the stricter standard applicable to decrees in foro was applied, it could not be said that H was bound, after proof, to fail to persuade the court to grant him a remedy. An application for financial provision on divorce should, except where parties were agreed, be supported by evidence and that such evidence should be considered by the judge or sheriff when deciding whether or not to grant the application. It was appropriate in all cases, except where otherwise agreed, that there should be an evidential basis to warrant the award. There was no such basis before the sheriff when he made an award of a capital sum. H's failure to obtemper the sheriff's order and disclose his assets had to be taken into account but did not of itself justify the award. Sworn testimony and affidavit evidence were required, giving a full, accurate and up to date explanation of why the amount claimed would be justified and reasonable. Opinion of the Court per Lord Hamilton.

ALI v. ALI (NO.2) 2001 S.C. 618, Lord Hamilton, Lord Marnoch and Lord Milligan, Ex Div.

6517. Divorce – financial provision – conduct of wife – husband rendered unfit for work – justification for unequal sharing

[Family Law (Scotland) Act 1985 (c.37) s.9(1)(a), s.10(6), s.11(7).]

In an action for divorce, the sheriff granted decree for payment by a husband (H) to his wife (W) of a capital sum, and ordered W to make over her one half pro indiviso share of the matrimonial home to H. W appealed, arguing that she should have received a larger capital sum, and that the sheriff had erred in law by treating H's loss of income as being a result of the adverse effects of W's conduct towards H. Such conduct was not, therefore, a special circumstance in terms of the Family Law (Scotland) Act 1985 s.10(6) justifying unequal sharing of matrimonial property. She argued that the conduct founded upon by the sheriff did not properly fall under s.11(7)(a), which should be interpreted as referring to conduct which had a direct effect on parties' resources and which was intended to, or which it was reasonably foreseeable would, have such effect.

Held, rejecting the appeal, that (1) when considering the fair sharing provision s.9(1)(a) and the special circumstances which might arise as the effect of conduct covered by s.11(7), it was not desirable to read in any element of intention or foreseeability. The issue was whether in fact the conduct had caused an adverse effect on resources; (2) the conduct need have no direct dealing with the resources in question. It was not unjust to hold that, where there was conduct by one party rendering the other party so ill as to be unable to work, the resulting diminution in resources was a result of that conduct, and (3) the sheriff had not erred in law.

BREMNER v. BREMNER (FINANCIAL PROVISION) 2000 S.C.L.R. 912, DJ Risk Q.C., Sheriff Principal, Sh Ct (Grampian, Highland and Islands).

6518. Divorce – financial provision – consensual variation of periodical allowance

[Divorce (Scotland) Act 1976 (c.39) s.5.]

Upon divorce in 1983 an order was made for the husband, H, to pay a periodical allowance to his wife, W, under the Divorce (Scotland) Act 1976 s.5(1) and (2). The order contained a provision allowing for increases in line with H's salary. The allowance was increased under a further agreement between H and W in 1986. H brought an action for variation of the allowance which was initially dismissed as incompetent. This was allowed on appeal by the Sheriff Principal however and W appealed.

Held, refusing the appeal, that the post decree agreement varying the amount payable could not affect the amount due under the decree. The statutory basis of the periodical allowance meant that it could not be determined by an agreement between the parties. Any such agreement would play a part in an application for variation but could not of itself determine the matter. Opinion of the Court per Lord Prosser.

MacDONNELL v. MacDONNELL 2001 S.C. 877, Lord Prosser, Lord Cowie, Lord Penrose, Ex Div.

6519. Divorce – financial provision – division of matrimonial property – inherited funds invested in matrimonial property

[Family Law (Scotland) Act 1985 (c.37) s.9(1)(b), s.10(6)(b).]

W raised an action of divorce against her husband, H, seeking, inter alia, (1) a residence order for their youngest child (aged 12); (2) to make permanent an interim interdict against H from molesting W, and (3) based on an equal division of the proceeds of sale of the matrimonial home, a capital sum of £227,632. H argued that (1) although his behaviour towards W in the past had been poor, this was a reaction to the breakup of the marriage in combination with a number of other stress factors at that time, and there was no cause for apprehension that the behaviour would recur; (2) the child should live with W and there was no need for a residence order, and (3) there were special circumstances justifying an unequal distribution of matrimonial property under the Family Law (Scotland) Act 1985 s.10(6)(b). W sought equal division of matrimonial property, arguing that H's income contribution had been matched by conversion to matrimonial property of some of her inherited income. W further argued that interruption to her career to care for the children had caused her economic disadvantage which should be taken into account under s.9(1)(b) of the Act.

Held, putting the case out by order to allow submissions on time to pay the capital sum, that (1) permanent interdict against molestation should not readily be granted. H's behaviour was primarily a result of the stress of the marriage breakup and, objectively, was unlikely to recur; (2) as the child had been upset by past conflict over contact, it was best to grant a residence order to formalise contact arrangements and give reassurance and security to the child; (3) both parties having inherited roughly the same amount of money, their contributions to matrimonial property from unearned income should be treated as roughly equal. Notwithstanding H's larger contribution towards the family home, the value of the home should be divided equally because funds were devoted to a matrimonial home in a particularly clear way. W should retain the value of inherited property which had merely undergone a change in form. The value of the home was to be shared equally, after deduction of certain sums representing inherited income and the value of a holiday home paid for by H, and (4) W had not proved quantifiable economic disadvantage.

CUNNINGHAM v. CUNNINGHAM 2001 Fam. L.R. 12, Lord Macfadyen, OH.

6520. Divorce – financial provision – fair sharing of matrimonial property – shareholding of company – spouse as beneficial owner

[Family Law (Scotland) Act 1985 (c.37) s.8(1)(aa); Requirements of Writing (Scotland) Act 1995 (c.7) s.1, s.1(2)(a)(iii), s.1(3), s.1(4).]

W raised an action of divorce against H on the grounds on the irretrievable breakdown of their marriage by reason of H's behaviour. W sought a capital sum of £400,000 and the transfer of H's one half pro indiviso share of the matrimonial home. The divorce was not opposed and arrangements for the care of one of the couple's children, still under the age of 16 had been agreed. The identity of the matrimonial property and the relevant date for calculating its net value were also agreed. H also had an interest in a company, M of which H owned the only two issued shares, and a valuation of £400,000 was agreed. The dispute centred on whether H held the beneficial interest in the entire holding or whether, as claimed be H, one of the two shares was held by H as nominee and in trust for a business associate, H, in recognition of H's funding of another company which had been absorbed into M. No formal documentation existed to support the contention that H was beneficially entitled to half and, apart from H and X, no witnesses were led who could confirm that such an agreement existed. H argued that X desired to remain anonymous in relation to M due to difficulties encountered in previous businesses caused by sectarian prejudice. Company paperwork for 1997-99 including director's reports and annual statements all indicated that H was sole director during that period and that he was the beneficial owner of the shares. In 1999, H appointed D as a director of M and transferred two shares in a subsidiary company to D, which, if the agreement with X existed, were half owned by X but X was not consulted. W argued that H and X were unreliable witnesses and that evidence concerning ownership of the holdings should require to be corroborated by independent sources. W further argued that if the agreement was found to have existed and been based on trust, then there was a requirement under the Requirements for Writing (Scotland) Act 1995 s.1 (2) (a) (iii) for such an agreement constituting a trust to be in writing.

Held, granting decree of divorce, ordering H to transfer his one half pro indiviso share of the matrimonial home to W, subject to him being discharged from liability under the standard security over the property, and awarding payment to W of a capital sum of £97,700 with interest at 5 per cent from the date of decree, that (1) H was, at the relevant date, beneficially entitled to only one of the two shares in M, with X being beneficially entitled to the other, giving the correct valuation of H's share in M and the subsidiary as £200,000 and, although the evidence led in explanation of why X had not become a shareholder, or at least insisted on a formal written record of the agreement, was unsatisfactory, however, that did not entitle the conclusion to be drawn that the agreement had not existed; (2) the discrepancies contained in the company records, whilst improper, were, when taken in context with other evidence, indicative of the fact that H regarded such discrepancies as a necessary consequence of X's desire to remain anonymous and did not point to the fact that the agreement had not existed; (3) the evidence regarding X's financial involvement with the absorbed company and the sale at nominal value to M supported the contention that X would have a beneficial interest in the ownership of M; (4) the terms of s.1 (2) (a) (iii) of the 1995 Act had to be read in conjunction with the rest of s.1 which allowed a trust to remain unwritten provided the criteria contained in s.1 (3) and s.1 (4) were met as was the case in this situation; (5) the transfer of the matrimonial home in terms of the Family Law (Scotland) Act 1985 s.8(1) (aa) was subject to H being released from all liabilities in respect of the standard security over the property, and (6) given H's financial situation, the equalisation payment represented by the capital sum award of £97,700 should be paid in instalments as set by the court.

McHUGH v. McHUGH 2001 Fam. L.R. 30, Lord Macfadyen, OH.

6521.   Divorce – financial provision – pension rights – valuation

[Divorce etc. (Pensions) (Scotland) Regulations 1996 (SI 1996 1901) Reg.3, Reg.3(1), Reg.3(5); Family Law (Scotland) Act 1985 (c.37) s.10(1).]

W raised an action of divorce against H craving payment of a capital sum of £50,000 based on an actuarial valuation of his occupational pension scheme with the fire service of £97,355. H pled to the relevancy of averments regarding the occupational pension scheme and the use of an actuarial valuation. H submitted that the Divorce etc. (Pensions) (Scotland) Regulations 1996 Reg.3(1) required the valuation of occupational pension schemes to be based on the cash equivalent value assuming the employee left their employment on the relevant date for the divorce. The relevant date being the date on which the parties had separated in 1992. The cash equivalent value of the occupational pension on that date was £57,422. H also submitted that W's pleadings relating the occupational pension scheme were irrelevant as lacking in specification as no mention was made in terms of the regulations of whether he had been an active or deferred member of the scheme or whether the scheme was salary related. MS argued that it was open to the court in terms of Reg.3(5) to use the actuarial valuation as a fairer method of valuation rather than the cash equivalent value which she agreed at £57,422. W also argued that even if the court considered the cash equivalent valuation to be the correct one in the circumstances, the difference between the two valuations amounted to special circumstances which would allow the court under the Family Law (Scotland) Act 1985 s.10(1) to depart from the usual practice of equal sharing of assets on divorce.

Held, sustaining H's plea to the relevancy to the extent of excluding the challenged averments, that (1) the method of valuation for occupational pensions set out in Reg.3 was mandatory and the relevant valuation was the cash equivalent valuation whether H was an active or deferred member and whether or not the pension was salary related, and (2) where Parliament had allowed the Secretary of State to make regulations which provided methods for the valuation of occupational pension scheme benefits on divorce it could not have intended that parties who felt the valuations unfair could side-step them by having the unfairness considered a special circumstance for a deviation from equal sharing under s.10(1).

STEWART v. STEWART 2001 S.L.T. (Sh Ct) 114, Sheriff Sir SST Young, Sh Ct (North Strathclyde).

6522. Divorce – financial provision – unequal division – special circumstances – financial support by parents – economic disadvantage of wife

[Family Law (Scotland) Act 1985 (c.37) s.10(6)(c).]

W raised an action of divorce and both parties lodged competing financial claims. W sought transfer of H's title in the matrimonial home and transfer of a joint endowment policy. H sought sale of the home and a lump sum payment from w's pension rights. A matrimonial home had been purchased in 1984 with £20,000 assistance from W's parents in return for a home in their remaining years. H lost his job in 1986 and the W supported the family. H failed to keep up mortgage payments and the home was repossessed in 1987, in 1992 a new home was purchased with a £13,000 deposit provided by W. For the next two years H led a separate social life, had affairs and contributed to the family upkeep only sporadically, they separated in 1995. W argued that the division should be in her favour because (1) she had suffered economic disadvantage; (2) she would continue to have the costs of raising the children, and (3) H had dissipated all of his income.

Held, granting decree of divorce and granting transfer orders in favour of W, that the parental contribution had to be taken into account. The evidence had not established dissipation of property by H in terms of the Family Law (Scotland) Act 1985 s.10(6)(c). There had been a lack of deliberate and positively wanton conduct. Fair account had to be taken of the economic advantage H derived and the disadvantage suffered by W and there was evidence to demonstrate that H had adversely affected the family's financial resources in terms of s.11(7)(a). Giving W sole title to the matrimonial home would be an appropriate division, along with which would transfer the endowment policy. Given the parties ages, income, earning prospects and pension arrangements there would be no interference in their pension provisions.

BUCHAN v. BUCHAN 2001 Fam. L.R. 48, Sheriff A Pollock, Sh Ct (Grampian, Highland and Islands).

6523. Family proceedings – matrimonial jurisdiction and judgments

EUROPEAN COMMUNITIES (MATRIMONIAL JURISDICTION AND JUDGMENTS) (SCOTLAND) REGULATIONS 2001, SSI 2001 36; made under the European Communities Act 1972 s.2. In force: March 1, 2001; £2.00.

These Regulations, which make provision in connection with the coming into force on March 1, 2001 of Council Regulation 1347/2000 ([2000] OJ L160/19) of May 29, 2000 on jurisdiction and enforcement of judgments in matrimonial matters and in matters of parental responsibility for children of both spouses, amend the Domicile and Matrimonial Proceedings Act 1973, the Child Abduction and Custody Act 1985, the Family Law Act 1986 and the Children (Scotland) Act 1995.

6524. Parental contact – allegation of child abuse – hearsay evidence of child – admissibility

See EVIDENCE: MT v. DT. §6217

6525. Sheriff courts – child support – non payment – remedies

ACT OF SEDERUNT (CHILD SUPPORT RULES) AMENDMENT 2001, SSI 2001 143; made under the Sheriff Courts (Scotland) Act 1971 s.32; and the Child Support Act 1991 s.40A. In force: April 2, 2001; £2.00.

This Act of Sederunt, which amends the Act of Sederunt (Child Support Rules) 1993 (SI 1993 920), inserts new rules relating to certain provisions of the Child Support Act 1991 to penalise the non payment of child support.

6526. Books

Cleland, Alison; Sutherland, Elaine E. – Children's Rights in Scotland. 2nd Ed. Paperback: £30.00. ISBN 0-414-01349-2. W.Green & Son.

Mays, Richard – Family Law: Cases and Materials. Paperback: £40.00. ISBN 0-414-01346-8. W.Green & Son.

FINANCIAL SERVICES

6527. Financial Services Authority – demands – regulated activity debt

BANKRUPTCY (FINANCIAL SERVICES AND MARKETS ACT 2000) (SCOTLAND) RULES 2001, SI 2001 3591 (S.19); made under the Financial Services and Markets Act 2000 s.372, s.428. In force: in accordance with rule 1; £1.75.

These Rules relate to demands made by the Financial Services Authority on an individual that he establish to the Authority's satisfaction that he has a reasonable prospect of being able to pay a regulated activity debt when it falls due. In addition, the Rules make provision for the form of a demand, relate to service of a demand and to the setting aside of a demand.

6528. Rehabilitation – rehabilitation of offenders

FINANCIAL SERVICES AND MARKETS ACT 2000 (SAVINGS, MODIFICATIONS AND CONSEQUENTIAL PROVISIONS) (REHABILITATION OF OFFENDERS) (SCOTLAND) ORDER 2001, SI 2001 3640 (S.23); made under the Financial Services and Markets Act 2000 s.426, s.427, s.428. In force: December 1, 2001; £2.00.

This Order makes amendments, savings and modifications that relate to the Rehabilitation of Offenders Act 1974. It also amends the Rehabilitation of Offenders Act 1974 (Exceptions) Order 1975 (SI 1975 1023), the Financial Services Act 1986 and the Banking Act 1987.

FISHERIES

6529. Fish – fish health – powers of veterinary inspector

FISH HEALTH AMENDMENT (SCOTLAND) REGULATIONS 2001, SSI 2001 409; made under the European Communities Act 1972 s.2. In force: November 29, 2001; £3.00.

These Regulations, which amend the Fish Health Regulations 1997 (SI 1997 1881), amend the definition of "the Minister" and insert a definition of "Scotland" to take account of devolution. They make drafting changes to clarify the scope of the powers conferred on a veterinary inspector and revoke the powers in relation to diseased fish. They also make amendments to reflect the restoration of the Great Britain Approved Zone brought about by Commission Decision 2000/188.

6530. Fish farms – diseases and disorders – order for destruction of fish stocks – requirement to pay compensation – reference to ECJ

See EUROPEAN UNION: Booker Aquaculture Ltd (t/a Marine Harvest McConnell) v. Secretary of State for Scotland (Reference to ECJ). §6501

6531. Fishing – conservation – prohibition of fishing for cockles

INSHORE FISHING (PROHIBITION OF FISHING FOR COCKLES) (SCOTLAND) AMENDMENT ORDER 2001, SSI 2001 449; made under the Inshore Fishing (Scotland) Act 1984 s.1. In force: January 1, 2002; £1.50.

This Order amends the Inshore Fishing (Prohibition of Fishing for Cockles) (Scotland) Order 1995 (SI 1995 1373). It extends the prohibition of fishing for cockles within the Solway Firth, so that it covers fishing by any method, including by means of any vehicle, equipment or manual gathering, and from any fishing boat.

6532. Fishing – conservation – prohibition on the use of mobile or active gear

INSHORE FISHING (PROHIBITION OF FISHING AND FISHING METHODS) (SCOTLAND) AMENDMENT ORDER 2001, SSI 2001 174; made under the Inshore Fishing (Scotland) Act 1984 s.1. In force: May 30, 2001; £2.00.

This Order, which amends the Inshore Fishing (Prohibition of Fishing and Fishing Methods) (Scotland) Order 1989 (SI 1989 2307), redefines the area and periods of prohibition of the use of mobile or active gear in and around the areas of Loch Torridon, the Northern Inner Sound and the Southern Inner Sound and permits dredging for scallops for a specified period and in a specified area around Loch Torridon and the Northern Inner Sound. The Order makes amendments by prohibiting fishing with a demersal trawler with a registered length greater than 12 metres or fishing with any trawl other than a single trawl for a specified period and in a specified area around the Southern Inner Sound, extending the area subject to a prohibition of the use of mobile or active gear between Mons Craig and Doolie Ness from one mile to two miles from the mean high water mark of ordinary spring tides and by introducing a ban on fishing by creel in an area north of Rona.

6533. Fishing – enforcement of Community quotas

SEA FISHING (ENFORCEMENT OF COMMUNITY QUOTA AND THIRD COUNTRY FISHING MEASURES) (SCOTLAND) ORDER 2001, SSI 2001 117; made under the Fisheries Act 1981 s.30. In force: April 25, 2001; £2.50.

This Order, which revokes the Sea Fishing (Enforcement of Community Quota and Third Country Fishing Measures) (Scotland) Order 2000 (SSI 2000 34), makes provision for the enforcement of certain Community restrictions and other obligations relating to sea fishing by Community vessels and third country vessels set out in Council Regulation 2848/2000 ([2000] OJ L334/1) which fixes total allowable catches and the quotas of Member States for 2001 and lays down certain conditions under which they may be fished. It authorises fishing by vessels of Norway and the Faroe Islands for specified descriptions of fish in certain specified areas within the fishery limits of Member States in 2001 and imposes requirements concerning fishing quotas and authorised zones, methods of fishing, the holding of licences and observance of licence conditions, the keeping of logbooks, the making of reports and similar matters.

6534. Fishing – Salmon fishery district – designation – Western Isles

WESTERN ISLES SALMON FISHERY DISTRICT DESIGNATION ORDER 2001, SSI 2001 151; made under the Salmon Act 1986 s.1, s.2, Sch.1. In force: April 26, 2001; £2.00.

This Order designates a specified area as a salmon fishery district to be known as the Western Isles Salmon Fishery District and abolishes the existing salmon fishery districts of Loch Roag, East Lewis, Fincastle, Clayburn, Resort, Mullanageren and Howmore which are superseded by it. In addition it makes provision for the annual close time applying to each part of the district and for the period during which fishing for and taking salmon by rod and line is permitted.

6535. Fishing – sea fishing offences – breach of licence – prohibition of fishing across boundaries – not undue interference in normal fishing activities

[Sea Fish Conservation Act 1967 (c.84) s.4, s.5, s.6; Council Regulation 93/2847 establishing a control system applicable to the common fisheries policy Art.4.]

W, as master of a fishing vessel was charged on summary complaint with fishing outwith the terms of his licence. The licensing scheme prevented a vessel fishing across a boundary between the North Sea and an adjacent area of west coast sea without first proceeding to port and obtaining a notice of variation. The Sheriff found that North Sea herring often swam into the west coast sea and when caught were wrongly classified as west coast herring. W was convicted and appealed arguing that the licensing powers in the Sea Fish Conservation Act 1967 s.4(5) and s.4 (6) did not permit the prohibition of fishing in both areas in a single voyage, and the prohibition was ultra vires because it constituted monitoring of fishing for purposes other than conservation and control and amounted to undue interference in normal fishing activities under the Council Regulation 93/2847 Art.4.

Held, refusing the appeal, that the scheme was wholly within the powers conferred by s.4, which under s.4(5) allowed for regulation of not only the area where fishing was authorised but also the extent to which a vessel on a particular voyage might fish in a particular area, and s.4(6) conferred an entirely general power to impose conditions. The licensing scheme was in accordance with and related to the basic aim of conservation, its aim being to stop the pursuit of North Sea herring past the line into the west area and thereby being classed as west area fish, creating a statistical distortion.

WEST v. COLLEY 2001 J.C. 104, Lord Johnston, Lord Allanbridge, Lord Kirkwood, HCJ Appeal.

6536. Fishing – sea fishing offences – fishing zones – jurisdiction – meaning of "Scottish zone" and "Scotland"

[Scotland Act 1998 (c.46) s.126 (1); Scottish Adjacent Waters Boundaries Order 1999 (SI 1999 1126) Art.3, Art.4; Sea Fishing (Enforcement of Community Control Measures) (Scotland) Order 2000 (SSI 2000 7) Art.1 (2), Art.3 (1).]

E, the master of a fishing vessel registered in the United Kingdom, was charged on summary complaint with an offence under the Sea Fishing (Enforcement of Community Control Measures) (Scotland) Order 2000 Art.3(1), which referred inter alia to fishing boats within the Scottish zone. The locus of the alleged offence was within the 200 mile fisheries limit established around Scotland but outwith the 12 mile limit of territorial waters. The accused's plea to the competency of the complaint was repelled and he appealed, arguing inter alia that (1) the Scottish Adjacent Waters Boundaries Order 1999 was fatally flawed as it failed to clarify that the "Scottish zone" lay to the north of the boundaries used in the order, and (2) the 2000 Order lacked the necessary precision required for the creation of a criminal offence as, by relying in Art.1 (2) on the definition of "Scotland" in the Scotland Act 1998 s.126 (1) the order was rendered fatally ambiguous in its extent.

Held, refusing the appeal, that (1) given the undoubted geography of Great Britain, of which the court had judicial knowledge, waters "adjacent to Scotland" had to be those lying to the north of the boundaries defined by Art.4 of the 1999 Order, and (2) there was no room for confusion between the "Scottish zone" and "Scotland" in the 2000 Order, each having their own separate and distinct meanings and Art.1 (2) being concerned with the application of the Scottish legal system.

ENRIQUEZ v. URQUHART 2001 S.L.T.1320, Lord Osborne, Lord Dawson, Lord Sutherland, HCJ Appeal.

6537. Fishing industry – grants

FISHERIES AND AQUACULTURE STRUCTURES (GRANTS) (SCOTLAND) REGULATIONS 2001, SSI 2001 140; made under the European Communities Act 1972 s.2. In force: May 12, 2001; £2.50.

These Regulations supplement specified Community structural assistance legislation which provides, inter alia, for assistance to be paid from the Financial Instrument for Fisheries Guidance in respect of certain categories of investments, projects and actions in the fisheries and aquaculture sector and the industry sector processing and marketing its products. The Regulations provide for and regulate the payment of grants and Community aid by the Scottish Ministers towards expenditure in respect of relevant operations which the Scottish Ministers have approved in accordance with these Regulations and the Community structural assistance legislation. They lay down a procedure for applications for the approval of relevant operations and expenditure to be made and approved for the purpose of the payment of Community aid and, if the Scottish Ministers so determine, grant in addition to that aid.

6538. Fishing vessels – carriage of nets and fishing gear

SEA FISH (SPECIFIED SEA AREAS) (REGULATION OF NETS AND OTHER FISHING GEAR) (SCOTLAND) AMENDMENT ORDER 2001, SSI 2001 250; made under the Sea Fish (Conservation) Act 1967 s.3. In force: August 1, 2001; £1.75.

This Order, which amends the Sea Fish (Specified Sea Areas) (Regulation of Nets and Other Fishing Gear) (Scotland) Order 2000 (SSI 2000 227), brings into effect additional technical conservation measures to further protect stocks of undersized fish. It exempts nets used for the purposes of fishing for queen scallops from the requirements of the 2000 Order and introduces a limitation upon the combined length of the codend and extension piece of certain fishing nets. It also prohibits the use of strengthening bags in these nets, and provides an exemption from this prohibition for nets used in or by boats for the purposes of fishing for Norway lobsters. In addition, the Order clarifies the provisions in the principal Order relating to the positioning of square mesh panels, twine thickness requirements and corrects the description of ICES Statistical Sub Area VI.

6539. Fishing vessels – control of satellite based vessel monitoring systems

SEA FISHING (ENFORCEMENT OF COMMUNITY SATELLITE MONITORING MEASURES) (SCOTLAND) ORDER 2000 AMENDMENT REGULATIONS 2001, SSI 2001 448; made under the European Communities Act 1972 s.2. In force: January 1, 2002; £1.75.

These Regulations amend the Sea Fishing (Enforcement of Community Satellite Monitoring Measures) (Scotland) Order 2000 (SSI 2000 20) which contain provisions for the enforcement of EC legislation requiring satellite monitoring of the position of fishing boats above a certain size. The amendments make it clear that no breach of the requirement relating to the installation and operation of satellite tracking devices occurs either when the satellite tracking device is switched off in port under conditions permitted by the relevant EC legislation or if there is a technical fault or non-function when the boat is in port or when the temporary period for which the relevant EC legislation allows fishing with a defective device has not yet expired. They also confer an additional enforcement power on a British sea-fishery officer in a case where there has been a failure of operation of the satellite tracking device on board a Scottish or relevant British fishing vessel.

6540. Salmon Conservation (Scotland) Act 2001 (asp 3) – Commencement Order
SALMON CONSERVATION (SCOTLAND) ACT 2001 (COMMENCEMENT) ORDER 2001, SSI 2001 116 (C.6); made under the Salmon Conservation (Scotland) Act 2001 s.3. Commencement details: bringing into force various provisions of the Act on April 15, 2001; £1.50.
This Order appoints April 15, 2001 as the date on which the Salmon Conservation (Scotland) Act 2001 will come into force.

6541. Salmon Conservation (Scotland) Act 2001 (asp 3)
This Act of the Scottish Parliament to makes further provision about the conservation of salmon and sea trout.
This Act received Royal Assent on February 14, 2001.

6542. Salmon fishings – deed of conditions – management of dam – breach of regulations concerning passage of salmon
[Salmon (Fish Passes and Screens) (Scotland) Regulations 1994 (SI 1994 2524) Reg.3.]
H and R entered into a deed of conditions in 1995 to regulate the future maintenance and management of an ancient dam or cauld known as Kelso Cauld. The deed provided that any disputes regarding the cauld would be referred to an arbiter. In 1996, following a breach in the cauld, the parties were unable to reach an agreement regarding repairs and restoration and the matter was referred to arbitration. The arbiter proposed to find R liable and a case was stated which asked whether the arbiter was entitled to find, given the terms of the deed of conditions, that R was liable to repair and restore the cauld to its original condition.
Held, answering the question in the negative, that (1) the deed, properly construed, only imposed an obligation on R to maintain the cauld to the standards set out in the Salmon (Fish Passes and Screens) (Scotland) Regulations 1994, which did not require the cauld to be restored to its original condition; (2) the purpose Reg.3 was to prevent dams being constructed or altered in such a way as to prevent salmon from passing upstream by virtue of water passing through the fabric of the dam, and (3) the breach in the cauld did not prevent the free movement of salmon and could not be construed as water passing through the structure or fabric of the dam, and, accordingly, there was no obligation upon R to repair or restore the cauld to its original condition, *Lyall v. Carnegy* (1900) 2 F. (Ct. of Sess.) 423 and *Hardie v. Walker* 1948 S.C. 674, [1949] C.L.Y. 4663, followed. Opinion of the Court per Lord Rodger, Lord-President.
HERITAGE FISHERIES LTD v. DUKE OF ROXBURGHE 2000 S.L.T. 800, Lord Rodger L.P., Lord Caplan, Lord Nimmo Smith, 1 Div.

6543. Shellfish – emergency prohibitions – amnesic shellfish poisoning
See FOOD. §6559 - §6590

6544. Shellfish – emergency prohibitions – amnesic, paralytic and diarrhetic shellfish poisoning
See FOOD. §6591

6545. Shellfish – emergency prohibitions – diarrhetic shellfish poisoning
See FOOD. §6592

6546. Shellfish – emergency prohibitions – paralytic shellfish poisoning
See FOOD. §6594 - 6604

6547. Ships – fishing vessels – grants – decommissioning
FISHING VESSELS (DECOMMISSIONING) (SCOTLAND) SCHEME 2001, SSI 2001 332; made under the Fisheries Act 1981 s.15. In force: June 29, 2001; £2.50.
This Scheme provides for the making of grants by the Scottish Ministers in respect of the decommissioning of fishing vessels. Applications for grant will be considered in respect of vessels meeting specified requirements including a requirement that to be eligible a vessel must be over 10m in length and licensed with a Category A licence.

FOOD

6548. Agricultural produce – coffee and chicory extracts – labelling requirements
COFFEE EXTRACTS AND CHICORY EXTRACTS (SCOTLAND) REGULATIONS 2001, SSI 2001 38; made under the Food Safety Act 1990 s.6, s.16, s.17, s.26, s.48. In force: March 17, 2001; £2.00.
These Regulations, which implement Directive 1999/4 ([1999] OJ L66/26) of the European Parliament and the Council relating to coffee extracts and chicory extracts, revoke and replace the Coffee and Coffee Products (Scotland) Regulations 1979 (SI 1979 383). They prescribe definitions and reserved descriptions for coffee extracts and chicory extracts, provide for the Regulations to apply to coffee extracts and chicory extracts ready for delivery to the ultimate consumer or to a catering establishment, prohibit the labelling of food with a reserved description other than food to which the description relates, require reserved descriptions and specified declarations to be applied to designated products, and prescribe the manner of marking or labelling to be employed. Certain provisions of the Food Labelling Regulations 1996 (SI 1996 1499), which govern the labelling of coffee extract and chicory extract products except so far as specifically provided for in these Regulations, are applied to these specific requirements. In addition, the regulations provide for penalties and enforcement, include a transitional provision and a defence in relation to exports in accordance with Directive 89/397 ([1989] OJ L186/23) on the official control of food stuffs and apply various provisions of the Food Safety Act 1990.

6549. Animal products – diseases and disorders – specified risk material
SPECIFIED RISK MATERIAL AMENDMENT (NO.2) (SCOTLAND) REGULATIONS 2001, SSI 2001 86; made under the European Communities Act 1972 s.2. In force: April 1, 2001; £1.75.
These Regulations, which amend the Specified Risk Material Regulations 1997 (SI 1997 2965), make provision for changes to the processing requirements at approved rendering plants in Scotland. They allow the mixing of specified risk material with other material at approved rendering plants providing all the material is kept, stored, handled and rendered as specified risk material and give effect to Commission Decision 2000/418 regulating the use of material presenting risks as regards transmissible spongiform encephalopathies.

6550. Animal products – diseases and disorders – specified risk material

SPECIFIED RISK MATERIAL AMENDMENT (NO.3) (SCOTLAND) REGULATIONS 2001, SSI 2001 288; made under the Food Safety Act 1990 s.16, s.17, s.19, s.26, s.48, Sch.1 para.2, Sch.1 para.3, Sch.1 para.5, Sch.1 para.6. In force: August 20, 2001; £2.00.

These Regulations, which amend the Specified Risk Material Regulations 1997 (SI 1997 2965), implement specified provisions of European Parliament and Council Regulation 999/2001 ([2001] OJ L147/1) laying down rules for the prevention, control and eradication of certain transmissible spongiform encephalopathies.

6551. Animal products – diseases and disorders – specified risk material

SPECIFIED RISK MATERIAL AMENDMENT (SCOTLAND) ORDER 2001, SSI 2001 287; made under the Animal Health Act 1981 s.1, s.10, s.11, s.83, Sch.2. In force: August 20, 2001; £2.00.

This Order amends the Specified Risk Material Order 1997 (SI 1997 2964) to implement European Parliament and Council Regulation 999/2001 ([2001] OJ L147/1) laying down rules for the prevention, control and eradication of certain transmissible spongiform encephalopathies. It provides a definition of vertebral column, excludes from the scope of the definition material derived from sheep and goats born, continuously reared and slaughtered in certain third countries and imposes new requirements for the import of carcasses of bovine animals containing vertebral column which are specified risk material.

6552. Animal products – food safety – intra-community trade – gelatine

GELATINE (INTRA-COMMUNITY TRADE) (SCOTLAND) REGULATIONS 2001, SSI 2001 169; made under the European Communities Act 1972 s.2. In force: May 21, 2001; £1.75.

These Regulations, which amend the Products of Animal Origin (Import and Export) Regulations 1996 (SI 1996 3124), implement Commission Decision 99/724 ([1999] OJ L290/32) in so far as it relates to trade between Member States of the the the European Community and imposes new or changed obligations on the UK. The Decision amends Annex II to Council Directive 92/118 ([1992] OJ L62/49) by imposing new requirements relating to gelatine intended for human consumption. The Regulations give power to food authorities in Scotland to issue, suspend, withdraw and cancel authorisations of collection centres and tanneries which supply raw materials for the manufacture of gelatine subject to the requirements of the Commission Decision.

6553. Animal products – origin marking – imports and exports

PRODUCTS OF ANIMAL ORIGIN (IMPORT AND EXPORT) AMENDMENT (SCOTLAND) REGULATIONS 2001, SSI 2001 257; made under the European Communities Act 1972 s.2. In force: July 3, 2001; £1.75.

These Regulations, which amend the Products of Animal Origin (Import and Export) Regulations 1996 (SI 1996 3124), implement provisions of Council Directive 99/78 ([1999] OJ L24/9) to extend the powers of authorised officers as regards products of animal origin which have been imported otherwise than in accordance with animal or public health conditions. They confer on authorised officers of the Scottish Ministers, the Food Standards Agency or a local authority the power in respect of intra-community trade, to prohibit the movement of products of animal origin which they have reasonable grounds for believing do not comply with animal or public health conditions relating to import into Great Britain or the European Community and also in respect of imports from third countries, to require the destruction or re-export of products of animal origin which they have reasonable grounds for believing do not comply with animal or public health conditions relating to import.

6554. Food safety – additives

MISCELLANEOUS FOOD ADDITIVES (AMENDMENT) (NO.2) (SCOTLAND) REGULATIONS 2001, SSI 2001 450; made under the Food Safety Act 1990 s.6, s.16, s.17, s.26, s.48, Sch.1 para.1. In force: January 15, 2002; £2.00.

These Regulations, which further amend the Miscellaneous Food Additives Regulations 1995 (SI 1995 3187) implement Directive 2001/5 ([2001] OJ L55/59) of the European Parliament and of the Council amending Directive 95/2 on food additives other than colours and sweeteners; and Commission Directive 2001/30 ([2001] OJ L146/1) amending Directive 96/77 laying down specific purity criteria on food additives other than colours and sweeteners. Subject to a transitional provision, the Regulations specify new purity criteria in relation to the additives specified in the Annex to Commission Directive 2001/30. They also add one new additive to the list in the 1995 Regulations; modify the list by adding four new additives to that list and specifying additional foods in which Glycerol esters of wood rosins may be contained; and modify the list of permitted carriers and carrier solvents by incorporating an E Number for Propan-1,2-diol.

6555. Food safety – additives

MISCELLANEOUS FOOD ADDITIVES (AMENDMENT) (SCOTLAND) REGULATIONS 2001, SSI 2001 103; made under the Food Safety Act 1990 s.16, s.17, s.26, s.48; and the Food safety Act 1990 Sch.1 para.1. In force: March 31, 2001; £1.75.

These Regulations, which amend the Miscellaneous Food Additives Regulations 1995 (SI 1995 3187) in relation to Scotland, implement Commission Directive 2000/63 ([2000] OJ L277/1) which amends Directive 96/77 ([1996] OJ L339/1) laying down specific purity criteria on food additives other than colours and sweeteners.

6556. Food safety – additives – colours

COLOURS IN FOOD AMENDMENT (SCOTLAND) REGULATIONS 2001, SSI 2001 422; made under the Food Safety Act 1990 s.6, s.16, s.17, s.26, s.48, Sch.1 para.1. In force: January 15, 2002; £1.50.

These Regulations amend the Colours in Food Regulations 1995 (SI 1995 3124) by bringing up to date a reference to Commission Directive 95/45 ([1995] OJ L226/1) laying down specific purity criteria concerning colours for use in foodstuffs so as to cover its amendment by Commission Directive 2001/50 ([2001] OJ L190/14) as regards the purity specifications for mixed carotenes and beta-carotene.

6557. Food safety – additives – sweeteners

SWEETENERS IN FOOD AMENDMENT (SCOTLAND) REGULATIONS 2001, SSI 2001 212; made under the Food Safety Act 1990 s.16, s.17, s.48, Sch.1 para.1. In force: June 30, 2001; £1.50.

These Regulations amend the Sweeteners in Food Regulations 1995 (SI 1995 3123) by bringing up to date a reference to Commission Directive 95/31 ([1995] OJ L178/1) on specific purity criteria so as to cover its amendment by Commission Directive 2000/51 ([2000] OJ L198/41) which substitutes a new specification for maltitol syrup.

6558. Food safety – beef – labelling – enforcement of schemes

BEEF LABELLING (ENFORCEMENT) (SCOTLAND) REGULATIONS 2001, SSI 2001 252; made under the European Communities Act 1972 s.2. In force: June 29, 2001; £2.00.

These Regulations, which revoke and replace the Beef Labelling (Enforcement) Regulations 1998 (SI 1998 616) in so far as they apply to Scotland, provide for the enforcement of the compulsory and voluntary beef labelling schemes established by European Parliament and Council Regulation 1760/2000 ([2000] OJ L204/1) which establishes a system for the identification and registration of bovine animals and regarding the labelling of beef and beef products, Commission Regulation 1825/2000 ([2000] OJ L216/8) laying down detailed rules for the application of the 2000 Regulation, and Commission Regulation 1141/97 ([1997] OJ L165/7) laying down detailed rules for the implementation of Council Regulation 820/97 as regards the labelling of beef and beef products.

6559. Food safety – emergency prohibitions – amnesic shellfish poisoning

FOOD PROTECTION (EMERGENCY PROHIBITIONS) (AMNESIC SHELLFISH POISONING) (EAST COAST) (SCOTLAND) ORDER 2001, SSI 2001 317; made under the Food and Environment Protection Act1985 s.1, s.24. In force: September 18, 2001 at 5 pm; £1.75.

This Order contains emergency prohibitions restricting various activities in order to prevent human consumption of food rendered unsuitable for that purpose by virtue of shellfish having been affected by the toxin which causes amnesic shellfish poisoning in human beings. It designates an area of sea off the east coast of Scotland within which taking scallops is prohibited and prohibits the movement of scallops out of the area.

6560. Food safety – emergency prohibitions – amnesic shellfish poisoning

FOOD PROTECTION (EMERGENCY PROHIBITIONS) (AMNESIC SHELLFISH POISONING) (EAST COAST) (SCOTLAND) REVOCATION ORDER 2001, SSI 2001 412; made under the Food and Environment Protection Act 1985 s.1. In force: November 7, 2001 at 5 pm in accordance with Art.1; £1.50.

This Order revokes the Food Protection (Emergency Prohibitions) (Amnesic Shellfish Poisoning) (East Coast) (Scotland) Order 2001 (SSI 2001 317), which prohibited fishing for or taking scallops within the area designated in the Schedule to that Order, movement of such scallops out of that area and landing, using in the preparation or processing for supply of food of, supplying and other specified activities in relation to, such scallops from the designated area. The effect of this Order is to remove the prohibitions in respect of the area of sea designated.

6561. Food safety – emergency prohibitions – amnesic shellfish poisoning

FOOD PROTECTION (EMERGENCY PROHIBITIONS) (AMNESIC SHELLFISH POISONING) (WEST COAST) (NO.11) (SCOTLAND) ORDER 2001, SSI 2001 420; made under the Food and Environment Protection Act 1985 s.1, s.24. In force: November 11, 2001 at 5 pm in accordance with Art.1 (1); £1.75.

This Order contains emergency prohibitions restricting various activities in order to prevent human consumption of food rendered unsuitable for that purpose by virtue of shellfish having been affected by the toxin which causes amnesic shellfish poisoning in human beings. It designates a further six areas of water off the West coast of Scotland within which taking scallops and the movement of scallops out of the area, are prohibited.

6562. Food safety – emergency prohibitions – amnesic shellfish poisoning

FOOD PROTECTION (EMERGENCY PROHIBITIONS) (AMNESIC SHELLFISH POISONING) (WEST COAST) (NO.12) (SCOTLAND) ORDER 2001, SSI 2001 423; made under the Food and Environment Protection Act 1985 s.1, s.24. In force: November 14, 2001 at 5 pm in accordance with Art.1 (1); £1.75.

This Order contains emergency prohibitions restricting various activities in order to prevent human consumption of food rendered unsuitable for that purpose by virtue of shellfish having been affected by the toxin which causes amnesic shellfish poisoning in human beings. It designates an area of sea off the West coast of Scotland within which taking scallops and the movement of scallops out of the area, is prohibited.

6563. Food safety – emergency prohibitions – amnesic shellfish poisoning

FOOD PROTECTION (EMERGENCY PROHIBITIONS) (AMNESIC SHELLFISH POISONING) (WEST COAST) (NO.13) (SCOTLAND) ORDER 2001, SSI 2001 425; made under the Food and Environment Protection Act 1985 s.1, s.24. In force: November 19, 2001 at 5 pm; £1.75.

This Order contains emergency prohibitions restricting various activities in order to prevent human consumption of food rendered unsuitable for that purpose by virtue of shellfish having been affected by the toxin which causes amnesic shellfish poisoning in human beings. It designates an area of sea off the West coast of Scotland within which taking scallops and the movement of scallops out of the area, is prohibited.

6564. Food safety – emergency prohibitions – amnesic shellfish poisoning

FOOD PROTECTION (EMERGENCY PROHIBITIONS) (AMNESIC SHELLFISH POISONING) (WEST COAST) (NO.14) (SCOTLAND) ORDER 2001, SSI 2001 451; made under the Food and Environment Protection Act 1985 s.1, s.24. In force: November 30, 2001 at 4 pm; £1.75.

This Order contains emergency prohibitions restricting various activities in order to prevent human consumption of food rendered unsuitable for that purpose by virtue of shellfish having been affected by the toxin which causes amnesic shellfish poisoning in human beings. It designates an area of water off the west coast of Scotland within which taking scallops and the movement of scallops out of the area is prohibited.

6565. Food safety – emergency prohibitions – amnesic shellfish poisoning

FOOD PROTECTION (EMERGENCY PROHIBITIONS) (AMNESIC SHELLFISH POISONING) (WEST COAST) (NO.2) (SCOTLAND) ORDER 2001, SSI 2001 281; made under the Food and Environmental Protection Act 1985 s.1, s.24. In force: August 3, 2001 at 5 pm; £1.75.

This Order, which contains emergency prohibitions restricting various activities in order to prevent human consumption of food rendered unsuitable for that purpose by virtue of shellfish having been affected by the toxin which causes amnesic shellfish poisoning in human beings, designates an area of sea off the west coast of Scotland within which taking scallops is prohibited and prohibits the movement of scallops out of that area.

6566. Food safety – emergency prohibitions – amnesic shellfish poisoning

FOOD PROTECTION (EMERGENCY PROHIBITIONS) (AMNESIC SHELLFISH POISONING) (WEST COAST) (NO.3) (SCOTLAND) ORDER 2001, SSI 2001 284; made under the Food and Environmental Protection Act 1985 s.1 Food and Environmental Protection Act 1985 s.24. In force: August 9, 2001 at 4 pm; £1.75.

This Order contains emergency prohibitions restricting various activities to prevent human consumption of food rendered unsuitable for that purpose by virtue of shellfish having been affected by the toxin which causes amnesic shellfish poisoning in human beings. It designates two areas off the west coast of Scotland within which taking scallops is prohibited and prohibits the movement of scallops out of those areas.

6567. Food safety – emergency prohibitions – amnesic shellfish poisoning

FOOD PROTECTION (EMERGENCY PROHIBITIONS) (AMNESIC SHELLFISH POISONING) (WEST COAST) (NO.4) (SCOTLAND) ORDER 2001, SSI 2001 289; made under the Food and Environment Protection Act 1985 s.1, s.24. In force: August 23, 2001 at 3pm; £1.75.

This Order contains emergency prohibitions restricting various activities in order to prevent human consumption of food rendered unsuitable for that purpose by virtue of shellfish having been affected by the toxin which causes amnesic shellfish poisoning in human beings. It designates three areas of sea off the west coast of

Scotland within which taking scallops is prohibited and prohibits the movement of scallops out of those areas.

6568. Food safety – emergency prohibitions – amnesic shellfish poisoning

FOOD PROTECTION (EMERGENCY PROHIBITIONS) (AMNESIC SHELLFISH POISONING) (WEST COAST) (NO.5) (SCOTLAND) ORDER 2001, SSI 2001 295; made under the Food and Environment Protection Act 1985 s.1, s.24. In force: August 30, 2001 at 5pm; £1.75.

This Order contains emergency prohibitions restricting various activities in order to prevent human consumption of food rendered unsuitable for that purpose by virtue of shellfish having been affected by the toxin which causes amnesic shellfish poisoning in human beings. It designates two areas of sea off the west coast of Scotland within which taking scallops is prohibited and prohibits the movement of scallops out of those areas.

6569. Food safety – emergency prohibitions – amnesic shellfish poisoning

FOOD PROTECTION (EMERGENCY PROHIBITIONS) (AMNESIC SHELLFISH POISONING) (WEST COAST) (NO.6) (SCOTLAND) ORDER 2001, SSI 2001 316; made under the Food and Environment Protection Act 1985 s.1, s.24. In force: September 18, 2001 at 5 pm; £1.75.

This Order contains emergency prohibitions restricting various activities in order to prevent human consumption of food rendered unsuitable for that purpose by virtue of shellfish having been affected by the toxin which causes amnesic shellfish poisoning in human beings. It designates an area of sea off the west coast of Scotland within which taking scallops is prohibited and also prohibits the movement of scallops out of the area.

6570. Food safety – emergency prohibitions – amnesic shellfish poisoning

FOOD PROTECTION (EMERGENCY PROHIBITIONS) (AMNESIC SHELLFISH POISONING) (WEST COAST) (NO.7) (SCOTLAND) ORDER 2001, SSI 2001 322; made under the Food and Environment Protection Act 1985 s.1, s.24. In force: September 20, 2001 at 3 pm; £1.75.

This Order contains emergency prohibitions restricting various activities in order to prevent human consumption of food rendered unsuitable for that purpose by virtue of shellfish having been affected by the toxin which causes amnesic shellfish poisoning in human beings. It designates an area of sea off the west coast of Scotland within which taking scallops is prohibited and prohibits the movement of scallops out of that area.

6571. Food safety – emergency prohibitions – amnesic shellfish poisoning

FOOD PROTECTION (EMERGENCY PROHIBITIONS) (AMNESIC SHELLFISH POISONING) (WEST COAST) (SCOTLAND) ORDER 2001, SSI 2001 273; made under the Food and Environment Protection Act 1985 s.1, s.24. In force: July 25, 2001 at 2 pm; £1.75.

This Order contains emergency prohibitions restricting various activities in order to prevent human consumption of food rendered unsuitable for that purpose by virtue of shellfish having been affected by the toxin which causes amnesic shellfish poisoning in human beings. The Order designates an area of sea off the west coast of Scotland within which taking scallops is prohibited and prohibits the movement of scallops out of that area.

6572. Food safety – emergency prohibitions – amnesic shellfish poisoning – partial revocation

FOOD PROTECTION (EMERGENCY PROHIBITIONS) (AMNESIC SHELLFISH POISONING) (WEST COAST) (NO.2) (SCOTLAND) PARTIAL REVOCATION

ORDER 2001, SSI 2001 10; made under the Food and Environment Protection Act 1985 s.1, s.24. In force: January 16, 2001 at 5 pm; £1.75.

This Order partially revokes the Food Protection (Emergency Prohibitions) (Amnesic Shellfish Poisoning) (West Coast) (No.2) (Scotland) Order 2000 (SSI 2000 291) by removing the prohibitions in respect of a designated area of sea.

6573. Food safety – emergency prohibitions – amnesic shellfish poisoning – partial revocation

FOOD PROTECTION (EMERGENCY PROHIBITIONS) (AMNESIC SHELLFISH POISONING) (WEST COAST) (NO.2) (SCOTLAND) PARTIAL REVOCATION ORDER 2001, SSI 2001 434; made under the Food and Environment Protection Act 1985 s.1, s.24. In force: November 23, 2001 at 4 pm; £1.75.

This Order partially revokes the Food Protection (Emergency Prohibitions) (Amnesic Shellfish Poisoning) (West Coast) (No. 2) (Scotland) Order 2001 (SSI 2001 281), which prohibited fishing for or taking scallops within the area designated in the Schedule to that Order, movement of such scallops out of that area and landing, using in the preparation or processing for supply of food of, supplying and other specified activities in relation to, such scallops from the designated area. The effect of this Order is to remove the prohibitions in respect of the area of sea designated.

6574. Food safety – emergency prohibitions – amnesic shellfish poisoning – partial revocation

FOOD PROTECTION (EMERGENCY PROHIBITIONS) (AMNESIC SHELLFISH POISONING) (WEST COAST) (NO.2) (SCOTLAND) PARTIAL REVOCATION (NO.2) ORDER 2001, SSI 2001 24; made under the Food and Environment Protection Act 1985 s.1, s.24. In force: February 1, 2001 at 2 pm; £1.75.

This Order, which is the seventh partial revocation of the Food Protection (Emergency Prohibitions) (Amnesic Shellfish Poisoning) (West Coast) (No.2) (Scotland) Order 2000 (SSI 2000 291), removes the prohibitions in respect of the designated area of sea.

6575. Food safety – emergency prohibitions – amnesic shellfish poisoning – partial revocation

FOOD PROTECTION (EMERGENCY PROHIBITIONS) (AMNESIC SHELLFISH POISONING) (WEST COAST) (NO.4) (SCOTLAND) PARTIAL REVOCATION ORDER 2001, SSI 2001 473; made under the Food and Environment Protection Act 1985 s.1, s.24. In force: December 19, 2001 at 4 pm; £1.50.

This Order amends the Food Protection (Emergency Prohibitions) (Amnesic Shellfish Poisoning) (West Coast) (No.4) (Scotland) Order 2001 (SSI 2001 289) which prohibited fishing for or taking scallops within the areas designated, movement of such scallops out of those areas and landing, using in the preparation or processing for supply of food of, supplying and other specified activities in relation to, such scallops from the designated areas. The effect of this Order is to remove the prohibitions in respect of the area of designated sea.

6576. Food safety – emergency prohibitions – amnesic shellfish poisoning – partial revocation

FOOD PROTECTION (EMERGENCY PROHIBITIONS) (AMNESIC SHELLFISH POISONING) (WEST COAST) (SCOTLAND) PARTIAL REVOCATION (NO.2) ORDER 2001, SSI 2001 413; made under the Food and Environment Protection Act 1985 s.1, s.24. In force: November 7, 2001 at 5 pm in accordance with Art.1; £1.75.

This Order is the second partial revocation of the Food Protection (Emergency Prohibitions) (Amnesic Shellfish Poisoning) (West Coast) (Scotland) Order 2001 (SSI 2001 273), which prohibited fishing for or taking scallops within the area designated in the Schedule to that Order, movement of such scallops out of that area and landing, using in the preparation or processing for supply of food of, supplying and other specified activities in relation to, such scallops from the designated area. The effect of this Order is to remove the prohibitions in respect of the area of sea designated.

6577. **Food safety – emergency prohibitions – amnesic shellfish poisoning – revocation**

FOOD PROTECTION (EMERGENCY PROHIBITIONS) (AMNESIC SHELLFISH POISONING) (WEST COAST) (NO.10) (SCOTLAND) REVOCATION ORDER 2001, SSI 2001 471; made under the Food and Environment Protection Act 1985 s.1. In force: December 19, 2001 at 4 pm; £1.50.

This Order revokes the Food Protection (Emergency Prohibitions) (Amnesic Shellfish Poisoning) (West Coast) (No.10) (Scotland) Order 2001 (SSI 2001 406) which prohibited fishing for or taking scallops within the area designated, movement of such scallops out of that area and landing, using in the preparation or processing for supply of food of, supplying and other specified activities in relation to, such scallops from the designated area. The effect of this Order is to remove the prohibitions in respect of the area of designated sea.

6578. **Food safety – emergency prohibitions – amnesic shellfish poisoning – revocation**

FOOD PROTECTION (EMERGENCY PROHIBITIONS) (AMNESIC SHELLFISH POISONING) (WEST COAST) (NO.11) (SCOTLAND) REVOCATION ORDER 2001, SSI 2001 470; made under the Food and Environment Protection Act 1985 s.1. In force: December 19, 2001 at 4 pm; £1.50.

This Order revokes the Food Protection (Emergency Prohibitions) (Amnesic Shellfish Poisoning) (West Coast) (No.11) (Scotland) Order 2001 (SSI 2001 420) which prohibited fishing for or taking scallops within the areas designated, movement of such scallops out of those areas and landing, using in the preparation or processing for supply of food of, supplying and other specified activities in relation to, such scallops from the designated areas. The effect of this Order is to remove the prohibitions in respect of the area of designated sea.

6579. **Food safety – emergency prohibitions – amnesic shellfish poisoning – revocation**

FOOD PROTECTION (EMERGENCY PROHIBITIONS) (AMNESIC SHELLFISH POISONING) (WEST COAST) (NO.13) (SCOTLAND) REVOCATION ORDER 2001, SSI 2001 468; made under the Food and Environment Protection Act 1985 s.1. In force: December 19, 2001 at 4 pm; £1.50.

This Order revokes the Food Protection (Emergency Prohibitions) (Amnesic Shellfish Poisoning) (West Coast) (No.13) (Scotland) Order 2001 (SSI 2001 425) which prohibited fishing for or taking scallops within the designated area, movement of such scallops out of that area and landing, using in the preparation or processing for supply of food of, supplying and other specified activities in relation to, such scallops from the designated area.

6580. **Food safety – emergency prohibitions – amnesic shellfish poisoning – revocation**

FOOD PROTECTION (EMERGENCY PROHIBITIONS) (AMNESIC SHELLFISH POISONING) (WEST COAST) (NO.2) (SCOTLAND) REVOCATION ORDER 2001, SSI 2001 134; made under the Food and Environment Protection Act 1985 s.1. In force: March 30, 2001 at 12.30 am; £1.75.

This Order revokes the Food Protection (Emergency Prohibitions) (Amnesic Shellfish Poisoning) (West Coast) (No.2) (Scotland) Order 2000 (SSI 2000 291) which prohibited fishing for or taking scallops within a designated area; movement of such scallops out of that area; and landing, using in the preparation of processing for supply of food of, supplying and other specified activities in relation to, such scallops from the designated area. In addition it revokes the Food Protection (Emergency Prohibitions) (Amnesic Shellfish Poisoning) (West Coast) (No.2) (Scotland) Partial Revocation Order 2000 (SSI 2000 313), the Food Protection (Emergency Prohibitions) (Amnesic Shellfish Poisoning) (West Coast) (No.2) (Scotland) Partial Revocation (No.2) Order 2000 (SSI 2000 346), the Food Protection (Emergency Prohibitions) (Amnesic Shellfish Poisoning) (West Coast) (No.2) (Scotland) Partial Revocation (No.3) Order 2000 (SSI 2000 378), the Food Protection (Emergency Prohibitions) (Amnesic Shellfish Poisoning) (West Coast) (No.2) (Scotland) Partial Revocation (No.4) Order 2000 (SSI 2000 404), the Food Protection (Emergency Prohibitions) (Amnesic Shellfish Poisoning) (West Coast) (No.2) (Scotland) Partial Revocation (No.5) Order 2000 (SSI 2000 435), the Food Protection (Emergency Prohibitions) (Amnesic Shellfish Poisoning) (West Coast) (No.2) (Scotland) Partial Revocation Order 2001 (SSI 2001 10) and the Food Protection (Emergency Prohibitions) (Amnesic Shellfish Poisoning) (West Coast) (No.2) (Scotland) Partial Revocation (No.2) Order 2001 (SSI 2001 24).

6581. Food safety – emergency prohibitions – amnesic shellfish poisoning – revocation

FOOD PROTECTION (EMERGENCY PROHIBITIONS) (AMNESIC SHELLFISH POISONING) (WEST COAST) (NO.3) (SCOTLAND) REVOCATION ORDER 2001, SSI 2001 444; made under the Food and Environment Protection Act 1985 s.1. In force: November 28, 2001 at 4 pm; £1.50.

This Order revokes the Food Protection (Emergency Prohibitions) (Amnesic Shellfish Poisoning) (West Coast) (No.3) (Scotland) Order 2001 (SSI 2001 284 as amended by SSI 2001 414), which prohibited fishing for or taking scallops within the area designated, movement of such scallops out of that area and landing, using in the preparation or processing of food, supplying and other specified activities in relation to, such scallops from the designated area. The effect of this Order is to remove the remaining prohibitions in respect of the area of sea designated.

6582. Food safety – emergency prohibitions – amnesic shellfish poisoning – revocation

FOOD PROTECTION (EMERGENCY PROHIBITIONS) (AMNESIC SHELLFISH POISONING) (WEST COAST) (NO.6) (SCOTLAND) ORDER 2001 REVOCATION ORDER 2001, SSI 2001 472; made under the Food and Environment Protection Act 1985 s.1. In force: December 19, 2001 at 4 pm; £1.50.

This Order revokes the Food Protection (Emergency Prohibitions) (Amnesic Shellfish Poisoning) (West Coast) (No.6) (Scotland) Order 2001 (SSI 2001 316) which prohibited fishing for or taking scallops within the area designated, movement of such scallops out of that area and landing, using in the preparation or processing for supply of food of, supplying and other specified activities in relation to, such scallops from the designated area. The effect of this Order is to remove the prohibitions in respect of the area of designated sea.

6583. Food safety – emergency prohibitions – amnesic shellfish poisoning – revocation

FOOD PROTECTION (EMERGENCY PROHIBITIONS) (AMNESIC SHELLFISH POISONING) (WEST COAST) (NO.6) (SCOTLAND) REVOCATION ORDER 2001, SSI 2001 9; made under the Food and Environmental Protection Act 1985 s.1. In force: January 16, 2001 at 5 pm; £1.50.

This Order revokes the Food Protection (Emergency Prohibitions) (Amnesic Shellfish Poisoning) (West Coast) (No.6) (Scotland) Order 2000 (SSI 2000 428) which prohibited fishing for or taking scallops within a designated area, movement of such scallops out of that area; and landing, using in the preparation or processing for supply of food of, supplying and other specified activities in relation to, such scallops from the designated area.

6584. Food safety – emergency prohibitions – amnesic shellfish poisoning – revocation

FOOD PROTECTION (EMERGENCY PROHIBITIONS) (AMNESIC SHELLFISH POISONING) (WEST COAST) (SCOTLAND) ORDER 2001 REVOCATION ORDER 2001, SSI 2001 442; made under the Food and Environment Protection Act 1985 s.1. In force: November 28, 2001 at 4 pm; £1.50.

This Order revokes the Food Protection (Emergency Prohibitions) (Amnesic Shellfish Poisoning) (West Coast) (Scotland) Partial Revocation Order 2001 (SI 2001 395) and the Food Protection (Emergency Prohibitions) (Amnesic Shellfish Poisoning) (West Coast) (Scotland) Partial Revocation (No.2) Order 2001 (SI 2001 413). It also revokes the Food Protection (Emergency Prohibitions) (Amnesic Shellfish Poisoning) (West Coast) (Scotland) Order 2001 (SI 2001 273) which prohibited fishing for or taking scallops within the area designated, movement of such scallops out of that area and landing, using in the preparation or processing for supply of food of, supplying and other specified activities in relation to, such scallops from the designated area. The effect of this Order is to remove the prohibitions in respect of the area of sea designated.

6585. Food safety – emergency prohibitions – amnesic shellfish poisoning – revocation

FOOD PROTECTION (EMERGENCY PROHIBITIONS) (AMNESIC SHELLFISH POISONING) (WEST COAST) (SCOTLAND) REVOCATION ORDER 2001, SSI 2001 11; made under the Food and Environment Protection Act 1985 s.1. In force: January 16, 2001 at 5 pm; £1.50.

This Order, which revokes the Food Protection (Emergency Prohibitions) (Amnesic Shellfish Poisoning) (West Coast) (Scotland) Order 2000 (SSI 2000 267), Food Protection (Emergency Prohibitions) (Amnesic Shellfish Poisoning) (West Coast) (Scotland) Partial Revocation Order 2000 (SSI 2000 434) and the Food Protection (Emergency Prohibitions) (Amnesic Shellfish Poisoning) (West Coast) (Scotland) Partial Revocation (No.2) Order 2000 (SSI 2000 441), removes the remaining prohibitions in respect of the area of sea designated.

6586. Food safety – emergency prohibitions – amnesic shellfish poisoning – scallops

FOOD PROTECTION (EMERGENCY PROHIBITIONS) (AMNESIC SHELLFISH POISONING) (WEST COAST) (NO.10) (SCOTLAND) ORDER 2001, SSI 2001 406; made under the Food and Environment Protection Act 1985 s.1, s.24. In force: November 6, 2001 at 5 pm; £1.75.

This Order contains emergency prohibitions restricting various activities in order to prevent human consumption of food rendered unsuitable for that purpose by virtue of shellfish having been affected by the toxin which causes amnesic shellfish poisoning in human beings. It designates a further area of sea off the West coast of Scotland within which taking scallops is prohibited and the movement of scallops out of the area.

6587. Food safety – emergency prohibitions – amnesic shellfish poisoning – scallops

FOOD PROTECTION (EMERGENCY PROHIBITIONS) (AMNESIC SHELLFISH POISONING) (WEST COAST) (NO.8) (SCOTLAND) ORDER 2001, SSI 2001 374; made under the Food and Environment Protection Act 1985 s.1, s.24. In force: October 10, 2001 at 5 pm; £1.75.

This Order contains emergency prohibitions restricting various activities in order to prevent human consumption of food rendered unsuitable for that purpose by virtue of shellfish having been affected by the toxin which causes amnesic shellfish poisoning in human beings. It designates two areas within which taking scallops is prohibited and prohibits the movement of scallops out of that area.

6588. Food safety – emergency prohibitions – amnesic shellfish poisoning – scallops

FOOD PROTECTION (EMERGENCY PROHIBITIONS) (AMNESIC SHELLFISH POISONING) (WEST COAST) (NO.9) (SCOTLAND) ORDER 2001, SSI 2001 388; made under the Food and Environment Protection Act 1985 s.1, s.24. In force: October 19, 2001 at 5 pm; £1.75.

This Order contains emergency prohibitions restricting various activities in order to prevent human consumption of food rendered unsuitable for that purpose by virtue of shellfish having been affected by the toxin which causes amnesic shellfish poisoning in human beings. It designates two further areas of sea off the west coast of Scotland within which taking scallops is prohibited and prohibits the movement of scallops out of the areas.

6589. Food safety – emergency prohibitions – amnesic shellfish poisoning – scallops – partial revocation

FOOD PROTECTION (EMERGENCY PROHIBITIONS) (AMNESIC SHELLFISH POISONING) (WEST COAST) (SCOTLAND) PARTIAL REVOCATION ORDER 2001, SSI 2001 395; made under the Food and Environment Protection Act 1985 s.1. In force: October 24, 2001 at 5 pm; £1.75.

This Order partially revokes the Food Protection (Emergency Prohibitions) (Amnesic Shellfish Poisoning) (West Coast) (Scotland) Order 2001 (SSI 2001 273) which prohibited fishing for or taking scallops within the designated area, movement of such scallops out of that area and landing, using in the preparation or processing for supply of food of, supplying and other specified activities in relation to, such scallops from the designated area. This Order removes the prohibitions in respect of the area of sea designated in the Schedule.

6590. Food safety – emergency prohibitions – amnesic, paralytic and diarrhetic shellfish poisoning

FOOD PROTECTION (EMERGENCY PROHIBITIONS) (AMNESIC, PARALYTIC AND DIARRHETIC SHELLFISH POISONING) (ORKNEY) (SCOTLAND) ORDER 2001, SSI 2001 282; made under the Food and Environmental Protection Act 1985 s.1, s.24. In force: August 3, 2001 at 5 pm; £1.75.

This Order, which contains emergency prohibitions restricting various activities in order to prevent human consumption of food rendered unsuitable for that purpose by virtue of shellfish having been affected by the toxins which cause amnesic, paralytic and diarrhetic shellfish poisoning in human beings, designates an area around Orkney within which taking scallops is prohibited and prohibits the movement of scallops out of that area.

6591. Food safety – emergency prohibitions – amnesic, paralytic and diarrhetic shellfish poisoning – partial revocation

FOOD PROTECTION (EMERGENCY PROHIBITIONS) (AMNESIC, PARALYTIC AND DIARRHETIC SHELLFISH POISONING) (ORKNEY) (SCOTLAND) PARTIAL REVOCATION ORDER 2001, SSI 2001 463; made under the Food and Environment Protection Act 1985 s.1, s.24. In force: December 14, 2001 at 5 pm; £1.50.

This Order amends the Food Protection (Emergency Prohibitions) (Amnesic, Paralytic and Diarrhetic Shellfish Poisoning) (Orkney) (Scotland) Order 2001 (SSI 2001 282) which prohibited fishing for or taking scallops within the designated area, movement of such scallops out of that area and landing, using in the preparation or processing for supply of food of, supplying and other specified activities in relation to, such scallops from the designated area.

6592. Food safety – emergency prohibitions – diarrhetic shellfish poisoning – scallops

FOOD PROTECTION (EMERGENCY PROHIBITIONS) (DIARRHETIC SHELLFISH POISONING) (ORKNEY) (SCOTLAND) ORDER 2001, SSI 2001 391; made under the Food and Environment Protection Act 1985 s.1, s.24. In force: October 22, 2001 at 5 pm; £1.75.

This Order contains emergency prohibitions restricting various activities in order to prevent human consumption of food rendered unsuitable for that purpose by virtue of shellfish having been affected by the toxin which causes diarrhetic shellfish poisoning in human beings. It designates an area of sea off the Orkney Islands within which the taking of scallops is prohibited and prohibits the movement of scallops out of the area.

6593. Food safety – emergency prohibitions – paralytic shellfish poisoning

FOOD PROTECTION (EMERGENCY PROHIBITION) (PARALYTIC SHELLFISH POISONING) (ORKNEY) (SCOTLAND) ORDER 2001, SSI 2001 195; made under the Food and Environment Protection Act 1985 s.1, s.24. In force: May 25, 2001 at 10.50pm in accordance with Art.1 (1); £1.75.

This Order contains emergency prohibitions restricting various activities to prevent human consumption of food rendered unsuitable for that purpose by virtue of shellfish having been affected by the toxin which causes paralytic shellfish poisoning in human beings. The Order designates an area within which taking scallops is prohibited, prohibits the movement of scallops out of that area and imposes other restrictions in relation to the use of any scallops taken from that area.

6594. Food safety – emergency prohibitions – paralytic shellfish poisoning

FOOD PROTECTION (EMERGENCY PROHIBITIONS) (PARALYTIC SHELLFISH POISONING) (EAST COAST) (NO.2) (SCOTLAND) ORDER 2001, SSI 2001 387; made under the Food and Environment Protection Act 1985 s.1, s.24. In force: October 19, 2001 at 5 pm; £1.75.

This Order contains emergency prohibitions restricting various activities in order to prevent human consumption of food rendered unsuitable for that purpose by virtue of shellfish having been affected by the toxin which causes paralytic shellfish poisoning in human beings. It designates areas within which taking scallops is prohibited and prohibits the movement of scallops out of these areas.

6595. Food safety – emergency prohibitions – paralytic shellfish poisoning

FOOD PROTECTION (EMERGENCY PROHIBITIONS) (PARALYTIC SHELLFISH POISONING) (EAST COAST) (SCOTLAND) ORDER 2001, SSI 2001 256; made under the Food and Environment Protection Act 1985 s.1, s.24. In force: June 29, 2001 at 4.00pm; £1.75.

This Order contains emergency prohibitions restricting various activities to prevent human consumption of food rendered unsuitable for that purpose by virtue of shellfish having been affected by the toxin which causes paralytic shellfish poisoning in human beings. The Order designates an area within which taking scallops is prohibited, prohibits the movement of scallops out of that area and imposes other restrictions in relation to the use of any scallops taken from that area.

6596. Food safety – emergency prohibitions – paralytic shellfish poisoning

FOOD PROTECTION (EMERGENCY PROHIBITIONS) (PARALYTIC SHELLFISH POISONING) (ORKNEY) (NO.2) (SCOTLAND) ORDER 2001, SSI 2001 241; made under the Food and Environment Protection Act 1985 s.1, s.24. In force: June 18, 2001 at 4.00pm; £1.75.

This Order contains emergency prohibitions restricting various activities to prevent human consumption of food rendered unsuitable for that purpose by virtue of shellfish having been affected by the toxin which causes paralytic shellfish poisoning in human beings. The Order designates an area within which taking scallops is prohibited, prohibits the movement of scallops out of that area and imposes other restrictions in relation to the use of any scallops taken from that area.

6597. Food safety – emergency prohibitions – paralytic shellfish poisoning

FOOD PROTECTION (EMERGENCY PROHIBITIONS) (PARALYTIC SHELLFISH POISONING) (ORKNEY) (NO.2) (SCOTLAND) REVOCATION ORDER 2001, SSI 2001 411; made under the Food and Environment Protection Act 1985 s.1. In force: November 7, 2001 at 5 pm in accordance with Art.1; £1.50.

This Order revokes the Food Protection (Emergency Prohibitions) (Paralytic Shellfish Poisoning) (Orkney) (No.2) (Scotland) Order 2001 (SSI 2001 241), which prohibited fishing for or taking scallops within the area designated in the Schedule to that Order, movement of such scallops out of that area and landing, using in the preparation or processing for supply of food of, supplying and other specified activities in relation to, such scallops from the designated area. The effect of this Order is to remove the prohibitions in respect of the area of sea designated.

6598. Food safety – emergency prohibitions – paralytic shellfish poisoning

FOOD PROTECTION (EMERGENCY PROHIBITIONS) (PARALYTIC SHELLFISH POISONING) (ORKNEY) (NO.3) (SCOTLAND) ORDER 2001, SSI 2001 255; made under the Food and Environment Protection Act 1985 s.1, s.24. In force: June 29, 2001 at 16.00pm; £1.75.

This Order contains emergency prohibitions restricting various activities to prevent human consumption of food rendered unsuitable for that purpose by virtue of shellfish having been affected by the toxin which causes paralytic shellfish poisoning in human beings. The Order designates an area within which taking scallops is prohibited, prohibits the movement of scallops out of that area and imposes other restrictions in relation to the use of any scallops taken from that area.

6599. Food safety – emergency prohibitions – paralytic shellfish poisoning

FOOD PROTECTION (EMERGENCY PROHIBITIONS) (PARALYTIC SHELLFISH POISONING) (WEST COAST) (SCOTLAND) ORDER 2001, SSI 2001 237; made under the Food and Environment Protection Act 1985 s.1, s.24. In force: June 15, 2001 at 5.00pm; £1.75.

This Order contains emergency prohibitions restricting various activities to prevent human consumption of food rendered unsuitable for that purpose by virtue of shellfish having been affected by the toxin which causes paralytic shellfish poisoning in human beings. The Order designates two areas within which taking scallops is prohibited, prohibits the movement of scallops out of that area and imposes other restrictions in relation to the use of any scallops taken from that area.

6600. Food safety – emergency prohibitions – paralytic shellfish poisoning – revocation

FOOD PROTECTION (EMERGENCY PROHIBITIONS) (PARALYTIC SHELLFISH POISONING) (EAST COAST) (NO.2) (SCOTLAND) REVOCATION ORDER 2001, SSI 2001 443; made under the Food and Environment Protection Act 1985 s.1. In force: November 28, 2001 at 4 pm; £1.50.

This Order revokes the Food Protection (Emergency Prohibitions) (Paralytic Shellfish Poisoning) (East Coast) (No.2) (Scotland) Order 2001 (SI 2001 387) which prohibited fishing for or taking scallops within the area designated, movement of such scallops out of that area and landing, using in the preparation or processing for supply of food of, supplying and other specified activities in relation to, such scallops from the designated area. The effect of this Order is to remove the prohibitions in respect of the area of sea designated.

6601. Food safety – emergency prohibitions – paralytic shellfish poisoning – revocation

FOOD PROTECTION (EMERGENCY PROHIBITIONS) (PARALYTIC SHELLFISH POISONING) (EAST COAST) (SCOTLAND) REVOCATION ORDER 2001, SSI 2001 462; made under the Food and Environment Protection Act 1985 s.1. In force: December 14, 2001 at 5 pm; £1.50.

This Order revokes the Food Protection (Emergency Prohibitions) (Paralytic Shellfish Poisoning) (East Coast) (Scotland) Order 2001 (SSI 2001 256) which prohibited fishing for or taking scallops within the designated area, movement of such scallops out of that area and landing, using in the preparation or processing for supply of food of, supplying and other specified activities in relation to, such scallops from the designated area.

6602. Food safety – emergency prohibitions – paralytic shellfish poisoning – revocation

FOOD PROTECTION (EMERGENCY PROHIBITIONS) (PARALYTIC SHELLFISH POISONING) (ORKNEY) (SCOTLAND) REVOCATION ORDER 2001, SSI 2001 294; made under the Food and Environment Protection Act 1985 s.1. In force: August 29, 2001 at 5 pm; £1.50.

These Regulations revoke the Food Protection (Emergency Prohibition) (Paralytic Shellfish Poisoning) (Orkney) (Scotland) Order 2001 (SSI 2001 195) which prohibited fishing for or taking scallops within the designated area, movement of such scallops out of that area and landing, using in the preparation or processing for supply of food of, supplying and other specified activities in relation to, such scallops from the designated area. This Order removes the prohibitions in respect of the area of sea designated in the Schedule to the principal Order.

6603. Food safety – emergency prohibitions – paralytic shellfish poisoning – revocation

FOOD PROTECTION (EMERGENCY PROHIBITIONS) (PARALYTIC SHELLFISH POISONING) (ORKNEY) (SCOTLAND) REVOCATION ORDER 2001, SSI 2001 53; made under the Food and Environment Protection Act 1985 s.1. In force: February 27, 2001 at 5 pm; £1.50.

This Order revokes the Food Protection (Emergency Prohibitions) (Paralytic Shellfish Poisoning) (Orkney) (Scotland) Order 2000 (SSI 2000 192) which prohibited fishing for or taking mussels, razor clams or scallops within the area designated, the movement of such mussels, razor clams or scallops out of that area and landing, using in the preparation or processing for supply of food of, supplying and other specified activities in relation to, such mussels, razor clams or scallops from the designated area. In addition, the Order revokes the the Food Protection (Emergency Prohibitions) (Paralytic Shellfish Poisoning) (Orkney) (Scotland) Partial Revocation Order 2000 (SSI 2000 413).

6604. Food safety – emergency prohibitions – paralytic shellfish poisoning – revocation

FOOD PROTECTION (EMERGENCY PROHIBITIONS) (PARALYTIC SHELLFISH POISONING) (WEST COAST) (SCOTLAND) REVOCATION ORDER 2001, SSI 2001 314; made under the Food and Environment Protection Act 1985 s.1. In force: September 13, 2001 at 3pm; £1.50.

This Order revokes the Food Protection (Emergency Prohibitions) (Paralytic Shellfish Poisoning) (West Coast) (Scotland) Order 2001 (SSI 2001 237) which prohibited fishing for or taking scallops within the areas designated, the movement of such scallops out of those areas and landing, using in the preparation or processing for supply of food of, supplying and other specified activities in relation to, such scallops from the designated areas. The effect of this Order is to remove the prohibitions in respect of the areas of sea designated.

6605. Food safety – emergency prohibitions – radioactivity in sheep – partial revocation

FOOD PROTECTION (EMERGENCY PROHIBITIONS) (RADIOACTIVITY IN SHEEP) PARTIAL REVOCATION (SCOTLAND) ORDER 2001, SSI 2001 313; made under the Food and Environment Protection Act 1985 s.1, s.24. In force: September 20, 2001; £1.75.

This Order partially revokes the Food Protection (Emergency Prohibitions) (Radioactivity in Sheep) Order 1991 (SI 1991 20) which contains emergency prohibitions restricting various activities in order to prevent human consumption of food which has been, or which may have been, rendered unsuitable for that purpose in consequence of the escape of radioactive substances from a nuclear reactor situated at Chernobyl in the Ukraine. The effect of this Order is to reduce the area which is subject to restriction.

6606. Food safety – inspections – charges – repackaging centres

MEAT (HYGIENE AND INSPECTION) (CHARGES) AMENDMENT (SCOTLAND) REGULATIONS 2001, SSI 2001 89; made under the Food Safety Act 1990 s.17, s.45, s.48. In force: April 2, 2001; £2.00.

These Regulations amend the Meat (Hygiene and Inspection) (Charges) Regulations 1998 (SI 1998 2095) by introducing new charges for meat inspections. They provide that, subject to certain provisions, the charge for inspections will be the lower of the standard charge and the time costs, provide for circumstances in which the Food Standards Agency can charge for increased costs on a time basis and make provision for charges at re-packaging centres and cold stores. In addition, the Regulations set the standard charge for ostriches, other rarities and any land mammals or birds.

GOVERNMENT ADMINISTRATION

6607. Budget (Scotland) Act 2001 (asp 4)

This Act of the Scottish Parliament makes provision, for financial year 2001/02, for the use of resources by the Scottish Administration and certain bodies whose expenditure is payable out of the Scottish Consolidated Fund, for authorising the payment of sums out of the Fund, for the maximum amount of relevant expenditure for the purposes of the Local Government (Scotland) Act 1973 s.94(5) and the maximum amounts of borrowing by certain statutory bodies; to make provision, for financial year 2002/03, for authorising the payment of sums out of the Fund on a temporary bases.

This Act received Royal Assent on March 15, 2001 and comes into force on March 15, 2001.

6608. Ministers – Scottish Ministers – agency arrangements

SCOTLAND ACT 1998 (AGENCY ARRANGEMENTS) (SPECIFICATION) ORDER 2001, SI 2001 3917 (S.20); made under the Scotland Act 1998 s.93, s.113. In force: January 28, 2002; £1.75.

This Order specifies functions of the Scottish Ministers for the purposes of the Scotland Act 1998 s.93 which allows a Minister of the Crown to make arrangements for any of that Minister's specified functions to be exercised on his or her behalf by the Scottish Ministers and allows the Scottish Ministers to make arrangements for any of their specified functions to be exercised on their behalf by a Minister of the Crown. The Order specifies the functions of the Scottish Ministers exercisable by the Scottish Ministers under the Environmental Protection (Controls on Ozone-Depleting Substances) Regulations 2001.

6609. Police and Fire Services (Finance) (Scotland) Act 2001 (asp 15)

This Act of the Scottish Parliament makes provision about the carrying forward by police authorities, joint police boards and joint fire boards of unspent balances from one financial year to the next.

This Act received Royal Assent on December 5, 2001.

6610. Public expenditure – Scottish Consolidated Fund – budget 2000/01

BUDGET (SCOTLAND) ACT 2000 (AMENDMENT) ORDER 2001, SSI 2001 7; made under the Budget (Scotland) Act 2000 s.6. In force: January 12, 2001; £2.00.

This Order amends the Budget (Scotland) Act 2000, which makes provision for payments out of the Scottish Consolidated Fund and the application of sums otherwise payable into that Fund, and for limits of the capital expenditure of and borrowing of local authorities and certain other public bodies, to increase the maximum amount for the purposes of the Local Government (Scotland) Act 1973 s.94, which provides for limits on the amount of capital expenses which may be incurred by local authorities in any financial year. It enables sums to be paid out of the Scottish Consolidated Fund for the purpose of meeting expenditure of the Scottish Ministers in connection with external relations initiatives, alters the maximum amounts which may be paid out of that Fund in connection with expenditure of the various parts of the Scottish Administration and of the Forestry Commissioners, the Food Standards Agency, the Scottish Parliamentary Corporate Body and Audit Scotland, and the maximum amounts of receipts which may be applied in connection with their expenditure and specifies further categories of receipts of certain parts of the Scottish Administration which may be applied to meet expenditure and the purposes for which that may be so applied.

6611. Public expenditure – Scottish Consolidated Fund – budget 2000/01

BUDGET (SCOTLAND) ACT 2000 (AMENDMENT) (NO.2) ORDER 2001, SSI 2001 68; made under the Budget (Scotland) Act 2000 s.6. In force: March 7, 2001; £2.00.

This Order amends the Budget (Scotland) Act 2000, which makes provision, for financial year 2000/01, for payments out of the Scottish Consolidated Fund and the application of sums otherwise payable into that Fund. In particular it amends the Act to alter the maximum amount for the purposes of the Local Government (Scotland) Act 1973 s.94 (5) (which provides for limits on the amount of capital expenses which may be incurred by local authorities in any financial year); amends the purposes for which sums may be paid out of the Scottish Consolidated Fund under the Scotland Act 1998 s65 (1) (c) (2) (a), so as to exclude the provision of grants to Scottish Universities for post mortem examinations; alters the maximum amounts which may be paid out of the Scottish Consolidated Fund in connection with expenditure of the various parts of the Scottish Administration and of the Forestry Commissioners, the Food Standards Agency, the Scottish Parliamentary Corporate Body and Audit Scotland, and the maximum amounts of receipts which may be applied in connection with their expenditure; provides that minor occupancy receipts of office holders in the Crown Office and Procurator Fiscal Service in respect of notional capital charging may not be applied for certain specified purposes instead of being paid into the Scottish Consolidated Fund and increases the amount of receipts of office holders in the Crown Office and Procurator Fiscal Service which may be applied for specific purposes instead of being paid into the Scottish Consolidated Fund.

HEALTH

6612. Health boards – membership and procedure

HEALTH BOARDS (MEMBERSHIP AND PROCEDURE) (SCOTLAND) REGULATIONS 2001, SSI 2001 302; made under the National Health Service (Scotland) Act 1978 s.2, s.105, s.108, Sch.1 para.2A, Sch.1 para.4, Sch.1 para.6, Sch.1 para.11. In force: September 28, 2001; £2.50.

These Regulations revoke in relation to Scotland the Health Boards (Membership and Procedure) (No.2) Regulations 1991 (SI 1991 809 as amended by SI 1993 1615, SI 1998 1459 and SI 1999 132). They make provision in relation to Boards established under the National Health Service (Scotland) Act 1978 as to the membership and procedure of these Boards. In addition, the Regulations deal with the remuneration of the members of Boards, provide for the circumstances in which a person may be disqualified from membership of a Board and deals with the appointment of a vice chairperson of committees and sub-committees of Boards.

6613. Medical profession – nurses – disciplinary procedures – right to fair hearing

See HUMAN RIGHTS: Tehrani v. United Kingdom Central Council for Nursing Midwifery and Health Visiting. §6703

6614. Medical profession – nurses, midwives and health visitors – professional conduct

NURSES, MIDWIVES AND HEALTH VISITORS (PROFESSIONAL CONDUCT) (AMENDMENT) RULES 2001 APPROVAL (SCOTLAND) ORDER 2001, SSI 2001 54; made under the Nurses, Midwives and Health Visitors Act 1997 s.19. In force: March 1, 2001; £1.75.

These Rules amend the Nurses, Midwives and Health Visitors (Professional Conduct) Rules 1993 (SI 1993 893) to allow the Health Committee of the UK Central Council for Nursing, Midwifery and Health Visiting to be made up of members of the Council and non Council members and to remove the restriction upon the Council which prevented it from choosing professional screeners who are not its members.

6615. National Health Service – charges – road traffic accidents

ROAD TRAFFIC (NHS CHARGES) AMENDMENT (SCOTLAND) REGULATIONS 2001, SSI 2001 466; made under the Road Traffic (NHS Charges) Act 1999 s.3, s.16, s.17. In force: January 28, 2002; £1.75.

These Regulations amend the Road Traffic (NHS Charges) Regulations 1999 (SI 1999 785) which provide for a scheme for the recovery from insurers and certain other persons of charges in connection with the treatment of road traffic casualties by the National Health Service. The Regulations increase the charges where the traffic casualty received NHS treatment but was not admitted to hospital from £354 to £402; increase the daily charge for NHS treatment where the traffic casualty is admitted to hospital from £435 to £494; and increases the maximum charge for treatment where the traffic casualty is admitted to hospital from £10,000 to £30,000. These increases apply to compensation payments made in respect of incidents occurring on or after January 28, 2002.

6616. National Health Service – dental services

NATIONAL HEALTH SERVICE (GENERAL DENTAL SERVICES) (SCOTLAND) AMENDMENT REGULATIONS 2001, SSI 2001 57; made under the National Health Service (Scotland) Act 1978 s.2, s.25, s.105, s.108. In force: April 1, 2001; £1.50.

These Regulations amend the National Health Service (General Dental Services) (Scotland) Regulations 1996 (SI 1996 177), which provide for arrangements under which dentists, to provide general dental services as part of the National Health Service in Scotland, increase the amount specified as the maximum cost, or likely cost, of care and treatment which a dentist may undertake without seeking the prior approval of the Scottish Dental Practice Board from £230 to £260.

6617. National Health Service – dental services

NATIONAL HEALTH SERVICE (GENERAL DENTAL SERVICES) (SCOTLAND) AMENDMENT (NO.2) REGULATIONS 2001, SSI 2001 368; made under the National Health Service (Scotland) Act 1978 s.2, s.25, s.28A, s.105, s.108. In force: November 7, 2001; £1.75.

These Regulations, which amend the National Health Service (General Dental Services) (Scotland) Regulations 1996 (SI 1997 177), remove the references to general anaesthesia which may no longer be provided under general dental services. They amend the definition of assistant to include those persons who are vocational trainees under the supervision of salaried dentists and provide that where a dentist applies for inclusion in Part A of the dental list the Health Board or primary care NHS trust may inspect the proposed practice premises before processing the application but where the premises have never before been inspected by the Health Board or PCT then there must be an inspection before the application can be processed. In addition, the Regulations replace postgraduate education allowances with continuing professional development allowance and adds a new matter being allowances in respect of practice improvements and allow the mixing of private dental treatment with general dental services, in order to prevent general anaesthesia from being administered privately in connection with treatment under general dental services.

6618. National Health Service – dental treatment – maximum charge

NATIONAL HEALTH SERVICE (DENTAL CHARGES) (SCOTLAND) AMENDMENT REGULATIONS 2001, SSI 2001 69; made under the National Health Service (Scotland) Act 1978 s.70, s.71, s.71A, s.105, s.108, Sch.11 para.3. In force: April 1, 2001; £1.75.

These Regulations amend the National Health Service (Dental Charges) (Scotland) Regulations 1989 (SI 1989 363) which provide for the making and recovery of charges for dental appliances supplied or repaired under the National Health Service, and for other dental treatment provided as part of NHS general dental services. They increase the maximum contribution which a patient may be required to make towards the aggregate cost of dental treatment and appliances under National Health Service (Scotland) Act 1978 Part II from £354 to £360, where the contract or arrangement leading to the provision of such treatment and the supply of such appliances is made on or after April 1, 2001.

6619. National Health Service – drugs and appliances – fees

NATIONAL HEALTH SERVICE (CHARGES FOR DRUGS AND APPLIANCES) (SCOTLAND) AMENDMENT REGULATIONS 2001, SSI 2001 67; made under the National Health Service (Scotland) Act 1978 s.69, s.75A, s.105, s.108. In force: April 1, 2001; £2.00.

These Regulations, which amend the National Health Service (Charges for Drugs and Appliances) (Scotland) Regulations 1989 (SI 1989 326), increase the charges for drugs and appliances supplied by doctors and pharmacists providing pharmaceutical services, and by Health Boards and NHS trusts to out-patients. They make amendments regarding the repayment of sums paid for pre-payment certificates and provide that the application of these Regulations shall be in respect of supplies made after March 31, 2001 or where examinations leading to the supply of an appliance take place after that date and in respect of repayments of sums for pre-payment certificates, where the pre-payment certificate itself was applied for after March 31, 2001.

6620. National Health Service – drugs and appliances – fees

NATIONAL HEALTH SERVICE (CHARGES FOR DRUGS AND APPLIANCES) (SCOTLAND) REGULATIONS 2001, SSI 2001 430; made under the National Health Service (Scotland) Act 1978 s.19, s.25, s.27, s.69, s.75, s.105, s.108. In force: December 14, 2001; £3.00.

These Regulations revoke the National Health Service (Charges for Drugs and Appliances) (Scotland) Regulations 1989 (SI 1989 326), the National Health Service (Charges for Drugs and Appliances) (Scotland) Amendment Regulations 1990 (SI 1990 468), the National Health Service (Charges for Drugs and Appliances) (Scotland) Amendment (No.2) Regulations 1990 (SI 1990 787), the National Health Service (Charges for Drugs and Appliances) (Scotland) Amendment Regulations 1991 (SI 1991 574), the National Health Service (Charges for Drugs and Appliances) (Scotland) Amendment Regulations 1992 (SI 1992 394), the Health Service (Charges for Drugs and Appliances) (Scotland) Amendment Regulations 1993 (SI 1993 552), the National Health Service (Charges for Drugs and Appliances) (Scotland) Amendment Regulations 1994 (SI 1994 697), the National Health Service (Charges for Drugs and Appliances) (Scotland) Amendment Regulations 1995 (SI 1995 699), the National Health Service (Charges for Drugs and Appliances) (Scotland) Amendment (No.2) Regulations 1995 (SI 1995 2739), the National Health Service (Charges for Drugs and Appliances) (Scotland) Amendment Regulations 1996 (SI 1996 740), the National Health Service (Charges for Drugs and Appliances) (Scotland) Amendment Regulations 1997 (SI 1997 697), the National Health Service (Charges for Drugs and Appliances) (Scotland) Amendment Regulations 1998 (SI 1998 609), the National Health Service (Charges for Drugs and Appliances) (Scotland) Amendment Regulations 1999 (SI 1999 612), the National Health Service (Charges for Drugs and Appliances) (Scotland) Amendment Regulations 2000 (SSI 2000 50), the National Health Service (Charges for Drugs and Appliances) (Scotland) Amendment (No.2) Regulations 2000 (SSI 2000 396) and the National Health Service (Charges for Drugs and Appliances) (Scotland) Amendment Regulations 2001 (SSI 2001 67). The Regulations, which also amend the National Health Service (General Medical Services, Pharmaceutical Services and Charges for Drugs and Appliances) (Scotland) Amendment Regulations 1996 (SI 1996 1504) and the National Health Service (Pilot Schemes for Personal Dental Services: Miscellaneous Provisions and Consequential Amendments) Regulations 1998 (SI 1998 2224), consolidate the provisions for the making and recovery of charges for drugs and appliances under or by virtue of the National Health Service (Scotland) Act 1978.

6621. National Health Service – general medical services – prescription of drugs

NATIONAL HEALTH SERVICE (GENERAL MEDICAL SERVICES) (SCOTLAND) AMENDMENT REGULATIONS 2001, SSI 2001 119; made under the National Health Service (Scotland) Act 1978 s.19, s.105, s.108. In force: April 30, 2001; £1.75.

These Regulations amend the National Health Service (General Medical Services) (Scotland) Regulations 1995 (SI 1995 416) which regulate the terms on which doctors provide general medical services under the National Health Service (Scotland) Act 1978. They remove nicotine replacement therapy items from Sch.10 to the 1995 Regulations which identifies those drugs and other substances not to be supplied by general medical practitioners or prescribed for supply in the course of pharmaceutical services.

6622. National Health Service – health boards – NHS 24

NHS 24 (SCOTLAND) ORDER 2001, SSI 2001 137; made under the National Health Service (Scotland) Act 1978 s.2, s.105. In force: April 6, 2001; £2.50.

This Order, which constitutes a Special Health Board for the whole of Scotland to be known as NHS 24, confers on the Board functions in providing advice, guidance and information on health and care services. It applies to the Board various provisions in enactments which apply to Health Boards in general including provisions as to funding, the keeping and auditing of accounts and the appointment and remuneration of Board members and staff. Provisions in certain other Acts of Parliament relevant to Health Boards are also applied as are provisions in various sets of Regulations.

6623. National Health Service – medical profession – doctors – choice of medical practitioner

NATIONAL HEALTH SERVICE (CHOICE OF MEDICAL PRACTITIONER) (SCOTLAND) AMENDMENT REGULATIONS 2001, SSI 2001 85; made under the National Health Service (Scotland) Act 1978 s.17F, s.105, s.108. In force: April 1, 2001; £2.00.

These Regulations amend the National Health Service (Choice of Medical Practitioner) (Scotland) Regulations 1998 (SI 1998 659) which relate to the right of a person to choose the doctor from whom that person is to receive primary medical services. The Regulations make amendments by replacing the definition of a "doctor's list" to extend it to include doctors performing personal medical services under a PMS agreement, introducing new definitions for "a PMS agreement", a "PMS provider" and "the PMS Regulations" and inserting a new regulation which provides that a person who has chosen a particular doctor will, in certain circumstances, continue to be included in the list of that doctor if the doctor transfers from a pilot scheme agreement to a PMS agreement.

6624. National Health Service – medical treatment – personal medical services

NATIONAL HEALTH SERVICE (PERSONAL MEDICAL SERVICES) (SCOTLAND) REGULATIONS 2001, SSI 2001 72; made under the National Health Service (Scotland) Act 1978 s.17E, s.24A, s.105, s.108. In force: April 1, 2001; £4.50.

These Regulations make provisions concerning arrangements to be made in relation to personal medical services provided under the National Health Service (Scotland) Act 1978 s.17C. Pilot scheme arrangements for the provision of personal medical services are already in operation under the National Health Service (Primary Care) Act 1997 and these Regulations allow these arrangements to be placed on a permanent footing. The Regulations ensure that the arrangements for personal medical services under an agreement will be similar in scope to the provision of general medical services, provide that personal medical services may only be performed by practitioners meeting certain requirements, provide for the keeping and maintenance of lists of patients and deal with the circumstances in which patients may be removed from lists or transferred to other lists, contain provisions allowing parties to agreements to become health service bodies and provide for enforcement of directions as to payments to be made by diligence. They provide for financial assistance to be given to certain bodies who seek to enter into agreements and provide for liabilities of deputies where deputising arrangements are made. In addition, they set out details of an agreement that must be published by a provider, lay down the conditions under which personal medical services may be performed and set out a dispute resolution procedure to be included in agreements.

6625. National Health Service – opticians – fees and payments

NATIONAL HEALTH SERVICE (OPTICAL CHARGES AND PAYMENTS) (SCOTLAND) AMENDMENT REGULATIONS 2001, SSI 2001 88; made under the National Health Service (Scotland) Act 1978 s.26, s.70, s.73, s.74, s.105, s.108, Sch.11 para.2, Sch.11 para.2A. In force: April 1, 2001; £2.00.

These Regulations amend the National Health Service (Optical Charges and Payments) (Scotland) Regulations 1998 (SI 1998 642), which provide for payments to be made by means of a voucher system, in respect of costs incurred by certain categories of persons in connection with the supply, replacement or repair of optical appliances. They amend the definition of "NHS sight test fee" to reflect the increase in fees for National Health Service sight tests payable to ophthalmic medical practitioners and opticians.

6626. National Health Service – opticians – provision of ophthalmic services

NATIONAL HEALTH SERVICE (GENERAL OPHTHALMIC SERVICES) (SCOTLAND) AMENDMENT REGULATIONS 2001, SSI 2001 62; made under the National Health Service (Scotland) Act 1978 s.26, s.105, s.106, s.108. In force: in accordance with Reg.1; £2.00.

These Regulations, which amend the National Health Service (General Ophthalmic Services) (Scotland) Regulations 1986 (SI 1986 965) which provide for arrangements under which ophthalmic medical practitioners and ophthalmic opticians provide general ophthalmic services under the National Health Service, insert new definitions of "day centre", "mobile practice" and "residential centre". The Regulations impose requirements that information in respect of mobile practices be included to the ophthalmic list kept, increase the amounts to which a person's eligibility for sight testing is assessed, from £70 to £71, provide that when a patient asks for a sight test, under general ophthalmic services, a contractor must ask the patient to produce satisfactory evidence of entitlement, unless, in cases other than where the patient is eligible by virtue of his lack of resources, the contractor already has satisfactory evidence and enable contractors to provide general ophthalmic services to patients attending day centres or in specified circumstances to patients at the place at which they normally reside.

6627. National Health Service – pharmaceutical services

NATIONAL HEALTH SERVICE (PHARMACEUTICAL SERVICES) (SCOTLAND) AMENDMENT REGULATIONS 2001, SSI 2001 70; made under the National Health Service (Scotland) Act 1978 s.27, s.105, s.108. In force: April 1, 2001; £1.75.

These Regulations, which amend the National Health Service (Pharmaceutical Services) (Scotland) Regulations 1995 (SI 1995 414), introduce definitions of "Charges Regulations", "directed services", "prescription forms" and "Remission of Charges Regulations" and amend the definition of "pharmaceutical services". They remove the provision of supplemental services from the arrangements for the provision of pharmaceutical services which must be made by a Health Board, provide that a pharmacist shall refuse to supply an order under a prescription where the pharmacist reasonably believes that the order is not genuine and require pharmacists who enter into an arrangement to provide "directed services" to comply with the terms and conditions of the arrangement.

6628. National Health Service (Primary Care) Act 1997 (c.46) – Commencement No.7 Order

NATIONAL HEALTH SERVICE (PRIMARY CARE) ACT 1997 (COMMENCEMENT NO.7) (SCOTLAND) ORDER 2001, SSI 2001 58 (C.1); made under the National Health Service (Primary Care) Act 1997 s.41. Commencement details: bringing into force various provisions of the Act on March 5, 2001; £2.00.

This Order, which amends the National Health Service (Primary Care) Act 1997 (Commencement No.4) Order 1998 (SI 1998 631) and the National Health Service (Primary Care) Act 1997 (Commencement No.5) Order 1998 (SI 1998 1998), brings into force certain provisions of the National Health Service (Primary Care) Act 1997, which insert new sub sections into the National Health Service (Scotland) Act 1978 to allow for arrangements to be made between specified bodies for the provision of personal medical services, on March 5, 2001.

6629. NHS trusts – establishment – Argyll and Clyde Acute Hospitals

ARGYLL AND CLYDE ACUTE HOSPITALS NATIONAL HEALTH SERVICE TRUST (ESTABLISHMENT) AMENDMENT ORDER 2001, SSI 2001 338; made under the National Health Service (Scotland) Act 1978 s.12A, s.105, Sch.7A para.1, Sch.7A para.3. In force: September 30, 2001; £1.50.

This Order, which amends the Argyll and Clyde Acute Hospitals National Health Service Trust (Establishment) Order 1998 (SI 1998 2716), reduces the number of trustees from five to two.

6630. NHS trusts – establishment – Ayrshire and Arran Acute Hospitals

AYRSHIRE AND ARRAN ACUTE HOSPITALS NATIONAL HEALTH SERVICE TRUST (ESTABLISHMENT) AMENDMENT ORDER 2001, SSI 2001 340; made under the National Health Service (Scotland) Act 1978 s.12A, s.105, Sch.7A para.1, Sch.7A para.3. In force: September 30, 2001; £1.50.

This Order, which amends the Ayrshire and Arran Acute Hospitals National Health Service Trust (Establishment) Order 1998 (SI 1198 2735), reduces the number of trustees from five to two.

6631. NHS trusts – establishment – Ayrshire and Arran Primary Care

AYRSHIRE AND ARRAN PRIMARY CARE NATIONAL HEALTH SERVICE TRUST (ESTABLISHMENT) AMENDMENT ORDER 2001, SSI 2001 339; made under the National Health Service (Scotland) Act 1978 s.12A, s.105, Sch.7A para.1, Sch.7A para.3. In force: September 30, 2001; £1.50.

This Order, which amends the Ayrshire and Arran Primary Care National Health Service Trust (Establishment) Order 1998 (SI 1998 2715), reduces the number of trustees from five to two.

6632. NHS trusts – establishment – Borders General Hospital

BORDERS GENERAL HOSPITAL NATIONAL HEALTH SERVICE TRUST (ESTABLISHMENT) AMENDMENT ORDER 2001, SSI 2001 341; made under the National Health Service (Scotland) Act 1978 s.12A, s.105, Sch.7A para.1, Sch.7A para.3. In force: September 30, 2001; £1.50.

This Order, which amends the Borders General Hospital National Health Service (Establishment) Order 1994 (SI 1994 2998), reduces the number of trustees from five to two.

6633. NHS trusts – establishment – Borders Primary Care

BORDERS PRIMARY CARE NATIONAL HEALTH SERVICE TRUST (ESTABLISHMENT) AMENDMENT ORDER 2001, SSI 2001 344; made under the National Health Service (Scotland) Act 1978 s.12A, s.105, Sch.7A para.1, Sch.7A para.3. In force: September 30, 2001; £1.50.

This Order, which amends the Borders Primary Care National Health Service Trust (Establishment) Order 1998 (SI 1998 2709), reduces the number of trustees from five to two.

6634. NHS trusts – establishment – Dumfries and Galloway Acute and Maternity Hospitals

DUMFRIES AND GALLOWAY ACUTE AND MATERNITY HOSPITALS NATIONAL HEALTH SERVICE TRUST (ESTABLISHMENT) AMENDMENT ORDER 2001, SSI 2001 345; made under the National Health Service (Scotland) Act 1978 s.12A, s.105, Sch.7A para.1, Sch.7A para.3. In force: September 30, 2001; £1.50.

This Order, which amends the Dumfries and Galloway Acute and Maternity Hospitals National Health Service Trust (Establishment) Order 1993 (SI 1993 2934), reduces the number of trustees from five to two.

6635. NHS trusts – establishment – Dumfries and Galloway Primary Care

DUMFRIES AND GALLOWAY PRIMARY CARE NATIONAL HEALTH SERVICE TRUST (ESTABLISHMENT) AMENDMENT ORDER 2001, SSI 2001 343; made under the National Health Service (Scotland) Act 1978 s.12A, s.105, Sch.7A para.1, Sch.7A para.3. In force: September 30, 2001; £1.50.

This Order, which amends the Dumfries and Galloway Primary Care National Health Service Trust (Establishment) Order 1998 (SI 1998 2714), reduces the number of trustees from five to two.

6636. NHS trusts – establishment – Fife Acute Hospitals

FIFE ACUTE HOSPITALS NATIONAL HEALTH SERVICE TRUST (ESTABLISHMENT) AMENDMENT ORDER 2001, SSI 2001 342; made under the National Health Service (Scotland) Act 1978 s.12A, s.105, Sch.7A para.1, Sch.7A para.3. In force: September 30, 2001; £1.50.

This Order, which amends the Fife Acute Hospitals National Health Service Trust (Establishment) Order 1998 (SI 1998 2714), reduces the number of trustees from five to two.

6637. NHS trusts – establishment – Fife Primary Care

FIFE PRIMARY CARE NATIONAL HEALTH SERVICE TRUST (ESTABLISHMENT) AMENDMENT ORDER 2001, SSI 2001 349; made under the National Health Service (Scotland) Act 1978 s.12A, s.105, Sch.7A para.1, Sch.7A para.3. In force: September 30, 2001; £1.50.

This Order amends the Fife Primary Care National Health Service Trust (Establishment) Order 1998 (SI 1998 2712) to reduce the number of trustees from five to two.

6638. NHS trusts – establishment – Forth Valley Acute Hospitals

FORTH VALLEY ACUTE HOSPITALS NATIONAL HEALTH SERVICE TRUST (ESTABLISHMENT) AMENDMENT ORDER 2001, SSI 2001 348; made under the National Health Service (Scotland) Act 1978 s.12A, s.105, Sch.7A para.1, Sch.7A para.3. In force: September 30, 2001; £1.50.

This Order amends the Forth Valley Acute Hospitals National Health Service Trust (Establishment) Order 1998 (SI 1998 2725) to reduce the number of trustees from five to two.

6639. NHS trusts – establishment – Forth Valley Primary Care

FORTH VALLEY PRIMARY CARE NATIONAL HEALTH SERVICE TRUST (ESTABLISHMENT) AMENDMENT ORDER 2001, SSI 2001 347; made under the National Health Service (Scotland) Act 1978 s.12A, s.105, Sch.7A para.1, Sch.7A para.3. In force: September 30, 2001; £1.50.

This Order amends the Forth Valley Primary Care National Health Service Trust (Establishment) Order 1998 (SI 1998 2713) to reduce the number of trustees from five to two.

6640. NHS trusts – establishment – Grampian Primary Care

GRAMPIAN PRIMARY CARE NATIONAL HEALTH SERVICE TRUST (ESTABLISHMENT) AMENDMENT ORDER 2001, SSI 2001 346; made under the National Health Service (Scotland) Act 1978 s.12A, s.105, Sch.7A para.1, Sch.7A para.3. In force: September 30, 2001; £1.50.

This Order amends the Grampian Primary Care National Health Service Trust (Establishment) Order 1998 (SI 1998 2720) to reduce the number of trustees from five to two.

6641. NHS trusts – establishment – Grampian University Hospitals

GRAMPIAN UNIVERSITY HOSPITALS NATIONAL HEALTH SERVICE TRUST (ESTABLISHMENT) AMENDMENT ORDER 2001, SSI 2001 350; made under the National Health Service (Scotland) Act 1978 s.12A, s.105, Sch.7A para.1, Sch.7A para.3. In force: September 30, 2001; £1.50.

This Order amends the Grampian University Hospitals National Health Service Trust (Establishment) Order 1998 (SI 1998 2718) to reduce the number of trustees from five to two.

6642. NHS trusts – establishment – Greater Glasgow Primary Care

GREATER GLASGOW PRIMARY CARE NATIONAL HEALTH SERVICE TRUST (ESTABLISHMENT) AMENDMENT ORDER 2001, SSI 2001 351; made under the National Health Service (Scotland) Act 1978 s.12A, s.105, Sch.7A para.1, Sch.7A para.3. In force: September 30, 2001; £1.50.

This Order amends the Greater Glasgow Primary Care National Health Service Trust (Establishment) Order 1998 (SI 1998 2719) to reduce the number of trustees from five to two.

6643. NHS trusts – establishment – Highland Acute Hospitals

HIGHLAND ACUTE HOSPITALS NATIONAL HEALTH SERVICE TRUST (ESTABLISHMENT) AMENDMENT ORDER 2001, SSI 2001 352; made under the National Health Service (Scotland) Act 1978 s.12A, s.105, Sch.7A para.1, Sch.7A para.3. In force: September 30, 2001; £1.50.

This Order amends the Highland Acute Hospitals National Health Service Trust (Establishment) Order 1998 (SI 1998 2722) to reduce the number of trustees from five to two.

6644. NHS trusts – establishment – Highland Primary Care

HIGHLAND PRIMARY CARE NATIONAL HEALTH SERVICE TRUST (ESTABLISHMENT) AMENDMENT ORDER 2001, SSI 2001 353; made under the National Health Service (Scotland) Act 1978 s.12A, s.105, Sch.7A para.1, Sch.7A para.3. In force: September 30, 2001; £1.50.

This Order amends the Highland Primary Care National Health Service Trust (Establishment) Order 1998 (SI 1998 2721) to reduce the number of trustees from five to two.

6645. NHS trusts – establishment – Lanarkshire Acute Hospitals

LANARKSHIRE ACUTE HOSPITALS NATIONAL HEALTH SERVICE TRUST (ESTABLISHMENT) AMENDMENT ORDER 2001, SSI 2001 357; made under the National Health Service (Scotland) Act 1978 s.12A, s.105, Sch.7A para.1, Sch.7A para.3. In force: September 30, 2001; £1.50.

This Order, which amends the Lanarkshire Acute Hospitals National Health Service Trust (Establishment) Order 1998 (SI 1998 2724), reduces the number of trustees from five to two.

6646. NHS trusts – establishment – Lanarkshire Primary Care

LANARKSHIRE PRIMARY CARE NATIONAL HEALTH SERVICE TRUST (ESTABLISHMENT) AMENDMENT ORDER 2001, SSI 2001 356; made under the National Health Service (Scotland) Act 1978 s.12A, s.105, Sch.7A para.1, Sch.7A para.3. In force: September 30, 2001; £1.50.

This Order, which amends the Lanarkshire Primary Care National Health Service Trust (Establishment) Order 1998 (SI 1998 2732), reduces the number of trustees from five to two.

6647. NHS trusts – establishment – Lomond and Argyll Primary Care

LOMOND AND ARGYLL PRIMARY CARE NATIONAL HEALTH SERVICE TRUST (ESTABLISHMENT) AMENDMENT ORDER 2001, SSI 2001 354; made under the National Health Service (Scotland) Act 1978 s.12A, s.105, Sch.7A para.1, Sch.7A para.3. In force: September 30, 2001; £1.50.

This Order, which amends the Lomond and Argyll Primary Care National Health Service Trust (Establishment) Order 1998 (SI 1998 2734), reduces the number of trustees from five to two.

6648. NHS trusts – establishment – Lothian Primary Care

LOTHIAN PRIMARY CARE NATIONAL HEALTH SERVICE TRUST (ESTABLISHMENT) AMENDMENT ORDER 2001, SSI 2001 355; made under the National Health Service (Scotland) Act 1978 s.12A, s.105, Sch.7A para.1, Sch.7A para.3. In force: September 30, 2001; £1.50.

This Order, which amends the Lothian Primary Care National Health Service Trust (Establishment) Order 1998 (SI 1998 2711), reduces the number of trustees from five to two.

6649. NHS trusts – establishment – Lothian University Hospitals

LOTHIAN UNIVERSITY HOSPITALS NATIONAL HEALTH SERVICE TRUST (ESTABLISHMENT) AMENDMENT ORDER 2001, SSI 2001 359; made under the National Health Service (Scotland) Act 1978 s.12A, s.105, Sch.7A para.1, Sch.7A para.3. In force: September 30, 2001; £1.50.

This Order amends the Lothian University Hospitals National Health Service Trust (Establishment) Order 1998 (SI 1998 2712) by reducing the number of trustees from five to two.

6650. NHS trusts – establishment – North Glasgow University Hospitals

NORTH GLASGOW UNIVERSITY HOSPITALS NATIONAL HEALTH SERVICE TRUST (ESTABLISHMENT) AMENDMENT ORDER 2001, SSI 2001 360; made under the National Health Service (Scotland) Act 1978 s.12A, s.105, Sch.7A para.1, Sch.7A para.3. In force: September 30, 2001; £1.50.

This Order amends the North Glasgow University Hospitals National Health Service Trust (Establishment) Order 1998 (SI 1998 2729) by reducing the number of trustees from five to two.

6651. NHS trusts – establishment – Renfrewshire and Inverclyde Primary Care

RENFREWSHIRE AND INVERCLYDE PRIMARY CARE NATIONAL HEALTH SERVICE TRUST (ESTABLISHMENT) AMENDMENT ORDER 2001, SSI 2001 361; made under the National Health Service (Scotland) Act 1978 s.12A, s.105, Sch.7A para.1, Sch.7A para.3. In force: September 30, 2001; £1.50.

This Order amends the Renfrewshire and Inverclyde Primary Care National Health Service Trust (Establishment) Order 1998 (SI 1998 2729) by reducing the number of trustees from five to two.

6652. NHS trusts – establishment – South Glasgow University Hospitals

SOUTH GLASGOW UNIVERSITY HOSPITALS NATIONAL HEALTH SERVICE TRUST (ESTABLISHMENT) AMENDMENT ORDER 2001, SSI 2001 362; made under the National Health Service (Scotland) Act 1978 s.12A, s.105, Sch.7A para.1, Sch.7A para.3. In force: September 30, 2001; £1.50.

This Order amends the South Glasgow University Hospitals National Health Service Trust (Establishment) Order 1998 (SI 1998 2730) by reducing the number of trustees from five to two.

6653. NHS trusts – establishment – Tayside Primary Care

TAYSIDE PRIMARY CARE NATIONAL HEALTH SERVICE TRUST (ESTABLISHMENT) AMENDMENT ORDER 2001, SSI 2001 363; made under the National Health Service (Scotland) Act 1978 s.12A, s.105, Sch.7A para.1, Sch.7A para.3. In force: September 30, 2001; £1.50.

This Order amends the Tayside Primary Care National Health Service Trust (Establishment) Order 1998 (SI 1998 2710) by reducing the number of trustees from five to two.

6654. NHS trusts – establishment – Tayside University Hospitals

TAYSIDE UNIVERSITY HOSPITALS NATIONAL HEALTH SERVICE TRUST (ESTABLISHMENT) AMENDMENT ORDER 2001, SSI 2001 364; made under the National Health Service (Scotland) Act 1978 s.12A, s.105, Sch.7A para.1, Sch.7A para.3. In force: September 30, 2001; £1.50.

This Order amends the Tayside University Hospitals National Health Service Trust (Establishment) Order 1998 (SI 1998 2728) by reducing the number of trustees from five to two.

6655. NHS trusts – establishment – West Lothian Healthcare

WEST LOTHIAN HEALTHCARE NATIONAL HEALTH SERVICE TRUST (ESTABLISHMENT) AMENDMENT ORDER 2001, SSI 2001 365; made under the National Health Service (Scotland) Act 1978 s.12A, s.105, Sch.7A para.1, Sch.7A para.3. In force: September 30, 2001; £1.50.

This Order amends the West Lothian Healthcare National Health Service Trust (Establishment) Order 1998 (SI 1998 7321) by reducing the number of trustees from five to two.

6656. NHS trusts – establishment – Yorkhill

YORKHILL NATIONAL HEALTH SERVICE TRUST (ESTABLISHMENT) AMENDMENT ORDER 2001, SSI 2001 366; made under the National Health Service (Scotland) Act 1978 s.12A, s.105, Sch.7A para.1, Sch.7A para.3. In force: September 30, 2001; £1.50.

This Order amends the Yorkhill National Health Service Trust (Establishment) Order 1992 (SI 1992 3321) by reducing the number of trustees from five to two.

6657. NHS trusts – membership and procedure

NATIONAL HEALTH SERVICE TRUSTS (MEMBERSHIP AND PROCEDURE) (SCOTLAND) REGULATIONS 2001, SSI 2001 301; made under the National Health Service (Scotland) Act 1978 s.12A, s.105, s.108. In force: September 28, 2001; £2.50.

These Regulations revoke in relation to Scotland the National Health Service Trusts (Membership and Procedure) (Scotland) Regulations 1991 (SI 1991 535 as amended by SI 1993 412, SI 1994 1408, SI 1998 1458 and SI 1999 1133). They contain provisions relating to the appointment, tenure of office, removal and qualifications of chairpersons and trustees, holding of meetings and the appointments of committees and sub-committees. In addition, the Regulations set out the matters that are required to be included in the standing orders being provisions as to the calling of meetings, quorum, conduct of meetings, voting, records, the procedure where there is a shared executive director post and for suspension and disqualification of members from meetings.

6658. Nurses – nursing agencies – registration – fees

NURSES AGENCIES (INCREASE OF LICENCE FEES) (SCOTLAND) REGULATIONS 2001, SSI 2001 216; made under the Nurses (Scotland) Act 1951 s.28, s.33. In force: August 1, 2001; £1.50.

These Regulations, which revoke the Nurse Agencies (Increase of Licence Fees) (Scotland) Regulations 1968 (SI 1968 247), increase to £175 the fee payable on making a first application to a local authority for an annual licence to carry on an agency for the supply of nurses and increase to £125 the fee payable on making a subsequent application in respect of that agency.

6659. Nursing homes – registration – fees

NURSING HOMES REGISTRATION (SCOTLAND) AMENDMENT REGULATIONS 2001, SSI 2001 215; made under the Nursing Homes Registration (Scotland) Act 1938 s.1A, s.4. In force: August 1, 2001; £1.75.

These Regulations amend the Nursing Homes Registration (Scotland) Regulations 1990 (SI 1990 1310) which make provision in respect of nursing homes under the Nursing Homes Registration (Scotland) Act 1938 by increasing the prescribed fee which a Health Board may impose in respect of applications for registration and for continuation of registration and related procedures.

6660. Pharmacy – relocation of pharmacy – "minor relocation" – "appreciable" effect on provision by other person

[National Health Service (Pharmaceutical Services) (Scotland) Regulations 1995 (SI 1995 414) Reg.5(6), Reg.5(10).]

B reclaimed against the decision of the Lord Ordinary refusing their petition for judicial review of a decision by A, an NHS trust, refusing their application for what they argued was a "minor relocation" under the National Health Service (Pharmaceutical Services) (Scotland) Regulations 1995 Reg.5(6) of their NHS contracted pharmacy. B argued that Reg.5(6) was designed to further the public interest, not the private interest of service providers, which were protected by Reg.5(10), and in considering those interests A had taken into account an irrelevant consideration. B referred to English authority and argued further that if there was ambiguity the provisions should be given a construction favouring freedom of trade.

Held, refusing the reclaiming motion, that A had fulfilled their duty under Reg.5(6) to consider whether what was proposed was a "minor relocation", including whether or not there was an "appreciable effect" on the pharmaceutical services provided by B "or by any other person" included on A's pharmaceutical lists. The Lord Ordinary was correct in stating that the term "minor relocation" was used differently in the regulations governing England and Wales, and in his reasons for his decision. Opinion of the Court per Lord McCluskey

BOOTS THE CHEMIST LTD v. AYRSHIRE AND ARRAN PRIMARY CARE NHS TRUST 2001 S.C. 479, Lord McCluskey, Lord Cowie, Lord Prosser, Ex Div.

HEALTH AND SAFETY AT WORK

6661. Animal products – diseases and disorders – specified risk material

RESTRICTION ON PITHING (SCOTLAND) REGULATIONS 2001, SSI 2001 73; made under the European Communities Act 1972 s.2. In force: in accordance with Reg.1; £1.75.

These Regulations, which give effect to Commission Decision 2000/418 ([2000] OJ L158/76), prohibit the use of the technique known as "pithing" in the slaughter of bovine, ovine or caprine animals for sale for human or animal consumption. They provide that all parts of the carcass of an illegally pithed animal are deemed to be specified risk material for the purposes of the Specified

Risk Material Order 1997 (SI 1997 2964) and the Specified Risk Material Regulations 1997 (SI 1997 2965), make a consequential amendment to the Welfare of Animals (Slaughter or Killing) Regulations 1995 (SI 1995 731), give a power of entry to persons appointed as inspectors by the relevant enforcement authority, create offences and penalties and specify who is to enforce them.

6662. **Employers liability – breach of statutory duty – meaning of "workplace" – meaning of "device"**

[Workplace (Health, Safety and Welfare) Regulations 1992 (SI 1992 3004) Reg.5(1), Reg.18; Provision and Use of Work Equipment Regulations 1992 (SI 1992 2932) Reg.5(1), Reg.6(1), Reg.2.]

B sought damages for an injury sustained when he trapped his right hand between two heavy doors at the premises of his employer, U, while closing them to enable machinery to start up. At proof B gave evidence that the locking mechanism was faulty due to a loose and misaligned bracket and that he had been using force on handles which were close to the edges of the doors, when his index and middle fingers became trapped. He pled cases under the Workplace (Health, Safety and Welfare) Regulations 1992 Reg.5(1) and Reg.18 and the Provision and Use of Work Equipment Regulations 1992 Reg.5(1) and Reg.6(1). U argued that the doors were neither "the workplace" nor "work equipment", and that although Reg.6 of the Work Equipment Regulations could apply in relation to the switch, the real cause of the accident emanated from B who allowed his fingers to extend and be trapped: the only regulation in issue was Reg.18 of the Workplace Regulations as a pure question of fact as to whether the doors were suitable.

Held, granting the decree, that (1) Reg.5(1) of the Workplace Regulations did not apply, the doors neither constituted "workplace" nor "device", but Reg.18 did apply as the doors had to be opened and closed many times and the position of the handles showed that they were not suitably constructed; (2) the doors fell within the definition of "work equipment" in the Work Equipment Regulations Reg.2 and were not "suitable" for their purpose by virtue of their faulty locking mechanism, the positioning of the handles and the faulty bracket; Reg.6 also applied and was conceded to impose an absolute duty; (3) U's breach of duty caused the accident and there was no contributory fault, and (4) solatium of £2,000 was appropriate where fractures to the fingers resulted in pain for a few weeks and residual discomfort in cold weather, together with £500 for services by B's wife in helping him dress.

BECK v. UNITED CLOSURES & PLASTICS PLC 2001 S.L.T.1299, Lord McEwan, OH.

6663. **Employers liability – breach of statutory duty – workman tripping over article or obstruction on floor**

[Workplace (Health, Safety and Welfare) Regulations 1992 (SI 1992 3004) Reg.12(3).]

S used a profile burner to cut metal plates. S would place the metal plate onto a low table, climb on top of the plate and use the burner. The burner had tubes attached, through which, oxygen and gas were supplied. S climbed down from the table, became entangled in those tubes and fell, injuring himself. S sought damages from B, arguing that the tubes were an obstruction or article which might cause a person to trip and B had breached the Workplace (Health, Safety and Welfare) Regulations 1992 Reg.12(3).

Held, that the tubes were not an obstruction, *Jenkins v. Allied Ironfounders Ltd* [1970] 1 W.L.R. 304, [1970] C.L.Y. 1076 followed, but were an article as they were easily visible objects on the floor. It was for B to show that their proper system of work meant it was not reasonably practicable to place such articles on the floor.

SIMMONS v. BRITISH STEEL PLC 2001 Rep. L.R. 82, Lord Hardie, OH.

6664. Employers liability – manual handling operations – risk of injury

[Provision and Use of Work Equipment Regulations 1992 (SI 1992 2932); Manual Handling Operations Regulations 1992 (SI 1992 2793); Manual Handling Operations Regulations 1992 (SI 1992 2793) Reg.4.]

M raised an action for damages against his employees in respect of an injury to his back sustained whilst trying to move a table in a dining hall in order to deal with water penetration in an emergency. Although the table was designed to fold and then be moved on castors, the folding mechanism was broken rendering the table difficult to move. M argued that his employers were in breach of the Provision and Use of Work Equipment Regulations 1992 Reg.6 by failing to maintain work equipment in good working order. F further argued that his employers were in breach of the Manual Handling Operations Regulations 1992 Reg.4 in that they had failed to take all reasonably practicable steps to ensure that manual handling operations were conducted without risk of personal injury to their employees. D, as M's employers, argued that the table was not a piece of work equipment in terms of the Provision and Use of Work Equipment Regulations 1992 and that they had not carried out a risk assessment under the Manual Handling Operations Regulations 1992 because they had not foreseen the need for the table to be moved and therefore the need for a manual handling operation.

Held, awarding damages of £2,956, that (1) the table was work equipment, had been inadequately maintained, the state of repair had resulted in M being injured and the local authority were, therefor, in breach of Reg.6, and (2) the table was intended to be moved by virtue of its folding mechanism and castors, the local authority should have foreseen that any attempt to move the table whilst in a poor state of repair would be likely to result in personal injury and they were accordingly in breach of Reg.4.

MacKIE v. DUNDEE CITY COUNCIL 2001 Rep. L.R. 62, Sheriff RA Davidson, Sh Ct (Grampian, Highland and Islands).

6665. Employers liability – psychiatric illness – employee committing suicide – work related stress

[Management of Health and Safety at Work Regulations 1992 (SI 1992 2051) Reg.3; Council Directive 89/391 EC on the introduction of measures to encourage improvements in health and safety of workers at work.]

F committed suicide when he was aged 39. His widow, C sought damages from his former employers, H, averring that F's suicide was caused by the stress to which he was subjected at work, that H had been negligent at common law, and were in breach of duty under the Management of Health and Safety at Work Regulations 1992. F had been employed as a senior training manager from 1990, based in a remote area. C averred that he had begun to suffer from depression late in 1992, prior to the death of his mother in February 1993. In April 1993 he had approached his manager, M, mentioning problems with his workload, and shortly after was certified unfit for work by his GP who identified "stress" as the cause. F was certified as fit for work two months later. Shortly before returning to work, F attended a session with a stress adviser to whom he was referred by H's personnel manager. He committed suicide two months after returning to work. C argued that (1) the common law duty of care of an employer needed to be interpreted in the light of the Council Directive 89/391, and the standard of care of a competent person under the Directive, rather than that of a reasonably careful employer, should apply; (2) given H's general knowledge of the possible effects of stress at work and in particular that F had been ill as a result of such stress, they were under a duty under Reg.3 to make an assessment of the risks at work; (3) H were under a duty to take protective steps following F's return to work, and (4) although the Regulations provided no civil right of action, they purported to implement the Framework Directive and such a right was required for proper implementation. H argued that psychiatric injury should be treated differently from physical injury and that only injury as a result of nervous shock was recoverable.

Held, granting H absolvitor, that (1) it was not proved that the job was such as to be likely to cause F psychological harm. It clearly did not for at least two years; (2) it was not proved that the initiating cause of F's illness was work related, though it was accepted that that was how F perceived it; (3) it was right in principle to treat the risk of psychiatric injury in the same way as the risk of physical injury when considering the duty of care of an employer to protect his employees; (4) nervous shock was not the only type of psychiatric injury that could give rise to an action in negligence, *Alcock v. Chief Constable of South Yorkshire* [1992] 1 A.C. 310, [1992] C.L.Y. 3250 distinguished as a secondary victim case. It would be unacceptable for the law to adopt a position which would allow an employer to continue exposing employees knowingly to conditions that could cause psychiatric illness; (5) it was common for statute and common law to impose different standards of care, and a pre-existing and co-existing common law duty setting a lower standard than the directive did not need to be interpreted as if it were the vehicle for the implementation of the directive; (7) given the limited extent to which H were aware of the severity of F's illness and his continued vulnerability, there was no clear evidence that the job was objectively harmful to his health. In 1993 the code of practice relative to the regulations only dealt with physical health and safety, and in the absence of a general practice of carrying out risk assessment in relation to stress at work, C's submissions on the impact of Reg.3 on the common law duty of care failed; (8) H were under a duty to moderate F's workload on his return at least until it could be proved that he was coping, but M's evidence was accepted that this was done, and (9) in the light of the preamble and other Commission documents on health and safety it was clear that at the time of enactment the Commission did not intend to address the issue of the impact of stress at work on mental health in the Framework Directive.

CROSS v. HIGHLANDS AND ISLANDS ENTERPRISE; *sub nom.* CROSS v. HIGHLAND AND ISLANDS ENTERPRISE; MacDONALD v. HIGHLANDS AND ISLANDS ENTERPRISE 2001 S.L.T. 1060, Lord Macfadyen, OH.

6666. Employers liability – safe system of working – duty owed to ship's master

[Merchant Shipping (Health and Safety: General Duties) Regulations 1984 (SI 1984 408).]

M, the widow of D, a ship's master, sued D's employers (G) for damages at common law, alleging G had negligently failed to devise and maintain a safe system of work, and under the Merchant Shipping (Health and Safety: General Duties) Regulations 1984, in respect of D's death during unloading of the vessel. M averred that, during unloading, a homemade tool was used to secure strops for lifting of cages by dockside cranes, which sometimes required a crew member to go beneath a raised cage. During such an operation a cage fell on D, killing him. G argued that (1) G did not owe D a duty of care because a ship's master was in a unique position, being in command of all shipboard operations, and because D was safety officer in charge it was not fair, just and reasonable to impose a duty on G; (2) there was nothing to suggest G were ever made aware of any risks attached to the system in use, which had been in operation for some years without incident, and there was no fair notice of how G could have foreseen any risk of injury, and (3) M's averments relating to situations where the homemade tool could not be used were irrelevant.

Held, allowing a proof before answer, that (1) there was no reason in principle or authority for a ship's master to be excluded from the employer's general duty of care to his employee, or from the particular duty to devise, maintain and enforce a safe system of work, and G owed D such a duty. Delegation of duty to a senior employee did not affect an employer's duties in law; (2) M's averments were sufficiently relevant. M had averred that had G taken an interest in the system prior to the accident, they would have foreseen the danger and been able to remedy the unsafe system; if this was proved G might be held responsible in law for the system in use on the ship, and (3) as M's pleadings simply amounted to a statement that the system in place did not obviate the need for someone to go under the cage from time to time, which might reflect on the general safety of the system and G's failure to remedy it, they were not irrelevant.

MacIVER v. J&A GARDNER LTD 2001 S.L.T. 585, Lord Carloway, OH.

HERITABLE PROPERTY AND CONVEYANCING

6667. **Damages – loss of profits – heritable property – inaccurate property inquiry certificate**

See DAMAGES: Maypark Properties Ltd v. Stirrat. §6419

6668. **Development plans – financial assistance – rural development – Highlands and Islands**

CROFTING COMMUNITY DEVELOPMENT SCHEME (SCOTLAND) REGULATIONS 2001, SSI 2001 208; made under the European Communities Act 1972 s.2. In force: June 29, 2001; £2.50.

These Regulations introduce measures to supplement Council Regulation 1257/1999 ([1999] OJ L160/80) on support for rural development from the European Agricultural Guidance and Guarantee Fund (EAGGF) and amending and repealing certain Regulations, Council Regulation 1260/1999 ([1999] OJ L161/1) laying down general provisions on the Structural Funds and Commission Regulation 1750/1999 ([1999] OJ L214/31) laying down detailed rules for the application of Council Regulation 1257/1999 on support for rural development from the European Agricultural Guidance and Guarantee Fund (EAGGF). The Community legislation referred to above provides for payment of assistance from the Guidance Section of the European Agricultural Guidance and Guarantee Fund for measures which promote rural development falling within the scope of Council Regulation 1257/1999. Measures relating to Objective 1 areas (which include the Highlands and Islands for transitional support under Objective 1) are subject to the provisions of Council Regulation 1260/1999. These Regulations set up the Crofting Community Development Scheme and enable the payment of financial assistance under the Single Programming Document for the Highlands and Islands Special Transitional Programme which, in accordance with Council Regulation 1260/1999, was approved by the European Commission on 8th August 2000. Financial assistance under the Regulations can be provided for the implementation of a development plan which achieves one of the objectives listed in Reg.3(2). An eligible applicant who wishes to benefit from financial assistance must prepare a development plan which must include the information listed at Reg.4(2). Applications can be made at any time. The Scottish Ministers may, however, suspend receipt of applications. The Regulations also make provision for the determination of applications by the Scottish Ministers; provide for the levels of financial assistance available including the maximum limits of financial assistance payable; provide for how financial assistance may be claimed and what evidence may be required in support of a claim; provide for retention of information and records; confer powers of entry and inspection for authorised persons to enforce the Regulations; make provision for the revocation of approval and the withholding or recovery of financial assistance; make provision for payment of interest on financial assistance recovered under these Regulations; and create offences of knowingly or recklessly making a false statement to obtain financial assistance or of obstructing authorised persons acting under the Regulations.

6669. **Disposition – description by reference to title of adjoining subjects – inconsistency with measurements and plan stated to be demonstrative only – bounding title**

The assignees of a development company (M) sought damages from a company who had sold an area of land to M, for breach of warrandice in the disposition to M. Following the purchase, the adjoining proprietors (D) had objected to building works begun by M as encroaching on their land. M then purchased the strip of land in question from D. The subjects originally sold were described as bounded inter alia by the property in D's title, and by reference to measurements and to a plan which was said to be demonstrative only. The pursuers averred that in terms of the measurements and plan, the disposition bore to convey the strip of land. The defenders sought dismissal, arguing that, properly construed, the disposition was a bounding description which did not bear to convey any part of the strip to M. The pursuers argued that the description of the subjects was not delimitative and the court had to look at all the elements of the description. Where the other descriptive elements were unclear the measurements within the dispositive clause would be preferred; a plan of the ground might be used insofar as consistent with these measurements, and did not require to be disregarded just because it was described as demonstrative.

Held, dismissing the action, that (1) in order to constitute a bounding title it was not necessary that the boundary in question be some physical feature or demarcation on the ground itself, and an imaginary geographical line, if specific and certain, was sufficient; (2) the disposition between the defenders and M employed a bounding description where it sought to define the boundary of the subjects; (3) the terms of the description did not make bald reference to the subjects being bounded by the property of others, but referred specifically to the previously recorded disposition of D's land which contained a bounding description, which was a competent way to create a bounding title stricto sensu, and (4) the terms of a plan expressed to be demonstrative and not taxative did not prevail against a written description constituting a bounding title, and it followed that the erroneous measurements did not prevail.

ROYAL & SUN ALLIANCE INSURANCE v. WYMAN-GORDON LTD 2001 S.L.T. 1305, Lord Eassie, OH.

6670. **Disposition – rectification – omission of right of pre-emption contained in missives – relevancy of averments of intention**

A company, owners of a farm, sought rectification of a disposition granted to a former employee and his wife, and an ancillary declarator. The parties had entered into missives which provided for a right of pre-emption in favour of the petitioners if the first respondent left their employment prior to repayment of sums due under a standard security. The missives were to cease to be enforceable two years after the date of entry. The disposition, executed five days after missives were concluded, did not include the right of pre-emption, and a clause imposing a duty on the petitioners to repurchase the property on notice had been made a real burden. The respondents argued inter alia that the petitioners' averments were irrelevant, as they referred to the common intention of the parties at the time of executing the disposition, rather than when the agreement was made, and as the disposition was revised and approved by the petitioners' solicitors, was read before it was signed and the date of entry also differed from the missives; that the petitioners could not seek to rely on the missives for the purpose of rectification once two years had passed; and that the prayer for declarator was incompetent.

Held, granting the order for rectification de plano and dismissing the prayer for declarator as incompetent, that (1) the petitioners had relevantly averred that the common intention expressed in the missives at the date they were concluded remained the common intention of the parties at the date of the disposition, and the disposition was intended to give effect to that intention; (2) rectification of the disposition by reference to the missives did not involve "enforcement" of the missives beyond the two year time limit; (3) given the admitted circumstances and the undisputed documents, the petitioners had discharged the onus on them to establish a prima facie case; (4) having regard to those factors and to the neutral character of the factors put forward by the respondents, the respondents had in principle no relevant defence to the application; (5) minor alterations to the terms in which the petitioners sought rectification could be made by the court ex proprio motu for clarification of the rectified deed, and (6) the petitioners' prayer for declarator was incompetent in a petition process.

RENYANA-STAHL ANSTALT v. MacGREGOR; *sub nom.* REYANA-STAHL ANSTALT v. MacGREGOR 2001 S.L.T. 1247, Lord Macfadyen, OH.

6671. Land registration – fees

FEES IN THE REGISTERS OF SCOTLAND AMENDMENT ORDER 2001, SSI 2001 163; made under the Land Registers (Scotland) Act 1868 s.25. In force: May 15, 2001; £1.50.

This Order, which amends the Fees on the Registers of Scotland Order 1995 (SI 1995 1945), makes additional provision for National Health Service trusts to qualify for abated fees in the Registers of Scotland when completing title to property following the reorganisation of those trusts.

6672. Land Registration (Scotland) Act 1979 (c.33) – Commencement No.15 Order

LAND REGISTRATION (SCOTLAND) ACT 1979 (COMMENCEMENT NO.15) ORDER 2001, SSI 2001 309 (C.14); made under the Land Registration (Scotland) Act 1979 s.30. Commencement details: bringing into force various provisions of the Act on April 1, 2002; £1.50.

This Order brings into force specified sections of the Land Registration (Scotland) Act 1979, which provide for the circumstances in which an interest in land shall be registerable, in the areas of the counties of Inverness and Nairn.

6673. Missives – servitude right for water pipe – waiver of right

E sought specific implement of missives whereby property was purchased by A, and E agreed to deliver a deed of servitude relating to the passage of a water pipe. E had been unable to provide a deed covering the full length of the pipe as it passed under a private road whose owners could not be traced. However E and A agreed that the title should be granted a non domino and title indemnity insurance obtained. A sought to resile which E contended was prevented by waiver of such rights in the missives.

Held, allowing a proof before answer, that (1) E's pleadings did not suggest that E was relying on the type of implied waiver expressly prohibited by the missives, but rather on the proposition that A had waived their right to resile based on E's failure to provide a deed of servitude in terms of the missives and the averments were relevant; (2) there was no objection in principle to the concept of conditional waiver and that waiver required a permanent, not temporary, abandonment of the right, but that is was possible for an inference that a party could permanently, but conditionally, waive a contractual right, and (3) it was not possible to affirm that E's averments were incapable of supporting the inference that A had abandoned their right to resile for lack of the deed of servitude, had accepted the alternative package put forward by E and only retained the right to resile if the terms of the alternative package proved unacceptable.

EVANS v. ARGUS HEALTHCARE (GLENESK) LTD 2001 S.C.L.R. 117, Lord Macfadyen, OH.

6674. Pre emption rights – non ambiguous nature of rights – condition unenforceable – cost unascertainable

G wanted to sell a former police station and the surrounding land as a dwelling house. The feu charter contained a real condition granting the right of pre-emption to the superior in the event of the property being sold at a price that did not exceed the original cost of the police station buildings. G sought declarator that this clause no longer had force and effect. Decree de plano was granted, the Lord Ordinary holding that the reference to "cost" did not meet the requirement of clarity since there was no mechanism or quantification of how to calculate that cost. P reclaimed.

Held, refusing the reclaiming motion, that the term "cost" was not ambiguous, it was clear that, regardless of any increase in value, the superior was not to pay more than the cost of the original police building. However, since there were no directions for ascertaining the "cost", and as it was not permissible to look outside the four corners of the deed for the extent of the restriction, it did not constitute a valid and enforceable real condition. Opinion of the Court per Lord Rodger, Lord President.

GRAMPIAN JOINT POLICE BOARD v. PEARSON 2001 S.C. 772, Lord Rodger L.P., Lord Caplan, Lord MacLean, 1 Div.

6675. Repairs – common repair scheme – statutory repairs – interdict against architect carrying out works – competency

[Housing (Scotland) Act 1987 (c.26) s.240(1).]

G was the owner occupier of a flat within a building containing three flats which were subject to a statutory repair notice issued by the local authority under the Housing (Scotland) Act 1987. Prior to the statutory notice being issued, G in conjunction with the other proprietors had, with the help of M, an architect, investigated the cost of a common repair scheme with improvement grant support under the Act. G had withdrawn from that course of action as the standard of repairs required in connection with an improvement grant was higher than those required to comply with a statutory repair notice. Following the issue of the repair notice, the other proprietors revived the proposal for the common repair scheme and instructed M to apply for an improvement grant. The grant application was successful and the work to repair the building was undertaken with M being appointed as consultant and G, along with the other proprietors, being liable for an equal share of the costs less his share of the improvement grant. G raised an action of interdict and interim interdict against M to prevent work proceeding, failing which G sought an order that works carried out should be undone by M as his own expense at least in so far as they affected G's flat. G argued that work of a higher standard than was required constituted a legal wrong against G as owner of the flat and that the works should not have been carried out without G's permission as required by s.240(1). The sheriff dismissed the action and the sheriff principal refused the appeal. G appealed to the Court of Session.

Held, refusing the appeal, that (1) an order for the works to be undone was inappropriate as completion of the works meant that M no longer worked for the proprietors under the repair grant scheme and could not, therefore, instruct any work to be carried out on the building without the owners' consent, and (2) any order of the type sought by G required to be clear and specific detailing precisely what work required to be undone and G's pleadings did not provide sufficient detail to enable such an order to be made.

Observed, that the sheriff was wrong to suggest that no authority existed in Scot's law for a court to direct that work be undone. Opinion of the Court as per Lord Cameron of Lochbroom.

GARDNER v. MacNEAL 2001 Hous. L.R. 8, Lord Rodger L.P., Lord Cameron of Lochbroom, Lord Caplan, Ex Div.

6676. Sale of land – option to purchase – consideration – provision of accommodation to sellers

M, a house-building company, raised an action against F and related family trustees, as proprietors of a piece of land, for declarator that an agreement between M and F had created a valid and binding option to purchase that land. M made a formal offer to F stating that, in return for an option over the land, M would provide a two bedroom bungalow within Hamilton up to the value of £60,000, which F would be entitled to live in rent free for life with no liability for council tax or other recurring property taxes. The offer also made provision for calculation of the consideration payable in the event of the option being purchased and bound M to take all necessary steps to promote and secure planning permission for a housing development on the land. F accepted the offer subject to the condition that the proposed bungalow had to be acceptable to F. M formally accepted that condition, the communications having been in writing and adopted as holograph. M argued that they had acted in good faith on the agreement, believing it to be binding from the outset, and had made certain payments to F in respect of fees and outlays incurred by F. In addition, M had incurred considerable expense promoting and subsequently obtaining outline planning permission for a development of 650 houses on the site. Without reference to M, F gratuitously disponed a one half pro indiviso share of the land to related family trustees. On discovering that, M raised the action. F sought dismissal of the action as irrelevant arguing that to have a concluded contract, the parties had to either fix a price or agree a mechanism for fixing the price. F argued that the provision of the bungalow required further negotiation and agreement between the parties and that the agreement could, therefore, not be concluded until an agreement regarding a specific property was in place. F claimed that no contract could be considered concluded unless its terms were enforceable by specific implement.

Held, refusing the motion to dismiss and allowing a proof before answer, that (1) it was clear from the form and terms of the missives and the subsequent formal variation of the missives, that the parties intended to be bound at that time by an enforceable agreement; (2) the missives were sufficient without further agreement between the parties to clearly identify the class of property which would represent the consideration for the option being granted; the effect of the requirement for F's approval was to add an additional criterion and there was no requirement for the missives to prescribe the mechanism for identification of a particular property, and (3) where a mechanism to ascertain the price was provided, the court should be reluctant to interfere unless the price could not be made certain even after application of the appropriate law. *Opinion*, that in Scots law a valid option to purchase could be created without any consideration.

MILLER HOMES LTD v. FRAME 2001 S.L.T. 459, Lord Hamilton, OH.

6677. **Servitudes – access – right arising by necessity – option to buy land incorporating part of seller's access**

M, through missives, granted an option to R to purchase a portion of M's farm land. Subsequently, R assigned its rights under the missives to I, a development company, which immediately informed M of its intention to exercise the option. M agreed to dispone the land subject to a reservation in favour of M of a servitude right of access to the portion of M's farm land not being sold as it would, by the sale, be otherwise landlocked. I raised an action of adjudication in implementation of the missives which was dismissed on the grounds that M's right of access implied by law arising out of the necessity of a landlocked property had the same effect as the insertion of such a right in the disposition. I reclaimed against the decision of the Lord Ordinary to dismiss the action.

Held, allowing the reclaiming motion and granting decree de plano, that although M had an implied right of access arising out of the necessity created by the sale to I, he was not entitled to commute that to a servitude right of access in the disposition to I as an implied right of access arising out of necessity would last only for as long as no other form of access existed to the land whereas an express grant of a right of access contained as a real burden in title deeds lasted, and was enforceable, in perpetuity, making the two rights fundamentally different, *Bowers v. Kennedy* 2000 S.C. 555, [2000] 9 C.L. 754 and *Walton Bros v. Glasgow Magistrates* (1876) 3 R. 1130, considered. *Observed*, that arguments made on behalf of I that an express grant would be wider in nature than the implied right which was restricted to the type and form of access used prior to the sale may be correct. Opinion of the Court per Lord Rodger, Lord President.

INVERNESS SEAFIELD DEVELOPMENT CO LTD v. MacKINTOSH 2001 S.C. 406, Lord Rodger L.P., Lord Cameron of Lochbroom, Lord Caplan, 1 Div.

6678. **Servitudes – constitution – real or personal right created – right of egress for fire escape**

M, heritable proprietors of retail premises, sought declarator that a minute of agreement entered into between their predecessors in title and S, neighbouring heritable proprietors, providing reciprocal rights of egress for fire escape purposes, were real rights or, if merely personal, that they had been assigned to and were assignable by M. S had served notice on M purporting to prohibit them from using the fire escape route and thereafter M received notice of S's application for listed building consent to block up the relevant doorways. S argued that (1) there was a basis in the provision laying on the party using the right of egress liability to pay for any damage caused, for inferring an element of delectus personae; and (2) the fact that the minute of agreement provided for recording did not make the right a servitude, because recording did not make real that which was not real.

Held, granting M decree de plano, that on balance, though the failure to use the term "servitude" and the failure to make express provision that the rights were to bind singular successors tended to support the inference that the minute was not intended to create servitudes, the proper inference to draw from the circumstances was that the parties to the agreement had intended to create reciprocal praedial servitudes. Support for that could be found in the facts that (a) the parties to the deed proceeded on the narrative that they were respectively heritable proprietors; (b) they set out in the deed descriptions of their respective properties in a sufficient form to serve as the identification of the dominant and servient tenements affected by servitudes; (c) the rights were designed to enhance the enjoyment of the respective heritable subjects as such, rather than to confer benefits personal to the parties and independent of their enjoyment of the heritable properties; (d) the nature of the rights was such that it was more likely that the parties would contemplate their continuation for the benefit of singular successors than their cessation on the first transmission of one or other of the two subjects; and (e) an entry clause, indicating that it was contemplated that the deed would be recorded in the Register of Sasines, and a warrandice clause, had been included, indicating an intention to create real rather than personal rights.

MOSS BROS GROUP PLC v. SCOTTISH MUTUAL ASSURANCE PLC 2001 S.C. 779, Lord Macfadyen, OH.

6679. Warranties – property inquiry certificate – breach of warranty

[Housing (Scotland) Act 1974 (c.45) s.16.]

N raised an action for damages of £30,000 against S in respect of an alleged breach of warranty. N entered into a full repairing and insuring lease of shop premises having first obtained a property search certificate from S which failed to mention that there was an outstanding notice attached to the property under the Housing (Scotland) Act 1974 s.16. N's share of the cost of repairs necessary under the notices, after deduction of a grant allowance, was £28,574.40. The action against S, and an associated search company was based on a warranty printed on the reverse of the certificate. N claimed that, had the certificate accurately reflected the true position with regard to the notice, they would either have taken steps to avoid liability for the repairs or taken the decision not to enter the lease. N based the assessment of their loss on the cost of the repairs. S, whilst agreeing that the certificate had been inaccurate, argued that the warranty was specific in limiting the method of assessment of loss in the event of a warranty claim and that N's pleadings were irrelevant. N argued that the wording of the warranty was more appropriate to the position were property was being sold and was insufficiently clear when applied to a lease to specifically exclude the approach taken in assessing loss.

Held, sustaining S's plea of irrelevance in respect of pleadings referring to loss based on the cost of repairs and putting the case out to order, that (1) although the terms of the warranty were more easily applied to a sale, the definitions of those terms given in the warranty allowed the warranty to be applied to a lease where, as in this case, that lease had been registered; (2) the warranty was offered by S to enhance the position available to their clients over that which would be available at common law and the language of the warranty defined the extent of the additional benefits offered by S making the appropriate method of assessing loss, the method specifically described in the warranty, and (3) N's averments relating to the cost of repairs were irrelevant when used as a primary measure of loss but could have been used to support an assessment of the true value of the lease as required by the warranty.

NATIONAL CHILDREN'S HOME AND ORPHANAGE TRUSTEES v. STIRRAT PARK HOGG 2001 S.C. 324, Lord Macfadyen, OH.

6680. Books

Conveyancing Statutes: 2001. Paperback: £24.00. ISBN 0-414-01427-8. W.Green & Son.

Paisley, Roderick – Land. Greens Law Basics. Paperback: £9.95. ISBN 0-414-01373-5.W.Green & Son.

Paisley, Roderick; Cusine, Sheriff D – Unreported Property Cases. Paperback: £85.00. ISBN 0-414-01338-7.W.Green & Son.

HIGHWAY CONTROL

6681. Access – roads – strip of land adjacent to public road – access refused by roads authority – judicial review – strip not forming part of public road

[Roads (Scotland) Act 1970 (c.20) s.29; Roads (Scotland) Act 1984 (c.54) s.1 (1).]

E were owners of an area of land adjacent to a public road, but separated from the metalled surface of that road by a strip of land owned by G, the roads authority. E wanted to develop its land and G were refusing access and egress over the strip, except in return for monetary consideration. E petitioned for judicial review of G's actions, seeking declarator that (1) it was entitled to take access over the strip, and (2) G were acting ultra vires in seeking to obtain value from E or from preventing E from taking access and egress. G argued that the strip was in their sole ownership and access and egress was something that they had the right to control or prevent, or for which to claim payment. The land for the road and the strip had been acquired compulsorily by G under the Roads (Scotland) Act 1970 s.29 and the road had been adopted under the Roads (Scotland) Act 1984 s.1 (1). E argued that all of the land appropriated by G must be considered as forming part of the road because it was purchased for that purpose, had been used for no other, and had not been declared surplus. E therefore had a right of access over the strip as part of a public road.

Held, rejecting the petition, that the purchase of land by G under s.29 of the 1970 Act was not the same as a dedication by G of the whole of that land for public passage. The strip had not been shown ever to have been subject to public rights of passage and was not included in the description given to the public road in the statutory list of roads. As E had failed to demonstrate any subsequent actings or circumstances amounting to such a dedication in respect of the strip, G were legally entitled to seek to obtain a consideration for access and egress.

ELMFORD LTD v. GLASGOW CITY COUNCIL 2001 S.C. 267, Lord Clarke, OH.

6682. Erskine Bridge Tolls Act 2001 (asp 12)

This Act of the Scottish Parliament restores, with retrospective effect (other than as regards criminal liability), the power to levy tolls conferred by the Erskine Bridge Tolls Act 1968 s.1 (1).

This Act received Royal Assent on September 13, 2001 and comes into force on September 13, 2001.

HOUSING

6683. Hostels – eviction – right of occupation – eviction without notice

[Rent (Scotland) Act 1984 (c.58).]

C, the occupier of a bed in a hostel for homeless persons who had been evicted, appealed against the decision of the sheriff principal ([1999] S.L.T. (Sh. Ct.) 102, [1999] C.L.Y. 6260) upholding the decision of the sheriff that she could not be regarded as having been a tenant or lessee of the premises. C's grounds of appeal were, inter alia, that the sheriff principal had erred in "(a) holding that the pursuer's averments failed to provide any basis for the importation into the contract of an implied condition that reasonable notice required to be given to terminate it; (b) holding that in the absence of an express contractual term as to reasonable notice of termination, the pursuer's contract for residential occupation of a local authority hostel for homeless persons gave the defenders a discretion to terminate it and eject her without notice or cause; (c) holding that in the circumstances where it was accepted that there was a contract for residential occupation between the parties, and that the normal rule was that such a contract could only be terminated on reasonable notice, it was incumbent on the pursuer to aver that such a term should be implied where not expressed, rather than for the defender to aver why it should be excluded; (d) in relying on the supposed analogy of the position with regard to contracts for occupation of hotel rooms, and in particular the case of *Cook v. Paxton* (1910) 48 S.L.R. 7, where it was accepted that the pursuer had a contract with the defenders, and in the absence of any admitted breach of that contract on her part; (e) in purporting to agree with the sheriff that from the provisions of the Rent (Scotland) Act 1984 it appeared to have been the view of Parliament that persons occupying hostel accommodation had no right to be evicted without notice, where the sheriff in fact held, rightly and on the contrary, that this provision did not deprive the pursuer of her common law rights not to be evicted without reasonable notice". The case called for a summar roll hearing at which it is understood that senior counsel for the respondents did not support the decision of the sheriff principal.

Held, pronouncing an interlocutor "in respect that agreement has been reached", inter alia allowing the appeal, restoring the interlocutor of the sheriff and remitting to the sheriff to proceed as accords. No opinions were issued.

CONWAY v. GLASGOW CITY COUNCIL 2001 S.L.T. 1472 (Note), Lord Cameron of Lochbroom, Lord Caplan, Lord Macfadyen, Ex Div.

6684. Housing associations – registered social landlords – specified bodies

HOUSING (SCOTLAND) ACT 2001 (REGISTERED SOCIAL LANDLORDS) ORDER 2001, SSI 2001 326; made under the Housing (Scotland) Act 2001 s.57. In force: November 1, 2001; £1.50.

This Order provides that specified bodies are to be treated as being housing associations which were registered in the register of housing associations maintained under the Housing Associations Act 1985 s.3.

6685. Housing associations – Scottish homes – transfer of property and liabilities

HOUSING (SCOTLAND) ACT 2001 (TRANSFER OF SCOTTISH HOMES PROPERTY ETC.) ORDER 2001, SSI 2001 396; made under the Housing (Scotland) Act 2001 s.85, s.109. In force: November 20, 2001; £2.00.

This Order makes provision for the transfer of certain property and liabilities of Scottish Homes to the Scottish Ministers.

6686. Housing benefit – rent officers – functions

RENT OFFICERS (HOUSING BENEFIT FUNCTIONS) (SCOTLAND) (AMENDMENT) ORDER 2001, SI 2001 1326 (S.4); made under the Housing Act 1996 s.122. In force: July 2, 2001; £1.50.

This Order amends the Rent Officers (Housing Benefit Functions) (Scotland) Order 1997 (SI 1997 1995) which confers functions on rent officers, in connection with housing benefit and rent allowance subsidy, and requires them to make determinations and redeterminations in respect of tenancies and licences of dwellings. It extends the relevant criteria that a rent officer must have regard to when determining a single room rent.

6687. Housing benefit – rent officers – functions

RENT OFFICERS (HOUSING BENEFIT FUNCTIONS) (SCOTLAND) (AMENDMENT) (NO.2) ORDER 2001, SI 2001 2318; made under the Housing Act 1996 s.122. In force: July 2, 2001; £1.50.

This Order amends the Rent Officers (Housing Benefit Functions) (Scotland) Order 1997 (SI 1997 1995) which confers functions on rent officers, in connection with housing benefit and rent allowance subsidy, and requires them to make determinations and redeterminations in respect of tenancies and licences of dwellings.

6688. Housing support grant – aggregate amount and apportionment

HOUSING SUPPORT GRANT (SCOTLAND) ORDER 2001, SSI 2001 129; made under the Housing (Scotland) Act 1987 s.191, s.192. In force: April 1, 2001; £2.00.

This Order, which fixes for the year 2001-2002 the aggregate amount of the housing support grants payable to some local authorities under the Housing (Scotland) Act 1987 s.191, provides for the aggregate amount to be divided into general and hostel portions. It prescribes the local authorities among whom the grants for the general portion will be apportioned, provides the method of calculation and prescribes the local authorities among whom the grants for the hostel portion will be apportioned and the method of calculation.

6689. Housing (Scotland) Act 2001 (asp 10) – Commencement No.1 Order

HOUSING (SCOTLAND) ACT 2001 (COMMENCEMENT NO.1, TRANSITIONAL PROVISIONS AND SAVINGS) ORDER 2001, SSI 2001 336 (C.15); made under the Housing (Scotland) Act 2001 s.109, s.113. Commencement details: bringing into force various provisions of the 2001 Act on October 1, 2001 and November 1, 2001; £2.00.

This Order brings into force various provisions of the Housing (Scotland) Act 2001.

6690. Housing (Scotland) Act 2001 (asp 10) – Commencement No.2 Order

HOUSING (SCOTLAND) ACT 2001 (COMMENCEMENT NO.2, TRANSITIONAL PROVISIONS, SAVINGS AND VARIATION) ORDER 2001, SSI 2001 397 (C.17); made under the Housing (Scotland) Act 2001 s.109, s.113. Commencement details: bringing into force various provisions of the 2001 Act on November 1, 2001; £1.75.

This Order amends the New Towns (Scotland) Act 1968, the Housing (Scotland) Act 1988, the Housing Act 1988, the Housing Act 1996, the Public Finance and Accountability (Scotland) Act 2001 and the Housing (Scotland) Act 2001 (Commencement No. 1, Transitional Provisions and Savings) Order 2001 (SSI 2001 336) to bring into force various provisions of the Housing (Scotland) Act 2001.

6691. Housing (Scotland) Act 2001 (asp 10) – Commencement No.3 Order

HOUSING (SCOTLAND) ACT 2001 (COMMENCEMENT NO.3, TRANSITIONAL PROVISIONS AND SAVINGS) ORDER 2001, SSI 2001 467 (C.21); made under the Housing (Scotland) Act 2001 s.109, s.113. Commencement details: bringing into force various provisions of the 2001 Act on December 19, 2001; £1.75.

This Order brings into force various provisions of the Housing (Scotland) Act 2001.

6692. Housing (Scotland) Act 2001 (asp 10)

This Act of the Scottish Parliament makes provision about housing, including provision about homelessness and the allocation of housing accommodation by social landlords, the tenants of social landlords, the regulation of social landlords, Scottish Homes, the strategic housing functions of the Scottish Ministers and local authorities and grants for improvement and repairs.

6693. Judgments and orders – interdict – interim interdict – notice to quit temporary accommodation served on wife as tenant – interdict raised by husband

[Housing (Scotland) Act 1987 (c.26) s.31, s.35.]

B raised an action against SLC for interdict to prevent them from evicting him and his dependants from temporary accommodation. B enrolled a motion for interim interdict. B argued that SLC, following an action for non-payment of rent in 1995, had persecuted him and that SLC had deliberately made unsuitable offers of permanent accommodation to B. He argued that, in light of the unsuitability of the accommodation offered, he should still be regarded as homeless and therefore entitled to remain in occupation of the temporary accommodation designated for homeless persons. SLC argued that B had no title to raise the action as the temporary accommodation had been allocated to B's wife only following a request from her solicitor indicating that she had separated from B and their differences were irreconcilable. Since allocation of the temporary accommodation to B's wife and four children, SLC had made three separate offers of permanent accommodation which all fell within the geographical areas indicated by her as acceptable. The latest offer had been within the same geographical area as the temporary accommodation, which would have allowed the children to remain at their schools. All three offers had been rejected without adequate explanation as to why they were deemed unacceptable. In all the circumstances, SLC argued that they were entitled to evict Mrs B and her dependants from the temporary accommodation.

Held, refusing the motion for interim interdict, that (1) B had no title to raise the action, not being a party to the tenancy in question; (2) SLC had fulfilled all its statutory obligations under the Housing (Scotland) Act 1987 s.31 and s.35 and were entitled to proceed with the eviction, and (3) any grievance which B may have had concerning his treatment by SLC since 1995 had no bearing on the instant application for interim interdict.

BROWN v. SOUTH LANARKSHIRE COUNCIL 2001 Hous. L.R. 34, Lord Clarke, OH.

6694. Local government finance – housing revenue account – contribution from general fund

HOUSING REVENUE ACCOUNT GENERAL FUND CONTRIBUTION LIMITS (SCOTLAND) ORDER 2001, SSI 2001 37; made under the Housing (Scotland) Act 1987 s.204. In force: March 15, 2001; £1.50.

This Order provides that local authorities may not include in their estimates for the year 2001-2002 any contribution from their general fund to their housing revenue account.

6695. Public sector tenancies – damages – dampness – delay effecting repairs – inconvenience – anxiety and loss

G, a local authority tenant, sought damages from GCC for the inconvenience, anxiety and loss caused by living in a property suffering from damp. On entering into occupation in 1987, the property appeared to be tenantable but over time it emerged that it was badly insulated and the window frames developed holes which let in moisture. G, a pensioner, contended that it was unreasonable for her to have to pay for the heating necessary to ward off the damp, which had proved ineffective in any event. G complained to GCC on several occasions between 1992 and 1997 when double glazing was eventually fitted. G adduced evidence from her son, a neighbour and an architect as to the state of the premises.

Held, granting decree, that the witnesses were sufficiently credible given the time scale involved. Notice of repair had effectively been given in 1992 but repairs had not been carried out in a reasonable time. G was therefore awarded £2,750 in damages on the basis of £500 per annum from her first complaint in 1992 to the carrying out of the work in 1997, with a further £250 for damage to clothing, carpets and furnishings. GCC had a contractual obligation to carry out the repairs and could not rely on lack of financial resources as a defence.

GALLOWAY v. GLASGOW CITY COUNCIL 2001 Hous. L.R. 59, Sheriff S Cathcart, Sh Ct (Glasgow and Strathkelvin).

6696. Public sector tenancies – repossession – antisocial behaviour

[Housing (Scotland) Act 1987 (c.26) s.48, s.48(1), Sch.3 Part I para.1, Sch.3 Part I para.3, Sch.3 Part I para.7; Human Rights Act 1998 (c.42) Sch.1 Part I Art.8.]

GCC sought recovery of possession of a top floor flat occupied by A and her children. There had been a series of incidents of deliberate flooding of her neighbours living in flats below, th storage of rubbish which was flung from windows which behaviour GCC argued was antisocial. A argued that GCC's action was unreasonable and no suitable transfer had been offered. A also contended that GCC's action constituted a violation of her right to family life in terms of the Human Rights Act 1998 (c.42) Sch.1 Part I Art.8.

Held, granting decree, that (1) the rent arrears, the flooding and A's behaviour and that of her children were sufficient to establish grounds for recovery of possession under Housing (Scotland) Act 1987 (c.26) Sch.3 Part I para.1 and para.7; (2) the ground contained in para.3 pertaining to deterioration of the flat had not been proved; (3) even allowing for the fact that A was a single mother with language, cultural and mental health difficulties, it had not been unreasonable in all the circumstances for the local authority to refuse to offer alternative accommodation; (4) a high degree of culpability was required to make it reasonable under s.48 of the 1987 Act to grant decree resulting in A being left homeless and that such a degree of culpability had been demonstrated, and (5) there was no breach of A's human rights as any interference had been justified under Sch.1 Part I Art.8(2) of the 1998 Act. Opinion, that if the case had been concerned solely with rent arrears, it would not have been reasonable to grant decree.

GLASGOW CITY COUNCIL v. AL-ABASSI 2001 Hous. L.R. 23, Sheriff S Cathcart, Sh Ct (Glasgow and Strathkelvin).

6697. Public sector tenancies – repossession – antisocial behaviour – negation of obligation to find alternate accommodation

[Housing (Scotland) Act 1987 (c.26) Sch.3 para.7.]

EDC raised proceedings to evict two secure tenants, C, founding on Housing (Scotland) Act 1987 Sch.3 para.7 which allowed the court to recover possession from tenants who were causing annoyance or nuisance. Decree was granted on the basis of C's behaviour over a number of years, which included excessive noise and quarrelling. It was also held that EDC were not obliged to find C alternative accommodation as it was clear C did not consider their behaviour unreasonable and would probably continue that behaviour elsewhere. C appealed, arguing that the sheriff had failed to distinguish between tenants when reviewing the evidence since more allegations had been made against the second defender than the first. Evidence was produced which included a petition by neighbours to the effect that C should not be evicted and purported to criticise the behaviour of other neighbour.

Held, refusing the appeal and answering the questions in the affirmative, that (1) it was clear from the sheriff's findings regarding quarrels and damage to the house that the first defender was guilty of conduct which was a nuisance or annoyance; (2) it was not open to the court to consider new evidence which threw a different light on the sheriff's conclusions and could not be tested in the way evidence was tested at proof, and (3) the reasons for the sheriff's conclusion that it was not reasonable for C to be rehoused made it difficult to quarrel with that decision.

EAST DUNBARTONSHIRE COUNCIL v. CAMERON 2000 Hous. L.R. 126, EF Bowen Q.C., Sheriff Principal, Sh Ct (Glasgow and Strathkelvin).

6698. Right to buy – withdrawal of offer by landlord

[Housing (Scotland) Act 1987 (c.26) s.71.]

S applied for a finding that ACC had failed to issue timeously either a notice to sell or a refusal, in accordance with the Housing (Scotland) Act 1987 s.71 (1) (a), following an application to purchase the house which she tenanted. ACC initially issued an offer to sell in accordance with the Act. However, following receipt of an anonymous letter suggesting that the property was no longer S's principal residence, ACC issued a notice withdrawing the offer to sell. S argued that the withdrawal of the offer to sell resulted in the same position under the Act as if an offer had never been made which then required ACC to timeously issue a notice of refusal. ACC argued that the offer to sell had been made timeously, that no attempt had been made by S to accept the offer or respond to the notice of withdrawal and that by making the offer to sell, there was no requirement under the Act to also issue a notice of refusal. ACC maintained that in circumstances where a timeous offer had been issued, s.71 did not apply. ACC further argued that S had made fraudulent misrepresentations on her application to purchase and was not, in fact, a secure tenant at the time the application was made.

Held, granting the application, that (1) the withdrawal of the offer by ACC was valid and successful and resulted in a position in terms of s.71 as if the offer had not been made, and (2) in the absence of a timeous notice of refusal, the tribunal had no jurisdiction to consider whether S had qualifying status at the time of the application or not, *East of Scotland Water Authority v. Livingstone* 1999 S.C. 65, [1999] C.L.Y. 6272, followed.

Observed that, the appropriate remedy for a local authority, where fraudulent misrepresentation could be proved, lay at common law in reduction of the application.

SMITH v. ABERDEEN CITY COUNCIL 2001 Hous. L.R. 17, Lord McGhie, LandsTr (Scot).

6699. Secure tenancies – housing associations – transfer of interest from qualifying to non-qualifying landlord – alteration to status of tenancy

[Housing (Scotland) Act 1987 (c.26) s.44; Housing (Scotland) Act 1988 (c.43) s.43, s.45.]

A housing association raised an action of removing against a tenant M, having previously served a notice to quit on her. M had entered into a secure tenancy in 1995 with a qualifying landlord in terms of the Housing (Scotland) Act 1987 s.44. On February 28, 1998 the landlord's interest in the property had transferred to K, a non-qualifying landlord by the Housing (Scotland) Act 1988 s.43. M argued that as s.45 of the 1998 Act, under which certain secure tenancies entered into prior to the commencement of the section should not be capable of being a secure tenancy if and for so long as the landlord's interest ceased to be held by a public body, did not apply to her tenancy, the security of tenure afforded her by the qualifying landlord continued notwithstanding the transfer of interest. The sheriff, and on appeal the sheriff principal, granted decree. The tenant appealed.

Held, refusing the appeal, that s.45 was not relevant. The existence of a secure tenancy was dependent on the landlord being a qualifying landlord in terms of s.43, and when K acquired the landlord's interest, the security of tenure flew off and M became merely an assured tenant under the 1988 Act.

KNOWES HOUSING ASSOCIATION LTD v. MILLAR 2002 S.C. 58, Lord Johnston, Lord Cameron of Lochbroom, Lord Prosser, Ex Div.

6700. Statutory nuisance – defective premises – condensation – injury to health

See NUISANCE: Robb v. Dundee City Council. §6827

HUMAN RIGHTS

6701. Convention Rights (Compliance) (Scotland) Act 2001 (asp 7) – Commencement Order

CONVENTION RIGHTS (COMPLIANCE) (SCOTLAND) ACT 2001 (COMMENCEMENT) ORDER 2001, SSI 2001 274 (C.12); made under the Convention Rights (Compliance) (Scotland) Act 2001 s.15. Commencement details: bringing into force various provisions of the Act on July 27, 2001; September 5, 2001 and October 8, 2001; £1.75.

This Order brings into force specified provisions of the Convention Rights (Compliance) (Scotland) Act 2001 on July 27, 2001, September 5, 2001 and October 8, 2001.

6702. Crime – breach of the peace – anti nuclear protestor laying in road – meaning of "crime"

[European Convention on Human Rights 1950 Art.7.]

S was charged with a breach of the peace caused by lying in a road outside a military base and, by doing so causing a disruption to traffic as a protest against the use of nuclear weapons. She lodged a minute raising a devolution issue that the offence of breach of the peace in Scottish law was not sufficiently or clearly defined so as to comply with the requirements of the European Convention on Human Rights 1950 Art.7. The magistrate held that no devolution issue existed but granted S leave to appeal. S argued on appeal that Art.7 required that a person would clearly know from the text of a law and the courts' interpretation of that law, what acts would constitute an offence. S submitted that the courts' interpretation of the offence of breach of the peace in Scotland, which was evident through an examination of leading case law, had become so wide that it could not reasonably be deemed to comply with the requirements of Art.7. The prosecution submitted that there was no devolution issue as the crime of breach of the peace was clearly defined. What was evident from an examination of the case law was that the method of committing the offence had wide variations but that did not alter the definition of the crime.

Held, refusing the appeal, that (1) the examination of the facts of one individual case in which a breach of the peace has been held to have been committed could not be used to provide a comprehensive definition of the crime of breach of the peace, (2) to constitute the crime, conduct severe enough to cause alarm to an ordinary person or threaten disturbance to a community was required; mere annoyance or irritation were insufficient but rather conduct which was genuinely alarming or disturbing to the reasonable person was required, (3) the definition of the crime found in the principle authorities was sufficient to meet the requirements of Art.7, and (4) although there were some borderline decisions within Scottish case law, provided the central nature and definition of the crime was borne in mind, there was no need for a major review of subsequent cases.

Observed, that although police officers have the discretion on whether or not to act in a particular set of circumstances, with actions in some circumstances resulting in a charge of breach of the peace and in others resulting in no further action, this could not be taken to reflect on the basic definition of what constituted a breach of the peace. Opinion, that whilst the statutory form of charge is sufficient, it may be more appropriate, bearing in mind the terms of the convention, to include specification of the conduct alleged to have caused the breach of the peace.

SMITH v. DONNELLY 2002 J.C. 65, Lord Coulsfield, Lord Caplan, Lord Osborne, HCJ Appeal.

6703. Disciplinary procedures – nurses – validity of procedures under ECHR Art.6(1)

[Nurses, Midwives and Health Visitors Act 1997 (c.24); European Convention on Human Rights 1950 Art.6(1).]

T was a qualified nurse on the register of the local authority in accordance with their duties under the Nurses, Midwives and Health Visitors Act 1997. Under the Act the council had power to take disciplinary proceedings against anyone on the register and to remove them from the register if a finding of misconduct was made. The council initiated proceedings against T. There was an unqualified right of appeal against any decision made. However T applied for judicial review of the decision to hold a meeting of the Professional Conduct Committee (PCC) to determine the charge of misconduct against her. She argued that it was unlawful because it was incompatible with her human rights under the European Convention on Human Rights 1950 as the PCC was not an independent and impartial tribunal.

Held, that the referral of charges to the council's PCC was not a breach of T's rights under Art.6(1) because the procedure had to be viewed as a whole and her right of appeal to the Court of Session met the requirements of Art.6(1).

TEHRANI v. UNITED KINGDOM CENTRAL COUNCIL FOR NURSING MIDWIFERY AND HEALTH VISITING 2001 S.C. 581, Lord Mackay of Drumadoon, OH.

6704. Right to fair trial – independent and impartial tribunal – effect on jury on indictment libelling bail aggravations

See CRIMINAL PROCEDURE: Boyd (John) v. HM Advocate. §6357

6705. Right to fair trial – judges – request to disclose whether a freemason

[European Convention on Human Rights 1950 Art.6(1).]

M was charged with theft. During police interviews, he made certain statements regarding the freemasons. At the intermediate diet, he lodged a plea that, as some police witnesses might be freemasons, unless the court could guarantee impartiality in relation to freemasonry, his right to an impartial and independent hearing under the European Convention on Human Rights 1950 Art.6(1) would be violated. M contended that he was entitled to ask the trial judge whether he was connected to the freemasons and that the judge would be obliged to answer. He further contended, with reference to the dictum of Lord Hope in *R. v. Bow Street Metropolitan Stipendiary Magistrate, ex p. Pinochet Ugarte (No.2)* [2000] 1 A.C. 119, [1999] C.L.Y. 39, that the trial judge should not only be impartial and unbiased, but should be clearly seen to be impartial and that the judicial oath was insufficient to prove impartiality.

Held, declaring that there was nothing to disclose which would give rise to concern regarding the sheriff's impartiality, that (1) there was no entitlement for accused persons to request positive declarations regarding membership of organisations, nor any duty for judges to reply to such requests, and (2) the judicial oath should be given the greatest weight and, if deemed insufficient in itself, then taken together with the ethical duty upon judges to disclose any conflict of interest in hearing a case, these two safeguards should provide sufficient proof of impartiality to satisfy the terms of Art.6(1).

STOTT v. MINOGUE 2001 S.L.T. (Sh Ct) 25, Sheriff IG McColl, Sh Ct (Tayside, Central and Fife).

6706. Right to fair trial – self incrimination – statutory requirement to identify driver

See CRIMINAL EVIDENCE: Brown (Margaret) v. Stott. §6319

6707. Right to liberty and security – mental patients rights – untreatable prisoners – continued detention – compatibility of domestic legislation with Convention rights

[Mental Health (Scotland) Act 1984 (c.36); Mental Health (Public Safety and Appeals) (Scotland) Act 1999 (asp.1) s.1; Human Rights Act 1998 Sch.1 Part I Art.5(1)(e).]

A appealed against the dismissal of his challenge (2001 S.C. 1, [2000] C.L.Y. 6472) to the lawfulness of a restriction order imposed following his conviction for homicide. A contended that the Mental Health (Public Safety and Appeals) (Scotland) Act 1999 s.1, amending the Mental Health (Scotland) Act 1984, was incompatible with the Human Rights Act 1998 Sch.1 Part I Art.5(1) (e) on the basis that (1) the second requirement for compulsory detention, as outlined in the leading case of *Winterwerp v. Netherlands (A/47)* (1982) 4 E.H.R.R. 228, was treatment, and A's condition was not amenable to treatment, and (2) the amendment was arbitrary since it was of application only to those subject to a restriction order.

Held, dismissing the appeal, that (1) Art.5 of the Convention permitted the detention of persons of unsound mind. To interpret the exception permitting detention as requiring an element of treatability before persons of unsound mind, who posed a danger to society, could be detained would not make sense. Furthermore, such an interpretation was not supported by the decision in *Winterwerp*, since the wording therein could equally well be applied to a case where confinement was required for public protection, *Winterwerp* considered, and (2) on the basis that the amendment complied with domestic law and Convention rights, it could not be described as an arbitrary measure despite the fact that its effect was restricted to a small group of people.

A v. SCOTTISH MINISTERS; D v. SCOTTISH MINISTERS; R v. SCOTTISH MINISTERS, [2001] UKPC D5, 2002 S.C. (P.C.) 63, Lord Hope of Craighead, PC (Sc).

6708. Surveillance – authorisation by public authorities

REGULATION OF INVESTIGATORY POWERS (PRESCRIPTION OF OFFICES, RANKS AND POSITIONS) (SCOTLAND) AMENDMENT ORDER 2001, SSI 2001 87; made under the Regulation of Investigatory Powers (Scotland) Act 2000 s.8, s.9, s.28. In force: April 1, 2001; £1.50.

This Order amends the Regulation of Investigatory Powers (Prescription of Offices, Ranks and Positions) (Scotland) Order 2000 (SSI 2000 343) by deleting the reference to the Scottish Crime Squad as a relevant public authority and to substitute a reference to the Operational and Intelligence Group of the Scottish Drug Enforcement Agency which is to replace the Scottish Crime Squad on April 1, 2001.

6709. Books

Loux, Andrea – Human Rights and Scots Law. Hardback: £30.00. ISBN 1-84113-044-3. Hart Publishing.

Reed, Lord – Practical Guide to Human Rights Law in Scotland. Paperback: £45.00. ISBN 0-414-01369-7. W.Green & Son.

IMMIGRATION

6710. Asylum – appeals – leave to appeal – time limits – date from which time runs

[Asylum and Immigration Appeals Act 1993 (c.23) s.9; Act of Sederunt (Rules of the Court of Session 1994) 1994 (SI 1994 1443) r.41.2.]

H, an Algerian national, sought leave of the court to lodge an application for leave to appeal against a decision of IAT in H's application for political asylum. H's application was refused by a special adjudicator on September 18, 2000, and H's appeal was refused by IAT on December 6. On December 27, IAT refused leave to appeal, but did not notify H until January 9, 2001. H's application for leave to appeal was lodged on February 5. The Home Secretary argued in terms of the Asylum and Immigration Appeals Act 1993 s.9 and Act of Sederunt (Rules of the Court of Session 1994) 1994 r.41.2 that leave to appeal should be refused because H's application should have been lodged within 42 days of the determination on December 6. Any risk of prejudice to H's case could be solved by recourse to judicial review.

Held, allowing receipt of the application, that while not dealt with by the 1994 Rules, there had to be some practical means of giving effect to the right of appeal, with leave, and the reasonable approach was that the 42 day period should run from the date of the refusal by IAT. Recourse to judicial review or to the dispensing power would be substituting a discretionary remedy for a right to apply, within a given time, for leave to appeal. Opinion of the Court per Lord Coulsfield

HAKIM v. SECRETARY OF STATE FOR THE HOME DEPARTMENT 2001 S.C. 789, Lord Coulsfield, Lord McCluskey, Lord Wheatley, Ex Div.

6711. Asylum – fear of persecution following assault on government official – assault not considered expression of "political opinion"

C, a Chinese national, was denied political asylum by the Secretary of State and sought reduction of the special adjudicator's subsequent decision rejecting his appeal. C had fled China following an assault on a local government official over the matter of a compulsory land purchase. It was accepted that C had a genuine fear of returning to China but had not established a well founded fear of persecution based on political opinion. C argued that "political opinion" needed to be interpreted widely to include situations where an asylum seeker had acted to preserve a fundamental human right such as the right to enjoy his own property. C also argued that the special adjudicator should have assumed that the Chinese authorities would have regarded C's actions as political and maintained that the adjudicator had erred in concluding that there had been no evidence to support the assertion that C's actions were an expression of political opinion.

Held, dismissing the petition, that "political opinion" was, correctly in this case, not interpreted too restrictively, the prosecution of C for the assault, even if the assault itself was treated as politically motivated, would not qualify as persecution for reasons of political opinion. Nor did it seem that any particular disadvantage would befall C as a direct result of the assault being seen to be politically motivated. The special adjudicator had not found that there was no evidence, but rather that the evidence did not support the conclusion that the assault was the expression of a political opinion.

CHEN v. SECRETARY OF STATE FOR THE HOME DEPARTMENT 2001 S.L.T. 703, Lord Kingarth, OH.

6712. Deportation – post deportation decision marriage – application to remain on basis of marriage – application refused

[Human Rights Act 1998 (c.42) Sch.1 Part 1 Art.8.]

A, a Pakistani national, entered the United Kingdom on a six month visitor visa and applied for asylum; it was denied and the refusal upheld under judicial review. A's deportation was ordered and he married a British citizen. The marriage was the basis for A's further application to remain; it was also refused. A was advised that deportation would not be considered a breach of the Human Rights Act 1998 Sch.1 Part 1 Art.8. A petitioned for reduction of the decision arguing that the decision letter had failed to give proper reasons or take account of the matters raised. A argued that S had failed to take into account the position of women in Pakistan, should A's wife join him there and the governmental advice to avoid all nonessential travel to Pakistan. A also argued that S had erred in considering the marriage only compassionately and had failed to give reasons as to why the circumstances were not exceptional enough.

Held, dismissing the petition, that S's decision had not been unreasonable. S had obviously taken all relevant matters into account, committed no error in law and made a decision within the discretionary area of judgment. The response was proportionate and taking account of the relevant authorities there had been no breach of Art.8.

AHMED (NASIM) v. SECRETARY OF STATE FOR THE HOME DEPARTMENT; *sub nom.* AHMED (NASIM), PETITIONER 2001 S.C. 705, Lord McEwan, OH.

INDUSTRY

6713. Enterprise zones – Highlands and Islands – area of operation – modification

HIGHLANDS AND ISLANDS ENTERPRISE AREA OF OPERATION (SCOTLAND) ORDER 2001, SSI 2001 126; made under the Enterprise and New Towns (Scotland) Act 1990 s.21. In force: April 1, 2001; £1.75.

This Order amends the Enterprise and New Towns (Scotland) Act 1990 by modifying the area within which the functions of Highlands and Islands Enterprise are exercisable by adding to the areas already specified all parishes in the local government area of Moray not already falling within the area of operation of Highlands and Islands Enterprise. The effect of this order is that the area of operation of Highlands and Islands Enterprise now includes the whole of the local government area of Moray.

INSOLVENCY

6714. Bankruptcy – sequestration – sale of assets – family home

[Bankruptcy (Scotland) Act 1985 (c.66) s.40(2).]

B, a debtor, was sequestrated in 1993 over expenses of £975 relating to an unsuccessful court action. He persistently refused to provide a list of his assets and liabilities, despite being ordained by a sheriff to do so, or to co-operate with the permanent trustee in any way, and as a result expenses of the administration amounted to £30,000. The permanent trustee sought authority to sell the family home. The free proceeds of any sale were likely to be about £40,000, of which B's wife was entitled to one half less expenses. The wife pled that authority to sell should be withheld or alternatively postponed for 12 months. The two children of the marriage also stayed in the home, the oldest, 18, attended college while the younger, aged 12, attended school a few miles away in Edinburgh. Both B and his wife had been unemployed for some time.

Held, granting decree, that (1) the Bankruptcy (Scotland) Act 1985 s.40(2) required that all circumstances of the case be taken into account, which included the public interest and B's behaviour, and it was in the public interest that the sequestration be brought to an end within a reasonable time, that expenses paid for by the public purse should be recouped and that B should not be seen to benefit from his recalcitrance; (2) the principal concern was the effect of the sale on the youngest child, but it was preferable that the house be sold sooner rather than later to end the uncertainty for the family, any important exams that the child might sit were some years away and though he would have to move to a less pleasant environment, he would be able to continue at the same school, and (3) it was appropriate to give the wife six months to find alternative accommodation.

RITCHIE v. BURNS; *sub nom.* BURNS TRUSTEE v. BURNS 2001 S.L.T. 1383, Lord Philip, OH.

6715. Directors – insolvent companies – reports on directors' conduct

INSOLVENT COMPANIES (REPORTS ON CONDUCT OF DIRECTORS) (SCOTLAND) (AMENDMENT) RULES 2001, SI 2001 768; made under the Insolvency Act 1986 s.411; and the Company Disqualification Act 1986 s.21. In force: April 2, 2001; £2.50.

These Rules substitute a new form D1 (Scot) in the Insolvent Companies (Reports on Conduct of Directors) (Scotland) Rules 1996 (SI 1996 1910). The new form is substantially the same as the previous form, but contains minor further requirements for information to be provided by office-holders to the Disqualification Unit of the Insolvency Service.

6716. Floating charges – arrestment subsequent to creation of floating charge – winding up 60 days after execution – effectiveness of arrestment

See CIVIL PROCEDURE: Customs and Excise Commissioners v. John D Reid Joinery Ltd. §6220

6717. Sequestration – standard security as payment of debt – inquiry into validity

Z, on a petition for sequestration, offered a standard security over three properties for payment of a debt due to Customs. The security offered would have ranked behind two other securities on two of the properties and behind one on the other. Z produced evidence detailing sufficiency of funds for Customs' debt, even if the other creditors enforced their claims. A proof was ordered. Customs appealed to the sheriff principal who refused the appeal and held that it was permissible to inquire into the validity and sufficiency of such a security. Customs then appealed to the Court of Session.

Held, allowing the appeal and directing the sheriff to award sequestration, that the sufficiency of the security had to be shown "forthwith" and once Z had appeared before the court to show cause why sequestration should not be awarded he was required to do so at that hearing. It was not unreasonable for Customs to regard the offer of security as unacceptable given the uncertainties, reliance on assertions by Z and the further steps required before the actual giving of a security. The lack of security in the interim was not envisaged by statute and as such did not meet the requirement of sufficient security being given forthwith.

Observed, that despite the memorandum being inapplicable in cases of adults, motions requesting support for the complainer had been granted.

CUSTOMS AND EXCISE COMMISSIONERS v. ZAOUI; *sub nom.* ADVOCATE GENERAL FOR SCOTLAND v. ZAOUI 2001 S.C. 448, Lord Prosser, Lord Allanbridge, Lord Milligan, Ex Div.

6718. Winding up – surplus assets – rights of untraced contributories

[Insolvency Act 1986 (c.45) s.148(1), s.193.]

The joint liquidators of A, having wound up the company, had a surplus available for distribution to its members. Despite strenuous efforts, the liquidators had been unable to trace all the members of the company and following an application under the Insolvency Act 1986 s.148(1), the court settled a list of contributories consisting of the details of contributories and personal representatives of contributories who had been traced. The joint liquidators then presented a note seeking a decision on whether the surplus funds could be distributed to the contributories and personal representatives of contributories as detailed in the list of contributories or whether the Insolvency Act 1986 s.193 required a portion of the surplus funds to be lodged in the name of the Accountant of Court in respect of those members who had not been traced.

Held, granting the prayer of the note and directing that the assets be distributed to those identified in the list of contributories settled by the court, that the application of s.193 suggested by counsel for the joint liquidators produced consistency between the rights of those identified in the list of contributories in a solvent winding up and their liabilities in an insolvent winding up; that by Parliament giving the courts the power to settle a list of contributories under s.148(1), they also intended the courts to have a decisive role in settling the distribution of surplus funds and accordingly the list of contributories settled by the court was definitive of those members entitled to share in the distributable assets of the company; and that s.193 did not apply to untraced members not included on the list of contributories.

JOINT LIQUIDATORS OF AUTOMATIC OIL TOOLS LTD, NOTERS 2001 S.L.T. 279, Lord Nimmo Smith, OH.

INSURANCE

6719. Health insurance – health insurance for employees – employer reaching settlement with insurers – employee entitled to settlement money

S, a former employee of U's, sued for payment of £5,000 allegedly due under an employee health insurance scheme. S became ill in 1995 and completed a claim form. S was dismissed in 1996 and reached a compromise with U in 1997 over the claim of unfair dismissal. S maintained that in 1996 U had granted a discharge to the insurance company with regard to S's claim of incapacity to work in return for £5,000. Under the terms of the scheme all monies should have been paid to S and as such S argued that U was holding the money in trust and had no title to it. U argued that S was not an incapacitated member under the insurance contract and averments of a trust were irrelevant. U also argued that the compromise reached with regard to the claim of unfair dismissal was an insuperable obstacle.

Held, allowing proof before answer, that the language of the discharge supported S's claim for entitlement to the sum and S had sufficiently shown that he was an incapacitated member in terms of the policy. It was also argued that the claim was not one arising out of, or under, the terms of S's termination of employment contract and as such was not covered by the terminology of the compromise.

SMITH v. UNUM LTD 2001 S.L.T. 184, Lord Osborne, OH.

6720. Insurance contracts – employers liability insurance – third party rights – interpretation of policy – payment of excess by employer contrary to statutory scheme

[Third Parties (Rights Against Insurers) Act 1930 (c.25) s.1 (1); Employers Liability (Compulsory Insurance) Act 1969 (c.57) s.1 (1).]

A's employer went into liquidation after he had sustained injuries at work. A sought damages from the company and its liquidators and was awarded the sum of £22,500. The sum was not paid and A raised an action against the insurers, I, under the Third Parties (Rights Against Insurers) Act 1930 s.1 (1). I sought dismissal of the action, relying on an excess of £25,000 contained in a schedule to the contract. A argued that the only schedule which purported to cover the date of the accident was dated after the accident, and the excess clause was not part of the contract. A maintained that even if it had been, it would have been either contrary to statute or an excess whereby I were liable to meet a claim and then recover the excess. I argued that the excess was of the sort where A's employer had to meet the excess and that such a clause was not excluded by statute at the relevant time.

Held, putting the case out by order, that in the absence of contrary documentation the court had to proceed on the basis of the documents before them, regardless of their dates. Although there was not a specific statutory prohibition at the time on conditions which would require A's employers to pay the first amount of any claim, it nonetheless ran contrary to a requirement set out in the Employers Liability (Compulsory Insurance) Act 1969 s.1 (1) since an employee would not be covered up to the value of the excess. However, even if the policy did contain that kind of excess, a provision in the policy, that the indemnity should be in accordance with "any law relating to compulsory insurance of liability", would protect A and cover any shortfall in relation to the statutory scheme, obliging I to grant indemnity, subject to a right to reclaim from A's employers. In other parts of the policy, the excess was of the kind where the employer would meet the excess, however the excess founded on here was such that it entitled A to look to I for satisfaction of the decree.

AITKEN v. INDEPENDENT INSURANCE CO LTD 2001 S.L.T. 376, Lord Macfadyen, OH.

6721. Insurance contracts – interpretation of policy – meaning of "arising from. . . employment"

D raised an action for damages against I for a fire in their home caused by work to I's roof. I called the tradesman, A, who carried out the work as a third party. A subsequently became the second defender, and he called his insurers with whom his wife held a policy. The terms of the policy specifically excluded all sums for which the policyholder or any member of her family became liable, which resulted from an accident arising out of the course of their employment, trade of profession. A argued that the roof repairs were being done as a favour to I and he did not expect payment. The insurers argued that A's main occupation was as a roofer and therefore the exclusion clause applied. The sheriff rejected the insurers' arguments and found them liable to indemnify A for any sums due. The insurers appealed to the Court of Session.

Held, refusing the appeal, that A was not acting in the course of his employment, but was merely carrying out repairs as a favour to I. As no remuneration was expected, nor paid, the exclusion clause did not apply and the insurers were liable to indemnify A.

Observed, that application of such exclusion clauses to the actings of Good Samaritans would prevent people doing favours out of love or friendship. Indeed, it was in the insurers' interests that such repairs done as favours were carried out by skilled persons rather than enthusiastic amateurs. Opinion of the Court per Lord Rodger, Lord President.

DIGNON v. IRVING 2001 S.C. 310, Lord Rodger L.P., Lord Caplan, Lord Reed, 1 Div.

6722. Insurance contracts – misrepresentation and nondisclosure in proposal form

G, an invoice factoring company sought declarator that S, an insurance syndicate were under obligation to indemnify G for losses as a result of fraudulent invoicing by their largest client. S argued that they were entitled to avoid the policy on the grounds that G had misrepresented the risk and not disclosed material facts in the proposal and breached the warranty. After proof, G argued that S had failed to plead actual reliance on nondisclosure or misrepresentation and, separately, had no case of breach of warranty. On the eve of judgment, G lodged a minute of amendment adding a conclusion for interest to be payable on any sum declared by the court to be due. S argued that there had been no judicial demand in the sense relevant for the running of interest.

Held, granting decree of declarator and payment, that the misrepresentation and reliance that S had to prove were not entirely distinct. S's averments could be read as implicitly offering to prove reliance and where G had not challenged that they could not now claim to have been deprived of the opportunity. S could not succeed on the breach of contract argument; the whole case on record concerned misrepresentation or nondisclosure. G's proposal had been a fair presentation of their business and its practices, and any misrepresentation or nondisclosure had not been shown to have been material, nor had it induced the making of the contract. Judicial demand had been effected in the instant case by the raising of the declaratory action.

GAELIC ASSIGNMENTS LTD v. SHARP; *sub nom.* GAELIC ASSIGNMENTS LTD v. SHARPE 2001 S.L.T. 914, Lord Hamilton, OH.

6723. Insurance contracts – professional indemnity insurance – breach of contract – decree against insured following withdrawal of defences – liability of insured – third party rights

[Third Parties (Rights Against Insurers) Act 1930 (c.25) s.1.]

Lenders raised an action against the professional indemnity insurers of a sequestrated solicitor, seeking damages for an alleged breach of contract. In 1990, the solicitor failed to obtain a first charge over heritable property owned by borrowers to whom the pursuers had advanced a loan. This resulted in an earlier security prevailing when it was called up in 1994. In 1995, the pursuers, having received nothing in respect of the debt due, raised a sheriff court action against the solicitor in which decree was granted after the insurers withdrew their cover and defences were dropped. In 1997 the solicitor was sequestrated. The pursuer thereafter raised an action against the insurers seeking indemnity in terms of the Third Parties (Rights Against Insurers) Act 1930 s.1. The insurers maintained that the solicitor had not acted in good faith and as such, was not covered by the policy, and that the decree in the pursuers' favour was insufficient to establish that the sums awarded related to matters covered by the policy. The Lord Ordinary held, inter alia, that the decree obtained against the solicitor was effectively determinative of the liability of the insurers, subject to the question of good faith, and allowed a proof concerned primarily with that matter. The insurers reclaimed.

Held, allowing the reclaiming motion and proof before answer, that (1) while the sheriff court decree would give the solicitor the necessary interest to sue his insurers, it would not prevent the insurer from reopening the matter in an action against them at his instance, and the pursuers stood in the solicitor's shoes; (2) the existence of a decree against a cautioner was not necessarily conclusive of the extent of his right to relief against the principal debtor and if the principal debtor failed to defend that action, or failed to do so successfully, he would have to indemnify the cautioner against the sum for which the cautioner was found liable, and (3) the insurers' withdrawal from the sheriff court action carried no implication that they accepted the validity of the pursuers' claim, and to hold that the insurers were not entitled to challenge the quantum of the claim would be inconsistent with the principle that insurers were bound to indemnify their insured only to the extent of his liability to the third party.

CHELTENHAM & GLOUCESTER PLC v. SUN ALLIANCE AND LONDON INSURANCE PLC; *sub nom.* CHELTENHAM & GLOUCESTER PLC v. ROYAL & SUN ALLIANCE INSURANCE CO 2001 S.C. 965, Lord Rodger L.P., Lord Abernethy, Lord Kirkwood, 1 Div.

INTELLECTUAL PROPERTY

6724. Designs – design right – competitor copying unique design – extent of interim interdict

[Copyright, Designs and Patents Act 1988 (c.48) s.227(1).]

UVG, an English company, designed and manufactured ambulance bodies. It applied for UK and European patents in relation to a design for access apparatus to ambulances combining a step and a ramp that was unlike any previous design. Having conducted trials of an ambulance incorporating UVG's design, the Scottish Ambulance Service invited tenders for the supply of ambulance conversions, referring to such a feature. The contract to supply some of the ambulances was to be awarded to AC, a competitor of UVG. UVG received information showing that AC's tender included a step ramp feature. UVG informed AC this would infringe its design right and sought an undertaking from AC that it would not do so. No undertaking was given. Following the commencement of proceedings for design infringement, UVG obtained an interdict unlimited in geographical scope. AC appealed.

Held, recalling the interdict but replacing it with one of similar terms limited to Scotland, that in the absence of any legislative provision to the contrary, interim relief in Scottish courts should be confined to acts in Scotland. Further, the Copyright, Designs and Patents Act 1988 s.227(1) did not widen the ordinary jurisdiction but defined a particular form of infringement of unregistered design right. A restricted interdict should be granted as neither the ambulance service nor the general public would suffer prejudice by its continued implementation and AC had been unable to offer caution.

UVG AMBULANCES LTD v. AUTO CONVERSIONS LTD [2000] E.C.D.R. 479, Lord Reed, OH.

6725. Patents – assignation – rights to "improvements" – new development patentable in own right

B reclaimed against a decision ([2000] R.P.C. 367, [2000] C.L.Y. 6520) to assoilzie A in his action seeking interdict and count, reckoning and payment in respect of A's manufacture and sales of a brake safety meter which B claimed to have patented.

Held, refusing the reclaiming motion and granting decree of declarator in favour of A, that (1) patent 321 did not constitute something distinct in character from application 311, but was rather an improvement of that invention; nor could it be said that patent 321, if embodied in a machine, would produce a different effect from that produced by the embodiment of application 311 in the same machine; patent 321 simply measured the brake fluid in a better and more efficient manner, (2) it was a recognised principle in Scottish law that acquirenda could competently be assigned, *Miller v. Muirhead* (1893) 21 R. 658 and *Reid v. Morison* (1892) 20 R. 510 followed, and so patents and applications which eventually devolved to M under the first assignation would automatically pass to A under the second assignation resulting in A becoming the beneficial owner of patent 321 when it was granted in 1996, (3) what constituted an improvement was a question of fact and it was not open to an appeal court to substitute its findings in fact for those of the judge at first instance unless it was proved that he had clearly misdirected himself in a material way, (4) the Lord Ordinary applied the appropriate test when determining the patent in suit, did not misdirect himself in the application of the test and that he did have sufficient evidence before him to reach the conclusion that A was well founded in their defence to the action of infringement. Opinion of the Court as per Lord Clarke.

Observed, that during the proof the Lord Ordinary had allowed much of the available time to be taken up in demonstrations and experiments, which he later dismissed as being of little relevance, rather than focusing on the main issues. This could have resulted in B feeling that the Lord Ordinary had misdirected himself as to what it was necessary for B to prove or rebut at the proof. However, it was impossible to determine if this was actually the case as the demonstrations and experiments had not been recorded and therefore did not form part of the evidence before the appeal court.

BUCHANAN v. ALBA DIAGNOSTICS LTD 2001 S.C.L.R. 307, Lord Rodger L.P., Lord Clarke, Lord Marnoch, 1 Div.

6726. Trade marks – infringement – interim interdict – trade mark registered by defenders abroad

[Trade Marks Act 1994 (c.26) s.11 (2) (a).]

S sought interim interdict against L, an American company, infringing its trade mark "SpeechWorks". The trade mark had been registered in the UK by R, a director of S, in 1999 in connection with computer software. L had been incorporated in 1994, had been using the name since 1996, had registered "SpeechWorks" as a trade mark in the US in 1999, and was seeking to register in Germany and France. L averred that it had used the name in marketing in the UK since 1997, and was planning an expansion into Europe, and would be exhibiting at a trade fair in London in 2000. L argued that (1) S's trade mark was invalid and liable to be set aside, and (2) whereas L had substantial goodwill overseas and in the UK, there was no evidence of S trading under the name, and the Trade Marks Act 1994 s.11 (2) (a) (honest use of own name) applied. S argued that it had a prima facie case and that the balance of convenience was in its favour, S having taken the proper steps to protect its trade mark. S accepted that it was a "start up" company, but argued that its business and trade under the name were growing. S was prepared to agree that any interim interdict should be suspended until after the trade fair to allow L to establish a different name, and to concede that interim interdict should not affect L's web site unless it was used to attract custom in the UK.

Held, refusing to grant interim interdict, that (1) it was inappropriate to express more than a tentative view on the likelihood of success, but S's registered trade mark made a prima facie case given that L's undisputed actings were capable of amounting to infringement; L would have to establish that s.11 (2) (a) applied. However, the likelihood of success was not so clear on one side or the other that it could materially influence the determination of the balance of convenience; (2) the balance of convenience did not favour interim interdict: (a) L was a substantial company which had successfully promoted "SpeechWorks" products since well before S was incorporated, and L's attempts at European expansion might be seen as a development of that success, whereas S was in the first phase of its business plan, its business remained local and much of it was based on R's personal reputation; and (b) S's concessions with regard to the trade fair and the web site gave credence to L's arguments that interim interdict would cause real difficulties, and it was hard to see how L could reasonably be expected to start using another name in the UK or how S could meet any damages awarded for wrongful use of interim interdict, whereas L was clearly in a position to pay damages to S for infringement. Opinion, that if interim interdict had been granted it would have been restricted to Scotland. Further submissions would have been required regarding L's web site.

SPEECHWORKS LTD v. SPEECHWORKS INTERNATIONAL INC [2000] E.T.M.R. 982, Lord Nimmo Smith, OH.

6727. **Trade marks – labelling – interim interdict granted to prevent reimports of goods with bar codes defaced**

[Council Directive 89/104 on trade marks.]

Perfumes which bore Z's registered trade mark were re-imported into Scotland from Singapore. Z brought proceedings for trade mark infringement and was given an undertaking by M that it would not perform further infringing acts in relation to that particular assignment of perfumes. Z then sought an interim interdict to prohibit all such acts in general.

Held, granting the interim interdict, that (1) the way in which the goods had arrived into the European Economic Area or into the hands of M had not been revealed; (2) the absence of bar codes on the goods made it very difficult to discover their provenance; (3) prima facie it would seem that the only reason for interfering with the bar codes was to conceal the true origin of the goods. The defacing or removal of those bar codes appeared to be designed to facilitate some invasion of the rights of Z under Council Directive 89/104, and (4) M, which said it had not inquired into the provenance of the goods, did not appear to have come to court with entirely clean hands and could not, therefore, claim that the balance of convenience favoured it.

ZINO DAVIDOFF SA v. M&S TOILETRIES LTD (NO.2) [2001] E.T.M.R. 10, Lord McCluskey, OH.

6728. Trade marks – parallel imports – infringement – relabelling by parallel importer

[Trade Marks Act 1994 (Denmark).]

B manufactured and marketed a medicinal product for which it held the patent under the trade name SEROXAT in all Member States, except France where it used the name DEROXAT to avoid confusion with another product. B sold DEROXAT in France for less than the price of SEROXAT. M was licensed by the Medicines Control Agency to import DEROXAT from France for sale in the UK under the generic name paroxetine. M also re-exported DEROXAT from France to Sweden, having first relabelled the product as SEROXAT. B sought interim interdict on the grounds that fixing the name SEROXAT to the re-exported product infringed its exclusive rights under the Trade Marks Act (Denmark) 1994 s.10.

Held, refusing the application, that M had an established market in Sweden for the relabelled product, which was a factor to be taken into account when considering the balance of convenience. It was not possible in the instant case to determine if M's sales had detracted from B's business or that of other parallel importers, nor was there any indication that the relabelling had caused problems in Sweden. The labelling clearly showed that the tablets carried one name but were marketed under another. As this was accepted by the market it was difficult to see how B's trade name could have been damaged. Until the ECJ decided the issues referred in the case of *Glaxo Group Ltd v. Dowelhurst Ltd (Infringement Action)* [2000] 2 C.M.L.R. 571, [2000] 4 C.L. 416 and other cases, it was undesirable for courts in the UK to reach decisions in this area of law that could be potentially in conflict, *Aventis Pharma AB v. Paranova Lakemedel AB* [2001] E.T.M.R. 60 and *Glaxo Group* considered.

BEECHAM GROUP PLC v. MUNRO WHOLESALE MEDICAL SUPPLIES LTD 2002 S.L.T. 263, Lord Nimmo Smith, OH.

6729. Books

Mr Justice Laddie; Prescott, Peter; Vitoria, Mary; Lane, Lindsay – Modern Law of Copyright and Designs. 3rd Ed. Hardback: £320.00. ISBN 0-406-90383-2. Butterworths Law.

INTERNATIONAL LAW

6730. Convention Rights (Compliance) (Scotland) Act 2001 (asp 7)

This Act of the Scottish Parliament amends certain enactments relating to the sentencing and release of life prisoners, the constitution and powers of the Parole Board, legal advice and assistance and legal aid, homosexual offences and the appointment and removal of the procurator fiscal of the Lyon Court which are or may be incompatible with the European Convention on Human Rights; and to enable further changes in the law where it is or may be incompatible with the Convention.

6731. International Criminal Court (Scotland) Act 2001 (asp 13) – Commencement Order

INTERNATIONAL CRIMINAL COURT (SCOTLAND) ACT 2001 (COMMENCEMENT) ORDER 2001, SSI 2001 456 (C.20); made under the International Criminal Court (Scotland) Act 2001 s.30. Commencement details: bringing into force various provisions of the 2001 Act on December 17, 2001; £1.50.

This Order brings the provisions of the International Criminal Court (Scotland) Act 2001, in so far as not already in force, into force on December 17, 2001.

6732. International Criminal Court (Scotland) Act 2001 (asp 13)

This Act of the Scottish Parliament makes provision for offences under the law of Scotland corresponding to offences within the jurisdiction of the International Criminal Court; enables assistance to be provided to that court in relation to investigations and prosecutions; makes provision in relation to the enforcement of sentences and orders of that court.

This Act received Royal Assent on September 24, 2001.

INTERNATIONAL TRADE

6733. Carriage – international carriage by air – timeous notification of damage to cargo – contracted carrier not "person entitled to delivery"

[Warsaw Convention on International Carriage by Air 1929 Art.26.]

CCM sought damages from CIL following water damage to cargo during transit. The cargo was governed by the Warsaw Convention on International Carriage by Air 1929 Art.26 provided that "the person entitled to delivery" must give written complaint of damage within 14 days. CIL were the contracted carriers but the actual transatlantic carriage was undertaken by a third party contracted by CIL. CCM maintained that the timeous notification of the damage to the third party by CIL satisfied the requirement under Art.26 since CIL could be considered both the contracting carrier and a "person entitled to delivery".

Held, putting the case out by order for CCM to consider amendment, that under a purposive interpretation of the Convention, the carrier, whether actual or contracting, could not also be the person entitled to delivery for the purpose of a claim of damages. Therefore CCM's argument that the actual carrier had undertaken to deliver the cargo to CIL, the contracting carrier, and should be considered a "person entitled to delivery" was irrelevant.

COMPAQ COMPUTER MANUFACTURING LTD v. CIRCLE INTERNATIONAL LTD 2001 S.C. 331, Lord McCluskey, OH.

6734. Infectious disease control – foot and mouth disease – import and export restrictions

IMPORT AND EXPORT RESTRICTIONS (FOOT-AND-MOUTH DISEASE) (SCOTLAND) (NO.3) AMENDMENT REGULATIONS 2001, SSI 2001 455; made under the European Communities Act 1972 s.2. In force: December 3, 2001 at 6 pm; £2.50.

These Regulations implement in Scotland Commission Decision 2001/848 ([2001] OJ L315/64) amending Commission Decision 2001/740 ([2001] OJ L277/30) concerning certain protection measures with regard to foot and mouth disease in the UK for the third time. They amend the restrictions on imports and exports of certain animals and animal products contained in the Import and Export Restrictions (Foot-and-Mouth Disease) (Scotland) (No.3) Regulations 2001 (SI 2001 429) to continue the effect of those restrictions, with amendments, until midnight on January 31, 2002.

6735. Infectious disease control – foot and mouth disease – import and export restrictions

IMPORT AND EXPORT RESTRICTIONS (FOOT-AND-MOUTH DISEASE) (SCOTLAND) (NO.3) AMENDMENT (NO.2) REGULATIONS 2001, SSI 2001 483; made under the European Communities Act 1972 s.2. In force: December 24, 2001 at 2 pm; £2.50.

These Regulations, which amend the Import and Export Restrictions (Foot-and-Mouth Disease) (Scotland) (No.3) Regulations 2001 (SSI 2001 429) and the Import and Export Restrictions (Foot-and-Mouth Disease) (Scotland) (No.3) Amendment Regulations 2001 (SI 2001 455), implement Commission Decision 2001/911 ([2001] OJ L337/39) amending for the fourth time Decision 2001/740 concerning certain protection measures with regard to foot and mouth disease in the UK. The Regulations make amendments to continue the effect of the restrictions until February 28, 2002. In addition, the Regulations permit the dispatch from Scotland of live pigs reared in certain areas of Scotland, as set out in the Schedule to these Regulations, subject to certain restrictions. They permit the multiple pick-up of animals destined for slaughter from holdings in certain areas, and where a sole occupancy licence applies. The Regulations also add Prestwick International Airport to the list of ports of import, remove the test requirements for donor bulls and boars at semen collection centres in those areas, and amend the certification requirements for horses dispatched from Great Britain.

6736. Books

D'arcy, Leo; Murray, Carol and Cleave, Barbara – Schmitthoff: Export Trade: the Law and Practice of International Trade. 10th Ed. Hardback: £65.00. ISBN 0-421-61950-3. Sweet & Maxwell.

LANDLORD AND TENANT

6737. Agricultural holdings – rent – retention of rent – validity of notice to quit referred to arbitration

[Agricultural Holdings (Scotland) Act 1991 (c.55) s.22(2)(d), s.60(1).]

A, the tenant of an agricultural holding, intimated to and thereafter withheld rent from, R, his landlord, for failure by R to repair farm buildings under the terms of their lease. R issued a written demand for payment of rent arrears, with which A failed to comply. R then served a notice to quit under the Agricultural Holdings (Scotland) Act 1991 s.22(2)(d). A requested that his entitlement to retain rent and the validity of the notice to quit should be referred to arbitration. R appealed, by way of stated case, against the decision of the arbiter that A was entitled to retain the rent and to allow a proof before answer. R argued that the question before the arbiter was one of liability for rent, which was specifically excluded from the remit of the arbiter under s.60(1) and that the wording of the joint submission by A and R to arbitration did not remedy that. R further argued that A had failed to relevantly aver that rent was not due at the date of issue of the notice to quit. The sheriff found in favour of R, and A appealed to the Court of Session.

Held, allowing the appeal in part, that (1) by retaining rent pending rectification of R's breach of contractual obligations, A was admitting liability for the rent. The question before the arbiter was not, therefore, one of liability for rent but whether the rent was due at the date of issue of the notice to quit, *Graham v. Wilson-Clarke* 1963 S.L.T. (Sh. Ct.) 2 overruled; (2) following the decision in *Brodie v. Ker* 1952 S.C. 216, [1952] C.L.Y. 3756, material breach of obligations under the lease by the landlord would justify retention of rent by the tenant; (3) nothing in s.22(2)(d) prevented the operation of common law principles allowing retention of rent for breach of obligations, and (4) for a notice to quit to be valid, rent must actually be due at the date of service. The case was remitted back to the sheriff to proceed as accords.

ALEXANDER v. ROYAL HOTEL (CAITHNESS) LTD; *sub nom.* ALEXANDER v. TAYLOR 2001 S.L.T. 17, Lord Cameron of Lochbroom, Lord Dawson, Lord Gill, Ex Div.

6738. Crofts – access – pertinent rights of access – no loss through non use for prescriptive period

[Prescription and Limitation (Scotland) Act 1973 (c.52).]

A Divisional Court held that a croft belonging to W, neighbouring that of K, had a pertinent right of access over two parts of K's croft. For one part, the right was for vehicular and pedestrian traffic and for the passage of stock. K appealed to the Land Court. The case turned on whether or not the pertinent rights had been lost through non-use for the prescriptive period of 20 years. K challenged the decision in *Smith v. Murray* 1990 S.L.C.R. 90, [1991] C.L.Y. 5707 as being wrong and sought to distinguish *Bowers v. Kennedy* 2000 S.C. 555, [2000] 9 C.L. 754 because there was no suggestion here that any right of access was a necessity. A pertinent had no basis in statute law and there was nothing in the Prescription and Limitation of Actions (Scotland) Act 1973 which afforded protection to a pertinent right.

Held, refusing the appeal, that the court's function was to determine the nature and extent of existing rights of access, not to create them. There was no basis for the proposition that established use of pertinent rights would only become legal rights when the court declared them to be so. There was evidence of established use of a pertinent right of access in 1960 and there was nothing to indicate a change of circumstances such that the right could no longer be established. Applying the case of *Smith*, the court was not persuaded that the right could be lost by prescription, even if there could be proved a non-use of the access for 20 years. Further, the court was entitled to consider the balance of hardship between the benefited and the burdened lands and, in that regard, there was sufficient evidence to justify the Divisional Court's finding.

KENNEDY v. KERSHAW 2000 S.L.C.R. 1, Lord McGhie, Land Ct (Full Ct).

6739. Crofts – boundaries – establishment of boundaries – appeal – rehearing not allowed – hearing de novo justified by court's treatment of evidence

[Scottish Land Court Rules 1992 (SI 1992 2656) r.78 to r.86.]

In an application for the determination of croft boundaries, the Divisional Court issued a decision against M. M appealed on the grounds that (1) the court had erred in not accepting historical evidence provided by M as being of paramount importance; (2) the court should have had greater regard to M's evidence as supported by her witness, and (3) the documentary evidence of the respondent (N) was conflicting or imprecise. M also sought a rehearing on the basis that she had pertinent and important new evidence regarding various maps, which maps the estate factor had failed to produce and lodge in process. The Full Court was not satisfied that the grounds of appeal stated were relevant and called a preliminary hearing to establish whether there was any proper basis for the appeal.

Held, refusing the motion for a rehearing but allowing a hearing de novo, that M had failed to bring her appeal within the Scottish Land Court Rules 1992 r.78 to r.86, dealing with rehearings. For such rules to apply, M would have had to have shown that she had been prevented from leading before the Divisional Court all the evidence she would like to have led, and that the interests of justice would be best served by allowing additional evidence. However, on the grounds of appeal, there was a statable case for appeal and there were sufficient grounds for criticising the Divisional Court's treatment of M's historical evidence, and sufficient evidence of confusion about the maps to justify the hearing of full submissions in the interests of justice. Evidence which was not allowed under the rehearing would be allowed in the new hearing.

MacDONALD v. MacNAB (NO.1) 2000 S.L.C.R. 133, Lord McGhie, DJ Houston, J Kinloch, Land Ct (Full Ct).

6740. Crofts – boundaries – establishment of boundaries – previous court decision – plea of res judicata upheld

S applied to the Land Court for an order determining the west and north boundaries of his croft. The same croft was already the subject of an order of a Divisional Court from 1953, which had issued an order declaring that the boundaries were as shown red on an estate plan. The plan had subsequently been mislaid. The landlord, M, did not lodge answers but the court asked to be addressed on the issues of competency and res judicata. On the plea of res judicata, S argued that M had not established the four essential elements of the plea, as outlined in *Murray v. Seath* 1939 S.L.T. 348, namely that there had to have been (1) proper judicial examination of the issue; (2) identity of the subject matter; (3) identity of the media concludendi, and (4) identity of the parties. S conceded that the parties may be the same in terms of their interests if not in terms of personnel.

Held, sustaining the pleas and refusing the application, that (1) the application was incompetent because one Divisional Court could not reinterpret the decision of another Divisional Court, and (2) applying the principles of *Murray*, the four prerequisites of a plea of res judicata had been established.

SUTHERLAND v. MacLEOD 2000 S.L.C.R. 18, J Kinloch, Land Ct (Div Ct).

6741. **Crofts – common grazings – apportionment of common grazings – validity of apportionment order – jurisdiction**

[Crofters (Scotland) Act 1993 (c.44) s.53(1).]

The Crofters Commission had made an order apportioning a part of common grazings. The Commission then made a reference to the court for a declaration as to whether the order was valid and effective, or null and void.

Held, that because of the Crofters (Scotland) Act 1993 s.53(1), the court had no jurisdiction to consider the reference or to review the general merits of an apportionment made by the Commission in the discharge of the Commission's functions under the Act.

CROFTERS COMMISSION v. WESTMINSTER (LIVERPOOL) TRUST CO 2000 S.L.C.R. 115, Lord McGhie, DJ Houston, DM Macdonald, Land Ct (Full Ct).

6742. **Crofts – common grazings – apportionment of common grazings to a non-crofter – status of apportionment as a croft**

[Crofters (Scotland) Act 1993 (c.44) s.3(5), s.47(10), s.52.]

M applied to the court for a determination of the status as a croft of an apportionment of part of common grazings. The apportionment had been granted to M's father (along with the let of non-crofting agricultural subjects) for the grazing of cows and sheep. M had subsequently taken an assignation of the lease. The Crofters Commission had granted M's application for an apportionment, but the landlords refused to recognise the apportionment as a croft.

Held, granting the application and continuing the application for a determination of fair rent, that the apportionment was a croft within the terms of the Crofters (Scotland) Act 1993, (1) although not a crofter, M had an unchallengeable legal right to share in the common grazings for the purposes of feeding his stock and was therefore "entitled" to share in the grazings, along with crofters, under s.47(10) and was entitled to apply for apportionment; (2) s.52 entitled the Commission to grant M the apportionment, and (3) therefore, the terms of s.3(5) were clear in providing that the land, even though apportioned to a non-crofter, would be deemed to be held under crofting tenure.

MacARTHUR v. TENTH DUKE OF ARGYLL'S TRUSTEES 2000 S.L.C.R. 94, Lord McGhie, DJ Houston, J Kinloch, Land Ct (Full Ct).

6743. **Crofts – common grazings – resumption of land – contaminated landfill site – valuation – deduction of negative amount relative to development – meaning of "deduct"**

[Crofters (Scotland) Act 1993 (c.44) s.21.]

HC applied to the court for resumption of 1.25 acres of land which had been used for many years as a landfill site, was full, was contaminated and in need of monitoring, and could be used only for landfill monitoring or for tree planting. On the matter of valuation under the Crofters (Scotland) Act 1993 s.21, M argued that (1) valuation should be based on what a site would have been worth in the absence of the development, notwithstanding that the development had precluded any use other than landfill monitoring or for planting trees, and (2) there should be deducted from the market value the negative value of the site attributable to its contamination, i.e. there would be an addition to the market value.

Held, refusing to make the deduction as sought but granting resumption and awarding £5,000 to M (being one half of the parties' agreed valuation of

£10,000), that (1) there was no evidence that the land was capable of being put to any use other than landfill monitoring or tree planting. Therefore, at the valuation date, i.e. the date of resumption, the market value had to reflect that restricted use, *Crofters Sharing in Oldshoremore Common Grazings v. Barr's Trustees* 1993 S.L.C.R. 56 distinguished, and (2) in refusing to make a determination of market value under s.21, the use of the word "deduct" in s.21 was deliberate and if Parliament had intended additions to be allowed, it would have said so.

HIGHLAND COUNCIL v. MacKENZIE 2000 S.L.C.R. 75, DJ Houston, Land Ct (Div Ct).

6744. Crofts – decrofting – entitlement of Crofters Commission to issue decrofting notice

[Crofters (Scotland) Act 1993 (c.44) s.12(2).]

M had applied to the Land Court under the Crofters (Scotland) Act 1993 s.12(2) as tenant of a croft, to have the owners grant him a conveyance of a house site. M then submitted a decrofting application to C which was dismissed since M was not registered as the tenant or owner. M was notified that C were processing an application from the owners for decrofting of the same area. M made written application as to the detrimental effect this would have on him and the crofting community and was assured, by telephone, that no decision would be taken by C until a determination was made on his Land Court application. M took no action to prevent a commission decision, however, the decision to decroft was taken and M's Land Court hearing was dismissed as incompetent. M sought judicial review arguing that the decrofting directions were procedurally unfair where he was not allowed a hearing. C argued that only an applicant could request a hearing and there was nothing in the 1993 Act giving them the power to postpone an application, if they were satisfied they had to grant it.

Held, reducing the decisions, that C had had a discretion to grant M a hearing under s.25(6). C were not bound to decide the owners' application within a particular time frame, they knew M's Land Court hearing had a date and was bound up with the owners application. The commission had acted wholly unfairly in reaching its decrofting decision in advance of the Land Court hearing. No tribunal acting fairly and reasonably, exercising quasi-judicial powers could have acted as they did.

MacINTYRE v. CROFTERS COMMISSION 2001 S.L.T. 929, Lord MacLean, OH.

6745. Crofts – determination of right of access in favour of applicant – applicant denied expenses – application necessitated by respondent's actions – offer to settle not precluding award of expenses

F had succeeded in his application for a determination that he had a right of access over a certain road, but the Divisional Court refused to award F expenses because S had gone to some length to reach a suitable agreement as to joint use of the road. F appealed.

Held, granting the appeal and awarding expenses to F, that (1) F had been obliged to make the application because S had been barring F from exercising his legal rights over the route; (2) there had been an obvious miscarriage of justice in the award and the Court would entertain the appeal, and (3) access was denied unless F agreed to the terms being offered, thereby forcing him to raise court proceedings and incur expense. Opinion, that an offer to settle an action need not justify a refusal of an award of expenses to the successful party unless the terms offered were as good as the result achieved by raising the action.

FINLAYSON v. STORNOWAY TRUST 2000 S.L.C.R. 158, Lord McGhie, DJ Houston, J Kinloch, Land Ct (Full Ct).

6746. Crofts – status of a cottar house – built on common grazings apportioned to a croft

N, the landlords of a croft, applied to the court for an order to determine the status of a former cottar house, and in particular whether it formed part of the croft or was a separate cottar subject. The house had been built on common grazings and occupied by a cottar. The common grazing land surrounding the house was subsequently apportioned to M, a crofter.

Held, finding that the solum and fabric of the house were owned by N and that M was the tenant of the solum of the house but had no rights in the fabric of the house, that the only way in which land could be permanently removed from crofting tenure was by resumption or decrofting. The solum of the house formed part of the apportionment to M and therefore formed part of his croft, although it could not be worked. The fabric of the house was a cottar subject in which M had no rights.

NORTH UIST ESTATE TRUST 1990 v. MORRISON 2000 S.L.C.R. 120, DJ Houston, Land Ct (Div Ct).

6747. Crofts – status of holding – not a "home farm"

[Small Landholders (Scotland) Act 1911 (1 & 2 Geo V, c.49); Crofters (Scotland) Act 1955 (c.21); Crofters (Scotland) Act 1993 (c.44).]

F, the landlord of the Mains of Hempriggs (M), sought to remove B from M on the grounds that M was a croft and had been sublet to B without consent of the Crofters Commission. B applied to the court to determine whether M was a croft. B maintained that because M had been a home farm on April 1, 1912 it was excluded from the terms of the Small Landholders (Scotland) Act 1911 and thus from the Crofters (Scotland) Act 1955 and the Crofters (Scotland) Act 1993. J, executors of the previous tenant, argued that B had no interest to sue because he had not proved title as subtenant and had no right to possession under the Crofting Acts or in any other way. B, referring to *Pottinger v. Hay* 1928 S.L.C.R. 14, argued, inter alia, that: in 1912, the subjects were occupied by L, the widow of S who had had a lease of the subjects for 30 years to 1912; the name "Mains" was indicative of a home farm; the dairy and pig house were of a higher standard than would be expected for a croft; and there was a supply of produce from M to the estate house between 1951 and 1956 which, B argued, suggested a continuation of established practice.

Held, finding that the subjects were a croft, that (1) where there were separate proceedings for his ejection under the Crofting Acts, B had an interest to establish that those Acts did not apply, and even if he could not have been a subtenant without the consent of the landlord, it was not clear that this would have had to be explicit. The evidence might justify an inference of tacit consent; (2) M was a croft; a home farm needed to be distinctive from other farms, and where it had been let on a normal tenancy with no evidence of special features, it would be difficult to view it as a home farm. The lease to L was inconsistent with home farm status and there was no reason to think that that changed with the succession of L or subsequent tenants; S had not been an employee on the estate; the dairy and pig house were consistent with a small holding; it was impossible to draw any inferences from the supply of food 40 years after the relevant date, particularly given the impact of two world wars on patterns of food supply; and unless there was an obligation to supply it would not have affected the substantive issue. Further there was no evidence that the tenants themselves ever had any doubt of its status as a croft.

BUDGE v. FORREST-JONES 2000 S.L.T. (Land Ct) 19, Lord McGhie, J Kinloch, DM Macdonald, Land Ct (Full Ct).

6748. Crofts – statutory rights of crofter – contracting out – statutory interpretation – approval of Land Court not required

[Crofters (Scotland) Act 1993 (c.44) s.5(3), s.12, s.19, s.21, s.37.]

N, landlords, prepared a reorganisation scheme for certain subjects which would make land available for crofting tenure, and applied to the Land Court to determine whether (1) prospective tenants could enter into agreements to renounce their rights under the Crofters (Scotland) Act 1993 s.12 to s.19, s.21 and s.37 (effectively relinquishing their rights to buy) without the approval of the court; and (2) singular successors of the crofters could be bound by such agreements. Section 5(3) of the Act provided that any "agreement made by a crofter by virtue of which he is deprived of any right ... (other than sections 12 to 19, 21 and 37) shall to that extent be void unless ... approved by the Land Court".

Held, answering question (1) in the affirmative and question (2) in the negative, that (1) the language of s.5(3) was tolerably clear and led to the conclusion that an agreement giving up the rights conferred by the specified sections was not struck at, which was neither surprising nor absurd where those sections permitted agreements which would have the effect of excluding any option to apply to the court, and approval of the court was not required; (2) such agreements included those reached by a party who, although only a prospective crofter at the time the agreement was made, was a crofter at the time any issue under the agreement came to be tested, were also included within s.5(3), and (3) agreements of the type in issue could not be created as conditions on crofting tenure and could not affect an assignee of a croft. On a plain reading of the sections, the rights were personal to whom they were purported to be given and exercise of such rights could not be excluded by the agreement or actings of a third party. There was no warrant for concluding that Parliament intended that a current crofter should be deemed to be the same person as his predecessor in title.

NATIONAL TRUST FOR SCOTLAND v. MacRAE 2000 S.L.T. (Land Ct) 27, Lord McGhie, DM Macdonald, J Kinloch, Land Ct (Full Ct).

6749. Land Court – expenses

Certain objections were taken to the Auditor of Court's taxation of expenses following a Land Court appeal, in particular relating to witness' expenses and a litigant's remuneration.

Held, allowing the appeal, that (1) witness fees were not to be treated as a claim by the witness but as a claim by the applicant, and it was not necessary that a payment to the witness had actually been made. Where a party could establish that a liability to pay such expenses had been incurred, that liability could be legitimately treated as an outlay, and (2) in assessing the appropriate rate of remuneration for a party litigant, there should be no distinction between free time and time taken as part of annual leave. The Auditor had to decide where there had and had not been loss of earnings. For valuation of a party's time, the best place to start was that party's normal rate of remuneration. The important aspect was the work actually done and not the time lost from another activity.

MacDONALD v. MacNAB (NO.2) 2000 S.L.C.R. 145, Lord McGhie, DJ Houston, J Kinloch, Land Ct (Full Ct).

6750. Leases – guarantee of tenant's obligations – assignable to subsequent landlords

W raised an action, as landlords of commercial premises for declarator and payment of sums said to be due under a guarantee granted by D, the parent company of the tenants. The guarantee was in favour of the previous owners, a development agency, and related to payment of rent, other monies due and all other obligations incumbent upon the tenants. D argued that the guarantee should be construed strictly and the references to the landlords as "the Agency" and to the tenants simply as "the tenants" reinforced the notion that although the tenants might change, the guarantee was in favour of the original landlords and their statutory successors alone.

Held, granting declarator, that the guarantee had to be interpreted in its transactional context taking account of other documentation relating to the lease which might help in determining the intention of the parties. The terms of the guarantee, read as a whole and construed narrowly were sufficient to permit assignation, the primary obligation related to the performance of obligations rather than in whose favour they were performed and it would be inappropriate to read this more restrictively than its own terms justified.

WAYDALE LTD v. DHL HOLDINGS (UK) LTD (NO.3) 2001 S.L.T. 224, Lord Hamilton, OH.

6751. Leases – rent reviews – determination by expert – expert not acting as arbiter

A were landlords of K. A and K could not agree the appropriate level of a rent review and appointed B under the terms of the lease, which provided for determination by an independent chartered surveyor acting as an expert and not an arbiter. B made his decision and A challenged it by way of judicial review. A argued that (1) B having acted as if an arbiter, he should therefore be treated as one and his decision was susceptible to judicial review; (2) B had introduced material which he was not entitled to take account without seeking the comments or observations of A and K; (3) B's determination was based on his own investigations into tenant demand and not on open market rental value as required by the lease, and (4) reduction was appropriate because A had been denied a chance to confront the evidence.

Held, dismissing the petition, that (1) the petition was competent because A were claiming that B acted as an arbiter; (2) the courts recognised a distinction between an arbiter and an expert. B was not an arbiter in any quasi judicial sense. Neither the terms of B's appointment, nor his subsequent conduct in inviting and considering written submissions, altered his status to that of arbiter. To decide otherwise would be to allow an expert to alter the terms of a lease to which he was not a party, and (3) as a valuer, B was entitled to undertake his own investigations and apply the results, together with his experience, in making his determination, *Arenson v. Casson Beckman Rutley & Co* [1977] A.C. 405, [1975] C.L.Y. 2318 referred to.

AGE LTD v. KWIK SAVE STORES LTD; *sub nom.* AGE LTD v. BROWN 2001 S.C. 144, Lord Hardie, OH.

6752. Leases – subtenancies – assignation of sublease – consent unreasonably withheld

SP, as tenant of a shop, obtained consent from C, the landlords, to confer a subtenancy on S on condition that the sublease was in the form supplied by C. It was also agreed that A, a subsidiary of a holding company of S, would occupy the premises. Subsequently, A ceased to be a subsidiary of S and was no longer in the same group of companies. S contacted C to indicate that they were willing to assign the sublease to A and requested C's consent in terms of cl.6.5(b) of the sublease. C refused to consent and indicated to S that they considered that, as S had shared possession of the property in an unlawful manner, the lease was rendered null and void and the premises reverted to C. SP raised an action of declarator that C had withheld their consent unreasonably, that C were not entitled to refuse consent to the assignation and that, as head landlord, C had no rights to enforce the terms of the sublease. C argued that, as the matter in question was an assignation by S in favour of A with the consent being sought of C, SP was not a party to the matter and thus had no title to sue. C further argued that the effect of the insertion of cl.6.5(b) in the sublease was to create a jus quaesitum tertio in favour of C, conferring upon them an absolute right of veto to the proposed assignation.

Held, granting decree de plano and putting the action out to further procedure as regards the financial standing of A, that C was not entitled to refuse consent to the assignation and that (1) the terms of the sublease could not serve to widen C's rights as head landlord to enforce the sublease; (2) for a jus quaesitum tertio to be created, it was essential that it was the clear intention of the contracting parties to confer such rights upon the tertius and that cl.6.5(b) did not create a jus quaesitum tertio in favour of C; (3) cl.3(12)(b) of the main lease did, by implication, require the C's consent to the assignation of the sublease subject to the proviso that it could not be withheld unreasonably, and (4) as SP were parties to the sublease which was the subject of the proposed assignation and further, that the assertion by C of a right to veto the assignation was linked to the claim by C for irritancy of the main lease, which SP was also a party to, SP had a clear interest and title to sue.

SEARS PROPERTIES NETHERLANDS BV v. COAL PENSION PROPERTIES LTD 2001 S.L.T. 761, Lord Eassie, OH.

6753. Rent – non payment – recompense sought from tenant – unjustified enrichment of informal occupier

C, landlords, sought recompense from G for several years' occupation of their shop premises, X, for which G had not paid rent. C had leased X to Y who had, with consent, assigned the lease to Z. On discovering that Z had ceased to trade from X and that G was in occupation, C entered into negotiations with G to secure a formal lease in C's favour. Those failed and C sent a letter to Z in 1995 intimating the annual rent for the following three year period. In 1997 C sent a notice to quit to Z and in 1998 called on him to ensure all rental arrears due were paid, declining G's invitation to enter into a lease and calling on him to vacate the subjects, which he did.

Held, dismissing the action, that (1) C's loss and G's gain had to arise from the same contract or transaction, but C's loss arose from their failure to take appropriate proceedings against Z and not from G's occupation. G was not lucratus by C's actions, and (2) the doctrine of recompense could not be invoked when another legal remedy was available to C, whether against G or a third party. C had not exhausted their remedies against Z, *Varney (Scotland) Ltd v. Lanark Burgh* 1974 S.C. 245, [1976] C.L.Y. 2991 followed. Opinion, on G's fallback position, that it was not correct in law that while G occupied the premises C were unable to recover rental income.

RENFREWSHIRE COUNCIL v. McGINLAY 2001 S.L.T. (Sh Ct) 79, Sheriff DJ Pender, Sh Ct (North Strathclyde).

6754. Rent – withholding of rent – property not in habitable condition

[Housing (Scotland) Act 1987 (c.26) s.113.]

M sought payment of unpaid rent withheld in part and then in whole by her tenant A who maintained that the premises she occupied were not in a reasonably habitable condition and as such M had failed in her duty under Housing (Scotland) Act 1987 s.113. The flat had damaged ceilings, walls and carpets as a result of a leaky roof. A sought complete abatement of the withheld rent.

Held, granting decree, that the flat was not reasonably fit for human habitation as injury to the defenders health was likely if she continued to live in the flat. Part of the rent had been correctly withheld, M having had sufficient time to effect repairs but M was entitled to rent owed previously.

MacLEOD v. ALEXANDER 2000 Hous. L.R.136, Sheriff TM Croan, Sh Ct (North Strathclyde).

6755. Books

Scottish Landlord & Tenant Fact Book. Looseleaf/ring bound. ISBN 0-414-01380-8. W.Green & Son.

LEGAL AID

6756. Childrens hearings – panels – persons to safeguard interests of children

PANELS OF PERSONS TO SAFEGUARD THE INTERESTS OF CHILDREN (SCOTLAND) REGULATIONS 2001, SSI 2001 476; made under the Children (Scotland) Act 1995 s.101, s.103. In force: January 23, 2002; £1.75.

These Regulations, which revoke the Social Work (Panels of Persons to Safeguard the Interests of Children) (Scotland) Regulations 1984 (SI 1984 1442), make provision for the continuation in each local government area of a panel or panels or persons to safeguard the interests of children in proceedings before a children's hearing or before the Sheriff for the purposes of the Children (Scotland) Act 1995. They provide that the local authority may establish more than one panel in its area, empower the local authority to consult with the chairman of the children's panel and the Sheriff Principal as to the experience which should be possessed by persons nominated to serve on any panel and set out the procedure to be followed by the local authority in seeking nominations and making appointments to panels to be established in its area.

6757. Civil legal aid

LEGAL AID (SCOTLAND) ACT 1986 AMENDMENT REGULATIONS 2001, SSI 2001 42; made under the Legal Aid (Scotland) Act 1986 s.13, s.37. In force: February 19, 2001; £1.50.

These Regulations, which amend the Legal Aid (Scotland) Act 1986 Sch. 2 Part I setting out those civil proceedings for which civil legal aid is available, add proceedings before the Proscribed Organisations Appeal Commission established under the Terrorism Act 2000 s.5. In addition, they remove a reference to the Restrictive Practices Court and update a reference to the EC Treaty.

6758. Civil legal aid – children's referral hearing – fees – uplift in solicitors fees justified

[Legal Aid (Scotland) Act 1986 (c.47); Civil Legal Aid (Scotland) (Fees) Regulations 1989 (SI 1989 1490) Reg.5(4); Act of Sederunt (Sheriff Court Ordinary Cause Rules) 1993 (SI 1993 1956).]

Following a children's referral hearing which lasted more than 30 days, involved numerous witnesses, and produced a 106 page judgment, the solicitors (S) for the mother applied for an uplift in fees in terms of the Civil Legal Aid (Scotland) (Fees) Regulations 1989 Reg.5(4). A hearing was held on the competency of the motion. S argued that the Regulations applied to all sheriff court causes. The Scottish Legal Aid Board (B) argued that the Legal Aid (Scotland) Act 1986 dealt separately with criminal, civil and children's legal aid; since the Regulations had specific provision for fee increases in ordinary and summary causes, but not for children's referrals, increases should be restricted to the types of cause specifically covered.

Held, allowing the appeal and granting a 25 per cent increase, that Reg.5(4) could apply to the instant case. Reading Reg.5(4) in light of the principle that the statute should be read as a whole, taken together with the fact that the Regulations were aimed at dealing with the unfairness of solicitors being unable to claim additional fees in certain circumstances, "Ordinary Roll" should be treated as including children's referral hearings. It should not be restricted to cases governed by the Act of Sederunt (Sheriff Court Ordinary Cause Rules) 1993, *L, Petitioners (No.3)* 1996 S.L.T. 928, [1996] C.L.Y. 7129 followed.

MUNRO, APPLICANT; *sub nom.* McCLURE, APPLICANT 2000 S.C.L.R. 920, Sheriff Brian Kearney, Sh Ct.

6759. Civil legal aid – income limits for eligibility

CIVIL LEGAL AID (FINANCIAL CONDITIONS) (SCOTLAND) REGULATIONS 2001, SSI 2001 123; made under the Legal Aid (Scotland) Act 1986 s.36. In force: April 9, 2001; £1.75.

These Regulations, which amend the Legal Aid (Scotland) Act 1986 increase certain of the financial limits of eligibility for civil legal aid. The income limits are increased to make eligible for civil legal aid, persons with a yearly disposable income of not more than £9,034 and to make eligible without payment of a contribution, persons with a yearly disposable income of not more than £2,723. In addition, they revoke the Civil Legal Aid (Financial Conditions) (Scotland) Regulations 2000 (SSI 2000 107).

6760. Criminal legal aid – legal representation – right to a fair trial – inadequacy of legal aid funding

[Human Rights Act 1998 (c.42) Sch.1 Part I Art.6 (3); Criminal Legal Aid (Fixed Payments) (Scotland) Regulations 1999 (SI 1999 491).]

NM and PM appealed against the successful appeal of the procurator fiscal (2000 S.L.T. 928, [2000] C.L.Y. 6089) from a decision to sustain their pleas in bar of trial and to dismiss the complaints against them on the ground of incompatibility with the Human Rights Act 1998 Sch.1 Part I Art.6(1) and Art.6(3). NM and PM had been allowed to withdraw pleas of not guilty to offences of assault and breach of the peace in order to state a plea in bar of trial. They contended that the inadequate legal aid funding they had been awarded under the Criminal Legal Aid (Fixed Payments) (Scotland) Regulations 1999, unfairly prejudiced them because their defence lawyers had a conflict of interest between serving the interests of their clients and their own concerns in being paid for work they had undertaken and they would fail to keep up professional standards because of the under funding. They submitted that the under funding was particularly acute given the need to raise the issue of devolution in their defence.

Held, dismissing the appeals, that the inadequacy of the legal aid funding was not incompatible with NM and PM's right to a fair trial given that the solicitors and counsel had agreed to act for them, continued to act for them even though funding had run out, showed no sign of withdrawing their representation. When compliance with Art.6(3) was being reviewed it was necessary to have regard to its basic purpose and accordingly the right to free legal representation could not be considered in isolation, *Artico v. Italy (A/37)* (1981) 3 E.H.R.R. 1 considered. It was up to the contracting state to chose the means by which the right under Art.6(3) was secured in the judicial system, *Imbrioscia v. Switzerland (A/275)* (1994) 17 E.H.R.R. 441, [1994] C.L.Y. 2407 considered. There was nothing to indicate that the solicitors acting for the appellants would fail to comply with their obligations under the professional codes of conduct in providing their clients with sound representation. However, it was noted that in a case where no legal representation was available as a result of the 1999 Regulations but under his Convention rights a defendant should be afforded representation then a breach might arise.

McLEAN v. BUCHANAN; *sub nom.* PROCURATOR FISCAL v. McLEAN; BUCHANAN v. McLEAN; McLEAN v. PROCURATOR FISCAL, [2001] UKPC D3, [2001] 1 W.L.R. 2425, Lord Hope of Craighead, Privy Council (Scotland).

6761. Criminal legal aid – life prisoners – availability

CRIMINAL LEGAL AID (SCOTLAND) (PRESCRIBED PROCEEDINGS) AMENDMENT REGULATIONS 2001, SSI 2001 381; made under the Legal Aid (Scotland) Act 1986 s.21. In force: October 15, 2001; £1.75.

These Regulations amend the Criminal Legal Aid (Scotland) (Prescribed Proceedings) Regulations 1997 (SI 1997 3069) so as to provide that criminal legal aid shall not be available for existing life prisoners, existing transferred life prisoners or transferred life prisoners who are the subject of a hearing to specify a notional punishment part. In addition, they provide that criminal legal aid shall be available for certain proceedings where those proceedings take place in a court designated as a drug court by the sheriff principal.

6762. Criminal legal aid – summary proceedings

CRIMINAL LEGAL AID (FIXED PAYMENTS) (SCOTLAND) AMENDMENT REGULATIONS 2001, SSI 2001 307; made under the Legal Aid (Scotland) Act 1986 s.33, s.41A. In force: October 15, 2001; £1.75.

The Regulations, which amend the Criminal Legal Aid (Fixed Payments) (Scotland) Regulations 1999 (SI 1999 491), provide that fixed payment criminal legal aid shall not apply to proceedings under the Extradition Act 1989 or the International Criminal Court Act 2001. They provide that the fixed payments set out in the 1999 Regulations shall not apply to proceedings which take place before a court designated as a drug court by the sheriff principal, that there shall be a fixed payment of £100 in respect of all work done up to and including the first appearance from custody and there shall be an additional fixed payment of £100 where an assisted person appearing before the drug court is under 21 years of age and is remanded in custody.

6763. Criminal legal aid – summary proceedings

CRIMINAL LEGAL AID (SCOTLAND) AMENDMENT REGULATIONS 2001, SSI 2001 306; made under the Legal Aid (Scotland) Act 1986 s.31, s.36. In force: October 15, 2001; £1.50.

These Regulations, which amend the Criminal Legal Aid (Scotland) Regulations 1996 (SI 1996 2555), provide that the duty solicitor scheme shall not apply to proceedings which take place in a court designated as a drug court by the sheriff principal.

6764. Legal advice – assistance by way of representation – employment tribunal proceedings

ADVICE AND ASSISTANCE (ASSISTANCE BY WAY OF REPRESENTATION) (SCOTLAND) AMENDMENT REGULATIONS 2001, SSI 2001 2; made under the Legal Aid (Scotland) Act 1986 s.9, s.37. In force: January 15, 2001; £1.75.

These Regulations make assistance by way of representation available in relation to proceedings before an adjudicator or the employment tribunal.

6765. Legal advice – assistance by way of representation – life prisoners

ADVICE AND ASSISTANCE (ASSISTANCE BY WAY OF REPRESENTATION) (SCOTLAND) AMENDMENT (NO.3) REGULATIONS 2001, SSI 2001 382; made under the Legal Aid (Scotland) Act 1986 s.9, s.37. In force: October 15, 2001; £1.75.

These Regulations amend the Advice and Assistance (Assistance by Way of Representation) (Scotland) Regulations 1997 (SI 1997 3070) to make assistance by way of representation available for existing life prisoners, existing transferred life prisoners and transferred life prisoners who are the subject of a hearing to specify a notional punishment part. They provide that assistance by way of representation for these proceedings shall be available without reference to the provisions of the Legal Aid (Scotland) Act 1986 which relate to financial limits on the availability of advice and assistance and payment of contributions towards advice and assistance. The Regulations also provide that assistance by way of representation shall not be available for certain proceedings, where those proceedings take place in a court designated as a drug court by the sheriff principal.

6766. Legal advice – assistance by way of representation – terrorism

ADVICE AND ASSISTANCE (ASSISTANCE BY WAY OF REPRESENTATION) (SCOTLAND) AMENDMENT (NO.2) REGULATIONS 2001, SSI 2001 43; made under the Legal Aid (Scotland) Act 1986 s.9, s.37. In force: February 19, 2001; £1.75.

These Regulations amend the Advice and Assistance (Assistance by Way of Representation) (Scotland) Regulations 1997 (SI 1997 3070) so as to make assistance by way of representation available for proceedings in connection with an application for a warrant of further detention, or extension of a warrant, under the Terrorism Act 2000 Sch.8. They provide that assistance by way of representation for these proceedings shall be available without reference to the provisions of the Legal Aid (Scotland) Act 1986 which relate to financial limits on the availability of advice and assistance and payment of contributions towards advice and assistance.

6767. Legal Aid Board – employment – solicitors

LEGAL AID (EMPLOYMENT OF SOLICITORS) (SCOTLAND) REGULATIONS 2001, SSI 2001 392; made under the Legal Aid (Scotland) Act 1986 s.26, s.27, s.37. In force: November 19, 2001; £1.75.

These Regulations make provision as to the employment by the Scottish Legal Aid Board of solicitors in accordance with the Legal Aid (Scotland) Act 1986 and as to the circumstances in which solicitors may be so employed. They provide that a solicitor may be employed to provide services to local organisations in certain circumstances. A solicitor so employed may also provide advice and assistance and legal aid. In addition, the Regulations provide that the Scottish Legal Aid Board may employ a solicitor to provide criminal legal assistance where the accused person is eligible to receive, and would be otherwise unable to secure the services of a solicitor to provide, such assistance.

6768. Legal Aid (Scotland) Act 1986 (c.47) – Commencement No.4 Order

LEGAL AID (SCOTLAND) ACT 1986 (COMMENCEMENT NO.4) ORDER 2001, SSI 2001 393 (C.16); made under the Legal Aid (Scotland) Act 1986 s.46. Commencement details: bringing into force various provisions of the 1986 Act on November 2, 2001; £1.50.

This Order provides for the coming into force of specified sections of the Legal Aid (Scotland) Act 1986 which relate to the employment of solicitors by the Scottish Legal Aid Board.

6769. Legal services – advice and assistance – income limits

ADVICE AND ASSISTANCE (FINANCIAL CONDITIONS) (SCOTLAND) REGULATIONS 2001, SSI 2001 124; made under the Legal Aid (Scotland) Act 1986 s.11, s.36, s.37. In force: April 9, 2001; £1.75.

These Regulations, which amend the Legal Aid (Scotland) Act 1986 in relation to any case where an application for advice and assistance is made on or after April 9, 2001, increase the disposable income limit for eligibility for advice and assistance from £180 to £186 a week. They increase the weekly disposable income above which a person is required to pay a contribution from £76 to £79 and prescribe the scale of contributions to be paid where the weekly disposable income exceeds £79 but does not exceed £186. In addition, the Regulations revoke, with savings, the Advice and Assistance (Financial Conditions) (Scotland) Regulations 2000 (SSI 2000 108).

6770. Legal services – representation by solicitors

LEGAL AID (SCOTLAND) ACT 1986 (AVAILABILITY OF SOLICITORS) REGULATIONS 2001, SSI 2001 464; made under the Legal Aid (Scotland) Act 1986 s.31, s.36. In force: February 6, 2002; £1.75.

These Regulations provide that where the Scottish Legal Aid Board makes a solicitor available to provide assistance by way of representation for certain proceedings in terms of Legal Aid (Scotland) Act 1986 s.31, an assisted person may only be represented by that solicitor. The Regulations apply to proceedings where a detained person appears before a sheriff under the Matrimonial Homes (Family Protection (Scotland) Act 1981 and the Protection from Abuse (Scotland) Act 2001 s.5.

LEGAL PROFESSION

6771. Law Society of Scotland – statutory functions – interdict against withdrawal of practising certificate

[Solicitors (Scotland) Act 1980 (c.46) s.40.]

H, a solicitor, raised an action for interdict against the Law Society seeking to prevent it from withdrawing his practising certificate, or from appointing a judicial factor to run his business on the recommendation of the Society's accountant, C, or during any time when C held that position. The sheriff dismissed the action as irrelevant and the sheriff principal adhered. H appealed to the Court of Session. H unsuccessfully had sought interim interdict on April 21, 1998; and later dropped his appeal. On April 24, C withdrew H's practising certificate under the Solicitors (Scotland) Act 1980 s.40(1). H lodged an appeal against the withdrawal, seeking a direction against C to restore the certificate, but following the lodging of answers by C there was no further procedure. H refused to allow officials of C to visit his office. Before the court, H confirmed that he was no longer attempting to interdict future actings of C, but wanted the reversal of C's decision of April 24 and the restoration of his practising certificate, arguing that the circumstances leading to the decision had made it wrongful. H argued that (1) the sheriff had not given him a fair hearing and his judgment made it clear he had prejudged the matter. In cases where malice was averred, special caution had to be observed before dismissing an action without proof; (2) the action had been raised prior to C's decision, and when interdict would have been the normal remedy. The Society had acted at its peril and could be obliged to reverse what it had done, and (3) there had been no alternative remedy available when the action was raised; H could not be expected to wait for the withdrawal of the certificate and then appeal and the action was not rendered inappropriate by subsequent events.

Held, refusing the appeal that (1) it was not competent to seek interdict as a context for establishing prior wrongdoing to be founded on in seeking a rectificatory remedy. The interdict sought would be incapable of execution or enforcement in any way at any time. The appropriate rectificatory remedy had to be sought in itself, although on similar averments and on the basis that C withdrew the certificate without having any right to do so, and (2) in any event, interdict became no longer appropriate once H's practising certificate had been withdrawn. Once it was withdrawn, s.40(2) and (3) provided remedies which had to be pursued in preference to other remedies at law, even if another remedy, like interdict, had been sought at a prior stage, *Green v. Lord Advocate* 1918 S.C. 667 distinguished.

Observed, that if the proceedings for interdict had a purpose running beyond the scope of the statutory remedies, seeking some lasting limitation on what C were entitled to do in future, then the statutory remedies would be insufficient and it was possible there were circumstances where interdict would be competent.

HILL v. COUNCIL OF THE LAW SOCIETY OF SCOTLAND 2000 S.L.T. 1389, Lord Prosser, Lord Clarke, Lord Marnoch, Ex Div.

6772. Solicitors – professional conduct – Scottish Solicitors' Discipline Tribunal – independence and impartiality of new tribunal

[European Convention on Human Rights 1950 Art.6(1).]

T, two solicitors, appealed against their striking off by the Scottish Solicitors' Discipline Tribunal. The Court of Session ordered a new tribunal to hear their appeal against that sanction on an agreed factual basis. The tribunal concluded that T be struck off and T appealed.

Held, refusing the appeals, that (1) there were no grounds for questioning the partiality of the tribunal and the European Convention on Human Rights 1950 Art.6(1) did not apply; (2) it was not within the remit of the new tribunal to re-open the issues of fact and guilt and they could only concern themselves with the sentence appropriate to the facts laid before them; (3) as the court had determined the matters which must be excluded from the remit, any further exclusions were at the discretion of the fiscal and did not require to be agreed by T; (4) T were offered adequate opportunity to lodge documentary material in support of a plea in mitigation or to lead mitigatory evidence and were fully aware of the basis for the findings of guilt based on the original tribunal proceedings so did not suffer prejudice; (5) there was no basis for T's claims of ill will on behalf of the tribunal which had been generous in allowing written formulations by T and neither was there any basis for claims that any steps taken by the tribunal were likely to confuse T or their advisors, and (6) there was no basis for the arguments made concerning delay. Opinion of the Court as per Lord Prosser.

GORDON COUTTS THOMSON (A FIRM) v. COUNCIL OF THE LAW SOCIETY OF SCOTLAND (NO.2) 2001 S.C.L.R. 61, Lord Prosser, Lord Allanbridge, Lord Kirkwood, Ex Div.

6773. Books

Scottish Lawyers Factbook. Looseleaf/ring bound: £145.00. ISBN 0-414-01343-3. W.Green & Son.
Solicitors Professional Handbook 2001. Paperback: £23.00. ISBN 0-414-01424-3. W.Green & Son.

LEGAL SYSTEMS

6774. Books

MacQueen, Hector – Gloag and Henderson: the Law of Scotland. 11th Ed. Hardback: £125.00. ISBN 0-414-01254-2. W.Green & Son.
Scots Law Times. Hardback: £255.00. ISBN 0-414-01418-9. W.Green & Son.

LEISURE INDUSTRY

6775. Recreational services – sports grounds – designation for the purposes of the Criminal Law (Consolidation) (Scotland) Act 1995

SPORTS GROUNDS AND SPORTING EVENTS (DESIGNATION) (SCOTLAND) AMENDMENT ORDER 2001, SSI 2001 209; made under the Criminal Law (Consolidation) (Scotland) Act 1995 s.18. In force: July 28, 2001; £1.50.

This Order amends the Sports Grounds and Sporting Events (Designation) (Scotland) Order 1998 (SI 1998 2314) which designates the sports grounds, the classes of sporting events played at those grounds and the classes of sporting events outside Great Britain for the purposes of the Criminal Law (Consolidation) (Scotland) Act 1995 Part II. As a result of the amendments, Boghead Park, Dumbarton ceases to be, and H.A.F.C. Stadium, Hamilton and Strathclyde Homes Stadium, Dumbarton become, designated sports grounds.

LICENSING

6776. Appeals – objections – competence of objector

[Licensing (Scotland) Act 1976 (c.66) s.17(5).]
B appealed against a decision by the licensing board to grant a provisional public house licence in the same area as its premises in Edinburgh. B argued, in response to preliminary pleas by the licensing board and the applicant, that it was a competent objector who had appeared at the hearing before the licensing board in terms of the Licensing (Scotland) Act 1976 s.17(5); that one of its directors objected in writing

and appeared at the hearing and was acting, at all times, on behalf of and representing B; and that as the names of both B and its directors were clearly stated on B's licence, the fact that the director was representing B was within the knowledge of the licensing board.

Held, sustaining the plea and dismissing the appeal, that (1) B was not a competent objector in terms of s.17(5) as no objections were lodged bearing B's name or openly purporting to be on behalf of B; (2) the director's name on B's licence was insufficient to rectify the director's failure to clearly intimate to the licensing board that the objection was being lodged on B's behalf, and (3) even if B had competently objected, it could not be considered to have appeared the hearing when the director had not clearly intimated to the licensing board that his appearance at the hearing was in his capacity as an agent of B.

BBW LEISURE LTD v. EDINBURGH CITY LICENSING BOARD 2001 S.L.T. (Sh Ct) 26, Sheriff AM Bell, Sh Ct (Lothian and Border).

6777. Entertainment licence – health and fitness club – meaning of "public entertainment"

B, a health club, appealed against the decision of L, a licensing board, to refuse to grant them an entertainment licence. B argued that the leisure, recreation, health and beauty facilities which they intended to provide from their premises amounted to "entertainment" in a widely accepted sense, which could be supported by the existence of similar premises in Edinburgh and Falkirk which had been granted licences. The question of whether an activity was "entertainment" within a statutory provision of national application could not vary with local conditions. L argued that it was in their discretion how to define entertainment.

Held, refusing the appeal, that where there was no definition for a particular word within a statute, words were to be given their ordinary meaning. In normal English, B's facilities and activities could be described as leisure, recreation, health and beauty facilities, and not entertainment. In the absence of a statutory definition of "public entertainment", it was open to L to decide whether B's premises could be classified as such, and the court was not persuaded that no reasonable board could have reached L's decision.

BANNATYNE'S HEALTH CLUB v. ABERDEEN CITY LICENSING BOARD 2000 S.L.T. (Sh Ct) 187, Sheriff AM Cowan, Sh Ct (Grampian, Highland and Islands).

6778. Gambling – licences and certificates – fees

GAMING ACT (VARIATION OF FEES) (NO.2) (SCOTLAND) ORDER 2001, SSI 2001 230; made under the Gaming Act 1968 s.48, s.51. In force: July 2, 2001; £1.75.

This Order, which amends the Gaming Act (Variation of Fees) (Scotland) Order 2001 (SSI 2001 83), sets fees to be charged in relation to the grant, renewal and transfer of gaming licences in Scotland. It decreases the fees to be charged in relation to the grant and transfer of gaming licences and increases the fees to be charged in relation to the renewal of gaming licences where gaming is restricted to the playing of bingo, as specified in the Schedule to the Order. Gaming fees are decreased by 26 per cent and 25 per cent respectively and gaming fees in relation to the renewal of licences where gaming is restricted to bingo are increased by 47 per cent. The fees in relation to the renewal of gaming licences and the grant and transfer of licences where gaming is restricted to bingo remain at the current level.

6779. Gambling – licences and certificates – fees

GAMING ACT (VARIATION OF FEES) (SCOTLAND) ORDER 2001, SSI 2001 83; made under the Gaming Act 1968 s.48, s.51. In force: March 29, 2001; £1.75.

This Order, which amends the Gaming Act (Variation of Fees) Order 1998 (SI 1998 456), specifies increases in the fees to be charged in relation to the grant, renewal and transfer of gaming licences in Scotland under the Gaming Act 1968. The fees are increased by approximately 8.5 per cent.

6780. Gambling – licences and certificates – fees

See LICENSING. §4303

6781. Licences – renewal – secondhand dealer – refusal to renew licence – competency of judicial review – same challenge pending before High Court

[Civic Government (Scotland) Act 1982 (c.45) s.24; Act of Sederunt (Rules of the Court of Session 1994) 1994 (SI 1994 1443) r.58(4).]

In 1994, S sought renewal of his second hand dealer licence. P refused the application. At appeal, the sheriff remitted the matter to P. P appealed to the Court of Session, which allowed the appeal and restored P's decision. S's licence remained valid throughout that time. S petitioned for judicial review of P's decision, claiming that it was ultra vires. He claimed compensation and damages for losses suffered because of the decision. In February 1997, S was convicted of trading without a licence and an appeal was pending in the High Court of Justiciary. P opposed S's petition on the grounds that (1) the question of damages, in the form raised by S, was not appropriate in a petition for judicial review, and (2) because the issues in the petition were the same as in the High Court, the petition was not competent, and in any event the court should decline to hear the issue out of respect for the High Court.

Held, repelling P's preliminary pleas except in relation to the damages claim, that (1) although it was competent to claim damages in a petition for judicial review, an order of damages could only be made in such form as could be sought in a petition. In a petition, it would not be competent for a petitioner to limit the order sought to a declarator of entitlement to damages; (2) the averments relating to compensation and damages could be excluded, because they were not an essential part of a petition for judicial review, and (3) the High Court and Court of Session had different functions and independent jurisdictions, and it was competent to raise proceedings in the Court of Session.

STEWART v. PERTH AND KINROSS DC (NO.2) 2001 S.C. 229, Lord Mackay of Drumadoon, OH.

6782. Licensed premises – extension of permitted hours – competency of renewed application within one year

[Licensing (Scotland) Act 1976 (c.66) s.64(9).]

C applied to G for an extension of its late night opening hours, Monday to Sunday, and for an afternoon extension on Sunday. G refused the former and granted the latter. C's agent applied under the Licensing (Scotland) Act 1976 s.64(9) for a direction that G could consider a fresh application within one year, but that application was refused. C then wrote to D, the clerk of G, asking for his agreement that the s.64(9) application had been unnecessary because part of the application had been granted and so did not constitute a refusal for the purposes of s.64(9), and that C were free to make a further application at G's next meeting. D responded that he did not agree and that a further application would be incompetent. C petitioned for judicial review, seeking an order that D place their application on the agenda and that it be considered by G, arguing that competency was an issue for G, not D, and that C were entitled to make representations on what was a real issue. G argued that D was competent to make a decision at his own hand on that issue. Any extension would be to hours that had been refused at the last meeting; the application would be incompetent and would be refused.

Held, allowing the petition and granting an order as sought, that (1) competency was a matter for G and could not be left to D, *Kelvinside Community Council v. Glasgow District Licensing Board* 1990 S.L.T. 725, [1990] C.L.Y. 5337 followed.; (2) s.64 permitted part grant and part refusal of an application, e.g. where an application was granted subject to restricted hours or where, as in the instant case, an element of a composite application was rejected, but (3) a further application had not yet been made and it would be speculative to say whether it would be barred by s.64(9).

CATSCRATCH LTD v. GLASGOW CITY LICENSING BOARD (NO.1); *sub nom.* CATSCRATCH LTD, PETITIONERS 2001 S.C. 218, Lord Penrose, OH.

6783. **Licensed premises – extension of permitted hours – fly posting – meaning of "undue public nuisance"**

[Town and Country Planning (Scotland) Act 1997 (c.8) s.187; Licensing (Scotland) Act 1976 (c.66) s.63(3).]

O, the owners of licenced premises (P) applied to Edinburgh Licensing Board (E) for a regular extension of permitted hours, under the Licensing (Scotland) Act 1976 s.64(3). P was operated as an entertainment venue, let to promoters for events organised by those promoters. The hours sought were the same as those granted in previous years and were within E's policy guidelines. The local authority objected on the grounds that there had been illegal fly posting for events at S. O questioned the relevance of the objection; the fly posting had been done by event organisers who were independent third parties. E granted the application, but subject to extended hours to 2 am and not 3 am as requested by O. O petitioned for judicial review, claiming that (1) the decision was irrational, and was one which no reasonable board could have reached. It was clear that the decision was influenced by the fly posting issue, and (2) fly posting was a contravention of the Town and Country Planning (Scotland) Act 1997 s.187 and was not a public nuisance. It was not proper to use the 1976 to attack fly posting.

Held, granting the petition and reducing E's order, that (1) when considering applications under s.64(3), the issue was whether the use of the premises for the sale of alcohol was likely to cause undue public nuisance or be a threat to public order and safety. In the instant case, E had no factual basis on which to conclude that it would. The fly posting was being done by independent third parties. *Bantop Ltd v. Glasgow District Licensing Board* 1990 S.L.T. 366, [1990] C.L.Y. 5334 followed; (2) fly posting was not a public nuisance for the purposes of s.64(3). There was no causal connection between the use of P for the sale of alcohol during the extended permitted hours and the fly posting, and (3) E's decision was irrational. There was nothing to suggest that restricting the hours to 2 am from 3 am would have any impact on the fly posting problem.

MARESQ (T/A LA BELLE ANGELE) v. EDINBURGH LICENSING BOARD 2001 S.C. 126, Lord Osborne, OH.

6784. **Licensed premises – extension of permitted hours – judicial review – extension refused on grounds of Sabbath observance – no prior notice to applicant of reasons – breach of natural justice**

[Law Reform (Miscellaneous Provisions) (Scotland) Act 1990 (c.40) s.47.]

M, a hotelier on the Isle of Lewis sought an extension of the licensing hours in the form of an additional two hours on Saturday night and four hours on a Sunday afternoon. The extension had been granted in 1996-1997, 1998-1999 and 1999-2000. W refused the application maintaining that M's evidence for the Saturday night extension did not demonstrate a need in the locality and under the Law Reform (Miscellaneous Provisions) (Scotland) Act 1990 s.47, they were not obliged to grant the extension. The Sunday afternoon extension was denied on the basis of W's local knowledge with regard to local tradition and opinion encouraging Sabbath observance. M sought judicial review of the decision arguing that W had breached natural justice in founding upon Sabbath observance without allowing M to address the matter. M argued that the decision was Wednesbury unreasonable and in light of the previous extensions M had a legitimate expectation to have it granted. M also argued that the demand she had demonstrated for the Saturday night extension should lead to a reduction of that decision.

Held, reducing the board's decision, that (1) on the facts as expressed by the demand from customers having spent the evening at the hotel and then waiting for a bus did constitute a need under s.47, and (2) in the absence of a clear policy communicated by the board as to their concerns it was not consistent with natural justice to fail to give an applicant an opportunity to address such as the board believed were the determining factors in their decision.

MacDONALD v. WESTERN ISLES LICENSING BOARD 2001 S.C. 628, Lady Paton, OH.

6785. Licensed premises – liquor licensing – fees

LIQUOR LICENSING (FEES) (SCOTLAND) ORDER 2001, SSI 2001 125; made under the Licensing (Scotland) Act 1976 s.8, s.135. In force: April 1, 2001; £2.00.

This Order, which revokes the Liquor Licensing (Fees) (Scotland) Order 1997 (SI 1997 1721), determines the fees payable from April 1, 2001 by applicants to a licensing board in respect of the matters listed in the Schedule to the Order. The fees are increased by approximately 13 per cent.

6786. Off licences – petrol stations – applications for provisional new licences – refusal – association between drink and driving

[Licensing (Scotland) Act 1976 (c.66) s.17 (1) (b).]

C, a licensing board, appealed against a sheriff's decision allowing the appeal of S, a supermarket operator, against the refusal to grant three applications for provisional new off sale licences. The relevant sites were joint ventures between S and a petrol company and each site comprised a petrol station run by the petrol company and a convenience shop run by S. C had found that the premises were neither suitable nor convenient for the sale of alcohol in terms of the Licensing (Scotland) Act 1976 s.17(1)(b) and had issued decision letters purportedly taking Government policy into account, basing the refusals on "insufficient separation within the premises of the sale of petrol and the sale of alcohol" and the creation of an unacceptable association between drinking and driving.

Held, dismissing the appeal, that C had failed to reveal any comprehensible reasons for its decisions, as there was no basis on which the sale of alcohol from the stores in question could be seen as suggesting that the supply of alcohol was an appropriate service for motorists as such or as weakening the Government message on drink driving, where the stores were not merely ancillary to the filling stations and had a preponderant body of customers who had nothing to do with cars or the filling stations.

SAFEWAY STORES PLC v. GLASGOW CITY LICENSING BOARD 2001 S.L.T. 1115, Lord Prosser, Lord Caplan, Lord Johnston, Ex Div.

6787. Off licences – refusal on grounds of public safety and overprovision – scale of operation

[Licensing (Scotland) Act 1976 (c.66) s.17 (1) (c), s.17 (1) (d).]

T applied to N for a licence for one of their petrol filling stations. It was proposed that the fast food area be replaced with a small off licence section. The application attracted objections from the public and community council with regard to overprovision in the area, road safety problems and exacerbation of the nuisance already caused by licensed premises. Five board members inspected the premises and N refused the application under the Licensing (Scotland) Act 1976 s.17 (1) (c) and (d). T appealed, arguing that N's decision had been fatally flawed relying as it did on the visual assessment of a minority of the board. T also maintained that the off licence section would not impact traffic levels negatively, because it would be a smaller operation than the fast food area and N had neglected to consider its size when considering overprovision in the area.

Held, refusing the appeal, that the visual assessment had only been part of N's collective decision making process which would also have included local knowledge. N was allowed to draw its own inferences from those sources. Although the off licence section proposed was on a small scale there was nothing to prevent its future expansion. N had provided an understandable

explanation as to why granting the licence would result in overprovision for the area.
TEXACO LTD v. NORTH LANARKSHIRE LICENSING BOARD (NO.2) [2001] 18 S.L.L.P. 18, Sheriff L Cameron, Sh Ct (South Strathclyde, Dumfries and Galloway).

6788. Off licences – renewal of licence refused – sale of alcohol to child – licensing board not entitled to infer applicant unfit

[Licensing (Scotland) Act 1976 (c.66) s.17 (1) (a).]
H, the holder of an off sale licence was refused a renewal by G under the Licensing (Scotland) Act 1976 s.17 (1) (a). The application was refused based on an incident involving the sale of alcohol to a 15 year old boy without an age check by one of H's assistants. H appealed successfully on the ground that G had no proper basis for finding H "not a fit and proper person to be the holder of a licence". G appealed to the Court of Session arguing that H had not given a satisfactory explanation as to why alcohol had been sold to a 15 year old and that they were entitled to take a similar view to that provided for in a criminal prosecution.
Held, refusing the appeal, that G's argument was misguided, the onus of a licence holder in a criminal case was clearly stated in the legislation whereas none existed in the instant case, and G's inference that H was not a "fit and proper person" to hold a licence was unwarranted.
HAMID v. GLASGOW CITY LICENSING BOARD 2001 S.C. 398, Lord Milligan, Lord Allanbridge, Lord Prosser, Ex Div.

6789. Statutory offences – sale of alcohol to underage person – training of employees – due diligence of licensee

FQR, the licence holder of a licensed shop, was found guilty under summary complaint of selling alcohol to a 15 year old girl. F's employee had asked the girl for identification and although none was provided, sold her alcohol in the belief that she had previously shown identification and been seen in a club for over 18s. The manager of the shop had undergone training in company policy which was to accept only Prove-It cards or passports as proof of age. F relied on the defence of due diligence under the Licensing (Scotland) Act 1976 s.67(2) in appealing against the conviction. F maintained that the manager's duties with regard to training and enforcing company policy were appropriate to his position and it had been reasonable for them to rely upon his discharge of those duties. F also argued that there had been nothing to suggest that they knew of his non-compliance or condoned it.
Held, refusing the appeal, that it had been shown that there was a local policy of subjective decision making with regard to selling alcohol and an effective training scheme would not only have ensured employees knew the rules, but would have instilled the importance of complying with those rules. An employer exercising due diligence would have implemented and monitored that system. On those grounds the justice had been entitled to hold that F had not exercised due diligence. Opinion of the Court per Lord Prosser.
FIRST QUENCH RETAILING LTD v. McLEOD 2001 S.L.T. 372, Lord Prosser, Lord Allanbridge, Lord Coulsfield, HCJ Appeal.

6790. Taxis – application for corporate licence – requirement to withdraw individual application – guidance at odds with policy

D entered a partnership and applied for a corporate taxi licence from E. As part of the application procedure, E, advised D by letter that under the terms of E's policy document on taxi licensing, he would be required to surrender his position on the waiting list for parties interested in obtaining an individual taxi licence. D, after protesting, agreed to withdraw from the individual list and the application for a corporate licence was granted. D subsequently petitioned for a judicial review of E's request for D to withdraw from the list, claiming that the guidance note issued in respect of the policy failed to mention the requirement regarding the individual list and so raised a legitimate expectation in D that he would be entitled to retain his position on that list, and further, that no reasonable authority, having issued such a guidance note, would insist on his removal from the waiting list in order for the corporate application to proceed. At a first hearing, the Lord Ordinary dismissed the petition as irrelevant relying on *R. v. Devon CC, ex p. Baker* [1995] 1 All E.R. 73, [1995] C.L.Y. 88 that for the petitioner to succeed, the guidance note must contain "a clear and unambiguous representation upon which it was reasonable for him to rely". D reclaimed against the dismissal of the petition.

Held, refusing the reclaiming motion, that (1) the letter merely notified D of the policy regarding corporate applications; it was D who made the decision to withdraw from the list based on that policy; it was open to D to retain his position on the list for an individual licence which would result in the corporate application being refused. The Lord Ordinary was incorrect in conceding that the contents of the letter were open to judicial review; (2) (per Lords Prosser and Clarke) the guidance note contained no clear and unambiguous statement regarding the position of the petitioner in relation to the waiting list that could be relied on and even if such a statement could be read into the guidance note, it fell short of the positive representation required in *Devon CC*, and (3) as counsel for the petitioner was not arguing that E did not have the power to adopt the licensing policy, there was no legal basis for a contention that it was acting unreasonably in enforcing it.

Observed, per Lord Prosser, that, generally speaking, guidance notes are not intended to be determinative of rights and in order to create a legitimate expectation based on a clear an unambiguous statement, it would require to be very clear indeed. *Observed*, per Lord Marnoch, that someone in the petitioner's position, reading the guidance note, might have formed a legitimate expectation that they would be entitled to remain on the individual list.

DOCHERTY v. EDINBURGH CITY COUNCIL 2001 S.L.T. 291, Lord Prosser, Lord Clarke, Lord Marnoch, Ex Div.

6791. Taxis – refusal to renew licence – reasonableness of conditions

[Civic Government (Scotland) Act 1982 (c.45) Sch.1 para.5.]

C, a taxi licence holder, appealed against the refusal by A, a licensing committee, to renew his application for the licence. By condition 29 of the licence, the holder was not to hire the taxi to the holder of a taxi driver licence or to any other person. A held that C was not a fit and proper person to be the holder of a licence in terms of the Civic Government (Scotland) Act 1982 Sch.1 para.5(3)(a)(ii), or that there was "other good reason for refusing the application" in terms of para.5(3)(d), as evidenced by his knowing and persistent breaches of condition 29. C had openly disclosed the hirer as a person with an interest in the running of his business. He understood that it was a common practice and had been acquiesced in by the committee for many years. He argued that condition 29 was a restraint of trade, a restriction of a licence holder's right to use his taxi as he chose and an unwarranted limitation on the commercial choices available in the use of that asset. A argued that it had the sole discretion to determine the reasonableness of conditions imposed under Sch.1, para.5(1).

Held, allowing the appeal and remitting the case to A for further consideration, that (1) A's power in terms of para.5(2) was to impose "reasonable conditions" and the court had the power to consider whether condition 29 was reasonable; (2) a breach of a condition did not by itself make C no longer a fit and proper person, and there was nothing to show that he had sought to defy A; (3) C's intention was crucial to A's argument but they had not sought to ascertain that and had based their decision on incorrect and obviously material fact, and (4) it was not appropriate to alter condition 29 and grant the application.

CHRISTIE v. ABERDEEN CITY COUNCIL LICENSING COMMITTEE 2001 S.L.T. (Sh Ct) 167, KA McLernan, Sh Ct (Grampian, Highland and Islands).

6792. Taxis – renewal of licence – refusal for good reason – overprovision – irrelevant consideration

[Civic Government (Scotland) Act 1982 (c.45) s.3(4), s.10(3), Sch.1, para.5(3)(d).]

B appealed against a sheriff's decision affirming the refusal by R of B's application for renewal of a taxi licence. B became unconditionally entitled to the licence for one year in terms of the Civic Government (Scotland) Act 1982 s.3(4) after R had failed competently to apply for an extension of time to consider B's application until they had reformulated their policy on issuing new licences. R's new policy restricted the number of new taxi licences. R thereafter purported to refuse B's original application under s.10(3) before recognising that their attempt to obtain an extension had been incompetent. When the application for renewal was considered, R refused B's application for renewal of the licence for "good reason" under Sch.1, para.5(3)(d) on the ground that was the first time it had been properly considered and, but for a technicality, would not have been granted under the new policy. R argued that overprovision was a proper ground for refusing to renew as well as grant a taxi licence.

Held, allowing the appeal and remitting the case to the sheriff to direct R to consider the application further, that (1) the sheriff erred in his construction of the 1982 Act. Overprovision was not a circumstance compelling a licensing authority to refuse to grant or renew a taxi licence under para.5(3), but it did constitute a circumstance in which an authority had a discretion to refuse to grant a licence under s.10(3). The assessment under s.10(3) had to be made in relation to the situation at the time an application fell to be considered, not, as R had, at a subsequent date. R were not entitled to have regard to a policy which they had not determined on at the time either when the application was received by them or at any time during the period when it ought to have been considered and a final decision reached. R's own failure to obtain an extension for consideration of the application could not be used as the basis for a good reason under para.5(3)(d). Opinion of the Court per Lord Cameron of Lochbroom

BARCLAY v. RENFREWSHIRE COUNCIL 2001 S.L.T. 647, Lord Cameron of Lochbroom, Lord Reed, Lord Wheatley, Ex Div.

6793. Taxis – taxi drivers – renewal of taxi licence and applicable considerations

M, the holder of two taxi licences, had been convicted of a series of road traffic offences. Following a complaint on behalf of the chief constable asserting that M was no longer a fit and proper person to hold a taxi licence, D's licensing committee suspended the two licences, a warning about M's driving record having previously been issued by the licensing committee in 1995. M successfully appealed to the sheriff who, in his judgment, followed the opinion of the court in *MacDowall v. Cunninghame DC* 1987 S.C. 217, [1987] C.L.Y. 4693 which held that a taxi driver's disregard for the law in relation to speeding offences should not be taken into consideration in determining whether a taxi licence should be granted or renewed. D appealed against the sheriff's decision arguing that the sheriff erred in concluding that M's speeding convictions and his other convictions relating to driving ability should be disregarded when determining if he was a fit and proper person to hold a taxi licence and that all the convictions, when taken together, indicated a pattern of behaviour which was relevant to the licensing committee.

Held, sustaining the appeal and restoring the decision of the licensing committee, that the licensing committee was correct in its consideration of M's convictions, not as being representative of M's ability to drive, but as indicative of a pattern of irresponsible behaviour and disregard for authority which suggested that M was not a fit person to hold a licence. In *MacDowall* the licence holder was guilty of speeding offences which was distinct from the instant case where M had been convicted of speeding, failure to comply with stop signs, failure to rectify a defective lamp, failure to produce documents and where M had also ignored a warning from the licensing committee, *MacDowall*, considered. Opinion of the Court per Lord Philip.

MIDDLETON v. DUNDEE CITY COUNCIL 2001 S.L.T. 287, Lord Philip, Lord Caplan, Lord Prosser, Ex Div.

LOCAL GOVERNMENT

6794. Competitive tendering – exemptions

LOCAL GOVERNMENT (EXEMPTION FROM COMPETITION) (SCOTLAND) AMENDMENT ORDER 2001, SSI 2001 431; made under the Local Government Act 1988 s.2, s.15. In force: December 17, 2001; £1.75.

The Local Government (Exemption from Competition) (Scotland) Order 1995 (SI 1995 678) modified the application of the Local Government Act 1988 Part I, in the period from March 31, 1995 to December 31, 2001. One of the effects of the principal order was to suspend compulsory competitive tendering under the 1988 Act in Scotland from March 31, 1995 until "the exemption end date", different such end dates being set for different authorities and different activities. This Order amends the principal order by substituting a new exemption end date of December 31, 2003 in each case and revokes Local Government (Exemption from Competition) (Scotland) Amendment Order 1999 (SI 1999 937) and Local Government (Exemption from Competition) (Scotland) Amendment Order 2000 (SSI 2000 206) which previously amended the principal Order.

6795. Competitive tendering – introduction of compulsory competitive tendering

LOCAL GOVERNMENT ACT 1988 (COMPETITION) (SCOTLAND) AMENDMENT REGULATIONS 2001, SSI 2001 432; made under the Local Government Act 1988 s.6, s.15. In force: December 17, 2001; £1.75.

The Local Government Act 1988 (Competition) (Scotland) Regulations 1997 (SI 1997 197) make provision for the introduction in Scotland of compulsory competitive tendering (CCT) in respect of functional work falling within certain activities which are defined activities for the purposes of the Local Government Act 1988. These Regulations amend the 1997 Regulations so as to delay the introduction of CCT until December 31, 2003 and revoke the Local Government Act 1988 (Competition) (Scotland) Amendment Regulations 2000 (SSI 2000 208).

6796. Competitive tendering – introduction of compulsory competitive tendering

LOCAL GOVERNMENT ACT 1988 (COMPETITION) (SCOTLAND) AMENDMENT (NO.2) REGULATIONS 2001, SSI 2001 446; made under the Local Government Act 1988 s.6, s.15. In force: December 16, 2001; £1.75.

The Local Government Act 1988 (Competition) (Scotland) Regulations 1997 (SI 1997 197) make provision as to the introduction in Scotland of compulsory competitive tendering (CCT) in respect of functional work falling within certain activities which are defined activities for the purposes of the Local Government Act 1988. These Regulations amend the Regulations so as to delay the introduction of CCT until December 31, 2003. The Local Government Act 1988 (Competition) (Scotland) Amendment Regulations 2000 (SSI 2000 208) and the Local Government Act 1988 (Competition) (Scotland) Amendment Regulations 2001 (SSI 2001 432) are revoked.

6797. Fire and civil defence authorities – determination of grants

CIVIL DEFENCE (SCOTLAND) REGULATIONS 2001, SSI 2001 139; made under the Civil Defence Act 1948 s.2, s.3, s.8. In force: April 1, 2001; £2.00.

These Regulations, which revoke the Civil Defence (Fire Services) (Scotland) Regulations 1949 (SI 1949 2167 as amended by SI 1968 548), the Civil Defence

(Grant) (Scotland) Regulations 1953 (SI 1953 1804 as amended by SI 1983 1651 and SI 1987 677), the Civil Defence (Police) (Scotland) Regulations 1954 (SI 1954 327), and the Civil Defence (General Local Authority Functions) (Scotland) Regulations 1993 (SI 1993 739), make provision for grants to be payable to police authorities by the Scottish Ministers towards expenses incurred by them in connection with the discharge of their civil defence functions. In addition, they amend the provision dealing with the estimate and determination of grant so as to reflect the position that civil defence grant is no longer demand led but instead is estimated by the Scottish Ministers at the outset.

6798. Local authorities – liability for acts and omissions of statutory successors

See NEGLIGENCE: Kirkpatrick v. Dumfries and Galloway Council. §6821

6799. Revenue support grant – determination for 2001/02

LOCAL GOVERNMENT FINANCE (SCOTLAND) ORDER 2001, SSI 2001 96; made under the Local Government Finance Act 1992 Sch.12 para.1, para.9. In force: February 8, 2001; £2.00.

This Order determines the amount of revenue support grant payable to each local authority in Scotland in respect of the financial year 2001/2002; determines the amount of non-domestic rate income to be distributed to each local authority in respect of that year; redetermines the amount of revenue support grant payable to each local authority in respect of the financial year 2000/2001; and makes consequential revocations in the Local Government Finance (Scotland) Order 2000 (SSI 2000 40).

6800. Revenue support grant – determination for 2001/02

LOCAL GOVERNMENT FINANCE (SCOTLAND) (NO.2) ORDER 2001, SSI 2001 260; made under the Local Government Finance Act 1992 Sch.12 para.1, para.9. In force: June 7, 2001; £2.00.

This Order, which amends the Local Government Finance (Scotland) Order 2001 (SI 2001 96), redetermines the amount of the revenue support grant payable to each local authority in respect of the financial year 2000 to 2001, and the amount of the revenue support grant payable to each local authority in Scotland in respect of the financial year 2001 to 2002. It determines the amount of non-domestic rate income to be distributed to each local authority in respect of the financial year 2001 to 2002.

6801. Scottish Local Authorities (Tendering) Act 2001 (asp 9)

This Act of the Scottish Parliament removes the time limit on the period during which the provisions about competition in the Local Government Act 1988 may be modified in relation to local authorities.

This Act comes into force on August 6, 2001.

MEDIA

6802. Books

Mckain, Bruce; Bonnington, Alistair – Scots Law for Journalists. 7th Ed. Paperback: £24.95. ISBN 0-414-01372-7. W. Green & Son.

MENTAL HEALTH

6803. Adults with Incapacity (Scotland) Act 2000 (asp 4) – Commencement No.1 Order

ADULTS WITH INCAPACITY (SCOTLAND) ACT 2000 (COMMENCEMENT NO.1) ORDER 2001, SSI 2001 81 (C.2); made under the Adults with Incapacity (Scotland) Act 2000 s.89. Commencement details: bringing into force various provisions of the Act on April 2, 2001 and April 1, 2002; £2.50.

This Order appoints April 2, 2001, and April 1, 2002, as the date for the coming into force of certain provisions of the 2000 Act.

6804. Mental patients – applications for authority to intromit – countersignatures

ADULTS WITH INCAPACITY (COUNTERSIGNATURES OF APPLICATIONS FOR AUTHORITY TO INTROMIT) (SCOTLAND) REGULATIONS 2001, SSI 2001 78; made under the Adults with Incapacity (Scotland) Act 2000 s.26. In force: April 2, 2001; £1.75.

These Regulations prescribe the classes of persons who may countersign an application made under the Adults with Incapacity (Scotland) Act 2000 s.26 and provide that a person who is a member of one of the classes may countersign an application made under that section.

6805. Mental patients – dispensing with intimation or notification – evidence

ADULTS WITH INCAPACITY (EVIDENCE IN RELATION TO DISPENSING WITH INTIMATION OR NOTIFICATION) (SCOTLAND) REGULATIONS 2001, SSI 2001 79; made under the Adults with Incapacity (Scotland) Act 2000 s.7, s.86. In force: April 2, 2001; £1.50.

These Regulations set out the evidence to be taken into account by the Public Guardian when deciding whether to dispense with intimation or notification to an adult for the purposes of the Adults with Incapacity (Scotland) Act 2000 s.11 (2). This evidence shall consist of two medical certificates stating that intimation or notification could be likely to pose a serious risk to the health of the adult. These certificates shall be prepared by medical practitioners independent of each other, and, where the incapacity of the adult is by reason of mental disorder, one of the two medical practitioners must be approved as having special experience in the diagnosis or treatment of mental disorder.

6806. Mental patients – local authorities – supervision of welfare attorneys

ADULTS WITH INCAPACITY (SUPERVISION OF WELFARE ATTORNEYS BY LOCAL AUTHORITIES) (SCOTLAND) REGULATIONS 2001, SSI 2001 77; made under the Adults with Incapacity (Scotland) Act 2000 s.10, s.86. In force: April 2, 2001; £1.75.

These Regulations prescribe the duties of the local authority acting under an order made by the sheriff in relation to supervision of a welfare attorney and prescribe the information to be provided by a welfare attorney to a local authority to enable it to carry out its supervisory function.

6807. Mental patients – medical practitioners certificates – accounts and funds

ADULTS WITH INCAPACITY (CERTIFICATES FROM MEDICAL PRACTITIONERS) (ACCOUNTS AND FUNDS) (SCOTLAND) REGULATIONS 2001, SSI 2001 76; made under the Adults with Incapacity (Scotland) Act 2000 s.26, s.86. In force: April 2, 2001; £1.75.

These Regulations prescribe the form of certificate from a medical practitioner to accompany an application to the Public Guardian under the Adults with Incapacity (Scotland) Act 2000 Part III for authority to intromit with funds. The certificate is completed by a medical practitioner who will confirm that the adult is incapable in relation to decisions about, or incapable of acting to safeguard or promote that adult's interest in, the funds.

6808. Mental patients – powers of attorney – certificates

ADULTS WITH INCAPACITY (CERTIFICATES IN RELATION TO POWERS OF ATTORNEY) (SCOTLAND) REGULATIONS 2001, SSI 2001 80; made under the Adults with Incapacity (Scotland) Act 2000 s.15, s.16. In force: April 2, 2001; £2.00.

These Regulations prescribe certificates for use in connection with the grant of continuing powers of attorney under the Adults with Incapacity (Scotland) Act 2000 s.15, and in connection with welfare powers of attorney under s.16 of that Act and prescribe the classes of persons, in addition to solicitors, who may issue a certificate under s.15 or s.16.

6809. Mental patients – public guardians – fees

ADULTS WITH INCAPACITY (PUBLIC GUARDIAN'S FEES) (SCOTLAND) REGULATIONS 2001, SSI 2001 75; made under the Adults with Incapacity (Scotland) Act 2000 s.7. In force: April 2, 2001; £1.75.

These Regulations, which set out the fees for certain services provided by the Public Guardian in connection with the Adults with Incapacity (Scotland) Act 2000, introduce charges for the registration of certain documents, the issue of certain certificates, and other miscellaneous charges.

NEGLIGENCE

6810. Accidents – road accident – tractor swinging out across central line of road – oncoming motorcyclist speeding – driver of tractor not negligent

H, a tractor driver towing a trailer, swung his tractor out to the right and over the central line of the road to turn left into a field. At that point G came round a blind bend at an excessive speed and collided with H. G, a motorcyclist, sought damages from H claiming that H had been negligent in crossing the central line in the road.

Held, that in the circumstances G was to blame for the accident as a result of the speed at which he was travelling in spite of road signs warning of agricultural vehicles.

GRIERSON v. HARVEY 2001 Rep. L.R. 84, Sheriff CB Miller, Sh Ct (South Strathclyde, Dumfries and Galloway).

6811. Clinical negligence – causation – inadequate anaesthesia

T, raised an action for damages against the health board for pain and suffering which she claimed were as a result of being improperly anaesthetised during a Caesarean section. T claimed that following the traumatic birth of her son she had suffered symptoms of depression, guilt and anxiety attributable to post traumatic stress disorder and had failed to bond with her son during the first four years of his life. Her sexual relationship with her husband had also been severely affected. Despite the severity of T's alleged symptoms, a significant amount of time had elapsed between the birth and the first reported symptoms in T's medical notes despite T receiving substantial amounts of medical treatment for gynaecological conditions in the years following the birth.

Held, granting decree of absolvitor, that (1) the events described by T as occurring during the operation were not based on facts, as it appeared that T had a powerful imagination which had, over the years, exaggerated the discomfort of the operation to such an extent that she subsequently began to experience post traumatic symptoms and the depression, anxiety and related symptoms could not, therefore, be directly attributed to the lack of adequate anaesthesia during the operation, and (2) had liability been established, an award of £1,500 would have been made in respect of discomfort and distress with interest at 7.5 per cent from July 3, 1992 to March 31, 1994, and at 4 per cent thereafter.

THOMSON v. LOTHIAN HEALTH BOARD 2001 S.C.L.R. 153, Lord MacLean, OH.

6812. Death – causation – asbestosis exposure – not cause of death

D was a plumber's mate who had worked in shipyards for both W and Y. D died in 1992, aged 75, and his daughter, C, sought damages from W and Y, averring that (1) D had died as a result of asbestosis; (2) D had been employed by W from 1942 to 1946, and by Y in 1946, then between 1956 and 1962, and again in 1965, and (3) D had been exposed to asbestos during those times. The principal issue at proof was cause of death.

Held, granting both defenders absolvitor, that (1) D had experienced significant exposure to asbestos during the course of his employment with both W and Y; (2) C had failed to prove that D had suffered from asbestosis. It was accepted by all experts that to support a diagnosis of asbestosis they would have to find features consistent with the condition which might remain constant or would deteriorate, and there was no evidence to satisfy this requirement. There was nothing in the radiographs or hospital records which could not be explained by other factors, given D's smoking and history of bronchitis, obstructive airways disease and emphysema, and (3) D died before his disease could be fully investigated and in the absence of a post mortem, no firm diagnosis of bronchial carcinoma was made and there was no evidence to prove that this was the cause of death, given that the preponderance of medical opinion was that he had died of pneumonia, which was more likely to have been caused by his smoking than by exposure to asbestosis. Opinion, that the damages which would have awarded were: solatium of £10,000 (35 per cent disablement for six years); £40,000 for death; £2,500 for services provided by his family; funeral expenses of £1,200.50; £500 for loss of society for D's wife who died two days after D; and loss of society for C £3,000.

COOK v. WYVERN STRUCTURES LTD (IN LIQUIDATION); *sub nom.* DURIE v. WYVERN STRUCTURES LTD 2001 S.L.T. 1212, Lord Nimmo Smith, OH.

6813. Duty of care – clubs – delictual liability of club to club member – liability of club officers as individuals

[Occupier's Liability (Scotland) Act 1960 (c.30); Unfair Contract Terms Act 1977 (c.50) s.16.]

H sustained major injuries in a go-karting accident when he collided with a wall of the building at W. H sought damages from W and five of its office bearers as representatives of the club and as individuals, and the motorsports association as the body responsible for the licensing and inspection of racing tracks. The basis of liability against W and office bearers was that they had been negligent in not providing crash protection in the area of the accident. The basis of liability against the motorsports association was that they had been negligent in licensing the track in the absence of adequate crash protection, whereas the association disputed it owed a duty of care. W contended that a club, and its office bearers as representatives of that club could not be held liable in delict to a club member.

Held, dismissing the action insofar as it was against W and the office bearers as representatives of the club since a member of a club could not sue the club in delict; allowing proof before answer on the action against the motorsports association and the committee members as individuals given their knowledge as averred by H coupled with their de facto assumption of the responsibility for taking executive decisions relating to track safety.

HARRISON v. WEST OF SCOTLAND KART CLUB 2001 S.C. 367, Lady Paton, OH.

6814. Duty of care – police officers – injury during training exercise – failure to show that additional precaution would have prevented injury

G, a former policeman, was injured after being struck by a baton during a training course and sought damages from his employers. G's right arm was bruised but he thereafter developed a serious psychological condition which rendered him unfit for work and his employment was terminated. G argued that the occurrence of an injury indicated a failure on the part of the training course officers to properly look after his welfare and, even if the risk of injury had been inevitable, given the nature of the course, it was the duty of the officers to minimise that injury. C argued that there was no direct connection between the incident and G's psychiatric illness, therefore it could not be shown that G's psychological condition was reasonably foreseeable.

Held, granting decree of absolvitor, that while there was no doubt that G was owed a duty of care as a participant in the training exercise, G had failed to show that there was action that the officers could have undertaken that would have prevented the bruising and not reduced the necessary realism of the training course.

GRANT v. CHIEF CONSTABLE OF GRAMPIAN POLICE 2001 Rep. L.R. 74, Lord Johnston, OH.

6815. Duty of care – police officers – injury during training exercise – well known risk that could have been avoided

F, a former policeman, sought damages after his wrists were injured during a training course that included training in the use of handcuffs, F thereafter became very depressed. F maintained that the risk of injury from training with handcuffs was well known at the time of his training course and that C had not taken the necessary precautions to prevent injury. C argued that F's depression could be attributable to other factors, not simply his handcuff injuries and as such, C could not be held liable.

Held, that the injury risks had been well known at the time of F's training course and C's lack of proper precautions rendered them liable in damages. F was predisposed to a severe reaction to a "trigger event" and on balance the depression was triggered by the handcuff injuries. C had to take F as he found him and was fully liable.

FRANKLIN v. CHIEF CONSTABLE OF GRAMPIAN POLICE 2001 Rep. L.R. 79, Lord McEwan, OH.

6816. Duty of care – road accidents – duty of driver to passenger – passenger engaged in criminal offence – passenger not disqualified from suing for injuries

[Road Traffic Act 1988 (c.52) s.178(1) (b).]

Cu sought £100,000 damages from Cl's estate for injuries sustained as a passenger in a road traffic accident. Cl died as a result of the accident. The car was owned by the mother of another passenger in the car, B, and the vehicle was provided for B's use. There was conflicting evidence regarding who had driven the car when the accident happened, but Cu accepted that the keys were in Cl's possession, that he refused to return them to B. B stated she had only gone in the car because she feared that otherwise it would have been stolen. Cl's insurance company accepted that the accident had been caused by Cl's negligence, but argued that Cu was not entitled to damages since he had been committing a criminal offence under the Road Traffic Act 1988 s.178(1) (b) by climbing into the car knowing that Cl was driving without the consent of the owner.

Held, putting the case out by order, that (1) cross examination of B should have taken place in the interests of fair play and failure to do so was prejudicial to Cu, however it was established that Cl was the driver, even though it could be considered there was a technical breach of s.178(1)(b) it could not be considered serious; (2) on a pragmatic approach to the issue of criminal conduct barring recovery of damages and on the facts Cl owed Cu a duty of care, and (3) Cu would be considered one third contributorily negligent. Cu knew or ought to have known that CI was unfit to drive given the quantity of alcohol he had consumed.

CURRIE v. CLAMP; *sub nom.* CURRIE v. CLAMP'S EXECUTOR 2002 S.L.T. 196, Lord Clarke, OH.

6817. Duty of care – roads authority – road accident – hazardous location – death of road user

S, the widow of D, together with her three children, sought damages from F, the First Minister, in respect of D's death, aged 45, on October 30, 1988. D was driving a vehicle which fell 20 feet down a sheer drop into a loch, after D swerved to avoid a bus which had crossed in front of his vehicle at a point where a trunk road narrowed to five metres and bent sharply around an outcrop of rock. A barrier and wall were situated at the road's edge, though not specifically designed to prevent cars leaving the road, but a space existed where the wall had degraded. S claimed that D had been driving at a reasonable speed, which was consistent with the evidence of a police officer, who also suggested that it was inevitable that a bus would have to cross onto the opposite side of the road when rounding the corner. Another officer stated that there was no reason why traffic lights could not have been erected at the locus. A temporary set was later erected until roadworks removed the hazard. S argued that the accident was reasonably foreseeable. Several incidents had occurred at the locus though no cars had left the road, and there should have been a sign warning buses of the hazard, a solid barrier, and traffic lights. In relation to damages for loss of support, S argued that the normal practice of taking a multiplier from the date of death would produce an unfair result where the award was being determined 12 years after the accident and all the pursuers had survived that period. S also sought loss of support based on the fact that prior to his death D had been successfully building up a building contractor's business, arguing that real increases in his earnings could have been expected after 1988.

Held, granting decree and putting the case out by order to determine interest, that (1) D had been driving at a reasonable speed and had come off the road while taking avoidance action; (2) the fact that many cars had travelled on the road without incident did not outweigh the factor that the hazardous locus made an accident almost inevitable, *Levine v. Morris* [1970] 1 W.L.R. 71, [1970] C.L.Y. 1867 applied; (3) S's averments relating to the risk of meeting tourist buses gave F adequate notice of a case to the effect that a sign could and should have been erected in relation to this particular hazard; (4) in fulfilling his duty of care, F's predecessor ought to have erected temporary traffic lights at the locus once the wall had become degraded, which could have been done at reasonable cost without material delay; (5) it was not for a judge at first instance to depart from normal practice; the appropriate multiplier was 11 based on the likelihood of D working until he was 60 but reducing his commitments in the final years; (6) the proper multiplicand was £30,000. S's earnings would be added and 30 per cent deducted from the total for D's own maintenance; then S's income would be deducted giving £206,580 as the figure for loss of support, of which £7,100 and £5,000 was awarded to two of D's children for bed and board. Loss of services was assessed at £1,000 per annum for 15 years; (7) loss of society was £15,000 to S, £2,000 to a child then aged 21 who had left home, £2,750 to a child then aged 20 who was still living at home, and £4,000 for a child then aged 15, two thirds to the past in each case. Funeral expenses were agreed at £1,323.34, and (8) problems in assessing interest arose from the delay between the accident and proof and further submissions on the matter were required.

SARGENT v. SECRETARY OF STATE FOR SCOTLAND; *sub nom.* SARGENT v. DEWAR 2001 S.C.L.R. 190, Lord Clarke, OH.

6818. Duty of care – schools – injury on school outing – foreseeability of accident – liability of school – level of duty of care as an independent school

C a pupil sought damages from his former school, M following an accident during a school trip to a golfing range. A teacher and golf professional were supervising, instructing pupils in covered bays. C was practising in one of the bays when another pupil, attempting to hit a bouncing ball, hit C in the face injuring him. C argued that M was vicariously liable for the teacher's failure to supervise and instruct the pupils correctly, maintaining the teacher ought to have known that there was a possibility that the boys would use the clubs in a way which presented a risk. C also argued that M was directly liable for the failure to provide an extra member of staff to supervise. The sheriff allowed proof before answer and M appealed. C argued that in considering the standard of care it was appropriate to distinguish cases involving local authority schools where resources might constrain the supervision available.

Held, allowing the appeal and dismissing the action, that there was no reason why the standard of care owed by a school to its pupils should be dependent upon the type of institution. The sheriff had erred when considering that in the absence of negligence, hitting a golf ball with a club in a location designed for just that activity would be in any way dangerous. The accident was not reasonably foreseeable and C's argument that the teacher should have anticipated it was not supported in any way. C's averments with regard to M's vicarious and direct liability were contradictory and mutually inconsistent and neither possibility gave rise to a relevant case of fault.

CUTHBERTSON v. MERCHISTON CASTLE SCHOOL 2001 S.L.T. (Sh Ct) 13, CGB Nicholson Q.C., Sheriff Principal, Sh Ct.

6819. Duty of care – solicitors – reliance on inaccurate report in granting loan – default by borrower – loss suffered as result of reliance upon report

N brought an action against P, averring breach of contract and delictual wrong. N had lent £135,000 to borrowers, with P acting as their solicitors, for the purchase of a flat subject to P confirming (1) the price, (2) that all loan conditions had been met, and (3) that the borrowers retained no interest in other subjects. P confirmed those matters in a report and the monies were advanced. The borrowers defaulted and N repossessed the flat. N discovered that the flat had not been purchased with the money but the borrowers had purchased the entire building two years earlier. There had been no purchase price and the borrowers had retained an interest in the building at the time of P's report. N averred that P had breached their contract by providing an inaccurate report and had not exercised reasonable care. N sought, as damages, the amount of loan outstanding after the sale of the flat and the amount of interest that N would have received if that money had been placed in the money market rather than loaned to P. P argued that N's loss had been incurred as a result of the borrowers default; not P's breach of contract or delict.

Held, allowing proof before answer, that where but for P's negligence in providing a false report there would have been no loan and where P's duty of care existed to protect N from default, there was no reason why the loss could not be seen to flow from the breach of duty and be the responsibility of P. Contractually, since the only loss N would suffer would be by default and since a negligent report might have increased that probability, the loss should have been reasonably contemplated by P.

NEWCASTLE BUILDING SOCIETY v. PATERSON ROBERTSON & GRAHAM 2001 S.C. 734, Lord Reed, OH.

6820. Local authorities – duty to maintain footpath – no duty to maintain to standard level

F raised an action for damages against G in respect of personal injuries sustained after he tripped whilst walking on a pavement which the local authority had a duty to maintain. The G raised a preliminary point arguing that F's pleadings did not give fair notice of the case being made against them, as there was no mention of the relative heights of the adjoining sections of pavement at the point where F tripped. F argued that it was sufficient to aver that the pavement had been broken and uneven, thereby rendering it dangerous and likely to result in tripping.

Held, dismissing F's pleadings as irrelevant and putting the case out to order, that (1) there was no obligation on a local authority to maintain a footpath to a completely uniform level, *Gordon v. Glasgow Corp* (Unreported, June 26, 1923) followed; (2) pleadings required to demonstrate that the level of unevenness was sufficient to be a foreseeable cause of injury which required specific averments concerning the different heights between adjoining parts of the pavement at the point where the trip occurred, (3) without sufficient averments, insufficient notice of the case against G had been given.

Observed, that F may have been able to avoid the normal rules of fair notice had the pleadings included averments indicating that the reason for not providing more specification on the condition of the pavement was due to the fact that the pavement had been repaired by the time F had sought legal advice regarding his injuries.

FOX v. GLASGOW CITY COUNCIL 2001 Rep. L.R. 59, Sheriff JA Taylor, Sh Ct (Glasgow and Strathkelvin).

6821. Local authorities – duty to maintain highway – road as land under Occupiers Liability (Scotland) Act 1960

[Occupiers Liability (Scotland) Act 1960 (c.30) s.2(1); Local Government etc (Scotland) Act 1994 (c.39) s.181, s.181 (3).]

K raised an action for damages against the local authority in respect of injuries sustained whilst walking on a road in a pedestrian area. K argued that the local authority were liable as statutory successors of the former Dumfries and Galloway regional council who had responsibility for the maintenance and repair of the road at the material time. K maintained that responsibility for the Regional Council's failure to inspect the road with a view to its maintenance had passed to the local authority by virtue of the Local Government etc (Scotland) Act 1994 s.181 (3) and that the local authority were also liable under the Occupiers Liability (Scotland) Act 1960 s.2(1). The local authority raised a preliminary plea to the relevance of K's pleadings arguing that (1) s.181 (3) applied only to positive acts in connection with the discharge of the council's functions and did not transfer liability to the local authority for omissions by the former regional council and, (2) in respect of s.2(1) were also irrelevant as the 1960 Act did not apply to roads which were maintained by public bodies.

Held, allowing proof, that (1) the purpose of s.181 was to effectively substitute the local authority for the former regional council meaning that s.181 (3) transferred liability for both acts and omissions by former regional council to the local authority, and (2) the 1960 Act did not apply to roads and streets where responsibility had, by statute, been conferred upon a public body and K's pleadings in that respect were irrelevant.

KIRKPATRICK v. DUMFRIES AND GALLOWAY COUNCIL 2001 S.C.L.R. 261, Sheriff Kenneth Barr, Sh Ct (South Strathclyde, Dumfries and Galloway).

6822. Professional negligence – solicitors – duty to disclose to lender information believed to be untrue

L sought damages from A for the alleged professional negligence of one of their solicitors (G) for failing to disclose information which would have affected the grant of loan to P. A contended that the information about which L complained had no causal connection between any alleged negligence and L's loss. P had hoped to develop the property for which the loan was obtained into a tennis centre. L's rules required information if the property was to be used for commercial purposes. P answered that question in the negative in the mortgage application form, and G made no comment despite having prior knowledge of P's aspirations, but which he knew were not likely to be achieved.

Held, granting A absolvitor, that (1) the question of any duty of disclosure had to be determined in relation to all the circumstances of the case taken as a whole. G was peculiarly well qualified both from his long association with P and his background knowledge of tennis funding to be able to accurately assess the likelihood of success in any commercial venture of that type and G was therefore entitled to exercise his professional judgment as he did. Any competent solicitor faced with similar circumstances and armed with the same level of specialist knowledge as G would have been likely to reach a similar decision, and (2) the causa causans of L's decision to expose themselves to risk by lending such a large sum to P was P's request for a loan coupled with the information supplied by, or on behalf of, P and the advice contained in the report on title. Had there been any material omission or inaccuracy contained in that information which led to L lending the money, when with fuller or more accurate information they would not have done so, and had G been found professionally negligent, there would have been a sufficient casual connection to link the negligence to the loss suffered by L.

LEEDS & HOLBECK BUILDING SOCIETY v. ALEX MORISON & CO (NO.2) 2001 S.C.L.R. 41, Lady Paton, OH.

6823. **Professional negligence – solicitors – financial provision on divorce – advice as to settlement**

D sought damages against M, a firm of solicitors, averring negligence and breach of contract in M's conduct of D's defence in divorce proceedings brought by D's exwife, W. By minute of agrement in 1989 D agreed to pay W aliment of £500 per month. W raised the divorce action in 1993 claiming a property transfer of the matrimonial home, which belonged wholly to D, a capital sum and a periodical allowance. D instructed M. Following D's retirement in October 1993, M enrolled a motion in the divorce action to vary the aliment, which was refused as incompetent and a subsequent action in Edinburgh sheriff court was abandoned for lack of jurisdiction. On May 20, 1994 W offered to settle the financial claims on divorce either by transfer of the house and contents with a capital payment of £18,500 and periodical allowance of £250 per month payable for two years from divorce, or transfer of the house and contents and a capital sum of £25,000. D refused the offer on M's recommendation. On September 29, 1995 the Lord Ordinary ordered the transfer of the matrimonial home to W and payment by D of £12,000 capital sum. W reclaimed and the court increased the capital sum to £33,239. The court's decision was based on the misapplication of *Wallis v. Wallis (Divorce: Financial Provision)* 1993 S.C. (H.L.) 49, [1994] C.L.Y. 2186, at first instance. D complained about M's failure (a) to advise D to accept W's offer; (b) to take proper and competent steps to vary the amount of aliment, and (c) in relation to W's reclaiming motion, to instruct counsel to consider lodging a cross appeal on grounds of the departure from equal sharing of matrimonial property. M argued D's claim should be dismissed as irrelevant because (1) there was no clear averment that it would have been reasonably foreseeable to a solicitor of ordinary competency, exercising reasonable care, that failure to accept the offer would result in adverse consequences for D; (2) D accepted junior counsel (C) had previously been instructed and had represented D, and where a solicitor had instructed appropriate counsel, liability could only arise where it was clear counsel's advice was "seriously wrong", and (3) D had failed to aver what C's response would have been to suggestion of a cross appeal, or the precise terms that a cross appeal might have taken, and had failed to aver what more favourable outcome would have been achieved.

Held, allowing proof before answer, that (1) D had not admitted that the advice given to reject the offer was based on C's advice, and M's argument therefore proceeded upon a factual basis disputed to a material extent and inquiry would be necessary; (2) while it was necessary for D to establish that a competent solicitor exercising reasonable care would have appreciated rejection of the offer would be likely to have adverse consequences, in the circumstances where the alleged negligence consisted in a failure to appreciate the implications of *Wallis* and where its proper comprehension would have shed a different light on the offer to settle, D had made sufficient averment to justify proof before answer; (3) it was possible to imply that any counsel exercising proper care and prudence would have acceded to the instruction if, once the misapplication of *Wallis* was appreciated, the necessity for a cross appeal became so clamant that the duty contended for by D arose, and (4) notwithstanding the difficulty of estimating the likely conduct of a court of superior instance if presented with a particular ground of appeal, it could not be said that the failure to appeal or cross appeal a judgment could never be a ground of professional negligence, and it could not be said at this stage that that branch of D's case would necessarily fail. As inquiry was needed on the other branches, it was expedient that inquiry embraced the whole course of the litigation and the advice given in connection with it.

DIBLE v. MORTON FRASER PARTNERSHIP 2001 Fam. L.R. 84, Lord Eassie, OH.

6824. Professional negligence – solicitors – mortgage lender relying on inaccurate report on title

See NEGLIGENCE: Newcastle Building Society v. Paterson Robertson & Graham. §6819

6825. Professional negligence – solicitors – settlement of claim for financial provision – relevancy

[Family Law (Scotland) Act 1985 (c.37) s.8, s.9(1)(b).]

P sought damages from D, the partners of a dissolved firm of solicitors, in respect of loss suffered as a result of entering a minute of agreement whereby P accepted a financial settlement which did not take into account her husband's (H) pension rights. P alleged that D had failed to give proper advice and averred inter alia that if they had done so she would have sought a settlement taking the pension rights into account, or sought financial provision on divorce. D sought dismissal, arguing that P's averments about resources available to H to make any payment under the Family Law (Scotland) Act 1985 s.8 were wholly unspecific. Further, the time for assessing the parties' resources would be when a s.8 order was made, which would be later than the relevant date for the date of separation and later than the date of the minute of agreement. P's averments regarding s.9(1)(b) left it impossible to tell what P was averring would fall to be added to any sum derived from the division of the matrimonial property. D were in no position to predict what would occur before the court at a future date.

Held, allowing a proof before answer, that P was claiming that, as a result of D's breach of contract, P had lost the right to advance a claim, and D's criticisms of P's pleadings suffered from a failure to appreciate the character of P's claim. The date of the breach of contract, ie. when the minute became effective in May 1992, constituted iniuria, and damnum crystallised at the same time as P suffered the loss of the right to make the claims surrendered in terms of the minute. The loss then had to be measured in terms of what the claim was worth when P surrendered it. Predictions about wholly unknowable factors were not necessary. P's averments were adequate, ie. that she would have sought a settlement taking account of the pension were properly to be read as a statement that she would have sought a settlement on the basis of proper advice about the relevance of H's pension rights, and failing any compromise, would have enforced her rights through an order of the court. P had averred with ample specification what the matrimonial property was, and P's averments regarding the possible application of s.9(1)(b) were such as to allow a court to make a decision on that factor.

DARRIE v. DUNCAN 2001 S.L.T. 941, Lord McCluskey, OH.

NUISANCE

6826. Building works – demolition of mutual gable wall – work carried out by independent contractors – liability of proprietors of demolished property

P was the owner of flats in a tenement building adjoining a tenement owned by D which D instructed be demolished. The mutual gable was exposed to the elements. Water penetration caused damage to P's property. P notified D and gave it an opportunity to rectify the problem by waterproofing the gable wall. D failed to take action, P carried out the work and raised an action to recover the cost of so doing. P based its claim on the fact that the actions taken by D, or on its behalf, of demolishing the adjoining property and then failing to weatherproof the mutual gable created a nuisance as a result of which P suffered loss. D argued that P's averments were irrelevant and, after debate, the sheriff pronounced an interlocutor repelling D's plea of irrelevance and allowing a proof. D appealed arguing that (1) P had failed to state in pleadings the basis on which its claim for nuisance was founded; (2) the sheriff had wrongly concluded that D's failure to respond to P's correspondence was a sound basis for the claim; (3) P had not set out its title to sue, and (4) P's averments of loss were lacking in specification and the matter should not be allowed to proceed to proof. D further argued that it should be excluded from liability as it had instructed the contractors to carry out the weatherproofing at the same time as the demolition and it was the contractor's failure to do so which resulted in P's loss.

Held, refusing the appeal and varying the sheriff's interlocutor by substituting a proof before answer for the proof simpliciter, that (1) where injurious consequences naturally flowed from operations resulting in damage to neighbouring property, the owner responsible for those operations must take steps to ensure that those consequences were rectified and instructing someone to carry out the work was insufficient to avoid liability, *GA Estates Ltd v. Caviapen Trustees Ltd (No.1)* 1993 S.L.T. 1037, [1993] C.L.Y. 4761 and *Noble's Trustees v. Economic Forestry (Scotland) Ltd* 1988 S.L.T. 662, [1988] C.L.Y. 4578, applied, *Borders RC v. Roxburgh DC* 1989 S.L.T. 837, [1989] C.L.Y. 3877, distinguished; (2) a decision on whether the sheriff's was correct in repelling a plea of irrelevance should to be determined following a proof before answer; (3) D's ground of appeal relating to title to sue related more to the question of quantification of damages and should be reserved until after proof, and (4) P had incorporated into pleadings a bill of quantities for the work actually carried out and two independent quotations from other building firms of higher amounts which were sufficient specification of loss to repel the D's plea.

POWRIE CASTLE PROPERTIES LTD v. DUNDEE CITY COUNCIL 2001 S.C.L.R. 146, RA Dunlop Q.C., Sheriff Principal, Sh Ct.

6827. Statutory nuisance – local authority housing – condensation – injury to health

[Environmental Protection Act 1990 (c.43) s.82.]

R leased a flat from D. R lodged an application under the Environmental Protection Act 1990 s.82, requiring D to abate condensation that adversely affected the premises, which R contended was prejudicial to her health and that of her three year old son. It was held at first instance that the condensation was due to R being unable to afford adequate heating for the flat so that D was not responsible for the statutory nuisance. R appealed.

Held, dismissing the appeal, that the appropriate test to determine statutory nuisance was to decide if the state of the premises was likely to be injurious to health or exacerbate a pre-existing condition. On the facts, R had not established such a link. Similarly, at common law, nuisance required an intolerable situation, mere discomfort would not suffice. The condition of the premises was due to R's inability to afford suitable heating and not the structure of the premises.

ROBB v. DUNDEE CITY COUNCIL 2001 Hous. L.R. 42, JF Wheatley Q.C., Sheriff Principal, Sh Ct.

OIL AND GAS INDUSTRY

6828. Oil pollution – claims against limitation fund – amendment of claim

See CIVIL PROCEDURE: Assuranceforeningen Skuld v. International Oil Pollution Compensation Fund (No.3). §6240

See PRESCRIPTION: Assuranceforeningen Skuld v. International Oil Pollution Compensation Fund (No.2). §6869

PARTNERSHIPS

6829. Dissolution – notice – diary entry by one representative of deceased partner – insufficient notice to other representatives

A and B were partners in a firm. The contract of copartnership provided that a surviving partner could purchase the share of a deceased partner on giving written notice to the deceased partner's representatives that he was to do so. B died and A and his three sisters (S) were appointed executors. On B's death, A had made a note to himself in the partnership diary that he intended to purchase B's share. S referred the matter to, and sought in the Court of Session an order that the partnership had dissolved on B's death. The arbiter referred the case to the Court of Session, asking whether (1) notice had to be given to each party who could at the time of B's death have become an executor of B, and (2) the diary entry was sufficient notice to "the representative" of B.

Held, answering question (1) in the affirmative and (2) in the negative, that relative to B, S stood in the same position as A, and A alone could not answer the description of "representative". "[T]he" used with "representative" indicated that notice was required to more than "a" representative. A representative could be the next of kin with an interest in the estate, or the executor(s) nominate or dative of a deceased.

MOFFAT v. LONGMUIR 2001 S.C. 137, Lord Cameron of Lochbroom, Lord Osborne, Lord Reed, Ex Div.

6830. Partners – partnerships – limited liability partnerships

LIMITED LIABILITY PARTNERSHIPS (SCOTLAND) REGULATIONS 2001, SSI 2001 128; made under the Limited Liability Partnerships Act 2000 s.14, s.15, s.16, s.17. In force: April 6, 2001; £4.00.

The Limited Liability Partnerships Act 2000 provided for the creation of limited liability partnerships and for the making of regulations concerning them. These Regulations, which amend the Companies Act 1985, the Insolvency Act 1986, the Requirements of Writing (Scotland) Act 1995 and the Criminal Procedure (Scotland) Act 1995, regulate limited liability partnerships by applying to them, with appropriate modifications, the appropriate provisions of the existing law which relate to companies and partnerships. They apply Scots law in relation to winding up and insolvency of limited liability partnerships and extend certain provisions of the Companies Act 1985 to limited liability partnerships in Scotland to ensure that such a limited liability partnership should be able to create create floating charges over its assets.

PENOLOGY

6831. Detention – legalised police cells – discontinuance

DISCONTINUANCE OF LEGALISED POLICE CELLS (PORTREE) RULES 2001, SSI 2001 64; made under the Prisons (Scotland) Act 1989 s.14, s.39. In force: March 31, 2001; £1.50.

These Rules provide for the discontinuance, as at March 31, 2001, of the police cells in the possession of the Northern Joint Police Board at Portree as a place in which prisoners may be detained before, during or after trial for any period not exceeding 14 days.

6832. Parole – Parole Board for Scotland – proceedings

PAROLE BOARD (SCOTLAND) RULES 2001, SSI 2001 315; made under the Prisoners and Criminal Proceedings (Scotland) Act 1993 s.20. In force: October 8, 2001; £3.00.

These Rules, which revoke the Parole Board (Scotland) Rules 1993 (SI 1993 2225 (S 235) and the Parole Board (Scotland) Rules 1995 (SI 1995 1273 (S.99) with savings, make provision with respect to the proceedings of the Parole Board for Scotland

6833. Prison discipline – right to fair trial – disciplinary proceedings not "criminal charges" – implications for parole

[Human Rights Act 1998 (c.42) Sch.1 Part I Art.6.]

M, a mandatory life prisoner charged with breaching prison rules and subjected to disciplinary proceedings, petitioned for judicial review of the decision of Scottish Ministers that he did not face a "criminal charge" and was therefore not entitled to rely on the provisions of the Human Rights Act 1998 Sch.1 Part I Art.6. M contended that by reason of the implications the results of the disciplinary proceedings could have on future parole board decisions on whether to recommend him for life licence, the disciplinary proceedings had a "criminal" character.

Held, dismissing the petition for judicial review, that the disciplinary proceedings did not involve the determination of a criminal charge, the proceedings being in the interest of maintaining prison discipline rather than being in the general public interest. Future parole board proceedings would not involve the determination of a criminal charge, and the disciplinary proceedings might not effect the board's decision. Even if they were of some effect, it would be in respect of assessing M's suitability for release on licence. A negative finding by the parole board was not a punishment for the disciplinary offence.

MATTHEWSON v. SCOTTISH MINISTERS *The Times*, October 24, 2001, Lord Reed, OH.

6834. Prisoners – ill treatment – confinement in inhumane and degrading conditions – absence of toilet – violation of human rights

[Human Rights Act 1998 (c.42) Sch.1 Part I Art.3.]

N, a remand prisoner in a Scottish prison, applied for an interim order that he be transferred to alternative conditions because the conditions of his detention were inhumane and contravened the Human Rights Act 1998 Sch.1 Part I Art.3. He contended that his cell, which he shared with another inmate for the bulk of each day, was too small and lacked adequate light and ventilation. His principal complaint was that the cell did not have a toilet and the provision for urination and defecation in vessels kept inside the cell was grossly inadequate. N further submitted that his confinement in the conditions he described had acutely exacerbated his facial eczema.

Held, granting the application, that N's confinement in the cell about which he complained was a violation of the rights guaranteed by Art.3. Although it was not practicable to transfer all the remand prisoners to accommodation which had better sanitation, N was entitled to have his case decided on its own merits. There had been no contention that it would be impracticable to transfer N and therefore the balance of convenience was biased in favour of making the order.

NAPIER v. SCOTTISH MINISTERS *The Times*, November 15, 2001, Lord Macfadyen, OH.

6835. Prisoners – status of prisoner – sentence imposed prior to commencement of law enabling additional days

[Criminal Procedure (Scotland) Act 1975 (c.21) s.25; Prisoners and Criminal Proceedings (Scotland) Act 1993 (c.9); Prison (Scotland) Amendment Rules 1993 (SI 1993 2227).]

S sought reduction, by way of judicial review, of the imposition by prison authorities of additional days on his term of imprisonment for breach of prison discipline. S had been sentenced in March 1993 to a total of 12 years imprisonment. On appeal in December 1993 the total time to be served was reduced to nine years backdated to November 1992. Relevant provisions of the Criminal Procedure (Scotland) Act 1993 came into force on October 1, 1993. The award of an additional 470 days to the sentence was made under the provisions derived from s.24 of the 1993 Act. S argued that the punishment regime for awarding additional days of sentence could not be applied to prisoners sentenced before the 1993 Act came into force. As S had originally been sentenced before that date, any punishment should have been by way of loss of remission and not the imposition of additional days. The prison authorities argued that S was being held by a warrant of the High Court dated December 1993 and as such came under the new regime. The Lord Ordinary dismissed the petition finding that the terms of the Criminal Procedure (Scotland) Act 1975 s.254 were determinative of the meaning to be given to "sentenced" as it applied to the phrase "existing prisoner" under the 1993 Act. The Lord Ordinary held that the effect of s.254 was that sentences on appeal were to be treated as different sentences from those at first instance bringing S within the regime imposed by the 1993 Act. S reclaimed.

Held, refusing the reclaiming motion, (Lord Marnoch dissenting) that (1) where an appeal court quashed a sentence, that sentence could no longer have any effect in determining which category the prisoner fell into as the prisoner's status changed from the date of the appeal, (2) the effect of the imposition of a new sentence on S by the appeal court was to make him a long term prisoner under the terms of the 1993 Act and subject to disciplinary procedures imposed by that Act. Per Lord Cameron of Lochbroom, (1) time spent by a person in custody pending the outcome of an appeal would count towards the sentence imposed on appeal only where that was affirmed by the High Court on appeal, and (2) by exercising a right to appeal, a convicted person could not consider his sentence as determined and a substitution of sentence on appeal had the effect of a new sentence rather that a continuation of the original sentence. Per Lord Marnoch (dissenting), the terms of the 1993 Act were clear without reference to s.254 and the relevant date for determination of whether S fell under the 1993 regime was the date on which he was initially sentenced in respect of the offence.

Observed, that it was doubtful whether a petition against the Scottish Ministers or their predecessors was competent in respect of their failure to quash awards of additional days sentence for breaches of prison discipline as they did not have the power to interfere with such decisions on S's behalf.

STEWART (JOHN) v. SCOTTISH MINISTERS; *sub nom* STEWART (JOHN) v. SECRETARY OF STATE FOR SCOTLAND 2001 S.C. 884, Lord Cameron of Lochbroom, Lord Marnoch, Lord Morison, Ex Div.

6836. Prisoners rights – right to liberty – revocation of licence – lawful detention – review by competent court

[Prisons (Scotland) Act 1989 (c.45) s.28(2); Scotland Act 1998 (c.46) s.57(2); European Convention on Human Rights 1950 Art.5.]

V sought reduction by judicial review of the Scottish Ministers' (S) decision to revoke a licence discharging him from prison. V had been released in 1998 after serving 13 of 29 years for assault, robbery and prison breaking. He was arrested in July 1999 and charged with being concerned in the supply of cannabis. On July 2, he was fully committed and refused bail, and on July 7, S revoked his licence under the Prisons (Scotland) Act 1989 s.28(2) without consulting the parole board (B), and V was recalled to custody. B later affirmed the decision. V argued that (1) the operative decision was that of S, and (2) S's decision was ultra vires of the Scotland Act1998 s.57(2) and the European Convention on Human Rights1950 Art.5 (right to liberty), because there was not a sufficient causal connection between the original conviction in 1984 and his deprivation of liberty in 1999 to justify the revocation.

Held, dismissing the petition, that (1) looking at the system as a whole, the decision to continue V's detention was that of B affirming the decision of S; B's decision could not be challenged as B was not yet subject to the Convention; (2) in assessing whether a prisoner was entitled to challenge the lawfulness of detention following revocation of a licence, a determinate sentence was to be regarded as falling within the same category of a mandatory life sentence. Therefore, unlike a discretionary sentence, there were no factors susceptible to change with the passage of time which could justify periodic review of the lawfulness of detention, and Art.5(4) (right to determine lawfulness of detention) was satisfied by V's original trial and sentence procedure, *Wynne v. United Kingdom (A/294-A)* (1995) 19 E.H.R.R. 333, [1995] C.L.Y. 2617 applied and *Weeks v. United Kingdom (A/114)* (1988) 10 E.H.R.R. 293, [1989] C.L.Y. 1916 referred to, and (3) even if V was entitled to independent review of S's decision, B had undertaken such a review.

VAREY v. SCOTTISH MINISTERS 2001 S.C. 162, Lady Paton, OH.

PENSIONS

6837. National Health Service – injury benefits – superannuation scheme

NATIONAL HEALTH SERVICE (SUPERANNUATION SCHEME, INJURY BENEFITS AND COMPENSATION FOR PREMATURE RETIREMENT) (SCOTLAND) AMENDMENT REGULATIONS 2001, SSI 2001 437; made under the Superannuation Act 1972 s.10, s.12, s.24, Sch.3. In force: December 18, 2001; £2.50.

These Regulations amend the National Health Service (Compensation for Premature Retirement) (Scotland) Regulations 1981 (SI 1981 1785), the National Health Service Superannuation Scheme Regulations 1995 (SI 1995 365) and the National Health Service (Scotland) (Injury Benefits) Regulations 1998 (SI 1998 1594). The amendments clarify that calculation of part-time service in relation to early retirement pensions is in accordance with E2, enable a member who leaves pensionable employment after March 30, 2000 with preserved rights to elect to receive an actuarially reduced pension and lump sum after attaining the age of 50, make provision for members to nominate someone other than their surviving spouse as the person who is to receive the lump sum payable on their death, with transitional protection for existing arrangements and clarify that where a preserved pension comes into payment and the person resumes employment within one month working more than 16 hours per week, the pension will be subject to suspension.

6838. Occupational pensions – firemens pension scheme – divorce – pension sharing

FIREMEN'S PENSION SCHEME (PENSION SHARING ON DIVORCE) (SCOTLAND) ORDER 2001, SSI 2001 310; made under the Fire Services Act 1947 s.26; the Fire Services Act 1959 s.8; and the Superannuation Act 1972 s.12, s.16. In force: October 5, 2001; £3.00.

This Order, which amends the Firemen's Pension Scheme 1992 (SI 1992 129) in relation to Scotland, relates to cases where firefighters are divorced, and stems from the pension sharing provisions in the Welfare Reform and Pensions Act 1999.

6839. Occupational pensions – local government pension scheme

LOCAL GOVERNMENT PENSION SCHEME (SCOTLAND) AMENDMENT REGULATIONS 2001, SSI 2001 460; made under the Superannuation Act 1972 s.7, s.12. In force: January 21, 2002; £1.75.

These Regulations amend the Local Government Scheme (Scotland) Regulations 1998 (SI 1998 366) in relation to Scottish Homes' employees who transferred into the employment of the Scottish Ministers on November 1, 2001. They provide that, notwithstanding their transfer, they may be members of the Local Government Pension Scheme.

6840. Occupational pensions – local government pension scheme – divorce – pension sharing

LOCAL GOVERNMENT PENSION SCHEME (PENSION SHARING ON DIVORCE) (SCOTLAND) REGULATIONS 2001, SSI 2001 23; made under the Superannuation Act 1972 s.7, s.12. In force: March 3, 2001; £3.00.

These Regulations amend the the Local Government Pension Scheme (Management and Investment of Funds) Regulations 1998 (SI 1998 366) and the Local Government Pension Scheme (Scotland) Regulations 1998 (SI 1998 2888) by inserting a new Part VI into the Local Government Pension Scheme (Management and Investment of Funds) Regulations 1998 (SI 1998 366) to allow for pension sharing on divorce.

6841. Occupational pensions – police pension scheme – divorce – pension sharing

POLICE PENSIONS (ADDITIONAL VOLUNTARY CONTRIBUTIONS AND INCREASED BENEFITS) (PENSION SHARING) (SCOTLAND) AMENDMENT REGULATIONS 2001, SSI 2001 461; made under the Police Pensions Act 1976 s.1. In force: January 21, 2002; £2.00.

These Regulations amend the Pensions (Purchase of Increased Benefits) Regulations 1987 (SI 1987 2215) and the Police Pensions (Additional Voluntary Contributions) Regulations 1991 (SI 1991 1304). The amendments relate to cases where police officers are divorced, and stem from the pension sharing provisions in the Welfare and Pensions Reform Act 1999 and associated subordinate legislation.

6842. Occupational pensions – police pension scheme – divorce – pension sharing

POLICE PENSIONS (PENSION SHARING ON DIVORCE) (SCOTLAND) AMENDMENT REGULATIONS 2001, SSI 2001 459; made under the Police Pension Act 1976 s.1. In force: January 21, 2002; £3.00.

This Order, which amends the Police Pensions Regulations 1987 (SI 1987 257), relates to cases where police officers are divorced, and stems from the pension sharing provisions in the Welfare Reform and Pensions Act 1999 and associated subordinate legislation.

6843. Pensions Appeal Tribunals – appeals

PENSIONS APPEAL TRIBUNALS (SCOTLAND) (AMENDMENT) RULES 2001, SI 2001 3207 (S.16); made under the Pensions Appeal Tribunals Act 1943 Sch.1 para.5. In force: December 1, 2001; £1.75.

These Rules, which amend the Pensions Appeal Tribunals (Scotland) Rules 1981 (SI 1981 500), provide for appeals against "specified decisions", the position and powers of the Deputy President of Pensions Appeal Tribunals for Scotland, the omission of some unnecessary words in defining what persons may represent an appellant and the statement of reasons for a decision of a Tribunal, including a decision to adjourn an appeal.

6844. Pensions Appeal Tribunals – rules

PENSIONS APPEAL TRIBUNALS (SCOTLAND) (AMENDMENT) RULES 2001, SSI 2001 410; made under the Pensions Appeal Tribunals Act 1943 Sch.1 para.5. In force: December 1, 2001; £1.75.

These Rules amend the Pensions Appeal Tribunals (Scotland) Rules 1981 (SI 1981 500) so as to reflect the amendments to the Pensions Appeal Tribunals Acts made by the Child Support, Pensions and Social Security Act 2000. They provide for appeals against "specified decisions", the position and powers of the Deputy President of Pensions Appeal Tribunals for Scotland, the omission of unnecessary words in defining what persons may represent an appellant and the statement of reasons for a decision of a Tribunal, including a decision to adjourn an appeal.

6845. Superannuation – National Health Service – divorce – pension sharing

NATIONAL HEALTH SERVICE (SCOTLAND) (SUPERANNUATION SCHEME AND ADDITIONAL VOLUNTARY CONTRIBUTIONS) (PENSION SHARING ON DIVORCE) AMENDMENT REGULATIONS 2001, SSI 2001 465; made under the Superannuation Act 1972 s.10, s.12, Sch.3. In force: January 28, 2002; £4.00.

These Regulations amend the National Health Service Superannuation Scheme (Scotland) Regulations 1995 (SI 1995 365) and the National Health Service Superannuation Scheme (Scotland) (Additional Voluntary Contributions) Regulations 1998 (SI 1998 1451) which provide for the superannuation of persons engaged in the National Health Service in Scotland and make provision for the payment of additional voluntary contributions by persons who are members of the NHS Superannuation Scheme, or by their employers, in order to secure additional pension benefits. The Regulations insert a new Part W into the 1995 Regulations setting out a new regime for pension sharing on divorce.

6846. Superannuation – teachers

TEACHERS' SUPERANNUATION (SCOTLAND) AMENDMENT REGULATIONS 2001, SSI 2001 291; made under the Superannuation Act 1972 s.9, s.12, Sch.3. In force: October 1, 2001; £2.00.

These Regulations, which amend the Teachers' Superannuation (Scotland) Regulations 1992 (SI 1992 280), introduce a new Regulation under which full time and part time further employment after retirement will be pensionable unless the teacher elects to opt-out.

6847. Superannuation – teachers – additional voluntary contributions

TEACHERS' SUPERANNUATION (ADDITIONAL VOLUNTARY CONTRIBUTIONS) (SCOTLAND) AMENDMENT REGULATIONS 2001, SSI 2001 292; made under the Superannuation Act 1972 s.9, s.12, Sch.3. In force: October 1, 2001; £1.75.

These Regulations, which make amendments to the Teachers' Superannuation (Additional Voluntary Contributions) (Scotland) Regulations 1995 (SI 1995 2814), make provision for pension benefits to a former spouse following a pension sharing order or agreement on divorce or nullity of marriage and have retrospective effect from December 1, 2000.

6848. Superannuation – teachers – pension sharing on divorce

TEACHERS' SUPERANNUATION (PENSION SHARING ON DIVORCE) (SCOTLAND) REGULATIONS 2001, SSI 2001 152; made under the Superannuation Act 1972 s.9, s.12, Sch.3. In force: May 14, 2001; £3.00.

These Regulations, which amend the Teachers' Superannuation (Scotland) Regulations 1992 (SI 1992 280), have retrospective effect from December 1, 2000 and insert a new Part J to allow for pension sharing on divorce.

PLANNING

6849. Compulsory purchase – back to back sale to developer – failure to take account of material considerations

[Town and Country Planning (Scotland) Act 1997 (c.8) s.189, s.191.]

To facilitate the effective redevelopment of an area and to prevent ransoming by property owners, G (a local authority) decided to acquire certain subjects by compulsory purchase, and to enter into a back to back agreement for the sale of that land to a developer (A). Prior to that decision, G had been in discussions with S in relation to the proposed redevelopment of that part of the subjects owned by S. S petitioned for judicial review of G's decision, seeking declarator that both the decision and the agreement with A were ultra vires, and reduction of the decision. They argued that (1) G had proceeded on a material misapprehension as to the facts and (2) G was acting ultra vires by unreasonably using compulsory purchase powers, ie. not in accordance with the Town and Country Planning (Scotland) Act 1997 s.189. G argued that it had acted intra vires and were proposing to use the powers in furtherance of an ongoing scheme for the proper planing and effective redevelopment of the subjects in accordance with the 1997 Act; even if it hadn't acted intra vires and the agreement with A fell to be reduced, the decision on the principle of compulsory purchase should not be reduced. A argued that it was incompetent to seek reduction of a decision by judicial review.

Held, allowing the petition and reducing the decision and the agreement, that (1) the court could entertain an application for reduction not only of a decision, but also of an agreement following on that decision, the validity of which depended on the legality of the decision; (2) s.189 and s.191 provided a statutory framework within which G could acquire land by compulsory purchase and agree, back to back, to sell it, provided that the acquisition and sale were reasonably necessary for planning purposes, and that in making the decisions, proper account was taken of all material considerations, and (3) G had failed to take account of all material considerations. It had decided that a single comprehensive redevelopment of the subjects was appropriate, without reference to previous negotiations with S's associated company, and without considering that company's proposals for redevelopment and comparing the merits of those proposals with those of A.

STANDARD COMMERCIAL PROPERTY SECURITIES LTD v. GLASGOW CITY COUNCIL 2001 S.C. 177, Lord Nimmo Smith, OH.

6850. Compulsory purchase – valuation

TOWN AND COUNTRY PLANNING (LIMIT OF ANNUAL VALUE) (SCOTLAND) ORDER 2001, SSI 2001 164; made under the Town and Country Planning (Scotland) Act 1997 s.100, s.275. In force: June 1, 2001; £1.50.

This Order, which revokes the Town and Country Planning (Limit of Annual Value) (Scotland) Order 1995 (SI 1995 3048), prescribes £24,725 as the limit of annual value for the purposes of the Town and Country Planning (Scotland) Act 1997 s.100 relating to the circumstances in which authorities may be obliged to purchase interests of owner-occupiers affected by planning proposals.

6851. Planning appeals – inquiry procedure – refusal to admit report lodged late – natural justice

[Town and Country Planning (Scotland) Act 1997 (c.8) s.237, s.239.]

C, a development company, appealed against the decision of a reporter, appointed by S, dismissing its appeal against refusal of planning permission for residential development of a playing field site. C and the school which owned the site had entered into negotiations for the development and an alternative sports facility at a site owned by the company. A pre-inquiry meeting was held in relation to the appeal and time limits for the lodging of cases and exchange of documents agreed. At the inquiry C moved to lead a report by an expert witness, assessing the suitability of the development site for continued use for the school's recreational and sports requirements, and the suitability of the company's site. The planning authority opposed the motion, arguing they would be prejudiced having had insufficient time to prepare and lead evidence in response. C offered no explanation for the late production of the report but offered an adjournment and to bear any resulting costs. The reporter refused to allow the report to be lodged or the expert to be led as a witness and following the inquiry the reporter decided that, although the site would constitute a brownfield site for the purposes of housing policy in the structure plan, its development for housing was not in accordance with the local plan and other relevant planning guidelines and policies. On appeal C claimed that the reporter had acted unreasonably in refusing to postpone the start of the inquiry to allow the expert's report to be received late. S argued that refusal to adjourn an inquiry was not a decision on the appeal, and an appeal under the Town and Country Planning (Scotland) Act 1997 s.237 and s.239 was not competent. C argued inter alia that the report contained information of overriding importance to the inquiry, that notice had been given that the issue dealt with in the report would be raised at the inquiry and any prejudice could have been overcome by allowing an adjournment at their expense and further, that the reporter erred in law in his interpretation and application of planning policies, and gave inadequate reasons for his views on the various policy questions.

Held, dismissing the appeal, that (1) a procedural decision could be founded on in an appeal against a final decision as vitiating that final decision; (2) the primary approach to cases like the present was to apply the principles of natural justice and to ask whether the reporter's actions unfairly deprived the appellants of a proper opportunity to present their case, bearing in mind that the procedural rules were designed to give all parties a fair opportunity to present their case and the importance of the evidence which had been rejected; (3) the expert's report had very little bearing on the real determining issues in the inquiry and the reporter had not acted unfairly or contrary to natural justice; (4) even if the report was substantially more important, the reporter had not erred in excluding it where the appellants were aware of the time limits proposed, the procedural rules gave ample opportunity for the preparation and submission of reports and C had never explained why the report was not presented at the time fixed or at the pre-inquiry meeting, and (5) the interpretation and application of planning policies were matters for the reporter in cases like the present, and the reporter had not erred in law and had adequately explained the reasons for his decisions.

CALA MANAGEMENT LTD v. SCOTTISH MINISTERS 2002 S.C. 42, Lord Coulsfield, Lord Caplan, Lord Marnoch, Ex Div.

6852. **Planning applications – general development procedure – telecommunications antennas**

TOWN AND COUNTRY PLANNING (GENERAL DEVELOPMENT PROCEDURE) (SCOTLAND) AMENDMENT ORDER 2001, SSI 2001 245; made under the Town and Country Planning (Scotland) Act 1997 s.30, s.32, s.275. In force: July 23, 2001; £1.75.

This Order, which amends the Town and Country Planning (General Development Procedure) (Scotland) Order 1992 (SI 1992 224), requires that applications for planning permission, in cases where the proposed development involves an antenna to be employed in a telecommunications system, are accompanied by a declaration that the development is designed to comply with the public exposure guidelines of the International Commission on Non-Ionising Radiation Protection.

6853. Planning applications – planning procedures – independence of planning authorities – compatibility with ECHR

[Planning (Listed Buildings and Conservation Areas) (Scotland) Act 1997 (c.9) s.58; Human Rights Act 1998 Sch.1 Part 1 Art.6.]

C, the owners of category A listed heritable subjects, sought judicial review of a decision by S to call in their application to a planning authority for listed building consent and of S's appointment of a reporter to hear a public inquiry in relation to that application. C had obtained planning permission in 1997 for demolition and replacement of the subjects. In 1999 a different application for planning permission was granted but an application for listed building consent was called in. Historic Scotland, an executive agency of S, had objected to the application. In November 1999, C lodged an application seeking to amend the 1997 grant of planning permission by substituting drawings approved in connection with the 1999 application but that was not determined timeously and C appealed to S in respect of the deemed refusal. A reporter was appointed to hold a public inquiry in respect of the application for listed building consent and S subsequently decided that a public inquiry should be held in relation to the November application, conjoined with the listed building inquiry under the same reporter. At a procedural meeting in relation to the first inquiry the reporter expressed his agreement with the view of Historic Scotland in relation to the other application that it was not lawful to substitute drawings of one replacement scheme for another. The Lord Ordinary, in reducing the decisions, held that neither S nor the reporter could be considered as an independent and impartial tribunal, having regard to the opposition by Historic Scotland, and that as the court did not have full jurisdiction in an appeal under the Planning (Listed Buildings and Conservation Areas) (Scotland) Act 1997 s.58, C's rights under the Human Rights Act 1998 Sch.1 Part 1 Art.6 had been infringed. S appealed and at a hearing following the decision in *R. (on the application of Holding & Barnes Plc) v. Secretary of State for the Environment, Transport and the Regions* [2001] UKHL 23, [2001] 2 W.L.R. 1389, [2001] 6 C.L. 497, C argued that notwithstanding that decision, in the present case there were insufficient safeguards to their interests in that either the reporter or the respondents would finally determine important issues in such a way that it would be beyond the powers of the court to review or correct what had been done.

Held, allowing the appeal and dismissing the petition, that the principles laid down in *Alconbury* were applicable, and in accordance with those principles there was no inevitable incompatibility with Art.6(1) of the 1998 Act in the decisions challenged as the powers of the court to deal with genuinely justiciable issues arising in the administrative procedures were sufficient to ensure compatibility.

COUNTY PROPERTIES LTD v. SCOTTISH MINISTERS 2002 S.C. 79, Lord Prosser, Lord Kirkwood, Lord Mackay of Drumadoon, Ex Div.

6854. Planning permission – aggregates "superquarry" – calling in of application – independent and impartial tribunal – conservation issue referred to objector

[Conservation (Natural Habitats etc.) Regulations 1994 (SI 1994 2716); European Convention on Human Rights 1950 Art.6(1); Council Directive 92/43 on the conservation of natural habitats and of wild fauna and flora.]

A company, R, raised a petition for judicial review against the Scottish Ministers, S, challenging (a) their failure to determine R's application for planning permission for the development of a "superquarry" at L, a site on the Isle of Harris, and (b) their decision to refer to Scottish Natural Heritage, H, the question of whether any part of L should be proposed as a candidate special area of conservation (cSAC). R applied to the planning authority, W, for permission in March 1991. In June 1993 W informed S that they were minded to grant the application; on H's recommendation S called in the application and a public local inquiry was held before a reporter, T, H being the principal objector. T reported to S in April 1999. S indicated that, prior to their determination, there would be a referral to H as to whether any part of L should be proposed as a cSAC in terms of Council Directive 92/43. The obligations to implement the Directive in Scotland fell to S as from July 1, 1999. In 1999 the European Commission found that the UK had proposed insufficient sites for cSACs. H was asked to make further proposals for possible cSACs, but L was not considered as a cSAC until S invited H to do so in July 2000. It would not have been possible to include L in the list of sites for consideration by the Commission by its next moderation seminar, given the timescale of consultation beforehand. R argued inter alia that S had acted ultra vires (1) by referring the classification of L to H, who could not give an impartial judgment; (2) by breaching the inquiry rules by undertaking further investigations without having reached the stage of disagreeing with T; (3) by acting irrationally in referring the application to H, which departed from normal procedure for identification of cSACs, whereby H identified possible sites, and by refusing to determine the application before the cSAC issue was determined, and (4) S were in breach of the European Convention on Human Rights 1950 Art.6. R accepted that S was only responsible for the delay from June 1993. S argued inter alia that there was no dispute or "contestation", nor would there be until S decided the application, thus Art.6 did not apply.

Held, granting certain declarators, that (1) there was no statutory timescale within which S had to determine an application for planning permission; however R had a legitimate expectation that S would determine the application within a reasonable time. What was reasonable depended on the particular circumstances, including complexity, the length of the public inquiry, and the change of administration following devolution. S had failed to determine the application within a reasonable time and had acted unfairly from a procedural point of view; (2) S had acted ultra vires insofar as the reference to H conveyed the appearance that they would not bring an impartial judgment to bear on the matter, and justice would not be seen to be done. However it was not ultra vires for S to undertake investigations to inform their decision as to whether there was agreement with T's findings in fact; (3) it would be unreasonable to preclude a third party, including a minister of S, from suggesting sites to H for evaluation. S were aware of the Commission's view that the deficiency in cSAC sites submitted by the UK was related to under representation of certain species which were present on L, and it could be argued that S would have failed in their duties in implementing the Directive if they had not referred L to H. However S's deferring of the decision on the application was irrational and ultra vires. If L were classified as a cSAC, planning permission would be reviewed as required by the Conservation (Natural Habitats etc.) Regulations 1994. Deferral of the decision to avoid potential liability to pay compensation to R, in respect of planning permission being later revoked or modified, was an improper consideration, and (4) Art.6 was applicable as (a) R's property rights, in the form of a 99 year lease of L, were clearly a civil right within the meaning of Art.6(1), and (b) if an appeal against refusal of planning permission was protected by Art.6 it would be astonishing if proceedings resulting from the calling in of an application were afforded less protection. There was a dispute involving R's civil rights, evidenced by an inquiry which heard evidence for and against the application. A breach of Art.6(1) had occurred in respect of the delay and in respect of the partiality issue.

LAFARGE REDLAND AGGREGATES LTD v. SCOTTISH MINISTERS 2001 S.C. 298, Lord Hardie, OH.

6855. **Planning permission – competing applications – difference between applications – planning judgment**

[Town and Country Planning (Scotland) Act 1997 (c.8) s.38, s.34(1) (h).]

In January 1999 B applied to the council for outline planning permission for a site. In February 1999 T applied for outline planning permission for a site near to that of B. B's application was deemed refused, and T's application was refused. Both B and T took appeals to the Scottish Ministers (M) and the appeals were conjoined. In the meantime, S applied for outline planning permission for a site which covered all of T's site as well as a large part of the additional land referred to in T's application. B requested that M call in S's application; M declined and B petitioned for judicial review seeking reduction of the declinature and interdict against the council from granting S's application. Interim interdict was refused. In October 1999, the council granted S's application. B adjusted their petition, and sought (1) declarator that M's declinature was ultra vires, and (2) suspension of the purported grant of permission to S. S argued that the petition was incompetent, B's adjustment being directed at something which had not happened at the time of the original petition. They also challenged B's title and interest to petition, because B had neither objected to S's application nor were they prejudiced by the granting of it. B argued that it was unreasonable for the council to make a decision when the conjoined appeals remained in dependence before M. They further argued that the council had been led into granting S's application by inaccurate and misleading information drawing distinctions between the applications of S and T that did not exist, and had not given adequate reasons why they had granted S's application after refusing T's.

Held, dismissing the petition, that (1) the petition was competent. Procedure for judicial review was sufficiently flexible to allow for what was an understandable reaction by B to a change in circumstances; (2) only where two competing applications were for the same site could the grant of permission be challenged on the ground that an appeal was in dependence; (3) although there was merit in B's argument that there was a material difference between the applications of T and S, it was not for the court to substitute its view for that of the council on what was essentially a matter of planning judgment. B had failed to satisfy the high standard required to demonstrate that the council's planning judgment was irrational or unreasonable in the *Wednesbury* sense, *James Aitken & Sons (Meat Producers) Ltd v. Edinburgh DC* 1990 S.L.T. 241, [1990] C.L.Y. 5943, *Trusthouse Forte (UK) Ltd v. Perth and Kinross DC* 1990 S.L.T. 737, [1990] C.L.Y. 5944, and *Henderson v. Argyll & Bute Council* 1998 S.L.T. 1224, [1998] C.L.Y. 6149 distinguished, and (4) B had no title to petition. The mere fact that B's appeal was conjoined with that of T for administrative convenience did not confer on B any rights they did not otherwise possess. B would have to have shown that M's decision was prejudicial both in the commercial sense and in the sense that it undermined B's appeal and rendered it pointless, *ASDA Stores Ltd v. Secretary of State for Scotland* 1999 S.L.T. 503, [1998] C.L.Y. 6151 distinguished.

Observed, that, per se, the fact that a petitioner was an applicant in a competing application, or had not made representations against the application challenged, would not prevent that petitioner from having title and interest.

BETT PROPERTIES LTD v. SCOTTISH MINISTERS 2001 S.C. 238, Lord Macfadyen, OH.

6856. **Planning permission – judicial review – delay – mora, taciturnity and acquiescence**

[Town and Country Planning (Scotland) Act 1997 (c.8) s.25; Environmental Assessment (Scotland) Regulations 1988 (SI 1988 1221).]

U, a local resident, brought an application for judicial review of a decision by FC to grant planning permission to developers for hotel and leisure facilities in St Andrews. U argued that FC should have required an environmental assessment statement to be prepared and had failed to give proper reasons for not doing so. FC contended that U had no locus standi and that there had been an unreasonable delay in bringing the application.

Held, dismissing the application, that although U did have a sufficient interest, because he was raising issues which he argued should have been dealt with by FC as matters of law, there was no justification for the delay of 19 weeks and the application would be dismissed on that basis. Obiter, with reference to the substantive claim, there was insufficient evidence to decide whether or not FC had made a decision about an environmental statement within the requisite time. Given the response of interested organisations in the area, such as the Architectural Heritage Society of Scotland, who had not raised the issue of an environmental statement, it could not be said that the decision not to require one was irrational.

UPRICHARD v. FIFE COUNCIL 2000 S.C.L.R. 949, Lord Bonomy, OH.

6857. Planning permission – permitted development – telecommunications development

TOWN AND COUNTRY PLANNING (GENERAL PERMITTED DEVELOPMENT) (SCOTLAND) AMENDMENT ORDER 2001, SSI 2001 244; made under the Town and Country Planning (Scotland) Act 1997 s.30, s.31, s.275. In force: July 23, 2001; £2.00.

This Order, which amends the Town and Country Planning (General Permitted Development) (Scotland) Order 1992 (SI 1992 223), restricts the range of development permitted under classes 67 and 68 without express planning permission being granted under the Town and Country Planning (Scotland) Act 1997.

6858. Planning permission – permitted development – telecommunications development

TOWN AND COUNTRY PLANNING (GENERAL PERMITTED DEVELOPMENT) (SCOTLAND) AMENDMENT (NO.2) ORDER 2001, SSI 2001 266; made under the Town and Country Planning (Scotland) Act 1997 s.30, s.31, s.275. In force: Art.3(1): July 22, 2001; remainder: July 23, 2001; £2.00.

This Order amends the Town and Country Planning (General Permitted Development) (Scotland) Order 1992 (SI 1992 223) and revokes the Town and Country Planning (General Permitted Development) (Scotland) Amendment Order 2001 (SSI 2001 244). It introduces transitional arrangements to deal with any development in accordance with Class 67 commenced and not completed before July 23, 2001 and restricts the range of development permitted under permitted under Class 67 and Class 68 of the 1992 Order without the requirement to obtain an express grant of planning permission under the Town and Country Planning (Scotland) Act 1997

6859. Planning permission – refusal – purchase notice by landowner – validity – judicial review

[Town and Country Planning (Scotland) Act 1972 (c.52) s.169, s.170; Town and Country Planning (General) (Scotland) Regulations 1976 (SI 1976 2022).]

In 1991 R, heritable proprietor of several plots of land on Arran, had sought outline planning permission for the erection of two houses on two plots. The applications were refused by the local authority, N, in December 1993. R's appeal to the Secretary of State was refused in December 1994. In February 1995 R served a purported purchase notice under the Town and Country Planning (Scotland) Act 1972 s.169 requiring N to purchase the two plots, claiming that the land was incapable of reasonably beneficial use in its existing state. N refused on the basis that the notice was invalid because it was dated over 12 months from the date of N's decision to refuse permission, and that R had invalidated the proforma notice by deleting from it a head of claim corresponding to s.169(1) (c) of the Act. R sought reduction of N's decision by judicial review, and declarators that N had effectively compulsorily purchased the plots of R's land covered by the notice. N argued inter alia that (1) R had delayed in raising the judicial review proceedings, to N's prejudice; (2) the notice was served out of time, and (3) the notice was invalid.

Held, granting reduction of the decision and the declarators, that (1) although there was substantial delay by R, it was not all her responsibility and N had handled the matter in a manner which was unhelpful. Any prejudicial effect was negligible; (2) R's notice was in time. In terms of the Town and Country Planning (General) (Scotland) Regulations 1976 the 12 months ran from the date of the decision to refuse planning permission, and as the reporter who heard R's appeal against the refusal had the power to grant planning permission, the relevant period ran from his decision in December 1994; (3) it was not essential for an owner's claims in terms of s.169 to be included in the notice itself. Whether the owner met the preconditions set out in s.169(1) could be established in various ways, and was essentially extraneous to the status of the purchase notice itself, and (4) N should have dealt with issues of validity by issuing a s.170(1) counternotice specifying why they did not intend to comply with the purchase notice. Having failed to do so, N were deemed to be authorised to acquire the land compulsorily, and to have served a notice to treat, in terms of s.170(4).

RESIDE v. NORTH AYRSHIRE COUNCIL 2001 S.L.T. 6, Lord Prosser, OH.

6860. Books

Collar, Neil – Green's Scottish Planning Factbook. Greens Professional Publishing. Looseleaf/ring bound: £149.00. ISBN 0-414-01381-6. W.Green & Son.

POLICE

6861. Grants – police authorities and joint police boards

POLICE GRANT (SCOTLAND) ORDER 2001, SSI 2001 74; made under the Police (Scotland) Act 1967 s.32. In force: April 1, 2001; £1.75.

This Order determines the aggregate amount of grants to be made under the Police (Scotland) Act 1967 s.32 to all police authorities and joint police boards for the financial year 2001/02 and the amount of such grants to be made to each police authority or joint police board.

6862. Occupational pensions – police pension scheme – divorce – pension sharing

See PENSIONS. §6841 - §6842

6863. Police Act 1997 (c.50) – Commencement No.8 Order

POLICE ACT 1997 (COMMENCEMENT NO.8) (SCOTLAND) ORDER 2001, SSI 2001 482 (C.24); made under the Police Act 1997 s.135. Commencement details: bringing into force various provisions of the 1997 Act on January 1, 2002 and February 1, 2002; £1.75.

This Order brings into force the Police Act 1997 s.120, which relates to the register to be maintained by the Scottish Ministers for the purposes of Part V of that Act, s.122(1)(2), which relates to the code of practice to be published in connection with the use of information provided to registered persons, and s.125, which relates to regulations made under the 1997 Act, Part V, on January 1, 2002 and February 1, 2002.

6864. Police officers – injury award – judicial review – appropriate test

P, a former police constable who had been discharged from the force on medical grounds sought reduction by judicial review of the decision of a medical referee, rejecting his appeal against a decision that he had not been disabled as a result of an injury sustained in the execution of his duty. The referee accepted that P had developed an anxiety disorder while working as a policeman, having had inter alia to deal with a number of stressful incidents in a short space of time, but concluded that nothing had taken place that was out of the ordinary for a policeman and his illness did not arise from an injury sustained in the execution of his duty.

Held, granting the reduction and remitting the case to the medical referee for redetermination in the light of the court's opinion, that (1) the relevant disablement had to have been caused or substantially contributed to by an "injury" as defined, and there had to be a substantial causal connection between the injury and the constable's duty, but while the mere fact that the condition manifested itself while the claimant was a serving policeman would be insufficient in itself to satisfy the causation test, it was not necessary that the work circumstances were the sole cause of the injury, nor did a particular vulnerability or susceptibility on the part of an individual constable prevent an award being made, and (2) in relying on the fact that the events causing the petitioner's illness were not out of the ordinary for a policeman, the medical referee had misdirected himself.

PHILLIPS v. STRATHCLYDE JOINT POLICE BOARD 2001 S.L.T. 1271, Lord Hamilton, OH.

PRESCRIPTION

6865. Negative – date from which time runs – induced error – damage to jetty – liability of vessel owner – meaning of "owner"

[Harbours, Docks, and Piers Clauses Act 1847 (10&11 Vict, c.27) s.74; Prescription and Limitation (Scotland) Act 1973 (c.52) s.6.]

BP appealed against a ruling (2000 S.L.T. 1374, [2000] C.L.Y. 6638) permitting reclaiming motions by the three defendants to three separate actions commenced by BP. BP sought to recover its losses following damage to an oil terminal caused when a vessel moved away from its berth. BP initially issued proceedings against S, as owners of the vessel, pursuant to the Harbours, Docks, and Piers Clauses Act 1847 s.74, whereby strict liability was imposed upon the owner of a vessel which caused damage to any harbour, dock, pier or quay. S initially admitted ownership of the vessel but eventually indicated that the owner was CTB. BP also issued proceedings against CTB, who maintained that the Prescription and Limitation (Scotland) Act 1973 s.6 was of application and that the action was consequently time barred. CTB further maintained that, at the relevant time, the vessel had been the subject of a bareboat charter to CTL. BP issued a further set of proceedings against CTL who also relied upon s.6 of the 1973 Act. The court dismissed the claim against CTL having accepted the plea of prescription.

Held, allowing the appeals, that (1) S had induced BP to believe, wrongly, that S was the relevant debtor in the obligation and not CTB. Having established that fact, the prescriptive period under the 1973 Act was suspended until the error became manifest at which point it began to run again, and (2) for the purposes of s.74 of the 1847 Act, the "owner" of a vessel meant the registered owner and did not include a charterer, even a bareboat charterer. Accordingly BP's claim against CTL had to be excluded from probation.

BP EXPLORATION OPERATING CO LTD v. CHEVRON SHIPPING CO; BP EXPLORATION OPERATING CO LTD v. CHEVRON TANKERS (BERMUDA) LTD; BP EXPLORATION OPERATING CO LTD v. CHEVRON TRANSPORT CORP; *sub nom.* BP EXPLORATION OPERATING CO LTD v. CHEVRON TRANSPORT (SCOTLAND), [2001] UKHL 50, [2001] 3 W.L.R. 949, Lord Hope of Craighead, HL.

6866. Negative – date from which time runs – missive of lease – defective building works – knowledge of claim

[Prescription and Limitation (Scotland) Act 1973 (c.52) s.11.]

In April 1997, C, tenant of a restaurant, raised an action for damages against his landlord, L, for breach of missives of lease as having prescribed. The sheriff dismissed the action, and the sheriff principal upheld that decision. C appealed. The alleged breach related to failures to carry out building works in respect of a kitchen ventilation system and the provision of fireproofing and soundproofing between upper and lower properties. The sheriff principal held that while there was insufficient material before the sheriff to establish that, when C discovered a failure in relation to the ventilation system in June 1990, C ought reasonably to have become aware of the other two matters, the obligation undertaken by L was a single contractual obligation relating to separating the properties, and the prescriptive period in respect of the whole obligation began to run in 1990.

Held, allowing the appeal and remitting the case to the sheriff to allow proof before answer on the remaining pleas, that nothing was disclosed in 1990 to indicate to C that anything was wrong with the fire safety provisions or soundproofing. Those defects were separate from the defects discovered in respect of ventilation provisions, and were only revealed after C's own investigations in 1992. Thus the defects derived from a failure to perform separate and distinct obligations. As a matter of law it was clear that contractual obligations could give rise to more than one default giving rise to an obligation to make reparation for loss, injury and damage, and so for the purposes of the Prescription and Limitation (Scotland) Act 1973 s.11, iniuria occurring at different times. *Sinclair v. MacDougall Estates Ltd* 1994 S.L.T. 76, [1994] C.L.Y. 6161, approved. Opinion of the Court per Lord Dawson.

COLE v. LONIE 2001 S.C. 610, Lord Cameron of Lochbroom, Lord Cowie and Lord Dawson, Ex Div.

6867. **Negative – date from which time runs – overdrafts – action for payment – obligation not enforceable until action raised**

[Prescription and Limitation (Scotland) Act 1973 (c.52) s.6(3).]

On December 13, 1995, R raised an action against H, the judicial factor of a former firm of solicitors (S), seeking payment of the debit balance of an overdraft facility granted to S on May 15, 1990. The facility letter made provision for repayment on demand. On October 2, 1990 R froze the facility. H argued that the Prescription and Limitation (Scotland) Act 1973 s.6(3) operated to extinguish the obligation to repay on the expiry of five years from the date on which the obligation became enforceable. As R had raised an action without demanding payment, the obligation must have become enforceable on its constitution on May 15, 1990. Alternatively, it became enforceable on October 2, when the facility was frozen. In either event, the obligation had prescribed.

Held, rejecting H's preliminary pleas, that there was no obligation to repay until the action was raised. As the debt was not enforceable until that date, the obligation had not prescribed.

Observed, that while it was unsatisfactory that there was a discrepancy between H's averments and his argument in court, as it was not a matter of material fact but was one of law, it was appropriate to deal with H's pleas on the basis of the argument presented.

ROYAL BANK OF SCOTLAND PLC v. HOME 2001 S.C. 224, Lord Philip, OH.

6868. **Negative – date from which time runs – reasonable awareness that loss had been suffered through negligence**

[Prescription and Limitation (Scotland) Act 1973 (c.52) s.11 (3).]

B, a building society, sought damages from C, solicitors, for alleged professional negligence. B averred that in four transactions in 1989 and 1990 where C had acted for them, borrowers had defaulted on loans for the purchase of heritable property from the same development and the subjects were then repossessed and resold at a loss in 1991 and 1992. In each transaction the seller was a developer and the buyers were employees of that developer. B further averred that C had failed to make proper inquiry about the borrowers or to report on the unusual nature of the transactions and the likely creditworthiness of the clients. The action was raised in June 2000. In response to a plea of prescription, B argued that it had made sufficient averments to support reliance on the Prescription and Limitation (Scotland) Act 1973 s.11 (3) as it had only become aware of the existence of a potential claim against C when C's files were passed to B's solicitors in June 1996 for an audit, and they could not with reasonable diligence have become aware that there was a claim prior to that date.

Held, dismissing the action, that this was not a case where B had any reason to know or suspect it had suffered loss at all, and to make a relevant case B would have had to set out facts and circumstances explaining why it could not, with reasonable diligence, have discovered prior to 1996 that it had suffered loss due to an act, neglect or default, *Glasper v. Rodger* 1996 S.L.T. 44 distinguished.

BRITANNIA BUILDING SOCIETY v. CLARKE 2001 S.L.T. 1355, Lord Macfadyen, OH.

6869. Negative prescription – claims against limitation fund – amendment of claim

[Merchant Shipping (Oil Pollution) Act 1971 (c.59) s.9.]

S, salmon farmers, raised a claim against the compensation fund in respect of the Braer oil tanker grounding which had prevented S from taking delivery from T of a contractual order of smolt. O, objectors to the claim, argued that S's claim was time barred. The Lord Ordinary had discharged the diet of proof after O, on the last date for lodging productions and witness lists, extensively amended their objections to include allegations of fraud in relation to faxes which allegedly constituted the orders for smolt. The pleadings were substantially amended and S now maintained that the faxes could be disregarded because B, chief executive of a group of companies which included S and T, had on behalf of S and T made an agreement that smolt would be delivered by T to S, and had also determined the price payable. O argued that the obligations allegedly constituted in that way were different obligations from those evidenced by the faxes and that was not a modification of the claim but a new claim based on a different contract, and the action was time barred under the Merchant Shipping (Oil Pollution) Act 1971 s.9.

Held, repelling the plea of time bar, that the test was whether the modified pleadings were presented on a fundamentally different basis. Whatever the position in a question between S and T, the present claim was still one under s.1 of the 1971 Act, consisting of alleged wasted expenditure and loss of profit resulting from S's inability to fulfil contractual obligations to take delivery of smolt in January and March 1993. The claim remained to be calculated by reference to quantities and price in exactly the same way as before, *Devos Gebroeder NV v. Sunderland Sportswear Ltd (No.2)* 1990 S.C. 291, [1990] C.L.Y. 5636 and *JG Martin Plant Hire Ltd v. MacDonald* 1996 S.L.T. 1192, [1996] C.L.Y. 6664 distinguished. Opinion, that had the claim for wasted expenditure prescribed, the claim for loss of profit would also have to, as the latter was not free standing and was integral with the wasted expenditure.

ASSURANCEFORENINGEN SKULD v. INTERNATIONAL OIL POLLUTION COMPENSATION FUND (NO.2) 2000 S.L.T. 1348, Lord Gill, OH.

6870. Positive – possession of heritable property – registration of title

[Land Registration (Scotland) Act 1979 (c.33) s.9.]

Title to a gap site was registered by M. S maintained that they were the rightful owners, there had been no prescriptive possession by M and sought reduction of the dispositions and an order for rectification under the Land Registration (Scotland) Act 1979 s.9. S founded on a title recorded in their favour in 1958. S maintained that the dispositions they were challenging were a non domino and M had not enjoyed possession "peaceably, and without judicial interruption" for the prescriptive period. S also argued that M's registration of title had been obtained by fraud or carelessness and demonstrated that they had made planning applications with regard to the site and had actually done some excavation. M maintained that they had been at the site to carry out general maintenance and had erected a fence.

Held, granting the decree, that S had taken active and obvious possession of the property and could be seen to have maintained that possession during the prescriptive period, unlike M who could not be said to have done the same. Any reasonably active possession would have brought to M's attention that someone else was in occupation of the property. M's assertions in their application for registration in relation to their record of possession were either erroneous or careless.

STEVENSON-HAMILTON'S EXECUTORS v. McSTAY (NO.2); *sub nom.* STEVENSON-HAMILTON'S TRUSTEES v. McSTAY 2001 S.L.T. 694, Judge TG Coutts Q.C., OH.

RATES

6871. Council tax – valuation – relevant decision regarding comparable dwelling

[Local Government (Scotland) Act 1992 (c.19) s.86(2); Council Tax (Alteration of Lists and Appeals) (Scotland) Regulations 1993 (SI 1993 290) Reg.5(6), Reg.15(1).]

The assessor of the Valuation Joint Board appealed against a decision of the Valuation Appeal Panel following on a reference to the panel under the Council Tax (Alteration of Lists and Appeals) (Scotland) Regulations 1993 Reg.15(1) of proposals for the alteration of the valuation list in relation to nine dwelling houses owned by the local authority. At the time of the reference all nine dwelling houses were entered in the list under band B. The proposals for alteration of the list were made by the taxpayers, who were the tenants of the houses, in terms of Reg.5(6) following a relevant decision made by the panel in relation to a comparable dwelling. The decision was that the dwelling houses should be in band A rather than band B.

Held, remitting the appeal to the panel for consideration, that (1) Part II of the 1993 Regulations contained provisions prescribing the manner of making proposals and the steps which the assessor required to take on receipt of a proposal. He might treat the proposal as invalid or, if he considered it to be valid he required to determine whether it was well founded or not; (2) any valuation which he carried out in connection with the proposal was required by Reg.13 to be carried out in accordance with the Local Government (Scotland) Act 1992 s.86(2) the same basis as that on which all valuations under the Act were carried out; (3) each proposal had to be looked at on its own merits, and there was nothing in either the Act or the regulations which provided that either the assessor or the panel was bound by the terms of a relevant decision; (4) the decision of the panel had to be read as indicating that they considered themselves bound to the relevant decision in question, or alternatively, that they were under no obligation to consider the valuation of the appeal subjects on their own merits, and (5) in those circumstances the panel erred in law and the appeal should be remitted back to them so that they might consider the valuations of the appeal subjects on their own merits.

ASSESSOR FOR HIGHLAND AND WESTERN ISLES VALUATION JOINT BOARD v. A; *sub nom.* ASSESSOR FOR HIGHLAND AND WESTERN ISLES VALUATION JOINT BOARD'S APPEAL, *Re* (NO.1); ASSESSOR FOR HIGHLAND AND WESTERN ISLES VALUATION JOINT BOARD v. FRASER 2001 S.C. 473, Lord Philip, Lord Rodger L.P., Lord Weir, 1 Div.

6872. Council tax – valuation list – inclusion – uninhabited croft – whether a "dwelling"

[Local Government Finance Act 1992 (c.14) s.72, s.81(1)(a).]

The tenant of a house on the Isle of Skye appealed against a decision of the Valuation Appeal Panel allowing an appeal against the inclusion of that property on the council tax valuation list for the area under the Local Government Finance Act 1992 s.72. The property was entered in the valuation list at April 1, 1993 and placed in band A. At that time they were occupied by the tenant's uncle who continued in occupation until his death in 1995. On his death the tenancy of the croft, of which the property formed part, passed to the present tenant and the property had been vacant and uninhabited since then. The tenant appealed on the ground that the property was in such a dilapidated state that it would not be classed as a dwelling in terms of s.72 of the Act. The panel allowed the appeal and found that the property should be removed from the valuation list. The assessor appealed. to the court against that decision.

Held, allowing the appeal and restoring the property to the list, that (1) in carrying out his duties under the Act the first step that the assessor required to take was to determine whether the property fell within the definition of a dwelling. If it did, he had to include in the valuation list and determine which valuation band should apply to it; (2) in the instant case the property was properly described as a dwelling. It was lived in until 1995 and in particular on April 1, 1993. There was no suggestion that its condition had altered materially since that date; (3) while it had no internal sanitation or running water, it was roofed, had external doors and most of the windows were glazed. There was an electricity supply, although it was disconnected and in need of modernisation. The panel had described the property as a dwelling house; (4) there was no provision in the Act, or in the regulations made under it, which provided for the exclusion of a dwelling from the valuation list on the ground that it was unsuitable for occupation. The valuation assumption as to reasonable repair was inconsistent with such an exclusion, and (5) therefore the panel erred in law in importing suitability for occupation as the test for inclusion in the valuation list.

ASSESSOR FOR HIGHLAND AND WESTERN ISLES VALUATION JOINT BOARD v. MacLEOD; *sub nom.* ASSESSOR FOR HIGHLAND AND WESTERN ISLES VALUATION JOINT BOARD'S APPEAL (NO.2), *Re* 2001 S.C. 476, Lord Philip, Lord Rodger L.P., Lord Weir, 1 Div.

6873. Non domestic rates – rate for 2001/02

NON-DOMESTIC RATE (SCOTLAND) ORDER 2001, SSI 2001 44; made under the Local Government (Scotland) Act 1975 s.7B, s.37. In force: April 1, 2001; £1.50.

This Order prescribes a rate of £0.47 as the non-domestic rate to be levied throughout Scotland in respect of financial year 2001 to 2002.

6874. Non domestic rates – rate for 2001/02

NON-DOMESTIC RATES (LEVYING) (SCOTLAND) REGULATIONS 2001, SSI 2001 71; made under the Local Government etc (Scotland) Act 1994 s.153. In force: April 1, 2001; £2.50.

These Regulations, which revoke the Non-Domestic Rates (Levying) (Scotland) Regulations 2000 (SSI 2000 92), make provision as to the amount payable in certain circumstances as non-domestic rates in respect of property in Scotland. They apply only to financial year 2001/02.

6875. Non domestic rates – rate relief – policy not to rate relief grant to licensed social clubs – whether proper exercise of discretion

[Local Government (Scotland) Act 1947 (c.43) s.238.]

R, a club, sought reduction of inter alia summary warrants and a decree of furthcoming by D, a council, in respect of unpaid rates. At a first hearing limited to certain issues, R argued that they were entitled to discretionary relief as a charity from 1993-1994 onwards and that at a meeting on February 22, 1994 D had either made no decision or implemented a fixed policy without having regard to R's particular circumstances, which was ultra vires and *Wednesbury* unreasonable. A decision made by D's committee, C, on December 21, 1993 was not challenged as R argued that the decision in February 1994 had abrogated, quashed or overturned this decision. D argued that R had failed to exhaust remedies as the Local Government (Scotland) Act 1947 s.238 provided machinery for appeal.

Held, putting the case out by order, that (1) the original decision taken on December 21, 1993 not to grant relief to the club in respect of rates on the licensed club premises had not been abrogated, quashed or overturned, and (2) as the club had not challenged the original decision, either for failure to make a decision or for implementation of a fixed policy without exercise of its discretion, the petition for judicial review was ill founded and fell to be dismissed.

Observed that, even if the club had challenged the decision of December 21, 1993 on either ground, it would have failed as there was nothing in the pleadings or productions to support such an argument and had the club's allegation of ultra vires, illegality or unreasonableness been well founded, the court would not be satisfied that the Local Government (Scotland) Act 1947 s.238 provided an adequate remedy. On a well founded complaint of ultra vires, the club would have been entitled to seek redress by way of judicial review and the delay in

bringing proceedings, although unsatisfactory, would not have been a bar to those proceedings.
ROYAL AIR FORCE ASSOCIATION CLUB v. DUMFRIES AND GALLOWAY COUNCIL 2001 S.C.L.R. 1, Lady Paton, OH.

6876. Non domestic rates – valuation – plant and machinery

VALUATION FOR RATING (PLANT AND MACHINERY) (SCOTLAND) AMENDMENT REGULATIONS 2001, SSI 2001 115; made under the Lands Valuation (Scotland) Act 1854 s.42. In force: April 1, 2001; £1.75.
These Regulations amend the Valuation for Rating (Plant and Machinery) (Scotland) Regulations 2000 (SSI 2000 58) by conferring exemption from rating on an additional class of plant and machinery, namely specified plant and machinery comprised in a combined heat and power station which is fully or partly exempt from climate change levy and which produces electrical power.

6877. Non domestic rates – valuation – two plots used by same business comprising two units for rating purposes

The issue arose as to whether land used for warehousing and offices fell to be considered for rating purposes as two separate units. The two premises were on opposite sides of a road but used by the same business. The first plot consisted of 39,000 square feet of dry goods warehousing and 14,150 square feet of offices. The other premises comprised a whisky bottling plant including a large underground storage space. Materials were transported between the plots across a public road by fork lift truck on average 20 times per day. The former premises had a shared exit that was also used by large, slow moving vehicles from the neighbouring plant.
Held, finding that there were two premises, that the fact that both plots shared a single function was not determinative of the matter. There was a clear separation between the two plots and each had its own recognisable curtilage. Separation was also enhanced by the need to cross a public road and the shared exit of the first plot. Furthermore, the fact that the premises could each be let separately was also indicative of there being two units for valuation purposes.
BURN STEWART DISTILLERS PLC v. ASSESSOR FOR LANARKSHIRE VALUATION JOINT BOARD [2001] R.A. 110, Lord McGhie, Lands Tr (Scot).

REPARATION

6878. Race discrimination – damages – direct discrimination – relevancy of pleadings – no averments as to knowledge of ethnic origin and application of discriminatory policy

[Race Relations Act 1976 (c.74) s.1 (1) (a).]
W, of gypsy ethnic origin, raised an action for damages against F, a publican who had asked him to leave his pub after W admitted that he was from a travellers' site. F explained in a letter to W that he operated a policy of not serving people from travellers' sites in order to avoid nasty incidents. W's action was raised, inter alia, under the Race Relations Act 1976 s.1 (1) (a). At a debate on preliminary pleas, F argued that W's averments based on s.1 (1) (a) (direct discrimination) were irrelevant, because it was not averred that the cause of W's exclusion was F's knowledge that W was of gypsy ethnic origin, nor that he had applied to him a policy directly discriminatory towards gypsies and which he knew to be so discriminatory. F knew that W was from the travellers' site, but no averments were made that he knew that a vast majority of people on that site were gypsies rather than "travellers". W argued it was sufficient to aver that W was of a different ethnic origin and was excluded whilst others not of that ethnic origin were not; discrimination could be inferred.
Held, excluding from probation averments relating to s.1 (1) (a), that (1) pleadings in the action fell to be treated as in any other civil action. To establish

direct discrimination, W had to aver and prove less favourable treatment on ethnic grounds, and it was necessary to aver that F knew or ought to have known that W was of a particular ethnic origin, despite there being no dispute that W had been treated less favourably than others. The word "travellers" was not synonymous with gypsies and W's averments were irrelevant in not specifying that F's exclusion of W was based on knowledge that W was a gypsy, *Commission for Racial Equality v. Dutton* [1989] Q.B. 783, [1989] C.L.Y. 267 referred to, and (2) even if such knowledge could be inferred from primary facts, it still had to be averred.

WHITE v. FERGUSON 2000 S.L.T. (Sh Ct) 179, Sheriff KA Ross, Sh Ct (Lothian and Border).

RIGHTS IN SECURITY

6879. Mortgage Rights (Scotland) Act 2001 (asp 11) – Commencement and Transitional Provision Order

MORTGAGE RIGHTS (SCOTLAND) ACT 2001 (COMMENCEMENT AND TRANSITIONAL PROVISION) ORDER 2001, SSI 2001 418 (C.18); made under the Mortgage Rights (Scotland) Act 2001 s.7. Commencement details: bringing into force various provisions of the 2001 Act on December 3, 2001; £1.50.

This Order appoints December 3, 2001 as the day on which the Mortgage Rights (Scotland) Act 2001 will come into force. It makes transitional provision in respect of notices, applications and proceedings referred to in s.1 (1) of the Act that have been served, made or commenced prior to December 3, 2001. The Act will not apply in those circumstances.

6880. Mortgage Rights (Scotland) Act 2001 (asp 11)

This Act of the Scottish Parliament provides for the suspension in certain circumstances of enforcement rights of a creditor in a standard security over property used for residential purposes and the continuation of proceedings relating to those rights and makes provision for notifying tenants and other occupiers of enforcement action by a creditor in a standard security.

This Act received Royal Assent on July 25, 2001.

6881. Mortgages – mortgage rights – prescribed notice

MORTGAGE RIGHTS (SCOTLAND) ACT 2001 (PRESCRIBED NOTICE) ORDER 2001, SSI 2001 419; made under the Mortgage Rights (Scotland) Act 2001 s.3. In force: December 3, 2001; £1.75.

This Order prescribes the notice that is to be sent to the Keeper of the Register of Inhibitions and Adjudications where an order is made by the court under the Mortgage Rights (Scotland) Act 2001 s.2. The Schedule to this Order sets out the notice that is to be sent.

6882. Standard securities – debts due by husband and wife whether solely or jointly – subsequent debt of husband

FW and JW were brothers, with AW and NW being their respective spouses. In 1991, FW and AW granted a standard security in joint names in favour of R, the bank, in respect of house finance. JW and NW also granted a standard security in joint names in 1991 in favour of R in respect of home improvements. By the terms of the standard conditions attached, both securities bound the signatories to repay to the bank, all sums, which might become due to the bank, either solely or jointly with any person or firm. By partnership letters dated 1992 and 1993, both FW and JW granted further security to R, with joint and several liability, in relation to financial obligations arising out of two businesses they were involved in. R brought actions against both brothers and their spouses for alleged default of the obligations under the standard securities. It was argued for R, that the obligations under the standard securities clearly included any indebtedness arising out JW and FW's involvement in their firm. As co-obligants under the standard securities, AW and NW were also liable for the business debts of FW and JW. On behalf of all the defendants, it was argued that the indebtedness to the bank arose out of separate and completely distinct documents, namely the partnership letters and that the actions as stated were irrelevant. AW and NW further claimed that it was unfair for their liabilities under the standard securities to have been extended to include the business debts of their spouses without notification by R that such an extension was taking place.

Held, allowing a proof before answer restricted to ascertaining the amounts properly due by the parties, that (1) the obligations to repay the debts to R arose directly from the terms of the standard securities which required repayment of all sums due or which might become due by the defendants and that those obligations were not restricted merely to indebtedness for the original house purchase/improvements, and (2) where no allegations had been made of misrepresentation or undue influence on AW and NW and with independent legal advice having been sought by both couples in the preparation of the standard securities, no reliance could be placed on the safeguards awarded to co-obligants in *Smith v. Bank of Scotland* 1997 S.C. (H.L.) 111, [1997] C.L.Y. 6087 which was not applied.

ROYAL BANK OF SCOTLAND PLC v. WILSON 2001 S.L.T. (Sh Ct) 2, RG Craik, Q.C., Sh Ct (Lothian and Border).

6883. **Standard securities – validity – property acquired and security executed after commencement of sequestration proceedings**

[Bankruptcy (Scotland) Act 1985 (c.66) s.32(6).]

H raised an action against A, the trustee on G's sequestrated estate, seeking declarator that a standard security granted by G in favour of H gave H, rather than A, a prior right to the security subjects. The petition for sequestration was lodged on October 15, 1991 but service was not effected until December 9. G did not contest the petition and sequestration was awarded on January 8, 1992, backdated to October 15, 1991. G had applied for the loan from H, and on October 23 G had answered a questionnaire to the effect that she had never been bankrupt, and had signed an application form on November 19 declaring that she would keep H informed of any change in circumstances relating to the mortgage. G did not inform H of the service of the petition and on December 12 G executed the standard security. The disposition in favour of G was delivered on December 31 and thereafter registered, but the Keeper refused to register the standard security. A registered a notice of title in his favour as trustee in June 1996. H argued that in making an advance to G in exchange for execution and delivery of the standard security, H acted in good faith and for value and its right or interest in the subjects was protected by the Bankruptcy (Scotland) Act 1985 s.32(6)(b)(ii). Alternatively payment of the loan was obtained in consequence of a fraudulent or negligent representation by G. Since assets acquired by G and passing to A were taken tantum et tale, A could not retain the benefit of the subjects. A sought dismissal, arguing that (1) whereas A had completed title to the subjects by registering notice of title, H had not registered the standard security and it had no effect whatsoever; (2) by s.32(6) ownership of the house had passed instantly to A, and G had no power validly to grant any security in favour of H and the standard security was therefore null and void; (3) H could not come within the terms of s.32(6)(b)(ii) because the holders of an unrecorded standard security could never have a "right or interest in" the property over which it was granted, and (4) G had made no fraudulent or negligent misrepresentations, having been unaware of the petition when completing the questionnaire. The tantum et tale principle applied only in cases of fraud, which was not averred.

Held, putting the case out by order to consider the precise wording of the declarator, that (1) s.32(6) could not have the effect of nullifying ab initio G's grant of the standard security to H. Section 32 only vested a personal title in the trustee in sequestration, it being for the trustee to adopt the appropriate means whereby his title might be made real in appropriate situations. The existence of s.32(6)(b)(ii) presupposed a power in the bankrupt acquirer to confer rights or interests in respect of property acquired after the date of sequestration, *Alliance & Leicester Building Society v. Murray's Trustee* 1995 S.L.T. (Sh Ct) 77, [1994] C.L.Y. 5915 not followed, and (2) a signed and delivered standard security, even though unrecorded, could constitute an "interest" in the property over which it was granted for the purposes of s.32(6)(b)(ii). That was an interest which A was required to respect and could not be defeated by registration of a notice of title. No view was expressed as to whether the Keeper was correct to refuse registration. Opinion, that the principle of tantum et tale was not limited to cases where the bankrupt was guilty of fraud and proof before answer would have been allowed on this part of the case. Any misrepresentation or other acting by a debtor which would otherwise vitiate his holding of the item of estate in question had his estate not been sequestrated, might come within the scope of the principle.

HALIFAX PLC v. GORMAN'S TRUSTEE 2000 S.L.T. 1409, Lord Eassie, OH.

SHIPPING

6884. **Harbours – accident causing damage – liability of charterer – meaning of "owner"**

See PRESCRIPTION: BP Exploration Operating Co Ltd v. Chevron Shipping Co. §6865

6885. **Harbours – harbour authority – duties and powers**

COMHAIRLE NAN EILEAN SIAR (AIRD MHOR, BARRA) HARBOUR EMPOWERMENT ORDER 2001, SSI 2001 262; made under the Harbours Act 1964 s.16. In force: July 10, 2001; £3.00.

This Order establishes Comhairle nan Eilean Siar as the harbour authority for a specified area at Aird Mhor on the island of Barra, na h'Eileanan an Iar. The Order authorises the Comhairle to construct specified works consisting of a breakwater, shipway and alignment structure and confers on the Comhairle duties and powers in relation to the works and the harbour.

6886. **Harbours – revision – constitution – Fraserburgh**

FRASERBURGH HARBOUR REVISION (CONSTITUTION) ORDER 2001, SSI 2001 457; made under the Harbours Act 1964 s.14. In force: December 12, 2001; £3.00.

This Order, which amends the Fraserburgh Harbour Revision Order 1985 and the Frasburgh Harbour Order Confirmation Act 1990 and repeals the Fraserburgh Harbour Order Confirmation Act 1975 and the Fraserburgh Harbour (No.2) Order Confirmation Act 1985, re-constitutes the Fraserburgh Harbour Commissioners in line with the recommendations of the Trust Ports Review, published by the Department of the Environment, Transport and the Regions in January 2000 and endorsed by the Scottish Ministers, increases the Commissioners' borrowing limit from £6 million to £8 million.

6887. **Harbours – revision – Lerwick**

LERWICK HARBOUR REVISION ORDER 2001, SSI 2001 232; made under the Harbours Act 1964 s.14. In force: June 15, 2001; £2.00.

This Order authorises Lerwick Port Authority to extend and improve the existing Roll-on Roll-off Ferry Terminal Pier at Holmsgarth, Lerwick.

6888. **Oil pollution – claims against limitation fund – caution for expenses – claimant on fund having status as pursuer**

See CIVIL PROCEDURE: Assuranceforeningen Skuld v. International Oil Pollution Compensation Fund (No.3). §6240

6889. **Oil pollution – compensation – offer containing time limit for reply – validity of late acceptance**

See CONTRACTS: Flaws v. International Oil Pollution Compensation Fund. §6298

6890. **Wrecks – protection – restricted area designation**

PROTECTION OF WRECKS (DESIGNATION) (NO.2) (SCOTLAND) ORDER 2001, SSI 2001 384; made under the Protection of Wrecks Act 1973 s.1. In force: December 1, 2001; £1.50.

This Order identifies the site in the Firth of Forth of what is thought to be a wreck of a vessel and, on account of the historical and archaeological importance of the vessel and its cargo, it designates an area 150m around the site as a restricted area so as to protect the site from unauthorised interference.

6891. **Wrecks – protection – restricted area designation**

PROTECTION OF WRECKS (DESIGNATION) (SCOTLAND) ORDER 2001, SSI 2001 242; made under the Protection of Wrecks Act 1973 s.1. In force: June 29, 2001; £1.50.

This Order identifies the site in Loch Inchard, near Kinlochbervie, Sutherland, of what is thought to be a wreck of a vessel and, on account of the historical and archaeological importance of the vessel and its cargo, it designates an area 300 metres around the site as a restricted area so as to protect the site from unauthorised interference.

SOCIAL SECURITY

6892. **Child support – imprisonment**

CHILD SUPPORT (CIVIL IMPRISONMENT) (SCOTLAND) REGULATIONS 2001, SI 2001 1236 (S.3); made under the Child Support Act 1991 s.40A. In force: April 24, 2001; £1.75.

The Child Support Act 1991 s.40A provides for a sheriff committing to prison a liable person who fails to pay under a liability order with imprisonment being in respect of an amount specified in the sheriff's warrant and specifies that the maximum period of imprisonment which the sheriff may impose is six weeks. These regulations set out the manner of determination of the amount of expenses of commitment and provide for the reduction in the period of imprisonment.

6893. **Disability living allowance – care component – meaning of "attention in connection with bodily functions"**

[Social Security Contributions and Benefits Act 1992 (c.4) s.72(1).]

MS, as appointee of her son IS, applied for disability living allowance for his chronic asthma and frequent bed wetting. The night care element of her claim was refused by the social security appeal tribunal and the social security commissioner, who founded on the dictum of Lord Hope in *Cockburn v. Chief Adjudication Officer* [1997] 1 W.L.R. 799, [1997] C.L.Y. 4625 in deciding that the disabilities suffered by IS did not necessitate the requirement for night-time attention in connection with his bodily functions at a level sufficient to meet the requirements of the Social Security Contributions and Benefits Act 1992 s.72(1). MS appealed against the commissioner's decision.

Held, sustaining the appeal and remitting the application to the tribunal for rehearing, that (1) the commissioner erred in excluding attention required by IS following upon completion of a bodily function, and (2) the approach taken on the other speeches given in the judgment in *Cockburn* was wider and all the circumstances of the case under reference to all the statutory provisions should be considered by the tribunal. Opinion of the Court per Lord Milligan.

STEWART v. SECRETARY OF STATE FOR SOCIAL SECURITY 2000 S.L.T. 826, Lord Milligan, Lord Caplan, Lord Rodger L.P., 1 Div.

6894. Income – capital – assessment

NATIONAL ASSISTANCE (ASSESSMENT OF RESOURCES) AMENDMENT (NO.2) (SCOTLAND) REGULATIONS 2001, SSI 2001 105; made under the National Assistance Act 1948 s.22. In force: Reg.5(2): April 11, 2001, remainder: April 9, 2001; £1.75.

These Regulations amend the National Assistance (Assessment of Resources) Regulations 1992 (SI 1992 2977) by inserting a definition for the term "permanent resident"; by increasing the capital limit set out in Reg.20 of the 1992 Regulations to £18,500; by increasing the capital limits set out in Reg.28(1) of the 1992 Regulations to £11,500 and £18,500 respectively; and by adding two new categories of capital to be disregarded under Sch.4.

6895. Income – capital – assessment

NATIONAL ASSISTANCE (ASSESSMENT OF RESOURCES) AMENDMENT (NO.3) (SCOTLAND) REGULATIONS 2001, SSI 2001 138; made under the National Assistance Act 1948 s.22. In force: Reg.5(3): April 12, 2001; Reg.6: April 6, 2001; remainder: April 9, 2001; £1.75.

These Regulations, which extend to Scotland only, amend the National Assistance (Assessment of Resources) Regulations 1992 (SI 1992 2977) by inserting a definition for the term "permanent resident". In addition, they increase the capital limits to £18,500 and revoke the National Assistance (Assessment of Resources) Amendment (No.2) (Scotland) Regulations 2001) (SSI 2001 105).

6896. Income – capital – assessment

NATIONAL ASSISTANCE (ASSESSMENT OF RESOURCES) AMENDMENT (SCOTLAND) REGULATIONS 2001, SSI 2001 6; made under the National Assistance Act 1948 s.22. In force: February 1, 2001; £1.50.

These Regulations make amendments as regards Scotland to the National Assistance (Assessment of Resources) Regulations 1992 (SI 1992 2977) so that, for the purpose of calculating a resident's capital, any ex-gratia payment of £10,000 made on or after February 1, 2001 by the Secretary of State in consequence of a person's imprisonment or internment by the Japanese during the Second World War shall be disregarded as capital when assessing the ability of a person to pay for accommodation arranged by local authorities under the Social Work (Scotland) Act 1968 and the Mental Health (Scotland) Act 1984 s.7.

SOCIAL WELFARE

6897. Community care – direct payments – children under 16

COMMUNITY CARE (DIRECT PAYMENTS) (SCOTLAND) AMENDMENT REGULATIONS 2001, SSI 2001 447; made under the Social Work (Scotland) Act 1968 s.12B. In force: December 20, 2001; £1.50.

These Regulations amend the Community Care (Direct Payments) (Scotland) Regulations 1997 (SI 1997 693) by inserting references to children entitled to services under the Children (Scotland) Act 1995 who are aged less than 16 years, and persons, other than a parent or person having parental responsibility, entitled to such services in respect of a child.

6898. Local authorities – residential accommodation – registration – fees

REGISTERED ESTABLISHMENTS (FEES) (SCOTLAND) ORDER 2001, SSI 2001 253; made under the Social Work (Scotland) Act 1968 s.64A, s.90, s.94. In force: August 1, 2001; £1.75.

This Order, which revokes the Registered Establishments (Fees) (Scotland) Order 2000 (SSI 2000 67) and re-enacts its provisions with amendments, increases as from August 1, 2001, the maximum levels for the fees chargeable by local authorities to applicants for registration and its annual continuation, variation of conditions of registration, and for issuing a new certificate of registration under the Social Work (Scotland) Act 1968 Part IV.

6899. Protection from Abuse (Scotland) Act 2001 2001 (asp 14)

This Act of the Scottish Parliament enables a power of arrest to be attached to interdicts granted to protect individuals from abuse and regulates the consequences of such attachment.

This Act received Royal Assent on November 6, 2001 and comes into force on February 6, 2002.

6900. Regulation of Care (Scotland) Act 2001 (asp 8) – Commencement No.1 Order

REGULATION OF CARE (SCOTLAND) ACT 2001 (COMMENCEMENT NO.1) ORDER 2001, SSI 2001 304 (C.13); made under the Regulation of Care (Scotland) Act 2001 s.81. In force: bringing in to force various provisions of the Act on October 1, 2001 and December 20, 2001; £1.50.

This Order brings into force specified provisions of the Regulation of Care (Scotland) Act 2001.

6901. Regulation of Care (Scotland) Act 2001 (asp 8)

This Act of the Scottish Parliament establishes the Scottish Commission for the Regulation of Care and the Scottish Social Services Council; to make provision for the registration and regulation of care services and for the registration, regulation and training of social service workers; to enable local authorities to make grants in respect of activities relating to child care and family support and to make direct payments to children in respect of certain care services; to enable the Scottish Ministers to delegate a power to make certain grants and loans for social work; to make further provision as respects payments by local authorities towards maintenance of certain children residing with and being cared for by persons other than their parents; to enable local authorities to provide and maintain residential accommodation in which nursing is provided; to make further provision as respects persons who have been looked after by local authorities; to amend the definition of "place of safety" in the Children (Scotland) Act 1995; to make further provision as respects the appointment for children of curators ad litem, reporting officers and safeguarders.

This Act received Royal Assent on July 5, 2001.

6902. Residential accommodation – sums for personal requirements

NATIONAL ASSISTANCE (SUMS FOR PERSONAL REQUIREMENTS) (SCOTLAND) REGULATIONS 2001, SSI 2001 100; made under the National Assistance Act 1948 s.22. In force: April 9, 2001; £1.75.

These Regulations, which revoke the National Assistance (Sums for Personal Requirements) (Scotland) Regulations 2000 (SSI 2000 80), set out the weekly sum which local authorities in Scotland are to assume, in the absence of special circumstances, that residents in accommodation arranged under the Social Work

(Scotland) Act 1968 or the Mental Health (Scotland) Act 1984 s.7 will need for their personal requirements. From April 9, 2001, all residents will be assumed to need £16.05 per week for their personal requirements.

6903. **Residential care – assessment of needs – prior disposal of capital – notional capital forming part of assessment**

[Social Work (Scotland) Act 1968 (c.49) s.12; National Assistance (Assessment of Resources) Regulations 1992 (SI 1992 2977) Reg.25.]

R, an elderly dementia sufferer, sought reduction by judicial review of F's refusal to fund her full time residential nursing care on the basis of its assessment of her notional capital. The Social Work (Scotland) Act 1968 s.12 imposed a duty on a local authority to promote social welfare, including the provision of residential accommodation. R's resources were assessed and, under the National Assistance (Assessment of Resources) Regulations 1992 Reg.25, she was found to possess capital that F was entitled to treat as disposed of for the purpose of reducing her liability. R had disponed the family home to her children for love, favour and affection prior to the diagnosis of dementia. R maintained that the house had been disponed without thought of future care costs. The Lord Ordinary held that F had been correct in its approach. R reclaimed, arguing (1) that aside from s.12(3A) and (3B) the 1968 Act showed that a person's capital was irrelevant when assessing need; (2) a person's resources should not be considered within the procedure for assessment of needs; (3) F was not entitled to decide that R did not need residential care on the basis of a calculation related to property she did not possess; (4) F had sought to extend the local government protection beyond the parliamentary limits and had put improper force on R's sons to pay; (5) F had applied the wrong test in giving weight to the gratuitous nature of the house transfer when the real test should have been the intention to decrease liability, and (6) a valuation of the property was not carried out therefore F had no basis for its decision.

Held, refusing the reclaiming motion (Lord Weir dissenting), that (1) the Act should be read as a whole and in reaching a decision, F was entitled to have regard to R's capital under the 1992 Regulations; (2) F had not erred in law in considering R's capital assets when deciding whether to arrange residential care; (3) F was entitled to take notional capital into account. Such a power being necessary to the application of the Act and the Regulations; (4) F's aim in reaching its decision was to ensure that R paid what a person in her position would be required to pay by Parliament; (5) F had applied the correct test, and (6) given the council tax band and lack of power to carry out a valuation F's approach was correct.

ROBERTSON v. FIFE COUNCIL 2001 S.C. 849, Lord Rodger L.P., Lord Bonomy, Lord Weir, 1 Div.

6904. **Residential care – duty of care once assessment completed – relevance of local authority resources – placement on waiting list and inactivity ultra vires**

[Social Work (Scotland) Act 1968 (c.49) s.12A.]

M, a 90 year old man with poor short term memory, restricted mobility, liability to fall and deafness was assessed by S under the Social Work (Scotland) Act 1968 s.12A. M was assessed as requiring 24-hour nursing care, placed on a waiting list for a residential nursing place and his son was informed that there might be a delay of seven or eight months due to lack of public funds. M sought judicial review of S's decision to delay the provision of residential nursing care. M could not afford that level of care in terms of the means testing regime and argued that S's decision was ultra vires.

Held, granting declarator and remitting the case to S to make specific nursing home provision for M, that once S had determined M's needs, s.12 imposed a duty on S to provide the necessary assistance to satisfy that need regardless of the resources available. The only relevant considerations were M's circumstances, including the ability to care adequately for himself without assistance from any outside agency. The resources of the local authority were relevant only in so far as they affected the way in which they met M's need for residential accommodation, S was not obliged to provide the optimum care, but S's decision to place M on a waiting list and take no action at all was ultra vires.

MacGREGOR v. SOUTH LANARKSHIRE COUNCIL 2001 S.C. 502, Lord Hardie, OH.

6905. Social services – Social Services Council – appointments, procedure and access to the register

SCOTTISH SOCIAL SERVICES COUNCIL (APPOINTMENTS, PROCEDURE AND ACCESS TO THE REGISTER) REGULATIONS 2001, SSI 2001 303; made under the Regulation of Care (Scotland) Act 2001 s.56, Sch.2 para.7. In force: October 1, 2001; £2.50.

These Regulations make provision concerning the membership and procedure of the Scottish Social Services Council, established under the Regulation of Care (Scotland) Act 2001 Part 3, and for access to the register maintained by the Council. They provide for the appointment and tenure of office of the convener and members of the Council, for disqualification for appointment, for resignations and for the termination of appointments by the Scottish Ministers. They also make provision for the payment of remuneration and allowances to the convener and members.

6906. Social services – Social Services Council – consultation on Codes of Practice

SCOTTISH SOCIAL SERVICES COUNCIL (CONSULTATION ON CODES OF PRACTICE) ORDER 2001, SSI 2001 424; made under the Regulation of Care (Scotland) Act 2001 s.53. In force: December 10, 2001; £1.75.

This Order prescribes, for the purposes of the Regulation of Care (Scotland) Act 2001 s.58, those persons or groups of persons whom the Scottish Social Services Council must consult before publishing a code of practice laying down standards of conduct and practice of social service workers or, in relation to such workers, of persons employing or seeking to employ them.

SUCCESSION

6907. Books

MacDonald, Ross – Introduction to the Scots Law of Succession 3rd Ed. Greens Concise Scots Law. Paperback: £32.00. ISBN 0-414-01436-7. W. Green & Son.
O'Donnell, David – Meston's Succession Opinions. Greens Practice Library. Hardback: £135.00. ISBN 0-414-01121-X. W. Green & Son.

TAXATION

6908. Air passenger duty – designated region – Highlands and Islands Enterprise

See TAXATION. §5177

6909. Enterprise Investment Scheme – regulation of care – revocation

SCOTLAND ACT 1998 (REGULATION OF CARE (SCOTLAND) ACT 2001) ORDER 2001, SI 2001 2478 (S.13); made under the Scotland Act 1998 s.107, s.112, s.113, s.114. In force: August 3, 2001; £1.50.

This Order revokes the Regulation of Care (Scotland) Act 2001 Sch.3 para.24 which would make modifications to the Finance Act 2000 Sch.14 and Sch.15 in relation to enterprise management incentives and the corporate venturing scheme.

6910. Public expenditure – use of resources

BUDGET (SCOTLAND) ACT 2001 (AMENDMENT) ORDER 2001, SSI 2001 480; made under the Budget (Scotland) Act 2000 s.7. In force: December 20, 2001; £2.50.

This Order amends the Budget (Scotland) Act 2001 which makes provision, for financial year 2001/02, for the use of resources by the Scottish Administration and certain bodies whose expenditure is payable out of the Scottish Consolidated Fund, for authorising the use of resources, and for limits on the capital expenditure of and borrowing of local authorities and certain other public bodies.

TRANSPORT

6911. Bus services – PSV Operater's Licence – conditions

TRANSPORT (SCOTLAND) ACT 2001 (CONDITIONS ATTACHED TO PSV OPERATER'S LICENCE AND COMPETITION TEST FOR EXERCISE OF BUS FUNCTIONS) ORDER 2001, SI 2001 2748 (S.14); made under the Scotland Act 1998 s.104, s.112, s.113. In force: July 25, 2001; £2.00.

This Order, which amends the Transport Act 1985, makes provision consequential on the Transport (Scotland) Act 2001. It provides additional grounds on which the traffic commissioner may attach conditions to a public service vehicle operator's licence. These grounds are where an operator has operated a local service in contravention of a written undertaking given to the traffic commissioner in terms of a quality partnership scheme, where an operator has provided a local service during a period when a quality contract scheme is in place and that service is not part of that scheme, where an operator has failed to make and implement the arrangements required by a ticketing scheme and where an operator has failed to provide an authority or authorities with information required by them.

6912. Passenger vehicles – local services – compulsory registration

PUBLIC SERVICE VEHICLES (REGISTRATION OF LOCAL SERVICES) (SCOTLAND) AMENDMENT REGULATIONS 2001, SSI 2001 251; made under the Public Passenger Vehicles Act 1981 s.60; and the Transport Act 1985 s.6, s.8. In force: July 1, 2001; £1.50.

These Regulations amend the Public Service Vehicles (Registration of Local Services) (Scotland) Regulations 2001 (SSI 2001 219) by correcting a reference to "paragraph 9 of the Schedule" which should have read "paragraph 10 of Schedule 1".

6913. Passenger vehicles – local services – compulsory registration

PUBLIC SERVICE VEHICLES (REGISTRATION OF LOCAL SERVICES) (SCOTLAND) REGULATIONS 2001, SSI 2001 219; made under the Public Passenger Vehicles Act 1981 s.60; and the Transport Act 1985 s.6, s.8. In force: July 1, 2001; £2.00.

These Regulations revoke and replace the Public Service Vehicles (Registration of Local Services) Regulations 1986 (SI 1986 1671 as amended by SI 1988 1879, SI 1989 1064 and SI 1993 2752) for Scotland. The Transport Act 1985 s.6 provides that particulars of local services are required to be registered with the traffic commissioner. These Regulations apply to applications received by the traffic commissioner on or after July 1, 2001. They set out the application procedure, stipulate the details to be provided to the traffic commissioner, provide for periods of notice on application for registration, variation or cancellation of a registration, for the variation of certain registered services without variation of the registration, for the traffic commissioner to cancel a registration where a service has been discontinued, for failure to operate a service in accordance with registered particulars to be disregarded for a period of 28 days in specified circumstances, for the display of fare tables, timetables, destinations and route numbers, stipulate the fees for applications to register or vary the registration of particulars of a service and exclude excursions and tours from the requirements of s.6 of the 1985 Act.

6914. Transport – transport policy – quality partnership schemes

EXISTING FACILITIES IN QUALITY PARTNERSHIP SCHEMES (SCOTLAND) REGULATIONS 2001, SSI 2001 218; made under the Transport (Scotland) Act 2001 s.4. In force: July 1, 2001; £1.75.

These Regulations, which amend the Transport (Scotland) Act 2001, make provision for existing facilities to form part of a quality scheme which were introduced by the Transport (Scotland) Act 2001 Part II. They provide that existing facilities may form part of a quality partnership scheme where they were provided for no more than 5 years before the scheme is proposed and that a local transport authority must, in carrying out the consultation process, specify the date on which the existing facilities were provided.

6915. Transport (Scotland) Act 2001 (asp 2) – Commencement No.1, Transitional Provisions and Savings Order

TRANSPORT (SCOTLAND) ACT 2001 (COMMENCEMENT NO.1, TRANSITIONAL PROVISIONS AND SAVINGS) ORDER 2001, SSI 2001 132 (C.7); made under the Transport (Scotland) Act 2001 s.81, s.84. Commencement details: bringing into force various provisions of the Act on April 1, 2001, July 1, 2001 and April 1, 2002; £2.00.

This Order brings into force various provisions of the Transport Act 2001 on April 1, 2001, July 1, 2001 and April 1, 2002.

6916. Transport (Scotland) Act 2001 (asp 2) – Commencement No.2 Order

TRANSPORT (SCOTLAND) ACT 2001 (COMMENCEMENT NO.2) ORDER 2001, SSI 2001 167 (C.9); made under the Transport (Scotland) Act 2001 s.84. Commencement details: bringing into force various provisions of the Act on May 1, 2001; £1.50.

This Order brings into force, on May 1, 2001, the Transport (Scotland) Act 2001 s.80 which provides that a director, manager, secretary or similar officer of a body corporate or a partner of a Scottish partnership may be required to pay a civil penalty under the Transport (Scotland) Act 2001 where an act or omission has been done with their consent or connivance or where the act or omission is attributable to them.

6917. Transport (Scotland) Act 2001 (asp 2)

This Act of the Scottish Parliament makes provision about transport, and amends the Chronically Sick and Disabled Persons Act 1970 s.21, Road Traffic Act 1988 s.40 and the Road Traffic Regulation Act 1984 s.26, s.28 and s.63.

This Act received Royal Assent on January 25, 2001.

UNJUSTIFIED ENRICHMENT

6918. Repetition – payment of advance freight under charterparty – abandonment of voyage

C chartered a vessel from A to carry sugar from Rouen to Umm Qasr. The voyage was abandoned and C sought damages from A for breach of contract under which decree was granted. C thereafter sought repetition of a sum paid to B, A's banker, on the grounds of unjustified enrichment. Alternatively they sought declarators that certain sums in A's accounts with B and a sum transferred were C's property on the grounds of constructive trust. C argued in support of the claim for repetition that the loan documentation between A and B constituted an absolute assignation and B received the advance for their own benefit. B argued that the obligation to complete the voyage or repay the advance was A's by virtue of contract and assignation would not impose a corresponding obligation on B.

Held, assoilzing B, that (1) the loan documentation indicated that the assignation was only in security, not absolute, therefore the advance monies were received by B for A and even if B had received the monies for their own benefit, that would not amount to unjustified enrichment; and (2) English law would not hold that A held the remaining balance of advance freight on constructive trust and even if constructive trust had arisen there was no evidence to suggest that B knew enough of the abandonment of the voyage to conclude that the advance freight would be repayable.

COMPAGNIE COMMERCIALE ANDRE SA v. ARTIBELL SHIPPING CO LTD (NO.2) 2001 S.C. 653, Lord Macfadyen, OH.

UTILITIES

6919. **Electricity supply industry – fossil fuel**

FOSSIL FUEL LEVY (SCOTLAND) AMENDMENT REGULATIONS 2001, SSI 2001 335; made under the Electricity Act 1989 s.33, s.60. In force: October 3, 2001; £1.75.

These Regulations amend the Fossil Fuel Levy (Scotland) Regulations 1996 (SI 1996 293) to take account of the changes in the electricity market with the commencement of the Utilities Act 2000. In addition, they update the definitions of the Director, licensed supplier and public electricity supplier and insert the definition of supply successor company.

VAT

6920. **Exemptions – supply of insurance – arrangement fee expressed as percentage of total price**

[Value Added Tax Act 1994 (c.23) Sch.9 Group 2 Note (5).]

C supplied and fitted double glazing with a warranty covering labour and material. It also supplied additional insurance to protect the warranty in the event of insolvency at a premium of £16 and an arrangement fee of 10 per cent of the contract price. C treated the premium and arrangement fee as exempt supplies of insurance amounts. Customs accepted that the premium was an exempt supply but decided that VAT was due on the arrangement fee and issued a notice of assessment. C appealed against the assessment and the VAT and duties tribunal held ([2000] B.V.C. 2146) that the use of a percentage based formula did not comply with the requirement for full disclosure in the Value Added Tax Act 1994 Sch.9 Group 2 Note (5) C appealed further, contending that the requirement for full disclosure was met by the use of the formula.

Held, dismissing the appeal, that Group 2 contained detailed requirements for disclosure so that customers would know the exact amount they had to pay. Note (5) required each amount to be individually set out so that even a simple formula based calculation did not comply with the specific notification required. Opinion of the Court per Lord Kirkwood.

CR SMITH GLAZIERS (DUNFERMLINE) LTD v. CUSTOMS AND EXCISE COMMISSIONERS; *sub nom.* CR SMITH GLAZIERS (DUNFERMLINE) LTD v. EDINBURGH VAT AND DUTIES TRIBUNAL [2001] S.T.C. 770, Lord Kirkwood, Lord Abernethy, Lord Cameron of Lochbroom, Ex Div.

6921. Repayments – overpaid VAT – three year cap – applicability to claim by repayment trader

[ValueAddedTax Act1994 (c.23) s.80(4);ValueAddedTax Regulations1995 (SI 1995 2518) Reg.29(1A).]

In 1998 a VAT tribunal held ([1998] B.V.C. 2239, [1998] C.L.Y. 6219) that G was not liable to VAT in respect of the cost of repair work carried out following the issue of statutory repair notices. As a consequence of that decision, Customs made some repayments but argued that its liability to repay was subject to the repayment cap imposed under the Value Added Tax Act 1994 s.80(4) so that claims for the years 1988 to 1992, inclusive, were not allowed. G appealed, contending that its status as a repayment trader during that time meant that the three year cap did not apply to the repayment of overpaid VAT and that its claims were valid as they referred to years prior to the coming into force of the Value Added Tax Regulations 1995 Reg.29(1A). Further, that it was incompatible with Community law to apply the three year limit to repayments and that Customs had exercised its discretion unreasonably by refusing repayments contrary to its own statement of December 4, 1996 that output tax charged in error to local authorities would be refunded.

Held, allowing the appeal in part, that the three year limit applied to amounts "paid" to Customs under s.80(4) with the three year period calculated by reference to the date of the payment. Each amount claimed was considered separately, having regard only to the date of the overpayment of a given return. In the circumstances, Customs was not liable to repay the amounts paid by G for the first four disputed periods. However, if the errors in the return for the fifth period had been corrected, G would have been a repayment trader due a repayment which was not subject to the three year limit and correction of the errors in the return was mandatory. Customs was not liable to repay the amount actually paid on the return but G could recover the balance of its claim for that period. The right to recover the amount actually paid on the last return was removed retrospectively and that was not a right enforceable under Community law, *Marks & Spencer Plc v. Customs and Excise Commissioners (No.1)* [2000] S.T.C. 16, [2000] 2 C.L. 541 distinguished. Customs had not exercised its discretion regarding the disputed claims and, even if it had, the tribunal had no jurisdiction to review the exercise of such a discretion.

GLASGOW CITY COUNCIL v. CUSTOMS AND EXCISE COMMISSIONERS (NO.2) [2000] B.V.C. 2363, J Gordon Reid Q.C., V&DTr.

6922. Supply of services – residential care – provision of medical, psychotherapeutic and curative treatment

[SocialWork (Scotland) Act1968 (c.49);ValueAddedTax Act1994 (c.23) Sch.9 Group 7 Item 4.]

CC, which operated four "residential establishments" providing vocational training and psychological services, appealed against the decision of the Commissioners that its business supplies were taxable supplies and liable to VAT at the standard rate. CC's four establishments were registered under the Social Work (Scotland) Act 1968, as amended.

Held, allowing the appeal, that the four establishments were "institutions" providing "care" for the purposes of the Value Added Tax Act 1994 Sch.9 Group 7 Item 4. It was apparent that the four establishments provided medical, psychotherapeutic and curative treatment and that whilst they were not hospitals, they did not amount to nursing or convalescent homes, *Kingscrest Associates Ltd v. Customs and Excise Commissioners* [2001] S.T.I. 1066 distinguished.

CATHOLIC CARE CONSORTIUM LTD v. CUSTOMS AND EXCISE COMMISSIONERS [2001] B.V.C. 2381, J Gordon Reid Q.C. (Chairman),V&DTr.

WATER INDUSTRY

6923. Water authorites – abstraction scheme – River Lochy

NORTH OF SCOTLAND WATER AUTHORITY (RIVER LOCHY ABSTRACTION SCHEME) WATER ORDER 2001, SSI 2001 369; made under the Water (Scotland) Act 1980 s.17, s.29, s.107. In force: October 9, 2001; £1.75.

This Order provides that the North of Scotland Water Authority may take water from the gravels adjacent to the river known as the River Lochy in the Lochaber Area of the Highland Council for the purposes of construction work undertaken for certain purposes. In addition, it revokes the County of Inverness (Allt Odhar, Spean Bridge) Water Order 1962 (SI 1962 651), the County of Inverness (River Loy, Corpach) Water Order 1964 (SI 1964 1769), the Argyll County Council (Allt Mor, Trislaig) Water Order 1968 (SI 1968 667), the Argyll Water Board (Allt Blaich Mhoir) Water Order 1968 (SI 1968 1121), the Argyll Water Board (Allt Meadhonach, Achaphubuil) Water Order 1970 (SI 1970 754) and the Highland Regional Council (Allt Beinn Chlianaig) Water Order 1977.

6924. Water authorities – duty to supply wholesome water – strict liability

[Water (Scotland) Act 1980 (c.45) s.8, s.10.]

W, a family, sought damages from E, a water authority, for injury sustained while using unwholesome water supplied to their home. W averred that contractors, C, acting on behalf of E, laid the mains and failed to swab all legs of the pipe installed, with the result that a dead fox lay undetected within the mains. W had a case at common law and also that E were in breach of duty under the Water (Scotland) Act 1980 s.8, which imposed strict liability. E argued that both cases were irrelevant. W argued that the duty under s.8 was owed to a limited class of persons, the owners and occupiers of premises within particular limits of supply, and there was no other enforceable remedy.

Held, putting the case put out by order, that (1) W's statutory case was irrelevant. Considered in its statutory context, the duty under s.8 was not a duty for the protection of a defined limited class, but was owed to every domestic customer within E's area, and W had other remedies either to sue at common law or seek compensation under s.10, which provided a remedy even though it referred to powers rather than duties. Further, s.8 did not create an absolute duty, *Read v. Croydon Corp* [1938] 4 All E.R. 631 referred to, and (2) W had undertaken to show that C did the work carelessly but had failed to aver why E should be held responsible, whether directly or vicariously, or even both as alternatives. Applying the test of the weaker alternative, W had (a) offered to prove that E engaged C to do the work but not that C were not competent to do the work, and (b) averred that the omission was by C but not that E had or should have had any knowledge of it. Given the small sums involved, W would be given the opportunity to move to amend without having to go to the Inner House.

WEIR v. EAST OF SCOTLAND WATER AUTHORITY 2001 S.L.T. 1205, Lord McCluskey, OH.

6925. Water quality – water supply

WATER SUPPLY (WATER QUALITY) (SCOTLAND) AMENDMENT REGULATIONS 2001, SSI 2001 238; made under the Water (Scotland) Act 1980 s.76B, s.76F, s.76J, s.101, s.109. In force: June 26, 2001; £1.50.

These Regulations amend the Water Supply (Water Quality) (Scotland) Regulations 2001 (SSI 2001 207) to correct the unintentional omission of the verb in Reg.8(1) and remove the date from Reg.36 to make it clear that the Regulation is commenced in accordance with Reg.1 (2) of the Regulations and comes into force on June 26, 2001.

6926. Water quality – water supply

WATER SUPPLY (WATER QUALITY) (SCOTLAND) REGULATIONS 2001, SSI 2001 207; made under the European Communities Act 1972 s.2; and the Water (Scotland) Act 1980 s.76B, s.76F, s.76J, s.101, s.109. In force: Reg.1: June 26, 2001; Reg.2: June 26, 2001; Reg.36: June 26, 2001; Reg.37: June 26, 2001; Reg.3: June 1, 2003; Reg.38: June 1, 2003; remainder: December 25, 2003; £6.50.

These Regulations, which are concerned with quality of water supplied in Scotland for drinking, washing and cooking, supplement the Water Act 1980 Part VIA; amend for a limited period the Water Supply (Water Quality) (Scotland) Regulations 1990 (SI 1990 119) and on December 25, 2003, revoke and replace those regulations.

6927. Water supply – sewerage – charges – reduction

DOMESTIC WATER AND SEWERAGE CHARGES (REDUCTION) (SCOTLAND) REGULATIONS 2001, SSI 2001 114; made under the Local Government etc. (Scotland) Act 1994 s.81. In force: April 1, 2001; £1.75.

These Regulations provide for reductions in water and sewerage charges in Scotland from April 1, 2001 until March 31, 2002. They make provision for a reduction in the water and sewerage charges due to a local authority for those in receipt of council tax benefit. The reduction applies to charges in a range from a threshold of £180 to the charges payable for properties in council tax Band E. There is no provision for reductions in charges that are due in the relevant year which fall either below £180 or above the B and E level. Within that range the Regulations provide that the proportion of the water and sewerage charge liability above the threshold attracts relief proportionate to council tax benefit received by virtue of the Social Security Contributions and Benefits Act 1992.

WORDS AND PHRASES

The table below is a cumulative guide to words and phrases judicially considered in 2001:

(N) refers to a case in the Northern Ireland section.

(S) refers to a case in the Scottish section.

aids, 2300
aircraft, 5386, 5386
an action founded on tort, 2511
arrising from ... employment, 6721 (S)
attention in connection with bodily functions, 6893(S)
bodily injury, 5385
business activity, 5579
capacity, 414
carriage, 5386
circumstances, 4251
college of, 5601
consequential provision, 3708
consideration, 5599
construction operations, 854
continuous use, 4653
control of, 549
crime, 6702(S)
criminal, 1137
custody, 313
date when grounds for application first arose, 53
deduct, 6743(S)
demand, 4948
detriment, 5771 (N)
device, 6662(S)
dismissal, 2234, 2295
driving, 1033
drunkenness, 1003
due proportion, 958
dwelling, 4148
false instrument, 1046
for reward, 5386
frozen products, 5620
goods or materials, 4945
grounds arising out of same circumstances, 6302(S)
hereditament, 4822
house, 4180
impropriety, 954
improvement, 4188
keeper, 324
knew or ought to have known, 3828
knowingly concerned, 1060
liable to pay, 896
limitations, 4219

locality, 5029
necessary, 574
normal day to day activities, 2242
occurrence, 3837
owner, 6865(S)
packaging, 2412
paid, 5199
passenger, 5386
persistent offender, 1377, 1378, 1380, 1384, 1394
persistent young offender, 1395
person charged with an offence, 5650(N)
pilot project, 769
possession, 1044
premises, 2429
protected building, 5559
public entertainment, 6777(S)
public place, 1033
rateable hereditament, 4806
reasonably obtained, 6103(S)
reconstruction, 5183
relevant business property, 5285
residing with, 5021
retirement, 5263
returned unsatisfied, 3737
road, 4449
roundsman, 4317
scotland, 6536(S)
scottish zone, 6536(S)
same damage, 609
sentence, 6409(S)
sewer, 5633
ship, 5269
supply, 1073
total and permanent invalidity, 4643
transaction in securities, 5174
undertakings, 755
undue public nuisance, 6783(S)
unnatural death, 27
violent offence, 1269
waste materials, 4654
wireless telegraphy apparatus, 6317(S)
within their area, 4374
workplace, 6662(S)

Law books

published during 2001

A-Z Essentials: Licensed Premises Management. Paperback: £27.50. ISBN 1-85524-611-2. Croner Publications.

A-Z of Scots Education Law. Paperback: £9.99. ISBN 0-11-497288-5. The Stationery Office Agencies.

Abeyratne, Ruwantissa–Aviation Trends in the New Millennium. Hardback: £69.95. ISBN 0-7546-1299-6. Ashgate Publishing Limited.

Abeyratne, Sonali–Banking and Debt Recovery in Emerging Markets: the Law Reform Context. Hardback: £60.00. ISBN 0-7546-2165-0. Ashgate Publishing Limited.

Abrams, Roger I.–Legal Bases. Paperback: £15.95. ISBN 1-56639-890-8. Temple University Press.

Ackerman, Marc J.–Clinician's Guide for Child Custody Evalations. Hardback: £39.50. ISBN 0-471-39260-X. John Wiley and Sons.

Adamantopoulos, Konstantinos; Pereyra-Friedrichsen, Maria Jesus; Branton, Jeremy–EU Anti-subsidy Law and Practice. Hardback: £80.00. ISBN 1-902558-32-4. Palladian Law Publishing Ltd.

Adams, Kenneth A.–Legal Usage in Drafting Corporate Agreements. Hardback: £58.95. ISBN 1-56720-410-4. Quorum Books.

Adams, Trevor–Business Law and Practice. Legal Practice Course. Hardback: £23.95. ISBN 0-85308-716-4. Paperback: £23.95. ISBN 0-85308-717-2. Jordans.

Ahdar, Rex J.–Law and Religion. Issues in Law and Society. Hardback: £55.00. ISBN 1-84014-745-8. Dartmouth. Paperback: £19.50. ISBN 1-84014-757-1. Ashgate Publishing Limited.

Ahdar, Rex J.–Worlds Colliding. Hardback: £50.00. ISBN 0-7546-2200-2. Dartmouth.

Akdeniz, Yaman; Walker, Clive–Internet, Law and Society. Paperback: £29.99. ISBN 0-582-35656-3. Prentice Hall.

Allan, Trevor–Constitutional Justice. Hardback: £40.00. ISBN 0-19-829830-7. Oxford University Press.

Alldridge, Peter–Personal Autonomy, the Private Sphere and Criminal Law. Hardback: £30.00. ISBN 1-901362-82-5. Hart Publishing.

Allen, Michael J.–Elliott and Wood's Cases and Materials on Criminal Law 8th Ed. Paperback: £27.95. ISBN 0-421-71740-8. Sweet & Maxwell.

Allott, Philip–Eunomia. Paperback: £16.99. ISBN 0-19-924493-6. Oxford University Press.

Alston, Philip–People's Rights-Reissue. Collected Courses of the Academy of European Law, Vol 9, No 2. Hardback: £40.00. ISBN 0-19-829875-7. Oxford University Press.

Alston, Philip–Peoples' Rights. Collected Courses of the Academy of European Law. Paperback: £16.99. ISBN 0-19-924365-4. Oxford University Press.

Alter, Karen–Establishing the Supremacy of European Law. Oxford Studies in European Law. Hardback: £40.00. ISBN 0-19-924347-6. Oxford University Press.

Amato, Giuliano; Laudati, Laraine L.–Anti-competitive Impact of Regulation. Hardback: £75.00. ISBN 1-84064-677-2. Edward Elgar.

Anderman, Steven D.–EC Competition Law and Intellectual Property Rights: the Regulation of Innovation. Paperback: £22.50. ISBN 0-19-829924-9. Oxford University Press.

Anderman, Steven D.–Law of Unfair Dismissal. 3rd Ed. Paperback: £24.95. ISBN 0-406-92181-4. Butterworths Law.

Andrews, Geraldine; Millett, Richard–Law of Guarantees. 3rd Ed. Hardback: £125.00. ISBN 0-7520-0589-8. Sweet & Maxwell.

Anthony and Berryman's Magistrates Court Guide 2002. Paperback: £35.00. ISBN 0-406-94598-5. Butterworths Law.

Anthony, Gordon–UK Public Law and European Law. Hardback: £30.00. ISBN 1-84113-148-2. Hart Publishing.

Appelbaum, Richard; Felstiner, William; Gessner, Volkmar–Rules and Networks. Hardback: £45.00. ISBN 1-84113-295-0. Paperback: £20.00. ISBN 1-84113-296-9. Hart Publishing.

Applebe, Gordon E.; Wingfield, Joy–Dale and Appelbe's Pharmacy, Law and Ethics 7th Ed. Paperback: £29.95. ISBN 0-85369-475-3. Pharmaceutical Press.

Aquino, Tracey–Q&A on Family Law. 3rd Ed. Questions and Answers. Paperback: £9.95. ISBN 1-85941-582-2. Cavendish Publishing Ltd.

Ashcroft, John; Ashcroft, Janet–Law for Business 14th Ed. Hardback: £32.00. ISBN 0-324-06053-X. South Western College Publishing.

Ashworth, Andrew; Mitchell, Barry–Rethinking English Homicide Law. Oxford Monographs on Criminal Law and Justice. Hardback: £40.00. ISBN 0-19-829904-4. Paperback: £16.99. ISBN 0-19-829915-X. Oxford University Press.

Askin, Kelly D.; Koenig, Dorean–Women and International Human Rights Law. Hardback: £257.50. ISBN 1-57105-094-9. Transnational Publishers, Inc.

Asouzu, Amazu A.–International Commercial Arbitration and African States. Cambridge Studies in International and Comparative Law. Hardback: £70.00. ISBN 0-521-64132-2. Cambridge University Press.

Attewell, P.B.–Ground Pollution. Paperback: £32.50. ISBN 0-419-21630-8. Spon Press.

Austen-Peters, A.O.–Custody of Investments: Law and Practice. Hardback: £110.00. ISBN 0-19-829858-7. Oxford University Press.

Austin, R.C.; Bonner, David; Whitty, Noel–Legal Protection of Civil Liberties. Paperback: £26.95. ISBN 0-406-55511-7. Butterworths Law.

Baatz, Nicholas; Clay, Robert; Walker, Steven J.–Technology and Construction Law Reports. Hardback: £220.00. ISBN 0-421-73890-1. Sweet & Maxwell.

Bagaric, Mirko–Punishment and Sentencing: a Rational Approach. Paperback: £19.95. ISBN 1-85941-631-4. Cavendish Publishing Ltd.

Bagshaw, Roderick; McBride, Nicholas–Tort Law. Longman Law Series. Paperback: £28.99. ISBN 0-582-35701-2. Longman.

Bailey, S.H.; Harris, D.J.; Jones, B.L.–Civil Liberties-cases and Materials 5th Ed. Paperback: £28.95. ISBN 0-406-90326-3. Butterworths Law.

Baker, Philip–Double Taxation Conventions and International Tax Law. 3rd Ed. Looseleaf/ringbound: £250.00. ISBN 0-421-67360-5. Sweet & Maxwell.

Ball, Caroline; McCormac, Kevin; Stone, Nigel–Young Offenders: Law, Policy and Practice 2nd Ed. Hardback: £60.00. ISBN 0-421-65710-3. Sweet & Maxwell.

Banaszak, Ronald–Fair Trial Rights of the Accused. Hardback: £41.50. ISBN 0-313-30525-0. Greenwood Press.

Bantekas, I; Nash, S.; Mackarel, M.–International Criminal Law. Paperback: £60.50. ISBN 1-85941-557-1. Cavendish Publishing Ltd.

Barber, Susan–Company Law: Textbook. 3rd Ed. Old Bailey Press Textbooks. Paperback: £14.95. ISBN 1-85836-399-3. Old Bailey Press.

Barendt, Eric; Firth, Alison–Yearbook of Copyright and Media Law: 5. Hardback: £95.00. ISBN 0-19-829919-2. Oxford University Press.

Bargate, Quentin; Shah, Martin—E-finance. Hardback: £135.00. ISBN 0-421-74790-0. Sweet & Maxwell.

Barkan; Bryjak—Essentials of Criminal Justice. Paperback: £32.99. ISBN 0-205-29518-5. Allyn & Bacon.

Barker, Craig—International Law and International Relations. IR for the 21st Century. Hardback: £45.00. ISBN 0-8264-5029-6. Paperback: £14.99. ISBN 0-8264-5028-8. Continuum Publishing Group.

Barker, Richard W.—Child Protection: Practice, Policy and Management. Paperback: £14.95. ISBN 1-85302-319-1. Jessica Kingsley Publishers.

Bateman, Mike—Tolley's Practical Guide to Risk Assessment. Paperback: £50.00. ISBN 0-7545-0749-1. Tolley Publishing.

Bates, Phil—Family Law. Butterworths Core Text. Paperback: £12.95. ISBN 0-406-92954-8. Butterworths Law.

Baumer, David; Poindexter, J. Carl—Cyberlaw and E-commerce. Paperback: £31.99. ISBN 0-07-112300-8. McGraw-Hill Publishing Company.

BDO Stoy Hayward's Orange Tax Guide 2001-02. Paperback: £45.00. ISBN 0-406-93911-X. Butterworths Tolley.

BDO Stoy Hayward's Yellow Tax Guide 2001-02. Paperback: £65.00. ISBN 0-406-93910-1. Butterworths Tolley.

Beale, Hugh—Contract Law. Casebooks for the Common Law of Europe, 2. Paperback: £32.50. ISBN 1-84113-237-3. Hart Publishing.

Beale, H.G.; Bishop, W.D.; Furmston, M.P.—Contract-cases and Materials 4th Ed. Paperback: £27.95. ISBN 0-406-92404-X. Butterworths Law.

Beale—Chitty on Contracts. 28th Ed. Common Law Library. Hardback: £38.00. ISBN 0-421-74140-6. Sweet & Maxwell.

Beaumont, Paul; Lyons, Carole; Walker, Neil—Convergence and Divergence in European Public Law. Hardback: £35.00. ISBN 1-84113-211-X. Hart Publishing.

Beck, M.—Law & Economics for Economists, Lawyers & Managers. Paperback. ISBN 0-631-21163-2. Blackwell Publishers.

Beck, Robert A.; Ambrosio, Thomas—International Law and the Rise of Nations. Paperback: £28.95. ISBN 1-889119-30-X. Chatham House Publishers of Seven Bridges Press, LLC.

Bederman, David J.—An International Law in Antiquity. Cambridge Studies in International and Comparative Law, 16. Hardback: £45.00. ISBN 0-521-79197-9. Cambridge University Press.

Bederman, David J.—Classical Canons. Applied Legal Philosophy. Hardback: £55.00. ISBN 0-7546-2161-8. Dartmouth.

Belknap, Joanne—Invisible Woman. 2nd Ed. Paperback: £23.99. ISBN 0-534-54209-3. Wadsworth.

Bell, A.—Nutcases: Employment Law. Paperback: £5.95. ISBN 0-421-74350-6. Sweet & Maxwell.

Bell, Cedric D.—Land: the Law of Real Property Textbook. 3rd Ed. Old Bailey Press Textbooks. Paperback: £14.95. ISBN 1-85836-410-8. Old Bailey Press.

Bellamy, Richard; Warleigh, Alex—Citizenship and Governance in the EU. Hardback: £50.00. ISBN 0-8264-5348-1. Paperback: £16.99. ISBN 0-8264-5347-3. Continuum International Publishing Group-Academic and Professional.

Bennett, Rebecca; Erin, Charles A.—HIV and AIDS Testing, Screening, and Confidentiality. Issues in Biomedical Ethics. Paperback: £14.99. ISBN 0-19-924314-X. Clarendon Press.

Bennion, F.A.R.—Understanding Common Law Legislation-Drafting and Interpretation. Hardback: £30.00. ISBN 0-19-924777-3. Oxford University Press.

Benson, Peter—Theory of Contract Law. Cambridge Studies in Philosophy and Law. Hardback: £40.00. ISBN 0-521-64038-5. Cambridge University Press.

Bercusson, Brian—European Labour Law. 2nd Ed. Butterworths Law in Context. Paperback: £36.95. ISBN 0-406-98254-6. Butterworths Law.

Bermann, George; Herdegen, Matthias; Lindseth, Peter–Transatlantic Regulatory Co-operation: Legal Problems and Political Prospects. Hardback: £60.00. ISBN 0-19-829892-7. Oxford University Press.

Berry, Christopher; Bailey, Edward; Schaw-Miller, Stephen–Personal Insolvency-law and Practice. 3rd Ed. Paperback: £145.00. ISBN 0-406-08153-0. Butterworths Law.

Beswick, Simon–Beswick and Wine: Buying and Selling of Private Companies and Businesses. 6th Ed. Paperback: Floppy disk: £60.00. ISBN 0-406-91164-9. Butterworths Law.

Beveridge, Fiona C.–Treatment and Taxation of Foreign Investment Under International Law. Melland Schill Studies in International Law. Hardback: £45.00. ISBN 0-7190-4309-3. Manchester University Press.

Bhat, Vasanthakumar N.–Medical Malpractice. Hardback: £53.95. ISBN 0-86569-279-3. Auburn House.

Biehl, Kathy; Calishain, Tara–Lawyer's Guide to Internet Legal Research. Paperback: £28.00. ISBN 0-8108-3885-0. Scarecrow Press.

Biggs, Hazel–Euthanasia, Death with Dignity and the Law. Hardback: £25.00. ISBN 1-84113-091-5. Hart Publishing.

Birds, John; Hird, Norma–Birds' Modern Insurance Law. 5th Ed. Paperback: £25.00. ISBN 0-421-71670-3. Sweet & Maxwell.

Blacam, Mark De–Judicial Review. Irish Law Library. Hardback: £110.00. ISBN 1-85475-214-6. Butterworths Law.

Black, Sharon–Telecommunications Law in the Internet Age. Hardback: £36.95. ISBN 1-55860-546-0. Hardback: £36.95. ISBN 1-55860-546-0. Morgan Kaufmann.

Black; Waller; White, Ken–Family Proceedings: a Guide for Urgent Business and Emergencies. Hardback: Floppy disk: £75.00. ISBN 0-406-99294-0. Butterworths Law.

Blackburn, Robert; Kennon, Andrew–Griffith & Ryle on Parliament-Functions, Practice and Procedures. 2nd Ed. Hardback: £60.00. ISBN 0-421-60910-9. Sweet & Maxwell.

Blackstone, Sir William; Morrison, Wayne J.–Blackstone Commentaries on Laws of England: Vols 1-4. Cavendish Commentaries. Hardback: £250.00. ISBN 1-85941-482-6. Cavendish Publishing Ltd.

Blakeney, Michael–Border Control of Intellectual Property Rights. Looseleaf/ring bound: £250.00. ISBN 0-421-71000-4. Sweet & Maxwell.

Bloxham, Donald–Genocide on Trial-War Crimes Trials and the Formation of Holocaust History and Memory. Hardback: £35.00. ISBN 0-19-820872-3. Oxford University Press.

Bobacka, Roger–Corporatism and the Myth of Consensus. Hardback: £50.00. ISBN 0-7546-2184-7. Dartmouth.

Bond, Robert–Negotiating International Software Licences and Data Transfer Agreement. International Business Negotiating Guides. Looseleaf/ring bound; Floppy disk: £210.00. ISBN 0-421-72910-4. Sweet & Maxwell.

Bonner, David; Hooker, Ian; White, Robin–Social Security: Legislation 2001: Vol 1, Non-means Tested Benefits. Paperback: £59.00. ISBN 0-421-82610-X. Sweet & Maxwell.

Booth, P.; Bloy, D.–Principles of Child Law 2nd Ed. Principles of Law. Paperback: £15.95. ISBN 1-85941-462-1. Cavendish Publishing Ltd.

Borgese, Elisabeth Mann; Chircop, Aldo; McConnell, Moira; Morgan, Joseph R.–Ocean Yearbook: Vol 14. Ocean Yearbook, Vol 14. Hardback: £61.50. ISBN 0-226-06617-7. University of Chicago Press.

Borrows, Jane–Current Issues in Securitisation. Special Reports. Hardback: £150.00. ISBN 0-7520-0585-5. Sweet & Maxwell.

Bouchet-Saulnier, Francois–Practical Guide to Humanitarian Law-1st English Language Ed. Hardback: £65.00. ISBN 0-7425-1062-X. Paperback: £27.00. ISBN 0-7425-1063-8. Rowman & Littlefield Publishers.

Bourne, C; Popat, P.–Guide to Civil Advocacy. 2nd Ed. Paperback: £19.95. ISBN 1-85941-562-8. Cavendish Publishing Ltd.

Bowers, John; Brown, Damian and Mead, Geoffrey–Employment Tribunal Practice and Procedure. 3rd Ed. Hardback: £75.00. ISBN 0-421-73950-9. Sweet & Maxwell.

Bowers, John–Employment Law and Human Rights. Special Reports. Hardback: £125.00. ISBN 0-421-73960-6. Sweet & Maxwell.

Bowers, John–Practice Notes on Termination of Employment. 4th Ed. Practice Notes. Paperback: £15.95. ISBN 1-85941-578-4. Cavendish Publishing Ltd.

Bowtle, Graeme; McGuinness, Kevin–Law of Ship Mortgages. Llyod's Shipping Law Library. Hardback: £175.00. ISBN 1-85978-997-8. LLP Professional Publishing.

Boyle, Fiona; Capps, Deveral; Plowden, Philip; Sandford, Clare–Practical Guide to Lawyering Skills. Paperback: £22.95. ISBN 1-85941-420-6. Cavendish Publishing Ltd.

Bradley, Ken–Point of Law: Health & Safety Act Explained. The Point of Law. Paperback: £25.00. ISBN 0-11-702810-X. The Stationery Office Books.

Bradshaw, Joseph–House Buying, Selling and Conveyancing. CD-ROM (software). ISBN 1-902646-84-3. Law Pack Publishing.

Brambley, S.–Pervasive and Core Topics. 9th Ed. Legal Practice Course. Paperback: £23.50. ISBN 0-85308-720-2. Jordans.

Bratton, William W.–Corporate Law and Economics. International Library of Essays in Law and Legal Theory (second Series). Hardback: £100.00. ISBN 0-7546-2086-7. Dartmouth.

Brennan, Lord; Blair, William–Bullen and Leake and Jacob's Precedents of Pleadings. 14th Ed. Hardback: £265.00. ISBN 0-421-73190-7. Sweet & Maxwell.

Brennan, Niamh; Hennessy, John–Forensic Accounting. Hardback: £149.00. ISBN 1-85800-203-6. Round Hall Ltd.

Bridge, Michael; Stevens, Robert–Cross-border Security and Insolvency. Oxford Law Colloquium Series. Hardback: £65.00. ISBN 0-19-829921-4. Oxford University Press.

Bridgeman, Jo; Monk, Daniel–Feminist Perspectives on Child Law. Paperback: £19.95. ISBN 1-85941-525-3. Cavendish Publishing Ltd.

Brinson, Dianne; Dara-Abrams, Benay; Dara-Abrams, Drew; Masek, Jennifer; McDunn, Ruth; White, Bebo–Exploring E-commerce and Internet Law. Advanced Website Architecture. Paperback: £35.99. ISBN 0-13-085898-6. Prentice Hall PTR.

Brockman, Joan–Gender in the Legal Profession: Fitting or Breaking the Mould. Law and Society. Hardback: £71.50. ISBN 0-7748-0834-9. University of British Columbia Press.

Brown, Damian; McMellen, Jeremy; Hendy, John; Wedderburn of Charlton, Lord–UK and EU Employee Consultation. Looseleaf/ring bound: £250.00. ISBN 0-421-70580-9. Sweet & Maxwell.

Brown, Ian–Conflict of Laws: Textbook. 2nd Ed. Old Bailey Press Textbooks. Paperback: £14.95. ISBN 1-85836-400-0. Old Bailey Press.

Brown, Travis–Popular Patents. Paperback: £15.20. ISBN 1-57886-010-5. Scarecrow Press.

Brownlie, Ian; Crawford, James; Lowe, Vaughan–British Year Book of International Law: Vol 70. 1999. Hardback: £110.00. ISBN 0-19-829914-1. Hardback: £110.00. ISBN 0-19-829914-1. Oxford University Press.

Bruce, Martha–Rights and Duties of Directors. 4th Ed. Paperback: £75.00. ISBN 0-406-94029-0. Butterworths Tolley.

Brunnee, Jutta; Hey, Ellen–Yearbook of International Environmental Law: Vol 10. 1999. Hardback: £110.00. ISBN 0-19-924278-X. Oxford University Press.

Brunnee, Jutta; Hey, Ellen–Yearbook of International Environmental Law: Vol 11. 2000. Yearbook of International Environmental Law. Hardback: £115.00. ISBN 0-19-924708-0. Oxford University Press.

Buck, A.R.; McLaren, John; Wright, Nancy E.–Land and Freedom-Law, Property Rights and the British Diaspora. Hardback: £45.00. ISBN 0-7546-2209-6. Ashgate Publishing Limited.

Bull, Ray–Children and the Law. Essential Readings in Developmental Psychology. Hardback: £60.00. ISBN 0-631-22682-6. Paperback: £15.99. ISBN 0-631-22683-4. Blackwell Publishers.

Bullis, Ronald–Sacred Calling, Secular Accountability. Hardback: £35.95. ISBN 1-58391-061-1. Paperback: £14.95. ISBN 1-58391-062-X. Brunner-Routledge.

Bunker, Matthew D.–Critiquing Free Speech. Hardback: £33.50. ISBN 0-8058-3751-5. Lawrence Erlbaum Associates, Inc.

Burca, Grainne de; Weiler, Joseph H.H.–European Court of Justice. Collected Courses of the Academy of European Law. Hardback: £40.00. ISBN 0-19-924602-5. Paperback: £16.99. ISBN 0-19-924601-7. Oxford University Press.

Burgess, Andrew–Tolley's Charity Investigations. Paperback: £37.95. ISBN 0-7545-0219-8. Tolley Publishing.

Burnett-Hall, Richard–Environmental Law: 1st Supplement. Paperback: £40.00. ISBN 0-421-59410-1. Sweet & Maxwell.

Burrows, Noreen–Devolution. Modern Legal Studies. Paperback: £23.95. ISBN 0-421-72280-0. Sweet & Maxwell.

Burton, Frank; Nelson-Jones, Rodney–Clinical Negligence Case Law. Hardback: £120.00. ISBN 0-406-91959-3. Butterworths Law.

Burton, William C.–Burton's Legal Thesaurus. £21.99. ISBN 0-07-137309-8. McGraw-Hill Publishing Company.

Bussiere, Elizabeth–(Dis)entitling the Poor. Paperback: £15.95. ISBN 0-271-01602-7. Penn State University Press.

Buti, Marco; Sestito, Paolo; Wijkander, Hans–Taxation, Welfare and the Crisis of Unemployment in Europe. Hardback: £55.00. ISBN 1-84064-511-3. Edward Elgar.

Butler, William E.–Russian-English Legal Dictionary. Hardback. ISBN 1-57105-194-5. Hardback: £116.99. ISBN 1-57105-194-5. Transnational Publishers, Inc.

Butt, Peter; Castle, Richard–Modern Legal Drafting. Hardback: £40.00. ISBN 0-521-80217-2. Paperback: £15.95. ISBN 0-521-00186-2. Cambridge University Press.

Butt, P.–Conveyancing. Hardback: £23.95. ISBN 0-85308-718-0. Jordans.

Byrne, John; Glover, Leigh; Martinez, Celia–Environmental Justice. Energy and Environmental Policy Series, Vol 8. Paperback: £22.95. ISBN 0-7658-0751-3. Paperback: £22.95. ISBN 0-7658-0751-3. Transaction Publishers.

Byrne, Raymond; Binchy, William–Annual Review of Irish Law: 1998. Hardback: £115.00. ISBN 1-85800-124-2. Round Hall Ltd.

Byrne, Raymond; Mccutcheon, J.Paul–Byrne & Mccutcheon: the Irish Legal System. 4th Ed. Paperback: £60.00. ISBN 1-85475-286-3. Butterworths Law.

Cahill, Mia L.–Social Construction of Sexual Harassment Law. Law, Justice and Power. Hardback: £45.00. ISBN 0-7546-2120-0. Dartmouth.

Caminos, Hugo–Law of the Sea. The Library of Essays in International Law, No. 3. Hardback: £110.00. ISBN 1-84014-090-9. Hardback: £94.50. ISBN 1-84014-090-9. Ashgate Publishing Limited.

Campbell, Euan; Rowe, Bernie–Practical Guide to Motor Accident Claims. Paperback: £85.00. ISBN 0-406-91780-9. Butterworths Law.

Campbell, Gordon–Heritage Law and Policy. Paperback: £55.00. ISBN 1-902558-27-8. Palladian Law Publishing Ltd.

Cane, Peter; Gardner, John –Relating to Responsibility. Hardback: £40.00. ISBN 1-84113-210-1. Hart Publishing.

Cannon–Irish Nutshells: Land Law. Paperback: £11.95. ISBN 1-85800-170-6. Round Hall Ltd.

Cartwright, A.L.–Return of the Peasant. Hardback: £50.00. ISBN 0-7546-2166-9. Ashgate Publishing Limited.

Cartwright, Peter–Consumer Protection and the Criminal Law-Law and Policy in the United Kingdom. Hardback: £45.00. ISBN 0-521-59080-9. Cambridge University Press.

Carty, Hazel–An Analysis of the Economic Torts. Hardback: £40.00. ISBN 0-19-825743-0. Oxford University Press.

Cassell, E.–Law of Trusts. Suggested Solutions. £6.95. ISBN 1-85836-396-9. Old Bailey Press.

Cassese, Antonio–International Law. 2nd Ed. Paperback: £21.99. ISBN 0-19-829998-2. Oxford University Press.

Castellino, Joshua–International Law of Self-determination: the Interplay of the Politics of Territorial Possession with Formulations of Post-colonial national Identity. Developments in International Law, 38. Hardback: £57.50. ISBN 90-411-1409-2. Martinus Nijhoff Publishers.

Catchpole, Mark–Employee Share Schemes. Paperback: £48.00. ISBN 1-902558-19-7. Palladian Law Publishing Ltd.

CCH Tax Handbook 2001-2002: Vol 2. Paperback: £40.00. ISBN 0-86325-562-0. Croner CCH Group Ltd.

Chandler, Peter–Waud's Employment Law 2000-2001. 13th Ed. Paperback: £25.00. ISBN 0-7494-3137-7. Kogan Page.

Chanock, Martin–Making of South African Legal Culture 1902-1936. Hardback: £60.00. ISBN 0-521-79156-1. Cambridge University Press.

Chapman, Alison–Tolley's Tax and the Business Car 2001-02. 5th Ed. Floppy disk: £44.95. ISBN 0-7545-1191-X. Tolley Publishing.

Chapman, Michael D.–Waterlow's Solicitors' & Barristers' Directory: 2001. Hardback: £59.00. ISBN 1-85783-906-4. Waterlow Professional Publishing.

Chappelle, Diane–Land Law 5th Ed. Foundation Studies in Law Series. Paperback: £26.99. ISBN 0-582-43818-7. Longman Higher Education.

Chaterjee, S.K.–International Engineering and Construction Contracts. Hardback: £40.00. ISBN 0-419-21670-7. Spon Press.

Chatterjee, Charles–Methods of Research in Law. 2nd Ed. Paperback: £9.95. ISBN 1-85836-386-1. Old Bailey Press.

Chatterton, David–Practice Notes on Wills. Practice Notes. Paperback: £15.95. ISBN 1-85941-663-2. Cavendish Publishing Ltd.

Cheatle, Kelvin–Mastering Human Resource Management. Palgrave Masters Series (Business). Paperback: £13.99. ISBN 0-333-79280-7. Palgrave, formerly Macmillan Press.

Chen, Lung-chu–An Introduction to Contemporary International Law. Hardback: £40.00. ISBN 0-300-08454-4. Paperback: £20.00. ISBN 0-300-08477-3. Yale University Press.

Chesterman, Simon–Just War or Just Peace? Oxford Monographs in International Law. Hardback: £40.00. ISBN 0-19-924337-9. Oxford University Press.

Chin, Gabriel J.–Immigration and the Constitution. Hardback: £150.00. ISBN 0-8153-3346-3. Garland Publishing, Inc.

Chinkin, Christine; Butegwa, Florence–Gender Mainstreaming in Legal and Constitutional Affairs-A Reference Manual for Governments and Other Stakeholders. Paperback: £8.99. ISBN 0-85092-653-X. Commonwealth Secretariat.

Christian, Charles–Virtual Lawyer-marketing, Selling and Delivering Legal Services Online. Paperback: £45.00. ISBN 0-406-92401-5. Butterworths.

Christie, Sarah–Inchoate Crimes. Greens Practice Library. Hardback: £65.00. ISBN 0-414-01390-5. W.Green & Son.

Christodoulidis, Emilios; Veitch, Scott–Lethe's Law. Hardback: £25.00. ISBN 1-84113-109-1. Hart Publishing.

Chuah, Jason C.T.–Statutes and Conventions on Private International Law. 2nd Ed. Paperback: £15.95. ISBN 1-85941-548-2. Cavendish Publishing Ltd.

Chuah, Jason–Law of International Trade. 2nd Ed. Paperback: £22.95. ISBN 0-421-74650-5. Sweet & Maxwell.

Clarke, Giles–Clarke: Offshore Tax Planning. 8th Ed. Paperback: £89.95. ISBN 0-406-93909-8. Butterworths Tolley.

Clayton, Patricia–Law for the Small Business. 10th Ed. Business Enterprise Guides. Paperback: £14.99. ISBN 0-7494-3614-X. Kogan Page.

Clayton, Richard; Tomlinson, Hugh–Fair Trial Rights. Paperback: £27.50. ISBN 0-19-924634-3. Oxford University Press.

Clayton, Richard; Tomlinson, Hugh–Privacy and Freedom of Expression. Paperback: £27.50. ISBN 0-19-924638-6. Oxford University Press.

Cleland, Alison; Sutherland, Elaine E.–Children's Rights in Scotland. 2nd Ed. Paperback: £30.00. ISBN 0-414-01349-2. W. Green & Son.

Clout, Imogen–Matrimonial Lawyer. 2nd Ed. Paperback: £29.50. ISBN 0-85308-736-9. Family Law.

Coates, Ross; Attwell, Nicholas–Practice Notes on Conveyancing. Practice Notes. Paperback: £15.95. ISBN 1-85941-453-2. Cavendish Publishing Ltd.

Coates, S.–Law of Tort. Suggested Solutions. £6.95. ISBN 1-85836-395-0. Old Bailey Press.

Cohen, David and Pett, David–New Employee Share Incentives. Special Reports. Hardback: £150.00. ISBN 0-421-72310-6. Sweet & Maxwell.

Cohen, Steve–Immigration Controls, the Family and the Welfare State. Paperback: £18.95. ISBN 1-85302-723-5. Jessica Kingsley Publishers.

Colbey, Richard–Practice Notes on Residential Tenancies. Practice Notes. Paperback: £15.95. ISBN 1-85941-452-4. Cavendish Publishing Ltd.

Cole, George; Gertz, Marc; Bunger, Amy–Criminal Justice System. Paperback: £30.99. ISBN 0-534-59472-7. Wadsworth.

Coleman, Jules L.–Hart's Postscript: Essays on the Postscript to The Concept of Law. 2nd Ed. Hardback: £40.00. ISBN 0-19-829908-7. Paperback: £14.99. ISBN 0-19-924362-X. Oxford University Press.

Coleman, Jules–Practice of Principle. Hardback: £25.00. ISBN 0-19-829814-5. Oxford University Press.

Coleman, Martin; Grenfell, Michael–Competition Act 1998: Law and Practice. Paperback: £45.00. ISBN 0-19-829956-7. Oxford University Press.

Coles, Joanne–Law of the European Union: Textbook. 3rd Ed. Old Bailey Press Textbooks. Paperback: £14.95. ISBN 1-85836-412-4. Old Bailey Press.

Collar, Neil–Green's Scottish Planning Factbook. Greens Professional Publishing. Looseleaf/ring bound: £149.00. ISBN 0-414-01381-6. W. Green & Son.

Collier–Conflict of Laws. 3rd Ed. Paperback: £27.95. ISBN 0-521-78781-5. Cambridge University Press.

Collins, Hugh; Ewing, Keith; McColgan, Aileen–Labour Law. Hardback: £50.00. ISBN 1-84113-235-7. Paperback: £25.00. ISBN 1-84113-236-5. Hart Publishing.

Collins, Matthew–Law of Defamation and the Internet. Hardback: £95.00. ISBN 0-19-924468-5. Oxford University Press.

Collins, Scott; Colville, Iain; Pengelly, Sarah–Guide to the Greater London Authority Act. Hardback: £48.00. ISBN 0-421-72700-4. Sweet & Maxwell.

Colman, Anthony; Lyon, Victor; Hopkins, Philippa–Practice and Procedure of the Commercial Court. 5th Ed. Lloyd's Commercial Law Library. Hardback: £150.00. ISBN 1-859-78300-7. LLP Professional Publishing.

Company Formation and Resolutions. CD-ROM (software). ISBN 1-902646-83-5. Law Pack Publishing.

Conant, Michael–Constitutional Structure and Purposes. Contributions in Legal Studies, No 98. Hardback: £58.95. ISBN 0-313-31669-4. Greenwood Press.

Constitutional Law. Suggested Solutions. £6.95. ISBN 1-85836-389-6. Old Bailey Press.

Convery, Jane–Constitutional Law Basics. 2nd Ed. Greens Law Basics. Paperback: £9.95. ISBN 0-414-01434-0. W. Green & Son.

Conveyancing Statutes: 2001. Paperback: £24.00. ISBN 0-414-01427-8. W.Green & Son.

Cook, Louise; Stilton, Ruth–Commercial Conveyancing. Legal Support Practitioner Series-the Law Society's NVQ in Legal Practice. Paperback: £25.00. ISBN 1-85941-447-8. Cavendish Publishing Ltd.

Cook, Michael–Cook on Costs 2001-a Guide to Legal Remuneration in Civil Contentious and Non-contentious Business. Paperback: £58.00. ISBN 0-406-94454-7. Butterworths Law.

Cooke, John–Law of Tort 5th Ed. Foundation Studies in Law Series. Paperback: £25.99. ISBN 0-582-43819-5. Longman.

Cooke, Julian; Young, Timothy; et al–Voyage Charters. 2nd Ed. Lloyd's Shipping Law Library. Hardback: £275.00. ISBN 1-85978-599-9. LLP Professional Publishing.

Coombes, A–Land Law. Suggested Solutions. £6.95. ISBN 1-85836-394-2. Old Bailey Press.

Cornish, Graham P.–Copyright: Interpreting the Law for Libraries and Information Services 3rd Rev Ed. The Library Association Copyright Guides. Paperback: £19.95. ISBN 1-85604-409-2. Library Association Publishing.

Cotterrell, Roger–Sociological Perspectives on Law: Vols 1 &2, Classical Foundations / Contemporary Debates. International Library of Essays in Law and Legal Theory (Second Series). Hardback: £195.00. ISBN 0-7546-2128-6. Dartmouth.

Cousins, Edward; Clarke, Ian–Law of Mortgages. 2nd Ed. Property and Conveyancing Library. Hardback: £165.00. ISBN 0-421-52950-4. Sweet & Maxwell.

Covey, Anne–Workplace Law Advisor. Paperback: £12.99. ISBN 0-7382-0374-2. Perseus Books.

Cracknell, D.G.–Company Law. Cracknell's Statutes Series. Paperback: £9.95. ISBN 1-85836-375-6. Old Bailey Press.

Cracknell, D.G.–Contract, Tort and Remedies. 2nd Ed. Cracknell's Statutes Series. Paperback: £9.95. ISBN 1-85836-377-2. Old Bailey Press.

Cracknell, D.G.–English Legal System. 3rd Ed. Cracknell's Statutes Series. Paperback: £9.95. ISBN 1-85836-378-0. Old Bailey Press.

Cracknell, D.G.–Equity and Trusts. 3rd Ed. Cracknell's Statutes Series. Paperback: £9.95. ISBN 1-85836-379-9. Old Bailey Press.

Cracknell, D.G.–Evidence. 4th Ed. Cracknell's Statutes Series. Paperback: £9.95. ISBN 1-85836-380-2. Old Bailey Press.

Cracknell, D.G.–Land: the Law of Real Property. 4th Ed. Cracknell's Statutes Series. Paperback: £9.95. ISBN 1-85836-381-0. Old Bailey Press.

Cracknell, D.G.–Obligations: the Law of Tort Textbook. 3rd Ed. Old Bailey Press Textbooks. Paperback: £14.95. ISBN 1-85836-415-9. Old Bailey Press.

Cracknell, D.G.–Obligations. 3rd Ed. Old Bailey Press Textbooks. Paperback: £14.95. ISBN 1-85836-414-0. Old Bailey Press.

Cracknell, D.G.–Succession: the Law of Wills and Estates. 4th Ed. Cracknell's Statutes Series. Paperback: £9.95. ISBN 1-85836-382-9. Old Bailey Press.

Craig, Victor; Miller, Kenneth–Employment Law: a Student Guide. Paperback: £23.95. ISBN 0-414-01450-2. W.Green & Son.

Cranston; Blair, William–Banks, Liabilities and Risk 3rd Ed. Hardback: £140.00. ISBN 1-85978-509-3. LLP Professional Publishing.

Crawford, David–Building Regulations and Your Business. And Your Business. Paperback: £17.99. ISBN 0-11-702709-X. The Stationery Office Books.

Crawford, James; Lowe, Vaughan–British Year Book of International Law: Vol 71. 2000. Hardback: £115.00. ISBN 0-19-924692-0. Oxford University Press Inc, USA.

Crime, State and Citizen. Hardback: £25.00. ISBN 1-872870-98-8. Waterside Press.

Criminal Law. Suggested Solutions. £6.95. ISBN 1-85836-391-8. Old Bailey Press.

Criminal Statutes: 2001. Paperback: £33.00. ISBN 0-414-01426-X. W.Green & Son.

Croall, Hazel–Understanding White Collar Crime Revised and Updated. Crime and Justice. Hardback: £50.00. ISBN 0-335-20428-7. Paperback: £16.99. ISBN 0-335-20427-9. Open University Press.

Croner's A-Z Essentials: Health and Safety. A-Z Essentials. Paperback: £25.00. ISBN 1-85524-609-0. Croner Publications.

Croner's A-Z Essentials: Managing People. A-Z Essentials. Paperback: £25.00. ISBN 1-85524-585-X. Croner Publications.

Croner's School Governor's Legal Guide. Paperback: £25.00. ISBN 1-85524-586-8. Croner Publications.

Cull, Lesley-Ann; Roche, Jeremy–Law and Social Work: Contemporary Issues for Practice. Paperback: £14.50. ISBN 0-333-94587-5. Palgrave, formerly Macmillan Press.

Curran, Patrick–Personal Injury Pleadings. 2nd Ed. Hardback: CD-ROM: £140.00. ISBN 0-421-72990-2. Sweet & Maxwell.

Curran, Susan–Land Use and Planning and Your Business. And Your Business. Paperback: £17.99. ISBN 0-11-702705-7. The Stationery Office Books.

Curzon, L.–Dictionary of Law. 6th Ed. Paperback: £26.99. ISBN 0-582-43809-8. Longman.

Curzon, L.B.–Q&A Jurisprudence. Questions and Answers. Paperback: £9.95. ISBN 1-85941-623-3. Cavendish Publishing Ltd.

Cuthbert, Mike–Q&A on European Union Law. Questions and Answers. Paperback: £9.95. ISBN 1-85941-418-4. Cavendish Publishing Ltd.

C.I.P.A Guide to the Patents Acts 5th Ed. Intellectual Property Library. Hardback: £310.00. ISBN 0-421-74950-4. Sweet & Maxwell.

D'arcy, Leo; Murray, Carol and Cleave, Barbara–Schmitthoff's Export Trade: the Law and Practice of International Trade. 10th Ed. International Student Edition. Paperback: £14.95. ISBN 0-421-60690-8. Hardback: £65.00. ISBN 0-421-61950-3. Sweet & Maxwell.

D'Costa, Roland–Executorship and Administration of Estates. Practice Notes. Paperback: £15.95. ISBN 1-85941-459-1. Cavendish Publishing Ltd.

Dakin, James; Beattie-Jones, Vanessa; Rabinowitz, Gavin–Loan and Security Documents. 2nd Ed. Hardback: £80.00. ISBN 0-85308-592-7. Jordans.

Darbyshire, Penny–Nutshells-English Legal System. Nutshells. Paperback: £5.50. ISBN 0-421-74280-1. Sweet & Maxwell.

Dashwood, Alan; Johnston, Angus–Future of the Judicial System of the European Union. Hardback: £35.00. ISBN 1-84113-241-1. Hart Publishing.

Dashwood, Alan; Ward, Angela; Spencer, John; Hillion, Christopher–Cambridge Yearbook of European Legal Studies: Vol 3, 2001. Hardback: £65.00. ISBN 1-84113-240-3. Hart Publishing.

Dashwood, Alan–EC External Relations Law in the Post-Maastricht Era. Hardback: £95.00. ISBN 0-421-59070-X. Sweet & Maxwell.

Daugherty, Richard F.–Special Education. Hardback: £83.95. ISBN 0-89789-726-9. Bergin & Garvey.

Davidson, Fraser P.–Arbitration. Hardback: £180.00. ISBN 0-414-01104-X. W.Green & Son.

Davies, Gareth–European Union Internal Market Law. Paperback: £30.95. ISBN 1-85941-688-8. Cavendish Publishing Ltd.

Davies, Karen–Understanding EU Law. Paperback: £12.95. ISBN 1-85941-611-X. Cavendish Publishing Ltd.

Davies, Margaret; Naffine, Ngaire–Are Persons Property? Applied Legal Philosophy. Hardback: £50.00. ISBN 0-7546-2032-8. Ashgate Publishing Limited.

Davis, Anthony C.R.–Tolley's Taxation on Corporate Insolvency. 4th Ed. Paperback: £46.95. ISBN 1-86012-325-2. Tolley Publishing.

Davis, Nigel; Smith, Graham; Sydenham, Angela–Agricultural Clients Precedent Handbook. Hardback: £70.00. ISBN 0-85308-386-X. Jordans.

de Burca, Grainne; Scott, Joanne–EU and the WTO. Hardback: £35.00. ISBN 1-84113-199-7. Hart Publishing.

de Burca, G.; Scott, J.–Constitution of the European Union. Butterworths Law in Context. Paperback: £16.95. ISBN 0-406-90579-7. Butterworths Law.

De Cruz, Peter–Comparative Healthcare Law. Paperback: £32.95. ISBN 1-85941-588-1. Cavendish Publishing Ltd.

De Than, Claire; Shorts, Edwin–Human Rights Law in the UK. 2nd Ed. Paperback: £26.95. ISBN 0-421-75460-5. Sweet & Maxwell.

De Wilde, Robin–Facts and Figures 2000. 5th Ed. Paperback: £28.00. ISBN 0-421-73760-3. Sweet & Maxwell.

De Wilde, Robin–Facts and Figures 2001 6th Ed. Paperback: £35.00. ISBN 0-421-82660-6. Sweet & Maxwell.

Deeks, Sarah–Tax Practice Management. Paperback: £61.95. ISBN 0-7545-0470-0. Tolley Publishing.

Delaney, Patrick; Hopkins, Debra–Wiley CPA Examination Review 2001: Business Law and Professional Responsibilities. Paperback: £29.50. ISBN 0-471-39791-1. John Wiley and Sons.

Dickson, Julie–Evaluation and Legal Theory. Hardback: £22.00. ISBN 1-84113-184-9. Paperback: £10.00. ISBN 1-84113-081-8. Hart Publishing.

Dillon, Sara–International Trade and Economic Law and the European Union. Paperback: £25.00. ISBN 1-84113-113-X. Hart Publishing.

DiMatteo, Larry A.–Equitable Law of Contracts-Standards and Principles. Hardback: £100.99. ISBN 1-57105-173-2. Transnational Publishers, Inc.

Dine, Janet–Company Law 4th Ed. Palgrave Law Masters. Paperback: £13.99. ISBN 0-333-94801-7. Palgrave, formerly Macmillan Press.

Dinstein, Yoram–War, Aggression and Self-defence. Hardback: £70.00. ISBN 0-521-79344-0. Paperback: £24.95. ISBN 0-521-79758-6. Cambridge University Press.

Dispute Settlement Reports 1998: Vol IX. World Trade Organization Dispute Settlement Reports. Hardback: £75.00. ISBN 0-521-80100-1. Paperback: £30.00. ISBN 0-521-80505-8. Cambridge University Press.

Dispute Settlement Reports 1998: Vol VIII. World Trade Organization Dispute Settlement Reports. Paperback: £30.00. ISBN 0-521-80504-X. Cambridge University Press.

Dispute Settlement Reports 1998: Vol VII. World Trade Organization Dispute Settlement Reports. Paperback: £30.00. ISBN 0-521-80503-1. Cambridge University Press.

Dispute Settlement Reports 1998. World Trade Organization Dispute Settlement Reports. Hardback: £75.00. ISBN 0-521-80096-X. Paperback: £30.00. ISBN 0-521-80501-5. Cambridge University Press.

Dispute Settlement Reports 1999: Volume III. World Trade Organization Dispute Settlement Reports. Hardback: £75.00. ISBN 0-521-80322-5. Cambridge University Press.

Dispute Settlement Reports 1999: Volume II. World Trade Organization Dispute Settlement Reports. Hardback: £75.00. ISBN 0-521-80321-7. Paperback: £30.00. ISBN 0-521-00564-7. Cambridge University Press.

Dispute Settlement Reports 1999: Volume I. World Trade Organization Dispute Settlement Reports. Hardback: £75.00. ISBN 0-521-80320-9. Paperback: £30.00. ISBN 0-521-00562-0. Cambridge University Press.

Dispute Settlement Reports 1999. World Trade Organization Dispute Settlement Reports. Paperback: £30.00. ISBN 0-521-00565-5. Cambridge University Press.

Dixon, Martin–Q&A Equity and Trusts. 3rd Ed. Questions and Answers. Paperback: £9.95. ISBN 1-85941-624-1. Cavendish Publishing Ltd.

Dodds, Malcolm–Family Law Textbook. 3rd Ed. Old Bailey Press Textbooks. Paperback: £14.95. ISBN 1-85836-408-6. Old Bailey Press.

Doherty, Michael–Jurisprudence. 2nd Ed. Old Bailey Press Textbooks. Paperback: £14.95. ISBN 1-85836-409-4. Old Bailey Press.

Dolton, Alan; Saunders, Glyn–Tolley's Tax Cases: 2001. Paperback: £59.95. ISBN 0-7545-1161-8. Tolley Publishing.

Dolton, Alan; Wareham, Robert–Tolley's Vat Cases: 2001. Paperback: £89.95. ISBN 0-7545-1159-6. Tolley Publishing.

Donohue, Laura K.–Counter-terrorist Law and Emergency Powers in the United Kingdom, 1922-2000. New Directions in Irish History. Hardback: £35.00. ISBN 0-7165-2687-5. Irish Academic Press.

Doolan, Brian–Lawless V Ireland (1957-1961): the First Case Before the European Court of Human Rights. Hardback: £50.00. ISBN 0-7546-2169-3. Dartmouth.

Doonan, Elmer–Drafting. Legal Skills. Paperback: £12.95. ISBN 1-85941-486-9. Cavendish Publishing Ltd.

Dorsen, Norman; Gifford, Prosser–Democracy and the Rule of Law. Hardback: £50.50. ISBN 1-56802-599-8. Congressional Quarterly Inc.

Douglas-Lewis, N.–Law and Governance. Paperback: £38.95. ISBN 1-85941-547-4. Cavendish Publishing Ltd.

Douglas, Gillian–Introduction to Family Law. Clarendon Law Series. Paperback: £14.99. ISBN 0-19-876541-X. Clarendon Press.

Douglas, John; Olshaker, Mark–Cases That Haunt Us. Hardback: £18.99. ISBN 0-684-85158-X. Simon & Schuster.

Drahos, Peter; Blakeney, Michael–IP in Biodiversity and Agriculture: Regulating the Biosphere. Perspectives on Intellectual Property, 9. Paperback: £45.00. ISBN 0-421-76630-1. Sweet & Maxwell.

Dreyfuss, Rochelle; Zimmerman, Diane L.; First, Harry–Expanding the Boundaries of Intellectual Property. Hardback: £40.00. ISBN 0-19-829857-9. Oxford University Press.

Dugdale, Anthony–Clerk & Lindsell on Torts. 18th Ed. Common Law Library. Hardback: £220.00. ISBN 0-421-69340-1. Sweet & Maxwell.

Dummett, Sir Michael–On Immigration and Refugees. Thinking in Action. Hardback: £30.00. ISBN 0-415-22707-0. Paperback: £7.99. ISBN 0-415-22708-9. Routledge, an imprint of Taylor & Francis Books Ltd.

Duxbury, Neil–Jurists and Judges. Paperback: £15.00. ISBN 1-84113-204-7. Hart Publishing.

Dyer, Joel–Perpetual Prisoner Machine. Paperback: £12.99. ISBN 0-8133-3870-0. Westview Press.

Earnshaw, Jill; Cooper, Cary L.–Stress and Employer Liability. Developing Practice. Paperback: £18.99. ISBN 0-85292-878-5. Chartered Institute of Personnel and Development (CIPD).

Economides, Kim; Betten, Lammy; Bridge, John; Tettenborn, Andrew; Shrubsall, Vivien–Fundamental Values. Hardback: £35.00. ISBN 1-84113-118-0. Hart Publishing.

Edwards, Martin; Malone, Michael–Tolley's Equal Opportunities Handbook. 2nd Ed. Paperback: £49.95. ISBN 0-7545-1395-5. Tolley Publishing.

Eeckhout, Piet; Tridimas, Takis–Yearbook of European Law: Vol 19. 1999/2000. Hardback: £110.00. ISBN 0-19-829939-7. Oxford University Press.

Egan, Michelle–Constructing a European Market-Standards, Regulation, and Governance. Hardback: £40.00. ISBN 0-19-924405-7. Oxford University Press.

Ehlermann, Claus-Dieter; Atanasiu, Isabella–European Competition Law Annual 2000: Vol 5. Hardback: £75.00. ISBN 1-84113-242-X. Hart Publishing.

Ehlermann, Claus-Dieter; Everson, Michelle–European Competition Law Annual 1999: Vol 4. Hardback: £75.00. ISBN 1-84113-224-1. Hart Publishing.

Ehrlich, Eugen–Fundamental Principles of the Sociology of Law. Paperback: £30.50. ISBN 0-7658-0701-7. Transaction Publishers.

Eisgruber, Christopher L.–Constitutional Self-government. Hardback: £30.95. ISBN 0-674-00608-9. Harvard University Press.

Ellig, Jerry–Dynamic Competition and Public Policy-Technology, Innovation, and Antitrust Issues. Hardback: £40.00. ISBN 0-521-78250-3. Cambridge University Press.

Elliot, Mark–Constitutional Foundations of Judicial Review. Hardback: £30.00. ISBN 1-84113-180-6. Hart Publishing.

Elliott, Catherine; Quinn, Frances–Contract Law. Paperback: £15.99. ISBN 0-582-43812-8. Longman Higher Education.

Elliott, Catherine; Quinn, Frances–Tort Law 3rd Ed. Paperback: £15.99. ISBN 0-582-43811-X. Longman Higher Education.

Elliott, Catherine–French Criminal Law. Hardback: £45.00. ISBN 1-903240-31-X. Paperback: £20.00. ISBN 1-903240-30-1. Willan Publishing.

Ellison, Robin; Rae, Maggie–Family Breakdown and Pensions. 2nd Ed. Paperback: £40.00. ISBN 0-406-91310-2. Butterworths.

Emmerson, Ben; Ashworth, Andrew–Human Rights and Criminal Justice. Paperback: £65.00. ISBN 0-421-63910-5. Sweet & Maxwell.

Endicott, Timothy–Vagueness in Law. Hardback: £40.00. ISBN 0-19-826840-8. Oxford University Press.

Engelman, Philip–Commercial Judicial Review. Hardback: £98.00. ISBN 0-421-62620-8. Sweet & Maxwell.

Epp, John–Building on the Decade of Disclosure in Criminal Procedure. Paperback: £48.40. ISBN 1-85941-659-4. Cavendish Publishing Ltd.

Epstein, Lee; Segal, Jeffrey A.; Spaeth, Harold J.; Walker, Thomas G.–Supreme Court Compendium. Hardback: £71.50. ISBN 1-56802-592-0. Congressional Quarterly Inc.

Evans, Carolyn–Freedom of Religion Under the European Convention on Human Rights. Oxford European Human Rights Series. Hardback: £40.00. ISBN 0-19-924364-6. Oxford University Press.

Evans, Judith; Templeman, Lord–Intellectual Property: Textbook. 1st Ed. Old Bailey Press Textbooks. Paperback: £14.95. ISBN 1-85836-355-1. Old Bailey Press.

Evans, Judith–English and European Legal Systems: Textbook. 2nd Ed. Old Bailey Press Textbooks. Paperback: £14.95. ISBN 1-85836-405-1. Old Bailey Press.

Evans, Judith–Law of International Trade Textbook . 3rd Ed. Old Bailey Press Textbooks. Paperback: £14.95. ISBN 1-85836-411-6. Old Bailey Press.

Evans, J.–English Legal System. Suggested Solutions. £6.95. ISBN 1-85836-392-6. Old Bailey Press.

Everall, Mark; Hamilton, Carolyn; Lowe, Nigel–International Child Abduction-law and Practice. Paperback (C format): £39.95. ISBN 0-406-00541-9. Butterworths Law.

Ewing, Keith David; Gearty, Conor Anthony–Struggle for Civil Liberties. Paperback: £14.99. ISBN 0-19-876251-8. Clarendon Press.

Facilities Management Handbook. Looseleaf in binder: £125.00. ISBN 0-7545-0230-9. Tolley Publishing.

Fallon, Richard H.–Implementing the Constitution. Hardback: £23.95. ISBN 0-674-00464-7. Harvard University Press.

Federal Regulatory Directory 10th Ed. Hardback: £130.50. ISBN 1-56802-503-3. CQ Press.

Fellows, R.F.; Fenn, Peter–JCT Standard Form of Building Contract 1998 Edition. Paperback: £18.99. ISBN 0-333-92535-1. Palgrave, formerly Macmillan Press.

Fenwick, Helen–Civil Liberties and Human Rights. 3rd Ed. Paperback: £24.95. ISBN 1-85941-493-1. Cavendish Publishing Ltd.

Fenwick, Helen–Q&A Civil Liberties and Human Rights. 2nd Ed. Questions and Answers. Paperback: £9.95. ISBN 1-85941-276-9. Cavendish Publishing Ltd.

Ferejohn, John; Rakove, Jack N.; Riley, Jonathan–Constitutional Culture and Democratic Rule. Murphy Institute Studies in Political Economy. Hardback: £47.50. ISBN 0-521-79022-0. Paperback: £17.95. ISBN 0-521-79370-X. Cambridge University Press.

Ferran, Eilis; Goodhart, Charles–Regulating Financial Services and Markets in the 21st Century. Hardback: £40.00. ISBN 1-84113-279-9. Hart Publishing.

Ferrera, John; Lichtenstein, Stephen; Reder, Margot–Cyberlaw: Text and Cases. Paperback: £34.99. ISBN 0-324-01297-7. South Western College Publishing.

Finch, Emily–Criminalisation of Stalking: Constructing the Problem and Evaluating the Solution. Paperback: £48.40. ISBN 1-85941-644-6. Cavendish Publishing Ltd.

Fisher, Jonathan; Bewsey, Jane–Law of Investor Protection 2nd Ed. Hardback: £95.00. ISBN 0-421-67300-1. Sweet & Maxwell.

Fitzpatrick, Peter–Modernism and the Grounds of Law. Cambridge Studies in Law and Society. Hardback: £37.50. ISBN 0-521-80222-9. Paperback: £13.95. ISBN 0-521-00253-2. Cambridge University Press.

Fitzsimmons, Jarlath; Mulcahy, Rory–Irish Nutshells-contract Law. Nutshells. Paperback: £11.95. ISBN 1-85800-171-4. Round Hall Ltd.

Fleck, Dieter–Handbook of Humanitarian Law in Armed Conflicts. Paperback: £27.50. ISBN 0-19-829867-6. Oxford University Press.

Fleck, Dieter–Handbook of the Law of Visiting Forces. Hardback: £65.00. ISBN 0-19-826894-7. Oxford University Press.

Fletcher, Ian F.; Mistelis, Loukas; Cremona, Marise–Foundations and Perspectives of International Trade Law. Paperback: £40.00. ISBN 0-421-74100-7. Sweet & Maxwell.

Flint, Michael F.–User's Guide to Copyright. 5th Ed. Paperback: £55.00. ISBN 0-406-91498-2. Butterworths Law.

Forde SC, Michael–Employment Law. 2nd Ed. Paperback: £68.00. ISBN 1-85800-188-9. Hardback: £108.00. ISBN 1-85800-221-4. Round Hall Ltd.

Fordham, Michael–Judicial Review Handbook: 2001. 3rd Ed. Hardback: £75.00. ISBN 1-84113-238-1. Hart Publishing.

Fosbrook, Deborah and Laing, Adrian C–Media Contracts Handbook. 2nd Ed. Hardback: £210.00. ISBN 0-421-66130-5. Sweet & Maxwell.

Fossey, Richard; Jarvis, Robin Garrett; Kemper, Elizabeth A.–Race, the Courts, and Equal Education. Readings on Equal Education, Vol 15. Hardback: £66.95. ISBN 0-404-10115-1. AMS Press.

Foster, Charles; Gilliat, Jacqui; Bourne, Charles; Popat, Prashant–Civil Advocacy 2nd Ed. Paperback: £24.95. ISBN 1-85941-562-8. Cavendish Publishing Ltd.

Francioni, Francesco–Environment, Human Rights and International Trade. Hardback: £35.00. ISBN 1-84113-217-9. Hart Publishing.

Franklin, Bob–New Handbook of Children's Rights. 2nd Ed. Hardback: £60.00. ISBN 0-415-25035-8. Paperback: £18.99. ISBN 0-415-25036-6. Routledge, an imprint of Taylor & Francis Books Ltd.

Frascogna, X.M.; Hetherington, H. Lee; Howell, Shawnasey–Business of Internet Law. Hardback: £15.95. ISBN 0-8230-7735-7. Watson-Guptill Publications.

Fredman, Sandra–Discrimination and Human Rights. Collected Courses of the Academy of European Law. Hardback: £40.00. ISBN 0-19-924245-3. Paperback: £16.99. ISBN 0-19-924603-3. Oxford University Press.

Freeman, M.D.A.–Current Legal Problems: Vol 53. 2000. Hardback: £60.00. ISBN 0-19-829940-0. Oxford University Press.

Freshfields: Guide to Financial Investigations and Disciplinary Proceedings. Paperback: £89.00. ISBN 0-406-91058-8. Butterworths Law.

Frieze, Steven–Practice Notes on Insolvency Law. Practice Notes. Paperback: £15.95. ISBN 1-85941-575-X. Cavendish Publishing Ltd.
Fuller, Graham–Purchasing Contracts. Chandos Business Guides: Procurement and Purchasing, 2. Paperback: £49.95. ISBN 1-902375-71-8. Chandos Publishing Ltd.
Furmston, Michael P.–Principles of Commercial Law 2nd Ed. Principles of Law. Paperback: £16.95. ISBN 1-85941-463-X. Cavendish Publishing Ltd.
Furmston, M.P.–Cheshire, Fifoot and Furmston's Law of Contract. 14th Ed. Paperback: £26.95. ISBN 0-406-93058-9. Butterworths Law.
Fyfe, Nicholas R.–Protecting Intimidated Witnesses. Hardback: £37.50. ISBN 0-7546-1335-6. Ashgate Publishing Limited.
Gallant, Simon; Epworth, Jennifer–Media Law and Risk Management: a Practical Guide. Hardback: £85.00. ISBN 0-421-59820-4. Sweet & Maxwell.
Gane, H.W.C; Stoddart, N.C.–Casebook on Scottish Criminal Law 3rd Ed. Paperback: £41.50. ISBN 0-414-01050-7.W.Green & Son.
Gantzias, George–Dynamics of Regulation: Global Control, Local Resistance. Hardback: £49.95. ISBN 1-84014-085-2. Ashgate Publishing Limited.
Garland, David–Culture of Control. Clarendon Studies in Criminology. Hardback: £19.99. ISBN 0-19-829937-0. Oxford University Press.
Garner, Bryan A.–Dictionary of Modern Legal Usage. 2nd Ed. Paperback: £14.99. ISBN 0-19-514236-5. Oxford University Press Inc, USA.
Garner, Bryan A.–Legal Writing in Plain English. Chicago Guides to Writing, Editing, and Publishing. Paperback: £9.50. ISBN 0-226-28418-2. Hardback: £25.50. ISBN 0-226-28417-4. University of Chicago Press.
Gaskell, Nicholas; Asariotis, Regina; Baatz, Yvonne–Bills of Lading: Law and Contracts. Hardback: £175.00. ISBN 1-85978-480-1. LLP Professional Publishing.
Gastinel, Eric; Milford, Mark–Legal Aspects of the Community Trade Mark. Hardback: £77.50. ISBN 90-411-9831-8. Kluwer Law International.
Genn, Hazel; Paterson, Alan–Paths of Justice in Scotland-What People in Scotland Think and Do about Going to Law. Paperback: £20.00. ISBN 1-841-13040-0. Hart Publishing.
George, Robert–In Defense of Natural Law. Paperback: £12.99. ISBN 0-19-924299-2. Oxford University Press.
George, Robert–Natural Law, Liberalism, and Morality. Paperback: £12.99. ISBN 0-19-924300-X. Oxford University Press.
Gerber, David–Law and Competition in Twentieth-century Europe. Paperback: £19.99. ISBN 0-19-924401-4. Oxford University Press.
Gerlis, Stephen M.–Practice Notes on County Court Procedure. Practice Notes. Hardback: £15.95. ISBN 1-85941-309-9. Cavendish Publishing Ltd.
Gerlis, Stephen; Blackford, Robert–Civil Practitioner's Handbook: 2001. Practitioner Series. Paperback: £50.00. ISBN 0-421-82640-1. Sweet & Maxwell.
Geva, Benjamin–Bank Collections and Payment Transactions-A Comparative Legal Analysis. Hardback: £75.00. ISBN 0-19-829853-6. Oxford University Press.
Gibson, Bryan–Introduction to the Magistrate's Court. 4th Ed. Paperback: £17.00. ISBN 1-872870-99-6.Waterside Press.
Gilchrist, Ian–Green's Scottish Early Years Manual. Greens Professional Publishing. Looseleaf/ring bound: £135.00. ISBN 0-414-01379-4.W.Green & Son.
Gillespie, J.–Immigration Appeals Practice: 2001. Hardback: £100.00. ISBN 0-85308-447-5. Jordans.
Gizzi, Julian; Hancox, Nicholas–Butterworths Education Law Manual. Looseleaf/ring bound: £125.00. ISBN 0-406-98171-X. Butterworths Law.
Goldberg, Richard; Lonbay, Julian–Pharmaceutical Medicine, Biotechnology, and European Law. Hardback: £45.00. ISBN 0-521-79249-5. Cambridge University Press.

Goldrein, Iain; Straker, Tim–Human Rights Torts-judicial Review and Human Rights. Looseleaf/ring bound: £95.00. ISBN 0-406-91721-3. Butterworths Law.

Gordley, James–Enforceability of Promises in European Contract Law. Cambridge Studies in International and Comparative Law, 17. Hardback: £55.00. ISBN 0-521-79021-2. Cambridge University Press.

Gordon, Richard; Ward, Tim; Eicke–Strasbourg Case Law: Leading Cases from the European Human Rights Reports. Hardback: £110.00. ISBN 0-421-74240-2. Sweet & Maxwell.

Gordon, Richard; Ward, Tim–Judicial Review and the Human Rights Act. Hardback: £65.00. ISBN 1-85941-430-3. Cavendish Publishing Ltd.

Gould IV, William B.–Labored Relations-Law, Politics, and the NLRB-a Memoir. Paperback: £15.95. ISBN 0-262-57155-2. The MIT Press.

Goulding, Paul–European Employment Law in the UK. Looseleaf/ring bound: £300.00. ISBN 0-421-65370-1. Sweet & Maxwell.

Goyder, Joanna–EU Distribution Law. 3rd Ed. Hardback: £65.00. ISBN 1-902558-29-4. Palladian Law Publishing Ltd.

Grabosky, Peter; Smith, Russell G.–Electronic Theft: Unlawful Acquisition in Cyberspace. Hardback: £30.00. ISBN 0-521-80597-X. Cambridge University Press.

Gray, James P.–Why Our Drug Laws Have Failed and What We Can Do about It. Hardback: £49.95. ISBN 1-56639-859-2. Paperback: £16.95. ISBN 1-56639-860-6. Temple University Press.

Gray, K.J.; Gray, Susan Francis–Butterworths Core Text: Land Law. 2nd Ed. Butterworths Core Text. Paperback: £12.95. ISBN 0-406-94685-X. Butterworths Law.

Gray, W. Robert–Four Faces of Affirmative Action. Contributions in Legal Studies, No 99. Hardback: £51.95. ISBN 0-313-31559-0. Greenwood Press.

Green, D.–Skills for Lawyers. Legal Practice Course. Paperback: £23.50. ISBN 0-85308-721-0. Jordans.

Greenberg, Janelle–Radical Face of the Ancient Constitution. Hardback: £45.00. ISBN 0-521-79131-6. Cambridge University Press.

Greene, Brendan–Essential Medical Law. Essential Law Series. Paperback: £5.50. ISBN 1-85941-546-6. Cavendish Publishing Ltd.

Greenfield, Steve; Osborn Guy–Law and Sport in Contemporary Society. Sport in the Global Society, No. 22. Hardback: £45.00. ISBN 0-7146-5048-X. Paperback: £18.50. ISBN 0-7146-8124-5. Frank Cass Publishers.

Greenfield, Steve; Robson, Peter; Osborn, Guy–Film and the Law. Paperback: £49.50. ISBN 1-85941-639-X. Cavendish Publishing Ltd.

Greenstreet, Ian–Stakeholder Pensions and Pooled Pension Investments. Special Reports. Hardback: £150.00. ISBN 0-421-73970-3. Sweet & Maxwell.

Grier, Nicholas–Banking Law in Scotland. Greens Practice Library. Hardback: £80.00. ISBN 0-414-01309-3. W.Green & Son.

Griffiths, Margaret; Griffiths, Ivor–Commercial Law: Textbooks. 2nd Ed. Old Bailey Press Textbooks. Paperback: £14.95. ISBN 1-85836-398-5. Old Bailey Press.

Grosse, Robert E.–Drugs and Money. Hardback: £48.95. ISBN 0-275-97042-6. Praeger Publishers.

Grubb, Andrew–Law of Tort. Butterworths Common Law. Hardback: £195.00. ISBN 0-406-89672-0. Butterworths Law.

Guide to Measured Term Contracts. Paperback: £40.00. ISBN 0-11-702554-2. The Stationery Office Agencies.

Gumpert, Benjamin; Kirk, Jonathan–Trading Standards: Law and Practice. Hardback: £80.00. ISBN 0-85308-713-X. Family Law.

Gunning, Jennifer–Assisted Conception. Hardback: £50.00. ISBN 0-7546-2149-9. Ashgate Publishing Limited.

Gup, Benton E.–New Financial Architecture: Banking Regulation in the 21st Century. Hardback: £50.50. ISBN 1-56720-341-8. Quorum Books.

Haigh, Simon P.–Contract Law in an E-commerce Age. Paperback: £38.00. ISBN 1-85800-224-9. Round Hall Ltd.

Haley, John–Antitrust in Germany and Japan. Hardback: £44.00. ISBN 0-295-97987-9. University of Washington Press.

Hall-Dick, Anne; Ballantine, Tom–Art of Family Law. Paperback: £14.95. ISBN 0-414-01371-9. Paperback: £14.95. ISBN 0-414-01371-9. W.Green & Son.

Hall-Dick, Anne; Ballantine, Tom–Science of Family Law. Paperback: £32.00. ISBN 0-414-01370-0. W.Green & Son.

Hall, Brendan; Burman, Ian; Everill, Lindsey–Planning and Surviving Your Retirement. Paperback: £48.00. ISBN 1-902558-23-5. Palladian Law Publishing Ltd.

Halliwell, Maragret–Equity and Trusts Textbook. 3rd Ed. Old Bailey Press Textbooks. Paperback: £14.95. ISBN 1-85836-406-X. Old Bailey Press.

Halson, Roger–Contract Law. LSL. Paperback: £29.99. ISBN 0-582-08647-7. Longman Higher Education.

Hammonds Suddards Edge–Dismissal. 2nd Ed. Legal Essentials. Paperback: £29.99. ISBN 0-85292-880-7. Chartered Institute of Personnel and Development (CIPD).

Hammonds Suddards Edge–Employment Tribunals. Legal Essentials. Paperback: £29.99. ISBN 0-85292-918-8. Chartered Institute of Personnel and Development (CIPD).

Hannibal, Martin; Hardy, Stephen–Road Traffic. Practice Notes. Paperback: £15.95. ISBN 1-85941-456-7. Cavendish Publishing Ltd.

Hannigan, Brenda–A Hannigan: A Practitioner's Guide to the Companies Act 1985. Paperback: £75.00. ISBN 0-406-98864-1. Butterworths Law.

Hardy, Stephen–Understanding TUPE-Essential Guide for Business Managers. Chandos Business Guides: Human Resources and Training, No. 5. Paperback: £39.95. ISBN 1-902375-67-X. Chandos Publishing Ltd.

Harker, Stephen–Matrimonial Conveyancing. 7th Ed. Paperback: £59.00. ISBN 0-421-82360-7. Sweet & Maxwell.

Harper, Mark; Baldwin, Camilla; Woelke, Andrea–Model Letters for Family Lawyers 2nd Ed. Paperback: Floppy disk: £50.00. ISBN 0-85308-623-0. Family Law.

Hart, C.–Civil Litigation. Hardback: £23.95. ISBN 0-85308-709-1. Jordans.

Hart, Gerry; Rayney, Peter–Tolley's Tax Planning for Family Companies and Owner-managed Businesses. 4th Ed. Paperback: £48.95. ISBN 0-7545-0713-0. Tolley Publishing.

Hartley, Hazel–Exploring Sport and Leisure Disasters Law: a Socio-legal Perspective. Paperback: £48.40. ISBN 1-85941-650-0. Cavendish Publishing Ltd.

Hartley, Trevor C.; McClean, J.D.; Morse, C.G.J.–Dicey and Morris on the Conflict of Laws: 1st Supplement to the 13th Edition. Paperback: £35.00. ISBN 0-421-75160-6. Sweet & Maxwell.

Hartley, William M.–Declarations of Trust. Paperback: £49.00. ISBN 0-7520-0605-3. Sweet & Maxwell.

Hatchick, Keith; Smith, Keith–Alternative Investment Market Handbook 2nd Ed. Hardback: £80.00. ISBN 0-85308-588-9. Jordans.

Hawken, Angela; Carroll, Stephen J.; Abrahamse, Allan F.–Effects of Third-party Bad Faith Doctrine on Automobile Insurance Costs and Compensation. Paperback: £10.95. ISBN 0-8330-3034-5. RAND.

Hayner, Priscilla B.–Unspeakable Truths. Hardback: £16.99. ISBN 0-415-92477-4. Routledge, an imprint of Taylor & Francis Books Ltd.

Hedges, Lawrence–Facing the Challenge of Liability in Psychotherapy. Hardback: Floppy disk. ISBN 0-7657-0290-8. Jason Aronson.

Hedley, Steve–Restitution. Paperback: £29.95. ISBN 0-421-74430-8. Sweet & Maxwell.

Hedley, William; Hedley, Richard–Bills of Exchange and Bankers' Documentary Credits. 4th Ed. Banking and Finance Law Library. Hardback: £150.00. ISBN 1-85978-545-X. LLP Professional Publishing.

Heines, M. Henry–Patent Empowerment for Small Corporations. Hardback: £53.95. ISBN 1-56720-452-X. Quorum Books.

Hendy, John; Ford, Michael–Munkman on Employers Liability. 13th Ed. Hardback: £105.00. ISBN 0-406-93247-6. Butterworths Law.

Henham, Ralph J.–Sentence Discounts and the Criminal Process. Hardback: £45.00. ISBN 0-7546-2018-2. Dartmouth.

Hennessy, C–Civil Court and Practice. Greens Concise Scots Law. Paperback: £32.00. ISBN 0-414-01283-6.W.Green & Son.

Hepburn, Samantha–Principles of Property Law 2nd Ed. Principles of Law. Paperback: £32.95. ISBN 1-87690-508-5. Cavendish Publishing (Australia) Pty Ltd.

Herring, Jonathan–Family Law: Issues and Debates. Hardback: £45.00. ISBN 1-903240-20-4.Willan Publishing.

Herring, Jonathan–Family Law. Longman Law Series. Paperback: £29.99. ISBN 0-582-38172-X. Longman Higher Education.

Herring, Jonathan–Family Law. Paperback: £20.00. ISBN 1-903240-19-0. Willan Publishing.

Herrup, Cynthia–House in Gross Disorder. Paperback: £8.99. ISBN 0-19-513925-9. Oxford University Press Inc, USA.

Hewitt, Ian–Joint Ventures. 2nd Ed. Hardback: Floppy disk: £130.00. ISBN 0-421-73980-0. Sweet & Maxwell.

Heyes, Anthony–Law and Economics of the Environment. Elgar Monographs. Hardback: £69.95. ISBN 1-84064-339-0. Edward Elgar.

Hickman, David–Lincoln Wills, 1532-1534. Publications of the Lincoln Record Society, 89. Hardback: £50.00. ISBN 0-90150-366-5. The Lincoln Record Society.

Hill, Mark–Ecclesiastical Law. 2nd Ed. Hardback: £68.00. ISBN 0-19-826890-4. Oxford University Press.

Hinchey, Patricia H.–Student Rights: Library Binding. Contemporary Education Issues. Hardback: £29.95. ISBN 1-57607-266-5. ABC Clio (Reference Books).

Hockton, Andrew–Law of Consent to Medical Treatment. Hardback: £85.00. ISBN 0-421-64760-4. Sweet & Maxwell.

Hoda, Anwarul–Tariff Negotiations and Renegotiations Under the GATT and the WTO-Procedures and Practices. Hardback: £45.00. ISBN 0-521-80449-3. Cambridge University Press.

Hodges, Susan; Hill, Christopher–Principles of Maritime Law: Case and Comment. Hardback: £120.00. ISBN 1-85978-998-6. LLP Professional Publishing.

Hoffman, Anthony–Civil Costs Cases: a Civil Guide. 2nd Ed. Paperback: £62.00. ISBN 0-421-72650-4. Sweet & Maxwell.

Hohfeld, W.N.; Campbell, David; Thomas, Philip–Fundamental Legal Conceptions As Applied in Judicial Reasoning by Wesley Newcomb Hohfeld. New Ed. Classical Jurisprudence Series. Hardback: £40.00. ISBN 1-85521-668-X. Dartmouth.

Holborn, Guy–Butterworths Legal Research Guide. 2nd Ed. Paperback: £19.95. ISBN 0-406-93023-6. Butterworths Law.

Hollander, Charles; Adams, Tom–Documentary Evidence. 7th Ed. Hardback: £130.00. ISBN 0-421-73820-0. Sweet & Maxwell.

Holtam, J.–Criminal Litigation. Hardback: £23.95. ISBN 0-85308-719-9. Jordans.

Holyoak; Torremans–Holyoak and Torremans: Intellectual Property Law. 3rd Ed. Butterworths Student Statutes. Paperback: £24.95. ISBN 0-406-93400-2. Butterworths Law.

Home and Family Solicitor. £19.99. ISBN 1-902646-30-4. Law Pack Publishing.

Homer, Arnold; Burrows, Rita–Tolley's Taxwise 2001-2002: II. Paperback: £38.95. ISBN 0-7545-1218-5. Tolley Publishing.

Honey, Gerard–Emergency and Security Lighting. Paperback: £19.99. ISBN 0-7506-5037-0. Butterworth-Heinemann.

Hooper, David–Reputations Under Fire-Winners and Losers in the Libel Business. Paperback: £14.99. ISBN 0-7515-2993-1. Warner.

Hopkins, Nicholas–Informal Acquisition of Rights in Land. Modern Legal Studies. Paperback: £23.95. ISBN 0-421-68100-4. Sweet & Maxwell.

House Buying, Selling and Conveyancing. £9.99. ISBN 1-902646-70-3. Law Pack Publishing.

Howarth, William; McGillivray, Donald–Water Pollution and Water Quality Law. Hardback: £65.00. ISBN 0-7219-1102-1. Shaw & Sons.

Howells, Geraint–Product Liability. Butterworths Common Law Series. Hardback: £195.00. ISBN 0-406-90050-7. Butterworths Law.

Hughes, Theodore E.; Klein, David–Executor's Handbook 2nd Ed. Hardback: £29.50. ISBN 0-8160-4426-0. Facts on File Inc.

Hughes, Theodore E.; Klein, David–Family Guide to Wills, Funerals & Probate 2nd Ed. Hardback: £29.50. ISBN 0-8160-4550-X. Facts on File Inc.

Hull, John–Commercial Secrecy: Law and Practice. 2nd Ed. Hardback: £120.00. ISBN 0-421-74770-6. Sweet & Maxwell.

Hunt, Murray; Singh, Rabinder–Practitioner's Guide to the Impact of the Human Rights Act 1998. Paperback: £22.00. ISBN 1-901362-49-3. Hart Publishing.

Huntley, John a K–Contract. Cases & Materials. Paperback: £45.00. ISBN 0-414-01281-X. W. Green & Son.

ICSA Paper 12-professional Stage 1: Corporate Law: Practice and Revision Kit (2001). Paperback: £10.95. ISBN 0-7517-5856-6. BPP Publishing Ltd.

ICSA Paper 3-foundation: Introduction to English and EC Law: Practice and Revision Kit (2001). Paperback: £10.95. ISBN 0-7517-5847-7. BPP Publishing Ltd.

ICSA Paper 7-pre-professional: Business Law: Practice and Revision Kit (2001). Paperback: £10.95. ISBN 0-7517-5851-5. BPP Publishing Ltd.

Imber, Michael; Van Geel, Tyll–Teacher's Guide to Education Law. 2nd Ed. Paperback: £22.50. ISBN 0-8058-3754-X. Lawrence Erlbaum Associates, Inc.

Informed Choice of Medical Services: Is the Law Just? Hardback: £35.00. ISBN 0-7546-1198-1. Ashgate Publishing Limited.

International Directory of Construction Law: 2001. £60.00. ISBN 1-84311-067-9. LLP Professional Publishing.

International IT and Telecoms Law Directory. £60.00. ISBN 1-84311-066-0. LLP Professional Publishing.

Iwobi, Andrew–Essential Succession. 2nd Ed. Essential Law Series. Paperback: £5.50. ISBN 1-85941-617-9. Cavendish Publishing Ltd.

Jack, Raymond; Malek, Ali–Documentary Credits. 3rd Ed. Hardback: £145.00. ISBN 0-406-91634-9. Butterworths Law.

Jackson, David–Enforcement of Maritime Claims. 3rd Ed. Lloyds Shipping Law Library. Hardback: £180.00. ISBN 1-85978-583-2. LLP Professional Publishing.

Jackson, Emily–Regulating Reproduction-Law, Technology and Autonomy. Paperback: £16.99. ISBN 1-84113-301-9. Hardback: £40.00. ISBN 1-84113-054-0. Hart Publishing.

Jackson, Emily–Regulation of Reproduction. Hardback: £25.00. ISBN 1-84113-054-0. Hart Publishing.

Jackson, Paul; Leopold, Patricia–O. Hood Phillips and Jackson's Constitutional and Administrative Law. 8th Ed. Paperback: £30.00. ISBN 0-421-57480-1. Sweet & Maxwell.

Jackson, R.P.; Legge, D.; Parry, J.; Ruddock, F.–Environmental Law and Techniques for the Built Environment. Paperback: £22.95. ISBN 1-85941-597-0. Cavendish Publishing Ltd.

Jacob–White Book Service 2001: Vols 1&2. Civil Procedure. Sweet & Maxwell Connections. Hardback: £225.00. ISBN 0-421-74570-3. Sweet & Maxwell.

Jain Ravi; Urban, L.V.; Stacey, Gary S.; Balbach, Harold–Environmental Assessment. 2nd Ed. Hardback: £65.99. ISBN 0-07-137008-0. McGraw-Hill Publishing Company.

James, Jennifer–Company Law. Questions and Answers. Paperback: £9.95. ISBN 1-85941-414-1. Cavendish Publishing Ltd.

James, Michael F.–Construction Law-Liability for the Construction of Defective Buildings. 2nd Ed. Building and Surveying Series. Paperback: £21.99. ISBN 0-333-79306-4. Palgrave, formerly Macmillan Press.

Jamieson, George–Summary Applications. Greens Practice Library. Hardback: £120.00. ISBN 0-414-01225-9. W. Green & Son.

Janis, Mark; Kay, Richard; Bradley, Anthony–European Human Rights Law. 2nd Ed. Paperback: £26.99. ISBN 0-19-876569-X. Oxford University Press.

Jazbec, Milan–Diplomacies of New Small States: the Case of Slovenia with Some Comparison from the Baltics. Hardback: £42.50. ISBN 0-7546-1706-8. Ashgate Publishing Limited.

Jefferson, Michael–Criminal Law 5th Ed. Foundation Studies in Law Series. Paperback: £25.99. ISBN 0-582-43814-4. Longman Higher Education.

Jess, Digby–Insurance of Commercial Risks: Law and Practice. 3rd Ed. Hardback: £150.00. ISBN 0-421-82440-9. Sweet & Maxwell.

Jessel, Christopher–Development Land-overage and Clawback. Hardback: £80.00. ISBN 0-85308-669-9. Jordans.

John Rayer–RSM Robson Rhodes: Personal Financial Planning Manual 2001-2002. 17th Ed. Paperback: £43.95. ISBN 0-406-93891-1. Butterworths Tolley.

Johnston, David; Zimmermann, Reinhard–Comparative Law of Unjust Enrichment. Hardback: £50.00. ISBN 0-521-80820-0. Cambridge University Press.

Jones, Alison; Sufrin, Brenda–Text, Cases, and Materials in EC Competition Law. Paperback: £32.99. ISBN 0-19-876329-8. Oxford University Press Inc, USA.

Jones, Alun–Jones on Extradition. 2nd Ed. Criminal Law Library. Hardback: £120.00. ISBN 0-421-69060-7. Sweet & Maxwell.

Jones, Brian–EMC Management. Paperback: £29.99. ISBN 0-7506-4584-9. Newnes.

Jones, Richard–Butterworths Compliance Series: Investigations and Enforcement. Butterworths Compliance Series. Paperback: £40.00. ISBN 0-406-93251-4. Butterworths Law.

Jones, Stephen–Understanding Violent Crime. Crime and Justice. Hardback: £50.00. ISBN 0-335-20418-X. Paperback: £15.99. ISBN 0-335-20417-1. Open University Press.

Jordan, Ronald R.; Quynn, Katelyn–Planned Giving: Management, Marketing and Law. 2nd Ed. Paperback: £46.50. ISBN 0-471-39027-5. John Wiley and Sons.

Jorgensen, Nina H. B.–Responsibility of States for International Crimes. Oxford Monographs in International Law. Hardback: £50.00. ISBN 0-19-829861-7. Oxford University Press.

Joseph, Sarah; Schultz, Jenny; Castan, Melissa–International Covenant on Civil and Political Rights: Cases, Materials and Commentary. Hardback: £75.00. ISBN 0-19-826774-6. Oxford University Press.

Kaczorowska, Alina–EU Law for Today's Lawyers. Paperback: £16.95. ISBN 1-85836-356-X. Old Bailey Press.

Kaczorowska, Alina–Public International Law Textbook. 2nd Ed. Old Bailey Press Textbooks. Paperback: £14.95. ISBN 1-85836-416-7. Old Bailey Press.

Kahn, Paul W.–Cultural Study of Law. Paperback: £9.00. ISBN 0-226-42255-0. University of Chicago Press.

Kamali–Dignity of Man-an Islamic Perspective. Hardback: £24.95. ISBN 1-903682-03-7. Paperback: £11.95. ISBN 1-903682-00-2. The Islamic Texts Society.

Kamali–Freedom, Equality and Justice in Islam. Paperback: £15.95. ISBN 1-903682-01-0. Hardback: £35.00. ISBN 1-903682-02-9. The Islamic Texts Society.

Kanda-Rovati, Veena–Succession: the Law of Wills and Estates Casebook. Old Bailey Press Leading Cases. Paperback: £9.95. ISBN 1-85836-423-X. Old Bailey Press.

Kanda-Rovati, Veena–Succession: the Law of Wills and Estates Textbook. 3rd Ed. Old Bailey Press Textbooks. Paperback: £14.95. ISBN 1-85836-418-3. Old Bailey Press.

Kane, Luan; Ashman, Linda–Sinclair: Warranties and Indemnities on Share and Asset Sales. 5th Ed. Hardback: £120.00. ISBN 0-421-70680-5. Sweet & Maxwell.

Keay, Andrew R.–McPherson's Law of Company Liquidation. Hardback: £140.00. ISBN 0-421-68420-8. Sweet & Maxwell.

Keenan, Denis–Smith and Keenan's English Law. Paperback: £26.99. ISBN 0-582-43816-0. Longman Higher Education.

Kelly, Gillian–Post Traumatic Stress Disorder and the Law. £38.00. ISBN 1-85800-201-X. Round Hall Ltd.

Kemp, Walter A.–Quiet Diplomacy in Action: the OSCE High Commissioner on National Minorities. Hardback: £28.00. ISBN 90-411-1651-6. Kluwer Law International.

Kennedy, Kevin–Competition Law and the WTO. Hardback: £130.00. ISBN 0-421-82450-6. Sweet & Maxwell.

Kent, Penelope–Law of the European Union. FRA. Hardback: £17.99. ISBN 0-582-42367-8. Longman Higher Education.

Khaled Abou El Fadl–Rebellion and Violence in Islamic Law. Hardback: £47.50. ISBN 0-521-79311-4. Cambridge University Press.

Killion, Susan Westrick; Dempski, Katherine–Quick Look Nursing: Legal and Ethical Issues in Nursing. Quick Look Nursing. Paperback: £18.50. ISBN 1-55642-505-8. Slack Incorporated.

Kimel, Dori–From Promise to Contract. Hardback: £30.00. ISBN 1-84113-212-8. Hart Publishing.

Kincaid, Peter–Privity. Hardback: £55.00. ISBN 0-7546-2089-1. Dartmouth.

King, Anthony–Does the United Kingdom Still Have a Constitution? Hamlyn Lectures. Paperback: £12.95. ISBN 0-421-74930-X. Sweet & Maxwell.

King, L.–Accounts for Solicitors. Legal Practice Course. Paperback: £23.95. ISBN 0-85308-715-6. Jordans.

King, Richard–Gutteridge and Megrah's Law of Bankers' Commercial Credits. £95.00. ISBN 1-85743-112-X. Europa Publications.

Kirkbride; Olowofoyeku–Law and Theory of Income Tax. Paperback: £24.95. ISBN 1-90349-900-3. Liverpool Academic Press.

Kitchen, David; Mellor, James; Meade, Richard–Kerly's Law of Trade Marks and Trade Names. 13th Ed. Hardback: £185.00. ISBN 0-421-45610-8. Sweet & Maxwell.

Kittichaisaree, Kriangsak–International Criminal Law. Paperback: £25.99. ISBN 0-19-876577-0. Oxford University Press.

Kjonstad, Asbjorn; Robson, Peter–Poverty and the Law. Onati International Series in Law and Society. Hardback: £35.00. ISBN 1-84113-190-3. Paperback: £20.00. ISBN 1-84113-191-1. Hart Publishing.

Klami, Hannu Tapani; Grans, Minna; Sorvettula, Johanna–Law and Truth: A theory of Evidence. Paperback: £25.00. ISBN 951-653-306-X. The Finnish Academy of Science and Letters.

Koskenniemi, Martti–Sources of International Law. The Library of Essays in International Law, No 5. Hardback: £90.00. ISBN 1-84014-097-6. Dartmouth.

Koutrakos, Panos–Trade, Foreign Policy and Defence in EU Constitutional Law. Hardback: £35.00. ISBN 1-84113-166-0. Hart Publishing.

Kramer, Ludwig–Casebook on EU Environmental Law 2nd Ed. Hardback: £30.00. ISBN 1-84113-172-5. Hart Publishing.

Kramer, Matthew H.–Rights, Wrongs and Responsibilities. Hardback: £42.50. ISBN 0-333-96329-6. Palgrave, formerly Macmillan Press.

Kraus, Jody S; Walt, Steven D.–Jurisprudential Foundations of Corporate and Commercial Law. Cambridge Studies in Philosophy and Law. Hardback: £35.00. ISBN 0-521-59157-0. Cambridge University Press.

Krebs, Thomas–Restitution At the Crossroads. Paperback: £38.95. ISBN 1-85941-646-2. Cavendish Publishing Ltd.

Kressel, Neil; Kressel, Dorit–Stack and Sway. Hardback: £19.99. ISBN 0-8133-9772-3. Westview Press.

Krieger, Heike–Kosovo Conflict and International Law: An Analytical Documentation 1974-1999. Cambridge International Documents Series, 11. Hardback: £80.00. ISBN 0-521-80071-4. Cambridge University Press.

Kutz, Christopher–Complicity: Ethics and Law for a Collective Age. Cambridge Studies in Philosophy and Law. Hardback: £37.50. ISBN 0-521-59452-9. Cambridge University Press.

Labareex, Robert–Federal Trade Commission. Hardback: £59.00. ISBN 0-8153-1296-2. Garland Publishing, Inc.

Lane, Robert–EC Competition Law. European Law. Paperback (C format): £9.99. ISBN 0-582-28976-9. Longman Higher Education.

Langlois, Anthony J.–Politics of Justice and Human Rights. Cambridge Asia-Pacific Studies. Hardback: £45.00. ISBN 0-521-80785-9. Paperback: £15.95. ISBN 0-521-00347-4. Cambridge University Press.

Langum, David J.–William M. Kunstler-The Most Hated Lawyer in America. Paperback: £18.95. ISBN 0-8147-5151-2. New York University Press.

Lasok, Dominick; Len, Juris–Law and Institutions of the European Union. 7th Ed. Paperback: £29.95. ISBN 0-406-90186-4. Butterworths Law.

Lasser–Profit from the New Tax Law. Paperback: £7.95. ISBN 0-471-09280-0. John Wiley and Sons.

Last Will and Testament 3rd Ed. Paperback: £9.99. ISBN 1-902646-85-1. Law Pack Publishing.

Last Will and Testament Kit. New Ed. Book: £9.99. ISBN 1-902646-22-3. Law Pack Publishing.

Last Will and Testament. 2nd Ed. CD-ROM: £17.01. ISBN 1-902646-21-5. Law Pack Publishing.

Lauterburg, Dominique–Food Law: Policy and Ethics. Paperback: £60.50. ISBN 1-85941-524-5. Cavendish Publishing Ltd.

Lauterpacht, E.; Greenwood, C. J.–International Law Reports Volume 117. International Law Reports. Hardback: £100.00. ISBN 0-521-66120-X. Cambridge University Press.

Lauterpacht, E.; Greenwood, C.J.–International Law Reports Volume 118. International Law Reports. Hardback: £110.00. ISBN 0-521-66121-8. Cambridge University Press.

Law of Consumer Protection and Fair Trading. 6th Ed. £25.95. ISBN 0-406-93062-7. Butterworths Law.

Law Update 2001. £9.95. ISBN 1-85836-385-3. Old Bailey Press.

Lawrence, Nick; Homer, Arnold; Burrows, Rita–Tolley's VATwise 2001-02. Paperback: £38.95. ISBN 0-7545-1292-4. Tolley Publishing.

Lawrence, Tim; Drake, Michael–Divorce and the Family Business 2nd Ed. Paperback: £39.50. ISBN 0-85308-646-X. Family Law.

Lazega, Emmanuel–Collegial Phenomenon. Hardback: £50.00. ISBN 0-19-924272-0. Oxford University Press.

Lee, N. Genell–Legal Concepts and Issues in Emergency Care. Hardback: £21.95. ISBN 0-7216-8324-X. WB Saunders.

Leiser, Burton M.; Campbell, Tom D.–Human Rights in Philosophy and Practice. Applied Legal Philosophy. Hardback: £65.00. ISBN 0-7546-2210-X. Ashgate Publishing Limited.

Letterman, G. Gregory–Basics of International Intellectual Property Law. The Basics of International Law. Hardback: £116.99. ISBN 1-57105-207-0. Transnational Publishers, Inc.

Leubsdorf, John–Man in His Original Dignity. Hardback: £40.00. ISBN 0-7546-2110-3. Ashgate Publishing Limited.

Levenson, Barry M.–Habeas Codfish. Hardback: £20.95. ISBN 0-299-17510-3. University of Wisconsin Press.

Lewis, Andrew; O'Dair, Richard–Law and Religion. Current Legal Issues, 4. Hardback: £70.00. ISBN 0-19-924660-2. Oxford University Press Inc, USA.

Lewis, Clive–Judicial Remedies in Public Law: 1st Supplement to the 2nd Edition. 2nd Ed. Paperback: £38.00. ISBN 0-421-76370-1. Sweet & Maxwell.

Lichtenstein, E–Contract Law. Suggested Solutions. £6.95. ISBN 1-85836-390-X. Old Bailey Press.

Lightman, Mr Justice and Moss, Gabr–Law of Receivers and Administrators of Companies. 3rd Ed. Hardback: £135.00. ISBN 0-421-67370-2. Sweet & Maxwell.

Lilley, Roy; Newdick, Christopher; Lambden, Paul–Understanding the Human Rights Act. Paperback: £30.00. ISBN 1-85775-494-8. Radcliffe Medical Press.

Livingston, Dorothy–Competition Act 1998: a Practical Guide. Act Book Series. Paperback: £50.00. ISBN 0-7520-0622-3. Sweet & Maxwell.

Lloyd's Law Reports: Medical. Hardback: £110.00. ISBN 1-85978-939-0. Lloyd's List.

Long, Colin–Global Telecommunications Law and Practice. 3rd Ed. Looseleaf/ring bound: £195.00. ISBN 0-421-65360-4. Sweet & Maxwell.

Lorenz, Edward C.–Defining Global Justice. Hardback: £45.95. ISBN 0-268-02550-9. Paperback: £23.50. ISBN 0-268-02551-7. University of Notre Dame Press.

Lorton, Roger–A-Z of Policing Law. 2nd Ed. Paperback: £20.00. ISBN 0-11-702812-6. The Stationery Office Books.

Loughlin, Paula–Civil Procedure. Paperback: £22.95. ISBN 1-85941-497-4. Cavendish Publishing Ltd.

Loux, Andrea–Human Rights and Scots Law. Hardback: £30.00. ISBN 1-84113-044-3. Hart Publishing.

Lowe, David–Pocket Guide to LGV Drivers' Hours and Tachograph Law. Paperback: £12.99. ISBN 0-7494-3572-0. Kogan Page.

Lupoi, Maurizio–Trusts. Cambridge Studies in International and Comparative Law, 12. Hardback: £65.00. ISBN 0-521-62329-4. Cambridge University Press.

Luxton, Peter–Law of Charities. Hardback: £145.00. ISBN 0-19-826783-5. Oxford University Press.

Lyons, Declan–Environmental Regulation and Your Business. Paperback: £14.99. ISBN 0-11-702700-6. The Stationery Office Books.

MacCoun, Robert J.; Reuter, Peter–Drug War Heresies-Learning from Other Vices, Times, and Places. Hardback: £50.00. ISBN 0-521-57263-0. Paperback: £18.95. ISBN 0-521-79997-X. Cambridge University Press.

Macdonald, Lynda–Managing E-mail and Internet Use: a Practical Guide to Employers' Obligations and Employees' Rights. Paperback: £35.00. ISBN 0-7545-1394-7. Tolley Publishing.

MacDonald, Ross–Introduction to the Scots Law of Succession 3rd Ed. Greens Concise Scots Law. Paperback: £32.00. ISBN 0-414-01436-7. W.Green & Son.

Macintyre, Ewan–Business Law. Paperback: £24.99. ISBN 0-273-64371-1. Longman Higher Education.

Mackie, Karl; Miles, David; Marsh, William–Commercial Dispute Resolution-an ADR Practice Guide. 2nd Ed. Hardback: £60.00. ISBN 0-406-91057-X. Butterworths Law.

Macmorran, Kenneth M.; Briden, Timothy–Handbook for Churchwardens and Parochial Church Councillors. Paperback (C format): £9.99. ISBN 0-264-67486-3. Continuum International Publishing Group-Mowbray.

MacNeil, Ian–Relational Theory of Contract: Selected Works of Ian MacNeil. Paperback: £35.00. ISBN 0-421-72240-1. Sweet & Maxwell.

MacQueen, Hector–Gloag and Henderson: the Law of Scotland. 11th Ed. Hardback: £125.00. ISBN 0-414-01254-2.W.Green & Son.

Magnus, Alan–Property Joint Ventures: Structures and Precedents. 2nd Ed. Hardback: Floppy disk: £195.00. ISBN 0-421-82500-6. Sweet & Maxwell.

Maine, Henry Sumner–Ancient Law. Paperback: £29.50. ISBN 0-7658-0795-5.Transaction Publishers.

Malanczuk, Peter–Akehurst's Modern Introduction to International Law. Paperback: £19.99. ISBN 0-415-24356-4. Hardback: £60.00. ISBN 0-415-24355-6. Routledge, an imprint of Taylor & Francis Books Ltd.

Malanczuk, Peter–Key Documents in International Law. Paperback: £17.99. ISBN 0-415-24688-1. Hardback: £50.00. ISBN 0-415-24687-3. Routledge, an imprint of Taylor & Francis Books Ltd.

Mandaraka-Sheppard, Aleka–Modern Admiralty Law. Paperback: £80.00. ISBN 1-85941-531-8. Cavendish Publishing Ltd.

Mann, Marin; Morse, Geoffrey–Palmer's Company Law Manual. Hardback: £150.00. ISBN 0-421-63840-0. Sweet & Maxwell.

Mantle, Greg–Helping Parents in Dispute. Hardback: £47.50. ISBN 0-7546-1638-X. Ashgate Publishing Limited.

Marmor, Andrei–Positive Law and Objective Values. Hardback: £30.00. ISBN 0-19-826897-1. Oxford University Press.

Mars, Gerald–Work Place Sabotage. The International Library of Criminology, Criminal Justice and Penology. Hardback: £95.00. ISBN 1-84014-788-1. Dartmouth.

Marshall, Audrey; McDonald, Margaret–Many-sided Triangle. Paperback: £19.95. ISBN 0-522-84943-1. Melbourne University Press.

Marshall, Enid–Gill: the Law of Arbitration. Paperback: £19.95. ISBN 0-421-68130-6. Sweet & Maxwell.

Martin, Jacqueline; Turner, Chris–Key Facts: Contract Law. Key Facts. Paperback: £4.99. ISBN 0-340-80181-6. Hodder & Stoughton Educational.

Martin, Jacqueline; Turner, Chris–Key Facts: Tort. Key Facts. Paperback: £4.99. ISBN 0-340-80182-4. Hodder & Stoughton Educational.

Martin, Jacqueline–Key Facts: Criminal Law. Key Facts. Paperback (B format): £4.99. ISBN 0-340-80180-8. Hodder & Stoughton Educational.

Martin, Jill–Hanbury & Martin: Modern Equity ISE. 16th Ed. Paperback: £14.95. ISBN 0-421-75320-X. Sweet & Maxwell.

Mason, J.K.–Forensic Medicine for Lawyers. 4th Ed. Paperback: £75.00. ISBN 0-406-91442-7. Butterworths Law.

Mastellone, Carlo H.–Handbook on Cross-border Industrial Sub-contracting. Aija Law Library, 11. Hardback: £140.00. ISBN 90-411-9826-1. Kluwer Law International.

Mather, Lynn; McEwen, Craig A.; Maiman, Richard J.–Divorce Lawyers At Work. Hardback: £39.95. ISBN 0-19-514515-1. Oxford University Press Inc, USA.

Matthews, John F.–Laying Down the Law. Hardback: £27.50. ISBN 0-300-07900-1.Yale University Press.

Matthews, Paul and Malek, Hodge M–Disclosure. Hardback: £135.00. ISBN 0-421-71660-6. Sweet & Maxwell.

Mayes, David G.; Berghman, Jos; Salais, Robert–Social Exclusion and European Policy. Hardback: £65.00. ISBN 1-84064-688-8. Edward Elgar.

Mayne, Susan; Malyon, Susan–Employment Law in Europe. Hardback: £95.00. ISBN 0-406-92360-4. Butterworths Law.

Mays, Richard–Family Law: Cases and Materials. Paperback: £40.00. ISBN 0-414-01346-8. W. Green & Son.

McBryde, William W.–Law of Contract in Scotland 2nd Ed. Hardback: £165.00. ISBN 0-414-01242-9. W. Green & Son.

McCaffrey, Stephen C.–Law of International Watercourses. Oxford Monographs in International Law. Hardback: £65.00. ISBN 0-19-825787-2. Oxford University Press.

McCall-Smith; Merry–Errors, Medicine and the Law. Hardback: £47.50. ISBN 0-521-80631-3. Paperback: £17.95. ISBN 0-521-00088-2. Cambridge University Press.

McCarthy, James J.; Canziani, Osvaldo F.; Leary, Neil A.; Dokken, David J.; Wite, Kasey S.–Climate Change 2001: Impacts, Adaptation, and Vulnerability. Paperback: £34.95. ISBN 0-521-01500-6. Cambridge University Press.

Mcdermott, Paul Anthony–Mcdermott: Contract Law. Irish Law Library. Hardback: £95.00. ISBN 1-85475-360-6. Butterworths Law.

McFadyen, Norman–Offences Against Justice. Scottish Criminal Law and Practice Series. Paperback: £40.00. ISBN 0-406-92322-1. Butterworths (Scotland).

McGee, Andrew–Modern Law of Insurance. Hardback: £175.00. ISBN 0-406-90385-9. Butterworths Law.

McGhee, Derek–Homosexuality, Law, and Resistance. Hardback: £55.00. ISBN 0-415-24902-3. Routledge, an imprint of Taylor & Francis Books Ltd.

McGrath, Michael–Liquor Licensing Law. Butterworth Irish Annotated Statutes. £85.00. ISBN 1-85475-365-7. Butterworths Law.

McInnis, Thomas N.–Christian Burial Case. Hardback: £56.95. ISBN 0-275-97027-2. Praeger Publishers.

Mckain, Bruce; Bonnington, Alistair–Scots Law for Journalists. 7th Ed. Paperback: £24.95. ISBN 0-414-01372-7. W. Green & Son.

McKendrick, Ewan–Sale of Goods. Hardback: £185.00. ISBN 1-85978-305-8. LLP Professional Publishing.

McKie, Simon; Ansley, Sharan–Tolley's Estate Planning 2000-01. Paperback: £57.95. ISBN 0-7545-0724-6. Tolley Publishing.

McKie, Simon; Anstey, Sharon–Tolley's Estate Planning 2001-02. Paperback: £64.95. ISBN 0-7545-1196-0. Tolley Publishing.

McMullen, John; Smith, Ian–Breach of Employment Contract and Wrongful Dismissal. Hardback: £65.00. ISBN 0-406-91411-7. Butterworths Law.

McMullen, John–Redundancy: Law and Practice. 2nd Ed. Hardback: £100.00. ISBN 0-421-68390-2. Sweet & Maxwell.

Mecklenberg, Keith–Telecommunications-law and Policy. Paperback: £24.95. ISBN 0-406-90580-0. Butterworths Law.

Medhurst–Brief and Practical Guide to EC Law. Paperback: £25.00. ISBN 0-632-05184-1. Blackwell Science (UK).

Mello, Robert de–Human Rights in the Public Sector. Spiral/comb bound: £129.00. ISBN 1-85978-931-5. LLP Professional Publishing.

Menikoff, Jerry–Law and Bioethics. Hardback: £48.25. ISBN 0-87840-838-X. Georgetown University Press.

Menkel-Meadow, Carrie–Mediation. International Library of Essays in Law and Legal Theory (second Series). Hardback: £125.00. ISBN 0-7546-2052-2. Ashgate Publishing Limited.

Mensah, Barbara–European Human Rights Case Summaries 1960-2000. Paperback: £95.00. ISBN 1-85941-649-7. Cavendish Publishing Ltd.

Mercantile Statutes: 2001. Paperback: £44.00. ISBN 0-414-01425-1. Sweet & Maxwell.

Merritt, Jonathan–Modern Business Law-principles and Practice. 2nd Ed. Paperback: £19.50. ISBN 1-90349-907-0. Liverpool Academic Press.

Meyer-Emerick, Nancy–Violence Against Women Act of 1994. Hardback: £47.95. ISBN 0-275-97084-1. Praeger Publishers.

Meyer, Howard N.–World Court in Action-Judging Among the Nations. Hardback: £57.00. ISBN 0-74250-923-0. Paperback: £20.95. ISBN 0-74250-924-9. Rowman & Littlefield Publishers.

Miele, Anthony L.–Patent Strategy. Hardback: £42.95. ISBN 0-471-39075-5. John Wiley and Sons.

Mildred, Mark–Product Liability: Law and Insurance. Hardback: £190.00. ISBN 1-85978-538-7. LLP Professional Publishing.

Miles, Michele G.–Business Appraiser and Litigation Support. Hardback: £60.95. ISBN 0-471-39410-6. John Wiley and Sons.

Milkovich, George; Newman, Jerry–Compensation 7th Ed. Paperback: £34.99. ISBN 0-07-112324-5. McGraw-Hill Publishing Company.

Miller, Chris–Planning and Environmental Protection. Paperback: £22.50. ISBN 1-84113-181-4. Hart Publishing.

Miller, Richard Lawrence–Whittaker-Struggles of a Supreme Court Justice. Contributions in Legal Studies, No 102. Hardback: £54.50. ISBN 0-313-31250-8. Greenwood Press.

Millett, Roger–Solicitors: an Industry Auditing and Accounting Guide. 2nd Ed. Hardback: £65.00. ISBN 1-84140-148-X. Accountancy Books.

Mills, Shaun–Constitutional and Administrative Law of the EC. Paperback: £24.95. ISBN 1-85941-223-8. Cavendish Publishing Ltd.

Mitchard, P.; Nairn, K.–International Commercial Arbitration. Looseleaf/ring bound. ISBN 0-7520-0659-2. Sweet & Maxwell.

Mitchels, Barbara; James, Helen–Child Care Protection Law and Practice. Practice Notes. Paperback: £15.95. ISBN 1-85941-455-9. Cavendish Publishing Ltd.

Moddelmog, William E.–Reconstituting Authority. Hardback: £27.95. ISBN 0-87745-736-0. University of Iowa Press.

Mohammad Hashim Kamali–Islamic Commercial Law. Paperback: £18.95. ISBN 0-946621-80-2. Hardback: £42.95. ISBN 0-946621-79-9. The Islamic Texts Society.

Molan, Michael T.–Administrative Law: Textbook. 3rd Ed. Old Bailey Press Textbooks. Paperback: £14.95. ISBN 1-85836-397-7. Old Bailey Press.

Molan, Michael T.–Constitutional and Administrative Law. 2nd Ed. Cracknell's Statutes Series. Paperback: £9.95. ISBN 1-85836-387-X. Old Bailey Press.

Molan, Michael T.–Constitutional Law: Textbook. 3rd Ed. Old Bailey Press Textbooks. Paperback: £14.95. ISBN 1-85836-401-9. Old Bailey Press.

Molan, Michael T.–Criminal Law: Textbook. 3rd Ed. Old Bailey Press Textbooks. Paperback: £14.95. ISBN 1-85836-403-5. Old Bailey Press.

Monkcom, Stephen–Law of Betting, Gaming and Lotteries. 2nd Ed. Hardback: £160.00. ISBN 0-406-90313-1. Butterworths Law.

Moore, Adam D.–Intellectual Property and Information Control. Hardback: £24.95. ISBN 0-7658-0070-5. Hardback: £24.95. ISBN 0-7658-0070-5. Transaction Publishers.

Moore, Sally Falk–Law As Process: an Anthropological Approach. 2nd Ed. Classics in African Anthropology. Paperback (C format): £14.95. ISBN 0-85255-910-0. James Currey Publishers.

Morgan, Derek–Issues in Medical Law and Ethics. Paperback: £29.95. ISBN 1-85941-591-1. Cavendish Publishing Ltd.

Morgan, Jill; Brand, Clive–Practice Notes on Business Tenancies. 4th Ed. Practice Notes. Paperback: £15.95. ISBN 1-85941-458-3. Cavendish Publishing Ltd.

Morgan, Richard; Burden, Kit–Morgan and Stedman on Computer Contracts. Hardback: £145.00. ISBN 0-421-74250-X. Sweet & Maxwell.
Morreim, E. Haavi–Holding Health Care Accountable. Hardback: £39.50. ISBN 0-19-514132-6. Oxford University Press Inc, USA.
Morris, Allison; Maxwell, Gabrielle–Restorative Justice for Juveniles-Conferencing, Mediation and Circles. Hardback: £25.00. ISBN 1-84113-176-8. Hart Publishing.
Morrison, Nigel–Sentencing Practice: Cases and Materials. Looseleaf/ring bound: £245.00. ISBN 0-414-01339-5. W.Green & Son.
Mowbray, John; Tucker, Lynton; Poidevin, Nicholas le; Simpson, Edwin–Lewin on Trusts. 17th Ed. Property and Conveyancing Library. Hardback: £195.00. ISBN 0-421-23390-7. Sweet & Maxwell.
Mr Justice Laddie; Prescott, Peter; Vitoria, Mary; Lane, Lindsay–Modern Law of Copyright and Designs. 3rd Ed. Hardback: £320.00. ISBN 0-406-90383-2. Butterworths Law.
Mulcahy, Leigh-Ann–Human Rights and Civil Practice. Hardback: £150.00. ISBN 0-421-70990-1. Sweet & Maxwell.
Munday, R.J.C.–Butterworths Core Text: Evidence. Butterworths Core Texts. Paperback: £12.95. ISBN 0-406-98570-7. Paperback: £12.95. ISBN 0-406-98570-7. Butterworths Law.
Munzer, Stephen–New Essays in the Legal and Political Theory of Property. Cambridge Studies in Philosophy and Law. Hardback: £37.50. ISBN 0-521-64001-6. Cambridge University Press.
Murdoch, John; Hughes, Will–Construction Contracts: Law and Management. 3rd Ed. Hardback: £60.00. ISBN 0-419-26170-2. Spon Press.
Murray, Fiona–EU Special Legal Relationships. Paperback: £55.00. ISBN 1-902558-43-X. Palladian Law Publishing Ltd.
Musson, Anthony–Expectations of the Law in the Middle Ages. Hardback: £50.00. ISBN 0-85115-842-0. The Boydell Press.
Mustill, Lord; Boyd, Stewart C.–Commercial Arbitration: 2000 Companion Volume. Hardback: £95.00. ISBN 0-406-92534-8. Butterworths Law.
Mwenda, Kenneth–Banking Supervision and Systematic Bank Restructuring: an International and Comparative Perspective. Hardback: £65.00. ISBN 1-85941-613-6. Cavendish Publishing Ltd.
Narain, Vrinda–Gender and Community. Hardback: £32.00. ISBN 0-8020-4869-2. University of Toronto Press Inc.
Nathanson, Stephen–Non-trial Advocacy: a Case Study Approach. Paperback: £12.95. ISBN 1-85941-612-8. Cavendish Publishing Ltd.
Ndekugri; O'Gorman–Law and Contractual Procedures for Construction Students. Paperback: £19.95. ISBN 0-406-90324-7. Paperback: £19.95. ISBN 0-406-90324-7. Butterworths Law.
Neale, Bren; Smart, Carol–Good to Talk? Paperback: £12.00. ISBN 1-903456-02-9. Young Voice.
Neill, Elizabeth–Rites of Privacy and the Privacy Trade: on the Limits of Protection for the Self. Paperback: £16.50. ISBN 0-7735-2113-5. Hardback: £42.50. ISBN 0-7735-2097-X. McGill-Queen's University Press.
Nemeth, Charles P.–Aquinas in the Courtroom. Contributions in Philosophy, 82. Hardback: £58.50. ISBN 0-313-31929-4. Paperback: £19.95. ISBN 0-275-97290-9. Greenwood Press.
Nesic, Miryana; Boulle, Laurence–Mediation: Principles, Process, Practice. Paperback: £49.00. ISBN 0-406-92747-2. Butterworths Law.
Nicholls, Doug–Employment Practice and Policies in Youth and Community Work. 2nd Ed. Paperback: £16.95. ISBN 1-898924-63-5. Russell House Publishing Ltd.
Nicholls, Paul; Ball, Paul–Tolley's Equal Opportunities Handbook: 1999-2000. 3rd Ed. Paperback: £47.00. ISBN 0-7545-0238-4. Tolley Publishing.

Nicolaidis, Kalypso; Howse, Robert–Federal Vision. Hardback: £55.00. ISBN 0-19-924501-0. Paperback: £19.99. ISBN 0-19-924500-2. Oxford University Press.

Niemeyer, Gerhart–Law Without Force: the Function of Politics in International Law. Paperback: £19.50. ISBN 0-7658-0640-1. Transaction Publishers.

Nonet, Philippe; Selznick, Philip–Law and Society in Transition: Toward Responsive Law. Paperback: £20.00. ISBN 0-7658-0642-8. Transaction Publishers.

Norrie, Alan–Norrie: Crime, Reason and History. 2nd Ed. Law in Context. Paperback: £21.95. ISBN 0-406-93246-8. Butterworths Law.

Nousainen, Kevat; Gunnarsson, Asa; Niemi-Kielanen, Johanna; Lundstrom, Karin–Responsible Selves. Hardback: £55.00. ISBN 0-7546-2160-X. Ashgate Publishing Limited.

O'Brien, John–International Law. Paperback: £36.95. ISBN 1-85941-630-6. Cavendish Publishing Ltd.

O'Donnell, David–Meston's Succession Opinions. Greens Practice Library. Hardback: £135.00. ISBN 0-414-01121-X. W. Green & Son.

O'Hare, John; Browne, Kevin–O'Hare & Hill: Civil Litigation. 10th Ed. Litigation Library. Paperback: £45.00. ISBN 0-421-82650-9. Sweet & Maxwell.

O'Malley, Thomas–Round Hall Guide to the Sources of Law. 2nd Ed. Paperback: £40.00. ISBN 1-85800-185-4. Round Hall Ltd.

O'Rourke, Raymond–European Food Law 2nd Ed. Paperback: £58.00. ISBN 1-902558-44-8. Palladian Law Publishing Ltd.

Obeng, M.–Jurisprudence and Legal Theory. Suggested Solutions. £6.95. ISBN 1-85836-393-4. Old Bailey Press.

Ogus, Anthony I.–Regulation, Economics and the Law. International Library of Critical Writings in Economics, 137. Book (details unknown): £115.00. ISBN 1-84064-482-6. Edward Elgar.

Okowa, Phoebe–State Responsibility for Transboundary Air Pollution in International Law. Oxford Monographs in International Law. Hardback: £65.00. ISBN 0-19-826097-0. Oxford University Press Inc, USA.

Omar, Paul J.–Directors' Duties and Liabilities. Association of European Lawyers. Hardback: £55.00. ISBN 0-7546-2009-3. Dartmouth.

Orlik, Michael–Introduction to Highway Law. 2nd Ed. Paperback: £21.95. ISBN 0-7219-1331-8. Shaw & Sons.

Osiel, Mark J.–Obeying Orders. Paperback: £24.95. ISBN 0-7658-0798-X. Transaction Publishers.

Osman, Christopher; et al–Butterworths Employment Law Guide. 3rd Ed. Paperback: £63.00. ISBN 0-406-90493-6. Butterworths Law.

Owen, Lynette–Selling Rights. Hardback: £40.00. ISBN 0-415-23508-1. Routledge, an imprint of Taylor & Francis Books Ltd.

Owens, Keith–Law for Non-law Students. 3rd Ed. Paperback: £25.95. ISBN 1-85941-671-3. Cavendish Publishing Ltd.

Page, Ed–Governing by Numbers. Hardback: £22.50. ISBN 1-84113-207-1. Hart Publishing.

Paisley, Roderick; Cusine, Sheriff D–Unreported Property Cases. Paperback: £85.00. ISBN 0-414-01338-7. W. Green & Son.

Paisley, Roderick–Land. Greens Law Basics. Paperback: £9.95. ISBN 0-414-01373-5. W. Green & Son.

Palmer, Julian–Animal Law 3rd Ed. Paperback: £29.95. ISBN 0-7219-0802-0. Shaw & Sons.

Palmer, Vernon Valentine–Mixed Jurisdictions Worldwide. Hardback: £60.00. ISBN 0-521-78154-X. Cambridge University Press.

Panesar, Sukhinder–General Principles of Property Law. Paperback: £19.99. ISBN 0-582-42332-5. Longman Higher Education.

Parr, Russell. L.–Intellectual Property Infringement Damages. 2nd Ed. Paperback: £46.50. ISBN 0-471-39050-X. John Wiley and Sons.

Parry, Helen; Cullen, Iain–Hedge Funds: Law and Regulation. Special Reports. Hardback: £150.00. ISBN 0-421-70570-1. Sweet & Maxwell.

Parsons, Andrew–Mental Health Law Compendium. Spiral/comb bound: £95.00. ISBN 1-85978-932-3. Monitor Press.

Pascoe, Susan–Land Law-A Student Friendly Introduction and Revision Guide. Law. Paperback: £9.95. ISBN 1-84285-003-2. Studymates Limited.

Paterson, Gerald–European Patent System. 2nd Ed. Hardback: £150.00. ISBN 0-421-58600-1. Hardback: £170.00. ISBN 0-421-58600-1. Sweet & Maxwell.

Patersons Licensing Acts 2002. Hardback: £190.00. ISBN 0-406-94566-7. Butterworths Law.

Peaple, Sheree–Storey: Conveyancing. 5th Ed. Paperback: £21.95. ISBN 0-406-93760-5. Butterworths Law.

Pearson, Philippa–Cohabitation Rights. Paperback: £9.99. ISBN 1-902646-52-5. Law Pack Publishing.

Peck, Lib; Cooper, Jonathan; Owers, Anne–Developing Key Privacy Rights. Justice-putting Rights Into Practice. Paperback: £15.00. ISBN 1-84113-168-7. Hart Publishing.

Pejovich, Svetozar–Economics of Property Rights. International Library of Critical Writings in Economics, 129. Hardback: £280.00. ISBN 1-84064-232-7. Edward Elgar.

Penton, John–Widening the Eye of the Needle. 2nd Ed. Conservation and Mission. Paperback: £10.95. ISBN 0-7151-7589-0. Church House Publishing.

Perry, Barbara–In the Name of Hate. Hardback: £50.00. ISBN 0-415-92772-2. Paperback: £13.99. ISBN 0-415-92773-0. Routledge, Inc.

Pertman, Adam–Adoption Nation-How the Adoption Revolution Is Transforming America. Paperback: £11.99. ISBN 0-465-05651-2. Basic Books.

Pettet, Ben–Company Law. Longman Law Series. Paperback: £27.99. ISBN 0-582-07716-8. Longman Higher Education.

Pettit, Philip–Equity and the Law of Trusts. 9th Ed. Paperback: £29.95. ISBN 0-406-93761-3. Butterworths Law.

Philips, Nevil; Craig, Nicholas–Merchant Shipping Act 1995. 2nd Ed. Paperback: £88.00. ISBN 1-85978-563-8. LLP Professional Publishing.

Phillips, E.; Walsh, C.; Dobson, P.–Law Relating to Theft. Legal Skills. Paperback: £23.95. ISBN 1-85941-200-9. Cavendish Publishing Ltd.

Phillips, Jim; Chapman, Bruce; Stevens, David–Between State and Market. Hardback: £52.50. ISBN 0-7735-2096-1. Paperback: £24.95. ISBN 0-7735-2112-7. McGill-Queen's University Press.

Picciotto, Sol–International Business Taxation. Law in Context. Paperback: £224.95. ISBN 0-406-93404-5. Butterworths Law.

Pierce, Jennifer; Purvis, Ian–Working with Technology: Funding, Protection and Exploitation. Hardback: £95.00. ISBN 0-421-59810-7. Sweet & Maxwell.

Pike, Christopher–Virtual Monopoly. Hardback: £19.99. ISBN 1-85788-284-9. Nicholas Brealey Publishing Ltd.

Pitt, Gwyneth–Employment Law. 4th Ed. Paperback: £21.95. ISBN 0-421-69010-0. Sweet & Maxwell.

Plender, Richard; Wilderspin, Michael–European Contracts Convention-The Rome Convention of the Choice of Contracts. 2nd Ed. Hardback: £125.00. ISBN 0-421-73860-X. Sweet & Maxwell.

Pollard, David; Parpworth, Neil; Hughes, David–Constitutional and Administrative Law-cases and Materials. 3rd Ed. Paperback: £34.95. ISBN 0-406-93056-2. Butterworths Law.

Polti, Mauro; Nesi, Giuseppe–Rome Statute of the International Criminal Court. Hardback: £55.00. ISBN 0-7546-2154-5. Ashgate Publishing Limited.

Porat, Ariel; Stein, Alex–Liability Under Uncertainty. Hardback: £50.00. ISBN 0-19-826797-5. Oxford University Press.

Porter, David S.; Openshaw, Vanessa–Business Management for Solicitors-Turning Your Practice Into a Business-New Ed. Paperback: £38.00. ISBN 1-85811-274-5. EMIS Professional Publishing.

Posner, Eric A.–Law and Economics. International Library of Essays in Law and Legal Theory (second Series). Hardback: £90.00. ISBN 0-7546-2098-0. Dartmouth.

Posner, Richard A.; Parisi, Francesco–Economics of Private Law: the Collected Economic Essays of Richard A. Posner: Vol 2. Economists of the 20th Century. Hardback: £75.00. ISBN 1-85898-642-7. Edward Elgar.

Posner, Richard A.; Parisi, Francesco–Economics of Public Law-The Collected Economic Essays of Richard A. Posner.Volume Three. Economists of the 20th Century. Hardback: £75.00. ISBN 1-85898-643-5. Edward Elgar.

Powell, Richard–Child Law. Paperback: £18.00. ISBN 1-872870-92-9. Waterside Press.

Power, Conor–Family Legislation Service. Looseleaf/ring bound: £295.00. ISBN 1-85800-163-3. Round Hall Ltd.

Priban, Jiri; Nelken, David–Law's New Boundaries-the Consequences of Legal Autopiesis. Applied Legal Philosophy. Hardback: £50.00. ISBN 0-7546-2202-9. Ashgate Publishing Limited.

Price, David–Legal and Ethical Aspects of Organ Transplantation. Hardback: £45.00. ISBN 0-521-65164-6. Cambridge University Press.

Price, Monroe E.; Verhulst, Stefaan–Parental Control of Television Broadcasting. LEA'S Communication Series. Hardback: £63.95. ISBN 0-8058-2978-4. Paperback: £31.95. ISBN 0-8058-3902-X. Lawrence Erlbaum Associates, Inc.

Professional Driver's Guide 2002. Paperback: £25.00. ISBN 1-85524-617-1. Croner Publications.

Purcell, Oliver Ryan–Milk Quotas. Paperback. ISBN 1-899738-73-8. Round Hall Ltd.

Pyke, James–A-Z of Civil Litigation. Paperback: £32.00. ISBN 0-7520-0608-8. Sweet & Maxwell.

Quarrel, John–Law of Pension Fund Investment. £49.95. ISBN 0-7545-0803-X. Tolley Publishing.

Quas, Jodi A.; Eisen, Mitchell L.; Goodman–Memory and Suggestibility in the Forensic Interview. Personality and Clinical Psychology Series. Hardback: £83.95. ISBN 0-8058-3080-4. Lawrence Erlbaum Associates, Inc.

Quinney, Richard–Critique of the Legal Order. Law and Society Series. Paperback: £20.95. ISBN 0-7658-0797-1. Transaction Publishers.

Radevsky, Anthony; Clark, Wayne–Radevsky and Clark: Tenant's Right of First Refusal. Hardback: £55.00. ISBN 0-406-91104-5. Butterworths Law.

Radford, Mike–Animal Welfare Law in Britain-Regulation and Responsibility. Hardback: £45.00. ISBN 0-19-826251-5. Paperback: £16.99. ISBN 0-19-826245-0. Oxford University Press.

Rammeloo, Stephan–Corporations in Private International Law. Oxford Monographs in Private International Law. Hardback: £75.00. ISBN 0-19-829925-7. Oxford University Press.

Ramsay, Vivian; Furst, Stephen–Keating on Building Contracts. 7th Ed. Hardback: £220.00. ISBN 0-421-56530-6. Sweet & Maxwell.

Ramsey, Rosalind; Szmuckler, George; Gerada, Clare; Mars, Sara–Mental Illness-A Handbook for Carers. 2nd Ed. Paperback: £15.95. ISBN 1-85302-934-3. Jessica Kingsley Publishers.

Ramsey, Rosalind; Szmuckler, George; Gerada, Clare; Mars, Sara–Mental Illness. Paperback: £14.95. ISBN 1-85302-934-3. Jessica Kingsley Publishers.

Rao, P.K.–International Environmental Law and Economics. Hardback: £60.00. ISBN 0-631-21892-0. Paperback: £19.99. ISBN 0-631-21893-9. Blackwell Publishers.

Ratner, Steven R.; Abrams, Jason S.–Accountability for Human Rights Atrocities in International Law. Oxford Monographs in International Law. Paperback: £16.99. ISBN 0-19-829871-4. Oxford University Press.

Rayer, John–RSM Robson Rhodes: Personal Financial Planning Manual: 2000-2001. 16th Ed. Paperback: £37.95. ISBN 0-406-91479-6. Butterworths Law.

Raz, Joseph–Value, Respect and Attachment. The Seeley Lectures, 4. Hardback: £37.50. ISBN 0-521-80180-X. Paperback (C format): £12.95. ISBN 0-521-00022-X. Cambridge University Press.

Reay, Rosamund–Evidence Textbook. 3rd Ed. Old Bailey Press Textbooks. Paperback: £14.95. ISBN 1-85836-407-8. Old Bailey Press.

Redmayne, Mike–Expert Evidence and Criminal Justice. Oxford Monographs on Criminal Law and Justice. Hardback: £35.00. ISBN 0-19-826780-0. Oxford University Press.

Reed, Lord–Practical Guide to Human Rights Law in Scotland. Paperback: £45.00. ISBN 0-414-01369-7. W. Green & Son.

Reed, O. Lee; Shedd, Peter; Morehead, Jere; Corley, Robert–Legal and Regulatory Environment of Business 12th Ed. Hardback: £95.99. ISBN 0-07-250399-8. McGraw-Hill Publishing Company.

Reid, Colin T.–Nature Conservation Law. 2nd Ed. Paperback: £40.00. ISBN 0-414-01355-7. W. Green & Son.

Reilly, Ben–Democracy in Divided Societies-electoral Engineering for Conflict Management. Theories of Institutional Design. Hardback: £40.00. ISBN 0-521-79323-8. Paperback: £14.95. ISBN 0-521-79730-6. Cambridge University Press.

Remuneration Strategy. Looseleaf/ring bound: £75.00. ISBN 0-406-90391-3. Butterworths Law.

Rent Review and Lease Renewal. Hardback: £60.00. ISBN 1-85978-964-1. LLP Professional Publishing.

Residential Letting Kit. Looseleaf/ring bound: £6.99. ISBN 1-902646-73-8. Law Pack Publishing.

Resumes for Law Careers-with Sample Cover Letters. 2nd Ed. VGM Professional Resumes. Book (details unknown): £7.99. ISBN 0-658-01723-3. McGraw-Hill Publishing Company.

Revenue Law. ISBN 1-85800-132-3. Round Hall Ltd.

Richards, Paul–Law of Contract. 5th Ed. Foundation Studies in Law Series. Paperback: £25.99. ISBN 0-582-43817-9. Longman.

Richardson, James; Thomas, David–Archbold: Criminal Pleading, Evidence and Practice: 2002. 50th Ed. Hardback: £235.00. ISBN 0-421-75370-6. Sweet & Maxwell.

Riles, Annelise–Rethinking the Masters of Comparative Law. Hardback: £40.00. ISBN 1-84113-289-6. Paperback: £25.00. ISBN 1-84113-290-X. Hart Publishing.

Robb, Cairo A. R.–International Environmental Law Reports. 2nd Ed. International Environmental Law Reports. Hardback: £120.00. ISBN 0-521-65035-6. Paperback: £45.00. ISBN 0-521-65967-1. Cambridge University Press.

Robb, Cairo–International Environmental Law Reports: Vol 3. 3rd Ed. International Environmental Law Reports, 3. Hardback: £200.00. ISBN 0-521-65036-4. Paperback: £80.00. ISBN 0-521-65966-3. Cambridge University Press.

Robert, Henry M.–Robert's Rules of Order 10th Ed. Hardback: £24.99. ISBN 0-7382-0384-X. Paperback: £12.99. ISBN 0-7382-0307-6. Perseus Books.

Robert, Henry M.–Robert's Rules of Order. Paperback: £12.99. ISBN 0-7382-0307-6. Perseus Books.

Robertson, Douglas; Rosenberry, Katharine–Home Ownership with Responsibility. Paperback: £12.95. ISBN 1-84263-057-1. York Publishing Services-Joseph Rowntree Foundation.

Rodger, Richard-Transformation of Edinburgh-Land, Property and Trust in the 19th Century. Hardback: £55.00. ISBN 0-521-78024-1. Cambridge University Press.

Rodway, Susan; Levene, Simon-Medical Negligence: Managing Medical Disputes. Hardback: £60.00. ISBN 1-902558-05-7. Palladian Law Publishing Ltd.

Roggenkamp, Martha M.; Ronne, Anita; Redgewell, Catherine; Guayo, Inigo del-Energy Law in Europe-National, EU and International Law and Institutions. Hardback: £165.00. ISBN 0-19-826068-7. Oxford University Press.

Rose, Adam; Leibowitz, David; Magnus, Adrian-Getting out of a Contract. Hardback: £39.95. ISBN 0-566-08161-X. Gower Publishing Limited.

Rose, Francis-Nutshells: Company Law. Nutshells. Paperback: £5.50. ISBN 0-421-73850-2. Sweet & Maxwell.

Rosenthal, Dennis-Guide to Consumer Credit Law and Practice. 2nd Ed. Paperback: £50.00. ISBN 0-406-90321-2. Butterworths Law.

Ross, Hamish-Law As a Social Institution. Legal Theory Today. Hardback: £22.00. ISBN 1-84113-230-6. Paperback: £10.00. ISBN 1-84113-231-4. Hart Publishing.

Ross, Jamie-Last Will and Testament Guide. £9.99. ISBN 1-902646-70-3. Law Pack Publishing.

Rostron, J.-Dictionary of Property and Construction Law. Paperback: £19.99. ISBN 0-419-26110-9. Hardback: £50.00. ISBN 0-419-26100-1. Spon Press.

Roth, Peter-Bellamy and Child: European Community Law of Competition 5th Ed. Hardback: £240.00. ISBN 0-421-56440-7. Sweet & Maxwell.

Rotherham, Craig-Proprietary Remedies in Context. Hardback: £27.50. ISBN 1-84113-165-2. Hart Publishing.

Rowland, Mark; White, Robin-Social Security Tribunals: the Legislation 2000: Vol 3. Administration, Adjudication and the European Dimension. £55.00. ISBN 0-421-82480-8. Sweet & Maxwell.

Rowland, Mark; White, Robin-Social Security: Legislation 2001: Vol III, Administration, Adjudication and the European Dimension. Paperback: £59.00. ISBN 0-421-82630-4. Sweet & Maxwell.

Rowley, J. William-Business Law International: Volume 1. Hardback: £120.00. ISBN 0-521-80100-1. Sweet & Maxwell.

Roznovschi, Mirela-Toward the Cyberlegal Culture. Hardback: £76.99. ISBN 1-57105-168-6. Transnational Publishers, Inc.

Rubenfeld, Jed-Freedom and Time. Hardback: £27.50. ISBN 0-300-08048-4. Yale University Press.

Ruegger, Maria-Hearing the Voice of the Child. Paperback: £16.95. ISBN 1-898924-82-1. Russell House Publishing Ltd.

Russell, Peter H.; O'Brien, David M.-Judicial Independence in the Age of Democracy. Constitutionalism and Democracy Series. Hardback: £58.95. ISBN 0-8139-2015-9. Paperback: £18.95. ISBN 0-8139-2016-7. University Press of Virginia.

Rutherford, L.; et al-Osborn's Concise Law Dictionary 9th Ed. Paperback: £9.95. ISBN 0-421-75340-4. Sweet & Maxwell.

Rutledge, Philip; Haines, Jason-Butterworths Compliance Series: Electronic Trading. Butterworths Compliance Series. Paperback: £50.00. ISBN 0-406-93750-8. Butterworths Law.

Ryley, Richard; Goodwyn, Edward-Employment Law for the Construction Industry. Hardback: £25.00. ISBN 0-7277-2784-2. Thomas Telford Ltd.

Sadler, Pauline-National Security and the D-Notice System. Hardback: £50.00. ISBN 0-7546-2170-7. Dartmouth.

Sadurski, Wojciech-Justice. International Library of Essays in Law and Legal Theory, Second Series. Hardback: £95.00. ISBN 0-7546-2088-3. Ashgate Publishing Limited.

Safferling, Christoph-Towards an International Criminal Procedure. Hardback: £60.00. ISBN 0-19-924350-6. Oxford University Press.

Salin, Patrick-Andre–Satellite Communications Regulations in the Early 21st Century. Utrecht Studies in Air and Space Law, 19. Hardback: £123.00. ISBN 90-411-1238-3. Martinus Nijhoff Publishers.

Salter, David; Bamber, Roger; Bird, Roger; Salter, David–Pensions and Insurance on Family Breakdown. Paperback: CD-ROM: £45.00. ISBN 0-85308-698-2. Family Law.

Samuel, Geoffrey–Law of Obligations and Legal Remedies. 2nd Ed. Paperback: £25.95. ISBN 1-85941-566-0. Cavendish Publishing Ltd.

Sanders, Michael–Joint Ventures Involving Tax-exempt Organizations: 2001 Cumulative Supplement. Paperback: £42.95. ISBN 0-471-39034-8. John Wiley and Sons.

Sands, Philippe; Klein, Pierre–Bowett: Law of International Institutions. 5th Ed. Paperback: £30.00. ISBN 0-421-53690-X. Sweet & Maxwell.

Sarooshi, Danesh–United Nations and the Development of Collective Security. Oxford Monographs in International Law. Paperback: £22.50. ISBN 0-19-829934-6. Oxford University Press.

Scannell, Yvonne–Law of Waste Management in Ireland. Hardback. ISBN 1-899738-85-1. Round Hall Ltd.

Schabas, William A.–An Introduction to the International Criminal Court. Hardback: £55.00. ISBN 0-521-80457-4. Paperback: £19.95. ISBN 0-521-01149-3. Cambridge University Press.

Schlueter, Thorsten–Banks As Financial Advisers. Studies in Comparative Corporate and Financial Law, 12. Hardback: £60.00. ISBN 90-411-9828-8. Kluwer Law International.

Schneid, Thomas–Legal Liabilities in Emergency Medical Services. Hardback: £30.00. ISBN 1-56032-899-1. Hardback: £30.00. ISBN 1-56032-899-1. Taylor & Francis.

Schonberg, Soren–Legitimate Expectations in Administrative Law. Hardback: £40.00. ISBN 0-19-829947-8. Oxford University Press.

School Governor's Legal Guide: 2002. Paperback: £25.00. ISBN 1-85524-618-X. Croner Publications.

Schulte-Nolke, Hans; Schulze, Reiner; Jones, Jackie–Casebook on European Consumer Law. Paperback: £25.00. ISBN 1-84113-227-6. Hart Publishing.

Sciarra, Silvana–Labour Law in the Courts. Hardback: £25.00. ISBN 1-84113-024-9. Hart Publishing.

Scots Law Times. Hardback: £255.00. ISBN 0-414-01418-9. W.Green & Son.

Scott-Hunt, Susan; Lim, Hilary–Feminist Perspectives on Equity and Trusts. Feminist Perspectives. Paperback: £19.95. ISBN 1-85941-606-3. Cavendish Publishing Ltd.

Scott, Craig–Torture As Tort. Hardback: £45.00. ISBN 1-84113-060-5. Hart Publishing.

Scottish Landlord & Tenant Fact Book. Looseleaf/ring bound. ISBN 0-414-01380-8. W.Green & Son.

Scottish Lawyers Factbook. Looseleaf/ring bound: £145.00. ISBN 0-414-01343-3. W.Green & Son.

Seiter, Richard P.–Correctional Administration-Integrating Theory and Practice. Paperback: £29.99. ISBN 0-13-087147-8. Prentice Hall.

Sellman, Pamela; Evans, Judith–Law of International Trade. 1st Ed. Old Bailey Press 150 Leading Cases Series. Paperback: £9.95. ISBN 1-85836-364-0. Old Bailey Press.

Selman, Andy; Hunter, Caroline–Best Value in Housing Management: Law and Practice in the Management of Social Housing. Arden's Housing Library. Paperback: £18.95. ISBN 1-898001-70-7. Lemos & Crane.

Serajuddin, Alamgir Muhammad–Shari'a Law and Society. Hardback: £13.95. ISBN 0-19-579666-7. OUP Pakistan.

Sergeant, Malcolm–Employment Law. Paperback: £24.99. ISBN 0-582-42375-9. Longman.

Shannon, Geoffrey; Dunne, Anne—Family Law Practitioner. Looseleaf/ring bound: £295.00. ISBN 1-85800-150-1. Round Hall Ltd.

Sheehan, Rosemary—Magistrates' Decision-making in Child Protection Cases. Hardback: £42.50. ISBN 0-7546-1505-7. Ashgate Publishing Limited.

Sheridan, Brian—EU Bio-technology Law & Practice. Paperback: £65.00. ISBN 1-902558-30-8. Palladian Law Publishing Ltd.

Sherman, Brad; Bently, Lionel—Intellectual Property Law-Reissue. Paperback: £32.99. ISBN 0-19-876343-3. Oxford University Press.

Short, Richard—Food Safety Law Procedures. Paperback: £59.95. ISBN 1-902375-64-5. Chandos Publishing Ltd.

Siddique, M.A.B.—International Migration Into the 21st Century. Hardback: £59.95. ISBN 1-84064-531-8. Edward Elgar.

Siegan, Bernard H.—Rights of Englishmen. New Studies in Social Policy. Hardback: £37.95. ISBN 0-7658-0057-8. Paperback: £24.95. ISBN 0-7658-0755-6. Transaction Publishers.

Sienho Yee; Wang Tieya—International Law in the Post-cold War World. Routledge Studies in International Law, 1. Hardback: £95.00. ISBN 0-415-23608-8. Routledge, an imprint of Taylor & Francis Books Ltd.

Simmons, A. John—Justification and Legitimacy. Hardback: £35.00. ISBN 0-521-79016-6. Paperback: £12.95. ISBN 0-521-79365-3. Cambridge University Press.

Simmons; Simmons—E-commerce Law-Doing Business on Line. Paperback: £55.00. ISBN 1-902558-45-6. Palladian Law Publishing Ltd.

Simor, Jessica—Human Rights Practice. Hardback: £198.00. ISBN 0-4216-2540-6. Sweet & Maxwell.

Simpson, Mark; Hoffman, Lord—Professional Negligence and Liability. Looseleaf/ring bound: £250.00. ISBN 1-85978-673-1. LLP Professional Publishing.

Sims, Nicholas—Evolution of Biological Disarmament. SIPRI Chemical & Biological Warfare Studies. Paperback: £25.00. ISBN 0-19-829578-2. Oxford University Press.

Singleton, Susan—Ecommerce: a Practical Guide to the Law. Hardback: £45.00. ISBN 0-566-08276-4. Gower Publishing Limited.

Singleton, Susan—Legal Guide to Online Business. Paperback: £9.99. ISBN 1-902646-77-0. Law Pack Publishing.

Skidmore, Paul; Novitz, Tania—Fairness At Work. Paperback: £23.00. ISBN 1-84113-083-4. Hart Publishing.

Skogly, Sigrun—Human Rights Obligations of the World Bank and the International Monetary Fund. Paperback: £65.00. ISBN 1-85941-665-9. Cavendish Publishing Ltd.

Slapper, Gary; Kelly, David—English Legal System 5th Ed. Paperback: £25.95. ISBN 1-85941-657-8. Cavendish Publishing Ltd.

Slapper, Gary; Kelly, David—Sourcebook on the English Legal System. 2nd Ed. Sourcebook Series. Paperback: £32.95. ISBN 1-85941-553-9. Cavendish Publishing Ltd.

Slapper, Gary—Organisational Proscecutions. Hardback: £40.00. ISBN 0-7546-2059-X. Dartmouth.

Smith, David—IR35 Defence Strategies: from Contracts to Commissioners. Paperback: £45.00. ISBN 0-7545-1426-9. Tolley Publishing.

Smith, Karen E.; Light, Margot—Ethics and Foreign Policy. LSE Monographs in International Studies. Hardback: £40.00. ISBN 0-521-80415-9. Cambridge University Press.

Smith, Lionel D.—Restitution. International Library of Essays in Law and Legal Theory (second Series). Hardback: £100.00. ISBN 0-7546-2057-3. Dartmouth.

Smits, Wendy; Stromback, Thorsten—Economics of the Apprenticeship System. Elgar Monographs. Hardback: £45.00. ISBN 1-84064-197-5. Edward Elgar.

Snyder, Francis–Regional and Global Regulation of International Trade. Hardback: £35.00. ISBN 1-84113-218-7. Hart Publishing.

Soares, Patrick–Non-resident Trusts. 6th Ed. Hardback: £175.00. ISBN 0-421-75970-4. Sweet & Maxwell.

Solicitors Professional Handbook 2001. Paperback: £23.00. ISBN 0-414-01424-3. W.Green & Son.

Somerville, Margaret–Death Talk. Hardback: £46.00. ISBN 0-7735-2201-8. Paperback: £17.95. ISBN 0-7735-2245-X. McGill-Queen's University Press.

Southern, David–Taxation of Corporate Debt and Financial Instruments. 4th Ed. Paperback: £62.95. ISBN 0-7545-0861-7. Tolley Publishing.

Spence, Charles F.–AIM/FAR 2002. Aviation Week. Paperback: Internet resource: £13.99. ISBN 0-07-137737-9. McGraw-Hill Publishing Company.

Spencer, John; Spencer, Maureen–Human Rights in a Nutshell. Nutshells. Paperback: £5.95. ISBN 0-421-75180-0. Sweet & Maxwell.

Stacy, Helen M.–Postmodernism and Law-Jurisprudence in a Fragmenting World. Applied Legal Philosophy. Hardback: £50.00. ISBN 1-84014-749-0. Dartmouth.

Stallworthy, Mark–Sustainability, Land Use and Environment. Paperback: £48.40. ISBN 1-85941-647-0. Cavendish Publishing Ltd.

Stamatoudi, Irina–Copyright and Multimedia Products. Cambridge Studies in Intellectual Property Rights. Hardback: £55.00. ISBN 0-521-80819-7. Cambridge University Press.

Standley, Kate–Family Law. 3rd Ed. Palgrave Law Masters. Paperback: £14.99. ISBN 0-333-94942-0. Palgrave, formerly Macmillan Press.

Status of Workers. Legal Essentials. Paperback: £29.99. ISBN 0-85292-931-5. Chartered Institute of Personnel and Development (CIPD).

Stevens, John and Pearce, Professor Robert–Land Law. 2nd Ed. Textbook Series. Paperback: £23.95. ISBN 0-421-69000-3. Sweet & Maxwell.

Steward, Clive–Taxation Simplified: 2001. Paperback: £9.99. ISBN 1-85252-368-9. Management Books 2000.

Stewart, William–Collins Dictionary of Law. 2nd Ed. Paperback: £9.99. ISBN 0-00-710294-1. Collins.

Stinchcombe, Arthur L.–When Formality Works-Authority and Abstraction in Law and Organizations. Hardback: £30.00. ISBN 0-226-77495-3. Paperback: £10.50. ISBN 0-226-77496-1. University of Chicago Press.

Stokke, Olav Schram–Governing High-seas Fisheries. Hardback: £65.00. ISBN 0-19-829949-4. Oxford University Press.

Storey, Tony; Lidbury, Alan–Criminal Law. Paperback: £15.99. ISBN 1-903240-25-5. Willan Publishing.

Strang, Heather; Braithwaite, John–Restorative Justice and Civil Society. Hardback: £47.50. ISBN 0-521-80599-6. Paperback: £17.95. ISBN 0-521-00053-X. Cambridge University Press.

Sunkin, Maurice; Ong, David M.; Wight, Robert–Sourcebook on Environmental Law. 2nd Ed. Sourcebook Series. Paperback: £25.95. ISBN 1-85941-586-5. Paperback: £33.95. ISBN 1-85941-586-5. Cavendish Publishing Ltd.

Sunnucks, James H.G.–Williams, Mortimer & Sunnucks-executors, Administrators and Probate. 18th Ed. Property and Conveyancing Library. Hardback: £235.00. ISBN 0-421-65330-2. Sweet & Maxwell.

Supiot, Alain–Beyond Employment. Hardback: £40.00. ISBN 0-19-924305-0. Paperback: £15.99. ISBN 0-19-924304-2. Oxford University Press.

Supperstone, Michael; Pitt-Payne, Timothy–Guide to the Freedom of Information Act 2000. Paperback: £35.00. ISBN 0-406-93145-3. Butterworths Law.

Surridge, Robert J.; Scott, Roselyn; Murphy, Brian; James, Natalie; John, Noleen–Houseman and Davies: Law of Life Assurance. 112th Ed. Hardback: £135.00. ISBN 0-406-93589-0. Butterworths Law.

Sykes, John and Wright, Patrick–Valuation and Commercial Assessment of Intellectual Property Assets. Hardback: £70.00. ISBN 0-421-57920-X. Sweet & Maxwell.

Tamanaha, Brian Z.–General Jurisprudence of Law and Society. Oxford Socio-Legal Studies. Hardback: £40.00. ISBN 0-19-924466-9. Paperback: £15.99. ISBN 0-19-924467-7. Oxford University Press.

Tarde, Gabriel–Penal Philosophy. Paperback: £33.50. ISBN 0-7658-0705-X. Transaction Publishers.

Tax Statutes and Statutory Instruments 2001-2002. Paperback: £73.00. ISBN 0-86325-559-0. Croner CCH Group Ltd.

Taylor, Ian–Procurement of Information Systems. Chandos Business Guides: Purchasing, 1. Paperback: £49.95. ISBN 1-902375-63-7. Paperback: £49.95. ISBN 1-902375-63-7. Chandos Publishing Ltd.

Taylor, Paul; Oliver, Timothy; Pether, Michael–Bingham and Berryman's Motor Claims Cases. 11th Ed. Hardback: £195.00. ISBN 0-406-93230-1. Butterworths Law.

Taylor, Paul–Taylor on Appeals. Criminal Law Library. Hardback: £110.00. ISBN 0-421-58990-6. Sweet & Maxwell.

Teff, Harvey–Medical Practice and Malpractice. The International Library of Medicine, Ethics and Law. Hardback: £110.00. ISBN 0-7546-2033-6. Hardback: £90.00. ISBN 0-7546-2033-6. Dartmouth.

Tessa, Shepperson–Residential Lettings. CD-ROM (software). ISBN 1-902646-82-7. Law Pack Publishing.

Tettenborn, Andrew–Law of Restitution in England and Ireland. 3rd Ed. Paperback: £28.95. ISBN 1-85941-567-9. Cavendish Publishing Ltd.

Thomas, P.A.; Knowles, John–Dane & Thomas: How to Use a Law Library. 4th Ed. Paperback: £14.95. ISBN 0-421-74410-3. Sweet & Maxwell.

Thurston, John–Practitioner's Guide to Powers of Attorney. 4th Ed. Paperback: £44.00. ISBN 0-7545-1270-3. Tolley Publishing.

Tigar, Michael–Law and the Rise of Capitalism 2nd Ed. Paperback: £15.00. ISBN 1-58367-030-0. New York University Press.

Tiley, John; Collison, David–Simon's Tiley and Collison: UK Tax Guide 2001-2002. 19th Ed. Paperback: £75.00. ISBN 0-406-94058-4. Butterworths Tolley.

Tingle, John; Garwood-Gowers, Austen–Healthcare Law: the Impact of the Human Rights Act 1998. Paperback: £48.40. ISBN 1-85941-670-5. Cavendish Publishing Ltd.

Todd–International Trade Law. Paperback: £45.00. ISBN 1-85978-573-5. LLP Professional Publishing.

Tolley's National Insurance Contributions 2001-02. Tolley's Tax Annuals. Paperback: CD-ROM: £54.95. ISBN 0-7545-1392-0. Tolley Publishing.

Tolley's Tax Computations: 2000-2001. Paperback: £54.95. ISBN 0-7545-0712-2. Tolley Publishing.

Tolley's Tax Planning: 2000-2001. Paperback: £125.00. ISBN 0-7545-0721-1. Tolley Publishing.

Tomlinson, Hugh; Shukla, Vena–Human Rights Cases of the Commonwealth. Hardback: £95.00. ISBN 0-406-91837-6. Butterworths Law.

Towse, Ruth–Creativity, Incentive and Reward-An Economic Analysis of Copyright and Culture in the Information Age. Hardback: £55.00. ISBN 1-84064-254-8. Edward Elgar.

Transfer Pricing: a UK Perspective. 2nd Ed. £65.00. ISBN 0-406-91901-1. Butterworths Law.

Treitel, Guenter H.; Reynolds, Francis M.B.–Carver: Bills of Lading. New Ed. Hardback: £210.00. ISBN 0-421-56470-9. Sweet & Maxwell.

Treverton, Gregory W.–Reshaping Intelligence for the 21st Century. Hardback: £24.95. ISBN 0-521-58096-X. Cambridge University Press.

Tromans, Stephen; Irvine, Gillian–Taking Responsibility. Business and Environment Practitioner Series. Paperback: £35.00. ISBN 1-85383-597-8. Earthscan.

Tshosa, Onkemetse–National Law and International Human Rights. Law, Social Change and Development Series. Hardback: £50.00. ISBN 0-7546-2175-8. Hardback: £50.00. ISBN 0-7546-2175-8. Ashgate Publishing Limited.

Tunick, Mark–Practices and Principles. Paperback: £12.95. ISBN 0-691-07079-2. Princeton University Press.

Tweedale, Geoffrey–Magic Mineral to Killer Dust. Paperback: £17.99. ISBN 0-19-924399-9. Oxford University Press.

Vaughn, Robert G.–Freedom of Information. International Library of Essays in Law and Legal Theory (second Series). Hardback: £100.00. ISBN 0-7546-2081-6. Ashgate Publishing Ltd.

Vidas, Davor–Protecting the Polar Marine Environment. Hardback: £45.00. ISBN 0-521-66311-3. Cambridge University Press.

Vincent, Robert; Clark, Jon; Mays, Ray; Francis, Amanda; Worsey, Mark–Charity Accounting and Taxation. 4th Ed. Paperback: £55.00. ISBN 0-406-98899-4. Butterworths Law.

Voller, Mike–Tolley's Taxation of Lloyd's Underwriters. 9th Ed. Hardback: £92.95. ISBN 0-7545-0705-X. Tolley Publishing.

von Lewinski, Silke; Reinbothe, Jong–WIPO Treaties 1996. 2nd Ed. Paperback: £75.00. ISBN 0-406-89669-0. Butterworths Law.

Waite, Andrew; Jewell, Tim–Environmental Law in Property Transactions. 2nd Ed. Paperback: £60.00. ISBN 0-406-92364-7. Butterworths Law.

Walker, Andrew–Conveyancing Textbook. 3rd Ed. Old Bailey Press Textbooks. Paperback: £14.95. ISBN 1-85836-402-7. Old Bailey Press.

Walker, Andrew–Conveyancing. Old Bailey Press Leading Cases. Paperback: £9.95. ISBN 1-85836-421-3. Old Bailey Press.

Walker, Campbell–Reading Bills of Rights in Changing Contexts. Hardback: £35.00. ISBN 1-84113-133-4. Hart Publishing.

Walker, Neil–Policing in a Changing Constitutional Order. Modern Legal Studies. Paperback: £19.95. ISBN 0-421-63370-0. Sweet & Maxwell.

Walker, Peter M.–Practice Notes on Consumer Law. Practice Notes. Paperback: £15.95. ISBN 1-85941-573-3. Cavendish Publishing Ltd.

Wallace, Rebecca M.M.–International Human Rights. 2nd Ed. Paperback: £26.95. ISBN 0-421-71030-6. Sweet & Maxwell.

Wallis, Peter; McCormac, Kevin; Niekirk, Paul–Wilkinson's Road Traffic Offences. 20th Ed. Hardback: £245.00. ISBN 0-421-82580-4. Sweet & Maxwell.

Walmsley–Butterworths Company Law Handbook. Hardback: £38.00. ISBN 0-406-94576-4. Butterworths Law.

Walton, Christopher; Percy, R.A.–Charlesworth and Percy on Negligence. 10th Ed. Common Law Library. Hardback: £225.00. ISBN 0-421-82590-1. Sweet & Maxwell.

Walton, Keith–Tolley's Capital Allowances 2000-01. Paperback: £49.95. ISBN 0-7545-0718-1. Tolley Publishing.

Ward, John–Judge: Irish Income Tax 2001-2002. Butterworth's Irish Tax Library. Paperback: £100.00. ISBN 1-85475-697-4. Butterworths Law.

Ward, Tim; Sedley; Gordon, Richard; Emmerson, Ben–Human Rights Law Reports-UK Cases: Vol 1. 2000. Hardback: £165.00. ISBN 0-421-73910-X. Sweet & Maxwell.

Wareham, Robert; Dolton, Alan–Tolley's Value Added Tax 2001-02. Paperback: £60.00. ISBN 0-7545-1517-6. Tolley Publishing.

Wareham, Robert; Dolton, Alan–Tolley's VAT Planning: 2000-2001. Paperback: £68.95. ISBN 0-7545-0725-4. Tolley Publishing.

Wareham, Robert; Dolton, Alan–Value Added Tax 2001-2002 2nd Ed. Paperback: £95.00. ISBN 0-7545-1071-9. Tolley Publishing.

Warren, Chief Justice Earl—Memoirs of Chief Justice Earl Warren. Paperback: £14.50. ISBN 1-56833-234-3. Cooper Square Press.

Weil, Roman L.—Litigation Services Handbook. 3rd Ed. Hardback: £118.00. ISBN 0-471-40309-1. John Wiley and Sons.

Weiler, Paul—Leveling the Playing Field. Paperback: £12.50. ISBN 0-674-00687-9. Harvard University Press.

Weinstein, Rebecca Jane—Mediation in the Workplace. Hardback: £56.95. ISBN 1-56720-336-1. Quorum Books.

Welfens, P.J.J.; Meyer, B.; Pfaffenberger, W.; Jasinski, P.; Jungmittag, A.—Energy Policies in the European Union. Hardback: £34.50. ISBN 3-540-41652-8. Springer-Verlag Berlin and Heidelberg GmbH & Co. KG.

Wells, Celia—Corporations and Criminal Responsibility. 2nd Ed. Oxford Monographs on Criminal Law and Justice. Hardback: £45.00. ISBN 0-19-826793-2. Paperback: £17.99. ISBN 0-19-924619-X. Oxford University Press.

West, Richard—Survival Guide for Claims Handlers. Paperback: £50.00. ISBN 0-406-91342-0. Butterworths Law.

West, Robin—Rights. International Library of Essays in Law and Legal Theory: Second Series -. Hardback: £130.00. ISBN 0-7546-2030-1. Ashgate Publishing Limited.

Whincop, Michael J.; Keyes, Mary—Policy and Pragmatism in the Conflict of Laws. Hardback: £50.00. ISBN 1-84014-753-9. Dartmouth.

Whincop, Michael J.—An Economic and Jurisprudential Genealogy of Corporate Law. Hardback: £45.00. ISBN 1-84014-773-3. Dartmouth.

Whisenhunt, William Benton—In Search of Legality-Mikhail M. Speranskii and the Codification of Russian Law. Hardback: £19.00. ISBN 0-88033-468-1. Columbia University Press.

Whish, Richard—Whish: Competition Law. 4th Ed. Paperback: £29.95. ISBN 0-406-00266-5. Butterworths Law.

Whitehead, Laurence—International Dimensions of Democratization-Europe and the Americas. 2nd Ed. Oxford Studies in Democratization. Paperback: £16.99. ISBN 0-19-924375-1. Oxford University Press.

Whitehouse, Chris; Hassall, Nicholas—Principles of Trust and Will Drafting. Paperback: £50.00. ISBN 0-406-91444-3. Butterworths Law.

Whitehouse, Chris; Watson, Loraine; Lakshmi, Narain; Baker, Tilly—Revenue Law-principles and Practice. 19th Ed. Paperback: £49.95. ISBN 0-406-93965-9. Butterworths Tolley.

Whiteman, Peter; Gammie, Malcolm; Herbert, Mark—Whiteman on Capital Gains Tax: 11th Supplement to the 4th Edition. British Tax Library. Paperback: £90.00. ISBN 0-421-68190-X. Sweet & Maxwell.

Whiteman, Peter; Goy, David; Sandison, Francis and; Sherry, Michael—Whiteman on Income Tax: 11th Supplement to the 3rd Edition. British Tax Library. Paperback: £90.00. ISBN 0-421-68180-2. Sweet & Maxwell.

Whiting, Raymond—Natural Right to die. Contributations in Legal Studies, No 101. Hardback: £51.95. ISBN 0-313-31474-8. Greenwood Press.

Whittington, Keith E.—Constitutional Interpretation. Paperback: £15.50. ISBN 0-7006-1141-X. University Press of Kansas.

Wickham, Gary; Pavlich, George—Rethinking Law Society and Governance. Onati International Series in Law and Society. Hardback: £45.00. ISBN 1-84113-293-4. Paperback: £20.00. ISBN 1-84113-294-2. Hart Publishing.

Widner, Jennifer A.—Building the Rule of Law. Hardback: £24.00. ISBN 0-393-05037-8. W.W. Norton.

Wilkinson, Chris—Joint Ventures and Shareholder Agreements. Paperback: £100.00. ISBN 0-406-93142-9. Butterworths Law.

Williams, Brian—Reparation and Victim-focused Social Work. Paperback: £15.95. ISBN 1-84310-023-1. Jessica Kingsley Publishers.

Willmore, C.—Environmental Law: Butterworth Core Text. Paperback: £12.95. ISBN 0-406-93406-1. Butterworths Law.

Wilson, Kate; James, Adrian–Child Protection Handbook. 2nd Ed. Hardback: £34.95. ISBN 0-7020-2584-4. Bailliere Tindall.

Wilson, Kate; James, Adrian–Child Protection Handbook. Hardback: £28.95. ISBN 0-7020-2584-4. Bailliere Tindall.

Wilson, Lee–Advertising Law Guide. Paperback: £14.95. ISBN 1-58115-070-9. Allworth Press.

Wilson, Lee–Copyright Guide. Paperback: £14.95. ISBN 1-58115-067-9. Allworth Press.

Windlesham, David James George Hennessy–Responses to Crime: Vol 4. Hardback: £50.00. ISBN 0-19-829844-7. Clarendon Press.

Windlesham, David James George Hennessy–Responses to Crime. Paperback: £16.99. ISBN 0-19-924741-2. Oxford University Press.

Winston, Kenneth–Fuller's Principles of Social Order. Paperback: £25.00. ISBN 1-84113-234-9. Hart Publishing.

Wintemute, Robert; Andenas, Mads–Legal Recognition of Same-sex Partnership. Paperback: £40.00. ISBN 1-84113-138-5. Paperback: £48.00. ISBN 1-84113-138-5. Hart Publishing.

Winter, Steven A.–Fair Housing Act. Paperback: £28.95. ISBN 0-471-39559-5. John Wiley and Sons.

Wood, Penny; Wikeley, Nick; Poynter, Richard; Bonn–Social Security Tribunals: the Legislation 2000: Vol 2. Income Support, Jobseeker's Allowance, Tax Credits and the Social Fund. £55.00. ISBN 0-421-82470-0. Sweet & Maxwell.

Woodhouse, Diana–Office of Lord Chancellor. Hardback: £22.00. ISBN 1-84113-021-4. Hart Publishing.

Word XP for Law Firms. Paperback: CD-ROM: £29.99. ISBN 0-7615-3394-X. Prima Tech.

Words and Phrases Supplement 2001. Paperback: £47.00. ISBN 0-406-94819-4. Butterworths Law.

Workman, Simon R.–Infrastructure Project Finance: a Legal and Financial Guide. Hardback: £70.00. ISBN 0-7277-2815-6. Thomas Telford Ltd.

World Trade Organization–Dispute Settlement Reports 1998: Vol IV. World Trade Organization Dispute Settlement Reports. Paperback: £30.00. ISBN 0-521-78896-X. Cambridge University Press.

World Trade Organization–Dispute Settlement Reports 1998: Vol IX. World Trade Organization Dispute Settlement Reports. Paperback: £30.00. ISBN 0-521-80505-8. Hardback: £75.00. ISBN 0-521-80100-1. Cambridge University Press.

World Trade Organization–Dispute Settlement Reports 1998: Vol VII. World Trade Organization Dispute Settlement Reports. Paperback: £30.00. ISBN 0-521-80503-1. Cambridge University Press.

World Trade Organization–Dispute Settlement Reports 1998. World Trade Organization Dispute Settlement Reports. Hardback: £65.00. ISBN 0-521-78329-1. Hardback: £75.00. ISBN 0-521-80099-4. Cambridge University Press.

World Trade Organization–Dispute Settlement Reports 1998. World Trade Organization Dispute Settlement Reports. Hardback: £75.00. ISBN 0-521-80097-8. Hardback: £75.00. ISBN 0-521-80098-6. Cambridge University Press.

World Trade Organization–Dispute Settlement Reports 1998. World Trade Organization Dispute Settlement Reports. Paperback: £30.00. ISBN 0-521-80502-3. Cambridge University Press.

World Trade Organization–World Trade Organization Agreements. World Trade Organization Schedules. Audio CD: £250.00. ISBN 0-521-79645-8. Cambridge University Press.

Wormald, Patrick–Making of English Law: King Alfred to the 12th Century: Vol 1. Paperback: £29.99. ISBN 0-631-22740-7. Blackwell Publishers.

Wright, Jane—Tort Law and Human Rights-The Impact of the ECHR on English Law. Hardback: £30.00. ISBN 1-84113-035-4. Hart Publishing.

WTO Dispute Settlement Procedures. Hardback: £60.00. ISBN 0-521-80448-5. Paperback: £20.00. ISBN 0-521-01077-2. Cambridge University Press.

York, Stephen; Tunkel, Daniel—Hammonds Suddards: E-commerce: a Guide to Electronic Business. 2nd Ed. Paperback: £95.00. ISBN 0-406-93395-2. Butterworths Law.

Your Rights on the Road. CD-ROM: £19.99. ISBN 1-902646-49-5. Law Pack Publishing.

Zander, Michael—Police and Criminal Evidence Act 1984 4th Ed. Hardback: £29.99. ISBN 0-421-67380-X. Sweet & Maxwell.

Zedalis, Rex J.—International Energy Law: Rules Governing Future Exploration, Exploitation and Use of Renewable Resources. Hardback: £60.00. ISBN 0-7546-2164-2. Ashgate Publishing Limited.

Zerbe Jr, Richard O.—Economic Efficiency in Law and Economics. New Horizons in Law and Economics. Hardback: £69.95. ISBN 1-84064-301-3. Edward Elgar.

Zilioli, Chiara; Selmayr, Martin—Law of the European Central Bank. Hardback: £50.00. ISBN 1-84113-245-4. Hart Publishing.

Zimmermann, Reinhard—Roman Law, Contemporary Law, European Law. Clarendon Law Lectures. Hardback: £25.00. ISBN 0-19-829913-3. Oxford University Press.

Zindani, Jeffrey—Health and Safety Law: a Modern Guide. Paperback: £65.00. ISBN 1-85811-217-6. EMIS Professional Publishing.

Zoellick, Bill—CyberRegs. AW Information Technology Series. Paperback: £30.99. ISBN 0-201-72230-5. Addison Wesley.

Zucker, Ross—Democratic Distributive Justice. Hardback: £42.50. ISBN 0-521-79033-6. Cambridge University Press.

INDEX 2001

abatement notices
noise
evidence, 01/2422
extent of specification of steps to be taken, 01/2423
methods of abatement
local authority's power to enter premises, 01/2424
noise measurement
relevance of British Standards, 01/2425
noise pollution
notice requirements
method of abatement, 01/2426
sewers and drains
environmental protection legislation
meaning of "premises", 01/2429
waste disposal
existence of statutory nuisance, 01/2427
Abolition of Poindings and Warrant Sales Act 2001 (asp 1), 01/6212S
abuse of process
civil proceedings
personal injury claim
effect of initiating fresh action, 01/5710NI
detention
substitution of one charge for another, 01/1091
disqualification orders
civil proceedings initiated by Secretary of State
estoppel, 01/708
equitable interest
failure to raise issues at previous hearing, 01/3781
professional negligence claim
court's approach to delay, 01/410
prosecutions
pursuing against complainant's wishes, 01/1093
repossession proceedings
pursuit of money judgment, 01/4839
retrials
successive trials, 01/1094
access to justice
compensation claim
statute bar
compatibility with ECHR, 01/411
Access to Justice Act 1999 (c.22)
Commencement No.6 and Transitional Provisions Order, 01/6
Commencement No.7, Transitional Provisions and Savings Order, 01/7
Commencement No.8 Order, 01/4255
accidents. *See also* **fatal accidents**
apportionment of responsibility

accidents *-cont.*
apportionment of responsibility *-cont.*
child carried in vehicle without adequate restraint, 01/4447
causation
toboggan rides
failure to warn, 01/1551
eyewitnesses
death of work colleague
risk of suffering psychiatric harm, 01/5352
road traffic
causation
collision with tractor in oncoming lane, 01/6810S
claimant driving without insurance
recovery in tort, 01/5349
cyclist emerging into path of oncoming vehicle, 01/4466
duty of driver to passenger
passenger engaged in criminal offence, 01/6816S
vehicle repairs
compensation for diminution in value, 01/1504
road traffic accidents
personal injuries
apportionment of liability, 01/4465
accountancy
books, 01/4
investment trusts
accounting methods, 01/3
accounts
annual accounts
valuation rules
Council Directive 2001/65, 01/1
annual audit letter
Wales, 01/4320
consolidated accounts
valuation rules
Council Directive 2001/65, 01/1
summary statement
Greater London Authority, 01/8
actions
causes of action
amendment to statement of case, 01/413
counterclaims
assignation of right, 01/6219S
settlement
offer subject to contract law, 01/6224S
sist of action pending arbitration
whether timeously pleading, 01/6258S
small claims
valuation of secondhand car
evidence regarding purchase price, 01/1550

Alliance & Leicester Group Treasury PLC (Transfer) Act 2001 (c.i), 01/368
alternative dispute resolution. *See* dispute resolution
ancient monuments
  consent forms
    Wales, 01/4649
Anguilla
  radio stations
    suspension of talk show
      violation of constitutional rights, 01/838
animal products. *See also* **agricultural produce; agriculture; animals**
  beef
    premiums, 01/131, 5660NI, 6110S
  diseases and disorders
    BSE
      monitoring, 01/5661NI
    ovine spongiform encephalopathy
      compensation, 01/310, 6114S
    specified risk material, 01/2812, 2813, 2814, 2815, 5662NI, 5663NI, 5818NI, 5819NI, 5820NI, 5821NI, 6112S, 6113S, 6549S, 6550S, 6551S, 6661S
      Wales, 01/309, 2816, 2817
  examination
    residues of veterinary medicinal products
      maximum residue limits, 01/2818
  food safety
    hygiene and inspections
      slaughtering, 01/5664NI
    intra-community trade
      gelatine, 01/2819, 5822NI, 6552S
  infectious disease control
    ruminant related fluid
      waste disposal, 01/138, 5665NI, 6115S
  intra-community trade
    gelatine
      Wales, 01/2849
  origin marking
    exports and imports, 01/2820, 5824NI, 6553S
      Wales, 01/2821
  waste disposal
    animal feed, 01/139, 5666NI, 6116S
      Wales, 01/140
animal welfare
  control of classical swine fever
    Council Directive 2001/89, 01/311
  protection of pigs
    minimum standards
      Commission Directive 2001/93, 01/314
      Council Directive 2001/88, 01/315
animals. *See also* **agriculture; animal products; birds; dogs**
  animal health
    diseases and disorders
      Council Directive 2001/10, 01/308
    import and export controls, 01/5823NI
    offspring of BSE infected cattle
      MAFF's discretion to slaughter, 01/130
  animal products
    meat and bone storage
      risk assessment requirements, 01/2416
  animal welfare

animals *-cont.*
  animal welfare *-cont.*
    cruelty to horses
      having custody of animals during disqualification period, 01/313
    farmed animals
      Wales, 01/312
    slaughter or killing, 01/316, 01/5707NI, 6207S
    transport cleansing and disinfection
      Wales, 01/317
    books, 01/331
  cattle
    artificial insemination, 01/147
      emergency licences, 01/148, 6121S
      Wales, 01/149
    extensification payment, 01/259, 5687NI
    identification and registration
      movement control, 01/6122S
    premiums
      administration, 01/150, 5671NI, 6123S
      slaughter premiums, 01/5688NI
      Wales, 01/260
  diseases and disorders
    animal products
      BSE, 01/133, 134, 6111S
    approved disinfectants, 01/318, 6208S
      Wales, 01/319
    BSE
      Wales, 01/135, 136
    foot and mouth disease
      infected areas, 01/5685NI
      Wales, 01/154
  dogs
    identification discs, 01/5708NI
    licensing
      identification, 01/5708NI
  domestic pets
    pet travel pilot scheme, 01/325
  feedingstuffs, 01/5667NI
    additives, 01/141, 5668NI, 6117S
    animal protein, 01/142, 5669NI, 6118S, 6119S
      Wales, 01/143
    official inspections
      Council Directive 2001/46, 01/322
    sampling and analysis, 01/144, 5670NI, 6120S
      Wales, 01/145
      Wales, 01/146
  food safety
    emergency prohibitions
      radioactivity in sheep, 01/6605S
  fur farming
    compensation scheme, 01/321
  infectious disease control
    approved disinfectants, 01/6209S
    foot and mouth disease, 01/219, 220, 221, 222
      ascertainment of value, 01/164, 165, 6125S, 6126S, 6127S, 6128S
      controlled areas, 01/5676NI, 5677NI, 5678NI, 5679NI, 6130S, 6131S, 6132S, 6133S, 6134S, 6135S, 6136S, 6137S, 6138S, 6139S, 6140S, 6141S, 6142S, 6143S, 6144S, 6145S, 6146S, 6147S, 6148S, 6149S, 6150S, 6151S, 6152S, 6153S, 6154S, 6155S, 6156S, 6157S,

broadcasting -*cont.*
  television
    European Broadcasting Union
      legality of membership rules, 01/781
    television licences
      increase in fees, 01/5324
  wireless telegraphy
    equipment
      exemptions, 01/5325
    licences, 01/5327
budget
  grants
    National Crime Squad, 01/4772
    National Criminal Intelligence Service, 01/4773
Budget Act (Northern Ireland) 2001 (c.7), 01/5838NI
Budget (No.2) Act (Northern Ireland) 2001 (c.16), 01/5800NI
Budget (Scotland) Act 2001 (asp 4), 01/6607S
building and engineering contracts. *See also* **arbitration**
  adjudication
    adjudicator not public authority, 01/855
    criteria for non enforcement of adjudicator's decision, 01/857
    failure to pass information to parties, 01/853
    installation of shop fittings
      meaning of construction operations, 01/854
    interpretation of contract
      jurisdiction of adjudicator, 01/6286S
    jurisdiction
      excluded operations, 01/6287S
    jurisdiction of adjudicator
      estoppel by convention, 01/945
      improper consideration for referral, 01/6288S
      insulation of pipework, 01/859
      power of court to review, 01/860
    notice of non payment
      jurisdiction of adjudicator, 01/861
    scope of jurisdiction, 01/863
    settlement agreement prior to adjudication request, 01/862
    validity of decision, 01/6289S
  adjudicators
    extent of jurisdiction, 01/858
  arbitration
    right to payment
      notice to withold payment, 01/6293S
  building contractors
    negligence
      interpretation of insurance and indemnity clauses, 01/865
    claim for overpayment, 01/946
  consulting engineers
    responsibility for certificate relating to roof design, 01/864
  ICE conditions of contract
    retention from sums due
      interest on retention, 01/6291S
  insurance
    duty to insure against negligence, 01/6294S

building and engineering contracts -*cont.*
  JCT forms of contract
    obligations under Building Regulations 1985, 01/868
    quality of workmanship
      interpretation of conditions, 01/876
  liability for negligence
    interpretation of exclusion clause, 01/947
  retention from sums due
    failure to pay, 01/6291S
  subcontractors
    refusal to complete work pending settlement of account, 01/872
  subcontracts
    time limit for claims
      interpretation, 01/6292S
  termination of contract
    loss of profit
      supervening insolvency, 01/948
  variation
    inclusion of overheads and profits
      loss from variation, 01/343
building regulations
  controlled services and fittings, 01/867
  local authorities
    requirements, 01/867
building societies
  Commission expenses
    fees, 01/2686
  derivatives
    investments, 01/2688
burden of proof
  discrimination
    sex discrimination, 01/2250
burglary
  juvenile offenders
    handling stolen goods, 01/1380
burials and cremation
  churchyards
    authorisation procedure, 01/1846
  disinterment
    title to sue, 01/6500S
  exhumation
    burial in consecrated ground
      right to widow to remove ashes, 01/3481
    reburial of national hero in Brazil, 01/1848
  fees
    parochial fees, 01/1849
business tenancies. *See also* **leases**
  compensation
    entitlement, 01/4151
    validity of tenant notices, 01/4158
  contract terms
    restrictions on use of airport, 01/5379
  derogation from grant
    tenant's profits
      landlord's right to set off, 01/4152
  distress levy
    overpayment
      right of equitable set off, 01/4153
  expiry of fixed term lease
    continued acceptance of rent, 01/4162
  forfeiture
    landlord's re entry of premises, 01/4154
  land registration

chemicals. *See* hazardous substances; pesticides

cheques

conversion

delivery to company recipient, 01/377

designation of payee

designation incomplete, 01/6214S

child abduction

custody

parties to Luxembourg Convention, 01/4067

child abuse. *See also* **sexual offences**

standard of proof required to determine perpetrator, 01/2549

child support

child maintenance

variation, 01/2551, 5786NI

child maintenance premium, 01/5950NI

collection and enforcement, 01/2552, 4982, 5787NI

consequential amendments

transitional provisions, 01/2553, 5788NI

decisions and appeals, 01/5789NI

information, evidence and disclosure, 01/5790NI

information, evidence and disclosure, maintenance arrangements and jurisdiction, 01/2555

jurisdiction, 01/5790NI

maintenance arrangements, 01/5790NI

maintenance arrears

voluntary payments, 01/5791NI

maintenance assessments

decisions and appeals, 01/5792NI

transitional provisions, 01/5792NI

maintenance calculation

procedure, 01/2556, 5793NI

special cases, 01/2557, 5794NI

temporary compensation scheme

recovery of arrears, 01/5796NI

variation applications, 01/5797NI

Child Support, Pensions and Social Security Act 2000 (c.19)

Commencement No.6 Order, 01/5118

Commencement No.7 Order, 01/2559

Commencement No.8 Order, 01/4983

Commencement No.9 Order, 01/4984

Commencement No.10 Order, 01/5119

Commencement No.4 Order, 01/5969NI

Commencement No.5 Order, 01/5970NI

Commencement No.6 Order, 01/6029NI

children. *See also* **childrens welfare; child abduction; child abuse; child benefit; child support**

adoption

father failing to attend court hearing

right to fair trial, 01/2539

fathers

notification of proceedings, 01/2541

removal from United States

care order in interest of children, 01/2538

right to family life

duty to investigate child's extended family, 01/2534

adoption orders

father's opposition to adoption by foster parents, 01/2531

children *-cont.*

care orders

likelihood of psychological damage to child, 01/2566

change of name

protection from family

relevant considerations, 01/2572

child abduction

risk of harm on return to New Zealand

standard of proof required, 01/2546

wrongful removal by mother, 01/2548

child protection

adoption

disclosure of information, 01/2527

local authorities powers and duties, 01/2573

assessment of risk

validity of care order, 01/2567

employment of teachers

restrictions, 01/2075

local authorities

reasonable cause to suspect child abuse, 01/2550

parental rights

apprehension of child without authorisation, 01/3488

child support

deduction from earnings orders

set off against subsequent arrears, 01/2554

imprisonment, 01/6892S

maintenance orders

periodical payments for school fees, 01/2558

childminders

application for registration, 01/2574

certificates of registration, 01/2575

information, advice and training, 01/2578

inspections, 01/2577

national standards, 01/2579

registration

annual fees, 01/2580

disqualification, 01/2576

fees, 01/6504S

Children's Commissioner

Wales, 01/2581

childrens hearings

appeals

computation of period for lodgement, 01/6505S

compatibility with ECHR, 01/6506S

legal aid

compatibility of non-availability with ECHR, 01/6507S

status as independent tribunal, 01/6506S

childrens homes

local authority registration

Wales, 01/2604

childrens welfare

childrens homes, 01/2603

contact orders

failure to make interim care order, 01/2565

family proceedings, 01/2626

conduct of litigation and rights of audience, 01/2605

grants, 01/2606

clinical negligence -*cont.*
  neo natal test
    failure to conduct Ortolani-Barlow test, 01/4457
  omissions
    failure to notice fracture revealed by X-ray
      date of actual knowledge, 01/4461
  wrongful birth
    measure of damages
      mother's care of disabled child, 01/4464
    severely disabled child
      interim payment, 01/1508
clubs
  delictual liability
    personal injuries
      sustained go-karting, 01/6813S
codes of practice
  immigration
    carriers liability, 01/3676, 3677
  local authorities
    conduct
      England, 01/4347
      Wales, 01/4348
    model codes of practice
      Wales, 01/4350
    National Park and Broads Authorities
      conduct, 01/4395
    Parish Councils
      conduct, 01/4369
    Police authorities
      conduct, 01/4397
  local education authorities
    school relations, 01/1958
  police interviews
    audio tape recordings
      terrorism, 01/1077
    video tape recordings
      terrorism, 01/5731NI
  police powers
    authorised officers
      terrorism, 01/1000, 1078
    drug testing provisions, 01/4781
    terrorism, 01/5732NI
  pollution control
    water pollution, 01/6499S
  public authorities
    conduct of members, 01/4398
    standards committees, 01/4399
  restrictions on employment
    employers liability, 01/2249
  trade union recognition
    ballots, 01/5763NI
cohabitation
  intestacy
    beneficial interest
      statement of future intention, 01/2431
Colchester Borough Council Act 2001 (c.ii), 01/4332
colleges
  further education
    Bell College of Technology
      designation, 01/6434S
      discharge of functions, 01/6435S
      governance, 01/6436S
    Northern College of Education

colleges -*cont.*
  Northern College of Education -*cont.*
    closure, 01/6431S
collisions at sea
  apportionment of blame
    failure to comply with traffic regulations, 01/4918
commercial law
  books, 01/696, 6272S
  title to goods
    establishing title against subsequent purchasers, 01/813
communications
  electronic communications
    unsolicited services, 01/915
community care
  direct payments
    children under 16, 01/6897S
    eligibility, 01/5120
    Wales, 01/5121
community charge. *See also* **council tax**
  administration and enforcement, 01/4804
  Wales, 01/4805
companies. *See also* **company law**
  business names, 01/698
  close companies
    loans to participators
      company assessable to tax on loan, 01/6037NI
  company registration
    striking off
      restoration to companies register, 01/703
  corporate personality
    lifting of corporate veil, 01/705
  designation
    National Air Traffic Services Ltd, 01/5394
    National Air Traffic Services (No.2) Ltd, 01/5395
  disqualification orders, 01/699
  local authorities
    revenue accounts and capital finance, 01/4345, 4346
  registration
    restoration to register
      competency of interlocutory order, 01/6273S
Company and Business Names (Chamber of Commerce, Etc.) Act 1999 (c.19)
  Commencement Order, 01/702
company law
  books, 01/752
  exemption
    EU political donations, 01/700
  open ended investment companies, 01/737
  unregistered companies
    political donations, 01/701
company name
  business names
    companies
      chambers of commerce, 01/698
compensation. *See also* **damages; measure of damages**
  diseases and disorders
    ovine spongiform encephalopathy, 01/310, 6114S

computers
  computer contracts
    damage to computerised accounts system
      recoverable heads of loss, 01/3701
conditions of employment. *See* **contract of employment**
confidential information. *See* **privilege**
confidentiality
  confidential information
    medical records
      disclosure of source's identity, 01/4413
    newspapers
      publication of information in public domain, 01/4414
  disclosure
    information conveyed in chambers during proceedings, 01/2622
  intellectual property
    Council Directive 2001/29, 01/3846
  sexual relationships
    obligation to prevent disclosure, 01/4415
  trade secrets
    knowledge acquired by employee
      degree of confidentiality, 01/4064
confiscation orders. *See also* **drug offences**
  drug trafficking
    matrimonial home
      spouse seeking to relitigate by appeal, 01/5
  enforcement
    restraint orders to aid enforcement of US order, 01/15
    Scottish orders in England and Wales, 01/1009
  statutory assumptions
    whether breach of human rights, 01/6327S
conflict of laws. *See also* **choice of forum; choice of law; judgments and orders; jurisdiction**
  books, 01/831
  choice of forum
    place of performance of contractual obligation, 01/802
    printed term within contract, 01/800
  choice of law
    Scottish/Italian contract for performance in Egypt, 01/6278S
    title to goods
      lex situs, 01/813
  exclusive distribution agreements
    characteristic performance of contract
      applicable law, 01/826
  foreign judgments
    enforceability
      order for security for costs, 01/818
    enforcement
      recovery of premiums, 01/817
  Taiwanese bankruptcy orders
    enforceability under Hong Kong law, 01/819
conservation. *See also* **conservation areas; environmental protection**
  birds
    protected species, 01/6481S
  fishing
    prohibition of fishing for cockles, 01/6531S

conservation -*cont.*
  fishing -*cont.*
    prohibition on the use of mobile or active gear, 01/6532S
  Isles of Scilly, 01/2357
Consolidated Fund Act 2001 (c.1), 01/2862
Consolidated Fund (No.2) Act 2001 (c.25), 01/2863
constitutional law. *See also* **Parliament**
  Bermuda
    constitution, 01/833
  books, 01/851, 6285S
  children
    adoption process
      non citizen adopting South African born child, 01/832
  Commonwealth of Dominica
    exclusive licences for telecom services
      protection of rights, 01/850
  education
    Canada
      provision for children in minority French speaking area, 01/836
  freedom of expression
    suspension of radio talk show
      violation of constitutional rights, 01/838
  Grenada
    confiscation of land
      compensation, 01/849
  local authorities
    conduct of referendums, 01/842, 843
  National Assembly for Wales
    nomonation papers
      welsh form, 01/2204
    transfer of functions, 01/845
    transfer of land, 01/2878
  Northern Ireland Assembly
    restoration of devolved government, 01/5715NI, 5716NI
    suspension of devolved government, 01/5717NI, 5718NI
  political parties
    registration
      fees, 01/847
      prohibited words and expressions, 01/848
  public authorities
    designation, 01/5719NI
  Scottish devolution
    road traffic enactments
      consequential modifications, 01/6279S
  Scottish Ministers
    agency arrangements, 01/6608S
    transfer of functions, 01/6283S, 6284S
  Scottish Parliament
    legislative competence, 01/6282S
  Secretary of State for Wales
    transfer of functions, 01/845
construction industry. *See also* **building and engineering contracts; construction law**
  building inspectors
    functions, 01/866
  Construction Industry Training Board
    levy on employers, 01/869, 5721NI
  Engineering Construction Board
    levy on employers, 01/870

customs duty -*cont.*
tobacco exports
reimbursement of levied tax
refusal on grounds of unjust enrichment, 01/5211
Cyprus
films
cinematic co-production agreements, 01/4417
damages. *See also* **measure of damages; compensation**
assessment
child in care
psychiatric harm, 01/1547
clinical negligence
cost of surrogacy
claim against public policy, 01/1520
wrongful birth
recovery of maintenance costs for disabled child, 01/1509
exemplary damages
misfeasance in public office, 01/1512
interim payments
admission of fault but not liability, 01/6415S
loss of profits
heritable property
inaccurate property inquiry certificate, 01/6419S
losses
foreseeability
inaccurate report by solicitors, 01/6819S
necessary services by relatives
valuation
relevancy, 01/6418S
offer to settle claim
offer subject to contract law, 01/6224S
rate of return
personal injuries, 01/1545
dangerous driving. *See also* **road traffic offences**
causing death
community punishment orders
unduly lenient sentence, 01/1253
unduly lenient sentence, 01/1262
disqualification
diabetic driver
existence of special reasons, 01/1265
sentence length
causing death by dangerous driving, 01/1255, 01/1259
data protection
access to health records
removal of cut off date, 01/3703
health records
access to information
removal of cut off date, 01/3703
Information Commissioner
notification from data controllers, 01/3704
personal data
unfair processing of customer data
breach of data protection principles, 01/3705
database right
EC law
directives

database right -*cont.*
EC law -*cont.*
directives -*cont.*
failure to implement Council Directive 96/9, 01/2460
debts
clients
indebtedness to solicitors
proportionality of professional fees, 01/631
deceit
paternity
actionable deceit between cohabitees, 01/5351
decrees
interim decree
motion during extrastatutory consensual hearing
no written intimation, 01/6260S
motions
motion enrolled outwith time limit
appropriateness of relief, 01/6223S
defamation
books, 01/1838
libel
abuse of process
basis of appeal, 01/1816
damages
summary disposal after judgment on liability, 01/1818
defence of fair comment, 01/1826
disclosure
source of leaked police report, 01/5744NI
electronic mail
weight of evidence supporting claim, 01/1819
fair comment
test established by common law, 01/1822
limitation period
articles posted on newspaper website, 01/1825
newspaper allegations of money laundering
defence of qualified privilege, 01/1829
photographs
effect of unintentional defamation, 01/1833
psychiatric report
unauthorised disclosure of confidential material, 01/1828
publication of newspaper article
availability of defence of qualified privilege, 01/1831
qualified privilege
multi jurisdictional publication, 01/1834
measure of damages
excessive award
TV allegation against nursing home, 01/6414S
newspapers
innuendo of criminal involvement, 01/6430S
publisher of defamatory statement
defence of qualified privilege, 01/1823
qualified privilege
journalists
public policy against extension of privilege, 01/1832
website operators

documentary evidence -*cont.*
patent infringement proceedings -*cont.*
disclosure by non party
relevance, 01/3866
dogs
causing injury
foreseeability as prerequisite for charge, 01/6324S
statutory duty
liability of deemed keeper for injury caused, 01/5743NI
Dogs (Amendment) Act (Northern Ireland) 2001 (c.1), 01/5709NI
domestic violence
husband responsible for wife's death
fostering under care order, 01/2564
dominant position. *See also* **competition law**
airports
ground handling licensing fees, 01/761
injunctions
online information services
evidence of unfair competition, 01/764
pension scheme
compulsory membership for medical specialists
compatibility with EC law, 01/763
postal services
mail interception
remail services, 01/4793
sole supplier of product
use of anti dumping procedure
validity under EC law, 01/766
double taxation
reliefs
dividends
dual resident companies, 01/5213
dual resident company, 01/5214
groups of companies, 01/5215
Jordan, 01/5216
Lithuania, 01/5217
drink driving offences. *See also* **road traffic offences**
breath specimens
failure to provide, 01/6331S
breath tests
evidence regarding reliability of intoximeter, 01/991
unreliable reading by intoximeter
discretion of police officer, 01/1131
causing death
excess alcohol
good character, 01/1226
defences
being in charge
no likelihood of driving, 01/6330S
disqualification
dangerous driving causing death, 01/1386
duress of circumstances, 01/1032
roads
restricted access routes
causeway not a "public place", 01/1033
sentence length
causing death by dangerous driving, 01/1272
driving licences
catergories of entitlement, 01/5397

driving licences -*cont.*
diseases and disorders
diabetes, 01/5398, 6050NI
disqualification
fees, 01/6051NI
motor vehicles, 01/5396
police powers
disclosure of information, 01/4783
refusal of renewal
medical grounds, 01/6052NI
renewal application fees
non driving related matters, 01/5400
drug offences. *See also* **confiscation orders**
bail
entry clearance status withdrawn
relevance of seriousness of offence, 01/6348S
coercion
supply to prisoner
threats of violence for failure to supply, 01/6329S
criminal evidence
sample testing
sufficient evidence of whole, 01/6316S
defences
jury directions
defence of incrimination and denial of involvement, 01/6386S
drug trafficking
confiscation orders
challenge by spouse, 01/5
foreign jurisdictions, 01/1035
importation of cannabis from Spain, 01/1274
importation of cocaine, 01/1388
seizure of proceeds
time limit for making detention order, 01/1138
forfeiture orders
money obtained from drug dealing
burden of proof, 01/5725NI
indictments
specification of controlled drug, 01/6354S
juvenile offenders
possession of heroin with intent to supply, 01/1405
listed drugs, 01/1038
prison officers
supply of drugs to prisoners, 01/1281
quantity involved
credit for guilty plea, 01/1276
sentence length
permitting premises or supplying drugs, 01/1286
possession with intent to supply
93 ecstasy tablets, 01/6315S
supply of cannabis
supply not commercial, 01/6399S
supply of drugs, 01/1288
supply of drugs
evidence of single occasion, 01/6332S
involuntary custodian
meaning of "supply", 01/1073
permitting premises to be used for supplying drugs, 01/1278
pleas

EC law -cont.
  Turkish national -cont.
    right of access to EU labour market -cont.
      direct effect of Council Decision 1/80, 01/
        2458
  utilities
    contracts, 01/5537
  VAT
    common system
      Council Directive 2001/41, 01/5610
    exemption for sporting activities
      compatibility with Council Directive 77/
        388, 01/5581
    supply of goods and services
      undertakings seeking refund from French
        tax authorities, 01/5589
  veterinary medicinal products
    Community code
      European Parliament and Council Directive
        2001/82, 01/326
  waste disposal
    incineration
      Council Directive 2000/76, 01/2414
  water
    water policy
      Council Directive 2000/60, 01/2419
  water pollution
    failure to fulfil obligations under Directive 91/
      676, 01/2420
  works of art
    resale rights
      Council Directive 2001/84, 01/4065
ecclesiastical law
  books, 01/1852
  Church of England
    periods of service, 01/1840
  ecclesiastical offences
    fees, 01/1850
  faculty proceedings
    fees, 01/1850
  legal officers
    fees, 01/1851
economic loss. *See* **damages**
economics
  books, 01/1853
education. *See also* **further education; higher
  education; schools; special educational
  needs; students; teachers**
  adjudication
    adjudicators inquiry procedure, 01/1854
  books, 01/2088, 6451S
  colleges
    closure
      Northern College of Education, 01/6431S
    funding
      Conservatoire for Dance and Drama, 01/
        1855
      Royal Agricultural College, 01/1856
  courses
    deregistration from entitlement to subsidy
      legitimate expectation, 01/428
  education action forums
    membership
      Barnsley, 01/1860
      Birmingham (Aston and Nechells), 01/1861

education -cont.
  education action forums -cont.
    membership -cont.
      Birmingham (Kitts Green and Shard End),
        01/1862, 1863
      Blackburn with Darwen, 01/1864
      Bridgwater, 01/1865
      Bristol, 01/1866
      CfBT/Lambeth, 01/1867
      East Basildon, 01/1868
      East Brighton, 01/1869
      East Middlesbrough, 01/1870
      Epicentre LEAP Ellesmere Port, 01/1871
      Hackney, 01/1872
      Halifax, 01/1873
      Herefordshire, 01/1874
      Kingston Upon Hull, 01/1875
      Leicester (South and West), 01/1876
      Leigh, 01/1877
      New Addington, 01/1878
      Newcastle, 01/1879
      Newham, 01/1880
      North East Lincolnshire, 01/1881
      North East Sheffield, 01/1882
      North Somerset, 01/1883
      North Southwark, 01/1884
      Nottingham (Bulwell), 01/1885
      Plymouth, 01/1886
      Salford and Trafford, 01/1887
      South Tyneside, 01/1888
      Thetford, 01/1889
  education action zones
    establishment
      Barnsley, 01/1860
      Birmingham (Aston and Nechells), 01/1861
      Birmingham (Kitts Green and Shard End),
        01/1862, 1863
      Blackburn with Darwen, 01/1864
      Bridgwater, 01/1865
      Bristol, 01/1866
      CfBT/Lambeth, 01/1867
      East Basildon, 01/1868
      East Brighton, 01/1869
      East Middlesbrough, 01/1870
      Epicentre LEAP Ellesmere Port, 01/1871
      Hackney, 01/1872
      Halifax, 01/1873
      Herefordshire, 01/1874
      Kingston Upon Hull, 01/1875
      Leicester (South and West), 01/1876
      Leigh, 01/1877
      New Addington, 01/1878
      Newcastle, 01/1879
      Newham, 01/1880
      North East Lincolnshire, 01/1881
      North East Sheffield, 01/1882
      North Somerset, 01/1883
      North Southwark, 01/1884
      Nottingham (Bulwell), 01/1885
      Plymouth, 01/1886
      Salford and Trafford, 01/1887
      South Tyneside, 01/1888
      Thetford, 01/1889
  education and training
    inspections

electricity industry
  agreements
    unfair dismissal
      revocation, 01/2339
  climate change levy, 01/5192
  dissolution
    Central Electricity Generating Board, 01/2205
    Electricity Council, 01/2206
  electricity generation
    non fossil fuel sources, 01/2211, 2212, 6458S
    wind and water generating stations
      consent, 01/2213
  electricity supply industry
    exemptions
      licences, 01/5539
    licences
      exemptions, 01/2216
  fossil fuel, 01/6919S
    calculation of levy, 01/2214
    electricity suppliers and distributors, 01/2215
  renewable energy sources
    internal market
      draft Council Directive, 01/2208, 2209
electricity supply industry
  licence holders
    statutory consultation, 01/5540
Electronic Communications Act (Northern Ireland) 2001 (c.9), 01/6040NI
emissions. *See also* **air pollution; noise**
  air pollution
    machinery
      Commission Directive 2001/63, 01/2354
    large combustion plants
      limitations
        European Parliament and Council Directive 2001/80, 01/2402
  national emission ceilings
    atmospheric pollutants
      European Parliament and Council Directive 2001/81, 01/2401
  passenger vehicles
    construction and use, 01/5443
employees
  local government
    code of conduct
      Wales, 01/101, 102
employers
  employers liability insurance
    payment of excess, 01/6720S
employers liability. *See also* **health and safety at work; vicarious liability**
  accident at work
    dishonest claimant
      no breach of statutory duty, 01/3299
  accidents
    laying of grit
      failure to ensure adequate safety for employee, 01/3303
  accidents at work
    foreseeable possibility of injury to employee, 01/4491
  custody officers
    injuries sustained during patrol in moving vehicle, 01/3298
  drivers

employers liability -*cont.*
  drivers -*cont.*
    rest periods
      adequacy of weekly checks on tachograph, 01/5401
  health and safety at work
    death of employee
      financial penalty, 01/1347
  injury at work
    operation of circular saw
      duty to give sufficient instructions, 01/3304
  manual handling operations
    risk of injury, 01/6664S
  psychiatric illness
    employee committing suicide, 01/6665S
  risk assessment
    scope of duty
      psychiatric illness, 01/6665S
  safe system of working
    duty owed to ship's master, 01/6666S
  social workers
    personal injuries
      handling of disabled persons, 01/3305
  statutory duty
    workman injured in tripping accident, 01/6663S
employment. *See also* **contract of employment; employment protection; part time employment**
  annual leave
    entitlement
      excluded classes of workers, 01/2219
  aviation industry
    working time
      Council Directive 2000/79, 01/2220
  books, 01/2350, 6479S
  casual workers
    employment agencies
      degree of control denoting employment relationship, 01/6467S
  collective agreements
    sickness insurance scheme
      compatibility with EC law, 01/2446
  collective agreements deductions
    incorporation of union negotiated agreement into contract, 01/2226
  complaints
    unfair dismissal
      electricity industry, 01/2339
  compromise agreements
    agreement purporting to prevent statutory claims
      breach of contract, 01/6459S
  conditions of employment
    annual leave, 01/2229
    police service, 01/4791
    teachers, 01/2049, 2050, 2051, 2052, 2053, 2054, 2055
  Construction Industry Training Board
    levy on employers, 01/869, 5721NI
  continuity of employment
    effect of void compromise agreement, 01/2230
  contract of employment

employment -cont.
transfer of undertakings -cont.
tender procedures
applicability of Council Directive 77/187, 01/2335
unfair dismissal
trade union official
authority to reach agreement with employer, 01/2347
wages
bank holidays
entitlement to additional day's wages, 01/6478S
whistleblowers
victimisation
jurisdiction to hear complaint, 01/2348
wrongful dismissal
compensation
loss of accrued rights, 01/2349
damages for manner of dismissal, 01/2253
summary dismissal without payment in lieu, 01/2323
Employment Appeal Tribunal
appeals
service by fax, 01/6466S
employment protection. *See also* **redundancy; transfer of undertakings; unfair dismissal**
continuity of employment, 01/2259
Employment Relations Act 1999 (c.26)
Commencement No.8 Order, 01/2260
Commencement No.8 (Amendment) Order, 01/2261
employment status
temporary employment
HGV drivers
applicable test of control, 01/2267
employment tribunals. *See also* **Employment Appeal Tribunals**
bias
appointment of tribunal members, 01/2269
rules of procedure, 01/2268
breach of contract claim
legality of chairman sitting alone, 01/2270
conciliation, 01/348
maximum deposits, 01/2272
power to call witnesses, 01/2276
procedure
disclosure of information, 01/2273, 2274, 6469S, 6470S
res judicata
application of principle, 01/6474S
vexatious litigants
restriction of proceedings order
discretion to grant order, 01/2275
energy. *See also* **electricity industry; gas industry; oil and gas industry**
energy conservation
building standards, 01/6295S
grants, 01/6482S
energy efficiency
fluorescent lighting
ballasts, 01/2363
renewable energy sources
electricity
Council Directive 2001/77, 01/2207

enforcement notices
agricultural land
deficiency in notice, 01/4690
infill of valley for agricultural hardstanding, 01/4689
amendment
risk of prosecution
permitted rights of use, 01/4696
change of use
gypsy status
inspector's findings of fact, 01/4691
previous lawful use as residential accommodation, 01/4692
retrospective legislation, 01/4693
green belt
construction of ancillary buildings
material considerations, 01/4695
land use
revocation of certificate, 01/4697
waste management
continued use of land without planning permission, 01/4699
enfranchisement
notice of claim
validity of landlord's counter notice, 01/4181
Enterprise Investment Scheme
regulation of care
revocation, 01/6909S
enterprise zones
modification
Highlands and Islands, 01/6713S
entrapment
supply of drugs
undercover police officers
right to fair trial, 01/1042
entry clearances. *See also* **immigration; illegal entrants**
applicant with criminal conviction
residual discretion to permit entry, 01/3668
dependants
exceptional compassionate circumstances, 01/3669
Zimbabwean national
refusal of entry
legitimate expectation, 01/3671
environment
air pollution
air quality reviews, 01/2351, 6480S
Wales, 01/2352
benzene and carbon monoxide limits
Council Directive 2000/69, 01/2353
motor vehicles emissions
Council Directive 2001/1, 01/2356
ancient monuments
conservation, 01/5774NI
books, 01/2421
contaminated land
access to database on sites
no requirement of disclosure, 01/2358
countryside access
local access forum
Wales, 01/2404
maps, 01/4767
Wales, 01/2405
dangerous preparations

environmental protection -cont.
  rural areas -cont.
    countryside stewardship
      arable options, 01/298
      stewardship, 01/6205S
  waste disposal
    foot and mouth disease
      Wales, 01/2379, 2382
    infectious disease control
      foot and mouth disease, 01/2380, 2381
  waste recycling payments, 01/2383
  water courses
    oil pollution, 01/2403
equal opportunities
  Equality Commission for Northern Ireland
    investigations
      time limits, 01/5768NI
    public authorities, 01/5766NI
equal pay. See also sex discrimination
  claims
    time limits
      compatibility with EC law, 01/2279
  collective agreements
    work of equal value
      justification for unequal pay, 01/2277
  comparators
    implied equality clause
      cause of action estoppel, 01/2278
equal treatment
  Council Directive 2000/78, 01/2282
  legal training
    priority accorded to males completing national
      service
        validity under EC law, 01/2285
  nurses
    pension schemes
      lawfulness of regulation, 01/2281
  part time employees
    prevention of less favourable treatment, 01/
      2283, 5767NI
  public authorities
    duties, 01/5719NI
  redundancy selection
    treatment for full and part time employees, 01/
      2284
  teachers
    part time employment
      pension scheme, 01/2280
Equatorial Guinea
  fisheries agreement
    Council Regulation 723/2001, 01/2797
equipment
  health and safety at work
    personal protective equipment, 01/3698
equitable interests in land. See cohabitation
equity. See also equitable interests in land;
  trusts
  agreements
    fiduciary duty
      purchasing freehold on behalf of tenants,
        01/2435
  assignment
    equitable assignment of choses in action, 01/
      2430
  books, 01/2441

equity -cont.
  equitable interest
    mortgages
      payment of equitable interest to redeem
        charge, 01/4871
  equitable interest in land
    debtor funding purchase of property, 01/5513
Erskine Bridge Tolls Act 2001 (asp 12), 01/
  6682S
estate agents
  sole selling rights
    entitlement to commission, 01/6104S
estoppel
  proprietary estoppel
    agreement for lease
      without prejudice negotiations, 01/4868
  unconscionability
    mistaken payment by bank
      extent of detriment, 01/2434
Ethical Standards in Public Life etc.
  (Scotland) Act 2000 (asp 7)
  Commencement No.1 Order, 01/6280S
  Commencement No.2 and Transitional Provisions
    Order, 01/6281S
ethics. See professional conduct
European Commission
  complaints
    discretion to discontinue, 01/2469
  funding of database project
    refusal to pay final instalment, 01/2473
European Community
  immunities and privileges
    North Atlantic Salmon Conservation
      Organization, 01/4070
  Principality of Andorra
    Exchange of Letters
      Council Regulation 2302/2001, 01/2476
  privileges
    European School, 01/2477
European Court of Justice
  appeals
    legality of CFI refusal to re-open oral hearing,
      01/2463
  jurisdiction
    provisional measures under TRIPs Agreement,
      01/2478
  preliminary reference
    judge's discretion to refer, 01/2480
  reference to
    improper implementation of Directive 93/53,
      01/6501S
  references
    proceedings for damages
      exclusive jurisdiction of Danish court, 01/
        824
European Economic Area
  consultation
    investment companies, 01/2697
European Parliament
  elections
    franchise of relevant citizens, 01/2100
European Patents. See patents
European Union. See also EC law
  books, 01/2522
  counterfeiting

European Union -cont.
  counterfeiting -cont.
    single currency, 01/2448
  European Social Fund
    transfer of functions
      National Assembly for Wales, 01/2481
  family law
    enforcement of judgments
      jurisdiction, 01/2625, 5799NI, 6523S
  ministers
    power to make regulations, 01/2871, 2872, 2873, 2874
  treaties
    African, Caribbean and Pacific Group of States, 01/4093
    Cotonou Agreement, 01/4093
    customs administration, 01/2520
    European School, 01/2521
    North Atlantic Salmon Conservation Organization, 01/2809
eviction. *See* possession of land
evidence. *See also* civil evidence; criminal evidence; discovery; documentary evidence; expert evidence; privilege; witnesses
  admissibility
    anonymised evidence
      right to fair trial, 01/396
    electronic copies of public records, 01/105
    expert evidence
      reports relating to banking management, 01/394
    expert witness friend of litigant, 01/395
    expert's report provided by friend of litigant, 01/393
    hearsay evidence
      statement of child, 01/6217S
    oral evidence on agreed boundary line, 01/4847
    secondary evidence
      effect on best evidence rule, 01/392
    secret surveillance evidence obtained by inquiry agent, 01/3299
  books, 01/409
  confidential information
    admissibility of evidence in civil proceedings, 01/390
  documentary evidence
    disclosure
      conduct tending to pervert course of justice, 01/398
  domain names
    unauthorised registration
      admissibility of without prejudice correspondence, 01/397
  expert evidence
    brittle bone disease
      expert's diagnosis unscientific, 01/400
    forgery of will
      evidence of lay witnesses, 01/403
    instruction of second expert, 01/402
  experts
    joint instruction, 01/557
  legal professional privilege
    statement disclosing criminal acts, 01/399

evidence -cont.
  letters of request
    criteria for allowing request for oral cross examination, 01/406
  single joint experts
    appropriateness
      cross examination, 01/405
excise duty. *See also* **Customs and Excise; customs duty; vehicle excise duty**
  air passenger duty
    amendment, 01/5175
  aircraft operators
    information
      air passenger duty, 01/5220
  cider, 01/5221
  designated region
    connected flights
      Isle of Man, 01/5176
    Highlands and Islands Enterprise, 01/5177
  excise duty points
    movement of excise goods, 01/5222
  gaming duty rates, 01/5223
  interest rates, 01/5277
  perry, 01/5221
  repayment of duty, 01/4296
  tobacco products, 01/5224
exemplary damages. *See* measure of damages
expenses
  caution
    company claimant
      statutory compensation scheme, 01/6240S
    undischarged bankrupt
      right to fair trial, 01/6241S
  caution for expenses
    insolvent EC national as pursuer, 01/6242S
  extra judicial settlement
    defender awarded expenses of principal action, 01/6243S
  motion for expenses
    competency, 01/6244S
  sheriff courts
    abandonment of action
      discretionary award, 01/6239S
  taxation
    notice of objections
      competency, 01/6245S
  tender
    summary causes
      small claims scale, 01/6246S
expert evidence. *See also* criminal evidence
  medical negligence
    judicial observation on proper procedure, 01/6218S
explosives
  carriage by rail
    prohibitions, 01/6046NI
  carriage by road, 01/6047NI
  landmines
    prohibited conduct
      Jersey, 01/4071
      overseas territories, 01/4072
exports
  export controls
    annulment proceedings
      locus standi of trade association, 01/2482

exports -*cont.*
  export controls -*cont.*
    dual use goods, 01/4124
      Council Regulation 458/2001, 01/4128
    petroleum
      Yugoslavia, 01/4126
    prohibitions, 01/4125
    weapons
      Yugoslavia, 01/4127
extradition
  books, 01/2526
  extradition crime
    conspiracy to murder
      requisite jurisdiction, 01/2524
    murder committed in India
      police impropriety in obtaining evidence, 01/2525
  habeas corpus
    murder committed in US
      risk of death penalty, 01/2523
  murder committed in US
    compatibility with ECHR, 01/2523
  parties to European Convention
    amendments, 01/4073
    fiscal offences, 01/4074
false imprisonment
  sentence length
    serious violent assault on victim during detention, 01/1297
  wrongful arrest
    wrong identification in warrant
      validity of arrest, 01/5650NI
Family Division
  disclosure
    proceedings in chambers, 01/2622
family law. *See also* **children; divorce; family proceedings**
  books, 01/2677, 6526S
  child protection
    adoption
      local authorities powers and duties, 01/2573
  children
    Children's Commissioner
      Wales, 01/2581
  childrens hearings
    panels
      curators ad litem and reporting officers, 01/6509S
      persons to safeguard interests of children, 01/6756S
  fostering and adoption
    protection from offenders
      Wales, 01/2641
  jurisdiction
    judgments and orders
      enforcement, 01/6523S
  maintenance orders
    reciprocal enforcement
      designation, 01/2649
      variation, 01/2650, 2651
  matrimonial law
    enforcement of judgements, 01/2625
    enforcement of judgments, 01/5799NI
    jurisdiction, 01/2625, 5799NI

family law -*cont.*
  reciprocal enforcement
    maintenance orders
      designation, 01/2649
      variation, 01/2650, 2651
Family Law Act (Northern Ireland) 2001 (c.12), 01/5798NI
Family Law Reform Act 1987 (c.42)
  Commencement No.3 Order, 01/2618
family proceedings
  allocation of proceedings, 01/2619, 2620
  children
    magistrates courts, 01/2624
  expert witnesses
    instructing expert witness without permission of court, 01/2621
  injunctions
    undertaking in damages
      third party restrained from dealing with property, 01/2623
  legal aid
    remuneration rates, 01/4232, 4233, 4234
  matrimonial proceedings, 01/2626
  parental orders, 01/2629
  practice directions
    committal applications, 01/2661
  proof of parentage
    blood tests, 01/2627
  rules, 01/2629
family provision. *See also* **succession**
  spouses
    provision determined by reference to situation on divorce, 01/5156
farming
  financial assistance
    provision of information, 01/5705NI
  grants
    application procedure, 01/6106S
  rural development
    financial assistance
      obligations, 01/5705NI
farming. *See* **agriculture**
farms
  farm subsidies
    review of decisions, 01/5674NI
  grants
    farm enterprise and farm improvement grants
      Wales, 01/162
fatal accident inquiries
  recommendations
    extent of sheriff's power to make, 01/6333S
fatal accidents
  measure of damages
    death of young husband, 01/1513
fees
  administration of benefits
    claims and payments, 01/4985
  agricultural produce
    seed potatoes
      certification of crops, 01/5702NI
  building societies
    Commission expenses, 01/2686
  carriage of goods
    vehicle type approvals, 01/5390
  certificates

fees *-cont.*
certificates *-cont.*
Arrest, Surrender of Deserters and Absentees, 01/356, 357
children
registration
day care, 01/2580, 6504S
county courts, 01/32
Court of Session
shorthand writers, 01/6235S
criminal record
registration, 01/2231, 2232
dentistry, 01/2960, 2961, 5844NI, 6618S
Wales, 01/2887
driving tests, 01/6066NI
drugs and appliances, 01/2963, 6619S, 6620S
Wales, 01/2964
ecclesiastical law
ecclesiastical offences, 01/1850
faculty proceedings, 01/1850
legal officers, 01/1851
parochial fees, 01/1849
fishing
licences
Moville and Louth, 01/5810NI
friendly societies
Commission expenses, 01/2739
gambling
Gaming Board, 01/4298, 5892NI
licences and certificates, 01/4303, 6778S, 6779S
renewal of licences, 01/4306
goods vehicles
tachographs, 01/5445
grants
budget statement
National Crime Squad, 01/4772
National Criminal Intelligence Service, 01/4773
Health and Safety Executive, 01/3313
heavy goods vehicles
international journey authorisations, 01/5416
Swiss permits, 01/5417
tests, 01/6061NI
industrial and provident societies, 01/2747
credit unions
registration, 01/2746
insolvency, 01/3764
insurance companies, 01/3802
land registration, 01/4863, 6671S
liquor licensing, 01/6785S
lotteries
Gaming Board, 01/4307
Maritime and Coastguard Agency, 01/4933, 4934
medicines
Isles of Scilly, 01/2937
registration, 01/2938
mergers
exemption, 01/773
messengers at arms, 01/6088S
motor vehicles
driving tests, 01/5420, 6067NI
tests, 01/5431, 6070NI
type approval, 01/5435, 6074NI

fees *-cont.*
National Lottery
licence fees
prescibed sum, 01/4311
nursing agencies
registration, 01/6658S
nursing homes
registration
fees, 01/6659S
partnerships
Limited Liability Partnerships, 01/4558
passenger vehicles, 01/6077NI
certificates, 01/5446
roadworthiness, 01/5446
tachographs, 01/5445
passports, 01/3689
pharmaceutical industry
registration of premises, 01/3104
planning permission
applications, 01/5926NI
applications and certificates, 01/4735
plant breeders rights, 01/3970
plant protection products, 01/288
plant varieties
seeds, 01/276
Wales, 01/277
public guardians
mental patients, 01/6809S
Public Record Office, 01/103, 104
registered designs
legal protection, 01/3977
registration
political parties, 01/847
residential accommodation
registration, 01/6898S
road works
inspections, 01/5869NI
Wales, 01/3350
roads
road works
inspections, 01/3349
sheriff courts
shorthand writers, 01/6093S
solicitors, 01/6089S
sheriff officers, 01/6092S
solicitors
Court of Session, 01/6236S
telecommunications systems
meters, 01/5347
veterinary medicines, 01/305, 306
wireless telegraphy
licence fees, 01/5326
fiduciary duty
good faith
directors
waiver of entitlement to clawback, 01/3742
solicitors
partnership with former client
failure to advise on need to obtain independent advice, 01/2437
films
cinematic co-production agreements
additional country
Cyprus, 01/4417
France, 01/4416

grants *-cont.*
  education *-cont.*
    mandatory awards, 01/1932
    Royal Ballet School, 01/1933
    schools for performing arts, 01/1934
    Yehundi Menuhin School, 01/1942
  education maintenance allowances, 01/1924, 1925
  education standards, 01/1926, 1927
    pre-school, 01/1928
    Wales, 01/1929
  energy conservation, 01/6482S
  Farm and Conservation Grant Scheme
    time extensions, 01/6124S
  farm enterprise grants
    Wales, 01/162
  farm waste grants
    nitrate vulnerable zones
      Wales, 01/161
  fire and civil defence authorities
    determination, 01/6797S
  fishing industry, 01/2803, 6537S
  fishing vessels
    eligibility, 01/2808, 5814NI, 6547S
  healthcare students
    eligibility, 01/1931
  housing payments, 01/5017
  housing relocation grants
    form of application
      Wales, 01/3407, 3408
    forms, 01/3405, 3406
  housing renewal grants
    forms, 01/3409, 3410
      Wales, 01/3411, 3412, 3413
    means test, 01/3414, 3415
      Wales, 01/3416
  housing renovation grants
    means test, 01/5873NI
    Wales, 01/3417
  housing support grant
    aggregate amount and apportionment, 01/6688S
  improvement grants
    Wales, 01/162
  local government finance
    central funds, 01/5894NI, 5895NI
  police grant, 01/6861S
  rural areas
    agricultural programmes
      time extensions, 01/6202S, 6204S
  rural development grants, 01/297, 299
  school access funds, 01/1925
  students, 01/5750NI
    disabled students, 01/1923, 5746NI
    eligibility, 01/1935, 2044, 5747NI, 5748NI
      European institutions, 01/1936, 1937
      full-time study, 01/1938
      higher education, 01/1939
      performing arts, 01/1940, 2045
    teacher training, 01/2081
    incentives
      Wales, 01/2082
    nursery education, 01/1964
grants, education
  mandatory awards, 01/1943

Greater London
  elections
    extension of polling hours, 01/2092
  Greater London Authority
    legal proceedings
      representation, 01/4336
Greater London Authority Act 1999 (c.29)
  Commencement No.10 Order, 01/4337
green belt
  conservation areas
    refusal to grant permission for accommodation, 01/4739
  development plans
    injunctive relief for breach of planning control, 01/4706
grievous bodily harm
  attempted murder, 01/1319
  criminal record
    inflicting serious injury on wife, 01/1326
  domestic violence
    inflicting serious injury on wife, 01/1325
  facial "glassing" injury
    discretionary sentence, 01/1338
  inflicting brain damage to daughter
    consideration of plea, 01/1320
  inflicting serious injury on victim, 01/1329, 1333
  sentence length
    attack on neighbour, 01/1331
    inflicting serious injury on victim, 01/1324, 1339
    premeditated attack with knife, 01/1337
    repeated attacks on police
      unduly lenient sentence, 01/1334
    road rage incident involving disqualified driver, 01/1330
    unprovoked attack resulting in severe brain injury, 01/1322
    violent attack on motorist, 01/1335
  spouses
    wounded partner intention to discontinue proceedings, 01/1089
Ground Rents Act (Northern Ireland) 2001 (c.5), 01/5943NI
guarantees. *See also* performance bonds
  debts
    classification of co-guarantee's claim for contribution, 01/961
  implied terms
    directors
      liabilities under guarantee, 01/2678
  security for trading debts
    non disclosure of dishonest trading, 01/694
  VAT and duty payments
    guarantors
      failure to make payments, 01/379
gypsies
  planning permission
    refusal for residential use of caravan
      right to private life, 01/4745
harassment
  conduct
    estranged spouse, 01/1050
    evidence of fear of violence, 01/1049
  intentional infliction of harm, 01/5353
  mental health

harassment -*cont.*
  mental health -*cont.*
    mental illness as defence, 01/1051
  newspaper publication
    probability of articles provoking racist
    reaction, 01/4418
  offensive behaviour
    behaviour amounting to course of conduct,
    01/1048
harbours
  harbour authority
    duties and powers, 01/6885S
  harbour development
    Portsmouth, 01/4920
  revision
    constitution
      Cowes, 01/4921
      Fraserburgh, 01/6886S
      King's Lynn Conservancy Board, 01/4922
      Yarmouth, 01/4923
    Fowey, 01/4924
    Lerwick, 01/6887S
    Poole, 01/4925
    Port of Tyne, 01/4926
    Swanage, 01/4927
hazardous substances. *See also* **chemicals;
pesticides**
  batteries and accumulators
    marking requirements, 01/2387
  health and safety at work
    controls, 01/3312
  marketing and use restrictions
    Commission Directive 2001/90, 01/2388
    Commission Directive 2001/91, 01/2389
  packaging
    labelling, 01/5722NI
  special waste, 01/2417
    Wales, 01/2418
health. *See also* **National Health Service;
medicine; mental health**
  appeals
    Family Health Services Appeal Authority
      documentary evidence, 01/2879
      procedure, 01/2880
  books, 01/3292
  dentists
    miscellaneous amendments, 01/2889
  health authorities
    membership and procedure, 01/2917, 2918,
    2919
  immunisation
    personal injuries
      compensation, 01/2925
  information
    Patient Information Advisory Group
      establishment, 01/3103
  injury benefits
    Health and Personal Social Services, 01/
    5843NI
  medical devices
    blood derivatives
      Council Directive 2000/70, 01/2936
  medical profession
    recognition of professional qualifications
      Council Directive 2001/19, 01/2932

health -*cont.*
  medicines
    control
      Isles of Scilly, 01/2937
    fees
      Isles of Scilly, 01/2937
  mental health
    discharge of patients
      judgments and orders, 01/2947
  National Blood Authority
    establishment and constitution, 01/2920
  National Health Service
    general medical services
      doctors and medical list, 01/2966
      supplementary list, 01/2973
  patients rights
    Patient Information Advisory Group
      establishment, 01/3103
  pharmaceutical services, 01/5857NI
  primary care
    extension
      Isles of Scilly, 01/2986
  tobacco
    manufacture and presentation
      Council Directive, 01/3291
Health Act 1999 (c.8)
  Commencement No.10 Order, 01/2903
  Commencement No.11 Order, 01/2904
**Health and Personal Social Services Act
(Northern Ireland) 2001 (c.3), 01/5848NI**
  Commencement No.1 Order, 01/5849NI
  Commencement No.2 Order, 01/5850NI
health and safety at work. *See also* **employers
liability; hazardous substances; industrial
injuries**
  accidents
    back injury
      no breach of statutory duty, 01/3299
    laying of grit
      obvious risk from ice, 01/3303
  books, 01/3321
  carriage of pressure equipment, 01/3307
  construction industry
    design regulations, 01/5864NI
  employees
    personal injuries
      tripping accident, 01/3306
  employers liability
    electrocution of employee
      failure to conduct risk assessment, 01/
      3296
    employee suffering burns resulting from
    explosion
      level of fine, 01/3300
    injury at work
      duty to give sufficient instructions, 01/
      3304
  equipments
    personal protective equipment, 01/3698
  fatal accidents
    breach
      appropriateness of fine, 01/1348
    collision between pedestrian employee and
    bus, 01/1349

health and safety at work -*cont.*
fatal accidents -*cont.*
death of employees during demolition work, 01/1350
genetically modified organisms
contained use, 01/5867NI
hazardous substances
batteries and accumulators
marking requirements, 01/2387
controls, 01/3312
packaging and labelling, 01/5722NI
Health and Safety Executive
legality of issuing prohibition notice, 01/3317
hospitals
accidents
extent of duty to protect employees, 01/4472
Italy's imposition of stringent standards
compatibility with Council Directive 89/655, 01/2506
manual handling operations
risk of injury, 01/6664S
merchant shipping and fishing vessels, 01/4928
safety signs and signals, 01/4929
minimum safety requirements
fire precautions, 01/5866NI
offshore installations
safety zones, 01/4553, 4554, 4555, 4556
radiation
employers duties, 01/3318, 5868NI
risk assessment
scope of employer's duty
psychiatric illness, 01/6665S
safe system of working
duty owed to ship's master, 01/6666S
ships, 01/4928
statutory duty
floor of workplace
article or obstruction on floor, 01/6663S
stress
constructive dismissal claim
effect on personal injury claim, 01/4494
work equipment
minimum safety requirements
Council Directive 2001/45, 01/3308
premises door as equipment, 01/6662S
workplace
premises door not "workplace", 01/6662S
Health and Social Care Act 2001 (c.15), 01/2905
Commencement No.1 Order
England, 01/2906
Wales, 01/2907
Commencement No.2 Order
England, 01/2908
Commencement No.3 Order
England, 01/2909
Commencement No.4 Order
England, 01/2910
Commencement No.5 Order, 01/2911
Commencement No.6 Order
England, 01/2912
Commencement No.7 Order
England, 01/2913

health authorities. *See also* **National Health Service**
change of name, 01/2914
dentistry
incentive scheme, 01/2888
establishment and abolition, 01/2915
functions and administration arrangements, 01/2916
prescribed functions
Wales, 01/2921
Retained Organs Commission
membership and procedure, 01/2922
establishment and constitution, 01/2923, 2924
health boards
membership and procedure, 01/6612S
Health services
drugs and appliances
fees, 01/5851NI
general medical services
doctors
prescription of drugs, 01/5852NI
issue of certificates, 01/5853NI
prescription of drugs
doctors, 01/5854NI
nurse prescribers, 01/5855NI
pharmaceutical services, 01/5857NI
travelling expenses
remission of charges, 01/5856NI
hearings
oral evidence
absence of up to date medical report, 01/563
right to fair trial
conduct of hearings in private, 01/564
heath and safety at work
radioactive substances
safety standards
clocks and watches, 01/3319
heavy goods vehicles
authorisation fees
Swiss permits, 01/5417
enforcement, 01/5415
international journeys
authorisation fees, 01/5416
testing
fees, 01/6061NI
notice of refusal, 01/6062NI
heritable property
books, 01/6680S
boundary title
description by reference
inconsistency with measurements and plan, 01/6669S
deed of conditions
management of salmon fishings
breach of dam, 01/6542S
pre emption rights
condition unenforceable, 01/6674S
repairs
common repair scheme
competency of interdict to stop, 01/6675S
searches
inaccurate certificate
damages for loss of profits, 01/6419S
title to land

heritable property -cont.
  title to land -cont.
    disputed title, 01/6247S
  warranties
    breach of warranty, 01/6679S
High Court
  judges
    increase in numbers, 01/5641NI
  jurisdiction, 01/47
    trespass to land, 01/565
higher education
  funding
    grants, 01/1858
  higher education corporations
    dissolution
      Bretton Hall, 01/1944
  Scottish Higher Education Funding Council
    designation
      UHI Millennium Institute, 01/6439S
highway control. *See also* **bridges; parking; roads**
  books, 01/3399
  road works
    charges
      occupation of the highway, 01/3348
    inspections
      maintenance, 01/5870NI
hire purchase. *See also* **consumer credit**
  title to goods
    innocent purchaser
      vehicle obtained by rogue on hire purchase, 01/917
holidays
  accommodation
    holiday property bond companies
      failure to provide suitable alternative apartment, 01/4275
  package holidays
    breach of contract
      award for disappointment, 01/4276
      foreseeability, 01/4277
    injuries sustained during excursion
      level of care of tour operator, 01/4282
    injuries sustained from defective sunbed
      standard of care, 01/4291
    personal injuries
      liability of tour operator, 01/4281
    poor weather conditions
      duty to warn, 01/4283
    provision of contractual services
      operator's failure to exercise reasonable care, 01/4279
    tour operator inability to comply with special request, 01/4278
    travel agents
      no strict liability for injury, 01/4284
  tour operators and travel agents
    non discriminatory pricing, 01/4286
    separate claims in contract and tort
      claims arising out of same facts, 01/4290
homelessness
  accommodation
    priority need
      Wales, 01/3420
    suitable accommodation

homelessness -cont.
  accommodation -cont.
    suitable accommodation -cont.
      temporary accommodation at seaside resorts, 01/3428
  asylum seekers
    eligibility for local authority housing, 01/3421
  harassment
    local authority duty to provide appropriate housing, 01/3422
  intentional homelessness
    domestic violence
      reasonableness of continued occupation, 01/3423
    local authorities
      duty to make proper enquiries, 01/3424
  legitimate expectation
    assurance of accommodation with security of tenure, 01/3426
  local connection
    date for determination, 01/3419
  priority needs
    spouse as dependant child, 01/3427
  settled accommodation
    local authority housing
      failure to make adequate inquiries, 01/3425
homosexuality
  children
    custody
      discrimination against gay father, 01/2587
hospitals. *See* **National Health Service**
House of Commons (Removal of Clergy Disqualification) Act 2001 (c.13), 01/841
House of Lords
  hereditary peers
    local government electors register, 01/5235
housing. *See also* **homelessness; housing benefit; right to buy**
  defective premises
    failure to disclose defect to subsequent purchaser, 01/3401
  grants
    disabled facilities, 01/3402, 3403
    Wales, 01/3404
  hostels
    eviction with out notice
      right of occupation, 01/6683S
  housing revenue account
    contribution from general fund, 01/6694S
    electronic notification of decisions
      Wales, 01/4392
  housing support grant
    aggregate amount and apportionment, 01/6688S
  local authority housing
    introductory tenancies
      fairness of review process, 01/3435
    right to buy
      written notice constituting "relevant outstanding matter", 01/3448
    statutory nuisance
      layout of council house, 01/4551
  multiple occupation grants
    failure to comply with conditions, 01/3437
  ownership

insurance -cont.
  reinsurance companies
    clause requiring separate account for premiums, 01/3835
  reinsurance contracts
    claims cooperation clause
      non compliance, 01/3839
    non disclosure
      avoidance for misrepresentation, 01/3834
  subrogation
    guarantees
      exclusion of rights of surety to subrogation, 01/3842
  third party insurance
    calculation for compensation payable, 01/3831
    liability for criminal act of motorist, 01/3843
insurance companies
  winding up
    valuation rules, 01/2753
insurance contracts
  limited liability partnerships
    threshold conditions
      variation, 01/2760
insurance policies. See insurance contracts
intellectual property. See also copyright; passing off; patents; trade marks
  agreements
    reasonableness
      restraints in settlement agreement, 01/3978
  books, 01/4066, 6729S
  copyright and confidential information
    Council Directive 2001/29, 01/3846
  registered designs
    Isle of Man, 01/3974
    legal protection, 01/3975, 3976
      fees, 01/3977
  trade marks
    registration
      classification, 01/4048
interdicts
  competency
    acts carried out pending appeal, 01/6771S
  interim interdict
    balance of convenience, 01/6247S
    infringement of trade mark, 01/6726S
    notice to quit
      interdict raised by spouse of tenant, 01/6693S
interest rates
  income tax, 01/5257
interest to sue
  occupier of disputed croft
    no formal right to occupy, 01/6747S
International Criminal Court Act 2001 (c.17), 01/4076
  Commencement Order, 01/4077
  Amendment, 01/4078
International Criminal Court (Scotland) Act 2001 (asp 13), 01/6732S
  Commencement Order, 01/6731S
international law. See also international trade; international organisations; United Nations
  anti-personnel landmines
    elimination of use

international law -cont.
  anti-personnel landmines -cont.
    elimination of use -cont.
      Council Regulation 1725/2001, 01/4113
  books, 01/4116
  continental shelf
    UK rights to natural resources, 01/4068
  fines
    forfeiture
      reparation orders, 01/4080
  International Criminal Court
    delivery proceedings
      forms, 01/4085
  landmines
    elimination of use
      Council Regulation 1724/2001, 01/4114
    prohibited conduct
      Jersey, 01/4071
  letters of request
    enforcement of letters rogatory
      request for international judicial assistance, 01/4083
  World Trade Organisation
    legal advice
      Advisory Centre for WTO Law, 01/4115
international organisations
  Organisation for the Prohibition of Chemical Weapons
    immunities, 01/4082
international trade. See also exports; imports
  anti-dumping activity
    Council Regulation 1515/2001, 01/4122
  books, 01/4138, 6736S
  carriage by air
    carriers liabilities
      person entitled to delivery, 01/6733S
  customs duty
    community transit
      entitlement to raise import duty, 01/4120
    fraud
      liability of principal, 01/4121
    preferential trade
      Council Regulation 1207/2001, 01/4136
    preferential trade concessions
      Bulgaria, Hugary and Romania
        Council Regulation 678/2001, 01/4137
  sanctions
    Iraq
      application to non residents, 01/4123
  statistics
    Council Decision 507/2001, 01/2510, 4118
  tariff duties
    suspension
      Council Regulation 1159/2001, 01/4119
internet
  domain names
    registration
      bad faith, 01/3874
      evidence of bad faith, 01/3870, 3871
      similarity to well known trade mark, 01/3875
    registration in bad faith
      celebrity's name constituted unregistered trade mark, 01/3873
    similarity

Land Court
appeals
  preliminary hearing to establish basis, 01/
    6739S
expenses
  party litigant's expenses, 01/6749S
  prior offer to settle, 01/6745S
  witness' expenses, 01/6749S
jurisdiction
  review of Crofters Commission apportionment
    order, 01/6741S
land drainage
environmental impact assessments, 01/5925NI
Internal Drainage Boards
  reorganisation
    Buckingham, 01/4710
    Denge and Southbrooks, 01/4711
    Holmewood and Stilton, 01/5628
    Pett, 01/4711
    River Ouzel, 01/4710
    Romney Marsh Levels, 01/4711
    Rother and Walland Marsh, 01/4711
    South Gloucestershire, 01/4712
    West Gloucestershire, 01/4712
    Whittlesey, 01/5629
    Whittlesey Fifth, 01/5629
    Yaxley, 01/5628
land registration
compulsory registration areas, 01/5944NI
district registries
  reorganisation, 01/4862
fees, 01/4863, 6671S
land registry
  fraud
    appropriate test for seeking indemnity, 01/
      4865
possession of land
  discretion to rectify land register, 01/4861
rules
  electronic communication, 01/4864
Land Registration (Scotland) Act 1979 (c.33)
Commencement No.15 Order, 01/6672S
landlord and tenant. *See also* **agricultural
holdings; assured tenancies; housing;
leaseholds; leases; public sector tenancies;
rent; service charges**
books, 01/4218, 6755S
claims
  applications, 01/594
defective gas fire
  extent of landlord's duty, 01/4163
eviction
  setting side
    oppression in execution of warrant, 01/
      4168
  stay of execution
    tenant's inability to apply following error,
      01/4169
forfeiture
  right of relief of equitable chargee, 01/4187
freeholds
  disputed valuation
    rejection of offer to settle, 01/4179
landlord's powers and duties
  covenants

landlord and tenant -*cont.*
landlord's powers and duties -*cont.*
  covenants -*cont.*
    liability upon transfer of freehold reversion,
      01/4173
  disrepair
    loss of enjoyment, 01/4212
  set off
    charge on rent deposit, 01/4175
leases
  validity of landlord's counter-notice, 01/4174
notices
  mistake
    effect on validity, 01/4156
possession orders
  setting aside execution of warrant
    oppressive conduct, 01/4166
rent arrears
  eviction
    award of statutory damages, 01/4164
repair covenants
  extent of repair obligations, 01/4211
  liability of tenants for cost, 01/4210
termination of tenancy
  notice to quit
    validity of notice, 01/4189
unlawful eviction
  attempt to pervert the course of justice, 01/
    1293
lands tribunal
documentary evidence
  disclosure of tribunal member's notes, 01/555
jurisdiction to award costs, 01/4177
order for costs
  enforceability, 01/4176
salaries, 01/5643NI
valuation
  option to obtain planning permission, 01/4678
law of the sea. *See also* **fisheries; navigation;
pollution control**
continental shelf
  UK rights to natural resources, 01/4068
Learning and Skills Act 2000 (c.21)
Commencement No.3 and Savings and
  Transitional Provisions Order, 01/1948
Commencement No.3 and Transitional Provisions
  Order
  Wales, 01/1949
Commencement No.4 Order
  Wales, 01/1950
leaseholds
enfranchisement
  tenant's notices
    procedural requirements, 01/4182
  valuation
    lack of mutual enforceability clause, 01/
      4184
houses
  leasehold enfranchisement
    meaning of "house", 01/4180
intermediate leaseholder
  gross rent calculation method
    compensation payable, 01/4178
leasehold valuation tribunals
  service charges

Legal Aid (Scotland) Act 1986 (c.47) *-cont.*
  Commencement No.4 Order *-cont.*
    Scotland, 01/6768S
legal executives
  free movement of services, 01/4260
legal methodology
  books, 01/4254
legal profession. *See also* **barristers; solicitors**
  barristers
    practising certificates, 01/4257
  books, 01/4273, 6773S
  free movement of services, 01/4260
  Law Society of Scotland
    statutory functions
      interdict against exercise, 01/6771S
  Legal Services Commission
    disclosure of information, 01/56
  licensed conveyancers
    disciplinary procedures, 01/4258
    Discipline and Appeals Committee
      procedure, 01/4259
  solicitors
    incorporated practices, 01/4266
legal representation. *See also* **legal aid**
  childrens hearings, 01/6508S
  defective representation
    inadequate cross examination in criminal trial, 01/6349S
  duty solicitors scheme
    committee's refusal to reselect solicitor, 01/4229
  freeing orders
    adjournment to allow parents to be represented, 01/2644
  housing possession cases
    adjournment pending grant of legal aid, 01/3439
  police stations
    consultation with solicitor in cell compatibility with ECHR, 01/3534
legal services
  assisted persons
    representation by solicitors, 01/6770S
  Community Legal Service
    assessment of financial resources, 01/4240, 4241, 4242
    funding, 01/4246, 4247
    counsel in family proceedings, 01/4248
  Criminal Defence Service, 01/1015, 4223
  recovery of costs, 01/4224
legal systems
  books, 01/4274, 5891NI, 6774S
legislation
  commencement
    sentencing transitional provisions, 01/6835S
  statutory interpretation
    compatibility with ECHR, 01/6475S
    unintended effect, 01/6413S
leisure industry
  books, 01/4292
  football grounds
    seating, 01/4288
  football spectators
    banning orders
      extension of powers, 01/1059

leisure industry *-cont.*
  package holidays
    tour operators and travel agents
      non discriminatory pricing, 01/4286
  personal injuries
    alleged negligence of tutor
      liability of tour operator, 01/4280
  sports grounds
    safety certificates, 01/4289
letters of credit
  deceit
    fraudulent endorsement, 01/5350
libel
  defence of fair comment
    objective test, 01/1821
  fair comment
    admissibility of contextual facts, 01/1820
  malice
    removal of issue from jury, 01/1827
  newspapers
    publication of reply to allegations
      summary judgments, 01/1830
  reputation
    holding company not damaged by allegations, 01/1835
Liberia
  United Nations
    sanctions, 01/4108
      Channel Islands, 01/4109
      Isle of Man, 01/4110
      overseas territories, 01/4111, 4112
libraries
  books, 01/4293
  public lending right
    scheme variations, 01/3973
licences. *See also* **driving licences; licensing**
  animals
    infectious disease control
      foot and mouth disease, 01/217, 218
  fishing
    conservation
      Channel Islands, 01/2800
    Foyle
      Carlingford, 01/5810NI
  National Lottery
    fees
      prescibed sum, 01/4311
  postal services
    penalties
      determination of turnover, 01/4800
  research
    Human Fertilisation and Embryology, 01/4896
  street trading, 01/5896NI
  vehicle licences
    refunds
      notice required, 01/6078NI
licensing
  alcohol
    permitted hours
      New Year's Eve 2001, 01/4294
    transfer of functions of justices' clerks to justices chief executives
      Isles of Scilly, 01/4295
  amusement machines
    medium-prize machines

New Zealand -cont.
patents
medical treatment
recognition of Swiss type claims, 01/3965
trustees in bankruptcy
abandonment of causes of action, 01/3786
newspapers
copyright
articles photocopied for internal use, 01/3857
NHS trusts
change of name
Avon and Western Wiltshire Mental Health Care, 01/2996
Greenwich Healthcare, 01/3062
Homerton Hospital, 01/2997
King's Mill Centre for Health Care Services, 01/3063
Norfolk and Norwich Health Care, 01/3064
North Middlesex Hospital, 01/3065
South Tees Acute Hospitals, 01/3066
Southern Derbyshire Mental Health, 01/3067
dissolution
Aylesbury Vale Community Healthcare, 01/2998
Barnet Community Healthcare, 01/2999
Bath and West Community, 01/3000
Bay Community Health, 01/3001
Calderdale Healthcare, 01/3002
Carlisle Hospitals, 01/3003
Central Manchester Healthcare, 01/3004
Central Nottinghamshire Healthcare, 01/3024
Central Sheffield University Hospitals, 01/3005
City and Hackney Community Services, 01/3006
Dorset Community, 01/3007
Ealing, Hammersmith and Fulham Mental Health, 01/3008
East Berkshire, 01/3009
East Gloucestershire, Gloucestershire Royal and Severn, 01/3069
Enfield Community Care, 01/2999
Essex and Herts Community, 01/3010
Exeter and District Community, 01/3011
First Community Health, 01/3012
Foundation, 01/3012
Guild Community Healthcare, North Sefton and the West Lancashire Community, 01/3070
Halton General Hospital, 01/3013
Haringey Health Care, 01/2999
Horizon, 01/3014
Huddersfield Health Care Services, 01/3002
Kingston and District Community, 01/3015
Lincoln District Healthcare, 01/3016
Manchester Children's Hospitals, 01/3004
Mancunian Community Health, 01/3017
Mid Essex Community and Mental Health, 01/3010
Newcastle City Health, 01/3018
Newham Community Health Services, 01/3006
North East Essex Mental Health, 01/3010
North East Lincolnshire, 01/3019

NHS trusts -cont.
dissolution -cont.
North Hampshire, Loddon Community, 01/3020
North Lakeland Healthcare, 01/3003
Northampton Community Healthcare, 01/3021
Northern General Hospital, 01/3005
Northumberland Mental Health, 01/3018
Norwich Community Health Partnership, 01/3022
Nottingham Community Health, 01/3023
Nottingham Healthcare, 01/3024
Oxfordshire Community Health, 01/3025
Plymouth Community Service, 01/3026
Premier Health, 01/3012
Ravensbourne Priority Health, 01/3027
Rockingham Forest, 01/3021
Salford Community Health Care, 01/3028
Scunthorpe and Goole Hospitals, 01/3019
Solihull Healthcare, 01/3029
South Lincolnshire Healthcare, 01/3016
Southern Derbyshire Community Health Services, 01/3030
Tameside and Glossop Community and Priority Services, 01/3071
Teddington Memorial Hospital, 01/3031
Tower Hamlets Healthcare, 01/3006
Warrington Commmunity Health Care, 01/3068
Warrington Hospital, 01/3013
West Berkshire Priority Care Service, 01/3009
West Cumbria Health Care, 01/3003
West Herts Community Health, 01/3014
Wigan and Leigh Health Services, 01/3032
Wrightington Hospital, 01/3032
establishment
5 Boroughs Partnership, 01/3068
Argyll and Clyde Acute Hospitals, 01/6629S
Ayrshire and Arran Acute Hospitals, 01/6630S
Ayrshire and Arran Primary Care, 01/6631S
Barnet, Enfield and Haringey Mental Health, 01/3033
Berkshire Healthcare, 01/3034
Borders General Hospital, 01/6632S
Borders Primary Care, 01/6633S
Buckinghamshire Mental Health, 01/3035
Calderdale and Huddersfield, 01/3036
Camden and Islington Mental Health, 01/3037
Central Manchester and Manchester Children's University Hospitals, 01/3038
Dumfries and Galloway Acute and Maternity Hospitals, 01/6634S
Dumfries and Galloway Primary Care, 01/6635S
Fife Acute Hospitals, 01/6636S
Fife Primary Care, 01/6637S
Forth Valley Acute Hospitals, 01/6638S
Forth Valley Primary Care, 01/6639S
Gloucestershire Hospitals and Gloucestershire Partnership, 01/3069
Grampian Primary Care, 01/6640S
Grampian University Hospitals, 01/6641S

nuisance -cont.
  private nuisance -cont.
    causes of action
      nuisance predating freehold acquisition, 01/
        4548
    floods
      occupier's duty to abate, 01/4547
  public nuisance
    birds
      interference with use of public footpath,
        01/4549
  statutory nuisance
    calculation of noise levels
      validity of abatement notice, 01/4550
    local authority housing
      condensation, 01/6827S
  tenants
    landlord's liability to third party, 01/4197
  tenements
    demolition of adjoining property, 01/6826S
nurses
  nursing agencies
    registration
      fees, 01/6658S
nursing homes
  registration
    fees, 01/6659S
obscenity
  importation of obscene materials
    evading prohibition, 01/1442
  indecent video recordings
    proof of knowledge video showed children,
      01/1060
occupation orders
  child respondent
    attachment of power of arrest, 01/2654
occupational pensions
  accidental benefits increase
    rectification, 01/4595
  armed forces
    disablement or death in service, 01/4589
  benefits
    revaluation percentages, 01/4596, 5908NI
  British Airways pension schemes
    disposable surplus, 01/4594
  Civil Aviation Authority pension scheme, 01/
    4597
  civil servants, 01/4598
  compensation
    calculation of loss, 01/2342
  compensation for premature retirement, 01/
    6837S
  compensation provision, 01/4599
  conversion of final salary schemes, 01/4625
  death in service benefits
    discretionary powers of trustees, 01/4601
  employers duties
    no unilateral absolution from accrued
      liabilities, 01/4626
  entitlement
    deferred pensions rights, 01/4602
  firemens pension scheme
    pension sharing on divorce, 01/4592, 6838S
  guaranteed minimum pensions
    increase, 01/4606, 5909NI

occupational pensions -cont.
  Inner London court staff, 01/4607, 4608
  local government
    discretionary payments, 01/5914NI
    injury benefits, 01/5914NI
    local government pension scheme
      pension sharing on divorce, 01/5911NI,
        6840S
  local government pension scheme, 01/4609,
    5910NI, 5913NI, 6839S
    employment, 01/4610
    fund management, 01/5912NI
    membership, 01/4611, 4612
    pension sharing on divorce, 01/5911NI, 6840S
  maladministration
    misinformation relating to entitlement, 01/
      4616
  merchant navy
    commencing dates of awards, 01/4644
  mistaken payment
    compensation for distressed caused, 01/
      5915NI
  National Health Service
    pension sharing on divorce, 01/6845S
  National Health Service pension scheme
    additional voluntary contributions, 01/4619
  Parliament
    pension sharing, 01/4620
    trustees, 01/4621
  part time employment
    access to scheme membership
      compatibility of time limits with EC law, 01/
        2279
  pensions management
    duty of care to beneficiaries, 01/4613
  Pensions Ombudsman
    early retirement
      determination of employee's eligibility, 01/
        4603
  perpetuities and contracting out, 01/4623,
    5916NI
  police pension scheme
    pension sharing on divorce, 01/6841S, 6842S
  public service pensions
    pension sharing
      exemption, 01/4622
  railway pension scheme
    railway workers, 01/4624
  retirement scheme
    calculation method based on gender, 01/4604
  Royal Ulster Constabulary, 01/5918NI
  superannuation
    Chief Executive to the Mental Health
      Commission, 01/5922NI
    pension sharing on divorce, 01/6848S
    teachers
      additional voluntary contributions, 01/
        6847S
      pension sharing on divorce, 01/6848S
  surplus
    valuation
      cost deduction inappropriate, 01/4629
  teachers, 01/4627, 5923NI
  transfer
    requirement for certification, 01/4628

occupational pensions -*cont.*
trustees in bankruptcy
superannuation schemes
time of vesting, 01/3734
occupiers liability
duty of care
duty to warn visitors against danger, 01/4504
footpaths
duty to maintain, 01/4498
local authorities
liability for highway, 01/6821S
local authority's duty to maintain coastal footpath, 01/4496
personal injuries
owner of servient tenement
duty to repair, 01/4503
sports
bowling alleys
sufficiency of warnings, 01/4285
off licences. *See also* **licensing**
offences
Official Secrets Act
applicability of defence of necessity, 01/1057
offences against the person. *See also* **assault; actual bodily harm; grievous bodily harm**
offensive weapons. *See also* **firearms**
offshore installations
pipelines
jurisdiction, 01/3316
safety
oil and gas industry, 01/4555
safety zones
oil and gas industry, 01/4553, 4554
oil. *See* **oil and gas industry**
oil and gas industry. *See also* **oil pollution; oil pollution**
income tax
reliefs
oil rig not a ship, 01/5269
offshore installations
safety, 01/4555, 4556
safety zones, 01/4553, 4554
petroleum
export controls
Yugoslavia, 01/4126
oil and gas production
habitats
wild birds
conservation, 01/2386
oil pollution
compensation
amendment of claim, 01/6869S
compensation scheme
validity of late acceptance, 01/6298S
International Convention on Oil Pollution 1990, 01/4940
ombudsmen
Assembly Ombudsman
salaries, 01/5654NI
Commissioner for Complaints
salaries, 01/5654NI
police
Royal Ulster Constabulary
complaints, 01/5930NI

opticians
general opthalmic services
opthalmic list, 01/3102
General Optical Council
membership, 01/3099
registration and enrolment, 01/3100
optical appliances
children leaving care, 01/3095
vouchers, 01/3093, 3094, 5860NI, 5861NI
Wales, 01/3096, 3097, 3098
provision of ophthalmic services, 01/5862NI
sight tests
eligibility
increase, 01/5862NI
origin marking
animal products
exports and imports, 01/2820, 5824NI, 6553S
PACE codes of practice. *See* **criminal evidence; police**
package holidays
tour operators and travel agents
non discriminatory pricing, 01/4286
parental contact. *See also* **contact orders; parental rights**
children
conflict of interest
appointment of guardian ad litem, 01/2589
in vitro fertilisation
lack of biological link to father, 01/2657
removal of child to Ghana
intention of mother, 01/2658
hearsay evidence of child's statement
admissibility, 01/6217S
parental leave
period of leave, 01/2289
parental responsibility
agreements
current contact details, 01/2659
father's concern for disabled child
history of conflict with mother, 01/2660
parental rights
deprivation of rights
blanket order, 01/6217S
parking. *See also* **highway control**
special parking areas
Barrow in Furness, 01/3331
Birmingham, 01/3332
Bournemouth, 01/3333
Brighton & Hove, 01/3334
Cumbria, 01/3335
Dartford, 01/3336
Dover, 01/3337
Herefordshire, 01/3338
Northampton, 01/3339
Oldham, 01/3340
Plymouth, 01/3341
Salford, 01/3342
Salisbury, 01/3343
Southend-on-Sea, 01/3344
Stoke-on-Trent, 01/3345
Taunton Deane, 01/3346
Three Rivers, 01/3347

race discrimination -*cont.*
gypsies -*cont.*
aiding unlawful act, 01/3492
exclusion from public house, 01/6878S
legal reasoning
drawing of inferences, 01/2298
psychiatric harm
measure of damages, 01/1534
public authorities
statutory duties, 01/3493
Race Equality Scheme, 01/3494
racial groups
English and Scots ethnicity, 01/6473S
termination of employment
meaning of "aids", 01/2300
time limits
basis of recruitment policy, 01/2299
victimisation
application of statutory test, 01/2301
refusal to give reference
pending hearing, 01/2302
Race Relations (Amendment) Act 2000 (c.34)
Commencement Order, 01/3495
railways. *See also* **public transport**
accessibility
disabled persons, 01/6080NI
exemption applications, 01/6081NI
exemptions, 01/5450, 5451, 5452, 5453,
5454, 5455, 5456, 5457, 5458, 5459,
5460, 5461
British Railways Board
membership, 01/5463
carriage by rail
dangerous goods
Commission Directive 2001/6, 01/5387
Channel Tunnel Rail Link
Stratford station, 01/5464
closure of operational passenger networks
St. Pancras station, 01/5465
explosives
carriage by rail, 01/6046NI
carriage by road, 01/6047NI
extension
London Underground
East London Line, 01/5473
insolvency
administration
protected companies, 01/5466
light railways
Greater Manchester
Ashton Moss variation, 01/5467
compulsory acquisition of land, 01/5468
Mumps surface crossing, 01/5469
Trafford Park, 01/5470
Leeds Supertram
compulsory acquisition of land, 01/5471
extension, 01/5472
London Underground
construction and maintenance, 01/5473
Norfolk
transfer of rights and liabilities, 01/5474
passengers
delayed train
contract terms of travel, 01/5475
railway infrastructure

railways. -*cont.*
railway infrastructure -*cont.*
levying of charges
Council Directive 2001/14, 01/5476, 5477
safety certification
Council Directive 2001/14, 01/5476, 5477
trans-European network
Council Directive 2001/16, 01/5478
railway pension scheme, 01/4624
safety
infrastructure controllers
audits, 01/5479
railway operators
railway safety case, 01/5479
Strategic Rail Authority
capital allowances, 01/5481
licence exemption, 01/5482
rape
cross examination
sexual history of complainer, 01/6318S
expert evidence
failure to obtain revised opinion, 01/6359S
false imprisonment
robbery of prostitute
consecutive sentence appropriate, 01/1457
indecent assault on daughter, 01/1464
probation orders
unduly lenient sentence, 01/1461
sentence length
breach of non molestation orders, 01/1462
indecent assault on child, 01/1460
rape of child, 01/1456
rape of children by father, 01/1455
victim devout Muslim virgin, 01/1463
rates. *See also* **community charge; council tax**
central rating list
designated persons and hereditaments, 01/
4803
Ineos Chlor Ltd, 01/4803
central rating lists
industry hereditaments
Wales, 01/4838
council tax
shared facilities in bedsitting accommodation,
01/4809
determination of rateable value, 01/5937NI,
5938NI
exemptions
student accommodation
primary purpose of account, 01/5939NI
non domestic rates
agricultural property, 01/4810, 4824
alteration of lists, 01/4811
Wales, 01/4812
alteration to rating list
meaning of "hereditament", 01/4822
appeals, 01/4811
Wales, 01/4812
billing authorities
calculation of contributions, 01/4813
Wales, 01/4814
calculation of contributions
amendment of rules, 01/4813
Wales, 01/4814
collection and enforcement, 01/4804

social welfare -cont.
  community care -cont.
    accommodation -cont.
      Wales, 01/5144
    direct payments
      children under 16, 01/6897S
    local authorities
      extent of duty to provide preferred
        accommodation, 01/5132
    direct payments
      disabled children, 01/5145
    disabled persons
      direct payments
        Wales, 01/5124
    food
      dried milk
        price increase, 01/5128
      milk, 01/6030NI
    health care
      private health care, 01/5130
      voluntary health care, 01/5130
    local authorities
      investigations into sexual abuse
        power to communicate to other
          organisations, 01/5131
    National Care Standards Commission
      fees and frequency of inspections, 01/5125
      membership and procedure, 01/5126
      registration, 01/5127
    nursing homes
      registration
        availability of premises, 01/5135
    residential accommodation
      registration
        fees, 01/6898S
        sums for personal requirements, 01/5137,
          6902S
        Wales, 01/5065
    residential care
      cancellation of registration, 01/5141
      care homes and nursing homes, 01/5138
      failure to place after assessment
        ultra vires, 01/6904S
      persons with learning disabilities
        assessment of care needs after hospital
          closure, 01/3289
      prior disposal of capital
        assessment of needs, 01/6903S
    social services
      community care
        accommodation, 01/5143
    Social Services Council
      appointments, procedure and access to the
        register, 01/6905S
      consultation on Codes of Practice, 01/6906S
    social work
      education and training
        transfer scheme, 01/5146
solemn procedure
  adjournment
    judicial justification for refusal
      complainer travelling from Canada, 01/
        6379S

solicitors. *See also* **legal advice; professional**
  negligence
  clients
    ascertainment of retainer, 01/4261
  conveyancing
    termination of retainer
      breach of duty, 01/4265
  disciplinary procedures
    proceedings arising from same facts
      abuse of process, 01/4264
  disciplinary tribunal
    power to refer case to OSS, 01/4270
  duty of care
    duty to judicial factor, 01/6086S
    execution of will
      cancellation of appointment with client, 01/
        4524
    inaccurate report to mortgage lender
      liability for losses on default, 01/6819S
  duty solicitors
    remuneration, 01/4249
  employment
    legal aid, 01/6767S
  fees
    Court of Session, 01/6236S
    sheriff courts, 01/6089S
  free movement of services, 01/4260
  incorporated practices, 01/4266
  legal aid
    employment, 01/6767S
  partners liabilities
    funds deposited in client account, 01/4267
  professional conduct
    disciplinary tribunal
      independence and impartiality, 01/6772S
  professional negligence
    acting for both parties in mortgage transaction
      extent of duty to disclose, 01/4523
    disclosure to lender, 01/6822S
    financial provision on divorce
      advice as to settlement, 01/6823S
    measure of damages
      loss of agricultural tenancy, 01/6420S
    wills
      inclusion of litigation costs in damages, 01/
        4537
  reliance on vendor's solicitors
    undertaking to redeem charge
      potential breach of duty, 01/4263
  undertakings
    subsequent change of instructions, 01/4272
    supervisory jurisdiction of court, 01/4271
South Africa
  freedom of expression
    constitutionality of offence of scandalising
      court, 01/3471
Special Commissioners
  appeals
    referrals, 01/5302
special educational needs
  Asperger's syndrome
    place child at school for learning difficulties
      validity of decision, 01/2027
  assessment

statutory offences -*cont.*
  school attendance -*cont.*
    parental sanction for failure to attend -*cont.*
      compatible with human rights, 01/6440S
  sentence length
    indecent photographs of children
      downloading images from internet, 01/6402S

statutory sick pay
  social security contributions
    appeals, 01/5003

stay of proceedings
  abuse of process
    destruction of video evidence, 01/1190
  case management
    orders for disclosure and exchange, 01/442
  delay
    lifting of automatic stay, 01/664
  relitigation of earlier proceedings
    payment of costs order, 01/666
  time limits
    effect of letter to court, 01/667

stop and search
  criminal evidence
    admissibility
      unlawfully obtained evidence inadmissible, 01/6320S

street trading
  form of licence, 01/5896NI
  penalties
    notices and procedure, 01/5897NI

Street Trading Act (Northern Ireland) 2001 (c.8), 01/5898NI
  Commencement Order, 01/5899NI

Street Works (Northen Ireland) Order 1995 (SI 1995 3210 (NI.19))
  Commencement No.5 Order, 01/5872NI

striking out. *See also* **abuse of process**
  abuse of process
    dispute only of academic interest, 01/430
    peremptory orders, 01/668
  cargo claims
    delay in low value cargo claim, 01/670
  causes of action
    statement of case, 01/669
  delay
    actions in absence of unless order, 01/674
    failure to comply with directions, 01/672
    failure to comply with rule
      court's discretion to strike out, 01/671
    effect of delay by party's solicitor, 01/673
  expert evidence
    reports relating to banking management, 01/394
  issue estoppel
    employment tribunals
      procedural fairness, 01/675
  judgments and orders
    failure to comply with order, 01/588
  professional negligence
    trustee's action against auditor of liquidated company, 01/677
  security for costs
    failure to comply with order, 01/679
  solicitors

striking out -*cont.*
  solicitors -*cont.*
    failure to lodge completed allocation questionnaire, 01/678
    standard of proof
      prospect of success, 01/680
    trial judges
      power to dismiss claim, 01/676

students
  allowances
    eligibility
      conditions and requirements, 01/6445S
  educational awards, 01/5750NI
  full time study
    work experience, 01/6449S
  grants
    disabled students, 01/1923, 5746NI
    eligibility, 01/1931, 1935, 2044, 5747NI, 5748NI
    European institutions, 01/1936, 1937
    full-time study, 01/1938
    performing arts, 01/1940, 2045
  higher education
    grants, 01/1939
  income related benefits, 01/5078, 6013NI
  loans, 01/6446S
    mortgage style repayment loans, 01/2046, 5751NI
    performing arts, 01/2045
    repayments, 01/2047, 5752NI, 6448S
  married students
    loans, 01/6447S
  part-time students
    loans, 01/6447S

subsidies
  farm subsidies
    review of decisions, 01/5674NI

succession. *See also* **administration of estates; family provision; wills**
  books, 01/5172, 6907S
  family provision
    challenge to will of former spouse
      existence of special circumstances, 01/5155
    spouses
      conclusive financial arrangement, 01/5157
  gifts
    inter vivos gift of house by parent
      presumption against double portions, 01/5152
  intestacy
    cohabitees
      provision for reasonable maintenance, 01/6034NI
    death resulting from road accident
      provision for dependants, 01/5160
    promises made to carer
      proprietary estoppel claim, 01/5158
  trust estate
    method of valuation, 01/5164
  valuation of property
    option to purchase
      value at time of death, 01/5163

summary causes
  appeals

terrorism -cont.
police powers
authorised officers
code of practice, 01/1078
code of practice, 01/5732NI
examining officers
codes of practice, 01/1000
proscribed organisations, 01/1079
deproscription, 01/1080
seizure, detention and forfeiture of assets, 01/5645NI
Proscribed Organisations Appeal Commission
human rights
procedure, 01/1081
procedure, 01/1082
restraint orders
High Court applications, 01/450
right to liberty and security
derogation by the UK, 01/3591
travel
disclosure of personal details, 01/1075
United Nations measures
powers and prohibitions, 01/4089
Channel Islands, 01/4090
Isle of Man, 01/4091
overseas territories, 01/4092
Terrorism Act 2000 (c.11)
Commencement No.3 Order, 01/1083
textile industry
textile imports
Taiwan
Council Regulation 2279/2001, 01/4130
theft. See also **burglary; fraud; robbery**
appropriation
company directors
act done on behalf of company, 01/1084
criminal evidence
sufficiency
possession of another's credit cards, 01/6321S
motor vehicles
fixing number plate to stolen trailer, 01/6340S
sentence length
racial aggravation, 01/6410S
Theft Act offences
evasion of excise duty
retrials, 01/1194
obtaining by deception
effect of agreement to defer payment, 01/1085
third countries
remuneration
officials of the European Communities
Council Regulation 2367/2001, 01/2310
time limits. See also **limitations**
childrens hearings
appeals
computation of period for lodgement, 01/6505S
prosecutions
110 day rule
justification for extension, 01/6346S
extension after abandonment, 01/6343S
justification for extension

time limits -cont.
prosecutions -cont.
justification for extension -cont.
mistaken desertion by prosecutor, 01/6345S
retrospective extension of time, 01/6342S
solemn procedure
pressure of business, 01/6344S
purchase notices
appellate decision the determination date, 01/6859S
title to land
deeds
validity
operation of estoppel, 01/2433
tenancies at will
adverse possession, 01/4892
torts. See also **defamation; negligence; nuisance; occupiers liability; passing off; trespass**
books, 01/5360
injurious falsehood
share sales
refusal to register, 01/743
malicious falsehood
limitations
extension of time limit to bring claim, 01/5354
misfeasance in public office
exemplary damages, 01/1512
tortious liability
misfeasance in public office, 01/5355
personal injuries
liability for dangerous animals, 01/4475
vicarious liability
Home Office detention centres
liability for acts of employee, 01/5358
trade marks. See also **passing off**
assignment of application
assignor dissolved company
validity of assignment, 01/3982
classification change
validity of application, 01/4046
Community trade marks
colours applied to inhalers
likelihood of confusion, 01/4012
distinctiveness
features of industrial goods, 01/3998
figurative mark, 01/3995
figurative mark made up of "THE", 01/3996
registration of figurative mark, 01/3992
registration of word "Electronica", 01/3993
registration of words "Poudre libre naturelle", 01/3991
shape of product, 01/4001
three dimensional mark applied to optical lenses, 01/3999
three dimensional mark used with other marks, 01/4000
word "Investor world", 01/3997
word combination mark "Baby-Dry", 01/4003
infringement
revocation of mark for non-use, 01/4009

trusts *-cont.*
trustees powers and duties *-cont.*
failure to keep pace with ordinary share index, 01/5531
recording made by former band member
entitlement to expenses incurred, 01/2436
trusts instruments
notarisation under Cayman Islands law, 01/5520
variation
beneficiaries
outright payment on attaining twentieth birthday, 01/5535
vested gifted property to trust, 01/5514
ultra vires
licensed premises
Scotland, 01/6875S
underwriting. *See* **Lloyds**
undue influence
mortgages
repossession
duty of bank to ensure independent advice taken, 01/4879
unemployment benefit. *See* **jobseekers allowance**
unfair dismissal
breach of contract
alteration in job description
relevance of underlying motive, 01/2341
compensation
computation of loss of pension benefits, 01/2342
disciplinary procedures
unauthorised use of company telephone by employee, 01/2343
ill health
compensatory award, 01/2345
misconduct
reasonableness
disciplinary procedures, 01/2344
part time lecturer
sex discrimination
business justification, 01/2319
police officers
transport constabulary
meaning of "maintained", 01/2346
poor attendance record
appellate body determining appeal without remission, 01/2340
public interest disclosure
protection for disclosure
relevant date, 01/6477S
redundancy selection
jurisdiction
jurisdiction to consider application from employee aged 65, 01/2308
unincorporated associations. *See also* **clubs; building societies; credit unions; friendly societies; industrial and provident societies**
delictual liability
motor racing association
adequacy of crash protection, 01/6813S
title to sue
club members suing club and third party, 01/6300S

United Nations
immunities and privileges
specialized agencies, 01/4094
international tribunals
Rwanda, 01/4095, 4097
Yugoslavia, 01/4096, 4097
sanctions
Afghanistan, 01/4098, 4099
Channel Islands, 01/4100, 4101
Isle of Man, 01/4102, 4103
overseas territories, 01/4104, 4105
Iraq
overseas territories, 01/4106, 4107
Liberia, 01/4108
Channel Islands, 01/4109
Isle of Man, 01/4110
overseas territories, 01/4111, 4112
universities
courses
criteria for removal of student, 01/2086
post graduate study
failure to progress, 01/2087
unjustified enrichment
repetition
payment of advance freight
abandonment of voyage, 01/6918S
urban areas
Commission for the New Towns
transfer of functions
Tees Barrage, 01/4770
utilities. *See also* **electricity industry; gas industry; water industry; water supply**
contracts, 01/5537
electricity and gas supply industries
energy efficiency, 01/5538
electricity supply industry
fossil fuel, 01/6919S
recovery of expenses
Leicestershire, 01/5541
Utilities Act 2000 (c.27)
Commencement No.4 Order and Transitional Provisions Order, 01/5542
Commencement No.5 Order and Transitional Provisions Order, 01/5543
Commencement No.6 and Transitional Provisions Order, 01/5544
VAT. *See also* **VAT and duties tribunals**
accounting
limits, 01/5545
acquisitions
registration limits
increase, 01/5593
apportionment
input tax
effect of out of country supplies, 01/5582
assessment
sale of land
application of relevant test, 01/5585
time limits
notice of assessment, 01/5547
books, 01/5627
buildings
change of use, 01/5549
business tenancies
supply of services, 01/5550

VAT -*cont.*
  commission
    sale of goods
      special provisions, 01/5596
  common system
    minimum standard rate
      Council Directive 2001/41, 01/5610
  companies
    business gifts
      amount increase, 01/5552
  company cars
    employee benefits
      fuel, 01/5553
  consideration
    sales promotion
      gift supplied under voucher scheme, 01/5554
    value of surrendered golf club, 01/5597
  consumer credit
    sale of goods
      interest free credit, 01/5555
  cultural services
    historic gardens not having status of museum, 01/5563
  discounts
    credit held on account for agents
      calculation of taxable amount, 01/5587
  excise duty
    evasion
      civil penalty giving rise to criminal charge, 01/5557
  exemptions
    alteration to listed building
      meaning of "protected building", 01/5559
    analysis of medical samples
      compatibility with Council Directive 77/388, 01/5560
    car parking fees
      applicability of Sixth Directive 77/388, 01/5561
    credit card protection plan
      block insurance, 01/5600
    exemption of trade associations, 01/5570
    grant of lease at peppercorn rate, 01/5579
    insurance transactions
      relationship between insurer and insured, 01/5564
    licences
      sale of cigarettes through vending machines, 01/5565
    professional bodies
      organisation's aims in public interest, 01/5566
    sale of land
      change to residential use, 01/5567
    Students' Union as integral part of university, 01/5562
    supply of animal feedingstuffs, 01/5625
    supply of insurance
      arrangement fee as percentage of contract price, 01/6920S
    supply of services
      standard rating supply ancillary to exempt supply, 01/5569
  France

VAT -*cont.*
  France -*cont.*
    rate on medicinal products
      validity under EC law, 01/5571
    Group 5, 01/5549
    imports
      non Member States
        payable as customs duty, 01/5573
    indirect taxes
      changes levied on traders engaged in tourism, 01/5574
    input tax
      Customs and Excise
        recovery of VAT on police vehicles, 01/5580
    distribution of college prospectuses
      taxable supplies, 01/5576
    exemptions
      for sporting facilities, 01/5581
    expensive sports cars for business use
      availability for private use, 01/5575
    partial deduction
      payments made to holding company by subsidiaries, 01/5578
    recovery of building works, 01/5608
    repayments
      taxable transactions in Italy, 01/5583
      three year cap, 01/5584
    sale of land and buildings
      right to deduct, 01/5577
    transfer of going concern
      right to deduct expenses on sale, 01/5586
  motor cars
    sale of goods
      commission, 01/5551
  partnership details forms
    registration, 01/5590
  place of supply
    groups of companies
      creation for financial advantage, 01/5588
  refunds
    art galleries, 01/5611
    museums, 01/5611
  registration
    capital assets
      cars sold by motor dealer in Ireland, 01/5594
    operating separate business from same premises
      validity of assessment, 01/5591
    partnership details forms, 01/5590
    validity
      best judgment assessment, 01/5592
  repayments
    Greater London Magistrates' Courts Authority, 01/5595
    overpaid VAT
      claim by repayment trader, 01/6921S
  retailer voucher schemes
    assessment of output tax, 01/5614
  returns
    electronic communications
      incentives, 01/5616
  sale of business item
    accountability on sale, 01/5548

voluntary arrangements -cont.
  individual voluntary arrangements -cont.
    nominee's fee -cont.
      discretionary power of court to refuse, 01/
        3790
      unjust enrichment, 01/3793
wages. See **remuneration**
  entitlement
    bank holidays
      additional   day   required   additional
        entitlement, 01/6478S
warrants
  search warrants
    Customs and Excise powers of search
      legality of execution, 01/6322S
    flaws rendering inadmissible, 01/6385S
Waste and Contaminated Land (Northern Ireland) Order 1997 (SI 1997 2778 (NI.19))
  Commencement No.5 Order, 01/5779NI
waste disposal. See also **contaminated land**
  incineration
    Council Directive 2000/76, 01/2414
  recycling
    payments, 01/2383
  special waste, 01/2417
    Wales, 01/2418
  waste management
    meaning of "controlled waste"
      compatibility with Council Directive 75/
        442, 01/2413
waste management
  non hazardous building waste
    restrictions on processing
      effect on freedom to export, 01/793
water industry
  abstraction scheme
    River Lochy, 01/6923S
  canals
    surface water
      discharge by sewage undertaker, 01/5632
  sewage treatment works
    validity of compulsory purchase order, 01/
      5630
  water abstraction
    River Lochy, 01/6923S
  water and sewerage
    charges
      reduction, 01/6927S
  water and sewerage undertakers
    duty to provide public sewerage services, 01/
      5631
  water authorities
    duty to supply wholesome water
      strict liability, 01/6924S
  water charges
    contractual liability
      discharge of charging agreement, 01/5634
  water companies
    competitive tendering
      provision of services, 01/5635
  water supply
    water quality, 01/5636, 6925S, 6926S
    Wales, 01/5637

water pollution. See also **sewers and drains; water industry; water supply**
  codes of practice, 01/6499S
  pollution control
    consent for discharges
      application procedure, 01/5777NI
water supply. See also **water pollution; land drainage**
Water (Northern Ireland) Order 1999 (1999 662 (NI.6))
  Commencement Order, 01/6083NI
weapons. See **firearms**
  anti-personnel landmines
    elimination of use
      Council Regulation 1725/2001, 01/4113
  decommissioning scheme
    amnesty period, 01/5720NI
  landmines
    elimination of use
      Council Regulation 1724/2001, 01/4114
weights and measures, 01/923
  equipment, 01/5713NI
    beltweighers, 01/924
    capacity measures, 01/925
    cold water meters, 01/926
    intoxicating liquor, 01/927
  metrication, 01/928
Welfare Reform and Pensions Act 1999 (c.30)
  Commencement   No.10,   and   Transitional
    Provisions Order, 01/5092
  Commencement No.11 Order, 01/5093
  Commencement No.12 Order, 01/5094
Welfare Reform and Pensions (Northern Ireland) Order 1999 (SI 1999 3147 (NI.11))
  Commencement No.7 and Transitional Provisions
    Order, 01/6027NI
  Commencement No.8 Order, 01/5924NI
  Commencement No.9 Order, 01/6028NI
whistleblowers
  unfair dismissal
    relevant date for statutory protection, 01/
      6477S
wills. See also **gifts; inheritance tax; succession; trusts**
  beneficiaries
    death of testator
      validity of disclaimer, 01/5153
    partnership agreement
      termination of onerous tenancy, 01/5154
  execution, capacity, knowledge and approval,
    01/5166
  knowledge and approval
    proof in solemn form
      implied revocation, 01/5165
  probate
    foreign jurisdictions
      legality of foreign grant of probate, 01/
        5168
    validity of will
      testator's knowledge at time signature
        witnessed, 01/5169
  residuary gifts
    directions regarding proceeds of Jersey bank
      accounts, 01/5170
  revocation